Standard & Poor's Stock and Bond Guide

This belongs to Shunda Lanae' Roberson

Standard & Poor's Stock and Bond Guide

1996 Edition

Standard & Poor's

McGraw-Hill

New York San Francisco Washington, D.C. Auckland Bogotá
Caracas Lisbon London Madrid Mexico City Milan
Montreal New Delhi San Juan Singapore
Sydney Tokyo Toronto

International Standard Serial Number

This book is printed on recycled paper containing a minimum of 50% total recycled fiber with 10% postconsumer de-inked fiber.

McGraw-Hill

A Division of The **McGraw·Hill** *Companies*

Standard & Poor's

The Publisher of the *Stock Guide* and the *Bond Guide* is Ron Oliver. The Editor is Frank LoVaglio.

1 2 3 4 5 6 7 8 9 0 MAL/MAL 9 0 1 0 9 8 7 6

ISBN 0-07-052238-1

The sponsoring editor for this book was David Conti, and the production supervisor was Thomas G. Kowalczyk. The front matter, introduction, and section opening materials were set by North Market Street Graphics.

Printed and bound by Malloy Lithographers, Inc.

CONTENTS

ABOUT THE AUTHOR

Standard & Poor's, a division of The McGraw-Hill Companies, is the nation's leading securities information company. It provides a broad range of services, including the respected bond and stock ratings, advisory services, data guides, and the most closely watched and widely reported gauge of stock market activity—the S&P 500 Stock Index. Standard & Poor's products are marketed around the world and used extensively by financial professionals and individual investors.

Standard & Poor's Stock and Bond Guide

INTRODUCTION

by Alan J. Miller, C.F.A.

The world's most inspired artist could not produce a great oil painting without brushes and palette, paints and canvas. The head chef at the most outstanding four-star restaurant on Paris' right bank could not cook a top-flight meal without the tools of the trade and proper ingredients: pots, pans and cutlery, fruits and vegetables, seasonings and spices. Even a cobbler could not manufacture a pair of first-class boots without hammer and nails, leather and twine.

Similarly, the most intelligent and serious investors could not select appropriate investments nor construct efficient portfolios for themselves without the right tools.

But what are the right tools for such serious investors?

The answer is more obvious than you might think. It is *information.* In today's information economy, what paints and brushes are to the artist, what spices and seasonings are to the cook, what leather and twine are to the cobbler, that is what comprehensive economic and financial information are to serious investors. Information which provides the investor with answers to such questions as:

What business is a company in?

How is the company capitalized and how well is it financed?

Is it highly leveraged?

What is its earnings growth record?

What has been its dividend-paying policy?

Are major institutions owners of its shares?

If one were to decide to invest in the company, how might that be accomplished?

Are its common shares listed and, if so, on which exchange?

Does it have any bonds outstanding?

What about preferred stocks?

Are any of these issues convertibles?

Are options available?

And what about mutual funds?

And annuities?

These, and dozens of questions like them, are the sort which serious investors, individual or institutional, must address if they are truly to do an effective job in managing their own assets or those entrusted to them.

To be sure, investors could, if they wanted, choose a random route of ignorance, hoping to get lucky by relying solely on a tip from a friend or neighbor, or they might throw darts at a page of stock market quotations, or they could buy the securities of companies whose names simply tickled their fancy. And from time to time they might even get lucky and generate a profit.

But over the long run, there is little doubt that such an approach would leave them worse off than when they started. Indeed, it is likely that they would be no more successful than would a painter who merely splattered paint on a canvas and wished for the best, or a chef who dumped a slew of meats, vegetables, and spices in a pot and hoped, thereby, to create a flavorful stew.

Sure, it *might* happen—just as a million monkeys randomly typing away at a million typewriters might someday produce a play of equivalent stature to Shakespeare's *Hamlet.* But don't bet on it.

No, a much better idea, and one adopted by virtually all investment professionals, is to attempt to seek out the most comprehensive and significant economic and financial information available, and to base investment decisions on a reasoned interpretation, evaluation, and analysis of such data. After all, in a rational world governed by the laws of cause and effect, that is the approach destined to maximize an investor's probability of success.

Which is where Standard & Poor's comes in.

Standard & Poor's

For generations, Standard & Poor's has been recognized as the leading purveyor of financial, economic, and business data to the investment community. The S&P 500 is among the most important and most widely reported benchmark indexes for investment professionals worldwide. Its products include *The Outlook,* one of the nation's leading investment advisory services; MarketScope, a respected, real-time investment advisory service for brokers; the Standard & Poor's Stock Market Encyclopedia; the Earnings Guide; the Trendline Chart Guide; the new Standard & Poor's Research Report, which provides "on-demand" investment information and guidance on over 5300 publicly-traded companies; and a whole host of other services that have proven all but indispensable to investment professionals. And not least of these are the Standard & Poor's monthly Stock and Bond Guides which provide hundreds of thousands of bits of information on more than 14,000 different securities—including common stocks, preferred stocks, annuities, mutual funds, and domestic and foreign bonds.

The Stock and Bond Guides have long been available only by subscription to individuals and institutions alike, but never before have individuals been able to purchase a combined year-end Stock and Bond Guide directly through a retail bookstore. Now all that has changed. *Standard & Poor's Stock and Bond Guide,* the first combined Standard & Poor's investment guide available to serious individual investors directly through retail outlets, is what you now hold in your hands.

This is an exceptional product, containing in just one source, a wealth of information designed to enable you to select the most appropriate securities for your own portfolio, no matter what your objectives.

The Common and Convertible Preferred Stock Guide

The first section of this book contains 50 columns of information on more than 5300 common and convertible preferred stocks—or approximately a quarter of a million bits of information on most of the equities in which you might be considering investing. Specifically:

1. The first column provides index numbers as a visual guide to the columnar data and indicates whether particular common stocks are components of the S&P 500 Stock Index, S&P MidCap 400, or S&P SmallCap 600. New this year, we have also added statistical data on each index, as well as on the S&P Super Composite 1500 Index. We have indicated where options are traded, along with footnotes indicating the exchanges on which those options trade and their monthly cycle.

2. The next column indicates the ticker symbols of stocks for the primary exchanges on which they trade. Supplementary symbols which appear on the ticker tape, such as "Pr" for preferred stocks, are also provided.

3. The name of the company appears here. This is not necessarily the exact corporate title of the company and may include abbreviations because of space limitations. When the name of the company is not followed by the designation of any particular issue of stock, it is the common stock which is being referred to.

If a check mark appears before the company name, a Standard & Poor's Research Report is available on the company.

This column also provides considerable additional information. For preferred stocks, call prices are shown in parentheses after the names of issues. Footnoted data indicate the years in which call prices decline. And various abbreviations indicate other provisions, for example, conversion terms of a preferred stock; whether or not it is participating or cumulative; when a stock is nonvoting; when a security is an American Depository Receipt; or the exercise terms of warrants.

Units of trading on the New York and American Stock Exchanges generally are 100 shares. When the unit is different for a particular issue (say 10, 25, or 50 shares), that fact is also indicated here.

4. This column indicates the markets in which the security trades. The primary exchange is the first market listed.

5. This column provides Standard & Poor's rankings for common stocks and ratings for convertible preferred stocks. These rankings and ratings represent some of the most valuable information in this book and merit special discussion.

Standard & Poor's Earnings and Dividend Rankings for Common Stocks

The investment process involves assessment of various factors—such as product and industry position, corporate resources, and financial policy—with results that make some common stocks more highly esteemed than others. In this assessment, Standard & Poor's believes that earnings and dividend performance is the end result of the interplay of those factors and that, over the long run, the record of this performance has a considerable bearing on relative quality. The rankings, however, do not pretend to reflect all the factors, tangible or intangible, that bear on stock quality. Even so, they are highly regarded, and many institutional investors will only buy stocks that carry Standard & Poor's highest rankings.

Relative quality of bonds or other debt—that is, degrees of protection for principal and interest—called *creditworthiness,* cannot be applied to common stocks; therefore, rankings are not to be confused with Standard & Poor's debt ratings which are arrived at by a necessarily different approach.

Growth and stability of earnings and dividends are key elements in establishing Standard & Poor's earnings and dividend rankings for common stocks, which are designed to capsulize the nature of the record in a single symbol. It should be noted, however, that the process also takes into consideration certain adjustments and modifications deemed desirable in establishing such rankings.

The point of departure in arriving at these rankings is a computerized scoring system based on per share earnings and dividend records of the most recent ten years. This is a period considered long enough to measure significant time segments of secular growth, to capture indications of basic change in trend as they develop, and to encompass the full peak-to-peak range of the business cycle.

Basic scores are computed for earnings and dividends, then adjusted by a set of predetermined modifiers for growth, stability within long-term trend, and cyclicality. Adjusted scores for earnings and dividends are then combined to yield a final score.

Further, the ranking system makes allowance for the fact that, in general, corporate size imparts certain recognized advantages from an investment standpoint. Conversely, minimum size limits (in terms of corporate sales volume) are set for the various rankings, but the system provides for making exceptions where the score reflects an outstanding earnings-dividend record.

The final score for each stock is measured against a scoring matrix determined by analysis of the scores of a large and representative sample of stocks. The range of scores in the array of this sample has been aligned with the following ladder of rankings:

- **A+** Highest
- **A** High
- **A−** Above Average
- **B+** Average
- **B** Below Average
- **B−** Lower
- **C** Lowest
- **D** In Reorganization
- **NR** No ranking because of insufficient data or because the stock is not amenable to the ranking process

The positions as determined above may be modified in some instances by special considerations, such as natural disasters, massive strikes, and nonrecurring accounting adjustments.

Bear in mind, however, that a ranking is not a forecast of future market performance, but is basically an appraisal of past performance of earnings and dividends, and relative current standing. Hence, these rankings should not be used as market recommendations: a high-score stock may at times be so overpriced as to justify its sale, while a low-score stock may be attractively priced for purchase.

Moreover, rankings based upon earnings and dividend records are no substitute for complete analysis. They cannot take into account potential effects of management changes, internal company policies not yet fully reflected in the earnings and dividend record, public relations standing, recent competitive shifts, and a host of other factors that may be relevant to investment status and decision. But they are an excellent place for the conscientious investor to begin.

Standard & Poor's Ratings for Preferred Stocks

Standard & Poor's preferred stock ratings are determined in an entirely different fashion. Unlike Standard & Poor's common stock rankings, these ratings are assessments of the capacity and willingness of an issuer to pay preferred stock dividends and any applicable sinking-fund obligations.

A preferred stock rating also differs from a bond rating inasmuch as it is assigned to an equity issue, which issue is intrinsically different from, and subordinated to, a debt issue. To reflect this difference, the preferred stock rating symbol will normally not be higher than the bond rating symbol assigned to, or that would be assigned to, the senior debt of the same issuer.

The preferred stock ratings are based on the following considerations:

1. Likelihood of payment, that is, the capacity and willingness of the issuer to meet the timely payment of preferred stock dividends and any applicable sinking-fund requirements in accordance with the terms of the obligation
2. Nature and provisions of the issue
3. Relative position of the issue in the event of bankruptcy, reorganization, or other arrangements affecting creditors' rights

Preferred stock ratings array as follows:

AAA This is the highest rating assigned by Standard & Poor's to a preferred stock issue and indicates an extremely strong capacity to pay the preferred stock obligations.

AA A preferred stock issue rated AA also qualifies as a high-quality fixed income security. The capacity to pay preferred stock obligations is very strong, although not as overwhelming as for issues rated AAA.

A An issue rated A is backed by a sound capacity to pay the preferred stock obligations, although it is somewhat more susceptible to the adverse effects of changes in circumstances and economic conditions.

BBB An issue rated BBB is regarded as backed by an adequate capacity to pay the preferred stock obligations. Whereas it normally exhibits adequate protection parameters, adverse economic conditions or changing circumstances are more likely to lead to a weakened capacity to make payments for a preferred stock in this category than for issues in the A category.

BB, B, CCC Preferred stocks rated BB, B, and CCC are regarded, on balance, as predominately speculative with respect to the issuer's capacity to pay preferred stock obligations. BB indicates the lowest degree of speculation and CCC the highest degree of speculation. While such issues will likely have some quality and protective characteristics, these are outweighed by large uncertainties or major risk exposures to adverse conditions.

CC This rating is reserved for a preferred stock issue in arrears on dividends or sinking-fund payments, but that is currently paying.

C A preferred stock rated C is a nonpaying issue.

D A preferred stock rated D is a nonpaying issue with the issuer in default on debt instruments.

NR This designation indicates that no rating has been requested, that there is insufficient information on which to base a rating, or that Standard & Poor's does not rate a particular type of obligation as a matter of policy.

Plus (+) or Minus (–) To provide more detailed indications of preferred stock quality, the ratings from AA to CCC may be modified by the addition of a plus or minus sign to show relative standing within the major rating categories.

Changes in Standard & Poor's common stock rankings and preferred stock ratings are highlighted by arrows showing the direction of change, up or down.

Now let's return to an explanation of the remaining columns in the Common and Preferred Stock Guide.

6–7. These columns indicate the number of financial institutions that hold the stock and the number of shares, in thousands, held. The data cover almost 4500 institutions, including investment companies, banks, insurance companies, college endowments, and money managers, as obtained from Vickers Stock Research Corporation.

8. In this column, the company's principal business is briefly described. Where a company is engaged in several lines of business, an attempt is made to list that line from which it obtains the greatest proportion of its revenues. In addition, an indication of the company's rank within its industry is given where possible.

9–14. The next six columns show the stock's price ranges during three discrete periods: for the 23 years 1971–1993 (columns 9–10); for the year 1994 (columns 11–12); and for the year 1995 (columns 13–14).

15. This column indicates the number of shares traded in December, 1995.

16–18. The next three columns show the stock's high, low, and closing prices in December, 1995. Prices for Canadian issues are quoted in Canadian dollars, when the primary exchanges on which these issues are traded are Canadian exchanges. When the closing quotation is a bid price, a "B" will follow the price in the "Last" column.

19. This column presents dividend yields, calculated by dividing the total indicated annual dividend rate by the closing price of the stock on December 29, 1995. The dividend rate used for this calculation is the latest dividend paid which may or may not include extras or stock dividends as indicated by the footnotes.

20. This column indicates the stock's latest price-earnings (or P-E) ratio, derived by dividing the closing price of the stock on December 29, 1995 by estimated 1995 earnings (where estimates are available) or by the last 12 months' earnings (where 1995 estimates are not available).

21–23. The total return value represents the price appreciation of a stock plus any cash dividends. To make the figures as close as possible to real portfolios, dividends are reinvested on the payment date, at that day's price. The total return figure, expressed as an annualized percentage, covers three time periods on a trailing basis: 12 months (column 21), 36 months (column 22), and 60 months (column 23).

24. This column (the first on the right-hand page) again provides index numbers as a visual guide to the columnar data. In addition, details of all stock dividends and stock splits effected during the previous five years are reported through symbols and footnotes. Adjustments are made for all stock dividends.

25. This column indicates that one or more cash dividends have been paid in each calendar year, without interruption, through 1995, beginning with the year listed.

26–32. The next seven columns provide data relating to the company's dividend policy. Where payments are being made at a regular established rate, that fact is noted in column 26 (Period) as follows: M = Monthly; Q = Quarterly; S = Semiannually; A = Annually. The amount of that regular payment is indicated in column 27 ($). The date of the latest payment appears in column 28 (Date) and the date on which the stock sells "ex dividend" (that is, the date on which the stock sells without the right to receive the latest declared dividend) appears in column 29 (Ex. Div.). Where stock dividends, no dividends, or dividends at no regular rate are being paid, those facts also appear in columns 26–29.

Column 30 provides total dividends paid in calendar 1995, including both regular and extras. Column 31 shows the latest total annual indicated rate based on the most recent quarterly or semiannual rate or on dividends paid during the last 12 months. And column 32 presents the total paid, including extras, in calendar 1994.

33–36. The next four columns provide important balance sheet information. Columns 33, 34, and 35 present Cash and Equivalents, Current Assets (including cash and equivalents), and Current Liabilities in millions of dollars. Column 36 indicates the date of that latest balance sheet information.

Where current balance sheet items are not of analytical significance, special calculations pertinent to the industry in which the company operates are presented, such as tangible "Book Value Per Share" for banks, "Net Asset Value Per Share" for investment trusts, and tangible "Equity Per Share" for insurance and finance companies. In such instances, intangibles such as goodwill, debt discount, and preferred liquidating value have been deducted.

37–39. The next three columns describe the company's capitalization: long-term debt in millions of dollars in column 37; preferred shares in thousands in column 38; and outstanding common shares in thousands in column 39.

40–49. The next ten columns present a record of the company's earnings per share for the last five years. Earnings generally are calculated on a "primary" basis as reported by the company, including discontinued operations but excluding extraordinary items.

Column 40 indicates the month in which the fiscal year ends so that you can tell exactly which periods you're looking at. Columns 41–45 present earnings per share for the years 1991–1995 and column 46 shows earnings per share for the last 12 months. Earnings for fiscal years ending March 31 or earlier are shown under the column of the preceding calendar year and "Last 12 Months" earnings indicate earnings through the period shown in the interim earnings column, when available, or annual, if not.

Where Standard & Poor's estimates are shown, they are the final product of careful analysis by industry specialists of available relevant information. They are unofficial, however, and responsibility for their accuracy cannot be assumed. Arrows denote changes in current estimates.

Interim earnings are shown, when available, for the longest accounting interval since the last fiscal year-end. Column 47 indicates the period for which interim earnings are being shown. Column 49 presents figures for that period in 1995 while column 48 presents figures for the same period in 1994 for comparative purposes.

50. Finally, the last column on the right-hand page again provides index numbers as a visual guide to the columnar data.

How to Use the Standard & Poor's Common and Convertible Preferred Stock Guide

We have outlined the wealth of information that is available on more than 5300 common and convertible preferred stocks in the Standard & Poor's Stock Guide—information relating to balance sheet data, stock price history, earnings records, dividend records, institutional ownership, and on and on. But how might an individual investor actually make use of all that? Let's look at two examples.

Suppose you were convinced that the timing was right to increase the amount of your funds committed to common or convertible preferred stocks and were interested primarily in ample and secure current income. Once you decided what you considered an adequate return, you'd thumb through the Stock Guide and select stocks yielding as much or more than your desired rate, as shown in the "% Dividend Yield" column near the extreme right of the left-hand page. By that one operation, alone, you would have run stocks through a preliminary screen and come up with a much more manageable list.

Now you'd probably want to know the prospects for maintaining dividends. By reference to the "Cash Dividends Each Year Since" column, adjacent on the next page, you could weed out those stocks whose record of consecutive dividend payments did not meet the standards you considered desirable.

Next you would have to decide if the stocks remaining on your list had adequate current protection. Among the various factors you would study in this connection would be annual and interim earnings and the company's financial position. In so doing, you'd be seeking answers to such questions as:

Do recent earnings cover dividend payments?

Have earnings been increasing or declining?

Is the company's balance sheet relatively clean with little long-term debt or is the company highly leveraged?

The measurement of earnings and dividends stability and growth provided by Standard & Poor's earnings and dividend rankings for common stocks and its ratings for preferred stocks are other helpful tools in the selection process. The fifth column on the left-hand page provides these rankings and ratings which have been discussed and explained at some length earlier in this introduction. Depending on the degree of conservatism you might wish to exercise, preferred stocks rated below A or common stocks ranked below B+ might be weeded out.

Having subjected your list to these various screenings, you might have perhaps a handful of issues remaining for further study. These securities should then be investigated in as thorough a fashion as possible. You'd still have a lot of work to do, but you'd have a huge head start in having eliminated hundreds, if not thousands, of companies which would not suit your needs. One place to begin the final phase of your search might be a Standard & Poor's Research Report, Standard & Poor's Investment Report, or a Standard & Poor's Street Report. Look for a check mark before the company name in order to find out companies for which reports are available.

Alternatively, suppose your objective was to invest for long-term capital appreciation rather than high current income. Again the Standard & Poor's Guide will be of tremendous help to you in getting started.

Instead of beginning with the dividend yield column, you might start by looking at the array of earnings-per-share statistics on the right-hand page. What you'd be looking for would be companies with consistent records of earnings growth, those whose earnings rose annually over the last five years, and those whose interim earnings for 1995 were greater than for the comparable period in 1994.

But just because a company's earnings were growing wouldn't necessarily mean that its common stock was attractive for purchase; the stock still might be overpriced. So you'd also want to look at the final column on the left-hand page to assure yourself that the stock's price-earnings ratio wasn't inordinately high.

Next, you'd want to look at the stock's Standard & Poor's ranking. And you'd probably want to review some of the balance sheet statistics to get a feeling for just how highly leveraged the company was.

In this situation (unlike the first in which you were seeking stocks providing ample, secure current income), you would end up with a small and manageable list of companies with good historic earnings growth records, selling at reasonable price-earnings multiples, and boasting satisfactory financial strength. Again you'd still have to do further research to ferret out the most attractive growth stocks to meet your objectives, but a good part of your job will have been done.

What have been outlined here are only two investor approaches: one suitable for an investor seeking high current income and the other appropriate for an investor more interested in long-term capital appreciation. But the data presented provide the basis for many other applications as well, which will become increasingly apparent to you as you use this book.

Standard & Poor's Preferred Stock Summary

The next section of this Standard & Poor's Guide provides data on more than 350 other nonconvertible preferred issues, including ticker symbols; exchanges on which these issues trade; call features; prices; dividend rates; payment dates; and yields. Perhaps most important, also included are the proprietary Standard & Poor's Preferred Stock Ratings, which have been discussed at some length earlier in this introduction.

Standard & Poor's Closed-End Fund Summary

The closed-end fund summary presents uniform data on more than 500 closed-end funds to make comparisons easy. You'll find all these facts on each closed-end fund: ticker symbol, fund name, exchange; fund type—24 kinds in all; dividends—latest payment, date, ex-dividend, year-to-date, regular distributions, capital gains distributions, indicated rate, yield %; price range—prior and current year to date, current month high/low and last; net assets—NAV premium/discount, latest NAV, common shares outstanding.

Standard & Poor's Mutual Fund Summary

Mutual funds are ideal investment vehicles for many investors who prefer to delegate the tasks of stock selection, asset allocation, and market timing to professional portfolio managers and who appreciate the additional benefits of broad diversification and liquidity which mutual funds provide. But how is one to determine *which* mutual fund may be most appropriate? Fortunately this guide can be of help to you on that score as well.

The next section of the Standard & Poor's Guide contains extensive information on more than 700 mutual funds arrayed in 25 columns. Here's what you'll be able to determine:

1. The name of the fund and the year in which it was originated or initially offered to the public.

2. The fund's principal objective: Growth, Income, Return on Capital, Stability or Preservation of Capital, or whether all objectives are treated equally.

3. The fund's type: Balanced, Bond, Common, Convertible Bond and Preferred, Flexible, Long-Term Governments (including GNMA, etc.), Global, Hedge, International, Leverage, Preferred, Precious Metals, Options, Specialized, Tax Free, or Short-Term Investments.

4. The fund's total net assets at market value less current liabilities (including cash equivalents) expressed in millions of dollars as of September 29, 1995.

5. The fund's cash and receivables plus U.S. Government securities, short-term commercial paper and short-term municipal and corporate bonds and notes, less current liabilities, expressed in millions of dollars as of September 29, 1995.

6. Whether or not the fund has IRA and Keogh plans available.

7–11. Performance results for the fund for each of the last five years, that is, the annual percentage change in net asset value per share in each of the years 1991–1995 after adjustment for all capital gains and dividends distributions, but excluding sales charges.

12. The minimum required initial purchase of shares exclusive of contractual plans (which is usually lower for retirement plans).

13. The maximum percentage sales charge, that is, the charge added to net asset value in computing the offering price.

18. The results of a $10,000 investment in the fund, assuming that all dividends and capital gains are reinvested. The calculation excludes any sales charge.

Standard & Poor's Variable Annuity/Life Investment Summary

An annuity is a contract between an insurance company and an annuitant whereby the insurance company guarantees to make fixed or variable payments to the annuitant at a future time, in exchange for a single or flexible premium.

Traditionally, annuities provided fixed payments over the course of an annuitant's lifetime in exchange for a single lump-sum premium payment, but a combination of rising inflation rates and increased life expectancies reduced the appeal of such products. As a result, in the late 1950s, the variable annuity was invented: This product is invested in assets (such as common stocks) which might be expected to rise in line with the rate of inflation, thereby providing some protection against declining purchasing power but at some increase in risk.

Variable annuities are variable in two senses:

1. they vary in what they are invested in (usually stocks, bonds, or money-market instruments); and
2. they vary in what they pay based upon fluctuations in their market value.

Since annuities are variable in both these senses, those who may be interested in purchasing them (usually for retirement) obviously need to find out something about the underlying terms of different annuities, the insurance companies marketing them, performance records, and so on. The Standard & Poor's Guide can help you in this area too.

The next section of the Standard & Poor's Guide contains information on 179 annuity vehicles arrayed in 14 columns. Here's what you'll be able to determine:

1. The name of the contract and the issuing company.

2. The investment vehicle, that is, what the underlying investment is.

3. Who the manager or submanager is.

4. The investment objective.

5. When the annuity was first offered.

6. Total assets (expressed in millions of dollars).

7–9. Fees and expenses, including separate account, fund, administrative, surrender, and sales charges.

10–13. Performance results, that is, annual percentage changes in unit values from 1992 through 1995.

14. Unit values as of December 27, 1995.

The Standard & Poor's Bond Guide

The next section of this book contains voluminous information on more than 6500 corporate bonds issued by more than 2300 different companies. Data relating to companies (including name, industry, fixed charges coverage, balance sheet figures, long-term debt outstanding, capitalization and debt-to-equity ratios) are referenced to the boldface headings at the top of the page. Data relating to individual issues (including exchanges where traded, descriptions, interest payment dates, recent rating history, redemption provisions, and others) are referenced to the second set of headings in lightface type.

Specifically, the following information is provided for *companies:*

1. The first company column provides the name of the issuing company and is footnoted to provide additional information relating to control, name changes, subsidiaries, and so on.

2. The next company column references the issuing company's principal business by industry code.

3–5. The next three company columns indicate fixed charges coverage for each of the three years 1992, 1993, and 1994. Figures represent the number of times available earnings (before income taxes and extraordinary charges or credits) cover fixed charges. Fixed charges include interest on funded debt, other interest, amortization of debt discount and expense, and similar charges.

6. The sixth company column indicates the month in which the fiscal year ends. For fiscal years ending March 31 or earlier, figures are shown under the columns of the preceding calendar year.

7–10. The next four company columns provide balance sheet data [cash and equivalents, current assets (including cash and equivalents), and current liabilities] in millions of dollars as of the annual or interim balance sheet date shown. (Note that utilities with a reasonable debt-to-property ratio often may report current liabilities in excess of current assets but that, in many instances, this is of no real significance since utilities have constant tax deferrals, high current debt maturity, and the ability to forecast revenues.)

11. The next company column shows the company's long-term debt in millions of dollars, that is, debt and certain obligations due after one year, including bonds, debentures, mortgages, and capitalized lease obligations. Increased debt resulting from new financing and offered subsequent to the latest balance sheet date is indicated by a five-pointed star (★).

12. The twelfth company column presents the company's capitalization in millions of dollars, that is, the sum of the stated values of common shareholders' equity, preferred and preference stock, total debt, and minority interest.

13. Finally, the last company column calculates total debt as a percentage of total capitalization, that is, total debt (including short-term debt) divided by total capital. This provides a measurement of the degree to which a company is leveraged.

Additionally, the following information is provided for *issues:*

1. The first issue column describes the specific bond, including coupon and maturity date. If the bond is traded on either the New York or American Stock Exchanges, that fact is noted as well.
2. The second issue column indicates the dates on which interest is payable. Symbols following interest dates note foreign issues payable in U.S. funds or currency of the issuing country and issues in default.
3. The next issue column presents Standard & Poor's debt ratings. These ratings differ from both common stock rankings and preferred stock ratings (previously described) and merit special discussion.

Standard & Poor's Corporate Debt Ratings

A Standard & Poor's debt rating is a current assessment of the creditworthiness of an obligor with respect to a specific obligation. This assessment may take into consideration obligors such as guarantors, insurers, or lessees.

Debt ratings are based on the following considerations:

1. Likelihood of default as evidenced by the capacity and willingness of the obligor as to the timely payment of interest and repayment of principal in accordance with the terms of the obligation
2. Nature and provisions of the obligation
3. Protection afforded by, and relative position of, the obligation in the event of bankruptcy, reorganization, or other arrangement under the laws of bankruptcy and other laws affecting creditors' rights.

Investment Grades: AAA, AA, A, BBB The top four categories (AAA, AA, A, and BBB) are commonly known as "Investment Grade" ratings. Under present commercial bank regulations issued by the Comptroller of the Currency, bonds rated in these categories are generally regarded as eligible for bank investments. (In addition, however, the Legal Investment Laws of various states may impose certain rating or other standards for obligations eligible for investment by savings banks, trust companies, insurance companies, and fiduciaries in general.)

AAA Debt rated AAA has the highest rating assigned by Standard & Poor's. Capacity to pay interest and repay principal is extremely strong.

AA Debt rated AA has a very strong capacity to pay interest and repay principal and differs from the higher rated issues only in small degree.

A Debt rated A has a strong capacity to pay interest and repay principal although it is somewhat more susceptible to the adverse effects of changes in circumstances and economic conditions than debt in higher rated categories.

BBB Debt rated BBB is regarded as having an adequate capacity to pay interest and repay principal. Whereas it normally exhibits adequate protection parameters, adverse economic conditions or changing circumstances are more likely to lead to a weakened capacity to pay interest and repay principal for debt in this category than in higher rated categories.

Speculative Grades: BB, B, CCC, CC, C Debt rated BB, B, CCC, CC, and C is regarded, on balance, as predominantly speculative with respect to capacity to pay interest and repay principal in accordance with the terms of the obligation. BB indicates the lowest degree of speculation and C the highest degree. Although such debt will likely have some quality and protective characteristics, these are outweighed by large uncertainties or major risk exposure to adverse conditions.

BB Debt rated BB has less near-term vulnerability to default than other speculative issues. However, it faces major ongoing uncertainties or exposure to adverse business, financial, or economic conditions which could lead to inadequate capacity to meet timely interest and principal payments. The BB rating category is also used for debt subordinated to senior debt that is assigned an actual or implied BBB– rating.

B Debt rated B has a greater vulnerability to default but currently has the capacity to meet interest payments and principal repayments. Adverse business, financial, or economic conditions will likely impair capacity or willingness to pay interest and repay principal. The B rating category is also used for debt subordinated to senior debt that is assigned an actual or implied BB or BB– rating.

CCC Debt rated CCC has a currently identifiable vulnerability to default and is dependent upon favorable business, financial, and economic conditions to meet the requirements of timely payment of interest and repayment of principal. In the event of adverse business, financial, or economic conditions, it is not likely to have the capacity to pay interest and repay principal. The CCC rating category is also used for debt subordinated to senior debt that is assigned an actual or implied B or B– rating.

CC The rating CC is typically applied to debt subordinated to senior debt that is assigned an actual or implied CCC rating.

C The rating C is typically applied to debt subordinated to senior debt that is assigned an actual or implied CCC– rating. The C rating may be used to cover a situation where a bankruptcy petition has been filed, but debt service payments are continued.

CI The rating CI is reserved for income bonds on which no interest is being paid.

D Debt rated D is in payment default. The D rating category is used when interest payments or principal repayments are not made on the date due even if the applicable grace period has not expired, unless Standard & Poor's believes that such payments will be made during such grace period. The D rating also is used upon the filing of a bankruptcy petition, if debt service payments are jeopardized.

Plus (+) or Minus (–) The ratings from AA to CCC may be modified by the addition of a plus (+) or minus (–) sign to show relative standing within the major categories.

r The 'r' is attached to highlight derivative, hybrid, and certain other obligations that Standard & Poor's believes may experience high volatility or high variability in expected returns due to noncredit risks. Examples of such obligations are: securities whose principal or interest return is indexed to equities, commodities, or currencies; certain swaps and options; and interest only and principal only mortgage securities. The absence of an 'r' symbol should not be taken as an indication that an obligation will exhibit no volatility or variability in total return.

NR This designation indicates that no public rating has been requested, that there is insufficient information on which to base a rating, or that Standard & Poor's does not rate a particular type obligation as a matter of policy.

Let's now return to an explanation of the remaining *issue* columns in the Bond Guide:

4–5. The next two issue columns indicate the date of the latest rating change and the previous rating.

6. The sixth issue column indicates whether or not the bond is eligible for purchase by banks.

7. The next issue column indicates the bond's form: Book-entry; Coupon only; Registered only; or Coupon or Registered, interchangeably.

8–13. The following six issue columns provide information regarding redemption provisions: the regular call price with beginning date (in parentheses) or ending date (columns 8–9); sinking-fund price with beginning date (in parentheses) or ending date (columns 10–11); and refund price with beginning date (in parentheses) or ending date (columns 12–13).

14. The next issue column indicates the amount of the issue outstanding (in millions of dollars) as of the latest available complete balance sheet date.

15–16. The next two issue columns reference the original underwriter and the year the issue was originally offered.

17–19. The following three issue columns indicate the bond's high and low price in 1995 and its last sale price as of December 29, 1995 (for listed issues) or bid price or Standard & Poor's valuation for over-the-counter issues or listed issues not traded on the last business day of the year.

20–21. Finally, the last two issue columns provide the bond's current yield and yield to maturity computed on the basis of the year-end price shown in column 19.

How to Use the Standard & Poor's Bond Guide

We have described the data available on more than 6500 corporate bonds in the Standard & Poor's Bond Guide—information relating to descriptions of corporate issuers and issues alike, balance sheet data, fixed charges coverage, long-term debt, capitalizations, redemption provisions, interest payment dates, debt ratings, underwritings, price history, current yields, yields to maturity and much, much more. But how can an individual investor actually use this information? Two examples follow.

A conservative investor might start with a consideration of Standard & Poor's bond ratings. Being conservative, she might limit her interest to investment grade bonds, those rated BBB or higher. Or she might set her sights even higher than that, screening out all bonds rated below A or even AA.

In addition to limiting her credit risk, however, she might want to limit her interest rate risk as well. So she might cut her list even further, eliminating those issues with maturities of longer than, say, seven years.

From among those issues, she next might search for those which provide the highest yields to maturity. As a preliminary cut, these are the issues which would appear to provide the greatest value within the context of her particular risk parameters.

Once she did these three things, the investor might check redemption provisions to make sure that what appear to be bargains aren't just fool's gold likely to be called away from her. Then, depending on her personal requirements (for liquidity, perhaps, or current income), she might check out the size of the issue, whether or not it was listed, current yield and interest payment dates.

Even once this was done, however, the investor still wouldn't know whether or not to place an order to purchase any particular issue—but she'd surely be a lot closer to making an intelligent decision. With just a few issues remaining after she completed these initial screens, she'd know exactly which bonds to investigate further and her project would be manageable.

An aggressive speculator, on the other hand, might address this issue the other way around: rather than starting out by screening for quality, he might screen for yield to maturity, looking for those issues providing the biggest payoffs—assuming they don't default. And he might want to increase his bet even further by assuming a big interest rate risk as well, screening out any issues with *less* than ten years to go to maturity.

But will these issues default? The investor now would examine such statistical data as fixed charges coverage, total debt as a percentage of capital, and the other balance sheet information provided in these tables. He, after all, would be looking for bargains too—but at the other end of the spectrum: poorly rated issues which would *not* be likely to default.

Not surprisingly, the issues this investor would be likely to come up with probably would carry low Standard & Poor's debt ratings—and that's when he'd have to be prepared to do a lot more work. Why are these bonds' ratings as low as they are, if fixed charges coverage, debt/capital ratios, and balance sheet data appear acceptable? Is there something qualitative he's missing?

Further research could provide the answers. Screening the Bond Guide wouldn't be the end of the job, but by reducing the number of issues to be investigated in depth down to a manageable number, it certainly would make the total job a whole lot easier.

The final sections of this Guide also provide extensive information on more than 450 Canadian and other foreign issues and over 400 convertible bonds, as well as Standard & Poor's debt ratings for hundreds of the largest state and municipal general obligations and revenue bonds.

Foreign Bonds

Information on foreign bonds is arrayed in 19 columns like this:

1–5. The first five columns provide a description of the bond, the coupon rate, the maturity date, and interest payment dates.

6. The next column indicates the Standard & Poor's Debt Rating. Debt obligations of issuers outside the United States and its territories are rated on the same basis as domestic corporate and municipal issues. The ratings measure the creditworthiness of the obligor but do not take into account currency exchange and related uncertainties.

7–9. The next three columns provide information relating to redemption provisions: callability, sinking fund, and refunding and other provisions.

10–12. In these three columns, you can determine who the underwriter of the issue was, the price at which the bonds initially were sold, and the year of the underwriting.

13. This column indicates the dollar amount of the issue outstanding (in millions).

14–18. Here's where you'll discover the bond's price history: the range from 1983 through 1994 in columns 14–15; the 1995 range in columns 16–17; and the closing price (or closing bid) in 1995 in column 18.

19. The last column provides a calculation of yield to maturity.

Selected Municipal Ratings

The Guide also provides Standard & Poor's debt ratings on several hundred municipal bonds. These ratings are determined on the same basis as the corporate debt ratings discussed earlier.

Convertible Bonds Statistical Analysis

Finally, the Guide provides considerable statistical data on over 400 different convertible bonds, arrayed in 24 columns. Here is what you'll be able to find out:

1–4. From these columns, you'll be able to determine the name of the issue, whether or not it's listed on the New York or American Stock Exchange, the coupon rate, interest payment dates, and maturity date.

5. The next column presents the Standard & Poor's debt rating, determined in the same manner as for all other bonds, as discussed earlier.

6. The next column indicates whether the bond is in bearer, registered, or book-entry form.

7. The seventh column shows the dollar amount of bonds outstanding (in millions).

8–11. The next four columns relate to the conversion feature. Column 8 indicates the year in which the conversion feature expires. Column 9 indicates the number of common shares into which each $1,000 bond is convertible. Column 10 is an alternative way of looking at the information in column 9: It shows the conversion price per common share. And column 11 indicates the annual dividend income which bondholders would receive, in lieu of interest income, if they were to convert their bonds into common stock (based upon current dividend rates).

12–14. The next three columns provide price information on the bond: the high and low prices at which the bond sold in 1995 (columns 12–13) and the last sale (or bid or asked price) for the bond in 1995.

15–16. The next two columns show current bond yields and yields to maturity based upon latest prices and bond coupon rates.

17–18. These two columns deal with the conversion value of the bond. Column 17 indicates the stock value of the bond, that is, the present market value of the total number of shares of common stock into which each $1,000 bond may be converted. Column 18 indicates the price at which the common stock would have to sell to equal the bond price.

19–20. The next two columns relate to the value of the underlying common stock into which the bond is convertible. Column 19 shows the common stock's last price (and indicates, incidentally, if the stock is traded on the New York or American Stock Exchange). Column 20 shows the stock's current price-earnings ratio, that is, the stock's latest price divided by the last 12 months earnings per share.

21–24. Finally, the last four columns provide earnings data on the underlying common stock: columns 22–24 indicate earnings per share in fiscal 1994, 1995, and the latest 12 months, respectively, while column 21 indicates the month in which the fiscal year ends.

How to Use the Convertible Bond Guide

The investor in convertible bonds typically seeks the best of two different worlds: (1) the assured income and more secure creditor position which attach to bond investment; and (2) the growth and inflation hedge characteristics which attach to equity ownership. In effect, he looks for the reward potential which attracts investors in common stocks while hoping to avoid at least some of the risk inherent in equity ownership.

Of course, in convertible bond investing, as in most human activities, "there ain't no such thing as a free lunch," and it is seldom that one can find the opportunity to acquire an attractive convertible bond selling at conversion value and providing a yield greater than that which would be available from the underlying common stock.

Nonetheless, there frequently are good opportunities among convertibles, even if there are no *perfect* investments. To find them, an investor should look for convertible bonds with the following two important characteristics:

1. They should be convertible into common stocks which themselves are attractive investments. (After all, what is the value of an option to acquire something you won't want?)
2. They should be selling at reasonable prices, that is, at prices which do not put too great a premium on the conversion privilege.

Turning first to the question of the underlying value of the common stock, the investor might peruse the last six columns on the convertible bond page. This would show whether or not the company was profitable, whether earnings rose or fell last year, the price at which the stock is selling, and whether that price represented a high or low multiple of earnings.

Such information is valuable but it is, admittedly, scanty, and the investor then would be well advised to turn to the data relating to the common stock in the Stock Guide section of this book. There he or she would be able to determine much more regarding the stock's earnings trend, its performance history, the company's capitalization, dividend-paying ability, and so on.

Once that is done and the investor decides that the stock is a possible candidate for investment, he or she must consider whether the company's convertible bond might provide a more attractive way to make that investment. In an ideal world, of course, the investor would be able to buy the bond at conversion value (rather than at a lesser value, because arbitrage activities would not allow a spread to persist), and the bond would be yielding more than the underlying common. But this is unlikely. More likely, he or she will have to pay *some* premium for the conversion privilege (although often a higher yield will be realized than could have been received on the common stock itself).

To evaluate this, the investor should investigate the column headed Stock Value of Bond. If the bond is not selling for too much more than this, then the conversion premium is small; but if the bond price is well above the stock value, then a big premium is being demanded for the conversion privilege. He or she could also get a feel for this by looking at the Conversion Parity column: If the stock is selling at close to its conversion price, then it wouldn't have too far to go before the bond would necessarily have to rise too; but if the gap is substantial, it would be possible that the stock could appreciate substantially while the bond did not.

Additionally, the investor ought to compare the bond's current yield and yield to maturity to the yield on the stock. If the yield on the bond is much higher than that on the stock, he or she might be willing to pay some significant premium for the convertible since, in effect, it would be possible to amortize the premium over time through the receipt of incremental interest income (relative to dividend income on the stock).

Summary

This is just a brief outline of what this Stock and Bond Guide contains and some of the ways in which it may be used by the individual investor. But the possibilities really are much greater than can be touched on in a short introduction. Thus, as you use this book, combining data from one section with information from another, and using it as the starting point for a more thorough investigation of the investment opportunities available to you, we have little doubt that you will discover a wealth of new uses and applications which will enable you to be an increasingly successful investor.

Good luck!

THE STOCK GUIDE

HOW TO USE THE STOCK GUIDE

It is necessary to read carefully the following instructions and those on Pages 4 and 5 to correctly interpret abbreviations and data in the Guide.

INDEX	Ticker Symbol	STOCKS NAME OF ISSUE (Call Price of Pfd. Stocks) Market	Com Rank & Pfd. Rating	Inst. Cos / Hold Shs (1,000)	PRINCIPAL BUSINESS	PRICE RANGE Historical High Low, Last Year High Low, Current Year High Low	Month Sales in 100s	Last Month Prices High Low Last	% Div. Yield	P-E Ratio	Total Return %
The index numbers are a visual guide to the columnar data. Stocks with options are indicated by ●; stocks in the S&P Indices are flagged with: ¶ for the S&P 500; # for the S&P MidCap 400; ✣ for the S&P SmallCap 600.	Ticker symbols are those of the exchange first listed in "Market" column. Supplementary symbols as would appear on the ticker tape after symbol, such as "Pr" for preferred stocks, etc., are indented.	Stocks for which **RESEARCH REPORTS, INVESTMENT REPORTS** or **STREET REPORTS** are available are flagged with a ✔ Names shown in this column are not necessarily the exact corporate title of the company. Also, because of space limitation, the occasional use of abbreviations has been necessary. Where the name of the company is not followed by the designation of any particular issue of its stock, it is the common or capital stock that is referred to. The Call Price of preferred stocks is shown in parentheses after the name of the issue; the footnoted data indicates year in which the call price declines. Abbreviations of various provisions, etc. are shown on Page 5. Unit of Trading for stocks on the New York Stock Exchange and American Stock Exchange is indicated as follows: 10—10 shares; 25—25 shares; 50—50 shares; all others 100 shares. The markets for each issue are indicated by standard abbreviations, as shown on Page 5. The primary exchange is the first market shown.	Standard & Poor's Rankings and Ratings are explained on pages xiii and xv. Directional arrows denote changes in the last 3 months.	The number of financial institutions—banks, investment, insurance, college endowments and "13F" money managers—that hold this stock and the number of shares (000 omitted) held. See explanation on Page 4.	This is the principal business of the company. Where a company is engaged in several lines of business every effort has been made to list that line from which it obtains the greatest proportion of its revenue. In addition, an indication of the company's rank in the industry is given where possible.	High and Low price ranges are for the calendar years indicated. Price ranges are not exclusive for the exchange on which the stock is currently traded, but are based on the best available data covering the period of the column head. Historical price ranges may be based on the best available high and low bid prices during the period, and should be viewed as reasonable approximations.	Trading volume is for the month indicated in hundreds of shares. NYSE & ASE companies are based on composite tape, all others are for primary exchange shown.	Last sales are closing quotations for the month indicated. When the closing quotation is a bid price, a 'B' will follow the 'Last' price. In the case of Canadian issues, prices are quoted in Canadian dollars provided the first exchange listed is a Canadian exchange.	Yields are derived by dividing total indicated dividend rate by price of stock. Such rate is based on latest dividend paid including (†), or excluding (e) extras as indicated by footnote. Additional symbols used: (s) including stock; and (‡) including extras and stock.	P-E Ratio (Price-Earnings Ratio)—See explanation on Page 4.	Total Return value represents the price appreciation of a stock with cash dividends reinvested on the pay date. The three values given are the annual compounded rate per year for the prior 12, 36 and 60 month period.

ALSO SEE OPPOSITE PAGE

HOW TO USE THE STOCK GUIDE

It is necessary to read carefully the following instructions and those on Pages 4 and 5 to correctly interpret abbreviations and data in the Guide.

INDEX	Cash Divs. Ea. Yr. Since	DIVIDENDS — Latest Payment — Per, $ Date, Ex. Div.	DIVIDENDS — -$- This Year, Total Ind. rate, -$- Last Year	FINANCIAL POSITION — Mil. $ — Cash & Equiv., Curr. Assets, Curr. Liabs., Balance Sheet Date	CAPITALIZATION — Long Term Debt Mil. $, Shs. 000 Pfd., Com.	Yrs. End	ANNUAL EARNINGS — -$- Per Share -$- Latest Five Years, Last 12 Mos.	INTERIM EARNINGS OR REMARKS — $ –Per Share –$ Period, Comparison	INDEX
Details of stock dividends and stock splits, effected during the past five years, are reported by symbol ♦ and footnotes which carry numerals corresponding to those in "Index" column. Adjustments have been made for all stock dividends.	One or more cash dividends have been paid each calendar year to date, without interruption, beginning with year listed.	Latest dividend payment, if at a regular established rate, it is so noted by M—Monthly, Q—Quarterly, S—Semi-Annually, or A—Annually. Date of disbursement of the latest payment. If an extra or stock dividend also is being paid, it is so indicated by footnote. The date shown is that on which the stock sells "ex-dividend"; that is the date on which it sells without the right to receive the latest declared dividend.	Payments made or declared payable thus far in the current calendar year, including both regular and extras, if any. Indicated Rates are usually based on most recent quarterly or semi-annual payments, or on dividends paid during the last 12 months. Total dividend payments, including extras if any, made in the preceding calendar year. For preferred dividend accumulations to latest payment due date, see "Financial Position" or Remarks column.	Cash & Equivalent, Current Assets, (includes cash/equiv) and Current Liabilities are given in millions of dollars (000,000) omitted, as 17.00—$17,000,000, 1.75—$1,750,000, 0.18—$175,000, etc. Where current balance sheet items are not of analytical significance, special calculations pertinent to the industry in which the company operates are presented, as tangible "Book Value per Share" for Banks, "Net Asset Value per Share" for Investment Trusts, and tangible "Equity per Share" (stockholders) for Insurance and Finance Companies. Intangibles such as goodwill, debt discount or pfd liquidating value have been deducted.	Long Term Debt is in millions of dollars, as 25.0—$25,000,000; 2.58—$2,580,000; 0.20—$200,000. It includes funded debt, long term bank loans, etc. Preferred and common stocks are in shares to the nearest thousands (000 omitted), as 150—150,000; 30—30,000; 2—1,500 (due to rounding). Outstanding shares exclude treasury stock. Figure shown under preferred shares column on company name line represents the combined number of preferred shares outstanding.		Earnings are in general on a "Primary" basis as reported by company, including discontinued operations but excluding extraordinary items. More detailed information on method of reporting and usage of standard footnotes can be found on Page 4. **Earnings for fiscal years ending March 31 or earlier are shown under the column of the preceding calendar year.** S&P Earnings Estimates are the final product of careful analysis by industry specialists of available relevant information. They are unofficial, however, and responsibility for their accuracy cannot be assumed. An arrow denotes changes in current estimate. Last 12 Mos. indicates 12 months earnings through period shown in interim earnings column, when available, or annual, if not.	Interim earnings are shown, when available, for the longest accounting interval since the last fiscal year-end. Also published in this column from time to time are references to SF provisions & divd arrears of pfds. See also Financial Position column for such notations.	The index numbers are a visual guide to the columnar data.

♦ **Stock Splits & Divs By Page Reference Index.**

UNIFORM FOOTNOTE EXPLANATIONS

To provide for consistency, eliminate repetition, and allow space for situations requiring further explanation, items recurring frequently that demand footnote explanation have been designated with specific symbols, which are explained on this page. Additional explanatory notations appear at the bottom of respective pages.

EARNINGS PER SHARE are in general on a 'Primary' basis as reported by company, excluding extraordinary items. If common equivalents are dilutive, the primary earnings are prefixed by symbol ∫. If potential dilution is significant, the extent is indicated for the latest year by reporting the "Fully Diluted" in the footnotes. Net operating values are shown for *mutual funds. Foreign* issues traded ADR are in dollars, converted at prevailing exchange rate. Specific footnotes used in earnings columns:

★ — Interim not comparable with annual earnings
§ — Net asset value
▵ — Excludes extraordinary income
▲ — Includes extraordinary income
□ — Excludes extraordinary charge
■ — Includes extraordinary charge
∫ — Primary earnings (includes dilutive common equivalents)
⋆ — Before tax loss carryforward
± — Combined various classes
△ — Comparison 1993–1994

® — Fully diluted earnings
ɪ — Partial year
b — Fixed charges & Pfd. & Pref. dividends Times Earned
c — Company only
d — Deficit
E — S&P estimate
f — Net investment income
j — Currency of country of origin
k — Net gain from operations
p — Pro forma reflecting acquisitions, mergers, etc.
P — Preliminary

LAST 12 MOS. indicates earnings computed through period shown in interim earnings column, unless otherwise footnoted. Where no interim period has been reported, last annual is given.

CHANGES IN S&P EARNINGS ESTIMATES are denoted by arrows showing the direction of change, up or down (↑↓). The indicator appears in the issue of the Stock Guide for the month in which the change occurred.

P-E RATIO—Ratio is derived by dividing current price by estimated new year earnings or last 12 months earnings if no estimate is available.

INSTITUTIONAL HOLDINGS—Figures in these columns show how many financial institutions hold the stock in question, and how many shares (000 omitted) are so held. This data cover almost 4,500 institutions, including investment companies, banks, insurance companies, college endowments, "13F" money managers, obtained from Vickers Stock Research Corporation, 226 New York Ave., Huntington, NY 11743.

CHANGES IN S&P COMMON STOCK RANKINGS AND PREFERRED STOCK RATINGS are highlighted by arrows showing the direction of change, up or down (↑↓). When a change is made, the indicator appears in the next three issues of the Stock Guide.

DIVIDENDS frequently include extra cash payments, stock, capital gains, payments on arrears for Pfd shares, or may be before deduction of foreign income taxes. These and other situations dictate the use of uniform footnotes, as follows:

ⓟ — Previous record (if any) not available
© — Dividend from capital gains
◉ — Excludes circled c type
‡ — Includes extras and stock
◆ — Divd. converted to U.S. funds
† — Includes extras
a — Dividend paid a/c arrears
e — Excluding extras
g — In Canadian funds, subject to 15% non-residence tax

h — Stock of another company
s — Also stock
t — Less tax country of origin
y — Based on last year's payment

OTHERS used in various columns:

± — Combined various classes
★ — Giving effect to new financing
p — Pro forma reflecting acquisitions, mergers, etc.

STOCKS WITH OPTIONS are indicated by ● in the index column preceding the ticker symbol. Numeric footnotes are used to show the exchanges on which the option trades and the cycle: 1—Jan, Apr, Jul, Oct; 2—Feb, May, Aug, Nov; 3—Mar, Jun, Sep, Dec.

STOCKS IN THE S&P Indices are flagged in the index column preceding the ticker symbol with: ¶ for the S&P 500; # for the MidCap400; ✜ for the SmallCap 600.

STOCK SPLITS & DIVIDENDS are indicated by ◆ in the "Index" column preceding the Dividend data. Details appear in footnotes which carry numerical symbols corresponding to those in the "Index" column. Adjustments of per share price ranges, dividends paid, book value, and earnings have been made for all stock splits and stock dividends.

ABBREVIATIONS USED

A	Asked Price
ADR	American Depositary Receipts
ADS	American Depositary Shares
B	Bid Price
Cl	Class
cm	Cumulative
Com	Common
Ctf	Certificates
Cv	Convertible
Dep	Depositary Receipts
Gtd	Guaranteed
L.P.	Ltd. Partnership
NC	Non-Callable
non-cm	Non-Cumulative
non-vtg	Non-Voting
Ord	Ordinary
Pfd	Preferred
Pr	Prior
Pref	Preference
Ptc	Participating
Red	Redeemable
Red restr	Redemption restriction
REIT	Real Estate Investment Trust
SBI	Shares of Beneficial Interest
Ser	Series
SF	Sinking Fund
shs	Shares
vtc	Voting Trust Certificates
Vtg	Voting

EXCHANGES REPRESENTED

Abbreviation	Exchange
Am	Amsterdam
AS	American
Au	Australian
B	Boston
BEL	Belgium
BSPA	Brazilian
Ch	Chicago
C	Cincinnati
CBOE	Chicago Board Options Exch
ECM	Emerging Company Marketplace
Lo	London
MA	Madrid
ME	Mexican
Mo	Montreal
ML	Milan
NNM	Nasdaq National Market
NSC	Nasdaq SmallCap
NY	New York
P	Pacific
Pa	Paris
Ph	Philadelphia
Ro	Rome
To	Toronto
Vc	Vancouver

Unit of Trading for stocks on the New York Stock Exchange and the American Stock Exchange is indicated as follows: (10)-10 shares; (25)-25 shares; (50)-50 shares; all others 100 shares.

¶ S&P 500 # MidCap 400 ✜ SmallCap 600 • Options

Index	Ticker	Name of Issue (Call Price of Pfd. Stocks)	Market	Com. Rank. & Pfd. Rating	Inst. Hold Cos	Inst. Hold Shs. (000)	Principal Business	Price Range 1971-93 High	1971-93 Low	1994 High	1994 Low	1995 High	1995 Low	Dec. Sales in 100s	December, 1995 Last Sale Or Bid High	Low	Last	%Div Yield	P-E Ratio	Total Return % Annualized 12 Mo	36 Mo	60 Mo
1	SPSC	**S&P Super Composite 1500 Index**		NR	..	...	U.S. equity performance indicator	....	....	....	....	134.43	111.17	....	134.43	130.43	133.24	2.2	16	...	...	...
2•[1]	SPIC	**S&P 500 Index**		NR	..	...	Broad large-cap indicator	471.29	60.96	482.85	435.86	622.88	457.20	....	622.88	605.05	615.93	2.3	17	37.6	15.3	16.6
3•[1]	SPMC	**S&P MidCap 400 Index**		NR	..	...	Broad mid-cap indicator	179.44	119.43	184.95	161.55	220.73	167.93	....	220.73	208.10	217.84	1.7	18	30.9	12.9	19.3
4•[1]	SPYC	**S&P SmallCap 600 Index**		NR	..	...	Broad small-cap indicator	....	....	94.17	92.84	122.69	92.45	....	121.22	116.24	121.10	1.0	24	30.0	13.7	21.5
5	ACOM	✓**A+ Network**	NNM	NR	30	2285	Paging,telemessaging svcs	19	11	15⅜	7½	16¼	11¼	6901	14¼	11¼	11¾	...	d	−16.1	...	...
6•[2]	AAM	✓**Aames Financial**	NY	NR	76	5267	Mortgage brokerage, California	13⅛	4⅜	10¾	7	36⅞	7¾	8341	34⅛	26⅞	27⅞	1.1	15	234	57.0	...
7	AAON	✓**AAON Inc**	NNM	NR	16	626	Mfr air-condition'g/heat'g eqp	7½	7/16	16⅝	6⅝	13⅝	4½	3287	6¾	4⅞	5¾	...	11	−45.4	62.4	...
✜8•[3]	AIR	✓**AAR Corp**	NY,Ch,Ph	B+	91	12110	Mkts aviation parts/service	37½	1¼	17⅜	11⅞	22	12⅛	6195	22	18⅛	22	2.2	27	81.4	27.9	20.3
9	ABAX	✓**Abaxis Inc**	NNM	NR	18	2258	Dvlp stge:blood analyzer sys	17½	3½	11½	3	9⅛	3¼	9259	7¾	5⅝	7	...	d	115	5.3	...
¶10•[4]	ABT	✓**Abbott Laboratories**	NY,B,C,Ch,P,Ph	A+	1173	394814	Diversified health care prod	34⅞	½	34	25⅜	44¾	30⅝	345587	42⅞	39¼	41⅝	2.0	19	28.9	13.3	16.1
11	ABCR	✓**ABC Rail Products**	NNM	NR	77	6613	Mfr orig'l&replace'mt rail prd	15	12	23¼	14⅛	27⅝	19⅜	18675	24⅜	21⅞	22⅛	...	15	1.7	...	...
12	ABMD	✓**ABIOMED, Inc**	NNM	C	13	406	Medical equip/cardiac sys	22¾	4¾	9	4	16	4⅞	6412	16	10	15	...	..	186	10.9	19.6
13•[5]	ABY	**Abitibi-Price**[53]	NY,To,Mo,P,Vc	C	99	29856	Newsprint,paper prods	28⅝	2 5/16	15¼	11⅜	19	12	38879	15⅞	13⅞	14½	...	..	7.7	10.0	9.3
✜14	ABM	✓**ABM Industries Inc**	NY,B,Ch,P,Ph	A	87	4719	Janitorial & building maint	21¾	1½	23⅞	17¼	28½	21	1652	28½	27¼	27¾	2.5	15	21.7	13.6	17.7
15	ALGEF	**ABN AMRO Holdings N.V.**[54]	Am	NR	..	...	Bank'g operations,Netherlands	73¾	30¾	73¾	54	73¼	53⅜	....	73¼	69¾	73⅛	4.0	..	...	...	...
16	ABRX	✓**ABR Information Services**	NNM	NR	40	2469	Healthcare benefits svcs	....	....	13½	6½	44	12	5442	44	33	44	...	..	245	...	...
17	ABRI	✓**Abrams Industries**	NNM	B+	13	575	Construct'n/mfg, real estate	7¾	¾	7⅞	4¼	5⅜	3⅞	146	5⅛	4⅜	4⅝B	2.6	d	5.5	7.3	12.6
18	ABTC	✓**ABT Building Products**	NNM	NR	54	3933	Mfr special build'g products	26½	15	30	11⅞	19¾	12	5166	15¼	14	14¼	...	9	9.6	...	...
19	ACLE	✓**Accel Intl**	NNM	C	13	895	Insurance:credit life/disab	14⅜	1 11/16	6	1¾	4⅞	1¾	2041	3	2⅜	2¾	...	46	37.5	−5.4	−17.2
20	AIF	✓**Acceptance Insur Cos**	NY,B,Ch,P,Ph	B−	65	5320	Hldg co: prop & casualty insur	54⅝	6	18	11⅛	17½	13⅛	6423	15½	14½	14⅞	...	30	1.7	15.6	−0.2
21	ACCS	✓**Access Health**	NNM	NR	35	2025	Healthcare ind market'g svcs	12⅛	2⅞	22⅜	7½	45½	14¼	50707	45½	32¼	44¼	...	..	149	102	...
22•[6]	AKLM	✓**Acclaim Entertainment**	NNM	NR	132	30238	Dvlp video game cartridges	31¾	1 15/16	27¼	12⅞	28⅝	10¾	434482	21¼	10¾	12⅜	...	14	−15.7	2.7	28.7
23	ACMM	✓**Accom Inc**	NNM	NR	21	715	Dgn/mfr digital video sys	....	....	....	....	9¾	6¼	5987	7⅝	6¼	6½	...	d	...	...	...
24	ASTF	✓**AccuStaff Inc**	NNM	NR	82	9484	Temporary personnel service	....	....	7⅜	5¼	44¼	6¾	44751	44¼	31¼	44	...	77	542	...	...
25	ACL	✓**ACE Limited**	NY,Ph	NR	..	...	Provides liability insurance	36	25½	31	20¾	40	21⅞	25505	40	35⅝	39¾	1.4	8	80.8	...	...
26	ACET	✓**Aceto Corp**	NNM	B+	46	2809	Mfrs & dstr chemicals	15⅞	5/16	15⅞	12	16⅜	12¼	1812	16⅜	15	16	2.3	11	36.3	5.0	21.9
27	AK	✓**Ackerley Communications**	AS	B−	27	1745	Brdcstg:pro basketball:adv	12	1¼	8⅜	5⅜	15⅞	6½	1171	15⅝	15	15¼	...	25	135	89.5	42.3
28	AMT	✓**Acme-Cleveland**	NY,Ch,Ph	B	93	4497	Mfr indus & telecom prod	35⅝	4½	15½	8¾	29¼	10¼	15930	23	15⅞	18¾	2.6	3	84.9	37.6	38.3
29	ACE	✓**Acme Electric**	NY	C	19	581	Pwr conv eq: transformers	11⅜	⅜	14	6½	38¾	7⅜	7454	9⅜	7⅝	9⅛	...	76	−29.8	15.0	12.8
✜30	ACME	✓**Acme Metals**	NNM	B−	78	6195	Producer steel/steel prod	26½	8	27¼	15	19¼	13¾	6610	16¾	13¾	14¼	...	6	−24.0	5.2	1.5
31	ACU	✓**Acme United**	AS,Ch	C	17	789	Medic eq:shears,scissors	19½	1⅜	4¼	2¾	4¼	2¾	1087	4	3¼	3⅞	...	..	19.2	−12.0	−3.5
32	ACO	✓**Acordia Inc**	NY,Ph	NR	45	3746	Hldg co:insurance brokerage	27⅝	14½	33½	23	34½	23½	744	29⅞	27⅞	29¾	2.4	16	−7.7	16.3	...
33	ACRO	**Acrodyne Communications**	NSC	NR	1	85	Dvlp,mfr transmitter equip	....	....	....	....	5⅜	1⅞	1745	4⅝	4⅛	4⅛	...	..	...	...	...
34	ACTM	✓**ACT Manufacturing**	NNM	NR	35	2115	Mfr electronic equip	....	....	....	....	19¾	9⅛	17090	15	9⅛	11⅛	...	17	...	...	...
35	ANET	✓**ACT Networks**	NNM	NR	35	2539	Mfr data commun ntwk prd	....	....	....	....	22½	5¾	39825	16¾	10⅜	15⅞	...	93	...	...	...
36•[7]	ACTL	✓**Actel Corp**	NNM	NR	87	8698	Dvlp programmable gate arrays	20½	9	14½	7¼	21	8	54120	14⅛	10½	10¾	...	d	32.3	...	...
37	ACZ	✓**Action Indus**	AS,B	C	10	949	Merchandising programs	18¼	½	3	1⅝	2⅛	7/16	3715	13/16	½	⅝	...	d	−67.7	−42.3	−27.5
38	ACVC	✓**Active Voice**	NNM	NR	45	1977	Mfr voice messaging softwr sys	20	15	24¾	15⅞	33	19⅝	4407	27½	24¼	27½	...	22	31.7	...	...
#39•[8]	ACN	✓**Acuson Corp**	NY	B	107	13911	Medical ultrasound imaging	40	5	18⅜	11¼	16¾	10⅛	12164	12⅞	11¼	12⅜	...	50	−23.8	−8.0	−14.2
40	ACX	✓**ACX Technologies**	NY,Ch	NR	89	8077	Mfr packag'g ceramic,alum'n pd	23⅜	5⅜	20⅜	15⅝	31⅜	13¾	20004	16⅝	13⅞	15⅛	...	14	−21.7	11.3	...
✜41	ACXM	✓**Acxiom Corp**	NNM	B+	93	10261	Computer-based mkting svcs	12⅛	2	15	9¼	32⅛	13⅝	27080	32⅛	25	27⅜	...	44	97.6	43.0	52.7
✜42	ADAC	✓**ADAC Laboratories**	NNM	B	63	8912	Nuclear medicine comput sys	82⅛	1½	14⅛	6⅛	13¾	7¼	12659	12¾	10¼	12⅛	4.0	19	64.5	−2.7	32.6
43	ADAM	**A.D.A.M. Software**	NNM	NR	1	388	Dvlp eductational softwr prd	....	....	....	....	14⅛	4⅜	19963	11½	4⅜	6½	...	d	...	...	...
44	AE	✓**Adams Res & Energy**	AS,B,Ch,Ph	B−	10	393	Oil&gas explor,dev,prod'n	70½	1¾	10¾	4⅜	10	4⅞	476	7⅜	5¾	7⅛	0.7	17	−27.2	11.1	26.2
45•[9]	ADPT	✓**Adaptec Inc**	NNM	B	320	43247	Mfr computer data flow sys	20	1⅛	24⅜	14	48⅜	21¾	207243	48⅜	37	41	...	20	79.2	49.2	78.4
#46•[10]	ADCT	✓**ADC Telecommunications**	NNM	B	292	49518	Telecommunications equip	22	1/32	25⅜	15⅞	49⅜	22⅝	99587	45¼	33¼	36½	...	39	46.0	48.1	43.8
✜47	ADDR	✓**Addington Resources**	NNM	C	65	8941	Mining,mkt bituminous coal	23	6	19¾	8	15½	8	4940	15⅛	13	14⅝	...	d	50.0	2.1	6.9
48	ADEX	✓**ADE Corp**	NNM	NR	..	...	Mfr semiconductor mfg eqp	....	....	....	....	18½	12	10674	16½	12	14½	...	15	...	...	...
49	AFLX	✓**ADFlex Solutions**	NNM	NR	53	5095	Flex-based interconnects	....	....	21¾	13½	31¼	16	4801	28½	25¾	26¾	...	20	56.2	...	...
50	PVD	**Administradora de Fondos ADS**[59]	[11]NY	NR	29	3343	Pension fund administ'r/Chile	....	....	19¾	18⅛	28¾	12¾	2665	27⅝	23⅜	27⅝	3.3	19	55.4	...	...
#51•[8]	ADBE	✓**Adobe Systems**	NNM,Ch	B	344	56727	Print,graphic software sys	37	1 7/16	38½	20½	74¼	27¼	337458	74¼	57	62	0.3	30	108	61.6	34.4
52•[2]	ADT	**ADT Limited**	NY,Ch,Ph	B−	137	78056	Security svcs/auctions	10⅜	5	11⅞	8½	15¼	9⅝	76839	15	13	15	...	18	41.2	24.6	...

Uniform Footnote Explanations-See Page 4. Other: [1]CBOE. [2]CBOE:Cycle 3. [3]Ph:Cycle 1. [4]Ph:Cycle 2. [5]CBOE,To:Cycle 1. [6]CBOE:Cycle 1. [7]P,Ph:Cycle 3. [8]P:Cycle 1. [9]ASE:Cycle 1. [10]P:Cycle 2. [11]Ph [51]Average of issues in index. [52]Rates from S&P monthly Earnings Guide. [53]1986 & prior prices in Canadian. [54]All data reported in Netherlands Guilder. [55]Approx. [56]®$1.68,'94. [57]Redemption of stk purch rt. [58]To be determined. [59]Ea ADS rep 1 com, no par. [60]Pfd in $M.

Splits ◆ Index	Cash Divs. Ea. Yr. Since	Dividends: Latest Payment Period $	Date	Ex. Div.	Total $ So Far 1995	Ind. Rate	Paid 1994	Financial Position Mil-$ Cash& Equiv.	Curr. Assets	Curr. Liab.	Balance Sheet Date	Capitalization Lg Trm Debt Mil-$	Shs. 000 Pfd.	Com.	Earnings $ Per Shr. Years End	1991	1992	1993	1994	1995	Last 12 Mos.	Interim Earnings Period	$ per Shr. 1994	1995	Index
1	....	....			2.856	2.91	....	Avg 5 yr proj growth:[51]14%[52]				.....	...	...	Dc	...	...	...	...	E8.44	....				1
2	....	....			13.788	14.19	13.18	Avg 5 yr proj growth:[51]12%[52]				.....	...	...	Dc	15.91	19.09	21.89	30.60	E36.65	35.15	12 Mo Sep	27.33	35.15	2
3	....	....			3.601	3.69	3.55	Avg 5 yr proj growth:[51]14%[52]				.....	...	...	Dc	6.14	7.06	7.91	9.73	E11.82	10.66	12 Mo Sep	9.27	10.66	3
4	....	....			1.132	1.19	1.08	Avg 5 yr proj growth:[51]16%[52]				.....	...	...	Dc	0.97	2.96	2.39	3.69	E5.06	4.20	12 Mo Sep	2.63	4.20	4
5	....	None Since Public			...	Nil	....	0.65	9.86	10.5	6-30-95	18.9	...	p10263	Dc	...	pd0.15	□d0.35	d0.68	....	d1.72	9 Mo Sep	d0.34	d1.38	5
6◆	1992	Q0.075	11-21-95	11-8	0.30	0.30	0.30	Equity per shr $9.56			9-30-95	23.1	...	8907	Je	p0.74	0.76	1.13	0.91	1.67	1.82	3 Mo Sep	0.37	0.52	6
7◆	....	None Paid			...	Nil	....	0.03	21.7	8.52	9-30-95	10.7	...	6113	Dc	0.07	0.25	0.44	0.81	....	0.52	9 Mo Sep	0.61	0.32	7
8	1973	Q0.12	12-5-95	10-27	0.48	0.48	0.48	28.6	311	59.5	8-31-95	119	...	15959	My	0.93	0.63	0.02	Δ□0.60	0.66	0.83	6 Mo Nov	0.26	0.43	8
9	....	None Since Public			...	Nil	....	10.7	12.3	1.58	9-30-95	.....	...	9797	Mr	d1.46	d1.30	d1.43	d1.24	....	d0.68	6 Mo Sep	d0.89	d0.33	9
10◆	1926	Q0.21	2-15-96	1-10	0.82	0.84	0.74	415	4077	3567	9-30-95	435	...	790444	Dc	Δ□1.27	1.47	1.69	1.87	E2.15	2.06	9 Mo Sep	1.34	1.53	10
11	....	None Since Public			...	Nil	....	....	73.6	39.7	10-31-95	50.5	...	7983	Jl	...	...	p0.72	□1.05	□1.46	1.48	3 Mo Oct	□0.25	0.27	11
12	....	None Since Public			...	Nil	....	9.82	13.7	1.93	9-30-95	.....	...	±6942	Mr	d0.79	±d0.60	±d0.31	±d0.05	....	0.02	6 Mo Sep	±d0.05	±0.02	12
13	1949	g0.10	1-2-96	11-24	g0.20	Nil	....	250	605	381	j12-31-94	479	977	p75715	Dc	d1.12	d3.19	d1.71	d0.66	....	j2.24	9 Mo Sep	d0.74	2.16	13
14◆	1965	Q0.17½	2-5-96	1-10	0.60	0.70	0.51½	1.04	199	102	7-31-95	31.2	6	9283	Oc	1.36	1.43	1.45	1.65	P1.85	1.85				14
15	....	[55]0.701		5-2	...	2.95	[55]0.701	Book Value $54.75			j12-31-93	19697	382503	293423	Dc	5.22	5.51	6.34	....	....	j6.34				15
16◆	....	None Since Public			...	Nil	....	24.2	27.2	13.1	7-31-95	.....	...	6532	Jl	*0.01	*0.16	0.21	0.33	0.40	0.44	3 Mo Oct	0.09	0.13	16
17	1960	Q0.03	1-3-96	12-7	0.12	0.12	0.12	5.67	30.0	19.4	10-31-95	50.7	...	2971	Ap	0.34	0.34	Δ0.42	0.46	d0.11	d0.16	6 Mo Oct	d0.01	d0.06	17
18	....	None Since Public			...	Nil	....	1.76	87.3	23.6	9-30-95	88.0	...	10604	Dc	...	p0.66	□1.50	1.70	....	1.60	9 Mo Sep	1.34	1.24	18
19	....	0.07	5-1-92	3-26	...	Nil	....	Equity per shr $4.78			9-30-95	18.7	...	4446	Dc	0.23	□d4.29	d1.19	d1.18	....	0.06	9 Mo Sep	d1.05	0.19	19
20◆	....	5%Stk	12-17-84	11-26	...	Nil	....	Equity per shr $8.80			9-30-95	49.0	...	15101	Dc	Δd12.76	d0.26	0.86	[56]1.71	....	0.49	9 Mo Sep	1.12	d0.10	20
21	....	None Since Public			...	Nil	....	11.7	18.9	8.70	9-30-95	0.40	...	★8101	Sp	0.21	0.24	0.20	d0.36	0.21	0.21				21
22◆	....	None Since Public			...	Nil	....	71.3	326	126	8-31-95	0.41	...	49700	Au	d0.21	0.37	0.63	1.00	0.86	0.86				22
23	....	None Since Public			...	Nil	....	0.41	10.2	5.70	6-30-95	0.10	p...	★6386	Sp	...	...	...	d0.20	Pd4.17	d4.17				23
24◆	....	None Since Public			...	Nil	....	3.62	31.1	24.3	10-01-95	p1.62	...	★15914	Dc	...	...	p0.13	0.35	....	0.57	9 Mo Sep	0.24	0.46	24
25	1993	Q0.14	1-19-96	12-27	0.50	0.56	0.42	Equity per shr $29.28			6-30-95	.....	...	46144	Sp	...	p0.21	p4.49	d0.95	P5.05	5.05				25
26◆	1985	S0.18	1-2-96	12-14	0.327	0.36	0.291	15.4	72.1	21.1	9-30-95	1.25	328	5293	Je	0.88	1.05	0.33	1.24	1.38	1.41	3 Mo Sep	0.19	0.22	26
27	1995	0.03	3-15-95	2-23	0.03	Nil	....	3.12	56.2	50.6	9-30-95	219	...	±15567	Dc	±d2.54	±0.21	□±0.19	±□0.57	....	0.62	9 Mo Sep	±0.28	±0.33	27
28	1936	Q0.12	11-17-95	11-1	0.48	0.48	0.44	44.7	96.0	46.3	9-30-95	0.69	161	6405	Sp	d0.52	*0.53	*0.77	□0.98	6.30	6.30				28
29	....	0.08	12-3-90	11-5	...	Nil	....	0.02	41.5	12.7	9-29-95	27.2	...	5004	Je	d1.60	0.13	Δd0.14	d1.17	0.20	0.12	3 Mo Sep	0.15	0.07	29
30	....	[57]0.02	4-6-92	3-10	...	Nil	....	204	336	117	6-25-95	271	...	11581	Dc	d0.43	□d0.53	1.15	□2.38	....	2.59	9 Mo Sep	□1.69	1.90	30
31	1990	0.05	3-5-93	2-8	...	Nil	....	0.18	33.0	10.6	9-30-95	15.2	...	3338	Dc	0.41	d0.16	d0.18	0.04	....	0.01	9 Mo Sep	0.03	Nil	31
32	1992	Q0.18	12-15-95	11-29	0.72	0.72	0.60	82.7	256	295	9-30-95	116	...	13951	Dc	1.41	1.53	□1.98	2.04	....	1.84	9 Mo Sep	1.32	1.12	32
33	....	None Since Public			...	Nil	....	0.74	3.64	2.37	9-30-95	1.00	...	2385	Dc	...	...	p0.01	pd0.32	....	....	9 Mo Sep	n/a	d0.09	33
34	....	None Since Public			...	Nil	....	10.8	49.7	19.7	9-30-95	0.39	...	8663	Dc	...	...	...	p0.65	....	0.66	9 Mo Sep	p0.44	p0.45	34
35	....	None Since Public			...	Nil	....	30.5	40.8	2.58	6-30-95	.....	...	7140	Je	0.43	0.01	d0.52	0.05	0.24	0.17	3 Mo Sep	0.04	d0.03	35
36	....	None Since Public			...	Nil	....	18.4	57.3	26.3	4-02-95	0.06	...	17292	Dc	...	pd0.02	p0.32	0.45	....	d0.16	9 Mo Sep	0.32	d0.29	36
37	....	0.06	6-15-87	5-26	...	Nil	....	1.10	28.2	16.6	9-30-95	7.62	...	5539	Je	0.44	0.44	d2.60	0.02	d0.67	d0.83	3 Mo Sep	d0.06	d0.22	37
38	....	None Since Public			...	Nil	....	8.26	21.5	3.52	9-30-95	.....	...	4526	Mr	0.38	0.42	0.88	1.11	....	1.24	6 Mo Sep	0.51	0.64	38
39	....	None Since Public			...	Nil	....	61.8	228	101	9-30-95	.....	...	27878	Dc	1.59	1.08	0.13	0.62	E0.25	0.31	9 Mo Sep	0.49	0.18	39
40◆	....	None Since Public			...	Nil	....	16.6	312	135	3-31-95	130	...	26774	Dc	...	□d0.85	0.51	0.76	....	1.12	9 Mo Sep	0.56	0.92	40
41◆	....	None Since Public			...	Nil	....	1.59	45.2	27.4	9-30-95	29.3	...	23491	Mr	0.11	0.30	0.38	0.54	....	0.63	6 Mo Sep	0.19	0.28	41
42◆	1992	Q0.12	1-8-96	12-27	0.48	0.48	0.48	5.53	108	53.8	7-02-95	.....	...	16512	Sp	0.06	0.81	1.10	1.06	P0.65	0.65				42
43	....	None Since Public			...	Nil	....	2.44	4.20	3.46	9-30-95	p....	p...	★5195	Mr	d0.98	d1.26	d1.14	d1.10	....	d0.94	6 Mo Sep	d0.62	d0.46	43
44◆	....	0.05	12-15-95	11-29	0.05	[58]0.05	0.03	2.41	60.6	56.4	9-30-95	10.4	...	4198	Dc	0.45	Δ0.18	0.36	0.72	....	0.42	9 Mo Sep	0.57	0.27	44
45◆	....	None Since Public			...	Nil	....	270	405	75.5	9-29-95	5.95	...	52448	Mr	0.35	0.95	1.10	1.75	E2.10	1.67	6 Mo Sep	0.67	0.59	45
46◆	....	None Since Public			...	Nil	....	226	409	67.6	7-31-95	.....	...	62609	Oc	0.41	0.39	0.58	□0.73	P0.94	0.94				46
47	....	None Since Public			...	Nil	....	1.62	16.4	23.5	9-30-95	35.4	...	14967	Dc	□d0.41	0.72	d1.04	d0.45	....	d1.23	9 Mo Sep	d0.47	d1.25	47
48	....	None Since Public			...	Nil	....	3.37	23.9	7.75	7-31-95	0.08	...	★7237	Ap	0.27	0.09	0.08	0.01	0.53	0.97	6 Mo Oct	0.03	0.47	48
49	....	None Since Public			...	Nil	....	21.4	49.5	14.7	9-30-95	1.07	...	7002	Dc	...	...	p0.48	1.26	....	1.31	9 Mo Sep	0.99	1.04	49
50	1995	[55]0.305		10-5	[55]0.898	0.90	....	19.7	28.6	20.9	12-31-94	.....	...	16645	Dc	1.49	1.13	1.08	□1.46	....	1.46				50
51◆	1988	Q0.05	10-20-95	10-4	0.20	0.20	0.20	474	604	137	9-01-95	.....	...	63819	Nv	1.13	0.93	p1.02	0.10	E2.05	0.70	9 Mo Aug	0.88	1.48	51
52◆	....	Wrrt	4-24-92	4-27	...	Nil	....	228	567	522	6-30-95	838	[60]5	131645	Dc	□1.04	0.80	0.80	0.76	....	0.83	9 Mo Sep	0.56	0.63	52

◆Stock Splits & Divs By Line Reference Index [6]4-for-3,'93. [7]1-for-4 REVERSE,'93:10%,'95. [10]2-for-1,'92. [14]2-for-1,'92. [16]3-for-2,'95. [20]1-for-4 REVERSE,'92. [22]3-for-2,'93. [24]2-for-1,'95. [26]6-for-5,'92:10%,'91,'95. [40]2-for-1,'95. [41]2-for-1,'92,'95. [42]1-for-3 REVERSE,'93. [44]1-for-2 REVERSE,'92. [45]2-for-1,'92,'94. [46]2-for-1,'93,'95. [51]2-for-1,'93. [52]1-for-10 REVERSE,'91.

¶ S&P 500
# MidCap 400
✤ SmallCap 600
• Options

Index	Ticker	Name of Issue (Call Price of Pfd. Stocks)	Market	Com. Rank. & Pfd. Rating	Inst. Hold Cos	Inst. Hold Shs. (000)	Principal Business	Price Range 1971-93 High	1971-93 Low	1994 High	1994 Low	1995 High	1995 Low	Dec. Sales in 100s	December, 1995 Last Sale Or Bid High	Low	Last	%Div Yield	P-E Ratio	Total Return % Annualized 12 Mo	36 Mo	60 Mo
1	ADTN	✔Adtran Inc	NNM	NR	44	4269	Dgn/svc digital transmision prd	...	...	23⅜	9	55½	20	30131	55½	44	54¼	...	78	146	...	...
2	AROS	✔Advance Ross[51]	NNM	B	44	2863	Oper value added tax refund sy	9⅜	3/16	15⅛	7⅜	29½	8⅝	4459	29⅛	24½	28⅛	...	27	189	101	62.9
3	AEIS	Advanced Energy Industries	NNM	NR	..	...	Thin film production eqp	...	...	...	...	11	8¼	17452	11	8¼	9	...	15	...	...	...
4	AVF	✔Advanced Financial	AS	NR	7	99	Mortgage banking services	6⅛	5/16	4⅛	1 1/16	1¾	9/16	1772	15/16	9/16	⅝	...	d	−44.4	−46.1	...
5	AVM	✔Advanced Magnetics	AS	↑B−	20	820	Mfr medical diagnostic prd	31¼	2⅞	17½	11½	29½	14¼	782	26⅝	24	26⅝	...	83	90.2	26.6	23.5
6	ADMS	✔Advanced Marketing Svcs	NNM	B−	21	1382	Warehouse club book supplier	18	1	7	4	10⅞	5¼	4484	10⅝	8¾	10¼	...	12	74.5	17.9	37.0
7	ADMG	✔Advanced Matls Group	NSC	NR	1	49	Mfr ind'l use foam products	8¼	3⅛	4⅝	9/16	1 7/16	¼	12326	1⅛	7/16	¾	...	d	0.0	...	...
8	AMA	✔Advanced Medical Inc	AS,Ch	NR	17	3194	Mfr infusion pumps/drug R&D	19¼	⅞	2⅞	⅜	4	1¾	10010	3¼	2¾	3	...	7	71.4	−31.3	−16.2
¶9•[1]	AMD	✔Advanced Micro Dev	NY,B,Ch,Ph	B−	402	56017	Major semiconductor mfr	41⅛	⅛	31¾	16¾	39¼	16⅛	311684	20⅝	16⅛	16½	...	6	−33.3	−2.6	28.3
10	API	✔Advanced Photonix'A'	AS	NR	6	1133	Dvlp radiation detection prd	10	3¼	4⅛	⅞	3	⅞	3139	3	2	2¾	...	d	76.1	−21.8	...
11	APOS	✔Advanced Polymer Sys	NNM	C	25	4316	Polymer-based delivery sys	16⅛	2	7¾	3⅝	8⅜	4	19103	6	4⅞	5½	...	d	24.0	−12.2	19.6
12	ASMIF	Advanced Semi Mat's	NNM	C	20	2627	Eq to mfr semicond devices	38¼	⅝	5	1⅝	61¼	4⅛	11106	54	47¼	49¼	...	16	1059	259	89.8
#13•[2]	ATLI	✔Advanced Technology Labs	NNM	C	109	9571	Medical ultrasound systems	63	12¾	19½	12½	28½	13	45765	28½	21	24½	...	d	38.0	...	...
14	ATMI	✔Advanced Technology Matr'l	NNM	NR	15	1492	Dvlp diamond semiconductors	7	5¾	7¼	4¼	16	5⅛	9189	10⅜	9½	10	...	..	73.9	...	...
15	ATH	Advanced Therapeutic Sys	AS	NR	..	...	Dvlp stge:pharmaceutical R&D	...	...	...	...	29	26½	2316	27⅞	26½	26¾	...	d	...	...	...
✤16•[3]	ATIS	✔Advanced Tissue Sci	NNM	NR	61	5864	Dvlp stage:cell technology	19¼	1¼	9½	4¼	15	5½	65809	12¼	8⅜	10⅛	...	d	22.7	−6.8	20.8
17•[4]	ADVNA	✔ADVANTA Corp Cl'A'	NNM	B	135	9166	Mkts consumer fin'l prod	46¾	13/16	41¾	24¼	48⅞	25½	19080	44	37½	38¼	0.9	13	38.9	22.7	63.4
18•[5]	ADVNB	✔ Cl'B'	NNM	B	147	15449		38½	7¾	37½	23¼	45	24½	25993	41½	35¾	36⅜	1.2	12	37.3	24.8	...
19	ADHC	✔Advantage Health[60]	NNM	NR	53	3112	Oper rehab ctrs,New England	20¾	8½	35	14	46¼	22¾	18678	46¼	33	43⅝	...	27	39.6	30.2	...
20	ADVS	Advent Software	NNM	NR	..	...	Invest mgmt software	...	...	...	...	24¾	14	16594	21	14	17¾	...	54	...	...	...
21	ADV	✔Advest Group	NY,B,Ch,Ph	B−	20	1425	Fin'l services hldg co	16¾	1⅝	6⅞	5	9¾	5	1438	9¼	8½	8½	...	12	65.9	14.8	29.0
✤22	AD	✔ADVO Inc	NY,Ph	B	111	14911	Direct mail advertis'g svcs	24¾	3	20	15	27½	16½	19396	27⅛	24⅞	26	0.4	23	53.7	9.0	22.7
23	AVC	✔Advocat Inc	NY,Ch	NR	47	4921	Oper nursing hmes&retire't ctrs	...	...	13½	8¼	13⅞	9½	2242	11½	10⅛	11⅛	...	12	−14.4	...	...
24	AEG	✔AEGON N.V. Ord[62]	NY,Ph	NR	52	3801	Life/health ins, invest prods	23⅜	5	25⅝	19¾	44¾	25½	3393	44¾	40⅞	44	2.5	16	80.3	44.0	36.0
25	AELNA	✔AEL Indus Cl'A'[64]	NNM	B−	17	429	Gov't defense electronics	19⅝	3/16	10	7	28⅛	8¾	1451	28⅛	26¾	27⅞	...	..	210	58.5	46.5
26	AEPI	✔AEP Industries	NNM	B	41	1987	Mfrs plastic film products	14⅛	2¾	21	11½	27¼	16¾	927	23¾	22	22	...	11	26.3	41.7	30.8
27	ARX	✔Aeroflex Inc	NY,Ch,Ph	B−	26	2589	Mfr military/ind'l products	14⅛	1/16	5	3⅜	5⅞	3⅜	6176	4½	3⅞	4¼	...	8	17.2	31.4	25.3
28	AIM	✔Aerosonic Corp	AS	B−	10	144	Mfg,overhaul aircraft instr	12⅜	1/16	3⅛	1⅞	2½	1 5/16	719	1 11/16	1 5/16	1 5/16	...	d	−34.4	−20.0	4.3
29	ARVX	✔Aerovox Inc	NNM	NR	34	1857	Mfr AC/DC pwr capacitors	12¼	2⅛	11	6¼	8⅞	5⅜	4788	6⅛	5⅝	5⅞	...	39	−19.0	0.7	18.6
30	CHGNF	AES China Generating'A'	NNM	NR	..	...	Dvlp stg:elec pwr plants china	...	...	17¼	8⅞	10¾	7½	8738	8⅝	7½	8	...	..	−21.0	...	...
#31	AESC	✔AES Corp	NNM	NR	135	28393	Oper pwr generat'g facilities	24⅜	10⅝	23¾	15¾	24	16	28647	24	20¼	23⅞	...	17	20.9	12.8	...
¶32•[5]	AET	✔Aetna Life & Casualty	NY,B,C,Ch,P,Ph	B−	584	89908	Multiline insurance business	68¼	10⅛	65¾	42¼	76¾	46¾	118351	73¾	68	69¼	4.0	28	53.3	19.9	18.3
33	ATRM	✔Aetrium Inc	NNM	NR	35	4858	Mfr integrated circuit mfr eq	8	5⅝	8⅝	5⅞	25¼	6⅝	28606	22	15¾	20	...	54	161	...	...
34	ACSA	✔Affiliated Computer Services'A'	NNM	NR	50	3508	Information processing svc	...	...	23½	16	38½	19¾	7690	38½	31½	37½	...	26	74.4	...	...
#35•[6]	AFL	✔AFLAC Inc	NY,B,Ch,P,Ph	A	365	48954	Insurance & broadcasting	34	5/16	36⅛	25¼	44¾	31⅞	42540	43⅝	40⅝	43½	1.2	12	34.0	18.3	24.6
36	AFPC	✔AFP Imaging	NSC	C	4	51	X-ray film,paper process eq	11½	¼	⅞	7/16	2½	⅝	1381	1⅝	1¼	1 7/16	...	12	130	36.7	23.5
37	AGSV	✔Ag Services of America	NNM	NR	19	622	Svcs to agricultural ind	10⅛	3¾	10½	6½	10	7¼	1032	9½	8⅛	9½	...	12	31.0	6.1	...
✤38•[7]	AG	✔AGCO Corp	NY,Ph	NR	219	22382	Mfr/dstr farm equipment	22⅞	3⅜	36¾	21½	54⅝	24¾	31289	52	43	51	0.1	8	70.2	94.1	...
39•	AEM	Agnico Eagle Mines	NY,To,Ch,Mo,Ph	B−	87	11864	Silver & gold mining prop	34¼	1⅝	14¾	8¼	14½	8⅞	12129	13	12¼	12½	0.8	..	17.4	44.6	17.3
40•[8]	AGPH	✔Agouron Pharmaceuticals	NNM	C	63	4328	Drugs for cancer and AIDS	24	3¼	16¾	9½	39¼	10⅞	35279	35⅞	28¼	32¾	...	d	185	36.1	40.4
41	ADC	✔Agree Realty	NY,Ch	NR	17	226	Real estate investment trust	...	...	19⅝	14⅝	17⅜	13½	2040	16½	14¼	14⅝	12.3	12	5.3	...	...
42	AHIS	✔AHI Healthcare Sys	NNM	NR	32	1448	Manage hlth care networks	...	...	...	...	16	5½	46368	13½	5½	5¾	...	d	...	...	...
¶43•[5]	AHM	✔Ahmanson (H F) & Co	NY,B,Ch,Ph,P	B	410	112031	Svg&Loan:Calif,Tx,FL,IL,NY	28¾	1⅞	22¾	15¼	28⅜	16	88458	28	25¾	26½	3.3	8	68.3	19.7	20.1
44	Pr D	6% cm Cv[71]Dep Pfd([72]51.50)	NY	BBB−	49	3538		51¾	47⅛	52	39¾	61⅜	40½	1602	61⅜	58½	59⅛	5.1	..	...	...	...
45	AHO	✔Ahold Ltd ADR[73]	NY,Ch	NR	43	1736	Retail food,Netherlands & U.S.	27⅜	19¼	30¾	24	41⅛	29⅝	2312	41⅛	39¼	41⅛	1.8	19	36.9	20.9	...
46	AHLN	Ahold nv[75]	Am	NR	30	1398	Retail food,Netherlands & U.S.	49⅞	10⅝	54	42¾	66	50¼	....	66	62¾	65½	1.2	..	...	...	...
47	ATS	✔Air-Cure Technologies	AS	NR	10	259	Design air pollut'n ctrl sys	10⅝	4	4⅞	2⅛	4¾	1¾	2910	4	3¼	3⅝	...	23	56.8	−10.2	−7.1
✤48	AEIC	✔Air Express Intl	NNM,Ch	B+	133	12944	Air freight forwarding	19⅝	1/32	20	12¼	26½	18½	11363	24⅜	22¼	23	0.9	15	18.9	10.8	38.8
¶49•[9]	APD	✔Air Products & Chem	NY,B,Ch,P,Ph	A	629	89858	Indust'l gases,eq,chemicals	49½	2 7/16	50⅜	38¾	59⅝	43⅞	58478	57½	51	52¾	2.0	16	22.3	7.5	16.2
#50	AWT	✔Air & Water Tech'A'	AS,Ph	NR	84	16525	Water/enviro treatm't svcs	30⅜	7¾	14¾	5¼	6⅞	4	6934	6⅜	5⅜	6⅛	...	d	4.3	−18.9	−19.8
#51•[10]	ABF	✔Airborne Freight	NY,B,Ch,P,Ph	B	152	18686	Int'l air express/freight	35¼	1 7/16	39⅞	18	29½	18⅜	21141	29¼	25	26⅝	1.1	27	33.3	15.3	10.7
52	AHT	✔AIRCOA Hotel Ptnrs L.P.'A'[81]	AS	NR	1	2	Own,oper hotel,resort prop	18⅝	¾	3⅝	2⅜	4⅛	1⅜	1376	2 3/16	1⅜	1 11/16	...	d	−43.8	19.0	−3.3

Uniform Footnote Explanations-See Page 4. Other: [1]P:Cycle 1. [2]Ph:Cycle 1. [3]P:Cycle 3. [4]ASE,CBOE:Cycle 1. [5]ASE:Cycle 1. [6]ASE:Cycle 2. [7]P:Cycle 2. [8]ASE,CBOE:Cycle 2. [9]Ph:Cycle 3. [10]CBOE:Cycle 2. [51]Vote Jan 10,CUC Int'l acq,0.833 com. [52]Fiscal Dec'91 & prior. [53]®$0.22,'94. [54]Spl div. [55]®$2.92,'94. [56]Stk dstr of SpaceLabs Inc,'92. [57]Excl special shares. [58]Fiscal Jan'92 & prior. [59]11 Mo Dec'92. [60]Healthsouth Corp plan acq,1.38-1.67 com. [61]®$0.71,'95. [62]Amer Reg Ctf. [63]In cash or stk. [64]Tracor Inc pian acq, $28. [65]®$0.55,'95. [66]®$1.36,'95. [67]®$0.12,'95. [68]®$0.60,'95. [69]®$4.70,'94. [70]Incl current amts. [71]Dep for 0.10 Cv 6% Ser'D'Pfd. [72]Fr 9-1-98. [73]Each ADR rep 1 com,NLG 1.25. [74]Incl $0.1596 in cash or stk,'94. [75]All data reported in Netherlands Guilder. [76]Fiscal Mar'93 & Prior. [77]12 Mo Dec'93. [78]®$1.21,'94. [79]Excl 10M shs held in trust. [80]®$1.74,'94. [81]Units.

Splits ◆ Index	Cash Divs. Ea.Yr. Since	Dividends Latest Payment Period $	Date	Ex. Div.	Total $ So Far 1995	Ind. Rate	Paid 1994	Financial Position Mil-$ Cash& Equiv.	Curr. Assets	Curr. Liab.	Balance Sheet Date	Capitalization Lg Trm Debt Mil-$	Shs. 000 Pfd.	Com.	Earnings $ Per Shr. Years End	1991	1992	1993	1994	1995	Last 12 Mos.	Interim Earnings Period	$ per Shr. 1994	1995	Index
1◆	....	None Since Public			...	Nil	....	60.2	128	10.8	9-30-95	20.0	...	37443	Dc	p0.19	p0.26	p0.25	p0.51	....	0.70	9 Mo Sep	p0.34	0.53	1
2◆	....	h....	11-27-64		...	Nil	....	19.6	53.1	24.5	9-30-95	7.26	17	7075	Dc	0.99	0.09	0.65	0.96	....	1.06	9 Mo Sep	0.66	0.76	2
3	....	None Since Public			...	Nil	....	0.73	33.7	17.5	9-30-95	p2.72	...	★21066	Dc	...	p0.01	p0.11	0.32	....	0.59	9 Mo Sep	0.29	0.56	3
4◆	....	None Paid			...	Nil	....	Equity per shr $0.53			9-30-95	13.3	372	3775	Mr	*[52]0.08	Δ0.33	Nil	d1.11	....	d1.05	6 Mo Sep	d0.46	d0.40	4
5◆	....	None Since Public			...	Nil	....	37.6	43.8	1.77	9-30-95	....	...	6754	Sp	d0.70	0.04	d0.36	0.13	Δ0.32	0.32				5
6	....	None Since Public			...	Nil	....	15.1	195	151	9-30-95	....	...	5410	Mr	0.34	0.53	0.03	0.60	....	0.83	6 Mo Sep	0.22	0.45	6
7	....	None Since Public			...	Nil	....	0.14	4.17	3.90	8-31-95	3.15	...	9174	Nv	...	...	d0.37	d0.31	....	d0.25	9 Mo Aug	d0.21	d0.15	7
8	....	None Since Public			...	Nil	....	6.87	49.2	22.3	9-30-95	63.2	333	16131	Dc	□d1.55	□d0.30	d0.29	[53]0.34	....	0.46	9 Mo Sep	0.20	Δ0.32	8
9	1995	[54]0.01	5-24-95	4-27	[54]0.01	Nil	....	493	1132	688	10-01-95	216	...	104270	Dc	1.53	2.57	2.30	[55]3.02	E2.75↓	2.71	9 Mo Sep	2.64	2.33	9
10	....	None Since Public			...	Nil	....	3.72	5.77	0.87	10-01-95	....	123	±10789	Mr	d0.77	d0.42	d0.55	d0.28	....	d0.19	6 Mo Sep	d0.13	d0.04	10
11	....	None Since Public			...	Nil	....	6.57	19.8	12.0	9-30-95	5.44	...	16580	Dc	d0.44	d0.45	d0.73	d0.65	....	d0.46	9 Mo Sep	d0.49	d0.30	11
12	....	None Since Public			...	Nil	....	45.1	259	221	j12-31-94	125	...	10571	Dc	0.64	d5.14	1.59	d0.51	....	3.00	9 Mo Sep	d0.78	2.73	12
13◆	....	h[56]....	6-26-92	6-29	...	Nil	....	16.1	239	96.6	9-29-95	15.8	...	13417	Dc	*2.09	0.67	d0.46	d1.53	....	d0.44	9 Mo Sep	d1.10	d0.01	13
14	....	None Since Public			...	Nil	....	11.2	18.7	6.28	9-30-95	3.28	...	★8690	Dc	pd0.22	pd0.29	pd0.18	0.35	....	0.01	9 Mo Sep	0.37	0.03	14
15	....	None Since Public			...	Nil	....	29.8	29.9	8.53	7-31-95	....	...	[57]3923	Jl	...	...	...	d6.22	d8.49	d8.49				15
16	....	None Since Public			...	Nil	....	22.5	24.3	5.35	9-30-95	0.03	...	33851	Dc	[58]d0.36	[59]d1.40	d0.67	d0.75	....	d0.70	9 Mo Sep	d0.58	d0.53	16
17◆	1989	Q0.09	12-19-95	11-29	0.291	0.36	0.217	Equity per shr $15.33			9-30-95	1104	★26	±41455	Dc	0.81	±1.39	□±1.95	±2.58	....	3.05	9 Mo Sep	±1.88	±2.35	17
18◆	1992	Q0.108	12-19-95	11-29	0.348	0.43	0.26	....	...	...		....	...	23977	Dc	0.81	±1.39	□±1.95	±2.58	....	3.05	9 Mo Sep	±1.88	±2.35	18
19	....	None Since Public			...	Nil	....	7.67	51.0	26.5	8-31-95	39.8	...	5650	Au	d0.51	□0.97	1.07	1.28	1.60	1.60				19
20	....	None Since Public			...	Nil	....	8.88	13.8	7.30	9-30-95	....	p...	★6619	Dc	0.16	0.14	0.24	0.17	....	0.33	9 Mo Sep	0.10	0.26	20
21	....	0.04	12-17-90	12-4	...	Nil	....	Equity per shr $8.66			9-30-95	37.8	...	8391	Sp	d0.70	d0.48	Δ0.56	0.34	[61]0.73	0.73				21
22◆	1993	Q0.02½	1-12-96	12-22	0.10	0.10	0.09½	54.5	156	96.8	9-30-95	....	...	20824	Sp	0.85	0.89	0.21	1.05	□1.14	1.14				22
23	....	None Since Public			...	Nil	....	1.15	22.6	14.5	9-30-95	7.26	...	5288	Dc	...	...	p0.65	p0.80	E0.97	0.91	9 Mo Sep	p0.56	0.67	23
24◆	1987	[63]0.33	10-4-95	9-13	[63]1.079	1.08	[63]0.778	1335	3793	8354	12-31-94	6093	32000	258980	Dc	1.93	2.09	2.15	2.47	....	2.68	9 Mo Sep	2.02	2.23	24
25	....	5%Stk	8-24-79	7-23	...	Nil	....	0.71	53.7	25.4	8-25-95	12.3	...	±4038	Fb	*2.69	±Δd0.52	±0.43	±0.46	....	0.10	9 Mo Nov	±0.34	±d0.02	25
26◆	1993	0.02½	10-6-95	9-20	0.09½	Nil	0.076	2.11	48.4	24.7	7-31-95	30.5	...	p4795	Oc	0.49	0.49	□1.01	1.55	P□1.99	1.99				26
27	....	5%Stk	5-27-86	5-7	...	Nil	....	12.2	43.4	10.6	9-30-95	11.8	...	11883	Je	d0.29	*0.09	0.26	0.57	[65]0.57	0.56	3 Mo Sep	0.06	0.05	27
28	....	0.00¾	2-25-77	2-24	...	Nil	....	0.04	10.4	3.63	10-31-95	2.99	...	3792	Ja	0.41	Δ0.44	0.23	d0.06	....	d0.33	9 Mo Oct	0.19	d0.08	28
29	....	None Since Public			...	Nil	....	0.42	45.0	17.9	9-30-95	25.0	...	5297	Dc	0.03	0.32	Δ0.57	0.56	....	0.15	9 Mo Sep	0.69	0.28	29
30	....	None Since Public			...	Nil	....	Equity per shr $11.36			12-29-93	....	...	★17500	Nv	...	...	...	....	....	....				30
31◆	1988	3%Stk	3-28-94	3-4	...	Nil	3%Stk	285	429	187	6-30-95	1136	...	75047	Dc	0.66	0.80	0.98	Δ1.30	....	1.39	9 Mo Sep	Δ0.95	1.04	31
32	1934	Q0.69	2-15-96	1-24	2.76	2.76	2.76	Equity per shr $60.36			9-30-95	1121	...	114315	Dc	4.59	□1.53	□d5.30	4.14	E2.50	2.08	9 Mo Sep	2.73	0.67	32
33◆	....	None Since Public			...	Nil	....	11.7	29.3	6.32	9-30-95	....	...	★8121	Dc	...	0.23	Δ0.53	0.17	....	0.37	9 Mo Sep	0.48	0.68	33
34	....	None Since Public			...	Nil	....	33.9	110	66.8	9-30-95	51.8	...	±13383	Je	0.42	0.52	0.84	1.08	[66]1.37	1.45	3 Mo Sep	0.33	0.41	34
35◆	1973	Q0.13	12-1-95	11-15	0.505	0.52	0.44½	Equity per shr $20.62			9-30-95	352	...	94753	Dc	1.46	1.75	Δ2.32	2.84	E3.50	3.40	9 Mo Sep	2.08	2.64	35
36	....	None Since Public			...	Nil	....	0.10	12.8	4.15	9-30-95	6.53	416	6535	Je	d0.25	d0.11	d0.26	d0.71	[67]0.13	0.12	3 Mo Sep	0.02	0.01	36
37◆	....	None Since Public			...	Nil	....	0.53	101	79.4	8-31-95	13.8	...	3604	Fb	0.42	0.53	0.54	[68]0.66	....	0.78	9 Mo Nov	0.71	0.83	37
38◆	1992	Q0.01	12-1-95	11-13	0.04	0.04	0.027	22.8	1397	836	9-30-95	684	...	23652	Dc	p1.37	p0.54	2.22	[69]6.13	....	6.77	9 Mo Sep	3.48	4.12	38
39	1983	t0.10	1-23-96	1-5	0.10	0.10	t0.10	172	191	33.6	j12-31-94	150	...	36764	Dc	d2.86	0.22	0.23	0.38	....	j0.52	9 Mo Sep	0.32	0.46	39
40	....	None Since Public			...	Nil	....	117	118	32.4	9-30-95	0.46	...	10422	Je	d1.42	d1.47	d1.40	d1.31	d1.77	d1.72	3 Mo Sep	d0.38	d0.33	40
41	1994	Q0.45	1-4-96	12-20	1.80	1.80	0.796	Equity per shr $9.03			9-30-95	[70]56.6	...	2638	Dc	...	...	p1.21	p1.25	....	1.27	9 Mo Sep	p0.89	0.91	41
42	....	None Since Public			...	Nil	....	38.4	50.6	32.3	p6-30-95	p0.12	...	★14523	Dc	pd0.01	pd0.05	p0.14	p0.13	....	d0.14	9 Mo Sep	p0.07	pd0.20	42
43	1968	Q0.22	12-1-95	11-8	0.88	0.88	0.88	Book Value $21.79			6-30-95	6170	4855	117482	Dc	2.06	Δ1.19	□d1.51	1.58	E3.50	3.21	9 Mo Sep	1.36	□2.99	43
44	1993	Q0.75	12-1-95	11-8	3.00	3.00	3.00	Cv into 2.05465 com, $24.335				....	5000	...	Dc	...	...	...	....	....	....				44
45◆	1983	0.219	10-17-95	9-12	0.719	0.72	[74]0.509	363	2031	2286	10-08-95	1954	...	124025	Dc	1.62	1.64	1.59	1.91	....	2.21	40 Wk Sep	1.35	1.65	45
46◆	....	0.585			...	0.81	....	535	3175	3300	j1-01-95	1949	...	120144	Dc	2.76	2.98	2.95	3.46	....	j3.46				46
47	....	None Since Public			...	Nil	....	0.18	29.8	25.4	9-30-95	1.51	...	7313	Dc	0.01	[76]d0.22	[77]d0.05	d0.04	....	0.16	9 Mo Sep	d0.03	0.17	47
48◆	1991	Q0.05	1-26-96	1-3	0.18	0.20	0.147	50.4	313	239	9-30-95	84.8	...	18574	Dc	*0.80	1.08	0.99	[78]1.28	E1.50↑	1.47	9 Mo Sep	0.91	1.10	48
49◆	1954	Q0.26	2-12-96	12-28	1.01	1.04	0.95	87.0	1332	1311	9-30-95	1194	...	[79]111683	Sp	2.22	□2.45	1.76	Δ2.06	3.29	3.29				49
50	....	None Since Public			...	Nil	....	9.06	178	180	7-31-95	313	1200	32018	Oc	d1.15	d0.40	d0.22	□d9.23	Pd0.35	d0.35				50
51	1974	Q0.075	12-5-95	11-17	0.30	0.30	0.30	14.1	321	236	9-30-95	476	79	21050	Dc	1.40	0.12	Δ1.66	[80]1.81	E1.00	1.05	9 Mo Sep	1.31	0.55	51
52	....	0.18	11-15-90	10-25	...	Nil	....	3.66	6.96	7.64	9-30-95	51.7	...	±6290	Dc	d0.66	d0.22	d0.02	d0.10	....	d0.30	9 Mo Sep	0.10	d0.10	52

◆Stock Splits & Divs By Line Reference Index [1]2-for-1,'95. [2]2-for-1,'94,'95. [4]1-for-10 REVERSE,'91. [5]3-for-2,'91. [13]No adj for stk dstr of Spacelabs Inc,'92. [17]3-for-2,'93. [18]3-for-2,'93. [22]5-for-4,'93. [24]2-for-1,'92:5-for-2,'95. [26]3-for-2,'94. [31]5-for-1,'91:Adj for 3%,'94:3-for-2,'94. [33]3-for-2,'95. [35]5-for-4,'93. [37]2-for-1,'94. [38]3-for-2,'94. [45]2-for-1,'93. [46]2-for-1,'90,'93. [48]3-for-2,'92,'94. [49]2-for-1,'92.

¶ S&P 500 # MidCap 400 ✣ SmallCap 600 • Options

Index	Ticker	Name of Issue (Call Price of Pfd. Stocks)	Market	Com. Rank. & Pfd. Rating	Inst. Hold Cos	Inst. Hold Shs. (000)	Principal Business	1971-93 High	1971-93 Low	1994 High	1994 Low	1995 High	1995 Low	Dec. Sales in 100s	December, 1995 Last Sale Or Bid High	Low	Last	%Div Yield	P-E Ratio	Total Return % Annualized 12 Mo	36 Mo	60 Mo
1•[1]	ARG	✔Airgas Inc	NY,Ch,Ph	B	145	19708	Dstr ind'l,medical,splty gases	23⅛	1 11/16	29⅞	19⅝	33¼	19⅝	12174	33¼	27⅞	33¼	...	30	54.7	46.6	60.9
2	FLY	✔Airlease Ltd L.P.	NY,Ch	NR	5	145	Leases commercial aircraft	20¾	8⅛	17	10⅞	18	13¼	1308	17⅞	17⅛	17¼	e11.6	12	45.4	32.4	22.5
3	ARSN	✔AirSensors Inc	NNM	B−	15	533	Mfr electr auto fuel mgmt sys	21¾	2¼	15¼	8	13¾	7½	5610	8¾	7½	8	...	20	−4.5	21.1	10.4
¶4•[2]	ATI	✔AirTouch Communications	NY,Ph	NR	923	272886	Wireless telecommun svcs	27¼	24⅜	30⅝	19⅞	35⅝	23⅞	268675	29⅞	26¼	28⅛	...	94	−4.3	...	...
5•[3]	AKS	✔AK Steel Holding	NY	NR	119	21633	Integrated steel producer	....	....	33¼	19¼	35⅝	21½	23495	35⅜	32⅛	34¼	...	2	12.8	...	...
6	Pr	7% cm Cv [54]'SAILS'[55]	NY	NR	57	6228		....	....	33⅝	26⅝	34⅞	24⅛	6989	34⅝	32	33½	6.4	..	...	...	...
7	AKRN	✔Akorn Inc	NNM	B−	17	1607	Dstr pharmaceutical products	4⅜	1⅛	4	2⅜	3⅝	2 1/16	4991	2½	2 1/16	2½	...	20	−21.2	8.6	5.7
8	AKZOY	✔Akzo Nobel N.V. ADS	NNM	NR	90	4832	Chemical,fiber,hlthcare prod	52¾	18⅞	63¾	48½	67⅜	52½	8154	58⅝	55¼	58	3.3	10	4.2	18.8	26.2
9	AXO	✔Alamco Inc	AS,Ch	B−	31	2569	Oil & gas explor,dev,prod'n	61¼	1¼	7¾	5½	8⅞	5⅝	260	8½	7⅝	8B	...	..	34.4	17.3	21.9
10	ALG	✔Alamo Group	NY	NR	42	6313	Mfr mowing/grounds mainten eq	16¼	11⅜	19¾	12	19½	15¾	1280	18¼	17⅛	18	2.2	13	13.3	...	...
11	ALTC	✔Alantec Corp[56]	NNM	NR	101	8737	Design/mfr switching hubs	....	....	34	9¼	61¾	24½	93594	61¾	40¾	58¼	...	66	72.6	...	...
#12•[4]	ALK	✔Alaska Air Group	NY,B,Ch,P,Ph	C	112	10967	Scheduled/charter airline sv	30½	1¾	18⅞	13⅛	21⅜	13½	32057	18⅞	16⅛	16¼	...	16	13.0	−0.3	−0.8
13	AWS	✔Alba-Waldensian	AS,Ch	B−	13	375	Hosiery: apparel:fabrics	23⅜	⅝	12⅛	9¾	11⅛	7½	217	8⅞	7½	7⅝	...	d	−32.2	0.0	−0.3
#14	AIN	✔Albany Intl 'A'	NY,Ph	B	153	23055	Mfr paper machine belt prod	23½	8	21¼	16⅛	26½	17⅛	20315	21⅜	17⅞	18⅛	2.2	14	−4.2	8.0	15.0
#15•[5]	ALB	✔Albemarle Corp	NY,Ph	NR	176	30433	Mfg ind'l chemicals	....	....	17⅝	12½	20	12¼	43353	19⅞	16⅝	19⅜	1.1	19	44.2	...	...
16	AOG	Alberta Energy	NY,Ch	B	44	10352	Oil&gas explor, dvlp prod'n	....	....	....	....	16¾	15	956	16¾	15⅜	16	...	..	...	...	...
¶17	ACV	✔Alberto-Culver Cl'B'	NY,B,Ch,Ph	A	197	4701	Hair care,health,beauty aids,	34¼	11/16	27⅜	19⅜	36½	25⅞	4104	36½	31⅞	34⅜	0.9	18	28.7	11.9	2.1
18	ACV.A	✔ Class'A'(1/10 vtg)	NY,Ph	A	85	7813	oper beauty supply stores	25¾	6⅜	24⅞	17¾	32⅜	23	3047	32⅜	28¼	30½	1.0	16	26.7	9.7	8.4
¶19•[6]	ABS	✔Albertson's, Inc	NY,B,Ch,P	A+	631	112381	Food supermkts: food-drug	29¾	5/16	30⅞	25⅛	34⅝	27¼	100432	34	30¾	32⅞	1.6	18	13.7	10.1	15.2
¶20•[7]	AL	✔Alcan Aluminium Ltd	[8]NY,To,B,C,Ch,Mo	B−	436	112819	Aluminum mfr/finished prod	25¼	3⅜	28⅛	19¾	36⅝	23⅜	71159	34½	29⅞	31⅛	1.9	12	24.5	23.5	12.2
21•[9]	ALA	✔Alcatel Alsthom ADS[58]	NY,Ph	NR	90	27757	Commun sys, energy, transp'tn	29½	21⅞	30¾	15⅜	22⅛	15⅜	29751	17⅝	16	17½	2.7	18	5.9	−8.6	...
22	ALCD	✔Alcide Corp	NNM	B−	14	361	R&D microbiocidal chemistry	82½	3⅛	11½	6¾	33	6¾	4095	29¼	20½	23¼	...	31	244	36.0	44.0
¶23•[3]	ASN	✔Alco Standard	NY,B,Ch,Ph	B+	473	70381	Dstr paper & office equipment	27⅜	13/16	32¾	24¾	47⅛	31	65468	47	42⅞	45⅝	1.2	27	46.8	38.5	25.1
24	Pr	Cm Cv [62]Dep Pfd Vtg([63]50)	NY	A−	37	1647		69⅜	50	75⅜	60	105⅛	70¾	8241	105⅛	96¼	100B	2.4	..	...	...	...
25	Pr B	$5.04 cm Cv Dep[66]Pfd Vtg(NC)	NY	A−	43	2854		....	....	....	....	88	77⅜	4049	87¼	82⅛	85½	5.9	..	...	...	...
26•[10]	ALDA	✔Aldila Inc	NNM	NR	37	2821	Mfr graphite golf shafts	18¼	7	19¼	9¾	11⅝	3¾	41564	4¾	4	4¼	...	9	−62.6	...	...
27	ALT	✔Alert Centre[68]	AS	NR	6	139	Sell,install security alarm sy	....	....	5⅞	1⅜	9¼	2	2376	9¼	9	9B	...	..	350	...	...
28	WS	Wrrt(Pur 1 com at$9.75)	AS	....	1	4		....	....	⅝	⅛	⅝	1/64	1811	1/16	1/64	1/64	...	..	...	...	...
✣29•[11]	AB	✔Alex Brown Inc	NY,Ph	B	117	6894	Invest't bank'g,brokerage	30½	6¾	30⅜	23¼	60¾	29½	14880	47¼	39¾	42¼	1.9	8	43.2	29.2	40.3
¶30•[10]	AAL	✔Alexander & Alex Sv	NY,B,P	B−	254	31993	Insurance brokerage & agency	42⅜	7⅛	22¾	14	26⅜	18½	13240	22¼	18⅝	19	0.5	16	−0.9	−8.3	−1.1
#31	ALEX	✔Alexander & Baldwin	NNM	A−	176	24667	Shipping,R.E.,agribusiness	39½	1 11/16	28¼	21¼	25½	20½	12450	24¼	22½	23	3.8	26	6.1	2.2	3.8
32	AEOK	✔Alexander Energy	NNM	B−	34	5902	Oil & gas expl,dev,prod'n	15⅜	1⅛	6⅞	4⅜	6¾	3⅜	19329	4⅝	3⅞	4½	...	d	−29.8	3.4	−1.3
33	ACH	✔Alexander Haagen Properties	AS,Ch	NR	78	8956	Real estate investment trust	18⅛	17⅝	18⅞	13½	16¾	10⅝	9446	12¾	10¾	12¼	11.8	d	−5.9	...	...
34	ALX	✔Alexander's, Inc	NY,B,Ch,Ph	NR	49	1949	Selling real-estate prop	77	2	60½	48⅞	70	49¾	660	70	62	69½	...	d	32.4	11.1	24.9
35	ALFA	✔Alfa Corp	NNM	A	40	3091	Insurance holding company	13⅜	7/16	12½	10	18¼	9¾	7230	18¼	10¾	16¾	2.3	21	57.4	15.1	33.5
36	AFN	✔Alfin Inc	AS,Ch	C	10	320	Mkts imported fragrances	40	5/16	2⅜	11/16	2⅛	⅝	2423	1½	1⅛	1 5/16	...	8	61.6	5.3	6.9
37	ALCO	Alico, Inc	NNM	B	40	1617	Citrus fruit: cattle-Florida	39	1½	22¾	16	26½	15	3740	26½	21¾	26¼	e0.6	21	59.8	10.1	7.9
38	MASK	✔Align-Rite Intl	NNM	NR	9	624	Mfr/mkt photomasks	....	....	....	....	18¼	10½	7056	13¾	10½	11½	...	11	...	...	...
39	AACIB	All Amer Communications'B'	NNM	NR	..	...	T.V.prd,music,news svcs	....	....	....	....	10⅝	8⅜	21859	10⅝	8⅜	8¾	...	8	...	...	...
40	SEMI	✔All Amer Semiconductor	NNM	B−	23	2182	Dstr electronic components	3⅞	9/16	3⅞	1½	3⅝	1½	26188	2⅝	2 3/16	2 5/16	...	29	19.4	13.9	21.4
41	ALCM	✔All-Comm Media	NSC	C	3	5	Sports technology & info svcs	28¾	⅝	23½	2½	9¾	1⅞	16519	5	1 15/16	3¼	...	d	−38.1	−34.4	...
42	Y	✔Alleghany Corp	NY,B,Ch,Ph	B	102	3994	Insur:title,prop:fin'l svcs	147½	5	149⅞	134⅛	199½	146⅛	423	199½	192	198	s...	12	36.1	20.0	23.2
#43•[12]	ALS	✔Allegheny Ludlum	NY,Ph	NR	150	33226	Major stainless steel mfr	24⅜	5	24⅞	17	23	16⅜	20407	19½	17½	18½	2.8	11	0.4	4.9	12.3
#44	AYP	✔Allegheny Power Sys	NY,B,C,Ch,P,Ph	A−	267	48115	Electric utility hldg co	28½	5⅞	26½	19¾	29¼	21½	54161	29¼	27⅝	28⅝	5.9	15	42.0	14.3	17.3
✣45•[13]	ALN	✔Allen Group	NY,B,Ch,P,Ph	B	167	20485	Elec telecom equip	29¼	15/16	25⅝	13½	39⅜	21¼	30419	26⅜	21¾	22⅜	0.9	17	...	...	...
¶46•[11]	AGN	✔Allergan, Inc	NY	NR	367	53246	Opthalmic/dermatologic prod	27¼	12¼	30⅞	20	33¾	25¾	37094	32¾	30⅜	32½	1.5	29	19.0	9.9	15.0
47	AC	✔Alliance Cap Mgmt L.P.	NY,Ph	NR	48	50379	Investment management svcs	27⅝	4⅞	27⅛	16½	23¼	15⅜	7523	23¼	21⅞	23⅛	7.5	12	40.6	18.0	33.5
48•[9]	CDS	✔Alliance Entertainment[77]	NY,Ph	NR	39	8801	Dstr pre-recorded music	7⅛	3¾	7¼	4⅝	11¼	4⅜	94393	11¼	9⅜	9½	...	30	100	27.1	...
49	ALLY	✔Alliance Gaming	NNM	C	15	1470	Coin gam'g machine operator	44⅜	15/16	10⅛	5⅛	8	2¾	19778	3¾	2¾	3	...	d	−59.2	−20.1	8.9
50	SCAN	Alliance Imaging	NSC	NR	12	2825	Magnetic resonance imaging	10¼	¾	1½	3/16	3⅜	7/16	3771	3	2⅝	2⅞	...	d	412	−2.1	...
✣51•[14]	ALLP	✔Alliance Pharmaceutical	NNM	C	68	8069	Dvlp,mfr med'l/pharmac'l prod	44	2	12¼	5⅝	14¼	4¼	37575	14¼	10⅞	13⅝	...	d	114	5.8	4.9
52•[15]	ALSC	✔Alliance Semiconductor	NNM	NR	175	23053	Mfr hi performance memory pd	4½	3⅜	14⅝	4	48¼	10½	367768	22½	10½	11⅝	...	9	−17.7	...	...

Uniform Footnote Explanations-See Page 4. Other: [1]CBOE:Cycle 1. [2]ASE,CBOE,P:Cycle 1. [3]NY:Cycle 3. [4]ASE:Cycle 1. [5]NY,P:Cycle 3. [6]Ph:Cycle 3. [7]ASE:Cycle 3,To:Cycle 2. [8]P,Ph,Vc [9]CBOE:Cycle 3. [10]CBOE:Cycle 2. [11]Ph:Cycle 1. [12]ASE,CBOE:Cycle 1. [13]ASE:Cycle 3. [14]ASE:Cycle 2. [15]ASE,CBOE,NY,P:Cycle 1. [51]Incl current amts. [52]To be determined. [53]®$8.30,'94. [54]Stock Appreceiation Income Linked Securities. [55]Fr 10-16-97 red for(min .8621)com re-spec cond.. [56]FORE Systems plan acq,1 com. [57]®$1.34,'94. [58]Ea ADS rep 0.2 ord FF40. [59]Approx,in cash or stk. [60]In cash or stk. [61]®$1.93,'92. [62]Dep for 0.01 shr Ser AA Cv Pfd. [63]Fr 1-9-2000. [64]Thru 1-2-96,then $3.25. [65]If com price exceeds $58.03 for 20 tdg days. [66]Dep for 0.01 shr Ser BB Cv Pfd. [67]Fr 9-25-95 to 10-1-98. [68]ADT Ltd(74.5%),plan mgr. [69]5 Mo Dec,'93. [70]®$4.05,'94. [71]Incl liab subj to reorg. [72]Fiscal Jul'92 & prior. [73]12 Mo Dec'93:Fiscal Jul'93 earned $5.36. [74]Stk dstr of Jackpot Enterprises. [75]Excl subsid pfd. [76]Stk dstr of TransPro Inc. [77]Metromedia Intl Grp plan acq. [78]10 Mo Sep'92. [79]Excl 1.3M Jr. Cv. Spl. Stk.

Splits ◆ Index	Cash Divs. Ea.Yr. Since	Dividends: Latest Payment Period $	Date	Ex. Div.	Total $ So Far 1995	Ind. Rate	Paid 1994	Financial Position Mil-$ Cash& Equiv.	Curr. Assets	Curr. Liab.	Balance Sheet Date	Capitalization Lg Trm Debt Mil-$	Shs. 000 Pfd.	Com.	Earnings $ Per Shr. Years End	1991	1992	1993	1994	1995	Last 12 Mos.	Interim Earnings Period	$ per Shr. 1994	1995	Index
1◆	....	None Since Public			...	Nil	....	....	193	111	9-30-95	327	...	31506	Mr	0.27	0.40	0.63	0.96	....	1.11	6 Mo Sep	0.43	0.58	1
2	1987	†Q0.50	2-15-96	12-27	†2.04	2.00	1.84	Equity per shr $15.50			9-30-95	28.7	...	4625	Dc	1.57	1.21	1.30	1.36	....	1.41	9 Mo Sep	1.06	1.11	2
3◆	....	None Since Public			...	Nil	....	0.09	19.6	7.64	10-31-95	[51]5.57	6	5650	Ap	d0.56	□d0.66	□0.31	0.32	0.40	0.41	6 Mo Oct	0.18	0.19	3
4	....	None Since Public			...	Nil	....	150	545	462	9-30-95	122	...	495413	Dc	...	p0.01	□0.09	0.20	E0.30	0.25	9 Mo Sep	0.19	0.24	4
5	1995	0.15	11-15-95	10-18	0.15	[52]....	....	347	878	375	9-30-95	325	7480	26260	Dc	...	...	p□d1.08	□[53]10.19	....	14.54	9 Mo Sep	□3.27	7.62	5
6	2995	Q0.538	1-15-96	12-13	2.153	2.153	....	Cv into 0.8621 com,$35.67				....	7480	...	Dc	...	...	...	....	....	....	Mand conv into 1 com 10-15-98			6
7	....	0.017	7-1-91	5-24	...	Nil	....	2.25	14.8	6.85	9-30-95	3.70	...	14923	Je	d0.39	d0.55	0.14	0.18	0.15	0.13	3 Mo Sep	0.05	0.03	7
8	1989	0.399	11-28-95	11-6	1.893	1.89	1.506	728	8234	5321	j12-31-94	3139	...	71070	Dc	4.39	4.26	□3.80	□4.86	....	5.67	9 Mo Sep	□3.91	Δ4.72	8
9	....	None Since Public			...	Nil	....	1.87	4.61	4.03	9-30-95	14.8	...	4694	Dc	Δd0.07	Δ0.37	0.45	0.35	....	Nil	9 Mo Sep	0.24	d0.11	9
10	1993	Q0.10	11-1-95	10-12	0.40	0.40	0.36	1.55	97.4	22.0	9-30-95	19.5	...	9577	Dc	0.95	1.07	1.08	1.20	....	1.37	9 Mo Sep	0.98	1.15	10
11	....	None Since Public			...	Nil	....	122	137	11.2	9-30-95	....	...	10912	Dc	...	...	p0.16	0.46	....	0.88	9 Mo Sep	0.26	0.68	11
12	....	0.05	11-5-92	10-8	...	Nil	....	144	354	443	9-30-95	561	...	13561	Dc	0.27	□d6.53	d2.51	1.68	E1.00↓	0.95	9 Mo Sep	2.07	1.34	12
13	....	0.05	9-28-84	9-7	...	Nil	....	0.08	28.9	9.49	10-01-95	12.9	...	1865	Dc	0.77	Δ0.74	0.54	1.05	....	d0.20	9 Mo Sep	0.91	d0.34	13
14	1987	Q0.10	1-2-96	11-29	0.37½	0.40	0.35	5.34	351	114	9-30-95	251	...	±30376	Dc	±0.41	±Δ□0.11	±0.58	±0.80	....	1.31	9 Mo Sep	±0.52	±1.03	14
15	1994	Q0.05½	1-1-96	12-13	0.20½	0.22	0.15	46.6	453	214	9-30-95	253	...	66068	Dc	...	p0.68	p0.27	p0.79	E1.00	0.82	9 Mo Sep	p0.71	0.74	15
16	1985	gA0.40	6-30-95	6-6	g0.40	0.40	g0.40	23.7	245	241	j12-31-94	562	...	74464	Dc	0.12	0.53	1.23	[57]1.36	....	j1.60	9 Mo Sep	1.11	1.35	16
17	1967	Q0.08	11-20-95	11-2	0.32	0.32	0.28	147	537	235	9-30-95	183	...	±27729	Sp	±1.06	±1.36	±1.44	±1.57	±1.89	1.89				17
18	1986	Q0.08	11-20-95	11-2	0.32	0.32	0.28	....	...	...		....	...	10963	Sp	1.06	±1.36	±1.44	±1.57	±1.89	1.89				18
19◆	1960	Q0.13	2-25-96	1-31	0.50	0.52	0.42	53.4	1252	1087	11-02-95	719	...	252856	Ja	0.97	□1.04	1.34	□1.65	E1.85	1.80	9 Mo Oct	□1.08	1.23	19
20	1939	tQ0.15	12-20-95	11-16	0.45	0.60	t0.30	89.0	3325	1660	9-30-95	1864	10400	225778	Dc	d0.25	d0.60	d0.54	0.34	E2.70	2.32	9 Mo Sep	0.15	□2.13	20
21	1903	[59]0.47	8-4-95	6-26	[59]0.47	0.47	[60]0.414	Equity per shr $3.86			j12-31-94	31377	...	142358	Dc	1.99	[61]1.95	1.68	Δ0.95	....	0.95				21
22◆	....	None Since Public			...	Nil	....	3.63	7.83	1.25	8-31-95	....	100	2788	My	Nil	0.08	*0.29	0.40	0.60	0.76	6 Mo Nov	0.23	0.39	22
23◆	1965	Q0.14	12-10-95	11-16	0.54	0.56	0.505	90.1	2161	1390	9-30-95	★1438	7902	112376	Sp	1.31	1.02	d0.10	0.55	1.67	1.67				23
24	1993	Q0.59⅜	1-2-96	12-14	2.37½	[64]2.375	2.37½	Cv into 1.1201 com,$44.64				....	3500	...	Sp	...	...	...	....	....	....	Red opt 1/9/96-1/9/2000 at 1.1201 com[65]			24
25	1995	Q1.26	1-1-96	12-14	0.938	5.04	....	Cv into .81965 com[67]				....	3400	...	Sp	...	...	...	....	....	....	Mand conv 10-1-98 re-spec cond.			25
26◆	....	None Since Public			...	Nil	....	19.9	31.2	5.69	9-30-95	20.0	...	16779	Dc	...	p0.28	□0.50	0.69	....	0.47	9 Mo Sep	0.55	0.33	26
27	....	None Since Public			...	Nil	....	10.3	17.7	15.5	9-30-95	33.4	...	9797	Dc	...	...	†[69]d0.39	d0.67	....	0.08	9 Mo Sep	d0.46	0.29	27
28	....	Terms&trad. basis should be checked in detail						Wrrts expire 8-6-98				....	...	3250	Dc	...	...	...	....	....	....				28
29	1986	Q0.20	11-9-95	10-26	0.75	0.80	0.65	Equity per shr $29.56			9-30-95	195	...	15517	Dc	3.36	3.72	5.61	[70]4.60	E5.60	5.39	9 Mo Sep	3.27	4.06	29
30	1922	Q0.02½	12-29-95	11-29	0.10	0.10	0.32½	1043	2318	2035	9-30-95	156	6700	±44442	Dc	□d0.25	±d2.20	Δ±0.40	□d3.45	E1.20	d1.26	9 Mo Sep	□d0.77	1.42	30
31	1902	Q0.22	12-7-95	11-7	0.88	0.88	0.88	52.5	290	224	9-30-95	410	...	45541	Dc	2.00	□1.31	1.45	1.62	E0.90	1.43	9 Mo Sep	1.12	0.93	31
32◆	....	None Since Public			...	Nil	....	2.82	7.85	8.68	9-30-95	48.5	...	12452	Dc	0.07	0.11	Δ0.14	Δd0.19	....	d0.26	9 Mo Sep	d0.04	d0.11	32
33	1994	Q0.36	1-20-96	12-27	1.44	1.44	1.44	Equity per shr $14.35			9-30-95	384	...	12024	Dc	...	p0.08	p0.06	0.14	....	d0.12	9 Mo Sep	0.11	d0.15	33
34	....	0.10	9-9-80	8-20	...	Nil	....	Equity per shr Neg			9-30-95	[71]182	...	5001	Dc	d0.84	[72]d26.69	[73]1.88	0.81	....	d0.82	9 Mo Sep	0.30	d1.33	34
35◆	1974	Q0.09½	12-1-95	11-13	0.37½	0.38	0.34¼	Equity per shr $7.52			9-30-95	105	...	40786	Dc	0.69	0.90	Δ1.04	0.81	....	0.81	9 Mo Sep	0.68	0.68	35
36	....	None Since Public			...	Nil	....	0.62	5.49	7.64	10-31-95	0.65	30	11519	Jl	d0.67	d0.42	d0.85	d0.14	0.12	0.16	3 Mo Oct	Nil	0.04	36
37	1973	†0.25	11-10-95	10-18	†0.25	0.15	†0.25	5.35	31.7	5.66	8-31-95	16.1	...	7028	Au	0.81	0.70	Δ0.42	1.10	1.27	1.27				37
38	....	None Since Public			...	Nil	....	16.2	24.6	7.23	9-30-95	1.31	...	4319	Mr	Δd0.02	Δd0.02	Δ0.51	1.01	....	1.01	6 Mo Sep	0.64	0.64	38
39	....	None Since Public			...	Nil	....	Equity per shr Neg			9-30-95	135	...	★±11343	Dc	d0.49	d0.18	±0.87	±0.07	....	1.11	9 Mo Sep	±d0.54	±0.50	39
40	....	None Since Public			...	Nil	....	0.22	80.8	29.0	9-30-95	34.4	...	17670	Dc	0.03	0.12	0.19	0.03	....	0.08	9 Mo Sep	0.10	0.15	40
41◆	....	h[74]....	7-31-90	7-12	...	Nil	....	0.83	2.83	3.43	9-30-95	2.72	...	3023	Je	d0.60	d1.80	d0.92	d2.12	0.06	d0.50	3 Mo Sep	0.51	d0.05	41
42◆	....	2%Stk	4-26-95	3-28	2%Stk	Stk	2%Stk	Equity per shr $177.40			9-30-95	385	...	7110	Dc	9.25	Δ9.20	14.09	19.73	....	17.02	9 Mo Sep	8.57	5.86	42
43◆	1987	Q0.13	12-29-95	11-28	0.49	0.52	0.48	59.4	432	189	10-01-95	★182	...	67470	Dc	0.63	□0.71	Δ1.06	0.26	E1.65↑	1.61	9 Mo Sep	d0.01	1.34	43
44◆	1935	Q0.42	12-29-95	12-14	1.65	1.68	1.64	5.35	535	566	9-30-95	2282	[75]...	120397	Dc	1.81	1.83	1.88	Δ1.86	E1.96	1.94	12 Mo Sep	Δ1.82	1.94	44
45◆	1991	h[76]....	10-10-95	10-11	h[76]0.15	0.20	0.16	11.0	173	87.3	9-30-95	31.0	...	26464	Dc	0.72	□0.81	Δ0.86	1.12	....	1.30	9 Mo Sep	0.79	0.97	45
46	1989	Q0.12	12-8-95	11-15	0.47	0.48	0.42	84.6	500	283	9-30-95	261	...	64468	Dc	d0.89	□1.56	1.65	1.73	E1.12	1.05	9 Mo Sep	1.19	0.51	46
47◆	1988	0.48	11-13-95	11-2	1.73	1.73	1.64	Equity per shr $3.87			9-30-95	3.48	...	80930	Dc	1.08	1.33	Δ0.95	1.70	E1.90↑	1.80	9 Mo Sep	1.27	1.37	47
48	....	None Since Public			...	Nil	....	0.53	409	283	9-30-95	237	...	34135	Dc	...	[78]0.10	□0.06	0.38	....	0.32	9 Mo Sep	0.20	0.14	48
49	....	None Paid			...	Nil	....	34.6	43.7	14.4	9-30-95	96.6	...	[79]11654	Je	d1.73	d0.51	d0.38	d1.28	d0.95	d1.06	3 Mo Sep	d0.18	d0.29	49
50	....	None Since Public			...	Nil	....	2.48	9.72	18.7	12-31-94	68.9	155	10614	Dc	0.32	0.15	d2.07	d2.68	....	d1.92	9 Mo Sep	d0.50	0.26	50
51	....	None Paid			...	Nil	....	18.9	22.7	4.84	9-30-95	1.49	1500	24875	Je	d1.24	d1.25	d1.39	d1.83	d1.35	d1.28	3 Mo Sep	d0.38	d0.31	51
52◆	....	None Since Public			...	Nil	....	172	202	19.1	p3-31-95	....	...	★37524	Mr	d0.19	0.08	0.33	0.69	....	1.31	6 Mo Sep	0.22	0.84	52

◆**Stock Splits & Divs By Line Reference Index** [1]2-for-1,'92,'93. [3]1-for-6 REVERSE,'93. [19]2-for-1,'93. [22]1-for-10 REVERSE, '92. [23]2-for-1,'95. [26]2-for-1,'94. [32]1-for-3 REVERSE,'91. [35]2-for-1,'93. [41]1-for-4 REVERSE,'95. [42]No adj for appx$41.81 dstr,'86:Adj to 2%,'95. [43]2-for-1,'93. [44]2-for-1,'93. [45]10%,'91:2-for-1,'93. [47]2-for-1,'93. [52]3-for-2,'95(twice).

¶ S&P 500
# MidCap 400
✜ SmallCap 600
• Options

Index	Ticker	Name of Issue (Call Price of Pfd. Stocks)	Market	Com. Rank. & Pfd. Rating	Inst. Hold Cos	Inst. Hold Shs. (000)	Principal Business	Price Range 1971-93 High	1971-93 Low	1994 High	1994 Low	1995 High	1995 Low	Dec. Sales in 100s	December, 1995 Last Sale Or Bid High	Low	Last	%Div Yield	P-E Ratio	Total Return % Annualized 12 Mo	36 Mo	60 Mo
✜1•[1]	ATK	✔Alliant Techsystems	NY,Ph	NR	94	7036	Mfr munitions/defense prod	31	8⅝	40⅝	21¾	53	34⅞	2425	53	49¾	50⅝	...	15	26.6	22.0	31.0
2	ALLA	✔Allied Capital Advisers	NNM	NR	16	1914	Investment advisers	5⅜	1⅜	5	3⅜	5⅜	3¼	2649	5¼	5	5¼	...	23	...	...	...
3	ALCC	✔Allied Capital Commercial	NNM	NR	46	2578	Real estate investment trust	19¾	14⅝	17¾	14⅜	19⅞	14¾	6377	19⅞	18¼	19¾	e8.5	12	33.6	12.0	...
4	ALLC	✔Allied Capital Corp	NNM	NR	24	995	Regulated invest co,SBIC	20¼	1⅜	15½	12¼	14¼	11⅛	3988	14¼	13¼	13⅝	†11.3	..	11.9	5.9	...
5	ALII	Allied Capital Corp II	NNM	NR	13	960	Closed-end management inv co	24½	12½	15½	13¼	19	13½	2312	19	16½	17⅛	e7.2	..	34.6	6.2	...
6	ALCL	✔Allied Capital Lending	NNM	NR	31	1124	Loans to small business	16	14½	15¾	9¾	13¼	9½	3776	13¼	12	13¼	e9.1	11	35.9	...	...
7	ADK	✔Allied Digital Tech	AS,Ch	NR	6	1550	Replication audio/video tapes	8½	4⅛	8¾	5⅛	7½	3⅝	1705	4½	3⅝	3⅞	...	d	−45.7	−9.9	...
8	WS.A	'A'Wrrt(Pur1com at$6.75)	AS	....	1	36		2	1	2	¾	1⅞	¼	1824	¾	¼	5/16	...	..	...	...	...
9	WS.B	'B'Wrrt(Pur1com at$7.50)	AS	....	..	...		1⅛	⅞	1⅜	7/16	1	⅛	595	⅜	⅛	3/16	...	..	...	...	...
✜10	ALGR	✔ALLIED Group	NNM	A	110	6844	Prop casualty insr/finl svcs	32¾	5⅝	31	22	36¾	23¼	10033	36	34	36	1.9	8	51.7	22.7	36.8
11	AHPI	✔Allied Healthcare Prod	NNM	NR	58	4157	Mfr medical gas equipment	12¾	6⅞	17½	12⅛	19½	14¼	9251	17¾	15½	16	1.8	11	5.0	14.4	...
12	HAUL	✔Allied Holdings	NNM	NR	38	2651	Auto/truck motor carrier	21¾	14	22½	10	12½	7¼	3021	10	8	8⅝	...	8	−27.0	...	...
13	AIB	✔Allied Irish Banks ADS[58]	NY,Ch	NR	21	1087	Major banking corp, Ireland	26½	16¼	27⅝	21½	34¾	23½	500	34¾	31½	32⅝	3.4	11	35.7	31.0	19.1
14	ADP	✔Allied Products	NY,B,Ch,P	†B−	60	5128	Metalwk'g/farm & indl mach	45½	1½	17⅜	12	24⅛	13⅜	2983	24⅛	20¼	24	0.4	12	70.3	100	48.1
15	ALR	✔Allied Research Corp	AS	B−	15	1115	Subsid mfrs defense prod	17½	⅛	9¼	2⅞	5	2½	2438	4	3⅛	4	...	d	−23.8	−32.7	7.1
16•[2]	AWIN	✔Allied Waste Ind	NNM	NR	37	5189	Integrated waste disposal	37½	⅝	6	3¼	10	3¾	15998	7¾	6⅜	7⅛	...	d	90.0	13.5	...
¶17•[3]	ALD	✔AlliedSignal Inc	NY,To,B,C,Ch,P,Ph	B+	708	242630	Aerospace,automotive,fibers	40⅛	7⅝	40¾	30⅜	49⅞	33⅜	108069	49⅞	46	47½	1.6	15	41.8	17.8	31.9
18	AFC	✔Allmerica Financial	NY,Ch,Ph	NR	3	105	Prop&casualty insur/finl svc	....	....	....	....	28⅝	21	33969	28⅝	25¾	27	0.7	9	...	...	...
19	APY	✔Allmerica Prop & Cas Cos	NY,Ph	B+	126	54260	Property-liability insurance	22⅛	¼	21⅞	14¼	27	16¾	7665	27	25	27	0.6	12	60.0	19.4	26.1
20	ALU	✔Allou Health&Beauty'A'	AS	B	23	1420	Dstr hlth & beauty aid prod	10½	1¾	11⅜	7	9¼	5¼	2782	6⅛	5¾	6	...	8	−22.6	−10.1	21.7
¶21•[4]	ALL	✔Allstate Corp	NY	NR	597	282095	Prop,liability life insurance	34¼	27	29⅞	22⅝	42⅜	23½	189252	42⅜	38⅞	41⅛	1.9	12	77.7	...	...
22	PME	Allstate Cp 6.76% Exch Nts '98	NY	A	45	3041	Exch Notes For Com Stock	....	....	....	....	46¾	34	8318	43⅜	38¼	41	5.6	..	...	...	...
¶23•[5]	AT	✔ALLTEL Corp	NY,B,Ch,P,Ph	A	437	71818	Telecommun/data process svc	31¼	2	31⅜	24	31⅛	23¼	77258	29⅞	27⅜	29½	3.5	16	1.7	10.6	16.0
24	Pr	$2.06 cm Cv C Pfd(27.50)	NY	A+	1	.7	dstr tel eqp/materials	178	18	182	149	177½	142	....	....	....	176B	1.2	..	...	...	...
25	JARS	✔Alltrista Corp	NNM	NR	74	5256	Mfr home canning products	20¾	12	21	16¼	24½	17¾	2178	18½	17¾	18	...	11	−10.0	...	...
✜26•[6]	ALW	✔Allwaste Inc	NY,Ph	B	76	14659	Vacuuming waste removal svc	12⅞	2½	7½	4⅜	6⅜	4⅛	28225	4⅞	4⅛	4¾	...	d	−9.5	−10.5	2.9
27	AHA	✔Alpha Indus	AS,B	B−	45	3210	Microwave comp. & devices	28⅛	3/16	7⅜	3	19⅝	6⅜	10108	15	10½	14⅛	...	30	117	62.2	41.4
28	ATGI	✔Alpha Technologies Grp	NNM	B−	15	906	Mapping database mgmt sys	18¾	13/16	5⅞	2⅝	13⅜	4⅞	12444	9¼	6⅞	7⅞	...	14	40.0	63.2	49.3
✜29•[3]	ALO	✔ALPHARMA INC 'A'	NY,Ch,Ph	B	88	9347	Pharmac'ls:animal health prod	29⅜	2 7/16	20⅝	12⅝	26⅜	16½	4672	26⅜	21⅞	26⅛	0.7	..	28.5	3.3	9.9
30	WS	Wrrt (Pur 1 Cl'A'com$21.945)	NY	....	..	...		....	....	....	....	11	6⅝	1117	11	7⅝	11	...	..	...	...	...
31	AGI	✔Alpine Group	AS,Ch	C	33	2610	Information display/coatings	21¼	¼	8¾	4⅛	6¾	4⅛	9984	5⅛	4¼	4⅜	...	d	...	...	...
32	ALTN	✔Alteon Inc	NNM	NR	42	5223	Dvlp diabetes & aging drugs	38¼	7¼	9¾	3⅝	16¼	5⅛	48198	16¼	8⅛	16⅛	...	d	193	8.1	...
#33•[7]	ALTR	✔Altera Corp	NNM,Ch	B−	290	38082	Mfrs integrated circuits	18	1 15/16	21⅝	10⅞	70⅞	19⅝	342650	59	43¼	49¾	...	27	133	105	56.1
34	ALRC	✔Alternative Resources	NNM	NR	97	10125	Provide info svcs personnel	....	....	15⅞	7	34	14¾	12356	31¾	28¼	30¼	...	52	104	...	...
35•[8]	ALRN	✔Altron Inc	NNM	B−	62	4800	Mfrs printed circuit boards	16⅜	1 3/16	16⅜	8	34¼	13½	25890	30¼	25¼	30	...	23	91.9	132	77.6
#36•[9]	AMX	✔Alumax Inc	NY	NR	259	38340	Produce aluminum products	21¾	16¾	35	21¼	37⅞	23¾	29636	34½	29⅛	30⅝	...	6	9.4	...	...
¶37•[10]	AA	✔Aluminum Co of Amer	NY,B,C,Ch,P,Ph	B−	696	140046	Leading U.S. aluminum prod'r	40⅜	6	45⅛	32⅛	60¼	36⅞	181272	59	49⅝	52⅞	1.7	11	26.0	16.7	15.6
¶38•[5]	AZA	✔ALZA Corp	NY,B,Ch,P	B	331	46454	Pharmaceutical research	55⅛	11/16	30¾	17	27	18⅛	90653	25⅛	21¾	24½	...	28	36.1	−17.5	1.0
39	AM	✔AM International	AS,Ch,Ph	NR	24	6467	Sell, svc graphic arts prod	10½	9⅜	12¼	8½	9⅜	5¾	1318	7¼	5¾	5¾	...	73	−35.4	...	...
40	WS	Wrrt (Pur 1 com at $18)	AS	....	5	181		1 7/16	½	1⅞	⅝	⅞	1/16	839	⅛	1/16	⅛	...	..	...	...	...
41•[8]	AU	✔Amax Gold Inc	NY,Ch,P,Ph	C	122	24038	Gold & silver mining,explor	21⅜	6	8¼	5⅝	7⅝	4½	51793	7⅝	6¼	7¼	...	d	26.1	−4.4	−12.5
42	Pr B	$3.75 Sr'B'Cv Pfd([67]52.625)	NY	BB	34	1288		....	....	56¼	47⅞	55⅞	42¾	806	55⅞	51	54½	6.9	..	...	...	...
43	WS	Wrrt (Pur 1 com at $21)	AS	....	3	82		2 7/16	½	15/16	1/16	¼	....	1673	1/32	....	....	...	..	...	...	...
44•[11]	ABK	✔AMBAC Inc	NY,Ph	NR	199	34532	Muni bond insurance co	49¾	20⅛	45	30¼	47⅞	36½	13887	47⅞	43¾	46⅞	1.3	10	29.2	5.0	...
45	AEN	✔AMC Entertainment	AS,Ch,P	B−	33	1470	Operates movie theatres	16⅛	3	13⅝	9¾	28¾	9⅞	9944	28¾	21¾	23⅜	...	12	106	55.2	55.2
46	Pr	$1.75 cm Cv Pfd([70]26)	AS	B	32	2640		....	....	26¼	20¼	49½	20¾	2927	49½	39¼	40¾	4.3	..	...	...	...
✜47	AIZ	✔Amcast Industrial	NY,Ch,Ph	B	92	5705	Technol-intensive metal prod	26⅜	3¾	25⅞	19⅜	22¼	16¾	4165	19⅜	18⅛	18¼	3.1	9	−10.0	8.3	26.0
✜48•[3]	ACOL	✔AMCOL Intl	NNM	A−	55	5580	World producer of bentonite	33	2 7/16	25¼	10½	18¼	11⅞	12240	16⅛	14⅛	14¼	2.0	15	−0.9	17.6	36.8
49	AMFI	✔Amcore Financial	NNM	A−	41	3224	Commercial banking,insur	20	3⅝	22¾	15¾	24	17	5109	23	19¾	20¼	3.0	16	15.8	14.9	30.1
¶50•[8]	AMH	✔Amdahl Corp	AS,B,Ch,P,Ph	C	281	52686	Mfr large computer sys, softwr	28	2¾	11⅛	5¼	13⅝	8⅛	69310	9¾	8⅛	8½	...	9	−22.7	7.0	−9.1
¶51•[12]	AHC	✔Amerada Hess	NY,To,B,C,Ch,P,Ph,Mo	B−	447	65380	Oil explor,prod,refining,mktg	59⅛	5⅝	52⅝	43¾	53⅝	43¼	67816	53⅝	47⅜	53	1.1	d	19.3	6.0	3.8
52	AFFFZ	✔Amer First Finl 1987-A Fd	NNM	NR	10	291	Banking, invest, acq finl inst	30	14½	25¾	18½	30¼	19½	1420	29¾	28¼	29¾	5.4	12	64.9	13.5	20.3

Uniform Footnote Explanations-See Page 4. Other: [1]NY,Ph:Cycle 2. [2]CBOE:Cycle 3. [3]Ph:Cycle 3. [4]ASE,CBOE,NY,Ph:Cycle 1. [5]P:Cycle 1. [6]ASE,Ph:Cycle 2. [7]NY,P:Cycle 3. [8]CBOE:Cycle 2. [9]ASE,Ph:Cycle 1. [10]CBOE:Cycle 1. [11]P:Cycle 2. [12]Ph:Cycle 2. [51]25 Wk Dec'92. [52]$0.60 payable in Allied Cap Lending stk,'95. [53]Incl subsid pfd. [54]Fiscal Dec'93 & prior. [55]If com exceeds $8.50 - 20 trad days(of30). [56]If com exceeds $8.50 - 20trad.days(of30). [57]®$3.19,'94. [58]Boston Scientific plan mgr, 3.4152 com. [59]Fiscal Mar'92 & prior. [60]9 Mo Dec'92. [61]Incl $0.05 redempt of Stk Pur Rt. [62]Stock or cash re-specified cond.. [63]Stk dstr of Polyvision Corp. [64]Accum on Pfd. [65]Stk dstr of Therapeutic Discovery Corp. [66]10 Mo Jul'94. [67]Fr 8-15-97,scale to $50 in 2004. [68]Special divd. [69]®$1.45,'95. [70]Fr 3-15-97,scale to $25 in 2001. [71]Approx.

Index	Splits ◆ Cash Divs. Ea.Yr. Since	Dividends Latest Payment Period $	Date	Ex. Div.	Total $ So Far 1995	Ind. Rate	Paid 1994	Financial Position Mil-$ Cash& Equiv.	Curr. Assets	Curr. Liab.	Balance Sheet Date	Capitalization Lg Trm Debt Mil-$	Shs. 000 Pfd.	Com.	Earnings $ Per Shr. Years End	1991	1992	1993	1994	1995	Last 12 Mos.	Interim Earnings Period	$ per Shr. 1994	1995	Index
1	....	None Since Public			...	Nil	....	19.8	446	342	10-01-95	373	...	12930	Mr	3.88	□d8.59	3.21	□d7.22	E3.50	d4.92	6 Mo Sep	□d0.74	1.56	1
2	....	None Paid			...	Nil	....	3.04	7.75	2.72	9-30-95	....	...	8990	Dc	0.07	d0.08	0.02	0.14	....	0.23	9 Mo Sep	0.10	0.19	2
3	1992	†0.17	1-31-96	12-26	†1.83	1.68	1.25	Equity per shr $13.76			9-30-95	61.2	...	13584	Dc	...	[51]0.30	0.95	1.42	....	1.69	9 Mo Sep	1.04	1.31	3
4	1963	†0.58	1-31-96	12-26	†[52]1.46	1.54	†1.35	Net Asset Val $8.60			9-30-95	81.3	[53]70	6186	Dc	§6.63	§6.70	§8.54	§7.15	....	....				4
5	1990	†0.48	1-31-96	12-26	†1.46	1.24	†1.22	Net Asset Val $15.41			9-30-95	....	...	6945	Dc	§13.45	§13.60	§13.87	§14.05	....	....				5
6	1994	†0.37¾	1-31-96	12-26	†1.202	1.20	1.10	Net Asset Val $7.59			9-30-95	....	...	4381	Dc	1.78	0.75	1.03	1.04	....	1.18	9 Mo Sep	0.77	0.91	6
7	....	None Since Public			...	Nil	....	0.56	42.6	32.9	7-31-95	49.2	...	13620	Jl	...	...	[54]0.25	□0.15	p0.05	d0.04	3 Mo Oct	p0.15	p0.06	7
8	....	Terms&trad. basis should			be checked in detail			Wrrts expire 7-28-97				....	...	1354	Jl	...	...	...	....	....	....	Callable at 5¢[55]			8
9	....	Terms&trad. basis should			be checked in detail			Wrrts expire 7-28-97				....	...		Jl	...	...	...	....	....	....	Callable at 5¢[56]			9
10◆	1985	Q0.17	12-26-95	12-13	0.68	0.68	0.60	Equity per shr $26.10			9-30-95	59.8	4883	9311	Dc	1.93	2.70	3.68	[57]4.48	....	4.70	9 Mo Sep	3.40	3.62	10
11	1993	Q0.07	1-15-96	12-27	0.28	0.28	0.24	1.11	59.7	24.9	9-30-95	64.4	...	★7797	Je	0.66	0.78	0.94	1.31	1.45	1.47	3 Mo Sep	0.30	0.32	11
12	....	None Since Public			...	Nil	....	7.32	51.9	46.0	9-30-95	110	...	7725	Dc	...	p1.00	□p1.78	□1.84	....	1.04	9 Mo Sep	1.28	0.48	12
13	1991	0.512	10-29-95	8-11	1.108	1.11	0.896	Book Value $15.41			12-31-94	1880	7200	664601	Dc	[59]1.57	‡[60]1.61	1.71	2.80	....	3.10	6 Mo Jun	1.28	1.58	13
14	1995	Q0.02½	12-29-95	11-21	0.075	0.10	....	1.52	112	72.5	9-30-95	0.10	115	9139	Dc	d5.62	□d3.11	□1.70	1.37	....	2.09	9 Mo Sep	1.35	2.07	14
15◆	....	5%Stk	11-6-92	10-8	...	Nil	....	35.3	64.9	51.9	9-30-95	10.7	...	4414	Dc	3.22	3.99	1.73	d2.49	....	d2.40	9 Mo Sep	d1.06	d0.97	15
16◆	....	None Since Public			...	Nil	....	9.47	49.2	56.4	9-30-95	191	436	30125	Dc	0.06	0.08	0.04	□d0.66	....	d0.36	9 Mo Sep	□d0.11	0.19	16
17◆	1887	Q0.19½	12-8-95	11-15	0.78	0.78	[61]0.67¼	545	4985	3630	9-30-95	1377	...	282853	Dc	d1.00	□1.90	□2.31	2.68	E3.10↓	2.99	9 Mo Sep	1.95	2.26	17
18	....	Plan qtly div			...	0.20	....	Equity per shr $29.04			6-30-95	★200	...	★48485	Dc	...	...	...	□p1.52	....	3.02	9 Mo Sep	p□0.64	p□2.14	18
19◆	1853	Q0.04	2-15-96	1-30	0.16	0.16	0.16	Equity per shr $23.72			9-30-95	....	...	61149	Dc	0.79	2.16	Δ4.08	□1.64	....	2.34	9 Mo Sep	□1.13	1.83	19
20	....	None Since Public			...	Nil	....	0.69	118	81.6	9-30-95	0.59	...	±5662	Mr	■0.51	0.60	0.73	0.80	....	0.78	6 Mo Sep	0.34	0.32	20
21	1993	Q0.19½	12-28-95	11-28	0.78	0.78	0.72	Equity per shr $25.88			9-30-95	1225	...	447615	Dc	...	p□d1.15	p2.99	1.08	E3.50↑	3.73	9 Mo Sep	0.71	3.36	21
22	1995	Q0.57½	1-15-96	12-27	1.131	2.30	....	Amt pay maturity based on PMI Group stk[62]				....	...	★9250	Dc	...	...	...	...	....	....	Due 4-15-98			22
23◆	1961	Q0.26	1-3-96	12-6	0.96	1.04	0.88	34.1	714	559	9-30-95	1853	509	189024	Dc	1.17	1.22	1.39	1.43	E1.85	1.61	12 Mo Sep	1.56	1.61	23
24	1977	Q0.51½	12-15-95	11-20	2.06	2.06	2.06	Cv into 5.963 common, $4.61				....	32	...	Dc	b4.02	b3.39	b3.64	....	....	....				24
25	....	None Since Public			...	Nil	....	1.93	94.6	41.5	10-01-95	30.0	...	7842	Dc	...	p0.78	□1.78	2.07	....	1.67	9 Mo Sep	1.87	1.47	25
26	....	None Since Public			...	Nil	....	4.03	97.9	71.0	8-31-95	163	...	39674	Au	0.09	0.33	0.28	0.36	d0.03	d0.03				26
27	....	0.02½	8-12-85	7-16	...	Nil	....	2.10	29.6	18.5	10-01-95	2.40	...	★9409	Mr	*0.02	d0.40	d1.53	0.36	....	0.47	6 Mo Sep	0.16	0.27	27
28	....	None Since Public			...	Nil	....	4.56	25.1	9.96	7-30-95	7.97	...	6042	Oc	d0.09	d0.67	*0.04	0.83	P0.57	0.57				28
29◆	1984	Q0.04½	1-19-96	1-3	0.18	0.18	0.18	8.67	254	145	9-30-95	220	...	±21651	Dc	0.30	±0.89	±0.40	□d0.08	....	0.05	9 Mo Sep	0.48	0.61	29
30	....	Terms&trad. basis should			be checked in detail			Wrrts expire 1-3-99				....	...	3600	Dc	...	...	...	...	....	....				30
31	....	h[63]....	6-13-95	6-14	h[63]...	[64]Nil	....	9.76	146	101	7-31-95	195	283	18227	Ap	Δd0.59	Δd1.20	□d1.26	□d2.16	d0.38	d0.19	6 Mo Oct	d0.22	□d0.03	31
32	....	None Since Public			...	Nil	....	29.7	31.1	2.12	9-30-95	0.54	...	★15223	Dc	0.02	d0.34	d0.59	d0.85	....	d0.84	9 Mo Sep	d0.63	d0.62	32
33◆	....	None Since Public			...	Nil	....	342	476	97.7	9-30-95	244	...	43500	Dc	0.44	0.28	0.51	0.34	E1.86	1.05	9 Mo Sep	0.57	1.28	33
34◆	....	None Since Public			...	Nil	....	18.8	41.8	9.05	9-30-95	....	...	15315	Dc	*d0.03	*®0.08	®0.24	®0.41	....	0.58	9 Mo Sep	®0.27	®0.44	34
35◆	....	None Since Public			...	Nil	....	34.3	76.8	23.5	9-30-95	4.62	...	9958	Dc	0.14	0.16	0.63	0.98	....	1.33	9 Mo Sep	0.70	1.05	35
36	....	None Since Public			...	Nil	....	179	1321	610	9-30-95	716	2333	44721	Dc	...	pd1.56	□d3.24	0.84	E4.95	5.02	9 Mo Sep	d0.07	4.11	36
37◆	1939	Q0.22½	11-25-95	11-1	0.90	0.90	0.80	996	5068	2430	9-30-95	1432	558	177210	Dc	■0.36	□0.12	0.01	□2.48	E4.75	5.65	9 Mo Sep	□0.41	3.58	37
38◆	....	[65].....	6-11-93	6-14	...	Nil	....	405	563	55.0	9-30-95	358	...	82488	Dc	±d0.88	±0.90	Δ□0.54	0.71	E0.87	0.83	9 Mo Sep	0.52	0.64	38
39	....	None Since Public			...	Nil	....	12.8	170	162	10-28-95	19.1	...	7009	Jl	...	...	...	‡[66]0.95	0.66	0.08	3 Mo Oct	0.04	d0.54	39
40	....	Terms&trad. basis should			be checked in detail			Wrrts expire 10-15-96				....	...	1095	Jl	...	...	...	...	....	....				40
41	1987	0.02	11-29-93	11-4	...	Nil	....	10.5	59.9	36.2	9-30-95	159	1840	p96411	Dc	0.35	□0.18	□d1.14	□d0.56	....	d0.60	9 Mo Sep	Δd0.21	d0.25	41
42	1994	Q0.93¾	11-15-95	10-30	3.75	3.75	0.93¾	Cv into 6.061 com,$8.25				....	...	...	Dc	...	...	...	...	....	....				42
43	....	Terms&trad. basis should			be checked in detail			Wrrts expire 1-8-96				....	...	4067	Dc	...	...	...	...	....	....				43
44	1991	Q0.15	12-6-95	11-8	0.555	0.60	0.49½	Equity per shr $37.14			9-30-95	224	...	35145	Dc	3.25	3.71	5.08	4.01	E4.50	4.32	9 Mo Sep	3.10	3.41	44
45	....	[68]1.14	9-8-92	8-18	...	Nil	....	136	160	73.1	9-28-95	261	4000	±16546	Mr	±d0.29	□±0.46	0.89	[69]1.63	....	1.99	6 Mo Sep	0.33	0.69	45
46	1994	Q0.43¾	12-15-95	11-29	1.75	1.75	1.371	Cv into 1.724 com, $14.50				....	4000	...	Mr	...	...	...	...	....	....				46
47	1936	Q0.14	12-22-95	11-30	0.54	0.56	0.50	1.29	103	55.0	8-31-95	29.7	...	8556	Au	1.04	d0.81	□1.44	1.72	2.02	2.06	3 Mo Nov	0.43	0.47	47
48◆	1937	Q0.07	1-3-96	12-6	0.25	0.28	0.23	1.25	124	37.5	9-30-95	117	...	19184	Dc	0.26	0.51	0.76	0.78	....	0.93	9 Mo Sep	0.52	0.67	48
49◆	1983	Q0.15	12-8-95	11-22	0.60	0.60	0.57	Book Value $13.09			9-30-95	22.0	...	14106	Dc	1.04	1.31	1.53	1.58	....	1.27	9 Mo Sep	1.16	0.85	49
50	1977	0.01¼	8-30-93	8-10	...	Nil	....	782	1412	558	9-29-95	80.0	...	119116	Dc	Δ0.04	d0.06	Δd5.17	0.63	E0.91	0.90	9 Mo Sep	0.29	0.56	50
51	1922	Q0.15	1-3-96	12-14	0.60	0.60	0.60	88.7	1867	1529	9-30-95	2867	...	93009	Dc	1.04	0.09	□d3.22	0.79	Ed0.13	d1.20	9 Mo Sep	0.70	d1.29	51
52	1989	[71]Q0.40	1-31-96	12-27	[71]1.60	1.60	1.60	Equity per shr $25.44			9-30-95	....	200	6011	Dc	3.20	3.15	0.36	2.36	....	2.41	9 Mo Sep	1.81	1.86	52

◆**Stock Splits & Divs By Line Reference Index** [10]3-for-2,'93. [15]Adj for 5%,'92. [16]1-for-2 REVERSE,'92. [17]2-for-1,'94. [19]3-for-1,'94. [23]2-for-1,'93. [29]3-for-2,'91. [33]2-for-1,'95. [34]2-for-1,'95. [35]3-for-2,'93,'95. [37]2-for-1,'95. [38]2-for-1,'91. [48]3-for-2,2-for-1,'93. [49]10%,'92:3-for-2,'93.

¶ S&P 500 · # MidCap 400 · ✣ SmallCap 600 · • Options

Index	Ticker	Name of Issue (Call Price of Pfd. Stocks)	Market	Com. Rank. & Pfd. Rating	Inst. Hold Cos	Inst. Hold Shs. (000)	Principal Business	Price Range 1971-93 High	1971-93 Low	1994 High	1994 Low	1995 High	1995 Low	Dec. Sales in 100s	December, 1995 Last Sale Or Bid High	Low	Last	%Div Yield	P-E Ratio	Total Return % Annualized 12 Mo	36 Mo	60 Mo
1	AFPFZ	✓Amer First Ptc/Pfd Eqty Mtg	NNM	NR	2	41	Invest in fed'l insured mtge	17¾	9¼	10¼	7	9⅛	7¾	1810	8¾	8⅜	8⅜	12.7	14	15.1	5.4	8.7
2	PF	✓Amer First Prep Fd 2 L.P.	AS	NR	2	4	Invest in fed'l insured mtge	19	11	14¼	9⅞	12⅝	10½	617	12	10½	10¾	14.4	16	4.9	−0.6	8.7
3	ATAXZ	✓Amer First Tax Exempt Mtg 2	NNM	NR	5	49	Invest-tax exempt mtg loans	20	6	9¼	7⅛	9⅜	7¾	1227	9	8½	8¾	8.6	14	15.9	9.0	15.6
✣4•[1]	AMER	✓America Online[54]	NNM,Ch	NR	199	58315	Provides online computer svcs	8¾	1⅜	14⅝	6	46¼	12⅜	365160	46¼	33½	37½	...	d	161	124	...
5•[2]	AWA	✓America West Airlines 'B'	NY	NR	92	16851	Regional airline service	....	....	16⅜	6⅜	19	6⅜	44321	19	16⅞	17	...	..	119	...	...
6	WS	Wrrt(Pur 1 com at $12.74)	NY	....	18	1332		....	....	7⅜	1½	8¾	1¾	5283	8¾	7¼	7¼	...	..	...	...	...
7	AAG	✓Amer Annuity Group	NY	NR	47	39682	Multiline insurance co	20	3	10⅝	8⅜	12	9⅛	4528	12	10⅞	12	0.6	10	26.2	24.2	25.8
8	BKC	✓Amer Bank, Conn	AS	B+	13	308	Savings bank, Connecticut	25½	1½	23¼	20⅛	27¼	18⅞	529	27¼	23½	27¼	4.8	13	40.0	20.2	24.7
✣9	ABIG	✓Amer Bankers Insur Grp	NNM	B+	162	13250	Hldg: life & casualty insur	30¾	5	26¾	19	39⅜	23⅜	17345	39⅜	35⅞	39	1.9	12	68.0	21.0	38.9
10	ABN	✓Amer Banknote	NY,Ph	NR	19	2152	Prints securities,currencies	10⅜	1½	6½	1¾	2½	1¼	20013	1⅝	1¼	1¼	...	d	−41.2	−41.9	−7.8
11	ABL	✓Amer Biltrite	AS,B,Ph	B+	21	654	Floor cover'g/elec tape prod	24⅞	1¾	30	21½	35¼	18⅞	1160	22¼	19	21¾	1.8	9	−18.5	34.6	36.8
12	BNGO	Amer Bingo & Gaming	NSC	NR	..	...	Manage bingo centers	....	....	6¾	5	6⅝	3	4640	4⅛	3½	3½	...	d	...	...	...
¶13•[3]	AMB	✓Amer Brands	NY,B,C,Ch,P,Ph	A	649	99518	Tobacco,life insurance	49⅞	3½	38⅜	29⅜	47¼	36⅝	73118	47¼	42	44½	4.5	16	24.6	8.8	6.7
14	Pr A	$2.67 cm Cv Pfd(30.50)vtg	NY,B	A	8	5	distilled bev,hardware	200¼	28¾	150¼	122½	182½	135	18	182½	173¾	181⅝B	1.5	..	...	...	...
15	ABCO	✓Amer Building	NNM	NR	57	4049	Mfr metal building sys	....	....	19⅝	9¼	27	15¾	19510	22⅝	20½	22½	...	10	35.3	...	...
16	ABP	✓Amer Business Prod	NY,Ch	A−	93	5070	Business supplies/printing	20⅞	1¼	17⅛	12½	28½	13¾	2692	28½	23½	28½	2.0	19	96.9	18.2	30.6
17	AMCV	✓Amer Classic Voyages	NNM	NR	58	4166	Oper cruises on U.S. waterways.	22⅝	9¾	19½	12	15¼	8¼	7893	10⅞	10⅛	10⅞	...	d	−14.8	−4.7	...
18	ACNS	Amer Communications Svcs	NSC	NR	3	12	Telecommun equip/svcs	....	....	....	....	8¼	3¼	802	7¼	5¼	5⅜	...	d	...	...	...
19	FLI	✓Amer Eagle Group	NY,Ch	NR	25	2339	Insur: spec prop & casualty	....	....	12¼	6½	12¼	8	813	11⅜	9¾	11⅛	1.4	10	40.7	...	...
20	AEOS	✓Amer Eagle Outfitters	NNM	NR	28	1002	Retail casual apparel/footwear	....	....	29¾	12½	23¾	5½	22149	10½	5½	5⅞	...	27	−55.7	...	...
21	ECGOF	✓Amer Eco Corp	NNM,To,Ch	NR	2	40	Dvlp stage: ecological svcs	46¼	1⅞	4¾	2 3/16	4¾	1⅝	17388	3¾	3¼	3½	...	17	42.5	−1.7	−34.1
22	ECOL	✓Amer Ecology	NNM	B−	26	1710	Disposal of low-level waste	33½	2 5/16	12½	5⅞	7¼	2⅞	4822	4¼	2⅞	3¼	3.1	d	−48.7	−30.9	−5.6
¶23•[4]	AEP	✓Amer Electric Pwr	NY,B,C,Ch,P,Ph	B+	487	59042	Utility holding co	40⅜	13½	37⅜	27¼	40⅝	31¼	64908	40⅝	37⅝	40½	5.9	14	32.0	14.9	16.0
24	AX	✓Amer Exploration(New)	AS	C	39	5353	Oil/gas explor'n,prod'n	70	10	18¾	8¾	12⅛	8⅛	16730	11⅞	10⅛	11⅜	...	d	30.0	−11.2	−19.5
25	Pr C	$2.25 cm Cv[63]Dep'C'Pfd([64]26.35)	AS	NR	5	198		....	....	29	24¼	28½	22	253	28⅜	26½	26⅞B	8.4	..	...	...	...
¶26•[5]	AXP	✓Amer Express	NY,To,B,C,Ch,P,Ph,Mo	B	955	317770	Travel & invest sv,insur,bk'g	40⅝	4½	33⅛	25	45⅛	29	205594	45⅛	40⅛	41⅜	2.2	13	...	...	...
27	AXD	Amer Exp 6.25% 'DECS' '96	NY	NR[66]	104	13677	Exch Notes For Com Stock	41	36¾	45¼	38¼	59⅞	40¾	9460	58½	53⅝	55½	4.1	..	36.9	...	...
28	FRI	✓Amer Family Restaurants[68]	AS,Ph	NR	6	572	Oper family style restaurants	....	....	5⅛	3½	6	2⅝	2682	6	5¼	5¾	...	19	61.4	...	...
29	AMFB	✓Amer Federal Bank	NNM	NR	50	5613	Savings bank South Carolina	12¼	⅝	13	10	16⅛	10¼	5482	15¼	14¼	15¼	1.8	10	51.9	33.4	74.1
30	AFIL	✓Amer Filtrona	NNM	B+	40	2496	Mfr filter/fiber/plastic prd	28½	2⅞	31½	25½	40¾	25¾	206	38¼	33	33½B	3.2	13	28.1	11.8	20.2
#31•[6]	AFG	✓Amer Finl Group	NY,B,Ch,P,Ph	B	128	17133	Property & casualty insurance	39¾	4⅝	33¼	21⅝	32⅛	22⅞	27929	30⅝	28⅜	30⅝	3.3	29	25.9	...	...
¶32•[2]	AGC	✓Amer General	NY,B,C,Ch,P,Ph	B+	618	145261	Hldg co:diversified fin'l	36½	1 3/16	30½	24⅞	39⅛	27½	101028	35	32¾	34⅞	3.6	10	27.5	10.7	23.0
33	PrC	6.00%'A'[69]Cv[70] 'MIPS'([71]50)	NY	A+	42	2454		....	....	....	....	57⅛	50	7514	52⅞	50¾	52⅜	5.7	..	...	...	...
¶34•[7]	AGREA	✓Amer Greetings Cl'A'	NNM	A	426	62325	Cards & gift wrappings	34¼	1⅝	34	25⅞	33	25½	247925	28⅛	26	27⅝	2.3	18	3.5	5.4	12.7
35•[8]	AHE	✓Amer Health Prop	NY,Ch,Ph	NR	75	5420	Real estate investment trust	37	12	27¼	18½	23¼	19⅜	11750	21⅝	19¾	21½	9.2	13	...	...	...
36	AHL	✓Amer Heritage Life	NY,Ch	A	55	3409	Insur hdg co: life, accident	25⅜	1 13/16	20⅛	16½	23¼	16¼	2189	23¼	19⅞	22⅞	3.1	12	29.9	8.1	21.8
¶37•[7]	AHP	✓Amer Home Products	NY,B,C,Ch,P,Ph	A+	1176	200556	Drugs, food,household/ware	86¼	10¾	67¼	55⅜	99⅞	61¾	104387	99⅞	91¼	97	3.2	15	58.5	16.6	17.8
38	Pr	$2.00 cm Cv Pfd (60) vtg	NY	NR	..	...	pkgd medicine,med prod	760	101	580	505¾	690	607	....	....	....	873B	0.2	..	...	...	...
39	AIFC	✓Amer Indem/Finl	NNM	B−	18	870	Property & casualty insur	25⅝	2¾	14¾	10	13¼	8¾	158	11¼	9½	10	3.0	13	1.5	20.7	27.2
40	IND	✓Amer Industrial Prop	NY,Ch	NR	11	196	REIT:self-liquid'g 12-31-97	15⅜	1½	2½	1¼	2½	1⅛	3262	2½	1¾	2	...	d	48.6	13.3	−0.6
41	AIA	✓Amer Ins Mtge Inv L.P.	AS,Ph	NR	10	42	Mortgage invest mgmt services	18⅝	3½	4⅞	3¼	3¾	3⅛	1230	3½	3⅛	3⅜	9.5	12	7.5	10.0	20.4
42	AII	✓Amer Ins Mtge Inv Ser 85[76]	AS,Ph	NR	11	41	Originate/acquire mtge loans	20¼	10	16⅛	12⅞	15	12⅞	2188	14⅝	14¼	14½	9.7	12	21.9	22.2	19.6
43	AIJ	Amer Ins Mtge Inv Ser 86[76]	AS	NR	13	59	Originate/acquire mtge loans	....	....	14⅜	11⅛	13⅜	11¼	1156	13⅜	12⅞	13	9.6	11	22.5	...	...
44	AIK	Amer Ins Mtge Inv Ser 88[76]	AS	NR	10	158	Originate/acquire mtge loans	....	....	15	11	13¾	11⅜	1198	13½	12⅞	12⅞	13.4	8	30.5	...	...
¶45•[4]	AIG	✓Amer Intl Group	NY,B,Ch,P	A+	1254	251614	Major int'l insur hldg co	66⅞	1 13/16	67⅛	54½	95½	64⅛	155016	95½	89⅞	92½	0.4	18	41.6	21.2	22.8
46	AIP	✓Amer Israeli Paper Ord	AS,B,Ch,Ph	NR	..	...	Paper mfg fr imported pulp	56	4	52	36½	59¾	41½	109	48¼	42½	42¾	4.9	7	−3.8	2.9	10.3
47	AMZ	✓Amer List	AS,Ch	B+	24	1103	Computerized student list	16¾	⅛	19¼	14½	30¾	16⅝	205	27⅝	25½	25½	3.9	17	58.0	37.7	26.5
✣48	AMSY	✓Amer Mgmt Systems	NNM	B+	136	18649	Computer sys mgmt/admin	15⅞	11/16	19¼	12	31¾	16½	19260	31¾	26⅛	30	...	31	66.1	26.6	30.1
49	ENQ	✓Amer Media Cl'A'	NY	NR	81	18645	Publish:personality journalism	21⅞	13½	19¼	13⅛	16⅛	4	18093	5	4	4½	e...	27	−46.9	−22.8	...
50	WS	Wrrt (Pur 1 Cl'A'at $27.78)	NY	....	9	2910		2⅝	1½	1⅞	1/16	11/16	1/32	680	1/16	1/32	1/32B	...	..	...	...	...
✣51•[2]	EMT	✓Amer Medical Response	NY,Ph	NR	168	15174	Provides ambulance services	29¼	8⅛	28⅞	21½	32½	22¾	12336	32½	27⅞	32½	...	26	17.6	21.5	...
52	SKYC	✓Amer Mobile Satellite	NNM	NR	65	9160	Dvlp/stg:satellite comm svc	22	20	21	11½	31¼	12½	19514	31¼	24½	30⅝	...	d	150	...	...

Uniform Footnote Explanations-See Page 4. Other: [1]ASE,CBOE,P:Cycle 1. [2]CBOE:Cycle 1. [3]ASE:Cycle 3. [4]CBOE:Cycle 2. [5]ASE,CBOE:Cycle 1. [6]Ph:Cycle 3. [7]ASE:Cycle 1. [8]Ph:Cycle 1. [51]Approx. [52]Approx:Incl return of cap,'95. [53]Incl return of cap,'94. [54]Plan MidCap 400 listing,SmallCap 600 delisting:eff Jan 5. [55]18 Wks Dec'94. [56]®$2.62,'94. [57]®$3.24,'94. [58]®$3.53,'94. [59]Fiscal Mar'93 & prior. [60]Redemption of stk purch rt,'95. [61]Incl redemption of stk purch rt,'95. [62]Subsud Pfd in $M. [63]Dep for 0.005 shr $450 cm Cv Pfd'C'. [64]Fr 12-31-97,scale to $25 in 2003. [65]Stk dstr of Lehman Bros Hldg Svc. [66]Rated "A+r" by S&P. [67]Stock or cash re-specified cond.. [68]Plan mgr/name chge, DenAmerica Corp. [69]Monthly Income Preferred Shrs. [70]Fr 5-31-2003. [71]Issued by subsid,Amer Genl Del L.L.C.. [72]Co opt conv right expire 5-31-2000 re-spec cond. [73]Stk dstr of Psychiatric Group. [74]Incl $0.4675 non-taxable,'94. [75]Est return of capital. [76]L.P. Units. [77]Incl proceeds from mtge disp & return of cap.

Common and Convertible Preferred Stocks

Index (Splits ◆)	Cash Divs. Ea. Yr. Since	Dividends: Latest Payment Period $	Date	Ex. Div.	Total $ So Far 1995	Ind. Rate	Paid 1994	Financial Position Mil-$ Cash& Equiv.	Curr. Assets	Curr. Liab.	Balance Sheet Date	Capitalization Lg Trm Debt Mil-$	Shs. 000 Pfd.	Com.	Earnings $ Per Shr. Years End	1991	1992	1993	1994	1995	Last 12 Mos.	Interim Earnings Period	$ per Shr. 1994	1995	Index
1	1987	[51]0.088	1-31-96	12-27	[52]1.059	1.06	[53]0.971	Equity per shr $9.69			9-30-95	9.61	...	5566	Dc	0.87	0.75	0.68	0.62	....	0.59	9 Mo Sep	0.46	0.43	1
2	1988	0.119	1-31-96	12-27	1.466	1.55	1.402	Equity per shr $11.47			9-30-95	....	...	1627	Dc	0.81	0.61	0.61	0.59	....	0.67	9 Mo Sep	0.49	0.57	2
3	1986	[51]0.06¼	1-25-96	12-27	[52]0.75	0.75	[53]0.75	Equity per shr $11.32			3-31-95	....	...	5246	Dc	0.71	0.09	0.52	0.60	....	0.62	9 Mo Sep	0.42	0.44	3
4◆	....	None Since Public			...	Nil	....	42.1	125	185	9-30-95	19.0	...	★80680	Je	*p0.03	*0.05	*0.06	0.10	d0.49	d0.64	3 Mo Sep	0.02	d0.13	4
5	....	None Since Public			...	Nil	....	250	412	489	9-30-95	377	...	±p48255	Dc	...	...	...	‡[55]0.17	....	....	9 Mo Sep	n/a	□1.06	5
6	....	Terms&trad. basis should			be checked in detail			Wrrts expire 8-25-99				....	...	10385	Dc	...	...	...	....	....	....				6
7	1989	A0.07	12-20-95	12-6	0.07	0.07	0.06	Equity per shr $7.53			6-30-95	168	...	p43067	Dc	d2.92	□d1.44	□1.14	□0.98	....	1.26	9 Mo Sep	□0.73	1.01	7
8	1982	Q0.33	12-22-95	12-6	1.32	1.32	1.32	Book Value $16.05			12-31-94	59.7	...	2269	Dc	1.94	1.83	2.76	[56]2.76	....	2.08	9 Mo Sep	2.07	1.39	8
9	1950	Q0.19	12-15-95	11-29	0.75	0.76	0.71	Equity per shr $23.93			9-30-95	236	...	20198	Dc	2.55	2.57	□2.85	2.74	....	3.39	9 Mo Sep	1.74	2.39	9
10	....	None Since Public			...	Nil	....	19.1	95.2	40.7	9-30-95	191	...	19111	Dc	0.26	□0.42	0.08	□d0.30	....	d0.80	9 Mo Sep	□d0.04	d0.54	10
11◆	1979	Q0.10	1-5-96	12-18	0.30	0.40	0.11¼	27.1	169	92.5	9-30-95	94.3	...	3684	Dc	Δ0.82	1.05	1.43	[57]3.25	....	2.56	9 Mo Sep	2.19	1.50	11
12	....	None Since Public			...	Nil	....	0.76	1.02	1.17	9-30-95	0.33	...	4083	Dc	...	...	p0.07	pd1.87	....	d2.02	9 Mo Sep	p0.06	d0.09	12
13	1905	Q0.50	12-1-95	11-2	2.00	2.00	1.99¼	393	3316	2348	9-30-95	1383	516	181491	Dc	3.91	4.29	□3.30	[58]3.63	E2.80	3.38	9 Mo Sep	2.30	□2.05	13
14	1979	Q0.66¾	12-10-95	11-2	2.67	2.67	2.67	Cv into 4.08 common				....	516	...	Dc	b3.85	b4.16	b3.54	b3.59	....	....				14
15	....	None Since Public			...	Nil	....	11.5	65.8	41.5	9-30-95	8.73	...	6219	Dc	...	...	pΔ□0.68	□1.81	....	2.34	9 Mo Sep	□1.25	1.78	15
16◆	1941	Q0.14	12-15-95	11-29	0.56	0.56	0.533	16.3	161	66.8	9-30-95	66.5	...	16368	Dc	1.03	□1.22	1.04	□1.22	....	1.51	9 Mo Sep	□0.82	1.11	16
17	1993	0.04	6-1-95	5-15	0.08	Nil	0.16	12.9	24.5	80.3	9-30-95	★110	...	13766	Dc	p0.37	[59]0.81	0.36	d0.07	....	d0.83	9 Mo Sep	0.04	d0.72	17
18	....	None Since Public			...	Nil	....	20.4	21.5	7.64		★191	★465	5853	Je	...	...	d1.82	d1.77	d3.30	d3.30				18
19	1994	Q0.04	1-19-96	1-3	0.12	0.16	0.06	Equity per shr $9.88			9-30-95	11.3	163	7051	Dc	*0.73	Δ0.83	1.27	1.16	....	1.15	9 Mo Sep	0.74	0.73	19
20	....	None Since Public			...	Nil	....	0.54	95.8	76.6	7-29-95	....	...	10000	Jl	...	...	p0.39	p0.79	0.68	0.22	3 Mo Oct	0.32	d0.14	20
21◆	....	None Since Public			...	Nil	....	0.87	12.8	6.35	11-30-94	4.98	...	6822	Nv	d16.20	Pd1.50	0.09	0.15	....	0.21	9 Mo Aug	0.21	0.27	21
22◆	1994	[60]0.01	4-15-95	4-4	[61]0.03½	0.10	0.10	2.62	24.0	30.6	9-30-95	35.3	72	7826	Dc	1.27	1.51	0.60	0.49	....	d4.52	9 Mo Sep	0.33	d4.68	22
23	1909	Q0.60	12-8-95	11-8	2.40	2.40	2.40	93.7	1339	1531	9-30-95	4846	[62]749	186285	Dc	2.70	2.54	1.92	2.71	E2.85	2.71	12 Mo Sep	2.93	2.71	23
24◆	....	None Since Public			...	Nil	....	6.44	20.6	28.5	9-30-95	37.0	4	11814	Dc	d4.50	Δd10.70	d2.80	Δd7.70	....	d3.98	9 Mo Sep	Δd3.29	Δ0.43	24
25	1994	Q0.56¼	12-29-95	12-14	2.25	2.25	1.68¾	Cv into 1.6667 com,$15.00				....	800	...	Dc	...	...	...	....	....	....				25
26◆	1870	Q0.22½	2-9-96	1-3	0.90	0.90	h[65]0.95	Equity per shr $14.89			9-30-95	6284	4000	484405	Dc	1.59	Δ0.83	2.92	2.75	E3.20	3.00	9 Mo Sep	2.09	2.34	26
27	1994	Q0.574	1-16-96	12-27	2.296	2.30	2.278	Amt pay maturity based on First Data Cp stk[67]				....	...	★23619	Dc	...	...	...	....	....	....	Due 10-1-96			27
28	....	None Since Public			...	Nil	....	2.20	5.05	10.2	6-28-95	16.3	...	6080	Sp	...	...	p0.11	0.30	P□0.30	0.30				28
29	1993	Q0.07	11-10-95	10-25	0.28	0.28	0.22	Book Value $9.71			9-30-95	93.4	...	10892	Dc	1.49	1.87	□1.25	1.37	....	1.56	9 Mo Sep	1.02	□1.21	29
30	1957	Q0.26½	11-24-95	11-8	1.03	1.06	0.98	36.1	77.6	24.9	9-30-95	0.65	...	3734	Dc	1.96	0.33	1.96	3.13	....	2.68	9 Mo Sep	2.43	1.98	30
31	1987	Q0.25	10-13-95	9-27	1.00	1.00	0.88	Equity per shr $14.37			9-30-95	p925	...	★59493	Dc	0.05	Δ1.28	4.81	0.01	....	1.05	9 Mo Sep	□1.35	Δ2.39	31
32◆	1929	Q0.31	12-1-95	11-2	1.24	1.24	1.16	Equity per shr $24.11			9-30-95	6147	...	204791	Dc	2.12	2.45	□1.15	2.45	E3.45	2.77	9 Mo Sep	2.27	2.59	32
33	1995	0.25	12-29-95	12-26	1.75	3.00	....	Cv into 1.2288 com,Amer Gen Cp,$40.69[72]				....	5000	...	Dc	...	...	...	....	....	....				33
34◆	1950	Q0.16	12-8-95	11-21	0.60	0.64	0.53	35.3	989	464	8-31-95	77.2	...	±74591	Fb	±1.40	±1.55	□±1.77	2.00	E1.50	1.52	9 Mo Nov	1.42	0.94	34
35	1987	Q0.49½	11-10-95	10-25	h[73]2.14	1.98	[74]2.29½	Equity per shr $14.43			9-30-95	p207	...	★23418	Dc	2.09	d0.37	2.71	0.46	E1.60	0.46	9 Mo Sep	1.17	1.17	35
36◆	1964	M0.06	1-19-96	1-4	0.70	0.72	0.64	Equity per shr $15.33			9-30-95	20.0	...	13886	Dc	1.27	1.42	1.59	1.71	....	1.98	9 Mo Sep	1.28	1.55	36
37	1919	Q0.77	12-1-95	11-9	3.02	3.08	2.94	2080	8038	4626	9-30-95	8492	59	312711	Dc	4.36	Δ3.66	4.73	4.97	E6.40	6.48	9 Mo Sep	3.67	5.18	37
38	1966	Q0.50	1-1-96	12-11	2.00	2.00	2.00	Cv into 9 common				....	38	...	Dc	b44.60	b39.51	b32.09	b15.10	....	....				38
39	1939	Q0.075	11-15-95	11-6	0.285	0.30	0.21	Equity per shr $19.27			9-30-95	....	...	1947	Dc	1.08	1.66	2.95	4.24	....	0.75	9 Mo Sep	1.57	d1.92	39
40	1986	[75]0.04	10-23-95	10-10	[75]0.04	Nil	....	Equity per shr $2.38			9-30-95	62.9	...	9075	Dc	Δd1.49	Δd2.06	□d0.59	□d0.47	....	d0.38	9 Mo Sep	d0.37	□d0.28	40
41	1985	Q0.08	2-1-96	12-27	0.32	0.32	1.42	Equity per shr $4.01			9-30-95	....	...	10000	Dc	0.45	0.38	0.44	0.32	....	0.29	9 Mo Sep	0.25	0.22	41
42	1986	0.12	2-1-96	12-27	1.54	1.40	†[77]2.09	Equity per shr $18.09			9-30-95	0.34	...	12079	Dc	1.02	1.22	1.52	1.29	....	1.26	9 Mo Sep	0.98	0.95	42
43	1994	0.11	2-1-96	12-27	1.25	1.25	†1.00	Equity per shr $17.64			9-30-95	0.50	...	9576	Dc	0.60	0.95	1.21	1.24	....	1.16	9 Mo Sep	0.95	0.87	43
44	1994	0.12	2-1-96	12-27	1.78	1.72	†0.97	Equity per shr $17.84			9-30-95	....	...	8802	Dc	0.65	0.90	1.13	1.24	....	1.54	9 Mo Sep	0.90	1.20	44
45◆	1969	Q0.08½	3-22-96	3-6	0.323	0.34	0.287	Equity per shr $39.50			9-30-95	9230	...	474092	Dc	3.24	Δ3.40	Δ4.03	4.58	E5.10	5.09	9 Mo Sep	3.36	3.87	45
46	1986	t[51]2.101	12-20-95	12-1	t[51]2.101	2.10	t1.037	2.83	126	97.0	12-31-94	22.9	...	3805	Dc	3.47	3.12	2.78	2.91	....	5.77	6 Mo Jun	0.11	2.97	46
47◆	1989	Q0.25	11-10-95	10-18	0.90	1.00	0.582	11.3	15.8	1.10	8-31-95	1.94	...	4565	Fb	0.65	0.77	1.00	1.36	....	1.49	6 Mo Aug	0.58	0.71	47
48◆	....	None Since Public			...	Nil	....	35.5	229	108	9-30-95	22.1	...	26610	Dc	0.50	Δ0.67	0.69	0.90	....	0.97	9 Mo Sep	0.63	0.70	48
49	1991	†7.00	1-3-95	1-4	†7.00	Nil	0.15	6.06	29.0	106	9-25-95	546	...	±41766	Mr	□±0.22	±0.47	±0.67	±□0.56	....	0.17	6 Mo Sep	±0.41	±0.02	49
50	....	Terms&trad. basis should			be checked in detail			Wrrts expire 5-15-97				....	...	★4860	Mr	...	...	...	....	....	....				50
51	....	None Since Public			...	Nil	....	39.0	138	72.0	9-30-95	8.55	...	19550	Dc	p0.57	p0.67	0.82	p1.05	....	1.27	9 Mo Sep	p0.77	0.99	51
52	....	None Since Public			...	Nil	....	55.4	69.6	45.0	9-30-95	41.4	...	24942	Dc	...	pd1.78	□pd2.03	d0.86	....	d1.33	9 Mo Sep	Δd0.61	d1.08	52

◆**Stock Splits & Divs By Line Reference Index** [4]2-for-1,'95(twice). [11]2-for-1,'94. [16]3-for-2,'91,'95. [21]1-for-10 REVERSE,'93. [22]3-for-2,'92. [24]1-for-10 REVERSE,'95. [26]No adj for Lehman Bros dstr(0.20 com)'94. [32]2-for-1,'93. [34]2-for-1,'93. [36]4-for-3,'92:3-for-2,'93. [45]3-for-2,'93,'95. [47]3-for-2,'93:10%,'94. [48]3-for-2,'92,'94:To split 3-for-2,ex Jan 8.

¶ S&P 500 # MidCap 400 ✣ SmallCap 600 • Options

Index	Ticker	Name of Issue (Call Price of Pfd. Stocks)	Market	Com. Rank. & Pfd. Rating	Inst. Hold Cos	Inst. Hold Shs. (000)	Principal Business	Price Range 1971-93 High	1971-93 Low	1994 High	1994 Low	1995 High	1995 Low	Dec. Sales in 100s	December, 1995 Last Sale Or Bid High	Low	Last	%Div Yield	P-E Ratio	Total Return % Annualized 12 Mo	36 Mo	60 Mo
1	ANAT	✓Amer Natl Insur	NNM	A	94	5037	Life insurance	63¼	5⅝	55	44¼	66¾	45½	2900	66½	60½	66½	3.8	9	48.9	13.1	24.7
2	AORI	✓Amer Oncology Res	NNM	NR	105	4941	Provides managed oncology svcs	....	....	....	....	49½	21	17167	49½	35¼	48⅝	...	87	...	...	...
3	APP	✓Amer Paging	AS,Ch,Ph	NR	38	1909	Wireless messaging svcs	....	....	14⅞	5⅞	8¾	6⅛	1862	7⅜	6⅜	6⅜	...	d	−1.9	...	...
#4•[1]	APCC	✓Amer Power Conversion	NNM	B	236	47288	Mfr constant pwr supply prod	24¾	¼	30½	14½	25⅞	9⅛	220780	11¼	9⅛	9½	...	12	−43.1	−12.4	32.3
5	APR	✓Amer Precision Indus	NY,Ch,Ph	B+	18	915	Ind'l process eq: electr comp	18	¼	8¼	6¼	14¾	7⅝	2193	12⅛	10¾	11⅛	2.3	18	49.6	16.4	−3.0
#6•[2]	APS	✓Amer President Cos	NY,B,Ch	B	162	16491	Major U.S. containership oper	30¼	5¼	34	19	31¾	21	25002	25½	21¾	23	1.7	10	5.6	7.9	25.6
7	AMRD	✓Amer Radio Systems'A'	NNM	NR	75	4884	Own,oper AM/FM radio stations	....	....	....	....	29¾	16½	14058	28½	21	28	...	..	...	...	...
8•[3]	ARN	✓Amer Re Corp	NY,Ch	NR	114	15131	Prop & casualty reinsurance	41¾	25¾	35¾	23½	45	29⅛	23774	45	39¼	40⅞	0.8	14	30.1	...	...
9	REA	✓Amer Real Estate Investment	AS	NR	3	84	Real estate investment trust	10	7¾	8⅞	6⅜	8¾	6⅝	289	8	7¾	7⅞	10.7	d	30.1	...	...
10	ACP	✓Amer R.E.Ptnrs L.P.	NY,Ch	NR	34	16814	Acquire,manage real estate	17½	6⅛	8⅝	7⅛	9⅜	6¾	3905	8¾	8⅛	8½	...	6	15.3	7.9	11.2
11	ARB	✓Amer Realty Tr SBI	NY,Ch	NR	11	103	Inv RE loons/own rental prop	72⅜	¾	13⅜	11⅛	15⅝	12⅞	113	15	14½	14¾	...	d	12.4	35.0	22.9
12	AMRC	✓Amer Recreation Ctrs[54]	NNM	B	18	1096	Bowling centers:catalog prod	11⅝	¼	7½	4½	7⅞	4½	3667	6⅝	6⅛	6⅜	3.9	9	32.3	5.0	4.5
13	AREE	✓Amer Resource	NSC	NR	2	202	Gold,copper mining & explor'n	14⅜	5	8⅜	3¼	4⅞	3½	1372	4½	3⅞	4½	...	d	0.0	...	...
14	RMC	✓Amer Restaurant Ptnrs'A'[55]	AS	NR	1	.1	Pizza Hut franchise	15⅛	7⅝	11⅞	5⅞	7	5½	254	6½	6	6	e10.6	10	11.0	−5.6	4.9
15	RICE	Amer Rice	NSC	NR	2	100	Rice producer	....	....	....	....	3¼	1¼	452	1⅝	1¼	1⅜	...	d	...	...	...
16	RAZR	✓Amer Safety Razor	NNM	NR	57	6699	Mfr shaving blades & razors	14½	10⅜	14½	10	14	7½	17310	8⅝	7½	7⅞	...	9	−40.6	...	...
17	ASE	✓Amer Science & Engr	AS,B	C	12	469	X-ray prod:rsch&engr svc	13⅞	11/16	6⅞	2⅞	8⅛	5⅝	2088	7⅞	6⅜	7⅝	...	d	19.6	9.1	7.7
18•[4]	SNIFF	✓Amer Sensors	NNM	NR	12	571	Indoor air quality monitor pd	....	....	21	8	18	3⅜	16986	5	3⅜	3⅝	...	..	−76.5	...	...
19	AMS	✓Amer Shared Hosp Sv	AS	C	8	641	Medical diagnostic imag'g eq	12⅛	1	3½	3/16	2¾	¼	1123	1½	1 3/16	1 5/16	...	d	200	−24.1	3.1
20•[5]	AMSWA	✓Amer Software'A'	NNM,Ph	B−	47	7369	Mkts IBM compatible softwr	19¾	2 3/16	6½	2⅝	8¾	2½	17392	6⅝	5⅞	6½	...	d	117	−7.0	−11.9
21•[6]	ASD	✓Amer Standard	NY,Ch,Ph	NR	110	39043	Air condit'g,bath fix,brake sy	....	....	....	....	32	19⅝	45330	31⅞	27½	28	...	51	...	...	...
¶22•[7]	ASC	✓Amer Stores	NY,B,Ch,P,Ph	A	428	85679	Operates supermkts,drug strs	24⅝	7/16	27¾	20⅞	30¾	23¼	61478	27½	25¾	26¾	2.1	12	1.0	9.1	16.9
23	AMK	✓Amer Techl Ceramics	AS,Ch	B−	11	287	Mfrs ceramic capacitors	10½	1	4⅜	3	17⅛	3⅜	1276	12⅛	9¾	10⅛	...	20	184	68.3	55.2
24	ATEL	✓Amer Telecasting	NNM	NR	50	3840	Operates CATV Systems	19¾	18	27	9¾	17¾	9	11510	14½	13½	14½	...	d	45.0	...	...
25	ATVC	✓Amer Travellers	NNM	B	99	8219	Life,accident,health,insur	20¾	1 15/16	18	10⅞	28⅝	15½	31986	28⅝	25	28⅛	...	14	73.1	56.2	18.3
26	AMGD	Amer Vanguard	NNM	B	6	64	Mfr agric-chem/dstr ind'l eqp	16¼	⅜	16½	5¾	9	4½	135	6¾	4½	6¾	...	9	−10.0	−2.4	8.4
27	AW	✓Amer Waste Svcs'A'	NY,Ch,Ph	NR	26	1877	Waste mgmt/disposal svcs	14⅞	1¾	3⅛	1½	5⅝	1⅛	30864	2⅝	2	2	...	d	23.1	−12.6	−30.5
#28	AWK	✓Amer Water Works	NY,B,Ch,Ph	A	151	13253	Water utility holding co	32¼	1 9/16	32¼	25¼	39¼	26¾	13461	39¼	31¾	38⅞	3.3	15	50.9	20.3	23.8
29	AHR	✓Americana Hotels/Rlty	NY,Ch,Ph	LIQ	19	2301	REIT:invests in hotels & resorts	28½	1¾	3	2¼	3⅝	2⅞	516	3⅜	3⅛	3¼	...	d	31.1	23.5	10.1
30•[8]	ACF	✓AmeriCredit Corp	NY,Ch	NR	80	12862	Provides used-car financing	23	2⅛	8⅛	5⅛	16¼	5¼	17439	13⅝	12	13⅝	...	14	142	52.1	27.0
31•[7]	ADA	✓AmeriData Technol	NY,Ch,Ph	NR	43	7627	Data/telecomm svc/alert'g prd	30½	1 9/16	23¼	9½	14⅛	6⅞	25982	10⅞	8¾	9⅝	...	13	−1.3	28.4	...
32	APU	✓AmeriGas Partners L.P.	NY,Ch	NR	17	505	Retail propane distributer	....	....	....	....	24⅝	21¼	9483	24¼	22	24¼	9.1	d	...	...	...
33	AMRN	Amerin Corp	NNM	NR	..	...	Mortgage insurance	....	....	....	....	28½	16	71252	28½	20¾	26¾	...	..	...	...	...
34	AQS	✓AmeriQuest Technol	NY,Ph	C	13	694	Mfr PC storage,mem subsys	47½	1¼	6	2⅝	3¼	⅝	26310	1	⅝	⅞	...	d	−73.1	−32.7	−17.2
35	ASHC	✓AmeriSource Health'A'	NNM	NR	105	9909	Wholesale dstr drug,hlth prod	....	....	....	....	34¼	19¾	8701	34¼	29	33	...	21	...	...	...
36	ASCA	✓Ameristar Casinos	NNM	NR	18	821	Own,oper casino-hotels	12¾	9	16¾	4½	10½	4½	7957	7⅛	5¾	6½	...	23	36.8	...	...
¶37•[7]	AIT	✓Ameritech Corp	NY,B,Ch,P,Ph	A−	861	201930	Tel sv:Ill,Ind,Mich,Oh,Wis	45⅝	10⅜	43⅛	36¼	59⅜	39⅞	123305	59⅜	54¾	58⅞	3.6	16	49.3	24.5	17.7
38	AWII	✓Ameriwood Indus Intl	NNM	B−	20	729	Mfr ready to assemble furniture	16½	1 11/16	19	7	9½	3⅞	4453	4¾	3⅞	3⅞	...	7	−45.1	−27.8	15.8
39	AMN	✓Ameron, Inc	NY	B−	67	1636	Mfr concrete & steel pipes	52½	4¼	43½	29	39	29⅛	1522	39	36	37⅝	3.4	12	32.7	6.5	3.0
40	AMES	✓Ames Department Stores	NNM	NR	16	1931	Discount department stores	4⅞	1	6½	1⅞	3¾	1⅛	30784	1⅞	1⅛	1⅜	...	2	−42.1	...	...
#41•[5]	AME	✓AMETEK, Inc	NY,B,Ch,P,Ph	B	145	18329	Mfr instruments/elec mtrs	19¾	1⅛	18¾	11⅝	19½	15¾	11827	19¼	17½	18¾	1.3	14	12.6	7.9	17.8
¶42•[9]	AMGN	✓Amgen Inc	NNM	B−	818	172913	Res/dev of biological prod	39⅛	5/16	30⅛	17⅜	59¾	28⅛	415919	59¾	49	59⅝	...	30	100	18.6	42.3
43	AML	✓Amli Residential Prop	NY,Ch	NR	69	6250	Real estate investment trust	....	....	23¼	17	20½	17	2804	20⅝	18¾	20	8.6	18	16.5	...	...
44	AMXI	✓AMNEX Inc	NSC	NR	10	1901	Provides tele operator svcs	200	1¼	3⅝	1 15/16	5¾	2⅜	12091	4⅝	3¼	4½	...	..	67.5	46.3	−39.4
¶45•[8]	AN	✓Amoco Corp	NY,To,B,C,Ch,P,Ph	B	1261	291936	International oil company	60⅜	6½	64⅛	50⅞	72⅝	56⅜	192362	72⅝	67⅞	71½	3.4	17	26.0	16.8	11.1
¶46•[8]	AMP	✓AMP Inc	NY,B,C,Ch,P,Ph	A−	818	168528	Solderless elec wire terminals	35¾	3	39¾	28⅞	46¼	35⅛	124030	42⅛	36⅞	38¼	2.4	19	7.3	12.9	14.9
47	PACE	✓Ampace Corp	NNM	NR	1	14	Trucking-gen'l commodities	....	....	....	....	5½	3	2084	3⅜	3	3	...	..	...	...	...
48	AIS.A	✓Ampal-Amer Israel'A'	AS,B	NR	30	1442	Loans/investments in Israel	13	⅜	13⅛	6¼	7⅛	5⅛	3176	5¾	5⅛	5¼	...	44	−17.6	2.1	27.4
49	WS	Wrrt(Pur 1'A'com at$16)	AS,Ch	....	2	1375		....	....	2¾	¼	13/16	¼	2084	½	¼	¼	...	..	...	...	...
50	AP	✓Ampco-Pittsburgh	NY,B,Ch,Ph	B−	46	6094	Air&liquid hndlg eq:metal pr	26¾	4⅜	9⅞	6⅛	11⅜	7¾	1353	11	9¼	10¾	e0.9	14	15.9	15.1	14.4
51•[10]	APH	✓Amphenol Corp'A'	NY	NR	169	21632	Mfr elec&fiberoptic connectors	16½	5⅛	25⅛	14⅛	30⅜	18¾	32481	24¼	20¾	24¼	...	19	1.0	49.6	...
52	AMPI	✓Amplicon, Inc	NNM	B+	25	1323	Lease/sell computers,elec eq	21	6¾	21½	17¼	17⅞	14	44	16	14¼	16	1.3	8	−6.1	2.7	16.7

Uniform Footnote Explanations-See Page 4. Other: [1]ASE,CBOE:Cycle 3. [2]P:Cycle 1. [3]P,Ph:Cycle 1. [4]CBOE:Cycle 3. [5]Ph:Cycle 1. [6]CBOE,NY:Cycle 1. [7]CBOE:Cycle 1. [8]CBOE:Cycle 2. [9]ASE:Cycle 1. [10]Ph:Cycle 3. [51]®$2.30,'94. [52]7 Wks Dec'93. [53]®$0.39,'94. [54]Fulcrum Cap Ptnrs plan acq,$7.50. [55]L.P. Income Pref Units. [56]100% non-taxable,'94. [57]Excl Cl'B'&Cl'C'Units. [58]®$2.33,'95. [59]Excl $50M subsid Pfd. [60]Liq div. [61]Incl. 19.8M Subordinated Units. [62]Fiscal Sep'93 & prior. [63]5 Wks Jan'93. [64]®$1.13,'94. [65]Combined AMP & Pamcor. [66]Spl div. [67]Incl common privately held.

Common and Convertible Preferred Stocks

Index (Splits ◆)	Cash Divs. Ea. Yr. Since	Dividends: Latest Payment Period $	Date	Ex. Div.	Total $ So Far 1995	Ind. Rate	Paid 1994	Financial Position Mil-$ Cash& Equiv.	Curr. Assets	Curr. Liab.	Balance Sheet Date
1	1923	Q0.63	12-15-95	11-29	2.40	2.52	2.24	Equity per shr $78.26			12-31-94
2	....	None Since Public			...	Nil	....	69.8	95.9	17.2	9-30-95
3	....	None Since Public			...	Nil	....	4.16	23.1	22.3	9-30-95
4◆	....	None Since Public			...	Nil	....	10.7	266	58.6	9-30-95
5	1973	Q0.06½	1-17-96	12-27	0.255	0.26	0.24½	0.25	26.3	10.6	9-30-95
6◆	1985	Q0.10	11-30-95	11-13	0.40	0.40	0.40	166	537	443	9-22-95
7	....	None Since Public			...	Nil	....	5.16	30.4	20.7	9-30-95
8	1995	Q0.08	12-29-95	12-13	0.32	0.32	....	Equity per shr $19.38			9-30-95
9	1994	Q0.21	12-5-95	11-22	0.83¼	0.84	0.721	Equity per shr $3.87			9-30-95
10	1987	0.12½	2-14-94	12-27	...	Nil	0.12½	Equity per shr $14.57			9-30-95
11◆	....	0.60	5-15-90	4-24	...	Nil	....	Equity per shr $18.01			9-30-95
12	1968	Q0.06¼	4-9-96	3-14	0.24½	0.25	0.23	11.4	13.6	11.3	8-31-95
13	....	None Since Public			...	Nil	....	9.67	13.8	14.0	6-30-95
14	1987	†0.26	10-27-95	10-10	†0.74	0.64	[56]1.07	1.12	2.07	4.17	9-26-95
15◆	....	None Paid			...	Nil	....	1.90	93.3	50.3	9-30-95
16	....	None Since Public			...	Nil	....	1.53	78.6	32.4	9-30-95
17	....	5%Stk	8-25-81	8-3	...	Nil	....	0.73	9.87	4.00	9-29-95
18◆	....	None Since Public			...	Nil	....	7.87	47.1	14.0	6-30-95
19	....	None Since Public			...	Nil	....	0.59	7.39	15.6	9-30-95
20	1986	0.08	9-26-94	8-30	...	Nil	0.24	35.2	61.1	25.2	10-31-95
21	....	None Since Public			...	Nil	....	54.4	1285	1299	9-30-95
22◆	1949	Q0.14	1-5-96	12-20	0.54	0.56	0.46	3.09	2059	1951	10-28-95
23	....	None Since Public			...	Nil	....	3.19	17.0	4.52	9-30-95
24	....	None Since Public			...	Nil	....	60.8	66.1	17.1	9-30-95
25	....	None Since Public			...	Nil	....	Equity per shr $13.31			9-30-95
26	....	0.05	12-1-89	11-9	...	Nil	....	0.32	16.7	6.45	9-30-95
27	....	None Since Public			...	Nil	....	6.24	28.9	15.5	9-30-95
28	1948	Q0.32	11-15-95	10-25	1.28	1.28	1.08	26.0	187	300	9-30-95
29	....	[60]0.50	3-6-95	2-16	[60]0.50	Nil	....	Equity per shr $3.76			9-30-95
30	....	None Since Public			...	Nil	....	Equity per shr $5.18			9-30-95
31◆	....	None Since Public			...	Nil	....	15.5	510	479	9-30-95
32	1995	0.55	11-18-95	11-8	0.996	2.20	....	0.05	179	147	p12-31-94
33	....	None Since Public			...	Nil	....	Equity per shr $9.88			9-30-95
34	....	None Since Public			...	Nil	....	0.21	94.5	90.7	9-30-95
35	....	None Since Public			...	Nil	....	32.2	773	530	9-30-95
36	....	None Since Public			...	Nil	....	8.91	14.5	20.1	9-30-95
37◆	1984	Q0.53	2-1-96	12-27	2.00	2.12	1.92	266	3420	4987	9-30-95
38◆	....	0.075	2-16-87	1-9	...	Nil	....	....	35.9	13.8	9-30-95
39	1939	Q0.32	11-21-95	10-24	1.28	1.28	1.28	8.36	218	86.2	8-31-95
40	....	None Paid			...	Nil	....	19.8	555	394	7-29-95
41◆	1942	Q0.06	12-22-95	12-6	0.24	0.24	0.24	10.7	259	238	9-30-95
42◆	....	None Since Public			...	Nil	....	992	1420	596	9-30-95
43	1994	Q0.43	11-20-95	11-7	1.71	1.72	1.05	Equity per shr $14.36			9-30-95
44◆	....	None Paid			...	Nil	....	0.60	29.1	27.4	9-30-95
45	1894	Q0.60	12-10-95	11-6	2.40	2.40	2.20	1127	6129	5451	9-30-95
46◆	1951	Q0.23	12-1-95	11-2	0.92	0.92	0.84	256	2287	1278	9-30-95
47◆	....	None Since Public			...	Nil	....	2.07	5.88	4.44	9-30-95
48	1995	[66]0.21	12-28-95	12-13	[66]0.21	Nil	....	Equity per shr $7.14			9-30-95
49	....	Terms&trad. basis should			be checked in detail			Wrrts expire 1-31-99			
50	1966	†0.075	1-31-96	1-10	0.10	0.10	0.10	15.3	85.8	22.0	9-30-95
51	....	None Since Public			...	Nil	....	3.55	215	111	9-30-95
52	1994	Q0.05	1-12-96	12-27	0.20	0.20	0.05	Equity per shr $15.96			9-30-95

Capitalization: Lg Trm Debt Mil-$	Shs. 000 Pfd.	Com.	Earnings $ Per Shr. Years End	1991	1992	1993	1994	1995	Last 12 Mos.	Interim Earnings Period	$ per Shr. 1994	1995	Index
12.4	...	26479	Dc	4.76	□6.37	7.00	8.12	....	7.46	9 Mo Sep	5.51	4.85	1
27.3	...	13738	Dc	...	...	...	p0.25	....	0.56	9 Mo Sep	p0.13	p0.44	2
87.3	...	±20029	Dc	...	...	±pd0.07	±d0.07	....	d0.63	9 Mo Sep	±d0.02	±d0.58	3
....	...	93178	Dc	0.17	0.30	0.53	0.77	E0.79	0.81	9 Mo Sep	0.52	0.56	4
2.35	...	7128	Dc	0.50	0.34	0.29	0.49	....	0.62	9 Mo Sep	0.35	0.48	5
498	...	p25666	Dc	□1.83	□2.43	2.65	[51]2.38	E2.30	2.23	9 Mo Sep	1.64	1.49	6
132	...	±14380	Dc	...	...	...	pd0.16	....	....	9 Mo Sep	n/a	±0.55	7
450	...	47050	Dc	p1.88	n/a	Δ□2.22	2.01	....	3.00	9 Mo Sep	1.30	□2.29	8
39.8	...	★1867	Dc	...	...	‡[52]0.10	[53]0.65	....	d0.09	9 Mo Sep	0.51	d0.23	9
205	1975	25667	Dc	Δ1.31	□0.84	1.60	1.64	....	1.41	9 Mo Sep	1.29	1.06	10
84.6	...	2929	Dc	Δd4.96	d3.95	Δd2.72	Δd0.90	....	d1.48	9 Mo Sep	Δd0.75	Δd1.33	11
26.7	...	5056	My	0.52	0.60	0.38	0.38	0.32	0.72	6 Mo Nov	0.01	0.41	12
13.3	...	13530	Dc	...	...	Δd3.59	d2.21	....	d1.78	9 Mo Sep	Δ0.06	0.49	13
10.7	...	[57]826	Dc	1.21	1.72	1.72	1.04	....	0.61	9 Mo Sep	0.98	0.55	14
94.1	3878	2444	Mr	...	...	Δd0.09	d0.83	....	d1.68	6 Mo Sep	d0.25	d1.10	15
110	...	±12093	Dc	...	p±0.36	□0.34	0.94	....	0.90	9 Mo Sep	0.65	□0.61	16
0.07	...	4411	Mr	d0.10	0.41	d0.83	d0.23	....	d0.07	6 Mo Sep	d0.11	0.05	17
0.36	...	10144	Je	...	...	...	0.32	0.25	0.02	3 Mo Sep	0.28	0.05	18
25.4	...	4244	Dc	Δ0.01	d3.39	d5.46	d1.80	....	d2.10	9 Mo Sep	Δd2.13	Δd2.43	19
....	...	±22265	Ap	0.75	0.80	0.23	d0.30	d0.30	d0.01	6 Mo Oct	d0.26	0.03	20
1757	...	76268	Dc	...	...	pd0.62	□d1.29	....	0.55	9 Mo Sep	d0.23	□1.61	21
2074	...	146368	Ja	□1.74	1.47	□1.85	[58]2.42	E2.15	2.24	9 Mo Oct	1.51	1.33	22
4.28	...	3874	Je	d0.21	0.10	0.25	0.26	Δ0.45	0.52	3 Mo Sep	Δ0.06	0.13	23
209	...	16392	Dc	...	pd0.37	pd0.46	d1.08	....	d2.55	9 Mo Sep	d0.60	Δ□d2.07	24
104	...	10569	Dc	1.09	1.03	1.39	1.71	....	1.98	9 Mo Sep	1.25	1.52	25
7.15	...	2309	Dc	0.15	0.82	0.98	0.52	....	0.75	9 Mo Sep	d0.07	0.16	26
8.53	...	±29916	Dc	±0.27	±0.21	±0.14	±0.07	....	d0.15	9 Mo Sep	±0.04	±d0.18	27
2270	[59]2067	33662	Dc	2.27	2.07	2.29	2.34	....	2.65	12 Mo Sep	2.27	2.65	28
3.15	...	6524	Dc	d0.22	0.20	0.05	d0.24	....	d0.20	9 Mo Sep	0.04	0.08	29
159	...	28314	Je	d1.15	d0.77	d0.66	0.16	0.95	0.97	3 Mo Sep	0.06	0.08	30
13.7	...	21458	Dc	d0.21	0.01	0.36	0.78	....	0.76	9 Mo Sep	0.58	0.56	31
655	...	[61]★39564	Sp	...	...	...	p1.49	Pd1.12	d1.12				32
....	p...	★24251	Dc	...	...	...	p0.13	....	....	9 Mo Sep	n/a	p0.38	33
6.69	2597	23792	Je	d2.89	d3.04	0.08	d1.33	d3.76	d3.96	3 Mo Sep	d0.10	d0.30	34
436	...	±22171	Sp	...	...	...	±pd7.13	±□1.54	1.54				35
67.3	...	20360	Dc	...	...	p[62]0.27	0.21	....	0.28	9 Mo Sep	0.30	□0.37	36
4547	...	553878	Dc	2.20	□2.51	2.78	□2.13	E3.75	3.66	9 Mo Sep	1.35	2.88	37
5.00	...	4188	Dc	d1.74	1.69	1.21	2.02	....	0.54	9 Mo Sep	1.27	d0.21	38
116	...	3948	Nv	2.01	1.53	d6.28	2.75	....	3.09	9 Mo Aug	1.86	2.20	39
60.7	...	20127	Ja	...	[63]d1.19	0.47	□0.86	....	0.82	9 Mo Oct	□d0.60	d0.64	40
150	...	33050	Dc	0.87	1.01	d0.17	□Δ1.05	E1.30	1.60	9 Mo Sep	□Δ0.76	□1.31	41
177	...	265999	Dc	0.34	1.22	Δ1.31	[64]1.14	E1.95	1.42	9 Mo Sep	1.12	1.40	42
210	...	11677	Dc	...	p0.34	p0.43	p1.00	....	1.10	9 Mo Sep	p□0.78	0.88	43
0.39	2570	19114	Dc	d15.30	d1.70	d0.01	0.02	....	0.02	9 Mo Sep	0.05	0.05	44
3775	...	496769	Dc	Δ2.36	□1.71	3.66	3.60	E4.30	4.42	9 Mo Sep	2.52	3.34	45
224	...	[65]217599	Dc	1.23	1.38	1.41	1.76	E2.00	1.95	9 Mo Sep	1.25	1.44	46
8.48	...	2800	Dc	...	...	...	p0.22	....	....	9 Mo Sep	n/a	0.02	47
80.4	1279	[67]±23454	Dc	*0.02	0.44	□0.22	0.27	....	0.12	9 Mo Sep	0.26	0.11	48
....	...	4000	Dc	...	...	...	....	....	....	Callable fr 2-1-96 without pymt to holder			49
....	...	9578	Dc	d1.43	□d0.20	d0.47	0.84	....	0.78	9 Mo Sep	0.67	0.61	50
195	...	47315	Dc	p0.58	0.26	0.58	□0.91	....	1.26	9 Mo Sep	□0.63	0.98	51
247	...	5874	Je	1.26	1.57	1.68	1.89	1.97	1.99	3 Mo Sep	0.43	0.45	52

◆**Stock Splits & Divs By Line Reference Index** [4]2-for-1,'91,'92,'93. [6]2-for-1,'94. [11]To split 2-for-1,ex Jan 16. [15]1-for-5 REVERSE,'94. [18]2-for-1,'95(ex'94). [22]2-for-1,'91,'94. [31]3-for-2,'93. [37]2-for-1,'94. [38]2-for-1,'93. [41]Stk dstr of Ketema Inc,'88. [42]3-for-1,'91:2-for-1,'95. [44]1-for-8 REVERSE,'91:1-for-10 REVERSE,'92. [46]2-for-1,'95. [47]43% stk div,'95.

¶ S&P 500 # MidCap 400 ✢ SmallCap 600 • Options

Index	Ticker	Name of Issue (Call Price of Pfd. Stocks)	Market	Com. Rank. & Pfd. Rating	Inst. Hold Cos	Inst. Hold Shs. (000)	Principal Business	Price Range 1971-93 High	1971-93 Low	1994 High	1994 Low	1995 High	1995 Low	Dec. Sales in 100s	December, 1995 Last Sale Or Bid High	Low	Last	%Div Yield	P-E Ratio	Total Return % Annualized 12 Mo	36 Mo	60 Mo
¶1•[1]	AMR	✔AMR Corp	NY,B,C,Ch,P,Ph	C	600	69230	Hldg co:American Airlines	107½	4⅞	72¾	48⅛	80¼	53⅜	140736	78½	72¼	74¼	...	11	40.4	4.5	8.9
2	AMM	✔AMRE Inc	NY,Ch,Ph	NR	18	4986	Siding,cabinet refacing	16⅛	2½	5⅞	3⅛	15	3⅛	33622	15	11½	14⅝	...	d	191	35.1	24.3
3	AXR	✔AMREP Corp	NY,B,Ch,P,Ph	B–	18	884	Land develop: dstr mag,books	23⅜	7/16	9¾	5½	8¼	5½	1592	6⅛	5½	5⅞	...	10	–4.1	6.4	9.4
✢4	AMMB	✔AMRESCO INC	NNM	B–	56	7112	Specialty financial svcs	12½	⅛	9¼	5½	13½	5⅞	58092	13⅜	11¾	12¾	1.6	21	109	52.5	39.7
✢5•[2]	ASZ	✔AMSCO Intl[53]	NY,Ph	NR	153	23538	Mfr infection control equip	30⅝	9½	12¼	6⅞	21⅝	8⅞	71598	18¾	13½	14⅞	...	15	63.0	–15.9	...
6•[3]	ASO	✔AmSouth Bancorp	NY,B,Ch,Ph	B+	160	22852	Comm'l bkg,Alabama,Florida	35⅞	3½	34⅞	25⅜	41⅜	25¾	18795	40¾	37½	40⅜	4.0	19	61.3	12.6	31.8
✢7•[4]	AMTC	✔Amtech Corp	NNM	B–	49	4241	Mfr electronic identif'n prd	32	4⅛	33¾	7⅝	10⅝	4⅝	27003	6⅞	4¾	5⅛	...	d	–46.6	–35.4	0.1
8	AMTR	✔Amtran, Inc	NNM	NR	28	1810	Provides scheduled airline svc	16½	7½	10¾	6¼	16¼	6	2434	13¾	11⅝	12¾	...	23	82.1	...	...
✢9	AMTL	✔AMTROL, Inc	NNM	NR	48	4226	Mfr prds for water ctrl sys	22¾	14½	22½	13½	20¼	14½	1616	17	14¾	15¼	1.3	11	–2.0	...	...
10	AMV	✔AmVestors Finl	NY,Ch	B–	57	4661	Life,accident,health insur	20⅜	2 3/16	12	8	12⅞	9¼	3070	11⅞	11⅛	11¾	...	8	24.6	4.7	28.0
11•[5]	AAP	Amway Asia Pacific	NY,Ch,Ph	NR	..	...	Dstr vehicle for Amway prd	36½	18	46⅝	24¾	45¾	28½	3691	35⅞	31⅝	35⅝	e1.8	24	12.7	...	...
12	AJL	✔Amway Japan Ltd ADS[54]	NY,Ch,Ph	NR	29	2757	Dstr Amway products in Japan	....	....	19	14⅜	23½	13¾	5930	21½	19⅞	20⅞	4.2	26	34.8	...	...
13	AMW	✔Amwest Insur Group	AS,Ch,P	B+	17	661	Hldg co:underwrite surety bds	15¾	7¾	14½	11⅛	18¼	11¾	506	17½	15	15¼	2.6	6	37.9	19.3	8.0
14	AMXX	AMX Corp	NNM	NR	..	...	Dgn/dvp remote control sys	....	....	....	....	9¾	6½	21186	9¾	6½	8¾	...	..	...	...	...
15	AAC	✔Anacomp, Inc	NY,B,Ch,P	B–	37	7259	Computer & micrograph svs	23¼	7/16	4¼	1¾	2⅜	1/64	152690	½	1/64	⅛	...	d	–91.9	–67.9	–38.7
#16•[6]	APC	✔Anadarko Petroleum	NY,B	B	361	42212	Oil & gas explor,dev,prod'n	51¾	18⅜	58½	37	54⅛	35⅝	52392	54⅛	47¼	54⅛	0.6	..	41.0	24.9	13.9
17	ANAD	✔ANADIGICS Inc	NNM	NR	54	2110	Dstr microwave commun eqp	....	....	....	....	33½	12	15797	21¾	14⅞	21¼	...	27	...	...	...
#18•[2]	ADI	✔Analog Devices	NY,B,Ch,P,Ph	↑B	284	52104	Electronic measure/contr pr	18⅝	⅛	24½	15⅝	39½	20	114212	38¾	32⅛	35⅜	...	24	52.9	51.7	51.4
19	ALOG	✔Analogic Corp	NNM	B	51	4109	Data conversion products	31⅛	1/16	20	14⅝	21¾	16	2847	21¼	16¾	18½	...	22	–0.7	8.7	18.0
20	AATI	✔Analysis & Technology	NNM	B+	18	485	Analysis,engin'g svc to govt	20¾	7⅛	18¾	13¾	16½	12	485	14½	13½	14⅜	1.8	18	–0.5	13.2	10.1
21	ANLY	✔Analysts Intl	NNM	B+	77	4408	Computer program'g serv's	23⅞	⅛	20¾	14½	33	19¾	2835	30¾	29½	30	2.0	19	49.4	23.6	30.0
22	ASIPY	✔Anangel-Amer Shiphldgs ADS[55]	NNM	NR	29	2534	Own/oper dry cargo vessels	18⅜	8¾	18⅝	13¼	15¼	10⅞	4001	11⅞	10⅞	11⅛	9.0	12	–19.4	3.3	11.0
23	SLOT	✔Anchor Gaming	NNM	NR	50	2752	Oper gaming machines,CO,NV	....	....	19½	10½	26½	15¼	10098	23¼	18⅞	22¾	...	15	54.2	...	...
24	ATOG	✔Andover Togs	NNM	B–	9	186	Mfrs children's sportswear	12½	¾	3	1¼	3⅜	1¼	650	1¾	1⅜	1⅜	...	28	–21.4	–23.9	8.5
25	AND	✔Andrea Electronics	AS,Ch	C	12	120	Devlp electr communic sys/eq	53¾	¼	28¼	9⅞	26¾	11⅜	4825	15½	11⅜	12⅛	...	d	–51.0	38.4	64.7
¶26•[7]	ANDW	✔Andrew Corp	NNM	B	359	22853	Telecomm antennas & lines	19⅜	1 15/16	35⅞	16	64½	34	90587	46	36½	38¼	...	22	7.1	53.4	51.4
27	ANDY	✔Andros Inc	NNM	B–	45	2595	Med/auto OEM instrument'n	21½	½	21¼	13½	19½	14¾	4269	17¼	15	15¼	...	41	–3.9	–6.2	16.9
28	ANRG	Anergen Inc	NNM	NR	14	333	Dvlp stge: immune sys drug R&D	31½	5	7	1⅞	5½	1¾	11868	4¾	2⅝	4¼	...	d	127	–24.8	...
29	ANM	✔Angeles Mtge Inv Tr L.P.[56]	AS	NR	4	42	Real estate investment trust	20	1⅛	6⅞	2½	7⅝	4⅝	1453	7½	6¼	7⅜	...	1	11.3	–21.6	–1.3
30	APT	✔Angeles Ptc Mtge'A'SBI	AS,Ch	NR	5	440	Real estate investment trust	20⅛	⅝	1 11/16	9/16	¾	7/16	189	9/16	½	½	...	d	–11.0	–18.8	1.0
#31	AGL	✔Angelica Corp	NY,Ch,Ph	B+	102	7347	Mfr/rental career apparel	40¼	2⅝	29½	24½	27½	19⅜	5895	22⅜	19⅜	20½	4.7	16	–19.1	–3.6	–4.4
¶32•[2]	BUD	✔Anheuser-Busch Cos[61]	NY,B,Ph	A+	784	163472	Largest U.S. brewer:baking	62	2⅞	55⅜	47⅛	68	50¾	83538	67½	65	66⅞	2.6	16	34.2	7.2	12.1
33•[7]	AXE	✔Anixter Intl	NY,Ch,Ph	B–	110	27514	Dstr wiring sys/networking prd	18¾	⅛	18⅛	11⅜	22⅛	16⅝	30738	18⅝	16⅝	18⅝	...	24	8.5	18.1	31.5
#34•[8]	ANN	✔AnnTaylor Stores	NY,Ch,Ph	NR	176	20699	Retail women's apparel/shoes	36½	12	44⅞	20½	38	9⅞	73989	12¾	9⅞	10⅜	...	..	–69.9	–19.0	...
35•[9]	ANTC	✔ANTEC Corp	NNM	NR	86	9443	Dvlp CATV transmission pd	30¼	18	38½	15	26¾	11⅛	34483	18	13⅝	18	...	d	1.4	...	...
36	ANT	✔Anthony Indus[63]	NY,B,Ch,P,Ph	B+	94	7867	Snow skis,fish tackle,ind prod	15¾	7/16	17½	13⅞	23¼	15⅛	8684	23¼	22⅛	23	1.9	17	48.9	37.3	43.8
37	ANU	✔Anuhco Inc	AS	NR	12	459	Motor freight transport'n	6	1	11⅞	4¾	10½	7	2912	8¾	7⅜	8¾	...	1	–18.6	48.2	...
#38•[10]	AOC	✔Aon Corp	NY,B,Ch,P	A–	315	50495	Insur hldg:accid,health,life	39	1¾	35¾	29¼	50⅞	31⅜	30172	50⅞	47	49⅞	2.7	14	62.0	16.4	21.3
39	Pr B	6.25%cm Cv[64]Ex Pfd([65]51.875)	NY	AA–	16	1545		56½	50	53⅜	45¼	65¼	46	655	65¼	62¾	63½	4.9	..	...	...	...
40	APAT	APA Optics	NSC	C	6	218	Dvlp optic/optoelectronic sys	8½	1½	5½	3½	8½	3	1155	7	5¼	5¾	...	d	56.0	24.2	1.8
41	APAC	✔APAC TeleServices	NNM	NR	1	10	Provides marketing svcs	....	....	....	....	34⅞	16	10344	34	30	33⅜	...	..	...	...	...
#42•[11]	APA	✔Apache Corp	NY,B,Ch	B–	347	54789	Oil,gas explor'n & prod'n	33½	1 11/16	29¼	22¼	31	22¼	94800	29⅝	25⅞	29½	0.9	74	21.7	18.6	16.8
43	AIV	✔Apartment Investment & Mgmt'A'	[12]NY	NR	31	2912	Real estate investment trust	....	....	18⅝	16¼	21¼	17⅛	17557	20⅛	18⅞	19⅜	8.6	..	23.3	...	...
44•[6]	APTS	✔Apertus Technologies	NNM	B–	44	5278	Data comm for telecomm ind	32½	⅞	12⅝	2¾	15	6¾	48302	10⅞	7	7¾	...	52	–23.5	32.8	44.0
45	APHT	✔Aphton Corp	NNM	C	27	1479	Immune sys biopharmaceutl R&D	25¾	5	27¾	6⅞	13	7⅞	3350	11	8¾	10	...	d	1.3	–19.6	...
✢46	APOG	✔Apogee Enterprises	NNM	B	74	6628	Auto glass: alum window sys	20⅛	¼	18½	11½	18¼	13	15653	17¼	13	17	2.0	14	–0.9	17.3	2.2
47	APGG	✔Apogee Inc	NNM	NR	40	2553	Outpatient mental hlth svcs	....	....	19¾	12	22¾	7	11269	10⅛	7⅜	9¼	...	15	–46.4	...	...
48	APOL	✔Apollo Group'A'	NNM	NR	35	5778	Adult higher education svcs	....	....	6⅛	5½	40½	6	16461	40½	30	39⅛	...	60	543	...	...
¶49•[13]	AAPL	✔Apple Computer	NNM	B+	541	68805	Personal computer systems	73¼	5⅜	43¾	24⅝	50⅛	31⅝	585736	40⅛	31⅝	31⅞	1.5	9	–18.4	–17.8	–4.7
50•[14]	APSO	✔Apple South	NNM	NR	157	18800	Oper full svc restaurants	17⅝	2 3/16	18¾	10¾	25⅞	11¾	68338	21½	17¾	21½	0.1	35	62.5	51.6	...
✢51•[6]	APPB	✔Applebee's Intl	NNM	NR	147	19396	Franchised restaur't operator	22½	2	25¼	11	31¾	13⅜	87727	28	20½	22¾	0.3	28	61.5	36.4	58.4
#52•[15]	APBI	✔Applied Bioscience	NNM	NR	74	17993	Toxicological testing svc	20⅛	1¾	7⅜	4⅝	7⅞	4⅛	13314	7¼	6⅛	6¾	...	d	22.7	–7.8	–7.4

Uniform Footnote Explanations-See Page 4. Other: [1]ASE:Cycle 2. [2]Ph:Cycle 3. [3]ASE,Ph:Cycle 3. [4]P:Cycle 3. [5]ASE,CBOE:Cycle 2. [6]CBOE:Cycle 2. [7]CBOE:Cycle 1. [8]NY,P:Cycle 3. [9]CBOE,NY:Cycle 2. [10]P:Cycle 1. [11]NY,Ph:Cycle 1. [12]Ch [13]ASE:Cycle 1. [14]CBOE:Cycle 3. [15]Ph:Cycle 1. [51]12 Mo Dec'91:fiscal Apr'91 earned$0.87. [52]Fiscal Oct'91 & prior. [53]STERIS Corp plan acq,0.46 com. [54]Ea ADS rep 0.5 com, no par. [55]Each ADS rep 1 ord Cl'A'shr,$1. [56]Plan name chge,Nova Capital Investment Trust. [57]To be determined. [58]Cl'B'shrs Cv into Cl'A',49-for-1. [59]Liq div. [60]Cl'B'Shrs Cv into Cl'A',49-for-1. [61]Plan spin-off,Campbell Taggart Inc. [62]®$3.88,'94. [63]Plan SmallCap 600 listing:eff Dec 30. [64]Co opt fr 11-1-96 exch for $50 amt 6.25%Cv2022. [65]Fr 11-1-96,scale to $50 in 2002. [66]5 Mo Dec'94.

Common and Convertible Preferred Stocks

Splits ◆ Index	Cash Divs. Ea. Yr. Since	Dividends: Latest Payment Period $	Date	Ex. Div.	Total $ So Far 1995	Ind. Rate	Paid 1994	Financial Position Mil-$: Cash& Equiv.	Curr. Assets	Curr. Liab.	Balance Sheet Date	Capitalization: Lg Trm Debt Mil-$	Shs. 000 Pfd.	Com.	Earnings $ Per Shr. Years End	1991	1992	1993	1994	1995	Last 12 Mos.	Interim Earnings Period	$ per Shr. 1994	1995	Index
1	....	0.10	2-15-80	1-28	...	Nil	....	1190	3863	5483	9-30-95	7158	159	76352	Dc	d3.54	□d6.35	□d2.05	2.26	E7.00	4.31	9 Mo Sep	3.95	□6.00	1
2	1988	0.03	7-21-95	6-21	0.09	Nil	0.12	18.9	44.5	36.2	10-01-95	0.25	...	13075	Dc	[51]0.38	0.59	0.07	0.11	....	d0.26	9 Mo Sep	d0.02	d0.39	2
3	....	None Paid			...	Nil	....	Equity per shr $8.49			10-31-95	62.3	...	7366	Ap	d0.65	d1.03	0.01	0.33	0.55	0.59	6 Mo Oct	0.24	0.28	3
4	1993	Q0.05	10-15-95	9-27	0.20	0.20	0.20	Equity per shr $4.08			9-30-95	141	...	★26365	Dc	[52]0.33	0.50	2.15	0.79	....	0.61	9 Mo Sep	0.79	0.61	4
5	....	None Since Public			...	Nil	....	90.8	284	108	10-01-95	102	...	32348	Dc	0.95	□1.13	0.50	□d1.64	E1.00	0.76	9 Mo Sep	d1.86	0.54	5
6◆	1943	Q0.40	1-2-96	12-6	1.52	1.60	1.40	Book Value $23.72			9-30-95	313	...	58501	Dc	2.17	2.55	3.10	2.25	....	2.18	9 Mo Sep	2.25	2.18	6
7◆	1993	0.02	3-28-95	3-1	0.02	Nil	0.08	26.9	67.4	15.2	9-30-95	2.64	...	14671	Dc	d0.40	0.51	Δ0.70	0.52	....	d0.12	9 Mo Sep	0.51	d0.13	7
8	....	None Since Public			...	Nil	....	70.8	136	137	6-30-95	118	...	11781	Dc	0.61	d0.24	0.28	0.30	....	0.55	9 Mo Sep	0.81	1.06	8
9	1993	Q0.05	11-15-95	11-2	0.20	0.20	0.20	5.71	59.8	19.4	9-30-95	....	...	7502	Dc	...	p1.29	□1.56	1.61	....	1.39	9 Mo Sep	1.35	1.13	9
10◆	....	0.075	4-13-95	3-13	0.075	Nil	....	Equity per shr $13.55			9-30-95	....	...	10135	Dc	1.83	□2.92	□2.62	1.32	....	1.47	9 Mo Sep	0.90	1.05	10
11	1994	†0.48	11-22-95	11-1	†0.96	0.64	0.64	221	353	156	8-31-94	8.92	...	59998	Au	p0.75	p1.05	p1.35	p1.38	P1.50	1.50				11
12	1994	0.396	12-11-95	8-28	0.877	0.88	0.578	751	893	448	8-31-95	....	...	149625	Au	0.47	0.45	0.51	0.69	0.79	0.79				12
13	1986	Q0.10	1-15-96	12-27	0.39	0.40	0.34	Equity per shr $17.80			9-30-95	12.5	...	2360	Dc	1.42	1.44	□1.70	1.91	....	2.37	9 Mo Sep	0.76	1.22	13
14	....	None Since Public			...	Nil	....	3.47	9.81	2.87	9-30-95	p0.04	p. . .	★7482	Mr	...	...	...	n/a	....	....	6 Mo Sep	n/a	p0.21	14
15	....	0.03	8-10-83	7-14	...	Nil	....	6.21	199	561	6-30-95	....	500	46178	Sp	*0.38	*0.38	*0.22	Δ0.10	....	d3.17	9 Mo Jun	Δ0.06	d3.21	15
16	1986	Q0.075	12-27-95	12-11	0.30	0.30	0.30	7.76	110	91.8	9-30-95	669	...	58987	Dc	0.59	0.49	Δ0.70	0.70	E0.39	0.28	9 Mo Sep	0.66	0.24	16
17	....	None Since Public			...	Nil	....	28.9	46.8	12.2	9-30-95	1.60	...	8006	Dc	...	...	0.42	0.34	....	0.80	9 Mo Sep	0.17	0.63	17
18◆	....	5%Stk	4-10-78	3-20	...	Nil	....	129	486	202	7-29-95	★280	...	76206	Oc	0.11	0.21	0.59	0.97	P1.50	1.50				18
19	1995	Q0.04	1-17-96	12-29	0.12	Nil	....	99.8	196	30.6	7-31-95	10.2	...	12424	Jl	0.91	0.78	1.01	1.18	1.02	0.85	3 Mo Oct	0.28	0.11	19
20	1972	A0.26	4-21-95	3-27	0.26	0.26	0.24	1.50	28.5	12.2	9-30-95	7.59	...	2419	Mr	0.67	0.91	1.06	1.12	....	0.79	6 Mo Sep	0.53	0.20	20
21◆	1988	Q0.15	2-15-96	1-29	0.54	0.60	0.49	15.0	60.1	18.9	9-30-95	....	...	7273	Je	0.79	0.76	1.15	1.10	1.55	1.59	3 Mo Sep	0.34	0.38	21
22	1988	0.50	10-6-95	9-1	1.00	1.00	†2.887	22.6	27.3	28.2	6-30-95	158	...	±15983	Je	1.81	1.21	1.08	±1.03	±0.80	0.94	3 Mo Sep	±0.15	±0.29	22
23	....	None Since Public			...	Nil	....	32.0	40.8	11.2	9-30-95	3.60	...	11488	Je	...	...	p0.59	p1.03	1.40	1.50	3 Mo Sep	0.33	0.43	23
24◆	....	None Since Public			...	Nil	....	0.91	37.7	23.8	8-31-95	4.09	...	4458	Nv	0.27	0.34	0.06	0.03	....	0.05	9 Mo Aug	d0.26	d0.24	24
25◆	....	0.026	1-15-90	12-20	...	Nil	....	2.34	4.26	0.34	9-30-95	....	...	3201	Dc	d0.19	d0.27	0.20	d0.83	....	d0.39	9 Mo Sep	d0.65	d0.21	25
26◆	....	None Since Public			...	Nil	....	45.1	311	87.9	9-30-95	44.7	...	39112	Sp	0.51	0.58	0.73	1.13	1.73	1.73				26
27	....	None Since Public			...	Nil	....	24.6	52.7	5.25	10-29-95	....	...	4597	Jl	d1.54	1.19	1.25	1.67	0.59	0.37	3 Mo Oct	0.25	0.03	27
28	....	None Since Public			...	Nil	....	13.2	13.8	1.90	9-30-95	0.80	...	14944	Dc	d0.96	d0.99	d1.12	d0.97	....	d0.71	9 Mo Sep	d0.71	d0.45	28
29	1996	0.10	2-13-96	1-18	0.10	[57]....	....	Equity per shr $11.80			9-30-95	2.00	...	[58]±2861	Dc	±1.93	d8.64	0.38	0.11	....	5.23	9 Mo Sep	0.05	▲5.17	29
30	1989	[59]14.50	12-3-93	12-6	...	Nil	....	Equity per shr $0.85			9-30-95	....	...	[60]±2576	Dc	±1.87	±d0.21	±1.45	±d0.13	....	d0.08	9 Mo Sep	d0.09	±d0.04	30
31	1954	Q0.24	1-1-96	12-13	0.94½	0.96	0.94	8.95	233	47.5	10-28-95	101	...	9142	Ja	2.43	Δ1.50	1.23	1.44	....	1.26	9 Mo Oct	1.16	0.98	31
32	1932	Q0.44	3-8-96	2-7	1.68	1.76	1.52	91.6	2038	1600	9-30-95	3157	...	254327	Dc	3.26	□3.48	2.17	[62]3.91	E4.10	4.11	9 Mo Sep	3.23	3.43	32
33◆	....	0.10	5-18-79	4-30	...	Nil	....	18.3	752	323	9-30-95	317	...	53567	Dc	Δd1.88	□d1.55	□0.19	3.85	....	0.77	9 Mo Sep	3.60	0.52	33
34	....	None Since Public			...	Nil	....	1.25	214	88.8	10-28-95	268	...	23084	Ja	□0.05	0.28	□0.66	□1.40	E0.05↓	0.37	9 Mo Oct	□1.05	0.02	34
35	....	None Since Public			...	Nil	....	3.32	263	107	9-30-95	146	...	22318	Dc	...	p0.31	p0.56	0.89	....	d0.12	9 Mo Sep	0.73	d0.28	35
36◆	1978	Q0.11	1-3-96	12-26	0.44	0.44	s0.419	4.04	285	120	9-30-95	53.6	...	16528	Dc	0.57	0.73	0.94	1.09	....	1.34	9 Mo Sep	0.84	1.09	36
37	....	None Paid			...	Nil	....	33.3	66.2	9.17	9-30-95	....	...	7140	Dc	▲5.66	0.60	0.85	8.00	....	7.69	9 Mo Sep	0.71	0.40	37
38◆	1950	Q0.34	11-15-95	10-31	1.34	1.36	1.26	Equity per shr $9.42			9-30-95	553	p14200	108029	Dc	2.47	□1.93	2.81	3.14	E3.58↑	3.42	9 Mo Sep	2.40	2.68	38
39	1994	Q0.78⅛	2-1-96	1-6	3.12½	3.125	3.12½	Cv into 1.22025 com,$40.97				....	1000	...	Dc	...	...	...	....	....	....				39
40	....	None Since Public			...	Nil	....	1.92	2.93	0.18	9-30-95	0.35	...	7986	Mr	d0.12	d0.09	d0.11	d0.06	....	d0.03	6 Mo Sep	d0.03	Nil	40
41	....	None Since Public			...	Nil	....	0.34	17.6	15.5	10-01-95	p1.96	...	★23100	Dc	...	...	...	p0.19	....	0.33	9 Mo Sep	p0.09	p0.23	41
42	1965	Q0.07	1-31-96	12-27	0.28	0.28	0.28	16.5	202	207	9-30-95	1058	...	77373	Dc	0.76	1.02	0.70	0.70	E0.40	0.39	9 Mo Sep	0.48	0.17	42
43	1994	Q0.41½	11-14-95	11-3	1.66	1.66	0.29	Equity per shr $12.75			9-30-95	p246	...	±★11641	Dc	...	...	p0.61	[66]0.42	....	....	9 Mo Sep	n/a	0.65	43
44	....	None Since Public			...	Nil	....	12.7	36.2	17.8	10-01-95	8.90	...	14005	Mr	d0.19	0.19	d0.70	0.69	....	0.15	6 Mo Sep	0.31	d0.23	44
45	....	None Since Public			...	Nil	....	Equity per shr $0.46			7-31-95	....	...	★12879	Ap	d0.12	d0.17	d0.20	d0.28	d0.32	d0.33	3 Mo Jul	d0.07	d0.08	45
46	1974	Q0.08½	11-16-95	10-27	0.32½	0.34	0.30½	14.7	265	137	9-02-95	79.7	...	13497	Fb	0.63	0.34	Δ0.25	0.97	....	1.23	9 Mo Nov	0.79	1.05	46
47	....	None Since Public			...	Nil	....	14.9	35.5	17.4	9-30-95	5.74	...	9620	Dc	...	...	pd0.11	0.06	....	0.63	9 Mo Sep	d0.14	0.43	47
48◆	....	None Since Public			...	Nil	....	52.6	87.5	46.1	11-30-95	1.72	...	±22103	Au	±*0.04	±Δ0.02	±0.08	±0.32	±0.62	0.65	3 Mo Nov	±0.17	±0.20	48
49	1987	Q0.12	12-15-95	11-21	0.48	0.48	0.48	952	5224	2325	9-30-95	303	...	122922	Sp	2.58	4.33	0.73	2.61	3.45	3.45				49
50◆	1992	Q0.006	11-30-95	11-13	0.022	0.02	0.014	5.21	18.4	24.1	10-01-95	104	...	p40000	Dc	0.12	0.19	0.32	0.51	....	0.61	9 Mo Sep	0.37	0.47	50
51◆	1991	A0.06	1-12-96	12-4	0.05	0.06	0.04	54.6	78.3	33.3	9-24-95	26.0	...	30996	Dc	0.22	0.27	□0.44	p0.62	....	0.82	9 Mo Sep	p0.47	p0.67	51
52◆	....	None Since Public			...	Nil	....	6.11	77.8	51.1	9-30-95	42.8	...	28976	Dc	0.51	0.22	d0.92	d0.36	....	d0.28	9 Mo Sep	d0.01	0.07	52

◆Stock Splits & Divs By Line Reference Index [6]3-for-2,'92. [7]3-for-2,'92:5-for-4,'93. [10]1-for-2.5 REVERSE,'93. [18]3-for-2,'95:To split 3-for-2,hldrs Jan 4. [21]3-for-2,'93. [24]10%,'91:5-for-4,'92. [25]5-for-1,'93. [26]2-for-1,'93:3-for-2,'92,'94,'95. [33]2-for-1,'95. [36]Adj to 5%,'94. [38]3-for-2,'94. [48]4-for-3,'95:3-for-2,'95. [50]3-for-2,'92,twice in'93,'94. [51]2-for-1,'93:3-for-2,'94. [52]2-for-1,'91,'92.

¶ S&P 500
# MidCap 400
✜ SmallCap 600
• Options

Index	Ticker	Name of Issue (Call Price of Pfd. Stocks)	Market	Com. Rank. & Pfd. Rating	Inst. Hold Cos	Inst. Hold Shs. (000)	Principal Business	Price Range 1971-93 High	1971-93 Low	1994 High	1994 Low	1995 High	1995 Low	Dec. Sales in 100s	December, 1995 Last Sale Or Bid High	Low	Last	%Div Yield	P-E Ratio	Total Return % Annualized 12 Mo	36 Mo	60 Mo
1•[1]	ADAX	✔Applied Digital Access	NNM	NR	70	6933	Test sys-telecom circuits	....	....	26¾	12	30½	10	28124	15	11½	11¾	...	32	−53.5	...	...
2	AINN	✔Applied Innovation	NNM	NR	42	3422	Mfr data commun products	12	13/16	16½	7½	31⅝	6⅞	23769	15⅞	9¼	11¾	...	23	−12.7	...	...
3•[2]	APM	✔Applied Magnetics	NY,B,P,Ph	C	60	10082	Computer eq & components	19⅞	5/16	7½	2⅛	19	2½	42652	19	12⅛	18⅝	...	..	521	19.6	17.7
¶4•[3]	AMAT	✔Applied Materials	NNM	B	642	70403	Reactors to mfr thin films	20	1/16	27¼	18⅛	59⅞	18½	784089	49⅞	38⅜	39⅜	...	15	83.6	68.4	72.1
5	AMBI	✔Applied Microbiology	NNM	B−	7	435	Biotech-antibacterial agents	6½	1⅛	6½	2⅝	5⅞	1⅜	10956	5	3⅜	3¾	...	d	25.0	−0.5	16.5
6	APMC	Applied Microsystems	NNM	NR	..	...	Software testing tools	....	....	....	....	10¾	6¾	18065	9¾	7	9	...	..	...	...	...
7	APW	✔Applied Power Cl'A'	NY	B+	105	10482	Mfr hydraulic ind'l/constr eq	27¼	5	25⅜	16¼	35⅛	22¾	10733	32⅜	27⅛	30	0.4	15	21.7	25.7	16.4
8	APSG	✔Applied Signal Technology	NNM	NR	14	1054	Mfr reconnaissance equipment	8¼	4¼	7¾	3¼	6⅜	3½	2913	5	3½	3⅝	...	30	−6.5	...	...
#9•[4]	APRA	✔Apria Healthcare Grp	NNM	NR	223	36018	Home hlth care svcs/products	28¼	9½	29½	14½	41⅝	19½	71030	30¼	25¾	28¼	...	..	21.5	7.1	...
10	APG	✔Aprogenex Inc	AS,Ch,Ph	NR	5	166	Dvlp stge diagnostic test sys	9½	5⅜	14⅝	5⅛	8⅝	1½	3747	2 3/16	1½	1 11/16	...	d	−77.5	...	...
11	APSI	✔APS Holding 'A'	NNM	NR	83	9149	Dstr auto replacement parts	20	15¼	31¼	17¾	30¼	17¼	8976	23¾	18½	22½	...	16	−20.4	...	...
12	ATR	✔AptarGroup Inc	NY,Ph	NR	123	11847	Mfr pkg compon'ts:pumps,valves	22	16	29	20⅛	38¼	24⅝	5631	38¼	35⅛	37⅜	0.7	20	32.8	...	...
✜13	WTR	✔Aquarion Co	NY,Ch,Ph	B+	61	1600	Water util/enviro test'g labs	36	8	28	21½	26	21⅝	1929	26	23⅜	25½	6.4	15	19.1	7.4	10.8
14	AQP	✔Aquila Gas Pipeline	NY	NR	37	3798	Natural gas gather'g/transpt'n	16⅜	10⅝	13¼	6¼	13	6⅝	6833	13	11¼	12⅞	0.4	24	59.3	...	...
15•[5]	ARA	✔Aracruz Celulose S.A. ADS[54]	NY,Ph	NR	59	7921	Produce eucalyptus kraft pulp	6⅞	4	11⅛	5⅝	13¾	7⅜	51225	9⅛	7½	7¾	...	14	−11.8	19.3	...
16•[2]	AKSEF	✔Arakis Energy	NNM	NR	39	4582	Acquis,dvlp O&G properties	9⅛	4¾	8½	3¼	26⅝	2 7/16	114212	4	2 7/16	3	...	d	−25.0	...	...
✜17	ARBR	✔Arbor Drugs	NNM	B+	101	12383	Operates drugstores in Mich	16⅞	2⅛	14⅞	10⅝	23¼	13½	16786	23¼	19½	21	1.3	22	55.5	14.3	18.3
18	AHCC	✔Arbor Health Care	NNM	NR	55	3868	Subacute/basic health care svs	19½	12¾	25	16¼	23½	15	5824	20	17⅜	17½	...	15	−12.5	...	...
19	ABR	✔Arbor Property Tr	NY,Ch	NR	14	1822	Real estate investment trust	13⅝	6⅝	10¾	7¼	9¾	5¾	7828	6⅜	5⅞	6⅛	11.4	32	−15.1	−2.9	−6.4
20	ARSW	✔Arbor Software	NNM	NR	..	...	Dvp multidemensional software	....	....	....	....	48½	17	14977	48½	38¾	47¼	...	..	...	...	...
21	ATV	✔ARC Intl	AS,To,Ch	B−	9	1461	Cable TV/movie theatre equip	6⅜	¼	4½	2	4	1¾	6271	2¼	1 13/16	2⅛	...	3	−29.2	31.4	19.4
22•[2]	ACA	✔Arcadian Corp	NY	NR	74	10569	Produce nitrogen fertilizers	....	....	....	....	24⅛	15½	24355	21⅜	18½	19⅜	...	8	...	...	...
23•[6]	APGR	✔Arch Communications Group	NNM	NR	116	14263	Provides paging services	19	6¾	23	12¾	30¾	15⅛	57440	26½	21½	24	...	..	38.1	34.4	...
24	ARCH	✔Arch Petroleum Inc	NNM	C	22	2315	Oil & gas exploration/dvlp	2⅞	1/16	2⅝	1 15/16	3	1 11/16	6431	2 3/16	1 11/16	2⅛	...	d	6.3	1.0	13.6
¶25•[1]	ADM	✔Archer-Daniels-Midland	NY,B,Ch,P,Ph	A+	712	281441	Process soybeans:flour mill'r	18¼	⅜	20⅛	13½	20	14¼	181182	18⅜	17⅛	18	s1.1	12	−2.5	9.0	13.1
26•[7]	RCM	✔ARCO Chemical	NY,Ch,P,Ph	NR	147	7827	Major commodity chem mfr	47¼	17	51	43⅛	50⅝	41¼	5118	48⅞	47½	48⅝	5.8	10	18.0	9.7	13.7
✜27•[8]	ACAT	✔Arctco Inc	NNM	B+	90	11122	Mfr snowmobiles&accessories	18⅛	2⅛	21¾	13⅜	19½	10⅜	12689	14⅛	12⅛	13	1.8	16	−31.4	18.7	38.9
28	ARDNA	Arden Group Cl'A'	NNM	B	11	582	West Coast food supermkts	73½	1⅛	55	32	65½	42½	113	61½	58	59½	...	12	38.4	19.3	7.2
29	ARTHF	Arethusa (Off-Shore) Ltd[60]	NNM	NR	..	...	Oper offshore drill'g rigs	16⅜	9½	12⅜	9⅝	29¼	11	52247	29¼	22½	28	...	26	197	...	...
30	AGII	✔Argonaut Group	NNM	B	104	7080	Ins hldg:workers comp,liab	35½	5	31¾	26¼	34½	27¾	1813	33¼	32½	32½	4.1	14	21.1	6.9	14.4
31•[2]	ARGY	✔Argosy Gaming	NNM	NR	68	6323	Operates riverboat casino	36¾	15¼	27	10	17½	7¼	12663	9⅛	7¼	7⅝	...	16	−33.0	...	...
32	ARGL	✔Argyle Television 'A'	NNM	NR	..	...	Own/oper&manage T.V.stations	....	....	....	....	18¼	15½	9408	18¼	15½	17½	...	d	...	...	...
33	AU	✔Ariel Resources	To	NR	4	900	Explor,dvlp precious metals	2¾	⅛	2½	1 5/16	4	1 1/16	8401	1 7/16	1 1/16	1¼	...	63	...	...	...
34	AZL	✔Arizona Land Income'A'	AS	NR	3	127	Real estate investment trust	10⅝	2⅝	4⅞	4	6¼	4⅛	11	4⅞	4¾	4¾B	...	30	34.3	19.0	14.5
35	AZD	Arizona Pub Svc 10%'[63]MIDS'[64]	NY	....[65]	..	...	Electric utility, Arizona	....	....	....	....	28¾	24¾	1558	27⅞	27⅜	27¾	9.0	..	...	...	...
✜36	ABFS	✔Arkansas Best	NNM	NR	71	14285	Genl truck'g:tire retreading	17⅛	8⅛	15¾	10⅛	13⅜	6⅝	33962	9¼	6⅝	7⅞	0.5	d	−32.0	−19.0	...
37	ART	✔Armatron Intl	AS,Ch	C	5	191	Mfr consumer prd/auto equip	17¾	15/16	1 5/16	11/16	1⅛	9/16	516	¾	⅝	11/16	...	d	−8.4	−31.4	−9.4
¶38•[9]	AS	✔Armco Inc	NY,B,C,Ch,P,Ph	C	229	72886	Steel producer & fabricator	41¾	3⅞	7⅜	4½	7¾	5⅜	44718	6	5⅜	5⅞	...	39	−6.0	−3.9	3.7
39	Pr	$2.10 cm Cv Pfd(40)vtg	NY,Ch,P	B−	15	449	oil field eq: insurance	52¾	13	29	19¾	26¼	20	197	24	23⅜	24	8.8	..	...	...	...
40	Pr A	$4.50 cm Cv 'B'Pfd(50)	NY,Ch	B−	13	359		50¾	27	51⅞	41	50⅜	41½	76	47⅞	47	47¼B	9.5	..	...	...	...
41	Pr B	$3.625cmCv'A'Pfd([66]52.5375)	NY	B−	26	2031		65¼	48½	58⅞	46	57¾	47⅝	547	49¾	47⅝	49¾	7.3	..	...	...	...
42	ARMR	✔Armor All Products	NNM	B+	85	9318	Mkts auto appearance prods	27¼	9	24	18	23⅜	15	4345	19	16¼	18⅛	3.5	19	−7.4	5.0	13.6
¶43•[1]	ACK	✔Armstrong World Indus	NY,B,Ch,P,Ph	B+	397	28461	Mfr floor cover'gs/bldg prd	55¼	6¼	57½	36	64⅛	38⅜	20007	64⅛	60⅛	62	2.3	15	65.3	29.8	24.1
#44	AIND	✔Arnold Indus	NNM	A	114	14161	Trucking-gen'l commodities	21¼	⅛	23½	18	20¾	15⅞	10488	18½	17⅜	17⅜	2.5	14	−11.0	4.9	18.1
45	HRT	✔Arrhythmia Research Tech	AS,Ph	C	12	309	Mkt cardiological medical prd	12¼	¾	8½	2¼	6¼	1⅞	2090	5⅜	3¾	4¼	...	85	70.0	−15.8	9.1
46	ARRS	✔Arris Pharmaceutical	NNM	NR	32	2938	Pharmaceutical R&D	7½	5½	7¾	4	15¼	5¾	22016	15¼	9¼	13½	...	d	125	...	...
47	AI	✔Arrow Automotive Indus	AS	B−	17	528	Rebuild auto replace parts	22¼	1 11/16	10	7	8	4¾	637	6¼	4¾	6¼	...	d	−13.8	2.8	14.9
#48•[10]	ARW	✔Arrow Electronics	NY,B,Ch,P	B−	282	40066	Dstr electronic components	43⅛	15/16	45⅛	33⅝	59¾	35⅛	67545	47½	39¼	43	...	10	20.3	14.2	57.9
49	ARRO	✔Arrow International	NNM	NR	100	6398	Mfr disposable catheters	29½	17½	35¼	18½	48¾	29¾	10484	44¼	39¼	39¾	0.4	26	17.3	15.7	...
50	ARRW	✔Arrow Transportation	NNM	NR	16	868	Transport bulk liquid chem'ls	7¾	5	9	4	5	⅞	3600	1¾	⅞	1¼	...	d	−71.4	...	...
51•[6]	ASFT	✔Artisoft Inc	NNM	NR	49	2578	Dvp local area ntwk softwr&sys	35	5¾	24½	7⅜	13⅞	5⅞	84700	9½	5⅞	6¼	...	d	−19.8	−26.3	...
52	ARTG	✔Artistic Greetings	NNM	B	12	587	Mail order stationery/gift pd	17½	11/16	6¼	2⅝	4⅜	2⅛	5266	3⅛	2¼	2½	...	d	−16.7	−32.2	−1.4

Uniform Footnote Explanations-See Page 4. Other: [1]Ph:Cycle 3. [2]CBOE:Cycle 1. [3]P:Cycle 1. [4]ASE:Cycle 2. [5]CBOE:Cycle 2. [6]CBOE:Cycle 3. [7]ASE:Cycle 1. [8]CBOE,Ph:Cycle 1. [9]Ph:Cycle 2. [10]ASE:Cycle 3. [51]Accum on pfd. [52]Fiscal Dec'91 & prior. [53]®$0.76,'94. [54]Ea ADS rep 5 Cl'B' ord, no par. [55]To be determined. [56]Fiscal Apr'93&prior:8 Mos Dec'93earn $0.01. [57]100% non-taxable,'94. [58]Fiscal Aug'94 & prior. [59]Fiscal Oct'91 & prior. [60]Diamond Offshore Drilling plan acq, .88 com. [61]Spl div. [62]Fiscal 92 & prior in Cdn$. [63]Monthly Income Debt Securities. [64]Jr Sub Deferrable Int Debs Sr'A'. [65]Rated BBB- by S&P. [66]To 10-14-96,scale to $50 in 2002. [67]Not rede'ble if com exceeds150%conv price20days. [68]®$4.64,'94. [69]®$2.31,'94.

Index	Cash Divs. Ea.Yr. Since	Dividends: Latest Payment Period $	Date	Ex. Div.	Total $ So Far 1995	Ind. Rate	Paid 1994	Financial Position Mil-$: Cash& Equiv.	Curr. Assets	Curr. Liab.	Balance Sheet Date	Capitalization: Lg Trm Debt Mil-$	Shs. 000 Pfd.	Com.	Earnings $ Per Shr. Years End	1991	1992	1993	1994	1995	Last 12 Mos.	Interim Earnings Period	$ per Shr. 1994	1995	Index
1	....	None Since Public			...	Nil	....	25.4	37.9	4.28	9-30-95	0.06	...	11881	Dc	...	...	pd0.07	p0.88	....	0.37	9 Mo Sep	p0.55	0.04	1
2◆	....	None Since Public			...	Nil	....	8.15	19.1	2.77	3-31-95	.....	...	15612	Dc	0.04	0.11	0.26	0.44	....	0.52	9 Mo Sep	0.24	0.32	2
3	....	5%Stk	4-10-89	3-6	...	Nil	....	48.2	128	134	9-30-95	3.25	...	★26223	Sp	d1.12	d1.51	d2.17	d2.39	0.08	0.08				3
4◆	....	None Since Public			...	Nil	....	700	2058	760	7-30-95	231	...	178342	Oc	0.19	0.27	0.61	Δ1.25	P2.56	2.56				4
5	....	None Paid			...	[51]Nil	....	3.69	9.40	3.39	9-30-95	0.73	2	18205	Je	[52]d0.18	pd1.09	d1.03	0.09	0.01	d0.07	3 Mo Sep	0.02	d0.06	5
6	....	None Since Public			...	Nil	....	2.20	11.3	8.56	9-30-95	p0.08	...	★6468	Dc	...	...	...	p0.01	....	....	9 Mo Sep	n/a	p0.15	6
7	1987	Q0.03	11-30-95	11-16	0.12	0.12	0.12	0.91	190	97.4	8-31-95	74.2	...	13408	Au	0.60	d1.87	□0.25	1.25	□1.82	1.97	3 Mo Nov	0.40	0.55	7
8	....	None Since Public			...	Nil	....	2.39	34.6	12.3	7-28-95	.....	...	7518	Oc	0.57	0.61	0.47	0.40	P0.12	0.12				8
9	....	None Since Public			...	Nil	....	19.6	393	216	9-30-95	468	...	49544	Dc	p0.64	1.31	1.71	p[53]0.79	....	....	9 Mo Sep	n/a	□d1.92	9
10	....	None Since Public			...	Nil	....	2.25	2.34	0.60	9-30-95	0.25	459	5155	Dc	d1.14	d1.24	d0.96	d1.96	....	d1.17	9 Mo Sep	d1.61	d0.82	10
11	....	None Since Public			...	Nil	....	4.74	339	121	7-25-95	195	...	13726	Ja	...	p0.64	□p1.03	2.36	....	1.41	9 Mo Oct	2.05	1.10	11
12	1993	Q0.07	11-28-95	11-3	0.26	0.28	0.23	13.5	224	123	9-30-95	55.7	...	17922	Dc	...	p1.18	pΔ1.31	1.65	....	1.90	9 Mo Sep	1.31	1.56	12
13	1890	Q0.40½	1-30-96	1-10	1.62	1.62	1.62	0.15	38.1	30.4	9-30-95	126	...	6847	Dc	d1.75	Δ1.51	1.76	1.87	....	1.71	9 Mo Sep	1.47	1.31	13
14	1994	Q0.01¼	12-20-95	12-1	0.05	0.05	0.05	6.47	76.4	79.3	9-30-95	175	...	29400	Dc	0.49	0.76	0.90	0.52	....	0.54	9 Mo Sep	0.39	0.41	14
15◆	1995	0.211	9-15-95	8-22	0.566	[55]....	....	922	1163	806	9-30-95	725	...	±1077920	Dc	±d0.84	±*0.01	±d0.41	±0.31	....	0.57	9 Mo Sep	±0.02	±0.28	15
16	....	None Paid			...	Nil	....	3.40	4.63	3.76	12-31-94	3.24	...	p23776	Dc	d0.36	d0.21	[56]d0.12	d0.17	....	d0.30	9 Mo Sep	d0.19	d0.32	16
17◆	1989	Q0.07	1-2-96	12-8	0.20	0.28	0.16	31.8	162	78.2	10-31-95	21.6	...	24826	Jl	0.59	0.65	0.29	0.57	0.94	0.96	3 Mo Oct	0.19	0.21	17
18	....	None Since Public			...	Nil	....	6.62	44.6	35.4	9-30-95	77.8	...	6887	Dc	p0.41	p0.65	p0.82	1.01	....	1.17	9 Mo Sep	0.68	0.84	18
19	1986	Q0.17½	2-15-96	12-27	0.80	0.70	[57]1.10	Equity per shr $2.10			9-30-95	131	...	12159	Dc	0.24	d0.02	□0.11	0.03	....	0.19	9 Mo Sep	Nil	0.16	19
20	....	None Since Public			...	Nil	....	5.06	7.71	5.48	9-30-95	p....	p....	★10505	Mr	...	...	...	0.04	....	0.10	6 Mo Sep	0.01	0.07	20
21	....	None Since Public			...	Nil	....	1.25	33.0	19.6	9-30-95	24.5	...	★12613	Dc	d1.05	□d0.61	0.05	0.43	....	0.62	9 Mo Sep	0.36	0.55	21
22	1995	0.05	11-13-95	11-1	0.05	[55]....	....	164	463	164	9-30-95	525	13813	30481	Dc	...	...	...	p0.77	....	2.30	9 Mo Sep	p0.84	p2.37	22
23	....	None Since Public			...	Nil	....	0.75	30.6	51.0	9-30-95	440	...	p19281	Dc	pd2.53	pd1.09	□d0.74	[58]d0.71	....	....	9 Mo Sep	□d0.54	□d1.49	23
24◆	....	None Paid			...	Nil	....	0.86	10.5	11.3	9-30-95	20.4	727	17141	Dc	[59]0.42	0.01	0.01	d0.12	....	d0.17	9 Mo Sep	d0.03	d0.08	24
25◆	1927	Q0.05	11-27-95	11-1	s0.121	0.20	s0.069	1141	3912	1412	9-30-95	2070	...	530169	Je	0.82	0.89	Δ0.95	0.88	1.48	1.51	3 Mo Sep	0.28	0.31	25
26	1987	Q0.70	12-1-95	11-7	2.65	2.80	2.50	152	1340	578	9-30-95	897	...	96399	Dc	1.96	□2.05	2.23	2.80	E5.10↓	4.86	9 Mo Sep	2.02	4.08	26
27◆	1992	Q0.06	12-1-95	11-15	0.24	0.24	0.187	34.5	202	65.5	9-30-95	.....	...	±29674	Mr	±0.46	±0.62	±0.94	±1.13	....	0.82	6 Mo Sep	±0.77	±0.46	27
28	....	0.30	8-24-87	8-11	...	Nil	....	44.4	62.7	22.2	9-30-95	6.04	...	±1314	Dc	±d0.15	±2.78	±4.14	±3.18	....	5.16	9 Mo Sep	±2.18	±4.16	28
29	1995	[61]3.00	7-28-95	7-12	[61]3.00	Nil	....	18.1	68.5	32.1	3-31-94	60.3	...	20333	Sp	...	pd0.24	d0.31	P0.18	P1.06	1.06				29
30◆	1989	Q0.33	11-21-95	11-3	1.28	1.32	1.12	Equity per shr $30.62			9-30-95	.....	...	24139	Dc	3.16	Δ3.32	3.48	3.00	....	2.31	9 Mo Sep	2.33	1.64	30
31	....	None Since Public			...	Nil	....	16.2	27.7	33.5	9-30-95	145	...	24333	Dc	...	p0.36	p0.38	0.40	....	0.47	9 Mo Sep	0.19	0.26	31
32	....	None Since Public			...	Nil	....	5.40	21.4	10.2	p6-30-95	p157	...	★11030	Dc	...	...	...	pd0.70	Ed0.35	....	6 Mo Jun	n/a	p□d0.22	32
33	....	None Paid			...	Nil	....	2.40	3.14	1.88	9-30-94	1.22	...	p14454	Sp	d0.01	[62]0.11	d0.05	0.02	....	0.02				33
34	1988	[61]0.75	4-18-95	3-27	[61]0.75	Nil	[61]0.40	Equity per shr $7.16			9-30-95	.....	...	±2533	Dc	±d1.08	±d0.01	±d0.06	±0.07	....	0.16	9 Mo Sep	±0.05	±0.14	34
35	1995	M0.208	12-29-95	12-26	2.417	2.50	....	Co option redm fr 1-31-2000 at $25				75.0	...	...	Dc	...	...	...	...	....	....	Mature 1-31-2025			35
36	1992	Q0.01	11-22-95	11-6	0.04	0.04	0.04	0.16	325	319	9-30-95	336	1495	19514	Dc	p□0.83	□0.99	□0.89	0.74	....	d0.17	9 Mo Sep	0.42	d0.49	36
37	....	4%Stk	1-21-63	12-31	...	Nil	....	0.34	6.84	1.75	6-30-95	4.72	...	2460	Sp	*0.06	d0.58	d0.63	d0.49	....	d0.35	9 Mo Jun	d0.57	d0.43	37
38	....	0.10	1-2-91	11-5	...	Nil	....	126	662	420	9-30-95	361	5397	106195	Dc	d3.89	□d4.37	□d3.32	0.57	E0.15	0.28	9 Mo Sep	0.52	0.23	38
39	1970	Q0.525	12-29-95	11-29	2.62½	2.10	1.57½	Cv into 1.27 com				....	1697	...	Dc	b1.12	bd1.97	bd2.51	b2.21	....	....				39
40	1983	Q1.12½	1-2-96	11-29	4.50	4.50	4.50	Cv into 2.22 com				....	1000	...	Dc	b1.12	bd1.97	bd2.51	b2.21	....	....				40
41	1992	Q0.906	12-29-95	11-29	4.531	3.625	2.71⅞	Cv into 6.78 com				....	2700	...	Dc	...	bd1.97	bd2.51	b2.21	....	....	Red rstr'n to 10-15-97[67]			41
42	1987	Q0.16	1-2-96	11-29	0.64	0.64	0.64	41.7	96.7	17.3	9-30-95	.....	...	21298	Mr	0.61	0.91	1.07	1.16	....	0.94	6 Mo Sep	0.51	0.29	42
43	1934	Q0.36	12-1-95	11-8	1.40	1.44	1.26	18.4	787	511	9-30-95	438	5478	p36839	Dc	0.77	□d2.03	1.32	[68]5.22	E4.15	3.74	9 Mo Sep	4.03	2.55	43
44◆	1972	Q0.11	12-1-95	11-8	0.44	0.44	0.41	26.1	67.2	50.4	9-30-95	.....	...	26636	Dc	0.89	0.97	1.13	□1.16	....	1.25	9 Mo Sep	□0.82	0.91	44
45	....	None Since Public			...	Nil	....	0.27	6.71	4.41	9-30-95	1.11	...	3581	Dc	0.14	Δ0.19	0.34	d0.95	....	0.05	9 Mo Sep	d0.75	0.25	45
46	....	None Since Public			...	Nil	....	27.1	27.9	12.0	9-30-95	1.99	...	8745	Dc	...	pd1.33	pd1.37	d0.97	....	d0.40	9 Mo Sep	d0.72	d0.15	46
47	....	0.10	1-4-88	12-7	...	Nil	....	0.44	56.0	15.7	9-30-95	18.9	...	2873	Je	*0.04	*0.95	0.36	□0.64	d0.09	d0.16	3 Mo Sep	0.19	0.12	47
48	....	0.05	10-13-86	9-18	...	Nil	....	77.6	1979	856	9-30-95	535	...	50603	Dc	0.28	□1.81	2.62	[69]2.40	E4.17	3.63	9 Mo Sep	1.89	3.12	48
49	1992	Q0.03½	12-15-95	11-28	0.14	0.14	0.12	9.45	96.7	43.8	8-31-95	20.5	...	23231	Au	p0.74	□1.07	1.06	1.29	1.52	1.56	3 Mo Nov	0.32	0.36	49
50	....	None Since Public			...	Nil	....	0.03	6.42	7.70	9-30-95	10.2	...	4133	Dc	d0.07	0.28	0.21	Nil	....	d0.13	9 Mo Sep	0.06	d0.07	50
51	....	None Since Public			...	Nil	....	38.3	68.8	9.67	9-30-95	.....	...	14464	Je	0.46	0.76	0.52	0.89	d0.41	d0.49	3 Mo Sep	0.11	0.03	51
52◆	1993	0.02½	9-15-94	8-26	...	Nil	0.075	3.49	24.6	25.9	9-30-95	5.09	...	6322	Dc	0.46	0.60	0.20	d0.07	....	d0.57	9 Mo Sep	Nil	d0.50	52

◆Stock Splits & Divs By Line Reference Index [2]3-for-2,'93:2-for-1,'94,'95. [4]2-for-1,'92,'93,'95. [15]3-for-2,'94:4-for-3,'95. [17]3-for-2,'91,'95. [24]2-for-1,'94. [25]3-for-2,'94:Adj to 5%,'95. [27]3-for-2,'93,'94. [30]3-for-1,'91. [44]2-for-1,'91,'93. [52]3-for-2,'91.

¶ S&P 500
\# MidCap 400
✤ SmallCap 600
• Options

Index	Ticker	Name of Issue (Call Price of Pfd. Stocks)	Market	Com. Rank. & Pfd. Rating	Inst. Hold Cos	Inst. Hold Shs. (000)	Principal Business	Price Range 1971-93 High	1971-93 Low	1994 High	1994 Low	1995 High	1995 Low	Dec. Sales in 100s	December, 1995 Last Sale Or Bid High	Low	Last	%Div Yield	P-E Ratio	Total Return % Annualized 12 Mo	36 Mo	60 Mo
1	ATA	✓Artra Group	NY,B,Ch,P,Ph	C	11	429	Paper & paper products	41¾	3	7¾	3¾	6⅛	3¼	10416	6⅛	3⅝	6⅛	...	d	19.5	17.8	−1.6
2	ARVI	✓ARV Assisted Living	NNM	NR	..	...	Oper assisted living facilities	....	....	....	....	15¼	9½	5082	11¾	9½	11¾	...	..	...	...	...
#3•[1]	ARV	✓Arvin Indus	NY,B,Ch	B−	135	12742	Auto pts,stereo,metals,video	39¾	2 7/16	33¾	22¾	24⅞	16⅛	20928	18⅛	16⅛	16½	4.6	24	−28.5	−15.9	3.3
¶4•[2]	AR	✓ASARCO Inc	NY,B,C,Ch,P,Ph	B−	336	33369	Producer non-ferrous metals	58½	10	34⅞	21⅜	36⅝	23⅝	66468	36⅝	29⅞	32	2.5	6	14.3	11.5	6.4
5•	ASND	✓Ascend Communications	NNM	NR	202	47781	Dvlp/mkt network access prods	....	....	11⅛	2⅞	81¼	9⅞	189900	81¼	61⅝	81⅛	...	..	670	...	...
6	GOAL	Ascent Entertainment Grp	NNM	NR	..	...	Diverse entmt/media co	....	....	....	....	16	13½	125047	16	13½	15¾	...	d	...	...	...
7	ASEAY	✓ASEA AB ADR[52]	NSC	NR	56	4444	Major Swedish electronics mfr	141½	21⅞	86½	67	101¼	72	1814	97½	91¾	96⅞	1.4	23	37.7	24.1	12.9
8	ACI	✓Ashland Coal	NY	NR	81	5118	Mines/process low sulfur coal	38	10	31¼	22½	30¾	20½	5918	22⅛	20½	21¼	2.2	9	−25.4	−4.9	−0.3
¶9•[3]	ASH	✓Ashland Inc	NY,B,C,Ch,P,Ph	B	387	36641	Petro/refining/chem/constr'n	43	5⅛	44½	31¼	38⅜	30⅜	19156	36½	34¾	35⅛	3.1	..	5.1	11.6	6.0
10	Pr	$3.125 cm Cv Pfd([55]51.88)	NY,Ch	BBB−	73	3333		63⅝	50	73⅛	53½	61¾	53	1496	60¼	58¼	58⅞	5.3	..	...	...	...
✤11•[4]	ASHW	✓Ashworth Inc	NNM	NR	36	2313	Design/mkt golf apparel	12	1	13¼	7⅜	10⅞	5	25450	6¾	5	5⅛	...	43	−34.9	−10.4	16.6
12	ARH	✓Asia Pac Resources Intl'A'	NY,Ch,Ph	NR	..	...	Pulp,paper,rayon fiber	....	....	....	....	10	4¼	20729	5	4½	4¾	...	d	...	...	...
13•[5]	PAP	Asia Pulp & Paper ADS[56]	NY,Ch	NR	55	19861	Mfr pulp & paper products	....	....	....	....	15	7¼	21109	10⅜	7¼	8⅛	...	10	...	...	...
14	ASMLF	ASM Litography Hldg NV	NNM	NR	..	...	Dvlp photolithography proj sys	....	....	....	....	58⅞	18	31202	44¼	33	33¼	...	43	...	...	...
✤15•[6]	ASPT	✓Aspect Telecommunications	NNM	NR	125	17126	Mfr phone call process'g sys	21⅝	2⅞	23	12	39¼	15⅜	48092	39¼	33¼	33½	...	33	91.6	65.7	54.0
16	ASBK	✓Aspen Bancshares	NNM	NR	11	222	Commercial banking, Colorado	12⅝	3⅝	14⅛	8⅝	15	8¾	383	14⅞	13⅛	13⅜	1.5	10	59.5	32.6	...
17	AZPN	✓Aspen Technology	NNM	NR	75	4898	Chem engineer'g software prd	....	....	20¼	13	37	17	10916	37	29½	33¾	...	42	70.9	...	...
18	ASR	✓ASR Investments	AS,Ch,P,Ph	NR	5	131	Real estate investment trust	60⅝	5⅞	15	7⅛	20½	10⅞	1987	17½	15⅜	15⅞	12.6	6	53.9	10.4	−7.6
19	AIC	✓Asset Investors Corp	NY,Ch	NR	18	2173	Mtge investments REIT	19¼	1¾	3½	1¾	3½	1⅝	14086	3⅛	2¾	2⅞	e9.7	5	71.8	...	...
20	ALF	✓Assisted Living Concepts	AS	NR	18	1332	Own/oper sr citizen housing	....	....	9⅜	8	16½	7½	2738	13⅜	12⅜	13⅛	...	..	54.4	...	...
21	ASBC	✓Associated Banc-Corp	NNM	A+	63	4857	Commercial banking,IL&WI	32	¾	30⅝	25	41	27⅜	4309	41	38½	40⅞	2.6	15	54.5	26.0	30.7
22	AEC	✓Associated Estates Realty	NY	NR	76	6823	Real estate investment trust	22⅛	19½	24⅜	18½	22	17	4582	21⅝	19	21½	8.0	17	11.1	...	...
#23•[7]	ASTA	✓AST Research	NNM	C	101	13445	Mfr personal computer sys	32¾	3⅛	33	10⅜	19⅛	7½	64267	10	7⅞	8½	...	d	−42.4	−27.2	−13.7
24	ATEA	✓Astea Intl	NNM	NR	24	2011	Customer interaction software	....	....	....	....	24¾	15	21470	23½	19¾	22⅞	...	65	...	...	...
✤25	ASTE	✓Astec Industries	NNM	B	62	3967	Asphalt mix plants,pav'g eqp	15¾	15/16	20⅛	11⅝	14¼	9¾	7749	11⅛	9¾	9⅞	...	5	−21.0	1.3	43.5
✤26•[8]	ASFC	✓Astoria Financial	NNM	NR	93	6944	Savings & loan, New York	30	25	34¾	25⅛	46⅝	26	24096	46⅝	43½	45⅝	...	11	79.3	...	...
27	ALOT	✓Astro-Med	NNM	B	30	1333	Specialty hi-speed printers	21½	¼	12¼	8¼	12½	8	1630	10¼	9¼	9¼	1.3	34	−9.8	−14.0	11.9
28	AIX	✓Astrotech Intl	AS	NR	20	513	Ptro refn'g maint svc of ASTs	10⅜	⅞	4	2	4⅜	2⅝	2895	4¼	3¼	3⅝	...	13	37.2	−10.4	26.8
29	ASYT	✓Asyst Technologies	NNM	NR	85	4348	Semiconductor mfr envro sys	12½	9	25¼	9¼	53½	20¾	7238	44¾	33	35¼	...	35	50.0	...	...
30	TCC	✓AT&T Capital[63]	NY	NR	65	5928	AT&T,NCR eqp leasing&finance	30⅜	21½	27⅜	19¾	40½	21⅜	4477	40	37¾	38¼	1.2	14	80.4	...	...
¶31•[8]	T	✓AT&T Corp[65]	NY,B,C,Ch,P,Ph	A−	1570	599858	Telecom svcs/business sys	65	14⅞	57⅛	47¼	68½	47⅝	462559	68½	64⅛	64¾	2.0	24	29.5	9.0	17.6
32	ATL	✓Atalanta/Sosnoff	NY,Ch	B	13	458	Inv't mgmt/brokerage svcs	15½	1⅞	9¼	5¼	14⅞	5½	1342	14⅞	9⅜	14½	...	15	165	41.6	54.5
33•[7]	ATC	✓Atari Corp	AS,B,Ch,Ph,P	C	28	2631	Microcomputers/video games	16⅜	½	8⅛	2⅞	4⅜	1⅛	34180	1 9/16	1⅛	1⅜	...	d	−63.9	6.9	−4.7
34	ACCX	✓Atchison Casting	NNM	NR	36	2620	Produce iron/steel castings	17⅞	12	20	13⅛	18¼	11	3045	14	11	12	...	5	−28.9	...	...
35	ATPC	Athey Products	NNM	C	19	990	Street sweepers:haul'g equip	12	3/16	9½	5¼	6½	4	463	4⅞	4	4¼	...	31	−21.6	−8.7	1.7
#36	ATG	✓Atlanta Gas Light[67]	NY	↓B+	157	16908	Natural gas utility,Georgia	21¼	2⅛	19½	14⅝	20	14⅞	10656	20	18¾	19¾	5.4	40	40.1	8.0	11.8
37	AAME	✓Atlantic American	NNM	B−	17	1009	Retail furniture strs/insurance	15¾	¼	2⅝	1¾	3	1⅞	1423	2⅜	2⅛	2 5/16	...	12	23.3	12.5	11.0
#38	ATE	✓Atlantic Energy	NY,B,Ch,Ph	A−	127	11188	Hldg co:Atlantic City Elec	25⅜	6	21¾	16	20⅛	17½	26658	20⅛	19⅛	19¼	8.0	17	18.5	1.3	10.9
39	LYX	Atlantic Rich 9% Exch Nts'97	NY	....[68]	127	26389	Exch Notes for Com Stock	....	....	32	23¾	28½	22⅛	15352	25⅝	22⅞	23⅜	9.5	..	−2.8	...	...
¶40•[8]	ARC	✓Atlantic Richfield	NY,To,B,C,Ch,P,Ph	B+	1120	103814	Integrated oil enterprise	142¼	11⅞	112⅜	92½	117⅞	100½	77844	115⅜	108⅜	110¾	e5.0	13	14.2	4.0	3.0
41	Pr A	$3.00 cm Cv Pref (82)vtg	NY,B,P,Ph	A	9	1	strong interest in Alaskan	910¼	81	736	648½	778½	708	....	....	....	753⅛B	0.4	..	...	...	...
42	Pr C	$2.80 cm Cv Pref(70)vtg	NY,B,Ch,P,Ph	A	30	147	north slope: copper	340	42½	263½	226½	280	242	15	274½	259¼	264½	1.1	..	...	...	...
#43•[5]	ASAI	✓Atlantic So'east Air	NNM	B+	163	17855	Regional commuter service	39	⅜	38¾	12¾	34¼	15¼	122679	26¾	20¾	21½	1.6	13	43.0	1.8	33.1
44	ATNI	Atlantic Tele-Network	NNM	NR	44	3339	Tele svc Virgin Islands/Guyana	25¾	9¾	14¼	7	12⅝	6	6512	11	10¼	10¾	...	9	27.2	−23.4	...
45	AGH	✓Atlantis Plastics	AS,Ch,P	NR	17	689	Hldg:Mfr plastics,furniture	8⅛	¾	7⅛	5¼	8⅛	3⅜	1900	5¼	3½	5¼	...	66	−5.0	3.4	31.4
46	ATLS	✓Atlas Air	NNM	NR	38	3579	Int'l air cargo carrier	....	....	....	....	24¼	12	14954	16¾	13¼	16¾	...	20	...	...	...
47	AZ	✓Atlas Corp	NY,B,Ch,P,Ph	C	33	4731	Gold mining,exploration	26½	2½	10	2	2½	1⅛	20106	1⅝	1¼	1⅜	...	d	−38.9	−34.4	−30.3
48	WS	Wrrt (Purch 1 Com at $15.625)	AS,P	....	5	49		15	⅝	3⅝	¾	1¼	½	815	⅞	½	11/16	...	..	...	...	...
49	ATP	Atlas Pacific Limited[71]	Au	NR	..	...	Gold mining/pearling	....	....	½	⅜	1¼	⅜	10	⅞	⅝	11/16	...	..	...	...	...
#50•[1]	ATML	✓Atmel Corp	NNM,Ch	NR	277	58933	Dvlp/mfr integrated circuits	9⅝	1 11/16	18⅞	8¼	36¾	15⅜	373961	30¼	19½	22⅜	...	20	31.2	77.6	...
✤51	ATO	✓Atmos Energy Corp	NY	B+	70	2950	Natural gas utility	21⅛	5⅛	20¼	15⅞	23	16⅛	2132	23	20⅝	23	4.2	19	45.0	19.9	23.3
52	ATSW	✓Atria Software	NNM	NR	72	9588	Dvl/mkt software products	....	....	15⅝	5¾	42¾	13	16540	42¾	36½	39⅛	...	..	165	...	...

Uniform Footnote Explanations-See Page 4. Other: [1]CBOE:Cycle 2. [2]ASE:Cycle 3. [3]Ph:Cycle 1. [4]ASE:Cycle 1. [5]CBOE:Cycle 3. [6]P:Cycle 3. [7]ASE:Cycle 2. [8]CBOE:Cycle 1.
[51]Excl $3.41M new 'pay-in-kind' pfd. [52]ADR equal 1 'B' ord shr, 50 SEK. [53]®$1.68,'94. [54]®$2.79,'94. [55]Fr 3-14-98,scale to $50 in 2003. [56]Ea ADS rep 4 ord shrs,US$0.50. [57]®$1.60,'94. [58]®$1.08,'94.
[59]Incl $0.05 non-taxable,'94. [60]1 Mo Dec '94 earned d$0.02. [61]To be determined. [62]7 Wks Dec'93. [63]AT&T plan sale of holdings in restructuring. [64]86% owned by AT&T Corp.
[65]Plan restructuring,form 3 seperate cos. [66]Spl div. [67]Plan form holding Co. [68]Rated "Ar" by S&P. [69]Stock or cash re-specified cond.. [70]Incl redemption stk purch rt. [71]All data reported in Australian dollars.

Index (Splits ◆)	Cash Divs. Ea. Yr. Since	Dividends: Latest Payment Period $	Date	Ex. Div.	Total $ So Far 1995	Ind. Rate	Paid 1994	Financial Position Mil-$ Cash& Equiv.	Curr. Assets	Curr. Liab.	Balance Sheet Date	Capitalization Lg Trm Debt Mil-$	Shs. 000 Pfd.	Com.	Earnings $ Per Shr. Years End	1991	1992	1993	1994	1995	Last 12 Mos.	Interim Earnings Period	$ per Shr. 1994	1995	Index
1	....	0.05½	9-5-86	7-25	...	Nil	....	0.08	46.1	115	9-28-95	11.1	[51]423	6730	Dc	d3.36	Δd9.05	Δd1.88	Δd5.30	....	d6.52	9 Mo Sep	d2.10	Δd3.32	1
2	....	None Since Public			...	Nil	....	2.31	8.28	2.56	9-30-95	15.3	2000	★7704	Mr	...	...	...	pd1.00	....	....	6 Mo Sep	n/a	pd0.33	2
3	1925	Q0.19	12-29-95	11-29	0.76	0.76	0.76	56.2	547	445	10-01-95	324	...	22301	Dc	0.81	□1.70	1.81	d0.73	E0.70↓	d1.51	9 Mo Sep	1.30	0.52	3
4	1987	Q0.20	12-1-95	11-2	0.70	0.80	0.40	229	1196	584	9-30-95	1120	...	42497	Dc	1.12	□d0.70	Δd1.70	1.53	E5.60	5.42	9 Mo Sep	0.38	4.27	4
5◆	....	None Since Public			...	Nil	....	209	248	18.6	9-30-95	....	...	54861	Dc	d0.42	d0.66	0.03	0.19	....	0.35	9 Mo Sep	0.13	0.30	5
6	....	None Since Public			...	Nil	....	8.94	55.2	68.4	p9-30-95	70.0	...	★29000	Dc	...	...	...	p0.23	....	d0.53	9 Mo Sep	p0.20	pd0.56	6
7◆	1989	1.318	6-2-95	4-28	1.318	1.32	1.091	112	115	7.80	j12-31-94	9.50	...	±91165	Dc	3.32	2.81	0.36	4.17	....	4.17				7
8	1988	Q0.11½	12-15-95	11-16	0.46	0.46	0.41½	1.45	130	107	9-30-95	188	.3	13750	Dc	2.40	2.01	□2.48	[53]1.72	....	2.32	9 Mo Sep	0.99	1.59	8
9	1936	Q0.27½	12-15-95	11-22	1.10	1.10	1.02½	52.0	2575	2094	9-30-95	1828	6000	63741	Sp	2.56	□d1.18	2.26	[54]2.94	0.08	0.08				9
10	1993	Q0.78⅛	12-15-95	11-22	3.12½	3.125	3.12½	Cv into 1.546 com,$32.343				....	...	5500	Sp	...	...	...	...	....	....				10
11	....	None Paid			...	Nil	....	1.24	45.5	15.4	7-31-95	5.39	...	11882	Oc	0.13	0.19	0.34	0.40	P0.12	0.12				11
12	....	None Since Public			...	Nil	....	48.3	136	188	12-31-94	771	...	±★182000	Dc	...	...	...	pd0.21	....	d0.04	3 Mo Mar	d0.16	0.01	12
13	....	None Since Public			...	Nil	....	652	1470	785	p12-31-94	1905	...	★761180	Dc	...	...	p0.39	p0.08	....	0.82	6 Mo Jun	d0.04	0.70	13
14	....	None Since Public			...	Nil	....	13.5	199	149	12-31-94	p11.5	...	★33000	Dc	d0.16	d0.54	0.49	0.77	....	0.77				14
15◆	....	None Since Public			...	Nil	....	116	163	32.1	9-30-95	55.0	...	20794	Dc	d0.09	*0.20	0.55	[57]0.82	....	1.02	9 Mo Sep	0.60	0.80	15
16◆	1992	Q0.05	1-3-96	12-20	0.16	0.20	0.136	Book Value $6.71			9-30-95	16.4	246	2979	Dc	0.61	0.59	0.82	[58]1.17	....	1.31	9 Mo Sep	0.87	1.01	16
17	....	None Since Public			...	Nil	....	26.0	52.6	16.7	9-30-95	4.04	...	7737	Je	0.20	0.21	0.24	0.44	0.70	0.81	3 Mo Sep	d0.05	0.06	17
18◆	1988	Q0.50	12-28-95	12-13	2.00	2.00	[59]0.50	Equity per shr $12.16			9-30-95	49.8	...	3154	Dc	6.25	d20.20	□d6.25	2.50	....	2.47	9 Mo Sep	1.93	1.90	18
19◆	1987	Q0.09	12-29-95	12-14	†0.37	0.28	†0.30	Equity per shr $3.12			9-30-95	....	...	24326	Dc	2.09	d2.30	□d1.90	0.92	....	0.58	9 Mo Sep	0.69	0.35	19
20	....	None Since Public			...	Nil	....	13.6	14.1	5.96	9-30-95	22.7	...	3000	Dc	...	...	pd0.13	[60]...	....	....	9 Mo Sep	n/a	d0.08	20
21◆	1970	Q0.27	11-15-95	11-2	0.972	1.08	0.848	Book Value $19.09			9-30-95	3.47	...	16501	Dc	1.86	*2.00	2.31	2.57	....	2.77	9 Mo Sep	1.87	2.07	21
22	1994	Q0.43	1-31-96	12-27	1.69	1.72	1.39	Equity per shr $6.62			9-30-95	162	225	13869	Dc	...	p1.16	p1.11	p1.24	....	1.27	9 Mo Sep	p□0.82	□0.85	22
23◆	....	None Since Public			...	Nil	....	135	814	457	9-30-95	123	...	44679	Je	2.13	2.16	d1.72	1.64	d3.07	d4.21	3 Mo Sep	d1.22	d2.36	23
24	....	None Since Public			...	Nil	....	35.0	51.2	12.1	9-30-95	2.63	...	10881	Dc	...	...	...	p0.18	....	0.35	9 Mo Sep	p0.17	p0.34	24
25◆	....	None Since Public			...	Nil	....	2.01	105	36.2	9-30-95	26.8	...	10092	Dc	0.56	0.82	1.07	2.38	....	2.01	9 Mo Sep	1.14	0.77	25
26	1995	0.20	12-1-95	11-13	0.40	[61]...	....	Book Value $40.24			9-30-95	1563	...	11303	Dc	...	...	†[62]0.37	3.70	....	4.03	9 Mo Sep	2.75	3.08	26
27◆	1991	Q0.03	1-3-96	12-20	0.12	0.12	0.12	8.04	31.4	4.99	10-28-95	0.19	...	5031	Ja	2.08	0.69	0.58	0.38	....	0.27	9 Mo Oct	0.34	0.23	27
28	....	None Paid			...	Nil	....	0.30	28.3	17.9	6-30-95	9.69	...	9929	Sp	0.37	0.46	0.14	0.10	P0.28	0.28				28
29	....	None Since Public			...	Nil	....	12.0	78.3	26.3	9-30-95	....	...	4955	Mr	0.03	0.60	0.75	0.31	....	1.01	6 Mo Sep	0.20	0.90	29
30	1993	Q0.11	11-30-95	11-8	0.31	0.44	0.37	Equity per shr $22.94			9-30-95	4320	...	[64]46969	Dc	...	p1.55	□1.67	2.14	....	2.69	9 Mo Sep	1.27	1.82	30
31	1881	Q0.33	2-1-96	12-27	1.32	1.32	1.32	4082	42197	34652	9-30-95	13073	...	1591865	Dc	0.40	2.86	□2.94	3.01	E2.71	2.62	9 Mo Sep	2.16	1.77	31
32	1995	[66]0.15	12-29-95	12-14	[66]0.30	Nil	....	Book Value $6.24			9-30-95	....	...	8812	Dc	0.48	0.65	0.91	0.65	....	0.97	9 Mo Sep	0.56	0.88	32
33	....	None Since Public			...	Nil	....	59.0	90.8	8.54	6-30-95	43.4	...	63643	Dc	Δ0.41	Δd1.29	d0.85	0.16	....	d0.04	9 Mo Sep	d0.14	d0.34	33
34	....	None Since Public			...	Nil	....	1.75	56.7	31.2	9-30-95	26.0	...	5514	Je	pd0.28	d0.86	0.40	□0.98	1.73	2.55	3 Mo Sep	0.42	1.24	34
35◆	....	5%Stk	7-22-94	7-1	...	Nil	5%Stk	4.14	22.9	2.59	9-30-95	0.10	...	3973	Dc	d0.63	Δd0.55	d0.08	0.35	....	0.14	9 Mo Sep	0.23	0.02	35
36◆	1939	Q0.26½	12-1-95	11-15	1.045	1.06	1.04	3.70	220	231	9-30-95	555	588	54900	Sp	1.04	1.13	1.08	1.17	0.50	0.50				36
37	....	0.02	8-15-88	6-24	...	Nil	....	Equity per shr $1.27			9-30-95	32.1	30	18690	Dc	Δd2.17	Δd0.06	Δ□0.15	Δ0.49	....	0.19	9 Mo Sep	0.17	d0.13	37
38◆	1919	Q0.38½	1-15-96	12-21	1.54	1.54	1.54	69.2	324	229	9-30-95	909	2015	52539	Dc	1.74	1.67	1.80	1.41	....	1.14	12 Mo Sep	1.82	1.14	38
39	1994	Q0.557	12-15-95	11-21	2.228	2.23	0.786	Amt pay maturity based on Lyondell Petro Cp stk[69]				....	...	★35000	Dc	...	...	...	...	....	....	Due 9-15-97			39
40	1927	Q1.37½	12-15-95	11-15	[70]5.60	5.50	5.50	2789	5387	3574	9-30-95	6724	873	160804	Dc	4.39	□7.39	1.66	5.63	E8.25	8.19	9 Mo Sep	3.73	6.29	40
41	1966	Q0.75	12-20-95	11-15	3.00	3.00	3.00	Cv into 6.8 common				....	78	...	Dc	b1.79	b2.56	b1.38	b2.21	....	....				41
42	1969	Q0.70	12-20-95	11-15	2.80	2.80	2.80	Cv into 2.4 common				....	795		Dc	b1.79	b2.56	b1.38	b2.21	....	....				42
43◆	1989	Q0.08½	12-15-95	11-29	0.34	0.34	0.32	198	220	63.4	9-30-95	128	...	32679	Dc	0.95	1.09	Δ1.35	1.54	E1.60↓	1.53	9 Mo Sep	1.21	1.20	43
44	1992	0.10	6-30-93	6-9	...	Nil	....	22.8	94.0	66.7	9-30-95	124	...	12273	Dc	□0.17	1.22	Δ0.25	1.07	....	1.27	9 Mo Sep	0.77	0.97	44
45	1994	0.02½	10-18-95	10-2	0.10	[61]....	0.075	3.69	60.2	28.3	9-30-95	120	20	±7093	Dc	Δ±d0.35	□±0.82	□±1.09	±0.83	....	0.08	9 Mo Sep	±0.50	±d0.25	45
46	....	None Since Public			...	Nil	....	77.3	93.3	35.8	9-30-95	239	...	19600	Dc	...	...	...	0.24	....	0.82	9 Mo Sep	0.02	0.60	46
47	....	0.12½	7-5-84	6-14	...	Nil	....	2.58	6.88	3.02	9-30-95	3.50	...	20035	Je	d1.06	d1.18	□d4.57	d1.19	d1.19	d0.97	3 Mo Sep	d0.31	d0.09	47
48◆	....	Terms&trad. basis should be checked in detail						....	...	...	....	....	...	2032	Warrants have no time limitation										48
49◆	....	None Paid			...	Nil	....	1.94	1.94	0.04	j12-31-94	....	...	24992	Dc	d0.06	d0.04	d0.01	0.02	....	j0.02				49
50◆	....	None Since Public			...	Nil	....	186	337	182	9-30-95	82.0	...	97109	Dc	0.15	0.19	0.37	0.66	E1.12	0.97	9 Mo Sep	0.47	0.78	50
51◆	1984	Q0.24	12-11-95	11-22	0.93	0.96	0.89	2.29	48.2	87.4	9-30-95	131	...	15519	Sp	0.80	0.97	1.45	0.97	1.22	1.22				51
52◆	....	None Since Public			...	Nil	....	40.0	44.9	13.7	9-30-95	....	...	14159	Dc	d0.32	d0.31	0.08	0.25	....	0.30	9 Mo Sep	0.16	0.21	52

◆**Stock Splits & Divs By Line Reference Index** [5]2-for-1,'95(twice):To split 2-for-1,ex Jan 8. [7]No adj for $28.65655 dstr,'91. [15]2-for-1,'95. [16]5-for-4,'94,'95. [18]1-for-5 REVERSE,'95. [19]No adj for stk dstr,'93. [21]10%,'93:5-for-4,'95. [23]2-for-1,'91. [25]2-for-1,'93. [27]3-for-2,'92. [35]Adj for 5%,'94. [36]2-for-1,'95. [38]2-for-1,'92. [43]3-for-2,'91:2-for-1,'93. [48]2-for-1,'89. [49]1-for-4 REVERSE'93. [50]2-for-1,'94,'95. [51]3-for-2,'94. [52]2-for-1,'95.

¶ S&P 500 · # MidCap 400 · ✤ SmallCap 600 · • Options

Index	Ticker	Name of Issue (Call Price of Pfd. Stocks)	Market	Com. Rank. & Pfd. Rating	Inst. Hold Cos	Inst. Hold Shs. (000)	Principal Business	Price Range 1971-93 High	1971-93 Low	1994 High	1994 Low	1995 High	1995 Low	Dec. Sales in 100s	December, 1995 Last Sale Or Bid High	Low	Last	%Div Yield	P-E Ratio	Total Return % Annualized 12 Mo	36 Mo	60 Mo
1	ATXI	✔Atrix International	NSC	NR	2	248	Copy mach mntr/vacuums,tools	2¼	¾	1 11/16	¾	1¼	¾	6072	⅞	¾	¾	...	13	–25.0	–11.0	...
2	ATWD	✔Atwood Oceanics	NNM	↑B–	45	3729	Contract offshore drilling	46¼	2½	14⅞	11	27	10⅜	13919	27	18½	25¼	...	24	113	39.8	13.6
✤3•[1]	ABPCA	✔Au Bon Pain'A'	NNM	NR	77	6276	Oper/franchise bakery cafes	29	9	26½	14⅜	17¼	5⅞	21443	10¼	8¼	8¼	...	d	–44.1	–31.4	...
4	VOX	✔Audiovox Cl'A'	AS,Ch	B	21	470	Auto sound/telephone equip	18⅜	1	18⅜	6¼	8⅛	4⅜	4352	6⅜	5¼	5⅜	...	d	–35.1	–8.1	37.0
5	ASW	✔Audits & Surveys Worldwide	AS	C	8	247	Intl marketing research svcs	12⅜	½	4¾	9/16	4½	1½	791	2	1½	1⅝	...	18	–50.9	–2.4	–4.1
✤6•[2]	AUG	✔Augat, Inc	NY,B,Ch,P,Ph	B–	123	13652	Mfr electromechanical comp	47½	3⅛	24⅞	16	24½	14½	33559	17½	15⅛	17⅛	0.9	14	–8.5	15.1	13.3
7•[3]	AURA	✔Aura Systems Inc	NNM	C	70	10769	Mfr actuators/display sys	12¼	1 5/16	9⅜	3¾	8¼	3	108221	5⅞	4½	5⅝	...	d	50.0	15.8	29.2
8	AUR	✔Aurora Electronics	AS,B	C	18	1666	Recycles integrated circuits	18	3⅝	9⅜	4¼	5⅛	1¾	10048	2⅜	1¾	2 1/16	...	d	–57.1	...	...
✤9•[1]	ASPX	✔Auspex Systems	NNM	NR	88	12856	Mfr client/server computer sys	15½	7½	10	3⅞	18¾	6½	52549	18⅜	14⅝	18¼	...	33	181	...	...
10	AUST	✔Austin's International	NSC	NR	3	29	Oper Texas-style restaurants	5½	2½	6¼	1½	2	⅝	3650	1½	⅝	¾	...	d	–57.1	–42.8	...
11	ANZ	Australia & N.Z. Bk ADS[55]	NY,Ch	NR	9	873	General banking/Fin'l svcs	....	....	16	15⅛	23¾	15½	9515	23¾	22⅜	23¼	4.6	11	54.7	...	...
12	SPJ	Austria (Republic) SIGNs	NY	....[58]	4	163	Stock Index Growth Notes	12⅞	9⅞	13¼	12	18	12⅝	5260	18	17	17⅝	...	..	36.9	14.5	...
✤13	ASM	✔Authentic Fitness	NY,Ph	NR	102	10986	Mfr swimwear/fitness apparel	16	6⅛	16	10⅞	23⅜	11⅞	11132	21¼	19⅜	20¾	...	23	48.3	24.7	...
14	ACAM	✔Autocam Corp	NNM	NR	14	726	Mfr specialty metal components	15	4⅝	20⅛	10¼	14½	9½	903	14½	13	14	s...	14	33.2	40.2	...
¶15•[4]	ACAD	✔Autodesk, Inc	NNM,Ch	B+	376	32486	Computer-aid design/draftg	31⅛	1 15/16	41½	21⅛	53	31¼	107968	39½	32¾	34¼	0.7	17	–10.5	15.3	7.3
16	AUTO	AutoInfo Inc	NNM	B–	22	3410	Auto parts data service	8⅞	1½	4½	2⅜	4⅛	2⅜	6378	3½	3⅛	3⅜	...	3	42.1	–10.8	–4.5
17	ASI	✔Automated Security Hldgs ADS[59]	[5]NY	NR	26	22317	Sell,svc electr security sys	8¾	2⅞	4½	1¾	2½	½	54326	1¼	9/16	¾	...	d	–62.5	–41.8	...
¶18•[6]	AUD	✔Automatic Data Proc	NY,B,Ch,P,Ph	A+	738	105387	Computer services	56⅞	1 5/16	59¾	47⅝	82⅜	57½	78132	82⅜	69⅝	74¼	1.1	26	27.7	12.1	24.0
19	APCO	Automobile Protection-APCO	NNM	NR	..	...	Extended vehicle svc contracts	2 1/16	9/16	2⅞	1 7/16	3⅜	1⅝	17133	3	2 7/16	2¾	...	..	25.0	47.6	32.5
20•[1]	TOTE	✔Autotote Corp Cl'A'	NNM	↓C	68	11983	Pari-mutuel wagering sys	28½	15/16	29¼	10⅝	14¼	2 7/16	63978	4	2⅝	2⅞	...	d	–74.5	–24.1	21.7
21•[7]	AZO	✔AutoZone Inc	NY,Ph	B+	247	63289	Retail auto parts stores	29½	5¾	30¾	21⅝	30⅛	22	48281	29⅞	27½	28⅞	...	30	20.9	14.9	...
22	AVN	✔Avalon Properties	NY,Ch	NR	162	23507	Real estate investment trust	21⅛	19½	24¼	18	23	17¾	12691	21⅝	19⅜	21½	6.9	19	6.5	...	...
23	AVNT	✔Avant Corp	NNM	NR	57	3847	Dvlp application software prd	....	....	....	....	51	12½	128947	44½	12½	19¼	...	29	...	...	...
24	AVE	✔AVEMCO Corp	NY,B,Ch	B+	56	4831	Insur/svcs for aviation ind	28	⅜	20¼	13⅜	18¼	14⅝	773	17	15¾	16	3.0	17	11.5	–8.8	1.5
25	AVR	Avenor Inc	To,Mo	C	46	8884	Paper & pulp:building prod	56⅛	3⅛	28¼	19	33⅜	22⅛	43296	25⅝	22⅛	23⅜	2.1	7	–15.8	1.6	...
¶26•[8]	AVY	✔Avery Dennison Corp	NY,Ch,P	B+	412	32363	Adhesives,labels,office prd	33¼	3⅛	36	26⅜	50⅛	33⅛	18862	50⅛	46½	50⅛	2.4	19	43.9	24.5	22.5
27	AVL	✔Aviall Inc	NY	NR	88	12882	Turbine engine overhaul, svcs	17⅛	14	19	7½	10⅛	5⅞	17577	10⅛	8⅛	9⅜	0.4	15	21.6	...	...
28•[9]	AVID	✔Avid Technology	NNM	NR	152	15246	Sell audio/video editing sys	27½	16	43¾	20½	49¼	16¾	265036	40	16¾	19	...	16	–42.0	...	...
29	AVV	✔Aviva Petroleum Dep[64]	AS	NR	1	255	Oil & gas explor,dvlp,prod'n	....	....	5⅛	4¾	7⅜	4	6	4½	4⅜	4¼B	...	d	–15.0	...	...
#30•[10]	AVT	✔Avnet, Inc	NY,B,Ch,P,Ph	A	336	31726	Distributor elec components	50	1⅞	45	30¾	55⅝	35¾	59285	49½	41¼	44¾	1.3	12	23.5	10.8	13.7
¶31•[1]	AVP	✔Avon Products	NY,B,C,Ch,P,Ph	B+	483	57886	Cosmetics,jewelry,gift prod	140	17⅞	63⅝	48⅜	78⅜	54	36295	78⅜	72¼	75⅜	2.9	18	31.3	14.0	26.5
32	AVND	✔Avondale Financial	NNM	NR	14	1360	Savings bank,Ill.	....	....	....	....	15¼	10	2124	15¼	14½	14½	...	..	...	...	...
33	AVDL	✔Avondale Industries	NNM	NR	40	5589	Ship construction, repairs	21¾	⅞	8½	6⅛	16⅜	7	5982	15½	13⅝	14½	...	8	90.2	88.8	19.3
34•[11]	AVX	✔AVX Corp	NY	NR	120	14388	Mfr passive electronic comp'ts	....	....	....	....	38	21⅛	51080	29⅜	21⅛	26½	0.8	18	...	...	...
35	AYD	✔Aydin Corp	NY,B,Ch,Ph	B	36	2115	Hi-tech communicns eq & sys	41⅝	1/16	14¼	10⅛	19⅜	11½	1454	15¾	14¾	15⅛	...	18	21.0	–1.9	4.0
36	AZC	✔Azco Mining	AS	NR	11	1779	Dvlp stge: copper mining	....	....	2⅞	1¾	2⅜	11/16	14823	1 1/16	11/16	13/16	...	d	–60.6	...	...
✤37•[11]	AZR	✔Aztar Corp	NY	NR	92	21445	Oper casino hotel facilities	10⅛	2⅜	7⅞	5⅜	10½	5⅝	23461	9⅛	7¾	7⅞	...	39	37.0	6.6	22.3
38	AZTC	✔Aztec Mfg Co	NNM	B	17	1194	Mfr electr prds/galvanizing	25⅜	⅛	6⅝	3⅞	5⅛	3⅛	3155	5⅛	3½	5	0.4	18	21.8	31.5	6.5
39	BHM	✔B&H Maritime Carriers	AS,Ch	NR	2	128	Own/oper dry&tank vessels	17½	⅝	1¾	¾	1¼	⅞	555	1⅛	15/16	1	...	d	–5.8	0.0	–30.9
40	BHO	✔B&H Ocean Carriers	AS,Ch	NR	8	850	Own/oper bulk cargo vessels	20¼	1⅞	5⅛	2	2⅞	1 15/16	2069	2⅝	2⅛	2⅜	...	d	18.2	8.9	–17.6
41	BAANF	Baan Co NV	NNM	NR	..	...	Dvlp ntwk/mgmt software	....	....	....	....	49⅛	21¼	13980	46⅛	40⅞	45¼	...	..	...	...	...
42•[3]	BSST	✔Baby Superstore	NNM	NR	95	6954	Retail non-food baby prod	....	....	31½	12	58½	29⅞	30198	58½	52	57	...	93	81.6	...	...
43	BYBI	Back Yard Burgers	NSC	NR	3	72	Oper fast-food restaurants	11¾	5½	6⅞	3	5	1½	4588	2 1/16	1½	1½	...	75	–52.0	...	...
44	BMI	✔Badger Meter	AS,Ch	B+	18	359	Fluid meters/accessories	24¼	4¼	28	19	27	22⅛	296	27	22⅞	26½	3.0	13	14.5	18.2	17.7
45	BZ	✔Bairnco Corp	NY,Ch,Ph	B–	33	3728	Food svc eqp,electr/ind'l prd	42¼	11/16	5½	3	6⅛	3⅞	7803	6⅛	5	5¾	3.5	8	45.7	–3.8	...
✤46•[3]	JBAK	✔Baker(J.) Inc	NNM	A–	111	13588	Self-svc footwear retailer	25⅞	3	22⅜	14½	15⅞	5⅜	26254	6½	5⅜	5¾	1.0	d	–61.4	–32.0	6.1
47	BKR	✔Baker (Michael)	AS,Ch,Ph	C	21	2322	Engr,oper & maint,constr	15¼	⅝	11	3	6⅜	3⅝	3097	5⅜	4⅛	5	...	d	37.9	–29.1	–7.1
¶48•[4]	BHI	✔Baker Hughes Inc	NY,B	B	491	100674	Oil,gas,mining equip/svcs	34¾	11⅛	22⅛	17	24⅞	16¾	234140	24⅞	20⅛	24⅜	1.9	36	38.4	10.6	1.6
49	BCP	✔Balchem Corp	AS	B+	5	35	Mfr specialty chemicals	7½	1	7¾	3⅝	11	5¼	418	9⅛	8½	9	0.4	20	44.8	9.3	23.4
✤50	BEZ	✔Baldor Electric	NY,Ch,Ph	A	139	10377	Industrial electric motors	16½	3/16	18⅜	14⅛	26½	17¼	6028	22¾	20	20⅛	1.8	18	16.0	19.7	29.8
51	BWINA	✔Baldwin & Lyons Cl'A'	NNM	B+	10	206	Insurance agent/broker	16½	⅜	20½	14	18¼	14½	8	17¾	15¾	16¾B	1.9	9	21.9	17.3	23.6
52	BWINB	✔ Class B(non-vtg)	NNM	B+	41	4344	insurance company	16¼	3⅝	15¾	13¾	17⅝	14¼	394	16½	15½	16¼	2.0	8	8.6	15.6	24.2

Uniform Footnote Explanations-See Page 4. Other: [1]CBOE:Cycle 1. [2]ASE:Cycle 1. [3]CBOE:Cycle 3. [4]P:Cycle 1. [5]Ph [6]Ph:Cycle 2. [7]CBOE,NY:Cycle 3. [8]Ph:Cycle 1. [9]ASE,NY:Cycle 3. [10]ASE:Cycle 2. [11]CBOE:Cycle 2. [51]®$2.21,'94. [52]Fiscal Dec'91 & prior. [53]12 Mo Sep'92. [54]50 Wk Mar'92. [55]Ea ADS rep 5 ord shrs, A $1.00 par. [56]Approx. [57]®$2.03,'94. [58]Rated "AAAr" by S&P. [59]Ea ADS rep 2 ord, 10 pence. [60]Stk dstr,1 com for every 48. [61]Fiscal Aug'94 & prior. [62]4 Mo Dec'94. [63]6 Wks Dec.'93. [64]Dep shrs ea rep 5 com. [65]78.4% owned by Kyocera Corp. [66]Special divd. [67]Pfd in M$. [68]®$0.41,'94. [69]®$0.27,'95. [70]To be determined. [71]®$0.15,'94. [72]®$1.46,'94.

Splits ◆ Index	Cash Divs. Ea.Yr. Since	Dividends: Latest Payment Period $	Date	Ex. Div.	Total $ So Far 1995	Ind. Rate	Paid 1994	Financial Position Mil-$ Cash& Equiv.	Curr. Assets	Curr. Liab.	Balance Sheet Date	Capitalization Lg Trm Debt Mil-$	Shs. 000 Pfd.	Com.	Earnings $ Per Shr. Years End	1991	1992	1993	1994	1995	Last 12 Mos.	Interim Earnings Period	$ per Shr. 1994	1995	Index
1	....	None Since Public			...	Nil	....	1.01	3.22	1.61	9-30-95	0.01	...	5654	Je	d0.11	d0.21	d0.12	0.08	0.06	0.06	3 Mo Sep	0.01	0.01	1
2	....	None Paid			...	Nil	....	14.1	34.5	19.1	6-30-95	36.3	...	6588	Sp	d1.07	d3.18	d0.27	0.94	P1.07	1.07				2
3	....	None Since Public			...	Nil	....	4.69	25.4	18.4	10-07-95	75.4	20	±11633	Dc	±0.30	±0.48	±0.60	±0.67	....	d0.03	9 Mo Sep	±0.48	±d0.22	3
4	....	None Since Public			...	Nil	....	4.36	230	46.7	8-31-95	70.2	50	±9039	Nv	d1.63	*0.64	*1.11	□[51]2.88	....	d1.14	9 Mo Aug	□2.96	d1.06	4
5	....	0.05	10-16-90	9-24	...	Nil	....	....	14.3	15.4	9-30-95	0.77	...	13095	Dc	Δ1.09	d1.78	Δd3.92	p0.11	....	0.09	9 Mo Sep	p0.03	p0.01	5
6	1994	Q0.04	11-30-95	11-8	0.16	0.16	0.08	24.0	217	95.0	9-30-95	25.8	...	19777	Dc	d1.21	0.36	0.83	1.36	....	1.24	9 Mo Sep	0.99	0.87	6
7	....	None Since Public			...	Nil	....	17.5	85.9	18.5	8-31-95	5.14	...	55576	Fb	d0.19	d0.36	d0.35	d0.07	....	d0.08	6 Mo Aug	d0.03	d0.04	7
8◆	....	h....	10-29-92	10-13	...	Nil	....	0.01	24.7	22.7	7-02-95	44.9	...	7508	Sp	Δ[52]d2.26	*Δ[53]d3.66	Δ0.04	d0.87	Pd1.79	d1.79				8
9	....	None Since Public			...	Nil	....	42.6	95.2	24.9	9-30-95	0.11	...	23423	Je	d0.98	0.25	0.36	0.34	0.51	0.56	3 Mo Sep	0.09	0.14	9
10	....	None Since Public			...	Nil	....	0.19	0.58	2.35	9-30-95	....	...	6714	Mr	‡[54]d0.13	d0.13	d0.23	d0.29	....	d0.22	6 Mo Sep	d0.16	d0.09	10
11	....	[56]0.599	1-29-96	12-12	0.937	1.08	0.64	Book Value $14.89			9-30-94	j4076	6000	1355683	Sp	1.07	d2.15	0.43	[57]2.07	....	2.07				11
12	....	None Paid			...	Nil	....	Int based on S&P 500,as defined				....	...	10000	$10 & contingent int pd at maturity							SIGNs mature 8-15-96			12
13◆	1995	0.01¼	1-3-96	11-29	0.01¼	Nil	....	0.09	178	147	9-30-95	33.4	...	20340	Je	p0.23	p0.43	0.56	□0.49	0.90	0.90	3 Mo Sep	0.10	0.10	13
14◆	....	5%Stk	12-8-95	11-16	10%Stk	Stk	....	0.04	11.3	9.16	6-30-95	13.3	...	5398	Je	pΔ0.37	p0.54	0.52	0.87	0.95	1.04	3 Mo Sep	0.15	0.24	14
15◆	1989	Q0.06	1-26-96	1-10	0.24	0.24	0.24	207	355	136	10-31-95	....	...	43315	Ja	1.16	0.88	1.25	1.14	E2.05	1.56	9 Mo Oct	0.99	1.41	15
16	....	None Paid			...	Nil	....	35.3	35.8	3.35	8-31-95	2.00	...	7758	My	0.33	*0.15	0.24	0.27	1.12	1.11	3 Mo Aug	0.06	0.05	16
17	1991	[60]....	7-15-94	7-6	...	Nil	[60]....	6.14	76.3	202	11-30-94	123	48630	119571	Nv	□0.40	0.78	0.07	d0.41	....	d0.71	9 Mo Aug	0.08	d0.22	17
18◆	1974	Q0.20	1-1-96	12-13	0.65	0.80	0.56	732	1246	567	9-30-95	394	...	144002	Je	1.63	1.84	2.08	□2.37	2.77	2.85	3 Mo Sep	0.49	0.57	18
19	....	None Paid			...	Nil	....	10.8	12.3	7.82	9-30-95	....	...	p9001	Dc	d0.18	d0.04	Δ[61]0.15	‡[62]0.04	....	....	9 Mo Sep	0.13	0.16	19
20◆	....	None Since Public			...	Nil	....	9.26	49.3	183	7-31-95	44.6	...	28942	Oc	d4.52	0.34	0.33	□d0.64	Pd1.72	d1.72				20
21◆	....	None Since Public			...	Nil	....	6.41	448	418	8-28-95	....	...	147052	Au	0.33	0.44	0.59	0.78	0.93	0.97	3 Mo Nov	0.19	0.23	21
22	1994	Q0.37	11-17-95	11-2	1.46	1.48	1.25	Equity per shr $14.77			9-30-95	310	...	28373	Dc	...	...	‡[63]0.12	1.10	....	1.13	9 Mo Sep	0.82	0.85	22
23	....	None Since Public			...	Nil	....	33.1	35.6	3.87	6-30-95	0.10	p...	9476	Dc	...	...	...	pd0.16	....	0.66	9 Mo Sep	d0.48	0.34	23
24◆	1970	Q0.12	1-19-96	12-20	0.45	0.48	0.44	Equity per shr $6.96			9-30-95	58.0	...	8688	Dc	1.34	0.82	Δ1.33	1.20	....	0.92	9 Mo Sep	0.91	0.63	24
25	....	gQ0.12	12-29-95	11-29	g0.24	0.48	....	107	901	308	j12-31-94	1672	...	p67083	Dc	d13.00	d4.82	d4.88	d1.07	....	j3.24	9 Mo Sep	d0.93	3.38	25
26	1964	Q0.30	12-20-95	12-4	1.11	1.20	0.99	3.90	763	549	9-30-95	438	...	53187	Dc	1.02	1.33	Δ1.44	1.97	E2.65	2.51	9 Mo Sep	1.45	1.99	26
27	1994	Q0.01	1-2-96	12-13	0.03	0.04	0.04	10.3	474	152	9-30-95	281	...	19442	Dc	...	p0.99	n/a	0.49	....	0.63	9 Mo Sep	0.30	0.44	27
28	....	None Since Public			...	Nil	....	87.7	270	80.4	9-30-95	3.00	...	20868	Dc	...	p0.23	0.38	1.10	....	1.18	9 Mo Sep	0.63	0.71	28
29	....	None Paid			...	Nil	....	1.93	5.90	6.09	9-30-95	6.93	...	31483	Dc	d8.80	d6.20	□d0.40	d0.08	....	d0.07	9 Mo Sep	d0.05	d0.04	29
30	1961	Q0.15	1-2-96	12-13	0.60	0.60	0.60	58.9	1687	530	9-29-95	438	...	43288	Je	1.72	1.42	1.91	□2.16	3.32	3.65	3 Mo Sep	0.69	1.02	30
31	1919	Q0.55	12-1-95	11-14	2.10	2.20	1.90	98.2	250	1254	9-30-95	114	...	67867	Dc	1.78	2.43	□3.32	□3.41	E4.20	4.06	9 Mo Sep	□1.84	2.49	31
32	....	None Since Public			...	Nil	....	Book Value $15.26			9-30-95	78.3	...	4232	Mr	...	...	p0.76	n/a	....	....	6 Mo Sep	n/a	0.47	32
33	....	0.23	12-17-90	11-27	...	Nil	....	33.0	151	99.6	9-30-95	60.6	...	14464	Dc	d9.76	d0.78	d0.61	0.59	....	1.79	9 Mo Sep	0.43	1.63	33
34	1995	0.05	11-10-95	10-26	0.05	0.20	....	122	522	199	9-30-95	9.28	...	[65]88000	Mr	0.24	*0.34	Δ0.41	0.87	E1.50	1.22	6 Mo Sep	0.42	0.77	34
35	....	[66]0.50	3-20-92	3-3	...	Nil	....	15.9	141	57.1	9-30-95	0.80	...	5122	Dc	2.13	1.40	d1.00	1.01	....	0.86	9 Mo Sep	0.75	0.60	35
36	....	None Paid			...	Nil	....	0.33	0.38	3.31	9-30-95	....	...	25513	Je	d0.06	d0.11	d0.11	d0.17	d0.19	d0.20	3 Mo Sep	d0.02	d0.03	36
37	....	None Since Public			...	Nil	....	48.9	92.0	95.7	9-28-95	455	[67]5	38253	Dc	Δ0.12	□Δ0.44	0.28	□[68]0.42	E0.20	0.11	9 Mo Sep	0.48	0.17	37
38◆	1969	0.02	3-24-95	3-6	0.02	0.02	0.02	0.05	15.2	8.36	8-31-95	6.11	...	5748	Fb	0.20	0.20	0.39	[69]0.28	....	0.28	9 Mo Nov	0.33	0.33	38
39◆	....	0.05	4-15-92	3-25	...	Nil	....	0.06	0.58	6.23	12-31-94	2.66	...	3080	Dc	d0.70	d4.21	d3.37	d2.19	....	d0.45	9 Mo Sep	d2.20	d0.46	39
40	1994	0.15	3-14-95	2-28	0.15	[70]....	†0.90	1.02	3.36	4.76	12-31-94	4.69	...	4080	Dc	d0.61	d1.25	d3.41	d1.07	....	d0.22	9 Mo Sep	d1.29	d0.44	40
41	....	None Since Public			...	Nil	....	4.98	60.4	61.4	p3-31-95	2.05	...	★42389	Dc	...	...	...	pNil	....	0.19	9 Mo Sep	Nil	0.19	41
42◆	....	None Since Public			...	Nil	....	30.7	99.7	38.9	7-26-95	★100	...	19181	Ja	0.05	0.10	0.25	0.44	....	0.61	9 Mo Oct	0.33	0.50	42
43	....	None Since Public			...	Nil	....	0.45	1.17	1.05	9-30-95	2.84	335	4197	Dc	...	p▲0.08	0.01	[71]0.20	....	0.02	9 Mo Sep	0.18	Nil	43
44	1934	Q0.20	12-14-95	11-29	0.782	0.80	0.71	0.22	35.2	18.9	9-30-95	1.00	...	±1756	Dc	±0.97	□±0.47	±1.27	±1.86	....	2.08	9 Mo Sep	±1.39	±1.61	44
45◆	1972	Q0.05	1-3-96	12-1	0.20	0.20	0.20	0.92	55.7	27.8	9-30-95	22.9	...	10328	Dc	0.41	0.70	d2.15	0.69	....	0.74	9 Mo Sep	0.51	0.56	45
46	1987	Q0.01½	2-2-96	1-12	0.06	0.06	0.06	2.66	403	168	10-28-95	230	...	13871	Ja	0.78	□1.25	1.70	[72]1.71	....	d2.35	9 Mo Oct	1.22	d2.84	46
47◆	....	0.01	11-1-83	10-12	...	Nil	....	5.74	98.7	74.7	9-30-95	1.40	...	±8364	Dc	0.60	0.67	□d1.84	d0.95	....	d0.70	9 Mo Sep	0.03	0.28	47
48	1987	Q0.11½	11-24-95	11-2	0.46	0.46	0.46	6.82	1565	580	9-30-95	798	...	142267	Sp	1.26	Nil	0.34	□0.85	□0.67	0.67				48
49◆	....	A0.03½	1-19-96	12-22	0.02¾	0.035	0.022	0.05	5.19	2.77	9-30-95	2.73	...	3121	Dc	0.25	0.05	0.20	0.27	....	0.46	9 Mo Sep	0.16	0.35	49
50◆	1938	Q0.09	1-2-96	12-8	0.33	0.36	0.267	36.8	205	67.5	9-30-95	25.4	...	27708	Dc	0.44	0.55	0.69	0.93	....	1.10	9 Mo Sep	0.67	0.84	50
51◆	1974	Q0.08	11-28-95	11-10	0.30	0.32	†0.33	Equity per shr $16.32			9-30-95	....	...	±14579	Dc	±1.19	□±1.37	±1.62	±1.37	....	1.97	9 Mo Sep	±1.10	±1.70	51
52◆	1986	Q0.08	11-28-95	11-10	0.30	0.32	†0.33	...	...	...		....	...	12103	Dc	±1.19	□±1.37	±1.62	±1.37	....	1.97	9 Mo Sep	±1.10	±1.70	52

◆Stock Splits & Divs By Line Reference Index [8]5-for-4,'92. [13]2-for-1,'94. [14]3-for-2,'94:Adj to 5%,Nov'95. [15]2-for-1,'94. [18]2-for-1,'91:To split 2-for-1,ex Jan 2. [20]3-for-2,'93:2-for-1,'93. [21]2-for-1,'92,'94. [24]3-for-2,'91. [38]Adj to 5%,'91. [39]No adj for spl $2.50 dstr,'91. [42]3-for-2,'95. [45]No adj for stk dstr of Keene Corp,'90. [47]2-for-1,'92. [49]4-for-3,'91:3-for-2,'94. [50]6-for-5,'94:3-for-2,'92,'95. [51]3-for-1,'93. [52]3-for-1,'93.

¶ S&P 500 # MidCap 400 ✣ SmallCap 600 • Options Index	Ticker	Name of Issue (Call Price of Pfd. Stocks)	Market	Com. Rank. & Pfd. Rating	Inst. Hold Cos	Inst. Hold Shs. (000)	Principal Business	Price Range 1971-93 High	1971-93 Low	1994 High	1994 Low	1995 High	1995 Low	Dec. Sales in 100s	December, 1995 Last Sale Or Bid High	Low	Last	%Div Yield	P-E Ratio	Total Return % Annualized 12 Mo	36 Mo	60 Mo
1	BPAO	✓Baldwin Piano & Organ	NNM	B–	30	1694	Mfrs pianos & electr organs	20	5½	18½	10¼	15¼	10¼	1474	13¼	12	12½	...	69	17.6	–9.3	14.0
2	BLD	✓Baldwin Technology'A'	AS,Ch,Ph	B–	50	9641	Mfrs eqp for printing indus	15⅜	1¾	6¾	4¼	6½	4¾	4140	5⅜	4¾	5	...	15	–7.0	3.6	5.5
¶3•[1]	BLL	✓Ball Corp	NY,B,Ch,P,Ph	B+	325	22024	Containers: metal:aerospace	48½	2	32⅛	24⅜	38¾	25¾	18160	30⅛	25¾	27¾	2.2	d	–10.9	–5.1	4.3
4	BTN	Ballantyne of Omaha	AS	NR	8	240	Mfr motion pic't proj/restr eq	...	...	...	...	8½	6½	1266	8⅛	6⅞	8	...	12	...	...	...
✣5•[2]	BMP	✓Ballard Medical Prod	NY,Ch,Ph	↑B+	91	10666	Mfr disposable medical prod	26½	11/16	15¼	8½	18⅛	10⅛	12691	18⅛	16⅝	17⅞	0.4	24	78.8	–4.2	19.5
¶6•[3]	BLY	✓Bally Entertainment[53]	NY,B,C,Ch,P,Ph	C	180	15639	Hlth clubs,casino,gaming eq	48⅝	1 5/16	9⅝	5¼	14	6	65343	14	12	14	...	26	129	26.8	42.6
✣7•[1]	BGII	✓Bally Gaming Intl[55]	NNM	NR	47	4061	Mfr/dstr gaming machines	25¼	8½	17⅞	7¼	12½	6⅛	12950	10	8	8⅛	...	37	–23.1	–13.9	...
8	BTEK	✓Baltek Corp	NNM	B–	12	248	Balsa wood pd/shrimp farm'g	19⅜	⅝	9¼	6½	10¼	6½	152	8⅝	8¼	8½	...	11	21.4	13.1	16.0
¶9•[4]	BGE	✓Baltimore Gas & El[56]	NY,B,C,Ch,P,Ph	A	428	55104	Utility: elec & gas service	27½	4	25½	20½	29	22	62049	29	26½	28½	5.5	14	35.7	13.2	16.3
¶10•[5]	ONE	✓Banc One Corp	NY,B,Ch,P,Ph	A+	677	190447	Comml bkg,Ohio,midwest	44¾	1⅝	38	24⅛	40⅛	25⅛	119217	40⅛	37	37⅝	3.6	12	53.4	6.2	23.6
11	BANF	✓BancFirst Corp	NNM	NR	25	1433	Commercial banking, Oklahoma	17½	14¼	17¼	12¼	22½	13¾	1422	20¼	18½	18⅝	1.5	10	35.3	...	...
12	BBV	✓Banco Bilbao Vizcaya ADS[57]	NY,Ch	NR	31	5988	Commercial banking,Spain	36¾	18⅞	26⅞	20¾	36⅛	23½	2360	36⅛	32⅜	35¾	3.0	15	53.6	26.6	13.1
13	BCH	✓Banco Cent Hispanoamer[58] ADS	[6]NY,To	NR	14	808	Gen'l bkg,Spain & worldwide	26¾	3⅝	12¾	9⅜	12¼	9¾	3856	10⅜	9¾	10⅛	3.6	14	–4.0	–2.2	–10.6
14	BPC	Banco Coml Portugues ADS[60]	NY	NR	21	3360	Commercial bank, Portugal	15½	10½	17	12	14	11⅞	1291	13¾	12¾	13⅛	2.6	11	5.1	7.7	...
15	AED	Banco de A Edwards ADS[62]	NY	NR	..	...	Commercial banking, Chile	...	...	...	...	19⅝	16⅛	7557	19⅝	17⅛	19⅝	...	25	...	...	...
16	BGALY	✓Banco de Galicia-Buenos Aires[64]	NNM	NR	53	6727	Commercial banking,Argentina	30⅜	16	33⅝	13¼	21½	5⅜	38004	21½	19½	20⅝	0.9	17	68.6	...	...
17•[7]	BFR	✓Banco Frances del Rio ADS[65]	NY,Ph	NR	62	6562	Commercial bank, Argentina	35¼	25⅜	41¼	16	27¾	8	21438	27¾	21½	26⅞	1.5	26	68.8	...	...
18	BGA	Banco Ganadero ADS[66]	NY,Ph	NR	10	822	Commercial banking-Colombia	...	...	27	24⅞	27¼	15⅝	2043	19⅜	16⅛	19	4.9	10	–20.6	...	...
19	BLX	✓Banco Latinoamer de Export'E'	NY,Ph	NR	..	...	Multi-national bank, Panama	45¾	20⅛	52	28½	46¾	23¾	2531	46¾	44½	46½	1.1	14	53.3	17.0	...
20	OHG	✓Banco O'Higgins ADS[67]	NY,Ch	NR	33	1439	Commercial bank, Chile	...	...	22½	14¼	23¾	13	6423	23	18½	23	3.0	21	38.7	...	...
21	BOU	Banco Osorno y La Union ADS[68]	NY,Ch	NR	60	3521	General banking-Chile	...	...	13⅝	10⅜	16⅛	8½	6641	14⅞	12⅝	13⅞	3.0	18	34.5	...	...
22	STD	✓Banco Santander ADS[69]	NY,Ch	NR	57	3897	Gen'l bkg,Spain & worldwide	64	33	52	34	49⅞	32½	2982	49⅞	44⅞	49¼	3.3	..	37.6	19.6	8.5
23	BWP	Banco Wiese ADS	NY,Ch,Ph	NR	41	3956	Commercial banking, Peru	...	...	12½	8¾	9⅜	5	7492	6⅝	5⅞	6¼	0.7	9	–29.6	...	...
#24•[8]	BOH	✓Bancorp Hawaii	NY,Ch,Ph	A	179	24293	Commercial bkg,Hawaii	35⅞	1⅞	34¾	24⅛	37⅛	24⅞	8113	36⅞	35	35⅞	3.1	12	46.3	10.9	17.2
25	BOMS	✓BancorpSouth	NNM	A	41	1827	Commercial banking, Tupelo	18½	2⅛	18⅛	14½	23⅞	16⅛	3923	22½	19	20¼	3.4	11	29.0	16.6	25.6
✣26•[9]	BTC	✓BancTec,Inc	NY	B–	99	8842	Computer processing checks	24¼	3⅜	27¼	18¼	22¾	14¾	12960	21	17¾	18½	...	16	–10.8	–1.8	22.8
27	BDG	✓Bandag, Inc	NY,B,Ch,Ph	A+	168	6077	Tread rubber: tire recap eqp	73¼	2½	63½	49⅛	65⅞	49	6973	54⅞	50½	54⅛	1.7	14	–9.5	–0.7	–7.6
28	BDG A	Cl'A'	NY,Ph	A+	110	5014		71	44¼	59⅜	44½	60½	47½	7682	53⅝	49⅜	53	1.7	14	0.8	–0.1	...
29	BMCC	✓Bando McGlocklin Capital	NNM	NR	10	272	Closed-end diversified inv co	16¼	5½	18½	12¼	15	11¼	2461	13	12	13	7.4	..	2.0	8.1	...
✣30	BGR	✓Bangor Hydro Electric	NY,Ph	B+	41	1305	Electric utility in Maine	24⅛	5½	19	9⅜	12⅞	9⅛	3848	12⅝	11¼	11½	6.3	41	29.6	–9.5	1.7
31	BAN	✓Banister Foundation	AS,To,Mo,B,Ph	B–	18	2949	Constr:util,PL,civil&ind'l	35½	3⅜	14⅞	9½	11¼	5⅜	626	6⅛	5⅜	6⅛	...	..	–38.8	–1.3	–3.3
¶32•[10]	BKB	✓Bank of Boston	NY,B,C,Ch,Ph,P	B–	555	77294	Comml bkg,Mass,northeast	38	3	29¼	22⅛	50⅛	25½	162591	48⅛	43¼	46¼	3.2	10	84.7	24.9	51.1
33•[11]	BMO	Bank of Montreal[73]	NY,To,Ch,Mo,Ph,Vc	B+	108	42606	General bkg,Canada	28	5	30¾	17¾	23⅛	17⅛	23148	23	21⅜	22⅝	...	..	30.1	5.9	...
¶34•[7]	BK	✓Bank of New York	NY,B,C,Ch,Ph	B	635	138421	Commercial bkg,New York	31¼	3⅝	33¼	25	49	28½	100843	48⅞	45⅜	48¾	3.0	11	68.6	26.7	46.9
35•[12]	BNS	Bank of Nova Scotia	To,Mo,Vc	B+	87	14502	General Banking, Canada	30¾	3½	33¼	23⅛	30⅜	24¼	107017	30⅜	28¾	29¾	4.2	9	16.4	13.1	...
36	BSO	✓Bank of Southington	AS	NR	3	.4	General banking, Connecticut	17⅜	6¾	9	6⅝	9⅝	6¼	103	9⅝	8⅝	9¼	s2.5	13	43.0	...	...
37•[7]	BKSO	✓Bank South Corp[76]	NNM	B–	101	14305	Comml bkg,Atlanta,Georgia	21⅛	1 3/16	21¼	14¾	32½	16¾	33906	32½	29½	30⅜	1.8	21	73.2	40.1	39.9
¶38•[7]	BAC	✓BankAmerica Corp	NY,B,C,Ch,P,Ph	B	911	221443	Commercial bank'g California	55½	5¼	50¼	38⅜	68½	39½	208650	68½	62¾	64¾	2.8	10	65.8	15.6	23.9
39	BANC	✓BankAtlantic Bancorp	NNM	B–	39	3007	Savings bank, Florida	14¼	⅜	13½	9⅝	20	11⅝	1016	18¾	18	18¾	1.2	10	56.3	55.3	74.2
40	BNKF	✓Bankers First Corp[79]	NNM	B	32	995	Savings & loan,Georgia	20¼	2¾	21¼	17¼	31½	18	4616	28½	27	27⅞	2.2	11	56.3	48.3	49.8
41•[9]	BLH	✓Bankers Life Holdings	NY,Ph	NR	54	3189	Individual hlth insurance prd	28¼	17	25¾	16½	21⅝	17½	8166	20¼	18	20¼	3.0	8	11.4	...	...
42	TBN.EC	✓Banker's Note	ECM	NR	5	118	Retail ladies sportswear	17	⅛	1¼	½	13/16	¼	867	7/16	¼	¼	...	d	–50.0	–42.5	–10.6
¶43•[13]	BT	✓Bankers Trust NY	NY,B,C,Ch,P,Ph	B+	488	51270	Commercial bkg,New York	83½	6⅜	84⅝	54¾	72	49¾	90516	69¼	65⅜	66½	6.0	32	21.4	3.9	15.1
44	BTB	Bankers Tr[81]6% Cap Sec(25)	AS	A	3	90	Convertible capital securities	25¾	24½	25	18⅜	24¼	19	12	23	22¾	22½B	8.4	..	...	...	...
45	BND	Bankers Tr[84]6.125%CapSec(25)	AS	A	3	355	Convertible capital securities	26⅛	23¾	25⅞	18⅜	25	19¾	17	23	22⅝	22⅝B	6.8	..	...	...	...
46	BKUNA	✓BankUnited Financial'A'	NNM	NR	4	140	Savings bank,Coral Gables, Fl	12¾	2⅜	8¼	4½	8¾	4¾	483	8	6	6⅛	...	4	28.9	–7.0	17.1
47	BAR	✓Banner Aerospace	NY,Ph	NR	28	7372	Sell aviation parts/aircraft	14⅛	3¾	6¼	3¾	6⅜	3½	1905	6	4¾	5¾	...	..	35.3	–0.7	–3.9
48	BPOP	✓BanPonce Corp	NNM	A	72	7581	General Bank'g,Puerto Rico	32¼	1¾	33¼	27	39⅞	28	3294	39½	38¼	38¾	3.1	10	43.0	13.8	25.7
#49	BNTA	✓Banta Corp	NNM	A–	227	14583	Printing/graphic/video svcs	37	11/16	38½	27	45⅛	28½	23689	45	41¾	44	1.5	17	49.6	19.0	23.9
50	VHT	✓Banyan Hotel Inv Fund[86]	AS	NR	..	...	Real estate investment trust	9½	⅛	½	⅛	1⅝	5/16	1945	1½	1	1 3/16	...	d	280	112	30.6
51	VMG	✓Banyan Mortgage Inv Fund	NY,Ch	NR	11	104	Real estate development	8¾	5/16	1¼	½	¾	⅜	14777	½	⅜	⅜	...	d	–18.8	–16.1	1.6
52	VST	✓Banyan Short Term Inc Tr SBI	AS	NR	4	664	Real estate investment trust	10⅞	¾	2⅛	1⅜	4½	7/16	3050	4½	7/16	9/16	...	1	191	57.8	47.3

Uniform Footnote Explanations-See Page 4. Other: [1]ASE:Cycle 2. [2]ASE:Cycle 1. [3]ASE,CBOE,NY:Cycle 1. [4]Ph:Cycle 1. [5]P:Cycle 2. [6]Ph [7]CBOE:Cycle 1. [8]ASE,P:Cycle 2. [9]CBOE:Cycle 2. [10]Ph:Cycle 2. [11]Mo:Cycle 1. [12]To:Cycle 3. [13]P:Cycle 1. [51]®$2.20,'94. [52]®$0.73,'95. [53]Plan spin-off,Bally's Health & Tennis. [54]Stk dstr of Bally's Health & Tennis Corp. [55]Vote Jan 9 Alliance Gaming mgr,cash & com. [56]Plan mgr,Potomac El Pwr,new hldg co,1 new co. [57]Each ADS equals one Ord shr,700 Pesetas. [58]Each ADS represents½ com shr. [59]Approx. [60]Ea ADS rep 1 ord,Escudos 1000. [61]Incl shrs hld by subsid. [62]Ea ADS rep 165 Sr A com,no par. [63]To be determined. [64]Ea ADS rep 4 ord Cl'B' shrs,Ps1.00. [65]Ea ADS rep 3 ord Ps.100. [66]Ea ADS rep 100 Cl'B'Ord,PS10.00. [67]Ea ADS rep 6 com,no par. [68]Ea ADS rep 220 Sr'A'com,no par. [69]Ea ADS rep 1 ord,440 peseta. [70]Incl proceeds from sale of rts. [71]®$0.60,'94. [72]®$3.67,'94. [73]Prices prior to 10-27-94 in Cdn $. [74]®$3.38,'95. [75]®$3.70,'94. [76]Approve NationsBank Corp acq,0.44 com. [77]®$5.33,'94. [78]®$1.89,'94. [79]Southtrust Corp plan acq, 1.126 com. [80]Conseco Inc owns 85%. [81]Fr 8-15-98 on int pymt dates. [82]Only upon int reset. [83]In M $. [84]Fr 6-1-98 on int pymt dates. [85]In M$. [86]Fund will terminate in 2001. [87]Liq div.

Index	Splits ◆ Cash Divs. Ea.Yr. Since	Dividends: Latest Payment Period $	Date	Ex. Div.	Total $ So Far 1995	Ind. Rate	Paid 1994	Financial Position Mil-$ Cash& Equiv.	Curr. Assets	Curr. Liab.	Balance Sheet Date	Capitalization Lg Trm Debt Mil-$	Shs. 000 Pfd.	Com.	Earnings $ Per Shr. Years End	1991	1992	1993	1994	1995	Last 12 Mos.	Interim Earnings Period	$ per Shr. 1994	1995	Index
1	. . . .	None Since Public			. . .	Nil	. . . .	0.80	68.8	34.8	9-30-95	4.48	. . .	3415	Dc	1.30	1.75	□1.81	0.10	. . . .	0.18	9 Mo Sep	0.60	0.68	1
2	. . . .	0.003	3-31-92	3-9	. . .	Nil	. . . .	13.2	115	62.9	9-30-95	33.2	. . .	±18034	Je	±0.40	±d0.41	□±Δ0.21	0.23	0.32	0.33	3 Mo Sep	±0.05	±0.06	2
3◆	1958	Q0.15	12-15-95	11-29	0.60	0.60	0.60	41.5	628	466	10-01-95	306	1787	30216	Dc	2.42	2.45	□d1.17	[51]2.35	Ed0.51	Nil	9 Mo Sep	1.64	d0.71	3
4	. . . .	None Since Public			. . .	Nil	. . . .	0.35	15.8	6.45	9-30-95	8.82	. . .	4000	Dc	. . .	. . .	. . .	p0.49	. . . .	0.65	9 Mo Sep	p0.33	p0.49	4
5◆	1992	0.08	1-3-96	12-14	. . .	0.08	0.06	45.7	75.0	4.21	9-30-95	. . . .	. . .	26561	Sp	0.35	0.50	0.68	0.55	[52]0.74	0.74				5
6	. . . .	h[54]. . . .	1-9-96	1-10	. . .	Nil	. . . .	158	210	159	6-30-95	1289	★14194	47212	Dc	Δd1.10	Δd0.05	□d0.27	□d1.08	E0.55	0.12	9 Mo Sep	□d0.85	Δ0.35	6
7	. . . .	None Since Public			. . .	Nil	. . . .	1.34	147	45.2	9-30-95	56.6	. . .	10800	Dc	0.48	0.50	Δd2.54	0.35	. . . .	0.22	9 Mo Sep	0.14	0.01	7
8	. . . .	0.075	1-18-91	1-7	. . .	Nil	. . . .	1.22	20.2	7.87	9-30-95	2.03	. . .	2523	Dc	0.32	d0.22	0.04	0.48	. . . .	0.76	9 Mo Sep	0.23	0.51	8
9◆	1910	Q0.39	1-2-96	12-7	1.54	1.56	1.50	28.1	725	807	9-30-95	2509	5502	147527	Dc	1.52	1.63	1.85	1.93	E2.05	1.99	12 Mo Sep	1.82	1.99	9
10◆	1935	Q0.34	1-2-96	12-13	1.33	1.36	1.212	Book Value $19.17			9-30-95	2677	4997	391285	Dc	2.12	2.38	Δ2.93	2.42	E3.20	2.50	9 Mo Sep	2.27	2.35	10
11	1994	Q0.07	10-16-95	10-4	0.28	0.28	0.24	Book Value $13.94			9-30-95	. . . .	. . .	6216	Dc	*Δ0.65	*1.70	Δ1.77	1.80	. . . .	1.93	9 Mo Sep	1.34	1.47	11
12	1989	0.256	10-31-95	10-4	1.08½	1.09	0.938	Book Value $19.51			12-31-94	1358	. . .	231000	Dc	4.64	2.74	2.15	2.37	. . . .	2.37				12
13	1978	[59]0.151	5-11-95	4-17	[59]0.362	0.36	0.275	Book Value $12.30			12-31-94	2907	. . .	163631	Dc	2.07	1.33	0.98	0.75	. . . .	0.75				13
14◆	1994	0.345	5-12-95	4-12	0.345	0.34	0.274	Book Value $9.36			12-31-94	468	. . .	[61]109686	Dc	1.47	1.64	1.17	1.07	. . . .	1.17	9 Mo Sep	0.76	0.86	14
15	. . . .	Plan annual div			. . .	[63]. . . .	. . . .	Book Value $5.62			6-30-95	434	p. . .	p5952642	Dc	0.52	0.51	0.55	0.68	. . . .	0.78	6 Mo Jun	0.33	0.43	15
16◆	1993	0.197	10-16-95	10-3	0.197	0.19	0.221	. . . .	. . .	. . .		273	. . .	185753	Je	0.13	1.13	1.40	P1.42	P1.25	1.25				16
17◆	1994	0.391	10-25-95	10-13	0.391	0.39	0.538	Book Value $11.50			6-30-95	p53.4	. . .	128224	Je	1.28	1.57	2.37	1.87	1.05	1.05				17
18	1995	[59]0.201		12-21	0.937	0.94	. . . .	. . . .	. . .	. . .		p418	479800	2310800	Dc	p±3.69	p±1.80	p±1.93	. . . .	. . . .	1.90	6 Mo JunΔ	p±0.61	p±0.58	18
19	1993	A0.53	2-15-95	1-31	0.53	0.53	0.45	Book Value $18.18			12-31-94	557	1724	20320	Dc	1.53	1.87	2.15	2.54	. . . .	3.24	9 Mo Sep	1.82	2.52	19
20	1995	0.684	4-18-95	3-16	0.684	0.68	. . . .	Book Value $8.14			12-31-94	414	. . .	236600	Dc	0.98	1.21	0.68	0.99	. . . .	1.10	9 Mo Sep	0.70	0.81	20
21	1995	[59]0.19½	8-17-95	8-14	[59]0.423	0.42	. . . .	Book Value $3.63			12-31-94	439	. . .	★12594315	Dc	0.22	0.17	0.22	□0.76	. . . .	0.76				21
22	1942	0.386	11-21-95	10-30	1.607	1.61	[70]5.938	Book Value $22.04			12-31-94	2075	. . .	160000	Dc	6.65	4.62	4.89	3.46	. . . .	. . . .	9 Mo Sep	n/a	3.22	22
23◆	1995	0.035	3-10-95	2-16	0.035	0.045	. . . .	Book Value $2.58			12-31-94	123	. . .	244304	Dc	0.57	0.28	0.36	0.56	. . . .	0.72	9 Mo Sep	0.38	0.54	23
24◆	1899	Q0.28	12-14-95	11-16	1.08½	1.12	1.04	Book Value $22.88			9-30-95	898	. . .	41522	Dc	2.69	Δ2.75	3.09	2.75	E2.90	2.54	9 Mo Sep	2.34	2.13	24
25◆	1945	Q0.17	1-2-96	12-13	0.60	0.68	0.54	Book Value $13.93			9-30-95	45.6	. . .	p20998	Dc	1.41	1.24	Δ1.50	1.60	. . . .	1.83	9 Mo Sep	1.10	1.33	25
26◆	. . . .	None Since Public			. . .	Nil	. . . .	1.94	153	116	9-24-95	39.3	. . .	p20131	Mr	1.18	Δ1.32	1.45	1.12	. . . .	1.16	6 Mo Sep	0.69	0.73	26
27◆	1976	Q0.22½	1-19-96	12-18	0.80	0.90	0.70	38.8	331	120	9-30-95	. . . .	. . .	±24419	Dc	±2.86	□±2.99	±2.88	±3.51	. . . .	3.82	9 Mo Sep	±2.47	±2.78	27
28	1992	Q0.22½	1-19-96	12-18	0.80	0.90	0.70	. . . .	. . .	. . .		. . . .	. . .	12322	Dc	±2.86	Δ±2.99	±2.88	±3.51	. . . .	3.82	9 Mo Sep	±2.47	±2.78	28
29	1987	Q0.24	1-31-96	12-27	0.96	0.96	†1.00	Net Asset Val $5.89			6-30-94	46.4	690	3924	Je	§4.29	§4.19	§6.35	§5.89	. . . .	. . . .				29
30	1925	Q0.18	1-20-96	12-28	1.02	0.72	1.32	3.61	36.4	73.3	9-30-95	288	197	7285	Dc	1.33	1.60	0.63	0.84	. . . .	0.28	12 Mo Sep	0.14	0.28	30
31	. . . .	g0.60	3-15-83	2-23	. . .	Nil	. . . .	45.4	228	193	j12-31-94	16.6	. . .	7751	Dc	1.12	1.21	1.63	[71]0.61	. . . .	j0.04	9 Mo Sep	0.37	d0.20	31
32	1784	Q0.37	11-24-95	11-2	1.28	1.48	0.93	Book Value $21.79			12-31-94	p2059	4594	p112205	Dc	Δd0.64	*2.10	Δ2.28	□[72]3.79	E4.45	4.40	9 Mo Sep	□2.75	3.36	32
33◆	1829	gQ0.33	11-29-95	11-6	g1.32	1.32	g1.20	Book Value $21.31			j10-31-95	2595	28000	263685	Oc	2.32	2.38	2.59	3.01	[74]3.45	j3.45				33
34◆	1785	Q0.36	11-2-95	10-18	1.36	1.44	1.09½	Book Value $25.27			9-30-95	1836	234	200030	Dc	0.64	2.23	2.87	[75]3.92	E4.55	4.48	9 Mo Sep	2.86	3.42	34
35	1834	gQ0.31	1-29-96	12-28	g1.24	1.24	g1.16	Book Value $22.70			j10-31-94	3016	44000	p229253	Oc	2.81	2.94	2.98	1.76	P3.38	j3.38				35
36◆	1993	s0.057	12-29-95	12-6	s0.224	0.23	0.20	Book Value $7.59			12-31-94	. . . .	. . .	1216	Dc	0.32	0.52	0.43	0.61	. . . .	0.74	9 Mo Sep	0.48	0.61	36
37	1993	Q0.14	1-2-96	12-13	0.55	0.56	0.43	Book Value $11.50			9-30-95	189	. . .	58786	Dc	d1.59	0.74	1.57	1.47	E1.45	1.34	9 Mo Sep	1.11	0.98	37
38	1989	Q0.46	12-14-95	11-20	1.84	1.84	1.60	Book Value $29.30			9-30-95	15882	p51185	369998	Dc	4.81	4.24	4.79	[77]5.36	E6.30	6.16	9 Mo Sep	3.95	4.75	38
39◆	1993	Q0.05½	1-19-96	1-3	0.202	0.22	0.193	Book Value $12.15			9-30-95	120	335	8471	Dc	Δd1.70	*2.46	2.02	[78]1.90	. . . .	1.97	9 Mo Sep	1.52	1.59	39
40	1989	Q0.15	11-15-95	10-27	0.60	0.60	0.45	Book Value $19.06			9-30-95	169	. . .	4755	Dc	□0.64	□Δ0.64	□1.72	□2.37	. . . .	2.54	9 Mo Sep	□1.76	1.93	40
41	1993	Q0.15	1-2-96	12-18	0.60	0.60	0.47	Equity per shr $12.00			9-30-95	273	. . .	[80]51124	Dc	. . .	p1.60	p□2.55	2.49	. . . .	2.40	9 Mo Sep	1.82	1.73	41
42	. . . .	None Since Public			. . .	Nil	. . . .	0.13	5.55	3.18	7-29-95	0.91	. . .	4407	Ja	d1.11	0.13	ΔNil	0.01	. . . .	d0.02	6 Mo Jul	0.04	0.01	42
43	1904	Q1.00	1-25-96	12-29	4.00	4.00	3.60	Book Value $53.39			9-30-95	8354	★12203	78688	Dc	7.75	8.82	□12.40	7.17	E2.10	1.86	9 Mo Sep	5.97	0.66	43
44	1993	Q0.37½	11-15-95	11-10	1.68¾	1.88	1.87½	Cv at hldrs opt into 1 Sr'P'Dep Pfd[82]				. . . .	[83]100	. . .	Dc	. . .	. . .	. . .	. . . .	. . . .	. . . .	Mature 8-15-2033			44
45	1993	Q0.383	12-1-95	11-28	1.625	1.53	1.906	Cv at hldrs opt into 1 Sr'O'Dep Pfd				. . . .	[85]150	. . .	Dc	. . .	. . .	. . .	. . . .	. . . .	. . . .	Mature 6-1-2033			45
46◆	1992	0.02½	6-30-94	6-14	. . .	Nil	0.05	Book Value $7.23			12-31-94	113	2679	±2040	Sp	±□0.65	±1.27	±1.42	±□0.19	P±1.77	1.77				46
47	. . . .	None Since Public			. . .	Nil	. . . .	. . . .	220	36.4	9-30-95	103	. . .	18002	Mr	0.34	d0.17	d0.65	0.03	. . . .	Nil	6 Mo Sep	0.11	0.08	47
48	1923	tQ0.30	1-2-96	12-13	t1.10	1.20	t1.00	Book Value $25.92			9-30-95	★869	4000	32922	Dc	2.15	2.79	Δ3.16	3.67	. . . .	3.97	9 Mo Sep	2.74	3.04	48
49◆	1927	Q0.16	2-1-96	1-17	0.56	0.64	0.52	9.31	276	120	9-30-95	103	. . .	20276	Dc	1.05	1.79	2.03	2.33	E2.60	2.54	9 Mo Sep	1.72	1.93	49
50	. . . .	0.22½	1-31-90	12-22	. . .	Nil	. . . .	Equity per shr $0.18			9-30-95	. . . .	. . .	12404	Dc	d0.52	d0.71	d0.05	d0.04	. . . .	d0.04	9 Mo Sep	d0.03	d0.03	50
51	. . . .	0.30	1-31-90	12-22	. . .	Nil	. . . .	Equity per shr $2.17			9-30-95	32.7	. . .	39822	Dc	d0.53	d0.14	0.03	d0.23	. . . .	d0.29	9 Mo Sep	d0.05	d0.11	51
52	. . . .	[87]3.95	12-22-95	12-26	[87]3.95	Nil	. . . .	Equity per shr $4.40			9-30-95	. . . .	. . .	6667	Dc	d0.61	d0.26	d0.23	0.27	. . . .	0.44	9 Mo Sep	0.23	0.40	52

◆**Stock Splits & Divs By Line Reference Index** [3]No adj for stk dstr of Alltrista,'93. [5]3-for-2,'91,'92:4-for-3,'93. [9]3-for-2,'92. [10]5=for-4,'93:10%,'92,'94. [14]6-for-5,'93. [16]15%,'94:18%,'95. [17]15%,'95. [23]2.06192-for-1,'95. [24]3-for-2,'91,'94. [25]15%,'93:2-for-1,'95. [26]3-for-2,'93. [27]2-for-1 in Cl'A','92. [33]2-for-1,'93. [34]2-for-1,'94. [36]10%,'94:Adj for 5%,'95. [39]15%,'93:5-for-4,'95. [46]10%,'92:15%,'92,'93. [49]3-for-2,'93.

¶ S&P 500 # MidCap 400 ✣ SmallCap 600 • Options Index	Ticker	Name of Issue (Call Price of Pfd. Stocks)	Market	Com. Rank. & Pfd. Rating	Inst. Hold Cos	Inst. Hold Shs. (000)	Principal Business	Price Range 1971-93 High	1971-93 Low	1994 High	1994 Low	1995 High	1995 Low	Dec. Sales in 100s	December, 1995 Last Sale Or Bid High	Low	Last	%Div Yield	P-E Ratio	Total Return % Annualized 12 Mo	36 Mo	60 Mo
✣1•	BNYN	✔Banyan Systems	NNM	NR	95	9418	Dvlp networking softwr prd	26½	10¼	19¾	12¾	19⅜	6	77349	12⅜	9⅜	10¼	...	d	–42.3	–18.9	...
2	BCS	✔Barclays plc ADS[51]	NY,B,Ch,Ph	NR	34	1533	Comm'l bkg,U.K.,world wide	39	18⅞	40	30	50¼	36	667	49⅛	45¼	45¼	3.3	10	20.8	29.2	15.4
¶3•[1]	BCR	✔Bard (C.R.)	NY,B,Ch,P	A–	324	38133	Hospital, surgical specialties	35⅞	1⅝	30½	22¼	32¼	25½	23559	32¼	28⅝	32¼	2.0	20	22.6	2.2	16.7
4	B	✔Barnes Group	NY,Ch	B	73	3272	Mfr prec mech springs:dstr	40¾	5½	39⅞	29½	45¾	35⅞	3127	38⅞	35⅞	36	4.4	9	–1.2	10.0	11.2
5•[2]	BKS	✔Barnes & Noble	NY,Ch	NR	192	16562	Retail bookstores/superstrs	34	20	31⅜	20	42¼	26⅛	64876	37	26⅛	29	...	25	–5.7	...	...
¶6•[3]	BBI	✔Barnett Banks Inc	NY,B,Ch,P	A–	487	49016	Comm'l bkg,Florida,Georgia	50⅜	2½	48⅛	37¼	62⅜	38¼	52924	62⅜	57⅜	59	3.2	11	57.4	16.6	30.7
7	Pr A	$4.50 cm Cv Pfd([54]52.25)	NY	BBB	54	1094		99	52¼	92	74	116¾	73⅞	1439	116¾	108	111½	4.0	..	...	...	...
8	BRN	✔Barnwell Indus	AS,To,Ch	B	12	202	O&G dev Cdn/water sys Hawaii	37½	3⅝	23⅝	18½	20⅛	15¾	173	17⅛	15¾	15⅞	...	32	–15.8	–0.3	–10.6
9	BRL	✔Barr Laboratories	AS,Ph	B–	38	2046	Mfr generic pharmaceuticals	37½	4	26¾	14⅞	30¾	17	2297	30¾	22⅞	29¾	...	41	22.1	41.5	27.7
10	BARZ	✔BARRA Inc	NNM	NR	22	913	Dvlp fin'l analysis software	15½	6⅛	9	5	17	7	3373	17	14	17	...	26	147	28.6	...
✣11•[4]	BRR	✔Barrett Resources	NY,Ch,Ph	B–	140	14646	Oil&gas explor,dev,prod'n	27½	2	22¾	10⅜	30⅝	16⅞	16564	30⅝	24⅝	29⅜	...	..	38.2	45.7	35.2
¶12•[5]	ABX	✔Barrick Gold	NY,To,P,Ph,Mo	A–	526	109724	Gold prod'n U.S./Canada	30⅜	11/16	31	19⅞	27⅝	19¾	174020	27⅝	25¾	26⅜	0.5	31	17.8	20.4	19.4
13	BIS	✔Barrister Info Sys	AS	C	4	21	Info sys to legal profession	108	7/16	13/16	5/16	2⅛	⅜	415	1⅝	1 5/16	1 7/16	...	d	283	24.2	–0.9
14	RGB	✔Barry (R.G.)	NY,Ch	B–	30	1439	Slippers, comfort footwear	9⅝	1 3/16	18½	7½	23⅝	7⅛	7109	23⅛	18⅝	19½	...	33	138	67.0	59.6
15•	BARY	✔Barry's Jewelers	NNM	NR	20	1246	Operates jewelry store chain	12½	1¼	8¾	3⅛	7⅛	2⅞	1755	4⅛	3⅝	4	...	6	–38.5	2.2	...
16	BASEB	Base Ten Sys Cl'B'[58]	NSC	B–	6	44	Electronics for defense indy	16⅞	1/16	9½	6½	13⅛	6⅝	21	12¼	11⅛	11½B	...	d	73.6	20.2	52.9
17	BASEA	✔ Class 'A'(1/10 vtg)	NNM	B–	14	355	alarms,intrusion,detractors	15	3/16	9¾	6¼	13¼	6⅝	5043	12	10⅝	11	...	d	69.2	18.4	54.5
18	BPILF	Basic Petroleum Intl	NNM	B–	7	488	Oil & gas explor,dev,prod'n	72⅞	1 5/16	13⅝	10⅛	31¼	10¾	716	26	23¾	25	...	28	133	46.5	33.2
19	BSNX	✔Basin Exploration	NNM	NR	47	5163	O&G dvlp,exploitat'n,prod'n	19½	8¼	13½	7½	11½	3	12902	5½	4⅜	4⅞	...	d	–54.1	–27.1	...
20	BAS	✔Bass ADS[59]	NY	NR	32	1373	Oper brewery,hotel,restaur'ts	23¼	13½	18½	15⅛	23	15½	22347	23	20¾	22¼	3.4	18	41.5	11.1	6.9
✣21	BSET	✔Bassett Furniture	NNM	B	168	6082	Mfr wood furniture for home	44	4	37¼	25¼	30¼	20⅛	9196	24½	22¼	23¼	3.4	14	–15.8	–9.5	9.6
22	BTI	✔B.A.T.Indus Ord ADR[60]	AS,B,Ch,Mo,P	NR	49	9407	Tobacco prod,fin'l svcs, insur	17¼	15/16	17	11⅜	18⅜	12⅞	13848	18⅜	16⅞	18⅜	4.4	13	45.4	10.6	...
#23•[6]	BMG	✔Battle Mtn Gold	NY,To,Ch,P,Ph	B–	193	35880	Operates gold & silver mines	29⅞	4½	13	8⅞	12⅜	7⅝	86736	9¼	8	8½	0.6	85	–22.3	20.0	5.3
24	Pr	$3.25 cm Cv Pfd([63]52.275)	NY,Ch	B+	44	1126		66	50	70½	56¾	62⅞	46½	1979	52¼	48¼	49⅝	6.5	..	...	...	...
¶25•[3]	BOL	✔Bausch & Lomb	NY,B,Ch,P,Ph	A–	374	38393	Vision care & instruments	60½	2⅛	53⅞	30⅝	44½	30⅞	129162	41	32¼	39⅝	2.6	18	21.0	–7.9	4.6
¶26•[7]	BAX	✔Baxter International[64]	NY,B,C,Ch,Ph,P	B+	760	191512	Mfr,dstr hospital/lab prod	40⅞	6	28⅞	21⅝	44¾	26¾	185046	42¾	39¾	41⅞	2.7	18	51.7	...	...
27	BYA	✔Bay Apartment Communities	NY,Ch,Ph	NR	115	10748	Real Estate Invest Trust	....	....	22¾	17¾	24½	16¾	6820	24½	21⅞	24¼	6.4	..	30.2	...	...
28	CJ	✔Bay Meadows Oper(Unit[66])	AS,Ch	NR	16	706	Turf racing:REIT	27½	1 11/16	21	12½	17¼	13¾	622	16	14	14⅝	4.4	18	–1.8	12.1	7.3
#29•[8]	BNET	✔Bay Networks[67]	NNM,Ch	NR	402	132887	Local area ntwrk computer eqp	21⅝	2⅞	29¼	12⅜	49⅞	18⅜	806363	47¼	34½	41⅛	...	48	108	48.9	...
30	BGC	✔Bay State Gas	NY,B,Ch	↓A–	62	2423	Natural gas, Massachusetts	32	3¾	28⅜	22½	29½	22¼	3014	29½	27⅛	27¾	5.4	16	25.9	9.9	13.6
31	BVFS	✔Bay View Capital	NNM	NR	61	5171	Svg & ln,California	27	10¾	26½	16¾	29¾	17¾	15483	29¼	27	28½	2.1	25	60.2	17.1	18.8
32•[8]	BBNK	✔BayBanks Inc	NNM	B+	238	13224	Comm'l bkg,Massachusetts	52¼	4¾	65¼	49¼	98½	52	77752	98½	82¾	98¼	2.4	14	92.7	39.0	52.2
33	BYX	✔Bayou Steel'A'	AS	NR	26	3633	Operates a steel minimill	13	1⅛	5	3¼	7½	3¾	4227	4½	3¾	3⅞	...	5	0.0	6.0	20.9
34	PORT	✔Bayport Restaurant Group	NNM	NR	12	1411	Oper seafood restaurants	34½	½	5⅛	2⅝	5⅛	2⅞	5911	4	3⅛	4	...	31	41.3	1.6	32.4
✣35•[6]	BBN	✔BBN Corp	NY,B,Ch,Ph	B–	94	10668	Research, consulting services	30	7/16	21½	10	48¾	14⅝	54759	48¾	37⅞	41⅛	...	13	194	104	56.5
36	BCG	BC Gas	To,Mo,Vc	B+	10	2545	Natural gas: Brit Columbia	17⅞	3⅜	17¼	13⅛	16	13⅛	7759	16	15⅛	16	5.6	13	26.1	8.3	...
37	BCE	BCE Inc	NY,To,C,Mo,Vc,B,Ch,P,Ph	B+	260	50622	Telecommun svcs & eq,Canada	43¼	12⅞	38¾	31⅝	35	29	45420	35	32¼	34½	◆...	..	16.9	10.4	8.0
38	BDMI	✔BDM Intl	NNM	NR	49	2356	Dvlp software svcs & prod	....	....	....	....	30½	18½	13031	30½	25¾	29	...	19	...	...	...
✣39•[9]	BEAV	✔BE Aerospace	NNM	NR	68	12256	Airline audio/video ctrl sys	16¾	4¾	11¾	7	11¼	5¼	16652	11¼	8⅞	10⅝	...	d	46.6	–4.3	6.5
40	BESIF	BE Semiconductor Indus	NNM	NR	..	...	Mfr semiconductor mfg eqp	....	....	....	....	16⅜	12⅜	92460	16⅜	12⅜	13	...	..	...	...	...
41	BCN	✔Beacon Properties	NY,Ch	NR	113	13360	Real estate investment trust	....	....	19½	17	23	17¼	9507	23	20⅛	23	7.3	..	33.3	...	...
#42•[6]	BSC	✔Bear Stearns Cos	NY,B,Ch	B+	255	85174	Investment bank'g,brokerage	23⅝	4½	22½	14	23⅜	14½	75101	22	19⅝	19⅞	s3.0	9	45.7	16.6	35.4
43	KBB	Bear Stearns Cos 'CUBS"98[72]	AS	NR	..	...	Customized Upside Basket Sec	....	....	....	....	4⅜	3¼	696	3⅝	3⅜	3½	...	..	...	...	...
44	MCP	Bear Stearns 5.50%MRK'CHIPS'	AS	NR	5	189	Merck Com-Link Hi Inc Ptc Sec	....	....	37	29⅝	45¾	36	478	45¾	44¾	45½	4.4	..	30.0	...	...
45	BOC	✔Beard Co	AS	NR	9	785	Carbon dioxide oper/R.E. dvlp	2⅜	1¾	2 5/16	1⅝	2¾	1⅝	344	2⅜	2⅛	2⅛	...	d	30.8	...	...
46	BER	✔Bearings, Inc	NY,Ch,Ph	B	92	8011	Dstr bearings & pwr transm'n	21⅞	3	25	18½	29⅝	18⅜	5395	29⅝	24⅝	29¼	1.9	19	35.2	27.9	22.9
47	BUTI	✔BeautiControl Cosmetics	NNM	B	26	1128	Mfr/mkt cosmetics,toiletries	21¾	2	15½	10¾	15½	9¼	1162	10	9¼	9½	4.4	12	–28.7	–3.4	–7.1
48	BZH	✔Beazer Homes USA	NY,Ch	NR	52	6503	Single family homebuilders	....	....	18¾	11⅛	20⅝	11½	6964	20⅝	18¼	20⅝	...	17	79.3	...	...
49	Pr A	$2.00 cm Cv [75]Ex Pfd([76]26.25)	NY	NR	8	697		....	....	....	....	31⅝	23¾	1775	31⅝	29⅝	31	6.5	..	...	...	...
#50•[6]	BEC	✔Beckman Instruments	NY,Ch	NR	190	19239	Mfr laboratory instruments	28¼	11⅞	32½	23	35⅞	26	9858	35⅞	34⅛	35⅜	1.2	20	28.8	16.3	20.7
¶51•[10]	BDX	✔Becton, Dickinson	NY,B,C,Ch,P,Ph	A+	537	55578	Health care pr:ind'l safety	42⅛	5⅛	49⅞	34	76	48	34620	76	69	75	1.2	21	57.3	25.9	17.1
52•[11]	BBBY	✔Bed Bath & Beyond	NNM	NR	186	30267	Domestics/home prd superstrs	35½	7	34½	22¾	39⅝	18	108178	39⅝	30	38¾	...	35	31.6	28.8	...

Uniform Footnote Explanations-See Page 4. Other: [1]Ph:Cycle 1. [2]ASE,CBOE:Cycle 1. [3]ASE:Cycle 1. [4]P:Cycle 3. [5]ASE:Cycle 1,To:Cycle 3. [6]CBOE:Cycle 1. [7]CBOE:Cycle 2. [8]CBOE:Cycle 3. [9]Ph:Cycle 2. [10]Ph:Cycle 3. [11]CBOE,NY:Cycle 2. [51]Each ADS equals 4 Ord shrs. [52]Incl 2.4M ESOP shrs. [53]®$4.66,'94. [54]Fr 4-15-96,scale to $50 in 2001. [55]®$0.49,'95. [56]Fiscal Sep'94 & prior. [57]®$0.80,'94. [58]Cv into 1 Cl'A' shr. [59]Each ADS rep 2 ord, 25 pence. [60]Each Sponsored ADR rep 2 ord, 25p. [61]Approx. [62]Incl curr amounts. [63]Fr 5-15-96,scale to $50 in 2003(in com stk). [64]Plan spin-off hospital-supply business. [65]9 Mo Dec'94. [66]Trades with 1 shr Calif Jockey Club. [67]Plan S&P 500 listing,MidCap 400 delisting:eff Jan 5. [68]Subsid Pfd in $M. [69]Excl shrs held by subsid. [70]Fiscal Jul'91&prior:7 Mo Feb'92 earned d$0.18. [71]Incl current amts. [72]Basket consists 23 co in 7 Industry grps. [73]Co can extend to 2-18-97. [74]®$0.21,'94. [75]Co opt fr 9-1-97 exch for $25amt8%Cv 2005. [76]Fr 9-1-98,scale to $25 in 2003. [77]Can be reduced re-spec. cond..

Index	Cash Divs. Ea.Yr. Since	Dividends: Latest Payment Period $	Date	Ex. Div.	Total $ So Far 1995	Ind. Rate	Paid 1994	Financial Position Mil-$ Cash& Equiv.	Curr. Assets	Curr. Liab.	Balance Sheet Date	Capitalization Lg Trm Debt Mil-$	Shs. 000 Pfd.	Com.	Earnings $ Per Shr. Years End	1991	1992	1993	1994	1995	Last 12 Mos.	Interim Earnings Period	$ per Shr. 1994	1995	Index
1	....	None Since Public			...	Nil	....	21.3	64.8	44.8	9-30-95	....	...	16748	Dc	0.19	0.50	0.70	0.27	Ed0.55	0.01	9 Mo Sep	0.02	d0.24	1
2	1986	0.637	10-12-95	8-18	1.50	1.50	1.088	Book Value $23.51			j12-31-94	3541	...	1635000	Dc	1.14	d1.29	1.15	4.52	....	4.52				2
3	1960	Q0.16	2-2-96	1-18	0.62	0.64	0.58	35.8	480	288	9-30-95	198	...	56899	Dc	1.08	1.42	□1.19	1.44	E1.65↓	1.31	9 Mo Sep	1.28	1.15	3
4	1934	Q0.40	12-8-95	11-28	1.60	1.60	1.45	16.7	181	78.4	9-30-95	78.1	...	6591	Dc	2.60	□0.94	0.70	3.20	....	4.07	9 Mo Sep	2.49	3.36	4
5	....	None Since Public			...	Nil	....	7.60	903	725	10-28-95	190	...	32958	Ja	...	p□0.01	0.30	0.81	E1.15	0.90	9 Mo Oct	d0.46	d0.37	5
6	1945	Q0.47	1-2-96	12-6	1.76	1.88	1.54	Book Value $24.84			9-30-95	1151	4266	[52]96990	Dc	1.71	□1.98	4.10	[53]4.79	E5.25	5.15	9 Mo Sep	3.55	3.91	6
7	1991	Q1.12½	12-31-95	12-6	4.50	4.50	4.50	Cv into 1.8868 com,$26.50				....	2000	...	Dc	b1.93	b3.37	b4.69	b5.04	....	....				7
8	1989	0.075	3-24-95	3-6	0.15	Nil	0.20	2.98	6.12	2.48	9-30-95	11.1	...	1322	Sp	1.26	Δ1.44	Δ1.81	1.90	0.49	0.49				8
9	....	None Since Public			...	Nil	....	52.8	116	55.9	9-30-95	20.4	...	9302	Je	0.57	d0.23	0.90	Δ0.26	□0.71	0.73	3 Mo Sep	0.21	0.23	9
10	....	None Since Public			...	Nil	....	17.5	33.6	18.4	9-30-95	0.41	...	7663	Mr	0.42	0.50	Δ0.45	[55]0.51	....	0.66	6 Mo Sep	0.24	0.39	10
11	....	None Paid			...	Nil	....	18.5	44.6	31.9	9-30-95	85.0	...	25071	Dc	0.17	Δ0.09	0.53	[56]0.37	....	....	9 Mo Sep	0.39	d0.23	11
12◆	1987	tS0.06	12-15-95	11-28	0.12	0.12	t0.10	458	656	289	12-31-94	396	...	353336	Dc	0.34	0.62	0.75	[57]0.81	E0.85	0.79	9 Mo Sep	0.63	0.61	12
13◆	....	None Since Public			...	Nil	....	0.05	5.35	3.11	9-29-95	2.64	...	6190	Mr	d1.92	d0.14	d0.53	d0.03	....	d0.02	6 Mo Sep	d0.04	Δd0.03	13
14◆	....	0.023	12-1-81	11-6	...	Nil	....	0.76	87.1	50.1	9-23-95	15.7	...	7393	Dc	d0.19	*0.46	0.57	0.54	....	0.59	9 Mo Sep	d0.05	Nil	14
15◆	....	None Paid			...	Nil	....	0.94	135	25.0	8-31-95	92.6	...	3971	My	...	...	‡d0.30	0.55	0.70	0.67	3 Mo Aug	d0.22	d0.25	15
16	....	0.021	2-22-80	1-14	...	Nil	....	8.20	18.9	4.20	7-31-95	3.54	...	±7652	Oc	±d3.65	*±0.14	±0.18	±0.03	....	d0.14	9 Mo Jul	±0.04	±d0.13	16
17	....	0.136	2-11-83	1-10	...	Nil	....	....	...	...		....	...	±7194	Oc	±d3.65	*±0.14	±0.18	±0.03	....	d0.14	9 Mo Jul	±0.04	±d0.13	17
18◆	....	20.00	9-9-85	8-26	...	Nil	....	3.36	13.7	6.25	12-31-94	....	...	6258	Dc	0.75	0.64	0.43	0.10	....	0.88	9 Mo Sep	0.03	0.81	18
19	....	None Since Public			...	Nil	....	2.52	11.4	14.2	6-30-95	81.0	...	10716	Dc	p0.51	0.57	0.67	0.34	....	d1.84	9 Mo Sep	0.30	d1.88	19
20	1990	0.511	2-22-96	12-26	0.723	0.75	0.66	851	1603	1431	j9-30-94	1199	...	873000	Sp	Δ1.62	1.41	1.09	1.27	....	1.27				20
21◆	1935	Q0.20	11-30-95	11-14	0.80	0.80	0.80	57.5	208	37.4	8-31-95	....	...	14048	Nv	1.37	1.90	1.79	□1.75	....	1.68	9 Mo Aug	□1.18	1.11	21
22◆	1928	[61]0.305	1-16-96	8-11	0.771	0.80	0.457	Equity per shr $4.64			12-31-94	[62]6130	...	3081600	Dc	0.52	0.90	1.14	1.22	....	1.37	9 Mo Sep	0.97	1.12	22
23	1985	S0.02½	8-15-95	7-28	0.05	0.05	0.05	32.9	119	71.0	9-30-95	159	2300	81092	Dc	d0.02	□d0.44	d0.10	0.02	E0.10	0.08	9 Mo Sep	0.02	0.08	23
24	1993	Q0.81¼	11-15-95	10-30	3.25	3.25	3.25	Cv into 4.762 com, $10.50				....	2000	...	Dc	...	...	...	....	....	....				24
25◆	1952	Q0.26	1-2-96	11-29	0.99½	1.04	0.93	285	1003	741	9-30-95	232	...	±57196	Dc	□±1.42	±2.84	±2.60	±0.23	E2.25↓	0.93	9 Mo Sep	±1.28	±1.98	25
26◆	1934	Q0.28¼	1-2-96	12-11	1.09	1.13	1.013	468	4304	2797	9-30-95	2358	...	271493	Dc	2.03	□2.15	Δ□d0.97	2.13	E2.35	2.31	9 Mo Sep	1.52	1.70	26
27	1994	Q0.39	1-12-96	12-27	1.54	1.56	0.82	Book Value $16.61			9-30-95	214	...	11544	Dc	...	...	p0.71	‡[65]0.65	....	....	9 Mo Sep	n/a	0.73	27
28	1972	0.40	12-31-95	12-15	0.65	0.65	0.60	15.5	19.9	12.4	9-30-95	....	...	5763	Dc	0.76	0.37	0.20	0.73	....	0.83	9 Mo Sep	0.24	0.34	28
29◆	....	None Since Public			...	Nil	....	606	1035	302	9-30-95	110	...	p182054	Je	*0.03	*0.12	0.29	p0.71	0.73	0.85	3 Mo Sep	0.21	0.33	29
30	1853	Q0.37½	12-1-95	11-14	1.49	1.50	1.45	2.76	66.9	118	9-30-95	199	p75	13357	Sp	1.32	1.41	1.75	1.85	1.71	1.71				30
31	1989	Q0.15	10-27-95	10-11	0.60	0.60	0.60	Book Value $29.55			9-30-95	732	...	7397	Dc	□1.41	□Δ0.89	□1.80	2.02	....	1.12	9 Mo Sep	1.44	0.54	31
32	1993	Q0.60	12-1-95	11-10	2.20	2.40	1.60	Book Value $43.74			9-30-95	64.8	...	19629	Dc	0.60	3.57	3.57	□5.65	E6.85	6.70	9 Mo Sep	□4.06	5.11	32
33	....	None Since Public			...	Nil	....	10.5	100	27.1	9-30-95	85.1	15	±12885	Sp	±d0.35	±d0.10	Δ±d0.50	±□0.34	±0.73	0.73				33
34◆	....	None Paid			...	Nil	....	2.30	9.35	4.54	9-25-95	10.7	2446	9722	Dc	d0.55	Δ0.17	Δ0.15	0.09	....	0.13	9 Mo Sep	0.10	0.14	34
35	....	0.03	8-20-92	7-29	...	Nil	....	98.5	165	63.4	9-30-95	73.5	[68]8	17684	Je	Δ0.49	Δ0.24	d2.05	d0.48	3.61	3.23	3 Mo Sep	d0.11	d0.49	35
36	1964	gQ0.22½	11-30-95	11-15	g0.90	0.90	g0.90	0.96	204	598	j12-31-94	911	3090	[69]45075	Dc	1.94	0.35	1.43	0.97	....	j1.25	9 Mo Sep	0.01	0.29	36
37	1881	gQ0.68	1-15-96	12-13	g2.72	2.72	g2.68	1367	8797	8305	j12-31-94	11434	18001	309291	Dc	4.01	4.21	jd2.44	j3.52	E2.15	j2.33	9 Mo Sep	2.56	1.37	37
38	....	None Since Public			...	Nil	....	48.7	250	166	9-30-95	2.75	...	±12718	Dc	0.05	□0.81	Δ0.92	1.20	....	1.50	9 Mo Sep	0.81	1.11	38
39	....	None Since Public			...	Nil	....	7.49	157	65.0	8-26-95	188	...	16216	Fb	[70]0.65	□1.03	0.35	d0.75	....	d0.20	9 Mo Nov	d0.78	d0.23	39
40	....	None Since Public			...	Nil	....	6.05	97.1	108	6-30-95	19.0	...	★25467	Dc	...	...	...	0.14	....	....	6 Mo Jun	n/a	d0.66	40
41	1994	Q0.42	11-21-95	11-8	1.64	1.68	0.56	Equity per shr $12.92			9-30-95	[71]176	...	20189	Dc	...	...	p0.74	p0.98	....	....	9 Mo Sep	n/a	0.81	41
42◆	1986	Q0.15	11-24-95	11-8	s0.586	0.60	s0.557	Equity per shr $17.48			9-29-95	4205	2319	118779	Je	1.02	2.22	2.72	2.75	1.70	2.14	3 Mo Sep	0.23	0.67	42
43	....	None Since Public			...	Nil	....	Payment at maturity at re-spec. cond.				....	...	★1200	Je	...	...	...	....	....	....	Mature 7-24-98			43
44	1994	Q0.504	11-11-95	10-11	2.014	2.01	1.511	Int based on Merck & Co com as defined				....	...	1250	Dc	...	...	...	....	....	....	Mature 2-11-97[73]			44
45	....	None Since Public			...	Nil	....	0.25	5.27	3.21	9-30-95	1.64	90	2652	Dc	...	pd2.48	□d5.72	[74]0.25	....	d0.14	9 Mo Sep	0.27	d0.12	45
46◆	1957	Q0.14	12-1-95	11-13	0.50	0.56	0.44	7.99	282	125	9-30-95	74.3	...	11798	Je	0.41	d0.16	0.82	1.12	1.47	1.57	3 Mo Sep	0.27	0.37	46
47◆	1989	Q0.10½	10-17-95	9-29	0.42	0.42	0.315	1.44	14.5	8.64	8-31-95	....	...	6264	Nv	0.71	0.65	0.44	Δ0.88	....	0.78	9 Mo Aug	Δ0.69	0.59	47
48	....	None Since Public			...	Nil	....	Book Value $15.82			6-30-95	160	p2000	p6548	Sp	...	...	p1.45	p1.76	P1.23	1.23				48
49	1995	Q0.50	12-1-95	11-16	0.639	2.00	....	Cv into 1.31 com,$19.05[77]				....	1800	...	Sp	...	...	...	....	....	....				49
50	1989	Q0.11	11-30-95	11-8	0.44	0.44	0.40	26.5	528	253	9-30-95	160	...	28862	Dc	1.32	1.53	□d1.21	□1.68	....	1.79	9 Mo Sep	□1.21	1.32	50
51◆	1926	Q0.23	1-2-96	12-14	0.82	0.92	0.74	240	1328	720	9-30-95	558	927	64254	Sp	2.43	2.57	□2.71	3.05	3.59	3.59				51
52◆	....	None Since Public			...	Nil	....	4.54	150	69.4	8-27-95	10.0	...	33946	Fb	p0.37	0.47	0.64	0.87	E1.10	1.04	9 Mo Nov	0.60	0.77	52

◆**Stock Splits & Divs By Line Reference Index** [12]2-for-1,'93. [13]1-for-6 REVERSE,'91. [14]4-for-3,'94,'95. [15]1-for-5 REVERSE,'94. [18]3-for-1,'94. [21]3-for-2,'92:5-for-4,'93. [22]2-for-1,'93:ADR rep 1 ord prior to 3-15-94. [25]2-for-1,'91. [26]No adj for stk dstr of Caremark Intl,'92. [29]2-for-1,'93,'94:3-for-2,'95. [34]1-for-4 REVERSE,'93. [42]Adj to 5%,'95. [46]3-for-2,'95. [47]3-for-2,'91. [51]2-for-1,'93. [52]2-for-1,'93.

¶ S&P 500
# MidCap 400
✣ SmallCap 600
• Options

Index	Ticker	Name of Issue (Call Price of Pfd. Stocks)	Market	Com. Rank. & Pfd. Rating	Inst. Hold Cos	Inst. Hold Shs. (000)	Principal Business	1971-93 High	1971-93 Low	1994 High	1994 Low	1995 High	1995 Low	Dec. Sales in 100s	Dec. 1995 Last Sale Or Bid High	Low	Last	%Div Yield	P-E Ratio	Total Return % Annualized 12 Mo	36 Mo	60 Mo
1	BED	✔Bedford Property Investors	NY,Ch,P	NR	13	1714	Invests in commercial RE	20	2	7¼	4⅞	7⅝	5⅛	1554	7⅝	6⅜	7⅛	5.9	22	31.5	31.8	14.8
2	BEII	✔BEI Electronics	NNM	↓B–	21	2468	Mfr defense/motion systems	11¾	5½	7¼	5	8½	4¾	1592	7⅝	6¼	7⅜	1.1	d	47.0	–1.5	6.3
3	BELF	✔Bel Fuse Inc	NNM	B–	25	1276	Mfr/sale of electronic parts	21½	1¾	9⅛	5¼	15	7¾	3418	11½	10	10½	...	9	37.7	–15.3	37.6
4	BELD	✔Belden & Blake Corp	NNM	NR	92	8121	Oil & gas explor,dvlp,prod'n	15	4⅞	15	9¾	19¼	11½	12601	18¼	15¾	17½	...	39	25.0	21.5	...
5	BWC	✔Belden Inc	NY,Ch	NR	155	18749	Mfr electrical wire,cable	18⅝	14¼	22½	16⅛	29⅞	19¾	22339	27⅛	25¼	25¾	0.8	15	16.7	...	...
6	BHY	Belding Heminway	NY,Ch	NR	22	1797	Thread,fabrics,hme sewing pd	...	...	8	6½	8¼	2¾	4247	3¾	2¾	3⅛	...	3	...	...	...
¶7•[1]	BEL	✔Bell Atlantic Corp	NY,B,Ch,P,Ph	A–	819	140778	Tel sv:NJ,Pa,Del,Md,Va,DC	69⅛	16¼	59⅝	48⅜	68⅞	48⅜	94998	68⅞	63⅜	66⅞	4.2	16	40.1	13.9	9.8
✣8	BELL	✔Bell Bancorp[53]	NNM	NR	73	4040	Savings & loan, Illinois	28⅞	12½	29½	21½	36	23	39261	36	32¼	35¾	1.3	27	52.4	19.1	...
9	BCMPY	✔Bell Cablemedia[54]	NNM	NR	64	12046	Cable TV/telecommun U.K.	...	...	26	16⅞	22½	14	10596	16¾	14	16	...	d	–20.0	...	...
10	BHW	✔Bell & Howell Holdings	NY	NR	71	8149	Info access/dissemin'tn sys,sv	...	...	...	...	29⅜	15½	17331	29⅜	26	28	...	d	...	...	...
✣11	BI	✔Bell Industries	NY,B,Ch,P,Ph	B–	77	3757	Dstr electronic components	28⅜	15/16	21¾	13⅛	25⅝	17¾	1691	22⅞	21⅝	22½	s...	12	20.3	36.7	21.9
12	BELM	✔Bell Microproducts	NNM	NR	35	3414	Mkt computer products	10	6¾	16	7½	14¼	7	25192	9¾	7	7¼	...	9	–37.0	...	...
✣13•[1]	BSPT	✔Bell Sports	NNM	NR	53	2575	Mfr/mkt bicycle helmets	49½	15	40½	12¾	18½	7	28033	8½	7	8	...	d	–41.8	–30.4	...
¶14•[2]	BLS	✔BellSouth Corp	NY,B,Ch,P,Ph	B+	917	299020	Tel sv:south,so central U.S.	32	9⅛	31¾	25¼	43⅞	26⅞	185908	43⅞	39¼	43½	3.3	20	66.9	23.7	15.3
15	BELW	✔Bellwether Exploration	NNM	B–	24	4745	Oil&gas explor'n,dvlp prod'n	34½	2	8¾	4⅝	6¾	4	2197	5¾	5⅛	5¾	...	..	24.3	8.5	15.9
16	BLM	✔Belmac Corp[56]	AS,Ph	C	12	69	Dvlp stage:pharmaceut'l prod	210	16¼	28¾	5	9⅜	2	4286	3⅛	2	2¼	...	d	–60.0	–65.5	–45.4
#17	BLC	✔Belo (A.H.)Cl'A'	NY,Ch,Ph	B+	188	18243	Newspaper publishing:brdcstg	26½	4⅛	28⅝	21⅝	36¾	27⅞	12583	35⅝	33	34¾	0.9	19	23.6	20.1	19.0
18	BGO	✔Bema Gold	AS	NR	31	10366	Explr,dvlp mineral properties	...	...	2½	1 7/16	2 5/16	1 5/16	23005	2 1/16	1 11/16	2	...	d	18.6	...	...
¶19	BMS	✔Bemis Co	NY,Ch,Ph	A	292	25456	Packaging,adhesive products	29⅝	11/16	25¾	20½	30	23	16839	26¼	24⅞	25⅝	2.5	16	8.2	2.8	13.3
20	BJICA	✔Ben & Jerry's Cl'A'	NNM	B+	39	927	Mfr ice cream/franch stores	33¾	4¼	21	9¼	20¾	9⅝	5253	17¼	14¾	14¾	...	..	49.4	–20.2	15.7
✣21	BHE	✔Benchmark Electronics	AS	NR	45	2112	Mfrs circuit boards	23⅞	3⅝	28	22½	31⅞	20¼	2274	29¼	23½	27½	...	18	13.4	18.9	42.8
¶22•[3]	BNL	✔Beneficial Corp	NY,B,Ch,P,Ph	B+	367	40335	Consumer financial svcs	40½	5⅞	44	34½	55½	37	25609	55½	46⅛	46⅝	4.0	12	23.3	18.3	21.9
23	Pr C	$5.50 cm Cv Pfd(100)vtg	NY(10)	A–	..	...		355	58½	385	324	478	349½	....	468½	468½	419⅝B	1.3	..	...	...	...
24	BNG	✔Benetton Group ADS[60]	NY,Ch,Ph	NR	16	749	Int'l mfr of casual apparel	32½	11½	36⅞	21½	24⅜	16	1144	24⅜	22⅝	23⅛	1.4	16	1.0	9.7	11.2
25	BTON	Benetton Group S.p.A[61]	ML	NR	..	...	Int'l mfr of casual apparel	26894⅞	7550	29850⅝	16950	19590	13800	....	19200	18300	18808	...	..	...	...	...
26	BE	✔Benguet Corp Cl'B'	NY,B,Ch,P,Ph	NR	9	877	Engin'g eq:Philippine gold	6⅛	7/16	1⅛	⅝	13/16	⅜	16705	9/16	⅜	⅜	...	20	–35.0	–18.5	–13.0
27	BNHN	✔Benihana Inc	NNM	B–	6	130	Japanese food restaurants	21½	½	6¾	2⅝	10¾	6½	388	10½	10⅜	10⅜	...	18	59.6	96.1	64.0
28	EYE	✔Benson Eyecare	NY,Ch,Ph	C	74	14303	Eyecare services/stores	12⅜	3/16	8½	6⅛	11⅛	7	40096	9⅛	7⅝	9	...	d	22.0	17.0	88.8
✣29•[4]	BNTN	✔Benton Oil & Gas	NNM	NR	99	13542	Oil & gas explor,dev,prod'n	18¾	1¼	9⅛	4¼	16⅛	8⅝	50276	16⅛	13½	15	...	54	70.2	38.7	13.1
#30•[5]	BBC	✔Bergen Brunswig 'A'	NY,B,Ch,Ph	A–	220	24640	Drug and health care dstr	25	¼	19⅞	13⅛	29⅛	19¼	16900	26	23½	24⅞	1.9	16	37.4	10.6	6.0
31	BKLY	✔Berkley (W.R.)	NNM	B+	132	14129	Regional insurance co's	50½	⅝	42	32½	55½	34½	18007	55½	44½	53¾	0.9	20	47.1	8.7	17.9
32	BRK	✔Berkshire Hathaway	NY(10),Ch	B	185	187	Insurance,shoes,investments	17800	38	21800	15150	33400	20250	42	33400	31300	32100	...	67	57.4	40.2	37.1
33	BRI	✔Berkshire Realty	NY,Ph	NR	48	2296	Real estate investment trust	12¾	7¼	12½	8¾	10⅝	8¾	8080	9¾	9¼	9⅝	9.4	16	15.4	13.1	...
34	WS	Wrrt(Pur1 com at$10.75)	NY	....	10	5		...	...	2¼	½	¾	5/16	209	11/16	½	½	...	..	...	...	...
35	BTZ	✔Berlitz International	NY	NR	32	1634	Language instruction svcs	17½	12	14⅝	12½	16½	12¼	323	16½	15⅞	16½	...	57	26.9	...	...
36	BRY	✔Berry Petroleum'A'	NY,Ch,Ph	B–	59	6516	Oil & gas dvlpmt prod'n	19	8	11⅜	8	10⅞	8¾	2436	10¾	10	10⅛	4.0	22	11.0	–0.9	–2.9
37	BGI.EC	✔Besicorp Group	ECM	B–	5	133	Own,dvlp pwr prod'n projects	9½	1	8⅜	5¾	14⅛	6⅜	356	11½	10	10¼	...	16	64.0	...	...
#38•[5]	BBY	✔Best Buy Co	NY,Ch,P,Ph	B	173	22168	Electronic/appliance stores	31½	1/16	45¼	19	33⅝	16	162458	20½	16	16¼	...	13	–46.5	9.5	55.5
39	BBYPrM	Best Buy Cap 6.50%'[66]MIPS'[67](NC)	[6]NY	NR	32	2177	Subsid of Best Buy Co	...	...	57	40	46⅞	34	9734	40½	37	37¾	8.6	..	...	...	...
40	BTV	✔BET Holdings'A'	NY,Ph	NR	54	4878	Black entert'nt cable TV ntwk	26⅜	12	21¼	13¼	23¾	14¾	1868	23¾	21⅞	22⅞	...	22	51.2	18.1	...
41	BEP	✔BET Public Ltd ADS[70]	NY,To,Ch	NR	17	1324	Industrial&commercial svcs	20½	5⅛	9½	6	8⅞	6¼	2611	7⅞	7⅛	7⅝	3.8	12	29.8	15.0	–4.7
42	BET	✔Bethlehem Corp	AS,Ch	C	5	139	Energy & environmental pr	9⅛	5/16	1½	¾	5⅝	⅞	638	3	2¼	2⅜	...	26	171	20.0	6.3
¶43•[1]	BS	✔Bethlehem Steel	NY,B,C,Ch,P,Ph	C	298	80254	Integrated steel company	48	4⅝	24¼	16¼	19⅛	12⅝	96692	14¾	13⅝	13⅞	...	11	–24.5	–5.4	–0.7
44	Pr	$5 cm Cv Pfd(50)	NY,Ph	B–	27	1057	serv'g heavy construction &	59⅞	12¾	55⅝	49¾	55⅛	48⅞	1112	52½	51⅛	51¾	9.7	..	...	...	...
45	Pr B	$2.50 cm Cv Pfd(25)	NY,Ch,Ph	B–	13	254	capital goods markets	29¾	6⅝	28¼	25¼	27⅞	24⅝	929	27¼	26	26⅝	9.4	..	...	...	...
46	BETT	✔Bettis Corp	NNM	NR	25	4466	Mfr actuators & controls	...	...	6¾	2⅝	5⅜	2¾	7693	5¼	4¾	5⅛	...	22	74.5	...	...
#47•[3]	BTL	✔Betz Laboratories	NY	A	218	20576	Water treatment chemicals	66¼	4⅞	53⅝	42¼	46⅝	38¾	20761	41⅛	38⅞	41	3.6	16	–6.0	–9.7	2.4
¶48•[7]	BEV	✔Beverly Enterprises	NY,B,Ch,P,Ph	B–	312	66030	Health care facilities	22½	3/16	16⅛	11¾	16⅛	9	150321	12½	9	10⅝	...	17	–27.4	–6.5	4.0
49	BHAG	✔BHA Group'A'	NNM	B+	48	4070	Aftermkt envir air poll'n ctrl	25	2¾	13½	8¼	15	11⅜	2395	14¼	13	13¼	0.9	13	9.2	–7.1	–2.7
50	BHC	✔BHC Communications'A'	AS	NR	92	5274	Own/oper VHF/UHF TV stations	82¾	40⅛	81¾	70⅛	95	71¾	910	95	89⅞	94½	...	45	31.4	18.3	17.1
51	BHCF	✔BHC Financial	NNM	NR	59	4907	Securities broker support svc	35½	11¼	29¾	8½	20⅛	8⅞	10060	19⅛	17¼	18	0.7	10	104	...	...
52	BIAC	BI Inc	NNM	B–	29	2043	Mfr electr ID/monitor'g sys	15½	1	6¼	3¾	9⅜	4⅜	6301	8¾	7½	7⅝	...	21	69.4	–5.4	–7.7

Uniform Footnote Explanations-See Page 4. Other: [1]CBOE:Cycle 1. [2]ASE:Cycle 1. [3]P:Cycle 1. [4]Ph:Cycle 1. [5]CBOE:Cycle 3. [6]Ch [7]P:Cycle 3. [51]100% non-taxable,'94. [52]Subsid pfd in $M. [53]Standard Fed Bancorp plan acq,$37.50. [54]Ea ADS rep 5 ord par 25p. [55]Fiscal Jun'93 & prior. [56]Aprv name chg,Bentley Pharmaceuticals. [57]Pfd in $M. [58]Fiscal Jun'91 & prior. [59]12 Mo Dec'92:Fiscal Jun'92 earned $1.11d. [60]Each ADS rep 2 Ord,Lire 500. [61]All data reported in Italian Lire. [62]Approx. [63]Fiscal Aug'93 & prior. [64]Incl $0.384 non-taxable,'94. [65]11 Mo Dec'93. [66]Monthly Income Preferred Shrs. [67]Can exchange for dep shrs re-spec cond. [68]Into com of Best Buy Co. [69]Cv right-can expire after 11-3-97, re-spec cond. [70]ADS's equal 4 Ord par 25p. [71]Fiscal Dec'93&prior. [72]5 Mo May. [73]®$2.30,'94. [74]Special divd.

Splits ◆ Index	Cash Divs. Ea.Yr. Since	Dividends: Latest Payment Period $	Date	Ex. Div.	Total $ So Far 1995	Ind. Rate	Paid 1994	Financial Position Mil-$: Cash& Equiv.	Curr. Assets	Curr. Liab.	Balance Sheet Date	Capitalization: Lg Trm Debt Mil-$	Shs. 000 Pfd.	Com.	Earnings $ Per Shr. Years End	1991	1992	1993	1994	1995	Last 12 Mos.	Interim Earnings Period	$ per Shr. 1994	1995	Index
1	1993	Q0.10½	1-31-96	1-11	†0.41	0.42	[51]0.33	Equity per shr $4.91			9-30-95	....	8333	6091	Dc	d0.91	Δd3.67	0.53	0.59	....	0.33	9 Mo Sep	0.44	0.18	1
2	1989	Q0.02	12-29-95	12-13	0.08	0.08	0.08	8.95	58.8	19.9	7-01-95	30.2	...	6779	Sp	0.94	1.05	0.56	d0.26	Pd0.65	d0.65				2
3	....	None Since Public			...	Nil	....	9.70	33.7	8.43	9-30-95	....	...	5051	Dc	d0.67	3.88	0.77	d0.32	....	1.18	9 Mo Sep	d0.51	0.99	3
4	....	None Since Public			...	Nil	....	18.0	56.1	30.0	9-30-95	110	24	11136	Dc	...	p0.99	p0.54	0.52	....	0.45	9 Mo Sep	0.40	0.33	4
5	1994	Q0.05	1-2-96	11-29	0.20	0.20	0.15	5.76	159	73.5	9-30-95	83.3	...	26110	Dc	...	p□1.05	p1.21	1.46	....	1.67	9 Mo Sep	1.00	1.21	5
6	....	None Since Public			...	Nil	....	0.83	50.6	24.6	9-30-95	45.6	20805	7409	Dc	...	...	...	1.00	....	0.97	9 Mo Sep	0.20	0.17	6
7	1984	Q0.70	2-1-96	1-8	2.79	2.80	2.74	140	3884	5283	9-30-95	6648	[52]85	437305	Dc	□3.41	□3.23	□3.39	□3.21	E4.22	4.07	9 Mo Sep	□2.49	3.35	7
8◆	1994	Q0.11¼	12-1-95	11-7	0.37½	0.45	0.15	Book Value $32.70			9-30-95	22.2	...	9152	Mr	p1.17	1.92	□1.66	1.32	....	1.34	6 Mo Sep	0.62	0.64	8
9	....	None Since Public			...	Nil	....	218	258	39.5	j12-31-94	188	...	310015	Dc	...	...	pd0.85	d0.86	....	d0.93	9 Mo Sep	d0.64	d0.71	9
10	....	None Since Public			...	Nil	....	7.85	235	292	4-01-95	525	...	18329	Dc	...	...	...	p□d0.27	....	d0.43	9 Mo Sep	p□0.34	0.18	10
11◆	1973	5%Stk	7-7-95	5-22	5%Stk	Stk	5%Stk	8.01	178	64.5	6-30-95	25.4	...	6849	Dc	0.10	0.06	□[55]d0.59	1.63	....	1.93	9 Mo Sep	1.26	1.56	11
12	....	None Since Public			...	Nil	....	1.77	122	25.2	9-30-95	43.7	...	8278	Dc	...	p0.10	0.45	0.86	....	0.77	9 Mo Sep	0.67	0.58	12
13	....	None Since Public			...	Nil	....	86.2	209	31.7	9-30-95	138	...	p14200	Je	p0.03	Δ0.77	□Δ0.88	1.27	d0.42	d0.82	3 Mo Sep	0.02	d0.38	13
14◆	1984	Q0.36	2-1-96	1-9	1.39½	1.44	1.38	726	4939	5709	9-30-95	7867	...	993464	Dc	□1.56	□1.69	□1.04	2.17	E2.23↑	2.23	9 Mo Sep	1.61	□1.67	14
15◆	....	None Paid			...	Nil	....	1.76	6.75	4.78	9-30-95	21.0	...	9045	Je	*0.11	*0.06	0.02	0.27	0.12	0.05	3 Mo Sep	0.07	Nil	15
16◆	....	None Since Public			...	Nil	....	0.58	10.1	8.80	9-30-95	....	[57]2	2978	Dc	[58]d3.60	[59]d23.70	d6.30	d1.60	....	d0.49	9 Mo Sep	d1.67	d0.56	16
17◆	1939	Q0.08	12-8-95	11-8	0.315	0.32	0.30	11.4	148	72.2	9-30-95	508	...	±38616	Dc	±0.33	±0.95	Δ±1.10	±1.70	E1.80	1.72	9 Mo Sep	±1.12	±1.14	17
18	....	None Paid			...	Nil	....	46.5	50.0	9.30	j12-31-94	....	...	62083	Dc	d0.10	d0.28	d0.03	d0.06	....	jd0.11	9 Mo Sep	0.02	d0.03	18
19◆	1922	Q0.16	12-1-95	11-13	0.64	0.64	0.54	23.1	431	215	9-30-95	158	...	52863	Dc	1.03	□1.11	□0.89	1.40	E1.65	1.55	9 Mo Sep	0.97	1.12	19
20◆	....	None Since Public			...	Nil	....	20.8	51.9	14.5	12-31-94	32.4	.9	±7177	Dc	±0.67	±1.07	±1.01	±d0.26	....	0.03	9 Mo Sep	±0.42	±0.71	20
21	....	None Since Public			...	Nil	....	5.84	43.9	8.38	9-30-95	....	....	4020	Dc	0.66	0.83	Δ1.10	1.41	....	1.54	9 Mo Sep	1.02	1.15	21
22◆	1929	Q0.47	12-31-95	11-29	1.80	1.88	1.62	Equity per shr $26.20			9-30-95	6964	1371	53024	Dc	2.90	□2.72	□3.45	3.28	E3.75	2.77	9 Mo Sep	3.13	2.62	22
23	1968	Q1.37½	1-31-96	12-28	5.50	5.50	5.50	Cv into 9 common				....	22	...	Dc	b1.21	b1.22	b1.28	b1.25	....	....				23
24	1990	0.328	6-12-95	5-19	0.328	0.33	0.341	250	1594	659	12-31-94	389	...	174554	Dc	1.76	1.54	1.48	1.49	....	1.49				24
25	1986	300.00	5-18-92	5-18	...	300.00	....	472835	1704445	892280	j12-31-91	486618	...	163554	Dc	1007.50	...	...	....	....	j1007.50				25
26	....	t[62]0.018	2-4-90	12-15	...	Nil	....	470	2345	969	j12-31-94	1294	220	±114143	Dc	±0.03	±d0.20	±0.29	±0.01	....	0.02	9 Mo Sep	Nil	±0.01	26
27	....	None Since Public			...	Nil	....	0.68	4.00	6.81	10-08-95	11.6	2	±5824	Mr	Δ±0.12	±0.16	±0.29	±0.42	....	0.57	27 Wk Oct	±0.14	±0.29	27
28	....	None Since Public			...	Nil	....	10.9	118	113	9-30-95	64.0	...	31862	Dc	pd0.33	d0.47	d0.16	0.41	....	d0.09	9 Mo Sep	0.40	d0.10	28
29◆	....	None Since Public			...	Nil	....	14.8	61.6	54.8	9-30-95	52.6	...	25118	Dc	*0.03	d0.22	d0.26	0.12	....	0.28	9 Mo Sep	0.07	0.23	29
30◆	1978	Q0.12	12-1-95	11-16	0.48	0.48	0.457	50.9	1667	1247	6-30-95	440	...	39816	Sp	1.43	1.54	□[63]0.75	1.45	P1.61	1.61				30
31◆	1975	Q0.12	1-5-96	12-15	0.47	0.48	0.43	Equity per shr $37.60			9-30-95	322	1000	★20148	Dc	2.61	Δ2.59	2.87	1.44	E2.75	2.64	9 Mo Sep	0.92	2.12	31
32	....	0.10	1-3-67	11-29	...	Nil	....	Equity per shr $13555.79			9-30-95	807	...	1194	Dc	384.00	355.00	□656.00	420.00	....	477.00	9 Mo Sep	342.00	399.00	32
33	1991	Q0.22½	11-15-95	10-30	0.89	0.90	[64]0.86	Equity per shr $10.50			9-30-95	168	...	25393	Dc	d0.16	0.29	0.26	0.23	....	0.59	9 Mo Sep	0.22	0.58	33
34	....	Terms&trad. basis should	be checked in detail					Wrrts expire 9-8-98				....	...	p3000	Dc	...	...	...	....	....	....				34
35	....	None Since Public			...	Nil	....	27.5	80.6	84.1	9-30-95	101	...	10033	Dc	pd12.08	pd1.04	p[65]d0.35	0.09	....	0.29	9 Mo Sep	d0.14	0.06	35
36	1987	Q0.10	12-29-95	12-13	0.40	0.40	0.40	26.0	37.5	7.58	9-30-95	....	...	±21932	Dc	±0.77	±0.46	±Nil	±d0.05	....	0.46	9 Mo Sep	±d0.12	±0.39	36
37◆	....	None Paid			...	Nil	....	1.81	4.07	1.60	9-30-95	3.51	...	2932	Mr	d1.72	3.29	Nil	□0.64	....	0.64	6 Mo Sep	d0.33	d0.33	37
38◆	....	None Paid			...	Nil	....	43.7	1601	1017	8-26-95	442	...	42670	Fb	0.33	0.57	□1.01	1.33	E1.30↓	1.30	9 Mo Nov	0.68	0.65	38
39	1994	M0.271	12-29-95	12-26	3.25	3.25	0.524	Cv into 1.111 com[68],$45[69]				....	...	★4000	Fb	...	...	...	....	....	....	Mandatory redemption re-spec cond			39
40	....	None Since Public			...	Nil	....	28.6	60.7	20.4	7-31-95	34.0	...	±19716	Jl	±0.50	±0.58	±0.61	±0.72	±1.00	1.06	3 Mo Oct	0.23	0.29	40
41	1896	[62]0.094	1-8-96	11-17	0.274	0.29	0.207	209	525	443	j4-01-95	154	...	934800	Mr	□d0.06	Δd0.24	0.41	0.65	....	0.65	6 Mo Sep	0.32	0.32	41
42	....	0.062	5-15-76	4-9	...	Nil	....	0.06	5.76	5.94	8-31-95	3.12	...	1889	My	d0.30	d0.68	[71]d2.13	‡[72]d0.52	0.08	0.09	3 Mo Aug	0.01	0.02	42
43	....	0.10	12-10-91	11-5	...	Nil	....	102	1551	1009	9-30-95	858	14242	112584	Dc	d10.41	□d2.73	d3.37	0.35	E1.30	1.24	9 Mo Sep	0.16	1.05	43
44	1983	Q1.25	12-10-95	11-8	5.00	5.00	5.00	Cv into 1.77 com,$28.25				....	2500	...	Dc	bd1.65	bd1.74	b1.43	b1.35	....	....				44
45	1983	Q0.62½	12-10-95	11-8	2.50	2.50	2.50	Cv into 0.84 com,$29.75				....	4000	...	Dc	bd1.65	bd1.74	b1.43	b1.35	....	....				45
46	....	None Since Public			...	Nil	....	0.83	23.6	14.3	9-30-95	10.5	...	8480	Dc	p0.62	p0.60	p0.44	0.24	....	0.23	9 Mo Sep	0.20	0.19	46
47	1958	Q0.37	2-8-96	1-23	1.46	1.48	1.42	22.4	237	94.3	9-30-95	95.5	489	27721	Dc	2.47	2.71	Δ2.05	[73]2.43	E2.60	2.52	9 Mo Sep	1.90	1.99	47
48	....	0.05	1-11-88	12-24	...	Nil	....	55.7	691	446	9-30-95	897	3000	98457	Dc	0.37	□0.04	□0.45	□0.79	E0.64↓	0.74	9 Mo Sep	0.59	0.54	48
49	1993	Q0.03	12-1-95	11-16	0.12	0.12	0.12	1.73	34.6	10.3	6-30-95	8.02	...	5495	Sp	0.61	0.75	0.67	0.75	P1.03	1.03				49
50	1993	[74]1.00	4-11-95	3-6	[74]1.00	Nil	....	1500	1729	209	9-30-95	93.5	...	±24302	Dc	±3.89	±4.09	±8.67	±3.71	....	2.08	9 Mo Sep	±2.83	±1.20	50
51◆	1993	Q0.03	11-15-95	10-30	0.11	0.12	0.08	Equity per shr $11.01			9-29-95	....	...	7028	Dc	1.50	2.29	1.84	1.40	....	1.79	9 Mo Sep	1.01	1.40	51
52	....	None Since Public			...	Nil	....	4.75	18.4	4.30	9-30-95	....	...	6660	Je	*0.10	*0.01	*0.22	Δ0.05	0.34	0.37	3 Mo Sep	0.06	0.09	52

◆**Stock Splits & Divs By Line Reference Index** [8]2-for-1,'94. [11]Adj to 5%,'95. [14]2-for-1,'95. [15]1-for-8 REVERSE,'94. [16]1-for-10 REVERSE,'95. [17]2-for-1,'95. [19]2-for-1,'92. [20]2-for-1,'92. [22]2-for-1,'93. [29]2-for-1,'91. [30]5-for-4,'91:Adj for 5%,'95. [31]3-for-2,'91. [37]1-for-10 REVERSE,'91. [38]3-for-2,'93:2-for-1,'94. [51]5-for-4,'93.

¶ S&P 500 # MidCap 400 ✣ SmallCap 600 • Options

Index	Ticker	Name of Issue (Call Price of Pfd. Stocks)	Market	Com. Rank. & Pfd. Rating	Inst. Hold Cos	Inst. Hold Shs. (000)	Principal Business	Price Range 1971-93 High	1971-93 Low	1994 High	1994 Low	1995 High	1995 Low	Dec. Sales in 100s	December, 1995 Last Sale Or Bid High	Low	Last	%Div Yield	P-E Ratio	Total Return % Annualized 12 Mo	36 Mo	60 Mo
1	BGF	**Big Flower Press Hldgs**	NY,Ph	NR	..	...	Prod ad circulars,TV listings	...	...	...	...	15⅞	14⅞	8248	15⅞	14⅞	15½	...	..	...	...	...
2	BIGO	**Big O Tires, Inc**[51]	NNM	B	12	266	Franchisor of auto prod strs	55	5/16	17⅞	12¾	16¼	12	2357	15⅛	13⅜	15	...	19	−1.6	3.3	38.3
3	BDY	✔**Bindley Western Indus**	NY,Ch,Ph	B	82	4997	Wholesaler of ethical drugs	20¾	5½	15⅝	11⅛	19½	13⅝	6252	18⅜	16⅜	17	0.5	12	12.0	11.1	6.9
4	BIN	✔**Binks Mfg**	AS,Ch	B−	31	1223	Mfr coatings application eq	44	5⅜	23¼	18½	26	18½	216	24¼	23½	23½	e1.7	17	28.8	6.2	−0.3
5	BDTC	✔**Bio-Dental Technologies**	NNM	NR	9	466	Dstr dental supplies/prod	6⅞	1	6¾	2¾	5⅜	2⅜	3994	3⅜	2⅝	3	...	d	−11.1	−0.7	...
6	BLSC	**Bio-Logic Systems**	NNM	B−	7	256	Computerized med test sys	9⅞	1 1/16	4	1¾	5⅝	2	982	5	3½	3⅝	...	12	70.6	−8.6	11.8
7	BIO.A	✔**Bio-Rad Labs Cl'A'**[53]	AS,Ch	B	85	2491	Research chems:med test:kits	32⅞	1 9/16	29¼	10¼	42⅝	24⅞	2322	42⅝	38⅝	42½	...	15	53.2	35.1	18.6
8	BIO.B	✔ **Class B Cv**	AS,Ch	B	8	60	hi technology instr	32⅞	3/16	28½	10¼	42¾	24¾	16	42¾	40	42⅛B	...	15	53.2	35.7	18.4
9	BTGC	✔**Bio-Technology Genl**	NNM	C	38	7389	Health prod thru biotechn'y	23¼	1	5⅞	1½	5	2	59763	5	3½	4½	...	d	128	−6.0	21.1
10•[1]	BCHXF	✔**BioChem Pharma**	NNM,To	NR	98	15942	R&D therapeutic prod	29⅞	7⅝	13⅝	8⅛	41⅛	12¼	159327	40½	30	40⅛	...	d	224	36.6	...
11	BICO	✔**Biocontrol Technology**	NSC	C	16	1591	Medl devices/bioremediation	13¼	⅛	4½	1 7/16	6⅜	1½	64303	4¾	3⅜	3⅝	...	d	98.3	2.1	75.0
12	BCL	✔**Biocraft Labs**	NY,B,Ch,Ph	B−	36	2176	Mfrs generic drug products	37⅝	7½	21¾	11¾	22½	12⅝	8067	15	12⅞	13¼	...	d	−22.1	−16.5	−2.5
13	BCRX	✔**BioCryst Pharm'l**	NNM	NR	14	906	R&D Pharmaceutical products	...	...	6¾	3⅜	13¾	4⅝	3605	10½	8½	9¼	...	d	100	...	...
#14•[2]	BGEN	✔**Biogen Inc**	NNM	B−	239	23627	Research/dev of biotech'gy	49¾	3¾	55¾	27¼	66½	32	301820	66½	52½	61½	...	..	50.9	8.6	16.2
15	BJCT	✔**Bioject Medl Technologies**	NNM	NR	24	3067	Dvlp stge:medl syringe R&D	9	1¾	5⅛	2	3½	1	14225	2¼	1¾	1⅞	...	d	−40.0	−26.0	−10.4
16	BLTI	✔**BIOLASE Technology**	NSC	NR	4	332	Mfr dental laser,endodontic eq	25	1 1/16	3½	⅝	4⅜	½	12092	3¾	1¾	3½	...	d	367	−41.0	...
¶17•[3]	BMET	✔**Biomet, Inc**	NNM,Ph	B+	330	60544	Mfr surgical implant devices	32⅜	3/16	14¼	9	19⅞	13⅛	124514	19⅞	17⅜	17⅞	...	24	28.8	3.8	14.3
18	BIPL	✔**Biopool Intl**	NSC	NR	5	78	R&D blood diagnostic prod	2⅞	1/16	1¾	15/16	3	⅝	4446	2 1/16	1⅜	1 9/16	...	20	61.2	−1.3	30.9
19	BSFE	**BioSafe Intl**	NSC	NR	1	53	Dvp stage:enviro mgt svc	...	...	...	...	5	3⅞	11639	4⅜	3⅞	4⅛	...	..	...	...	...
20	BSTC	**BioSpecifics Technologies**	NNM	NR	10	193	Pharmaceutical R&D	19	3¼	13¼	6	8¾	2½	4492	5	2½	4	...	..	−54.9	−8.7	...
21	BVF	✔**Biovail Corp Intl**	AS	NR	10	1228	R&D ctrl released pharma'l pd	...	...	10¼	4¼	77½	6⅞	6799	77½	52	77¼	...	..	913	...	...
22	BWI	✔**BioWhittaker Inc**	NY	NR	34	4558	Dvlp/mfr biomedical prod	14	5	8⅛	5¾	8½	6¼	2776	8⅛	6⅜	7⅝	...	12	15.1	−3.6	...
✣23•[4]	BIR	✔**Birmingham Steel**	NY,Ch,Ph	B	120	18716	Mini-mills:steel/steel pr	27¾	5⅛	32⅝	18¾	22¾	14	40572	15½	14	14⅞	2.7	9	−25.9	−13.7	13.8
24	BHA	✔**Biscayne Apparel**	AS	C	17	1362	Apparel manufacturing	75¼	¼	3⅜	2	2⅜	¾	1071	1⅛	¾	1	s...	d	−54.8	−2.6	12.0
✣25	BSYS	✔**BISYS Group**	NNM	NR	133	17177	Data processing svc to banks	24½	9⅞	22⅜	17	31⅛	17½	22178	31⅛	27½	30¾	...	d	43.9	16.9	...
#26•[1]	BJS	✔**BJ Services**	NY,Ch,Ph	NR	228	26488	O&G well pressure pump'g svc	31⅝	10	22½	16¼	29½	15½	33535	29½	24¾	29	...	63	74.4	23.2	6.9
27	WS	**Wrrt(Pur 1 com at $30)**	NY	....	60	2407		...	...	...	...	7⅞	3	8356	7⅞	4⅞	7⅝	...	..	...	...	...
¶28•[5]	BDK	✔**Black & Decker Corp**	NY,B,C,Ch,P,Ph	B	412	66485	Mfr power tools/home prod	42⅜	8	25¾	17	38⅛	22⅞	60576	38⅛	33⅝	35¼	1.1	18	48.1	27.2	33.5
#29	BKH	✔**Black Hills Corp**	NY,B,Ch,Ph	A	84	3260	Electric utility:coal mining	32¼	1⅞	22¾	17¾	26⅛	19¾	2244	26⅛	24⅝	24¾	5.4	14	24.0	1.9	10.3
30	BL	✔**Blair Corp**	AS,B,Ch,P,Ph	B+	107	5682	Mail order:apparel&furnish'gs	70¾	3⅛	46⅞	36½	40	27⅝	1910	31⅝	29⅛	31⅝	†7.3	10	−15.3	−12.6	2.5
31	BCO	✔**Blessings Corp**	AS,B,Ch,Ph	B+	39	2360	Mfg plastic film:geriatic pr	12⅜	5/16	17⅞	12⅛	14¾	9½	578	10¾	9½	10⅜	3.9	15	−24.0	8.7	15.3
¶32•[6]	HRB	✔**Block (H & R)**	NY,B,Ch,P,Ph	A	559	73816	Tax,computer & personal serv	42¾	11/16	48¾	33	48⅞	33⅜	91699	45⅝	39¼	40½	3.2	40	11.8	3.8	17.1
33	BLOCA	**Block Drug'A'non-vtg**	NNM	A	89	4634	Denture, dental care pr: drugs	54¼	1⅝	36⅞	27⅜	39	31¼	4041	39	34	34¾	s3.2	8	10.0	−6.3	6.2
34	BDR	**Blonder Tongue Labs**	AS	NR	..	...	'Private Cable' ind electr sys	...	...	...	...	10⅝	9½	59556	10⅝	9½	9¾	...	16	...	...	...
35	BLT.B	✔**Blount Intl Cv'B'**[61]	NY	B	10	110	Constr'n timber cutting prd	19¼	9/16	31⅞	17⅜	35⅛	25⅛	14	31½	31⅛	31¼	1.1	12	−1.2	48.8	44.8
36	BLT.A	✔ **Class'A' (1/10 vtg)**	NY,Ch	B	97	3983	ind'l,pwr sporting equip	19¼	1 3/16	32	17⅝	35⅛	24½	5655	31⅛	25	26¼	1.4	10	−16.8	41.2	40.8
37	BTH	✔**Blyth Industries**	NY,Ch	NR	65	10578	Mfr,mkt candle products	...	...	14⅜	8¼	29½	13⅜	7521	29½	26⅜	29½	...	40	108	...	...
✣38•[7]	BMC	✔**BMC Industries**	NY,Ch,Ph	B	135	18906	Precision etched prod:optics	7	⅝	8⅜	4⅞	23⅝	7¾	20987	23⅝	16⅝	23¼	0.2	30	209	120	88.6
#39•[8]	BMCS	✔**BMC Software**	NNM	B+	301	50089	Dvlp IBM compatible softwr	42⅛	2⅝	35½	20⅛	51½	27	89015	43¾	39	42¾	...	18	52.1	7.8	24.2
✣40•[9]	BMCW	✔**BMC West**	NNM	NR	77	5402	Dstr/retail bldg materials	21½	3⅞	30½	12	17¼	11¼	13133	15	12¼	14¾	...	16	9.3	36.2	...
¶41•[1]	BOAT	✔**Boatmen's Bancshares**	NNM	A	418	51292	Comm'l bkg,Missouri,IL,TN,DE	33½	3⅞	35	26⅛	42⅝	26⅞	89339	42⅝	38½	40⅞	3.6	12	60.3	18.5	26.6
#42	BOBE	✔**Bob Evans Farms**	NNM	A	143	16728	Restaurants sausage prod	22⅝	5/16	23½	19	21¾	15⅞	52967	19¼	15⅞	19	1.7	15	−5.8	1.2	13.4
43	BOCI	✔**Boca Research**	NNM	NR	64	5343	Mfr computer peripheral prod	14¾	5½	9¼	4¼	36½	8	22632	31	23	26½	...	28	203	...	...
44	BNP	✔**Boddie-Noell Properties**	AS,Ch	NR	11	287	REIT: Hardee's Food System	17⅛	8½	15¾	12½	13⅞	11¼	699	12¾	12⅛	12½	9.9	22	4.7	6.8	16.1
¶45•[5]	BA	✔**Boeing Co**	NY,B,C,Ch,P,Ph	A−	1067	204194	Mfr jet airplanes: missiles	61⅞	¾	50⅛	42⅛	80	44⅜	208894	80	72⅜	78⅜	1.3	63	69.1	28.3	13.8
46	BGN	**Bogen Communic Intl**	AS	NR	1	39	Mfr telecommunications prod	...	...	...	...	6	2⅞	1090	4⅛	2⅞	3	...	..	...	...	...
47	BGN.E	**Unit**[64]	AS	NR	..	...		...	...	...	...	6¾	4½	10	5	4½	4B	...	..	...	...	...
48	WS	**Wrrt(Pur 1 com at$5.50)**	AS	....	1	80		...	...	...	...	1 3/16	¼	2114	⅞	¼	⅝	...	..	...	...	...
¶49•[5]	BCC	✔**Boise Cascade**	NY,B,C,Ch,P,Ph	B−	397	34697	Leading mfr of forest prod	52⅜	5	30½	19	47½	26¼	99193	37⅜	31½	34½	1.7	6	32.4	20.7	8.7
50	Pr G	**7.48%**[66] **Dep**[67]**'ACES'**[68]	NY	↑BB+[69]	38	7204		24	20⅜	26¾	19	39	23½	3533	31½	27	28⅝	5.5	..	...	...	...
51	BOP	✔**Boise Cascade Office Products**[10]	NY,Ch	NR	52	5123	Distribute office products	...	...	...	...	43½	21¾	9594	43½	36⅛	42¾	...	38	...	...	...
52	BOKF	✔**BOK Financial**	NSC	NR	18	357	Commercial banking, Oklahoma	57¼	5¾	25⅝	17⅞	24½	18⅞	446	23½	19½	23	s...	10	19.8	7.6	...

Uniform Footnote Explanations-See Page 4. Other: [1]CBOE:Cycle 1. [2]ASE,CBOE,P:Cycle 1. [3]ASE,CBOE:Cycle 1. [4]NY:Cycle 1. [5]CBOE:Cycle 2. [6]ASE:Cycle 1. [7]Ph:Cycle 1. [8]CBOE,P:Cycle 2. [9]P:Cycle 2. [10]Ph [51]Mgmt grp plans acq,$16.50. [52]®$1.20,'94. [53]1/10 vtg. [54]Fiscal Jan'94 & prior. [55]11 Mo Dec '94. [56]Stk dstr of Pancretec. [57]Excl 1.5M restricted com. [58]Fiscal Jan'92 & prior. [59]12 Mo Mar'93. [60]Incl 4.85M Cl'A'spec. shrs. [61]Cv into 1 Cl'A'. [62]®$0.51,'94. [63]Incl $0.61132 non-taxable,'94. [64]1 shr com & 2 Redm Wrrts. [65]If com min $10.00 - 20 con trad days. [66]Automatically Convertible Equity Sec. [67]Ref fr7-15-97$21.225(in stk)to9-15-97aft$21.125. [68]Dep for 0.10 shr Conv Pref stk Sr'G'. [69]Note:'r'added to derivative/hybrid secur ratings. [70]84.6% owned by Boise Cascade. [71]7 Mo Dec'91. [72]®$1.94,'94.

Index	Splits ◆ Cash Divs. Ea.Yr. Since	Dividends: Latest Payment Period $	Date	Ex. Div.	Total $ So Far 1995	Ind. Rate	Paid 1994	Financial Position Mil-$ Cash& Equiv.	Curr. Assets	Curr. Liab.	Balance Sheet Date	Capitalization Lg Trm Debt Mil-$	Shs. 000 Pfd.	Com.	Earnings $ Per Shr. Years End	1991	1992	1993	1994	1995	Last 12 Mos.	Interim Earnings Period	$ per Shr. 1994	1995	Index
1	....	None Since Public			...	Nil	....	2.16	203	148	p9-30-95	p305	...	★16173	Je	...	...	...	....	p0.44	....	3 Mo Sep	n/a	p0.28	1
2◆	....	None Paid			...	Nil	....	0.85	35.6	13.8	9-30-95	17.4	...	3318	Dc	0.50	0.80	□0.55	0.80	....	0.79	9 Mo Sep	0.44	0.43	2
3	1990	Q0.02	12-11-95	11-28	0.08	0.08	0.08	24.9	618	422	9-30-95	68.8	...	11133	Dc	1.61	Δ1.02	0.88	[52]1.34	....	1.41	9 Mo Sep	0.97	1.04	3
4◆	1947	Q0.10	11-1-95	10-16	†0.50	0.40	0.30	6.56	171	65.8	8-31-95	41.9	...	3089	Nv	0.39	Δ0.46	0.44	1.11	....	1.35	9 Mo Aug	0.83	1.07	4
5	....	None Since Public			...	Nil	....	0.24	8.96	6.06	9-30-95	0.52	...	6416	Mr	*0.02	*0.19	0.27	d0.07	....	d0.29	6 Mo Sep	0.08	d0.14	5
6◆	....	None Since Public			...	Nil	....	2.82	9.05	2.12	2-28-95	0.81	...	4148	Fb	0.08	0.02	0.13	0.18	....	0.30	6 Mo Aug	Nil	0.12	6
7	....	None Paid			...	Nil	....	7.56	197	87.1	9-30-95	25.7	...	±8151	Dc	±1.04	±1.96	±0.35	±1.93	....	2.86	9 Mo Sep	±1.41	±2.34	7
8	....	None Since Public			...	Nil	....	Cv into 1 Cl'A'				....	...	1766	Dc	±1.04	±1.96	±0.35	±1.93	....	2.86	9 Mo Sep	±1.41	±2.34	8
9	....	None Since Public			...	Nil	....	11.9	20.5	5.01	9-30-95	....	...	43257	Dc	d0.38	d0.38	d0.63	Δd0.23	....	d0.10	9 Mo Sep	Δd0.13	ΔNil	9
10	....	None Since Public			...	Nil	....	31.9	132	58.2	j12-31-94	80.1	...	p47334	Dc	0.37	d0.32	[54]d0.21	[55]d0.30	Ed0.15	d0.27	9 Mo Sep	d0.21	d0.18	10
11	....	h[56]....	11-16-83	11-18	...	Nil	....	7.21	9.31	0.83	9-30-95	0.05	5	36944	Dc	d0.08	d0.23	d0.45	d0.43	....	d0.81	9 Mo Sep	d0.30	d0.68	11
12	1989	0.10	11-22-94	10-12	...	Nil	0.10	1.84	89.8	36.2	9-30-95	51.4	...	14180	Mr	d0.48	0.42	Δ0.43	d0.17	....	d0.29	6 Mo Sep	d0.06	□d0.18	12
13	....	None Since Public			...	Nil	....	13.0	13.4	0.69	9-30-95	0.03	...	[57]9498	Dc	...	...	pd1.27	pd1.02	....	d0.97	9 Mo Sep	d0.79	d0.74	13
14	....	None Since Public			...	Nil	....	285	317	42.9	9-30-95	29.1	...	35471	Dc	0.15	1.12	0.93	d0.15	E0.15↑	0.43	9 Mo Sep	d0.45	0.13	14
15	....	None Paid			...	Nil	....	2.48	4.53	1.48	9-30-95	....	...	13270	Mr	[58]d0.43	[59]d0.35	d0.39	d0.43	....	d0.51	6 Mo Sep	d0.15	d0.23	15
16◆	....	None Since Public			...	Nil	....	1.83	2.66	0.61	9-30-95	0.01	...	11236	Dc	d0.80	d1.52	d1.57	Δd0.45	....	d0.34	9 Mo Sep	d0.26	d0.15	16
17◆	....	None Since Public			...	Nil	....	76.3	386	69.1	8-31-95	....	...	115301	My	0.35	0.46	0.56	0.61	0.69	0.75	6 Mo Nov	0.32	0.38	17
18	....	None Paid			...	Nil	....	1.68	5.13	1.35	9-30-95	0.56	...	7929	Dc	d0.07	Δ0.06	0.05	0.09	....	0.08	9 Mo Sep	0.07	0.06	18
19	....	None Since Public			...	Nil	....	9.21	10.9	3.54	p9-30-95	14.3	...	11569	Dc	...	...	...	pd0.01	....	....	9 Mo Sep	n/a	d0.40	19
20◆	....	None Paid			...	Nil	....	4.28	7.16	0.96	10-31-95	....	...	4883	Ja	0.32	*0.29	0.28	0.02	....	0.02	9 Mo Oct	d0.01	d0.01	20
21◆	....	None Since Public			...	Nil	....	3.95	12.2	11.4	j12-31-94	6.61	...	[60]±8274	Dc	d2.65	d2.94	1.09	1.82	....	j1.05	9 Mo Sep	1.10	0.33	21
22	....	None Since Public			...	Nil	....	0.56	34.3	10.5	7-31-95	3.16	...	10759	Oc	p0.38	0.42	0.17	0.32	P0.64	0.64				22
23◆	1988	Q0.10	11-7-95	10-25	0.40	0.40	0.40	2.85	323	146	9-30-95	158	...	28538	Je	d0.42	1.11	0.60	Δ0.86	1.74	1.61	3 Mo Sep	0.42	0.29	23
24◆	....	5%Stk	5-31-95	5-18	5%Stk	Stk	5%Stk	1.83	69.2	45.9	9-30-95	12.7	...	10741	Dc	Δd0.07	Δ□Nil	Δ0.41	0.22	....	d0.11	9 Mo Sep	0.14	d0.19	24
25	....	None Since Public			...	Nil	....	13.2	54.0	43.0	9-30-95	....	...	23337	Je	pd0.92	□d2.64	Δ0.23	0.86	d0.27	d0.22	3 Mo Sep	0.17	0.22	25
26	....	None Since Public			...	Nil	....	1.84	257	204	9-30-95	260	...	28012	Sp	p1.88	d0.08	0.94	□0.69	0.46	0.46				26
27	....	Terms&trad. basis should	be checked in detail					Wrrts expire 4-13-2000				....	...	4800	Sp	...	...	...	....	....	....				27
28	1937	Q0.10	12-29-95	12-13	0.40	0.40	0.40	112	2097	2010	10-01-95	1677	150	86010	Dc	0.81	□d1.11	□1.00	1.37	E1.95	1.77	9 Mo Sep	0.69	1.09	28
29◆	1942	Q0.33½	12-1-95	11-8	1.34	1.34	1.32	16.4	41.0	30.5	9-30-95	166	...	14418	Dc	1.66	1.73	1.66	1.66	....	1.75	12 Mo Sep	1.64	1.75	29
30	1931	Q0.35	12-15-95	11-20	2.30	2.30	†2.05	1.23	279	132	9-30-95	....	...	9322	Dc	3.37	3.82	3.34	4.07	....	3.24	9 Mo Sep	2.82	1.99	30
31◆	1976	Q0.10	3-1-96	1-31	0.40	0.40	0.34¼	3.34	36.9	27.1	10-07-95	23.4	...	10124	Dc	0.92	Δ0.93	1.00	1.20	....	0.68	40 Wk Oct	0.93	0.41	31
32◆	1962	Q0.32	1-2-96	12-8	1.25¾	1.28	1.15¼	69.2	387	248	10-31-95	....	...	103912	Ap	1.30	1.49	1.68	1.88	1.01	1.02	6 Mo Oct	d0.04	d0.03	32
33◆	1971	s0.282	1-2-96	11-29	s1.041	1.126	s0.973	26.2	291	218	9-30-95	11.8	...	±20798	Mr	±2.77	±2.98	±2.31	±2.43	....	4.64	6 Mo Sep	±1.17	±3.38	33
34	....	None Since Public			...	Nil	....	0.16	23.6	25.4	p9-30-95	0.33	...	★7919	Dc	...	p0.09	p0.23	p0.48	....	0.60	9 Mo Sep	p0.38	p0.50	34
35◆	1971	0.102	1-2-96	12-13	0.347	0.35	0.30	62.9	278	124	8-31-95	96.7	...	±19028	Fb	Δ±d0.29	□±0.40	Δ±0.73	±2.07	....	2.54	9 Mo Nov	±1.64	±2.11	35
36◆	1983	0.11	1-2-96	12-13	0.38	0.38	0.333	....	...	...		....	...	13101	Fb	Δ±d0.29	□±0.40	Δ±0.73	±2.07	....	2.54	9 Mo Nov	±1.64	±2.11	36
37◆	....	None Since Public			...	Nil	....	4.53	91.7	33.2	7-31-95	27.8	...	★30702	Ja	...	...	p0.37	0.49	....	0.73	9 Mo Oct	0.35	0.59	37
38◆	1994	Q0.01¼	1-3-96	12-18	0.04	0.05	0.00½	18.9	86.5	45.5	9-30-95	....	...	26936	Dc	0.37	0.31	Δ0.40	[62]0.52	....	0.78	9 Mo Sep	0.33	0.59	38
39◆	....	None Since Public			...	Nil	....	121	217	140	9-30-95	....	...	50622	Mr	0.94	1.25	1.08	1.52	E2.35	1.64	6 Mo Sep	0.91	1.03	39
40◆	....	None Since Public			...	Nil	....	6.06	148	53.0	9-30-95	118	40	9481	Dc	0.21	□0.62	1.14	1.62	....	0.92	9 Mo Sep	1.35	0.65	40
41◆	1873	Q0.37	1-1-96	11-28	1.39	1.48	1.27	Book Value $21.71			9-30-95	563	12	129372	Dc	2.04	2.25	3.07	3.40	E3.35	3.41	9 Mo Sep	2.36	2.37	41
42◆	1964	Q0.08	12-1-95	11-30	0.30½	0.32	0.28	7.86	51.7	99.3	10-27-95	2.33	...	42638	Ap	Δ0.80	0.94	1.03	1.15	1.27	1.27	6 Mo Oct	0.65	0.65	42
43	....	None Since Public			...	Nil	....	0.17	48.3	13.8	9-30-95	....	...	8506	Dc	p0.48	p0.73	0.33	0.68	....	0.95	9 Mo Sep	0.47	0.74	43
44	1987	Q0.31	11-15-95	10-30	1.24	1.24	[63]1.24	Equity per shr $7.91			9-30-95	66.8	...	3017	Dc	1.03	1.11	0.86	0.80	....	0.56	9 Mo Sep	0.70	0.46	44
45	1942	Q0.25	3-1-96	2-7	1.00	1.00	1.00	4201	12305	7148	9-30-95	2355	...	343146	Dc	4.56	□4.57	3.66	2.51	E1.25	0.97	9 Mo Sep	2.05	0.51	45
46	....	None Since Public			...	Nil	....	1.24	16.8	13.7	9-30-95	0.13	...	5759	Dc	...	...	...	p0.04	....	....	9 Mo Sep	n/a	d0.91	46
47	....	....			....	....	....	....	....	...		....	...	1500	Dc	...	...	...	....	....	....				47
48	....	Terms&trad. basis should	be checked in detail					Wrrts expire 10-7-2000				....	...	3660	Dc	...	...	...	....	....	....	Callable at $0.01[65]			48
49	1935	Q0.15	1-15-96	12-27	0.60	0.60	0.60	74.4	1163	859	9-30-95	1497	7121	48134	Dc	d2.46	□d4.79	d3.17	d3.08	E5.60↓	5.10	9 Mo Sep	d3.40	4.78	49
50	1993	Q0.39½	1-15-96	12-27	1.58	1.58	1.58	Cv into 0.801 com $26.375				....	7500	...	Dc	...	...	...	....	....	....	Mand Cv into 1 com 10-15-97			50
51	....	None Since Public			...	Nil	....	34.0	327	170	9-30-95	....	...	[70]31139	Dc	...	...	...	p0.95	....	1.13	9 Mo Sep	p0.81	p0.99	51
52◆	....	3%Stk	11-27-95	11-15	3%Stk	Stk	3%Stk	Book Value $10.28			9-30-95	....	250000	19818	Dc	‡[71]0.99	1.51	Δ1.77	[72]2.13	....	2.30	9 Mo Sep	1.56	1.73	52

◆**Stock Splits & Divs By Line Reference Index** [2]1-for-5 REVERSE,'92. [4]Adj to 2%,Jul'93. [6]3-for-2,'91. [16]1-for-2 REVERSE,'92:1-for-4 REVERSE,'94. [17]2-for-1,'91(twice). [20]2-for-1,'92. [21]Vote Jan 2 on 3-for-1 stk split. [23]3-for-2,'92. [24]Adj for 5%,'95:No adj for dstr of $1.60&$1 in debs,'89(ex'90). [29]3-for-2,'92. [31]3-for-2,'91:2-for-1,'94. [32]2-for-1,'91. [33]Adjj to 3%,'95. [35]3-for-2,'95. [36]3-for-2,'95. [37]2-for-1,'95. [38]2-for-1,'94,'95. [39]2-for-1,'95. [40]3-for-2,'94. [41]2-for-1,'93. [42]4-for-3,'92. [52]1-for-100 REVERSE,'91:Adj to 3%,'95.

¶ S&P 500 # MidCap 400 ✢ SmallCap 600 • Options Index	Ticker	Name of Issue (Call Price of Pfd. Stocks)	Market	Com. Rank. & Pfd. Rating	Inst. Hold Cos	Inst. Hold Shs. (000)	Principal Business	Price Range 1971-93 High	1971-93 Low	1994 High	1994 Low	1995 High	1995 Low	Dec. Sales in 100s	December, 1995 Last Sale Or Bid High	Low	Last	%Div Yield	P-E Ratio	Total Return % Annualized 12 Mo	36 Mo	60 Mo
1	BBD.B	Bombardier Inc Cl'B'	To,Mo	A–	74	42498	Mfr aircraft/transport eq	10½	3/16	12⅝	8⅞	18⅛	11¼	124959	18⅛	17	18	e1.1	22	49.2	46.4	...
✢2•[1]	BBA	✔Bombay Company	NY,Ch,Ph	B–	88	19630	Sell furniture/leather goods	32⅞	⅛	32¾	8¾	11	4¾	39528	7	5⅜	6⅜	...	d	–37.8	–22.6	...
3	BNSOF	Bonso Electronics Intl	NNM	B–	1	70	Mfr electronics scales/prod	7½	⅜	12¾	4½	5⅜	2⅛	3108	2¾	2⅛	2⅛	...	5	–57.5	77.8	13.5
4	BONT	✔Bon-Ton Stores	NNM	NR	43	2583	Department stores eastern U.S.	15½	4	14⅛	6⅜	12¼	4¾	6252	6⅛	4¾	5	...	9	–54.0	–9.5	...
✢5•[2]	BMTN	✔Boomtown Inc	NNM	NR	41	3842	Oper western style casino, NV	32½	10	21¼	12⅛	16¼	4¾	20115	6⅞	4¾	5	...	d	–68.3	–28.6	...
6	BORAY	Boral Ltd ADS[55]	NNM	NR	8	305	Constr'n prod/oil&gas prod'n	24½	13¼	26⅜	18¾	21¾	18¼	61	20¼	19	20⅛	6.1	13	0.8	15.2	4.9
7•[3]	BCU	✔Borden Chem/Plastics L.P.	NY,Ch	NR	63	1634	Produces chem & PVC resins	24	7½	26⅜	9⅞	25½	12¼	57690	15⅜	12¼	12⅝	...	2	–25.3	15.3	25.9
8•[4]	BGP	✔Borders Group	NY,Ch,Ph	NR	157	29923	Operates book superstores	....	....	....	....	21⅞	13⅞	36679	19⅛	15⅜	18½	...	d	...	...	...
9	BWA	✔Borg-Warner Automotive	NY,Ch	NR	142	21312	Auto powertrain components	28	20½	34	21⅝	33⅞	22⅜	6170	32¼	29½	32	1.9	11	30.7	...	...
10	BOR	✔Borg-Warner Security	NY,Ch,Ph	NR	64	17042	Provides protective services	22⅞	18	22	8¼	13	5½	5598	13	11⅝	12½	...	78	37.0	...	...
#11•[5]	BORL	✔Borland Intl	NNM,Ch	C	90	12473	Design/mkt computer software	86¾	9⅝	16	6	20⅝	6⅛	171469	20⅝	16	16½	...	41	169	–10.3	–11.9
12	SAM	Boston Beer 'A'	NY,Ph	NR	..	...	Largest craft brewer U.S.	....	....	....	....	33	20	20530	28¼	21½	23¾	...	..	...	...	...
13	BOS	✔Boston Celtics L.P.	NY,B,Ch,Ph	NR	15	25	Professional basketball team	23⅞	10⅜	24⅛	18½	28⅜	19¾	464	24⅛	22⅞	23⅛	6.5	3	11.6	18.5	15.1
14•[5]	BOST	✔Boston Chicken	NNM	NR	160	24179	Oper,franchise food svc strs	25½	17¾	24¼	13½	35⅞	14½	227048	35¾	30⅝	32⅛	...	51	82.3	...	...
15	BSE	✔Boston Edison	NY,B,Ch,P,Ph	B+	166	17648	Electric utility:Boston area	32⅝	7	29⅞	21½	29½	23⅛	16292	29½	27½	29½	6.4	12	32.7	8.7	15.6
¶16•[6]	BSX	✔Boston Scientific	NY,Ph	NR	409	74039	Dvlp,mfr medical devices	23⅝	9⅜	17⅞	11⅞	49⅜	16⅝	81212	49⅜	37⅜	49¼	...	..	194	35.9	...
17•[7]	BSTN	✔Boston Technology	NNM	NR	97	9256	Voice process'g communic sys	14⅜	1 15/16	18⅝	7⅝	21¼	9⅜	53883	15⅝	12⅜	12¾	...	51	–19.4	9.8	44.8
18	BFD	BostonFed Bancorp	AS	NR	..	...	Savings bank, Massachusetts	....	....	....	....	12¾	10	7186	12	11⅝	11¾	...	..	...	...	...
#19•[8]	BOW	✔Bowater, Inc	NY,B,Ch,P,Ph	B–	284	35935	Mfrs newsprint,coated paper	44½	14⅞	29⅝	20⅜	54⅜	26⅜	140576	40⅝	32¼	35½	1.7	6	36.8	16.6	14.5
20	Pr B	7%Sr'B"PRIDES'[59]([60]23.911)	NY	↑BBB–[61]	53	4410		....	....	27¼	21	45	23¾	16894	34½	28	30½	5.4	..	...	...	...
21	BWL.A	✔Bowl America Cl'A'	AS,Ch	B+	23	1116	Bowling centers	12⅛	¼	10	7⅞	9	7¼	259	8	7¼	7⅝	5.0	13	–0.6	–7.3	3.1
22	BOM	✔Bowmar Instrument	AS,B,P,Ph	B–	15	577	Electromechanical compon'ts	44⅞	¼	4⅜	2½	4	2¼	5348	3	2 5/16	2½	...	5	–13.0	5.6	29.4
23	Pr	$3.00 cm Cv Sr vtg Pfd([63]25)	AS	NR	1	19		72	25	56	37⅛	52	33	42	41	34¾	33½B	9.0	..	...	...	...
✢24	BNE	✔Bowne & Co	AS,B,Ch,P,Ph	↓B	96	7976	Fin'l,corp,legal printing	24⅜	⅜	28½	15⅜	20⅞	15⅜	6549	20⅞	19⅛	20	1.8	15	24.7	12.6	17.9
✢25•[7]	BOXXB	✔Box Energy 'B'[64]	NNM	NR	49	3003	Oil&gas explor,dvlp,prod'n	19½	8⅝	14⅛	7½	11¼	7⅝	19807	9¼	8¼	8⅝	...	45	–15.9	–0.5	...
26	BOYD	✔Boyd Bros.Transport'n	NNM	NR	8	700	Flatbed trucking services	....	....	13	9½	12¼	6	331	8¾	6	7¼	...	13	–23.7	...	...
27•[9]	BYD	✔Boyd Gaming	NY,Ch	NR	42	3498	Own,operate casino-hotels	26	12⅞	19⅜	10½	18⅝	10	9761	11⅞	10	11⅝	...	19	5.7	...	...
28	BPT	✔BP Prudhoe Bay Royalty[65]	NY,Ch,Ph	NR	34	7592	Royalties of oil/gas prop	35½	23⅞	27	15¾	19	13	12300	15¼	14¼	14½	11.0	9	–0.2	–15.8	–4.9
29•[10]	BLE	✔Bradlees, Inc	NY,Ph	D	38	3252	Discount department stores	20⅛	10⅝	17¼	10⅞	12	⅞	24682	1⅝	1	1⅛	...	d	–89.7	–58.5	...
30	BPRXA	✔Bradley Pharmaceuticals'A'	NNM	NR	12	192	RX-OTC Pharmaceuticals	4⅛	1½	4½	2⅛	4¾	15/16	19567	1 11/16	1	1⅛	...	d	–69.6	–28.6	...
31	BTR	✔Bradley Real Estate	NY,Ch	NR	71	6824	Real estate investment trust	32½	13/16	19¼	13⅝	16⅞	13⅛	5541	14⅜	13⅛	13½	9.8	14	–3.1	–1.9	6.9
32	BRCOA	✔Brady(W.H.)'A'non-vtg	NNM	A–	74	8680	Mfrs adhesives & coatings	14⅜	3⅜	16⅜	14⅛	27	15⅝	4726	27	25	27	1.5	20	69.6	33.1	26.6
33	BRA	✔Brandon Systems	AS	B+	44	2144	Temp computer personnel svc	12⅞	3½	19⅛	11⅝	25⅝	17¼	1144	25⅝	22½	25⅝	1.3	19	46.5	37.6	36.3
34	BDN	✔Brandywine Rlty Trust SBI	AS	NR	..	...	Real estate investment trust	11⅛	5/16	6	1⅝	4¾	3⅜	242	3½	3⅜	3½	e5.6	d	11.8	148	59.0
35•[11]	BRS.A	Brascan Ltd Cv'A'Ord	AS,To,Ch,Mo,Vc	NR	66	12940	Canadian invest't mgmt co	31⅞	4¾	15½	11⅞	17⅞	12⅛	3688	17⅞	16⅝	17⅝	◆...	..	32.4	28.7	14.2
36	BRE	✔BRE Properties Cl'A'	NY,Ch	NR	73	4598	Real estate investment trust	39⅞	2⅞	34⅝	29⅞	36¼	29⅝	2830	36¼	32⅝	35⅝	7.1	17	27.2	11.8	17.7
37•[12]	BDT	✔Breed Technologies	NY,Ph	NR	102	7866	Mfr airbag sys crash sensors	21¾	10¾	44	15¼	29	16⅜	20634	20⅜	18½	18½	1.1	8	–35.0	4.0	...
✢38	BREN	✔Brenco, Inc	NNM	B	67	5674	Bearings for RR freight cars	25	3⅛	14	8¼	14½	9¾	3502	10¾	10⅛	10¼	2.7	9	–9.9	21.3	16.7
39	BRBK	✔Brenton Banks	NNM	B+	33	1427	Commercial bkg,Iowa	20⅞	2¼	20½	17½	22¾	17¾	1527	22¾	19¾	21¼	2.3	18	18.5	8.7	21.8
40	BPTM	✔Bridgeport Machines	NNM	NR	24	1943	Metal cutting machine tools	....	....	10¼	8¼	21	9⅜	3584	21	17	21	...	14	130	...	...
¶41•[12]	BGG	✔Briggs & Stratton	NY,B,Ch,Ph	A–	354	21213	Mfr small gas engines:locks	44¾	6⅞	45⅛	30½	44⅛	32¼	9650	44⅛	41	43⅜	2.4	14	...	...	...
42	CBA	✔Brilliance China Automotive	NY,Ph	NR	..	...	Minibus manufacturer in China	34¾	13½	20	7½	8⅝	3⅛	9453	4¼	3¼	3⅞	2.1	19	–50.1	–49.6	...
#43•[13]	EAT	✔Brinker Intl	NY,Ch,Ph	B+	242	51093	Limited menu restaurants	30⅞	1 11/16	33⅝	15	20⅞	11⅞	43610	15¾	14¾	15⅛	...	16	–16.6	–4.8	17.8
44	BH	Bristol Hotel	NY	NR	..	...	Own/oper hotels Southern U.S.	....	....	....	....	24¾	20½	38137	24¾	20½	24⅜	...	..	...	...	...
¶45•[2]	BMY	✔Bristol-Myers Squibb	NY,B,C,Ch,P,Ph	A+	1308	264462	Pharmaceutical,medical prod	90⅛	3⅞	61	50	87⅛	57¾	212966	87⅛	80⅜	85⅞	3.5	17	52.0	13.2	9.7
46	Pr	$2 cm Cv Pfd (50)vtg	NY,B,P	NR	7	.5	non-prescp hlth pr: toiletries	371	25	244	214	359½	330	8	359½	358	364⅛B	0.5	..	...	...	...
47	BVSI	✔Brite Voice Systems	NNM	B	45	3767	Mfr voice data/audiotex sys	14¼	2½	19¾	7⅝	24½	12	12722	17¾	13¼	13⅞	...	26	–23.4	70.2	29.9
48•[12]	BAB	✔British Airways ADS[72]	NY,Ch,P,Ph	NR	108	7183	Major int'l U.K. airline	69	16⅛	74⅛	54⅞	76⅜	56¼	5405	73⅝	70⅛	72¾	3.0	10	33.8	20.5	27.5
49	BRG	✔British Gas ADS[74]	NY,B,Ch,P,Ph	NR	69	5688	Major gas supplier in UK	54¼	8⅝	54⅛	39	50½	34½	4798	39⅞	34½	39⅛	5.9	12	–14.4	2.5	4.4
50•[13]	BP	✔British Petrol ADS[75]	NY,B,Ch,P,Ph	NR	399	44352	Major integrated world oil	86¼	4½	85¼	58⅜	103⅞	75⅝	62783	103⅞	96¼	102⅛	2.8	17	32.3	35.7	11.1
51•[14]	BSY	British Sky Broadcstg Gp ADS[76]	[15]NY	NR	123	18005	Pay TV svcs U.K./Ireland	....	....	25¼	23¾	40	22⅞	13494	39¾	35½	37⅝	0.9	40	59.7	...	...
52•[16]	BST	✔British Steel ADS[77]	NY,Ch	NR	83	14855	Largest steel producer in U.K.	27¾	7	27¼	18⅛	30¼	22⅝	60175	26¼	23¼	25⅝	5.5	5	11.6	47.7	8.1

Uniform Footnote Explanations-See Page 4. Other: [1]Ph:Cycle 3. [2]CBOE:Cycle 3. [3]NY:Cycle 2. [4]CBOE,NY,Ph:Cycle 2. [5]CBOE:Cycle 1. [6]CBOE:Cycle 2. [7]ASE:Cycle 1. [8]P:Cycle 3. [9]Ph:Cycle 2. [10]ASE:Cycle 2. [11]Mo:Cycle 1. [12]Ph:Cycle 1. [13]P:Cycle 1. [14]CBOE,NY:Cycle 1. [15]Ch,Ph [16]NY:Cycle 1. [51]®$0.69,'94. [52]Stk dstr of Tandy Brands Accessories. [53]Fiscal Jun'93 & prior. [54]12 Mo Jan'95,prior fiscal Jun'94 $0.60.. [55]Ea ADS rep 8 Ord shrs, par A.$0.50. [56]Incl proceeds from sale of rts,'94. [57]To be determined. [58]Inc current amts. [59]Dep for 0.25 shr'7%'PRIDES,Sr,B Cv Pfd. [60]Fr 1-1-97,scale to $23.50 in'98. [61]Note:'r'added to derivative/hybrid secur ratings. [62]®$0.27,'94. [63]Fr 1-1-98. [64]non-vtg. [65]Units of Beneficial Int. [66]Incl liabs subj to reorg. [67]Spl div. [68]©$0.01,'95. [69]Incl $0.23 non-taxable:©$0.09,'94. [70]3 Mo Mar'93. [71]Stk dstr of Strattec Security Corp,'95. [72]Full paym't ADR's equal 10 Ord par 25p. [73]Approx. [74]Full pay't ADS's equal 10 Ord par 25p. [75]ADS's equal 12 Ord par 25 pence. [76]Ea ADS rep 6 Ord Shrs, 50 pence. [77]Full paym't ADS's equal 10 Ord par 50p.

Splits ◆ Index	Cash Divs. Ea.Yr. Since	Dividends: Latest Payment Period $	Date	Ex. Div.	Total $ So Far 1995	Ind. Rate	Paid 1994	Financial Position Mil-$ Cash& Equiv.	Curr. Assets	Curr. Liab.	Balance Sheet Date	Capitalization Lg Trm Debt Mil-$	Shs. 000 Pfd.	Com.	Earnings $ Per Shr. Years End	1991	1992	1993	1994	1995	Last 12 Mos.	Interim Earnings Period	$ per Shr. 1994	1995	Index
1◆	1984	g†0.052	1-31-96	1-10	g†0.197	0.20	g0.14⅜	Equity per shr $4.96			j1-31-95	p1211	1258	±p331676	Ja	±0.37	±0.43	±0.56	±[51]0.72	....	j0.83	9 Mo Oct	±0.50	±0.61	1
2◆	....	h[52]....	1-11-91	1-14	...	Nil	....	0.80	106	18.5	10-28-95	....	...	37270	Ja	0.20	0.29	[53]0.23	[54]d0.25	....	d0.37	9 Mo Oct	0.13	0.01	2
3◆	....	None Paid			...	Nil	....	0.16	10.9	6.14	3-31-95	0.07	...	2826	Mr	0.06	0.24	0.66	0.95	....	0.47	6 Mo Sep	0.58	0.10	3
4	....	None Since Public			...	Nil	....	4.16	179	78.4	7-29-95	116	...	±11313	Ja	±p0.93	±0.64	±Δ0.80	±1.23	....	0.58	9 Mo Oct	±d0.03	±d0.68	4
5	....	None Since Public			...	Nil	....	17.7	29.5	20.3	6-30-95	107	...	9230	Sp	p0.72	p0.61	□0.65	d0.89	Pd0.31	d0.31				5
6	1992	0.628	11-10-95	10-5	1.228	1.23	[56]1.252	58.3	1463	1394	j6-30-95	900	...	1100804	Je	1.47	1.02	1.28	0.72	1.52	1.52				6
7	1989	0.90	11-14-95	11-1	5.73	[57]....	2.06	65.3	214	170	9-30-95	200	...	36750	Dc	1.39	0.73	d0.04	3.94	....	5.95	9 Mo Sep	1.87	□3.88	7
8	....	None Since Public			...	Nil	....	41.5	883	730	10-22-95	8.70	...	37518	Ja	...	...	...	p0.48	....	d4.00	9 Mo Oct	pd0.18	p■d4.66	8
9	1994	Q0.15	11-15-95	10-30	0.60	0.60	0.57½	14.1	233	214	9-30-95	139	...	23415	Dc	...	pd0.12	p□1.41	2.75	....	3.05	9 Mo Sep	1.90	2.20	9
10	....	None Since Public			...	Nil	....	17.4	184	190	9-30-95	476	...	23172	Dc	p1.16	p1.30	p1.50	0.56	....	0.16	9 Mo Sep	0.53	0.13	10
11	....	None Paid			...	Nil	....	85.3	115	77.0	9-30-95	17.1	...	29912	Mr	d4.29	d1.87	d2.62	d0.43	E0.40	d2.09	6 Mo Sep	1.84	0.18	11
12	....	None Since Public			...	Nil	....	....	26.2	18.3	p9-30-95	[58]p1.95	...	±★19182	Dc	...	...	...	±p0.29	....	....	9 Mo Sep	n/a	±p0.26	12
13	1987	1.50	7-21-95	6-28	1.50	1.50	1.50	139	147	63.5	9-30-95	50.0	...	5641	Je	1.69	1.19	0.80	3.61	2.43	8.51	3 Mo Sep	d0.33	5.75	13
14◆	....	None Since Public			...	Nil	....	41.2	63.3	23.3	10-01-95	307	...	★57767	Dc	d0.14	d0.20	0.06	0.38	E0.63	0.59	9 Mo Sep	0.26	0.47	14
15	1890	Q0.47	2-1-96	1-8	1.82	1.88	1.76	29.0	386	545	9-30-95	1160	p2190	47890	Dc	1.96	2.10	2.28	2.41	E2.50	2.48	12 Mo Sep	2.39	2.48	15
16	....	None Since Public			...	Nil	....	162	460	139	9-30-95	9.12	...	151746	Dc	*0.44	0.57	0.70	0.81	E0.48	0.33	9 Mo Sep	0.64	0.16	16
17	....	None Paid			...	Nil	....	15.2	69.0	27.2	10-31-95	0.97	...	25353	Ja	d0.11	0.13	0.27	0.50	....	0.25	9 Mo Oct	0.36	0.11	17
18	....	None Since Public			...	Nil	....	Book Value $13.01			4-30-95	146	...	★6613	Dc	...	...	...	p0.81	....	....	4 Mo Apr	n/a	p0.02	18
19	1984	Q0.15	1-2-96	12-7	0.60	0.60	0.60	207	619	286	9-30-95	817	3573	39068	Dc	1.15	Δd2.64	d1.84	d0.59	E5.77↓	4.11	9 Mo Sep	d1.04	□3.66	19
20	1994	Q0.41⅛	1-2-96	12-27	1.64½	1.645	1.065	Cv into 0.82 com, $28.659				....	4894	...	Dc	...	...	...	b0.81	....	....	Mandatory conversion into 1 com 1-1-98			20
21◆	1969	Q0.09½	2-14-96	1-8	0.37	0.38	0.36	7.31	9.38	2.43	10-01-95	....	...	±5743	Je	±0.72	±0.65	±0.69	±0.66	±0.57	0.57	3 Mo Sep	±d0.02	±d0.02	21
22	....	None Since Public			...	Nil	....	0.37	11.1	8.45	7-01-95	0.46	120	p6685	Sp	0.05	0.20	0.06	[62]0.28	P0.54	0.54				22
23	1992	Q0.75	12-29-95	12-13	3.00	3.00	3.00	Cv into 13.33 com, $1.875				....	120	...	Sp	...	...	...	....	....	....				23
24	1941	Q0.09	1-10-96	12-27	0.36	0.36	0.315	31.8	168	53.5	7-31-95	2.83	...	17391	Oc	0.84	1.65	2.05	1.80	P1.34	1.34				24
25	....	None Since Public			...	Nil	....	43.0	50.7	6.76	9-30-95	55.1	...	±20803	Dc	p0.09	0.92	0.10	±0.44	....	0.19	9 Mo Sep	±0.42	±0.17	25
26	....	None Since Public			...	Nil	....	0.60	10.6	8.56	9-30-95	8.65	...	3823	Dc	p0.30	p0.39	p0.60	p0.80	....	0.55	9 Mo Sep	p0.71	0.46	26
27	....	None Since Public			...	Nil	....	46.3	88.4	133	9-30-95	564	...	56999	Je	...	...	p0.43	Δ0.19	0.64	0.61	3 Mo Sep	0.10	0.07	27
28	1989	0.375	10-25-95	10-19	1.598	1.60	1.483	Equity per shr $14.65			9-30-95	....	...	21400	Dc	4.05	3.03	2.39	1.48	....	1.65	9 Mo Sep	1.05	1.22	28
29	1992	0.15	4-1-95	3-9	0.30	Nil	0.60	File bankruptcy Chapt 11				[66]379	...	11418	Ja	p1.79	p2.25	□1.19	□0.51	....	d7.17	9 Mo Oct	□d0.95	d8.63	29
30	....	None Since Public			...	Nil	....	0.80	9.77	10.4	9-30-95	5.39	...	±7640	Dc	±d0.41	±d0.30	±0.17	±0.27	....	d0.44	9 Mo Sep	±0.15	±d0.56	30
31◆	1961	Q0.33	12-29-95	12-7	1.32	1.32	1.29	Equity per shr $12.13			9-30-95	34.7	...	11227	Dc	0.38	0.40	0.82	1.05	....	0.95	9 Mo Sep	0.72	0.62	31
32◆	1984	Q0.10	1-31-96	1-3	0.30	0.40	0.237	94.9	177	39.5	10-31-95	1.82	29	±21843	Jl	0.71	□0.39	0.78	0.85	1.28	1.35	3 Mo Oct	0.23	0.30	32
33◆	1989	Q0.08½	1-12-96	12-21	0.28	0.34	0.23½	17.7	30.0	4.35	7-02-95	....	...	4460	Sp	0.46	0.60	0.69	1.10	P1.32	1.32				33
34	1994	[67]Q0.05	1-30-96	1-24	†1.20	0.20	†0.87	Book Value $4.18			9-30-95	8.96	...	1856	Dc	d3.61	Nil	1.33	Δd0.21	....	d0.86	9 Mo Sep	Δ0.33	d0.32	34
35	1965	gQ0.26	11-30-95	10-30	g1.04	1.04	g1.04	Equity per shr $18.63			j12-31-94	1072	15145	87861	Dc	d0.60	d1.56	1.01	1.17	....	j1.90	9 Mo Sep	0.81	1.54	35
36	1970	Q0.63	12-21-95	12-6	[68]2.52	2.52	[69]2.40	Book Value $21.98			10-31-95	113	...	10971	Jl	1.94	2.56	3.02	2.04	2.15	2.11	3 Mo Oct	0.50	0.46	36
37	1994	Q0.05	1-22-96	12-20	0.20	0.20	0.05	29.2	134	57.2	9-30-95	1.91	...	31507	Je	*0.08	0.13	0.59	1.56	2.30	2.34	3 Mo Sep	0.36	0.40	37
38	1959	Q0.07	1-2-96	12-13	0.26	0.28	0.21	9.23	50.1	10.2	9-30-95	8.24	...	10151	Dc	0.46	0.20	0.43	0.88	....	1.11	9 Mo Sep	0.64	0.87	38
39◆	1988	Q0.12	10-31-95	10-17	0.45	0.48	0.44	Book Value $15.38			9-30-95	40.9	...	7687	Dc	1.52	1.67	1.80	1.27	....	1.19	9 Mo Sep	1.11	1.03	39
40	....	None Since Public			...	Nil	....	3.81	77.8	35.0	4-01-95	3.10	...	5660	Mr	...	‡[70]0.26	0.63	1.48	....	1.48	6 Mo Sep	0.65	0.65	40
41◆	1929	Q0.26	1-2-96	11-29	h[71]1.01	1.04	0.91	37.0	406	184	10-01-95	75.0	...	28927	Je	1.26	1.78	2.43	□3.54	3.62	3.12	3 Mo Sep	0.39	d0.11	41
42	1993	Q0.02	10-30-95	10-12	0.08	0.08	0.08	387	1219	702	j12-31-94	20.5	...	±17391	Dc	p0.34	p0.84	1.03	0.20	....	0.20				42
43◆	....	None Since Public			...	Nil	....	16.5	66.3	103	9-27-95	103	...	76566	Je	0.41	0.51	0.69	0.83	0.98	0.94	3 Mo Sep	0.25	0.21	43
44	....	None Since Public			...	Nil	....	22.6	45.4	41.7	p9-30-95	183	...	★15928	Dc	...	...	...	p0.54	....	....	9 Mo Sep	n/a	p0.44	44
45	1900	Q0.75	2-1-96	1-3	2.96	3.00	2.92	2184	6610	4211	9-30-95	632	20	504567	Dc	3.95	□4.26	3.80	3.62	E5.10	4.05	9 Mo Sep	3.43	3.86	45
46	1968	Q0.50	3-1-96	1-31	2.00	2.00	2.00	Cv into 4.24 common				....	22	...	Dc	n/a	n/a	d28.39	b23.01	....	....				46
47	....	None Since Public			...	Nil	....	4.87	44.4	19.8	9-30-95	0.10	...	11470	Dc	0.30	d0.39	d0.25	0.68	....	0.54	9 Mo Sep	0.22	0.08	47
48	1987	[73]0.642	2-6-96	11-17	2.102	2.15	1.797	1163	2415	2320	j3-31-95	4429	...	955718	Mr	6.13	3.64	4.63	4.27	E7.00↓	5.31	6 Mo Sep	4.30	5.34	48
49	1987	[73]1.052	12-23-95	10-24	[73]2.291	2.29	2.387	1563	4675	3382	j12-31-94	2753	...	4338000	Dc	5.10	2.39	d0.98	2.65	E3.30	2.65				49
50	1917	0.806	2-6-96	11-17	2.548	2.83	1.755	188	8897	8589	j12-31-94	5705	12706	5502619	Dc	1.68	d1.80	2.03	5.41	E6.00	5.84	9 Mo Sep	3.97	4.40	50
51	1995	0.248	11-22-95	9-1	0.248	0.33	....	63.7	547	540	6-30-95	1273	...	★1715054	Je	...	...	...	p0.67	0.83	0.94	3 Mo Sep	0.17	0.28	51
52	1989	[73]0.497	1-25-96	11-28	1.25	1.42	0.32½	623	2877	1390	j4-01-95	386	...	2018287	Mr	d0.30	d0.99	0.51	3.71	....	5.72	6 Mo Sep	1.03	3.04	52

◆**Stock Splits & Divs By Line Reference Index** [1]2-for-1,'92,'95. [2]3-for-2,'92(twice),'93,'94. [3]1-for-6 REVERSE,'94. [14]2-for-1,'94. [21]2-for-1,'95. [31]1-for-2 REVERSE,'94. [32]3-for-1,'95. [33]5-for-4,'91,'92. [39]3-for-2,'94. [41]2-for-1,'94. [43]3-for-2,'91(twice),'93,'94.

¶ S&P 500 # MidCap 400 ✣ SmallCap 600 • Options

Index	Ticker	Name of Issue (Call Price of Pfd. Stocks)	Market	Com. Rank. & Pfd. Rating	Inst. Hold Cos	Inst. Hold Shs. (000)	Principal Business	Price Range 1971-93 High	1971-93 Low	1994 High	1994 Low	1995 High	1995 Low	Dec. Sales in 100s	December, 1995 Last Sale Or Bid High	Low	Last	%Div Yield	P-E Ratio	Total Return % Annualized 12 Mo	36 Mo	60 Mo
1•[1]	BTY	✔British Telecommn ADR[51]	NY,P	NR	112	4462	Telecomm'n svcs in UK	74⅞	6	71¾	53⅞	65½	52½	13615	58⅞	52½	56½	5.2	12	−0.7	2.7	4.9
✣2•[2]	BBTK	✔BroadBand Technologies	NNM	NR	90	6551	Mfr telecommunications equip	52¼	18	33½	11	31¾	15¾	30129	19¼	15¾	16¼	...	d	−45.8	...	...
3	BWY WS	Broadway Stores Wrrt[53]	NY	....	8	126	Operates department stores	5¾	1⅜	4½	1¾	2⅛	⅛	758	5/16	⅛	⅛	...	..	...	...	...
4	BKE	✔Brock Exploration[55]	AS,P	B−	12	1014	Oil & gas explor/prod'n	14¾	.01	4⅛	2 5/16	4½	2¾	624	3¾	3⅛	3B	...	43	−17.2	22.7	9.9
5	BWAY	✔Brockway Standard Hldgs	NNM	NR	25	2764	Mfr steel containers	...	...	...	...	17¾	14½	3049	16¼	15½	15½B	...	8	...	...	...
✣6•[3]	BROD	✔Broderbund Software	NNM,Ch	NR	215	18896	Dvlp personal computer softwr	29⅝	5½	47¼	15¾	78¾	42¼	247093	65½	53¼	60¾	...	32	30.6	41.6	...
7	BHP	✔Broken Hill Prop ADR[58]	NY,Ch,Ph	NR	68	4685	Petroleum,minerals,steel	44	3⅝	56¾	40⅞	59⅞	47¼	1765	57¾	54½	56½	2.6	32	13.0	27.2	20.5
8	BGL	✔Brooke Group Ltd	NY,Ch	NR	14	1297	Major cigarette mfr	12⅝	1¼	5⅜	1¼	14	3⅛	8129	9⅛	6⅜	9	3.3	1	...	...	...
#9	BU	✔Brooklyn Union Gas	NY,Ch,Ph	A−	174	14073	Natural gas dstr: NY City	28½	3⅝	28⅝	21½	29⅝	22	11611	29⅝	27¼	29¼	4.9	15	39.8	15.9	15.0
10	BKST	✔Brookstone Inc	NNM	NR	37	3506	Retail specialty consumer prd	18½	9½	16½	5⅞	9¼	4⅞	8037	9¼	6⅜	8¼	...	30	24.5	...	...
11•[4]	BTRE	✔Brooktree Corp	NNM	NR	64	9865	Design/dvlp integrated circuits	21	8	11¾	5¾	21¾	7¾	22596	13¾	10⅝	12⅛	...	17	47.0	7.5	...
12•[5]	BEAN	✔Brothers Gourmet Coffees	NNM	NR	34	2427	Wholesale/retail coffee prod	21¾	15¾	18	9¾	15¼	3½	15101	4⅜	3⅝	3⅝	...	d	−65.5	...	...
¶13	BF.B	✔Brown-Forman Cl'B'[60]	NY,B,Ch,P	A	258	25273	Large whisky marketer	30⅝	13/16	32½	26⅛	40¾	29⅜	8623	39½	36½	36½	2.8	16	19.8	13.4	12.9
14	BF.A	✔ Class 'A' vtg	NY,B,Ch	A	47	13178	imported wines,Lenox china	30⅛	13/16	32¼	26¾	40¼	29⅞	554	39⅜	37⅜	37⅜	2.8	17	24.1	14.7	13.3
¶15	BG	✔Brown Group	NY,Ch,Ph	B−	195	11388	Mfr/retailer shoes: fabric	44¼	4½	38⅞	30⅝	33⅜	12½	15394	15¾	13⅞	14¼	7.0	26	−50.7	−15.9	−2.9
16	BNS	✔Brown & Sharpe Mfg'A'	NY,Ch	C	24	2649	Measuring instr: mach tools	26⅛	2⅝	8	5¼	12⅛	5⅝	595	10¼	9½	10¼	...	d	60.8	15.7	1.4
¶17•[6]	BFI	✔Browning-Ferris Indus	NY,B,Ch,P,Ph	A−	713	142275	Solid & liquid waste mgmt sv	49¼	11/16	32⅞	24¼	40⅝	27⅛	163464	31⅞	28¼	29⅜	2.3	15	4.8	5.8	8.5
18	BFE	Browning-Ferris 7.25% 'ACES'[62]	NY	NR	45	4477	Automatic Com Exch Securities	...	...	...	...	39½	29¾	19251	34⅞	29¾	31⅜	8.2	..	...	...	...
19	BRT	✔BRT Realty Trust SBI	NY,Ch	NR	9	272	Real estate investment trust	27⅜	1 5/16	4⅞	3	4¾	3¼	1080	4½	4¼	4¼	...	12	25.9	15.6	12.3
¶20•[7]	BC	✔Brunswick Corp	NY,B,C,Ch,P,Ph	B	377	69224	Marine, recreation products	30¼	⅞	25⅜	17	24	16¼	58594	24	21¼	24	2.1	18	27.7	16.7	25.0
#21	BW	✔Brush Wellman	NY,B,Ch,Ph	B−	113	10114	Beryllium products & eq comp	44½	1 1/16	18⅝	13⅜	23⅝	14½	7989	17⅞	16	17¼	2.3	13	4.9	6.6	6.6
22	BTF	✔BT Office Prod Intl	NY,Ch,Ph	NR	31	6631	Distributor of office prod	...	...	...	...	16	11	10312	16	11⅝	16	...	..	...	...	...
23	BKI	Buckeye Cellulose	NY,Ph	NR	..	...	Mfr,mkt cellulose pulps	...	...	...	...	23	18½	12129	23	21	22	...	..	...	...	...
24	BPL	✔Buckeye Ptnrs L.P.	NY,Ch	NR	56	1088	Refined petrol'm pipeline sys	41⅝	17¾	41	30⅞	37	30	4408	36¾	33⅝	34⅛	8.2	9	8.4	14.1	15.6
25•[5]	BAE	✔Buenos Aires Embotell'a ADS[65]	NY	NR	110	7392	PepsiCo bottler Argentina	45½	22½	49¼	28¼	34⅞	19⅞	26137	26½	20¼	20⅝	2.2	17	−32.7	...	...
26	GBI	✔Bufete Industrial S.A. ADS[66]	NY,Ph	NR	40	2892	Engineer,constr'n svcs-Mexico	41	23	54¾	22½	29½	5	8054	15¾	12¾	15	...	d	−48.7	...	...
#27•[2]	BOCB	✔Buffets Inc	NNM	B+	136	25229	Operates buffet-style rest'ts	26¼	1 1/16	27½	7⅞	15½	8⅞	43458	15½	12⅞	13¾	...	17	41.0	−5.0	17.4
28	BFX	✔Buffton Corp	AS	B−	10	270	Elec prod, fittings, cable	9⅛	½	3¼	1⅛	2 7/16	1 1/16	1158	2 1/16	1½	1 11/16	...	d	22.7	24.5	14.0
29	BWAI	Builders Warehouse Assn	NSC	NR	1	.1	Dsgn/dvlp PC sys	129	42	51	10½	13½	2½	2930	9⅜	5⅜	6⅝	...	d	−41.1	...	...
30	BNBGA	✔Bull & Bear Group 'A'	NSC	B−	1	13	Invest mgmt,brokerage svcs	22⅛	5/16	3½	1½	2⅝	1¼	1002	1 15/16	1⅝	1⅝	...	6	8.3	−3.6	7.6
31•[8]	BCF	✔Burlington Coat Factory	NY,Ch,Ph	B+	96	13174	Off-price apparel stores	24½	3½	28⅜	10¼	14⅜	8½	20534	11⅝	10	10¼	...	37	−9.9	−11.9	18.4
#32•[9]	BUR	✔Burlington Industries	NY,Ph	NR	129	44975	Mfr fabrics/textile prod	16⅞	10⅞	17⅛	9¼	14¼	9⅝	15334	14¼	12¾	13⅛	...	13	32.9	−2.1	...
¶33•[5]	BNI	✔Burlington Northern SantaFe[68] [10]	NY,B,C	NR	624	106654	RR,o/g,pipelines,forest prod	84¼	6¾	66⅝	46½	84¾	45½	189220	82¾	73⅞	78	1.5	14	62.1	21.1	22.4
¶34•[11]	BR	✔Burlington Resources	NY,Ch,Ph	NR	571	88092	Oil & gas,explor,dvlp	53⅞	23⅜	49⅝	33⅛	42¼	33⅝	94655	41⅜	38¼	39¼	1.4	d	13.0	...	...
35	BRU	✔Burlington Res CoalSeamGasRty[70] [12]	NY	NR	29	845	Royalty int:natural gas prod'n	26½	20½	25	14⅛	17⅝	12¼	17238	14⅜	12¼	13⅛	11.6	8	−5.7	...	...
36	BPP	✔Burnham Pacific Prop	NY,Ch,Ph	NR	54	4668	Real estate investment trust	21½	5⅝	19⅛	12⅝	14½	9½	19508	10⅝	9½	9⅝	10.4	13	−14.5	−6.7	5.7
37•[5]	BBRC	✔Burr-Brown Corp	NNM	B−	110	8425	Mfr microelec data devices	12	2¾	10⅜	3⅞	41¼	6⅝	27686	28¾	17¾	25½	...	19	191	97.6	42.8
38	BOA	✔Bush Boake Allen	NY,Ch	NR	73	5861	Produce flavors & fragrances	...	...	27	15¼	32¾	23⅜	6159	32¾	26¼	27⅜	...	18	4.3	...	...
39	BSH	✔Bush Indus Cl'A'	NY,Ch	B	44	3491	Ready-to-assemble furniture	17⅛	1 9/16	26¾	13⅝	19⅞	10⅛	3091	19⅞	16⅞	19⅝	0.5	16	23.5	68.0	57.4
40	BOBJY	Business Objects ADS[72]	NNM	NR	42	4406	Dvp decision support software	...	...	38¼	17½	54	28¾	9441	49¼	38	48⅜	...	65	31.6	...	...
41	BRCP	Business Records Cp Hldg	NNM	B−	41	2242	Provides info & data svcs	33¾	2⅞	37	29⅜	43	32	1682	39½	37	39½	...	23	16.2	23.9	26.4
42	BUTL	✔Butler International	NNM	NR	16	649	Technical,aviation mgmt svc	48	1⅞	7⅛	4⅜	8½	4	14733	6¼	4¼	5⅜	...	20	−10.4	19.8	−0.9
✣43	BWIP	✔BW/IP Inc	NNM	NR	129	19777	Mfr fluid transfer & ctrl sys	30¾	13⅜	25¾	15	20¼	14	18853	16½	14½	16½	2.7	14	3.2	−14.0	...
44	CATX	✔C.ATS Software	NNM	NR	23	1565	Dvlp client/server software	...	...	...	...	16¼	6	6485	7½	6	7⅛	...	13	...	...	...
45•[13]	CCBL	✔C-COR Electrs[74]	NNM	B−	69	6446	CATV equip-amplifiers	10	15/16	36½	6¾	36¼	16¾	39660	30½	20½	23½	...	27	−31.9	49.4	66.7
46•[14]	CUBE	✔C-Cube Microsystems	NNM	NR	76	10558	Video compression solutions	...	...	12⅜	7½	65	7½	189954	65	39¾	62½	...	..	617	...	...
47	CPCL	✔C.P. Clare	NNM	NR	67	3260	Dvlp semiconductor equip	...	...	...	...	27⅞	16	10918	25¼	16½	20½	...	31	...	...	...
48	CTEX	✔C-TEC Corp	NNM	B−	68	6901	Tel svc in Penna/Cable TV	33½	1 7/16	31	18	32¼	19⅛	26168	32¼	26¾	31	...	67	61.0	30.3	16.4
49	CDTC	✔Cable Design Technologies	NNM	NR	63	3684	Mfr elec data transmisn cables	11¼	9¾	19¾	9¾	48¾	14½	11731	48¾	39½	44	...	30	167	...	...
50•[2]	CWP	✔Cable & Wireless ADS[75]	NY,Ch,Ph	NR	94	13695	Intl telecommunications svcs	25⅛	10⅞	25	16½	22¼	16¾	175311	22⅛	20	21⅛	2.2	23	22.3	13.2	14.1
51	TTV	✔Cabletel Communications	AS	NR	..	...	Dstr communications equip	...	...	9⅝	3	8¼	2½	3622	3⅛	2½	3	...	..	−61.3	...	...

Uniform Footnote Explanations-See Page 4. Other: [1]ASE,CBOE:Cycle 1. [2]CBOE:Cycle 2. [3]CBOE,P:Cycle 3. [4]Ph:Cycle 3. [5]CBOE:Cycle 1. [6]ASE:Cycle 3. [7]CBOE:Cycle 3. [8]Ph:Cycle 1. [9]ASE:Cycle 1. [10]Ch,P,Ph [11]Ph:Cycle 2. [12]Ph [13]ASE,CBOE:Cycle 3. [14]ASE,CBOE,NY:Cycle 2. [51]Full pay't ADR's equal 10 Ord par 25p. [52]Approx. [53]Wrrt(Pur 1 com at $17). [54]If com exceeds $25.50 30 con. trad. days. [55]Key Production plan acq, 0.69 com. [56]Fiscal Mar'93 & prior. [57]12 Mo Dec'93. [58]ADR's represent'g 4 com par A$1. [59]Stk dstr of MAI Sys Corp,'95. [60]Non-vtg. [61]■$1.02,'91. [62]Browing-Ferris Pur contract&5.125%U.S. Treasury Note. [63]®$0.35,'95. [64]100% non-taxable,'94. [65]Ea ADS rep 2 Ord Cl'B',p0.01. [66]Ea ADS rep 3 Ord Ptc Ctf(3'L'shrs&1'B'shr). [67]'94&prior represents Builders W'hse(Old). [68]Inst. Hldgs not avail. [69]®$4.38,'94. [70]Trust Units. [71]Incl $0.4665 non-taxable,'94. [72]Ea ADS rep 2 com,FF/1.00 par. [73]®$2.18,'94. [74]Plan SmallCap 600 listing:eff Dec 30. [75]Each ADS rep 3 ord shrs,50p. [76]®$0.35,'94.

Splits ◆	Dividends							Financial Position				Capitalization			Earnings $ Per Shr.							Interim Earnings			
	Cash Divs.	Latest Payment			Total $			Mil-$					Shs. 000		Years								$ per Shr.		
Index	Ea.Yr. Since	Period $	Date	Ex. Div.	So Far 1995	Ind. Rate	Paid 1994	Cash& Equiv.	Curr. Assets	Curr. Liab.	Balance Sheet Date	Lg Trm Debt Mil-$	Pfd.	Com.	End	1991	1992	1993	1994	1995	Last 12 Mos.	Period	1994	1995	Index
1	1985	[52]1.251	2-20-96	1-3	[52]2.934	2.95	2.704	1400	4367	5090	j3-31-95	3361	...	6234918	Mr	5.78	2.99	4.24	4.50	....	4.78	9 Mo Sep	2.37	2.65	1
2	....	None Since Public			...	Nil	....	75.0	82.4	28.5	9-30-95	0.06	...	13147	Dc	pd1.55	pd1.54	pd1.89	d1.85	....	d2.18	9 Mo Sep	d1.27	d1.60	2
3	....	Terms&trad. basis should			be checked in detail			Wrrts expire 10-8-99				....	...	2500	Ja	...	...	...	....	....	....	Co can accelerate expiration date[54]			3
4	....	None Since Public			...	Nil	....	2.39	4.28	1.22	9-30-95	9.43	...	3829	Dc	0.06	[56]0.22	Δ[57]0.08	0.04	....	0.07	9 Mo Sep	0.01	0.04	4
5	....	None Since Public			...	Nil	....	3.54	63.4	44.0	3-31-95	p50.1	...	★5991	Sp	...	...	...	p□0.95	P1.85	1.85				5
6◆	....	None Since Public			...	Nil	....	127	153	32.6	8-31-95	....	...	20632	Au	0.38	0.50	0.68	0.55	1.72	1.88	3 Mo Nov	0.57	0.73	6
7◆	1959	0.74¾	12-8-95	11-7	1.493	1.49	1.282	232	6105	5357	j5-31-95	6134	...	1936195	My	▲2.63	1.15	2.32	2.52	2.28	1.77	6 Mo Nov	2.14	1.63	7
8◆	1995	h[59]Q0.075	12-20-95	12-14	h[59]0.30	0.30	....	17.0	86.9	99.3	9-30-95	397	...	18497	Dc	d6.91	Δd4.39	Δ□d0.74	□8.90	....	8.26	9 Mo Sep	□0.92	0.28	8
9◆	1949	Q0.35½	2-1-96	12-28	1.39	1.42	1.35	40.5	310	211	9-30-95	721	72	48788	Sp	1.45	1.35	1.73	1.85	1.90	1.90				9
10	....	None Since Public			...	Nil	....	1.08	35.1	15.3	7-29-95	2.90	...	7675	Ja	Δp0.30	Δp0.56	pΔ0.88	0.66	....	0.28	9 Mo Oct	d0.48	d0.86	10
11	....	None Since Public			...	Nil	....	41.5	86.1	26.6	6-24-95	7.03	...	16603	Sp	0.64	0.76	1.73	0.12	P0.72	0.72				11
12	....	None Since Public			...	Nil	....	....	54.3	60.5	9-29-95	....	...	±11202	Dc	...	±p0.43	p0.54	0.20	....	d4.42	9 Mo Sep	d0.01	d4.63	12
13◆	1960	Q0.26	1-1-96	11-30	0.992	1.04	0.946	39.2	797	309	10-31-95	273	1178	±68996	Ap	±1.74	±1.76	±1.88	□±2.04	±2.15	2.26	6 Mo Oct	±1.12	±1.23	13
14◆	1945	Q0.26	1-1-96	11-30	0.992	1.04	0.946	....	....	...		....	...	28988	Ap	±1.74	±1.76	±1.88	□±2.04	±2.15	2.26	6 Mo Oct	±1.12	±1.23	14
15	1923	Q0.25	1-2-96	12-14	1.45	1.00	1.60	28.7	527	319	10-28-95	107	...	17932	Ja	□0.92	0.27	□d1.70	2.24	E0.55	0.30	9 Mo Oct	1.77	d0.17	15
16◆	....	0.08	12-31-90	12-6	...	Nil	....	5.01	203	121	9-30-95	58.1	...	±8695	Dc	±d0.86	±d1.74	±d0.45	±d2.37	....	d0.68	9 Mo Sep	±d1.71	±d0.02	16
17	1950	Q0.17	1-5-96	12-15	0.68	0.68	0.68	198	1422	1414	9-30-95	2411	...	212602	Sp	■[61]0.42	1.11	1.15	□1.52	1.93	1.93				17
18	1996	1.256	1-2-96	12-27	...	2.58	....	6-30-98 exch for Browing-Ferris com re-spec cond.				....	...	★10000	Sp	...	...	...	....	....	....				18
19	....	0.16	10-2-90	9-10	...	Nil	....	Equity per shr $7.72			9-30-95	43.7	1	7347	Sp	d1.42	Δd1.27	d0.56	d0.01	[63]0.37	0.37				19
20	1969	Q0.12½	12-15-95	11-17	0.50	0.50	0.44	260	1233	650	9-30-95	316	...	95948	Dc	d0.27	□0.41	□0.57	1.35	E1.37	1.28	9 Mo Sep	1.16	1.09	20
21	1972	Q0.10	1-2-96	12-13	0.34	0.40	0.23	23.3	192	62.6	9-29-95	17.8	...	16236	Dc	□d1.72	0.65	0.40	1.14	....	1.30	9 Mo Sep	0.86	1.02	21
22	....	None Since Public			...	Nil	....	5.69	292	148	9-30-95	76.2	...	33400	Dc	...	...	...	p0.27	....	....	9 Mo Sep	n/a	p0.32	22
23	....	None Since Public			...	Nil	....	3.66	142	43.3	p9-30-95	p215	...	★21310	Je	...	...	...	....	p1.67	....	3 Mo Sep	n/a	p0.62	23
24	1987	Q0.70	11-30-95	11-8	2.80	2.80	[64]2.80	17.0	39.9	26.9	9-30-95	214	...	12030	Dc	±2.51	□±2.85	□±3.43	±□3.96	....	3.94	9 Mo Sep	□3.01	2.99	24
25	1993	0.46	12-26-95	12-14	0.46	0.46	0.46	94.9	195	194	j9-30-94	111	...	±72500	Sp	...	1.45	1.56	±1.48	P±1.24	1.24				25
26	1994	0.088	7-25-94	7-12	...	Nil	0.088	30.6	310	205	12-31-94	26.8	...	262596	Dc	0.25	0.90	*Δ0.96	Δd0.02	....	d0.02				26
27◆	....	None Since Public			...	Nil	....	11.6	25.6	56.7	10-04-95	5.00	...	31161	Dc	0.38	0.51	0.66	0.71	E0.82	0.78	40 Wk Oct	0.60	0.67	27
28	....	None Since Public			...	Nil	....	0.01	5.43	2.61	9-30-95	....	...	5685	Sp	d0.59	d1.11	0.06	0.37	d0.22	d0.22				28
29◆	....	None Since Public			...	Nil	....	0.16	1.69	0.77	8-31-95	0.04	3	1207	My	0.48	0.48	d5.16	[67]d5.40	d0.27	d0.53	3 Mo Aug	0.22	d0.04	29
30	....	None since 1968			...	Nil	....	2.60	3.33	0.38	9-30-95	....	...	±1249	Dc	±d0.07	*±0.03	±0.32	±0.05	....	0.28	9 Mo Sep	±d0.05	±0.18	30
31◆	....	None Since Public			...	Nil	....	35.2	664	419	9-30-95	83.3	...	41149	Je	0.62	0.78	Δ1.05	1.12	0.37	0.28	3 Mo Sep	d0.18	d0.27	31
32	....	None Since Public			...	Nil	....	30.4	766	320	7-01-95	886	...	64913	Sp	0.38	□d2.42	*□1.19	□1.46	P1.05	1.05				32
33◆	1940	Q0.30	1-2-96	12-4	1.20	1.20	1.20	62.0	1414	2286	9-30-95	4164	6879	141876	Dc	□d3.96	□3.35	3.06	□[69]4.48	E5.65	5.41	9 Mo Sep	□2.97	□3.90	33
34◆	1988	Q0.13¾	1-2-96	12-13	0.55	0.55	0.55	19.8	234	315	9-30-95	1278	...	126599	Dc	1.54	1.95	1.96	1.20	Ed2.00	d1.96	9 Mo Sep	0.78	d2.38	34
35	1993	0.37½	12-14-95	11-30	1.524	1.52	1.881	Equity per shr $14.74			9-30-95	....	...	8800	Dc	...	p1.44	0.74	1.87	....	1.59	9 Mo Sep	1.43	1.15	35
36	1966	Q0.25	12-29-95	12-13	1.33	1.00	[71]1.41½	Equity per shr $11.93			9-30-95	148	...	17192	Dc	0.40	0.13	0.77	0.84	....	0.73	9 Mo Sep	0.69	0.58	36
37◆	....	None Since Public			...	Nil	....	82.8	187	65.7	9-30-95	1.95	...	16269	Dc	d0.67	0.07	0.19	0.45	....	1.38	9 Mo Sep	0.37	1.30	37
38	....	None Since Public			...	Nil	....	8.39	197	98.7	9-25-95	6.11	...	19215	Dc	...	...	p1.03	p1.33	....	1.55	9 Mo Sep	p1.02	1.24	38
39◆	1992	Q0.02½	11-20-95	11-2	0.10	0.10	0.064	1.96	55.0	25.3	9-30-95	11.0	...	±8764	Dc	±0.28	±0.32	±0.82	±1.29	....	1.23	9 Mo Sep	±0.93	±0.87	39
40	....	None Since Public			...	Nil	....	30.8	40.9	10.4	12-31-94	0.09	...	15678	Dc	d0.06	d0.06	0.04	0.34	....	0.74	9 Mo Sep	0.16	0.56	40
41	....	None Paid			...	Nil	....	36.2	86.7	26.1	9-30-95	0.52	...	6441	Dc	*1.04	Δ1.48	Δ0.53	[73]2.25	....	1.74	9 Mo Sep	1.71	1.20	41
42◆	....	None Since Public			...	Nil	....	4.38	90.1	31.0	9-30-95	56.6	2368	5994	Dc	d1.02	d1.07	d0.50	0.25	....	0.27	9 Mo Sep	0.23	0.25	42
43	1991	Q0.11	1-3-96	12-11	0.42	0.44	0.36	5.49	223	98.1	9-30-95	64.4	...	24275	Dc	1.38	□1.75	0.18	1.03	E1.16	1.02	9 Mo Sep	0.77	0.76	43
44	....	None Since Public			...	Nil	....	27.1	32.2	11.7	9-30-95	....	...	5805	Dc	d1.01	0.33	0.34	0.52	....	0.56	9 Mo Sep	0.38	0.42	44
45◆	....	None Since Public			...	Nil	....	1.38	61.1	32.8	9-29-95	2.01	...	9552	Je	d0.39	0.25	0.37	0.43	0.84	0.88	3 Mo Sep	0.23	0.27	45
46◆	....	None Since Public			...	Nil	....	....	85.4	20.7	9-30-95	★76.1	...	32234	Dc	...	...	pd0.02	0.16	E0.63	0.52	9 Mo Sep	0.09	0.45	46
47	....	None Since Public			...	Nil	....	9.04	44.3	25.6	9-30-95	4.10	...	★7607	Mr	...	...	...	pΔ0.31	....	0.67	6 Mo Sep	0.06	0.42	47
48	....	0.076	5-25-89	5-3	...	Nil	....	174	244	90.1	6-30-95	286	...	±27445	Dc	d0.75	d0.13	□d0.33	□±4.58	....	0.46	9 Mo Sep	□±4.91	±0.79	48
49◆	....	None Since Public			...	Nil	....	2.43	85.8	45.4	10-31-95	56.3	...	9719	Jl	...	...	p0.79	0.98	1.29	1.49	3 Mo Oct	0.30	0.50	49
50◆	1990	[52]0.153	3-11-96	12-8	0.449	0.46	0.399	991	2238	1745	j3-31-95	1340	...	2195402	Mr	0.78	1.08	1.05	0.56	....	0.93	6 Mo Sep	0.56	0.93	50
51	....	None Since Public			...	Nil	....	....	14.1	10.3	j9-30-95	0.57	...	4575	Dc	d0.19	d0.12	0.11	[76]0.37	....	j0.19	9 Mo Sep	0.28	0.10	51

◆**Stock Splits & Divs By Line Reference Index** [6]2-for-1,'94. [7]10%,'95. [8]No adj for stk dstr,'93. [9]3-for-2,'93. [13]3-for-1,'94. [14]3-for-1,'94. [16]4-for-3 in new Cl'B','88. [27]3-for-2,'91:2-for-1,'93. [29]1-for-4 REVERSE,'93:1-for-6 REVERSE,'95:1-for-2 REVERSE,'95. [31]3-for-2,'92,'93. [33]No adj for stk dstr Burlington Res'88. [34]No adj for stk dstr of El Paso Nat Gas,'92. [37]3-for-2,'95. [39]3-for-2,'94:5-for-4,'95. [42]1-for-6 REVERSE,'92. [45]2-for-1,'94. [46]2-for-1,'95. [49]To split 3-for-2,ex Jan 2. [50]2-for-1,'93.

¶ S&P 500 # MidCap 400 ✣ SmallCap 600 • Options

Index	Ticker	Name of Issue (Call Price of Pfd. Stocks)	Market	Com. Rank. & Pfd. Rating	Inst. Hold Cos	Inst. Hold Shs. (000)	Principal Business	Price Range 1971-93 High	1971-93 Low	1994 High	1994 Low	1995 High	1995 Low	Dec. Sales in 100s	December, 1995 Last Sale Or Bid High	Low	Last	%Div Yield	P-E Ratio	Total Return % Annualized 12 Mo	36 Mo	60 Mo
¶1•[1]	CS	✓Cabletron Systems	NY,Ch,Ph	B	452	48014	Mfr computer interconnectn eq	47⅝	2¾	53	33	87¾	37⅜	94395	82⅝	70⅝	81	...	27	73.7	34.3	79.2
2•[2]	CVC	✓Cablevision Sys'A'[52]	AS,Ch	C	108	9017	Operates CATV Systems	72	9⅞	67⅞	39	69¾	48¾	18351	58⅜	53⅜	54¼	...	d	9.6	16.7	28.7
3	Pr	8.50% [53]Dep CvExch Pfd([54]25.70)	AS	↑B	..	...		....	....	....	....	28⅝	25	33054	28⅝	26⅞	27¼	7.8	..	...	...	...
#4•[3]	CBT	✓Cabot Corp	NY,B,Ch,P	↑B+	246	22108	Carbon black: oil & gas	29¼	1 3/16	29¼	24⅜	58¾	28	23755	54⅝	46⅝	53⅞	1.3	12	90.3	38.1	...
✣5	COG	✓Cabot Oil & Gas 'A'	NY,Ch,Ph	NR	114	15638	Oil & gas explor,dev,prod'n	27	10¼	23¾	13⅜	17	12⅜	7714	15¾	14	14⅝	1.1	d	6.6	−5.4	−0.7
6	CACH	✓Cache, Inc	NNM	B−	17	1029	Women's apparel spec'ty strs	43⅝	½	8½	4¼	8¼	3¼	5495	3⅝	3⅜	3⅜	...	13	−34.1	−26.0	...
7	CACI	✓CACI Int'l	NNM	B	39	2701	Prof svs,analysis/computer	19¼	1/16	12	5⅝	13⅞	8¾	5092	12⅜	11½	11⅞	...	15	20.3	40.2	36.6
8	CADBY	✓Cadbury Schweppes ADS[57]	NNM	NR	54	4898	Soft drinks,candy,food prod	38⅜	6¾	32½	25	35⅜	24⅝	6460	34¾	32½	33¼	3.3	17	31.5	12.7	12.0
9	CADE	✓Cade Industries	NNM	B−	10	776	Aircraft engineer'g,mfg svcs	3	½	1⅛	9/16	⅞	½	6625	11/16	½	⅝	...	d	0.0	−10.6	−13.4
#10•[4]	CDN	✓Cadence Design Sys	NY,Ch,Ph	B	230	41641	Softwr for computer-aid-eng'g	23⅛	2⅜	14½	6⅞	42⅜	12⅞	58881	42⅜	33¼	42	...	34	212	43.5	22.2
11	CDMS	✓Cadmus Communication	NNM	B+	54	2437	Print'g & graphic arts svcs	28½	4⅛	19½	13½	29⅞	14½	9292	29⅞	25	27	0.7	21	70.4	47.6	34.5
12•[5]	CAER	✓Caere Corp	NNM	B	51	3089	Mfr info recognit'n softwr	24½	5½	19⅝	6¼	18¼	7⅛	29746	9½	7⅛	7⅛	...	65	−60.4	−26.9	−0.3
13	CGL.A	✓Cagle's Inc 'A'	AS,Ch	B	26	669	Poultry producer: food dstr	12½	5/16	22⅝	10¾	24⅝	13¾	707	15¾	13⅞	14	0.9	6	−21.4	34.6	54.7
14	CAWS	✓CAI Wireless Systems	NNM	NR	50	8647	Own/oper wireless cable sys	....	....	16½	7	16¼	7¼	28534	10¼	8⅝	9⅝	...	d	32.8	...	...
15•[6]	CLD	✓Caldor Corp	NY,Ch,Ph	D	114	11786	Retail-genl merchandise strs	35¼	12⅝	32½	21⅜	24¼	3¼	40662	4⅝	3¼	3¼	...	d	−85.2	−50.9	...
✣16•[7]	CGNE	✓Calgene Inc	NNM	C	54	6967	Recombinant-DNA plant tech	20⅝	4¼	15⅜	6⅜	9⅝	4¼	52722	5⅜	4¼	4⅝	...	d	−32.7	−37.1	−5.1
#17•[8]	CCC	✓Calgon Carbon	NY,Ph	NR	120	20014	Mkts activated carbons/svcs	30¾	5½	15⅜	9⅞	13¾	10	10182	12⅞	11⅝	12	e2.5	d	27.0	−9.9	−9.2
18	CLI	✓Cali Realty	NY,Ch	NR	80	8025	Real estate investment trust	....	....	17⅞	14⅞	22	15⅜	8636	22	19¾	21⅞	7.8	19	58.1	...	...
19	COOK	✓Calif Culinary Academy	NNM	NR	9	134	Oper chef training school	7½	5⅝	8⅛	5	8¼	4⅜	2164	7⅝	6½	7⅝	...	d	7.0	...	...
#20•[9]	CE	✓Calif Energy	NY	B−	161	27866	Dvlp geothermal energy pwr	21¾	1 5/16	19½	15¼	21½	15⅜	21571	20½	18⅜	19½	...	16	26.8	5.5	19.3
✣21•[3]	CAL	✓Calif Federal Bank'A'[63]	NY,B,Ch,P	C	126	31334	Savings & loan Calif/R.E. dev	210	5	16¾	9¼	16⅝	9½	35772	16	15	15¾	...	12	...	...	...
22	Pr	7 3/4% non-cm Cv Pfd'A'([65]25)	NY	B	22	649		27¼	16⅛	23	19½	25¼	19⅜	1199	24⅞	23⅞	24⅜	8.0	..	...	...	...
23	CFHC	✓Calif Finl Hldg	NNM	B	22	842	Savings & loan, California	19⅜	5⅞	19½	12	22	12	716	20⅞	20¼	20½	2.1	35	71.8	29.1	31.0
✣24•[7]	CMIC	✓Calif Microwave	NNM	B	108	10790	Electr commun transmiss eq	31¼	¼	38¼	16½	39¾	16¼	41977	21¾	16¼	16⅝	...	d	−56.1	0.3	18.5
25	CT	✓Calif REIT SBI	NY,B,P,Ch	NR	5	88	Real estate investment trust	14⅜	1⅝	2⅜	1⅝	1⅞	1⅛	802	1½	1⅛	1½	...	38	−7.7	−4.7	−1.5
26	CWT	✓Calif Water Svc	NY	A−	49	733	Water service in California	41¼	5⅜	41	29⅜	35¼	29⅝	1070	35¼	32⅝	32¾	6.2	15	11.2	6.5	11.1
27	CNEBF	Call-Net Enterprises'B'[66]	NNM	NR	18	5458	Long-dist telecomn,Canada	9	8⅞	10¼	3⅜	9¼	4	191	8½	7	8B	...	d	137	...	...
#28•[10]	ELY	✓Callaway Golf	NY,Ph	NR	231	25888	Develop,mfr golf clubs	16⅜	2¼	21¾	12⅛	22⅝	11¼	140354	22⅝	18½	22⅝	0.9	17	35.2	76.1	...
#29	CZM	✓CalMat Co	NY,Ch,P,Ph	B	94	11236	Cement,concrete,stone prod	46⅛	1 7/16	25⅝	16⅞	21⅜	16⅜	13875	18⅞	17	18¼	2.2	38	8.9	−4.0	1.6
30	CPP	✓Calprop Corp	AS,Ch	C	8	302	Home builder: rentals	10⅞	1/16	1½	½	1⅜	⅝	1700	15/16	⅝	13/16	...	41	29.9	−13.4	−26.8
31	CN	✓Calton,Inc	AS,Ch,P,Ph	NR	12	9007	Single-family home bldr	153¾	1 5/16	3⅛	⅝	1 1/16	5/16	10472	7/16	5/16	7/16	...	7	−53.4	−55.6	...
32	CADA	CAM Data Systems	NSC	NR	2	8	Cash register/inventory ctr sy	5¾	½	3¾	1⅞	4⅛	1⅞	532	4	3⅜	4	...	19	60.0	3.3	39.8
33	CWKTF	Cam-Net Communic Ntwk	NNM	NR	6	672	Long dist voice/data commn svc	14⅞	2 5/16	10	2¼	4⅜	⅝	105681	1⅝	⅝	13/16	...	d	−64.9	−59.3	−24.5
34	CBEX	✓Cambex Corp	NNM	↓C	19	1991	Mfr IBM-compatible equip	23½	1/16	6¼	3¼	13⅛	3⅜	13330	8⅞	6¾	7⅝	...	d	118	−21.9	13.9
35	CBJ	✓Cambior Inc	AS,To,Mo	NR	87	21332	Gold exploration/mining	....	....	16⅛	10¼	14⅛	9¼	5686	11¾	10⅜	10⅞	...	d	−3.3	...	...
36	WS.A	Wrrt(Pur 1 com $25[70]Cdn)	AS	....	5	61		....	....	2½	1	1½	7/16	20	7/16	7/16	⅜B	...	..	...	...	...
37	CBM	✓Cambrex Corp	AS,Ch	B	79	5333	Producer of specialty chems	24	4	27¼	19¾	43⅝	26⅝	5726	41⅜	36⅞	41⅜	0.5	15	58.5	35.6	60.7
✣38	CAM	✓Camco International	NY,Ch	NR	170	20718	Provides oilfield equip&svcs	17⅛	15	21⅝	16	28⅜	16⅝	17132	28⅜	23⅛	28	0.7	21	50.7	...	...
39	CPT	✓Camden Property Trust	NY	NR	119	11988	Real estate investment trust	27⅝	22	27	20⅛	25	20⅛	8075	24	20⅝	23¾	7.7	26	5.3	...	...
40	CAML	Camelot Corp	NSC	C	9	498	Publish,retail CD-Rom prod	....	2	1⅛	1 1/16	7⅞	1	48387	5⅛	3½	3⅝	...	d	225	17.6	10.2
41	CABP	✓Cameron Ashley Bldg Prod	NNM	NR	32	4223	Building materials distrib	....	....	18¾	9	16¼	7½	7861	10⅝	8¼	10¼	...	9	−28.1	...	...
42	CMRN	Cameron Financial	NNM	NR	11	1056	Savings & loan, MO	....	....	....	....	15½	10	3116	14¾	13¾	14⅜	...	..	...	...	...
43	CCH	Campbell Resources	NY,To,B,Ch,P,Mo	B−	38	37948	Natural resources, Canada	16⅞	¼	13/16	⅜	1⅛	9/16	79593	1⅛	13/16	1	...	..	77.9	42.7	23.8
¶44•[6]	CPB	✓Campbell Soup	NY,To,B,Ch,P,Ph	B	543	60701	Canned soup & other foods	45⅜	2¾	46	34¼	61¼	41	47626	61¼	55⅛	60	2.3	21	38.7	15.3	18.5
45	CMPO	✓Campo Electr Appliances/Comp	NNM	NR	20	1740	Retail consumer electronics	17¼	6¾	18½	7⅞	12⅞	2⅞	15005	4⅛	2⅞	3	...	d	−71.1	...	...
46•[11]	CM	Canadian Imperial Bk	To,Mo,Vc	↑B+	108	31666	Gen'l bkg,Canada & worldwide	37	8⅛	36¼	28	41⅜	31⅜	171017	41⅜	38¼	40⅝	3.9	10	26.3	20.3	...
47	CMW	Canadian Marconi	AS,To,B,Mo,Ch,Ph	B	19	1570	Avionics, telecommunications	23½	⅝	12¾	10	11	8⅝	282	10½	8⅞	10	...	..	−4.8	−0.2	6.4
48	CNI PP	Canadian Natl[75] Railway[76]	NY	NR	..	...	Railroad oper Canada & U.S.	....	....	....	....	15¾	14½	115565	15¾	14⅞	15	◆1.0	..	...	...	...
49	CXY	Canadian Occidental Petrol	AS,To,B,Ph	B−	106	13863	Oil,gas,chemical: metal	25¾	1 1/16	25¼	16	35⅜	21½	7627	35	31½	32¾	◆...	..	49.5	20.5	23.9
50•[12]	CP	Canadian Pacific,Ord[13]	NY,To,Mo,Vc,B,C	B−	282	154067	Transportation/Natural Res	24⅜	3½	18½	14	18⅞	13⅜	42427	18½	17⅛	18⅛	◆...	..	23.4	15.9	4.1
51•[14]	WINEA	✓Canandaigua Wine Cl'A'[79]	NNM,Ch	B	131	13830	Domestic wine producer	32	3	38½	20¼	53	29¾	41977	33½	29¾	32⅝	...	15	−14.1	25.5	46.9

Uniform Footnote Explanations-See Page 4. Other: [1]ASE,NY,P:Cycle 1. [2]CBOE:Cycle 3. [3]CBOE:Cycle 1. [4]ASE,CBOE:Cycle 2. [5]ASE:Cycle 2. [6]NY:Cycle 2. [7]ASE:Cycle 1. [8]Ph:Cycle 2. [9]P:Cycle 3. [10]ASE,CBOE,NY:Cycle 2. [11]Vc:Cycle 3. [12]Ph:Cycle 1,To:Cycle 2. [13]Ch,P,Ph [14]ASE,CBOE:Cycle 1. [51]®$2.24,'95. [52]Time Warner Inc plan acq. [53]Dep for 0.10 shr 8.50% Sr I cm Cv Exch Pfd. [54]Fr 11-1-99,scale to $25 in 2001. [55]Fr 1-8-96. [56]®$1.84,'94. [57]Each ADS rep 4 Ord par 25p. [58]Incl proceeds from sale of rts. [59]Fiscal Dec'92. [60]7 Mo Mar'94. [61]Incl current amts. [62]Fiscal Aug'93 & prior. [63]Approve form holding co, Cal Fed Bancorp. [64]Stk dstr,0.10 new Goodwill Partic shr. [65]Fr 3-31-96. [66]Non-vtg. [67]®$0.58,'93. [68]Dstr of 0.1 Cl B ptnrshp. [69]®$0.20,'95. [70]Fr 3-28-96 can be exercised by U.S. Citizens. [71]®$1.95,'94. [72]Incl $0.076 return of cap:$0.4896 non-tax,'94. [73]Excl restrcted com. [74]To be determined. [75]Installment Receipts(1st install't 60.2% Paid). [76]2nd (39.8% paid). [77]®$3.85,'94. [78]Pfd in M$. [79]0.10 vtg. [80]®$2.13,'95.

Index (Splits ◆)	Cash Divs. Ea.Yr. Since	Dividends: Latest Payment Period $	Date	Ex. Div.	Total $ So Far 1995	Ind. Rate	Paid 1994	Financial Position Mil-$: Cash& Equiv.	Curr. Assets	Curr. Liab.	Balance Sheet Date	Capitalization: Lg Trm Debt Mil-$	Shs. 000 Pfd.	Com.	Earnings $ Per Shr. Years End	1991	1992	1993	1994	1995	Last 12 Mos.	Interim Earnings Period	$ per Shr. 1994	1995	Index
1◆	....	None Since Public			...	Nil	....	260	534	120	8-31-95	....	....	71964	Fb	0.83	1.18	1.68	[51]2.27	E3.00	2.83	9 Mo Nov	1.63	2.19	1
2	....	None Since Public			...	Nil	....	Equity per shr Neg			9-30-95	3226	★14611	±23964	Dc	±d10.32	±d11.17	±d10.83	±d13.72	Ed13.00	d16.19	9 Mo Sep	±d7.82	±d10.29	2
3	1996	0.31⅞	1-2-96	12-13	...	2.125	....	Cv into 0.3707 Cl'A' com, $67.44[55]				....	12000	...	Dc	...	...	...	....	....	....				3
4◆	1931	Q0.18	12-8-95	11-21	0.64	0.72	0.54	34.5	681	441	6-30-95	314	75	37946	Sp	2.90	1.59	□0.90	[56]1.96	P4.35	4.35				4
5	1990	Q0.04	11-30-95	11-14	0.16	0.16	0.16	1.96	37.9	44.0	9-30-95	240	1826	22780	Dc	0.01	0.11	0.10	d0.25	....	d3.96	9 Mo Sep	d0.10	d3.81	5
6◆	....	None Since Public			...	Nil	....	0.69	22.1	13.0	9-30-95	6.10	...	9091	Dc	*0.04	*0.12	Δ0.42	0.53	....	0.26	9 Mo Sep	0.34	0.07	6
7	....	None Since Public			...	Nil	....	0.78	64.3	38.9	9-30-95	....	...	10100	Je	0.10	0.40	0.29	□0.60	0.77	0.80	3 Mo Sep	0.18	0.21	7
8◆	1985	0.325	12-1-95	9-22	[58]1.723	1.09	0.996	366	1434	1340	j12-31-94	404	1	833900	Dc	2.07	1.62	1.84	1.97	....	1.93	24 Wk Jun	0.79	0.75	8
9	....	None Paid			...	Nil	....	0.05	14.0	5.51	9-30-95	6.73	...	21686	Dc	0.17	0.12	Δd0.05	0.01	....	d0.01	9 Mo Sep	Nil	d0.02	9
10◆	....	8.6%Stk	6-7-88	5-26	...	Nil	....	125	213	193	9-30-95	7.81	...	53895	Dc	d0.37	0.80	d0.20	0.56	E1.25↓	1.11	9 Mo Sep	0.16	0.71	10
11	1941	Q0.05	12-5-95	11-15	0.20	0.20	0.20	0.13	88.4	56.3	9-30-95	53.9	...	★7531	Je	0.50	0.65	0.76	Δ0.79	1.21	1.29	3 Mo Sep	0.16	0.24	11
12◆	....	None Since Public			...	Nil	....	45.4	60.0	6.18	9-30-95	....	...	13232	Dc	0.54	0.68	d0.10	0.18	....	0.11	9 Mo Sep	0.23	0.16	12
13◆	1992	Q0.03	12-15-95	11-29	0.12	0.12	0.10	1.35	41.6	20.5	9-30-95	20.2	...	5023	Mr	0.36	Δ0.99	1.65	2.67	....	2.24	6 Mo Sep	1.33	0.90	13
14	....	None Since Public			...	Nil	....	Equity per shr $1.22			9-30-95	316	188	37829	Mr	...	p[59]d0.33	†[60]d0.61	d0.93	....	d1.67	6 Mo Sep	d0.24	d0.98	14
15	....	None Since Public			...	Nil	....	File bankruptcy Chapt 11				222	...	16964	Ja	p1.37	□2.54	□2.50	2.65	Ed2.50↓	0.06	9 Mo Oct	0.31	□d2.28	15
16	....	None Since Public			...	Nil	....	10.2	25.7	23.1	9-30-95	17.5	...	30264	Je	d2.54	d1.42	d1.13	d1.71	d1.04	d1.03	3 Mo Sep	d0.35	d0.34	16
17◆	1987	Q0.075	1-2-96	12-8	†0.76½	0.30	0.16	34.2	138	59.4	9-30-95	5.73	...	40419	Dc	0.94	□0.70	0.47	d0.21	....	d0.11	9 Mo Sep	0.28	0.38	17
18	1994	Q0.42½	1-19-96	1-2	1.636	1.70	0.135	Book Value $9.94			9-30-95	[61]118	...	p14494	Dc	...	...	p1.03	p1.11	....	1.17	9 Mo Sep	p0.85	0.91	18
19	....	None Since Public			...	Nil	....	1.79	5.66	5.70	9-30-95	0.33	...	3102	Je	p0.02	p0.36	□[62]0.46	Δd0.04	0.05	d0.10	3 Mo Sep	0.02	d0.13	19
20◆	....	4%Stk	1-17-91	12-11	...	Nil	....	Equity per shr $4.51			9-30-95	1958	...	50050	Dc	0.75	□0.92	Δ1.00	□0.95	....	1.20	9 Mo Sep	□0.77	1.02	20
21◆	....	h[64]....	7-28-95	7-31	h[64]...	Nil	....	Book Value $12.22			9-30-95	2851	5525	49200	Dc	d27.15	□d7.74	d5.98	□d3.82	E1.30	1.32	9 Mo Sep	□d4.15	0.99	21
22	1993	Q0.484	11-15-95	10-30	1.937	1.94	1.93¾	Cv into 0.952 Cl'A'com,$26.25				....	3800	...	Dc	...	...	...	....	....	....				22
23◆	1984	Q0.11	11-15-95	10-30	0.44	0.44	0.44	Book Value $18.05			9-30-95	121	...	4659	Dc	1.65	Δ1.62	2.04	0.96	....	0.58	9 Mo Sep	0.71	0.33	23
24	....	None Since Public			...	Nil	....	2.66	214	83.4	9-30-95	75.5	...	15848	Je	±0.93	±0.56	±0.98	±1.20	d0.51	d0.52	3 Mo Sep	0.32	0.31	24
25	1969	0.05	8-26-94	8-8	...	Nil	0.10	Equity per shr $3.07			9-30-95	8.35	...	9157	Dc	■d0.39	d1.13	d0.89	Nil	....	0.04	9 Mo Sep	Nil	0.04	25
26	1931	Q0.51	11-15-95	10-30	2.04	2.04	1.98	15.7	48.5	36.6	9-30-95	149	139	6259	Dc	2.42	2.18	2.70	2.44	....	2.23	12 Mo Sep	2.59	2.23	26
27	....	None Since Public			...	Nil	....	158	190	54.8	j12-31-94	140	...	±★49108	Dc	d0.65	0.18	d0.16	d1.62	....	jd2.38	9 Mo Sep	d0.68	d1.44	27
28◆	1993	Q0.05	11-20-95	10-26	0.20	0.20	0.10	80.7	218	84.2	9-30-95	....	...	68673	Dc	0.12	0.32	Δ[67]0.59	1.07	....	1.33	9 Mo Sep	0.80	1.06	28
29	1909	Q0.10	1-3-96	12-11	0.40	0.40	0.40	1.22	87.2	58.6	9-30-95	84.4	...	23166	Dc	0.81	□d0.45	Δ0.36	0.81	....	0.48	9 Mo Sep	0.56	0.23	29
30	....	0.03	6-30-81	6-4	...	Nil	....	Equity per shr $2.38			9-30-95	11.0	3571	4816	Dc	d2.63	Δd4.86	Δd0.70	d0.44	....	0.02	9 Mo Sep	d0.24	0.22	30
31◆	....	[68]....	12-28-87	12-29	...	Nil	....	Equity per shr $1.13			8-31-95	2.35	...	26371	Nv	±d25.60	±d22.80	n/a	0.16	....	0.06	9 Mo Aug	0.11	0.01	31
32	....	None Paid			...	Nil	....	3.02	5.39	2.05	9-30-95	....	...	1931	Sp	d0.25	0.33	0.37	0.14	[69]0.21	0.21				32
33	....	None Paid			...	Nil	....	0.12	13.5	24.6	j2-28-95	9.37	...	14692	Fb	d0.39	d0.78	d2.08	d1.94	....	jd1.94				33
34◆	....	None Paid			...	Nil	....	3.25	27.2	16.3	8-31-95	....	...	8914	Au	0.70	1.13	d0.28	0.07	d1.14	d1.14				34
35	1987	gS0.07	12-15-95	11-21	g0.14	0.14	g0.14	166	252	82.4	j3-31-94	122	...	★51587	Dc	0.45	d0.13	0.36	P0.05	....	jd0.01	6 Mo Jun	0.22	0.16	35
36	....	Terms&trad. basis should	be checked in detail					Wrrts expire 6-28-96				....	...	2750	Dc	...	...	...	....	....	....				36
37	1989	Q0.05	11-24-95	11-8	0.20	0.20	0.20	7.15	145	64.9	9-30-95	112	...	7443	Dc	±0.01	±1.27	1.64	[71]1.96	....	2.84	9 Mo Sep	1.41	2.29	37
38	1994	Q0.05	11-21-95	10-27	0.20	0.20	0.20	42.4	342	146	9-30-95	82.4	...	24154	Dc	...	pd1.75	□0.79	1.13	....	1.34	9 Mo Sep	0.85	1.06	38
39	1993	Q0.46	1-17-96	12-22	1.82	1.84	[72]1.72	Book Value $18.68			9-30-95	[61]262	...	14515	Dc	...	p0.42	p0.58	p0.82	....	0.90	9 Mo Sep	p0.55	0.63	39
40	....	None Paid			...	Nil	....	0.65	1.43	1.08	7-31-95	....	1189	[73]12772	Ap	d0.01	d0.36	d0.24	d0.27	d0.35	d0.34	3 Mo Jul	d0.06	d0.05	40
41	....	None Since Public			...	Nil	....	3.19	136	55.5	7-31-95	33.9	...	8711	Oc	...	0.67	1.14	1.40	P1.15	1.15				41
42	1995	0.07	10-27-95	10-11	0.07	[74]....	....	Book Value $15.80			6-30-95	....	...	3027	Sp	...	...	...	p0.67	....	....	9 Mo Jun	n/a	p0.53	42
43	....	2%Stk	6-8-84	5-21	...	Nil	....	29.0	42.2	6.36	j9-30-95	10.6	...	124142	Dc	0.03	d0.01	d0.03	0.05	....	j0.09	9 Mo Sep	0.02	0.06	43
44◆	1902	Q0.34½	1-31-96	1-10	1.24	1.38	1.12	69.0	1969	2514	10-29-95	852	...	249138	Jl	1.58	1.95	□1.02	2.51	2.80	2.89	3 Mo Oct	0.79	0.88	44
45	....	None Since Public			...	Nil	....	3.32	89.2	70.7	8-31-95	20.3	...	5567	Au	...	p0.45	p0.68	0.91	□d0.19	d0.19				45
46	1890	g0.40	1-29-96	12-22	g1.48	1.60	g1.32	Book Value $30.48			j10-31-94	3441	55501	p216286	Oc	3.93	d0.59	2.99	3.52	P4.18	j4.18				46
47	1972	g0.07	12-7-94	11-14	...	Nil	g0.21	208	341	78.8	j3-31-95	8.11	...	23938	Mr	1.18	1.01	1.31	0.20	....	j0.29	6 Mo Sep	d0.19	d0.10	47
48	....	Plan qtly div			...	0.20	....	....	1229	1540	j9-30-95	p1303	...	★82259	Dc	...	...	...	p[77]4.06	....	....	9 Mo Sep	n/a	pd13.14	48
49	1975	gQ0.12½	1-1-96	12-7	g0.42½	0.50	g0.40	55.5	307	261	j9-30-95	615	...	67387	Dc	0.35	0.26	0.10	1.44	....	j2.07	9 Mo Sep	1.00	1.63	49
50	1944	gQ0.12	1-29-96	12-22	g0.32	0.48	g0.32	1287	2619	2162	j12-31-94	4748	[78]15	341800	Dc	d2.87	d1.50	d0.60	1.16	E1.45	j0.78	9 Mo Sep	0.87	0.49	50
51◆	....	None Since Public			...	Nil	....	4.18	402	175	8-31-95	199	...	±19612	Au	±0.84	±1.08	±1.30	±0.74	±[80]2.14	2.14				51

◆**Stock Splits & Divs By Line Reference Index** [1]2.5-for-1,'94. [4]2-for-1,'94:To split 2-for-1,ex Mar 25. [6]1-for-4 REVERSE,'93. [8]5-for-2,'91. [10]3-for-2,'95. [12]2-for-1,'92. [13]5-for-4,'94:2-for-1,'95. [17]2-for-1,'91. [20]Adj to 4%,'91(ex '90). [21]1-for-5 REVERSE,'93. [23]10%,'93. [28]2-for-1,'93,'94,'95. [31]Reorg,1-for-20 REVERSE,'93. [34]3-for-2,'91:2-for-1,'92. [44]2-for-1,'91. [51]3-for-2,'91,'92.

¶ S&P 500 # MidCap 400 ✣ SmallCap 600 • Options Index	Ticker	Name of Issue (Call Price of Pfd. Stocks)	Market	Com. Rank. & Pfd. Rating	Inst. Hold Cos	Inst. Hold Shs. (000)	Principal Business	Price Range 1971-93 High	1971-93 Low	1994 High	1994 Low	1995 High	1995 Low	Dec. Sales in 100s	December, 1995 Last Sale Or Bid High	Low	Last	%Div Yield	P-E Ratio	Total Return % Annualized 12 Mo	36 Mo	60 Mo
1	CTH.EC	✔Cancer Treatment Hldgs	ECM	NR	5	77	Oper radiation treatment ctrs	9½	1	3⅝	1⅜	4¼	1 9/16	871	2⅝	2¼	2½	...	36	42.9	−23.1	−5.1
2	CLZR	✔Candela Corp[51]	NNM	C	12	1675	Mfrs scientific/medic lasers	25	1 11/16	4¼	1⅜	5⅞	1 7/16	3274	5¼	4	4⅞	...	d	225	−14.3	−25.9
3	CNMCD	✔Canmax Inc(New)	NSC	NR	7	352	Retailer softwr/hardwr tech	16¼	16¼	19⅜	4⅜	7¾	2	7197	4	2	2½	...	d	−52.9	...	...
4	CANXA	✔Cannon Express'A'	NNM	B+	15	730	Trucking-gen'l commodities	14	1 9/16	16	10¾	16	8½	147	10½	8½	9B	...	8	−23.4	10.1	12.9
5	BIKE	✔Cannondale Corp	NNM	NR	64	4214	Mfr bicycles/accessories	...	...	14½	9¾	19½	10¼	3927	17⅝	14	15⅞	...	10	54.9	...	...
6	CANNY	✔Canon Inc ADR[54]	NNM	NR	52	1648	Business mach, cameras,optic	71⅛	1 1/16	92½	68⅝	95⅜	72	1330	94¼	88¾	91⅜	0.6	51	7.7	18.8	15.2
7	CAB	✔Capco Automotive	NY,Ph	NR	46	7594	Mfr manual transmissions	...	...	14¼	9⅝	11¾	6⅛	10582	8⅛	6⅛	7⅛	2.2	9	−40.1	...	...
8	CCBT	✔Cape Cod Bank & Trust	NNM	B	21	562	Comm'l bkg,Massachusetts	52	2 7/16	32	20½	41¾	24¾	125	41¼	39½	39½	3.4	10	60.3	26.6	33.8
9	CABK	✔Capital Bancorp[56]	NNM	NR	16	493	Commercial banking, Missouri	23	12	24¾	19	38	21½	730	38	36	37	2.1	14	76.7	35.7	...
¶10•[1]	CCB	✔Capital[57]Cities/ABC[58]	NY,B,Ch,P,Ph	A	874	118921	Radio/TV brdcstg:publish'g	64⅜	13/16	86½	60¼	126⅞	80¾	62221	126⅛	122⅜	123⅜	0.2	25	45.4	34.5	21.7
11•[2]	COF	✔Capital One Financial	NY	NR	221	35684	Bank card issuer/svcs	...	...	16⅝	13⅞	29⅝	15⅜	48163	26⅞	22¾	23⅞	1.3	14	50.7	...	...
12	CPH	✔Capital Pacific Hldgs	AS,Ph	NR	12	556	Builds single family homes	14⅞	¾	4⅛	1⅞	3⅜	1⅞	686	3¼	2⅛	3⅛	...	..	41.6	16.8	8.4
✣13	KRE	✔Capital Re	NY	NR	80	5796	Financial debt reinsurer	29	17⅛	27⅜	18½	31⅝	22	1749	31⅝	29⅞	30¾	0.8	11	14.8	14.6	...
14	CRA	Cap Rlty Inv TaxExFdLP I[62]	AS	NR	3	23	First mortgage loan svcs	13¼	10⅞	12¾	9⅜	13½	9⅞	809	13¼	12½	13	8.2	27	45.8	...	...
15	CRB	Cap Rlty Inv TaxExFdLP II[62]	AS	NR	3	12	First mortgage loan svcs	12⅞	9¼	12⅜	9⅛	13⅛	9⅝	766	12¾	12	12⅝	8.5	21	44.0	...	...
16	CRL	Cap Rlty Inv TaxExFdLP III[63]	AS	NR	7	31	Inv in tax exempt bonds	15	11	13⅜	9⅛	14	10⅛	1062	13¾	13⅛	13½	9.5	19	54.2	...	...
✣17	CAF	✔Capitol American Finl	NY	NR	57	3887	Health & accident insurance	32	16¾	24⅞	20¾	24⅜	19½	3464	22¾	20⅜	22⅝	1.6	9	4.5	−6.5	...
18	CATA	✔Capitol Transamerica	NNM	B+	26	1233	Ins hldg:property & casualty	18⅛	1/16	17¼	13⅜	20½	13⅞	2045	20½	17½	20¼	e1.8	13	42.7	18.7	27.0
19	KAP	CapMAC Holdings	NY	NR	..	...	Finl guaranty insurance	...	...	...	...	25½	20	35276	25½	20	25⅛	0.3	13	...	...	...
20	CMO	✔Capstead Mortgage	NY,Ch,Ph	NR	76	8540	Mtge investments REIT	28⅝	7⅞	28⅛	11⅛	24½	11⅛	11297	24½	22⅛	22⅞	7.2	14	126	6.6	32.7
21	Pr A	$1.60 cm Cv Pfd([65]16.40)	NY	NR	1	2		38½	10½	37¼	15	32½	15¾	61	32½	29¼	29B	5.5	..	...	...	...
22	Pr B	$1.26 cm Cv Pfd([66]12.50)	NY	NR	24	1941		15	13	14¾	9¾	13½	10⅛	7553	13⅝	12⅞	13	9.7	..	...	...	...
23	CCT	✔Capstone Capital	NY,Ch,Ph	NR	21	1648	Real estate investment trust	...	...	18⅛	14¾	19⅜	15¼	22013	19⅜	18	19⅛	9.3	..	34.0	...	...
24	DOSE	✔Capstone Pharmacy Svc	NNM	C	20	633	Pharmaceutical prod/svcs	11⅜	⅞	5¼	2 1/16	8⅛	2¾	13788	8⅛	5¾	7½	...	d	90.5	12.6	28.7
25	CSH	✔Capsure Holdings	NY	NR	67	6781	Insurance:spcl prop & casualty	19⅝	4¼	16⅛	12⅛	18⅛	12⅜	3059	18⅛	14	17⅝	...	16	25.9	9.0	30.0
✣26	CSAR	✔Caraustar Industries	NNM	NR	104	13852	Mfr recycled paperboard/prd	20¼	13¼	22½	15	23	15¾	13185	21½	19¼	20	2.4	13	−9.2	6.2	...
27	CGGI	✔Carbide/Graphite Group	NNM	NR	39	3911	Mfr graphite electrode pds	...	...	...	...	17¼	12¼	9154	16	13¾	14⅜	...	4	...	...	...
#28•[3]	CAH	✔Cardinal Health	NY,Ch	A−	319	26769	Wholesale dstr drug,hlth prod	38⅝	3⅜	48¼	33¼	58⅛	41½	41843	57¼	50⅞	54¾	0.2	26	19.3	33.0	26.3
29	CARH	✔Career Horizons	NNM	NR	58	3654	Temporary personnel service	...	...	21	13¾	33¾	15½	9022	33¾	27¾	33¾	...	25	114	...	...
30•[4]	CK	✔Caremark International	NY	NR	242	47863	Alternate site hlth care svcs	20¾	11⅞	26¾	15¾	23⅜	16	71884	19⅞	17¾	18⅛	0.2	17	4.5	7.3	...
31	CTND	✔Caretenders Healthcorp	NNM	NR	11	595	Home health svcs/adult care	36¼	4⅝	15⅝	6½	9	5⅛	3149	6¾	5⅝	5⅞	...	13	−18.2	−23.5	−13.1
#32	CSL	✔Carlisle Cos	NY,Ch,Ph	B+	124	7997	Rubber, plastics, metal prod	34½	1 3/16	36⅛	30¼	43⅝	34½	3891	42¾	39⅞	40⅜	2.2	15	16.6	23.5	26.0
33	CPA	✔Carlisle Plastics Cl'A'	NY,Ch,Ph	NR	31	3065	Mfr plastic bags/containers	12⅞	3⅜	8⅞	3¾	6⅜	4⅛	3555	4⅞	4⅜	4½	...	30	9.1	−5.0	...
34	CCTVY	✔Carlton Communic ADS[70]	NNM	NR	23	1477	Mfrs TV prod in U.K./U.S.	32⅛	10⅞	30⅞	24¾	34⅜	27¼	2851	31¼	29	30⅜	2.5	18	10.9	12.6	19.1
35	CCMPr	Carlton Commun[71]'X-CAPS'([72]26)	NY	A−	..	...	Mfr TV prod in U.K./U.S.	25⅜	23⅝	25¼	19⅛	24⅞	20⅛	1904	24⅞	23⅞	24⅝	8.1	..	...	...	...
36	KML	✔Carmel Container Sys	AS,Ch	NR	2	.3	Israeli packaging mfr	14⅛	1¾	11⅞	7⅜	17	7	382	12¾	9⅛	9⅛	...	5	19.7	17.5	32.3
✣37	CKE	✔Carmike Cinemas'A'	NY	B	119	7386	Oper motion picture theatres	20¾	5	24⅜	16⅜	25½	18¾	12701	25¼	22	22½	...	18	1.7	16.1	19.1
38•[5]	CCL	✔Carnival Corp'A'	NY,Ch,P,Ph	B+	331	111714	Cruise ships,hotel,casino	25	4⅛	26⅛	19⅛	27⅛	20	105289	26	22¾	24⅜	1.5	15	20.5	15.9	30.5
39	CAFC	✔Carolina First Corp	NNM	NR	16	456	Bank hldg co, South Carolina	13⅜	6⅜	15	10⅞	19⅜	12⅛	8098	19⅜	15¼	17½	1.6	d	45.3	26.0	25.5
¶40	CPL	✔Carolina Pwr & Lt	NY,B,C,Ch,P,Ph	A−	393	47700	Elec serv No & So Carolinas	34⅝	5¼	30	22½	34⅝	26⅛	42743	34⅝	32¾	34½	5.3	14	36.8	14.1	15.2
41	CPD	Carolina Pwr & Lt 8.55%[74]'QUICS'[75]	NY	....[76]	2	22	Elec serv No & So Carolinas	...	...	...	...	27¼	25	1394	27¼	26¼	26⅞	8.0	..	...	...	...
#42	CRS	✔Carpenter Technology	NY,Ch,P,Ph	B+	177	12286	Stainless,high-alloy steels	29⅛	3⅞	33¼	26⅝	44	26⅝	10400	43⅛	39⅜	41⅛	3.2	13	57.0	22.1	18.4
43	CGF	✔Carr-Gottstein Foods	NY,Ph	NR	39	6489	Food,drug retailer-Alaska	15⅝	10¼	10⅝	5½	8⅝	5⅛	11645	5¾	5⅛	5⅝	...	11	−10.0	...	...
44	CRE	✔Carr Realty[78]	NY,Ch	NR	83	7686	Real estate investment trust	27½	20	24½	17⅜	24⅝	16¾	8766	24⅝	21⅜	24⅜	7.2	24	49.3	...	...
45	CARN	✔Carrington Laboratories	NNM,Ch	B−	36	1501	Mfr pharmac'l prod/drug R&D	41¼	3¼	14¼	8	40¾	10	19662	32½	21¾	31	...	d	199	37.7	37.8
46•[6]	CRP	✔Carson Pirie Scott	NY,Ch	NR	80	13401	Oper retail department strs	14¾	10¾	22¼	14⅛	20¾	15	9243	20¾	19	19⅞	...	5	12.0	...	...
#47•[5]	CAR	✔Carter-Wallace	NY,B,Ch,Ph	B	116	15190	Drug and toiletry products	45⅞	13/16	26⅜	9⅞	13⅞	10⅛	15412	13⅛	10⅞	11⅜	1.4	18	−13.8	−30.2	−7.1
48•[5]	CSCC	✔Cascade Communications	NNM	NR	136	19336	Mfr data commun ntwk prd	...	...	32½	7½	92½	28⅝	159403	92½	67	85¼	...	..	167	...	...
49	CASC	✔Cascade Corp	NNM	B+	79	4943	Hydraulically actuated equip	12¾	⅜	12⅝	8⅞	17¼	11⅜	4277	14¾	13½	14	†2.6	10	23.3	8.4	18.8
✣50	CGC	✔Cascade Natural Gas	NY,Ch,Ph,P	B	55	1561	Nat'l gas dstr: Wash, Ore	19½	3⅜	18⅛	12¾	17½	13	3656	17½	15¾	16	6.0	21	15.8	7.4	12.9
51•[7]	CSE	✔Case Corp	NY,Ph	NR	218	50258	Mfr farm,constr'n equipment	...	...	21½	18¼	45⅞	20½	54764	45⅞	39½	45¾	0.4	11	125	...	...
✣52•[5]	CASY	✔Casey's Genl Stores	NNM	B+	149	17386	Convenience-style gen'l strs	12⅜	1¾	15⅜	10⅜	25⅜	14⅜	34234	23¼	19⅛	21⅞	0.5	22	46.5	38.6	53.3

Uniform Footnote Explanations-See Page 4. Other: [1]CBOE:Cycle 2. [2]CBOE:Cycle 3. [3]ASE:Cycle 3. [4]ASE,CBOE,NY,Ph:Cycle 1. [5]CBOE:Cycle 1. [6]Ph:Cycle 2. [7]ASE:Cycle 1. [51]Formerly Candela Laser. [52]Fiscal Aug'92 & prior. [53]10 Mo Jun'93. [54]ADRs rep 5 shrs com par 50 yen. [55]Approx. [56]Union Planters Corp plan acq, 1.185 com. [57]Vote Jan 4 Walt Disney Co mgr,1 com & $65 cash. [58]Plan S&P 500 delisting:eff Jan 5. [59]Incl curr amts. [60]Southmark Corp owns 87.3%. [61]Subsid Pfd in $M. [62]Beneficial Assignee Ctf. [63]Sr'A'Beneficial Assignee Ctf. [64]®$2.00,'94. [65]From 11-7-94. [66]Fr 12-3-97. [67]6 Mo Dec,'94. [68]Fiscal March'93 & prior. [69]12 Mo Jun'93. [70]ADS's equal 2 Ord par 25p. [71]Co opt exch for pref shrs re-specified cond. [72]Fr 10-7-98,scale to $25 in 2003. [73]Incl shrs hld by subsid. [74]Quarterly Income Capital Securities. [75]Sr'A' Subordinated Deferrable Int Debs. [76]Rated A- by S&P. [77]®$2.70,'95. [78]Plan name chg,CarrAmerican Realty. [79]Incl $0.4376 non-taxable,'94. [80]Fiscal Nov'94 & prior. [81]24% owned by Tenneco Inc. [82]®$0.68,'94.

Splits ◆ Index	Cash Divs. Ea.Yr. Since	Dividends: Latest Payment Period $	Date	Ex. Div.	Total $ So Far 1995	Ind. Rate	Paid 1994	Financial Position Mil-$ Cash& Equiv.	Curr. Assets	Curr. Liab.	Balance Sheet Date	Capitalization Lg Trm Debt Mil-$	Shs. 000 Pfd.	Com.	Earnings $ Per Shr. Years End	1991	1992	1993	1994	1995	Last 12 Mos.	Interim Earnings Period	$ per Shr. 1994	1995	Index
1	....	None Since Public			...	Nil	....	0.93	4.39	1.85	8-31-95	0.17	...	3496	My	Nil	Δ0.11	d0.03	d0.09	0.15	0.07	3 Mo Aug	0.11	0.03	1
2	....	None Since Public			...	Nil	....	3.04	14.1	6.25	9-30-95	0.32	...	5239	Je	*0.27	*0.51	d1.78	0.12	d0.30	d0.07	3 Mo Sep	d0.25	d0.02	2
3◆	....	None Paid			...	Nil	....	0.33	1.97	2.55	7-31-95	0.25	...	4935	Oc	d0.30	d0.60	d0.30	d1.54	Pd0.79	d0.79				3
4◆	....	None Since Public			...	Nil	....	20.6	31.4	15.5	9-30-95	39.4	...	±4328	Je	0.48	□0.49	0.47	Δ±0.86	±1.35	1.18	3 Mo Sep	±0.37	±0.20	4
5	....	None Since Public			...	Nil	....	2.85	68.7	24.9	9-30-95	5.50	...	8529	Je	0.28	[52]d1.08	□[53]d0.73	d0.73	□1.18	1.64	3 Mo Sep	d0.43	0.03	5
6	1949	[55]0.258		12-26	0.568	0.52	0.525	6030	14700	9463	12-31-94	3123	...	830103	Dc	2.60	1.87	1.20	1.80	....	1.80				6
7	1995	Q0.04	12-15-95	11-29	0.16	0.16	....	26.4	89.1	42.8	9-30-95	....	...	11061	Dc	0.10	0.81	1.22	1.17	....	0.77	9 Mo Sep	0.78	0.38	7
8	1938	Q0.34	10-31-95	10-19	1.12	1.36	0.35	Book Value $23.44			12-31-94	....	...	2265	Dc	2.08	0.76	1.78	3.41	....	3.99	9 Mo Sep	2.27	2.85	8
9	1941	Q0.19	11-2-95	10-24	0.74	0.76	0.69	Book Value $18.01			9-30-95	26.0	28	3087	Dc	2.29	1.80	2.06	1.90	....	2.64	9 Mo Sep	1.30	2.04	9
10◆	1976	Q0.05	12-29-95	12-13	0.25	0.20	0.11	1310	2962	1290	10-01-95	514	...	153892	Dc	□2.23	□2.35	□2.85	4.42	E5.00	4.77	9 Mo Sep	2.86	3.21	10
11	1995	Q0.08	11-22-95	11-3	0.24	0.32	....	Equity per shr $8.48			9-30-95	[59]2492	...	66157	Dc	...	...	p1.37	1.44	....	1.73	9 Mo Sep	1.04	1.33	11
12	....	None Since Public			...	Nil	....	Equity per shr $4.02			8-31-95	145	...	[60]14995	Fb	d4.13	d6.05	Δ0.04	Δ0.12	....	Nil	9 Mo Nov	Δ0.12	Nil	12
13	1992	Q0.06	12-28-95	12-19	0.21	0.24	0.20	Equity per shr $26.15			9-30-95	90.7	[61]75	14805	Dc	2.14	2.16	2.43	2.69	....	2.91	9 Mo Sep	2.06	2.28	13
14	1994	0.09	2-29-96	12-27	1.04	1.07	1.00	Equity per shr $13.77			9-30-95	....	...	2280	Dc	...	0.12	0.20	0.44	....	0.48	9 Mo Sep	0.30	0.34	14
15	1994	0.09	2-29-96	12-27	1.04	1.07	1.00	Equity per shr $14.32			9-30-95	....	...	3239	Dc	...	0.09	Δ0.37	0.42	....	0.60	9 Mo Sep	0.26	0.44	15
16	1993	0.10	2-14-96	12-27	1.31	1.28	1.631	Equity per shr $15.15			9-30-95	....	...	5258	Dc	...	0.42	0.49	0.61	....	0.73	9 Mo Sep	0.37	0.49	16
17	1993	Q0.09	11-16-95	10-31	0.36	0.36	0.32	Equity per shr $15.04			9-30-95	30.0	...	17454	Dc	Δ1.77	2.19	2.36	2.50	....	2.51	9 Mo Sep	1.95	1.96	17
18◆	1984	†0.10	1-15-96	12-26	0.345	0.364	†0.40	Equity per shr $11.80			9-30-95	....	...	7374	Dc	1.28	1.16	1.60	1.26	....	1.53	9 Mo Sep	1.06	1.33	18
19	....	Plan qtly div			...	0.08	....	Equity per shr $17.54			9-30-95	15.0	...	★15478	Dc	...	p0.62	0.96	1.23	....	1.88	9 Mo Sep	0.56	1.21	19
20◆	1985	0.56	12-29-95	12-15	1.64	1.64	2.14	Equity per shr $12.64			9-30-95	4687	31130	23070	Dc	1.95	2.25	2.45	[64]2.04	E1.65↑	1.52	9 Mo Sep	1.60	1.08	20
21	1989	Q0.40	12-29-95	12-15	1.60	1.60	1.60	Cv into 0.9 com				....	623	...	Dc	b1.67	b1.12	b1.11	b1.09	....	....				21
22	1992	0.10½	12-29-95	12-15	1.26	1.26	1.26	Cv into 0.3196 com				....	30277	...	Dc	...	b1.12	b1.11	b1.09	....	....				22
23	1994	Q0.44½	11-15-95	10-30	1.74	1.78	0.42½	Equity per shr $16.29			9-30-95	p117	...	★9535	Dc	...	...	...	‡[67]0.80	....	....	9 Mo Sep	n/a	1.15	23
24	....	None Paid			...	Nil	....	4.95	23.1	8.61	8-31-95	4.25	...	13324	Fb	0.31	d0.26	d0.14	d1.86	....	d1.30	6 Mo Aug	d0.61	Δd0.05	24
25	....	None Paid			...	Nil	....	Equity per shr $9.61			9-30-95	34.0	...	15409	Dc	0.79	0.91	1.08	0.95	....	1.09	9 Mo Sep	0.71	0.85	25
26	1993	Q0.12	1-8-96	12-18	0.42	0.48	0.36	20.1	126	61.7	9-30-95	83.4	...	25584	Dc	0.99	Δ1.01	Δ1.20	1.38	....	1.57	9 Mo Sep	0.96	1.15	26
27	....	None Since Public			...	Nil	....	37.2	144	35.5	10-31-95	98.6	...	7391	Jl	...	...	0.57	□d0.11	3.71	3.66	3 Mo Oct	0.38	□0.33	27
28◆	1983	Q0.03	1-15-96	12-27	0.12	0.12	0.108	62.2	1776	1159	9-30-95	208	...	p48355	Je	1.07	[68]1.42	[69]1.14	0.86	2.01	2.10	3 Mo Sep	0.39	0.48	28
29	....	None Since Public			...	Nil	....	0.93	105	56.9	9-30-95	....	...	±5986	Je	...	...	p0.60	p0.81	1.29	1.37	3 Mo Sep	0.32	0.40	29
30	1993	0.04	12-15-95	11-28	0.04	0.04	0.04	26.0	616	498	9-30-95	330	...	80888	Dc	...	0.39	1.06	1.08	E1.05	d0.91	9 Mo Sep	0.71	d1.28	30
31◆	....	None Since Public			...	Nil	....	1.42	20.2	7.09	9-30-95	6.65	...	3119	Mr	d0.20	d0.30	0.20	0.40	....	0.46	6 Mo Sep	0.20	0.26	31
32◆	1950	Q0.22	12-1-95	11-15	0.84	0.88	0.76	18.9	287	129	9-30-95	70.0	...	15408	Dc	d0.55	1.61	1.83	2.30	....	2.69	9 Mo Sep	1.75	2.14	32
33	....	None Since Public			...	Nil	....	3.83	129	66.0	9-30-95	190	...	±17704	Dc	p□±0.54	±□d0.35	□Δ±0.33	□±0.17	....	0.15	9 Mo Sep	±□0.07	±0.05	33
34	1987	[55]0.462	4-24-96	2-2	[55]0.731	0.77	0.621	271	880	528	j9-30-94	253	372808	227353	Sp	□1.04	□1.22	1.28	1.70	....	1.70				34
35	1993	Q0.50	12-15-95	12-12	2.00	2.00	2.00	....	...	...		....	6000	...	Sp	...	...	...	....	....	....				35
36	....	t0.18	5-2-88	4-11	...	Nil	....	1.10	52.1	36.1	6-30-95	15.8	...	[73]2520	Dc	0.52	0.02	0.88	1.27	....	1.83	9 Mo Sep	1.03	1.59	36
37	....	None Since Public			...	Nil	....	11.5	26.4	49.9	9-30-95	173	...	±11163	Dc	±0.75	±0.80	Δ±1.50	±2.00	....	1.23	9 Mo Sep	±1.65	±0.88	37
38◆	1988	Q0.09	12-14-95	11-28	0.315	0.36	0.285	148	289	663	8-31-95	1072	...	±284788	Nv	±0.31	□±1.00	±1.12	±1.35	±P1.59	1.59				38
39◆	1994	Q0.07	2-1-96	1-10	s0.231	0.28	s0.186	Book Value $9.35			9-30-95	25.3	1504	6274	Dc	0.49	0.54	0.86	d0.90	....	d0.83	9 Mo Sep	0.69	0.76	39
40◆	1937	Q0.45½	2-1-96	1-8	1.76	1.82	1.70	14.9	635	588	9-30-95	2684	1437	153889	Dc	2.26	2.36	2.10	2.03	E2.40	2.33	12 Mo Sep	2.10	2.33	40
41	1995	Q0.534	12-29-95	12-26	1.484	2.14	....	Co option redm fr 4-21-2000 at $25				125	...	...	Dc	...	...	...	....	....	....	Mature 6-30-2025			41
42◆	1907	Q0.33	12-7-95	10-31	1.26	1.32	1.20	10.6	241	123	9-30-95	195	456	16441	Je	1.76	□0.82	□1.56	□2.27	[77]2.81	3.23	3 Mo Sep	0.28	0.70	42
43	....	None Since Public			...	Nil	....	0.22	73.1	76.2	10-01-95	132	...	15302	Dc	...	p*0.56	□Δ0.30	0.55	....	0.51	9 Mo Sep	0.39	0.35	43
44	1993	Q0.43¾	11-24-95	11-8	1.75	1.75	[79]1.75	Equity per shr $6.78			9-30-95	270	...	13384	Dc	p1.07	n/a	□0.41	1.06	....	1.02	9 Mo Sep	0.82	0.78	44
45	....	None Since Public			...	Nil	....	6.98	15.6	2.65	9-30-95	3.08	11	8430	Dc	*0.08	*0.02	*0.05	[80]0.18	....	d0.04	9 Mo Sep	0.13	d0.09	45
46	....	None Since Public			...	Nil	....	133	545	151	7-29-95	273	...	16347	Ja	...	p1.63	p1.65	2.48	....	4.34	9 Mo Oct	0.51	2.37	46
47◆	1883	Q0.04	11-28-95	11-2	0.16	0.16	0.333	60.2	320	213	9-30-95	19.8	...	±46113	Mr	±1.00	±1.03	□±0.58	d1.22	E0.65	d0.28	6 Mo Sep	d1.02	d0.08	47
48◆	....	None Since Public			...	Nil	....	52.2	80.9	20.8	9-30-95	....	...	27894	Dc	...	...	pd0.12	0.34	....	0.69	9 Mo Sep	0.19	0.54	48
49◆	1954	Q0.09	12-15-95	11-21	†0.42	0.36	0.30	22.6	89.8	35.6	10-30-95	14.0	...	11928	Ja	0.60	0.64	□0.49	1.02	....	1.44	9 Mo Oct	0.71	1.13	49
50◆	1964	Q0.24	2-15-96	1-10	0.96	0.96	0.96	2.77	23.3	42.8	9-30-95	100	195	9105	Dc	1.14	0.63	Δ1.05	0.60	....	0.75	9 Mo Sep	0.09	0.24	50
51	1994	Q0.05	1-30-96	12-27	0.20	0.20	0.05	59.0	3053	2176	9-30-95	1112	1540	[81]71066	Dc	...	...	pd0.31	p□2.32	E4.00	....	9 Mo Sep	n/a	□3.55	51
52◆	1990	Q0.02½	2-15-96	1-30	0.09	0.10	0.078	10.5	49.8	91.7	10-31-95	55.9	...	26126	Ap	0.41	0.52	0.60	[82]0.73	0.88	0.98	6 Mo Oct	0.54	0.64	52

◆**Stock Splits & Divs By Line Reference Index** [3]1-for-5 REVERSE,'95. [4]5-for-4,'91:2-for-1 in Cl'B','93. [10]10-for-1,'94. [18]5-for-4,'91:3-for-2,'92:10%,'95. [20]3-for-2,'95. [28]5-for-4,'91,'94. [31]1-for-5 REVERSE,'95. [32]2-for-1,'93. [38]2-for-1,'94. [39]Adj to 5%,'95. [40]2-for-1,'93. [42]2-for-1,'95. [47]3-for-1,'92. [48]2-for-1,'95. [49]2-for-1,'95. [50]3-for-2,'93. [52]2-for-1,'94.

¶ S&P 500 # MidCap 400 ✣ SmallCap 600 • Options

Index	Ticker	Name of Issue (Call Price of Pfd. Stocks)	Market	Com. Rank. & Pfd. Rating	Inst. Hold Cos	Inst. Hold Shs. (000)	Principal Business	Price Range 1971-93 High	1971-93 Low	1994 High	1994 Low	1995 High	1995 Low	Dec. Sales in 100s	December, 1995 Last Sale Or Bid High	Low	Last	%Div Yield	P-E Ratio	Total Return % Annualized 12 Mo	36 Mo	60 Mo
✣1	PWN	✔Cash Amer Intl	NY,Ch,Ph	B+	93	19805	Acquire,operate pawnshops	12⅞	3¼	10⅛	7½	9¾	4⅝	18925	6⅜	5⅜	5½	0.9	12	−38.4	−20.1	−5.0
2•[1]	CSNO	✔Casino America	NNM	NR	61	3752	Oper casino gaming facilities	21⅝	4⅜	25	7	17½	5⅛	21596	6⅝	5½	6⅛	...	7	−22.2	−7.2	...
3	CSDS	✔Casino Data Systems	NNM	NR	37	2606	Dvp casino act'g/playr info sy	22⅜	4⅝	24	10½	26¾	7⅝	41636	26¾	16¾	25	...	43	123	...	...
✣4•[2]	CMAG	✔Casino Magic	NNM	NR	45	3564	Oper gaming casino,Mississippi	28⅜	1 11/16	17¼	4⅝	7⅝	3	52141	4½	3	3⅛	...	d	−40.5	−24.2	...
✣5•[3]	CTA	✔CasTech Aluminum Group	NY,Ch,Ph	NR	75	8242	Mfr cast aluminum sheet	...	...	16¾	12¼	21⅞	12⅜	8680	16¼	12⅞	13½	...	8	−3.6	...	...
6	CAS	✔Castle (A.M.)	AS,Ch	B	68	6621	Metals service dstr centers	11⅝	13/16	16⅜	11⅛	28¼	12¼	1186	28¼	24¼	28⅛	2.1	12	109	59.6	35.4
7	CCS	Castle & Cooke Inc	NY	NR	..	...	Real estate dvlp't/resorts	...	...	...	...	18¼	15	6758	18¼	15	16¾	...	d	...	...	...
8	CECX	✔Castle Energy Corp	NNM	B−	31	3217	Oil & gas explor,dev,prod'n	87½	3	19	7¼	14¼	7	2910	9	7⅝	8⅞	...	3	−28.6	3.7	−23.0
9	LTG	✔Catalina Lighting	NY,Ch,Ph	NR	28	2120	Mkts light'g prod/ceil'g fans	15¼	1⅝	12⅞	6¾	9⅝	3½	4222	5½	4⅝	4¾	...	95	−41.5	−3.3	16.1
✣10	POS	✔Catalina Marketing	NY	NR	117	7167	Electronic coupon mktg sys	50¼	20	56¼	41¼	64⅞	40	6261	64⅞	57¾	62¾	...	33	13.3	17.9	...
11	CLYS	Catalyst Intl	NNM	NR	..	...	Warehouse mgmt software	...	...	...	...	14	10	17471	14	10	11½	...	..	...	...	...
12	CTAL	✔Catalytica Inc	NNM	NR	33	7686	Pollution ctrl catalysts,sys	9¼	4¾	8¼	2	5¾	2	5645	4⅝	3⅝	4⅜	...	d	75.0	...	...
13•[4]	CDX	✔Catellus Development	NY,Ch,P	C	100	20451	Real estate development	15	5¾	8½	5⅜	6⅞	5¼	28177	6⅜	5⅝	5⅞	...	d	9.3	−1.4	−9.9
14	Pr A	$3.75 Sr'A'cm Cv Pfd([54]52.63)	NY,Ch	B−	31	1509		63⅞	50	59¼	45⅛	52	44⅞	909	49⅜	46½	48	7.8	..	...	...	...
¶15•[5]	CAT	✔Caterpillar Inc	NY,B,C,Ch,P,Ph	B	754	131695	Earthmoving mchy: diesel eng	73¼	12¾	60¾	44⅜	75¼	48¼	121174	63⅛	57¼	58¾	2.4	11	10.0	31.0	40.3
16	CATH	✔Catherines Stores	NNM	NR	48	6249	Sell large-size women's apparel	21½	8	18¼	6¼	13¼	7¼	4959	9	8	8¼	...	12	−8.3	−23.9	...
✣17•[6]	CACOA	✔Cato Corp'A'	NNM	B−	89	13158	Women's apparel stores	24¾	⅜	21½	5½	8⅞	5	16173	7¾	6½	7¾	2.1	19	9.3	−20.2	82.7
18	CAV	✔Cavalier Homes	NY,Ch,Ph	B	44	2527	Produce factory built homes	12¾	1⅛	13⅝	7¾	22¼	7¾	8454	22¼	18¼	20¾	0.6	16	144	32.9	78.6
#19•[7]	CBI	✔CBI Indus[55]	NY,Ch,P,Ph	B	151	30870	Ind'l gases/constr svc	47¼	5⅛	35⅞	20	34	19	126504	33½	31¼	32⅞	1.5	28	32.0	7.5	6.0
20	CBL	✔CBL & Associates Prop	NY,Ch	NR	87	14408	Real estate investment trust	20	17¾	21	16⅞	22⅜	18⅞	4653	22⅜	20½	21¾	7.3	19	16.8	...	...
21	CBTSY	CBT Group ADS[56]	NNM	NR	62	5094	Dvlp business software	...	...	...	...	57	16	9434	57	46	53	...	..	...	...	...
22	CCAM	✔CCA Industries	NNM	B	16	584	Mfr,dstr hlth & beauty aid prd	8⅛	¼	9⅛	3⅜	4¼	1 1/16	13643	1½	1 1/16	1¼	...	63	−68.8	−13.6	23.3
✣23	CCBF	✔CCB Financial	NNM	A	105	4136	Comm'l bkg,North Carolina	42½	2 5/16	44½	32¾	56½	34	9654	56½	49½	55½	2.7	12	65.2	21.2	30.0
24	CCHIA	✔CCH Inc'A'[57]	NNM	B	94	8168	Tax & business law reports	35½	2 3/16	21	15	55⅞	15¼	14288	55½	54½	55¼	1.3	74	242	47.1	20.6
✣25	CDI	✔CDI Corp	NY,Ch,Ph	B	83	6664	Engr'g & technical services	18⅝	1/16	19⅞	10¼	26⅝	13½	6816	19½	17⅝	18	...	14	−5.3	29.1	23.6
26	FSL	✔CE Franklin Ltd[58]	AS,Mo	NR	4	205	Dstr oil field supplies	5⅞	3⅝	5	1¾	2 7/16	1⅛	1308	1½	1¼	1½	...	d	−33.3	...	...
27	CGS	✔CEC Resources	AS	NR	2	143	O&G acq,dvlp,prodn-Cdn	...	...	...	...	6½	3⅞	148	5⅝	5⅜	5⅝	...	..	...	...	...
28	FUN	✔Cedar Fair L.P.	NY,Ch,Ph	NR	82	4495	Own,operate amusem'nt parks	36⅝	5¾	36⅝	26¾	37⅛	28⅛	6852	37⅛	34	37	6.2	12	36.3	16.8	32.1
29	CELI	✔Cel-Sci Corp	NNM	C	10	28	Finances biomed/tec research	91⅞	2½	18⅛	3½	7¾	2¼	14614	3¾	2⅜	3⅝	...	d	−4.2	−36.5	−10.5
30	CLDN	✔Celadon Group	NNM	NR	43	3352	Long-haul trucking svcs	...	...	21	12	18¾	7¾	15450	11	7¾	9	...	d	−39.0	...	...
31	CCL	Celanese Canada	To,Mo	B+	10	4400	Fibers, chems, industrial prod	20⅞	13/16	26	20	29¼	22	2258	26	24⅜	25	†e6.2	7	10.3	28.9	...
32	CEGE	✔Cell Genesys	NNM	NR	43	6059	Gene tech'nlgy hlth care prod	22¼	8⅝	19¾	6½	10⅛	3¾	21562	10⅛	7½	10	...	d	48.1	...	...
✣33•[8]	CPRO	✔CellPro Inc	NNM	NR	64	5774	Dvlp cell separation systems	36½	7¼	36¼	9⅝	16¾	8⅛	24944	16¾	11¾	16	...	d	17.4	−7.9	...
34•[9]	CLST	✔CellStar Corp	NNM	NR	81	6457	Dstr/sell cellular phones	17½	11½	23¼	9⅛	37⅛	17⅛	35886	29	22½	26	...	22	12.4	...	...
✣35	COMMA	✔Cellular Communications'A'[61]	NNM	B−	156	11377	Oper cellular telephone sys	48½	29¾	55¾	43¾	55	44½	67823	50½	46⅜	49¾	...	47	−3.4	15.0	...
36•[10]	CTSC	✔Cellular Technical Svcs	NNM	NR	50	3459	Softwr for cellular phone ind	15⅞	2	24¾	8¼	31	13	27490	24½	18½	23¼	...	d	67.6	101	...
37	CTRX	✔Celtrix Pharmaceuticals	NNM	NR	20	1616	Dvlp stge: Pharmaceutical R&D	19¼	5¼	11⅞	2	3¼	1¼	19858	2¾	1 11/16	2½	...	d	2.5	−34.8	...
38	CEMX	✔CEM Corp	NNM	B+	29	1845	Mfr microwave test equip	15½	4⅜	13⅝	9¾	14½	11	1899	14½	12¾	13¼	...	15	20.5	8.9	5.8
39	CTN	✔Centennial Technologies	AS,Ph	NR	7	201	Mfr printer font cartridges	...	...	6⅝	2⅞	20¾	5⅛	8681	20¾	16¼	18⅞	...	82	211	...	...
✣40	CFCX	✔Center Financial	NNM	NR	59	4097	Saving bank, Connecticut	17⅜	1⅞	18	9¼	19⅝	9¾	12422	18½	17	17½	1.1	11	80.5	28.7	52.6
41•[11]	CX	✔Centerior Energy	NY	B−	155	54772	Hldg co:Cleve Elec/Toledo Ed	27¾	12	13⅜	8	11¼	8½	76466	9⅞	8½	8⅞	9.0	6	11.7	−16.7	−5.7
42	CNT	✔CenterPoint Properties	AS,Ch	NR	83	8078	Real estate investment trust	18⅝	18	21½	17½	23¾	17¾	3107	23⅜	21⅝	23⅛	6.7	34	28.8	...	...
43	CXP	✔Centex Construction Prod	NY,Ph	NR	79	9964	Produce/mkt cement & wallboard	...	...	14⅜	8⅞	15	10½	4622	14⅝	13⅞	14⅜	...	10	30.7	...	...
¶44•[12]	CTX	✔Centex Corp	NY,B,Ch	B+	260	18986	Home bldg,constr'n prd,S & L	45¼	1 5/16	45¾	20⅛	36	21⅞	27115	36	32⅝	34¾	0.6	20	54.8	3.8	19.0
✣45	CGRM	✔Centigram Communications	NNM	B−	42	3498	Mfr audio info process'g sys	39¾	3¾	43	10	25⅛	12¼	15765	22	17¾	19¾	...	d	6.8	18.9	...
#46•[8]	CNTO	✔Centocor Inc	NNM,Ch	C	162	31402	Develops diagnostic test kits	60¼	4	18¾	8⅞	33⅛	9⅝	497462	33⅛	13⅜	30⅞	...	d	87.1	24.5	6.9
¶47•[11]	CSR	✔Central & So. West	NY,B,C,Ch,P,Ph	A−	518	83621	Integ elec utility hldg co	34¼	5⅜	30⅞	20⅛	28½	22⅜	58885	28½	26⅞	27⅞	6.2	13	33.2	4.3	11.9
48	CETV	Central Euro Media Enter'A'	NNM	NR	..	...	Own,oper TV stations-Europe	...	...	17¼	12⅞	27¼	7¾	17219	22¾	17¾	20½	...	..	45.1	...	...
#49•[7]	CFBS	✔Central Fidelity Banks	NNM	A	128	14703	Commercial bkg,Virginia	35¼	1⅝	34½	23¾	34¼	24¼	10916	34¼	31¼	32	3.8	16	34.7	9.5	27.6
✣50	CNH	✔Central Hudson Gas&El	NY,B,Ch,P,Ph	B	116	6035	Utility:elec & gas, NY State	39⅞	11	30⅜	22⅞	31⅞	25⅜	5779	31⅞	30	30⅞	6.8	12	25.6	7.2	12.4
#51	CNL	✔Central La Elec	NY,B,Ch,Ph	A−	121	7536	Electric sv in Louisiana	27⅛	6⅜	25⅝	20⅞	28⅛	22	5665	28⅛	25½	26⅞	5.6	13	27.0	10.1	15.2
#52	CTP	✔Central Maine Power	NY,B,Ch,Ph,P	B	123	9641	Utility supplies electricity	24½	7⅞	15	10⅝	15⅛	10¼	20367	15⅛	13½	14⅜	6.3	d	17.6	−8.8	2.8

Uniform Footnote Explanations-See Page 4. Other: [1]CBOE,P,Ph:Cycle 3. [2]ASE,CBOE,NY,P:Cycle 2. [3]Ph:Cycle 2. [4]ASE,CBOE:Cycle 3. [5]ASE:Cycle 2. [6]CBOE:Cycle 2. [7]Ph:Cycle 3. [8]CBOE:Cycle 1. [9]ASE,CBOE:Cycle 2. [10]CBOE:Cycle 3. [11]P:Cycle 2. [12]NY:Cycle 1. [51]®$1.15,'95. [52]®$3.43,'94. [53]®$0.74,'94. [54]Fr 2-16-96,scale to $50 in 2003. [55]Praxair Inc offer,$33 to Jan 16. [56]Ea ADS rep 1 ord, par IR 37.5p. [57]Wolters Kluwer NV offer,$55.50 to Jan 4. [58]Formerly Franklin Supply Co Ltd. [59]Fiscal Sep'92 & prior. [60]12 Mo Jun,'93. [61]Redeemable at re-specified cond.. [62]Excl 0.03M nonredeemable Cl'C' com. [63]®$0.14,'95. [64]Excl subsid pfd. [65]Subsid pfd in $M. [66]®$1.86,'94. [67]100% non-taxable,'94.

Splits ◆ Index	Cash Divs. Ea.Yr. Since	Dividends: Latest Payment: Period $	Date	Ex. Div.	Total $: So Far 1995	Ind. Rate	Paid 1994	Financial Position Mil-$: Cash& Equiv.	Curr. Assets	Curr. Liab.	Balance Sheet Date	Capitalization: Lg Trm Debt Mil-$	Shs. 000: Pfd.	Com.	Earnings $ Per Shr. Years: End	1991	1992	1993	1994	1995	Last 12 Mos.	Interim Earnings: Period	$ per Shr. 1994	1995	Index
1◆	1988	Q0.01¼	11-22-95	11-6	0.05	0.05	0.05	6.98	183	14.5	9-30-95	136	...	28731	Dc	*0.43	0.45	0.48	0.54	....	0.45	9 Mo Sep	0.35	□0.26	1
2◆	....	None Since Public			...	Nil	....	10.0	15.4	29.8	7-31-95	135	...	14923	Ap	...	...	0.71	1.28	[51]1.16	0.89	6 Mo Oct	0.55	0.28	2
3◆	....	None Since Public			...	Nil	....	10.1	24.7	3.29	9-30-95	....	...	9125	Dc	pd0.03	p0.10	0.50	0.77	....	0.58	9 Mo Sep	0.57	0.38	3
4◆	....	None Since Public			...	Nil	....	37.7	53.4	34.2	9-30-95	137	...	35272	Dc	d0.07	0.31	1.32	d0.10	....	d0.20	9 Mo Sep	0.16	0.06	4
5	....	None Since Public			...	Nil	....	0.10˙	117	47.3	9-30-95	56.3	...	12940	Mr	...	...	p1.22	Δ2.10	....	1.81	6 Mo Sep	1.28	0.99	5
6◆	1934	Q0.15	11-17-95	11-8	0.54	0.60	0.33	0.85	178	80.9	9-30-95	47.2	...	11155	Dc	0.02	Δ0.31	0.63	1.40	....	2.26	9 Mo Sep	0.98	1.84	6
7	....	None Since Public			...	Nil	....	Equity per shr $27.05			10-07-95	210	4	20000	Dc	...	...	...	p0.36	....	d5.05	40 Wk Oct	p0.12	pd5.29	7
8◆	....	0.12	1-16-90	12-22	...	Nil	....	13.0	212	194	6-30-95	30.3	...	6684	Sp	d21.20	d8.22	Δ8.12	[52]3.48	....	3.56	9 Mo Jun	1.72	1.80	8
9	....	None Since Public			...	Nil	....	1.65	92.9	27.3	6-30-95	52.2	...	6994	Sp	d0.34	0.39	0.69	[53]0.75	P0.05	0.05				9
10	....	None Since Public			...	Nil	....	28.6	60.1	39.7	9-30-95	....	...	9625	Mr	0.51	0.81	1.24	1.71	....	1.89	6 Mo Sep	0.88	1.06	10
11	....	None Since Public			...	Nil	....	0.19	7.38	4.43	9-30-95	p34.0	p...	★8117	Dc	...	...	...	p0.16	....	0.03	9 Mo Sep	p0.23	p0.10	11
12	....	None Since Public			...	Nil	....	6.47	10.6	4.82	9-30-95	2.06	...	★19128	Dc	...	pd0.36	pd0.66	d0.61	....	d0.62	9 Mo Sep	d0.44	d0.45	12
13	....	None Since Public			...	Nil	....	Equity per shr $2.34			9-30-95	540	6450	72967	Dc	0.09	0.02	□d0.87	d0.36	Ed0.05	d0.38	9 Mo Sep	d0.07	d0.09	13
14	1993	Q0.93¾	2-15-96	1-30	3.75	3.75	3.75	Cv into 5.5187 com, $9.06				....	3450	...	Dc	...	...	...	....	....	....				14
15◆	1914	Q0.35	2-20-96	1-18	1.50	1.40	0.45	897	8304	5874	9-30-95	4589	...	197519	Dc	d2.00	□d1.08	□3.36	4.70	E5.40	5.57	9 Mo Sep	3.32	4.19	15
16	....	None Since Public			...	Nil	....	3.25	62.6	38.1	7-29-95	8.14	...	7659	Ja	0.70	0.70	0.91	0.71	....	0.72	9 Mo Oct	0.70	0.71	16
17◆	1992	Q0.04	1-1-96	12-14	0.16	0.16	0.13	41.3	165	63.8	10-28-95	....	...	±28427	Ja	0.43	□0.74	0.84	±0.62	....	0.41	9 Mo Oct	±0.52	±0.31	17
18◆	1989	Q0.03	11-15-95	10-27	0.106	0.12	0.064	14.4	51.2	36.3	9-29-95	4.49	...	5979	Dc	0.03	0.52	0.78	0.97	....	1.32	9 Mo Sep	0.71	1.06	18
19◆	1913	Q0.12	12-15-95	11-20	0.48	0.48	0.48	35.7	541	352	9-30-95	716	4235	38295	Dc	1.54	□1.79	d1.07	1.20	E1.18	1.19	9 Mo Sep	0.74	0.73	19
20	1994	Q0.39¾	1-11-96	12-22	1.56¾	1.59	1.36¾	Equity per shr $13.51			9-30-95	376	...	20827	Dc	...	p0.71	p0.94	1.05	....	1.15	9 Mo Sep	0.75	□0.85	20
21	....	None Since Public			...	Nil	....	16.2	25.2	13.2	6-30-95	....	...	★8260	Dc	d2.19	d0.43	d0.08	0.23	....	0.51	9 Mo Sep	0.11	0.39	21
22	....	None Paid			...	Nil	....	2.13	13.9	6.22	8-31-95	0.18	...	±6795	Nv	±0.12	±0.15	±0.32	±0.35	....	0.02	9 Mo Aug	±0.27	±d0.06	22
23◆	1934	Q0.38	1-2-96	12-13	1.40	1.52	1.30	Book Value $27.73			9-30-95	80.9	...	14952	Dc	2.81	3.30	□3.50	4.06	....	4.76	9 Mo Sep	2.03	2.73	23
24◆	1936	Q0.17½	10-24-95	9-27	0.70	0.70	0.70	32.3	294	327	9-30-95	....	...	±33036	Dc	±0.89	□±d0.39	±0.19	±0.55	....	0.75	9 Mo Sep	±0.16	±0.36	24
25	....	0.013	11-2-70	10-16	...	Nil	....	3.84	262	109	9-30-95	68.3	...	19815	Dc	d0.39	0.17	0.40	1.13	....	1.28	9 Mo Sep	0.76	0.91	25
26	....	None Since Public			...	Nil	....	....	39.1	32.7	j6-30-95	0.35	...	7064	Je	0.69	[59]d0.38	▲[60]1.51	0.33	Nil	jd0.04	3 Mo Sep	0.09	0.05	26
27	....	None Since Public			...	Nil	....	....	2.03	0.55	j8-31-95	....	...	1500	Nv	...	...	pΔ0.65	0.72	....	j....	9 Mo Aug	n/a	0.45	27
28	1987	Q0.57½	2-15-96	1-2	2.26¼	2.30	2.06¼	1.55	19.8	43.9	10-01-95	53.2	...	22965	Dc	1.68	1.96	2.75	2.79	....	3.03	12 Mo Sep	2.80	3.03	28
29◆	....	None Since Public			...	Nil	....	3.72	4.35	0.27	6-30-95	0.72	...	p4922	Sp	d0.40	d0.40	d0.60	d1.10	....	d1.15	9 Mo Jun	0.75	0.70	29
30	....	None Since Public			...	Nil	....	0.87	65.6	42.4	9-30-95	47.3	...	7751	Je	□d0.02	d0.04	d0.09	0.61	d0.05	d0.18	3 Mo Sep	0.21	0.08	30
31◆	1983	g†0.70	1-3-96	11-30	g0.53	1.55	g†1.257	172	318	81.7	j12-31-94	....	...	40734	Dc	0.81	0.88	1.48	2.46	....	j3.43	9 Mo Sep	1.52	2.49	31
32	....	None Since Public			...	Nil	....	60.8	64.2	7.58	9-30-95	7.97	...	13922	Dc	pd0.16	pd0.62	d0.80	d1.07	....	d1.34	9 Mo Sep	d0.78	d1.05	32
33	....	None Since Public			...	Nil	....	82.8	88.2	5.47	9-30-95	0.33	...	14185	Mr	d1.25	d1.23	d1.27	d1.45	....	d1.28	6 Mo Sep	d0.57	d0.40	33
34	....	None Since Public			...	Nil	....	6.41	263	189	8-31-95	7.13	...	19271	Nv	...	p0.34	p0.71	0.88	....	1.18	9 Mo Aug	0.59	0.89	34
35	....	None Since Public			...	Nil	....	204	215	35.2	9-30-95	353	42560	[62]13004	Dc	□d0.56	*d0.09	Δ0.27	0.40	....	1.05	9 Mo Sep	0.35	1.00	35
36◆	....	None Since Public			...	Nil	....	9.40	12.0	1.29	9-30-95	....	...	10787	Dc	d0.27	d0.19	d0.14	0.15	....	d0.02	9 Mo Sep	0.13	d0.04	36
37	....	None Since Public			...	Nil	....	18.2	18.9	2.13	9-30-95	0.41	...	13719	Mr	d4.82	d2.71	d1.64	d1.57	....	d1.22	6 Mo Sep	d0.74	d0.39	37
38	....	None Since Public			...	Nil	....	5.42	18.0	3.53	9-30-95	1.52	...	3633	Je	0.54	0.41	0.57	0.70	0.85	0.87	3 Mo Sep	0.16	0.18	38
39◆	....	None Since Public			...	Nil	....	0.67	21.3	9.28	9-30-95	0.56	...	6069	Je	0.04	0.08	0.15	0.14	[63]0.16	0.23	3 Mo Sep	0.03	0.10	39
40	1995	Q0.05	11-13-95	11-1	0.20	0.20	....	Book Value $14.30			12-31-94	319	...	p12682	Dc	d0.48	0.58	Δ0.75	0.53	....	1.53	9 Mo Sep	0.18	1.18	40
41	1986	Q0.20	11-15-95	10-25	0.80	0.80	0.80	235	854	905	9-30-95	3792	[64]...	148032	Dc	1.71	1.50	d6.51	1.38	E1.54↑	1.53	12 Mo Sep	d5.83	1.53	41
42	1994	Q0.39	1-22-96	12-22	1.54½	1.56	1.219	Equity per shr $10.88			6-30-95	p123	p2273	10111	Dc	...	pd0.61	pd0.33	0.41	....	0.69	9 Mo Sep	0.27	0.55	42
43	....	None Since Public			...	Nil	....	13.1	79.0	43.7	9-30-95	12.5	...	22973	Mr	...	p0.08	p...	0.95	E1.45	1.21	6 Mo Sep	0.54	0.80	43
44◆	1973	Q0.05	1-5-96	12-12	0.20	0.20	0.20	Equity per shr $24.47			9-30-95	322	...	28299	Mr	1.11	1.91	2.60	3.04	E1.75	1.57	6 Mo Sep	2.24	0.77	44
45	....	None Since Public			...	Nil	....	58.6	85.6	17.1	7-01-95	0.28	...	6592	Sp	0.67	0.49	1.00	1.18	Pd0.55	d0.55				45
46◆	....	None Since Public			...	Nil	....	126	168	58.6	9-30-95	232	...	58368	Dc	d5.72	d4.90	d1.79	d2.55	Ed0.90	d1.49	9 Mo Sep	d1.71	d0.65	46
47◆	1947	Q0.43	11-30-95	11-6	1.72	1.72	1.70	61.0	1483	2247	9-30-95	3001	[65]326	192398	Dc	1.99	2.03	Δ1.39	2.08	E2.13	2.11	12 Mo Sep	1.50	2.11	47
48	....	None Since Public			...	Nil	....	28.7	64.3	28.1	6-30-95	p19.8	...	★±18196	Dc	...	...	pd5.23	pd2.29	....	....	9 Mo Sep	n/a	d0.86	48
49◆	1969	Q0.30	1-2-96	12-13	1.16	1.20	1.09	Book Value $19.62			9-30-95	754	...	40102	Dc	1.87	2.25	2.66	2.17	....	1.96	9 Mo Sep	2.21	2.00	49
50	1903	Q0.525	2-1-96	1-8	2.09	2.10	2.07	41.8	147	89.2	9-30-95	389	810	17442	Dc	2.40	2.65	2.68	2.68	....	2.68	12 Mo Sep	2.73	2.68	50
51◆	1935	Q0.37½	11-15-95	10-26	1.49	1.50	1.45	18.5	72.2	113	9-30-95	361	377	22425	Dc	1.92	1.93	1.78	[66]1.92	....	2.10	12 Mo Sep	2.01	2.10	51
52	1943	Q0.22½	1-31-96	1-8	0.90	0.90	[67]0.90	61.7	231	159	9-30-95	628	1456	32443	Dc	1.82	1.85	1.65	d1.04	....	d1.43	12 Mo Sep	1.33	d1.43	52

◆**Stock Splits & Divs By Line Reference Index** [1]2-for-1,'92. [2]3-for-2,'93,'94. [3]3-for-2,'95. [4]3-for-1,'93. [6]3-for-2,'94. [8]1-for-2 REVERSE,'93. [15]2-for-1,'94. [17]3-for-2,'93. [18]5-for-4,'92,'93,'95. [19]3-for-2,'91. [23]3-for-2,'92. [24]2-for-1 in Cl'B','91. [29]1-for-10 REVERSE,'95. [31]3-for-1,'94. [36]2-for-1,'94. [39]3-for-2,'95. [44]2-for-1,'92. [46]2-for-1,'91. [47]2-for-1,'92. [49]3-for-2,'91,93. [51]2-for-1,'92.

¶ S&P 500 # MidCap 400 ✤ SmallCap 600 • Options

Index	Ticker	Name of Issue (Call Price of Pfd. Stocks)	Market	Com. Rank. & Pfd. Rating	Inst. Hold Cos	Inst. Hold Shs. (000)	Principal Business	Price Range 1971-93 High	1971-93 Low	1994 High	1994 Low	1995 High	1995 Low	Dec. Sales in 100s	December, 1995 Last Sale Or Bid High	Low	Last	%Div Yield	P-E Ratio	Total Return % Annualized 12 Mo	36 Mo	60 Mo
1	ECP	✔Central Newspapers 'A'	NY,Ch,Ph	B	92	9715	Newspaper publishing	27¾	13⅞	30	24⅝	32⅝	24⅛	8338	32⅝	29¼	31⅜	2.2	18	17.6	13.7	15.5
2	PK	✔Central Parking	NY,Ph	NR	..	...	Oper parking facilities	...	...	...	...	29½	18	2150	29½	26⅛	28¾	0.3	30	...	...	...
3	CRLC	✔Central Reserve Life	NNM	B+	19	724	Life,small group health ins	14⅛	5/16	8⅞	6¾	10	7⅛	411	9¾	9¼	9⅝	5.0	8	26.8	7.8	22.3
4	CETPrD	Central Sec$2cmCv D Pfd(27.50)	AS	NR	1	294		44	22½	50	44½	63	50½	...	...	...	58B	3.4	..	...	...	...
5	CTFC	✔Central Tractor Farm & Country	NNM	NR	41	3169	Agricultural spcl retailer	...	...	17¼	14¼	16	6¾	5311	11¼	9	10¼	...	21	−29.3	...	...
6	TPH	✔Central Trans Rental [51]Gp ADS	NY,Ch	NR	11	1165	Rent freight transport'n equip	31⅛	1½	3½	1⅜	2⅝	⅝	27292	⅞	⅝	⅝	...	d	−54.5	−66.3	...
✤7	CV	✔Central VT Pub Svc	NY,Ch,Ph	B	68	2866	Electricity in Vt., N.H.	25¾	3½	22	12⅛	14⅜	13¼	4625	14⅜	13⅜	13⅜	6.0	9	9.0	−12.3	1.6
✤8	CBC	✔Centura Banks	NY,Ch,Ph	A	100	5402	Comm'l bkg, No Carolina	24⅝	11⅝	25¼	18	35½	22½	3986	35½	33¾	35⅛	2.8	14	52.2	24.2	27.0
9•[1]	CTYA	✔Century Communic'ns'A'	NNM,B,Ch,Ph	C	92	17380	Owns/operates CATV systems	13⅞	2½	12	6¼	10½	7¼	13996	9⅛	7¾	8	...	d	6.7	3.7	15.2
#10•[2]	CTL	✔Century Tel Enterp	NY,Ch,Ph	A	290	45190	Tel svc in parts of 14 states	33⅜	15/16	32¼	21⅞	33⅛	27	31004	32⅛	29⅝	31¾	1.0	16	7.4	6.0	10.0
✤11•[1]	CEPH	✔Cephalon Inc	NNM	NR	114	18360	R&D neurodegenerative diseases	19½	7	19½	7½	41½	5¾	152329	41½	27⅛	40¾	...	d	406	50.3	...
12	CRDN	✔Ceradyne Inc	NNM	C	10	1354	Mfr advanced tech ceramics	21¼	2	3⅝	1½	7⅝	2¼	8265	6	4⅞	5⅝	...	52	153	31.5	5.4
¶13•[1]	CEN	✔Ceridian Corp	NY,To,B,C,Ch,P,Ph	C	410	43035	Computer serv/eq: finance co	64⅜	4¾	27½	18½	47½	26⅛	71880	43⅜	36⅝	41¼	...	24	54.9	...	...
14	Pr	5.50% cm Cv[56]Dep[57]Ex Pfd([58]51.10)	NY	BB−	49	3635		51½	49⅝	65½	50½	106¼	61½	4001	97½	82½	92½	3.0	..	...	...	...
✤15•[3]	CERN	✔Cerner Corp	NNM	B	160	17119	Devl,mkts clinical info sys	22⅞	13/16	24¾	11¾	36	20	156293	27	20	20½	...	31	−7.3	16.2	75.9
16	CPLX	✔Cerplex Group	NNM	NR	18	1086	Repair electronic equip	...	...	16¼	9¼	12	4½	5627	9	7	7¾	...	d	−22.5	...	...
17	CRTN	✔Certron Corp	NSC	C	2	78	Audio magnetic tape products	8⅜	¼	1¼	½	1⅛	⅝	718	15/16	⅝	⅝	...	d	−16.7	−24.2	−7.8
18	CES.SA	CESP-Companhia Energetica[59]	BSPA	NR	..	...	Electric/gas distr,SaoPoulo	...	...	...	...	41½	20	...	22½	21½	22	...	..	...	...	...
19	ENV	✔CET Environmental Svcs	AS	NR	4	149	Enviro consult'g/enginrg svc	...	...	...	...	9½	4⅞	1152	9½	8⅛	9⅜	...	24	...	...	...
20	PROI	✔CFI ProServices	NNM	NR	35	2213	Software prod for fin'l indus	15¼	8	15¾	9⅞	17¾	9¼	2221	15	12½	14⅞	...	24	8.2	...	...
21	CFX	✔CFX Corp	AS,Ch	NR	18	646	Savings bank,New Hampshire	14	3½	12⅛	9¾	17½	10	2663	17	14⅝	15⅝	se4.4	15	65.6	32.6	37.1
22	CTU	✔Chad Therapeutics	AS	NR	19	812	Mfr respiratory care devices	6¼	...	5¾	3¾	16½	4½	4430	16½	14½	15⅝	...	45	255	...	...
23	CCCFF	✔Chai-Na-Ta Corp	NNM,To	NR	6	417	Produce,process,dstr Ginseng	7⅛	4½	5⅛	2½	2⅞	1⅜	7745	2⅝	2	2⅜	...	..	−9.5	−14.5	...
✤24•[4]	CHB	✔Champion Enterprises	NY,B,Ch,P,Ph	B−	118	8922	Mfr'd homes/midsize buses	65	15/16	20⅜	8¾	31	13⅝	7709	31	28⅜	30⅞	...	17	101	81.7	80.9
25	CHC	✔Champion Healthcare	AS	NR	10	523	Health care facilities	...	...	10	7½	9⅛	4¾	1891	5¾	4¾	5¼	...	d	−33.6	...	...
26	CHMP	✔Champion Industries	NNM	NR	20	249	Commercial print'g/office prd	13	6⅜	23¾	11½	25½	19¼	882	24¼	22¼	22¾	0.9	39	2.8	...	...
¶27•[3]	CHA	✔Champion Intl	NY,B,C,Ch,P,Ph	B−	542	82957	Building mtls,paper prod	44⅝	9⅜	40	28	60¼	36⅛	187478	47¼	39½	42	0.5	5	16.0	13.8	11.1
28	CREB	✔Champion Parts	NSC	C	11	369	Rebuilder of auto parts	20	1 5/16	5	2⅞	3¾	¼	4160	⅝	¼	⅜	...	d	−88.0	−52.5	−32.9
29	CHANF	Chandler Insurance Ltd	NNM	B−	6	1024	Casualty re-insur-truck'g ind	13¼	2⅛	7	4⅛	6¾	4⅝	701	6¾	6¼	6¼	...	13	28.2	11.6	−0.8
30	CSM	✔Chaparral Steel Co[68]	NY,Ch,Ph	NR	..	...	Own/oper steel minimill	15⅝	5⅝	12¼	6½	16¾	7½	4363	16¾	10½	16¾	1.2	17	140	21.3	24.8
¶31•[5]	CHRS	✔Charming Shoppes	NNM,Ph	B+	250	62995	Women's specialty stores	19½	1/32	14	5¾	6¾	2 1/16	297938	3½	2 5/16	2⅞	...	d	−56.1	−45.5	−11.2
32	CHT	✔Chart House Enterpr	NY,Ch,Ph	NR	30	4706	Full-svc restaurant chain	15½	5½	15¾	5¾	9⅜	5⅝	4325	6⅝	5⅝	6	...	11	−34.2	−3.2	−8.3
33	CTI	✔Chart Industries	NY	NR	20	2317	Mfr custom-built indl equip	16⅝	4⅞	5¾	3	8⅞	3¾	3101	7⅝	6½	7⅝	3.7	16	99.5	−11.3	...
34	SAIL	✔Charter Bancshares	NSC	B−	10	2990	General banking Texas	15⅜	2 1/16	14¾	12	20⅞	13⅛	89	20⅞	19¼	19⅝B	s1.6	13	60.2	24.9	...
✤35•[6]	COFI	✔Charter One Finl	NNM	NR	137	16547	Savings bank,Ohio	25	3⅜	24	17¾	33⅜	18⅞	40838	33⅜	30	30⅝	2.6	10	68.2	21.0	42.6
36	CHTR	✔Charter Power Systems	NNM	NR	45	2205	Mfrs battery power systems	14½	3¼	18½	9¾	31¾	17½	9329	28¾	24¼	28¾	0.4	14	58.3	73.8	37.2
37	CSI	✔Chase Brass Indus	NY,Ch	NR	42	2481	Mfr,dstr brass rod	...	...	10⅛	8⅝	15	9¼	1649	13⅝	12	12⅝	...	9	32.9	...	...
38	CCF	✔Chase Corp	AS,Ph	B	5	215	Protective coatings & tapes	5	½	4	1⅝	5⅝	3⅛	643	5⅝	4½	4¾	2.1	11	38.6	44.9	...
¶39•[7]	CMB	✔Chase Manhattan[69]	NY,B,C,Ch,P,Ph	B	615	122435	Commercial bkg,New York	49½	9¾	40	30⅜	66⅝	32⅝	168383	64⅛	58½	60⅜	3.0	11	81.0	32.4	49.0
40	WS	Wrrt(Pur1com at$34.612)	NY	...	42	444		10⅛	5	9⅝	4½	32¼	3¾	6051	29¾	24½	26⅛	...	..	...	...	...
41	CPJ	✔Chateau Properties	NY	NR	62	3634	Real estate investment trust	22¾	18⅝	24¼	18¼	22⅞	18	3176	22⅞	20¾	22½	7.1	24	11.7	...	...
42	CHTT	✔Chattem Inc	NNM	B	24	3452	Consumer prod/spec'lty chem	32	1 3/16	8¾	4⅝	6¼	4	3272	4¾	4¼	4⅝	...	3	−7.5	−24.0	5.6
43	CHS	✔Chaus (Bernard) Inc	NY,B,Ch,Ph	C	17	2552	Designs women's apparel	25⅛	1⅝	6⅛	1⅝	6⅝	2⅞	14440	4	3½	3⅝	...	d	−27.5	−19.7	14.1
44	FLYAF	✔CHC Helicopter Cl'A'	NNM	NR	13	2917	Helicopter transport'n/svcs	7	6½	9⅜	3	4¾	2¼	...	3½	3½	3½B	◆...	..	−9.8	...	...
45	CTCQ	Check Technology	NNM	B−	14	1765	Computerized check print'g	15¼	1½	5⅞	3	10¼	5	5036	10¼	8	9⅞	...	30	88.1	80.2	29.7
✤46	CHKR	✔Checkers Drive-In Restr	NNM	NR	46	3025	Own/franchise fast-food restr	17⅜	3½	12¼	2⅛	4	15/16	93384	1⅜	15/16	1	...	d	−55.4	−45.9	...
47	CKFR	✔Checkfree Corp	NNM	NR	64	3376	Electronic commerce mkt serv	...	...	...	...	29⅜	16	36125	28⅝	20⅛	21½	...	..	...	...	...
48	CMEL	✔Checkmate Electronics	NNM	NR	27	1522	Mfr,mkt check readers	11¾	8½	11	5¾	18	7	2968	16¼	14½	14¾	...	31	111	...	...
49•[8]	CKP	✔Checkpoint Sys	NY	B−	94	10350	Electronic detection sys	20⅛	⅛	21½	10¾	39	15⅞	20634	39	30¾	37⅜	...	45	95.4	29.7	32.6
✤50	CAKE	✔Cheesecake Factory	NNM	NR	86	6575	Oper casual dining restaurants	23⅞	13⅜	24⅝	13½	30¼	13¾	11560	23½	20	21½	...	27	39.8	12.8	...
51	CCG	✔Chelsea GCA Realty	NY,Ph	NR	104	10717	Real estate investment trust	30¼	25⅝	30½	23⅛	30½	23⅛	3811	30¼	27⅞	30	7.7	18	19.2	...	...
✤52	CHE	✔Chemed Corp	NY,Ch,Ph	B+	109	3182	Specialty chem:health care pr	44⅝	3	36⅛	30¼	40¼	30⅜	3311	40¼	38½	38⅞	5.4	9	22.9	20.8	24.8

Uniform Footnote Explanations-See Page 4. Other: [1]CBOE:Cycle 2. [2]P:Cycle 1. [3]CBOE:Cycle 3. [4]ASE:Cycle 1. [5]Ph:Cycle 1. [6]Ph:Cycle 2. [7]ASE:Cycle 3. [8]P:Cycle 2. [51]Ea ADS rep 3 ord, 10p. [52]®$1.80,'94. [53]12 Mos Dec, fiscal Jun'91 earned $0.10d. [54]Stk dstr of Control Data Systems,'92. [55]®$1.40,'94. [56]Dep for 0.01 shr cm Cv Exch Pfd stk. [57]Co opt fr 12-3-95 exch for$50 amt 5.50%Cv 2008. [58]Fr 12-31-96,scale to $50 in'98. [59]All data reported in Reais. [60]Last com divd Jun'90. [61]Pfd shs in millions. [62]Fiscal May'92 & prior. [63]6 Mo Nov'93. [64]®$0.26,'94. [65]Fiscal Feb'92 & prior. [66]44 Wks Dec'92. [67]Pfd in $M. [68]81% owned by Texas Indus. [69]Approve mgr w/Chemical Banking,1.04 com. [70]®$5.84,'94. [71]5 Wk Dec'93.

Splits ◆ Index	Cash Divs. Ea. Yr. Since	Dividends: Latest Payment Period $	Date	Ex. Div.	Total $ So Far 1995	Ind. Rate	Paid 1994	Financial Position Mil-$ Cash& Equiv.	Curr. Assets	Curr. Liab.	Balance Sheet Date	Capitalization Lg Trm Debt Mil-$	Shs. 000 Pfd.	Com.	Earnings $ Per Shr. Years End	1991	1992	1993	1994	1995	Last 12 Mos.	Interim Earnings Period	$ per Shr. 1994	1995	Index
1	1949	Q0.17	1-10-96	12-27	0.59	0.68	0.50	126	201	63.6	9-24-95	2.68	...	±55067	Dc	0.98	□0.88	1.21	1.55	....	1.76	9 Mo Sep	1.18	1.39	1
2	1996	0.03	1-5-96	12-27	...	0.10	....	15.2	27.5	23.6	6-30-95	....	...	★11378	Sp	0.25	0.50	0.48	0.84	P0.97	0.97				2
3	1980	Q0.12	12-26-95	12-6	0.48	0.48	0.44	Book Value $7.99			9-30-95	8.62	...	4037	Dc	0.82	0.85	0.57	1.14	....	1.16	9 Mo Sep	0.85	0.87	3
4	1984	Q0.50	2-1-96	1-10	2.00	2.00	2.00	Cv into 2.962 com				....	398	...	Dc	...	...	...	....	....	....				4
5	....	None Since Public			...	Nil	....	2.07	90.9	34.1	7-29-95	16.0	...	10577	Oc	...	...	p0.52	□0.57	P0.50	0.50				5
6	1989	0.663	10-12-93	8-6	...	Nil	....	9.15	138	818	4-30-95	....	...	110715	Ap	□3.39	3.03	d1.94	d13.66	d1.46	d1.46				6
7◆	1944	Q0.20	11-15-95	10-27	0.80	0.80	1.42	14.7	41.5	46.5	9-30-95	120	281	11591	Dc	1.65	1.71	1.64	1.08	....	1.49	9 Mo Sep	0.70	1.11	7
8	1990	Q0.25	3-15-96	2-27	0.85	1.00	0.74	Equity per shr $18.26			9-30-95	586	...	21976	Dc	0.62	1.70	2.14	2.35	....	2.61	9 Mo Sep	1.70	1.96	8
9◆	....	3%Stk	12-1-93	11-4	...	Nil	....	168	212	115	8-31-95	1751	...	±73759	My	±d0.92	□±d0.69	±d0.50	±d0.53	±d1.01	d1.14	3 Mo Aug	±d0.18	±d0.31	9
10◆	1974	Q0.08¼	12-15-95	11-29	0.33	0.33	0.32	10.0	94.0	183	9-30-95	★575	91	59032	Dc	0.80	□1.25	1.35	[52]1.88	E1.96↑	2.13	9 Mo Sep	1.22	1.47	10
11	....	None Since Public			...	Nil	....	71.6	79.1	15.3	9-30-95	22.5	...	23073	Dc	[53]d0.22	d0.80	d1.77	d2.13	Ed1.40	d1.65	9 Mo Sep	d1.58	d1.10	11
12	....	None Since Public			...	Nil	....	0.26	10.6	3.98	9-30-95	0.71	...	p7524	Dc	d0.18	d0.33	d0.42	d0.30	....	0.11	9 Mo Sep	d0.20	0.21	12
13	....	h[54]....	8-31-92	9-1	...	Nil	....	192	426	370	9-30-95	12.6	47	46000	Dc	Δd0.21	□d8.24	□d0.52	[55]1.43	E1.75↓	1.80	9 Mo Sep	1.00	1.37	13
14	1994	Q0.68¾	12-29-95	12-13	2.75	2.75	2.819	Cv into 2.20 com,$22.72				....	4720	...	Dc	...	...	...	....	....	....				14
15◆	....	None Since Public			...	Nil	....	118	200	34.1	9-30-95	30.1	...	32237	Dc	0.17	0.35	0.50	0.65	....	0.67	9 Mo Sep	0.44	0.46	15
16	....	None Since Public			...	Nil	....	1.48	74.8	25.8	9-30-95	66.2	...	13119	Dc	...	...	p0.16	□0.20	....	d2.03	9 Mo Sep	□0.40	d1.83	16
17	....	None Paid			...	Nil	....	1.82	3.48	0.55	7-31-95	....	...	3128	Oc	d0.08	*0.02	*d0.02	d0.05	....	d0.24	9 Mo Jul	d0.04	d0.23	17
18	....	None Paid			...	[60]Nil	....	107	936	3982	j12-31-94	3859	[61]45157	48541652	Dc	8.12	d2.72	d4.90	3.45	....	j3.45				18
19	....	None Since Public			...	Nil	....	0.16	15.4	8.38	9-30-95	0.76	...	4914	Dc	...	...	...	p0.33	....	0.39	9 Mo Sep	p0.27	p0.33	19
20	....	None Since Public			...	Nil	....	8.39	18.2	6.48	9-30-95	....	p10	4490	Dc	d0.87	0.24	0.56	0.71	....	0.61	9 Mo Sep	0.50	0.40	20
21◆	1987	‡0.343	1-19-96	12-20	s0.437	0.69	s0.514	Book Value $10.70			9-30-95	76.7	...	7442	Dc	Δ0.05	0.59	0.79	0.86	....	1.02	9 Mo Sep	0.60	0.76	21
22◆	....	5%Stk	10-21-94	10-3	...	Nil	5%Stk	2.59	7.85	1.54	9-30-95	....	...	9558	Mr	*0.04	*0.09	0.20	0.27	....	0.35	6 Mo Sep	0.12	0.20	22
23◆	....	1.66%Stk	8-19-94	7-29	...	Nil	Stk	1.44	22.2	20.3	j2-28-95	★10.5	...	14401	Nv	0.08	[62]0.17	‡[63]d0.11	[64]0.30	....	j0.28	9 Mo Aug	0.10	0.08	23
24◆	....	0.02½	7-15-74	6-24	...	Nil	....	9.30	111	113	9-30-95	1.28	...	15306	Dc	[65]d0.05	[66]0.20	0.77	1.75	....	1.80	9 Mo Sep	1.48	1.53	24
25	....	None Since Public			...	Nil	....	7.85	47.7	36.4	9-30-95	152	[67]81	4262	Dc	...	...	pd4.30	d1.69	....	d2.24	9 Mo Sep	d0.18	□d0.73	25
26◆	1993	Q0.05	12-22-95	11-29	0.20	0.20	0.16	1.81	14.0	3.59	7-31-95	1.69	...	5067	Oc	...	p0.39	0.46	0.53	P0.58	0.58				26
27	1940	Q0.05	1-11-96	12-13	0.20	0.20	0.20	343	1554	1162	9-30-95	2777	...	96512	Dc	0.14	□d0.15	□d1.75	0.38	E7.80↓	6.76	9 Mo Sep	d0.64	5.74	27
28	....	0.02	7-25-85	7-2	...	Nil	....	0.22	23.1	30.1	10-01-95	0.78	...	3655	Dc	□d0.06	d2.13	0.50	d1.60	....	d4.74	9 Mo Sep	d0.66	d3.80	28
29	....	None Since Public			...	Nil	....	Equity per shr $8.43			9-30-95	....	...	6942	Dc	0.09	0.24	0.53	0.36	....	0.48	9 Mo Sep	0.24	0.36	29
30	1988	Q0.05	11-30-95	11-1	0.20	0.20	0.20	9.05	186	66.2	8-31-95	81.0	...	29685	My	0.63	0.25	d0.06	0.41	0.67	1.01	6 Mo Nov	0.23	0.57	30
31◆	1976	0.02¼	7-15-95	6-27	0.068	Nil	0.09	66.7	508	278	10-28-95	15.8	...	103131	Ja	0.55	0.75	Δ0.70	0.42	Ed0.50	d0.26	9 Mo Oct	0.37	d0.31	31
32	....	None Since Public			...	Nil	....	0.24	7.77	16.9	9-30-95	55.2	...	8213	Dc	0.54	0.04	□0.50	0.52	....	0.56	9 Mo Sep	0.46	0.50	32
33	1993	Q0.07	12-15-95	11-29	0.28	0.28	0.28	0.65	48.8	28.3	9-30-95	18.6	...	9949	Dc	p0.46	0.73	0.08	d0.15	....	0.49	9 Mo Sep	d0.19	0.45	33
34◆	1993	Q0.08	1-15-96	12-28	s0.267	0.32	s0.209	Book Value $8.29			9-30-95	43.1	14	±6281	Dc	±0.70	±1.11	Δ±0.82	±1.21	....	1.55	9 Mo Sep	±0.86	±1.20	34
35◆	1988	Q0.20	11-21-95	10-31	0.75	0.80	0.59	Book Value $18.89			9-30-95	1456	...	p44904	Dc	2.06	2.21	Δ2.67	2.92	E3.15↑	3.10	9 Mo Sep	2.18	2.36	35
36	1987	Q0.02¾	10-20-95	10-4	0.11	0.11	0.11	1.03	72.9	40.5	7-31-95	8.74	...	★6250	Ja	0.50	□d0.11	1.08	1.50	....	2.09	9 Mo Oct	1.12	1.71	36
37	....	None Since Public			...	Nil	....	12.4	51.2	19.1	9-30-95	18.3	...	±10061	Dc	...	...	p±0.64	p±1.30	....	1.49	12 Mo Sep	±1.37	±1.49	37
38	1993	A0.10	11-30-95	10-27	0.10	0.10	0.08	0.11	11.5	6.48	8-31-95	6.46	...	3572	Au	0.28	0.28	0.24	0.36	0.43	0.43				38
39	1848	Q0.45	11-15-95	10-26	1.75	1.80	1.46	Book Value $32.93			12-31-94	p5518	56000	p178956	Dc	3.12	3.46	Δ1.89	[70]5.87	E5.60↓	5.18	9 Mo Sep	4.76	4.07	39
40	....	Terms&trad. basis should			be checked in detail			Wrrts expire 6-30-96				....	...	3315	Dc	...	...	...	....	....	....				40
41	1994	0.40	1-15-96	12-20	1.50	1.60	1.20	Equity per shr $4.10			9-30-95	136	...	6093	Dc	...	...	□[71]d0.01	1.05	....	0.94	9 Mo Sep	0.79	□0.68	41
42◆	1922	†20.00	6-11-93	6-14	...	Nil	....	2.60	29.8	18.9	8-31-95	81.5	...	7292	Nv	1.20	1.60	□0.20	□0.50	....	1.80	9 Mo Aug	0.38	□1.68	42
43	....	None Since Public			...	Nil	....	0.22	51.2	64.9	9-30-95	21.7	...	★26134	Je	d0.66	*0.19	d0.60	d2.55	d1.40	d0.94	3 Mo Sep	d0.48	d0.02	43
44	1992	gA0.10	10-30-95	9-27	g0.10	0.10	g0.10	....	154	85.6	j4-30-95	232	10000	±11627	Ap	±0.95	±0.26	±0.28	±d0.41	d0.09	jNil	6 Mo Oct	0.81	0.90	44
45	....	None Since Public			...	Nil	....	5.61	16.9	2.53	6-30-95	0.15	...	6112	Sp	0.34	0.11	0.15	0.29	P0.33	0.33				45
46◆	....	None Since Public			...	Nil	....	5.64	19.5	45.1	9-11-95	41.8	...	51520	Dc	p0.10	p0.25	p0.31	d0.14	....	d0.34	9 Mo Sep	Nil	d0.20	46
47	....	None Since Public			...	Nil	....	13.4	89.2	8.51	9-30-95	7.45	...	31363	Dc	Δ0.05	Nil	0.04	0.02	....	0.01	9 Mo Sep	0.01	Nil	47
48	....	None Since Public			...	Nil	....	8.28	23.6	4.37	9-30-95	0.39	...	5078	Dc	0.09	0.14	0.81	0.29	....	0.48	9 Mo Sep	0.20	0.39	48
49	....	None Since Public			...	Nil	....	19.9	123	32.4	9-24-95	35.9	...	14150	Dc	0.05	0.45	0.16	0.58	....	0.84	9 Mo Sep	0.35	0.61	49
50◆	....	None Since Public			...	Nil	....	7.85	22.3	10.6	10-01-95	....	...	10853	Dc	p0.23	p0.58	0.51	0.69	....	0.81	9 Mo Sep	0.49	0.61	50
51	1994	Q0.57½	1-22-96	12-27	2.08	2.30	1.68	Equity per shr $15.34			9-30-95	90.8	...	11485	Dc	...	p0.81	Δp0.35	1.49	....	1.71	9 Mo Sep	1.06	1.28	51
52	1971	Q0.52	12-8-95	11-20	2.06	2.08	2.04	34.2	220	151	9-30-95	88.0	...	9850	Dc	5.27	1.60	Δ1.82	4.46	....	4.49	9 Mo Sep	1.91	1.94	52

◆**Stock Splits & Divs By Line Reference Index** [7]3-for-2,'93. [9]Adj to 3%, Nov'93. [10]3-for-2,'93. [15]2-for-1,'92,'93,'95. [21]Adj to 5%,'94,'95:3-for-2,'95. [22]2-for-1,'93:Adj for 5%,'94:3-for-2,'95. [23]Adj to 1.66%,'94. [24]2-for-1,'95. [26]5-for-4,'94,'95:To split 5-for-4,ex Jan 23. [31]2-for-1,'92. [34]Adj to 5%,'95. [35]3-for-2,'92,'93. [42]3-for-1,'91. [46]3-for-2,2-for-1,'92:3-for-2,'93. [50]3-for-2,'94.

¶ S&P 500 # MidCap 400 ✣ SmallCap 600 • Options Index	Ticker	Name of Issue (Call Price of Pfd. Stocks)	Market	Com. Rank. & Pfd. Rating	Inst. Hold Cos	Inst. Hold Shs. (000)	Principal Business	Price Range 1971-93 High	1971-93 Low	1994 High	1994 Low	1995 High	1995 Low	Dec. Sales in 100s	December, 1995 Last Sale Or Bid High	Low	Last	%Div Yield	P-E Ratio	Total Return % Annualized 12 Mo	36 Mo	60 Mo
1	CMFB	✔Chemfab Corp	NNM	B	29	2049	Hi-performance coat'd fabrics	28½	1½	14	10¼	21½	12½	302	21	19¼	21	...	19	66.3	22.2	1.0
¶2•[1]	CHL	✔Chemical Banking Corp	NY,B,C,Ch,P	B–	724	186364	Commercial bkg,NYC&Texas	56¼	9⅝	42⅛	33⅝	64¾	35¾	184714	62½	56⅞	58¾	3.4	9	67.5	19.3	46.2
3	CHERB	✔Cherry Corp'B'	NNM	B–	38	1268	Electro-mechanical products	17	2½	17¼	10⅞	16¼	9½	815	10½	9½	9½	...	8	–32.1	–10.5	8.1
4	PHD.EC	✔Chesapeake Bio Labs'A'	ECM	NR	..	...	Mfr pharmac'l,medical prod/svc	3¼	1	4⅜	1⅞	2⅞	1³⁄₁₆	913	1⅝	1³⁄₁₆	1⅜	...	8	–47.6	...	...
#5•[2]	CSK	✔Chesapeake Corp	NY,Ch,Ph	B–	218	16872	Kraft paper, board: containers	29⅛	2⅞	35⅞	22¼	39	27½	25043	30⅛	27½	29⅝	2.7	8	–8.0	16.7	20.4
6	CHK	✔Chesapeake Energy	NY,Ch,Ph	NR	72	8856	Oil & gas developm't/prod'n	4¼	1½	11½	1⁷⁄₁₆	33¼	6⅝	36427	33¼	27¼	33¼	...	51	207	...	...
7	CPK	✔Chesapeake Utilities	NY	B	24	461	Natural gas dstr Del & Md	17⅝	1½	15¼	12⅜	15½	12⅛	1086	15⅛	14½	14⅝	6.2	8	21.4	10.7	11.5
¶8•[1]	CHV	✔Chevron Corp	NY,B,C,Ch,P,Ph,Vc	B	1087	304632	Major integrated int'l oil	49⅜	5	47⅜	39⅞	53⅝	43⅜	223908	53⅝	48¾	52⅜	3.8	18	22.7	19.9	12.5
9•[3]	CYE	✔Cheyenne Software	AS,Ph	B–	156	25262	Computer software/equipment	26⅞	⁹⁄₁₆	30⅜	6	27⅞	12⅜	67433	27⅞	21⅜	26⅛	...	34	90.0	27.8	64.2
10	JNS	✔Chic by H.I.S. Inc	NY,Ch,Ph	NR	61	6150	Design,mfr casual apparel	15½	9	16	9	12⅛	4¾	12583	6	4¾	5½	...	55	–41.3	...	...
11	DOCKS	✔Chicago Dock & Canal Trust	NNM	NR	24	2313	Real estate investment trust	37½	7¾	12	8¾	14½	9½	970	11	9¾	11	0.4	d	7.7	7.6	2.6
12	CHML	✔Chicago Miniature Lamp	NNM	NR	16	1297	Mfr miniature light prd	....	....	....	....	25½	12½	4217	25½	20	23	...	..	...	...	...
13	CVR	✔Chicago Rivet & Mach	AS,Ch	B+	15	116	Mfr rivets, fasteners: mchy	30⅝	10¾	34⅜	25⅞	34⅞	25¾	71	30⅜	28⅛	29	e4.1	8	16.2	10.2	14.8
14	CHCS	✔Chico's FAS	NNM	NR	28	876	Retail private label clothing	19	7	17¼	4¼	8½	4	12733	5	4¼	4⅜	...	55	–12.5	...	...
15	CFCM	Chief Consol Mining	NSC,P	C	8	82	Mine leasing operations,Utah	15⅜	¹³⁄₁₆	6⅞	3⅜	11⅜	5	3195	11⅜	6¾	11	...	d	126	32.3	35.9
16	CID	✔Chieftain Intl	AS,To	NR	44	5117	Oil & gas explor'n/prod'n	25	11½	18	10	17⅞	10⅛	1296	17⅞	16¾	17¾	...	d	71.1	1.7	–0.8
17	GSSPr	Chieftain Intl Fd $1.8125 Cv Pfd[54]	AS	B–	23	1094	Subsid of Chieftain Intl	32½	23¾	28⅞	19¼	27½	19⅞	1527	27½	25	25¼	7.2	..	...	...	...
18	AAHSC	✔Children's Broadcasting	NSC	NR	14	2383	Dvlp childrens radio prgms	7⅞	1	6⅜	3¼	8¼	3⅝	7161	7⅞	5⅞	6¼	...	d	51.5	...	...
19	KIDS	✔Childrens Comp Svcs	NNM	NR	17	5679	Educ/treatment/corrections	13	³⁄₁₆	3¼	1	4	1⅞	1810	3⅝	3⅛	3½	...	18	64.7	67.1	–1.4
20	CDCR	✔Childrens Discovery Centers	NNM	B–	48	5746	Operates day care centers	50	3	14¾	8½	17⅝	4	33541	8¼	4	5⅛	...	9	–53.9	11.0	–8.5
21	CHR	Chilgener S.A. ADS[55]	NY,Ch,Ph	NR	61	5428	Electricity generation, Chile	....	....	30½	23	34⅞	18¾	7634	26	23⅝	25	2.6	21	4.9	...	...
22	TIR	✔China Tire Holdings Ltd	NY	NR	..	...	Mfr motor vehicle tires	29	12¼	28	10	13⅞	4¾	21413	8¼	4¾	8	1.0	9	–22.3	...	...
23	CYD	China Yuchai Intl	NY,Ch,Ph	NR	..	...	Mfr diesel engines	....	....	10½	10	13¾	6⅞	7365	9⅛	6⅞	8⅛	1.2	..	–21.7	...	...
✣24	CHPS	✔Chips/Technologies	NNM,Ch	B–	64	7609	Mkts microcomputer chips	37¾	2¾	7⅝	3⅝	15⅞	6¼	97075	11⅜	8⅞	9	...	14	28.6	29.7	4.4
✣25•[4]	CQB	✔Chiquita Brands Intl	NY,B,Ch,P,Ph	B–	122	40150	Meat packing,bananas	50¾	¹³⁄₁₆	19⅜	11¼	18⅛	12⅛	22388	14¼	13¼	13¾	1.5	43	3.3	–4.2	–13.3
26	Pr A	$2.875 cm[57]Cv'A'Pfd(NC)	NY	B	23	2204		....	....	59¼	39½	53⅝	39¼	1481	46	44½	45⅛	6.4	..	...	...	...
#27•[5]	CHIR	✔Chiron Corp	NNM,Ch	C	215	15525	Therapeutic/diagnostic prod	86⅞	4⅜	96	50¾	113¾	47¾	127448	113¾	96¼	110½	...	d	37.3	25.2	20.1
28	CHF	✔Chock Full O'Nuts	NY,B,Ch,Ph	B–	42	4596	Process mkt coffee, tea	17⅛	1³⁄₁₆	8⅜	4⅞	7¼	5	5576	5⅞	5⅛	5¼	s...	12	–3.1	–9.7	4.0
#29•[6]	CCN	✔Chris-Craft Indus	NY,B,Ch,P,Ph	B–	150	11943	TV stations,video,chemicals	40⅞	¹⁄₁₆	40¼	31⅛	46¼	32⅛	6900	43⅝	40⅛	43¼	s...	48	32.0	16.0	16.9
30	Pr B	$1.40 cm Cv Pfd(40)vtg	NY,P	NR	3	3	plastic:foam rubber	971	3⅝	....	....	1248¾	850	....	....	....	1340½B	0.1	..	...	...	...
31	CST	✔Christiana Cos	NY,B,Ch,Ph	B–	27	548	Mfr indl prod/warehse/R.E.	37¼	⁹⁄₁₆	34⅝	24⅝	31¾	22	531	25	22	22½	...	13	–28.6	–14.8	4.9
32	CRC	✔Chromcraft Revington	NY	NR	52	5336	Design,mfr furniture	25¼	10	26¾	18½	27⅛	20	1230	27⅛	24¼	26⅝	...	13	23.8	11.9	...
¶33•[6]	C	✔Chrysler Corp	NY,To,B,C,Ch,P,Ph,Mo	B–	762	223385	Third largest auto maker	58⅜	1⁵⁄₁₆	63½	43⅛	58⅛	38¼	239779	55⅝	51¾	55⅛	4.4	13	15.0	21.6	38.5
34	CHSE	CHS Electronics	NSC	NR	1	.4	Wholesale computer equip/pd	....	....	....	....	5¾	3½	5571	5¾	4⅜	4½	...	21	...	...	...
¶35•[7]	CB	✔Chubb Corp	NY,B,Ch,P,Ph	A	643	61678	Property-casualty insurance	96⅜	4	83⅛	68⅝	100⅝	76⅛	33204	100⅝	96⅝	96¾	2.0	14	27.2	5.0	14.7
#36	CHD	✔Church & Dwight	NY,Ch,Ph	A	98	9726	Arm&Hammer,sodium bicarb	35¾	1¹⁄₁₆	29¼	16⅝	24⅞	17	8327	19½	18	18½	2.4	19	6.5	–14.2	2.1
37	CHY	✔Chyron Corp	NY,Ch	NR	8	636	Electr TV titling,graphic eq	11⅝	¹⁄₁₆	¾	⁷⁄₁₆	3	⅜	19160	2⅞	2⅛	2¾	...	46	529	54.2	54.4
38	CIBR	✔CIBER Inc	NNM	NR	18	1178	Computer info tech sys/svs	....	....	11⅛	7¾	34¼	9⅛	34598	31½	18¼	23⅜	...	37	137	...	...
39	CDCO	✔CIDCO Inc	NNM	NR	146	12205	Dgn/Dvp network svcs tel equip	....	....	32½	15	39¾	21¾	49935	28	22½	25½	...	18	–13.0	...	...
¶40•[6]	CI	✔CIGNA Corp	NY,B,Ch,P,Ph	B+	569	61454	Multi-line insur hldg co	77¼	14⅞	74	57	115	62¼	65105	113⅜	103	103¼	2.9	d	71.2	27.6	26.9
41	CER	✔CILCORP, Inc	NY,B,Ch,P,Ph	B+	107	2035	Hldg co:Central Illinois Lt	43¾	10	37½	28¾	44¾	31⅞	4612	44¾	39½	42⅜	5.8	13	42.4	8.8	11.3
42	CIMC	✔CIMCO Inc[63]	NNM	C	16	879	Mfrs plastic components	16	5¾	7½	4	10¾	3⅜	3958	10¾	9⅜	10¼	...	d	128	7.5	0.5
43•[6]	CSN	✔Cincinnati Bell	NY,C,Ch	B+	206	26545	Tel service in Ohio,Ky,Ind	35	1¹⁵⁄₁₆	20⅛	15⅜	35¼	16⅞	23274	35¼	29⅞	34¾	2.3	87	105	30.9	12.5
44•[8]	CINF	✔Cincinnati Financial	NNM	A	163	18071	Insurance holding co	63⅝	¾	55½	43¾	66¾	48⅜	8508	66¾	61¼	65¼	s2.1	16	43.1	8.8	23.3
45	JRL	Cincinnati G&E8.28%Jr SubDebs	NY	BBB+	..	...	Subsid of CINergy Corp	....	....	....	....	26⅜	24⅞	1491	26⅜	25¼	25⅝	8.1	..	...	...	...
46	CNMW	✔Cincinnati Microwave	NNM	C	58	9194	Mfrs radar warning devices	15½	¾	12	2⅛	21⅝	3½	73423	7	4	4½	...	d	14.3	14.5	30.5
¶47•[9]	CMZ	✔Cincinnati Milacron	NY,B,C,Ch,P	B–	219	23683	Machine tools: plastics mchy	46¾	2¼	27⅝	18⅝	33⅝	19⅞	12446	26¼	23⅞	26¼	1.4	8	11.5	19.4	22.4
✣48	CPX	✔Cineplex Odeon	NY,To,Ch,Ph	C	34	5150	Oper motion picture theatres	24¾	1⅛	4⅛	2¼	2⅞	1⅜	29506	1¾	1⅜	1½	...	d	–42.9	–5.0	–7.8
49	CINE	✔Cinergi Pictures Entertain	NNM	NR	29	5077	Dvlp,produce motion pictures	....	....	9¾	4⅝	11⅜	2½	30868	4⅛	2½	2½	...	d	–60.6	...	...
¶50	CIN	✔CINergy Corp	NY,B,C,Ch,P,Ph	B	472	85544	Hldg:elec & natural gas	29⅝	5⅞	27¾	20¾	31⅛	23⅜	37355	31⅛	29¼	30⅝	5.6	14	38.4	9.9	10.5
#51	CTAS	✔Cintas Corp	NNM	A+	238	18986	Sales & rental of uniforms	34	2⅞	36¼	29¾	48	33½	26322	46⅛	42½	44½	0.4	31	27.8	19.8	21.3
52	CPCI	✔Ciprico Inc	NNM	C	10	1072	Mfrs microcomputer parts	11⅝	1¾	6½	3½	18⅛	4½	9234	18⅛	12¼	17¼	...	96	273	81.7	44.4

Uniform Footnote Explanations-See Page 4. Other: [1]ASE:Cycle 3. [2]ASE:Cycle 2. [3]CBOE:Cycle 3. [4]Ph:Cycle 3. [5]ASE,CBOE,NY,P,Ph:Cycle 1. [6]CBOE:Cycle 1. [7]CBOE,NY:Cycle 1. [8]ASE:Cycle 1. [9]Ph:Cycle 2. [51]©$0.03,'94. [52]9 Mo Nov'94. [53]Excl subsid pfd. [54]Cm:callable$26.2083 to 1-1-97,scale to$25in2001. [55]Ea ADS rep 4 com, no par. [56]®$0.47,'95. [57]Co opt fr2-15-97to2-15-2001Cv into com re-spec cond. [58]®$0.42,'95. [59]?1.68,'94. [60]As reported,incl Chrysler Financial. [61]®$9.10,'94. [62]Subsid pfd in $M. [63]Hanna(M.A.)offer, $10.50. [64]Incl 49.2M sub restricted vtg shrs. [65]Incl current amts. [66]®$0.17,'95.

Index	Cash Divs. Ea. Yr. Since	Latest Payment Period $	Date	Ex. Div.	Total $ So Far 1995	Ind. Rate	Paid 1994	Mil-$ Cash & Equiv.	Curr. Assets	Curr. Liab.	Balance Sheet Date	Lg Trm Debt Mil-$	Shs. 000 Pfd.	Com.	Years End	1991	1992	1993	1994	1995	Last 12 Mos.	Interim Earnings Period	$ per Shr. 1994	1995	Index
1	....	None Since Public			...	Nil	....	3.28	35.6	9.03	10-01-95	7.09	...	5271	Je	1.13	0.86	0.67	0.74	1.00	1.09	3 Mo Sep	0.16	0.25	1
2	1827	Q0.50	1-31-96	1-3	1.88	2.00	1.58	Book Value $41.90			9-30-95	7537	30000	250038	Dc	0.11	3.90	Δ5.63	4.64	E6.55†	5.61	9 Mo Sep	3.98	□4.95	2
3◆	....	0.03	10-5-90	9-17	...	Nil	....	3.14	126	76.0	8-31-95	36.7	...	±12284	Fb	*0.42	Δ0.84	Δ±1.02	±1.36	....	1.14	9 Mo Nov	±0.95	±0.73	3
4	....	None Paid			...	Nil	....	0.09	2.69	0.70	9-30-95	0.13	...	3980	Mr	Δd0.04	Δ0.06	Δ0.13	0.14	....	0.17	6 Mo Sep	0.02	0.05	4
5	1933	Q0.20	2-15-96	1-10	0.76	0.80	0.72	0.30	301	144	9-30-95	371	...	23899	Dc	0.75	□0.63	0.44	1.58	E3.85	3.56	9 Mo Sep	0.90	2.88	5
6◆	....	None Since Public			...	Nil	....	29.3	75.1	70.7	9-30-95	145	...	17678	Je	0.10	0.20	d0.07	0.24	0.63	0.65	3 Mo Sep	0.13	0.15	6
7	1960	Q0.22½	1-6-96	12-6	0.89½	0.90	0.87½	0.49	14.9	18.6	9-30-95	26.1	...	3710	Dc	0.73	1.02	Δ1.10	1.23	....	1.77	12 Mo Sep	1.40	1.77	7
8◆	1912	Q0.50	12-11-95	11-15	1.92½	2.00	1.85	1317	7587	8798	9-30-95	4472	...	652234	Dc	1.85	□3.26	1.95	2.60	E2.87	3.03	9 Mo Sep	1.64	2.07	8
9◆	....	None Since Public			...	Nil	....	41.8	82.2	16.0	9-30-95	....	...	37497	Je	*0.04	*0.18	0.53	0.82	0.97	0.78	3 Mo Sep	0.38	0.19	9
10	....	None Since Public			...	Nil	....	6.32	178	48.9	8-05-95	86.6	...	9754	Oc	...	*p0.97	*p0.90	Δ1.03	P0.10	0.10				10
11	1962	Q0.01	3-1-96	2-13	0.04	0.04	[51]0.04	Equity per shr $14.39			10-31-95	28.0	...	5784	Ap	0.71	▲7.82	d0.39	0.02	□d0.50	d0.40	6 Mo Oct	d0.03	0.07	11
12	....	None Since Public			...	Nil	....	7.95	23.6	8.75	8-27-95	0.86	...	10470	Nv	...	...	...	p[52]0.31	....	....	9 Mo Aug	n/a	0.47	12
13	1932	Q0.30	12-20-95	12-1	†1.75	1.20	†1.55	7.22	15.2	3.14	9-30-95	....	...	587	Dc	1.25	1.62	2.39	3.25	....	3.79	9 Mo Sep	2.18	2.72	13
14◆	....	None Since Public			...	Nil	....	0.59	10.9	9.47	10-01-95	2.20	...	7777	Dc	...	p0.34	p0.61	0.41	....	0.08	9 Mo Sep	0.52	0.19	14
15	....	0.05	12-1-49	11-3	...	Nil	....	1.37	1.41	0.16	6-30-95	....	6	4758	Dc	d0.07	d0.05	d0.20	d0.24	....	d0.31	9 Mo Sep	d0.09	d0.16	15
16	....	None Since Public			...	Nil	....	102	108	4.69	12-31-94	....[53]	...	10912	Dc	d0.58	0.04	d0.01	d1.32	....	d1.43	9 Mo Sep	d0.39	d0.50	16
17	1992	Q0.453	12-31-95	12-13	1.81¼	1.813	1.81¼	Cv into 1.25 Chieftain Intl com,$20				....	2400	...	Dc	...	...	...	....	....	....				17
18	....	None Since Public			...	Nil	....	0.07	1.27	4.67	9-30-95	0.18	290	6132	Dc	±d0.35	±d0.63	d0.70	d0.84	....	d1.07	9 Mo Sep	d0.51	d0.74	18
19	....	None Since Public			...	Nil	....	0.70	4.42	2.42	9-30-95	6.16	...	10758	Mr	d0.55	d1.90	0.08	0.19	....	0.20	6 Mo Sep	0.07	□0.08	19
20◆	....	None Paid			...	Nil	....	11.4	16.6	5.11	9-30-95	16.7	3	6204	Dc	d0.28	d0.33	0.35	0.57	....	0.55	9 Mo Sep	0.36	0.34	20
21	1994	0.095	11-27-95	10-31	0.644	0.64	0.204	27.2	93.4	87.8	12-31-94	330	...	247964	Dc	0.95	0.93	1.01	1.20	....	1.20				21
22	1993	Q0.02	12-31-95	12-13	0.10	0.08	0.09¼	76.8	141	47.4	12-31-93	6.86	...	±9100	Dc	...	p1.44	0.76	P0.92	....	0.92				22
23	1995	0.05		9-14	0.05	0.10	....	78.9	145	89.9	p9-30-94	13.3	...	★35340	Dc	...	...	p0.38	....	....	....	9 Mo SepΔ	n/a	p0.81	23
24	....	None Since Public			...	Nil	....	54.3	77.1	16.3	9-30-95	1.98	...	20280	Je	d0.71	d4.00	d3.13	0.16	[56]0.50	0.63	3 Mo Sep	0.07	0.20	24
25	1985	Q0.05	12-7-95	11-17	0.20	0.20	0.20	224	995	634	9-30-95	1320	p3523	54209	Dc	2.55	d5.48	d0.99	□d1.07	....	0.32	9 Mo Sep	□d0.37	□1.02	25
26	1994	Q0.71⅞	12-7-95	11-17	2.87½	2.875	2.324	Cv into 2.6316 com,$19				....	2000	...	Dc	...	...	...	....	....	....				26
27	....	None Since Public			...	Nil	....	149	602	361	9-30-95	412	...	p41557	Dc	*d22.12	□d3.18	0.55	0.53	Ed12.90	Ed13.31	9 Mo Sep	0.66	d13.18	27
28◆	....	3%Stk	7-27-95	7-7	3%Stk	Stk	3%Stk	4.74	109	16.9	10-31-95	108	...	10736	Jl	0.89	d0.37	d0.11	0.73	[58]0.45	0.44	3 Mo Oct	0.09	0.08	28
29◆	....	3%Stk	4-4-95	3-16	3%Stk	Stk	3%Stk	1525	1771	248	9-30-95	....	352	±29168	Dc	2.00	2.25	5.11	[59]2.17	E0.90	1.05	9 Mo Sep	1.70	0.58	29
30	1977	S0.70	9-29-95	9-13	1.40	1.40	1.40	Cv into 30.9929				....	282	...	Dc	b35.55	b39.40	...	....	....	....				30
31	....	0.10	12-2-81	11-9	...	Nil	....	4.31	15.7	12.6	9-30-95	36.3	...	5196	Je	2.30	1.01	0.57	0.59	1.98	1.79	3 Mo Sep	0.46	0.27	31
32	....	None Since Public			...	Nil	....	....	41.9	17.8	9-30-95	6.63	...	5729	Dc	p0.80	p1.15	1.55	1.91	....	2.03	9 Mo Sep	1.39	1.51	32
33	1984	Q0.60	1-12-96	12-13	1.80	2.40	0.90	Equity per shr $21.80			9-30-95	[60]9105	200	382561	Dc	□d2.22	□1.47	□6.77	[61]10.11	E4.30	6.01	9 Mo Sep	6.92	2.82	33
34	....	None Since Public			...	Nil	....	9.51	173	155	9-30-95	0.52	...	p15165	Dc	...	...	...	d0.02	....	0.22	9 Mo Sep	d0.01	0.23	34
35	1902	Q0.49	1-9-96	12-20	1.93	1.96	1.81	Equity per shr $57.38			9-30-95	1165	...	87211	Dc	6.32	6.96	□3.91	Δ5.95	E7.00	7.44	9 Mo Sep	4.19	5.68	35
36	1901	Q0.11	12-1-95	11-10	0.44	0.44	0.44	13.6	122	100	9-29-95	7.50	...	19608	Dc	1.34	1.45	□1.46	0.31	E1.00	0.31	9 Mo Sep	0.43	0.43	36
37	....	2%Stk	3-1-90	2-1	...	Nil	....	6.95	33.4	13.5	9-30-95	6.37	...	89080	Dc	d1.71	0.01	0.02	d0.10	....	0.06	9 Mo Sep	d0.12	0.04	37
38	....	None Since Public			...	Nil	....	0.61	24.0	13.9	9-30-95	0.30	...	★7734	Je	0.10	0.11	0.23	0.44	0.55	0.63	3 Mo Sep	0.14	0.22	38
39	....	None Since Public			...	Nil	....	33.0	119	35.7	9-30-95	....	...	14122	Dc	...	...	p0.38	0.90	....	1.44	9 Mo Sep	0.62	1.16	39
40	1867	Q0.76	1-10-96	12-11	3.04	3.04	3.04	Equity per shr $69.25			9-30-95	1068	...	75939	Dc	□6.34	□4.70	3.25	7.66	Ed0.85	1.54	9 Mo Sep	5.14	d0.98	40
41	1921	Q0.615	12-20-95	11-20	2.46	2.46	2.46	5.58	154	123	9-30-95	331	[62]66	13266	Dc	3.14	2.48	2.60	2.50	....	3.28	12 Mo Sep	2.60	3.28	41
42	....	None Since Public			...	Nil	....	3.80	36.7	38.3	10-31-95	....	...	2970	Ap	0.85	0.37	0.50	d0.41	d0.52	d0.22	6 Mo Oct	d0.37	d0.07	42
43	1879	Q0.20	2-1-96	12-29	0.80	0.80	0.80	136	449	410	9-30-95	491	...	66389	Dc	0.63	□0.56	d0.93	□1.15	E0.40	0.26	9 Mo Sep	□0.83	d0.06	43
44◆	1954	Q0.34	1-15-96	12-13	s1.308	1.36	1.181	Equity per shr $45.13			9-30-95	278	...	53028	Dc	2.80	3.23	Δ3.75	3.72	....	4.11	9 Mo Sep	2.87	3.26	44
45	....	Plan qtly div			...	2.07	....	Co option redm fr 6-30-2000 at $25				★100	...	...	Dc	...	...	...	....	....	....	Mature 6-30-2025			45
46	....	0.15	12-16-86	11-25	...	Nil	....	0.61	37.6	19.9	10-01-95	0.73	...	15595	Dc	d0.85	□d0.54	d0.12	d0.94	Ed0.35↓	d0.64	9 Mo Sep	d0.58	d0.28	46
47	1923	Q0.09	12-12-95	11-21	0.36	0.36	0.36	43.7	688	373	10-07-95	329	60	34268	Dc	d3.67	*0.58	□d1.41	1.10	E3.25↓	1.46	9 Mo Sep	0.72	1.08	47
48	....	None Since Public			...	Nil	....	1.68	20.0	83.7	9-30-95	389	...	[64]±114757	Dc	d1.38	d0.48	d0.07	d0.13	....	d0.30	9 Mo Sep	d0.06	d0.23	48
49	....	None Since Public			...	Nil	....	Equity per shr $5.24			6-30-95	[65]143	...	p14192	Dc	...	...	pd0.64	0.30	....	d1.29	9 Mo Sep	0.14	d1.45	49
50◆	1853	Q0.43	11-15-95	10-26	1.72	1.72	1.72	87.4	862	1072	9-30-95	2695	8018	157210	Dc	2.21	2.04	d0.39	1.30	E2.12	1.62	12 Mo Sep	0.36	1.62	50
51◆	1984	A0.20	4-3-95	3-6	0.20	0.20	0.17	61.2	260	101	8-31-95	120	...	47047	My	0.73	Δ0.79	0.97	1.12	1.34	1.46	6 Mo Nov	0.63	0.75	51
52	....	0.20	11-29-90	11-14	...	Nil	....	4.69	9.70	3.13	9-30-95	0.04	...	2271	Sp	d0.19	0.20	d0.87	d0.16	[66]0.18	0.18				52

◆Stock Splits & Divs By Line Reference Index [3]2-for-1 in Cl'A','94. [6]2-for-1,'94:3-for-2,'95. [8]2-for-1,'94. [9]3-for-2,'92,'93,'94. [14]2-for-1,'94. [20]1-for-8 REVERSE,'91. [28]Adj to 3%,'95. [29]Adj to 3%,'95. [44]3-for-1,'92:Adj for 5%,'95. [50]3-for-2,'92. [51]3-for-2,'91:2-for-1,'92.

¶ S&P 500 # MidCap 400 ✣ SmallCap 600 • Options

Index	Ticker	Name of Issue (Call Price of Pfd. Stocks)	Market	Com. Rank. & Pfd. Rating	Inst. Hold Cos	Inst. Hold Shs. (000)	Principal Business	1971-93 High	1971-93 Low	1994 High	1994 Low	1995 High	1995 Low	Dec. Sales in 100s	December, 1995 Last Sale Or Bid High	Low	Last	%Div Yield	P-E Ratio	Total Return % Annualized 12 Mo	36 Mo	60 Mo
1	CIP	✔CIPSCO Inc[51]	NY,B,C,Ch,Ph	A–	144	8871	Hldg co:Central Ill Public Svc	33¾	8½	30⅝	25¼	39	27	7830	39	36¾	39	5.2	17	53.1	15.5	20.2
2	CRK	✔Circle K Corp	NY,Ch	NR	38	6100	Operate convenience stores	....	....	....	....	27⅜	13¾	6597	27⅜	23¼	25⅜	...	17	...	...	...
✣3•[1]	CCON	✔Circon Corp	NNM	B–	67	4610	Video equip for medical use	50	2⅜	14¼	8½	24¼	11	43418	23½	19	20¼	...	d	80.0	–3.1	14.6
¶4•[2]	CC	✔Circuit City Stores	NY,P,Ph	A	497	69150	Retailer:video eq,appliances	33⅞	1/32	27½	16½	38	21	158272	30¾	26⅝	27⅝	0.4	14	29.7	2.7	34.9
5	CSYI	✔Circuit Systems	NNM	B–	15	993	Mfr printed circuit boards	9⅛	⅞	8⅞	4⅜	7⅞	3	14900	7⅞	5	6¼	...	12	22.0	12.6	31.9
#6•[3]	CIR	✔Circus Circus Enterp	NY,B,Ch,P	B+	327	70338	Casino-hotels,Las Vegas,Reno	49⅜	2¼	40¾	19¾	36⅛	23½	97839	28⅝	25⅝	27⅞	...	21	17.4	–9.2	9.3
#7•[4]	CRUS	✔Cirrus Logic	NNM	B–	246	47491	Mkt semiconductor controllers	19⅞	4	22⅜	10½	61⅛	11⅛	571761	29½	18⅞	19¾	...	15	70.4	4.0	18.3
8	CISI	✔C.I.S. Technologies	NNM	B–	31	4170	Process med'l insur claims	7⅞	¾	4⅛	1 15/16	4½	2	33210	4	2⅞	3¼	...	30	36.8	–23.0	–2.8
¶9•[5]	CSCO	✔cisco Systems	NNM,Ch	B	943	223497	Mfr computer network prod	32⅞	1⅛	40¾	18¾	89⅜	32⅜	1212384	85¾	69½	74⅝	...	43	113	56.8	93.5
10	CDL	✔Citadel Holding	AS,B,Ch	NR	11	811	Real estate development	60¾	7½	12½	2 1/16	3⅛	2	10147	2½	2⅛	2⅜	...	d	–5.0	–50.0	–34.7
11	CITA	✔CITATION Computer Sys	NNM	NR	13	585	Mfr microcomputer lab info sys	15⅝	5½	8	4½	7⅝	3⅝	3262	5⅝	3⅞	5⅝	...	d	–18.2	–20.0	...
12	CAST	✔Citation Corp	NNM	NR	58	5497	Mfr iron/steel castings	....	....	13¼	8	19	9¼	43011	16⅜	9¼	12	...	9	–5.9	...	...
¶13•[6]	CCI	✔Citicorp	NY,B,C,Ch,P,Ph	B–	1050	303056	Commercial bkg,New York	39¾	8¼	47¾	36⅛	74	38½	453685	72⅞	63⅜	67¼	1.8	10	64.2	49.6	41.7
14	CZF	CitiSave Financial	AS	NR	1	31	Savings & loan, Louisiana	....	....	....	....	15⅞	10	747	14¾	14¼	14¾	2.0	..	...	...	...
15	CZC	✔Citizens Corp	NY	NR	49	4248	Insur-personal prop, casualty	27⅛	18¾	20¾	14¾	19⅝	16⅛	4651	19⅝	18½	18⅝	1.1	10	21.5	...	...
16	CIA	✔Citizens Inc'A'	AS,Ch	B–	20	391	Life Insurance hldg co	10	3/16	9⅛	6⅞	15⅝	7⅛	1193	9⅛	8⅜	9⅛	...	54	8.1	22.5	18.1
17	CSGI	✔Citizens Security Grp	NSC	NR	5	96	Sells property,casualty insur	4	2⅜	4¾	3¼	5⅝	3⅛	278	5⅝	4¾	5⅝	...	8	73.1	17.1	12.4
18	CZN.A	✔Citizens Util[56]'A'	NY,Ph	A+	136	12574	Elec, teleph, water, gas sv	17¾	⅜	16⅛	11¾	13⅝	10¼	28256	13¼	12⅜	12¾	s...	17	40.0	20.0	34.6
19	CZN.B	✔ Class'B'	NY,Ph	A+	113	5384	broad geographic area	17⅝	1	16¼	11⅞	13⅝	10⅜	26532	13⅜	12⅜	12¾	s...	17	38.9	20.9	34.3
20	CTXS	Citrix Systems	NNM	NR	..	...	Multi-user applicat'n svr sys	....	....	....	....	35	15	70269	35	15	32½	...	..	...	...	...
#21•[7]	CYN	✔City National	NY,Ch,Ph	C	132	19183	Comm'l bkg,Beverly Hills,Calif	28	7/16	12⅛	7⅛	15⅝	9¾	18516	14⅛	13¼	14	2.0	14	37.8	30.3	3.8
22	CKR	✔CKE Restaurants	NY,Ch	B–	50	6868	Fast svc restaurant chain	17¾	2⅜	14⅜	6½	18	6⅜	9371	18	15¼	16	0.5	41	135	25.3	21.0
23	CKSG	CKS Group	NNM	NR	..	...	Marketing commun svcs	....	....	....	....	39	17	50893	39	17	39	...	..	...	...	...
#24•[8]	CLE	✔Claire's Stores	NY,B,Ch,P	A–	148	12654	Women's specialty retail strs	23⅞	1/16	23⅛	9½	23	11¼	44189	20	16¾	17⅝	0.7	13	54.4	17.9	13.6
✣25	CLC	✔CLARCOR Inc	NY	B+	108	8728	Mfr filtration/consumer prod	22⅝	1	22⅜	15⅞	27	18⅝	4551	21⅞	19	20⅜	3.1	14	3.6	6.1	11.2
26	CLFY	✔Clarify Inc	NNM	NR	..	...	Dvp client/server software	....	....	....	....	32¾	13	9203	30	24½	30	...	..	...	...	...
#27•[8]	CMH	✔Clayton Homes	NY,Ch,Ph	B+	237	59171	Produces/finances mfrd hms	15¾	11/16	17⅛	9⅞	23⅝	11¼	50506	23⅜	20⅛	21⅜	0.4	22	78.5	22.1	38.8
28•[6]	CCU	✔Clear Channel Commun	NY,Ch	B–	194	17215	Oper TV/radio stations	18½	1¼	26	15¾	44¼	25⅛	14054	44¼	38	44⅛	...	54	78.9	89.8	76.1
29	CLNTF	✔Clearnet Communic 'A'[59]	NNM	NR	13	2102	Wireless communic svc,Canada	....	....	12	6⅞	18⅛	5	23382	18⅛	14	16	...	d	133	...	...
#30	CLF	✔Cleveland-Cliffs	NY,Ch	B	190	10478	Produce/process iron ore	46¼	6	45½	34	46¾	36⅛	5118	41⅛	38	41	3.2	9	16.0	11.3	16.4
31	CLDR	✔Cliffs Drilling	NNM	B–	49	2608	Contract drill'g o&g wells	17½	6½	14	10½	16⅜	11¼	4253	16⅜	14	14¾B	...	..	21.6	6.0	5.6
¶32•[9]	CLX	✔Clorox Co	NY,B,C,Ch,P,Ph	A	471	26032	Household pr: spec foods	55⅝	2¾	59½	47	79¼	55¼	20198	79¼	70½	71⅝	3.0	18	25.8	19.5	18.0
33	CTMEQ	✔ClothesTime Inc	NNM	D	30	5485	Young women's apparel strs	24½	1⅜	8⅜	3½	4	⅜	68159	1¾	⅜	⅝	...	d	–83.9	–61.8	–17.7
✣34	CMT	✔CMAC Investment	NY,Ph	NR	153	10037	Private mortgage insurance	35⅛	18	30⅝	23¼	55¾	28¾	6277	50¾	42½	44	0.5	11	51.1	21.5	...
35	CMX	✔CMI Corp Cl'A'	NY,B,Ph	B–	35	4472	Automated roadbldg eq,dstr	22½	⅝	9⅞	4¾	8¼	4¼	5250	6	4⅞	5⅛	...	6	–19.6	12.2	40.4
#36•[9]	CML	✔CML Group	NY,Ch,Ph	B	126	28533	Specialty retailer	32⅜	1 1/16	22⅝	8½	11⅛	3⅝	86675	6¼	3⅝	5	2.0	d	–50.6	–38.9	12.2
#37•[10]	CMS	✔CMS Energy	NY,B,C,Ch,P,Ph	B	256	50791	Hldg:elec&gas in Michigan	39⅝	4⅛	25	19⅝	30	22⅝	36738	30	27¼	29⅞	3.2	13	34.7	22.5	4.3
38	CPG	✔CMS Energy Cl'G'	NY,Ch	NR	16	1215	Natl gas dstr,storage,transp'tn	....	....	....	....	18⅞	16⅛	4168	18⅞	17¾	18⅞	5.9	12	...	...	...
39•[11]	CNA	✔CNA Financial[62]	NY,B,Ch,P,Ph	B–	..	...	Insurance holding company	108¾	2¼	82¼	60	123¼	64¾	7197	117	111⅝	113½	...	15	76.0	4.4	10.7
40	CNBE	✔CNB Bancshares	NNM	A	43	3231	Comm'l bkg,Indiana, Ky	28¼	3	30½	26⅞	30⅝	25	2835	28½	26	28½	s2.8	14	11.9	20.6	24.3
41•[12]	CNXS	✔CNS Inc	NNM	NR	51	4667	Mfr nasal breathing device	7⅛	11/16	5	2 1/16	24¾	4⅜	45535	16⅜	13¾	15⅛	...	29	241	132	63.1
42	COA	✔Coachmen Indus	NY,Ch,Ph	B–	65	4837	Mfr recreational vehicles	39⅝	½	18⅜	11¾	23¾	13⅝	5418	23¾	19½	21¾	1.3	10	46.1	11.6	45.1
43	CRV	✔Coast Distribution Sys	AS,Ch	B	21	1501	Wholesale distr R.V.parts	11	1½	9	6	7⅞	5¾	1335	6⅛	5¾	6	...	8	–23.8	5.4	24.6
✣44•[7]	CSA	✔Coast Svgs Finl	NY,Ch,Ph,P	B–	89	12629	Savings banks,California	22	1⅝	19	12⅜	34⅝	13½	19019	34⅝	29	34⅝	...	20	152	46.6	70.9
¶45•[13]	CGP	✔Coastal Corp	NY,B,C,Ch,P,Ph	B+	451	63154	Refining & marketing of oil	39⅝	1	33¾	24¾	37¾	25⅛	56169	37¾	33¼	37	1.1	16	47.1	16.8	4.4
46	Pr A	$1.19 cm Cv A Pfd (33)vtg	NY,B	BB	2	.1	natural gas, oil & gas,	128	10¼	119	95½	119	108⅞	....	....	....	133¾B	0.9	..	...	...	...
47	Pr B	$1.83 cm Cv B Pfd (50)vtg	NY	BB	3	.9	coal mining, chemicals	135	14½	....	....	138¼	104½	1	138¼	138¼	136½B	1.3	..	...	...	...
48•[9]	DR	✔Coastal Physician Grp	NY,Ch	NR	81	8221	Physician recruit'g/mgmt svs	40	11	42	26⅜	30⅝	12¼	16663	14¾	13	13½	...	..	–49.8	–20.9	...
49	PAR	✔Coastcast Corp	NY,Ch,Ph	NR	29	1419	Mfr metal golf clubheads	19⅞	15¾	33⅞	10⅝	13⅝	7½	8636	10¾	9⅛	10⅛	...	13	–12.0	...	...
50	COBR	✔Cobra Electronics	NNM	C	17	1348	Consumer & ind'l electronics	23½	⅜	3⅞	1¾	3⅜	1½	5478	3⅜	2½	3	...	d	60.0	–10.1	–1.6
✣51•[14]	CBRA	✔Cobra Golf[66]	NNM	NR	109	6882	Mfr,mkt golf clubs	18	10½	41½	12½	39¼	20	219216	35⅞	26¾	35⅝	...	21	–3.1	...	...
✣52	COKE	✔Coca-Cola Bott Consol	NNM	B–	62	2560	Soft drink distributor	58	1⅞	37¼	24	35⅞	26	1763	35½	33½	35	2.9	21	38.9	31.6	17.3

Uniform Footnote Explanations-See Page 4. Other: [1]ASE,Ph:Cycle 2. [2]P:Cycle 1. [3]ASE:Cycle 3. [4]CBOE,NY,P:Cycle 3. [5]CBOE,Ph:Cycle 1. [6]CBOE:Cycle 1. [7]CBOE:Cycle 2. [8]NY:Cycle 2. [9]Ph:Cycle 1. [10]NY:Cycle 3. [11]ASE:Cycle 2. [12]CBOE,NY:Cycle 1. [13]ASE,CBOE:Cycle 3. [14]ASE,CBOE,NY,P,Ph:Cycle 1. [51]Approve mgr w/Union Elec form Ameren Cp,1.03 com. [52]Subsid pfd. [53]®$6.40,'94. [54]To be determined. [55]82.3% owned by Hanover Insurance Co. [56]Cv into 1 shr Cl'B'. [57]®$0.74,'94. [58]Special divd. [59]non-vtg. [60]Excl subsid pfd. [61]Excl 7.6M class'G'com. [62]Loews Corp holds 83%. [63]®$1.85,'94. [64]®$0.70,'94. [65]Excl $0.6M subsid Pfd. [66]Amer Brands plan mgr,$36.

Splits ◆	Dividends							Financial Position				Capitalization			Earnings $ Per Shr.							Interim Earnings			
Index	Cash Divs. Ea. Yr. Since	Latest Payment Period $	Date	Ex. Div.	Total $ So Far 1995	Ind. Rate	Paid 1994	Mil-$ Cash& Equiv.	Curr. Assets	Curr. Liab.	Balance Sheet Date	Lg Trm Debt Mil-$	Shs. 000 Pfd.	Com.	Years End	1991	1992	1993	1994	1995	Last 12 Mos.	Period	$ per Shr. 1994	1995	Index
1	1947	Q0.51	12-10-95	11-15	2.03	2.04	1.99	9.19	209	144	9-30-95	479	[52]800	34070	Dc	2.11	2.13	2.51	2.46	....	2.30	12 Mo Nov	2.50	2.30	1
2	....	None Since Public			...	Nil	....	35.3	250	327	7-31-95	177	...	24267	Ap	...	...	...	p0.94	□1.20	1.50	6 Mo Oct	0.56	0.86	2
3	....	None Since Public			...	Nil	....	23.8	94.4	22.1	9-30-95	71.9	...	12336	Dc	*0.45	*0.77	Δ0.25	0.47	....	d0.37	9 Mo Sep	0.35	d0.49	3
4◆	1979	Q0.03	1-15-96	12-27	0.11	0.12	0.09	46.6	1805	1086	8-31-95	300	...	97234	Fb	0.83	1.15	1.36	1.72	E1.95↓	1.85	9 Mo Nov	0.86	0.99	4
5	....	None Paid			...	Nil	....	0.21	18.8	9.94	10-31-95	12.7	...	5322	Ap	0.10	□0.36	0.59	0.95	0.42	0.52	6 Mo Oct	0.28	0.38	5
6◆	....	None Since Public			...	Nil	....	74.7	133	113	10-31-95	740	...	102891	Ja	1.23	□1.41	1.34	1.59	E1.32	1.34	9 Mo Oct	1.23	0.98	6
7◆	....	None Since Public			...	Nil	....	163	605	297	9-30-95	40.7	...	63140	Mr	0.41	0.41	Δ0.70	0.97	....	1.32	6 Mo Sep	0.44	0.80	7
8	....	None Since Public			...	Nil	....	0.02	19.6	4.82	9-30-95	4.41	2384	30200	Dc	0.06	0.12	Δ0.02	0.08	....	0.11	9 Mo Sep	0.06	0.09	8
9◆	....	None Since Public			...	Nil	....	598	1290	477	10-29-95	....	...	276252	Jl	0.17	0.33	0.66	1.19	1.52	1.74	3 Mo Oct	0.37	0.59	9
10	....	None Since Public			...	Nil	....	Equity per shr $2.93			9-30-95	16.2	1329	6004	Dc	0.81	0.62	d11.56	d26.45	....	d1.10	9 Mo Sep	d25.16	0.19	10
11	....	None Since Public			...	Nil	....	2.30	11.2	5.56	9-30-95	0.49	...	3730	Mr	0.60	0.73	0.36	d0.49	....	d0.76	6 Mo Sep	0.22	d0.05	11
12	....	None Since Public			...	Nil	....	....	72.9	44.8	7-02-95	p60.0	...	★17421	Sp	...	...	p0.34	p1.02	P1.27	1.27				12
13	1994	Q0.30	11-17-95	10-27	1.20	1.20	0.45	Book Value $37.99			9-30-95	18956	★26451	425062	Dc	Δd3.22	1.35	Δ3.82	□[53]7.15	E7.10	7.49	9 Mo Sep	□4.95	5.29	13
14	1995	0.075	12-29-95	12-13	0.15	[54]0.30	....	Book Value $14.58			9-30-95	....	...	965	Dc	...	...	...	p0.72	....	....	11 Wk Sep	n/a	0.25	14
15	1993	Q0.05	2-15-96	1-30	0.20	0.20	0.20	Equity per shr $18.17			9-30-95	....	...	[55]36023	Dc	p0.53	p2.36	p2.32	□1.15	....	1.92	9 Mo Sep	□0.74	1.51	15
16	....	0.023	3-31-73	3-21	...	Nil	....	Equity per shr $2.43			9-30-95	0.79	...	±19945	Dc	*±0.22	±0.25	±0.35	±0.25	....	0.17	9 Mo Sep	±0.20	±0.12	16
17	....	0.02	5-28-92	5-8	...	Nil	....	Equity per shr $6.91			9-30-95	1.22	1250	1662	Dc	d0.04	0.31	Δ0.51	0.57	....	0.69	9 Mo Sep	0.39	0.51	17
18◆	....	1.6%Stk	12-29-95	11-29	6.2%Stk	Stk	4.95%Stk	17.9	225	426	9-30-95	1072	...	±228864	Dc	±0.59	±0.60	±0.64	±0.74	....	0.75	9 Mo Sep	±0.54	±0.55	18
19◆	....	1.6%Stk	12-29-95	11-20	6.2%Stk	Stk	4.95%Stk	....	...	...		....	...	71115	Dc	±0.59	±0.60	±0.64	±0.74	....	0.75	9 Mo Sep	±0.54	±0.55	19
20	....	None Since Public			...	Nil	....	3.25	5.41	2.96	9-30-95	0.09	p...	★11391	Dc	...	...	...	p0.02	....	....	9 Mo Sep	n/a	p0.05	20
21	1994	Q0.07	11-16-95	11-2	0.26	0.28	0.05	Book Value $7.97			9-30-95	25.0	...	45538	Dc	d0.66	d1.84	d0.17	0.81	E0.97	0.98	9 Mo Sep	0.60	0.77	21
22	1988	S0.04	10-20-95	10-2	0.08	0.08	0.10	11.0	44.6	61.4	11-06-95	70.5	...	18485	Ja	0.72	□d0.17	□0.24	0.07	....	0.39	40 Wk Nov	0.10	0.42	22
23	....	None Since Public			...	Nil	....	1.51	9.14	6.60	8-31-95	0.40	...	★12339	Nv	0.02	0.02	0.03	0.03	....	0.09	9 Mo Aug	0.01	0.07	23
24	1984	Q0.03	11-15-95	10-30	0.12	0.12	0.11½	37.8	86.2	31.0	10-28-95	....	...	±21071	Ja	□0.16	±0.71	±1.15	±1.15	....	1.32	9 Mo Oct	±0.37	±0.54	24
25◆	1921	Q0.16	1-26-96	1-10	0.633	0.64	0.62¼	26.3	120	38.9	9-02-95	36.3	...	14822	Nv	1.26	□1.10	1.16	Δ1.39	....	1.48	9 Mo Aug	Δ0.91	1.00	25
26	....	None Since Public			...	Nil	....	4.62	9.73	6.32	9-30-95	0.45	p...	9257	Dc	...	...	...	pd0.18	....	0.14	9 Mo Sep	pd0.22	p0.10	26
27◆	1995	Q0.02	1-24-96	12-29	0.064	0.08	....	Equity per shr $6.02			9-30-95	41.0	...	94854	Je	0.41	0.46	0.60	Δ[57]0.75	0.92	0.97	3 Mo Sep	0.19	0.24	27
28◆	....	[58]0.512	7-14-89	6-26	...	Nil	....	9.04	60.6	41.6	9-30-95	300	...	34568	Dc	0.04	0.15	0.30	0.64	....	0.82	9 Mo Sep	0.39	0.57	28
29	....	None Since Public			...	Nil	....	93.9	105	4.79	j4-30-95	0.13	...	±488765	Ap	...	...	...	p0.04	d0.01	jd0.23	6 Mo Oct	0.01	d0.21	29
30	1989	Q0.32½	12-27-95	12-8	1.30	1.30	1.22½	133	276	96.7	9-30-95	57.9	...	11898	Dc	4.55	□2.57	4.55	3.54	E4.35	4.88	9 Mo Sep	2.27	3.61	30
31	....	None Since Public			...	Nil	....	0.76	39.8	23.0	9-30-95	....	1150	4109	Dc	d2.19	0.11	0.21	0.80	....	0.11	9 Mo Sep	0.69	Nil	31
32	1968	Q0.53	11-15-95	10-25	2.02	2.12	1.86	128	503	426	9-30-95	253	...	52276	Je	0.98	□2.01	3.05	3.94	3.78	3.90	3 Mo Sep	1.00	1.12	32
33	....	None Since Public			...	Nil	....	File bankruptcy Chapt 11				3.03	...	14190	Ja	0.37	0.58	0.56	d0.79	....	d1.10	9 Mo Oct	d0.19	d0.50	33
34	1993	Q0.05	12-1-95	11-3	0.20	0.20	0.20	Equity per shr $25.53			9-30-95	....	800	11097	Dc	1.81	2.79	Δ2.78	3.41	....	3.96	9 Mo Sep	2.48	3.03	34
35	....	0.05	12-31-81	12-10	...	Nil	....	1.57	91.1	20.4	9-30-95	28.1	5	20382	Dc	d0.29	0.08	0.37	1.07	....	0.87	9 Mo Sep	1.05	0.85	35
36◆	1991	Q0.02½	3-21-96	3-4	0.09½	0.10	0.08	2.10	218	82.8	10-28-95	86.4	...	49128	Jl	*0.39	Δ0.65	1.11	1.00	□d0.42	d0.74	3 Mo Oct	0.02	d0.30	36
37	1989	Q0.24	11-22-95	11-6	0.90	0.96	0.78	37.0	742	1380	9-30-95	2864	[60]...	[61]91131	Dc	□d3.26	d3.72	1.90	2.09	E2.25	2.26	12 Mo Sep	2.05	2.26	37
38	1995	0.28	11-22-95	11-6	0.56	1.12	....	....	...	...		....	...	7587	Dc	...	...	...	p1.66	....	1.63	9 Mo Sep	p1.41	p1.38	38
39	....	0.14½	6-3-74	5-6	...	Nil	....	Equity per shr $98.80			9-30-95	3012	2	61798	Dc	9.80	Δd10.79	4.26	0.51	E7.65	10.76	9 Mo Sep	d1.02	9.23	39
40◆	1936	5%Stk	11-20-95	10-26	s0.781	0.80	s0.736	Equity per shr $16.15			9-30-95	154	...	17808	Dc	1.20	1.65	Δ1.75	[63]1.89	....	2.00	9 Mo Sep	1.33	1.44	40
41◆	....	None Paid			...	Nil	....	12.2	30.9	7.96	9-30-95	....	...	17380	Dc	d0.09	d0.07	d0.11	d0.18	....	0.53	9 Mo Sep	d0.10	0.61	41
42	1982	Q0.07	11-30-95	11-7	0.28	0.28	0.24	27.0	103	45.8	9-30-95	12.4	...	7454	Dc	d1.88	1.13	1.74	2.01	....	2.21	9 Mo Sep	1.43	1.63	42
43	....	None Paid			...	Nil	....	1.60	68.3	15.5	9-30-95	38.2	...	5140	Dc	d0.42	0.35	0.53	[64]0.71	....	0.72	9 Mo Sep	0.80	0.81	43
44	....	0.10	8-31-90	8-13	...	Nil	....	Book Value $21.42			9-30-95	724	...	18579	Dc	2.68	Δ2.27	0.94	d0.35	E1.70↑	1.05	9 Mo Sep	d0.14	1.26	44
45	1977	Q0.10	1-1-96	11-28	0.40	0.40	0.40	64.6	2278	2298	9-30-95	3516	[65]8181	±105015	Dc	±0.92	±d1.23	±□1.02	±2.05	E2.35	2.13	9 Mo Sep	±1.31	±1.39	45
46	1968	Q0.29¾	12-15-95	11-28	1.19	1.19	1.19	Cv into 3.6125 com & 0.1 Cl'A'				....	63	...	Dc	b1.22	b0.61	b1.24	b1.51	....	....				46
47	1973	Q0.45¾	12-15-95	11-28	1.83	1.83	1.83	Cv into 3.6125 com & 0.1 Cl'A'				....	84	...	Dc	b1.22	b0.61	b1.24	b1.51	....	....				47
48	....	None Since Public			...	Nil	....	17.5	235	107	9-30-95	114	...	23730	Dc	0.65	0.84	1.03	p0.74	E0.10	d0.31	9 Mo Sep	p0.73	d0.32	48
49	....	None Since Public			...	Nil	....	31.6	45.9	6.36	9-30-95	....	...	9092	Dc	...	p0.14	p0.52	1.08	....	0.77	9 Mo Sep	0.86	0.55	49
50	....	3%Stk	6-1-84	5-8	...	Nil	....	0.04	38.6	33.6	9-30-95	....	...	6227	Dc	d0.90	□d1.39	d0.70	d0.24	....	d0.21	9 Mo Sep	d0.09	d0.06	50
51◆	....	None Since Public			...	Nil	....	27.1	99.0	12.7	9-30-95	....	...	18617	Dc	...	p0.22	p0.50	1.21	....	1.71	9 Mo Sep	0.95	1.45	51
52	1967	Q0.25	12-8-95	11-21	1.00	1.00	1.00	2.72	65.3	64.8	10-01-95	420	...	±9294	Dc	±0.24	□±d0.23	±1.60	□±1.52	....	1.69	9 Mo Sep	□±1.41	±1.58	52

◆**Stock Splits & Divs By Line Reference Index** [4]2-for-1,'93. [6]2-for-1,'91:3-for-2,'93. [7]2-for-1,'95. [9]2-for-1,'91,'92,'93,'94. [18]3-for-2,'92:2-for-1,'93:Adj to 1.6% Nov,'95. [19]3-for-2,'92:2-for-1,'93:Adj to 1.6% Nov,'95. [25]3-for-2,'92. [27]5-for-4,'92,'93,'94,'95. [28]5-for-4,'92,'93,'94:2-for-1,'95. [36]2-for-1,'91,'92:3-for-2,'93. [40]10%,'92,'94:Adj to 5%,'95. [41]2-for-1,'95. [51]2-for-1,'94.

¶ S&P 500
\# MidCap 400
✜ SmallCap 600
• Options

Index	Ticker	Name of Issue (Call Price of Pfd. Stocks)	Market	Com. Rank. & Pfd. Rating	Inst. Hold Cos	Inst. Hold Shs. (000)	Principal Business	Price Range 1971-93 High	1971-93 Low	1994 High	1994 Low	1995 High	1995 Low	Dec. Sales in 100s	December, 1995 Last Sale Or Bid High	Low	Last	%Div Yield	P-E Ratio	Total Return % Annualized 12 Mo	36 Mo	60 Mo
¶1•[1]	KO	✔**Coca-Cola Co**	NY,B,C,Ch,P,Ph	A+	1238	655271	Major soft drink/juice co	45⅜	1⅞	53½	38⅞	80⅜	48¾	412275	80⅜	70⅝	74¼	1.2	31	43.7	21.8	28.1
#2•[1]	CCE	✔**Coca-Cola Enterprises**	NY,B,P,Ph	B–	181	50649	Largest Coca-Cola bottler	21¼	10½	19½	14	29⅞	17¾	31402	29½	25¾	26⅞	0.2	45	47.7	31.2	12.4
3•[2]	KOF	✔**Coca-Cola FEMSA ADS**	NY,Ch	NR	60	6002	Coca-Cola bottler,mkt,Mexico	33¾	20½	38⅜	20	27⅜	12⅞	31300	21⅛	18	18½	0.6	22	–24.2	...	...
4	CODA	✔**Coda Energy Inc**[53]	NNM	B–	62	9194	Oil & gas acq,dev,prod'n	177½	1¼	7½	4½	8¼	5⅛	20968	7⅝	6⅞	7⅜	...	32	24.0	21.7	27.7
5	CODL	✔**Code Alarm**	NNM	C	17	493	Mfr automobile security sys	24⅛	4	12⅜	8⅜	10¼	6⅛	1240	7⅝	6⅛	6¼	...	d	–28.6	1.4	3.5
✜6•[1]	CDE	✔**Coeur d'Alene Mines**	NY,Ch,Ph,P	B–	105	9518	Mining claims:gold & silver	36	1 1/16	23½	14⅜	21⅝	14½	18904	19⅛	16⅝	17⅛	0.9	..	6.2	16.9	2.7
7	CXIPY	**Coflexip**[54] **ADS**[55]	NNM	NR	99	12780	Mfr offshore flexible pipe	17⅜	16	24⅜	16¼	30¼	11⅞	20735	19⅛	15⅜	18⅞	1.5	30	–16.3	...	...
✜8•[3]	CGNX	✔**Cognex Corp**	NNM	B	162	32312	Mfr machine vision systems	8⅞	1¼	14	5⅞	38½	10½	85835	38½	27	34¾	...	81	168	98.8	57.3
9	CGN	✔**Cognitronics Corp**	AS,Ch	C	11	291	Voice processing equipment	18⅜	3/16	5¼	1⅜	7¼	2⅛	2733	7¼	5¾	6¾	...	29	273	–25.6	6.9
10•[4]	COHR	✔**Coherent, Inc**	NNM	B–	86	6397	Laser sys: optical, medical	26¾	1 11/16	17½	11½	44½	16½	34243	44½	37	40½	...	23	138	54.4	37.5
11	COHT	**Cohesant Technologies**	NNM	NR	..	...	Dvp spray finishing eqp	....	....	4¾	4⅜	4⅛	2⅜	2308	3⅜	2⅜	2⅜	...	11	...	...	...
12	COHU	✔**Cohu Inc**	NNM,Ch	B+	49	3103	Electronic devices & TV eq	11¼	5/16	11⅜	7⅝	36	10⅞	6104	29¼	23½	25½	0.6	13	143	98.9	61.9
13	CLQ	✔**Cold Metal Products**	NY,Ch	NR	26	2159	Intermediate steel processor	....	....	10½	6⅜	7⅞	4¼	2701	5⅛	4⅜	4¾	...	7	–32.1	...	...
14	CNJ	✔**Cole National**	NY,Ph	NR	56	7328	Retail:gift/eyewear prod	....	....	13½	8⅝	14⅛	8¼	3937	14⅛	12⅛	13⅞	...	5	52.1	...	...
15	CTFG	✔**Cole Taylor Financial Grp**	NNM	NR	33	1565	Commercial banking/fin svc	....	....	22⅞	13	31¼	16½	4611	31¼	26½	29⅞	0.9	20	44.0	...	...
16	CLN	✔**Coleman Co**	NY,Ph	NR	83	4246	Mfr outdoor recreat'n prod	30½	19½	36⅛	25⅜	39⅞	31	5368	35¾	34	35⅛	...	19	–1.1	8.5	...
17	CM	✔**Coles Myer Ltd ADR**[57]	NY,Ch	NR	18	648	Supermkt/dept strs,Australia	34¾	19⅛	30⅛	22⅝	28⅜	24⅛	165	26⅜	25⅜	24⅞B	5.1	11	–1.6	4.7	...
¶18•[1]	CL	✔**Colgate-Palmolive**	NY,B,C,Ch,P,Ph	B+	799	90879	Household & personal care	67¼	5½	65⅜	49½	77⅜	58	87700	76⅞	68⅞	70¼	2.7	67	13.9	10.8	16.7
✜19•[5]	CGEN	✔**Collagen Corp**	NNM	B	69	4533	Biomedical pr: human tissue	34	4⅛	31¾	17	28½	15	10139	21¼	17¾	21⅛	0.7	d	0.2	–2.4	...
✜20•[6]	COFD	✔**Collective Bancorp, Inc**	NNM	B	94	9602	Savings & loan,New Jersey	25⅜	1 5/16	23⅞	15½	27¾	15¾	17252	26¾	25⅛	25⅜	3.2	10	59.1	12.8	54.2
21	CKC	✔**Collins & Aikman**	NY,Ch	NR	43	11311	Auto prd/interior furnish'g	....	....	11	7⅝	9⅜	5¾	15678	7	6⅜	6⅝	...	5	–17.2	...	...
22	CNB	✔**Colonial BancGroup**	NY,Ch,Ph	B+	49	3448	Commercial bkg,Alabama	28¼	4¾	25	17¾	33	19½	2607	33	29⅜	32¼	2.8	9	67.3	21.9	39.5
23•[7]	CDT	✔**Colonial Data Tech**	AS,Ph	NR	72	5861	Mkt phone call identifiers	4½	7/16	15⅜	3⅞	27¼	12¼	54510	23	15⅝	20½	...	28	36.7	180	95.4
24	CGES	✔**Colonial Gas**	NNM	B+	39	1526	Utility: gas sv in Mass	26½	4⅞	23¾	18¼	21½	18	2823	21½	20	20¼	6.3	17	12.0	3.9	13.3
25	CLP	✔**Colonial Properties Tr**	NY,Ch,Ph	NR	82	10902	Real estate investment trust	23⅞	20½	23¾	20½	26¼	22⅛	4677	26¼	24½	25½	7.5	21	23.4	...	...
26•[8]	COT	✔**Coltec Industries**	NY,Ph	NR	138	65531	Mfr aerospace/automotive prd	21¾	14⅛	21⅞	16	18¾	10⅛	28190	12¼	10⅞	11⅝	...	11	–32.1	–14.9	...
¶27•[5]	CG	✔**Columbia Gas System**	.[9]NY,To,B,C,Ch,P	NR	273	30634	Utility holding co:nat'l gas	56½	12⅞	30¾	21½	44⅛	23⅛	36051	44⅛	42¾	43⅞	...	8	83.8	31.9	–0.7
¶28•[10]	COL	✔**Columbia/HCA Hlthcare**	NY	NR	1020	280404	Health care facilities/svcs	33⅞	9¾	45¼	33¼	54	35⅜	219222	54	50¼	50¾	0.2	21	37.1	37.2	34.1
29•[11]	COB	✔**Columbia Laboratories**	AS,Ph	NR	45	6379	Dvlp,mkt pharmaceutical prod	19⅝	1⅜	6¾	4	9⅞	4	20686	9	6¾	9	...	d	80.0	19.7	14.2
30	EGY	✔**Columbus Energy**	AS	NR	13	763	Oil & gas explor, dev, prod'n	9⅞	2¾	9⅜	7⅝	8¼	5¼	761	5¾	5¼	5⅜	...	22	–22.3	2.5	12.3
31	CLB	✔**Columbus Realty Trust**	NY,Ch,Ph	NR	73	6630	Real estate investment trust	17⅜	17¼	21¾	17⅛	20⅛	16	4398	19⅞	18¼	19⅜	7.7	22	13.5	...	...
32	CSJ	**Columbus SoPwr 8.375% Sub Db**[63]	NY	....[64]	..	...	Electric utility,Ohio	....	....	....	....	26⅞	24⅝	6216	26⅞	25⅜	26⅛	8.0	..	...	...	...
✜33•[12]	COMR	✔**Comair Holdings**	NNM	A–	139	15710	Passenger/pkge air transp	23	5/16	18⅛	9⅛	37	9⅞	79131	37	26½	26⅞	1.0	15	148	37.8	49.6
34	CMRO	✔**Comarco Inc**	NNM	B	26	1462	High technology computer sys	15¼	1/16	9⅛	4⅜	15⅝	7⅞	10257	15⅝	12⅞	14½	...	20	68.1	38.1	50.5
¶35•[8]	CMCSK	✔**Comcast Cl'A'Spl(non-vtg)**	NNM	B–	390	146489	CATV,sound communic sys	26	4⅛	24	14	22⅜	13¾	341861	19¾	17¾	18⅛	0.5	d	19.9	15.0	17.9
36•[8]	CMCSA	✔ **Cl'A'vtg**	NNM,Ch	B–	227	34881	music,telecom sys	28⅛	1/32	24¼	13¾	22½	13¾	49787	19¼	17½	17⅝	0.5	d	16.2	11.4	7.7
37	CMCAF	**Comcast UK Cable Partners'A'**	NNM	NR	..	...	CATV sys in England	....	....	20⅝	14⅝	19¼	11¾	17384	13⅛	11¾	12½	...	..	–18.0	...	...
38	CMDL	✔**Comdial Corp**	NNM	B	28	3177	Mfr of telecomm systems	99⅜	1⅛	12⅜	5⅜	15⅜	6	31189	10½	6⅝	9⅛	...	7	13.2	82.5	40.1
#39•[13]	CDO	✔**Comdisco, Inc**	NY,B,Ch	↑B	166	25481	Remarket/lease IBM comp eq	23⅛	1/32	16⅛	11⅞	23¾	14⅝	19640	23¾	21⅞	22⅝	1.2	13	51.8	36.2	17.8
¶40•[6]	CMA	✔**Comerica Inc**	NY	A–	352	61795	Comm'l Bkg,Detroit,Michigan	35¼	2¼	31¼	24⅛	42¾	24⅛	69423	42¾	34¾	40	3.5	11	69.9	13.0	29.0
41	CFS	✔**Comforce Corp**[68]	AS	C	8	128	Dstr of costume jewelry	123¾	⅝	8⅛	1⅞	9¼	1 9/16	4244	9¼	4½	9¼	...	d	208	131	35.8
42•[14]	CLT	✔**Cominco Ltd**	AS,To,B,Mo,Ph,Vc	C	75	12659	Lead, zinc mines: fertilizer	27¼	6⅛	19⅜	14	21⅞	14⅞	677	21⅜	20⅛	20⅝	...	..	17.0	15.2	4.1
43	COBA	✔**Commerce Bancorp**	NNM	B+	55	3168	Commercial banking, New Jersey	16⅜	4	22⅝	14	25⅝	15½	7347	23¾	21¾	22⅛	s2.9	11	26.3	28.7	43.9
44	CBSH	✔**Commerce Bancshares**	NNM	A+	107	13373	Commercial bkg,Missouri	30¼	2¼	30⅜	25⅜	38¼	25¾	5560	38¼	37¼	38¼	s1.8	13	62.5	18.0	27.8
45	CGI	✔**Commerce Group Inc**	NY	NR	49	4486	Prop & casualty insur/mtg fin	23	17½	22¾	13¼	21⅞	14¾	10284	21⅞	20½	20⅝	1.2	7	39.2	...	...
46	CAX	✔**Commercial Assets**	AS	NR	14	709	Real estate investment trust	6⅞	6⅛	7⅜	5½	6½	5½	2112	6	5½	5⅝	e11.6	9	7.8	...	...
✜47	CFB	✔**Commercial Federal**	NY,Ch,Ph	B–	121	8463	Svgs bank,Nebraska,Colorado	28½	1⅝	27⅞	17½	38⅜	20⅜	9586	38⅜	36¼	37¾	...	13	80.3	28.4	77.9
48	TEC	✔**Commercial Intertech**	NY,Ch	B+	94	7213	Engineered metal components	19⅛	1⅜	20⅜	12	22¾	15⅞	7041	19⅜	17¼	18⅛	3.0	10	1.2	14.0	18.4
✜49	CMC	✔**Commercial Metals**	NY,Ch	B+	98	7242	Metal processor, ind'l mfg	30	1	29⅛	21	29	23	8610	25⅛	23	24¾	1.9	9	–2.1	9.8	17.7
50	NNN	✔**Commercial Net Lease Rlty**	NY,Ph	NR	52	2338	Real estate investment trust	15	7	14½	11⅞	13¾	11¾	2541	13¼	12¾	12¾	9.1	12	13.9	10.7	14.1
✜51•[4]	CELS	✔**CommNet Cellular**	NNM	C	107	10074	Cellular tele systems svcs	30	3½	29⅞	15¼	30¾	21¼	24748	29¼	25⅞	28⅞	...	..	–1.3	24.4	23.6
52•[15]	CALC	✔**Commonwealth Aluminum**	NNM	NR	46	6907	Mfr aluminum sheet	....	....	....	....	24⅞	14	18151	18½	15¼	15½	1.3	6	...	...	...

Uniform Footnote Explanations-See Page 4. Other: [1]CBOE:Cycle 2. [2]CBOE:Cycle 1. [3]P,Ph:Cycle 2. [4]P:Cycle 2. [5]ASE:Cycle 2. [6]Ph:Cycle 2. [7]ASE,NY: Cycle 3. [8]Ph:Cycle 1. [9]Ph [10]ASE,CBOE:Cycle 2. [11]CBOE:Cycle 3. [12]NY:Cycle 3. [13]P:Cycle 1. [14]To:Cycle 3. [15]NY,CBOE:Cycle 1. [51]100% non-taxable,'94. [52]Coca-Cola Co owns 43.8%. [53]Enron Corp plan acq, $8. [54]Ea ADS rep 0.5 ord shr FF10. [55]Plan name chg,Coflexip Stena Offshore Group. [56]In cash or stk,'95. [57]Ea new ADR rep 8 ord shrs A$0.50(old ADR rep 3). [58]Incl ESOP Pref. [59]®$3.56,'94. [60]®$2.74,'94. [61]Incl $0.4118 non-taxable,'94. [62]Pfd in $M. [63]Jr Sub Deferrable Int Debs Sr'A'. [64]Rated BBB+ by S&P. [65]®$0.66,'94. [66]Return of cap. [67]Incl return of cap. [68]Formerly Lori Corp. [69]To be determined. [70]®$2.10,'94. [71]2 Mo Dec,'93. [72]®$1.72,'95. [73]Incl $0.19266 non-taxable,'94.

Index	Cash Divs. Ea.Yr. Since	Latest Payment Period $	Date	Ex. Div.	Total $ So Far 1995	Ind. Rate	Paid 1994	Cash& Equiv.	Curr. Assets	Curr. Liab.	Balance Sheet Date	Lg Trm Debt Mil-$	Shs. 000 Pfd.	Com.	Years End	1991	1992	1993	1994	1995	Last 12 Mos.	Interim Earnings Period	1994	1995	Index
1◆	1893	Q0.22	12-15-95	11-29	0.88	0.88	0.78	1925	6112	7815	9-30-95	880	...	1254362	Dc	1.21	□1.43	□1.68	1.98	E2.37↓	2.29	9 Mo Sep	1.54	1.85	1
2	1986	Q0.01¼	12-28-95	12-14	0.05	0.05	[51]0.05	....	1009	844	9-29-95	4251	1000	[52]128493	Dc	■d0.79	□d0.11	d0.11	0.52	E0.60↓	0.73	9 Mo Sep	0.43	0.64	2
3	1994	0.10½	7-26-95	7-10	0.10½	0.11	0.15	17.2	109	166	12-31-94	100	...	±475000	Dc	*±1.85	□*±1.10	*1.33	0.84	....	0.84				3
4	....	None Paid			...	Nil	....	4.45	16.7	11.4	9-30-95	108	...	22089	Dc	0.11	0.02	0.07	0.15	....	0.23	9 Mo Sep	0.09	0.17	4
5	....	None Since Public			...	Nil	....	0.26	30.2	16.5	9-30-95	10.1	...	2320	Dc	d0.24	d1.16	0.63	d0.58	....	d1.50	9 Mo Sep	0.60	d0.32	5
6	1988	A0.15	4-21-95	4-4	0.15	0.15	0.15	84.8	132	19.5	9-30-95	p174	...	p20468	Dc	d0.94	d0.05	Δd0.87	d0.26	....	0.04	9 Mo Sep	d0.15	0.15	6
7	1994	[56]0.293	8-7-95	6-19	[56]0.293	0.29	0.231	139	412	370	12-31-94	227	...	15552	Dc	1.09	0.88	1.05	1.16	....	0.63	6 Mo Jun	0.69	0.16	7
8◆	....	None Since Public			...	Nil	....	85.7	123	15.0	10-01-95	.....	...	38772	Dc	0.27	0.18	0.32	0.43	....	0.43	9 Mo Sep	0.30	0.30	8
9◆	....	None Paid			...	Nil	....	3.62	9.95	3.20	9-30-95	0.39	...	3376	Dc	*0.26	0.51	□d0.72	d0.09	....	0.23	9 Mo Sep	d0.02	0.30	9
10	....	None Since Public			...	Nil	....	44.7	185	78.2	9-30-95	5.14	...	10955	Sp	0.02	0.28	Δ0.49	1.11	1.75	1.75				10
11	....	None Since Public			...	Nil	....	1.19	6.95	2.02	8-31-95	.....	...	2636	Nv	...	...	...	p0.16	....	0.21	9 Mo Aug	pΔ0.12	0.17	11
12◆	1978	Q0.04	1-19-96	11-29	0.14½	0.16	0.11½	20.4	77.8	25.8	9-30-95	.....	...	9005	Dc	0.33	□0.43	0.81	1.15	....	1.93	9 Mo Sep	0.78	1.56	12
13	....	None Since Public			...	Nil	....	3.05	104	50.4	9-30-95	34.3	...	7172	Mr	...	p0.52	□p0.75	0.96	....	0.71	6 Mo Sep	0.46	0.21	13
14	....	None Since Public			...	Nil	....	8.99	148	101	10-28-95	186	...	10422	Ja	...	...	p1.29	□2.62	....	2.64	9 Mo Oct	□0.36	0.38	14
15	1994	Q0.07	1-11-96	12-27	0.26	0.28	0.10	Book Value $10.14			9-30-95	116	...	14553	Dc	0.61	0.67	0.91	1.26	....	1.47	9 Mo Sep	0.91	1.12	15
16	....	None Since Public			...	Nil	....	19.9	423	155	9-30-95	316	...	26577	Dc	p0.69	1.07	1.30	□1.26	....	1.83	9 Mo Sep	□1.30	□1.87	16
17◆	1983	0.588	12-1-95	10-16	s1.261	1.26	1.172	167	3332	2141	j7-31-95	1865	12669	1069000	Jl	□1.88	1.74	1.65	3.45	2.20	2.20				17
18◆	1895	Q0.47	11-15-95	10-23	1.76	1.88	1.54	277	2579	1842	9-30-95	3011	[58]6216	145583	Dc	0.77	2.92	□3.38	[59]3.82	E1.05	1.14	9 Mo Sep	2.91	0.23	18
19	1994	S0.075	1-15-96	12-13	0.15	0.15	0.10	21.2	42.7	42.2	9-30-95	.....	...	8972	Je	d0.45	0.11	□0.95	0.50	0.93	d0.16	3 Mo Sep	0.14	d0.95	19
20◆	1987	Q0.20	10-26-95	10-12	0.70	0.80	0.60	Book Value $15.71			9-30-95	.....	...	20362	Je	1.02	1.67	Δ2.29	2.89	2.80	2.67	3 Mo Sep	0.78	0.65	20
21	....	None Since Public			...	Nil	....	4.59	341	237	10-28-95	550	...	69416	Ja	...	...	pd1.31	□d0.39	E1.35↓	1.49	9 Mo Oct	□d0.97	0.91	21
22	1982	Q0.22½	11-14-95	11-3	0.90	0.90	0.80	Book Value $16.74			9-30-95	41.4	...	12267	Dc	*±1.45	±2.05	±Δ□2.48	±[60]2.85	....	3.48	9 Mo Sep	±1.72	2.35	22
23	....	None Since Public			...	Nil	....	34.9	70.8	5.35	9-30-95	.....	...	15407	Dc	Nil	0.03	0.10	0.30	....	0.73	9 Mo Sep	0.18	0.61	23
24◆	1937	Q0.32	12-15-95	11-29	1.27½	1.28	1.25½	7.25	39.8	82.0	9-30-95	72.4	...	8336	Dc	±1.11	1.38	1.52	1.36	....	1.21	12 Mo Sep	1.63	1.21	24
25	1994	Q0.47½	11-13-95	11-2	1.90	1.90	[61]1.73	Equity per shr $14.72			9-30-95	324	...	13044	Dc	...	p0.72	□p0.19	1.18	....	1.24	9 Mo Sep	0.88	0.94	25
26	....	None Since Public			...	Nil	....	10.8	485	254	10-01-95	977	...	69979	Dc	p0.82	□1.11	□0.94	□1.35	....	1.08	9 Mo Sep	□0.98	0.71	26
27	....	0.58	5-15-91	4-19	...	Nil	....	....	....	....		p2000	[62]p400	50576	Dc	Δd15.72	□1.79	3.01	□4.87	E5.45	4.99	9 Mo Sep	□3.42	3.54	27
28◆	1993	Q0.03	3-1-96	1-30	0.12	0.12	0.12	75.0	3728	2445	9-30-95	6198	...	±445157	Dc	□0.92	□1.18	□1.74	□2.13	E2.37	2.19	9 Mo Sep	□1.52	□1.58	28
29	....	None Since Public			...	Nil	....	3.15	5.43	4.38	9-30-95	.....	3	25957	Dc	d1.17	d0.51	d0.40	d0.59	....	d0.12	9 Mo Sep	d0.36	0.11	29
30◆	....	None Paid			...	Nil	....	2.31	5.39	3.93	8-31-95	1.60	...	3090	Nv	0.02	0.68	Δ0.83	0.67	....	0.25	9 Mo Aug	0.58	0.16	30
31	1994	Q0.37½	1-16-96	12-27	1.50	1.50	1.127	Equity per shr $13.74			9-30-95	122	...	11524	Dc	...	p0.60	p0.66	0.89	....	0.89	9 Mo Sep	0.67	0.67	31
32	....	Plan qtly div			...	2.09	....	Co option redm fr 9-27-2000 at $25				75.0	...	...	Dc	...	...	...	.....	.....	....	Mature 9-30-2025			32
33◆	1987	Q0.07	11-10-95	10-30	0.23	0.28	0.173	132	164	89.7	9-30-95	75.5	...	29611	Mr	0.45	0.69	0.89	0.97	E1.85	1.45	6 Mo Sep	0.56	1.04	33
34	....	0.003	4-1-85	3-19	...	Nil	....	9.71	20.0	7.08	7-30-95	.....	...	4617	Ja	Δ0.50	0.60	0.45	[65]0.68	....	0.74	9 Mo Oct	0.47	0.53	34
35◆	1987	Q0.023	3-28-96	3-5	0.093	0.09	[66]0.093	828	1492	1146	9-30-95	6619	...	±239918	Dc	±d0.87	±□d1.08	□±d0.46	□±d0.32	Ed0.35	d0.26	9 Mo Sep	□±d0.19	±□d0.13	35
36◆	1977	Q0.023	3-28-96	3-5	[67]0.093	0.09	[66]0.093	....	....	....		.....	...	39103	Dc	±d0.87	±□d1.08	□±d0.46	□±d0.32	....	d0.26	9 Mo Sep	□±d0.19	±□d0.13	36
37	....	None Since Public			...	Nil	....	2.32	5.39	26.3	p6-30-94	13.0	...	★±39729	Dc	...	...	...	...	....	....	6 Mo JunΔ	±pd0.29	±d0.27	37
38◆	....	None Since Public			...	Nil	....	1.75	31.9	13.5	10-01-95	3.14	...	8088	Dc	d0.15	*0.06	0.36	□0.42	....	1.31	9 Mo Sep	□0.32	1.21	38
39◆	1977	Q0.07	12-8-95	11-15	0.25	0.28	0.24	Equity per shr $13.10			9-30-95	2457	3626	52271	Sp	1.13	□0.33	Δ0.98	0.77	1.73	1.73				39
40◆	1936	Q0.35	1-2-96	12-13	1.34	1.40	1.20	Book Value $22.29			9-30-95	4949	...	114556	Dc	2.52	1.92	2.85	3.28	E3.52↑	3.44	9 Mo Sep	2.46	2.62	40
41	....	1.20	7-1-73	6-11	...	Nil	....	0.05	3.11	6.26	6-30-95	....	10	3356	Dc	d2.25	pd11.20	Δd0.45	Δd5.80	....	d10.56	9 Mo Sep	d1.38	Δd6.14	41
42	....	g0.15	12-29-95	12-11	g0.15	[69]....	....	46.1	632	304	j12-31-94	505	2583	79495	Dc	d0.56	d0.42	d1.46	1.62	....	j1.62	9 Mo Sep	0.78	0.78	42
43◆	1984	sQ0.16¼	10-16-95	9-28	s0.642	0.65	s0.588	Book Value $13.95			9-30-95	23.0	417	10680	Dc	0.88	1.35	1.73	[70]2.28	....	2.11	9 Mo Sep	1.76	1.59	43
44◆	1936	s0.171	12-15-95	11-28	s0.686	0.686	s0.599	Book Value $23.52			9-30-95	15.7	...	37724	Dc	1.92	2.21	2.49	2.71	E2.86	2.78	9 Mo Sep	2.03	2.10	44
45	1994	Q0.06	12-15-95	11-29	0.23	0.24	0.15	Equity per shr $13.58			9-30-95	.....	...	37146	Dc	1.37	Δ1.47	1.98	3.23	....	2.94	9 Mo Sep	2.42	2.13	45
46	1993	Q0.17	12-29-95	12-14	†0.88	0.65	0.33	Equity per shr $7.39			9-30-95	.....	...	10125	Dc	...	...	†[71]0.07	0.49	....	0.64	9 Mo Sep	0.33	0.48	46
47	1995	0.10	1-12-96	12-27	0.10	[69]....	....	Book Value $22.46			9-30-95	1629	...	p14300	Je	*1.26	□5.19	2.43	Δd0.44	2.11	2.98	3 Mo Sep	0.04	0.91	47
48◆	1936	Q0.135	12-15-95	11-29	0.51	0.54	0.477	42.8	252	157	7-31-95	75.1	1054	15423	Oc	□0.93	Δ0.65	0.79	1.50	P[72]1.82	1.82				48
49◆	1964	Q0.12	1-25-96	1-3	0.48	0.48	0.479	21.0	534	268	8-31-95	158	...	15388	Au	0.84	0.87	1.46	1.75	2.52	2.78	3 Mo Nov	0.44	0.70	49
50	1985	Q0.29	11-15-95	10-13	1.16	1.16	[73]1.14	Equity per shr $11.36			9-30-95	72.9	...	11664	Dc	0.85	0.95	0.95	1.04	....	1.07	9 Mo Sep	0.78	0.81	50
51	....	None Since Public			...	Nil	....	41.0	57.6	17.7	9-30-95	246	...	13470	Sp	d6.00	d2.44	□d2.30	d1.45	□0.17	0.17				51
52	1995	Q0.05	11-17-95	11-1	0.15	0.20	....	2.77	224	68.4	9-30-95	38.8	...	10190	Dc	...	...	...	p1.42	....	2.56	9 Mo Sep	p1.73	2.87	52

◆**Stock Splits & Divs By Line Reference Index** [1]2-for-1,'92. [8]2-for-1,'92,'93,'95. [9]3-for-2,'92. [12]2-for-1,'93,'95. [17]12.5%,'88:0.84 new ADR-for-1 old,'93:Adj for 2%,'95. [18]2-for-1,'91. [20]4-for-3,'92:3-for-2,'93. [24]3-for-2,'92. [28]1-for-4 REVERSE,'91. [30]10%,'94,'95. [33]3-for-2,'92,'93,'95. [35]3-for-2,'94. [36]3-for-2 in Cl'A' spl stk,'89,'94. [38]1-for-3 REVERSE,'95. [39]Adj for 5%,'92:3-for-2,'95. [40]3-for-2,'91:2-for-1,'93. [43]Adj to 5%,Dec'94. [44]3-for-2,'93:Adj for 5%,'95. [48]3-for-2,'94. [49]4-for-3,'93.

¶ S&P 500 # MidCap 400 ✤ SmallCap 600 • Options Index	Ticker	Name of Issue (Call Price of Pfd. Stocks) Market	Com. Rank. & Pfd. Rating	Inst. Hold Cos	Inst. Hold Shs. (000)	Principal Business	Price Range 1971-93 High	1971-93 Low	1994 High	1994 Low	1995 High	1995 Low	Dec. Sales in 100s	December, 1995 Last Sale Or Bid High	Low	Last	%Div Yield	P-E Ratio	Total Return % Annualized 12 Mo	36 Mo	60 Mo
✤1	CES	✓Commonwealth Energy Sys..NY,B,Ch,P	B+	112	2411	Hldg co: gas & elec sv,Mass	50½	8⅜	46	35⅜	47⅝	35⅜	1698	47⅝	44½	44¾	6.7	11	32.5	9.1	14.6
2	CABL	✓Communic Cable[51] .... NNM	B–	18	447	Mfr specialty electr cable	15¾	1 13/16	14⅞	8½	12¾	7	4144	12¾	11½	12¼	s. . .	15	27.4	17.2	13.2
3	CSII	✓Communic Sys .... NNM	B+	45	3022	Telephone eq:tel sys:CATV	15½	1⅝	14	9½	20	12	6632	16¾	14¾	15¾	1.8	16	28.3	28.5	. . .
4	CCAI	✓Community Care of Amer .... NNM	NR	24	2600	Dvlp/oper rural hlthcr centers	. . . .	. . . .	. . . .	. . . .	14⅝	9½	3731	13	9¾	10½	. . .	. .	. . .	. . .	. . .
✤5	CYH	✓Community Hlth Sys........NY,Ch,Ph	NR	213	18359	Operate acute care hospitals	19¼	7⅛	27¾	17½	42¾	26¼	12333	36¼	32⅞	35⅝	. . .	28	34.4	40.2	. . .
¶6•[1]	CMY	✓Community Psych Ctrs ....NY,B,Ch,P	B	272	36968	Acute psychiatric hospitals	40	⅛	19	9¼	13¾	10⅛	38140	12¼	10⅞	12¼	. . .	d	15.4	7.2	–14.6
7	BLP	✓Compania Boliviana De Energia [2]NY,Ch	NR	29	1522	Bolivian elec power co	30½	9/16	26	21½	33¼	19½	1467	33¼	26	33¼	2.3	17	51.1	48.1	50.6
8	CCUUY	Compania Cervecerias ADS[54]........ NNM	NR	34	1900	Mfr,bottle,dstr beer in Chile	29½	12⅜	36¼	18¼	28½	16⅝	14043	24⅞	21⅝	23¼	1.8	27	–4.6	17.0	. . .
9•[3]	CTC	✓Compania de Telecom Chile ADS... [4]NY	NR	149	4973	Telecommunications svc,Chile	104	12⅞	133¾	75	93⅜	48	24905	83½	72½	82⅞	e2.3	20	7.1	15.4	44.5
¶10•[5]	CPQ	✓Compaq Computer........NY,B,Ch,P	B	878	178972	Portable personal computers	25¼	9/16	42⅛	24⅛	56¾	31⅛	551978	50½	43⅜	48	. . .	12	19.6	43.8	20.6
11	CPDN	✓CompDent Corp........ NNM	NR	73	6791	Provides managed dental svcs	. . . .	. . . .	. . . .	. . . .	42¾	14½	20163	42¾	33¾	41½	. . .	. .	. . .	. . .	. . .
12	CTT	✓Competitive Technologies .... AS,B	C	8	566	Technology mgmt,education sv	25⅜	2 3/16	8¾	5⅝	9⅞	4½	2919	9⅞	8¼	8⅝	. . .	26	27.8	–5.6	9.9
13	CMP	✓Comprehensive Care ....NY,Ch,Ph	C	13	672	Mgmt health care facilities	300¾	⅝	12½	2½	10	5	2237	9⅜	8	8⅝	. . .	d	60.5	–14.4	–7.2
14	COEV	Comprehensive Envir'l Sys........NSC	NR	6	39	Asbestos abatement/waste mgmt	187½	3⅛	28¾	6¼	7½	1	15481	2¼	1	1¼	. . .	d	–84.0	–64.8	–36.9
✤15•[6]	CLIX	✓Compression Labs........ NNM	C	53	5784	Video teleconferencing sys	35¼	2¼	16⅛	6⅛	11⅜	6	25013	7¾	6	6¼	. . .	d	–20.6	–17.5	–10.7
16	CTK	✓Comptek Research Inc ....AS	C	23	1156	Electr tactical sys-US Navy	22⅝	1⅞	25½	11¼	19	8	2273	10½	8	8⅜	. . .	d	–49.3	–21.4	33.7
✤17•[7]	CPU	✓CompUSA Inc ....NY	NR	156	15727	Oper computer superstores	40½	15	22¼	6¾	44⅜	14¾	88038	38½	28⅛	31⅛	. . .	19	113	3.6	. . .
18	CSIN	✓Computational Systems .... NNM	NR	25	1025	Dgn predictive maint prod/svcs	. . . .	. . . .	. . . .	. . . .	17¼	12½	3816	15½	14¾	15½	. . .	24	. . .	. . .	. . .
¶19•[3]	CA	✓Computer Assoc Intl........NY,B,Ph	B+	695	141898	Systems software packages	29½	½	33⅞	18¼	70½	31¼	195356	70½	55⅞	56⅞	0.2	d	82.2	63.0	63.4
20	CCEE	✓Computer Concepts........NSC	NR	11	619	Dvlp software/hardware prod	9⅜	3⅝	5⅜	⅝	5	¼	290081	3½	2⅛	2⅝	. . .	d	258	–23.0	. . .
21	CDSI	✓Computer Data Systems ....NNM,B	A–	35	1925	Data processing & prof svs	19½	1/16	24	8¾	16	8½	3360	16	12⅞	13	0.8	9	38.2	14.1	29.7
22	CLRI	✓Computer Language Rsch .... NNM	B	34	1255	Software for inc tax svcs	35	2⅝	12½	6¾	15	7¼	3856	15	11¼	14	2.9	14	26.7	62.2	42.9
23	CMSX	✓Computer Mgmt Sciences........ NNM	NR	13	267	Dvlp custom software	. . . .	. . . .	. . . .	. . . .	22¼	14	6502	20½	17¼	17¾	. . .	29	. . .	. . .	. . .
24•[8]	CMNT	✓Computer Network Technology..... NNM	B–	54	6252	Computer sys info transm'n eq	11⅜	1	12⅜	5⅛	12¾	4	46933	6⅜	4	4½	. . .	14	–35.7	–7.2	13.6
¶25•[9]	CSC	✓Computer Sciences..........NY,B,Ch,P,Ph	B+	422	45904	Provides computer services	33⅜	½	52⅝	31⅝	75¼	46½	43707	75¼	68¾	70¼	. . .	28	39.5	39.5	33.7
26	TSK	✓Computer Task Group........NY,Ph	B–	40	4357	Computer svs:mkt systems	18⅝	1/16	10⅜	6⅝	22	8⅛	3661	22	18½	19¾	0.5	17	149	35.3	20.5
27	CPTL	✓Computer Telephone Cl'1' .... NNM	B	12	935	Network communic svcs	3⅝	1/16	3¼	9/16	19½	2⅝	11712	16¼	12	13½	. . .	52	342	177	66.7
28•[10]	CVN	✓Computervision Corp ....NY	NR	97	30646	Workstation-based softw,svcs	12⅜	2⅛	5⅜	2½	15½	3⅝	94985	15½	11½	15¼	. . .	32	321	40.9	. . .
29	LLB	✓Computrac Inc........AS,Ch	C	12	1295	Software for legal profess'n	11⅝	15/16	1 7/16	7/16	2⅞	⅞	2062	2½	2	2½	. . .	23	150	22.1	17.3
30	CTRN	✓Computron Software........ NNM	NR	56	2710	Dgn/dvp data mgmt software	. . . .	. . . .	. . . .	. . . .	21¾	12¾	15199	18½	14¾	18	. . .	53	. . .	. . .	. . .
#31•[7]	CPWR	✓Compuware Corp ....NNM,Ch	NR	187	29901	Dvlp systems software prod	34¼	19¼	49¼	24½	43	17½	54010	23	18¼	18½	. . .	12	–49.0	–9.8	. . .
#32•[1]	CQ	✓Comsat Corp........NY,B,Ch,P,Ph	B	251	35297	Global telecommunications	35¼	5¾	30	17½	24⅝	17⅝	41500	20¾	18¼	18⅝	4.2	11	2.5	–3.5	13.2
33	CSRE	✓Comshare, Inc .... NNM	B–	30	1074	Timesharing computer serv	16⅞	5/16	9⅞	6	26¾	8⅞	11824	26¾	21	26	. . .	37	180	43.6	19.6
34	CMRE	✓Comstock Resources .... NNM	C	17	2265	Oil/gas explor & devel	24	⅞	5¾	2¾	5⅝	2¾	27308	5⅝	4⅝	5⅝	. . .	. .	69.8	40.4	9.2
✤35•[3]	CMVT	✓Comverse Technology........ NNM	B–	96	9502	Dvlp,mkt computer systems	21¾	5/16	15⅝	8	26	11	37351	23⅜	19⅝	20	. . .	28	75.8	5.2	60.5
¶36•[11]	CAG	✓ConAgra Inc........NY,B,Ch,P,Ph	A+	573	117385	Prepared foods:agri-products	36½	⅛	33⅛	25½	41¾	29¾	97073	41¾	39⅝	41¼	2.3	19	34.1	10.0	13.4
37	CTRA	✓Concentra Corp........ NNM	NR	19	1589	Dvp engineering software	. . . .	. . . .	. . . .	. . . .	14¼	7¼	5528	11	8¾	8¾	. . .	14	. . .	. . .	. . .
38	LENS	✓Concord Camera .... NNM	C	11	865	Mfr,import camera/photo eqp	11¼	1⅜	9⅜	1⅞	6⅝	2⅛	29140	5⅛	3⅛	4½	. . .	27	112	–19.9	3.7
39	CIS	✓Concord Fabrics Cl'A' ....AS,Ch	B–	12	440	Woven & knitted fabrics	10⅝	½	10⅝	6¾	7¼	3⅝	567	4¼	3⅝	4¼	. . .	d	–41.4	–6.0	1.2
40	CIS.B	Class B Cv(10 votes) ....AS	B–	6	197		10⅝	1⅝	10	7	6¾	3⅝	19	4	3⅝	4	. . .	d	–42.9	–7.2	1.3
41	CPLNY	Concordia Paper Holdings ADS[59].. NNM	NR	19	1177	Mfr recycle paper boxboard	. . . .	. . . .	10½	10	15¼	7⅞	868	9	7⅞	7⅞	. . .	9	–22.2	. . .	. . .
✤42	COE	✓Cone Mills ....NY,Ph	NR	90	15520	Prod apparel fabrics/home prd	19⅝	10	17¼	11⅛	14⅜	10⅝	20422	11⅞	10¾	11¼	. . .	23	–2.2	–8.1	. . .
43	CONE	Conestoga Bancorp[60] .... NNM	NR	13	801	Savings & loan, New York	. . . .	. . . .	14⅜	9¾	20⅜	12	3894	20⅜	19⅞	20⅛	. . .	26	73.0	. . .	. . .
44	CGM	✓Congoleum Corp 'A' ....NY,Ph	NR	39	3311	Mfr resilient vinyl flooring	. . . .	. . . .	. . . .	. . . .	15⅝	8	4885	12⅛	10	10¾	. . .	7	. . .	. . .	. . .
45	CNMD	✓Conmed Corp .... NNM	B–	62	7561	Mfr disposable medical prod	17⅜	1¼	13⅝	4½	27⅛	9⅝	10280	27⅛	20½	25	. . .	30	86.4	55.5	38.0
✤46	CNE	✓Connecticut Energy ....NY,Ph	A–	55	1949	Gas utility in south'n Conn	26½	4⅝	25	18⅝	22½	18½	1813	22½	19¾	22¼	5.8	14	26.0	4.7	13.4
47	CTG	✓Connecticut Nat Gas........NY,Ch	A–	51	1243	Gas Service, Connecticut	32⅜	4⅞	31¾	21⅞	25¼	21¼	2308	25⅛	22⅝	23⅜	6.3	14	0.7	–0.1	12.6
48	CTWS	✓Connecticut Wtr Svc........ NNM	B+	20	324	Hldg co,water utility,Conn	31⅞	7¾	28	22¾	28¼	22¾	262	28	27½	27½	6.1	13	22.3	8.5	15.0
#49•[5]	CNR	✓Conner Peripherals[63] ....NY,Ch,Ph	NR	140	31510	Mfr Winchester disk drives	31¼	6½	20½	9	24	9¼	101525	24	18⅜	21	. . .	21	127	0.4	–1.5
¶50•[1]	CRR	✓Conrail Inc........NY,B,Ch,P	B	574	64405	Major freight railroad sys	67½	10	69¼	48⅛	74⅜	50½	83218	72½	67½	70	2.4	13	44.1	16.2	30.3
51•[11]	CNC	✓Conseco Inc........NY,Ch,Ph	B+	106	10293	Hldg co:life insurance	75¾	1¾	66¼	35⅞	63⅛	32½	19756	63⅛	57	62⅝	0.1	13	42.1	11.2	56.2
52	PrD	Series'D'cm Cv Pfd([67]52.275) ......NY,Ch	B+	53	2232		68	49	60⅞	38	53½	35	6283	53½	50¼	53	6.1	. .	. . .	. . .	. . .

Uniform Footnote Explanations-See Page 4. Other: [1]Ph:Cycle 1. [2]Ph [3]CBOE:Cycle 1. [4]Ch,Ph [5]P:Cycle 1. [6]ASE,CBOE:Cycle 1. [7]CBOE:Cycle 2. [8]P:Cycle 2. [9]CBOE:Cycle 3. [10]CBOE,NY,Ph:Cycle 1. [11]ASE:Cycle 3. [51]Kuhlman Corp offer,$12 to Jan 22. [52]Redemption of stk purch rt,'95. [53]Spl div. [54]Each ADS rep 5 ord,no par. [55]Approx. [56]®$3.74,'94. [57]®$3.21,'94. [58]Stk dstr of University Genetics. [59]Ea ADS rep 5 Ord. [60]Dime Svgs Bank plan mgr,$21.25. [61]®$0.92,'94. [62]10 Mo Dec'93. [63]Seagate Tech plan acq, 0.442 com. [64]®$1.77,'94. [65]®$3.56,'94. [66]®$5.00,'94. [67]To 1-21-97 scale to $50 in 2003.

Index	Cash Divs. Ea.Yr. Since	Dividends: Latest Payment Period $	Date	Ex. Div.	Total $ So Far 1995	Ind. Rate	Paid 1994	Financial Position Mil-$ Cash& Equiv.	Curr. Assets	Curr. Liab.	Balance Sheet Date	Capitalization Lg Trm Debt Mil-$	Shs. 000 Pfd.	Com.	Earnings $ Per Shr. Years End	1991	1992	1993	1994	1995	Last 12 Mos.	Interim Earnings Period	$ per Shr. 1994	1995	Index
1	1947	Q0.75	2-1-96	1-8	3.00	3.00	2.98	3.61	136	239	9-30-95	397	155	10763	Dc	1.82	3.83	4.37	4.59	....	4.19	12 Mo Sep	4.89	4.19	1
2◆	....	3%Stk	4-30-95	3-27	3%Stk	Stk	8%Stk	3.11	20.4	4.56	7-31-95	4.29	...	2574	Oc	0.06	0.40	0.66	Δ0.51	P0.80	0.80				2
3◆	1985	Q0.07	1-2-96	12-20	0.26	0.28	0.22	12.7	44.5	10.0	9-30-95	0.07	...	9171	Dc	0.48	Δ0.62	0.75	0.75	....	0.99	9 Mo Sep	0.52	0.76	3
4	....	None Since Public			...	Nil	....	5.35	21.3	17.2	9-30-95	32.0	...	6958	Dc	...	...	...	pd0.13	....	....	9 Mo Sep	n/a	p□0.18	4
5◆	....	None Since Public			...	Nil	....	11.2	148	78.8	9-30-95	209	...	19498	Dc	Δ0.85	0.95	1.10	□0.73	....	1.29	9 Mo Sep	0.94	1.50	5
6	1974	[52]0.01	4-14-95	3-27	[52]0.01	Nil	[53]0.01	38.7	199	135	8-31-95	33.8	...	43340	Nv	0.98	0.52	d0.58	0.24	Ed0.11	d0.08	9 Mo Aug	0.11	d0.21	6
7	1987	Q0.19	12-15-95	11-29	0.76	0.76	0.72	48.0	61.0	8.07	12-31-94	....	...	4199	Dc	1.34	1.96	2.34	1.84	....	1.91	9 Mo Sep	1.53	1.60	7
8	1993	[55]0.148	1-23-96	12-27	0.543	0.42	0.298	33.2	147	64.6	12-31-93	80.1	...	261000	Dc	0.87	0.96	1.10	....	....	0.86	9 Mo SepΔ	0.65	0.79	8
9	1990	[55]0.379	2-23-96	2-1	1.894	1.92	1.79	115	399	376	12-31-94	1151	...	±859034	Dc	±2.74	±3.55	±4.08	±[56]4.42	....	4.16	3 Mo Mar	±1.15	±0.89	9
10◆	....	None Since Public			...	Nil	....	1120	6578	2764	9-30-95	300	...	265800	Dc	0.50	0.86	1.82	[57]3.23	E3.90	3.49	9 Mo Sep	2.33	2.59	10
11	....	None Since Public			...	Nil	....	37.1	43.0	19.9	9-30-95	....	...	10017	Dc	...	...	...	p0.46	....	....	9 Mo Sep	n/a	p□0.47	11
12	....	h[58]....	6-2-86	5-23	...	Nil	....	4.96	5.58	0.48	7-31-95	....	2	5815	Jl	d0.26	d0.19	d0.35	d0.11	0.34	0.33	3 Mo Oct	d0.02	d0.03	12
13◆	....	1.00	2-23-89	1-24	...	Nil	....	0.80	5.33	21.3	8-31-95	4.64	...	2657	My	Δd22.70	d2.10	d5.30	d3.60	d5.11	d4.47	3 Mo Aug	d1.14	d0.50	13
14◆	....	None Paid			...	Nil	....	1.34	5.28	2.00	7-31-95	0.27	...	4777	Ap	d5.00	d1.80	d1.30	Δ0.30	d3.50	d3.97	6 Mo Oct	0.55	0.08	14
15	....	None Since Public			...	Nil	....	11.0	99.9	51.3	9-30-95	1.16	...	15461	Dc	d1.55	d0.29	d0.30	0.01	....	d0.10	9 Mo Sep	d0.03	d0.14	15
16◆	1985	0.04	9-3-93	8-9	...	Nil	....	0.08	10.8	6.39	9-29-95	2.44	...	4481	Mr	0.39	0.18	d1.13	d0.22	....	d0.35	6 Mo Sep	d0.05	d0.18	16
17	....	None Since Public			...	Nil	....	199	704	448	9-23-95	115	...	21019	Je	d1.58	□0.71	0.67	d0.92	1.21	1.68	3 Mo Sep	d0.17	0.30	17
18	....	None Since Public			...	Nil	....	8.75	21.9	7.13	9-29-95	0.02	...	4734	Dc	...	...	...	p0.46	....	0.64	9 Mo Sep	0.22	0.40	18
19◆	1990	S0.07	1-12-96	12-20	0.133	0.14	0.113	208	1245	1478	9-30-95	p48.1	...	241647	Mr	0.61	0.96	1.56	1.71	Ed0.50	d0.75	6 Mo Sep	0.18	d2.28	19
20◆	....	None Since Public			...	Nil	....	3.51	8.04	9.12	6-30-95	0.95	...	57334	Dc	d0.07	d0.40	d0.51	d0.51	....	d0.72	9 Mo Sep	d0.07	d0.28	20
21◆	1976	S0.05	8-29-95	8-9	0.10	0.10	0.10	0.26	54.8	31.1	9-30-95	....	...	5760	Je	0.64	0.65	0.97	1.31	1.36	1.46	3 Mo Sep	0.28	0.38	21
22	1983	Q0.10	11-22-95	11-6	0.40	0.40	0.36	32.1	43.4	16.8	9-30-95	1.13	...	14105	Dc	0.28	Δ0.40	0.61	0.79	....	1.03	9 Mo Sep	0.65	0.89	22
23	....	None Since Public			...	Nil	....	1.06	5.17	1.65	9-30-95	....	...	★4939	Dc	0.04	0.13	0.19	0.45	....	0.61	9 Mo Sep	0.37	0.53	23
24	....	None Paid			...	Nil	....	29.3	61.5	17.3	9-30-95	0.07	...	22903	Dc	0.13	0.21	0.26	d0.21	....	0.33	9 Mo Sep	d0.34	0.20	24
25◆	....	0.003	3-28-69	3-7	...	Nil	....	26.2	1068	668	9-29-95	421	...	55642	Mr	1.37	1.55	Δ1.77	2.09	E2.50	2.25	6 Mo Sep	0.86	1.02	25
26	1976	A0.10	5-26-95	5-2	0.10	0.10	0.10	12.3	82.9	31.7	9-29-95	4.47	...	10236	Dc	0.10	0.56	d2.62	0.52	....	1.15	9 Mo Sep	0.37	1.00	26
27◆	....	None Paid			...	Nil	....	3.32	8.93	3.05	9-30-95	....	...	9436	Mr	d0.11	0.07	0.01	0.16	....	0.26	6 Mo Sep	0.05	0.15	27
28	1993	0.01	8-27-93	8-6	...	Nil	....	31.9	162	277	10-01-95	p219	...	★62609	Dc	pd1.52	pd6.09	d11.89	0.20	....	0.47	9 Mo Sep	0.09	0.36	28
29	....	0.05	1-22-88	12-29	...	Nil	....	5.57	7.04	0.99	10-31-95	0.29	...	6196	Ja	d0.20	0.05	d0.90	0.03	....	0.11	9 Mo Oct	0.01	0.09	29
30	....	None Since Public			...	Nil	....	53.5	72.6	16.7	p9-30-95	0.12	...	20698	Dc	...	...	...	pNil	....	0.34	9 Mo Sep	pd0.19	p0.15	30
31	....	None Since Public			...	Nil	....	98.5	312	175	9-30-95	....	...	42407	Mr	pd0.74	1.03	1.52	1.30	....	1.50	6 Mo Sep	0.27	0.47	31
32◆	1970	Q0.19½	12-11-95	11-8	0.78	0.78	0.76	16.5	306	202	9-30-95	594	...	47486	Dc	□1.88	1.09	Δ1.82	1.64	E1.65	0.74	9 Mo Sep	1.34	0.44	32
33◆	....	None Since Public			...	Nil	....	2.02	37.9	38.6	9-30-95	p....	...	★9365	Je	0.77	■d1.40	d0.22	0.03	0.63	0.71	3 Mo Sep	0.09	0.17	33
34	....	None Since Public			...	Nil	....	0.97	11.9	27.2	9-30-95	57.0	3100	12769	Dc	d0.51	d0.09	□0.25	□d0.07	....	0.01	9 Mo Sep	□Nil	0.08	34
35◆	....	None Paid			...	Nil	....	125	183	33.6	9-30-95	60.0	...	21259	Dc	*0.20	Δ0.32	0.65	0.57	....	0.72	9 Mo Sep	0.38	0.53	35
36◆	1976	Q0.23¾	3-1-96	1-31	0.86	0.95	0.74¾	92.2	6476	5828	8-27-95	2414	p14196	238472	My	1.42	1.50	□1.58	1.81	2.06	2.20	6 Mo Nov	0.94	1.08	36
37	....	None Since Public			...	Nil	....	17.0	23.2	8.04	3-31-95	0.12	...	5259	Mr	...	...	pd0.67	0.74	....	0.62	6 Mo Sep	0.19	0.07	37
38	....	None Since Public			...	Nil	....	3.28	37.8	19.3	9-30-95	0.79	...	10942	Je	0.64	d0.48	d0.99	d0.09	0.12	0.17	3 Mo Sep	0.05	0.10	38
39◆	....	0.05	4-1-70	3-13	...	Nil	....	2.36	60.9	16.3	9-03-95	20.0	...	±3615	Au	±0.22	±0.05	±1.30	±1.80	±□d0.75	d0.75				39
40	....	....			...	Nil	....	Cv into 1 Cl'A'				....	...	1509	Au	±0.22	±0.05	±1.30	±1.80	±□d0.75	d0.75				40
41	....	None Since Public			...	Nil	....	0.60	8.20	7.02	9-30-94	26.7	...	★45000	Dc	...	...	0.49	P0.92	....	0.92				41
42	....	None Since Public			...	Nil	....	0.75	240	128	10-01-95	162	384	27380	Dc	p®0.29	□1.67	1.68	□1.20	....	0.48	9 Mo Sep	□0.96	0.24	42
43	1995	0.10	11-30-95	10-27	0.20	Nil	....	Book Value $16.19			9-30-95	....	...	4814	Mr	...	p1.13	n/a	[61]0.93	....	0.79	6 Mo Sep	0.49	0.35	43
44	....	None Since Public			...	Nil	....	23.2	103	44.8	9-30-95	90.0	...	±10000	Dc	...	...	±p[62]0.98	±1.75	....	1.45	9 Mo Sep	±1.11	±0.81	44
45◆	....	None Since Public			...	Nil	....	1.60	45.3	13.1	9-29-95	27.8	...	11096	Dc	0.46	0.42	d0.15	0.56	....	0.83	9 Mo Sep	0.39	0.66	45
46	1850	Q0.32½	12-29-95	12-6	1.30	1.30	1.29½	4.64	49.1	51.2	9-30-95	119	...	8870	Sp	1.38	1.43	1.50	1.58	1.60	1.60				46
47	1851	Q0.37	12-22-95	12-6	1.48	1.48	1.48	3.04	55.7	63.3	9-30-95	150	146	9931	Sp	Δ1.50	1.75	1.76	1.85	1.71	1.71				47
48	1956	Q0.42	12-8-95	11-29	1.68	1.68	1.65	0.13	9.92	12.3	9-30-95	54.5	44	2948	Dc	1.80	1.87	2.00	2.08	....	2.20	12 Mo Sep	2.09	2.20	48
49	....	None Since Public			...	Nil	....	349	1203	444	9-30-95	528	...	53714	Dc	1.57	2.19	d9.03	[64]2.10	E1.00	1.41	9 Mo Sep	1.26	Δ0.57	49
50◆	1987	Q0.42½	12-15-95	11-28	1.60	1.70	1.40	81.0	1187	1238	9-30-95	2037	...	82618	Dc	d2.70	3.28	□2.74	[65]3.90	E5.55	5.44	9 Mo Sep	2.07	3.61	50
51◆	1988	Q0.02	1-2-96	12-18	0.29	0.08	0.50	Equity per shr Neg			9-30-95	921	5750	20237	Dc	□4.30	□5.59	□9.86	□[66]5.15	E4.90	7.15	9 Mo Sep	□5.16	7.16	51
52	1993	Q0.81¼	1-15-96	12-27	3.25	3.25	3.25	Cv into 0.7843 com, $63.75				....	5000	...	Dc	...	...	...	...	....	....				52

◆**Stock Splits & Divs By Line Reference Index** [2]10%,'91:Adj to 3%,'95. [3]No adj for stk dstr of Hector Commun,'90:2-for-1,'93. [5]4-for-3,'92:3-for-2,'93. [10]3-for-1,'94. [13]1-for-10 REVERSE,'94. [14]1-for-10 REVERSE,'92,'95. [16]2-for-1,'92. [19]3-for-2,'95. [20]1-for-4 REVERSE,'92. [21]2-for-1,'93. [25]3-for-1,'94. [27]5-for-4,'95:3-for-2,'95:2-for-1,'95. [32]2-for-1,'93. [33]3-for-2,'95. [35]1-for-10 REVERSE,'93. [36]3-for-2,'91. [39]2-for-1 in new Cl'B'. [45]3-for-2,'94,'95. [50]2-for-1,'92. [51]2-for-1,'91,'92.

¶ S&P 500 # MidCap 400 ✣ SmallCap 600 • Options

Index	Ticker	Name of Issue (Call Price of Pfd. Stocks)	Market	Com. Rank. & Pfd. Rating	Inst. Hold Cos	Inst. Hold Shs. (000)	Principal Business	Price Range 1971-93 High	1971-93 Low	1994 High	1994 Low	1995 High	1995 Low	Dec. Sales in 100s	December, 1995 Last Sale Or Bid High	Low	Last	%Div Yield	P-E Ratio	Total Return % Annualized 12 Mo	36 Mo	60 Mo
1	CSEP	✔Consep Inc	NNM	NR	19	1863	Dvp/mfr pest control prods	...	...	6¼	2⅛	4⅜	2	3788	3¼	2⅜	2¾	...	d	-8.3	...	...
2	CSIM	✔Consilium Inc	NNM	C	27	2992	Factory mgmt software & svcs	27½	5½	10½	3¾	15⅛	7	9128	14⅝	10½	11⅞	...	..	58.3	7.3	-10.1
3	CDLI	Consol Delivery & Logistics	NNM	NR	..	...	Ground/air delivery	...	...	...	...	13½	10	16849	11½	10	11	...	..	...	...	...
¶4•[1]	ED	✔Consolidated Edison	NY,B,C,Ch,P,Ph	A	472	77731	Utility:el,gas,steam-NYC	37¾	1½	32⅜	23	32¼	25½	81638	32¼	28⅜	31¾	6.4	11	34.1	5.7	13.6
5	Pr B	6% cm Cv Pref B (100)	NY	A-	11	1		455	34¾	397	388	387	345	...	...	...	412¾B	1.5	..	...	...	...
¶6•[2]	CNF	✔Consolidated Freightways	[3]NY,B,Ch,P	B-	271	30932	Trucking: air freight	41¼	2⅞	29¼	17⅞	28¾	20¼	57972	28¾	25¼	26½	1.5	16	21.8	14.1	18.1
7	COGI	✔Consolidated Graphics	NNM	NR	24	1899	Commercial printing services	...	...	22½	9¾	26⅛	9½	12035	26⅛	23	26	...	29	131	...	...
8	CHCA	✔Consolidated Hlth Care Assoc	NSC	C	..	...	Provides physical therapy svcs	12¾	⅛	1⅝	7/16	1⅛	¼	5363	⅜	¼	¼	...	d	-67.9	-44.3	-8.5
¶9•[4]	CNG	✔Consolidated Nat Gas	[3]NY,To,B,C,Ch,P	B+	457	40524	Integrated natural gas sys	55⅜	4¼	47	33⅜	46¼	33⅝	48913	46¼	43¾	45⅜	4.3	..	34.9	4.2	5.4
#10•[5]	CDP	✔Consolidated Papers	NY,Ch,Ph	B+	205	11974	Enamel printing paper	54¼	1 1/16	52⅜	36¼	65⅜	44⅞	12476	62	53	56⅛	2.6	12	26.9	15.4	11.4
11	COPI	✔Consolidated Products	NNM	NR	47	3841	Drive-in type restaurants	8⅛	¾	9¾	7	15¼	8⅛	5732	15¼	14⅛	14¾	...	17	91.4	41.8	60.8
12	CYNXF	Consolidated Ramrod[54] Gold[55]	NSC,To	C	10	727	Mineral resource prop	10⅜	5/16	10½	4¾	5⅛	1	19152	1½	1	1¼	...	d	-71.0	...	...
13	PIPE	✔Consolidated Stainless	NNM	NR	5	18	Mfr stainless steel pipe	4⅜	3¼	6⅝	3½	14½	5⅛	4270	10	8	9	...	15	75.9	...	...
14•[6]	CNS	✔Consolidated Stores	NY,B,Ch,P,Ph	B	218	47279	Retails close-out mdse	23⅝	1⅞	20¼	11½	25⅝	15¾	34073	25⅝	21½	21⅝	...	17	18.5	6.3	41.0
15	COTG	✔Consolidated Technology Grp	NSC	NR	3	69	Mfr precision electronic instr	...	...	7	½	1⅜	¼	25945	¾	¼	¼	...	..	-60.0	...	...
16	CTO	✔Consolidated Tomoka Land	AS	B	17	5453	Fla citrus,resorts,RE devel	28	1½	15⅝	11⅞	17¼	11½	145	17¼	15¾	17	2.9	21	45.1	14.3	12.8
17•[7]	DIN	✔Consorcio G Grupo Dina ADS[57]	NY,Ph	NR	37	6588	Mfr trucks & buses in Mexico	29⅞	15	31	7⅞	9½	1¾	16345	2½	1¾	1⅞	...	d	-81.3	...	...
18	DIN.L	Cl'L'ADS[58]	NY,Ph	NR	29	4034		...	...	13⅛	6⅜	7⅝	15/16	27812	1⅜	15/16	1⅜	...	d	-82.6	...	...
19	CFIN	✔Consumers Finl	NNM	B-	6	116	Insur hldg: credit, life	8⅝	¾	3½	2	4¼	2	763	4	3⅜	3⅜B	...	d	50.0	20.8	-2.7
✣20	CONW	✔Consumers Water	NNM	B+	49	1332	Owns water utilities	22½	3¾	18¾	15¼	19	14½	1595	19	16¾	18¼	6.6	13	15.3	8.4	13.1
21	CAI.A	✔Contl Airlines'A'	NY,Ph	NR	22	469	Domestic, int'l air service	30¼	16	30¾	8⅛	46⅞	7	917	46⅞	38⅝	42½	...	d	360	...	...
22•[8]	CAI.B	✔ Cl'B'	NY,Ph	NR	73	9845		30½	13	27¼	7½	47½	6½	30506	47½	39	43½	...	7	390	...	...
23	CAN	✔Contl Can	NY	B	29	1185	Food pckg/engineering svcs	40⅜	⅜	25½	18¾	29⅛	14⅝	2131	17⅞	14⅝	16⅜	...	61	-21.6	-9.0	...
24	CCIR	✔Contl Circuits	NNM	NR	14	633	Computer eq & components	...	...	...	...	17¾	9¾	7810	17	15¼	16¼	...	16	...	...	...
✣25	CON	✔Contl Homes Hldg	NY,Ch,Ph	B	67	4932	Builds single-family homes	24¼	1½	23⅛	11½	24⅞	11	14647	24⅞	18⅜	24⅝	0.8	10	110	14.5	67.9
26	CUO	✔Contl Materials	AS,Ch	B-	11	166	Bldg mtls: mineral pr: mfg	38¼	2½	14	7⅞	13⅜	10⅞	193	12½	12	12⅛	...	16	7.8	14.3	14.2
✣27	CNU	✔Continuum Co	NY	B	100	8486	Software for insur industry	25¾	1/32	30½	18	41¾	27	12997	41¾	33⅝	39½	...	24	32.2	17.3	23.1
✣28•[9]	CDAT	✔Control Data Systems	NNM,Sg	NR	81	10845	Dvlp tailored computer sys	14⅛	7	11⅜	5⅜	21⅜	5⅞	47445	21⅜	16¼	19⅝	...	d	186	29.1	...
29	CVE	✔Converse Inc	NY,Ch	NR	44	14176	Mfr athletic footwear,apparel	...	...	12⅝	9¼	11¾	3½	8584	4⅝	3½	4⅛	...	d	-63.3	...	...
30	COV	✔Convest Energy Corp	AS,Ch	C	13	425	Oil & gas explor,dev,prod'n	29¼	⅜	8½	4¼	4¾	3	740	4	3⅛	3¾	...	d	-15.5	-17.3	-8.6
31	CGR	✔Cooker Restaurant	NY,Ch	NR	29	2699	Owns/operates restaurants	24	2⅞	13¼	5⅞	13⅛	6⅛	1783	11⅜	9⅝	11¼	0.4	21	77.6	-19.1	23.8
32	RON	✔Cooper Cameron	NY	NR	55	16323	Oil & gas ind services/prod	...	...	...	...	35½	18½	13497	35½	25⅞	35½	...	d	...	...	...
33	CCTI	✔Cooper & Chyan Technology	NNM	NR	..	...	Dvlp circuit board dgn softwr	...	...	...	...	16¼	10¾	22083	16¼	10¾	15¾	...	..	...	...	...
34	COO	✔Cooper Cos	NY,P	C	15	1536	Mfrs health care prod	86¼	13/16	10½	1 5/16	11¼	5¼	10735	8	6	7½	...	..	11.1	30.5	-7.2
¶35•[4]	CBE	✔Cooper Indus	NY,B,Ch,P	A-	454	76436	Mfr elec equip&auto prod	59⅜	2¼	52¼	31⅝	40½	32⅞	57011	37⅝	34⅛	36¾	3.6	15	...	...	...
36	CXW	Cooper Ind 6.00%'DECS'1998	NY	....[64]	..	...	Exch Notes For Com Stock	...	...	...	...	13¾	13¼	55236	13¾	13¼	13¾	5.9	..	...	...	...
¶37•[10]	CTB	✔Cooper Tire & Rubber	NY,Ch,Ph	A	356	51065	Auto/truck tires,rubber prd	39⅝	3/16	29½	21⅝	29⅝	22¼	43330	25¾	23¾	24⅝	1.2	18	3.7	-10.2	23.9
¶38•[5]	ACCOB	✔Coors (Adolph)Cl'B'[66]	NNM	B-	216	13755	Western brewer:ceramic,food	35½	9½	20⅞	14¾	23¼	15⅛	26503	23¼	20⅛	22⅛	2.3	20	36.8	...	...
39	CPRT	✔Copart Inc	NNM	NR	58	5289	Auctions salvage vehicles	...	...	18⅝	12	27	16¾	17930	27	20¾	26¼	...	37	57.9	...	...
40•[11]	CPLY	✔Copley Pharmaceutical	NNM	NR	41	2348	Mfr off-patent pharmac'l prd	53¾	12⅝	39½	12¾	21¼	13	7869	15¼	13¼	13¾	...	d	3.8	-16.0	...
41	COP	✔Copley Properties	AS,Ch	NR	12	569	Real estate investment trust	22⅞	7⅝	10¾	9¼	13⅜	9⅜	2527	13⅜	12⅝	12⅞	8.4	30	44.8	21.7	16.9
42•[12]	COPY	CopyTele Inc	NNM	NR	36	3234	Dvlp stge:data display sys	20¾	1 7/16	13½	3¾	11⅛	5⅜	21040	10⅝	8¾	9⅝	...	d	48.1	-8.9	11.5
✣43•[5]	CORR	✔Cor Therapeutics	NNM	NR	91	10456	Cardiovascular biopharma R&D	22	7½	17¼	9	19½	7¾	55148	12½	7¾	8⅜	...	d	-20.2	-17.2	...
#44•[13]	CRH	✔Coram Healthcare	NY	NR	122	16590	Health care services	...	...	19⅛	10½	26¾	3	50353	5⅞	4⅛	4⅜	...	d	-73.1	...	...
45	CDA	✔Cordiant[71] ADS	NY,Ch,Ph	NR	26	33408	Int'l advertising services	343¾	4⅜	8⅝	5⅝	6¾	3¾	39592	4⅜	3¾	4	...	d	-40.7	-16.0	-26.6
#46•[6]	CORD	✔Cordis Corp[74]	NNM	B-	239	13229	Specialized medical devices	50½	1 7/16	61¾	36	112¼	57¼	70040	107	92¾	100½	...	32	64.8	40.3	34.3
✣47	CRI	✔Core Indus	NY,Ch	B-	61	4275	Electr,agric,veh,constr prod	18¾	1 3/16	15½	8⅝	14¼	9¾	4146	14¼	12⅜	12⅞	1.9	30	34.9	17.4	21.4
48	CRLBF	Core Laboratories N.V.	NNM	NR	..	...	Oil & gas industry svcs	...	...	...	...	13¾	9½	3969	12¾	10	12	...	18	...	...	...
49•[9]	COSFF	✔Corel Corp	NNM	NR	65	9679	Dvlp,mkt graphics software	13⅝	3⅝	16¾	10⅝	19½	10⅛	43932	18	12¾	13	...	23	-5.5	37.1	...
50	CSTF	COREStaff Inc	NNM	NR	..	...	Temporary personnel service	...	...	...	...	38¾	23	18994	38¾	31¼	36½	...	66	...	...	...
¶51•[4]	CFL	✔CoreStates Financial	NY,Ph	B+	463	79150	Comml bkg,Philadelphia,Pa,NJ	30¼	2 7/16	29⅛	22⅞	49½	25⅝	53865	40⅛	36¾	37⅞	4.4	12	49.1	15.4	24.7
52	CRM	Corimon [78]ADS	NY,Ch	NR	26	1501	Mfr constr prd,chem,food prd	15	5⅞	23½	7⅞	9⅜	3⅛	7329	4	3⅛	3¼	...	4	-64.9	...	...

Uniform Footnote Explanations-See Page 4. Other: [1]ASE:Cycle 2. [2]NY:Cycle 3. [3]Ph [4]ASE:Cycle 1. [5]P:Cycle 1. [6]Ph:Cycle 1. [7]CBOE:Cycle 2. [8]ASE,CBOE:Cycle 3. [9]CBOE:Cycle 1. [10]NY,Ph:Cycle 2. [11]Ph:Cycle 3. [12]ASE:Cycle 3. [13]P:Cycle 2. [51]Restated from $0.21,'91. [52]®$1.00,'94. [53]Excl $3 in sub debs,'90. [54]1994 & prior prices in Cdn$. [55]Plan name chg,Ramrod Gold Ltd. [56]Fiscal Jul'94 & prior. [57]Ea ADS rep 4 com, no par. [58]Ea ADS rep 4'L' shrs,no par. [59]8 Mo Dec'93. [60]®$1.45,'94. [61]®$1.82,'95. [62]Edisto Resources owns 72%. [63]Stk dstr of Gardner Denver Machinery,'94. [64]Rated A-r by S&P. [65]Stock or cash re-specified cond.. [66]Non-vtg. [67]Fiscal Jan'94 & prior. [68]11 Mo Dec'94. [69]©$0.1651,'94. [70]Incl debt under negotiation. [71]ADS's represent'g 3 Ord shr par 25p. [72]From sale of rights. [73]Excl Defr. shrs. [74]Johnson & Johnson plan mgr, $109. [75]1993 & prior in Can.$. [76]®$0.63,'94. [77]®$1.73,'94. [78]Ea ADS rep 35 Com Bs10.

Index (Splits ◆)	Cash Divs. Ea. Yr. Since	Dividends: Latest Payment: Period $	Date	Ex. Div.	Total $: So Far 1995	Ind. Rate	Paid 1994	Financial Position Mil-$: Cash& Equiv.	Curr. Assets	Curr. Liab.	Balance Sheet Date	Capitalization: Lg Trm Debt Mil-$	Shs. 000: Pfd.	Com.	Earnings $ Per Shr. Years: End	1991	1992	1993	1994	1995	Last 12 Mos.	Interim Earnings: Period	$ per Shr. 1994	1995	Index
1	....	None Since Public			...	Nil	....	3.56	16.3	6.36	9-30-95	0.97	...	7570	Dc	...	pd0.80	pd1.01	d0.97	....	d0.49	9 Mo Sep	d0.50	d0.02	1
2	....	None Since Public			...	Nil	....	12.0	20.2	11.1	7-31-95	....	...	7684	Oc	[51]d0.15	d0.77	d0.75	d0.85	P0.08	0.08				2
3	....	None Since Public			...	Nil	....	2.01	26.6	50.5	9-30-95	p3.20	...	★6630	Dc	...	...	...	p0.11	....	....	9 Mo Sep	n/a	p0.32	3
4	1885	Q0.51	12-15-95	11-13	2.04	2.04	2.00	430	1469	1072	9-30-95	4066	★6568	234951	Dc	2.32	2.46	2.66	2.98	E2.85↑	2.98	12 Mo Sep	2.98	2.98	4
5	1968	Q1.50	2-1-96	1-8	6.00	6.00	6.00	Cv into 13 common, $7.6923				....	53	...	Dc	b2.56	b2.68	b2.85	b3.03	....	....				5
6	1995	†0.01	11-10-95	11-2	0.40	0.40	....	102	1188	1082	9-30-95	496	956	43536	Dc	d1.52	□d0.58	0.87	□[52]1.11	E1.70	1.65	9 Mo Sep	□0.71	1.25	6
7	....	None Since Public			...	Nil	....	2.28	27.4	11.0	9-30-95	15.1	...	5492	Mr	0.28	0.74	1.06	0.90	....	0.89	6 Mo Sep	0.47	0.46	7
8	....	None Paid			...	Nil	....	0.01	2.43	2.28	9-30-95	1.02	1727	14002	Dc	0.08	d0.13	d0.16	d0.53	....	d0.44	9 Mo Sep	d0.10	d0.01	8
9	1944	Q0.48½	2-15-96	1-10	1.94	1.94	1.94	26.4	851	936	9-30-95	1298	...	93375	Dc	1.94	2.19	Δ2.03	1.97	E0.20↓	0.08	9 Mo Sep	1.18	d0.71	9
10	1934	Q0.37	11-17-95	11-2	1.43	1.48	1.28	3.71	341	230	9-30-95	264	...	44580	Dc	2.10	□1.15	1.46	1.97	E4.90	4.17	9 Mo Sep	1.32	3.52	10
11◆	....	†[53]2.637	11-27-90	11-28	...	Nil	....	1.35	14.5	29.0	9-27-95	28.3	...	13684	Sp	0.50	0.55	0.62	0.80	0.86	0.86				11
12	....	None Paid			...	Nil	....	0.23	1.01	9.06	j6-30-95	9.32	...	p26311	Je	d0.30	d0.29	d0.24	d0.33	d0.53	jd0.53				12
13◆	....	None Since Public			...	Nil	....	0.09	26.9	9.81	9-30-95	15.6	...	4212	Dc	...	p0.07	p0.17	d0.07	....	0.60	9 Mo Sep	0.02	0.69	13
14	....	None Since Public			...	Nil	....	14.7	559	221	10-28-95	140	...	47724	Ja	±0.44	±0.78	±0.90	1.15	....	1.24	9 Mo Oct	0.36	0.45	14
15	....	None Paid			...	Nil	....	1.89	28.0	37.4	9-30-95	15.8	81	24725	Dc	d0.05	d0.03	Δ0.12	[56]d0.61	....	....	9 Mo Sep	n/a	d0.26	15
16◆	1976	S0.25	8-14-95	7-28	0.45	0.50	0.35	Equity per shr $4.51			9-30-95	29.8	...	6261	Dc	*0.32	*0.40	Δ0.08	1.01	....	0.80	9 Mo Sep	0.21	Nil	16
17	1995	0.047	1-10-95	12-21	0.047	Nil	....	53.4	516	188	12-31-94	499	...	±258026	Dc	*3.96	*1.88	*1.56	*d2.33	....	d2.97	3 Mo Mar	d0.06	d0.70	17
18	1995	0.047	1-10-95	12-21	0.047	Nil	....	....	...	...		....	...	54226	Dc	...	*1.88	*1.56	*d2.33	....	d2.97	3 Mo Mar	d0.06	d0.70	18
19	1981	0.05	5-1-94	4-11	...	Nil	0.05	Equity per shr $4.41			9-30-95	2.70	481	2619	Dc	d1.26	0.02	□d0.46	Δd0.62	....	d0.39	9 Mo Sep	Δd0.62	d0.39	19
20	1951	Q0.30	2-26-96	2-7	1.18½	1.20	1.16½	3.75	31.3	46.2	9-30-95	150	11	8448	Dc	1.74	1.14	0.80	1.22	....	1.43	12 Mo Sep	1.29	1.43	20
21	....	None Since Public			...	Nil	....	603	1241	2030	9-30-95	1715	p471	±27578	Dc	...	n/a	[59]d2.33	d23.76	....	d14.20	9 Mo Sep	d3.69	5.87	21
22	....	None Since Public			...	Nil	....	....	...	...		....	...	21277	Dc	...	n/a	[59]d2.33	d23.76	E6.20↑	d14.20	9 Mo Sep	d3.69	5.87	22
23	....	0.02½	9-1-60	8-10	...	Nil	....	13.2	256	192	9-30-95	137	...	3196	Dc	2.92	Δ□1.01	0.33	□[60]1.50	....	0.27	9 Mo Sep	□1.38	0.15	23
24	....	None Since Public			...	Nil	....	2.04	22.1	13.4	7-31-95	1.36	...	7130	Jl	...	...	0.37	p0.48	0.99	1.05	3 Mo Oct	0.24	0.30	24
25	1990	Q0.05	1-12-96	12-28	0.20	0.20	0.20	Equity per shr $14.78			8-31-95	★199	...	6950	My	0.03	Δ0.27	1.38	2.11	[61]1.99	2.42	6 Mo Nov	1.09	1.52	25
26	....	None Paid			...	Nil	....	0.41	31.4	19.5	9-30-95	....	...	1130	Dc	0.51	0.12	□1.18	1.21	....	0.74	9 Mo Sep	0.52	0.05	26
27	....	0.01	4-15-86	3-24	...	Nil	....	25.0	140	77.2	9-30-95	18.1	...	19201	Mr	0.81	Δ0.60	d1.79	1.38	E1.65	1.58	6 Mo Sep	0.63	0.83	27
28	....	None Paid			...	Nil	....	83.6	201	102	9-30-95	....	...	12880	Dc	d4.14	d12.03	0.66	d6.87	....	d6.26	9 Mo Sep	d0.21	0.40	28
29	....	None Since Public			...	Nil	....	4.17	219	79.6	9-30-95	120	...	16692	Dc	...	...	p0.58	p0.96	....	d1.90	9 Mo Sep	p1.04	d1.82	29
30◆	....	0.20	5-23-86	5-5	...	Nil	....	1.96	11.1	20.6	9-30-95	16.1	...	[62]p16599	Dc	0.58	0.45	d2.42	d1.77	....	d1.04	9 Mo Sep	d0.35	0.38	30
31◆	1991	0.05	2-24-95	2-6	0.05	0.05	0.05	0.79	2.30	6.81	10-01-95	29.9	...	7155	Dc	0.38	0.52	0.45	Δ0.34	....	0.54	9 Mo Sep	0.24	0.44	31
32	....	None Since Public			...	Nil	....	12.8	601	313	9-30-95	306	...	25146	Dc	...	...	...	pd0.14	....	d0.56	9 Mo Sep	pd0.09	p□d0.51	32
33	....	None Since Public			...	Nil	....	1.65	7.51	4.27	9-30-95	....	p...	★11632	Dc	0.04	0.04	0.10	0.03	....	0.03	9 Mo Sep	0.03	0.03	33
34◆	....	0.30	1-15-88	12-28	...	Nil	....	8.79	42.6	40.5	7-31-95	43.6	...	11477	Oc	Δd3.15	Δd2.94	Δd4.74	d0.45	P0.01	0.01				34
35	1947	Q0.33	1-2-96	12-5	1.32	1.32	h[63]1.32	8.40	2038	1280	9-30-95	1882	...	107875	Dc	3.04	□2.71	2.75	d0.64	E2.45↑	0.81	9 Mo Sep	d1.27	0.18	35
36	....	Plan qtly div			...	0.81	....	Amt pay maturity based on Wyman-GordanCo stk[65]				....	...	15000	Dc	...	...	...	....	....	....	1-1-99			36
37◆	1950	Q0.075	12-22-95	11-28	0.27	0.30	0.23	29.4	464	169	9-30-95	33.2	...	83650	Dc	0.96	□1.30	1.22	1.54	E1.35	1.41	9 Mo Sep	1.07	0.94	37
38◆	1970	Q0.12½	12-15-95	11-28	0.50	0.50	0.50	12.7	347	294	10-01-95	195	...	±37903	Dc	*±0.64	±□0.17	±d1.10	±1.52	E1.10	1.25	9 Mo Sep	±1.26	±0.99	38
39	....	None Since Public			...	Nil	....	13.8	48.0	15.2	7-31-95	3.15	...	12390	Jl	...	...	p0.18	□0.30	0.65	0.72	3 Mo Oct	0.13	0.20	39
40◆	....	None Since Public			...	Nil	....	17.4	110	46.3	9-30-95	5.40	...	19064	Dc	0.28	0.83	[67]0.34	[68]0.78	....	d0.02	9 Mo Sep	0.76	d0.04	40
41	1985	Q0.27	12-26-95	12-8	1.06	1.08	[69]0.94	Equity per shr $10.65			9-30-95	41.6	...	3584	Dc	Nil	d0.42	d0.09	d0.15	....	0.43	9 Mo Sep	d0.43	0.15	41
42◆	....	None Since Public			...	Nil	....	8.72	8.75	0.23	7-31-95	....	...	25782	Oc	d0.06	d0.08	d0.12	d0.14	....	d0.11	9 Mo Jul	d0.11	d0.08	42
43	....	None Since Public			...	Nil	....	94.4	97.4	15.0	12-31-94	4.67	...	19236	Dc	d0.62	d0.86	d1.27	d2.07	....	d0.43	9 Mo Sep	d1.54	0.10	43
44	....	None Since Public			...	Nil	....	40.5	304	267	9-30-95	[70]450	...	40369	Dc	p1.39	p1.85	p0.89	d3.33	....	d7.89	9 Mo Sep	d3.30	□d7.86	44
45◆	....	[72]1.856	4-26-91	4-8	...	Nil	....	137	829	854	j12-31-94	232	...	[73]220122	Dc	d3.80	d17.58	0.21	0.29	....	d0.66	6 Mo Jun	0.14	d0.81	45
46	....	None Paid			...	Nil	....	92.6	288	92.7	9-30-95	1.35	...	16512	Je	0.68	1.67	2.00	Δ2.27	3.00	3.19	3 Mo Sep	0.70	0.89	46
47	1943	Q0.06	1-2-96	12-7	0.24	0.24	0.30	1.14	108	28.0	8-31-95	32.6	...	p10684	Au	0.17	□d2.53	0.88	1.02	0.39	0.43	3 Mo Nov	0.21	0.25	47
48	....	None Since Public			...	Nil	....	0.53	30.7	15.9	6-30-95	p6.79	...	★9467	Dc	...	...	...	p0.39	....	0.67	9 Mo Sep	p0.24	p0.52	48
49◆	....	None Paid			...	Nil	....	79.8	162	12.1	8-31-95	....	...	48905	Nv	0.34	0.35	[75]0.66	[76]0.70	....	0.56	9 Mo Aug	0.46	0.32	49
50	....	None Since Public			...	Nil	....	6.60	56.9	40.6	6-30-95	p47.0	p...	★11449	Dc	...	...	...	p0.41	....	0.55	6 Mo Jun	p0.17	p0.31	50
51◆	1844	Q0.42	1-1-96	12-4	1.36	1.68	1.20	Book Value $16.67			9-30-95	1862	...	139052	Dc	2.10	□2.27	□2.80	□[77]1.75	E3.20↑	3.01	9 Mo Sep	□0.97	2.23	51
52	1992	0.024	6-15-94	5-20	...	Nil	0.056	24687	46951	46640	j3-31-95	15310	...	1028449	Mr	*0.43	0.35	0.15	0.02	....	0.82	6 Mo Sep	d0.61	0.19	52

◆**Stock Splits & Divs By Line Reference Index** [11]10%,'91,'92,'94(twice),'95. [13]3-for-2,'95. [16]2-for-1,'92. [30]Reorg & 1-for-2 REVERSE,'90. [31]1-for-3 REVERSE,'91:2-for-1,'92. [34]1-for-3 REVERSE,'95. [37]2-for-1,'92. [38]No adj for stk dstr,'92. [40]3-for-2,'93. [42]2-for-1,'91. [45]1-for-10 REVERSE,'92. [49]2-for-1,'93:3-for-2,'94. [51]2-for-1,'93.

¶ S&P 500 # MidCap 400 ✥ SmallCap 600 • Options

Index	Ticker	Name of Issue (Call Price of Pfd. Stocks)	Market	Com. Rank. & Pfd. Rating	Inst. Hold Cos	Inst. Hold Shs. (000)	Principal Business	Price Range 1971-93 High	1971-93 Low	1994 High	1994 Low	1995 High	1995 Low	Dec. Sales in 100s	December, 1995 Last Sale Or Bid High	Low	Last	%Div Yield	P-E Ratio	Total Return % Annualized 12 Mo	36 Mo	60 Mo
1	CBN.EC	Cornerstone Bank	ECM	NR	1	84	General banking, Connecticut	....	....	....	....	11⅜	8½	32	11¼	10⅞	10⅞B	1.7	7	...	...	...
2	CGA	✓Cornerstone Natural Gas	AS	NR	9	555	Nat'l gas process'g,transp	10¾	¼	3¼	1 7/16	3¼	1 9/16	1007	2½	2 3/16	2¼	...	75	33.4	72.7	...
¶3•[1]	GLW	✓Corning Inc	NY,B,Ch,P,Ph	A–	571	135302	Sp'lty mat,commun,csmr prd/sv	43⅛	3⅛	35	27⅝	37⅜	24⅛	112465	32	29¾	32	2.3	d	7.3	–2.6	9.6
4	GLWPrM	Corning Del L.P. 6%[51]'MIPS'([52]51.80)	[2]	A	94	5893	Subsid of Corning Inc	....	....	52½	46⅛	55½	43⅞	7110	50⅞	49	50⅜	6.0	..	...	...	...
5	AGR	Corporacion Banc Espana ADS[53]	NY	NR	26	3109	General banking, Spain	23⅛	17	23⅞	17⅛	20½	14	804	20½	19⅛	20⅛	4.0	10	25.0	...	...
6•[3]	CEXP	✓Corporate Express	NNM	NR	195	38903	Office products supplier	....	....	16⅜	10⅝	30¾	11½	93659	30¾	22⅝	30⅛	...	..	132	...	...
7	CTZ	✓Corpus Christi Bancshares	AS,Ph	B–	5	71	General banking, Texas	15¼	6	11¾	8¾	13	8⅝	175	12	10¾	11⅞	2.1	11	24.6	...	...
✥8	CXC	✓Corrections Corp Amer	NY,Ch,Ph	B–	96	10849	Supplies prison mgmt svcs	8¼	1½	8⅞	4½	38⅞	8	22077	38⅞	30⅜	37⅛	...	..	405	127	58.4
9	WS	Wrrt(Pur 1 com at$8.50)	NY	....	7	215		4½	½	10⅜	3⅝	68⅝	8¼	301	68⅝	52¾	65¾	...	..	...	...	...
10	CO	✓Corrpro Co	NY,Ch	NR	35	1265	Corrosion ctrl engineer'g svc	21	11	24¼	11⅝	19¼	5⅛	8046	6⅝	5¼	6¼	...	d	–56.5	...	...
11	CBS	Cort Business Services	NY	NR	..	...	Rental furniture/access	....	....	....	....	17¾	12	6727	17¾	15	16½	...	..	...	...	...
12	CORX	✓Cortex Pharmaceuticals	NSC	NR	13	1510	Dvlp stge:therapeutic drug R&D	23¾	1 9/16	10¼	2½	6⅞	1⅝	10686	5¼	2⅜	4⅜	...	d	55.7	–19.7	18.5
13	CRVL	✓CorVel Corp	NNM	NR	36	2051	Workers compensation services	26¼	8¾	31	16¾	38⅛	19⅞	1154	38⅛	31¼	38⅛	...	26	37.4	41.8	...
14	COSCB	Cosmetic Center Cl'B'(vtg)[56]	NNM	↓B	12	396	Retails cosmetic/beauty aids	18¾	3⅛	20½	12½	14	6¼	1146	8	6¼	7	...	..	–48.1	–20.6	...
15	COSCA	✓ Cl'A'	NNM	↓B	19	547		18¾	3⅛	21	12¾	14	5¾	7635	8⅜	6½	6¾	...	..	–49.1	–22.0	7.3
16•[4]	COTTF	✓Cott Corp	NNM,To	NR	77	11017	Mfr beverages/snack foods	37¾	4⅜	31⅜	8¾	13¼	5	91917	6½	5	5½	◆...	..	–42.9	–24.3	...
17	CSLI	Cotton States Life Ins	NNM	B+	11	295	Insurance: life,health	7¾	1⅜	7¾	5¼	9⅞	6½	664	9¾	9	9	1.8	8	41.4	22.3	11.9
18•[5]	CCR	✓Countrywide Credit Indus	NY,B,Ch,P	B+	225	82617	Services mtge loans	23⅜	1/32	19⅛	12⅜	26¾	12½	134152	22½	19	21⅝	s1.5	11	72.5	15.8	43.9
19	COU	✓Courtaulds, plc ADR[59]	AS,B,Ch	NR	9	1024	Rayon yarn, British Isles	10½	⅞	8⅝	6¾	8	5⅜	336	6⅝	5⅝	5⅞B	4.1	15	–7.5	–10.9	2.9
20	CUZ	✓Cousins Properties	NY,Ph	NR	68	10852	Real estate develop: jt vent	21¼	3/16	18	15⅛	20½	16½	2479	20½	18⅛	20¼	5.3	20	31.7	17.9	21.0
21	CVTI	✓Covenant Transport 'A'	NNM	NR	36	1857	Long-haul trucking svcs	....	....	20½	16	19⅞	10⅝	5488	13	11¼	12	...	17	–39.2	...	...
✥22•[5]	CVTY	✓Coventry Corp	NNM	NR	155	22627	Hlth benefit svcs/oper HMO's	22⅛	3½	26¾	15¾	31	11	195894	22⅝	17¼	20⅝	...	30	–15.8	22.7	...
23•[6]	COX	✓Cox Communications'A'	NY,Ch,Ph	NR	233	50043	Cable TV/communic svcs	....	....	....	....	21½	14	39470	20⅝	18	19½	...	d	...	...	...
24	CPAK	✓CPAC Inc	NNM	B+	19	1104	Chem/equip for imaging indus	8¼	5/16	13	6¼	15⅞	10	1527	15¼	13½	14⅛	...	14	31.1	32.6	30.0
25	CPBI	✓CPB Inc	NNM	A–	31	994	Commercial banking, Hawaii	33	8¼	29½	22¼	35½	23½	239	33½	30½	32	3.0	12	32.3	9.3	17.9
¶26•[7]	CPC	✓CPC Intl	NY,B,C,Ch,P,Ph	A+	750	87672	International food processor	51⅝	2⅞	55⅝	44¼	74½	51⅝	53554	74½	68	68⅝	2.2	19	33.6	13.0	13.6
#27	CPY	✓CPI Corp	NY,Ch,Ph	B+	132	11716	Photo studio/lab,elec publ'g	34¾	3⅜	21⅞	14	22⅛	13¾	4861	21¼	15¾	16	3.5	14	–0.7	–2.2	–7.8
28	CRAA	✓CRA Managed Care	NNM	NR	25	2340	Mgmt & consulting services	....	....	....	....	25¼	16	4528	24	21⅜	21⅞	...	..	...	...	...
#29•[8]	CBRL	✓Cracker Brl Old Ctry	NNM	A	188	18833	Restaurant & gift stores	34¼	7/16	29⅛	17½	24⅝	15¾	74348	19¼	17⅛	17¼	0.1	16	–4.1	–15.3	16.3
30	CRFT	✓Craftmade Intl	NNM	NR	16	966	Mkt ceiling fans,light kits	13¼	2	12⅜	8⅞	10⅜	6⅛	1344	7⅜	6¼	6¾	0.6	12	–29.5	–0.4	19.9
31	CRG	✓Craig Corp[63]	NY,B,Ch,P,Ph	C	26	1814	Supermkt chain,real estate	26⅝	¾	12⅞	8⅜	10⅜	8¾	959	9⅞	9¼	9⅞	...	90	12.9	6.7	–4.0
32	Pr	Cl'A' com[64]Pref (1 Vote)	NY	B–	8	603	banking investment in Calif	18	6⅝	12⅝	8½	9½	8⅜	543	9⅛	8½	9	...	..	...	...	...
¶33•[5]	CR	✓Crane Co	NY,B,Ch,P,Ph	B+	259	15725	Mfr industrial,consumer prd	30⅞	1 11/16	29½	24⅛	39½	25⅞	19242	38⅜	33⅝	36⅞	2.0	15	42.2	19.4	15.6
34	CRD.B	✓Crawford & Co Cl'B'	NY,Ch,Ph	A	60	9812	Insur co claim,risk,mgmt svcs	30	¼	17	14⅜	17¾	14½	1553	16⅝	15¾	16¼	3.3	16	14.0	–8.4	2.5
35	CRD.A	✓ Class'A' (non-vtg)	NY	A	35	10467		29¼	10	17¾	14⅜	17¾	14½	2189	16⅛	15⅝	16	3.6	16	14.5	–7.7	3.5
¶36•[8]	CYR	✓Cray Research	NY,B,Ch	B–	239	20295	Scientific computer/software	135¾	15/16	33¾	14⅝	29¼	14⅝	19058	24⅞	22¾	24⅝	...	d	60.2	3.6	–4.2
37	CAP.EC	✓Creative Computer Appl	ECM	B–	2	16	Hlthcare ind info systems	11	¼	4	7/16	3⅛	1 1/16	1276	2	1⅝	1 11/16	...	..	–41.3	4.0	40.1
38	MALL	✓Creative Computers	NNM	NR	49	3033	Direct mkt computer products	....	....	....	....	33	15¼	25790	26⅜	15¼	18¼	...	22	...	...	...
39•[3]	CREAF	Creative Technology[66]	NNM	NR	..	...	IBM compatible audio/video pd	19¼	5⅜	24	9¾	14⅜	5⅞	67695	11½	8⅝	8⅝	...	48	–38.9	–3.6	...
40•[9]	CMOS	✓Credence Systems	NNM	NR	146	19080	Mfr semiconductor test eqp	10	6⅝	18⅝	9⅝	41½	13	64397	31¼	22	22⅞	...	16	117	...	...
41	BAP	Credicorp Ltd	NY	NR	..	...	Banking,insur,fin'l svc Peru	....	....	....	....	18½	14¾	7459	17¾	15¾	17¼	...	..	...	...	...
42	CACC	✓Credit Acceptance	NNM	NR	119	14360	Auto dealers financial svcs	13	2 3/16	19⅝	10	29¼	16	53681	23	19	20¾	...	33	17.7	56.8	...
43	CRLP	Credit Lyonnais[68]	Pa	NR	..	...	Intl banking:France	901	385	856	370	446	203⅛	....	296	234	235	4.3	d	...	...	...
44•[7]	CEI	✓Crescent Real Estate Eq	NY,Ph	NR	111	15698	Real estate investment trust	....	....	30	24½	35⅞	25	6071	35⅞	33¼	34⅛	6.4	25	41.4	...	...
#45•[5]	CF	✓Crestar Financial	NY	B+	256	18413	Commercial bkg,Virginia	46½	2¾	49¾	36⅛	61	37	11224	61	56⅞	59⅛	3.0	12	62.3	19.0	38.6
46	CFR	✓CRI Liquidating REIT[70]	NY,Ph	NR	23	249	Real estate investment trust	13⅜	7¾	8¾	4⅛	5	3¼	4639	3⅝	3⅜	3⅝	⊙19.3	9	49.6	13.1	11.4
47	CMM	✓CRIIMI MAE	NY,Ph	NR	34	1795	Real estate investment trust	12¾	6¼	12	6½	9¼	6¾	11719	9¼	8¼	8⅜	11.2	13	43.7	5.1	12.0
48	CGW	✓Cristalerias de Chile ADS[73]	NY,Ch,Ph	NR	28	2419	Mfr glass containers,Chile	....	....	31	15¾	25⅞	13	4375	22⅞	21⅜	22¼	1.5	17	37.5	...	...
49	CXIM	✓Criticare Systems	NNM	B–	10	648	Mfr patient monitor'g instr	12½	1 11/16	2⅝	1¾	4⅜	1⅝	12997	4⅜	3⅛	3¼	...	..	67.8	–1.3	7.6
50	CKT	Crocker Realty Trust	AS	NR	2	174	Real estate investment trust	....	....	....	....	9⅛	6⅝	195	9	8½	8⅞	1.0	..	...	...	...
51	WS	Wrrt[74](Pur1 com at $10[75])	AS	....	..	...		....	½	1	9/16	1⅛	7/16	845	¾	7/16	½	...	..	...	...	...
#52•[10]	CNK	✓Crompton & Knowles	NY,Ch,Ph	A+	205	29023	Spec chemicals,ind'l mchy	27¼	5/16	24⅛	13⅞	20	12	34315	13½	12⅝	13¼	4.1	15	–16.3	–13.4	11.7

Uniform Footnote Explanations-See Page 4. Other: [1]CBOE:Cycle 2. [2]NY [3]CBOE:Cycle 1. [4]CBOE,P:Cycle 2. [5]Ph:Cycle 1. [6]CBOE,NY:Cycle 3. [7]P:Cycle 1. [8]P:Cycle 3. [9]ASE,NY,Ph:Cycle 2. [10]P:Cycle 2. [51]Monthly Income Preferred Shrs. [52]Fr 8-5-98. [53]Ea ADS rep 0.5 com,500 Spanish Pesetas. [54]®$0.26,'94. [55]Extended from 9-14-96. [56]Perfumania Inc plan acq,$13. [57]®$0.57,'95. [58]®$1.94,'93. [59]ADR equals 1 ord shr. [60]Approx. [61]©$0.3128,'94. [62]Incl current amts. [63]Entitled to 30 votes. [64]$5.00 liquidation preference. [65]Stk dstr of Cray Computer Corp. [66]Ord shrs, par $0.25(Singapore dollars). [67]To be determined. [68]All data reported in French francs. [69]®$3.67,'93. [70]Liquidating asset fund. [71]Approx,incl $1.33 return of cap. [72]Incl $1.635 non-taxable:©$0.6033,'94. [73]Ea ADS rep 3 ord, no par. [74]Issued by Crocker Realty Investors. [75]Pur com of Crocker Realty Trust.

Index	Cash Divs. Ea.Yr. Since	Dividends: Latest Payment Period $	Date	Ex. Div.	Total $ So Far 1995	Ind. Rate	Paid 1994	Financial Position Mil-$ Cash& Equiv.	Curr. Assets	Curr. Liab.	Balance Sheet Date	Capitalization Lg Trm Debt Mil-$	Shs. 000 Pfd.	Com.	Earnings $ Per Shr. Years End	1991	1992	1993	1994	1995	Last 12 Mos.	Interim Earnings Period	$ per Shr. 1994	1995	Index
1	1995	0.047	1-16-96	1-2	0.093	0.19	....	Book Value $9.61			12-31-94	....	1	850	Dc	d0.29	0.98	Δ1.88	0.01	....	1.64	9 Mo Sep	d0.72	0.91	1
2	....	None Since Public			...	Nil	....	1.01	15.5	18.1	9-30-95	21.4	...	12516	Dc	d0.46	d0.97	Δd3.71	0.02	....	0.03	9 Mo Sep	Nil	0.01	2
3◆	1881	Q0.18	12-29-95	12-14	0.72	0.72	0.69	109	1818	1035	10-08-95	1473	250	229255	Dc	*1.66	□*1.40	d0.09	1.32	Ed0.29	d0.46	40 Wk Oct	1.18	d0.60	3
4	1994	0.25	12-29-95	12-26	3.00	3.00	1.333	Cv into 1.2821 com, $39				....	6500	...	Dc	...	...	...	....	....	....	Mand red'm re-specified cond.			4
5	1993	0.387	11-13-95	10-18	0.803	0.80	0.736	Equity per shr $15.75			12-31-94	7788	...	125500	Dc	...	p1.95	1.80	1.98	....	1.98				5
6◆	....	None Since Public			...	Nil	....	13.2	291	141	8-26-95	p104	...	★50191	Fb	...	...	pd0.09	Δ0.14	....	0.27	6 Mo Aug	0.02	0.15	6
7◆	1993	Q0.06¼	1-24-96	1-5	0.25	0.25	0.18¾	Book Value $9.59			9-30-95	....	...	1600	Dc	*0.26	*0.95	1.38	1.08	....	1.12	9 Mo Sep	0.73	0.77	7
8◆	....	Wrrt	9-14-92	8-31	...	Nil	....	1.26	46.9	44.1	9-30-95	64.0	...	31866	Dc	d0.10	0.13	0.17	[54]0.26	....	0.32	9 Mo Sep	0.19	0.25	8
9	....	Terms&trad. basis should			be checked in detail			Wrrts expire 9-14-97[55]				....	...	1870	Dc	...	...	...	....	....	....				9
10	....	None Since Public			...	Nil	....	1.07	66.2	27.8	9-30-95	31.4	...	6026	Mr	...	p0.74	p1.01	0.43	....	d0.74	6 Mo Sep	0.47	d0.70	10
11	....	None Since Public			...	Nil	....	0.06	10.6	3.92	9-30-95	p63.0	...	★10011	Dc	...	...	...	p0.83	....	....	9 Mo Sep	n/a	p0.75	11
12◆	....	None Since Public			...	Nil	....	3.06	4.00	0.51	9-30-95	1.01	260	6160	Je	d1.00	d0.90	d0.25	d0.95	d1.13	d1.05	3 Mo Sep	d0.24	d0.16	12
13	....	None Since Public			...	Nil	....	15.2	36.0	8.04	9-30-95	....	...	4436	Mr	0.43	0.61	1.01	1.30	....	1.45	6 Mo Sep	0.61	0.76	13
14	....	None Since Public			...	Nil	....	1.32	66.7	33.6	9-30-95	0.42	...	±4284	Sp	0.60	±0.68	±0.82	±0.95	±0.06	0.06				14
15	....	None Since Public			...	Nil	....	....	...	...		....	...	2721	Sp	0.60	±0.68	±0.82	±0.95	±0.06	0.06				15
16◆	1991	gQ0.02½	11-30-95	11-17	g0.10	0.10	g0.09	43.9	350	217	j1-28-95	★245	...	59667	Ja	0.21	0.25	0.62	[57]0.58	....	j0.24	9 Mo Oct	0.60	0.26	16
17◆	1974	Q0.04	1-2-96	12-13	0.128	0.16	0.104	Equity per shr $11.24			9-30-95	....	...	3395	Dc	0.39	0.62	□Δ0.75	1.01	....	1.09	9 Mo Sep	0.83	0.91	17
18◆	1978	Q0.08	1-22-96	12-27	0.32	0.32	0.313	Equity per shr $11.97			8-31-95	5479	...	101883	Fb	0.88	1.65	[58]1.97	0.96	E1.95	1.60	9 Mo Nov	0.75	1.39	18
19	1913	[60]0.06	2-6-96	12-8	0.24	0.24	0.219	87.0	867	746	j3-31-95	155	3500	402700	Mr	Δ0.66	0.57	0.30	0.40	....	0.40				19
20	1980	Q0.27	12-21-95	12-6	0.99	1.08	[61]0.90	Equity per shr $9.88			9-30-95	91.9	...	28087	Dc	0.53	0.86	0.53	0.97	....	1.04	9 Mo Sep	0.68	0.75	20
21	....	None Since Public			...	Nil	....	0.19	30.5	6.61	9-30-95	64.7	...	±13350	Dc	*0.05	0.18	±0.39	±0.69	....	0.70	9 Mo Sep	±0.50	±0.51	21
22◆	....	None Since Public			...	Nil	....	75.4	114	132	12-31-94	65.1	...	p32150	Dc	Δd3.19	Δ0.41	0.79	0.96	E0.70	0.63	9 Mo Sep	0.75	0.42	22
23	....	None Since Public			...	Nil	....	Equity per shr Neg			9-30-95	[62]★2388	...	±270164	Dc	...	...	p0.02	pd0.17	....	d0.17	9 Mo Sep	pd0.04	pd0.04	23
24◆	1990	0.052	11-4-94	9-19	...	Nil	0.208	2.51	30.7	11.4	9-30-95	8.92	...	5341	Mr	0.57	0.65	0.67	0.76	....	1.00	6 Mo Sep	0.37	0.61	24
25	1958	Q0.24	1-19-96	12-27	0.90	0.96	0.88	Book Value $24.72			9-30-95	....	...	5244	Dc	2.51	2.81	Δ3.02	2.58	....	2.68	9 Mo Sep	1.94	2.04	25
26◆	1920	Q0.38	1-25-96	12-28	1.46	1.52	1.34	183	2414	2099	9-30-95	972	2143	145750	Dc	2.40	□2.47	2.95	2.25	E3.65	3.54	9 Mo Sep	1.35	2.64	26
27	1985	Q0.14	11-27-95	11-9	0.56	0.56	0.56	9.49	93.3	92.6	11-11-95	54.8	...	13867	Ja	1.80	1.54	Δ0.76	1.05	....	1.18	40 Wk Nov	0.21	0.34	27
28	....	None Since Public			...	Nil	....	0.79	28.2	15.5	9-30-95	5.00	...	7352	Dc	...	...	...	p0.63	....	....	9 Mo Sep	n/a	□0.66	28
29◆	1972	Q0.00½	1-2-96	12-13	0.02	0.02	0.02	45.7	118	78.7	10-27-95	22.9	...	60235	Jl	0.45	0.61	0.78	Δ0.94	1.09	1.11	3 Mo Oct	0.26	0.28	29
30	1994	Q0.01	1-15-96	12-28	0.04	0.04	0.03	0.37	18.4	8.97	9-30-95	....	32	3299	Je	0.06	0.31	0.48	0.69	0.55	0.55	12 Mo Sep	0.74	0.55	30
31	....	0.031	1-31-80	12-21	...	Nil	....	21.6	21.9	0.29	6-30-95	....	...	±5935	Sp	*0.70	Δ□d1.26	d0.93	□0.16	....	0.11	9 Mo Jun	□0.36	0.31	31
32	....	None Since Public			...	Nil	....	....	...	...		....	...	1600	Sp	*0.70	Δ□d1.26	d0.93	....	....	d0.49	9 Mo JunΔ	d0.08	□0.36	32
33◆	1939	Q0.18¾	12-14-95	12-1	0.75	0.75	0.75	0.42	531	255	9-30-95	306	...	30163	Dc	□1.42	0.79	1.62	1.86	E2.45	2.37	9 Mo Sep	1.30	1.81	33
34	1965	Q0.135	11-21-95	11-8	0.54	0.54	0.50	41.3	237	111	9-30-95	10.1	...	±34882	Dc	±1.05	±1.13	□±1.06	±1.14	....	1.00	9 Mo Sep	±0.87	±0.73	34
35	1990	Q0.14½	11-21-95	11-8	0.58	0.58	0.56	....	...	...		....	...	17418	Dc	±1.05	±1.13	□±1.06	±1.14	....	1.00	9 Mo Sep	±0.87	±0.73	35
36	....	h[65]....	11-29-89	11-30	...	Nil	....	32.0	487	258	9-30-95	92.7	...	25521	Dc	4.15	d0.56	2.33	2.16	....	d7.57	9 Mo Sep	1.78	d7.95	36
37◆	....	None Paid			...	Nil	....	0.38	2.67	1.60	8-31-95	0.03	...	2736	Au	*0.06	*0.06	*0.02	0.06	Nil	Nil				37
38	....	None Since Public			...	Nil	....	22.6	95.8	49.7	9-30-95	0.64	...	9750	Dc	d0.13	Δ0.01	d0.06	0.29	....	0.83	9 Mo Sep	0.06	0.60	38
39◆	....	None Since Public			...	Nil	....	126	378	176	6-30-94	0.22	...	86447	Je	0.12	0.01	0.55	1.11	P0.30	0.18	3 Mo Sep	0.20	0.08	39
40◆	....	None Since Public			...	Nil	....	82.7	157	37.8	7-31-95	....	...	21259	Oc	0.19	d0.73	0.37	0.94	P1.45	1.45				40
41	....	Plan annual div			...	[67]....	....	Equity per shr $8.39			6-30-95	47.0	...	43739	Dc	...	...	...	p0.95	....	....	6 Mo Jun	n/a	p0.82	41
42◆	....	None Since Public			...	Nil	....	Equity per shr $4.16			9-30-95	[62]64.3	...	45542	Dc	p0.13	p0.20	0.30	0.49	....	0.63	9 Mo Sep	0.35	0.49	42
43	....	10.00	7-1-93	7-1	...	10.00	....	Book Value 961			j6-30-93	130000	14000	45779	Dc	90.00	Pd49.00	...	....	....	jd77.30	6 Mo Jun	3.40	d24.90	43
44	1994	0.55	11-1-95	10-16	2.05	2.20	0.79	Equity per shr $17.61			9-30-95	290	...	23144	Dc	...	...	pd1.09	p1.05	....	1.39	9 Mo Sep	p0.71	1.05	44
45	1870	Q0.45	11-21-95	11-2	1.75	1.80	1.53	Book Value $29.24			9-30-95	380	...	37666	Dc	0.98	2.32	[69]3.68	4.47	E5.00	4.84	9 Mo Sep	3.34	3.71	45
46	1989	0.10	9-29-95	9-14	[71]1.92	0.70	[72]2.73	Equity per shr $3.83			9-30-95	....	...	30423	Dc	1.08	0.95	0.91	0.89	....	0.41	9 Mo Sep	0.77	0.29	46
47	1989	Q0.23½	12-29-95	12-14	0.92	0.94	1.16	Equity per shr $9.03			9-30-95	....	...	30407	Dc	□0.78	0.79	0.78	1.07	....	0.63	9 Mo Sep	0.90	0.46	47
48	1994	[60]0.073		12-26	0.324	0.33	0.163	81.0	132	20.9	12-31-94	14.4	...	61600	Dc	0.94	1.67	0.99	1.30	....	1.30				48
49	....	None Since Public			...	Nil	....	1.63	17.5	4.29	9-30-95	3.60	...	6712	Je	0.19	d0.03	0.02	0.01	0.02	0.01	3 Mo Sep	0.02	0.01	49
50	....	Plan annual div			...	0.09	....	Equity per shr $4.58			9-30-95	202	...	14285	Dc	...	...	...	p0.31	....	....	9 Mo Sep	n/a	p0.17	50
51	....	Terms&trad. basis should			be checked in detail			Wrrts expire 1-20-98				....	...	2300	Dc										51
52◆	1933	Q0.135	11-24-95	11-1	0.525	0.54	0.46	2.91	304	171	9-30-95	64.0	...	48059	Dc	0.73	□0.87	1.00	1.00	E0.90	0.93	9 Mo Sep	0.76	0.69	52

◆**Stock Splits & Divs By Line Reference Index** [3]2-for-1,'92. [6]3-for-2,'95. [7]4-for-1,'93. [8]2-for-1,'95. [12]1-for-5 REVERSE,'95. [16]3-for-1,'91:2-for-1,'92,'93. [17]5-for-4,'95. [18]Adj to 5%,'93:3-for-2,'92,'94. [22]2-for-1,'94. [24]5-for-4,'95. [26]2-for-1,'92. [29]3-for-2,'91,'92,'93. [33]No adj for stk dstr,'88. [37]1-for-5 REVERSE,'91. [39]2-for-1,'94. [40]3-for-2,'95. [42]3-for-2,'93:2-for-1,'93,'94. [52]2-for-1,'92.

¶ S&P 500 # MidCap 400 ✤ SmallCap 600 • Options

Index	Ticker	Name of Issue (Call Price of Pfd. Stocks)	Market	Com. Rank. & Pfd. Rating	Inst. Hold Cos	Inst. Hold Shs. (000)	Principal Business	Price Range 1971-93 High	1971-93 Low	1994 High	1994 Low	1995 High	1995 Low	Dec. Sales in 100s	December, 1995 Last Sale Or Bid High	Low	Last	%Div Yield	P-E Ratio	Total Return % Annualized 12 Mo	36 Mo	60 Mo
1	CRNSF	Cronos Group	NNM	NR	..	...	Leases marine containers	....	....	....	....	11⅞	9¾	28281	11⅞	9¾	11¾	...	15	...	...	...
#2	ATX.A	✔Cross (A.T.) Cl'A'	AS,B,Ch,P,Ph	B	111	9512	Fine writing instruments	41	1 15/16	17⅝	12½	17½	12⅞	3827	16¾	14⅞	15⅛	4.2	22	23.7	−0.3	−4.3
✤3	XTO	✔Cross Timbers Oil	NY,Ph	NR	75	11761	Oil & gas dvlpmt, prod'n	18⅞	12⅞	16⅝	12½	18⅛	13¼	6093	17¾	16⅝	17⅝	1.7	61	21.0	...	...
4	CRT	✔Cross Timbers Royalty Tr	NY,Ph	NR	10	1133	Royalty interest O&G prop	17	10	14¾	9½	11⅞	9½	5254	10¾	9⅝	10⅛	9.2	10	11.4	−3.6	...
5	CROS	✔Crossmann Communities	NNM	NR	21	1107	Builder single-family homes	12	9½	14⅛	5¼	19	5¼	3884	19	16¾	18¾	...	12	257	...	...
6	COM	✔Crowley, Milner & Co	AS,Ch	B−	7	66	Retail merchandiser,Mich	24⅛	2⅞	11⅞	4½	6	3	616	6	5	5⅝	...	d	9.8	−7.2	−4.2
7	CWN	✔Crown Amer Realty Tr	NY,Ch	NR	111	19048	Real estate investment trust	17½	14½	15½	12¼	14⅛	6½	51016	8	6⅝	7⅞	10.2	d	−35.8	...	...
8	CNP.A	✔Crown Centl Pet 'A'	AS,Ch	C	33	840	Independent producer,refiner	43⅞	3¼	24¼	12⅜	17⅞	11⅞	627	15¼	13⅞	14¾	...	d	13.5	1.2	−8.0
9	CNP.B	✔ Class B (1/10 vtg)	AS,Ch	C	33	2549	&marketer of petrol prd	40¾	7⅝	23⅛	11⅝	17¾	11⅝	834	15⅛	13⅜	14⅝	...	d	19.4	6.4	−7.2
¶10•[1]	CCK	✔Crown Cork & Seal	NY,B,Ch,P,Ph	B+	449	57362	Metal cans,closures:mchy	41⅞	1½	41⅞	33½	50⅝	33½	80529	42⅝	39⅞	41¾	...	44	8.4	1.4	17.2
11	CRW	✔Crown Crafts	NY,Ch,P	B	59	4266	Mfr home furnshings prod	20⅞	⅛	21⅞	14⅛	18	11¼	1724	12⅞	11¼	11½	1.0	11	−23.3	−13.2	1.3
12	CLL.EC	✔Crown Laboratories	ECM	NR	2	1486	Mfr/dvlp spcl food products	....	....	5	1½	3⅜	1 3/16	3167	1⅞	1 3/16	1¾	...	d	−36.4	...	...
13	CRO	✔Crown Pac Partners L.P.	NY,Ch,Ph	NR	5	62	Mfr dstr lumber products	....	....	21⅝	21½	21⅝	17	7767	19⅛	17⅜	18⅛	11.3	..	−8.4	...	...
14	CRRS	✔Crown Resources Corp	NNM,To	C	39	7274	Gold,silver,mineral mining	11⅛	⅝	7⅛	3⅜	5⅝	3⅜	21569	5½	4¼	4⅞	...	d	27.4	−10.5	−14.6
15	CVAN	✔Crown Vantage	NNM	NR	119	4710	Produce paper prods	....	....	....	....	27	13	22309	17½	13¼	14¼	...	..	...	...	...
16	RVR	✔Cruise America	AS,Ch	C	11	1197	Rental/sale of RV vehicles	13¼	2⅝	5¼	2⅜	5⅞	3⅜	835	5⅝	5⅛	5⅜	...	15	62.3	−0.8	13.3
17	CMSI	✔Cryomedical Sciences	NNM	NR	28	2033	Dvlp low-temp medical prod	19½	1 7/16	4¾	1 13/16	4	1 15/16	36296	3	1 15/16	2	...	d	−37.2	−39.4	6.4
18	COR	✔Crystal Oil	AS	B−	20	1916	Oil & gas explor prod'n	76500	12½	33¾	20⅛	34½	29⅛	172	30⅝	29¼	30⅛	...	12	2.1	9.8	17.0
19	CSFC	✔CSF Holdings[53]	NNM	B	43	2306	Saving bank,Florida,Calif	20¾	⅝	21⅝	14¾	40	18⅜	861	40	39	39⅝	...	11	117	38.2	87.5
20	CSPI	✔CSP Inc	NNM	B	18	1047	Array processor,software pkg	23¼	4½	10½	7⅛	9½	7	1593	9½	8¾	9	...	24	20.0	−3.5	11.9
21	CSS	✔CSS Industries	NY,Ph	B	48	3802	Business forms,metal contnrs	21¼	3/16	21	15½	24¾	15¼	692	22	20⅝	22	...	16	29.4	15.1	16.6
22	CLR	✔CST Entertainment	AS,Ch	C	13	3717	Film colorizing/licensing	29½	11/16	2½	¾	1½	7/16	20317	¾	7/16	9/16	...	d	−57.2	−35.2	−25.0
¶23•[2]	CSX	✔CSX Corp	NY,B,C,Ch,P,Ph	↑B+	663	119183	RR hldg:Transportation	44⅛	3⅛	46¼	31⅝	46⅛	34¾	70388	46⅛	43	45⅝	2.3	17	36.5	12.0	26.7
24	CFS	CT Finl Services	To,Mo	B+	4	407	Savings & loan svcs Cdn	27	2¾	20½	17⅛	24¾	18	3790	24⅜	22½	24	e3.3	13	39.8	18.1	...
25	CTLI	✔CTL Credit	NNM	NR	26	2161	Offer consumer loans/svcs	13¼	10	14¼	7⅜	17¾	8⅞	2216	14⅛	12¾	13⅝	...	10	73.0	...	...
26	CTS	✔CTS Corp	NY,Ch,Ph	B	50	2139	Electronic components/subsys	57¾	6½	31	19½	37¾	27⅜	526	37¾	36	37¾	1.6	12	37.3	32.8	19.8
27	CUBN	✔CU Bancorp	NNM	B−	21	1297	Commercial bkg,California	18⅛	3¼	8	5¾	10¼	6¾	1302	10¼	9⅜	10¼	0.8	17	53.4	43.6	4.2
28	CUB	✔Cubic Corp	AS,B,Ch,Ph	B	48	1573	Electronics:elevator:fare sys	34⅝	⅞	23¾	17⅜	28⅝	17⅛	973	28⅝	23¾	28⅜	1.9	32	55.1	21.2	16.9
¶29•[3]	CU	✔CUC Intl	NY,Ch,Ph	B	520	151364	Member based consumer svcs	26½	1 3/16	23⅞	16⅝	39¼	21¾	124248	38	29¼	34⅛	...	42	53.7	41.7	50.7
30	CUC	✔Culbro Corp	NY,Ch	B−	38	1595	Tob,plastic&nursery prod/RE	58½	3	17½	12⅞	51⅞	11¾	1023	51	49	49⅛	...	22	261	43.9	28.7
✤31	CFBI	✔Cullen Frost Bankers	NNM	B	130	6838	Commercial bkg,Texas	40¼	4¾	39¼	28½	51½	29¾	4314	51¼	48¾	50	2.8	13	65.6	27.9	59.7
32	CUL	Culligan Water Tech	NY	NR	9	1470	Mfr water purification sys	....	....	....	....	24¼	23¼	31834	24¼	23¼	24¼	...	..	...	...	...
¶33•[4]	CUM	✔Cummins Engine	NY,B,Ch,P	B−	341	29015	Mfr diesel engines,components	54⅜	5⅞	57⅝	35⅞	48⅝	34	23636	39⅜	36¾	37	2.7	9	−16.9	−0.7	16.1
34	CW	✔Curtiss-Wright	NY,B,Ch,P,Ph	B	58	4034	Process eq,aerospace,nuclear	70½	5	37¼	32⅞	53¾	35⅛	294	53¾	47¼	53¾	1.9	14	51.7	23.4	21.2
✤35	CSTM	✔Custom Chrome	NNM	NR	66	4391	Wholesale Harley-Davidson Pts	27	6	28	12¼	26½	15¾	6588	24⅝	22⅞	23⅛	...	15	39.1	34.5	...
36	CUS	✔Customedix Corp	AS,B,Ch	B−	11	119	Health/dental care prod	172½	1	4⅜	2⅜	3¼	1¾	709	2	1¾	2	...	9	−23.8	−11.4	−8.5
37	CVI	✔CV REIT Inc[56]	NY,Ch	NR	10	289	Real estate investment trust	27	7/16	11½	8⅜	11¼	8⅞	1984	11¼	10⅛	11¼	9.6	11	40.4	...	...
38	CVB	✔CVB Financial	AS	B+	20	354	Comm'l bkg,California	21	⅞	14⅞	10¼	15½	12⅝	337	15⅛	13¾	15⅛	2.1	12	17.1	37.3	22.4
39	CWM	✔CWM Mortgage Hldgs	NY,Ch	NR	83	8625	Invest in single-family mtgs	19½	3⅛	11¾	7	17¼	8½	34354	17¼	14⅞	17	7.8	14	120	56.2	34.8
40	CYAN	Cyanotech Corp	NSC	NR	7	374	Dvlp algae related products	2¼	¼	1 11/16	13/16	15	1 1/16	15464	14¼	9½	12	...	..	815	134	...
41	CBXC	✔Cybex Computer Products	NNM	NR	21	640	Dvlp/mkt computer eqp	....	....	....	....	26	12	14430	19½	12	14¼	...	16	...	...	...
42	CYS	✔CyCare Systems	NY,Ch	C	52	3974	Medic computer svs & sys	17⅜	4	15⅞	7¾	39½	14½	7449	28½	23	25⅝	...	32	64.0	58.0	34.8
43	CYI	✔Cycomm Intl(New)	AS,Ch	NR	4	190	Dvlp,mfr special electr Prd	23¾	14¾	20	2½	12¾	3¾	11380	5⅝	4⅛	4¼	...	d	−43.3	...	...
44	CYDS	✔Cygne Designs	NNM	NR	44	3578	Design mfr womens apparel	20¾	10	27	10	14	⅝	35735	1¾	⅝	15/16	...	d	−92.9	...	...
#45•[5]	CY	✔Cypress Semiconductor	NY	B	266	65527	Mfrs integrated circuits	12¼	3	12⅛	6⅝	27¾	10¾	446007	15⅞	11½	12⅝	...	11	9.4	41.8	17.3
¶46•[6]	CYM	✔Cyprus Amax Minerals	NY,Ph	B−	479	58291	Mineral resources expl,min'g	36⅜	7⅜	33⅜	23⅛	32⅛	24¼	58542	28½	25½	26⅛	3.1	20	3.5	−2.3	9.1
✤47•[7]	CYRX	✔Cyrix Corp	NNM,Ch	NR	100	8035	Mfr computer processor prd	41⅜	16	47½	18½	49¾	16¾	215514	36¼	21⅜	23	...	14	17.9	...	...
✤48	CYRK	✔Cyrk Inc	NNM	NR	65	7037	Design,mfr promotional prgm pd	23	10	44¾	20½	41¼	7	8895	10⅝	9⅜	9¾	...	25	−77.6	...	...
✤49•[8]	CYT	✔Cytec Industries	NY,Ph	NR	178	6468	Integrated chemical prod'n	14	13⅛	41⅞	12⅝	64¼	31¾	6628	64¼	60¾	62⅜	...	12	57.4	...	...
50	CYTO	✔Cytogen Corp	NNM	C	47	7362	Cancer biochem treatment sys	34¼	3	7	2⅜	6½	2⅞	55021	5½	4½	5¼	...	d	35.5	−34.9	−13.8
✤51	CYTR	✔CytRx Corp	NNM	NR	32	1739	Pharmaceutical research	11¾	7/16	8¼	1¼	3⅜	⅞	76760	1 3/16	⅞	1⅛	...	d	−12.2	−38.7	4.4
52	DNFC	✔D&N Finl Corp	NNM	C	20	718	Savings & loan,Michigan	19¼	2½	10	6⅝	13½	7¼	5251	12½	11¾	12⅛	...	11	73.2	13.7	32.2

Uniform Footnote Explanations-See Page 4. Other: [1]Ph:Cycle 1. [2]P:Cycle 2. [3]Ph:Cycle 2. [4]NY:Cycle 3. [5]CBOE:Cycle 3. [6]CBOE:Cycle 1. [7]ASE,CBOE,P:Cycle 2. [8]ASE:Cycle 2.
[51]Incl $0.868 non-taxable,'94. [52]Fiscal Jan'93 & prior. [53]Nations Bank Corp offer,$39.50. [54]Excl subsid pfd. [55]Spl $ dstr,excl dstr of $3.111CvNote,'89. [56]Plan spin-off,Hillcoast Dvlmt Corp. [57]©$0.20988,'94.
[58]Fiscal Dec'92 & prior. [59]®$0.73,'95. [60]®$0.60,'94. [61]®$2.51,'94.

Splits ◆ Index	Cash Divs. Ea.Yr. Since	Dividends: Latest Payment Period $	Date	Ex. Div.	Total $ So Far 1995	Ind. Rate	Paid 1994	Financial Position Mil-$ Cash& Equiv.	Curr. Assets	Curr. Liab.	Balance Sheet Date	Capitalization Lg Trm Debt Mil-$	Shs. 000 Pfd.	Com.	Earnings $ Per Shr. Years End	1991	1992	1993	1994	1995	Last 12 Mos.	Interim Earnings Period	$ per Shr. 1994	1995	Index
1	....	None Since Public			...	Nil	....	Equity per shr $6.86			9-30-95	p81.2	p...	★8615	Dc	1.62	0.44	0.68	0.58	....	0.78	9 Mo Sep	0.71	0.91	1
2	1952	Q0.16	2-12-96	1-23	0.64	0.64	0.64	57.8	120	36.6	9-30-95	....	...	±16522	Dc	1.26	0.64	d0.21	0.62	....	0.70	9 Mo Sep	0.28	0.36	2
3	1993	Q0.075	1-15-96	12-27	0.30	0.30	0.30	3.61	27.3	26.5	9-30-95	239	...	18207	Dc	...	p0.45	pd0.02	0.19	....	0.29	9 Mo Sep	0.12	Δ0.22	3
4	1992	0.07	1-16-96	12-27	1.002	0.93	1.06	Equity per shr $7.66			9-30-95	....	...	6000	Dc	...	1.22	1.28	1.12	....	1.06	9 Mo Sep	0.79	0.73	4
5	....	None Since Public			...	Nil	....	Equity per shr $6.11			9-30-95	15.5	...	6082	Dc	...	p0.61	p1.06	1.28	....	1.57	9 Mo Sep	0.86	1.15	5
6◆	....	0.06¼	1-25-91	1-7	...	Nil	....	0.25	27.2	23.2	10-28-95	9.65	...	966	Ja	d2.57	d3.88	0.44	0.85	....	d0.48	9 Mo Oct	d2.54	d3.87	6
7	1993	Q0.20	12-15-95	11-15	1.10	0.80	[51]1.40	Equity per shr $4.40			9-30-95	551	...	27428	Dc	...	p[52]0.27	p0.31	0.55	Ed0.55	d0.52	9 Mo Sep	0.26	Δd0.81	7
8	....	0.10	5-22-92	4-28	...	Nil	....	47.6	234	158	9-30-95	129	...	±9953	Dc	d0.61	Δd1.35	d0.44	±d3.63	....	d1.02	9 Mo Sep	±d2.57	□±0.04	8
9	....	0.10	5-22-92	4-28	...	Nil	....	....	....	....		....	...	5136	Dc	d0.61	Δd1.35	d0.44	±d3.63	....	d1.02	9 Mo Sep	±d2.57	±□0.04	9
10◆	....	0.001	8-31-56	8-8	...	Nil	....	58.0	1954	1754	9-30-95	1163	...	90611	Dc	1.48	1.79	□2.08	1.47	E0.96	1.21	9 Mo Sep	1.02	0.76	10
11	1989	Q0.03	12-19-95	12-1	0.12	0.12	0.12	0.44	94.0	26.4	10-01-95	57.0	...	7944	Mr	0.91	0.89	1.08	1.31	....	1.10	6 Mo Sep	0.52	0.31	11
12	....	None Since Public			....	Nil	....	1.77	2.02	1.35	9-30-95	1.45	.2	13803	Dc	...	d0.11	d0.09	d0.15	....	d0.27	9 Mo Sep	d0.08	d0.20	12
13	1995	Q0.51	11-14-95	10-30	1.58½	2.04	....	10.7	110	44.5	9-30-95	326	...	±18134	Dc	...	...	±p2.38	p1.07	....	....	9 Mo Sep	n/a	0.69	13
14	....	None Paid			...	Nil	....	8.60	9.06	0.33	9-30-95	15.0	...	13166	Dc	d0.09	Δd1.27	d0.14	0.27	....	d0.10	9 Mo Sep	0.29	d0.08	14
15	....	None Since Public			...	Nil	....	14.8	233	137	9-24-95	582	...	p8917	Dc	...	...	...	pd6.29	....	....	9 Mo Sep	n/a	p0.88	15
16	....	None Since Public			...	Nil	....	7.34	28.2	27.7	10-31-95	22.3	...	5716	Ap	0.64	d0.09	d0.14	d0.55	0.03	0.37	6 Mo Oct	1.13	1.47	16
17	....	None Since Public			...	Nil	....	1.18	6.45	3.11	9-30-95	0.02	...	24854	Je	d0.18	d0.26	d0.29	d0.12	d0.09	d0.08	3 Mo Sep	d0.02	d0.01	17
18◆	....	180.00	7-3-84	6-11	...	Nil	....	67.7	68.8	62.7	9-30-95	p60.2	33500	2654	Dc	0.70	0.09	0.40	1.68	....	2.53	9 Mo Sep	d0.49	0.36	18
19◆	....	0.01	1-28-82	12-29	...	Nil	....	Book Value $22.98			12-31-94	p647	[54].5	11399	Dc	Δ0.98	Δ□3.66	□3.74	□3.24	....	3.51	9 Mo Sep	□2.54	□2.81	19
20	....	None Since Public			...	Nil	....	17.6	24.5	1.61	8-25-95	....	...	2922	Au	0.39	0.61	0.70	0.61	0.14	0.37	3 Mo Nov	d0.15	0.08	20
21◆	....	0.05	4-30-70	4-14	...	Nil	....	3.79	162	95.4	9-30-95	8.14	...	10656	Dc	1.69	1.87	1.43	2.05	....	1.39	9 Mo Sep	1.57	0.91	21
22	....	None Since Public			...	Nil	....	0.04	2.43	2.88	9-30-95	....	...	26204	Je	Δd0.31	Δd0.21	Δd0.18	Δd0.08	Δd0.06	d0.07	3 Mo Sep	d0.01	d0.02	22
23◆	1922	Q0.26	12-15-95	11-21	0.92	1.04	0.88	563	1810	2664	9-30-95	2564	...	210484	Dc	□d0.38	0.10	1.73	3.11	E2.65	2.76	9 Mo Sep	1.97	1.62	23
24	1865	g†1.50	12-22-95	12-17	g†2.30	0.80	g0.80	Equity per shr $18.99			j12-31-94	3906	10000	119361	Dc	1.76	1.52	1.22	1.64	....	j1.92	9 Mo Sep	1.21	1.49	24
25	....	None Since Public			...	Nil	....	Equity per shr $13.17			9-30-95	....	...	3456	Dc	...	p1.36	p1.30	1.42	....	1.40	9 Mo Sep	1.04	1.02	25
26	1930	Q0.15	2-5-96	12-27	0.60	0.60	0.40	29.6	123	47.9	10-01-95	15.6	...	5207	Dc	0.82	0.37	□1.27	2.70	....	3.21	9 Mo Sep	1.82	2.33	26
27	....	Q0.02	11-27-95	11-9	0.08	0.08	....	Book Value $7.01			9-30-95	....	...	4587	Dc	d0.83	d1.90	0.47	0.56	....	0.60	9 Mo Sep	0.40	0.44	27
28	1971	S0.26½	9-1-95	8-9	0.53	0.53	0.53	24.1	208	89.1	9-30-95	39.0	...	5987	Sp	2.15	1.11	3.66	Δ0.39	0.90	0.90				28
29◆	....	[55]0.988	6-6-89	6-7	...	Nil	....	160	606	103	10-31-95	14.3	...	182294	Ja	0.17	0.37	0.51	0.67	....	0.81	9 Mo Oct	0.48	0.62	29
30	....	0.20	10-5-92	9-14	...	Nil	....	0.69	107	33.4	9-02-95	87.5	...	4384	Nv	0.74	0.43	□0.24	0.27	....	2.21	9 Mo Aug	0.01	1.95	30
31◆	1993	Q0.35	12-15-95	11-29	1.14	1.40	0.67	Book Value $29.53			9-30-95	....	...	11190	Dc	0.02	1.66	Δ3.48	3.33	....	3.84	9 Mo Sep	2.48	2.99	31
32	....	None Since Public			...	Nil	....	1.70	125	74.7	10-31-95	p32.1	...	★19389	Ja	...	...	...	pd1.30	....	....	9 Mo Oct	n/a	pd0.62	32
33◆	1948	Q0.25	12-15-95	11-29	1.00	1.00	0.62½	77.0	1363	920	10-01-95	148	...	40100	Dc	Δd2.48	□1.77	□4.95	6.11	E4.00	6.15	9 Mo Sep	4.43	4.47	33
34◆	1974	Q0.25	12-15-95	11-29	1.00	1.00	1.00	81.5	154	33.4	9-30-95	10.3	...	5059	Dc	4.21	4.29	□d0.58	□3.86	....	3.74	9 Mo Sep	□2.73	2.61	34
35	....	None Since Public			...	Nil	....	5.91	51.0	7.37	7-31-95	19.7	...	5050	Ja	□*0.33	*0.78	Δ1.10	1.27	....	1.50	9 Mo Oct	1.07	1.30	35
36◆	....	None Since Public			...	Nil	....	0.29	15.2	4.54	9-30-95	6.68	...	3296	Je	0.26	d0.45	0.20	0.27	0.24	0.23	3 Mo Sep	0.02	0.01	36
37	1976	Q0.27	1-17-96	1-2	1.08	1.08	[57]1.06	Equity per shr $9.60			9-30-95	37.5	...	7967	Dc	Δ0.40	Δ1.35	1.29	0.79	....	1.07	9 Mo Sep	0.50	0.78	37
38◆	1990	Q0.08	1-23-96	1-4	0.313	0.32	0.284	Book Value $8.11			9-30-95	9.91	...	8113	Dc	1.01	1.12	1.15	1.24	....	1.30	9 Mo Sep	0.90	0.96	38
39	1985	Q0.33	12-1-95	10-25	1.17	1.32	0.72	Equity per shr $8.18			9-30-95	172	...	40887	Dc	0.78	0.36	0.13	0.86	....	1.18	9 Mo Sep	0.59	0.91	39
40	....	None Paid			...	Nil	....	0.96	2.49	1.04	9-30-95	0.60	1997	9521	Mr	d0.13	Δ[58]0.01	0.02	0.05	....	0.09	6 Mo Sep	0.03	0.07	40
41	....	None Since Public			...	Nil	....	28.5	35.6	1.70	9-30-95	....	...	5905	Mr	0.17	0.28	0.44	[59]0.82	....	0.90	6 Mo Sep	0.37	0.45	41
42	....	None Since Public			...	Nil	....	16.7	29.3	9.64	9-30-95	3.17	...	5100	Dc	0.11	0.27	d1.39	0.60	....	0.81	9 Mo Sep	0.42	0.63	42
43◆	....	None Since Public			...	Nil	....	2.45	4.46	1.84	j5-31-95	0.07	...	3594	My	d2.70	d1.75	d2.35	d3.50	d1.90	jd1.88	3 Mo Aug	d0.09	d0.07	43
44	....	None Since Public			...	Nil	....	15.2	128	95.8	4-29-95	1.34	...	12437	Ja	0.02	0.59	0.92	0.93	....	d3.84	9 Mo Oct	0.56	d4.21	44
45◆	....	None Since Public			...	Nil	....	184	345	144	10-02-95	95.3	...	83828	Dc	0.43	d0.28	0.10	[60]0.61	E1.15†	0.93	9 Mo Sep	0.43	0.75	45
46	1988	Q0.20	2-1-96	1-8	0.70	0.80	†0.90	163	1139	822	9-30-95	1638	4667	92946	Dc	0.72	□d6.31	1.85	1.69	E1.30	0.83	9 Mo Sep	1.01	0.15	46
47	....	None Since Public			...	Nil	....	49.7	128	57.3	9-30-95	63.6	...	19178	Dc	0.78	0.49	1.06	1.88	E1.60	1.91	9 Mo Sep	1.25	1.28	47
48	....	None Since Public			...	Nil	....	63.4	120	11.4	9-30-95	0.01	...	10737	Dc	...	p0.44	p1.18	3.20	....	0.39	9 Mo Sep	2.73	d0.08	48
49	....	None Since Public			...	Nil	....	49.3	392	332	9-30-95	p111	p4	★16428	Dc	...	p2.14	pd7.83	[61]3.15	....	5.36	9 Mo Sep	1.99	4.20	49
50	....	None Since Public			...	Nil	....	11.3	14.3	5.31	9-30-95	....	...	p36601	Dc	d0.98	d0.75	d1.38	d1.38	....	d1.68	9 Mo Sep	d0.90	d1.20	50
51◆	....	None Paid			...	Nil	....	27.1	27.5	1.11	9-30-95	....	...	31632	Dc	0.12	Nil	d0.10	d0.24	....	d0.34	9 Mo Sep	d0.17	d0.27	51
52	....	0.075	10-25-90	10-2	...	Nil	....	Book Value $9.18			9-30-95	207	...	6741	Dc	0.96	□1.43	□d8.44	0.46	....	1.15	9 Mo Sep	0.33	1.02	52

◆**Stock Splits & Divs By Line Reference Index** [6]2-for-1,'94. [10]3-for-1,'92. [18]1-for-100 REVERSE,then 10-for-1,'92. [19]3-for-2,'92,'93:5-for-4,'92,'95. [21]2-for-1,'93. [23]2-for-1,'95.
[29]No adj for $2.222cash & $3.111 note dstr,'89:3-for-2, '91, '92, '93, '95. [31]10%,'93. [33]2-for-1,'93. [34]No adj for $30 dstr,'90. [36]1-for-10 REVERSE,'91. [38]10%,'92,'93,95:Vote 10% stk div,ex Jan 4.
[43]1-for-5 REVERSE,'95. [45]2-for-1,'95. [51]Hldrs vote Feb 5 on 1-for-4 REVERSE.

¶ S&P 500 # MidCap 400 ✣ SmallCap 600 • Options

Index	Ticker	Name of Issue (Call Price of Pfd. Stocks)	Market	Com. Rank. & Pfd. Rating	Inst. Hold Cos	Inst. Hold Shs. (000)	Principal Business	Price Range 1971-93 High	1971-93 Low	1994 High	1994 Low	1995 High	1995 Low	Dec. Sales in 100s	December, 1995 Last Sale Or Bid High	Low	Last	%Div Yield	P-E Ratio	Total Return % Annualized 12 Mo	36 Mo	60 Mo
1	DHI	✔D.R.Horton	NY	NR	53	6678	Single-family home constr'n	11⅛	4⅜	12¼	5⅞	11⅞	5¾	8871	11⅞	9⅞	11¾	s. . .	15	115	33.5	. . .
2	DTII	✔D T Industries	NNM	NR	37	5020	Mfr spcl machines/metal prd	. . . .	. . . .	17½	10¾	14	8½	5950	13½	12⅞	13½	0.6	13	23.6	. . .	. . .
3•[1]	DAI	✔Daimler-Benz Aktieng ADS[53]	NY,Ch,Ph	NR	57	4830	Mfr autos,electr/aerospc prd	48¾	40⅝	55¼	43¼	51¾	43⅛	8961	51⅜	49¼	50⅞	1.1	d	6.9	. . .	. . .
4	DZTK	✔Daisytek Intl	NNM	NR	44	1901	Dstr office/computer access eq	. . . .	. . . .	. . . .	. . . .	33	15	3359	32¼	29¾	30¾	. . .	22	. . .	. . .	. . .
5	DKAI	✔DAKA Intl	NNM	B–	82	5240	Food service,restaurants	175	2½	16⅜	11⅛	34¼	14½	27567	29⅜	20½	27½	. . .	14	84.9	30.1	57.8
6	DKT	✔Dakota Mining	AS	NR	21	8502	Gold & silver mining	45⅛	1⅜	3⅛	1	2	1 1/16	9888	1¾	1 1/16	1½	. . .	d	9.1	–21.6	. . .
7	DAKT	✔Daktronics Inc	NNM	NR	4	199	Mfg info display sys	. . . .	. . . .	10	4¾	7½	4⅜	1485	5⅛	4⅜	4½	. . .	24	–10.0	. . .	. . .
8	DLS.EC	✔Dallas Gold&Silver Exchange	ECM	B–	1	.2	Sells jewelry & bullion prod	10½	⅛	3⅜	1 13/16	2¼	1	339	1½	1	1¼	. . .	18	–41.2	–3.1	51.6
✣9•[2]	DS	✔Dallas Semiconductor	NY,Ph	B	150	17936	Mfrs hi performance circuits	19	4⅛	20⅛	13⅜	24⅞	15	16107	22⅝	20¾	20¾	0.5	17	28.3	17.1	28.3
✣10•[3]	DMRK	✔Damark International'A'	NNM	NR	47	3493	Direct market catalog sales	23¾	3¾	31	5¾	9	5½	16355	7½	6½	7½	. . .	. .	–6.3	1.7	. . .
11	DFIN	Damen Financial	NNM	NR	. .	. . .	Savings bank,Illinois	. . . .	. . . .	. . . .	. . . .	12¼	10	4779	11¾	11¼	11⅜	. . .	. .	. . .	. . .	. . .
✣12	DM	✔Dames & Moore Inc	NY	NR	69	10182	Environmental/engineer'g svcs	22¾	14	21¼	12½	16	11⅛	7145	13¼	11⅞	12⅛	1.0	14	–14.9	–10.0	. . .
¶13•[4]	DCN	✔Dana Corp	NY,B,Ch,P	B	400	68460	Mfr parts for auto industry	30⅛	2 5/16	30¾	19⅝	32⅝	21⅜	29218	31	28½	29¼	3.1	11	28.5	10.8	19.3
#14•[5]	DHR	✔Danaher Corp	NY,B,Ch,P	B	221	38645	Mfr hand tools,auto parts	19⅝	3/16	26⅝	18	34⅜	24¼	15026	33¾	30	31¾	0.3	18	20.5	33.8	32.2
✣15	DAN	✔Daniel Indus[57]	NY,Ch,Ph	B–	68	6905	Measure, contr fluid devices	25½	1 3/16	13¾	9⅞	16½	12⅝	7987	14⅜	13	14¼	1.3	d	8.9	8.5	–1.1
16	DHC	✔Danielson Holding	AS,Ch	NR	34	3480	Investment co/insurance	8⅞	2⅜	9¾	6	8	6⅝	1448	7¼	6¾	6⅞	. . .	43	–3.5	25.2	19.0
17•[6]	DANKY	Danka Business Systems ADR[58]	NNM	NR	185	34896	Dstr office equip,east'n U.S.	20	4⅜	23⅜	16¾	38½	21⅜	48717	37	32½	37	0.3	41	77.2	100	. . .
¶18•[7]	DRI	✔Darden Restaurants	NY	NR	360	98257	Oper family style restaurants	. . . .	. . . .	. . . .	. . . .	12⅛	9⅛	83433	12⅛	11¼	11⅞	0.7	. .	. . .	. . .	. . .
19	DARTA	✔Dart Group Cl'A'	NNM	B–	50	697	Discount book&auto parts strs	178½	3⅝	90	70	100	73	254	95	88¼	93½	0.1	62	19.7	9.5	5.5
20	DDII	✔Data Documents	NNM	NR	. .	. . .	Dgn custom business forms	. . . .	. . . .	. . . .	. . . .	9⅞	8	3175	8¾	8	8⅝	. . .	20	. . .	. . .	. . .
¶21•[8]	DGN	✔Data General	NY,B,Ch,P,Ph	C	214	27871	General purpose computers	76	3⅛	12	6⅝	14¾	6¾	34121	14¾	12⅛	13⅝	. . .	d	36.3	6.2	26.2
22	DRAI	✔Data Research Associates	NNM	NR	27	1178	Provides library automat'n sys	14¾	7	13	8½	20¾	8⅜	5030	20¾	16⅞	18¾	. . .	19	103	16.9	. . .
23	DATX	✔Data Translation	NNM	C	34	2917	Mfr microcomputer products	12½	1 5/16	9¾	3½	21	8⅜	16758	21	15¾	16¼	. . .	30	71.3	56.4	63.9
24	DTLN	Data Transmission Ntwk	NNM	NR	25	1040	Agricultural market info svc	27¼	5½	27½	16⅛	50¼	16½	2035	50¼	43	49¼	. . .	d	190	51.6	32.6
25	DKEY	Datakey Inc	NNM	C	12	777	Mfrs electronic access keys	12	2¼	4⅛	2¼	8¾	2½	5731	7¼	4⅞	5	. . .	56	81.8	17.0	–2.8
26	DLGX	✔Datalogix Intl	NNM	NR	46	4316	Computer sys consult'g/svcs	. . . .	. . . .	. . . .	. . . .	26½	8	13450	12¾	10¾	12⅝	. . .	20	. . .	. . .	. . .
27	DC	✔Datametrics Corp	AS	↓C	18	1137	Dvlp/mfr computer periph'ls	10⅜	1/16	6⅜	2⅜	11¾	3¾	13311	8¾	7⅜	7⅞	. . .	d	70.3	81.7	90.6
28	DPT	✔Datapoint Corp	NY,B,Ch,P,Ph	C	13	810	Mfr data process'g systems	67½	¾	7½	1¼	2⅜	1	8926	1⅜	1	1¼	. . .	d	–33.3	–31.4	–1.9
29	DTM	✔Dataram Corp	AS,B,Ph	↓C	15	469	Minicomputer related products	19¾	1/64	9⅛	4⅛	9⅜	4½	3677	7½	5⅝	6⅜	. . .	d	0.0	–13.2	16.7
#30•[9]	DSCP	✔Datascope Corp	NNM	B	99	6668	Electronic medical instru't'n	41¾	9/16	19¾	12	27¼	15½	18318	26	21⅞	24	. . .	22	45.5	–1.5	17.7
31	DSTM	✔Datastream Systems	NNM	NR	54	3083	Dvlp personal computer softwr	. . . .	. . . .	. . . .	. . . .	26½	7½	25546	20½	14¾	19	. . .	37	. . .	. . .	. . .
32	DWRX	✔DataWorks Corp	NNM	NR	. .	. . .	Dvlp resource mgmt,info softwr	. . . .	. . . .	. . . .	. . . .	15	10¾	8402	14½	10¾	12⅝	. . .	66	. . .	. . .	. . .
33	DTSI	✔Datron Systems	NNM	B	19	959	Satellite commun/radar sys	17½	2	12½	7¼	20½	9¾	1602	19¾	17¼	17¾	. . .	12	42.0	47.8	26.4
34	DATM	✔Datum Inc	NNM	B–	17	816	Mfr tim'g/frequency devices	16¾	½	10⅝	3¾	19⅛	8¼	6231	12⅛	9¾	10¼	. . .	64	10.8	48.6	38.7
#35	DAPN	✔Dauphin Deposit	NNM	A	101	6126	Comm'l bkg,Pennsylvania	28	3	27½	22½	31¾	23	9414	31¾	28¾	28¾	3.7	14	26.2	11.4	21.0
36	DVCO	✔DavCo Restaurants	NNM	NR	32	5371	Franchises Wendy's Intl	17¾	11¼	18½	12¼	14½	8½	7137	12⅜	8½	8⅝	. . .	7	–29.6	. . .	. . .
37•[10]	DAVD	✔Davidson & Associates Inc	NNM	NR	93	9862	Dvlp educational software	13½	6½	17½	7¼	39¼	12⅜	91406	28⅛	16	22	. . .	73	32.8	. . .	. . .
38	DWW	✔Davis Water & Waste	NY,Ch,Ph	C	18	774	Sewage/water treat,pump eq	25⅝	½	10	6⅛	17½	8¼	1810	17½	13⅜	14½	2.0	10	55.6	35.1	11.7
39	DAVX	✔Davox Corp	NNM	C	17	804	Computer-aid commun'n sys	13⅛	1⅛	5⅝	2	13¼	5⅜	8082	12¾	10	11⅞	. . .	20	116	77.5	39.5
40	DAWK	✔Daw Technologies	NNM	NR	14	1103	Dgn cleanroom sys/svc	4¼	1	8⅜	3¼	10⅝	5⅜	18518	7⅜	5⅝	5¾	. . .	. .	3.4	. . .	. . .
41	DWSN	✔Dawson Geophysical	NNM	B–	33	1591	Seismic data for oil/gas ind	19½	3	13½	7¼	15½	8½	3139	10	8½	9⅜	. . .	17	–10.7	24.4	22.7
42	DXR	✔Daxor Corp	AS	B–	12	422	Operates human sperm bank	37	1/16	8⅛	5½	8⅞	5⅝	500	7¼	6⅜	6⅞	. . .	25	19.6	–1.2	26.5
43	DAYR	✔Day Runner	NNM	NR	35	3355	Mfr personal organizer prd	21¾	7½	22¼	11	35¼	12	13123	35¼	27½	34½	. . .	24	103	55.1	. . .
¶44•[11]	DH	✔Dayton Hudson	NY,B,Ch,P,Ph	A	606	56657	Depart/disc/spec stores	85	1⅝	86⅞	64⅞	80½	63¼	65285	76⅛	71¼	75	2.3	15	9.9	2.3	8.6
45	DAY	Dayton Mining	AS	NR	35	17442	Precious metal explor,dvlp	. . . .	. . . .	. . . .	. . . .	4½	3¼	7197	4½	3⅝	4	. . .	d	. . .	. . .	. . .
46	DDL	✔DDL Electronics	NY,P,Ph	C	12	920	Mfrs printed circuit boards	13⅛	5/16	2½	¾	3⅛	1	8222	2⅞	2⅜	2⅝	. . .	24	75.0	41.0	10.1
47	DER	De Rigo ADS[67]	NY,Ch	NR	. .	. . .	Mfr sunglasses/eyeglass frames	. . . .	. . . .	. . . .	. . . .	23⅜	16	12859	23⅜	21⅛	22¾	. . .	23	. . .	. . .	. . .
#48•[6]	DF	✔Dean Foods	NY,Ch	A	213	17574	Milk & dairy: food items	33½	⅜	33½	25¼	31¾	26¼	24687	29¾	26¾	27½	2.6	15	–3.2	0.8	3.0
¶49•[12]	DWD	✔Dean Witter, Discover & Co	NY,Ch	NR	628	105442	Provides financial svcs/prod	46½	27	43⅛	31½	58¼	33½	136622	52½	46½	47	1.4	9	42.8	. . .	. . .
50	DEBS	✔Deb Shops	NNM	B–	33	2166	Women's apparel stores	21⅞	4⅜	7⅜	3	5⅛	2⅞	2128	3¾	3⅜	3⅜	5.8	d	–9.5	–23.2	–11.2
51	EJD	✔DeBartolo Realty	NY,Ch	NR	156	36420	Real estate investment trust	. . . .	. . . .	15½	13	15⅛	12	33889	13¾	12⅞	13	9.7	22	–2.7	. . .	. . .
52	DBRSY	✔DeBeers Cons Mns ADR[68]	NSC	NR	85	11814	Diamond mining	32⅝	2⅛	27	19¼	31¾	19¾	10036	31¾	27¾	30¼	2.5	23	34.7	41.8	14.0

Uniform Footnote Explanations-See Page 4. Other: [1]CBOE:Cycle 1. [2]Ph:Cycle 1. [3]CBOE:Cycle 2. [4]NY:Cycle 1. [5]Ph:Cycle 3. [6]P:Cycle 2. [7]CBOE,NY:Cycle 1. [8]P:Cycle 3. [9]ASE,P,Ph:Cycle 3. [10]CBOE,Ph:Cycle 2. [11]P:Cycle 1. [12]ASE,CBOE,P,Ph:Cycle 1. [51]Fiscal Dec'92 & prior. [52]12 Mo Sep'93. [53]Ea ADS rep 0.10 Ord Bearer shr DM 50. [54]Incl current amts. [55]®$1.18,'95. [56]16 Wks Dec'93. [57]Moorco Int'l Inc plan acq,$11.90 cash & 0.3 co. [58]Ea ADR rep 4 ord, 5p. [59]Approx. [60]Stk dstr of Intelogic Trace Inc. [61]Accum on pfd. [62]32 Wks Sep'93. [63]®$0.25,'94. [64]Fiscal Dec'93 & prior. [65]®$5.52,'95. [66]10 Mo Feb'92. [67]Ea ADS rep 1 Ord Shr,Lit 500. [68]ADR equal DeBeers/Centenary linked unit.

Splits ◆ Index	Cash Divs. Ea.Yr. Since	Dividends: Latest Payment Period $	Date	Ex. Div.	Total $ So Far 1995	Ind. Rate	Paid 1994	Financial Position Mil-$ Cash& Equiv.	Curr. Assets	Curr. Liab.	Balance Sheet Date	Capitalization Lg Trm Debt Mil-$	Shs. 000 Pfd.	Com.	Earnings $ Per Shr. Years End	1991	1992	1993	1994	1995	Last 12 Mos.	Interim Earnings Period	$ per Shr. 1994	1995	Index
1◆	....	9%Stk	6-30-95	5-24	9%Stk	Stk	6%Stk	Equity per shr $4.05			9-30-95	170	...	25442	Sp	p0.30	p[51]0.43	[52]0.48	0.69	0.80	0.80				1
2	1994	Q0.02	12-15-95	11-28	0.08	0.08	0.06	0.97	73.7	58.2	9-24-95	41.4	...	9000	Je	...	...	p0.57	□1.10	0.94	1.05	3 Mo Sep	0.14	0.25	2
3	1994	0.576	5-31-95	5-18	0.576	0.58	0.362	8635	36798	16346	12-31-94	[54]19034	...	51299	No current fin'l info							6 Mo Jun	0.49	d2.22	3
4	....	None Since Public			...	Nil	....	0.19	96.6	43.0	9-30-95	17.0	...	6304	Mr	...	...	p0.76	1.17	....	1.39	6 Mo Sep	0.51	0.73	4
5◆	....	None Since Public			...	Nil	....	11.0	62.2	41.6	9-30-95	73.9	12	p6927	Je	*Δ0.30	1.24	Δ1.36	1.55	[55]2.03	1.99	3 Mo Sep	0.40	0.36	5
6◆	....	None Since Public			...	Nil	....	1.94	11.3	12.0	9-30-95	0.57	...	26535	Dc	d12.19	d2.74	‡[56]d0.10	d0.33	....	d0.17	9 Mo Sep	d0.32	d0.16	6
7	....	None Since Public			...	Nil	....	0.29	21.6	9.97	7-29-95	1.87	...	4191	Ap	...	...	p0.36	0.62	0.23	0.19	6 Mo Oct	0.14	0.10	7
8	....	None Paid			...	Nil	....	0.98	2.19	0.88	9-30-95	0.89	...	5830	Dc	0.01	d0.03	0.04	Δ0.03	....	0.07	9 Mo Sep	0.01	0.05	8
9	1995	Q0.02½	12-1-95	11-13	0.10	0.10	....	79.2	161	32.7	10-01-95	....	...	26345	Dc	0.58	0.71	0.95	1.09	....	1.24	9 Mo Sep	0.81	0.96	9
10	....	None Since Public			...	Nil	....	15.5	102	79.5	9-30-95	....	...	8980	Dc	0.15	□d0.45	0.67	0.59	....	0.01	9 Mo Sep	0.17	d0.41	10
11	....	None Since Public			...	Nil	....	Book Value $13.30			p3-31-95	46.3	...	★3968	Nv	...	...	...	p0.45	....	....	4 Mo Mar	n/a	p0.15	11
12	1992	Q0.03	1-2-96	12-14	0.12	0.12	0.12	27.0	188	86.2	9-29-95	28.1	...	22686	Mr	p1.18	1.03	0.97	□0.83	....	0.87	6 Mo Sep	□0.47	0.51	12
13◆	1936	Q0.23	12-15-95	11-29	0.90	0.92	0.83	Equity per shr $10.81			9-30-95	1304	...	101386	Dc	0.17	□0.49	□1.39	2.31	E2.65	2.67	9 Mo Sep	1.71	2.07	13
14◆	1993	Q0.02	1-26-96	12-26	0.08	0.08	0.06	10.5	553	537	9-29-95	176	...	58483	Dc	0.24	0.55	□0.93	1.40	E1.80	1.72	9 Mo Sep	0.98	1.30	14
15	1948	Q0.04½	12-18-95	11-29	0.18	0.18	0.18	3.90	109	43.4	9-30-95	8.57	...	12083	Sp	d0.18	0.70	0.42	0.11	d1.06	d1.06				15
16	....	None Since Public			...	Nil	....	Equity per shr $4.03			9-30-95	....	...	15360	Dc	0.01	Δ0.13	Δ0.17	□0.20	....	0.16	9 Mo Sep	0.18	0.14	16
17◆	1993	[59]0.06¼	1-24-96	12-15	0.118	0.12	0.091	86.8	367	174	3-31-95	234	...	191352	Mr	□0.51	0.64	0.58	0.80	....	0.90	6 Mo Sep	0.37	0.47	17
18	1995	0.04	5-1-96	4-8	0.04	0.08	....	39.9	334	490	8-27-95	304	...	158544	My	...	...	...	pΔ0.75	p0.31	0.07	6 Mo Nov	p0.27	0.03	18
19	1965	Q0.033	12-13-95	11-27	0.133	0.13	0.133	113	365	243	10-31-95	30.8	...	±2074	Ja	□3.46	Δ□1.91	d4.10	d39.57	E1.50	d11.70	9 Mo Oct	d34.98	d7.11	19
20	....	None Since Public			...	Nil	....	4.84	75.1	28.7	p6-30-95	74.3	...	★8303	Dc	...	...	...	□p0.15	....	0.44	9 Mo Sep	p0.14	p0.43	20
21	....	None Paid			...	Nil	....	182	599	379	7-01-95	155	...	37281	Sp	2.62	d1.91	d1.73	d2.45	Pd1.23	d1.23				21
22	....	None Since Public			...	Nil	....	6.40	21.9	8.64	6-30-95	....	...	3647	Sp	0.60	0.75	0.67	0.80	P0.99	0.99				22
23◆	....	None Since Public			...	Nil	....	13.6	32.9	12.6	8-31-95	....	...	★7621	Nv	d0.26	d0.59	d1.01	0.06	....	0.55	9 Mo Aug	d0.01	0.48	23
24	....	None Since Public			...	Nil	....	0.32	7.22	19.5	9-30-95	40.9	...	3313	Dc	0.43	0.41	0.20	d0.49	....	d0.19	9 Mo Sep	d0.34	d0.04	24
25	....	None Paid			...	Nil	....	6.58	9.07	0.75	7-01-95	....	150	2830	Dc	0.45	0.08	d0.07	d0.06	....	0.09	9 Mo Sep	d0.11	0.04	25
26	....	None Since Public			...	Nil	....	40.1	56.4	12.0	9-30-95	....	...	10967	Je	...	...	...	p0.16	0.59	0.62	3 Mo Sep	Nil	0.03	26
27	....	7½%Stk	3-21-80	2-26	...	Nil	....	14.8	26.8	3.48	7-30-95	0.86	p...	★11998	Oc	0.13	0.30	Δ0.09	Nil	Pd0.84	d0.84				27
28◆	....	h[60]....	8-12-85	8-13	...	[61]Nil	....	5.74	60.1	87.9	10-28-95	69.7	1896	13391	Jl	*Δd0.42	*d1.62	*d0.97	□d6.69	d2.29	d1.92	3 Mo Oct	d0.50	d0.13	28
29◆	....	None Since Public			...	Nil	....	0.46	33.4	15.3	10-31-95	1.90	...	3824	Ap	0.38	0.80	0.76	Δd0.22	d0.34	d0.22	6 Mo Oct	0.21	0.33	29
30◆	....	None Paid			...	Nil	....	61.4	148	34.9	9-30-95	....	...	16107	Je	0.55	0.47	0.97	0.97	1.07	1.09	3 Mo Sep	0.17	0.19	30
31◆	....	None Since Public			...	Nil	....	1.71	10.2	3.77	9-30-95	0.03	...	★8105	Dc	0.05	0.06	0.10	0.30	....	0.52	9 Mo Sep	0.21	0.43	31
32	....	None Since Public			...	Nil	....	1.44	11.9	13.2	9-30-95	p0.34	p...	★5638	Dc	d0.24	d0.86	0.22	□d0.27	....	0.19	9 Mo Sep	□d0.30	□0.16	32
33	....	None Since Public			...	Nil	....	0.11	36.2	19.0	9-30-95	1.20	...	2598	Mr	1.32	d3.32	Δ1.94	1.51	....	1.53	6 Mo Sep	0.45	0.47	33
34	....	None Since Public			...	Nil	....	0.01	34.7	18.0	9-30-95	9.54	...	4003	Dc	Δ0.22	d0.89	0.03	0.34	....	0.16	9 Mo Sep	0.32	0.14	34
35◆	1910	Q0.26½	1-12-96	12-20	1.00	1.06	0.92	Equity per shr $17.29			9-30-95	40.6	...	30739	Dc	1.83	1.93	2.15	2.18	....	2.09	9 Mo Sep	1.65	1.56	35
36	....	None Since Public			...	Nil	....	0.29	6.82	23.0	7-01-95	47.8	...	6588	Sp	...	pd0.63	p[62]0.59	0.98	P1.18	1.18				36
37◆	....	None Since Public			...	Nil	....	26.6	61.5	20.9	9-30-95	....	...	34741	Dc	...	p0.13	0.21	0.15	....	0.30	9 Mo Sep	0.05	0.20	37
38	1995	0.15	1-5-96	12-21	0.22	0.29	....	3.05	65.9	34.1	10-31-95	14.3	...	3229	Ap	d0.38	d0.26	Δ0.06	d1.64	1.06	1.42	6 Mo Oct	0.56	0.92	38
39	....	None Since Public			...	Nil	....	11.4	16.5	10.2	9-30-95	0.06	...	6799	Dc	■d1.44	d0.66	0.07	d1.01	....	0.60	9 Mo Sep	d1.18	0.43	39
40	....	None Paid			...	Nil	....	0.17	24.1	9.34	9-30-95	0.14	...	12318	Dc	...	0.06	0.12	[63]0.26	....	0.02	9 Mo Sep	0.21	d0.03	40
41	....	None Since Public			...	Nil	....	5.44	10.8	1.15	9-30-95	....	...	4149	Sp	*0.11	*0.31	*0.62	0.74	0.54	0.54				41
42	....	None Since Public			...	Nil	....	37.2	37.8	6.61	9-30-95	....	...	4771	Dc	d0.35	0.66	0.42	0.35	....	0.28	9 Mo Sep	0.29	0.22	42
43	....	None Since Public			...	Nil	....	10.3	60.3	18.2	9-30-95	0.01	...	6218	Je	0.72	0.77	Δ[64]0.87	Δ0.97	1.25	1.44	3 Mo Sep	0.30	0.49	43
44	1965	Q0.44	12-10-95	11-16	1.74	1.76	1.68	177	5720	4329	10-28-95	4968	416	71901	Ja	3.86	5.02	4.99	[65]5.77	E4.95	4.76	9 Mo Oct	1.96	0.95	44
45	....	None Paid			...	Nil	....	5.94	11.7	0.99	j3-31-95	78.2	...	29930	Dc	‡[66]d0.04	d0.09	d0.03	d0.07	....	jd0.11	3 Mo Mar	Nil	d0.04	45
46	....	0.06	4-4-89	3-13	...	Nil	....	2.46	10.6	9.29	9-30-95	7.14	...	16312	Je	Δd3.03	d3.34	Δd0.50	d0.55	Δd0.15	0.11	3 Mo Sep	d0.19	0.07	46
47	....	None Since Public			...	Nil	....	27.1	138	67.4	6-30-95	5.74	...	★44500	Dc	...	0.10	0.35	0.71	E1.00	0.90	6 Mo Jun	0.52	0.71	47
48◆	1941	Q0.18	12-15-95	11-15	0.70	0.72	0.66	3.88	598	388	8-27-95	227	...	40125	My	0.41	1.53	1.73	Δ1.78	2.01	1.82	6 Mo Nov	0.93	0.74	48
49	1993	Q0.16	1-2-96	11-29	0.60½	0.64	0.47½	Equity per shr $26.70			9-30-95	6873	...	170474	Dc	...	p□2.65	p3.54	4.35	E5.20	4.76	9 Mo Sep	3.46	3.87	49
50	1984	Q0.05	11-14-95	10-27	0.20	0.20	0.20	33.2	70.4	13.2	10-31-95	2.02	.5	12845	Ja	0.55	0.46	0.33	d0.21	....	d0.37	9 Mo Oct	d0.37	d0.53	50
51	1994	Q0.315	1-20-96	12-27	1.26	1.26	0.56	Equity per shr $0.75			9-30-95	[54]1381	...	55329	Dc	...	...	p0.35	p□0.49	E0.60	0.55	9 Mo Sep	p□0.35	□0.41	51
52	1941	0.22½	11-9-95	9-13	0.747	0.75	0.76	487	2119	1122	j12-31-94	3.00	3667	380205	Dc	Δ2.81	Δ1.99	Δ1.30	1.29	....	1.29	No interim report			52

◆**Stock Splits & Divs By Line Reference Index** [1]Adj to 9%,'95:7-for-5,'95. [5]1-for-10 REVERSE,'92. [6]1-for-12.43452 REVERSE,'93. [13]2-for-1,'94. [14]2-for-1,'95. [17]2-for-1,'93,'94. [23]2-for-1,'95. [28]No adj for Intelogic spinoff'85. [29]3-for-1,'92. [30]3-for-1,'92. [31]2-for-1,'95. [35]2-for-1,'92. [37]2-for-1,'95. [48]3-for-2,'91.

¶ S&P 500 # MidCap 400 ✣ SmallCap 600 • Options Index	Ticker	Name of Issue (Call Price of Pfd. Stocks)	Market	Com. Rank. & Pfd. Rating	Inst. Hold Cos	Inst. Hold Shs. (000)	Principal Business	Price Range 1971-93 High	1971-93 Low	1994 High	1994 Low	1995 High	1995 Low	Dec. Sales in 100s	December, 1995 Last Sale Or Bid High	Low	Last	%Div Yield	P-E Ratio	Total Return % Annualized 12 Mo	36 Mo	60 Mo
1	DII	✔**Decorator Indus**	AS	B	13	469	Mfr & dstr of draperies	12¾	7/16	12⅜	7⅛	10⅛	7⅛	1509	8½	8	8	3.5	6	13.7	4.0	47.2
¶2•[1]	DE	✔**Deere & Co**	NY,B,C,Ch,P,Ph	B	720	223488	Lgst mfr farm eq:constr mchy	26⅛	3¼	30¼	20⅜	36	21⅝	177495	36	32	35¼	2.3	13	66.2	38.8	22.0
3	DEFI	✔**Defiance Inc**	NNM	B–	31	2084	Mfrs vehicle engine parts	12¼	⅜	10⅛	5½	8	5⅜	5167	7⅝	5⅜	6	2.7	6	–7.3	45.3	61.3
✣4	SEEDB	✔**DEKALB Genetics'B'**	NNM	NR	76	3770	Agricultural genetic R & D	44¾	12	36	24½	50	25¾	3483	46	44¼	45⅛	1.8	22	72.1	24.1	9.2
5	DEL	✔**Del Electronics Corp**	AS,Ch	↑B+	9	192	Mfr hi-voltage pwr supplies	7¼	1/16	8	4⅝	6¾	4¾	2564	6½	6⅛	6½	s. . .	16	44.0	14.7	18.0
6	DLI	✔**Del Laboratories**	AS	B+	16	669	Drugs and cosmetics	12½	11/16	19¼	10⅝	25¾	17⅝	121	20⅞	19¾	20⅜B	0.7	15	8.0	36.4	36.5
#7•[2]	DELL	✔**Dell Computer Corp**	NNM	B	269	54139	Dvlp/mfr IBM compatible PC's	25	1 9/16	23¾	9⅝	49⅜	19¾	512114	44⅛	28⅞	34⅝	. . .	12	65.3	13.1	42.9
#8	DEW	✔**Delmarva Pwr & Lt**	NY,B,Ch,P,Ph	B+	161	14280	Elec & gas: Delaware, Md, Va	25⅞	4¾	23⅝	16⅞	23⅝	17⅞	12726	23¼	22	22¾	6.8	13	35.4	6.3	12.7
9	DLFI	✔**Delphi Fin'l Group 'A'**	NNM	NR	43	4003	Ins hldg:life,disability,accid	25¾	5¾	25¼	16½	23¾	16	9539	23¾	20¼	21¼	. . .	10	18.1	14.9	18.7
¶10•[3]	DAL	✔**Delta Air Lines**	NY,B,C,Ch,P,Ph	B–	412	45484	Domestic, Int'l air service	85¾	12¾	57⅞	39½	81¼	50¼	102683	79⅞	71¾	73⅝	0.3	11	47.3	14.1	6.8
11	Pr C	**Series'C'cm Cv[54]Dep Pfd([55]NC)**	NY	B+	138	12345		59⅜	49¼	56¼	41	63⅛	43¾	24723	62¼	58⅛	59⅜	5.9	. .	. . .	. . .	. . .
12	DLP	✔**Delta and Pine Land**	NY	NR	68	6322	Produce cotton planting seed	13½	9	14½	9¼	37¼	12¾	7722	37¼	28	36¾	0.4	50	184	. . .	. . .
13	DGAS	✔**Delta Natural Gas**	NNM	B	17	172	Dstr nat'l gas,Kentucky	23½	5¾	21¾	15¾	18¾	15½	307	18	17⅜	17⅜	6.4	18	15.7	5.4	14.6
14	DPTR	✔**Delta Petroleum**	NSC	NR	1	34	Oil&gas explor,dvlp,prod'n	9⅜	3	8½	3⅝	8½	5	9734	7¾	6¾	7⅛	. . .	d	3.6	. . .	. . .
✣15•[4]	DLW	✔**Delta Woodside Ind**	NY,Ch,Ph	B–	76	12463	Mfr/sale fabrics & apparel	25¼	3⅝	12½	8⅞	11⅜	6⅛	10127	6⅞	6⅛	6⅝	6.0	22	–27.8	–19.4	9.8
¶16•[5]	DLX	✔**Deluxe Corp**	NY,B,Ch,P,Ph	A	389	56056	Imprinted bank checks: forms	49	1½	38	25⅝	34	25¾	69612	29¾	26⅞	29	5.1	26	14.5	–10.9	0.4
17	DRTE	✔**Dendrite International**	NNM	NR	47	2167	Manage large sales forces	. . . .	. . . .	. . . .	. . . .	22¾	13⅝	7074	21	17	18	. . .	45	. . .	. . .	. . .
#18•[6]	XRAY	✔**DENTSPLY International**	NNM	B+	147	21321	Mfr dental/medl x-ray equip	55	2¾	47	28¼	40¼	31¼	23644	40¼	35½	40	0.8	19	27.1	–6.2	46.5
19	DEPCB	✔**DEP Corp'B'**	NSC	C	11	446	Mfr/dstr personal care prod	16½	2½	6	2½	3¼	1	2103	1¾	1	1¼	. . .	d	–56.5	–55.4	–22.6
20	DFS	✔**Department 56**	NY	NR	192	14604	Design,dstr collectibles/gifts	29⅞	18	40	26	48	32⅝	25664	41⅞	32⅝	38⅜	. . .	17	–0.6	. . .	. . .
✣21	DEPS	✔**Deposit Guaranty**	NNM	A–	101	4520	Comm'l bkg,Mississippi	35¾	3⅞	34½	25½	51½	29½	7764	51½	44½	44½	3.0	11	53.1	24.1	39.7
22	DEPO	**DepoTech Inc**	NNM	NR	24	1271	Mfr drug delivery sys	. . . .	. . . .	. . . .	. . . .	21¾	12	8335	21¾	15½	19¼	. . .	d	. . .	. . .	. . .
23	DES	**Desc S.A. ADS[59]**	NY,Ch	NR	20	1163	Auto pts,chemicals,R.E.,Finl	. . . .	. . . .	34¼	19⅞	23¾	5¾	7203	14⅜	11¼	14¼	3.4	d	–39.7	. . .	. . .
✣24•[7]	DESI	✔**Designs Inc**	NNM	NR	58	3949	Retails branded casual apparel	25¼	1 3/16	17½	6⅝	11¼	6¾	31683	8⅛	6⅞	7	. . .	9	–3.4	–25.5	18.4
25	DTOP	✔**Desktop Data**	NNM	NR	38	1268	Computer-based info svcs	. . . .	. . . .	. . . .	. . . .	38	15	15898	29½	21¼	24½	. . .	. .	. . .	. . .	. . .
26	DSO	✔**DeSoto Inc**	NY,Ch,Ph	C	28	1813	Detergent prod/mfr	52½	4	8⅝	3	6¼	2¾	3223	4	2¾	3½	. . .	d	16.7	–22.4	–15.5
27•[8]	ENG	✔**Destec Energy**	NY,Ch,Ph	NR	61	8273	Utility mgmt svc/pwr generat'n	28⅝	13	15⅝	9	16⅛	9½	5271	14⅜	13⅝	13¾	. . .	14	34.1	–3.7	. . .
28	DDC	✔**Detroit Diesel**	NY,Ch	NR	68	5773	Mfr heavy-duty diesel engines	36⅞	20	35⅝	18⅛	24⅞	17	9750	19⅝	18⅛	18⅝	. . .	10	–9.1	. . .	. . .
¶29•[8]	DTE	✔**Detroit Edison[61]**	NY,B,C,Ch,Ph	↓B+	401	51714	Electric & steam utility	37⅛	7½	30¼	24¼	34⅞	25¾	83684	34⅞	32¾	34½	6.0	12	41.0	8.7	11.3
30	DTD	**Detroit Edison 8.50% 'QUIDS'[62]**	NY	. . . .[63]	. .	. . .	Quarterly Income Debt Sec	. . . .	. . . .	. . . .	. . . .	26½	24⅝	348	26½	25⅝	26¼	8.1	. .	. . .	. . .	. . .
31	DEVC	✔**Devcon International**	NNM	B–	25	1812	Construction svcs/concrete	27½	4⅝	9¾	5¾	10¼	5½	1148	8	7	8	. . .	d	0.0	–5.6	–14.5
32	DDR	✔**Developers Diversified Rlty**	NY,Ch	NR	145	14033	Real estate investment trust	31⅞	22	33⅜	26⅜	32⅛	26⅛	10302	32⅛	28¼	30	7.2	21	2.6	. . .	. . .
✣33	DVN	✔**Devon Energy**	AS,Ph	NR	130	16666	Oil & gas devel prod'n	27¼	3⅝	26½	16	26	16¾	7802	26	23⅝	25½	0.5	47	44.5	20.6	20.0
34	DEVN	✔**Devon Group**	NNM	B	103	5201	Computer typeset/print svcs	20¼	3¾	29¾	16½	45¾	22	17923	38½	26¾	29	. . .	9	–1.5	33.4	36.0
✣35	DV	✔**DeVRY INC**	NY	NR	91	10774	Tech'l/MBA degree schools	15	4⅜	16¾	11¾	28⅛	15¼	5856	28⅛	25⅞	27	. . .	28	76.8	40.2	. . .
36	DWL	✔**DeWolfe Cos**	AS	NR	6	77	Sell residential prop/mtg svc	6¼	3	6¾	3¼	6⅜	3⅞	446	5⅞	5⅛	5¾	. . .	72	15.0	19.4	. . .
#37•[9]	DEX	✔**Dexter Corp**	NY,B,Ch	↑B+	156	19843	Specialty chemicals:fiber	34¾	2 1/16	26	19⅞	26⅞	20⅜	10901	26⅞	23⅜	23⅝	3.7	14	18.3	0.2	6.1
38	DHTK	✔**DH Technology**	NNM	B+	62	6070	Mfrs dot matrix printheads	12	1 5/16	17⅜	11	24¾	13⅞	2601	24¾	21½	24½	. . .	21	53.8	39.0	34.5
39	DRL	✔**DI Industries**	AS,Ph	C	11	900	Onshore contract drilling	26¾	⅝	1 5/16	¾	1 1/16	⅝	3024	¾	⅝	¾	. . .	d	–7.6	0.0	–7.8
40	DMM.B	**Dia Met Minerals'B'**	AS	NR	9	632	Nonmetallic mineral explor	. . . .	. . . .	. . . .	. . . .	11	7⅝	86	10	9	9⅜	. . .	. .	. . .	. . .	. . .
41	DMM.A	**Cl'A'**	AS	NR	7	217		. . . .	. . . .	. . . .	. . . .	10	7⅜	109	9½	8¼	9B	. . .	. .	. . .	. . .	. . .
42	DHSM	✔**Diagnostic Health Svcs**	NSC	NR	4	271	Medical services,management	4	1⅝	3⅛	⅞	5⅜	1⅞	6974	5⅜	3⅞	5¼	. . .	25	110	. . .	. . .
#43	DP	✔**Diagnostic Products**	NY,Ch,Ph	B+	104	3445	Medical immunodiagnostic kits	53¾	3⅛	26⅝	17¾	44⅞	24¼	3197	37⅞	34½	37⅞	1.3	23	45.5	11.2	4.7
44	DRS.A	✔**Diagnostic/Retr'l Cv'A'[69]**	AS	B	13	980	Anti-sub warfare comput sys	17	1⅛	5¼	3	8	4	754	8	7¼	8	. . .	14	93.9	37.7	45.0
45	DRS.B	✔ **Class'B'(1/10 vtg)**	AS	B	5	577		14⅞	1	5⅛	3	7⅞	3⅞	554	7⅞	7	7¾	. . .	14	92.3	34.0	47.3
¶46•[9]	DL	✔**Dial Corp**	NY,B,C,Ch,P,Ph	B+	374	58037	Consumer prod transpt'n mfr	25⅜	4⅞	24	19¼	30⅜	20⅞	73924	30⅜	25⅞	29⅝	2.2	. .	37.3	. . .	. . .
47	DLGC	✔**Dialogic Corp**	NNM	NR	76	5250	Call process'g sys softwr, hrdwr	. . . .	. . . .	23½	10¾	44¼	16	25550	44¼	30	38½	. . .	41	69.2	. . .	. . .
48•[3]	DIMD	✔**Diamond Multimedia Systems**	NNM	NR	76	7180	Dvlp computer add-in subsystems	. . . .	. . . .	. . . .	. . . .	43	16½	143712	43	30¼	35⅞	. . .	d	. . .	. . .	. . .
49	DO	✔**Diamond Offshore Drilling**	NY,Ch,Ph	NR	2	123	Contract drilling O&G wells	. . . .	. . . .	. . . .	. . . .	34½	23⅜	48368	34½	28⅜	33¾	. . .	d	. . .	. . .	. . .
#50•[3]	DRM	✔**Diamond Shamrock**	NY,P	NR	192	23647	Oil & gas refining,mktg	28½	7⅜	30	23⅜	28⅞	23⅛	23155	25⅞	24¼	25⅞	2.2	15	1.7	15.3	8.4
51	DNA	✔**Diana Corp**	NY,B,Ch,Ph	B–	18	554	Invest co: telecom/food dstr	13⅝	1½	14	5⅜	26⅞	3¾	17859	26⅞	13⅜	26⅝	. . .	d	366	83.1	59.7
52	DCPI	✔**dick clark productions**	NNM	B	16	697	Dvlp & produce TV programs	8¼	2¾	10¾	5¼	10¼	7½	473	10¼	9	9¼	. . .	19	19.4	32.2	25.3

Uniform Footnote Explanations-See Page 4. Other: [1]ASE:Cycle 3. [2]Ph:Cycle 2. [3]CBOE:Cycle 1. [4]CBOE:Cycle 3. [5]P:Cycle 1. [6]CBOE:Cycle 2. [7]P:Cycle 2. [8]Ph:Cycle 1. [9]ASE:Cycle 1. [51]®$1.30,'94. [52]®$1.57,'94. [53]®$4.01,'95. [54]Dep for 0.001 shr Ser'C'Cv Pfd. [55]If com price exceeds$82.125-20 trad'g days. [56]Fiscal Dec'93 & prior. [57]6 Mo Jun'94. [58]Fiscal Mar'92 & prior. [59]Ea ADS rep 4 Sr'C' shrs, no par. [60]75% owned by Dow Chemical. [61]Plan hldg co,DTE Energy. [62]Jr Sub Deferrable Int Debs. [63]Rated BBB by S&P. [64]Can be deferred by co re-spec cond.. [65]®$0.90,'92. [66]Fiscal Mar'94 & prior. [67]12 Mo Dec'94. [68]®$1.19,'94. [69]Cv into 1 Cl'B'. [70]®$2.34,'94.

Index (Splits ◆)	Cash Divs. Ea.Yr. Since	Dividends: Latest Payment Period $	Date	Ex. Div.	Total $ So Far 1995	Ind. Rate	Paid 1994	Financial Position Mil-$ Cash& Equiv.	Curr. Assets	Curr. Liab.	Balance Sheet Date	Capitalization Lg Trm Debt Mil-$	Shs. 000 Pfd.	Com.	Earnings $ Per Shr. Years End	1991	1992	1993	1994	1995	Last 12 Mos.	Interim Earnings Period	$ per Shr. 1994	1995	Index
1◆	1993	Q0.07	12-15-95	11-28	0.27	0.28	0.23	5.18	12.2	4.45	9-30-95	0.60	...	1916	Dc	d0.06	0.84	1.25	[51]1.43	....	1.30	9 Mo Sep	1.09	0.96	1
2◆	1937	Q0.20	2-1-96	12-27	0.75	0.80	0.683	Equity per shr $10.46			7-31-95	2377	...	261915	Oc	d0.09	0.16	□0.80	2.34	P2.71	2.71				2
3	1995	Q0.04	12-5-95	11-13	0.16	0.16	....	0.30	34.4	19.6	9-30-95	21.3	...	6558	Je	d0.16	0.15	0.54	Δ0.81	0.98	0.99	3 Mo Sep	0.22	0.23	3
4	1989	Q0.20	12-8-95	11-21	0.80	0.80	0.80	3.00	175	94.6	8-31-95	85.0	...	±5187	Au	2.84	1.94	0.59	□2.11	2.04	2.04				4
5◆	....	3%Stk	12-21-95	12-21	6%Stk	Stk	6%Stk	0.71	26.9	6.36	10-28-95	11.4	...	4198	Jl	0.35	0.35	0.38	0.25	0.39	0.41	3 Mo Oct	0.09	0.11	5
6◆	1973	Q0.03½	1-2-96	11-15	0.13¼	0.14	0.121	5.43	74.2	35.9	9-30-95	40.0	...	4188	Dc	0.50	0.68	□0.87	1.19	....	1.37	9 Mo Sep	0.95	1.13	6
7◆	....	None Since Public			...	Nil	....	571	1943	997	10-29-95	113	60	93081	Ja	0.71	1.30	d0.53	[52]1.69	E2.90	2.67	9 Mo Oct	1.00	1.98	7
8	1921	Q0.38½	1-31-96	1-10	1.54	1.54	1.54	37.4	243	288	9-30-95	876	2881	60720	Dc	Δ1.44	1.69	1.76	1.67	....	1.77	12 Mo Sep	1.59	1.77	8
9	....	None Since Public			...	Nil	....	Equity per shr $17.24			9-30-95	351	...	±11736	Dc	±1.42	□±2.38	□±4.36	±2.14	....	2.13	9 Mo Sep	±1.79	±1.78	9
10	1949	Q0.05	12-1-95	11-7	0.20	0.20	0.20	1632	3141	3575	9-30-95	3048	6776	51157	Je	d7.73	d10.60	□d10.54	d10.32	Δ[53]4.07	6.54	3 Mo Sep	Δ1.00	3.47	10
11	1992	Q0.87½	12-1-95	11-7	3.50	3.50	3.50	Cv into 0.7605 com,$65.75				....	20000	...	Je	...	...	...	....	....	....	Co opt redeem for 0.7605 com fr 7-1-95			11
12◆	1993	Q0.04	12-15-95	11-29	0.13	0.16	0.12	5.57	29.8	19.3	8-31-95	11.3	...	12868	Au	0.52	0.67	0.70	0.60	0.77	0.73	3 Mo Nov	d0.19	d0.23	12
13	1964	Q0.28	12-15-95	11-28	1.12	1.12	1.11½	0.16	2.17	14.9	9-30-95	23.6	...	1882	Je	0.73	1.52	1.60	1.50	1.04	0.96	12 Mo Sep	1.42	0.96	13
14	....	None Paid			...	Nil	....	0.44	0.78	3.76	9-30-95	....	...	4061	Je	...	d1.40	[56]d0.63	‡[57]d0.45	Δd1.33	d0.89	3 Mo Sep	d0.64	d0.20	14
15	1988	Q0.10	12-6-95	11-21	0.40	0.40	0.40	0.83	372	80.2	9-30-95	237	...	24428	Je	1.27	1.62	□1.06	d0.70	0.42	0.30	3 Mo Sep	0.17	0.05	15
16	1921	Q0.37	12-4-95	11-16	1.85	1.48	1.46	51.9	430	370	9-30-95	114	...	82626	Dc	2.18	2.42	1.71	1.71	E1.10↓	1.62	9 Mo Sep	1.22	1.13	16
17	....	None Since Public			...	Nil	....	24.5	37.3	11.6	9-30-95	0.03	...	10676	Dc	...	...	...	p0.24	....	0.40	9 Mo Sep	p0.10	p0.26	17
18◆	1994	Q0.08¼	1-9-96	12-26	0.30	0.33	0.075	4.24	245	100	9-30-95	90.1	...	26951	Dc	[58]0.58	1.42	□1.14	2.23	....	2.10	9 Mo Sep	1.45	1.32	18
19	....	None Since Public			...	Nil	....	5.93	37.0	71.7	10-31-95	3.71	...	±6251	Jl	Δ0.70	0.98	0.18	d0.57	d4.32	d4.39	3 Mo Oct	0.01	d0.06	19
20	....	None Since Public			...	Nil	....	5.54	164	115	9-30-95	80.0	...	21545	Dc	...	p0.70	1.16	1.67	....	2.22	9 Mo Sep	1.48	□2.03	20
21◆	1938	Q0.33	1-2-96	12-13	1.16	1.32	1.03	Book Value $26.57			9-30-95	....	...	19549	Dc	2.04	2.67	3.77	3.80	....	3.98	9 Mo Sep	2.75	2.93	21
22	....	None Since Public			...	Nil	....	7.04	7.88	7.19	9-30-95	2.39	...	11269	Dc	pd0.07	pd0.52	pd0.78	pd1.26	....	d0.95	9 Mo Sep	pd0.91	pd0.60	22
23	....	Plan annual div			...	0.48	....	732	2583	2936	j12-31-94	2101	...	±273091	Dc	Δ±1.11	Δ±1.03	□±1.78	□±d1.90	....	d1.51	6 Mo Jun	0.35	0.74	23
24◆	....	None Since Public			...	Nil	....	18.4	85.8	27.1	10-28-95	0.50	...	15766	Ja	0.40	0.84	Δ0.36	1.06	E0.80	1.04	12 Mo Oct	0.30	1.04	24
25	....	None Since Public			...	Nil	....	32.4	35.9	13.7	9-30-95	0.06	14	8502	Dc	...	...	...	pd0.06	....	0.16	9 Mo Sep	d0.07	0.15	25
26◆	....	0.04	4-29-91	3-20	...	Nil	....	0.43	14.8	27.1	9-30-95	....	583	4679	Dc	d0.10	□d0.54	d1.83	d0.42	....	d1.02	9 Mo Sep	d0.37	d0.97	26
27	....	None Since Public			...	Nil	....	388	581	137	9-30-95	....	...	[60]58523	Dc	1.39	Δ1.41	1.67	1.84	....	1.02	9 Mo Sep	1.33	0.51	27
28	....	None Since Public			...	Nil	....	11.4	673	512	9-30-95	89.6	...	24677	Dc	...	p0.67	p1.17	1.52	....	1.85	9 Mo Sep	1.11	1.44	28
29	1909	Q0.51½	1-15-96	12-13	2.06	2.06	2.06	12.3	817	814	9-30-95	3974	3376	145120	Dc	3.64	3.79	3.34	2.67	E2.80	2.90	12 Mo Sep	2.90	2.90	29
30	1995	Q0.53⅛	12-29-95	12-26	0.97	[64]2.125	....	Co option redm fr 6-30-98 at $25				105	...	...	Dc	...	...	...	....	....	....	Mature 9-30-2025			30
31	....	0.05	10-19-92	9-24	...	Nil	....	1.28	25.0	18.1	9-30-95	15.5	...	4431	Dc	d0.37	d0.32	Δd2.11	0.46	....	d0.24	9 Mo Sep	0.42	d0.28	31
32	1993	Q0.54	12-29-95	12-13	2.16	2.16	2.32	Equity per shr $14.06			9-30-95	424	★400	18965	Dc	p0.63	p0.93	p1.22	□1.35	....	1.45	9 Mo Sep	1.00	□1.10	32
33	1993	Q0.03	12-29-95	12-13	0.12	0.12	0.12	11.1	27.6	15.7	9-30-95	97.0	...	22097	Dc	d1.99	[65]0.94	Δ0.92	0.64	....	0.54	9 Mo Sep	0.56	0.46	33
34	....	None Since Public			...	Nil	....	12.6	85.7	31.6	9-30-95	2.05	...	7369	Mr	0.69	1.43	1.83	2.94	....	3.42	6 Mo Sep	1.32	1.80	34
35◆	....	None Since Public			...	Nil	....	31.0	62.3	65.8	9-30-95	21.0	...	16615	Je	□d1.42	Δ0.37	0.57	0.73	0.89	0.95	3 Mo Sep	0.18	0.24	35
36	....	None Paid			...	Nil	....	0.78	31.4	28.0	9-30-95	3.80	...	3292	Dc	0.47	0.42	0.46	0.18	....	0.08	9 Mo Sep	0.31	0.21	36
37	1957	Q0.22	1-10-96	12-13	0.88	0.88	0.88	61.6	456	202	9-30-95	224	...	24517	Dc	d0.29	1.58	□1.40	1.56	....	1.69	9 Mo Sep	1.18	1.31	37
38◆	....	None Since Public			...	Nil	....	30.5	58.8	13.3	9-30-95	1.96	...	8266	Dc	0.62	0.75	0.82	1.00	....	1.18	9 Mo Sep	0.73	0.91	38
39	....	None Since Public			...	Nil	....	3.02	36.9	30.8	9-30-95	11.2	...	38669	Dc	d0.08	d0.09	[66]d0.07	[67]d0.08	....	d0.14	9 Mo Sep	d0.08	d0.14	39
40	....	None Since Public			...	Nil	....	10.6	11.6	0.71	4-30-95	....	...	±26915	Ja	...	...	...	n/a	....	....				40
41	....	None Since Public			...	Nil	....	....	...	...		....	...	5383	Ja	...	...	...	n/a	....	....				41
42	....	None Since Public			...	Nil	....	0.56	5.24	3.78	9-30-95	4.99	...	4700	Dc	Δ0.01	Δd0.02	d0.22	0.12	....	0.21	9 Mo Sep	0.08	0.17	42
43	1988	Q0.12	11-15-95	10-30	0.46	0.48	0.40	16.0	90.3	21.6	9-30-95	....	...	13357	Dc	1.49	1.26	1.04	[68]1.24	....	1.66	9 Mo Sep	0.87	1.29	43
44	....	None Since Public			...	Nil	....	21.0	58.0	20.7	9-30-95	30.7	...	±5502	Mr	±d1.01	±0.20	±0.30	±0.50	....	0.57	6 Mo Sep	±0.21	±0.28	44
45	....	None Since Public			...	Nil	....	....	...	...		....	...	2195	Mr	±d1.01	±0.20	±0.30	±0.50	....	0.57	6 Mo Sep	±0.21	±0.28	45
46◆	1936	Q0.16	1-2-96	11-29	0.61	0.64	0.58	17.5	1127	2152	9-30-95	731	382	94068	Dc	■d0.74	□0.38	□1.65	1.61	E0.08	0.15	9 Mo Sep	1.22	d0.24	46
47	....	None Since Public			...	Nil	....	41.1	88.2	17.5	9-30-95	2.42	...	15386	Dc	...	...	p0.69	p0.94	....	0.94	9 Mo Sep	p0.69	0.69	47
48	....	None Since Public			...	Nil	....	20.9	188	110	p9-30-95	3.23	...	★35065	Dc	...	...	...	p0.72	....	d0.64	9 Mo Sep	0.70	d0.66	48
49	....	None Since Public			...	Nil	....	....	106	42.3	p6-30-95	....	...	★50000	Dc	...	...	...	pd0.31	....	d0.16	9 Mo Sep	pd0.22	pd0.07	49
50	1987	Q0.14	12-7-95	11-16	0.56	0.56	0.53	24.4	485	298	9-30-95	607	1725	29031	Dc	1.39	□0.92	□1.04	[70]2.45	....	1.73	9 Mo Sep	1.96	1.24	50
51◆	....	5%Stk	1-5-96	12-14	...	Stk	5%Stk	8.37	31.5	12.5	10-14-95	6.86	...	3922	Mr	d0.25	Δ0.48	Δ□0.88	d0.18	....	d0.15	28 Wk Oct	d0.10	d0.07	51
52	....	None Since Public			...	Nil	....	Equity per shr $4.29			9-30-95	....	...	±8279	Je	±0.35	±0.37	±0.39	±Δ0.59	±0.49	0.50	3 Mo Sep	±Nil	±0.01	52

◆**Stock Splits & Divs By Line Reference Index** [1]2-for-1,'93. [2]3-for-1,'95. [5]Adj to 3%,Dec'95. [6]4-for-3,'94:2-for-1,'95. [7]3-for-2,'92:2-for-1,'95. [12]4-for-3,'95. [18]2-for-1,'92. [21]2-for-1,'92. [24]3-for-2,'92,'93. [26]No adj for special $24 & $11.50 dstrs,'90. [35]2-for-1,'95. [38]3-for-2,'95. [46]No adj for stk dstr of GFC Fin'l,'92:2-for-1,'94. [51]Adj to 5%,'95.

¶ S&P 500 # MidCap 400 ✧ SmallCap 600 • Options Index	Ticker	Name of Issue (Call Price of Pfd. Stocks)	Market	Com. Rank. & Pfd. Rating	Inst. Hold Cos	Inst. Hold Shs. (000)	Principal Business	Price Range 1971-93 High	1971-93 Low	1994 High	1994 Low	1995 High	1995 Low	Dec. Sales in 100s	December, 1995 Last Sale Or Bid High	Low	Last	%Div Yield	P-E Ratio	Total Return % Annualized 12 Mo	36 Mo	60 Mo
#1•[1]	DBD	✔Diebold, Inc	NY,B,Ch,P	A–	243	18561	Auto teller machines/sec sys	41⅛	1 13/16	46¾	33⅞	62⅛	33	19243	62⅛	52	55⅜	1.7	23	35.9	30.7	33.3
✧2•[2]	DGII	✔Digi International	NNM	B+	99	8321	Data commun hardwr/softwr	26¼	2⅞	22½	11¼	30¼	17⅛	23500	24	17⅛	19	...	14	–3.2	–7.5	22.4
3	DGC	✔Digicon Inc	AS	NR	32	7407	Serves oil indy:seismic data	18¾	6	9⅜	2¾	8¾	3⅛	6820	8¾	5⅞	8	...	31	125	–15.2	...
4	WS	Wrrt (pur 1 com at $18)[51]	AS	....	9	99		7½	⅜	2¼	3/16	9/16	1/16	146	5/16	1/16	1/32B	...	..	...	...	...
5	DCT	✔Digital Comm Tech	AS	NR	6	261	Video tape duplicating svcs	9¼	1	8¾	2	2¾	1	3336	1⅜	1 1/16	1 3/16	...	d	–42.4	–5.5	–20.6
¶6•[3]	DEC	✔Digital Equipment	NY,B,C,Ch,P,Ph	C	502	99259	Mfr data processing eq	199½	7⅝	38⅛	18¼	65	31⅛	250732	65	55⅝	64⅛	...	35	88.6	24.2	2.9
7	DLNK	✔Digital Link	NNM	NR	55	4833	Mfr digital access products	....	....	29½	7¾	34	13¾	15705	18	14	14⅛	...	22	–47.7	...	...
✧8•[4]	DMIC	✔Digital Microwave	NNM	C	49	7961	Microwave radio/fiber optics	34½	4½	29⅜	8½	20¾	9½	29966	12⅞	9½	10	...	d	–50.6	26.0	–10.8
9	DGT	✔Digitran Systems[53]	AS	C	15	1105	Dvlp simulator/enginr'g softwr	11½	2½	....	....	....	....	....	....	....	....	...	..	...	...	...
10	Pr	8%'A'cm Cv[54]Pfd([53])	AS	NR	1	13		22¼	7	....	....	....	....	....	....	....	....	...	..	...	...	...
¶11•[5]	DDS	✔Dillard Dept Str'A'	NY,Ch	A+	435	85579	Dept stores in southwest US	52⅞	5/16	37⅝	25½	33⅞	24	67265	29⅞	27¼	28½	0.4	12	10.1	–16.8	–0.1
12	DMC	✔DIMAC Corp[55]	AS	NR	38	3251	Direct marketing services	....	....	13⅞	10	27½	11¾	3157	27⅜	26⅝	27	...	28	114	...	...
13	DMK	✔Dimark Inc	AS,Ph	B+	34	2864	Hldg co:mail mktg print svc	14¾	⅝	15⅞	9¼	16	9⅞	2531	14¾	13⅜	14½	...	24	30.7	74.2	65.7
14•[6]	DME	✔Dime Bancorp	NY,Ch,Ph	NR	157	48598	Savings bank, New York	27	1½	10¾	7⅜	13⅜	7⅜	55591	11⅝	10¾	11⅝	...	15	50.0	26.4	40.5
✧15	DMN	✔DiMon Inc	NY	NR	110	14432	Tobacco dealer/cut flowers	....	....	....	....	18¾	13¾	8439	18¾	16¾	17⅝	3.1	d	...	...	...
16	DIO	✔Diodes, Inc	AS,Ch	B–	10	254	Semiconductor devices	8¼	¼	10	4⅜	19⅝	4⅞	6390	13¾	10½	10½	...	14	110	86.3	56.3
✧17	DNEX	✔Dionex Corp	NNM	B+	122	5248	Mfr ion chromatography sys	44½	9½	39	31¼	58½	37	4915	58½	56	56¾	...	21	53.4	12.4	22.9
18	DGI	Disc Graphics	AS,Ph	NR	..	...	Mfr/printer specialty packag'g	....	....	....	....	4⅞	2⅞	1709	3⅝	2⅞	3¼	...	20	...	...	...
19	DAP	✔Discount Auto Parts	NY	NR	68	5760	Auto parts stores, Florida	31⅛	18	27⅝	13⅞	33⅞	17¾	9078	31¼	24¾	31⅛	...	23	62.7	6.0	...
20•[7]	ZONE	✔Discovery Zone	NNM	NR	43	3044	Indoor child recreat'n ctrs	34¼	11	24¼	11⅜	12⅜	2½	48854	4⅛	2⅞	3⅛	...	5	–74.2	...	...
21	DSLGF	✔Discreet Logic	NNM	NR	64	9562	Film/video visual effects	....	....	....	....	32¼	14⅛	24381	32	21½	25	...	..	...	...	...
¶22•[3]	DIS	✔Disney (Walt) Co	NY,B,C,Ch,P,Ph	A	1185	254606	Amusement parks: films, TV	47⅞	15/16	48⅝	37¾	64¼	45	245437	63	58⅝	58⅞	0.6	23	29.8	10.8	19.0
✧23	DXYN	✔Dixie Yarns	NNM	B–	51	5083	Mfrs yarn & thread products	33¾	1⅛	11¼	6¾	7⅜	3⅜	10722	4⅜	3¾	3⅞	...	d	–44.6	–32.3	–16.6
24	DXT	✔Dixon Ticonderoga	AS,Ch,Ph	B–	11	279	Writ'g/art prod:indust'l prod	18⅝	⅛	10⅜	6⅛	11⅛	5½	2117	7⅞	5½	7¾	...	24	–15.1	1.1	15.6
25	DIYH	✔D.I.Y. Home Warehouse	NNM	NR	17	595	Oper home improvement ctrs	16½	9¾	16½	5¼	8½	3½	5786	4¾	3½	3½	...	7	–44.0	...	...
26	DLBI	✔DLB Oil & Gas	NNM,Ch	NR	13	1628	Oil & gas explor & dev	....	....	....	....	10½	7⅞	5710	9⅝	8¾	9⅝	...	d	...	...	...
27	TUNE	✔DMX Inc	NNM	C	34	8791	Cable audio program'g svcs	9⅛	1⅝	4¾	1½	4	2	40295	3	2⅛	2 7/16	...	d	–2.5	–23.2	–1.0
28	DNAP	✔DNA Plant Technology	NNM	C	29	2417	Agricultural biotechnology	21¼	2½	5⅝	2⅜	3½	⅝	71471	1	⅝	13/16	...	d	–69.8	–45.9	–24.2
29	DNXX	✔DNX Corp	NNM	NR	13	1425	R&D transgenic animals/prd	15½	3	6½	3	5¼	2¾	4929	3⅝	3⅜	3⅝	...	d	–19.4	–18.7	...
30•[8]	DFS	Dofasco, Inc	To,Mo	B–	71	10414	Canadian steel producer	32⅝	6⅝	26⅜	17⅛	20⅜	16	34142	19	16¾	17¼	4.6	8	–4.9	21.9	...
31	DPKG	✔Dolco Packaging	NNM	NR	12	197	Mfr plastic foam packaging	15⅜	1 5/16	16	12⅜	27	11¾	303	21	18½	19¼B	...	7	48.1	54.1	...
#32•[4]	DOL	✔Dole Food Co	NY,B,Ch,P	B	209	36852	Processed/fresh foods: R.E.	48	5½	35½	22½	38⅝	23	23421	38⅝	32	35	1.1	17	...	...	...
#33•[5]	DG	✔Dollar General	NY,Ph	↑A	258	45929	Self-service discount stores	22¼	⅛	24⅜	15⅝	34	19½	134544	27¾	19½	20¾	1.0	16	–11.3	24.0	56.5
34	DLTR	✔Dollar Tree Stores	NNM	NR	40	3656	Operates discount stores	....	....	....	....	36¼	15	15362	31¼	22	24¾	...	26	...	...	...
35	DOMZ	Dominguez Services	NNM	NR	7	31	Water supply svcs-Calif	22¼	9⅜	21½	14¾	18¾	16	192	18¾	17	18½B	6.3	10	18.1	11.4	12.0
¶36•[9]	D	✔Dominion Resources	NY,B,C,Ch,P,Ph	A–	438	68867	Hldg co:elec service in Va	49½	6⅞	45⅜	34⅞	41⅝	34⅞	46433	41⅝	39⅝	41¼	6.3	14	22.2	7.6	12.7
37	DOM	✔Dominion Res Black Warrior Tr [10]	NY,Ch	NR	11	226	Invest trust/royalty interest	....	....	20⅛	16⅞	20⅛	17¼	5759	18⅞	17½	17⅝	15.1	..	18.0	...	...
38	DTX	Dominion Textile	Mo,To	B–	24	9558	Lgst Canadian textile mfr	25½	5	9¾	5¾	10¼	6⅛	6851	7⅜	6⅛	6¾	3.0	13	–13.6	–6.2	...
39•[11]	DTC	Domtar, Inc	NY,To,B,Ch,Mo,Vc	C	68	47659	Pulp/paper,constrn mtls:chem	18¾	2 5/16	7⅛	4¾	10⅞	6¾	7138	8⅛	6⅞	7⅝	...	..	10.9	25.3	–0.6
#40	DCI	✔Donaldson Co	NY,B,Ch	A+	158	14701	Engine air cleaners, mufflers	22⅛	11/16	26¼	20	28	22½	8100	25⅜	24⅛	25⅛	1.1	17	7.5	12.5	19.5
41	DLJ	Donaldson,Lufkin&Jenrette	NY,Ch,Ph	NR	1	84	Investment/merchant bank svcs	....	....	....	....	33½	27	15314	33½	29	31¼	1.6	12	...	...	...
¶42•[6]	DNY	✔Donnelley(RR)& Sons	NY,B,Ch,P,Ph	A–	531	112058	Large commercial printer	33¾	2	32½	26⅞	41¼	28⅞	52812	41	36¾	39⅜	1.8	20	35.9	8.4	17.0
43	DON	✔Donnelly Corp Cl'A'	AS,Ch	B	43	2312	Mfrs automotive glass prod	22¼	6¼	20¼	13¼	18	13¾	1115	15⅝	14	14¾	2.7	12	–2.0	–0.6	16.8
44	DNKY	✔Donnkenny Inc	NNM	NR	69	10513	Mfr womens sportswear/sleepwr	9¾	5¾	13⅜	5⅛	18¼	6¾	56456	18¼	16⅜	18⅛	...	21	143	...	...
45	DSYT	✔Dorsey Trailers	NNM	NR	21	1308	Mfr truck trailers	....	....	18⅜	12⅛	15½	5⅛	4719	7¼	5⅛	5¼	...	3	–64.4	...	...
46	TREE	✔Doubletree Corp	NNM	NR	84	9810	Hotel mgmt/franchisor	....	....	22¼	13	26⅜	16¼	5505	26⅜	20½	26¼	...	32	45.8	...	...
47	DOVTV	✔DOVatron Intl	NNM	NR	101	5779	Contract electronics mfr	30¼	14¾	32¼	18	35½	17½	14698	34¾	29½	33¾	...	33	28.6	...	...
48	DOVE	✔Dove Audio	NSC	NR	3	45	Produce audio books/films	....	....	11	8½	13¼	6⅝	16527	13¼	9½	12⅞	...	40	...	...	...
¶49•[6]	DOV	✔Dover Corp	NY,B,Ch,P,Ph	A	488	74729	Elevators:petrol eq:ind'l pr	31	¾	33½	24⅞	41¾	25⅞	63658	38⅞	35⅛	36⅞	1.6	15	44.2	18.7	15.5
¶50•[7]	DOW	✔Dow Chemical	NY,To,B,C,Ch,P,Ph	B	1027	154380	Chem/metals/plastics/pkg	75¾	8	79¼	56½	78	61⅜	156991	72⅞	68⅞	70¼	4.3	10	9.0	12.1	13.5
¶51•[12]	DJ	✔Dow Jones & Co	NY,B,Ch,P,Ph	A	311	36923	Business pubs & fin'l news	56¼	2 7/16	41⅞	28⅛	40⅛	30⅝	22576	40⅛	37	39⅞	2.3	20	30.9	16.4	14.4
✧52	DSL	✔Downey Financial	NY,B,Ch,P	B–	53	5110	Savings & loan,California	26⅜	7/16	20⅝	13⅜	24⅜	14⅛	5403	24⅜	21½	21¾	2.1	20	66.8	19.3	13.6

Uniform Footnote Explanations-See Page 4. Other: [1]P,Ph:Cycle 2. [2]ASE,Ph:Cycle 1. [3]ASE,CBOE:Cycle 1. [4]P:Cycle 3. [5]P:Cycle 2. [6]ASE:Cycle 3. [7]CBOE:Cycle 3. [8]Mo:Cycle 3. [9]Ph:Cycle 1. [10]Ph [11]Mo:Cycle 2. [12]Ph:Cycle 3. [51]Min $18 max $22.50. [52]□$8.25,'91. [53]ASE trad'g halted 6-7-93. [54]Fr 12-31-93. [55]Heritage Media plan acq, $28. [56]11 Mo July'92. [57]Stk dstr of Castle & Cooke. [58]Fiscal Jan'92 & prior. [59]Subsid Pfd. [60]Incl $0.172949 return of cap. [61]®$0.46,'94. [62]Incl 5.2M restricted shrs.

Splits ◆ Index	Cash Divs. Ea.Yr. Since	Dividends: Latest Payment Period $	Date	Ex. Div.	Total $ So Far 1995	Ind. Rate	Paid 1994	Financial Position Mil-$ Cash& Equiv.	Curr. Assets	Curr. Liab.	Balance Sheet Date	Capitalization Lg Trm Debt Mil-$	Shs. 000 Pfd.	Com.	Earnings $ Per Shr. Years End	1991	1992	1993	1994	1995	Last 12 Mos.	Interim Earnings Period	$ per Shr. 1994	1995	Index
1◆	1954	Q0.24	12-8-95	11-15	0.96	0.96	0.88	72.0	367	175	9-30-95	....	...	30528	Dc	1.20	□1.37	1.60	2.09	E2.40	2.38	9 Mo Sep	1.50	1.79	1
2◆	....	None Since Public			...	Nil	....	41.3	93.3	14.5	6-30-95	....	...	13494	Sp	0.65	0.82	Δ1.02	1.15	P1.38	1.38				2
3◆	....	None Since Public			...	Nil	....	3.49	54.6	44.0	10-31-95	26.7	...	11135	Jl	Δd0.06	0.75	d0.15	d1.47	0.25	0.26	3 Mo Oct	0.06	0.07	3
4	....	....			...	Nil	....	Wrrts expire 7-1-96				....	...	454	Jl	...	...	...	....	....	....				4
5◆	....	None Paid			...	Nil	....	2.78	10.8	9.33	9-30-95	0.48	...	5961	Je	0.06	0.07	0.14	□0.13	d0.05	d0.05	3 Mo Sep	0.04	0.04	5
6	....	None Paid			...	Nil	....	1501	7102	3921	9-30-95	1013	4000	150811	Je	■[52]d5.08	■d18.50	d1.93	□d15.43	Δ0.15	1.85	3 Mo Sep	Δd1.44	0.26	6
7	....	None Since Public			...	Nil	....	22.2	37.9	8.38	9-30-95	....	...	8868	Dc	0.23	0.28	0.31	0.48	....	0.63	9 Mo Sep	0.30	0.45	7
8	....	None Since Public			...	Nil	....	3.17	87.4	41.6	9-30-95	4.73	...	15763	Mr	d1.64	d0.55	d1.81	0.14	....	d0.13	6 Mo Sep	0.31	0.04	8
9	....	None Since Public			...	Nil	....	0.33	3.25	2.72	10-31-95	0.33	458	±9408	Ap	±0.12	±0.19	±d0.10	±d0.14	±d0.21	d0.20	6 Mo Oct	d0.06	d0.05	9
10	1993	0.28	3-15-93	3-1	...	Nil	....	Cv into 2 com, $3.50				....	460	...	Ap	...	...	...	....	....	....				10
11◆	1969	Q0.03	2-1-96	12-27	0.12	0.12	0.09	59.4	2990	1253	10-28-95	1172	4	±113046	Ja	±1.84	±2.11	±2.14	±2.23	E2.30	2.27	12 Mo Oct	2.16	2.27	11
12	....	None Since Public			...	Nil	....	....	36.9	31.7	9-30-95	44.6	...	6491	Dc	...	...	p0.29	□0.64	....	0.98	9 Mo Sep	□0.43	□0.77	12
13◆	....	None Since Public			...	Nil	....	8.22	21.0	8.10	8-31-95	1.25	...	9162	Fb	0.18	0.39	0.38	0.52	....	0.61	9 Mo Nov	0.28	0.37	13
14	....	0.15	9-11-90	8-8	...	Nil	....	Book Value $9.76			9-30-95	4465	...	99662	Dc	d10.27	□0.44	p1.00	□p1.12	E0.80	0.70	9 Mo Sep	□0.97	0.55	14
15	1995	Q0.135	12-15-95	12-1	0.40½	0.54	....	60.7	1043	767	9-30-95	342	...	38230	Je	...	p1.57	p1.81	pd0.17	d0.79	d0.59	3 Mo Sep	d0.04	0.16	15
16	....	None Paid			...	Nil	....	0.47	23.7	11.2	9-30-95	0.26	170	4958	Dc	*0.05	*0.07	0.34	0.46	....	0.78	9 Mo Sep	0.33	0.65	16
17◆	....	None Since Public			...	Nil	....	45.8	87.4	24.5	9-30-95	0.08	...	6701	Je	1.69	1.78	2.02	2.21	2.69	2.77	3 Mo Sep	0.55	0.63	17
18	....	None Since Public			...	Nil	....	0.57	9.89	5.06	p6-30-95	3.30	...	5147	Dc	...	...	...	p0.11	....	0.16	9 Mo Sep	p0.05	p0.10	18
19	....	None Since Public			...	Nil	....	3.35	103	51.1	8-29-95	p39.7	...	★16413	My	0.48	p0.66	p0.91	1.03	1.48	1.37	6 Mo Nov	0.81	0.70	19
20◆	....	None Since Public			...	Nil	....	14.2	36.1	182	9-30-95	139	...	57490	Dc	pd0.04	pd0.16	0.08	□d0.41	E0.65	d2.31	9 Mo Sep	□d0.18	d2.08	20
21◆	....	None Since Public			...	Nil	....	35.7	62.3	26.3	p7-31-95	0.12	...	★26748	Jl	...	‡[56]0.01	...	0.02	0.31	0.05	3 Mo Oct	0.06	d0.20	21
22◆	1957	Q0.09	2-16-96	12-29	0.34½	0.36	0.28¾	Equity per shr $12.68			9-30-95	2984	...	524844	Sp	1.19	1.52	□1.23	2.04	2.60	2.60				22
23	1954	0.05	12-9-94	11-21	...	Nil	0.20	1.99	163	59.5	9-30-95	201	...	±11194	Dc	□±d2.88	±0.65	±0.41	±d0.24	....	d0.36	9 Mo Sep	±d0.28	±d0.40	23
24	....	0.02½	12-1-89	11-13	...	Nil	....	1.51	55.0	36.1	9-30-95	14.5	...	3193	Sp	d0.22	0.11	Δ0.11	1.06	0.33	0.33				24
25	....	None Since Public			...	Nil	....	0.72	43.4	23.9	9-30-95	25.1	...	7625	Dc	...	p0.35	p0.51	0.56	....	0.51	9 Mo Sep	0.45	0.40	25
26	....	None Since Public			...	Nil	....	18.3	23.4	4.30	9-30-95	....	...	13000	Dc	0.03	0.19	0.31	0.59	....	d0.44	9 Mo Sep	0.49	d0.54	26
27	....	None Paid			...	Nil	....	5.42	8.76	2.87	6-30-95	1.63	...	39581	Sp	d0.26	d0.90	d0.52	d0.48	....	d0.50	9 Mo Jun	d0.34	d0.36	27
28	....	None Since Public			...	Nil	....	3.71	8.05	4.19	9-30-95	0.78	1380	40695	Dc	d0.75	d0.99	d1.67	d1.02	....	d0.52	9 Mo Sep	d0.87	d0.37	28
29	....	None Since Public			...	Nil	....	4.40	12.3	11.2	12-31-94	8.50	...	8456	Dc	■d1.07	d0.69	d2.23	d0.76	....	d0.38	9 Mo Sep	□d0.57	□d0.19	29
30	1994	gQ0.20	1-1-96	12-12	g0.70	0.80	g0.20	532	1454	343	j12-31-94	781	10131	84891	Dc	d0.73	d2.96	1.41	2.33	....	j2.12	9 Mo Sep	1.66	1.45	30
31◆	....	None Paid			...	Nil	....	0.01	14.5	6.44	9-30-95	2.84	1825	1466	Dc	Δd2.22	*0.35	2.09	2.70	....	2.97	9 Mo Sep	1.83	2.10	31
32◆	1991	h[57]....	12-28-95	12-29	h[57]0.40	0.40	0.40	31.2	1060	666	10-07-95	1098	...	59833	Dc	2.24	□1.09	1.30	1.14	E2.10	d0.02	9 Mo Sep	1.12	d0.04	32
33◆	1975	Q0.05	12-15-95	11-24	0.19	0.20	0.152	4.15	610	379	10-31-95	3.42	1716	57626	Ja	0.34	0.54	0.72	1.07	E1.28	1.18	9 Mo Oct	0.59	0.70	33
34	....	None Since Public			...	Nil	....	3.24	72.5	57.0	9-30-95	14.1	...	16605	Dc	p[58]0.13	p0.38	p0.42	□0.74	....	0.94	9 Mo Sep	0.15	0.35	34
35	1963	Q0.29	12-15-95	11-22	1.16	1.16	1.10	Equity per shr $20.86			9-30-95	7.44	4	1004	Dc	1.32	1.53	1.99	1.92	....	1.92	12 Mo Sep	2.00	1.92	35
36◆	1925	Q0.64½	12-20-95	11-29	2.58	2.58	2.55	153	915	1080	6-30-95	4780	[59]5940	173511	Dc	2.94	Δ2.66	3.12	2.81	E3.00	2.44	9 Mo Sep	2.59	2.22	36
37	1994	0.66	12-8-95	11-27	2.656	2.66	[60]0.907	Equity per shr $15.90			9-30-95	....	...	7850	Dc	...	...	...	n/a	....	....	9 Mo Sep	n/a	2.01	37
38	....	gQ0.05	1-12-96	12-11	g0.20	0.20	....	56.1	551	224	j6-30-95	445	2728	41473	Je	d4.07	d2.31	0.68	0.70	0.70	j0.52	3 Mo Sep	0.13	d0.05	38
39◆	....	2½%Stk	12-15-91	11-19	...	Nil	....	87.0	888	353	j12-31-94	1168	874	127448	Dc	d1.69	d1.36	d0.90	[61]0.56	....	j2.23	9 Mo Sep	0.30	1.97	39
40◆	1956	Q0.07	12-13-95	12-1	0.28	0.28	0.28	28.2	249	126	10-31-95	13.6	...	25815	Jl	0.84	0.92	1.01	Δ1.17	1.45	1.49	3 Mo Oct	0.35	0.39	40
41	....	Plan qtly div			...	0.50	....	Equity per shr $18.77			6-30-95	★868	2250	[62]★58479	Dc	...	...	...	1.98	....	2.70	9 Mo Sep	1.35	2.07	41
42◆	1911	Q0.18	12-1-95	11-8	0.68	0.72	0.60	19.2	1867	1066	9-30-95	1629	...	153628	Dc	1.32	1.51	□1.16	1.75	E2.00	1.90	9 Mo Sep	1.18	1.33	42
43◆	1988	Q0.10	1-1-96	12-13	0.34	0.40	0.32	5.76	113	60.5	9-30-95	97.6	53	±7798	Je	0.59	1.00	*0.94	*±0.87	±1.42	1.20	3 Mo Sep	±d0.01	±d0.23	43
44◆	....	None Since Public			...	Nil	....	0.85	129	32.3	9-02-95	69.8	...	13952	Nv	0.37	0.61	□0.74	□0.75	....	0.85	9 Mo Aug	□0.60	0.70	44
45	....	None Since Public			...	Nil	....	2.40	36.2	24.4	9-30-95	7.88	...	4989	Dc	...	...	p0.52	p1.53	....	1.58	9 Mo Sep	p1.01	p1.06	45
46	....	None Since Public			...	Nil	....	12.0	38.5	18.7	9-30-95	....	...	19371	Dc	...	...	p0.52	0.73	....	0.82	9 Mo Sep	0.55	0.64	46
47	....	None Since Public			...	Nil	....	12.4	103	67.9	9-30-95	34.4	...	8097	Dc	...	p0.81	1.07	0.46	....	1.01	9 Mo Sep	0.90	1.45	47
48	....	None Since Public			...	Nil	....	2.45	10.7	4.12	6-30-95	0.85	214	3934	Dc	d0.72	0.38	0.03	0.04	....	0.32	9 Mo Sep	d0.13	0.15	48
49◆	1947	Q0.15	12-15-95	11-24	0.56	0.60	0.49	160	1314	1068	9-30-95	★502	...	113578	Dc	1.08	Δ1.12	1.39	1.77	E2.45	2.34	9 Mo Sep	1.28	1.85	49
50	1911	Q0.75	1-30-96	12-27	2.80	3.00	2.60	4638	12149	6078	9-30-95	5026	1549	261784	Dc	3.46	□0.99	2.33	3.37	E7.30	6.89	9 Mo Sep	2.57	6.09	50
51	1906	Q0.23	12-1-95	10-30	0.92	0.92	0.84	4.76	326	538	9-30-95	279	...	±97064	Dc	0.71	□1.17	1.48	□1.83	E2.00	1.94	9 Mo Sep	□1.23	1.34	51
52◆	1986	5%Stk	12-22-95	12-7	s0.457	0.46	0.457	Book Value $22.02			9-30-95	213	...	16973	Dc	1.47	2.47	Δ1.68	1.39	....	1.08	9 Mo Sep	1.06	0.75	52

◆**Stock Splits & Divs By Line Reference Index** [1]3-for-2,'93,'94. [2]2-for-1,'91:3-for-2,'92. [3]1-for-3 REVERSE,'95. [5]1-for-8 REVERSE,'92. [11]3-for-1,'92. [13]6-for-5,'91:10%,'92,'93:2-for-1,'93:5-for-4,'95. [17]To split 2-for-1,ex Jan 2. [20]2-for-1,'93. [21]2-for-1,'95. [22]4-for-1,'92. [31]3-for-2,'94. [32]No adj for stk dstr of Castle & Cooke,'95. [33]10%,'91:5-for-4,'92,'93(twice),'94,'95. [36]3-for-2,'92. [39]Adj for 2.5%,'91. [40]3-for-2,'92:2-for-1,'94. [42]2-for-1,'92. [43]5-for-4,'92. [44]2-for-1,'95. [49]2-for-1,'95. [52]Adj for 5%,'95.

¶ S&P 500
# MidCap 400
✣ SmallCap 600
• Options

Index	Ticker	Name of Issue (Call Price of Pfd. Stocks)	Market	Com. Rank. & Pfd. Rating	Inst. Hold Cos	Inst. Hold Shs. (000)	Principal Business	Price Range 1971-93 High	1971-93 Low	1994 High	1994 Low	1995 High	1995 Low	Dec. Sales in 100s	December, 1995 Last Sale Or Bid High	Low	Last	%Div Yield	P-E Ratio	Total Return % Annualized 12 Mo	36 Mo	60 Mo
1	DPL	✓DPL Inc	NY,B,C,Ch,Ph	B+	246	34670	Hldg co:Dayton Pwr & Lt	21⅞	4¾	21⅝	18⅜	25⅝	20	16680	25⅝	24	24¾	5.0	16	28.4	14.5	21.6
2	DQE	✓DQE	NY,B,C,Ch,P,Ph	B+	225	27855	Hldg: Duquesne Light	24⅝	7⅛	23	18⅜	30¾	19⅝	38735	30¾	28⅝	30¾	4.2	14	65.0	19.4	19.3
✣3	DRV	✓Dravo Corp	NY,B,Ch,Ph	B–	75	9146	Domestic natural resources	33⅛	5¾	13⅜	9½	14¾	10	4116	12¼	11½	12	...	d	11.6	11.6	3.2
4	DRC	✓DRCA Medical Corp	AS,Ch	NR	7	230	Out-patient diagnostic ctrs	12	¼	3¾	2¼	6⅛	2¼	2171	3½	2¾	3⅜	...	23	35.0	–10.4	–9.3
✣5•[1]	DBRN	✓Dress Barn	NNM	B+	88	9848	Women's apparel stores	23½	1¼	14	8¼	11	8¼	27375	9⅞	9	9⅞	...	12	–6.0	–19.1	6.0
¶6•[2]	DI	✓Dresser Industries	NY,B,C,Ch,P,Ph	B	507	135078	Energy & nat'l resources mkt	28½	3⅛	24⅞	18½	25⅛	18½	186971	24¾	22¾	24⅜	2.8	21	31.3	...	...
7	DW	✓Drew Industries	AS	B–	17	1026	Mfr specialty building prod	14	¾	11¼	8¼	16⅜	8⅜	699	15⅜	13¾	14	...	10	...	...	...
8	DRXR	✓Drexler Technology	NNM	C	19	1572	Optical data products	26⅜	5/16	8¼	4¼	16	4⅞	18607	16	13⅛	15¼	...	d	209	57.9	29.9
#9•[3]	DRYR	✓Dreyer's Gr Ice Cr	NNM	B	91	4906	Ice cream mfr & dstr	36¾	3	29⅛	21¼	40	24¼	8724	34	29⅞	33¼	0.7	..	36.1	12.9	10.6
10	DRFNY	✓Driefontein Consol ADR[55]	NSC	NR	53	11323	Gold mining, South Africa	20½	1⅝	17	9⅜	15½	10⅜	18273	12¾	10⅜	12⅜	3.3	11	–15.2	27.9	4.0
11	DRH	✓Driver-Harris	AS	C	6	107	Elec & heat resisting alloys	13⅝	1 15/16	7¼	5	6½	4¾	75	6	5¾	5⅞	...	12	20.5	4.7	–6.3
12	DEMP	✓Drug Emporium	NNM	C	27	3677	Discount drug store chain	16⅜	3⅝	6⅝	4	5⅝	3½	9608	4¼	3½	4⅛	...	17	–23.3	–9.8	–10.7
¶13•[4]	DIGI	✓DSC Communications	NNM	B	658	92841	Digital tel switch'g sys	36⅝	5/16	37⅞	17⅞	64	30⅛	715531	43¼	30⅛	36⅞	...	21	0.7	49.3	61.6
14	DSGIF	DSG International Ltd	NNM	NR	..	...	Mfr disposable diapers	28¼	13½	29¾	16⅛	19½	8½	7686	12⅞	11⅛	12½	2.0	18	–26.5	–14.9	...
15•[5]	DSPC	✓DSP Communications	NNM	NR	50	4657	Dvlp chip sets for telecomm	...	...	...	...	49	10	27674	49	34	43⅝	...	67	...	...	...
16•[6]	DSPG	✓DSP Group	NNM	NR	56	3059	Dvlp digital speech softwr prd	...	...	27¼	12¼	26	7¾	33481	14½	10¾	11½	...	13	–41.0	...	...
17	DSPT	✓DSP Technology	NNM	B	10	370	Mfr measurm't/ctrl instr	7¼	½	6⅜	2¾	8⅛	4⅜	2966	7½	6	7	...	14	33.3	5.3	51.6
18	DST	✓DST Systems	NY,Ch	NR	..	...	Info processing/softwr svcs	...	...	...	...	31¾	21	41276	31¾	26	28½	...	34	...	...	...
19	DUAL	✓Dual Drilling	NNM	NR	47	7093	Domestic/intl offshore drill'g	17½	8⅞	13⅝	8¼	11⅝	7	20022	11⅝	9⅞	11⅜	...	d	30.0	...	...
20	DUCK	✓Duckwall-Alco Stores	NNM	NR	24	2123	Retail-genl merchandise strs	...	...	9½	9	11⅞	8¾	3994	10¼	9½	10¼	...	7	13.9	...	...
21	DCO	✓Ducommun Inc	AS,B	B–	17	1137	Mfg svcs to aerospace indus	47½	⅞	5⅜	2¾	10½	4⅝	1519	10¼	9⅜	9⅞	...	13	97.5	32.4	21.4
22	DCR	✓Duff & Phelps Credit Rating	NY	NR	48	3140	Financial credit rating svcs	...	...	12½	7⅝	16	8½	1720	15½	14¼	14⅜	0.8	13	48.7	...	...
¶23•[2]	DUK	✓Duke Power	NY,B,C,Ch,P,Ph	A–	589	82962	Electric utility-Carolinas	44⅞	5	43	32⅞	47⅞	37⅜	41818	47⅞	44⅞	47⅜	4.3	15	29.9	14.4	14.6
24	DRE	✓Duke Realty Inv	NY,Ch,Ph	NR	137	14256	Real estate inv trust	26¾	10	28¼	20¼	31¾	25	7622	31⅜	27⅝	31⅜	6.2	21	26.1	31.9	...
¶25•[7]	DNB	✓Dun & Bradstreet	NY,B,Ch,P,Ph	A	776	125027	Bus info:publish:mkt:TV	71¾	3⅜	64	51⅞	65½	48½	54510	65½	61¼	64¾	4.1	17	23.0	8.3	13.8
26	DPX	✓Duplex Products	AS	C	42	5232	Continuous business forms	23⅝	15/16	11¾	8	9¼	6¾	2573	8⅛	7⅜	8⅛	...	d	–4.4	–6.3	–3.9
27	DUP.A	duPont of Canada Cl'A'	To,Mo	B+	11	2367	Owned 75% by du Pont (E.I.)	17	1	20⅛	14¾	24½	16½	2081	24½	23	24	1.8	12	30.6	25.2	...
¶28•[1]	DD	✓duPont(El)deNemours	NY,B,C,Ch,P,Ph	B+	1238	327114	Large chemical co:oil & gas	54⅞	9⅜	62⅜	48¼	73	52⅝	217622	70¼	66⅛	69⅞	3.0	12	30.4	17.1	17.7
29•[8]	DUR	✓Duracell Intl	NY,Ch,Ph	NR	358	66893	Mfr alkaline batteries	38⅛	15	47¼	36	55	36¾	66537	54⅞	47¾	51¾	2.0	27	24.6	17.9	...
30	DUCR	✓Duracraft Corp	NNM	NR	73	4884	Mfr household products	25¼	14	46¾	23½	46¼	20	11755	26¼	21¼	25⅛	...	16	–22.7	...	...
31	DRKN	✓Durakon Industries	NNM	B–	46	3328	Mfr plastic truckbed liners	22¾	2	19¾	15¾	17¾	11¼	1747	14	12¼	12½	...	9	–27.5	–0.7	40.9
#32	DURI	✓Duriron Co	NNM	B+	145	14192	Corrosion resist process eq	19⅜	13/16	20	14⅜	30¼	17	21055	28¾	22½	23⅜	2.0	20	36.3	15.6	16.5
33	DUSA	✓DUSA Pharmaceuticals	NNM	NR	4	146	Dvlp stge:pharmaceutical R&D	15¼	3¼	5⅝	3¼	7⅝	2¾	27039	7⅝	5½	6⅝	...	d	35.9	2.0	...
#34•[9]	DFI	✓Duty Free Intl	NY,Ph	B+	81	10259	Oper'duty-free'retail strs	56¼	5⅛	20	8¾	16¼	7	11092	16¼	13⅜	16	1.3	29	48.3	–4.8	4.9
35	DVI	✓DVI Inc	NY,Ch,Ph	B	39	4536	Finance/lease medical equip	14¼	⅞	11½	8	14¾	10⅝	4182	14¾	13⅛	14	...	19	30.2	24.5	5.9
36	DYC	✓Dycam Inc	AS	NR	1	.2	Dvlp digtal cemeras & equip	...	...	6	1½	2⅝	½	853	⅞	9/16	9/16	...	d	–65.4	...	...
37	DY	✓Dycom Industries	NY,Ch,Ph	C	14	1791	Telecommun & electrical svcs	16¾	7/16	4⅛	2	8½	2½	3827	6	5⅛	5⅝	...	11	114	6.7	–7.4
38	DBG	✓Dyersburg Corp	NY	NR	33	4256	Mfr/mkt fleece fabrics	9⅞	5½	8¾	5⅛	6¼	4¼	13645	6¼	4½	5	0.8	11	–16.0	–9.5	...
39	BOOM	Dynamic Materials	NSC	B–	7	110	Explosion metal working	26¼	5/16	3⅝	1⅞	3	1⅝	3036	3	2½	2¾	...	11	15.8	5.0	5.9
40	DYA	✓Dynamics Corp Amer	NY,Ch	B–	35	1910	Appliances,metal fab,power	33¼	¼	21	13	26¾	19½	498	25⅞	23⅛	24½	0.8	14	23.5	23.7	22.4
41	DRCO	✓Dynamics Research	NNM,B	B	19	1167	Mfr encoders: computer svs	8⅜	1/16	4¾	2¾	9½	2¾	4619	9½	5¾	8½	...	33	209	41.3	26.0
42	DYMO	✓Dynamotion/ATI[60]	NSC	NR	4	9	Mfr spcl prod for electr ind	25	3¼	7	3	4½	1	3578	3	1	1	...	d	–66.7	–45.0	...
✣43•[10]	DYTC	✓Dynatech Corp	NNM	B	122	11008	Communic&med'l pr,sci instr	21¾	3/16	16¾	7⅞	22¾	13½	24084	17¾	14½	17	...	23	3.3	13.8	11.5
44	EFMC	✓E for M Corp[61]	NNM	NR	15	1955	Medical equipment & supplies	12¾	3¾	8¼	3⅜	12⅛	4¼	113	12⅛	11¾	11¾B	...	30	154	4.7	...
45	EZM.A	✓E-Z EM Inc'A'	AS	B–	17	767	Mfr diagnostic imag'g prod	17¼	3⅞	5⅞	3⅞	13⅛	3¼	381	10⅛	9½	9¾	s...	81	143	19.8	32.4
46	EZM.B	Cl'B'(non-vtg)	AS	B–	17	770		8	4⅛	6⅛	3⅝	12⅝	3⅝	263	9⅝	9¼	9⅝	...	80	155	25.9	...
47	EZS	✓E-Z Serve Corp	AS	NR	10	16432	Retail/wholesale gasoline	5½	¾	3	1	1¾	15/16	865	1 7/16	1¼	1 5/16	...	15	23.5	–3.0	...
48	EGFC	✓Eagle Financial	NNM	NR	36	1800	Savings&loan,Connecticut	19⅝	6⅛	21½	16⅝	27¾	17½	819	27¾	25¼	26¼	3.5	11	62.0	36.0	42.0
✣49•[11]	EAGL	✓Eagle Hardware & Garden	NNM	NR	46	1986	Oper home improvement ctrs	40½	9⅜	18¼	7⅝	10	6	29211	8½	7¼	7½	...	d	–3.2	–33.7	...
50	EPII	Eagle Pacific Indus	NSC	NR	3	232	Mfr 'PVC'pipe/tubing	5¼	¼	3⅝	1⅝	3⅜	1⅜	2758	2	1⅜	1 7/16	...	d	...	...	...
51	EGPT	✓Eagle Point Software	NNM	NR	37	1148	Design/mkt computer software	...	...	...	...	24¼	13	5320	22¼	17¼	21½	...	..	...	...	...
52	EUSA	Eagle USA Airfreight	NNM	NR	..	...	Air freight forwarding svcs	...	...	...	...	26¼	16½	33335	26¼	18¼	26¼	...	26	...	...	...

Uniform Footnote Explanations-See Page 4. Other: [1]ASE,CBOE:Cycle 1. [2]Ph:Cycle 1. [3]P:Cycle 3. [4]ASE:Cycle 1. [5]CBOE:Cycle 2. [6]CBOE:Cycle 1. [7]ASE:Cycle 2. [8]ASE,NY,P:Cycle 3. [9]Ph:Cycle 2. [10]P:Cycle 1. [11]ASE,CBOE,Ph:Cycle 2. [51]Subsid pfd. [52]Excl subsid pfd. [53]Stk dstr of Leslie Bldg Prods,'94. [54]Fiscal Aug'92 & prior, 12 Mo Dec $0.87. [55]ADR equal 1 ord shr. [56]Approx. [57]Stk dstr of Arrow Electronics. [58]Incl $0.40 non-taxable,'94. [59]Fiscal Oct'93 & prior. [60]Formerly Cybernetics Products. [61]Marquette Electronics (80%)plan mgr. [62]®$2.38,'95. [63]®$0.24,'94.

Index (Splits ◆)	Cash Divs. Ea.Yr. Since	Dividends: Latest Payment Period $	Date	Ex. Div.	Total $ So Far 1995	Ind. Rate	Paid 1994	Financial Position Mil-$ Cash& Equiv.	Curr. Assets	Curr. Liab.	Balance Sheet Date	Capitalization Lg Trm Debt Mil-$	Shs. 000 Pfd.	Com.	Earnings $ Per Shr. Years End	1991	1992	1993	1994	1995	Last 12 Mos.	Interim Earnings Period	$ per Shr. 1994	1995	Index
1◆	1919	Q0.31	12-1-95	11-10	1.24	1.24	1.18	170	405	210	9-30-95	1089	[51]229	106952	Dc	1.15	1.34	1.42	1.54	E1.60	1.60	9 Mo Sep	1.27	1.33	1
2◆	1913	Q0.32	1-1-96	12-7	0.887	1.28	1.12	25.2	266	318	9-30-95	1363	[52]...	77543	Dc	1.67	1.78	Δ1.78	1.99	E2.20	2.18	12 Mo Sep	1.86	2.18	2
3	....	0.12½	5-22-87	4-28	...	Nil	....	0.18	40.2	33.6	9-30-95	59.1	225	14704	Dc	d1.95	Δ0.52	d0.18	□d0.28	....	d0.12	9 Mo Sep	□0.26	0.42	3
4	....	None Since Public			...	Nil	....	0.03	6.04	2.77	9-30-95	1.63	...	5270	Dc	0.01	0.10	d0.15	0.08	....	0.15	9 Mo Sep	0.06	0.13	4
5	....	None Since Public			...	Nil	....	70.3	173	64.2	10-28-95	3.50	...	22381	Jl	0.68	0.74	0.86	0.73	0.82	0.80	3 Mo Oct	0.29	0.27	5
6◆	1948	Q0.17	12-20-95	11-29	0.68	0.68	0.68	252	2109	1712	7-31-95	464	...	182519	Oc	*1.04	□0.26	p0.74	1.98	P□1.17	1.17				6
7	....	h[53]....	8-5-94	7-25	...	Nil	h[53]....	5.82	21.3	12.8	9-30-95	0.34	...	4956	Dc	0.37	[54]0.80	1.19	1.12	....	1.47	9 Mo Sep	0.86	1.21	7
8	....	None Since Public			...	Nil	....	2.28	3.25	1.03	9-30-95	....	...	8800	Mr	d0.52	d0.51	d0.37	d0.27	....	d0.18	6 Mo Sep	d0.19	d0.10	8
9	1990	Q0.06	1-9-96	12-27	0.24	0.24	0.24	2.46	144	55.8	9-30-95	137	1008	12900	Dc	1.05	Δ0.94	1.15	0.07	E0.02↓	0.27	9 Mo Sep	0.16	0.36	9
10	1974	[56]0.12½	2-23-96	12-27	0.513	0.41	0.54	573	868	769	j6-30-95	....	...	204000	Je	0.85	0.97	□0.80	1.06	1.15	1.15				10
11	....	0.05	7-7-71	6-9	...	Nil	....	0.05	12.1	9.02	9-30-95	2.56	...	1296	Dc	*d3.23	d3.50	d1.54	d0.75	....	0.48	9 Mo Sep	d0.83	0.40	11
12	....	0.04	7-1-92	5-26	...	Nil	....	0.57	155	82.5	8-26-95	54.9	...	13183	Fb	d0.36	d0.20	0.10	d0.41	....	0.25	9 Mo Nov	d0.56	0.10	12
13◆	....	None Since Public			...	Nil	....	534	1143	439	9-30-95	217	...	115354	Dc	d1.31	0.13	0.76	1.39	E1.75↓	1.66	9 Mo Sep	0.94	1.21	13
14	1993	0.25	7-12-94	6-8	...	0.25	0.25	32.9	53.9	13.4	12-31-92	2.48	...	8315	Dc	1.26	1.36	P1.60	P2.00	....	0.70	9 Mo Sep	1.58	0.28	14
15	....	None Since Public			...	Nil	....	40.4	47.5	7.50	9-30-95	....	...	8834	Dc	...	...	...	p0.35	....	0.65	9 Mo Sep	0.20	0.50	15
16	....	None Since Public			...	Nil	....	30.4	45.2	5.93	9-30-95	....	...	9439	Dc	...	...	d0.08	0.44	....	0.86	9 Mo Sep	0.27	0.69	16
17	....	None Paid			...	Nil	....	2.34	7.44	2.30	10-31-95	....	...	2154	Ja	0.40	0.43	0.12	0.40	....	0.51	9 Mo Oct	0.25	0.36	17
18	....	None Since Public			...	Nil	....	10.8	160	118	p6-30-95	33.7	...	★50000	Dc	...	...	...	p0.69	E0.83	....	6 Mo Jun	n/a	p0.39	18
19	....	None Since Public			...	Nil	....	45.4	73.6	19.5	9-30-95	139	...	15766	Dc	...	pd0.30	p□0.25	d1.09	....	d1.03	9 Mo Sep	d0.69	d0.63	19
20	....	None Since Public			...	Nil	....	0.82	87.7	35.2	10-29-95	14.0	...	3999	Ja	pd0.41	p0.66	p0.96	1.51	....	1.53	9 Mo Oct	p0.53	0.55	20
21◆	....	h[57]....	3-24-88	3-25	...	Nil	....	3.00	32.8	21.5	9-30-95	41.8	...	4473	Dc	Δ0.58	Δ0.66	Δ0.48	0.48	....	0.79	9 Mo Sep	0.37	0.68	21
22	1994	Q0.03	12-8-95	11-21	0.12	0.12	0.03	Equity per shr Neg			9-30-95	6.50	...	5590	Dc	...	...	p1.10	1.12	....	1.15	9 Mo Sep	0.84	0.87	22
23	1926	Q0.51	12-18-95	11-15	2.00	2.04	1.92	136	1098	653	9-30-95	3695	12610	204859	Dc	2.60	2.21	2.80	2.88	E3.10	3.26	12 Mo Sep	3.00	3.26	23
24◆	1988	Q0.49	11-30-95	11-14	1.92	1.96	[58]1.84	Equity per shr $22.22			9-30-95	412	...	24152	Dc	d0.80	p0.84	p1.19	1.53	....	1.47	9 Mo Sep	1.19	1.13	24
25	1934	Q0.66	12-8-95	11-16	2.63	2.64	2.56	515	2106	2117	9-30-95	....	...	169347	Dc	2.85	3.10	□2.42	3.70	E3.80	3.74	9 Mo Sep	2.47	2.51	25
26	....	0.12	10-6-92	9-14	...	Nil	....	11.4	90.7	25.2	7-29-95	4.86	...	7490	Oc	0.55	d0.07	Δ0.19	□d1.19	Pd0.25	d0.25				26
27◆	1979	gQ0.10½	1-31-96	12-27	g0.39	0.42	g0.283	300	726	330	j12-31-94	84.5	1	92288	Dc	0.60	0.88	0.71	1.68	....	j1.94	9 Mo Sep	1.26	1.52	27
28	1904	Q0.52	12-14-95	11-13	2.03	2.08	1.82	1541	11604	13476	9-30-95	5971	2373	555323	Dc	2.08	□1.43	□0.83	4.00	E5.78	5.42	9 Mo Sep	3.05	4.47	28
29	1992	Q0.26	12-15-95	11-29	1.04	1.04	0.88	37.3	855	386	9-30-95	380	...	118432	Je	□0.50	□1.43	□1.04	1.68	1.95	1.95	3 Mo Sep	0.44	0.44	29
30	....	None Since Public			...	Nil	....	23.1	112	39.4	9-30-95	2.26	...	6337	Dc	0.21	0.62	1.27	2.03	....	1.59	9 Mo Sep	1.49	1.05	30
31	....	None Since Public			...	Nil	....	13.6	47.2	17.6	9-30-95	1.77	...	6520	Dc	d0.50	1.22	1.82	1.82	....	1.46	9 Mo Sep	1.39	1.03	31
32◆	1935	Q0.11½	12-1-95	11-1	0.46	0.46	0.42	19.6	174	59.8	9-30-95	42.4	...	19046	Dc	1.03	□0.69	□0.87	0.90	E1.15	1.22	9 Mo Sep	0.65	0.97	32
33	....	None Since Public			...	Nil	....	8.79	8.91	0.57	9-30-95	....	...	★8439	Dc	...	d0.23	d0.44	d0.66	....	d0.64	9 Mo Sep	d0.49	d0.47	33
34◆	1992	Q0.05	11-20-95	11-2	0.20	0.20	0.20	45.6	193	73.2	7-30-95	118	...	27244	Ja	1.08	1.08	1.01	d0.91	....	0.56	9 Mo Oct	d1.04	0.43	34
35	....	None Since Public			...	Nil	....	Equity per shr $7.23			9-30-95	197	...	9642	Je	0.37	0.51	0.10	d0.13	0.61	0.73	3 Mo Sep	0.08	0.20	35
36	....	None Since Public			...	Nil	....	1.57	3.64	0.25	9-30-95	....	...	3121	Dc	d0.16	0.02	0.13	d0.30	....	d0.66	9 Mo Sep	0.01	d0.35	36
37	....	5%Stk	12-21-87	12-1	...	Nil	....	6.22	27.6	19.5	10-31-95	12.3	...	8552	Jl	d0.19	d0.54	□d3.41	d0.91	0.52	0.52	3 Mo Oct	0.11	0.11	37
38	1992	Q0.01	11-20-95	11-8	0.04	0.04	0.04	0.97	61.4	16.2	9-30-95	77.6	...	14196	Sp	p0.62	□0.72	□0.74	0.74	0.46	0.46				38
39	....	None Paid			...	Nil	....	0.01	6.70	2.42	9-30-95	0.21	...	2495	Dc	®0.28	Δd0.06	[59]0.02	0.31	....	0.26	9 Mo Sep	0.21	0.16	39
40	1978	S0.10	9-1-95	8-3	0.20	0.20	0.20	1.21	51.5	23.8	9-30-95	0.44	...	±3830	Dc	d0.34	□0.78	□0.68	2.25	....	1.73	9 Mo Sep	1.85	1.33	40
41◆	....	s0.009	4-13-84	3-26	...	Nil	....	0.52	37.2	17.4	9-09-95	1.80	...	5575	Dc	0.61	0.70	0.33	0.04	....	0.26	36 Wk Sep	d0.18	0.04	41
42◆	....	None Paid			...	Nil	....	....	0.60	12.2	9-30-95	0.45	1020	1759	Dc	0.28	d0.52	d1.72	d2.96	....	d6.80	9 Mo Sep	d0.16	d4.00	42
43◆	....	None Since Public			...	Nil	....	30.3	184	76.3	9-30-95	22.1	...	18328	Mr	0.72	0.90	d1.62	□1.13	E0.75	0.63	6 Mo Sep	0.48	d0.02	43
44	....	None Since Public			...	Nil	....	2.77	92.3	41.8	9-30-95	2.71	64	6346	Dc	0.64	0.46	□d0.29	d0.33	....	0.39	9 Mo Sep	d0.37	0.35	44
45◆	....	3%Stk	3-16-95	2-17	3%Stk	Stk	3%Stk	3.89	46.4	13.0	9-02-95	0.88	...	±8845	My	0.05	0.52	0.18	0.03	0.18	0.12	3 Mo Aug	0.12	0.06	45
46◆	....	3%Stk	3-16-95	2-17	3%Stk	Stk	....	....	...	...		....	...	4785	My	0.05	0.52	0.18	0.03	0.18	0.12	3 Mo Aug	0.12	0.06	46
47	....	None Since Public			...	Nil	....	23.2	76.5	72.7	9-24-95	75.4	76	67854	Dc	d3.34	d2.55	Δ0.06	0.07	....	0.09	9 Mo Sep	0.04	0.06	47
48◆	1987	Q0.23	12-1-95	11-13	0.86	0.92	0.709	Book Value $20.73			9-30-95	73.2	...	4460	Sp	1.25	1.55	1.79	□2.14	□[62]2.41	2.41				48
49◆	....	None Since Public			...	Nil	....	4.18	161	107	10-27-95	100	...	22900	Ja	0.09	0.26	0.50	d0.28	....	d0.19	9 Mo Oct	0.33	0.42	49
50◆	....	None Paid			...	Nil	....	0.27	19.4	18.0	9-30-95	12.2	1384	4080	Dc	d0.09	d0.20	□d0.21	[63]0.27	....	d0.29	9 Mo Sep	0.34	d0.22	50
51	....	None Since Public			...	Nil	....	14.9	19.0	3.05	9-30-95	0.71	...	4912	Je	...	...	...	p0.10	p0.51	....	3 Mo Sep	n/a	0.14	51
52	....	None Since Public			...	Nil	....	0.18	21.5	14.4	9-30-95	p....	...	★8223	Sp	...	...	...	....	p1.02	1.02				52

◆**Stock Splits & Divs By Line Reference Index** [1]3-for-2,'92. [2]3-for-2,'95. [6]No adj for stk dstr of INDRESCO Inc,'92. [13]2-for-1,'94. [21]No adj for stk dstr,'88. [24]1-for-4.2 REVERSE,'93. [27]3-for-1,'94. [32]3-for-2,'94. [34]2-for-1,'91. [41]10%,'92,'93,'94. [42]1-for-4 REVERSE,'95. [43]2-for-1,'95. [45]Adj to 3%,'95. [46]Adj to 3%,'95. [48]10%,'93,'95. [49]3-for-2,'92. [50]1-for-4 REVERSE,'91.

¶ S&P 500 # MidCap 400 ✤ SmallCap 600 • Options Index	Ticker	Name of Issue (Call Price of Pfd. Stocks)	Market	Com. Rank. & Pfd. Rating	Inst. Hold Cos	Inst. Hold Shs. (000)	Principal Business	Price Range 1971-93 High	1971-93 Low	1994 High	1994 Low	1995 High	1995 Low	Dec. Sales in 100s	December, 1995 Last Sale Or Bid High	Low	Last	%Div Yield	P-E Ratio	Total Return % Annualized 12 Mo	36 Mo	60 Mo
1	ETCO	✔Earth Technology[51]	NNM	C	16	1807	Enviro/tech consult'g svcs	10¾	2½	16½	7¼	8½	4¼	27451	8	5¾	7⅞	...	d	–1.6	21.6	22.3
2	ESCO	✔Easco Inc	NNM	NR	43	3992	Mfr extrude & aluminum prod	....	....	....	....	17	6	5136	8¾	7⅛	8⅝	0.5	8	...	...	...
3	EBAY	✔Eastbay Inc	NNM	NR	27	772	Athletic footw'r/eqp catalogs	....	....	....	....	24¾	15	5735	24¾	19	19¾	...	24	...	...	...
4	NGT	Eastern AmerNatlGasTr'SPERs'[52]	NY	NR	10	254	Secure Principal Ener Receipt	26¼	20½	24⅞	14½	18	14½	4541	16½	15	16	10.0	9	19.5	...	...
5	EML	✔Eastern Co	AS,Ch	B+	26	1127	Mfrs locks & metal products	14½	2¼	17⅝	11⅝	15½	11	1095	12⅜	11¼	12¼	3.8	12	–4.2	10.3	4.1
¶6•[1]	EFU	✔Eastern Enterprises	NY,B,C,Ch,P,Ph	B+	254	14977	Boston Gas/river barging	35¼	5½	28	22¼	35½	25¼	7967	35½	32⅛	35¼	4.2	13	40.3	15.0	11.4
✤7	EUA	✔Eastern Util Assoc	NY,B,Ch,P	↓B	135	13342	Util hldg co: Mass & RI elec	41¾	8	27¾	21⅛	25¼	21¼	12824	24⅝	22⅝	23⅝	6.8	15	15.8	4.7	6.1
8	EGP	✔EastGroup Properties SBI	NY	NR	22	876	Real estate investment trust	40	3⅝	21⅛	16½	22⅜	17¼	824	22⅜	20⅝	21⅜	8.8	16	28.1	16.9	23.5
¶9•[2]	EMN	✔Eastman Chemical	NY,Ph	NR	578	49486	Mfr chemical plastic,fiber prd	48⅛	42⅞	56	39½	69½	48½	59926	67⅛	59⅝	62⅜	2.7	9	25.2	...	...
¶10•[3]	EK	✔Eastman Kodak	NY,B,C,Ch,P,Ph	B	1126	204040	Photograph apparatus,chem	71	18¼	56⅜	40⅝	70⅜	47⅛	153160	70⅜	65⅜	67	2.4	17	46.7	22.9	14.7
¶11•[3]	ETN	✔Eaton Corp	NY,B,Ch,P,Ph	B+	522	53922	Electronic/electric sys,eqp:	55⅜	4	62⅛	43⅞	62½	45¼	31216	56⅛	53¼	53⅝	3.0	10	10.5	13.4	20.0
✤12	EAVN	✔Eaton Vance[56]	NNM,B	A–	100	3103	Advisor to mutual funds,dstr	41¼	¼	37½	24½	39¼	27¼	3087	29½	27¾	28¼	2.4	9	...	...	...
13	ECC	✔ECC International	NY,Ch,Ph	B–	39	2515	Computer-contr simulators	14⅝	1/16	17½	4⅝	13¼	9⅜	5875	11⅛	9⅝	11	...	11	8.6	56.4	21.6
¶14•[4]	ECH	✔Echlin Inc	NY,B,Ch,P	↑A–	432	39393	Auto elec,brake replacem't pts	34⅝	3¾	35¼	24½	39⅝	29⅞	42966	38¼	36⅛	36½	2.2	14	22.9	19.5	30.9
¶15•[5]	ECO	✔Echo Bay Mines	AS,To,B,Ch,P,Mo,Vc	B–	278	36266	Mining:gold & silver	30⅛	3⅛	15⅛	9¾	11½	8⅝	113529	11¼	10⅛	10¼	0.8	d	–5.0	28.1	4.7
16	DISH	✔EchoStar Communications'A'	NNM	NR	40	2828	Mfr satellite TV prod	....	....	....	....	25¾	12	22220	25¾	14¾	24¼	...	d	...	...	...
17•[6]	ECILF	ECI Telecom Ltd	NNM	NR	137	23718	Electronic telecommun sys	26⅞	3/16	28½	11½	24¼	11¼	142129	24¼	19⅝	22¾	0.6	20	77.5	8.5	48.8
18•[7]	ECK	✔Eckerd Corp	NY,Ch	NR	194	32223	Operates drug store chain U.S.	19¼	12¾	32	17⅞	44⅝	24½	44147	44⅝	40½	44⅝	...	16	51.9	...	...
19	EECN	✔Ecogen Inc	NNM	C	28	3112	Dvlps biological pesticides	14½	1	8⅜	2¼	3⅞	⅝	67096	1⅝	1 1/16	1 7/16	...	d	–56.6	–42.0	–5.2
¶20•[8]	ECL	✔Ecolab Inc	NY,Ch,Ph	B	265	28885	Comm'l cleaning&sanitizing	23⅞	4	23½	19¼	31¾	20	14874	31¾	28⅝	30	1.9	20	45.8	21.0	25.9
21	EEI	✔Ecology/Environment'A'	AS,Ch	B+	25	683	Evironm'l consult'g/test'g	28½	8⅛	15⅛	8¾	9⅝	7⅛	3075	8½	7⅛	8⅜	3.8	22	–2.3	–11.6	–7.4
22	EDEL	✔Edelbrock Corp	NNM	NR	30	1433	Custom auto accessories	....	....	16¾	12¼	17	11¼	675	15¾	14	15¾	...	12	23.5	...	...
23•[9]	EBS	✔Edison Bros Stores	NY,Ch,Ph	D	89	7654	Apparel,footwr strs/enter'nt	49⅛	2¾	32⅛	16⅞	18½	1⅞	36921	2½	1⅞	1⅞	...	d	...	...	...
24	EDS	✔Edisto Resources	AS,Ch,Ph	NR	37	10140	Oil & gas explor,dev,prod'n	435	3¾	9⅝	5⅜	8⅝	5	4580	7⅜	5	7⅛	...	20	11.8	4.5	...
25	WS	Wrrt (Pur 1 com $9.74)	AS	....	12	171		5	1 11/16	4	9/16	2	1/16	1987	15/16	3/16	11/16	...	..	...	...	...
26	EDI	✔Editek Inc	AS	C	10	313	Mfr diagnostic screen'g tests	51⅝	⅜	5⅜	1¼	4	2½	5566	3¼	2⅝	2⅞	...	d	–19.3	–32.9	35.7
27	EDO	✔EDO Corp	NY,B,Ch	C	20	788	Electr eq:military,marine	23	7/16	7¼	2⅞	6	3	2744	5½	4½	5	...	d	48.1	–3.8	7.1
28	EAIN	✔Education Alternatives	NNM	NR	50	3720	School mgmt/consulting svcs	48¾	2⅜	39	9¾	19	3⅞	32623	6⅛	4	4½	...	d	–69.5	–40.6	...
29	EDNTF	Edunetics Ltd[64]	NNM	NR	..	...	Dvp science/math teachg softwr	13¾	8¾	14	1¼	2 3/16	13/16	12765	1 13/16	13/16	1¾	...	d	25.0	...	...
#30•[6]	AGE	✔Edwards(AG)Inc	NY,B,Ch,P	A	199	26062	Security broker: inv banker	25¾	⅛	28⅞	16½	27	17½	34649	26⅞	22⅝	23⅞	2.7	9	37.1	11.2	25.6
¶31•[10]	EGG	✔EG&G Inc	NY,B,Ch,Ph,P	A–	247	31832	Scientific equip,sys & svcs	26¾	⅞	19	13¾	24½	13	25884	24½	19	24¼	e2.3	24	74.3	9.5	12.4
32•[11]	EGGS	✔Egghead Inc	NNM	B–	65	11149	Retailer of PC computer softw	30¾	6⅝	12⅛	6⅛	14¼	5¾	35527	8¾	5¾	6⅜	...	d	–45.5	–13.7	–8.0
33	EKC	✔Ek Chor China Motorcycle	NY	NR	..	...	Joint venture motorcycle mfr	38⅞	17¾	37½	13⅝	20¾	11	6342	14½	11¼	11⅝	1.1	9	–16.2	...	...
34	EKO	✔Ekco Group	NY,B,Ch,P,Ph	B–	55	8810	Mfrs kitchen/household prod	54⅝	1½	8⅛	5⅞	6⅞	5⅜	11577	6¼	5⅞	5⅞	1.4	11	–10.5	–15.6	17.7
35	ELCH	✔El Chico Restaurants	NNM	B–	27	1919	Mexican restaur'ts:franch	16¼	2½	17¾	8⅛	12⅝	7⅝	3453	9½	9	9½	...	10	11.8	–9.0	29.3
#36•[12]	EPG	✔El Paso Natural Gas	NY,Ph	NR	236	22337	Natural gas pipeline system	40⅜	19	41⅞	29⅝	32½	24¾	15563	31⅝	28⅜	28¾	4.6	12	–0.2	1.7	...
37•[3]	ELN	✔Elan Corp ADS[67]	NY,Ch,Ph	NR	217	24315	Res/dev drug formulat'n tech	44⅛	3	47⅞	30⅛	51	32⅞	36009	51	46⅜	48⅝	...	20	37.9	12.5	29.2
38	WS A	Wrrt(Pur 1 Ord shr [69]$39.26)[70]	NY	....	12	1611		....	....	....	....	19	11	2683	19	15	16¼	...	..	...	...	...
39	ELBTF	Elbit Ltd	NNM	NR	6	76	Mfr computerized sys/prod	54	3⅝	44¼	17	24¾	13⅛	1613	16¾	13⅜	16	1.5	21	–18.1	–29.3	3.9
40	ELK	✔Elcor Corp	NY,B,Ch,Ph	B–	69	4365	Roofing & industrial products	36½	¼	25¾	14⅛	23⅞	13	2106	21¾	20¼	21¾	...	19	37.4	7.6	35.5
41	ELB	✔Eldorado Bancorp	AS	↑B	16	515	Comm'l bkg,California	14⅝	2⅝	11⅜	6⅛	17	9	451	17	15⅜	16⅛	2.0	13	101	29.3	19.9
42	ELGT	Electric & Gas Technology	NNM	C	11	466	Mfr electrical/gas ind equip	8⅝	⅛	4¾	1⅛	3⅝	1 13/16	6793	3	2¾	2⅞	...	29	53.3	...	...
43	ELRC	✔Electro Rent	NNM	B+	41	8160	Rental/lease electr test eq	9	7/16	11⅞	7⅝	22	10⅞	1739	22	20	21¾	...	16	101	48.5	39.5
44•[2]	ESIO	✔Electro Scientific Ind	NNM	B–	101	6459	Computer-control laser sys	26	2½	21⅝	8⅝	41½	17½	14350	30½	24¾	29¼	...	20	44.4	79.4	46.2
45	EIF	Electrochemical Ind(Frutarom)	AS	NR	1	2	Mfr/dstr chemical products	3⅞	1 1/16	3⅞	2¼	4¾	2⅝	672	2⅞	2⅝	2⅝B	...	5	–18.9	7.1	13.8
46•[3]	EGLS	✔Electroglas Inc	NNM	NR	151	15750	Mfr semicondctor mfg equip	14⅜	6⅞	25¼	11½	40¼	13⅝	39310	30	19¾	24½	...	14	50.7	...	...
47	ELMG	✔Electromagnetic Sci	NNM	B–	36	3946	Mfr microwave products	19¾	3/16	12½	7¾	17⅝	9½	5135	12	10⅝	11	...	26	–9.3	13.6	10.7
#48•[13]	ERTS	✔Electronic Arts	NNM	B+	233	42219	Dvlp/mkt entertain't softwr	42	1 9/16	33½	12¾	42¼	15⅜	326073	34⅛	22⅜	26⅛	...	25	35.7	7.6	62.5
49	EA	✔Electronic Assoc[73]	NY,B,Ch,Ph	C	12	414	Contract mfr electr pr & sys	16⅜	¾	8¾	1⅛	11¾	4¼	29016	6⅛	4¾	5⅛	...	d	–37.9	50.6	22.3
50•[3]	EFII	✔Electronics For Imaging	NNM	NR	149	22731	Dvlp publish'g system softwr	11⅞	6⅜	14¾	6⅝	50⅛	12	52544	46	35½	43¾	...	35	220	66.4	...
51	ELSI	✔Electrosource Inc	NSC	NR	22	968	Mfr rechg storage batteries	7⅛	3/16	4⅝	2¾	4½	1 3/16	122068	2½	1 5/16	1 7/16	...	d	–51.6	–15.4	5.0
52•[14]	ELF	✔Elf Aquitaine[74] ADS	NY,Ch	NR	159	24330	Int'l integrated oil & gas co	39⅞	27½	39⅜	31¼	42⅛	31⅜	20006	37¼	32¾	36¾	2.7	20	8.2	6.3	...

Uniform Footnote Explanations-See Page 4. Other: [1]Ph:Cycle 1. [2]CBOE:Cycle 3. [3]CBOE:Cycle 1. [4]P:Cycle 3. [5]P,Vc:Cycle 1. [6]CBOE:Cycle 2. [7]ASE:Cycle 2. [8]NY:Cycle 1. [9]NY:Cycle 2. [10]Ph:Cycle 3. [11]ASE,CBOE:Cycle 3. [12]ASE:Cycle 1. [13]ASE:Cycle 3. [14]ASE,NY:Cycle 1. [51]Tyco Intl offer,$8 to Jan 11. [52]Dep Unit int E.AmerNatGasTr&$20U.S.GvtObl(2013). [53]Excl subsid pfd. [54]Stk dstr of Eastman Chemical Co,'94. [55]®$2.42,'94. [56]Non-vtg. [57]Stk dstr of Investors Finl Svcs,'95. [58]Subsid pfd. [59]Fiscal Dec'93 & prior. [60]10 Mo Oct'94. [61]Stk dstr of Dave & Buster's Inc. [62]Long term debt classified as curr.. [63]6 Mo Dec'93. [64]Natl Education plan acq,$2. [65]Fiscal May'91 & prior. [66]12 Mo Dec'92:Fiscal May'92 earned $0.22d. [67]Each ADS rep 1 ord shr P.IR 0.04. [68]Excl Executive shrs. [69]Plus $0.05 per ADR issuance fee. [70]Fr 8-12-95. [71]To be determined. [72]Stk dstr of Tech Electro Ind. [73]Approve name chg, EA Industries. [74]Each ADS rep 0.5 ord shr FF50.

Index	Splits ◆ Cash Divs. Ea.Yr. Since	Dividends: Latest Payment Period $	Date	Ex. Div.	Total $ So Far 1995	Ind. Rate	Paid 1994	Financial Position Mil-$ Cash& Equiv.	Curr. Assets	Curr. Liab.	Balance Sheet Date	Capitalization Lg Trm Debt Mil-$	Shs. 000 Pfd.	Com.	Earnings $ Per Shr. Years End	1991	1992	1993	1994	1995	Last 12 Mos.	Interim Earnings Period	$ per Shr. 1994	1995	Index
1	....	None Since Public			...	Nil	....	4.57	65.1	33.4	8-25-95	14.6	...	8698	Au	d1.38	d0.17	0.65	d0.52	d0.06	d0.06				1
2	1995	Q0.01	11-30-95	11-13	0.02	0.04	....	7.49	84.7	49.8	9-30-95	85.0	...	10243	Dc	...	...	...	p1.01	....	1.14	9 Mo Sep	p0.80	0.93	2
3	....	None Since Public			...	Nil	....	0.02	37.2	13.0	6-30-95	p1.09	...	★5771	Je	...	...	...	....	p0.78	0.81	3 Mo Sep	p0.23	p0.26	3
4	1993	0.38	12-15-95	11-28	1.597	1.60	1.902	Liq date 5-15-2013				....	...	★5900	Dc	...	...	n/a	P1.82	....	1.82				4
5◆	1940	Q0.11½	12-15-95	11-21	0.46	0.46	0.46	2.04	23.7	5.54	9-30-95	0.42	...	2776	Dc	1.01	□1.10	1.01	0.95	....	1.00	9 Mo Sep	0.67	0.72	5
6	1974	Q0.37	1-3-96	11-29	1.40	1.48	1.40	117	377	158	9-30-95	359	...	20174	Dc	□1.30	Δ1.67	□d1.43	2.46	....	2.67	9 Mo Sep	1.52	1.73	6
7	1928	Q0.40	11-15-95	10-30	1.58½	1.60	1.51½	23.7	161	145	9-30-95	445	[53]...	20379	Dc	1.58	2.00	2.44	2.41	E1.60	1.52	12 Mo Sep	2.51	1.52	7
8	1978	Q0.47	12-29-95	12-14	1.84	1.88	1.74	Equity per shr $19.22			9-30-95	76.0	...	4227	Dc	2.28	d1.49	2.61	1.74	....	1.33	9 Mo Sep	1.55	1.14	8
9	1994	Q0.42	1-2-96	12-14	1.62	1.68	1.20	66.0	1442	866	9-30-95	1205	...	80326	Dc	...	p2.72	p□2.46	4.05	E6.75	6.53	9 Mo Sep	2.80	5.28	9
10◆	1902	Q0.40	1-2-96	11-29	1.60	1.60	[54]1.70	1333	7069	4422	9-30-95	653	...	342107	Dc	0.05	Δ3.06	□2.02	□[55]2.45	E3.85	3.66	9 Mo Sep	□1.65	2.86	10
11◆	1923	Q0.40	11-24-95	11-2	1.50	1.60	1.20	39.0	2067	1111	9-30-95	1147	...	77600	Dc	1.10	□2.03	□2.57	4.40	E5.25↓	5.12	9 Mo Sep	3.25	3.97	11
12◆	1976	Q0.17	11-13-95	10-27	h[57]0.65	0.68	0.60	66.3	89.9	24.6	7-31-95	60.1	...	±9280	Oc	±1.74	±2.49	±3.09	Δ±3.00	P3.27	3.27				12
13	....	0.05	7-28-92	6-22	...	Nil	....	3.61	64.9	23.1	9-30-95	15.6	...	7686	Je	0.67	d0.50	d0.17	0.57	0.93	0.97	3 Mo Sep	0.17	0.21	13
14	1950	Q0.20½	1-18-96	1-3	0.80½	0.82	0.74½	27.7	1076	486	8-31-95	482	...	59658	Au	0.75	1.15	1.60	Δ2.06	2.60	2.60	3 Mo Nov	0.54	0.54	14
15	1983	tS0.038	12-31-95	12-13	0.075	0.08	0.075	197	251	57.3	9-30-95	116	[58]p1149	126384	Dc	0.07	d0.30	0.03	0.07	Ed0.30	d0.34	9 Mo Sep	0.12	d0.29	15
16	....	None Since Public			...	Nil	....	68.6	111	18.5	9-30-95	375	1617	p±33809	Dc	...	...	...	pd0.02	....	d0.21	9 Mo Sep	p0.04	pd0.15	16
17◆	1990	t0.05	8-30-95	8-14	t0.10	0.13	t0.16	103	324	84.0	12-31-94	1.79	...	75714	Dc	0.47	0.60	Δ0.68	1.01	E1.17	1.12	9 Mo Sep	0.74	0.85	17
18	....	None Since Public			...	Nil	....	9.37	964	580	10-28-95	814	...	★34955	Ja	...	p0.70	p□1.80	□2.41	E2.85	2.80	9 Mo Oct	□1.04	□1.43	18
19	....	None Since Public			...	Nil	....	5.56	15.8	7.08	7-31-95	....	260	29686	Oc	d0.80	d1.26	[59]d0.68	†[60]d0.25	....	d0.71	9 Mo Jul	d0.24	d0.70	19
20◆	1936	Q0.14	1-16-96	12-27	0.50	0.56	0.44	27.7	356	278	9-30-95	104	...	64628	Dc	□d4.13	1.03	□Δ1.20	1.25	E1.50	1.34	9 Mo Sep	1.02	1.11	20
21◆	1987	S0.16	1-12-96	12-20	0.32	0.32	s0.276	15.4	42.5	9.05	10-28-95	0.76	...	±4077	Jl	±1.29	±1.08	±1.12	□±1.13	±0.52	0.38	3 Mo Oct	±0.27	±0.13	21
22	....	None Since Public			...	Nil	....	10.7	35.2	15.0	9-30-95	4.32	...	5240	Je	0.02	0.39	0.54	Δ0.79	1.32	1.32	3 Mo Sep	0.23	0.23	22
23◆	1934	h[61]....	6-29-95	6-30	h[61]0.73	Nil	1.24	File bankruptcy Chapt 11				[62]....	...	22087	Ja	2.83	□3.27	1.01	0.93	....	d4.45	9 Mo Oct	0.15	d5.23	23
24◆	....	None Since Public			...	Nil	....	43.9	124	85.1	9-30-95	16.3	...	12954	Dc	d136.80	d39.80	[63]0.44	0.55	....	0.35	9 Mo Sep	0.55	0.35	24
25	....	Terms&trad. basis should			be checked in detail			Wrrts expire 6-29-96				....	...	1977	Dc	...	...	...	....	....	....				25
26	....	None Paid			...	Nil	....	0.42	3.33	1.57	9-30-95	....	...	10233	Dc	d0.31	d0.35	d0.56	d0.49	....	d0.43	9 Mo Sep	d0.34	d0.28	26
27	1976	0.07	6-30-94	6-3	...	Nil	0.21	19.3	60.0	26.2	9-30-95	42.5	71	5805	Dc	Δ0.05	0.78	□d1.54	d4.30	....	d2.40	9 Mo Sep	d1.75	0.15	27
28	....	None Since Public			...	Nil	....	18.8	19.8	14.5	9-30-95	0.56	...	7489	Je	d1.06	d0.44	0.18	0.33	d1.09	d1.40	3 Mo Sep	d0.03	d0.34	28
29	....	None Since Public			...	Nil	....	0.07	3.88	5.30	12-31-92	0.33	...	★6000	Dc	d0.29	0.36	P0.42	....	....	d0.47	9 Mo SepΔ	0.44	d0.45	29
30◆	1971	Q0.16	1-2-96	11-29	0.56	0.64	0.56	Equity per shr $15.78			8-31-95	....	...	62412	Fb	1.88	2.06	2.57	2.00	E2.60	2.41	9 Mo Nov	1.49	1.90	30
31◆	1965	Q0.14	2-9-96	1-17	0.57	0.56	0.56	64.3	443	355	10-01-95	★115	...	48129	Dc	1.45	□1.56	□1.41	d0.10	E1.02	1.09	9 Mo Sep	d0.32	0.87	31
32	....	None Since Public			...	Nil	....	55.9	315	201	9-30-95	0.42	...	17540	Mr	0.92	0.41	d0.03	0.15	....	d0.12	6 Mo Sep	d0.12	d0.39	32
33	1993	0.05	12-28-95	11-29	0.13	0.13	0.10	48.1	49.2	0.21	12-31-94	....	...	17098	Dc	...	0.92	0.89	1.20	....	1.27	6 Mo Jun	0.58	0.65	33
34	1995	Q0.02	1-10-96	12-29	0.06	0.08	....	0.21	126	49.6	10-01-95	133	1519	18383	Dc	0.60	0.75	□0.11	0.57	....	0.53	9 Mo Sep	0.32	0.28	34
35	....	None Since Public			...	Nil	....	0.08	3.20	7.15	9-30-95	7.87	...	4094	Dc	[65]0.28	[66]0.03	0.64	0.88	....	0.94	9 Mo Sep	0.62	0.68	35
36	1992	Q0.33	1-2-96	12-6	1.29¼	1.32	1.18¼	24.5	324	540	9-30-95	768	...	34213	Dc	p1.97	2.12	2.46	2.45	E2.50	2.46	9 Mo Sep	1.80	1.81	36
37◆	....	0.032	6-11-84	5-14	...	Nil	....	110	152	17.3	j3-31-95	98.3	...	[68]31618	Mr	0.70	1.01	□d1.43	1.90	E2.40	2.12	6 Mo Sep	0.86	1.08	37
38	....	Terms&trad. basis should			be checked in detail			Wrrts expire 8-12-98				....	...	3923	Mr	...	...	...	....	....	....				38
39	1986	t0.06	1-8-96	12-20	t0.21	0.24	t0.27	101	607	366	12-31-94	41.2	...	20532	Dc	2.15	1.76	□2.24	1.57	....	0.77	9 Mo Sep	1.47	0.67	39
40	....	Q0.06	2-14-96	1-9	0.06	[71]....	....	2.01	49.4	22.0	9-30-95	17.2	...	8730	Je	d2.14	Δ*0.59	Δ1.92	Δ1.58	1.08	1.14	3 Mo Sep	0.35	0.41	40
41◆	1986	Q0.08	1-10-96	12-22	0.291	0.32	0.073	Book Value $10.61			9-30-95	....	...	3038	Dc	0.91	0.91	d0.57	0.85	....	1.29	9 Mo Sep	0.59	1.03	41
42	....	h[72]....	8-5-92	8-3	...	Nil	....	0.64	16.8	12.2	10-31-95	6.04	...	8270	Jl	0.23	0.05	0.13	d0.71	0.11	0.10	3 Mo Oct	0.05	0.04	42
43◆	....	None Since Public			...	Nil	....	Equity per shr $8.27			8-31-95	....	...	11800	My	0.52	0.62	Δ0.57	0.99	1.20	1.34	3 Mo Aug	0.29	0.43	43
44	....	None Since Public			...	Nil	....	32.8	97.4	17.0	8-31-95	....	...	8626	My	0.20	d1.00	0.37	1.23	1.53	1.47	6 Mo Nov	0.69	0.63	44
45◆	....	None Paid			...	Nil	....	46.7	162	92.3	12-31-92	146	...	p50588	Dc	0.03	0.09	Pd0.15	P0.08	....	0.52	6 Mo Jun	d0.10	0.34	45
46◆	....	None Since Public			...	Nil	....	91.5	152	34.3	9-30-95	....	...	17958	Dc	...	p0.32	p1.07	1.31	....	1.75	9 Mo Sep	0.98	1.42	46
47	....	None Since Public			...	Nil	....	6.08	58.3	24.3	9-30-95	4.26	...	7004	Dc	Δ0.79	0.10	0.20	0.58	....	0.43	9 Mo Sep	0.35	0.20	47
48◆	....	None Since Public			...	Nil	....	91.6	220	81.1	9-30-95	....	...	52433	Mr	0.36	0.65	0.90	1.07	E1.05	0.78	6 Mo Sep	0.36	0.07	48
49	....	2%Stk	1-23-67	12-27	...	Nil	....	1.47	32.1	24.1	9-30-95	5.13	...	14976	Dc	d1.43	d0.97	d1.26	d0.95	....	d3.10	9 Mo Sep	d0.20	d2.35	49
50◆	....	None Since Public			...	Nil	....	127	164	27.2	9-30-95	....	...	24889	Dc	0.05	0.37	0.52	0.86	....	1.27	9 Mo Sep	0.55	0.96	50
51	....	None Paid			...	Nil	....	0.96	3.87	3.01	9-30-95	7.55	...	27267	Dc	d0.15	d0.20	d0.03	d0.61	....	d1.17	9 Mo Sep	d0.15	d0.71	51
52	1960	1.00	7-17-95	5-31	1.00	1.00	0.903	4341	18030	14577	12-31-94	8288	[53]...	264347	Dc	3.78	2.21	0.25	□d0.01	E1.80	d0.01				52

◆**Stock Splits & Divs By Line Reference Index** [5]3-for-2,'91. [10]No adj for stk dstr 0.25 of Eastman Chem,'94. [11]2-for-1,'93. [12]2-for-1,'92:No adj for stk dstr Inv Finl Svcs,'95. [17]2-for-1,'91,'92,'93. [20]2-for-1,'94. [21]Adj for 5%,'94. [23]No adj for stk dstr Dave & Buster's,'95. [24]Reorg, 1-for-20 REVERSE,'93. [30]3-for-2,'91:5-for-4,'92,'94. [31]2-for-1,'92. [37]3-for-2,'92. [41]10%,'95. [43]3-for-2,'92,'94,'95. [45]6-for-5,'91. [46]2-for-1,'95. [48]2-for-1,'92,'93. [50]2-for-1,'95.

¶ S&P 500 # MidCap 400 ✣ SmallCap 600 • Options Index	Ticker	Name of Issue (Call Price of Pfd. Stocks)	Market	Com. Rank. & Pfd. Rating	Inst. Hold Cos	Inst. Hold Shs. (000)	Principal Business	Price Range 1971-93 High	1971-93 Low	1994 High	1994 Low	1995 High	1995 Low	Dec. Sales in 100s	December, 1995 Last Sale Or Bid High	Low	Last	%Div Yield	P-E Ratio	Total Return % Annualized 12 Mo	36 Mo	60 Mo
1	ELJ	✔Eljer Industries	NY,Ph	NR	28	1657	Mfr plumbing/building prod	34¾	4½	9¼	5⅛	12	3¾	7920	12	7¾	10¾	...	d	95.5	7.1	8.1
2	EBY	✔Elsag Bailey Process Auto N.V.	NY,Ph	NR	..	...	Mfr process control systems	21⅞	17¾	28¾	19¼	34⅛	22⅛	13395	28⅞	26	26⅞	...	17	7.5	...	...
3	ELT	✔Elscint Ltd[51]	NY,Ch,Ph	NR	10	1896	Scient/nuclear medical/instr	28¾	7/16	5⅛	1¾	3½	1¾	10573	2¾	2⅛	2⅜	...	15	18.8	−30.7	1.1
4	ENL	Elsevier NV[52] ADS[53]	NY	NR	20	2617	Publishing/information svcs	....	....	22⅛	19⅝	28	18⅞	4187	28	25½	26⅝	2.0	9	33.6	...	...
5	ELS	✔Elsinore Corp[55]	AS,B,Ch,P	D	11	2144	Hotels/casino:resort	85⅝	⅝	6⅛	1⅜	2¾	1/16	3887	⅝	1/16	⅝	...	d	−64.3	−3.1	−12.9
6	ELTN	✔Eltron Intl	NNM	NR	37	3133	Mfg bar code label printers	....	....	12	3¼	38¾	9¼	7576	38¾	31¾	35½	...	41	265	...	...
7	ELXS	✔ELXSI Corp	NNM	B−	14	733	Restaurants/video inspect eq	300	¾	9¼	4¾	7¾	4⅞	3140	6⅜	4⅞	6⅛	...	7	19.5	8.8	21.2
8	AKO	Embotelladora Andina ADS[57]	NY,Ch	NR	41	4690	Produce soft drinks,Chile	....	....	28	17⅞	39⅝	19¾	7391	37¼	32¼	36⅛	0.7	30	43.9	...	...
#9•[1]	EMC	✔EMC Corp	NY	B	440	117312	Mfr board-level computer prod	19½	7/16	24	12½	27⅜	13	243898	18	15⅛	15⅜	...	11	−30.5	37.2	62.9
10	EMCI	EMC Insurance Group	NNM	B	30	1525	Hldg co:multi-line insur	15⅛	4⅛	10¾	8½	15¼	9½	180	13¾	12¼	13¾	4.1	9	51.2	24.7	21.1
11	EMCR	✔EmCare Holdings	NNM	NR	46	3270	Physician provider mgmt svc	....	....	14¾	11	27⅜	13⅛	8350	27⅜	22⅞	24	...	24	68.4	...	...
12	ESC	Emeritus Corp	AS	NR	..	...	Oper long-term care communit's	....	....	....	....	15⅜	11¼	10433	15⅛	11¼	11⅝	...	..	...	...	...
¶13•[2]	EMR	✔Emerson Electric	NY,B,C,Ch,P,Ph	A+	990	148668	Mfr electric/electronic prdts	62⅜	7	65⅞	56⅛	81¾	61½	70458	81¾	77	81¾	2.4	20	34.5	17.1	...
14	MSN	✔Emerson Radio	AS	NR	29	5326	Consumer electronic prod	....	....	2⅞	2¼	3¾	1⅜	11822	2¼	1⅜	1 15/16	...	19	−26.2	...	...
15	EMMS	✔Emmis Broadcasting'A'	NNM	NR	71	6425	Own/oper FM radio stations	....	....	16¾	11	35	13½	23173	31	26¾	31	...	46	118	...	...
16	EMR	Emperor Gold	Vc	NR	..	...	Gold/mineral mining explor'n	1¾	1/16	1⅞	⅝	1 9/16	¾	3710	1 7/16	1 1/16	1 5/16B	...	..	...	...	...
17	EMPI	✔Empi Inc	NNM	B	43	4956	Mfr biomedical/diagnostic sys	34¼	7/16	21¼	7	27⅛	7	18383	27⅛	18½	25½	...	42	176	11.6	68.5
18	EDE	✔Empire Dist Elec	NY,B,Ch	A−	56	2533	Utility:El svc in MO,KS,OK,AK	24⅞	4⅞	20½	15	19¾	15⅞	4433	19½	17¾	17⅞	7.2	14	20.9	1.2	9.8
19	EMP	✔Empire of Carolina	AS,B	C	10	83	Design,mfr toys/seasonal pd	12⅜	1 13/16	6⅞	5⅜	12⅞	6	1123	7⅜	6	7	...	d	5.7	2.5	21.7
20	ESOL	✔Employee Solutions	NSC	NR	14	1094	Staff leasing co	7½	3⅞	12⅞	5¼	36½	6¾	45888	36½	21½	34	...	81	369	...	...
21	EOC	Empresa Nac'l De Electric ADS[60]	NY,Ch	NR	52	5298	Major elec utility in Chile	....	....	29	22⅛	29	18¼	26681	23⅜	20	22¾	6.9	16	−8.4	...	...
22•[3]	ELE	✔Empresa Nac'l Elec ADS[62]	NY,Ch,Ph	NR	130	9716	Major elec utility in Spain	48¼	12	55⅞	40	57⅞	37	7412	57⅞	54	57¼	1.8	13	46.1	24.1	24.3
23•[4]	ICA	✔Empresas ICA Sociedad ADS[63]	NY,Ph	NR	73	9412	Largest contrust'n co,Mexico	29⅝	15	34½	14⅞	15¾	3⅞	81071	11⅛	9¼	10¼	1.0	85	−37.6	−16.6	...
24	MDAa.M	Empresas La Moderna, SA[64]	ME	NR	..	...	Mfr cigarettes/packaging	....	....	28	16⅝	30⅝	13⅞	....	30⅝	26⅞	29⅞	0.7	..	...	...	...
25•[1]	ELM	✔Empresas La Moderna SA ADS[65]	[5]NY	NR	17	1100	Mfr cigarettes/packaging	....	....	37⅛	14½	19	7⅜	16158	16⅜	13½	15½	...	53	−11.4	...	...
26	TL	Empresas Telex-Chile ADS[66]	NY,Ch	NR	37	1958	Telecommunications svc-Chile	....	....	21¼	9¾	14¼	5⅛	11423	10½	8⅛	10⅜	0.9	25	−1.3	...	...
27	ENCD	✔ENCAD Inc	NNM	NR	36	1463	Mfr color inkjet printers	6	5	19¾	4⅝	29⅞	11⅜	13463	20¼	16¼	17½	...	13	34.6	...	...
28	EMI.EC	✔Encore Marketing Intl	ECM	NR	1	.3	Mkt'g membership data info svc	3⅛	9/16	1⅝	5/16	2⅛	¼	452	2⅛	5/16	2⅛	...	d	209	...	...
29	WIRE	✔Encore Wire	NNM	NR	27	3016	Mfr copper electrical wire	13¼	6½	20¾	10¾	17¾	9¼	6249	10¾	9¼	9¾	...	29	−42.6	−0.8	...
✣30	EGN	✔Energen Corp	NY,Ch,Ph	A	96	3631	Gas serv in central Alabama	26¾	2 7/16	23⅞	19¼	25⅛	20⅛	4106	25⅛	23¼	24⅛	4.8	14	24.6	15.6	11.1
31	EVI	✔Energy Ventures	NY,Ch	B−	107	9260	Oil & gas ind services/equip	26	½	16¼	11¼	25¼	11⅞	7185	25¼	21	25¼	...	38	120	38.5	8.9
32	EWST	✔Energy West	NNM	B+	9	71	Gas utility in Montana	9¼	⅞	9¼	7⅜	9½	7½	399	9½	8⅛	9⅜	4.3	15	19.3	15.0	18.6
33	EI	✔EnergyNorth Inc	NY,Ch	A−	25	562	Hldg co:dstr nat'l gas N.H.	22¼	3⅝	22¼	15¼	18⅜	15½	482	18⅜	17¼	17¾	6.5	14	16.7	5.2	7.0
34	ENI	✔Enersis S.A. ADS[67]	NY,Ch,Ph	NR	98	6964	Electric utility - S. America	23½	18	33¼	16¾	34½	18¾	17217	29½	25⅞	28½	3.2	21	8.4	...	...
¶35•[1]	EC	✔Engelhard Corp	NY,B	B	369	62738	Specialty chems/metals	20	3⅜	21	13⅞	32½	14⅞	52647	23⅜	20¾	21¾	1.7	22	52.7	14.7	34.5
36	EASI	✔Engineered Support Sys	NNM	B−	12	248	Military ground support sys	15¾	1	4⅝	3⅜	8	3¾	3927	7	6	6¾	0.3	11	74.5	44.3	9.4
37	ENC	✔English China Clays[68] ADR	NY	NR	6	494	Ind'l minerals/bldg mat'ls	33	15⅞	24	15	19⅞	13	394	15⅝	13	15	5.5	16	−7.5	−1.3	0.6
✣38	EFS	✔Enhance Financial Svcs Grp	NY,Ph	NR	68	9265	Muni/asset-backed debt reinsr	24⅞	15½	20⅝	15½	27	15⅞	7171	27	23½	26⅝	1.4	14	59.5	13.5	...
39	E	ENI S.p.A. ADS[70]	NY,Ch	NR	..	...	Oil&gas explor,dvlp,prod'n	....	....	....	....	34¾	30½	71851	34¾	30½	34¼	...	10	...	...	...
#40	EBF	✔Ennis Business Forms	NY,Ch,Ph	A	106	8457	Business forms: paper items	21⅜	3/16	16⅛	11⅝	14½	12	4079	13	12⅛	12¼	4.9	10	9.0	−6.0	4.8
¶41•[1]	ENE	✔Enron Corp	NY,To,B,C,Ch,P,Ph	B+	705	136657	Major nat'l gas pipeline sys	37	2⅛	34⅝	26¾	39⅜	28	102774	39⅜	35	38⅛	2.2	18	30.0	20.2	26.6
42	Pr J	$10.50 cm Cv 2nd Pfd(100)	NY	†BBB	11	73	oil & gas explor & prod'n	500¾	117¼	455	376¾	502	393	1	502	502	520½B	2.0	..	...	...	...
43	EXG	6.25% Exch Nts,'98	NY	....[74]	..	...		....	....	....	....	24⅜	22⅝	27866	24⅜	22⅝	24	5.7	..	...	...	...
44	EPP	✔Enron Global Pwr/Pipeln LLC	NY,Ch,Ph	NR	85	5916	Power plant/natl gas pipeline	....	....	24⅞	21⅜	27	20	6998	25¼	24¼	24⅞	3.3	16	17.0	...	...
45	ENP	✔Enron Liquids Pipeline L.P.	NY	NR	18	236	Liquid natl gas pipeline sys	32¾	23	34½	23	26⅞	23⅞	3260	24½	23⅞	24⅜	10.3	14	11.0	7.1	...
46•[1]	EOG	✔Enron Oil & Gas	NY,Ch	NR	140	21524	Oil & gas explor,dev,prod'n	27	8⅛	24⅝	17⅜	25⅜	17⅛	118794	24⅞	20½	24	0.5	25	27.9	21.9	19.9
47•[6]	ESV	✔ENSCO Intl[79]	NY,Ph	B−	157	42589	Offshore contract drill'g	121	½	19¼	10¾	23	11¼	58816	23	16¾	23	...	35	93.7	72.3	17.0
¶48•[7]	ENS	✔ENSERCH Corp	NY,To,B,C,Ch,Ph	B	278	44610	Oil & Nat Gas:expl,dvlp,distr	40	7¼	19⅛	12⅛	18⅝	12⅝	31890	16⅝	15¼	16¼	1.2	41	30.3	4.3	...
49	EEX	✔Enserch Exploration	NY,B,P	B−	34	13935	Oil & gas explor,dev prod'n	21⅝	6¼	11	5¾	14⅞	9¼	22524	11⅝	10½	11⅝	...	89	20.8	15.7	6.5
¶50•[8]	ETR	✔Entergy Corp	NY,B,C,Ch,P	B	484	147036	Owns five operating utilities	39⅞	7¾	37⅜	21¼	29¼	20	173786	29¼	26½	29¼	6.2	12	43.8	0.2	8.4
51	ETP	✔Enterprise Oil ADS[83]	NY	NR	6	560	Oil & gas explor dev prod'n	23¾	18½	21¾	17⅜	20¼	15⅝	226	18½	16⅛	18B	4.5	31	4.7	1.6	...
52	ESIX	Enterprise Systems	NNM	NR	..	...	Dvlp hlthcr mgmt software	....	....	....	....	37¾	16	12979	37¾	24¾	30½	...	..	...	...	...

Uniform Footnote Explanations-See Page 4. Other: [1]CBOE:Cycle 1. [2]ASE:Cycle 3. [3]ASE,CBOE,NY:Cycle 3. [4]ASE,CBOE,NY:Cycle 1. [5]Ch,Ph [6]ASE,NY:Cycle 3. [7]P:Cycle 2. [8]CBOE:Cycle 3.
[51]Plan reorg,form 3 new public cos. [52]Ea ADS rep 2 ord, DF1.10. [53]Own 50% interest in Reed Elsevier plc. [54]Proportionate shr of Reed Elsevier(in pounds). [55]ASE trading halted 11-1-95.
[56]Debt subj to acceleration. [57]Ea ADS rep 6 com,no par. [58]®$1.10,'94. [59]®$1.28,'94. [60]Ea ADS rep 30 com, no par. [61]Approx. [62]ADS's represent 1 shr nominal value 800 Ptas.
[63]Ea ADS rep 1 ord Participat'g ctf. [64]All data reported in New Mexican Pesos. [65]Ea ADS rep 4 ptc ctf ea rep Cl 1'A'com. [66]Ea ADS rep 2 com, no par. [67]Ea ADS rep 50 com,no par.
[68]Each sponsored ADR rep 3 ord. [69]Dstr of Camas plc in cash or stk,'94. [70]Ea ADS rep 10 ord, Lit. 1,000. [71]To be determined. [72]Excl subsid Pfd. [73]®$1.70,'94. [74]Rated BBB+ by S&P. [75]Exchangeable Notes.
[76]5 Mo Dec'92. [77]Pfd in $M. [78]63% owned by Enron Corp. [79]Plan MidCap 400 listing:eff Jan 5. [80]100% non-taxable,'94. [81]83.4% owned by Enserch Corp. [82]Subsid Pfd in M$. [83]Ea ADS rep 3 ord shrs, 25p.

Splits ◆ Index	Cash Divs. Ea. Yr. Since	Dividends: Latest Payment Period $	Date	Ex. Div.	Total $ So Far 1995	Ind. Rate	Paid 1994	Financial Position Mil-$ Cash& Equiv.	Curr. Assets	Curr. Liab.	Balance Sheet Date	Capitalization Lg Trm Debt Mil-$	Shs. 000 Pfd.	Com.	Earnings $ Per Shr. Years End	1991	1992	1993	1994	1995	Last 12 Mos.	Interim Earnings Period	$ per Shr. 1994	1995	Index
1	....	0.07	1-14-91	12-24	...	Nil	....	7.70	174	147	10-01-95	85.5	...	7137	Dc	d8.46	□d0.30	0.55	d1.72	....	d2.37	9 Mo Sep	0.99	0.34	1
2	....	Plan annual div			...	....	....	39.4	480	352	12-31-94	238	...	23400	Dc	*d0.19	*0.71	Δ0.88	1.04	....	1.60	9 Mo Sep	0.52	□1.08	2
3	....	None Paid			...	Nil	....	36.3	206	78.3	12-31-94	2.67	...	79567	Dc	0.24	0.26	Δ0.27	0.13	....	0.16	9 Mo Sep	0.11	0.14	3
4	1995	0.169	10-17-95	8-18	0.518	0.52	....	2.50	216	267	[54]j12-31-94	14.5	...	657428	Dc	...	...	2.34	3.06	....	3.06				4
5◆	....	None Paid			...	Nil	....	File bankruptcy Chapt 11				[56]56.7	...	15892	Dc	d0.02	d0.01	□d0.19	Δd0.84	....	d1.30	9 Mo Sep	d0.59	d1.05	5
6◆	....	None Since Public			...	Nil	....	18.4	32.0	4.24	9-30-95	0.92	...	6726	Dc	d0.18	d0.13	0.25	0.50	....	0.86	9 Mo Sep	0.30	0.66	6
7◆	....	None Since Public			...	Nil	....	....	10.5	9.32	9-30-95	14.1	...	4792	Dc	0.25	0.68	0.72	0.79	....	0.88	9 Mo Sep	0.55	0.64	7
8	1994	0.068	10-23-95	9-26	0.251	0.25	0.099	16.4	111	65.8	12-31-94	20.3	...	351531	Dc	...	...	p0.22	1.02	....	1.19	9 Mo Sep	0.63	0.80	8
9◆	....	None Since Public			...	Nil	....	209	1140	308	9-30-95	247	...	216016	Dc	0.09	0.17	0.65	[58]1.18	E1.40	1.37	9 Mo Sep	0.82	1.01	9
10	1982	Q0.14	12-15-95	11-24	0.53	0.56	0.52	Equity per shr $11.90			9-30-95	....	...	10763	Dc	0.91	0.02	Δ0.70	1.29	....	1.53	9 Mo Sep	0.90	1.14	10
11	....	None Since Public			...	Nil	....	7.60	38.8	22.0	9-30-95	2.80	...	8009	Dc	...	...	p0.22	□0.89	....	0.99	9 Mo Sep	0.67	0.77	11
12	....	None Since Public			...	Nil	....	9.05	10.9	4.71	p7-31-95	65.9	...	★11000	Dc	...	...	...	pd0.66	....	....	7 Mo Jul	n/a	pd0.49	12
13	1947	Q0.49	12-11-95	11-15	1.84	1.96	1.60	117	3784	3281	9-30-95	209	...	224004	Sp	2.83	2.96	3.15	□4.04	□4.16	4.16				13
14	....	None Since Public			...	Nil	....	14.3	95.7	36.6	9-30-95	20.9	10	40253	Mr	...	...	pd1.51	0.16	....	0.10	6 Mo Sep	0.02	d0.04	14
15	....	None Since Public			...	Nil	....	1.91	30.6	11.9	8-31-95	143	...	±10670	Fb	...	pd0.64	p0.35	±0.70	....	0.68	6 Mo Aug	0.56	0.54	15
16◆	....	None Since Public			...	Nil	....	0.02	0.02	0.27	j12-31-94	....	...	4508	Dc	n/a	n/a	n/a	n/a	....	n/a				16
17◆	....	None Paid			...	Nil	....	16.3	45.6	5.85	9-30-95	1.80	...	8601	Dc	0.30	0.48	1.08	0.39	....	0.61	9 Mo Sep	0.44	0.66	17
18◆	1944	Q0.32	12-15-95	11-29	1.28	1.28	1.28	4.32	42.1	30.1	9-30-95	195	3300	15150	Dc	1.43	1.26	1.16	[59]1.32	....	1.29	12 Mo Sep	1.25	1.29	18
19	....	0.12½	11-15-89	10-25	...	Nil	....	2.51	92.3	31.4	9-30-95	21.5	...	5195	Dc	Δ0.68	□1.20	Δ0.23	0.05	....	d0.53	9 Mo Sep	0.09	d0.49	19
20◆	....	None Since Public			...	Nil	....	3.14	11.8	7.53	9-30-95	....	...	★6500	Dc	...	...	0.04	0.08	....	0.42	9 Mo Sep	0.03	0.37	20
21	1994	[61]0.316		10-13	[61]1.564	1.56	0.269	340	492	3678	12-31-94	1397	...	8202000	Dc	0.86	1.10	0.80	1.40	....	1.45	3 Mo Mar	0.26	0.31	21
22	1989	[61]0.51	1-30-96	1-2	0.933	1.03	0.777	48.0	1488	4076	12-31-94	3016	...	260006	Dc	3.76	3.56	3.14	4.00	....	4.41	6 Mo Jun	1.90	2.31	22
23	1993	0.10	5-3-95	4-7	0.10	0.10	0.164	631	1286	712	12-31-94	1026	...	104378	Dc	1.48	1.70	1.85	0.12	....	0.12				23
24◆	....	Plan annual div			...	0.22	....	571	2191	1896	p9-30-93	748	...	★453280	Dc	Δ0.05	Δ0.48	...	....	....	j0.75	9 Mo Sep	Δ0.31	□0.58	24
25	1994	0.265	5-23-94	5-5	...	Nil	0.265	166	768	651	12-31-94	232	...	460228	Dc	*0.06	*0.61	1.12	0.20	....	0.29	9 Mo Sep	0.58	0.67	25
26	1994	0.049	9-15-95	8-23	0.089	0.09	0.026	47.4	127	81.4	12-31-94	67.0	...	111684	Dc	0.07	0.17	0.37	0.42	....	0.42				26
27	....	None Since Public			...	Nil	....	8.91	28.7	5.35	9-30-95	....	...	5541	Dc	...	*0.43	Δ0.70	1.10	....	1.38	9 Mo Sep	0.79	1.07	27
28	....	None Since Public			...	Nil	....	1.42	14.5	13.1	8-31-95	3.47	1824	3232	My	□0.57	0.08	Δd0.51	d0.62	d0.35	d0.41	3 Mo Aug	0.07	0.01	28
29	....	None Since Public			...	Nil	....	2.28	59.4	20.7	9-30-95	26.0	...	7102	Dc	0.50	0.64	0.45	0.98	....	0.34	9 Mo Sep	0.69	0.05	29
30	1943	Q0.29	12-1-95	11-13	1.14	1.16	1.10	36.7	119	138	9-30-95	132	...	10910	Sp	1.42	Δ1.54	1.77	2.19	1.77	1.77				30
31	....	1.12½	4-23-84	4-24	...	Nil	....	9.37	233	77.7	9-30-95	129	...	18497	Dc	0.52	0.01	0.49	□0.37	....	0.67	9 Mo Sep	□0.21	0.51	31
32◆	1960	Q0.10	1-3-96	12-6	0.39	0.40	0.36½	0.21	8.33	10.5	9-30-95	10.1	...	2280	Je	0.51	0.39	0.59	Δ0.57	0.68	0.63	12 Mo Sep	0.55	0.63	32
33◆	1983	Q0.29	12-15-95	11-29	1.13	1.16	1.09	0.58	17.8	28.2	9-30-95	30.1	...	3209	Sp	0.27	1.22	1.74	1.74	1.30	1.30				33
34	1993	0.18½	12-11-95	11-15	0.905	0.90	0.593	69.7	361	282	12-31-94	196	...	6279693	Dc	1.39	1.61	0.90	1.36	....	1.36				34
35◆	1981	Q0.09	12-29-95	12-11	0.35	0.36	0.307	45.0	563	391	9-30-95	212	...	144051	Dc	0.58	□0.67	□0.11	0.82	E0.97	0.95	9 Mo Sep	0.58	0.71	35
36	1995	0.01	1-31-96	12-27	0.01	0.02	....	0.13	15.3	11.3	7-31-95	2.95	...	2963	Oc	0.20	d0.07	0.15	0.21	....	0.63	9 Mo Jul	0.09	0.51	36
37	1920	0.27	12-22-95	9-29	0.824	0.82	[69]0.908	215	527	266	j12-31-94	305	...	305335	Dc	1.83	1.25	0.91	0.94	....	0.94				37
38	1992	Q0.09	12-22-95	12-14	0.36	0.36	0.32	Equity per shr $23.54			9-30-95	79.8	...	17236	Dc	1.85	2.07	2.09	1.49	....	1.90	9 Mo Sep	1.51	1.92	38
39	....	Plan annual div			...	[71]....	....	3054	20477	23688	6-30-95	8351	...	7999205	Dc	1.09	d0.80	0.18	2.48	E3.45	3.11	6 Mo Jun	1.37	2.00	39
40◆	1973	Q0.15	2-1-96	1-10	0.59	0.60	0.57	30.2	62.6	12.8	8-31-95	0.36	...	16440	Fb	Δ1.08	1.21	1.16	1.22	....	1.18	9 Mo Nov	0.89	0.85	40
41◆	1935	Q0.21¼	12-20-95	11-29	0.81¼	0.85	0.76¼	106	2017	1862	9-30-95	3425	[72]1386	251625	Dc	1.08	□1.39	1.32	[73]1.80	E2.10	1.98	9 Mo Sep	1.37	1.55	41
42	1983	2.901	1-2-96	12-6	10.922	10.50	10.50	Cv into 13.652 common				....	1417	...	Dc	b1.54	b0.68	...	....	....	....				42
43	....	Plan qtly div			...	1.36	....	Exch for com Enron O&G(or cash)re-spec cond				....	...	[75]★10000	Dc	...	...	...	....	....	....	Mature 12-13-1998			43
44	1995	Q0.20½	12-15-95	11-28	0.82	0.82	....	22.3	26.2	6.84	9-30-95	....	...	20840	Dc	...	...	p1.13	p1.45	....	1.60	9 Mo Sep	p1.06	1.21	44
45	1992	Q0.63	2-14-96	1-29	2.52	2.52	2.52	1.70	22.5	17.8	9-30-95	153	...	5650	Dc	p1.95	p[76]1.01	p1.50	1.86	....	1.78	9 Mo Sep	1.07	0.99	45
46◆	1990	Q0.03	1-31-96	1-11	0.12	0.12	0.12	8.46	192	157	9-30-95	264	[77]19	[78]159800	Dc	0.36	0.63	0.86	0.93	E0.95	0.96	9 Mo Sep	0.66	0.69	46
47◆	....	None Since Public			...	Nil	....	90.5	168	85.4	9-30-95	163	...	60595	Dc	d0.56	d1.12	Δ0.36	0.61	....	0.65	9 Mo Sep	0.47	0.51	47
48	1926	Q0.05	12-4-95	11-15	0.20	0.20	[80]0.20	8.74	431	616	9-30-95	948	175	68468	Dc	0.07	□d0.39	0.70	1.36	E0.40↓	1.25	9 Mo Sep	0.02	d0.09	48
49	1985	0.075	1-3-94	12-9	...	Nil	0.075	1.35	59.4	127	9-30-95	235	...	[81]125874	Dc	d0.48	d0.20	d0.04	p0.25	....	0.13	9 Mo Sep	p0.05	d0.07	49
50	1988	Q0.45	12-1-95	11-8	1.80	1.80	1.80	719	2613	2197	9-30-95	7058	[82]961	227756	Dc	2.64	2.48	Δ2.62	1.49	E2.35↑	2.05	9 Mo Sep	1.56	2.12	50
51	1993	0.326	11-8-95	9-22	0.806	0.81	0.65	409	564	229	j12-31-94	995	12000	492333	Dc	1.37	0.84	0.75	0.55	....	0.58	6 Mo Jun	0.05	0.08	51
52	....	None Since Public			...	Nil	....	1.08	10.1	5.82	6-30-95	....	...	★7029	Dc	0.11	0.16	0.15	0.01	....	0.06	9 Mo Sep	d0.11	d0.06	52

◆**Stock Splits & Divs By Line Reference Index** [5]1-for-5 REVERSE,'91. [6]2-for-1,'95. [7]1-for-25 REVERSE,'92. [9]3-for-2,'92:2-for-1,'93(twice). [16]1-for-5 REVERSE,'92. [17]3-for-2,'91:2-for-1,'93. [18]2-for-1,'92. [20]To split 2-for-1,ex Jan 16. [24]5-for-1,'93. [32]2-for-1,'94. [33]Adj to 3%,'91. [35]3-for-2, '92, '93, '95. [40]3-for-2,'91. [41]2-for-1,'91,'93. [46]2-for-1,'94. [47]1-for-4 REVERSE,'94.

¶ S&P 500 # MidCap 400 ✣ SmallCap 600 • Options Index	Ticker	Name of Issue (Call Price of Pfd. Stocks)	Market	Com. Rank. & Pfd. Rating	Inst. Hold Cos	Inst. Hold Shs. (000)	Principal Business	1971-93 High	1971-93 Low	1994 High	1994 Low	1995 High	1995 Low	Dec. Sales in 100s	December, 1995 Last Sale Or Bid High	Low	Last	%Div Yield	P-E Ratio	Total Return % Annualized 12 Mo	36 Mo	60 Mo
1	EEC	✓Environmental Elements	NY	C	16	1416	Design air pollut'n ctrl sys	22½	3⅞	5⅜	3⅛	3½	1⅝	2464	2	1¾	2	...	d	−38.5	−39.4	−35.0
2	EVTC	✓Environmental Technologies	NNM	NR	10	272	Mkt, sale of refrigerants	8¼	4¾	8⅝	5⅛	14⅞	7½	5834	10¼	8½	9¼	...	17	7.2	15.5	...
3	ETC	✓Environmental Tectonics	AS,Ch	C	4	50	Mfr specialty systems	8⅜	⅝	6⅛	2⅜	4⅜	2¼	1318	3⅜	2 5/16	3⅛	...	d	−19.4	−1.3	−3.6
4	ENSO	✓EnviroSource Inc	NNM	C	50	11296	Indust'l svc to steel ind/mfg	16½	⅛	4½	2¾	4¾	2½	12346	3¼	2¾	3	...	9	−11.1	−14.2	−5.6
✣5•[1]	ENVY	✓Envoy Corp	NNM	NR	42	4972	Hlth care transact'n svcs	17¾	10	23	16¼	24¼	7¼	18988	18¾	13½	17¼	...	d	−17.1	16.3	...
✣6•	ENZ	✓Enzo Biochem	AS,Ph	†B−	35	1694	Enzymes: DNA research	27⅛	9/16	18⅞	7¼	24⅝	9	56289	24⅝	17⅝	19¼	...	d	95.2	45.6	62.5
7	ENZN	✓ENZON Inc	NNM	C	22	4671	Dvlp stge:biopolymer R&D	17	1¼	5⅝	1½	4⅛	1 11/16	23473	2⅞	1 15/16	2⅛	...	d	15.2	−35.0	−23.8
8	EOT	✓EOTT Energy Partners L.P.	NY,Ch,Ph	NR	17	377	Gather/mkt crude oil	...	...	20⅛	14¾	18½	12¾	7809	18¼	17⅝	18¼	10.4	d	28.4	...	...
9	EPIC	✓Epic Design Technology	NNM	NR	72	8436	Dvlp integrated circuits	...	...	12⅜	6½	24¼	9	14200	23	19¾	21	...	..	90.3	...	...
10•[2]	EPT	✓Epitope Inc	AS,Ch,Ph	C	48	1944	Diagnostic reagents,AIDS R&D	27½	1⅞	26	13¼	21⅞	9½	29803	18	10½	16½	...	d	−25.4	−4.8	12.3
11	EKR	✓EQK Realty Inv I SBI	NY,Ch	NR	18	4174	Closed-end real estate inv tr	18¼	1½	2¾	1¾	2¼	1⅜	2411	1¾	1⅜	1½	...	d	−20.0	−14.2	−8.2
12	ENET	✓EqualNet Holding	NNM	NR	22	1841	Long distance telephone svc	...	...	...	...	21	6¾	19381	21	6¾	7¼	...	28	...	...	...
#13•[3]	EFX	✓Equifax Inc	NY,Ch,Ph	A−	375	86080	Risk mgmt & fin'l ctrl svs	13¾	½	15¼	11	21¾	12⅝	57114	21¾	19⅝	21⅜	1.5	23	67.2	32.9	24.9
14•[4]	EQ	✓Equitable Cos	NY	NR	181	42838	Insurance/financial services	31½	7⅛	30	16¾	26½	17	74916	25	22½	24	0.8	14	32.6	21.1	...
15	EIC	✓Equitable of Iowa	NY,Ch	A−	139	14950	Life insurance: dept strs	39⅜	1⅛	39¼	26⅜	38⅜	27¾	8166	36	31	32⅛	1.7	10	17.0	15.6	55.6
16	EQT	✓Equitable Resources	NY,B,Ch,Ph	B+	191	22533	Oil & gas expl:Nat'l gas dstr	44¼	2 1/16	38¾	25½	31⅜	25⅞	11007	31⅜	29¼	31¼	3.8	25	20.5	1.2	8.1
17	ECII	✓Equity Corp Intl	NNM	NR	45	2830	Funeral service:cemetery	...	...	15½	12⅝	25¼	13	6390	24½	19¼	23¾	...	40	77.6	...	...
18	ENNS	Equity Inns	NNM	NR	70	10332	Real estate investment trust	...	...	14½	8⅞	12½	9½	7414	12	11	11½	9.0	16	16.5	...	...
19	EQR	✓Equity Residential Prop Tr	NY,Ch,Ph	NR	188	30724	Real estate investment trust	36¾	26	35⅛	25¾	31⅞	24⅞	17800	31⅞	30⅛	30⅝	7.7	25	14.8	...	...
20	EQVN	EquiVision Inc[56]	NSC	NR	2	7	Oper opthalmology centers	3½	3	6	2¾	8¼	3½	6245	6⅞	5¾	6	...	40	20.0	...	...
21•[5]	ERICY	✓Ericsson(LM)Tel'B'ADR[57]	NNM	NR	426	256183	Worldwide telecommunic'ns	15⅛	⅝	15⅞	10	26¼	13½	805588	23¾	17½	19½	0.8	23	44.6	44.8	21.1
22	ERLY	ERLY Indus	NNM	B−	13	601	Rice,wine:agric chem	10½	⅝	10¼	7⅛	10½	6⅛	264	7⅝	6⅝	6¾	...	5	3.5	43.8	...
23	ERNS	✓Ernst Home Center	NNM	NR	19	1658	Bldg mtls, home improv strs	...	...	18¼	8	14¾	2⅝	9810	4⅛	2⅝	3⅛	...	d	−65.5	...	...
24	ESE	✓ESCO Electronics[59]	NY	NR	53	6360	Mfr electronic/defense prod	12⅞	2⅝	13⅜	6½	9¾	6⅝	3349	9¾	7⅞	9⅜	...	d	25.0	4.9	14.6
25	EDSE	ESELCO Inc	NNM	A−	10	178	Electric utility-Michigan	23⅝	3⅝	23½	20⅞	25	20⅝	264	23½	23	23B	s4.5	15	13.5	14.5	18.8
26	ESP	✓Espey Mfg & Electr	AS	B−	13	245	Electronic pwr supply,syst's	38	¾	15¼	12½	14¼	11⅝	170	13¼	12¾	12⅞	5.4	42	8.4	−1.6	5.8
27	ESF	Espirito Santo Finl ADS[60]	NY,Ch,Ph	NR	35	6047	Financial Svcs-Portugal	18⅛	13⅛	19¾	12⅛	14⅛	8½	19572	12⅛	8¾	11⅞	4.6	24	−6.8	...	...
28	ESST	✓ESS Technology	NNM	NR	..	...	Dvlp mixed signal semiconductors	...	...	...	...	39⅝	13¼	61951	39	22¼	23	...	38	...	...	...
29	ESSF	✓ESSEF Corp	NNM	B−	27	2796	Mfr reinforced plastic prod	20	2	18¼	12¾	18½	14	669	16¾	15¾	15¾	...	14	3.3	5.9	41.8
30	ESX	✓Essex Bancorp	AS	NR	2	7	Savings bank southeast	40	1½	7½	1⅝	6¼	⅝	882	2⅞	1⅝	1⅞	...	..	−53.1	−25.3	−43.0
31	ESEX	Essex Corp	NSC	C	6	119	Info technology/sys support	12¼	1⅛	2¾	1	3⅞	1⅛	753	2¾	2⅛	2½	...	d	100	0.0	17.3
32	ECGC	✓Essex County Gas	NNM	A	15	81	Distribute nat'l gas,Mass	30½	4¾	28½	24	25¾	22	127	25¾	25	25¾	6.2	13	14.3	8.2	13.6
33	ESS	✓Essex Property Trust	NY,Ch,Ph	NR	31	2541	Real estate investment trust	...	...	19⅝	14⅝	19¾	14⅝	2427	19¾	18½	19¼	8.7	19	40.4	...	...
34	ESL	✓Esterline Technologies	NY,Ch,Ph	†B−	74	4183	Printed circuits mfr equip	39½	1¼	14¾	6⅝	30⅜	12½	8866	24	19⅛	23¾	...	9	72.7	25.6	32.8
35	ETEC	✓Etec Systems	NNM	NR	..	...	Mask pattern generation eqp	...	...	...	...	14¼	9⅛	9976	12½	9⅛	11¼	...	18	...	...	...
✣36	ETH	✓Ethan Allen Interiors	NY,Ph	NR	107	11859	Mfr,retail home furniture	31½	16¼	32	19½	25	17¼	7705	22⅛	19⅜	20⅜	...	14	−14.7	...	...
#37•[3]	EY	✓Ethyl Corp	NY,B,Ch,P,Ph	NR	222	57146	Mfr fuel additives/pharm'l pds	33	1 3/16	19⅝	9½	13⅛	9½	61604	13⅛	12⅛	12⅜	4.0	17	...	...	...
38	ETW	✓E'town Corp	NY	B+	50	1852	Water service in New Jersey	35¾	6⅛	32	23½	30½	24¾	1890	30½	28⅜	30⅛	6.8	14	22.4	10.8	12.6
39	ETS.EC	✓ETS International	ECM	NR	2	26	Pollution control prods/svcs	3¼	15/16	2 5/16	1	2¼	1¼	876	1 9/16	1 5/16	1½	...	..	−20.0	−10.1	...
40	ETZ	Etz Lavud Ltd Ord	AS,Ch	NR	..	...	Laminates & wood products	18⅜	⅝	15¾	6⅜	10¼	6⅜	329	7	6⅜	6¾	4.1	8	−3.3	−10.1	−4.5
41	ETZ.A	Cl'A'vtg	AS	NR	..	...		13¼	5⅛	11⅞	5½	8½	5⅜	292	6	5⅝	5⅞	4.8	7	−3.7	−9.0	...
42	EVAN	✓Evans Inc	NNM	C	18	2779	Women's fur & apparel stores	18¼	½	3⅞	1¾	2⅜	1	1591	1⅝	1¼	1⅜	...	d	−35.3	−18.1	4.1
43	ESCC	✓Evans&Sutherl'd Computer	NNM	B−	52	5802	Computer graphics/softw sys	50½	3⅜	21	11¼	25¼	11¼	7070	24½	20½	22¼	...	16	...	...	...
44	EWR	✓Evans Withycombe Res	NY,Ch,Ph	NR	89	7641	Real estate investment trust	...	...	21½	17⅞	21⅝	18⅜	5748	21⅝	18⅞	21½	7.1	..	13.7	...	...
45	EJ	✓Everest/Jennings[66] Intl[67]	AS	C	7	41	Manufacture wheelchairs	17½	1 3/16	1 7/16	7/16	1 3/16	7/16	1965	11/16	7/16	9/16	...	d	12.4	−24.6	...
46	EVGM	✓Evergreen Media Corp'A'	NNM	NR	130	15323	Own, operates radio stations	23¾	16	18½	11¾	36½	14	51708	32¾	23¾	32	...	d	82.9	...	...
47	EVER	✓Evergreen Resources	NNM	B−	14	784	Oil & gas explor,dev,prod'n	325	1¼	10¾	5¼	6	3½	5500	5⅝	3⅞	5	...	d	−4.8	−20.0	12.7
48	EWB	✓E.W. Blanch Holdings	NY	NR	61	5852	Reinsurance intermediary	23½	16½	23	15¾	23⅜	16½	4724	23⅜	21¼	23⅜	1.7	18	17.8	...	...
#49•[6]	EXBT	✓Exabyte Corp	NNM,Ch	NR	137	10834	Mfr 8mm cartridge tape subsys	40⅝	6⅝	24	14	21⅝	10	59062	15⅛	12¼	14⅝	...	d	−31.6	−6.0	2.0
50•[7]	EXAR	✓Exar Corp	NNM	B−	108	8276	Mfrs integrated circuits	23	2⅞	24½	14⅜	40¼	13¾	56672	21½	13¾	14¾	...	10	−35.9	−6.7	23.5
51	EXC	✓Excel Industries	NY,Ph	B+	73	7564	Mfr vehicle window systems	21	4¼	20¼	12⅞	15⅛	11½	6668	14	11⅜	14	3.1	9	5.3	−5.0	12.0
52	XEL	✓Excel Realty Trust	NY,Ch,Ph	NR	53	5360	Real estate investment trust	21¼	17⅝	22¼	15⅝	21⅛	16⅜	4677	21⅛	19½	20½	8.7	14	40.4	...	...

Uniform Footnote Explanations-See Page 4. Other: [1]P:Cycle 3. [2]ASE:Cycle 2. [3]P:Cycle 1. [4]ASE,NY:Cycle 1. [5]CBOE,NY,Ph:Cycle 1. [6]ASE,CBOE:Cycle 2. [7]CBOE,P:Cycle 1. [51]Incl 7M subord units. [52]Incl curr amts. [53]®$1.53,'94. [54]Incl $0.0814 return of cap,'94. [55]Incl current amts. [56]Colkitt Oncology plan mgr/name chg,EquiMed Inc. [57]ADR equal 1 ord Cl'B'. [58]®$1.74,'95. [59]Trust Receipts. [60]Ea ADS rep 1 ord,$10 par. [61]Excl subsid pfd. [62]Stk dstr of Albemarle Corp. [63]Subsid pfd in $M. [64]®$1.94,'94. [65]Stk dstr of Tripos Inc,'94. [66]Ltd vtg. [67]Reclassified fr Cl'A' Nov '93. [68]Pfd in $M. [69]®$1.46,'94.

Index	Splits ◆ Cash Divs. Ea. Yr. Since	Dividends: Latest Payment Period $	Date	Ex. Div.	Total $ So Far 1995	Ind. Rate	Paid 1994	Financial Position Mil-$ Cash& Equiv.	Curr. Assets	Curr. Liab.	Balance Sheet Date	Capitalization Lg Trm Debt Mil-$	Shs. 000 Pfd.	Com.	Earnings $ Per Shr. Years End	1991	1992	1993	1994	1995	Last 12 Mos.	Interim Earnings Period	$ per Shr. 1994	1995	Index
1	....	0.03	6-1-92	4-24	...	Nil	....	5.34	25.5	20.9	9-30-95	2.76	...	6881	Mr	0.77	□d1.53	d0.98	0.01	....	d0.13	6 Mo Sep	d0.28	d0.42	1
2	....	None Since Public			...	Nil	....	1.22	14.8	5.67	6-30-95	0.72	...	4000	Sp	d0.24	*0.65	0.37	0.42	....	0.56	9 Mo Jun	0.31	0.45	2
3	....	None Paid			...	Nil	....	....	15.5	13.1	8-25-95	0.29	...	2927	Fb	0.30	0.13	d0.50	d0.49	....	d0.17	6 Mo Aug	d0.28	0.04	3
4	....	None Paid			...	Nil	....	3.31	49.4	87.5	9-30-95	257	...	40194	Dc	d1.51	d0.52	□d0.73	0.26	....	0.32	9 Mo Sep	0.10	0.16	4
5◆	....	None Since Public			...	Nil	....	8.46	18.7	5.26	9-30-95	....	...	p11248	Dc	0.61	0.38	0.41	p0.36	....	d0.14	9 Mo Sep	p0.32	d0.18	5
6	....	5%Stk	7-31-95	6-29	5%Stk	Stk	....	15.5	35.3	4.55	10-31-95	4.76	...	21372	Jl	□d0.90	Δd0.09	Δd0.34	Δ0.24	0.26	d0.56	3 Mo Oct	0.86	0.04	6
7	....	None Since Public			...	Nil	....	8.78	9.71	6.46	9-30-95	....	109	26329	Je	d0.90	d1.46	d1.15	d0.71	d0.26	d0.26	3 Mo Sep	d0.07	d0.07	7
8	1994	Q0.47½	11-14-95	10-27	1.80	1.90	0.883	1.89	478	471	9-30-95	4.73	...	[51]±17000	Dc	...	...	p0.97	p1.13	....	d3.10	9 Mo Sep	p0.90	□d3.33	8
9◆	....	None Since Public			...	Nil	....	24.8	28.4	6.37	6-30-95	....	...	12048	Sp	d0.11	...	0.06	0.12	P0.07	0.07				9
10	....	None Since Public			...	Nil	....	21.3	24.7	4.15	9-30-95	3.64	...	12491	Sp	d0.64	d0.83	d1.67	d1.56	d1.56	d1.56				10
11	....	0.10	1-31-91	12-11	...	Nil	....	Equity per shr Neg			9-30-95	81.4	...	9264	Dc	d1.97	d1.16	□d0.22	d0.37	....	d0.77	9 Mo Sep	d0.23	d0.63	11
12	....	None Since Public			...	Nil	....	4.03	26.6	16.2	9-30-95	0.06	...	6024	Je	...	...	...	p0.24	p0.38	0.26	3 Mo Sep	p0.15	p0.03	12
13◆	1913	Q0.08¼	12-15-95	11-21	0.315	0.33	0.30¼	75.5	384	297	9-30-95	258	...	p156754	Dc	□0.33	0.52	■0.43	0.81	....	0.92	9 Mo Sep	0.57	0.68	13
14	1992	Q0.05	12-22-95	11-30	0.20	0.20	0.20	Equity per shr $16.27			12-31-94	[52]4627	p60	184662	Dc	pd2.50	d0.08	1.19	□[53]1.70	E1.75	1.78	9 Mo Sep	□1.25	1.33	14
15◆	1889	Q0.135	12-14-95	11-24	0.525	0.54	0.46½	Equity per shr $22.32			9-30-95	281	...	31757	Dc	Δ1.09	□2.06	2.95	3.11	....	3.23	9 Mo Sep	2.32	2.44	15
16◆	1950	Q0.29½	12-1-95	11-13	1.18	1.18	1.15	29.7	291	458	9-30-95	415	...	34981	Dc	2.05	1.92	2.27	1.76	....	1.27	12 Mo Sep	2.03	1.27	16
17	....	None Since Public			...	Nil	....	1.62	12.7	7.08	9-30-95	39.6	...	9798	Dc	...	...	p0.51	□0.59	....	0.60	9 Mo Sep	0.43	0.44	17
18	1994	Q0.26	1-29-96	12-27	0.96	1.04	0.483	Equity per shr $9.46			9-30-95	16.6	...	14907	Dc	...	...	p0.57	0.60	....	0.70	9 Mo Sep	0.51	0.61	18
19	1993	Q0.59	1-12-96	12-27	2.11	2.36	[54]1.95½	Equity per shr $16.95			9-30-95	[55]1099	★6620	34504	Dc	...	...	p1.08	1.34	....	1.24	9 Mo Sep	1.05	0.95	19
20	....	None Since Public			...	Nil	....	1.28	9.70	5.03	9-30-95	23.4	...	8676	Dc	...	Nil	d0.07	0.12	....	0.15	9 Mo Sep	0.07	□0.10	20
21◆	1967	0.157	6-5-95	5-9	0.157	0.158	0.121	11892	51214	33184	j12-31-94	4891	...	±872000	Dc	0.19	0.08	0.38	0.60	E0.85	0.79	9 Mo Sep	0.35	0.54	21
22◆	....	5%Stk	8-15-64		...	Nil	....	2.74	118	70.4	9-30-95	104	...	4276	Mr	Δd4.72	Δd3.23	Δ1.09	[58]1.84	....	1.33	6 Mo Sep	1.12	0.61	22
23	....	None Since Public			...	Nil	....	8.61	195	100	7-29-95	105	...	12259	Oc	...	...	p0.77	Δ0.56	....	d0.29	9 Mo Jul	pΔ0.67	d0.18	23
24	....	None Since Public			...	Nil	....	3.28	220	143	6-30-95	25.0	...	10999	Sp	d6.03	0.12	0.47	0.72	Pd2.76	d2.76				24
25◆	1921	Q0.26	2-15-96	1-30	s1.015	1.04	s0.971	0.27	6.99	10.8	12-31-94	15.5	...	1414	Dc	1.35	1.39	1.46	1.56	....	1.59	9 Mo Sep	1.12	1.15	25
26	1977	A0.70	11-21-95	10-25	0.70	0.70	0.60	12.0	25.7	2.29	9-30-95	....	...	1339	Je	1.80	1.35	1.18	Δ0.85	0.37	0.31	3 Mo Sep	0.13	0.07	26
27◆	1994	0.55	6-14-95	6-6	0.55	0.55	0.65	Book Value $2.44			12-31-94	831	[61]...	30887	Dc	p1.98	p2.15	1.88	0.95	....	0.50	6 Mo Jun	0.84	0.39	27
28	....	None Since Public			...	Nil	....	14.7	33.7	13.4	6-30-95	....	...	★34831	Dc	0.09	0.08	0.01	0.22	....	0.61	9 Mo Sep	0.13	0.52	28
29	....	None Since Public			...	Nil	....	0.52	50.7	24.0	6-30-95	19.9	...	p5200	Sp	Δ0.38	▲1.22	1.08	1.22	P1.13	1.13				29
30	....	0.50	2-14-92	12-26	...	Nil	....	Book Value $13.27			9-30-95	33.3	2250	1050	Dc	d7.16	d17.10	d8.08	Δd7.22	....	....	9 Mo Sep	n/a	Δd2.58	30
31	....	None Since Public			...	Nil	....	0.18	2.52	2.50	9-24-95	0.33	...	3586	Dc	d0.38	d0.20	d1.04	d0.26	....	d0.66	9 Mo Sep	d0.14	d0.54	31
32	1915	Q0.40	1-1-96	12-13	1.56	1.60	1.52	0.14	10.9	21.5	8-31-95	21.3	3	1607	Au	1.48	1.79	1.95	2.12	2.00	2.00				32
33	1994	Q0.42½	1-16-96	12-27	1.67¾	1.68	0.49¾	Equity per shr $13.05			9-30-95	136	...	6275	Dc	...	...	p1.02	p1.02	....	1.04	9 Mo Sep	p0.79	□0.81	33
34	....	0.18	7-31-86	6-30	...	Nil	....	22.1	142	106	10-31-95	35.5	...	6659	Oc	1.12	0.76	d3.90	1.15	2.53	2.53				34
35	....	None Since Public			...	Nil	....	23.6	75.4	52.1	p7-31-95	p13.3	p...	★16508	Jl	...	...	...	....	p0.61	0.61				35
36	....	None Since Public			...	Nil	....	7.73	177	57.5	9-30-95	119	...	14377	Je	...	pd0.23	p1.12	1.53	Δ□1.56	1.47	3 Mo Sep	Δ0.40	0.31	36
37◆	1957	Q0.12½	1-1-96	12-13	0.50	0.50	h[62]0.525	24.3	388	145	9-30-95	312	...	118434	Dc	1.75	□2.27	□1.52	0.83	E0.75	0.64	9 Mo Sep	0.62	0.43	37
38◆	1881	Q0.51	12-21-95	12-5	2.04	2.04	2.04	1.78	30.6	82.1	9-30-95	154	[63]12	7458	Dc	2.32	2.21	2.59	[64]1.95	....	2.22	12 Mo Sep	1.92	2.22	38
39	....	None Paid			...	Nil	....	0.03	6.06	5.66	8-31-95	0.85	...	12476	My	*Nil	0.01	d0.08	0.01	0.04	0.01	3 Mo Aug	0.01	d0.02	39
40◆	1990	t0.15	1-9-95	12-13	0.15	0.28	t0.27½	27.0	159	75.7	j12-31-92	38.4	...	±3218	Dc	1.25	0.71	...	....	....	0.87	9 Mo SepΔ	0.53	0.69	40
41	1992	t0.15	1-9-95	12-13	t0.19	0.28	t0.27½	....	...	...		....	...	1744	Dc	1.25	0.71	...	....	....	0.87	9 Mo Sep	0.53	0.69	41
42	....	0.01	10-14-87	9-21	...	Nil	....	0.16	31.4	17.8	8-26-95	9.61	...	4918	Fb	d0.52	*0.21	Δ0.09	d2.45	....	d2.80	6 Mo Aug	d0.51	d0.86	42
43	....	h[65]....	6-1-94	6-2	...	Nil	h[65]....	94.6	156	46.4	9-29-95	18.0	...	8699	Dc	Δ1.07	Δ0.78	Δ0.22	Δd0.65	....	1.36	9 Mo Sep	Δd0.24	Δ1.77	43
44	1994	Q0.38	1-11-96	12-27	1.49	1.52	0.18	Equity per shr $12.37			9-30-95	241	...	16104	Dc	...	...	p0.40	p0.51	....	....	9 Mo Sep	n/a	0.73	44
45	....	0.05	6-9-89	5-22	...	Nil	....	0.24	38.5	33.0	9-30-95	35.9	28004	72266	Dc	d1.87	d2.07	d5.96	d0.14	....	d0.13	9 Mo Sep	d0.05	d0.04	45
46	....	None Since Public			...	Nil	....	1.41	49.2	20.0	9-30-95	207	1610	±18695	Dc	...	pd1.46	d6.72	□d0.55	....	d1.02	9 Mo Sep	d0.22	d0.69	46
47	....	None Paid			...	Nil	....	4.07	5.57	1.39	9-30-95	....	[68]8	5674	Mr	d0.08	0.15	0.01	d0.13	....	d0.13	6 Mo Sep	d0.06	d0.06	47
48	1993	Q0.10	12-1-95	11-8	0.40	0.40	0.32	6.49	31.6	20.3	9-30-95	0.35	...	13208	Dc	p0.50	p0.75	p0.97	1.22	....	1.28	9 Mo Sep	1.07	1.13	48
49	....	None Since Public			...	Nil	....	59.5	190	55.3	9-30-95	0.81	...	21780	Dc	1.51	0.95	0.76	1.48	Ed0.50	d0.29	9 Mo Sep	1.06	d0.71	49
50◆	....	None Since Public			...	Nil	....	67.4	116	28.2	9-30-95	....	...	9818	Mr	1.15	1.33	Δ1.50	d1.25	E1.50↓	0.46	6 Mo Sep	d1.01	0.70	50
51	1984	Q0.11	1-19-96	1-3	0.44	0.44	0.34	44.0	188	88.0	9-30-95	32.3	...	10703	Dc	0.02	□0.47	1.23	[69]1.60	....	1.54	9 Mo Sep	1.24	1.18	51
52	1993	Q0.44½	1-15-96	12-27	1.75	1.78	1.69	Equity per shr $15.91			9-30-95	201	...	13115	Dc	...	p0.85	0.55	1.27	....	1.44	9 Mo Sep	0.95	1.12	52

◆**Stock Splits & Divs By Line Reference Index** [5]No adj for First Data mgr/dstr,'95. [9]2-for-1,'95. [13]2-for-1,'95. [15]2-for-1,'92,'93. [16]3-for-2,'93. [21]4-for-1,'95. [22]15%,'95. [25]3-for-2,'93:Adj to 3%,'95. [27]2-for-1,'94. [37]No adj for stk dstr of Albemarle Corp,'94:No adj for stk dstr of First Colony Corp,'93. [38]3-for-2,'91. [40]2-for-1 in Cl'A','91. [50]3-for-2,'94.

Index	Ticker	Name of Issue (Call Price of Pfd. Stocks)	Market	Com. Rank. & Pfd. Rating	Inst. Hold Cos	Inst. Hold Shs. (000)	Principal Business	Price Range 1971-93 High	1971-93 Low	1994 High	1994 Low	1995 High	1995 Low	Dec. Sales in 100s	December, 1995 Last Sale Or Bid High	Low	Last	%Div Yield	P-E Ratio	Total Return % Annualized 12 Mo	36 Mo	60 Mo
1	XLTC	✔Excel Technology	NNM	NR	15	1864	Mfr laser products & systems	8	2⅞	7¾	4⅜	7⅛	3⅜	30605	7⅛	5⅞	6⅝	...	24	39.5	26.8	...
2	ER	✔Executive Risk	NY,Ch	NR	52	4806	Underwrites liab insur	...	...	15⅞	10⅞	29	13⅝	2164	29	25⅝	29	0.3	14	114	...	...
3	EXTL	✔Executive Telecard Ltd	NNM	NR	17	728	Intl telephone calling svc	13⅝	1 3/16	11⅝	3⅛	9⅛	3⅛	18192	7⅞	5¾	6	...	d	35.1	19.9	16.4
4	XL	✔EXEL Limited	NY,Ph	NR	111	22628	Provides excess liability insur	52¼	25½	45⅜	36	65½	38⅝	11016	65½	59¼	60⅞	2.6	12	59.1	11.9	...
5•[1]	EX	✔Exide Corp	NY	NR	148	16390	Mfr starting, ignit'n batteries	29⅜	20	56¼	26½	57½	29½	19291	48	44⅜	45⅞	0.2	25	−17.0	...	...
6	XUPS	✔Exide Electronics Group	NNM	B−	52	3306	Mfr power supply products	27¼	6	25¾	14½	25½	13⅞	15275	16¾	13⅞	14¾	...	18	−14.5	−14.1	16.9
7	EXGN	✔Exogen Inc	NNM	NR	26	2191	Dvp/mfr medical devices	...	...	...	...	20¾	11	6872	20¾	16¼	19¼	...	d	...	...	...
8	EXPD	✔Expeditors Intl,Wash[53]	NNM	B+	105	9699	Int'l air freight forward'g	17⅞	2 7/16	23¼	15	28¼	19¾	10763	26¾	22¾	26⅛	0.5	20	22.1	21.2	24.3
9	XPRT	✔Expert Software	NNM	NR	47	3030	Dvlp/mkt computer software	...	...	...	...	24¼	12	13708	17	12¾	14	...	33	...	...	...
10	EXAM	✔Express America Hldgs	NNM	NR	17	1944	Hldg co-mortgage banking	18	7½	11¾	3½	6⅞	3⅛	9516	5¼	3⅛	3½	...	d	−12.5	−34.6	...
✣11	ESRX	✔Express Scripts 'A'	NNM	NR	81	5090	Health care management svcs	23½	6¼	38¼	22	55	25	6011	55	41¼	51	...	45	45.7	46.5	...
12	EXTR	✔Exstar Financial	NNM	NR	10	1114	Casualty insur hld/underwrit'g	18¼	8¾	11½	3½	5⅛	⅞	3252	2	1	1⅛	...	d	−70.0	−56.6	...
13	STAY	Extended Stay Amer	NNM	NR	..	...	Own/oper lodging facilities	...	...	...	...	28	13	88369	28	13	27½	...	..	...	...	...
14	EXX.A	✔EXX Inc Cl'A'	AS	B−	8	72	Toys,machinery,electr mtrs	3⅝	3/16	34⅞	1⅝	26⅞	5	3235	8	5	5¼	...	5	−69.6	58.1	84.3
15	EXX.B	Cl'B'	AS	B−	7	17		...	...	34	8⅞	25¾	4½	749	7⅝	4½	4⅞	...	4	−71.9	...	...
¶16•[2]	XON	✔Exxon Corp	NY,B,C,Ch,P,Ph	B+	1434	504658	World's leading oil co	69	6⅞	67⅜	56⅛	86	60⅛	339495	86	77⅛	80½	3.7	16	37.8	14.5	14.5
17	EZPW	✔EZCORP Inc'A'	NNM	NR	37	1759	Acquire, operate pawnshops	28	9	17½	9½	12¼	4⅛	20188	5⅞	4¼	4¾	...	d	−55.3	−41.3	...
18	FBTC	✔F B & T Financial[55]	NNM	NR	1	23	General banking, Virginia	16	15	16⅝	13⅜	33	14¾	372	33	32¼	32½	s1.9	17	139	...	...
19	FMBN	✔F&M Bancorp	NNM	B+	14	260	General banking, Maryland	22¼	13⅝	29	20⅞	30	25½	261	30	28¾	29¾	s2.7	16	14.0	28.4	...
20	FMN	✔F&M National Corp	NY,Ch	A	42	1918	Commercial bkg,Virginia	17½	2⅞	17¾	14⅝	20	15¼	2199	20	18⅜	20	3.2	14	32.8	10.7	22.2
21	FIT	✔Fab Indus	AS,Ph	A−	51	2728	Warp knit textile producer	36¾	¼	36⅛	30	32¾	29	1469	31⅞	29½	31⅞	2.2	16	5.2	4.4	16.8
✣22	FCA.A	✔Fabri-Centers Amer'A'	NY,Ch,Ph	B−	72	5529	Fabric/housewares retail strs	23⅝	9/16	9⅜	5⅞	16⅛	7⅞	6842	15	12¼	13¼	...	15	53.8	24.1	9.7
23	FCA.B	Cl'B'(non-vtg)	NY	B−	39	5169		...	...	...	...	13⅞	9¾	8021	12⅜	9¾	10¾	...	12	...	...	...
24	FACE	Facelifters Home Systems[56]	NNM	NR	9	274	Kitchen cabinet refacing prd	6½	¾	8½	4⅛	13⅞	5⅜	16483	13⅞	10⅛	13½	0.1	..	84.3	81.9	...
25	FAC	✔Factory Stores of America	NY,Ph	NR	68	2939	Real estate investment trust	29½	23	28⅞	19⅜	23¼	12¼	26829	18⅛	12¼	13⅛	15.5	17	−33.3	...	...
26	FAHNF	Fahnestock Viner Hldgs'A'	NNM	B−	21	2129	Securities brokerage svcs	9⅞	1 1/16	9⅞	5¾	10½	6¼	1900	9⅜	8⅛	9¼	1.6	7	50.6	12.8	51.1
27	FAI	FAI Insurances Ltd ADS[60]	NY	NR	4	103	Insur/fin'l svcs, Australia	18¼	1½	5	2⅝	2¾	1⅞	931	2⅝	2	2⅝	2.3	d	−2.9	22.2	−7.8
28	FICI	✔Fair Isaac & Co	NNM	B+	75	3546	Dvlp credit evaluation sys	11¼	1¾	28⅝	10½	30¾	17	2189	29¼	24¾	25⅞	0.2	26	−3.2	61.6	62.6
29	FA	✔Fairchild Corp 'A'	NY,Ch,P	C	17	2735	Aerospace fastners/Ind Prd	17⅛	⅝	4⅞	2⅝	8¾	2	9526	8¾	7⅜	8½	...	d	143	21.4	7.5
30	FENPrA	Fairchild Indus$3.60cmCv[62]Pfd	NY,B,Ch	B−	1	5	Subsid of Fairchild Corp	53¼	23⅛	38¾	35½	44	35½	37	44	42	41B	8.8	..	...	...	...
31	FFD	✔Fairfield Communities	NY	NR	23	1682	Dvlp/oper resort,home dvlpm'tsd2=np	4⅝	2¾	7	4	8¼	4½	8662	7⅜	5⅞	7⅛	...	12	26.7	...	...
32	FB	✔Falcon Building Products'A'	NY	NR	29	3442	Mfr constr'n/hme improv prd	...	...	12⅛	10	11¾	7⅜	7372	9¾	8⅛	9⅝	...	9	−12.5	...	...
33	FAL	✔Falcon Cable Sys L.P.[64]	AS	NR	25	1883	Cable TV system,Calif	22⅛	6⅛	14⅛	5¾	11½	6⅛	1785	11½	10½	11	...	d	80.7	6.8	15.0
34	FLCN	✔Falcon Drilling	NNM	NR	27	3939	Contract drilling:oil/gas	...	...	...	...	15¼	9	22066	15¼	12⅝	15	...	63	...	...	...
35	FCP	✔Falcon Products	NY	B+	48	4723	Contract furniture:food sv eq	15⅞	⅜	11⅜	8⅜	13⅜	10	2630	13¼	12⅜	13⅛	0.8	16	26.4	12.0	36.0
36	FBAR	Family Bargain	NSC	NR	3	24	Oper off-price retail stores	94½	7⅛	8¼	2 7/16	2⅝	⅝	9034	1 11/16	1 1/16	1⅜	...	d	−48.2	−43.0	...
#37•[3]	FDO	✔Family Dollar Stores	NY,B,Ch,P,Ph	A−	141	35845	Self-service retail stores	24⅝	1/16	18⅜	9⅞	19¾	10⅞	40873	16⅜	13½	13¾	2.9	13	17.7	−14.3	21.3
38	FNL	✔Fansteel Inc	NY,Ch	↑B	26	2932	Mfrs specialty metal prod	19⅜	1 1/16	8	6⅛	8¼	5¾	1102	7⅛	6⅝	6⅞	...	17	10.4	−1.5	−5.6
39	FEB	✔Far East National Bank	AS	NR	6	176	Commercial banking, Calif	8⅝	4¼	8	5½	10⅜	6¼	368	10⅜	8½	10⅜	...	11	56.9	47.7	...
40	FRA	✔Farah Inc	NY,B,Ch,P,Ph	↓C	44	4995	Mfr men, boys & girls apparel	49¼	2⅜	21⅞	6⅝	9	4¾	8035	6⅜	4¾	4¾	...	d	−33.3	−12.6	10.6
41	FARC	✔Farr Co	NNM	C	19	1129	Filters & filtration systems	16¼	7/16	7⅜	4⅛	9½	5⅞	1277	8	7	8	...	12	36.2	7.2	−4.8
#42•[4]	FAST	✔Fastenal Co	NNM	B+	146	20246	Fasteners/constrn supply strs	15⅞	¾	23	14½	43	19⅞	45180	42¾	38¼	42¼	0.0	63	102	57.4	59.1
✣43	FAY	✔Fay's Inc	NY,Ch,Ph	↑A−	71	5256	Discount super drug stores	12⅝	⅛	8	6	9⅜	6¼	12307	8¼	6½	7½	2.7	17	20.7	2.9	5.6
✣44•[5]	FJC	✔Fedders Corp	NY,B,Ch,P,Ph	↑B−	65	5762	Air conditioners:heat transf	26⅝	1 5/16	5¾	3⅜	7⅞	4¾	22590	5¾	5	5¾	1.4	8	7.0	29.3	12.4
45	FJA	Cl'A' (non-vtg)	NY	↑B−	54	5323		...	...	4⅜	3¼	5½	3⅝	17383	4⅜	3⅞	4¼	1.9	6	6.4	...	...
¶46•[2]	FDX	✔Federal Express	NY,B,Ch,P	B−	434	44848	Air-van package delivery sv	75½	3	80¾	53½	86	58½	64784	82⅝	68½	73⅞	...	13	23.1	11.4	17.0
¶47•[6]	FRE	✔Federal Home Loan	NY,Ch,P	NR	723	144658	Provides Residential Mtg fds	56¾	10⅛	62⅞	47	83⅝	49⅞	80897	83⅝	76⅛	83½	1.4	15	70.2	22.2	41.6
#48•[7]	FMO	✔Federal-Mogul	NY,Ch,P,Ph	B−	173	20379	Mfr bearings:transmis'n pr	30	3	37⅝	18⅝	23¾	16¾	27899	21½	19	19⅝	2.4	16	1.1	9.0	9.5
¶49•[8]	FNM	✔Federal Natl Mtge	NY,B,C,Ch,P,Ph	A−	1262	225587	Provides residential mtg fds	86⅛	2⅛	90⅜	68⅛	126	68¾	181776	126	109¼	123⅞	2.2	14	75.9	21.5	32.0
¶50•[7]	FBO	✔Federal Paper Board[72]	NY,B,Ch,P,Ph	B	364	37245	Boxboards & folding cartons,	33⅞	1⅞	32	20⅜	53	26⅝	80654	52⅜	50⅛	51⅞	3.1	10	85.5	32.9	28.6
51	Pr B	$1.20 cm Cv Pfd(20.00)vtg	NY	NR	1	.1	pulp,bleached paperboard	164¾	12¼	145½	102	258	141½	1	258	258	260½B	0.5	..	...	...	...
52	FRT	✔Federal Rlty Inv Tr SBI	NY,Ch	NR	141	17687	Real estate investment trust	30¼	1 11/16	29½	19⅝	23⅝	19¾	7828	23½	21¾	22¾	7.2	30	17.9	3.9	17.5

¶ S&P 500 # MidCap 400 ✣ SmallCap 600 • Options

Uniform Footnote Explanations-See Page 4. Other: [1]P,Ph:Cycle 2. [2]CBOE:Cycle 1. [3]Ph:Cycle 1. [4]ASE:Cycle 2. [5]NY:Cycle 1. [6]ASE:Cycle 1. [7]P:Cycle 1. [8]Ph:Cycle 3. [51]®$1.69,'94. [52]®$1.05,'04. [53]Plan SmallCap 600 listing:eff Jan 3. [54]9 Mo Sep,'91. [55]F&M Natl plan acq. [56]AMRE Inc plan acq, $11.28. [57]Incl $0.035 non-taxable:©$0.028,'94. [58]9 Mo Dec'93. [59]®$0.93,'94. [60]Each ADR rep 5 ord shrs $0.10(Aust'l). [61]Special divd. [62]Cm:Callable at $45. [63]®$1.05,'94. [64]Units of Benef Int. [65]Spl div(Approx). [66]Fiscal Dec'91 & prior. [67]4 Mo Apr'92:12 Mo Apr'93loss&12.07. [68]8 Mo Aug'91. [69]8 Mo Aug,'91. [70]L-T-D as of 12-31-94. [71]®$1.46,'94. [72]Intl Paper prop acq,cash or stk to Jan 2. [73]®$1.52,'94. [74]Incl $0.7512 non-taxable,'94.

Common and Convertible Preferred Stocks

Splits ◆ Index	Cash Divs. Ea. Yr. Since	Dividends: Latest Payment Period $	Date	Ex. Div.	Total $ So Far 1995	Ind. Rate	Paid 1994	Financial Position Mil-$ Cash& Equiv.	Curr. Assets	Curr. Liab.	Balance Sheet Date	Capitalization Lg Trm Debt Mil-$	Shs. 000 Pfd.	Com.	Earnings $ Per Shr. Years End	1991	1992	1993	1994	1995	Last 12 Mos.	Interim Earnings Period	$ per Shr. 1994	1995	Index
1	....	None Since Public			...	Nil	....	12.6	32.6	10.4	9-30-95	5.31	409	8322	Dc	d0.47	d2.03	0.41	0.22	....	0.28	9 Mo Sep	0.17	0.23	1
2	1995	Q0.02	12-29-95	12-13	0.08	0.08	....	Equity per shr $14.58			9-30-95	25.0	...	±11496	Dc	...	...	p2.40	±[51]1.80	....	2.11	9 Mo Sep	±1.24	±1.55	2
3◆	....	None Since Public			...	Nil	....	2.23	7.46	9.22	9-30-95	0.61	...	14406	Mr	0.02	0.05	0.10	d0.39	....	d0.28	6 Mo Sep	d0.03	0.08	3
4	1992	Q0.40	10-26-95	10-10	1.39	1.60	1.23	Equity per shr $32.42			11-30-94	....	...	51953	Nv	4.83	5.01	6.82	2.65	E5.25	4.56	9 Mo Aug	2.71	4.62	4
5	1994	Q0.02	12-13-95	11-20	0.08	0.08	0.08	51.6	1407	787	10-01-95	1165	...	20578	Mr	...	□p0.49	□1.56	□0.28	E1.85	d0.62	6 Mo Sep	□0.68	d0.22	5
6	....	None Since Public			...	Nil	....	2.02	184	88.0	6-30-95	62.3	10	8373	Sp	Δd1.29	0.82	Δ1.25	[52]1.10	P0.84	0.84				6
7	....	None Since Public			...	Nil	....	6.86	8.92	0.68	3-31-95	0.02	p...	★9475	Sp	...	...	pd0.32	pd0.48	Pd0.93	d0.93				7
8◆	1993	S0.06	12-15-95	11-29	0.12	0.12	0.10	27.0	187	108	9-30-95	....	...	12013	Dc	0.87	0.93	0.85	1.08	....	1.30	9 Mo Sep	0.76	0.98	8
9	....	None Since Public			...	Nil	....	17.1	23.7	5.42	9-30-95	....	...	7146	Dc	...	...	d0.47	0.38	....	0.42	9 Mo Sep	0.29	0.33	9
10	....	None Since Public			...	Nil	....	Equity per shr $1.77			6-30-95	....	...	4878	Sp	p‡[54]2.04	1.42	d0.47	□d1.35	....	d1.24	9 Mo Jun	d0.38	d0.27	10
11◆	....	None Since Public			...	Nil	....	4.70	128	75.7	9-30-95	....	...	±15023	Dc	±p0.26	±0.36	±0.55	±0.84	....	1.13	9 Mo Sep	±0.60	±0.89	11
12	....	None Since Public			...	Nil	....	Equity per shr $1.14			9-30-95	2.46	...	5498	Dc	p0.78	p0.37	0.35	d0.45	....	d0.40	9 Mo Sep	d0.21	d0.16	12
13	....	None Since Public			...	Nil	....	124	124	1.62	9-30-95	....	...	★21471	Dc	...	...	...	n/a	....	....	9 Mo Sep	n/a	pd0.13	13
14◆	....	0.01½	10-1-82	9-13	...	Nil	....	5.10	13.4	4.41	9-30-95	....	...	±2708	Dc	0.16	0.19	0.22	±0.99	....	1.18	9 Mo Sep	±0.53	±0.72	14
15	....	None Since Public			...	Nil	....	....	...	...		....	...	677	Dc	0.15	0.18	0.22	±0.99	....	1.18	9 Mo Sep	±0.53	±0.72	15
16	1882	Q0.75	12-11-95	11-9	3.00	3.00	2.91	2537	17498	18583	9-30-95	8362	8000	1241678	Dc	4.45	Δ□3.82	4.21	4.07	E5.08	5.36	9 Mo Sep	2.54	3.83	16
17	....	None Since Public			...	Nil	....	2.84	114	8.39	6-30-95	41.5	...	±11987	Sp	*0.20	0.33	0.56	±0.15	P±d1.32	d1.32				17
18◆	1994	Q0.154	11-15-95	10-30	s0.601	0.62	0.533	Book Value $11.60			9-30-95	....	...	1237	Dc	...	1.02	1.90	1.87	....	1.95	9 Mo Sep	1.36	1.44	18
19◆	1992	Q0.20	11-1-95	10-18	s0.781	0.80	s0.743	Book Value $14.03			9-30-95	....	...	4413	Dc	Δ1.42	1.73	1.84	1.92	....	1.87	9 Mo Sep	1.36	1.31	19
20◆	1970	Q0.16	1-23-96	12-21	0.61	0.64	s0.574	Book Value $11.36			9-30-95	3.51	...	16551	Dc	1.08	1.24	1.30	1.31	....	1.46	9 Mo Sep	0.92	1.07	20
21◆	1976	Q0.17½	12-21-95	12-6	0.68½	0.70	0.64	58.2	120	15.0	9-02-95	0.69	...	5926	Nv	2.52	2.65	2.75	2.44	....	1.96	9 Mo Aug	1.65	1.17	21
22◆	....	0.024	6-12-87	5-18	...	Nil	....	12.8	403	147	10-28-95	195	...	±18481	Ja	0.95	Δ0.12	Δ0.10	0.63	....	0.91	9 Mo Oct	±d0.13	±0.15	22
23	....	None Since Public			...	Nil	....	....	...	...		....	...	9213	Ja	0.95	Δ0.11	Δ0.09	0.63	....	0.91	9 Mo Oct	±d0.13	±0.15	23
24	1994	0.00½	12-15-95	11-29	0.02	0.02	0.00½	2.58	8.95	6.47	9-30-95	1.66	...	3399	Mr	d0.78	*0.13	0.31	d0.13	....	0.09	6 Mo Sep	d0.24	d0.02	24
25	1993	Q0.51	1-11-96	12-18	2.01	2.04	[57]1.89	Equity per shr $16.34			9-30-95	159	...	11814	Dc	...	p1.69	‡[58]0.86	□1.11	....	0.78	9 Mo Sep	0.96	0.63	25
26	1993	A0.15	2-24-95	2-6	0.15	0.15	0.15	10.3	671	574	9-30-95	0.03	...	±11930	Dc	±0.83	±1.18	±1.59	±[59]0.96	....	1.26	9 Mo Sep	±0.88	±1.18	26
27	1994	0.032	5-1-95	3-30	0.032	0.06	0.064	576	1431	939	j6-30-95	j413	...	306140	Je	d2.27	d0.76	d0.13	0.02	d1.07	d1.07				27
28◆	1989	S0.02	12-15-95	11-29	0.075	0.04	0.07	14.2	47.8	23.4	9-30-95	1.93	...	12311	Sp	0.24	0.33	0.44	0.80	1.00	1.00				28
29	....	[61]0.20	10-11-91	9-24	...	Nil	....	56.6	280	179	10-01-95	503	...	±16103	Je	Δ±1.07	Δd1.42	□d2.70	□1.70	Δd2.12	d1.97	3 Mo Sep	d0.42	d0.27	29
30	1981	Q0.90	1-17-96	12-29	3.60	3.60	3.60	Cv into $27.18				....	1132	...	Je	b1.54	...	...	....	....	....	Redeem 10% ea Jan 31,$45			30
31	....	None Paid			...	Nil	....	Equity per shr $5.42			12-31-94	....	...	p9972	Dc	...	‡0.11	±0.65	[63]1.11	....	0.62	9 Mo Sep	1.04	0.55	31
32	....	None Since Public			...	Nil	....	6.80	81.6	84.2	9-30-95	119	...	±20071	Dc	...	...	±□p1.01	p±1.30	....	1.13	9 Mo Sep	±p0.99	±0.82	32
33	1987	[65]0.386	3-31-95	3-20	[65]0.386	Nil	....	Equity per shr Neg			9-30-95	170	...	6399	Dc	d1.62	d1.39	d0.85	d1.12	....	d0.28	9 Mo Sep	d0.83	0.01	33
34	....	None Since Public			...	Nil	....	7.19	46.9	33.0	9-30-95	p176	...	★35067	Dc	...	...	...	p0.21	....	0.24	9 Mo Sep	0.08	0.11	34
35◆	1994	Q0.02½	1-17-96	12-29	0.073	0.10	0.041	6.93	35.3	8.20	4-29-95	1.29	...	9507	Oc	0.42	0.48	0.51	0.65	P0.84	0.84				35
36◆	....	None Paid			...	Nil	....	0.14	36.7	17.0	10-28-95	29.8	3200	4008	Ja	[66]d0.36	‡[67]0.14	pd0.17	pd1.13	....	d1.63	9 Mo Oct	Δpd0.58	d1.08	36
37◆	1976	Q0.10	1-15-96	12-13	0.38½	0.40	0.33	8.85	475	210	8-31-95	....	...	56744	Au	0.72	1.00	1.15	Δ1.10	1.03	1.03				37
38	1973	0.10	9-12-95	8-30	0.30	Nil	0.40	8.70	38.3	17.7	9-30-95	0.02	...	8599	Dc	d1.55	0.61	Δ0.10	0.42	....	0.41	9 Mo Sep	0.32	0.31	38
39◆	....	....			...	Nil	....	Book Value $7.11			12-31-94	5.31	...	5136	Dc	0.93	0.95	0.75	0.63	....	0.91	6 Mo Jun	0.21	0.49	39
40	....	0.22	12-1-86	10-28	...	Nil	....	2.98	134	80.5	8-04-95	12.1	...	10133	Oc	d0.93	d1.52	0.02	1.16	Pd1.28	d1.28				40
41	....	0.06	3-6-92	2-14	...	Nil	....	0.25	40.6	18.9	9-30-95	14.6	...	3793	Dc	d0.83	□d1.12	□0.39	d0.10	....	0.66	9 Mo Sep	d0.21	0.55	41
42◆	1991	A0.02	2-28-95	2-8	0.02	0.02	0.02	2.58	74.8	14.1	9-30-95	....	...	37939	Dc	0.18	0.24	0.31	0.49	....	0.67	9 Mo Sep	0.35	0.53	42
43◆	1975	Q0.05	1-5-96	12-20	0.20	0.20	0.20	1.63	229	141	10-28-95	75.4	...	20595	Ja	0.44	0.56	□0.50	0.62	....	0.43	9 Mo Oct	0.33	0.14	43
44◆	....	Q0.02	3-1-96	2-14	0.04	0.08	....	57.7	99.4	43.3	8-31-95	4.52	...	±40087	Au	[68]d0.32	■d0.70	d0.05	Δ0.49	0.72	0.76	3 Mo Nov	d0.03	0.01	44
45◆	....	Q0.02	3-1-96	2-14	0.04	0.08	....	....	...	...		....	...	18831	Au	[69]d0.32	■d0.70	d0.05	Δ0.49	0.72	0.76	3 Mo Nov	d0.03	0.01	45
46	....	None Since Public			...	Nil	....	207	1730	1737	8-31-95	1319	...	56495	My	0.11	d2.11	□2.01	3.65	5.27	5.56	6 Mo Nov	2.61	2.90	46
47◆	1989	Q0.30	12-29-95	12-7	1.20	1.20	1.04	Equity per shr $25.80			12-31-94	[70]44746	34500	180762	Dc	3.08	3.29	4.07	Δ5.32	E5.75	5.46	9 Mo Sep	□4.02	4.16	47
48	1936	Q0.12	12-11-95	11-28	0.48	0.48	0.48	22.2	904	427	9-30-95	467	2526	34996	Dc	d0.36	d0.01	1.13	[71]1.55	E1.20↓	1.22	9 Mo Sep	1.27	0.94	48
49◆	1956	Q0.68	11-25-95	10-27	2.72	2.72	2.40	Equity per shr $34.97			12-31-94	144628	...	272802	Dc	□5.33	□6.01	□7.44	□7.80	E8.60	8.34	9 Mo Sep	□5.81	□6.35	49
50	1948	Q0.40	1-15-96	12-27	1.40	1.60	1.00	0.29	438	337	9-09-95	816	2210	47183	Dc	1.83	Δ1.82	0.34	[73]1.55	E5.05	4.68	36 Wk Sep	0.46	3.59	50
51	1972	Q0.30	3-15-96	2-27	1.20	1.20	1.20	Cv into 5.02 shrs common				....	52	...	Dc	b1.76	b2.40	b1.15	b1.69	....	....				51
52	1962	Q0.41	1-12-96	12-28	1.59½	1.64	[74]1.56½	Equity per shr $10.29			9-30-95	469	...	32148	Dc	Δ0.25	□0.41	Δ0.60	0.67	....	0.76	9 Mo Sep	0.47	0.56	52

◆**Stock Splits & Divs By Line Reference Index** [3]10%,'92,'93(twice),'94,'95. [8]2-for-1,'93. [11]2-for-1,'94. [14]4-for-1(3 Cl'A',1 Cl'B'),'94. [18]Adj for 5%,'95. [19]Adj for 5%,'95. [20]Adj for 2.5%,'94. [21]2-for-1,'91. [22]3-for-2,'91:2-for-1 in Cl'B','95. [28]2-for-1,'95. [35]3-for-2,'93:10%,'95. [36]1-for-3 REVERSE,'92:1-for-6 REVERSE,'94. [37]2-for-1,'92. [39]12%,'93:10%,'93,'94. [42]2-for-1,'92,'95. [43]5-for-4,'92. [44]3-for-2 in Cl'A':5-for-4 in Cl'A','95. [45]5-for-4,'95. [47]3-for-1,'92. [49]To split 4-for-1,hldrs Jan 8.

¶ S&P 500 # MidCap 400 ✣ SmallCap 600 • Options Index	Ticker	Name of Issue (Call Price of Pfd. Stocks)	Market	Com. Rank. & Pfd. Rating	Inst. Hold Cos	Inst. Hold Shs. (000)	Principal Business	Price Range 1971-93 High	1971-93 Low	1994 High	1994 Low	1995 High	1995 Low	Dec. Sales in 100s	December, 1995 Last Sale Or Bid High	Low	Last	%Div Yield	P-E Ratio	Total Return % Annualized 12 Mo	36 Mo	60 Mo
#1•[1]	FSS	✓Federal Signal	NY,B,Ch,P,Ph	A+	184	23789	Special trucks,tools,signals	21	3/16	21 3/8	16 7/8	25 7/8	19 5/8	14831	25 7/8	22 5/8	25 7/8	1.9	22	27.6	20.1	23.5
¶2•[2]	FD	✓Federated Dept Stores	NY,Ph	NR	481	172706	Operates department strs-U.S.	25	11 1/4	25 1/4	18	30 1/8	17 7/8	188339	29 1/8	26 1/8	27 1/4	...	36	41.6	11.1	...
3	WS.C	Wrrt'C'(Pur1com $25.93)	NY,Ph	....	35	2716		....	....	6	4 1/2	10 1/4	3 3/4	3660	8 7/8	7 1/4	8	...	..	...	...	...
4	WS.D	Wrrt'D'(Pur1com $29.92)	NY,Ph	....	28	3739		....	....	6 1/2	5	10 3/8	4 1/4	4441	9 1/4	7 1/4	8 1/8	...	..	...	...	...
5	FEIC	FEI Co	NNM	....	25	2396	Mfr semiconductor mfg eqp	....	....	....	....	14 1/2	8 3/4	4818	12	8 3/4	10 3/4	...	26	...	...	...
6	FLCO	FelCor Suite Hotels	NNM	NR	96	7160	Real estate investment trust	....	....	23 3/4	17	31 3/4	18 1/2	84528	31 3/4	24 3/4	27 3/4	6.4	..	53.5	...	...
7	FGP	✓Ferrellgas Partners L.P.	NY,Ch,Ph	NR	32	1115	Retail marketer of propane	....	....	22 3/4	19 3/4	23 1/8	19 3/4	6669	23 1/8	21 1/8	23 1/8	8.6	42	22.2	...	...
#8•[3]	FOE	✓Ferro Corp	NY,B,Ch	B+	153	20285	Chemical specialties	34 3/4	2 1/16	35 7/8	21 5/8	30 5/8	21 3/8	13727	23 3/8	21 1/2	23 3/8	2.3	14	−1.0	−2.6	16.1
9	FFP	✓FFP Partners L.P.	AS	NR	4	16	Retail operations:food & gas	12 3/4	13/16	6 3/4	3 1/4	8 5/8	5 3/8	493	7 1/2	7	7	12.4	6	26.7	32.8	43.9
10	FFFC	✓FFVA Financial	NNM	NR	18	770	Savings bank, Va	....	....	20 3/4	16 1/4	29 1/4	18 5/8	1006	29	26 3/4	27 1/2	2.2	..	52.3	...	...
11	FFYF	✓FFY Financial	NNM	NR	22	494	Savings bank,Youngstown,Ohio	15 1/8	12 1/4	22 1/8	13 3/8	23 3/8	17 1/2	3803	21 1/4	20 5/8	21	2.9	16	16.6	...	...
#12•[4]	FHPC	✓FHP Int'l Corp	NNM	B	187	32928	Multi-state HMO services	30	2 1/2	31	20 1/4	30	19 1/2	64214	29 3/8	27 1/4	28 1/2	...	..	10.7	13.2	19.8
13	FIA	✓Fiat SpA ADR[54]	NY,Ch,Ph	NR	15	1407	Mfr automobiles,farm equip	45 1/4	10 1/8	23	12 1/4	21 1/8	14 7/8	1269	16 1/2	15	15 3/4	0.7	17	−11.2	23.8	2.9
14	FOCS	✓FiberChem Inc	NSC	NR	7	119	Mfr fiber optic chem'l sensors	4 1/2	1/2	3 3/8	3/4	1 9/16	5/8	14018	1 1/16	3/4	1	...	d	17.8	−13.0	1.9
✣15	FBD	✓Fibreboard Corp	AS,Ch,Ph	B−	56	2893	Building products/resorts	17 7/8	13/16	19 3/4	11 7/8	27	13 3/4	5398	23	19 5/8	22 3/8	...	2	64.1	87.8	84.6
16	FFFL	✓Fidelity Fedl Svgs Bk Fla	NNM	NR	12	707	Savings bank, Florida	9 1/8	9 1/8	13 5/8	9 1/8	17	10 1/4	2232	16 3/4	16 1/4	16 1/4	3.7	22	86.8	...	...
✣17	FNF	✓Fidelity Natl Finl	NY,Ph	B+	50	3168	Title insurance/services	27 1/4	1 5/16	26 7/8	9 3/4	19	9 7/8	7722	19	15 5/8	18 5/8	1.7	93	71.2	18.6	51.1
✣18•[5]	FLD	✓Fieldcrest Cannon	NY,Ch	B	116	7401	Household textile products	43	3 1/4	34 3/8	22 1/2	25 3/8	15 3/4	16544	21 3/4	15 3/4	16 1/2	...	d	−34.7	−2.9	20.5
#19•[6]	FITB	✓Fifth Third Bancorp	NNM	A+	217	23636	Comm'l bkg,Cincinnati,Ohio	59	1 5/16	55	45	76 1/2	47	41523	76 1/2	70 5/8	73 1/4	2.1	17	56.5	14.8	29.7
✣20	FIGIA	✓Figgie Intl Cl'A' 0.05 vtg	NNM	C	80	10099	Mfrs industrial consumer	27 1/2	10 1/2	14 1/2	4 5/8	14 1/8	5 7/8	13772	11 7/8	9 7/8	10 3/8	...	d	69.4	−13.6	−3.5
21	FLH	✓Fila Holdings ADS	NY	NR	58	5124	Market athletic footwear & pd	19	12 1/8	19 7/8	12 1/2	51 1/4	17 3/4	18211	48 1/8	41 3/8	45 1/2	0.3	23	132	...	...
✣22	BSMT	✓Filene's Basement	NNM	NR	51	7529	Off-price apparel retailer	37	6 3/4	11 3/4	4 1/2	6 5/8	2 3/16	49781	3 5/8	2 3/16	2 5/16	...	d	−52.6	−51.0	...
✣23•[7]	FILE	✓FileNet Corp	NNM	B	127	8652	Document mgmt systems	37 1/2	5	29 1/4	14 1/4	51	25 1/4	45173	49 3/4	38 1/4	47	...	39	74.9	29.3	42.1
24	FI	✓FINA,Inc Cl'A'	AS,Ch	B	42	1085	Integrated oil: petrochemical	45 1/2	10 1/4	39 7/8	32	50 7/8	34 1/4	645	50 3/4	48	50 1/2	4.8	10	65.4	27.5	11.0
25	FIF	✓Financial Federal	AS	NR	22	1804	Equipment financing/leasing	19 1/2	10	19 1/2	12 3/4	22 3/4	16 1/2	563	22 3/4	21 5/8	22 3/8	...	18	24.3	13.0	...
26	FSA	✓Financial Sec Assurance Hldg	NY,Ph	NR	41	7017	Insure asset-backed securities	....	....	22 3/4	18 3/4	27 3/4	19	4430	26 1/8	24 1/2	24 7/8	1.3	12	21.5	...	...
#27•[8]	FHT	✓Fingerhut Companies	NY,Ch,Ph	NR	182	38756	Catalog mktg-consumer prod	30 5/8	6 1/8	33 1/4	14	17 7/8	10 7/8	44777	14 7/8	12 1/2	13 7/8	1.2	21	−8.8	−2.1	12.7
28	FNLY	✓Finlay Enterprises	NNM	NR	41	1517	Retail fine jewelry	....	....	....	....	18 1/4	11	3105	16	11 1/2	11 3/4	...	14	...	...	...
29•[9]	FNV	✓FINOVA Group	NY,Ph	NR	193	21437	R.E. financing/insurance	32	17 7/8	39	28 1/4	49 1/2	30 5/8	10037	49 1/8	44 5/8	48 1/4	1.8	14	45.3	26.9	...
30	FFOX	✓Firefox Communications	NNM	NR	43	2257	Dvlp internetworking softwr pd	....	....	....	....	30	15	29256	26 1/8	21	23 1/2	...	84	...	...	...
31	FACT	First Albany Cos	NNM	B−	10	231	Investment bank & brokerage	9 3/4	1 3/4	7 5/8	5 5/8	11	6 5/8	1095	11	9	10B	s1.9	14	71.6	36.5	50.3
32	ALRT	✓First Alert	NNM	NR	78	5971	Mfr residential safety prods	....	....	22 1/2	8 1/2	18 1/2	8 1/4	54494	10 3/4	8 5/8	8 5/8	...	10	−37.3	...	...
33	FATN	✓First Amer (Tenn)	NNM	B−	152	9902	Comm'l bkg,Tennessee	34 5/8	4 7/8	35	26 1/8	50 1/4	26 7/8	33615	50 1/4	45 1/4	47 3/8	2.4	12	80.7	23.6	51.2
✣34	FAF	✓First Amer Finl	NY,Ch,Ph	B	68	7148	Title insurance	39 1/4	9/16	37 1/2	16	27 1/2	16 1/2	3526	27 1/2	22 3/4	26 3/4	2.2	d	63.1	4.5	...
¶35•[4]	FBS	✓First Bank System	NY,B,Ch,P,Ph	B−	391	73530	Comml bkg,MN,upper midwest	37 1/8	6 1/4	39	29 3/8	53 3/4	32 5/8	80857	52 5/8	49	49 5/8	2.9	12	54.8	25.7	35.1
36	Pr X	$3.5625 cm Cv'91A Pfd([57]52.1375)	NY	BBB+	34	1415		68 5/8	49 3/4	69 1/2	58 3/8	93	58	262	90 1/8	85 1/4	85 3/4	4.2	..	...	...	...
37	FBA	✓First Banks America	NY,B,Ch,P	B−	11	22	Commercial bkg,Dallas, Texas	31878 1/4	1 7/8	26 1/4	13 1/8	18 3/4	9	1840	13 7/8	9 7/8	12 1/4	...	d	−6.7	−22.4	28.4
38	FBBC	✓First Bell Bancorp	NNM	NR	25	3303	Savings & loan, Pennsylvania	....	....	....	....	13 3/4	11 3/4	3692	13 1/2	13 1/8	13 3/8	...	14	...	...	...
#39	FBR	✓First Brands Corp	NY,Ph	NR	185	19563	Mfr home/auto consumer prod	35 1/2	14 1/2	37 1/2	31 1/2	47 7/8	32 3/4	10898	47 7/8	44 1/8	47 5/8	1.0	23	41.5	19.8	19.2
40	FCC	✓First Central Finl	AS	B+	17	1569	Property & casualty insurance	8 1/2	3 5/8	7 3/4	5 1/2	7 3/4	5 3/4	824	6 7/8	6 3/8	6 5/8	1.8	7	−7.1	11.7	3.7
¶41•[7]	FCN	First Chicago NBD	NY	NR	..	...	Commercial banking, Midwest	....	....	....	....	42 1/2	38	146672	42 1/2	38	39 1/2	3.3	10	...	...	...
42	Pr V	5 3/4%cm Cv[61]Dep Pfd([62]51.725)	[10]NY	BBB+	36	4107		58 3/4	47 5/8	56 3/4	45 1/2	71 3/8	47	12984	71 3/8	65	67	4.3	..	...	...	...
43	FND	First Chi NBD[63]5.50%[64]'DECS'97	NY	NR	21	4240	Exch Notes For Com Stock	....	....	44	16 1/4	23 1/2	12 3/8	4948	20 3/8	17 3/4	18	11.1	..	1.4	...	...
44	FCNCA	✓First Citizens BancShares'A'	NNM	B+	48	802	Full svc bank,Raleigh,NC	63 1/2	18 1/2	46 1/2	40	55 1/2	42	807	55 1/2	52 3/4	55 1/8	1.6	11	31.9	4.9	23.2
45	FIR	✓First Citizens BancStock[66]	AS,Ch	NR	3	7	General banking, Louisiana	16 7/8	15 5/8	21	16 1/8	50 3/4	19 5/8	23	47 1/2	46 1/2	47 3/8B	e1.3	17	145	...	...
46	FCT	✓First City Bancorp[67]	AS	NR	7	52	Commercial banking, Tenn	12 1/2	3 5/8	12 1/2	10	26 1/4	10 1/8	141	25 1/2	25	25 3/8	0.8	31	145	47.9	46.4
47	FCL	✓First Colony	NY	NR	179	28620	Hldg co:life insur,annuity prd	37 7/8	23 3/4	26 3/8	19	29	20 1/2	14700	26 1/8	23 7/8	25 3/8	1.6	11	12.7	−6.7	...
48	FCOM	✓First Commerce	NNM	B+	128	11535	Comm'l bkg,Louisiana,MS	32 1/4	2 1/16	30	21 3/4	34 1/2	22	16821	33 3/4	31 1/2	32	4.4	12	53.9	12.8	39.8
✣49	FCLR	✓First Commercial Corp[70]	NNM	A	60	5442	Comm'l bkg,Little Rk,Arkansas	20 1/2	3/8	22 3/4	17 3/8	33 1/4	20 3/8	5351	33 1/4	29 5/8	33	s2.5	16	71.5	25.9	37.8
50	FCWI	First Commonwealth	NNM	NR	..	...	Managed dental benefits	....	....	....	....	27 1/4	15	5902	27 1/4	21 1/2	26	...	41	...	...	...
51	FCF	✓First Commonwealth Finl	NY	A	38	1299	General banking, Pennsylvania	17 5/8	8 1/2	20 1/4	13 1/2	17 7/8	13 1/8	1981	17 7/8	16 5/8	17 1/2	4.1	13	34.0	10.0	...
¶52•[1]	FDC	✓First Data	NY,Ph	NR	637	128481	Credit-card processing svcs	42 1/4	21 1/4	50 5/8	40 1/2	71 1/4	46	125881	70	64 1/4	66 7/8	0.2	30	41.1	26.9	...

Uniform Footnote Explanations-See Page 4. Other: [1]ASE:Cycle 2. [2]CBOE,NY:Cycle 2. [3]Ph:Cycle 1. [4]ASE,CBOE:Cycle 3. [5]CBOE:Cycle 3. [6]Ph:Cycle 2. [7]CBOE:Cycle 1. [8]NY:Cycle 1. [9]ASE:Cycle 1. [10]Ch [51]Return of Capital. [52]®$1.45,'94. [53]®$0.64,'95. [54]Each ADR rep 5 ord shrs,lit.1000. [55]®$3.00,'94. [56]®$3.52,'94. [57]To 1-1-97,scale to $50 in 2002. [58]®$0.90,'94. [59]Pfd in $M. [60]®$3.62,'94. [61]Dep for 0.01 shr 5 3/4% cm Cv Pfd Ser'B'. [62]Fr 4-1-97. [63]Debt exchangeable for common stock. [64]Formerly First Chicago. [65]Stock or cash re-specified cond. [66]Whitney Hldg plan acq, $49.95. [67]First American Corp plan acq,$26.50. [68]®$1.20,'94. [69]®$2.19,'94. [70]Centura Banks plan acq,0.63 com.

Index	Cash Divs. Ea.Yr. Since	Latest Payment Period $	Date	Ex. Div.	Total $ So Far 1995	Ind. Rate	Paid 1994	Mil-$ Cash& Equiv.	Curr. Assets	Curr. Liab.	Balance Sheet Date	Lg Trm Debt Mil-$	Shs. 000 Pfd.	Com.	Years End	1991	1992	1993	1994	1995	Last 12 Mos.	Interim Period	$ per Shr. 1994	1995	Index
1◆	1948	Q0.12½	1-3-96	12-6	0.48	0.50	0.40½	1.14	247	190	9-30-95	40.1	...	45286	Dc	0.68	Δ0.75	0.86	1.02	....	1.17	9 Mo Sep	0.72	0.87	1
2	....	None Since Public			...	Nil	....	158	7142	3882	10-28-95	5943	...	202595	Ja	p0.21	□1.19	□1.56	1.41	E0.75	d0.13	9 Mo Oct	0.63	d0.91	2
3	....	Terms&trad. basis should			be checked in detail			Wrrts expire 12-19-99				....	...	8983	Ja	...	...	...	....	....	....				3
4	....	Terms&trad. basis should			be checked in detail			Wrrts expire 12-19-2001				....	...	8983	Ja	...	...	...	....	....	....				4
5	....	None Since Public			...	Nil	....	14.5	36.3	7.57	9-30-95	3.50	...	7170	Dc	d0.06	0.08	Δ0.24	d0.04	....	0.41	9 Mo Sep	d0.05	0.40	5
6	1994	0.46	1-30-96	12-8	1.76½	1.77	0.272	Equity per shr $18.82			6-30-95	p180	...	★21403	Dc	...	...	p1.22	p1.69	....	....	9 Mo Sep	n/a	p1.27	6
7	1994	[51]Q0.50	12-14-95	11-28	[51]2.00	2.00	0.65	14.6	154	136	10-31-95	347	...	±31135	Jl	...	...	p0.91	p1.29	0.76	0.55	3 Mo Oct	d0.02	d0.23	7
8◆	1939	Q0.135	12-10-95	11-13	0.54	0.54	0.54	90.8	509	257	9-30-95	163	1407	27302	Dc	0.05	1.90	□1.83	[52]1.52	E1.70	1.65	9 Mo Sep	1.11	1.24	8
9	1994	0.30	12-12-95	11-24	0.87	0.87	0.37	9.29	32.2	34.2	9-24-95	5.50	...	±3638	Dc	d0.19	0.16	□0.28	Δ0.97	....	1.21	9 Mo Sep	Δ0.69	0.93	9
10	1995	Q0.15	1-18-96	12-29	0.60	0.60	....	Book Value $29.24			9-30-95	34.3	...	2852	Dc	...	...	p1.71	1.57	....	...	9 Mo Sep	n/a	1.64	10
11	1993	Q0.15	11-16-95	10-27	0.525	0.60	0.42½	Book Value $19.88			9-30-95	....	...	5435	Je	...	p0.86	n/a	Δ1.20	1.33	1.33	3 Mo Sep	0.32	0.32	11
12◆	....	None Since Public			...	Nil	....	455	676	743	9-30-95	320	21120	40297	Je	1.37	1.00	1.33	1.71	[53]0.29	0.19	3 Mo Sep	0.38	0.27	12
13	1995	0.107	8-16-95	7-12	0.107	0.11	....	Equity per shr $17.25			12-31-94	6847	930168	3284370	Dc	2.15	0.84	d1.30	0.91	....	0.91				13
14	....	None Paid			...	Nil	....	1.18	3.17	0.45	6-30-95	0.01	206	20240	Sp	d0.47	d0.26	d0.37	d0.35	....	d0.12	9 Mo Jun	d0.32	d0.09	14
15◆	....	None Since Public			...	Nil	....	147	264	152	9-30-95	6.99	...	8396	Dc	□d5.25	1.15	1.33	[55]3.01	....	10.52	9 Mo Sep	2.51	10.02	15
16◆	1994	Q0.15	1-16-96	12-27	0.545	0.60	†0.25	Book Value $11.62			9-30-95	85.7	...	6710	Dc	...	...	...	0.80	....	0.75	9 Mo Sep	0.60	0.55	16
17◆	1987	Q0.077	2-14-96	1-31	0.287	0.308	0.28	Equity per shr $6.42			9-30-95	136	...	11139	Dc	0.58	1.17	2.37	Δ0.65	....	0.20	9 Mo Sep	Δ0.82	□0.37	17
18	....	0.10	10-1-90	9-17	...	Nil	....	5.87	446	155	9-30-95	365	1500	8913	Dc	0.30	□1.81	□2.29	3.02	Ed0.65↓	0.88	9 Mo Sep	1.99	d0.15	18
19◆	1952	Q0.39	1-12-96	12-27	1.36	1.56	1.16	Book Value $24.59			9-30-95	431	...	66909	Dc	2.33	2.75	3.28	3.80	E4.30	4.20	9 Mo Sep	2.80	3.20	19
20	1986	0.06	12-15-93	11-24	...	Nil	....	29.1	235	150	9-30-95	211	...	±18364	Dc	±1.72	±1.61	±Δd10.44	±d9.41	....	d7.08	9 Mo Sep	±d3.04	±d0.71	20
21	1994	0.15	7-13-95	6-29	0.15	0.15	0.129	37.1	369	200	6-30-95	59.6	...	★132500	Dc	0.93	1.12	Δ1.05	1.70	....	2.00	6 Mo Jun	0.77	1.07	21
22	....	None Since Public			...	Nil	....	0.24	149	91.6	7-29-95	38.9	...	20523	Ja	□0.81	□0.87	Δd0.20	□0.05	....	d0.18	9 Mo Oct	□0.20	d0.03	22
23	....	None Since Public			...	Nil	....	52.8	121	42.5	10-01-95	....	...	12852	Dc	0.75	d0.76	0.71	1.37	....	1.21	9 Mo Sep	0.63	0.47	23
24◆	1987	Q0.60	12-13-95	11-29	2.30	2.40	1.80	4.16	726	576	9-30-95	474	...	±31205	Dc	±1.36	□±0.78	±2.26	±3.27	....	4.99	9 Mo Sep	±2.13	±3.85	24
25◆	....	None Since Public			...	Nil	....	Equity per shr $10.59			7-31-95	172	...	5484	Jl	0.50	1.00	0.87	1.03	1.21	1.27	3 Mo Oct	0.29	0.35	25
26	1994	Q0.08	12-7-95	11-20	0.32	0.32	0.16	Equity per shr $23.21			9-30-95	....	2000	26225	Dc	2.40	1.90	d5.44	2.32	....	2.09	9 Mo Sep	2.03	1.80	26
27◆	1990	Q0.04	11-22-95	10-31	0.16	0.16	0.16	63.4	879	540	9-29-95	146	...	45950	Dc	1.07	1.19	1.50	0.91	....	0.67	9 Mo Sep	0.66	0.42	27
28	....	None Since Public			...	Nil	....	1.48	253	203	10-28-95	201	...	7523	Ja	...	...	...	p0.60	....	0.83	9 Mo Oct	pd1.51	pd1.28	28
29	1992	Q0.22	1-2-96	11-29	0.82	0.88	0.72	Equity per shr $29.56			9-30-95	5403	...	27264	Dc	pd2.74	2.31	1.77	2.94	....	3.40	9 Mo Sep	2.10	2.56	29
30	....	None Since Public			...	Nil	....	16.6	28.6	4.73	9-30-95	0.16	...	6735	Dc	d0.06	0.03	d0.05	0.08	....	0.28	9 Mo Sep	0.03	0.23	30
31◆	1992	s0.048	11-22-95	11-6	s0.186	0.19	s0.168	Equity per shr $8.00			9-29-95	1.79	...	4530	Sp	0.52	1.21	1.14	0.96	0.71	0.71				31
32◆	....	None Since Public			...	Nil	....	2.00	138	48.0	9-30-95	39.8	...	24043	Dc	...	...	p0.32	□0.79	....	0.91	9 Mo Sep	□0.42	0.54	32
33	1992	Q0.28	11-30-95	11-13	1.06	1.12	0.88	Book Value $25.55			9-30-95	260	...	p29610	Dc	0.73	1.74	□3.93	3.48	....	3.84	9 Mo Sep	2.56	2.92	33
34◆	1909	Q0.15	1-12-96	12-27	0.60	0.60	0.60	Equity per shr $19.43			9-30-95	87.4	...	11412	Dc	±0.31	±4.55	±Δ5.47	1.66	....	d0.45	9 Mo Sep	1.91	d0.20	34
35	1930	Q0.36¼	12-15-95	11-29	1.45	1.45	1.16	Book Value $20.33			9-30-95	3127	8099	129796	Dc	2.13	Δ1.10	2.39	[56]3.57	E4.15	4.19	9 Mo Sep	2.43	3.05	35
36	1991	Q0.891	12-31-95	12-4	3.562	3.56	3.562	Cv into 1.7256 com,$28.975				....	2134	...	Dc	b1.91	b2.26	...	....	....	....				36
37◆	....	37.50%	12-1-84	11-20	...	Nil	....	Book Value $10.05			6-30-95	9.07	...	±3884	Dc	Δd3.00	Δ0.45	0.15	d0.30	....	d0.52	9 Mo Sep	d0.34	d0.56	37
38	....	None Since Public			...	Nil	....	Book Value $13.50			9-30-95	....	...	8596	Dc	...	...	...	p0.97	....	p0.97				38
39	1990	Q0.12½	1-20-96	12-27	0.40	0.50	0.32	9.52	296	189	9-30-95	197	...	20851	Je	□2.21	□1.91	2.41	2.71	□2.01	2.06	3 Mo Sep	0.68	0.73	39
40	1989	Q0.03	2-9-96	12-29	0.12	0.12	0.10	Equity per shr $6.15			9-30-95	6.51	...	5994	Dc	*0.38	0.53	0.80	[58]0.97	....	1.02	9 Mo Sep	0.75	0.80	40
41	....	Plan qtly div			...	1.32	....	....	...	...		5283	[59]611	320807	Dc	...	p0.60	p3.90	p[60]3.67	....	3.83	6 Mo Jun	p1.84	p2.00	41
42	1993	Q0.71⅞	1-1-96	12-6	2.87½	2.87	2.87½	Cv into 0.9324 com,$53.625				....	4000	...	Dc	...	...	b0.99	b2.00	....	....				42
43	1994	Q0.499	11-15-95	10-27	1.994	1.99	1.496	Amt pay maturity based on NEXTEL commun stk[65]				....	...	★6500	Dc	...	...	...	....	....	....	Due 2-15-97			43
44	1987	Q0.22½	1-6-96	12-14	0.80	0.90	0.70	Book Value $47.32			9-30-95	23.6	...	±10700	Dc	±3.12	±5.45	±5.73	±5.13	....	5.12	9 Mo Sep	±3.86	±3.85	44
45◆	1993	†0.20	12-29-95	12-13	†0.59	0.60	†0.543	Book Value $20.51			9-30-95	....	...	1266	Dc	1.19	1.74	2.46	2.65	....	2.74	9 Mo Sep	2.00	2.09	45
46◆	1991	Q0.05	11-1-95	10-12	0.20	0.20	0.20	Book Value $10.69			9-30-95	6.23	373	1340	Dc	▲0.62	0.94	Δ0.80	[68]1.28	....	0.83	9 Mo Sep	0.89	0.44	46
47	1993	Q0.10	1-1-96	12-13	0.38	0.40	0.27½	Equity per shr $26.54			9-30-95	175	3200	49302	Dc	p2.06	Δ3.32	4.12	2.10	....	2.37	9 Mo Sep	1.89	2.16	47
48◆	1935	Q0.35	1-10-96	12-13	1.20	1.40	1.05	Book Value $17.94			6-30-95	88.6	2397	p38130	Dc	1.56	2.88	3.48	[69]2.25	E2.73	2.22	9 Mo Sep	1.91	1.88	48
49◆	1981	Q0.21	1-2-96	12-13	s0.748	0.841	0.641	Book Value $14.76			9-30-95	11.5	...	25402	Dc	1.49	1.67	1.84	1.96	....	2.08	9 Mo Sep	1.45	1.57	49
50	....	None Since Public			...	Nil	....	4.78	9.06	6.43	9-30-95	....	p...	★3363	Dc	pΔ0.16	pΔ0.27	p0.36	p0.47	....	0.63	9 Mo Sep	p0.38	p0.54	50
51◆	1987	Q0.18	1-12-96	12-27	0.64	0.72	0.555	Book Value $11.06			9-30-95	5.61	...	22372	Dc	0.97	1.15	Δ1.22	1.28	....	1.32	9 Mo Sep	0.86	0.90	51
52	1992	Q0.03	1-15-96	12-28	0.12	0.12	0.12	Equity per shr Neg			9-30-95	633	...	p222947	Dc	1.13	1.30	1.56	1.87	E2.25	2.10	9 Mo Sep	1.29	1.52	52

◆**Stock Splits & Divs By Line Reference Index** [1]3-for-2,'91,'92:4-for-3,'94. [8]3-for-2,'92. [12]10%,'91. [15]2-for-1,'95. [16]10%,'95. [17]10%,'91:4-for-3,'92:3-for-2,'93(twice):Vote 10% stk div,ex Jan 10. [19]To split 3-for-2,ex Jan 16. [24]2-for-1,'95. [25]To split 3-for-2,ex Jan 31. [27]2-for-1,'93. [31]Adj to 5%,Nov,'95. [32]2-for-1,'94. [34]Adj for 4%,'92. [37]1-for-15 REVERSE,'95. [45]10%,'94. [46]10%,'92. [48]3-for-2,'93:5-for-4,'93. [49]10%,'92:3-for-2,'94:Adj to 7%,'95. [51]2-for-1,'94.

¶ S&P 500 # MidCap 400 ✣ SmallCap 600 • Options

Index	Ticker	Name of Issue (Call Price of Pfd. Stocks)	Market	Com. Rank. & Pfd. Rating	Inst. Hold Cos	Inst. Hold Shs. (000)	Principal Business	Price Range 1971-93 High	1971-93 Low	1994 High	1994 Low	1995 High	1995 Low	Dec. Sales in 100s	December, 1995 Last Sale Or Bid High	Low	Last	%Div Yield	P-E Ratio	Total Return % Annualized 12 Mo	36 Mo	60 Mo
1	FES	✔First Empire State	AS	A+	92	2823	Comm'l bkg,Buffalo,New York	159	2¾	165	134½	218	136	474	218	206	218	1.3	13	62.5	19.1	33.5
2	FTFC	✔First Federal Capital	NNM	B	29	1403	Savings Bank,Wisconsin	18⅛	1 7/16	19	12¾	19¾	14	3746	18½	17¾	18	3.1	12	19.9	22.0	61.5
3	FAB	✔First Federal of Alabama	AS	NR	9	138	General banking Jasper, AL	17⅜	4	16	13⅝	19⅜	13⅜	273	19	17½	18	4.0	12	38.1	12.7	37.8
4	FFEC	✔First Fed of Eau Clair	NNM	NR	20	1747	Savings bank, Wis	....	....	10½	8¼	15⅜	9¾	6639	15⅜	14⅜	15¼	...	..	53.0	...	...
¶5•[1]	FFB	✔First Fidelity[53] Bancorp[54]	NY,Ch	B	328	25277	Commercial banking,NJ,Penn	52⅜	7⅞	48¼	40½	80	44¼	30415	80	72½	75⅜	2.7	14	75.4	23.1	38.2
6	Pr B	$2.15 cm Cv B Pfd (25)	NY,Ch	BBB	24	523		40½	15	37¾	32	62	34¼	884	62	56⅜	58¼	3.7	..	...	...	...
✣7	FFHC	✔First Finl Corp Wis	NNM	A	100	11376	Svg & loan,Wisconsin	19¾	⅝	17¼	13¼	23¾	13½	11110	23¾	20¾	23	2.1	11	78.4	29.7	57.7
8	FFCH	✔First Finl Hldgs	NNM	B+	22	824	Svgs & loan,Carleston S.C.	18¼	2 5/16	17¾	13	22½	13¾	1091	20½	19	19¼	3.3	13	30.2	24.6	34.1
9	FHWN	✔First Hawaiian	NNM	A	93	10412	Commercial bkg,Hawaii	31¼	1 11/16	31¼	23	31¼	23	10245	30¼	27⅞	30	3.9	12	33.9	7.1	11.9
10	FISB	✔First Indiana Corp	NNM	B+	35	1173	Commercial bkg,Indiana	19¾	2⅛	19	14¼	27⅝	15¾	1380	27	25½	25¾	2.2	11	62.6	30.6	52.5
11	FR	✔First Industrial Rlty Tr	NY,Ch,Ph	NR	81	9169	Real estate investment trust	....	....	23¾	17	22⅞	17¼	8278	22⅞	20⅝	22½	8.5	35	38.9	...	...
¶12•[2]	I	✔First Interstate[57] Bancorp[58] .	[3]NY,B,C,Ch	B	549	54132	Comml bkg,Western U.S.	70⅜	8⅞	85	62⅜	142⅛	67¼	75110	142⅛	134⅝	136½	2.3	12	109	47.5	46.7
13	FIFS	✔First Investors Finl Svcs Grp	NNM	NR	..	...	Pur retail install't contracts	....	....	....	....	11¾	8⅛	11914	10½	8⅛	8⅛	...	23	...	...	...
14	FRME	✔First Merchants Corp	NNM	A+	24	1472	Commercial banking, Indiana	20⅞	4½	22½	18⅝	26¾	20⅞	516	26¾	25¾	25¾	3.1	14	27.5	14.7	27.3
✣15	FMBC	✔First Michigan Bank	NNM	A+	56	2309	Commercial bkg,Michigan	20⅛	1⅜	23⅜	18½	30	21⅝	3564	30	27¼	27¾	s3.0	15	35.6	32.3	35.5
16	FMBI	✔First Midwest Bancorp	NNM	A–	52	3030	Comm'l bkg,Illinois	28¼	2 7/16	28¾	22	29¾	23¼	2360	29⅜	28¾	28⅞	2.6	16	30.7	16.0	18.7
✣17•[4]	FRM	✔First Mississippi	NY,B,Ch,P,Ph	↑B	242	11581	Indl & agricultural chemicals	30⅜	5/16	25	12¾	41⅜	20¼	12085	27⅛	23⅞	26½	1.5	10	...	...	...
18	FMOR	✔First Mortgage	NNM	NR	11	1080	Mortgage banking services	9½	4¼	9¼	4	6⅛	4	364	6⅛	5¼	5¾B	...	16	43.8	9.4	...
19	FMBD	✔First Mutual Bancorp	NNM	NR	17	1581	Savings bank,Central IL	....	....	....	....	14¾	10	6676	14¾	13	13⅝	...	20	...	...	...
20	FNH	First Natl Bankshares(LA)	AS	NR	3	31	General banking, Louisiana	....	....	....	....	16¾	7	118	15⅝	14⅞	15	0.7	14	...	...	...
21	FNGB	✔First Northern Capital[60]	NNM	B+	18	639	Savings bank N.E. Wisconsin	16	3⅛	15½	11¾	16⅞	11¾	593	16½	15¼	16½	3.4	17	34.7	7.6	22.9
#22•[5]	FOA	✔First of America Bk	NY,Ch,Ph	↓A–	216	21669	Commercial bkg,Michigan	43¼	3⅞	40⅛	29¾	46⅛	29½	16637	45⅛	41¾	44⅜	4.0	12	55.5	11.6	20.5
23•[6]	FPNX	First Pacific Networks	NSC	NR	28	2741	Dvlp single wire telecomn svcs	26½	4⅛	16½	3¼	5½	13/16	119260	1¾	13/16	1¼	...	d	–68.5	–52.7	...
24	FFPB	✔First Palm Beach Bancorp	NNM	NR	33	1321	General banking, Florida	16⅜	13¾	20½	13¾	25	17⅛	9402	23¼	21⅛	21⅛	1.9	19	28.3	...	...
25	FRC	✔First Republic Bancorp	NY,P	B–	54	6041	Thrift & loan svcs,Calif	17	4	16½	9⅞	14⅜	9⅞	3843	13¼	11¼	13⅛	...	88	26.5	10.7	26.8
26	FWWB	✔First Svgs Bk Wash Bancorp	NNM	NR	..	...	Savings bank, WA	....	....	....	....	13¼	10	14431	13¼	12¾	13⅛	...	18	...	...	...
#27•[7]	FSCO	✔First Security	NNM	A	169	26641	Comm'l bkg,UT,ID,WY,OR	30¾	4¼	32¾	21½	38½	21¾	38592	38½	34½	38½	2.9	13	74.9	15.9	33.3
28	SRCE	✔First Source Corp	NNM	A+	29	7090	Commercial bkg,Indiana	16⅝	1 3/16	16⅞	14⅛	24	16⅜	545	24	23	23½	s1.4	14	48.7	23.6	38.7
29	FSFC	✔First Southeast Finl	NNM	NR	10	381	General banking, S.Carolina	14	11¾	16¼	11½	20¾	12¾	1105	19¼	18¼	19	2.5	22	49.5	...	...
30	FSTH	First Southern Bancshares	NNM	NR	3	129	Savings & loan, Alabama	....	....	....	....	15½	10	1056	15½	14¾	15¼	2.6	..	...	...	...
31	FSNM	✔First State Bancorporation	NNM	NR	8	582	General banking, New Mexico	10	8⅜	11¾	8¼	13	9¼	280	12¾	12	12B	1.7	10	35.5	...	...
32	FTSP	✔First Team Sports	NNM	NR	56	3556	Mfr in-line roller skates	11⅞	7/16	13⅞	4⅜	31¾	10¾	42103	18¾	14½	15¼	...	12	60.3	35.1	39.3
#33•[5]	FTEN	✔First Tenn Natl	NNM	A–	188	14099	Comm'l bkg,Tennessee	47¼	2½	47¾	37	61¾	39¼	22127	61¾	58¼	60½	3.5	13	53.8	22.8	38.9
¶34•[4]	FTU	✔First Union Corp	NY,Ph	A	578	96080	Comml bkg,NC,southeast	53⅛	2¼	48	39	59½	41⅜	116092	59½	53⅞	55⅝	3.7	10	38.6	12.1	34.0
35	FUR	✔First Union RE EqSBI	NY,Ch,Ph	NR	52	4078	Ohio real estate invest trust	27⅜	2½	10¼	6⅛	8⅝	6½	9299	7¼	6⅞	7	6.3	23	11.4	–2.8	7.6
36	UNTD	✔First United Bancshrs	NNM	A–	13	372	Commercial bkg,Arkansas	29½	10½	33	26½	43	28½	100	43	40	40B	2.2	14	35.3	23.3	31.8
37•[8]	FUS	✔First USA	NY,Ph	NR	331	54508	Credit card issuer & processor	39¾	4¾	46⅝	26½	55⅝	32	87158	48⅞	43⅜	44⅜	0.5	15	38.7	56.3	...
38	Pr	6.25% [65]PRIDES([66]32.373)	NY,Ch	BB–	41	3383		....	....	43⅛	27½	48½	31¼	3337	42½	38¾	39½	5.0	..	...	...	...
#39	FVB	✔First Virginia Banks	NY,B,Ch,Ph	A	152	9369	Commercial bkg,Virginia	41	2⅝	40⅜	31⅝	44	32	5962	43⅞	40⅝	41¾	3.4	13	34.3	7.9	27.1
40	FWSH	First Wash Realty Trust	NNM	NR	11	998	Real estate investment trust	....	....	....	....	18½	17	3451	18½	17¼	18⅛	10.8	..	...	...	...
41	FWV	First West Virginia Bancorp	AS	NR	4	34	Commerc'l banking,Wheeling WV	....	....	....	....	22	14¼	15	22	21½	22	2.7	13	...	...	...
42	KIDD	First Years	NNM	NR	14	481	Mkts products for infants	14	1 13/16	19½	8½	24	16¾	273	22½	20½	21¾	0.8	14	12.6	22.3	26.7
43•[9]	FSR	✔Firstar Corp	NY,B,Ch	B+	199	31519	Comml banking,Wis,Il,MN,AZ	37¼	1¼	35⅜	25⅛	41	26¼	30383	40½	39⅛	39⅝	3.4	13	54.9	11.8	27.5
44	FBIC	✔Firstbank of Illinois	NNM	A	45	2735	General banking,Illinois	26⅛	3⅜	25⅞	22⅝	31½	25½	1454	31½	30¼	30⅞	2.9	13	24.2	10.9	25.1
✣45	FBP	✔Firstbank Puerto Rico	NY	NR	26	2155	Comml bank,Puerto Rico	11½	1 7/16	12⅞	9	24⅜	10⅞	2570	23	19	22⅜	...	4	95.6	70.2	69.6
46	FED	✔FirstFed Financial	NY,Ch	C	51	6749	Svgs&loan,California	26¾	1⅞	17¼	10⅛	18½	11⅛	5776	15¾	13⅝	14⅛	...	17	22.8	–8.6	1.9
47	FRST	✔FirsTier Financial[67]	NNM	A–	86	6349	Commercial bkg,Nebraska	37½	2 5/16	35	28	46	29½	2652	46	43¼	44	2.7	14	45.3	17.5	39.9
✣48	FMER	✔FirstMerit Corp	NNM	A	78	5908	Comm'l bkg,Akron,Ohio	30¾	2¼	27¾	21¾	30½	21⅜	9331	30½	27⅞	30	3.6	21	21.9	10.7	22.1
#49•[10]	FISV	✔FIserv Inc	NNM	B+	238	32194	Data process'g services	23¾	3⅜	23¾	18	31	21	45133	30¼	26¼	30	...	28	34.8	25.2	28.5
✣50•[2]	FSH	✔Fisher Scientific Intl	NY,Ph	NR	161	13792	Mfr/dstr scientific equip	36⅛	13¾	38¾	22⅞	34¾	24⅝	7141	34⅜	32½	33⅜	0.2	54	33.9	3.3	...
✣51	FLST	✔Flagstar Companies	NNM	NR	50	8995	Food & vending services	29⅝	8½	12¾	5½	7⅞	2⅞	39229	4⅛	2⅞	3⅛	...	d	–53.7	–45.9	–25.0
52	BDL	✔Flanigan's Enterprises	AS,Ch	B–	4	28	Liquor strs:cocktail lounges	20½	11/16	6⅜	2⅛	4¾	2¼	356	4	3⅛	4	...	7	60.0	–23.3	39.8

Uniform Footnote Explanations-See Page 4. Other: [1]CBOE:Cycle 3. [2]CBOE:Cycle 1. [3]P,Ph [4]P:Cycle 1. [5]Ph:Cycle 2. [6]CBOE,P:Cycle 1. [7]ASE,NY:Cycle 3. [8]ASE:Cycle 2. [9]Ph:Cycle 1. [10]Ph:Cycle 3. [51]®$15.71,'94. [52]To be determined. [53]Approve First Union Corp acq,1.35 com. [54]Plan S&P 500 delisting:eff Dec 30. [55]®$5.11,'94. [56]Inc current amts. [57]Wells Fargo plan offer,0.66 com:Co rejects. [58]First Bank system plan acq,2.6 com. [59]Stk dstr of FirstMiss Gold. [60]Formerly First North'n Svg Bk. [61]®$0.85,'94. [62]®$2.80,'94. [63]®$1.06,'94. [64]®$1.03,'95. [65]Pfd Redeemable Increased Div Equity Sec. [66]Fr 5-20-97. [67]First Bank System plan acq, .8829 com. [68]®$2.00,'94. [69]®$0.59,'95.

Splits ◆ Index	Cash Divs. Ea.Yr. Since	Dividends: Latest Payment Period $	Date	Ex. Div.	Total $ So Far 1995	Ind. Rate	Paid 1994	Financial Position Mil-$ Cash& Equiv.	Curr. Assets	Curr. Liab.	Balance Sheet Date	Capitalization Lg Trm Debt Mil-$	Shs. 000 Pfd.	Com.	Earnings $ Per Shr. Years End	1991	1992	1993	1994	1995	Last 12 Mos.	Interim Earnings Period	$ per Shr. 1994	1995	Index
1	1979	Q0.70	12-29-95	11-29	2.50	2.80	2.20	Book Value $119.53			9-30-95	196	40	6444	Dc	9.32	13.41	13.87	[51]16.35	E17.31	18.03	9 Mo Sep	11.82	13.50	1
2◆	1990	Q0.14	12-7-95	11-14	0.55	0.56	0.481	Book Value $14.44			9-30-95	271	...	p6563	Dc	*1.15	Δ1.85	2.13	□1.64	....	1.57	9 Mo Sep	□1.25	1.18	2
3	1987	Q0.18	12-15-95	12-6	0.72	0.72	0.72	Book Value $15.20			6-30-95	18.9	...	848	Je	1.26	1.55	0.06	1.33	1.39	1.55	3 Mo Sep	0.31	0.47	3
4	1995	0.05	12-12-95	12-1	0.05	[52]....	....	Book Value $13.85			6-30-95	122	...	6987	Dc	...	...	...	n/a	....	....	9 Mo Sep	n/a	0.69	4
5	1812	Q0.50	11-7-95	10-26	2.00	2.00	1.76	Book Value $27.38			12-31-94	p677	p5213	p81772	Dc	3.37	3.89	Δ4.63	[55]5.21	E5.60	5.51	9 Mo Sep	3.87	4.17	5
6	1988	Q0.538	1-1-96	11-22	2.15	2.15	2.15	Cv into 0.7801 com				....	4788	...	Dc	b2.21	b3.49	b5.11	b3.91	....	....				6
7◆	1981	Q0.12	12-31-95	12-13	0.48	0.48	0.40	Book Value $11.60			9-30-95	528	...	29609	Dc	0.80	Δ1.21	1.88	1.91	....	2.15	9 Mo Sep	1.25	1.49	7
8◆	1986	Q0.16	11-27-95	11-8	0.58	0.64	0.50	Book Value $14.50			9-30-95	128	...	6306	Sp	0.98	1.10	Δ1.77	1.88	1.47	1.47				8
9	1929	Q0.29½	12-15-95	11-29	1.18	1.18	1.18	Book Value $18.38			9-30-95	225	...	31118	Dc	2.55	2.70	Δ2.41	2.25	E2.48	2.27	9 Mo Sep	1.78	1.80	9
10◆	1987	Q0.14	12-15-95	12-5	0.56	0.56	0.48¾	Book Value $20.44			9-30-95	214	...	6878	Dc	1.43	Δ1.53	2.11	1.44	....	2.25	9 Mo Sep	1.04	1.85	10
11	1994	0.48¾	1-22-96	12-27	1.89	1.91	0.47¼	Equity per shr $14.46			9-30-95	[56]309	★1500	18881	Dc	...	...	p0.66	p0.99	....	0.64	9 Mo Sep	p0.74	0.39	11
12	1958	Q0.80	11-30-95	11-2	3.10	3.20	2.75	Book Value $47.95			9-30-95	1368	1750	75744	Dc	d5.24	3.23	□Δ6.68	8.71	E11.25	10.98	9 Mo Sep	6.09	8.36	12
13	....	None Since Public			...	Nil	....	Book Value $3.58			6-30-95	p....	p...	★5567	Ap	d0.03	0.04	d0.09	0.11	0.27	0.35	3 Mo Jul	0.03	0.11	13
14◆	1894	Q0.20	12-20-95	12-4	0.973	0.80	0.707	Book Value $15.09			9-30-95	....	...	5050	Dc	1.39	1.53	Δ1.65	1.81	....	1.91	9 Mo Sep	1.35	1.45	14
15◆	1977	Q0.21	1-31-96	12-27	s0.742	0.84	s0.613	Book Value $13.12			9-30-95	6.58	...	18187	Dc	1.20	1.36	1.57	1.75	....	1.87	9 Mo Sep	1.30	1.42	15
16	1983	Q0.19	1-4-96	12-8	0.74	0.76	0.66	Book Value $17.89			9-30-95	....	...	12349	Dc	1.42	1.43	1.68	1.67	....	1.85	9 Mo Sep	1.38	1.56	16
17◆	1973	Q0.10	12-13-95	11-24	h[59]0.38¾	0.40	0.38¾	51.2	208	94.7	9-30-95	83.3	...	20820	Je	0.27	0.21	d1.17	Δ0.88	2.80	2.65	3 Mo Sep	0.74	0.59	17
18◆	....	None Since Public			...	Nil	....	Equity per shr $4.09			9-30-95	....	...	5883	Mr	0.58	0.89	0.83	d0.09	....	0.36	6 Mo Sep	d0.11	0.34	18
19	1995	Q0.07	1-19-96	1-8	0.07	[52]....	....	Book Value $15.12			9-30-95	....	...	4700	Dc	...	...	...	p0.69	....	0.69	6 Mo Jun	Nil	Nil	19
20	1995	0.06	1-31-96	1-10	0.10	0.10	....	Book Value $8.22			9-30-95	....	...	2018	Dc	0.04	□0.39	Δ0.88	3.17	....	1.07	9 Mo Sep	3.05	0.95	20
21◆	1984	Q0.14	11-15-95	11-1	0.56	0.56	0.52	Book Value $15.66			3-31-95	....	...	4502	Dc	1.07	1.33	Δ1.31	0.91	....	0.99	9 Mo Sep	0.66	0.74	21
22	1864	Q0.44	1-30-96	1-5	1.70	1.76	1.62	Book Value $26.13			3-31-95	p490	...	p63279	Dc	3.32	□2.86	4.20	3.69	E3.80	3.56	9 Mo Sep	2.82	2.69	22
23	....	None Since Public			...	Nil	....	0.68	6.24	6.62	9-30-95	0.29	...	25325	Mr	Δd0.26	d1.03	d1.76	d1.31	....	d1.57	6 Mo Sep	d0.41	d0.67	23
24	1995	Q0.10	1-12-96	12-27	0.20	0.40	....	Book Value $20.10			6-30-95	161	...	5274	Sp	...	...	n/a	1.05	P1.11	1.11				24
25◆	....	3%Stk	3-15-94	2-14	...	Nil	3%Stk	Equity per shr $14.55			9-30-95	621	...	7363	Dc	1.59	1.52	1.55	[61]0.92	....	0.15	9 Mo Sep	0.71	d0.06	25
26	1996	0.05	1-12-96	12-27	...	[52]....	....	Book Value $13.29			3-31-95	62.7	...	★10911	Mr	...	...	...	p0.72	....	0.72				26
27◆	1935	Q0.28	12-4-95	11-15	1.12	1.12	1.04	Book Value $18.39			9-30-95	857	11	50056	Dc	1.76	2.22	2.38	[62]2.81	E2.90	2.89	9 Mo Sep	2.11	2.19	27
28◆	1973	Q0.08	11-15-95	11-2	s0.30	0.32	0.267	Book Value $12.41			9-30-95	21.8	...	11961	Dc	1.05	□1.21	1.38	1.52	....	1.66	9 Mo Sep	1.12	1.26	28
29	1994	Q0.12	11-6-95	10-25	0.38	0.48	0.18¾	Book Value $16.97			9-30-95	1.60	...	4101	Je	...	...	...	n/a	0.91	0.87	3 Mo Sep	0.23	0.19	29
30	1995	0.12½	11-2-95	10-19	0.22½	0.40	....	Book Value $15.39			9-30-94	p5.38	...	2050	Dc	...	...	p1.28	....	....	....	9 Mo Sep	n/a	p0.38	30
31◆	1994	Q0.05	12-20-95	11-20	0.154	0.20	0.064	Book Value $8.92			9-30-95	5.75	...	1963	Dc	...	p0.60	1.26	[63]1.18	....	1.17	9 Mo Sep	0.87	0.86	31
32◆	....	None Since Public			...	Nil	....	1.43	42.5	20.1	8-31-95	2.57	...	5718	Fb	0.35	0.54	0.11	[64]1.07	....	1.32	6 Mo Aug	0.55	0.80	32
33◆	1895	Q0.53	1-1-96	12-13	1.88	2.12	1.68	Book Value $21.67			9-30-95	★263	...	33575	Dc	2.69	3.19	4.26	4.56	E4.75	4.73	9 Mo Sep	3.34	3.51	33
34	1914	Q0.52	12-15-95	11-28	1.96	2.08	1.72	Book Value $24.63			9-30-95	6041	...	170410	Dc	2.55	pΔ2.25	4.73	4.98	E5.70	5.31	9 Mo Sep	3.94	4.27	34
35◆	1962	Q0.11	2-1-96	12-28	0.40	0.44	0.48	Equity per shr $6.81			9-30-95	248	...	18435	Dc	1.01	1.02	□0.84	0.36	E0.30	1.88	9 Mo Sep	0.27	1.79	35
36◆	1979	Q0.22	12-27-95	12-6	0.85	0.88	0.74	Book Value $22.47			9-30-95	11.1	...	5159	Dc	1.76	2.44	Δ2.79	2.72	....	2.87	9 Mo Sep	2.07	2.22	36
37◆	1992	Q0.06	11-13-95	10-27	0.18	0.24	0.10	Equity per shr Neg			9-30-95	2717	5750	59106	Je	±p0.04	0.30	0.73	□1.69	2.74	3.00	3 Mo Sep	0.57	0.83	37
38	1994	Q0.498	11-20-95	10-27	1.992	1.99	1.367	Cv into 0.8333 com, $38.25				....	5750	...	Je	...	...	...	....	....	....	Mandatory conversion into one com 5-20-98			38
39◆	1960	Q0.35	1-8-96	12-27	1.34	1.40	1.26	Book Value $22.23			9-30-95	0.78	71	33945	Dc	2.17	3.02	3.57	3.51	E3.35	3.35	9 Mo Sep	2.63	2.47	39
40	1995	Q0.48¾	11-15-95	10-30	1.95	1.95	....	Equity per shr $22.89			9-30-95	124	2278	3169	Dc	...	...	...	pd0.93	....	....	9 Mo Sep	pn/a	pd0.96	40
41◆	1995	2%Stk	12-15-95	11-29	s0.412	0.588	....	Book Value $14.67			9-30-95	....	...	775	Dc	0.80	0.94	Δ1.51	1.66	....	1.73	9 Mo Sep	1.31	1.38	41
42◆	1991	A0.17	6-1-95	5-9	0.17	0.17	0.17	0.63	31.4	11.5	9-30-95	0.13	...	2256	Dc	0.85	0.86	0.35	1.33	....	1.57	9 Mo Sep	1.12	1.36	42
43◆	1940	Q0.34	11-15-95	10-26	1.32	1.36	1.16	Book Value $20.63			9-30-95	776	19	74993	Dc	2.13	2.62	3.15	3.22	....	3.02	9 Mo Sep	2.25	2.05	43
44◆	1974	Q0.22	1-1-96	12-13	0.86	0.88	0.78	Book Value $18.35			9-30-95	0.16	...	9836	Dc	1.69	1.93	Δ2.16	2.36	....	2.47	9 Mo Sep	1.74	1.85	44
45◆	....	Q0.08	12-29-95	12-13	0.16	[52]....	....	Book Value $7.92			12-31-94	191	...	15051	Dc	□0.56	□0.74	Δ0.73	□2.01	....	5.45	9 Mo Sep	□d1.48	1.96	45
46◆	....	None Since Public			...	Nil	....	Book Value $17.494			9-30-95	1010	...	10610	Dc	2.61	Δ1.66	d0.19	d2.32	....	0.82	9 Mo Sep	d2.61	0.53	46
47◆	1935	Q0.30	1-2-96	12-14	1.12	1.20	1.04	Book Value $20.30			9-30-95	168	...	18523	Dc	1.92	2.37	2.73	3.00	....	3.10	9 Mo Sep	2.18	2.28	47
48◆	1939	Q0.27	12-11-95	11-22	1.02	1.08	0.98½	Book Value $16.18			9-30-95	....	...	33604	Dc	1.58	2.02	2.19	2.22	....	1.46	9 Mo Sep	1.60	0.84	48
49◆	....	None Since Public			...	Nil	....	Equity per shr Neg			9-30-95	373	...	44858	Dc	0.57	0.67	0.80	0.95	....	1.06	9 Mo Sep	0.73	0.84	49
50	1992	Q0.02	1-5-96	12-19	0.08	0.08	0.08	15.2	388	234	9-30-95	★466	...	16253	Dc	p0.51	1.66	2.00	[68]2.18	....	0.62	9 Mo Sep	1.63	0.07	50
51◆	....	None Since Public			...	Nil	....	86.6	241	342	9-30-95	2012	6300	42434	Dc	d3.05	□d2.35	□d39.23	□7.38	....	d0.66	9 Mo Sep	□7.06	Δd0.98	51
52	....	0.10	3-30-88	3-9	...	Nil	....	0.48	2.15	1.86	7-01-95	0.56	...	891	Sp	d1.63	0.89	0.99	0.43	P[69]0.60	0.60				52

◆**Stock Splits & Divs By Line Reference Index** [2]4-for-3,'92:2-for-1,'93:10%,'94. [7]2-for-1,'92,'93. [8]2-for-1,'93. [10]5-for-4,'92,'93:4-for-3,'94. [14]3-for-2,'93,'95. [15]4-for-3,'94:Adj to 5%,'95. [17]No adj for stk dstr of FirstMiss Gold,'95. [18]5-for-4,'93. [21]2-for-1,'92. [25]Adj for 3%,'94. [27]3-for-2,'91,'92. [28]5-for-4,'92:3-for-2,'93,'95. [31]5-for-4,'95. [32]3-for-2,'95. [33]3-for-2,'92. [35]Adj for 4%,'91(ex'90). [36]2-for-1,'92. [37]2-for-1,'93. [39]3-for-2,'92. [41]Adj for 2%,'95. [42]2-for-1,'91:3-for-1,'92:To split 2-for-1,ex Jan 2. [43]2-for-1,'92. [44]3-for-2,'95. [45]10%,'92:3-for-2,'93(twice),'95. [46]5-for-4,'91. [47]2-for-1,'92:3-for-2,'94. [48]2-for-1,'93. [49]3-for-2,'91,'92,'93. [51]1-for-5 REVERSE,'93.

¶ S&P 500 # MidCap 400 ✢ SmallCap 600 • Options Index	Ticker	Name of Issue (Call Price of Pfd. Stocks)	Market	Com. Rank. & Pfd. Rating	Inst. Hold Cos	Inst. Hold Shs. (000)	Principal Business	Price Range 1971-93 High	1971-93 Low	1994 High	1994 Low	1995 High	1995 Low	Dec. Sales in 100s	December, 1995 Last Sale Or Bid High	Low	Last	%Div Yield	P-E Ratio	Total Return % Annualized 12 Mo	36 Mo	60 Mo
¶1•[1]	FLT	✓Fleet Financial Group	NY,B,Ch,Ph	B+	487	101160	Comm'l bkg,RI,ME,NY,CT,MA	37⅞	2 5/16	41⅜	29⅞	43¼	29⅞	181880	43¼	38⅜	40¾	4.2	10	30.3	11.3	33.0
2	WS	Wrrt (Pur 1 com at$43.875)	NY	....	20	259		....	....	....	....	13	3⅛	2084	13	9⅞	12	...	..	...	...	...
3	WS.A	Wrrt (Pur 1 com at$24.78)	NY,Ch	....	34	166		....	....	7	2	16⅜	2⅜	1523	16⅜	12⅞	14¾	...	..	...	...	...
¶4•[2]	FLE	✓Fleetwood Enterpr	NY,B,Ch,P,Ph	B+	310	27759	Recreat'l vehicle/Mfr hous'g	26⅞	⅞	27¼	17⅞	26⅜	17¾	36061	26⅜	24	25¾	2.3	15	40.3	5.5	21.3
¶5•[3]	FLM	✓Fleming Cos	NY,B,Ch,Ph,P	B+	292	26559	Whlse food to affil stores	45⅞	4¼	30	22⅝	29⅞	19⅛	35728	25¾	20	20⅝	5.8	16	−7.9	−8.4	−6.6
6	FCC.A	Fletcher Challenge Cda'A'	To,Mo,Vc	↑B−	43	8709	Canadian mfr timber products	25⅞	1 13/16	23¼	16	24¾	17	26077	22¾	19¾	21¾	1.1	13	25.7	13.0	...
7	FFS	✓Fletcher Challenge Forest ADS	NY	NR	24	1706	Oper wood/forestry division	18½	16⅜	19⅞	10½	15⅞	11½	4435	14⅝	13	14⅜	2.7	23	25.1	...	...
8	FLC	Fletcher Challenge Ord ADS	NY	NR	22	1852	Fin'l operations division	19¼	17¼	28¼	16⅜	31⅝	22⅝	3398	25⅛	22¾	23⅛	3.5	9	2.6	...	...
9	FLXS	✓Flexsteel Indus	NNM	B	39	3229	Quality upholstered furniture	17½	11/16	18½	9½	13¼	10¼	3110	11⅝	10¼	10¼	4.7	18	−16.1	−4.1	6.8
10	FLEXF	Flextronics Intl	NNM	NR	..	...	Mfr circuit boards	....	....	16½	8¾	30¼	13	18258	30¼	24¾	30	...	43	87.5	...	...
#11•[4]	FSI	✓Flightsafety Intl	NY,B,Ch	A	175	16700	Aircraft & marine training	65¼	¼	44¼	33½	52⅝	37½	8085	52½	50	50¼	1.1	19	23.9	7.3	2.1
12	FNRI	✓Flores & Rucks	NNM,Mo	NR	39	5158	Oil&gas explor,dev,prod'n	....	....	10½	8¾	15¼	9¼	5321	15¼	12⅛	14½	...	..	46.8	...	...
13	FLA	✓Florida East Coast Indus	NY,B,Ch	B	80	1728	Hldg co:Fla RR,land hldgs	77½	3⅝	77⅝	57⅝	80¾	64⅛	2567	68⅞	64⅛	68¼	0.6	22	4.0	12.6	9.5
14	FPD	Florida P&L 8.75%'QUIDS'[55]	NY	NR	..	...	Quarterly Income Debt Sec	....	....	....	....	27¼	25	234	27¼	26⅜	27⅛	8.1	..	...	...	...
#15	FPC	✓Florida Progress	NY,B,C,Ch,P,Ph	A−	308	34909	Hldg co:electric utility	36⅜	3⅝	33⅝	24¾	35¾	29⅜	35601	35¾	33¾	35⅜	5.7	14	25.1	9.4	13.9
16	FPU	✓Florida Public Utilities	AS,Ch,Ph	B+	9	235	Natural/propane gas,elec svc	24½	3	18⅞	15¾	20	16	111	19¼	18¼	18⅞	6.1	12	25.9	5.2	10.4
17	FRK	✓Florida Rock Indus	AS	B	71	4676	Concrete & aggregates	41¾	13/16	34½	23¾	30	26¼	681	29¼	26½	29¼	1.7	12	9.3	7.7	11.8
✢18	FLOW	✓Flow International	NNM	B	63	5101	Mfrs waterjet cutt'g systems	13¼	1	8½	4⅝	13¼	6½	21429	9⅝	7⅞	9⅜	...	18	33.9	13.7	44.3
#19•[4]	FLO	✓Flowers Indus	NY,B,Ch,Ph	B+	150	28119	Baked,convenience,snack food	14⅝	7/16	13½	10⅝	15⅜	11¼	39935	13⅜	12⅛	12⅛	4.7	16	3.9	1.5	10.3
✢20	FLK	✓Fluke Corp	NY,Ch,P	↑B	72	3913	Test & measure instr'ts/sys	34⅜	1⅛	32	24⅝	42½	27¾	10691	37¾	32	37¾	1.6	17	28.9	13.9	26.9
¶21•[5]	FLR	✓Fluor Corp	NY,B,C,Ch,P,Ph	↑B+	572	51041	Engr'g & constrn: coal,lead	71	3⅝	56¼	40⅛	68	42¾	45128	68	63¾	66	1.0	24	53.0	18.3	13.4
22	FLRO	✓FluoroScan Imaging Sys	NNM	NR	9	485	Mfr low-intensity x-ray equip	....	....	8⅜	5⅝	10⅝	5¾	3983	7¾	5⅞	6½	...	18	10.6	...	...
23	FFIC	Flushing Financial	NNM	NR	..	...	Savings bank, New York	....	....	....	....	15⅝	13¾	21855	15⅝	14⅛	15⅜	...	..	...	...	...
¶24•[3]	FMC	✓FMC Corp	NY,B,C,Ch,P,Ph	↑B	349	25303	Chemicals/machinery	72	9	65⅛	45½	80	57⅛	18724	75⅛	67⅛	67⅝	...	12	17.4	11.5	16.8
25	FGL	✓FMC Gold	NY,Ch,Ph	NR	45	3950	Gold/silver min'g,process'g	17⅝	3⅞	7⅛	2⅞	6¾	2¾	6201	4⅞	4⅛	4⅛	1.2	d	34.0	0.2	−13.3
26	FMXI	✓Foamex International	NNM	NR	54	9949	Mfr polyurethane foam prd	17	15	20¾	7¼	11⅜	6⅜	18221	7⅞	6⅝	7⅜	...	13	−24.4	...	...
27•[1]	FDLNB	✓Food Lion Inc Cl'B'[63]	NNM	A−	73	15753	Oper food supermarket chain	18⅛	1/32	7½	5⅛	6½	5	54051	5⅞	5⅜	5⅝	1.6	16	10.1	−10.4	−7.6
28•[1]	FDLNA	✓ Class'A'non-vtg	NNM	A−	90	28948		18⅛	1/16	7⅜	5	6⅝	4⅞	96643	6⅛	5½	5¾	1.7	16	10.8	−8.7	−6.7
29	FSM	✓Foodarama Supermkts	AS,Ch	C	14	259	Shop-Rite food chain	38⅝	2	14½	10⅜	13	9¾	35	10⅞	10	10B	...	12	−9.1	−14.1	−14.6
30	FBAI	✓Foodbrands America	NNM	NR	35	3575	Mfr precook meat/topp'g prod	437	7¼	15¼	6	15⅝	7¼	5907	13¼	10⅜	12	...	d	52.4	−9.1	...
✢31•[6]	FM	✓Foodmaker Inc	NY,Ph	NR	44	11214	Oper Jack-in-Box,Chi-Chi rstr	18½	7½	10¾	3⅜	7¼	3¼	59424	6¼	4⅞	6	...	d	45.5	−22.7	...
32	FOOT	✓Foothill Independent Banc	NNM	B+	13	197	Commercial banking, Calif	9¾	3½	8⅞	6⅞	9¼	7	523	8⅜	7¾	8	...	9	16.9	20.5	20.6
33	FGAS	✓Forcenergy Gas Exploration	NNM	NR	21	5849	Oil & gas explor,dvlp,prod'n	....	....	....	....	11½	9¼	4033	11½	10⅜	11	...	..	...	...	...
¶34•[7]	F	✓Ford Motor	NY,To,B,C,Ch,P,Ph,Mo	B−	1039	472697	Second largest auto maker	33⅛	1¾	35⅛	25⅝	32⅞	24⅝	571334	30	27⅞	28⅞	4.8	7	8.1	15.1	21.7
35	Pr	8.40% cm Cv[67]Dep Pfd([68]51.68)	NY,Ph	A	249	24913		110¾	50⅝	116¾	84⅛	107½	80¾	3126	97¼	90⅞	94¾	4.4	..	...	...	...
36•[8]	FORE	✓FORE Systems	NNM	NR	88	8335	Mfr high-performace ntwk prd	....	....	35¾	8	67¾	25½	178653	67¾	52	59½	...	..	71.2	...	...
37	FCOA	✓Foremost Corp,Amer	NNM	B	82	5902	Mobile home & RV insurance	54⅞	1 3/16	38¼	30¼	52¾	35¼	3372	52¾	48½	50¾	2.1	12	48.8	21.8	31.8
38	FCE.A	✓Forest City Enterp Cl'A'	AS,Ch	NR	51	2476	R.E. dev & const	56¾	1 5/16	43⅜	27¾	39½	29	1312	33⅝	32⅛	32⅜	0.8	d	9.6	21.6	17.9
39	FCE.B	Class B Cv	AS,Ch	NR	24	701		58½	13	46⅜	29½	39⅜	29⅞	431	33⅞	32	32	0.8	d	7.5	21.7	17.8
#40•[6]	FRX	✓Forest Labs	AS,B,Ch,P,Ph	B+	310	36951	Pharmaceutical mfr & dstr	47⅞	1/16	52½	40	52¼	40⅜	20162	45⅞	42⅛	45¼	...	20	−3.7	3.8	13.2
41	FOIL	✓Forest Oil	NNM	C	49	13506	Oil & natural gas explor/dev	29⅞	1	4¾	1⅞	3¼	1⅜	87803	3¼	2½	2¾	...	d	18.4	−4.1	−11.7
✢42	FSNR	✓Forschner Group	NNM	B	48	3586	Dstr'Swiss Army Knife' prod	18¼	2⅜	16¼	10¼	13	10	3947	12⅝	11⅛	12⅜	...	23	−1.0	2.5	15.6
43•[5]	FORT	✓Fort Howard	NNM	NR	97	51344	Mfr sanitary tissue prod	....	....	....	....	23¼	12	28343	23¼	18¾	22½	...	49	...	...	...
44	AGFIB	Fortis-AG[70] Group[71]	BEL	NR	..	...	Intl insurance/banking	3688	1378	2790	2300	3580	2470	....	3580	3425	3575	...	..	...	...	...
45	AMEVN	Fortis-N.V.[73] AMEV[71]	Am	NR	..	...	Intl insurance/banking	89¼	42⅞	79¼	66½	109¾	69⅝	....	108½	103¾	107½	...	..	...	...	...
46	FPX	✓Fortune Petroleum	AS,Ch	NR	16	662	Oil&gas explor,devl,prod'n	10⅝	1¼	3⅝	1⅜	4⅞	1 5/16	18233	4⅞	3¾	4⅞	...	d	152	−0.8	10.2
47	WS	Wrrt(Pur 1.43com at$2.61)	AS	....	3	103		....	....	1 11/16	3/16	3½	¼	3918	3½	2⅝	3⅜	...	..	...	...	...
48	FRL	✓Forum Retirem't[74] Ptnrs	AS,Ch	NR	1	15	Owns retirement living ctrs	14¼	¼	3	1⅝	2⅞	1⅞	379	2⅞	2½	2⅞	...	..	27.8	56.5	13.1
¶49•[9]	FWC	✓Foster Wheeler	NY,B,Ch,P,Ph	A	324	23389	Engineering/constr'n svcs	35⅞	1 9/16	45⅛	26⅝	43½	29⅜	31803	43½	39½	42½	1.8	34	42.9	16.4	15.3
#50•[2]	FH	✓Foundation Health	NY	NR	250	46824	Administers health care svcs	44¾	6⅝	46	29¾	46¾	26⅜	52168	46¾	39	43¼	...	39	35.2	4.4	38.8
51	GUSH	✓Fountain Oil	NNM	NR	11	208	Oil & gas acq,dvlp	....	....	5	2½	7⅜	3⅜	16052	5½	3⅝	4⅛	...	d	...	...	...
52	FPI	✓Fountain Powerboat Ind	AS	C	9	164	Mfr/sells sport/fishing boats	28½	1½	6⅝	2¼	8¼	4½	439	5¾	5¼	5⅜	...	10	0.0	10.4	21.9

Uniform Footnote Explanations-See Page 4. Other: [1]ASE:Cycle 1. [2]ASE:Cycle 2. [3]NY:Cycle 2. [4]Ph:Cycle 2. [5]CBOE:Cycle 1. [6]CBOE:Cycle 2. [7]CBOE:Cycle 3. [8]Ph:Cycle 1. [9]P:Cycle 1. [51]Pfd in $M. [52]®$3.2. [53]Fiscal Dec'91 & prior. [54]12 Mo Jun'92. [55]Jr Sub Deferrable Int Debs. [56]Can be deferred by co re-spec cond.. [57]Redm restrn(8.2102%)to 3-1-97. [58]Subsid pfd. [59]Fiscal Sep'92 & prior. [60]12 Mo Apr'93. [61]®$4.65,'94. [62]FMC Corp owns 80%. [63]Vtg. [64]3 Mo Dec'91. [65]L-T-D as of 12-31-94. [66]®$4.44,'94. [67]Dep for 0.001 shr Ser'A'cm Cv Pfd. [68]Fr 12-7-97. [69]®$2.14,'95. [70]All data reported in Belgium Francs. [71]Own 50% Fortis. [72]Current data not available. [73]All data reported in Dutch Guilders. [74]L.P. Pfd Dep Units. [75]78.7% owned by Forum Grp. [76]CP. [77]Fiscal Oct'93 & prior. [78]10 Mo Aug,'94.

Splits ◆ Index	Cash Divs. Ea.Yr. Since	Dividends: Latest Payment Period $	Date	Ex. Div.	Total $ So Far 1995	Ind. Rate	Paid 1994	Financial Position Mil-$ Cash& Equiv.	Curr. Assets	Curr. Liab.	Balance Sheet Date	Capitalization Lg Trm Debt Mil-$	Shs. 000 Pfd.	Com.	Earnings $ Per Shr. Years End	1991	1992	1993	1994	1995	Last 12 Mos.	Interim Earnings Period	$ per Shr. 1994	1995	Index
1	1791	Q0.43	1-1-96	11-29	1.60	1.72	1.30	Equity per shr $23.63			9-30-95	p6734	[51]p682	p245800	Dc	0.67	1.61	3.01	3.75	E4.20	4.19	9 Mo Sep	2.70	3.14	1
2	....	Terms&trad. basis should be checked in detail						Wrrts expire 1-26-2001				....	...	2500	Dc	...	...	...	....	....	....				2
3	....	Terms&trad. basis should be checked in detail						Wrrts expire 1-18-96				....	...	★1200	Dc	...	...	...	....	....	....				3
4◆	1965	Q0.15	2-14-96	1-3	0.58	0.60	0.53	Equity per shr $13.92			10-29-95	0.30	...	46084	Ap	0.69	0.88	1.23	□1.46	1.82	1.75	6 Mo Oct	1.08	1.01	4
5	1927	Q0.30	12-8-95	11-16	1.20	1.20	1.20	4.75	1597	1316	10-07-95	1636	...	37662	Dc	Δ2.06	□[52]3.33	□1.02	1.51	E1.30	1.29	40 Wk Oct	1.23	1.01	5
6	....	Q0.15	12-15-95	11-29	0.40	0.25	....	35.7	485	352	j6-30-94	392	...	p124189	Je	[53]d0.44	[54]d0.69	d0.26	0.21	P0.97	j1.62	3 Mo Sep	Nil	0.65	6
7	1994	0.196	11-15-95	10-17	0.393	0.39	0.354	37.0	138	149	j6-30-95	377	...	600000	Je	...	...	p1.33	0.30	0.62	0.62				7
8	1994	0.409	11-15-95	10-17	s0.82	0.82	0.739	213	2903	2310	j6-30-95	3033	...	1541000	Je	...	...	p0.96	2.85	2.63	2.63				8
9	1938	Q0.12	1-8-96	12-21	0.48	0.48	0.48	14.3	68.4	22.1	9-30-95	0.07	...	7211	Je	□0.27	0.24	0.87	Δ0.91	0.73	0.57	3 Mo Sep	0.22	0.06	9
10	....	None Since Public			...	Nil	....	29.1	80.7	46.1	3-31-94	1.13	...	p11902	Mr	...	p0.12	P0.48	P0.51	....	0.70	6 Mo Sep	0.32	0.51	10
11	1976	Q0.14	2-8-96	1-12	0.50	0.56	0.42	221	295	86.4	9-30-95	38.4	...	30855	Dc	2.11	2.39	2.01	2.35	E2.70	2.68	9 Mo Sep	1.60	1.93	11
12	....	None Since Public			...	Nil	....	....	15.2	34.5	9-30-95	165	...	15044	Dc	...	...	p0.04	pd0.64	....	....	9 Mo Sep	n/a	0.05	12
13	1980	Q0.10	12-29-95	12-13	0.40	0.40	0.40	18.8	64.2	37.3	9-30-95	....	...	9052	Dc	3.21	2.67	Δ2.31	3.85	....	3.11	9 Mo Sep	2.90	2.16	13
14	....	Plan qtly div			...	[56]2.188	....	Co opt redm $27 to 2-28-97 then $25[57]				61.1	...	...	Dc	...	...	...	....	....	....	Mature 11-1-2025			14
15◆	1937	Q0.505	12-20-95	12-1	2.02	2.02	1.99	9.40	669	513	9-30-95	1579	[58]1385	96147	Dc	2.13	2.06	Δ2.22	2.28	E2.50↑	2.50	12 Mo Sep	2.22	2.50	15
16	1942	Q0.29	1-2-96	12-13	1.16	1.16	1.15	2.52	12.6	17.2	9-30-95	23.5	6	1460	Dc	1.43	1.47	1.22	1.18	....	1.52	12 Mo Sep	1.23	1.52	16
17◆	1978	S0.25	1-2-96	12-14	0.50	0.50	0.50	0.93	78.8	57.6	9-30-95	9.65	...	9487	Sp	0.22	0.42	0.85	1.82	2.51	2.51				17
18	....	None Since Public			...	Nil	....	1.84	73.3	24.5	10-31-95	37.2	...	14418	Ap	d0.08	*0.23	*0.30	Δ0.18	0.53	0.52	6 Mo Oct	0.27	0.26	18
19◆	1971	Q0.143	11-17-95	11-1	0.557	0.57	0.53	31.8	189	147	7-01-95	121	...	57612	Je	0.47	0.61	0.71	0.53	0.75	0.78	3 Mo Sep	0.11	0.14	19
20	1989	Q0.15	2-16-96	1-24	0.58	0.60	0.54	24.4	187	54.7	10-27-95	17.0	...	8047	Ap	0.46	[59]2.16	[60]1.28	1.10	1.86	2.28	6 Mo Oct	0.69	1.11	20
21	1974	Q0.17	1-16-96	12-21	0.60	0.68	0.52	433	1293	1072	7-31-95	26.5	...	83024	Oc	1.97	□0.47	2.03	2.32	P2.78	2.78				21
22	....	None Since Public			...	Nil	....	4.63	8.36	1.16	6-30-95	....	...	3473	Dc	...	0.15	0.52	0.57	....	0.37	9 Mo Sep	0.51	0.31	22
23	....	None Since Public			...	Nil	....	Book Value $15.89			6-30-95	....	...	★8625	Dc	...	...	...	p0.80	....	....	6 Mo Jun	n/a	p0.15	23
24◆	....	0.55	3-31-86	3-3	...	Nil	....	101	1749	1684	9-30-95	995	...	36696	Dc	□4.77	□3.24	□1.11	[61]4.66	E5.80	5.64	9 Mo Sep	3.99	4.97	24
25	1987	A0.05	12-31-95	12-5	0.05	0.05	0.05	0.03	100	22.2	9-30-95	....	...	[62]73484	Dc	0.10	0.20	d0.70	Nil	....	d0.06	9 Mo Sep	d0.01	d0.07	25
26	....	None Since Public			...	Nil	....	25.6	405	213	10-01-95	713	...	25846	Dc	...	□p0.30	□pd0.25	0.98	....	0.59	9 Mo Sep	0.74	0.35	26
27◆	1971	Q0.024	10-24-95	10-5	0.095	0.09	0.088	168	1197	733	9-09-95	675	...	±479020	Dc	±0.43	±0.37	±0.01	±0.32	....	0.35	36 Wk Sep	±0.21	±0.24	27
28◆	1983	Q0.024	10-24-95	10-5	0.097	0.10	0.09	....	...	...		....	...	240578	Dc	±0.43	±0.37	±0.01	±0.32	....	0.35	36 Wk Sep	±0.21	±0.24	28
29	....	0.12½	10-2-79	9-17	...	Nil	....	4.57	37.3	47.2	7-29-95	18.6	136	1118	Oc	d0.49	0.64	d1.84	d0.58	....	0.82	9 Mo Jul	d0.87	□0.53	29
30	....	None Paid			...	Nil	....	4.93	95.3	63.9	9-30-95	164	...	12454	Dc	[64]0.68	d4.63	□0.32	□d1.57	....	d4.07	9 Mo Sep	d0.42	d2.92	30
31	....	None Since Public			...	Nil	....	14.3	77.8	133	7-09-95	440	...	38726	Sp	p0.57	□0.67	□d1.15	□d0.94	Pd1.77	d1.77				31
32◆	1989	0.09	1-30-95	1-9	0.091	Nil	s0.364	Book Value $7.58			9-30-95	0.22	...	3947	Dc	1.04	0.89	Δ0.82	0.89	....	0.94	9 Mo Sep	0.61	0.66	32
33	....	None Since Public			...	Nil	....	0.57	19.3	35.2	9-30-95	108	...	★18250	Dc	...	...	...	pd0.13	....	0.04	9 Mo Sep	pd0.26	pd0.09	33
34◆	1983	Q0.35	12-1-95	10-30	1.23	1.40	0.91	Equity per shr $15.50			12-31-94	[65]65207	69	±p1074089	Dc	d2.40	□d0.73	2.27	[66]4.97	E4.25↓	4.60	9 Mo Sep	3.50	3.13	34
35	1992	Q1.05	12-1-95	10-30	4.20	4.20	4.20	Cv into 3.2654 com, $15.312				....	46000	...	Dc	...	...	...	....	....	....				35
36◆	....	None Since Public			...	Nil	....	32.8	83.4	30.9	9-30-95	....	...	★31608	Mr	...	...	p0.09	0.27	....	0.36	6 Mo Sep	0.09	0.18	36
37	1978	Q0.27	12-15-95	11-13	1.08	1.08	1.08	Equity per shr $23.68			9-30-95	97.8	...	10182	Dc	0.90	2.25	3.01	2.80	....	4.24	9 Mo Sep	1.76	3.20	37
38	1994	0.25	12-15-95	11-29	0.25	0.25	0.20	Equity per shr $20.38			7-31-95	1924	...	±8992	Ja	±d0.69	±1.41	±0.25	±Δd2.06	....	d2.09	9 Mo Oct	Δ±d0.36	±Δd0.39	38
39	1994	0.25	12-15-95	11-29	0.25	0.25	0.20	Cv into 1 Cl'A'				....	...	3830	Ja	±d0.69	±1.41	±0.25	Δd2.06	....	d2.09	9 Mo Oct	Δ±d0.36	Δ±d0.39	39
40◆	....	2%Stk	7-2-73	5-30	...	Nil	....	124	359	65.9	9-30-95	....	...	45294	Mr	1.13	1.42	1.75	[69]2.15	E2.30↓	2.33	6 Mo Sep	1.01	1.19	40
41◆	....	3%Stk	6-10-91	5-14	...	Nil	....	3.42	22.2	31.0	9-30-95	182	2881	48552	Dc	Δ±d3.21	±0.36	□d0.53	□d2.49	....	d1.75	9 Mo Sep	□d1.23	d0.49	41
42	....	None Paid			...	Nil	....	0.69	74.7	21.3	9-30-95	....	...	8187	Dc	0.45	0.80	Δ1.04	1.16	....	0.55	9 Mo Sep	0.81	0.20	42
43	....	None Since Public			...	Nil	....	0.44	299	277	9-30-95	3011	...	63371	Dc	...	...	...	pd0.20	....	0.46	9 Mo Sep	□d0.44	□0.22	43
44	....	....			...	[72]....	....	Equity per shr 2,138			j12-31-94	1100	...	±35396	Dc	239.00	242.00	242.00	285.00	....	j285.00				44
45	....	....			...	[72]....	....	Equity per shr 75.43			j12-31-93	332	...	70578	Dc	7.75	817.00	8.12	....	....	j8.12				45
46◆	....	None Paid			...	Nil	....	2.67	3.43	4.64	9-30-95	1.69	...	9382	Dc	d0.92	d0.28	d2.06	d1.12	....	d1.05	9 Mo Sep	d0.37	d0.30	46
47	....	Terms&trad. basis should be checked in detail						Wrrts expire 9-28-98				....	...	1800	Dc	...	...	...	....	....	....				47
48	....	0.09	2-14-91	12-24	...	Nil	....	4.69	9.16	7.98	9-30-95	48.2	...	[75]15285	Dc	d2.64	d0.69	□d0.17	0.02	....	0.01	9 Mo Sep	0.02	0.01	48
49	1960	Q0.19½	12-15-95	11-13	0.77	0.78	0.72	[76]519	1486	1089	9-29-95	★655	...	★40068	Dc	1.22	□1.28	1.62	1.83	E1.25	2.03	9 Mo Sep	1.31	1.51	49
50◆	....	None Since Public			...	Nil	....	Equity per shr $6.47			9-30-95	224	...	57062	Je	1.33	2.02	2.05	2.84	0.90	1.11	3 Mo Sep	0.48	0.69	50
51◆	....	None Since Public			...	Nil	....	4.79	5.29	1.10	8-31-95	....	...	10834	Au	d1.00	d1.00	[77]d0.50	[78]d0.50	d0.91	d0.91				51
52◆	....	None Since Public			...	Nil	....	0.23	5.98	5.54	9-30-95	6.81	...	3029	Je	d1.50	d0.66	0.04	d1.00	0.68	0.56	3 Mo Sep	0.26	0.14	52

◆**Stock Splits & Divs By Line Reference Index** [4]2-for-1,'93. [15]3-for-2,'92. [17]No adj for spinoff'86. [19]3-for-2,'95. [24]No adj for recap:$80 & 1 new com'86. [27]3-for-2,'92. [28]3-for-2,'92. [32]Adj for 5%,'93:10%,'95. [34]2-for-1,'94. [36]2-for-1,'95. [40]2-for-1,'91. [41]Adj to 3%,May,'91. [46]1-for-4 REVERSE'93. [50]3-for-2,'92. [51]1-for-25 REVERSE,'94. [52]1-for-2 REVERSE,'94.

¶ S&P 500 # MidCap 400 ✣ SmallCap 600 • Options

Index	Ticker	Name of Issue (Call Price of Pfd. Stocks)	Market	Com. Rank. & Pfd. Rating	Inst. Hold Cos	Inst. Hold Shs. (000)	Principal Business	Price Range 1971-93 High	1971-93 Low	1994 High	1994 Low	1995 High	1995 Low	Dec. Sales in 100s	December, 1995 Last Sale Or Bid High	Low	Last	%Div Yield	P-E Ratio	Total Return % Annualized 12 Mo	36 Mo	60 Mo
1	FRTH	✔Fourth Financial[51]	NNM	A–	75	5737	Comm'l bkg,Wichita,Kansas	31½	2 7/16	33	25	42⅛	29⅝	16995	42⅛	37½	40⅞	e3.6	18	35.6	15.1	23.8
2	FOX	✔FoxMeyer Health	NY,B,C,Ch,P,Ph	B–	89	8371	Whsle dstr drug,beauty aids	52¼	10¼	18¾	13¼	28⅜	14⅜	10300	28⅜	25¾	26¾	...	15	...	...	...
3	Pr	$5 cm Cv Pfd(50:SF50)	NY,Ch	B–	9	67		77	29	52½	48¼	55¾	49¼	953	55¾	52¾	54½	9.2	..	...	...	...
4	FPO	✔FPA Corp	AS	C	11	406	Community devel:leisure sv	14	1/16	3⅜	1¼	2 1/16	1	593	1 1/16	1	1	...	11	–20.0	13.3	51.6
¶5•[1]	FPL	✔FPL Group	NY,B,C,Ch,P,Ph	B	649	82847	Hldg co:Fla Pwr & Lt	41	6¾	39⅛	26⅞	46½	34	64602	46½	43⅛	46⅜	3.8	15	40.1	14.2	16.7
6	FFA	✔Franchise Finance Cp Amer	NY,Ch,Ph	NR	61	4861	Real estate investment trust	....	....	22	16½	23⅜	17⅛	13623	23⅛	19¾	22⅝	8.0	17	40.2	...	...
7	FKKY	Frankfort First Bancorp	NNM	NR	8	711	Savings bank,Kentucky	....	....	....	....	13¼	11⅝	1199	13¼	12¼	13¼	2.7	..	...	...	...
8	FAD	✔Franklin Adv R.E. Inc Fd'A'[55]	AS,Ch	NR	3	1436	Real estate investment trust	....	....	8⅜	5¼	6½	5	234	5⅜	5	5	11.3	11	–1.7	...	...
9	FSVB	✔Franklin Bank N.A.	NNM	B–	13	316	Commercial bank, Michigan	14⅞	2⅛	9¼	6⅞	13	7¾	1757	13	11⅝	13	s1.8	13	74.9	28.2	47.4
10	FELE	✔Franklin Electric	NNM	B+	44	2407	Mfr special purpose elec mtrs	37¼	4¼	36½	24½	34½	28¼	846	33	28¼	33	1.2	15	2.8	13.0	29.7
11	FEP	✔Franklin Electronic Pub	NY	B–	70	3158	Dvlp,mkt computers/elec prd	20¾	1⅜	21½	10½	44¼	20¼	7446	44¼	26¾	29½	...	20	43.9	26.7	56.7
✣12	FNQ	✔Franklin Quest	NY,Ph	NR	153	12066	Provides training seminars&prd	35¼	14⅝	40½	27¼	35⅞	17⅞	20673	19½	17⅞	19½	...	11	–34.5	–1.3	...
13	FIN	✔Franklin R.E. Income Fd[59]	AS,Ph	NR	..	...	Real estate investment trust	....	....	6⅜	4⅛	5⅞	4⅛	955	5⅜	4⅞	5	10.0	12	22.3	...	...
#14•[2]	BEN	✔Franklin Resources	NY,B,Ch,P	A	276	24855	Mut'l fd inv advisory & svcs	51⅞	1/64	51	33⅝	58	33	27658	54¼	46¾	50⅜	0.9	16	43.2	11.3	29.0
15	FSN	✔Franklin Select R.E. Inc Fd'A'	AS	NR	..	...	Real estate investment trust	....	....	5¾	3	4⅝	3¾	1066	4⅜	4	4⅛	10.7	15	16.2	...	...
16	FOH.A	✔Fredericks of Hollywood'A'	NY,Ch,Ph	B	22	1881	Apparel stores, mail order	17⅛	¼	6⅛	3⅝	6¼	4	504	4⅞	4	4¼	1.2	14	4.0	–15.1	...
17	FOH.B	Cl'B'	NY	B	21	4359		7¼	4¾	5⅞	2⅞	6½	3½	883	4¾	3⅞	3⅞	1.3	13	4.4	...	...
18	FSCNY	✔Free St Con Gld Mines ADR[64]	NSC	NR	53	14764	Gold mining,South Africa	19⅝	4	18½	10¾	14⅞	7¼	16067	9	7¼	7¼	4.7	10	–49.8	25.1	5.3
19•[3]	FTX	✔Freeport McMoRan(New)	[4]NY,B,C,Ch,P	NR	233	19336	Mineral dv:gold,copper,sulphur	135¾	11	130½	96¾	145½	24	17944	40½	35⅝	37	1.0	d	...	...	...
¶20•[5]	FCX	✔Freep't McMoRan Copper&Gold'B'	[4]NY	NR	188	39457	Explor'n/mining in Indonesia	....	....	....	....	30¾	22⅝	60928	30¾	26¾	28⅛	3.2	27	...	...	...
21•[1]	FCX.A	✔ Cl'A'	NY,Ph	NR	284	42844		27⅜	2 3/16	27½	19⅝	30½	19⅞	83316	30½	26¾	28	3.2	31	38.2	11.8	32.2
22	Pr	7%cm Cv[67]Dep[68]Ex Pref(26.225)	NY	BB	55	5391		33⅜	25	31¾	22⅜	31¼	22⅞	5351	31¼	28¼	28¾	6.1	..	...	...	...
23	Pr A	$1.25 cm Cv[69]Dep Pfd([70]25)	NY	BB	87	11107		25½	20	26⅞	19¾	28¾	19⅞	6406	28¾	26⅛	27¼	4.6	..	...	...	...
24	FMR	✔Freeport McMoRan O/G Rlty[72]	NY,P,Ph	NR	41	3053	Royalties of oil & gas prop	11⅝	2¼	7¾	1¾	6¼	3⅝	10090	5	4	4⅞	e...	16	16.0	9.2	18.9
25•[6]	FRP	✔Freeport McMoRan Res L.P.	[4]NY,B,Ch,P	NR	66	9117	Prod phosphate fertilizer	31¼	14¾	20½	13⅜	20⅜	14½	18875	19⅝	18½	18½	13.0	14	43.8	15.9	11.3
✣26	FMT	✔Fremont Genl	NY,Ph	B	124	9959	Insur hldg: workers compen	26⅛	1¾	23⅝	19½	37¼	17⅛	15726	37¼	34¼	36¾	2.2	10	96.3	30.3	41.2
27	FEI	✔Frequency Electrs	AS,Ch,P,Ph	C	13	1793	Electronic control prod	36	⅛	5⅞	2⅞	6½	3⅛	9339	6½	3¼	6⅜	...	d	39.7	13.4	9.8
28	FRN	✔Fresenius USA	AS,B,Ch,Ph	B–	48	3639	Dispose med pr:kidney mach	147½	⅝	9	5¼	19⅞	8⅝	2937	19⅞	17	19⅞	...	41	130	59.1	73.9
29	FRES	✔Fresh America	NNM	NR	11	512	Food distribution mgmt svc	....	....	10⅛	7¼	9¾	4⅛	4660	9¾	7⅞	9⅝	...	..	26.2	...	...
✣30	SALD	✔Fresh Choice	NNM	NR	33	956	Oper casual restaurants, Calif	33¼	13	32½	9	12½	5⅛	15637	7¾	6	6¼	...	d	–35.9	–34.8	...
31	FRD	✔Friedman Indus	AS	B–	15	987	Steel coils into plate/sheet	7⅞	13/16	4⅜	3⅜	4⅝	3½	839	4	3½	3⅞	s4.6	8	14.3	29.6	21.0
32	FRDM	✔Friedman's Inc'A'	NNM	NR	73	5048	Retail fine jewelry	16	9	19	10¾	25	16	10155	23¾	18½	19¼	...	20	13.2	...	...
33	FRS	✔Frisch's Restaurants	AS,Ch,Ph	B+	34	1916	Operates coffee shops,motels	32⅞	1	14¼	8⅜	10⅜	7⅞	1822	10⅛	8⅝	9	s2.6	30	5.1	–20.3	5.0
34•[3]	FRTZ	✔Fritz Companies	NNM	NR	166	19965	Freight transportation svcs	15¼	7½	23⅝	13	43¾	22⅝	37771	43	35¼	41½	...	87	85.2	50.4	...
35	FAJ	✔Frontier Adjusters of Amer	AS,Ch	B+	6	154	Franchises insurance adjusters	6⅛	1⅜	3¾	2⅜	3⅛	2 3/16	583	2⅞	2½	2½	5.5	12	2.3	–9.4	–0.1
#36•[7]	FRO	✔Frontier Corp	NY,B,Ch,Ph	B+	355	88933	Diversified Telecom Svcs	25⅛	2 3/16	25¼	20¼	30	19¼	76622	30	25⅝	30	2.8	32	42.1	21.4	16.5
✣37	FTR	✔Frontier Insurance Gr	NY,Ch,Ph	B+	87	5859	Property & casualty insur	33⅜	2⅝	37½	16¾	33¾	20¼	5045	33¾	31⅛	32	1.5	13	48.2	10.7	31.0
✣38	FFEX	✔Frozen Food Express	NNM	A–	42	3872	Transp by refrig mtr carrier	15	3/16	15	11	13⅞	8½	6123	10⅛	8⅝	8¾	1.4	14	–25.4	–3.7	36.6
39	FTC	✔Fruehauf Trailer	NY,Ph	NR	41	15569	Mfr truck trailers/parts	17¾	3	7⅞	3⅜	4½	1⅜	49871	1⅞	1⅜	1⅞	...	d	–46.4	–26.6	...
¶40•[8]	FTL	✔Fruit of The Loom'A'	NY,Ch,P,Ph	NR	263	55610	Global mfr of family apparel	49⅝	3⅞	33	23	27¾	16½	87581	25⅛	19¼	24¼	...	d	–10.2	–21.0	24.1
41•[9]	FSII	✔FSI International	NNM	B–	134	17708	Mfr semiconductor mfg equip	6½	13/16	14¾	5	38½	12½	54961	24¼	17¾	20¼	...	16	53.6	73.8	82.7
42•[7]	FTPS	✔FTP Software	NNM	NR	171	19658	Dvlp internetworking softwr pd	27¾	19	33½	11½	40⅝	20¼	175822	40⅝	28¼	29	...	27	–11.1	...	...
43	FUSE	Fuisz Technologies	NNM	NR	..	...	Dvp stg:pharmaceut'l R&D	....	....	....	....	15¼	12	38361	15¼	12	15¼	...	..	...	...	...
44	FUJIY	✔Fuji Photo Film ADR[80]	NSC	NR	53	3843	Photo films,papers,products	58½	15/16	50½	38¾	59	39½	2918	59	49	58⅛	0.6	23	25.9	11.4	9.2
#45	FULL	✔Fuller (HB)	NNM	B+	132	7232	Industrial adhesives	53¼	1 1/16	42¼	27¾	39¾	29¾	10260	39¼	32	34¾	1.8	16	6.4	–4.4	12.8
46	FFC	✔Fund Amer Enterpr[83] Hldgs[84]	.[10]NY,B,Ch	NR	91	4610	Mortgage/finl svcs	92½	24⅛	79½	60	76	66	2860	75½	69⅜	74½	...	9	2.3	...	...
47	FQE	✔Fuqua Enterprises	NY,Ch	B	37	1164	Manufacture leather products	27¼	⅝	25⅜	19½	24¾	18¼	1417	20⅞	18⅝	18⅝	...	11	–10.8	4.9	16.0
48	FCY	✔Furon Co	NY,Ch	B+	70	6232	Mfr non-metallic ind'l pr	19	5/16	23¼	14¼	23⅜	15½	4827	20½	17⅛	20	1.2	14	–12.0	12.6	15.9
49	CHI	✔Furr's/Bishop's Inc'A'	NY	NR	3	2	Operates cafeterias	3⅝	⅜	1	⅛	¾	⅛	2246	¼	⅛	¼	...	d	25.1	–40.8	...
50	Pr	Series A cm Cv Pfd(9)	NY	NR	6	79		6½	½	⅞	⅛	⅜	⅛	3566	3/16	⅛	⅛	...	..	...	...	...
51•[9]	FUSN	✔Fusion Systems	NNM	NR	91	5961	Mfr ultraviolet curing sys	....	....	35	14½	38	21½	18590	33½	26¾	28	...	16	5.7	...	...
✣52	GKSRA	✔G & K Services Cl'A'	NNM	A–	99	11564	Rents & launders textile prod	16	3/16	17¼	12½	26	15	10591	25¾	22¾	25½	0.3	27	55.1	38.1	32.0

Uniform Footnote Explanations-See Page 4. Other: [1]Ph:Cycle 3. [2]P:Cycle 2. [3]CBOE:Cycle 2. [4]Ph [5]Ph:Cycle 2. [6]ASE:Cycle 3. [7]CBOE:Cycle 1. [8]NY:Cycle 2. [9]CBOE:Cycle 3. [10]P,Ph
[51]Boatmen's Bancshares plan acq,1 com. [52]®$2.74,'94. [53]Stk dstr of Ben Franklin Retail Stores. [54]Subsid pfd in $M. [55]Plan mgr w/Franklin Sel RE Fd 1.2 shs. [56]Incl 0.12M Sr'B'com. [57]®$0.81,'94.
[58]®$1.52,'95. [59]Plan mgr w/Franklin Sel RE Fd 1.286 shs. [60]Incl 0.32M Sr'B' com. [61]®$3.20,'95. [62]Incl 0.19M Sr'B'com. [63]®$0.30,'95. [64]Each ADR rep 1 ord shr,R0.50.
[65]Stk dstr of Freeport-McMoran Copper & Gold. [66]Stk dstr of Freeport McMoRan C&G,McMoRan O&G,'94. [67]To 7-31-96,scale $25 in 2002. [68]Co opt fr 8-1-94 exch for $25 amt 7% Cv 2007.
[69]Dep for 0.05 shr Step-Up Cv Pfd stk. [70]Fr 8-1-96 to 8-1-99 red re-spec cond,aft at $25. [71]Thru 8-1-96,then $1.75. [72]Units of Ben Int. [73]Return of capital. [74]100% non-taxable,'94.
[75]Freeport-McMoRan Inc owns 51%. [76]®$2.73,'94. [77]Fiscal Dec'94 & prior. [78]12 Mo May'95. [79]®$0.79,'94. [80]ADR represents 2 shrs,par 50 yen. [81]Oct'93 & prior. [82]23 Wk Mar'94:Oct'94 earned $2.52.
[83]Approve conclusion of liquid'n plan. [84]Co offer for 0.5M com,$71 to Jan 10. [85]To be determined.

Index (Splits ◆)	Cash Divs. Ea. Yr. Since	Dividends: Latest Payment Period $	Date	Ex. Div.	Total $ So Far 1995	Ind. Rate	Paid 1994	Financial Position Mil-$: Cash& Equiv.	Curr. Assets	Curr. Liab.	Balance Sheet Date	Capitalization: Lg Trm Debt Mil-$	Shs. 000 Pfd.	Com.	Earnings $ Per Shr. Years End	1991	1992	1993	1994	1995	Last 12 Mos.	Interim Earnings Period	$ per Shr. 1994	1995	Index
1	1925	†0.10	1-31-96	1-10	1.21	1.48	1.04	Book Value $17.22			9-30-95	190	248	27649	Dc	1.24	2.17	Δ2.26	[52]2.83	....	2.26	9 Mo Sep	2.07	1.50	1
2	....	h[53]....	9-29-95	9-8	h[53]...	Nil	....	34.3	1226	781	9-30-95	468	4704	16532	Mr	Δ0.91	d0.24	1.10	1.52	E1.85	1.55	6 Mo Sep	0.19	0.22	2
3	1983	Q1.25	1-15-96	1-4	5.00	5.00	5.00	Cv into 1.869 com,$26.75				....	924	...	Mr	b1.75	b0.79	b1.49	b1.45	....	....	SF 88,000 ea Jan 15,$50			3
4	....	0.067	3-8-82	2-5	...	Nil	....	Equity per shr $1.06			9-30-95	44.6	...	11696	Je	d1.67	Δd0.55	d1.32	Δd0.07	0.10	0.09	3 Mo Sep	0.04	0.03	4
5	1944	Q0.44	12-15-95	11-21	1.76	1.76	1.88	103	1146	1529	9-30-95	3338	[54]501	184878	Dc	1.48	2.65	2.30	2.91	E3.15	3.16	12 Mo Sep	2.91	3.16	5
6	1994	Q0.45	11-20-95	11-8	1.80	1.80	0.60	Equity per shr $12.42			9-30-95	243	...	40251	Dc	...	...	p0.88	0.64	....	1.32	9 Mo Sep	0.32	1.00	6
7	1995	0.09	1-15-96	12-27	0.09	0.36	....	Book Value $14.66			9-30-95	4.36	...	3450	Je	...	...	...	....	n/a	....	3 Mo Sep	n/a	0.15	7
8	1994	Q0.143	1-12-96	12-27	0.63	0.57	0.48¾	Equity per shr $8.48			9-30-95	5.28	...	[56]±3138	Dc	0.57	0.50	0.59	0.41	....	0.45	9 Mo Sep	0.36	0.40	8
9◆	1993	5%Stk	1-22-96	1-3	s0.237	0.24	s0.216	Book Value $8.66			12-31-94	22.5	...	2994	Dc	1.83	□0.50	Δ0.82	[57]0.89	....	1.01	9 Mo Sep	0.75	0.87	9
10◆	1993	Q0.10	11-24-95	11-8	0.38	0.40	0.29	27.7	107	47.1	9-30-95	20.0	...	6252	Dc	*1.57	*1.85	Δ2.37	2.84	....	2.24	9 Mo Sep	2.04	1.44	10
11	....	None Paid			...	Nil	....	5.35	58.4	17.2	9-30-95	....	...	7782	Mr	0.47	0.94	1.06	[58]1.56	....	1.45	6 Mo Sep	0.67	0.56	11
12	....	None Since Public			...	Nil	....	35.0	120	32.2	8-31-95	4.52	...	21771	Au	p0.61	p0.93	1.10	1.40	1.71	1.72	3 Mo Nov	0.56	0.57	12
13	1994	Q0.12½	1-12-96	12-27	0.50	0.50	0.37½	Equity per shr $8.17			9-30-95	1.95	...	[60]±4319	Dc	0.51	0.32	0.36	0.39	....	0.41	9 Mo Sep	0.29	0.31	13
14◆	1981	Q0.11	1-15-96	12-27	0.40	0.44	0.32	396	533	200	6-30-95	382	...	80945	Sp	1.25	1.59	2.12	3.00	P[61]3.24	3.24				14
15	1994	Q0.11	1-12-96	12-27	0.44	0.44	0.30	Equity per shr $8.19			9-30-95	....	...	[62]±5569	Dc	0.51	0.28	0.23	0.27	....	0.28	9 Mo Sep	0.18	0.19	15
16◆	1988	0.02½	1-2-96	12-13	0.05	0.05	0.05	11.4	35.6	14.3	9-02-95	1.36	...	±8858	Au	0.58	0.57	0.53	±Δd0.11	±[63]0.31	0.31				16
17	1993	0.02½	1-2-96	12-13	0.05	0.05	0.05	....	...	...		....	...	5903	Au	0.58	0.57	0.53	±Δd0.11	±0.31	0.31				17
18	1986	0.022	1-3-96	11-1	0.592	0.34	0.902	86.1	688	610	j3-31-95	234	1535	118983	Mr	1.56	1.07	1.13	0.75	....	0.75				18
19◆	1995	0.09	12-1-95	11-13	h[65]0.09	0.36	h[66]1.876	28.7	219	205	9-30-95	301	p1002	28066	Dc	□4.08	7.02	□d4.44	□2.22	Ed1.12	13.06	9 Mo Sep	□1.38	12.22	19
20	1995	0.22½	11-1-95	10-12	0.22½	0.90	....	33.5	663	493	9-30-95	976	29404	±202009	Dc	□±0.56	±0.66	±0.16	±0.38	E1.05	0.91	9 Mo Sep	±0.18	±0.71	20
21◆	1988	0.22½	11-1-95	10-12	0.67½	0.90	0.60	....	...	...		....	...	84100	Dc	□±0.56	±0.66	±0.16	±0.38	....	0.91	9 Mo Sep	±0.18	±0.71	21
22	1992	Q0.43¾	11-1-95	10-12	1.75	1.75	1.75	Cv into 0.992 Cl'A'com, $25.20				....	8976	...	Dc	...	b1.15	...	....	....	....				22
23	1993	Q0.31¼	11-1-95	10-12	1.25	[71]1.25	1.25	Cv into 0.813 com,$30.75				....	...	14000	Dc	...	...	...	....	....	....				23
24	1995	0.008	10-10-95	7-27	†0.32¼	Nil	....	Freeport-McMoRan(prop)				....	...	14975	Dc	2.57	1.07	0.42	Nil	....	0.31	9 Mo Sep	Nil	0.31	24
25	1986	[73]Q0.60	11-15-95	10-27	[73]2.415	2.40	[74]2.40	23.9	200	117	9-30-95	347	...	[75]103554	Dc	□1.34	0.20	□d2.14	0.81	....	1.36	9 Mo Sep	0.55	1.10	25
26◆	1977	Q0.20	1-31-96	12-27	0.545	0.80	0.673	Equity per shr $22.40			9-30-95	746	...	16929	Dc	2.28	Δ2.57	2.78	[76]3.25	....	3.68	9 Mo Sep	2.42	2.85	26
27	....	None Since Public			...	Nil	....	18.9	44.9	3.55	10-31-95	11.8	...	4846	Ap	d1.07	0.08	d1.42	d0.85	Δd0.84	d0.17	6 Mo Oct	Δd0.43	0.24	27
28◆	....	None Since Public			...	Nil	....	3.16	112	104	9-30-95	28.6	200	21738	Dc	Δd0.18	0.04	0.18	0.31	....	0.48	9 Mo Sep	0.22	0.39	28
29	....	None Since Public			...	Nil	....	9.31	16.5	5.09	9-29-95	0.21	...	3518	Dc	...	...	p0.46	p0.65	....	....	9 Mo Sep	n/a	0.35	29
30	....	None Since Public			...	Nil	....	0.81	4.29	9.13	9-03-95	0.16	...	5517	Dc	0.23	0.40	0.61	0.58	....	d0.55	36 Wk Sep	0.57	d0.56	30
31◆	1972	Q0.04½	2-23-96	1-17	s0.209	0.18	s0.168	0.43	26.9	6.68	9-30-95	5.80	...	5832	Mr	0.09	0.14	Δ0.28	0.42	....	0.47	6 Mo Sep	0.18	0.23	31
32	....	None Since Public			...	Nil	....	8.34	96.1	18.1	6-30-95	22.4	...	±12038	Sp	...	±pd2.97	±p0.23	±0.63	P0.97	0.97				32
33◆	1956	Q0.058	1-10-96	12-27	s0.231	0.231	0.222	0.54	9.50	18.3	9-17-95	26.3	...	6884	My	0.48	0.77	0.79	0.74	0.35	0.30	3 Mo Aug	0.17	0.12	33
34◆	....	None Since Public			...	Nil	....	70.3	430	366	8-31-95	34.5	...	33600	My	p0.32	p0.64	0.66	[77]0.87	[78]0.34	0.48	3 Mo Aug	0.22	0.36	34
35	1984	Q0.03½	12-8-95	11-16	0.13	0.14	†0.11½	1.76	3.44	0.55	9-30-95	....	...	4610	Je	0.23	0.17	0.19	0.22	0.22	0.22	3 Mo Sep	0.06	0.06	35
36◆	1926	Q0.21¼	2-1-96	1-10	0.83	0.85	0.81	45.1	505	533	9-30-95	633	228	157069	Dc	Δ1.18	□1.04	1.21	□1.50	E0.95↓	1.19	9 Mo Sep	□0.87	Δ□0.56	36
37◆	1992	Q0.12	1-18-96	12-27	0.48	0.48	0.44	Equity per shr $16.41			9-30-95	....	...	13018	Dc	±1.52	±1.77	Δ±2.03	±1.31	....	2.38	9 Mo Sep	±0.69	±1.76	37
38◆	1971	Q0.03	12-1-95	11-20	0.12	0.12	0.096	3.59	61.5	32.0	9-30-95	6.00	...	16242	Dc	0.34	0.45	0.58	0.72	....	0.64	9 Mo Sep	0.55	0.47	38
39	....	None Since Public			...	Nil	....	5.15	103	126	9-30-95	78.0	...	39198	Dc	d3.63	d5.36	Δd6.60	d0.07	....	d0.10	9 Mo Sep	0.03	□Nil	39
40	....	None Since Public			...	Nil	....	14.4	1262	306	9-30-95	1499	...	±75890	Dc	1.60	□2.48	□Δ2.80	0.79	Ed2.00↓	0.48	9 Mo Sep	1.37	1.06	40
41◆	....	None Since Public			...	Nil	....	111	201	54.9	8-26-95	0.05	...	20316	Au	d0.38	d0.36	0.34	0.54	1.13	1.27	3 Mo Nov	0.21	0.35	41
42	....	None Since Public			...	Nil	....	83.8	118	19.9	9-30-95	1.80	...	26421	Dc	p0.24	p0.34	0.65	[79]0.80	....	1.06	9 Mo Sep	0.51	0.77	42
43	....	None Since Public			...	Nil	....	0.50	0.65	1.40	p9-30-95	p0.02	p...	★12026	Dc	...	...	...	pd0.70	....	....	9 Mo Sep	n/a	pd0.40	43
44◆	1950	0.162	12-26-95	9-26	0.49	0.33	0.273	7331	12200	4126	3-31-95	730	...	514626	Mr	2.87	2.44	[81]2.21	‡[82]1.18	....	2.52				44
45◆	1953	Q0.16	2-9-96	1-23	0.62½	0.64	0.57½	4.35	389	243	8-31-95	156	46	14005	Nv	2.00	2.55	□1.55	2.20	E2.22	2.38	9 Mo Aug	1.59	□1.77	45
46◆	....	0.20	12-20-95	12-7	0.20	[85]....	....	Equity per shr $86.54			9-30-95	456	...	7534	Dc	Δ□4.87	□2.77	5.68	□1.20	....	7.97	9 Mo Sep	□2.61	□9.38	46
47	....	0.04	10-18-88	9-27	...	Nil	....	Equity per shr $17.31			9-30-95	34.5	...	3834	Dc	1.23	1.63	Δ2.09	2.48	....	1.74	9 Mo Sep	1.76	1.02	47
48	1976	Q0.06	2-2-96	1-17	0.24	0.24	0.24	2.65	99.3	44.3	10-28-95	23.8	...	8886	Ja	d2.65	0.84	0.92	1.27	....	1.42	9 Mo Oct	0.94	1.09	48
49	....	None Since Public			...	Nil	....	1.42	15.2	280	10-03-95	....	6392	±11326	Dc	d3.46	*d0.93	d15.33	d2.54	....	d2.91	9 Mo Sep	d1.83	d2.20	49
50	....	0.30½	7-30-91	7-9	...	Nil	....	Cv into 0.827 Cl'A'com,$10.88				....	6392	...	Dc	...	...	...	....	....	....	Accum $4.9725 to 10-31-95			50
51	....	None Since Public			...	Nil	....	40.4	81.3	14.4	9-30-95	....	...	7700	Dc	0.45	0.12	0.93	2.58	....	1.73	9 Mo Sep	2.20	1.35	51
52◆	1968	Q0.01¾	1-2-96	12-12	0.07	0.07	0.07	3.05	87.3	42.4	7-01-95	76.5	...	±20408	Je	±Δ0.35	±0.43	±0.55	±0.73	±0.90	0.94	3 Mo Sep	±0.21	±0.25	52

◆**Stock Splits & Divs By Line Reference Index** [9]Adj to 5%,Dec'94. [10]No adj for spl $25(cash or stk)dstr,'89. [14]2-for-1,'92. [16]3-for-2,'91:1-for-3 REVERSE,then 2-for-1 in Cl'B','93. [19]2-for-1,'92:1-for-6 REVERSE,'95:No adj for stk dstr Freeport-McMoran Copper&Gold'95. [21]2-for-1,'92. [26]3-for-2,'93:10%,'95:To split 3-for-2,ex Feb 8. [28]1-for-10 REVERSE,'91. [31]Adj to 5%,'95. [33]Adj to 4%,'95. [34]2-for-1,'95. [36]2-for-1,'94. [37]Adj for 5%,'92:10%,'91,'93:3-for-2,'94. [38]3-for-2,'92:4-for-3,'92,'93:5-for-4,'95. [41]2-for-1,'95. [44]10%,'91. [45]3-for-2,'92. [46]No adj for stk dstr,'93. [52]3-for-2,'94.

¶ S&P 500 # MidCap 400 ✣ SmallCap 600 • Options Index	Ticker	Name of Issue (Call Price of Pfd. Stocks)	Market	Com. Rank. & Pfd. Rating	Inst. Hold Cos	Inst. Hold Shs. (000)	Principal Business	Price Range 1971-93 High	1971-93 Low	1994 High	1994 Low	1995 High	1995 Low	Dec. Sales in 100s	December, 1995 Last Sale Or Bid High	Low	Last	%Div Yield	P-E Ratio	Total Return % Annualized 12 Mo	36 Mo	60 Mo
1	GLR	✔G & L Realty Corp	NY,Ch,Ph	NR	15	757	Real estate investment trust	18¼	16¾	17¾	12⅝	13½	8⅛	5785	10⅞	9⅝	10⅜	12.0	11	−9.3	...	...
2	GBP	✔Gables Residential Trust	NY,Ch	NR	78	6591	Real estate investment trust	....	....	26⅜	18¾	23¼	17½	10140	23⅛	21¾	22⅞	8.4	18	19.6	...	...
3	GADZ	✔Gadzooks Inc	NNM	NR	..	...	Spcl retailer casual apparel	....	....	....	....	26	14	7480	26	20¾	25¼	...	38	...	...	...
4	GNA	✔Gainsco Inc	AS,Ch	B+	78	7229	Property & casualty insur	14½	⅝	8½	6⅞	12⅜	7	8473	12⅜	9⅞	11⅜	s0.4	16	70.5	11.3	49.0
5	GTV	✔Galaxy Cablevision L.P.	AS	NR	6	190	Liquidating assets	26	7⅝	18½	7⅜	7⅝	2 1/16	1156	3⅛	3	3⅛	...	..	98.9	63.3	33.9
✣6	GNL	✔Galey & Lord Inc	NY	NR	51	8653	Mfr cotton apparel fabrics	15	8½	23½	12¾	16	9½	2360	11¾	10¼	10¾	...	24	−22.5	−9.0	...
✣7	AJG	✔Gallagher(Arthur J.)	NY,Ch	A−	95	7307	Ins brokerage,risk mgmt svc	37⅜	6⅞	36⅜	28⅛	38	30⅛	3268	38	32⅝	37¼	2.7	15	22.1	12.7	13.1
8•[1]	GAL	✔Galoob (Lewis) Toys	NY,Ch,P	C	30	3823	Develops,mkts,dstr toy prod	18¾	2¼	10⅝	4¼	13¾	5¼	17226	13¾	10⅝	11¾	...	65	100	55.5	37.7
9	Pr	$1.70 cm Cv[56]Dep[57]ExPfd(20.68)	[2]NY	NR	12	1096		20⅜	5⅜	16	10½	21⅜	11⅛	261	21⅜	19¾	20⅞	...	..	...	...	...
10	GBL	✔Gamma Biologicals	AS,Ch	B−	18	787	Blood transfusion prod	17¼	2	7⅛	3⅞	5	3⅞	4294	4⅞	4⅛	4⅝	2.2	16	5.2	4.3	14.0
11•[3]	GANDF	Gandalf Technologies	NNM,To	C	61	11496	Electr data communic prod	21¾	1⅛	3	½	20	1¼	545507	20	14½	17	...	..	1136	77.1	46.0
12	GNDR	✔Gander Mountain	NNM	↓C	24	932	Retails outdoor clothing,eqp	15	5½	19⅝	10¼	18¼	3½	9002	8¾	5⅞	6⅝	...	d	−60.4	−15.6	3.5
¶13•[4]	GCI	✔Gannett Co	NY,B,Ch,P,Ph	A	678	97495	Newspapers: TV/radio:adv	58¼	3⅝	59	46⅛	64⅞	49½	69098	64⅞	59⅛	61⅜	2.3	18	18.5	8.4	14.2
¶14•[5]	GPS	✔Gap Inc	NY,B,Ch,P,Ph	A	468	60889	Apparel specialty stores	59⅜	¼	49⅜	28⅞	51	29¾	116633	47¼	41⅛	42	1.1	18	39.6	9.8	22.2
15	GAN	✔Garan Inc	AS,Ch	B+	48	2343	Knitted/woven apparel	37⅜	1⅞	33	15½	19⅜	14⅞	1095	18	16⅜	16⅞	e4.7	16	10.1	−17.5	12.4
16	GRDG	✔Garden Ridge	NNM	NR	38	2596	Retail home & seasonal prd	....	....	....	....	39	15	5218	39	35	38¾	...	53	...	...	...
17	GARN	✔Garnet Resources	NNM	NR	33	5427	Oil & gas exploration,devel'nt	17	2¾	5	3	3½	1	14408	1⅝	1¼	1 9/16	...	d	−53.7	−28.4	−25.9
18•[3]	GART	✔Gartner Group'A'	NNM	NR	145	17858	Res'r/analysis of info tech Ind	9⅜	5½	19¾	8	48¼	17¾	42777	48¼	41¼	47⅞	...	86	148	...	...
19•[4]	GSNX	✔GaSonics International	NNM	NR	83	7237	Dvlp photoresist removal eq	....	....	14	6½	27	10⅛	32641	19	11½	13½	...	11	30.1	...	...
20•[6]	GATE	✔Gateway 2000	NNM	NR	129	13664	Direct mkt personal computers	21½	15	24¾	9¼	37½	16	348310	28⅝	20⅝	24½	...	13	12.6	...	...
#21•[7]	GMT	✔GATX Corp	NY,B,Ch,P,Ph	A−	233	17268	Railcar leas'g/equip financ'g	42¼	10¼	44⅝	38¼	54¼	40⅜	7700	51⅛	48¼	48⅝	3.3	11	21.2	19.9	18.2
22	Pr	$2.50 cm Cv Pfd (63)vtg	NY,Ch	NR	4	10	tank terminals, shipping	101	28½	103	101	124½	107¾	....	....	....	121⅝B	2.1	..	...	...	...
23	Pr A	$3.875 cm Cv Pfd([61]51.9375)	NY,Ch	BBB−	53	1801		56	33¾	56⅜	49⅞	63	50½	1262	59⅝	57⅜	57½	6.7	..	...	...	...
24•[5]	GCR	✔Gaylord Container'A'	AS,Ch	NR	101	18958	Mfr paper packaging prod	22	1⅞	9¾	4⅜	15½	6⅝	102263	10¾	7⅜	8	...	3	−6.5	35.4	20.9
25	WS	Wrrt([62]Pur 1 Cl'A'at $0.0001)[63]	AS	....	53	13987		4	1⅜	8⅛	3⅛	11⅞	6½	9237	9⅜	7⅛	7½	...	..	...	...	...
26•[5]	GET	✔Gaylord Entertainment 'A'	NY,Ph	NR	198	36998	Entert'nt,cable TV, broadc'stg	27⅝	9¾	31	18½	29	20¼	29503	27¾	24⅝	27¾	1.2	38	44.0	17.0	...
27	GCX	✔GC Companies	NY,Ch	NR	91	4327	Oper motion picture theatres	40	32	38½	24¾	35¼	26	1898	34¼	31⅞	33½	...	30	27.0	...	...
28	GCREF	GCR Hldgs Ltd	NNM	NR	..	...	Property & casualty insurance	....	....	....	....	23¼	18½	69119	23¼	18½	22½	11.0	7	...	...	...
29	GEHL	✔Gehl Co	NNM	B−	23	2202	Mfr farm,constr'n,indus equip	16¾	2¼	8½	5⅜	9⅝	6¼	1945	7¾	7⅛	7⅛	...	5	9.6	33.4	−4.8
30	GEC	✔GEICO Corp[64]	NY,B,Ch,Ph,P	A	169	49850	Property & casualty insurance	67⅝	7/16	57⅝	47⅝	70	47⅝	12134	70	69⅜	69⅞	1.5	20	43.0	3.9	18.4
31	GSC	✔Gelman Sciences	AS	B	58	4296	Lab health devices: filters	10⅝	7/16	15⅞	9⅞	25¼	11⅝	1831	25¼	23⅜	25¼	...	26	66.9	67.1	48.0
32	GELX	GelTex Pharmaceuticals	NNM	NR	..	...	Dvp stage:pharmaceutical R&D	....	....	....	....	12½	9½	8617	12½	10½	12¼	...	d	...	...	...
33	GMSTF	Gemstar Intl	NNM	NR	..	...	TV/video recording prods	....	....	....	....	41¾	12	6701	34¾	27¼	28⅜	...	44	...	...	...
#34•[5]	GY	✔GenCorp	NY,B,C,Ch,P,Ph	B	153	20915	Aerospace,auto,polymer prods	40	2½	16⅜	9⅞	14⅛	10	12121	12⅞	11⅛	12¼	4.9	..	10.5	8.1	20.7
35•[4]	GNE	✔Genentech[66] Inc[67]	NY	NR	5	585	Health care pr-gene-splic'g	65¼	4⅜	53½	41¾	53	44½	29611	53	50⅞	53	...	39	14.6	12.3	18.3
36	GACC	✔Genl Acceptance	NNM	NR	34	1298	Offer consumer loans/svcs	....	....	....	....	37	14	18828	29¼	14	15½	...	18	...	...	...
37	GA	✔Genl Automation	AS	C	5	65	Multi-user microcomputers	25¾	5/16	1 7/16	¼	1 1/16	7/16	2134	15/16	9/16	⅞	...	d	27.4	8.4	18.5
38	GBND	✔Genl Binding	NNM	B+	48	3707	Mfr business machines & sup	30¼	2 1/16	22	14⅜	23	14¼	3949	22¾	19¼	19¾	2.1	17	7.8	3.3	8.1
39	GCABY	Genl Cable plc ADS[68]	NNM	NR	26	4456	Cable TV systems,UK	....	....	....	....	16½	12⅞	3927	15⅜	14¼	15	...	d	...	...	...
40	GNCMA	✔Genl Communication'A'	NNM	B	29	3665	Long distance telecom svcs	5½	⅞	5⅞	3⅛	5⅛	3¼	6938	5⅛	4¼	5⅛	...	18	29.1	31.6	22.3
41•[3]	GDC	✔Genl DataComm Ind	NY,B,Ch,P	B	95	10444	Data communic'n netwk/eq	21	1/16	34⅞	8¼	35⅞	9¼	36696	20⅜	15⅝	17⅛	...	d	−48.7	44.9	53.6
¶42•[1]	GD	✔Genl Dynamics	NY,B,C,Ch,P,Ph,Mo	B	330	36090	Armored/space launch vehicles	60	1⅜	47⅝	38	63	42⅜	26690	63	58⅞	59⅛	2.5	15	40.1	26.8	54.5
¶43•[5]	GE	✔Genl Electric	NY,B,C,Ch,P,Ph	A+	1753	865969	Consumer/ind'l prod,broad'cst	53½	3¾	54⅞	45	73⅛	49⅞	479535	73⅛	67½	72	2.6	19	43.5	22.2	23.8
44	JOB	✔Genl Employ Enterpr	AS	B−	8	103	Personnel placement service	6¾	½	10⅛	1⅝	8¾	4½	893	5¾	4⅞	5¼	...	11	−18.3	42.4	17.0
45	GGP	✔Genl Growth Properties	NY	NR	124	16155	Real estate investment trust	26	19¼	22⅝	19¼	22⅝	18⅛	15102	21¾	18½	20¾	8.3	26	0.5	...	...
46	GH	✔Genl Host	NY,B,Ch,P,Ph	B−	55	7242	Specialty retailer:lawn prod	23¼	9/16	6⅝	3⅝	7⅝	3⅞	36496	5	3⅞	4	s...	31	−7.2	−17.4	1.0
47	GHW	✔Genl Housewares	NY,B,Ch,Ph	B	30	2046	Mfr cookware & giftware	29¾	¼	16⅜	9¾	16⅜	8½	3229	10⅜	8½	8⅝	3.7	13	−37.4	−18.6	−2.7
48•[7]	GIC	✔Genl Instrument	NY,P,Ph	NR	450	100686	Supplies CATV/commun equip	30⅛	5¾	34⅝	21¼	41⅝	18¼	159287	26½	22	23⅜	...	19	−22.1	21.9	...
49	GKI	✔Genl Kinetics	AS	C	6	266	Mfr govt communic/electr equip	11⅜	⅛	2⅝	7/16	1⅝	1/16	824	⅞	9/16	⅝	...	d	25.0	−46.1	−34.2
50	GMGC	✔Genl Magic	NNM	NR	34	1350	Dvlp stge:spcl softwr tech	....	....	....	....	32	9⅞	27042	14⅛	10⅜	10⅝	...	..	...	...	...
51	GMW	✔Genl Microwave	AS	B−	9	385	Electron measure/control eq	18¼	5/16	10⅛	7	9¼	6⅞	32	7⅞	7¾	7¾	...	d	10.7	5.1	4.6
¶52•[4]	GIS	✔Genl Mills	NY,B,C,Ch,P,Ph	A	695	101767	Consumer foods,restaurants	75⅞	3½	62¼	49⅜	64⅝	47¼	69957	58½	54½	57¾	3.3	26	...	...	...

Uniform Footnote Explanations-See Page 4. Other: [1]CBOE:Cycle 2. [2]Ch [3]CBOE:Cycle 1. [4]P:Cycle 1. [5]CBOE:Cycle 3. [6]ASE,CBOE,P:Cycle 3. [7]Ph:Cycle 3. [51]Incl current amts. [52]Liq div. [53]Liq div:100% non-taxable,'94. [54]In liquidation. [55]®$1.41,'94. [56]Dep for 0.10 shr $17cm Cv Exch Pfd. [57]Thru 10-1-96,scale to $20 in '99. [58]Fiscal Jul'91 & prior,8 Mo Mar'92 earn $d0.63. [59]Incl $0.025 redemption of Purch Rt. [60]®$3.78,'94. [61]To 7-31-95,scale to $50 in'99. [62]Exercisable fr 7-31-96:spl exercise 7-31-95. [63]Callable re-specified cond.. [64]Berkshire Hathaway (51%) plan acq, $70. [65]®$1.24,'93. [66]Callable Putable com stk: hldrs put option $60. [67]Red by Roche Hld,$62.50-$82 incr qtly to6-30-99. [68]Each ADS rep 4 Ord par 25p. [69]®$13.99,'93. [70]Spl div. [71]Incl $0.72 non-taxable,'94. [72]10 Mo Dec'91. [73]Stk dstr of Darden Restaurants,'95.

Splits ◆	Cash Divs.	Dividends						Financial Position				Capitalization			Earnings $ Per Shr.							Interim Earnings			
		Latest Payment			Total $			Mil-$			Balance	Lg Trm	Shs. 000		Years						Last	$ per Shr.			
Index	Ea.Yr. Since	Period $	Date	Ex. Div.	So Far 1995	Ind. Rate	Paid 1994	Cash& Equiv.	Curr. Assets	Curr. Liab.	Sheet Date	Debt Mil-$	Pfd.	Com.	End	1991	1992	1993	1994	1995	12 Mos.	Period	1994	1995	Index
1	1994	Q0.31	1-15-96	12-27	1.34	1.24	1.30	Equity per shr $4.68			9-30-95	91.2	...	4062	Dc	...	p0.76	p0.87	0.77	....	0.93	9 Mo Sep	0.50	□0.66	1
2	1994	Q0.48	1-12-96	12-27	1.83	1.92	1.22½	Equity per shr $11.17			9-30-95	[51]348	...	★15183	Dc	...	p0.33	p0.71	p□1.23	....	1.24	9 Mo Sep	p□0.92	0.93	2
3	....	None Since Public			...	Nil	....	0.56	16.9	12.9	p7-29-95	p0.11	p...	★4943	Ja	0.05	0.20	0.36	0.49	....	0.67	9 Mo Oct	0.25	0.43	3
4◆	1991	Q0.01¼	1-15-96	12-27	s0.038	0.05	s0.034	Equity per shr $4.35			9-30-95	1.75	...	21512	Dc	0.39	0.60	0.61	0.69	....	0.72	9 Mo Sep	0.51	0.54	4
5	1994	[52]1.00	5-5-95	5-8	[52]6.20	Nil	[53]12.69	Liq Val per shr $3.49			9-30-95	....	...	2142	Dc	d0.87	d1.66	d1.36	....	....	[54]....				5
6	....	None Since Public			...	Nil	....	4.44	182	46.8	9-30-95	162	...	11762	Sp	p0.47	□1.14	1.12	□1.56	□0.44	0.44				6
7	1985	Q0.25	1-15-96	12-27	0.97	1.00	0.84	70.2	389	366	9-30-95	....	...	15552	Dc	1.31	1.57	2.02	2.17	....	2.51	9 Mo Sep	1.38	1.72	7
8	....	None Since Public			...	Nil	....	3.76	108	55.7	9-30-95	18.3	184	10077	Dc	d1.14	d0.59	d1.47	[55]1.51	....	0.18	9 Mo Sep	0.96	d0.37	8
9	....	0.42½	4-1-92	3-10	...	Nil	....	Cv into 1.185 com,$16.875				....	1840	...	Dc	bd1.18	bd0.38	...	....	....	....	Accum %6.375 to 1-1-96			9
10	1994	Q0.02½	1-23-96	1-4	0.10	0.10	0.10	3.54	11.6	1.36	9-30-95	0.01	...	4546	Mr	*0.12	d0.20	0.28	0.32	....	0.29	6 Mo Sep	0.14	0.11	10
11	....	None Since Public			...	Nil	....	11.8	56.2	35.1	3-31-95	11.9	...	★41399	Mr	[58]d0.48	d1.24	d2.27	0.05	....	0.08	6 Mo Sep	d0.03	Nil	11
12◆	....	None Since Public			...	Nil	....	2.82	127	64.2	7-01-95	69.0	200	3243	Je	0.55	0.79	0.02	Δ0.48	d3.69	d4.56	3 Mo Sep	0.44	d0.43	12
13	1929	Q0.35	1-2-96	12-13	1.37	1.40	1.33	35.5	676	595	9-24-95	542	...	140206	Dc	2.00	□2.40	2.72	3.23	E3.40	3.36	9 Mo Sep	2.17	2.30	13
14◆	1976	Q0.12	12-26-95	11-29	0.48	0.48	0.46	441	1252	653	10-28-95	p128	...	143859	Ja	1.62	1.47	1.78	2.20	E2.30	2.20	9 Mo Oct	1.38	1.38	14
15◆	1963	†0.40	11-30-95	11-14	†1.00	0.80	†1.00	23.0	81.8	12.5	6-30-95	3.10	...	5070	Sp	2.03	3.03	3.32	1.84	P1.08	1.08				15
16	....	None Since Public			...	Nil	....	3.48	36.8	13.7	7-30-95	....	...	7480	Ja	...	...	...	p0.69	....	0.73	6 Mo Jul	0.03	0.07	16
17	....	None Paid			...	Nil	....	2.17	5.48	2.29	9-30-95	19.4	...	11492	Dc	d0.20	d1.01	□d0.29	d0.67	....	d0.63	9 Mo Sep	d0.16	d0.12	17
18◆	....	None Since Public			...	Nil	....	91.1	218	212	9-30-95	....	...	±42776	Sp	d0.37	d0.20	□0.13	±0.32	±0.56	0.56				18
19◆	....	None Since Public			...	Nil	....	31.7	64.5	15.0	3-31-95	....	...	13163	Sp	d0.05	0.08	0.33	0.87	P1.21	1.21				19
20	....	None Since Public			...	Nil	....	163	779	444	9-30-95	13.2	...	72633	Dc	...	p1.03	p1.41	1.22	....	1.95	9 Mo Sep	0.72	1.45	20
21	1919	Q0.40	12-31-95	12-13	1.60	1.60	[59]1.52½	Equity per shr $26.40			12-31-94	p1873	3438	p20091	Dc	3.56	□0.82	2.99	[60]3.88	E4.55	4.63	9 Mo Sep	2.80	3.55	21
22	1969	Q0.62½	12-1-95	11-13	2.50	2.50	2.50	Cv into 2.50 common				....	49	...	Dc	n/a	b0.92	b1.17	b1.25	....	....				22
23	1989	Q0.96⅞	2-1-96	1-10	3.87½	3.875	3.87½	Cv into 1.1494 com,$43.50				....	3395	...	Dc	n/a	b0.92	b1.17	b1.25	....	....				23
24	....	None Since Public			...	Nil	....	7.20	263	169	6-30-95	689	...	±54050	Sp	■d11.68	±d8.54	□Δd1.40	d1.57	P2.44	2.44				24
25	....	Terms&trad. basis should			be checked in detail			Wrrts expire 11-3-2002				....	...	31846	Sp	...	...	...	....	....	....				25
26◆	1991	Q0.08	12-18-95	11-30	s0.312	0.32	0.248	8.35	202	265	9-30-95	200	...	±91799	Dc	0.02	0.33	□0.41	0.69	E0.73	1.01	9 Mo Sep	0.60	0.92	26
27	....	None Since Public			...	Nil	....	98.2	103	112	7-31-95	3.76	...	7813	Oc	...	...	n/a	1.73	P1.11	1.11				27
28	....	Plan qtly div			...	2.48	....	Equity per shr $15.30			9-30-95	p106	...	★25665	Sp	...	...	...	....	p3.17	3.17				28
29	....	0.04	6-30-91	6-10	...	Nil	....	4.44	108	28.9	9-30-95	51.3	...	6211	Dc	□d2.89	d3.05	0.04	0.82	....	1.39	9 Mo Sep	0.65	1.22	29
30◆	1977	Q0.27	12-27-95	11-30	1.08	1.08	1.00	Equity per shr $25.75			9-30-95	433	...	67529	Dc	2.70	2.39	□4.01	□2.98	E3.45	3.46	9 Mo Sep	□2.16	2.64	30
31◆	....	None Paid			...	Nil	....	3.29	47.2	14.1	10-31-95	5.18	...	7831	Jl	0.02	□d0.15	0.47	□0.78	0.92	0.97	3 Mo Oct	0.19	0.24	31
32	....	None Since Public			...	Nil	....	10.6	10.9	1.24	6-30-95	0.55	p...	★10127	Dc	...	...	...	pd0.27	....	d0.37	6 Mo Jun	pd0.28	pd0.38	32
33	....	None Since Public			...	Nil	....	13.9	16.5	9.02	6-30-95	....	...	★30012	Mr	0.32	0.35	0.42	0.51	....	0.65	6 Mo Sep	0.06	0.20	33
34	1937	Q0.15	11-30-95	10-30	0.60	0.60	0.60	27.0	453	329	8-31-95	420	...	33405	Nv	1.00	0.70	[65]1.35	□d0.41	....	Nil	9 Mo Aug	□0.55	0.96	34
35	....	....			...	Nil	....	825	1133	230	9-30-95	176	...	118779	Dc	0.39	±0.18	±0.50	±1.04	E1.35†	1.15	9 Mo Sep	±0.89	±1.00	35
36	....	None Since Public			...	Nil	....	Equity per shr $4.71			9-30-95	83.9	...	6022	Dc	...	...	...	p0.60	....	0.87	9 Mo Sep	p0.42	p0.69	36
37	....	None Paid			...	Nil	....	0.42	5.49	6.17	6-30-95	1.45	...	7392	Sp	Δ0.02	□d0.08	Δd0.13	Δd0.04	....	d0.26	9 Mo Jun	Δd0.06	d0.28	37
38	1975	Q0.10½	12-21-95	11-17	0.42	0.42	0.40½	5.19	180	83.3	9-30-95	43.9	...	±15735	Dc	±0.80	±1.06	±0.95	±1.00	....	1.16	9 Mo Sep	±0.86	±1.02	38
39	....	None Since Public			...	Nil	....	11988	23797	15733	j12-31-94	p24627	...	★253360	Dc	...	...	...	pd0.95	....	pd0.95				39
40	....	None Paid			...	Nil	....	2.96	26.0	20.5	9-30-95	9.59	...	±23836	Dc	d0.12	0.02	0.17	0.30	....	0.29	9 Mo Sep	0.24	0.23	40
41	....	None Since Public			...	Nil	....	18.4	116	52.8	9-30-95	23.4	...	±20516	Sp	0.04	0.17	0.36	□d0.11	d1.40	d1.40				41
42◆	1979	Q0.37½	2-9-96	1-17	1.47½	1.50	1.35	993	1970	858	10-01-95	186	...	62980	Dc	6.03	▲10.78	▲[69]14.01	3.75	E3.85	4.59	9 Mo Sep	2.84	3.68	42
43◆	1899	Q0.46	1-25-96	12-27	1.64	1.84	1.44	Equity per shr $8.37			9-30-95	49853	...	1670275	Dc	□2.55	2.76	□3.03	2.77	E3.90	3.24	9 Mo Sep	2.32	2.79	43
44◆	1996	[70]0.05	1-17-96	12-11	...	Nil	....	3.23	5.09	2.84	9-30-95	....	...	2196	Sp	d0.71	d0.29	0.03	0.30	0.48	0.48				44
45	1993	Q0.43	1-31-96	12-27	1.64	1.72	[71]1.54	Equity per shr $8.22			9-30-95	[51]655	...	27273	Dc	...	p0.61	p0.87	□0.65	....	0.81	9 Mo Sep	□0.43	0.59	45
46◆	1974	5%Stk	4-7-95	3-13	5%Stk	Stk	s0.086	26.4	186	156	11-05-95	176	...	22140	Ja	□0.73	Δ0.12	d2.58	0.39	....	0.13	9 Mo Oct	d0.04	d0.30	46
47	1981	Q0.08	12-29-95	12-13	0.32	0.32	0.32	0.08	48.6	11.4	6-30-95	36.6	...	3989	Dc	1.20	Δ1.34	0.91	0.80	....	0.68	9 Mo Sep	0.37	0.25	47
48◆	....	None Since Public			...	Nil	....	20.0	797	488	9-30-95	709	...	122776	Dc	p[72]d0.57	□d0.42	Δ0.74	□2.01	....	1.26	9 Mo Sep	□1.32	0.57	48
49◆	....	None Paid			...	Nil	....	0.33	6.12	3.54	8-31-95	9.76	...	6509	My	0.45	d1.68	d0.88	d0.85	d0.24	d0.13	3 Mo Aug	d0.10	0.01	49
50	....	None Since Public			...	Nil	....	108	112	9.27	9-30-95	1.15	...	25598	Dc	pd0.29	pd0.69	pd1.11	pd1.36	....	....	9 Mo Sep	d0.90	d0.63	50
51	1994	[70]0.25	2-9-94	1-20	...	Nil	[70]0.25	1.14	14.3	3.72	9-02-95	2.59	...	1198	Fb	0.84	*0.11	0.76	0.14	....	d0.55	6 Mo Aug	d0.13	d0.82	51
52	1898	Q0.47	2-1-96	1-8	h[73]1.88	1.88	1.88	16.7	1001	1305	8-27-95	1335	...	158597	My	2.87	2.99	3.10	2.95	2.33	2.21	6 Mo Nov	1.90	1.78	52

◆**Stock Splits & Divs By Line Reference Index** [4]3-for-2,'91,'92:Adj to 5%,Sep'95. [12]10%,'91. [14]2-for-1,'91. [15]2-for-1,'92. [18]2-for-1,'94,'95. [19]3-for-2,'95. [26]2-for-1,'93:Adj for 5%,'95. [30]5-for-1,'92. [31]3-for-2,'93,'94. [42]2-for-1,'94. [43]2-for-1,'94. [44]15%,'94,'95. [46]Adj to 5%,'95. [48]2-for-1,'94. [49]2-for-1,'91.

¶ S&P 500 # MidCap 400 ✣ SmallCap 600 • Options

Index	Ticker	Name of Issue (Call Price of Pfd. Stocks)	Market	Com. Rank. & Pfd. Rating	Inst. Hold Cos	Inst. Hold Shs. (000)	Principal Business	Price Range 1971-93 High	1971-93 Low	1994 High	1994 Low	1995 High	1995 Low	Dec. Sales in 100s	December, 1995 Last Sale Or Bid High	Low	Last	%Div Yield	P-E Ratio	Total Return % Annualized 12 Mo	36 Mo	60 Mo
¶1•[1]	GM	✓Genl Motors[51]	NY,To,B,C,Ch,P,Ph,Mo	B–	1063	441187	Largest mfr automotive prods	57⅛	14½	65⅜	36⅛	53⅛	37¼	451820	53⅛	48½	52⅞	2.3	8	28.5	19.9	12.0
2•[2]	GME	✓Genl Motors Cl'E'[53]	NY,B	A+	649	180173	Computer systems/svcs	35⅞	7/16	39½	27½	52⅝	36⅞	132738	52⅝	48⅞	52	1.0	27	36.2	17.7	24.0
3	Pr C	Series'C'Cv[54]Dep Pfd([55]51.95)	NY	↑BBB+	259	18150		59⅜	48¼	59⅝	53½	74⅜	55⅞	21574	74⅜	69½	73¼	4.4	..	...	...	...
4•[3]	GMH	✓Genl Motors Cl'H'[56]	NY,B	B+	348	67581	High technology electronics	42⅜	13⅛	40⅜	31	50	33¼	48733	50	46⅜	49⅛	1.9	18	43.5	26.6	26.1
5•[3]	GNCI	✓Genl Nutrition	NNM	NR	275	68641	Oper chain hlth prod stores	15¼	4⅞	16¼	7¾	26½	11¼	114490	24¾	19	23	...	31	60.2	...	...
6	GPSX	Genl Parcel Service	NSC	NR	5	101	Pick-up/shipping/delivery svc	9	3	7	3¼	6⅛	2¾	610	3⅞	3⅝	3⅝	...	d	–23.7	–5.2	–5.3
7	GPH	✓Genl Physics	NY,Ch	NR	18	1819	Training/tech'l svc-nuclear ind	16¾	3⅜	5	2⅜	3⅝	2⅛	2130	3⅜	3	3¼	7.4	15	40.5	–11.5	...
¶8•[4]	GPU	✓Genl Public Util	NY,B,C,Ch,P,Ph	B	446	72581	Util hldg co: N.J. & Penna.	34¾	1 11/16	31⅝	23¾	34	26¼	69492	34	31½	34	5.5	12	37.0	13.6	15.3
¶9•[5]	GRN	✓Genl Re Corp	NY,B,Ch,P,Ph	A	753	68272	Hldg: reinsur:prop/casual	133⅜	4½	129⅛	101¾	158¼	121⅝	45143	158¼	149¾	155	1.3	17	26.2	11.1	12.9
10	GSCN	✓Genl Scanning	NNM	NR	27	1794	Dvp/mfr laser systems	....	....	....	....	13¾	8	15246	12½	8	10	...	14	...	...	...
¶11•[6]	GSX	✓Genl Signal	NY,B,Ch,P,Ph	B	320	36204	Control equipment & systems	36¾	4⅜	38	30⅛	42½	28	23084	33⅞	31	32⅜	3.0	15	2.8	4.7	15.4
12	GCO	✓Genesco Inc	NY,B,Ch,Ph	C	42	6966	Apparel & footwear:shoe strs	39¾	2⅜	5⅝	1⅝	4⅞	2	11133	4¼	3⅜	3½	...	5	86.7	–27.3	1.5
13	GENBB	Genesee Corp'B'	NNM	B	36	698	Beer and ale	61	6¼	44	35	49½	34½	439	48	44	44	†4.4	28	25.0	7.9	13.5
✣14•[5]	GHV	✓Genesis Hlth Ventures	NY,Ch,Ph	NR	158	12982	Provide geriatric hlth svcs	24⅛	6¼	32	21¾	37½	25⅜	21494	37½	32¼	36½	...	24	17.7	31.6	...
15•[7]	GENIZ	✓Genetics[61] Institute[62] Dep[63] Shrs	NNM	C	69	6089	Mfr/R&D Pharmaceutical prod	62½	13¼	49¾	34½	57½	31¼	27866	57½	43¾	53½	...	d	47.6	20.3	5.7
16•[8]	GNV	✓Geneva Steel Co 'A'	NY,Ch,Ph	NR	60	5982	Integrated steel producer	21	6½	21⅜	12¼	16	6⅜	25917	7⅞	6⅝	6⅞	...	29	–48.1	–12.8	–8.6
17	GECM	✓Genicom Corp	NNM	C	22	3451	Mfrs/mkts computer printers	16½	⅞	3¼	1	6	2	26394	5⅛	4⅜	5⅛	...	12	116	72.4	38.7
18	GDX.A	✓Genovese Drug Str'A'	AS,Ch	A	42	1740	Drug & gen mdse chain	10⅝	3/16	11½	8⅛	12½	8⅝	1373	11⅝	10½	11¼	2.1	12	16.3	25.6	35.8
19	GEN	✓GenRad, Inc	NY,B,Ch,P,Ph	C	47	7705	Electr test & measurement pr	46⅜	1½	7⅛	4⅛	10⅛	4⅝	10088	9⅞	8¼	9¾	...	19	100	28.2	43.1
20•[1]	GNSA	✓Gensia, Inc	NNM	NR	64	12934	Dvlp cardiovascular drugs	47	3⅛	25¾	4	6⅝	2	48281	5⅝	3¾	5¼	...	d	27.3	–39.9	–2.9
✣21•[9]	GNTX	✓Gentex Corp	NNM	B	85	6494	Mfr optical/elec devices	35¼	7/16	35¼	18	27½	15¾	18497	25	21	22	...	21	–7.4	32.5	54.5
¶22•[10]	GPC	✓Genuine Parts	NY,B,Ch	A+	482	79294	Distrib auto replacement parts	39	3⅜	39⅜	33⅝	42	35½	30633	42	39¾	41	3.1	16	16.0	10.2	13.6
#23•[11]	GENZ	✓Genzyme Corp-Genl Div	NNM	C	269	26068	Biological health care prod	66½	5¾	38¼	24	70	27¼	244373	70	51¼	62⅜	...	34	105	13.2	17.8
24	GDYN	✓Geodynamics Corp	NNM	B	19	575	Software for govt/military	17¼	6¼	9½	6	13⅛	7	551	12⅛	11	12⅛	2.3	17	64.0	17.5	7.2
25•[6]	GON	✓Geon Co	NY	NR	132	23265	Mfr polyvinyl chloride resins	24⅜	17¾	31⅝	23¼	31⅜	23⅜	10997	26¾	24⅛	24⅜	2.1	19	–8.8	...	...
#26•[6]	GGC	✓Georgia Gulf Corp	NY,Ch,Ph	NR	179	22951	Integrated chemical producer	59⅞	4⅞	43¼	21⅝	40¾	26⅝	25980	36¾	30½	30⅝	1.0	7	–20.4	11.5	25.3
¶27•[12]	GP	✓Georgia-Pacific	NY,B,C,Ch,P,Ph	B–	682	61211	Plywood,lumber,paper,gyps'm	75	13¼	79	56¾	95¾	65¾	133220	77⅝	65¾	68⅝	2.9	6	–1.0	6.8	16.1
✣28•[13]	GOTK	✓Geotek Communications	NNM	NR	77	8121	Telecom service provider	17⅝	¾	16	6⅜	10	5½	86629	7¾	5⅞	6¼	...	d	–26.8	14.7	33.3
29	GEOW	✓GeoWaste, Inc	NSC	C	11	5409	Enviro svcs/leases o&g prop	6¾	¼	¾	⅜	2⅛	7/16	12098	1 5/16	13/16	1¼	...	16	150	–1.6	27.2
✣30•[14]	GRB	✓Gerber Scientific	NY,B,Ch,P,Ph	B	97	15893	Computer draft/cutting sys	24⅛	1/16	16⅜	11⅞	19½	12⅝	9664	17⅛	14⅝	16⅛	2.0	18	30.3	15.3	15.7
31	GEMC	✓Geriatric & Medl Cos	NNM	B–	16	1331	Diversified health care svcs	5⅝	1/16	3⅝	1⅝	3⅛	1 13/16	3618	2½	2 1/16	2⅜	...	8	–20.8	9.4	18.6
✣32•[1]	GOG	✓Gerrity Oil & Gas	NY,Ch	NR	46	7882	Oil & gas devel & prod'n	18¾	3⅛	12¼	3⅞	5⅛	2⅝	13179	4⅞	3¾	4	...	d	0.0	–33.7	–3.9
33	Pr	Cv[68]Dep Pfd([69]26.05)	NY	B	15	2102		....	....	17⅜	12	13½	10	3089	11¼	10¼	10⅝	14.1	..	...	...	...
34	GTY	✓Getty Petroleum	NY,B,Ch,Ph	B–	41	1885	Dstr gasoline: stations	25	3/16	16⅞	10⅝	15	10¾	3986	15	13	13⅜	0.9	12	15.3	9.8	1.1
35	GCHI	✓Giant Cement Holding	NNM	NR	64	7166	Mfr portland/masonary cement	....	....	15	11⅛	13⅞	8¾	10884	11⅞	10¼	11½	...	10	–3.2	...	...
¶36•[5]	GFS.A	✓Giant Food Cl'A'[70]	AS,B,Ch,P,Ph	A–	272	26488	Supermkts: DC, Md, Va area	36¼	7/16	26⅜	19½	35⅛	21⅝	16037	33¾	31¼	31½	2.3	19	47.7	15.4	5.0
37	GPO	✓GIANT GROUP	NY,B,Ch	C	22	1871	Cement-southeastern mkt	20½	2⅞	14⅝	6¾	9⅛	5⅝	3564	9⅛	6⅜	9⅛	...	8	28.1	–6.4	11.2
38	GI	✓Giant Industries	NY	B–	51	5532	Oil & gas explor,devel,prod'n	15	3⅝	10¾	6¾	12¼	6⅝	2869	12¼	10⅝	12¼	1.6	22	82.3	31.6	13.7
39	ROCK	✓Gibralter Steel	NNM	NR	24	1992	Processor value-added steel pd	14½	11	16¼	9¾	14¼	10	1898	12¾	12	12⅛	...	13	18.3	...	...
#40•[14]	GIBG	✓Gibson Greetings	NNM	↓B	115	13434	Mfr greet'g cards/wrappings	32	10⅜	23⅝	11¾	16⅛	8	14818	16⅛	14¾	16	...	d	9.9	–3.8	–6.9
¶41•[15]	GIDL	✓Giddings & Lewis	NNM	NR	249	26282	Mfr automated machine tools	29¾	6⅛	28	13¾	18⅞	14½	36014	16⅝	15¼	16½	e0.7	17	13.4	–13.3	14.3
42	GILTF	Gilat Satellite Networks	NNM	NR	..	...	Mfr satellite stations & hubs	17¼	11	15	8	29⅛	12	10384	27¼	23⅝	25¼	...	28	85.3	...	...
43	GILBA	✓Gilbert Assoc'A'[70]	NNM	B–	54	3310	Engr/consult'g svs: voice eq	31	2⅝	18¾	12	15½	11½	3436	15¼	12	12½	6.4	4	0.3	–8.8	–7.5
44•[10]	GILD	✓Gilead Sciences	NNM	NR	101	17659	Nucleotide pharmaceut'l R&D	22¼	9½	14¼	6⅝	34¼	9¼	58681	34¼	21¾	32	...	d	246	24.1	...
¶45•[5]	G	✓Gillette Co	NY,B,C,Ch,P,Ph	↑A+	1021	303915	Shaving, personal care: pens	31⅞	1⅛	38¼	28⅞	55⅜	35⅜	162168	55⅜	49⅝	52⅛	1.2	28	40.6	23.2	29.4
46	GISH	✓Gish Biomedical	NNM	B	23	1097	Mfr disposable medical prod	17⅜	¼	7⅛	4¾	9¼	5⅞	1127	8½	7⅜	7¾	...	22	19.2	–4.0	–3.2
47	GBCI	✓Glacier Bancorp	NNM	A+	18	645	Savings bank,Montana	21⅛	1 7/16	18¾	14½	22	15	182	21	19½	20¼	e3.2	11	53.0	23.0	44.0
48	HOO	✓Glacier Water Services	AS	NR	18	1803	Oper drink'g wtr vending sys	15⅞	8	20½	13	22⅞	18⅜	496	20⅛	18⅝	18½B	...	21	–3.9	17.6	...
✣49•[1]	GLG	✓Glamis Gold Ltd	NY,Ch,Ph	B–	38	4771	Explor,dev gold mineral prop	9¾	1/16	10⅛	5½	9⅜	5½	23269	6⅞	6⅛	6¼	◆...	..	–27.9	21.6	19.8
#50	GLT	✓Glatfelter (P. H.)	AS,Ch	B	151	32127	Mfr printing/writing paper	29⅞	5/16	19⅜	14⅝	23⅝	15⅜	13233	19⅛	15⅞	17⅛	4.1	11	14.7	2.4	–1.1
51•[15]	GLX	✓Glaxo Wellcome plc[72] ADR	NY,Ch,P,Ph	NR	250	41489	Ethical pharmaceuticals	35¼	¼	21⅝	15⅞	28⅜	18¾	110459	28¼	26½	28⅛	3.6	18	43.6	8.0	12.1
52	GLE	✓Gleason Corp	NY,Ch	B–	45	1961	Bevel gear mchy: tooling	47¼	4⅜	16½	10¾	37¼	14⅝	2513	35⅞	32¼	32½	1.5	12	121	33.1	19.8

Uniform Footnote Explanations-See Page 4. Other: [1]CBOE:Cycle 3. [2]CBOE,Ph:Cycle 3. [3]CBOE:Cycle 1. [4]NY:Cycle 2. [5]ASE:Cycle 3. [6]Ph:Cycle 2. [7]NY,P:Cycle 2. [8]CBOE:Cycle 2. [9]P:Cycle 3. [10]P:Cycle 2. [11]ASE,CBOE,NY:Cycle 1. [12]Ph:Cycle 1. [13]CBOE,P:Cycle 2. [14]Ph:Cycle 3. [15]ASE:Cycle 2. [51]Plan spin-off,Electronic Data Systems. [52]L-T-D as of 12-31-94. [53]½ vtg:GM option to exch for GM stk. [54]Dep for 0.1 shr Series'C'cm Cv Pfd. [55]Fr 2-19-96,scale to $50 in 2002. [56]Vtg:co option to exch for com fr'96. [57]®$0.74,'93. [58]Subsid pfd in $M. [59]Pfd in $M. [60]®$1.26,'94. [61]Each Dep shr rep 1 com. [62]Amer Hm Prd opt,call$50 1-16-92 to $85 12-31-96. [63]Fr 12-31-96 red opt at re-specified cond.. [64]64% owned by American Home. [65]Fiscal Nov '93 & prior. [66]®$0.27,'94. [67]One shr Genzyme Corp-Tissue Repair Stk,'94. [68]Dep for 0.125 shr $12 Cv Pfd. [69]Fr 5-23-96,scale to $25 in 2003. [70]Non-vtg. [71]1994 & prior earnings in $Cdn. [72]Sponsored ADR's rep 2 Ord shrs 50p.

Splits ◆ Index	Cash Divs. Ea.Yr. Since	Dividends: Latest Payment Period $	Date	Ex. Div.	Total $ So Far 1995	Ind. Rate	Paid 1994	Financial Position Mil-$ Cash& Equiv.	Curr. Assets	Curr. Liab.	Balance Sheet Date	Capitalization Lg Trm Debt Mil-$	Shs. 000 Pfd.	Com.	Earnings $ Per Shr. Years End	1991	1992	1993	1994	1995	Last 12 Mos.	Interim Earnings Period	$ per Shr. 1994	1995	Index
1	1915	Q0.30	12-9-95	11-14	1.10	1.20	0.80	Equity per shr Neg			12-31-94	[52]37490	p23938	p749399	Dc	□d8.85	□d4.85	2.13	□6.20	E6.75↓	7.06	9 Mo Sep	□4.46	5.32	1
2◆	1984	Q0.13	12-9-95	11-14	0.52	0.52	0.48	....	...	...		....	...	438902	Dc	Δ1.17	1.33	1.51	1.71	E1.95	1.89	9 Mo Sep	1.22	1.40	2
3	1992	Q0.81¼	2-1-96	12-28	3.25	3.25	3.25	Cv into 1.4078 Cl'E',$35.517				....	31881	...	Dc	...	b0.93	b1.61	b1.96	....	....				3
4	1986	Q0.23	12-9-95	11-14	0.92	0.92	0.80	....	...	...		....	...	96142	Dc	Δ1.26	□d0.11	2.30	□2.70	E2.75	2.67	9 Mo Sep	□2.06	2.03	4
5◆	....	None Since Public			...	Nil	....	....	193	126	7-22-95	240	...	p86992	Ja	pd0.09	□...	□[57]0.39	□0.57	....	0.74	36 Wk Oct	□0.38	0.55	5
6	....	None Paid			...	Nil	....	0.01	2.58	3.94	6-30-95	6.21	100	3759	Dc	d0.88	d0.41	d0.22	d0.26	....	d1.78	9 Mo Sep	d0.06	d1.58	6
7	1992	Q0.06	11-30-95	11-16	0.24	0.24	0.24	0.53	35.9	18.9	9-30-95	12.3	...	10335	Dc	p1.00	0.02	0.28	0.15	....	0.22	9 Mo Sep	0.09	0.16	7
8◆	1987	Q0.47	2-28-96	1-24	1.86	1.88	1.77½	45.0	838	1099	9-30-95	2537	[58]562	★119921	Dc	Δ1.96	2.27	2.65	1.42	E2.80	3.67	12 Mo Sep	1.22	3.67	8
9	1934	Q0.49	12-29-95	12-20	1.96	1.96	1.92	Equity per shr $69.59			6-30-95	156	1728	82028	Dc	7.46	Δ6.84	Δ8.11	7.97	E9.25	9.57	9 Mo Sep	5.57	7.17	9
10	....	None Since Public			...	Nil	....	21.2	56.2	16.1	9-30-95	....	...	10100	Dc	0.09	0.17	0.12	0.48	....	0.70	9 Mo Sep	0.24	0.46	10
11◆	1940	Q0.24	1-18-96	1-8	0.96	0.96	0.90	4.50	686	352	9-30-95	504	...	47436	Dc	1.41	□0.23	□1.47	1.71	E2.18	0.33	9 Mo Sep	1.64	0.26	11
12	....	0.17	4-30-73	4-9	...	Nil	....	22.6	163	57.6	10-31-95	76.7	[59]8	24351	Ja	0.01	□0.40	□d2.16	d3.35	....	0.78	9 Mo Oct	d3.97	0.16	12
13	1934	Q0.35	1-2-96	12-13	†1.90	1.95	†1.60	40.7	68.8	18.1	10-28-95	....	...	±1616	Ap	±3.71	±4.64	±□0.21	±2.55	Δ±3.50	1.60	6 Mo Oct	Δ±2.35	±0.45	13
14	....	None Since Public			...	Nil	....	7.60	149	43.7	6-30-95	298	...	14670	Sp	□0.56	□0.80	1.00	Δ□[60]1.33	P□1.55	1.55				14
15	....	None Since Public			...	Nil	....	262	327	34.9	9-30-95	....	...	[64]26770	Dc	■d1.05	d1.80	[65]d0.81	d0.71	....	d0.31	9 Mo Sep	d0.26	0.14	15
16	....	None Since Public			...	Nil	....	6.79	136	112	6-30-95	333	400	±33608	Sp	±1.17	±d0.87	±d0.80	□±d1.57	P±0.24	0.24				16
17	....	None Since Public			...	Nil	....	0.53	110	66.8	10-01-95	60.0	...	10837	Dc	Δd1.58	Δ0.03	d0.30	0.23	....	0.43	9 Mo Sep	0.18	0.38	17
18◆	1977	Q0.06	1-4-96	12-20	0.218	0.24	0.198	1.30	107	73.9	8-18-95	33.7	...	±11085	Ja	0.62	0.66	0.75	0.84	E0.95	0.80	40 Wk Nov	0.46	0.42	18
19	....	0.05	10-15-85	9-25	...	Nil	....	8.39	66.9	41.1	9-30-95	49.0	...	19966	Dc	d2.22	d0.42	■d2.42	[66]0.28	....	0.52	9 Mo Sep	0.21	0.45	19
20◆	....	None Since Public			...	Nil	....	21.9	44.0	16.1	9-30-95	0.02	1600	32309	Dc	d1.25	d1.36	d2.40	d1.89	....	d1.23	9 Mo Sep	d1.76	d1.10	20
21◆	....	None Since Public			...	Nil	....	31.8	52.6	11.8	9-30-95	....	...	16852	Dc	□0.12	0.31	0.59	0.97	....	1.03	9 Mo Sep	0.71	0.77	21
22◆	1948	Q0.315	1-2-96	12-6	1.233	1.26	1.12¾	29.9	1696	457	9-30-95	10.9	...	122835	Dc	1.81	1.92	□2.08	2.33	E2.50↓	2.47	9 Mo Sep	1.66	1.80	22
23	....	[67]....	12-23-94	12-27	...	Stk	[67]....	44.6	184	48.9	6-30-95	128	...	★29255	Dc	*0.50	*d1.38	d0.25	p1.22	E1.85	1.51	9 Mo Sep	p1.13	1.42	23
24	1987	Q0.07	1-8-96	12-21	0.28	0.28	0.28	6.40	23.3	6.68	9-01-95	0.15	...	2662	My	1.35	0.77	0.80	0.38	0.73	0.70	3 Mo Aug	0.21	0.18	24
25	1993	Q0.12½	12-15-95	11-29	0.50	0.50	0.50	31.6	262	198	9-30-95	92.8	...	24889	Dc	...	p□d0.92	p□0.08	□2.06	E1.30	1.71	9 Mo Sep	□1.41	1.06	25
26◆	1995	Q0.08	1-5-96	12-20	0.24	0.32	....	3.33	196	121	9-30-95	276	...	37736	Dc	1.75	1.18	Δ□1.01	2.88	E4.72↓	5.26	9 Mo Sep	1.52	3.90	26
27	1927	Q0.50	12-4-95	11-8	1.90	2.00	1.60	375	2950	2308	9-30-95	4268	...	91817	Dc	□d0.92	□d0.69	□d0.21	□3.66	E11.15↓	11.01	9 Mo Sep	□1.77	9.12	27
28	....	None Paid			...	Nil	....	101	184	52.0	9-30-95	109	...	51459	Dc	d0.20	d0.26	d1.55	d0.90	....	d1.26	9 Mo Sep	d0.61	d0.97	28
29	....	None Paid			...	Nil	....	3.64	4.89	1.60	9-30-95	6.79	...	18663	Dc	d0.15	d0.10	d0.01	0.06	....	0.08	9 Mo Sep	0.03	0.05	29
30	1978	Q0.08	11-30-95	11-13	0.32	0.32	0.28	6.52	151	59.6	10-31-95	7.44	...	23512	Ap	0.34	0.31	0.35	Δ0.61	0.76	0.88	6 Mo Oct	0.30	0.42	30
31◆	....	0.012	2-4-88	1-12	...	Nil	....	0.56	67.6	39.3	8-31-95	123	...	15406	My	*0.14	□0.08	0.16	d0.09	0.27	0.30	3 Mo Aug	0.05	0.08	31
32	....	None Since Public			...	Nil	....	0.16	12.7	14.6	9-30-95	136	380	13781	Dc	0.30	0.50	Δ0.78	□d0.27	....	d0.86	9 Mo Sep	□d0.05	d0.64	32
33	1994	Q0.37½	11-15-95	10-25	1.50	1.50	0.75	Cv into 1.299 com,$19.25				....	3036	...	Dc	...	...	...	....	....	....				33
34	1995	0.03	1-9-96	12-27	0.03	0.12	....	38.8	75.1	85.4	7-31-95	54.4	...	12645	Ja	d0.98	d0.29	Δ0.74	□Δ0.55	....	1.15	9 Mo Oct	Δ□0.05	0.65	34
35	....	None Since Public			...	Nil	....	2.35	36.7	21.1	9-30-95	8.13	...	10000	Dc	d0.61	d0.57	0.51	0.92	....	1.11	9 Mo Sep	0.73	0.92	35
36	1960	Q0.18½	12-1-95	11-1	0.73½	0.74	0.71½	236	519	332	8-12-95	195	...	±59334	Fb	1.47	1.37	Δ1.53	1.59	E1.70	1.66	36 Wk Nov	0.90	0.97	36
37◆	....	0.10	10-1-79	9-10	...	Nil	....	45.7	47.0	4.29	9-30-95	1.52	...	5058	Dc	d1.31	d1.18	d0.51	3.22	....	1.18	9 Mo Sep	d0.07	d2.11	37
38	1995	Q0.05	2-6-96	1-22	0.20	0.20	....	34.5	89.9	42.7	9-30-95	112	...	11316	Dc	d0.54	d0.20	□0.51	0.37	....	0.57	9 Mo Sep	0.17	0.37	38
39	....	None Since Public			...	Nil	....	2.83	91.3	27.1	9-30-95	65.1	...	10163	Dc	...	p0.59	p0.72	0.87	....	0.94	9 Mo Sep	0.67	0.74	39
40	1984	0.10	12-15-94	11-23	...	Nil	0.40	1.10	358	260	9-30-95	52.1	...	16090	Dc	2.61	Δ□0.50	1.61	d1.77	Ed2.90	d3.42	9 Mo Sep	d1.70	d3.35	40
41◆	1989	Q0.03	12-29-95	12-6	†0.12½	0.12	0.12	6.86	509	217	10-01-95	100	...	34422	Dc	*0.92	1.16	1.31	1.40	E1.00↑	1.43	9 Mo Sep	0.70	0.73	41
42	....	None Since Public			...	Nil	....	12.2	36.4	8.22	6-30-95	0.02	...	★10034	Dc	d0.21	0.08	0.53	0.73	....	0.89	9 Mo Sep	0.46	0.62	42
43	1943	Q0.20	12-11-95	11-13	0.80	0.80	0.80	34.3	83.5	26.6	9-29-95	0.80	...	±6293	Dc	±0.42	±1.19	±□0.90	±d1.66	....	3.40	9 Mo Sep	±d1.78	±3.28	43
44	....	None Since Public			...	Nil	....	81.4	83.3	9.60	6-30-95	4.78	...	★22841	Mr	d0.40	d0.88	d1.37	d1.65	....	d1.71	6 Mo Sep	d0.75	d0.81	44
45◆	1906	Q0.15	3-5-96	1-30	0.57½	0.60	0.48	68.5	2863	1801	9-30-95	550	162	443757	Dc	0.97	1.16	□0.96	1.57	E1.85	1.78	9 Mo Sep	1.12	1.33	45
46	....	None Since Public			...	Nil	....	5.33	16.2	2.12	9-30-95	....	...	3105	Je	0.59	0.54	0.54	0.41	0.52	0.36	3 Mo Sep	0.13	d0.03	46
47◆	1985	Q0.16	1-25-96	1-9	†0.654	0.64	†0.516	Book Value $11.84			9-30-95	111	...	3054	Dc	1.01	1.40	1.70	1.68	....	1.79	9 Mo Sep	1.25	1.36	47
48	....	None Since Public			...	Nil	....	0.06	4.16	3.51	9-30-95	10.2	...	3342	Dc	p0.42	0.54	0.62	0.80	....	0.89	9 Mo Sep	0.61	0.70	48
49	1990	gA0.06	9-29-95	9-11	g0.06	0.06	g0.06	10.2	22.7	3.16	9-30-95	....	...	26387	Je	0.28	0.10	0.05	[71]0.32	0.10	0.04	3 Mo Sep	0.04	d0.02	49
50◆	1946	Q0.17½	2-1-96	1-10	0.70	0.70	0.70	6.04	152	86.5	9-30-95	150	...	43527	Dc	1.67	1.27	□0.46	d2.67	E1.55	d1.63	9 Mo Sep	0.06	1.10	50
51◆	1959	0.67	11-2-95	9-22	1.008	1.01	0.88	2763	4648	2130	j6-30-94	298	...	3049397	Je	□1.13	1.20	1.29	1.29	E1.55	1.35	6 Mo DecΔ	0.70	0.76	51
52	1990	Q0.12½	11-17-95	11-1	0.50	0.50	0.40	8.18	99.8	49.2	9-30-95	24.6	...	5177	Dc	1.16	□d4.35	d0.56	1.41	....	2.80	9 Mo Sep	0.61	2.00	52

◆**Stock Splits & Divs By Line Reference Index** [2]2-for-1,'92. [5]2-for-1,'93,'95. [8]2-for-1,'91. [11]2-for-1,'93. [18]10%,'91,'92,'93,'94,'95. [20]3-for-2,'92. [21]2-for-1,'93. [22]3-for-2,'92. [26]No adj for reorg,'90(dstr $$30&$8.50deb). [31]5-for-4,'91,'92. [37]3-for-2,'92. [41]2-for-1,'92. [45]2-for-1,'91,'95. [47]10%,'92,'93,'94,'95. [50]2-for-1,'92. [51]2-for-1,'91.

¶ S&P 500 · # MidCap 400 · ✣ SmallCap 600 · • Options

Index	Ticker	Name of Issue (Call Price of Pfd. Stocks)	Market	Com. Rank. & Pfd. Rating	Inst. Hold Cos	Inst. Hold Shs. (000)	Principal Business	Price Range 1971-93 High	1971-93 Low	1994 High	1994 Low	1995 High	1995 Low	Dec. Sales in 100s	December, 1995 Last Sale Or Bid High	Low	Last	%Div Yield	P-E Ratio	Total Return % Annualized 12 Mo	36 Mo	60 Mo
1•[1]	GEMS	✓Glenayre Technologies	NNM	B	260	28576	Mfr telecommunications eqp	24⅝	1	28⅛	14½	73¾	24⅛	81167	63½	51	62¼	...	41	144	163	102
2•[2]	GLN	✓Glendale Federal Bank	NY	NR	135	33447	Savings bank, California	9⅜	6¼	13½	5⅛	18	8¾	81430	18	15⅞	17⅝	...	13	85.5	...	...
3	Pr E	8.75% Cv'E' Pfd([51]26.09375)	NY	CCC+	53	5806		26¾	23	36	19½	46	26½	9333	46	41⅞	45¼	4.8	..	...	...	...
4	GLIA	Gliatech Inc	NNM	NR	..	...	Dvlp postoperative med devices	....	....	....	....	9⅞	7⅞	5484	9½	8¼	8⅜	...	..	...	...	...
5	GRT	✓Glimcher Realty Trust	NY,Ch	NR	111	12384	Real estate investment trust	....	....	22½	18⅛	22⅜	16½	19459	18⅛	16½	17¼	11.1	14	−5.9	...	...
6	GML	✓Global DirectMail	NY,Ch	NR	87	7079	Direct mkt computer/office pd	....	....	....	....	30⅜	17½	8947	30	25¾	27½	...	34	...	...	...
✣7	GIX	✓Global Industrial Tech	NY	NR	169	16425	Minerals&refract'y prd/ind eq	15½	6⅜	15½	10¼	19⅝	10⅞	11019	19⅝	17⅜	18⅞	...	11	38.5	27.4	...
8	GLBL	✓Global Industries	NNM	NR	75	5604	Provides offshore O&G svcs	23	13	25¾	13¼	30¾	19¼	7393	30¾	26½	30	...	16	29.0	...	...
#9	GLM	✓Global Marine	NY	NR	191	115005	Oil & gas contract drilling	10¾	⅜	5	3½	8⅞	3⅜	225525	8⅞	6¾	8¾	...	29	133	60.3	19.3
10•[2]	GNR	✓Global Natural Res	NY,Ch,Ph	C	81	19273	Oil&gas:US,Indonesia,Canada	20⅜	2¾	9⅝	6⅜	12⅜	7	8723	10½	9⅝	10½	...	d	25.4	18.1	11.8
11	GLO	✓Global Ocean Carriers	AS	NR	4	552	Ocean shipping fleet	15½	1½	4⅞	2 1/16	4⅞	3	491	4⅛	3⅜	3¾	...	d	20.0	23.9	−2.7
12	GNK	✓Globalink Inc	AS,Ph	NR	31	1581	Dvlp translation software	8⅝	5¾	17⅜	7⅛	16⅝	6	6452	9⅝	6	6½	...	d	−54.8	...	...
13	GSTRF	Globalstar Telecommunications	NNM	NR	..	...	Global telecommunications	....	....	....	....	38½	11½	18837	38½	27½	37	...	..	...	...	...
14	GNUC	✓GNI Group, Inc	NNM	↑B	23	2428	Environmental services	11½	¾	8	2⅝	8¼	3¾	1977	7	6	6⅝	...	12	55.9	−4.6	18.2
15	VCR	✓Go-Video	AS,Ch,P	B−	12	638	Dvlp, mkt consumer electrs prd	24⅛	½	3	1¼	2⅜	1⅛	10034	1¾	1⅛	1¼	...	d	−35.5	−26.3	−18.6
16	WS	Wrrt(Pur 1 com at $8.25)	AS	NR	1	.3		4½	⅛	9/16	1/64	⅜	1/64	464	⅛	1/16	1/16	...	..	...	...	...
17	GG.A	✓Goldcorp Inc 'A'[60]	NY,To,Ch,Mo	NR	17	2167	Gold mining, exploration	....	....	6⅞	4⅞	12⅝	4⅞	2310	12½	10⅜	11¾	...	..	125	...	...
18	GG.B	Class'B'[62]	NY,Ch	NR	..	...		....	....	6⅞	5¾	12¼	5½	8	11¾	11⅝	11½B	...	..	96.7	...	...
19	GEGP	Golden Eagle Group	NSC	NR	..	...	Int'l ocean/air freight fwdg	5⅝	2½	4⅝	1¼	2⅞	1⅜	1094	2⅜	1¾	2	...	11	33.3	−17.0	...
20	GLDC	✓Golden Enterprises	NNM	B	22	1331	Snack foods:bolts&fasteners	16½	5/16	8¼	6⅝	9¾	6¾	1140	9⅛	8	8⅛	5.8	20	27.9	6.6	8.9
21	CHIK	✓Golden Poultry Co	NNM	B−	17	1227	Producer/dstr poultry prod	10½	2½	8	5½	9	5½	986	9	8	8¾	0.5	21	53.1	10.8	10.3
22	GSR	✓Golden Star Resources	AS,Ch	NR	41	10491	Explor,mine gold S. America	15⅛	8¼	17¼	7⅝	9	4½	10998	5⅞	5	5	...	d	...	...	...
23	GTRO	✓Golden Tri Roy. & Oil	NSC	NR	2	3	Envir/ener sv,oil royl US&Aust	120½	1 9/16	3¼	1⅜	3⅜	1⅜	1675	3¼	2¾	3¼	...	9	32.5	2.2	−6.7
¶24•[3]	GDW	✓Golden West Finl	NY,B,Ch,P	↓B+	301	40159	Savings&loan,CA,CO,KS,TX	50⅜	9/16	46	34¼	57½	34¾	18381	56¼	51¼	55¼	0.7	14	56.3	10.6	18.2
25	GV	✓Goldfield Corp	AS,Ch	C	7	736	Elect'l constr,silver min'g	4⅜	¼	⅝	5/16	½	¼	7238	⅜	¼	¼	...	d	−19.9	−23.7	0.0
26	SG	✓Goldwyn, Samuel Co	AS	NR	18	1392	Prod'n,dstr films/TV programs	257½	5¾	13	5	9¾	2⅜	18033	6⅛	2⅜	4⅝	...	d	−28.8	−23.3	−18.0
27	GLFE	✓Golf Enterprises	NNM	NR	20	1382	Golf course operator	....	....	15	10¼	14¼	6¾	2646	8¾	7	7¼	...	14	−37.0	...	...
28•[1]	GGUY	✓Good Guys Inc	NNM	B+	76	10180	Retails consumer electr prod	30	1 1/16	20½	10½	13⅞	8⅝	16956	10⅜	8⅝	9	...	9	−22.6	−4.2	0.3
29	GTIM	✓Good Times Restaurants	NSC	NR	4	205	Limited menu,fast-food svc	6	1½	2⅛	1⅛	2	½	6829	11/16	½	½	...	d	−65.2	−39.4	...
✣30	GDMK	✓GoodMark Foods	NNM	B	50	3795	Produces & Mkts meat snacks	10¾	3½	16¾	7⅜	19	13¼	3306	18¾	16¾	17¾	0.9	19	11.9	36.1	30.3
¶31•[4]	GR	✓Goodrich (B.F.)	NY,B,C,Ch,P,Ph	B−	314	21426	Aerospace prd/spcl chemicals	69	12½	48⅜	39	72⅝	41⅝	17142	70¼	65¼	68	3.2	16	60.1	17.4	18.6
32	GDP	✓Goodrich Petroleum	NY,B,Ch,P,Ph	C	16	1208	Oil, gas explor & develop	54½	1¾	2⅞	13/16	1⅜	11/16	10762	15/16	¾	13/16	...	..	−13.3	−28.8	−18.4
¶33•[5]	GT	✓Goodyear Tire & Rub	NY,B,C,Ch,P,Ph	B	624	104425	Mfr tire & rubber products	47¼	5⅜	49¼	31⅝	45⅜	33	93519	45⅜	42⅜	45⅜	2.2	11	37.1	12.6	38.8
34	GDYS	✓Goody's Family Clothing	NNM	NR	38	3076	Sells Moder'tly-priced apparel	25	10	20	7½	14¾	8⅛	7275	11⅜	8⅜	8¾	...	13	−6.6	−27.2	...
35	GRC	✓Gorman-Rupp	AS	B+	44	3769	Mfr pumps:constr'n,ind'l use	20⅜	1 3/16	20	15⅛	18¼	13	765	15⅞	14⅜	15½	3.4	15	−7.7	−3.8	14.6
✣36	GOT	✓Gottschalks Inc	NY,Ch,Ph,P	B−	29	2000	Retail dept str chain,Calif	26⅜	6⅛	13	7	8⅜	5⅛	4963	6⅝	5⅛	5¼	...	..	−27.6	−16.4	−17.1
#37•[6]	GULD	✓Goulds Pumps	NNM	B+	130	14689	Centrifugal liq hdlg pumps	29⅜	2⅞	26½	19⅛	26	19⅝	16525	26	23⅝	25	e3.2	19	27.1	3.7	8.9
38	GTSI	✓Government Technology Svcs	NNM	NR	32	1953	Resell computer prod to govt	16	4	14¾	9¼	11	3⅜	11509	4⅝	3⅜	4⅜	...	d	−58.3	−12.4	...
¶39•[7]	GRA	✓Grace (W.R.)[69]	NY,B,C,Ch,P,Ph	B−	481	78715	Specialty chems:energy:mfg	45	9	46¾	35¼	71⅝	38¼	99539	63¼	56¾	59⅛	0.8	35	55.1	18.8	24.1
40	GGG	✓Graco Inc	NY,Ch	A−	80	8256	Specialized pump & spray eq	24¼	13/16	24⅝	16¾	38¼	19¾	3395	36	30	30½	2.4	14	47.9	33.5	21.0
41	GHM	✓Graham Corp	AS,Ch	B−	10	198	Vacuum & heat transfer eq	41	2 7/16	14⅞	9⅝	16	9	1223	16	13¼	15¾	...	d	53.7	3.5	6.9
42	GFI	✓Graham-Field Health	NY,Ch,Ph	↓C	25	3101	Mfr/dstr med/surg equip	20½	1¾	6½	2⅞	4⅝	2¾	12737	3½	2⅞	3⅜	...	d	−3.6	−16.3	2.4
¶43•[5]	GWW	✓Grainger (W.W.)	NY,B,Ch,P,Ph	A	443	31574	Natl dstr indus/comm'l prod	66¾	2⅞	69⅛	51½	67⅝	55½	17304	67⅝	65¼	66¼	1.4	18	16.1	5.1	16.5
✣44•[8]	GC	✓GranCare Inc	NY	NR	104	9723	Hlth care/rehab facilities	24	8¾	22½	14¾	19⅛	12¾	9971	15⅝	13½	14½	...	17	−15.9	−11.3	...
✣45•[9]	GND	✓Grand Casinos	NY,Ch	NR	130	19113	Develop/manage casinos	34⅝	3	21⅞	8	28⅛	9⅛	34764	26⅞	22⅝	23¼	...	13	151	28.6	...
46•[10]	GRM	✓Grand Metropolitan ADS[71]	NY,Ch,Ph	NR	77	14524	Food & drink prod/retailing	37¼	22⅜	30	23⅛	29	22½	10860	28⅞	26⅝	28¾	3.4	14	18.8	4.9	...
47	GXL	✓Granges Inc(New)	AS,To,Ph	↑B−	19	7950	Mineral explor'n,devel	14¾	13/16	3⅜	1⅜	2⅜	1 7/16	4281	1⅞	1 9/16	1⅝	...	..	−10.3	2.7	6.5
#48	GCCO	✓Granite Construction	NNM	B	109	6230	Heavy constr contractor U.S.	33¼	15½	26¼	16	31⅞	18	13819	31⅞	26½	31½	e1.0	23	56.4	15.4	8.9
49	GRPH	✓Graphic Industries	NNM	B	44	2708	Commercial/fin'l printing	16⅞	2¾	12½	7⅛	13⅜	8⅜	4317	13⅜	10⅜	12¼	0.6	13	21.9	21.5	19.6
50	GCS	✓Gray Communications Systems	NY,Ch	NR	10	311	TV broadcstg/newspaper publish	154⅝	5⅜	11⅛	8⅜	24⅜	10⅝	1185	19⅜	16⅜	17⅞	0.4	37	64.8	32.0	...
51	GRH	✓GRC International	NY,B,Ch,P	B−	38	3622	Research svcs/testing, softwr	45⅜	5/16	16½	7⅜	39⅝	11⅜	8550	39⅝	30	38⅜	...	85	223	84.4	72.7
52	GAMI	Great Amer Mgmt & Inv	NSC	↑B−	22	378	Mfg,AG chem/fert,fin'l svcs	40⅜	⅛	38	29	49	33½	161	49	41¼	49	...	4	47.9	24.0	15.0

Uniform Footnote Explanations-See Page 4. Other: [1]CBOE:Cycle 3. [2]CBOE:Cycle 1. [3]Ph:Cycle 2. [4]CBOE:Cycle 2. [5]ASE:Cycle 1. [6]NY:Cycle 3. [7]ASE:Cycle 2. [8]Ph:Cycle 3. [9]ASE,CBOE,P:Cycle 2. [10]ASE,P:Cycle 1. [51]Fr 10-1-98,scale to $25 in 2003. [52]Fr 9-30-94. [53]Incl current amts. [54]100% non-taxable,'94. [55]□$1.08,'94. [56]9 Mo Dec'94. [57]One wrrt for ea 10 com held. [58]Fiscal Jul'93 & prior. [59]12 Mo Mar'95:Jul'94 earn$0.01. [60]Sub vtg shrs. [61]®$1.07,'94. [62]Multi vtg shrs. [63]Stk dstr of Guyanor Resources Ltd S.A.. [64]22 Wk Dec'92. [65]12 Mo Mar'92. [66]Fiscal'94 & prior refl. Patrick Petrol. [67]Spl div. [68]Incl redemption of stk purch rt. [69]Plan spin-off,Natl Medical Care. [70]Fiscal Jul'91 & prior. [71]Ea Am shr rep 4 ord,50 pence. [72]Approx. [73]Fiscal Jun'92 & prior. [74]Year Dec'93:yr Jun'93 earn $0.95. [75]Special div. [76]Fiscal Jul'92 & prior. [77]12 Mo Dec'93:fiscal Jul 93 earned d$3.23.

Splits ◆ Index	Cash Divs. Ea.Yr. Since	Dividends: Latest Payment Period $	Date	Ex. Div.	Total $ So Far 1995	Ind. Rate	Paid 1994	Financial Position Mil-$ Cash& Equiv.	Curr. Assets	Curr. Liab.	Balance Sheet Date	Capitalization Lg Trm Debt Mil-$	Shs. 000 Pfd.	Com.	Earnings $ Per Shr. Years End	1991	1992	1993	1994	1995	Last 12 Mos.	Interim Earnings Period	$ per Shr. 1994	1995	Index
1◆	....	None Paid			...	Nil	....	115	267	59.9	9-30-95	....	...	39914	Dc	0.02	d0.28	□0.73	0.85	....	1.51	9 Mo Sep	0.61	1.27	1
2	....	None Since Public			...	Nil	....	Book Value $15.25			6-30-95	3524	8050	40734	Je	...	...	pd4.21	Δd6.48	Δ1.28	1.37	3 Mo Sep	0.12	0.21	2
3	1994	Q0.547	1-2-96	11-29	2.18¾	2.19	2.223	Cv into 2.137 com, $11.70[52]				....	7000	...	Je	...	...	...	....	....	....				3
4	....	None Since Public			...	Nil	....	5.40	6.00	2.06	6-30-95	....	p...	★7120	Dc	...	...	...	pd1.30	....	....	6 Mo Jun	n/a	pd0.53	4
5	1994	Q0.481	1-16-96	12-27	1.897	1.92	1.273	Equity per shr $13.13			9-30-95	[53]304	...	21880	Dc	...	p0.50	p0.83	p1.17	....	1.24	9 Mo Sep	p0.84	0.91	5
6	....	None Since Public			...	Nil	....	31.1	203	70.9	9-30-95	6.41	...	36709	Dc	...	...	...	p0.61	....	0.82	9 Mo Sep	p0.44	p0.65	6
7	....	None Since Public			...	Nil	....	19.1	273	183	7-31-95	p3.90	...	22715	Oc	pd0.18	□pd1.85	p□0.78	1.02	P1.70	1.70				7
8	....	None Since Public			...	Nil	....	28.5	84.2	24.2	9-30-95	22.1	...	9454	Mr	p0.95	1.58	Δ1.33	2.15	....	1.86	6 Mo Sep	1.57	1.28	8
9	....	None Since Public			...	Nil	....	88.3	174	63.5	9-30-95	225	...	165451	Dc	0.01	Δ0.24	d0.17	□0.03	E0.30	0.27	9 Mo Sep	□d0.01	0.23	9
10	....	None Paid			...	Nil	....	21.8	36.4	21.3	9-30-95	7.70	...	29544	Dc	d1.66	d0.12	0.16	d0.28	....	d0.24	9 Mo Sep	d0.16	d0.12	10
11	1994	0.05	4-22-94	4-4	...	Nil	[54]0.05	6.52	8.07	7.96	12-31-94	19.3	...	4096	Dc	Δ0.31	0.08	d0.24	d3.88	....	d1.76	6 Mo Jun	d1.81	0.31	11
12	....	None Since Public			...	Nil	....	2.84	11.0	3.26	9-30-95	0.47	...	5301	Dc	...	d0.09	0.10	□[55]d0.47	....	d0.64	9 Mo Sep	0.04	d0.13	12
13	....	None Since Public			...	Nil	....	Equity per shr $9.21			12-31-94	....	...	★10000	Dc	...	...	...	‡p[56]0.73	....	....				13
14	....	0.01¼	7-28-83	7-18	...	Nil	....	0.34	8.57	8.44	9-30-95	13.5	...	6559	Je	0.06	0.20	0.42	d0.34	0.47	0.55	3 Mo Sep	0.04	0.12	14
15	....	[57]Wrrt	3-19-90	3-20	...	Nil	....	0.16	14.9	8.74	9-30-95	....	...	11301	Mr	d0.16	d0.13	[58]0.01	[59]0.08	....	d0.05	6 Mo Sep	0.07	d0.06	15
16	....	Terms&trad. basis should			be checked in detail			Wrrts expire 3-9-97				....	...	1955	Jl	...	...	...	....	....	....	Callable at $0.50			16
17	1994	gA0.05	5-23-95	5-11	g0.05	0.05	g†0.10	90.2	137	46.9	j12-31-94	26.5	...	±31124	Dc	...	p0.11	p0.57	[61]1.11	....	j0.16	9 Mo Sep	1.08	0.13	17
18	1994	gA0.05	5-23-95	5-11	g0.05	0.05	g†0.10	....	...	...		....	...	1670	Dc	...	p0.11	p0.57	[61]1.11	....	j0.16	9 Mo Sep	1.08	0.13	18
19	....	None Paid			...	Nil	....	0.19	7.53	6.52	9-30-95	....	...	5307	Dc	...	...	d0.04	0.07	....	0.19	9 Mo Sep	0.03	0.15	19
20	1968	Q0.11¾	10-25-95	10-4	0.46¼	0.47	0.45¼	16.6	33.4	8.42	8-31-95	0.65	...	12262	My	0.35	0.38	0.40	0.25	0.42	0.41	6 Mo Nov	0.20	0.19	20
21◆	1986	Q0.01	11-22-95	11-6	0.04	0.04	0.039	3.05	75.9	43.8	9-30-95	6.39	...	14518	Je	0.21	□d0.13	0.53	0.27	0.19	0.41	3 Mo Sep	0.06	0.28	21
22	....	h[63]....		3-14	h[63]...	Nil	....	20.1	23.8	4.44	9-30-95	....	...	22727	Dc	...	‡[64]d1.14	d0.10	d0.42	....	d0.55	9 Mo Sep	d0.07	d0.20	22
23◆	....	5%Stk	10-15-90	9-5	...	Nil	....	0.03	0.97	0.16	9-30-95	....	...	3819	Dc	Nil	Nil	d0.18	0.15	....	0.37	9 Mo Sep	d0.05	0.17	23
24	1977	Q0.09½	12-11-95	11-13	0.35	0.38	0.31	Book Value $35.08			9-30-95	9163	...	58641	Dc	3.76	4.46	4.28	3.71	E3.95	3.66	9 Mo Sep	2.91	2.86	24
25	....	0.05	8-31-63		...	Nil	....	5.36	7.85	1.47	9-30-95	....	339	26855	Dc	0.16	0.04	Δd0.13	d0.04	....	d0.05	9 Mo Sep	d0.02	d0.03	25
26◆	....	None Since Public			...	Nil	....	Equity per shr $0.03			9-30-95	77.1	...	8489	Mr	p[65]d0.60	0.18	Δ0.20	d2.37	....	d3.44	6 Mo Sep	d0.38	□d1.45	26
27	....	None Since Public			...	Nil	....	3.06	13.7	11.2	9-30-95	59.6	...	6489	Dc	...	...	p0.41	p□0.33	....	0.52	9 Mo Sep	□0.35	0.54	27
28◆	....	None Since Public			...	Nil	....	18.4	166	91.7	9-30-95	....	...	13581	Sp	0.93	0.29	0.60	1.06	1.06	1.06				28
29◆	....	None Paid			...	Nil	....	0.37	1.52	0.79	6-30-95	0.21	...	6898	Sp	d0.44	d0.43	d0.21	d0.04	....	d0.17	9 Mo Jun	d0.03	d0.16	29
30◆	1993	Q0.04	2-1-96	1-10	0.14	0.16	0.11	0.10	31.7	12.3	8-27-95	21.7	...	7827	My	0.17	0.38	0.56	□0.88	1.20	0.95	6 Mo Nov	0.74	0.49	30
31	1939	Q0.55	1-2-96	12-6	2.20	2.20	1.65	53.9	960	657	9-30-95	386	...	26132	Dc	d3.50	□d0.69	4.68	2.63	E4.35	4.08	9 Mo Sep	1.97	3.42	31
32	....	Wrrt	1-25-80	1-9	...	Nil	....	1.03	2.44	1.88	9-30-95	11.0	1099	41805	Dc	d0.53	d1.79	d0.63	□[66]d0.72	....	....	9 Mo Sep	p0.08	Δp0.04	32
33◆	1937	Q0.25	12-15-95	11-14	0.95	1.00	0.75	223	4544	3005	9-30-95	1288	...	152430	Dc	*0.62	□2.57	□3.33	3.75	E4.00↓	3.96	9 Mo Sep	2.85	3.06	33
34◆	1995	[67]0.01	6-6-95	4-27	[67]0.01	Nil	....	14.3	140	104	10-28-95	16.3	...	16125	Ja	p0.77	1.00	0.86	0.43	....	0.70	9 Mo Oct	0.06	0.33	34
35◆	1935	Q0.13	12-8-95	11-8	0.52	0.52	0.49	2.20	69.1	22.8	9-30-95	3.48	...	8593	Dc	0.89	□0.93	1.03	1.09	....	1.01	9 Mo Sep	0.92	0.84	35
36	....	None Since Public			...	Nil	....	4.53	167	124	10-28-95	35.4	...	10417	Ja	0.44	d0.77	d0.26	0.15	....	0.01	9 Mo Oct	d0.66	d0.80	36
37	1948	[68]Q0.20	1-15-96	1-3	0.80	0.80	0.80	9.96	331	192	9-30-95	88.3	...	21265	Dc	□1.51	□1.04	□1.12	0.86	E1.30	1.25	9 Mo Sep	0.68	1.07	37
38	....	None Since Public			...	Nil	....	0.05	238	190	9-30-95	....	...	6806	Dc	1.49	0.91	1.30	0.37	....	d1.06	9 Mo Sep	0.98	d0.45	38
39	1934	Q0.12½	12-11-95	10-31	1.175	0.50	1.40	80.9	1764	1947	9-30-95	1256	74	97299	Dc	2.50	□d1.17	0.28	0.88	E1.68↓	2.65	9 Mo Sep	d0.22	1.55	39
40◆	1970	Q0.18	2-7-96	12-29	0.64	0.72	3.26	0.65	139	85.1	9-29-95	12.6	15	11503	Dc	0.79	□0.97	0.82	1.32	....	2.20	9 Mo Sep	0.88	1.76	40
41	1989	0.07	1-4-93	11-9	...	Nil	....	0.11	16.1	9.46	9-30-95	4.31	...	1054	Dc	0.79	□Δ1.24	0.39	□d8.01	....	d3.19	9 Mo Sep	□d4.69	0.13	41
42	....	None Since Public			...	Nil	....	3.07	50.8	18.2	9-30-95	20.1	...	14082	Dc	0.40	0.10	Δd0.26	d0.18	....	d0.11	9 Mo Sep	d0.04	0.03	42
43◆	1965	Q0.23	12-1-95	11-2	0.89	0.92	0.78	22.9	1099	515	9-30-95	4.41	...	50856	Dc	2.37	2.58	2.88	2.50	E3.65	2.67	9 Mo Sep	2.48	2.65	43
44	....	None Since Public			...	Nil	....	29.0	218	103	9-30-95	320	...	22943	Dc	0.69	1.08	□1.00	1.08	....	0.88	9 Mo Sep	0.75	0.55	44
45◆	....	None Since Public			...	Nil	....	66.7	101	111	10-01-95	★666	...	33653	Dc	p[70]0.08	0.13	0.71	0.87	....	1.77	9 Mo Sep	0.69	1.59	45
46	1988	[72]0.611	4-15-96	1-8	0.965	0.98	0.855	986	4204	3235	j9-30-94	2291	12235	2084475	Sp	Δ2.31	Δ2.14	□1.22	2.04	E2.00	2.04				46
47	....	None Paid			...	Nil	....	33.7	50.0	7.55	j9-30-95	....	...	46043	Dc	d0.79	Nil	0.08	0.20	....	j0.13	9 Mo Sep	0.25	0.18	47
48	1990	Q0.075	1-19-96	12-27	†0.40	0.30	0.20	56.3	279	210	9-30-95	41.7	...	11899	Dc	1.51	0.34	Δ0.30	1.66	E1.35	2.21	9 Mo Sep	1.37	1.92	48
49	1987	Q0.01¾	1-5-96	12-18	0.07	0.07	0.07	23.7	140	86.8	10-31-95	86.0	...	±11077	Ja	0.01	0.41	0.65	0.80	....	0.93	9 Mo Oct	0.58	0.71	49
50◆	1992	Q0.02	12-20-95	12-6	0.08	0.08	†0.067	0.28	11.1	10.8	9-30-95	52.5	...	4397	Dc	0.43	[73]d0.08	[74]0.55	0.59	....	0.48	9 Mo Sep	0.38	0.27	50
51	....	None Paid			...	Nil	....	0.02	41.7	21.6	9-30-95	2.35	...	9133	Je	d0.33	0.43	0.60	Δ0.65	0.54	0.45	3 Mo Sep	0.16	0.07	51
52	1995	[75]0.90	1-3-95	12-12	[75]0.90	Nil	....	46.6	301	211	9-30-95	307	...	9196	Dc	3.40	[76]3.56	□[77]d9.25	□5.83	....	13.12	9 Mo Sep	□d0.73	6.56	52

◆**Stock Splits & Divs By Line Reference Index** [1]3-for-2,'95(twice):To split 3-for-2,ex Jan 2. [21]10%,'93,'94. [23]1-for-20 REVERSE,'93:1-for-2.5 REVERSE,'95. [26]1-for-5 REVERSE,'92:1-for-4 REVERSE,'93. [28]2-for-1,'91. [29]1-for-4 REVERSE,'92. [30]2-for-1,'94. [33]2-for-1,'93. [34]3-for-2,'93. [35]3-for-2,'92,'94. [40]3-for-2,'94:To split 3-for-2,ex Feb 8. [43]2-for-1,'91. [45]10%,'92:3-for-2,'95. [50]10-for-1,'91:3-for-2,'95.

¶ S&P 500
\# MidCap 400
✣ SmallCap 600
• Options

Index	Ticker	Name of Issue (Call Price of Pfd. Stocks)	Market	Com. Rank. & Pfd. Rating	Inst. Hold Cos	Inst. Hold Shs. (000)	Principal Business	Price Range 1971-93 High	1971-93 Low	1994 High	1994 Low	1995 High	1995 Low	Dec. Sales in 100s	December, 1995 Last Sale Or Bid High	Low	Last	%Div Yield	P-E Ratio	Total Return % Annualized 12 Mo	36 Mo	60 Mo
¶1•[1]	GAP	✔Great Atl & Pac Tea	NY,B,C,Ch,P,Ph	B–	232	14158	Food super markets	65⅜	3½	27⅜	17⅜	29	17⅝	7053	24⅝	21¼	23	0.9	22	25.4	0.6	–10.2
2	GTFN	✔Great Financial	NNM	NR	50	4461	General banking,Kentucky	....	....	19⅛	10	24⅛	14⅞	5816	24⅛	22⅞	23½	1.7	..	63.9	...	...
¶3•[2]	GLK	✔Great Lakes Chemical	NY,B,Ch,P	A+	494	50922	Bromine & brominated chem	84	5/16	82	48¾	74⅝	55¾	24060	74⅝	69½	72	0.6	16	27.5	2.6	18.7
4	GNI	✔Great North'n Iron Ore[52]	NY,Ch	NR	21	149	Royalty income from mines	80¼	8¾	50	35	49¼	39⅞	859	46	44½	44½	11.2	9	16.7	–2.6	10.3
5	GPWC	Great Pines Water	NSC	NR	..	...	Processes,mkt bottled water	6	3¾	5⅜	1⅛	4	1⅞	1501	3¼	2¼	2 5/16	...	d	15.6	...	...
6	GWALY	Great Wall Electr Int. ADS[53]	NNM	NR	4	231	Mfr,mkt electronic prod	10½	8	9⅝	3¾	4½	3⅛	829	4⅛	3⅝	3⅝	4.6	5	–13.6	...	...
¶7•[3]	GWF	✔Great Westn Finl	NY,B,C,Ch,P,Ph	B–	411	117398	Savings & loan,Calif,Fla	25⅛	1 11/16	21⅛	15¼	27⅛	16	81131	27⅛	24½	25⅜	3.6	16	61.5	22.0	22.8
8	Pr	8.75%cmCv[54]DepPfd([55]52.1875)	NY	BBB–	49	1251		63⅞	47¾	63¼	50	68¼	50	1487	68¼	63	64¾	6.8	..	...	...	...
9	APGI	✔Green(A.P.)Indus	NNM	NR	41	2709	Mfr,install refractory prod	26⅝	7⅜	20½	16½	24	17	743	20¼	18¾	19½	1.4	9	5.5	25.0	14.8
✣10	GMP	✔Green Mountain Pwr	NY,Ph	A–	48	941	Electricity in Vermont	36⅝	3⅜	31¼	23⅜	28⅝	23⅞	1620	28⅝	27⅜	27¾	7.6	12	8.8	1.5	12.4
#11•[4]	GNT	✔Green Tree Finl	NY,B,Ch,Ph	B+	422	117091	Purchases hous'g contracts	15⅝	11/16	17½	10¾	32⅜	14¾	158208	28⅝	22	26⅜	0.9	15	78.1	66.2	83.7
12	GBX	✔Greenbrier Cos	NY,Ch	NR	59	4208	Railroad transp'n eqp/leas'g	....	....	19½	14	17¾	10½	2339	13	11	12⅛	2.0	10	–24.1	...	...
✣13	GFII	✔Greenfield Industries	NNM	NR	164	15665	Mfr expendable cutting tools	20¾	15½	24½	18¼	35½	20¾	8903	32½	30¾	31¼	0.5	17	34.3	...	...
14•[3]	GNPT	✔Greenpoint Finl	NNM	NR	154	27592	Savings bank, New York	....	....	25¼	17½	29¾	20⅜	80589	27⅜	24⅝	26¾	3.0	11	32.9	...	...
15	GMAI	✔Greg Manning Auctions	NSC	NR	1	.5	Conducts public auction svs	4⅞	2⅜	3⅛	2⅛	3	1½	10401	3	1 15/16	2 3/16	...	d	–7.9	...	...
16	GBC	Greif Bros[57] Cl'A'	Ch	B+	62	7412	Ship'g containers/containerbrd	23½	1⅛	23¼	18⅝	28⅞	21⅛	873	27¼	25⅞	26⅞	†1.6	11	28.2	16.2	...
17	GII	✔Greiner Engineering[58]	NY,B,Ch,P,Ph	B+	26	1527	Architect,engr'g,design sv	19⅜	7/16	17⅜	9¾	14	8⅛	4794	14	9	13½	2.2	d	35.5	–6.8	1.1
18	GREY	Grey Advertising	NNM	↓B	58	504	Advertising agency	192	2¾	196	144	209	144	41	203	190	200	1.9	d	40.4	17.0	12.3
19•[5]	BUS	✔Greyhound Lines	AS,Ph	NR	57	25977	Nationwide bus transportation	22¾	6½	12½	1⅝	5⅝	1¼	37181	4½	3⅞	4¼	...	d	116	–28.4	...
20	GGE	✔Griffin Gaming & Entmt	AS,Ph	NR	21	809	Oper casino/hotel facilities	19⅜	2½	9⅜	3¾	19⅝	4	4763	12¼	11	11	...	3	171	32.9	28.6
✣21•[6]	GFF	✔Griffon Corp	NY,B,Ch,Ph	B–	111	21420	Home furnish'gs,electr equip	123¾	⅞	9¾	6⅝	9½	7⅜	7306	9	8⅜	9	...	13	9.1	14.5	43.1
22	Pr I	2nd[59]Pfd'I'Cv(10)vtg	NY	NR	3	172	specialty plastic films	24	1	9¾	7⅛	9½	7⅝	129	9¼	8¾	9	s...	..	...	...	...
23	GRST	✔Grist Mill	NNM	B	41	2295	Mfr natural cereal/snacks	14⅛	5/16	11¼	4⅜	13⅜	7⅜	11164	10¼	7⅜	7⅜	...	11	–22.4	–9.7	25.4
24	GROS	✔Grossman's Inc	NNM	C	37	11465	Retail lumber,bldg material	24¾	1¾	4¾	1⅞	2⅞	15/16	39126	1½	15/16	1⅛	...	6	–55.0	–36.1	–11.9
✣25•[6]	GWTI	✔Groundwater Technology	NNM	B	71	3302	Groundwater cleanup svcs	32½	11	15¾	11½	19¼	11½	15699	19¼	13¼	14	...	30	5.7	–8.0	–12.5
26	GRTK	✔Group Technologies	NNM	NR	11	1311	Mfr,engineer,test electr prd	....	....	10½	5	8	1⅞	5691	4	1⅞	2½	...	d	–61.5	...	...
27	GRE.EC	✔Grove Real Estate Asset Tr	ECM	NR	1	10	Real estate investment trust	....	....	11	8¼	9	7¼	428	8⅞	7⅝	8⅛	11.2	..	4.4	...	...
28	GBE	✔Grubb & Ellis	NY,B,Ch	C	16	814	R.E.broker: mtge: R.E.	63⅛	1⅞	4¼	1⅝	2¾	1⅞	2336	2¼	1⅞	2	...	4	–5.9	–23.0	–16.7
29	ATY	✔Grupo Casa Autrey ADS[62]	NY,Ch,Ph	NR	46	4517	Dstr pharmac'l/consumer prd	24¾	17	36½	22¼	23	8	6386	15⅜	13⅜	13⅜	0.8	21	–41.7	...	...
30	EKT	Grupo Elektra GDS[63]	NY,Ch,Ph	NR	5	241	Specialty retailer, Mexico	....	....	21¾	13¼	14⅜	3¾	7034	9½	5⅞	8¾	...	88	–36.1	...	...
31•[3]	GEM	✔Grupo Embotellador Mex GDS[64]	[7]NY,Ch	NR	12	7027	Soft drink bottler, Mexico	....	....	31⅛	12⅞	14½	5⅝	10148	10¾	8½	9	...	d	–37.4	...	...
32	GFVb.M	Grupo Financiero InverMex[65]	ME	NR	..	...	Bank,credit financial svcs	6⅛	3⅜	7¾	4	4⅛	1¾	....	1⅞	1⅞	1⅞	...	..	...	...	...
33	SFN	✔Grupo Financiero Serfin ADS[66]	NY,Ph	NR	35	4964	Commercial banking,fin,Mexico	29¾	24⅜	37¼	7½	8⅜	2¼	35871	4⅛	3¼	3⅜	...	d	–57.8	...	...
34	GID	Grupo Indl Durango ADS[67]	NY,Ch	NR	23	1618	Corrugated containers/paper pd	....	....	26½	12⅝	14¼	3⅞	2520	7⅜	6⅛	6⅝	...	d	–53.9	...	...
35	MSK	✔Grupo Indl Maseca ADS[68]	NY,Ch	NR	21	1467	Producer of corn flour	....	....	30¼	13¾	16⅞	6⅞	6007	10	8½	9⅛	3.3	13	–45.1	...	...
36	CEL.D	Grupo Iusacell S.A.'D'ADS[69]	NY,Ch,Ph	NR	22	572	Wireless telecommun,Mexico	....	....	31¼	15½	16	7⅜	3156	9½	8	8	...	d	–55.2	...	...
37	CEL	✔ Sr 'L' ADS[70]	NY,Ch,Ph	NR	42	3899		....	....	33½	18½	18¾	8¾	9283	11⅜	9¼	10⅛	...	d	–47.7	...	...
38•[2]	GMD.B	✔Grupo Mex de Desarrollo'B'ADS[71]	[7]NY	NR	23	2073	Infrastructure projects,Mexico	26¼	16¾	27⅝	7	7¾	1¾	8513	2½	1⅞	2¼	...	d	–71.4	...	...
39	GMD	Series'L'ADS[72]	NY,Ch,Ph	NR	27	3024		26½	17¼	28⅛	8⅝	9⅛	2	24743	3⅛	2½	2¾	...	d	–69.4	...	...
40	RC	✔Grupo Radio Centro ADS[73]	NY,Ch,Ph	NR	22	1533	Radio broadcasting-Mexico	27⅞	14½	29⅝	12½	14⅛	6⅛	4112	8⅝	6⅞	7½	3.3	21	–42.9	...	...
41	SDK	Grupo Sidek S.A. 'L' ADS[75]	NY,Ch,Ph	NR	22	3507	Resort mgmt/steel mini-mills	....	....	22¾	9	10¼	2	17892	2⅞	2⅛	2¼	5.8	d	–78.6	...	...
42	SDK.B	Cl'B' ADS[76]	NY,Ch	NR	4	670		....	....	18½	8	8¾	1½	10972	2⅛	1⅝	1⅝	8.0	d	–82.4	...	...
43	SIM	Grupo Simec ADS[77]	AS	NR	37	3755	Oper steel mini-mill, Mexico	33	13⅛	33¾	13⅞	15⅜	3⅜	7266	7¼	5⅜	6¼	...	d	–60.9	...	...
44	STRb.M	Grupo Situr'B'[78]	ME	NR	..	...	Hotel & resort dvlp,mgmt/R.E.	9½	3¼	12¼	6½	10⅛	1 11/16	....	2 7/16	2¼	2⅜	...	..	...	...	...
45•[8]	TV	✔Grupo Televisa S.A.GDS[79]	NY,Ch,Ph	NR	133	19324	TV/radio production,Mexico	72	63½	73¾	29	32⅜	12⅛	169115	24½	20⅝	22½	1.9	94	–31.5	...	...
46•[3]	GTR	✔Grupo Tribasa S.A. ADS[80]	NY,Ch,Ph	NR	48	2314	Highway constr'n, Mexico	37	15½	40¼	16½	16⅞	4⅞	186477	7⅞	6	7½	...	14	–57.7	...	...
47	GRYP	✔Gryphon Holdings	NNM	NR	39	4494	Insur hldg:prop & casualty	14	13	15¼	12¾	19⅜	12⅝	11148	19⅜	17¼	19¼	...	14	46.7	...	...
48	GSES	✔GSE Systems	NNM	NR	13	845	Dvlp/dgn energy/mfr software	....	....	....	....	16¾	14	3109	14¾	14	14B	...	..	...	...	...
49	GST	✔GST Telecommunications	AS,Ch	NR	14	1220	Telecommunications sys/svcs	....	....	7	3¼	7¾	3½	19706	7⅜	6⅛	7	...	d	60.0	...	...
50	GTBX	✔GT Bicycles	NNM	NR	..	...	Mfr,mkt bicycles	....	....	....	....	14¾	8½	14939	10⅛	8½	9¼	...	..	...	...	...
51	GTIS	GT Interactive Software	NNM	NR	..	...	Publish/distrib software	....	....	....	....	16½	12¼	124343	16½	12¼	14	...	..	...	...	...
¶52•[9]	GTE	✔GTE Corp	NY,B,C,Ch,P,Ph	B+	1163	395245	Lgst indep telephone sys:mfg	39⅞	5⅜	35¼	29½	45⅛	30	260769	45⅛	42⅛	43⅞	4.3	17	52.0	14.6	14.5

Uniform Footnote Explanations-See Page 4. Other: [1]ASE:Cycle 1. [2]CBOE:Cycle 3. [3]CBOE:Cycle 1. [4]CBOE,Ph:Cycle 3. [5]ASE,CBOE:Cycle 2. [6]NY:Cycle 1. [7]Ph [8]ASE,CBOE:Cycle 1. [9]ASE:Cycle 3. [51]9 Mo Dec'94. [52]Tr Ctfs. [53]Ea ADS rep 50 ord,HK $0.10. [54]Dep for⅕ shr 8.75% cm Cv Pfd. [55]Fr 5-1-96,scale to $50 in 2001. [56]Fiscal Jun'93. [57]Non-vtg. [58]URS Corp plan acq, cash & com. [59]$0.25 cash or $0.25 shr common. [60]6 Mo Dec'94. [61]Redemption of stk purch rt. [62]Ea ADS rep 4 ord shrs,no par. [63]Ea GDS rep 2 ord Ptc Ctf(ea rep 2'B'&1'L'shr). [64]Global Dep shrs,rep 2ord Ptc Ctf rep1B,1L&1Dshr. [65]All data reported in New Mexican Pesos. [66]Ea ADS rep 4 Sr'L'shrs,no-par. [67]Ea ADS rep 2 ord ptcf ctf. [68]Ea ADS rep 15 sr'B'com,no par. [69]Ea ADS rep 10 Sr'D'com, no par. [70]Ea ADS rep 10 Sr'L'Com, no par. [71]Ea ADS rep 1 Sr'B'Shr,no par. [72]Ea ADS rep 1 Sr L Shr,no par. [73]Ea ADS rep 9 non-Redm Ord Ptc ctf. [74]Approx. [75]Ea ADS rep 4 Sr'L'shrs,no par. [76]Ea ADS rep 4 Sr'B'shrs,no par. [77]Ea ADS rep 20 series'B' shrs,no par. [78]All data reported in New Pesos. [79]Global Dep Shrs,rep 2 ord Ptc Ctf rep 1A,L&D shr. [80]Ea ADS rep 2 ord shrs, no-par. [81]Fiscal Aug'93 & prior. [82]13 Mo Sep'94. [83]Pfd in M$,excl $109M subsid Pfd.

Splits ◆ Index	Cash Divs. Ea.Yr. Since	Dividends: Latest Payment Period $	Date	Ex. Div.	Total $ So Far 1995	Ind. Rate	Paid 1994	Financial Position Mil-$ Cash& Equiv.	Curr. Assets	Curr. Liab.	Balance Sheet Date	Capitalization Lg Trm Debt Mil-$	Shs. 000 Pfd.	Com.	Earnings $ Per Shr. Years End	1991	1992	1993	1994	1995	Last 12 Mos.	Interim Earnings Period	$ per Shr. 1994	1995	Index
1	1986	Q0.05	2-1-96	1-8	0.20	0.20	0.80	132	1192	1119	9-09-95	700	...	38220	Fb	1.85	□d2.58	0.10	□d4.36	E1.05↓	0.98	40 Wk Nov	□d4.51	0.83	1
2	1994	Q0.10	11-22-95	11-1	0.38	0.40	0.08	Book Value $18.53			9-30-95	....	...	14923	Dc	...	p0.72	n/a	‡[51]1.05	....	....	9 Mo Sep	n/a	1.07	2
3◆	1973	Q0.11½	1-30-96	12-27	0.42½	0.46	0.38	151	1055	432	9-30-95	298	...	64740	Dc	2.23	3.27	3.82	4.00	E4.50	4.42	9 Mo Sep	2.95	3.37	3
4	1934	1.40	1-31-96	12-27	4.75	5.00	3.60	4.53	7.19	2.12	9-30-95	....	...	1500	Dc	6.07	5.59	3.66	4.14	....	5.21	9 Mo Sep	2.98	4.05	4
5	....	None Since Public			...	Nil	....	0.33	1.15	1.84	6-30-95	3.84	...	2374	Dc	...	p0.04	pd0.16	d0.41	....	d0.16	6 Mo Jun	d0.29	d0.04	5
6	1994	0.087	2-15-95	1-9	0.087	0.17	0.206	9.91	174	149	3-31-95	28.0	...	925859	Mr	Δ1.15	...	0.50	0.79	....	0.79				6
7	1972	Q0.23	11-30-95	11-1	0.92	0.92	0.92	Book Value $14.11			3-31-95	p2434	1178	p136655	Dc	2.25	Δ0.30	0.28	1.69	E1.55	1.66	9 Mo Sep	1.08	1.05	7
8	1991	Q1.09⅜	2-1-96	1-10	4.37½	4.375	4.37½	Cv into 2.451 com,$20.40				....	2250	...	Dc	...	...	...	....	....	....				8
9◆	1993	Q0.07	12-18-95	11-29	0.28	0.28	0.24	11.0	156	75.8	9-30-95	34.5	...	4037	Dc	d1.24	□d0.79	1.62	□1.65	....	2.26	9 Mo Sep	□0.98	1.59	9
10	1951	Q0.53	12-29-95	12-18	2.12	2.12	2.12	0.06	26.4	44.7	9-30-95	67.1	91	4793	Dc	2.45	2.54	2.20	2.23	....	2.25	12 Mo Sep	2.29	2.25	10
11◆	1986	Q0.06¼	12-31-95	12-13	0.203	0.25	0.117	Equity per shr $6.67			9-30-95	638	...	137176	Dc	0.50	□0.60	0.91	1.30	E1.80↑	1.64	9 Mo Sep	0.97	1.31	11
12	1994	Q0.06	12-14-95	11-17	0.24	0.24	0.06	Equity per shr $6.84			8-31-95	228	...	14160	Au	...	...	p0.78	□1.02	1.18	1.18				12
13	1993	Q0.04	12-29-95	12-6	0.13	0.16	0.09	....	173	58.7	9-30-95	129	...	16256	Dc	...	p*0.46	□2.27	1.35	....	1.80	9 Mo Sep	0.97	1.42	13
14	1994	Q0.20	11-30-95	11-21	0.80	0.80	0.60	Book Value $16.70			9-30-95	....	...	53465	Dc	...	...	p[56]1.67	2.38	E2.55	2.44	9 Mo Sep	1.80	1.86	14
15	....	None Since Public			...	Nil	....	0.96	14.4	12.3	6-30-95	0.35	...	4086	Je	...	0.31	0.30	0.17	d0.28	d0.30	3 Mo Sep	d0.03	d0.05	15
16◆	1926	Q0.06	1-1-96	12-8	†0.40	0.42	†0.34	42.5	194	41.6	7-31-95	8.18	...	±24075	Oc	0.84	1.18	0.96	1.32	P2.39	2.39				16
17	1989	Q0.075	11-27-95	11-9	0.30	0.30	0.28	14.8	59.0	23.2	9-30-95	0.16	...	4698	Dc	0.75	0.86	0.88	0.82	....	d0.47	9 Mo Sep	0.57	d0.72	17
18	1965	Q0.93¾	12-27-95	12-13	3.56¼	3.75	3.31¼	140	671	665	9-30-95	33.0	32	±1177	Dc	±3.51	±13.18	±13.46	±d17.51	....	d15.96	9 Mo Sep	±8.52	±10.07	18
19	....	None Since Public			...	Nil	....	0.81	62.4	113	9-30-95	176	...	58163	Dc	...	1.10	□0.65	Δd7.58	....	d3.14	9 Mo Sep	□d4.69	d0.25	19
20	....	None Since Public			...	Nil	....	47.5	68.8	39.1	9-30-95	216	...	7941	Dc	d10.35	d13.25	d25.35	Δd15.10	....	3.97	9 Mo Sep	Δd17.20	1.87	20
21◆	....	©Wrrt	7-1-69	5-23	...	Nil	....	21.9	212	97.8	9-30-95	16.1	1670	30919	Sp	*Δ0.51	□0.66	0.48	0.80	0.71	0.71				21
22	....	[59]....	6-30-95	6-13	0.25	Stk	[59]....	Cv into 1 common				....	1677	...	Sp	n/a	n/a	...	....	....	....				22
23◆	....	None Since Public			...	Nil	....	5.14	21.5	11.8	8-31-95	3.15	...	6697	My	0.25	0.51	0.54	0.16	0.66	0.67	6 Mo Nov	0.27	0.28	23
24	....	0.227	2-15-82	1-26	...	Nil	....	4.94	168	128	9-30-95	49.5	...	25856	Dc	0.17	0.24	d2.66	d0.07	....	0.18	9 Mo Sep	d0.03	0.22	24
25	....	None Since Public			...	Nil	....	24.0	96.2	19.5	7-29-95	....	...	6906	Ap	1.10	1.30	0.76	d0.03	0.80	0.46	6 Mo Oct	0.41	0.07	25
26	....	None Since Public			...	Nil	....	1.22	104	90.0	10-01-95	....	...	15733	Dc	...	...	p0.77	0.30	....	d0.50	9 Mo Sep	0.40	d0.40	26
27	1994	Q0.22¾	1-18-96	12-21	0.90	0.91	0.23	Equity per shr $7.12			9-30-95	1.18	...	525	Dc	...	...	...	‡[60]0.30	....	....	9 Mo Sep	n/a	0.49	27
28◆	1993	[61]0.05	1-29-93		...	Nil	....	14.5	26.4	21.0	9-30-95	26.8	287	8873	Dc	d14.75	d17.01	d5.08	d0.05	....	0.46	9 Mo Sep	d1.18	d0.67	28
29	1994	0.111	5-26-95	5-10	0.111	0.11	0.178	17.5	206	114	12-31-94	....	...	106060	Dc	1.03	*0.65	*1.05	0.64	....	0.64				29
30	1995	0.084	5-4-95	4-12	0.084	Nil	....	19.6	273	171	12-31-94	18.0	...	411232	Dc	±▲p0.25	±▲p0.56	±▲p0.62	*0.10	....	0.10				30
31	....	None Since Public			...	Nil	....	8.41	126	157	12-31-94	149	...	352220	Dc	...	p▲±1.18	±1.24	±d0.38	....	d0.38				31
32	....	None Paid			...	Nil	....	3.49	3.49	...	j12-31-94	....	...	732381	Dc	...	0.40	0.80	0.05	....	j0.05				32
33	1994	0.321	4-14-94	3-24	...	Nil	0.321	Book Value $3.93			12-31-94	4664	...	±501020	Dc	...	p0.10	1.72	d1.41	....	d1.41				33
34	....	None Since Public			...	Nil	....	127	602	485	12-31-94	1670	...	46610	Dc	...	...	pd0.64	d5.82	....	d5.82				34
35	1995	0.172	5-1-95	4-12	0.172	0.30	....	33.1	205	91.2	12-31-94	47.6	...	918405	Dc	0.88	0.82	0.96	0.69	....	0.69				35
36	....	None Since Public			...	Nil	....	25.0	91.4	129	12-31-94	92.6	...	±981614	Dc	...	...	±Δp0.10	d0.72	....	d0.72				36
37	....	None Since Public			...	Nil	....	....	...	...		....	...	142566	Dc	...	...	±Δp0.10	d0.72	....	d0.72				37
38	....	None Since Public			...	Nil	....	9.78	401	372	12-31-94	291	...	±45250	Dc	Δ0.89	*1.81	Δ0.43	d0.49	....	d1.52	3 Mo Mar	0.11	d0.92	38
39	....	Stk	12-30-94	12-12	...	Stk	Stk	....	...	...		....	...	9583	Dc	*0.89	*1.81	Δ0.43	Pd2.29	....	d3.32	3 Mo Mar	0.11	d0.92	39
40	1994	0.131	9-15-95	9-6	0.249	0.25	[74]0.494	5.67	38.4	28.3	12-31-94	0.26	...	133011	Dc	0.72	p1.04	0.24	0.36	....	0.36				40
41	....	Plan annual div			...	0.13	....	108	763	1063	12-31-94	681	...	±437104	Dc	±0.70	±0.77	±1.45	±d1.52	....	d1.52				41
42	....	Plan annual div			...	0.13	....	....	...	...		....	...	170771	Dc	±0.70	±0.77	±1.45	±d1.52	....	d1.52				42
43	....	None Since Public			...	Nil	....	44.1	125	170	12-31-94	154	...	±414301	Dc	p1.34	*1.42	1.46	d3.80	....	d3.80				43
44	....	....			...	Nil	....	105	1308	588	j12-31-93	1697	...	±716391	Dc	...	...	...	....	....	....				44
45	1994	0.072	2-21-95	2-6	0.072	0.43	0.355	462	1550	296	12-31-94	1160	...	927000	Dc	...	p±1.48	□±0.60	±0.24	....	0.24				45
46	....	None Since Public			...	Nil	....	224	353	555	12-31-94	374	...	141859	Dc	...	p2.80	p2.82	0.53	....	0.53				46
47	....	None Since Public			...	Nil	....	Equity per shr $12.92			9-30-95	25.5	...	6648	Dc	1.64	1.67	Δ1.53	0.77	....	1.36	9 Mo Sep	0.52	1.11	47
48	....	None Since Public			...	Nil	....	13.7	39.4	22.0	9-30-95	....	...	4225	Dc	...	...	...	p0.80	....	....	9 Mo Sep	n/a	0.83	48
49	....	None Since Public			...	Nil	....	5.06	12.2	3.07	9-30-94	....	...	11911	Sp	d0.01	d0.11	[81]d0.18	[82]d0.33	Pd0.78	d0.78				49
50	....	None Since Public			...	Nil	....	4.21	59.8	7.10	p6-30-95	25.0	...	★9765	Dc	...	...	...	p0.59	....	....	9 Mo Sep	n/a	p0.29	50
51	....	None Since Public			...	Nil	....	10.1	134	127	9-30-95	p....	...	★59296	Dc	...	...	...	p0.32	....	....	9 Mo Sep	n/a	p0.17	51
52	1936	Q0.47	1-1-96	11-20	1.88	1.88	1.88	487	5649	8476	9-30-95	12157	[83]10	968620	Dc	1.75	□1.90	□1.03	2.55	E2.60	2.60	9 Mo Sep	1.83	1.88	52

◆**Stock Splits & Divs By Line Reference Index** [3]2-for-1,'92. [9]3-for-2,'93. [11]2-for-1,'93,'94,'95. [16]2-for-1,'95. [21]No adj for stk dstr,'92. [23]3-for-2,'92. [28]1-for-5 REVERSE,'93.

¶ S&P 500 # MidCap 400 ✣ SmallCap 600 • Options Index	Ticker	Name of Issue (Call Price of Pfd. Stocks)	Market	Com. Rank. & Pfd. Rating	Inst. Hold Cos	Inst. Hold Shs. (000)	Principal Business	Price Range 1971-93 High	1971-93 Low	1994 High	1994 Low	1995 High	1995 Low	Dec. Sales in 100s	December, 1995 Last Sale Or Bid High	Low	Last	%Div Yield	P-E Ratio	Total Return % Annualized 12 Mo	36 Mo	60 Mo
1•[1]	GTK	✔GTECH Holdings	NY	NR	135	23332	Computerized lottery systems	45⅞	17⅜	38⅞	15⅛	30¾	18⅛	33622	28½	24⅛	26	...	93	35.9	−12.3	...
2	GGTI	✔GTI Corp	NNM	B	31	3155	Electr comp'nts: circuit bds	41¾	½	29¼	7¾	23⅝	9½	25176	18¼	10½	17¾	...	35	7.6	−13.0	52.9
3	GUAR	Guarantee Life Cos	NNM	NR	..	...	Group life/health insur	....	....	....	....	16¾	13	58239	16¾	13	15¾	1.3	..	...	...	...
4	GNC	✔Guaranty National	NY	NR	67	11463	Property & casualty insurance	24¾	12⅝	18¾	13¾	19	13¾	3156	15½	14½	15⅜	3.3	16	−8.9	−5.2	...
5	GPI	✔Guardsman Products	NY,Ch	B+	33	1614	Ind'l coat'gs/consumer polish	17⅝	1⅛	16⅝	9	15¼	9⅞	3721	14⅛	12½	13⅜	2.7	19	10.9	6.8	12.8
6	GUC	✔Gucci Group N.V.	NY,Ph	NR	..	...	Mfr personal luxury accessor's	....	....	....	....	39¼	22	35831	39¼	33¾	39⅛	...	33	...	...	...
7	GEST	✔Guest Supply	NNM	B−	49	3594	Personal care prod for hotels	20	1 9/16	13⅞	8¾	23¾	11⅛	5497	23¾	21¼	22⅝	...	32	83.0	77.6	49.3
8	GDT	✔Guidant Corp	NY,Ph	NR	205	53133	Dgn/mfr cardiological equip	....	....	16⅛	14½	42⅝	15½	95732	42⅝	36	42¼	0.2	33	169	...	...
✣9	GFD	✔Guilford Mills	NY,Ch,Ph	B+	107	8381	Knit fabric mfr	28½	¼	24⅛	18½	28⅜	20	7980	22⅞	20	20⅜	2.9	9	−5.0	−3.9	15.9
10•[2]	GOU	Gulf Canada Resources	AS,To,Mo	NR	55	40102	Oil/gas explor,dev,prod,mktg	21	2 1/16	4⅜	2⅝	5⅛	2½	14234	4¼	3⅞	4⅛	...	d	40.4	9.0	−13.0
11•[3]	GSMS	✔Gulf South Medical Supply	NNM	NR	101	11939	Dstr medical supplies	....	....	19¾	8	32½	10⅜	21424	30¾	23½	30¼	...	52	65.4	...	...
12	GUL	✔Gull Laboratories	AS	C	7	302	Mfr medl diagnostic test kits	8½	13/16	5⅞	3⅛	6½	4	573	5	4¼	4¾	...	37	−2.6	...	...
13	GUN	✔Gundle/SLT Environmental	AS,Ch,Ph	NR	29	5328	Mfg polyethylene lining prod	25	3⅞	8½	4½	8⅝	4⅞	4074	5⅞	5¼	5½	...	d	5.9	−12.3	−15.1
14•[3]	GPTA	✔Gupta Corp	NNM	NR	46	1941	Dvlp client/server softwr prd	35¼	13½	31¾	6¾	13½	4⅞	22936	7	4⅞	5⅛	...	d	−58.6	...	...
15•[3]	GYMB	✔Gymboree Corp	NNM,Ch	NR	237	22824	Retail young childrens apparel	26¼	10	33	17⅜	37¼	18	137932	24⅞	18	20⅝	...	20	−28.9	...	...
16	HACH	✔Hach Co	NNM	A	24	386	Environm'l test eq/chemicals	25⅝	13/16	17	12¾	20⅜	12¾	508	17½	15½	17¼	1.4	19	34.4	−9.5	16.2
17•[3]	HDCO	✔Hadco Corp	NNM	B	67	5955	Mfrs printed circuits	11½	2⅞	9⅝	5⅞	35⅞	8⅜	15280	30¾	25¼	28⅛	...	14	196	44.9	47.7
18•[3]	HAE	✔Haemonetics Corp	NY,Ch,Ph	NR	137	19560	Mfr blood collection systems	28½	11	27⅝	14	23⅛	12⅞	10894	18	16⅝	17¾	...	14	0.7	−10.3	...
19	HN	✔Hafslund Nycomed ADS[58]	NY	NR	39	3682	Intl pharmaceutical R&D	29¼	14½	20¾	14¾	32⅜	19	5628	27	24⅝	26¼	2.3	19	31.2	9.5	...
✣20	HGGR	✔Haggar Corp	NNM	NR	74	5298	Mfr,mkt men's apparel	25½	15½	40½	20½	26¼	15¾	5793	18¾	17¼	18	1.1	16	−24.2	−2.8	...
21	HAHN	✔Hahn Automotive Warehouse	NNM	NR	15	702	Retail/wholesale auto parts	13⅝	9⅝	16	11	15⅛	5⅜	2313	6¼	5⅜	6	...	d	−58.1	...	...
22	HX	✔Halifax Corp	AS	↑B	4	8	Electric svc/facility support	10¾	3⅝	9	6⅜	7⅜	5⅞	89	7	6¼	7	3.7	13	0.5	1.4	7.6
¶23•[3]	HAL	✔Halliburton Co[60]	NY,To,B,C,Ch,Ph	B−	594	89718	Oil well svcs:engr & constr	86½	7¾	37¼	27⅞	50⅞	32⅞	97953	50⅞	43½	50⅝	2.0	25	56.0	24.2	5.6
24	HAF.EC	✔Hallmark Finl Svcs	ECM	NR	2	26	Retail non-standard auto insur	9½	¼	13/16	3/16	1½	¼	1370	1⅜	13/16	1	...	10	221	26.0	−16.7
25	HEP	✔Hallwood Energy Ptnrs L.P.[62]	AS	NR	16	51	Oil & gas explor,dev prod'n	197½	6½	8⅝	4⅞	6¼	3¾	3936	4⅝	3¾	3⅞	20.3	d	−10.1	−10.4	−3.1
26	HWG	✔Hallwood Group	NY,B,Ch,Ph,P	C	13	123	Investment co/merchant bank'g	1715⅝	14	21	7½	14½	6½	848	9⅞	7½	7¾	...	d	−3.1	−30.4	−17.3
27	HRY	✔Hallwood Rlty Ptnrs L.P.(New)	AS	NR	11	1	Acquire,manage real estate	37½	3⅛	19⅜	7½	16¾	9⅜	204	16¾	14⅜	16½	...	d	46.7	55.7	−8.0
28	HDG	✔Halsey Drug	AS,Ch	↓C	11	432	Mfrs generic drug products	11¼	1⅛	5⅜	1½	4¼	1¼	6381	4¼	3¼	3½	...	d	67.6	−28.7	7.9
29	JQH	✔Hammons(John Q)Hotels'A'	NY,Ch	NR	41	5368	Own,manage upscale hotels	....	....	16⅞	12½	16½	7⅞	10682	10	7⅞	9¼	...	10	−32.1	...	...
30	HAI	✔Hampton Indus	AS	C	11	583	Mens/boys shirts: casual wear	14⅜	5/16	7	4¾	7⅜	4⅝	436	5⅜	4⅞	4⅞	...	41	0.0	−16.8	6.2
#31	HKF	✔Hancock Fabrics	NY	NR	105	14189	Fabric retailer/wholesaler	27¾	5⅝	10	6½	11¾	7¾	4639	10⅝	9	9	3.6	20	7.9	−4.2	−11.8
32	HBHC	✔Hancock Holding	NNM	NR	34	904	Commercial banking, Miss	36¼	14¼	33	26¼	38	28¾	1109	37½	36	37½	2.7	12	34.2	11.9	...
¶33•[4]	HDL	✔Handleman Co	NY,B,Ch,P	↓B+	235	23322	Dstr recorded music & books	24	7/16	14	10	11⅞	5⅜	41438	7	5⅝	5¾	3.5	22	−47.3	−22.1	−12.1
✣34	HNH	✔Handy & Harman	NY,B,Ch,Ph	B−	95	8226	Precious mtls:auto prod:elec	34½	2¼	17⅝	13	16¾	13⅝	7645	16⅝	15	16½	1.5	25	7.3	10.9	5.6
35	HGR	✔Hanger Orthopedic Grp	AS,Ch	C	14	2623	Orthotic/prosthetic rehab svc	17½	1½	6⅞	2½	3⅞	2 3/16	4228	3⅛	2⅝	2¾	...	d	−4.3	−31.0	−11.3
#36•[5]	MAH	✔Hanna (M.A.)Co	NY,B,Ch	B	169	20272	Polymers/specialty chemical	27⅞	7	28⅞	21⅜	30	23	14303	28	25¼	28	2.1	15	18.6	16.1	20.1
#37	HRD	✔Hannaford Bros	NY,B,Ch,Ph	A+	164	15650	Food dstr: partner supermkts	28⅝	5/16	26⅝	19¾	29	23⅞	13494	25¼	23⅞	24⅝	1.7	15	−3.3	5.3	8.0
38	HNV	✔Hanover Direct	AS,B,Ch,P,Ph	B−	49	11031	Direct mkt catalog sales	29⅜	⅝	7⅞	3¼	3¾	1½	46530	2	1½	1 9/16	...	d	−54.6	−11.5	−7.0
39•[4]	HAN	✔Hanson plc ADR[67]	NY,B,Ch,P,Ph	NR	364	150219	Indust'l mgmt co:U.K. & U.S.	23¼	9	22½	17⅝	19¾	14¼	1199789	15½	14¼	15¼	6.9	10	...	...	...
40	WS.B	Cl'B'Wrrt(Pur 1 ord at 287p)	AS,Ph	....	..	...		⅝	¼	11/16	5/16	⅜	1/16	69313	⅛	1/16	⅛	...	..	...	...	...
41	HAPY	✔Happiness Express	NNM	NR	22	739	Mfr children's room decor	....	....	18⅛	9	15⅝	3⅝	17005	4⅝	3⅝	4⅜	...	6	−68.8	...	...
42	HRBC	✔Harbinger Corp	NNM	NR	27	2497	Dvp business info software	....	....	....	....	29½	12	35790	29½	20½	23	...	77	...	...	...
43	HARB	Harbor Federal Svgs Bk	NNM	NR	9	379	Savings bank,Florida	10	10	20¼	11	27¾	15½	1901	27¾	25¼	27½	3.3	14	85.2	...	...
44	HBT	✔Harbourton Finl Svcs L.P.	NY,Ph	NR	..	...	Mtge broker/investment co	10¼	4⅜	5	13/16	2⅜	1	2070	1¾	1⅜	1½	...	d	50.0	−40.9	−25.4
45	HARC	✔Harcor Energy	NNM	C	18	3607	Oil & gas expl,devel,prod'n	50	⅝	4¼	2¾	4⅜	1⅞	4199	2¾	2⅛	2⅝	...	d	−16.0	−9.1	3.7
¶46•[6]	H	✔Harcourt General	NY,B,Ch,P	B+	374	39601	Retail stores, publishing,	46⅛	5/16	39½	30¼	45¾	32⅜	23469	43⅜	40	41⅞	1.6	19	20.8	...	...
47	Pr A	Ser[73]A cm Cv Stk(NC)	NY,Ch	NR	6	229	theatres,insurance	46	6⅜	42	34⅞	49⅛	37⅜	170	46	43	45⅜	1.7	..	...	...	...
48	HRDG	✔Harding Lawson Assoc Grp	NNM	B	33	2695	Hazardous waste consult svcs	26	4⅞	10	5¼	7⅝	5¼	2330	7⅜	5⅞	6	...	9	5.5	−18.3	−17.6
49	HDNG	✔Hardinge Inc	NNM,NSC	NR	44	3126	Mfr machine tools, lathes	....	....	....	....	26¾	18¾	1763	26	24½	26	2.6	13	...	...	...
50	HEC	✔Harken Energy	AS	C	26	12085	Oil & gas expl,dev,prod'n	25½	¾	2¾	15/16	2½	1⅜	21560	1¾	1½	1¾	...	d	0.0	−17.6	7.0
¶51•[7]	JH	✔Harland (John H.)	NY,B,Ch	A	251	18411	Bank stationer: checks, etc.	30¾	1 1/16	24¾	19⅜	23⅝	19⅛	18668	21¼	19¾	20⅞	4.9	13	10.0	−3.5	6.3
#52•[8]	HDI	✔Harley-Davidson	NY,Ch,Ph	B+	274	41859	Manufactures motorcycles	23¾	15/16	29⅞	21⅝	30⅛	22	56498	28⅞	25½	28¾	0.7	20	3.8	14.9	43.9

Uniform Footnote Explanations-See Page 4. Other: [1]ASE,CBOE:Cycle 3. [2]Mo:Cycle 2. [3]CBOE:Cycle 1. [4]CBOE:Cycle 3. [5]NY:Cycle 3. [6]CBOE:Cycle 2. [7]NY,Ph:Cycle 3. [8]Ph:Cycle 2. [51]To be determined. [52]Fiscal Jun'92 & prior. [53]12 Mo Sep'93. [54]Stk dstr of USANA Inc. [55]Fiscal Dec'91 & prior. [56]Fiscal Mar'94 & prior. [57]12 Mo Dec'94. [58]Ea ADS rep 1 Cl'B'shr,NOK 5. [59]Incl restricted A shrs. [60]Plan spin-off Highlands Ins,10 new com. [61]Stk dstr of Highlands Ins Gr. [62]Units. [63]100% non-taxable,'94. [64]Dstr of $10 amt debs. [65]Excl 16M LP units. [66]®$1.50,'94. [67]ADR's representing 5 Ord shrs par 25p. [68]Approx. [69]Stk dstr of U.S. Inds,'95. [70]®$1.58,'94. [71]Pfd units. [72]■$3.41,'91. [73]Divd rt $0.03 plus amt pd on com.

Index	Splits ◆ Cash Divs. Ea.Yr. Since	Dividends Latest Payment Period $	Date	Ex. Div.	Total $ So Far 1995	Ind. Rate	Paid 1994	Financial Position Mil-$ Cash& Equiv.	Curr. Assets	Curr. Liab.	Balance Sheet Date	Capitalization Lg Trm Debt Mil-$	Shs. 000 Pfd.	Com.	Earnings $ Per Shr. Years End	1991	1992	1993	1994	1995	Last 12 Mos.	Interim Earnings Period	$ per Shr. 1994	1995	Index
1	....	None Since Public			...	Nil	....	5.56	173	162	8-26-95	339	...	43277	Fb	p0.64	p1.02	1.29	□0.05	....	0.28	9 Mo Nov	□0.94	1.17	1
2	....	0.03	9-17-82	8-24	...	Nil	....	3.55	71.4	27.8	9-30-95	5.26	8	8952	Dc	0.45	0.93	1.32	0.52	....	0.51	9 Mo Sep	0.47	0.46	2
3	....	Plan qtly div			...	0.20	....	Equity per shr $20.03			9-30-95	......	...	★9569	Dc	...	...	...	p1.93	....	....	9 Mo Sep	n/a	p1.03	3
4	1992	Q0.12½	12-29-95	12-6	0.50	0.50	0.50	Equity per shr $11.60			9-30-95	115	...	14961	Dc	1.44	1.62	Δ1.54	1.86	....	0.95	9 Mo Sep	1.42	0.51	4
5	1918	Q0.09	12-18-95	11-30	0.33	0.36	0.32	7.69	83.9	31.2	6-30-95	35.6	...	9522	Dc	d0.04	0.27	Δ0.58	0.70	....	0.69	9 Mo Sep	0.58	0.57	5
6	....	Plan annual div			...	[51]....	....	51.0	172	130	7-31-95	p1.24	...	★58500	Ja	d1.03	d0.72	d0.51	0.38	E1.20	0.83	6 Mo Jul	0.10	0.55	6
7◆	....	None Since Public			...	Nil	....	1.54	55.5	32.4	6-30-95	17.5	...	6111	Sp	*0.03	*0.07	*0.21	0.59	P0.70	0.70				7
8	1995	Q0.02½	12-18-95	11-8	0.05	0.10	....	14.2	366	663	9-30-95	......	...	71911	Dc	...	...	p0.38	p1.06	....	1.29	9 Mo Sep	p0.75	0.98	8
9◆	1973	Q0.15	12-8-95	11-22	0.60	0.60	0.60	16.0	285	108	7-02-95	167	...	14081	Sp	Δ1.02	[52]1.85	[53]1.53	1.82	P2.41	2.41				9
10	....	g0.10	4-1-92	2-27	...	Nil	....	559	715	330	j3-31-95	1329	85505	p218815	Dc	d0.84	d2.16	d0.37	d1.39	....	jd1.11	9 Mo Sep	d0.54	d0.26	10
11◆	....	None Since Public			...	Nil	....	1.53	43.8	10.9	9-30-95	......	...	13730	Dc	...	...	p0.31	0.45	....	0.58	9 Mo Sep	0.32	0.45	11
12	....	h[54]....	4-21-93	4-22	...	Nil	....	0.05	7.44	4.81	9-30-95	1.78	...	6564	Dc	0.10	0.20	d0.06	d0.05	....	0.13	9 Mo Sep	d0.06	0.12	12
13	....	None Since Public			...	Nil	....	7.00	141	64.5	9-30-95	50.6	...	17193	Dc	[55]0.83	0.05	[56]0.49	[57]0.28	Ed0.25	d0.20	9 Mo Sep	0.26	d0.22	13
14	....	None Since Public			...	Nil	....	23.7	43.8	20.3	9-30-95	10.5	...	12281	Dc	0.01	0.17	0.44	d2.00	....	d1.20	9 Mo Sep	d1.51	d0.71	14
15◆	....	None Since Public			...	Nil	....	51.7	106	24.4	7-30-95	......	...	24911	Ja	0.14	0.32	0.57	0.88	....	1.03	9 Mo Oct	0.54	0.69	15
16◆	1972	Q0.06	1-30-96	1-11	0.19	0.24	0.152	18.1	50.1	11.5	10-28-95	......	...	11363	Ap	0.53	0.68	0.76	Δ0.80	0.81	0.89	6 Mo Oct	0.41	0.49	16
17	....	None Since Public			...	Nil	....	38.5	87.0	45.9	7-29-95	2.77	...	9922	Oc	0.52	0.75	0.76	0.93	P1.98	1.98				17
18◆	....	None Since Public			...	Nil	....	8.43	164	45.9	9-30-95	25.2	...	28741	Mr	0.63	0.87	1.09	1.18	....	1.25	6 Mo Sep	0.58	0.65	18
19	1991	0.603	7-11-95	5-17	0.603	0.60	0.515	267	785	654	12-31-94	699	...	[59]±97835	Dc	1.83	1.59	1.51	1.36	....	1.36				19
20	1993	Q0.05	11-13-95	10-26	0.20	0.20	0.20	1.26	220	66.7	6-30-95	68.8	...	8547	Sp	...	p1.64	1.88	2.95	P1.14	1.14				20
21◆	....	4%Stk	5-1-95	4-4	4%Stk	Stk	....	0.21	96.0	30.6	6-30-95	50.0	...	4387	Sp	...	p0.77	pΔ0.87	1.00	Pd0.31	d0.31				21
22	1984	Q0.06½	12-10-95	11-20	0.26	0.26	0.25	0.09	13.2	5.38	9-30-95	6.13	...	1168	Mr	0.59	0.57	0.71	0.72	....	0.56	6 Mo Sep	0.34	0.18	22
23	1947	h[61]....	1-23-96	1-24	1.00	1.00	1.00	70.8	1894	1002	9-30-95	232	...	114387	Dc	■0.25	□d1.15	d1.43	1.56	E2.00	1.96	9 Mo Sep	0.44	0.84	23
24	....	None Since Public			...	Nil	....	Equity per shr $0.42			9-30-95	0.70	...	10662	Dc	*0.04	d0.09	0.04	0.06	....	0.10	9 Mo Sep	0.04	0.08	24
25	1985	Q0.20	1-31-96	12-27	0.80	0.80	[63]0.80	4.83	16.1	20.6	9-30-95	37.8	...	±9977	Dc	0.42	0.24	1.30	d1.36	....	d2.50	9 Mo Sep	0.09	d1.05	25
26◆	....	[64]....	5-3-89	5-16	...	Nil	....	Equity per shr $2.47			7-31-95	48.6	250	1594	Jl	d2.96	Δd19.00	d1.04	Δd3.68	Δd3.60	d3.95	3 Mo Oct	d0.92	d1.27	26
27◆	....	0.62½	2-14-92	12-24	...	Nil	....	Equity per shr $24.83			9-30-95	177	...	1748	Dc	d25.45	Δd16.10	d10.75	d10.38	....	d5.82	9 Mo Sep	d8.61	Δd4.05	27
28	....	5%Stk	12-15-89	11-9	...	Nil	....	0.07	10.7	11.3	9-30-95	6.28	...	8470	Dc	0.26	0.13	□d1.53	d0.80	....	d0.25	9 Mo Sep	d0.39	0.16	28
29	....	None Since Public			...	Nil	....	33.6	40.3	44.5	9-30-95	378	...	[65]±6336	Dc	...	...	p0.28	□p0.48	....	0.93	9 Mo Sep	p□0.38	0.83	29
30◆	....	0.025	12-31-73	12-4	...	Nil	....	0.03	114	62.8	9-30-95	18.5	...	4587	Dc	d0.13	0.32	d0.53	0.22	....	0.12	9 Mo Sep	d0.32	d0.42	30
31◆	1987	Q0.08	1-15-96	12-27	0.32	0.32	0.32	7.75	192	52.0	10-29-95	48.0	...	21508	Ja	□1.03	0.57	0.26	0.48	E0.45	0.47	9 Mo Oct	0.27	0.26	31
32◆	1937	Q0.25	12-15-95	12-1	0.96	1.00	0.92	Book Value $24.73			9-30-95	2.96	...	8881	Dc	2.21	2.74	3.15	2.88	....	3.02	9 Mo Sep	2.12	2.26	32
33	1963	Q0.05	1-10-96	12-22	0.44	0.20	0.44	2.92	611	282	10-28-95	200	...	33584	Ap	0.72	1.21	1.32	0.83	0.84	0.26	6 Mo Oct	0.49	d0.09	33
34	1905	Q0.06	12-1-95	11-13	0.24	0.24	0.20	3.81	187	155	9-30-95	107	...	14104	Dc	d2.47	0.84	Δ0.64	1.18	....	0.66	9 Mo Sep	0.93	0.41	34
35	....	None Paid			...	Nil	....	1.07	26.3	6.51	9-30-95	23.3	.3	8291	Dc	□d0.03	□0.03	□Δ0.18	d0.32	....	d0.18	9 Mo Sep	0.05	0.19	35
36◆	1944	Q0.14½	12-12-95	11-22	0.55	0.58	0.51	119	607	361	9-30-95	232	...	35562	Dc	□0.19	□1.06	0.07	□[66]1.52	E1.83	3.34	9 Mo Sep	□1.07	2.89	36
37◆	1948	Q0.10½	12-21-95	12-6	0.42	0.42	0.38	31.6	203	180	9-30-95	215	...	42260	Dc	1.08	1.21	Δ1.33	1.50	....	1.67	9 Mo Sep	1.10	1.27	37
38	....	5%Stk	9-12-84	8-15	...	Nil	....	7.69	164	118	9-30-95	69.7	713	92550	Dc	Δd4.46	Δd0.06	0.17	0.16	....	d0.13	9 Mo Sep	0.07	□d0.22	38
39	1986	[68]0.289	1-12-96	12-15	h[69]1.007	1.05	0.941	6815	9933	6704	j9-30-94	5255	...	5173075	Sp	Δ1.93	1.98	1.14	[70]1.66	E1.50	1.63	9 Mo Jun	1.17	1.14	39
40	....	Terms&trad. basis should			be checked in detail			Wrrts expire 9-30-97				....	...	565203	Sp	...	...	...	....	....	....				40
41	....	None Since Public			...	Nil	....	1.07	43.6	8.19	9-30-95	....	...	8154	Mr	...	...	p0.72	p1.12	....	0.71	6 Mo Sep	p0.75	0.34	41
42	....	None Since Public			...	Nil	....	12.3	19.2	5.94	9-30-95	....	298	10048	Dc	...	...	...	pd0.42	E0.30	....	9 Mo Sep	n/a	0.06	42
43	1994	Q0.22½	11-20-95	10-25	0.90	0.90	0.33¾	Book Value $15.78			9-30-95	66.0	...	4911	Sp	...	...	...	n/a	2.03	2.03				43
44	1989	0.05	4-8-94	3-25	...	Nil	0.10	Net Asset Val $1.11			9-30-95	50.6	...	[71]41903	Dc	1.32	0.62	d0.70	□d1.23	....	d1.03	9 Mo Sep	0.19	0.39	44
45◆	....	None Since Public			...	Nil	....	8.35	10.8	6.47	9-30-95	63.1	65	8631	Dc	d0.51	d0.40	d0.23	□d0.27	....	d0.77	9 Mo Sep	□d0.28	□d0.78	45
46◆	1953	Q0.17	1-31-96	1-9	0.65	0.68	0.61	493	1626	781	7-31-95	824	p1451	±72823	Oc	[72]d3.88	Δ1.44	2.15	2.22	P2.16	2.16				46
47	1982	Q0.195	1-31-96	1-9	0.74½	0.778	0.701	Cv into 1 common				....	1504	...	Oc	n/a	n/a	n/a	....	....	....				47
48	....	None Since Public			...	Nil	....	12.3	50.0	14.6	8-31-95	......	...	4845	My	0.94	0.81	0.10	0.21	0.62	0.64	6 Mo Nov	0.37	0.39	48
49	1995	Q0.17	12-8-95	11-21	0.47	0.68	....	4.70	113	19.6	9-30-95	3.01	...	6409	Dc	...	...	...	p1.28	....	1.98	9 Mo Sep	p1.41	p2.11	49
50	....	None Since Public			...	Nil	....	7.69	9.06	4.56	9-30-95	13.3	187	66930	Dc	d0.38	*Nil	d0.09	d0.14	....	d0.12	9 Mo Sep	d0.03	d0.01	50
51	1932	Q0.255	11-30-95	11-14	1.02	1.02	0.98	7.11	134	95.7	9-30-95	115	...	30608	Dc	□1.33	1.59	1.62	1.68	E1.60	1.59	9 Mo Sep	1.28	1.19	51
52◆	1993	Q0.05	12-22-95	12-13	0.18	0.20	0.14	25.5	429	243	9-24-95	......	...	77270	Dc	0.52	□0.75	□0.24	1.37	E1.45	1.40	9 Mo Sep	1.04	1.07	52

◆Stock Splits & Divs By Line Reference Index [7]3-for-2,'95. [9]3-for-2,'92. [11]2-for-1,'95. [15]2-for-1,'94. [16]3-for-2,'92:5-for-4,'91,'94. [18]2-for-1,'93. [21]Adj for 4%,'95. [26]No adj for dstr of $10 debs, '89:1-for-4 REVERSE,'95. [27]1-for-5 REVERSE,'95. [30]10%,'92,'93. [31]2-for-1,'91. [32]2-for-1,'91. [36]3-for-2,'94. [37]2-for-1,'92. [45]1-for-10 REVERSE,'91. [46]No adj for stk dstr of GC Co's,'93. [52]2-for-1,'92,'94.

¶ S&P 500 # MidCap 400 ✣ SmallCap 600 • Options Index	Ticker	Name of Issue (Call Price of Pfd. Stocks)	Market	Com. Rank. & Pfd. Rating	Inst. Hold Cos	Inst. Hold Shs. (000)	Principal Business	Price Range 1971-93 High	1971-93 Low	1994 High	1994 Low	1995 High	1995 Low	Dec. Sales in 100s	December, 1995 Last Sale Or Bid High	Low	Last	%Div Yield	P-E Ratio	Total Return % Annualized 12 Mo	36 Mo	60 Mo
1	HGIC	✓Harleysville Group	NNM	B+	59	4326	Insur hldg:prop/casualty	32¾	7⅝	30¼	19¾	33	23½	4885	33	28¼	32⅜	2.3	11	37.2	10.3	19.5
2	HRN	✓Harlyn Products	AS	↓B–	9	262	Mfrs gold & silver jewelry	5	¼	5	3½	4⅜	⅞	1263	1 13/16	⅞	1	...	d	–75.0	–26.3	–19.3
3	HAR	✓Harman International	NY,Ch,Ph	B	186	12193	Audio video sys components	27⅞	4¼	36¼	23⅜	49¾	32⅜	6335	45½	39¾	40⅛	0.5	14	23.4	45.4	44.3
✣4	HRMN	✓Harmon Indus	NNM	B	51	3189	Railroad communic/ctrl prod	23¼	¼	24¼	16½	20½	13⅜	2741	18¼	14¼	15¾	1.0	16	–17.5	10.1	33.7
5	HLIT	✓Harmonic Lightwaves	NNM	NR	30	3137	Dvlp CATV transmission prd	....	....	....	....	20½	7¾	21164	13	8¼	11	...	38	...	...	...
¶6•[1]	HPH	✓Harnischfeger Indus	NY,B,Ch,P	B	332	33773	Mfr paper mach/min'g eq/sys	29¾	5⅛	28⅜	18½	39⅜	26	61036	34⅞	28⅝	33¼	1.2	25	20.8	20.7	15.7
7	HLD	✓Harold's Stores	AS	B	10	652	Retail:ladies&mens apparel	8⅛	1 11/16	13	6¾	12⅜	9⅝	223	12⅜	11⅞	12⅛	...	22	30.1	45.0	45.2
8	HARG	✓Harper Group	NNM	B+	83	10558	Int'l ocean/air freight fwdg	24⅝	1 9/16	18¼	12½	20	15	8755	18½	16⅞	17¾	1.2	16	23.9	6.5	7.2
¶9•[2]	HET	✓Harrah's Entertainment	NY,Ph	NR	403	76535	Hotel & casino operations	55	3	55¼	25⅞	45⅞	22⅛	85401	26½	23⅜	24¼	...	18	...	...	...
¶10•[2]	HRS	✓Harris Corp	NY,B,Ch,P,Ph	B+	380	27560	Gov't Sys/communications	60¼	3¼	52¼	37¾	61⅜	40½	31652	57¾	52¼	54⅝	2.5	13	...	...	...
11	HARS	Harris Savings Bank	NNM	NR	14	271	Savings bank,Pennsylvania	....	....	20	10	20½	13	782	20½	19¼	20	2.6	23	52.7	...	...
12	HARY	✓Harry's Farmers Market	NNM	NR	12	386	Owns perishable food mega strs	31¼	14¼	29¼	6½	11	2½	8783	4¼	2½	3⅛	...	d	–67.1	...	...
#13	HSC	✓Harsco Corp	NY,B,Ch,P,Ph	B+	230	13697	Ind'l serv,engin prd, defense	45	2⅞	46⅜	38⅜	60½	39⅝	6886	60½	58	58⅛	2.6	16	46.3	19.9	23.6
14	HOPS	Hart Brewing	NNM	NR	..	...	Brewer:specialty beer	....	....	....	....	22½	14	51231	22½	14	15¼	...	29	...	...	...
15	HHS	✓Harte-Hanks Communications	NY,Ph	NR	49	9245	Newspapers,direct mktg, TV	13	10⅛	14⅜	11¾	22⅝	12⅜	4611	22⅝	19½	19¾	0.4	18	53.7	...	...
#16	HSB	✓Hartford Stm Boiler Ins	NY,Ch,Ph	B+	187	10810	Insurance/engineering svcs	63¾	1 7/16	53⅜	35⅞	50⅜	39¼	8730	50⅜	45⅝	50	4.6	17	31.4	–0.5	5.1
✣17	HMX	✓Hartmarx Corp	NY,B,Ch	B–	109	16014	Apparel manufacturing/mktg	34¾	2 3/16	7⅜	5	6⅞	4¼	13340	4⅝	4¼	4⅜	...	63	–25.5	–11.2	–11.6
18	HRVY	✓Harvey Entertainment	NNM	NR	20	693	Film entertain't/merchandis'g	12	7⅛	19½	8¼	18¼	6¼	7002	8½	6¼	7½	...	33	–45.5	...	...
19	HVY	✓Harveys Casino Resorts	NY,Ch,Ph	NR	36	1943	Own/oper hotel casino	....	....	17¾	10½	23¾	12¾	2068	18⅛	15	18	0.9	28	38.4	...	...
¶20•[3]	HAS	✓Hasbro Inc	AS,B,P	B+	364	59780	Mfrs toys & games	40⅛	1/16	36⅝	27⅞	35¼	28⅜	53536	32⅝	30	31	1.0	17	7.5	–1.5	25.6
21	HSKL	✓Haskel Intl 'A'	NNM	NR	11	1925	Mfr hydraulic pumps	....	....	12½	9⅜	11¼	5	3492	6¼	5¼	5⅞	4.8	37	–37.6	...	...
22	HMF	✓Hastings Mfg	AS	B–	7	37	Mfr automotive replace't parts	53¼	4⅜	38	21¼	28¼	17¼	39	22¼	20¾	20¾	1.9	d	–3.9	–11.5	–9.0
23	HATH	✓Hathaway Corp	NNM	B–	10	257	Electronic sys & components	10¼	1/16	4⅛	2⅜	3⅛	1⅞	2060	2 7/16	1⅞	2¼	4.4	d	–15.2	6.6	1.6
✣24•[4]	HAUS	✓Hauser Chemical Research	NNM	↓B–	39	3380	Natural chemical processor	31	1/16	10½	4¼	6⅝	4¼	7313	5¼	4¼	4½	...	d	–5.3	–46.9	11.4
25	HAVN	✓Haven Bancorp	NNM	NR	25	1121	General banking, New York	13⅛	9¼	17⅝	11⅛	25⅜	12⅞	18682	25⅜	21⅝	23⅜	1.7	12	84.3	...	...
26	HAVT	✓Haverty Furniture	NNM	B	65	4661	Retail furniture stores	19⅝	1¼	19¼	10¾	15	9⅝	6229	15	13⅜	13⅞	2.2	13	26.4	11.6	27.1
27	HA	Hawaiian Airlines 'A'	AS,Ph	NR	3	649	Regional airline service	....	....	....	....	13½	1⅝	6881	3	2 3/16	2 5/16	...	..	...	...	...
#28	HE	✓Hawaiian Elec Indus	NY,B,Ch,P,Ph	A–	135	9866	Hldg:electric/finl svc,Hawaii	44⅝	7⅛	36½	29⅞	39¾	32⅛	10362	39½	37¾	38¾	6.2	15	29.3	8.3	10.8
29	HWKB	✓Hawkeye Bancorp[58]	NNM	B	67	4086	Commercial bkg,Iowa	20½	1	21⅜	15½	27	18⅝	5691	27	25⅜	26⅝	2.9	15	50.9	22.2	36.8
✣30	HAY	✓Hayes Wheels International[59]	NY	NR	92	6953	Mfr original equip wheels	30⅞	18⅛	35½	18¼	27¼	15¼	10877	26¾	25½	25⅝	0.2	15	24.6	10.0	...
31•[5]	HBOC	✓HBO & Co	NNM	B	271	32031	Hospital information system	23⅛	2	36¾	18¾	86½	32⅞	122263	86½	73¾	76⅝	0.2	d	121	86.6	94.5
32	HCC	✓HCC Insurance Hldgs	NY,Ch	NR	73	6263	Prop & casualty insur,agency	23⅞	8	22¼	15	38	19¾	6822	38	30¾	37	...	20	76.2	41.8	...
33	HCIA	✓HCIA Inc	NNM	NR	61	3954	Health care info services	....	....	....	....	47	14	7735	47	39¼	46¾	...	..	...	...	...
34	HRG	✓He-Ro Group	NY,Ch,Ph	NR	9	43	Mfr/mkt women's apparel	22½	1⅞	2⅛	1	1¾	⅜	1855	⅝	⅜	⅜	...	d	–67.5	–59.3	...
35	HRP	✓Health & Retirement Prop Tr	NY,Ch,Ph	NR	97	12028	Real estate investment trust	16¾	6¾	16½	13	16⅞	13¼	45694	16⅞	15⅝	16¼	8.6	15	31.7	21.5	27.3
#36•[1]	HCR	✓Health Care & Retirement	NY,Ph	NR	224	26045	Long-term care/rehab svcs	22¼	8½	30¼	21¼	36⅛	25⅛	18971	36⅛	33¼	35	...	23	16.7	29.8	...
37	HCP	✓Health Care Prop Inv	NY,B,Ch	NR	174	15662	Real estate investment trust	33⅝	9½	32⅝	26¼	35¼	28	6249	35¼	33½	35⅛	6.3	12	24.8	19.8	25.0
38	HCN	✓Health Care REIT	NY,Ch	NR	54	2028	Real estate investment trust	27	6⅛	25⅜	19¾	23⅛	15½	4954	18¼	17¼	18	11.6	11	–1.4	3.9	16.5
39	HCH	✓Health-Chem[64]	AS,B	B–	11	753	Indust'l & health care prod	33¾	5/16	4⅝	2½	3⅛	1 5/16	1394	1⅝	1⅜	1½	...	50	–52.0	–6.1	11.4
40•[5]	HII	✓Health Images	NY,Ch	B	40	3992	Outpatient MRI centers,svcs	17⅜	2	7¾	4½	8	4¾	4297	7⅞	7	7¼	1.4	d	22.5	–4.9	–7.5
41•	HMA	✓Health Mgmt Associates'A'	NY,Ph	B	244	62139	Oper acute care hospitals	13	3⅛	17¾	12	27	15⅝	35837	27	22⅞	26⅛	...	30	56.9	54.1	...
42	HPI	✓Health Professionals	AS,Ch	C	14	1589	Health care personnel svcs	13⅛	⅛	1¼	5/16	1	1/16	13844	½	⅛	⅜	...	d	20.2	–64.7	–32.2
43•[4]	HQ	✓Health Systems Intl	NY	NR	80	8411	Manage HMO's western U.S.	22	10	36¾	20	34¼	24⅞	9254	34¼	31⅝	32⅛	...	18	46.9	19.7	...
#44•[2]	HCCC	✓HealthCare COMPARE	NNM	B	243	24051	Hlthcare utiliz'n review svc	44	1⅞	34⅜	15½	47⅞	27⅝	111411	47⅞	39¼	43½	...	23	28.9	13.5	39.6
45	HR	✓Healthcare Realty Tr	NY,Ph	NR	69	5916	Real estate investment trust	23½	17¾	22½	18¼	23¼	18⅜	6136	23¼	20⅝	23	8.1	16	19.1	...	...
46•[5]	HDYN	✓Healthdyne Inc[66]	NNM	B–	52	6708	Electronic medical eq-baby	41¼	1⅞	9	5½	11½	3⅞	18070	9½	7⅝	8⅝	...	d	...	...	...
47	HPS	✓HealthPlan Services	NY,Ph	NR	28	3015	Managed healthcare srvices	....	....	....	....	27	14	5408	27	23½	25	...	..	...	...	...
#48•[4]	HS	✓Healthsource Inc	NY,Ph	B	266	55296	Multi-state HMO services	14⅛	1 7/16	21⅛	12¾	36	15⅛	60654	36	29⅞	36	...	44	77.1	59.7	69.0
#49•[6]	HRC	✓HEALTHSOUTH Corp	NY,Ch,Ph	B	289	74911	Medical rehabilitation svc	18⅝	2	19¾	11¾	32⅜	16⅜	121384	32⅜	26½	29⅛	...	27	69.7	33.0	30.6
50	HPP	✓Healthy Planet Prod	AS,Ch	B–	10	91	Dsgn,mkt stationery/card prd	134	¼	9¾	7	14¾	7⅝	2654	10	7¾	8½	...	8	6.3	14.8	12.3
✣51•[2]	HRTT	✓Heart [69]Technology[70]	NNM	NR	113	12605	Atherosclerosis treatment prd	31	7¾	26¾	13¾	33¼	15½	21438	33¼	25¾	32⅞	...	35	66.5	21.4	...
52	HTL	✓Heartland Partners L.P. 'A'[71]	AS	NR	8	701	Real estate development	14⅞	6¼	14⅝	10½	12⅝	8⅞	371	10¼	8⅞	10¼	...	d	–9.9	8.6	2.6

Uniform Footnote Explanations-See Page 4. Other: [1]Ph:Cycle 2. [2]CBOE:Cycle 2. [3]P:Cycle 1. [4]CBOE:Cycle 1. [5]P:Cycle 2. [6]NY:Cycle 3. [51]Excl. 1.5M employee comp. shares. [52]Stk dstr of Promus Hotel Corp,'95. [53]Stk dstr of Harris Computer Sys,'94. [54]Incl 8.5M owned by Harris Fin'l. [55]®$0.80,'94. [56]15 Wks Dec'94. [57]Subsid pfd in $M. [58]Mercantile Bancorporation plan acq, 0.585 com. [59]Varity Corp(46%)plan mgr. [60]49.3% owned by AMBAC Inc. [61]Incl $0.08052 non-taxable:©$0.16632,'94. [62]®$1.02,'93. [63]©$1.2896,'94. [64]Plan spin-off, Transderm Labs. [65]Incl $0.1421 non-taxable,'94. [66]Plan form new co w/Tokos,Medical,1 new com. [67]Stk dstr of Healthdyne Info Entmt,'95. [68]Pfd in $M. [69]Boston Scientific plan acq. [70]Plan SmallCap 600 delisting:eff Dec 30. [71]Units.

Splits ◆ Index	Cash Divs. Ea.Yr. Since	Dividends: Latest Payment Period $	Date	Ex. Div.	Total $ So Far 1995	Ind. Rate	Paid 1994	Financial Position Mil-$ Cash& Equiv.	Curr. Assets	Curr. Liab.	Balance Sheet Date	Capitalization Lg Trm Debt Mil-$	Shs. 000 Pfd.	Com.	Earnings $ Per Shr. Years End	1991	1992	1993	1994	1995	Last 12 Mos.	Interim Earnings Period	$ per Shr. 1994	1995	Index
1◆	1986	Q0.19	12-29-95	12-13	0.72	0.76	0.66	Equity per shr $23.12			6-30-95	98.0	...	13581	Dc	2.05	2.14	□2.50	1.40	....	2.92	9 Mo Sep	0.68	2.20	1
2◆	....	0.015	8-1-77	7-6	...	Nil	....	0.34	28.5	18.2	9-30-95	1.30	...	4753	Je	0.34	0.25	0.35	0.32	d0.39	d0.69	3 Mo Sep	0.11	d0.19	2
3◆	1994	Q0.05	11-29-95	11-13	0.136	0.20	0.076	8.80	606	291	9-30-95	314	...	16252	Je	d2.15	0.37	0.99	□1.89	□2.72	2.82	3 Mo Sep	0.26	0.36	3
4	1994	0.075	12-15-95	11-28	0.15	0.15	0.15	0.67	54.4	22.7	9-30-95	8.02	...	6806	Dc	*0.08	*0.90	1.11	1.16	....	0.99	9 Mo Sep	0.91	0.74	4
5	....	None Since Public			...	Nil	....	22.3	38.2	5.56	9-30-95	0.21	...	9824	Dc	...	...	...	pd0.29	....	0.29	9 Mo Sep	pd0.29	0.29	5
6	1988	Q0.10	1-5-96	12-21	0.40	0.40	0.40	182	1112	615	7-31-95	467	...	[51]48593	Oc	2.08	1.95	d0.67	□0.70	P□1.32	1.32				6
7◆	....	None Since Public			...	Nil	....	0.18	31.3	18.8	10-28-95	0.54	...	4719	Ja	0.16	0.26	0.37	0.45	....	0.56	9 Mo Oct	0.27	0.38	7
8◆	1977	S0.11	3-15-96	2-13	0.22	0.22	0.20	22.2	202	152	9-30-95	30.6	...	16249	Dc	1.05	0.30	1.15	1.02	....	1.10	9 Mo Sep	0.74	0.82	8
9◆	....	h[52]....	6-30-95	7-3	h[52]...	Nil	....	72.8	177	216	9-30-95	699	...	102633	Dc	0.33	Δ0.51	□0.89	□0.84	E1.38	0.87	9 Mo Sep	□1.09	1.12	9
10	1941	Q0.34	12-1-95	11-15	1.30	1.36	h[53]1.18	64.3	1758	1012	9-30-95	476	...	39218	Je	0.50	□2.00	2.82	□3.07	3.95	4.08	3 Mo Sep	0.73	0.86	10
11	1994	Q0.13	11-14-95	10-27	0.51	0.52	0.272	Book Value $13.07			6-30-95	....	...	[54]11192	Dc	...	p1.19	p1.59	0.85	....	0.89	9 Mo Sep	0.63	0.67	11
12	....	None Since Public			...	Nil	....	0.06	10.4	12.6	8-02-95	27.9	1222	±6164	Ja	±0.28	±0.25	±d0.86	d1.09	....	d1.79	9 Mo Oct	d0.83	d1.53	12
13	1939	Q0.38	2-15-96	1-10	1.48	1.52	1.40	58.3	515	406	9-30-95	182	...	25325	Dc	2.91	□3.52	Δ3.23	3.45	E3.65	3.83	9 Mo Sep	2.33	2.71	13
14	....	None Since Public			...	Nil	....	....	2.63	2.17	p9-30-95	p....	...	★8200	Dc	...	...	p0.13	p0.34	....	0.52	9 Mo Sep	p0.24	p0.42	14
15◆	1995	0.017	12-15-95	11-29	0.067	0.07	....	7.42	114	75.7	9-30-95	228	...	29876	Dc	Δd0.38	0.13	□d2.33	[55]0.83	....	1.08	9 Mo Sep	0.54	0.79	15
16	1871	Q0.57	1-25-96	1-8	2.22	2.28	2.14	Equity per shr $16.38			9-30-95	53.3	...	20335	Dc	3.53	□2.71	□0.63	2.54	E3.00	2.91	9 Mo Sep	1.88	2.25	16
17	....	0.15	11-15-91	10-28	...	Nil	....	1.42	304	81.5	8-31-95	186	...	32726	Nv	d1.74	d8.59	0.20	□0.62	E0.07	0.05	9 Mo Aug	□d0.01	d0.58	17
18	....	None Since Public			...	Nil	....	3.15	6.84	0.37	9-30-95	....	...	3629	Dc	d0.17	d0.20	d0.27	d0.02	....	0.23	9 Mo Sep	d0.04	0.21	18
19	1994	Q0.04	12-1-95	11-13	0.16	0.16	0.12	9.52	27.5	27.6	8-31-95	101	...	9398	Nv	0.42	1.04	0.67	0.58	....	0.65	9 Mo Aug	0.48	0.55	19
20◆	1981	Q0.08	2-16-96	1-31	0.31	0.32	0.27	53.8	1730	1240	10-01-95	150	...	87673	Dc	0.94	□2.01	2.22	□2.01	E1.80	1.65	9 Mo Sep	□1.16	0.80	20
21	1995	Q0.07	12-12-95	11-28	0.35	0.28	....	8.58	28.7	7.80	8-31-95	2.90	...	±4728	My	...	...	...	p0.08	0.23	0.16	3 Mo Aug	0.18	0.11	21
22	1940	Q0.10	12-15-95	11-28	0.40	0.40	0.40	0.52	27.3	14.7	6-30-95	5.37	...	389	Dc	1.10	d1.13	□2.46	1.16	....	d3.59	9 Mo Sep	1.10	d3.65	22
23	1993	0.10	9-15-95	8-23	0.10	0.10	0.22	6.53	19.1	7.22	9-30-95	....	...	4266	Je	0.25	0.39	0.21	1.20	0.19	d0.01	3 Mo Sep	0.02	d0.18	23
24	....	None Paid			...	Nil	....	20.1	38.6	4.16	10-31-95	0.20	...	10543	Ap	0.08	0.31	0.80	0.98	d0.26	d0.67	6 Mo Oct	0.09	d0.32	24
25	1995	Q0.10	1-19-96	12-28	0.10	0.40	....	Book Value $20.71			9-30-95	....	...	4508	Dc	...	pd0.48	d0.09	d0.94	....	1.93	9 Mo Sep	d1.56	1.31	25
26◆	1935	Q0.075	11-24-95	11-9	0.30	0.30	0.27½	1.39	241	92.9	9-30-95	112	...	±11621	Dc	±0.27	±0.53	±0.91	±1.10	....	1.11	9 Mo Sep	±0.68	±0.69	26
27	....	None Since Public			...	Nil	....	7.43	43.6	89.8	9-30-95	18.3	...	±8514	Dc	...	...	...	†[56]d0.65	....	....	9 Mo Sep	n/a	pd0.42	27
28	1901	Q0.60	12-11-95	11-9	2.37	2.40	2.33	Equity per shr $29.17			9-30-95	1293	[57]91	29513	Dc	2.40	d0.48	1.88	2.60	E2.65	2.87	9 Mo Sep	1.86	2.13	28
29	1991	Q0.19	1-2-96	12-8	0.64	0.76	0.50	Book Value $12.72			9-30-95	39.7	...	13461	Dc	Δ1.33	Δ1.49	1.64	1.78	....	1.75	9 Mo Sep	1.31	1.28	29
30	1993	Q0.01½	1-3-96	12-14	0.06	0.06	0.06	4.20	163	114	7-31-95	122	...	17574	Ja	p0.61	p0.96	p□1.40	1.70	....	1.73	9 Mo Oct	1.31	1.34	30
31◆	1982	Q0.04	1-22-96	12-27	0.16	0.16	0.158	16.8	193	180	9-30-95	....	...	39780	Dc	d0.13	0.43	0.59	0.85	....	d0.87	9 Mo Sep	0.57	d1.15	31
32◆	....	None Since Public			...	Nil	....	Equity per shr $15.86			9-30-95	16.3	...	11339	Dc	±pΔ0.37	p±0.66	1.13	1.55	....	1.89	9 Mo Sep	1.11	1.45	32
33	....	None Since Public			...	Nil	....	44.7	61.3	8.65	9-30-95	....	...	[60]8950	Dc	...	...	...	0.19	....	0.46	9 Mo Sep	0.14	0.41	33
34	....	None Since Public			...	Nil	....	0.30	30.0	21.5	8-31-95	6.80	...	6717	My	p1.69	p1.26	pd0.35	d4.55	d0.65	d0.62	3 Mo Aug	d0.04	d0.01	34
35	1987	Q0.35	2-20-96	1-8	1.37	1.40	[61]1.32	Equity per shr $10.43			9-30-95	p273	...	★65690	Dc	1.01	1.02	□1.10	□0.98	E1.11	0.92	9 Mo Sep	□0.91	0.85	35
36◆	....	None Since Public			...	Nil	....	14.3	127	142	9-30-95	149	...	30840	Dc	Δp0.55	p0.81	Δ[62]1.03	1.26	E1.55	1.48	9 Mo Sep	0.92	1.14	36
37◆	1985	Q0.55	11-20-95	11-1	2.14	2.20	1.98	Equity per shr $11.94			9-30-95	265	...	28546	Dc	1.14	1.38	1.66	1.87	....	2.83	9 Mo Sep	1.38	2.34	37
38	1971	Q0.52	11-20-95	11-1	2.07½	2.08	[63]2.01	Equity per shr $15.91			9-30-95	57.0	...	11724	Dc	1.92	1.91	2.15	2.17	....	1.61	9 Mo Sep	1.66	1.10	38
39	....	None Paid			...	Nil	....	0.29	17.1	7.36	9-30-95	16.4	...	7982	Dc	Δd0.04	Δ0.22	Δ0.33	Δ0.18	....	0.03	9 Mo Sep	0.12	d0.03	39
40	1989	Q0.02½	3-1-96	2-14	0.08½	0.10	0.07	3.15	36.9	35.4	9-30-95	44.9	...	11388	Dc	0.49	0.53	0.32	d0.10	....	d0.02	9 Mo Sep	0.24	0.32	40
41◆	....	None Since Public			...	Nil	....	99.5	183	47.8	6-30-95	74.6	...	69164	Sp	±0.23	Δ±0.34	±0.49	□±0.69	P0.88	0.88				41
42◆	....	None Since Public			...	Nil	....	0.07	3.53	4.42	6-30-95	4.31	...	21710	Sp	d0.31	d0.60	d0.25	d0.49	....	d0.32	9 Mo Jun	d0.21	d0.04	42
43	....	None Since Public			...	Nil	....	536	673	501	9-30-95	257	...	±48292	Dc	...	±p0.88	±0.48	±1.77	....	1.83	9 Mo Sep	±1.29	±1.35	43
44◆	....	None Since Public			...	Nil	....	129	163	18.3	9-30-95	....	...	34549	Dc	0.50	0.51	1.08	1.45	E1.88	1.78	9 Mo Sep	1.05	1.38	44
45	1993	Q0.46½	11-15-95	10-31	1.83	1.86	[65]1.75	Equity per shr $18.01			9-30-95	93.0	...	12971	Dc	...	p1.27	p1.40	1.33	....	1.43	9 Mo Sep	0.95	1.05	45
46	....	h[67]....	11-6-95	11-7	h[67]...	Nil	....	30.0	68.5	16.3	9-30-95	3.34	...	16115	Dc	0.67	d0.22	0.57	1.05	....	d0.30	9 Mo Sep	1.10	d0.25	46
47	....	None Since Public			...	Nil	....	45.7	63.3	33.3	9-30-95	1.25	...	13395	Dc	...	...	...	p0.69	....	....	9 Mo Sep	n/a	p0.49	47
48◆	....	None Since Public			...	Nil	....	181	447	285	9-30-95	130	[68]100	63518	Dc	0.28	0.35	0.48	0.62	E0.83	0.76	9 Mo Sep	0.45	0.59	48
49◆	....	None Since Public			...	Nil	....	93.2	494	195	9-30-95	1386	...	97360	Dc	0.43	0.50	0.11	0.70	E1.07	0.67	9 Mo Sep	0.54	0.51	49
50	....	None Paid			...	Nil	....	2.68	6.50	1.11	9-30-95	....	255	1736	Dc	d0.19	0.49	0.25	0.56	....	1.08	9 Mo Sep	0.33	0.85	50
51	....	None Since Public			...	Nil	....	44.8	71.9	7.21	9-30-95	11.0	...	17625	Dc	pd0.34	d0.88	d0.13	0.77	....	0.94	9 Mo Sep	0.21	0.38	51
52	....	None Since Public			...	Nil	....	Equity per shr $10.43			9-30-95	....	...	2142	Dc	d0.35	d0.26	d0.02	d1.20	....	d1.50	9 Mo Sep	d1.23	d1.53	52

◆Stock Splits & Divs By Line Reference Index [1]3-for-2,'91. [2]5-for-4,'91. [3]Adj for 5%,'95. [7]10%,'92,'93,'94. [8]3-for-2,'92. [9]2-for-1,'93:3-for-2,'93. [15]3-for-2,'95. [20]3-for-2,'92. [26]3-for-2,'93. [31]2-for-1,'94. [32]3-for-2,'94. [36]2-for-1,'93. [37]2-for-1,'92. [41]3-for-2,'92,'93,'94,'95. [42]2-for-1,'92. [44]2-for-1,'91. [48]3-for-2,'92:2-for-1,'94,'95. [49]3-for-2,'92:2-for-1,'95.

¶ S&P 500 # MidCap 400 ✣ SmallCap 600 • Options Index	Ticker	Name of Issue (Call Price of Pfd. Stocks)	Market	Com. Rank. & Pfd. Rating	Inst. Hold Cos	Inst. Hold Shs. (000)	Principal Business	Price Range 1971-93 High	1971-93 Low	1994 High	1994 Low	1995 High	1995 Low	Dec. Sales in 100s	December, 1995 Last Sale Or Bid High	Low	Last	%Div Yield	P-E Ratio	Total Return % Annualized 12 Mo	36 Mo	60 Mo
1	HART	✔Heartland Wireless Commun	NNM	NR	33	2945	Oper wireless cable TV sys	....	....	15¾	9½	31½	11¾	7673	30¼	27¾	29¾	...	d	143	...	...
✣2•[1]	HECHA	✔Hechinger Co Cl'A'	NNM	B–	108	19307	Retail home centers	27¼	½	16½	9	13½	3⅜	52443	4⅞	4¼	4⅜	3.7	d	–58.8	–22.4	–9.1
3	HECHB	✔ Class'B'	NNM	B–	12	600	for do-it-yourself mkt	27¼	3/16	16¼	9	13½	3⅞	1985	5	4¼	4⅞	1.2	d	–55.3	–20.1	–7.4
✣4•[2]	HL	✔Hecla Mining	NY,B,Ch,P,Ph	C	124	20120	Silver producer: lead,gold	35⅞	3⅛	15	9¼	13	6⅝	75055	7⅝	6¾	6⅞	...	d	–33.7	–2.3	–3.3
5	Pr B	Sr'B'cm Cv Pfd([51]52.45)	NY,Ch	B–	18	1056		59⅛	45¾	58¼	44⅜	53	38¾	1600	42½	39⅛	40	8.8	..	...	...	...
6	HBCCA	✔Heftel Broadcasting'A'	NNM	NR	40	2246	Spanish language radio brdcst	....	....	16⅜	9½	21¾	9⅞	3997	18½	14½	17½	...	52	75.0	...	...
7	HEII	✔HEI Inc	NNM	B–	12	212	Miniature thick film hybrids	11	5/16	6⅝	4	7⅛	4⅛	3821	6⅛	5¼	5⅜	...	13	19.4	5.1	70.3
8	HEI	✔HEICO Corp	AS,B,P,Ph	B–	18	429	Mfr jet aircraft engine parts	23⅜	5/16	11½	8⅛	19¾	8¼	418	19	18	19	0.9	19	159	21.9	16.7
#9•[3]	HMY	✔Heilig-Meyers	NY,Ch,P	A+	240	38951	Retail furniture stores	39	3/16	38⅜	23¼	29	16	58270	21⅛	16	18⅜	1.5	18	–24.1	–3.3	25.1
10	HNW	✔Hein-Werner	AS	C	17	567	Auto service/repair equip	14¼	2¼	7⅝	3¾	5⅞	4¼	630	4¾	4¼	4½	s...	24	0.6	4.2	2.3
¶11•[4]	HNZ	✔Heinz (H.J.)	NY,B,Ch,Ph	A+	686	216632	Major mfr of processed foods	32⅜	1	26	20½	34⅞	24¼	137625	34⅞	31⅝	33⅛	3.2	20	41.0	7.9	11.2
12	Pr	$1.70 3d cm Cv 1st Pfd(28)[52]	NY,B	NR	1	.8	ketchup,soups,baby foods	400	25½	333	288	410	323½	....	....	....	298⅛B	0.6	..	...	...	...
13	HST	✔Heist(C.H.)Corp	AS	B	17	706	Indl maintenance/temp svc	11¼	1⅞	8	5⅝	11½	6½	273	7¼	6½	7	...	11	1.8	–2.8	3.9
14	HELE	✔Helen of Troy Ltd	NNM	B	52	4354	Hair care appliances	20¾	1/32	19¼	12½	21¼	16¼	2943	21	18	21	...	12	23.5	6.8	...
✣15	HC	✔Helene Curtis Ind	NY,B,Ch,Ph	B+	80	4111	Beauty/hair care toiletries	47⅜	½	36⅜	22¾	34½	27½	3007	31⅞	27¾	31⅝	1.0	16	–2.5	–8.3	5.2
16	HHGR	✔Helian Health Group[53]	NNM	NR	11	796	Oper out-patient surgery ctrs	10⅜	3¾	6¾	4⅛	6	2½	2106	5½	4⅞	5¼	...	d	18.9	–11.7	–4.0
17•[5]	HELX	✔Helix Technology	NNM	B+	85	5037	Mfr of cryogenic equipment	9½	3/16	19	6¾	55¾	14¾	15612	41½	28	39½	2.5	19	133	111	90.5
18	HELO	✔Hello Direct	NNM	NR	10	949	Mkt telecommunications eqp	....	....	....	....	18½	5	7741	7¾	5	6¾	...	12	...	...	...
19	HHH	✔Helm Resources	AS,Ch	C	3	10	Mkts thermoplastic resins	101¼	7/16	2	⅝	1⅛	7/16	971	15/16	11/16	11/16	...	d	–8.4	–25.1	...
¶20•[6]	HP	✔Helmerich & Payne	NY,B,Ch,Ph	B	242	17373	Contract driller:o&g prod'n	54⅛	2 5/16	31⅜	24¾	31¼	24¼	9464	30¼	27	29¾	1.7	74	17.6	9.3	4.8
21	HLM	✔Helmstar Group	AS,Ch	C	1	2	Merchant banking	13⅜	¼	⅞	½	1¼	⅜	949	1 3/16	¾	1	...	7	100	10.1	14.9
22	HEMA	✔HemaCare Corp	NSC	C	8	560	Therapeutic blood services	14¼	¾	7¾	2½	4⅞	2	5271	4⅜	3½	3¾	...	d	7.1	–15.7	16.5
23•[7]	HEM	✔Hemlo Gold Mines	AS,To,Ph,Mo	NR	81	20795	Gold mining Ontario, Canada	12⅜	5⅜	11⅞	8½	12⅛	7⅝	15445	10⅜	9	9⅜	◆...	..	–5.6	19.4	...
24	JKHY	✔Henry(Jack) & Assoc	NNM	B	45	3142	Data process'g svcs to banks	12¾	⅜	11⅞	6½	25½	8¾	9456	25½	22⅛	24¾	0.9	33	155	42.4	107
25•[2]	HERB	✔Herbalife Intl	NNM	B	61	3275	Weight ctrl/hlth care prod	18½	⅜	31	14¼	17¾	6¾	32754	9½	7¼	8⅝	7.0	14	–43.1	–6.9	70.7
¶26•[2]	HPC	✔Hercules, Inc	NY,B,Ch,P,Ph	B	494	86962	Chemical & plastics prod'r	38¼	4⅛	40½	32⅛	62¼	38¼	65439	59⅝	54⅝	56⅜	1.6	20	50.2	42.2	42.6
27	HERS	✔Heritage Finl Svcs	NNM	A–	32	1423	Commercial banking,Illinois	17½	4⅞	19¾	15¾	19½	15¾	208	19½	18¾	19¼	2.3	12	20.5	14.7	25.6
28•[8]	HTG	✔Heritage Media'A'	AS,Ch,Ph	NR	141	12780	Broadcasting, in-store adv	23	5⅝	27⅝	15¾	32½	23¾	20521	27⅜	24¾	26	...	16	–3.7	48.1	14.9
¶29•[9]	HSY	✔Hershey Foods	NY,B,Ch,P,Ph	A	428	25939	Mfr chocolate,candy,pasta	55⅞	1 7/16	53½	41⅛	67⅞	48	22209	67⅞	61¼	65	2.2	19	35.5	14.8	14.4
¶30•[3]	HWP	✔Hewlett-Packard	NY,B,C,Ch,P,Ph	A	1296	287361	Electr data:measure/test instr	44⅝	1⅞	51¼	36	96⅝	49	498283	88⅛	74¾	83¾	1.0	18	66.1	36.0	40.9
31	HXL	✔Hexcel Corp	NY,Ch,P	NR	41	12122	Honeycomb cores: plastics	43	1⅞	6⅝	2¾	12¼	4¼	8160	11¼	9⅜	11¼	...	d	173	9.3	0.5
32	HEMT	✔HF Bancorp	NNM	NR	10	1670	Savings & loan,California	....	....	....	....	10¼	7¾	8941	10⅛	9⅜	9⅞	...	..	...	...	...
#33•[10]	HFS	✔HFS Inc	NY,Ch,Ph	NR	272	47471	Hotel Franchisor/services	26⅞	8	33½	20¾	82¼	25	56026	82¼	69⅝	81¾	...	61	...	...	...
34	HGI	✔HGI Realty	NY,Ch,Ph	NR	132	11139	Real estate investment trust	25⅜	22½	29	20⅞	26⅜	20⅝	10182	24	21⅝	22⅞	e8.8	15	–5.5	...	...
✣35	HLO	✔Hi-Lo Automotive	NY,Ch,Ph	NR	49	4895	Retail auto parts/accessories	21½	9⅜	14⅝	9¼	11⅝	4½	13764	5⅝	4½	5⅛	...	13	–47.4	–36.6	...
36	HSI	✔Hi-Shear Indus	NY,Ch,Ph	C	23	3030	Mfr aerospace technology sys	24⅛	2 1/16	6¾	3⅞	8⅛	3⅞	728	7⅞	6¾	7¼	...	d	87.1	12.3	–2.8
37	HSR	✔Hi-Shear Technology	AS,Ch,Ph	NR	14	231	Electr/ordnance prod&sys	....	....	14¾	3⅜	15	5¼	6049	9	5¼	6⅛	...	d	–53.3	...	...
#38•[5]	HIB	✔Hibernia Corp Cl'A'	NY,Ch,Ph	B–	147	33460	Commercial bkg,Louisiana	26	1 9/16	9⅛	7¼	11	6⅞	40152	10⅞	10⅛	10¾	2.6	10	42.6	26.4	11.9
39	HSBK	✔Hibernia Savings Bk	NNM	NR	10	62	Savings bank,Massachusetts	11⅝	13/16	13⅛	9	18¼	10⅛	256	17½	15¾	16¼	1.7	9	57.8	47.5	65.5
40	HICKA	Hickok Inc 'A'	NSC	↑B+	1	.2	Mfr auto diagnostic equip	12⅜	2	18½	9	22½	14½	75	20	16½	16½B	1.2	11	–2.1	15.7	42.1
41	HWYM	✔HighwayMaster Communic	NNM	....	41	2591	Wireless communic svcs-trucking	....	....	....	....	22¾	7½	13131	12⅜	9	10⅜	...	d	...	...	...
42	HIW	✔Highwoods Properties	NY,Ch,Ph	NR	125	13510	Real estate investment trust	....	....	21⅝	18½	28½	19⅞	6092	28½	26⅛	28¼	6.4	..	43.2	...	...
✣43	HRH	✔Hilb,Rogal & Hamilton	NY	B+	72	5885	Operates insurance agencies	20⅝	5⅜	13⅜	11	14⅜	10½	4168	14⅜	13¼	13⅜	4.5	16	14.3	0.0	2.2
44	HILI	✔Hilite Industries	NNM	NR	9	326	Mfr automotive components	....	....	10⅜	6¾	11¾	6	660	11	10	10	...	13	37.9	...	...
45•[2]	HB	✔Hillenbrand Indus	NY,B,Ch,Ph	A	175	25168	Burial caskets,hosp eq,lugg.	48⅝	11/16	43⅝	26⅝	34⅛	27	11899	34⅛	32⅛	33⅞	1.8	21	23.5	–3.4	13.6
46	HDS	✔Hills Stores	NY	NR	68	7725	Regional discount retailer	21⅝	17½	23	18	24⅞	7⅛	12564	12	8⅝	9⅞	...	d	–51.8	...	...
47	Pr	Sr'A'vtg cm Cv Pfd(20)	NY	NR	10	704		20½	17¾	22¾	18¼	24⅜	7½	402	11⅞	8¾	9⅜	...	..	...	...	...
¶48•[8]	HLT	✔Hilton Hotels[59]	NY,B,Ch,P,Ph	B+	310	20977	Own/manage hotels & casinos	115½	1⅛	74	49¾	79¾	60⅜	41962	65¼	60⅝	61½	2.0	19	–6.8	15.1	14.2
49	HRSH	✔Hirsch Intl Corp'A'	NNM	NR	18	843	Distrib embroidery machines	....	....	7⅝	5½	15¼	6¾	2642	15	11	12¾	...	13	88.9	...	...
50•[5]	HIT	✔Hitachi,Ltd ADR[60]	NY,B,Ch,P,Ph	NR	96	4214	Elec eq, ind mchy: Japan	145	2⅜	110⅞	72	114⅛	82⅞	3527	104⅜	94¼	100½	1.0	26	2.9	20.3	5.0
51	HMG	✔HMG/Courtland Prop	AS	NR	5	66	Real estate investment trust	25¼	2⅛	13¾	6½	8½	7½	15	8	7½	7½	...	d	–9.1	19.7	9.6
52	HMII	✔HMI Industries	NNM	B+	19	893	Vacuum cleaners:metal tubing	14⅜	9/16	19⅛	12½	17	11¼	410	12¾	11¼	12	2.9	10	–21.3	27.3	22.1

Uniform Footnote Explanations-See Page 4. Other: [1]Ph:Cycle 3. [2]ASE:Cycle 3. [3]CBOE:Cycle 2. [4]CBOE:Cycle 3. [5]CBOE:Cycle 1. [6]NY:Cycle 3. [7]ASE,CBOE:Cycle 2. [8]P:Cycle 1. [9]ASE:Cycle 2. [10]ASE,CBOE:Cycle 3. [51]Fr 7-1-96,scale to $50 in 2003. [52]0.50 vtg. [53]TheraTx Inc plan acq. [54]Stk dstr of National Gaming,'94. [55]Pfd in $M. [56]Spl div. [57]29 Wks Dec'94. [58]®$2.73,'94. [59]Plan spin-off,gaming opers. [60]ADR's represent'g 10 com par yen 50.

Index	Splits ◆ Cash Divs. Ea.Yr. Since	Dividends: Latest Payment Period $	Date	Ex. Div.	Total $ So Far 1995	Ind. Rate	Paid 1994	Financial Position Mil-$ Cash& Equiv.	Curr. Assets	Curr. Liab.	Balance Sheet Date	Capitalization Lg Trm Debt Mil-$	Shs. 000 Pfd.	Com.	Earnings $ Per Shr. Years End	1991	1992	1993	1994	1995	Last 12 Mos.	Interim Earnings Period	$ per Shr. 1994	1995	Index
1	....	None Since Public			...	Nil	....	37.2	61.4	10.9	9-30-95	139	...	12569	Dc	...	...	pd0.04	d0.30	....	d1.13	9 Mo Sep	d0.13	d0.96	1
2	1983	Q0.04	11-17-95	10-25	0.16	0.16	0.16	62.0	604	363	10-28-95	401	...	±42325	Ja	±0.66	±d0.63	±0.59	±d0.24	....	d0.84	9 Mo Oct	±0.69	±0.09	2
3	1978	Q0.016	11-17-95	10-25	0.064	0.06	0.064	....	....	...		....	...	11457	Ja	±0.66	±d0.63	±0.59	±d0.24	....	d0.84	9 Mo Oct	±0.69	±0.09	3
4	....	0.05	12-21-90	11-15	...	Nil	....	7.16	59.7	22.4	9-30-95	31.2	2300	48254	Dc	d0.51	□d1.59	d0.48	□d0.72	Ed2.30	d2.76	9 Mo Sep	□d0.22	d2.26	4
5	1993	Q0.87½	1-1-96	12-8	3.50	3.50	3.50	Cv into 3.2154 com, $15.55				....	2300	...	Dc	...	...	...	....	....	....				5
6	....	None Since Public			...	Nil	....	15.0	35.5	12.5	6-30-95	72.1	336	±10061	Sp	...	...	±pd0.14	±0.05	P±0.34	0.34				6
7	....	None Since Public			...	Nil	....	5.26	9.98	1.60	8-31-95	....	...	3802	Au	d0.04	0.57	0.66	0.34	0.52	0.40	3 Mo Nov	0.18	0.06	7
8◆	1976	S0.08¼	2-8-96	1-11	0.143	0.17	0.136	6.29	21.1	7.92	7-31-95	6.90	...	2539	Oc	0.86	d0.24	0.38	Δ0.58	P1.01	1.01				8
9◆	1975	Q0.07	2-17-96	1-12	0.27	0.28	0.23	11.9	844	301	8-31-95	359	...	48562	Fb	0.65	0.84	1.12	1.34	E1.00↓	1.08	9 Mo Nov	1.04	0.78	9
10◆	....	5%Stk	1-26-96	1-3	5%Stk	Stk	5%Stk	0.04	38.6	17.9	9-30-95	12.5	...	2501	Dc	d2.10	d1.00	Δd0.94	0.33	....	0.19	9 Mo Sep	0.27	0.13	10
11◆	1911	Q0.26½	1-10-96	12-18	0.98½	1.06	0.90	190	3265	2778	11-01-95	2330	36	369661	Ap	1.42	1.60	□1.36	1.57	1.59	1.69	6 Mo Oct	0.78	0.88	11
12	1976	Q0.42½	1-1-96	12-18	1.70	1.70	1.70	Cv into 9 common				....	36	...	Ap	b5.12	b5.73	b4.62	b4.19	b3.81	....				12
13◆	....	None Paid			...	Nil	....	2.43	24.4	7.51	10-01-95	9.19	...	2873	Dc	0.70	0.44	0.17	0.11	....	0.64	40 Wk Sep	d0.29	0.24	13
14◆	....	0.16	8-3-77	7-15	...	Nil	....	30.3	93.3	37.8	5-31-94	....	...	6351	Fb	1.03	1.77	□1.07	P1.65	....	1.80	6 Mo Aug	0.60	0.75	14
15	1986	Q0.08	11-27-95	11-8	0.30	0.32	0.24	4.57	421	249	8-31-95	144	...	±9896	Fb	±2.04	±2.33	□±1.51	±2.02	....	1.95	12 Mo Aug	±1.83	±1.95	15
16	....	None Since Public			...	Nil	....	5.43	14.8	4.23	8-31-95	5.31	...	5475	Nv	0.26	0.35	d0.55	0.26	....	d0.13	9 Mo Aug	0.22	d0.17	16
17◆	1987	Q0.25	11-8-95	10-23	0.58	1.00	0.29	16.2	47.1	13.5	9-30-95	....	...	9777	Dc	0.33	0.30	Δ0.51	1.08	E2.07	1.82	9 Mo Sep	0.74	1.48	17
18	....	None Since Public			...	Nil	....	7.28	16.7	2.11	9-30-95	0.04	...	4897	Dc	d3.45	d1.44	0.32	0.39	....	0.56	9 Mo Sep	0.37	□0.54	18
19◆	....	None since 1962			...	Nil	....	0.02	3.07	6.60	9-30-95	4.82	43	2369	Dc	d4.05	Δd3.00	Δ0.11	□d1.25	....	d1.27	9 Mo Sep	□d0.38	d0.40	19
20	1959	Q0.12½	3-1-96	2-13	0.50	0.50	0.49	19.7	115	69.6	9-30-95	....	...	24764	Sp	0.88	0.45	1.01	Δ0.86	0.40	0.40				20
21	....	None Since Public			...	Nil	....	Equity per shr $1.42			9-30-95	....	...	5548	Dc	d0.48	0.17	d0.23	d0.18	....	0.15	9 Mo Sep	d0.11	0.22	21
22	....	None Paid			...	Nil	....	1.39	3.26	1.19	9-30-95	0.42	...	5905	Dc	d0.07	d0.25	d0.55	d0.45	....	d0.15	9 Mo Sep	d0.33	d0.03	22
23	1987	gS0.10	12-15-95	11-15	g0.20	0.20	g†0.35	132	215	108	j12-31-94	....	...	96823	Dc	0.15	0.43	0.47	0.67	....	j0.37	9 Mo Sep	0.51	0.21	23
24◆	1990	Q0.05¾	12-12-95	11-17	0.23	0.233	0.19½	8.62	18.3	18.7	9-30-95	....	...	11746	Je	0.21	0.36	Δ0.45	0.52	0.66	0.76	3 Mo Sep	0.15	0.25	24
25	1992	Q0.15	11-2-95	10-24	0.81	0.60	0.76	80.6	149	64.2	9-30-95	1.35	...	29885	Dc	0.33	0.79	1.47	1.50	....	0.63	9 Mo Sep	1.35	0.48	25
26◆	1913	Q0.23	3-25-96	3-6	0.84	0.92	0.747	82.6	960	722	9-30-95	248	...	109971	Dc	■0.67	1.23	□1.62	2.29	E2.80	2.95	9 Mo Sep	1.52	2.18	26
27◆	1987	Q0.11	11-14-95	10-26	0.44	0.44	0.36	Book Value $9.82			9-30-95	1.50	...	7939	Dc	0.96	1.18	1.34	1.50	....	1.56	9 Mo Sep	1.11	1.17	27
28◆	....	None Since Public			...	Nil	....	6.54	90.8	87.8	9-30-95	347	...	17709	Dc	Δd2.40	□d1.51	Δd0.32	0.15	....	1.67	9 Mo Sep	d0.64	0.88	28
29	1930	Q0.36	12-15-95	11-17	1.37	1.44	1.25	27.3	1054	1307	10-01-95	154	...	±77414	Dc	±2.43	±2.69	□±3.31	±2.12	E3.40	2.37	9 Mo Sep	±1.83	±2.08	29
30◆	1965	Q0.20	1-10-96	12-18	0.70	0.80	0.55	2825	14872	9678	7-31-95	665	...	511800	Oc	1.51	□1.75	2.33	3.07	P4.63	4.63				30
31	....	0.11	11-16-92	10-27	...	Nil	....	....	126	110	10-01-95	68.2	...	18094	Dc	0.58	□Δd2.99	Δd12.34	d4.10	....	d0.30	9 Mo Sep	d3.75	0.05	31
32	....	None Since Public			...	Nil	....	Book Value $13.18			9-30-95	70.0	...	.6613	Je	...	...	...	....	n/a	....	3 Mo Sep	n/a	0.03	32
33◆	....	h[54]....	11-28-94	11-29	...	Nil	h[54]....	41.2	205	148	p9-30-95	302	[55]80	50956	Dc	pd0.20	□0.46	□0.69	1.06	....	1.34	9 Mo Sep	0.84	1.12	33
34	1993	†Q0.505	1-19-96	12-27	†1.626	2.02	1.75½	Equity per shr $18.32			9-30-95	446	...	18422	Dc	...	p0.70	p1.08	1.42	....	1.55	9 Mo Sep	1.00	1.13	34
35	....	None Since Public			...	Nil	....	2.18	121	40.9	6-30-95	57.2	...	10734	Dc	□0.80	0.89	0.64	0.85	E0.40	0.43	9 Mo Sep	0.69	0.27	35
36	....	0.05½	8-30-90	8-20	...	Nil	....	0.94	35.2	13.5	8-31-95	10.1	...	5855	My	d3.01	*0.36	d1.41	d0.96	d0.09	d0.11	3 Mo Aug	d0.06	d0.08	36
37	....	None Since Public			...	Nil	....	0.44	10.2	3.98	8-31-95	0.33	...	6527	My	...	...	p0.10	d0.38	0.01	d0.01	3 Mo Aug	0.03	0.01	37
38	1993	Q0.07	11-21-95	10-25	0.25	0.28	0.19	Book Value $5.64			9-30-95	8.84	...	119253	Dc	□d5.12	□d0.27	0.58	0.78	E1.03	0.89	9 Mo Sep	0.64	0.75	38
39◆	1995	Q0.07	2-1-96	1-19	0.22	0.28	....	Book Value $13.68			12-31-94	9.00	...	1447	Dc	d1.23	1.21	2.15	1.41	....	1.77	9 Mo Sep	1.04	1.40	39
40◆	1989	[56]0.10	12-25-96	12-29	[56]0.285	0.20	0.15	0.70	14.2	6.08	9-30-95	....	...	±1193	Sp	±0.48	±1.02	±1.27	±1.30	±1.50	1.50				40
41	....	None Since Public			...	Nil	....	29.2	40.4	6.27	9-30-95	11.2	...	22022	Dc	...	...	...	pd1.18	....	d1.17	9 Mo Sep	pd1.06	□d1.05	41
42	1994	Q0.45	11-22-95	11-8	1.75	1.80	0.50	Equity per shr $18.30			9-30-95	182	...	19401	Dc	...	...	p0.80	□[57]0.77	....	....	9 Mo Sep	n/a	□1.14	42
43	1987	Q0.15	12-29-95	12-13	0.57	0.60	0.50	33.6	88.6	92.3	9-30-95	8.84	...	14085	Dc	0.57	0.71	0.61	0.77	....	0.82	9 Mo Sep	0.68	0.73	43
44	....	None Since Public			...	Nil	....	0.56	21.8	11.8	9-30-95	18.0	...	4900	Je	0.19	0.31	0.53	0.66	0.74	0.76	3 Mo Sep	0.19	0.21	44
45◆	1948	Q0.15	11-24-95	10-18	0.60	0.60	0.57	164	605	260	9-02-95	209	...	70757	Nv	1.22	Δ1.47	2.04	1.26	E1.65	1.72	9 Mo Aug	0.69	1.15	45
46	....	None Since Public			...	Nil	....	4.63	616	508	10-28-95	280	3483	9799	Ja	...	...	p2.14	[58]2.87	....	d0.09	9 Mo Oct	0.49	d2.47	46
47	....	None Since Public			...	Nil	....	Cv into 1 com, $20				....	3483	...	Ja	...	...	...	....	....	....	Mand red 10-5-2008,$20			47
48	1946	Q0.30	12-22-95	12-6	1.20	1.20	1.20	378	634	465	9-30-95	1098	...	48324	Dc	1.76	2.17	Δ2.14	2.52	E3.20	3.05	9 Mo Sep	1.73	2.26	48
49◆	....	5%Stk	8-10-94	7-13	...	Nil	5%Stk	7.70	26.1	14.4	7-31-95	2.55	...	±5957	Ja	0.18	0.43	p0.61	0.82	....	1.01	9 Mo Oct	0.61	0.80	49
50	1951	0.462	12-26-95	9-26	0.998	1.00	0.937	24761	67145	41459	3-31-95	11371	...	3287404	Mr	2.78	2.00	1.95	3.70	....	3.91	6 Mo Sep	1.46	1.67	50
51	....	0.15	9-28-90	9-10	...	Nil	....	Equity per shr $16.40			9-30-95	8.36	...	1167	Dc	d0.75	0.47	1.37	d2.62	....	d2.05	9 Mo Sep	d0.66	d0.09	51
52◆	1969	Q0.08¾	1-5-96	12-18	0.346	0.35	0.325	0.78	50.2	27.9	6-30-95	12.8	...	4876	Sp	0.68	0.63	1.01	Δ1.32	P1.15	1.15				52

◆**Stock Splits & Divs By Line Reference Index** [8]10%,'95:Vote 10% stk div,ex Jan 11. [9]3-for-2,'92(twice),'93(once). [10]Adj to 5%,Dec'94. [11]3-for-2,'95. [13]3-for-2,'91. [14]3-for-2,'92. [17]2-for-1,'93,'94. [19]1-for-15 REVERSE,'93. [24]3-for-2,'92,'93:4-for-3,'94. [26]3-for-1,'95. [27]2-for-1,'92. [28]1-for-4 REVERSE,'92. [30]2-for-1,'95. [33]2-for-1,'94:Vote Jan 22 on 2-for-1 stk split. [39]3-for-2,'95. [40]2-for-1,'95. [45]2-for-1,'92. [49]5-for-4,'95. [52]3-for-2,'92,'94.

¶ S&P 500 # MidCap 400 ✣ SmallCap 600 • Options Index	Ticker	Name of Issue (Call Price of Pfd. Stocks)	Market	Com. Rank. & Pfd. Rating	Inst. Hold Cos	Inst. Hold Shs. (000)	Principal Business	Price Range 1971-93 High	1971-93 Low	1994 High	1994 Low	1995 High	1995 Low	Dec. Sales in 100s	December, 1995 Last Sale Or Bid High	Low	Last	%Div Yield	P-E Ratio	Total Return % Annualized 12 Mo	36 Mo	60 Mo
1	HMNF	✔**HMN Financial**	NNM	NR	26	2052	Savings & loan, Minnesota	...	...	13¾	9¼	16¼	10¾	2049	16	15⅛	16	...	16	48.8	...	...
2	HNCS	✔**HNC Software**	NNM	NR	46	2401	Dvlp client/server softwr prd	...	...	...	...	49	14	31876	48½	31¼	47¾	...	68	...	...	...
3	HOEN	**Hoenig Group**	NNM	NR	10	488	Global securities broker, svcs	8⅝	3¼	4⅞	3¼	4⅜	2⅝	5595	4⅜	3¾	4⅛	2.4	..	25.9	−1.3	...
4	HOGN	✔**Hogan Systems**[51]	NNM	B	49	7102	Software prod for bank'g ind	26¼	2	10⅞	5⅛	13⅞	4⅝	70372	13⅞	8⅞	13⅝	...	23	114	37.1	44.7
5	HOL.A	✔**Holco Mtge Accept I**	AS	NR	2	2	Invest in GNMA ctfs	7½	1½	3⅜	1⅜	2⅝	11⁄16	102	1	¾	⅞B	...	10	−63.8	−14.4	−1.8
6	HOLI	✔**Hollinger Intl'A'**	NNM	NR	31	5081	Newspaper publishing	...	...	15	10	13	9¼	12522	12	9¾	10½	1.0	18	−4.4	...	...
7	HOC	✔**Holly Corp**	AS,Ph	B	51	5684	Petroleum refin'g & mktg	41	½	33⅜	23¾	28½	21¼	1662	23	21¼	22⅝	e1.8	17	−11.9	−7.7	1.7
8•[1]	HWCC	✔**Hollywood Casino'A'**	NNM	NR	47	4807	Casino gaming operations	32¾	12	15¼	4½	10¼	3⅝	17779	5½	3⅝	4¼	...	39	−16.3	...	...
9•[2]	HLYW	✔**Hollywood Entertainment**	NNM	NR	157	24746	Oper video rental superstores	7¼	2⁵⁄16	18½	5	35	7⅜	359923	17⅛	7⅜	8⅜	...	20	−47.2	...	...
✣10•[3]	HPRK	✔**Hollywood Park**	NNM	NR	61	6753	Horse racing track	35	2¼	30¾	9¼	15	9	12003	10½	9	10	...	d	−4.2	5.1	−18.8
11	HLPH	✔**Holophane Corp**	NNM	NR	62	5195	Mfr lighting fixtures,systems	11⅝	9⅝	12⅞	9½	23½	11⅜	8741	23½	19⅞	21¾	...	19	81.3	...	...
12	HBFW	✔**Home Bancorp**	NNM	NR	9	381	Savings bank, Indiana	...	...	...	...	16	10	551	15¾	14½	15¼	...	..	...	...	...
13	HBENB	✔**Home Beneficial**[53]**Cl'B'**	NNM	B+	65	6428	Hldg:life,accident,health	29	1⁹⁄16	23	19½	25½	19	2162	25½	23½	24	3.5	11	23.1	2.3	12.2
¶14•[4]	HD	✔**Home Depot**	NY,B,Ch,P,Ph	A	997	268063	Bldg mtls,home improv strs	51½	³⁄16	48¼	36½	50	36⅝	301452	48	42⅞	47¾	0.4	32	3.4	−1.7	30.7
15	HHCA	✔**Home Health Corp of Amer**	NNM	NR	..	...	Home health care svcs	...	...	...	...	11¼	7	12834	11¼	7	11	...	23	...	...	...
16	HME	✔**Home Properties of NY**	NY,Ch	NR	38	3772	Real estate investment trust	...	...	19⅞	17⅞	20	16½	5488	17¾	16⅝	17⅛	9.8	24	−3.6	...	...
#17•[5]	HSN	✔**Home Shopping Network**	NY,B,Ch,P,Ph	B−	150	36732	Retail mdse via own TV ntwk	47	2⅞	15⅛	9½	10⅞	6½	71271	10⅛	8⅞	9	...	d	−6.5	...	...
18	HMCI	✔**HomeCorp Inc**	NNM	NR	10	47	Savings bank, Rockford, IL	15½	5	18½	9¾	17¾	10¼	30	17¼	16½	16½B	...	38	61.0	17.3	22.7
19	HPX	✔**Homeplex Mtge Invmts**	NY,Ph	NR	3	40	Real estate investment trust	10¾	¹³⁄16	1½	1	2⅛	1	6330	1⅝	1⅜	1½	2.0	d	52.7	−13.1	−10.7
¶20•[5]	HM	✔**Homestake Mining**	NY,B,Ch,P,Ph	B−	369	59344	Mining:gold,lead,zinc	24⅛	1⅜	24⅞	16⅛	19⅛	14¾	131105	16⅞	15⅜	15½	1.3	62	−10.3	13.2	−2.5
21	HTBB	✔**HomeTown Buffet**	NNM	NR	66	5322	Franchise buffet style restr	20⅜	10	19¼	8¼	15¼	7¾	16161	11¼	9¾	11	...	22	16.4	...	...
#22	HONI	✔**HON Indus**	NNM	A−	86	7824	Mfr office furn/hm bldg prod	29¼	⁷⁄16	34	24	31¼	23	4757	28	23¼	23¼	2.1	14	−13.2	1.2	11.4
23•[6]	HMC	✔**Honda Motor ADR**[57]	NY,B,Ch,P,Ph	NR	34	2273	Autos,trucks,motorcycles	37½	⁷⁄16	37¾	27⅛	42½	27½	2480	42½	36⅜	41¾	0.6	34	18.2	26.1	18.3
24	HOG	✔**Hondo Oil & Gas**	AS,Ch,P,Ph	C	22	609	Oil & gas explor:refinery	28½	2⅛	22	5¾	24⅜	8½	2557	17	13⅝	13⅞	...	d	13.3	16.1	14.7
¶25•[7]	HON	✔**Honeywell, Inc**	NY,B,C,Ch,P,Ph	B	562	89533	Computer/ind'l control sys	39⅜	2³⁄16	36⅞	28¼	49½	30¾	50659	48⅝	45	48⅝	2.1	20	61.4	18.6	...
26•[2]	HKT	✔**Hong Kong Telecom ADR**[58]	NY,Ch,P	NR	174	22721	Telecommun svcs,Hong Kong	22⅝	5½	22⅛	16	21½	16	52786	18	16¾	17⅝	4.7	18	−4.0	19.8	23.6
27	HH	✔**Hooper Holmes**	AS	B+	32	2990	Health care/info services	18⅛	2⅝	14¾	5¾	10¾	6½	2338	9	7⅞	8⅛	0.5	d	26.0	−18.5	0.1
28	HMN	✔**Horace Mann Educators**	NY	NR	132	20056	Insur hldg:prop,cslty,life	32½	17⅜	28¾	19⅛	31¼	20⅛	11569	31¼	28½	31¼	1.2	12	37.7	4.0	...
#29•[2]	HHC	✔**Horizon/CMS Healthcare**	NY,Ph	B	270	35220	Long-term care facilities	20⅞	1⅛	30	18¾	28¼	16⅝	75139	25½	21⅝	25¼	...	d	−9.0	24.0	75.9
30	HRZB	✔**Horizon Financial**	NNM	NR	17	395	Savings bank,Bellingham,Wash	15⅞	3¼	15½	10½	13¾	10¾	1561	13¾	13	13	2.5	12	18.9	5.1	11.0
31	HMH	✔**Horizon Mental Health Mgmt**	AS	NR	30	1665	Managed mental hlth programs	...	...	...	...	19	9⅞	777	18½	16½	16⅝	...	19	...	...	...
32•[4]	HRL	✔**Hormel Foods**	NY,Ch,Ph	A+	154	17826	Meat packing: conven'ce food	25½	¹⁵⁄16	26¾	18¾	28	22⅞	9527	25⅛	23⅞	24⅝	2.4	16	−2.6	4.2	7.7
✣33•[8]	HOSS	✔**Hornbeck Offshore Svcs**[61]	NNM	B−	92	9989	Marine svcs to oil & gas ind	24¾	³⁄16	18⅝	11½	20⅛	8⅞	23618	20⅛	17¾	19⅝	...	39	58.6	46.4	25.7
34•[9]	HSM	✔**Horsham Corp**[62]	NY,Ch,Ph	NR	122	49961	Gold mining/RE/Oil refining	15½	5⅞	16½	12	15	11⅝	43476	14⅛	13⅛	13⅜	0.5	23	5.4	17.4	11.8
35	HSS	✔**Hospital Staffing Svcs**	NY,Ph	C	18	1402	Recruitment svcs hlthcare ind	16⅝	⅞	4⅛	1⅜	2⅝	⅞	3876	2¼	1⅝	2⅛	...	d	30.8	−24.2	−9.5
36	HPT	✔**Hospitality Properties Trust**	NY,Ph	NR	33	3025	Real estate investment trust	...	...	...	...	27	24⅜	3673	26¾	24⅜	26¾	8.2	..	...	...	...
37•[6]	HMT	✔**Host Marriott**	NY,B,Ch,P,Ph	C	226	104839	Hotel/land development	43¾	1³⁄16	13¾	8¼	13⅞	9⅛	68673	13¾	11½	13⅛	...	d	...	...	...
38	Pr A	**$4.125cm Cv**[66]**Dep Pfd(**[67]**52.48)**	NY	C	5	11		168	50	260	165	246⅝	190⅜	...	...	...	217B	...	..	...	...	...
39	HMS	**Host Marriott Services**	NY	NR	..	...	Food & beverage concessions	...	...	...	...	7	6¼	6592	7	6¼	7	...	..	...	...	...
#40•[10]	HTN	✔**Houghton Mifflin**	NY,B,Ch	A−	228	11426	Publ textbooks: trade books	50⅜	1½	53	36⅛	54¾	39⅝	14971	43⅛	39¾	43	2.2	d	−3.5	5.5	14.1
41	HF	✔**House of Fabrics**	NY,B,Ch,P	D	22	3212	Retails fabrics, notions, etc.	41½	1⅜	8⅛	¾	1¼	⅜	15481	½	⅜	⅜	...	d	−62.5	−69.5	−52.3
¶42•[11]	HI	✔**Household Intl**	NY,B,Ch,P	B+	489	67244	Finance & banking services	40½	4⅞	39¾	28½	68⅜	35⅞	77499	67¼	56¾	59½	2.3	14	65.5	30.4	34.1
43	HBI	✔**Houston Biotechnology**	AS	NR	4	114	R&D biopharmaceutical prod	6⅛	1¾	3⅛	¾	1¹⁄16	⁵⁄16	1959	⅝	⅜	⁷⁄16	...	d	−50.1	...	...
¶44•[12]	HOU	✔**Houston Indus**	NY,B,C,Ch,P,Ph	B+	480	116948	Elec utility hldg co:Texas	24⅞	5½	23⅞	15	24½	17¾	102412	24½	22⅞	24¼	6.2	14	46.0	9.4	13.9
45	HOV	✔**Hovnanian Enterpr Cl'A'**	AS,Ch,P,Ph	↓B−	33	3207	Multifamily home builder	19¼	1¾	16	4¾	8¼	5	8081	7⅞	6¼	7½	...	12	46.3	−14.2	21.1
46	HWL	✔**Howell Corp**	NY,Ch	B−	28	1800	Oil & gas explor,devel,prod	33	⅝	13⅝	10½	16⅜	10⅜	1972	14½	12	14⅜	1.1	35	18.7	7.9	5.4
47	HOW	✔**Howell Indus**	AS	B	12	308	Auto steel parts,seat guides	37⅞	⅝	33¼	26⅝	31	23⅝	148	24¾	24	24⅜	4.1	12	−4.9	0.2	3.1
48	HOWT	**Howtek Inc**	NNM	C	14	575	Computer colorgraphic sys	27¾	2½	11⅜	6	11½	6½	14679	8¾	6½	6⅞	...	d	−24.7	−23.3	8.3
49	HPRI	✔**HPR Inc**	NNM	NR	39	1740	Dvlp/mkt heathcare softwr	...	...	...	...	37½	16	2789	37½	28	30⅛	...	72	...	...	...
50	HRE	✔**HRE Properties**	NY,Ch,Ph	NR	23	358	RE inv tr: purch/lease back	27¾	9	16¼	13¼	14⅝	13	1161	14⅛	13⅛	13⅛	8.8	18	4.6	13.1	13.9
✣51	HSE	✔**HS Resources**	NY,Ch	NR	68	6667	Oil & gas dvlp,prod'n/pipeline	29	12¾	24¾	17⅛	17½	12⅝	6501	13¾	12⅝	12⅞	...	92	−25.9	−2.8	...
52	HNP	**Huaneng Power Intl ADS**[75]	NY,Ph	NR	78	13820	Dvlp,oper coal-fired pwr plants	...	...	20⅛	14½	20¼	12¼	10622	16¼	14⅜	14⅜	...	30	−1.7	...	...

Uniform Footnote Explanations-See Page 4. Other: [1]ASE,P:Cycle 2. [2]ASE,CBOE:Cycle 1. [3]CBOE:Cycle 3. [4]Ph:Cycle 2. [5]CBOE:Cycle 1. [6]Ph:Cycle 1. [7]CBOE:Cycle 2. [8]NY:Cycle 1. [9]CBOE,NY:Cycle 1. [10]P:Cycle 1. [11]ASE:Cycle 1. [12]NY:Cycle 3. [51]Continuum Co plan acq, cash & com. [52]To be determined. [53]Non-voting. [54]Incl current amts. [55]Stk dstr of Silver King Communication,'93. [56]Fiscal Aug'92 & prior. [57]ADRs represent'g 2 com,par yen 50. [58]Each ADR represent 10 ord, HK$0.50. [59]Approx. [60]®$2.13,'94. [61]Tidewater Inc plan acq, .667 com. [62]Sub vtg shrs. [63]®$1.68,'94. [64]Incl current amt. [65]Stk dstr of Host Marriott Svcs. [66]Dep for 0.001 shr Series'A'cm Cv Pfd. [67]To 1-15-97,scale to $50 in 2002. [68]Liabs subject to compromise. [69]Incl curr amts. [70]Excl $100M subsid Pfd. [71]®$3.50,'94. [72]Subsid Pfd in $M. [73]Feb'94 & prior. [74]Incl $0.55 non-taxable,'94. [75]Ea ADS rep 40 N ord shrs,par Rmb 1.00.

Index (◆ Splits)	Cash Divs. Ea.Yr. Since	Dividends: Latest Payment Period $	Date	Ex. Div.	Total $ So Far 1995	Ind. Rate	Paid 1994	Financial Position Mil-$ Cash & Equiv.	Curr. Assets	Curr. Liab.	Balance Sheet Date	Capitalization Lg Trm Debt Mil-$	Shs. 000 Pfd.	Com.	Earnings $ Per Shr. Years End	1991	1992	1993	1994	1995	Last 12 Mos.	Interim Earnings Period	$ per Shr. 1994	1995	Index
1	....	None Since Public			...	Nil	....	Book Value $16.80			9-30-95	68.9	...	5321	Dc	...	...	p0.97	p0.86	....	1.02	9 Mo Sep	p0.63	0.79	1
2	....	None Since Public			...	Nil	....	14.4	20.5	4.61	9-30-95	....	...	★7300	Dc	...	...	...	p0.31	....	0.70	9 Mo Sep	p0.14	p0.53	2
3	1993	Q0.02½	12-29-95	12-13	0.12½	0.10	†0.12½	Equity per shr $3.31			9-30-95	....	...	9755	Dc	p0.25	0.38	0.45	0.25	....	0.03	9 Mo Sep	0.25	0.03	3
4	1991	0.17	6-16-94	5-24	...	Nil	0.17	4.75	51.2	29.1	9-30-95	....	...	14509	Mr	0.14	0.38	Δ0.39	0.43	....	0.60	6 Mo Sep	0.10	0.27	4
5	1988	Q0.01	12-1-95	10-30	0.05	[52]....	0.96	Equity per shr $1.03			9-30-95	8.92	...	564	Dc	0.38	0.16	0.20	0.24	....	0.09	9 Mo Sep	0.22	0.07	5
6	1994	Q0.02½	1-15-96	12-27	0.10	0.10	0.02½	16.8	89.7	87.7	3-31-95	310	...	±23345	Dc	...	...	±p0.08	±0.63	E0.60	0.48	9 Mo Sep	±0.46	±0.31	6
7◆	1988	†0.15	1-12-96	12-27	0.40	0.40	0.37½	28.1	156	129	10-31-95	58.1	...	8254	Jl	1.42	0.33	□2.42	2.51	Δ1.51	1.37	3 Mo Oct	Δ0.88	0.74	7
8	....	None Since Public			...	Nil	....	49.4	88.6	68.5	9-30-95	419	...	24720	Dc	d0.97	d1.81	□0.02	0.08	....	0.11	9 Mo Sep	0.43	0.46	8
9◆	....	None Since Public			...	Nil	....	65.3	95.1	30.6	9-30-95	0.52	...	36004	Dc	p0.02	p0.09	p0.14	0.32	....	0.41	9 Mo Sep	0.21	0.30	9
10◆	....	0.048	3-31-92	3-9	...	Nil	....	27.0	64.6	56.7	9-30-95	15.6	27	18370	Dc	*0.30	*0.25	0.25	0.10	....	d0.03	9 Mo Sep	d0.02	d0.15	10
11◆	....	None Since Public			...	Nil	....	8.98	57.0	32.5	9-30-95	25.1	...	11471	Dc	...	pΔ0.59	p0.81	0.82	....	1.12	9 Mo Sep	0.79	1.09	11
12	....	None Since Public			...	Nil	....	Book Value $16.15			6-30-95	....	...	3303	Sp	...	...	...	p0.90	....	....	9 Mo Jun	n/a	0.22	12
13◆	1906	Q0.21	12-8-95	11-15	0.83	0.84	0.79½	Equity per shr $29.53			9-30-95	....	...	±17439	Dc	±2.51	□±2.50	±2.35	±2.04	....	2.12	9 Mo Sep	±1.51	±1.59	13
14◆	1987	Q0.05	12-22-95	12-6	0.19	0.20	0.15	130	2727	1822	10-29-95	291	...	476818	Ja	0.60	0.82	1.01	1.32	E1.50	1.47	9 Mo Oct	1.00	1.15	14
15	....	None Since Public			...	Nil	....	0.66	21.5	9.55	p6-30-95	6.72	p...	★7514	Je	...	...	...	....	p0.44	0.48	3 Mo Sep	0.06	0.10	15
16	1994	Q0.42	11-21-95	11-8	1.65¾	1.68	0.26	Equity per shr $14.43			9-30-95	[54]85.6	...	5408	Dc	...	...	p0.86	p0.84	....	0.71	9 Mo Sep	p0.65	0.52	16
17	....	h[55]....	1-13-93	1-14	...	Nil	....	20.4	237	206	9-30-95	116	...	±90681	Dc	Δ±d0.11	□±[56]0.42	□d0.18	□0.19	Ed0.30	d0.39	9 Mo Sep	□0.17	d0.41	17
18◆	....	None Paid			...	Nil	....	Book Value $17.84			9-30-95	....	...	1126	Dc	1.87	1.43	Δ1.01	□0.54	....	0.44	9 Mo Sep	□0.86	0.76	18
19	1994	0.03	1-17-96	12-27	0.02	0.03	0.03	Equity per shr $1.90			9-30-95	8.81	...	9717	Dc	0.81	d1.93	□d2.66	d0.47	....	d0.24	9 Mo Sep	d0.14	0.09	19
20	1946	Q0.05	11-21-95	11-8	0.20	0.20	0.17½	240	378	88.9	9-30-95	185	...	137959	Dc	□d1.57	d1.31	0.38	0.57	E0.25	0.24	9 Mo Sep	0.49	0.16	20
21◆	....	None Since Public			...	Nil	....	3.60	7.59	19.0	10-04-95	★57.7	...	11580	Dc	d0.57	d0.66	0.21	0.31	....	0.50	40 Wk Oct	0.21	0.40	21
22	1955	Q0.12	12-1-95	11-21	0.48	0.48	0.44	28.5	180	115	9-30-95	45.1	...	30383	Dc	1.02	1.18	Δ1.39	□1.74	....	1.65	9 Mo Sep	□1.16	1.07	22
23	1949	0.11¾	12-20-95	9-27	0.257	0.26	0.239	2272	15304	14127	3-31-95	6598	...	974178	Mr	1.00	0.67	0.48	1.42	....	1.23	3 Mo Jun	0.48	0.29	23
24	....	None Paid			...	Nil	....	0.16	0.67	2.90	6-30-95	82.2	...	13309	Sp	d3.58	d4.37	d1.83	d0.85	....	d0.64	9 Mo Jun	d0.60	d0.39	24
25◆	1928	Q0.26	12-18-95	11-29	1.01	1.04	0.97	229	2707	1967	10-01-95	565	...	126978	Dc	2.35	□2.88	2.40	2.15	E2.50	2.44	9 Mo Sep	1.34	1.63	25
26◆	1989	[59]0.399	1-8-96	11-14	0.766	0.82	0.357	4792	9590	11437	j3-31-95	....	...	11152786	Mr	0.66	0.75	0.87	1.01	....	1.01				26
27◆	1974	0.01	11-24-95	11-8	0.06	0.04	0.30	1.86	53.0	29.9	9-30-95	27.6	...	6707	Dc	0.70	0.73	0.54	0.40	....	d1.85	9 Mo Sep	0.29	d1.96	27
28	1992	Q0.09	12-15-95	11-29	0.36	0.36	0.29	Equity per shr $9.34			12-31-94	100	...	p23358	Dc	□1.57	□2.48	2.67	□[60]2.23	....	2.65	9 Mo Sep	□1.63	2.05	28
29	....	None Since Public			...	Nil	....	48.5	498	208	8-31-95	573	...	51074	My	*0.24	0.44	0.66	pd0.66	p0.79	d0.12	6 Mo Nov	p0.30	d0.61	29
30◆	1988	Q0.08	2-5-96	1-5	0.32	0.32	0.298	Book Value $11.16			3-31-95	....	...	p6537	Mr	0.94	□1.25	1.25	1.16	....	1.09	6 Mo Sep	0.61	0.54	30
31	....	None Since Public			...	Nil	....	3.17	10.0	7.56	8-31-95	2.50	...	3561	Au	...	...	...	p0.25	p0.90	0.90				31
32	1928	Q0.15	2-15-96	1-17	0.58	0.60	0.50	208	650	219	7-29-95	17.0	...	76682	Oc	1.13	1.24	□1.31	1.54	P1.57	1.57				32
33	....	None Paid			...	Nil	....	19.6	33.3	9.46	9-30-95	17.9	...	13166	Dc	0.18	0.01	□0.92	0.60	....	0.51	9 Mo Sep	0.41	0.32	33
34	1993	A0.07	6-30-95	6-13	0.07	0.07	0.06	394	856	417	6-30-95	1199	...	±102309	Dc	0.70	0.41	0.42	[63]1.81	E0.59	0.32	9 Mo Sep	1.90	0.41	34
35	....	None Paid			...	Nil	....	2.01	18.6	11.3	8-31-95	1.00	...	6350	Nv	0.57	d0.54	d1.04	□d2.02	....	d1.16	9 Mo Aug	Δd0.79	0.07	35
36	1995	0.55	1-30-96	12-20	0.24	2.20	....	Equity per shr $23.69			6-30-95	[64]p23.4	...	★11750	Dc	...	...	...	....	....	....	8 Mo Sep	n/a	p2.15	36
37◆	1978	h[65]....	12-29-95	1-2	h[65]...	Nil	....	Equity per shr $4.20			9-08-95	1925	4	159288	Dc	0.80	0.64	pd0.51	□d0.13	Ed0.12	d0.28	36 Wk Sep	d0.05	□d0.20	37
38	1992	1.031	7-15-93	6-28	...	Nil	....	Cv into 2.8736 com,$17.40				....	3500	...	Dc	...	...	...	....	....	0.52				38
39	....	None Since Public			...	Nil	....	41.0	119	171	9-08-95	408	...	31858	Dc	...	...	...	pd0.20	....	....	36 Wk Sep	n/a	p0.15	39
40	1908	Q0.24	11-22-95	11-6	0.93	0.96	0.87	110	449	156	9-30-95	226	...	14470	Dc	1.75	□1.35	□2.27	□3.79	Ed0.50↓	2.71	9 Mo Sep	□4.30	3.22	40
41◆	....	0.06	7-2-90	6-4	...	Nil	....	File bankruptcy Chapt 11				[68]204	...	13697	Ja	1.44	0.37	d2.16	d6.96	....	d2.45	9 Mo Oct	d6.30	d1.79	41
42◆	1926	Q0.34	1-15-96	12-27	1.28½	1.36	1.21½	Equity per shr $21.21			9-30-95	[69]11154	[70]1902	98115	Dc	1.58	1.97	□2.91	[71]3.52	E4.15	4.09	9 Mo Sep	2.45	3.02	42
43	....	Wrrt	2-11-94	2-14	...	Nil	Wrrt	0.54	0.55	0.72	9-30-95	0.16	...	5639	Dc	...	pd1.03	d1.10	d0.84	....	d0.54	9 Mo Sep	d0.68	d0.38	43
44◆	1922	Q0.37½	3-9-96	2-14	1.50	1.50	1.50	64.5	446	873	9-30-95	3558	[72]402	262672	Dc	1.64	Δ1.32	1.60	□1.66	E1.70	4.49	9 Mo Sep	□1.62	4.45	44
45	....	None Since Public			...	Nil	....	Equity per shr $7.19			7-31-95	382	...	±23729	Oc	Δ0.07	0.43	□[73]0.87	0.50	P0.61	0.61				45
46	1975	Q0.04	11-29-95	11-13	0.16	0.16	0.16	6.19	72.2	72.8	9-30-95	98.2	690	4932	Dc	d1.58	0.09	0.18	0.10	....	0.41	9 Mo Sep	0.07	0.38	46
47	1984	Q0.25	11-15-95	10-17	1.00	1.00	1.00	5.18	19.3	6.58	10-31-95	....	...	623	Jl	1.72	2.28	2.56	Δ2.09	2.21	2.05	3 Mo Oct	0.66	0.50	47
48	....	None Since Public			...	Nil	....	0.26	15.0	4.62	9-30-95	5.26	...	7947	Dc	d0.67	0.49	d0.10	0.11	....	d0.38	9 Mo Sep	0.01	d0.48	48
49	....	None Since Public			...	Nil	....	8.49	15.9	4.78	6-30-95	1.93	p...	★6822	Je	...	...	...	....	p0.37	0.42	3 Mo Sep	0.02	0.07	49
50	1970	Q0.29	1-23-96	12-29	1.14	1.16	[74]1.10	Equity per shr $15.79			7-31-95	62.3	...	5362	Oc	0.58	0.30	d0.94	0.26	P0.72	0.72				50
51	....	None Since Public			...	Nil	....	1.08	9.64	15.6	9-30-95	124	...	10893	Dc	p0.18	□0.69	0.93	0.53	....	0.14	9 Mo Sep	0.43	0.04	51
52	....	None Since Public			...	Nil	....	690	831	215	12-31-94	822	...	±5000000	Dc	...	...	±p0.77	±0.48	....	0.48				52

◆**Stock Splits & Divs By Line Reference Index** [7]No adj for recap,'85:Spl $ dstr,'89. [9]3-for-2,'94:2-for-1,'95. [10]7-for-4,'92:5-for-4,'93. [11]3-for-2,'95. [13]2-for-1,'92. [14]3-for-2,'91,'92:4-for-3,'93. [18]3-for-2,'93. [21]3-for-2,'94. [25]2-for-1,'92. [26]3-for-1,'94. [27]3-for-2,'92. [30]5-for-4,'92:15%,'93:10%,'91,'94. [37]No adj for stk dstr of Marriott Int,'93. [41]2-for-1,'91. [42]No adj for stk dstr,'89:2-for-1,'93. [44]2-for-1,'95.

¶ S&P 500 # MidCap 400 ✤ SmallCap 600 • Options

Index	Ticker	Name of Issue (Call Price of Pfd. Stocks)	Market	Com. Rank. & Pfd. Rating	Inst. Hold Cos	Inst. Hold Shs. (000)	Principal Business	Price Range 1971-93 High	1971-93 Low	1994 High	1994 Low	1995 High	1995 Low	Dec. Sales in 100s	December, 1995 Last Sale Or Bid High	Low	Last	%Div Yield	P-E Ratio	Total Return % Annualized 12 Mo	36 Mo	60 Mo
#1	HUB.B	✓Hubbell Inc Cl'B'	NY,Ch	A	271	17595	Electrical wiring devices:	57⅛	2 7/16	59⅞	50	66⅛	49⅝	5016	66⅛	60¾	65¾	2.9	19	41.9	13.5	18.0
2	HUB.A	✓ Class A com (20 votes)	NY	A	70	3740	industrial controls & gear	55	2 7/16	55¼	47⅛	62⅛	48⅛	385	62⅛	58¾	62⅛	3.0	18	42.4	13.0	17.9
3	HUBC	✓HUBCO Inc	NNM	A	53	3707	Commercial bkg,New Jersey	16⅞	½	15⅞	12½	22⅛	14⅝	5144	22⅛	19⅝	22⅛	2.7	11	55.5	32.0	61.7
4	HFI	✓Hudson Foods Cl'A'	NY,Ch	B	125	13131	Produces/mkts poultry prod	14⅛	3¼	17⅞	7⅜	20	12¾	17443	17½	15¾	17¼	0.5	14	−0.1	24.9	27.9
5	HGC	✓Hudson General	AS	B−	17	574	Aviation svcs:land devel	28	¾	20⅜	13⅜	34½	15⅝	486	34½	31	32½	1.5	8	114	52.1	13.2
6	HBC	Hudson's Bay Co	To,Mo	B	43	4968	Retail dept stores,Canada	41⅛	9¾	40⅜	22⅞	28¾	19⅛	19331	21¼	19⅛	19⅝	4.7	18	−18.6	−9.6	...
✤7	HUF	✓Huffy Corp	NY,Ch	B+	87	8681	Mfr/dstr consumer products	24⅜	11/16	19½	14	15⅞	10	10694	11⅝	10⅛	10⅛	3.4	60	−31.3	−11.4	2.5
✤8	HUG	✓Hughes Supply	NY	B	62	3009	Fla distr elect, plumb'g:mfg	21⅞	1 3/16	32¼	15⅞	29⅛	17¾	4497	29⅛	26¼	28⅛	1.3	13	55.0	24.6	24.6
9	HUGO	✓Hugoton Energy	NNM	NR	27	4147	Oil & gas explor,devlp,prod'n	....	....	15½	8	10½	6	6025	9¼	8¼	8¾	...	d	6.1	...	...
10	HGSI	✓Human Genome Sciences	NNM	NR	50	4702	R&D human gene products	27¾	12	20¾	14	38¼	12¼	23373	38¼	23¾	38¼	...	d	164	...	...
¶11•[1]	HUM	✓Humana Inc	NY,B,Ch,P,Ph	B+	358	105190	Provides managed hlth plans	35⅛	3/16	25⅜	15⅞	28	17	166278	27⅞	25⅜	27⅜	...	23	18.4	...	...
12	HTC	Hungarian Tel & Cable	AS	NR	11	266	Dvp stage:telecomm svcs	16¼	7	41½	9½	19	9¼	5233	12	9½	10⅝	...	d	−3.4	−3.6	...
13	HUN	✓Hunt Mfg[59]	NY,Ph	A−	74	7043	Mfr/dstr office & art prod	24⅞	⅜	18¼	13	18⅜	12⅝	9410	17½	13⅝	17⅜	2.2	18	32.1	12.9	11.0
#14•[2]	JBHT	✓Hunt(JB)Transport	NNM	B+	120	16152	Motor carrier,gen'l freight	26¾	5⅛	25¾	15	20⅛	12¾	18822	17⅛	14⅝	16¾	1.2	67	8.4	−8.8	9.3
15	HCO	✓Huntco Inc'A'	NY,Ch	NR	63	4368	Intermediate steel processor	42¼	16	42½	16¾	26½	12⅜	5993	17⅝	12⅝	15⅜	0.8	73	−25.4	...	...
16	HTD	Huntingdon Intl ADR[60]	NY,Ch,Ph	NR	23	3493	Biological safety evaluat'n	34¼	1¾	11½	1⅞	6½	2	4008	5⅞	5⅛	5½	...	d	110	−33.1	−24.7
17•[3]	HBAN	✓Huntington Bancshares	NNM	A−	132	23289	Commercial bkg,Ohio	21	15/16	21⅛	15⅞	25⅜	16⅛	31047	25⅜	22¾	24	3.3	12	62.2	24.5	41.8
18	HWY	✓Huntway Ptnrs L.P.	NY,Ch	NR	1	25	Refines liq asphalt prod	13⅞	11/16	3⅛	⅝	1⅛	¼	7055	⅝	⅜	7/16	...	d	−36.4	−33.7	−28.7
19	HURC	✓Hurco Companies	NNM	C	25	1922	Machine tools-microproc'r	28½	1¾	4¾	2¼	7¼	2¾	4621	7¼	4⅝	5¼	...	..	31.3	−17.2	−9.1
20	HTCH	✓Hutchinson Technology	NNM	B−	61	2643	Mfr parts for computer equip	51¼	5	41	21½	91	23½	26174	54¾	41	42¼	...	11	69.0	−1.9	36.2
21	HYBD	✓Hycor Biomedical	NNM	B−	18	3839	Medical diagnostic products	8⅝	⅜	6⅛	3¾	5⅛	3¼	8189	4⅝	4⅜	4⅜	...	19	6.1	−6.6	1.8
22	HYDEA	Hyde Athletic Indus'A'	NNM	B−	16	588	Athletic/recreat'l footwear	14½	1/16	8	4½	5½	3⅝	1258	4¼	3¾	3¾	...	8	−23.1	−24.8	−2.4
23	HYDEB	Cl'B'	NNM	B−	17	737		12¾	4⅞	7⅜	4¼	5½	3⅝	3467	4¼	3¾	4⅛	...	8	−13.2	...	...
24	HTEC	Hydron Technologies	NNM	B−	20	1408	Dvlp,mkt polymer based prod	14½	¼	7⅛	2	5½	1¾	14592	2¼	1¾	1¾	5.7	13	−62.0	12.6	25.9
✤25	HYSW	✓Hyperion Software	NNM	NR	124	14724	Dvlp business info software	13⅞	5⅝	20⅛	9	28⅜	15⅝	40621	22½	18¼	21¼	...	30	9.5	21.2	...
26	IBAH	✓IBAH Inc	NNM	NR	16	2444	Dvlp stge:drug delivery sys	6⅛	2¾	4¾	2¼	6⅜	1¾	12253	6⅜	4⅝	6¼	...	d	163	19.9	...
#27•[4]	IBP	✓IBP, Inc	NY,Ch,P,Ph	NR	372	42094	Produces beef/pork products	26¼	10¾	35½	22⅝	67¼	29⅛	109326	62½	43⅝	50½	0.4	9	45.0	36.9	21.1
28	IBSF	IBS Financial	NNM	NR	35	3553	Saving & loan, New Jersey	....	....	10½	9	17⅛	9¾	14044	16⅝	14½	15	1.6	16	56.2	...	...
29	ICF	✓ICF Kaiser International	NY,Ch	C	17	7136	Environmental consult'g svcs	18½	3¾	5	2	5	3⅛	8420	4¼	3⅛	4¼	...	d	36.0	−10.9	−18.6
30•[5]	ICN	✓ICN Pharmaceuticals	NY,Ch	NR	101	13366	Mfr specialty/generic prod	32	2 3/16	24⅞	12⅞	24⅛	12	33284	20⅛	17¼	19¼	s1.4	d	27.3	29.6	27.4
31•[6]	ICOS	✓ICOS Corp	NNM,Ch	NR	40	2291	Dvlp stge:biopharmaceut'l R&D	21½	4¾	6⅛	3⅜	8⅛	3⅜	20489	7⅝	5⅞	7⅜	...	d	111	−1.6	...
32	IDBEF	ID Biomedical	NSC,Vc	NR	8	1936	Medical products R&D	12⅝	4¾	7½	3¼	11	3¾	3892	7	5⅛	5⅞	...	d	15.3	...	...
#33	IDA	✓Idaho Power	NY,B,Ch,P,Ph	B	147	8282	Hydroelectric utility	33	9⅛	30⅝	21¾	30	23⅜	9904	30	28¾	30	6.2	15	36.4	9.9	10.2
34	IDX	✓Identix Inc	AS,Ch,Ph	C	27	2912	Mfr computerized ID systems	9⅜	1¼	4	2 5/16	16¾	2⅞	15819	12½	10	11	...	d	267	68.2	40.6
✤35•[7]	IQ	✓IDEON Group	NY,Ch,Ph	↓B−	103	24742	Credit card enhancement svcs	35⅞	1/16	20¾	13¾	21⅜	7⅜	14990	10⅞	7½	10⅛	2.0	d	−42.8	3.9	8.3
36	IEX	✓IDEX Corp	NY,Ch,Ph	NR	144	10309	Mfr fluid handl'g/indl prod	24	6⅜	29¼	22⅝	44¼	27⅝	2728	43¼	40⅛	40¾	1.6	19	50.9	38.4	42.3
✤37•[8]	IDXX	✓IDEXX Laboratories	NNM	NR	222	32503	Mfr animal biomedical test prd	16	3⅜	18⅝	12⅝	47½	16⅞	38427	47½	42¼	47	...	86	164	79.8	...
38	IDXC	IDX Systems	NNM	NR	..	...	Health care info sys	....	....	....	....	34¾	18	23825	34¾	24¾	34¾	...	..	...	...	...
39	IECE	✓IEC Electronics	NNM	NR	34	1684	Mfr electronic products & sys	18	10⅜	21¼	7½	11¼	6⅜	9332	9⅜	8¾	8¾	...	14	2.9	...	...
40	IES	✓IES Industries[63]	NY,B,Ch,P,Ph	B+	123	7381	Electric & natural gas	34¼	8	31⅜	24¾	28½	20⅜	21766	28½	26⅛	26½	7.9	12	13.6	4.1	6.9
41	IEU	IES Util 7.875%JrSubDebs[65]	NY	NR	..	...	Subsid of IES Industries	....	....	....	....	25½	25	17804	25½	25	25⅜	7.8	..	...	...	...
42	IFRS	✓IFR Systems	NNM	B−	30	2458	Mfrs communic'ns test eqp	16	4¼	10¾	6½	14½	9	2913	10	9¼	9¼	...	21	2.8	3.9	9.0
43	IGEN	✓IGEN Inc	NNM	NR	31	3065	Mfr/mkt diagnostic systems	....	....	12⅜	4⅞	8	4⅜	15474	6⅛	4⅝	5⅞	...	d	14.6	...	...
44	IG	✓IGI Inc	AS,B,Ch	B−	21	1282	Mfr animal health prod	32	⅝	14⅜	8	17½	6⅜	14023	12⅜	6⅜	8¼	...	d	...	...	...
✤45•[9]	IHOP	✓IHOP Corp	NNM	NR	105	8651	Oper Intl House Pancake restr	31¼	9⅜	33¾	22½	30½	20½	12423	26½	24¼	26	...	15	−3.7	10.8	...
46•[10]	IISLF	I.I.S. Intellig't Info[67]	NNM	B	9	392	Mfr computer peripheral eqp	34	11/16	26	2⅜	4¼	1 13/16	8074	2¼	1 13/16	2	...	d	−20.0	−50.1	−9.1
#47•[9]	IC	✓Illinois Central Corp	NY,Ph	NR	315	39480	Major freight railroad sys	36	5⅝	38⅝	28⅝	43	30¾	35062	43	36¾	38⅜	3.0	13	27.9	20.0	38.9
¶48•[9]	ITW	✓Illinois Tool Works	NY,B,Ch	A+	533	83600	Fasteners,tools, plastic items	40½	1 11/16	45½	37	65½	39¾	37445	63½	56¼	59	1.2	18	38.5	23.7	21.1
#49	ILN	✓Illinova Corp	NY,B,C,Ch,P,Ph	B	280	46402	Hldg co: Illinois Power	44¾	12¾	22⅝	18⅛	30	21¼	29953	30	28⅛	30	3.7	13	44.5	12.9	14.1
50	DISK	✓Image Entertainment	NNM	B−	20	1482	Dstr home video programs	14⅞	⅛	9	5⅜	8⅞	6	50865	8⅞	6⅝	7½	...	14	1.7	8.5	0.2
51•[11]	IMS	Imasco Ltd	To,Mo,Vc	A	66	13975	Tobacco,food,retail,fin'l svc	20⅞	15/16	22⅛	16	27¼	19⅜	30336	26¾	24	26½	3.6	12	39.3	14.2	...
52	IMAXF	✓Imax Corp	NNM,To	NR	16	1850	Design,dstr project'n/sound sy	....	....	13¾	8	26⅛	6½	10291	23¾	19¼	22¾	...	d	164	...	...

Uniform Footnote Explanations-See Page 4. Other: [1]CBOE:Cycle 2. [2]P:Cycle 2. [3]CBOE,Ph:Cycle 1. [4]ASE,Ph:Cycle 2. [5]ASE:Cycle 3. [6]CBOE:Cycle 3. [7]P:Cycle 1. [8]ASE,CBOE:Cycle 3. [9]Ph:Cycle 3. [10]CBOE,P:Cycle 3. [11]Mo:Cycle 1. [51]®$1.64,'94. [52]®$2.67,'95. [53]®$1.76,'95. [54]6 Mo Dec,'92. [55]Stk dstr of Galen Health Care,'93. [56]Fiscal Aug'91 & prior. [57]12 Mo Dec'92. [58]9 Mo Dec'93. [59]Co offer for 3.2M com,$17 to Jan 24. [60]ADR rep 5 ord shares. [61]Fiscal Oct'93 & prior. [62]12 Mo Dec'94,fiscal Oct'94 earned $0.63. [63]Plan mgr w/Interstate Pwr&WPL Hldgs,.98 new co. [64]Subsid pfd in $M. [65]Jr Sub Deferrable Int Debs Sr'A'. [66]Stk dstr of Novavax Inc. [67]Ord Shrs. [68]Subsid Pfd in $M. [69]Pfd in $M.

Splits ◆ Index	Cash Divs. Ea.Yr. Since	Dividends: Latest Payment Period $	Date	Ex. Div.	Total $ So Far 1995	Ind. Rate	Paid 1994	Financial Position Mil-$ Cash& Equiv.	Curr. Assets	Curr. Liab.	Balance Sheet Date	Capitalization Lg Trm Debt Mil-$	Shs. 000 Pfd.	Com.	Earnings $ Per Shr. Years End	1991	1992	1993	1994	1995	Last 12 Mos.	Interim Earnings Period	$ per Shr. 1994	1995	Index
1◆	1934	Q0.47	1-11-96	12-20	s1.78	1.88	1.60	76.1	491	296	9-30-95	2.70	...	±32911	Dc	±2.73	□±2.83	±2.00	±3.20	....	3.56	9 Mo Sep	±2.34	±2.70	1
2◆	1934	Q0.47	1-11-96	12-20	s1.78	1.88	1.60	....	...	...		.....	...	5784	Dc	±2.73	□±2.83	±2.00	±3.20	....	3.56	9 Mo Sep	±2.34	±2.70	2
3◆	1952	Q0.15	12-1-95	11-15	0.60	0.60	0.36	Book Value $9.56			9-30-95	25.0	...	13110	Dc	0.67	1.05	1.37	[51]1.69	....	2.00	9 Mo Sep	1.03	1.34	3
4◆	1986	Q0.02	1-11-96	12-26	0.08	0.08	0.08	2.16	297	116	9-30-95	130	...	±30073	Sp	0.39	0.10	0.67	±1.08	±1.21	1.21				4
5	....	S0.25	1-3-96	12-6	0.50	0.50	....	9.29	31.4	34.5	9-30-95	29.0	...	1145	Je	*2.33	*0.90	□d1.65	Δ5.86	[52]3.69	3.91	3 Mo Sep	0.19	0.41	5
6◆	1938	gQ0.23	1-31-96	1-4	g0.92	0.92	g0.89	22.0	2675	979	j1-31-95	1126	...	57635	Ja	1.61	2.32	2.72	Δ2.65	....	j1.12	9 Mo Oct	1.42	d0.11	6
7◆	1950	Q0.08½	2-1-96	1-10	0.34	0.34	0.34	2.35	182	101	9-30-95	56.8	...	13433	Dc	1.52	□0.92	□d0.30	1.20	....	0.17	9 Mo Sep	1.05	0.02	7
8	1976	Q0.09	2-23-96	2-8	0.27	0.36	0.21	0.95	282	107	10-31-95	106	...	6584	Ja	d0.97	0.54	1.35	[53]1.78	....	2.24	9 Mo Oct	1.31	1.77	8
9	....	None Since Public			...	Nil	....	5.14	15.3	6.45	9-30-95	95.0	...	19697	Dc	...	pd0.01	p0.12	d0.07	....	d0.25	9 Mo Sep	0.02	□d0.16	9
10	....	None Since Public			...	Nil	....	52.7	54.7	4.23	9-30-95	4.99	...	18189	Dc	...	†[54]d0.41	0.15	0.47	....	d1.78	9 Mo Sep	0.86	d1.39	10
11◆	1976	h[55]. . . .	3-5-93	3-8	...	Nil	....	945	1143	894	9-30-95	.....	...	161888	Dc	[56]2.26	Δ[57]0.49	0.56	1.10	E1.20	1.17	9 Mo Sep	0.80	0.87	11
12	....	None Paid			...	Nil	....	7.98	11.2	11.7	6-30-95	9.03	...	3001	Dc	...	[58]d0.19	d0.80	d2.13	....	d3.79	6 Mo Jun	d0.74	d2.40	12
13	1965	Q0.09½	2-15-96	2-5	0.38	0.38	0.36	3.19	98.5	32.6	9-03-95	3.56	...	15975	Nv	0.60	0.83	0.93	Δ1.07	....	0.98	9 Mo Aug	Δ0.71	0.62	13
14◆	1985	Q0.05	11-22-95	11-1	0.20	0.20	0.20	4.37	193	216	9-30-95	294	...	38692	Dc	□0.85	Δ1.03	1.00	1.05	E0.25↓	0.40	9 Mo Sep	0.77	0.12	14
15	1993	Q0.03	12-8-95	11-22	0.11	0.12	0.09	1.58	82.6	20.8	10-31-95	62.2	...	±8940	Ap	±Δd0.16	±0.04	±□0.61	±0.92	±1.11	0.21	6 Mo Oct	±0.48	±d0.42	15
16	1989	0.072	7-13-94	6-10	...	Nil	0.22	1.07	54.9	26.0	j9-30-94	40.0	...	98547	Sp	1.28	1.02	0.55	d5.55	....	d5.55				16
17◆	1912	Q0.20	1-2-96	12-12	s0.771	0.80	0.648	Book Value $11.02			9-30-95	1622	...	133642	Dc	1.05	1.25	1.76	1.78	E1.95	1.67	9 Mo Sep	1.40	1.29	17
18	....	0.10	8-29-90	8-8	...	Nil	....	1.72	14.3	16.0	9-30-95	90.8	...	11673	Dc	0.26	d1.24	d1.60	d0.26	....	d0.57	9 Mo Sep	d0.16	d0.47	18
19	....	0.02	11-23-92	10-20	...	Nil	....	1.15	44.1	22.0	7-31-95	30.1	...	5418	Oc	0.43	d1.05	d3.89	d1.07	P0.04	0.04				19
20	....	None Since Public			...	Nil	....	31.7	90.5	36.2	9-24-95	34.9	...	5447	Sp	1.12	2.72	1.58	1.08	3.84	3.84				20
21	....	None Paid			...	Nil	....	6.35	18.3	3.14	9-30-95	.....	...	8060	Dc	0.01	0.41	0.26	0.34	....	0.23	9 Mo Sep	0.26	0.15	21
22◆	....	None Since Public			...	Nil	....	8.30	59.6	12.5	9-29-95	5.92	...	±6217	Dc	0.20	□0.71	±0.76	±0.46	....	0.49	9 Mo Sep	±0.26	±0.29	22
23	....	None Since Public			...	Nil	....	....	...	...		.....	...	3515	Dc	0.19	□0.71	±0.76	±0.46	....	0.49	9 Mo Sep	±0.26	±0.29	23
24	1995	Q0.02½	12-29-95	12-13	0.10	0.10	....	4.93	10.6	0.76	9-30-95	.....	...	22640	Dc	d0.06	d0.07	d0.07	0.16	....	0.14	9 Mo Sep	0.10	0.08	24
25◆	....	0.69			...	Nil	....	41.1	69.9	35.8	12-31-94	.....	...	15682	Je	0.24	0.31	0.29	0.55	P0.70	0.70	3 Mo Sep	0.11	0.12	25
26	....	None Since Public			...	Nil	....	8.48	22.8	18.0	9-30-95	2.51	1000	14352	Dc	pd0.33	d0.40	d0.77	d1.76	....	d0.26	9 Mo Sep	d1.78	d0.28	26
27◆	1988	Q0.05	1-12-96	12-6	0.20	0.20	0.20	146	1116	664	9-30-95	306	...	47386	Dc	0.03	1.34	Δ1.62	3.79	E5.75↓	6.24	9 Mo Sep	2.17	4.62	27
28	1995	0.06	12-13-95	11-15	0.21	0.24	....	Book Value $14.33			9-30-95	.....	...	10478	Sp	...	...	0.81	n/a	0.92	0.92				28
29	....	None Since Public			...	Nil	....	29.3	227	145	8-31-95	121	.2	21233	Fb	±d2.25	±0.16	□d0.83	d0.18	....	d0.13	6 Mo Aug	d0.07	d0.02	29
30◆	1985	sQ0.069	12-20-95	12-4	s0.271	0.277	s0.24	32.3	310	112	9-30-95	170	...	30213	Dc	1.45	1.59	0.99	■d7.92	....	d7.39	9 Mo Sep	1.05	1.58	30
31	....	None Since Public			...	Nil	....	27.7	28.7	3.90	9-30-95	.....	...	32234	Dc	d0.31	d0.34	d0.71	d0.88	....	d0.74	9 Mo Sep	d0.66	d0.52	31
32◆	....	None Paid			...	Nil	....	0.69	1.41	1.43	j3-31-95	.....	...	10610	Mr	d0.19	d0.19	d0.44	d0.60	....	jd0.06	6 Mo Sep	d0.34	0.20	32
33	1917	Q0.46½	11-20-95	10-23	1.86	1.86	1.86	7.65	139	169	9-30-95	673	825	37612	Dc	1.56	1.55	2.14	1.80	....	2.06	12 Mo Sep	1.94	2.06	33
34	....	None Paid			...	Nil	....	6.75	19.5	5.72	9-30-95	0.13	...	23204	Je	d0.28	d0.24	d0.20	d0.14	d0.04	d0.01	3 Mo Sep	d0.02	0.01	34
35	1989	Q0.05	12-29-95	12-19	0.20	0.20	0.20	63.8	271	237	9-30-95	.....	...	27982	Dc	1.02	0.75	[61]1.10	[62]d1.25	....	d3.74	9 Mo Sep	Δ0.60	d1.89	35
36◆	1995	Q0.16	1-31-96	1-10	0.56	0.64	....	3.28	168	72.7	9-30-95	179	...	19126	Dc	*0.94	□1.07	1.31	1.72	....	2.18	9 Mo Sep	1.25	1.71	36
37◆	....	None Since Public			...	Nil	....	202	267	32.0	9-30-95	.....	...	36480	Dc	0.16	0.18	0.29	0.40	....	0.55	9 Mo Sep	0.27	0.42	37
38	....	None Since Public			...	Nil	....	10.3	49.8	50.5	p9-30-95	2.90	...	★19687	Dc	...	...	...	p0.13	....	0.32	9 Mo Sep	p0.19	p0.38	38
39	....	None Since Public			...	Nil	....	8.44	34.4	18.2	6-30-95	7.46	...	7387	Sp	...	p0.16	□1.45	1.51	P0.62	0.62				39
40	1950	Q0.525	1-1-96	12-6	2.10	2.10	2.10	4.43	123	340	9-30-95	540	[64]18	29454	Dc	1.85	1.92	2.45	2.34	....	2.18	12 Mo Sep	2.40	2.18	40
41	1995	0.098	12-29-95	12-26	0.098	1.97	....	Co option redm fr 12-31-2000 at $25				★50.0	...	...	Dc	...	...	...	....	....	....	Mature 12-31-2025			41
42	....	0.075	6-6-88	5-9	...	Nil	....	0.14	39.3	15.7	9-30-95	4.91	...	5492	Je	0.71	0.30	0.17	0.19	0.41	0.45	3 Mo Sep	0.03	0.07	42
43	....	None Since Public			...	Nil	....	18.3	23.2	6.01	9-30-95	0.33	...	14763	Mr	...	p0.12	pd0.22	d0.40	....	d0.65	6 Mo Sep	d0.01	d0.26	43
44◆	....	h[66]. . . .	12-12-95	12-13	h[66]. . .	Nil	....	0.89	18.4	9.67	9-30-95	7.83	...	9202	Dc	0.01	0.01	d0.46	0.03	....	d0.31	9 Mo Sep	0.17	d0.17	44
45	....	None Since Public			...	Nil	....	2.38	24.3	19.4	9-30-95	91.5	...	9358	Dc	□0.73	□0.98	1.15	1.60	....	1.69	9 Mo Sep	1.03	1.12	45
46◆	....	t0.013	12-29-89	12-18	...	Nil	....	3.91	60.6	16.6	12-31-94	.....	...	13948	Dc	0.47	0.56	0.85	d0.66	....	d1.34	9 Mo Sep	d0.39	d1.07	46
47◆	1992	Q0.29	1-9-96	12-15	1.00	1.16	0.84	13.2	112	193	9-30-95	358	...	41217	Dc	1.64	Δ1.70	□2.14	2.67	E2.95↓	3.04	9 Mo Sep	1.84	□2.21	47
48◆	1933	Q0.17	1-26-96	12-27	0.62	0.68	0.54	102	1495	794	9-30-95	282	...	117553	Dc	1.63	1.72	1.83	2.45	E3.30↑	3.15	9 Mo Sep	1.70	2.40	48
49	1991	Q0.28	2-1-96	1-8	1.00	1.12	0.80	16.5	415	553	9-30-95	1803	[68]319	75644	Dc	1.04	1.23	d1.08	2.09	E2.30	2.35	12 Mo Sep	1.76	2.35	49
50◆	....	None Since Public			...	Nil	....	Equity per shr $1.29			9-30-95	0.03	...	13477	Mr	0.04	d1.44	□0.26	□0.51	....	0.55	6 Mo Sep	□0.17	0.21	50
51◆	1912	gQ0.24	12-29-95	11-27	g0.96	0.96	g0.78	Equity per shr $6.98			j12-31-94	5833	[69]135	p233408	Dc	1.28	1.49	1.63	2.09	....	j2.30	9 Mo Sep	1.46	1.67	51
52	....	None Since Public			...	Nil	....	52.9	87.2	54.5	6-30-95	68.8	[69]1	14076	Dc	...	...	pd0.04	pd1.12	....	d0.35	9 Mo Sep	pd0.62	0.15	52

◆Stock Splits & Divs By Line Reference Index [1]Adj to 5%,'95. [2]Adj to 5%,'95. [3]10%,'91,'93:3-for-2,'95. [4]3-for-2,'95. [6]No adj for stk dstr of Markborough ptys,'90. [7]3-for-2,'91. [11]3-for-2,'91:No adj for stk dstr of Galen Health Care,'93. [14]3-for-2,'92. [17]10%,'93:5-for-4,'92,'94:Adj to 5%,'95. [22]2-for-1 in Cl'B','93. [25]2-for-1,'95. [27]To split 2-for-1,hldrs Dec 28:To split 2-for-1,ex Jan 22. [30]10%,15%,'91:Adj to 1.248%,Dec'95. [32]2-for-1,'95. [36]3-for-2,'95. [37]2-for-1,'93,'95. [44]No adj for stk dstr Novavax Inc. [46]3-for-1,'93. [47]3-for-2,'92. [48]2-for-1,'93. [50]1-for-14.857 REVERSE,'91. [51]2-for-1,'95.

¶ S&P 500 # MidCap 400 ✣ SmallCap 600 • Options Index	Ticker	Name of Issue (Call Price of Pfd. Stocks)	Market	Com. Rank. & Pfd. Rating	Inst. Hold Cos	Inst. Hold Shs. (000)	Principal Business	Price Range 1971-93 High	1971-93 Low	1994 High	1994 Low	1995 High	1995 Low	Dec. Sales in 100s	December, 1995 Last Sale Or Bid High	Low	Last	%Div Yield	P-E Ratio	Total Return % Annualized 12 Mo	36 Mo	60 Mo
#1•[1]	IGL	✓IMC Global	NY,Ch,Ph	NR	269	54239	Mfrs chemical fertilizer	34	11¼	24⅝	15⅜	40⅞	20⅝	94598	40⅞	35	40¾	0.8	18	89.3	25.4	19.7
2	IMCL	✓ImClone Systems	NNM	NR	18	3432	Biopharmaceutical research	28	5	6⅝	⅝	9	5/16	76954	9	4⅞	7⅝	...	d	876	−10.1	...
✣3	IMR	✓IMCO Recycling	NY,Ch,Ph	NR	89	6704	Aluminum can recycling svcs	16¾	1	16⅞	12⅛	24½	13⅜	3420	24½	22	24½	e0.6	25	69.5	19.9	30.7
4	IMEX	Imex Medical Systems	NSC	C	2	66	Mfr med'l monitoring instr	3¼	5/16	1⅜	⅝	1 1/16	⅝	1549	¾	⅝	¾	...	d	9.2	−18.3	9.8
5	ICCC	✓ImmuCell Corp	NSC	NR	6	201	Antibody-base prevention prd	3½	⅜	2⅜	1	2¾	1	3228	2⅝	1⅝	2 7/16	...	d	130	23.9	35.6
✣6	IMUL	✓ImmuLogic Pharmaceutical	NNM	NR	79	11906	Drug R&D:allergies/immune sys	25	7½	15¼	6	19¼	6¼	40655	19¼	11¾	19¼	...	d	166	18.7	...
✣7•[2]	IMNR	✓Immune Response Corp	NNM	NR	45	3532	R&D:immune sys pharmac'ls	62¾	2¾	13¾	5⅜	8⅜	2⅝	35375	6⅜	3⅝	5½	...	d	1.1	−32.4	13.1
8•[3]	IMNX	✓Immunex Corp[53]	NNM	C	81	9189	Immunological bio products	68	4	19¾	10¾	18½	9¾	39927	17½	16	16½	...	d	10.0	−31.1	−13.8
9•[3]	IMMU	Immunomedics Inc	NNM	C	31	3814	Cancer imaging/therapy MOAB	17	1⅜	6½	2⅞	8½	2⅛	24574	6	4⅝	6	...	d	65.5	−15.7	13.0
10	IMNT	✓IMNET Systems	NNM	NR	41	2875	Document mgmt software	...	...	...	...	29¾	12	6470	26¾	20½	24	...	d	...	...	...
✣11	IMD	✓Imo Industries	NY,Ph	C	74	9973	Mfr instr/controls:engin'g pr	23	3⅞	12½	6¾	11⅞	5¾	8791	7½	6¼	6⅞	...	3	−35.3	15.2	−8.1
12	IBAN	✓Imperial Bancorp	NNM	B−	54	2898	Commercial bkg,California	22⅞	1⅛	18⅝	11⅝	25	11⅜	7872	25	22¾	24½	s...	20	114	54.9	22.7
13•[4]	ICI	✓Imperial Chem Ind ADR[55]	NY,B,P	B+	111	12079	Leading int'l chemical co	108⅛	10¾	54½	44	53	43½	12697	48	44½	46¾	4.1	10	4.4	...	...
14	IMH	Imperial Credit Mtge Hldgs	AS	NR	..	...	Real estate investment trust	...	...	...	...	13¼	12	7468	13¼	12	13¼	...	..	...	...	...
15	IHK	✓Imperial Holly Corp	AS	NR	20	3541	Ref beet/cane sugar:sweet'nrs	58¾	5⅜	11¾	7⅜	10¼	5¼	1537	6⅞	5¼	5¾	...	d	−30.7	−17.3	−17.1
16	IMO	Imperial Oil Ltd	AS,To,B,Mo,Ph	B	200	24715	Canadian oil:Exxon owns 70%	61⅝	15½	36	29	39	32	12997	36⅛	33¾	36⅛	◆...	..	15.3	13.8	−0.3
17	ITLA	Imperial Thrift & Loan	NNM	NR	..	...	Special'd lend'g&deposit svcs	...	...	...	...	12¾	10	8973	12¾	11¾	12¼	...	d	...	...	...
18•[5]	INFS	✓In Focus Systems	NNM	NR	79	7123	Mfr LCD project'n panel prod	28¾	5½	31	10¼	38	17¾	44683	38	30	36⅛	...	20	35.7	44.4	26.8
19	IHHI	✓In Home Health Inc	NNM	B−	19	668	Home health/nursing services	7⅛	⅝	3⅝	1 13/16	3⅛	1¾	11813	2⅝	2 1/16	2⅜	...	24	26.7	−25.0	10.1
20•[6]	INAC	✓InaCom Corp	NNM	B	64	6538	Franchise/oper computer str	25½	6¼	21	6⅞	15¼	7	39002	15¼	11	14⅛	...	15	98.2	0.3	5.1
21	INBR	✓INBRAND Corp	NNM	NR	44	3079	Mfr disposable incontinerce pd	14⅜	9⅜	20¾	10¼	18¾	10	5424	18	15	16½	...	18	22.2	...	...
¶22•[7]	N	✓Inco Ltd	NY,To,B,C,Ch,Mo,Ph,P	B−	347	70143	Producer of nickel & copper	46¾	7⅞	31¼	21⅜	38	23½	52937	36½	32⅝	33¼	1.2	16	17.7	16.1	8.1
23	IOT	✓Income Opportunity Rlty	AS	NR	2	.4	Real estate investment trust	78	1¾	20⅞	15⅛	20⅝	19	55	19⅝	19	19⅝B	3.1	d	3.8	53.1	51.2
24	ICNT	Incomnet Inc	NSC	C	22	2749	Long dist telephone reseller	30¼	½	14¾	6	24½	2½	48816	8¼	4⅜	4½	...	11	−65.9	−6.4	32.3
25	INCL	✓InControl Inc	NNM	NR	20	4831	Implant atrial defibrillator	...	...	12	9⅜	18½	8¾	2690	15¼	12	14¾	...	d	55.3	...	...
26	ISR	✓Incstar Corp	AS,Ch	B−	18	2300	Medical RIA test kits	16	1½	3⅞	1 11/16	5¼	1½	2025	4⅜	3¾	4⅛	...	..	145	−13.5	−4.7
27	IPI	✓INCYTE Pharmaceuticals	AS,Ch,Ph	NR	29	1836	Bio-pharmaceutical R&D	11⅞	7½	16¼	6⅝	25⅛	12⅞	13374	25⅛	17⅛	25	...	d	75.4	...	...
28	IBCP	✓Independent Bank	NNM	A	19	565	Commercial banking,Michigan	22⅛	5⅜	23¾	17⅝	28¾	22⅜	261	27¾	26¾	26¾	s3.6	11	28.7	20.5	39.3
29	IBK	Independent Bankshares	AS	NR	3	3	Bank holding, Texas	42⅛	1½	7⅛	5⅞	11¼	5¼	13	10¾	10⅝	10⅝B	1.1	17	86.2	44.7	...
30	INDHK	✓Independent Ins.[60] Gr[61]	NNM	B−	43	2702	Hldg:indust'l& ordinary life	22¾	2⅝	16¾	9¾	27½	11	2998	27½	26¾	27¼	0.9	22	135	22.0	15.0
#31	IEI	✓Indiana Energy	NY,Ch,Ph	B+	98	4383	Hldg co:gas service, Indiana	24⅞	2 5/16	23⅜	17½	24⅛	17⅝	3668	24⅛	22⅝	23⅞	4.6	16	22.7	13.9	15.5
32	INDGF	Indigo N.V.	NNM	NR	..	...	Mfr offset color printing sys	...	...	20¾	13	64¾	7	29313	13	9½	10½	...	d	−31.7	...	...
33	IHII	Industrial Holdings	NNM	NR	10	306	Dstr values,pipe to petrol ind	5	2⅝	5¼	2¼	4¾	2⅞	3169	4⅛	3¼	4⅛	...	19	15.8	4.4	...
34	NTZ	✓Industrie Natuzzi ADS[62]	NY,Ph	NR	86	7423	Mfr contemporary furniture	28	13	36	24¾	46¾	30⅝	5135	46¾	43	45⅜	0.1	24	35.8	...	...
35	INFR	✓Inference Corp 'A'	NNM	NR	47	3105	Dvlp client/server software	...	...	...	...	20½	11	18298	20½	16¾	19	...	50	...	...	...
36•[8]	INF	✓Infinity Broadcasting'A'	NY,Ch,Ph	NR	200	37365	Own/operate radio stations	23¾	3⅛	22½	13½	38½	20⅛	44529	38½	31	37¼	...	53	84.1	73.8	...
#37•[2]	IRIC	✓Information Resources	NNM	B−	121	21974	Data base prod mktg info svc	44¾	7⅝	39¾	11¼	18⅝	10	41351	12¾	11⅜	12⅜	...	d	−6.6	−25.4	...
38	ISDI	✓Information Storage Devices	NNM	NR	49	4972	Dvp/mkt integrated circuits	...	...	...	...	29⅛	8	46331	18¼	8	11⅛	...	15	...	...	...
#39•[9]	IFMX	✓Informix Corp	NNM	B	440	123243	Mkts database mgmt softw	13⅝	5/16	16⅛	7⅛	34⅜	14⅝	470021	30¾	24⅛	30	...	43	99.4	56.5	124
40	IFRA	✓Infrasonics Inc	NNM	B−	12	1088	Mfr respiratory care prod	13⅝	1¾	6	2⅜	7⅛	2⅜	10587	6⅝	5	6	...	d	100	−19.5	6.5
¶41•[10]	IR	✓Ingersoll-Rand	NY,B,Ch,P,Ph	B+	473	72037	Std mchny,eqp:bear'gs,tools	39⅞	7⅛	41⅝	29½	42⅜	28⅜	58244	38⅜	33⅝	35⅛	2.1	14	12.0	7.5	16.3
¶42•[11]	IAD	✓Inland Steel Indus	NY,B,C,Ch,P,Ph	C	270	32502	Integrated steel producer	58⅝	14½	42	29⅜	36¾	21¼	30844	27½	24½	25⅛	0.8	10	−27.3	3.4	0.8
43	INMC	✓Inmac Corp[65]	NNM	B−	26	2550	Mkts data communic'ns	25⅛	2¾	9¾	3	11⅝	4¼	69876	11⅝	9	11½	...	28	137	56.8	23.7
44	ISER	✓InnoServ Technologies	NNM	B−	9	469	Medical diagnostic imag'g sv	10⅛	2¼	6	3¼	4⅝	2	1698	4⅝	2	4	...	d	23.1	−4.2	2.6
45	INVX	✓Innovex Inc	NNM	↑B	34	2241	Thin-film disk drive pd	13⅜	1/32	11⅛	5	24¾	9⅝	24102	21⅛	15¼	15¼	1.0	11	42.5	69.0	48.2
46	INVR	Innovir Laboratories	NSC	NR	1	.3	Dvlp stge: biopharm'l R&D	6⅜	4	9⅛	5¾	12½	1¾	36140	4⅜	2¾	4⅛	...	d	−50.7	...	...
47	IMMI	✓InPhyNet Medical Mgmt	NNM	NR	37	1829	Physician mgmt svcs	...	...	14½	9¾	25¼	11⅜	13411	25¼	17¾	24	...	26	111	...	...
✣48•[2]	IO	✓Input/Output Inc	NY,Ph	NR	189	18523	Mfr seismic data acquis'n sys	12¼	2¾	27¼	11⅞	57¾	22	17099	57¾	45½	57¾	...	39	141	119	...
49	IFS	✓Insignia Financial Grp'A'	NY	NR	45	4540	Real estate management svcs	24¼	16	24¼	15½	38½	19¼	9947	38½	33⅛	38½	...	63	85.5	...	...
50	INSGY	Insignia Solutions ADS[68]	NNM	NR	..	...	Dvlp/mkt software solutions	...	...	...	...	22	11¼	13534	22	11¼	11¾	...	20	...	...	...
51	INSL	✓Insilco Corp	NNM	NR	40	2275	Auto,tele'n,elec prd/publish'g	15¼	11¾	29	13⅝	41¼	23¼	4186	33¼	30	31⅞	...	d	32.8	...	...
✣52•[12]	INSUA	✓Insituform Technol'A'	NNM	B−	71	6484	Mkts sewer/PL repair process	26½	1⅛	15⅜	10½	16⅝	11⅛	14270	11⅞	11⅛	11⅝	...	23	0.0	−22.5	23.8

Uniform Footnote Explanations-See Page 4. Other: [1]NY,P:Cycle 1. [2]CBOE:Cycle 2. [3]ASE:Cycle 3. [4]NY:Cycle 1. [5]CBOE,NY:Cycle 1. [6]Ph:Cycle 1. [7]ASE:Cycle 1,To:Cycle 2. [8]CBOE:Cycle 3. [9]ASE:Cycle 2. [10]NY:Cycle 3. [11]Ph:Cycle 3. [12]P:Cycle 3. [51]Fiscal Mar'92 & prior. [52]12 Mo Dec'92. [53]Amer Home Prod(55%)prop acq,$14.50:Co rejects. [54]7 Mo Dec'93. [55]ADR equals 4 ord shrs,1'. [56]To be determined. [57]100% non-taxable,'94. [58]Incl redeemable shrs. [59]Special divd incl redemption of stk purch rt. [60]Non-vtg. [61]American General plan acq, $27.50 cash &/or stk. [62]Ea ADS rep 1 ord shr Lit.250. [63]Stk dstr of VideOcart Inc. [64]®$1.70,'94. [65]Micro Warehouse plan acq. [66]®$1.39,'95. [67]Pfd in $M. [68]Ea ADS rep 1 ord,0.20p.

Splits ◆ Index	Cash Divs. Ea.Yr. Since	Dividends: Latest Payment Period $	Date	Ex. Div.	Total $ So Far 1995	Ind. Rate	Paid 1994	Financial Position Mil-$ Cash& Equiv.	Curr. Assets	Curr. Liab.	Balance Sheet Date	Capitalization Lg Trm Debt Mil-$	Shs. 000 Pfd.	Com.	Earnings $ Per Shr. Years End	1991	1992	1993	1994	1995	Last 12 Mos.	Interim Earnings Period	$ per Shr. 1994	1995	Index
1◆	1995	Q0.08	12-29-95	12-13	0.28	0.32	....	218	591	291	9-30-95	516	...	59496	Je	1.93	□2.06	□d2.72	□d0.07	□2.15	2.29	3 Mo Sep	□0.37	0.51	1
2	....	None Since Public			...	Nil	....	2.30	2.60	6.01	9-30-95	3.94	...	13766	Dc	[51]d1.81	[52]d1.56	d1.58	d1.12	....	d0.36	9 Mo Sep	d1.18	d0.42	2
3	1995	Q0.03½	12-15-95	11-28	†0.20½	0.14	....	10.7	35.3	19.1	9-30-95	15.0	...	11754	Dc	0.52	0.67	0.70	0.73	....	1.00	9 Mo Sep	0.49	0.76	3
4	....	None Paid			...	Nil	....	0.12	4.73	1.52	9-30-95	....	...	6865	Je	0.05	0.08	d0.04	0.03	d0.06	d0.08	3 Mo Sep	Nil	d0.02	4
5	....	None Paid			...	Nil	....	1.47	2.57	0.66	9-30-95	0.65	...	2292	Dc	d0.69	d0.11	d0.01	d0.06	....	d0.03	9 Mo Sep	d0.03	Nil	5
6	....	None Since Public			...	Nil	....	49.7	50.5	7.27	12-31-94	....	...	★19516	Dc	d1.20	d0.70	d1.30	d1.70	....	d1.26	9 Mo Sep	d1.25	d0.81	6
7	....	None Since Public			...	Nil	....	49.3	50.1	1.33	9-30-95	....	...	16762	Dc	d0.23	d2.19	d0.95	d1.05	....	d1.09	9 Mo Sep	d0.80	d0.84	7
8◆	....	None Since Public			...	Nil	....	14.3	47.4	29.6	9-30-95	4.87	...	39602	Dc	0.05	d5.21	[54]d9.58	d0.85	Ed0.50	d0.37	9 Mo Sep	d0.71	d0.23	8
9	....	None Since Public			...	Nil	....	29.4	30.4	4.41	9-30-95	....	205	32777	Je	d0.20	d0.05	d0.32	d0.50	d0.38	d0.39	3 Mo Sep	d0.10	d0.11	9
10	....	None Since Public			...	Nil	....	35.7	42.7	2.72	9-30-95	....	...	8318	Je	...	...	d1.28	d1.73	d0.98	d0.60	3 Mo Sep	d0.37	0.01	10
11	....	0.12½	10-15-92	9-21	...	Nil	....	2.31	194	116	9-30-95	231	...	17084	Dc	0.68	□d3.26	□d14.95	□0.54	....	2.69	9 Mo Sep	□0.32	□2.47	11
12◆	....	5%Stk	2-24-95	2-13	5%Stk	Stk	5%Stk	Book Value $15.70			9-30-95	5.90	...	13794	Dc	0.20	0.89	0.08	0.49	....	1.20	9 Mo Sep	0.31	1.02	12
13◆	1927	0.771	10-17-95	8-28	1.932	1.93	1.787	1759	4972	2608	j12-31-94	1522	...	724000	Dc	5.71	d5.54	1.14	1.59	E4.75	3.16	6 Mo Jun	Δ1.08	Δ2.65	13
14	....	Plan qtly div			...	[56]....	....	Equity per shr $10.59			9-30-95	....	...	★4250	Dc	...	...	...	pd0.65	....	....	9 Mo Sep	n/a	p0.17	14
15	1988	0.04	5-16-95	5-3	0.08	Nil	0.16	38.8	189	102	9-30-95	95.3	...	10307	Mr	d0.28	□0.01	d0.78	d0.52	....	d0.59	6 Mo Sep	d0.01	Δd0.08	15
16	1891	gQ0.50	1-1-96	11-30	g1.85	2.00	g†4.80	528	3280	1789	j9-30-95	1964	...	191186	Dc	0.84	1.01	j1.44	1.85	E2.93	j2.70	9 Mo Sep	1.33	2.18	16
17	....	None Since Public			...	Nil	....	Book Value $9.11			9-30-95	0.75	...	★5200	Dc	1.08	0.55	1.12	0.93	....	d0.91	9 Mo Sep	0.83	d1.01	17
18	....	None Since Public			...	Nil	....	35.1	88.7	20.1	9-30-95	....	...	10793	Dc	0.53	0.42	0.53	0.89	....	1.85	9 Mo Sep	0.43	1.39	18
19	....	None Since Public			...	Nil	....	1.95	18.3	16.7	6-30-95	2.55	...	p9393	Sp	0.11	0.15	□0.07	0.02	P0.10	0.10				19
20	....	None Since Public			...	Nil	....	15.4	443	356	9-30-95	23.7	...	10013	Dc	0.56	1.25	Δ1.23	d0.22	....	0.95	9 Mo Sep	d0.46	0.71	20
21◆	....	None Since Public			...	Nil	....	....	21.2	14.9	9-30-95	14.1	...	7840	Je	0.23	0.34	Δd0.18	0.81	0.96	0.90	3 Mo Sep	0.23	0.17	21
22	1934	tQ0.10	12-1-95	10-31	0.40	0.40	t0.40	76.6	1472	675	9-30-95	807	7734	118061	Dc	0.74	d0.21	0.22	0.15	E2.05	2.20	9 Mo Sep	d0.68	1.37	22
23◆	1985	Q0.15	12-31-95	12-13	0.60	0.60	[57]0.60	Equity per shr $30.58			9-30-95	20.3	...	[58]791	Dc	Δd9.97	d0.64	Δ0.09	d0.36	....	d1.55	9 Mo Sep	d0.09	d1.28	23
24	....	None Since Public			...	Nil	....	4.74	20.3	14.5	9-30-95	1.40	...	13600	Dc	Nil	*Δd0.29	Δd0.20	0.42	....	0.42	9 Mo Sep	0.28	0.28	24
25	....	None Since Public			...	Nil	....	26.1	27.8	2.80	9-30-95	2.35	...	13779	Dc	...	...	p1.23	pd1.83	....	d1.83	9 Mo Sep	pd1.37	pd1.37	25
26◆	....	[59]7.50	1-16-90	1-17	...	Nil	....	0.01	21.8	6.63	9-29-95	1.26	...	16363	Dc	*□0.23	0.30	0.02	d0.28	....	Nil	9 Mo Sep	d0.11	0.17	26
27	....	None Since Public			...	Nil	....	11.6	12.1	3.56	9-30-95	0.06	...	★9654	Dc	...	pd0.49	d2.26	d1.68	....	d1.51	9 Mo Sep	d1.16	d0.99	27
28◆	1974	sQ0.24	1-31-96	1-3	s0.648	0.96	0.714	Book Value $16.60			9-30-95	....	...	2709	Dc	□1.71	1.94	2.14	2.19	....	2.42	9 Mo Sep	1.60	1.83	28
29◆	1994	Q0.03	11-30-95	11-13	0.11¼	0.12	0.068	Book Value $12.82			9-30-95	1.07	17	1039	Dc	0.13	Δ0.73	Δ0.91	0.37	....	0.64	9 Mo Sep	0.48	0.75	29
30	1939	Q0.06	12-1-95	11-8	0.24	0.24	0.24	Equity per shr $25.49			9-30-95	5.40	...	±13165	Dc	2.18	□d1.15	□0.49	0.84	....	1.23	9 Mo Sep	0.53	0.92	30
31◆	1946	Q0.27½	12-1-95	11-13	1.08	1.10	1.04	0.02	84.5	112	9-30-95	176	...	22562	Sp	1.11	1.16	1.62	1.53	1.46	1.46				31
32	....	None Since Public			...	Nil	....	7.69	27.7	58.3	3-31-94	p....	p...	★50000	Dc	p0.01	pd0.36	pd0.84	Pd0.61	....	d0.40	9 Mo Sep	d0.63	d0.42	32
33	....	None Paid			...	Nil	....	0.08	13.1	10.4	9-30-95	3.10	...	3091	Dc	d1.39	0.17	0.27	0.01	....	0.22	9 Mo Sep	d0.05	0.16	33
34	1994	0.06	7-13-95	6-29	0.06	0.06	0.061	54.5	238	105	12-31-94	6.47	...	28183	Dc	0.84	0.77	1.32	1.69	....	1.93	6 Mo Jun	0.78	1.02	34
35	....	None Since Public			...	Nil	....	24.7	31.8	6.88	10-31-95	....	...	7395	Ja	...	...	...	p0.18	....	0.38	9 Mo Oct	p0.07	0.27	35
36◆	....	None Since Public			...	Nil	....	9.21	94.3	48.9	9-30-95	553	...	±55793	Dc	...	□d0.20	0.23	0.49	....	0.71	9 Mo Sep	0.28	0.50	36
37	....	h[63]....	10-31-90	10-15	...	Nil	....	35.6	155	101	9-30-95	4.22	...	27355	Dc	0.63	0.78	Δ0.82	□d0.34	....	d0.61	9 Mo Sep	□d0.17	d0.44	37
38	....	None Since Public			...	Nil	....	76.9	92.6	12.0	9-30-95	2.67	...	10384	Dc	d3.22	d2.87	Nil	0.63	....	0.74	9 Mo Sep	0.38	0.49	38
39◆	....	None Since Public			...	Nil	....	211	414	218	10-01-95	....	...	134567	Dc	Δ0.11	0.38	0.42	0.49	E0.70	0.65	9 Mo Sep	0.32	0.48	39
40◆	....	None Paid			...	Nil	....	6.73	19.8	1.82	9-30-95	....	...	10444	Je	0.09	0.19	0.13	0.06	d0.13	d0.10	3 Mo Sep	Nil	0.03	40
41◆	1910	Q0.18½	12-1-95	11-13	0.74	0.74	0.72	197	2450	1423	9-30-95	1384	...	108906	Dc	1.45	□1.11	□1.56	2.00	E2.45	2.39	9 Mo Sep	1.26	1.65	41
42	....	Q0.05	2-1-96	1-5	0.15	0.20	....	182	1272	584	9-30-95	870	3200	48772	Dc	d9.88	□d5.83	d1.96	[64]1.81	E2.65↑	2.90	9 Mo Sep	1.15	2.24	42
43	....	0.05	4-12-89	3-28	...	Nil	....	10.5	102	48.1	10-28-95	20.5	...	10579	Jl	0.72	0.10	d1.47	0.17	0.42	0.42	3 Mo Oct	0.10	0.10	43
44◆	1988	0.04	11-17-94	11-1	...	Nil	†0.31	0.92	19.4	15.4	7-31-95	0.06	...	5036	Ap	0.11	d1.37	0.76	□0.32	d0.81	d0.51	6 Mo Oct	d0.29	0.01	44
45◆	1993	Q0.04	11-30-95	11-13	0.16	0.16	0.147	22.5	32.2	3.87	9-30-95	1.17	...	7074	Sp	0.10	0.02	0.55	0.52	[66]1.40	1.40				45
46	....	None Since Public			...	Nil	....	3.25	3.28	0.65	6-30-95	0.61	773	3736	Sp	d6.24	d13.49	□d8.73	d1.12	Pd1.42	d1.42				46
47	....	None Since Public			...	Nil	....	3.47	77.0	33.0	p6-30-95	6.86	...	★16659	Dc	...	...	p0.69	p0.82	....	0.92	9 Mo Sep	p0.59	□0.69	47
48◆	....	None Since Public			...	Nil	....	0.21	151	55.3	8-31-95	p....	...	★20784	My	0.50	0.54	0.61	1.05	1.31	1.50	6 Mo Nov	0.58	0.77	48
49	....	None Since Public			...	Nil	....	Equity per shr $8.03			9-30-95	97.1	[67]15	±★12900	Dc	...	p0.79	□0.68	0.71	....	0.61	9 Mo Sep	0.51	0.41	49
50	....	None Since Public			...	Nil	....	22.6	29.8	23.2	9-30-95	0.37	p...	★11118	Dc	0.15	0.02	d2.54	0.42	....	0.58	9 Mo Sep	0.25	0.41	50
51	....	None Since Public			...	Nil	....	3.46	179	120	9-30-95	184	...	9572	Dc	...	...	pd7.09	□d3.09	....	d0.50	9 Mo Sep	d2.41	0.18	51
52	....	None Since Public			...	Nil	....	14.3	76.2	29.2	9-30-95	52.9	...	p27102	Dc	*1.77	d0.45	Δ0.34	0.60	....	0.51	9 Mo Sep	0.50	0.41	52

◆Stock Splits & Divs By Line Reference Index [1]2-for-1,'95. [8]No adj for spl $23 dstr,'93. [12]Adj to 5%,'95. [13]No adj for stk dstr of Zeneca Group plc,'93. [21]3-for-2,'94. [23]1-for-4 REVERSE,'91. [26]No adj for spl $7.49 dstr, '90. [28]Adj for 5%,'95. [29]5%,'93:4-for-3,'95. [31]3-for-2,'93. [36]3-for-2,'93(twice),'95. [39]2-for-1,'92,'93,'95. [40]1-for-2 REVERSE,'91. [41]2-for-1,'92. [44]10%,'93. [45]3-for-2,'95. [48]2-for-1,'94:To split 2-for-1,ex Jan 10.

¶ S&P 500
\# MidCap 400
✤ SmallCap 600
• Options

Index	Ticker	Name of Issue (Call Price of Pfd. Stocks)	Market	Com. Rank. & Pfd. Rating	Inst. Hold Cos	Inst. Hold Shs. (000)	Principal Business	Price Range 1971-93 High	1971-93 Low	1994 High	1994 Low	1995 High	1995 Low	Dec. Sales in 100s	December, 1995 Last Sale Or Bid High	Low	Last	%Div Yield	P-E Ratio	Total Return % Annualized 12 Mo	36 Mo	60 Mo
1	INSO	✔INSO Corp	NNM	NR	82	8301	Mkt/dvp textual info software	....	....	17⅞	7½	47½	16½	16132	47½	39½	42½	...	..	152	...	...
✤2	III	✔Insteel Industries Inc	NY	B	39	2953	Mfrs wire & wire products	12¾	2⅞	12⅛	6⅞	8⅞	6⅜	3220	7	6⅜	6⅞	3.5	9	−2.0	−8.7	14.3
3	ININ	✔InStent Inc	NNM	NR	39	3364	Mfr specialized medical prod	....	....	....	....	18½	12½	10556	16	12½	15	...	d	...	...	...
4	ISN	✔Instron Corp	AS,B,Ch	B	27	1990	Material testing equip	18⅜	7/16	13⅛	9½	14½	11⅛	654	14½	12⅛	13½	1.2	18	12.6	11.8	11.3
✤5	IAAI	✔Insurance Auto Auctions	NNM	NR	90	8250	Sells insur recovered vehicles	45½	11	38⅝	24½	36	6½	10252	11¼	8¾	10¾	...	36	−65.0	−20.9	...
✤6	IN	✔Integon Corp	NY,Ph	NR	74	8035	Nonstandard auto insurance	34⅞	13½	20⅞	12	21¼	11¾	14656	21¼	16¾	20⅝	1.7	13	65.3	−5.7	...
7	Pr	$3.875 cm Cv Pfd ([52]52.33)	NY	BB+	27	977		....	....	52½	44½	61¼	43⅝	2299	61¼	53⅞	60	6.5	..	...	...	...
8	ITG	✔Integra Finl Corp[53]	NY	B+	133	15534	Commercial banking, Penna	50¾	3⅞	49¾	38⅜	64⅝	36⅞	15573	64⅝	61⅛	63⅛	3.2	13	62.9	19.1	36.7
9	IBIN	✔Integrated Brands 'A'	NSC	NR	3	62	Sells ice cream/franch stores	4	½	1⅝	¾	2⅛	1	4059	1⅜	1	1 1/16	...	15	−10.5	−22.1	9.1
✤10•[1]	ICST	✔Integrated Circuit Sys	NNM	B	52	2946	Design, mfr integrated circuits	25	4⅜	15¾	6¾	18⅞	7⅜	21944	14⅝	10¾	12⅜	...	23	57.1	−6.0	...
#11•[2]	IDTI	✔Integrated Device Tech	NNM,Ch	B−	275	53129	Mfrs integrated circuits	9⅞	1 9/16	17¼	8	33½	12¼	463099	17¼	12¼	12⅞	...	8	−14.1	57.4	50.2
✤12•[3]	IHS	✔Integrated Health Svcs	NY,Ch	NR	191	18394	Oper geriatric medl facilities	31⅜	13¾	41⅛	28⅛	42½	19⅝	42564	26⅜	21⅞	25	0.1	10	−36.5	1.4	...
13	IMSC	✔Integrated Measurement Sys	NNM	NR	20	1507	Dgn/mfr test software	....	....	....	....	16⅝	11	15867	15¾	13	14¾	...	31	...	...	...
14	ISSI	✔Integrated Silicon Solution	NNM	NR	99	6294	Mfrs integrated circuits	....	....	....	....	73¼	13	196035	24	15	16¾	...	9	...	...	...
15	INTS	✔Integrated Systems Inc	NNM	↑B	57	3288	Dvlp CAE/CASE software prod	17¼	5¼	19⅜	8⅜	42	17¾	12158	39½	34¾	39	...	68	114	80.6	28.8
¶16•[4]	INTC	✔Intel Corp	NNM	B	1608	489761	Semiconductor memory circts	37⅛	1/16	36¾	28	78⅜	31½	1553046	64	55⅛	56¾	0.3	14	77.0	37.2	43.4
17•[5]	ITR	✔IntelCom Group	AS,Ch,Vc	NR	84	12880	Telecommunications services	25⅝	2½	25¼	9½	14⅛	6⅝	35702	12½	9⅝	12¼	...	d	−7.5	37.8	...
18	ICOMF	Intelect Communications[57]	NNM	B−	20	2319	Manufactures sporting arms	16	⅛	3¼	1¾	6⅝	1⅞	10769	5½	3⅞	5½	...	43	162	77.2	86.0
19	ICL	✔Intellicall Inc	NY,Ph	NR	24	1379	Mfr/mkt pay telephones	18½	3	9⅝	3¾	7¼	3	4764	4⅛	3¼	3¾	...	d	−6.3	−10.6	−16.5
20	ITC.EC	✔Intelligent Controls	ECM	NR	1	2	Mfr ind'l monitoring,ctrl eqp	....	....	....	....	6½	3⅛	239	4¼	3¾	4	...	40	...	...	...
#21•[6]	INEL	✔Intelligent Electronics	NNM	NR	114	19143	Dstr/sell computer prod	30⅜	1¼	27⅝	7½	14⅝	6	61948	8¼	6	6	6.7	d	−25.1	−16.7	−7.2
22	INS	✔Intelligent Systems	AS,P	C	5	570	Personal computer enhanc'mt	32¾	⅞	2½	1¾	2¾	1⅜	952	2⅜	2⅛	2⅛	...	d	0.0	9.4	...
23	IPR	✔Inter-City Products	AS,To	NR	23	4233	Mfr heat/cooling equip,pipe	8¼	2¼	3⅞	2⅛	2¾	13/16	15278	1 5/16	13/16	1 3/16	...	d	−47.2	−39.6	−15.5
✤24	IFG	✔Inter-Regional Fin. Gr.	NY,B,Ch	B−	63	3601	Brokerage/investm't bkg svcs	22⅝	⅞	21¾	13⅜	27⅛	14⅞	5554	27⅛	25¼	25¼	1.7	11	77.2	33.5	52.9
25	INTL	✔Inter-Tel Inc	NNM	B	68	7472	Mfr electronic telecommun eqp	25¾	11/16	12⅛	6	19¾	6⅞	19483	17	14⅝	15⅜	...	22	113	50.1	72.9
26	ICAR	✔Intercargo Corp	NNM	B+	31	4501	Underwriters specialized insur	17	3¼	12¼	7¼	14¾	8	3181	10½	8¼	10	1.8	10	23.5	−5.5	18.1
27	ISB	✔Interchange Finl Svcs	AS	A−	21	707	Commercial banking,New Jersey	21¾	1⅞	16¾	14	23	14⅝	230	21¼	20¼	21	3.4	10	46.6	20.9	33.2
28	ISS	✔INTERCO Inc	NY,Ph	NR	74	49921	Mfr residential furniture	54	6⅝	15¾	6⅛	9¼	5½	18679	9¼	8	9	...	25	...	...	...
29•[7]	IDC	✔Interdigital Communications	AS,Ph	C	48	4887	Wireless digital communic prd	20⅝	2⅜	7⅞	2	12⅞	4¾	96997	9½	7⅛	7⅜	...	8	5.4	−7.3	11.0
✤30	IFSIA	✔Interface Inc'A'	NNM	A−	87	11999	Mfr carpet/tile	19¾	3¼	17	9¾	18	11⅝	16628	17⅜	15⅞	17	1.4	17	42.5	11.7	14.5
31	INTF	✔Interface Systems	NNM	↓B−	20	1338	Document mgmt sys/com prod	11	⅝	10	3⅞	13½	4	27323	13½	6	12¾	1.3	..	77.3	...	...
¶32•[8]	INGR	✔Intergraph Corp	NNM	C	221	19302	Computer graphics systems	40½	3⅞	11¼	7⅜	18½	8⅛	68532	18¼	14⅞	15¾	...	d	93.8	5.9	2.9
✤33•[9]	INTM	✔Interim Services	NNM	NR	116	11250	Temporary help services	....	....	28¼	20	35½	22⅝	14579	35½	31¾	34¾	...	25	44.0	...	...
34	IK	✔Interlake Corp	NY,B,Ch,P	NR	32	7054	Diversified ind'l mfg co	61¾	2⅜	3¾	1½	3¼	1⅝	8954	2½	1¾	2½	...	d	42.9	−10.6	−6.5
35	IRC.EC	✔Interline Resources	ECM	NR	10	541	Natl gas gathering/oil prod'n	9¼	6¾	9½	3⅞	6⅝	2½	2457	5	4	4⅜	...	d	−2.8	...	...
36	INLQ	✔INTERLINQ Software	NNM	NR	14	1644	Dvlp mtge lending software	9¼	6	9	3⅜	4⅜	2⅞	8586	3⅝	3	3½	...	d	−6.7	...	...
✤37•[10]	IMG	✔Intermagnetics Genl	AS	B	36	1613	Mfr superconductive mtls	17¼	2¼	19¾	9½	27⅛	10	32025	27⅛	19⅜	21	...	50	69.7	52.8	39.7
✤38•[11]	INMT	✔Intermet Corp[62]	NNM	C	71	12357	Iron foundry-auto indus	19	3⅝	10½	4¾	14⅛	6¼	15464	12½	9½	10½	...	70	50.0	2.9	18.3
39	ICM	Internacional De Ceramica ADS[63]	NY	NR	10	881	Mfr glazed ceramic tile-Mexico	....	....	21¾	20	21½	4¼	835	5¾	5⅛	5½	...	d	−73.2	...	...
40	IAL	✔Intl Aluminum	NY,B,Ch,P	B+	50	1694	Mfr & sale aluminum prod	30¾	1	31¼	23⅝	36¾	28	898	29⅜	28⅛	28¾	3.5	10	−3.2	16.3	9.0
¶41•[1]	IBM	✔Intl Bus. Machines	[12]NY,To,B,C,Ch,P,Ph	B−	1422	277782	Lgst mfr business machines	175⅞	37⅝	76⅜	51⅜	114⅝	70¼	595818	97¼	87¾	91⅜	1.1	8	24.2	24.8	−1.0
42•[3]	ICTL	✔Intl Cabletel	NNM	NR	165	24737	Telecommunications svcs	23⅛	1⅞	25	13	28⅞	20¼	22788	25⅞	23⅝	24½	...	d	19.7	77.6	...
43•[8]	KCN	✔Intl Colin Energy	NY,To,Ch	NR	44	4800	Oil&gas explor,dev,prod'n	21⅜	2¾	15½	6	7½	4⅜	4114	5⅛	4½	4¾	...	..	−25.5	...	...
#44	INDQA	✔Intl Dairy Queen 'A'	NNM	B+	111	9077	Lmtd menu stores: franch'g	25¾	1/16	18½	15¾	24¾	16	9688	24¾	22¼	22¾	...	16	37.9	4.8	6.9
✤45•[9]	FAM	✔Intl Family Entert'nt 'B'	NY,Ph	NR	96	17459	Oper cable TV'Family Channel'	25⅛	9⅛	22¼	12⅛	20⅝	12⅜	14048	19¼	16⅛	16⅜	...	33	33.7	6.0	...
¶46•[13]	IFF	✔Intl Flavors/Fragr	NY,B,C,Ch,P,Ph	A+	539	59403	Dev&mfr flavor&fragr prod	39⅞	5½	47⅞	35⅝	55⅞	45⅛	43952	55⅞	47¾	48	2.8	21	5.3	12.8	17.8
#47•[10]	IGT	✔Intl Game Technology	NY,Ch,Ph	B	186	47698	Coin oper video/reel games	41⅜	7/16	34	14⅞	17	10¾	209407	12⅝	10¾	10¾	1.1	15	−31.2	−22.3	43.3
48	IMAK	✔Intl Imaging Materials	NNM	NR	81	4839	Mfr thermal transfer ribbons	20½	14	33¾	15	32¼	18	6637	28½	24¼	25¼	...	25	−23.5	...	...
49	IJIN	✔Intl Jensen	NNM	NR	24	1298	Mfr loudspeakers & compon'ts	16	6	10¼	6½	12	6⅝	2542	7¾	6⅝	6¾	...	11	−28.9	−5.5	...
50	ILI	✔Intl Lottery	AS,Ch,Ph	NR	5	32	Mfr instant lottery machines	....	....	13⅛	6⅞	13⅝	5¾	1472	10¾	7⅜	8⅜	...	36	−4.3	...	...
#51	IMC	✔Intl Multifoods	NY,Ch,P	B+	148	10524	Diversified food prod/svcs	31½	3¾	19⅛	15⅛	23⅞	17⅝	6690	23⅞	18⅞	20⅛	4.0	13	17.0	−6.1	−0.1
52•[11]	MURXF	✔Intl Murex Technologies	NNM,Ch	NR	13	662	Mfr medical diagnostic prod	17⅜	2⅞	6½	3¼	5½	2½	11879	3¼	2⅝	3⅛	...	d	−10.7	−24.5	−6.5

Uniform Footnote Explanations-See Page 4. Other: [1]CBOE:Cycle 1. [2]CBOE,NY,Ph:Cycle 2. [3]CBOE:Cycle 3. [4]ASE,CBOE,P:Cycle 1. [5]ASE,CBOE:Cycle 3. [6]ASE,CBOE,P:Cycle 3. [7]P:Cycle 3. [8]ASE:Cycle 1. [9]NY:Cycle 2. [10]ASE,CBOE:Cycle 1. [11]ASE:Cycle 2. [12]Mo [13]CBOE:Cycle 2. [51]10 Mo Dec'91. [52]Fr 9-16-97,scale to $50 in 2003. [53]National City plan acq,2 com. [54]®$0.43,'95. [55]®$1.71,'94. [56]Incl redemption stk purch rt. [57]Formerly Challenger Int'l Ltd. [58]Fiscal Oct'91 & prior. [59]Stk dstr of Converse & Florsheim Shoe,'94. [60]Fiscal Mar'94 & prior. [61]Special divd. [62]GWM Inc prop acq,$13.50. [63]Ea ADS rep 5 Ltd Vtg Units(rep 1'D'&1'L'shr). [64]Excludes non-recurring charge. [65]Stk dstr of Pembina Ltd. [66]Fiscal June'92 & prior. [67]®$1.05,'94.

Index	Splits ◆ Cash Divs. Ea.Yr. Since	Dividends Latest Payment Period $	Date	Ex. Div.	Total $ So Far 1995	Ind. Rate	Paid 1994	Financial Position Mil-$ Cash& Equiv.	Curr. Assets	Curr. Liab.	Balance Sheet Date	Capitalization Lg Trm Debt Mil-$	Shs. 000 Pfd.	Com.	Earnings $ Per Shr. Years End	1991	1992	1993	1994	1995	Last 12 Mos.	Interim Earnings Period	$ per Shr. 1994	1995	Index
1◆	....	None Since Public			...	Nil	....	53.5	62.9	13.9	9-30-95	....	...	12952	Dc	...	p0.15	p0.24	p0.48	....	0.27	9 Mo Sep	p0.33	0.12	1
2◆	1986	Q0.06	1-2-96	12-13	0.24	0.24	0.24	0.76	78.3	49.9	6-30-95	25.0	...	8377	Sp	Δ0.26	0.67	0.80	Δ0.45	P0.76	0.76				2
3	....	None Since Public			...	Nil	....	1.26	1.98	0.28	3-31-95	....	...	★9683	Dc	§[51]d0.09	d0.23	d0.44	d0.37	....	d0.25	9 Mo Sep	d0.27	d0.15	3
4	1973	Q0.04	1-5-96	12-6	0.14	0.16	0.12	2.75	75.8	35.8	9-30-95	15.2	...	6339	Dc	0.82	0.59	0.39	0.72	....	0.77	9 Mo Sep	0.37	0.42	4
5	....	None Since Public			...	Nil	....	7.57	44.6	30.1	9-30-95	28.7	...	11270	Dc	p0.35	0.61	0.74	0.98	E0.30	0.47	9 Mo Sep	0.72	0.21	5
6◆	1992	Q0.09	12-15-95	11-29	0.36	0.36	0.36	Equity per shr $7.13			9-30-95	151	1438	15705	Dc	p1.08	□p1.84	Δ2.53	Δ1.38	....	1.59	9 Mo Sep	Δ1.19	□1.40	6
7	1994	Q0.96⅞	12-15-95	11-29	3.87½	3.875	0.614	Cv into 2.625 com,$19.05				....	1250	...	Dc	...	...	...	....	....	....				7
8	1989	Q0.50	12-1-95	11-13	1.95	2.00	1.70	Book Value $32.75			9-30-95	1263	...	32917	Dc	2.89	4.54	Δ4.50	5.01	E4.90	4.80	9 Mo Sep	3.84	3.63	8
9	....	None Since Public			...	Nil	....	2.11	14.5	10.7	9-30-95	5.32	...	9953	Dc	0.15	0.11	0.04	0.09	....	0.07	9 Mo Sep	0.12	0.10	9
10◆	....	None Since Public			...	Nil	....	28.6	70.8	12.5	9-30-95	3.41	...	11293	Je	0.33	0.43	1.15	1.11	[54]0.45	0.54	3 Mo Sep	0.26	0.35	10
11◆	....	None Since Public			...	Nil	....	352	538	173	10-01-95	231	...	77253	Mr	d0.41	0.09	0.61	1.04	E1.68	1.34	6 Mo Sep	0.47	0.77	11
12	1995	0.02	1-10-96	12-27	0.02	0.02	....	35.7	268	165	9-30-95	692	...	21508	Dc	0.82	□1.04	□1.36	[55]1.96	E2.48↓	2.39	9 Mo Sep	1.39	□1.82	12
13	....	None Since Public			...	Nil	....	5.02	17.4	4.88	3-31-95	0.12	...	★6699	Dc	0.12	0.13	0.02	0.30	....	0.48	9 Mo Sep	0.18	0.36	13
14	....	None Since Public			...	Nil	....	41.6	62.8	18.0	3-31-95	2.87	...	★16593	Sp	...	...	...	p0.34	P1.79	1.79				14
15	....	None Since Public			...	Nil	....	22.1	38.8	16.2	8-31-95	....	...	9747	Fb	d0.85	0.37	0.44	0.60	....	0.57	9 Mo Nov	0.38	0.35	15
16◆	1992	Q0.04	3-1-96	1-30	0.14	0.16	[56]0.11¼	1954	8024	4162	9-30-95	401	...	821200	Dc	0.98	1.24	2.60	2.62	E4.18	3.49	9 Mo Sep	2.19	3.06	16
17◆	....	None Paid			...	Nil	....	11.4	59.8	69.6	6-30-95	114	1600	24469	Sp	d0.65	d0.40	d0.39	d1.56	Pd3.25	d3.25				17
18	....	0.10	2-3-86	1-13	...	Nil	....	3.00	15.1	8.83	10-31-94	2.24	...	10583	Oc	d0.15	Δ0.16	0.10	0.26	....	0.13	9 Mo Jul	0.19	0.06	18
19	....	None Since Public			...	Nil	....	3.57	43.0	33.8	9-30-95	1.10	...	7678	Dc	d0.70	d3.71	d0.17	d1.91	....	d0.90	9 Mo Sep	d1.27	d0.26	19
20	....	None Since Public			...	Nil	....	0.10	4.85	2.44	9-30-95	0.39	...	3211	Dc	*0.02	*0.03	□0.15	0.09	....	0.10	9 Mo Sep	0.07	0.08	20
21◆	1993	Q0.10	12-1-95	11-13	0.40	0.40	0.36	32.6	663	633	10-28-95	75.2	...	34537	Ja	[58]1.11	□0.06	1.18	0.23	Ed0.42↓	d0.57	9 Mo Oct	0.35	d0.45	21
22	....	0.10	9-19-89	8-25	...	Nil	....	1.07	10.5	6.16	9-30-95	0.05	...	5313	Dc	d0.27	d0.56	d0.07	d1.30	....	d0.23	9 Mo Sep	d1.08	d0.01	22
23	....	None Since Public			...	Nil	....	13.7	322	177	12-31-94	170	...	38822	Dc	d1.13	d0.40	d1.32	d0.29	....	d0.75	9 Mo Sep	d0.08	d0.54	23
24◆	1992	Q0.107	12-5-95	11-17	0.427	0.427	0.373	Equity per shr $17.73			9-30-95	42.7	...	12102	Dc	*Δ1.67	2.69	3.78	2.03	....	2.29	9 Mo Sep	1.74	2.00	24
25	....	None Since Public			...	Nil	....	38.5	90.0	19.0	9-30-95	....	...	12761	Dc	d0.53	0.37	0.45	0.58	....	0.69	9 Mo Sep	0.37	0.48	25
26◆	1992	S0.09	9-15-95	9-6	0.18	0.18	0.18	Equity per shr $5.68			9-30-95	9.74	...	7641	Dc	0.77	0.88	0.30	0.65	....	0.97	9 Mo Sep	0.43	0.75	26
27	1981	Q0.18	1-19-96	12-18	0.71½	0.72	0.70	Book Value $13.94			9-30-95	1.25	...	2697	Dc	1.26	1.79	□1.80	2.05	....	2.11	9 Mo Sep	1.53	1.59	27
28◆	....	h[59]....	11-18-94	11-21	...	Nil	h[59]....	61.4	438	125	9-30-95	381	...	50120	Dc	...	...	0.88	0.74	....	0.36	9 Mo Sep	0.76	0.38	28
29	....	None Since Public			...	Nil	....	69.1	79.7	16.7	9-30-95	0.72	105	44387	Dc	d0.39	d0.95	d1.11	d0.38	....	0.94	9 Mo Sep	d0.51	0.81	29
30	1977	Q0.06	11-24-95	11-8	0.24	0.24	0.24	3.03	280	112	10-01-95	p208	250	±18269	Dc	±0.52	±0.71	±0.75	±0.82	....	1.01	9 Mo Sep	±0.53	±0.72	30
31	1994	Q0.04	11-20-95	10-12	0.16	0.16	0.16	4.74	24.8	12.6	6-30-95	0.30	...	4212	Sp	0.16	0.35	0.41	□0.71	P0.04	0.04				31
32	....	None Since Public			...	Nil	....	41.0	486	248	9-30-95	27.5	...	46282	Dc	1.47	0.18	Δd2.56	d1.56	Ed1.05↓	d1.55	9 Mo Sep	d1.15	d1.14	32
33	....	None Since Public			...	Nil	....	0.73	173	120	9-29-95	....	...	11514	Dc	...	p0.77	[60]1.14	1.24	....	1.42	9 Mo Sep	0.85	1.03	33
34◆	....	[61]45.00	9-28-89	9-29	...	Nil	....	23.9	250	153	10-01-95	441	40	22816	Dc	d1.31	□d0.84	d1.18	□d1.84	....	d1.48	40 Wk Sep	□d0.30	□0.06	34
35	....	None Since Public			...	Nil	....	2.27	5.53	5.28	9-30-95	2.44	...	13950	Dc	0.01	0.01	Δ0.01	d0.05	....	d0.02	9 Mo Sep	d0.02	0.01	35
36	....	None Since Public			...	Nil	....	14.8	17.4	5.63	9-30-95	....	...	5981	Je	0.06	*0.27	*0.47	□0.46	d0.19	d0.20	3 Mo Sep	d0.01	d0.02	36
37◆	....	3%Stk	6-15-95	5-24	3%Stk	Stk	....	16.5	62.8	9.59	8-27-95	39.8	...	11734	My	0.29	0.43	0.32	Δ0.10	0.35	0.42	6 Mo Nov	0.09	0.16	37
38	1985	0.04	8-19-93	7-30	...	Nil	....	14.6	121	87.0	10-01-95	61.1	...	24738	Dc	0.42	□d0.06	d0.83	d0.45	....	0.15	9 Mo Sep	0.18	0.78	38
39	....	None Since Public			...	Nil	....	23.7	81.7	66.4	12-31-94	71.9	...	87856	Dc	p±0.90	p*±1.61	p*±0.82	d3.40	....	d3.40				39
40	1966	Q0.25	1-10-96	12-18	1.00	1.00	1.00	6.66	89.6	21.2	9-30-95	0.31	...	4257	Je	1.46	0.21	0.85	Δ1.74	3.18	2.82	3 Mo Sep	0.85	0.49	40
41	1916	Q0.25	12-9-95	11-8	1.00	1.00	1.00	6951	37642	29016	9-30-95	★11186	2611	p568723	Dc	□d0.99	Δd12.03	□d14.02	5.02	E[64]10.90	6.25	9 Mo Sep	2.96	4.19	41
42◆	....	None Since Public			...	Nil	....	342	369	94.3	9-30-95	505	...	30201	Dc	...	§d1.13	d0.83	d0.98	....	d2.18	9 Mo Sep	d0.70	d1.90	42
43	....	h[65]....	10-8-93	9-22	...	Nil	....	2.71	12.8	7.04	j9-30-95	65.8	...	12868	Dc	0.23	[66]0.51	1.23	0.70	....	j0.24	9 Mo Sep	0.63	0.17	43
44◆	....	None Since Public			...	Nil	....	40.5	96.9	36.4	8-25-95	25.0	...	±22810	Nv	±1.05	±1.12	±1.19	±1.30	E1.40	1.41	9 Mo Aug	±1.03	±1.14	44
45◆	....	None Since Public			...	Nil	....	40.6	212	93.2	9-30-95	164	220	±32319	Dc	1.08	1.17	□0.49	±0.38	....	0.49	9 Mo Sep	±0.25	±0.36	45
46◆	1956	Q0.34	1-11-96	12-22	1.24	1.36	1.08	285	1048	261	9-30-95	12.1	...	110966	Dc	1.47	□1.53	1.78	2.03	E2.24↓	2.27	9 Mo Sep	1.64	1.88	46
47◆	1993	Q0.03	12-1-95	10-30	0.12	0.12	0.12	258	573	79.9	6-30-95	112	...	129087	Sp	0.26	0.54	0.96	[67]1.07	P0.71	0.71				47
48	....	None Since Public			...	Nil	....	0.06	32.6	20.0	10-03-95	2.96	...	8954	Mr	0.29	0.50	0.71	1.10	....	1.02	6 Mo Sep	0.51	0.43	48
49	....	None Since Public			...	Nil	....	2.39	117	68.6	8-31-95	15.9	...	5714	Fb	1.59	0.93	Δd0.08	1.21	....	0.59	6 Mo Aug	0.69	0.07	49
50	....	None Since Public			...	Nil	....	....	10.7	12.4	9-30-95	0.49	1335	3210	Dc	...	...	p0.34	d0.32	....	0.23	9 Mo Sep	d0.16	0.39	50
51◆	1923	Q0.20	1-15-96	12-26	0.80	0.80	0.80	15.1	430	277	8-31-95	164	37	18024	Fb	□2.00	2.13	d0.72	3.16	E1.60↓	1.88	6 Mo Aug	1.91	0.63	51
52	....	None Since Public			...	Nil	....	16.5	70.0	33.4	9-30-95	0.37	...	16279	Dc	d0.62	d1.17	0.16	0.85	....	d0.21	9 Mo Sep	0.74	d0.32	52

◆**Stock Splits & Divs By Line Reference Index** [1]2-for-1,'95. [2]10%,'91,'92,'93. [6]10%,'92. [10]3-for-2,'93. [11]2-for-1,'95. [16]2-for-1,'93,'95. [17]1-for-5 REVERSE,'93. [21]2-for-1,'92. [24]3-for-2,'95. [26]2-for-1,'91. [28]No adj for stk dstr Converse & Florsheim Shoe,'94. [34]No adj for spl $45 dstr,'89. [37]5-for-4,'94:Adj to 3%,'95. [42]4-for-3,'95. [44]3-for-1,'91. [45]To split 5-for-4,ex Jan 8. [46]3-for-1,'94. [47]2-for-1,'91,'92,'93. [51]3-for-2,'91.

¶ S&P 500 # MidCap 400 ✢ SmallCap 600 • Options

Index	Ticker	Name of Issue (Call Price of Pfd. Stocks)	Market	Com. Rank. & Pfd. Rating	Inst. Hold Cos	Inst. Hold Shs. (000)	Principal Business	Price Range 1971-93 High	1971-93 Low	1994 High	1994 Low	1995 High	1995 Low	Dec. Sales in 100s	December, 1995 Last Sale Or Bid High	Low	Last	%Div Yield	P-E Ratio	Total Return % Annualized 12 Mo	36 Mo	60 Mo
¶1•[1]	IP	✔Intl Paper	NY,B,C,Ch,P,Ph,Mo	B+	813	191639	Mfr paper,pulp&wood prod	39¼	7⅛	40¼	30⅜	45¾	34⅛	240432	38⅜	35	37⅞	2.6	8	4.6	7.8	9.9
✢2•[2]	IRF	✔Intl Rectifier	NY,B,Ch,P	B–	165	34695	Power semiconductors	12⅝	½	12¼	6½	26	11⅛	64388	26	21⅝	25	...	27	116	65.0	37.6
3	IRI	✔Intl Remote Imaging	AS	B–	11	159	Mfr urinalysis workstation	50	⅝	7⅛	3⅞	8⅞	5¼	2089	8	6⅞	7⅞	...	d	50.0	28.1	31.1
4	IRM.A	Intl Road Dynamics 'A'	Vc	NR	..	...	Mfr traffic mgmt,monitor'g sys	....	....	1⅜	11/16	1	⅝	660	¾	⅝	11/16B	...	d	...	...	...
5	ISH	✔Intl Shipholding	NY	B+	44	3106	Ocean freight transportation	19⅞	1½	18½	14¾	21¾	15⅜	1853	20¾	19⅛	20¾	1.2	14	35.7	14.4	7.3
6•[3]	ISP	✔Intl Specialty Products	NY,Ph	NR	62	13888	Mfr specl derivative chemicals	18	5¾	8½	5⅜	11	6⅜	11794	11	9⅞	10⅞	...	18	61.7	7.6	...
7	ITX	✔Intl Technology	NY,B,Ch,Ph	C	67	15871	Waste mgmt services	27⅜	1⅞	4½	2	3⅞	2¼	31581	2⅞	2¼	2¾	...	d	–4.3	–19.4	–18.7
8	Pr	7% cm Cv Dep[51]Ex[52]Pfd([53]26.225)	NY	B	18	1118		25⅛	21¼	22⅝	15½	22⅛	15¾	6139	17⅝	16⅛	17⅝	9.9	..	...	...	...
9	ITB	✔Intl ThoroughBred	AS,Ch	↑B–	8	397	Operates racetracks:breeding	225	1⅞	8¼	2½	7¼	2⅝	2852	4¼	3¼	4	...	18	47.7	14.8	1.6
10	INB	Intl Thunderbird Gaming	Vc	NR	..	...	Mfr slot machines, gaming prd	4⅛	3/16	2¾	15/16	6⅜	1 3/16	12710	5⅞	4½	4¾B	...	16	...	...	...
11	IVCO	Intl Vitamin	NSC	NR	1	4	Dvlp,mfr vitamin products	....	....	5½	2⅜	3½	2	4463	3	2	2 7/16	...	35	–15.2	...	...
12	INCC	Internet Communications	NSC	NR	4	163	Telecommunication equip,svcs	16	2	11¼	3⅛	7⅝	3¼	4872	6⅜	3⅝	4¼	...	d	3.0	17.4	...
13	INPH	✔Interphase Corp	NNM	C	21	1735	Mfrs microcomputer prod	17¼	2½	13¼	4	18⅛	8⅛	3713	15½	11½	11⅝	...	21	34.8	18.4	18.4
14	INTP	✔Interpoint Corp	NNM	↑B	16	436	Mfr microcircuit compon'ts	12½	1⅛	13¾	6¾	12½	7	6235	12⅜	8¾	9⅜	...	12	13.6	6.0	15.2
15	IPX	✔Interpool, Inc	NY	NR	64	5214	Leases dry cargo containers	20½	14	20⅝	11½	18½	13¼	2476	18½	16¼	17⅞	...	11	18.2	...	...
16	Pr	5.75% Cv Pfd ([59]103.675)	NY	NR	..	...		....	....	....	....	94¼	88⅜	899	94¼	89⅜	93B	6.2	..	...	...	...
¶17•[4]	IPG	✔Interpublic Grp Cos	NY,To,Ch	A+	454	61532	Worldwide advertis'g agencies	35¾	⅜	35⅞	27½	43⅜	31¾	42412	43⅜	37⅞	43⅜	1.4	20	35.1	8.8	22.2
18•[4]	ISLI	✔INTERSOLV	NNM	C	110	15701	Mkt softw tools for IBM eqp	20¾	4½	18¼	8⅝	26¼	8¾	53010	14⅜	10⅝	12⅞	...	..	–28.5	2.4	7.1
✢19	IBC	✔Interstate Bakeries	NY,Ph	NR	99	14927	Largest independent U.S.baker	21⅛	13¾	15⅛	11⅝	23⅜	13⅜	6633	23⅜	21	22⅜	2.2	28	73.9	9.1	...
20	IGC	✔Interstate Genl L.P.	AS,P	NR	6	49	Homebuild'g/real estate dvlp	13½	1 15/16	9¼	6	7½	2⅞	1795	3½	2⅞	3¼	...	d	...	...	...
21	IJL	✔Interstate/Johnson Lane	NY,Ch	B–	18	697	Securities brokerage	15¾	1⅝	11⅞	7¼	11⅛	7⅝	1226	10⅝	10	10⅝	1.1	11	38.8	14.6	38.7
✢22	IPW	✔Interstate Power[62]	NY,B,Ch,P,Ph	B+	79	1404	Elec & gas: Iowa, Minn, Ill	35¼	10½	30¼	20⅞	33¼	23	2998	33¼	31	33⅛	6.3	13	52.5	10.8	13.9
23	II	✔Intersystems Inc	AS,Ch	C	5	225	Mkts thermoplastic resins	11	9/16	2¼	1	2 7/16	1	3087	2 7/16	1⅜	2⅛	...	d	88.9	9.4	...
24	WS	Wrrt(Pur 1 com at $3.50)	AS	....	2	23		1¼	3/16	⅞	3/16	⅝	⅛	64	⅝	5/16	9/16	...	..	...	...	...
25	ITN	✔InterTan Inc	NY,Ch,Ph	NR	57	8286	Retails consumer electronics	62¾	4½	8⅞	4⅝	10⅛	6⅝	5750	8¼	7⅛	7¼	...	9	–12.1	–10.9	–19.6
26	ITP	✔Intertape Polymer Group	AS,To	NR	58	3777	Mfr plastic packag'g prod	14	7¾	18¼	12½	33⅝	15¾	4563	33⅝	30⅞	31⅜	◆...	..	102	50.0	...
✢27•[5]	INTV	✔InterVoice	NNM	B	108	10406	Mfr phone voice response sys	22½	⅜	17	5⅞	26⅜	12⅜	59761	24½	18½	19	...	19	39.4	34.9	58.5
28	IBI	✔Intimate Brands 'A'	NY,Ph	NR	2	83	Sell intimat apprl/per care pd	....	....	....	....	18½	13¾	109921	16⅞	13¾	15	3.2	17	...	...	...
29	INET	✔Intrenet Inc	NSC	B–	8	1766	Genl/spcl trucking services	4⅝	½	4¾	3¼	6	1¼	13963	3⅛	1¼	1¾	...	11	–58.8	20.5	...
30•[1]	INTU	✔Intuit Inc	NNM	NR	171	26607	Dvlp financial softwr prd	23¼	10	36⅝	13½	89¼	29¾	146100	87¾	67¼	78	...	d	134	...	...
✢31•[6]	IVCR	✔Invacare Corp	NNM	B	152	13474	Home healthcare medical eqp	16⅛	13/16	18⅛	12⅝	29¾	16⅛	25988	29¾	24½	25¼	e0.2	25	49.5	28.0	37.8
32	IVC	INVESCO PLC ADS[70]	NY,Ch,Ph	NR	24	3041	Investment management svcs	....	....	....	....	41⅛	31⅜	555	41	38⅛	38¾	2.0	17	...	...	...
33	ITGI	✔Investment Tech Group	NNM	NR	24	2858	Securities executn/analysis sv	....	....	16½	4¾	10	5½	3413	9¾	8½	9¼	...	12	54.2	...	...
34	IFIN	✔Investors Finl Svcs	NNM	NR	..	...	Asset admin svcs	....	....	....	....	21⅛	16½	9336	21⅛	19¼	20¾	...	19	...	...	...
35	IIG	✔Investors Ins Group	AS	↓C	6	100	Dvlp, mkt annuity insurance pd	11¾	⅛	2⅝	1 9/16	2⅜	⅞	821	1 5/16	⅞	1 1/16	...	d	–37.0	–9.6	16.3
36	ITIC	✔Investors Title Co	NNM	B+	10	174	Land title/mortgage insur	17¾	11/16	9½	6½	11	6	497	11	10¼	10½B	0.8	10	57.0	19.9	18.2
37•[7]	IOMG	✔Iomega Corp	NNM	C	41	3289	Mfr computer disk drives	18⅜	1	3⅝	1⅝	53¾	3¼	392098	53¾	38¾	48⅝	...	..	1368	108	64.6
38	ILT.EC	✔Ion Laser Technology	ECM	C	3	62	Mfr air-cooled lasers	3⅜	3/16	1¾	9/16	4⅜	9/16	11680	4	2¾	3¾	...	d	567	26.0	...
✢39•[8]	ION	✔Ionics Inc	NY,Ch,Ph	B+	134	8531	Water purify equip:wtr & chem	34¼	¾	31⅜	21⅜	45½	26¼	6143	45½	43	43½	...	34	41.2	10.0	24.8
40	IPT	✔IP[73] Timberlands[74] Cl'A'[75]	NY,B,Ch,P	A	..	...	Timber resource in U.S.	30⅛	14¾	31⅛	21½	26½	19¾	4844	22¼	20	20⅞	e13.8	4	21.9	23.3	24.1
#41	IPL	✔IPALCO Enterprises	NY,B,C,Ch,Ph,P	B+	197	11704	Hldg:electr sv,Indianapolis	40	6	35⅜	28¼	38¾	29⅞	18657	38¾	37⅛	38⅛	5.7	15	35.0	8.7	13.9
42	IPCI	✔IPC Information Systems	NNM	NR	28	2293	Specialized telecommun sys	....	....	16¼	11	19¼	11¼	7724	19¼	14¼	16½	...	13	40.4	...	...
43	IPLSA	IPL Systems, Cl'A'	NNM	↓C	11	352	Mfr computer systems	34¾	⅞	9¾	2⅛	7⅞	2	7758	4⅛	2⅞	3⅛	...	d	34.2	–33.8	–26.6
44	IPSCF	IPSCO Inc[79]	NNM,To	B	35	9092	Mfr steel/steel products	25¼	5⅛	21¼	15¾	21½	15½	61	21½	20	20½B	◆...	..	23.9	13.3	...
45	IQSW	✔IQ Software	NNM	NR	11	214	Dvlp report writing software	19¼	6	16½	5¾	17¾	9¾	3346	13¾	9¾	11¼	...	d	9.8	–10.6	...
46	IRATA	✔Irata Inc'A'	NNM	NR	1	19	Oper self-svc photo booths	....	....	5¼	4½	5¾	4⅜	3946	5⅜	4½	5⅜	...	d	7.2	...	...
47	IRS	IRSA Inversiones y Rep GDS[80]	NY,Ch	NR	34	2082	Real estate dvlp - Argentina	....	....	26⅞	24½	26½	14½	5316	25½	21⅝	25½	...	12	2.0	...	...
48	IRT	✔IRT Property	NY,Ch	NR	74	7717	Real estate investment trust	16¼	1 3/16	11¾	8¾	10⅜	9	12973	9½	9⅛	9¼	9.7	15	0.0	–0.3	13.5
49	IAC	✔Irvine Apartment Communities	NY	NR	77	10770	Real estate investment trust	17⅞	16⅜	21¾	14¼	20⅜	15	8105	20⅜	17⅞	19¼	7.4	37	28.2	...	...
50	IRSN	✔Irvine Sensors	NSC	C	20	757	Mfr infrared sensors/elec pd	12	⅛	10⅝	4¾	10⅜	5¼	15766	7⅞	5½	6¼	...	d	22.0	7.7	102
51	ISBF	✔ISB Financial	NNM	NR	35	2917	Savings bank, Louisiana	....	....	....	....	17	10	3106	16	14⅞	15	2.0	..	...	...	...
52	OREX	✔Isolyser Co	NNM	NR	68	6910	Mfr disposable medical prod	....	....	12	6½	23	8⅛	96345	16¼	10	14	...	d	54.8	...	...

Uniform Footnote Explanations-See Page 4. Other: [1]CBOE:Cycle 1. [2]CBOE:Cycle 3. [3]ASE:Cycle 2. [4]NY:Cycle 1. [5]CBOE,NY:Cycle 1. [6]ASE:Cycle 3. [7]CBOE:cycle 2. [8]ASE,P:Cycle 1. [51]Dep for 0.01 shr 7% cm Cv Exch Pfd. [52]Co opt fr 9-30-96 exch for $25 amt 7% Cv 2008. [53]Fr 9-30-96 scale to $25 in 2003. [54]®$0.05,'94. [55]Fiscal Jan,'93. [56]6 Mo Jul,'93. [57]To be determined. [58]®$1.30,'94. [59]Fr 12-15-96 scale to $100 in 2003. [60]Stk dstr of Equus Gaming LP,'95. [61]®$0.91,'95. [62]Plan mfr w/IES Indus&WPL Hldgs,1.11 new co. [63]Dstr of 0.25 wrrt,'91. [64]If com price equal/exceeds $5-30 trad days. [65]®$0.65,'95. [66]®$1.35,'94. [67]®$0.40,'94. [68]Fiscal Sep,'93 & prior. [69]Spl div. [70]Ea ADS represent 10 Ord shr,par 25p. [71]Excl 10M Spl deferred shs. [72]®$1.79,'94. [73]Ltd ptnshp,dep units. [74]Int'l Paper holds 84%. [75]Rt to earnings sharply declines 12/31/99. [76]Return of Cap. [77]100% non-taxable,'94. [78]Subsid pfd in $M. [79]All prices prior to 1992 in $Cdn. [80]Ea GDS rep 10 com,P$1 par. [81]Approx. [82]Incl $0.0821 non-taxable:©$0.03864,'94. [83]Incl $0.7992 non-taxable,'94. [84]Accum on Pfd.

Index (Splits ◆)	Cash Divs. Ea.Yr. Since	Dividends: Latest Payment Period $	Date	Ex. Div.	Total $ So Far 1995	Ind. Rate	Paid 1994	Financial Position Mil-$: Cash& Equiv.	Curr. Assets	Curr. Liab.	Balance Sheet Date	Capitalization: Lg Trm Debt Mil-$	Shs. 000 Pfd.	Com.	Earnings $ Per Shr. Years End	1991	1992	1993	1994	1995	Last 12 Mos.	Interim Earnings Period	$ per Shr. 1994	1995	Index
1◆	1946	Q0.25	12-15-95	11-21	0.92	1.00	0.84	372	6102	5365	9-30-95	5474	...	260758	Dc	□1.81	□0.59	1.17	□1.73	E4.70↓	4.10	9 Mo Sep	□1.12	3.49	1
2◆	....	0.053	10-1-81	9-4	...	Nil	....	53.5	237	94.9	9-30-95	39.2	...	50472	Je	□0.65	0.23	d0.08	0.39	0.84	0.93	3 Mo Sep	0.16	0.25	2
3◆	....	None Since Public			...	Nil	....	6.36	12.0	2.35	9-30-95	....	...	5937	Dc	*0.05	*0.10	0.26	0.28	....	d0.29	9 Mo Sep	0.17	d0.40	3
4	....	None Since Public			...	Nil	....	0.38	6.65	3.34	j11-30-94	0.51	.2	8029	Nv	0.13	0.08	d0.08	d0.09	....	jd0.09				4
5◆	1988	Q0.062	12-15-95	11-29	0.182	0.25	0.16	42.5	100	82.6	9-30-95	324	...	6684	Dc	2.13	□0.77	□1.01	1.95	....	1.47	9 Mo Sep	1.40	0.92	5
6	1992	0.02½	1-17-95	12-27	0.02½	Nil	0.05	134	340	197	10-01-95	354	...	97798	Dc	0.56	□0.57	0.30	□0.46	....	0.59	9 Mo Sep	□0.39	0.52	6
7	....	None Since Public			...	Nil	....	15.4	174	87.8	9-30-95	50.1	24	36068	Mr	d0.26	Δd0.38	d0.09	d0.52	....	d0.29	6 Mo Sep	d0.16	0.07	7
8	1993	Q0.43¾	12-29-95	12-13	1.75	1.75	1.75	Cv into 4.28 com, $5.84				....	2400	...	Mr	...	...	...	....	....	....				8
9◆	....	None Since Public			...	Nil	....	15.2	20.1	11.9	9-30-95	14.5	362	9551	Je	*0.40	d1.33	Δd3.48	0.26	0.25	0.23	3 Mo Sep	Nil	d0.02	9
10	....	None Paid			...	Nil	....	0.97	5.91	3.20	j12-31-94	1.17	...	p16500	Dc	d0.05	d0.08	d0.14	[54]0.06	....	j0.30	9 Mo Sep	d0.05	0.19	10
11	....	None Paid			...	Nil	....	0.46	21.0	10.1	7-31-95	0.02	...	13257	Jl	...	p[55]0.03	‡p[56]0.06	p0.11	0.06	0.07	3 Mo Oct	0.03	0.04	11
12	....	None Since Public			...	Nil	....	0.33	6.75	4.84	7-31-95	....	...	2391	Ja	0.20	d0.06	0.14	d0.78	....	d1.02	9 Mo Oct	0.02	d0.22	12
13	....	None Since Public			...	Nil	....	11.1	27.7	3.87	7-31-95	0.13	...	4621	Oc	0.77	0.39	d0.94	d0.06	P0.55	0.55				13
14	....	None Since Public			...	Nil	....	0.17	32.2	18.2	7-31-95	3.36	...	3825	Oc	0.53	0.43	0.50	0.43	P0.77	0.77				14
15	1996	0.04½	1-16-96	12-28	...	[57]....	....	Equity per shr $10.10			9-30-95	478	664	17302	Dc	...	p1.15	1.29	[58]1.39	....	1.59	9 Mo Sep	1.00	Δ1.20	15
16	1996	1.214	12-15-95	12-1	1.214	5.75	....	Cv into 4.279 com, $23.37				....	664	...	Dc	...	...	...	....	....	....				16
17◆	1971	Q0.15½	3-15-96	2-26	0.60½	0.62	0.54½	333	2517	2424	9-30-95	260	...	78225	Dc	1.30	□1.50	□1.67	□1.53	E2.20	1.71	9 Mo Sep	□1.12	1.30	17
18	....	None Since Public			...	Nil	....	32.9	72.8	49.9	10-31-95	....	...	19483	Ap	d2.11	0.48	d1.00	d2.42	0.83	0.04	6 Mo Oct	0.19	d0.60	18
19	1991	Q0.12½	2-1-96	1-10	0.50	0.50	0.50	....	303	315	11-18-95	370	...	37031	My	p1.19	□1.49	□1.46	0.78	1.05	0.81	6 Mo Nov	0.61	0.37	19
20◆	1994	h[60]....	2-6-95	2-7	h[60]...	Nil	0.10	Equity per shr $3.66			9-30-95	71.8	...	10257	Dc	0.05	d1.47	Δ0.56	0.66	....	d0.11	9 Mo Sep	0.66	d0.11	20
21	1994	Q0.03	12-1-95	11-8	0.12	0.12	0.12	Equity per shr $9.37			9-30-95	28.8	...	5946	Sp	d0.04	*1.05	*1.54	Δ1.20	[61]0.94	0.94				21
22	1948	Q0.52	12-20-95	11-16	2.08	2.08	2.08	1.56	67.6	87.2	9-30-95	189	761	9564	Dc	2.84	1.74	1.73	1.92	....	2.51	12 Mo Sep	2.13	2.51	22
23	....	[63]Wrrt	10-15-91	10-16	...	Nil	....	0.04	4.76	4.94	9-30-95	4.83	...	4367	Dc	d1.39	d1.30	0.03	d0.19	....	d0.18	9 Mo Sep	d0.05	d0.04	23
24	....	Terms&trad. basis should			be checked in detail			Wrrts expire 12-31-99				....	...	762	Dc	...	...	...	....	....	....	Fr 9-23-93:expiration date can be shortened[64]			24
25	....	None Since Public			...	Nil	....	13.4	220	74.8	9-30-95	67.8	...	10815	Je	*1.04	□d5.04	d12.20	2.09	[65]0.81	0.78	3 Mo Sep	d0.18	d0.21	25
26	1993	g0.10	3-30-95	3-17	g0.10	0.10	g0.12	n/a	78.6	39.6	j6-30-95	p43.5	...	★11800	Dc	0.62	0.59	0.95	[66]1.41	....	j1.94	9 Mo Sep	0.98	1.51	26
27◆	....	None Paid			...	Nil	....	14.2	49.7	16.3	8-31-95	....	...	15747	Fb	0.16	0.45	0.64	0.15	....	0.99	9 Mo Nov	d0.07	0.77	27
28	1995	Q0.12	12-12-95	11-29	0.12	0.48	....	10.6	490	343	10-28-95	350	...	±250000	Ja	...	...	...	p0.67	E0.88	0.72	9 Mo Oct	p0.28	p0.33	28
29	....	None Paid			...	Nil	....	1.60	30.5	29.1	9-30-95	14.4	...	13198	Dc	d0.13	d0.05	Δ0.16	[67]0.52	....	0.16	9 Mo Sep	0.45	0.09	29
30◆	....	None Since Public			...	Nil	....	191	259	98.1	7-31-95	4.43	...	44201	Jl	0.21	0.25	[68]0.37	d5.37	d1.11	d0.23	3 Mo Oct	d1.36	d0.48	30
31◆	1994	[69]Q0.01¼	1-16-96	12-28	†0.034	0.05	0.01¼	6.42	194	81.6	9-30-95	107	...	±29158	Dc	±0.53	±0.63	±0.75	±0.89	....	1.02	9 Mo Sep	±0.59	±0.72	31
32	1995	0.276	10-18-95	8-24	0.834	0.76	....	104	282	122	12-31-94	64.2	...	[71]262978	Dc	0.43	0.38	1.48	[72]1.90	....	2.31	6 Mo Jun	0.88	1.29	32
33	....	None Since Public			...	Nil	....	Equity per shr $2.11			9-30-95	2.12	...	18390	Dc	...	...	p0.45	d0.45	....	0.75	9 Mo Sep	d0.58	0.62	33
34	....	None Since Public			...	Nil	....	Book Value $7.77			7-31-95	....	...	★6144	Oc	...	...	...	p0.86	Pp1.09	1.09				34
35	....	0.12	3-7-70	2-17	...	Nil	....	Equity per shr Neg			9-30-95	8.00	...	2763	Dc	*0.23	0.11	d0.31	□d1.15	....	d0.67	9 Mo Sep	□d0.80	d0.32	35
36	1983	Q0.02	12-15-95	11-29	0.08	0.08	0.08	Equity per shr $7.55			9-30-95	....	...	2801	Dc	0.28	Δ□0.53	0.81	1.10	....	1.09	9 Mo Sep	0.82	0.81	36
37◆	....	None Since Public			...	Nil	....	....	112	95.0	10-01-95	0.92	...	19432	Dc	0.60	0.23	Δd0.93	d0.10	....	Nil	9 Mo Sep	d0.17	d0.07	37
38	....	None Paid			...	Nil	....	0.04	2.10	1.29	6-30-95	0.84	...	3862	Mr	*0.04	d0.16	0.04	d0.07	....	d0.05	6 Mo Sep	d0.04	d0.02	38
39◆	....	None Paid			...	Nil	....	11.1	111	56.5	9-30-95	0.09	...	14138	Dc	0.73	0.93	0.98	1.09	E1.30	1.27	9 Mo Sep	0.79	0.97	39
40	1985	[76]Q0.72	11-15-95	10-27	†[76]6.88	[75]2.88	[77]2.88	7.79	319	12.4	9-30-95	1.24	...	46446	Dc	3.09	3.42	5.94	5.49	....	5.40	9 Mo Sep	4.05	3.96	40
41	1934	Q0.54	1-15-96	12-20	2.15	2.16	2.10	6.79	161	270	9-30-95	669	[78]52	37844	Dc	2.72	2.35	2.00	2.46	E2.55	2.67	12 Mo Sep	2.48	2.67	41
42	....	None Since Public			...	Nil	....	18.6	101	55.5	6-30-95	....	...	10522	Sp	...	...	p0.10	p1.11	P1.26	1.26				42
43	....	None Since Public			...	Nil	....	3.62	12.5	6.13	9-30-95	....	...	±5588	Dc	±1.73	±0.56	Δ±d0.49	±d2.80	....	d2.36	9 Mo Sep	±d1.01	±d0.57	43
44	1988	gQ0.12	12-29-95	12-6	g0.48	0.48	g0.48	81.1	342	183	j12-31-94	341	...	27081	Dc	2.53	0.98	1.42	2.13	....	j3.09	9 Mo Sep	1.36	2.32	44
45	....	None Since Public			...	Nil	....	11.0	18.8	3.03	7-31-95	....	...	4223	Ja	0.39	0.70	0.60	0.41	....	d0.61	9 Mo Oct	0.22	d0.80	45
46	....	None Since Public			...	Nil	....	0.15	0.90	3.39	9-30-95	....	...	±4043	Je	...	...	d0.39	d0.64	d0.24	d0.30	3 Mo Sep	0.01	d0.05	46
47◆	1995	[81]0.873	12-13-95	11-27	s[81]0.873	[57]....	....	106	130	8.02	6-30-95	37.8	...	113815	Je	...	...	...	p1.64	2.19	2.19				47
48	1978	Q0.22½	12-1-95	11-20	0.88½	0.90	[82]0.84	Equity per shr $7.81			9-30-95	223	...	25656	Dc	Δ0.59	□0.74	□0.72	Δ0.35	....	0.60	9 Mo Sep	Δ0.22	0.47	48
49	1994	Q0.35½	11-30-95	11-1	1.39	1.42	[83]1.11	Equity per shr $7.89			9-30-95	543	...	16975	Dc	...	p0.30	p0.34	0.62	....	0.52	9 Mo Sep	0.47	□0.37	49
50	....	None Paid			...	[84]Nil	....	0.37	4.20	1.88	7-02-95	0.09	15	14888	Sp	d0.04	d0.08	d0.12	d0.18	Pd0.20	d0.20				50
51	1995	0.075	1-17-96	12-29	0.15	0.30	....	Book Value $1595			9-30-95	30.5	...	7381	Dc	...	...	p1.34	....	....	....	9 Mo Sep	n/a	p0.85	51
52◆	....	None Since Public			...	Nil	....	19.2	67.7	24.4	9-30-95	p18.8	...	★30140	Dc	...	...	pd0.02	□d0.11	....	d0.08	9 Mo Sep	Δd0.11	d0.08	52

◆**Stock Splits & Divs By Line Reference Index** [1]2-for-1,'95. [2]2-for-1,'95. [3]1-for-5 REVERSE,'93. [5]5-for-4,'95. [9]1-for-20 REVERSE,'92. [17]2-for-1,'92. [20]No adj for stk dstr Equus Gaming,'95. [27]2-for-1,'93. [30]2-for-1,'95. [31]2-for-1,'91,'95. [37]5-for-4,'94:To split 3-for-1,ex Feb 1. [39]2-for-1,'95. [47]Adj for 2.8%,'95. [52]2-for-1,'95.

¶ S&P 500 # MidCap 400 ✤ SmallCap 600 • Options Index	Ticker	Name of Issue (Call Price of Pfd. Stocks)	Market	Com. Rank. & Pfd. Rating	Inst. Hold Cos	Inst. Hold Shs. (000)	Principal Business	Price Range 1971-93 High	1971-93 Low	1994 High	1994 Low	1995 High	1995 Low	Dec. Sales in 100s	December, 1995 Last Sale Or Bid High	Low	Last	%Div Yield	P-E Ratio	Total Return % Annualized 12 Mo	36 Mo	60 Mo
1	ISO	✔Isomedix Inc	NY,Ch	↑B+	52	4510	Sterilizat'n of med devices	28	3⅝	20¼	14¾	18	12⅝	5034	15½	13¾	14⅜	...	13	−8.7	−18.4	3.9
2	ISG	ISS-Intl Service Sys ADS[51]	NY,Ch	NR	15	1734	Cleaning & maintenance svcs	....	....	14⅛	12⅝	16	9⅞	160	11⅞	10½	11¼B	1.2	15	−14.8	...	...
3	IMI	✔Istituto Mobiliare Ital ADS[52]	NY,Ch,Ph	NR	34	8365	Banking/Finance svcs Italy	....	....	25¾	16⅞	20⅜	15	4513	19¼	17⅛	18⅞	2.6	11	7.6	...	...
4	INZ	✔Istituto Nazionale ADS[55]	NY,Ph	NR	10	13274	Multiple-line insurance	....	....	15⅞	12¾	14⅞	11¾	404	12⅝	11¾	12½	...	27	−1.2	...	...
5	ITEX	Itex Corp	NSC	NR	3	12	Manages barter concerns	....	....	5	1 15/16	8⅛	2	6674	7¼	6¼	6⅝	...	16	159	...	...
6	ITII	✔ITI Technologies	NNM	NR	79	7360	Mfr wireless secuity sys	....	....	23⅝	15⅝	29¾	20¼	6834	29¾	24½	29¾	...	27	34.5	...	...
✤7•[1]	ITRI	✔Itron Inc	NNM	NR	89	7775	Mfr wireless communications pd	18	13½	23½	14	34½	18	11624	34½	27¼	33¾	...	42	68.8	...	...
¶8	ITT	ITT Corp (New)	NY	NR	..	...	Hospitality/enter/info svc	....	....	....	....	53⅛	47½	85011	53⅛	47½	53	...	..	...	...	...
9	ESI	✔ITT Educational Svcs	NY,Ch	NR	20	1969	Oper technical skill schools	....	....	10⅜	10	25	9½	1374	25	20½	24⅝	...	30	146	...	...
¶10	HIG	✔ITT Hartford Group	NY	NR	..	...	Multi-line insurance	....	....	....	....	50⅛	47⅜	101967	50⅛	47⅜	48⅜	3.3	12	...	...	...
¶11	IIN	ITT Industries	NY	NR	2	88	Auto/defense elec/fluid tech	....	....	....	....	24¼	21¼	124086	24¼	21¼	24	2.5	..	...	...	...
#12•[2]	IVX	✔IVAX Corp[60]	AS,Ch,Ph	B−	225	31728	Pharm,personal care prod	41⅜	15/16	38⅛	14⅞	32¼	19⅛	98692	28¾	26½	28½	0.3	26	54.5	0.9	41.5
13	IWRK	✔Iwerks Entertainment	NNM	NR	23	2419	Prod movie-based spcl theaters	37	18	29¼	3⅞	6⅞	2⅞	16449	6⅞	5⅞	6⅜	...	d	38.2	...	...
✤14	JJSF	✔J & J Snack Foods	NNM	↓B	58	3909	Mfrs frozen snack foods	20¾	3⅝	20¾	10⅞	13⅜	10	4028	12⅜	11	11	...	18	−5.4	8.4	5.9
15•[3]	JL	✔J & L Specialty Steel	NY,Ch,Ph	NR	122	15085	Mfr flat roll stainless steel	16⅝	14	20¼	12⅞	27¼	14⅞	19261	18¾	15	18¾	1.9	9	−2.0	...	...
16•[2]	J	✔Jackpot Enterprises	NY	B	48	2090	Slot mach in Nev retail strs	23¼	1	14½	7	13⅞	7¾	7212	13¾	11½	11⅝	2.8	16	60.1	−6.3	21.3
17	JLN	✔Jaclyn, Inc	AS,Ch	C	10	333	Popular priced handbags	13½	1 7/16	15¼	4⅜	6	3½	472	4⅜	3¾	4⅜	...	d	−21.9	−15.7	−3.9
18	JACO	✔Jaco Electronics	NNM	B−	11	122	Dstr electronic components	8	½	6½	3¾	18½	4¼	10854	14¼	11½	11½	...	12	198	44.9	57.6
#19	JEC	✔Jacobs Engr Group	NY,Ph	↑B+	130	13438	Full-service engr organiz'n	36½	½	26⅞	16⅞	25¾	17¼	9654	25⅜	23⅜	25	...	20	41.8	−1.1	14.8
20	JCBS	✔Jacobson Stores	NNM	B−	23	1933	Specialty department stores	43½	⅞	15	10	12	8	2229	9½	8¼	9	5.6	38	−12.3	−11.2	−0.8
21	JLT	✔Jalate Ltd	AS,Ch	NR	2	5	Design/mkt women's sportswear	....	....	12½	6½	7¾	2⅞	3690	4	2⅞	3⅛	...	d	−58.3	...	...
¶22•[4]	JR	✔James River Corp	NY,B,Ch,P	B−	366	64364	Chem treated spec paper prod	43¾	1 1/16	24¾	15⅝	37⅜	20¼	225870	33¾	22	24⅛	2.5	27	...	...	...
23	Pr L	Dep[62]cm Cv[63]Exch Pfd([64]51.05)	NY,Ch	BB+	46	1984		52½	34⅛	46	37⅞	53	39⅜	12970	51¾	44¾	46⅜	7.5	..	...	...	...
24	Pr P	9% [65]Dep[66]'DECS'([67]17.6381)	NY,Ch	BB+	56	14720		....	....	23⅞	17⅛	35	20	37256	32	21⅞	23⅜	6.6	..	...	...	...
25	Pr K	$3.375cmCv[68]Ex K Pfd([69]50.675)	NY,Ch	BB+[70]	30	884		67½	32½	45¼	37⅜	52⅛	37¾	2417	50⅜	44¼	45¾B	7.4	..	...	...	...
✤26•[5]	JBM	✔Jan Bell Marketing	AS,Ch,Ph	↓C	46	8618	Design,mfr fine jewelry	34	2 5/16	10⅜	3¾	4¼	2 3/16	16753	3	2 5/16	2½	...	d	−36.5	−50.2	−18.9
27	WS	Jan Bell Marketing Wrrt	AS,Ch	....	..	...		....	....	....	....	½	3/16	226	½	3/16	⅜B	...	..	...	...	...
28•[6]	JANNF	Jannock Ltd[72]	NNM,To,Mo	B−	26	1322	Brick, vinyl prod, steel prd	25¾	1 1/16	22⅞	10⅜	13	9¼	298	10	9¼	9¼	...	..	−9.8	−6.1	...
29	JASN	✔Jason Inc	NNM	NR	41	8446	Mfr auto trim&finish'g prod	10⅝	11/16	12	8	11	6	4017	7⅜	6	6½	...	12	−23.5	2.0	12.7
30	JACC	✔Jayhawk Acceptance	NNM	NR	22	2166	Provides used car financing	....	....	....	....	16	8¼	22663	12¾	8¼	9⅛	...	51	...	...	...
31	JDN	✔JDN Realty	NY,Ch	NR	74	5309	Real estate investment trust	....	....	23¾	17⅞	22½	18	5298	22½	20¼	22⅜	8.1	22	21.5	...	...
32	JEAN	✔Jean Philippe Fragrances	NNM	NR	39	2749	Mkts imported fragrances	18	¾	12⅞	6¾	11⅞	7¼	5203	9⅛	8⅛	8⅛	...	11	14.0	−12.8	28.0
33	JEFG	✔Jefferies Group	NNM	B	55	2617	Equity securities broker	40½	7¾	45¾	28½	48½	28½	1729	48½	42½	47¼	0.4	10	60.3	36.9	35.0
34	JBNK	✔Jefferson Bankshares	NNM	A−	48	2948	Commercial bkg,Virginia	23	3¼	23¼	17⅛	23½	19⅛	3484	23½	20⅛	20¼	3.8	13	8.3	8.8	22.9
¶35•[7]	JP	✔Jefferson-Pilot	NY,B,C,Ch,P,Ph	A	341	29147	Insurance hldg co, life	38⅝	2⅝	36¾	28⅞	48¼	33⅝	16008	48¼	45⅞	46½	2.8	16	38.7	17.3	27.3
36	NBX	Jefferson-Pilot 7.25% 'ACES'	NY	NR	..	...	Automatic Com Exch Securities	....	....	....	....	75⅞	72½	5736	75⅞	72½	73⅛	7.2	..	...	...	...
37•[8]	JJSC	✔Jefferson Smurfit	NNM,Ch	NR	92	62981	Produce paperboard & pkg prd	....	....	23⅛	12⅜	20⅜	9	52474	11½	9	9½	...	4	−43.7	...	...
38	JS	Jefferson Smurfit Grp ADS[73]	NY,Ph	NR	4	8413	Produce paper&board/pkg prd	....	....	....	....	33¼	24	100	26¾	24	23B	3.0	3	...	...	...
39	JC	✔Jenny Craig	NY,Ph	NR	38	3190	Weight loss centers/svcs	33⅞	10⅛	11½	4⅜	10⅝	6½	8264	10⅝	9⅜	9⅞	...	20	33.9	−14.2	...
40	FORMF	✔JetForm Corp	NNM	NR	26	2754	Design, dvlp software products	12½	4	11½	6	20¼	7	9909	19⅝	14⅛	14⅛	...	..	98.2	...	...
41	JET	✔Jetronic Indus	AS	B−	6	166	Mfr electr eq:furniture strs	10	⅛	1¾	⅜	1⅛	7/16	1801	11/16	7/16	9/16	...	d	−10.1	−3.5	0.0
42	JCC	Jilin Chemical Ind ADS[76]	NY,Ph	NR	21	981	Chemical pd-Republic of China	....	....	....	....	25⅝	17¾	4764	21½	18½	21½	...	..	...	...	...
43	JHPC	✔Jim Hjelms Private Coll'n	NSC	NR	2	24	Design/mfr bridal apparel	7½	⅜	3½	1½	2 1/16	¾	412	1⅜	1⅛	1⅛	...	d	−40.0	−22.7	...
44	JLGI	✔JLG Indus	NNM	B	96	9335	Mobile aerial lifts:cranes	7⅜	15/16	10½	6⅛	30½	8½	10279	30½	26¾	29¾	0.1	17	224	118	63.6
45•[7]	JA	✔John Alden Financial	NY	NR	131	16207	Insurance hldg:life & health	36¾	13¾	42⅛	23½	32⅛	15	28174	21⅝	19⅞	20⅞	2.1	17	−29.5	−4.5	...
46•[7]	JNC	✔John Nuveen 'A'	NY,Ph	NR	53	2951	Mkt,manage tax-free invest pd	41⅝	15⅛	27⅜	19	27⅛	20½	3289	27	24	24¾	2.9	15	11.2	1.0	...
¶47•[1]	JCI	✔Johnson Controls	NY,B,Ch,P,Ph,NSC	↑A−	396	25028	Mfr bldg controls:auto prod	59⅛	1 11/16	61¾	44⅞	69¾	45¾	17496	69¾	65⅞	68¾	2.4	15	44.0	18.6	26.9
¶48•[9]	JNJ	✔Johnson & Johnson	NY,To,B,C,Ch,P,Ph	A+	1408	386278	Health care products	58¾	4¾	56½	36	92⅜	53⅝	238476	92⅜	85⅛	85½	1.5	23	58.3	22.0	21.8
49	JWAIA	✔Johnson Worldwide'A'	NNM	NR	46	3818	Recreational prod/inking	31½	8	26½	18¼	24¾	19	2035	23	21¾	22½	...	18	20.0	10.9	1.1
✤50	JII	✔Johnston Industries	NY,Ch	↑B	35	1887	Mfrs ind'l/apparel textiles	13⅛	¼	13¾	8¼	12	7⅜	2344	8¼	7⅜	8⅛	4.9	20	−21.1	0.8	25.1
51	JAII	✔Johnstown America Indus	NNM	NR	74	6825	Mfr railroad freight cars	26¼	14	30¼	10½	16¾	4¼	16953	5⅝	4¼	5	...	6	−68.8	...	...
#52•[2]	JNY	✔Jones Apparel Group	NY,Ch,Ph	NR	180	16336	Design,dstr womens apparel	42	13⅝	35¾	22	39⅝	22⅝	25871	39⅝	33½	39⅜	...	17	55.9	2.1	...

Uniform Footnote Explanations-See Page 4. Other: [1]Ph:Cycle 1. [2]CBOE:Cycle 3. [3]Ph:Cycle 2. [4]NY:Cycle 3. [5]ASE,CBOE:Cycle 1. [6]Mo:Cycle 3. [7]ASE:Cycle 1. [8]CBOE,NY:Cycle 2. [9]CBOE:Cycle 1. [51]Ea ADS rep 0.5'B'shr,DKK 20. [52]Ea ADS rep 3 com, LIT 5000. [53]In billions,incl current amts. [54]Fiscal Mar'91 & prior. [55]Ea ADS rep 10 ord shrs, Lit. 1000 par. [56]To be determined. [57]9 Mo Dec'92. [58]83.3% owned by ITT Corp. [59]Inc current amts. [60]Comb w/Hafslund Nycomed form IVAX NYCOMED (54%). [61]Stk dstr of Crown Vantage Inc. [62]Dep for 0.25shr of $14Cv Exch Pfd. [63]Co opt exch for $50 amt 7% Cv 2017. [64]Thru 9-30-95,scale to $50 in'97. [65]Dep for 0.01 shr Sr P'DECS'. [66]Dividend Enhanced Cv Stk. [67]Fr 7-1-97. [68]Co opt exch for $50 amt 6.75%Cv2016. [69]Thru 10-31-95,scale to $50 in'96. [70]Note:'r'added to derivative/hybrid secur ratings. [71]Fiscal Dec'93 & prior. [72]Jun'94 & prior prices in Canadian $. [73]Ea ADS rep 10 Nominal Value, IR 25p. [74]Fiscal Jan'94 & prior. [75]®$0.24,'95. [76]Ea ADS rep 100 Cl'H' ord shrs,RMB 1.00. [77]®$4.27,'95.

Splits ◆ Index	Cash Divs. Ea.Yr. Since	Dividends: Latest Payment Period $	Date	Ex. Div.	Total $ So Far 1995	Ind. Rate	Paid 1994	Financial Position Mil-$ Cash& Equiv.	Curr. Assets	Curr. Liab.	Balance Sheet Date	Capitalization Lg Trm Debt Mil-$	Shs. 000 Pfd.	Com.	Earnings $ Per Shr. Years End	1991	1992	1993	1994	1995	Last 12 Mos.	Interim Earnings Period	$ per Shr. 1994	1995	Index
1	....	None Since Public			...	Nil	....	28.4	37.5	2.23	9-30-95	9.00	...	6983	Dc	0.79	1.08	1.08	1.20	....	1.07	9 Mo Sep	0.92	0.79	1
2	1995	0.172	5-17-95	4-18	0.172	0.14	....	68.8	345	339	12-31-94	103	...	29764	Dc	...	...	±p0.90	0.73	....	0.73				2
3	1994	0.497	6-12-95	5-11	0.497	0.50	0.538	Book Value $22.94			12-31-94	[53]j35467	...	600000	Dc	■[54]0.80	1.50	□Δ1.46	□1.80	....	1.80				3
4	1995	0.17	8-4-95	7-17	0.17	[56]....	....	Equity per shr $16.97			12-31-94	....	...	4000000	Dc	...	0.08	0.28	0.47	....	0.47				4
5	....	None Paid			...	Nil	....	1.52	3.02	1.51	7-31-95	....	...	5678	Jl	...	0.21	Δ0.07	Δ0.23	0.41	0.41				5
6	....	None Since Public			...	Nil	....	0.23	26.4	7.30	9-30-95	....	...	8914	Dc	...	‡[57]d2.54	d0.13	□0.55	....	1.09	9 Mo Sep	0.32	0.86	6
7	....	None Since Public			...	Nil	....	40.9	90.1	25.4	9-30-95	....	...	12162	Dc	d0.31	Δd0.58	0.46	0.67	....	0.81	9 Mo Sep	0.44	0.58	7
8	....	None Since Public			...	Nil	....	Equity per shr $19.97			6-30-95	667	...	119000	Dc	...	...	...	p0.07	....	....	6 Mo Jun	n/a	p0.32	8
9	....	None Since Public			...	Nil	....	0.72	90.3	63.1	9-30-95	....	...	[58]12000	Dc	...	...	p0.69	0.71	....	0.83	9 Mo Sep	0.65	0.77	9
10	....	Plan qtly div			...	1.60	....	Equity per shr $40.39			6-30-95	598	...	119000	Dc	...	...	...	pΔ5.31	E4.00	4.92	6 Mo Jun	p2.45	p2.06	10
11	....	Plan qtly div			...	0.60	....	n/a	2999	2961	6-30-95	[59]1866	...	119000	Dc	...	...	...	p□2.75	....	....	6 Mo Jun	n/a	p▲4.55	11
12◆	1993	S0.04	12-1-95	11-8	0.08	0.08	0.06	29.5	607	188	9-30-95	290	...	117818	Dc	*0.19	0.65	1.17	□0.77	E1.10	0.77	9 Mo Sep	□0.67	0.67	12
13	....	None Since Public			...	Nil	....	13.5	24.4	19.4	9-30-95	1.91	...	10455	Je	d0.15	0.04	0.18	d1.05	d1.32	d1.23	3 Mo Sep	d0.08	0.01	13
14	....	None Since Public			...	Nil	....	14.5	44.5	16.5	9-30-95	5.01	...	9126	Sp	0.67	0.55	0.80	0.82	0.61	0.61				14
15	1994	Q0.09	1-24-96	1-8	0.36	0.36	0.36	66.6	299	179	9-30-95	14.5	...	38670	Dc	...	p0.59	□1.15	1.39	E2.15	2.23	9 Mo Sep	1.02	1.86	15
16◆	1987	Q0.08	11-24-95	11-8	0.32	0.32	0.32	34.7	38.2	5.17	9-30-95	....	...	9302	Je	Δ0.22	Δ0.45	0.80	d0.50	0.72	0.75	3 Mo Sep	0.16	0.19	16
17	1969	0.12½	2-15-95	1-9	0.12½	Nil	0.50	7.28	25.0	8.49	9-30-95	....	...	2691	Je	0.31	0.52	Δd0.42	0.59	d0.86	d0.91	3 Mo Sep	0.14	0.09	17
18◆	....	None Since Public			...	Nil	....	0.42	58.2	22.4	9-30-95	p8.35	...	★3792	Je	d0.40	0.12	0.55	Δ0.46	0.78	0.99	3 Mo Sep	0.11	0.32	18
19◆	....	0.028	12-15-83	11-15	...	Nil	....	41.9	369	255	9-30-95	17.8	...	25508	Sp	0.86	1.11	1.15	0.75	1.27	1.27				19
20	1960	Q0.12½	1-10-96	12-13	0.50	0.50	0.50	3.80	157	58.6	10-28-95	129	...	5779	Ja	0.73	0.68	0.52	0.71	....	0.24	9 Mo Oct	d0.81	d1.28	20
21	....	None Since Public			...	Nil	....	0.43	14.6	7.59	9-30-95	....	...	3391	Dc	...	p0.03	p0.37	0.53	....	d0.11	9 Mo Sep	0.64	Nil	21
22	1973	Q0.15	12-29-95	12-13	h[61]0.60	0.60	0.60	43.7	1898	1131	9-24-95	2457	3631	84808	Dc	0.66	□d1.82	d0.40	d0.72	E0.88↓	0.26	9 Mo Sep	d0.31	0.67	22
23	1987	Q0.87½	1-2-96	12-15	3.50	3.50	3.50	Cv into 1.25 com,$40				....	4000	...	Ap	b0.94	b0.69	b0.29	b0.74	....	....				23
24	1994	Q0.388	1-2-96	12-15	1.55¼	1.553	0.397	Cv into .8547 com,$20.1825				....	16667	...	Dc	...	...	...	b0.74	....	....	Mandatory conversion into 1 com 7-1-98			24
25	1987	Q0.84⅜	2-1-96	1-16	3.37½	3.375	3.37½	Cv into 1.2269 com,$40.75				....	2000	...	Ap	b0.94	b0.69	b0.29	b0.74	....	....				25
26	....	None Since Public			...	Nil	....	9.35	145	46.6	10-28-95	17.5	...	25812	Ja	0.33	0.59	[71]d1.40	d2.92	....	d2.73	9 Mo Oct	d0.60	d0.41	26
27	....	Terms&trad. basis should			be checked in detail			Wrrts expire 12-18-98				....	...	700	Ja	...	...	...	....	....	....				27
28	1945	gQ0.20	1-2-96	11-29	g0.80	0.80	g0.80	6.60	312	178	j12-31-94	149	1454	30258	Dc	d1.25	1.06	d0.05	0.88	....	j0.86	9 Mo Sep	0.58	0.56	28
29◆	....	5%Stk	5-6-88	4-26	...	Nil	....	0.29	116	62.7	9-29-95	124	...	20098	Dc	0.28	0.32	□0.52	□0.55	....	0.56	9 Mo Sep	□0.39	0.40	29
30	....	None Since Public			...	Nil	....	Book Value $2.28			9-30-95	7.49	...	20478	Dc	...	...	...	pd0.13	....	0.18	9 Mo Sep	pd0.14	p0.17	30
31	1994	Q0.45½	1-16-96	12-27	1.78½	1.82	0.89	Equity per shr $16.04			9-30-95	113	...	10012	Dc	...	...	p1.63	p0.93	....	1.03	9 Mo Sep	p0.70	0.80	31
32◆	....	None Since Public			...	Nil	....	5.63	65.4	30.6	9-30-95	0.77	...	9268	Dc	0.27	0.50	0.70	0.70	....	0.75	9 Mo Sep	0.46	0.51	32
33	1988	Q0.05	12-15-95	11-13	0.20	0.20	0.20	Book Value $32.59			9-29-95	59.8	...	5598	Dc	1.74	3.82	Δ5.37	3.25	....	4.54	9 Mo Sep	2.55	3.84	33
34◆	1935	Q0.19	1-31-96	1-3	0.74	0.76	0.68	Book Value $14.53			9-30-95	0.02	...	15194	Dc	1.19	1.54	1.64	1.49	....	1.54	9 Mo Sep	1.11	1.16	34
35◆	1913	Q0.32	3-1-96	2-7	1.247	1.28	1.12	Equity per shr $28.08			9-30-95	....	...	71201	Dc	2.28	2.66	□2.91	3.28	E3.00	3.53	9 Mo Sep	2.35	2.60	35
36	....	Plan qtly div			...	5.256	....	Exch for com NationsBank(or cash)re-spec cond				....	...	★1650	Dc	...	...	...	....	....	....	Mature 1-21-2000			36
37	....	None Since Public			...	Nil	....	15.2	719	655	9-30-95	2244	...	110989	Dc	...	...	d1.38	□0.12	E2.30	1.92	9 Mo Sep	□d0.15	□1.65	37
38	1995	0.226	10-31-95	10-5	0.226	0.70	....	1365	2782	1801	12-31-94	1521	304	538286	Dc	□4.27	□1.26	Δ[74]1.01	□9.15	....	9.15				38
39	1992	0.15	4-8-94	3-25	...	Nil	0.30	59.8	87.4	41.2	6-30-95	....	...	25196	Je	p1.45	□1.64	1.35	0.02	0.46	0.49	3 Mo Sep	0.13	0.16	39
40◆	....	None Since Public			...	Nil	....	28.7	42.8	4.81	j4-30-95	0.10	2264	8246	Ap	d0.23	d0.29	0.33	d0.08	[75]0.29	j0.34	6 Mo Oct	0.10	0.15	40
41	....	None Paid			...	Nil	....	0.26	9.56	5.20	10-31-95	4.32	...	3604	Ja	d1.64	*0.02	0.05	0.01	....	d0.17	9 Mo Oct	Nil	d0.18	41
42	....	Plan annual div			...	....	....	21.4	240	330	12-31-94	270	...	★3289327	Dc	...	...	...	....	....	....				42
43◆	....	None Since Public			...	Nil	....	0.01	3.89	2.93	1-31-95	....	...	1143	Oc	0.15	d0.24	0.12	Δd0.07	....	d0.07	9 Mo Jul	Δ0.12	0.12	43
44◆	1993	Q0.01	1-4-96	12-13	0.03⅛	0.04	0.02½	13.0	84.6	39.2	7-31-95	2.26	...	14275	Jl	d0.23	d0.21	0.22	0.68	1.46	1.73	3 Mo Oct	0.27	0.54	44
45	1993	Q0.11	1-19-96	12-27	0.43	0.44	0.38	Equity per shr $19.01			9-30-95	94.6	150	25247	Dc	pΔ2.35	p2.71	Δ3.29	□2.95	....	1.26	9 Mo Sep	□2.61	0.92	45
46	1992	Q0.18	12-15-95	11-29	0.68	0.72	0.64	Equity per shr $8.47			9-30-95	....	...	±36821	Dc	p1.21	□1.66	1.76	1.52	....	1.67	9 Mo Sep	1.15	1.30	46
47	1901	Q0.41	1-2-96	12-6	1.56	1.64	1.44	104	2064	1910	9-30-95	630	.3	41121	Sp	2.19	2.86	□3.16	3.80	[77]4.53	4.53				47
48◆	1905	Q0.33	12-5-95	11-10	1.28	1.32	1.13	1338	8084	4311	10-01-95	2108	...	647626	Dc	2.19	□2.46	2.74	3.12	E3.70	3.59	9 Mo Sep	2.53	3.00	48
49	....	None Since Public			...	Nil	....	8.94	185	63.9	9-29-95	68.9	...	±8116	Sp	±1.40	±0.96	±d0.15	±1.51	±1.25	1.25				49
50◆	1988	Q0.10	12-11-95	11-22	0.40	0.40	0.369	16.7	115	57.2	9-30-95	103	...	10565	Je	d0.10	0.62	0.81	0.60	0.74	0.40	3 Mo Sep	0.16	d0.18	50
51	....	None Since Public			...	Nil	....	10.9	156	125	p9-30-95	306	...	9754	Dc	...	p0.31	p0.72	0.58	....	0.87	9 Mo Sep	0.38	0.67	51
52	....	None Since Public			...	Nil	....	10.9	369	110	10-01-95	10.6	...	26246	Dc	p1.25	1.59	Δ1.85	2.08	....	2.34	9 Mo Sep	1.69	1.95	52

◆**Stock Splits & Divs By Line Reference Index** [12]3-for-2,'91(twice). [16]Adj to 5%,'92:10%,'93. [18]10%,'95:4-for-3,'95. [19]2-for-1,'91. [29]3-for-2,'92:5-for-4,'91,'93,'94. [32]3-for-2,'92. [34]2-for-1,'93. [35]3-for-2,'92,'95. [40]3-for-2,'93. [43]1-for-3 REVERSE,'95. [44]2-for-1,'95(twice). [48]2-for-1,'92. [50]3-for-2,'94.

¶ S&P 500 · # MidCap 400 · ✤ SmallCap 600 · • Options

Index	Ticker	Name of Issue (Call Price of Pfd. Stocks)	Market	Com. Rank. & Pfd. Rating	Inst. Hold Cos	Inst. Hold Shs. (000)	Principal Business	Price Range 1971-93 High	1971-93 Low	1994 High	1994 Low	1995 High	1995 Low	Dec. Sales in 100s	December, 1995 Last Sale Or Bid High	Low	Last	%Div Yield	P-E Ratio	Total Return % Annualized 12 Mo	36 Mo	60 Mo
1	JOIN	✓Jones Intercable	NNM	C	35	1656	Cable television systems	20⅞	⅛	17½	10¾	17½	11¾	1538	13	11¾	12½	...	d	5.3	−1.3	11.9
2	JOINA	✓ Class A (1/10 vtg)	NNM	C	54	12187		20⅞	2⅞	18	11	17½	11⅝	6436	13¼	11⅝	12⅜	...	d	3.1	−1.0	10.9
3	JTV	✓Jones Intercable Inv Cl'A'[51]	AS,Ch	NR	14	187	Acquire,operate CATV system	17½	6⅜	13	8⅝	13⅞	10⅜	1814	12⅝	12	12⅜	4.8	77	21.1	12.5	25.6
4	JMED	✓Jones Medical Indus	NNM	B+	43	2526	Mfr brand/generic drug prod	17½	1 5/16	15½	6⅜	24¾	6¼	14915	24¾	20½	24⅛	0.5	30	268	52.5	31.0
5	JPS	✓Jones Plumbing Sys	AS	LIQ	6	1065	Mfg/dstr plumbing repair prod	13¼	13/16	2⅞	1⅛	1⅜	7/16	...	...	...	...	...	..	−53.8	−24.6	−12.9
6	JOSB	✓Jos.A. Bank Clothiers	NNM	NR	19	4722	Retail mens & womens clothing	...	...	10¾	3¾	4⅞	1½	8759	2½	1½	2	...	d	−50.0	...	...
¶7•[1]	JOS	✓Jostens Inc	NY,B,Ch,Ph	B+	292	29644	School class rings,yearbook	38⅝	⅞	20	15⅛	25⅛	17¾	12797	25⅛	24	24¼	3.6	21	33.7	2.4	−2.3
8	JOL	✓Joule Inc	AS	↑B−	13	452	Office/engineering temp help	13	11/16	3⅜	1 5/16	5⅛	1 13/16	301	5⅛	4	5	...	19	150	41.9	43.8
9	JPFS	✓JP Foodservice	NNM	NR	48	8769	Dstr to food service industry	...	...	11½	9¼	19¾	9¼	12464	19¾	18	19½	...	20	111	...	...
10	JPR	✓JP Realty	NY,Ph	NR	72	9661	Real estate investment trust	...	...	22½	17⅜	22⅜	17⅜	4340	22⅜	19¾	21⅞	7.7	18	16.8	...	...
✤11	JSBF	✓JSB Financial	NNM	NR	80	5130	Savings bank, New York	26⅞	10⅝	27½	22	34¼	23¾	7315	32⅞	31⅛	31⅝	3.2	15	37.2	18.5	23.6
✤12	JUNO	✓Juno Lighting	NNM	A−	129	14907	Mfrs recessed/track light'g	21	1⅝	21	16¼	21	14	16215	16½	15	16	2.0	14	−7.6	−1.1	15.8
13	JPI	✓Jupiter[53] Natl[54]	AS	NR	15	214	Textile mfr/venture cap invest	30⅞	⅛	29⅝	19⅞	31½	19⅞	68	30	29½	30	...	13	37.1	30.2	49.7
✤14	JSTN	✓Justin Indus	NNM	B+	76	7133	Bldg mtl:leather gds,towers	25⅜	5/16	16¾	9¾	12⅛	9½	11046	11⅜	10¾	11	1.5	11	−4.5	−14.1	22.5
¶15•[2]	KM	✓K mart	NY,B,C,Ch,P,Ph	↓B+	590	295573	Operates discount dept strs	28⅛	5	22	12½	16¼	5⅞	1377829	8⅛	5⅞	7⅛	...	..	−42.9	−30.3	−8.1
✤16	KSWS	✓K Swiss Inc 'A'	NNM	B	45	3132	Dvlp/mkt athletic footwear	30¼	10½	25¾	18¼	21	9¾	2987	12	9¾	10⅞	e0.7	9	−47.3	−19.6	−8.1
17	KCC	✓K-III Communications	NY,Ph	NR	..	...	Edu/spcl interest publis'g svc	...	...	...	...	12⅝	10	14112	12⅝	11½	12⅛	...	..	...	...	...
18	KTII	✓K-Tron Intl	NNM	C	20	1035	Digital process ctr feeders	20¾	2¾	12¼	8¼	11½	4½	1059	6⅝	5½	6¼	...	d	−41.9	−21.2	−2.9
19	KV.B	✓K-V Pharmaceutical Cl'B'[56]	AS,Ph	C	14	830	Mfr drugs for major firms	21⅛	3/16	11½	4⅝	13⅜	5¼	1946	13⅜	8⅝	13⅜	...	..	155	5.9	11.2
20	KV.A	Cl'A' 1/20 vtg	AS,Ph	C	16	1231		19⅛	7¼	11½	4⅜	13⅜	5⅛	5308	13⅜	8⅜	13⅜	...	..	155	5.9	...
21	KHLR	✓Kahler Realty[58]	NNM	B−	17	740	Lodg'g,formal wear, laundry	11½	1 15/16	14¾	6½	14⅛	7	1690	12⅞	11¼	12	1.3	36	45.1	61.7	24.9
22•[3]	KLU	✓Kaiser Aluminum	NY,Ch,Ph	NR	70	16948	Aluminum mfr/fabricated prd	14¾	6⅜	12½	8¼	21	10⅛	32576	15¾	12⅜	13⅛	...	d	25.0	16.7	...
23	Pr D	8.255% PRIDES[59]([60]11.9925)	NY	CCC[61]	34	7057		...	...	12	9¼	17⅛	10⅛	2991	15	12⅞	13⅛	7.4	..	...	...	...
24	KRSC	✓Kaiser Ventures	NNM	NR	31	2088	Waste management services	20¼	2	17½	5½	13	5¼	2782	13	10⅝	13	...	..	136	−0.6	18.8
✤25	KAMNA	✓Kaman Corp Cl'A'[62]	NNM	B	95	9484	Technology/indust/prod & svc	21⅜	⅝	11⅛	8½	13⅜	10	6176	11½	10½	11⅛	4.0	d	6.2	8.9	12.7
26	KPP	✓Kaneb Pipe Line Ptnrs[64]L.P.[65]	NY	NR	15	564	Pipeline & terminaling svcs	28⅛	13¾	28⅜	20½	25	20⅝	2500	25	23¾	24	9.2	11	25.3	14.2	20.8
27	KPU	✓ Preference 'B' Units	NY	NR	..	...		...	...	...	...	22⅝	21⅝	3439	22½	22	22½	9.8	..	...	...	...
28	KAB	✓Kaneb Services	NY,B,Ch,P,Ph	B−	47	14072	Ind svcs, pipelines & terminals	40⅛	1¼	4⅛	1⅞	2¾	1½	25360	2⅝	1⅞	2¼	...	32	12.5	−11.5	−9.7
29	KNK	✓Kankakee Bancorp	AS	NR	9	200	Savings bank, Illinois	19¼	13½	19½	15	21¼	15	197	20⅜	18⅛	18⅞	2.1	16	23.9	...	...
#30	KLT	✓Kansas City Pwr & Lt	NY,B,C,Ch,Ph	B+	181	15324	Supplies elec to K.C. suburbs	26¼	5⅜	23⅞	18⅝	26⅝	21½	17630	26⅝	24⅜	26¼	5.9	14	20.4	12.3	16.1
#31•[4]	KSU	✓Kansas City So. Ind	NY,B,Ch,P,Ph	B	200	27538	RR fin'l svcs,mutual funds,RE	51½	⅜	52⅝	29⅞	48⅝	31	26465	47⅜	45½	45¾	0.7	21	48.8	24.8	41.2
✤32	KAS	✓Kasler Hldg	NY	B−	39	3225	Heavy contstr in west'n U.S.	15½	3½	10¾	3⅞	6¾	4⅜	5455	6¾	5⅜	6⅜	...	43	50.0	−12.3	−5.7
33	KT	✓Katy Indus	NY,B,Ch,Ph,P	B−	41	3139	Indus machin'y&components	45	2	26⅞	7½	10⅞	7	2034	10⅛	9⅛	9¼	2.7	5	13.5	2.5	7.7
34	KTZ	✓Katz Media	AS	NR	40	4535	Broadcast media advert'g svcs	...	...	...	...	21⅞	14⅝	1998	17⅝	15½	17⅝	...	..	...	...	...
¶35•[5]	KBH	✓Kaufman & Broad Home	NY,Ph	B+	217	17661	Single-family home builder	25	5⅜	25½	12⅛	16	10⅞	20429	15	12¾	14⅞	2.0	23	16.9	−1.3	12.8
36	HWK	✓Kaufman (H.W.) Finl Grp[70]	AS,Ch	B+	7	164	Insurance brokerage & agency	5⅜	2 3/16	5	3¾	8¼	4⅛	342	8⅛	8	8⅛	2.0	14	115	65.8	34.3
#37	KDN	✓Kaydon Corp	NY,Ch,Ph	A−	146	13416	Mfrs bear'gs/filtration prod	32	1⅞	25¼	19¾	31⅝	22¾	4019	30¾	28½	30⅜	1.6	14	28.6	11.0	14.1
✤38	KCS	✓KCS Energy Inc	NY	B	79	4749	Oil & gas explor,prod'n,mkt	32¾	13/16	29	12¼	22¼	9⅞	7667	16¾	13⅜	15	0.8	8	−6.2	11.5	51.7
✤39	KEA	✓Keane Inc	AS	↑B+	114	9904	Computer software services	21	1/16	27¼	18	30⅞	18¼	14273	29⅞	18¼	22⅛	...	18	−3.8	23.6	27.7
40	KEI	✓Keithley Instruments	NY	B−	27	1870	Mfr electronic test instr/sys	9⅞	1¼	5½	4½	18	4⅞	3863	17⅛	14⅜	16¾	0.7	25	259	46.0	35.2
41	KOGC	✓Kelley Oil & Gas	NNM	NR	37	6193	Oil & gas explor,dev,prod'n	...	...	...	...	6⅜	15/16	124394	1⅞	15/16	1 5/16	...	d	...	...	...
¶42•[6]	K	✓Kellogg Co	NY,B,C,Ch,P,Ph	A+	566	163601	Convenience food products	75⅜	2⅝	60¾	47⅜	79½	52½	38894	79½	75⅛	77¼	2.0	23	35.5	7.3	18.0
✤43	KWD	✓Kellwood Co	NY,B,Ch,Ph	B	158	17685	Mfrs & mkts apparel	27⅜	1 7/16	26⅞	19⅛	22⅞	16½	17886	20⅞	19⅛	20⅜	2.9	49	0.1	8.0	26.1
#44	KELYA	✓Kelly Services'A'[62]	NNM	A	170	15832	Temporary help services	36⅝	5/16	32	23	37	24½	12653	28½	25¾	27¾	2.9	15	4.6	−4.5	3.5
✤45•[7]	KMET	✓KEMET Corp	NNM	NR	166	22757	Mfr tantalum/ceramic capacitrs	10	5	14⅞	7	36⅛	12⅞	117767	30½	20¾	23⅞	...	20	60.5	50.5	...
#46•[5]	KEM	✓Kemper[72]Corp[73]	NY,Ch,Ph	B	169	16733	Insur & fin'l hldg	51⅞	1 13/16	64⅝	35⅜	49¾	38	22510	49¾	49¼	49⅝	1.9	12	...	...	...
47•[8]	KWND	✓KENETECH Corp	NNM	NR	56	9687	Dvlp wind energy technology	21¾	14⅜	29½	9¼	16¾	1	50522	3½	1	1⅝	...	d	−88.2	...	...
#48•[9]	KMT	✓Kennametal, Inc	NY,B,Ch	B+	234	18245	Tungsten-base carbide prod	23	2½	29⅝	21⅛	41⅛	23	23394	33¾	30½	31¾	1.9	12	36.9	34.8	38.4
49	KCP	✓Kenneth Cole Productions'A'	NY,Ch,Ph	NR	50	5242	Design,mkt footwear/handbags	...	...	11½	5¼	22½	9⅛	4944	21⅜	18¼	18¾	...	26	98.3	...	...
50	KNSY	Kensey Nash	NNM	NR	..	...	Dgn/dvp arterial seal'g device	...	...	...	...	13½	12	28364	13½	12	12½	...	..	...	...	...
✤51	KNT	✓Kent Electronics	NY,Ch,Ph	B+	139	7453	Dstr variety wiring products	19⅛	2⅝	27	17⅝	59⅞	25⅝	13060	59⅞	51¾	58⅜	...	33	123	54.0	50.1
52	KESI	✓Kentucky Electric Steel	NNM	NR	24	3230	Oper steel mini-mill	13¼	10⅛	14⅜	7½	12	7⅝	4030	9½	7⅝	8¼	...	9	−5.7	...	...

Uniform Footnote Explanations-See Page 4. Other: [1]NY:Cycle 3. [2]CBOE:Cycle 3. [3]P,Ph:Cycle 1. [4]P:Cycle 3. [5]Ph:Cycle 1. [6]ASE:Cycle 3. [7]CBOE:Cycle 1. [8]P:Cycle 2. [9]Ph:Cycle 3. [51]L.P.units. [52]Incl $0.44225 non-taxable,'94. [53]Jun '94 & prior co reported on Net Asset Val basis. [54]Johnston Industries plan acq,$32.875. [55]Fiscal Dec'92 & prior. [56]Conv into Cl'A'shr for shr. [57]Accum on Pfd. [58]Plan spin-off,Kahler Mgmt Corp. [59]Pfd Redeemable Increased Div Equity Sec. [60]Fr 12-31-96,in com stk scale to $11.75 12-31-97. [61]Note:'r'added to derivative/hybrid secur ratings. [62]Non-vtg. [63]®$0.93,'92. [64]Sr Pref Units. [65]Redeemable at re-specified cond.. [66]Incl 7.25MSr Pref Uts/4.65MPref Uts/1MPref'B'Ut. [67]Pref units. [68]Incl redemption of stk purch rt. [69]Fiscal Oct'91 & prior. [70]Approve AJK Enterprises acq, $8.20. [71]®$0.52,'95. [72]Zurich Ins plan acq MidCap400 delist eff Jan 5. [73]Plan spin-off,KemperSec,name chge to CAPMARC Inc. [74]Stk dstr of Everen Capital Corp. [75]Excl subsid pfd.

Index	Cash Divs. Ea.Yr. Since	Dividends: Latest Payment Period $	Date	Ex. Div.	Total $ So Far 1995	Ind. Rate	Paid 1994	Financial Position Mil-$ Cash& Equiv.	Curr. Assets	Curr. Liab.	Balance Sheet Date	Capitalization Lg Trm Debt Mil-$	Shs. 000 Pfd.	Com.	Earnings $ Per Shr. Years End	1991	1992	1993	1994	1995	Last 12 Mos.	Interim Earnings Period	$ per Shr. 1994	1995	Index
1	....	5%Stk	5-7-85	4-1	...	Nil	....	Book Value $5.58			8-31-95	482	...	±31271	My	Δd3.71	*±1.30	□±d2.82	±d1.43	±d0.16	d0.87	3 Mo Aug	±0.51	±d0.20	1
2	....	5%Stk	5-7-85	4-1	...	Nil	....	....	...	...		....	...	26158	My	Δd3.71	*±1.30	□±d2.82	±d1.43	±d0.16	d0.87	3 Mo Aug	±0.51	±d0.20	2
3◆	1987	0.15	2-15-96	11-29	0.60	0.60	0.60	Equity per shr $1.17			9-30-95	25.3	...	8323	Dc	d0.86	5.24	d0.01	0.07	....	0.16	9 Mo Sep	0.05	0.14	3
4◆	1989	Q0.03	1-2-96	12-13	0.10½	0.12	0.10	5.66	23.8	10.9	9-30-95	....	2	9394	Dc	0.36	0.40	Δ0.65	0.60	....	0.81	9 Mo Sep	0.46	0.67	4
5	....	0.04	10-10-86	9-8	...	Nil	....	File bankruptcy Chapt 7				0.24	...	5768	Dc	d0.44	Δ0.17	d0.19	d0.18	....	d0.87	6 Mo Jun	d0.12	d0.81	5
6	....	None Since Public			...	Nil	....	0.04	56.9	31.2	4-29-95	31.1	...	6790	Ja	Δd0.50	*0.40	Δ0.34	0.22	....	d1.12	9 Mo Oct	0.13	d1.21	6
7	1960	Q0.22	12-1-95	11-13	0.88	0.88	0.88	2.36	251	232	9-30-95	53.9	...	38563	Je	1.58	1.50	□d0.18	d0.36	□1.12	1.14	3 Mo Sep	□0.04	0.06	7
8	....	None Since Public			...	Nil	....	0.07	8.90	6.43	9-30-95	0.46	...	3610	Sp	0.08	0.13	d0.93	0.20	0.26	0.26				8
9	....	None Since Public			...	Nil	....	15.4	215	112	7-01-95	147	...	15932	Je	...	...	...	p0.58	□0.59	0.97	3 Mo Sep	d0.16	0.22	9
10	1994	Q0.42	12-28-95	12-13	1.637	1.68	[52]1.52½	Equity per shr $11.55			9-30-95	106	...	16036	Dc	...	p0.86	p0.91	p1.12	....	1.24	9 Mo Sep	p0.78	0.90	10
11	1990	Q0.25	11-22-95	11-6	1.00	1.00	0.72	Book Value $31.87			9-30-95	....	...	10503	Dc	1.00	1.89	Δ1.57	2.02	....	2.10	9 Mo Sep	1.38	1.46	11
12◆	1987	Q0.08	1-15-96	12-13	0.30	0.32	0.26	65.1	110	10.3	8-31-95	8.13	...	18505	Nv	0.69	0.83	0.98	1.23	....	1.12	9 Mo Aug	0.92	0.81	12
13◆	....	©1.30	12-26-86	11-20	...	Nil	....	13.9	60.8	28.0	9-30-95	56.3	...	1919	Je	§9.78	§[55]17.59	§20.49	§[53]20.73	3.06	2.32	3 Mo Sep	0.25	d0.49	13
14◆	1984	Q0.04	1-5-96	12-21	0.16	0.16	0.16	3.39	276	82.3	9-30-95	71.4	...	26699	Dc	0.73	0.98	Δ1.29	1.33	....	1.03	9 Mo Sep	0.92	0.62	14
15◆	1913	0.12	12-11-95	11-7	0.60	Nil	0.96	470	10574	6509	10-25-95	3658	655	459363	Ja	2.01	2.06	□d2.05	0.63	E0.05↓	d0.03	9 Mo Oct	0.32	d0.34	15
16	1994	0.02	1-15-96	12-27	0.08	0.08	0.06	27.1	92.7	8.01	9-30-95	0.55	...	±6578	Dc	1.34	□1.49	1.87	2.20	....	1.20	9 Mo Sep	1.98	0.98	16
17	....	None Since Public			...	Nil	....	20.8	235	287	p6-30-95	p1103	5290	★128230	Dc	...	...	...	pd0.51	....	....	6 Mo Jun	n/a	pd0.57	17
18	....	None Since Public			...	Nil	....	2.51	48.5	63.9	9-30-95	0.19	...	3104	Dc	1.23	1.27	Δd0.62	d2.22	....	d5.23	9 Mo Sep	d0.18	d3.19	18
19◆	....	0.004	12-18-80	12-5	...	[57]Nil	....	0.22	18.4	7.60	9-30-95	10.8	241	±11485	Mr	d0.07	0.06	d0.78	±d0.52	....	0.03	6 Mo Sep	d0.42	0.13	19
20	....	None Since Public			...	Nil	....	....	...	...		....	...	6793	Mr	d0.07	0.06	d0.78	±d0.52	....	0.03	6 Mo Sep	d0.42	0.13	20
21◆	1993	Q0.04	1-26-96	1-2	0.13	0.16	0.08	2.88	12.8	25.3	10-01-95	125	...	4229	Dc	*0.07	Δd1.26	0.49	0.14	....	0.33	9 Mo Sep	0.62	0.81	21
22	....	0.05	12-15-92	11-23	...	Nil	....	11.2	894	515	9-30-95	799	★9725	71638	Dc	2.03	0.47	□d2.25	□d2.09	....	d0.16	9 Mo Sep	□d1.53	0.40	22
23	1994	Q0.24¼	1-2-96	12-13	0.97	0.97	0.604	Cv into 0.8333 com,$14.10				....	8000	...	Dc	...	...	...	....	....	....	Mandatory conversion into one com 12-31-97			23
24	....	None Paid			...	Nil	....	10.4	13.2	6.97	9-30-95	5.52	...	10464	Dc	0.11	0.14	0.16	□0.21	....	0.07	9 Mo Sep	0.16	0.02	24
25	1972	Q0.11	1-16-96	12-28	0.44	0.44	0.44	3.17	418	222	9-30-95	76.5	286	±18419	Dc	±0.93	±[63]0.95	±d1.63	±d0.93	....	d0.88	9 Mo Sep	±0.60	±0.65	25
26	1990	Q0.55	11-14-95	9-13	2.20	2.20	2.20	6.94	20.0	21.8	9-30-95	69.0	...	[66]±16060	Dc	2.20	2.20	2.20	2.20	....	2.20	9 Mo Sep	1.65	1.65	26
27	....	Plan qtly div			...	2.20	....	....	...	...		....	...	[67]★4650	Dc	...	...	...	....	....	....				27
28	....	0.02	7-1-86	6-10	...	Nil	....	28.2	73.8	46.3	9-30-95	126	1558	33669	Dc	Δd0.71	Δd0.19	0.46	0.02	....	0.07	9 Mo Sep	0.03	Δ0.08	28
29	1995	Q0.10	12-1-95	11-13	0.40	0.40	....	Book Value $24.80			9-30-95	....	...	1447	Dc	...	...	□2.09	1.44	....	1.17	9 Mo Sep	1.11	0.84	29
30◆	1921	Q0.39	12-20-95	11-27	1.54	1.56	1.50	46.3	189	256	9-30-95	836	906	61902	Dc	1.58	1.35	1.66	1.64	E1.85	1.86	12 Mo Sep	1.63	1.86	30
31◆	1978	Q0.075	1-2-96	11-29	0.22½	0.30	[68]0.31¼	14.6	428	392	9-30-95	1038	1243	40612	Dc	□1.08	1.43	□2.16	2.32	E2.15	1.82	9 Mo Sep	1.95	1.45	31
32◆	1989	0.05	2-15-94	1-25	...	Nil	0.05	25.2	95.4	43.0	8-31-95	5.18	...	29484	Nv	[69]d0.03	p0.65	p0.30	0.02	....	0.15	9 Mo Aug	0.05	0.18	32
33	1991	Q0.06¼	1-22-96	12-27	0.25	0.25	†14.18¾	20.7	98.0	57.4	9-30-95	9.63	...	8763	Dc	Δ0.82	0.12	□d0.02	d0.98	....	2.04	9 Mo Sep	d1.00	2.02	33
34	....	None Since Public			...	Nil	....	2.22	72.0	53.9	9-30-95	178	...	13667	Dc	...	...	...	pd0.10	....	....	9 Mo Sep	n/a	d0.01	34
35	1986	Q0.075	11-28-95	11-10	0.30	0.30	0.30	Equity per shr $12.41			8-31-95	904	1300	32391	Nv	0.80	0.78	±0.96	1.16	E0.65	0.67	9 Mo Aug	0.77	0.28	35
36◆	1988	A0.164	4-8-95	3-16	0.164	0.164	0.149	13.2	44.8	43.1	9-30-95	0.60	...	3441	Dc	0.19	0.36	0.38	0.52	....	0.59	9 Mo Sep	0.40	0.47	36
37◆	1986	Q0.12	1-2-96	12-14	0.44	0.48	0.40	42.2	138	48.9	9-30-95	8.00	...	16560	Dc	1.47	□1.47	1.60	□1.87	....	2.18	9 Mo Sep	□1.37	1.68	37
38◆	1992	Q0.03	2-20-96	1-11	0.12	0.12	0.08	1.66	99.4	56.8	6-30-95	80.4	...	11486	Sp	0.23	0.30	1.19	1.97	P1.94	1.94				38
39◆	....	0.005	5-27-86	5-6	...	Nil	....	22.1	113	15.7	9-30-95	7.50	...	±16155	Dc	±0.54	±0.56	±0.76	±1.15	....	1.23	9 Mo Sep	±0.87	±0.95	39
40◆	1964	Q0.03⅛	12-29-95	12-19	0.11¼	0.125	0.10	3.89	39.7	20.1	9-30-95	6.04	...	±7259	Sp	±0.60	d1.77	Δ0.48	0.13	0.66	0.66				40
41	....	None Since Public			...	Nil	....	6.31	20.1	33.6	9-30-95	142	4677	43668	Dc	...	...	...	pd1.54	....	d1.42	9 Mo Sep	pd1.02	pd0.90	41
42◆	1923	Q0.39	12-14-95	11-29	1.50	1.56	1.40	464	1743	1441	9-30-95	718	...	217427	Dc	2.51	□2.86	2.94	3.15	E3.35	3.26	9 Mo Sep	2.45	2.56	42
43◆	1962	Q0.15	12-15-95	11-29	0.60	0.60	0.60	15.6	533	286	10-31-95	140	...	21171	Ap	0.71	1.26	1.39	1.71	[71]0.53	0.42	6 Mo Oct	1.04	0.93	43
44◆	1962	Q0.20	12-11-95	11-22	0.78	0.80	0.70	137	550	229	10-01-95	....	...	±38013	Dc	±1.02	±1.04	±1.18	±1.61	E1.81	1.78	9 Mo Sep	±1.13	±1.30	44
45◆	....	None Since Public			...	Nil	....	6.03	129	116	9-30-95	68.7	...	±38115	Mr	±pd0.76	±0.44	±□0.46	Δ±0.80	....	1.17	6 Mo Sep	±0.34	±0.71	45
46	1968	Q0.23	11-30-95	11-7	h[74]0.92	0.92	0.92	Equity per shr $34.97			9-30-95	357	[75]6631	34985	Dc	4.25	□d3.83	Δ5.00	1.97	E4.00	d0.31	9 Mo Sep	2.26	d0.02	46
47	....	None Since Public			...	Nil	....	26.3	245	136	9-30-95	152	102	36534	Dc	0.34	□Δ0.05	d0.22	d0.03	....	d0.25	9 Mo Sep	0.06	d0.16	47
48◆	1944	Q0.15	11-24-95	11-8	0.60	0.60	0.59	12.6	414	228	9-30-95	78.2	...	26624	Je	1.00	0.60	0.92	□0.45	2.58	2.69	3 Mo Sep	0.40	0.51	48
49◆	....	None Since Public			...	Nil	....	17.2	36.6	10.5	9-30-95	6.00	...	±13067	Dc	...	...	p0.34	0.60	....	0.72	9 Mo Sep	p0.49	0.61	49
50	....	None Since Public			...	Nil	....	....	1.32	16.5	9-30-95	0.10	...	★7160	Je	...	...	...	pd1.34	....	....	3 Mo Sep	n/a	pd0.75	50
51◆	....	None Since Public			...	Nil	....	105	189	34.5	9-30-95	....	...	11896	Mr	0.69	0.80	0.97	1.32	....	1.75	6 Mo Sep	0.60	1.03	51
52	....	None Since Public			...	Nil	....	0.20	36.1	24.1	7-01-95	7.72	...	4869	Sp	...	p0.95	1.23	1.06	P0.95	0.95				52

◆**Stock Splits & Divs By Line Reference Index** [3]No adj for spl cash dstr,'92. [4]2-for-1,'91. [12]2-for-1,'92. [13]1-for-4 REVERSE,'91:2-for-1,'94. [14]3-for-2,'92:2-for-1,'93. [15]2-for-1,'92. [19]2-for-1 in Cl'A','91. [21]2-for-1,'93. [30]2-for-1,'92. [31]2-for-1,'92,'93. [32]3-for-2,'91. [36]10%,'94,'95. [37]2-for-1,'92. [38]3-for-2,'92:2-for-1,'93(twice). [39]3-for-2,'93,'94. [40]2-for-1,'95. [42]2-for-1,'91. [43]3-for-2,'94. [44]5-for-4,'93. [45]2-for-1,'95. [48]2-for-1,'94. [49]2-for-1,'95. [51]3-for-2,'95.

¶ S&P 500 # MidCap 400 ✤ SmallCap 600 • Options

Index	Ticker	Name of Issue (Call Price of Pfd. Stocks)	Market	Com. Rank. & Pfd. Rating	Inst. Hold Cos	Inst. Hold Shs. (000)	Principal Business	Price Range 1971-93 High	1971-93 Low	1994 High	1994 Low	1995 High	1995 Low	Dec. Sales in 100s	December, 1995 Last Sale Or Bid High	Low	Last	%Div Yield	P-E Ratio	Total Return % Annualized 12 Mo	36 Mo	60 Mo
1	KYF	**Kentucky First Bancorp**	AS	NR	2	51	Savings bank, Kentucky	...	...	...	...	13	10	370	12¾	12¼	12¼B	4.1	..	...	...	...
2	KPC	**Kentucky Pwr 8.72% Sr'A'Debs**[51]	NY	....[52]	..	...	Subsid of Amer Elec Pwr	...	...	...	...	26⅝	24¼	460	26⅝	25¼	26¼B	8.3	..	...	...	...
3	KWN	✔**Kenwin Shops**	AS	NR	5	25	Ladies & children apparel	24	2¾	6⅛	2 7/16	4½	1⅝	134	3	2¼	2¼	...	d	−12.2	−26.9	−11.9
4	KERA	✔**KeraVision Inc**	NNM	NR	16	1699	Dvlp stage:eyecare medical prd	...	...	...	...	13¾	9	5985	13	10¾	12½	...	d	...	...	...
5	KER	**Kerr-Addison Mines**	To	B	8	2457	Canada gold mine: invests	30¾	5⅝	26	22⅛	28	19	1189	27⅜	26	27⅜	2.2	22	11.2	24.1	...
6	KGM	✔**Kerr Group**	NY,B,Ch	C	17	1820	Glass containers: closures	22	4⅜	10⅝	8	10⅜	6½	1546	10⅜	8½	10	...	d	21.2	15.4	14.9
7	Pr D	**$1.70 cm CvB PfdSerD(20)**	NY	NR	5	171	packaging products	30⅝	11⅞	22	19⅛	20⅝	16⅜	523	19½	16⅜	18½	9.2	..	...	...	...
¶8•[1]	KMG	✔**Kerr-McGee**	NY,To,B,C,Ch,P,Ph	B	443	38204	Petroleum, chemicals,coal	56	15⅞	51	40	64	44	36775	64	57¼	63½	2.6	d	41.0	16.0	11.0
9	KEQU	✔**Kewaunee Scientific**	NNM	C	11	274	Furniture & eqp for labs	15¾	1¼	4¼	2	3½	2⅛	1402	3⅜	2⅝	3¼	...	18	57.6	−2.4	−3.3
10	KEG	✔**Key Energy Group**	AS	NR	14	1168	Provides oil field services	6⅛	2	5¾	4⅜	6½	4⅛	2622	6½	5⅜	6½	...	19	40.5	42.4	...
¶11•[2]	KEY	✔**KeyCorp**	NY	A+	516	103578	Commercial bkg,Ohio,Nthn US	37¼	2⅛	33¾	23⅝	37¼	24¾	73934	37¼	35¼	36¼	4.0	11	53.1	7.1	...
12	KES	✔**Keystone Consol Ind**	NY,Ch	B−	21	759	Mfr steel & wire products	25¾	1 11/16	18	10	15⅛	11⅛	241	12¾	11⅛	11½	...	18	−17.1	5.7	0.9
✤13	KSTN	✔**Keystone Financial**	NNM	A−	88	6573	General banking, Pennsylvania	34½	8⅝	32¼	27¼	34	26¼	11263	32¼	29½	30	4.8	12	8.3	5.5	20.0
14	KHG	✔**Keystone Heritage Group**	AS	A−	23	605	Commercial banking, PA	27¼	10¼	28½	24	31⅞	23	38	31½	30¾	30½B	3.1	13	31.6	52.5	49.0
#15•[3]	KII	✔**Keystone Intl**	NY,B,Ch	B+	156	21894	Mfrs flow control prod & sys	35⅜	7/16	29½	16¾	23	16¾	16249	21¼	18⅞	20	3.7	20	14.3	−4.0	−1.9
16	KPI	✔**Killearn Properties**[55]	AS,Ph	B−	4	27	Develop communities:Florida	23½	1/16	6	4⅛	6⅝	4⅛	487	5⅝	5	5	...	9	12.5	14.5	4.2
17	KBALB	✔**Kimball Intl Cl'B'**	NNM	A−	86	4970	Furniture,pianos,organs	34½	2 7/16	32½	21⅜	28¾	23¾	4182	26½	24¾	25¼	3.6	13	7.1	1.8	10.7
¶18•[4]	KMB	✔**Kimberly-Clark**	NY,B,C,Ch,P,Ph	A+	721	105004	Consumer products:newsprint	63¼	2 5/16	60	47	83	47¼	205420	83	73¾	82¾	2.2	20	...	...	...
19	KIM	✔**Kimco Realty**	NY,Ph	NR	134	27533	Real estate investment trust	26⅛	12⅞	25⅞	22	28⅛	23⅝	5393	28⅛	26¾	27¼	5.7	21	14.0	17.1	...
20	KVN	✔**Kimmins Environ'l Svcs**	NY,Ch	B−	12	816	Environmen'l svcs/waste mgmt	9½	2	2¾	1⅜	6⅜	1½	8423	2⅞	2⅛	2½	...	31	66.7	...	...
21	KIN	✔**Kinark Corp**	AS,B,P	B−	17	839	Chemical packag'g/dstr:mfg	10⅞	½	4⅞	3	4	2¼	1317	2⅞	2¼	2⅞	...	d	−6.0	−14.8	−6.0
22	KCLC	✔**Kinder-Care Learning Ctrs**	NSC	NR	72	17756	Operates day care centers	17¼	⅛	16½	10⅞	14⅝	11⅛	11895	12⅞	11¾	12⅝	...	12	8.6	156	74.5
23	KNCI	✔**Kinetic Concepts**	NNM	B	91	9365	Mfr & rents therapeutic beds	13⅞	2¼	7⅛	3⅜	13⅛	6¼	5273	12¼	11	12	1.3	19	81.0	9.2	30.1
¶24•[5]	KWP	✔**King World Prod'ns**	NY,B,P,Ph	B+	315	23723	Dstr/synd'n of TV programs	43¾	1⅛	44⅛	32½	44½	32½	24804	40¼	38½	38⅞	...	12	13.9	3.4	9.9
25	KINN	✔**Kinnard Investments**	NNM,Ch	B−	7	337	Securities broker/dealer	8	¾	5¼	1⅞	4⅜	1 15/16	1817	3⅞	3⅝	3⅝	...	17	95.4	−8.3	27.0
26	KGC	✔**Kinross Gold**	NY,To,Ch,Ph,Vc	B−	78	30973	Acquis/dev of precious metals	4¼	¼	6	3	8⅞	3⅞	4312	8¼	7⅝	7⅝	...	..	45.2	82.7	48.3
✤27•[6]	KEX	✔**Kirby Corp**	AS,B,Ch,Ph	B−	103	13801	Tows freight by barge:insur	45¾	⅞	23⅜	15½	19¾	13	10386	17⅞	15¼	16¼	...	45	−15.0	9.9	16.0
28	KIT	✔**Kit Mfg**	AS	B−	10	269	Mobile hms:recr'l vehicles	23⅜	1	19½	8¼	14¼	9⅞	472	14¼	11	14	...	12	20.4	20.5	22.9
29•[7]	KLAC	✔**KLA Instruments**	NNM,Ch	B−	258	48417	Electro-optical test sys	14⅛	1 3/16	27	12¼	48¾	23¼	269325	36¾	26	26	...	18	4.3	65.5	42.9
30	KFBI	✔**Klamath First Bancorp**	NNM	NR	1	20	Savings & loan, Oregon	...	...	...	...	13¾	10	13277	13¾	13⅛	13¾	1.5	..	...	...	...
31	KVU	✔**Kleer-Vu Industries**	AS	C	8	90	Plastic transparent items	34¾	13/16	11⅜	4	10¼	4⅛	650	6⅜	4¾	4⅞	...	d	−48.7	...	...
32	KLLM	✔**KLLM Transport Sv**	NNM	B	29	1934	Temp-controlled transport	24	6⅜	20	14	16	9	6055	11½	10⅜	10½	...	28	−30.0	−17.9	9.3
33•[8]	KLM	✔**KLM Royal Dutch Air**	NY,B,Ch,P,Ph	NR	68	4321	Worldwide air transport	27¾	2½	32½	21¼	39¼	24⅝	7099	36	34¼	35¼	...	10	47.8	38.1	26.8
34	KDX	**Klondex Mines Ltd**	Vc	NR	1	84	Acq,explore natural res prop	2⅞	⅛	1⅞	⅝	1¾	11/16	660	1⅝	15/16	1B	...	d	...	...	...
35	KLOFY	✔**Kloof Gold Mining ADR**[65]	NSC	NR	43	9829	South Africa gold mining	16⅛	13/16	17⅞	8⅜	14¾	9	20587	10	9	9⅜	3.7	8	−33.2	23.4	2.6
✤36	KNE	✔**KN Energy**	NY,Ch	B	138	12683	Nat'l gas,mineral resources	37⅜	6⅝	26⅞	20¾	30¼	20¼	4865	30¼	28⅞	29⅛	3.6	18	37.0	20.3	18.8
37	KNAP	✔**Knape & Vogt Mfg**	NNM	B+	47	1610	Mfr home furnishing items	20½	1 9/16	20½	14½	19¾	12¾	1214	18	15⅛	17⅜	3.8	14	−5.0	12.5	22.1
¶38•[9]	KRI	✔**Knight-Ridder Inc**	NY,B,Ch,P	A−	331	32096	Newspapers:business info svs	65	3⅜	61	46½	66⅝	50½	33363	66⅝	61⅞	62½	2.4	21	24.9	5.1	9.2
39	KNGT	✔**Knight Transportation**	NNM	NR	30	1708	Trucking-gen'l commodities	...	...	15¾	12	16⅞	11⅜	2120	15½	13¾	13¾B	...	23	−3.5	...	...
40	KNA	✔**Knogo North America**	AS	NR	12	568	Electronic detector systems	...	...	...	...	8	2⅜	2482	7⅜	6⅜	7	...	..	...	...	...
41	KE	✔**Koger Equity**	AS,Ch	NR	48	10365	Real estate investment trust	20¾	3¼	10½	6⅛	10⅝	6½	8110	10⅝	9⅜	10⅝	...	8	49.1	36.4	7.4
42	WS	**Wrrt(Pur 1 com at $8)**	AS	....	17	24		3½	2⅛	3¾	1¾	3½	1⅝	673	3½	2⅞	3⅜	...	..	...	...	...
#43•[1]	KSS	✔**Kohl's Corp**	NY,Ph	NR	250	28802	Oper family oriented dept strs	52⅛	13¼	55¼	39⅛	55⅛	38	20866	55	50½	52½	...	27	32.1	21.4	...
44	KOL	✔**Kollmorgen Corp**	NY,Ch,Ph	B−	32	4039	Motor/ctrls,elec optic instr	36¾	1 3/16	9¾	5¼	12	5⅝	3050	11	9	11	0.7	26	102	24.6	10.4
✤45•[3]	KMAG	✔**Komag Inc**	NNM	B−	197	18177	Mfr thin film computer disks	24½	6	28⅞	15¾	74⅞	22¼	137439	57	43⅞	46⅛	...	12	79.1	39.5	32.9
46	KOR	**Koor Indus Ltd ADS**[68]	NY	NR	..	...	Telecommun,electr,chem,food	...	...	...	...	20⅞	16⅝	9833	20⅞	17½	20¼	1.0	9	...	...	...
47	KEP	**Korea Electric Power ADS**[70]	NY,Ch,Ph	NR	89	24919	Electric utility-Korea	...	...	22	19	27	17⅜	71699	27	24⅜	26¾	1.2	24	27.7	...	...
48	KEP Pr	**Partial Dividend ADS**[71]	NY	NR	2	3		...	...	...	...	26⅝	21½	7770	26⅝	24⅜	26½	...	..	...	...	...
49	KRT	✔**Kranzco Realty Trust**	NY,Ph	NR	64	3573	Real estate investment trust	27	19¾	24	16⅝	19½	14	16835	15⅜	14⅛	14¾	13.0	16	−13.4	−3.0	...
¶50•[4]	KR	✔**Kroger Co**	NY,B,C,Ch,Ph	B	468	71033	Supermkt/convenience stores	59	3⅝	26⅞	19⅜	37¾	23⅜	53870	37¾	33⅛	37⅜	...	14	56.5	35.9	22.1
51	KRON	✔**Kronos Inc**	NNM	NR	62	2962	Mfr data collection systems	24	11¾	27	14½	50½	24½	1879	49	43¼	47½	...	31	77.6	30.2	...
52	KRUG	✔**KRUG International**	NNM	B−	9	718	Aerospace/marine/housewares	13⅞	⅛	5	2 1/16	4¾	2⅝	2902	3¼	3	3¼	...	11	12.5	16.6	26.8

Uniform Footnote Explanations-See Page 4. Other: [1]CBOE:Cycle 1. [2]Ph:Cycle 3. [3]P:Cycle 3. [4]ASE:Cycle 1. [5]P:Cycle 2. [6]NY:Cycle 2. [7]NY,Ph:Cycle 3. [8]CBOE:Cycle 3. [9]Ph:Cycle 1.
[51]Jr Sub Deferrable Int Debs. [52]Rated BBB by S&P. [53]Restated from $4.90. [54]Stk dstr of Keycon Indus Inc. [55]Digital Communications prop acq,$8:Co rejects. [56]Restated by company.
[57]Stk dstr of Schweitzer-Mauduit Intl Inc. [58]12 Mo Dec'91. [59]Stk dstr of Cumberland Holdings,'92. [60]Redemption of stk purch rt. [61]Fiscal Dec'92 & prior. [62]21 wk May,'93. [63]®$0.24,'94. [64]Approx.
[65]ADR equal 1 ord shr. [66]Fiscal Feb'94 & prior. [67]At prices scaling fr $1.92-$5.24, at 6-99. [68]Ea ADS rep 0.20 Ord Shrs, NIS 0.001. [69]Excl 12.9M Deferred shrs. [70]Ea ADS rep 0.5 com,5,000 Won.
[71]Ea ADS rep 0.5 com 5,000 won. [72]To be determined. [73]Incl current amts. [74]6 Mo Dec'92. [75]Special dstr. [76]®$2.19,'94.

Index	Cash Divs. Ea.Yr. Since	Dividends: Latest Payment Period $	Date	Ex. Div.	Total $ So Far 1995	Ind. Rate	Paid 1994	Financial Position Mil-$ Cash& Equiv.	Curr. Assets	Curr. Liab.	Balance Sheet Date	Capitalization Lg Trm Debt Mil-$	Shs. 000 Pfd.	Com.	Earnings $ Per Shr. Years End	1991	1992	1993	1994	1995	Last 12 Mos.	Interim Earnings Period	$ per Shr. 1994	1995	Index
1	....	Plan qtly div			...	0.50	....	Book Value $14.06			9-30-95	0.33	...	1389	Je	...	...	...	....	n/a	....	3 Mo Sep	n/a	p0.11	1
2	....	Plan qtly div			...	2.18	....	Co option redm fr 4-20-2000 at $25				40.0	...	...	Dc	...	...	...	....	....	....	Mature 6-30-2025			2
3	....	0.05	8-14-87	7-27	...	Nil	....	0.30	6.01	3.20	p7-31-95	0.05	...	p557	Dc	d1.39	0.65	d1.59	d6.59	....	d6.28	9 Mo Sep	d3.90	d3.59	3
4	....	None Since Public			...	Nil	....	46.8	47.2	2.13	9-30-95	0.14	...	12261	Dc	...	...	...	pd0.74	....	d0.75	9 Mo Sep	d0.57	pd0.58	4
5	1940	gQ0.15	12-14-95	11-21	g0.60	0.60	g0.60	240	250	0.45	j12-31-94	....	...	17593	Dc	0.18	1.75	1.78	1.09	....	j1.25	9 Mo Sep	0.75	0.91	5
6	....	0.11	9-15-90	8-27	...	Nil	....	0.27	49.3	21.2	9-30-95	50.0	487	3933	Dc	d0.93	d0.96	□d0.32	0.70	....	d0.62	9 Mo Sep	0.69	d0.63	6
7	1979	Q0.42½	12-29-95	12-6	1.70	1.70	1.70	Cv into 1.4545 com,$13.75				....	487	...	Dc	b0.50	b1.26	b0.82	b1.44	....	....				7
8	1941	Q0.41	1-2-96	11-29	1.52	1.64	1.52	102	798	594	9-30-95	577	...	51600	Dc	2.10	□d0.53	1.57	1.74	Ed0.69↓	d0.78	9 Mo Sep	1.35	d1.17	8
9	....	0.04	9-25-92	9-4	...	Nil	....	0.01	17.9	9.85	10-31-95	3.41	...	2367	Ap	0.03	0.33	d1.04	d0.09	d0.46	0.18	6 Mo Oct	d0.55	0.09	9
10	....	None Since Public			...	Nil	....	0.66	11.1	8.46	9-30-95	14.5	...	6913	Je	p0.29	n/a	Δ0.33	0.26	0.33	0.35	3 Mo Sep	0.09	0.11	10
11◆	1963	Q0.36	12-15-95	11-24	1.44	1.44	1.28	Book Value $16.19			9-30-95	4048	1280	p236757	Dc	[53]0.61	2.51	p2.89	3.45	E3.40↑	3.23	9 Mo Sep	2.66	Δ2.44	11
12	....	h[54]....	3-2-84	3-5	...	Nil	....	....	84.4	81.9	9-30-95	15.3	...	5637	Dc	*1.75	□0.92	0.14	1.35	....	0.65	9 Mo Sep	1.39	0.69	12
13	1985	Q0.36	1-20-96	1-8	1.36	1.44	1.28	Book Value $18.96			9-30-95	180	...	24099	Dc	2.27	2.33	2.49	2.20	....	2.52	9 Mo Sep	1.60	1.92	13
14◆	1984	Q0.24	11-10-95	10-27	0.94	0.96	0.84	Book Value $18.68			9-30-95	11.6	...	3054	Dc	1.41	1.68	□1.72	2.22	....	2.43	9 Mo Sep	1.61	1.82	14
15	1972	Q0.18½	2-21-96	2-5	0.74	0.74	0.73½	12.5	334	129	9-30-95	59.4	...	35410	Dc	□0.66	1.22	Δ1.12	0.94	E1.00	0.98	9 Mo Sep	0.68	0.72	15
16	....	None Paid			...	Nil	....	Equity per shr $12.34			7-31-95	20.0	...	1439	Ap	0.45	0.06	[56]0.27	Δ0.13	0.43	0.56	6 Mo Oct	0.53	0.66	16
17	1954	Q0.23	1-15-96	12-21	0.88	0.92	0.84	117	322	118	9-30-95	0.76	...	±20959	Je	1.42	1.83	1.45	±1.71	±1.97	1.97	3 Mo Sep	±0.40	±0.40	17
18◆	1935	Q0.45	1-3-96	12-6	h[57]1.79	1.80	1.75	235	3692	3971	p6-30-95	2176	...	p279137	Dc	3.18	□2.15	3.18	3.33	E4.10↑	3.66	9 Mo Sep	2.67	3.00	18
19◆	1992	Q0.39	1-16-96	12-28	1.44	1.56	1.333	Equity per shr $9.61			9-30-95	349	500	33686	Dc	[58]d0.67	0.83	□1.17	□1.17	....	1.31	9 Mo Sep	□0.87	1.01	19
20	....	h[59]....	9-30-92	10-1	...	Nil	....	0.37	40.6	31.1	9-30-95	18.2	...	±20217	Dc	0.17	0.01	0.13	0.06	....	0.08	9 Mo Sep	0.09	0.11	20
21	....	[60]0.01	11-1-90	10-9	...	Nil	....	0.13	6.95	9.88	9-30-95	7.45	...	3747	Dc	1.00	0.38	Δ0.21	0.11	....	d0.52	9 Mo Sep	0.16	d0.47	21
22◆	....	None Since Public			...	Nil	....	10.5	34.6	77.5	9-22-95	153	...	19454	My	d0.99	[61]d0.21	Δ[62]d1.71	□0.97	1.07	1.09	16 Wk Sep	0.15	0.17	22
23	1989	Q0.038	11-16-95	11-6	0.15	0.15	0.15	49.9	131	35.7	9-30-95	....	...	44269	Dc	0.49	0.63	□Δ0.18	Δ1.44	....	0.64	9 Mo Sep	Δ1.25	0.45	23
24	....	None Since Public			...	Nil	....	447	589	111	8-31-95	....	...	36753	Au	□2.38	2.43	2.65	2.33	3.14	3.14				24
25◆	1992	0.02½	1-31-95	1-9	0.02½	Nil	0.10	Equity per shr $3.94			9-30-95	1.72	...	6255	Dc	1.17	0.76	0.64	d0.54	....	0.22	9 Mo Sep	d0.32	0.44	25
26	....	None Since Public			...	Nil	....	115	147	22.6	j12-31-94	5.15	470	★102813	Dc	0.03	0.17	0.11	[63]0.27	....	j0.23	9 Mo Sep	0.15	0.11	26
27	....	0.10	9-5-89	8-8	...	Nil	....	17.7	105	70.7	9-30-95	159	...	26385	Dc	0.61	□0.60	0.86	0.58	....	0.36	9 Mo Sep	0.34	0.12	27
28	....	None Paid			...	Nil	....	0.81	17.4	8.99	7-31-95	....	...	1111	Oc	Nil	0.99	0.02	1.61	P1.21	1.21				28
29◆	....	None Since Public			...	Nil	....	104	372	130	9-30-95	....	...	50421	Je	d0.29	■d0.38	0.18	0.68	1.20	1.45	3 Mo Sep	0.27	0.52	29
30	1996	0.05	1-22-96	1-3	...	0.20	....	Book Value $12.84			3-31-95	....	...	★12233	Sp	...	...	...	p□0.54	....	....	6 Mo Mar	n/a	p□0.25	30
31◆	1992	0.066	1-15-93	12-24	...	Nil	....	0.32	17.3	8.76	9-30-95	14.8	900	2676	Dc	0.33	Δ0.64	d1.63	d1.56	....	d1.94	9 Mo Sep	d1.67	d2.05	31
32◆	....	None Paid			...	Nil	....	....	41.0	23.7	9-30-95	64.8	...	4509	Dc	0.83	1.23	1.09	1.15	....	0.38	9 Mo Sep	0.90	0.13	32
33	....	[64]0.806	8-22-95	8-11	0.806	Nil	....	3239	4942	3120	j3-31-95	8165	11750	85126	Mr	Δ0.79	Δd6.10	Δ0.73	3.30	E3.50	3.27	6 Mo Sep	3.00	2.97	33
34	....	None Paid			...	Nil	....	0.64	0.65	0.05	j6-30-95	....	...	5160	Dc	n/a	n/a	d0.03	d0.03	....	jd0.04	6 Mo Jun	d0.01	d0.02	34
35	1970	[64]0.112	2-23-96	12-27	0.428	0.35	0.397	238	356	437	j6-30-95	....	...	138600	Je	1.03	0.94	1.13	1.49	1.14	1.14	No interim reporting			35
36◆	1937	Q0.26	12-29-95	12-13	1.01	1.04	0.97	22.9	234	239	9-30-95	320	70	27962	Dc	0.21	1.28	p1.09	0.52	....	1.61	12 Mo Sep	0.43	1.61	36
37◆	1934	Q0.16½	12-1-95	11-15	0.66	0.66	0.63	1.33	63.0	12.1	9-30-95	39.4	...	±5881	Je	±0.96	±1.14	±0.95	±1.39	±1.40	1.23	3 Mo Sep	±0.43	±0.26	37
38	1941	Q0.37	1-6-96	12-26	1.48	1.48	1.44	17.7	479	428	9-24-95	593	...	48514	Dc	2.55	□2.65	2.68	3.15	E3.00	3.70	9 Mo Sep	2.16	□2.71	38
39	....	None Since Public			...	Nil	....	0.13	9.70	8.39	9-30-95	1.20	...	9102	Dc	0.11	0.17	0.30	0.49	....	0.60	9 Mo Sep	0.35	0.46	39
40	....	None Since Public			...	Nil	....	Equity per shr $3.86			9-30-95	0.76	...	5684	Dc	...	...	p[66]0.10	n/a	....	....	9 Mo Sep	n/a	0.18	40
41	....	0.12	10-23-91	9-24	...	Nil	....	Equity per shr $17.05			9-30-95	256	...	17751	Dc	d0.43	0.07	0.18	0.24	....	1.37	9 Mo Sep	0.17	1.30	41
42	....	Terms&trad. basis should			be checked in detail			Wrrts expire 6-30-99				....	...	644	Dc	...	...	...	....	....	....	Callable qtly fr 12-31-93 to 6-30-99[67]			42
43	....	None Since Public			...	Nil	....	3.27	478	260	10-28-95	260	...	36859	Ja	Δp0.75	□0.88	□1.52	1.87	E1.95	1.76	9 Mo Oct	0.94	0.83	43
44	1943	Q0.02	12-1-95	11-15	0.08	0.08	0.08	12.8	97.3	68.3	9-30-95	36.9	23	9692	Dc	d3.97	d1.14	0.25	0.18	....	0.42	9 Mo Sep	0.05	0.29	44
45◆	....	None Since Public			...	Nil	....	202	309	69.9	10-01-95	....	...	★25204	Dc	*0.74	0.79	d0.46	2.54	E4.00	3.41	9 Mo Sep	1.94	2.81	45
46	....	Plan semi-annual div			...	0.20	....	247	1635	1206	6-30-95	p423	...	[69]±★15117	Dc	2.47	2.86	2.14	1.86	....	2.23	9 Mo Sep	1.61	1.98	46
47	1995	[64]0.271		12-27	[64]0.314	0.31	....	325	2296	3879	6-30-95	9184	...	★623171	Dc	p0.59	0.84	0.46	1.04	....	1.10	6 Mo Jun	0.49	0.55	47
48	....	Plan annual div			...	[72]....	....	....	...	...		....	...	6977	Dc	...	...	...	....	....	....				48
49	1993	Q0.48	1-17-96	12-26	1.92	1.92	1.88	Equity per shr $15.74			9-30-95	[73]202	11	10324	Dc	p0.84	‡[74]0.11	1.16	0.96	....	0.95	9 Mo Sep	0.69	0.68	49
50◆	....	†[75]40.00	12-2-88	12-5	...	Nil	....	43.9	2076	2479	10-07-95	3505	...	123618	Dc	□1.12	□1.11	□1.60	□[76]2.37	E2.70	2.59	9 Mo Sep	□1.56	□1.78	50
51	....	None Since Public			...	Nil	....	21.4	57.2	30.4	9-30-95	....	...	5181	Sp	0.55	*0.81	Δ0.76	0.93	1.54	1.54				51
52◆	....	Wrrt	1-31-95	2-1	Wrrt	Wrrt	5%Stk	2.09	26.8	13.9	9-30-95	12.9	...	5052	Mr	Δ0.28	0.52	0.28	0.40	....	0.29	6 Mo Sep	0.27	0.16	52

◆**Stock Splits & Divs By Line Reference Index** [11]2-for-1,'93. [14]10%,'91:5-for-4,'94. [18]2-for-1,'92. [19]3-for-2,'95. [22]No adj for'93 reorg. [25]6-for-5,'91. [29]2-for-1,'95. [31]10%,'92(twice):6-for-5,'93. [32]4-for-3,'92. [36]No adj for '85 spinoff:3-for-2,'93. [37]10%,'91,'92,'94. [45]To split 2-for-1,ex Jan 11. [50]No adj for spl dstr of $40 & debs,'88. [52]Adj for 5%,Nov'93:10%,'94.

¶ S&P 500 · # MidCap 400 · ✥ SmallCap 600 · • Options

Index	Ticker	Name of Issue (Call Price of Pfd. Stocks)	Market	Com. Rank. & Pfd. Rating	Inst. Hold Cos	Inst. Hold Shs. (000)	Principal Business	Price Range 1971-93 High	1971-93 Low	1994 High	1994 Low	1995 High	1995 Low	Dec. Sales in 100s	December, 1995 Last Sale Or Bid High	Low	Last	%Div Yield	P-E Ratio	Total Return % Annualized 12 Mo	36 Mo	60 Mo
1	KU	✓KU Energy	NY,B,Ch,P	A	131	6940	Electric utility: coal based	32¾	6⅝	29¼	24½	30⅝	26	6684	30⅝	28¾	30	5.6	17	15.8	8.2	12.3
2	KUB	Kubota Corp ADR[51]	NY,B,Ch,Ph	NR	11	203	Agricul mchy,pipe,Japan	195	5½	160	103	142	122	13	131	127	127	0.9	36	−4.9	15.5	6.0
✥3	KUH	✓Kuhlman Corp	NY,Ch	B−	69	6952	Transformers,metal prod	22⅛	1 11/16	19⅜	11	13½	10⅜	6920	12½	10⅞	12½	4.8	23	1.0	2.3	9.3
4•[1]	KLIC	✓Kulicke & Soffa Ind	NNM	B−	148	17119	Equip to mfr semiconduct'rs	17⅜	1/16	11	4¾	45⅜	9⅛	75131	29½	22	23¼	...	10	128	96.1	55.8
5	KMAC	Kushi Macrobiotics	NSC	NR	..	...	Dvlp stge:dvp natural food prd	....	....	....	....	6¼	3	4286	5	3	4	...	..	...	...	...
6	KYO	✓Kyocera Corp[53] ADR	NY,B,Ch	NR	69	1343	Ceramic products,elec/other	126	⅝	154¼	104	184	123	1183	162½	144½	149¼	0.6	28	1.3	29.3	12.5
✥7	KZ	✓Kysor Indl	NY,Ch	†B	62	2692	Truck eq:commer'l refrig'n	23½	1	22⅜	15	25¼	20	2012	24½	21½	24¼	2.5	9	13.1	12.9	30.4
✥8•[1]	LA	✓L.A. Gear, Inc	NY,Ch,Ph	C	45	2687	Athletic footwear	50⅝	1⅝	10¼	4⅝	5⅛	1½	33407	1⅞	1⅝	1⅝	...	d	−67.5	−45.7	−34.6
9•[2]	LQI	✓La Quinta Inns	NY,B,Ch	B−	236	32527	Motor inn operator	16	1/16	25⅞	12¾	30¾	19½	26292	28½	24⅝	27⅜	0.4	28	31.6	69.2	53.5
✥10	LZB	✓La-Z Boy Chair	NY,Ch,P,Ph	A−	85	4621	Mfr of reclining chairs	38⅞	1 1/16	40	25¼	33½	25⅝	6242	32⅛	28⅞	30⅞	2.5	15	−1.0	9.9	16.1
11	LB	✓LaBarge Inc	AS	B−	17	1819	Mfr electronic devices/cable	8⅝	⅜	2¼	1	4⅜	1 3/16	4132	3⅞	3	3½	...	39	180	34.5	51.5
12	LABS	✓LabOne Inc	NNM	B	27	796	Lab svcs to life insur indus	39¼	8¾	24¼	14½	16	10⅝	2494	15¼	12½	14¾	4.9	48	0.3	6.5	10.6
13	LBC	Laboratorio Chile ADS[55]	NY,Ch,Ph	NR	19	321	Mfr,dstr pharmaceutical prod	....	....	23⅛	12⅞	23¾	11	2442	13¾	11⅝	12⅝	1.7	18	−41.2	...	...
#14•[3]	LH	✓Laboratory Corp Amer Hldgs	NY,Ch,Ph	NR	119	29822	Clinical lab svcs in U.S.	30⅞	7⅜	15¾	10⅝	15½	8⅛	22777	9⅜	8¼	9⅜	...	..	−27.2	−19.0	−2.2
15	WS	Wrrt(Pur 1 com at $22)[56]	NY	....	36	3599		....	....	....	....	2⅞	9/16	3834	13/16	9/16	11/16	...	..	...	...	...
16	LG	✓Laclede Gas	NY,Ch,Ph	B	63	2710	Distr nat gas in St. Louis	25	2⅞	25⅝	18¼	23⅛	18⅜	2757	23⅛	21	21¼	5.9	17	14.5	8.2	14.0
17	LCLD	✓Laclede Steel	NNM	B−	26	1147	Semi & finished steel prods	27½	2 7/16	18¾	9⅝	14½	6	4217	7⅝	6	7½	...	6	−25.0	−23.1	−1.5
18	BOOT	✓LaCrosse Footwear	NNM	NR	17	1332	Mfr/dsgn protective footwear	....	....	14¾	10¾	12	8	2483	10¾	8½	8¾	1.0	16	−19.7	...	...
19	LADF	✓LADD Furniture	NNM	B−	60	3726	Mfrs & mkts furniture	74¼	12¾	35¼	14⅝	19⅞	12¼	5384	13⅝	13⅛	13⅛	2.7	d	−31.8	−26.1	−5.9
20	LUCK	✓Lady Luck Gaming'A'	NNM	NR	17	3312	Own,oper,dvlp casinos	19	7¼	13¾	2¼	2¾	1½	5525	2	1⅝	1⅝	...	d	−40.9	...	...
21•[4]	LAF	✓Lafarge Corp	NY,B,Ch,Mo,Ph	B−	119	14941	Major cement producer	22⅞	6¾	27¼	16¼	22¼	16⅝	15603	19½	17¾	18⅝	2.1	10	7.7	9.0	9.4
¶22•[5]	LDW.B	✓Laidlaw Inc Cl'B'[57]	NY,Ch,Ph	B+	216	74729	Waste mgmt/transport'n svc	24⅝	2 1/16	8½	5½	10¼	7⅝	103030	10¼	9⅛	10¼	◆...	21	30.4	6.1	−9.3
23•[5]	LDW.A	✓ Cl'A' vtg	NY,Ch,Ph	B+	25	5234		24½	2¼	8¼	5⅝	10⅛	7¾	603	10⅛	9	9⅞	◆...	21	29.7	3.9	−10.1
24	UXL	Laidlaw One 5.75% Ex Nts 2000	NY	....[58]	..	...	Subsid of Laidlaw Inc	....	....	....	....	26⅜	21¼	3905	26⅜	22⅝	25⅞B	4.7	..	...	...	...
25	LHP	✓Lakehead Pipe Line Ptnrs L.P.[60]	[6]NY,Ch	NR	34	473	Own/oper oil&gas pipeline sys	33¼	20⅞	34	25½	30⅝	22	11102	26½	24	25½	10.0	19	5.6	10.0	...
26•[7]	LRCX	✓Lam Research	NNM,Ch	B	281	25515	Mfrs plasma etching equip	36¾	2	46¾	22¾	73⅜	35¼	216746	57¼	45⅝	45¾	...	12	18.8	49.2	69.0
27	LMS	✓Lamson & Sessions	NY,Ch,Ph,P	C	40	6924	Mfr PVC electr prod/other	21¼	1¾	8⅝	4¾	8	5¼	4372	8	7	7¾	...	13	29.2	12.1	14.1
#28•[8]	LANC	✓Lancaster Colony	NNM	A	178	15963	Mfr food/auto prod	35⅝	7/16	39¼	28¼	38	28¾	15736	38	33¾	37¼	1.8	16	30.7	22.2	45.6
#29	LNCE	✓Lance, Inc	NNM	B+	102	10760	Snack foods: vending	28¼	1⅝	22¾	16¼	20	15¾	21715	16½	15¾	16⅜	5.9	22	−2.7	−6.8	−0.3
30	LAN	✓Lancer Corp	AS	B−	17	557	Mfr beverage dispensing sys	12⅝	2 5/16	15¼	9½	16	10¼	323	14½	13	14	...	17	19.7	41.5	40.5
31	LNCT	✓Lancit Media Productions	NNM	NR	31	1863	Dvlp original T.V. program's	15¾	1½	16⅝	11¼	18⅛	10⅝	5639	13¾	10⅝	11⅞	...	59	−11.0	46.8	...
32	LAND	✓Landair Services	NNM	NR	29	1704	Truck'g svcs/freight forward'g	21½	14¾	24½	14¼	17½	11¼	2535	14½	12	13¼	...	24	−13.1	...	...
33	LDR	✓Landauer Inc	AS,Ch	B+	57	4658	Provides radiation monitor svc	21⅜	4⅝	17	13⅛	22⅛	16¼	2849	22⅛	19⅛	21¾	5.1	18	40.3	14.5	13.9
34	LMBC	✓Landmark Bancorp[64]	NNM	B	5	49	General banking,California	14½	4½	10	6¼	18½	8¼	968	18½	17¼	17⅞	...	16	121	56.4	17.4
✥35•[9]	LMRK	✓Landmark Graphics	NNM	†B	115	13348	Computer sys for o&g explor'n	26¾	7⅜	35¼	16	28½	17¾	22158	24	19¾	23¼	...	27	29.2	20.2	10.7
36•[1]	LDRY	✓Landry's Seafood Restaurants	NNM	NR	100	17677	Oper seafood restaurants	12⅛	6	15⅜	8⅝	22¼	12½	28338	17⅞	14¼	17	...	32	20.5	...	...
#37•[10]	LE	✓Lands' End	NY,Ch,Ph	B+	109	7077	Mkts men/women's apparel	23¾	4½	27¾	13⅝	19½	12⅞	13995	15	12⅞	13⅝	...	16	−2.7	0.1	14.9
✥38•[11]	LSTR	✓Landstar System	NNM	NR	153	11511	Transport'n svcs/trucking	22⅛	12¼	36	19¾	37¾	21¼	13164	27½	23¾	26¾	...	13	−15.7	...	...
39	LNOPF	LanOptics Ltd	NNM	NR	..	...	Mfr local area netwk products	24¼	13½	18¾	5⅛	21¼	6	18851	21¼	17⅝	19½	...	28	140	2.7	...
40	LII	✓Larizza Industries[66]	AS	B−	12	718	Mfr auto/defense components	16⅞	½	9⅝	3¾	6½	3¾	995	6½	6⅜	6⅜	...	10	56.0	37.1	53.7
41	LSREF	LaSalle Re Holdings	NNM	NR	..	...	Prop & casualty reinsurance	....	....	....	....	23¼	19¼	14410	23¼	19¾	22⅞	4.4	..	...	...	...
42	LAS	✓Laser Indus Ltd, Ord	AS,Ch,Ph	NR	8	995	Surgical laser instruments	31⅝	2⅛	9¾	4⅜	12⅝	4⅞	12159	11¼	8¾	10⅞	...	13	102	21.9	25.5
43	LSR	✓Laser Technology	AS,Ch	NR	7	268	Mfr laser speed/distance instr	6½	2⅜	7½	2⅝	6⅜	2½	3909	4⅝	3¼	4½	...	32	50.0	...	...
44	WS	Wrrt (Pur 1 com at $6[70])	AS	....	2	16		1¾	5/16	2	7/16	1⅞	7/16	1166	1	7/16	⅝	...	..	...	...	...
45	LMTS	✓LaserMaster Technologies	NNM	NR	27	1880	Laser printer hardwr/softwr	19¾	2	18¾	5⅞	8	4⅝	17906	6½	5⅛	5⅝	...	d	−15.1	34.5	−7.9
46	LSCP	✓Laserscope	NNM	C	16	759	Mfr surgical laser systems	31½	3¼	7⅛	3⅛	5⅛	1⅜	15028	2 3/16	1⅜	1 15/16	...	d	−48.3	−27.1	−39.7
47	LASXC	✓Lasertechnics Inc	NSC	C	8	5170	Mfr laser marking sys	8⅞	⅛	2⅝	1	2½	1	30302	2⅛	1 9/16	1 11/16	...	d	42.1	1.3	17.6
48	LSO	✓LASMO plc ADS[72]	NY	NR	12	5247	Oil & gas explor,dvlp,prod'n	7½	4⅝	7½	5⅛	8¾	6½	1040	8¼	7⅜	8	...	..	21.7	...	...
✥49•[10]	LSCC	✓Lattice Semiconductor	NNM	NR	156	15580	Mkt program'ble logic devices	26¾	3¼	20⅛	14	43	16⅜	122773	33⅝	27⅝	32⅝	...	19	91.9	26.8	54.0
50	EL	Lauder (Estee) Co	NY	NR	..	...	Mfr,mkt skin care,fragrance pd	....	....	....	....	36¾	26	32059	36½	32⅞	34⅞	1.0	..	...	...	...
51	LWR	✓Lawrence Ins Group	AS	NR	9	200	Property-casualty insurance	11⅝	3½	4⅜	1½	1⅞	⅝	465	1	⅞	15/16	...	10	...	−51.2	...
#52	LAWS	✓Lawson Products	NNM	A−	97	4617	Dstr fasteners, maint parts	35¼	11/16	31	21¾	28½	23	3461	25	23¾	24½	2.1	14	−1.1	2.5	−1.7

Uniform Footnote Explanations-See Page 4. Other: [1]CBOE:Cycle 1. [2]NY,Ph:Cycle 2. [3]P:Cycle 2. [4]Ph:Cycle 2. [5]ASE:Cycle 3. [6]Ph [7]P:Cycle 3. [8]NY:Cycle 3. [9]ASE:Cycle 1. [10]CBOE:Cycle 3. [11]Ph:Cycle 1. [51]ADR's equal 20 com shrs,par 50 Yen. [52]34 Wks Dec,'94. [53]ADR's equal to 2 com par 50 yen. [54]®$1.81,'94. [55]Ea ADS rep 20 com no par. [56]Wrrts only exercisable on 4-28-2000. [57]Non-vtg. [58]Rated BBB+r by S&P. [59]Exchangeable Notes. [60]Preference Units. [61]100% non-taxable,'94. [62]Incl 20.1M Pref Units. [63]®$3.06,'95. [64]California State Bank plan acq,cash & stk. [65]Spl div. [66]Approve Collins & Aikman acq, $6.50. [67]®$0.66,'94. [68]Fiscal Dec,'91 & prior. [69]12 Mo Sep,'92. [70]Fr 1-11-94. [71]At re-specified cond.. [72]Ea ADS rep 3 ord,25p. [73]To be determined.

Splits ◆ Index	Cash Divs. Ea.Yr. Since	Dividends Latest Payment Period $	Date	Ex. Div.	Total $ So Far 1995	Ind. Rate	Paid 1994	Financial Position Mil-$ Cash& Equiv.	Curr. Assets	Curr. Liab.	Balance Sheet Date	Capitalization Lg Trm Debt Mil-$	Shs. 000 Pfd.	Com.	Earnings $ Per Shr. Years End	1991	1992	1993	1994	1995	Last 12 Mos.	Interim Earnings Period	$ per Shr. 1994	1995	Index
1	1939	Q0.42	12-15-95	11-20	1.68	1.68	1.64	28.1	172	120	9-30-95	546	400	37818	Dc	2.13	1.96	2.11	2.01	....	1.79	12 Mo Sep	2.04	1.79	1
2	1949	0.504	12-19-95	9-27	1.203	1.20	1.019	1624	8722	6533	3-31-95	3259	...	1409655	Mr	0.45	Δ0.69	1.13	3.02	....	3.52	6 Mo Sep	2.67	3.17	2
3	1990	Q0.15	1-10-96	12-7	0.60	0.60	0.60	3.80	126	76.9	9-30-95	76.3	...	13177	Dc	1.21	1.05	□d0.29	p0.73	....	0.54	9 Mo Sep	0.66	□0.47	3
4◆	....	0.02	7-8-85	6-10	...	Nil	....	38.2	160	56.2	9-30-95	0.16	...	19315	Sp	Δd0.08	Δd0.78	0.67	0.63	2.38	2.38				4
5	....	None Since Public			...	Nil	....	2.83	3.73	0.13	9-30-95	....	184	2789	Dc	...	...	...	‡[52]d0.04	....	....	9 Mo Sep	n/a	d0.87	5
6	1960	0.416	12-28-95	9-27	0.902	0.90	0.848	2578	5174	1450	3-31-95	525	...	186951	Mr	2.18	2.24	3.84	5.32	....	5.32				6
7	1936	Q0.15	1-25-96	1-8	0.58	0.60	0.50	17.9	122	69.5	9-30-95	26.5	799	5579	Dc	d0.35	1.52	□1.62	[54]2.12	....	2.62	9 Mo Sep	1.51	2.01	7
8	....	None Since Public			...	Nil	....	25.1	168	36.1	8-31-95	50.0	...	22936	Nv	d3.49	d3.76	d1.75	d1.29	Ed1.15	d1.73	9 Mo Aug	d0.56	d1.00	8
9◆	1993	Q0.02½	12-16-95	12-4	0.10	0.10	0.075	3.69	35.3	83.8	9-30-95	486	...	52467	Dc	□0.03	□d0.17	Δ□0.41	0.78	....	0.98	9 Mo Sep	0.64	□0.84	9
10	1963	Q0.19	12-8-95	11-15	0.72	0.76	0.68	15.9	334	102	10-28-95	64.9	...	18525	Ap	1.30	1.39	1.50	Δ1.90	2.01	2.05	6 Mo Oct	0.90	0.94	10
11	....	0.03	11-2-84	10-1	...	Nil	....	0.32	24.3	14.7	10-01-95	3.78	...	15296	Je	*0.05	Δ□0.05	0.13	0.16	0.09	0.09	3 Mo Sep	0.01	0.01	11
12	1991	Q0.18	12-1-95	11-17	0.72	0.72	0.72	39.0	51.5	5.44	9-30-95	....	...	13054	Dc	1.02	1.02	0.80	0.43	....	0.31	9 Mo Sep	0.31	0.19	12
13	1994	0.097	9-18-95	8-23	0.218	0.22	0.263	24.7	71.2	52.5	12-31-94	....	...	300218	Dc	0.64	0.92	0.67	0.71	....	0.71				13
14	1990	Wrrt	4-28-95		Wrrt	Wrrt	0.16	25.0	591	312	9-30-95	959	...	122909	Dc	1.05	0.43	1.26	0.36	....	0.06	9 Mo Sep	0.26	□d0.04	14
15	....	Terms&trad. basis should			be checked in detail			Wrrts expire 4-28-2000				....	...	13824	Dc	...	...	...	....	....	....				15
16◆	1946	Q0.315	1-2-96	12-7	1.24	1.26	1.22	1.56	108	128	9-30-95	154	78	17420	Sp	1.28	1.17	1.61	1.42	1.27	1.27				16
17	....	0.10	6-17-91	5-28	...	Nil	....	0.16	156	52.2	9-30-95	120	...	4056	Dc	d2.05	d1.86	□0.77	1.10	....	1.29	9 Mo Sep	0.43	0.62	17
18	1995	0.09	1-31-96	12-27	0.09	0.09	....	0.02	66.2	32.5	9-30-95	4.89	20	6668	Dc	...	...	p0.82	0.98	....	0.55	9 Mo Sep	0.72	0.29	18
19◆	1993	Q0.04½	12-19-95	11-30	0.27	0.36	0.36	2.91	145	60.2	9-30-95	140	...	7727	Dc	d2.01	0.72	0.51	0.57	....	d3.58	9 Mo Sep	0.86	d3.29	19
20	....	None Since Public			...	Nil	....	21.3	33.6	196	9-30-95	3.93	434	29286	Dc	...	±pd0.01	±□0.43	Δd1.51	....	d0.96	9 Mo Sep	d0.42	Δ0.13	20
21	1983	Q0.10	12-1-95	11-13	0.37½	0.40	0.30	127	737	300	9-30-95	278	8491	60512	Dc	±d0.90	□±d0.63	±0.10	±1.18	....	1.83	9 Mo Sep	±0.71	±1.36	21
22	1969	gQ0.04	11-15-95	10-30	g0.16	0.16	g0.16	147	719	552	8-31-95	1669	633	±p294151	Au	±d1.41	□±0.52	±d1.05	±0.33	±0.48	0.48				22
23	1975	gQ0.04	11-15-95	10-30	g0.16	0.16	g0.16	....	...	...		....	...	47632	Au	±d1.41	□±0.52	±d1.05	±0.33	±0.48	0.48				23
24	....	Plan qtly div			...	1.22	....	Exch for com U.S.Filter(or cash)re-spec cond				....	...	[59]★2966	Au	...	...	...	....	....	....	Mature 12-31-2000			24
25	1992	Q0.64	11-14-95	10-27	2.56	2.56	[61]2.51	134	168	105	9-30-95	378	...	[62]24003	Dc	p1.21	p2.13	2.36	2.61	....	1.36	9 Mo Sep	2.24	0.99	25
26◆	....	None Since Public			...	Nil	....	112	549	198	9-30-95	92.0	...	27380	Je	0.33	0.49	0.79	1.55	[63]3.27	3.73	3 Mo Sep	0.61	1.07	26
27	....	0.05	12-10-85	11-18	...	Nil	....	1.58	98.3	56.0	9-30-95	41.6	...	13292	Dc	d1.05	□d1.47	d0.44	d0.43	....	0.58	9 Mo Sep	d0.51	0.50	27
28◆	1963	Q0.17	12-29-95	12-6	0.61	0.68	0.49¼	0.48	279	92.1	9-30-95	31.6	...	29584	Je	□0.69	1.06	1.52	1.97	2.35	2.36	3 Mo Sep	0.51	0.52	28
29	1945	Q0.24	11-15-95	10-30	0.96	0.96	0.96	54.1	124	36.2	9-09-95	....	...	30347	Dc	1.21	1.25	□1.00	0.88	....	0.73	36 Wk Sep	0.64	0.49	29
30◆	....	None Since Public			...	Nil	....	1.01	31.5	12.9	9-30-95	4.11	...	3872	Dc	0.20	Δ0.29	0.61	0.78	....	0.83	9 Mo Sep	0.73	0.78	30
31	....	None Since Public			...	Nil	....	5.50	16.7	5.38	9-30-95	1.16	...	6178	Je	d0.11	d0.10	d0.25	0.01	0.20	0.20	3 Mo Sep	0.01	0.01	31
32	....	None Since Public			...	Nil	....	0.03	21.7	19.3	9-30-95	32.8	...	5864	Dc	p0.04	p0.30	p0.46	0.66	....	0.55	9 Mo Sep	0.63	0.52	32
33◆	1990	Q0.27½	1-11-96	12-27	1.00	1.10	0.88	6.98	15.8	14.6	6-30-95	....	...	8477	Sp	0.88	0.93	0.95	1.05	P1.19	1.19				33
34◆	....	[65]0.20	6-1-95	5-10	[65]0.20	Nil	5%Stk	Book Value $11.00			9-30-95	....	...	1867	Dc	0.03	0.15	0.73	0.96	....	1.12	9 Mo Sep	0.64	0.80	34
35	....	None Since Public			...	Nil	....	73.5	138	37.4	9-30-95	10.8	...	17428	Je	0.94	d0.67	0.49	0.36	0.77	0.85	3 Mo Sep	d0.06	0.02	35
36◆	....	None Since Public			...	Nil	....	33.7	39.4	11.1	9-30-95	0.42	...	18050	Dc	...	pΔ0.23	p0.28	0.40	....	0.53	9 Mo Sep	0.32	0.45	36
37◆	1987	0.10	12-29-93	11-30	...	Nil	....	3.20	308	227	10-27-95	0.26	...	33690	Ja	0.77	0.93	Δ1.18	1.03	E0.85↓	0.83	9 Mo Oct	0.34	0.14	37
38	....	None Since Public			...	Nil	....	7.26	181	128	9-30-95	77.9	...	12778	Dc	...	p□0.78	□1.14	1.90	....	2.11	9 Mo Sep	1.33	1.54	38
39	....	None Since Public			...	Nil	....	1.95	4.47	1.07	9-30-92	0.07	...	★5700	Dc	p0.36	0.77	P0.71	P0.50	....	0.69	9 Mo Sep	0.35	0.54	39
40	....	1.25	1-2-89	12-12	...	Nil	....	0.84	49.3	34.0	9-30-95	34.5	...	22088	Dc	d1.22	Δ0.11	0.90	Δ[67]0.68	....	0.63	9 Mo Sep	0.53	0.48	40
41	....	Plan qtly div			...	1.00	....	Equity per shr $15.75			9-30-95	....	...	★22727	Dc	...	...	...	n/a	....	....	9 Mo Sep	n/a	p3.04	41
42	....	None Since Public			...	Nil	....	5.03	28.6	14.5	3-31-95	10.4	...	5889	Dc	0.01	Δ0.26	0.38	0.67	....	0.83	9 Mo Sep	0.51	0.67	42
43◆	....	None Paid			...	Nil	....	3.61	8.23	0.43	6-30-95	0.45	...	4990	Sp	[68]d0.01	[69]Nil	□0.20	0.01	P0.14	0.14				43
44	....	Terms&trad. basis should			be checked in detail			Wrrts expire 1-11-98				....	...	1380	Sp	...	...	...	....	....	....	Callable fr 7-11-93 at $0.05[71]			44
45	....	None Since Public			...	Nil	....	0.23	40.4	27.6	9-30-95	1.45	...	11246	Je	d0.24	Δd0.02	d0.07	0.57	0.02	d0.18	3 Mo Sep	0.12	d0.08	45
46	....	None Since Public			...	Nil	....	3.34	20.1	6.15	9-30-95	0.02	...	7016	Dc	d0.79	d0.66	0.09	d0.13	....	d0.22	9 Mo Sep	d0.17	d0.26	46
47	....	None Paid			...	Nil	....	0.45	8.96	11.2	9-30-95	0.04	2210	±29576	Dc	d0.08	d0.14	d0.12	d0.33	....	d0.38	9 Mo Sep	d0.18	±d0.23	47
48	1995	0.06	5-15-95	3-24	0.06	[73]....	....	593	1102	451	j12-31-94	1686	70000	965000	Dc	d0.16	d2.36	d0.35	d0.11	....	0.08	6 Mo Jun	d0.12	0.07	48
49◆	....	None Since Public			...	Nil	....	113	178	39.8	9-30-95	....	...	★22003	Mr	0.61	0.94	1.19	1.41	....	1.69	6 Mo Sep	0.65	0.93	49
50	....	Plan qtly div			...	0.34	....	184	1335	893	p9-30-95	63.9	p3600	★±115000	Je	...	...	...	....	±p0.90	....	3 Mo Sep	n/a	±p0.37	50
51	1987	0.04	11-19-93	10-12	...	Nil	....	Equity per shr Neg			9-30-95	0.30	...	14121	Dc	0.51	□0.09	...	d0.50	....	0.09	9 Mo Sep	d0.53	0.06	51
52	1973	Q0.13	1-17-96	12-29	0.50	0.52	0.48	33.2	95.5	16.9	9-30-95	....	...	11765	Dc	1.23	1.13	Δ1.32	1.55	....	1.73	9 Mo Sep	1.08	1.26	52

◆Stock Splits & Divs By Line Reference Index [4]2-for-1,'95. [9]3-for-2,'93,'94(twice). [16]2-for-1,'94. [19]1-for-3 REVERSE,'95. [26]3-for-2,'93. [28]3-for-2,'92:4-for-3,'93,'94. [30]3-for-2,'95. [33]2-for-1,'92. [34]Adj to 5%,'94. [36]2-for-1,'95. [37]2-for-1,'94. [43]1-for-4 REVERSE,'92. [49]3-for-2,'93.

¶ S&P 500 # MidCap 400 ✣ SmallCap 600 • Options Index	Ticker	Name of Issue (Call Price of Pfd. Stocks)	Market	Com. Rank. & Pfd. Rating	Inst. Hold Cos	Inst. Hold Shs. (000)	Principal Business	Price Range 1971-93 High	1971-93 Low	1994 High	1994 Low	1995 High	1995 Low	Dec. Sales in 100s	December, 1995 Last Sale Or Bid High	Low	Last	%Div Yield	P-E Ratio	Total Return % Annualized 12 Mo	36 Mo	60 Mo
#1•[1]	LAW	✓Lawter Intl	NY,Ch	A–	142	17836	Printing ink vehicles, resin	15½	1 11/16	13¾	10¾	14⅜	10¼	8100	12	10⅝	11⅝	3.4	17	–2.9	–2.4	10.2
2	LTI	✓Lawyers Title	NY	NR	67	4884	Title insurance svcs	21¾	5⅜	19½	9¾	19¼	10½	2280	19¼	16⅞	19⅛	1.0	14	84.3	26.8	...
3	LKI	✓Lazare Kaplan Intl	AS	C	20	1157	Cutter/merchant diamonds	27	2¾	9⅞	7⅛	9½	6⅛	504	9	6¾	7⅞	...	d	–16.5	8.3	–9.6
4•[2]	LCI	✓LCI International	NY,Ch	NR	165	43003	Long-dist telecommunications	10⅝	4⅝	13⅜	6⅜	20⅞	10⅛	22458	20½	17½	20½	...	..	57.1	...	...
5	Pr	5% cm Cv[51]Exch Pfd([52]25.50)	NY	B–	48	3358		32	25½	36	22	54⅜	27½	472	53½	47¼	53½	2.3	..	...	...	...
6	LDIC	✓LDI Corporation	NNM	B–	22	2191	Buy,sell,lease,svc computers	17⅜	6	7¼	3¼	4¼	1¾	2769	3¼	1¾	2⅜	...	d	–36.7	–29.7	–26.8
7	LFCT	✓Leader Financial	NNM	NR	81	4183	General banking, TN,NE	17⅜	14½	29¾	17	39½	20¾	7623	39½	36⅞	37⅜	1.6	10	89.8	...	...
8	LEA	✓Lear Seating	NY,Ph	NR	123	46633	Mfr auto/light truck seat sys	....	....	22⅛	15½	32½	16⅝	18947	29⅞	27¼	29	...	18	47.8	...	...
9	LBMSY	Learmouth & Burchett Mgt ADS[53]	NNM	NR	..	...	Mgmt software pds	....	....	....	....	10½	8¾	16220	10⅛	8¾	8⅞	...	d	...	...	...
10	LTRE	Learning Tree Intl	NNM	NR	..	...	Provides educat'n/train'g svcs	....	....	....	....	17¼	12	62315	17¼	12	15⅝	...	27	...	...	...
11	LRI	✓LeaRonal Inc	NY,Ch	B+	77	4055	Chemicals, electroplat proc	21¼	¾	19⅝	14⅝	28⅞	17¾	3822	28⅛	23	23	2.7	15	26.1	20.3	20.1
12	LECE	✓Leasing Edge	NSC	NR	..	...	Mkt info process'g/commun eq	22	3½	5½	2⅝	3¼	1	2663	1⅞	1 9/16	1 11/16	...	d	–35.0	–35.1	...
13	LSSI	✓Leasing Solutions	NNM	NR	22	2189	Leases processing/commun equip	13	3¾	12¾	5⅝	16¼	6⅜	5655	16	14⅝	15	...	17	118	...	...
14	TLF	✓Leather Factory	AS	NR	10	550	Mfr,dstr leather products	7⅞	5¼	7¼	3½	4⅝	2¼	1742	3	2¼	2 7/16	...	15	–42.7	...	...
✣15	LECH	✓Lechters Inc	NNM	B	88	9023	Sells housewrs/kitchen items	25¼	5⅝	19	10¾	19	5½	40249	7⅝	5½	6⅜	...	21	–61.6	–28.4	–5.1
16	LCRY	✓LeCroy Corp	NNM	NR	..	...	Mfr oscilloscope products	....	....	....	....	19¼	10½	8359	19¼	14	18½	...	29	...	...	...
17	LECT	LecTec Corp	NNM	↓B–	11	361	Mfr medical electrodes/tapes	13⅝	2⅝	10½	6½	14¼	7	2058	12¼	8¾	11	...	d	57.1	4.3	33.1
#18	LEE	✓Lee Enterprises	NY,Ch	A–	163	19966	Newspaper publish:radio,TV	17½	9/16	19⅛	15¾	23⅛	16¾	5739	23⅛	20⅞	23	2.1	19	38.7	17.5	15.8
19	LPH	✓Lee Pharmaceuticals	AS,B,Ch,P	C	8	340	Nail care:orthodontic pr	19⅜	¾	2 1/16	7/16	1	¼	2846	7/16	5/16	⅜	...	d	–40.0	–33.1	–17.8
20	LGTO	✓Legato Systems	NNM	NR	26	1655	Dvlps/mkts network mgmt sftwr	....	....	....	....	39¾	19	4303	39¾	30	31	...	45	...	...	...
✣21	LM	✓Legg Mason Inc	NY,B,Ph	B+	83	8850	Regional securities broker	25¼	5¼	25¼	18⅛	31⅜	20½	7257	30⅜	27⅜	27½	1.7	14	34.1	12.0	24.9
#22•[3]	LEG	✓Leggett & Platt	NY,Ch,P,Ph	A	278	44362	Mfr springs,etc for furn,bed	25⅛	¼	24¾	16⅝	26⅞	17	40736	24⅝	19⅞	24¼	1.6	15	43.5	14.0	32.7
23	LEI	✓Lehigh Group[55]	NY,B,Ch,P,Ph	C	13	1415	Interior construction mgmt	301⅞	½	1¼	9/16	¾	3/16	2332	5/16	3/16	¼	...	1	–59.1	–29.8	–33.7
24	AYN	Lehman Br Amgen'YEELD"97	AS	NR	9	181	Yield Enh'd Eq Link Debt Sec	48¾	45¼	52	39	61⅜	50¼	237	61⅜	59½	60¾B	4.8	..	24.4	...	...
25	SXT	Lehman Br G1 Tele'SUNS' 2000	AS	NR	..	...	Stock Upside Note Sec	....	....	25⅞	21⅝	24⅝	20½	188	24	21⅞	24	...	..	8.5	...	...
26•[4]	LEH	✓Lehman Br Holdings	NY	NR	299	74402	Investment banking svcs	....	....	20⅞	13¾	24⅝	14½	69361	22⅞	20	21¼	0.9	12	45.5	...	...
27	MUY	Lehman Br Micron'YEELD"97	AS	NR	1	29	Yield Enh'd Eq Link Debt Sec	....	....	19¾	16¾	25¾	18⅝	86	24⅜	23⅜	23⅞B	6.7	..	30.4	...	...
28	LYN	Lehman Br Oracle'YEELD"96	AS	NR	6	70	Yield Ehn'd Eq Link Debt Sec	34	28⅝	38	30	47¼	35¼	825	47¼	44½	46¼	5.0	..	31.8	...	...
29	BKG	Lehman Br Reg'l Bk'SUNS' 1996	AS	NR	..	...	Stock Upside Note Sec	....	....	25	23⅜	35⅛	24¼	185	35⅛	34	35⅛	...	..	44.8	...	...
30•[5]	LEN	✓Lennar Corp	NY,B,Ch,P,Ph	A–	158	17203	Bldr residential communities	24	¼	25⅛	14¼	25½	15¼	15388	25½	22	25⅛	0.4	13	60.4	10.8	35.7
31	LHSPF	Lernout & Hauspie Speech Pds	NNM	NR	..	...	Dvlp advanced speech tech	....	....	....	....	31⅞	11	63360	31⅞	11	28	...	d	...	...	...
32	LESL	✓Leslie's Poolmart	NNM	NR	48	3218	Retail swimming pools/prd	12	4½	14	7¾	16⅝	12⅛	4079	14	12½	14	...	20	16.5	23.6	...
33	LUK	✓Leucadia National	NY,Ch,P,Ph	B	114	7804	Consumer finance,life insur	25⅝	1/16	23⅛	17⅜	29⅝	21½	28756	28¾	24½	25	0.5	19	12.5	10.0	36.3
34•[6]	LEVL	✓Level One Communications	NNM	NR	45	4758	Design,dvlp,mkt circuit prod	24½	11⅜	32¼	11¼	27¼	12	15323	24	17	18	...	36	12.5	...	...
35	LEV	✓Leviathan Gas PL[63]Ptnrs LP[64]	NY,Ch	NR	32	837	Oper nat'l gas pipeline systems	32¼	20½	32	22½	29⅜	21⅞	5966	29⅜	25	28⅜	8.5	16	37.3	...	...
✣36•[7]	LFI	✓Levitz Furniture	NY	NR	43	6491	Retail furniture stores	18¾	10⅞	20¼	6¼	9¼	2½	39433	3⅞	2¾	3⅜	...	d	–55.0	...	...
37	LXP	✓Lexington Corporate Prop	NY	NR	18	461	Real estate investment trust	11⅜	8¼	11	8⅝	11⅜	8⅝	2798	11¼	10	11¼	9.6	30	41.2	...	...
38	LXK	Lexmark Intl Group'A'	NY	NR	..	...	Mfr laser & inkjet printers	....	....	....	....	22⅜	15½	35964	20⅛	15½	18¼	...	..	...	...	...
#39	LGE	✓LG&E Energy	NY,B,Ch,P,Ph	B+	159	9673	Hldg co:Louisville Gas&Elec	43⅜	9⅝	41	33⅝	43½	36⅜	12465	43½	41⅛	42¼	5.3	14	21.1	12.4	16.5
40	LBY	✓Libbey Inc	NY	NR	105	14997	Produce glass tableware	17⅝	11⅞	19⅞	14	24¼	14⅜	3560	23¾	22¼	22½	1.3	11	33.3	...	...
41	LBI	✓Liberte Investors	NY,B,Ch,P,Ph	NR	12	1909	Real estate investment trust	35⅞	⅜	2⅝	1	2¼	1½	3178	2¼	2	2¼	...	d	38.5	77.0	–3.0
✣42	LBNA	✓Liberty Bancorp(OK)	NNM	B–	60	4967	Comm'l bkg,Oklahoma	187⅜	6¼	33½	26½	39¾	29¼	3587	38	36¼	37¼	2.1	15	32.6	9.1	39.3
43	LC	✓Liberty Corp	NY,Ch,Ph	B+	88	6944	Insurance hldg: TV: S&L	34¾	1 13/16	29⅞	23⅞	34¼	24⅜	3774	33⅞	32¾	33¾	2.0	26	37.5	8.4	12.8
44	L	✓Liberty Financial Cos	NY,Ch	NR	39	1711	Asset management svcs	....	....	....	....	30¼	23⅞	2568	30¼	29⅛	30¼	2.0	..	...	...	...
45	LRY	✓Liberty Property Trust	NY,Ch,Ph	NR	140	17750	Real estate investment trust	....	....	20⅜	17⅜	21¾	18⅜	20900	20¾	19¼	20¾	7.7	26	16.0	...	...
46	LDAKA	✓LIDAK Pharmaceuticals'A'	NNM	NR	12	1051	Dvlp stge:pharmaceut'l R&D	9⅞	¼	7	1¼	7½	1 9/16	21666	4½	3⅝	3⅞	...	d	139	70.6	48.8
47	LIFB	✓Life Bancorp	NNM	NR	36	2588	Savings bank, Norfolk, Va	....	....	10¼	8⅛	16¾	8⅞	12251	15⅜	14⅜	15	2.9	..	65.1	...	...
✣48	LPG	✓Life Partners Group	NY	NR	130	19113	Hldg co:life insurance	23⅜	16¾	22	15⅜	23¼	12⅛	36586	13¾	12⅛	13⅝	0.9	13	–36.6	...	...
✣49	LRE	✓Life Re	NY	NR	76	10915	Provides life&hlth reinsurance	39¼	19⅛	23¼	14⅞	25	16½	6668	25	21⅝	25	1.1	12	48.0	–3.3	...
50	LTEK	✓Life Technologies	NNM	B+	71	4980	Dvlp,mfr,life science prod	29	8⅜	20¼	15	27½	17½	2155	27½	23	27¼	0.7	20	41.0	9.3	11.9
51•[1]	LUSA	✓Life USA Holdings	NNM	NR	44	2257	Life insurance/annuity prd	20	4½	18½	6½	11⅜	7⅛	18423	8⅝	7¾	8	...	11	12.3	–10.1	...
52	LIFC	✓LifeCell Corp	NSC	NR	11	1164	Dvlp stge:human cell prod	16¼	6½	9¾	1⅜	5½	1⅝	2077	3¼	2	2½	...	d	25.0	–35.9	...

Uniform Footnote Explanations-See Page 4. Other: [1]Ph:Cycle 3. [2]CBOE:Cycle 3. [3]ASE:Cycle 3. [4]ASE,CBOE,NY,P:Cycle 1. [5]ASE:Cycle 2. [6]ASE,CBOE:Cycle 2. [7]CBOE:Cycle 1.
[51]Fr 8-31-95 co opt exch for$25 amt 5% Cv 2003. [52]Fr 8-31-96,scale to $25 in'98. [53]Ea ADS rep 2 Ord, 10p. [54]®$1.13,'94. [55]Consol Technology Grp,plan acq. [56]Co can extend to 1-22-97.
[57]Fiscal Dec'93 & prior. [58]11 Mos Nov'94. [59]Co can extend to 8-8-97. [60]Co can extend to 12-19-96. [61]Incl curr amts. [62]®$1.21,'94. [63]Preference units. [64]Convertible and redeemable re specified cond..
[65]Incl 9.04M pref units. [66]Fiscal Jun'92. [67]Subsid Pfd. [68]Incl current amts.

Splits ◆ Index	Cash Divs. Ea.Yr. Since	Dividends: Latest Payment Period $	Date	Ex. Div.	Total $ So Far 1995	Ind. Rate	Paid 1994	Financial Position Mil-$: Cash& Equiv.	Curr. Assets	Curr. Liab.	Balance Sheet Date	Capitalization: Lg Trm Debt Mil-$	Shs. 000 Pfd.	Com.	Earnings $ Per Shr.: Years End	1991	1992	1993	1994	1995	Last 12 Mos.	Interim Earnings Period	$ per Shr. 1994	1995	Index
1◆	1959	Q0.10	12-1-95	11-14	0.40	0.40	0.40	72.4	172	86.3	9-30-95	4.10	...	45066	Dc	0.61	0.62	Δ0.02	0.66	....	0.68	9 Mo Sep	0.48	0.50	1
2	1993	Q0.05	12-15-95	11-29	0.18	0.20	0.12	Equity per shr $19.65			9-30-95	5.21	...	8886	Dc	...	...	4.31	0.80	....	1.40	9 Mo Sep	0.58	1.18	2
3	....	0.12½	11-12-81	10-23	...	Nil	....	1.03	91.5	31.1	8-31-95	26.4	...	6148	My	*0.44	d0.48	d0.15	0.49	d0.18	d0.13	3 Mo Aug	0.08	0.13	3
4◆	....	None Since Public			...	Nil	....	....	189	111	9-30-95	277	4600	64316	Dc	...	p□d0.44	□d0.10	0.01	....	0.08	9 Mo Sep	0.36	0.43	4
5	1993	Q0.31¼	11-30-95	11-8	1.25	1.25	1.25	Cv into 0.658 com, $38				....	4600	...	Dc	...	...	...	....	....	....				5
6◆	1993	0.04	1-28-94	1-6	...	Nil	0.04	Equity per shr $7.01			10-31-95	266	...	6764	Ja	1.54	1.03	d3.65	d2.76	....	d2.96	9 Mo Oct	d0.43	d0.63	6
7	1995	Q0.15	1-1-96	12-13	0.45	0.60	....	Book Value $23.10			9-30-95	526	...	9870	Dc	...	p0.74	□0.57	3.33	....	3.65	9 Mo Sep	2.39	2.71	7
8	....	None Paid			...	Nil	....	15.2	1144	1146	9-30-95	1132	...	★56237	Dc	...	...	p0.74	1.26	....	1.66	9 Mo Sep	0.73	□1.13	8
9	....	None Since Public			...	Nil	....	3.20	15.8	13.5	7-31-95	0.53	...	★25300	Ap	d0.36	0.02	0.20	d0.10	d0.80	d0.12	6 Mo Oct	d0.62	0.06	9
10	....	None Since Public			...	Nil	....	10.0	21.3	22.8	9-30-95	0.27	...	★13872	Sp	0.11	0.17	d0.08	d0.04	0.57	0.57				10
11	1963	Q0.15½	10-31-95	10-13	0.60½	0.62	0.55	38.3	102	22.9	8-31-95	0.46	...	8821	Fb	0.90	Δ1.00	1.18	1.40	....	1.59	6 Mo Aug	0.65	0.84	11
12◆	....	Wrrt	8-7-95	7-27	Wrrt	Wrrt	....	Equity per shr $2.78			6-30-95	2.34	230	3076	Dc	0.91	0.93	0.11	d1.67	....	d1.81	9 Mo Sep	0.20	0.06	12
13	....	None Since Public			...	Nil	....	Equity per shr $4.60			9-30-95	140	...	6248	Dc	0.18	0.43	0.66	0.75	....	0.89	9 Mo Sep	0.51	0.65	13
14	....	None Since Public			...	Nil	....	0.43	12.7	2.96	9-30-95	7.33	...	9853	Dc	...	0.09	□0.14	0.15	....	0.16	9 Mo Sep	0.11	0.12	14
15◆	....	None Since Public			...	Nil	....	5.71	174	50.9	10-28-95	74.8	...	17155	Ja	0.80	0.90	0.65	0.20	....	0.31	9 Mo Oct	d0.41	d0.30	15
16	....	None Since Public			...	Nil	....	1.41	40.2	18.4	6-30-95	p0.25	p...	★5255	Je	d0.29	0.04	d0.03	d0.24	0.56	0.64	3 Mo Sep	0.06	0.14	16
17◆	....	5%Stk	7-29-94	7-11	...	Nil	5%Stk	0.42	6.13	1.60	9-30-95	....	...	3798	Je	0.26	0.25	0.20	0.17	0.04	d0.01	3 Mo Sep	0.02	d0.03	17
18◆	1960	Q0.12	1-2-96	12-14	0.44	0.48	0.42	10.9	105	117	9-30-95	75.5	...	±47407	Sp	0.68	0.83	0.88	1.08	1.24	1.24				18
19	....	None Since Public			...	Nil	....	0.03	5.74	2.94	3-31-95	3.44	...	4135	Sp	d0.95	d0.04	d0.09	d0.16	....	d0.17	9 Mo Jun	d0.09	d0.10	19
20	....	None Since Public			...	Nil	....	47.8	54.3	7.67	9-30-95	....	...	7994	Dc	d0.27	d0.52	0.03	0.27	....	0.69	9 Mo Sep	0.10	0.52	20
21◆	1983	Q0.12	1-8-96	12-12	0.45	0.48	0.41	Equity per shr $14.84			9-30-95	68.0	...	13975	Mr	1.86	2.61	2.98	[54]1.30	....	1.93	6 Mo Sep	0.65	1.28	21
22◆	1939	Q0.10	1-2-96	11-21	0.36	0.40	0.23	7.50	599	266	9-30-95	171	...	84003	Dc	0.56	0.82	1.05	1.39	E1.60	1.56	9 Mo Sep	1.02	1.19	22
23◆	....	None Paid			...	Nil	....	0.46	6.91	4.39	9-30-95	2.17	...	10339	Dc	Δd5.95	d0.04	Δ0.20	0.45	....	0.44	9 Mo Sep	Δd0.04	d0.05	23
24	1994	Q0.735	1-15-96	12-27	2.941	2.94	2.337	Int&prin based on 6 1/2%per shr Amgen Inc stk				....	...	★1150	Dc	...	...	...	....	....	....	Matures 1-15-97[56]			24
25	....	....			...	....	....	Int fr 4-10-95,re-specified cond.				....	...	★1300	Dc	...	...	...	....	....	....	Mature 4-10-2000			25
26	1994	Q0.05	11-30-95	11-13	0.20	0.20	†0.17½	Equity per shr $26.22			8-31-95	12897	21000	104558	Nv	...	...	p[57]3.08	□[58]0.81	E1.80	1.59	9 Mo Aug	□0.49	1.27	26
27	1994	Q0.401	11-1-95	10-11	1.603	1.603	0.418	Int&Prin based on 9.125%per shr Micron Tech stk as defined				....	...	★1700	Dc	...	...	...	....	....	....	Matures 8-1-97[59]			27
28	1994	Q0.578	12-12-95	11-28	2.31	2.31	2.643	Int&prin based on 7.25% per shr Oracle sys stk as defined				....	...	★2000	Dc	...	...	...	....	....	....	Matures 12-12-96[60] co can extend to 12-19-96			28
29	....	....			...	....	....	Amt pay maturity based on 'Sec're-spec cond.				....	...	★1593	Dc	...	...	...	....	....	....	Mature 12-5-96			29
30◆	1978	Q0.02½	2-15-96	2-1	0.10	0.10	0.09½	Equity per shr $16.26			8-31-95	[61]401	...	±35826	Nv	±0.70	±0.95	±1.51	±Δ1.89	E1.95	1.87	9 Mo Aug	Δ±1.42	±1.40	30
31	....	None Since Public			...	Nil	....	2.37	7.40	27.7	9-30-95	★13.3	...	★13798	Dc	d2.22	d2.94	d1.67	d2.47	....	d2.14	9 Mo Sep	d1.76	d1.43	31
32◆	....	5%Stk	10-13-95	8-29	5%Stk	Nil	5%Stk	0.11	46.2	30.6	9-30-95	18.2	...	6319	Dc	0.17	0.33	0.48	0.70	....	0.70	9 Mo Sep	1.07	1.07	32
33◆	1993	0.12½	12-29-95	12-13	0.12½	0.125	0.12½	Equity per shr $17.61			9-30-95	[61]526	...	60123	Dc	2.00	2.68	Δ1.99	[62]1.22	....	1.34	9 Mo Sep	0.82	0.94	33
34◆	....	None Since Public			...	Nil	....	33.4	59.6	17.5	9-30-95	3.37	...	12836	Dc	...	p0.18	p0.35	0.60	....	0.50	9 Mo Sep	0.49	0.39	34
35	1993	Q0.60	11-14-95	10-27	2.40	2.40	2.40	5.93	12.7	42.8	9-30-95	104	...	[65]12184	Dc	...	p[66]2.15	p2.09	2.03	....	1.78	9 Mo Sep	1.74	1.49	35
36	....	None Since Public			...	Nil	....	8.28	206	180	9-30-95	410	...	29621	Mr	...	p□0.03	Δ□0.48	□0.13	....	d0.29	6 Mo Sep	□0.13	d0.29	36
37	1994	Q0.27	11-14-95	10-26	1.08	1.08	1.05	Equity per shr $10.50			9-30-95	117	...	9255	Dc	...	p0.25	0.48	0.59	....	0.37	9 Mo Sep	0.46	0.24	37
38	....	None Since Public			...	Nil	....	37.3	658	388	9-30-95	215	p...	±★69612	Dc	...	±d1.12	±d0.34	±d0.46	....	0.04	9 Mo Sep	±0.13	±□0.63	38
39◆	1913	Q0.555	1-16-96	12-27	2.16¾	2.22	2.098	132	452	427	9-30-95	647	[67]2468	33072	Dc	2.57	2.34	2.70	□3.39	....	3.06	12 Mo Sep	□3.23	3.06	39
40	1993	Q0.075	12-21-95	12-8	0.30	0.30	0.30	2.35	128	75.3	9-30-95	214	...	15000	Dc	...	p□2.03	p□1.58	1.78	....	1.97	9 Mo Sep	1.21	1.40	40
41	....	0.21	5-25-90	5-8	...	Nil	....	Equity per shr $2.54			9-30-95	....	...	12154	Je	d5.67	d3.68	d2.94	□d1.34	d0.23	d0.19	3 Mo Sep	d0.04	Nil	41
42	1993	Q0.20	11-17-95	11-1	0.80	0.80	†0.60	Equity per shr $27.20			9-30-95	....	...	9477	Dc	*0.57	*1.49	Δ2.28	2.64	....	2.51	9 Mo Sep	2.11	1.98	42
43◆	1941	Q0.17	1-2-96	12-13	0.65	0.68	0.60½	Equity per shr $19.81			9-30-95	275	1865	20025	Dc	1.90	2.48	□2.62	1.22	....	1.28	9 Mo Sep	1.85	1.91	43
44	1995	Q0.15	12-6-95	11-20	0.45	0.60	....	Equity per shr $25.21			9-30-95	229	328	27515	Dc	...	...	p1.68	p2.32	....	....	9 Mo Sep	n/a	1.93	44
45	1994	Q0.40	1-15-96	12-27	1.60	1.60	0.43	Equity per shr $10.31			9-30-95	p411	...	★28348	Dc	...	...	p1.02	p0.80	....	0.81	9 Mo Sep	p0.64	0.65	45
46	....	None Paid			...	Nil	....	11.6	12.3	1.34	6-30-95	....	...	±29925	Sp	d0.27	d0.26	d0.35	d0.19	Pd0.35	d0.35				46
47	1995	Q0.11	11-30-95	11-15	0.44	0.44	....	Book Value $14.33			9-30-95	287	...	10911	Dc	...	...	...	n/a	....	....	9 Mo Sep	n/a	0.69	47
48	1993	Q0.03	12-15-95	11-21	0.11	0.12	0.08	Equity per shr $11.02			9-30-95	221	...	27878	Dc	...	p1.66	2.05	□1.43	....	1.05	9 Mo Sep	1.34	0.96	48
49	1993	Q0.07	12-14-95	11-24	0.28	0.28	0.24	Equity per shr $17.47			9-30-95	[68]140	...	14568	Dc	p1.72	□3.45	2.50	2.21	....	2.18	9 Mo Sep	1.56	1.53	49
50	1991	Q0.05	1-19-96	12-13	0.20	0.20	0.20	24.2	142	49.8	9-30-95	2.49	...	15460	Dc	0.82	1.03	1.10	1.21	....	1.39	9 Mo Sep	0.91	1.09	50
51	....	None Since Public			...	Nil	....	Equity per shr $7.07			9-30-95	36.0	...	20268	Dc	*0.33	0.69	0.79	0.71	....	0.73	9 Mo Sep	0.56	0.58	51
52	....	None Since Public			...	Nil	....	3.71	4.60	0.73	9-30-95	....	265	4300	Dc	±d0.56	±d0.70	±d0.80	d0.90	....	d1.08	9 Mo Sep	d0.63	d0.81	52

◆**Stock Splits & Divs By Line Reference Index** [1]4-for-3,'91. [4]2-for-1,'94,'95. [6]Adj for 5%,'91. [12]1-for-8 REVERSE,'94. [15]2-for-1,'92. [17]Adj to 5%,'94. [18]2-for-1,'95. [21]5-for-4,'93. [22]2-for-1,'92,'95. [23]1-for-35 REVERSE,'91. [30]2-for-1,'92:3-for-2,'94. [32]Adj for 5%,'95. [33]2-for-1,'93,'95. [34]3-for-2,'94. [39]3-for-2,'92. [43]2-for-1,'91.

¶ S&P 500 · # MidCap 400 · ✤ SmallCap 600 · • Options

Index	Ticker	Name of Issue (Call Price of Pfd. Stocks)	Market	Com. Rank. & Pfd. Rating	Inst. Hold Cos	Inst. Hold Shs. (000)	Principal Business	1971-93 High	1971-93 Low	1994 High	1994 Low	1995 High	1995 Low	Dec. Sales in 100s	Dec. 1995 Last Sale Or Bid High	Low	Last	%Div Yield	P-E Ratio	Total Return % Annualized 12 Mo	36 Mo	60 Mo
1	LCUT	✓Lifetime Hoan	NNM	NR	47	3812	Mfr household cutlery/prod	10	4⅝	11⅛	7⅜	12¼	8½	2432	9½	8⅝	9¼	...	13	5.0	28.9	...
2	LIHRY	Lihir Gold ADS[51]	NNM	NR	..	...	Gold mining,exploration	...	...	...	...	24⅞	21⅜	576	22¼	21⅜	21⅝B	...	..	...	...	...
✤3	LVC	✓Lillian Vernon	AS	B	54	3054	Direct mail catalog sales	18⅞	4⅛	22⅝	14½	22¼	12⅞	4266	14¾	12⅞	13⅜	2.1	14	−8.6	0.8	7.2
¶4•1	LLY	✓Lilly (Eli)	NY,B,C,Ch,P,Ph	A	852	378890	Ethical drugs:agri chemicals	45¼	4⅛	33⅛	23⅝	57	31¼	299770	57	48⅞	56¼	2.4	25	78.2	26.8	13.4
5	HYU	Lilly Ctgnt Pymt Units[52]	AS	NR	8	109		5¾	.01	1/16	.01	1/32	....	193	1/64	...	...	...	..	...	...	...
✤6	LI	✓Lilly Industries'A'	NY,Ph	A−	85	10323	Dvlp & mfr indus'l coatings	16⅛	¼	18	11¾	15	11	4598	14⅝	12½	12¾	2.5	13	−1.5	10.7	30.7
¶7•2	LTD	✓Limited Inc	NY,B,Ch,P,Ph	A+	549	190061	Women's apparel stores	32⅞	1/32	22⅜	16¾	23¼	15⅞	283072	17¾	15⅞	17⅛	2.3	16	−2.8	−13.5	0.8
✤8•3	LNCR	✓Lincare Holdings[53]	NNM	NR	233	25103	In-home respiratory svcs	25½	6⅝	29	18¾	35¼	21	86799	28½	24¼	25	...	15	−12.3	18.9	...
9	LECOA	✓Lincoln Electric 'A'	NNM	B−	24	3445	Mfr arc welding products	...	...	...	...	37¼	21½	13023	25	21½	24	2.0	9	...	...	...
¶10•1	LNC	✓Lincoln Natl Corp	NY,B,C,Ch,P,Ph	B+	443	67763	Multiline insurance hldg co	48¼	4¾	44⅜	34⅝	53¾	34⅝	37785	53¾	46	53¾	3.4	19	58.5	17.6	26.6
11	Pr	$3.00 cm Cv A Pfd (80)vtg	NY,Ch	NR	4	1	life,accid,health,prop/cas	366	38½	347	282	391	319	1	391	391	430B	0.7	..	...	...	...
#12•4	LTEC	✓Lincoln Telecommun	NNM	A	121	10328	Telephone serv, Nebraska	20½	1⅛	20	13¾	21½	14½	19922	21½	18¾	21⅛	2.8	18	36.8	22.8	13.9
13	LNDL	✓Lindal Cedar Homes	NNM	B	9	252	Pre-cut home packages	7½	⅛	6	3	5	3¼	2249	4¾	4	4½	...	10	44.0	−4.5	10.6
14	LIND	✓Lindberg Corp	NNM	B−	26	1903	Heat treating of metals	17⅛	9/16	8¾	4⅛	7½	5¼	2024	7	6⅛	6¾	4.1	7	3.8	29.4	9.5
✤15	LINZ	✓Lindsay Mfg	NNM	NR	76	2717	Mfr elec pwr irrigation sys	44	4½	37	27⅞	39	28¼	5261	39	35½	38½	...	16	28.3	8.1	28.4
#16•5	LLTC	✓Linear Technology Corp	NNM	B+	357	61238	Mfrs integrated circuits	19¾	1 7/16	25¾	18¼	45⅝	23	145207	45¼	36	39¼	0.4	31	59.4	48.0	66.0
✤17•3	LIPO	✓Liposome Co	NNM	C	99	18057	Lipid/liposome drug tech	27⅝	⅞	10¾	4¾	21¾	7⅞	124877	21¾	16¾	20	...	d	139	19.4	43.8
18	LIQB	✓Liqui-Box Corp	NNM	A	58	1879	Plastic packaging & pkg sys	40½	¾	38½	31¼	36¾	27¼	755	30½	28½	29⅝	1.5	15	−5.5	2.5	10.8
19	LFA	✓Littlefield, Adams	AS	↑B−	9	147	Imprinted leisurewear	21⅜	⅛	27⅞	3½	7⅜	1⅛	2284	2⅜	1⅛	1½	...	d	−74.5	−46.4	35.2
#20•6	LIT	✓Litton Indus	NY,B,C,Ch,P,Ph	B	237	36727	Defense & marine systems	71⅜	1 3/16	74¾	28¼	46	32½	23521	45⅝	41⅜	44½	...	15	...	...	...
21	LSKI	✓Liuski International	NNM	NR	13	372	Dstr computer peripherals/prd	13⅜	5⅜	13⅝	3⅞	5½	2⅜	6124	3⅜	2 7/16	3¼	...	d	−17.2	−24.7	...
✤22•7	LCA	✓Living Centers of America	NY,Ph	NR	163	11117	Oper long-term hlth centers	27¾	11	34¼	25⅛	38¼	25¼	13047	35	30½	35	...	28	4.9	18.8	...
¶23•8	LIZ	✓Liz Claiborne	NY,Ph	A−	350	68235	Designer womens apparel	50⅜	13/16	26⅝	15⅝	30	14⅜	64869	30	26¾	27½	1.6	18	75.7	−11.5	0.1
24	LRT	✓LL&E Royalty Tr UBI	NY,B,P	NR	26	1082	Royalties of oil & gas prop	17⅛	1⅜	5⅞	4	4⅜	3	7006	3⅝	3⅛	3⅝	10.2	10	−8.4	11.7	17.5
25	LHC	✓LNH REIT[56]	NY,Ch	NR	8	114	Real estate investment trust	34⅜	4⅝	9¼	6⅛	7⅞	5¾	404	7⅞	7⅛	7⅝	e7.9	25	44.4	19.8	27.2
26	L	Loblaw Cos	To,Mo,Vc	A−	24	3522	Food retailer & wholesaler	24	1¼	26	19½	31½	23¼	4275	31½	30	30⅞	1.2	18	30.8	17.1	...
¶27•9	LMT	✓Lockheed Martin	NY	NR	710	168427	Aerospace/defense systems	...	...	...	...	79½	50	78890	79½	73⅛	79	1.8	16	...	...	...
#28•10	LOC	✓Loctite Corp	NY,B,Ch,P,Ph	A	225	14831	Chemical sealants, adhesives	50⅞	1 9/16	46¾	35	50⅞	43⅜	12574	49¾	46⅞	47½	2.1	18	4.4	3.8	12.1
29•8	LWNGF	✓Loewen Group	NNM	B+	201	29467	Oper funeral homes/svcs	27¼	8¼	27⅜	22	41¾	23⅛	135507	27⅜	23⅝	25¼	♦...	23	−2.4	19.0	19.2
¶30•6	LTR	✓Loews Corp	NY,B,Ch,P,Ph	A−	413	61525	Insurance sub:tobacco:hotels	67½	¾	51⅜	42¼	79⅞	43⅜	40498	79⅞	76¼	78⅜	1.3	13	82.2	10.2	10.9
31	RDHS	✓Logan's Roadhouse	NNM	NR	20	891	Own/oper casual dining rest	...	...	...	...	18¾	13½	1660	17½	15¾	17¼	...	26	...	...	...
32	LGWX	✓Logic Works	NNM	NR	..	...	Client/server database prod	...	...	...	...	19½	11	12920	17¼	11¼	12½	...	..	...	...	...
33	LGN	✓Logicon Inc	NY,B,Ch,Ph	↑A	100	7057	Electr sys/hi-tech svs	15⅛	3/16	16⅝	12⅝	32⅛	15	5136	29¼	25⅞	27½	0.7	18	85.5	42.3	49.0
34•11	LOJN	✓LoJack Corp	NNM	B−	73	10540	Mfr stolen vehicle track'g svs	8⅞	1¼	11⅜	5⅛	17½	5⅜	67802	11½	9¼	11⅛	...	32	107	50.7	25.6
35	LOMK	✓Lomak Petroleum	NNM	NR	49	3473	Oil & gas production	9¾	15/16	9½	6⅝	10	5½	31281	10	8⅜	9¾	...	35	47.2	31.9	24.3
36	LOFSY	London & Overseas Freight ADS[62]	[12]	NR	20	2853	Operates fleet of oil tankers	15¼	13½	16½	13	16	11	431	12¼	11½	11½B	0.7	10	−18.7	...	...
37	LCE	✓Lone Star Indus	NY,B,Ch,P,Ph	NR	72	9629	Cement,concrete,sand,gravel	41⅜	1⅜	19¾	1⅞	25¼	17¼	5323	25¼	24⅛	25	...	10	44.8	109	54.3
38	WS	Wrrt(Pur 1com at$18.75)	NY	....	15	132		...	...	9½	6	9⅞	6	862	9⅝	8⅝	9	...	..	...	...	...
39•6	STAR	✓Lone Star Steakhouse/Saloon	NNM	NR	213	26246	Own/oper full svc restaurants	30¼	3⅜	29¼	16½	45	18½	82490	40¾	34⅞	38⅜	...	35	95.5	29.2	...
40•8	LISB	✓Long Island Bancorp	NNM	NR	97	16315	Savings bank, New York	...	...	17⅛	11½	28⅝	14	36900	26¾	25⅛	26⅜	1.5	15	87.2	...	...
41•13	LIL	✓Long Island Light'g	NY,B,C,Ch,P,Ph	B	163	39343	Elec & gas service in N.Y.	29⅝	3¾	24¼	15	17¾	13¼	175508	17½	15⅝	16⅜	10.9	8	18.2	−6.0	2.9
42	Pr I	5.75% cm Cv I Pfd(100)	NY,Ch	BB+	2	..	mainly a residential area	159⅞	35	150	98	91	91	2	91	91	95½B	6.0	..	...	...	...
43	LOHO	✓Longhorn Steaks	NNM	NR	43	2985	Oper full-svc restaurants	25½	6¼	12½	7¾	18¾	8½	5454	18¼	15½	17¾	...	36	106	−7.6	...
¶44	LDG	✓Longs Drug Stores	NY,Ch,Ph	A−	201	8504	Self-service drug store chain	48½	7⅝	39⅞	30¼	48¼	28¼	13109	48¼	39⅝	47⅞	2.3	19	56.2	13.8	8.7
#45•6	LFB	✓Longview Fibre	NY,Ph	B	173	23595	Logs,board,paper & cv prod	23	1⅝	23⅝	14¾	19⅝	13¼	14075	18⅛	16	16¼	e3.7	11	3.6	−0.1	13.5
¶46•8	LOR	✓Loral Corp	NY,B,Ch,P,Ph	A+	589	138307	Military electronic systems	19⅜	⅛	21⅜	16¾	36¼	18¼	114371	36¼	32⅜	35⅜	0.9	18	89.2	47.7	35.9
47	LOTO	✓Lottery Enterprises	NNM	NR	12	184	Mfr lottery-ticket vend'g mach	23¾	8⅝	15½	3⅞	4⅜	½	17503	1¼	½	1⅛	...	d	−73.5	...	...
48	LD	✓Louis Dreyfus Natural Gas	NY,Ch	NR	53	6083	Oil&gas acq'n dvlp, prod'n	18¾	14⅞	23¼	12¼	16½	11¼	4262	15⅝	13½	15⅛	...	18	15.2	...	...
¶49•14	LLX	✓Louisiana Land/Exp	NY,To,B,C,Ch,P,Ph	B−	319	28974	Oil/gas prod'n,explor'n,dev	63¾	16¾	47⅛	35⅛	43	31¼	25763	43	38⅝	42⅞	0.6	88	17.4	9.6	2.9
¶50•15	LPX	✓Louisiana Pacific	NY,B,Ch,P,Ph	B+	361	53066	Lumber,plywood & pulp	42⅛	1⅝	48	25¾	30½	20⅞	73298	27⅛	22⅞	24¼	2.3	12	−9.1	−5.8	24.0
¶51•16	LOW	✓Lowe's Cos	NY,B,Ch,P	A−	479	80935	Dstr bldg mtls: consum'r gds	30	1 3/16	41⅜	26⅝	38⅞	26	107995	34½	30⅛	33½	0.6	23	−2.7	40.4	42.4
52	LEIX	✓Lowrance Electronics	NNM	B−	6	896	Mfrs & mkts sonar equip	13	1¼	9¾	3¼	7¼	3¾	290	5	4¼	5	...	12	8.1	7.7	23.4

Uniform Footnote Explanations-See Page 4. Other: [1]ASE:Cycle 1. [2]ASE,CBOE:Cycle 2. [3]CBOE:Cycle 2. [4]P:Cycle 1. [5]P:Cycle 2. [6]CBOE:Cycle 3. [7]ASE:Cycle 3. [8]CBOE:Cycle 1. [9]P,Ph:Cycle 3. [10]Ph:Cycle 3. [11]CBOE,NY:Cycle 3. [12]NNM [13]NY:Cycle 3. [14]Ph:Cycle 2. [15]ASE:Cycle 2. [16]Ph:Cycle 1. [51]Ea ADS rep 20 ord,par K0.10. [52]Pymts based on Hybritech's operat'g results. [53]Coram Healthcare Corp plan acq, 1.54 com. [54]Subsid pfd in $M. [55]Stk dstr of Western Atlas Inc. [56]EastGroup Properties plan acq. [57]Incl $1.33 non-taxable,'94. [58]Pfd in $M. [59]®$4.83,'94. [60]Fiscal '93 & prior in $Cdn. [61]To be determined. [62]Ea ADS rep 10 ord shrs,$0.25. [63]Approx. [64]®$1.71,'95. [65]®$1.39,'94.

Splits ◆ Index	Cash Divs. Ea.Yr. Since	Dividends: Latest Payment Period $	Date	Ex. Div.	Total $ So Far 1995	Ind. Rate	Paid 1994	Financial Position Mil-$ Cash& Equiv.	Curr. Assets	Curr. Liab.	Balance Sheet Date	Capitalization Lg Trm Debt Mil-$	Shs. 000 Pfd.	Com.	Earnings $ Per Shr. Years End	1991	1992	1993	1994	1995	Last 12 Mos.	Interim Earnings Period	$ per Shr. 1994	1995	Index
1◆	....	None Since Public			...	Nil	....	0.25	68.3	21.4	9-30-95	....	...	11257	Dc	0.55	0.55	0.62	0.75	....	0.74	9 Mo Sep	0.46	0.45	1
2	....	None Since Public			...	Nil	....	Equity per shr $0.67			6-30-95	....	...	★900000	Dc	...	...	...	n/a	....	....	6 Mo Jun	n/a	p0.01	2
3	1992	Q0.07	12-1-95	11-13	0.28	0.28	0.24	12.6	93.5	24.6	8-26-95	3.61	...	9749	Fb	1.02	1.15	1.35	1.38	....	0.95	9 Mo Nov	0.95	0.52	3
4◆	1885	Q0.34¼	3-11-96	2-13	1.13	1.37	1.25	1055	4110	5315	9-30-95	2118	...	p551530	Dc	2.25	□1.41	□0.84	2.22	E2.30↑	3.88	9 Mo Sep	1.72	3.38	4
5	....	....			...	Nil	....	Payable ea Dec 31 '86 thru'95				....	...	p12934	Dc	...	...	...	....	....	....				5
6◆	1957	Q0.08	1-2-96	12-8	0.31	0.32	0.267	16.7	76.5	39.4	8-31-95	21.0	...	±22655	Nv	±0.27	±0.54	±0.70	±1.00	....	0.97	9 Mo Aug	±0.68	±0.65	6
7	1970	Q0.10	12-12-95	11-29	0.40	0.40	0.36	275	3017	800	10-28-95	650	...	358180	Ja	1.11	1.25	1.08	1.25	E1.05	2.80	9 Mo Oct	0.53	2.08	7
8◆	....	None Since Public			...	Nil	....	16.0	41.4	22.9	12-31-94	6.72	...	27124	Dc	p0.13	□0.64	1.01	1.34	....	1.68	9 Mo Sep	0.96	1.30	8
9	1995	Q0.12	1-15-96	12-27	0.20	0.48	....	14.4	380	205	9-30-95	85.0	...	±24901	Dc	0.67	d2.12	Δd1.87	±2.19	....	2.72	9 Mo Sep	±1.57	±2.10	9
10◆	1920	Q0.46	2-1-96	1-8	1.72	1.84	1.64	Equity per shr $33.48			9-30-95	622	41	103961	Dc	2.30	3.90	□4.06	3.37	E2.85	4.81	9 Mo Sep	2.47	3.91	10
11	1965	Q0.75	3-5-96	2-13	3.00	3.00	3.00	Cv into 8 common				....	43	...	Dc	b3.32	b5.87	b5.90	b6.24	....	....				11
12◆	1937	Q0.15	1-10-96	12-26	0.56	0.60	0.52	n/a	78.1	101	9-30-95	74.0	[54]4	36605	Dc	0.83	0.90	□1.01	1.03	....	1.21	9 Mo Sep	0.72	0.90	12
13◆	....	0.018	6-20-80	6-2	...	Nil	....	4.11	17.6	8.69	10-01-95	1.23	...	4047	Dc	*0.45	0.42	□0.21	0.25	....	0.46	9 Mo Sep	0.13	0.34	13
14	1956	Q0.07	12-1-95	11-8	0.25	0.28	0.21	0.12	29.7	16.1	9-30-95	20.6	...	4727	Dc	0.03	0.20	Δd0.60	0.92	....	0.99	9 Mo Sep	0.73	0.80	14
15◆	....	None Since Public			...	Nil	....	23.3	43.7	15.9	8-31-95	....	...	4368	Au	1.91	2.28	2.21	Δ2.31	2.48	2.48				15
16◆	1992	Q0.04	11-15-95	10-25	0.15	0.16	0.12½	284	354	67.9	10-01-95	....	...	73796	Je	0.24	0.35	0.50	0.75	1.11	1.26	3 Mo Sep	0.24	0.39	16
17	....	None Since Public			...	Nil	....	79.3	86.1	13.1	9-30-95	4.56	276	29681	Dc	d0.22	□d0.43	d1.18	□d1.64	....	d1.68	9 Mo Sep	d1.16	d1.20	17
18◆	1977	Q0.11	1-15-96	12-27	0.41	0.44	0.40	7.86	56.2	16.1	9-30-95	....	...	6232	Dc	1.48	1.73	2.00	2.06	....	1.92	9 Mo Sep	1.73	1.59	18
19◆	....	0.027	6-15-83	5-24	...	Nil	....	0.08	7.43	6.98	9-30-95	0.02	...	2280	Dc	d0.15	d0.01	0.10	0.29	....	d0.18	9 Mo Sep	0.35	d0.12	19
20◆	....	h[55]....	3-17-94	3-18	...	Nil	h[55]....	212	1503	1308	10-31-95	104	411	46243	Jl	1.44	4.22	□4.41	□d2.69	2.84	2.93	3 Mo Oct	0.68	0.77	20
21	....	None Since Public			...	Nil	....	0.45	86.0	41.7	9-30-95	20.8	...	4381	Dc	p0.77	p1.00	0.91	0.23	....	d0.49	9 Mo Sep	0.41	d0.31	21
22	....	None Since Public			...	Nil	....	17.9	227	192	9-30-95	182	...	20191	Sp	p0.90	p1.16	1.46	1.77	1.27	1.27				22
23	1984	Q0.11¼	12-4-95	11-9	0.45	0.45	0.45	310	1022	275	9-30-95	1.15	...	74039	Dc	2.61	2.61	Δ1.54	1.06	E1.55	1.20	9 Mo Sep	1.10	1.24	23
24	1983	0.043	1-16-96	1-3	0.349	0.37	0.51	Equity per shr $0.33			9-30-95	....	...	18991	Dc	0.44	0.27	0.44	0.51	....	0.37	9 Mo Sep	0.40	0.26	24
25	1981	Q0.15	12-29-95	12-14	†1.08	0.60	†[57]1.96	Equity per shr $10.85			9-30-95	....	...	★2584	Dc	1.11	d0.98	d0.70	0.12	....	0.31	9 Mo Sep	0.33	0.52	25
26	1956	gQ0.09	12-30-95	12-13	g0.32	0.36	g0.26	216	1119	1089	j12-31-94	666	711	p79891	Dc	1.17	0.88	1.07	1.51	....	j1.71	9 Mo Sep	1.00	1.20	26
27	1995	Q0.35	12-29-95	11-29	1.05	1.40	....	122	8013	5969	9-30-95	2892	[58]1000	199152	Dc	p3.05	p□3.31	p3.99	p□[59]5.32	E5.00	3.07	9 Mo Sep	□3.97	1.72	27
28◆	1962	Q0.25	1-2-96	12-6	0.92	1.00	0.81	69.4	376	240	9-30-95	4.44	...	34839	Dc	1.98	1.99	1.92	2.33	E2.60	2.53	9 Mo Sep	1.73	1.93	28
29◆	1991	g0.05	6-30-95	6-14	g0.09	0.10	g0.06	35.2	175	121	9-30-95	687	...	48070	Dc	0.61	0.77	[60]1.01	0.97	....	1.10	9 Mo Sep	0.69	0.82	29
30◆	1967	Q0.25	12-1-95	11-1	0.62½	1.00	0.50	Equity per shr $61.79			9-30-95	4242	...	117832	Dc	6.57	Δd0.17	4.64	2.23	E6.00	9.33	9 Mo Sep	1.56	8.66	30
31	....	None Since Public			...	Nil	....	3.41	4.36	2.73	10-01-95	1.77	...	3145	Dc	...	...	p0.17	p0.51	....	0.67	9 Mo Sep	p0.39	p0.55	31
32	....	None Since Public			...	Nil	....	1.39	7.19	5.76	6-30-95	p....	p...	★10665	Dc	Nil	0.01	0.05	0.07	....	0.07	9 Mo Sep	0.09	0.09	32
33◆	1980	Q0.05	1-9-96	12-15	0.17	0.20	0.15	42.7	122	38.0	9-30-95	....	...	13856	Mr	0.87	1.02	Δ1.36	1.38	....	1.57	6 Mo Sep	0.59	0.79	33
34	....	None Paid			...	Nil	....	26.1	34.0	6.75	8-31-95	1.03	...	21624	Fb	d0.38	d0.23	□0.02	0.16	E0.35	0.30	6 Mo Aug	0.03	0.17	34
35◆	1995	0.01	12-29-95	12-14	0.01	[61]....	....	2.40	14.4	12.7	9-30-95	113	200	12063	Dc	0.02	0.08	0.18	0.25	....	0.28	9 Mo Sep	0.18	0.21	35
36	1994	[63]0.02	1-19-96	12-26	0.08	0.08	0.08½	32.2	33.5	10.1	3-31-95	52.1	...	73351	Mr	1.53	0.43	1.02	1.13	....	1.13				36
37◆	....	Q0.05	12-15-95	11-29	0.15	Nil	....	46.9	152	61.7	9-30-95	78.0	...	12073	Dc	d0.64	d3.03	□d2.42	p1.76	....	2.49	9 Mo Sep	p1.15	1.88	37
38	....	Terms&trad. basis should	be checked in detail					Wrrts expire 12-31-2000				....	...	4000	Dc	...	...	...	....	....	....				38
39◆	....	None Since Public			...	Nil	....	111	127	25.4	9-05-95	....	...	37564	Dc	p0.04	0.17	0.46	0.82	....	1.09	36 Wk Sep	0.54	0.81	39
40	1995	Q0.10	2-14-96	1-11	0.40	0.40	....	Equity per shr $19.66			6-30-95	584	...	26504	Sp	...	...	pd2.15	pΔ1.15	P[64]1.73	1.73				40
41	1989	Q0.44½	1-1-96	12-13	1.78	1.78	1.78	245	1089	961	9-30-95	4723	24125	119383	Dc	2.15	2.14	2.15	2.15	E2.10	1.92	9 Mo Sep	1.94	1.71	41
42	1989	Q1.43¾	2-10-96	1-12	5.75	5.75	5.75	Cv into 5.8309 common				....	20	...	Dc	b1.41	b1.40	b1.40	b1.44	....	....				42
43	....	None Since Public			...	Nil	....	2.39	9.17	8.96	9-30-95	....	...	6623	Dc	p0.47	p0.62	0.53	0.23	....	0.50	9 Mo Sep	0.14	0.41	43
44	1961	Q0.28	1-10-96	12-1	1.12	1.12	1.12	25.6	421	271	10-26-95	9.05	...	19936	Ja	2.71	2.58	Δ2.41	2.35	E2.52	2.54	9 Mo Oct	1.52	1.71	44
45	1937	Q0.15	1-10-96	12-20	†0.60	0.60	0.52	....	209	166	10-31-95	409	...	51751	Oc	0.32	0.62	0.78	0.64	1.47	1.47				45
46◆	1976	Q0.08	3-15-96	2-26	0.31	0.32	0.29	111	1859	1325	9-30-95	1832	...	172321	Mr	1.00	□1.03	1.36	1.69	E1.95↑	1.85	6 Mo Sep	0.71	0.87	46
47◆	....	5%Stk	7-29-94	6-27	...	Nil	5%Stk	2.88	11.0	8.42	9-30-95	0.55	...	7911	Dc	d0.48	0.02	0.38	d1.13	....	d2.22	9 Mo Sep	0.44	d0.65	47
48	....	None Since Public			...	Nil	....	6.42	34.9	28.2	9-30-95	307	...	27800	Dc	...	p0.41	0.11	0.39	....	0.83	9 Mo Sep	0.18	0.62	48
49	1935	Q0.06	12-15-95	11-29	0.24	0.24	1.00	7.60	155	154	9-30-95	712	...	33481	Dc	0.74	□d0.04	Δ□0.43	d6.80	E0.49	d6.31	9 Mo Sep	d0.14	0.35	49
50◆	1973	Q0.14	12-1-95	11-13	0.54½	0.56	0.48½	125	678	510	9-30-95	184	...	107888	Dc	0.52	1.63	□2.32	3.15	E2.10	0.04	9 Mo Sep	2.38	d0.73	50
51◆	1961	Q0.05	1-31-96	1-12	0.18½	0.20	0.17	143	1706	1082	10-31-95	★849	...	160809	Ja	■0.05	0.58	0.89	[65]1.44	E1.45	1.45	9 Mo Oct	1.16	1.17	51
52	....	None Since Public			...	Nil	....	0.29	32.3	18.2	10-31-95	12.2	...	3352	Jl	d0.72	*0.48	0.88	d0.20	0.42	0.43	3 Mo Oct	d0.36	d0.35	52

◆**Stock Splits & Divs By Line Reference Index** [1]3-for-2,'93:10%,'92,'94,'95. [4]2-for-1,'95. [6]Adj to 5%,'92:3-for-2,'93,'94. [8]2-for-1,'93. [10]2-for-1,'93. [12]2-for-1,'94. [13]5-for-4,'92:10%,'91,'93. [15]3-for-2,'91. [16]2-for-1,'92,'95. [18]3-for-1,'92. [19]3-for-2,'93. [20]2-for-1,'92:No adj for stk dstr Western Atlas,'94. [28]2-for-1,'91. [29]2-for-1,'91. [30]2-for-1,'95. [33]2-for-1,'91,'95. [35]1-for-15 REVERSE,'92. [37]No adj for reorg, '94. [39]2-for-1,'92,'93. [46]2-for-1,'93,'95. [47]Adj for 5%,'94. [50]3-for-2,'92:2-for-1,'93. [51]2-for-1,'92,'94.

¶ S&P 500 # MidCap 400 ✤ SmallCap 600 • Options

Index	Ticker	Name of Issue (Call Price of Pfd. Stocks)	Market	Com. Rank. & Pfd. Rating	Inst. Hold Cos	Inst. Hold Shs. (000)	Principal Business	Price Range 1971-93 High	1971-93 Low	1994 High	1994 Low	1995 High	1995 Low	Dec. Sales in 100s	December, 1995 Last Sale Or Bid High	Low	Last	%Div Yield	P-E Ratio	Total Return % Annualized 12 Mo	36 Mo	60 Mo
✤1	LSB	✔LSB Industries	NY,Ch	B–	38	3388	Chemicals, climate control eqp	12⅜	11/16	10	5¼	6⅞	3⅝	5996	4⅞	3¾	4⅜	1.4	d	–21.5	–14.4	34.9
2	PrC	$3.25 cm Cv[52]Ex'C'Pfd([53]52.28)	NY	NR	8	332		....	....	....	....	38⅝	30¼	838	33⅝	31½	33½	9.7	..	...	...	...
3	LYTS	✔LSI Industries	NNM	↑B	38	2206	Mfrs outdoor lighting sys	10⅞	2 1/16	8⅜	5⅜	22	7⅜	10092	16½	14¼	16	e1.0	19	121	81.6	51.1
¶4•[1]	LSI	✔LSI Logic	NY,Ch	B–	449	113508	Mfr integrated circuits(ASICs)	10⅝	2 7/16	22¾	7¾	62½	18¼	710751	48	30	32¾	...	18	59.1	82.3	60.8
5	LTC	✔LTC Properties	NY	NR	101	11977	Real estate investment trust	14⅜	9¾	15⅛	11⅞	15½	12½	12971	15½	14⅝	15	8.4	14	23.6	23.8	...
6•[2]	LTV	✔LTV Corp	NY	NR	221	75403	Steel prod'n/energy prd	16¼	10	21¼	14	17⅞	12⅝	66150	15	13¼	13¾	...	8	–16.7	...	...
7	WS	Sr'A'Wrrt[57]	NY	....	33	445		4¼	3	6¼	3½	4⅛	2¼	5568	2¾	2¼	2⅜	...	..	...	...	...
#8•[3]	LZ	✔Lubrizol Corp	NY,B,Ch,Ph	B+	334	44261	Spec'lty chemicals/agric R&D	36⅜	7	38⅝	28½	37⅜	25½	49873	29⅞	25½	27¾	3.5	12	–14.4	3.4	6.3
¶9	LUB	✔Luby's Cafeterias	NY,Ch	A	229	10581	Cafeteria style restaurants	25⅞	⅜	24⅝	21⅝	23¼	18½	8569	23	21½	22¼	3.2	14	0.4	2.6	7.9
#10•[4]	LUC	✔Lukens Inc	NY,B,Ch,P,Ph	↑B+	145	11823	Mfr plate steels,ind'l prod	52⅞	2⅜	39¾	26⅛	35½	25¾	7634	29⅞	26¾	28¾	3.5	14	6.1	–9.6	5.1
11	LUM	✔Lumex, Inc	AS	B–	14	844	Mfr hospital furniture/eq	33⅜	¼	14⅜	9	15⅛	8⅝	3640	10¼	8⅝	9⅜	...	d	–29.2	–12.8	14.0
12	LUMI	Lumisys Inc	NNM	NR	..	...	Dgn/mfr precision digitizers	....	....	....	....	11¼	7	23975	11¼	7⅝	11¼	...	28	...	...	...
13	LUND	✔Lund International	NNM	NR	26	1255	Mfr truck van accessory prd	20	1¾	27½	15½	26½	10¼	4806	13¾	12	12	...	9	–26.2	15.1	40.5
14	LUR	✔Luria (L)& Son	NY,B,Ch	B–	26	1821	Catalog showrooms,Florida	19	3¼	14⅞	5⅞	8⅞	4⅝	2888	6⅝	4⅝	5⅛	...	d	–14.6	–17.1	–1.4
15	LUX	✔Luxottica Group ADS[59]	NY,Ch,Ph	NR	70	6379	Design/mfr eyeglass frames	32⅞	8	36⅝	27⅝	59¾	31⅛	6496	59¾	52½	58½	0.6	31	74.8	34.9	45.6
16	LXU.EC	✔Luxtec Corp	ECM	↓C	1	8	Mfr fiber optic surgical instr	16¼	5/16	10⅛	1¾	7¼	2½	290	4	3⅜	3½	...	d	–9.7	13.8	41.1
17	LVMHY	✔LVMH Moet Henn Lou Vttn ADS[60]	NNM	NR	33	1971	Prod's wine,spirits,luxury prd	31⅞	3¾	33¾	22¾	41⅞	29¾	1773	41⅞	37⅝	41⅞	1.5	15	34.5	26.1	19.8
18	LXR	✔LXR Biotechnology	AS,Ch	NR	5	475	Dvlp stge:biopharm'l R&D	....	....	6	11/16	3	¾	4679	2	1¼	1¾	...	d	116	...	...
✤19	LDL	✔Lydall, Inc	NY	B+	108	10608	Engineered fiber materials	11¾	¼	18⅝	10⅛	28½	14¾	6804	28½	22	22¾	...	20	42.3	32.1	41.2
20	LGL	✔Lynch Corp	AS	B	18	175	Transport'n & fin'l svcs: commun	34⅞	¾	32⅞	22	84¾	30	191	64½	57¾	58½	...	18	98.3	33.0	32.0
#21•[5]	LYO	✔Lyondell Petrochem	NY,Ch,Ph	NR	218	43132	Petrochemical refin'g/mktg	33½	13⅛	33	20⅝	29⅛	21⅛	21992	25⅜	22⅜	22⅞	3.9	5	–8.3	2.0	15.2
22	MHMY	✔M.H.Meyerson & Co	NNM	NR	..	...	Broker/dealer, underwriter	....	....	6½	⅞	2⅞	⅞	4157	2⅛	1⅞	2	...	d	52.4	...	...
23	MACD	✔MacDermid, Inc	NNM	↑A–	34	1406	Indust'l metal finish'g chems	34¾	2¼	42	24	60⅛	36½	168	60⅛	54	59½	1.0	15	64.2	33.9	25.2
24	MAC	✔Macerich Co	NY,Ch	NR	87	11375	Real estate investment trust	....	....	21⅝	18⅛	21⅞	19¼	7699	20½	19¼	20	8.4	24	1.0	...	...
#25•[6]	MFI	✔MacFrugals Bargains Closeouts	NY,Ph	B	157	22559	'Close out'mdse retail strs	30⅜	1/16	21¼	13⅛	20¼	11½	12161	14	13⅛	14	...	9	–28.2	0.0	10.2
26	MKIE	✔Mackie Designs	NNM	NR	18	1038	Dvlp/mfr audio mixers	....	....	....	....	16¼	11	1920	12¼	11	11¼	...	16	...	...	...
27	MNS	✔MacNeal-Schwendler	AS,Ch	B	82	8514	Softw for computer-aid-eng'g	23	4¼	15⅜	9⅝	19⅝	10	4893	16	14⅝	16	4.0	13	63.2	7.5	12.5
28•[6]	MACR	✔Macromedia Inc	NNM	NR	135	26407	Dvlp software authoring tools	8⅞	6⅜	13⅞	3¾	63¾	10⅝	157047	63¾	40	52¼	...	..	284	...	...
29	SHOO	✔Madden (Steven) Ltd	NSC	NR	2	8	Mkt fashion footwear for women	8	5	6	1½	10⅛	3⅞	52464	9⅛	7	8⅛	...	20	58.5	...	...
30	MAD	✔Madeco S.A. ADS[69]	NY	NR	72	2952	Mfr copper/aluminum prd-Chile	29¼	15	41¼	23¼	31⅝	16½	6119	27	24	27	2.2	28	3.4	...	...
31•[1]	MYS	✔Maderas y Sinteticos ADS[70]	NY	NR	56	2683	Mfr particle board, Chile	28¼	14⅞	34¾	22½	25¼	11½	9018	19⅝	16¾	19½	1.6	25	–23.2	...	...
32•[2]	MADGF	Madge Networks N.V.	NNM	NR	33	4931	Dvlp,mfr computer products	15	8	19⅝	9⅞	48⅝	11½	54034	48⅝	37¼	44¾	...	43	269	...	...
33	MDSN	✔Madison Gas & Elec	NNM	A–	56	1168	Util:elec & gas in Wisconsin	36¾	7⅛	35	31	35	30½	1917	35	32⅞	35	5.4	15	16.8	8.3	16.1
34	MAFB	✔MAF Bancorp	NNM	NR	42	1293	Savings bank, Chicago	22¼	2¾	21⅞	16⅜	26¼	17	3526	25½	24⅞	25	1.3	9	57.4	28.9	48.8
35	MFO	Mafco Consolidated Group	NY	NR	38	2012	Mfr cigars/licorice extract	....	....	....	....	29¼	16¾	3692	21	17	18	...	20	...	...	...
✤36•[3]	MGL	✔Magellan Health Svcs[72]	AS	NR	118	20352	Operates hospitals	27	4⅝	28½	19	24¼	13⅞	34044	24¼	18⅛	24	...	d	15.7	45.0	...
✤37•[7]	MCU	✔Magma Copper[73]	NY,Ch	NR	196	20118	Copper mining & refining	18⅝	3⅝	18¾	12¾	28	13⅞	157042	28	27⅝	27⅞	...	7	70.2	29.8	43.2
38	Pr D	5.625% cm CvSr'D'Pfd([74]51.969)	NY,Ch	BB+	29	1186		56¼	45¾	69⅞	54¼	96⅛	54½	4964	96⅛	95⅜	96⅛	2.9	..	...	...	...
39	Pr E	6% cm Cv Sr'E'Pfd([75]52.10)	NY,Ch	BB+	21	1181		59	48⅞	72⅝	57	100¼	56⅞	4844	100¼	99⅜	100¼B	3.0	..	...	...	...
✤40	MAGI	✔Magna Group, Inc	NNM	B+	103	8643	Retail bkg,Ill & Missouri	20¼	3	21½	16¾	26⅜	17⅛	7136	24⅞	23	23¾	3.4	13	39.3	15.9	26.8
41•[7]	MGA	✔Magna Intl Cl'A'	NY,To	B	254	27913	Mfrs automotive parts	50	1 11/16	54	31⅛	48⅞	31¾	28329	45¾	42¾	43¼	◆...	..	16.8	19.5	85.5
#42•[8]	MAG	✔MagneTek Inc	NY,Ch,Ph	B–	102	17353	Mfrs diverse group elec prod	25½	6¾	16¾	12⅜	16½	7⅞	35011	8⅞	7⅞	8⅛	...	d	–39.8	–22.2	–4.5
43	MPM.EC	✔Magnum Petroleum	ECM	NR	1	.3	Oil & gas explor'n dvlp,prod	8	2	5¼	2⅛	5	2¾	2314	3¼	2¾	2⅞	...	d	–35.2	...	...
44	NOW	MAI Systems	AS	NR	12	724	Computer software/services	....	....	....	....	12¼	5¾	2702	7¼	5¾	6¾	...	5	...	...	...
45	MAIDY	M.A.I.D. ADS[77]	NNM	NR	..	...	Supply business info	....	....	....	....	18⅜	12¾	23877	18⅜	12¾	14½	...	76	...	...	...
✤46•[5]	MAIL	✔Mail Boxes Etc	NNM	B+	45	3665	Postal & business svc ctrs	21	1⅝	12	6⅝	15¾	8	6089	14⅞	12½	12½	...	18	22.0	–9.3	12.6
47	MLWL	✔Mail-Well Inc	NNM	NR	17	2957	U.S.lrgst envlp mfr/printer	....	....	....	....	14	10½	9156	12¼	10⅝	12¼	...	..	...	...	...
48	MAP	✔Maine Public Service	AS	B	23	513	Electric pwr northern Maine	31¼	4¼	27⅜	20½	23⅞	19⅞	427	21¾	20⅝	21⅜	8.6	9	12.0	0.5	7.1
49	MAL	✔Malan Realty Investors	NY,Ch,Ph	NR	28	1758	Real estate investment trust	....	....	17½	13⅜	16¼	12	4915	13¾	12	12⅜	13.7	..	3.1	...	...
¶50•[1]	MKG	✔Mallinckrodt Group	NY,B,C,Ch,P,Ph	B	405	57565	Hlth care prd/spcl chem	46⅝	2¼	38½	28⅜	41⅞	29⅛	42571	36⅜	34	36⅜	1.7	15	25.9	3.7	8.6
51	MLRC	✔Mallon Resources	NNM	NR	8	244	O&G mineral explor,dvl,prod	8½	⅛	4½	1⅜	2¾	1	6162	1⅞	1	1½	...	d	0.0	–36.6	–10.6
52	MANA	✔Manatron Inc	NNM	B–	6	9	Data process sys to local gvt	9⅛	1 3/16	5¼	3	3⅝	1⅞	945	3	1⅞	2	...	d	–40.7	–8.1	7.3

Uniform Footnote Explanations-See Page 4. Other: [1]CBOE:Cycle 1. [2]ASE,CBOE:Cycle 2. [3]Ph:Cycle 2. [4]P,Cycle 3. [5]NY:Cycle 3. [6]P:Cycle 1. [7]CBOE:Cycle 2. [8]P:Cycle 3. [51]®$1.46,'94. [52]Co opt fr 6-15-96 exch for $50 amt 6.50%Cv2018. [53]Fr 6-15-96. [54]®$0.92,'94. [55]6 Mo Dec,'93. [56]®$1.27,'94. [57]Wrrt to purch 0.5582 com at $16.28. [58]®$1.32,'94. [59]Each ADS rep 1 ord,1000 lire. [60]Ea ADS rep 0.2 ord. [61]®$2.80,'94. [62]Stk dstr of Corcap Inc. [63]®$1.88,'94. [64]®$3.50,'95. [65]Incl $0.1653 non-taxable,'94. [66]Incl current amts. [67]Redemption of stk purch rt. [68]Fiscal Jun'93 & prior. [69]Ea ADS rep 10 ord, no par. [70]Ea ADS rep 30 ord, no par. [71]Approx. [72]Formerly Charter Medical. [73]Broken Hill Prop offer, $28 to Jan 4. [74]Fr 7-20-96,scale to $50 in 2003. [75]Fr 12-1-96,scale to $50 in 2003. [76]®$5.16,'95. [77]Ea ADS rep 4 ord shrs par 0.01P.

Index (Splits ◆)	Cash Divs. Ea. Yr. Since	Dividends: Latest Payment Period $	Date	Ex. Div.	Total $ So Far 1995	Ind. Rate	Paid 1994	Financial Position Mil-$ Cash& Equiv.	Curr. Assets	Curr. Liab.	Balance Sheet Date	Capitalization Lg Trm Debt Mil-$	Shs. 000 Pfd.	Com.	Earnings $ Per Shr. Years End	1991	1992	1993	1994	1995	Last 12 Mos.	Interim Earnings Period	$ per Shr. 1994	1995	Index
1	1993	S0.03	1-2-96	12-13	0.06	0.06	0.06	1.43	123	55.2	9-30-95	98.2	942	12915	Dc	d0.48	0.94	0.77	[51]1.54	....	d0.41	9 Mo Sep	1.85	d0.10	1
2	1993	Q0.81¼	12-15-95	11-29	3.25	3.25	3.25	Cv into 4.3 com				....	915	...	Dc	...	...	...	....	....	....				2
3◆	1988	Q0.04	11-13-95	11-2	†0.183	0.16	s0.09	1.34	43.5	25.0	9-30-95	7.06	...	7622	Je	d0.15	d0.65	0.23	0.55	0.79	0.83	3 Mo Sep	0.24	0.28	3
4◆	....	None Since Public			...	Nil	....	671	1090	347	9-30-95	272	...	p129029	Dc	0.10	d1.24	0.55	[54]0.99	E1.84	1.65	9 Mo Sep	0.68	1.34	4
5	1992	Q0.315	1-26-96	12-27	1.18½	1.26	1.08	Equity per shr $9.26			9-30-95	111	...	18296	Dc	...	0.10	0.75	0.99	....	1.07	9 Mo Sep	0.74	0.82	5
6	....	None Since Public			...	Nil	....	911	2141	1044	9-30-95	149	500	104982	Dc	...	pd2.05	‡[55]3.21	[56]1.29	E1.75	1.76	9 Mo Sep	0.91	1.38	6
7	....	Terms&trad. basis should be checked in detail						Wrrts expire 6-29-98				....	...	8500	Dc	...	...	...	....	....	....				7
8◆	1935	Q0.24	12-8-95	11-8	0.93	0.96	0.89	28.8	650	241	9-30-95	196	...	63226	Dc	1.79	1.81	□1.25	2.67	E2.38↓	2.70	9 Mo Sep	2.13	2.16	8
9	1965	Q0.18	1-2-96	12-13	0.67½	0.72	0.615	12.4	20.2	99.5	8-31-95	....	...	23335	Au	1.18	1.19	1.31	Δ1.45	1.55	1.57	3 Mo Nov	0.35	0.37	9
10◆	1940	Q0.25	11-17-95	11-2	1.00	1.00	1.00	7.17	328	183	9-30-95	250	495	14733	Dc	1.68	2.31	□0.95	[58]1.37	E2.10	2.44	9 Mo Sep	0.68	1.75	10
11	....	0.02	8-20-90	7-16	...	Nil	....	5.93	61.9	39.8	9-30-95	10.5	...	4325	Dc	0.86	1.01	d0.02	0.81	....	d0.34	9 Mo Sep	0.68	d0.47	11
12	....	None Since Public			...	Nil	....	2.98	9.40	3.49	9-30-95	....	p...	★6234	Dc	d1.74	0.22	0.16	0.34	....	0.40	9 Mo Sep	0.22	0.28	12
13	....	None Paid			...	Nil	....	11.0	27.0	4.18	9-30-95	4.59	...	4398	Je	0.11	0.47	0.90	1.20	1.58	1.40	3 Mo Sep	0.40	0.22	13
14	....	3%Stk	4-27-84	4-2	...	Nil	....	1.34	84.9	46.5	10-28-95	0.79	...	±5424	Ja	±0.22	±0.64	±0.26	±0.03	....	d0.87	9 Mo Oct	±d0.62	±d1.52	14
15◆	1990	0.335	7-17-95	7-3	0.335	0.33	0.317	96.5	331	131	12-31-94	8.52	...	44585	Dc	1.16	1.01	1.20	1.74	....	1.90	3 Mo Mar	0.41	0.57	15
16◆	....	None Paid			...	Nil	....	0.02	3.96	2.59	7-31-95	....	...	p2439	Oc	*0.17	*0.19	*0.08	0.11	Pd4.19	d4.19				16
17◆	1988	0.187	12-11-95	11-28	0.622	0.62	0.425	11791	34511	15174	j12-31-94	9556	...	86955	Dc	1.80	1.34	1.48	[61]2.81	....	2.81				17
18	....	None Since Public			...	Nil	....	0.65	0.73	0.96	9-30-95	0.24	...	7495	Dc	...	...	d0.77	d0.94	....	d0.82	9 Mo Sep	d0.77	d0.65	18
19◆	....	h[62]....	7-11-88	7-13	...	Nil	....	25.4	81.1	34.1	9-30-95	7.79	...	17290	Dc	0.47	0.52	Δ0.57	0.86	....	1.15	9 Mo Sep	0.62	0.91	19
20	....	0.05	1-30-89	1-3	...	Nil	....	27.3	106	76.2	9-30-95	73.6	...	1379	Dc	Δ1.08	Δ1.54	□3.35	□[63]1.94	....	3.21	9 Mo Sep	□1.27	2.54	20
21	1989	Q0.22½	12-15-95	11-21	0.90	0.90	0.90	44.0	784	757	9-30-95	732	...	80000	Dc	2.78	□0.32	Δ0.06	2.78	E5.12↓	5.79	9 Mo Sep	1.51	4.52	21
22	1994	0.03	5-13-94	4-7	...	Nil	0.03	Equity per shr $2.30			7-31-95	....	...	5008	Ja	0.24	0.29	0.47	d0.11	....	d0.03	9 Mo Oct	Nil	0.08	22
23	1946	Q0.15	1-1-96	12-13	0.60	0.60	0.60	7.95	90.6	45.7	9-30-95	19.3	...	2796	Mr	2.03	2.16	□2.18	□[64]3.55	....	3.90	6 Mo Sep	□1.72	2.07	23
24	1994	Q0.42	12-5-95	11-21	1.66	1.68	[65]0.87	Equity per shr $5.31			9-30-95	[66]401	...	★19376	Dc	...	...	p0.73	p0.73	....	0.84	9 Mo Sep	p0.44	□0.55	24
25	....	[67]0.01	8-28-90	8-17	...	Nil	....	18.0	292	147	10-29-95	120	...	25527	Ja	1.12	0.37	1.07	1.37	E1.55	0.54	9 Mo Oct	0.47	d0.36	25
26	....	None Since Public			...	Nil	....	18.4	36.4	8.19	9-30-95	....	...	12875	Dc	...	...	...	p0.63	....	0.70	9 Mo Sep	p0.47	p0.54	26
27	1978	Q0.16	3-6-96	2-14	0.64	0.64	0.64	12.2	50.8	35.9	10-31-95	56.6	...	13421	Ja	d0.12	1.03	0.86	d2.27	....	1.21	9 Mo Oct	d2.74	0.74	27
28◆	....	None Since Public			...	Nil	....	102	115	16.5	9-30-95	....	...	35054	Mr	...	pd0.02	0.15	0.19	....	0.37	6 Mo Sep	0.09	0.27	28
29	....	None Paid			...	Nil	....	2.26	7.90	1.46	6-30-95	....	...	5578	Dc	...	0.04	[68]d0.03	d0.13	....	0.41	9 Mo Sep	d0.22	0.32	29
30	1994	0.445	5-22-95	4-26	0.445	0.60	0.605	4.74	247	230	12-31-94	44.9	...	337750	Dc	0.93	0.94	1.00	0.98	....	0.98				30
31	1993	0.139	6-7-95	5-9	0.139	0.32	[71]0.37½	6.14	100	27.4	12-31-94	13.9	...	684000	Dc	1.44	0.93	0.94	0.79	....	0.79				31
32	....	None Since Public			...	Nil	....	5.45	35.9	29.2	3-31-93	1.27	p...	★30841	Dc	0.10	0.27	P0.56	P0.74	E1.05	0.98	9 Mo Sep	0.54	0.78	32
33◆	1909	Q0.47½	12-15-95	11-29	1.89	1.90	1.87	0.32	51.1	44.3	9-30-95	128	...	10720	Dc	2.28	2.18	2.26	2.29	....	2.33	12 Mo Sep	2.29	2.33	33
34◆	1994	Q0.08	1-3-96	12-13	0.298	0.32	0.073	Book Value $19.92			9-30-95	20.1	...	5494	Je	*0.84	*1.50	□Δ2.20	2.22	2.55	2.79	3 Mo Sep	0.48	0.72	34
35	....	None Since Public			...	Nil	....	99.3	219	86.7	10-01-95	231	...	23237	Dc	...	...	...	p0.57	....	0.89	9 Mo Sep	p0.48	0.80	35
36	....	None Since Public			...	Nil	....	106	306	214	9-30-95	539	...	28415	Sp	pd1.43	pd1.50	□d1.75	□d1.78	d1.54	d1.54				36
37	....	Wrrt	12-29-88	12-30	...	Nil	....	62.0	396	241	9-30-95	582	4000	46376	Dc	d3.51	□1.37	□0.42	1.54	....	3.75	9 Mo Sep	0.85	3.06	37
38	1993	Q0.703	12-15-95	11-24	2.81¼	2.813	2.812	Cv into 3.448 com $14.50				....	1800	...	Dc	...	...	...	....	....	....				38
39	1993	Q0.75	12-15-95	11-24	3.00	3.00	3.00	Cv into 3.5945 com, $13.91				....	1800	...	Dc	...	...	...	....	....	....				39
40◆	1980	Q0.20	12-10-95	11-13	0.80	0.80	0.76	Book Value $15.59			9-30-95	93.7	2	27902	Dc	0.28	□Δ1.36	1.53	1.69	....	1.81	9 Mo Sep	1.22	1.34	40
41	1992	gQ0.27	1-15-96	12-27	g1.08	1.08	g0.93	404	1493	966	j7-31-95	★615	...	±61435	Jl	±0.59	2.91	3.09	4.18	[76]5.20	j5.04	3 Mo Oct	1.33	1.17	41
42	....	None Since Public			...	Nil	....	1.31	468	179	9-30-95	370	...	24700	Je	1.47	□1.22	□1.09	d1.84	□0.29	d0.08	3 Mo Sep	0.23	d0.14	42
43	....	None Since Public			...	Nil	....	2.38	2.69	0.27	9-30-95	....	655	p9819	Dc	d0.12	d0.30	d0.55	d0.44	....	d0.45	9 Mo Sep	d0.15	d0.16	43
44◆	....	None Since Public			...	Nil	....	5.14	16.1	16.3	9-30-95	1.17	...	6686	Dc	...	...	...	Δ0.50	....	1.25	9 Mo Sep	0.03	Δ0.78	44
45	....	None Since Public			...	Nil	....	Equity per shr $1.79			9-30-95	3.06	...	★91717	Dc	0.01	0.01	0.01	0.02	....	0.19	9 Mo Sep	0.04	0.21	45
46◆	....	None Since Public			...	Nil	....	15.5	39.6	10.7	10-31-95	1.36	...	11151	Ap	0.37	0.46	0.56	0.49	0.60	0.69	6 Mo Oct	0.24	0.33	46
47	....	None Since Public			...	Nil	....	23.0	208	101	p9-30-95	310	...	12473	Dc	...	...	...	p0.47	....	....	9 Mo Sep	n/a	p1.04	47
48	1944	Q0.46	1-1-96	12-13	1.84	1.84	1.84	0.89	15.4	10.1	9-30-95	36.1	...	1617	Dc	2.62	2.93	3.19	2.99	....	2.35	9 Mo Sep	2.17	1.53	48
49	1994	Q0.42½	1-22-96	12-27	1.70	1.70	0.42½	Equity per shr $12.01			9-30-95	172	...	3571	Dc	...	...	p0.84	p0.64	....	....	9 Mo Sep	n/a	0.46	49
50◆	1971	Q0.15½	12-29-95	12-13	0.57½	0.62	0.51½	88.2	1038	786	9-30-95	★602	98	76530	Je	1.24	1.63	□d1.56	1.33	2.32	2.38	3 Mo Sep	0.44	0.50	50
51	....	None Paid			...	Nil	....	1.26	2.51	2.62	9-30-95	9.34	1501	7800	Dc	d0.99	d0.06	d0.22	d0.24	....	d0.26	9 Mo Sep	d0.08	□d0.10	51
52◆	....	5%Stk	11-18-94	10-7	...	Nil	5%Stk	0.24	11.5	7.60	10-31-95	4.49	...	2989	Ap	0.16	0.19	Δ0.05	0.11	0.15	d0.83	6 Mo Oct	0.10	d0.88	52

◆**Stock Splits & Divs By Line Reference Index** [3]Adj for 5%,'94:3-for-2,'95. [4]2-for-1,'95. [8]2-for-1,'92. [10]3-for-2,'92. [15]2-for-1,'92. [16]1-for-10 REVERSE,'92. [17]5-for-1,'94:10%,'94. [19]2-for-1,'92,'95:3-for-2,'93. [28]2-for-1,'95. [33]3-for-2,'92:3-for-2,'92:To split 3-for-2,hldrs Feb 1. [34]3-for-2,'93:10,'95. [40]Adj to 5%,'91(ex,'90). [44]5-for-4,'95. [46]4-for-3,'91:2-for-1,'92. [50]3-for-1,'91. [52]Adj to 5%,'94.

¶ S&P 500 # MidCap 400 ✢ SmallCap 600 • Options

Index	Ticker	Name of Issue (Call Price of Pfd. Stocks)	Market	Com. Rank. & Pfd. Rating	Inst. Hold Cos	Inst. Hold Shs. (000)	Principal Business	Price Range 1971-93 High	1971-93 Low	1994 High	1994 Low	1995 High	1995 Low	Dec. Sales in 100s	December, 1995 Last Sale Or Bid High	Low	Last	%Div Yield	P-E Ratio	Total Return % Annualized 12 Mo	36 Mo	60 Mo
✢1	MTW	✔Manitowoc Co	NY,Ph	B	82	4876	Mfr heavy-lift cranes:shipyd	37½	1⅞	32⅜	21½	30⅝	21	2744	30⅝	29⅛	30⅝	3.3	..	46.1	10.0	15.1
¶2•[1]	MNR	✔Manor Care	NY,B,Ch,P,Ph	A–	342	32677	Nursing hms(elderly):motels	26⅝	1/16	29⅝	23¼	35⅝	27½	22824	35½	32¾	35	0.3	22	24.2	15.2	25.7
#3•[2]	MAN	✔Manpower Inc	NY	NR	294	68977	Worldwide employment svcs	17⅞	11⅛	29⅞	16⅞	34¼	24⅛	133370	28⅝	24⅛	28⅛	0.5	17	0.5	25.8	...
4	MHC	✔Manufactured Home Communities	NY	NR	116	20680	Real estate investment trust	24⅛	12⅞	24	15	19⅞	13¾	14617	18¼	16½	17½	6.7	26	–3.0	...	...
5•[3]	MVL	✔Manville Corp	NY	NR	87	21877	Bldg,constrn,paper products	10⅞	4	10⅛	7	15¼	8¼	21306	13⅜	12½	13	...	12	38.7	20.9	29.9
6	WS	Wrrt(Purch 1com at$9.40)	NY,Ch	....	15	1505		4⅝	9/16	2⅜	1⅛	6	1	6189	4	3¼	3⅞	...	..	...	...	...
#7•[4]	MDA	✔MAPCO, Inc	NY,B,Ch,P,Ph	A–	219	21693	Coal,LP-gas pipeline:crude	65⅜	3⅛	64¾	49¾	59¼	48⅞	15072	54⅝	51⅝	54⅝	1.8	16	8.6	1.5	7.0
8	MAPS	✔MapInfo Corp	NNM	NR	56	2394	Dvlp desktop mapping software	....	....	27½	14¾	40	17¾	4564	22¾	18½	20	...	31	–20.8	...	...
9	MCAM	✔Marcam Corp	NNM	↓C	69	6069	Mkt IBM-compatible software	32	7½	14¾	7¾	20¾	7¾	14176	20¾	14¾	15¼	...	d	58.4	–19.5	–9.4
✢10	MCS	✔Marcus Corp	NY,Ph	A	87	7515	Hotels:restaurants:theatres	18⅜	7/16	19⅝	16	27⅜	17⅛	3055	27⅜	22¾	27⅜	1.0	13	54.1	28.8	41.9
11	MARPS	✔Marine Petrol Tr[53]	NSC	NR	7	76	Oil & gas royalties-Gulf Oil	45	5	15½	12	13½	10¼	172	11½	10¼	10¼	10.5	10	–7.7	8.8	7.8
✢12•[5]	MRNR	✔Mariner Health Group	NNM	NR	123	17348	Subacute health care services	22	11	27⅛	15½	22⅛	8⅝	67801	17	13⅛	16¾	...	26	–21.6	...	...
13	MRSA	✔Marisa Christina	NNM	NR	33	2956	Mfr womens/childrens cloth'g	....	....	15¾	9⅛	18	9⅝	4628	17¼	16⅝	17	...	15	63.9	...	...
14	TUG	✔Maritrans Inc	NY	NR	27	4878	U.S.coast marine transporter	10¼	1¾	6⅛	4	6½	5⅛	3217	5⅞	5¼	5⅞	3.4	13	8.9	34.0	–1.6
15	MCT	✔Mark Centers Trust	NY,Ph	NR	48	4978	Real estate investment trust	20⅜	14⅛	15⅞	12	14¼	9⅝	9455	11½	9⅝	11⅜	12.7	22	0.2	...	...
#16•[6]	IV	✔Mark IV Industries	NY,Ch	B+	188	35785	Power transfer eqp/audio prod	23½	1/32	22	14⅞	23¾	16⅝	15830	20¾	17⅝	19¾	s0.6	13	15.3	16.5	41.3
17	MVII	✔Mark VII	NNM	B–	45	2938	Interstate truckload carrier	19½	3⅛	15¼	9⅛	20⅝	11⅛	8043	16½	15½	15½B	...	18	37.0	28.1	32.8
✢18	MTWN	✔Mark Twain Bancshrs	NNM	A	79	3529	Commercial bkg, St.Louis, MO	31¾	1¼	31	24	39½	26	6530	39¼	37	38¾	2.8	14	49.9	24.9	41.9
19	MAKL	✔Markel Corp	NNM	B	74	1668	Insurance broker/underwriter	40½	7½	44½	37½	75½	40¾	1330	75½	70½	75½	...	15	84.1	34.7	45.1
20	MTY	✔Marlton Technologies	AS	B–	6	992	Mfr custom trade show exhibits	29	⅜	1¾	13/16	2⅛	⅞	526	1½	1 3/16	1 5/16	...	10	40.0	–20.6	11.8
21	MARQA	✔Marquette Electronics'A'	NNM	B+	41	3294	Medl electronic equip & sys	23½	13⅛	23½	15	23¾	13	4774	21	19	20¼	...	22	–12.9	2.6	...
¶22•[1]	MAR	✔Marriott International	NY	NR	429	62952	Hotels,food service mgmt	29	22¾	32⅛	24⅝	39⅞	27¾	45319	39⅞	36¼	38¼	0.7	21	38.3	...	...
¶23•[4]	MMC	✔Marsh & McLennan	NY,B,Ch,P	A+	491	50171	Insur brokerage & agency serv	97⅝	7⅝	88¾	71¼	90⅛	76⅛	23605	90⅛	86½	88¾	3.6	15	16.0	2.5	6.7
24	MARSA	✔Marsh Supermkts'A'	NNM	A	22	1680	Food chain, Indiana & Ohio	23½	1	12¼	9½	15¾	9¾	355	14	13¼	13¼	3.3	12	31.1	2.5	–2.9
#25•[7]	MRIS	✔Marshall & Ilsley	NNM	A–	145	31345	Commercial bkg,Wisconsin	26	1⅜	24	17¾	26½	18	20471	26½	24¾	26	2.5	13	35.3	10.1	25.8
✢26	MI	✔Marshall Indus	NY,Ch,P,Ph	B+	153	12418	Dstr electronic comp:tools	25⅛	¼	29½	20¼	38¼	24⅜	14666	35⅝	31½	32⅛	...	12	24.8	20.0	26.3
27	MLE	✔Martin Lawrence Ltd Editions	NY,Ch	C	7	305	Publishes,retails artworks	13¾	½	1¼	7/16	1⅜	7/16	2439	13/16	½	9/16	...	d	28.6	–25.8	–28.5
28	MLM	✔Martin Marietta Materials	NY,Ch,Ph	NR	70	8032	Aggregates/bldg materials	....	....	25⅞	17	22⅛	16½	2864	22⅛	20¼	20⅝	2.1	15	20.6	...	...
29•[8]	MRV	✔Marvel Entertainment Grp[61]	NY,Ph	NR	..	...	Comic books,trading cards,toys	35¾	2¼	30⅜	13½	17¾	10½	35839	13⅜	11⅜	13	...	52	–7.1	4.4	...
¶30•[9]	MAS	✔Masco Corp	NY,B,Ch,P	B	472	99103	Bldg & home improv't prod	40⅞	2⅜	39⅞	21¼	31½	22½	73171	31⅜	28¾	31⅜	2.4	18	40.1	4.4	15.3
31•[2]	MSX	✔MascoTech, Inc	NY,Ch	B–	83	10527	Mfr oil field/ind'l prod	28⅛	1½	27⅞	11	13¾	10	14989	11⅜	10⅜	10⅞	1.5	d	–15.4	–1.9	19.8
32	Pr	Divd Enhanced Cv Pfd([62]20.30)	NY	BB–[63]	55	5481		25⅜	19	25¼	12⅝	15¼	11⅜	6383	13	11⅜	12½	9.6	..	...	...	...
33•[10]	MSLD	✔Masland Corp	NNM	NR	83	7494	Mfr auto carpet,vinyl floor pd	20¾	15⅜	23⅜	11⅝	16	11½	10111	14⅞	13½	14	1.4	10	–5.3	...	...
34	MXC	✔MATEC Corp	AS	C	9	263	Steel cable:electr:instr	8⅞	9/16	4¾	3⅜	4¾	3⅞	144	4¼	3⅞	4	...	50	–13.5	7.2	–3.1
✢35	MSC	✔Material Sciences	NY,Ch,Ph	↑B	101	10957	Steel coil protective coat'gs	17⅜	3⅞	17¾	13¾	22⅜	12⅛	11429	14⅞	12⅞	14⅞	...	18	–8.5	14.4	26.0
36	MLK	✔Matlack Systems	NY,Ch,Ph	NR	35	3598	Bulk commodities trucking	11	2 1/16	11¾	9	12¼	8¼	1414	10⅛	8⅝	8¾	...	12	–12.5	17.0	27.7
37	MATX	✔Matrix Pharmaceutical	NNM	NR	53	3929	Dvlp stge:protein matrix R&D	18¼	5¼	15½	9	19	9½	21748	19	13¾	18¾	...	d	45.6	24.4	...
38	MC	✔Matsushita El Ind[65] ADR	NY,B,Ch,P,Ph	NR	64	1570	Japan mfr consumer elec eq	219	6¼	188	134¾	172½	131½	771	166	147¼	164½	0.7	d	2.1	21.8	8.0
¶39•[9]	MAT	✔Mattel, Inc	NY,B,Ch,P,Ph	B	643	179016	Design,mfg,market toys	19⅝	1⅝	23⅝	16½	31⅛	19¾	115746	31⅛	27⅝	30¾	0.8	19	54.2	25.9	36.5
40	MTSN	✔Mattson Technology	NNM	NR	55	8521	Mfr semiconductor mfg equip	....	....	10⅞	6	31⅝	8	23468	23	13	15	...	25	68.8	...	...
41	NUT	✔Mauna Loa Macadamia'A'[67]	NY,Ch	NR	11	87	Owns macadamia nut orchards	11½	3⅞	5¼	2½	2⅞	2¼	4364	2⅝	2¼	2½	8.0	21	7.8	–13.6	–13.4
42	MAVK	✔Maverick Tube	NNM,Ch	NR	28	3243	Mfr welded tube for o&g ind	16¾	4⅜	10¾	6¾	10½	6⅛	4411	7⅞	6⅛	7¾	...	d	–16.2	–0.5	...
43	MAXE	✔Max & Erma's Restaurants	NNM	B	15	759	Family style restr:Franch'g	8⅝	½	9¾	6	8⅜	5¾	1233	6¾	5¾	5⅞	...	12	–6.8	9.9	21.6
44	MAXC	✔Maxco Inc	NNM	B–	9	628	Auto prod/constr supplies	8⅝	7/16	11¾	7¼	10¾	7	1646	8⅜	7⅝	7¾	...	41	–7.5	23.4	32.8
45•[11]	MAXI	✔Maxicare Health Plans	NNM	NR	104	8741	Multi-state HMO services	14½	6⅜	16½	9½	27¾	14	83951	27¾	21⅛	26⅞	...	16	78.4	27.4	...
#46•[12]	MXIM	✔Maxim Integrated Prod	NNM	B	232	50197	Mfr,mkt integrated circuits	12¼	1 5/16	17⅞	10⅞	41⅞	14⅛	162636	39⅜	27¾	38½	...	50	144	84.2	73.3
47	MXIS	✔Maxis Inc	NNM	NR	77	3594	Dvlp personal computer softwr	....	....	....	....	50	16	37436	43¼	29¼	38	...	69	...	...	...
48•[13]	MXTR	✔Maxtor Corp[70]	NNM	C	58	10948	Mfrs Winchester disk drives	33⅞	1⅝	8⅝	2⅝	7¼	3⅞	27884	6⅝	6¼	6⅝	...	d	17.8	–21.8	5.8
49	MXWL	✔Maxwell Labs	NNM	B–	22	760	Defense/comm'l electr sys	25¼	5⅛	10½	6¾	11	6½	1342	9¼	8	8¼	...	..	13.8	–5.4	–0.9
#50	MXM	✔MAXXAM Inc	AS,B,Ch,P,Ph	C	73	2572	Alum'n/forest prod:RE mgmt	67½	2⅛	44½	29½	67⅝	27¼	2878	40	33	35¼	...	30	13.7	9.3	2.7
51	MAM	✔Maxxim Medical	NY,Ch,Ph	B	62	3537	Mfr medical/therapy products	24¼	4	20½	11½	17	12¼	3812	17	15¼	16¾	...	62	18.6	3.5	28.0
¶52•[2]	MA	✔May Dept Stores	NY,B,C,Ch,P,Ph	A+	836	182000	Large department store chain	46½	1¾	45⅛	32¼	45⅜	32⅞	104285	44⅞	41	42⅛	2.7	13	30.7	8.5	...

Uniform Footnote Explanations-See Page 4. Other: [1]Ph:Cycle 1. [2]CBOE:Cycle 3. [3]CBOE,P:Cycle 1. [4]P:Cycle 1. [5]NY,Ph:Cycle 2. [6]NY:Cycle 2. [7]ASE,Ph:Cycle 3. [8]ASE,CBOE,NY:Cycle 1. [9]ASE:Cycle 1. [10]Ph:Cycle 3. [11]ASE:Cycle 3. [12]P:Cycle 2. [13]CBOE:Cycle 1. [51]Fiscal Jun'93 & prior. [52]12 Mo Dec'94,Jun'94 earned $1.61. [53]Units of int. [54]Incl $0.4676 non-taxable,'94. [55]Incl current amts. [56]7 Mo Dec'93. [57]®$1.30,'94. [58]®$2.48,'94. [59]®$0.98,'95. [60]®$0.93,'94. [61]80.6% owned by MacAndrews & Forbes. [62]Fr 7-1-96 payable in com stk, scale to $20in'97. [63]Note:'r'added to derivative/hybrid secur ratings. [64]Pfd in $M. [65]Each ADR equal 10 com yen 50 par. [66]®$0.60,'93. [67]L.P. Dep Unit. [68]Excl 1.5M Cl B units. [69]®$0.86,'95. [70]Hyundai Electronics offer,$6.70 to Jan 5. [71]®$1.00,'94. [72]Excl ESOP Shs. [73]®$2.92,'94.

Splits ◆ Index	Cash Divs. Ea. Yr. Since	Dividends: Latest Payment Period $	Date	Ex. Div.	Total $ So Far 1995	Ind. Rate	Paid 1994	Financial Position Mil-$ Cash& Equiv.	Curr. Assets	Curr. Liab.	Balance Sheet Date	Capitalization Lg Trm Debt Mil-$	Shs. 000 Pfd.	Com.	Earnings $ Per Shr. Years End	1991	1992	1993	1994	1995	Last 12 Mos.	Interim Earnings Period	$ per Shr. 1994	1995	Index
1	1945	Q0.25	12-10-95	11-29	1.00	1.00	1.00	14.1	107	72.3	9-30-95	....	...	7674	Dc	1.50	0.80	□[51]0.65	[52]0.16	....	0.24	9 Mo Sep	1.32	1.40	1
2◆	1975	Q0.022	11-27-95	11-13	0.088	0.09	0.088	32.9	217	197	8-31-95	360	...	62450	My	0.56	□1.16	□1.09	1.29	1.51	1.63	6 Mo Nov	0.79	0.91	2
3	1994	S0.07	12-14-95	11-22	0.06	0.14	0.11	56.4	1157	753	6-30-95	123	...	75248	Dc	d0.73	□d0.54	d0.66	1.12	E1.70	1.56	9 Mo Sep	0.76	1.20	3
4◆	1993	Q0.29½	1-12-96	12-27	1.18	1.18	1.105	Equity per shr $10.85			9-30-95	199	...	24373	Dc	...	p0.71	0.70	0.70	....	0.68	9 Mo Sep	0.60	0.58	4
5	1992	1.04	6-24-93	6-14	...	Nil	....	410	1166	633	9-30-95	1453	9231	123000	Dc	Δd0.24	□0.22	□Δ0.31	□0.33	....	1.05	9 Mo Sep	□0.31	1.03	5
6	....	Terms&trad. basis should be checked in detail						Wrrts expire 6-5-96				....	...	7000	Dc	...	...	...	....	....	....				6
7	1965	Q0.25	12-29-95	12-7	1.00	1.00	1.00	27.2	454	371	9-30-95	795	...	29498	Dc	4.20	3.37	4.24	2.64	....	3.48	9 Mo Sep	1.39	2.23	7
8	....	None Since Public			...	Nil	....	28.9	38.5	5.03	6-30-95	0.14	...	5631	Sp	0.09	0.10	0.41	0.61	P0.65	0.65				8
9	....	None Since Public			...	Nil	....	10.9	70.2	66.0	6-30-95	25.2	...	11053	Sp	0.64	1.02	0.25	d0.09	Pd3.05	d3.05				9
10◆	1983	A0.267	7-31-95	7-13	0.267	0.27	0.227	27.5	44.2	57.3	8-17-95	98.1	...	±19619	My	0.68	0.79	0.95	Δ1.07	1.23	2.10	6 Mo Nov	0.74	1.61	10
11	1966	0.29	12-28-95	11-28	1.082	1.08	1.48½	1.72	2.20	0.91	9-30-95	....	...	2000	Je	1.46	0.95	1.21	1.57	1.07	1.08	3 Mo Sep	0.30	0.31	11
12	....	None Since Public			0.34	Nil	....	2.13	93.6	35.8	9-30-95	38.1	...	20467	Dc	...	p□d0.17	p0.47	□0.45	E0.65	0.58	9 Mo Sep	□0.21	□0.34	12
13	....	None Since Public			...	Nil	....	10.2	42.9	10.5	9-30-95	....	...	8434	Dc	...	...	p1.03	□p1.12	....	1.15	9 Mo Sep	p□0.79	0.82	13
14	1994	Q0.05	12-13-95	11-22	0.11	0.20	0.02	38.2	69.7	29.6	9-30-95	105	...	11667	Dc	d0.13	0.27	d0.94	0.52	....	0.46	9 Mo Sep	0.36	0.30	14
15	1993	Q0.36	12-8-95	11-16	1.44	1.44	[54]1.44	Equity per shr $8.43			9-30-95	[55]106	...	8543	Dc	...	...	Δ‡[56]0.18	0.68	....	0.51	9 Mo Sep	0.52	0.35	15
16◆	1990	Q0.03	1-2-96	12-13	s0.115	0.12	s0.10	0.90	830	406	8-31-95	638	...	59975	Fb	□0.89	□1.05	□1.14	□[57]1.40	E1.55	1.50	9 Mo Nov	□1.09	1.19	16
17	....	None Since Public			...	Nil	....	0.17	57.5	42.0	9-30-95	0.73	...	4862	Dc	0.35	d0.13	d2.33	0.49	....	0.88	9 Mo Sep	0.32	0.71	17
18◆	1970	Q0.27	11-10-95	10-18	1.08	1.08	0.96	Book Value $16.43			9-30-95	19.4	...	16060	Dc	1.55	1.98	2.28	[58]2.54	....	2.85	9 Mo Sep	1.86	2.17	18
19	....	None Since Public			...	Nil	....	Equity per shr $28.07			9-30-95	118	...	5413	Dc	2.68	4.64	4.23	3.33	....	5.08	9 Mo Sep	2.51	4.26	19
20	....	0.15	11-13-79	10-30	...	Nil	....	1.55	7.65	4.32	9-30-95	1.07	...	3905	Dc	*0.06	*0.03	*d0.03	0.13	....	0.13	9 Mo Sep	0.10	0.10	20
21	....	None Since Public			...	Nil	....	2.96	177	74.7	7-31-95	8.09	...	±42226	Ap	0.64	0.93	Δ1.08	1.16	1.21	0.92	6 Mo Oct	0.60	0.31	21
22	1993	Q0.07	1-15-96	12-26	0.28	0.28	0.28	269	1372	1500	9-08-95	687	...	125187	Dc	...	p1.10	□p1.27	1.51	E1.85	1.74	36 Wk Sep	0.96	1.19	22
23	1923	Q0.80	2-14-96	1-9	2.97½	3.20	2.80	383	1611	1478	9-30-95	411	...	73159	Dc	4.18	□4.21	4.52	□5.19	E5.80	5.35	9 Mo Sep	□4.21	4.37	23
24◆	1960	Q0.11	2-5-96	1-17	0.44	0.44	0.44	10.2	132	99.3	10-14-95	151	...	±8396	Mr	±1.25	±1.26	Δ±1.01	±[59]1.02	....	1.10	28 Wk Oct	±0.56	±0.64	24
25◆	1938	Q0.16½	12-14-95	11-28	0.64½	0.66	0.59	Book Value $10.40			12-31-94	p495	349	p93974	Dc	1.50	□1.73	1.87	Δ[60]0.95	E1.94	1.15	9 Mo Sep	1.23	1.43	25
26◆	....	5%Stk	3-25-82	2-19	...	Nil	....	1.33	369	108	8-31-95	39.0	...	17279	My	1.02	1.12	1.38	1.91	2.32	2.76	6 Mo Nov	1.04	1.48	26
27	....	None Since Public			...	Nil	....	0.67	15.0	4.58	9-30-95	0.10	225	5894	Dc	d1.81	d0.66	d1.13	d0.73	....	d0.66	9 Mo Sep	d0.53	d0.46	27
28	1994	Q0.11	12-29-95	11-29	0.44	0.44	0.22	....	279	200	9-30-95	★173	...	46079	Dc	...	...	□p1.05	□1.30	....	1.40	9 Mo Sep	□1.02	1.12	28
29◆	....	None Since Public			...	Nil	....	24.7	498	281	9-30-95	563	...	101573	Dc	□0.17	0.33	0.55	0.60	E0.25	0.27	9 Mo Sep	0.46	□0.13	29
30	1944	Q0.19	2-5-96	1-3	0.73	0.76	0.69	84.6	2033	635	9-30-95	1656	...	160592	Dc	0.30	1.21	1.45	1.22	E1.75	1.20	12 Mo Sep	1.69	1.20	30
31	1993	Q0.04	11-20-95	10-11	0.14	0.16	0.10	21.4	438	185	9-30-95	728	10800	55670	Dc	d0.31	0.48	□0.63	Δd4.00	....	d4.35	9 Mo Sep	Δ0.96	0.61	31
32	1993	Q0.30	1-1-96	12-14	1.20	1.20	1.20	Cv into 0.806 com, $24.81				....	10800	...	Dc	...	...	...	....	....	....	Mand conv into 1 com 7-1-97			32
33	1994	Q0.05	12-8-95	11-21	0.20	0.20	0.20	12.4	119	66.0	9-30-95	76.8	...	13441	Je	...	...	p0.89	1.47	1.53	1.34	3 Mo Sep	0.28	0.09	33
34	....	†0.10	2-28-92	2-10	...	Nil	....	0.50	14.1	6.16	10-01-95	2.18	...	2764	Dc	0.42	d0.25	Δ0.04	d0.04	....	0.08	9 Mo Sep	d0.09	0.03	34
35◆	....	None Since Public			...	Nil	....	3.09	62.1	32.7	8-31-95	7.34	...	15355	Fb	0.63	□0.67	0.79	1.10	....	0.84	9 Mo Nov	0.86	0.60	35
36◆	....	None Since Public			...	Nil	....	2.85	38.5	26.0	9-30-95	33.0	...	8801	Sp	d0.33	□0.26	0.50	0.69	0.74	0.74				36
37	....	None Since Public			...	Nil	....	19.3	19.9	2.84	12-31-94	0.76	[64]13	★15892	Dc	n/a	d0.60	d1.18	d1.86	....	d2.25	9 Mo Sep	d1.39	d1.78	37
38	1950	0.525	12-18-95	9-27	1.146	1.15	†1.147	18425	47559	29200	3-31-95	14506	...	2097257	Mr	4.60	1.60	1.10	4.60	....	d3.01	6 Mo Sep	1.14	d6.47	38
39◆	1990	Q0.06	1-3-96	12-13	0.228	0.24	0.182	101	2079	1209	9-30-95	464	864	220849	Dc	□0.79	0.92	□[66]0.62	1.12	E1.60	1.26	9 Mo Sep	0.94	1.08	39
40◆	....	None Since Public			...	Nil	....	49.1	65.3	11.4	10-01-95	....	...	13675	Dc	...	...	pd0.13	0.29	....	0.59	9 Mo Sep	0.19	0.49	40
41	1986	Q0.05	2-15-96	12-27	0.20	0.20	0.35	0.01	4.28	3.57	9-30-95	0.22	...	[68]7500	Dc	0.13	0.17	0.20	0.06	....	0.12	9 Mo Sep	Nil	0.06	41
42	....	None Since Public			...	Nil	....	0.53	59.7	22.7	6-30-95	18.5	...	7440	Sp	0.54	d0.47	0.58	0.07	Pd0.31	d0.31				42
43◆	....	s0.003	12-30-83	12-9	...	Nil	....	0.64	1.92	5.37	8-06-95	21.0	...	4097	Oc	0.11	0.25	0.35	0.47	P0.50	0.50				43
44	....	None Paid			...	Nil	....	0.88	57.5	28.6	9-30-95	36.4	34	4245	Mr	0.38	0.26	2.06	[69]0.88	....	0.19	6 Mo Sep	0.77	0.08	44
45	....	None Paid			...	Nil	....	95.4	129	60.7	9-30-95	0.83	...	17365	Dc	□0.14	□0.66	0.02	0.73	....	1.64	9 Mo Sep	0.12	1.03	45
46◆	....	None Since Public			...	Nil	....	102	193	69.9	9-30-95	....	...	59890	Je	0.19	0.24	0.29	0.38	0.58	0.78	3 Mo Sep	0.13	0.32	46
47	....	None Since Public			...	Nil	....	45.0	56.9	8.07	9-30-95	....	...	10844	Mr	0.12	0.01	0.20	0.40	....	0.55	6 Mo Sep	0.12	0.27	47
48	....	None Since Public			...	Nil	....	19.4	317	306	9-30-95	101	...	±53032	Mr	0.27	1.46	d8.00	d1.63	Ed1.75	d1.40	6 Mo Sep	±d1.34	±d1.11	48
49◆	....	5%Stk	1-21-94	12-27	...	Nil	5%Stk	0.88	30.2	12.2	10-31-95	1.66	...	2702	Jl	1.00	d1.50	0.38	d0.63	0.12	0.02	3 Mo Oct	0.12	0.02	49
50	....	5%Stk	11-17-75	9-24	...	Nil	....	131	1146	587	9-30-95	1620	670	8708	Dc	6.08	d0.77	□d13.95	□d12.35	....	1.16	9 Mo Sep	□d9.80	3.71	50
51	....	None Since Public			...	Nil	....	1.18	119	50.4	7-30-95	92.5	...	8092	Oc	0.57	0.75	0.94	Δ[71]1.05	....	0.27	9 Mo Jul	Δ0.78	Nil	51
52◆	1911	Q0.285	12-15-95	11-29	1.11½	1.14	1.01	28.0	5420	2109	10-28-95	3456	[72]...	248970	Ja	2.01	2.35	2.77	[73]3.06	E3.20	3.10	9 Mo Oct	1.47	1.51	52

◆**Stock Splits & Divs By Line Reference Index** [2]3-for-2,'92. [4]2-for-1,'94. [10]3-for-2,'95. [16]3-for-2,'92:Adj to 5%,'95. [18]3-for-2,'93. [24]1-for-2 REVERSE in Cl'A',2-for-1 in Cl'B','91. [25]3-for-1,'93. [26]2-for-1,'94. [29]2-for-1,twice in'92,once in'93. [35]3-for-2,'92,'94. [36]3-for-2,'94. [39]3-for-2,'92:5-for-4,'91,'94,'95. [40]2-for-1,'95. [43]5-for-4,'93:10%,'95. [46]2-for-1,'94,'95. [49]Adj to 5%,'93. [52]2-for-1,'93.

¶ S&P 500 / # MidCap 400 / ✣ SmallCap 600 / • Options — Index	Ticker	Name of Issue (Call Price of Pfd. Stocks)	Market	Com. Rank. & Pfd. Rating	Inst. Hold Cos	Inst. Hold Shs. (000)	Principal Business	Price Range 1971-93 High	1971-93 Low	1994 High	1994 Low	1995 High	1995 Low	Dec. Sales in 100s	December, 1995 Last Sale Or Bid High	Low	Last	%Div Yield	P-E Ratio	Total Return % Annualized 12 Mo	36 Mo	60 Mo
1•[1]	MAY	✓Maybelline Inc[51]	NY	NR	77	5637	Cosmetics & personal care prod	31	16¾	33	15⅜	36¾	16½	63810	36¾	26	36¼	0.9	29	116	10.0	...
¶2•[2]	MYG	✓Maytag Corp	NY,B,Ch,P	B–	357	60851	Mfrs major home appliances	32⅜	4	20⅛	14	21½	14½	113178	21½	19⅝	20¼	2.8	d	39.0	14.5	18.2
3•[3]	MBI	✓MBIA Inc	NY,Ch,Ph	NR	359	34250	Insurance for muni bonds	81¼	10⅝	65¼	47¼	77½	55⅜	16634	77½	73½	75	1.8	12	35.7	7.5	23.8
¶4•[4]	KRB	✓MBNA Corp	NY,Ch,Ph	NR	578	110296	Bank hldg/credit card svc'g	25¼	7⅝	27⅜	19¼	43⅝	22⅜	100341	40⅜	34⅜	36⅞	2.3	16	60.2	35.8	...
5	MCX	✓MC Shipping	AS,Ph	NR	5	79	Inv/owns 2nd hand cargo ships	15⅝	2⅛	5⅝	2⅞	4½	3¼	3347	3¾	3¼	3⅜	4.1	10	–1.7	–1.7	–5.4
6	MNI	✓McClatchy Newspapers'A'	NY,Ch,P,Ph	B	65	5724	Publish newsp CA,WA,Alaska	30⅞	13¼	27¼	20⅜	24⅛	19⅛	2026	23¼	20⅝	22⅞	1.7	19	7.5	7.2	7.0
#7•[5]	MCCRK	✓McCormick[52] & Co	NNM	A	218	39596	Spices, flavoring, tea, mixes	30¼	1 5/16	24¾	17¾	26⅝	18⅛	51582	24½	22⅞	24⅛	2.3	19	34.4	–3.9	15.6
¶8•[3]	MDR	✓McDermott Intl	NY,B,C,Ch,P,Ph	B–	290	45835	Offshore oil & gas constr	46⅝	7⅜	27½	19⅜	29⅛	15⅜	97654	22⅛	18⅛	22	4.5	31	–7.3	2.4	2.4
9	MDEPrA	$2.20cmCvAPfd(31.25:SF[53])1/2vtg	[6]NY	BB+	31	553	Steam gen eqp:tubular goods	47½	17½	33¼	27⅜	32⅛	26⅞	516	30⅞	28⅜	28⅜	7.8	..	...	...	...
10	JRM	✓McDermott (J.Ray) S.A.	NY,Ch,Ph	NR	104	7469	Marine constr'n svcs o&g ind	17¾	4⅛	22⅝	15⅜	28⅝	15	20994	18¼	15¾	17⅞	...	..	–18.8	17.1	28.4
11	MDD	✓McDonald & Co Invest	NY,B	B	44	1526	Investm't bank'g/brokerage	16	3½	16⅞	11⅛	18⅜	11	1670	18¼	17⅜	18	1.9	9	63.3	17.5	41.1
¶12•[1]	MCD	✓McDonald's Corp	NY,To,B,C,Ch,P,Ph	A+	1124	391651	Fast food restaurant:franch'g	29⅝	¾	31½	25½	48	28⅝	311211	48	43¾	45⅛	0.6	23	53.3	23.4	26.8
13	MCZ	McDonald's Corp 8.35% 'QUIDS'	NY	....[58]	2	19	Qtly Income Debt Securities	....	....	....	....	27	25½	1096	27	26	26½	7.9	..	...	...	...
¶14•[7]	MD	✓McDonnell Douglas	NY,B,C,Ch,P,Ph	B+	515	63643	Aircraft/aerospace/missiles	39½	2½	48⅝	34⅛	92⅛	46½	37726	92⅛	87	92	0.9	15	96.0	83.5	50.5
15	MCFE	✓McFarland Energy	NNM	B–	22	2455	Oil & gas expl & prod'r	28¾	1½	8¾	4	8¼	5⅞	1496	8¼	7¼	7⅝	...	3	27.1	26.7	–1.6
¶16•[3]	MHP	✓McGraw-Hill Companies	NY,B,Ch,P,Ph	[59]	499	32868	Books:educ/info svs:publ:TV	86⅛	2¾	77¼	62½	87⅝	63⅝	18307	87⅝	83¼	87⅛	2.8	20	33.6	15.4	14.6
¶17•[8]	MCIC	✓MCI Communications	NNM	B	817	377267	Telecommun'ns network,svcs	29⅞	⅛	29	17¼	27½	17⅜	522200	27½	25¾	26⅛	0.2	33	44.5	9.8	23.1
#18•[7]	MCK	✓McKesson Corp	NY	NR	226	23946	Dstr drugs, toiletries/hm pd	....	....	33½	30⅛	53¼	31⅞	16145	52½	48½	50⅝	2.0	17	58.4	...	...
#19	MCN	✓MCN Corp	NY,Ph	NR	247	31683	Natural gas dstr,Michigan	18⅜	8½	20¼	16⅞	23½	16⅜	16078	23½	21½	23¼	4.0	16	38.2	22.5	23.7
20	MRI.B	McRae Indus Cv 'B'[61]	AS	B+	4	13	Mfr elect sys/combat boots	9	1/16	10½	6¾	8	5⅞	14	8	6⅝	7½B	...	10	13.2	7.0	9.6
21	MRI.A	✓ Class 'A' (1/10 vtg)	AS	B+	11	121		9⅛	1⅝	10¾	6¾	8⅜	5¾	365	8⅜	6¼	7¾	4.5	10	16.4	12.3	14.8
✣22	MWT	✓McWhorter Technologies	NY	NR	72	5817	Produce ind'l resin products	....	....	19¼	13¼	16⅜	14	4700	15⅜	14	14¾	...	15	–0.8	...	...
23	MDQ	✓MDC Corp Cl'A'[62]	AS,To	NR	21	10261	Advertising/mktg svcs	....	....	....	....	2⅛	13/16	6101	1 1/16	13/16	1 1/16	...	..	...	...	...
✣24	MDC	✓M.D.C. Hldgs	NY,Ch,P	B–	54	8480	Home bldg,mtge banking	22½	⅛	7⅞	4½	8⅛	4⅞	11560	7¼	6⅝	7⅛	1.7	8	45.0	22.4	87.9
25	MDLI	✓MDL Information Sys	NNM	NR	64	6739	Chemical info mgmt softwr	13¼	6½	9½	5¼	26¼	8	21362	26¼	21⅞	23	...	30	188	...	...
26	MDTC	✓MDT Corp	NNM	B–	29	3120	Mfr sterility assurance sys	15⅛	2⅞	7⅛	4¼	8	4½	6170	6	4½	4⅞	...	98	–13.3	–12.4	–0.5
27	MDU	✓MDU Resources Group	NY,Ch,P	B+	118	4120	Gas & elec utility:coal,o&g	22⅛	3⅝	21½	16⅞	23⅛	17⅛	7698	21⅜	19¾	19⅞	5.5	15	16.9	9.9	14.1
¶28•[8]	MEA	✓Mead Corp	NY,B,C,Ch,P,Ph	B–	439	37244	Mfr paper,lumber,wood prod	49½	3⅞	53¼	39⅛	64⅛	48⅝	51145	57½	50½	52¼	2.1	8	9.0	12.8	17.8
29	MIG	Meadowbrook Insurance Grp	NY	NR	..	...	Alternat'e Mkt risk mgmt ins	....	....	....	....	33⅞	21	4817	33⅞	26	33½	0.2	31	...	...	...
30	MSS	✓Measurement Specialties	AS	↑B–	5	138	Mfr temp,distance,pressure eq	6½	1	5⅛	1⅞	7	3	3619	5½	4	4¼	...	21	30.8	...	...
#31•[7]	MX	✓Measurex Corp	NY,B,Ch,P,Ph	B–	154	13477	Ind'l process control sys	35⅞	2⅛	23⅝	17¼	36	22⅛	20531	29½	25	28¼	1.6	18	29.7	18.4	12.5
✣32•[1]	MEDA	✓Medaphis Corp	NNM	NR	248	38287	Hospital/Dr. acc rec mgmt svcs	16⅞	6	24	11¾	38½	20¼	82155	38½	31	37	...	..	58.2	45.9	...
33	MDXR	✓Medar Inc	NNM	B–	49	3539	Quality control equip	13	1⅜	16¾	9	16½	6¾	8588	8⅝	7⅝	7⅞	...	d	–35.7	3.4	39.3
34	MEDX	✓Medarex Inc	NNM	NR	16	634	Dvlp stage:AIDS,cancer R & D	17¼	4¾	8⅛	2½	7⅝	2¾	13364	7⅛	5⅝	7⅛	...	d	165	–4.8	...
35	MCTH	✓MedCath Inc	NNM	NR	32	2536	Cardiology/cardiovascular svcs	....	....	16	14	25¾	11	11328	21½	17½	21	...	41	43.6	...	...
36•[9]	MRE	✓Medco Research	AS,Ch,Ph	C	34	3073	R&D pharmaceutical/med prod	33⅝	9/16	16⅛	9½	15⅝	9½	7506	11⅝	9½	10⅜	...	d	–8.8	–15.2	12.0
37•[10]	MDV	✓Medeva ADR	AS,Ch	NR	43	6025	Pharmaceut'ls U.K. & abroad	22⅛	5⅜	11⅞	7¼	18⅜	10	3049	17⅛	15⅜	17	1.4	19	70.8	12.8	...
38	MDVL	Medeva plc[67]	Lo	NR	..	...	Pharmaceut'ls U.K. & abroad	383	42	187	117	296	162	....	276	253	268	0.3	..	...	...	...
39	MDEX	✓Medex Inc	NNM	↓B+	45	3400	Mfg specialized medical prod	39½	1/16	19¾	11¼	13¾	9½	10384	11½	10⅝	11¼	1.4	45	–13.8	–12.2	–7.1
40	MDBK	✓Medford Savings Bank	NNM	NR	25	1195	General Banking, Mass	19⅜	3¼	20¼	12	23¼	13½	1462	22½	20½	21½	e2.8	11	51.4	31.1	41.3
#41	MEG.A	✓Media General Cl'A'	AS,Ch,P,Ph	B	150	14739	Newspaper:newsprint:TV	50½	1 13/16	30¼	21⅜	38⅜	27¼	6039	31¼	29⅛	30⅜	1.6	16	8.2	23.1	12.2
42	TST	✓Media Logic	AS	C	11	242	Mfr computer-based test eq	21½	3/16	6	1 5/16	9⅝	1¼	10649	8⅝	5⅝	8¼	...	d	230	–16.0	75.3
43•[10]	MCSY	✓Medic Computer Systems	NNM	NR	134	9640	Mkt physician practice mgmt sys	14¾	5¼	31	13¼	70	28⅞	34439	70	57	60½	...	48	108	66.4	...
44	MGCC	✓Medical Graphics	NNM	B–	17	704	Computerized diagnostic sys	18½	1¾	8¼	5¼	6¾	4⅜	1698	5⅝	4⅜	4⅞	...	d	–10.2	–8.8	8.7
45	MPS	Medical Polymers Tech	Vc	NR	..	...	Mfr dental/medical products	3⅝	1/16	2⅛	⅝	⅞	1/32	8500	⅛	1/32	1/32B	...	d	...	...	...
46	MRA	✓Medical Resource Co Amer(New)	[11]AS	NR	7	45	Hlth care svcs,retirement ctrs	20⅝	1¼	12½	4⅜	13⅜	5	1144	12	9⅜	10⅛	...	9	62.0	...	...
47	MSYS	✓Medical Tech Systems	NNM	B	19	525	Mfr medication dispens'g sys	23	⅞	9¾	5½	9⅛	¾	16145	2 1/16	¾	⅞	...	d	–85.1	–54.0	–26.2
48	MDCL	MedicalControl Inc	NNM	NR	5	65	Healthcare cost mgmt svcs	6⅛	3⅝	9⅝	3¼	10½	4¾	1053	5⅜	5	5	...	..	–45.9	...	...
49	MDK	✓Medicore,Inc	AS	C	7	227	Mfr electro-mechanical eqp	13⅜	⅜	3¼	¾	7½	2⅜	4629	5¾	3¼	4¾	...	16	94.9	68.1	42.3
✣50•[12]	MEDI	✓MedImmune Inc	NNM	NR	46	4503	Drug R&D-infectious diseases	55	9¼	13¼	3⅜	21½	3½	76882	21½	12¾	20	...	d	433	–1.2	...
51	MED	✓MEDIQ Inc	AS,B	C	21	5398	Health care services	9⅞	1⅛	4⅝	3¼	6⅛	3¾	4171	4⅝	4⅛	4¼	...	d	15.0	–8.2	35.7
52	Pr	Ser'A' Cv Pfd(NC)vtg	AS	NR	1	114	Medical products	9¾	1⅛	4¼	3	5⅞	3¾	32	4½	4⅛	4⅜B	...	..	...	...	...

Uniform Footnote Explanations-See Page 4. Other: [1]CBOE:Cycle 3. [2]CBOE,NY:Cycle 1. [3]Ph:Cycle 2. [4]ASE,CBOE:Cycle 3. [5]Ph:Cycle 3. [6]Ch,Ph [7]P:Cycle 2. [8]CBOE:Cycle 1. [9]ASE:Cycle 1. [10]CBOE:Cycle 2. [11]Ph [12]ASE:Cycle 3. [51]L'Oreal S.A. offer,$36.75 to Jan 16. [52]Non-vtg. [53]SF at $31.25. [54]Plus $0.10 in cash. [55]Payable upon presentation of ctfs. [56]68.6% owned by McDermott Intl. [57]Fiscal Jul'92 & prior. [58]Rated AA- by S&P. [59]S&P is a division of the McGraw-Hill Companies; common not ranked, pfd not rated. [60]Subsid Pfd in M$. [61]Cv into 1 Cl'A'. [62]Subsidinate vtg shrs. [63]®$0.87,'94. [64]Fiscal Aug'91 & prior. [65]12 Mo Dec'92:Fiscal Aug'92 earned $0.04. [66]®$0.85,'94. [67]All data reported in British pounds. [68]Fiscal May '92 & prior. [69]®$0.24,'94. [70]Stk dstr of Viragen Inc.

Splits ◆	Cash Divs. Ea.Yr.	Dividends Latest Payment			Total $			Financial Position Mil-$				Capitalization	Shs. 000		Earnings $ Per Shr. Years							Interim Earnings	$ per Shr.		
Index	Since	Period $	Date	Ex. Div.	So Far 1995	Ind. Rate	Paid 1994	Cash& Equiv.	Curr. Assets	Curr. Liab.	Balance Sheet Date	Lg Trm Debt Mil-$	Pfd.	Com.	End	1991	1992	1993	1994	1995	Last 12 Mos.	Period	1994	1995	Index
1	1993	Q0.08	1-2-96	12-7	0.30	0.32	0.26	10.1	106	82.4	9-30-95	110	...	13732	Dc	p1.25	□0.90	1.25	1.07	....	1.25	9 Mo Sep	0.97	1.15	1
2	1946	Q0.14	12-15-95	11-29	0.51½	0.56	0.50	135	1005	359	9-30-95	537	...	107949	Dc	0.75	□d0.08	0.48	□1.42	Ed0.10	d0.13	9 Mo Sep	□1.25	□d0.30	2
3	1987	Q0.34½	1-15-96	12-19	1.27½	1.38	1.09	Equity per shr $47.39			9-30-95	299	...	41911	Dc	3.74	4.62	Δ5.80	6.18	E6.40	6.35	9 Mo Sep	4.65	4.82	3
4◆	1991	Q0.21	1-1-96	12-13	0.81	0.84	0.70	Equity per shr $7.11			9-30-95	2509	★6000	148500	Dc	1.00	1.15	1.39	1.77	E2.30	2.15	9 Mo Sep	1.22	1.60	4
5	....	Q0.03½	1-17-96	1-3	0.075	0.14	....	15.2	18.8	15.4	9-30-95	24.8	...	6120	Dc	0.42	d0.62	d0.21	0.18	....	0.33	9 Mo Sep	0.10	0.25	5
6	1930	Q0.09½	1-2-96	12-6	0.37	0.38	0.318	15.7	110	77.1	9-30-95	273	...	±29961	Dc	±0.83	±□1.05	±1.10	±1.58	E1.20	1.26	9 Mo Sep	±1.11	±0.79	6
7◆	1929	Q0.14	1-19-96	12-27	0.52	0.56	0.48	30.5	695	702	8-31-95	350	...	±81175	Nv	0.98	1.16	□1.22	0.75	E1.30	0.64	9 Mo Aug	0.79	0.68	7
8	1955	Q0.25	1-1-96	12-13	1.00	1.00	1.00	178	1562	1375	9-30-95	580	2875	54351	Mr	1.67	□1.29	□1.57	□0.05	E0.70	0.38	6 Mo Sep	□d0.08	0.25	8
9	1978	Q0.55	1-1-96	12-13	2.20	2.20	2.20	Cv into 1 com of McDermott Int'l[54]				....	2819	...	Mr	...	...	...	....	....	....	SF 5% ea Mar 31,$31.25			9
10	....	[55]0.51	1-31-95		[55]0.51	Nil	....	68.0	602	571	9-30-95	336	3653	[56]40154	Mr	d1.31	[57]0.62	...	....	....	....	6 Mo Sep	n/a	0.21	10
11◆	1983	Q0.08½	11-27-95	11-13	0.33	0.34	0.31	Equity per shr $13.59			9-30-95	25.0	...	8894	Mr	1.48	1.92	2.38	1.47	....	2.02	6 Mo Sep	0.42	0.97	11
12◆	1976	Q0.068	12-15-95	11-28	0.263	0.27	0.234	318	913	1938	9-30-95	3979	3500	696279	Dc	1.18	1.30	1.45	1.68	E1.95	1.89	9 Mo Sep	1.25	1.46	12
13	1995	Q0.522	12-31-95	12-13	1.199	2.09	....	Co opt redm fr 12-3-97 at $25				450	...	...	Dc	...	...	...	....	....	....				13
14◆	1950	Q0.20	1-2-96	11-29	0.80	0.80	0.467	Equity per shr $35.85			9-30-95	2558	...	112024	Dc	3.68	□6.48	3.37	5.05	E6.00	5.95	9 Mo Sep	3.66	4.56	14
15	....	0.045	1-17-78	12-14	...	Nil	....	5.75	10.8	3.52	9-30-95	5.84	...	5233	Dc	d1.54	0.18	Δd0.30	0.29	....	2.53	9 Mo Sep	0.10	2.34	15
16	1937	Q0.60	12-12-95	11-24	2.40	2.40	2.32	4.92	1323	1084	9-30-95	657	2	50025	Dc	3.03	□3.13	0.23	4.10	....	4.47	9 Mo Sep	3.09	3.46	16
17◆	1990	S0.02½	12-8-95	11-15	0.05	0.05	0.05	1235	4477	3898	9-30-95	2905	...	±681275	Dc	1.01	1.11	□1.12	1.32	E0.80	0.59	9 Mo Sep	1.11	0.38	17
18	1995	Q0.25	1-2-96	11-29	1.00	1.00	....	766	2769	1800	9-30-95	456	...	44322	Mr	...	...	p2.87	▲9.20	E2.95	9.19	6 Mo Sep	1.39	1.38	18
19◆	1989	Q0.23¼	11-24-95	11-8	0.90	0.93	0.86¾	16.8	408	439	9-30-95	812	[60]100	66262	Dc	0.71	1.05	1.24	1.31	E1.50	1.21	12 Mo Sep	1.44	1.21	19
20	....	0.02½	7-22-83	7-5	...	Nil	....	3.02	18.1	5.90	10-28-95	....	...	±2731	Jl	±0.92	±0.80	±0.81	±0.97	±0.80	0.76	3 Mo Oct	±0.17	±0.13	20
21	1985	Q0.08¾	12-29-95	12-6	0.35	0.35	0.35	....	...	...		....	...	1779	Jl	±0.92	±0.80	±0.81	±0.97	±0.80	0.76	3 Mo Oct	±0.17	±0.13	21
22	....	None Since Public			...	Nil	....	2.13	74.4	34.9	7-31-95	30.1	...	10964	Oc	...	...	p0.93	p0.78	....	1.02	9 Mo Jul	p0.49	0.73	22
23	....	None Paid			...	Nil	....	1.74	46.8	36.7	j2-28-95	39.1	...	p61082	Nv	d0.09	0.04	0.04	0.08	....	j0.05	9 Mo Aug	0.04	0.01	23
24	1994	Q0.03	11-10-95	11-1	0.11	0.12	0.06	Equity per shr $10.45			9-30-95	345	...	19467	Dc	Δd0.62	□0.22	Δ0.45	[63]0.94	....	0.90	9 Mo Sep	0.73	0.69	24
25	....	None Since Public			...	Nil	....	5.34	25.5	15.6	9-30-95	1.90	...	8348	Mr	...	p0.78	Nil	0.48	....	0.78	6 Mo Sep	0.01	0.31	25
26	....	None Since Public			...	Nil	....	1.05	69.9	41.1	9-30-95	10.1	...	6769	Mr	0.06	0.39	Δ0.18	0.04	....	0.05	6 Mo Sep	Nil	0.01	26
27◆	1937	Q0.27¼	1-1-96	12-12	1.072	1.09	1.047	37.1	150	152	9-30-95	233	171	28478	Dc	1.31	1.21	Δ1.33	1.37	....	1.36	9 Mo Sep	1.02	1.01	27
28	1940	Q0.28	12-1-95	11-7	1.09	1.12	1.00	337	1470	825	10-01-95	704	...	53784	Dc	□1.12	Δ0.63	2.08	□11.39	E6.30	14.01	9 Mo Sep	2.20	4.82	28
29	....	Plan qtly div			...	0.08	....	Equity per shr $9.85			9-30-95	p8.01	...	★8320	Dc	...	...	...	p0.69	....	1.09	9 Mo Sep	p0.55	p0.95	29
30	....	None Paid			...	Nil	....	0.28	5.45	3.71	6-30-95	....	...	3529	Mr	0.04	Δ0.24	□d0.28	0.09	....	0.20	6 Mo Sep	d0.02	0.09	30
31	1984	Q0.11	1-10-96	12-28	0.44	0.44	0.44	47.4	177	93.9	9-03-95	40.0	...	15588	Nv	0.02	*0.04	0.46	Δ0.31	P1.60	1.60				31
32◆	....	None Since Public			...	Nil	....	13.2	147	94.1	9-30-95	85.3	...	p46105	Dc	0.23	Δ□0.29	0.40	0.57	....	0.11	9 Mo Sep	0.40	d0.06	32
33	....	None Since Public			...	Nil	....	0.67	31.7	9.42	9-30-95	8.99	...	8772	Dc	*0.11	*0.20	0.47	0.49	....	d0.25	9 Mo Sep	0.42	d0.32	33
34	....	None Since Public			...	Nil	.....	9.63	9.94	2.28	6-30-95	0.05	...	9614	Dc	d0.15	d0.79	d0.86	d1.00	....	d0.74	9 Mo Sep	d0.81	d0.55	34
35	....	None Since Public			...	Nil	....	18.4	23.9	5.48	6-30-95	12.9	...	8683	Sp	...	...	...	p0.44	□P0.51	0.51				35
36	....	None Since Public			...	Nil	....	28.9	33.7	3.19	9-30-95	....	...	11097	Dc	[64]0.07	[65]0.08	d0.32	d0.40	....	d0.44	9 Mo Sep	d0.22	d0.26	36
37◆	1991	0.094	10-16-95	8-4	0.241	0.24	0.187	22.1	161	122	12-31-94	3.27	...	279327	Dc	0.63	0.78	0.70	[66]0.89	....	0.89				37
38	1991	0.75	5-31-91		...	0.75	....	28.3	112	67.7	j6-30-95	19.1	...	290800	Dc	8.40	0.13	0.12	0.15	....	j0.16	6 Mo Jun	0.05	0.06	38
39	1978	S0.08	10-6-95	9-21	0.16	0.16	0.16	6.12	50.5	12.7	9-30-95	3.43	...	6166	Je	0.98	1.15	0.69	Δ1.03	0.28	0.25	3 Mo Sep	0.21	0.18	39
40◆	1988	†0.27	1-15-96	12-13	†0.66	0.60	†0.585	Book Value $15.52			12-31-94	25.6	...	4405	Dc	Δ0.39	Δ0.87	1.56	1.78	....	2.03	9 Mo Sep	1.28	1.53	40
41	1923	Q0.12	12-15-95	11-28	0.36	0.48	0.44	17.8	133	106	9-24-95	129	...	±26456	Dc	±d2.39	Δ±0.70	0.98	4.45	E1.85	1.77	9 Mo Sep	3.99	1.31	41
42◆	....	None Paid			...	Nil	....	6.62	10.9	0.87	9-30-95	....	...	6130	Mr	0.24	1.01	0.15	□d2.01	....	d1.44	6 Mo Sep	d1.28	d0.71	42
43	....	None Since Public			...	Nil	....	45.0	93.2	23.4	9-30-95	....	...	11695	Dc	p0.46	1.01	Δ0.58	0.94	....	1.25	9 Mo Sep	0.64	0.95	43
44	....	None Paid			...	Nil	....	0.11	15.7	5.87	9-30-95	....	...	2473	Dc	0.33	0.27	0.35	0.27	....	d0.61	9 Mo Sep	0.24	d0.64	44
45	....	None Paid			...	Nil	....	0.04	0.53	0.29	9-30-95	0.80	...	11725	Je	pd0.18	[68]d0.01	d0.14	d0.20	d0.29	d0.27	3 Mo Sep	d0.06	d0.04	45
46◆	....	None Since Public			...	Nil	....	10.6	14.4	2.16	9-30-95	0.90	...	3504	Dc	pd7.15	p1.85	0.40	0.40	....	1.10	9 Mo Sep	0.45	1.15	46
47◆	....	None Paid			...	Nil	....	0.55	12.3	34.0	9-30-95	1.13	6500	3993	Mr	0.45	0.61	0.68	d0.32	....	d3.73	6 Mo Sep	0.36	d3.05	47
48	....	None Since Public			...	Nil	....	3.69	7.11	7.11	9-30-95	0.11	...	3891	Dc	0.12	Δ0.24	0.28	[69]0.26	....	0.01	9 Mo Sep	0.18	d0.07	48
49	....	h[70]....	11-7-86	11-10	...	Nil	....	2.37	10.9	6.47	9-30-95	1.21	...	5455	Dc	*d0.33	Δd0.20	Nil	0.16	....	0.30	9 Mo Sep	0.09	0.23	49
50	....	None Since Public			...	Nil	....	22.5	32.3	7.79	12-31-94	2.09	...	14618	Dc	0.11	d0.51	d0.96	d1.29	....	d1.31	9 Mo Sep	d0.88	d0.90	50
51	1992	0.03	8-10-94	7-21	...	Nil	0.09	0.50	100	74.9	3-31-95	249	6401	17792	Sp	0.18	□d0.33	□0.18	d0.30	Pd0.20	d0.20				51
52	1992	0.018	8-10-94	7-21	...	Nil	0.054	Cv into 1 com				....	6418	...	Sp	n/a	n/a	n/a	....	....	....				52

◆**Stock Splits & Divs By Line Reference Index** [4]2-for-1,'93:3-for-2,'94. [7]2-for-1,'92. [11]6-for-5,'93. [12]2-for-1,'94. [14]3-for-1,'95. [17]2-for-1,'93. [19]2-for-1,'94. [27]3-for-2,'95. [32]2-for-1,'95. [37]5-for-2,'92. [40]2-for-1,'94. [42]2-for-1,'93. [46]1-for-5 REVERSE,'95. [47]1-for-4 REVERSE,'92.

¶ S&P 500
\# MidCap 400
✤ SmallCap 600
• Options

Index	Ticker	Name of Issue (Call Price of Pfd. Stocks)	Market	Com. Rank. & Pfd. Rating	Inst. Hold Cos	Inst. Hold Shs. (000)	Principal Business	Price Range 1971-93 High	1971-93 Low	1994 High	1994 Low	1995 High	1995 Low	Dec. Sales in 100s	December, 1995 Last Sale Or Bid High	Low	Last	%Div Yield	P-E Ratio	Total Return % Annualized 12 Mo	36 Mo	60 Mo
1•[1]	MSNS	✓**MediSense Inc**	NNM	NR	130	16331	Mfr blood glucose monitor'g sy	....	....	26	12	32	13⅞	47697	32	24⅜	31⅝	...	21	45.4	...	...
2	MT	✓**Meditrust SBI**	NY,Ch,Ph	NR	208	27216	REIT:health care facilities	34⅝	11⅝	35⅞	28¾	35½	29	19007	35	32½	34⅞	7.7	14	26.8	13.1	21.9
3	MPTR	✓**MedPartners/Mullikin**[52]	NNM	NR	88	5735	Multi-state HMO services	....	....	....	....	34½	13	91286	34½	28	33	...	..	...	...	...
4	MBS	✓**MedQuist Inc**	AS,Ph	NR	12	283	Mgmt & info svcs to hospitals	7¾	4	9	4½	10⅛	6⅜	2235	8⅛	6¾	8⅛	...	11	14.0	8.4	...
5	MEDS	✓**Medstone Intl**[53]	NNM	B–	15	962	Mkts kidney stone treat't eq	42	⅞	6⅜	3¼	12¾	4⅞	15403	12¾	8⅞	10½	...	13	78.7	15.2	...
¶6•[1]	MDT	✓**Medtronic, Inc**	NY,B,Ch,P,Ph	A+	773	215052	Cardiac pacemakers:med.serv	26⅛	½	28	17¼	60	26¼	123485	57⅞	51⅜	55⅞	0.5	36	102	35.3	40.3
✤7	MSA	✓**Medusa Corp**	NY	NR	104	7312	Mfr portland/masonry cement	32¾	7⅜	36½	18⅜	28½	21⅜	6035	27⅜	24	26½	1.9	12	16.9	31.8	27.4
8	MEGO	✓**Mego Financial**	NNM	NR	21	1442	Consumer financial svcs	3⅛	⅛	4¾	2⅛	11⅛	3⅝	5148	7⅞	6	7⅛	...	19	78.1	96.6	95.4
9	MTWO	✓**Melamine Chemicals**	NNM	C	16	1060	Specialty chem,melamine	15	4½	12¼	4½	10¾	7	2859	9½	8½	9½	...	14	–7.3	15.0	11.5
¶10•[2]	MEL	✓**Mellon Bank Corp**	NY,B,Ch,P	B–	579	82985	Comm'l bkg,Pittsburgh,Penn	48⅜	9⅝	40⅜	30	56½	30⅝	66983	56½	51¾	53¾	4.1	12	83.8	19.7	32.0
11	MPMTS	**Mellon Ptc Mtg Tr 85/10**[59]	NNM	NR	11	394	Real estate investment trust	12	3¼	6	3¼	4	2	2659	2½	2⅛	2 3/16	e11.0	d	18.7	20.0	19.0
¶12•[3]	MES	✓**Melville Corp**	NY,B,Ch,P,Ph	A–	470	89678	Footwear:apparel,hlth strs	57¾	1 3/16	41⅝	29½	39⅞	28⅝	88236	32¼	28⅝	30¾	4.9	d	6.4	–13.2	–2.1
13	MEM	✓**MEM Co**	AS	C	11	660	Mfr men's/women's toiletries	21⅛	2	6⅜	3¾	4⅝	2¾	120	3⅛	2¾	2¾	...	d	–26.7	–17.4	–10.4
14•[4]	WFR	✓**MEMC Electronic Materials**	NY,Ch,Ph	NR	80	12356	Produce silicon wafers	....	....	....	....	40	22½	52367	40	31¼	32⅝	...	..	...	...	...
15	MHM	✓**Mental Health Mgmt**	AS	NR	16	1299	Mnge psychiatric dept in hosp	4⅞	3⅝	7⅜	2½	3¾	1¾	326	2⅝	1¾	1 13/16	...	d	–29.3	...	...
✤16•[5]	MNTR	✓**Mentor Corp**	NNM	B	106	16793	Medical devices/hlth care pr	14⅞	1/16	9⅜	6⅜	23⅜	8½	29344	23¼	16¾	23	0.4	28	171	50.5	29.8
#17•[5]	MENT	✓**Mentor Graphics**	NNM,Ch	C	169	43888	Computer-aided engin'g sys	26	5¼	17¼	9⅜	22⅞	12⅜	89519	20¼	16⅛	18¼	...	22	20.2	32.5	8.7
#18•[6]	MTL	✓**Mercantile Bancorp**	NY,Ph	B+	227	18763	Commercial bkg,Missouri	37⅝	6⅛	39¼	29½	47	31¼	16511	46½	43½	46	2.9	12	52.7	17.6	31.9
#19	MRBK	✓**Mercantile Bankshares**	NNM	A	153	17061	Comm'l bkg,Baltimore, MD	23⅞	1 5/16	23⅛	17¾	29½	19½	17838	29½	27½	27⅞	3.3	13	46.8	11.9	19.7
¶20•[7]	MST	✓**Mercantile Stores**	NY,B,Ch,P,Ph	B+	305	16018	Department stores, branches	53⅜	4½	57	30½	49	39⅛	9006	46¾	45¼	46¼	2.3	16	19.8	12.7	12.3
21•[8]	MERCS	✓**Mercer Intl SBI**	NNM	B	82	5970	Natl Res,acq cos,finl svcs	14⅞	2⅜	24⅝	6⅝	27¾	12	43183	23⅛	19	20½	...	5	46.4	46.2	42.4
22	MGP	✓**Merchants Group**	AS	B–	31	2015	Property & casualty insurance	17¾	6½	17⅛	13⅞	20	14⅜	466	17¾	16¾	17¾	1.1	d	16.9	8.1	14.3
23	MBNY	✓**Merchants NY Bancorp**	NNM	A–	15	270	Commercial Bank,New York	68	4½	27½	25	33	25¼	136	32½	31	31½	3.8	14	27.8	15.3	9.9
¶24•[4]	MRK	✓**Merck & Co**	NY,B,C,Ch,P,Ph	A+	1559	633898	Ethical drugs/specialty chem	56⅝	2⅝	39½	28⅛	67¼	36⅜	531848	67¼	61¼	65⅝	2.1	24	74.5	17.7	20.5
25	MAX	✓**Mercury Air Group**	AS,B	B	17	1360	Airport ancillary svs:electr	7½	⅛	7	3¼	11	6¼	1705	9	8¼	8¾	0.5	11	49.3	67.8	39.7
26•[9]	MFN	✓**Mercury Finance**	NY,Ph	A–	242	92212	Consumer finance/insurance	13⅝	1 3/16	12¾	7⅜	16⅝	8¼	65059	14⅝	11⅞	13¼	2.3	21	59.7	25.4	48.3
27	MRCY	✓**Mercury General**	NNM	A–	90	9047	Underwrites auto ins,Calif	39½	5⅜	31½	25½	49¾	28¼	16725	49¾	46¼	47¾	1.7	16	72.0	23.4	38.0
28•[8]	MERQ	✓**Mercury Interactive**	NNM	NR	87	9249	Mfr software testing prod	23	13	21¾	7	29	11¾	34534	24¾	17½	18¼	...	63	37.7	...	...
¶29	MDP	✓**Meredith Corp**	NY,Ch,P,Ph	B	266	15996	Magazines, broadcasting,RE	21¾	9/16	24⅝	19⅜	42½	22⅝	9551	42¼	39⅛	41⅞	1.0	31	80.6	48.6	30.9
#30•[6]	MRDN	✓**Meridian Bancorp**[65]	NNM	A–	166	21809	Comm'l Bkg,Phila,Pa	35¾	3½	33¼	25½	47⅞	26¼	39010	47⅞	44⅞	46½	3.2	15	80.8	18.7	43.7
31	MIGI	✓**Meridian Insurance Gp**	NNM	B	24	1628	Property & casualty insur	13¼	3½	12⅛	9½	15½	10	797	15¼	14¼	14⅞	1.9	9	48.4	14.3	25.7
32	MPD	✓**Meridian Point Rlty IV**[66]	AS	NR	3	38	Real estate investment trust	10	¼	2⅜	1 1/16	1 13/16	1 1/16	1124	1 13/16	1⅝	1¾	...	d	33.4	67.1	4.9
33	MPF	✓**Meridian Point Rlty VI**[67]	AS	NR	..	...	Real estate investment trust	10¼	⅝	1¾	½	1	½	393	15/16	13/16	⅞	...	d	55.7	–8.0	–23.2
34	MPG	✓**Meridian Point Rlty VII**[68]	AS	NR	..	...	Real estate investment trust	10	⅝	1¾	7/16	1	½	494	1	⅞	⅞	...	d	40.0	0.0	–19.7
35	MPH	✓**Meridian Point Rlty VIII**	AS	NR	2	5	Real estate investment trust	9	½	3⅝	¾	2⅝	1⅛	374	1⅝	1⅜	1⅝	17.2	d	20.5	30.3	–21.2
36	MSPO	✓**Meridian Sports**	NNM	NR	12	365	Marine,recreation products	....	....	11¼	7¼	11⅛	4½	8089	6	4¾	5⅛	...	..	–41.4	...	...
37	MERS	✓**Meris Laboratories**	NNM	NR	22	2291	Oper medical testing labs	21	2¼	5½	2½	5½	¾	12724	1 11/16	1	1 3/16	...	d	–60.4	–53.4	...
✤38•[10]	MSEL	✓**Merisel, Inc**	NNM	B	75	11110	Wholesale computer products	18½	1⅝	22½	6¼	8½	3⅞	53660	5¼	4⅛	4⅜	...	d	–48.5	–24.1	11.8
39	MMSI	✓**Merit Medical Systems**	NNM	NR	11	470	Mfr disposable medical prod	21½	2⅞	6⅞	3⅞	11	4¼	7324	8½	5⅝	6¾	...	84	63.6	–2.4	8.5
✤40	MRLL	✓**Merrill Corp**	NNM	B	79	4994	Typesett'g,print'g,dstr svcs	28	1 15/16	32½	13¾	21¼	14	6075	19	15¼	16	0.8	15	–6.6	3.3	34.1
¶41•[4]	MER	✓**Merrill Lynch**	NY,B,C,Ch,P,Ph	B+	494	86372	Investment,finance,insurance	51¼	1 9/16	45⅝	32¼	64¾	34⅝	209190	57⅞	49⅞	51	2.0	9	44.1	21.7	40.5
42	MIT	**Merrill Lynch & Co 'MITTS''97**	NY,Ph	NR	4	5255	Mkt Index Target-Term Secs	11	9¾	11⅛	10¼	14⅞	10½	879	14⅞	14⅜	14⅝	...	..	39.3	13.5	...
43	MIE	**Merrill Lynch & Co 'MITTS''98**	NY	NR	3	121	Mkt Index Target-Term Secs	10⅞	9½	10⅞	9⅝	13¾	10	291	13¾	13	13¼	...	..	32.5	...	...
44	MML	**Merrill Lyn 6.50% 'STRYPES'**	NY	NR	15	1188	Struct Yld Prd Exch For Stk	....	....	....	....	58	48	3043	55	48⅞	51⅝B	6.0	..	...	...	...
45	MEE	**Merrill Lyn Euro 'MITTS''99**	NY	....[71]	..	...	Mkt Index Target-Term Secs	10⅛	10	10⅛	8½	10⅛	8½	935	10⅛	9¾	10	...	..	17.6	...	...
46	MLC	**Merrill Lyn Gl Tel'MITTS''98**	NY	....[71]	4	3247	Mkt Index Target-Term Secs	10¾	9⅞	10⅝	8¼	9⅞	8	3788	9¾	9⅜	9¾	...	..	18.2	...	...
47	MRM	✓**Merrimac Industries**	AS	B	12	364	Mfr/design signal components	13¾	3⅝	12¾	7⅜	12⅜	7⅞	416	11⅛	9⅝	11	3.6	12	47.8	20.2	19.3
48	MGR	✓**Merry-Go-Round Ent**	NY,Ch,Ph	D	31	9248	Specialty fashion stores	22	1 5/16	4¼	⅝	2¼	¼	61133	½	¼	¼	...	d	–62.5	–73.7	–51.7
49	MRY	✓**Merry Land & Invest**	NY,Ph	NR	163	16022	Real estate dev,invest'ts	22⅛	2 5/16	24½	16¼	24	18⅞	20159	24	21⅝	23⅝	5.9	21	16.2	26.0	50.1
50	Pr	**$1.75 Sr'A'cm Cv Pfd([74]Stk)**	NY	BBB	17	346		30¾	24⅞	32⅞	22	32	25⅛	45	32	28⅞	32	5.5	..	...	...	...
51	PrC	**$2.15 Sr'C'cm Cv Pfd([75]Stk)**	NY	BBB	24	2149		....	....	....	....	29	24¼	6274	29	26¾	28¾	7.5	..	...	...	...
✤52•[1]	MESA	✓**Mesa Air Group**	NNM	B	98	22905	Western U.S. commuter airline	24	¾	23	6	12	4⅞	55382	9½	8¼	9	...	21	–1.4	–16.3	36.5

Uniform Footnote Explanations-See Page 4. Other: [1]CBOE:Cycle 2. [2]NY:Cycle 3. [3]P:Cycle 2. [4]ASE,CBOE:Cycle 1. [5]ASE,P:Cycle 1. [6]ASE:Cycle 3. [7]Ph:Cycle 3. [8]CBOE:Cycle 1. [9]NY:Cycle 2. [10]CBOE:Cycle 3. [51]Incl $0.3306 non-taxable,'94. [52]Formerly MedPartners Inc. [53]Plan spin-off, Endocare Inc. [54]Stk dstr of Cardiac Science. [55]Stk dstr of UroGen Corp. [56]®$0.81,'94. [57]®$1.76,'94. [58]®$0.13,'94. [59]Plan liquid'n in'95. [60]Incl $0.60 return of cap,'95. [61]Incl $2.34 return of cap,'94. [62]®$1.30,'95. [63]®$2.35,'94. [64]Δ$1.46,'91. [65]Corestates Financial plan acq, 1.225 com. [66]Plan mgr/Meridian Indus Tr,0.1431 new com. [67]Plan mgr/Meridian Indus Tr,0.07598 new com. [68]Plan mgr/Meridian Indus Tr,0.07444 new com. [69]Excl 4.4M unallocated ESOP,shrs. [70]®$4.74,'94. [71]Rated "A+r" by S&P. [72]Incl liab subj to compromise. [73]©$0.00125,'94. [74]Fr 6-30-98 redeemable for 1.34 com re-spec cond.. [75]Fr 3-31-2000 redeem for 1.136 com re-spec cond.

Index	Cash Divs. Ea.Yr. Since	Dividends: Latest Payment Period $	Date	Ex. Div.	Total $ So Far 1995	Ind. Rate	Paid 1994	Financial Position Mil-$ Cash& Equiv.	Curr. Assets	Curr. Liab.	Balance Sheet Date	Capitalization Lg Trm Debt Mil-$	Shs. 000 Pfd.	Com.	Earnings $ Per Shr. Years End	1991	1992	1993	1994	1995	Last 12 Mos.	Interim Earnings Period	$ per Shr. 1994	1995	Index
1	....	None Since Public			...	Nil	....	26.0	68.6	31.5	3-31-95	0.44	...	±17494	Mr	...	...	p0.61	1.34	....	1.50	6 Mo Sep	0.62	0.78	1
2	1986	0.68¼	11-15-95	10-27	2.70	2.70	[51]2.62	Equity per shr $20.54			9-30-95	750	...	★51037	Dc	□1.75	1.95	2.03	2.28	E2.55↑	2.49	9 Mo Sep	1.66	□1.87	2
3	....	None Since Public			...	Nil	....	19.7	73.8	25.8	6-30-95	18.6	...	16043	Dc	...	...	...	pd0.13	....	0.28	9 Mo Sep	pd0.25	p0.16	3
4	....	None Since Public			...	Nil	....	0.49	15.9	12.4	9-30-95	29.0	...	2397	Dc	0.50	0.56	0.62	0.58	....	0.75	9 Mo Sep	0.40	0.57	4
5	....	h[5455]....	1-15-96	12-27	...	Nil	....	16.8	22.8	2.63	9-30-95	....	...	5447	Dc	0.18	0.22	0.10	[56]0.82	....	0.82	9 Mo Sep	0.58	0.58	5
6◆	1977	Q0.06½	1-26-96	1-3	0.23¼	0.26	0.18¾	413	1198	391	10-27-95	p14.2	...	232307	Ap	0.56	0.68	□0.89	1.01	1.27	1.56	6 Mo Oct	0.59	0.88	6
7◆	1991	Q0.12½	12-8-95	11-27	0.50	0.50	0.50	50.5	124	72.9	9-30-95	61.3	...	16320	Dc	□0.50	0.56	Δ1.12	[57]1.81	....	2.31	9 Mo Sep	1.28	1.78	7
8	....	None Paid			...	Nil	....	Book Value $1.72			5-31-95	62.2	300	18088	Au	*0.22	0.22	Δ0.12	[58]0.14	....	0.38	9 Mo May	0.12	0.36	8
9	....	0.06	2-28-92	2-10	...	Nil	....	6.44	22.8	7.50	9-30-95	....	...	5450	Je	0.40	d0.28	d0.66	d0.46	0.60	0.68	3 Mo Sep	0.09	0.17	9
10◆	1895	Q0.55	11-15-95	10-27	2.00	2.20	1.57	Book Value $14.78			9-30-95	1642	18000	141309	Dc	3.11	4.64	p2.73	2.42	E4.50↑	3.39	9 Mo Sep	2.35	3.32	10
11	1985	0.10	12-30-95	12-19	†[60]1.53	0.24	†[61]3.09	Equity per shr $3.15			9-30-95	....	...	8645	Dc	0.70	d1.21	0.37	0.10	....	d0.14	9 Mo Sep	0.20	d0.04	11
12	1916	Q0.38	11-1-95	10-20	1.52	1.52	1.52	80.1	3067	2367	9-30-95	332	6307	105088	Dc	3.20	□1.34	3.00	2.75	Ed5.60	1.87	9 Mo Sep	0.78	d0.10	12
13	....	0.05	8-13-90	6-25	...	Nil	....	0.23	37.3	25.0	9-30-95	3.62	...	2580	Dc	0.02	d1.67	d1.00	d0.52	....	d0.74	9 Mo Sep	d0.80	d1.02	13
14	....	None Since Public			...	Nil	....	54.4	473	224	9-30-95	86.8	...	41400	Dc	...	...	...	p□1.02	....	....	9 Mo Sep	n/a	p2.01	14
15	....	None Since Public			...	Nil	....	3.63	12.2	6.12	6-30-95	11.6	...	3310	Sp	...	pd7.44	0.17	□d0.40	....	d0.44	9 Mo Jun	□d0.24	d0.28	15
16◆	1987	Q0.02½	10-20-95	9-27	0.10	0.10	0.02½	11.9	84.9	28.8	9-30-95	0.11	...	24714	Mr	0.21	d0.14	0.51	[62]0.71	....	0.82	6 Mo Sep	0.32	0.44	16
17	1988	0.06	8-12-93	7-26	...	Nil	....	186	279	96.6	9-30-95	52.6	...	55454	Dc	d1.43	d1.13	d0.69	0.53	E0.85	0.82	9 Mo Sep	0.28	0.57	17
18◆	1909	Q0.33	1-2-96	12-7	1.27	1.32	1.087	Book Value $25.43			9-30-95	304	15	55298	Dc	2.57	2.91	3.32	3.74	E4.00	4.01	9 Mo Sep	2.68	2.95	18
19◆	1909	Q0.23	12-30-95	12-20	0.86	0.92	0.74	Book Value $15.59			9-30-95	25.8	...	46894	Dc	1.56	1.67	1.80	1.88	E2.15↑	2.11	9 Mo Sep	1.40	1.63	19
20	1940	Q0.26½	12-15-95	11-28	1.05	1.06	1.02	79.0	1314	356	10-28-95	257	...	36844	Ja	3.10	□2.36	Δ2.35	□2.84	E2.90	2.86	9 Mo Oct	□1.22	1.24	20
21	....	2½%Stk	5-21-90	5-1	...	Nil	....	86.8	176	84.7	6-30-95	12.9	...	p13498	Dc	0.75	0.99	Δ1.34	Δ4.04	....	4.23	9 Mo Sep	3.46	3.65	21
22	1993	Q0.05	12-1-95	11-7	0.20	0.20	0.20	Equity per shr $20.99			9-30-95	....	...	3214	Dc	2.91	2.31	Δ2.12	0.36	....	d1.35	9 Mo Sep	0.22	d1.49	22
23◆	1932	Q0.30	12-21-95	12-8	1.10	1.20	0.90	Equity per shr $18.98			9-30-95	....	...	4977	Dc	1.31	1.32	1.59	2.15	....	2.26	9 Mo Sep	1.73	1.84	23
24◆	1935	Q0.34	1-2-96	12-6	1.24	1.36	1.14	2917	7754	5661	9-30-95	1337	...	1231318	Dc	1.83	□2.12	1.87	[63]2.38	E2.70	2.61	9 Mo Sep	1.77	2.00	24
25◆	1995	Q0.01	11-1-95	10-16	0.038	0.04	....	0.53	41.2	20.7	9-30-95	20.0	...	5371	Je	0.40	...	0.62	0.75	0.76	0.80	3 Mo Sep	0.18	0.22	25
26◆	1989	Q0.075	12-1-95	11-13	0.255	0.30	0.193	Book Value $1.23			6-30-95	459	...	173237	Dc	0.19	0.26	Δ0.37	0.49	E0.63	0.59	9 Mo Sep	0.36	0.46	26
27◆	1986	Q0.20	12-28-95	12-12	0.80	0.80	0.70	Equity per shr $19.47			9-30-95	25.0	...	27435	Dc	2.41	3.06	3.52	2.43	....	2.97	9 Mo Sep	1.88	2.42	27
28	....	None Since Public			...	Nil	....	82.0	94.8	11.9	9-30-95	....	...	15592	Dc	...	pd0.34	0.12	0.38	E0.29	0.25	9 Mo Sep	0.24	0.11	28
29◆	1930	Q0.10	12-15-95	11-28	0.40	0.40	0.36	9.47	238	278	9-30-95	80.6	...	±27552	Je	Δ±[64]1.01	□0.03	0.61	0.95	±□1.44	1.36	3 Mo Sep	□±0.39	0.31	29
30	1828	Q0.37	12-1-95	11-13	1.45	1.48	1.34	Book Value $21.90			9-30-95	515	...	57823	Dc	2.40	2.55	Δ2.61	□2.80	E3.05	2.91	9 Mo Sep	□2.03	2.14	30
31	1992	Q0.07	1-5-96	12-19	0.27	0.28	0.24	Equity per shr $16.03			9-30-95	....	...	6776	Dc	1.18	□1.52	Δ1.45	1.35	....	1.75	9 Mo Sep	0.70	1.10	31
32	....	0.075	9-28-90	9-14	...	Nil	....	Equity per shr $2.83			9-30-95	30.3	...	7466	Dc	d0.42	d1.02	Δd0.54	d0.38	....	d0.31	9 Mo Sep	d0.08	□d0.01	32
33	....	0.032	9-30-92	9-15	...	Nil	....	Equity per shr $10.58			9-30-95	25.1	6977	3526	Dc	d1.10	d2.23	d0.69	d0.45	....	d0.17	9 Mo Sep	d0.13	□0.15	33
34	....	0.041	9-30-92	9-15	...	Nil	....	Equity per shr $12.74			9-30-95	41.0	9376	3733	Dc	d3.31	d1.21	d1.10	d1.81	....	d1.73	9 Mo Sep	d0.08	□Nil	34
35	1994	0.07	12-29-95	12-15	0.28	0.28	0.22	Equity per shr $26.87			9-30-95	32.3	5274	1610	Dc	d3.97	Δd3.39	d0.44	d1.89	....	d2.46	9 Mo Sep	d0.37	□d0.94	35
36	....	None Since Public			...	Nil	....	3.30	58.8	78.9	9-30-95	....	...	8000	Dc	...	...	pd0.95	p0.90	....	....	9 Mo Sep	n/a	d3.64	36
37	....	None Since Public			...	Nil	....	2.34	17.5	16.0	6-30-95	10.8	...	7961	Dc	0.42	0.11	d1.26	d0.58	....	d0.72	9 Mo Sep	d0.52	d0.66	37
38	....	None Since Public			...	Nil	....	1.47	1249	974	9-30-95	263	...	29863	Dc	0.43	0.67	1.00	0.38	....	d0.30	9 Mo Sep	0.46	d0.22	38
39◆	....	None Since Public			...	Nil	....	0.17	18.7	9.21	9-30-95	1.98	...	6779	Dc	0.22	0.19	0.28	0.19	....	0.08	9 Mo Sep	0.22	0.11	39
40◆	1993	Q0.03	1-15-96	12-27	0.12	0.12	0.11½	2.86	75.4	39.3	10-31-95	7.05	...	7825	Ja	0.86	1.12	Δ1.65	1.50	....	1.07	9 Mo Oct	1.41	0.98	40
41◆	1961	Q0.26	11-22-95	11-1	1.01	1.04	0.89	Equity per shr $30.35			9-29-95	16156	47	[69]175717	Dc	3.01	□4.18	□6.14	[70]4.75	E5.50	4.72	9 Mo Sep	3.98	3.95	41
42	....	....			...	....	....	Int based on S&P 500,as defined				....	...	7750	Dc	...	...	...	....	....	....	Due 8-29-97			42
43	....	....			...	....	....	Int based on S&P 500,as defined				....	...	1600	Dc	...	...	...	....	....	....	Due 7-31-98			43
44	....	Plan qtly div			...	3.12	....	At maturity MGIC Com or Cash re spec cond.				....	...	★5000	Dc	...	...	...	....	....	....	Mature 8-15-98			44
45	....	....			...	....	....	Int based on European Portfolio,as defined				....	...	★3100	Dc	...	...	...	....	....	....	Due 6-30-99			45
46	....	....			...	....	....	Int based on Global Tel Portfolio Val as defined				....	...	★11000	Dc	...	...	...	....	....	....	Due 10-15-98			46
47	1988	Q0.10	12-15-95	11-30	0.40	0.40	0.40	5.51	12.1	1.56	9-30-95	....	...	1625	Dc	0.58	0.22	1.14	0.81	....	0.95	40 Wk Oct	0.54	0.68	47
48◆	1990	0.013	11-26-93	11-5	...	Nil	....	File bankruptcy Chapt 11				[72]244	...	53931	Ja	±0.43	0.71	d0.85	d3.45	....	d3.34	9 Mo Oct	d1.34	d1.23	48
49	1987	Q0.35	12-29-95	12-13	1.40	1.40	[73]1.25	Equity per shr $13.81			9-30-95	304	9282	33849	Dc	0.94	1.07	1.30	1.10	....	1.14	9 Mo Sep	0.81	0.85	49
50	1993	Q0.43¾	12-29-95	12-13	1.75	1.75	1.75	Cv into 1.34 com,$18.65				....	4000	...	Dc	...	...	...	....	....	....				50
51	1995	Q0.538	12-29-95	12-13	1.714	2.15	....	Cv into 1.136 com,$22				....	4000	...	Dc	...	...	...	....	....	....				51
52◆	....	None Since Public			...	Nil	....	99.2	176	55.6	9-30-95	78.4	...	33467	Sp	*0.38	0.50	Δ0.73	Δ0.75	0.42	0.42				52

◆**Stock Splits & Divs By Line Reference Index** [6]2-for-1,'91,'94,'95. [7]3-for-2,'93. [10]3-for-2,'94. [16]2-for-1,'95. [18]3-for-2,'94. [19]3-for-2,'93. [23]2-for-1,'95. [24]3-for-1,'92. [25]No adj for spl $4 dstr,'90:10%,'95. [26]2-for-1,'92:4-for-3,'91(twice),'93:3-for-2,'95. [27]2-for-1,'92. [29]2-for-1,'95. [39]3-for-2,'91. [40]2-for-1,'92. [41]2-for-1, '93. [48]3-for-2,'91(twice). [52]3-for-2,'92 twice:2-for-1,'93.

¶ S&P 500 # MidCap 400 ✣ SmallCap 600 • Options

Index	Ticker	Name of Issue (Call Price of Pfd. Stocks)	Market	Com. Rank. & Pfd. Rating	Inst. Hold Cos	Inst. Hold Shs. (000)	Principal Business	Price Range 1971-93 High	1971-93 Low	1994 High	1994 Low	1995 High	1995 Low	Dec. Sales in 100s	December, 1995 Last Sale Or Bid High	Low	Last	%Div Yield	P-E Ratio	Total Return % Annualized 12 Mo	36 Mo	60 Mo
✣1•[1]	MXP	✓Mesa Inc	NY,B,Ph	C	86	13543	Oil & gas explor,dev,prod'n	91¼	2½	8½	3⅝	6⅛	3	81751	4	3⅛	3¾	...	d	−21.1	0.0	...
2	MTR	✓Mesa Royalty Tr UBI	NY,B,Ch,Ph	NR	11	924	Royalty interests,oil & gas	49	17	47½	42½	43½	38	532	39	38	38⅞	8.2	12	−1.8	18.8	7.0
3	MSB	✓Mesabi Tr Ctfs SBI	NY,B,Ch	NR	16	2590	Royalties from Res. Mining	18¼	1	3⅞	2⅝	4⅛	2⅞	3492	3⅞	3½	3½	7.4	14	25.0	39.8	13.7
4	MCC	✓Mestek Inc	NY,B,Ch,Ph	B	30	1180	Climate control eqp:engin'g	31½	2¼	10½	9	14⅝	9½	1243	11¾	10¾	11¾	...	10	17.5	9.3	9.0
5	MPR	✓Met-Pro Corp	AS,Ph	B+	27	1084	Pollution control,fluid hdlg	15⅝	¼	11⅞	8⅝	14⅝	10¾	1601	14⅝	12⅝	14½	2.1	15	37.5	20.9	12.7
6	METG	META Group	NNM	NR	..	...	Computer eqp research svcs	...	...	...	...	33¼	18	58516	33¼	20¾	30⅝	...	..	...	...	...
7	MESW	Meta-Software	NNM	NR	..	...	Library generation software	...	...	...	...	20½	15	8850	19½	15	16¾	...	..	...	...	...
8	MTLC	Metalclad Corp	NSC	C	20	2617	Insulation contracting svcs	5¾	1	4⅛	2 5/16	5½	1⅛	77108	5½	3¾	4	...	d	39.1	−3.9	22.7
9	META	✓Metatec Corp	NNM	NR	26	1914	Compiles,dstr info on CD ROM	16½	1¼	16	8¼	14¾	8¼	6325	11¾	8¼	11	...	26	15.8	30.1	...
10	MTLS	MetaTools Inc	NNM	NR	..	...	Dgn computer graphic sys	...	...	...	...	30	12	72129	30	12	26	...	..	...	...	...
11•[2]	MEOHF	✓Methanex Corp	NNM,Ch	NR	101	27692	Prod Methanol, synthetic gas	10⅝	6	18⅞	7¾	15¼	6	118709	8¼	7	7¼	...	3	−42.1	−1.4	...
12	METHA	✓Methode Electronics'A'	NNM	B+	115	22103	Electronic component devices	9⅞	¾	13⅝	8¾	16½	8⅝	17078	16¼	13¾	14¼	1.1	17	31.2	28.5	46.1
13	MTRA	✓Metra Biosystems	NNM	NR	28	3774	Mfr medical diagnostic prd	...	...	...	...	21⅞	10	10314	21¼	16¾	17¼	...	d	...	...	...
14	MBN	✓Metrobank[55]	AS	B+	21	699	Comml bkg,Los Angeles,Calif	14½	5½	17⅜	10½	33⅛	15¼	503	33⅛	27¾	31¼	1.9	17	112	55.4	46.5
15•[3]	MCLL	✓Metrocall Inc	NNM	NR	70	4874	Provides local paging svcs	25¼	12½	20	12	30	14½	39294	24½	18½	19⅛	...	d	15.9	...	...
16	MGS	MetroGas S.A. Cl'B'ADS[56]	NY,Ch,Ph	NR	25	3462	Gas distribution-Argentina	...	...	13⅛	10	11¾	7¼	1217	9¾	8¾	9¾	7.4	..	4.4	...	...
17•[4]	MMG	✓Metromedia Intl Grp	AS,B,Ch,P,Ph	C	51	3930	Consumer prd/commun/pic dstr	38⅜	11/16	13¾	5¾	19½	8⅝	45092	17½	13½	14	...	..	60.0	3.8	6.2
18	MET	✓Metropolitan Realty	AS	NR	3	10	Real estate investment trust	10	4⅛	6⅜	5⅛	8⅞	5⅝	98	8⅝	8⅛	8½B	†5.8	25	57.7	27.5	27.8
#19•[5]	FMY	✓Meyer (Fred) Inc	NY,Ph	B	126	12503	Regional gen'l mdse retailer	38½	9½	42½	29¼	33⅜	17⅜	18796	23⅝	21⅜	22½	...	32	−26.8	−10.4	13.6
20	MFRI	✓MFRI, Inc	NNM	B−	22	971	Mfr air pollut'n filter bags	11	3⅝	9¼	4¾	7½	4	839	7⅜	6¼	6¼	...	13	25.0	−3.7	−0.8
21•[6]	MFST	✓MFS Communications	NNM	NR	176	18048	Telecommunications svc in U.S.	57¾	20	41½	20½	53¾	28¾	58263	53¾	44¾	53¼	...	d	60.2	...	...
22•[7]	MOGN	✓MGI PHARMA, Inc	NNM	C	25	2949	Develop,mkt pharmaceuticals	25¼	2¾	14¾	5¼	6¾	3⅝	15451	5	4⅜	4⅜	...	d	−29.0	−27.2	−0.3
23	MGI	✓MGI Properties	NY,Ph	NR	64	3927	Real estate investment trust	23½	2⅞	16⅝	13⅜	16¾	13⅝	3037	16¾	15¾	16¾	5.7	19	26.0	20.7	26.3
24•[7]	MTG	✓MGIC Investment	NY,Ph,Ch	NR	326	56733	Provides private mtge insur	35¾	13⅝	34¼	25	62	32¾	45214	58⅜	49½	54¼	0.3	17	61.9	30.4	...
25•[7]	MGG	✓MGM Grand	NY	NR	60	7146	Hotel/casino & airline oper	49¾	8¾	39⅝	22⅝	32⅜	22¾	15290	26¼	22¾	23	...	33	−6.6	4.8	18.7
26	MHO	✓M/I Schottenstein Homes	NY,Ch,Ph	NR	42	2100	Single family homebuilder	18½	13	18¼	6¾	12½	6⅜	2741	12¼	10½	11¾	...	11	70.9	...	...
27	MAJ	✓Michael Anthony Jewelers	AS,Ch,Ph	B−	27	4042	Mfr handcrafted gold jewelry	16	2¼	9½	4⅝	6⅞	2⅜	5257	3⅛	2½	2⅝	...	..	−59.6	−14.0	−1.8
#28	MIKL	✓Michael Foods	NNM	NR	101	9317	Processing/dstr food prod	23⅝	6½	13¼	7⅞	14½	9	7067	12⅛	10¾	11⅝	1.7	13	22.8	7.2	−2.9
✣29•[5]	MIKE	✓Michaels Stores	NNM	B	151	15387	Specialty retail stores	39	2½	46½	29½	37	11	42757	17½	13	13¾	...	..	−61.4	−23.5	29.7
30	MCRL	✓Micrel Inc	NNM	NR	46	3344	Mfr,mkt integrated circuits	...	...	15½	9	32½	12⅜	6042	20¾	15½	19½	...	29	36.8	...	...
31	MIFGY	Micro Focus Grp ADS[63]	NNM	NR	9	1779	Design computer compilers/eqp	46	13⅛	20	11½	13¾	8⅜	415	9¼	8⅜	8⅜	...	d	−35.0	−41.2	...
32	MLIN	✓Micro Linear	NNM	NR	56	6006	Dvp/mfr integrated circuits	...	...	9¾	6⅝	18⅝	7⅞	52315	12⅜	9	10¼	...	16	34.4	...	...
#33•[8]	MWHS	✓Micro Warehouse	NNM	NR	191	22516	Direct mkt computer products	21⅜	9	36¼	17¾	56⅞	26¾	105981	53¼	39	43¼	...	32	21.4	58.1	...
✣34•[9]	MICA	✓MicroAge Inc	NNM	↓B	68	7269	Franchises computer stores	26⅝	2 3/16	32½	9¼	15	7¼	24471	9⅞	7¼	8⅛	...	..	−31.6	17.6	4.6
✣35•[10]	MCHP	✓Microchip Technology	NNM	NR	212	24078	Mfr microcontrollers/spcl prd	17⅜	3⅛	31⅝	12⅞	45	21¾	92127	40½	32½	36½	...	29	30.4	...	...
36	MCDY	✓Microdyne Corp	NNM	B	52	4557	Communic/local area ntwk sys	33¾	⅛	10⅝	3⅜	31¼	10⅛	54337	23⅞	14¾	17	...	18	60.0	37.8	39.2
¶37•[11]	MU	✓Micron Technology	NY,Ch,Ph	B	625	107140	Mfr microcomputer parts	12¾	11/16	23	8⅞	94¾	21¼	1222444	55¾	38⅞	39⅝	0.5	8	75.9	120	81.4
38	NOIZ	Micronetics Wireless[66]	NSC	NR	4	123	Mfr noise test'g/microwave prd	4¼	5/16	3½	1	4¾	1 5/16	1327	2⅝	2	2	...	50	25.5	47.4	32.0
39	MCRN	✓Micronics Computers	NNM	NR	36	5577	IBM compatible system boards	9¾	2⅞	6⅛	3½	5⅞	3¼	13876	4⅜	3¼	3½	...	d	−17.6	−8.0	...
40	MCRS	✓MICROS Systems	NNM	B	64	5756	Mfr point-of-sale computer sys	26	¾	41¼	22½	49¾	27¾	13862	49¾	41	49¼	...	33	35.9	36.5	71.6
41	MSCC	✓Microsemi Corp	NNM	B−	22	2805	Mfr silicon semiconductors	11¾	1/16	6	4	14¾	4½	27406	11⅞	8½	8⅝	...	12	76.9	56.5	56.9
¶42•[12]	MSFT	✓Microsoft Corp	NNM,Ch	B+	1224	201887	Software for microcomputers	49	1 3/16	65⅛	39	109¼	58¼	1033479	94¾	85⅛	87¾	...	34	42.0	26.6	39.4
43	MTMI	✓Microtek Medical	NNM	NR	10	201	Mfr surgical & medical prod	14½	5	7¾	4⅛	9¼	4¼	2514	9¼	6¼	8½	...	27	58.1	−10.9	...
44	MOL	✓Microtel Intl	AS,Ch	C	9	375	Mfr telecommunic test equip	14⅞	3/16	1 7/16	½	1 11/16	9/16	7672	1⅜	13/16	1¼	...	63	100	5.6	−7.8
45	MTST	✓Microtest Inc	NNM	NR	48	3411	Local area netwk cabling prd	19¼	4½	26	7	25½	9¼	37281	15½	9¼	10	...	35	−61.5	−10.9	...
46•[4]	MTSI	✓MicroTouch Systems	NNM	NR	57	2985	Supplies touch screen-based sys	10⅛	4⅜	47½	5⅞	45¼	11½	24000	15¼	11½	12⅛	...	43	−73.6	20.0	...
47	MPDI	Microwave Power Devices	NNM	NR	12	1452	Dvlp/mfr linear power amplifiers	...	...	...	...	15	7¼	23241	15	9⅞	11⅛	...	..	...	...	...
48	MIAM	✓Mid Am Inc	NNM	A−	37	1568	Commercial banking,Ohio	13¼	1¾	13⅝	11⅛	17	12¾	4644	17	16⅜	16⅜	3.9	14	37.8	27.4	26.8
49	MAA	✓Mid-Amer Apart Communities	NY,Ch	NR	81	7108	Real estate investment trust	...	...	27	19¾	26⅞	21⅝	5426	25¼	22⅝	24¾	8.1	23	6.3	...	...
50	MAB	✓Mid-America Bancorp	AS,Ch,Ph	A−	27	1169	Commercial banking, Kentucky	19¼	1 13/16	19⅝	15⅞	18⅞	15	330	18¼	17⅜	18	se3.2	19	21.4	17.8	25.9
51	MDI	✓Mid-America Realty Inv	NY,Ch	NR	36	2845	Real estate investment trust	22	8½	10¾	6⅞	9	6½	3449	8	7⅜	7¾	11.4	25	19.4	1.7	−2.6
52•[13]	MAW	✓Mid-American Waste Sys	NY,Ph	NR	66	12793	Nonhazardous solid waste mgmt	27¼	6⅞	10¼	4⅜	7⅛	3¼	31561	4⅛	3¼	3½	...	..	−49.1	−34.6	−27.0

Uniform Footnote Explanations-See Page 4. Other: [1]ASE:Cycle 1. [2]CBOE:Cycle 1. [3]ASE:Cycle 2. [4]CBOE:Cycle 3. [5]P:Cycle 3. [6]ASE,CBOE,P:Cycle 2. [7]ASE:Cycle 3. [8]ASE,Ph:Cycle 2. [9]CBOE:Cycle 2. [10]CBOE,NY:Cysle 1. [11]CBOE,P:Cycle 1. [12]ASE,P:Cycle 1. [13]Ph:Cycle 2. [51]Dstr of 1 wrrt. [52]Fiscal Dec'92 & prior. [53]12 Mo May'93. [54]®$0.32,'94. [55]Approve Comerica Inc acq,0.7889 com. [56]Ea ADS rep 10 Cl'B'shrs, 1 peso. [57]Fiscal Aug,'93 & prior data of Actava Group. [58]©$0.299,'94. [59]Incl current amts. [60]Tracinda Corp owns 72.9% com. [61]Fiscal Jun'93 & prior. [62]®$1.76,'95. [63]Ea ADS rep 1 ord, par 10p. [64]Fiscal Sep'93 & prior. [65]®$3.90,'95. [66]Formerly Micronetics Inc. [67]12 Mo Dec'94:Fiscal Jun'94 earned d$0.08. [68]®$0.75,'94. [69]®$1.21,'94. [70]Incl $0.544 non-taxable,'94. [71]Incl $0.56 non-taxable,'94.

Splits ◆ Index	Cash Divs. Ea.Yr. Since	Dividends: Latest Payment Period $	Date	Ex. Div.	Total $ So Far 1995	Ind. Rate	Paid 1994	Financial Position Mil-$ Cash& Equiv.	Curr. Assets	Curr. Liab.	Balance Sheet Date	Capitalization Lg Trm Debt Mil-$	Shs. 000 Pfd.	Com.	Earnings $ Per Shr. Years End	1991	1992	1993	1994	1995	Last 12 Mos.	Interim Earnings Period	$ per Shr. 1994	1995	Index
1◆	....	1.87½	2-15-90	1-2	...	Nil	....	161	205	168	9-30-95	1135	...	64050	Dc	d2.05	d2.31	d2.61	d1.42	Ed1.05	d1.06	9 Mo Sep	d1.21	d0.85	1
2	1980	0.217	1-31-96	12-27	3.29	3.20	3.697	Equity per shr $10.85			9-30-95	....	...	1864	Dc	2.52	1.62	3.15	3.74	....	3.29	9 Mo Sep	3.06	2.61	2
3	1990	0.09	11-20-95	10-26	0.255	0.26	0.24	....	...	...	10-31-95	....	...	13120	Ja	0.12	0.08	0.25	0.23	....	0.25	9 Mo Oct	0.17	0.19	3
4	....	[51]....	9-22-86	8-25	...	Nil	....	0.93	91.8	38.0	9-30-95	0.19	...	9015	Dc	0.95	Δ0.57	0.46	1.02	....	1.19	9 Mo Sep	0.67	0.84	4
5◆	1992	A0.30	5-12-95	4-3	0.30	0.30	0.167	7.19	29.4	11.6	10-31-95	1.99	...	4655	Ja	0.53	0.42	0.53	0.81	....	0.97	9 Mo Oct	0.59	0.75	5
6	....	None Paid			...	Nil	....	2.63	12.7	16.8	9-30-95	....	p...	★5094	Dc	...	...	...	pd0.99	....	....	9 Mo Sep	n/a	p0.20	6
7	....	None Paid			...	Nil	....	8.03	14.4	16.8	9-30-95	....	...	★9500	Dc	...	...	...	p0.22	....	....	9 Mo Sep	n/a	p0.24	7
8	....	None Paid			...	Nil	....	1.06	4.40	7.15	p8-31-95	0.59	...	20913	My	d0.19	[52]d0.68	[53]d0.79	d0.56	d1.13	d1.01	3 Mo Aug	d0.16	d0.04	8
9	....	None Paid			...	Nil	....	6.79	13.6	4.76	9-30-95	0.14	...	7041	Dc	d0.13	d0.11	0.25	[54]0.33	....	0.42	9 Mo Sep	0.16	0.25	9
10	....	None Since Public			...	Nil	....	1.62	5.82	3.02	9-30-95	p....	p...	★11220	Dc	...	...	...	pd0.26	....	....	9 Mo Sep	n/a	pd0.09	10
11	....	None Paid			...	Nil	....	384	612	166	6-30-95	338	...	p194798	Dc	0.12	d0.20	0.06	2.24	....	2.21	9 Mo Sep	1.05	1.02	11
12◆	1983	Q0.04	1-31-96	1-10	0.12	0.16	0.058	44.5	117	35.5	7-31-95	....	...	±35159	Ap	0.23	0.13	±0.45	±0.61	±0.75	0.82	6 Mo Oct	±0.34	±0.41	12
13	....	None Since Public			...	Nil	....	31.4	33.1	1.78	9-30-95	0.03	...	9660	Je	...	d1.09	d0.87	d0.69	d1.08	d1.06	3 Mo Sep	d0.20	d0.18	13
14◆	1987	Q0.15	10-30-95	10-12	0.60	0.60	0.545	Book Value $13.06			12-31-94	....	...	5377	Dc	1.05	1.10	1.15	1.47	....	1.81	9 Mo Sep	1.00	1.34	14
15	....	None Since Public			...	Nil	....	3.45	23.5	18.1	6-30-95	p114	...	★14619	Dc	...	p0.32	p□d0.11	□d0.14	....	d1.04	9 Mo Sep	0.23	d0.67	15
16	1995	0.428	11-8-95	10-25	0.719	0.72	....	4.21	175	301	12-31-94	20.0	...	512530	Dc	...	...	p1.72	1.00	....	....	6 Mo Jun	n/a	0.20	16
17	1976	0.09	1-3-94	12-10	...	Nil	0.09	12.0	386	361	p5-31-95	253	...	40776	Fb	d3.08	Δ0.64	□[57]d2.52	pd2.18	....	....	3 Mo May	n/a	pd0.55	17
18	1989	†Q0.07	12-29-95	12-14	†0.34	0.49	†0.63	Equity per shr $9.03			9-30-95	....	...	4532	Dc	0.43	0.47	0.60	0.57	....	0.34	9 Mo Sep	0.52	0.29	18
19	....	None Since Public			...	Nil	....	41.7	742	462	11-04-95	688	...	26704	Ja	1.80	2.21	□2.50	0.25	....	0.70	9 Mo Oct	d0.05	0.40	19
20	....	None Since Public			...	Nil	....	0.10	37.1	18.9	7-31-95	7.28	...	4654	Ja	0.25	0.41	0.54	0.27	....	0.47	9 Mo Oct	0.24	0.44	20
21	....	None Since Public			...	Nil	....	183	389	241	9-30-95	610	15095	62021	Dc	...	pd0.30	d0.30	d2.42	Ed4.25	d4.10	9 Mo Sep	d1.48	d3.16	21
22	....	None Paid			...	Nil	....	14.1	15.8	2.28	9-30-95	....	...	12740	Dc	d0.94	d0.83	d1.03	d0.82	....	d0.60	9 Mo Sep	d0.59	d0.37	22
23	1972	Q0.24	1-12-96	1-3	0.90	0.96	[58]0.86	Equity per shr $15.52			8-31-95	[59]76.1	...	11496	Nv	0.66	0.77	0.75	1.26	E0.90	1.19	9 Mo Aug	0.92	0.85	23
24◆	1991	Q0.04	12-1-95	11-8	0.16	0.16	0.16	Equity per shr $17.32			9-30-95	35.9	...	58615	Dc	1.34	1.74	2.16	2.70	....	3.28	9 Mo Sep	1.93	2.51	24
25	....	None Since Public			...	Nil	....	96.0	185	121	9-30-95	559	...	[60]48775	Dc	d0.40	d0.48	d2.47	1.52	....	0.69	9 Mo Sep	1.13	0.30	25
26	....	None Since Public			...	Nil	....	Equity per shr $10.85			9-30-95	151	...	8800	Dc	...	p1.05	p1.87	1.32	....	1.05	9 Mo Sep	0.93	0.66	26
27	....	None Since Public			...	Nil	....	0.13	62.6	16.6	10-28-95	18.8	...	8333	Ja	0.35	d0.06	0.23	[61]0.34	....	....	9 Mo Oct	0.33	0.03	27
28◆	1987	Q0.05	11-20-95	11-2	0.20	0.20	0.20	2.29	95.9	69.0	9-30-95	70.6	...	19332	Dc	1.07	0.20	d0.84	0.79	E0.90	0.87	9 Mo Sep	0.55	0.63	28
29	....	None Since Public			...	Nil	....	6.58	465	224	7-30-95	199	...	21354	Ja	□0.90	1.22	1.53	[62]1.77	....	0.02	9 Mo Oct	0.69	d1.06	29
30	....	None Since Public			...	Nil	....	14.8	36.7	9.84	9-30-95	2.70	...	8851	Dc	0.05	0.12	Δ0.04	0.38	....	0.68	9 Mo Sep	0.23	0.53	30
31	....	None Since Public			...	Nil	....	88.8	116	58.3	1-31-95	0.31	...	p15029	Ja	1.55	1.64	1.52	0.91	....	d0.08	6 Mo Jul	0.51	d0.48	31
32	....	None Since Public			...	Nil	....	30.0	47.4	9.07	9-30-95	3.30	...	12262	Dc	*0.16	*0.17	Nil	0.24	....	0.64	9 Mo Sep	0.12	0.52	32
33◆	....	None Since Public			...	Nil	....	51.8	285	80.0	9-30-95	0.45	...	★30928	Dc	p0.21	p0.39	0.64	1.01	....	1.34	9 Mo Sep	0.71	1.04	33
34◆	....	None Since Public			...	Nil	....	14.1	450	348	7-30-95	3.84	...	14305	Oc	0.50	0.59	[64]1.15	1.22	P0.02	0.02				34
35◆	....	None Since Public			...	Nil	....	43.9	151	86.1	9-30-95	15.1	...	33861	Mr	p0.02	0.19	0.62	1.05	....	1.24	6 Mo Sep	0.48	0.67	35
36	....	0.03	12-18-87	11-9	...	Nil	....	4.59	94.2	53.6	10-01-95	17.0	...	12790	Sp	0.76	d0.15	0.10	0.35	0.96	0.96				36
37◆	1992	Q0.05	1-18-96	12-26	0.17½	0.20	0.08½	607	1530	953	11-30-95	122	...	207004	Au	0.03	0.03	0.52	1.91	[65]3.95	4.71	3 Mo Nov	0.75	1.51	37
38	....	None Since Public			...	Nil	....	0.23	2.23	0.74	6-30-95	0.17	...	2845	Mr	d0.20	*0.05	Δ0.04	Δ0.01	....	0.04	6 Mo Sep	0.02	0.05	38
39	....	None Since Public			...	Nil	....	20.5	84.1	22.5	9-30-94	3.26	...	13100	Sp	1.05	0.74	0.90	0.20	Pd0.95	d0.95				39
40	....	None Since Public			...	Nil	....	23.7	73.4	34.1	9-30-95	6.16	...	7871	Je	0.44	0.53	0.74	1.10	1.46	1.49	3 Mo Sep	0.38	0.41	40
41	....	0.06	1-16-87	12-19	...	Nil	....	3.56	70.5	32.2	7-02-95	48.6	...	7694	Sp	Δ0.24	Δ0.14	Δ0.23	d0.28	P0.74	0.74				41
42◆	....	None Since Public			...	Nil	....	5064	6417	1759	9-30-95	....	...	592306	Je	0.83	1.20	1.57	1.88	2.32	2.59	3 Mo Sep	0.51	0.78	42
43	....	None Since Public			...	Nil	....	0.14	15.6	10.1	8-31-95	1.86	...	4593	Nv	p0.08	□p0.42	0.20	0.11	....	0.32	9 Mo Aug	0.09	0.30	43
44	....	None Paid			...	Nil	....	0.37	8.26	3.97	9-30-95	0.35	...	13363	Dc	d0.60	d0.49	[61]d0.89	[67]d0.03	....	0.02	9 Mo Sep	d0.05	Nil	44
45	....	None Since Public			...	Nil	....	31.6	43.7	7.01	12-31-94	....	...	8032	Dc	0.40	1.05	d0.34	0.64	....	0.29	9 Mo Sep	0.43	0.08	45
46◆	....	None Since Public			...	Nil	....	43.1	73.4	10.4	9-30-95	0.03	...	7987	Dc	0.21	0.38	0.31	[68]0.77	E0.28↓	0.41	9 Mo Sep	0.53	0.17	46
47	....	None Since Public			...	Nil	....	0.52	24.5	9.55	9-30-95	p8.98	...	★10375	Dc	...	...	...	p0.08	....	....	9 Mo Sep	n/a	pd0.25	47
48◆	1950	Q0.16	12-29-95	12-6	0.635	0.64	0.60	Book Value $8.33			9-30-95	50.2	1446	19051	Dc	*0.41	Δ1.08	1.26	[69]1.16	....	1.16	9 Mo Sep	0.87	0.87	48
49	1994	Q0.50	10-31-95	10-20	2.00	2.00	[70]1.21	Equity per shr $18.71			9-30-95	303	...	10947	Dc	...	p0.58	p0.54	Δ0.94	....	1.06	9 Mo Sep	Δ0.38	0.50	49
50◆	1950	3%Stk	12-15-95	11-3	‡0.631	0.58	‡0.613	Book Value $14.09			9-30-95	80.8	...	9091	Dc	1.01	1.07	1.27	1.38	....	0.94	9 Mo Sep	0.94	0.50	50
51	1987	Q0.22	11-22-95	11-6	0.88	0.88	[71]0.88	Equity per shr $9.87			9-30-95	65.9	...	8281	Dc	0.37	0.23	0.27	d0.02	....	0.31	9 Mo Sep	d0.02	0.31	51
52◆	1993	0.00½	9-15-93	8-26	...	Nil	....	14.9	43.9	42.9	9-30-95	307	...	27985	Dc	0.83	0.80	d0.98	□0.37	....	0.01	9 Mo Sep	□0.34	d0.02	52

◆Stock Splits & Divs By Line Reference Index [1]1-for-5 REVERSE,'92. [5]Adj for 5%,'91:3-for-2,'95. [12]2-for-1,'93:3-for-2,'95. [14]10%,'94. [24]2-for-1,'93. [28]3-for-2,'91. [33]2-for-1,'94. [34]3-for-2,'94. [35]2-for-1,'93:3-for-2,'94(twice). [37]5-for-2,'94:2-for-1,'95. [42]3-for-2,'91,'92:2-for-1,'94. [46]2-for-1,'94. [48]3-for-2,'92:10%,'92,'94,'95. [50]10%,'91:Adj to 3%,'95. [52]3-for-2,'91.

¶ S&P 500 # MidCap 400 ✣ SmallCap 600 • Options

Index	Ticker	Name of Issue (Call Price of Pfd. Stocks)	Market	Com. Rank. & Pfd. Rating	Inst. Hold Cos	Inst. Hold Shs. (000)	Principal Business	Price Range 1971-93 High	1971-93 Low	1994 High	1994 Low	1995 High	1995 Low	Dec. Sales in 100s	December, 1995 Last Sale Or Bid High	Low	Last	%Div Yield	P-E Ratio	Total Return % Annualized 12 Mo	36 Mo	60 Mo
1•[1]	MME	✔Mid Atlantic Medical Svcs	NY,Ch,Ph	NR	209	32899	Health care mgmt services	14	¼	30¼	12⅛	26⅛	16½	36020	24½	22⅜	24¼	...	19	7.8	53.5	51.3
2	MRR	✔Mid-Atlantic Realty Trust	AS	NR	33	2480	Real estate investment trust	11	9	10⅜	7⅜	9½	7½	2255	9	8⅜	8⅝	10.7	15	17.4	...	...
3	MOCNF	✔Mid Ocean Ltd	NNM	NR	..	...	Prop/catastrophe reinsurance	34¾	24½	30½	22¼	38¾	24½	27174	38¾	36½	37⅛	2.7	8	40.8	...	...
4	MIDS	✔Mid-South Insurance[52]	NNM	B	15	1486	Life,accident,health insur	11⅛	9/16	10	8½	15½	8¾	1717	15⅜	15	15B	1.9	52	70.5	36.4	37.1
#5	MEC	✔MidAmerican Energy	NY	NR	105	13374	Electric & gas utility	...	...	...	...	17⅛	13⅝	20179	17⅛	16⅜	16¾	7.2	14	...	...	...
6	MCCI	✔MIDCOM Communications	NNM	NR	33	4277	Long distance telephone svc	...	...	...	...	19½	11	3688	18½	15½	18¼	...	d	...	...	...
7	MIDD	✔Middleby Corp	NNM	B–	13	663	Food preparation equip	10	1/16	4⅞	2⅝	9¾	3⅞	6276	9¾	7½	9½	...	23	138	61.6	50.3
8	MLA	✔Midland Co	AS	A–	34	647	Insurance,transpt'n,sportswr	50⅝	1 5/16	45⅛	34	51	43	55	50	48½	48⅞B	1.3	12	13.2	4.3	11.5
9	MRIX	✔Midland Resources	NSC	NR	..	...	Oil & gas explor dev, prod'n	3¼	⅜	3	1⅛	5⅜	2¼	2458	3½	2½	3⅛B	...	d	31.6	71.0	...
10•[2]	MIDL	✔Midlantic Corp[54]	NNM	B–	219	19907	Commercial bkg,New Jersey	52⅛	2⅞	31⅞	24	66⅛	26¼	54960	66⅛	57⅝	65⅝	2.0	15	152	47.7	67.9
11	MSL	✔MidSouth Bancorp	AS	NR	1	1	General banking, Louisiana	7⅜	6⅝	9⅜	6½	19¾	8⅛	100	15½	14⅞	15⅜	...	12	81.3	...	...
12	Pr	8.28%[57]Adj[58]Rt'A'cmCvPfd([59]14.25)	AS	NR	..	...		...	...	...	...	24	13⅜	34	21½	21	20¾B	5.7	..	...	...	...
13	MEH	✔Midwest Express Holdings	NY	NR	38	1462	Passenger jet airline	...	...	...	...	31	18	7193	30⅛	27¼	28	...	12	...	...	...
14	EQM	✔Midwest R.E.Shop'g Ctr L.P.	NY,Ch	NR	4	81	Real estate investments	10⅞	1⅝	2⅜	½	⅞	3/16	8942	⅜	3/16	3/16	...	d	−36.8	−41.6	−33.9
15	MKS	✔Mikasa Inc	NY,Ch	NR	39	3141	Dvlp, mkt tableware/gift prd	...	...	16⅞	12½	17⅝	12⅝	3418	14	12⅝	13½	...	10	−15.6	...	...
16	MPI	✔Milestone Properties	NY,Ch	NR	1		Real estate development	5½	2	5⅛	3⅝	3¾	1⅛	371	1⅞	1⅛	1⅜	...	3	...	...	...
17	Pr A	$0.78 cm[61]Cv Ser'A'Pfd(10.00)	NY	NR	1	34		7⅞	3½	7¾	2½	4¼	1⅜	1291	2½	1⅝	1⅞	...	..	...	...	...
#18•[3]	MLHR	✔Miller (Herman)	NNM	↓B–	136	14530	Office furniture & systems	31	⅜	35	23⅜	32⅜	19¼	17065	31¾	27¼	30	1.7	88	16.7	20.7	14.4
19	MLR	✔Miller Industries	NY	NR	36	2069	Mfr towing & recovery equip	...	...	16¾	10½	26½	14½	2778	26½	21¾	24¾	...	26	59.7	...	...
20•[4]	MICCF	Millicom Intl Cellular S.A.	NNM	NR	..	...	Cellular telephone ntwrk	23½	20¼	32¼	18¾	35¾	20½	19666	32¼	28	30½	...	d	4.3	...	...
¶21•[2]	MIL	✔Millipore Corp	NY,Ch,Ph	B+	368	37804	Separations technology sys	24	2¾	28½	19¼	41½	22⅞	22870	41½	36⅝	41⅛	0.8	22	71.7	34.4	19.7
22	MLS	✔Mills Corp	NY,Ch	NR	47	3580	Real estate investment trust	...	...	24	16½	20⅝	15⅛	7942	18½	16⅝	17	11.1	27	7.7	...	...
23	MILT	✔Miltope Group	NNM	C	17	1238	Computer eq for the military	23¾	2	5⅛	2¼	4⅞	2½	2336	3¼	2½	2¾	...	d	−37.5	−16.4	1.9
24	MNES	✔Mine Safety Appl	NNM	B	62	2650	Safety & health protect'n eq	62	2¼	46¼	39½	55	41	1064	49½	41	48	2.3	14	12.8	8.3	1.7
25•[5]	MTX	✔Minerals Technologies	NY,Ph	NR	195	21789	Mkts specialty minerals & prd	32	16	31⅜	24	43¼	27¼	14095	38⅜	34	36½	0.3	21	34.3	22.6	...
26	MNMD	✔MiniMed Inc	NNM	NR	19	1971	Mfr medication infusion systems	...	...	...	...	13½	7¾	19826	13⅜	10¼	12½	...	..	...	...	...
¶27•[4]	MMM	✔Minnesota Min'g/Mfg	NY,B,C,Ch,P,Ph	A+	1024	272852	Scotch tapes: coated abrasives	58½	10¾	57⅛	46⅜	69⅞	50¾	166108	69⅞	63¼	66⅜	2.8	20	29.9	13.7	12.8
#28	MPL	✔Minnesota Pwr & Lt	NY,B,Ch,P,Ph	B+	129	4155	Electric utility	36½	6⅜	33	24¾	29¼	24¼	9582	29⅛	27⅝	28⅜	7.2	11	19.9	0.6	8.3
29	MNTX	✔Minntech Corp	NNM	B	37	3752	Mfrs dialysis eqp & supplies	18¼	⅞	16½	10	23⅝	11½	10918	23⅝	18½	19⅝	0.5	27	29.9	10.9	26.0
30	MNRCY	✔Minorco ADR[65]	NSC	NR	41	5190	Invest in Intl firms,min'g	22¾	1⅝	27¾	17¾	29¾	20⅛	3455	29¾	28⅛	28⅝	2.1	27	23.9	32.6	16.7
#31•[6]	MIR	✔Mirage Resorts	NY,B,Ch,P	B–	347	67815	Hotel-casino complex	25	1/16	27	16⅝	35⅛	19¾	34829	34¾	31⅛	34½	...	21	69.3	37.8	36.4
32	MAENF	Miramar Mining	NNM,To	↑B–	60	14369	Acq,explor,dvlp mineral prop	6⅞	3/16	7⅞	4⅞	7½	4⅞	3883	5⅝	4⅞	4⅞	...	..	−18.8	...	...
33	MSW	✔Mission West Prop[69]	AS,B,P	NR	7	107	Real estate business trust	18½	½	7	3⅝	7¼	4⅞	145	5⅜	4⅞	4¾B	...	d	−26.9	11.2	−10.1
34•[4]	MISS	✔Mississippi Chemical	NNM	NR	88	8972	Prod/supp nitrogen fertilizers	...	...	19¼	14¾	25⅛	15⅜	29348	25⅛	22	23¼	1.4	9	38.0	...	...
35•[5]	MND A	✔Mitchell Energy/Dev'A'	NY,B,P,Ph	B	64	4911	Oil & gas:pipeline:real estate	45⅝	1	22⅞	14½	19⅜	14⅞	2613	19	17⅞	18½	2.6	43	21.7	6.3	2.2
36•[5]	MND B	✔ Cl'B' non-vtg	NY	B–	77	11170		27⅜	13	23¼	14½	19⅛	15	6710	18⅞	17⅜	18¾	2.8	44	19.0	11.8	...
37	MLT	✔Mitel Corp	NY,To,B,Ch,Mo,P,Ph	B	50	19622	Telecommunications eq	41	⅝	7½	2⅞	6⅞	3½	33195	6⅞	6¼	6½	...	..	79.3	58.7	45.4
38	MBK	✔Mitsubishi Bank Ltd ADS[70]	NY,Ch,Ph	NR	15	5990	Commercial banking, Japan	29¼	10½	28	21¾	25¼	19⅜	3680	25	22¼	24⅜	0.3	..	0.9	10.0	9.6
39	MITY	✔Mity-Lite Inc	NNM	NR	8	507	Mfr folding leg tables	...	...	9½	5¼	9⅞	7⅜	1946	8⅞	7⅜	7⅜	...	13	−7.8	...	...
40	MKRL	MK Rail	NNM	NR	26	4412	Locomotive mfr,re-mfr parts	...	...	21	8½	10⅝	3¾	24542	5¼	3¾	3¾	...	..	−61.5	...	...
41	MLFB	MLF Bancorp	NNM	NR	38	2101	Savings bank, Pennsylvania	...	...	16¾	12¼	24⅝	13⅜	8190	22¾	21	22¼	2.5	14	72.5	...	...
42	MMI	✔MMI Companies	NY	NR	52	3701	Insurance/risk mgmt svcs	16¾	13⅛	16	12⅛	26	14⅞	3029	25½	23¼	24	0.8	11	53.9	...	...
¶43•[7]	MOB	✔Mobil Corp	NY,To,B,C,Ch,P,Ph	B+	1420	207861	Int'l oil/gas explor'n,devlp	84¾	7⅝	87⅛	72	116⅝	82¾	157805	116⅝	104⅜	111¾	3.3	17	36.3	26.4	19.0
44	MBLE	✔Mobile Gas Service	NNM	↓B+	18	412	Natural gas, Mobile,Ala.	26	2⅞	28¾	19¼	22¾	19¼	461	22¾	22	22½	4.8	18	18.5	5.9	17.7
45•[8]	MTEL	✔Mobile Telecommun Tech	NNM	NR	204	28753	Telecommun/paging services	39	4⅛	26¼	14⅝	36⅜	18¾	172306	23⅜	19¼	21⅜	...	d	10.3	16.2	27.9
46•[4]	MBLM	✔MobileMedia Corp	NNM	NR	80	8148	Provides paging svcs	...	...	...	...	29¼	18½	61635	28	21⅞	22¼	...	..	...	...	...
47	MOCO	✔Modern Controls	NNM	B+	28	2005	Mfr specialized test instr	21¼	½	9¼	5¾	11⅛	6⅛	3728	11⅛	10⅛	10⅞	2.2	21	81.7	3.5	6.7
48	MODM	✔Modern Medl Modalities	NSC	NR	..	...	Leases'MRI','CT Scan'equip	...	...	8	5	9	1	4085	2½	1¾	2⅜	...	..	−70.3	...	...
#49	MODI	✔Modine Mfg	NNM	A	137	10633	Auto parts: heating: air-cond	30¼	⅝	31¼	23¾	40½	23¾	19400	32	23¾	24	2.5	10	−15.0	11.1	23.1
✣50•[9]	MOHK	✔Mohawk Industries	NNM	NR	80	16609	Mfr resident'l/commer'l carpet	34¾	7¼	36½	10¾	19¼	10⅞	12990	17½	13½	15⅝	...	22	25.0	3.8	...
✣51•[2]	MB	✔Molecular Biosystems	NY,Ch,Ph	C	50	3508	Organic & biochemical R&D	40⅞	½	20¾	8⅝	11⅜	5¼	12828	7⅞	6½	6⅞	...	d	−36.0	−27.1	−15.7
52	MDYN	✔Molecular Dynamics	NNM	NR	30	3097	Mfr image acquis/analysis inst	24¼	10¼	14½	4¾	10	4⅞	13556	6½	4⅞	6¼	...	d	0.0	...	...

Uniform Footnote Explanations-See Page 4. Other: [1]ASE:Cycle 3. [2]ASE:Cycle 1. [3]NY:Cycle 2. [4]CBOE:Cycle 1. [5]P:Cycle 3. [6]ASE:Cycle 2. [7]CBOE:Cycle 2. [8]CBOE:Cycle 3. [9]P:Cycle 2. [51]Incl $0.24 non-taxable:©$0.06,'94. [52]Trigon Blue Cross/Shield plan acq, $15.67. [53]Pfd in $M. [54]Approve PNC Bank Corp acq,2.05 com. [55]®$5.11,'94. [56]To be determined. [57]Thru 12-31-95,min 6% max 10%. [58]Rate set at 10% after 8-1-2005. [59]Fr 8-1-2000. [60]Stk dstr of Union Property Investors. [61]Cum to 12-31-92. [62]Scale to 0.625 com in'95. [63]9 Mo Apr. [64]Incl current amts. [65]Ea. Sponsored ADR repr 1 ord shr. [66]Fiscal Jun'93 & prior:Fiscal Jun'94 earned $0.99. [67]Fiscal Nov 92 & prior. [68]13 Mo Dec'93. [69]Plan liquidation. [70]Each ADS rep 1 ord,par 50y.

Splits ◆ Index	Cash Divs. Ea. Yr. Since	Dividends: Latest Payment Period $	Date	Ex. Div.	Total $ So Far 1995	Ind. Rate	Paid 1994	Financial Position Mil-$: Cash& Equiv.	Curr. Assets	Curr. Liab.	Balance Sheet Date	Capitalization: Lg Trm Debt Mil-$	Shs. 000 Pfd.	Com.	Earnings $ Per Shr. Years End	1991	1992	1993	1994	1995	Last 12 Mos.	Interim Earnings Period	$ per Shr. 1994	1995	Index
1◆	....	None Since Public			...	Nil	....	201	273	131	9-30-95	0.21	...	46436	Dc	0.23	0.32	□0.56	1.15	E1.30	1.28	9 Mo Sep	0.82	0.95	1
2	1993	Q0.23	12-15-95	11-29	0.89	0.92	[51]0.85	Equity per shr $3.67			9-30-95	143	...	6118	Dc	...	p0.05	p0.19	0.46	....	0.57	9 Mo Sep	0.28	Δ0.39	2
3	1995	Q0.25	10-5-95	9-21	0.75	1.00	....	Equity per shr $25.34			4-30-95	....	...	±36319	Oc	...	...	±p2.60	±2.41	P4.90	4.90				3
4◆	1967	Q0.07	11-22-95	10-27	0.28	0.28	0.233	Equity per shr $7.49			9-30-95	....	...	5447	Dc	0.94	0.93	1.18	1.06	....	0.29	9 Mo Sep	0.75	d0.02	4
5	1995	Q0.30	12-1-95	11-6	0.60	1.20	....	32.0	331	522	9-30-95	1385	[53]140	100752	Dc	...	...	p1.43	1.27	....	1.20	9 Mo Sep	p1.03	p0.96	5
6	....	None Since Public			...	Nil	....	0.63	63.8	65.1	9-30-95	23.4	...	14817	Dc	...	...	...	pd0.39	Ed0.37↓	....	9 Mo Sep	n/a	p□d0.45	6
7	....	0.02	3-25-91	2-26	...	Nil	....	0.96	46.2	25.7	9-30-95	42.7	...	8388	Dc	d0.90	d0.23	0.41	0.36	....	0.42	9 Mo Sep	0.22	0.28	7
8	1961	Q0.15½	1-11-96	12-27	0.61	0.62	0.57	Equity per shr $49.79			9-30-95	42.8	...	3020	Dc	3.02	3.98	Δ4.27	3.09	....	3.98	9 Mo Sep	1.37	2.26	8
9	....	None Since Public			...	Nil	....	0.19	1.30	2.65	9-30-95	4.39	...	3374	Dc	d0.15	d0.06	Δ0.02	0.10	....	d0.02	9 Mo Sep	0.10	d0.02	9
10	1994	Q0.32	11-13-95	10-30	1.18	1.28	0.40	Book Value $21.83			12-31-94	p369	...	p52442	Dc	d14.36	0.08	Δ2.51	□[55]5.18	E4.35	4.62	9 Mo Sep	□3.76	3.20	10
11◆	....	0.06	1-2-96	12-14	0.08	[56]....	5%Stk	Book Value $7.08			9-30-95	1.07	187	961	Dc	*0.41	*0.72	Δ0.76	1.21	....	1.29	9 Mo Sep	0.88	0.96	11
12	....	Plan qtly div			...	1.18	....	Cv into 1 com				....	187	...	Dc	...	...	...	....	....	....				12
13	....	None Since Public			...	Nil	....	9.25	22.2	39.9	9-30-95	....	...	6429	Dc	...	...	...	p0.71	....	2.32	9 Mo Sep	p0.70	p2.31	13
14	1987	Q0.07	11-15-95	9-27	0.28	[56]....	†1.20	Equity per shr $0.37			9-30-95	37.0	...	10700	Dc	0.04	d0.73	d1.70	d0.79	....	d0.92	9 Mo Sep	0.08	d0.05	14
15	....	None Since Public			...	Nil	....	30.7	235	25.9	9-30-95	60.0	...	22280	Dc	1.03	1.09	1.23	1.34	....	1.33	9 Mo Sep	0.78	0.77	15
16◆	....	h[60]....	11-20-95	11-21	h[60]...	Nil	....	0.33	36.4	61.3	6-30-95	47.8	3513	1187	Dc	d0.88	d0.96	d2.06	d1.28	....	0.56	9 Mo Sep	d0.88	0.96	16
17	1991	Q0.19½	2-15-96	12-27	0.78	....	0.78	Cv into 1 com thru 6-30-93[62]				....	3550	...	Dc	...	...	...	....	....	....				17
18	1945	Q0.13	1-15-96	12-14	0.52	0.52	0.52	17.2	311	212	9-02-95	97.5	...	24893	My	0.55	□d0.14	0.88	1.60	0.18	0.34	3 Mo Aug	0.32	0.48	18
19	....	None Since Public			...	Nil	....	1.43	40.7	22.2	10-31-95	0.07	...	6492	Ap	...	...	...	pΔ[63]0.64	Δ0.91	0.97	6 Mo Oct	Δ0.42	0.48	19
20	....	None Since Public			...	Nil	....	31.6	75.4	90.2	12-31-94	105	...	★47995	Dc	pd3.10	pd1.71	0.77	0.23	....	d0.43	3 Mo Mar	0.53	d0.13	20
21◆	1966	Q0.08	1-26-96	12-27	0.31	0.32	0.29	33.3	277	195	9-30-95	107	...	44554	Dc	1.09	□0.71	□0.68	1.03	E1.85	1.52	9 Mo Sep	0.89	1.39	21
22	1994	Q0.47¼	1-16-96	12-28	1.89	1.89	0.84	Equity per shr $4.45			9-30-95	[64]658	...	16906	Dc	...	...	p0.42	p0.37	....	0.62	9 Mo Sep	0.02	□0.27	22
23	....	None Since Public			...	Nil	....	0.21	29.8	8.41	10-01-95	19.5	...	5867	Dc	0.57	0.74	0.02	d2.65	....	d2.16	9 Mo Sep	d0.58	d0.09	23
24	1918	Q0.27	12-10-95	11-15	1.06	1.08	0.94	54.2	248	69.0	9-30-95	15.4	23	5783	Dc	2.92	□1.86	1.73	2.58	....	3.41	9 Mo Sep	1.78	2.61	24
25	1993	Q0.02½	12-14-95	11-13	0.10	0.10	0.10	14.1	192	68.2	10-01-95	80.9	...	22649	Dc	p0.80	Δ0.97	1.25	1.48	....	1.72	9 Mo Sep	1.06	1.30	25
26	....	None Since Public			...	Nil	....	27.6	40.2	8.63	9-29-95	....	...	11393	Dc	...	...	...	pd0.10	....	0.04	9 Mo Sep	d0.11	0.03	26
27◆	1916	Q0.47	12-12-95	11-21	1.88	1.88	1.76	344	7613	3826	9-30-95	1213	...	419645	Dc	2.63	□2.82	2.91	3.13	E3.40	3.35	9 Mo Sep	2.34	2.56	27
28	1945	Q0.51	12-1-95	11-13	2.04	2.04	2.02	96.4	278	284	9-30-95	622	483	31315	Dc	2.46	Δ2.31	2.20	2.06	....	2.60	12 Mo Sep	1.74	2.60	28
29◆	1994	A0.10	9-29-95	9-13	0.10	0.10	0.10	4.07	24.7	5.57	9-30-95	....	...	6541	Mr	0.58	0.72	0.78	0.90	....	0.73	6 Mo Sep	0.46	0.29	29
30	1956	0.206	11-17-95	9-29	0.59	0.59	0.54	1633	2838	1139	12-31-94	976	...	225318	Je	□1.14	Δ1.22	Δ[66]1.25	1.07	....	1.07				30
31◆	....	0.006	7-10-78	6-27	...	Nil	....	35.0	188	140	9-30-95	258	...	91443	Dc	Δ0.80	Δ□0.53	□0.58	□1.32	E1.65	1.65	9 Mo Sep	□0.98	□1.31	31
32◆	....	None Paid			...	Nil	....	82.4	93.9	8.27	j12-31-94	0.21	...	p40715	Dc	d0.10	[67]d0.13	[68]0.03	0.37	....	j0.34	9 Mo Sep	0.32	0.29	32
33	1981	0.05	2-26-93	2-5	...	Nil	....	Equity per shr $10.25			8-31-95	33.0	...	1369	Nv	d0.59	d0.56	d0.73	□d1.62	....	d1.97	9 Mo Aug	Δ0.31	d0.04	33
34	1995	Q0.08	11-15-95	10-27	0.32	0.32	....	32.0	122	54.0	9-30-95	0.03	...	★23148	Je	...	...	...	p1.10	2.34	2.50	3 Mo Sep	0.27	0.43	34
35	1976	Q0.12	1-4-96	12-19	0.48	0.48	0.48	13.1	240	206	7-31-95	787	...	±52040	Ja	0.95	□±0.77	□±0.49	±0.87	....	0.43	9 Mo Oct	±0.70	±0.26	35
36	1992	Q0.13¼	1-4-96	12-19	0.53	0.53	0.53	....	...	...		....	...	28823	Ja	0.95	□±0.77	□±0.49	±0.87	....	0.43	9 Mo Oct	±0.70	±0.26	36
37	....	None Since Public			...	Nil	....	150	336	113	j9-29-95	36.9	1635	105864	Mr	d0.12	d0.01	0.16	0.27	....	j0.44	6 Mo Sep	0.05	0.22	37
38	1989	0.036	12-18-95	9-26	0.078	0.08	0.073	Book Value $8.43			3-31-95	15130	...	2880669	Mr	0.19	0.16	□0.13	0.14	....	0.14				38
39	....	None Since Public			...	Nil	....	5.80	8.81	1.00	9-30-95	....	...	3076	Mr	...	p0.23	p0.46	p0.55	....	0.56	6 Mo Sep	p0.28	0.29	39
40	1994	0.04	3-20-95	2-15	0.08	Nil	0.08	1.12	155	54.3	9-30-95	104	10	17563	Dc	...	...	p0.23	pd2.47	....	....	9 Mo Sep	n/a	d0.71	40
41	1995	Q0.14	12-6-95	11-17	0.36	0.56	....	Book Value $21.53			9-30-95	368	...	7274	Mr	...	...	p0.47	0.97	....	1.59	6 Mo Sep	0.26	0.88	41
42	1993	Q0.05	1-17-96	12-28	0.19	0.20	0.15	Equity per shr $16.84			9-30-95	49.8	...	9620	Dc	p1.62	Δpd0.05	1.90	1.73	....	2.26	9 Mo Sep	1.21	1.74	42
43	1902	Q0.92½	12-11-95	11-2	3.62½	3.70	3.40	597	11724	13698	9-30-95	4793	94	394473	Dc	4.65	□3.13	5.07	□4.28	E6.50	5.22	9 Mo Sep	□3.00	3.94	43
44	1943	Q0.27	1-1-96	12-13	1.06	1.08	1.02	0.73	12.9	19.0	6-30-95	57.5	...	3209	Sp	1.48	1.96	1.79	1.78	P1.26	1.26				44
45	....	None Since Public			...	Nil	....	29.2	91.7	76.4	9-30-95	270	3750	54050	Dc	d0.36	d0.09	0.40	d0.76	Ed0.78	d0.80	9 Mo Sep	d0.32	d0.36	45
46	....	None Since Public			...	Nil	....	4.70	37.6	67.0	9-30-95	345	...	±32187	Dc	...	...	...	pd1.38	....	....	9 Mo Sep	n/a	pd1.03	46
47◆	1984	Q0.06	2-16-96	1-31	0.20	0.24	0.20	5.83	9.59	1.79	9-30-95	....	...	4542	Dc	0.59	0.55	0.39	0.39	....	0.52	9 Mo Sep	0.28	0.41	47
48	....	None Since Public			...	Nil	....	0.98	4.45	3.83	9-30-95	7.68	...	3088	Dc	p0.07	p0.12	p0.13	pΔ0.10	....	....	9 Mo Sep	n/a	d0.12	48
49◆	1959	Q0.15	12-7-95	11-22	0.58	0.60	0.505	17.8	345	208	9-26-95	53.2	...	29642	Mr	0.93	□1.12	Δ1.41	2.24	E2.40	2.27	6 Mo Sep	1.04	1.07	49
50◆	....	None Since Public			...	Nil	....	....	542	221	9-30-95	438	...	33063	Dc	p0.70	□0.86	p1.19	0.99	....	0.72	9 Mo Sep	0.76	0.49	50
51	....	None Paid			...	Nil	....	25.7	28.0	3.96	9-30-95	8.26	...	13291	Mr	d0.05	d1.20	d1.58	d1.02	....	d1.49	6 Mo Sep	d0.32	d0.79	51
52	....	None Since Public			...	Nil	....	19.4	35.3	6.27	9-30-95	....	...	10073	Dc	0.01	0.26	0.39	d0.47	....	d0.07	9 Mo Sep	d0.50	d0.10	52

◆**Stock Splits & Divs By Line Reference Index** [1]3-for-2,'93:2-for-1,'94. [4]6-for-5,'91,'93,'94. [11]Adj for 5%,'94:4-for-3,'95. [16]No adj for stk dstr Union Property Inv,'95. [21]2-for-1,'95. [27]2-for-1,'94. [29]3-for-2,'91(twice). [31]5-for-2,'93. [32]May'95 & prior pricing in Cdn dollars. [47]3-for-2,'91. [49]2-for-1,'93. [50]3-for-2,'93.

¶ S&P 500 # MidCap 400 ✥ SmallCap 600 • Options

Index	Ticker	Name of Issue (Call Price of Pfd. Stocks)	Market	Com. Rank. & Pfd. Rating	Inst. Hold Cos	Inst. Hold Shs. (000)	Principal Business	Price Range 1971-93 High	1971-93 Low	1994 High	1994 Low	1995 High	1995 Low	Dec. Sales in 100s	December, 1995 Last Sale Or Bid High	Low	Last	%Div Yield	P-E Ratio	Total Return % Annualized 12 Mo	36 Mo	60 Mo
#1•[1]	MOLX	✔Molex Inc	NNM	A	268	22396	Terminals,connectors,switch	24½	3/16	28¾	19⅜	37	24¾	28544	35¼	30½	31¾	0.2	24	15.4	24.4	23.4
2•	MOLXA	Cl'A'(non-vtg)	NNM	A	206	34505		22⅜	8⅜	27	19⅜	34½	23⅝	35465	34¼	29	30⅝	0.2	23	22.2	25.7	23.1
3•[2]	MOL.A	Molson Cos Cl'A'	To,Mo	B	28	3447	Brewer:chem specialities	36	3⅞	28⅞	17¾	24½	18⅜	7517	23	21⅜	22½	3.2	38	18.6	−4.7	...
4	MOL.B	Class'B' (vtg)	To,Mo	B	4	477	retail lumber & bldg mat'ls	36	4	28¼	18	24½	19	495	23½	22	22¾	3.2	39	20.0	−4.1	...
5•[1]	MLTN	✔Molten Metal Technology	NNM	NR	108	11127	Enviro tech/waste recovery	27½	10	31	16	41¼	13¾	36232	38¾	29¼	32⅝	...	d	94.8	...	...
6	MCCO	✔Monaco Coach	NNM	NR	27	961	Mfr motor coaches	16	10	16⅞	12¾	16¾	8	2295	10¾	8¾	9	...	7	−40.5	...	...
7	MMO	✔Monarch Mach Tool	NY,B,Ch	B−	36	2073	Lathes for metal-wkg indy	32¾	2⅛	12½	9	15¼	9⅛	793	13⅛	11⅜	12½	1.6	..	28.8	3.6	6.0
8	MONE	✔Money Store	NNM,Ch,Ph	NR	141	28513	Consumer & commercial loans	4⅞	1 13/16	5⅞	4⅛	22⅛	4¾	99918	20	15½	15⅝	0.5	19	228	77.3	...
9	WVQ	Monongahela Pwr 8% 'QUIDS'	NY	....[51]	..	...	Qtly Income Debt Securities	....	....	....	....	26¼	24⅜	2277	26¼	25⅜	26	7.7	..	...	...	...
10	MNRO	✔Monro Muffler Brake	NNM	NR	46	2907	Provides auto repair services	15⅞	9⅛	20	14¼	19	13⅝	611	15¼	13¾	13⅞	s...	13	−13.2	9.0	...
¶11•[1]	MTC	✔Monsanto Co	NY,B,C,Ch,P,Ph	A−	788	77585	Major chemical producer	76	8¼	86½	66½	124¾	68¼	71922	124¾	114¼	122½	2.3	19	82.0	33.7	24.8
#12	MTP	✔Montana Power	NY,B,C,Ch,P,Ph	B+	220	15877	Utility: electric & gas	28⅜	8⅜	25⅞	21¾	24⅛	21⅛	35524	23⅛	21¾	22⅝	7.1	13	4.9	1.2	9.2
13	MNT	✔Montedison S p A ADS[52]	NY,Ch	NR	21	1566	Int'l chemical concern	29	½	10⅛	5¼	8⅜	5¾	2528	6⅞	5¾	6½	...	d	−8.8	−4.6	−9.0
14	MBBC	✔Monterey Bay Bancorp	NNM	NR	8	1072	General banking, California	....	....	....	....	13⅛	8½	3098	12⅜	11⅝	11⅝	...	..	...	...	...
15	MOG.B	✔Moog, Inc Cl'B'	AS	B−	7	17	Mfr electrohydraulic ctrl sys	30⅞	13/16	15⅛	9¾	18	11⅝	120	18	15¼	18	...	18	23.1	37.8	13.0
16	MOG.A	✔ Class'A'(Ltd-vtg)	AS,B	B−	30	2677		31	1 13/16	9⅝	7	17½	8⅝	1859	17½	14	17¼	...	17	86.5	42.2	23.0
¶17•[3]	MCL	✔Moore Corp Ltd	NY,To,B,Ch,Mo,P	B−	274	37188	Produces business forms	33¾	7⅞	20⅞	16¼	23½	17½	25924	18⅞	17½	18¾	5.0	7	3.4	7.9	1.4
18	MHCO	✔Moore-Handley,Inc	NNM	B−	4	116	Dstr hardware/building prod	19¼	3½	5½	3	5¾	3½	54	3⅝	3½	3⅝B	...	8	−14.7	−8.6	−1.9
19	MMD	✔Moore Medical Corp	AS,Ch,Ph	B−	25	1071	Dstr drugs,med'l/beauty prod	33¼	5/16	18	10⅜	13⅜	8½	1925	11¾	10⅜	10¾	...	13	−16.5	−9.0	22.6
20	MOOV	✔Moovies Inc	NNM	NR	27	2184	Video specialty stores	....	....	....	....	23¼	10	31269	16¼	10	13½	...	29	...	...	...
21	MG	✔Morgan Group	AS	NR	9	171	Transport svcs-mfg homes,RVS	9½	6¾	10	7	10⅝	7	630	8⅜	7¾	8⅜	1.0	10	20.8	...	...
¶22•[4]	JPM	✔Morgan (J.P.)	NY,B,C,Ch,P,Ph	B+	911	116477	Comm'l&wholesale bkg,NY	79⅜	7¾	72	55⅛	82½	56⅛	96839	82⅜	78½	80¼	4.0	13	48.7	11.2	17.4
23	MOR	✔Morgan Keegan Inc	NY,Ch,Ph	B	54	5009	Hldg:regional brokerage	10	1 3/16	9	7⅞	13⅞	7⅞	3099	13⅞	12⅛	12⅝	1.9	10	54.5	25.0	58.0
24	MGN	✔Morgan Products Ltd	NY,Ch	C	30	3789	Mfrs,dstr building products	30¾	5⅜	9	4½	7⅞	5⅛	1596	6⅛	5⅝	5⅞	...	d	−4.1	−7.3	−1.2
25	MSZ	Morgan Stan Fin 7.80% Cp Uts[54]	NY	NR	13	250	Deb & Pur contract equity unit	....	....	25⅜	19⅜	25¼	20⅝	8582	25¼	24¼	25¼	7.7	..	31.2	...	...
26	MSU	Morgan Stan Fin 7.82% Cp Uts[55]	NY	NR	14	548	Deb & Pur contract equity unit	25½	24½	25⅝	19¾	25½	20¾	5992	25½	24⅜	25⅛	7.8	..	29.1	...	...
27	MSP	Morgan Stan Fin 8.20% Cp Uts[56]	NY	NR	..	...	Deb & Pur contract equity unit	....	....	....	....	26	24	11070	26	25	26	7.9	..	...	...	...
28	MSE	Morgan Stan Fin 8.40% Cp Uts[57]	NY	NR	7	188	Deb & Pur contract equity unit	....	....	....	....	26⅛	24⅜	5282	26⅛	25¼	26	8.1	..	...	...	...
29	MSV	Morgan Stan Fin 9% Cp Uts[58]	NY	NR	9	54	Deb & Pur contract equity unit	....	....	....	....	26⅞	24¾	1454	26½	26	26½	8.5	..	...	...	...
¶30•[5]	MS	✔Morgan Stanley Group	NY,B,Ch,P,Ph	B+	334	36954	Invest't banking,brokerage	89⅝	12¾	80⅜	55	99¾	57¾	96444	89¼	77⅜	80⅝	1.6	12	36.0	14.9	26.3
31	MXT	Morgan StanGp 6.00%Tele'PERQS'[63]	[6]	NR	7	185	Telefonos de Mexico'PERQS'	....	....	64	42⅛	47	30¾	1917	39	33¾	35⅝	10.6	..	−17.8	...	...
32	IGS	Morgan StanGp 6.50% IGT'PERQS'[65]	[7]	NR	4	59	Int'l Game Tech 'PERQS'	....	....	21¾	15⅝	18⅜	12⅛	2395	14¼	12⅛	12¼	10.1	..	−18.7	...	...
33	XPC	Morgan StanGp 7%CiscoSy'PERQS'[67]	[6]	NR	9	223	Cisco Systems'PERQS'	....	....	32¾	30⅜	43¾	31⅜	1055	42⅞	40⅝	41½	5.4	..	36.7	...	...
34	MR	✔Morgan's Foods	AS,Ch	C	12	1817	Ky Fried Chicken franchise	13½	⅜	3	1 3/16	1½	9/16	8750	¾	9/16	⅝	...	10	−52.4	−28.2	−9.0
35•[8]	MRN	✔Morrison Knudsen	NY,B,Ch,P	NR	177	17285	Constr/engin'g:mining:mfr	30⅜	1 13/16	29⅞	12¼	13	4	101425	6¼	4	4½	...	d	−63.8	−39.1	−24.4
#36•[9]	RI	✔Morrison Restaurants	NY	A	149	16660	Public & contract food svcs	26¼	1/16	29¾	20⅞	27⅞	12½	25797	17	12½	14	2.6	11	−41.6	−6.8	15.2
¶37•[5]	MII	✔Morton International	NY	B+	558	92692	Specialty chems,salt,airbags	33½	10½	37¼	25½	36⅛	26¼	77094	36⅛	33⅞	35⅞	1.4	18	29.0	23.0	50.8
38	MSCM	✔MOSCOM Corp	NNM	B−	18	608	Telecommun's mgmt sys	9¼	1¼	12⅜	4⅛	11¼	5¾	13062	8¼	6	8⅛	0.5	74	−2.6	22.5	9.9
✥39	MOSI	✔Mosinee Paper	NNM	B	59	4004	Paper & paper products	34½	1/16	32¾	22½	26¾	21¼	2153	26⅛	23¼	25¾	1.4	14	26.5	12.2	9.7
40	MOTO	✔Moto Photo	NSC	C	10	209	One-hour photo processing	6⅜	7/16	3⅜	1⅞	2⅞	1 7/16	2319	1⅞	1½	1 9/16	...	20	−34.2	−7.9	20.1
¶41•[10]	MOT	✔Motorola, Inc	NY,B,Ch,P,Ph	A	1533	357477	Semiconductors:communic eq	53¾	2⅛	61⅛	42⅛	82½	51½	895913	62½	56	57	0.7	18	−2.6	30.3	35.4
42	MOVI	✔Movie Gallery	NNM	NR	82	6824	Own,oper video stores	....	....	32½	14	50	21	47657	34¾	23	30½	...	26	20.8	...	...
43	MSI	✔Movie Star Inc	AS	C	11	1200	Mfr women's apparel	3⅝	3/16	2	1	1¼	3/16	5068	7/16	5/16	⅜	...	d	−66.7	−35.2	−24.2
44	MPSI	MPSI Systems	NSC	B−	2	109	Testing&simulat'n softwr prd	86¼	1¼	7	2¼	9¼	1¾	90	6½	4¾	6¼	...	9	...	...	...
✥45	MSCA	✔M.S. Carriers	NNM	B+	107	8398	Motor carrier,gen'l freight	26½	4	28½	17¾	25¼	15¼	10049	20¼	18½	20	...	17	−5.9	0.4	17.4
46	MSFI	✔MS Financial	NNM	NR	16	1513	Auto loan financing svcs	....	12	....	....	13⅞	5⅜	21866	7½	5⅜	6⅞	...	10	...	...	...
47	MSM	MSC Industrial Direct'A'	NY	NR	..	...	Mkt industrial prd to indl co	....	....	....	....	27⅝	19	54299	27⅝	19	27½	...	47	...	...	...
48	MSR	✔MSR Exploration	AS,To,Vc	NR	2	39	Oil/gas explor,dev,prod'n	18	¼	2¼	½	2 3/16	15/16	1533	1¼	1	1⅛	...	d	−47.1	14.5	−12.9
49	MTIC	MTI Technology	NNM	NR	19	2628	Design/mfr storage software	....	....	10	3	4⅝	1⅜	28673	2½	1 9/16	2⅜	...	d	−34.5	...	...
50	MTLI	✔MTL Inc	NNM	NR	24	2285	Bulk transport truck'g svc	....	....	18⅜	10½	16¼	11¼	1830	14	12¾	14	...	8	19.1	...	...
51	MTSC	✔MTS Systems	NNM	B+	58	2411	Mfr testing systems: services	32½	¾	32½	20¼	35½	22	4145	35¼	31	33	1.9	14	53.4	18.2	19.0
✥52	MLI	✔Mueller Industries	NY,Ch,Ph	NR	118	10334	Mfr fabricated steel prod	18⅝	3½	19⅜	13½	29½	14¼	8737	29½	23½	29¼	...	13	99.3	37.0	...

Uniform Footnote Explanations-See Page 4. Other: [1]CBOE:Cycle 1. [2]Vc:Cycle 1. [3]NY:Cycle 1,To:Cycle 2. [4]Ph:Cycle 3. [5]Ph:Cycle 2. [6]AS [7]AS,Ph [8]Ph:Cycle 1. [9]NY:Cycle 1. [10]ASE:Cycle 1. [51]Rated 'A' by S&P. [52]ADS's represent'g 10 ord shrs par 1000 lire. [53]®$0.73,'94. [54]Ea rep$25 amt 7.80% Sub Deb 2-28-2014&Pur cont. [55]Ea rep $25 amt 7.82%Sub Deb 11-30-2013&Pur cont.. [56]Ea rep $25 amt 8.20%Sub Deb 11-30-2015&Pur cont. [57]Ea rep$25 amt 8.40% Sub Deb 8-30-2015 &Pur cont. [58]Ea rep $25 amt 9% Sub Deb 2-28-2015&Pur cont. [59]Incl ESOP pfd. [60]Fiscal Dec'91 & prior. [61]®$4.03,'95. [62]Fiscal Jan'95 & prior. [63]Perfromance Equity-Linked Red Qtly-Pay Sec. [64]Co can exted to 10-8-97. [65]Performance Equity-Linked Red Qtrly-Pay Sec. [66]Co can extend to 7-8-97. [67]Performance Equity-Linked Red Qtly-Pay Sec. [68]Co can extend to 11-22-97. [69]Excl $1.3M subsid pfd.

Index	Cash Divs. Ea. Yr. Since	Dividends: Latest Payment Period $	Date	Ex. Div.	Total $ So Far 1995	Ind. Rate	Paid 1994	Financial Position Mil-$ Cash& Equiv.	Curr. Assets	Curr. Liab.	Balance Sheet Date	Capitalization Lg Trm Debt Mil-$	Shs. 000 Pfd.	Com.	Earnings $ Per Shr. Years End	1991	1992	1993	1994	1995	Last 12 Mos.	Interim Earnings Period	$ per Shr. 1994	1995	Index
1◆	1976	Q0.01½	1-25-96	12-27	0.039	0.06	0.026	253	703	247	9-30-95	8.35	...	±100737	Je	±0.67	±0.69	□±0.76	±0.96	±1.24	1.31	3 Mo Sep	±0.28	±0.35	1
2◆	1990	Q0.01½	1-25-96	12-27	0.039	0.06	0.026	....	...	...		....	...	50649	Je	±0.67	±0.69	□±0.76	±0.96	±1.24	1.31	3 Mo Sep	±0.28	±0.35	2
3◆	1950	gQ0.18	1-1-96	12-4	g0.72	0.72	g0.72	110	973	875	j3-31-95	545	...	±57732	Mr	±2.25	±2.76	±2.13	±1.49	....	j0.59	6 Mo Sep	±1.40	±0.50	3
4◆	1944	gQ0.18	1-1-96	12-4	g0.72	0.72	g0.72	....	...	...		....	...	14517	Mr	±2.25	±2.76	±2.13	±1.49	....	j0.59	6 Mo Sep	±1.40	±0.50	4
5	....	None Since Public			...	Nil	....	91.0	104	13.4	9-30-95	22.9	...	22516	Dc	...	pd0.52	d0.69	d0.67	....	d0.30	9 Mo Sep	d0.47	d0.10	5
6	....	None Since Public			...	Nil	....	0.24	20.1	14.2	12-31-94	....	...	4401	Dc	...	p0.69	0.87	1.33	....	1.21	9 Mo Sep	1.01	0.89	6
7	1913	Q0.05	12-1-95	11-16	0.20	0.20	0.20	1.71	68.9	32.6	9-30-95	8.00	15	3745	Dc	0.30	d1.94	Δd0.26	d0.39	....	0.09	9 Mo Sep	d0.35	0.13	7
8◆	1992	Q0.021	12-1-95	12-4	0.068	0.08	0.047	Equity per shr $4.39			9-30-95	961	...	51328	Dc	0.33	0.34	0.48	0.62	....	0.81	9 Mo Sep	0.42	0.61	8
9	....	Plan qtly div			...	2.00	....	Co opt redm fr 6-19-2000 at $25				40.0	...	...	Dc	...	...	...	....	....	....				9
10◆	....	5%Stk	8-7-95	6-21	5%Stk	Stk	5%Stk	4.72	23.7	20.2	9-30-95	32.0	92	6858	Mr	0.76	0.81	0.90	1.18	E1.10	1.01	6 Mo Sep	0.84	0.67	10
11	1925	Q0.69	12-12-95	11-8	2.70	2.76	2.47	144	4179	2964	9-30-95	1685	...	116278	Dc	2.33	□3.67	4.10	5.32	E6.40	6.22	9 Mo Sep	4.81	5.71	11
12	1935	Q0.40	2-1-96	1-10	1.60	1.60	1.60	17.0	236	284	9-30-95	618	1920	54579	Dc	2.03	2.02	1.98	2.00	....	1.79	12 Mo Sep	2.11	1.79	12
13	1994	0.353	2-3-94	1-6	...	Nil	0.353	619	8339	12429	12-31-94	3397	736730	5321974	Dc	0.45	d0.36	d3.70	d0.36	....	d0.36				13
14	....	None Since Public			...	Nil	....	Book Value $13.55			9-30-95	47.1	...	3594	Dc	...	...	p0.95	n/a	....	....	9 Mo Sep	n/a	0.14	14
15	....	0.05	10-5-88	9-2	...	Nil	....	7.05	272	105	6-30-95	177	100	±7726	Sp	±0.97	±d0.88	□±0.66	Δ±0.22	P±1.00	1.00				15
16	....	0.07	10-5-88	9-2	...	Nil	....	....	...	...		....	...	6048	Sp	±0.97	±d0.88	□±0.66	Δ±0.22	P±1.00	1.00				16
17	1934	tQ0.23½	1-2-96	11-29	0.94	0.94	t0.94	590	1378	530	6-30-95	74.2	...	99819	Dc	0.91	d0.02	d0.78	1.22	E2.70	2.86	9 Mo Sep	0.82	2.46	17
18	....	None Since Public			...	Nil	....	0.13	40.3	27.0	9-30-95	4.02	...	2165	Dc	d0.43	0.59	0.36	0.65	....	0.43	9 Mo Sep	0.52	0.30	18
19	....	None Paid			...	Nil	....	0.05	77.9	28.3	9-30-95	....	...	2881	Dc	*0.19	0.80	1.08	1.21	....	0.80	9 Mo Sep	0.96	0.55	19
20	....	None Since Public			...	Nil	....	7.19	11.3	5.04	p9-30-95	3.32	...	8161	Dc	...	...	...	p0.36	....	0.47	9 Mo Sep	p0.23	p0.34	20
21	1994	Q0.02	1-16-96	12-28	0.08	0.08	0.08	4.80	21.1	12.9	9-30-95	2.74	1494	±2574	Dc	±d1.04	±*0.15	±0.71	±[53]0.75	....	0.87	9 Mo Sep	±0.59	±0.71	21
22	1892	Q0.81	1-12-96	12-21	3.00	3.24	2.72	Book Value $51.34			9-30-95	9450	2694	187544	Dc	Δ5.63	Δ5.66	□8.48	6.02	E6.35	5.59	9 Mo Sep	5.05	4.62	22
23◆	1984	Q0.06	1-15-96	12-13	0.167	0.24	0.193	Equity per shr $7.30			10-31-95	....	...	20128	Jl	0.38	1.25	1.44	1.46	1.17	1.28	3 Mo Oct	0.33	0.44	23
24	....	None Since Public			...	Nil	....	1.42	89.9	25.2	9-30-95	39.5	...	8645	Dc	d0.96	d1.20	0.11	d1.10	....	d0.10	9 Mo Sep	d1.13	d0.13	24
25	1994	Q0.48¾	11-30-95	11-13	1.95	1.95	1.582	Pur cont:pur0.125 7.80% cm Pfd 8-30-2013,$25				....	...	★8000	Dc	...	...	...	....	....	....	Red fr 2-28-99 Debs $25:Pur cont $0.025			25
26	1994	Q0.489	11-30-95	11-13	1.95½	1.96	1.96	Pur cont:pur0.125 7.82%cm Pfd 5-30-2013,$25				....	...	29688	Dc	...	...	...	....	....	....	Red fr 11-30-98 Debs $25:Pur cont $0.025			26
27	1995	0.239	11-30-95	11-13	0.239	2.05	....	Pur cont:pur0.125 8.20% cm Pfd 5-30-2015,$25				....	...	★6000	Dc	...	...	...	....	....	....	Red fr 11-30-2000 Debs$25:pur cont $0.025			27
28	1995	0.694	11-30-95	11-13	0.694	2.10	....	Pur cont:pur0.125 8.40% cm Pfd 2-28-2015,$25				....	...	★7000	Dc	...	...	...	....	....	....	Red fr8-30-2000 Debs$25:pur cont $0.025			28
29	1995	Q0.56¼	11-30-95	11-13	1.74⅜	2.25	....	Pur cont:pur 0.125 9% cm Pfd 8-30-2014,$25				....	...	★5350	Dc	...	...	...	....	....	....	Red fr 2-28-2000 Debs $25:Pur cont $0.025			29
30◆	1986	Q0.32	10-26-95	10-4	0.96	1.28	1.20	Equity per shr $52.37			8-31-95	9111	[59]11994	77647	Nv	[60]5.93	5.90	9.59	[61][62]4.18	E6.90	....	7 Mo Aug	n/a	4.80	30
31	1995	Q0.94½	1-1-96	12-13	3.89½	3.78	....	Int based on TeleFonos de Mex com as defined				....	...	★2000	Dc	...	...	...	....	....	....	Mature 10-1-97[64]			31
32	1994	Q0.309	1-1-96	12-13	1.235	1.24	0.292	Int based on Int Game Tech com as defined				....	...	★1750	Dc	...	...	...	....	....	....	Mature 7-1-97[66]			32
33	1995	Q0.562	11-15-95	10-27	2.28	2.25	....	Int based on Cisco Systems com as defined				....	...	★1500	Dc	...	...	...	....	....	....	Mature 11-15-97[68]			33
34	....	0.04	6-21-74	5-24	...	Nil	....	3.02	3.67	4.06	11-05-95	10.7	...	17816	Fb	Nil	d0.01	Δd0.04	d0.02	....	0.06	36 Wk Nov	0.01	0.09	34
35◆	1973	Q0.20	1-3-95	11-17	0.20	Nil	0.80	63.3	655	714	9-30-95	....	...	33046	Dc	1.30	□0.44	1.15	d10.75	Ed1.25	d14.80	9 Mo Sep	d1.05	d5.10	35
36◆	1936	Q0.092	10-31-95	10-11	0.355	0.37	0.337	8.71	70.8	121	9-02-95	76.0	...	34579	My	0.71	0.87	1.00	1.20	1.73	1.33	3 Mo Aug	0.67	0.27	36
37◆	1989	Q0.13	12-11-95	11-22	0.48	0.52	0.407	76.2	1240	568	9-30-95	219	...	148360	Je	0.95	0.98	□0.86	1.51	1.96	2.00	3 Mo Sep	0.41	0.45	37
38	1990	S0.02	7-24-95	6-30	0.04	0.04	0.04	5.39	11.6	2.43	9-30-95	....	...	6822	Dc	0.30	0.01	d0.59	d0.06	....	0.11	9 Mo Sep	d0.09	0.08	38
39◆	1942	Q0.09	2-1-96	1-16	0.172	0.364	0.327	0.79	71.4	37.9	9-30-95	90.0	[69]...	7863	Dc	0.11	□...	1.22	□1.65	....	1.85	9 Mo Sep	□1.08	1.28	39
40	....	None Paid			...	Nil	....	0.82	9.42	10.8	9-30-95	7.97	1000	7786	Dc	d0.03	d0.04	d0.10	d0.07	....	0.08	9 Mo Sep	d0.11	0.04	40
41◆	1942	Q0.10	1-17-96	12-13	0.40	0.40	0.26½	994	10050	7384	9-30-95	1961	...	590963	Dc	0.86	□1.08	1.78	2.65	E3.14	3.08	9 Mo Sep	1.79	2.22	41
42	....	None Since Public			...	Nil	....	3.12	12.0	26.5	9-30-95	0.55	...	11856	Dc	...	...	p0.56	p0.70	....	1.17	9 Mo Sep	p0.44	0.91	42
43	....	0.027	4-30-72	4-7	...	Nil	....	0.10	48.7	26.0	6-30-95	22.5	...	13960	Je	0.08	0.02	0.16	Δd0.30	d0.36	d0.48	3 Mo Sep	0.04	d0.08	43
44◆	....	None Paid			...	Nil	....	1.31	8.21	6.26	9-30-95	....	...	2752	Sp	d15.73	d6.54	Δ1.21	0.53	0.72	0.72				44
45◆	....	None Since Public			...	Nil	....	3.36	45.4	45.8	9-30-95	38.3	...	12878	Dc	0.73	0.97	Δ1.13	1.31	....	1.17	9 Mo Sep	0.93	0.79	45
46	....	None Since Public			...	Nil	....	Book Value $4.19			9-30-95	....	...	10800	Dc	...	...	...	p0.48	....	0.70	9 Mo Sep	0.36	0.58	46
47	....	None Since Public			...	Nil	....	....	...	...		p....	...	±★31263	Au	...	...	...	....	±p0.58	0.58				47
48	....	None Paid			...	Nil	....	0.30	2.07	0.93	9-30-95	5.47	...	14412	Dc	d0.63	Δd0.09	Δd0.05	Δd0.07	....	d0.07	9 Mo Sep	Δd0.05	d0.05	48
49	....	None Since Public			...	Nil	....	2.45	59.6	38.8	9-30-95	29.9	...	19420	Mr	...	pd1.77	p0.18	d1.34	....	d1.71	6 Mo Sep	d0.02	d0.39	49
50	....	None Since Public			...	Nil	....	0.72	30.5	21.8	12-31-94	25.7	...	4516	Dc	0.40	□0.90	1.44	1.61	....	1.68	9 Mo Sep	1.23	1.30	50
51	1967	Q0.16	1-2-96	12-6	0.56	0.64	0.56	8.74	132	67.0	9-30-95	11.4	...	4679	Sp	2.25	1.07	2.27	1.85	2.30	2.30				51
52◆	....	None Since Public			...	Nil	....	31.2	206	81.2	9-30-95	62.7	...	17335	Dc	d2.25	Δ0.81	1.01	1.41	....	2.18	9 Mo Sep	0.92	1.69	52

◆Stock Splits & Divs By Line Reference Index [1]5-for-4,'92,'95:5-for-4 in Cl'A','94. [2]5-for-4,'92,'94,'95. [3]3-for-2,'91. [4]3-for-2,'91. [8]3-for-2,'94,'95:5-for-2,'95. [10]Adj to 5%,'95. [23]4-for-3,'91:3-for-2,'92,'93,'95. [30]2-for-1,'91. [35]2-for-1,'92. [36]3-for-2,'92,'93. [37]3-for-1,'94. [39]10%,'95. [41]2-for-1,'93,'94. [44]1-for-10 REVERSE,'93. [45]2-for-1,'92. [52]2-for-1,'95.

¶ S&P 500 # MidCap 400 ✣ SmallCap 600 • Options Index	Ticker	Name of Issue (Call Price of Pfd. Stocks)	Market	Com. Rank. & Pfd. Rating	Inst. Hold Cos	Inst. Hold Shs. (000)	Principal Business	Price Range 1971-93 High	1971-93 Low	1994 High	1994 Low	1995 High	1995 Low	Dec. Sales in 100s	December, 1995 Last Sale Or Bid High	Low	Last	%Div Yield	P-E Ratio	Total Return % Annualized 12 Mo	36 Mo	60 Mo
1	LABL	✔Multi-Color Corp	NNM	C	12	258	Printed product labels	17¼	5	10¾	5½	6	2¼	1706	3½	2¼	2⅜	...	d	−56.8	−34.0	−21.1
2•[1]	MUL	✔Multicare Cos	NY,Ph	NR	99	7332	Long-term/special hlthcare sv	18¼	10	21¾	15	24¼	16¾	7429	24¼	20¼	24	...	20	23.1	...	...
3	MUN	✔Munsingwear Inc	NY,Ph	NR	17	214	Intimate apparel:mens wear	18⅞	¼	8⅞	4½	9⅝	6¼	741	7½	6¼	6½	...	d	−8.8	−6.7	87.4
#4•[2]	MUR	✔Murphy Oil	NY,B,Ch,P,Ph	B	237	32408	International integrated oil	64	4⅛	49⅛	37⅞	45⅜	37½	13370	42½	39⅜	41½	3.1	30	1.9	8.7	4.5
✣5•[3]	MLG	✔Musicland Stores	NY,Ph	NR	95	21644	Sell pre-recrd music,video prd	23⅜	10⅛	22½	8¾	11	3¾	51311	6⅜	3¾	4¼	...	d	−55.3	−27.2	...
✣6	MM	✔Mutual Risk Management	NY	NR	..	...	Provides risk mgmt services	32¾	11⅜	29¾	21⅛	45¾	24⅞	4909	45¾	39¾	45¾	0.9	22	77.7	22.4	...
✣7•[4]	MYCO	✔Mycogen Corp	NNM	↓C	61	11324	Mfrs & markets biopesticides	20¾	4½	12	8	17¼	7¾	16394	17¼	11¾	17	...	d	113	6.7	5.9
✣8	MYE	✔Myers Indus	AS	A	77	6999	Tire svc eqp:plastic prod	18½	3/16	16¾	11¾	16¾	11⅞	2554	16¾	15¾	16⅜	1.0	16	48.4	9.8	26.8
#9•[4]	MYL	✔Mylan Labs	NY,B,Ch,P	A−	379	61485	Pharmaceutical products	25⅛	1/64	19⅞	10⅜	24½	16½	83837	24½	21¾	23½	0.7	21	33.5	6.7	29.6
10•[3]	MYLX	✔Mylex Corp	NNM	C	66	5089	Mfr computer/electronic prod	7¾	1/16	11¾	3⅝	20⅝	8	47656	20¼	17⅜	19⅛	...	27	84.3	45.2	60.2
11	MYR	✔MYR Group[56]	NY,Ch,Ph	B	23	1362	Transmiss'n sys for elec util	29½	⅞	10¼	7⅜	11⅞	8	1039	11½	10	10⅝	1.8	11	30.3	−3.0	−1.3
12	MYGN	✔Myriad Genetics	NNM	NR	..	...	R&D human gene products	....	....	....	....	39	18	6112	35	26¼	32⅝	...	d	...	...	...
13	MYSW	✔MySoftware Co	NNM	NR	29	1702	Dvlp small bus software	....	....	....	....	15½	10½	2984	15½	10¾	12¾	...	35	...	...	...
14•[5]	NA	✔Nabisco Holdings'A'	NY,Ch,Ph	NR	197	49464	Mfr,dstr packaged foods	....	....	....	....	32⅝	24½	96305	32⅝	28	32⅝	1.7	26	...	...	...
#15•[1]	NBR	✔Nabors Industries	AS,To,Ch,Ph	B−	198	50970	Contract drill'g & services	36⅞	⅜	7⅞	5¾	11⅜	6⅛	77619	11⅜	9½	11¼	...	19	69.8	21.6	17.0
16	NRC	✔NAC Re Corp	NY,Ph	B+	118	15951	Hldg co:reinsurance	44¾	7¾	34	24	39	28¼	6085	36¼	31⅝	36	0.6	15	12.7	−2.9	11.2
¶17	NC	✔NACCO Indus Inc Cl'A'	NY,B,Ch,Ph	B+	192	2906	Forklifts,sm applncs/Coal mng	70½	2 5/16	64	45¾	64	46⅞	2373	59	55¼	55½	1.3	8	17.4	3.4	14.5
18	NATL	✔NAI Technologies	NNM	B−	19	1742	Computer periph:electr instr	11½	1/32	7¼	2⅛	3½	1⅛	14691	2 1/16	1⅛	1½	...	d	−44.2	−37.2	−5.7
¶19•[6]	NLC	✔Nalco Chemical	NY,B,Ch,P	A	368	49536	Specialty chemicals	42¼	3¼	37⅞	29¾	38⅝	28⅛	38726	30¾	29¼	30⅛	3.3	14	−7.4	−2.0	4.6
20	NTAIF	Nam Tai Electronics	NNM	NR	9	812	Mfr electronic products	21¼	½	15½	9⅜	17¼	7⅞	7316	13⅞	10¾	11¾	0.2	9	9.5	−10.6	32.6
21	NAN	✔Nantucket Indus	AS,B	C	10	286	Mfr hosiery & underwear	14½	1/16	7⅝	2¾	6⅛	2½	1332	3	2½	2¾	...	d	−37.1	−42.2	−3.3
✣22	NAFC	✔Nash Finch Co	NNM	A−	78	4845	Dstr food & non-food prod	27½	2	18½	15	20¾	15¼	6601	19¾	17¾	18¼	e3.9	12	18.9	3.4	5.2
✣23•[4]	NSH	✔Nashua Corp	NY,To,B,Ch,Ph	B−	63	4575	Office copy & computer prod	44⅞	4¼	30⅞	19⅜	21	12¼	5228	16½	12⅞	13⅝	5.3	d	−31.3	−19.1	−14.5
24	NAB	Natl Australia Bk ADR[59]	NY,Ch	NR	49	2759	Commercial banking,Australia	43⅛	12⅛	46⅝	37⅛	47½	38½	8559	47½	43⅞	45¼	6.7	10	18.4	27.0	25.3
✣25•[4]	NAK	✔Natl Auto Credit	NY,Ch	B	82	8920	Insur replacement rentals	22⅜	3⅝	15	9⅜	19¼	10	8959	17⅞	14¾	16¼	...	23	35.4	29.4	17.9
26	NBT	Natl Bancshares Texas	AS	NR	4	178	Commercial banking, Laredo	....	....	....	....	11⅜	7¼	262	10¾	10⅛	10¼	...	8	...	...	...
27	POPS	✔Natl Beverage	NNM	NR	13	666	Mfr,bottle softdrinks	12½	3¾	9¾	4⅛	7½	4¾	1329	6	4¾	5⅜	...	7	−10.4	2.6	...
28	NCMC	✔Natl Capital Mgmt	NNM	C	1	.1	Real estate dev, invest'ts	42	1 11/16	3⅞	2 7/16	3⅛	1⅛	370	1¾	1¼	1¼B	...	d	−52.4	−30.7	−11.1
¶29•[4]	NCC	✔Natl City Corp	NY,Ch,Ph	A−	399	87445	Comml bkg,Ohio,midwest	28⅛	2 7/16	29	23¾	33¾	25¼	47105	33¾	32	33⅛	4.0	11	39.3	15.9	22.7
30	Pr	8% cm Cv[61]Dep Pfd([62]52)	NY	BBB+	36	1024		74½	48¾	70½	59	80½	61¼	1326	80½	76½	78¾	5.1	..	...	...	...
31	NCBC	✔Natl Commerce Bancorp	NNM	A	69	7656	Commercial bkg,Tennessee	24¾	½	24¼	20½	27¼	22¾	2616	26⅝	25¾	26¼	2.9	14	14.9	14.2	29.6
32	NLCS	✔Natl Computer Sys	NNM	B+	93	9397	Optical mark/read process eq	23⅝	⅛	16¾	10¼	22	14⅞	11864	22	18¼	18⅞	1.9	18	24.2	7.4	18.0
✣33•[7]	NDC	✔Natl Data	NY,Ch	B	151	19022	Telep/computer svs: billing	23⅜	15/16	17⅝	10⅜	28	15⅜	16037	26⅞	23¾	24¾	1.2	28	48.7	46.5	29.1
34	NEC	✔Natl Education	NY,B,Ch,P	C	100	27049	Vocational training:hm/resid	30⅞	1/16	7⅜	3¾	8¾	2½	23727	8⅜	6⅜	8¼	...	d	100	6.9	14.2
#35	NFG	✔Natl Fuel Gas	NY,B,Ch	B+	172	12116	Natural gas utility hldg co	36⅞	3¾	36¼	25¼	33⅞	25	7097	33⅞	31¾	33⅝	4.8	17	39.0	10.1	13.6
36	NLG	✔Natl Gas & Oil	AS	↑B+	15	957	Hldg: natural gas in Ohio	11¾	11/16	12¼	9¼	12⅛	9½	352	10¼	9½	9¾	s2.4	23	−10.0	10.6	12.5
37	TEE	✔Natl Golf Properties	NY,Ch	NR	68	6983	Real estate investment trust	22¼	17½	23	17	24¼	19⅛	2641	24¼	21½	22⅞	7.2	18	17.3	...	...
38	NHI	✔Natl Health Investors	NY,Ph	NR	112	8273	Real estate investment trust	29⅝	20	29⅜	25¾	33¾	23	14636	33¾	30¾	33⅛	8.5	13	38.9	25.0	...
39	Pr	8.50%cm Cv Pfd(NC)	NY	NR	25	1997		....	....	27	22¾	31	22¼	2359	31	27½	30¾	6.9	..	...	...	...
40	NHC	✔Natl Healthcare L.P.	AS,Ph	NR	10	729	Health care ctrs/home care	29⅛	7⅜	30¼	24¾	39⅜	22⅞	243	39⅜	36⅜	39	5.3	16	60.9	42.7	33.0
41	NHCI	✔Natl Home Centers	NNM	NR	10	533	Retail home/building products	14¼	9¼	14	2¾	4½	2⅛	3119	3⅛	2⅛	2⅛	...	d	−29.2	...	...
42	NHHC	✔Natl Home Health Care	NNM	B−	12	231	Home health care services	7½	½	3¾	1¾	7⅛	2¾	2570	7⅛	5¼	5⅜	...	16	53.6	12.7	25.2
43	NIRTS	Natl Inc Rlty Tr SBI	NNM	NR	5	6	Real estate investment trust	69¼	3⅜	11⅜	9⅞	11¼	10½	592	11⅛	10¾	11⅛	7.2	d	21.9	62.0	34.7
44	NATI	✔Natl Instruments	NNM	NR	48	3809	Dvlp virtual instrument softwr	....	....	....	....	22¾	14½	7165	20¼	17⅞	20¼	...	25	...	...	...
45	NM	✔Natl Media Corp	NY,Ch	C	34	4899	Provides direct market'g svcs	31¾	½	11⅝	3¼	21⅛	4½	24688	21⅛	16½	21	...	60	310	30.3	64.9
46	NPD	✔Natl Patent Devel	AS,B,Ch,P,Ph	C	20	1887	Environmental technol & svs	268	8	19½	6	10¾	6½	10057	10¾	8½	8½	...	d	...	...	...
47	NATP	Natl Power plc[69]	Lo	NR	2	96	Elec generation&sale,U.K.	510	188	520	402	552	418	....	467	418	449½	2.4	..	...	...	...
48	NP	Natl Power PLC ADS[70]	NY	NR	25	2505	Elec generation&sale U.K.	....	....	....	....	35⅜	26¼	1262	29¼	26¼	28	4.0	10	...	...	...
49	NP.PP	1st [71]Installm't[72]ADS[73]	NY	NR	35	11273		....	....	....	....	16¾	9	38073	11½	9	9¼	8.8	..	...	...	...
#50	NPK	✔Natl Presto Indus	NY,B,Ch,Ph	B+	116	3157	Mfr,distr small appliances	83	3⅜	48	39⅛	48	38¾	3788	42¼	38¾	39¾	e4.9	13	1.5	−4.9	3.9
✣51	NRE	✔Natl Re Corp	NY,Ph	NR	119	11854	Property & casualty reinsurance	39⅝	17	31¾	22¼	38	25¾	3257	38	33	38	0.5	19	49.1	10.1	...
52	NLP	✔Natl Realty L.P.	AS	NR	11	4	Real estate investments	97½	7¼	30¾	25	38	30	134	38	34¼	34B	e2.4	17	15.3	22.2	33.8

Uniform Footnote Explanations-See Page 4. Other: [1]CBOE:Cycle 3. [2]P:Cycle 2. [3]CBOE,NY:Cycle 1. [4]ASE:Cycle 1. [5]ASE,CBOE,NY:Cycle 3. [6]Ph:Cycle 3. [7]Ph:Cycle 2. [51]2 Mo Dec'91. [52]Excl 0.35M shrs subject to redemption. [53]Fiscal Dec'94 & prior. [54]12 Mo Aug'95. [55]®$0.51,'94. [56]Formerly Myers(L.E.) Gr. [57]®$1.95,'94. [58]®$1.19,'94. [59]ADS's represent 5 Ord par A$1. [60]Approx. [61]Dep for⅕ shr 8% cm Cv Pfd. [62]Fr 5-1-96,scale to $50 in 2001. [63]®$0.75,'95. [64]Incl $0.231 non-taxable,'94. [65]®$2.28,'94. [66]If com exceed$27.625 20 trad.days(out of30). [67]®$1.80,'94. [68]Stk dstr of 1 com & 1 wrrt of American Drug Co. [69]All data reported in British pence. [70]Ea ADS rep four ord shrs. [71]1st Installm't ADS(37% paid). [72]Full pay't ADS rep four Ord, 50p. [73]2nd pay't (35%)2-6-96,3rd(28%)9-17-96.

Index (Splits ◆)	Cash Divs. Ea. Yr. Since	Dividends: Latest Payment Period $	Date	Ex. Div.	Total $ So Far 1995	Ind. Rate	Paid 1994	Financial Position Mil-$ Cash & Equiv.	Curr. Assets	Curr. Liab.	Balance Sheet Date	Capitalization Lg Trm Debt Mil-$	Shs. 000 Pfd.	Com.	Earnings $ Per Shr. Years End	1991	1992	1993	1994	1995	Last 12 Mos.	Interim Earnings Period	$ per Shr. 1994	1995	Index
1	....	None Since Public			...	Nil	....	0.02	10.5	26.8	10-01-95	0.01	...	2173	Mr	0.03	Δ0.56	d2.02	□d3.93	....	d3.31	6 Mo Sep	□d0.47	0.15	1
2	....	None Since Public			...	Nil	....	49.3	134	33.9	9-30-95	233	...	17677	Dc	...	p0.47	p0.69	□1.07	....	1.20	9 Mo Sep	□0.78	0.91	2
3	....	None Paid			...	Nil	....	0.07	25.4	18.4	10-07-95	0.02	...	2027	Dc	†[51]d0.07	0.59	d0.16	□d0.20	....	d0.08	9 Mo Sep	d0.13	d0.01	3
4	1961	Q0.32½	12-1-95	11-13	1.30	1.30	1.30	59.7	512	394	9-30-95	199	...	44834	Dc	d0.28	*1.93	Δ1.94	2.37	E1.40	1.39	9 Mo Sep	1.97	0.99	4
5	....	None Since Public			...	Nil	....	1.30	701	460	9-30-95	446	...	34297	Dc	p0.57	□0.83	□1.03	0.51	....	d3.94	9 Mo Sep	d0.20	d4.65	5
6◆	1991	Q0.10	11-24-95	11-8	0.34	0.40	0.29	Equity per shr $11.18			9-30-95	14.0	2952	[52]13359	Dc	0.92	□1.18	1.55	1.80	....	2.11	9 Mo Sep	1.34	1.65	6
7	....	None Since Public			...	Nil	....	17.6	79.9	21.2	8-31-95	....	3	19425	Au	d0.27	d2.09	d2.66	[53]0.11	[54]d0.83	d0.84	3 Mo Nov	d0.39	d0.40	7
8◆	1966	Q0.04	1-2-96	12-6	0.149	0.16	0.135	4.26	98.9	26.5	9-30-95	17.7	...	16884	Dc	0.69	0.84	Δ0.94	1.06	....	1.00	9 Mo Sep	0.74	0.68	8
9◆	1983	Q0.04	1-15-96	12-27	†0.207	0.16	0.113	180	338	39.7	9-30-95	8.58	...	120063	Mr	0.35	0.61	0.62	1.01	E1.10	1.07	6 Mo Sep	0.47	0.53	9
10	....	None Paid			...	Nil	....	32.6	71.7	13.2	9-30-95	0.27	...	14867	Dc	d0.19	d0.25	d0.35	[55]0.53	....	0.70	9 Mo Sep	0.33	0.50	10
11◆	1989	Q0.047	12-15-95	11-28	0.182	0.19	0.165	0.34	62.0	45.6	9-30-95	15.5	...	3176	Dc	1.23	1.03	0.49	0.65	....	0.93	9 Mo Sep	0.46	0.74	11
12	....	None Since Public			...	Nil	....	26.2	26.5	2.71	p6-30-95	0.78	p...	★8134	Je	Nil	pd0.05	pd0.16	pd0.80	pd1.19	d1.22	3 Mo Sep	pd0.29	d0.32	12
13	....	None Since Public			...	Nil	....	8.46	11.2	2.76	9-30-95	....	...	4219	Dc	...	...	...	p0.26	....	0.36	9 Mo Sep	p0.12	p0.22	13
14	1995	Q0.13¾	1-1-96	12-13	0.27½	0.55	....	133	1612	1232	9-30-95	4400	...	±265000	Dc	...	...	p0.64	p1.10	E1.25	1.20	9 Mo Sep	p0.66	□0.76	14
15	....	0.06	7-19-82	6-24	...	Nil	....	15.5	188	138	6-30-95	53.7	...	84103	Sp	±0.44	±0.52	±0.50	±0.01	P±0.58	0.58				15
16◆	1989	Q0.05	1-10-96	12-22	0.18	0.20	0.16	Equity per shr $24.15			9-30-95	★318	...	★19117	Dc	2.20	Δ0.57	2.30	[57]1.99	E2.35	2.96	9 Mo Sep	1.46	2.43	16
17	1947	Q0.18	12-15-95	11-29	0.71	0.72	0.67½	30.9	743	481	9-30-95	735	...	±8966	Dc	2.31	□2.71	□1.30	□5.06	E6.60	7.09	9 Mo Sep	□2.57	□4.60	17
18◆	....	4%Stk	3-14-94	2-18	...	Nil	4%Stk	1.44	28.1	30.8	9-30-95	0.25	...	7459	Dc	0.63	0.80	0.80	d1.69	....	d1.68	9 Mo Sep	d1.26	d1.25	18
19◆	1928	Q0.25	3-8-96	2-15	0.99	1.00	0.94½	39.8	380	290	9-30-95	249	400	67264	Dc	1.82	1.90	□2.03	[58]1.25	E2.15	1.86	9 Mo Sep	0.96	1.57	19
20◆	1994	0.01½	4-21-95	3-27	0.01½	0.02	0.01	19.6	47.9	21.5	6-30-95	....	...	8125	Dc	0.76	0.47	0.87	1.09	....	1.39	9 Mo Sep	0.85	1.15	20
21	....	None Paid			...	Nil	....	0.03	17.9	4.25	8-26-95	10.4	5	2986	Fb	0.29	0.15	d3.81	d1.15	....	d0.35	6 Mo Aug	d0.70	0.10	21
22	1965	†0.20	12-8-95	11-29	†0.74	0.72	†0.73	7.04	326	225	10-07-95	82.4	...	10876	Dc	1.75	1.85	1.46	1.42	....	1.58	40 Wk Oct	1.09	1.25	22
23	1986	0.18	10-3-95	9-8	0.72	0.72	0.72	12.2	109	67.9	9-30-95	68.6	...	6374	Dc	0.09	□0.84	d3.02	0.34	....	d0.79	9 Mo Sep	0.29	d0.84	23
24	1985	[60]1.57	2-2-96	12-26	2.927	3.01	2.185	Book Value $22.72			9-30-94	2945	...	1368785	Sp	2.72	1.94	2.82	4.71	....	4.71				24
25	....	5%Stk	6-8-90	5-21	...	Nil	....	Equity per shr $8.26			10-31-95	13.3	...	25833	Ja	0.68	0.66	0.72	0.87	....	0.72	9 Mo Oct	0.67	0.52	25
26	....	None Since Public			...	Nil	....	Book Value $7.53			9-30-95	1.99	3319	4469	Dc	...	...	1.09	1.25	....	1.24	9 Mo Sep	0.92	Δ0.91	26
27	....	None Paid			...	Nil	....	26.6	100	64.4	7-29-95	42.8	150	9300	Ap	0.13	0.53	d0.72	1.37	0.81	0.83	6 Mo Oct	0.63	0.65	27
28◆	....	0.45	11-20-84	11-5	...	Nil	....	0.24	7.75	9.49	9-30-95	2.52	...	1651	Dc	d0.60	d1.02	d0.81	d0.57	....	d0.61	9 Mo Sep	d0.62	d0.66	28
29◆	1936	Q0.33	11-1-95	10-11	1.30	1.32	1.18	Book Value $18.22			9-30-95	1216	744	147258	Dc	p1.46	2.09	2.41	2.70	E2.93	2.95	9 Mo Sep	1.99	2.24	29
30	1991	Q1.00	11-1-95	10-11	4.00	4.00	4.00	Cv into 2.384 com, $20.97				....	3965	...	Dc	...	...	...	....	....	....				30
31◆	1939	Q0.19	1-1-96	11-29	0.68	0.76	0.60	Book Value $11.22			9-30-95	437	...	24805	Dc	1.23	1.38	1.58	1.77	....	1.90	9 Mo Sep	1.29	1.42	31
32	1976	Q0.09	1-3-96	12-13	0.36	0.36	0.36	4.31	103	67.5	10-31-95	24.7	...	15537	Ja	0.96	1.03	d0.16	0.88	....	1.04	9 Mo Oct	0.74	0.90	32
33◆	1977	Q0.075	11-30-95	11-13	0.298	0.30	0.293	88.5	155	54.6	8-31-95	18.1	...	22696	My	d0.80	0.41	0.47	□0.57	[63]0.76	0.87	6 Mo Nov	0.33	0.44	33
34	....	0.018	3-24-78	2-27	...	Nil	....	24.5	115	80.0	9-30-95	64.8	...	35123	Dc	0.18	0.02	d0.32	d2.16	....	d2.74	9 Mo Sep	d2.31	d2.89	34
35	1903	Q0.40½	1-15-96	12-27	1.60	1.62	1.56	12.8	189	393	9-30-95	474	...	37438	Sp	1.63	1.94	2.15	Δ2.23	2.03	2.03				35
36◆	1970	s0.058	12-18-95	11-22	s0.233	0.23	0.233	1.57	12.9	10.1	9-30-95	11.4	...	6861	Dc	0.31	□0.32	0.30	0.50	....	0.43	9 Mo Sep	0.35	0.28	36
37	1993	Q0.41	11-14-95	10-27	1.591	1.64	[64]1.44⅜	Equity per shr $16.87			9-30-95	131	...	10622	Dc	...	p0.95	p0.84	1.12	....	1.24	9 Mo Sep	0.86	0.98	37
38	1992	0.70	2-9-96	12-27	2.53	2.80	2.33	Equity per shr $12.74			9-30-95	328	2739	18735	Dc	0.29	1.60	1.95	[65]2.35	....	2.63	9 Mo Sep	1.72	2.00	38
39	1994	Q0.53⅛	1-2-96	12-20	1.594	2.125	1.853	Cv into 0.905 com, $27.625				....	4000	...	Dc	...	...	...	....	....	....	Fr 2-15-99 redm for 0.905 com[66]:			39
40◆	1984	Q0.52	2-15-96	12-27	1.88	2.08	†2.27	28.0	107	55.1	9-30-95	220	...	7827	Dc	2.45	1.28	4.85	[67]2.02	....	2.48	9 Mo Sep	1.37	1.83	40
41	....	None Since Public			...	Nil	....	0.14	42.5	17.4	7-31-95	33.8	...	7142	Ja	0.19	0.44	0.46	0.21	....	d0.06	9 Mo Oct	0.20	d0.07	41
42	....	None Paid			...	Nil	....	8.58	18.0	4.05	10-31-95	....	...	4718	Jl	0.34	0.39	0.18	d0.47	0.30	0.34	3 Mo Oct	0.06	0.10	42
43◆	1979	Q0.20	12-29-95	12-19	0.555	0.80	0.582	Equity per shr $20.38			9-30-95	143	...	3402	Dc	Δd1.14	d1.89	Δd0.78	d0.07	....	d0.11	9 Mo Sep	d0.10	Δd0.14	43
44	....	None Since Public			...	Nil	....	45.2	96.5	25.6	9-30-95	12.3	...	21471	Dc	0.17	0.13	0.55	0.71	....	0.80	9 Mo Sep	0.49	0.58	44
45	....	0.02½	1-15-91	12-24	...	Nil	....	16.2	63.3	33.8	9-30-95	3.74	256	14883	Mr	d0.44	0.48	d0.72	d0.05	....	0.35	6 Mo Sep	d0.12	0.28	45
46◆	....	h[68]....	8-15-94	8-16	...	Nil	h[68]....	6.84	79.8	49.2	9-30-95	19.7	...	±5634	Dc	±Δ0.16	±Δd3.44	±Δd1.84	d2.56	....	d1.02	9 Mo Sep	Δd1.40	□0.14	46
47	1991	1.20	8-12-93	6-7	...	10.60	....	38500	116200	89500	j9-25-94	68000	...	1279383	Mr	28.60	32.90	40.90	....	....	j42.70	6 Mo SepΔ	12.60	□14.40	47
48◆	1992	[60]0.357	1-19-96	12-1	1.04	1.11	0.81	531	1308	1084	j3-26-95	645	...	1186175	Mr	1.99	1.96	2.44	2.67	....	2.78	27 Wk Sep	0.91	1.02	48
49	1995	[60]0.357	1-19-96	12-1	0.751	0.81	....	....	...	...		....	...	127836	Mr	...	...	...	....	....	....				49
50	1994	†2.15	3-10-95	2-22	†2.15	1.95	1.90	199	266	42.8	10-01-95	....	...	7351	Dc	4.98	3.53	2.55	2.92	....	3.00	9 Mo Sep	1.27	1.35	50
51	1992	Q0.05	12-29-95	12-13	0.17	0.20	0.16	Equity per shr $21.29			9-30-95	211	...	16866	Dc	2.37	□1.85	3.42	□1.59	....	1.98	9 Mo Sep	□1.66	2.05	51
52◆	1993	†3.20	1-2-96	12-13	0.60	0.80	†1.30	Equity per shr Neg			9-30-95	334	...	2139	Dc	Δd16.42	Δd3.98	Δd3.40	2.30	....	1.97	9 Mo Sep	d1.33	d1.66	52

◆**Stock Splits & Divs By Line Reference Index** [6]3-for-2,'93. [8]5-for-4,'92,'94:10%,'91,'93,'95. [9]2-for-1,'92:3-for-2,'95. [11]4=for-3,'95. [16]3-for-2,'91. [18]3-for-2,'93:Adj to 4%,'94. [19]2-for-1,'91. [20]2-for-1,'92. [28]1-for-3 REVERSE,'95. [29]2-for-1,'93. [31]3-for-2,'92,'93. [33]3-for-2,'95. [36]3-for-2,'94:Adj to 3%,'95. [40]No adj for stk dstr,'91. [43]10%,'93,'94,'95. [46]1-for-4 REVERSE, '95. [48]5-for-2,'95. [52]1-for-4 REVERSE,'91:To split 3-for-1,ex Jan 16.

¶ S&P 500
# MidCap 400
✣ SmallCap 600
• Options

Index	Ticker	Name of Issue (Call Price of Pfd. Stocks)	Market	Com. Rank. & Pfd. Rating	Inst. Hold Cos	Inst. Hold Shs. (000)	Principal Business	Price Range 1971-93 High	1971-93 Low	1994 High	1994 Low	1995 High	1995 Low	Dec. Sales in 100s	December, 1995 Last Sale Or Bid High	Low	Last	%Div Yield	P-E Ratio	Total Return % Annualized 12 Mo	36 Mo	60 Mo
1	NRVH	✓Natl R.V.Holdings	NNM	NR	8	800	Design,mfr motorhomes	12¾	6	14	7¼	13	6¾	2542	13	11⅛	11⅝	...	9	52.5	...	...
¶2•[1]	NSM	✓Natl Semiconductor	NY,B,C,Ch,P,Ph	B–	433	97337	Integ circuits & transistors	22¼	11/16	25	14⅜	33⅝	16½	287659	24	20⅝	22⅛	...	10	13.5	27.2	36.8
¶3•[2]	NSI	✓Natl Service Indus	NY,B,Ch,P	A	325	29008	Lighting eq:textile rental	30⅜	1½	28⅜	24¾	33⅞	24⅞	18548	33⅞	30⅝	32⅜	3.6	16	30.9	12.6	9.3
4	NSD	✓Natl-Standard	NY,B,Ch	C	19	2551	Mfr steel wire prod:machinery	48¼	1	14	7⅝	16¾	9⅝	2303	11⅜	9⅝	10⅞	...	8	–9.4	58.1	38.6
5•[1]	NS	✓Natl Steel 'B'	NY,Ph	NR	71	20483	Mfg flat rolled carbon steel	20⅝	10⅜	22⅞	11½	18⅞	11¾	10196	13⅛	11¾	12⅞	...	6	–14.9	...	...
6	NSCI	Natl Surgery Centers	NNM	NR	..	...	Oper ambulatory surgery ctrs	...	...	...	...	23½	18	7564	23½	19⅝	23	...	32	...	...	...
7•[3]	NVAL	✓Natl Vision Associates	NNM	NR	29	1081	Retail optical vision ctrs	26½	6¾	7⅞	3½	5¾	2⅞	24563	4⅛	2⅞	3	...	..	–22.6	–51.3	...
8	NW	✓Natl Westminster ADS[53]	NY,B,Ch,Ph	NR	36	1168	Genl bkg,U.K. & worldwide	56⅜	20⅞	55½	38¾	64¾	43¾	3279	62⅞	56¾	60¾	3.8	10	32.8	23.8	21.4
¶9•[4]	NB	✓NationsBank Corp	NY,B,Ch,P,Ph	A–	813	166776	Comm'l bkg, Southeast,N.C.	58	3⅜	57⅜	43⅜	74¾	44⅝	131326	74¾	67⅞	69⅝	3.3	10	61.1	13.9	28.1
10	NHP	✓Nationwide Health Prop	NY,Ch,Ph	NR	161	13976	REIT:health care facilities	42½	9¾	42¾	31⅝	42⅛	34⅞	5304	42⅛	39½	42	6.9	16	24.1	17.0	29.1
11	NAI	✓Natural Alternatives Intl	AS	B	16	663	Mfr vitamins & natl supplem'ts	13⅜	1 5/16	12⅜	3⅞	12⅞	4	5516	8¾	7	8	...	17	88.2	15.1	32.8
✣12	NATR	✓Nature's Sunshine Prod	NNM	B+	60	4280	Direct sale health rel'd pr	13⅜	¼	16⅜	10	28	9¾	12340	25¾	22	25¼	0.8	30	138	48.4	72.6
✣13•[5]	NAUT	✓Nautica Enterprises	NNM	B+	165	16277	Mfr men's robes,sportswear	18⅛	⅛	21⅝	13	45½	16⅜	44754	45½	35	43¾	...	33	116	87.4	89.9
¶14•[6]	NAV	✓Navistar Intl	NY,B,C,Ch,P,Ph	↑B–	240	31948	Heavy & medium duty trucks	455	17½	26⅝	12¼	17½	9	80520	12⅜	10⅜	10⅝	...	6	–29.8	–23.5	–12.9
15	Pr D	Cv Jr D[57]Pref(25)	NY	NR	1			36¾	5¾	8½	4	10	5	47	10	9	8B	...	..	...	...	...
16	Pr G	$6 cm Cv G Pfd(50)	NY	B+	31	1995		61	19	54¾	49¼	55¼	50⅞	589	55	53¼	54¼	11.1	..	...	...	...
✣17•[7]	NBTY	✓NBTY Inc	NNM	B–	48	8012	Mfr vitamins,food supplem'ts	21½	1/32	24¼	4¾	8⅜	4	30208	5⅝	4⅝	4¾	...	18	–13.6	–18.8	64.4
#18	NCH	✓NCH Corp	NY,Ch,Ph	B+	107	3764	Cleaning & other chemicals	78¼	12⅛	67	56⅝	66⅞	52¾	1617	57⅞	54⅛	57¾	e2.1	13	–9.1	–1.9	4.5
19•[6]	NMG	✓Neiman-Marcus Group	NY,Ph	NR	65	12991	Operates dept/specialty strs	45½	10⅛	18¾	13	23½	13	5064	23½	20¾	23½	...	28	79.7	11.7	12.4
#20•[8]	NELL	✓Nellcor Puritan Bennett	NNM	↑B+	270	24285	Electr patient monitor'g sys	36	7	34	24¼	62¼	31½	41174	62¼	55½	58	...	d	77.1	23.9	33.4
21	NPTH	✓Neopath Inc	NNM	NR	37	3392	Dvp stage:medical image tech	...	...	...	...	28¼	11	18260	23½	18½	23¼	...	d	...	...	...
22•[9]	NEOP	✓Neoprobe Corp	NNM	NR	37	5797	Dvlp stge:cancer treatment R&D	8¼	5⅛	7½	1 3/16	19⅛	1½	35369	16⅞	14⅝	16⅛	...	d	1159	39.0	...
23	NERAY	Nera AS ADS	NNM	NR	30	2370	Wireless telecomm eqp/svcs	...	...	...	...	37	26⅜	2428	33⅝	31½	32½	...	..	...	...	...
24•[10]	NETC	✓NETCOM On-Line Comm Svcs	NNM	NR	72	5699	Internet connectivity provider	...	...	29¼	13	91½	19	110732	74	34¾	36	...	d	29.7	...	...
25•[3]	NETF	✓NetFRAME Systems	NNM	NR	35	1952	Mfr specialized computer sys	23¾	8¼	17½	7⅛	7⅞	4¼	32763	6½	5	5¼	...	d	–30.3	–32.3	...
26•[11]	NETM	✓NetManage Inc	NNM	NR	151	24771	Dvlp,mkt'window'softwr prd	9¼	4	22½	5⅝	34	13	278188	34	20¾	23¼	...	33	8.2	...	...
27	NSCP	✓Netscape Communications	NNM	NR	59	3548	Dvlp softwr prd for Internet	...	...	...	...	174	28	235701	174	116¼	139	...	d	...	...	...
28	NTSR	NetStar Inc	NNM	NR	12	606	Dvlp stg:design/mkt netwks eq	...	...	...	...	27	8⅜	32499	23¼	15¾	18¼	...	d	...	...	...
29	NTAP	Network Appliance	NNM	NR	..	...	Network data storage devices	...	...	...	...	41¾	13½	29781	41¾	29¾	40⅛	...	d	...	...	...
30•[9]	NCDI	✓Network Computing Devices	NNM	NR	44	5690	Computer network systems	19	6¼	8¾	3¼	12	3⅞	39344	9⅜	7	7⅛	...	d	67.6	–22.4	...
✣31•[9]	NWK	✓Network Equip Tech	NY,Ch,Ph	↑B–	134	19029	Mfr,mkt communic products	34⅜	4	24¾	7⅜	42	19¾	26021	33¾	27⅜	27⅜	...	15	11.2	43.6	36.6
✣32•[3]	NETG	✓Network General	NNM	NR	159	15887	Local area netwk softwr prd	25½	4	26⅛	13⅞	46½	22¾	59057	42⅜	32	33⅜	...	33	31.5	22.6	31.5
33•[9]	NPIX	✓Network Peripherals	NNM	NR	92	7185	Dvlp local area ntwk prd	...	...	29	6	32¼	8¼	44637	13¾	10⅛	11¾	...	17	–58.4	...	...
34	NWSS	✓Network Six	NNM	NR	8	165	Computer software/systems	16½	¼	17½	9¼	12½	2⅞	6739	5	2⅞	3⅛	...	45	–71.6	...	...
35	NSIX	Neuromedical Systems	NNM	NR	..	...	Dvlp stg:Cancer R&D	...	...	...	...	21½	15	123964	21½	15	20⅛	...	..	...	...	...
#36	NVP	✓Nevada Power	NY,B,Ch,P	B+	113	8464	Elec in Las Vegas & vicinity	26¾	3¼	24⅜	17⅛	22⅞	19⅛	14058	22½	21⅝	22¼	7.2	14	17.3	5.2	8.3
37	DDDDF	New Dimension Software	NNM	NR	..	...	Dvlp system software prod	25¼	12	24½	3	8¼	3⅜	4978	5¼	4	4¼	...	d	–2.9	–39.3	...
✣38	NEB	✓New England Bus Svc	NY,Ch	A–	99	12516	Standardized business forms	30¼	1 13/16	21¾	16¼	23¾	16¾	11205	23½	20	22	3.6	27	24.6	12.1	17.1
#39	NES	✓New England El Sys	NY,B,Ch,P,Ph	A–	263	21944	Hldg co: electric service	43⅜	6	39	28⅞	40	29⅝	43762	40	38⅛	39⅝	6.0	13	32.1	7.3	17.3
40	NEW	✓New England Inv Cos L.P.	NY,Ch	NR	13	21154	Provides invest't mgmt svcs	23⅞	6¾	23⅝	15⅛	22⅜	15⅜	743	21⅜	20¼	21⅛	9.1	17	49.2	27.0	26.7
41	NIB	New Iberia Bancorp	AS	NR	..	...	Commercial banking, Louisiana	...	...	...	...	23¾	14	83	23¾	23¼	23¼B	1.3	20	...	...	...
42	NIIS	✓New Image Industries	NNM	NR	18	1012	Designs computer imaging prd	22¼	⅝	16¾	3½	5⅜	1½	10312	3	1⅝	2 5/16	...	d	–42.2	...	...
✣43	NJR	✓New Jersey Resources	NY,Ch,Ph	B+	98	4701	Supplies gas in New Jersey	29½	4⅜	27⅜	19¾	30½	21½	6178	30½	27¾	30⅛	5.0	21	44.5	14.0	18.1
44	NJST	✓New Jersey Steel	NNM	C	26	1311	Operates a steel minimill	27	8¼	19¼	12¾	15⅜	8¼	2236	10½	8¼	9½	...	11	–35.9	–17.2	–0.3
45	NZ	✓New Mexico/Ariz Land	AS	B–	13	289	Real estate,mineral explor'n	43¼	3	9⅜	7	13⅝	6⅞	228	12¼	11⅜	12	...	5	84.4	19.5	21.4
46•[12]	NPR	✓New Plan Rlty Tr SBI	NY,Ch	NR	122	6484	Real estate investment trust	26⅜	½	24½	18¾	23	19⅝	17343	21⅞	20¾	21¾	6.4	18	18.1	3.0	11.4
47	NEWI	✓New West Eyeworks	NSC	NR	4	126	Specialty eyewear retailer	7¾	7	8½	2⅞	5¾	3⅛	2038	5	4	4⅝	...	d	42.3	...	...
48•[13]	NWCG	✓New World Communic Grp'A'	NNM	NR	102	18516	Dvp/distrib T.V. programs	...	...	16	8⅜	25	11⅝	41013	17⅞	15⅛	17½	...	d	47.4	...	...
49	NWPC	✓New World Power	NNM	NR	32	3136	Renewable elect pwr sys, svcs	12¾	7	13¾	6	7½	1¼	8008	2⅜	1½	1¾	...	d	–76.7	–41.1	...
50	NYB	✓New York Bancorp	NY,Ch,Ph	NR	39	2914	Savings bank, New York	24½	2 7/16	23⅛	16¾	22½	16	2987	22½	20¼	22½	3.6	26	24.3	14.5	54.5
#51	NGE	✓New York State E&G	NY,B,Ch,Ph	B	223	27535	Utility: electric & gas	38½	10	30½	17¾	26¾	19	39149	26⅜	25⅜	25⅞	5.4	11	45.5	–0.5	7.4
¶52•[14]	NYT.A	✓New York Times Cl'A'	AS,B,Ch,P,Ph	B+	326	49494	Newspapers,mag's,TV,CATV	49⅝	1⅛	29½	21¼	30⅞	20⅛	41879	30⅝	28⅝	29⅝	1.9	21	39.2	6.8	10.0

Uniform Footnote Explanations-See Page 4. Other: [1]CBOE:Cycle 2. [2]Ph:Cycle 3. [3]CBOE:Cycle 1. [4]Ph:Cycle 2. [5]CBOE. [6]NY:Cycle 1. [7]P:Cycle 3. [8]NY,P:Cycle 1. [9]CBOE:Cycle 3. [10]CBOE,NY:Cycle 1. [11]CBOE,P:Cycle 1. [12]ASE:Cycle 2. [13]ASE,CBOE:Cycle 3. [14]P:Cycle 1. [51]®$1.11,'95. [52]®$1.92,'95. [53]ADS's representing 6 Ord shrs. [54]Approx. [55]®$6.06,'94. [56]©$0.0975,'94. [57]Divds cm at 120% of cash declared on com stk. [58]4 Mo Dec'92. [59]9 Mo Dec'94. [60]®$1.37,'95. [61]®$0.60,'94. [62]Subsid Pfd stk in M$. [63]100% non-taxable,'94. [64]Incl 29M Prin Unit Hldrs. [65]Stk dstr of Styles on Video Inc,'93. [66]Subsid pfd in $M. [67]Incl $0.213133 non-taxable:©$0.037551,'94. [68]Fiscal Sep'92 & prior.

Splits ◆ Index	Cash Divs. Ea.Yr. Since	Dividends: Latest Payment Period $	Date	Ex. Div.	Total $ So Far 1995	Ind. Rate	Paid 1994	Financial Position Mil-$ Cash& Equiv.	Curr. Assets	Curr. Liab.	Balance Sheet Date	Capitalization Lg Trm Debt Mil-$	Shs. 000 Pfd.	Com.	Earnings $ Per Shr. Years End	1991	1992	1993	1994	1995	Last 12 Mos.	Interim Earnings Period	$ per Shr. 1994	1995	Index
1	....	None Since Public			...	Nil	....	1.95	22.3	5.69	8-31-95	2.11	4	3136	My	...	d0.98	0.61	1.16	□[51]1.12	1.31	6 Mo Nov	0.55	Δ0.74	1
2	....	None Paid			...	Nil	....	373	1160	617	8-27-95	118	345	135600	My	d1.56	d1.24	0.98	Δ1.98	[52]2.02	2.22	6 Mo Nov	0.96	1.16	2
3	1937	Q0.29	1-11-96	12-27	1.12	1.16	1.08	83.0	640	203	8-31-95	26.8	...	48354	Au	0.65	1.50	1.52	1.67	1.93	1.98	3 Mo Nov	0.43	0.48	3
4	....	0.10	4-2-87	2-27	...	Nil	....	2.06	58.9	48.4	9-30-95	34.2	...	5385	Sp	d5.36	d1.34	□d0.92	d0.86	1.37	1.37				4
5	....	None Since Public			...	Nil	....	121	856	636	9-30-95	504	15	±43288	Dc	d8.11	Δ□d3.61	□d7.55	4.33	E2.03	2.61	9 Mo Sep	3.66	Δ1.94	5
6	....	None Since Public			...	Nil	....	15.2	26.0	8.50	p6-30-95	20.0	...	★5307	Dc	...	...	...	p□0.60	....	0.73	9 Mo Sep	p□0.42	p0.55	6
7◆	....	None Since Public			...	Nil	....	3.52	35.2	18.4	9-30-95	35.5	...	20562	Dc	pd0.26	0.07	d0.59	0.02	....	Nil	9 Mo Sep	0.06	0.04	7
8	1920	[54]0.84½	10-24-95	8-11	[54]2.291	2.29	1.888	Book Value $32.49			j12-31-94	5199	160000	1715601	Dc	Δ0.28	1.06	3.10	5.89	....	5.89				8
9	1903	Q0.58	12-20-95	11-29	2.08	2.32	1.88	Book Value $38.38			9-30-95	15741	2518	270922	Dc	0.76	4.60	Δ5.00	[55]6.12	E7.05	6.72	9 Mo Sep	4.66	5.26	9
10	1986	Q0.72½	12-6-95	11-8	2.82½	2.90	[56]2.62½	Book Value $19.26			9-30-95	184	...	19360	Dc	□1.68	2.00	□2.33	2.47	....	2.62	9 Mo Sep	1.85	2.00	10
11	....	None Paid			...	Nil	....	1.38	14.5	5.50	9-30-95	1.04	...	5280	Je	0.07	0.18	0.21	0.38	0.39	0.48	3 Mo Sep	0.02	0.11	11
12◆	1988	Q0.05	11-30-95	11-15	0.20	0.20	0.182	16.1	46.7	22.6	9-30-95	....	...	12263	Dc	0.37	0.48	0.60	0.67	....	0.84	9 Mo Sep	0.49	0.66	12
13◆	....	None Paid			...	Nil	....	34.0	161	37.7	8-31-95	0.20	...	19851	Fb	0.44	0.60	0.90	1.15	....	1.31	6 Mo Aug	0.39	0.55	13
14◆	....	3.00	1-15-81	12-22	...	Nil	....	Equity per shr $8.90			7-31-95	573	4977	±75197	Oc	d7.70	d9.50	□d8.63	0.72	P1.83	1.83				14
15	....	None Paid			...	Nil	....	Cv into 0.3125 com				....	179	...	Oc	bd0.21	bd0.38	bd1.52	....	....	....				15
16	1987	Q1.50	1-15-96	1-3	6.00	6.00	6.00	Cv into 0.133 com, $375				....	4800	...	Oc	bd0.21	bd0.38	bd1.52	....	....	....				16
17◆	....	None Paid			...	Nil	....	10.4	67.7	27.1	9-30-95	10.9	...	19478	Sp	0.09	0.28	0.53	0.38	0.26	0.26				17
18	1965	†1.30	12-15-95	11-29	†2.20	1.20	†2.05	117	403	121	10-31-95	3.80	...	8040	Ap	5.19	4.77	4.53	3.77	4.29	4.34	6 Mo Oct	2.24	2.29	18
19	1987	0.05	1-31-95	1-6	0.05	Nil	0.20	12.6	754	471	10-28-95	275	1500	38002	Jl	±d0.45	±d0.21	□±0.78	d0.35	0.70	0.84	3 Mo Oct	0.33	0.47	19
20	....	None Since Public			...	Nil	....	108	352	169	10-01-95	....	...	p28467	Je	1.05	1.31	1.50	1.22	2.20	d0.19	3 Mo Sep	0.35	d2.04	20
21	....	None Since Public			...	Nil	....	28.0	29.7	1.98	9-30-95	0.29	...	9794	Dc	...	...	n/a	pd1.94	....	d1.59	9 Mo Sep	pd1.39	pd1.04	21
22	....	None Since Public			...	Nil	....	19.1	20.1	1.92	9-30-95	1.24	...	16972	Dc	pd0.48	d0.41	d1.13	d1.18	....	d0.76	9 Mo Sep	d0.96	d0.54	22
23	....	None Since Public			...	Nil	....	12.7	169	107	3-31-95	p58.4	...	★13114	Dc	...	...	...	0.96	....	....	3 Mo Mar	n/a	0.27	23
24	....	None Since Public			...	Nil	....	35.8	41.0	11.3	9-30-95	....	...	★11095	Dc	...	‡[58]Nil	0.04	d0.02	....	d1.13	9 Mo Sep	0.01	d1.10	24
25	....	None Since Public			...	Nil	....	35.3	63.6	14.1	9-30-95	....	...	13586	Dc	d0.41	0.29	0.53	0.42	Ed0.55	d0.69	9 Mo Sep	0.50	d0.61	25
26◆	....	None Since Public			...	Nil	....	56.8	80.1	20.1	6-30-95	....	...	39932	Dc	...	0.03	0.17	0.41	E0.70	0.63	9 Mo Sep	0.25	0.47	26
27◆	....	None Since Public			...	Nil	....	123	143	35.5	9-30-95	2.09	p...	38956	Dc	...	...	...	‡[59]d0.26	Ed0.02	....	9 Mo Sep	n/a	d0.09	27
28	....	None Since Public			...	Nil	....	3.68	6.90	5.11	6-30-95	0.08	...	★8825	Sp	...	...	d0.63	d0.85	Pd0.90	d0.90				28
29	....	None Since Public			...	Nil	....	2.75	11.4	5.01	p10-27-95	p....	p...	★15887	Ap	...	...	...	....	pd0.38	d0.13	6 Mo Oct	pd0.14	p0.11	29
30	....	None Since Public			...	Nil	....	37.8	81.7	26.2	9-30-95	1.08	...	15802	Dc	p0.12	0.43	Δ0.55	d0.68	....	d0.20	9 Mo Sep	d0.70	d0.22	30
31	....	None Since Public			...	Nil	....	103	219	65.9	9-24-95	68.6	...	19661	Mr	d0.76	d0.71	d0.38	[60]1.44	....	1.87	6 Mo Sep	0.25	0.68	31
32	....	None Since Public			...	Nil	....	99.4	140	33.7	9-30-95	....	...	21838	Mr	0.56	0.55	0.53	1.14	....	1.02	6 Mo Sep	0.45	0.33	32
33	....	None Since Public			...	Nil	....	54.0	66.1	5.20	9-30-95	....	...	11180	Dc	...	...	0.05	0.62	....	0.68	9 Mo Sep	0.41	0.47	33
34	....	None Paid			...	Nil	....	0.20	18.1	11.8	9-30-95	0.25	714	2845	Dc	0.09	*0.19	Δ0.43	[61]0.68	....	0.07	9 Mo Sep	0.57	d0.04	34
35	....	None Since Public			...	Nil	....	8.19	9.82	5.53	9-30-95	6.27	p...	★27251	Dc	...	...	...	pd0.84	....	....	9 Mo Sep	n/a	pd0.90	35
36	1951	Q0.40	11-1-95	10-10	1.60	1.60	1.60	65.1	213	181	9-30-95	786	2113	46744	Dc	1.05	1.47	1.76	1.82	E1.65	1.55	12 Mo Sep	1.84	1.55	36
37	....	None Since Public			...	Nil	....	35.3	49.9	19.5	12-31-93	0.58	...	10972	Dc	0.23	0.68	0.09	Pd2.02	....	d0.95	9 Mo Sep	d1.02	0.05	37
38	1965	Q0.20	11-24-95	11-8	0.80	0.80	0.80	25.9	83.8	34.3	9-30-95	....	...	14889	Je	1.24	□1.02	0.93	1.01	1.07	0.81	3 Mo Sep	0.30	0.04	38
39	1947	Q0.59	1-2-96	12-7	2.33	2.36	2.27	7.80	501	538	9-30-95	1639	[62]147	64924	Dc	2.77	2.85	2.93	3.07	E3.10	2.97	12 Mo Sep	3.44	2.97	39
40	1987	Q0.48	2-15-96	12-27	1.72	1.92	[63]1.66	11.9	101	82.6	6-30-95	....	...	[64]31880	Dc	1.50	1.46	p1.46	1.13	....	1.25	9 Mo Sep	1.24	1.36	40
41	1995	0.075	10-2-95	9-20	0.15	0.30	....	Book Value $11.11			9-30-95	....	...	2000	Dc	0.92	1.33	1.52	1.37	....	1.17	9 Mo Sep	1.16	0.96	41
42	....	h[65]....	4-15-93	2-2	...	Nil	....	1.81	10.9	5.42	9-30-95	....	...	4791	Je	d3.00	d0.26	1.27	d0.08	d1.61	d1.78	3 Mo Sep	0.03	d0.14	42
43	1951	Q0.38	1-2-96	12-13	1.52	1.52	1.52	1.07	186	106	9-30-95	352	[66]21	17793	Sp	0.83	1.64	1.72	Δ1.89	1.41	1.41				43
44	....	0.15	8-1-91	7-9	...	Nil	....	....	42.2	33.9	8-31-95	19.2	...	5921	Nv	d0.66	*0.12	Δd0.63	0.44	....	0.86	9 Mo Aug	d0.12	0.30	44
45◆	....	5%Stk	11-1-84	10-9	...	Nil	....	Equity per shr $10.87			9-30-95	13.7	...	2728	Dc	0.11	Δd0.54	0.47	1.45	....	2.57	9 Mo Sep	0.59	1.71	45
46	1942	Q0.34¾	1-17-96	12-29	1.36½	1.39	[67]1.32½	Equity per shr $10.71			10-31-95	p244	...	p57441	Jl	1.05	1.08	0.89	1.06	1.19	1.21	3 Mo Oct	0.29	0.31	46
47	....	None Paid			...	Nil	....	0.13	4.79	8.22	9-30-95	0.37	5	3763	Dc	d4.27	d1.67	Δd0.57	d0.43	....	d0.49	9 Mo Sep	d0.12	d0.18	47
48	....	None Since Public			...	Nil	....	96.8	363	213	9-30-95	987	1525	±68583	Dc	...	pd0.59	pd0.89	d0.81	....	d0.79	9 Mo Sep	d0.50	d0.48	48
49	....	None Since Public			...	Nil	....	1.85	21.5	16.3	9-30-95	21.4	375	11611	Dc	pd0.38	[68]0.73	Nil	d0.90	....	d0.50	9 Mo Sep	d0.72	d0.32	49
50◆	1990	Q0.20	1-26-96	1-10	0.80	0.80	0.781	Book Value $12.55			9-30-95	422	...	12139	Sp	0.37	□1.83	2.18	Δ2.39	0.87	0.87				50
51	1910	Q0.35	11-15-95	10-23	1.40	1.40	2.00	6.63	249	245	9-30-95	1617	7905	71503	Dc	2.36	2.40	2.08	2.37	E2.45	2.58	12 Mo Sep	2.06	2.58	51
52	1958	Q0.14	12-15-95	11-29	0.56	0.56	0.56	77.4	461	491	9-30-95	638	18	±96437	Dc	±0.61	±□d0.14	±0.07	±2.05	E1.40	1.48	9 Mo Sep	±1.63	±1.06	52

◆**Stock Splits & Divs By Line Reference Index** [7]3-for-2,'92. [12]3-for-2,'92:4-for-3,'93:10%,'95. [13]3-for-2,'92,'93,'95. [14]1-for-10 REVERSE,'93. [17]3-for-1,'92:2-for-1,'92,'93. [26]2-for-1,'94,'95. [27]Vote Jan 23 on 2-for-1 stk split. [45]10%,'95. [50]3-for-2,'93:10%,'94.

¶ S&P 500 # MidCap 400 ✣ SmallCap 600 • Options Index	Ticker	Name of Issue (Call Price of Pfd. Stocks)	Market	Com. Rank. & Pfd. Rating	Inst. Hold Cos	Inst. Hold Shs. (000)	Principal Business	Price Range 1971-93 High	1971-93 Low	1994 High	1994 Low	1995 High	1995 Low	Dec. Sales in 100s	December, 1995 Last Sale Or Bid High	Low	Last	%Div Yield	P-E Ratio	Total Return % Annualized 12 Mo	36 Mo	60 Mo
1	NEWB	✔Newberry Bancorp	NNM	NR	1	12	General banking, Michigan	7½	¾	5¼	3	5⅝	3½	184	5⅝	4¼	5½	...	4	48.3	50.7	17.3
2•[1]	NN	✔Newbridge Networks	NY,To,Ph	NR	181	21192	Mfr digital networking prod	73⅞	1½	68¾	26½	45⅜	25	107380	44¾	38½	41⅜	...	..	6.8	26.4	93.0
3	NEWC	✔Newcor Inc	NNM	B	17	1294	Specialized ind'l mchy	20½	11/16	12¼	7	10¼	6¼	4108	10¼	7⅞	8⅛	2.5	43	11.3	−4.1	15.5
¶4•[2]	NWL	✔Newell Co	NY,Ch,Ph	A+	520	110184	Mfr,mkt consumer products	26½	3/16	23⅞	18⅞	27¼	20¼	35188	27¼	25	25⅞	1.9	18	24.0	9.3	18.3
✣5	NFX	✔Newfield Exploration	NY,Ch	NR	85	10094	Oil&gas explor,devlp, prod'n	18½	15¾	26	17⅜	32⅛	18	1839	29¾	26⅝	27	...	32	34.2	...	...
6	NHL	✔Newhall Land/Farming[53]	NY,Ch,P	B−	45	14839	Agriculture,real estate	35¾	⅞	17¼	12	17	12⅛	12845	17	13⅜	17	2.4	22	45.7	9.3	4.7
7•[3]	NGC	✔Newmont Gold[55]	NY,B,Ch,P,Ph	B+	..	...	Gold min'g/process'g,Nevada	57½	8⅝	50	33⅜	44¼	31⅞	16335	44¼	40⅜	43¾	1.1	34	25.6	13.4	2.1
¶8•[4]	NEM	✔Newmont Mining	NY,B,Ch,P,Ph	B	429	66891	Gold min'g:explor,dev,prod	81⅞	6¼	48⅛	33⅞	46¼	33⅛	89855	46	42½	45⅜	1.1	34	28.4	14.0	9.0
9	NR	✔Newpark Resources	NY	B−	95	7596	Oil & gas ind enviro svcs	11	2⅛	23¾	7⅞	24¾	14	5763	22⅞	18	22¼	...	21	−2.7	29.0	39.0
10	NEWP	✔Newport Corp	NNM	B−	36	3716	Mfr laser/electro-optic eqp	33	⅛	8¼	5	12⅜	7	4507	8⅝	7⅝	8⅛	0.5	16	7.0	17.3	3.8
11•[5]	NWS	✔News Corp Ltd ADS[57]	NY,B,Ch,Ph	NR	267	100356	Newspapers:TV broadcasting	31⅝	2¾	30½	15	25⅛	14⅜	109006	23	21	21⅜	0.4	16	...	...	...
12•[6]	NXGN	✔Nexgen Inc[60]	NNM	NR	32	587	Dvlp high-performance ntwk prd	....	....	....	....	31	12¼	75255	16⅛	12¼	12¾	...	d	...	...	...
13	NXTR	✔NeXstar Pharmaceuticals	NNM	NR	37	4662	R&D pharmaceutical products	....	....	12	4¼	19	5½	24242	19	11½	16¼	...	d	189	...	...
#14•[7]	CALL	✔NEXTEL Communic'ns'A'	NNM	NR	188	52089	Provides mobile commun svcs	54⅞	9	46¾	13¼	21¾	9⅜	270455	17⅜	14⅝	14¾	...	d	0.0	−5.3	...
15	NEXT	NextHealth Inc	NNM	C	19	2732	Alcohol/drug rehab centers	31½	3⅝	4⅜	2¾	4⅞	2⅞	4455	4¾	2⅞	3⅛	...	d	8.7	−9.7	−24.4
16	NFC	✔NFC plc[63] ADS	AS	NR	5	232	Road freight/distribution:RE	25⅜	7½	21½	11¾	15	9⅝	146	11⅞	9⅝	10¼	5.8	32	−18.4	−18.2	0.4
17	NGL	✔NGC Corp	NY	NR	62	9018	Integrated natural gas svcs	13⅛	10⅛	12¼	8	11¾	8⅜	8479	9⅝	8⅝	8⅞	0.6	..	−14.1	...	...
18	NHPI	✔NHP Inc	NNM	NR	26	8853	Real estate management svcs	....	....	....	....	18⅝	12	5267	18⅝	15⅝	18½	...	9	...	...	...
19	NHSL	✔NHS Financial[66]	NNM	B	6	64	Savings & loan,California	9⅜	3¾	11⅛	7	10¼	7⅝	370	10	8½	10	1.6	28	29.6	29.9	16.1
¶20•[8]	NMK	✔Niagara Mohawk Pwr	NY,B,C,Ch,P,Ph	B	320	71772	Electric-gas utility in N.Y.	25½	7⅝	20⅝	12	15⅝	9½	134930	10½	9½	9½	11.8	7	−26.5	−15.5	−1.5
¶21•[9]	GAS	✔NICOR Inc	NY,B,C,Ch,P,Ph	B+	325	24141	Utility hldg: natural gas	31⅝	7½	29¼	21⅞	28½	21¾	15691	27¾	24⅞	27½	4.7	15	27.1	8.8	9.7
¶22•[9]	NKE	✔NIKE, Inc Cl'B'[67]	NY,Ch,P,Ph	A	517	79120	Athletic footwear	45⅛	1 11/16	38¼	23⅛	70⅜	34⅜	95616	70⅜	57⅞	69⅝	0.9	21	89.5	20.0	30.4
23	NMBS	Nimbus CD Intl	NNM	NR	..	...	Produces compact disc	....	....	....	....	9¾	7	8022	9¼	7⅛	8⅛	...	20	...	...	...
#24•[1]	NIN	✔Nine West Group	NY,Ch	NR	227	31035	Design/mkt women's footwear	35	17½	35	23¾	48¾	26⅜	59425	46¾	33	37½	...	..	32.2	...	...
25	NTT	Nippon Tel & Tel ADS[69]	NY,Ch,Ph	NR	..	...	Telecommunications svcs, Japan	....	....	46⅜	40⅞	46⅜	35¼	2916	43½	38	41	0.6	..	−1.3	...	...
#26	NI	✔NIPSCO Industries	NY,B,C,Ch,Ph	B+	327	31933	Util hldg co:Elec/nat'l gas	34⅞	8	33	26⅛	38½	29¼	15033	38½	36¾	38¼	4.4	15	34.2	18.6	20.7
27•[3]	NL	✔NL Industries, Inc	NY,B,C,Ch,P,Ph	C	74	7765	Mfr commodity chemicals	486¼	3⅜	13¼	4⅜	17½	10⅞	7017	13	12⅛	12⅛	...	12	0.0	35.5	6.4
28	NMRR	✔NMR of America	NNM	B	10	133	Manage magnetic resonance sys	8⅝	1⅜	5⅛	2¼	5½	3¼	7561	3¾	3¼	3½	...	10	−15.2	20.5	3.1
29	NNBR	✔NN Ball & Roller	NNM	NR	49	4951	Mfr steel balls/rollers	....	....	9½	6¼	19½	8⅛	13142	19½	15⅛	17½	1.2	24	119	...	...
#30•[10]	NBL	✔Noble Affiliates	NY,B,Ch,P,Ph	B	226	36782	Oil & gas explor'n,prod'n	32⅞	1 3/16	32¼	22½	30½	21¼	57231	30½	26¾	29⅞	0.5	d	22.7	21.7	16.9
✣31•[2]	NDCO	✔Noble Drilling Corp	NNM	NR	176	70964	Contr drill'g oil/gas wells	11½	1⅝	9⅛	5¼	9⅛	5	163480	9⅛	7¼	9	...	d	56.5	26.0	6.3
32	NCTI	Noise Cancellation Tech	NNM	C	38	7531	Dvlp electr noise reduct'n sys	6	⅛	3	7/16	1 9/16	½	82681	¾	9/16	⅝	...	d	17.7	−46.0	7.4
33	NKID	✔Noodle Kidoodle[72]	NNM,Ch,P	↓C	26	2157	Toys: wholesale & retail	28¾	⅛	7½	5¼	14⅝	4	4843	14	11¼	13½	...	d	151	44.2	34.0
¶34•[10]	NAE	✔NorAm Energy	NY,B,C,Ch,P,Ph	B	256	43036	Integrated nat'l gas utility	29⅞	3⅛	9	5¼	9	5⅛	63368	9	8	8⅞	3.2	23	71.9	5.0	−13.5
35	Pr A	$3cmCv[73]Exch A Pfd([74]50.90)	NY,Ch	BB−	22	296	chemical,petroleum products	59	29½	40	29⅝	40⅛	29½	518	39½	37⅜	39¼	7.6	..	...	...	...
✣36	NRNDE	✔Norand Corp	NNM	NR	79	5951	Mfr sales/inventory data sys	28¾	15½	40¾	26¾	48¼	11	24451	16	11	11¾	...	..	−66.5	...	...
37•[11]	NOR	Noranda Inc	To,Mo,Vc	B−	94	22651	Metal mining/mfg:forest pr	38	6½	27⅞	22⅜	30	21½	33435	29⅛	27⅜	28⅛	3.6	12	12.9	20.6	...
38•[12]	NRD	✔Nord Resources	NY,B,Ch,P	C	34	6372	World wide ore expl/dev	21⅝	1 11/16	7⅜	4¼	7⅛	1⅞	18245	2⅜	1⅞	2⅜	...	d	−62.7	−27.1	−19.2
39	NAT WS	Nordic Amer Tanker Ship Wrrt	AS	....	..	...	Wrrt:(Pur 1 com at $10.21)	....	....	....	....	5⅛	3⅜	1460	4⅛	3⅜	3½	...	..	...	...	...
#40	NDSN	✔Nordson Corp	NNM	A	111	4402	Industrial application eqp	57	3½	63	52	61	53¾	3448	58	55¾	56¼	1.3	20	−5.6	7.3	20.2
¶41•[13]	NOBE	✔Nordstrom, Inc	NNM,Ch	A+	401	43636	Dept stores:upscale apparel	53	⅜	49¾	31	45¼	35	92587	41½	38¼	40½	1.2	18	−1.8	3.4	13.1
42	NXA	✔Norex America	AS,Ch	B−	11	356	Interests in O&G,shipping ind	11	1¼	11¼	8⅝	12⅝	9	155	12⅝	12	12½	...	13	37.0	13.6	14.7
¶43•[14]	NSC	✔Norfolk Southern	NY,B,C,Ch,Ph,P	A	702	75993	RR hldg co:motor carrier	72⅜	5⅝	74¾	58½	81⅝	60½	34626	81⅝	76⅜	79⅜	2.6	15	34.0	11.4	17.2
44	NRLD	Norland Medical Systems	NNM	NR	17	1049	Bone disorder diagnosis eqp	....	....	....	....	24½	10½	5496	23¼	19½	23¼	...	..	...	...	...
45	NRL	✔Norrell Corp	NY,Ph	NR	62	4401	Temporary personnel services	....	....	19¾	14	34	18	4951	33⅜	28⅛	29⅜	0.8	21	58.3	...	...
46	NHY	✔Norsk Hydro A.S. ADS[78]	NY,B,Ch,Ph	NR	133	16008	Fertilizers:oil,gas:metals	41¾	8½	41	28⅜	46⅜	35	17301	42¼	40⅜	41⅞	1.3	12	9.4	25.7	8.3
47	NRRD	✔Norstan, Inc	NNM	B	37	2271	Digital commun,info proc sys	18¾	⅜	20½	14¼	26	17	2147	25¾	23	25¼	...	15	44.3	19.0	31.2
48	NTK	✔Nortek Inc	NY,B,Ch,P,Ph	C	53	3949	Mfr comm'l,resid'l bldg prd	19¼	15/16	13½	7⅞	12¼	7⅜	5700	12¼	9½	11¾	...	10	3.3	39.0	32.7
49•[14]	NBIO	✔North Amer Biologicals	NNM	B	91	11760	Blood plasma prod/med R&D	6¾	⅜	8½	3	11¾	6¼	33412	11	8¼	10¾	...	17	50.9	55.2	60.8
✣50•[4]	NAC	✔North American Mtge	NY,Ph	NR	97	11947	Mortgage banking services	34¾	11½	33¾	13⅝	26	14½	23276	25	20⅜	21¼	1.1	11	43.4	11.4	...
✣51•[15]	NVX	✔North American Vaccine	AS,Ch,Ph	NR	58	8169	Dvlp immunobiological prod	18	1	15½	7¾	15½	5¼	25340	15½	10⅝	14⅛	...	83	68.7	15.7	56.6
52	NAWC	✔North Amer Watch	NNM	NR	30	2767	Mfr, dstr quality watches	14¼	10½	14⅝	11¾	19¾	13⅛	1810	19¾	18⅝	19¼	0.5	10	35.9	...	...

Uniform Footnote Explanations-See Page 4. Other: [1]P:Cycle 3. [2]NY:Cycle 3. [3]Ph:Cycle 2. [4]Ph:Cycle 3. [5]CBOE,NY,Ph:Cycle 1. [6]CBOE,NY:Cycle 3. [7]CBOE:Cycle 2. [8]ASE:Cycle 3. [9]P:Cycle 1. [10]ASE:Cycle 2. [11]Mo:Cycle 2. [12]Ph:Cycle 1. [13]ASE:Cycle 1. [14]CBOE:Cycle 3. [15]ASE,CBOE:Cycle 3. [51]®$2.22,'95. [52]Co revised earnings from $1.03 in'91. [53]Ltd Ptnrshp(Dep Rect). [54]100% non-taxable,'94. [55]89.2% owned by Newmont Mining. [56]Fiscal Jul'92 & prior. [57]Each ADS represents 4 Ord. [58]Pfd in M$:Excludes subsid Pfd. [59]Excl 123M spl div, incl 967M ltd vtg ord shs. [60]Advanced Micro Devices plan acq, 0.80 com. [61]Mar'94 & prior. [62]12 Mo Dec'94. [63]Each ADS rep 5 Var Vtg Ord shr,5p. [64]Approx. [65]Incl curr amt. [66]Formerly New Horizons Svgs & Ln. [67]Ltd vtg. [68]Fiscal Dec'94 & prior. [69]Ea ADS rep .005 com, par y50,000. [70]Excl subsid pfd stk. [71]®$0.47,'95. [72]Formerly Greenman Bros. [73]Co opt exch for $50amt 6% Cv 2012. [74]Thru 3-14-95,scale to $50 in'97. [75]®$1.42,'94. [76]Stk dstr of Shanley Oil. [77]□$3.37,'91. [78]Each ADR rep 1 ord,Nok25. [79]®$1.34,'94.

Splits ◆ Index	Cash Divs. Ea.Yr. Since	Dividends: Latest Payment Period $	Date	Ex. Div.	Total $ So Far 1995	Ind. Rate	Paid 1994	Financial Position Mil-$ Cash& Equiv.	Curr. Assets	Curr. Liab.	Balance Sheet Date	Capitalization Lg Trm Debt Mil-$	Shs. 000 Pfd.	Com.	Earnings $ Per Shr. Years End	1991	1992	1993	1994	1995	Last 12 Mos.	Interim Earnings Period	$ per Shr. 1994	1995	Index
1	....	None Paid			...	Nil	....	Book Value $3.92			9-30-95	11.0	...	1173	Dc	d0.10	0.32	0.12	▲1.55	....	1.56	9 Mo Sep	d0.02	d0.01	1
2◆	....	None Since Public			...	Nil	....	371	647	123	j7-30-95	2.93	...	82961	Ap	d0.18	0.14	0.81	1.98	[51]2.31	j2.23	6 Mo Oct	1.08	1.00	2
3◆	1991	Q0.05	2-7-96	1-10	0.20	0.20	0.20	0.08	46.0	19.1	7-31-95	27.5	...	4680	Oc	[52]0.80	0.98	□1.16	d0.47	P0.19	0.19				3
4◆	1946	Q0.12	12-4-95	11-16	0.46	0.48	0.39	17.6	974	562	9-30-95	550	...	158555	Dc	0.91	□1.05	1.05	1.24	E1.45	1.38	9 Mo Sep	0.85	0.99	4
5	....	None Since Public			...	Nil	....	7.88	23.5	28.4	9-30-95	0.20	...	17165	Dc	...	p0.98	0.98	0.80	....	0.84	9 Mo Sep	0.60	0.64	5
6	1936	Q0.10	12-11-95	11-29	0.40	0.40	[54]0.40	Equity per shr $3.09			9-30-95	157	...	36172	Dc	0.82	0.47	0.35	0.42	....	0.76	9 Mo Sep	0.18	0.52	6
7	1986	Q0.12	12-7-95	11-22	0.48	0.48	†0.48	123	335	194	9-30-95	604	2875	96622	Dc	1.20	□0.83	Δ1.08	0.70	....	1.27	9 Mo Sep	0.55	1.12	7
8◆	1934	Q0.12	12-7-95	11-22	0.48	0.48	0.48	123	335	194	9-30-95	604	3	p94127	Dc	1.11	□1.04	Δ0.92	0.70	E1.35↑	1.27	9 Mo Sep	0.55	1.12	8
9◆	....	5%Stk	12-31-95	11-28	5%Stk	Stk	....	1.18	46.3	18.3	9-30-95	44.3	...	10631	Dc	□0.59	0.55	0.25	0.90	....	1.09	9 Mo Sep	0.62	0.80	9
10	1978	S0.02	1-5-96	12-13	0.04	0.04	0.04	2.30	45.8	24.9	9-30-95	6.29	...	8678	Dc	0.50	[56]d2.04	d0.53	0.47	....	0.50	9 Mo Sep	0.25	0.28	10
11◆	1984	0.039	10-17-95	9-19	0.076	0.08	h0.086	1212	5391	3794	j6-30-95	8017	[58]503	[59]2896353	Je	□0.75	□1.11	□1.52	Δ1.76	Δ1.36	1.37	3 Mo Sep	0.29	0.30	11
12	....	None Since Public			...	Nil	....	26.3	66.0	46.3	9-30-95	....	...	33219	Je	d0.68	d0.69	d0.55	d0.84	d1.82	d2.25	3 Mo Sep	d0.19	d0.62	12
13	....	None Since Public			...	Nil	....	25.8	56.3	17.8	9-30-95	9.59	...	24026	Dc	...	d0.38	d0.75	d0.71	....	d1.29	9 Mo Sep	d0.48	d1.06	13
14	....	None Since Public			...	Nil	....	507	577	353	9-30-95	1481	8163	193239	Dc	□d0.58	d0.16	[61]d0.73	[62]d1.55	Ed2.00	d2.19	9 Mo Sep	d1.04	d1.68	14
15	....	None Since Public			...	Nil	....	5.28	7.26	7.09	9-30-95	1.07	...	8556	Dc	□1.18	0.04	d1.27	d0.33	....	d0.66	9 Mo Sep	d0.28	d0.61	15
16◆	1990	[64]0.212	4-12-96	2-15	[64]0.598	0.59	0.445	206	718	506	j10-01-94	175	...	692854	Sp	□1.20	1.19	0.98	0.85	....	0.32	28 Wk Apr	0.45	d0.08	16
17	1994	Q0.01¼	1-2-96	12-14	0.038	0.05	0.05	27.6	542	478	9-30-95	★525	...	104865	Dc	±p0.52	±p0.64	±□0.53	p0.21	....	....	9 Mo Sep	n/a	0.66	17
18	....	None Since Public			...	Nil	....	4.72	18.6	20.1	9-30-95	[65]20.5	...	12256	Dc	...	...	...	p0.81	....	2.12	9 Mo Sep	p0.84	□2.15	18
19◆	1993	Q0.04	1-15-96	12-28	0.155	0.16	0.139	Book Value $9.51			12-31-94	25.0	...	2523	Dc	□0.20	Δ0.35	1.28	1.00	....	0.36	9 Mo Sep	0.80	0.16	19
20	1991	Q0.28	11-30-95	11-2	1.12	1.12	1.09	104	874	640	9-30-95	3457	14832	144332	Dc	1.49	1.61	1.71	1.00	E1.45↓	0.71	12 Mo Sep	1.78	0.71	20
21◆	1954	Q0.32	2-1-96	12-27	1.27½	1.28	1.25	18.7	235	522	9-30-95	419	206	50318	Dc	1.86	1.91	2.01	2.07	E1.90	1.93	12 Mo Sep	2.09	1.93	21
22◆	1984	Q0.15	1-3-96	12-6	0.50	0.60	0.40	179	2203	1145	8-31-95	14.1	300	±142968	My	±1.89	±2.15	±2.37	±1.98	±2.72	3.36	6 Mo Nov	±1.29	±1.93	22
23	....	None Since Public			...	Nil	....	0.13	28.2	20.4	6-30-95	p25.0	...	★20655	Mr	...	...	...	p0.36	....	0.41	6 Mo Sep	p0.17	p0.22	23
24	....	None Since Public			...	Nil	....	23.4	581	201	7-29-95	587	...	34928	Ja	p0.93	p1.52	Δp1.43	[68]1.85	....	....	6 Mo Jul	0.70	0.49	24
25◆	1995	0.104	12-22-95	9-27	s0.227	0.23	....	6544	18419	24897	3-31-95	48692	...	15600	Mr	0.52	0.44	0.25	0.30	....	0.30				25
26	1987	Q0.42	2-20-96	1-29	1.56	1.68	1.44	18.5	260	587	9-30-95	1176	[70]350	62629	Dc	1.94	2.00	2.31	2.48	E2.60	2.66	12 Mo Sep	2.45	2.66	26
27◆	....	0.05	9-30-92	9-10	...	Nil	....	153	550	261	9-30-95	751	...	51071	Dc	*d0.40	□d0.88	Δ□d1.63	d0.47	....	1.05	9 Mo Sep	d0.52	1.00	27
28	....	None Since Public			...	Nil	....	5.90	19.1	8.98	9-30-95	16.3	...	6282	Mr	*0.37	d0.08	0.29	[71]0.49	....	0.37	6 Mo Sep	0.23	0.11	28
29◆	1994	Q0.053	9-15-95	8-30	0.196	0.21	0.071	....	22.9	8.28	9-30-95	....	...	14472	Dc	...	...	p0.45	□0.65	....	0.74	9 Mo Sep	□0.48	0.57	29
30	1975	Q0.04	11-21-95	11-3	0.16	0.16	0.16	22.3	89.1	112	9-30-95	402	...	50066	Dc	0.44	0.93	0.26	0.06	Ed0.01↓	d0.11	9 Mo Sep	0.30	0.13	30
31	....	None Since Public			...	Nil	....	86.0	190	74.4	9-30-95	126	4025	94516	Dc	Δd0.48	d0.53	Δ0.32	0.11	Ed0.02	d0.18	9 Mo Sep	0.17	d0.12	31
32	....	None Paid			...	Nil	....	0.26	3.40	4.59	9-30-95	....	...	89137	Dc	d0.04	d0.25	d0.24	d0.26	....	d0.14	9 Mo Sep	d0.18	d0.06	32
33	....	5%Stk	9-12-73	8-20	...	Nil	....	6.55	27.2	12.4	10-28-95	....	...	5369	Ja	□0.71	0.32	0.13	d0.65	....	d2.74	9 Mo Oct	d0.73	d2.82	33
34	1953	Q0.07	12-15-95	11-16	0.28	0.28	[54]0.28	7.34	382	766	9-30-95	1475	2600	124534	Dc	0.05	□d0.30	□0.26	□0.34	E0.38	0.36	12 Mo Sep	□0.13	0.36	34
35	1987	Q0.75	12-15-95	11-16	3.00	3.00	[54]3.00	Cv into 1.7467 com,$28.625				....	2600	...	Dc	b1.01	b0.93	b1.14	b1.49	....	....				35
36	....	None Since Public			...	Nil	....	5.32	124	88.7	6-03-95	....	...	7500	Au	...	p0.68	1.81	1.40	P0.01	0.01				36
37	1930	gQ0.25	12-15-95	11-22	g1.00	1.00	g1.00	1010	4385	2061	j12-31-94	★3241	13160	p227496	Dc	d1.04	0.10	d0.41	[75]1.45	....	j2.37	9 Mo Sep	0.88	1.80	37
38	....	h[76]....	12-22-83	11-16	...	Nil	....	5.72	22.9	36.0	9-30-95	1.52	...	15838	Dc	d0.90	Δd0.66	□d0.54	d1.02	....	d1.27	9 Mo Sep	d0.14	d0.39	38
39	....	Terms&trad. basis should be checked in detail						Wrrt expire 9-30-97				....	...	11732	Dc	...	...	...	....	....	....				39
40◆	1969	Q0.18	1-3-96	11-29	0.64	0.72	0.56	7.16	285	153	7-30-95	17.9	...	18086	Oc	1.77	2.03	□2.13	2.45	P2.84	2.84				40
41	1971	Q0.12½	12-15-95	11-29	0.50	0.50	0.38½	52.3	1812	1017	10-31-95	390	...	81172	Ja	1.66	1.67	1.71	2.47	E2.30	2.20	9 Mo Oct	1.62	1.35	41
42	1993	0.10	3-19-93	3-4	...	Nil	....	12.1	55.4	54.0	6-30-95	31.5	...	6296	Je	□1.91	0.18	5.20	1.99	0.95	0.95				42
43	1901	Q0.52	12-11-95	11-1	2.08	2.08	1.92	287	1340	1181	9-30-95	1691	...	129768	Dc	□[77]3.57	3.94	Δ3.94	4.90	E5.30↓	5.38	9 Mo Sep	3.59	4.07	43
44	....	None Since Public			...	Nil	....	Equity per shr $4.82			3-31-95	....	...	★4000	Dc	...	...	...	p0.03	....	0.18	9 Mo Sep	p0.31	p0.46	44
45	1994	Q0.06	1-2-96	12-15	0.24	0.24	0.06	4.62	119	70.2	7-30-95	0.20	...	11070	Oc	0.56	0.15	□0.46	Δ1.39	P1.41	1.41				45
46	1985	0.562	6-14-95	4-26	0.562	0.56	0.417	8303	34555	22369	j12-31-94	19159	...	229073	Dc	d0.36	Δd0.49	1.94	Δ2.61	E3.58	4.22	6 Mo Jun	Δ1.19	2.80	46
47	....	0.033	7-3-78	6-12	...	Nil	....	2.32	101	58.8	10-28-95	27.3	...	4246	Ap	1.10	0.94	1.25	□1.41	1.61	1.70	6 Mo Oct	0.71	0.80	47
48	....	0.02½	2-1-91	12-21	...	Nil	....	108	339	149	9-30-95	220	...	±12223	Dc	Δd2.57	Δd1.93	□d1.00	Δ[79]1.35	....	1.22	9 Mo Sep	Δ0.99	0.86	48
49	....	None Paid			...	Nil	....	2.45	52.0	22.4	9-30-95	34.9	...	19551	Dc	0.14	d0.04	Δ0.25	□0.49	....	0.63	9 Mo Sep	0.35	0.49	49
50	1992	Q0.06	11-15-95	11-1	0.24	0.24	0.24	Equity per shr $7.31			9-30-95	501	...	15128	Dc	p1.19	p2.37	3.17	0.53	....	1.93	9 Mo Sep	0.45	1.85	50
51◆	....	None Since Public			...	Nil	....	11.7	12.9	6.29	9-30-95	....	2000	30078	Dc	d0.26	d0.40	d0.44	d0.14	....	0.17	9 Mo Sep	d0.42	d0.11	51
52	1994	Q0.02½	10-31-95	10-12	0.09½	0.10	0.06	2.04	192	62.6	7-31-95	40.0	...	±5991	Ja	...	±p1.32	□±1.61	±2.32	....	2.02	9 Mo Oct	±1.45	±1.15	52

◆Stock Splits & Divs By Line Reference Index [2]2-for-1,'93. [3]3-for-2,'93. [4]2-for-1,'94. [8]No adj for $33 & stk dstr,'87:1.2481-for-1,'94. [9]Adj for 5%,'95. [11]2-for-1,'94:No adj for dstr Spons ADR,'94. [16]1-for-5 REVERSE,'91. [19]10%,'91:15%,'95. [21]2-for-1,'93. [22]2-for-1,'95. [25]Adj for 2%,'95. [27]No adj for:dstr of pfd,'86,dstr of Baroid,'88. [29]3-for-2,'95(twice). [40]2-for-1,'91. [51]2-for-1,'92.

¶ S&P 500 # MidCap 400 ✣ SmallCap 600 • Options Index	Ticker	Name of Issue (Call Price of Pfd. Stocks)	Market	Com. Rank. & Pfd. Rating	Inst. Hold Cos	Inst. Hold Shs. (000)	Principal Business	Price Range 1971-93 High	1971-93 Low	1994 High	1994 Low	1995 High	1995 Low	Dec. Sales in 100s	December, 1995 Last Sale Or Bid High	Low	Last	%Div Yield	P-E Ratio	Total Return % Annualized 12 Mo	36 Mo	60 Mo
1	NCG	✔North Carolina Nat Gas	NY	A–	46	779	Natural gas distributor	29⅜	2 1/16	27⅜	19¾	25¾	20½	1197	25¾	22¾	25	4.9	14	24.2	7.5	16.5
2	NCEB	✔North Coast Energy	NSC	C	6	122	Oil&gas explor,dev,prod'n	2⅞	3/16	2⅛	1 1/16	1⅝	½	305	1 1/16	15/16	15/16	...	d	–25.0	–9.8	10.7
3	NEIC	North East Insurance	NSC	C	2	14	Casualty & property insur	4¾	¼	2⅝	1¼	2⅛	¾	2079	1¾	1	1	...	d	–30.4	58.7	–4.4
4	NET	✔North Europn Oil Rty Tr	NY,B,Ch	NR	34	1980	Oil,gas royalty,W Germany	30⅛	5¼	17¼	12½	14¾	12⅛	3972	13⅛	12⅛	12¾	10.2	9	10.1	–1.5	4.4
5	NFB	✔North Fork Bancorp	NY,Ph	B–	103	9230	Comm'l bkg,Long Island,NY	25¾	2 5/16	16⅞	12½	25¼	13½	13708	25¼	23⅛	25¼	2.4	15	85.3	55.6	36.9
6	NBF	✔Northbay Financial[51]	AS	NR	8	112	Savings & loan, California	13⅝	4	16⅜	11½	15¼	12⅝	442	15¼	15	15¼	2.9	26	13.4	15.8	34.9
#7	NU	✔Northeast Utilities	NY,B,C,Ch,P,Ph	B	268	41030	Utility hldg co:Conn, Mass	28⅞	5½	25¾	20⅜	25⅜	21	63720	24⅝	23½	24¼	7.3	11	22.6	4.1	11.6
8	NBP	✔Northern Border Ptnrs L.P.	NY,Ch	NR	40	1380	Natural gas pipeline transpt'n	28¼	24⅜	29⅜	20½	25⅝	20⅞	6764	24⅞	23¼	23⅜	9.4	12	23.5	...	...
¶9	NSP	✔Northern States[54] Pwr[55]	NY,B,C,Ch,P,Ph	A–	368	20021	Elec & gas util:WI,MN,ND,SD	47⅞	7⅝	47	38¾	49½	42½	26277	49½	46⅞	49⅛	5.5	14	15.7	10.5	14.2
10	NTI	✔Northern Technol Intl	AS,Ch	NR	8	45	Mfr corrosion inhibiting prd	4	1	6⅜	2⅜	8⅞	3¼	1799	5⅜	4¾	5¼	1.9	13	15.8	19.6	...
¶11•[1]	NT	✔Northern Telecom Ltd	[2]NY,To,B,Ch,P,Ph	B	364	58137	Telecommunication equip	49¼	2 7/16	37¾	26	44¼	31½	156359	44¼	39⅞	43	1.0	23	31.8	1.1	10.3
#12•[3]	NTRS	✔Northern Trust	NNM	B+	247	37825	Comm'l bkg,Chicago, Ill.	50½	2 5/16	43¼	32¼	56	31¾	43039	56	52⅛	56	2.2	15	62.0	12.6	26.0
13	NGX	Northgate Explor	NY,To,B,Ch,Ph,Mo	C	13	2545	Cdn gold,copper,silver min'g	14¾	½	1⅜	⅝	1¼	⅝	5704	1	⅞	⅞	...	..	27.4	20.5	–6.9
14	CBRYA	✔Northland Cranberries'A'	NNM	NR	38	3366	Grows & sells cranberries	19¾	4¼	20½	11	20	12¼	4772	19¾	17	17¾	e1.6	..	36.2	12.8	35.2
¶15•[4]	NOC	✔Northrop Grumman	NY,B,Ch,P,Ph	B–	362	33552	Aerospace: aircraft:missile	56⅝	1 9/16	47⅜	34½	64¼	39¾	13631	64¼	61	64	2.5	13	53.6	27.7	32.5
16•[5]	NWAC	✔Northwest Airlines'A'	NNM	NR	112	31047	Domestic, int'l air service	....	....	21⅜	11½	52½	15⅞	84666	52½	46	51	...	13	224	...	...
✣17	NWNG	✔Northwest Natural Gas	NNM	B+	107	4322	Gas utility, Oreg. & Wash.	38¾	5¾	36½	28¼	34¼	27½	9735	33¾	30¼	33	5.5	14	19.4	10.3	11.3
18	NWSB	Northwest Savings Bank	NNM	NR	13	557	Savings bank, PA	....	....	20	14½	27	15	2531	25½	23¼	24¼	2.5	..	69.0	...	...
19	NWTL	✔Northwest Teleprod'ns	NNM	↓B–	7	68	Advertising/educat'l video's	9¼	7/16	5	2¼	4¼	1⅞	127	3¾	3½	3½B	...	d	40.0	0.0	–6.8
20	NPS	✔Northwestern Pub Svc	NY,Ch,Ph	A	60	1079	Elec & nat gas in Neb, S.D.	33½	6⅜	29⅝	24½	28⅜	24¼	2344	28¼	26⅝	28	6.3	13	13.7	6.3	13.4
✣21	NWSW	✔Northwestern Steel & Wire	NNM	NR	46	2382	Mini-mill:steel,rod,wire prod	10⅞	7¼	13⅛	5½	10¼	5¾	9193	8¾	7¾	8⅛	...	8	38.3	...	...
22	NRTY	✔Norton McNaughton	NNM	NR	62	6297	Design/mfr women's clothing	....	....	22¾	12½	23¼	10¾	5539	14	10¾	11⅛	...	8	–21.9	...	...
23	NRWA	NORWEB[63] plc[64]	Lo	NR	..	...	Elec utility:N.W. England	768	204¼	864	585	1205	611	....	1035	1006	1025	2.0	..	...	...	...
¶24•[6]	NOB	✔Norwest Corp	NY,B,C,Ch,P,Ph	A–	618	192348	Comm'l banking,Minneapolis	29	1 15/16	28¼	21	34¾	22⅝	131575	34¾	32½	33	2.9	12	47.9	18.2	29.5
25	NPPI	✔Norwood Promotional Prd	NNM	NR	20	1914	Mkt custom-imprinted products	13¾	11	14¼	9¼	19¼	11¼	26134	19¼	16¼	17	...	15	44.7	...	...
26•	NVA	Nova Corp	NY,To,Ph,Mo	↑B	164	95481	Petrochem:gas PL:petroleum	13⅝	3	11¼	6¾	9⅝	7	123771	8½	7½	8	...	..	–11.6	7.5	3.3
#27•[7]	NOV	✔NovaCare	NY,Ph	B	149	22946	Speech/physical therapy svcs	30¼	1 15/16	19⅛	7⅛	9⅞	5	84164	6⅜	5	5⅛	...	6	–30.5	–39.4	–13.0
28	NVDM	✔Novadigm Inc	NNM	NR	30	2257	Dvlp mgmt software applications	....	....	....	....	28½	15	12389	28½	21¾	28⅜	...	d	...	...	...
29	NOX	Novavax Inc	AS	NR	..	...	Pharma'l delivery sys R&D	....	....	....	....	5	3	7442	5	3	3¾	...	..	...	...	...
¶30•[8]	NOVL	✔Novell Inc	NNM,Ch	B+	559	166511	Personal computer ntwk sys	35¼	3/16	26¼	13¾	23¼	13¾	762962	17	14⅛	14¼	...	16	–17.4	–20.9	11.7
✣31•[9]	NVLS	✔Novellus Systems	NNM,Ch	NR	188	14207	Mfr of semiconductor equip	37	2¾	56½	25¾	87¼	42¾	131273	64½	51	54	...	13	5.6	44.2	36.5
✣32•[6]	NOVN	✔Noven Pharmaceuticals	NNM	NR	63	7537	Transdermal drug delivery sys	15½	1¼	19¼	10¼	12⅜	6½	17449	11½	9¾	11¼	...	d	–7.2	–4.4	45.1
33	NOVI	✔Novitron Intl	NNM	C	11	679	Medical elec monitor'g eqp	12¾	7/16	7⅝	2⅞	6⅛	2⅞	1663	4⅛	2⅞	3¾	...	d	–26.8	–28.3	35.1
34	NVO	✔Novo-Nordisk A/S ADR[67]	NY,B,Ch,P,Ph	NR	54	4615	Ind'l enzymes: insulin	24¾	1 11/16	27⅝	21⅞	34½	22¼	1237	34½	31¼	34¼	0.6	17	47.0	17.4	18.3
35	NPCI	✔NPC Intl	NNM	B	54	3494	Pizza Hut franchise	14⅞	1⅞	7½	5	8½	4⅞	6449	8	6½	7¼	...	d	38.1	5.1	–16.4
✣36	NSBI	✔N.S. Bancorp[69]	NNM	NR	65	3494	Savings & loan,Illinois	34⅞	7⅜	33	25¼	39½	26⅛	7424	39½	38½	38¾	0.8	15	51.4	9.0	37.2
✣37	NSS	✔NS Group	NY,Ch	C	36	6000	Mfrs specialty steel prod	15⅞	3¼	7¾	4	5¼	1⅞	7144	2⅞	2	2½	...	d	–41.2	–12.6	–16.7
✣38•[8]	NTN	✔NTN Communications	AS	C	42	1758	Viewer response TV network	75	⅛	10¼	4¼	8¼	4	30255	5	4	4½	...	d	–26.5	–1.8	...
39	NKOT	✔Nu-kote Holding'A'	NNM	NR	95	14397	Mfr office/home printing prd	11⅛	5¾	13¼	7½	22½	10⅜	28172	20½	16	17	...	d	32.4	26.7	...
40	NTBM	Nu-Tech Bio-Med	NSC	NR	2	.3	Dvlp stge:oncology lab R&D	....	....	8	6⅞	15	7½	5264	15	13½	14⅞	...	d	...	...	...
41	NUCM	✔Nuclear Metals	NNM	C	8	271	Mfr depleted uranium parts	38¾	5¼	21	10⅛	16¾	10½	580	14	10½	12	...	d	–9.4	22.0	16.0
¶42•[3]	NUE	✔Nucor Corp	NY,B,Ch,P,Ph	A	486	52486	Steel joists,angles,rounds	57¼	¼	72	48¾	63¼	42	62594	57¼	49⅝	57⅛	0.5	19	6.3	14.5	30.5
43	NEV	✔Nuevo Energy	NY,Ch	C	104	8168	Oil & gas explor,dev,prod'n	28½	7	24⅜	16½	25	15¼	9375	23¾	20	22⅜	...	d	27.0	12.1	22.8
44	NUI	✔NUI Corp	NY,Ch	B	54	2335	Hldg:gas sv in N.J.,Florida	29¾	5¼	28¾	13½	17¾	14¼	4400	17¾	16⅛	17½	5.1	29	30.8	–5.3	8.6
45	NMC	✔Numac Energy	AS,To,B,Ph,Mo	B–	19	3220	Canada oil/gas:field constr	23	1 11/16	7⅛	5⅛	6	3¾	1404	4⅝	3¾	4¼	...	..	–26.1	–1.9	–4.1
46	NUMR	✔NUMAR Corp	NNM	NR	29	2986	Mfr'MRI'tool for o&g ind	....	....	17½	8½	13	8	4406	12¼	10¾	11⅛	...	d	27.1	...	...
47	NINE	✔Number Nine Visual Tech	NNM	NR	40	2148	Dvlp/supply software prds	....	....	....	....	25¾	7½	23580	11¾	7½	8¾	...	24	...	...	...
48	NVUE	✔nVIEW Corp	NNM	NR	20	1053	Mfr flat panel LCD projectn pd	31½	3½	9½	3⅜	9⅞	3¼	7055	4½	3¼	3⅝	...	d	–57.4	–11.6	...
49	NVR	✔NVR Inc	AS	NR	41	10300	Single-family home builder	11⅛	8½	11¼	5⅛	11⅝	5⅜	10656	11¼	9⅝	10	...	11	81.8	...	...
50	WS	Wrrt (Pur 1 com$8.80)	AS	....	17	654		5⅜	3¼	5¾	⅜	3½	⅝	1637	2⅞	1¾	2	...	..	...	...	...
51	NYCO	✔NYCOR, Inc[71]	NNM	B–	16	787	Mfr heating/cooling sys parts	10	2	5½	2⅛	5⅞	2⅛	3291	5⅛	4⅝	5⅛	...	d	105	31.6	15.9
52	NYM	✔NYMAGIC, Inc	NY	B	48	4987	Marine/liab ins underwriter	39¾	3⅝	25⅝	15⅞	18⅞	15⅜	7696	17¼	16⅛	17	2.4	11	–5.3	–12.9	–7.6

Uniform Footnote Explanations-See Page 4. Other: [1]CBOE:Cycle 3,To:Cycle 1. [2]Mo,Vc [3]CBOE:Cycle 1. [4]CBOE:Cycle 2. [5]ASE,CBOE,NY:Cycle 3. [6]P:Cycle 1. [7]P:Cycle 2. [8]ASE:Cycle 2. [9]CBOE,NY,P:Cycle 3. [51]Bank of the West plan acq, $15.75. [52]Susid pfd in $M. [53]Incl 6.4M sub units. [54]Approve mgr, Wisc Energy. [55]Approve hldg co, Primergy Corp, 1.626 com. [56]®$3.16,'94. [57]In cash or stock. [58]Fiscal Mar'94 & prior. [59]5 Mo Aug'95. [60]®$2.87,'94. [61]8 Mo Jun'95. [62]Excl subsid pfd. [63]All data reported in British pence. [64]Acq offers by Cen&S.W./Houston Ind & N.W. Water. [65]®$2.41,'94. [66]®$1.10,'95. [67]Ea ADR rep 0.25 'B'shr, DKR 20 par. [68]Spl div. [69]MAF Bancorp plan acq,cash & com. [70]3 Mo Dec,'93. [71]Vote Mar 26,Fedders Corp plan acq,$6.25.

Splits ◆ Index	Cash Divs. Ea.Yr. Since	Dividends: Latest Payment Period $	Date	Ex. Div.	Total $ So Far 1995	Ind. Rate	Paid 1994	Financial Position Mil-$ Cash& Equiv.	Curr. Assets	Curr. Liab.	Balance Sheet Date	Capitalization Lg Trm Debt Mil-$	Shs. 000 Pfd.	Com.	Earnings $ Per Shr. Years End	1991	1992	1993	1994	1995	Last 12 Mos.	Interim Earnings Period	$ per Shr. 1994	1995	Index
1◆	1969	Q0.30½	12-15-95	11-29	1.22	1.22	1.16	1.64	30.9	30.6	9-30-95	62.0	...	6477	Sp	1.31	1.79	1.84	1.76	1.84	1.84				1
2◆	....	None Since Public			...	Nil	....	0.80	3.98	4.26	9-30-95	8.09	773	8034	Mr	d0.02	Nil	Nil	d0.05	....	d0.06	6 Mo Sep	d0.09	d0.10	2
3	....	None Since Public			...	Nil	....	Equity per shr $1.81			9-30-95	....	...	2987	Dc	d0.18	d0.49	0.16	d0.32	....	d0.17	9 Mo Sep	d0.08	0.07	3
4	1976	Q0.35	11-22-95	11-8	1.43	1.30	1.01	2.95	2.95	2.91	7-31-95	....	...	8314	Oc	1.51	1.55	1.24	1.06	P1.43	1.43				4
5	1994	Q0.15	2-15-96	1-17	0.50	0.60	0.25	Book Value $10.98			9-30-95	25.0	...	24818	Dc	d3.36	0.16	1.05	1.25	....	1.64	9 Mo Sep	1.20	1.59	5
6◆	1991	Q0.11	10-18-95	10-2	0.44	0.44	0.335	Book Value $12.63			9-30-95	61.6	...	2751	Je	1.01	1.40	1.29	Δ1.06	0.67	0.58	3 Mo Sep	0.24	0.15	6
7	1927	Q0.44	12-29-95	11-29	1.76	1.76	1.76	51.2	889	1070	9-30-95	3844	[52]472	135562	Dc	2.12	2.02	Δ1.60	2.30	E2.20	2.25	12 Mo Sep	2.40	2.25	7
8	1994	Q0.55	11-14-95	10-27	2.20	2.20	2.20	30.5	53.9	46.8	9-30-94	425	...	[53]26200	Dc	...	p1.77	p1.98	P2.00	E1.90	1.95	9 Mo Sep	1.50	1.45	8
9	1910	Q0.67½	1-20-96	12-28	2.67	2.70	2.61	46.0	625	859	9-30-95	1545	2400	68099	Dc	3.29	Δ2.31	3.02	3.46	E3.50	3.77	12 Mo Sep	3.53	3.77	9
10	1989	0.10	12-18-95	11-30	0.10	0.10	0.075	2.83	4.77	0.52	8-31-95	....	...	4249	Au	0.19	0.27	0.29	0.30	0.42	0.42				10
11	1965	tQ0.11	12-29-95	12-6	t0.42	0.44	t0.36	407	5728	3611	9-30-95	1312	.2	253920	Dc	2.03	2.17	d3.54	1.60	E1.90	1.75	9 Mo Sep	0.72	0.87	11
12◆	1896	Q0.31	1-2-96	12-6	1.04	1.24	0.88	Book Value $22.37			9-30-95	458	51	55460	Dc	2.29	2.64	2.96	[56]3.17	E3.65	3.43	9 Mo Sep	2.48	2.74	12
13	....	g[57]0.50	7-20-88	6-6	...	Nil	....	20.6	22.3	5.08	j12-31-94	0.06	...	29496	Dc	d3.17	d0.30	d0.26	0.05	....	j0.18	9 Mo Sep	0.01	0.14	13
14	1988	Q0.07	11-16-95	11-2	†0.26	0.28	0.26	0.36	11.7	10.6	8-31-95	45.5	...	±6629	Au	0.41	±0.51	±0.67	±[58]0.36	±[59]d0.56	....				14
15	1951	Q0.40	12-9-95	11-22	1.60	1.60	1.60	32.0	2371	1868	9-30-95	1433	...	49416	Dc	□5.69	2.56	1.99	0.72	E4.90	1.48	9 Mo Sep	3.17	3.93	15
16	....	None Since Public			...	Nil	....	1459	2796	3023	9-30-95	4089	4285	±90422	Dc	...	...	pd1.01	[60]2.92	E4.00	3.96	9 Mo Sep	2.75	3.79	16
17	1952	Q0.45	11-15-95	10-27	1.77	1.80	1.76	2.91	55.5	98.6	9-30-95	271	455	14781	Dc	1.01	1.11	2.61	2.44	....	2.35	12 Mo Sep	2.00	2.35	17
18	1995	Q0.15	11-15-95	10-27	0.55	0.60	....	Book Value $15.47			6-30-95	0.10	...	★3450	Je	...	...	...	p1.16	[61]0.94	....	3 Mo Sep	n/a	0.40	18
19	....	0.06	9-27-91	8-26	...	Nil	....	0.15	4.01	4.03	9-30-95	2.71	...	1356	Mr	d0.23	0.22	0.40	0.03	....	d0.08	6 Mo Sep	0.03	d0.08	19
20	1947	Q0.44	12-1-95	11-13	1.71½	1.76	1.67	8.90	58.3	45.3	9-30-95	190	[62]51	8877	Dc	1.88	1.77	1.96	2.00	....	2.12	12 Mo Sep	1.99	2.12	20
21	....	None Since Public			...	Nil	....	5.45	180	87.5	10-31-95	165	...	24411	Jl	...	pd0.90	p0.42	0.40	1.07	1.09	3 Mo Oct	0.17	0.19	21
22	....	None Since Public			...	Nil	....	0.21	61.8	20.9	8-04-95	....	...	8011	Oc	...	...	p0.56	□1.28	....	1.40	9 Mo Jul	□0.81	0.93	22
23	....	14.10	10-4-93	8-12	...	20.00	....	19280	47840	31340	j12-31-94	15300	...	172750	Mr	0.51	64.60	76.00	....	....	j76.00				23
24◆	1939	Q0.24	12-1-95	11-1	0.90	0.96	0.76½	Book Value $13.72			9-30-95	12686	2129	p353053	Dc	1.46	□1.74	2.13	[65]2.45	E2.80	2.67	9 Mo Sep	1.82	2.04	24
25	....	None Since Public			...	Nil	....	2.17	45.5	14.4	9-02-95	p31.9	...	★5556	Au	...	p0.59	p0.83	0.93	[66]1.11	1.11				25
26	1962	gQ0.08	2-15-96	1-24	g0.30	0.32	g0.24	14.0	929	1103	j12-31-94	3449	...	478172	Dc	d2.99	j0.39	j0.47	j1.24	jE1.73	j1.77	9 Mo Sep	0.80	1.33	26
27◆	....	None Since Public			...	Nil	....	116	354	112	9-30-95	191	...	65540	Je	0.64	0.75	0.93	0.90	0.95	0.90	3 Mo Sep	0.17	0.12	27
28	....	None Since Public			...	Nil	....	1.01	6.13	2.25	3-31-95	....	...	★16827	Mr	...	d0.18	d0.38	d1.40	....	d1.17	6 Mo Sep	d0.15	0.08	28
29	....	None Since Public			...	Nil	....	5.02	5.05	0.12	p9-30-95	....	...	★9888	Dc	...	...	...	pd0.65	....	....	9 Mo Sep	n/a	pd0.59	29
30◆	....	None Since Public			...	Nil	....	1230	1878	495	7-29-95	....	...	370387	Oc	0.55	0.81	d0.11	0.56	P0.90	0.90				30
31	....	None Since Public			...	Nil	....	163	299	62.6	9-30-95	....	...	16485	Dc	1.15	0.44	1.10	2.72	....	4.27	9 Mo Sep	1.82	3.37	31
32	....	None Since Public			...	Nil	....	26.0	30.1	1.74	9-30-95	....	...	19648	Dc	d0.25	d0.21	d0.21	d0.28	....	d0.37	9 Mo Sep	d0.20	d0.29	32
33◆	....	None Since Public			...	Nil	....	1.41	11.3	5.82	9-30-95	0.08	...	3966	Mr	0.12	0.34	d0.28	d0.06	....	d0.22	6 Mo Sep	0.11	d0.05	33
34◆	1982	0.193	5-16-95	4-24	0.193	0.19	0.132	668	1741	753	12-31-94	511	...	±37515	Dc	1.14	1.36	1.40	1.57	....	2.01	9 Mo Sep	1.02	1.46	34
35◆	1995	[68]0.422	8-30-95	8-9	[68]0.422	Nil	....	6.63	16.7	38.0	9-26-95	82.9	...	24513	Mr	±0.40	±0.35	±0.45	±d0.63	....	d0.58	9 Mo Sep	±0.27	±0.32	35
36	1991	Q0.08	12-29-95	12-6	0.32	0.32	0.32	Book Value $36.92			9-30-95	62.7	...	6100	Dc	2.46	3.61	3.31	1.87	....	2.57	9 Mo Sep	1.42	2.12	36
37	....	0.03	3-27-92	2-28	...	Nil	....	11.3	123	57.4	9-30-95	167	...	13809	Sp	d1.53	□d0.99	□d0.44	Δ0.84	□d0.36	d0.36				37
38◆	....	None Paid			...	Nil	....	3.94	29.5	10.0	9-30-95	0.01	163	22428	Dc	Δd0.43	d0.23	d0.08	0.03	....	d0.06	9 Mo Sep	0.05	d0.04	38
39◆	....	None Since Public			...	Nil	....	7.90	216	109	6-30-95	92.3	...	21482	Mr	Δ□0.02	□0.58	0.47	□d0.69	....	d0.34	6 Mo Sep	d0.05	0.30	39
40	....	None Since Public			...	Nil	....	2.99	3.15	0.50	9-30-95	0.37	...	1742	Dc	d1.05	d2.10	d1.46	d2.15	....	d1.12	9 Mo Sep	d1.69	d0.66	40
41	1989	0.20	3-5-93	2-12	...	Nil	....	1.03	23.6	7.22	6-30-95	1.06	...	2383	Sp	0.60	0.40	Δd3.18	d4.43	Pd0.03	d0.03				41
42◆	1973	Q0.07	2-9-96	12-27	0.255	0.28	0.17½	259	829	463	9-30-95	125	...	87473	Dc	0.75	0.92	1.42	2.60	E3.05	3.18	9 Mo Sep	1.71	2.29	42
43	....	None Since Public			...	Nil	....	7.19	32.5	16.6	9-30-95	120	15	11717	Dc	0.45	0.30	0.70	d1.76	....	d1.57	9 Mo Sep	0.28	0.47	43
44	1923	Q0.22½	12-15-95	11-15	0.90	0.90	1.42½	3.60	81.5	111	9-30-95	222	...	9201	Sp	0.55	1.68	1.70	1.25	0.60	0.60				44
45	....	....			...	Nil	....	44.1	88.7	45.0	j12-31-94	196	...	93385	Dc	d2.34	0.08	0.18	0.28	....	0.03	9 Mo Sep	0.30	0.05	45
46	....	None Since Public			...	Nil	....	8.24	11.9	3.06	9-30-95	0.27	...	8273	Dc	...	...	pd0.51	d0.63	....	d0.65	9 Mo Sep	d0.39	d0.41	46
47	....	None Since Public			...	Nil	....	8.52	64.2	25.0	9-30-95	0.09	...	8757	Dc	0.17	0.20	0.05	0.23	....	0.36	9 Mo Sep	0.09	0.22	47
48◆	....	None Paid			...	Nil	....	0.24	26.0	7.53	9-30-95	....	...	4904	Dc	0.36	d0.48	d0.13	0.52	....	d0.70	9 Mo Sep	0.38	d0.84	48
49	....	None Since Public			...	Nil	....	Equity per shr $2.31			9-30-95	349	...	15385	Dc	...	...	±[70]d0.35	Δ0.57	....	0.88	9 Mo Sep	□0.44	Δ0.75	49
50	....	Terms&trad. basis should	be checked in detail					Wrrts expire 9-30-96				....	...	4117	Dc	...	...	...	....	....	....				50
51◆	....	0.04	9-1-92	8-7	...	Nil	....	1.12	20.7	14.5	9-30-95	5.99	1150	±7565	Dc	±0.30	±0.48	Δ±0.21	±d0.17	....	d0.65	9 Mo Sep	d0.12	d0.60	51
52	1989	Q0.10	1-9-96	12-27	0.40	0.40	0.40	Equity per shr $16.14			9-30-95	3.71	...	11284	Dc	2.06	1.33	Δ1.17	0.85	....	1.52	9 Mo Sep	0.52	1.19	52

◆**Stock Splits & Divs By Line Reference Index** [1]3-for-2,'92. [2]2-for-1,'91:15%,'94. [6]3-for-2,'91:15%,'92:10%,'93,'94:6-for-5,'94. [12]3-for-2,'92. [24]2-for-1,'93. [27]2-for-1,'91. [30]2-for-1,'91,'92. [33]3-for-2,'93. [34]4-for-1,'94. [35]2-for-1 in Cl'B','91. [38]1-for-20 REVERSE,'91. [39]2-for-1,'95. [42]2-for-1,'92,'93. [48]2-for-1,'91. [51]1-for-2 REVERSE,'91.

¶ S&P 500
\# MidCap 400
✣ SmallCap 600
• Options

Index	Ticker	Name of Issue (Call Price of Pfd. Stocks) Market	Com. Rank. & Pfd. Rating	Inst. Hold Cos	Inst. Hold Shs. (000)	Principal Business	Price Range 1971-93 High	1971-93 Low	1994 High	1994 Low	1995 High	1995 Low	Dec. Sales in 100s	December, 1995 Last Sale Or Bid High	Low	Last	%Div Yield	P-E Ratio	Total Return % Annualized 12 Mo	36 Mo	60 Mo
1	NYNCY	**NYNEX CableComms[51]Grp[52]ADS Unit**.. [1]	....	48	6923	Telecommunications/Cable TV,UK	....	....	....	....	23¼	17¼	3753	19¾	17¼	17⅜	...	..	...	...	...
¶2•[2]	NYN	✔**NYNEX Corp** ....NY,B,Ch,P,Ph	B+	775	168824	Tel svc:NY & New England	49	14⅝	41⅜	33¼	54	35⅞	143112	54	46⅞	54	4.4	19	54.9	15.6	15.7
✣3•[3]	OAK	✔**Oak Indus**....NY,B,Ch,P,Ph	B–	124	11093	Mfr electr controls/circuits	192½	1⁹⁄₁₆	29⅞	15⅝	32	16½	52884	24¼	16½	18⅝	...	10	–19.0	16.2	42.9
4•[4]	OAKT	✔**Oak Technology** .... NNM	NR	111	10977	Mfr hi performance CD-ROM prod	....	....	....	....	59	14	94418	48¼	36¾	42¼	...	23	...	...	...
5•[5]	OO	✔**Oakley Inc** ....NY	NR	78	8148	Mfr sport sunglasses & goggles	....	....	....	....	39¼	23	25653	34⅝	28⅝	34	...	32	...	...	...
✣6	OH	✔**Oakwood Homes**....NY,Ch,Ph	↑A–	180	15997	Mobile home mfr/retailer/prk	28¾	¼	29⅞	19¼	42½	21⅝	12992	42½	38⅛	38⅜	0.2	20	56.3	22.7	45.9
7	OAS	✔**Oasis Residential** ....NY,Ch	NR	149	15388	Real estate investment trust	26	21¾	28⅝	18¾	24⅝	19½	11759	23¼	20⅝	22¾	7.2	18	–0.4	...	...
8	Pr A	**$2.25 Sr 'A'cm Cv Pfd**.... NY	NR	29	1791		....	....	....	....	26¾	24⅝	2124	26⅛	24⅞	25¾	8.7	..	...	...	...
9	OSII	**Objective Sys Integrators**.... NNM	NR	..	...	Dvlp client/server softwr prd	....	....	....	....	54¾	19	80620	54¾	39¼	54¾	...	..	...	...	...
¶10•[6]	OXY	✔**Occidental Petrol'm** .NY,To,B,C,Ch,P,Ph	B–	572	168837	Major diversified energy co	39⅝	7⅜	22⅜	15⅛	24⅜	18	256112	22⅝	20⅛	21⅜	4.7	12	16.3	12.6	8.4
11	Pr A	**$3 cm Cv CXY-Ind Pfd([55]51.50)** ..NY,Ch	BBB–	70	8769		....	....	51¼	39⅞	66⅛	44½	27265	65¾	60⅜	62⅛B	4.8	..	...	...	...
12	OSYS	✔**OccuSystems Inc** .... NNM	NR	83	7174	Hlth care cost mgmt svcs	....	....	....	....	21¾	14	10834	20¼	18¼	20	...	40	...	...	...
✣13•[7]	OII	✔**Oceaneering Intl**.... NY,Ph	B–	85	14705	Offshore oil/gas field serv	24¾	⅞	14⅝	9¾	13	7¾	29171	13	10⅜	12⅞	...	59	25.6	2.0	3.2
14	OCE.B	✔**Ocelot Energy'B'**[57] .... Mo,To	NR	10	1913	O&G explor,dvlp prod'n,Canada	9⅞	6¾	9¾	6½	8½	5⅞	....	....	....	....	...	..	–20.3	...	...
#15•[7]	OCTL	✔**Octel Communications**.... NNM	B	139	18496	Mfr voice process'g systems	37½	7	30	15½	42⅝	18	60144	35¼	29½	32¼	...	24	57.8	15.4	22.9
#16•[8]	OEA	✔**OEA Inc** ....NY,Ch,Ph	B+	127	9339	Auto airbag initiators	37	³⁄₁₆	32	21⅞	33⅜	23½	9840	30¼	26⅞	29⅞	0.8	24	26.9	10.4	18.7
17•[8]	OXE	✔**OEC Medical Sys**....NY,Ch,Ph	NR	34	6657	Mfr med diagnostic imag'g eq	146¼	5¼	7⅞	5	10½	5½	4152	10½	9⅜	9¾	...	11	50.0	...	...
#18•[8]	ODP	✔**Office Depot**....NY,Ph	NR	451	131492	Office supply strs/rental eqp	23⅞	1½	27	18⅞	32⅛	19	351293	25	19	19⅝	...	23	–14.7	15.9	46.0
19•[9]	OMX	✔**OfficeMax Inc**....NY,Ch	NR	289	69904	Oper office prod superstores	....	....	17⅝	14⅜	26½	14⅝	97757	23⅛	17⅝	22⅜	...	15	29.6	...	...
¶20•[6]	OG	✔**Ogden Corp** ....NY,B,Ch,Ph,P	B+	309	28160	Support services	44⅝	3⅞	24⅜	17¾	24½	18⅜	64449	22¾	21	21⅜	5.8	14	23.3	4.1	...
21	Pr	**$1.875 [60]cm Cv Pfd(50)1/2vtg** .... NY	NR	1	.1	aviation,environ'l svc	243	22⅛	137	115	139	113½	....	....	....	127¾B	†2.6	..	...	...	...
22	OGLE	✔**Oglebay Norton** .... NNM	B–	26	883	Mining/diversified transport	38	9⅝	31¾	21¾	38¾	30	182	38¾	36	37¼	3.2	6	26.4	21.8	8.4
23	OAR	✔**Ohio Art**....AS	B	7	34	Mfr toys:plastic prod	62½	2⅜	36	21	56	28	238	56	42	53	†0.9	40	85.5	2.3	27.4
24	OCAS	✔**Ohio Casualty** .... NNM	B+	152	19562	Hldg: full multiple insur line	36	1¹⁵⁄₁₆	33¾	26½	39	28¼	9662	39	37¼	38¾	3.9	16	46.0	12.5	19.5
¶25•[7]	OEC	✔**Ohio Edison**.... NY,B,C,Ch,P,Ph	B	355	58045	Utility:electric sv-Ohio,PA	27⅞	9⅜	22¾	16½	23¾	18½	54275	23¾	22½	23½	6.4	12	33.7	7.6	14.3
26	OPJ	**Ohio Power 8.16% Jr Sub Debs** ....NY	....[63]	..	...	Contr by Amer Elec Pwr	....	....	....	....	26⅛	24½	1400	26⅛	25⅜	25¾	7.9	..	...	...	...
✣27	OHM	✔**OHM Corp** ....NY,Ch,Ph	C	59	4600	Chem waste monitor'g sys	36¼	2⅞	19½	5⅞	14⅞	6¾	18429	8½	7⅛	7⅜	...	d	–11.9	–1.1	–6.1
28	ODC	✔**Oil Dri Amer Cl'A'**....NY,Ch	A–	52	3211	Absorbent minerals,cat bx,etc	25	⅞	23⅜	17⅛	18⅝	14	1351	16¼	14⅞	15⅝	2.0	16	–6.9	–8.7	–2.8
#29	OGE	✔**Oklahoma Gas & Elec**[64] NY,B,C,Ch,P,Ph	A–	203	8973	Utility:el sv-OK,Westn AR	44	11½	37¼	29⅜	43⅝	32½	11352	43⅝	40⅜	43	6.2	14	40.3	16.2	9.6
30•[10]	OKEN	✔**Old Kent Finl**.... NNM	A+	142	12920	Commercial bkg,Michigan	35¾	2⅜	34	27¾	41⅝	28⅝	22730	41⅝	39	41⅛	3.1	13	54.8	14.1	28.2
31	OLDB	✔**Old Natl Bancorp(Ind)**.... NNM	A–	48	3630	Commercial bkg,Indiana	36	8	36	34¼	35⅞	33¾	1971	34¾	33¾	34¾	s2.6	16	7.8	15.3	21.4
32•[11]	ORI	✔**Old Republic Intl** ....NY,Ch,Ph	B+	190	38936	Insur:life,disab,prop,casual	27⅝	⅞	24½	18⅞	35½	21	30422	35½	33⅝	35½	1.5	11	72.1	15.3	32.7
33•[10]	OLCMF	**Olicom A/S**.... NNM	NR	..	...	Mfr computer softwr & hardwr	29	8¾	12⅝	6¾	16⅛	8⅝	21551	15½	12⅝	15¼	...	18	52.5	–11.5	...
#34•[12]	OLN	✔**Olin Corp**.... NY,B,C,Ch,P,Ph	B	276	19442	Chem,metals & defense pr	68¼	6½	60⅛	46	77⅛	48⅜	18041	77⅛	71⅜	74¼	3.2	13	49.0	23.5	21.0
#35•[12]	OLS	✔**Olsten Corp**....NY	B+	258	25723	Provide temp work forces	32	¹⁄₃₂	38⅞	28⅛	42¼	28¼	13867	40½	36¾	39½	0.8	19	25.1	17.5	39.6
36	WS	**Wrrt(6 ws)pur1.27'B'$27** .... NY	....	5	1798		2⅝	1⁹⁄₁₆	3⅞	2¹⁄₁₆	4⅞	2¼	400	4½	3⅞	4⅜	...	..	...	...	...
37•[10]	OLYM	✔**Olympic Financial Ltd**.... NNM	NR	110	13908	Purchases,sells,svc auto loans	9	3	6½	4¼	30⅝	5⅞	168600	23½	14¼	16¼	...	16	165	45.7	...
38	ZEUS	✔**Olympic Steel** .... NNM	NR	31	2174	Dstr stainless steel prods	....	....	16½	10	11½	7½	6804	9⅛	7½	8¾	...	5	–15.7	...	...
39	OMGI	✔**OM Group**.... NNM	NR	136	11168	Produce specialty chemicals	21	14	24¾	18¾	33½	21¾	16464	33⅛	29½	33⅛	1.1	17	41.3	...	...
✣40•[13]	OMEG	✔**Omega Environmental**.... NNM	NR	40	1993	Undergrnd storage tanks svcs	14½	1½	13⅛	4¼	5⅝	3	21794	4⅛	3⅛	3⅜	...	d	–37.2	–5.0	...
41	OHI	✔**Omega Healthcare Investors** .... NY	NR	94	7139	Real estate investment trust	25½	18⅝	26½	22⅜	27¼	23½	7062	26⅞	24¼	26⅝	8.9	15	22.7	20.1	...
42	OMM	✔**OMI Corp**....NY,Ch,Ph	C	80	21134	Operates fleet of cargo ships	11⅞	1¾	8	5¾	8¾	5	8506	6½	5½	6½	...	d	4.0	14.7	4.6
43	OMG.EC	**Omni MultiMedia Group** ....ECM	NR	1	48	Softwr duplication/pkg svcs	....	....	....	....	8⅝	4½	1361	7⅝	7	7⅝	...	64	...	...	...
✣44•[14]	OCR	✔**Omnicare, Inc** .... NY,B,Ch,Ph	↑B+	204	23705	Long-term care pharmacy svcs	24¾	2⅝	22⅝	13½	45⅜	20½	22944	45⅜	37¼	44¾	0.2	53	104	45.0	62.6
#45•[7]	OMC	✔**Omnicom Group**....NY,Ch,Ph	↑A	302	50188	Major int'l advertising co	23¾	2¾	26⅞	21⅞	37½	25	34756	37½	33	37¼	1.9	20	47.4	25.2	30.6
46	ASGN	✔**On Assignment**.... NNM	NR	59	3452	Provides temporary lab svcs	15	7	16¾	10½	34½	15	6513	34½	29	32¾	...	40	105	43.9	...
47	ONTC	✔**ON Technology**.... NNM	NR	33	2336	Dvlp workgroup software	....	....	....	....	20	11½	10593	15	11½	13	...	38	...	...	...
48	ONCS	✔**Oncogene Science**.... NNM	C	28	2939	Human cancer research	11⅛	1¹⁄₁₆	4⅛	2¼	10¾	2½	47610	10¾	6⅜	9½	...	d	280	17.4	40.3
49	ONC	✔**ONCOR Inc**.... AS,Ch	C	55	9332	DNA-based tests	12⅝	½	10⅝	3¾	8⅝	3½	25863	5½	3¾	4½	...	d	–2.7	–13.7	2.2
50	ONM	✔**OncorMed Inc** ....AS	NR	9	920	Genetic testing services	....	....	9⅝	6	12¼	5½	1353	8⅛	5½	6	...	d	...	...	...
51	OLP	✔**One Liberty Properties** ....AS	NR	11	144	Real estate investment trust	18⅛	5⅞	11¼	9⅛	14⅛	10¼	53	13⅝	12¾	12⅞B	9.3	11	31.7	25.1	34.8
52	Pr	**$1.60 cm Cv Pfd([75]17.10)[76]** ....AS	NR	6	99		17¾	10	17½	15⅞	17⅛	15¾	31	16⅞	16½	16½B	9.7	..	...	...	...

Uniform Footnote Explanations-See Page 4. Other: [1]NNM [2]CBOE,NY:Cycle 1. [3]ASE:Cycle 3. [4]CBOE:cycle 3. [5]CBOE,Ph:Cycle 2. [6]CBOE:Cycle 2. [7]P:Cycle 1. [8]ASE:Cycle 1. [9]ASE,CBOE,NY,P:Cycle 3. [10]CBOE:Cycle 1. [11]Ph:Cycle 2. [12]ASE:Cycle 2. [13]CBOE:Cycle 2,NY:Cycle 1. [14]P,Ph:Cycle 3. [51]Ea ADS rep 10 Units. [52]Ea Unit rep:1NYNEX CableComms Grp Plc&1Gp Inc. [53]Incl $0.176 non-taxable,'94. [54]Com or cash re-spec cond.. [55]Fr 1-1-97,scale to $50 in 2004. [56]Sub to adj:based on Cdn Oxy com mult. by 1.766. [57]Oct'95 & prior pricing in $U.S.. [58]Stk dstr of Focal Surgery Inc. [59]®$1.54,'94. [60]Addl ptc 150% of amt qtly com div exceeds $0.667. [61]®$2.69,'94. [62]Excl $71M Subsid Pfd. [63]Rated BBB+ by S&P. [64]Plan form hldg co. [65]®$2.01,'94. [66]®$2.44,'94. [67]®$3.54,'94. [68]®$1.61,'94. [69]Fiscal June'93 & prior. [70]Fiscal Dec'94:yr end June'94 $0.02. [71]Incl $0.044 non-taxable,'94. [72]9 Mo Dec,'92. [73]®$0.59,'94. [74]®$1.53,'94. [75]Thru 7-1-96,scale to $16.50 in'98. [76]From 7-1-99,hldrs opt $16.50 for 90 days.

Splits ◆ Index	Cash Divs. Ea.Yr. Since	Dividends: Latest Payment Period $	Date	Ex. Div.	Total $ So Far 1995	Ind. Rate	Paid 1994	Financial Position Mil-$ Cash& Equiv.	Curr. Assets	Curr. Liab.	Balance Sheet Date	Capitalization Lg Trm Debt Mil-$	Shs. 000 Pfd.	Com.	Earnings $ Per Shr. Years End	1991	1992	1993	1994	1995	Last 12 Mos.	Interim Earnings Period	$ per Shr. 1994	1995	Index
1	....	None Since Public			...	Nil	....	47.0	105	149	9-30-95	58.5	...	925000	Dc	...	...	...	pd0.84	....	....	9 Mo Sep	n/a	0.02	1
2◆	1984	Q0.59	2-1-96	1-8	2.36	2.36	2.36	130	3889	5577	9-30-95	7759	...	429991	Dc	1.49	3.20	□d0.66	1.89	E2.80	2.43	9 Mo Sep	1.42	□1.96	2
3◆	....	0.30	3-10-83	2-17	...	Nil	....	19.5	133	60.8	9-30-95	99.3	...	17584	Dc	0.35	Δ0.65	1.47	2.31	E1.80↓	d1.99	9 Mo Sep	1.36	□d2.94	3
4	....	None Since Public			...	Nil	....	146	199	32.5	9-30-95	3.10	...	19424	Je	0.43	d0.62	d1.09	0.30	1.35	1.81	3 Mo Sep	0.16	0.62	4
5	....	None Since Public			...	Nil	....	16.5	55.9	20.7	9-30-95	0.04	...	35700	Dc	...	...	...	p0.79	....	1.07	9 Mo Sep	p0.64	p0.92	5
6◆	1976	Q0.02	11-22-95	11-3	0.08	0.08	0.08	Equity per shr $13.68			6-30-95	226	...	22145	Sp	0.77	1.00	1.26	1.54	P1.97	1.97				6
7	1994	Q0.41	11-21-95	11-8	1.64	1.64	[53]1.43	Equity per shr $23.52			9-30-95	206	4165	16238	Dc	...	p0.43	p0.79	1.24	....	1.27	9 Mo Sep	0.94	□0.97	7
8	1995	Q0.56¼	11-15-95	10-30	1.006	2.25	....	Cv into 1.0146 com, $24.64				....	4000	...	Dc	...	...	...	....	....	....	Co opt red fr 4-30-2001[54]			8
9	....	None Since Public			...	Nil	....	2.19	18.6	10.3	9-30-95	....	p...	★30038	Je	Nil	0.02	0.07	0.13	0.23	0.18	3 Mo Sep	0.09	0.04	9
10	1975	Q0.25	1-15-96	12-7	1.00	1.00	1.00	118	2160	2033	9-30-95	5271	26495	318449	Dc	Δ1.04	□d1.65	□0.84	d0.36	E1.75	1.31	9 Mo Sep	d0.30	1.37	10
11	1994	Q0.75	1-1-96	12-7	3.00	3.00	1.992	Cv into Occid Pete[56]				....	10250	...	Dc	...	...	...	....	....	....				11
12	....	None Since Public			...	Nil	....	28.6	51.4	13.7	9-30-95	17.3	...	16847	Dc	...	...	...	p0.31	....	0.50	9 Mo Sep	0.15	□0.34	12
13	....	0.05	12-31-77	11-28	...	Nil	....	12.5	106	52.8	9-30-95	33.0	...	23131	Mr	0.70	0.82	0.62	0.23	....	0.22	6 Mo Sep	0.33	0.32	13
14	....	None Since Public			...	Nil	....	9.58	28.1	27.3	j12-31-94	78.4	...	±27732	Dc	...	±0.20	±0.50	±0.50	....	j0.75	9 Mo Sep	±0.40	±0.65	14
15	....	None Since Public			...	Nil	....	54.9	216	72.5	9-30-95	0.51	...	24673	Je	1.00	1.14	Δ1.19	0.54	1.26	1.36	3 Mo Sep	0.15	0.25	15
16◆	1990	A0.25	12-8-95	11-27	0.25	0.25	0.20	19.3	74.9	12.2	7-31-95	....	...	20490	Jl	0.60	0.75	0.72	0.88	1.04	1.23	3 Mo Oct	0.11	0.30	16
17◆	....	h[58]....	10-1-93	10-4	...	Nil	....	14.9	59.2	21.2	9-30-95	....	...	12787	Dc	1.49	d1.56	d0.26	0.69	....	0.92	9 Mo Sep	0.44	0.67	17
18◆	....	None Since Public			...	Nil	....	63.1	1404	788	9-30-95	405	...	155256	Dc	*0.12	*0.27	0.45	0.69	....	0.84	9 Mo Sep	0.48	0.63	18
19◆	....	None Since Public			...	Nil	....	371	1072	574	10-21-95	....	...	82301	Ja	...	...	p0.11	0.40	E1.50	1.44	9 Mo Oct	0.18	1.22	19
20	1972	Q0.31¼	1-5-96	12-12	1.25	1.25	1.25	126	954	508	9-30-95	2055	50	48917	Dc	1.01	□1.41	□1.43	□[59]1.55	E1.50	1.32	9 Mo Sep	□1.18	0.95	20
21	1968	0.838	12-29-95	12-12	†3.35	3.35	†3.35	Cv into 5.976 common,$8.366				....	55	...	Dc	b1.32	b1.61	b1.48	....	....	....				21
22	1958	Q0.30	12-8-95	11-27	1.20	1.20	1.00	26.4	67.1	40.2	9-30-95	52.8	...	2469	Dc	2.04	□d11.82	2.89	5.98	....	6.23	9 Mo Sep	4.32	4.57	22
23	1930	Q0.06	2-6-96	1-4	†0.48	0.48	†0.30	0.50	21.7	9.35	9-30-95	5.03	...	481	Dc	5.05	6.68	0.82	1.66	....	1.33	9 Mo Sep	d0.78	d1.11	23
24◆	1923	Q0.38	12-10-95	11-29	1.52	1.52	1.46	Equity per shr $29.33			9-30-95	65.0	...	35590	Dc	3.01	Δ2.70	2.41	□[61]2.70	E2.50	1.87	9 Mo Sep	□2.34	1.51	24
25	1930	Q0.37½	12-29-95	12-5	1.50	1.50	1.50	113	593	1021	9-30-95	2877	[62]6682	152569	Dc	1.60	1.70	Δ0.01	1.97	E2.03	2.04	12 Mo Sep	0.02	2.04	25
26	....	Plan qtly div			...	2.04	....	Co option redm fr 10-18-2000 at $25				★85.0	...	...	Dc	...	...	...	....	....	....	Mature 9-30-2025			26
27	....	None Since Public			...	Nil	....	29.3	245	85.0	9-30-95	119	...	26607	Dc	d0.57	□d0.28	0.35	d0.49	....	d0.61	9 Mo Sep	0.34	0.22	27
28	1970	Q0.08	3-15-96	2-14	0.32	0.32	0.29	8.91	49.8	16.0	10-31-95	20.4	...	±6813	Jl	1.00	1.00	1.34	1.41	1.15	0.95	3 Mo Oct	0.41	0.21	28
29	1908	Q0.66½	1-30-96	1-8	2.66	2.66	2.66	4.53	347	304	9-30-95	845	839	40355	Dc	3.27	2.42	2.78	3.01	E3.05	3.05	12 Mo Sep	2.12	3.05	29
30◆	1937	Q0.32	12-15-95	11-13	s1.22	1.28	1.124	Book Value $22.07			9-30-95	★1.01	...	p45329	Dc	2.20	2.62	2.99	3.19	E3.25	3.26	9 Mo Sep	2.35	2.42	30
31◆	1984	5%Stk	2-20-96	2-1	s0.92	0.92	s0.876	Book Value $17.49			9-30-95	81.5	...	22700	Dc	1.72	2.00	2.10	[65]2.08	....	2.20	9 Mo Sep	1.52	1.64	31
32◆	1942	Q0.13	12-18-95	12-6	0.51	0.52	0.47	Equity per shr $28.90			9-30-95	309	p25633	52159	Dc	2.47	3.09	Δ2.69	[66]2.55	....	3.16	9 Mo Sep	1.82	2.43	32
33	....	None Since Public			...	Nil	....	41.5	80.7	12.2	12-31-93	0.15	...	15775	Dc	p0.21	0.67	0.85	P0.86	....	0.84	9 Mo Sep	0.62	0.60	33
34	1926	Q0.60	12-8-95	11-8	2.40	2.40	2.20	5.60	1054	789	9-30-95	426	1000	24624	Dc	d0.92	□2.17	d4.52	[67]3.65	E5.70	5.48	9 Mo Sep	2.64	4.47	34
35◆	1977	Q0.08	12-1-95	11-16	0.32	0.32	0.24	19.5	491	199	10-01-95	125	...	±42825	Dc	±0.62	±0.87	±□d0.30	±[68]1.67	E2.07	1.99	9 Mo Sep	±1.16	±1.48	35
36	....	Terms&trad. basis should be checked in detail						Wrrts expire 10-31-96				....	...	4530	Dc	...	...	...	....	....	....				36
37	....	None Since Public			...	Nil	....	Equity per shr $8.08			9-30-95	157	1109	21774	Dc	...	□d0.36	[69]d0.11	[70]0.17	....	1.04	9 Mo Sep	0.02	□0.89	37
38	....	None Since Public			...	Nil	....	3.71	203	41.6	9-30-95	160	...	8600	Dc	...	...	p0.86	p1.05	....	1.78	9 Mo Sep	pd0.08	0.65	38
39	1994	Q0.09	11-30-95	11-15	0.36	0.36	0.28	6.47	191	84.0	6-30-95	54.7	...	12419	Dc	pd0.94	1.16	1.43	1.63	....	1.95	9 Mo Sep	1.20	1.52	39
40	....	None Since Public			...	Nil	....	1.28	68.0	30.7	9-30-95	12.2	...	35696	Mr	d0.66	d0.89	pd0.32	d0.55	....	d0.44	6 Mo Sep	d0.12	d0.01	40
41	1992	Q0.59	11-15-95	10-31	2.36	2.36	[71]2.20	Equity per shr $20.51			9-30-95	195	...	16405	Dc	...	‡[72]0.68	1.78	1.70	....	1.73	9 Mo Sep	1.32	1.35	41
42	1990	0.07	1-21-93	12-21	...	Nil	....	29.2	61.5	59.3	9-30-95	239	...	31041	Dc	0.92	d0.37	d0.29	d1.24	....	d1.36	9 Mo Sep	d0.25	d0.37	42
43	....	None Since Public			...	Nil	....	0.74	5.97	4.66	9-30-95	1.06	...	2752	Mr	...	d0.96	0.32	0.08	....	0.12	6 Mo Sep	d0.03	0.01	43
44◆	1989	Q0.02½	12-7-95	11-16	0.10	0.10	0.09	43.6	152	37.1	9-30-95	87.8	...	26315	Dc	0.25	0.67	Δ0.47	[73]0.60	....	0.84	9 Mo Sep	0.41	0.65	44
45◆	1986	Q0.17½	1-4-96	12-13	0.64	0.70	0.62	254	1943	2105	9-30-95	513	...	75258	Dc	1.04	Δ1.16	1.40	□[74]1.57	E1.84	1.76	9 Mo Sep	□1.05	1.24	45
46	....	None Since Public			...	Nil	....	6.32	15.6	2.62	9-30-95	....	...	4847	Dc	0.25	0.38	0.50	0.68	....	0.81	9 Mo Sep	0.48	0.61	46
47	....	None Since Public			...	Nil	....	34.9	43.6	10.2	9-30-95	1.69	...	10170	Dc	...	...	...	pd0.59	....	0.34	9 Mo Sep	pd0.68	p0.25	47
48	....	None Since Public			...	Nil	....	26.8	29.1	2.98	9-30-95	....	...	17689	Sp	d0.17	d0.31	d0.21	d0.35	d0.25	d0.25				48
49	....	None Since Public			...	Nil	....	10.8	23.5	7.89	9-30-95	0.96	...	20961	Dc	d0.45	d0.64	d0.71	d1.01	....	d0.86	9 Mo Sep	d0.71	d0.56	49
50	....	None Since Public			...	Nil	....	2.50	2.72	0.98	9-30-95	0.72	...	4948	Dc	...	...	...	d0.90	....	d1.23	9 Mo Sep	d0.62	d0.95	50
51	1992	Q0.30	1-3-96	12-13	0.85	1.20	†0.83	Equity per shr $12.14			9-30-95	4.92	809	1416	Dc	3.17	0.74	0.74	1.04	....	1.19	9 Mo Sep	0.78	0.93	51
52	1990	Q0.40	1-3-96	12-13	1.60	1.60	1.60	Cv into 0.825 com,$20				....	809	...	Dc	b3.30	b1.72	...	....	....	....				52

◆**Stock Splits & Divs By Line Reference Index** [2]2-for-1,'93. [3]1-for-5 REVERSE,'93. [6]5-for-4,'91:3-for-2,'92. [16]3-for-1,'92. [17]1-for-5 REVERSE,'91:No adj for stk dstr,'93. [18]2-for-1,'92:3-for-2,'93,'94. [19]3-for-2,'95. [24]2-for-1,'94. [30]3-for-2,'92:Adj for 5%,'95. [31]Adj to 5%,'95. [32]10%,'91:2-for-1,'92. [35]3-for-2,'93. [44]2-for-1,'95. [45]2-for-1,'95.

¶ S&P 500
\# MidCap 400
✚ SmallCap 600
• Options

Index	Ticker	Name of Issue (Call Price of Pfd. Stocks)	Market	Com. Rank. & Pfd. Rating	Inst. Hold Cos	Inst. Hold Shs. (000)	Principal Business	Price Range 1971-93 High	1971-93 Low	1994 High	1994 Low	1995 High	1995 Low	Dec. Sales in 100s	December, 1995 Last Sale Or Bid High	Low	Last	%Div Yield	P-E Ratio	Total Return % Annualized 12 Mo	36 Mo	60 Mo
1	ONPR	✔One Price Clothing Strs	NNM	B+	31	3697	Off-price apparel stores	15⅝	2¼	20	6⅞	8½	2¾	11868	4¼	2¾	3	...	d	−60.0	−36.1	5.1
2	OCQ	✔Oneida Ltd	NY,B,Ch	↑B+	82	4903	Table&cookware:indus.wire	19⅜	1⅛	17	12⅛	17⅝	12⅞	4045	17⅝	15⅜	17⅝	2.7	11	41.5	13.9	18.6
3	ONA	✔Oneita Industries	NY,Ch,Ph	NR	35	3518	Mfr activewr for screenprint'g	23¾	4	11⅞	6	12¾	6⅛	3045	7¼	6⅛	6½	...	16	−39.5	−19.3	5.9
¶4•[1]	OKE	✔ONEOK Inc	NY,B,Ch,P,Ph	B	245	13080	Natural gas dstr: oil & gas	26¼	4⅞	20⅜	15¾	24¾	17⅛	9273	23⅞	22⅛	22⅞	5.1	14	34.2	13.6	15.6
5	ONTK	✔OnTrak Systems	NNM	NR	45	2314	Semiconductor mfg eqp	....	....	....	....	34¾	14	24132	22¾	14	14½	...	81	...	...	...
6	OKP	O'okiep Copper ADR[51]	AS	NR	1	43	Mines in Rep of So Africa	108¾	3	13¾	7⅛	27½	9¼	2344	14¼	9¼	10¼	...	12	−6.1	12.5	9.1
7	OPAL	✔Opal Inc	NNM	NR	34	1381	Mfr semiconductor devices	....	....	....	....	25¼	11	20935	17	11	12¾	...	14	...	...	...
8	OPEN	✔Open Environment	NNM	NR	43	2376	Dvlp client/server softwr prd	....	....	....	....	23¼	6½	36782	21¼	9½	13¾	...	81	...	...	...
9	OCC	✔Oppenheimer Cap L.P.	NY,Ch,Ph	NR	36	2570	Investment advisory svcs	30	6	28¾	18½	28¾	19¾	4970	28½	26⅞	27⅞	e7.8	13	56.5	17.8	26.0
10•[2]	OPTI	✔OPTi Inc	NNM	NR	75	6052	Supplies core logic chipsets	13	6	19¾	10¾	29	8⅛	38847	10¾	8⅛	8⅛	...	7	−48.4	...	...
11	OCLI	✔Optical Coating Lab	NNM	B	32	2023	Optical thin film coatings	13⅛	9/16	7¾	5⅛	15⅜	6⅛	13305	14¾	10⅜	11⅛	1.1	15	83.6	6.1	19.5
12•[3]	ODSI	✔Optical Data Systems	NNM	NR	86	6715	Mfr computer network'g prd	11⅝	4	14⅞	5⅜	43¼	12¾	65617	26	19¾	25¼	...	30	71.4	46.7	...
13	OPPCF	✔Optima Petroleum	NNM	C	9	1036	Dvlp/acq petrol/nat gas props	6⅜	2¼	5½	3	4	2	7506	3	2⅛	2⅞	...	d	−28.9	1.1	...
¶14•[4]	ORCL	✔Oracle Corp	NNM,Ch	B	805	235363	Mkts database mgmt softwr	25⅛	9/16	31	17½	48¾	26⅝	848410	47⅝	39⅞	42⅜	...	39	41.2	66.3	74.6
15	OJ	✔Orange-Co	NY,Ch,P	B−	27	2249	Citrus groves,juice products	12½	½	6½	5⅛	8⅜	5⅜	1315	8¼	7⅝	7¾	...	9	37.8	8.9	9.7
✚16	ORU	✔Orange/Rockland Util	NY,B,Ch,Ph	↓A−	86	2678	Elec & gas util: NY State	47½	7⅛	41¼	28⅜	37⅜	30⅞	3397	37⅜	35¼	35¾	7.2	14	20.6	1.9	9.8
17	ORVX	✔OraVax Inc	NNM	NR	8	907	Dvlp stge:antibody products	....	....	....	....	16¾	7¼	10665	12½	9½	11¾	...	d	...	...	...
18	ORBT	Orbit International	NSC	↓C	17	1202	Apparel,electronic equipment	13¼	1/16	5	1½	2½	¾	7478	1	13/16	⅞	...	d	−50.0	−50.0	−23.7
19	OE	✔Orbital Engine ADS[55]	NY,Ph	NR	15	961	Two-stroke engine technology	30½	10	14⅝	7⅝	9⅞	6¼	17440	7¼	6¼	6½	...	d	−18.8	−28.1	...
✚20•[5]	ORBI	✔Orbital Sciences Corp	NNM	B−	80	8207	Dvlp/mfr aerospace products	23½	9¼	26½	14	22	12⅛	33766	16¼	12⅛	12¾	...	..	−32.0	0.0	−2.2
21	ORBKF	Orbotech Ltd Ord	NNM	NR	2	267	Mfr/svc electro-optical sys	21¾	2⅝	14¾	7⅛	14⅜	8	5728	13⅜	11½	11¾	...	11	44.6	−3.9	12.1
22	OSHC	✔Orchard Supply Hardware Strs	NNM	NR	44	2635	Oper hardware superstrs, Calif	17¾	11	15½	6¼	22½	6¾	14167	22½	19½	20⅝	...	17	185	...	...
23	OREM	✔Oregon Metallurgical	NNM	C	33	2446	Produces reactive alloys	40	¼	8⅜	4⅜	13½	6	5632	11½	9¾	11⅜	...	..	54.2	41.7	8.7
#24•[1]	OS	✔Oregon Steel Mills	NY,Ch,Ph	B	110	13365	Mfr steel plate,steel pipe	38⅝	7⅜	27⅜	14⅛	19¾	13⅛	13990	14⅛	13⅛	13⅞	4.0	13	−4.2	−13.6	−7.1
25	ORLY	✔O'Reilly Automotive	NNM	NR	46	2922	Oper automotive parts stores	32½	17½	35¼	23¼	33⅝	23	7268	30½	27½	29	...	20	19.6	...	...
26•[6]	ORG	✔Organogenesis Inc	AS,Ch,Ph	NR	29	2695	Dvlp living organ equivalent	21¼	3⅜	16	6⅞	22½	7½	115050	22½	13⅝	18½	...	d	18.8	39.0	28.9
27	OBT	✔Oriental Bank & Trust	NY	NR	16	1227	Savings bank, Puerto Rico	18½	1½	16½	9⅞	18¼	10⅞	1425	17⅛	15	16½	3.0	9	53.7	40.8	49.1
28	OAU	✔Original Sixteen To One Mine	P	NR	8	185	Gold mining, California	6¾	⅜	7½	3¾	5¼	2⅝	144	4	3¾	3⅞	...	11	...	...	...
29	OHC.A	✔Oriole Homes[58]Cv'A'	AS,B,Ph	B	15	389	Homes & condominium apts	19½	1 9/16	12⅜	6½	8	5¼	338	6⅜	5⅜	6¼	...	18	−2.9	−12.5	4.6
30	OHC.B	✔ Class 'B'(1/10 vtg)	AS	B	20	1319	in south Florida area	17½	4⅜	12½	6	8	5⅛	1310	6¼	5⅛	6⅛	...	18	−6.2	−12.4	4.9
✚31	OC	✔Orion Capital	NY,B,Ch	B	132	9148	Ins hldg:property & casualty	37½	2⅝	35¼	28⅛	45¼	34¼	4972	45⅛	42	43⅜	2.1	9	26.2	18.2	34.5
32	ONSI	Orion Network Systems	NNM	NR	15	1837	Satellite communic systems	....	....	....	....	14¼	6¾	19681	8¾	6¾	8⅜	...	d	...	...	...
33•[5]	ORN	✔OrNda Healthcorp	NY	NR	165	26978	Oper health care facilities	16	2⅞	22⅜	10½	24	11⅛	99829	24	19¼	23¼	...	15	87.9	38.5	31.1
34	OROA	OroAmerica Inc	NNM	NR	21	1877	Mfr,dstr 14 karat gold jewelry	15½	11¾	18	5½	8¾	3½	3411	4⅞	4	4⅞	...	20	−30.4	...	...
35	ORTL	✔Ortel Corp	NNM	NR	50	2500	Mfr linear fiberoptic prod	....	....	29¾	13	26¾	8½	20610	14	10½	11¼	...	20	−57.1	...	...
36	OCAI	✔Orthodontic Centers of Amer	NNM	NR	62	4487	Manage orthodontic centers	....	....	12½	11	48¼	11⅝	14438	48¼	31¼	48¼	...	54	294	...	...
37	OFIXF	Orthofix International	NNM	NR	..	...	Bone fracture treatment prd	12¾	7¾	13	8¾	20½	7	13074	9½	7	7⅜	...	d	−34.4	−8.9	...
¶38•[7]	ORX	✔Oryx Energy Co	NY	NR	327	71922	Oil & gas explor'n/prod'n	54⅞	16¼	20	10⅝	14¾	9⅞	120186	14	12¾	13⅜	...	9	16.3	−11.1	−16.4
39	OSBN	✔Osborn Communications	NNM	NR	25	3138	Owns,oper radio/TV stations	30	3	7¾	6	11⅛	6	2149	8½	7½	8½	...	d	13.3	19.3	−7.4
40•[8]	OSH.A	Oshawa Grp Cl'A'[60]	To,Mo	A	29	5553	Food dstr & retailer: mdsr	35⅝	¾	24½	17⅛	24⅛	18	7206	24⅛	22⅜	24	2.2	15	33.8	4.2	...
✚41	GOSHA	✔Oshkosh B'Gosh Cl'A'	NNM	B	122	7250	Clothing manufacturer	44	12½	21¾	12¼	18	11½	8774	17½	14⅞	17½	1.6	21	27.2	−2.8	−3.0
42	OSH	✔Oshman's Sporting Gds	AS	C	14	601	Retails sporting goods	26	1⅝	9⅜	5½	15⅛	5¾	968	13⅜	11	11¼	...	39	40.6	6.3	16.7
43	OSM	✔Osmonics, Inc	NY	B+	57	4916	Reverse osmosis/ultrafiltrtn	15⅛	1/16	16⅝	13½	21¼	13¼	1445	21¼	17⅞	20⅜	...	24	40.5	16.9	24.4
44	OSTX	✔Ostex Intl	NNM	NR	46	2847	Dvp stge:osteoporosis treatm't	....	....	....	....	25	8	8347	19¾	16	19¼	...	..	...	...	...
✚45	OSL	✔O'Sullivan Corp	AS	B	61	4925	Mfr molded plastic products	17	3/16	10¾	8⅝	12⅜	9¼	2111	10⅞	9⅞	10⅜	3.1	13	13.8	7.8	9.8
46•[9]	OSU	✔O'Sullivan Industries Hldg	NY,Ch	NR	55	9454	Ready-to-assemble furniture	....	....	25⅝	8¾	13⅛	5⅞	19425	7	5⅞	6⅝	...	21	−43.6	...	...
47	OTRX	✔OTR Express	NNM	NR	9	481	Trucking-gen'l commodities	6½	2¾	9¾	5¾	10¼	4¼	804	4¾	4¼	4½	...	28	−52.6	11.5	...
48	OFCP	✔Ottawa Financial	NNM	NR	7	342	Savings bank, Michigan	....	....	13½	10	16⅜	10½	2066	15¾	15⅜	15⅝	2.0	22	52.2	...	...
49	OTTR	✔Otter Tail Power	NNM	A−	62	1007	Electric sv: Minn/Dakotas	41¼	7⅛	34¾	29½	37¾	30¾	2206	37¾	35	35¾	4.9	15	14.1	7.8	11.7
#50•[10]	OSSI	✔Outback Steakhouse	NNM	NR	209	25977	Oper full-svc restaurants	26⅛	3⅜	32	22⅝	37⅞	22⅞	60298	36⅝	33¾	35⅞	...	31	53.5	24.4	...
¶51•[4]	OM	✔Outboard Marine	NY,B,Ch,P,Ph	B−	230	16029	Leading mfr outboard motors	46	4½	25⅞	17⅜	22⅞	18	7141	21¼	19¾	20⅜	2.0	8	7.8	0.1	11.2
52	OUTL	✔Outlook Group	NNM	B	21	1480	Printing,graphic,pack'g svcs	24½	8¼	13	9¼	12	5¾	5242	7⅞	5¾	6¼	...	d	−45.7	−29.7	...

Uniform Footnote Explanations-See Page 4. Other: [1]Ph:Cycle 2. [2]ASE,CBOE,NY:Cycle 3. [3]CBOE:Cycle 2. [4]CBOE:Cycle 3. [5]ASE,CBOE:Cycle 3. [6]CBOE,NY:Cycle 1. [7]ASE,CBOE:Cycle 1. [8]To:Cycle 2. [9]ASE:Cycle 3. [10]ASE,CBOE,P:Cycle 2. [51]ADR equal 1 ord shr. [52]Approx. [53]Fiscal Jun'92 & prior. [54]12 Mo Dec'93:Fiscal Jun'93 earned $1.59. [55]Ea ADS rep 8 ord, A$0.50. [56]®$0.33,'93. [57]Spl div. [58]Cv into 1 Cl'B' shr. [59]®$1.51,'95. [60]Non-vtg. [61]®$2.33,'95.

Splits ◆ Index	Cash Divs. Ea.Yr. Since	Dividends: Latest Payment Period $	Date	Ex. Div.	Total $ So Far 1995	Ind. Rate	Paid 1994	Financial Position Mil-$ Cash& Equiv.	Curr. Assets	Curr. Liab.	Balance Sheet Date	Capitalization Lg Trm Debt Mil-$	Shs. 000 Pfd.	Com.	Earnings $ Per Shr. Years End	1991	1992	1993	1994	1995	Last 12 Mos.	Interim Earnings Period	$ per Shr. 1994	1995	Index
1◆	....	None Since Public			...	Nil	....	2.27	46.2	31.1	9-30-95	4.00	...	10317	Dc	Δ0.45	0.66	0.84	0.42	....	d0.07	9 Mo Sep	0.31	d0.18	1
2	1936	Q0.12	12-29-95	12-7	0.48	0.48	0.48	3.20	242	117	10-28-95	76.5	89	11000	Ja	0.90	□0.36	1.01	1.24	....	1.60	9 Mo Oct	0.74	1.10	2
3◆	....	5%Stk	3-10-93	2-22	...	Nil	....	1.07	120	53.5	7-01-95	23.9	...	6878	Sp	0.68	1.24	d0.43	d0.98	P0.40	0.40				3
4	1939	Q0.29	11-15-95	10-27	1.13	1.16	1.12	12.5	194	174	8-31-95	351	180	27020	Au	1.33	1.21	1.43	1.34	1.58	1.60	3 Mo Nov	0.29	0.31	4
5	....	None Since Public			...	Nil	....	36.1	50.0	5.59	9-30-95	1.28	...	7167	Je	...	0.01	0.06	0.24	0.17	0.18	3 Mo Sep	0.10	0.11	5
6	....	[52]0.273	2-9-96	1-3	0.094	Nil	....	....	45.3	59.8	j12-31-94	2.88	...	7000	Dc	1.07	0.46	d0.90	0.89	....	0.89				6
7	....	None Since Public			...	Nil	....	28.1	47.0	6.94	9-30-95	....	...	8644	Dc	...	Nil	0.23	0.61	....	0.94	9 Mo Sep	0.47	0.80	7
8	....	None Since Public			...	Nil	....	19.5	31.5	8.26	9-30-95	0.08	...	7445	Dc	...	...	0.08	0.07	....	0.17	9 Mo Sep	0.04	0.14	8
9	1987	0.62½	11-30-95	10-27	†2.35	2.18	†2.17½	Book Value $2.71			4-30-95	....	...	15235	Ap	1.43	1.57	1.74	2.04	2.02	2.22	6 Mo Oct	1.04	1.24	9
10	....	None Since Public			...	Nil	....	53.8	99.3	18.8	3-31-95	2.05	...	10515	Dc	0.62	0.99	0.84	1.17	....	1.16	9 Mo Sep	0.77	0.76	10
11	1991	S0.06	12-15-95	11-29	0.12	0.12	0.12	12.4	65.9	35.1	7-31-95	46.9	...	9409	Oc	□0.16	Δ0.69	d0.65	0.51	P0.73	0.73				11
12◆	....	None Since Public			...	Nil	....	24.2	59.4	9.96	9-30-95	....	...	16144	Dc	0.14	0.34	0.30	0.52	....	0.83	9 Mo Sep	0.35	0.66	12
13	....	None Paid			...	Nil	....	0.40	2.09	2.02	j9-30-95	5.43	...	10177	Dc	d0.38	d0.23	d0.05	d0.56	....	jd0.62	9 Mo Sep	0.03	d0.03	13
14◆	....	None Since Public			...	Nil	....	577	1434	875	8-31-95	81.3	...	434614	My	d0.03	0.14	□0.32	0.64	1.00	1.08	6 Mo Nov	0.35	0.43	14
15	....	†0.10	2-1-96	1-3	...	Nil	....	0.85	47.3	17.8	9-30-95	31.3	...	10298	Sp	d0.14	0.58	□0.17	0.32	0.89	0.89				15
16	1908	Q0.64½	11-1-95	10-12	2.57	2.58	2.54	5.08	221	208	9-30-95	360	469	13654	Dc	3.12	3.15	3.06	2.50	....	2.49	12 Mo Sep	2.68	2.49	16
17	....	None Since Public			...	Nil	....	29.3	29.4	3.87	9-30-95	0.49	...	7587	Dc	...	...	...	pd2.61	....	d1.26	9 Mo Sep	pd2.33	d0.98	17
18	....	h....	5-14-71	3-25	...	Nil	....	7.10	36.4	31.8	9-30-95	7.41	...	5886	Dc	d0.78	[53]0.46	[54]d0.49	d2.75	....	d3.87	9 Mo Sep	d1.89	d3.01	18
19◆	....	1.33%Stk	10-30-92	9-23	...	Nil	....	60.6	80.9	18.1	j6-30-95	19.2	...	323178	Je	0.38	0.43	0.19	d0.30	d0.14	d0.14				19
20	....	None Since Public			...	Nil	....	18.4	160	66.8	6-30-95	95.2	...	22663	Dc	*0.10	0.33	Δ[56]0.37	0.28	....	0.02	9 Mo Sep	0.23	□d0.03	20
21	1993	t0.99	1-25-93	10-20	...	Nil	....	13.4	72.8	46.7	12-31-94	0.28	...	12085	Dc	0.23	d4.26	Δ0.31	0.74	....	1.11	9 Mo Sep	0.51	0.88	21
22	....	None Since Public			...	Nil	....	15.9	156	79.2	10-29-95	133	800	6984	Ja	...	p□0.76	□1.57	0.17	....	1.21	9 Mo Oct	0.31	1.35	22
23	....	0.31	3-28-91	3-1	...	Nil	....	0.53	87.4	29.8	6-30-95	22.6	...	10911	Dc	d0.44	□d0.38	d0.38	d0.18	....	0.06	9 Mo Sep	d0.19	0.05	23
24	1988	Q0.14	11-30-95	11-8	0.56	0.56	0.56	9.60	241	150	9-30-95	240	...	19422	Dc	1.97	1.04	0.75	0.60	E1.10	0.75	9 Mo Sep	0.33	0.48	24
25	....	None Since Public			...	Nil	....	4.12	71.5	26.6	9-30-95	p0.44	...	★10352	Dc	0.73	□0.89	1.01	1.28	....	1.48	9 Mo Sep	1.00	1.20	25
26◆	....	None Since Public			...	Nil	....	15.3	16.1	1.00	9-30-95	....	250	13639	Dc	d0.62	d0.55	d0.87	d0.91	....	d0.94	9 Mo Sep	d0.69	d0.72	26
27◆	1992	tQ0.12½	1-4-96	12-13	t0.324	0.50	†t0.16	Book Value $9.12			6-30-94	92.9	...	6105	Je	0.21	*0.34	1.38	1.82	P1.78	1.85	3 Mo Sep	0.41	0.48	27
28	1995	[57]0.05	9-10-95	8-11	[57]0.05	Nil	....	0.03	2.92	1.21	9-30-95	0.17	...	3517	Dc	d0.14	*0.11	Δ0.39	0.04	....	0.36	9 Mo Sep	d0.07	0.25	28
29	1992	0.20	1-12-95	12-23	0.20	Nil	0.30	Equity per shr $16.49			9-30-95	90.0	...	±4626	Dc	±1.36	±1.17	□±0.79	±0.89	....	0.34	9 Mo Sep	±0.43	±d0.12	29
30	1992	0.22½	1-12-95	12-23	0.22½	Nil	0.35	....	...	...		....	...	2732	Dc	±1.36	±1.17	□±0.79	±0.89	....	0.34	9 Mo Sep	±0.43	±d0.12	30
31◆	1978	Q0.23	1-2-96	12-13	0.83	0.92	0.74	Equity per shr $29.40			9-30-95	209	...	14046	Dc	3.75	□3.61	Δ3.88	3.85	....	4.62	9 Mo Sep	2.78	3.55	31
32	....	None Since Public			...	Nil	....	63.0	69.3	58.0	9-30-95	227	19	10806	Dc	d0.35	d0.40	d0.85	d0.86	....	d2.64	9 Mo Sep	d0.64	d2.42	32
33	....	None Paid			...	Nil	....	4.96	404	398	8-31-95	p1032	1330	★58878	Au	0.91	□d4.86	0.52	□d1.29	[59]1.53	1.53				33
34	....	None Since Public			...	Nil	....	0.51	72.6	34.4	10-27-95	3.38	...	6248	Ja	...	p0.98	□p1.78	0.67	....	0.25	9 Mo Oct	0.47	0.05	34
35	....	None Since Public			...	Nil	....	43.3	62.8	7.98	7-31-95	....	...	11244	Ap	0.12	Δ0.15	0.23	0.30	0.55	0.56	6 Mo Oct	0.26	0.27	35
36◆	....	None Since Public			...	Nil	....	47.6	65.5	9.53	9-30-95	3.59	...	10437	Dc	...	...	p0.57	p0.44	....	0.89	9 Mo Sep	p0.21	0.66	36
37	....	None Since Public			...	Nil	....	15.2	29.4	6.53	12-31-92	0.74	...	p12238	Dc	p0.57	0.61	P0.71	P0.84	....	d1.29	9 Mo Sep	0.58	d1.55	37
38	1988	0.10	12-10-93	11-15	...	Nil	....	12.0	298	627	9-30-95	978	...	104430	Dc	0.08	□0.74	□d1.01	□d0.68	E1.51	1.58	9 Mo Sep	□d0.82	□1.44	38
39◆	....	None Since Public			...	Nil	....	2.18	10.2	7.02	9-30-95	44.5	...	5276	Dc	±d2.38	d1.30	d0.50	□d0.21	....	d0.01	9 Mo Sep	□d0.40	□d0.20	39
40	1960	gQ0.13	12-10-95	11-14	g0.51½	0.52	g0.49½	54.6	663	377	j1-28-95	124	...	±p37308	Ja	0.96	1.14	±1.35	±1.41	....	j1.57	40 Wk Oct	±1.06	±1.22	40
41	1985	Q0.07	12-1-95	11-15	0.28	0.28	0.37¾	0.98	163	53.0	9-30-95	17.8	...	±12456	Dc	±1.62	±□1.08	±0.31	±0.50	E0.85	0.83	9 Mo Sep	±0.38	±0.71	41
42	....	0.05	1-11-91	12-21	...	Nil	....	0.41	140	80.2	10-28-95	37.7	...	5818	Ja	Δd0.70	d0.03	d3.36	0.05	....	0.29	9 Mo Oct	d0.62	d0.38	42
43◆	....	None Since Public			...	Nil	....	37.6	82.3	21.8	9-30-95	12.6	...	12766	Dc	0.43	Δ0.45	0.63	0.79	....	0.86	9 Mo Sep	0.57	0.64	43
44	....	None Since Public			...	Nil	....	30.3	31.1	0.91	9-30-95	....	...	12433	Dc	...	...	pd0.23	pd0.47	....	....	9 Mo Sep	Nil	d0.31	44
45	1960	Q0.08	1-12-96	12-13	0.30	0.32	0.28	11.9	92.4	29.8	9-30-95	1.79	...	16511	Dc	0.09	0.66	Δ0.59	0.16	....	0.78	9 Mo Sep	0.04	0.66	45
46	....	None Since Public			...	Nil	....	0.20	117	25.6	9-30-95	52.0	...	16820	Je	...	...	p1.04	Δp0.78	0.49	0.32	3 Mo Sep	0.25	0.08	46
47	....	None Since Public			...	Nil	....	0.02	6.11	10.8	12-31-94	14.6	...	1825	Dc	0.14	0.32	□0.45	0.70	....	0.16	9 Mo Sep	0.50	d0.04	47
48	1994	Q0.08	12-29-95	12-4	0.31	0.32	0.07	Book Value $14.23			9-30-95	18.2	...	5541	Dc	...	...	p0.73	0.25	....	0.70	9 Mo Sep	0.07	0.52	48
49	1938	Q0.44	12-9-95	11-13	1.76	1.76	1.72	1.40	67.3	71.0	9-30-95	166	388	11180	Dc	2.15	2.17	2.23	2.34	....	2.38	12 Mo Sep	2.23	2.38	49
50◆	....	None Since Public			...	Nil	....	20.8	34.9	41.0	9-30-95	26.3	...	43725	Dc	p0.17	0.34	0.58	0.88	E1.17	1.09	9 Mo Sep	0.63	0.84	50
51	1937	Q0.10	11-24-95	11-8	0.40	0.40	0.40	58.3	502	249	9-30-95	177	...	20015	Sp	*d4.42	0.10	□d8.42	2.42	[61]2.56	2.56				51
52	....	None Since Public			...	Nil	....	0.05	37.8	9.75	8-31-95	29.9	...	4649	My	0.92	1.14	1.07	0.95	0.26	d0.36	6 Mo Nov	0.53	d0.09	52

◆**Stock Splits & Divs By Line Reference Index** [1]3-for-2,'94. [3]Adj to 5%,'93. [12]2-for-1,'95. [14]2-for-1,'93:3-for-2,'95. [19]Adj for 1.333%,'92. [26]5-for-4,'95. [27]10%,'91:8-for-7,'92:3-for-2,'93:4-for-3,'94:5-for-4,'95. [31]5-for-4,'92,'93. [36]To split 2-for-1,ex Jan 2. [39]1-for-2 REVERSE,'94. [43]3-for-2,'91,'94. [50]2-for-1,'92:3-for-2,'91,'94.

¶ S&P 500 # MidCap 400 ✜ SmallCap 600 • Options

Index	Ticker	Name of Issue (Call Price of Pfd. Stocks)	Market	Com. Rank. & Pfd. Rating	Inst. Hold Cos	Inst. Hold Shs. (000)	Principal Business	Price Range 1971-93 High	1971-93 Low	1994 High	1994 Low	1995 High	1995 Low	Dec. Sales in 100s	December, 1995 Last Sale Or Bid High	Low	Last	%Div Yield	P-E Ratio	Total Return % Annualized 12 Mo	36 Mo	60 Mo
#1	OSG	✔**Overseas Shiphldg**	NY,B,Ch,P,Ph	↓B–	126	15013	Major internat'l shipowner	27⅜	2 3/16	26¾	17¼	23⅞	17	3615	20⅛	18¾	19	3.2	d	–16.4	6.9	6.4
2	OWEN	✔**Owen Healthcare**	NNM	NR	36	6880	Manage hospital pharmacies	...	...	...	...	27⅝	12	17184	27⅝	19¾	27⅝	...	69	...	...	...
¶3•[1]	OCF	✔**Owens-Corning**	NY,B,Ch,P,Ph	B–	324	40556	Glass fiber/polyester resins	82½	8⅞	46	27¾	47⅛	30¼	29984	46¾	43⅝	44⅞	...	10	43.6	8.1	22.9
4•[2]	OI	✔**Owens-Illinois**	NY	NR	129	60363	Mfr glass/plastic packag'g prd	14½	7⅞	13⅝	10¼	14¾	10⅛	29977	14¾	12⅝	14½	...	11	33.3	14.1	...
✜5	OMI	✔**Owens & Minor**	NY,Ch,Ph	A–	110	16228	Hospital supply:drug distr	15⅝	3/16	18⅛	13¼	14⅞	11⅝	10031	13⅜	12⅛	12¾	1.4	d	–7.7	10.6	24.7
6•[2]	OXHP	✔**Oxford Health Plans**	NNM	NR	254	34102	Hlth benefit svcs N.Y. area	28	3½	41¾	19¾	83¾	38½	83572	75½	69¼	73⅞	...	53	81.8	79.1	...
✜7	OXM	✔**Oxford Indus**	NY,Ch	B+	84	5131	Mfr wearing apparel	27⅛	1¾	34¾	21⅞	22	16	2657	19¼	16½	16¾	4.8	58	–21.9	–3.4	23.3
8	OXFD	✔**Oxford Resources Cl'A'**	NNM	NR	50	2737	Automobile leasing svcs	10½	9¾	14	8½	28	10¾	8118	26⅛	22½	22½	...	21	102	...	...
9	OXIS	✔**OXIS International**	NNM	C	8	408	Drug devel:human/veter	43¼	1½	4⅜	1⅜	4½	1⅛	7097	2	1⅜	1¾	...	d	0.0	–21.6	–1.4
10	PCMS	✔**P-COM Inc**	NNM	NR	47	7327	Wireless telecommun svcs	...	...	...	...	22⅞	7½	43943	20	15½	20	...	d	...	...	...
¶11•[3]	PCAR	✔**PACCAR Inc**	NNM	B+	298	16405	Mfr trucks,ind'l/oilfield eq	61⅛	2¾	61¾	40	54⅝	39¼	38062	51¾	40½	42⅛	e2.4	7	2.1	3.5	15.3
¶12•[4]	PET	✔**Pacific Enterprises**	NY,B,C,Ch,P,Ph	B–	377	40807	Hldg co:natl gas-So'n Cal	61¼	13⅞	24½	19¼	28⅝	21	21614	28⅝	26½	28¼	4.8	14	42.8	20.8	–1.7
¶13•[5]	PCG	✔**Pacific Gas & Elec**	NY,B,C,Ch,P,Ph,Vc	B	519	174656	Elec & gas util:North'n Calif	36¾	8½	35	21⅜	30⅝	24¼	146539	28⅞	27½	28⅜	6.9	10	24.4	1.0	8.8
14	PGP	✔**Pacific Gateway Prop**	AS	C	11	824	Real estate investments	20½	2⅛	4⅝	2⅞	4⅛	2 7/16	1123	2⅞	2½	2⅞	...	..	–14.8	3.9	–14.4
15	PAG	✔**Pacific Gulf Properties**	AS,Ch	NR	21	1505	Real estate investment trust	...	...	18½	12¾	16¾	13	3468	16¾	14½	16¼	9.8	..	20.7	...	...
16•[5]	PPSI	✔**Pacific Physician Svcs**[56]	NNM	NR	68	5897	Ntwk Dr.grps/staffing svcs	27½	5⅜	30¾	10¼	19	10¾	58351	18⅞	16⅛	18	...	27	14.3	15.5	...
✜17•[6]	PSX	✔**Pacific Scientific**	NY,Ch	B–	72	4204	Mfr elec mtrs,ctrls,safetydvc	20	3/16	23¾	10¾	27⅜	14⅛	6068	26⅞	24⅜	25	0.5	25	22.0	47.9	45.1
¶18•[7]	PAC	✔**Pacific Telesis Group**	NY,Ch,P,Ph	B+	701	174329	Tel svc:Calif & Nevada	59¼	12⅞	58	28¼	34⅜	25⅝	256749	34⅜	30⅛	33½	6.5	14	...	...	...
#19•[8]	PHSYB	✔**PacifiCare Health Sys'B'**	NNM	B+	216	19989	Health maintenance svcs	50	20	75	37¼	91	44	70272	91	82¾	87	...	24	34.6	26.2	...
20	PHSYA	✔ **Cl'A'**	NNM	B+	129	4311		57½	1 5/16	79½	37¼	89⅜	44½	8426	89⅜	80½	87	...	24	36.7	21.3	40.1
¶21•[9]	PPW	✔**PacifiCorp**	NY,B,C,Ch,P,Ph	B+	460	102059	Utility: electric service	25¼	6⅞	19½	15⅞	21⅝	17½	102920	21⅝	19⅝	21⅛	5.1	13	22.6	8.2	5.4
22	PCQ	**PacifiCorp 8.375% 'QUIDS'**[58]	NY	....[59]	1	2	Qtly Income Debt Securities	...	...	...	...	26⅝	25	2047	26⅝	25¾	26⅛	8.0	..	...	...	...
23	PCX	**PacifiCorp 8.55%'QUIDS'**[58]	NY	NR	..	...	Qtly Income Debt Securities	...	...	...	...	26¼	25¼	2691	26¼	25½	25⅞	8.3	..	...	...	...
24	PRCA	**Packaging Research**	NSC	C	3		Mfr food processing eqp	510	⅝	7⅝	4⅞	6⅞	1⅛	1685	2⅛	1⅛	1⅞	...	d	–70.0	23.3	24.6
25	PGG	✔**Page America Group**	AS,Ch,Ph	C	16	968	Provides radio paging svcs	8⅞	1¼	5¾	2¾	4¼	⅛	9635	7/16	⅛	⅛	...	d	–95.7	–68.8	...
26•[1]	PAGE	✔**Paging Network**	NNM,Ch	NR	257	93594	Provides paging svcs in U.S.	17¼	5¼	17⅛	10⅜	26	12½	111316	25¼	21½	24⅜	...	d	49.3	34.8	...
#27•[6]	PWJ	✔**Paine Webber Group**	NY,B,Ch,P,Ph	B	145	36245	Major securities broker	23⅛	7/16	19¾	12¾	23⅛	14⅜	38454	22¾	19⅝	20	2.4	31	37.1	11.1	30.0
28	SIS	**Paine Webber Gp Stk Index Sec**	AS	NR	2	814	Stock Index Return Securities	10⅛	8⅞	9⅝	8½	11⅜	8½	796	11⅜	10½	11	...	..	27.5	...	...
29•[6]	PAIR	✔**PairGain Technologies**	NNM	NR	113	11489	Mfr telecommunications prd	22¼	9¼	16¼	6⅞	56	13¼	45599	56	45	54¾	...	63	262	...	...
¶30•[10]	PLL	✔**Pall Corp**	NY,B,P	A	421	76495	Fine filters,fluid contr eq	24⅛	⅛	20¼	13⅝	27⅞	18⅜	44291	27⅞	25½	26⅞	1.6	25	45.1	12.0	20.3
31	PWIR	✔**Palmer Wireless 'A'**	NNM	NR	44	5438	Oper celular telephone sys	...	...	...	...	24½	14¼	4940	22⅜	19¾	22	...	d	...	...	...
32	PAM	✔**Pamida Holdings**	AS,Ch	NR	12	1227	Operates department stores	6½	2½	7⅞	2¾	7¾	2¼	1129	3⅞	3	3⅛	...	11	–45.7	–3.7	–4.8
33	PANA	✔**Panaco Inc**	NNM	NR	18	2159	Oil & gas explor,dev,prod'n	5⅞	1	4⅝	2½	5¼	3⅝	13684	4⅝	4	4⅜	...	22	9.2	33.3	26.4
34•[11]	PB	✔**Panamerican Beverages'A'**	NY,Ch	NR	..	...	Soft drink bottler Latin Amer	39¼	25½	45⅜	23⅝	34¾	15	23335	34½	29⅝	32	1.0	19	3.2	...	...
35	SPOT	**PanAmSat Corp**	NNM	NR	39	5272	Satellite communication svcs	...	...	...	...	22⅜	12¼	42616	22⅜	17	22	...	d	...	...	...
36	PCP	**PanCanadian Petroleum**	To,Mo,Vc	↑B+	18	4559	Crude oil & natural gas	48⅜	1¾	44¾	37	54	37	3151	53¼	50	53¼	1.5	26	35.5	21.0	...
37	PAMX	✔**Pancho's Mexican Buffet**	NNM	B–	20	1376	Cafeteria-style restaurants	15⅞	⅜	12¾	6⅜	7	2⅝	6426	3⅛	2⅝	2⅞	2.1	d	–54.6	–31.4	–10.5
38	PNDA	✔**Panda Project**	NNM	NR	19	373	Dvlp stge:semiconductor tech	...	...	11⅜	5¼	51¾	11	9958	31¼	19¾	21¾	...	d	97.7	...	...
¶39•[12]	PEL	✔**Panhandle East'n**	NY,To,B,C,Ch,P,Ph	B	506	98394	Operates natural gas lines	52¼	9¾	25½	18¼	28⅞	18¾	52874	28⅞	27⅛	27⅞	3.2	14	46.2	23.5	23.6
40	PTC	✔**PAR Technology**	NY,Ch,Ph	B–	16	977	Retail/defense computer prod	29½	2⅜	9¼	6⅛	10¾	5⅞	1503	9⅞	8¾	9	...	18	35.8	15.3	27.9
41	PRDM	✔**Paradigm Technology**	NNM	NR	49	2706	Dvlp/mfr semiconductor devices	...	...	...	...	37¼	12	28097	19¼	12	13½	...	..	...	...	...
42	PAO	✔**Paragon Group**	NY,Ch,Ph	NR	53	5518	Real estate investment trust	...	...	21⅜	16¼	19½	15¼	9154	17⅝	15⅜	17⅜	10.7	..	11.3	...	...
✜43•[10]	PTB	✔**Paragon Trade Brands**	NY,Ch	NR	78	10187	Mfr infant disposable diapers	31⅜	15	36½	11⅝	23⅞	12⅜	10114	23⅞	20⅛	23⅜	...	d	79.8	...	...
44	PLLL	✔**Parallel Petroleum**	NNM	B–	14	1560	Oil & gas:acq,dvlp,drilling	8⅛	1/32	4⅞	2¾	3⅛	1⅜	7408	2	1 7/16	1¾	...	..	–39.4	29.9	11.6
#45•[13]	PMTC	✔**Parametric Technology**	NNM,Ph	NR	335	54433	Mechanical design softwr prd	44¾	2	40¼	21½	72½	32	172160	71	57	66½	...	55	91.4	39.6	71.9
46	PARQ	✔**ParcPlace-Digitalk**	NNM	NR	45	3093	Dvlp softwr development sys	...	...	24½	13⅜	22¼	6⅝	22306	11¾	8⅛	8½	...	d	–60.7	...	...
47	PRXL	**PAREXEL Intl**	NNM	NR	..	...	Pharmaceutical R&D	...	...	...	...	36	18¾	13438	36	21¾	33¼	...	d	...	...	...
48	PKE	✔**Park Electrochemical**	NY,Ch	B+	87	4432	Printed circuit materials	13	¼	17⅞	11½	34⅛	14	4661	33	28⅜	33	1.0	17	127	76.6	47.1
49	PRK	✔**Park National Corp**	AS,Ch	NR	26	1631	General Banking, Ohio	43½	13¼	42½	34½	54½	42⅜	205	48½	46⅝	47⅝B	2.9	16	15.4	...	...
50	PKOH	✔**Park-Ohio Indus**	NNM	B–	52	4539	Consum/ind.prod./containers	29	2⅜	18⅛	12⅜	16½	10⅛	6531	16½	12¾	16⅛	...	10	25.2	47.7	41.2
#51	PKD	✔**Parker Drilling**	NY,B,Ch,Ph	C	110	34625	Land contract drilling sv	36¾	1 5/16	6⅜	4⅜	6⅜	4⅜	31297	6¼	5	6⅛	...	88	36.1	9.8	–2.3
¶52•[13]	PH	✔**Parker-Hannifin**	NY,B,Ch,P,Ph	B+	409	48787	Fluid pwr systems & comp	32⅝	2½	31⅜	22⅝	41½	27⅝	59637	37¾	32⅞	34¼	2.1	11	15.1	25.1	19.5

Uniform Footnote Explanations-See Page 4. Other: [1]Ph:Cycle 3. [2]CBOE:Cycle 2. [3]NY:Cycle 2. [4]ASE:Cycle 1. [5]ASE:Cycle 3. [6]CBOE:Cycle 1. [7]P:Cycle 1. [8]CBOE,P:Cycle 2. [9]P:Cycle 2. [10]CBOE:Cycle 3. [11]ASE,CBOE:Cycle 1. [12]Ph:Cycle 1. [13]Ph:Cycle 2. [51]®$0.81,'94. [52]Incl current amts. [53]Excl subsid pfd. [54]Incl $0.336 non-taxable,'94. [55]11 Mo Dec'94. [56]MedPartners/Mullikin plan acq,.66667 com. [57]Stk dstr of PacTel Corp,'94. [58]Junior Subordinated Deferrable Interest Debs. [59]Rated A-by S&P. [60]®$0.30,'94. [61]12 Mo Dec'91. [62]6 Mo Dec'94. [63]®$1.52,'94.

Index (◆ Splits)	Cash Divs. Ea. Yr. Since	Dividends: Latest Payment Period $	Date	Ex. Div.	Total $ So Far 1995	Ind. Rate	Paid 1994	Financial Position Mil-$ Cash & Equiv.	Curr. Assets	Curr. Liab.	Balance Sheet Date	Capitalization Lg Trm Debt Mil-$	Shs. 000 Pfd.	Com.	Earnings $ Per Shr. Years End	1991	1992	1993	1994	1995	Last 12 Mos.	Interim Earnings Period	$ per Shr. 1994	1995	Index
1	1973	Q0.15	11-28-95	10-30	0.60	0.60	0.60	193	259	78.4	9-30-95	1123	...	36227	Dc	1.67	ΔNil	0.55	d0.17	Ed0.20	d0.40	9 Mo Sep	d0.05	d0.28	1
2	....	None Since Public			...	Nil	....	21.5	104	30.4	8-31-95	....	...	16990	Nv	...	...	...	p0.40	....	0.40	9 Mo Aug	0.45	p0.45	2
3◆	....	0.35	9-15-86	8-26	...	Nil	....	20.0	1030	1015	9-30-95	798	...	50880	Dc	□d12.58	Δ1.68	Δ2.40	Δ1.70	E4.50↑	4.35	9 Mo Sep	Δ0.71	3.36	3
4	....	None Since Public			...	Nil	....	169	1214	920	9-30-95	2746	263	119550	Dc	□d3.25	□0.81	□0.13	0.64	E1.28	0.82	9 Mo Sep	1.05	1.23	4
5◆	1926	Q0.04½	12-29-95	12-20	0.18	0.18	0.17	0.22	693	306	9-30-95	368	1	30859	Dc	0.41	□0.71	Δ0.62	0.15	....	d0.02	9 Mo Sep	d0.03	d0.20	5
6◆	....	None Since Public			...	Nil	....	305	455	349	9-30-95	....	...	34282	Dc	*0.16	*0.26	0.46	[51]0.82	E1.40	1.29	9 Mo Sep	0.54	1.01	6
7	1960	Q0.20	12-2-95	11-13	0.80	0.80	0.72	10.3	294	152	9-01-95	46.8	...	8705	My	0.62	1.42	1.70	2.23	1.22	0.29	6 Mo Nov	1.26	0.33	7
8	....	None Since Public			...	Nil	....	Equity per shr $2.86			9-30-95	[52]1207	...	±★14813	Je	±d0.13	±0.01	±0.42	±0.66	±0.98	1.08	3 Mo Sep	±0.20	±0.30	8
9	....	None Since Public			...	Nil	....	1.01	3.13	3.79	9-30-95	0.42	643	12124	Dc	d0.04	d0.07	d0.30	d0.88	....	d0.66	9 Mo Sep	d0.90	d0.68	9
10◆	....	None Since Public			...	Nil	....	18.8	44.2	10.6	9-30-95	....	...	16534	Dc	...	...	...	pd0.59	....	d0.17	9 Mo Sep	pd0.39	0.03	10
11◆	1943	Q0.25	3-5-96	2-15	†3.00	1.00	†1.87	Equity per shr $34.12			9-30-95	1106	...	38861	Dc	Δ1.02	1.68	3.66	5.26	E6.25	6.30	9 Mo Sep	3.79	4.83	11
12	1909	Q0.34	11-15-95	10-18	1.34	1.36	1.26	368	1035	913	9-30-95	1279	[53]1101	84688	Dc	■d1.45	d7.57	2.06	1.95	E2.10	2.15	9 Mo Sep	1.37	1.57	12
13	1919	Q0.49	1-15-96	12-13	1.96	1.96	1.94	339	3386	3097	9-30-95	8207	p27592	419027	Dc	2.24	2.58	2.33	2.21	E2.90	2.71	12 Mo Sep	2.45	2.71	13
14	....	0.15	6-28-90	5-21	...	Nil	....	Equity per shr Neg			9-30-95	61.8	...	3893	Dc	*▲2.04	d0.73	Δd0.07	□7.10	....	6.72	9 Mo Sep	d0.10	d0.48	14
15	1994	Q0.40	1-10-96	12-28	1.56	1.60	[54]0.96	Equity per shr $13.78			9-30-95	[52]205	...	4857	Dc	...	...	n/a	□[55]0.63	....	....	9 Mo Sep	n/a	0.30	15
16◆	....	None Since Public			...	Nil	....	59.6	120	46.5	7-31-95	69.7	...	16247	Jl	0.36	0.46	0.57	0.54	□0.63	0.67	3 Mo Oct	0.15	0.19	16
17◆	1992	Q0.03	1-2-96	12-13	0.12	0.12	0.06	4.96	106	35.8	9-29-95	64.9	...	11023	Dc	0.73	0.50	Δ0.67	0.85	....	1.01	9 Mo Sep	0.56	0.72	17
18◆	1984	Q0.54½	2-1-96	12-27	2.18	2.18	h[57]2.18	72.0	2667	3892	9-30-95	5232	...	428435	Dc	2.58	2.83	□0.53	2.73	E2.45	2.53	9 Mo Sep	2.12	□1.92	18
19	....	None Since Public			...	Nil	....	812	962	641	9-30-95	11.9	...	±30883	Sp	1.10	±1.78	±2.25	Δ±3.02	±3.62	3.62				19
20◆	....	None Since Public			...	Nil	....	....	....	...		....	...	12306	Sp	1.10	±1.78	±2.25	Δ±3.02	P±3.62	3.62				20
21	1947	Q0.27	2-15-96	1-18	1.08	1.08	1.08	16.0	734	1354	9-30-95	3707	p8299	284277	Dc	1.86	d1.42	Δ1.59	1.51	E1.65↑	1.63	9 Mo Sep	1.10	1.22	21
22	1995	Q0.523	12-29-95	12-26	1.227	2.09	....	Co option redm fr 5-31-2000 at $25				110	...	...	Dc	...	...	...	....	....	....	Mature 6-30-20335			22
23	....	Plan qtly div			...	2.14	....	Co option redm fr 5-31-1997 at $25				55.8	...	...	Dc	...	...	...	....	....	....	Mature 12-31-2025			23
24◆	....	None Paid			...	Nil	....	0.29	6.09	7.09	9-30-95	3.37	...	3097	Dc	d0.20	pd1.78	0.87	[60]0.34	....	d0.40	9 Mo Sep	0.32	d0.42	24
25◆	....	None Paid			...	Nil	....	0.80	3.80	54.7	9-30-95	0.09	286	8052	Dc	[61]d2.14	□Δd1.51	d2.50	d1.55	....	d2.34	9 Mo Sep	d0.79	d1.58	25
26◆	....	None Since Public			...	Nil	....	256	307	108	9-30-95	1150	...	102224	Dc	d0.11	□d0.07	d0.20	d0.18	....	d0.33	9 Mo Sep	d0.16	d0.32	26
27◆	1975	Q0.12	1-4-96	11-30	0.48	0.48	0.46	Equity per shr $14.90			9-30-95	2423	3500	97437	Dc	2.10	2.83	3.11	0.41	E0.65	d0.26	9 Mo Sep	0.67	Nil	27
28	....	....			...	....	....	Based on S&P Midcap 400 as defined				....	...	2800	Dc	...	...	...	....	....	....	Due 6-2-2000			28
29	....	None Since Public			...	Nil	....	68.8	105	11.5	9-30-95	....	...	15077	Dc	pd0.45	pd0.22	p0.60	0.56	....	0.87	9 Mo Sep	0.37	0.68	29
30◆	1974	Q0.10½	11-10-95	10-25	0.42	0.42	0.37	86.6	489	278	10-28-95	64.8	...	114614	Jl	0.69	Δ0.77	0.68	0.86	□1.04	1.08	3 Mo Oct	□0.12	0.16	30
31	....	None Since Public			...	Nil	....	6.31	23.3	14.3	9-30-95	187	...	±23369	Dc	...	...	...	pd0.08	....	d0.23	9 Mo Sep	p0.17	0.02	31
32	....	None Since Public			...	Nil	....	10.8	244	141	10-29-95	268	2	5005	Ja	±0.01	±0.46	±□d0.48	±0.51	....	0.28	9 Mo Oct	±d0.11	±Δd0.34	32
33	....	0.03	4-15-91	4-16	...	Nil	....	1.47	4.49	2.60	9-30-95	8.87	...	11137	Dc	d0.19	d0.07	d0.02	Δ0.29	....	0.20	9 Mo Sep	□0.22	0.13	33
34	1993	Q0.08	12-20-95	11-29	0.32	0.32	0.28	159	287	156	12-31-93	33.4	...	★±39946	Dc	...	±p1.58	±1.46	P±1.80	E1.70	1.82	9 Mo Sep	±1.15	±1.17	34
35	....	None Since Public			...	Nil	....	27.2	39.0	12.7	6-30-95	527	269	±p100000	Dc	...	...	...	p±0.11	....	d0.14	9 Mo Sep	p±0.13	p±d0.12	35
36	1960	gQ0.20	12-29-95	12-6	g0.80	0.80	g0.80	40.5	341	301	j12-31-94	291	...	p125269	Dc	■0.38	1.37	1.85	2.30	....	j2.06	9 Mo Sep	1.78	1.54	36
37	1980	Q0.01½	12-12-95	11-24	0.12	0.06	0.24	1.20	4.38	5.47	9-30-95	8.71	...	4398	Sp	d0.83	0.67	Δ0.48	0.47	d1.22	d1.22				37
38	....	None Paid			...	Nil	....	24.8	26.6	1.96	9-30-95	....	...	8109	Mr	...	d0.14	d0.54	d1.25	....	d2.12	6 Mo Sep	d0.52	d1.39	38
39◆	1937	Q0.22½	12-15-95	11-9	0.88½	0.90	0.84	80.3	805	956	9-30-95	2251	...	150127	Dc	0.86	1.74	1.29	1.51	E2.00↑	1.86	9 Mo Sep	1.16	1.51	39
40	....	None Since Public			...	Nil	....	4.03	53.0	11.3	9-30-95	....	...	7689	Dc	0.20	0.30	0.32	0.46	....	0.51	9 Mo Sep	0.27	0.32	40
41	....	None Since Public			...	Nil	....	26.7	38.1	10.1	9-30-95	5.14	...	6595	Dc	...	...	...	‡p[62]0.23	....	....	9 Mo Sep	n/a	p0.58	41
42	1994	Q0.46½	11-28-95	11-14	1.86	1.86	0.33	Equity per shr $13.78			9-30-95	[52]218	...	14697	Dc	...	...	...	p0.76	....	....	9 Mo Sep	n/a	0.62	42
43	....	None Since Public			...	Nil	....	3.08	96.6	72.3	9-24-95	....	...	11599	Dc	p1.62	p1.55	Δp2.61	2.16	....	d0.44	9 Mo Sep	2.00	d0.60	43
44	....	None Since Public			...	Nil	....	0.19	1.00	0.75	9-30-95	10.4	...	14854	Dc	*0.02	*0.03	□0.03	0.03	....	Nil	9 Mo Sep	0.04	0.01	44
45◆	....	None Since Public			...	Nil	....	309	400	82.0	9-30-95	....	...	62997	Sp	0.19	0.37	0.75	1.14	1.20	1.20				45
46	....	None Since Public			...	Nil	....	29.4	39.1	12.4	9-30-95	....	...	11217	Mr	...	d0.53	0.30	0.45	....	d0.84	6 Mo Sep	0.21	d1.08	46
47	....	None Since Public			...	Nil	....	3.62	39.5	28.3	9-30-95	0.72	p...	★6922	Je	d0.97	0.33	d2.97	Δ0.35	d12.61	d11.31	3 Mo Sep	d1.16	0.14	47
48◆	1985	Q0.08	2-6-96	1-5	0.26	0.32	0.18	41.2	104	47.0	8-27-95	....	...	11532	Fb	0.19	0.27	1.01	[63]1.60	....	1.97	9 Mo Nov	1.14	1.52	48
49◆	1986	Q0.35	1-2-96	12-6	1.20	1.40	1.13	Book Value $18.31			9-30-95	....	...	7150	Dc	Δ2.07	Δ2.28	Δ2.48	2.80	....	2.99	9 Mo Sep	2.14	2.33	49
50	....	0.05	9-15-86	8-25	...	Nil	....	2.71	153	63.2	9-30-95	91.8	...	10964	Dc	■d1.83	□d1.28	0.90	1.49	....	1.67	9 Mo Sep	0.97	1.15	50
51	....	0.01	2-17-87	1-28	...	Nil	....	22.1	78.4	22.3	8-31-95	1.75	...	55726	Au	0.06	d0.21	d0.20	d0.53	0.07	0.07				51
52◆	1949	Q0.18	12-1-95	11-20	0.707	0.72	0.667	47.0	1250	640	9-30-95	237	...	74152	Je	0.82	Δ□0.88	0.89	□0.71	2.96	3.14	3 Mo Sep	0.59	0.77	52

◆Stock Splits & Divs By Line Reference Index [3]No adj for recap:$52 & $35 debs,1 new shr,'86. [5]3-for-2,'91,'93,'94. [6]2-for-1,'93,'95. [10]2-for-1,'95. [11]15%,'94. [16]3-for-2,'93. [17]2-for-1,'95. [18]No adj for stk dstr PacTel Corp,'94. [20]2-for-1 in Cl'B','92. [24]1-for-20 REVERSE,'92. [25]1-for-10 REVERSE,'91. [26]3-for-2,'93:2-for-1,'95. [27]3-for-2,'91,'94. [30]3-for-2,'91(twice):4-for-3,'92. [39]No adj for spinoff'86. [45]3-for-2,'91:2-for-1,'92,'93. [48]2-for-1,'95. [49]2-for-1,'91,'94. [52]3-for-2,'95.

¶ S&P 500 # MidCap 400 ✣ SmallCap 600 • Options Index	Ticker	Name of Issue (Call Price of Pfd. Stocks)	Market	Com. Rank. & Pfd. Rating	Inst. Hold Cos	Inst. Hold Shs. (000)	Principal Business	Price Range 1971-93 High	1971-93 Low	1994 High	1994 Low	1995 High	1995 Low	Dec. Sales in 100s	December, 1995 Last Sale Or Bid High	Low	Last	%Div Yield	P-E Ratio	Total Return % Annualized 12 Mo	36 Mo	60 Mo
#1•[1]	PDP	✔Parker & Parsley Petrol	NY,Ch,Ph	B	208	25609	Oil & gas explor,dev,prod'n	35⅞	5¼	28¼	19⅛	23¼	16¼	21979	22	18½	22	0.5	d	11.2	17.8	...
2	PRLX	✔Parlex Corp	NNM	B–	8	171	Mfrs electronic components	20½	2	15½	5¼	18¾	7¼	745	11¼	7¼	10	...	22	–25.9	38.7	25.2
3	PTREF	✔PartnerRe Ltd	NNM	NR	2	139	Prop catastrophe re-insur	23½	19½	22¼	18½	28⅜	18¾	85659	27⅝	23¾	27½	1.8	8	35.0	...	...
4	PYA	✔Partners Preferred Yld'A'	AS	NR	3	17	Real estate investment trust	14⅞	7¼	14¼	11½	15⅞	12¼	705	15⅝	14⅝	15	e7.2	13	35.6	22.2	...
5	PYB	✔Partners Preferred Yld'A' II	AS	NR	7	52	Real estate investment trust	16	6¾	15¼	12	16	12⅝	547	15⅜	14⅜	14⅝	e7.7	13	17.3	18.2	...
6	PYC	✔Partners Preferred Yld'A' III	AS	NR	3	3	Real estate investment trust	18	7¾	16	14⅛	17⅜	14⅛	169	16⅝	15⅞	15⅞	e8.6	12	21.3	22.6	...
7	PATK	✔Patrick Indus	NNM	B–	31	2061	Dstr wall/ceiling panels:mfg	13⅝	⅛	15⅝	7¾	14½	8¼	4806	14½	13	14¼	1.1	8	79.3	59.5	61.3
8	PAH	Patriot Amer Hospitality	NY,Ph	NR	50	5454	Real estate investment trust	....	....	....	....	25¾	23¼	16798	25¾	23⅝	25¾	7.5	19	...	...	...
9	PBIX	Patriot Bank	NNM	NR	..	...	Savings bank, PA	....	....	....	....	13⅛	12¼	44245	13⅛	12¼	12⅞	...	..	...	...	...
10	PAT	✔Patten Corp	NY,Ch	B	29	3850	Sells undeveloped rural land	16⅜	5/16	3¾	2¾	5¾	2¾	3806	4⅞	4¼	4¾	s...	15	61.1	24.9	69.4
✣11	PDCO	✔Patterson Dental	NNM	B+	100	7749	Dstr dental supplies & equip	21⅞	10½	24⅜	15¾	29½	20	14429	28¼	25½	27	...	23	32.5	18.4	...
12	PTEN	✔Patterson Energy	NNM	NR	9	178	Oil&gas contract drilling	7¾	6½	7⅞	6	14⅝	6	8623	14¼	11⅜	14⅛	...	13	106	...	...
13	PRL	✔Paul Revere	NY,Ph	NR	49	4618	Provides disability insurance	26½	22⅛	25½	13¾	21⅜	14⅜	3485	21⅜	19	20¾	1.2	12	42.7	...	...
✣14	PXR	✔Paxar Corp	NY	B	57	6831	Mfr/mkts product ID systems	11⅜	3/16	10⅛	7⅝	16⅛	7⅝	4312	15¼	12¾	13¼	...	20	67.2	11.6	61.5
15	PXN	Paxson Communications 'A'	AS	NR	8	204	Radio/TV broadcstg,programs	....	....	16	10⅛	16⅝	9	1309	16⅝	14½	15¼	...	..	...	...	...
#16•[2]	PAYX	✔Paychex,Inc	NNM	B+	245	28228	Computer payroll acctg svcs	25⅛	1	27⅛	19	49⅞	25¾	62214	49⅞	39¾	49⅞	0.7	50	89.1	49.1	58.2
✣17•[3]	PCS	✔Payless Cashways	NY	NR	76	25902	Bldg Mtls,home improv strs	16¾	11	19⅝	8¼	10	3⅝	42899	4⅝	3⅞	4¼	...	6	–53.4	...	...
18	PQT	✔PC Quote	AS,Ph	B–	6	155	Stock price data-base svc	11⅜	⅝	3⅛	1	27½	1 1/16	47029	21⅞	10	15⅞	...	72	1005	163	81.2
19	PCSS	PC Service Source	NNM	NR	7	491	Dstr computer repair parts	....	....	10	5⅝	12¼	5¼	972	9	6¾	9	...	d	0.0	...	...
20	PCAI	✔PCA Intl	NNM	B–	29	3848	Portrait photographers	22	¾	12½	8¼	14¼	8⅜	5156	11¼	8⅜	11	2.5	14	8.8	–14.0	16.5
21	PDSF	✔PDS Financial	NNM	NR	2	398	Finance gaming eqp.furniture	....	....	7⅛	4⅝	5¾	1	6112	2	1⅜	1½	...	d	–72.7	...	...
22	IEC	✔PEC Israel Economic	NY,Ph	NR	48	3296	Fin/organize co's in Israel	34¼	2¾	34¾	23⅛	28¼	20¼	1524	24⅝	21	24⅛	...	21	–13.5	–4.7	29.2
23	PY	Pechiney ADS[59]	NY,Ch	NR	..	...	Aluminum production/products	....	....	....	....	18¾	16¾	9906	18¾	16¾	16⅞	...	..	...	...	...
¶24•[4]	PE	✔PECO Energy	NY,B,C,Ch,P,Ph	B	494	85719	Elec & gas:Phila/S.E. Penna	33½	9	30	23⅝	30¼	24¼	81476	30¼	28⅞	30⅛	5.8	11	28.5	8.6	13.7
25	PEDX	✔Pediatrix Medical Group	NNM	NR	34	1710	Physician mgmt svs-NICU	....	....	....	....	28½	18½	17910	28½	19⅞	27½	...	..	...	...	...
26	PMFG	✔Peerless Mfg	NNM	B	19	307	Control eq for nat'l gas ind	25	1 7/16	16½	9	12¾	9¼	662	10½	9¼	9⅜	5.3	d	–13.7	2.3	–4.2
27•[5]	PGU	✔Pegasus Gold	AS,Ch,Mo,Ph	C	116	20721	Gold & silver mining	28⅛	3⅜	24¾	10⅝	14¾	10	35072	14¾	12⅞	13⅞	...	d	22.0	0.7	2.5
28	PORL	Peninsular/Oriental Steam Nav[61]	Lo	NR	..	...	UK/int'l:svcs,ship'g,constrn	741	290	746	583	618	454	....	487	454	476	6.4	..	...	...	...
29	PNN	✔Penn Engr & Mfg	AS,Ch	B+	32	978	Captive fasteners: DC motors	47⅞	4¼	52½	39⅝	100½	42½	177	97	79	97	e1.1	12	135	41.8	41.7
30	PNF	✔Penn Traffic	NY	NR	60	7195	Food supermkt chain,NY, Pa	45¾	11¾	44⅝	34⅜	39½	10¾	8172	17	13⅛	15	...	d	–60.0	–19.3	–2.6
31	PVIR	✔Penn Virginia	NNM	B–	60	1488	Nat'l resources:O&G:Inv'mnt	69	8¾	40½	30	34½	27½	1243	33	32	32¼	5.6	11	11.9	3.2	–1.5
32	PFG	✔PennCorp Financial Group	NY,Ph	NR	148	19121	Accident,sickness,life insur	22⅞	13¾	19¾	12¼	29⅞	13	38231	29⅞	24⅝	29½	0.4	12	134	21.6	...
33	Pr	$3.375 cm Cv Pfd([62]52.36)	NY	BB–	36	1558		....	....	....	....	72⅛	50½	6783	72⅛	63¼	71⅜	4.7	..	...	...	...
¶34•[6]	JCP	✔Penney (J.C.)	NY,B,C,Ch,Ph,P	A–	784	171977	Dept stores,disc:mail order	56⅜	4⅞	59	41⅛	50	39⅞	110513	48⅞	43⅞	47⅝	4.0	12	13.9	11.3	21.7
35	PFSB	✔PennFed Financial Svcs	NNM	NR	25	1870	Savings bank, New Jersey	....	....	13¼	8⅞	15⅝	10	4544	14⅞	14⅛	14¾	...	14	42.2	...	...
✣36	PNT	✔Penna Enterprises	NY,Ch,Ph	B	54	1565	Natural gas & water dstr	60¾	9⅜	33	26⅞	38⅛	27⅛	2183	38⅛	36⅝	37⅞	5.8	..	48.5	14.3	10.6
37	PEI	✔Penna RE Inv Tr SBI	AS	NR	52	2093	Real estate investment trust	30⅜	2	25⅜	17⅝	23⅝	18½	1811	21¾	19½	20¾	9.1	16	22.7	5.8	15.8
¶38•[3]	PZL	✔Pennzoil Co.	NY,To,B,C,Ch,P,Ph	B–	356	26531	Integrated oil co: mining	95	8½	56⅜	43	50⅞	34⅝	30067	43⅛	39½	42¼	2.4	d	1.3	0.0	–3.4
39	PSO	✔Penobscot Shoe	AS	B–	6	79	Mfr casual sport footwear	10¼	⅜	6	4	5	4⅛	258	4⅞	4⅜	4½B	4.4	16	7.5	–2.6	15.5
40	PNRL	✔Penril DataComm Ntwks	NNM	↓C	19	1953	Data networking equipment	11⅝	⅜	7½	2⅛	11¼	2⅛	32231	11¼	7⅜	8½	...	d	258	21.5	7.8
#41	PNTA	✔Pentair, Inc	NNM	A–	147	11695	Mfr indl eqp/specialty prod	41¼	3/16	44¾	32¼	53	39¾	10599	53	48¼	49¾	e1.6	17	20.5	25.8	27.5
42	PNTK	✔Pentech International	NNM	B	28	3345	Mkts writing/drawing prod	9⅞	⅜	6¾	3½	4¼	1⅞	16050	2¾	2	2	...	d	–46.7	–25.7	–17.6
43	PNDL	Pentland Group plc[67]	Lo	NR	1	122	Mkt/dstr branded goods	217	2⅜	123	84	147	102	....	115½	108	113	2.0	..	...	...	...
✣44	PENW	✔PENWEST Ltd	NNM	B	54	1690	Mfr paper making chemicals	37¼	1 13/16	26½	17½	27	18¼	2682	26¼	23¼	24¾	0.8	24	28.0	6.2	–0.7
45•[7]	PBCT	✔People's Bank	NNM	NR	67	7059	Savings bank,Bridgeport,CT	10¼	1½	16⅛	8⅜	23⅛	11⅜	20630	21⅛	18½	19	3.8	11	66.4	52.2	51.1
46	PCTV	✔People's Choice TV	NNM	NR	80	7417	Operate wireless cable TV Sys	43	10½	38¾	15¼	30½	15	8039	22½	18	19	...	d	16.9	...	...
¶47	PGL	✔Peoples Energy	NY,B,C,Ch,P,Ph	B+	256	13185	Gas utility in Chicago	62⅞	7	32⅛	23¼	32	24¼	10309	32	30⅛	31¾	5.7	18	30.7	8.0	13.2
48	PHBK	✔Peoples Heritage Finl Gr	NNM	NR	101	8388	Svgs bank,Portland,Maine	22¼	1⅞	15⅛	10⅛	22⅞	11¾	17327	22⅞	20½	22¾	2.6	12	95.6	36.0	51.5
49	PTEL	✔Peoples Telephone Co	NNM	B–	40	5460	Oper private pay tel system	13¾	2	15¼	3½	5⅜	2⅛	29426	3	2⅛	2 5/16	...	d	–45.6	–31.4	–2.6
50•[8]	PSFT	✔PeopleSoft Inc	NNM	NR	144	30963	Mfr human resource mgmt softwr	10⅛	4¼	19¾	6½	47	15	88304	45½	36¾	43	...	98	123	85.2	...
¶51•[9]	PBY	✔Pep Boys-Man,Mo,Ja	NY,B,Ch,P,Ph	A+	358	34351	Retail chain: auto parts, etc.	27⅜	3/16	36⅞	25⅛	34¾	21⅞	35873	27⅞	25¼	25⅝	0.7	18	–16.4	5.1	22.2
52	PPO	✔Pepsi-Cola Puerto Rico Bott'B'	[10]NY,Ch	NR	19	1514	Bottle/dstr soft drink prod	....	....	....	....	14¼	10⅜	11316	14⅛	10½	11½	...	14	...	...	...

Uniform Footnote Explanations-See Page 4. Other: [1]AS:CBOE 3. [2]Ph:Cycle 3. [3]CBOE:Cycle 1. [4]P:Cycle 1. [5]CBOE:Cycle 2,MS:Cycle 1. [6]ASE:Cycle 2. [7]CBOE,NY:Cycle 1. [8]ASE,CBOE,NY,P:Cycle 1. [9]NY:Cycle 1. [10]Ph [51]Excl subsid pfd. [52]4 Mo Dec'93 earned $0.12. [53]®$2.64,'94. [54]®$1.00,'94. [55]®$0.97,'94. [56]®$1.16,'94. [57]83% owned by Textron Inc. [58]®$0.75,'94. [59]Ea ADS rep 0.5 Ord'A'shr,FF100. [60]To be determined. [61]Deferred stk:All data reported in British pence. [62]Fr 7-16-98 scale to $50 in 2005. [63]®$4.05,'94. [64]Excl $50M subsid pfd. [65]©$1.235,'94. [66]®$2.52,'94. [67]All data reported in British pence. [68]®$1.72,'94. [69]Incl current amts. [70]Fiscal Dec'91 & prior. [71]9 Mo Sep'92.

Splits ◆ Index	Cash Divs. Ea.Yr. Since	Dividends: Latest Payment Period $	Date	Ex. Div.	Total $ So Far 1995	Ind. Rate	Paid 1994	Financial Position Mil-$ Cash& Equiv.	Curr. Assets	Curr. Liab.	Balance Sheet Date	Capitalization Lg Trm Debt Mil-$	Shs. 000 Pfd.	Com.	Earnings $ Per Shr. Years End	1991	1992	1993	1994	1995	Last 12 Mos.	Interim Earnings Period	$ per Shr. 1994	1995	Index
1◆	1987	S0.05	9-15-95	7-27	0.10	0.10	0.10	17.8	126	125	9-30-95	571	[51]...	35131	Dc	0.77	1.05	Δ1.13	□d0.47	....	d2.71	9 Mo Sep	□d0.15	d2.39	1
2	....	None Since Public			...	Nil	....	0.12	14.8	6.53	10-01-95	2.65	...	2371	Je	d0.68	d0.17	0.13	0.44	0.61	0.46	3 Mo Sep	0.16	0.01	2
3	1994	Q0.12½	12-1-95	11-13	0.45	0.50	0.40	Equity per shr $20.37			12-31-94	....	...	50845	Dc	...	...	[52]...	[53]2.70	....	3.58	9 Mo Sep	1.95	2.83	3
4	1992	†0.42	1-12-96	12-27	†1.26	1.08	†1.00	Equity per shr $11.32			9-30-95	....	...	±4062	Dc	0.53	0.78	0.93	[54]1.08	....	1.13	9 Mo Sep	0.83	0.88	4
5	1992	†0.39	1-12-96	12-27	†1.25	1.12	†1.22	Equity per shr $11.98			9-30-95	....	...	±4062	Dc	0.51	0.87	1.01	[55]1.06	....	1.11	9 Mo Sep	0.84	0.89	5
6	1992	†0.41	1-12-96	12-27	†1.49	1.36	1.24	Equity per shr $11.67			9-30-95	....	...	±1663	Dc	0.52	0.80	1.15	[56]1.33	....	1.31	9 Mo Sep	1.05	1.03	6
7◆	1995	Q0.04	1-3-96	12-13	0.08	0.16	....	0.60	62.6	20.4	9-30-95	26.9	...	5952	Dc	d0.04	0.32	1.11	1.46	....	1.71	9 Mo Sep	1.07	1.32	7
8	1996	0.48	1-30-96	12-27	...	1.92	....	Equity per shr $16.63			9-30-95	p0.15	...	★15090	Dc	...	...	...	p1.25	....	1.36	12 Mo Sep	n/a	p1.36	8
9	....	None Since Public			...	Nil	....	Book Value $13.69			6-30-95	9.50	...	★3769	Dc	...	...	...	p0.54	....	....	6 Mo Jun	n/a	p0.27	9
10◆	....	5%Stk	3-30-95	3-9	5%Stk	Stk	4%Stk	Equity per shr $3.12			10-01-95	69.2	...	19522	Mr	0.07	0.17	0.24	0.30	....	0.32	6 Mo Sep	0.17	0.19	10
11◆	....	None Since Public			...	Nil	....	22.8	148	48.2	10-28-95	3.10	3564	17676	Ap	p0.31	p0.38	□0.62	0.87	1.10	1.19	6 Mo Oct	0.51	0.60	11
12	....	None Since Public			...	Nil	....	5.41	18.5	12.8	9-30-95	10.4	...	3159	Dc	*0.10	*Δ0.36	0.95	1.01	....	1.10	9 Mo Sep	0.60	0.69	12
13	1994	Q0.06	12-31-95	12-6	0.24	0.24	0.24	Equity per shr $25.68			9-30-95	0.01	...	[57]45000	Dc	1.40	□1.71	1.91	2.04	....	1.75	9 Mo Sep	1.72	1.43	13
14◆	....	None Paid			...	Nil	....	5.77	72.6	28.7	9-30-95	23.1	...	22144	Dc	0.20	0.42	0.43	0.53	....	0.68	9 Mo Sep	0.38	0.53	14
15◆	....	None Since Public			...	Nil	....	57.9	75.1	8.64	9-30-95	230	749	±34475	Dc	...	...	±pd0.36	±pd0.24	....	....	9 Mo Sep	n/a	d0.50	15
16◆	1988	Q0.09	11-22-95	10-25	0.27	0.36	0.18	93.6	137	30.2	8-31-95	....	...	45381	My	0.22	0.31	0.45	0.63	0.87	0.99	6 Mo Nov	0.43	0.55	16
17	....	None Since Public			...	Nil	....	4.50	455	337	8-26-95	641	406	±39914	Nv	...	p0.91	□±0.16	±□1.17	E0.70	0.52	9 Mo Aug	±0.77	±0.12	17
18	....	None Paid			...	Nil	....	1.04	3.04	3.53	9-30-95	0.26	...	7137	Dc	d0.08	*0.01	0.03	0.04	....	0.22	9 Mo Sep	d0.02	0.16	18
19	....	None Since Public			...	Nil	....	0.72	22.7	8.32	9-30-95	8.88	...	3897	Dc	d0.06	0.09	0.30	0.46	....	d0.23	9 Mo Sep	0.34	d0.35	19
20◆	1991	Q0.07	1-12-96	12-13	0.28	0.28	0.28	0.50	20.6	31.0	10-29-95	....	...	7482	Ja	0.89	□1.07	0.31	0.56	....	0.77	9 Mo Oct	0.12	0.33	20
21	....	None Since Public			...	Nil	....	Equity per shr $1.76			9-30-95	7.82	...	3120	Dc	p0.25	p0.17	p0.30	p[58]0.87	....	d1.47	9 Mo Sep	p0.79	d1.55	21
22◆	....	None Paid			...	Nil	....	Book Value $19.40			9-30-95	....	...	18759	Dc	1.40	1.89	□2.30	Δ1.60	....	1.16	9 Mo Sep	Δ1.36	0.92	22
23	....	Plan annual div			...	[60]....	....	746	4414	3364	p6-30-95	2830	...	★82731	Dc	...	...	...	pd4.66	....	....	6 Mo Jun	n/a	p0.78	23
24	1902	Q0.43½	12-20-95	11-13	1.65	1.74	1.54½	199	829	1271	9-30-95	4314	3702	221976	Dc	2.15	1.90	2.45	1.76	E2.65	2.68	12 Mo Sep	1.78	2.68	24
25	....	None Since Public			...	Nil	....	44.4	56.7	5.03	9-30-95	0.77	...	13048	Dc	...	...	...	p0.46	....	....	9 Mo Sep	n/a	p0.38	25
26	1954	Q0.12½	11-24-95	11-8	0.50	0.50	0.50	2.08	14.5	6.05	9-30-95	....	...	1447	Je	Δ0.43	0.68	0.11	0.54	0.85	d0.21	3 Mo Sep	0.72	d0.34	26
27	1988	t0.10	1-4-94	12-27	...	Nil	t0.10	66.7	137	51.2	9-30-95	122	...	34668	Dc	0.37	Δd0.29	0.30	d1.69	....	d0.10	9 Mo Sep	d1.67	d0.08	27
28◆	1936	13.50	11-4-92		...	30.50	....	Equity per shr 394			j12-31-94	155400	127100	602600	Dc	Δ31.00	32.90	68.50	38.50	....	j38.50				28
29	1967	†1.175	12-15-95	11-29	†2.00	1.10	†1.52½	13.3	57.8	12.8	9-30-95	....	...	1707	Dc	2.29	Δ3.71	Δ4.06	6.12	....	7.81	9 Mo Sep	4.09	5.78	29
30	....	None Since Public			...	Nil	....	41.3	523	379	10-28-95	1338	...	10839	Ja	□d1.03	□0.39	□0.76	□1.97	....	d4.06	9 Mo Oct	□1.25	d4.78	30
31	1984	Q0.45	12-19-95	11-27	1.80	1.80	†2.00	3.06	11.2	7.87	9-30-95	22.5	...	4262	Dc	0.29	□d3.39	2.40	3.15	....	2.94	9 Mo Sep	2.34	2.13	31
32	1993	Q0.03	12-29-95	12-13	0.06	0.12	0.04	Equity per shr $8.83			9-30-95	199	2300	22880	Dc	p1.40	□1.35	□1.71	1.82	....	2.46	9 Mo Sep	1.30	1.94	32
33	1995	Q0.43¾	1-16-96	12-28	0.82½	3.375	....	Cv into 2.212 com,$22.60				....	2000	...	Dc	...	...	...	....	....	....				33
34◆	1922	Q0.48	2-1-96	1-8	1.86	1.92	1.62	321	10419	5199	10-28-95	4023	1000	223672	Ja	□0.98	3.15	Δ□3.79	[63]4.29	E3.95↓	3.87	9 Mo Oct	2.51	2.09	34
35	....	None Since Public			...	Nil	....	Book Value $16.64			9-30-95	86.1	...	5344	Je	...	...	...	....	1.08	1.05	3 Mo Sep	0.34	0.31	35
36	1946	Q0.55	12-15-95	11-29	2.20	2.20	2.20	0.76	42.6	87.0	9-30-95	155	[64]...	5766	Dc	1.53	1.61	1.82	2.17	....	0.03	12 Mo Sep	2.31	0.03	36
37	1962	Q0.47	2-15-96	1-29	1.88	1.88	[65]1.88	Equity per shr $5.97			8-31-95	123	...	8676	Au	1.27	1.01	1.62	2.39	1.29	1.29				37
38	1925	Q0.25	12-15-95	11-28	2.50	1.00	3.00	50.9	629	865	9-30-95	1987	...	46319	Dc	□1.73	□0.72	□3.80	□d6.16	Ed5.84	d6.24	9 Mo Sep	□d5.92	d6.00	38
39	1976	Q0.05	12-15-95	11-21	0.20	0.20	0.20	3.85	11.3	1.18	8-25-95	....	...	1482	Nv	d0.17	0.60	0.45	0.34	....	0.28	9 Mo Aug	0.14	0.08	39
40◆	1992	0.02	12-30-93	12-10	...	Nil	....	3.60	35.0	16.7	10-31-95	0.44	...	9156	Jl	1.01	0.16	0.02	0.19	d1.02	d1.06	3 Mo Oct	d0.13	d0.17	40
41◆	1976	Q0.20	11-30-95	10-26	†0.83	0.80	0.72	26.6	653	248	9-30-95	242	1882	18460	Dc	2.20	□2.15	2.26	[66]2.62	E2.90	3.82	9 Mo Sep	1.77	2.97	41
42	....	None Since Public			...	Nil	....	0.55	46.2	27.0	6-30-95	....	...	10858	Sp	0.34	0.23	0.34	0.40	Pd0.10	d0.10				42
43◆	....	1.31¼			...	2.25	....	26860	55220	26240	j12-31-94	2460	...	36112	Dc	Δ4.71	15.79	2.74	6.56	....	j6.56				43
44	1992	Q0.05	12-1-95	11-15	0.20	0.20	0.20	5.33	48.9	19.7	8-31-95	58.6	...	6770	Au	1.17	□1.01	0.88	0.86	1.03	1.03	3 Mo Nov	0.25	0.25	44
45	1993	Q0.18	11-15-95	10-30	0.64	0.72	0.47	Book Value $11.90			12-31-94	745	666	36615	Dc	d2.79	*0.14	Δ1.17	Δ[68]1.88	....	1.68	9 Mo Sep	Δ1.53	1.33	45
46	....	None Since Public			...	Nil	....	Equity per shr $8.54			9-30-95	[69]194	500	12840	Dc	...	pd1.50	pd1.73	d2.20	....	d4.40	9 Mo Sep	d1.32	Δd3.52	46
47	1937	Q0.45	1-12-96	12-20	1.80	1.80	1.79½	178	383	284	9-30-95	622	...	34937	Sp	2.05	2.06	2.11	2.13	1.78	1.78				47
48	1994	Q0.15	11-10-95	11-1	0.52	0.60	0.24	Book Value $14.18			9-30-95	276	...	16945	Dc	d2.58	d0.58	1.00	1.52	....	1.92	9 Mo Sep	1.09	1.49	48
49◆	....	None Since Public			...	Nil	....	9.11	28.7	31.1	9-30-95	103	5000	15883	Dc	0.25	0.28	0.37	d1.17	....	d2.38	9 Mo Sep	d0.31	□d1.52	49
50◆	....	None Since Public			...	Nil	....	102	201	118	9-30-95	1.62	...	49140	Dc	0.05	0.12	0.17	0.28	....	0.44	9 Mo Sep	0.18	0.34	50
51	1950	Q0.04¾	1-22-96	1-4	0.18½	0.19	0.16½	17.1	418	333	10-28-95	381	...	62046	Ja	0.69	0.90	1.06	□1.32	E1.40	1.33	9 Mo Oct	□1.02	1.03	51
52	1995	†0.24	12-27-95	12-20	†0.24	[60]....	....	2.51	30.8	28.9	6-30-95	7.65	...	±★21500	Sp	[70]0.01	‡[71]1.99	1.82	0.98	P0.83	0.83				52

◆**Stock Splits & Divs By Line Reference Index** [1]Reorg & 2-for-1,'91. [7]3-for-2,'93:2-for-1,'94. [10]Adj to 5%,'95. [11]3-for-2,'94. [14]5-for-4,'91,'92,'93(twice),'94,'95. [15]3-for-2,'95. [16]3-for-2,'92,'93,'95. [20]3-for-2,'92. [22]2-for-1,'92. [28]Adj for rts issue,'91. [34]2-for-1,'93. [40]4-for-3,'91. [41]3-for-2,'93. [43]Adj for 29% scrip issue,'89. [49]3-for-2,'93. [50]2-for-1,'94,'95.

¶ S&P 500 / # MidCap 400 / ✣ SmallCap 600 / • Options Index	Ticker	Name of Issue (Call Price of Pfd. Stocks)	Market	Com. Rank. & Pfd. Rating	Inst. Hold Cos	Inst. Hold Shs. (000)	Principal Business	Price Range 1971-93 High	1971-93 Low	1994 High	1994 Low	1995 High	1995 Low	Dec. Sales in 100s	December, 1995 Last Sale Or Bid High	Low	Last	%Div Yield	P-E Ratio	Total Return % Annualized 12 Mo	36 Mo	60 Mo
¶1•[1]	PEP	✔PepsiCo Inc	NY,B,C,Ch,P,Ph	A+	1344	473772	Soft drink:snack fd/food svc	43⅝	1¹⁄₁₆	41⅛	29¼	58¾	33⅞	294107	58¾	53⅝	55⅞	1.4	23	55.3	11.8	18.7
2	PRCP	✔Perceptron Inc	NNM	NR	39	3467	Laser-based sensor/image sys	8⅞	3½	16⅞	7⅞	28	9⅞	16848	28	21½	22¼	...	22	50.2	62.5	...
3	PERC	✔Perclose Inc	NNM	NR	..	...	Dvp vascular surgery sys	....	....	....	....	19⅛	12¾	17939	19⅛	12¾	19⅛	...	..	...	...	...
4	PFGC	✔Performance Food Group	NNM	NR	37	1736	Market,dstr food products	24¾	14	24¼	9¾	25½	12¼	1692	24½	23¾	23¾	...	23	90.0	...	...
5	PCR	✔Perini Corp	AS,B,Ch	C	32	2135	Construction:R.E. develop	44	3	13⅞	9⅛	13⅜	7⅞	2310	9⅜	7⅞	8¼	...	d	−12.0	−20.2	2.3
6	Pr	$2.125[51]Dep Cv[52]Ex Pfd([53]25.524)	AS	NR	7	188		28⅛	11½	24⅞	21	25⅛	20½	230	21¾	21	21⅛	10.1	..	...	...	...
7	PERI	✔Periphonics Corp	NNM	NR	27	2148	Mfr voice processing systems	....	....	....	....	29½	14	19231	27¾	22½	27¾	...	28	...	...	...
¶8•[2]	PKN	✔Perkin-Elmer	NY,B,Ch,P,Ph	↑B	304	32504	Analytical instruments, optics	41⅛	7¼	39½	25¼	40¼	25¾	46642	40¼	35⅝	37¾	1.8	23	49.1	4.9	13.8
9	PFR	✔Perkins Family Rest L.P.	NY,Ch,Ph	B+	18	190	Family style restaurant svc	23⅝	7⅜	21⅞	9⅞	13½	10¼	3431	12¼	11⅛	11½	11.3	10	20.5	−5.4	6.8
10	PERLF	Perle Systems	NNM	B	10	2149	Computer systems/services	5	3	4½	2½	9¼	3	491	6	4⅞	5	...	..	66.7	8.0	38.1
11	PBT	✔Permian Basin Rty Tr[57]	NY,B,Ch,P,Ph	NR	15	486	Royalty oil interests,Texas	25	3½	6½	3¾	4¾	3	12934	3½	3	3¼	7.7	12	−15.8	0.8	3.6
#12•[3]	PRGO	✔Perrigo Co	NNM	NR	186	35245	Mfr store brand pharmac'l prd	34⅞	8	34¼	10⅞	14⅜	10½	70294	13⅝	11½	11⅞	...	22	−2.1	−19.0	...
✣13•[4]	PBIO	✔PerSeptive Biosystems	NNM	NR	58	7497	Biomolecule purificat'n sys	29	7	32¼	3¾	12⅝	4⅛	24216	10⅛	8⅜	8½	...	d	65.9	−25.1	...
14	PGA	✔Personnel Group of America	NY,Ch,Ph	NR	14	2153	Personnel staffing services	....	....	....	....	15	11	15461	15	12¼	14⅝	...	19	...	...	...
15	TPMI	✔Personnel Management	NNM	NR	6	133	Provides temporary help svcs	....	....	13⅛	7¾	18¾	5¼	3751	10	5¼	7⅞	...	21	−28.8	...	...
16•[5]	IIT	Perusahaan PT IndoSat ADS[58]	[6]NY,Ch	NR	142	9678	Intl telecommun svc Indonesia	....	....	40¾	31¼	40⅝	29½	10627	37⅝	33½	36½	1.5	26	3.5	...	...
17	VETS	✔Pet Practice	NNM	NR	14	2160	Owns/oper veterinary care ctrs	....	....	....	....	15⅛	9	16417	11¾	9⅞	10¼	...	..	...	...	...
18	PLDIF	Petersburg Long Distance	NNM	NR	40	8671	Investment co:telecommun sv	13	5⅝	12½	6¼	7½	4⅜	28489	5¼	4⅝	4¾	...	d	−24.0	...	...
19	WIKD	Pete's Brewing Co	NNM	NR	..	...	Brewer:specialty beers	....	....	....	....	27¾	12½	46206	25	12½	14	...	..	...	...	...
20•[7]	PST	✔Petrie Stores[60]	NY,B,Ch,P	LIQ	77	12428	Selling assets	40	4⅜	29⅛	21⅝	22⅞	2½	19766	3⅛	2½	2¾	...	d	−87.4	−51.9	−29.2
21	PCZ	Petro-Canada	NY,Ch,Ph	NR	44	13209	Oil&gas explor,dvlp,prodn	....	....	....	....	11½	10⅛	292	11½	11⅜	11½	...	..	...	...	...
22	PCZ PP	1st [62]Installment[63]	NY,Ch,Ph	NR	36	18769		....	....	....	....	5¾	4¼	15189	5¾	5⅜	5¾	...	..	...	...	...
23	PETD	Petroleum Development	NNM	B−	8	1727	Oil&gas explor,dev,prod'n	12⅛	⅛	2½	1¹⁄₁₆	1⅝	⅞	4289	1⅝	1⅛	1⅝	...	12	36.9	11.0	25.1
24•[3]	PGSAY	Petroleum Geo-Svcs A/S ADS[64]	NNM	NR	142	21894	Marine seismic data svcs	18⅞	9½	25½	12⅜	34⅛	16⅜	72858	25⅝	19½	25	...	20	37.0	...	...
25	HEAT	✔Petroleum Heat & Pwr'A'	NNM	NR	43	5770	Retail dstr heat'g oil	12¾	7	9½	6⅝	9¼	6½	8870	8⅛	6¾	8⅛	7.4	d	0.0	−1.8	...
26	PLIT	✔Petrolite Corp	NNM	B	64	3797	Spec chem,eq,processes-wax	48½	5¼	37½	26	32½	22	12680	29	22	28½	3.9	52	14.2	3.4	9.7
27•[8]	PETM	✔PETsMART Inc	NNM,Ch	NR	197	33546	Pet food/supplies superstores	24	12	25⅞	14⅜	36⅛	20⅞	71146	33½	28½	31	...	d	32.2	...	...
¶28•[9]	PFE	✔Pfizer, Inc	NY,B,C,Ch,P,Ph	A−	1269	413538	Health care,csmr prd,sp chem	43½	2⅝	39¾	26⅝	66⅞	37¼	273844	66⅞	58¼	63	1.7	25	67.2	22.8	28.8
29	PHAM	✔Phamis Inc	NNM	NR	49	3054	Dvp/mkt healthcare softwr	....	....	18⅜	12	31	14⅞	6654	30½	26¼	29¾	...	40	78.3	...	...
✣30	PMRX	✔Pharmaceutical Mktg Svcs	NNM	NR	47	2796	Mktg svcs/prd to pharm'l cos	30½	13	17¾	6¾	16¼	7¾	13549	15⅛	12⅜	15⅛	...	36	68.1	−8.1	...
✣31•[5]	PRX	✔Pharmaceutical Resources	NY,Ch,P,Ph	B−	54	2864	Mfr prescript'n generic drugs	27¼	2⅝	16¾	6¼	13⅛	6⅞	11743	8	6⅞	7½	...	..	−13.0	−5.5	12.7
¶32	PNU	✔Pharmacia & Upjohn	NY	NR	..	...	R&D pharmaceutical/hlth prd	....	....	....	....	40¼	32⅜	314620	40¼	35⅜	38¾	2.8	22	...	...	...
33	PCOP	Pharmacopeia Inc	NNM	NR	..	...	Pharmaceutical R&D	....	....	....	....	24½	16	40833	24½	16	24¼	...	..	...	...	...
34	PCYC	Pharmacyclics Inc	NNM	NR	..	...	Dvlp stge:pharmaceutical R&D	....	....	....	....	16¾	12	1001	16	13¼	14	...	d	...	...	...
35	PARS	✔Pharmos Corp	NSC	C	24	3058	Drug delivery system R&D	52	1⅛	7⅞	1¹⁄₁₆	3¼	½	35953	1¾	1⅛	1½	...	d	9.3	−47.7	−0.4
¶36•[10]	PD	✔Phelps Dodge	NY,B,C,Ch,P,Ph	B	581	53261	Largest US copper prod'r	55⅝	6½	65	47⅝	70½	51⅞	81994	68¼	59¾	62¼	2.9	6	5.1	13.1	21.8
#37	PHH	✔PHH Corp	NY,B,Ch,Ph	A−	227	12685	Mgmt svs to co's:fleet,reloc	47	2⅝	43¼	33	48	34⅛	6530	47½	44½	46¾	2.9	11	38.8	8.1	18.1
✣38	PSC	✔Phila Suburban	NY,B,Ch,Ph	B+	53	1605	Water svc in suburban Phila	20¾	5⅜	19⅝	17⅛	21½	17⅜	1318	21½	19⅜	20¾	5.6	14	24.4	15.5	19.2
¶39•[9]	MO	✔Philip Morris Cos	NY,B,C,Ch,P,Ph	A+	1606	518627	Cigarettes,food prod,brew'g	86⅝	1⁷⁄₁₆	64½	47¼	94⅜	55¾	367203	94⅜	86¼	90¼	4.4	14	65.9	10.4	16.9
40•[1]	PHI	✔Philippine Long D Tel ADS[73]	NY,B,Ch,P	NR	148	22563	Tel service in Philippines	85¼	½	81¼	50⅛	77½	48¼	17046	58	50⅝	54⅛	0.4	13	−3.0	15.1	44.3
41	Pr A	Global Dep[75] Cv Pfd(NC)	NY	BB	44	5906		....	....	54⅜	49¼	68⅝	48	8340	55	49⅝	51¾B	6.8	..	...	...	...
42•[11]	PHG	Philips Electronics[76]NV	NY,Ch,P,Ph	NR	333	82344	World-wide mfr operations	27⅜	6	33⅞	21	53⅜	29⅝	126122	39¾	34⅛	35⅞	1.9	8	23.5	50.9	25.5
¶43•[12]	P	✔Phillips Petroleum	NY,To,B,C,Ch,P,Ph	B	606	139841	Domestic integ oil: chems	37⅜	4⅜	37¼	25½	37⅛	29⅞	93364	34⅞	32	34⅛	3.6	17	7.5	14.6	9.7
✣44•[13]	PVH	✔Phillips-Van Heusen	NY,B,Ch,Ph	A	116	17528	Apparel mfr & retailer	37½	⅜	39	14	18	9⅛	21688	10⅝	9¼	9⅞	1.5	..	−35.9	−29.1	7.7
45	DUF	✔Phoenix Duff & Phelps	NY,Ph	NR	74	10443	Invest mgmt/finl advisory svcs	22⅞	12	22	7⅞	13¼	6	32911	7¼	6⅝	6⅞	e2.9	..	...	...	...
46	Pr	$1.50 Sr A cm Cv[81]Ex Pfd([82]25)	NY	NR	..	...		....	....	....	....	25¾	24⅜	4393	25¾	24¾	25¼	5.9	..	...	...	...
47	PHX	✔Phoenix Network	AS,Ch	C	15	1063	Provides telecom'n mgmt svcs	8½	¹⁵⁄₁₆	6⅞	2¼	4⅝	1⅞	6994	4	3¼	3⅝	...	..	34.9	50.5	17.4
✣48	PHN	✔Phoenix Resource Cos	AS	NR	66	6283	Oil&gas explor,prod'n Egypt	9½	³⁄₁₆	12	5¾	20½	9⅜	4040	17½	16⅛	17¼	0.5	25	48.4	41.7	62.0
49•[7]	PTEC	✔Phoenix Technologies	NNM	B−	50	5442	Mfr IBM compatible software	18¾	1¼	8⅛	4	16⅛	6⅛	63691	16⅛	11	15¾	...	27	100	42.0	43.1
50	PHOC	✔Photo Control	NNM	B−	11	131	Photo & flash equipment	12	³⁄₁₆	8¾	5¾	6¼	3¼	2361	3⅞	3½	3⅝	...	d	−39.6	−20.7	3.3
51	PHTN	Photon Dynamics	NNM	NR	..	...	Flat panel display repair sys	....	....	....	....	12¼	6⅞	8603	10	6⅞	8	...	..	...	...	...
52	PLAB	✔Photronics, Inc	NNM	B	78	4390	Manufacture,mkt'photo masks'	12	¹¹⁄₁₆	20	9⅞	41¼	17⅞	20243	33½	26¼	26¾	...	16	42.5	54.1	34.6

Uniform Footnote Explanations-See Page 4. Other: [1]CBOE:Cycle 1. [2]P:Cycle 3. [3]ASE,CBOE:Cycle 3. [4]CBOE,NY:Cycle 3. [5]CBOE:Cycle 2. [6]Ph [7]Ph:Cycle 3. [8]Ph:Cycle 2. [9]ASE:Cycle 3. [10]ASE:Cycle 1. [11]NY:Cycle 1. [12]ASE:Cycle 2. [13]CBOE:Cycle 3. [51]Dep for⅒ shr $21.25 cm Cv Exch Pfd. [52]Co opt to exch for $25amt 8½%Cv2012. [53]Thru 6-14-96,scale to $25 in'97. [54]Subsid Pfd. [55]Fiscal Jul'92 & prior. [56]100% non-taxable,'94. [57]Unit Benef. Int. [58]Ea ADS rep 10'B'shr,par 500 Rupiah. [59]9 Mo Dec'91. [60]Approve liquidation. [61]Liq stk dstr of Toys R Us. [62]1st Installment (41.9% paid). [63]2nd pay't(29.1%) 9-26-96,3rd(29%) 3-24-97. [64]Ea ADS rep 1 ord shr, NOK 5. [65]®$0.56,'94. [66]Fiscal Dec'92 & prior. [67]12 Mo Jun'93. [68]®$1.60,'94. [69]Incl liabs under mgmt programs. [70]Sub pfd in $M. [71]Incl redempt of Stk Pur Rt. [72]As reported,incl finance subsid. [73]Ea ADS repr 1 com,par P5. [74]®$3.39,'94. [75]Ea GDS rep 1 Sr III Cv Pfd. [76]Philips Incandescent Lamp Works Holding Co.. [77]To be determined. [78]Stk dstr of Duff & Phelps CR Rating Co,'94. [79]Fiscal Dec'93 & prior data of Duff & Phelps Corp. [80]®$0.62,'94. [81]Co opt fr 11-1-97 exch for $25 amt 6% Cv 2015. [82]Fr 11-2-2000. [83]8 Mo Dec'91:Fiscal Apr'91 earned,$d0.15.

Splits ◆ Index	Cash Divs. Ea.Yr. Since	Dividends: Latest Payment Period $	Date	Ex. Div.	Total $ So Far 1995	Ind. Rate	Paid 1994	Financial Position Mil-$ Cash& Equiv.	Curr. Assets	Curr. Liab.	Balance Sheet Date	Capitalization Lg Trm Debt Mil-$	Shs. 000 Pfd.	Com.	Earnings $ Per Shr. Years End	1991	1992	1993	1994	1995	Last 12 Mos.	Interim Earnings Period	$ per Shr. 1994	1995	Index
1	1952	Q0.20	1-2-96	12-6	0.76	0.80	0.68	1376	5547	5459	9-09-95	8691	...	787925	Dc	1.35	□1.61	1.96	□2.22	E2.45	2.42	9 Mo Sep	□Δ1.58	1.78	1
2◆	....	None Since Public			...	Nil	....	10.8	28.5	5.22	9-30-95	0.01	...	6504	Dc	d0.38	0.38	0.45	0.83	....	1.03	9 Mo Sep	0.52	0.72	2
3	....	None Since Public			...	Nil	....	7.37	8.26	1.34	9-30-95	0.61	p...	★9095	Mr	...	...	...	pd1.04	....	....	6 Mo Sep	n/a	pd0.69	3
4	....	None Since Public			...	Nil	....	2.80	83.6	51.9	9-30-95	33.2	...	6161	Dc	0.16	□0.54	0.90	0.71	....	1.05	9 Mo Sep	0.55	0.89	4
5	....	0.20	12-18-90	11-20	...	Nil	....	6.66	307	287	9-30-95	74.7	100	4719	Dc	0.27	d4.69	0.24	d0.42	....	d6.43	9 Mo Sep	d0.57	d6.58	5
6	1987	Q0.53⅛	12-15-95	11-20	2.12½	2.125	2.12½	Cv into 0.662 com,$37.75				....	1000	...	Dc	b0.91	bd0.94	b1.56	b1.04	....	....				6
7	....	None Since Public			...	Nil	....	9.05	42.4	13.4	8-31-95	....	[54]626	★6727	My	0.13	0.31	0.09	□0.44	0.65	0.99	6 Mo Nov	0.21	0.55	7
8	1971	Q0.17	1-2-96	11-29	0.68	0.68	0.68	48.4	573	338	9-30-95	29.2	...	42268	Je	d0.47	p[55]0.81	□0.54	1.14	1.57	1.63	3 Mo Sep	0.35	0.41	8
9	1987	Q0.32½	2-15-96	12-27	1.30	1.30	[56]1.30	1.47	15.0	30.2	9-30-95	60.0	...	10491	Dc	1.47	1.48	1.21	1.16	....	1.13	9 Mo Sep	0.93	0.90	9
10◆	....	None Paid			...	Nil	....	3.04	12.7	7.55	j8-31-95	....	...	★6723	My	0.12	0.22	0.28	0.40	0.50	j0.08	6 Mo Nov	0.24	d0.18	10
11	1981	0.026	1-16-96	12-27	0.261	0.25	0.341	Southland Royalty (prop)				....	...	46609	Dc	0.51	0.45	0.40	0.35	....	0.27	9 Mo Sep	0.25	0.17	11
12◆	....	None Since Public			...	Nil	....	0.17	301	118	9-30-95	98.1	...	76188	Je	p0.26	0.41	0.58	0.71	0.58	0.55	3 Mo Sep	0.19	0.16	12
13	....	None Since Public			...	Nil	....	26.5	66.1	47.9	6-30-95	27.2	4	p13284	Sp	pd0.76	pd0.56	d0.10	d2.88	Pd1.88	d1.88				13
14	....	None Since Public			...	Nil	....	5.40	45.4	18.9	9-30-95	....	...	8000	Dc	...	...	...	p0.49	....	0.78	9 Mo Sep	p0.31	0.60	14
15◆	....	None Since Public			...	Nil	....	d0.05	6.65	3.26	7-31-95	2.43	...	1991	Oc	...	...	p0.68	p0.65	P0.37	0.37				15
16	1995	0.22	12-22-95	11-7	0.539	0.54	....	366	478	47.6	12-31-94	20.1	...	1035500	Dc	1.12	p1.23	p1.28	1.40	....	1.40				16
17	....	None Since Public			...	Nil	....	26.4	28.7	8.55	p3-29-95	p10.9	p...	★8359	Dc	...	...	...	pd0.29	....	0.03	9 Mo Sep	d0.75	pd0.43	17
18	....	None Since Public			...	Nil	....	56.7	61.3	22.3	j12-31-94	....	5447	30012	Dc	‡[59]d0.01	d1.02	d1.26	d0.89	....	jd0.50	9 Mo Sep	d0.56	d0.17	18
19	....	None Since Public			...	Nil	....	0.18	11.1	11.0	9-30-95	0.02	p...	★10161	Dc	...	...	...	p0.08	....	....	9 Mo Sep	n/a	p0.11	19
20◆	1968	[61]....	8-15-95	8-16	[61]...	Nil	0.20	Liq Val Per shr $3.47			10-28-95	....	...	52350	Ja	0.34	0.32	Δd1.04	d8.75	....	d3.38	9 Mo Oct	d8.71	d3.34	20
21	1991	gQ0.05	1-1-96	11-29	g0.20	0.20	g0.14¾	....	1255	930	j6-30-95	1289	...	246667	Dc	d3.08	0.04	0.66	1.06	....	j0.75	9 Mo Sep	0.84	0.53	21
22	1996	g0.05	1-1-96	11-29	...	0.20	....	....	...	...		....	...	134473	Dc	...	...	...	....	....	....	9 Mo Sep	0.84	0.53	22
23	....	None Paid			...	Nil	....	2.33	4.94	5.07	9-30-95	2.70	...	11041	Dc	0.08	0.16	Δ0.11	0.08	....	0.14	9 Mo Sep	0.03	0.09	23
24◆	....	None Since Public			...	Nil	....	23.2	149	99.4	12-31-94	70.8	...	25883	Dc	...	p0.68	0.97	1.74	....	1.24	9 Mo Sep	1.61	1.11	24
25	1992	Q0.15	1-2-96	12-13	0.588	0.60	0.55	16.2	102	94.2	9-30-95	362	208	±25466	Dc	d1.64	d0.81	□d0.53	□d0.34	....	d1.17	9 Mo Sep	d0.48	d1.31	25
26	1931	Q0.28	1-26-96	1-3	1.12	1.12	1.12	30.1	151	69.4	7-31-95	40.0	...	11333	Oc	1.30	1.45	□1.82	Δ0.62	P0.55	0.55				26
27◆	....	None Since Public			...	Nil	....	85.6	263	135	7-30-95	55.6	...	49595	Ja	Δd0.29	*0.09	Δ0.13	0.09	....	d0.08	9 Mo Oct	d0.19	d0.36	27
28◆	1901	Q0.26	12-21-95	11-8	1.04	1.04	0.94	1670	6137	5799	10-01-95	358	...	636154	Dc	1.07	□1.63	1.03	2.09	E2.50	2.39	9 Mo Sep	1.55	1.85	28
29	....	None Since Public			...	Nil	....	24.8	34.0	12.1	9-30-95	0.24	...	5778	Dc	*0.20	*0.07	d0.64	[65]0.60	....	0.74	9 Mo Sep	0.41	0.55	29
30	....	None Since Public			...	Nil	....	58.7	104	35.3	9-30-95	70.3	...	13085	Je	pd0.17	[66]0.48	[67]0.54	0.36	0.40	0.42	3 Mo Sep	d0.06	d0.04	30
31	....	0.02	7-5-89	5-26	...	Nil	....	18.4	49.7	13.5	7-01-95	4.53	p...	★18172	Sp	d3.61	*0.39	Δ0.01	Δ0.29	P0.04	0.04				31
32	1996	Q0.27	2-1-96	1-8	...	1.08	....	1662	4872	2871	p6-30-95	868	7	503723	Dc	...	p1.36	p1.08	p[68]1.62	E1.80	1.68	6 Mo Jun	p0.84	p0.90	32
33	....	None Since Public			...	Nil	....	7.93	8.66	2.90	9-30-95	0.71	p...	★9651	Dc	...	...	...	pd1.18	....	....	9 Mo Sep	n/a	pd0.85	33
34	....	None Since Public			...	Nil	....	3.95	4.11	1.67	p6-30-95	p2.18	...	★8216	Je	...	...	...	....	pd1.65	d1.59	3 Mo Sep	pd0.37	pd0.31	34
35◆	....	None Paid			...	Nil	....	9.31	10.1	2.53	9-30-95	....	...	29131	Dc	±pd1.80	d2.28	d1.24	d1.19	....	d0.66	9 Mo Sep	d0.91	d0.38	35
36◆	1987	Q0.45	12-8-95	11-15	1.80	1.80	1.68¾	530	1534	620	9-30-95	620	...	69310	Dc	3.93	□4.28	2.66	3.81	E10.30	8.81	9 Mo Sep	2.92	7.92	36
37	1959	Q0.34	1-31-96	1-3	1.32	1.36	1.24	Equity per shr $30.51			10-31-95	[69]4227	...	17165	Ap	2.78	2.92	3.25	3.64	4.15	4.36	6 Mo Oct	1.96	2.17	37
38	1939	Q0.29	12-1-95	11-10	1.14	1.16	1.10	6.36	31.2	31.2	9-30-95	190	[70]6	12073	Dc	0.62	□0.60	1.27	1.35	....	1.47	9 Mo Sep	1.03	1.15	38
39	1928	Q1.00	1-10-96	12-13	[71]3.48½	4.00	2.85½	Equity per shr Neg			9-30-95	[72]14247	...	834736	Dc	□4.24	5.45	□4.06	5.45	E6.50	6.26	9 Mo Sep	4.17	□4.98	39
40◆	1953	0.052		12-13	0.215	0.21	t0.235	8176	20466	10011	j12-31-94	26969	206600	53800	Dc	3.29	3.79	3.38	[74]3.44	....	4.15	9 Mo Sep	1.99	2.70	40
41	1995	0.87½	1-16-96	12-13	3.50	3.50	....	Cv into 0.8565 com,$58.38				....	4250	...	Dc	...	...	...	....	....	....	Mand conv fr 11-22-98 re-spec. cond.			41
42	1994	0.682	5-31-95	5-3	0.682	[77]0.69	0.229	2824	29896	18405	j12-31-94	6179	...	338452	Dc	▲2.34	d1.60	Δ1.38	3.40	E4.60↓	4.62	9 Mo Sep	Δ1.83	Δ3.05	42
43	1934	Q0.30½	12-1-95	11-1	1.19½	1.22	1.12	143	2442	2778	9-30-95	2876	...	262068	Dc	Δ□0.38	□1.04	□0.94	1.85	E2.05	1.99	9 Mo Sep	1.23	1.37	43
44◆	1970	Q0.038	12-4-95	11-8	0.18¾	0.15	0.15	15.6	509	229	7-31-95	240	...	26723	Ja	1.15	1.42	□1.60	1.11	E0.04	0.23	9 Mo Oct	0.74	d0.14	44
45◆	1993	Q0.05	12-11-95	11-16	†1.94	0.20	h[78]0.16	9.67	47.8	23.1	p6-30-95	30.5	3105	43447	Dc	□p0.62	□1.00	[79]1.30	p[80]0.65	....	....	6 Mo Jun	n/a	p0.23	45
46	1995	0.14	12-11-95	11-16	0.14	1.50	....	Cv into 3.11 com $8.03				....	3105	...	Dc	...	...	...	....	....	....				46
47	....	None Paid			...	Nil	....	9.53	23.5	12.3	9-30-95	....	2570	14451	Dc	[83]d0.15	d0.12	d0.33	□d0.09	....	0.03	9 Mo Sep	d0.10	0.02	47
48◆	1994	Q0.02	12-29-95	12-13	0.08	0.08	0.05	20.4	35.2	9.71	9-30-95	....	...	15596	Dc	□d0.15	0.87	□0.90	0.79	....	0.69	9 Mo Sep	0.57	0.48	48
49	....	None Since Public			...	Nil	....	30.6	47.4	14.1	6-30-95	0.12	...	13815	Sp	*d0.13	0.16	0.19	0.48	P0.58	0.58				49
50◆	....	None Since Public			...	Nil	....	0.33	8.76	2.37	9-30-95	0.64	...	1619	Dc	0.12	0.49	0.49	0.28	....	d0.30	9 Mo Sep	0.41	d0.17	50
51	....	None Since Public			...	Nil	....	0.30	8.78	8.07	9-30-95	0.59	p...	★6688	Sp	...	...	...	....	p0.07	0.07				51
52◆	....	None Since Public			...	Nil	....	54.6	80.0	23.9	7-31-95	1.85	...	11600	Oc	0.89	0.55	0.59	Δ1.01	P1.66	1.66				52

◆**Stock Splits & Divs By Line Reference Index** [2]3-for-2,'95. [10]2-for-1,'94. [12]2-for-1,'93. [15]10%,'95. [20]No adj for stk dstr Toys R Us,'95. [24]2-for-1,'94. [27]3-for-2,'95. [28]2-for-1, '91, '95. [35]1-for-4 REVERSE,'93. [36]No adj for spl $10 dstr,'89:2-for-1,'92. [40]15%,'92. [44]2-for-1,'91. [45]3-for-2,'93:No adj for stk dstr Duff & Phelps CR Ratings'94. [48]1-for-10 REVERSE,'92:2-for-1,'95(twice). [50]5-for-4,'93. [52]3-for-2,'95.

¶ S&P 500
\# MidCap 400
✣ SmallCap 600
• Options

Index	Ticker	Name of Issue (Call Price of Pfd. Stocks)	Market	Com. Rank. & Pfd. Rating	Inst. Hold Cos	Inst. Hold Shs. (000)	Principal Business	Price Range 1971-93 High	1971-93 Low	1994 High	1994 Low	1995 High	1995 Low	Dec. Sales in 100s	December, 1995 Last Sale Or Bid High	Low	Last	%Div Yield	P-E Ratio	Total Return % Annualized 12 Mo	36 Mo	60 Mo
1	PPH	✔PHP Healthcare	NY	C	19	1418	Provides hlth care services	13¾	1 7/16	6¾	3½	28⅞	4⅞	22199	28⅞	20⅝	25	...	..	331	51.2	29.8
✣2•[1]	PHYC	✔PhyCor Inc	NNM	NR	204	30736	Oper mult-special medl clinics	13⅝	3⅜	18⅝	11¼	51	16⅜	97546	51	43¾	50½	...	84	236	109	...
3•[2]	PCAM	✔Physician Corp of Amer	NNM	NR	138	19310	Oper HMO's Florida & Texas	26	7½	30¼	18½	28	13½	76071	18½	14¾	17	...	34	−13.9	...	...
4	PHYN	✔Physician Reliance Network	NNM	NR	88	6345	Oncology practice mgmt	....	....	21	14	43	17¼	19751	43	35¼	39¾	...	75	104	...	...
5	PHSV	✔Physicians Health Svcs'A'	NNM	NR	59	3291	Provides HMO svcs Conn & NY	21¼	12	27½	19	43¼	22	14872	42½	35	37	...	22	38.3	...	...
6	PRG	✔Physicians Resource Group	NY,Ch,Ph	NR	24	2503	Physician practice mgmt svcs	....	....	....	....	24⅛	12¼	3575	23⅜	17¾	19⅞	...	..	...	...	...
7	PHYS	Physio-Control Intl	NNM	NR	..	...	Dgn emergency cardiac pds	....	....	....	....	18⅜	14⅜	135428	18⅜	14⅜	17⅞	...	..	...	...	...
8	PIC	✔Piccadilly Cafeterias	NY	↓B	35	2979	Cafeterias in south & so'west	26¼	4⅜	15½	7½	10⅞	7⅝	1552	10¼	9½	9½	5.1	22	23.7	−2.8	6.7
9	PPI	✔Pico Products	AS,Ch	B−	7	273	Electr devices for CATV ind	23¼	3/16	4½	2 3/16	3⅛	1½	1746	1 15/16	1½	1 13/16	...	23	−21.6	17.2	42.1
10	PICM	✔Picom Insurance	NNM	NR	5	289	Hlthcare liability insurance	15½	7/16	16⅞	11	21¾	10	606	21¾	18¾	21¾	...	9	97.7	...	...
✣11•[3]	PCTL	✔PictureTel Corp	NNM	NR	125	25727	Mfr visual communications sys	27½	1 9/16	12¼	5	43⅞	11⅛	78162	43⅞	34¾	43⅛	...	..	260	51.7	48.4
12	PDB	Piedmont Bancorp	AS	NR	..	...	Svgs bank, North Carolina	....	....	....	....	13	10	28647	13	10	12½	3.2	18	...	...	...
✣13	PNY	✔Piedmont Natl Gas	NY,Ch,Ph	A−	119	5723	Natural gas dstr, Carolinas	26⅜	1 15/16	23⅜	18	24⅞	18¼	5550	24⅞	23	23¼	4.7	16	30.0	12.5	16.4
✣14•[4]	PIR	✔Pier 1 Imports	NY,Ch,P,Ph	↑B+	134	27773	Import specialty stores	13¼	¼	10⅛	6¾	12⅜	7¾	49125	12⅜	10¼	11⅜	1.4	20	47.3	1.3	25.6
15	CHX	✔Pilgrim's Pride	NY,Ch,Ph	B−	29	2157	Produces,mkts chicken prd	15⅜	3⅝	10½	6⅜	9⅞	6⅝	2456	7⅛	6⅝	6⅞	0.9	d	−28.1	3.9	4.8
✣16	PTX	✔Pillowtex Corp	NY,Ph	NR	33	3105	Mfr bedroom textile products	20⅝	9	21¼	8⅞	13⅛	8	3710	13	11⅜	11⅝	...	15	24.5	...	...
17	PA	✔PIMCO Advisors'A'	NY	NR	22	1350	Mutual fd mgmt/advisory svc	....	....	18	15⅝	21¼	16⅞	2221	21¼	20⅜	20⅞	9.0	19	38.9	...	...
18	PKTN	✔Pinkerton's Inc	NNM	B−	56	5128	Security/investigation svcs	36	14	22	14	21½	14¾	2417	20¾	18	19½	...	d	−1.3	−2.4	−3.0
19	PNCL	✔Pinnacle Micro	NNM	NR	23	915	Mfr optical storage systems	15	6⅝	13⅝	6⅛	19⅝	5⅞	15144	19½	14½	14½	...	..	126	...	...
20	PCLE	✔Pinnacle Systems	NNM	NR	72	5931	Dgn/mfr video processing equip	....	....	15½	9¾	35½	9¾	21424	33	23	24¾	...	46	65.0	...	...
#21•[5]	PNW	✔Pinnacle West Capital	NY,B,C,Ch,P,Ph	B	285	60627	Hldg:Arizona Pub Svc	32¾	5	22⅞	16	28⅞	19⅝	46426	28⅞	27	28¾	3.5	13	52.2	15.6	25.5
22	PIO	✔Pioneer Electron ADR[55]	NY,B,Ch,Ph	NR	15	684	High fi stereo audio/Japan	43⅜	⅞	30⅛	21¾	24⅜	15⅝	1824	18⅞	16⅞	18¼	1.0	d	−23.1	−5.3	−7.8
23	PFS	✔Pioneer Financial Svcs	NY,Ch	B−	38	2865	Life,accident,health insur	26⅜	3¾	14¾	8½	18⅝	8¾	6404	18⅝	16⅛	18½	1.0	8	115	54.7	24.9
24	Pr	$2.125 cmCv[57]ExPfd([58]25.85)	NY,Ch	NR	3	6		41½	12½	27⅞	22⅛	31¼	22⅜	326	31¼	29⅝	31	6.9	..	...	...	...
✣25	PIOG	✔Pioneer Group	NNM	A−	137	12864	Mutual fund underwrtr,gold mng	13½	¼	25⅜	12⅜	29⅝	17¾	9584	27¾	25¾	27¼	1.5	32	27.0	60.1	51.0
¶26•[6]	PHB	✔Pioneer Hi-Bred Intl	NY,Ph	B+	374	48087	Hybrid seed corn	39½	1¾	40½	29½	60⅛	32½	35175	60⅛	53¾	55⅝	1.4	26	67.6	29.2	38.1
27	PRR	Pioneer Railcorp	Ch	NR	1		Railroad shipping transport'n	2 3/16	⅞	3	1 5/16	4½	2	310	3⅜	2¼	3	...	43	34.4	...	...
✣28	PIOS	✔Pioneer Std Electr	NNM	B+	129	13544	Dstr electronic components	11	3/16	13⅛	8¼	19¼	10⅝	30734	15¼	13	13¼	0.9	11	25.4	27.8	38.4
✣29•[7]	PJC	✔Piper Jaffray Cos Inc	NY,Ch,Ph	↓B	55	4709	Broker:inv bkg:money mgmt	18¾	2 3/16	18⅜	9⅜	17	9⅝	3492	14⅜	12⅝	13¾	2.2	d	38.8	4.2	32.5
¶30•[8]	PBI	✔Pitney Bowes	NY,B,Ch,P,Ph	A+	554	114936	Postage meters: mailing sys	44½	13/16	46⅜	29¼	48¼	30	73126	48¼	44½	47	2.6	18	48.9	8.6	22.7
31	Pr	$2.12 cm Cv Pref(28)vtg	NY,Ch	NR	5	2	copying & dictating sys	347¾	23⅛	366	251	351¾	251	....	....	....	376B	0.6	..	...	...	...
32	PDM	✔Pitt-DesMoines Inc	AS	B−	40	992	Steel fabricating, contract'g	60	3⅞	36½	26	39¼	31½	86	39¼	37	38¼B	2.6	7	15.8	4.9	7.9
33•[9]	PITC	✔Pittencrieff Communic	NNM	NR	42	2514	Mobile radio communic svcs	41½	14	30¼	4½	7	3⅛	28443	4⅛	3¼	3¾	...	d	−23.8	...	...
34	PW	✔Pitts & W Va RR SBI	AS	NR	3	6	Real estate investment trust	8⅜	4	7⅞	6⅞	7½	6½	71	7½	7⅛	7⅛B	7.7	13	10.2	9.3	12.5
35	PZM	✔Pittston Minerals Group	NY	NR	64	5220	Coal & minerals mining	24½	11½	30½	17¼	26	9⅜	7425	14¾	12⅞	13⅞	4.7	7	−43.2	...	...
¶36•[10]	PZS	✔Pittston Services Group	[11]NY,B,C,Ch,P	B	330	34602	Air Freight/security svcs	47	8½	31¼	21⅜	32⅝	22½	22912	32⅝	30⅜	31⅜	0.6	14	19.3	...	...
37	PRY	✔Pittway Corp	AS	NR	31	1623	Alarms,security prd/pack'g	44⅜	18½	40¾	31½	67⅜	37½	290	67⅜	62⅛	66⅜	0.6	24	73.3	...	...
38	PRY.A	✔ Class'A'	AS	NR	86	8076		40¾	15½	40⅝	31⅜	69	37½	1079	69	64	67¾	0.7	25	73.4	28.3	35.9
39	PIXR	Pixar	NNM	NR	..	...	Digital animation studio/films	....	....	....	....	49½	22	155115	42¼	22	28⅞	...	..	...	...	...
40	PIXT	✔PixTech Inc	NNM	NR	9	422	Dgn/dvp field emission displays	....	....	....	....	10½	6⅜	3384	10¼	9¾	9¾	...	d	...	...	...
41	PZZI	Pizza Inn	NSC	NR	10	924	Oper/franchises pizza restr	5¾	3/16	5	2½	4½	2 5/16	5875	4½	4⅛	4½	...	19	75.6	...	...
¶42•[12]	PDG	✔Placer Dome Inc	NY,To,Mo	B−	444	79582	Mining:gold,silver,copper	33⅛	2⅝	28¼	18⅛	29½	18⅜	110831	26⅜	23¾	24⅛	1.2	80	11.0	31.6	10.1
✣43•[13]	PLX	✔Plains Resources	AS,Ph	C	57	9525	Oil & gas expl,devel,prod'n	30¾	2½	8	5⅜	11	5½	11036	9¼	7⅜	9	...	56	63.6	0.9	8.9
44•[14]	PLNR	✔Planar Systems	NNM	NR	79	8408	Mfr electrolumins'*displays	9¾	7	23¾	8¾	25¾	14¾	14152	20¼	15¾	19⅛	...	20	−14.5	...	...
45	POLY	Planet Polymer Technologies	NSC	NR	1	10	Dvlp stg:specialty chemical	....	....	....	....	8¾	3	8544	8¾	4⅝	8	...	d	...	...	...
46	PLT	✔Plantronics Inc	NY	NR	82	7483	Mfr telephone headsets	....	....	32¼	14½	37⅞	22	2432	36⅛	34¼	36⅛	...	15	23.5	...	...
47	PMAT	✔Plasma & Materials Technologies	NNM	NR	31	3118	Dgn/mfr plasma etching eqp	....	....	....	....	21¼	9	16907	15	9½	11¼	...	d	...	...	...
48	SIGN	✔Plasti-Line	NNM	B−	15	731	Mfr illuminated outdr signs	20½	3½	10⅞	4¾	9⅛	4¾	848	8¾	8	8½	...	d	70.0	0.0	12.3
✣49•[2]	PSQL	✔Platinum Software	NNM	NR	71	9894	Dvlp finl mgmt,info softwr pd	39¾	9⅜	25¼	3½	16⅞	4¾	56069	6¾	4¾	5⅝	...	d	−56.3	−32.5	...
✣50•[15]	PLAT	✔PLATINUM technology	NNM	NR	143	22781	Dvlp educational softwr prd	25¼	7¼	23¾	10	26	13½	138322	18¾	14¾	18⅜	...	d	−16.5	−2.0	...
51	PBYP	✔Play-By-Play Toys&Novelties	NNM	NR	15	1519	Dgn/dvp stuffed toys	....	....	....	....	16⅜	10¾	6935	16⅜	13⅜	14⅝	...	16	...	...	...
52	PLAA	✔Playboy Enterprises'A'(vtg)	[11]NY,B,Ch,P	C	15	444	Magazine,clubs,cable prog'g	16⅜	1	11	6	9⅝	7⅝	130	9⅜	8⅝	8¾	...	63	−7.9	4.7	18.5

Uniform Footnote Explanations-See Page 4. Other: [1]P,Ph:Cycle 3. [2]CBOE:Cycle 1. [3]Ph:Cycle 1. [4]NY:Cycle 3. [5]P:Cycle 1. [6]ASE:Cycle 3. [7]ASE,Ph:Cycle 2. [8]ASE:Cycle 1. [9]CBOE:Cycle 2. [10]Ph:Cycle 2. [11]Ph [12]Ph,To:Cycle 3. [13]ASE,CBOE:Cycle 1. [14]Ph:Cycle 3. [15]CBOE:Cycle 3. [51]®$0.08,'95. [52]12 Mo Dec'94,prior fiscal Sep earned $0.19. [53]To be determined. [54]Subsid pfd in $M. [55]ADR representing 1 shr,par 50 yen. [56]®$1.58,'94. [57]Co opt to exch for$25 amt8.50%Cv 2014. [58]To 7-14-95,scale to $25 in'99. [59]Excl subsid Pfd. [60]Stk dstr of Aptar Group Inc. [61]10 Mo Dec'94.

Common and Convertible Preferred Stocks

Index (Splits ◆)	Cash Divs. Ea.Yr. Since	Dividends: Latest Payment Period $	Date	Ex. Div.	Total $ So Far 1995	Ind. Rate	Paid 1994	Financial Position Mil-$ Cash& Equiv.	Curr. Assets	Curr. Liab.	Balance Sheet Date	Capitalization Lg Trm Debt Mil-$	Shs. 000 Pfd.	Com.
1◆	....	None Paid			...	Nil	....	3.29	49.4	33.4	10-31-95	22.1	...	10846
2◆	....	None Since Public			...	Nil	....	31.1	216	89.9	9-30-95	73.7	...	35388
3◆	....	None Since Public			...	Nil	....	224	323	283	9-30-95	106	...	38592
4	....	None Since Public			...	Nil	....	33.1	76.2	20.1	6-30-95	0.63	...	20854
5	....	None Since Public			...	Nil	....	121	164	93.7	9-30-95	....	...	±9264
6	....	None Since Public			...	Nil	....	17.9	26.2	8.88	9-30-95	2.35	...	9558
7	....	None Since Public			...	Nil	....	3.40	64.6	37.0	9-30-95	p15.1	...	★16755
8	1947	Q0.12	1-2-96	12-6	0.48	0.48	0.48	....	12.8	57.4	9-30-95	18.0	...	10333
9	....	None Since Public			...	Nil	....	0.25	17.1	13.7	10-31-95	0.27	...	3682
10◆	....	None Paid			...	Nil	....	Equity per shr $19.49			12-31-94	....	...	3239
11◆	....	None Since Public			...	Nil	....	65.7	216	87.2	9-30-95	1.08	...	32502
12	....	Plan qtly div			...	0.40	....	Book Value $13.59			6-30-95	13.0	...	★2645
13◆	1956	Q0.27½	1-12-96	12-20	1.08½	1.10	1.02½	7.21	99.3	118	7-31-95	312	...	28742
14◆	1986	Q0.04	2-26-96	2-8	0.059	0.16	0.10	37.6	374	120	8-26-95	140	...	39433
15	1987	Q0.01½	12-29-95	12-6	0.06	0.06	0.06	11.9	193	105	9-30-95	183	...	27589
16	1995	0.05	12-20-95	11-29	0.05	[53]....	....	0.49	237	87.0	9-30-95	197	...	10618
17	1995	Q0.47	11-15-95	10-26	1.649	1.88	....	47.8	116	49.7	9-30-95	....	...	±73082
18	....	None Since Public			...	Nil	....	34.6	166	81.0	9-08-95	34.3	.2	8343
19◆	....	None Since Public			...	Nil	....	2.42	28.1	11.4	9-30-95	0.02	...	7862
20	....	None Since Public			...	Nil	....	60.2	71.6	5.35	9-30-95	....	...	★7223
21	1993	Q0.25	12-1-95	10-30	0.92½	1.00	0.82½	52.9	489	559	9-30-95	2520	[54]269	87429
22◆	1989	0.063	12-27-95	9-26	0.187	0.19	0.21¼	895	3198	1562	3-31-95	377	...	179573
23	1994	Q0.04½	1-12-96	12-27	0.17¼	0.18	0.11¼	Equity per shr $13.76			6-30-95	33.2	849	10011
24	1989	Q0.53⅛	1-12-96	12-27	2.12½	2.125	2.12½	Cv into 1.6 com,$15.625				....	885	...
25◆	1979	Q0.10	12-8-95	11-29	0.40	0.40	0.315	33.7	81.2	75.1	9-30-95	13.3	...	24815
26◆	1935	Q0.20	1-10-96	12-27	0.74	0.80	0.62	84.0	770	280	8-31-95	18.0	...	83487
27◆	....	None Since Public			...	Nil	....	0.37	2.03	2.76	9-30-95	7.09	[59]...	4256
28◆	1965	Q0.03	2-1-96	12-29	0.097	0.12	0.071	18.8	293	131	9-30-95	80.3	...	22451
29◆	1971	Q0.075	12-12-95	11-24	0.30	0.30	0.60	Equity per shr $8.65			6-30-95	54.4	...	17444
30◆	1934	Q0.30	12-12-95	11-21	1.20	1.20	1.04	137	2066	3411	9-30-95	1051	104	151596
31	1979	Q0.53	1-1-96	12-13	2.12	2.12	2.12	Cv into 8 common				....	110	...
32	1988	Q0.25	12-29-95	12-13	1.00	1.00	0.90	2.31	148	66.9	9-30-95	....	...	2322
33	....	None Since Public			...	Nil	....	0.70	13.7	20.5	9-30-95	2.57	...	14205
34	1964	Q0.14	12-29-95	12-8	0.55	0.55	0.55	Equity per shr $6.07			9-30-95	....	...	1510
35	1993	Q0.16¼	12-1-95	11-13	0.65	0.65	0.65	27.6	201	258	9-30-95	84.5	161	8406
36◆	1990	Q0.05	12-1-95	11-13	0.20	0.20	0.20	41.3	465	378	9-30-95	57.3	...	41574
37◆	1990	[60]Q0.10	1-3-96	12-13	0.40	0.40	0.40	29.8	395	221	9-30-95	8.76	...	±13941
38◆	1990	Q0.12½	1-3-96	12-13	0.50	0.50	0.50	....	...	...		....	...	11315
39	....	None Since Public			...	Nil	....	6.33	8.26	6.65	p9-30-95	....	...	★37387
40	....	None Since Public			...	Nil	....	20.3	23.7	7.95	9-30-95	5.87	...	8112
41	....	None Paid			...	Nil	....	2.03	9.56	6.06	6-25-95	11.0	...	13527
42	1987	tQ0.075	12-18-95	11-15	0.30	0.30	t0.27	299	581	262	9-30-95	411	...	239036
43	....	None Since Public			...	Nil	....	5.07	46.4	52.7	9-30-95	150	39	15326
44	....	None Since Public			...	Nil	....	34.5	64.4	14.6	3-31-95	....	...	★10224
45	....	None Since Public			...	Nil	....	5.10	5.18	0.41	9-30-95	....	...	5014
46	....	None Since Public			...	Nil	....	17.2	70.8	35.5	9-30-95	65.1	...	8221
47	....	None Since Public			...	Nil	....	40.6	53.4	4.74	9-30-95	....	...	8239
48	....	None Since Public			...	Nil	....	0.01	46.2	24.3	10-01-95	11.2	...	3674
49◆	....	None Since Public			...	Nil	....	21.5	41.1	20.4	9-30-95	....	2722	13346
50◆	....	None Since Public			...	Nil	....	29.5	130	107	9-30-95	....	...	p47847
51	....	None Since Public			...	Nil	....	16.5	41.1	15.0	7-31-95	0.15	...	4841
52	....	0.03	7-16-82	6-28	...	Nil	....	1.05	95.3	81.7	9-30-95	0.69	...	±19990

Index	Earnings $ Per Shr. Years End	1991	1992	1993	1994	1995	Last 12 Mos.	Interim Earnings Period	$ per Shr. 1994	1995	Index
1◆	Ap	0.45	0.43	d0.38	d0.93	[51]0.09	0.23	6 Mo Oct	0.02	0.17	1
2◆	Dc	*0.08	d0.86	*0.30	0.48	E0.60	0.56	9 Mo Sep	0.35	0.43	2
3◆	Dc	d0.04	0.48	1.14	1.30	E0.50	0.81	9 Mo Sep	0.96	0.47	3
4	Dc	...	...	...	[52]0.21	....	0.53	9 Mo Sep	Δ0.14	0.46	4
5	Dc	1.16	1.36	1.31	1.52	....	1.68	9 Mo Sep	1.12	1.28	5
6	Dc	...	...	...	p0.64	....	....	9 Mo Sep	n/a	p0.09	6
7	Dc	...	...	...	p0.73	....	....	9 Mo Sep	n/a	p0.31	7
8	Je	0.90	d2.51	0.49	0.70	0.40	0.43	3 Mo Sep	0.09	0.12	8
9	Jl	d0.36	0.02	d0.08	0.21	0.12	0.08	3 Mo Oct	0.04	Nil	9
10◆	Dc	□4.13	□2.81	□3.66	1.59	....	2.35	9 Mo Sep	1.06	1.82	10
11◆	Dc	*0.15	Δ0.27	Δ0.24	0.15	....	0.44	9 Mo Sep	0.07	0.36	11
12	Je	...	...	...	....	p0.71	0.71				12
13◆	Oc	0.89	1.39	1.45	1.35	P1.45	1.45				13
14◆	Fb	0.68	0.59	0.15	0.60	....	0.57	9 Mo Nov	0.36	0.33	14
15	Sp	0.54	d1.24	□0.81	1.13	d0.29	d0.29				15
16	Dc	...	p0.84	p1.32	0.73	....	0.76	9 Mo Sep	0.63	0.66	16
17	Dc	...	...	p1.15	p1.08	....	1.08	9 Mo Sep	p0.81	0.81	17
18	Dc	1.66	1.04	0.39	d1.24	....	d1.04	9 Mo Sep	0.40	0.60	18
19◆	Dc	p0.15	p0.15	p0.28	0.35	....	0.12	9 Mo Sep	0.28	0.05	19
20	Je	...	...	...	pd0.21	0.44	0.54	3 Mo Sep	0.07	0.17	20
21	Dc	■d2.15	1.80	Δ1.95	2.30	E2.20	2.49	12 Mo Sep	2.07	2.49	21
22◆	Mr	1.19	*0.43	Δ0.09	d0.07	....	d0.27	6 Mo Sep	d0.04	d0.24	22
23	Dc	1.02	d2.85	1.51	[56]2.36	....	2.46	9 Mo Sep	1.64	1.74	23
24	Dc	...	...	...	....	....	....				24
25◆	Dc	0.58	0.59	0.73	Δ1.16	....	0.86	9 Mo Sep	1.07	0.77	25
26◆	Au	1.15	1.68	□1.53	2.40	2.16	2.16				26
27◆	Dc	*0.03	0.04	□0.08	0.09	....	0.07	9 Mo Sep	0.11	0.09	27
28◆	Mr	0.29	0.63	0.87	1.09	....	1.16	6 Mo Sep	0.51	0.58	28
29◆	Sp	1.16	2.21	2.29	1.41	Pd0.82	d0.82				29
30◆	Dc	1.84	□1.98	2.22	□2.50	E2.65↓	3.79	9 Mo Sep	□1.80	3.09	30
31	Dc	b2.11	b2.37	...	....	....	....				31
32	Dc	3.19	2.02	0.45	5.19	....	5.92	9 Mo Sep	3.16	3.89	32
33	Dc	...	p0.27	p0.15	d0.89	....	d0.60	9 Mo Sep	d0.51	d0.22	33
34	Dc	0.55	0.55	0.55	0.55	....	0.55	9 Mo Sep	0.42	0.42	34
35	Dc	...	p2.97	d4.47	d7.50	....	1.95	9 Mo Sep	d8.44	1.01	35
36◆	Dc	□d0.77	p0.73	1.28	2.11	E2.25	2.16	9 Mo Sep	1.50	1.55	36
37◆	Dc	±1.85	±3.42	Δ±2.24	±3.22	....	2.72	9 Mo Sep	±2.56	±2.06	37
38◆	Dc	±1.85	±3.42	Δ±2.24	±3.22	....	2.72	9 Mo Sep	±2.56	±2.06	38
39	Dc	...	...	...	pd0.06	....	....	9 Mo Sep	n/a	p0.08	39
40	Dc	...	...	...	pd0.51	....	d1.45	9 Mo Sep	pd0.28	pd1.22	40
41	Je	...	d0.07	Δ0.11	0.18	0.22	0.24	3 Mo Sep	0.04	0.06	41
42	Dc	d1.00	0.47	0.45	0.44	E0.30↓	0.26	9 Mo Sep	0.33	0.15	42
43	Dc	d1.59	d0.32	d1.77	0.04	....	0.16	9 Mo Sep	d0.02	0.10	43
44	Sp	d0.09	*0.25	*0.65	0.77	P0.98	0.98				44
45	Dc	...	...	d0.22	d0.18	....	d0.36	9 Mo Sep	d0.12	d0.30	45
46	Mr	...	p0.48	d6.55	2.38	....	2.48	6 Mo Sep	1.24	1.34	46
47	Dc	...	...	...	p[61]d0.75	....	d0.44	9 Mo Sep	pd0.46	pd0.15	47
48	Dc	0.25	□0.65	0.77	d1.31	....	d1.28	9 Mo Sep	0.04	0.07	48
49◆	Je	0.03	0.11	d1.52	d4.80	d0.44	d0.76	3 Mo Sep	Nil	d0.32	49
50◆	Dc	0.25	0.43	0.14	d0.16	Ed0.31	d1.69	9 Mo Sep	0.31	d1.22	50
51	Jl	...	...	...	p0.41	0.63	0.89	3 Mo Oct	0.06	0.32	51
52	Je	*±0.12	*±0.10	±0.02	±d0.86	±0.03	0.14	3 Mo Sep	±d0.06	±0.05	52

◆**Stock Splits & Divs By Line Reference Index** [1]5-for-4,'91:2-for-1,'95. [2]3-for-2,'94,'95. [3]2-for-1,'93. [10]10%,'93,'94. [11]2-for-1,'95. [13]2-for-1,'93. [14]No adj for stk dstr'85:Adj to 5%,'95. [19]3-for-2,'95. [22]2-for-1,'91. [25]2-for-1,'93,'94. [26]3-for-1,'92. [27]2-for-1,'95. [28]3-for-2,'93,'94,'95. [29]2-for-1,'91,'93. [30]2-for-1,'92. [36]No adj for reorg/dstr Pittston Minerals,'93. [37]No adj for stk dstr of Aptar Group,'93. [38]No adj for stk dstr of Aptar Group,'93. [49]3-for-2,'93. [50]2-for-1,'91.

¶ S&P 500 # MidCap 400 ✤ SmallCap 600 • Options

Index	Ticker	Name of Issue (Call Price of Pfd. Stocks)	Market	Com. Rank. & Pfd. Rating	Inst. Hold Cos	Shs. (000)	Principal Business	1971-93 High	1971-93 Low	1994 High	1994 Low	1995 High	1995 Low	Dec. Sales in 100s	December, 1995 Last Sale Or Bid High	Low	Last	%Div Yield	P-E Ratio	Total Return % Annualized 12 Mo	36 Mo	60 Mo
		Playboy Enterprises'A'(vtg) (Cont.)																				
1	PLA	✓ Cl 'B' non-vtg	NY,Ph	C	36	4816		13	3⅜	13	6	10⅝	7⅜	6241	8½	7½	8⅜	...	60	−17.3	3.7	16.7
✤2•[1]	PLAY	✓Players International	NNM	B−	114	18019	Services & prod to gaming ind	18⅜	½	19⅞	9⅝	23	10⅜	38347	13½	10½	10⅝	...	9	−27.2	38.9	35.6
3•[2]	PYX	✓Playtex Products	NY,Ch	NR	61	9191	Mfr personal care products	...	...	13⅛	6⅜	12½	6½	27634	8⅝	6⅞	7½	...	16	5.3	...	...
4•[3]	PLC	✓PLC Systems	AS	NR	36	1683	Heart laser technology	9	3	7⅜	3¼	20⅝	3⅝	15670	19¼	16	16⅝	...	d	264	29.7	...
✤5	PLXS	✓Plexus Corp	NNM	B	21	1531	Mfr electronic components	22¼	2	18	8	19	8½	1968	17	16⅛	16⅝	...	19	95.6	3.5	41.2
6	GFX	✓PLM Equip Growth Fd L.P.	AS	NR	1	.9	Own/lease transport'n equip	20	12½	16⅜	12¼	12¾	6⅝	1182	8⅝	6⅝	6⅞	33.5	11	−30.8	−6.0	0.9
7	GFY	✓PLM Equip Growth Fd II L.P.	AS	NR	3	3	Own/lease transport'n equip	17	9	12¼	7¼	8½	4½	971	5½	4½	4½	35.1	d	−23.2	−7.2	−5.4
8	GFZ	✓PLM Equip Growth Fd III L.P.	AS,Ph	NR	8	9	Own/lease transport'n equip	16⅞	9	12⅛	7⅜	8⅝	4½	1364	5⅝	4½	4⅞	32.8	23	−19.8	−6.8	...
9	PLM	✓PLM International	AS	NR	15	2780	Fin'l svcs/leasing	11⅜	1½	3⅞	2⅛	4⅛	2½	2581	3⅞	3½	3¾	...	7	42.9	27.4	−2.8
10•[4]	PCL	✓Plum Creek Timber L.P.	NY,Ch,Ph	NR	78	4699	Mfr,sell raw timber/wood prd	26¾	6⅜	32½	19⅝	26¾	19⅞	18987	24	21⅞	23⅞	8.2	10	28.6	26.2	39.8
✤11	PGI	✓Ply Gem Industries, Inc	NY,Ch,P	B	83	6692	Building mtls: home imp prods	18⅜	5/16	25⅞	17	21¼	14½	6081	18⅞	16	16¼	0.7	..	−9.1	9.2	24.3
12	PLR.A	✓Plymouth Rubber'A'vtg	AS	B−	4	33	Plastic & rubber specialties:	8¼	11/16	9⅝	5¼	12	7⅛	27	10⅛	10	10⅛	...	9	39.8	41.6	45.8
13	PLR.B	Class B Com, non-vtg	AS	B−	3	58	tapes,films,rubber bands	6⅞	7/16	9½	5⅝	12⅛	7	33	10½	9¾	10	...	9	46.7	39.1	46.2
14	PMC	✓PMC Capital	AS	NR	22	823	Loans to small businesses	15	3	17⅜	11⅞	13½	10¾	1454	13⅛	12½	12⅝	e8.2	11	0.7	6.4	30.6
15	PCC	✓PMC Commercial Tr	AS	NR	12	873	Real estate investment trust	15¼	15	15⅜	11¼	17⅛	11¾	1151	17⅛	15¼	16¼	e8.7	12	51.4	...	...
16•[5]	PMA	✓PMI Group	NY,Ch	NR	235	25905	Private mortgage insurer	...	...	...	...	53½	34	36407	48¾	40¾	45¼	0.4	12	...	...	...
17	PMTS	✓PMT Services	NNM	NR	59	4995	Svc electronic credit card sys	...	...	11¼	7¾	34¾	8⅜	15703	34¾	27¾	30¼	...	44	246	...	...
¶18•[6]	PNC	✓PNC Bank Corp	NY,Ch	B	507	137931	Comml bkg,Penn,mid Atlantic	36⅝	2¼	31⅝	20	32⅝	21⅛	213180	32⅝	28⅛	32¼	4.3	13	61.4	9.5	30.7
19	Pr C	$1.60cm Cv C Pfd(20)vtg	NY	BBB+	2	6		60	14	50⅜	35⅜	50⅛	35¼	5	50⅛	50	53⅞B	3.0	..	...	...	...
20	Pr D	$1.80cm Cv D Pfd(20)vtg	NY	NR	3	7		60	15½	51⅝	35	52½	35¾	61	52½	47¼	53⅞B	3.3	..	...	...	...
21	POBR	✓Poe & Brown	NNM	B+	54	3800	General insurance agency	21¼	2⅝	22¾	17	25¼	20¼	2219	25¼	24	24⅞	1.9	15	23.1	17.1	34.7
✤22•[7]	PPP	✓Pogo Producing	NY,B,Ch,P,Ph	B−	134	25743	Oil&gas explor,dev,prod'n	39⅜	2½	24¼	15⅝	29	16	31650	29	23⅛	28¼	0.4	81	63.5	41.2	36.6
23	PKX	Pohang Iron & Steel ADS[53]	NY,Ch,Ph	NR	58	3417	Steel production, Korea	...	...	37⅞	25	35½	20	18064	25⅝	20	21⅞	1.0	18	−25.4	...	...
24	PII	✓Polaris Industries	NY,Ch,P,Ph	NR	84	4387	Mfrs snowmobiles & ATV's	25⅝	4¾	34⅞	19⅜	34⅜	25	16936	31¼	27⅝	29⅜	e1.8	13	−0.9	31.3	30.3
¶25•[3]	PRD	✓Polaroid Corp	NY,B,C,Ch,P,Ph	B	303	38425	Photographic equip & film	74¾	7⅛	36¾	29¼	49⅝	29	43530	49⅝	46	47⅜	1.3	d	45.7	16.2	18.5
#26•[4]	PMS	✓Policy Mgmt Systems	NY,Ch,Ph	C	155	16249	Computer softw for insur co's	87¼	8	47¾	25¾	54¼	37¾	10456	48¾	43⅝	47⅝	...	20	12.1	−15.9	3.0
27	POLXF	Polydex Pharmaceuticals	NSC	C	4	687	Pharmac'ls:animal health prod	13	⅜	3	⅝	1½	½	15828	13/16	½	⅝	...	d	−13.5	−31.0	−2.0
28	PLG	PolyGram N.V.	NY,Ph	NR	121	8244	Produce/mkt recorded music	40⅛	15¼	46⅞	37⅜	66½	45⅞	17265	62⅝	49⅞	52⅝	0.9	21	14.6	30.2	26.0
29	PM	✓PolyMedica Industries	AS	NR	25	1403	Mfr polyurethane-based medl pd	16⅝	5	6⅜	3⅛	10⅞	4	5516	7⅛	5½	6	...	15	33.3	−22.6	...
30	PLY	✓Polyphase Corp	AS,Ph	†B−	5	353	Food/elec/forestry eq,comput's	10⅝	⅛	7⅜	3	4¾	1¾	6049	4¾	3⅞	4	...	15	10.3	42.8	84.3
31	PLI	✓PolyVision Corp	AS	NR	27	901	Mfr visual display products	116¼	8⅜	13⅛	5⅝	10¼	1¾	2103	2¼	1⅞	2 1/16	...	d	−75.5	−39.6	−35.7
32	PBK	✓PONCEBANK	NY,Ch	B−	7	494	Commercial bkg,Puerto Rico	13¼	2¼	9⅞	7⅛	12⅞	7½	2414	12	11⅛	11½	3.1	7	49.9	39.0	23.1
✤33	PESC	✓Pool Energy Services	NNM	NR	79	9593	Oil&gas well servicing oper	18⅛	5¼	10½	6¼	9⅞	6⅝	8013	9⅞	8¾	9½	...	d	35.7	13.5	0.3
✤34	POP	✓Pope & Talbot	NY,B,Ch,P	B−	91	7835	Tissue:diapers:pulp:lumber	29⅞	2	32⅝	15¼	17⅞	12½	8445	15	12½	13¼	5.7	d	−11.6	−2.4	2.1
35	PSI	✓Porta Systems	AS,B,Ch,P	C	19	1327	Mfr telecommunications eq	26	⅛	12¾	4½	6¼	9/16	13423	1⅛	11/16	11/16	...	d	−86.3	−64.1	−46.6
36	PCW	PortaCom Wireless	Vc	NR	..	...	Cellular,wireless commun svc	10⅝	1¼	8¾	4⅞	5½	1⅜	2480	2	1⅜	1 7/16B	...	..	...	...	...
37	PTG	✓Portage Industries	AS	B−	8	855	Mfr:extruded plastic sheet	7½	1¼	4¾	2 5/16	4¼	2¼	2271	4¼	2¼	3⅝	...	15	52.6	27.5	15.7
38	POR	✓Portec Inc	NY,Ch,Ph	B−	23	1844	RR prod,mat'l hldg/constr eq	17⅛	1 11/16	15⅜	9⅜	14	9½	782	10	9½	9⅝	...	7	−23.8	28.3	44.7
#39	PGN	✓Portland Genl Corp	NY,B,C,Ch,P,Ph	B	197	23228	Hldg co:Portland Gen'l El	36¾	10¾	20½	16⅜	29¼	18⅞	27040	29¼	27⅝	29⅛	4.1	18	59.6	23.7	17.3
40	PGB	Portland Genl Elec 8.25% 'QUIDS'[59]	NY	....[60]	..	...	Quarterly Income Debt Sec	...	...	...	...	26⅜	24¾	1388	26⅜	25½	25⅞B	8.0	..	...	...	...
41	PT	Portugal Telecom ADS[62]	NY,Ch,Ph	NR	70	8952	Telecommun svcs, Portugal	...	...	...	...	20⅛	17¾	18131	19⅛	18⅜	19	1.9	23	...	...	...
42	POSI	✓Positron Corp	NNM	NR	4	8	Mfr medical imaging devices	7	5¾	7⅜	4¼	5¼	1	5082	2¾	1 11/16	1 11/16	...	d	−64.5	...	...
43	PPS	✓Post Properties	NY,Ph	NR	147	11776	Real estate investment trust	33⅝	27¼	33¼	27⅜	32¼	28½	10217	32¼	30	31⅞	6.1	21	7.4	...	...
44•	POT	Potash Corp Saskatchewan	[8]NY,To,Ch	NR	282	25517	Mine & produce potash	25⅝	10¾	42⅛	22¼	79	32⅜	49824	73¼	62⅞	70⅞	...	19	116	56.3	43.4
¶45•[5]	PCH	✓Potlatch Corp	NY,B,Ch,P,Ph	B+	258	13990	Lumber, plywood, papers	51⅞	4⅞	49½	35½	44⅛	37⅛	16619	41½	38⅝	40	4.2	10	11.2	−0.1	10.3
46	PEQ	Potomac Edison 8.00% 'QUIDS'	NY	....[66]	..	...	Qtly Income Debt Securities	...	...	...	...	26⅜	24⅝	832	26⅜	25⅝	25¾	7.8	..	...	...	...
#47•[9]	POM	✓Potomac Electric Pwr[67]	NY,B,Ch,P,Ph	B+	229	24475	Utility: el sv DC,MD,VA	29⅝	4¼	26⅝	18¼	26¼	18⅜	29296	26¼	24⅜	26¼	6.3	38	53.7	10.1	12.4
48	Pr	$2.44 cm Cv '66 Pfd (50)	NY,B,Ph	A−	1		Wash DC & areas of Md & Va	173½	23½	123⅝	100	113½	113½	...	...	...	154⅜B	1.6	..	...	...	...
49	POWL	✓Powell Indus	NNM	†B	28	2711	Electrical dstr eq: controls	16½	½	7½	5⅛	8⅜	5½	5858	8⅜	7⅛	8¼	...	15	50.0	5.6	−5.8
50	ATP	Power Control Technologies	NY	NR	41	4639	Mfr aerospace/defense subsys	...	...	...	...	8⅜	4¾	4995	8¼	7⅝	8	...	12	...	...	...
51	PWGN	PowerGen plc[68]	Lo	NR	..	...	Elec generation&sale,U.K.	577½	196	602	448	605	457½	....	537	495	532½	2.1	..	...	...	...

Uniform Footnote Explanations-See Page 4. Other: [1]ASE,CBOE:Cycle 1. [2]ASE:Cycle 1. [3]CBOE:Cycle 1. [4]ASE:Cycle 2. [5]NY:Cycle 3. [6]Ph:Cycle 2. [7]NY,P:Cycle 2. [8]Mo [9]CBOE:Cycle 2. [51]Excl $7M subsid pfd. [52]®$2.56,'94. [53]Ea ADS rep 0.25 com, par 5000 won. [54]Approx. [55]Philips NV owns 75% of com. [56]Fiscal Dec'94 & prior. [57]®$1.20,'94. [58]Subsid Pfd. [59]Jr Sub Deferrable Int Debs. [60]Rated BBB+ by S&P. [61]Payment period can be extended re-spec cond.. [62]Ea ADS rep 1 ord shr,par PTE 1,000. [63]Incl $0.612 non-taxable,'94. [64]Incl current amts. [65]Dec'93 & prior in Can Funds 1.4028. [66]Rated A by S&P. [67]Plan mgr,Baltimore G&E,new hldg co,.997new co. [68]All data reported in British pence.

Splits ◆ Index	Cash Divs. Ea. Yr. Since	Dividends: Latest Payment Period $	Date	Ex. Div.	Total $ So Far 1995	Ind. Rate	Paid 1994	Financial Position Mil-$ Cash& Equiv.	Curr. Assets	Curr. Liab.	Balance Sheet Date	Capitalization Lg Trm Debt Mil-$	Shs. 000 Pfd.	Com.	Earnings $ Per Shr. Years End	1991	1992	1993	1994	1995	Last 12 Mos.	Interim Earnings Period	$ per Shr. 1994	1995	Index
1	....	None Since Public			...	Nil	....	....	...	...		....	...	15276	Je	*±0.12	*±0.10	±0.02	±d0.86	±0.03	0.14	3 Mo Sep	±d0.06	±0.05	1
2◆	....	None Paid			...	Nil	....	139	155	35.8	9-30-95	150	...	29404	Mr	d0.35	d0.85	Δ0.61	1.45	....	1.16	6 Mo Sep	0.76	0.47	2
3	....	None Since Public			...	Nil	....	55.8	179	109	9-30-95	728	...	50880	Dc	...	p0.45	Δ□d12.67	0.97	....	0.47	9 Mo Sep	0.90	□0.40	3
4	....	None Since Public			...	Nil	....	8.86	12.5	2.03	9-30-95	0.03	...	15894	Dc	d0.48	d2.76	d0.31	d0.18	....	d0.10	9 Mo Sep	d0.16	d0.08	4
5◆	....	None Since Public			...	Nil	....	3.57	103	31.6	9-30-95	41.7	7	6494	Sp	0.59	0.80	0.40	0.46	0.89	0.89				5
6	1989	Q0.57½	2-15-96	12-27	2.30	2.30	2.30	Equity per shr $3.08			9-30-95	23.0	...	5810	Dc	1.52	d1.27	0.27	d0.01	....	0.63	9 Mo Sep	0.09	0.73	6
7	1991	Q0.40	2-15-96	12-27	1.60	1.60	1.60	Equity per shr $2.86			9-30-95	27.0	...	7431	Dc	0.03	d1.53	0.60	d0.12	....	d0.02	9 Mo Sep	d0.09	0.01	7
8	1991	Q0.40	2-15-96	12-27	1.60	1.60	1.60	Equity per shr $3.51			9-30-95	41.0	...	9906	Dc	Nil	d1.24	d0.10	d0.05	....	0.21	9 Mo Sep	d0.03	0.23	8
9	....	0.10	11-1-91	10-11	...	Nil	....	Equity per shr $4.36			9-30-95	59.3	...	11568	Dc	0.30	d2.41	0.14	□d0.32	....	0.54	9 Mo Sep	□d0.42	0.44	9
10◆	1989	Q0.49	11-29-95	11-13	1.90	1.96	1.62	85.1	170	62.5	9-30-95	517	...	40608	Dc	0.37	1.34	1.92	2.36	....	2.29	9 Mo Sep	1.71	1.64	10
11	1977	Q0.03	12-1-95	11-7	0.12	0.12	0.12	4.57	182	66.3	10-02-95	109	...	14574	Dc	0.39	0.56	0.76	d0.62	....	0.08	9 Mo Sep	d0.66	0.04	11
12◆	....	0.057	2-16-70	1-27	...	Nil	....	....	18.4	16.8	9-01-95	3.06	...	±1865	Nv	±d1.25	*±0.93	*±0.78	Δ±0.93	....	1.16	9 Mo Aug	Δ±0.65	±0.88	12
13◆	....	0.057	2-16-70	1-27	...	Nil	....	....	...	...		....	...	1054	Nv	±d1.25	*±0.93	*±0.78	Δ±0.93	....	1.16	9 Mo Aug	Δ±0.65	±0.88	13
14	1984	†0.32½	1-15-96	12-27	†1.11½	1.04	†0.98	Equity per shr $5.44			9-30-95	78.5	[51]...	10831	Dc	0.63	0.79	0.87	1.12	....	1.20	9 Mo Sep	0.68	0.76	14
15	1994	†0.43½	1-15-96	12-27	†1.24½	1.42	0.72	Equity per shr $13.87			9-30-95	2.35	...	3458	Dc	...	...	...	0.93	....	1.32	9 Mo Sep	0.64	1.03	15
16	1995	0.05	1-16-96	12-27	0.10	0.20	....	Equity per shr $23.39			9-30-95	....	...	35000	Dc	1.60	3.21	1.71	3.03	....	3.64	9 Mo Sep	2.28	2.89	16
17◆	....	None Since Public			...	Nil	....	0.06	3.68	4.12	7-31-95	p....	...	★8312	Jl	...	...	pΔ0.20	Δ0.53	0.59	0.69	3 Mo Oct	0.10	0.20	17
18◆	1865	Q0.35	10-24-95	10-12	1.40	1.40	1.31	Book Value $19.62			9-30-95	9616	865	229225	Dc	1.97	□2.36	□3.14	[52]2.57	E2.40	1.90	9 Mo Sep	2.45	1.78	18
19	1984	Q0.40	1-2-96	11-30	1.20	1.60	1.60	Cv into 1.667 com,$12				....	393	...	Dc	b1.78	b2.05	b2.27	b2.25	....	....				19
20	1985	Q0.45	1-2-96	11-30	1.35	1.80	1.80	Cv into 1.667 com,$12				....	501	...	Dc	b1.78	b2.05	b2.27	b2.25	....	....				20
21◆	1986	Q0.12	11-20-95	11-8	0.48	0.48	0.42	32.0	87.9	77.0	9-30-95	7.48	...	8682	Dc	0.93	0.25	0.95	1.56	....	1.64	9 Mo Sep	1.18	1.26	21
22	1994	Q0.03	11-30-95	11-8	0.12	0.12	0.06	7.43	64.8	23.7	9-30-95	164	...	32977	Dc	Δ0.37	0.66	0.76	□0.82	E0.35	0.34	9 Mo Sep	□0.73	0.25	22
23	1995	[54]0.183		12-27	[54]0.218	0.22	....	2353	6820	5535	6-30-95	4174	...	★93732	Dc	0.38	0.52	0.96	1.33	....	1.23	6 Mo Jun	1.32	1.22	23
24◆	1987	Q0.13	11-15-95	10-30	†4.267	0.52	1.68	2.59	193	228	9-30-95	....	...	27324	Dc	±1.10	±1.15	±1.50	±p1.98	....	2.30	9 Mo Sep	p1.27	1.59	24
25	1952	Q0.15	12-23-95	11-21	0.60	0.60	0.60	66.7	1420	615	10-01-95	547	...	45440	Dc	▲12.54	2.06	□1.45	2.49	Ed2.75↓	0.58	9 Mo Sep	1.27	d0.64	25
26	....	None Since Public			...	Nil	....	63.8	205	64.8	9-30-95	27.9	...	19436	Dc	2.21	2.55	d2.46	d0.46	E2.40	0.23	9 Mo Sep	1.12	1.81	26
27	....	None Paid			...	Nil	....	0.52	2.80	1.66	7-31-95	0.40	2994	28042	Ja	*d0.03	*d0.02	d0.05	d0.04	....	d0.04	9 Mo Oct	d0.01	d0.01	27
28	1991	0.46	5-5-95	4-17	0.46	0.46	0.339	753	5168	3629	j12-31-94	337	...	[55]180000	Dc	1.53	1.65	1.83	2.36	....	2.49	6 Mo Jun	0.83	0.96	28
29◆	....	5%Stk	10-28-94	10-18	...	Nil	5%Stk	12.7	23.0	3.52	9-30-95	24.5	...	6821	Mr	d1.03	d0.56	d0.06	0.26	....	0.40	6 Mo Sep	0.05	0.19	29
30	....	None Since Public			...	Nil	....	0.32	44.3	36.2	6-30-95	23.4	...	12619	Sp	Δ0.31	d0.35	Δ0.25	Δd0.28	P0.26	0.26				30
31◆	....	None Since Public			...	Nil	....	0.28	16.2	8.51	7-31-95	0.86	1020	8301	Ap	1.95	0.45	0.45	[56]d3.60	d0.67	d0.70	6 Mo Oct	d0.20	d0.23	31
32◆	1995	t0.09	11-22-95	11-3	t0.25	0.36	10.99%Stk	Book Value $11.35			12-31-94	64.2	...	5802	Dc	d1.43	0.38	1.35	1.62	....	1.65	9 Mo Sep	1.04	1.07	32
33	....	None Since Public			...	Nil	....	3.61	83.5	56.1	9-30-95	16.5	...	14064	Dc	0.19	□d0.22	0.46	d0.94	....	d0.99	9 Mo Sep	0.15	0.10	33
34	1948	Q0.19	11-15-95	10-26	0.76	0.76	0.76	4.48	182	80.7	9-30-95	177	...	13364	Dc	□d0.44	d0.19	□1.85	[57]1.21	....	d1.00	9 Mo Sep	0.95	d1.26	34
35	....	None Since Public			...	Nil	....	1.44	35.9	84.8	9-30-95	....	...	7307	Dc	1.30	d2.56	d1.38	d5.61	....	d5.01	9 Mo Sep	d2.66	□d2.06	35
36	....	None Paid			...	Nil	....	0.52	0.72	4.41	9-30-95	....	...	★19556	Mr	...	d0.17	d0.24	d0.49	....	....	6 Mo Sep	n/a	d0.12	36
37	....	None Since Public			...	Nil	....	0.02	8.55	7.15	10-01-95	2.25	...	2269	Dc	d0.27	Δd0.37	0.25	0.29	....	0.24	9 Mo Sep	0.22	0.17	37
38◆	....	0.112	12-1-86	11-4	...	Nil	....	3.96	36.6	16.6	9-30-95	9.75	...	4308	Dc	*0.13	1.36	1.04	1.49	....	1.41	9 Mo Sep	1.19	1.11	38
39	1948	Q0.30	1-15-96	12-21	1.20	1.20	1.20	10.3	302	360	9-30-95	874	[58]1197	50824	Dc	d1.06	1.93	1.88	1.99	E1.65	1.36	9 Mo Sep	1.51	0.88	39
40	....	Plan qtly div			...	[61]2.063	....	Co option redm fr 10-10-2000 at $25				75.0	...	...	Dc	...	...	...	...	....	....	Mature 12-31-2035			40
41	....	Plan annual div			...	0.37	....	75.4	794	1142	12-31-94	1398	...	±★190000	Dc	...	...	0.33	0.83	....	0.83				41
42	....	None Since Public			...	Nil	....	0.18	4.65	3.26	9-30-95	....	...	3637	Dc	...	pd0.89	d3.50	d1.03	....	d1.20	9 Mo Sep	d0.77	d0.94	42
43	1993	Q0.49	1-15-96	12-27	1.92	1.96	[63]1.80	Equity per shr $13.97			9-30-95	[64]p324	...	★21577	Dc	...	p0.33	p1.00	□1.32	....	1.55	9 Mo Sep	□0.97	□1.20	43
44	1990	gQ0.36	2-15-96	1-23	g1.44	1.44	g0.90	83.9	425	203	9-30-95	772	...	★45105	Dc	1.17	1.50	[65]1.59	2.12	E3.65	3.36	9 Mo Sep	1.59	2.83	44
45	1939	Q0.41½	12-4-95	11-13	1.61½	1.66	1.57	42.6	397	272	9-30-95	601	...	29109	Dc	1.92	2.71	□1.31	1.68	E3.85	3.63	9 Mo Sep	0.76	2.71	45
46	1995	Q0.50	12-29-95	12-26	1.00	2.00	....	Co option redm fr 6-30-2000 at $25				45.5	...	...	Dc	...	...	...	....	....	....	Mature 9-30-2025			46
47	1904	Q0.41½	12-29-95	11-27	1.66	1.66	1.66	21.9	534	568	9-30-95	1983	5460	118493	Dc	1.87	Δ1.66	1.95	1.79	E0.70	0.69	12 Mo Sep	1.73	0.69	47
48	1966	Q0.61	12-1-95	11-2	2.44	2.44	2.44	Cv into 5.88 common,$8.51				....	9	...	Dc	b2.01	b1.66	...	....	....	....				48
49	....	None Since Public			...	Nil	....	3.58	73.9	29.6	7-31-95	5.35	...	10543	Oc	0.69	0.81	□0.43	0.42	P0.54	0.54				49
50	....	None Since Public			...	Nil	....	13.7	108	71.8	9-30-95	6.50	20	20656	Dc	...	...	...	p0.30	....	0.65	9 Mo Sep	p0.13	p0.48	50
51	1992	3.95	11-12-93	9-20	...	11.10	....	35600	65200	76700	j10-02-94	25000	...	784002	Mr	31.00	36.50	44.00	....	....	j45.09	6 Mo SepΔ	9.71	10.80	51

◆**Stock Splits & Divs By Line Reference Index** [2]3-for-2,'95. [5]3-for-2,'92. [10]3-for-1,'93. [12]10% in Cl'B','95. [13]10%,'95. [17]To split 2-for-1,ex Jan 16. [18]2-for-1,'92. [21]5-for-4,'91. [24]2-for-1,'93:3-for-2,'95. [29]Adj for 5%,'94. [31]1-for-15 REVERSE,'95. [32]11%,'93. [38]10%,'92,'93,'94.

¶ S&P 500 # MidCap 400 ✤ SmallCap 600 • Options Index	Ticker	Name of Issue (Call Price of Pfd. Stocks)	Market	Com. Rank. & Pfd. Rating	Inst. Hold Cos	Inst. Hold Shs. (000)	Principal Business	Price Range 1971-93 High	1971-93 Low	1994 High	1994 Low	1995 High	1995 Low	Dec. Sales in 100s	December, 1995 Last Sale Or Bid High	Low	Last	%Div Yield	P-E Ratio	Total Return % Annualized 12 Mo	36 Mo	60 Mo
1	PWG	PowerGen PLC ADS[51]	NY	NR	23	3170	Elec generation&sale,U.K.	....	....	....	....	38	29½	23930	34¼	31¼	34	3.2	11	...	...	...
2	PWG.PP	1st[52]Installm't[53]ADS[54]	NY	NR	37	6665		....	....	....	....	18⅜	11⅜	5923	14⅜	12¼	13B	8.5	..	...	...	...
¶3	PPL	✔PP&L Resources	NY,B,C,Ch,Ph,P	A–	177	33086	Hldg co:Penn Pwr & Lt	31	6½	27¼	18⅝	26½	17⅞	64594	25¼	24⅜	25	6.7	17	35.9	–2.2	3.3
¶4•1	PPG	✔PPG Indus	NY,B,Ch,P,Ph	A–	651	97252	Coatings&chem/flat glass	38⅛	1 11/16	42⅛	33¾	47⅞	34⅞	59156	47⅞	43¾	45¾	2.6	12	26.7	15.7	17.9
5	PLU	✔Pratt & Lambert United[56]	NY	B	49	4146	Mfr paints,chemical coat'gs	24⅞	1 13/16	20⅜	14¾	35⅛	17½	2888	35⅛	34⅝	34⅞	1.8	48	90.1	38.5	29.8
6	PHC	✔Pratt Hotel Corp	AS	C	6	140	Hotel & casino,Atlantic City	56¼	15/16	7	3¼	5⅛	2⅛	1083	2⅞	2⅛	2¼	...	d	–47.1	1.9	–2.1
¶7•2	PX	✔Praxair Inc	NY	NR	497	98193	Ind'l gases/spcl coatings	18⅝	13⅝	24⅝	16¼	34⅛	19¾	103112	34⅛	28⅝	33⅝	1.0	19	66.1	29.2	...
8	PPD	✔Pre-Paid Legal Svcs	AS,Ch,Ph	B–	25	3524	Sells legal svc contracts	16⅜	¼	2⅜	1¼	10⅞	1 11/16	22847	10⅞	7⅝	10⅜	...	34	436	103	88.3
#9	PCP	✔Precision Castparts	NY,Ch,Ph	A–	169	18661	Castings for aircraft engines	28⅝	3/16	27½	18	40	19⅝	13270	40	35	39¾	0.6	22	99.2	49.2	13.2
10	PCSN	Precision Standard	NNM	NR	14	721	Aircraft maintenance/systems	6⅛	⅜	5	1⅝	2⅝	1	3712	1 7/16	1	1	...	2	–52.9	–2.0	–4.4
¶11•3	PMI	✔Premark Intl	NY,B	B+	478	45188	Mfr Tupperware,food eqp prod	41⅞	6⅜	48	33⅝	54¾	38½	41470	52⅛	49⅜	50⅝	2.1	13	12.8	36.6	45.7
12	PI	✔Premdor Inc	NY,To,Mo	NR	25	6871	Mfr,dstr wood doors	11⅞	7¾	14⅜	6⅞	8⅞	6¾	685	8¼	7⅝	7¾	...	..	10.7	...	...
13	PRMO	✔Premenos Technology	NNM	NR	47	2923	Dvp software pds/svcs	....	....	....	....	47	18	23973	46	24¾	26⅜	...	..	...	...	...
✤14	PRBC	✔Premier[60]Bancorp[61]	NNM	B–	104	12132	Commercial bkg,Louisiana	18⅝	2¼	18⅛	15¼	24½	15⅝	11256	24½	22¾	23⅜	...	12	50.7	23.8	58.7
15	PRE	✔Premier Industrial	NY,Ch,Ph	A	137	13311	Electronics & ind'l distr'n	30¾	⅜	28¼	17⅝	26⅛	21¾	9144	25⅝	23¾	24½	2.0	18	6.7	–0.4	10.5
16	PRNI	✔Premiere Radio Networks	NNM	NR	12	468	Produce,dstr radio programs	8¾	4⅜	11¾	6½	29¼	6¾	3918	18½	15½	16¾	...	25	139	44.9	...
17	PRMS	✔Premisys Communications	NNM	NR	47	4822	Mfr access prd telecomm ind	....	....	....	....	57¼	15¾	65992	57¼	45½	56	...	..	...	...	...
18•4	PREZ	✔President Casinos	NNM	NR	59	7931	Own riverboat/dockside casinos	33⅛	6⅛	27	6¼	10⅛	1⅝	49653	2½	1⅝	1¾	...	d	–80.3	–43.1	...
19	PDL.B	✔Presidential Rlty Cl'B'	AS	NR	10	397	Real estate investment trust	14¾	1⅝	8⅝	6¼	8½	5¾	220	6¼	5¾	5⅞	10.2	5	–17.8	27.4	27.7
20	PDL.A	Class A	AS	NR	2	2		18⅝	1¾	8½	6⅜	8⅝	6¾	36	7	6¾	6⅝B	9.1	5	–8.9	26.8	20.5
21	PRS.B	✔Presidio Oil[63]Cl'B'[64]	AS	C	4	76	Interest in oil&gas wells	16⅝	1 1/16	2½	⅝	⅝	1/64	400	1/64	1/64	1/64	...	d	–91.6	–67.8	–57.3
22	PRS.A	✔ Class 'A'(1/20 vtg)	AS	C	19	5268		9¼	9/16	2⅜	⅜	⅝	1/64	639	1/16	1/64	1/64	...	d	–87.5	–58.0	–55.6
23	PDC	✔Presley Cos 'A'	NY,Ph	NR	27	3421	Home building/community dvlp	17⅜	1¾	4½	1⅞	2⅞	1¼	6224	2	1¼	1¾	...	d	–33.3	–23.3	...
24•5	PRST	✔Presstek Inc	NNM	NR	55	1797	Dvlp stge:color imaging sys	13	1 13/16	25⅞	7¼	100	21½	58411	100	79	94½	...	..	273	119	76.1
25	PRIA	✔PRI Automation	NNM	NR	78	4850	Mfr semiconductor mfg equip	....	....	17½	13½	46¼	13¼	14314	43½	33⅞	35⅛	...	30	123	...	...
26	PR	✔Price Communications	AS,B,Ch,P	NR	20	3895	Own/oper TV stations	6¾	1/32	6	2¾	9	4⅞	5740	8⅛	7⅝	8	...	4	57.1	57.3	110
¶27•6	PCCW	✔Price/Costco Inc[67]	NNM	NR	406	116751	Wholesale cash & carry mdsg	65¼	11/16	21⅝	12½	18¾	12	282066	17⅜	13⅝	15¼	...	22	...	...	...
28	RET	✔Price REIT	NY	NR	36	2992	Real estate investment trust	33½	29	35¼	27¼	32½	27⅝	2180	29⅞	27¾	27¾	9.6	14	3.0	...	...
29	PC	✔PriCellular Corp'A'	AS,Ch	NR	35	4779	Oper cellular telephone sys	....	....	7¾	7¼	14⅞	5¼	4488	14½	11⅞	13	...	d	72.1	...	...
30	PRF	Pride Co $2.60cm Cv L.P.	NY	NR	2	181	Gathers/refines petrol prod	27⅝	6½	9⅛	3½	6¼	1⅝	2997	2¼	1⅝	2¼	...	..	...	...	...
✤31	PRDE	✔Pride Petroleum Svcs	NNM	NR	119	20227	Oil & gas well svcs in U.S.	8⅝	2⅛	6¼	4⅝	11	4¾	29674	11	9¾	10⅝	...	20	113	40.0	13.6
32•3	PRMA	✔Primadonna Resorts	NNM	NR	68	5853	Own,oper casino-hotels	36	18	33	20	26¼	14¼	10754	17½	14¼	14¾	...	19	–35.2	...	...
✤33	PMK	✔Primark Corp	NY,P,Ph	NR	91	10429	Fin'l info/hlth care svcs	29⅛	4¾	15	11	30¼	12¾	22928	30¼	26⅞	30	...	38	126	27.1	35.8
✤34	PDQ	✔Prime Hospitality	NY	NR	104	22888	Own,manage hotel chain	6⅜	1½	9	5⅜	11	7¼	10040	10	9⅜	10	...	20	37.9	67.6	...
35	PMGI	✔Prime Management Group[73]	NSC	NR	9	446	Property mgmt,maintenance svcs	....	....	5¾	2½	4	2¼	378	3	2¼	2¼	...	d	...	...	...
36	PMP	✔Prime Motor Inns L.P.	NY,Ch,Ph	NR	1	8	Owns/operates motor inns	21¾	¼	1¾	⅜	13/16	5/16	1698	½	⅜	7/16	...	d	–22.2	15.9	–29.4
37	AAH	Prime Residential	NY	NR	62	8513	Real estate investment trust	....	....	16⅝	14	18¾	14¼	6985	18¾	17	18½	8.6	16	35.2	...	...
38	PRNS	✔Prins Recycling	NNM	NR	15	1038	Conducts recycling svcs	5	1¼	6⅝	1¼	19¾	6	45028	11¼	7⅛	7½	...	d	22.4	...	...
39	PTNX	✔Printronix Inc	NNM	B–	34	2282	Minicomputer printers	23⅝	2 5/16	28¾	4⅜	38¾	13½	11721	18¾	13½	14	...	9	–46.7	64.7	20.1
40	PRZ	✔Prism Entertainment	AS	B–	5	68	Dstr pre-recorded video tapes	13¾	¾	3⅜	1⅝	3½	⅛	918	⅛	⅛	⅛	...	1	–93.3	–69.1	–45.1
¶41•2	PG	✔Procter & Gamble	NY,B,C,Ch,P,Ph	A	1259	330162	Hshld,personal care,food prod	58⅞	7	64⅝	51¼	89½	60⅝	176102	88	82⅛	83	1.9	22	35.6	18.0	16.8
42•7	PRCY	✔ProCyte Corp	NNM	NR	32	2093	Dvlp stge:pharmaceutical prd	17½	4¼	15⅛	2¼	3⅜	2	28854	3	2⅛	2¾	...	d	–6.3	–34.5	–12.6
✤43	PROP	✔Production Operators	NNM	B+	87	5782	Oil & gas field service	34¾	½	28⅞	21¼	33½	22	1750	33½	29¾	33	0.8	49	47.2	8.9	19.3
44	MDB	✔Professional Bancorp	AS	B–	4	129	Commercial banking, California	16⅛	3⅝	12⅝	7⅛	16⅛	7⅝	134	13¾	12	12½	s...	9	55.3	–1.1	18.1
45	PRO.EC	✔Professional Dental Tech	ECM	NR	3	191	Mfr/dstr dental equipment	5½	2¼	3⅝	2	2⅜	¾	630	1¼	¾	15/16	...	..	–57.2	–35.5	...
✤46	PRFT	✔Proffitts Inc	NNM	NR	97	6087	Oper specialty dept stores	36¾	4¾	25¾	14¾	34¼	20¾	11351	28⅜	24½	26¼	...	15	20.0	6.5	38.0
47	PROG	✔Programmer's Paradise	NNM	NR	12	745	Mkt microcomputer software	....	....	....	....	12⅜	6¾	5087	8¾	6¾	6¾	...	11	...	...	...
✤48	PRGS	✔Progress Software	NNM	NR	115	9635	Database mgmt sys/softwr	30¾	12½	28⅜	13½	38	18⅝	21970	38	31	37½	...	27	97.6	10.4	...
#49•1	PGR	✔Progressive Corp,Ohio	NY,Ch,Ph	B+	245	47430	Insur subsid: hi risk auto	46⅛	1/16	40½	27¾	49½	34¾	31673	49½	44¼	48⅞	0.5	16	38.9	20.0	24.2
50	PJTV	✔Projectavision Inc	NSC	NR	12	795	Dvlp stge:projection TV R&D	16¾	15/16	11⅛	3⅛	6⅛	1 7/16	27464	4⅞	3⅛	4¾	...	d	40.7	–2.1	...
51	PS	✔Proler Intl	NY,Ch	C	32	2762	Upgrades ferrous/scrap metal	29⅞	3⅝	14¾	5⅝	8⅞	6¼	1066	7⅝	7	7½	...	8	20.0	2.3	–8.5
#52•4	PRH	✔Promus Hotel	NY,Ch	NR	168	32987	Own, oper hotels	....	....	....	....	26⅜	20⅜	25682	23¼	21⅝	22¼	...	28	...	...	...

Uniform Footnote Explanations-See Page 4. Other: [1]Ph:Cycle 2. [2]ASE:Cycle 1. [3]CBOE:Cycle 1. [4]CBOE:Cycle 2. [5]ASE,CBOE,P,Ph:Cycle 1. [6]P:Cycle 1. [7]P:Cycle 2. [51]Ea ADS rep four ord shrs. [52]Full pay't ADS rep four Ord, 50p. [53]2nd pay't(36%)2-6-96,3rd(27%)9-17-96. [54]1st Installm't ADS(37% paid). [55]Approx. [56]Sherwin Williams offer,$35 to Jan 5. [57]®$0.70,'94. [58]®$0.24,'94. [59]®$0.27,'93. [60]Approve Banc One Corp acq,0.617761 com. [61]Plan SmallCap 600 delisting:eff Jan 3. [62]©$0.28,'94. [63]Cv into Cl'A'shr for shr. [64]Tom Brown Inc plan acq. [65]Incl current amts. [66]®$0.12,'94. [67]Plan dstr of real-estate operations. [68]Incl $0.334848 non-taxable,'94. [69]Accum $9.40 to 11/28/95. [70]Specified cond. [71]Stk dstr of Mich Consol Gas. [72]5 Mo Dec,'92. [73]FirstService Corp plan acq, .08 com. [74]®$1.33,'95. [75]®$3.48,'95.

Splits ◆ Index	Cash Divs. Ea.Yr. Since	Dividends: Latest Payment Period $	Date	Ex. Div.	Total $ So Far 1995	Ind. Rate	Paid 1994	Financial Position Mil-$ Cash& Equiv.	Curr. Assets	Curr. Liab.	Balance Sheet Date	Capitalization Lg Trm Debt Mil-$	Shs. 000 Pfd.	Com.	Earnings $ Per Shr. Years End	1991	1992	1993	1994	1995	Last 12 Mos.	Interim Earnings Period	$ per Shr. 1994	1995	Index
1◆	1992	0.425	12-29-95	12-1	1.103	1.10	0.86	157	760	979	j4-02-95	250	...	725264	Mr	2.16	2.22	2.62	3.21	....	3.21				1
2	1995	[55]0.425	12-29-95	12-1	[55]1.103	1.10	....	....	...	...		....	...	76522	Mr	...	...	...	....	....	....				2
3◆	1946	Q0.41¾	1-1-96	12-6	1.67	1.67	1.66½	104	667	635	9-30-95	2827	3814	159061	Dc	2.00	2.02	2.07	1.41	....	1.44	12 Mo Sep	1.94	1.44	3
4◆	1899	Q0.30	12-12-95	11-8	1.18	1.20	1.12	118	2375	1580	9-30-95	745	...	196044	Dc	Δ0.95	1.51	□1.39	2.43	E3.80	3.69	9 Mo Sep	1.71	2.97	4
5	1905	Q0.16	1-2-96	11-14	0.61	0.64	0.60	2.94	152	81.8	9-30-95	75.9	...	10660	Dc	0.85	0.92	1.10	[57]0.71	....	0.73	9 Mo Sep	1.06	1.08	5
6◆	....	None Paid			...	Nil	....	27.5	54.2	43.4	9-30-95	327	...	5187	Dc	d3.50	d6.38	□d2.19	d0.87	....	d0.97	9 Mo Sep	0.04	d0.06	6
7	1992	Q0.08	12-15-95	12-5	0.32	0.32	0.28	12.0	890	1016	9-30-95	936	...	139872	Dc	p0.84	□p0.64	□1.06	1.45	E1.80	1.76	9 Mo Sep	1.06	1.37	7
8	....	None Paid			...	Nil	....	15.0	21.1	2.17	9-30-95	....	51	20746	Dc	0.02	0.04	0.02	[58]0.26	....	0.31	9 Mo Sep	0.20	0.25	8
9◆	1978	Q0.06	1-2-96	11-29	0.24	0.24	0.18	9.00	200	88.9	10-01-95	9.70	...	20426	Mr	1.78	0.06	□1.29	1.45	E1.85	1.64	6 Mo Sep	0.74	0.93	9
10	....	None Paid			...	Nil	....	....	55.8	54.3	9-30-95	0.91	...	12452	Dc	Δd0.23	*0.09	□0.58	0.67	....	0.46	9 Mo Sep	0.09	d0.12	10
11◆	1987	Q0.27	1-5-96	12-13	0.94	1.08	0.68	88.8	1403	1013	9-30-95	198	...	61212	Dc	1.63	□0.07	2.57	3.39	E4.05	3.86	9 Mo Sep	2.04	2.51	11
12	....	None Since Public			...	Nil	....	16.5	284	80.9	j12-31-94	144	...	36318	Dc	d0.09	[59]0.28	0.57	0.78	....	j0.69	9 Mo Sep	0.57	0.48	12
13	....	None Since Public			...	Nil	....	62.8	70.5	9.57	9-30-95	0.97	...	10542	Dc	d0.03	d0.01	0.03	0.28	....	0.14	9 Mo Sep	0.14	Nil	13
14◆	....	0.25	12-21-95	12-5	0.50	Nil	....	Book Value $14.34			9-30-95	285	...	34911	Dc	*0.54	*1.41	Δ2.38	2.08	....	2.02	9 Mo Sep	1.57	1.51	14
15◆	1950	Q0.12½	1-10-96	12-20	0.44	0.50	0.40	157	460	72.7	8-31-95	6.50	...	83042	My	0.86	0.91	1.02	1.10	1.28	1.35	6 Mo Nov	0.62	0.69	15
16	....	None Since Public			...	Nil	....	6.65	11.4	2.59	9-30-95	1.56	...	3637	Dc	0.44	0.44	d0.17	0.64	....	0.66	9 Mo Sep	0.59	0.61	16
17◆	....	None Since Public			...	Nil	....	43.0	51.0	5.51	6-30-95	0.11	...	23472	Je	...	...	...	p0.04	0.18	0.28	3 Mo Sep	0.02	0.12	17
18◆	....	None Since Public			...	Nil	....	23.3	32.4	37.7	8-31-95	108	...	30195	Fb	p0.13	p0.39	Δ0.33	□d0.54	....	d0.54	9 Mo Nov	□d0.36	d0.36	18
19	1980	Q0.15	12-29-95	12-6	0.60	0.60	[62]0.60	Equity per shr $2.90			9-30-95	33.3	...	±3523	Dc	±0.45	±0.57	□±0.46	±Δ1.28	....	1.24	9 Mo Sep	Δ±0.44	±0.40	19
20	1980	Q0.15	12-29-95	12-6	0.60	0.60	[62]0.60	....	...	...		....	...	479	Dc	±0.45	±0.57	□±0.46	±Δ1.28	....	1.24	9 Mo Sep	Δ±0.44	±0.40	20
21	....	None Since Public			...	Nil	....	8.54	16.2	276	9-30-95	[65]246	...	±28535	Dc	d2.68	d0.92	d0.27	d0.91	....	d1.11	9 Mo Sep	d0.69	d0.89	21
22	....	0.02½	11-30-92	10-30	...	Nil	....	....	...	...		....	...	25318	Dc	d2.58	d0.82	d0.27	d0.91	....	d1.11	9 Mo Sep	d0.69	d0.89	22
23	....	None Since Public			...	Nil	....	Equity per shr $2.00			9-30-95	263	...	±52196	Dc	p0.45	d0.57	d2.75	±0.11	....	d0.26	9 Mo Sep	±0.08	±Δd0.29	23
24◆	....	None Paid			...	Nil	....	1.79	9.53	1.85	12-31-94	....	...	14388	Dc	d0.33	*0.19	0.07	[66]0.12	....	0.13	9 Mo Sep	0.07	0.08	24
25	....	None Since Public			...	Nil	....	18.5	48.1	10.2	6-30-95	0.19	...	p6958	Sp	...	...	pd0.62	0.71	P1.16	1.16				25
26◆	....	None Paid			...	Nil	....	3.68	12.3	8.61	9-30-95	22.0	...	9822	Dc	...	...	Δd0.25	1.15	....	1.84	9 Mo Sep	0.22	0.91	26
27◆	....	None Since Public			...	Nil	h....	45.7	1702	1693	9-03-95	1095	...	195235	Au	2.68	p1.07	p1.01	d0.51	0.68	0.71	3 Mo Nov	0.22	0.25	27
28	1993	0.68	12-29-95	12-7	2.67	2.67	[68]2.56	Equity per shr $26.82			9-30-95	93.8	...	±8290	Dc	...	p1.63	±1.84	±2.07	....	2.01	9 Mo Sep	±1.54	±1.48	28
29◆	....	None Since Public			...	Nil	....	100	107	17.9	9-30-95	314	...	±22801	Dc	...	...	±pd1.45	±d0.10	....	d0.22	9 Mo Sep	±0.19	±0.07	29
30	....	0.35	5-29-92	5-11	...	[69]Nil	....	0.04	34.5	46.5	12-31-94	52.3	4700	5250	Cv into 1 com unit fr 7-1-95							Co call opt fr 7-1-97[70]			30
31	....	None Since Public			...	Nil	....	13.1	77.7	48.8	9-30-95	58.8	...	24809	Dc	0.22	d0.05	Δ0.13	0.30	....	0.54	9 Mo Sep	0.20	0.44	31
32	....	None Since Public			...	Nil	....	5.23	16.8	12.4	9-30-95	154	...	30785	Dc	...	p0.93	p1.00	0.86	....	0.77	9 Mo Sep	0.70	0.61	32
33◆	....	h[71]0.34½	5-13-88	6-1	...	Nil	....	11.8	172	198	9-30-95	267	675	★22744	Dc	0.02	0.30	□0.34	0.62	....	0.80	9 Mo Sep	0.45	□0.63	33
34	....	None Since Public			...	Nil	....	60.1	102	33.0	9-30-95	289	...	30965	Dc	...	[72]0.04	Δ0.24	Δ0.57	E0.50	0.59	9 Mo Sep	Δ0.41	Δ□0.43	34
35	....	None Since Public			...	Nil	....	1.22	2.08	1.28	9-30-95	0.44	...	2234	Dc	...	...	p0.25	p0.09	....	d0.08	9 Mo Sep	p0.27	0.10	35
36	....	0.52	8-14-90	6-25	...	Nil	....	1.88	4.03	3.48	9-30-95	65.6	...	4000	Dc	■d15.30	d0.72	d0.30	d1.16	....	d0.61	9 Mo Sep	d0.78	d0.23	36
37	1994	Q0.40	11-15-95	10-27	1.60	1.60	0.138	Equity per shr $11.06			9-30-95	[65]230	...	8959	Dc	...	...	p0.69	p0.77	....	1.13	9 Mo Sep	p□0.09	Δ0.45	37
38	....	None Since Public			◆0.04	Nil	....	1.32	20.3	25.3	9-30-95	11.3	...	10225	Dc	Nil	0.02	d0.27	d1.06	....	d0.84	9 Mo Sep	0.24	0.46	38
39◆	....	None Since Public			...	Nil	....	12.2	52.3	16.3	9-29-95	....	...	5156	Mr	d1.84	d0.51	0.39	[74]1.34	....	1.61	6 Mo Sep	0.57	0.84	39
40	....	None Since Public			...	Nil	....	Equity per shr $3.09			10-31-95	4.12	...	2213	Ja	d1.04	0.01	Δ0.56	d0.18	....	0.12	9 Mo Oct	d0.47	d0.17	40
41◆	1891	Q0.40	11-15-95	10-18	1.50	1.60	1.32	1993	11386	8693	9-30-95	5018	p33218	686325	Je	2.46	2.62	□0.25	3.09	[75]3.71	3.86	3 Mo Sep	1.12	1.27	41
42	....	None Since Public			...	Nil	....	38.5	39.0	0.84	9-30-95	....	...	13118	Dc	d0.66	d0.79	d0.80	d0.97	....	d0.55	9 Mo Sep	d0.74	d0.32	42
43	1976	Q0.07	2-15-96	1-10	0.26	0.28	0.24	1.19	48.5	17.8	9-30-95	46.0	...	10127	Sp	0.99	1.37	1.13	Δ1.18	0.67	0.67				43
44◆	....	5%Stk	7-21-95	6-21	5%Stk	Stk	....	Book Value $14.62			9-30-95	4.74	...	1198	Dc	1.27	1.64	0.84	0.82	....	1.45	9 Mo Sep	0.43	1.06	44
45	....	None Since Public			...	Nil	....	0.82	5.29	3.37	7-31-95	0.70	...	14100	Oc	0.04	0.07	0.05	0.02	....	Nil	9 Mo Jul	0.03	0.01	45
46	....	None Paid			...	Nil	....	1.17	275	141	10-29-95	272	...	10246	Ja	0.78	1.02	Δ□0.62	1.46	....	1.73	9 Mo Oct	0.30	0.57	46
47	....	None Since Public			...	Nil	....	21.1	39.3	17.1	9-30-95	....	...	4704	Dc	0.34	0.09	0.10	0.35	....	0.63	9 Mo Sep	0.13	0.41	47
48◆	....	None Since Public			...	Nil	....	84.2	124	47.1	8-31-95	0.06	...	12812	Nv	0.53	0.76	1.00	1.12	E1.40	1.14	9 Mo Aug	0.76	0.78	48
49◆	1965	Q0.05½	12-31-95	12-6	0.22	0.22	0.21	Equity per shr $18.14			9-30-95	676	3500	72064	Dc	0.41	Δ2.09	3.59	3.59	E3.10	3.74	9 Mo Sep	2.25	2.40	49
50◆	....	None Since Public			...	Nil	....	4.76	5.37	0.56	9-30-95	....	386	12439	Dc	d0.29	d0.27	d0.26	d0.47	....	d0.36	9 Mo Sep	d0.35	d0.24	50
51	....	0.06½	10-15-91	9-23	...	Nil	....	1.78	8.12	4.26	10-31-95	....	...	4714	Ja	d3.47	d2.10	Δd0.51	0.06	....	0.89	9 Mo Oct	d0.44	0.39	51
52	....	None Since Public			...	Nil	....	1.86	44.8	63.0	9-30-95	204	...	51374	Dc	...	...	...	p0.65	....	0.79	9 Mo Sep	p0.58	p0.72	52

◆**Stock Splits & Divs By Line Reference Index** [1]5-for-2,'95. [3]2-for-1,'92. [4]2-for-1,'94. [6]1-for-10 REVERSE,'92. [9]3-for-2,'94. [11]2-for-1,'94. [14]10%,'93. [15]3-for-2,'93. [17]2-for-1,'95. [18]2-for-1,'93:3-for-2,'93. [24]5-for-4,'94:2-for-1,'95. [26]5-for-4,'95. [27]No adj for mgr w/Costco,2.13 new shrs'93. [29]5-for-4,'95. [33]No adj for'88 dstr. [39]3-for-2,'94. [41]2-for-1,'92. [44]Adj for 5%,'95. [48]2-for-1,'95. [49]3-for-1,'92. [50]2-for-1,'92.

¶ S&P 500 # MidCap 400 ✣ SmallCap 600 • Options

Index	Ticker	Name of Issue (Call Price of Pfd. Stocks)	Market	Com. Rank. & Pfd. Rating	Inst. Hold Cos	Inst. Hold Shs. (000)	Principal Business	Price Range 1971-93 High	1971-93 Low	1994 High	1994 Low	1995 High	1995 Low	Dec. Sales in 100s	December, 1995 Last Sale Or Bid High	Low	Last	%Div Yield	P-E Ratio	Total Return % Annualized 12 Mo	36 Mo	60 Mo
1	PNET	✔ProNet Inc	NNM	B–	79	4534	Wireless communications svcs	19¼	2½	17⅜	10½	32¼	13⅝	10019	31	28	29½	...	d	103	61.5	41.9
2	PCT	✔Property Cap Tr	AS,Ph	NR	21	1139	Real estate investment trust	27⅛	2¼	6⅝	5⅛	9	5¾	2281	9	8½	8⅝	5.6	9	58.8	37.8	13.6
✣3	PL	✔Protective Life Corp	NY,Ch	B+	170	17691	Hldg:life,gr accid & health	26¼	1	24⅜	18½	31⅜	21⅜	7008	31¼	28¼	31¼	2.0	12	46.3	32.0	37.3
✣4•[1]	PDLI	✔Protein Design Labs	NNM	NR	74	4982	Antibody technology R&D	26⅝	5⅞	29⅞	13¾	26¾	13⅛	25571	24	16⅜	23⅛	...	d	39.1	24.4	...
5	PZA	✔Provena Foods	AS,Ch,Ph	B–	3	22	Process/dstr spec'ty food prd	7⅜	1¾	3¼	2¼	5⅜	2¼	616	4	3⅜	3½	5.1	44	50.0	25.8	4.1
6	PVY	✔Providence Energy	AS	B	41	1047	Natural gas service, R.I.	25⅛	3⅜	19⅛	14⅝	17½	14⅝	1153	17¼	16⅛	17	6.4	16	11.8	7.7	8.5
✣7	PRBK	✔Provident Bancorp	NNM,C,P,Ph	B+	59	2678	Commercial banking,Ohio	34	3⅛	36½	27¾	51½	30½	8484	51½	43	47	2.3	12	45.5	43.7	43.9
8	PBKS	✔Provident Bankshares	NNM	NR	56	2771	Comm'l bkg, Maryland	21	2⅝	26⅜	17⅜	35¼	20¾	4922	31¾	29½	29½	s2.2	15	50.2	34.6	56.9
#9	PVT	✔Provident Companies[53]	NY	B	137	20707	Life, group, accid insur	31⅞	3⅝	31⅞	21½	33⅞	20½	5533	33⅞	28⅛	33⅞	2.1	12	55.7	5.6	15.1
¶10•[2]	PVN	✔Providian Corp	NY,B,C,Ch	↓A–	480	63841	Insur hldg:ord/ind'l life	44⅞	3⅜	38⅛	28⅝	42⅞	30⅞	29522	42⅞	39¾	40¾	2.5	10	32.9	5.4	17.1
11	PRXM	✔Proxima Corp	NNM	NR	52	2534	Mfr desktop projection prod	19	5½	39⅝	8	35⅛	13⅞	35450	24	17¾	22⅛	...	15	–23.9	...	...
12	RE	Prudential Reinsurance Hldgs	NY,Ch	NR	1	39	Treaty&facultative reinsurance	...	...	...	...	23½	16¾	35176	23½	20⅞	23⅜	0.5	14	...	...	...
13	PSB	✔PS Business[54] Parks'A'	AS,Ch	NR	3	.9	Real estate investment trust	16¾	11½	16¼	14¼	18⅞	14½	184	18⅞	17⅛	18⅝	e4.1	16	43.9	22.1	...
14	PSG	✔PS Group Inc	NY,B,Ch,P,Ph	C	30	2078	Aircraft leas'g/fuel dstr	72¼	2¾	14¾	8⅞	12	8½	1983	12	9¾	10¾	...	d	0.0	8.7	–21.8
15	PSCX	✔PSC Inc	NNM	B–	41	4317	Bar code scanning equip	13½	¾	13¾	5½	15¾	8⅝	18016	10¼	8⅝	9¼	...	93	–28.2	–4.9	27.5
16	PCOR	✔PSICOR Inc[57]	NNM	B+	23	1109	Perfusion svcs to hospitals	19⅛	2⅛	11¾	8¼	18	8½	1243	17½	17¼	17¼	...	60	73.1	7.3	11.6
17•[3]	PSIX	✔PSINet Inc	NNM	NR	41	3847	Leading Internet svc provider	...	...	...	...	29	12	188385	29	20¼	22⅞	...	..	...	...	...
18	PSTV	✔PST Vans	NNM	NR	22	1057	Trucking-gen'l commodities	...	...	...	...	16⅞	4⅛	5109	6¼	4⅛	4⅝	...	5	...	...	...
19	PMD	✔Psychemedics Corp	AS	NR	20	812	Laboratory testing, svcs	6⅛	⅜	4⅜	1⅞	10¾	2½	13355	6¼	4⅞	5¾	...	64	73.6	19.4	50.3
20	TLK	P.T. Telekomunikasi ADS[58]	NY	NR	..	...	Telecommun svcs, Indonesia	...	...	...	...	25½	18	51201	25½	20⅞	25¼	0.4	26	...	...	...
21	TPIFY	P.T. Tri Polyta Indonesia ADS[59]	NNM	NR	29	3875	Polyproplene resins, plastics	...	...	30¾	21	26¼	10	21785	14	10	13¾	...	10	–41.5	...	...
#22	PSR	✔Public Svc[60]Colorado[61]	NY,B,C,Ch,Ph,P	B+	266	22448	Elec & nat'l gas:Denver area	33⅜	9¾	32⅛	24¾	35⅞	29	15311	35⅞	33¾	35⅜	5.8	14	27.3	14.4	16.9
¶23•[4]	PEG	✔Public Svc Enterpr	NY,B,C,Ch,P,Ph	B+	494	90503	Hldg co:Public Svc Elec&Gas	36⅛	7	32	23⅞	30⅝	26	96349	30⅝	29	30⅝	7.1	12	24.8	7.2	10.6
#24	PNM	✔Public Svc New Mexico	NY,B,Ch	B	171	23816	Utility:electric,gas,water	39¼	7⅝	13⅝	11	18¼	12⅛	25630	18¼	17	17⅝	...	9	35.6	12.5	16.0
✣25	PGS	✔Public Svc No Car	NY	B+	64	2992	Natural gas: Raleigh-Durham	20⅛	1 13/16	17¾	13½	18¾	14	3979	18¾	16¼	17⅞	4.8	15	30.1	6.3	17.5
26	PSA	✔Public Storage	NY,Ch,Ph	NR	136	14154	R.E.invest tr:mini-warehouse	21¾	6¼	16¾	13	19¾	13½	14918	19½	17⅜	19	4.6	19	39.4	28.9	24.4
27	Pr X	8.25% cm Cv Pfd (NC)	NY	NR	15	610		28	24¾	29½	23¾	33⅜	24½	755	33¼	30	32½	6.3	..	...	...	...
28	PSK	✔Public Storage Prop'A' IX[54]	AS,Ch	NR	11	11	Real estate investment trust	20¼	10	18⅝	16⅛	18¼	16	298	18¼	16¾	18	e6.7	12	15.7	20.8	...
29	PSL	✔Public Storage Prop'A' X	AS,Ch	NR	5	6	Real estate investment trust	18⅝	8⅛	18⅜	16	18¾	16⅜	152	17¾	17	17¼	8.1	10	14.1	18.5	...
30	PSM	✔Public Storage Prop'A' XI	AS,Ch	NR	5	6	Real estate investment trust	18¾	8⅜	17½	14⅞	17⅞	15	195	17¾	16⅞	17¼	7.9	12	26.0	23.3	...
31	PSN	✔Public Storage Prop'A' XII	AS,Ch	NR	6	6	Real estate investment trust	18¼	8⅛	17¼	14¾	19¾	15¼	139	19¾	18½	18⅞	e7.0	11	32.8	23.1	...
32	PSP	✔Public Storage Prop'A' XIV	AS	NR	8	10	Real estate investment trust	18⅝	9¼	17⅞	15¼	18½	15¼	189	18	17¼	17⅝	7.7	11	21.4	18.8	...
33	PSQ	✔Public Storage Prop'A' XV	AS,Ch	NR	7	11	Real estate investment trust	15½	7⅜	17¼	13½	18¼	15⅜	199	18¼	17⅛	17⅛	e7.0	12	18.0	30.3	...
34	PSU	✔Public Storage Prop'A' XVI	AS,Ch	NR	10	49	Real estate investment trust	16⅜	8¼	15	12⅞	16⅛	12¾	400	16⅛	15¼	15½	7.0	12	27.5	19.4	...
35	PSV	✔Public Storage Prop'A' XVII	AS,Ch	NR	10	63	Real estate investment trust	16	6⅜	16¼	12¾	18	14⅛	436	17⅜	16¼	16⅝	e7.5	13	26.6	34.1	...
36	PSW	✔Public Storage Prop'A' XVIII	AS,Ch	NR	8	50	Real estate investment trust	15¼	5⅝	16⅜	12	17⅞	14	414	17⅞	17	17	e7.1	13	29.4	29.5	...
37	PSY	✔Public Storage Prop'A' XIX	AS	NR	4	6	Real estate investment trust	12¼	3¾	12¼	9	14¼	11⅛	452	14	13¼	13½	e5.3	19	27.3	38.1	...
38	PSZ	✔Public Storage Prop'A' XX	AS,Ch	NR	4	2	Real estate investment trust	14⅜	6	15	11¼	17	12⅞	309	17	16⅛	16⅛	e6.9	13	35.8	29.2	...
39	PUL	✔Publicker Indus	NY,B,Ch,Ph	C	17	1461	Industrial products & svcs	11¾	⅝	2⅜	1⅛	2⅜	1½	2661	2⅜	1⅝	2⅜	...	..	11.8	33.4	18.9
40	PRN	✔Puerto Rican Cement	NY,Ch	B+	56	2655	Lgst mfr of cement in P.R.	27¼	13/16	33¼	24½	35¼	27½	319	34¼	32¼	33⅛	2.1	11	20.4	13.7	21.8
#41	PSD	✔Puget Sound P&L[74]	NY,B,Ch,P	B+	147	15899	Electricity in west'n Wash	29¾	9⅛	24⅞	16½	24	20⅛	12598	24	23⅛	23¼	7.9	13	24.7	3.1	10.6
42	PLFC	✔Pulaski Furniture	NNM	B	23	866	Mfr,sells wooden furniture	25	¾	27	16	21⅜	16	1069	19¾	16¾	18½	3.5	12	16.0	0.2	5.5
43	PTZ	✔Pulitzer Publishing	NY,Ch	B+	104	3752	Newspapers:TV/radio brdcstg	33⅛	12⅛	32¼	26⅜	53	30¾	2235	48	45	47¾	1.1	16	50.7	29.7	33.9
¶44•[5]	PHM	✔Pulte Corp	NY,B,Ch,P,Ph	A–	230	12974	Homebuilding/fin'l services	41⅜	1/16	38⅝	18⅛	34⅝	20⅛	14652	34⅝	30¾	33⅝	0.7	19	49.2	4.8	30.1
45	PRSW	Pure Software	NNM	NR	37	3037	Dvlp,mkt software prod	...	...	...	...	43¾	17	4309	38	31½	32¼	...	d	...	...	...
46	PURS	✔Purus Inc	NNM	NR	6	64	Enviro tech ind compound recov	150	117½	130	11¼	17¼	1⅞	1323	2½	2⅛	2⅛	...	d	–83.8	...	...
47	PXRE	✔PXRE Corp	NNM	NR	111	7375	Reinsurance:prop,casualty	38¼	5	29¼	18½	29¾	21	7085	27¼	24⅛	26½	2.7	5	–4.2	21.1	28.4
48	PYR.EC	✔Pyrocap International	ECM	NR	1	10	Mfr specialty chemicals	...	...	5⅜	⅞	2⅝	⅞	155	1 5/16	1	1 3/16	...	d	–33.3	...	...
49•[6]	PYXS	✔Pyxis Corp	NNM,Ch	NR	196	29096	Mfr point-of-use dstr systems	38⅞	7	37¾	16	26⅞	11¾	142781	15½	12⅞	14⅝	...	15	–25.9	–6.0	...
50•[7]	AQM	✔QMS Inc	NY,Ch,P	↓C	25	2148	Mfr intelligent graphic prod	26¾	6	10¾	6⅞	9⅜	3¼	15833	5⅛	4¼	4½	...	d	–50.0	–29.3	–20.9
51	QSNDF	QSound Labs	NSC,To	NR	7	1056	License/mkt 3-D sound tech	23⅝	⅝	4½	1 15/16	5⅛	2½	21009	3½	2¾	3	...	d	8.9	15.3	–21.3
52	QDRX	✔Quadrax Corp	NSC	NR	8	793	Dvlp stge:composit mat'ls	43¾	3⅛	7¾	1 9/16	3⅝	11/16	54169	1⅛	11/16	⅞	...	d	–65.4	–57.8	–45.5

Uniform Footnote Explanations-See Page 4. Other: [1]CBOE:Cycle 2. [2]NY:Cycle 3. [3]CBOE,Ph:Cycle 1. [4]ASE:Cycle 3. [5]Ph:Cycle 1. [6]ASE:Cycle 1. [7]NY,Ph:Cycle 2. [51]Incl $0.005 redempt of Stk Pur Rt. [52]®$3.13,'94. [53]Formerly Provident Life & Accident. [54]Public Storage plan acq,cash or com. [55]®$0.96,'94. [56]Spl div. [57]Baxter Healthcare offer,$17.50 to Jan 3. [58]Ea ADS rep 20 Sr'B',500 Rupiah. [59]Ea ADS rep 10 com, 1,000 Rupiah. [60]Southwestern Pub Sv plan mgr,1 com new Co. [61]Plan form new hldg co,New Century Energies. [62]Pfd of sub. [63]If com exceeds $14.85-20 trad days. [64]®$1.33,'94. [65]®$1.28,'94. [66]®$1.11,'94. [67]®$1.22,'94. [68]®$1.20,'94. [69]®$1.09,'94. [70]®$0.89,'94. [71]®$0.92,'94. [72]®$0.45,'94. [73]®$0.81,'94. [74]Plan mgr w/Washington Energy,form new co. [75]®$3.94,'94.

Index	Cash Divs. Ea. Yr. Since	Dividends: Latest Payment Period $	Date	Ex. Div.	Total $ So Far 1995	Ind. Rate	Paid 1994	Financial Position Mil-$ Cash& Equiv.	Curr. Assets	Curr. Liab.	Balance Sheet Date	Capitalization Lg Trm Debt Mil-$	Shs. 000 Pfd.	Com.	Earnings $ Per Shr. Years End	1991	1992	1993	1994	1995	Last 12 Mos.	Interim Earnings Period	$ per Shr. 1994	1995	Index
1	....	None Since Public			...	Nil	....	37.7	52.1	14.2	9-30-95	99.3	...	6412	Dc	*0.20	0.43	0.40	0.16	....	d0.35	9 Mo Sep	0.13	d0.38	1
2	1969	Q0.12	12-22-95	12-7	0.44	0.48	0.32	Equity per shr $10.70			10-31-95	67.8	...	9054	Jl	d1.23	Δd2.61	d0.08	0.45	Δ0.58	0.98	3 Mo Oct	0.08	□0.48	2
3◆	1926	Q0.16	12-1-95	11-15	[51]0.62	0.64	0.55	Equity per shr $16.58			9-30-95	141	...	28775	Dc	1.31	□1.56	2.07	2.57	....	2.71	9 Mo Sep	1.89	2.03	3
4	....	None Since Public			...	Nil	....	97.7	98.7	3.27	12-31-94	....	...	15248	Dc	0.03	d0.07	d0.47	d0.37	....	d0.52	9 Mo Sep	d0.28	d0.43	4
5	1988	Q0.04½	12-31-95	12-6	0.18	0.18	0.17¼	0.01	4.67	1.92	9-30-95	0.96	...	2708	Dc	0.30	d0.02	d0.01	0.12	....	0.08	9 Mo Sep	0.07	0.03	5
6	1849	Q0.27	11-15-95	10-30	1.08	1.08	1.07	1.28	38.1	38.3	9-30-95	74.5	80	5668	Sp	0.56	1.15	1.39	1.46	1.09	1.09				6
7◆	1985	Q0.27½	11-24-95	11-8	1.05	1.10	0.94	Book Value $23.99			9-30-95	508	371	15646	Dc	p0.93	□3.00	3.09	[52]3.40	....	4.03	9 Mo Sep	2.52	3.15	7
8◆	1988	Q0.16	11-10-95	10-26	s0.567	0.64	0.40	Book Value $21.71			9-30-95	263	...	7893	Dc	0.46	0.64	□1.29	1.72	....	2.04	9 Mo Sep	1.26	1.58	8
9	1925	Q0.18	12-8-95	11-15	0.72	0.72	1.04	Equity per shr $32.39			9-30-95	200	1042	45390	Dc	□±2.53	±2.49	d2.03	2.71	E2.75	2.16	9 Mo Sep	2.11	1.56	9
10◆	1941	Q0.25	3-15-96	2-28	0.90	1.00	0.80	Equity per shr $26.64			9-30-95	699	...	95212	Dc	2.67	3.14	3.12	3.02	E4.00	3.23	9 Mo Sep	2.31	2.52	10
11	....	None Since Public			...	Nil	....	13.7	65.3	11.7	9-30-95	....	...	6674	Mr	0.75	0.94	0.61	1.91	....	1.53	6 Mo Sep	0.81	0.43	11
12	1995	0.03	12-4-95	11-16	0.03	0.12	....	Equity per shr $18.41			9-30-95	....	...	50793	Dc	2.11	d1.23	2.53	0.21	....	1.67	9 Mo Sep	d0.04	1.42	12
13	1991	Q0.19	1-12-96	12-27	†1.60	0.76	1.60	Equity per shr $9.71			9-30-95	1.00	...	534	Dc	1.03	1.40	1.16	[55]1.16	....	1.18	9 Mo Sep	0.91	0.93	13
14	....	[56]1.50	12-30-95	12-13	[56]1.50	Nil	....	23.7	59.1	33.8	9-30-95	108	...	6068	Dc	d4.38	d11.33	d3.53	1.19	....	d0.34	9 Mo Sep	1.88	0.35	14
15	....	None Paid			...	Nil	....	6.44	34.7	16.5	9-30-95	0.53	...	9984	Dc	0.26	0.59	0.25	0.08	....	0.10	9 Mo Sep	0.50	0.52	15
16	....	None Since Public			...	Nil	....	0.37	30.9	10.9	3-31-95	0.19	...	4323	Sp	0.72	0.93	1.02	1.02	P0.29	0.29				16
17	....	None Since Public			...	Nil	....	30.3	40.5	21.3	9-30-95	16.4	...	★37652	Dc	...	...	...	pd0.38	....	....	9 Mo Sep	n/a	d0.81	17
18	....	None Since Public			...	Nil	....	0.77	14.5	22.8	12-31-94	17.1	...	★4200	Dc	...	...	...	pΔ1.66	....	0.97	9 Mo Sep	pΔ1.10	0.41	18
19	....	None Paid			...	Nil	....	6.62	8.76	0.71	9-30-95	....	...	19780	Dc	d0.12	d0.03	0.05	0.09	....	0.09	9 Mo Sep	0.07	0.07	19
20	....	Plan annual div			...	0.09	....	325	716	785	6-30-95	1561	...	★9333333	Dc	p0.28	p0.35	p0.56	p0.86	....	0.98	6 Mo Jun	p0.39	p0.51	20
21	1995	0.411	8-29-95	5-22	0.411	Nil	....	12.6	103	85.2	12-31-94	....	...	★257500	Dc	...	0.03	1.16	1.61	....	1.45	9 Mo Sep	1.11	0.95	21
22	1907	Q0.51	2-1-96	1-10	2.03	2.04	2.00	6.29	456	829	9-30-95	1080	2877	63329	Dc	2.48	2.16	2.43	2.57	E2.55	2.66	12 Mo Sep	2.62	2.66	22
23	1907	Q0.54	12-29-95	12-5	2.16	2.16	2.16	66.8	1465	1722	9-30-95	5288	[62]11800	244698	Dc	2.43	2.17	Δ2.48	2.78	E2.65↓	2.62	12 Mo Sep	2.54	2.62	23
24	....	0.38	2-24-89	1-30	...	Nil	....	98.0	258	172	9-30-95	729	130	41774	Dc	0.32	d2.67	d1.64	1.77	....	1.93	12 Mo Sep	d1.07	1.93	24
25◆	1958	Q0.21¼	1-1-96	12-7	0.83½	0.85	0.80½	0.99	42.3	104	9-30-95	101	...	18766	Sp	0.70	1.09	0.90	1.17	1.16	1.16				25
26	1981	Q0.22	12-29-95	12-13	0.88	0.88	0.85	Equity per shr $13.26			6-30-95	58.5	★13412	42043	Dc	0.81	0.90	0.98	1.05	....	1.02	9 Mo Sep	0.79	0.76	26
27	1993	Q0.516	12-29-95	12-13	2.062	2.063	2.06¼	Cv into 1.6835 com,$14.85				....	2000	...	Dc	...	...	...	...	....	....	Fr 7-1-98 red for 1.6835 com[63]			27
28	1991	Q0.30	1-12-96	12-27	†1.38	1.20	1.56	Equity per shr $9.84			9-30-95	0.10	...	2488	Dc	1.24	2.24	1.69	[64]1.70	....	1.47	9 Mo Sep	1.28	1.05	28
29	1991	Q0.35	1-12-96	12-27	1.40	1.40	1.40	Equity per shr $9.85			9-30-95	2.23	...	±2398	Dc	1.05	1.16	1.34	[65]1.62	....	1.70	9 Mo Sep	1.20	1.28	29
30	1991	Q0.34	1-12-96	12-27	1.36	1.36	1.36	Equity per shr $10.53			9-30-95	....	...	±2563	Dc	0.90	0.99	1.23	[66]1.39	....	1.43	9 Mo Sep	1.04	1.08	30
31	1991	†0.65	1-12-96	12-27	1.32	1.32	1.27	Equity per shr $11.61			9-30-95	....	...	±2471	Dc	1.09	1.19	1.30	[67]1.56	....	1.70	9 Mo Sep	1.12	1.26	31
32	1991	Q0.34	1-12-96	12-27	1.36	1.36	1.36	Equity per shr $11.62			9-30-95	....	...	±3229	Dc	1.02	1.27	1.34	[68]1.52	....	1.62	9 Mo Sep	1.13	1.23	32
33	1992	†0.52	1-12-96	12-27	†1.32	1.20	†1.12	Equity per shr $12.28			9-30-95	....	...	±3109	Dc	0.55	0.83	1.16	[69]1.40	....	1.43	9 Mo Sep	1.05	1.08	33
34	1991	Q0.27	1-12-96	12-27	1.08	1.08	1.08	Equity per shr $11.62			9-30-95	....	...	±4369	Dc	0.51	0.75	1.10	[70]1.12	....	1.32	9 Mo Sep	0.84	1.04	34
35	1992	†0.49	1-12-96	12-27	1.20	1.24	†1.07	Equity per shr $10.64			9-30-95	4.55	...	±4089	Dc	0.29	0.36	0.79	1.14	....	1.26	9 Mo Sep	0.85	0.97	35
36	1991	†0.54	1-12-96	12-27	1.16	1.20	0.97	Equity per shr $12.02			9-30-95	4.50	...	±4096	Dc	0.14	0.61	0.76	[71]1.16	....	1.35	9 Mo Sep	0.86	1.05	36
37	1992	†0.48	1-12-96	12-27	†0.85	0.72	†0.46	Equity per shr $11.94			9-30-95	....	...	±4220	Dc	d0.38	d0.04	0.24	[72]0.55	....	0.73	9 Mo Sep	0.42	0.60	37
38	1991	†0.58	1-12-96	12-27	†1.24	1.12	†1.04	Equity per shr $12.45			9-30-95	....	...	±1233	Dc	0.07	0.35	0.71	[73]1.00	....	1.24	9 Mo Sep	0.73	0.97	38
39	....	5%Stk	9-30-77	8-25	...	Nil	....	2.47	28.2	28.0	9-30-95	8.52	...	14861	Dc	d0.20	d0.30	d0.65	d0.15	....	Nil	9 Mo Sep	d0.14	0.01	39
40◆	1986	tQ0.17	2-15-96	1-10	t0.68	0.68	t0.60	8.64	59.3	13.6	9-30-95	36.8	...	5419	Dc	1.77	1.74	Δ□2.14	2.76	....	2.94	9 Mo Sep	1.82	2.00	40
41	1943	Q0.46	11-15-95	10-19	1.84	1.84	1.84	11.1	288	303	9-30-95	928	5912	63641	Dc	2.21	2.16	2.00	1.64	E1.85	1.82	12 Mo Sep	1.62	1.82	41
42	1977	Q0.16	1-2-96	12-13	0.60	0.64	0.56	0.50	72.4	23.6	7-09-95	30.8	...	2837	Oc	0.63	0.91	1.53	Δ0.96	P1.56	1.56				42
43◆	1918	Q0.135	11-1-95	10-5	0.54	0.54	0.464	85.8	169	62.3	9-30-95	115	...	±16383	Dc	±0.74	□±1.66	Δ±1.50	□±2.45	....	3.00	9 Mo Sep	□±1.46	±2.01	43
44	1977	Q0.06	1-2-96	12-13	0.24	0.24	0.24	Equity per shr $27.26			9-30-95	★655	...	26953	Dc	□1.71	□2.66	□2.78	□5.94	E1.75	2.77	9 Mo Sep	□4.37	1.20	44
45	....	None Since Public			...	Nil	....	38.1	47.5	12.2	9-30-95	0.12	...	15495	Dc	...	...	...	p0.08	....	d0.47	9 Mo Sep	d0.07	pd0.62	45
46◆	....	None Since Public			...	Nil	....	0.18	8.45	2.64	9-30-95	....	...	636	Dc	...	pd25.00	pd11.10	d23.20	....	d16.40	9 Mo Sep	d12.80	d6.00	46
47	1989	Q0.18	12-4-95	11-16	0.63	0.72	0.37½	Equity per shr $22.85			9-30-95	67.8	...	8745	Dc	0.25	Δd0.49	3.34	[75]4.89	....	4.97	9 Mo Sep	3.46	3.54	47
48	....	None Since Public			...	Nil	....	0.03	1.00	0.96	5-31-95	0.63	546	5339	Au	...	d0.15	d0.36	d0.40	Pd0.12	d0.12				48
49◆	....	None Since Public			...	Nil	....	84.9	161	65.2	9-30-95	3.13	...	36441	Dc	d0.03	0.38	0.68	0.92	....	0.97	9 Mo Sep	0.67	0.72	49
50	....	None Since Public			...	Nil	....	7.43	99.7	64.2	9-29-95	25.6	...	10677	Sp	1.60	d0.27	d0.31	0.28	d4.15	d4.15				50
51	....	None Since Public			...	Nil	....	1.13	3.12	1.75	j12-31-94	3.10	...	15828	Dc	d0.56	d0.34	d0.14	d0.22	....	jd0.21	9 Mo Sep	d0.20	d0.19	51
52◆	....	None Since Public			...	Nil	....	2.37	4.57	2.79	6-30-95	0.54	...	16350	Dc	d4.90	d5.10	d2.20	d2.09	....	d1.22	9 Mo Sep	d1.40	d0.53	52

◆**Stock Splits & Divs By Line Reference Index** [3]2-for-1,'95. [7]3-for-2,'93. [8]Adj for 5%,'95. [10]2-for-1,'93. [25]3-for-2,'93. [40]3-for-1,'92. [43]10%,'93:5-for-4,'95. [46]1-for-10 REVERSE,'95. [49]2-for-1,'94. [52]1-for-10 REVERSE,'94.

¶ S&P 500
# MidCap 400
✣ SmallCap 600
• Options

Index	Ticker	Name of Issue (Call Price of Pfd. Stocks)	Market	Com. Rank. & Pfd. Rating	Inst. Hold Cos	Inst. Hold Shs. (000)	Principal Business	Price Range 1971-93 High	1971-93 Low	1994 High	1994 Low	1995 High	1995 Low	Dec. Sales in 100s	December, 1995 Last Sale Or Bid High	Low	Last	%Div Yield	P-E Ratio	Total Return % Annualized 12 Mo	36 Mo	60 Mo
✣1	QCHM	✓Quaker Chemical	NNM	B+	53	3480	Specialty chemical prod	26	13/16	19½	14¾	19	11	9602	16½	11	13½	5.0	13	–21.8	–10.9	–3.0
2	QFAB	✓Quaker Fabric	NNM	NR	29	1402	Mfr woven upholstery fabrics	14	12	17	12¼	12¾	7½	5509	9½	8⅝	8¾	...	10	–31.4	...	...
¶3•[1]	OAT	✓Quaker Oats	NY,To,B,Ch,P,Ph	A–	432	57345	Human & pet food processor	38½	1⅜	42½	29¾	37½	30⅜	114234	37⅜	34⅛	34½	3.3	6	15.5	4.8	...
#4•[2]	KSF	✓Quaker State Corp	NY,B,Ch,P,Ph	B–	129	13893	Motor oil,lubricants:coal	36½	7⅞	16⅛	12⅝	16½	12⅛	13363	13⅝	12⅝	12¾	3.1	28	–5.5	7.6	7.9
5•[3]	QCOM	✓QUALCOMM Inc	NNM	NR	209	28790	Mfr digital wireless commun pd	43⅜	6¼	33¾	15	54¾	20½	260311	44⅝	35	43	...	81	75.5	47.7	...
6	QDIN	Quality Dining	NNM	NR	44	2794	Own/oper quick serv restr	....	....	13⅝	10¾	26⅞	11⅝	11054	26⅞	23½	24¼	...	29	...	...	...
7	QFCI	✓Quality Food Centers	NNM	NR	54	4838	Supermarket chain, Wash	46	3¼	25¼	19	26¾	19	5797	22½	19½	22	...	18	–7.2	–14.3	2.8
✣8	NX	✓Quanex Corp	NY,Ch,Ph	B	109	9118	Mfr specialty steel tubing	31¾	2⅛	27¼	17	26⅝	18	11432	19¾	18¼	19⅜	3.1	9	–13.1	3.1	12.7
#9•[4]	QNTM	✓Quantum Corp	NNM,Ch,Ph	B–	202	36254	Mfrs rigid disk drives	18⅛	1¾	20¼	11⅝	28½	13¾	172110	19⅝	15⅞	16⅛	...	10	7.1	1.9	5.4
✣10•[5]	QHRI	✓Quantum Hlth Resources	NNM	NR	116	11229	Chronic disease mgmt svcs	32	12	42¾	26½	32	8	43976	10⅜	8	9¾	...	61	–65.3	–27.0	...
11	KRG	✓Quantum Restaurant Group	NY,Ch	NR	42	5342	Own/oper full svc restaurants	19¼	8	12½	7	14⅞	9⅝	4156	13¼	10¾	11¼	...	d	4.7	–9.6	...
12•[3]	QDEK	✓Quarterdeck Corp	NNM	C	60	9585	Dvlp computer software prod	26⅝	1 15/16	4⅛	1⅞	39½	2¾	383805	39½	22⅝	27½	...	..	780	90.1	...
13•[6]	PQB	Quebecor Cl'A'[54]	AS,To,B,Mo	B+	18	4010	Print'g,publish'g,forest prod	16⅛	7/16	15⅞	11⅝	16	11⅞	366	15⅝	14⅝	15¼	...	..	27.3	6.8	20.3
14	PRW	Quebecor Printing[56]	NY	NR	17	2943	Commercial printing svcs	....	....	....	....	17⅛	16⅝	43526	17⅛	16⅝	16⅞	0.9	17	...	...	...
15	QCSB	✓Queens County Bancorp	NNM	NR	63	2671	Savings bank, Queens,N.Y.	23	16⅝	32⅛	21¾	43	24¼	6517	42	38¼	39½	1.5	12	53.5	...	...
16	QMED	✓Quest Medical	NNM	↓C	17	1221	Surgical tapes,tubing	11⅝	1¼	7⅜	4⅛	15	4½	9061	11⅜	9¾	10⅜	...	d	108	24.2	40.6
#17•[7]	STR	✓Questar Corp	NY,Ch,Ph	A–	222	29916	Nat'l gas dstr:oil/gas:mfg	44	3⅞	35¼	26⅝	33¾	26⅛	15119	33¾	32¼	33½	3.5	16	26.5	12.2	18.1
✣18•[8]	BQR	✓Quick & Reilly Group	NY,B,Ch,Ph	A–	96	11079	Hldg:discount brokerage svcs	16⅞	3⅝	16⅛	10½	30¾	12⅛	21804	26⅞	20¼	20½	e1.4	9	67.6	32.3	41.6
19	QRSI	✓QuickResponse Services	NNM	NR	59	5939	Merchandise mgmt database svc	32	12	25¾	9¼	27	11	6640	25¼	17	18⅜	...	12	53.1	...	...
20•[3]	QKTN	✓Quickturn Design Sys	NNM	NR	59	3625	Mfr intg circuit emulation sys	14¼	12	16½	5¼	13¾	6	14002	10½	8⅞	10	...	22	–26.6	...	...
21	QUIK	✓Quiksilver, Inc	NNM	B	86	5084	Designs/dstr casual clothing	30	3⅜	18⅛	9¾	36⅛	14	19316	36⅛	31½	34⅛	...	24	122	85.3	20.0
22	QTRN	✓Quintiles Transnational	NNM	NR	82	9477	Contract pharma'l/biotech resh	....	....	15⅜	8⅛	46	14½	21218	46	33¼	41	...	83	174	...	...
23	QUIX	✓Quixote Corp	NNM	B–	51	3716	CD/CD-ROM prd:hwy safety prd	20¾	⅛	22¾	10¾	13¼	7¼	9503	8¼	7¼	7¾	3.1	d	–27.9	–16.2	11.9
24•[9]	QHGI	✓Quorum Health Group	NNM	NR	112	17510	Own, oper acute care hospitalsd2=nsp	....	....	23	15	24	17	30558	22½	19¾	22	...	18	15.0	...	...
25	RBIN	✓R & B Inc	NNM	NR	26	1929	Mkt replacement auto parts	12	4	10½	5¼	9⅝	5¾	6507	7	6⅛	6⅝	...	11	10.4	–1.8	...
26	RACO	✓Racotek Inc	NNM	NR	34	3314	Mobile data commun prd/svcs	10½	7	14⅜	2¾	7⅞	3⅛	20054	6	5	5⅛	...	d	57.7	...	...
27	RADAF	Radica Games	NNM	NR	..	...	Dvp/mfr casino theme games	....	....	11½	4⅝	5⅜	1⅛	14032	2⅛	1⅛	1¼	...	d	–75.6	...	...
28	RSYS	✓RadiSys Corp	NNM	NR	..	...	Dgn embedded computer solut'ns	....	....	....	....	15	10	3761	13¼	10	11¾	...	35	...	...	...
29	BRD	✓Ragan (Brad)	AS,Ch	B–	12	533	Tire retreading: retail strs	49⅝	5	34	27	35	30	2	35	34½	35B	...	33	9.4	19.5	10.5
30	RAIL	✓RailAmerica Inc	NSC	NR	2	77	Operates short-line railroads	3¾	1½	4¾	1⅜	5¼	2⅞	7734	4	3¼	3⅝	...	11	20.8	6.5	...
31	RNBO	✓Rainbow Technologies	NNM	B+	31	1647	Dvlp computer security prod	32¾	1¼	24	9½	26¾	13⅝	10145	25½	21⅝	21⅝	...	20	60.2	3.1	25.8
32•[10]	RAH	✓Ralcorp Holdings	NY	NR	166	17845	Mfr food prod/oper resorts	....	....	24⅛	13½	28	21⅜	8166	26	23⅜	24¼	...	24	9.0	...	...
¶33•[10]	RAL	✓Ralston-Purina Group	NY,B,C,Ch,P,Ph	B+	430	56589	Pet food,agricul pd,batteries	60⅛	4⅛	46⅜	33½	67	43½	36755	67	61	62⅜	1.9	23	...	...	...
34	RGI.EC	✓Randers Group	ECM	B–	1	.6	Engineer'g/constr'n mgmt svcs	2 7/16	¼	1 5/16	5/16	1¼	⅜	1127	9/16	⅜	7/16	...	d	–12.6	–25.6	–1.4
#35•[11]	RGO	✓Ranger Oil Ltd	NY,To,B,Ch,Ph,Mo	B	125	34855	Oil & gas explor & prod'n	20⅞	⅞	7⅛	4¾	7½	5	20935	6½	5⅝	6¼	1.3	d	7.6	6.7	–0.6
36	RANKY	✓Rank Organisation ADR[63]	NSC,To	NR	15	2685	Leisure:TV,Film prod,hotels	13¾	1 3/16	13¾	10¾	14⅝	11½	8501	14⅝	12½	14⅝	3.8	25	20.8	27.0	15.9
37•[12]	RATL	✓Rational Software	NNM	C	62	8926	Develop softwr/computer sys	22⅞	2¼	10⅛	4⅛	24	7⅛	38303	24	16¼	22⅜	...	49	214	13.3	41.5
38	RCH	✓Rauch Industries[64]	AS	B+	18	903	Mfr Christmas ornaments	11⅜	1 5/16	10¼	8½	12¾	8½	2144	12¾	9⅝	12⅝	0.6	14	45.5	17.4	26.8
39	RMA	Rauma Oy ADS[65]	NY	NR	19	3470	Mfr industrial prd-Finland	....	....	....	....	26¼	17¾	4138	20⅞	18¾	18⅞	...	15	...	...	...
40	RAWL	✓Rawlings Sporting Goods	NNM	NR	44	4040	Supplier of team sports equip	....	....	14¾	10⅝	14⅜	6	12009	8⅛	6	7¾	...	13	–45.6	...	...
¶41•[5]	RYC	✓Raychem Corp	NY,B,Ch,Ph	B–	299	38725	Plastic & elastomeric insul'n	54⅞	3½	42⅜	32⅜	59¾	32½	31276	59¾	52¼	56⅞	0.6	42	61.4	11.7	21.4
✣42•[2]	RJF	✓Raymond James Finl	NY,Ch,Ph	A–	98	8096	Invest firm & brokerage	20¼	1½	18¾	13⅛	25¼	13¾	4693	25¼	21⅛	21¼	1.8	10	56.2	15.5	34.1
#43•[10]	RYN	✓Rayonier Inc	NY,Ph	NR	275	23598	Mfg/logs,timber&wood prods	....	....	35	26¾	40⅝	28¼	18672	38½	31½	33⅜	3.0	7	17.8	...	...
44	LOG	✓Rayonier[68] Timberlands[69] Cl'A'	NY,Ph	NR	15	59	Marketing & sale of timber	43¾	14⅝	40	27⅝	38¼	24⅞	9057	32½	24⅞	26¾	23.6	5	–9.7	12.8	27.9
45	RAY	✓Raytech Corp	NY,Ch	D	13	692	Energy absorb'g & transm'n pr	33⅝	½	5⅞	2⅞	4⅝	2¼	800	3⅜	2⅞	2⅞	...	1	–36.1	–5.2	15.9
¶46•[13]	RTN	✓Raytheon Co	NY,B,C,Ch,P,Ph	A+	751	178729	Defense&comm'l electr:constr	34¼	1¼	34½	30¼	47¼	31½	69735	47¼	44	47¼	1.6	15	51.1	25.1	25.5
✣47•[14]	RCSB	✓RCSB Financial	NNM	NR	76	6731	Savings bank, New York	21¾	5¼	21½	14¾	25⅞	15⅜	24554	24⅛	21⅞	23¾	2.0	11	57.3	29.7	27.9
✣48•[3]	RDRT	✓Read-Rite Corp	NNM	NR	246	34131	Supply thinfilm record'g heads	32	8⅝	19⅞	10⅞	49½	14	267085	28⅝	22¼	23¼	...	9	23.2	–8.4	...
49•[15]	RDA	✓Reader's Digest Assn'A'	NY,Ch,Ph	↑A–	254	34012	Magazine/book publishing	56⅜	21	49⅜	39⅞	52	38¼	14771	51¼	46¾	51¼	3.5	23	9.2	1.5	15.1
50	RDB	✓ Cl 'B'(vtg)	NY,Ph	↑A–	72	5450		54	35⅞	46	37	47⅞	36¾	1233	47¼	44	47¼	3.8	21	10.4	0.4	...
51	RDIC	✓ReadiCare, Inc	NNM,Ch,Ph	C	21	3002	Operates health care ctrs	16¾	1 3/16	2⅛	1⅛	4	1	2155	3⅜	2⅞	3¼	...	33	117	4.2	–6.3
52•[16]	RB	✓Reading & Bates	NY,B,Ch,P,Ph	C	129	43795	Offshore contract drilling	995⅞	3⅞	7¾	5⅜	15⅜	5½	95131	15⅜	13⅛	15	...	..	161	53.8	11.4

Uniform Footnote Explanations-See Page 4. Other: [1]Ph:Cycle 1. [2]ASE:Cycle 3. [3]CBOE:Cycle 1. [4]NY:Cycle 2. [5]P:Cycle 1. [6]Mo:Cycle 2. [7]Ph:Cycle 2. [8]CBOE,Ph:Cycle 1. [9]ASE,Ph:Cycle 1. [10]CBOE:Cycle 3. [11]To:Cycle 1. [12]CBOE,NY:Cycle 1. [13]CBOE:Cycle 2. [14]ASE:Cycle 2. [15]ASE,CBOE:Cycle 1. [16]P:Cycle 3. [51]®$2.15,'95. [52]®$1.52,'95. [53]®$1.31,'94. [54]Multiple vtg shrs. [55]Excl $35.8M sub-vtg shrs. [56]Sub Vtg Shrs. [57]Pfd in $M. [58]®$1.44,'95. [59]9 Mo Dec,'91. [60]®$0.27,'94. [61]Stk dstr of Ralcorp Hldgs Inc. [62]®$2.63,'95. [63]Each Sponsored ADR rep 2 ord, 25p. [64]Syratech Corp plan acq, $13. [65]Ea ADS rep 1 ord shr,FIM 10. [66]Fiscal Dec'93. [67]12 Mo Aug'94. [68]L.P. Dep Units,L.P. to dissolve by 12/31/2035. [69]Rt to timber(income)sharply declines in 2001. [70]100% non-taxable,'94. [71]®$2.24,'94. [72]®$2.39,'94.

Index	Splits ◆ Cash Divs. Ea.Yr. Since	Dividends: Latest Payment Period $	Date	Ex. Div.	Total $ So Far 1995	Ind. Rate	Paid 1994	Financial Position Mil-$ Cash& Equiv.	Curr. Assets	Curr. Liab.	Balance Sheet Date	Capitalization Lg Trm Debt Mil-$	Shs. 000 Pfd.	Com.	Earnings $ Per Shr. Years End	1991	1992	1993	1994	1995	Last 12 Mos.	Interim Earnings Period	$ per Shr. 1994	1995	Index
1	1954	Q0.17	1-30-96	1-10	0.68	0.68	0.62	6.77	89.4	57.2	9-30-95	10.2	...	8853	Dc	□1.20	1.33	d0.19	1.03	....	1.03	9 Mo Sep	0.74	0.74	1
2	....	None Since Public			...	Nil	....	0.20	46.9	20.5	9-30-95	43.3	...	8021	Dc	...	p0.55	□p0.75	1.15	....	0.84	9 Mo Sep	0.83	0.52	2
3◆	1906	Q0.285	1-15-96	12-13	1.14	1.14	1.08	174	1319	1845	9-30-95	1055	1190	134310	Je	1.33	1.63	■□1.97	1.68	□6.00	6.00	3 Mo Sep	□0.45	0.45	3
4	1931	Q0.10	12-15-95	11-13	0.40	0.40	0.40	29.9	267	170	9-30-95	★171	...	32824	Dc	Δ0.58	□d1.15	0.50	0.66	E0.45↓	0.63	9 Mo Sep	0.58	0.55	4
5◆	....	None Since Public			...	Nil	....	27.0	191	58.7	3-26-95	27.1	...	★62349	Sp	d0.27	d0.11	0.25	0.28	P0.53	0.53				5
6	....	None Since Public			...	Nil	....	2.24	6.12	9.47	8-06-95	p10.3	...	★8563	Oc	...	...	p0.61	p0.59	pP0.85	0.85				6
7◆	1993	0.05	2-24-95	1-30	0.05	Nil	0.20	10.2	56.9	53.0	9-09-95	168	...	14430	Dc	1.06	1.28	1.33	1.34	....	1.26	36 Wk Sep	0.91	0.83	7
8	1988	Q0.15	12-29-95	12-13	0.60	0.60	0.56	45.7	238	152	7-31-95	134	...	13431	Oc	1.02	□0.28	0.18	0.96	□P[51]2.20	2.20				8
9◆	....	None Since Public			...	Nil	....	159	1373	744	10-01-95	423	...	52817	Mr	1.05	2.05	0.06	[52]1.72	E1.70	0.10	6 Mo Sep	2.27	0.65	9
10	....	None Since Public			...	Nil	....	73.5	176	22.2	12-31-94	86.3	...	15712	Dc	0.45	0.67	1.07	[53]1.37	E0.16	0.43	9 Mo Sep	1.02	0.08	10
11	....	None Since Public			...	Nil	....	5.10	46.1	18.2	10-01-95	25.9	...	6367	Dc	p±d3.12	□0.58	0.74	d0.05	....	d0.60	9 Mo Sep	0.46	d0.09	11
12	....	None Since Public			...	Nil	....	30.3	44.2	17.4	6-30-95	0.22	...	p24413	Sp	0.63	0.45	0.06	d1.06	P0.16	0.16				12
13◆	1976	gS0.18	12-11-95	11-10	g0.33	0.36	g0.24	199	1274	723	j12-31-94	1220	...	[55]30261	Dc	0.39	▲1.43	1.15	[53]1.34	....	j1.95	9 Mo Sep	0.83	1.44	13
14	....	Plan semi-annual div			...	0.16	....	....	833	581	9-30-95	p868	...	±★113450	Dc	...	±0.72	±0.82	±0.87	....	0.98	9 Mo Sep	±0.60	±0.71	14
15◆	1994	Q0.15	11-15-95	10-30	0.30	0.60	0.10	Book Value $33.66			9-30-95	19.5	...	6302	Dc	...	p1.79	p2.05	3.03	....	3.39	9 Mo Sep	2.17	2.53	15
16◆	....	3%Stk	5-23-94	5-2	...	Nil	3%Stk	3.66	15.3	7.21	9-30-95	p11.0	...	★7754	Dc	0.21	0.04	Δ0.12	d0.33	....	d1.82	9 Mo Sep	d0.20	d1.69	16
17◆	1935	Q0.29½	12-11-95	11-15	1.16	1.18	1.13	2.70	124	151	9-30-95	451	[57]6	40630	Dc	1.63	Δ1.79	2.03	2.16	E2.10	1.19	12 Mo Sep	2.92	1.19	17
18◆	1981	†0.15	4-1-96	2-28	†0.249	0.28	‡0.225	Equity per shr $10.55			8-25-95	....	...	24953	Fb	0.98	1.23	1.69	1.66	....	2.27	9 Mo Nov	1.16	1.77	18
19	....	None Since Public			...	Nil	....	25.0	32.2	4.94	9-30-95	....	...	8268	Dc	...	pd0.15	□0.57	1.67	....	1.60	9 Mo Sep	0.47	0.40	19
20	....	None Since Public			...	Nil	....	26.4	59.2	22.3	9-30-95	3.78	...	13563	Dc	d0.68	d1.07	d0.63	0.32	....	0.45	9 Mo Sep	0.32	0.45	20
21	....	None Since Public			...	Nil	....	0.98	72.5	30.6	7-31-95	3.39	...	6692	Oc	1.02	0.05	0.69	Δ1.07	P[58]1.45	1.45				21
22◆	....	None Since Public			...	Nil	....	13.4	79.9	43.7	9-30-95	20.1	...	★21342	Dc	0.14	0.23	0.29	0.38	....	0.50	9 Mo Sep	0.27	0.39	22
23	1993	S0.12	1-5-96	11-29	0.22	0.24	0.21	0.51	45.6	33.6	9-30-95	77.3	...	7863	Je	d0.43	□1.07	1.20	1.44	0.73	d0.84	3 Mo Sep	0.25	d1.32	23
24	....	None Since Public			...	Nil	....	27.6	248	103	9-30-95	★430	...	47872	Je	...	...	p□0.74	p0.96	1.14	1.20	3 Mo Sep	0.23	0.29	24
25	....	None Since Public			...	Nil	....	0.77	64.9	11.4	9-30-95	47.9	...	7982	Dc	p0.56	p0.53	0.65	0.41	....	0.63	9 Mo Sep	0.31	0.53	25
26	....	None Since Public			...	Nil	....	18.8	22.2	1.64	9-30-95	....	...	23874	Dc	‡[59]d0.75	d1.41	d1.79	d0.49	....	d0.51	9 Mo Sep	d0.35	d0.37	26
27	....	None Since Public			...	Nil	....	6.34	16.1	4.64	1-31-94	0.01	...	★22780	Oc	p0.04	p0.09	p0.48	P0.81	P□d0.91	d0.91				27
28	....	None Since Public			...	Nil	....	0.28	14.4	6.89	9-30-95	0.94	4336	6009	Dc	0.01	0.08	0.20	0.35	....	0.34	9 Mo Sep	0.24	0.23	28
29	....	0.03	11-22-91	11-4	...	Nil	....	0.12	118	74.1	9-30-95	....	...	2191	Dc	d2.35	□0.42	□1.85	1.75	....	1.06	9 Mo Sep	1.69	1.00	29
30	....	None Since Public			...	Nil	....	2.84	9.77	4.42	9-30-95	16.7	100	4659	Dc	0.22	0.21	Δd0.06	[60]0.29	....	0.32	9 Mo Sep	0.15	0.18	30
31	....	None Since Public			...	Nil	....	35.6	54.8	7.73	9-30-95	2.68	...	7320	Dc	0.80	0.95	1.06	0.99	E1.10	1.22	9 Mo Sep	0.66	0.89	31
32	....	None Since Public			...	Nil	....	....	183	150	6-30-95	320	...	33340	Sp	...	...	p□1.20	p1.28	P1.00	1.00				32
33◆	1934	Q0.30	12-8-95	11-16	1.20	1.20	h[61]1.20	73.9	1917	2092	6-30-95	1539	4600	105912	Sp	3.34	□2.82	p□2.56	□2.12	P□[62]2.76	2.76				33
34	....	None Paid			...	Nil	....	0.39	2.39	1.95	9-30-95	1.12	...	14116	Dc	0.01	d0.02	0.04	d0.02	....	d0.01	9 Mo Sep	d0.01	Nil	34
35	1990	tA0.08	4-17-95	3-27	0.08	0.08	t0.08	46.5	77.2	104	12-31-94	50.0	...	98590	Dc	0.06	0.24	0.21	0.06	....	d0.03	9 Mo Sep	0.06	d0.03	35
36◆	1954	0.249	10-25-95	9-22	0.556	0.56	0.141	132	707	622	j10-31-94	771	227700	829200	Oc	0.53	□0.47	0.55	0.58	....	0.58				36
37◆	....	None Since Public			...	Nil	....	37.2	61.2	18.9	9-30-95	0.04	...	15739	Mr	0.39	0.03	d1.17	0.37	....	0.46	6 Mo Sep	0.13	0.22	37
38◆	1992	Q0.02	12-15-95	11-29	0.08	0.08	0.077	....	62.2	30.1	9-30-95	11.6	...	3696	Dc	0.75	0.77	Δ0.84	d0.01	....	0.88	9 Mo Sep	0.22	1.11	38
39	....	Plan annual div			...	....	....	74.0	981	891	12-31-94	95.0	...	★54000	Dc	d2.81	d0.38	d0.02	0.99	....	1.27	4 Mo Apr	0.15	0.43	39
40	....	None Since Public			...	Nil	....	1.34	61.8	13.8	8-31-95	43.9	...	7671	Au	...	...	p[66]0.84	p[67]0.83	0.60	0.60				40
41	1977	Q0.08	12-13-95	11-6	0.32	0.32	0.32	147	809	285	9-30-95	258	...	44118	Je	d0.63	□d0.43	Δ0.19	0.04	□d0.49	1.35	3 Mo Sep	□d1.12	0.72	41
42◆	1985	Q0.09½	1-2-96	12-7	0.36	0.38	0.32	Equity per shr $12.31			6-30-95	13.1	...	20570	Sp	1.26	1.89	2.28	1.97	P2.23	2.23				42
43	1994	Q0.25	12-29-95	12-6	1.00	1.00	0.72	10.8	400	198	9-30-95	483	...	29647	Dc	p1.50	□pd2.77	1.77	2.36	E4.80	4.22	9 Mo Sep	1.76	3.62	43
44	1986	Q1.58	12-29-95	11-28	6.64	[69]6.32	†[70]9.20	0.19	49.6	13.2	9-30-95	0.51	...	±40000	Dc	±3.93	±4.49	±4.45	±6.41	....	5.66	9 Mo Sep	±4.91	±4.16	44
45	....	0.05	3-17-88	2-22	...	Nil	....	File bankruptcy Chapt 11				33.7	...	3230	Dc	0.36	1.04	□2.60	2.52	....	3.78	9 Mo Sep	2.20	3.46	45
46◆	1964	Q0.18¾	1-29-96	1-4	0.75	0.75	0.72½	207	5559	4266	10-01-95	1480	...	242372	Dc	2.24	2.36	2.56	[71]2.26	E3.20	3.12	9 Mo Sep	1.46	2.33	46
47	1994	Q0.12	2-1-96	1-10	0.42	0.48	0.10	Book Value $18.60			11-30-94	p616	2989	p14060	Nv	d2.24	0.80	d4.50	[72]2.81	....	2.16	9 Mo Aug	2.32	1.67	47
48	....	None Since Public			...	Nil	....	138	339	187	6-30-95	48.0	...	46172	Sp	1.04	1.59	0.02	0.43	P2.60	2.60				48
49	1990	Q0.45	11-1-95	10-19	1.65	1.80	1.45	269	1270	1153	9-30-95	....	289	±107814	Je	±1.74	±1.95	±□2.16	□±2.34	±2.35	2.26	3 Mo Sep	±0.59	±0.50	49
50	1992	Q0.45	11-1-95	10-19	1.65	1.80	1.45	....	...	...		....	...	21716	Je	±1.74	±1.95	±□2.16	□±2.34	±2.35	2.26	3 Mo Sep	±0.59	±0.50	50
51	....	None Since Public			...	Nil	....	1.30	9.18	3.37	8-31-95	....	...	8205	Fb	0.20	0.09	Δd1.13	0.05	....	0.10	6 Mo Aug	0.05	0.10	51
52◆	....	0.25	3-31-86	3-11	...	Nil	....	34.4	92.8	78.6	9-30-95	96.7	2985	61246	Dc	Δ□d0.45	d0.04	0.05	d0.39	....	0.01	9 Mo Sep	d0.27	0.13	52

◆**Stock Splits & Divs By Line Reference Index** [3]No adj for dstr of Fisher-Price,'91:2-for-1,'94. [5]2-for-1,'94. [7]2-for-1,'91. [9]3-for-2,'91. [13]2-for-1,'92. [15]3-for-2,'94. [16]Adj for 3%,'94. [17]2-for-1,'91. [18]Adj for 5%,Dec,'93:3-for-2,'95(twice). [22]2-for-1,'95. [33]2-for-1,'91:Stk dstr Ralcorp Hldgs,'94:Stk dstr of Ralston-Continental Baking Gr,'93. [36]5-for-4,'94. [37]1-for-3 REVERSE,'95. [38]3-for-2,'92,'93. [42]3-for-2,'91,'92,'93. [46]2-for-1,'92,'95. [52]1-for-5 REVERSE,'92.

¶ S&P 500
\# MidCap 400
✣ SmallCap 600
• Options

Index	Ticker	Name of Issue (Call Price of Pfd. Stocks)	Market	Com. Rank. & Pfd. Rating	Inst. Hold Cos	Inst. Hold Shs. (000)	Principal Business	Price Range 1971-93 High	1971-93 Low	1994 High	1994 Low	1995 High	1995 Low	Dec. Sales in 100s	December, 1995 Last Sale Or Bid High	Low	Last	%Div Yield	P-E Ratio	Total Return % Annualized 12 Mo	36 Mo	60 Mo
		Reading & Bates (Cont.)																				
1	Pr	$1.625 cm Cv Pfd([51]26.1375)	NY	B–	39	2620		35½	25½	28	20½	45½	20¼	5062	45½	39⅞	45	3.6	..	...	...	...
2	RCT	✓Real Est Inv Tr,Cal[53]	NY,Ch	NR	36	1487	Real estate investment trust	20¾	6¼	18¾	15¼	19⅞	14¾	2569	19⅞	17⅞	19⅞	7.1	18	36.5	24.9	19.9
3	O	✓Realty Income	NY,Ph	NR	34	1470	Real estate investment trust	....	....	18⅛	15¼	22½	16⅜	9796	22½	19⅛	22½	e8.3	..	49.6	...	...
4	RRF	✓Realty Refund SBI	NY,Ch	NR	4	12	Real estate investment trust	23½	6¾	9	7	8⅝	4⅜	624	5⅝	4⅜	5⅝	12.4	d	–27.8	–2.3	–6.5
5	RA	✓Reckson Associates Realty	NY	NR	50	4584	Real estate investment trust	....	....	....	....	29⅝	24	10549	29⅝	27½	29⅜	7.9	..	...	...	...
6	RCOT	✓Recoton Corp	NNM	↑B	77	7190	Home entertain't accessories	17⅜	1/32	23⅝	12	29	13½	6581	19¼	17½	18¾	...	16	0.0	27.9	77.9
7	RL	✓Red Lion Hotels	NY	NR	58	7186	Oper full service hotels	....	....	....	....	24⅜	15¾	31868	18	15¾	17½	...	18	...	...	...
8	RED	✓Red Lion Inns L.P.	AS	NR	15	801	Own,oper Red Lion hotels	29	10½	28⅞	21⅛	24½	20½	1135	23¼	22⅜	22⅝	9.7	18	15.0	11.4	24.1
9	REDI	✓Reddi Brake Supply	NNM	NR	16	1695	Retail auto parts stores	6¾	1⅜	6¾	3¾	7¼	1 15/16	25445	2¾	2 3/16	2⅜	...	d	–53.1	–14.1	...
10	HOOK	✓Redhook Ale Brewery	NNM	NR	25	495	Brewer of craft beer	....	....	....	....	35	17	5621	27¾	24¾	26	...	46	...	...	...
11	RDL	✓Redlaw Industries	AS,To,Ch	C	7	257	Auto pts mfr,fdry,seating	29⅜	⅝	5½	2¾	4	1½	2128	2 5/16	1½	1⅝	...	d	–56.7	–11.9	5.4
12	WS.B	Wrrt(Pur 1 com at $2.80)	AS	....	3	82		3⅝	¼	3	⅞	1¾	½	185	9/16	½	9/16	...	..	...	...	...
13	RDMN	✓Redman Industries	NNM	NR	86	6037	Produce manufactured homes	21	15	26½	14½	33¾	15¾	9499	33¾	28	33¾	...	11	98.5	...	...
14	REB	✓Redwood Empire Bancorp	AS,Ch	NR	11	413	Commercial banking, California	13¾	7	14⅝	7	10⅛	5⅝	945	8½	7½	8	...	d	12.3	1.7	...
15	Pr	7.80%CvPerpetual'A'Pfd([57]10.55)	AS	NR	1	203		14¼	10	14⅞	8	11¼	6	458	11	10⅜	10¾B	7.3	..	...	...	...
16	RWTI	✓Redwood Trust	NNM	NR	30	2906	Real estate investment trust	....	....	....	....	22⅜	15½	10959	20½	17¼	18¼	...	..	...	...	...
¶17•[1]	RBK	✓Reebok Intl	NY,B,Ch,P,Ph	B+	405	55571	Markets athletic footwear	38⅝	2⅞	40¼	28⅜	39⅝	24⅛	118748	28⅜	24⅛	28¼	1.1	11	–28.6	–5.9	20.2
18	RUK	Reed Intl P.L.C.[59] ADS[60]	NY,Ph	NR	6	1146	Publishing/information svcs	....	....	25⅛	24¼	31¼	22¾	2862	31¼	29¾	29⅞B	2.5	22	25.1	...	...
19	REED	✓Reeds Jewelers	NNM	B	14	333	Retail jewelry store chain	10¾	2½	11	6⅜	12¼	7¼	38	10½	9¾	10⅛	...	10	53.1	45.7	31.4
20	REF	✓REFAC Technology Develop	AS,Ch,Ph	B	15	837	Int'l transfer of technology	15½	¼	11⅞	5⅝	7⅜	5⅝	4065	7¼	6	6⅝	7.5	13	19.3	17.2	31.1
✣21	RBC	✓Regal Beloit	AS,Ch	B+	115	12758	Cutting tools:pwr transm'ns	13¼	7/16	15½	11¼	23⅛	12⅛	6752	23⅛	20⅝	21¾	1.8	14	69.7	33.4	30.9
✣22	REGL	✓Regal Cinemas	NNM	NR	120	10672	Motion picture exhibiter	9½	5¾	17½	9	30¼	11⅜	29507	30¼	25	29¾	...	35	73.5	...	...
23•[2]	RHS	✓Regency Health Services	NY	NR	89	7714	Provide nurs'g/hlthcare svcs	14⅛	6½	19⅜	7⅝	16½	9¼	14519	10⅞	9⅝	10⅛	...	13	–12.0	1.7	...
24	REG	✓Regency Realty	NY	NR	44	3416	Real estate investment trust	19⅜	15¾	18⅞	15⅛	18⅜	15¼	2101	17¼	16⅜	17¼	9.2	23	13.8	...	...
✣25•[3]	REGN	✓Regeneron Pharmaceuticals	NNM	NR	49	3388	Drug R&D:neurological diseases	23¼	7¾	17⅜	3	16½	3⅛	40221	14⅛	11	12¾	...	d	300	5.0	...
26	REGA	✓Regional Acceptance	NNM	NR	29	1827	Auto loan financing svcs	7¾	4¾	10⅞	5⅞	13¼	6⅜	10277	9¾	8¼	9¾	...	..	38.0	...	...
#27	RGBK	✓Regions Financial	NNM	A+	175	13466	Commercial bkg,Alabama	38⅜	2¼	36¾	29¾	45	31	23807	45	41¾	43	3.1	12	43.7	11.7	22.9
28	RGIS	✓Regis Corp	NNM	NR	69	4674	Operate hair salons in malls	13¾	5⅞	16½	10⅝	25¼	14	10988	24⅝	20¾	24	0.4	18	65.9	36.3	...
29	RGA	✓Reinsurance Group of Amer	NY	NR	81	5077	Mkts life reinsurance	34⅞	25⅞	28⅞	21⅞	36⅝	23⅞	3334	36⅝	30¼	36⅝	0.8	14	55.6	...	...
30•[2]	RELY	✓Reliance Bancorp	NNM	NR	50	4836	General banking, New York	....	....	14	8½	15¼	10⅛	9497	14⅝	13	14⅝	3.1	14	49.1	...	...
31	REL	✓Reliance Group Hldgs	NY,B,Ch,Ph	B–	116	31825	Hldg co:Ins,investments R.E.	11½	3½	8⅛	4⅞	9¼	4⅞	35808	9¼	8⅛	8⅝	3.7	12	69.2	15.4	19.1
32	RS	✓Reliance Steel & Aluminum	NY,Ch	NR	36	1947	Process,dstr metal products	....	....	16⅜	10½	20¾	11⅜	1124	20¾	18⅝	20⅝	e0.5	11	63.5	...	...
33•[4]	RLR	✓ReliaStar Financial	NY,Ch,Ph	B+	230	24303	Insurance/financial services	38¾	1 15/16	34½	27	44½	29	11942	44½	40¾	44⅜	2.3	11	57.0	21.6	40.5
34	RLV	✓Reliv' International	AS	NR	4	182	Sell nutritional, diet prod	13⅞	4	5¼	2	3⅞	1 3/16	3340	2¼	1 3/16	2⅛	0.5	30	–7.7	...	...
35	RMDY	✓Remedy Corp	NNM	NR	37	2801	Dvlp client/server softwr prd	....	....	....	....	71¼	23	11489	71¼	54¼	59¼	...	93	...	...	...
36	RRR	✓Renaissance Commun	NY,Ch	NR	95	12216	Own/oper T.V. stations	....	....	20⅝	12⅛	26⅜	17⅜	8892	22⅜	20⅛	22⅛	...	13	26.0	...	...
37	RHG	Renaissance Hotel Group N.V.	NY	NR	..	...	Intl hotel management	....	....	....	....	25½	17	4799	25½	21	25½	...	..	...	...	...
38	RENS	✓Renaissance Solutions	NNM	NR	24	2172	Computer sys consult'g/svcs	....	....	....	....	26¾	9½	8450	17¾	13	14¼	...	29	...	...	...
39	RNREF	RenaissanceRe Holdings	NNM	NR	..	...	Prop catastrophe reinsurance	....	....	....	....	33⅛	19½	9624	33⅛	27¼	30⅜	2.1	5	...	...	...
40	RXT	✓Renal Treatment Ctrs	NY	NR	115	9390	Outpatient dialysis centers	22	10½	25¾	11½	47	20¾	18434	47	39¾	44	...	40	102	...	...
41	RCII	✓Renters Choice	NNM	NR	35	6851	Rent/sell household prds	....	....	....	....	18¼	3⅜	49819	18	11⅝	13¾	...	28	...	...	...
42	RENT	✓Rentrak Corp	NNM	B–	17	1565	Dstr prerecd video cassettes	11⅛	⅞	9⅜	4⅝	8¾	4½	14990	6⅛	4⅝	4⅞	...	33	–36.3	–9.3	0.3
43	RPAPF	Repap Enterprises[69]	NNM	C	100	36575	Mfr, mkt premium coated paper	13⅜	1⅛	5⅛	2 7/16	9	4	140991	5⅝	4	4⅜	...	..	–11.8	38.0	–0.3
44•[1]	RGEN	✓Repligen Corp	NNM	C	23	2170	Biochem/biocatalytic prod	30¼	4¾	8	1⅝	3⅛	⅞	27142	1⅜	⅞	1⅛	...	d	–35.7	–50.9	–38.0
45•[5]	REP	✓Repsol S.A.[70] ADS[71]	NY,Ch,Ph	NR	..	...	Integrated oil co in Spain	31⅜	16¼	35	26	34¼	26⅜	220617	33⅛	31⅜	32⅞	2.9	10	29.9	14.7	12.5
46	REPT	✓Reptron Electronics	NNM	NR	18	647	Dstr electronic components	....	....	13½	6¾	18⅛	8¾	1644	18⅛	15¼	15¼	...	14	64.9	...	...
47	RAUT	✓Republic Automotive	NNM	B–	33	1750	Auto parts distributor	13	2¼	18½	11¾	16¾	11½	5068	13½	12¼	12⅞	...	19	–2.8	10.7	19.7
48	REPS	✓Republic Engineered Steels	NNM	NR	30	6283	Major engineered steel prod	....	....	....	....	8½	4¼	8653	5½	4¼	4⅝	...	d	...	...	...
✣49	RGC	✓Republic Group	NY,Ch	B	52	3487	Mfr recycle paper board/gypsum	13⅝	1/16	15⅜	7¼	14⅛	9⅜	4479	14⅛	12¾	14	2.1	12	46.8	30.9	46.7
50•[6]	RWIN	✓Republic Industries	NNM	C	62	6982	Non-hazardous solid waste svc	27½	⅜	4⅛	2½	36⅛	3	110755	36⅛	26¾	36⅛	...	..	...	...	...
¶51•[7]	RNB	✓Republic New York	NY,B,Ch,Ph	B+	268	27376	Comm'l bkg,NY & worldwide	53¾	2 1/16	52¼	41⅞	65	44¾	32485	65	60⅝	62⅛	2.3	13	41.8	12.3	16.7

Uniform Footnote Explanations-See Page 4. Other: [1]ASE:Cycle 1. [2]CBOE:Cycle 2. [3]ASE,Ph:Cycle 2. [4]ASE,CBOE:Cycle 1. [5]CBOE:Cycle 3. [6]CBOE:Cycle 1. [7]Ph:Cycle 2. [51]Fr 9-30-96,scale to $25 in 2003. [52]100% non-taxable,'94. [53]BRE Properties plan acq,0.57 com. [54]©$0.28,'93. [55]Incl $0.25467 non-taxable,'94. [56]Cash or stk. [57]Fr 2-16-96,scale to $10 in2003. [58]To be determined. [59]Ea ADS rep 2 ord, 25p. [60]Own 50% interest in Reed Elsevier plc. [61]Proportionate shr of Reed Elsevier. [62]Fiscal Jun'93&prior:12 Mo Dec'93 earn$0.99. [63]25 Wks Dec'93. [64]Incl current amts. [65]®$1.26,'95. [66]Steinberg Gp owns 50% com. [67]®$3.00,'94. [68]®$0.40,'95. [69]Subordinate vtg shrs. [70]Each ADS rep 1 ord, 500 Ptas. [71]Instituto Nacional de Hidrocarburos owns 70.5%. [72]Approx. [73]Stk dstr of Republic Environmental Systems Inc. [74]®$5.61,'94.

Index (Splits ◆)	Cash Divs. Ea.Yr. Since	Dividends: Latest Payment Period $	Date	Ex. Div.	Total $ So Far 1995	Ind. Rate	Paid 1994	Financial Position Mil-$ Cash& Equiv.	Curr. Assets	Curr. Liab.	Balance Sheet Date	Capitalization Lg Trm Debt Mil-$	Shs. 000 Pfd.	Com.	Earnings $ Per Shr. Years End	1991	1992	1993	1994	1995	Last 12 Mos.	Interim Earnings Period	$ per Shr. 1994	1995	Index
1	1993	Q0.406	12-29-95	12-13	1.62½	1.625	[52]1.62½	Cv into 2.899 com,$8.625				....	2600	...	Dc	...	...	...	...	....	....				1
2	1969	[54]Q0.35½	1-18-96	12-27	1.42	1.42	1.35	Equity per shr $11.09			9-30-95	83.8	...	9358	Dc	1.14	1.28	1.13	1.16	....	1.13	9 Mo Sep	0.86	0.83	2
3	1994	0.15½	1-26-96	12-21	1.82½	1.86	0.60	Equity per shr $15.84			9-30-95	57.2	...	p22836	Dc	...	...	p0.89	0.78	....	....	9 Mo Sep	n/a	0.91	3
4	1971	Q0.10	12-15-95	11-28	0.60	0.70	[55]0.78	Equity per shr $7.42			10-31-95	20.9	...	1021	Ja	1.72	d4.45	0.94	0.66	....	d4.38	9 Mo Oct	0.51	d4.53	4
5	1995	Q0.578	12-29-95	12-13	1.336	2.31	....	Equity per shr $4.72			3-31-95	p84.5	...	★9279	Dc	...	...	...	p1.10	....	....	3 Mo Mar	n/a	p0.30	5
6◆	....	None Since Public			...	Nil	....	6.03	120	45.0	9-30-95	4.70	...	11153	Dc	0.34	0.58	0.86	1.12	....	1.20	9 Mo Sep	0.70	0.78	6
7	....	None Since Public			...	Nil	....	71.2	122	61.5	9-30-95	219	...	31313	Dc	...	...	...	p0.83	....	1.00	9 Mo Sep	p0.68	p0.85	7
8	1987	Q0.55	11-15-95	10-27	2.20	2.20	[52]2.20	....	0.18	134	9-30-95	9.73	...	4134	Dc	0.71	0.72	□0.76	0.69	....	1.26	9 Mo Sep	0.50	1.07	8
9	....	None Since Public			...	Nil	....	1.01	33.2	21.1	9-30-95	8.22	...	16538	Je	0.15	d0.09	Δd0.24	d1.16	Nil	d0.04	3 Mo Sep	0.03	d0.01	9
10	....	None Since Public			...	Nil	....	32.7	36.2	6.21	9-30-95	1.86	p1290	7683	Dc	0.23	0.39	Δ0.51	0.41	E0.57	0.38	9 Mo Sep	0.34	0.31	10
11◆	....	g[56]0.12½	7-31-79	7-10	...	Nil	....	0.13	1.47	7.21	j9-30-94	15.6	7	4527	Sp	d6.65	d5.47	d2.05	d0.15	Pd0.43	jd0.43				11
12	....	Terms&trad. basis should			be checked in detail			Wrrts expire 9-12-2001				.....	...	3903	Sp	...	...	...	...	....	....				12
13	....	None Since Public			...	Nil	....	30.9	96.8	73.3	9-29-95	1.91	...	6987	Mr	...	...	□0.63	2.75	....	3.10	6 Mo Sep	1.32	1.67	13
14◆	1993	0.03½	11-15-94	10-26	...	Nil	0.14	Book Value $9.27			9-30-95	12.0	575	2679	Dc	0.91	1.11	1.54	d1.31	....	d0.71	9 Mo Sep	0.13	0.73	14
15	1993	Q0.19½	11-15-95	11-6	0.78	0.78	0.78	Cv into 0.8421 com,$11.875				....	500	...	Dc	...	...	...	...	....	....				15
16	1995	0.26	1-16-96	12-27	0.20	[58]Nil	....	Equity per shr $13.14			9-30-95	6.50	...	5516	Dc	...	...	...	n/a	....	....	9 Mo Sep	n/a	0.41	16
17	1987	Q0.075	1-3-96	12-11	0.30	0.30	0.30	104	1562	628	9-30-95	255	...	75576	Dc	2.37	1.24	2.53	3.02	E2.70	2.67	9 Mo Sep	2.38	2.03	17
18	1995	0.251	10-17-95	8-28	0.749	0.75	....	2.30	136	88.7	[61]j12-31-94	36.4	3800	562586	Dc	...	...	1.04	1.35	....	1.35				18
19◆	....	None Since Public			...	Nil	....	0.14	66.3	15.9	8-31-95	33.5	...	4216	Fb	0.26	0.50	0.76	0.98	....	1.00	6 Mo Aug	0.18	0.20	19
20	1992	0.50	12-20-95	12-6	0.50	0.50	0.50	4.67	10.1	1.36	9-30-95	....	...	5295	Dc	0.45	0.40	□0.77	Δ0.55	....	0.51	9 Mo Sep	Δ0.34	0.30	20
21◆	1961	Q0.10	1-15-96	12-27	0.37	0.40	0.29½	10.7	103	35.5	9-30-95	3.89	...	20535	Dc	0.28	0.47	□0.70	1.13	....	1.51	9 Mo Sep	0.80	1.18	21
22◆	....	None Since Public			...	Nil	....	3.36	7.68	14.1	9-28-95	79.3	...	17504	Dc	...	p0.37	0.58	□0.53	....	0.85	9 Mo Sep	□0.37	□0.69	22
23	....	None Since Public			...	Nil	....	27.5	98.2	62.1	9-30-95	★178	...	16648	Dc	p*0.40	*0.62	*□[62]0.81	□0.01	....	0.79	9 Mo Sep	□d0.24	0.54	23
24	1994	Q0.39½	11-27-95	11-8	1.58	1.58	1.37½	Equity per shr $14.36			9-30-95	123	4	6615	Dc	...	...	†[63]0.14	0.80	....	0.75	9 Mo Sep	0.64	0.59	24
25	....	None Since Public			...	Nil	....	25.5	30.6	14.1	9-30-95	7.03	...	±★21839	Dc	pd0.29	d1.24	±d2.41	±d1.62	....	d1.11	9 Mo Sep	±d1.32	±d0.81	25
26◆	....	None Since Public			...	Nil	....	Equity per shr $2.34			9-30-95	[64]49.6	...	15007	Dc	...	p0.26	pΔ0.33	p0.47	....	....	9 Mo Sep	n/a	0.40	26
27◆	1968	Q0.33	1-2-96	12-13	1.29	1.32	1.16	Book Value $24.19			9-30-95	574	...	46033	Dc	2.16	2.60	3.01	3.40	E3.71	3.65	9 Mo Sep	2.52	2.77	27
28	....	0.02½	12-5-95	11-17	0.05	0.10	....	1.24	35.1	45.1	6-30-95	38.0	...	11392	Je	d0.56	0.47	0.41	0.39	[65]1.29	1.37	3 Mo Sep	0.28	0.36	28
29	1993	Q0.07	11-30-95	11-7	0.26	0.28	0.24	Equity per shr $20.07			9-30-95	....	...	16820	Dc	2.27	2.41	2.24	2.36	....	2.70	9 Mo Sep	1.53	1.87	29
30	1994	Q0.11½	1-19-96	1-3	0.41½	0.46	0.10	Book Value $16.37			6-30-95	40.0	...	9315	Je	...	...	p0.64	p0.73	1.03	1.06	3 Mo Sep	0.23	0.26	30
31	1986	Q0.08	1-1-96	12-13	0.32	0.32	0.32	Equity per shr $2.80			9-30-95	690	...	[66]113310	Dc	Δd2.00	Δd0.52	□0.92	0.38	....	0.72	9 Mo Sep	0.28	□0.62	31
32	1995	Q0.02½	1-5-96	12-20	†0.15	0.10	....	3.55	165	54.0	9-30-95	43.8	...	10272	Dc	...	...	p0.99	1.71	....	1.94	9 Mo Sep	1.39	1.62	32
33◆	1936	Q0.25	11-10-95	10-19	0.97½	1.00	0.87½	Equity per shr $33.28			9-30-95	238	1971	36257	Dc	1.70	□2.07	□2.63	[67]3.21	....	4.07	9 Mo Sep	2.37	3.23	33
34	1994	0.00½	10-15-95	9-28	0.01	0.01	0.01½	2.08	5.85	3.27	9-30-95	1.29	...	9355	Dc	0.22	0.34	□0.31	0.09	....	0.07	9 Mo Sep	0.07	0.05	34
35	....	None Since Public			...	Nil	....	51.3	61.0	7.07	9-30-95	0.18	...	8449	Dc	...	0.02	0.26	0.41	....	0.64	9 Mo Sep	0.27	0.50	35
36◆	....	None Since Public			...	Nil	....	11.2	121	96.5	9-30-95	60.4	...	30037	Dc	...	...	p0.25	□0.46	....	1.77	9 Mo Sep	□0.03	1.34	36
37	....	None Since Public			...	Nil	....	10.0	61.2	57.2	p6-30-95	136	...	30100	Je	...	...	...	p0.56	p0.78	....	3 Mo Sep	n/a	0.26	37
38	....	None Since Public			...	Nil	....	11.4	18.9	2.81	9-29-95	.....	...	5969	Dc	...	...	...	p0.44	....	0.49	9 Mo Sep	p0.31	p0.36	38
39	1995	0.16	12-5-95	11-17	0.16	0.64	....	Equity per shr $15.77			6-30-95	p72.4	p...	★25200	Dc	...	...	...	4.24	....	6.72	9 Mo Sep	2.73	5.21	39
40	....	None Since Public			...	Nil	....	3.61	54.2	18.0	9-30-95	36.5	...	10863	Dc	...	p0.33	p0.60	0.90	....	1.09	9 Mo Sep	0.61	0.80	40
41◆	....	None Since Public			...	Nil	....	Equity per shr $1.10			6-30-95	p10.4	...	★24028	Dc	...	...	p0.10	p0.31	....	0.50	9 Mo Sep	p0.18	0.38	41
42	....	None Paid			...	Nil	....	6.78	38.2	33.7	9-30-95	0.56	...	12127	Mr	d0.03	*d0.13	0.08	[68]0.41	....	0.15	6 Mo Sep	0.21	d0.05	42
43	....	g0.07	10-26-90	9-24	...	Nil	....	27.2	440	417	j12-31-94	2101	2256	121940	Dc	d3.47	d2.77	d2.50	d0.75	....	j0.79	9 Mo Sep	d0.86	□0.68	43
44	....	None Since Public			...	Nil	....	11.6	16.0	8.94	6-30-95	.....	...	15359	Mr	d1.14	d0.93	d1.53	d2.08	....	d1.47	6 Mo Sep	d0.84	d0.23	44
45	1990	[72]0.444	1-18-96	1-4	0.837	0.95	0.636	903	4674	4324	12-31-94	1920	...	300000	Dc	2.44	2.09	1.87	2.45	E3.25	2.45				45
46	....	None Since Public			...	Nil	....	0.85	92.8	26.9	9-30-95	49.2	...	6048	Dc	...	...	p0.72	1.03	....	1.06	9 Mo Sep	0.78	0.81	46
47	....	0.04	1-23-86	12-26	...	Nil	....	2.95	74.4	25.9	9-30-95	27.1	...	3388	Dc	*0.59	0.73	□0.90	1.22	....	0.69	9 Mo Sep	0.95	0.42	47
48	....	None Since Public			...	Nil	....	2.43	274	119	9-30-95	267	...	19707	Je	...	...	...	Δpd1.25	d0.78	d0.10	3 Mo Sep	d0.92	d0.24	48
49	1992	Q0.075	12-15-95	11-28	0.255	0.30	0.21	8.77	31.8	16.0	9-30-95	24.8	...	10571	Je	Δd0.04	0.18	0.31	0.73	1.10	1.15	3 Mo Sep	0.25	0.30	49
50	....	h[73]....	4-26-95	4-27	h[73]...	Nil	....	2.95	15.8	10.5	6-30-95	18.0	...	p61639	Dc	p0.21	d0.53	d0.67	Δ0.40	....	0.33	9 Mo Sep	0.29	0.22	50
51◆	1975	Q0.36	1-1-96	12-13	1.41	1.44	1.26	Book Value $41.26			9-30-95	4159	8503	56209	Dc	3.95	4.42	5.20	[74]5.79	E4.85	4.61	9 Mo Sep	4.28	3.10	51

◆Stock Splits & Divs By Line Reference Index [6]4-for-3,'92,'93:3-for-2,'94. [11]1-for-5 REVERSE,'91. [14]Adj to 3%,'93. [19]10%,'94,'95. [21]2-for-1,'94. [22]3-for-2,'94,'95. [26]5-for-4,'94:3-for-2,'95. [27]10%,'93. [33]2-for-1,'93. [36]3-for-2,'95. [41]3-for-2,'95:2-for-1,'95. [51]3-for-2,'91.

¶ S&P 500 # MidCap 400 ✣ SmallCap 600 • Options

Index	Ticker	Name of Issue (Call Price of Pfd. Stocks)	Market	Com. Rank. & Pfd. Rating	Inst. Hold Cos	Inst. Hold Shs. (000)	Principal Business	Price Range 1971-93 High	1971-93 Low	1994 High	1994 Low	1995 High	1995 Low	Dec. Sales in 100s	December, 1995 Last Sale Or Bid High	Low	Last	%Div Yield	P-E Ratio	Total Return % Annualized 12 Mo	36 Mo	60 Mo
1	REFR	✔Research Frontiers	NSC	C	11	307	Light flow control devices	11	13/16	11¼	4⅝	16⅞	5⅛	11682	13¾	8½	10	...	d	56.9	39.3	56.7
2•[1]	RMED	✔Research Medical[51]	NNM	B+	83	5782	Mfr specialized medical prod	28	⅛	14¾	7½	30½	13	8638	29⅝	26⅝	27	...	32	96.4	17.3	23.7
3	RESM	✔ResMed Inc	NNM	NR	32	2706	Mfr sleep disorder eqp	...	...	...	...	18	9¾	10026	14½	10½	13	...	19	...	...	...
4	RII	✔Resort Income Investors	AS	NR	8	208	Assets in liquidation	13¼	6¼	14	8⅜	10½	1	5570	1⅜	1	1¼	...	d	−85.6	−43.0	−21.0
✣5•[2]	RSND	✔Resound Corp	NNM	NR	51	3083	Mfr hearing aid devices	25	8	23½	5	10⅝	6¾	10782	8⅛	6⅞	7¼	...	d	−26.6	...	...
6	REMI	✔Resource Bancshares Mtg Gp	NNM	NR	45	6825	Mortgage banking services	10⅛	6	9⅝	6⅝	18¼	6⅝	2795	14¼	13½	14¼	s...	17	97.5	...	...
7	RMR	✔Resource Mortgage Capital	NY,Ch,Ph	NR	51	2868	Real estate investment trust	32½	1⅞	30	9½	21⅝	10⅜	8615	21⅝	19⅝	20	9.6	12	99.4	10.6	45.6
✣8•[3]	RESP	✔Respironics Inc	NNM	B	89	7609	Home med'l respiratory prod	15½	1 3/16	12¼	8	22¼	10½	16487	21¼	17	21	...	30	79.0	13.4	36.4
9	ROIX	✔Response Oncology	NNM,Ph	C	18	313	Cancer patient lab research	125	15/16	16¼	8⅛	21¼	7½	2724	14	9⅝	12½	...	74	50.4	−7.3	42.1
10	RCA	✔Retirement Care Assoc	NY	NR	24	1334	Oper retirement/nursing centers	5⅜	5/16	12	5¼	17⅞	6¾	10088	13½	9⅝	10⅛	s...	23	50.1	...	...
11•[4]	RTRSY	✔Reuters Hldgs ADS[53]	NNM,Ch	NR	364	60746	International news agency	42⅝	4⅛	48⅜	39	58⅞	38⅜	76262	57⅝	52¼	55⅛	1.5	24	27.8	23.9	25.4
#12•[5]	RXR	✔Revco D.S.[54]	NY,Ph	NR	190	40281	Oper drug store chain	17⅛	7⅛	24½	13⅞	28⅜	17½	135551	28⅜	27⅛	28¼	...	26	21.5	46.4	...
13	RSC	✔Rex Stores	NY,B,Ch,P,Ph	↑B	88	5839	Retails consumer electronics	24	2⅜	23¼	14⅜	18¾	12¼	1972	17¾	16⅛	17¾	...	12	11.8	27.8	40.4
14	RXSD	✔Rexall Sundown	NNM	NR	26	1599	Mkt vitamins/supplements	20¼	7	22	7¼	22½	8¼	22073	22½	17½	22	...	..	126	...	...
15	REXMY	✔Rexam Plc ADR[55]	NSC,To,Mo	NR	10	1443	Packaging products,services	8⅛	⅞	7⅞	6¼	8⅜	4⅞	2259	5⅝	4⅞	5⅜B	4.5	11	−13.8	−9.7	4.8
✣16	RXL	✔Rexel Inc	NY,B,Ch,P,Ph	C	76	6756	Dstr elec mater'l for constr	20½	3/16	8⅝	5⅝	14⅞	5¾	12895	14⅞	12⅝	13½	...	20	116	...	...
17•[2]	RXN	✔Rexene Corp	NY	NR	53	7795	Thermoplastic/petro prod	4¼	2⅜	18	2⅞	15⅝	8⅞	51328	12¼	9⅝	10¾	...	3	−9.5	42.1	...
¶18•[6]	RLM	✔Reynolds Metals	NY,B,C,Ch,P,Ph	B−	431	49318	Aluminum mfg,finished pr	70	6	59⅜	40⅜	64¾	46¼	52978	58½	52⅝	56⅞	2.5	10	18.8	4.7	2.6
19	Pr D	7%[58]PRIDES([59]48.077)	NY	BBB[60]	88	11305		...	...	55½	44⅝	56½	45⅝	4469	52⅞	48½	50⅝	6.5	..	...	...	...
#20•[7]	REY	✔Reynolds & Reynolds'A'	NY,Ch,Ph	B+	294	28809	Mfr business forms: EDP sys	23	¾	26⅝	19¾	39⅝	22⅞	22761	39⅝	35⅜	38⅞	1.2	21	61.7	49.5	60.8
21	RFP	✔RF Power Products	AS,Ch	NR	8	1136	Mfr radio frequency pwr sys	...	...	4⅜	1	8⅜	2	8308	6¼	5⅛	5½	...	61	57.1	...	...
22	RFSI	RFS Hotel Investors	NNM	NR	121	22401	Real estate investment trust	14¾	10¼	18¾	11⅜	16½	13	32567	16	14¼	15⅜	8.1	13	12.8	...	...
23	RHD	✔Rhodes Inc	NY,Ch,Ph	NR	47	3922	Retail furniture stores	16¾	8¾	20¼	8¼	13	8½	5974	11⅛	9⅝	9¾	...	11	−15.2	...	...
24	RP	✔Rhone-Poulenc ADR[62]	NY,Ch	NR	39	5858	Chemicals,medic,agric,consum	29	22⅝	27⅝	21	25⅝	19⅜	17923	21¾	19⅝	21⅜	2.1	12	−4.8	...	...
25•[8]	RPR	✔Rhone-Poulenc Rorer	NY,B,Ch,P,Ph	B+	186	29446	Health care products	69⅜	3¼	42⅝	30½	54½	35⅞	26443	54½	47⅞	53¼	2.3	16	50.0	7.6	11.3
26•[3]	RIBI	✔Ribi ImmunoChem Res	NNM	C	50	6366	Develop anti-tumor agents	13⅞	1 1/16	11⅛	3⅜	6½	3⅜	32375	6½	3⅞	6	...	d	47.0	−11.5	20.6
✣27	RCHF	✔Richfood Hldgs	NNM	NR	110	14075	Wholesale food distributor	17½	1⅞	18½	13⅜	29¼	15¾	15190	28¼	25½	26¾	0.4	20	69.3	38.2	42.4
28	RHT	✔Richton Intl	AS	C	5	45	Distr sprinkler irrigation sys	27½	7/16	6½	1⅞	4⅛	2⅜	791	3½	3	3⅜	...	8	−6.9	31.0	8.4
29•[9]	RIDE	✔Ride Inc	NNM	NR	30	2265	Mkt snowboards & accessories	...	...	5⅞	2 5/16	35⅞	5	70502	35⅞	21	32⅝	...	56	514	...	...
30	RJL	✔Rigel Energy	AS,To,Ph,Mo	NR	39	6448	Oil&gas explor,dev,prod'n	18¾	4⅛	16⅜	9¾	11⅛	8	410	9	8	8¾	...	..	−11.9	3.8	...
✣31•[6]	RIGS	✔Riggs Natl Corp	NNM	C	82	8775	Comm'l bkg,Washington,D.C.	41½	3¾	11¼	7½	14⅝	7⅞	24417	14⅝	12⅝	13	...	6	60.0	9.1	6.6
32	RTST	✔Right Start	NNM	NR	12	3312	Mail order: baby products	8⅜	3	5¼	1⅞	5⅛	2	2800	5⅛	4¼	4⅞	...	d	132	4.1	...
33	RIT	✔RightCHOICE Managed Care'A'[66]	NY,Ch	NR	37	2495	Manage hlth care,Missouri	...	...	15¾	10	18⅞	11½	3131	13⅛	12⅜	13	...	10	−3.7	...	...
34	ROM	✔Rio Algom Ltd	AS,To,B,Ph,Mo	B−	67	12036	Mng:uran'm,copper,molybdenum	23⅛	4⅛	20	15¾	21⅝	16⅛	116	19⅞	18¼	18¼	...	..	2.4	14.9	16.1
35•[10]	RIOH	✔Rio Hotel & Casino	NNM	B−	91	10021	Operates gaming resorts	19⅛	1¾	18⅛	11⅝	16⅝	11	15607	12½	11⅜	11⅞	...	15	−2.1	4.6	38.0
36	RSR	✔Riser Foods Cl'A'	AS,Ch	NR	31	2879	Hldg:Food retail&wholesale	15⅞	5¾	9¾	6⅛	16⅜	6¾	1450	16⅜	14¾	16⅛	1.2	11	123	34.7	13.4
37	RCHI	✔Risk Capital Holdings	NNM	NR	32	7314	Reinsurance:prop,casualty	...	...	...	...	23⅜	19⅞	6612	23⅜	19⅞	23⅜	...	..	...	...	...
¶38•[11]	RAD	✔Rite Aid	NY,B,Ch,P,Ph	A−	432	71711	Discount drug stores	24⅛	5/16	24	15¾	34⅜	22	153652	34⅜	30	34¼	2.0	18	52.9	20.8	16.6
39	RIVL	✔Rival Co	NNM	NR	78	7314	Mfr small househld appliances	20⅝	9⅛	26¼	14½	23	14	3031	23	20¾	22⅛	0.9	15	31.4	33.4	...
40	RSGI	Riverside Group, Inc	NNM	↑B−	11	267	Hldg:prop/cas & life insur	16¼	11/16	11	5¼	6¾	3⅜	398	4¼	3⅜	3⅜	...	4	−35.7	4.0	−1.4
41	RVW	✔Riverwood Intl[67]	NY,Ph	NR	59	12061	Mfr packaging & paper prod	17¼	11⅞	19¼	14	26¼	15½	15289	19½	18¼	19⅛	0.8	38	24.4	14.1	...
42	RVFD	✔Riviana Foods	NNM	NR	26	2478	Process/mkt rice products	...	...	...	...	14⅞	11⅝	3721	13½	12⅜	13¼	2.7	10	...	...	...
43•[12]	RN	✔RJR Nabisco Holdings(New)	NY,Ch,Ph	NR	506	204383	Mfr tobacco/food products	65	21⅞	40⅝	26½	33⅜	25	174433	31¾	28½	30¾	4.9	14	12.1	−9.0	...
44	RLI	✔RLI Corp	NY	B+	58	3282	Property/contact lens insur	22⅞	⅜	22¼	15⅞	25	16¼	1399	25	24	25	2.1	34	55.5	11.1	20.1
45	RTI	✔RMI Titanium	NY,Ch	NR	19	4267	Produce titanium metal prod	130	13¾	21¼	2	10⅜	3⅛	3278	8	7	8	...	d	60.0	−23.0	−30.7
✣46	RDM	✔Roadmaster Industries	NY	NR	33	3481	Mfr bicycles/fitness equip	5¼	⅜	4⅝	2¾	4	2⅛	25931	3⅛	2⅛	2⅜	...	d	−34.5	8.2	34.9
¶47•[13]	CBB	✔Roadway[70] Services[71]	NY,Ch,Ph	↓B+	253	18406	Hldg:motor freight carrier	77¾	3⅝	74¼	46	56¾	42	11160	51⅜	48⅝	48⅞	2.9	96	−11.3	−9.0	7.4
48	RESC	✔Roanoke Electric Steel	NNM	B	40	2669	Mfr merchant steel products	11⅛	2½	12⅜	8½	17½	10⅛	2239	17½	14½	16⅝	e2.6	7	68.3	34.1	29.7
49	ROBN	✔Robbins & Myers	NNM	B	51	2418	Electric motors, fans, pumps	24¼	1⅝	20½	16½	35	17	759	33	28½	30	1.2	13	76.0	22.6	28.3
50	RBDS	✔Roberds Inc	NNM	NR	23	1705	Retail home furnishing prod	15¼	11	15¼	7	13	7¼	4235	11	8¼	9	...	7	10.8	...	...
51	RHI	✔Robert Half Intl	NY,Ch,Ph	B	172	18240	Personnel placement services	15	1/64	26¾	12¾	44⅝	19⅝	13731	44⅝	39⅛	41⅞	...	34	73.6	87.4	79.0
52	MOND	✔Robert Mondavi 'A'	NNM	NR	82	5001	Produces premium wines	14¼	8	12⅜	6¼	34¾	10¼	6671	32½	27	27⅝	...	17	135	...	...

Uniform Footnote Explanations-See Page 4. Other: [1]Ph:Cycle 3. [2]ASE,CBOE:Cycle 3. [3]CBOE:Cycle 3. [4]ASE,CBOE:Cycle 2. [5]Ph:Ccycle 3. [6]P:Cycle 2. [7]NY:Cycle 1. [8]ASE:Cycle 1. [9]CBOE,NY:Cycle 2. [10]CBOE:Cycle 1. [11]Ph:Cycle 1. [12]ASE:Cycle 3. [13]P:Cycle 1. [51]Formerly Research Indus. [52]12 Mo Dec'91:Fiscal Apr'91 earned d$0.18. [53]Each ADS represents 6 ord shrs par 2.5p. [54]Rite Aid offer for 35M com,$27.50 to Jan 16. [55]ADR rep 1 ord shr. [56]Stk dstr of Worldtex Inc,'92. [57]To be determined. [58]Pfd Redeemable Increased Div Equity Sec. [59]Fr 12-31-96,in com stock. [60]Note:'r'added to derivative/hybrid secur ratings. [61]Excl 10M Cl'B' privately held. [62]Ea ADS rep 1 ord shr FF 25. [63]Excl subsid Pfd. [64]Fiscal Apr'93 & prior. [65]®$0.27,'94. [66]dba Alliance Blue Cross Blue Shield. [67]Investor Group plan acq, $20.25. [68]81.5% owned by Manville Corp. [69]7.5M shrs owned by USX. [70]Plan spin-off Roadway Express. [71]Approve name chg to Caliber System. [72]Stk dstr of Roadway Express,'96. [73]®$2.17,'95. [74]Stk dstr of BF Enterpr.

Splits ◆ Index	Cash Divs. Ea.Yr. Since	Dividends: Latest Payment Period $	Date	Ex. Div.	Total $ So Far 1995	Ind. Rate	Paid 1994	Financial Position Mil-$ Cash& Equiv.	Curr. Assets	Curr. Liab.	Balance Sheet Date	Capitalization Lg Trm Debt Mil-$	Shs. 000 Pfd.	Com.	Earnings $ Per Shr. Years End	1991	1992	1993	1994	1995	Last 12 Mos.	Interim Earnings Period	$ per Shr. 1994	1995	Index
1◆	....	None Since Public			...	Nil	....	6.23	6.31	0.11	9-30-95	....	...	9465	Dc	d0.20	d0.19	d0.24	d0.33	....	d0.33	9 Mo Sep	d0.19	d0.19	1
2◆	....	None Paid			...	Nil	....	6.91	29.2	2.69	9-30-95	0.15	...	9505	Je	0.27	0.44	□0.57	0.62	0.81	0.85	3 Mo Sep	0.16	0.20	2
3	....	None Since Public			...	Nil	....	26.8	38.0	5.33	9-30-95	0.83	...	7031	Je	d0.04	0.08	0.22	0.34	0.63	0.67	3 Mo Sep	0.08	0.12	3
4	1989	0.37½	5-15-95	4-24	0.75	Nil	1.50	Liq Val per shr $5.53			9-30-95	....	...	4156	Dc	1.24	1.17	1.47	0.96	....	d1.94	6 Mo Jun	0.29	d2.61	4
5	....	None Since Public			...	Nil	....	13.5	50.2	39.1	10-01-95	24.0	...	15535	Dc	...	pd0.08	p0.35	d0.95	....	d1.54	9 Mo Sep	0.22	d0.37	5
6◆	....	5%Stk	8-31-95	8-11	5%Stk	Stk	5%Stk	Equity per shr $6.03			9-30-95	66.7	...	14538	Dc	...	p1.18	0.87	1.25	....	0.82	9 Mo Sep	0.99	0.56	6
7	1988	Q0.48	1-31-96	12-27	1.20	1.92	3.02	Equity per shr $14.31			6-30-95	973	1350	20118	Dc	1.60	2.73	3.12	2.64	....	1.61	9 Mo Sep	2.22	1.19	7
8◆	....	None Since Public			...	Nil	....	13.9	55.3	13.9	9-30-95	5.44	...	16819	Je	0.26	0.32	0.43	0.27	0.67	0.71	3 Mo Sep	0.14	0.18	8
9◆	....	None Since Public			...	Nil	....	3.43	19.8	5.86	6-30-95	....	28	6986	Dc	[52]d5.00	*0.05	0.10	d0.35	....	0.17	9 Mo Sep	d0.24	0.28	9
10◆	....	5%Stk	2-15-95	1-26	5%Stk	Stk	5%Stk	2.85	27.0	24.9	9-30-95	40.1	300	10554	Je	0.12	0.02	0.11	0.31	0.40	0.44	3 Mo Sep	0.13	0.17	10
11◆	1984	0.227	9-15-95	8-18	0.853	0.85	0.664	595	943	785	j12-31-94	64.0	...	1668106	Dc	±1.54	□±1.40	±1.62	2.04	E2.35	2.22	6 Mo Jun	0.99	1.17	11
12	....	None Since Public			...	Nil	....	8.30	1237	742	11-18-95	720	...	67288	My	...	...	0.35	0.77	□0.95	1.07	6 Mo Nov	□0.18	0.30	12
13	....	None Since Public			...	Nil	....	3.61	195	123	10-31-95	31.3	...	8984	Ja	±0.45	±0.72	±1.10	±1.40	....	1.51	9 Mo Oct	0.53	0.64	13
14◆	....	None Since Public			...	Nil	....	1.15	41.2	11.9	8-31-95	0.45	...	19913	Au	...	p0.20	p0.46	0.32	0.22	0.22				14
15◆	1947	0.102	11-28-95	9-15	0.237	0.24	0.21½	379	1171	1119	j12-31-94	213	89820	500000	Dc	□0.44	0.38	Δ0.42	0.47	....	0.47				15
16◆	....	h[56]....	12-14-92	12-15	...	Nil	....	17.2	284	173	3-31-95	87.5	...	24114	Dc	□0.12	d0.82	Δ0.40	0.38	....	0.69	9 Mo Sep	0.30	□0.61	16
17	....	0.04	1-4-96	12-19	...	[57]....	....	44.4	197	82.8	9-30-95	175	...	18745	Dc	...	n/a	d2.38	□1.84	....	4.27	9 Mo Sep	0.57	3.00	17
18	1942	Q0.35	1-2-96	11-29	1.10	1.40	0.75	248	2346	1268	9-30-95	1907	13000	63587	Dc	2.60	□d1.83	d5.38	1.42	E5.60	5.17	9 Mo Sep	0.45	4.20	18
19	1994	Q0.82¾	1-2-96	11-29	3.31	3.31	2.271	Cv into 0.82 com,$57.623				....	10000	...	Dc	...	...	...	....	....	....	Mandatory conversion into one com 12-31-97			19
20◆	1953	Q0.12	1-12-96	12-21	0.40	0.48	0.33	18.4	188	126	9-30-95	173	...	[61]41029	Sp	0.53	Δ0.81	□1.20	1.51	1.85	1.85				20
21	....	None Since Public			...	Nil	....	0.57	8.27	3.56	8-31-95	0.35	...	11641	Nv	...	d0.07	Δ0.03	Δ0.10	....	0.09	9 Mo Aug	Δ0.06	0.05	21
22	1993	Q0.31	11-15-95	11-3	1.18	1.24	0.97	Equity per shr $13.96			9-30-95	2.42	...	24294	Dc	...	...	p0.84	0.94	....	1.18	9 Mo Sep	0.75	0.99	22
23	....	None Since Public			...	Nil	....	0.83	71.4	84.2	8-31-95	45.8	...	9273	Fb	...	p0.30	0.92	1.18	....	0.86	9 Mo Nov	0.92	0.60	23
24	1993	0.44	8-3-95	6-28	0.44	0.44	0.328	4347	45907	36057	j12-31-94	19807	[63]924	314000	Dc	pΔ1.01	0.84	0.65	1.20	....	1.72	9 Mo Sep	0.74	1.26	24
25◆	1939	Q0.30	11-30-95	11-8	1.20	1.20	1.12	56.1	2188	1415	9-30-95	872	2	134279	Dc	2.37	Δ2.99	2.96	2.45	E3.25	3.26	9 Mo Sep	1.28	2.09	25
26	....	None Since Public			...	Nil	....	6.84	7.75	1.06	9-30-95	....	...	18886	Dc	d0.31	d0.27	d0.25	d0.20	....	d0.28	9 Mo Sep	d0.14	d0.22	26
27◆	1991	Q0.03	12-30-95	12-13	0.10½	0.12	0.09	1.00	179	128	10-14-95	49.3	...	p31250	Ap	±0.45	±0.66	±0.75	±0.81	±1.19	1.31	24 Wk Oct	±0.48	0.60	27
28	....	0.11	10-30-79	10-17	...	Nil	....	0.41	21.9	16.8	9-30-95	8.35	...	2949	Dc	d0.46	■d2.85	■[64]d0.32	0.34	....	0.45	9 Mo Sep	0.44	0.55	28
29◆	....	None Since Public			...	Nil	....	11.5	39.5	12.5	9-30-95	....	100	p10479	Dc	...	...	p□0.10	[65]0.29	....	0.58	9 Mo Sep	0.13	0.42	29
30	....	None Since Public			...	Nil	....	3.09	19.8	17.1	j12-31-94	22.4	...	35543	Dc	0.19	0.28	0.64	0.74	....	j0.35	9 Mo Sep	0.62	0.23	30
31	....	0.05	5-15-91	4-24	...	Nil	....	Book Value $8.62			9-30-95	218	4000	30266	Dc	Δd4.79	d0.86	d3.65	0.72	....	2.37	9 Mo Sep	0.55	2.20	31
32	....	None Since Public			...	Nil	....	0.70	10.5	4.77	8-31-95	....	...	6300	My	p0.26	0.14	0.16	0.03	d0.33	d0.33	3 Mo Aug	0.01	0.01	32
33	....	None Since Public			...	Nil	....	290	373	250	9-30-95	70.0	...	±18682	Dc	...	...	±□p1.51	±p1.49	....	1.28	9 Mo Sep	p±1.21	±1.00	33
34	1961	gS0.30	12-4-95	11-15	g0.60	0.60	g0.60	386	794	257	j12-31-94	279	906	51959	Dc	0.51	0.85	0.73	1.48	....	j2.48	9 Mo Sep	0.89	1.89	34
35	....	None Paid			...	Nil	....	19.3	29.6	19.6	9-30-95	100	...	21294	Dc	*Nil	*0.37	□0.60	0.74	....	0.81	9 Mo Sep	0.59	0.66	35
36	1995	0.05	1-9-96	12-27	0.05	0.20	....	3.52	135	102	10-21-95	72.0	...	±9637	Je	1.20	0.99	Δ0.75	Δ0.18	1.42	1.53	16 Wk Oct	0.27	0.38	36
37	....	None Since Public			...	Nil	....	Book Value $19.85			9-30-95	....	...	16876	Dc	...	...	...	....	....	....	3 Mo Sep	n/a	d0.01	37
38◆	1968	Q0.17	10-30-95	10-19	0.68	0.68	0.60	28.3	1535	688	12-02-95	971	...	83758	Fb	1.43	1.51	0.11	1.67	E1.95†	1.85	9 Mo Nov	1.04	1.22	38
39	1993	Q0.05	12-15-95	12-5	0.18	0.20	0.16	0.43	151	86.5	9-30-95	42.0	...	9724	Je	p0.61	□0.81	□1.20	1.51	1.47	1.52	3 Mo Sep	0.46	0.51	39
40	....	0.066	6-28-85	6-10	...	Nil	....	Equity per shr $5.63			9-30-95	29.6	...	5267	Dc	d1.49	Δd1.29	Δ0.13	0.79	....	0.90	9 Mo Sep	0.07	0.18	40
41	1992	Q0.04	12-28-95	12-13	0.16	0.16	0.16	42.5	468	347	9-30-95	1018	...	[68]65683	Dc	pΔ0.02	0.78	□0.05	□0.16	....	0.50	9 Mo Sep	□0.34	0.68	41
42	1995	Q0.09	1-8-96	11-16	0.25	0.36	....	15.2	101	57.9	7-02-95	2.37	...	15883	Je	0.74	0.75	0.98	□0.80	1.23	1.29	3 Mo Sep	0.13	0.19	42
43◆	1995	Q0.37½	1-1-96	12-13	1.12½	1.50	....	354	4524	3515	9-30-95	9524	41770	272694	Dc	1.10	□2.75	□d0.25	□2.05	E2.25	1.86	9 Mo Sep	□1.67	□1.48	43
44◆	1976	Q0.13	1-15-96	12-27	0.50	0.52	0.456	Equity per shr $15.52			9-30-95	52.3	...	7849	Dc	1.78	1.83	Δ1.94	d0.67	....	0.74	9 Mo Sep	d1.25	0.16	44
45◆	....	0.25	9-1-91	7-26	...	Nil	....	0.10	113	28.1	9-30-95	68.0	...	[69]15326	Dc	pd39.20	d9.70	□d8.10	□d1.45	....	d0.40	9 Mo Sep	□d1.59	□d0.54	45
46	....	None Since Public			...	Nil	....	5.13	391	251	9-30-95	229	...	49802	Dc	*0.07	*0.15	0.26	0.16	....	d0.19	9 Mo Sep	0.16	d0.19	46
47	1956	h[72]....	1-12-96	1-16	1.40	1.40	1.40	37.2	675	842	9-09-95	....	...	39069	Dc	3.27	3.73	Δ□3.02	0.50	....	0.51	9 Mo Sep	0.15	0.16	47
48◆	1978	Q0.11	11-22-95	11-3	0.37	0.44	†0.407	8.14	78.5	36.9	7-31-95	17.6	...	8066	Oc	0.03	0.33	0.60	Δ1.10	P2.51	2.51				48
49◆	1989	Q0.08¾	1-31-96	1-10	0.30	0.35	0.30	10.2	110	77.7	8-31-95	61.8	...	5202	Au	1.00	1.50	□1.18	1.21	Δ[73]2.19	2.39	3 Mo Nov	0.55	0.75	49
50	....	None Since Public			...	Nil	....	1.67	49.5	28.8	9-30-95	49.8	...	5909	Dc	...	p0.93	p0.91	1.12	....	1.34	9 Mo Sep	0.69	0.91	50
51◆	....	h[74]....	8-3-87	6-22	...	Nil	....	31.7	117	49.5	9-30-95	2.09	...	28587	Dc	Δ0.18	0.18	0.46	0.92	....	1.24	9 Mo Sep	0.66	0.98	51
52	....	None Since Public			...	Nil	....	0.90	148	30.9	6-30-95	113	...	±★14475	Je	0.39	0.69	0.83	0.75	1.39	1.59	3 Mo Sep	0.11	0.31	52

◆**Stock Splits & Divs By Line Reference Index** [1]3-for-2,'93:5-for-4,'94. [2]3-for-2,'91. [6]10%,'95:Adj for 5%,'95. [8]2-for-1,'92,'95. [9]1-for-5 REVERSE,'95. [10]Adj to 5%,'95. [11]2-for-1,'94. [14]2-for-1,'93. [15]2-for-1,'92. [16]No adj for stk dstr of Worldtex,'92. [20]2-for-1,'94. [25]No adj for rt dstr,'90:2-for-1,'91. [27]2-for-1,'93. [29]2-for-1,'95. [38]2-for-1,'91. [43]1-for-5 REVERSE,'95. [44]5-for-4,'95. [45]1-for-10 REVERSE,'94. [48]3-for-2,'95. [49]2-for-1,'92. [51]2-for-1,'94.

¶ S&P 500 # MidCap 400 ✣ SmallCap 600 • Options

Index	Ticker	Name of Issue (Call Price of Pfd. Stocks)	Market	Com. Rank. & Pfd. Rating	Inst. Hold Cos	Inst. Hold Shs. (000)	Principal Business	Price Range 1971-93 High	1971-93 Low	1994 High	1994 Low	1995 High	1995 Low	Dec. Sales in 100s	December, 1995 Last Sale Or Bid High	Low	Last	%Div Yield	P-E Ratio	Total Return % Annualized 12 Mo	36 Mo	60 Mo
✣1•[1]	RPCX	✔**Roberts Pharmaceutical**	NNM	B–	78	4155	Dvlp/mkt proprietary drugs	42½	2½	40	19¾	46½	15½	42423	19¾	16¼	17¾	...	..	–44.5	–6.4	30.2
2	RHH	✔**Robertson-Ceco Corp**	NY,Ch,Ph	C	18	2775	Mfr,dstr construction prod	800⅜	2½	4	2⅜	7⅛	2¼	1893	6	4⅝	5⅛	...	9	57.7	–20.8	–41.4
3	ROBV	✔**Robotic Vision Sys**	NNM	B–	52	2867	3-D sensor-based robotic sys	17⅛	7/16	8⅛	4⅜	27¾	5½	57929	27¾	19⅝	24⅛	...	40	311	...	71.5
4	RCI	✔**ROC Communities**	NY,Ch,Ph	NR	118	10133	Real estate investment trust	27⅛	20	24⅝	18⅛	24	18⅝	5097	24	22⅛	24	6.5	25	22.8	...	...
5	RGS	✔**Rochester Gas & El**	NY,B,Ch,P	B	155	13115	Electric/gas utility, NY	29⅞	7⅞	26⅜	19¾	24⅛	20	18271	24⅛	22⅜	22⅝	8.0	10	18.3	3.7	11.0
6	RKTN	✔**Rock-Tenn 'A'**	NNM	NR	49	4315	Mfr recycled paperb'rd/contain	....	....	18¾	13½	19¼	15¼	3601	16¾	15¾	16¼	1.8	12	–1.3	...	...
7•[2]	RCP	✔**Rockefeller Ctr Prop**[52]	NY,B,Ch,P,Ph	NR	46	4848	Real estate investment trust	22½	6½	8⅜	3¾	8⅜	4⅛	23404	7¾	7⅜	7⅝	...	d	60.8	12.9	–6.9
¶8•[1]	ROK	✔**Rockwell Intl**	NY,To,B,C,Ch,P,Ph	A–	600	81518	Electronics,auto,aerospace pd	38½	2¼	44⅛	33½	53	35	71681	53	49	52⅞	2.2	16	51.0	25.5	17.2
9	Pr	**$4.75 cm Cv A Pfd(100)vtg**	NY,B,Ph	AA–	1	.1	vehicle parts: textile machy	732	48	700	625	885	865	....	....	....	1046⅞B	0.5	..	...	...	...
10	Pr B	**$1.35 cm Cv B Pfd (36)vtg**	NY	AA–	3	6	lgst mfr printing presses	265	16	313	220	368	268	5	368	360	380¾B	0.4	..	...	...	...
11	RMCF	✔**Rocky Mtn Choc Factory**	NSC	B–	17	817	Mfr gourmet chocolate prod	17⅝	1⅝	15¼	11½	19	11¾	2217	12¾	11¾	12	...	23	–11.1	31.7	29.9
12	RR	✔**Rodman&Renshaw Cap**	NY,Ch	C	10	214	Securities broker/fin'l svcs	13	3¼	7⅞	3⅝	5	1⅜	1412	1¾	1⅜	1¾	...	d	–53.3	–31.7	–12.9
13	RCMIF	✔**Rogers Cantel MobComm'B'**	[3]NNM,To	NR	81	10980	Cellular telephone svc Canada	31¾	15⅞	31⅞	22¼	29⅜	20⅜	7114	26½	22½	26½	...	..	–7.0	11.7	...
14•[4]	RCI.B	**Rogers Commun Cl'B'**[62]	To	C	72	27649	CATV in Can.,U.S.,Ireland	24⅞	9/16	24	17¼	18⅞	11½	81618	16	13¾	15¼	...	d	–19.2	2.3	...
15	RCI.A	✔ **Cl'A'Cv**	To,Mo	C	4	1072	provid'g entnmt,info svcs	25⅝	¼	25¼	18⅞	20	12⅜	487	16⅞	14⅝	16½	...	d	–17.5	2.4	...
16	ROG	✔**Rogers Corp**	AS,B	B–	56	4340	Polymeric mtls: eng'd comp	18⅝	1¼	25½	12¼	31½	21¾	1993	24⅝	21¾	21¾	...	13	–11.2	47.4	20.9
¶17•[2]	ROH	✔**Rohm & Haas**	NY,B,Ch,P,Ph	B+	351	49795	Mfr specialty chem & plastics	62	4⅝	68½	53¼	64⅞	49½	33050	64⅞	60⅜	64⅜	2.5	16	15.7	8.7	16.0
#18•[5]	RHR	✔**Rohr Inc**	NY,B,Ch,P,Ph	B–	99	13847	Jet engine pod assemblies	39	2	12⅛	8	16⅞	9¾	18083	15⅛	13½	14⅜	...	24	40.2	7.3	–2.1
#19	REN	✔**Rollins Environ Sv**	NY,B,Ch,P,Ph	↓C	123	33176	Industrial waste disposal	20¾	⅝	6⅜	4	5½	2¾	41589	3¼	2¾	2⅞	...	d	–34.3	–38.7	–19.7
#20	ROL	✔**Rollins Inc**	NY,B,Ch,P,Ph	A–	153	13981	Pest controls/protective svcs	27¾	2⅛	30¾	22⅛	28⅝	18⅞	11462	22⅛	20	22⅛	2.5	16	–0.4	–0.5	11.4
✣21•[6]	RLC	✔**Rollins Truck Leasing**	NY,B,Ch,P,Ph	↑A	118	25217	Truck, trailer leasing	14	5/16	14⅜	10⅞	14½	9¼	16728	11¼	10	11⅛	1.6	12	–0.7	5.6	29.1
22	ROMC	✔**Romac Intl**	NNM	NR	24	989	Personnel placement service	....	....	....	....	23½	12½	2473	23½	19½	23½	...	48	...	...	...
✣23•[7]	RFED	✔**Roosevelt Finl**	NNM	NR	176	25698	Savings bank,Missouri	16⅛	21/16	18¼	12⅜	19½	14⅝	44416	19½	16⅝	19⅜	2.9	12	34.6	31.0	58.6
✣24	ROPR	✔**Roper Industries**	NNM	NR	94	9710	Mfr fluid handl'g/ctrl prd	39	5¾	34	18	40½	21	2549	38	35½	36¾	0.8	24	54.3	60.8	...
✣25•[8]	ROST	✔**Ross Stores**	NNM	B	126	18357	Apparel,shoes,linen retailer	24⅝	3⅝	17¾	10¾	21½	9½	46075	21½	18⅛	19⅛	1.3	14	73.2	–0.3	25.8
26	RTEC	**Ross Technology**	NNM	NR	..	...	Mfr hi-performance circuits	....	....	....	....	17⅛	9	22983	15¼	9	9¾	...	..	...	...	...
27•[9]	ROTC	✔**Rotech Medical**	NNM	B+	112	7538	Out-patient hlth care svcs	20⅜	1¼	29	13½	33	21⅝	20543	30½	25½	27½	...	20	–5.2	26.0	37.4
28	ROTO	✔**Roto-Rooter Inc**	NNM	A–	42	1785	Sewer/drain cleaning services	30	13½	32	19⅜	37¾	19¼	466	34	30½	32¾	2.1	18	63.4	15.0	17.0
29	RMI	✔**Rotonics Manufacturing**	AS,Ch	B–	6	137	Mfr,mkt plastic containers	10⅛	3/16	1 13/16	¾	3	1⅛	3239	2 7/16	1½	1⅞	...	9	42.9	28.9	38.0
30•[10]	ROU	✔**Rouge Steel 'A'**	NY,Ph	NR	55	6722	Integrated domestic steel mfr	....	....	34¼	19¾	30¾	19¾	4956	24½	19¾	23¾	0.5	5	–17.4	...	...
31	RSE	✔**Rouse Co**	NY,Ph	B–	114	33130	Real estate acquis/dvlp	29¾	7/16	20	16¼	22⅝	17⅝	8480	20⅜	18⅝	20⅜	3.9	d	12.3	9.4	11.4
32	Pr A	**$3.25 cm Cv Sr'A'Pfd([69]NC)**	NY,Ph	↑BBB–	53	3046		59½	49¼	54¼	47¼	55¾	47⅛	945	53	49¾	51⅝	6.3	..	...	...	...
¶33•[2]	RDC	✔**Rowan Cos**	NY,B,Ch,P	C	266	78359	Contract drilling:aircraft sv	23½	11/16	9¼	5¾	10	5⅜	117761	10	7½	9⅝	...	d	54.0	6.9	–3.1
34	ROW	✔**Rowe Furniture**	NY,Ph	B	20	1618	Mfr living room furniture	10⅜	3/16	12⅞	4⅝	6⅛	3⅞	3112	5⅛	4⅜	4½	1.8	8	–8.5	21.9	53.7
✣35•[11]	RAM	✔**Royal Appliance Mfg**	NY,Ph	NR	39	3531	Assemble,mkt vacuum cleaners	31	4½	6¼	3¼	4⅝	2½	13333	3¼	2½	2½	...	d	–25.9	–44.0	...
36•[4]	RY	**Royal Bank Canada**[70]	Mo,To,Vc	↑B+	105	32226	Banking:Canada&worldwide	29¼	5⅝	31⅞	25⅛	31¼	20½	445	23¾	21⅞	23	5.4	7	–14.7	2.3	...
37•[12]	RCL	✔**Royal Caribbean Cruises**	NY	NR	..	...	Operates passenger cruise line	27½	15⅝	30½	23⅝	28½	20⅞	8287	24½	20⅞	22	2.1	9	–18.7	...	...
¶38•[13]	RD	✔**Royal Dutch Petrol**	NY,B,C,Ch,P,Ph	A	1136	150004	Owns 60% Royal Dutch/Shell	108⅛	5⅝	116¾	96⅞	141¾	107¼	103344	141¾	129	141⅛	3.3	16	36.1	25.7	18.2
39	RGLD	✔**Royal Gold Inc**	NSC	C	15	775	Gold mining,U.S.	18¼	1/32	9½	7⅛	9½	5⅝	1320	8½	7½	7⅞	...	d	0.0	37.9	83.8
40	RYO	✔**Royal Oak Mines**	AS,To,Ph	NR	77	26340	Gold mining	7	½	5½	2⅞	4½	2¾	64712	4	3½	3½	...	..	9.8	34.5	...
41	RPB	✔**Royal Palm Beach**[73] **Col**[74]	AS	NR	3	24	Company liquidating assets	13⅛	⅜	1 3/16	¾	2	¾	573	1½	¾	¾	...	d	0.0	–5.0	–2.6
42	KPN	**Royal PTT Nederland ADS**[76]	NY,Ph	NR	13	252	Postal/telecom sv, Netherlands	....	....	....	....	36¼	34⅜	9916	36¼	35⅜	36¼	3.6	13	...	...	...
43	RES	✔**RPC Inc**	NY,B	B–	40	3765	Svc oil&gas eqp/mfr boats	13⅜	1¾	9	6¼	9⅝	6¾	994	9⅝	8	9⅛	...	13	14.1	13.4	1.4
#44	RPOW	✔**RPM, Inc**	NNM	A+	177	27105	Protective coatings: fabrics	15½	3/16	15¾	13	17¼	14¼	33801	17¼	16⅛	16½	2.9	19	16.7	7.3	16.0
45	RPS	✔**RPS Realty Trust**	NY,Ch,Ph	NR	34	4414	Real estate investment trust	7½	3⅛	4½	3½	5⅛	4	8624	4¾	4¼	4⅝	6.9	58	20.5	4.8	7.5
46	RTWI	✔**RTW Inc**	NNM	NR	30	2055	Managed healthcare svcs/prd	....	....	....	....	30½	13	1829	28	24½	26¼	...	30	...	...	...
47	RTZ	✔**RTZ Corp plc**[78] **ADS**[79]	NY,Ch,Ph	NR	53	2944	Hldg co:mining,metals,energy	49¼	2⅝	58½	48¼	60	45½	1021	60	57	57½	3.2	15	14.1	15.7	15.5
¶48•[8]	RBD	✔**Rubbermaid, Inc**	NY,B,Ch,P,Ph	A+	490	71460	Mfr plastic/rubber housewre	38¼	⅝	35¾	23⅝	34¼	24¾	120648	28½	24¾	25½	2.2	62	–6.9	–6.0	5.5
#49	RDK	✔**Ruddick Corp**	NY,Ch	A	106	28138	Food supermkts,thread/yarn	12	⅛	11½	7⅞	14⅛	9⅜	12788	12¾	9⅝	11½	†2.1	14	25.8	7.2	18.9
50	RULE	✔**Rule Indus**[80]	NNM	B–	14	504	Marine,hardware pr: export sv	13⅛	2	16¾	8¼	15½	6¼	718	15½	14⅝	15	...	..	20.0	28.2	24.6
51	RURL	✔**Rural/Metro Corp**	NNM	NR	69	3240	Emergency ambulance/fire svcs	20¾	12½	21¼	13¼	26½	16¾	3554	24¾	22½	22⅝	...	23	17.5	...	...
✣52•[11]	RUS	✔**Russ Berrie & Co**	NY,Ch	B	81	7780	Mkts variety of gift items	30½	8⅝	15⅝	12¾	15⅞	12	2274	14¼	12¼	12⅝	4.8	18	–3.2	–5.8	9.8

Uniform Footnote Explanations-See Page 4. Other: [1]CBOE:Cycle 1. [2]ASE:Cycle 1. [3]Mo [4]To:Cycle 1. [5]Ph:Cycle 3. [6]P:Cycle 1. [7]ASE:Cycle 3. [8]P:Cycle 2. [9]AS,Ph:Cycle 3. [10]P:Cycle 3. [11]CBOE:Cycle 3. [12]ASE,P:Cycle 3. [13]ASE:Cycle 2. [51]4 Mo Dec,'93. [52]Investor group plan acq, $8. [53]Incl $0.256 non-taxable:©$0.02,'94. [54]®$3.36,'95. [55]9.8985 com & 9.8985 nontransferable Cv'A'. [56]3.6 com & 3.6 nontransferable Cv'A'. [57]Accum on pfd. [58]®$0.49,'95. [59]Redemption of stk purch rt. [60]Fiscal Jun'93 & prior. [61]12 Mo Dec'94. [62]Non-vtg. [63]Excl shrs hld by subsid. [64]®$1.38,'94. [65]®$0.68,'94. [66]8 Mo Mar'94. [67]To be determined. [68]100% non-taxable,'94. [69]Spcl redm fr 3-1-96 (in com) re-spec cond.. [70]Sep'95 & prior prices in Cdn$. [71]Approx. [72]Proportionate shr of group B/S. [73]Ltd partnership. [74]Regency Homes plan mgr:Co rejects. [75]Liq divd. [76]Ea ADS rep 1 ord,NLG 10. [77]®$0.81,'95. [78]Ea ADS rep 4 ord,10p. [79]Plan business combination w/CRA Ltd. [80]Greenfield Indus plan acq,$15.30. [81]®$1.18,'94.

Splits ◆ Index	Cash Divs. Ea.Yr. Since	Dividends: Latest Payment: Period $	Date	Ex. Div.	Total $: So Far 1995	Ind. Rate	Paid 1994	Financial Position Mil-$: Cash& Equiv.	Curr. Assets	Curr. Liab.	Balance Sheet Date	Capitalization: Lg Trm Debt Mil-$	Shs. 000: Pfd.	Com.	Earnings $ Per Shr. Years: End	1991	1992	1993	1994	1995	Last 12 Mos.	Interim Earnings: Period	$ per Shr. 1994	1995	Index
1	....	None Since Public			...	Nil	....	31.9	94.5	84.4	9-30-95	16.2	...	18531	Dc	d0.58	*d0.68	0.46	1.04	E0.07	d0.31	9 Mo Sep	0.73	d0.62	1
2◆	....	6.601	9-16-85	8-26	...	Nil	....	18.2	81.7	76.8	9-30-95	42.2	...	16214	Dc	d142.41	d81.02	Δd4.05	d1.38	....	0.56	9 Mo Sep	d1.27	0.67	2
3	....	None Paid			...	Nil	....	11.6	26.0	7.96	6-30-95	....	...	p14543	Sp	d0.38	*0.02	0.14	0.24	P0.61	0.61				3
4	1993	Q0.39	1-15-96	12-27	1.55	1.56	1.51	Equity per shr $15.59			9-30-95	83.6	...	12424	Dc	...	...	‡[51]0.25	0.80	....	0.95	9 Mo Sep	0.55	0.70	4
5	1944	Q0.45	1-25-96	12-29	1.80	1.80	1.76	26.1	253	171	9-30-95	717	970	38424	Dc	1.60	1.86	2.00	1.79	....	2.38	12 Mo Sep	1.71	2.38	5
6	1994	Q0.075	11-17-95	11-2	0.30	0.30	0.18¾	7.04	174	66.1	6-30-95	★147	...	±30086	Sp	...	...	p0.90	±1.21	P±1.33	1.33				6
7	1985	0.15	4-24-95	3-31	0.15	Nil	[53]0.65	Equity per shr $9.03			9-30-95	752	...	38261	Dc	1.02	Δ0.97	□1.05	□0.66	Ed5.00↓	d4.12	9 Mo Sep	0.43	d4.35	7
8	1948	Q0.29	12-11-95	11-9	1.10	1.16	1.04	665	5805	4111	9-30-95	1776	105	±216984	Sp	2.57	□2.16	2.55	2.87	[54]3.42	3.42				8
9	1967	Q1.18¾	1-1-96	11-29	4.75	4.75	3.56¼	Cv into 19.797[55]shares,$5.05				....	25	...	Sp	b4.91	b5.48	b9.60	b7.54	b5.34	....				9
10	1969	Q0.33¾	1-1-96	11-29	1.35	1.35	1.013	Cv into 7.2[56]shares,$5				....	80	...	Sp	b4.91	b5.48	b9.60	b7.54	b5.34	....				10
11	....	None Since Public			...	[57]Nil	....	0.09	3.84	2.38	8-31-95	3.55	...	2957	Fb	d0.10	0.18	0.43	[58]0.51	....	0.53	6 Mo Aug	0.22	0.24	11
12	1993	[59]0.01	12-31-93	1-3	...	Nil	[59]....	Equity per shr $1.81			9-30-95	2.50	...	6646	Dc	d0.37	0.46	[60]0.06	[61]d4.83	....	d2.78	9 Mo Sep	d4.30	d2.25	12
13	....	None Since Public			...	Nil	....	Equity per shr Neg			j12-31-94	1088	...	±93894	Dc	±d0.45	±d1.86	±d1.61	±d0.02	....	j0.08	9 Mo Sep	±d0.05	±0.05	13
14	....	0.009	7-30-82	7-12	...	Nil	....	Equity per shr Neg			j12-31-94	4175	42683[63]	±176863	Dc	±d0.76	±d1.30	±d1.89	±d1.16	....	jd1.81	9 Mo Sep	±d0.69	±d1.34	14
15	....	g†0.007	8-4-80	7-18	...	Nil	....	Cv into Cl'B'shr for shr				....	...	56240	Dc	±d0.76	±d1.30	±d1.89	±d1.16	....	jd1.81	9 Mo Sep	±d0.69	±d1.34	15
16◆	....	0.01½	2-12-92	1-9	...	Nil	....	14.1	52.6	19.2	10-01-95	4.80	...	7133	Dc	d0.38	□d4.27	1.05	[64]1.42	....	1.65	9 Mo Sep	1.05	1.28	16
17	1927	Q0.41	12-1-95	11-1	1.56	1.64	1.44	60.0	1422	774	9-30-95	619	2659	67294	Dc	2.45	□2.53	□1.74	3.79	E4.10	3.91	9 Mo Sep	3.12	3.24	17
18	....	0.05	10-31-75	9-24	...	Nil	....	48.9	588	189	10-29-95	540	...	18110	Jl	1.74	0.08	□d1.71	0.38	□0.68	0.61	3 Mo Oct	0.10	0.03	18
19	1984	0.02½	9-20-93	8-16	...	Nil	....	38.7	109	58.4	9-30-95	134	...	60376	Sp	0.43	0.53	0.20	Δd0.17	d0.30	d0.30				19
20◆	1961	Q0.14	12-8-95	11-8	0.56	0.56	0.50	95.5	221	66.3	9-30-95	....	...	35853	Dc	0.89	1.07	1.25	1.39	E1.36	1.15	9 Mo Sep	1.14	0.90	20
21◆	1976	Q0.04½	12-15-95	11-13	0.16½	0.18	0.14	22.7	111	54.1	9-30-95	553	...	44955	Sp	0.45	0.53	0.66	0.86	0.91	0.91				21
22	....	None Since Public			...	Nil	....	9.53	17.7	4.35	9-30-95	0.82	...	4813	Dc	...	...	...	p0.23	....	0.49	9 Mo Sep	p0.22	0.48	22
23◆	1988	Q0.14	11-30-95	11-13	0.56	0.56	0.43	Book Value $11.50			9-30-95	2345	1301	40277	Dc	□0.52	1.02	□1.97	□[65]0.70	E1.60	1.60	9 Mo Sep	□0.19	1.09	23
24◆	1992	Q0.075	10-27-95	10-11	0.22½	0.30	0.14	4.57	62.2	18.6	4-30-95	28.3	...	14907	Oc	0.47	0.37	1.29	□1.39	P1.54	1.54				24
25	1994	Q0.06	1-2-96	12-6	0.23	0.24	0.15	23.6	389	247	10-28-95	37.9	...	24355	Ja	1.13	1.32	1.14	1.49	....	1.40	9 Mo Oct	0.98	0.89	25
26	....	None Since Public			...	Nil	....	0.70	37.6	57.3	10-02-95	p....	p...	★20370	Mr	...	...	‡[66]d2.92	d1.47	....	0.08	6 Mo Sep	d1.16	0.39	26
27	....	None Since Public			...	Nil	....	2.77	74.1	59.3	10-31-95	....	...	12071	Jl	0.43	0.60	0.77	0.99	1.27	1.36	3 Mo Oct	0.28	0.37	27
28	1985	Q0.17	12-8-95	11-20	0.64	0.68	0.58	12.7	52.3	53.7	9-30-95	8.42	...	5127	Dc	1.18	1.33	1.59	1.73	....	1.86	9 Mo Sep	1.20	1.33	28
29	1996	0.04	1-29-96	1-8	...	[67]....	....	0.02	11.1	3.88	9-30-95	7.31	...	14155	Je	d0.09	0.09	d0.05	Δ0.13	0.24	0.21	3 Mo Sep	0.06	0.03	29
30	1994	Q0.03	1-26-96	1-10	0.09	0.12	0.04	76.5	497	187	9-30-95	....	...	±21736	Dc	...	...	p□2.98	5.21	E4.40	5.27	9 Mo Sep	3.86	3.92	30
31	1978	Q0.20	12-22-95	12-13	0.80	0.80	[68]0.68	Equity per shr Neg			9-30-95	2560	4505	47921	Dc	Δ0.05	□d0.33	□d0.27	□d0.14	....	d0.13	9 Mo Sep	□d0.16	□d0.15	31
32	1993	Q0.81¼	10-2-95	9-13	3.25	3.25	3.25	Cv into 2.353 com, $21.25				....	4505	...	Dc	...	...	...	...	....	....				32
33	....	0.01	9-5-86	8-8	...	Nil	....	88.5	265	68.2	9-30-95	248	...	84782	Dc	□d0.53	d1.01	d0.17	d0.27	Ed0.23	d0.49	9 Mo Sep	d0.07	d0.29	33
34◆	1954	Q0.02	1-12-96	12-20	0.08	0.08	0.057	1.45	32.5	17.6	8-27-95	....	...	13538	Nv	d0.04	0.11	Δ0.33	0.47	....	0.57	9 Mo Aug	0.32	0.42	34
35◆	....	None Since Public			...	Nil	....	....	101	49.0	9-30-95	53.1	...	23999	Dc	p1.08	0.81	d0.35	0.06	....	d0.59	9 Mo Sep	d0.04	d0.69	35
36	1870	gQ0.31	2-23-96	1-22	g1.18	1.24	g1.16	Equity per shr $18.97			j10-31-94	3477	75100	314155	Oc	2.92	d0.05	0.46	3.19	P3.49	j3.49				36
37	1993	Q0.13	12-28-95	11-29	0.48	0.46	0.40	34.8	109	313	6-30-95	★969	...	63481	Dc	0.08	1.17	1.80	□2.25	....	2.43	9 Mo Sep	□1.91	2.09	37
38	1947	[71]1.996	10-4-95	9-18	[71]4.648	4.65	4.119	4462	13804	10809	[72]j12-31-94	2290	2	536074	Dc	5.69	6.15	5.15	7.11	E8.81	9.53	9 Mo Sep	4.34	6.76	38
39	....	None Since Public			...	Nil	....	8.75	9.92	0.61	9-30-95	....	...	14686	Je	d1.00	d0.07	d0.06	d0.11	d0.14	d0.11	3 Mo Sep	d0.04	d0.01	39
40	....	None Since Public			...	Nil	....	183	246	49.0	j6-30-95	....	...	114495	Dc	p0.25	p0.18	0.19	0.22	....	j0.12	9 Mo Sep	0.27	0.17	40
41	....	[75]0.25	12-15-92	11-23	...	Nil	....	Net Asset Val $0.69			6-30-95	1.51	...	4486	Sp	0.31	0.09	0.17	d0.12	....	d0.20	9 Mo Jun	d0.09	d0.17	41
42	....	Plan semi-annual div			...	1.32	....	1275	3940	2872	6-30-95	2807	...	462211	Dc	2.02	1.97	1.98	2.54	....	2.86	6 Mo Jun	1.24	1.56	42
43	....	None Since Public			...	Nil	....	23.5	63.6	24.2	9-30-95	....	...	14541	Dc	*0.37	*0.23	Δ0.46	0.61	....	0.70	9 Mo Sep	0.42	0.51	43
44◆	1969	Q0.12	10-31-95	10-19	0.456	0.48	0.424	38.7	435	153	8-31-95	424	...	75293	My	0.55	0.58	0.66	0.74	[77]0.86	0.87	3 Mo Aug	0.26	0.27	44
45	1989	Q0.08	1-25-96	12-22	0.32	0.32	[68]0.32	Equity per shr $6.29			9-30-95	....	...	28492	Dc	0.45	Δ0.27	0.11	0.55	....	0.08	9 Mo Sep	0.59	0.12	45
46	....	None Since Public			...	Nil	....	Equity per shr $5.00			9-30-95	10.2	...	7797	Dc	0.13	0.03	0.27	0.74	....	0.88	9 Mo Sep	0.50	0.64	46
47	1988	[71]0.65	12-22-95	10-20	[71]1.856	1.86	1.016	1128	2280	1693	j12-31-94	636	10800	1067175	Dc	□2.32	1.50	1.60	3.57	....	3.95	6 Mo Jun	1.62	2.00	47
48◆	1941	Q0.14	12-1-95	11-8	0.51½	0.56	0.46¼	50.4	1010	441	9-30-95	11.0	...	157438	Dc	1.02	□1.04	1.32	1.42	E0.41↓	1.18	9 Mo Sep	1.08	0.84	48
49◆	1976	Q0.06	1-1-96	11-29	†0.25	0.24	†0.21½	19.0	299	231	10-01-95	120	...	46374	Sp	0.62	0.65	Δ0.63	0.68	0.84	0.84				49
50	....	None Paid			...	Nil	....	0.04	29.7	18.0	8-31-95	32.6	...	3586	Au	d1.49	d0.07	d0.21	[81]1.27	□0.03	0.03				50
51	....	None Since Public			...	Nil	....	4.07	58.2	21.5	9-30-95	62.2	...	9246	Je	d0.26	0.33	0.63	0.71	□0.92	0.97	3 Mo Sep	0.18	0.23	51
52◆	1986	Q0.15	12-1-95	11-20	0.60	0.60	0.60	27.6	201	42.8	9-30-95	....	...	21554	Dc	0.98	2.69	0.61	0.25	....	0.72	9 Mo Sep	0.16	0.63	52

◆**Stock Splits & Divs By Line Reference Index** [2]1-for-16.5 REVERSE,'93. [16]2-for-1,'95. [20]3-for-2,'92. [21]3-for-2,'92,'94. [23]3-for-1,'94. [24]2-for-1,'93. [34]3-for-2,'93(twice),'94(twice). [35]2-for-1,'92. [44]3-for-2,'92:5-for-4,'95. [48]2-for-1,'91. [49]2-for-1,'91,'95. [52]3-for-2,'93.

¶ S&P 500 # MidCap 400 ✣ SmallCap 600 • Options

Index	Ticker	Name of Issue (Call Price of Pfd. Stocks)	Market	Com. Rank. & Pfd. Rating	Inst. Hold Cos	Inst. Hold Shs. (000)	Principal Business	Price Range 1971-93 High	1971-93 Low	1994 High	1994 Low	1995 High	1995 Low	Dec. Sales in 100s	December, 1995 Last Sale Or Bid High	Low	Last	%Div Yield	P-E Ratio	Total Return % Annualized 12 Mo	36 Mo	60 Mo
¶1•[1]	RML	✓Russell Corp	NY,Ch,P,Ph	A–	234	18386	Athletic wear, knit gds, cloth	40⅝	5/16	32⅝	24	31¼	22	16138	27¾	26	27¾	1.7	20	–10.4	–2.2	5.6
2	RXM	✓RX Medical Services	AS	NR	2	16	Medical facilities/svcs	42½	5	6½	¾	2¼	11/16	2874	15/16	11/16	11/16	...	d	–54.2	–69.0	...
¶3	RYAN	✓Ryan's Family Stk Hse	NNM	B+	223	31449	Cafeteria-style restaurants	16	5/16	9⅛	5⅜	8½	6⅛	74326	7½	6⅜	7	...	12	–1.8	–13.7	4.0
¶4•[2]	R	✓Ryder System	NY,B,Ch,P,Ph	B	356	71615	Equip leasing/transp'n svcs	43	13/16	28	19⅞	26⅛	21	28558	25¾	23¼	24¾	2.4	14	16.7	...	...
✣5	RYK	✓Rykoff-Sexton Inc	NY,Ph,P	B–	80	11009	Dstr to food service industry	23⅝	1 5/16	18	14⅛	24¾	14⅞	8874	19½	15⅝	17½	0.3	30	8.1	12.0	7.9
✣6•[3]	RYL	✓Ryland Group	NY,B,Ch,P,Ph	B+	99	12630	Constr single family homes	33	13/16	25⅝	12⅞	17½	12¼	13353	14⅝	12¼	14	4.3	..	–1.1	–9.6	0.3
7	RM	✓RYMAC Mtge Invest	AS,Ch,Ph	NR	4	25	Real estate investment trust	12⅜	1	1 9/16	⅝	1¾	15/16	3269	1⅜	1	1⅛	...	d	20.4	–37.8	–25.0
8	RYR	✓Rymer Foods	NY,Ch	NR	13	1307	Portion-contr food entrees	35½	⅞	4½	1⅝	3¼	⅝	14440	1⅛	⅝	1	...	d	–65.2	–10.1	–28.9
✣9•[4]	SIII	✓S3 Inc	NNM	NR	165	43800	Mfr accelerators/software prd	10⅜	3¾	9⅝	3¼	22	7⅝	223345	19½	15⅞	17⅝	...	28	129	...	...
10	SAB	✓Saba Petroleum	AS	NR	1	4	Oil & gas production	6¾	1	4	1⅜	8¼	2⅛	1185	8	7	7⅝	...	64	239	...	...
11	SBR	✓Sabine Royalty Tr UBI	NY,Ph	NR	32	1133	Royalties of oil & gas prop	27½	10	14¾	9¾	10½	7¾	6969	8⅜	7¾	8	12.9	7	–10.8	–6.9	4.4
¶12•[5]	SAFC	✓SAFECO Corp	NNM	A–	408	86486	Hldg co: fire & casualty ins	33⅜	1½	29⅞	23⅜	39¼	25⅛	72656	39¼	34¼	34½	3.1	13	37.6	9.2	20.0
13•[6]	SFE	✓Safeguard Scientifics	NY,B,Ch,Ph	B	64	2539	Computer products & services	10½	7/16	11⅞	7⅝	51½	11⅜	7761	50⅜	42¾	49½	...	56	337	108	72.4
14•[4]	SFSK	✓Safeskin Corp	NNM	NR	28	2002	Mfr disposable latex gloves	16½	12	17¾	12¼	20½	10¼	10233	20	15¾	17	...	15	12.4	...	...
15	SAFT	✓Safety 1st Inc	NNM	NR	48	2354	Dvlp,mkt child safety prod	33½	9¼	33¼	20¼	29½	13½	12396	20¾	13½	14¾	...	16	–49.6	...	...
¶16•[3]	SK	✓Safety-Kleen	NY,B,Ch,Ph	B+	256	39489	Parts cleaning sv:auto,farm	37⅞	1 1/16	18½	12¾	18⅛	12⅞	31665	15⅝	14	15½	2.3	18	6.4	–11.0	–8.0
17	SAFE	✓SafetyTek Corp	NNM	B–	18	685	Mfrs/mkts pressure sensors	14¼	1⅛	14¼	7	18¼	8⅝	2055	16½	13¼	15	...	15	66.7	41.9	58.5
18•[7]	SWY	✓Safeway Inc	NY,Ch,Ph	NR	259	37557	Food supermarket chain	22¾	9⅝	31⅞	19¼	51½	30⅝	24902	51½	45⅝	51½	...	20	62.8	57.2	33.0
19	WS	Wrrt(3.58wrrt pur 1com $3.7691)	[8]NY	NR	14	102		5¼	2	7⅞	4⅜	13⅛	7½	1191	13⅛	11⅝	13⅛	...	..	...	...	...
20	SGA	✓Saga Communications'A'	AS	NR	43	4453	Own,oper AM&FM radio stations	17	11	14	8¾	18⅛	11⅜	3014	16½	14	16¼	...	41	45.6	...	...
21	SPM.A	Saga Petroleum ADS'A'[56]	NY,Ch	NR	6	227	Oil & gas explor,dvlp,prod'n	...	...	...	...	14⅞	12¼	313	13	12½	12⅜B	2.2	20	...	...	...
22	SPM.B	ADS'B'[57]	NY	NR	6	1170		...	...	...	...	14⅜	11⅞	323	13	12	12B	2.3	19	...	...	...
23	SGM	✓Sahara Gaming	AS	NR	8	219	Oper hotel-casinos	18¾	9⅝	12⅜	3	7⅞	2	3774	2⅞	2	2 7/16	...	d	–25.0	...	...
24	STFR	✓St. Francis Capital	NNM	NR	42	2262	Savings bank, Wisconsin	15½	12⅝	18¼	13½	26	13¾	4244	26	22¾	23¼	...	11	69.8	...	...
25	SJP	✓St. Joe Paper	NY,Ph	B–	98	27356	Forest prod,RR,sugar,communic	55	25½	62⅝	49⅛	68	52½	2161	57¾	53½	55	0.4	22	0.9	13.9	14.9
✣26	SJK	✓St. John Knits	NY,Ph	NR	130	6305	Mfr women's clothing	23¼	13¼	32¼	21¼	54¼	28⅝	5663	54¼	46½	53⅛	0.4	22	84.1	...	...
27	SAJ	✓St. Joseph Lt & Pwr	NY,Ch	A–	51	819	Utility:elec,natural gas in Mo	37⅞	5½	30¼	25	36½	27⅛	703	36½	30¾	35½	5.2	12	33.7	7.3	11.1
¶28•[4]	STJM	✓St. Jude Medical	NNM,Ch	B+	449	50898	Heart valve:electro med dev	37	1/16	27⅜	16½	43¼	23⅝	138333	43¼	37¾	43	...	24	60.5	16.5	14.1
✣29	MARY	✓St. Mary Land Exploration	NNM	NR	57	4138	Oil & gas explor,dvlp,prod'n	18	11	14⅜	10⅞	15	10⅞	3736	15	13¼	14	1.1	d	8.0	9.3	...
✣30•[4]	SPBC	✓St. Paul Bancorp	NNM	NR	86	6162	Savings bank, Illinois	20⅝	3¾	24⅛	16¼	28⅜	17⅜	12882	26	24⅞	25½	1.2	14	50.9	21.2	38.2
¶31•[4]	SPC	✓St. Paul Cos	NY	A–	545	69366	General line of insurance	49	3⅞	45½	37¾	59⅜	43½	41605	58⅛	54⅞	55⅝	2.9	11	28.9	16.8	16.1
32	SPCPrM	6.00%[61] Cv[62]'MIPS'([63]50)	NY	AA	41	2107		...	...	...	...	59½	50	1089	58⅜	55½	56¼	5.3	..	...	...	...
33	SLT	✓Salant Corp	NY,Ch	NR	31	8877	Mfr slacks,jeans,outerwear	28⅞	1¼	9⅜	4⅜	6⅜	2¾	6644	4⅛	3⅜	3⅞	...	d	–29.5	–25.5	25.4
34	WS	Wrrt'B'(Pur 1com at$16)	AS	....	7	388		13/16	¼	13/16	1/64	⅛	1/64	244	1/16	1/64	1/64	...	..	...	...	...
35	SBS	✓Salem Corp	AS,B,Ph	†B	15	286	Heavy eq: coal/metal ind'y	14⅝	1 9/16	17⅜	12	29	15¾	355	22	17⅞	21	2.9	12	30.5	37.9	49.3
¶36•[9]	SB	✓Salomon Inc	NY,B,Ch,P,Ph	B	415	55756	Invest bank'g:mineral trad'g	59⅜	3	52¾	35	43¼	32¼	112105	36⅜	33⅞	35⅜	1.8	9	–2.7	–0.3	9.4
37	MEK	Salomon Inc 5% MSFI'ELKS'	AS	NR	8	34	Microsoft Com Equity-Link Sec	82¾	76¾	96	79¼	106	92	100	106	103½	104	3.8	..	17.0	...	...
38	HLK	Salomon Inc 5.25% HWP'ELKS'	AS	NR	15	633	Hewlett Pack Equity/Link Sec	77¾	75¾	87	74½	102½	85⅝	458	102½	100¼	100½	4.0	..	20.6	...	...
39	PLK	Salomon Inc 6.125% PRI 'ELKS'	AS	NR	5	79	Promus Com Equity-Link Sec	...	...	49⅜	29⅞	45½	34	276	38	35⅜	36B	8.4	..	14.2	...	...
40	AEK	Salomon Inc 6.50% AMGN'ELKS'	AS	NR	8	303	Amgen Inc Equity-Linked Sec	...	...	53½	41	65¼	51⅜	163	65¼	62½	64¾B	4.9	..	30.8	...	...
41	DLK	Salomon Inc 6.75% DEC'ELKS'	AS	NR	4	155	Digital Eqp Equity-Linked Sec	40⅜	36⅝	39¼	23⅞	48	32½	847	48	46⅛	47½	5.3	..	48.7	...	...
42	OLK	Salomon Inc 7.25% ORCL'ELKS'	AS	NR	7	229	Oracle Sy Com Equity-Link Sec	34¼	28¾	38⅜	28¾	46⅜	35⅜	834	46⅜	45	45⅝	5.0	..	26.2	...	...
43	SEK	Salomon Inc 7.625% SNPL'ELKS'	AS	NR	5	301	Snapple BV Com Equity-Link Sec	...	...	29¼	15¼	15¾	14¾	166	15¼	14⅞	15⅛	14.0	..	10.2	...	...
44	SAN	✓San Carlos Milling[72]	AS	NR	3	4	Philippine cane sugar prod	7⅝	⅝	1⅜	⅛	...	...	...	...	...	...	...	..	...	...	...
45	SDO	✓San Diego Gas & El	NY,B,Ch,P,Ph	A–	168	20059	Elec-gas utility	27¾	4½	25	17½	23⅞	19⅛	22355	23⅞	21⅞	23¾	6.6	13	30.0	6.8	7.9
46	SJT	✓San Juan Basin Rty Tr	NY,Ch,P	NR	46	21517	Royalty gas interest,N.M.	19¾	4¾	9⅞	5⅞	7⅜	5⅝	19733	6⅝	5¾	6¼	4.8	18	9.0	2.2	10.9
47	SNDCF	Sand Technology Sys'A'	NNM	B–	2	139	Mkt/svc computer peripheral pr	11⅛	¼	2⅞	1⅜	9	1	31520	9	2¾	4½	...	..	188	17.8	64.4
48	SAFM	✓Sanderson Farms	NNM	B	43	2210	Prod,mkt chicken/food items	16⅜	4½	14⅞	9⅜	14⅝	10	6293	11	10⅛	10½	1.9	13	–26.1	0.7	10.6
49	SNDK	SanDisk Corp	NNM	NR	..	...	Dgn flash mem storage pd	...	...	...	...	31	10	28315	23½	13½	15	...	..	...	...	...
50	SNDS	✓Sands Regent	NNM	B	16	610	Casino-hotel Reno Nevada	22¼	3¾	14½	6¼	8	4½	4920	6¼	5⅛	5⅛	3.9	d	–21.2	–17.5	–1.8
51	SDY	✓Sandy[74] Corp[75]	AS	B–	12	301	Mkts corp train'g programs	16½	½	9⅜	5⅝	13¼	6¾	556	13¼	11⅞	12⅛	1.3	21	75.5	26.9	62.7
✣52•[10]	FIL	✓Sanifill Inc	NY,Ch,Ph	B	148	15708	Non-hazardous waste landfills	33⅜	8⅝	25⅝	20	34⅛	22⅜	14542	34	32⅞	33⅜	...	24	37.6	26.1	7.0

Uniform Footnote Explanations-See Page 4. Other: [1]ASE:Cycle 1. [2]P:Cycle 2. [3]Ph:Cycle 3. [4]CBOE:Cycle 1. [5]NY:Cycle 2. [6]NY,Ph:Cycle 2. [7]ASE,CBOE,P:Cycle 3. [8]Ch,Ph [9]Ph:Cycle 1. [10]P,Cycle 3. [51]®$1.28,'94. [52]Stk of Safeguard Bus.Sys. [53]®$0.94,'94. [54]®$2.02,'94. [55]9 Mo Sep'92. [56]Ea ADS rep 1'A'shr,NOK 15. [57]Ea ADS rep 1'B'shr,NOK 15. [58]To be determined. [59]68%owned-Alfred I. duPont testamentary trust. [60]®$4.93,'94. [61]Isued by subsid St. Paul Cos L.L.C.. [62]Monthly Income Preferred Shrs. [63]Fr 6-1-1999,If less then 5% shrs outstanding. [64]Co opt conv right expire 5-31-99 re-spec cond. [65]Or prior based on re-pymt Cv Debs re-spec cond. [66]Co can extend to 11-8-96. [67]Co can extend to 1-8-97. [68]Co can extend to 3-22-97. [69]Co can extend to 2-8-97. [70]Can extend to 8-9-96. [71]Co can extend to 10-28-96. [72]ASE trading halted 5-4-94. [73]9 Mo Sep'91. [74]Vote Jan 4 Automatic Data Processing acq,$12. [75]Westcott Communications Inc plan acq,$11.

Splits ◆ Index	Cash Divs. Ea.Yr. Since	Dividends: Latest Payment: Period $	Date	Ex. Div.	Total $: So Far 1995	Ind. Rate	Paid 1994	Financial Position Mil-$: Cash& Equiv.	Curr. Assets	Curr. Liab.	Balance Sheet Date	Capitalization: Lg Trm Debt Mil-$	Shs. 000: Pfd.	Com.	Earnings $ Per Shr.: Years End	1991	1992	1993	1994	1995	Last 12 Mos.	Interim Earnings: Period	$ per Shr.: 1994	1995	Index
1	1963	Q0.12	11-20-95	11-2	0.48	0.48	0.42	3.73	649	279	10-01-95	188	...	38951	Dc	1.38	1.99	1.19	1.96	E1.40	1.67	9 Mo Sep	1.25	0.96	1
2◆	....	None Paid			...	Nil	....	0.05	2.79	26.9	6-30-95	0.58	1843	8943	Dc	d5.64	d3.72	d4.09	d2.05	....	d1.90	6 Mo Jun	d0.75	d0.60	2
3	....	None Since Public			...	Nil	....	1.64	10.9	110	9-27-95	....	...	53454	Dc	0.44	Δ0.53	0.53	0.57	E0.61	0.59	9 Mo Sep	0.45	0.47	3
4	1976	Q0.15	12-20-95	11-15	0.60	0.60	0.60	96.6	805	1114	9-30-95	2318	...	79211	Dc	0.05	1.51	□d0.51	1.95	E1.80	1.73	9 Mo Sep	1.47	□1.25	4
5◆	1995	Q0.03	1-3-96	12-13	0.06	0.06	....	16.9	370	244	10-28-95	133	...	14801	Ap	0.95	□0.87	Δd1.35	□0.50	2.24	0.59	6 Mo Oct	2.02	0.37	5
6	1975	Q0.15	1-30-96	1-10	0.60	0.60	0.60	Equity per shr $19.35			9-30-95	811	965	15667	Dc	0.53	1.66	d0.34	Δ[51]1.29	E0.10	1.35	9 Mo Sep	Δ1.18	1.24	6
7	1989	0.003	9-29-95	9-18	0.003	Nil	0.04	Equity per shr $1.19			9-30-95	11.1	...	5211	Dc	1.52	d0.36	□d4.62	0.15	....	d0.14	9 Mo Sep	0.14	d0.15	7
8	....	0.188	3-25-77	3-7	...	Nil	....	....	34.9	5.54	7-29-95	34.6	...	10752	Oc	d2.09	d3.80	□d3.35	0.61	....	d0.25	9 Mo Jul	0.56	d0.30	8
9◆	....	None Since Public			...	Nil	....	91.6	196	67.2	9-30-95	24.0	...	46348	Dc	...	p0.16	Δ0.41	0.14	....	0.63	9 Mo Sep	0.03	0.52	9
10	....	None Since Public			...	Nil	....	0.16	4.45	13.6	9-30-95	★22.9	...	4190	Dc	0.17	0.13	d0.02	0.13	....	0.12	9 Mo Sep	0.06	0.05	10
11	1983	0.067	12-29-95	12-13	1.027	1.03	1.197	Equity per shr $0.40			9-30-95	....	...	14579	Dc	1.52	1.31	1.43	1.20	....	1.13	9 Mo Sep	0.90	0.83	11
12◆	1933	Q0.26½	1-22-96	1-3	1.02	1.06	0.94	Equity per shr $28.66			9-30-95	1087	...	125969	Dc	2.07	2.48	Δ3.39	2.50	E2.65	3.01	9 Mo Sep	1.74	2.25	12
13◆	....	h[52]....	3-4-80	3-5	...	Nil	....	6.40	429	232	9-30-95	204	...	14649	Dc	0.75	0.65	0.21	[53]1.03	....	0.88	9 Mo Sep	0.97	0.82	13
14	....	None Since Public			...	Nil	....	5.45	41.1	13.0	9-30-95	4.75	...	12467	Dc	0.14	0.69	1.12	1.13	....	1.13	9 Mo Sep	0.82	0.82	14
15	....	None Since Public			...	Nil	....	0.02	60.1	32.9	9-30-95	....	...	7146	Dc	...	p0.44	p0.71	0.95	....	0.94	9 Mo Sep	0.81	0.80	15
16◆	1979	Q0.09	12-28-95	12-12	0.36	0.36	0.36	37.6	218	175	9-09-95	298	...	57869	Dc	0.90	Δ0.78	d1.76	0.87	E0.85	0.90	36 Wk Sep	0.58	0.61	16
17	....	None Since Public			...	Nil	....	0.15	12.5	5.30	9-30-95	0.84	...	3210	Je	0.08	0.54	d1.90	0.86	0.99	1.03	3 Mo Sep	0.20	0.24	17
18	....	None Since Public			...	Nil	....	48.7	1430	1800	9-09-95	1940	...	106593	Dc	□0.69	□0.83	1.02	□[54]2.05	E2.60	2.48	36 Wk Sep	□1.35	1.78	18
19	....	Terms&trad. basis should be checked in detail						Wrrts expire 11-24-96				....	...	4643	Dc	...	...	...	....	....	....				19
20◆	....	None Since Public			...	Nil	....	3.75	16.3	11.5	9-30-95	34.6	...	±6422	Dc	p[55]0.12	□d0.33	0.13	0.36	....	0.40	9 Mo Sep	0.26	0.30	20
21	1991	0.268	6-12-95	5-9	0.268	0.27	0.24	1327	2385	2537	j12-31-94	5893	...	±128609	Dc	±0.96	±0.31	±0.40	±0.63	....	0.63				21
22	1991	0.268	6-12-95	5-9	0.268	0.27	0.24	....	...	...		....	...	32152	Dc	±0.96	±0.31	±0.40	±0.63	....	0.63				22
23◆	....	None Since Public			...	Nil	....	28.5	46.4	73.9	6-30-95	355	7873	6194	Sp	...	pd1.52	d0.26	d2.74	....	d5.31	9 Mo Jun	d0.78	□d3.35	23
24	1995	0.10	11-22-95	11-8	0.10	[58]....	....	Book Value $21.35			6-30-95	332	...	6107	Sp	...	pΔ0.57	p1.02	1.16	P2.10	2.10				24
25	1990	Q0.05	12-29-95	12-13	0.20	0.20	0.20	119	293	90.7	9-30-95	0.77	...	[59]30499	Dc	0.90	0.51	Δ0.39	1.38	....	2.55	9 Mo Sep	0.76	1.93	25
26	1994	Q0.05	2-9-96	1-9	0.20	0.20	0.15	11.6	49.5	12.6	7-30-95	....	...	8227	Oc	0.64	1.02	1.35	1.82	P2.38	2.38				26
27	1949	Q0.46	11-17-95	11-1	1.84	1.84	1.80	10.0	34.3	16.9	9-30-95	73.1	...	3906	Dc	2.44	2.23	1.98	2.81	....	3.02	9 Mo Sep	2.48	2.69	27
28◆	1992	0.067	8-24-94	8-4	...	Nil	0.20	152	476	152	9-30-95	140	...	69971	Dc	1.17	1.41	1.55	1.13	E1.80	1.38	9 Mo Sep	1.10	1.35	28
29	1993	Q0.04	11-13-95	11-1	0.16	0.16	0.16	1.01	9.73	6.74	9-30-95	14.8	...	8759	Dc	p0.56	2.16	Δ0.39	0.43	....	d0.03	9 Mo Sep	0.65	0.19	29
30◆	1987	Q0.075	11-16-95	10-27	0.30	0.30	0.30	Book Value $20.08			9-30-95	267	...	18741	Dc	1.51	2.00	2.03	1.70	....	1.82	9 Mo Sep	1.27	1.39	30
31◆	1872	Q0.40	1-17-96	12-27	1.57½	1.60	1.47½	Equity per shr $37.84			9-30-95	620	5152	84532	Dc	4.68	Δd2.84	4.92	[60]5.12	E5.00	5.53	9 Mo Sep	3.59	4.00	31
32	1995	0.25	12-29-95	12-26	1.87½	3.00	....	Cv into 0.8475 St. Paul com,$59[64]				....	4140	...	Dc	...	...	...	....	....	....	Mand redemption 5-31-2025[65]			32
33	....	0.10	7-24-84	7-3	...	Nil	....	1.44	212	111	9-30-95	110	...	14653	Dc	d5.52	d5.13	Δ2.67	d0.53	....	d0.50	9 Mo Sep	0.30	0.33	33
34	....	Terms&trad. basis should be checked in detail						Wrrts expire 9-22-96				....	...	2370	Dc	...	...	...	....	....	....				34
35◆	1992	Q0.15	1-15-96	12-27	0.40	0.60	0.40	11.4	62.2	37.2	9-30-95	1.92	...	1865	Dc	0.85	*1.70	□1.07	1.96	....	1.75	9 Mo Sep	1.02	0.81	35
36	1960	Q0.16	1-2-96	12-14	0.64	0.64	0.64	Equity per shr $27.23			6-30-95	17459	1325	106387	Dc	3.90	4.18	□7.34	d4.31	E3.80	0.58	9 Mo Sep	d2.67	2.22	36
37	1994	Q0.998	11-1-95	10-11	3.994	3.99	3.972	Int based on Microsoft Cp com as defined				....	...	★1500	Dc	...	...	...	....	....	....	Mature 11-1-96[66]			37
38	1994	Q1.002	1-1-96	12-13	4.01	4.01	3.185	Int based on Hewlett-Packard com as defined				....	...	★1700	Dc	...	...	...	....	....	....	Mature 1-1-97[67]			38
39	1994	Q0.754	12-15-95	11-28	3.017	3.02	2.329	Int based on Promus Co com as defined				....	...	★1000	Dc	...	...	...	....	....	....	Mature 3-15-97[68]			39
40	1994	Q0.79⅝	11-1-95	10-11	3.18½	3.19	2.557	Int based on Amgen Inc com as defined				....	...	★1300	Dc	...	...	...	....	....	....	Mature 2-1-97[69]			40
41	1993	Q0.633	11-2-95	10-11	2.531	2.53	2.531	Int based on Digital Eqp com as defined				....	...	★1600	Dc	...	...	...	....	....	....	Mature 8-2-96[70]			41
42	1994	Q0.576	1-21-96	1-3	2.302	2.30	2.302	Int based on Oracle Sys Corp com as defined				....	...	★2000	Dc	...	...	...	....	....	....	Mature 10-21-96[71]			42
43	1994	Q0.529	11-1-95	10-11	2.116	2.12	1.587	Int based on Snapple Bev Corp com as defined				....	...	★2200	Dc	...	...	...	....	....	....	Mature 2-1-97[69]			43
44◆	....	t0.088	9-17-90	8-13	...	Nil	....	2.89	143	696	j9-30-94	....	...	5000	Sp	[73]0.03	▲d0.50	d0.55	0.12	....	0.12	No interim report			44
45◆	1909	Q0.39	1-15-96	12-6	1.55	1.56	1.51	140	470	691	9-30-95	1396	4565	116539	Dc	1.76	1.77	1.81	1.17	E1.90	1.91	12 Mo Sep	1.16	1.91	45
46	1981	0.009	1-16-96	12-27	0.299	0.30	0.533	Equity per shr $1.52			9-30-95	....	...	46609	Dc	0.45	0.68	0.79	0.49	....	0.34	9 Mo Sep	0.42	0.27	46
47	....	None Since Public			...	Nil	....	10.6	17.6	8.12	j7-31-94	....	...	4432	Jl	1.03	0.51	0.12	0.27	P0.16	j0.14	3 Mo Oct	0.04	0.02	47
48◆	1987	Q0.05	10-24-95	9-29	0.20	0.20	0.20	1.80	58.7	12.5	7-31-95	57.0	...	13613	Oc	0.55	0.39	0.88	1.14	P0.80	0.80				48
49	....	None Since Public			...	Nil	....	30.9	47.1	15.0	9-30-95	....	p...	★21356	Dc	...	...	...	pd0.23	....	....	9 Mo Sep	n/a	p0.32	49
50◆	1991	Q0.05	12-15-95	11-20	0.20	0.20	0.20	10.9	14.8	17.2	9-30-95	16.0	...	4499	Je	0.68	0.96	1.27	1.76	d2.54	d2.47	3 Mo Sep	0.19	0.26	50
51	1992	0.04	8-15-95	7-28	0.12	0.16	0.14	8.87	21.9	10.5	8-31-95	....	...	2327	Au	0.35	Δ0.78	0.57	0.71	0.58	0.58				51
52	....	None Since Public			...	Nil	....	4.63	61.3	52.1	9-30-95	210	...	21428	Dc	0.91	0.67	0.83	1.12	E1.40	1.35	9 Mo Sep	0.78	1.01	52

◆**Stock Splits & Divs By Line Reference Index** [2]1-for-5 REVERSE,'91:1-for-4 REVERSE,'93. [5]5-for-4,'95. [9]2-for-1,'93,'95. [12]2-for-1,'95. [13]2-for-1,'94:3-for-2,'95. [16]3-for-2,'91. [20]5-for-4,'95. [23]5-for-4,'94. [28]3-for-2,'95. [30]3-for-2,'94. [31]2-for-1,'94. [35]3-for-2,'94. [44]No adj for 60% stk div,'92. [45]2-for-1,'92. [48]3-for-2,'95. [50]2-for-1,'93.

¶ S&P 500 # MidCap 400 ✜ SmallCap 600 • Options

Index	Ticker	Name of Issue (Call Price of Pfd. Stocks)	Market	Com. Rank. & Pfd. Rating	Inst. Hold Cos	Inst. Hold Shs. (000)	Principal Business	Price Range 1971-93 High	1971-93 Low	1994 High	1994 Low	1995 High	1995 Low	Dec. Sales in 100s	December, 1995 Last Sale Or Bid High	Low	Last	%Div Yield	P-E Ratio	Total Return % Annualized 12 Mo	36 Mo	60 Mo
✜1	SANM	✔**Sanmina Corp**	NNM	NR	126	8300	Mfr electronic circuit boards	29½	10	31½	15¼	57¼	25¾	21568	56	47¾	51⅞	...	26	93.0	...	...
2	SANO	✔**Sano Corp**	NNM	NR	..	...	Dvp stge:transderm'l deliv sys	...	...	...	...	12¾	11	9478	12¾	11	11½	...	d	...	...	...
3	SAR	✔**Santa Anita Rlty(UNIT[51])**	NY,Ch,Ph	B–	31	2286	Turf racing: comm'l dev:R.E.	35	2⅛	20¾	13¼	17¾	11¾	5454	13¼	11⅞	11⅞	6.7	d	–5.9	–5.8	–4.2
4•[1]	SCOC	✔**Santa Cruz Operation**	NNM	NR	47	5556	Provides open sys software	13	4¾	11½	4⅞	15	5½	48607	8⅜	5⅞	6¼	...	d	–37.5	...	...
¶5•[2]	SFR	✔**Santa Fe Energy Res**	NY	NR	268	51320	Oil & gas explor,dev,prod'n	22⅜	7	10	7½	10⅝	7⅞	21861	10	9⅛	9⅝	...	80	18.5	5.3	–6.8
6	Pr	**7% cm Cv Pfd([52]NC)**	NY	B	29	3250		23	16	21½	15⅛	20	16⅛	2726	19¾	18¾	19⅛	7.3	..	...	...	...
7	Pr A	**8.25%[53]'DECS'([54]9.058)**	NY	B	22	9774	Divd Enhanced Cv Stock	...	...	10¼	8⅜	10¾	8½	380	10⅛	9¾	9⅞	7.4	..	...	...	...
8	SFF	**Santa Fe Energy Tr 'SPERs'**	NY	NR	10	148	Secure Principal Ener Receipt	23⅝	17⅝	21¾	14¼	19	15¼	2855	17⅞	17⅛	17½	9.1	..	32.0	8.0	...
¶9•[3]	GLD	✔**Santa Fe Pacific Gold**	NY,Ch,Ph	NR	398	77693	Explor,dvlp gold properties	...	...	17⅞	12¼	14	8⅞	86282	13⅛	11¾	12⅛	0.4	35	–7.2	...	...
10	SFL	✔**Santa Fe Pac Pipeline[55]**	NY,Ch,Ph	NR	52	1721	Refined petrol pipeline svcs	40¾	20	40	30	37⅞	30½	1805	37¼	35	36⅝	8.2	12	19.0	3.8	9.5
11	ISA	**Santa Isabel ADS[58]**	NY,Ch,Ph	NR	29	2269	Supermarket chain Chile & Peru	...	...	...	...	25⅝	17¼	4701	25⅝	24	24	0.7	38	...	...	...
12	SMO	✔**Santa Monica Bank**	AS	C	16	458	Commercial bkg, Calif	36⅛	9/16	10¾	7⅛	14	7⅛	1109	13⅞	12⅛	13¾	...	34	89.7	16.8	–1.4
¶13•[2]	SLE	✔**Sara Lee Corp**	NY,C,B,Ch,P,Ph	A	833	232694	Processed foods:consumer pr	32½	11/16	26	19⅜	33¾	24¼	147020	33¾	31½	32	2.4	19	29.3	3.5	17.8
14	STMI	✔**Satellite Tech Mgmt**	NNM	NR	19	355	Mfr satellite communic sys	13½	3⅝	15⅛	5⅞	23	10¼	6881	19⅞	14⅝	19¼	...	38	41.3	24.4	...
15	BFS	✔**Saul Centers**	NY,Ch	NR	55	4358	Real estate investment trust	20¼	17½	19⅝	13⅝	17¾	13½	13179	14⅜	13½	13⅝	11.4	21	2.8	...	...
#16	SFI	✔**Savannah Foods & Ind**	NY,Ph	↓B–	85	8786	Refined sugar	33	13/16	15⅜	10	14⅝	9	6138	13	11⅜	11⅜	0.9	d	–16.6	–5.0	–11.7
17	SAVLY	**Saville Systems ADS[62]**	NNM	NR	..	...	Telecom indus billing sys	...	...	...	...	17⅜	9½	36213	17⅜	13⅝	14¼	...	34	...	...	...
18	SPEI	✔**Savoy Pictures Entertainment[63]**	NNM	NR	63	14585	Finance,dstr motion pictures	22	14½	21	6	9⅝	4¾	17043	7⅛	6	6¼	...	d	3.1	...	...
19	SAYT	✔**Sayett Group**	NSC	NR	6	119	Mfr high tech projection eqp	10½	1⅞	6¼	2⅛	3¼	9/16	5308	1	9/16	9/16	...	d	–79.1	–40.2	...
#20•[4]	SBA	✔**Sbarro Inc**	NY,Ph	B+	137	9718	Italian fast food restaurants	33⅜	2½	29½	21¼	27⅞	19⅞	12611	23⅛	21¼	21½	3.5	21	–10.5	0.3	1.7
¶21•[5]	SBC	✔**SBC Communications**	NY,B,Ch,P,Ph	A	999	218116	Tel svc:Ark,Kan,Mo,Okl,Tex	47	9⅛	44⅜	36¾	58½	39⅝	129134	58½	54⅛	57¼	2.9	19	41.9	16.9	15.9
22	SBM	✔**SBM Industries**	AS	B–	6	14	Dstr watch batteries/publish'g	9⅝	¾	20¾	3¾	14⅝	3⅞	611	4¼	3⅞	4	...	80	–64.0	1.1	3.5
23	SCK	✔**SC Bancorp**	AS	C	15	1316	Commercial banking, Calif	12	4¾	6	3½	6¾	4⅛	7411	6⅛	5⅞	6⅛	...	77	53.1	5.3	...
#24•[6]	SCG	✔**SCANA Corp**	NY,B,C,Ch,P,Ph	A–	236	45561	Hldg co: electric & gas	26⅛	4⅜	25⅛	20½	28⅝	20⅝	36173	28⅝	25⅞	28⅝	5.0	17	46.9	19.8	17.9
25	SCF	✔**Scandinavia Co**	AS,Ch	NR	1	12	Investment co	10¾	3/16	1 11/16	⅞	3⅞	1 1/16	7471	3⅞	2⅛	2¼	...	4	80.0	108	–9.7
26	SBTVF	**Scandinavian Broadcstg Sys**	NNM	NR	..	...	TV broadcast'g Scandinavia	22½	12	28¾	19⅛	29½	19½	7047	24¼	21¼	21⅞	...	d	6.7	...	...
¶27•[5]	SCE	✔**SCEcorp**	NY,B,C,Ch,P,Ph	B+	546	152047	Hldg co for So'n Cal Edison	25¾	3⅝	20½	12⅜	18	14⅜	268772	17¾	14⅞	17⅝	5.7	11	24.7	–1.0	5.3
28	SRL	✔**Sceptre Resources**	AS,To,Mo	↑B–	31	16318	Oil/gas explor,dev,prod'n	67½	2½	11⅜	6¼	7⅞	5	299	6	5⅛	5⅞	...	..	–7.8	11.4	–28.4
29	SGK	✔**Schawk Inc'A'**	NY,Ch	B–	18	10911	Mfrs filtration elements	20½	5	13⅜	8¼	11¼	5⅞	2321	6⅞	5⅞	6⅝	3.9	26	–34.8	–9.6	5.0
30	ESH	✔**Scheib (Earl)**	AS	C	20	1935	Chain-auto paint shops	24⅜	1⅛	6¼	3½	8¾	4⅞	2423	8¾	6⅜	7¾	...	d	31.9	2.0	–7.3
31	HSIC	✔**Schein (Henry)**	NNM	NR	..	...	Market healthcare pds	...	...	...	...	29½	16	20184	29½	22¾	29½	...	..	...	...	...
32	SCHR	✔**Scherer Healthcare**	NNM	C	12	1018	Health care products/services	38	9	23	17⅝	20	2	377	4½	2½	2⅝	...	d	–86.9	–50.0	–29.0
#33•[2]	SHR	✔**Scherer (R.P.)**	NY,Ph	NR	230	21733	Mfr drug delivery systems	38⅞	18	45½	31¾	50¼	37¼	16308	49⅛	43⅛	49⅛	...	26	8.0	8.8	...
¶34•[7]	SGP	✔**Schering-Plough**	NY,B,C,Ch,P,Ph	A+	1104	242657	Pharmaceut'l/consumer prod	35½	3⅛	38	27¼	60¾	35½	199967	60¾	53¼	54¾	2.1	20	51.8	22.7	23.3
¶35•[1]	SLB	✔**Schlumberger Ltd**	NY,B,C,Ch,P,Ph	B+	1034	149257	Oilfield svs: electronics	87⅛	3⅞	63	50	70½	50⅛	141863	70½	63⅝	69¼	2.2	26	40.6	9.3	6.6
36	SCHN	✔**Schnitzer Steel Ind'A'**	NNM	NR	45	2741	Recycles steel/mfr steel prd	30¾	18	33¼	17½	31	17⅜	2535	31	29	30½	0.7	11	58.8	...	...
#37•[8]	SCHL	✔**Scholastic Corp**	NNM	NR	177	10095	Publish child'ns books,edu mtl	54¼	22½	52½	33¾	78¼	47¾	17875	78¼	68½	77¾	...	29	51.0	33.2	...
38	SHLR	✔**Schuler Homes**	NNM	NR	77	8831	Residential homebldg,Hawaii	30¼	9¾	29¼	13½	14¼	7¾	7411	9⅛	7¾	7¾	...	10	–43.2	–20.6	...
#39•[9]	SHLM	✔**Schulman (A.)**	NNM	A	189	23575	Plastic mfr/merchant resins	28¼	¼	29¾	21	32¾	17¼	56427	22½	17½	22½	1.5	16	–15.6	0.7	7.1
40	SHC	✔**Schult Homes Corp**	AS,Ch	B	30	1641	Design/build manufact'd homes	19⅜	1	17⅞	10⅝	17¾	9¾	1158	17¾	16¼	17½	0.9	14	41.8	1.6	33.7
41	SAVO	✔**Schultz Sav-O Stores**	NNM	A–	31	2138	Food wholesaler/supermkts	9⅜	⅜	10⅛	7⅝	15½	9¾	361	15½	14¾	14¾	2.2	13	54.6	31.7	20.7
#42•[3]	SCH	✔**Schwab(Chas)Corp**	NY,Ch,P,Ph	NR	224	73649	Discount brokerage/svcs	12¾	⅞	12⅜	7⅞	29	11	195922	24¼	16½	20⅛	0.8	20	72.5	51.9	64.7
43	SWM	**Schweitzer-Mauduit Intl**	NY	NR	..	...	Mfr tobacco-related paper	...	...	...	...	25⅞	20⅜	64958	23⅝	20⅜	23⅛	2.6	..	...	...	...
44	SRVPrT	**SCI Fin $3.125[68]'TECONS'([69]52.50)**	NY	BBB	48	3151	Subsid Service Corp Intl	...	...	52¼	50	76	52⅛	1477	74	71½	74	4.2	..	...	...	...
✜45•[8]	SCIS	✔**SCI Systems**	NNM	B+	167	16244	Electronic prod/systems	23⅜	1/16	22¼	12⅝	38	17	127726	38	29⅜	31	...	17	73.4	19.6	31.1
✜46•[3]	SCLN	✔**SciClone Pharmaceuticals**	NNM	NR	38	3183	Dvlp stge:mkt therapeutic drugs	27⅛	5⅝	24⅝	4⅜	9¾	3¾	44332	5¾	3¾	5⅛	...	d	–21.9	–31.9	...
¶47•[10]	SFA	✔**Scientific-Atlanta**	NY,B,C,Ch,Ph	B+	347	59027	Electronic instr & commun eq	19½	3/16	23¼	12½	24⅞	11⅜	86917	17	13¾	15	0.4	27	–27.0	5.1	30.2
48•[1]	SGIH	✔**Scientific Games Hldgs**	NNM	NR	109	9416	Mfr instant lottery tickets	12	7	25½	10⅝	40¾	17¾	19303	39¼	32¼	37¾	...	26	49.7	...	...
49	STIZ	✔**Scientific Technologies**	NNM	B+	15	584	Mfr electr equip/software	10⅛	15/16	7⅝	3¼	24	4	1206	16	11	11½	1.2	19	145	89.1	55.4
50•[11]	SCIO	✔**Scios Nova**	NNM,Ph	C	65	11300	Biotechnology R & D	29¾	4¼	11⅛	5	8¾	2⅞	58042	4½	3¼	4¼	...	d	–31.0	–22.5	–13.7
51•[2]	SCIXF	**Scitex Corp, Ord**	NNM	NR	111	15488	Imaging, comput graphics	44⅜	⅞	26⅞	15¼	24¾	12	53075	16	13⅜	13⅝	3.8	..	–14.7	–29.4	0.0
52	SCP	✔**Scope Indus**	AS,P	B–	15	177	Waste mat recycl'g, o & g	41⅞	1/16	26⅜	23⅜	32½	23⅛	15	32¼	31⅜	32B	1.6	18	38.2	6.6	0.7

Uniform Footnote Explanations-See Page 4. Other: [1]CBOE:Cycle 2. [2]ASE:Cycle 1. [3]CBOE:Cycle 3. [4]ASE:Ph:Cycle 3. [5]P:Cycle 1. [6]P,Ph:Cycle 1. [7]P:Cycle 2. [8]CBOE:Cycle 1. [9]P,Cycle 3. [10]P:Cycle 3. [11]ASE,P:Cycle 3. [51]Trades with 1 shr of Santa Anita Operating. [52]HRO on change of ownership of co. [53]Divd Enhanced Cv Stock. [54]Fr 5-15-97 in com stk. [55]L.P. Units. [56]100% non-taxable,'94. [57]Incl 11M pref units. [58]Ea ADS rep 15 com, no par. [59]®$1.57,'95. [60]Incl $0.76 non-taxable,'94. [61]Dec'92 & prior. [62]Ea ADS rep 1 Ord shr. [63]Silver King Communic plan mgr, .2 com. [64]11 Mo Dec'92. [65]Subsid pfd. [66]®$2.37,'95. [67]®$1.37,'94. [68]Term Cv Shrs Sr'A'. [69]Fr6/7/97-1•/99 re-spec cond scale to$50 2004. [70]Into Service Corp Int com. [71]If SCI com 125% Cv price 20 out 30 trad days. [72]®$1.56,'95.

Splits ◆ Index	Cash Divs. Ea.Yr. Since	Dividends: Latest Payment Period $	Date	Ex. Div.	Total $ So Far 1995	Ind. Rate	Paid 1994	Financial Position Mil-$ Cash& Equiv.	Curr. Assets	Curr. Liab.	Balance Sheet Date	Capitalization Lg Trm Debt Mil-$	Shs. 000 Pfd.	Com.	Earnings $ Per Shr. Years End	1991	1992	1993	1994	1995	Last 12 Mos.	Interim Earnings Period	$ per Shr. 1994	1995	Index
1	....	None Since Public			...	Nil	....	29.7	69.1	28.5	7-01-95	1.11	...	p8453	Sp	...	pd0.01	□1.03	d0.40	P2.02	2.02				1
2	....	None Since Public			...	Nil	....	2.73	2.77	1.78	6-30-95	p....	p...	★8817	Dc	d0.09	d0.16	d0.31	d0.71	....	d0.06	9 Mo Sep	d1.17	d0.52	2
3	1977	Q0.20	1-26-96	1-3	0.80	0.80	1.08	Equity per shr $2.74			9-30-95	115	...	11271	Dc	0.89	0.66	0.04	0.21	....	d3.09	9 Mo Sep	0.60	d2.70	3
4	....	None Since Public			...	Nil	....	49.6	107	43.7	6-30-95	0.26	...	30955	Sp	...	p0.32	0.47	0.45	Pd0.20	d0.20				4
5	1990	0.04	10-22-93	9-24	...	Nil	....	41.8	141	125	9-30-95	344	15700	90300	Dc	0.29	d0.07	d0.94	0.06	E0.12	0.09	9 Mo Sep	0.05	0.08	5
6	1992	Q0.35	3-1-96	1-30	1.40	1.40	1.40	Cv into 1.3913 com, $14.37				....	5000	...	Dc	...	b0.83	...	....	....	....	Mand conv 5-2-97 at re-specified cond.			6
7	1994	Q0.183	2-15-96	1-26	0.732	0.732	0.344	Cv into 0.8474 com$10.473				....	10700	...	Dc	...	...	...	....	....	....	Mandatory conversion into one com 5-15-98			7
8	1993	Q0.40	11-30-95	11-10	1.60	1.60	1.60	Liq date 2-15-2008				....	...	6300	Dc	...	...	...	....	....	....				8
9	1995	A0.05	6-30-95	5-30	0.05	0.05	....	65.2	200	65.5	9-30-95	200	...	131449	Dc	...	...	p0.34	0.46	E0.35	0.37	9 Mo Sep	0.34	0.25	9
10	1989	Q0.75	11-14-95	10-27	2.95	3.00	[56]2.80	43.2	88.8	27.5	6-30-95	355	...	[57]±19148	Dc	3.10	□2.77	2.13	3.93	....	3.19	9 Mo Sep	2.99	2.25	10
11	....	Plan annual div			...	0.17	....	8.45	48.6	48.7	3-31-95	p9.30	...	★315142	Dc	0.34	0.41	0.48	0.53	....	0.63	3 Mo Mar	0.10	0.20	11
12◆	....	0.15	10-1-92	9-10	...	Nil	....	Book Value $8.83			9-30-95	2.00	...	7077	Dc	±1.70	±d1.33	±d1.55	0.07	....	0.40	9 Mo Sep	0.13	0.46	12
13◆	1946	Q0.19	1-1-96	11-29	0.68	0.76	0.64	222	5287	4913	9-30-95	1873	4570	483861	Je	1.07	1.54	1.40	□0.44	[59]1.62	1.66	3 Mo Sep	0.33	0.37	13
14	....	None Since Public			...	Nil	....	10.6	32.7	8.64	9-30-95	4.40	...	5812	Dc	Δ0.81	0.81	Δd0.47	0.28	....	0.51	9 Mo Sep	0.15	0.38	14
15	1993	Q0.39	1-31-96	1-12	1.56	1.56	[60]1.56	Equity per shr Neg			9-30-95	268	...	11879	Dc	...	p0.39	p0.43	□0.87	....	0.65	9 Mo Sep	□0.73	0.51	15
16	1924	Q0.02½	12-29-95	12-6	0.21	0.10	0.54	10.8	258	175	7-02-95	112	...	26238	Sp	1.43	□[61]1.03	Δ0.56	0.22	Pd0.13	d0.13				16
17	....	None Since Public			...	Nil	....	0.32	9.83	5.15	9-30-95	0.06	...	★17504	Dc	d0.03	d0.02	Nil	0.34	....	0.42	9 Mo Sep	0.24	0.32	17
18	....	None Since Public			...	Nil	....	Equity per shr Neg			9-30-95	51.7	...	30042	Dc	...	[64]0.06	d0.71	d2.58	....	d2.63	9 Mo Sep	d1.30	d1.35	18
19	....	None Since Public			...	Nil	....	0.81	2.94	0.94	9-30-95	....	...	6353	Dc	0.14	d0.24	0.12	d0.41	....	d0.57	9 Mo Sep	d0.18	d0.34	19
20◆	1993	Q0.19	1-5-96	12-19	0.73	0.76	0.613	68.4	77.6	24.5	10-08-95	....	...	20342	Dc	1.07	1.18	Δ1.40	1.63	E1.05↓	1.54	40 Wk Oct	0.99	0.90	20
21◆	1984	Q0.41¼	2-1-96	1-8	1.63¼	1.65	1.56¼	455	3790	5283	9-30-95	5660	...	609860	Dc	□1.93	2.17	□2.39	2.74	E3.10	2.96	9 Mo Sep	2.03	□2.25	21
22	....	s0.097	3-22-83	2-22	...	Nil	....	0.20	5.99	3.29	9-30-95	1.40	...	2028	Dc	d0.41	d0.14	0.02	0.55	....	0.05	9 Mo Sep	0.48	d0.02	22
23	....	0.20	1-15-92	12-10	...	Nil	....	Book Value $5.98			9-30-95	....	...	7469	Dc	0.69	d0.40	□d0.78	0.49	....	0.08	9 Mo Sep	0.39	d0.02	23
24◆	1946	Q0.36	1-1-96	12-6	1.43¼	1.44	1.40	104	435	504	9-30-95	1535	1145	103359	Dc	1.69	1.42	1.86	1.59	E1.70	1.56	12 Mo Sep	1.38	1.56	24
25	....	0.23	4-24-89		...	Nil	....	No Recent Finl Reporting				....	...	...	Ja	d8.62	d0.26	P1.32	P0.34	....	0.54	6 Mo Jul	0.13	0.33	25
26	....	None Since Public			...	Nil	....	46.5	85.7	40.3	3-31-95	★136	...	13478	Dc	...	pd0.86	d0.23	d0.22	....	d3.12	9 Mo Sep	d0.28	d3.18	26
27◆	1909	Q0.25	1-31-96	1-3	1.00	1.00	1.21	545	2675	3358	9-30-95	6751	[65]18350	445289	Dc	1.61	1.66	1.43	1.52	E1.65	1.64	12 Mo Sep	1.53	1.64	27
28◆	....	None Paid			...	Nil	....	0.26	46.6	52.3	j12-31-94	172	...	56686	Dc	d22.90	d0.04	0.43	0.43	jE0.35	j0.15	9 Mo Sep	0.41	0.13	28
29	1977	tQ0.06½	11-15-95	10-30	0.26	0.26	t0.26	1.15	54.8	29.2	9-30-95	79.5	...	±19256	Dc	±0.43	±0.47	±0.14	±p0.64	....	0.26	9 Mo Sep	p0.56	0.18	29
30	1981	0.04½	10-15-93	9-29	...	Nil	....	5.51	12.3	6.46	10-31-95	....	...	4568	Ap	d0.03	0.33	□Nil	d0.40	d1.22	d0.84	6 Mo Oct	0.30	0.68	30
31	....	None Since Public			...	Nil	....	4.96	177	83.0	7-01-95	p10.3	...	★18316	Dc	...	...	...	p0.50	....	....	6 Mo Jun	n/a	p0.25	31
32	....	None Paid			...	Nil	....	1.76	15.3	17.0	9-30-95	4.94	30	4289	Mr	d0.37	d0.38	Δd1.17	d2.39	....	d2.10	6 Mo Sep	d0.48	d0.19	32
33	....	None Since Public			...	Nil	....	29.2	219	101	9-30-95	192	...	23362	Mr	□d1.59	□Δ1.17	□1.27	1.83	....	1.89	6 Mo Sep	0.84	0.90	33
34◆	1952	Q0.29	11-28-95	11-1	1.12½	1.16	0.99	337	1930	2219	9-30-95	86.3	...	367568	Dc	1.51	□Δ1.80	□2.12	2.41	E2.80	2.28	9 Mo Sep	1.87	1.74	34
35	1957	Q0.37½	1-5-96	12-14	1.35	1.50	1.20	1238	4005	2866	6-30-95	447	...	241882	Dc	3.42	2.75	□2.40	2.21	E2.72	2.64	9 Mo Sep	1.57	2.00	35
36	1994	Q0.05	11-24-95	11-7	0.20	0.20	0.20	1.60	98.6	41.8	8-31-95	64.7	...	±7889	Au	d0.50	d0.75	0.42	1.47	2.82	2.82				36
37	....	None Since Public			...	Nil	....	0.49	380	184	8-31-95	175	...	±15738	My	±1.29	±1.08	±1.77	□±2.04	±[66]2.38	2.70	6 Mo Nov	±1.00	±1.32	37
38	....	None Since Public			...	Nil	....	Equity per shr $8.48			9-30-95	57.5	...	20874	Dc	p0.68	p0.80	p1.49	[67]1.47	....	0.81	9 Mo Sep	1.17	0.51	38
39◆	1968	Q0.08½	11-1-95	10-19	0.34	0.34	0.297	144	491	128	8-31-95	75.1	11	37579	Au	1.14	1.18	□1.04	1.19	1.43	1.43				39
40	1992	Q0.04	11-20-95	11-1	0.16	0.16	0.16	4.30	37.6	36.5	9-30-95	1.14	...	3731	Je	0.98	1.29	1.16	1.60	1.16	1.26	3 Mo Sep	0.40	0.50	40
41◆	1960	Q0.08	11-24-95	11-8	0.22	0.32	0.10	15.6	55.1	30.4	10-07-95	17.3	3	4654	Dc	0.43	0.45	0.88	1.05	....	1.18	40 Wk Oct	0.70	0.83	41
42◆	1989	Q0.04	11-15-95	10-30	0.14	0.16	0.093	Equity per shr $3.17			9-30-95	216	...	174678	Dc	0.28	0.47	□0.70	0.77	E1.00	0.92	9 Mo Sep	0.58	0.73	42
43	....	Plan qtly div			...	0.60	....	1.40	127	98.7	p6-30-95	91.0	...	16045	Dc	...	...	...	p1.66	....	....	6 Mo Jun	n/a	p0.95	43
44	1994	M0.26	12-29-95	12-26	3.125	3.125	0.15⅝	Cv into 1.6617 com, $30.09[70]				....	3000	...	Dc	...	...	...	....	....	....	Spcl Red fr 6-7-97 to 12-5-99[71]			44
45	....	None Since Public			...	Nil	....	20.1	947	579	9-24-95	194	...	29490	Je	Δ0.16	0.18	1.09	0.76	[72]1.63	1.78	3 Mo Sep	0.36	0.51	45
46	....	None Since Public			...	Nil	....	35.7	40.6	4.23	9-30-95	....	...	16807	Dc	d0.41	d0.73	d0.89	d1.02	....	d0.86	9 Mo Sep	d0.81	d0.65	46
47◆	1976	Q0.01½	12-20-95	11-29	0.06	0.06	0.06	50.5	585	247	9-29-95	0.76	...	76241	Je	■0.02	0.23	□0.33	0.45	0.83	0.55	3 Mo Sep	0.16	d0.12	47
48◆	....	None Since Public			...	Nil	....	17.0	48.7	13.0	9-30-95	0.65	...	12918	Dc	...	p0.10	0.47	1.21	....	1.47	9 Mo Sep	0.95	1.21	48
49	1988	Q0.03½	12-1-95	11-16	0.13	0.14	0.10	5.95	15.6	4.29	9-30-95	0.05	...	9608	Dc	0.10	0.14	0.26	0.39	....	0.61	9 Mo Sep	0.27	0.50	49
50	....	None Since Public			...	Nil	....	26.4	29.1	15.7	9-30-95	1.25	16	36006	Dc	d1.18	d5.76	d1.05	d0.79	....	d0.76	9 Mo Sep	d0.64	d0.61	50
51	1990	t0.13	9-7-95	8-21	t0.39	0.52	t0.52	289	759	191	12-31-94	0.18	...	42790	Dc	2.70	3.02	Δ2.10	1.49	....	0.04	9 Mo Sep	1.02	d0.43	51
52	1976	0.50	1-8-96	11-29	0.35	0.50	0.30	5.35	9.02	3.82	9-30-95	....	...	1234	Je	1.19	d0.51	d8.77	1.24	1.15	1.78	3 Mo Sep	0.24	0.87	52

◆**Stock Splits & Divs By Line Reference Index** [12]6-for-5,'91. [13]2-for-1,'92. [20]3-for-2,'94. [21]2-for-1,'93. [24]2-for-1,'95. [27]2-for-1,'93. [28]1-for-10 REVERSE,'92. [34]2-for-1,'95. [39]3-for-2,'92:5-for-4,'94. [41]2-for-1,'95. [42]3-for-2,'91,'93,'95:2-for-1,'95. [47]3-for-2,'92:2-for-1,'94. [48]2-for-1,'95.

¶ S&P 500 # MidCap 400 ✤ SmallCap 600 • Options

Index	Ticker	Name of Issue (Call Price of Pfd. Stocks)	Market	Com. Rank. & Pfd. Rating	Inst. Hold Cos	Inst. Hold Shs. (000)	Principal Business	1971-93 High	1971-93 Low	1994 High	1994 Low	1995 High	1995 Low	Dec. Sales in 100s	Dec. 1995 Last Sale Or Bid High	Low	Last	%Div Yield	P-E Ratio	Total Return % Annualized 12 Mo	36 Mo	60 Mo
1	SCOP	Scopus Technology	NNM	NR	..	...	Info mgmt software sys	...	...	...	...	28¾	12	15991	28¾	19¼	25¼	...	..	...	...	...
2	SCT	✓Scotsman Industries	NY,Ph	NR	84	5928	Mfr refrigeration products	15	4⅝	18¼	13	20	15⅛	2235	17¾	16⅜	17⅝	0.6	11	3.5	23.7	22.3
3	SCOT	✓Scott/Stringfellow Finl	NNM,Ch	B+	4	35	Regional securities broker	13½	5⅝	13⅜	11	14¾	11	102	14¾	13½	13¾B	2.9	11	26.2	15.1	25.9
✤4	SMG	✓Scotts Co 'A'	NY	NR	114	11546	Mfr lawn,golf turf care prd	24½	13½	20¼	14½	24	15⅝	9678	20½	19¼	19⅝	...	18	24.0	2.7	...
5	SGD	✓Scott's Liquid Gold	NY,Ph	B–	11	831	Mfr household chemical prod	11	¼	9¼	3⅜	6⅛	2½	3534	3⅜	2⅝	2⅞	3.5	11	–49.1	39.5	44.7
6	POOL	✓SCP Pool	NNM	NR	..	...	Dstr swimming pools/prod	...	...	...	...	11¼	9¾	4558	10¾	10	10½	...	..	...	...	...
7	SSP	✓Scripps(E.W.)'A'	NY,Ch,Ph	B+	120	20260	Newspapers:TV/radio:CATV	30⅞	13	31	23	40⅝	26¾	13716	40⅜	37½	39⅜	1.3	27	34.4	19.8	20.8
8	SCOMC	SCS/COMPUTE Inc[53]	NSC	↓C	12	534	Income tax & acct'g software	10¼	1¾	3⅜	1½	6¾	1¾	9795	6¾	2⅜	6⅜	...	51	234	12.1	21.7
9	SDLI	✓SDL Inc	NNM	NR	68	4017	Semiconductors & circuits	...	...	...	...	35½	16	7394	25¾	21¾	24	...	..	...	...	...
10	SCRA	✓Sea Containers Ltd Cl'A'[54]	NY	B	35	4360	Marine cargo containers	28⅜	12⅝	18	11¾	20¼	13⅛	3542	17¾	17	17⅝	4.4	2	40.1	4.7	...
11	SCR B	✓ Cl'B'	NY,Ch,Ph	B	16	484		37⅛	6	18¼	12	20	13⅜	318	18⅜	16⅞	17¼	4.1	2	35.9	3.1	0.6
12	Pr D	$4.125cmCv Pfd([55]50.41:SF50)	NY,Ch	B+	1	51		119⅝	34½	57½	15⅜	...	...	...	...	...	56B	7.4	..	...	...	...
13	Pr E	$4.00 cm Cv Pfd([57]52.40)	NY	B+	25	1087		59⅝	42½	53	40½	49¾	40½	679	46¾	43¼	43¾	9.1	..	...	...	...
14	SEB	✓Seaboard Corp	AS([50])	B	35	224	Food prodn:poultry,pork:bank'g	257	4⅝	205	158¼	306	159	23	268¾	242¼	265B	0.4	12	64.8	13.6	17.6
15	SBCFA	✓Seacoast Banking FL'A'	NNM	A–	27	887	Commercial bkg,Florida	22½	5½	20	16⅛	25¼	16¼	1896	24¼	21¾	21¾	2.8	14	29.6	17.5	24.4
16	CKOR	✓SEACOR Holdings	NNM	NR	37	2814	Oper fleet o&g svc vessels	28	13	23½	17¾	28	18	26270	28	22½	27	...	24	36.7	23.4	...
17	SFLD	✓Seafield Capital Corp	NNM	NR	55	2819	Insurance/hlth testing labs	48¼	3⅝	41¼	30¾	40⅝	32⅛	1158	36	33¼	34	3.5	d	2.6	4.5	13.6
#18•[1]	SEG	✓Seagate Technology	NY,Ch,Ph	B	369	60364	Computer magnetic disc drives	45¾	4	28¾	18⅝	54¾	23⅝	229405	54¾	43⅜	47½	...	10	97.9	36.0	32.2
¶19•[2]	VO	✓Seagram Co. Ltd	NY,To,B,Ch,Ph,Mo	A–	494	112596	Produce, mkt distilled spirits	30⅞	1⅝	32⅝	26¼	39½	25½	92880	36⅝	34¼	34½	1.7	55	18.6	12.6	11.6
#20•[3]	SGO	✓Seagull Energy	NY,B,Ch,Ph,P	B–	174	29491	Natural gas explr,prodn	32⅞	2 7/16	29¾	17⅝	22½	15¼	35040	22¼	18½	22¼	...	..	15.6	12.4	8.9
#21	SEE	✓Sealed Air	NY,B,Ch	A–	201	30843	Protective packaging mtl	16	½	18⅛	13⅜	30¾	18	25320	30¾	25¼	28	...	23	61.6	31.1	35.6
22	SRCO	✓Sealright Co	NNM	B+	59	3683	Paperboard/plastic containers	26¾	10	20¾	12	19¾	10½	5720	11½	10½	11⅛	4.3	22	–41.8	–17.9	–7.9
23	SCC	Sears Canada	To,Mo	B	15	9291	Mail order/dept stores	16½	4¼	10	6½	8½	5½	18210	6⅜	5½	6	4.0	18	–19.9	–1.4	...
¶24•[4]	S	✓Sears,Roebuck	NY,B,C,Ch,P,Ph	B–	936	267916	Large retailer gen mdse:insur	61⅝	14⅜	55⅛	42⅛	61¼	29⅝	189847	40¾	37¾	39	2.4	16	...	...	...
25	FOTO	✓Seattle FilmWorks	NNM	B	36	2535	Mail order:film proc'g/eqp	6⅝	¼	13⅝	6	23¾	10⅞	5135	21¾	18	20¾	...	28	87.7	72.5	63.4
26	SEWY	✓Seaway Food Town	NNM	B	18	565	Food supermkts Ohio, Mich	25	1 3/16	12¾	9½	17¼	9½	137	17¼	16	16½B	2.4	8	65.7	17.4	4.7
27	SECM	✓Secom General	NNM	B–	4	40	Mfr custom tooling	41⅜	15/16	3¾	2	4⅛	1⅝	1692	3⅛	2½	2¾	...	10	18.9	–13.5	8.8
28	SECD	✓Second Bancorp	NNM	A–	13	166	General banking,Ohio	21⅜	6¾	22	20⅜	30	20⅛	98	29⅞	28¼	28¾B	2.6	12	41.3	25.7	38.6
29	SCUR	Secure Computing	NNM	NR	..	...	Computer security sys	...	...	...	...	64½	16	21107	64½	47½	56	...	..	...	...	...
30	SFBM	✓Security Bancorp	NNM	NR	15	163	Svgs bank:Billings, Montana	23¼	4¼	20¾	17¼	21¼	17¼	462	21⅛	20	21	e2.8	13	18.7	22.1	30.1
31	SECP	✓Security Capital	NNM	NR	54	2598	Savings & loan, Wisconsin	25	25	51¾	34	62¼	41¾	8531	62¼	59¼	60¼	...	23	42.5	...	...
32	SCN	✓Security Capital Ind Tr	NY,Ch,Ph	NR	115	23798	Real estate investment tr	...	...	18¼	11½	17¾	14½	6664	17⅝	16⅛	17½	5.8	30	9.9	...	...
33	PTR	✓Security Cap Pacific Tr	NY,Ch,Ph	NR	157	30089	Real estate investment trust	21⅝	1½	21¾	15½	20½	16⅜	12294	20½	19	19¾	6.3	23	15.3	15.2	24.6
34	Pr A	7% cm Cv Sr'A'Pfd([66]25)	NY	BBB+	61	8057		28	25⅛	29¼	20	25⅝	21¼	1479	25⅝	24	24½	7.1	..	...	...	...
35	SRC	✓Security-Connecticut Corp	NY	NR	74	5753	Life insurance/annuity prod	...	...	24½	18	28½	22	9120	27⅛	25⅛	27⅛	1.8	9	25.0	...	...
36	SDTI	✓Security Dynamics Technologies	NNM	NR	62	7156	Dvlp,mkt computer security pds	...	...	10⅛	7	58¼	8⅞	36942	58¼	42¾	54½	...	..	539	...	...
37	SEER	✓Seer Tech	NNM	NR	38	1514	Dvlp/designs software prd	...	...	...	...	22	10¾	16209	15	10¾	12½	...	28	...	...	...
✤38	SEIC	✓SEI Corp	NNM	B+	87	11017	Diversified investment services	27¼	2⅛	28½	16¾	24½	16¾	5730	23¾	21	21¾	0.9	23	27.2	14.0	15.6
✤39•[5]	SEI	✓Seitel Inc	NY,Ph	B	96	5032	Acquires,mkts seismic data	15⅞	¾	37	13⅜	35½	18⅞	24087	35½	24⅞	35⅜	...	27	63.6	49.3	30.0
40	SLS	✓Selas Corp of Amer	AS,B,Ch,Ph	B–	11	460	Heat processing equipment	19¼	1 7/16	15⅝	9½	10	7⅛	1335	9⅞	7⅞	9¾	2.5	17	1.3	–2.5	4.8
✤41	SIGI	✓Selective Insurance Gr	NNM	B	120	7587	Property/casualty insurance	31	1¼	30¾	23	38⅜	24½	5762	38¼	35½	35½	3.2	10	48.5	23.0	28.2
42	SEM	✓Semiconductor Pkg Materials	AS	NR	17	1062	Mfr fine wire/metal ribbon	9	1½	7	3	14¼	5¾	10834	9⅝	8¼	9¼	...	19	57.4	47.2	...
43	SMTL	✓Semitool Inc	NNM	NR	47	3910	Mfrs semiconductor mfg equip	...	...	...	...	36¾	8⅝	21267	17½	12½	13	...	11	...	...	...
44	SMTC	Semtech Corp	NNM	B–	28	1816	Mfr silicon rectifiers	12½	⅞	3⅜	1 13/16	31¾	2⅝	24992	25⅝	16⅜	19½	...	21	609	121	81.1
45	SNTKY	Senetek Plc ADS[71]	NSC	NR	7	1066	Dvlp stge:biotechnology R&D	10¼	¼	6⅛	1¾	2⅞	1 1/16	56608	1⅞	1 1/16	1 5/16	...	d	–28.9	7.3	–2.6
#46•[6]	SRM	✓Sensormatic Elect	NY,Ch,Ph	B+	355	62128	Electronic article surveil sys	35	⅛	39¼	26	38¼	16¼	204495	21½	16¼	17⅜	1.3	18	–50.3	–5.4	12.0
47•[4]	SEPR	✓Sepracor Inc	NNM	NR	83	12986	Pharmaceut'l prd/drug R&D	15¾	6	9⅝	3¾	22⅞	4	58041	19	13⅝	18⅜	...	d	346	22.5	...
#48	SQA.A	✓Sequa Corp Cl'A'	NY	C	93	3039	Mfr jet engine components	88⅜	17⅞	39¾	17⅝	32⅛	21⅞	2489	31⅛	28	30½	...	d	20.2	0.4	–10.9
49	SQA.B	✓ Class B (10 votes)	NY	C	17	1112	specialty instr & chemicals	91½	8⅞	40¼	21	40	23	257	40	38½	39½	...	d	45.0	8.0	–9.4
50	Pr	$5 cm Cv Pfd(100)vtg	NY	NR	11	441		115½	51½	75	53	67½	51	35	61	58	58	8.6	..	...	...	...
#51•[6]	SQNT	✓Sequent Computer Sys	NNM	B–	171	27865	Parallel multiprocess sys	34	4¾	20⅝	11⅛	25⅞	13¾	176269	16¾	13¾	14½	...	13	–28.4	–11.1	–4.0
52	SEQS	✓Sequoia Systems	NNM	↑B–	16	1402	Mfr high-perform computer sys	18⅜	1⅜	6⅞	3⅛	10	3½	31259	6⅛	5	5¼	...	13	47.4	32.6	0.5

Uniform Footnote Explanations-See Page 4. Other: [1]ASE:Cycle 3. [2]P:Cycle 2,To:Cycle 1. [3]Ph:Cycle 2. [4]CBOE:Cycle 1. [5]CBOE:Cycle 2. [6]ASE:Cycle 1. [51]®$1.35,'94. [52]®$1.64,'93. [53]Thomson Corp offer,$6.75 to Jan 25. [54]0.10 vtg. [55]Thru 4-15-96,scale to $50 in'96:SF fr 2001. [56]Mand Red by Apr 15,2011. [57]To 7-14-96,scale to $50 in 2001. [58]®$1.24,'94. [59]®$3.06,'95. [60]Stk dstr Allstate Corp,'95. [61]®$0.29,'94. [62]®$2.01,'94. [63]To be determined. [64]Incl $0.1371 non-taxable,'94. [65]Incl $0.31815 non-taxable,'94. [66]Fr 11-30-2003. [67]Incl current amts. [68]®$1.10,'94. [69]®$2.66,'94. [70]®$0.22,'95. [71]Ea ADS rep 1 ord,5p. [72]Fiscal May '92 & prior.

Splits ◆ Index	Cash Divs. Ea.Yr. Since	Dividends: Latest Payment Period $	Date	Ex. Div.	Total $ So Far 1995	Ind. Rate	Paid 1994	Financial Position Mil-$ Cash& Equiv.	Curr. Assets	Curr. Liab.	Balance Sheet Date	Capitalization Lg Trm Debt Mil-$	Shs. 000 Pfd.	Com.	Earnings $ Per Shr. Years End	1991	1992	1993	1994	1995	Last 12 Mos.	Interim Earnings Period	$ per Shr. 1994	1995	Index
1	....	None Since Public			...	Nil	....	2.09	10.9	5.33	9-30-95	....	p...	★11268	Mr	0.01	0.03	0.07	0.10	....	0.08	6 Mo Sep	0.04	0.02	1
2	1989	Q0.02½	1-15-96	12-27	0.10	0.10	0.10	11.5	132	63.6	10-01-95	84.7	2000	8964	Dc	d0.24	0.90	1.06	[51]1.49	....	1.54	9 Mo Sep	1.35	1.40	2
3◆	1987	Q0.10	1-12-96	12-27	0.40	0.40	0.375	Book Value $12.45			9-29-95	....	...	2124	Je	0.83	1.53	[52]1.65	1.40	1.00	1.29	3 Mo Sep	0.28	0.57	3
4	....	None Since Public			...	Nil	....	10.7	329	135	7-01-95	243	10000	18672	Sp	p0.89	*0.84	□1.07	□1.27	P1.11	1.11				4
5	1994	0.10	4-7-95	3-20	0.10	0.10	0.10	5.15	15.3	11.1	9-30-95	11.4	...	10021	Dc	*0.14	Δ0.01	0.30	0.57	....	0.27	9 Mo Sep	0.42	0.12	5
6	....	None Since Public			...	Nil	....	4.48	57.7	30.3	p6-30-95	p31.1	...	★4123	Dc	...	...	...	p0.58	....	....	6 Mo Jun	n/a	p0.95	6
7	1922	Q0.13	12-8-95	11-21	0.50	0.52	0.44	52.6	354	262	9-30-95	63.5	...	±80020	Dc	±0.87	□±1.43	±1.72	±1.61	....	1.45	9 Mo Sep	±1.32	±1.16	7
8	....	None Since Public			...	Nil	....	2.26	7.89	13.4	7-31-95	7.50	100	2564	Ja	0.47	Δd2.92	d1.36	0.14	....	0.13	9 Mo Oct	d2.03	d2.04	8
9	....	None Since Public			...	Nil	....	21.8	41.4	9.94	9-30-95	....	...	7069	Dc	...	...	...	p0.51	....	....	9 Mo Sep	n/a	0.56	9
10	1992	Q0.19¼	11-21-95	11-1	0.77	0.77	0.77	Equity per shr $20.98			9-30-95	553	5847	±11068	Dc	1.95	Δ1.95	±2.66	±1.50	....	8.83	9 Mo Sep	±1.16	±8.49	10
11◆	1978	Q0.17½	11-21-95	11-1	0.70	0.70	0.70	....	...	...		....	...	2180	Dc	1.95	1.95	±2.66	±1.50	....	8.83	9 Mo Sep	±1.16	±8.49	11
12	1986	Q1.03⅛	1-16-96	12-27	4.12½	4.125	4.12½	Cv into 3.22 Cl'B'com,$15.53				....	55	...	Dc	b1.28	b1.30	...	....	....	....	SF 7.5% fr Ap 2001,$50[56]			12
13	1991	Q1.00	1-16-96	12-27	4.00	4.00	4.00	Cv into 1.73 Cl'B'com, $28.91				....	2193	...	Dc	b1.28	b1.30	...	....	....	....				13
14	1959	Q0.25	12-29-95	12-15	1.00	1.00	1.00	222	455	150	9-09-95	306	...	1488	Dc	14.28	20.89	10.63	23.67	....	22.06	36 Wk Sep	16.32	14.71	14
15	1940	Q0.15	1-2-96	12-15	0.52	0.60	0.48	Book Value $14.15			9-30-95	....	...	±4268	Dc	±0.92	±1.45	±Δ1.60	±1.44	....	1.52	9 Mo Sep	±1.06	±1.14	15
16	....	None Since Public			...	Nil	....	29.4	59.1	18.8	9-30-95	p114	...	★8100	Dc	0.51	0.05	□1.46	[58]1.35	E1.15	1.27	9 Mo Sep	0.94	0.86	16
17	1924	Q0.30	12-1-95	11-17	1.20	1.20	1.20	81.5	124	15.6	6-30-95	0.01	...	6441	Dc	0.65	Δ0.16	0.82	d0.75	....	d0.67	9 Mo Sep	d0.16	d0.08	17
18	....	None Since Public			...	Nil	....	1247	2612	1003	9-29-95	540	...	72903	Je	Δ0.95	0.92	2.80	3.08	[59]3.52	4.66	3 Mo Sep	0.30	1.44	18
19◆	1937	tQ0.15	12-29-95	12-13	0.60	0.60	t0.58	231	5834	3538	7-31-95	2955	...	373147	Ja	1.92	1.26	□1.03	□2.18	E0.63↓	0.95	9 Mo Oct	□1.66	Δ0.43	19
20◆	....	None Since Public			...	Nil	....	12.5	93.4	87.0	9-30-95	538	...	36204	Dc	0.23	Δ0.17	0.76	0.09	E0.21↑	d0.27	9 Mo Sep	0.25	d0.11	20
21◆	....	†10.00	5-11-89	5-12	...	Nil	....	7.63	199	160	9-30-95	169	...	42174	Dc	0.44	0.54	□0.66	□0.94	E1.20	1.16	9 Mo Sep	□0.67	0.90	21
22	1986	Q0.12	11-30-95	11-14	0.48	0.48	0.46	0.71	82.7	38.3	9-30-95	76.3	...	11072	Dc	1.44	□1.45	1.00	1.20	E0.50	0.73	9 Mo Sep	1.11	0.64	22
23	1961	gQ0.06	12-15-95	11-10	g0.24	0.24	g0.24	54.4	1799	872	j12-31-93	734	...	p94944	Dc	d0.34	d1.04	0.05	P0.47	....	j0.34	9 Mo Sep	d0.03	d0.16	23
24◆	1935	Q0.23	1-2-96	11-28	h[60]1.43	0.92	1.60	469	25336	14392	9-30-95	9434	10438	389850	Dc	3.71	□d5.65	□6.68	Δ3.16	E2.50	4.62	9 Mo Sep	1.92	3.38	24
25◆	....	None Since Public			...	Nil	....	9.91	16.5	8.00	9-30-95	....	...	7154	Sp	0.29	0.36	0.43	0.54	0.73	0.73				25
26	1964	Q0.10	11-10-95	10-27	0.40	0.40	0.36	7.40	63.6	57.5	8-26-95	48.4	...	2193	Au	0.54	□1.02	0.48	□1.05	2.04	2.04				26
27◆	....	None Paid			...	Nil	....	0.04	10.9	9.90	6-30-95	4.98	...	4260	Sp	*0.45	Δ0.09	d1.27	[61]0.31	P0.28	0.28				27
28◆	1940	Q0.19	1-31-96	1-10	0.57	0.76	0.627	Book Value $17.22			9-30-95	12.5	715	2558	Dc	1.57	1.68	1.97	[62]2.22	....	2.43	9 Mo Sep	1.61	1.82	28
29	....	None Since Public			...	Nil	....	0.32	4.99	2.93	9-30-95	p....	p...	★6070	Dc	...	...	...	p0.43	....	....	9 Mo Sep	n/a	pd0.28	29
30	1987	†0.19¾	9-29-95	9-12	†0.48¼	0.59	†0.58	Book Value $17.69			6-30-95	19.5	...	1479	Je	1.09	1.25	1.64	1.82	1.80	1.68	3 Mo Sep	0.53	0.41	30
31	1995	0.15	11-30-95	11-13	0.15	[63]....	....	Book Value $57.54			9-30-95	431	...	9681	Je	...	...	p1.82	1.05	2.53	2.66	3 Mo Sep	0.61	0.74	31
32	1994	Q0.253	2-19-96	2-6	0.93½	1.01	[64]0.63¾	Equity per shr $12.35			9-30-95	324	5400	★81410	Dc	...	...	p0.56	0.57	....	0.59	9 Mo Sep	0.41	0.43	32
33	1970	Q0.31	2-15-96	1-31	1.15	1.24	†[65]1.01	Book Value $13.36			9-30-95	376	13400	72211	Dc	0.21	0.46	0.66	0.66	....	0.86	9 Mo Sep	0.46	0.66	33
34	1993	Q0.43¾	12-29-95	12-13	1.75	1.75	1.75	Cv into 1.2162 com, $20.556				....	8000	...	Dc	...	...	...	....	....	....				34
35	1994	Q0.12	1-31-96	1-9	0.48	0.48	0.36	Equity per shr $36.36			9-30-95	[67]65.0	...	8556	Dc	...	p2.84	□p2.75	2.94	....	2.99	9 Mo Sep	2.20	2.25	35
36◆	....	None Since Public			...	Nil	....	32.2	39.2	5.18	9-30-95	....	...	★13444	Dc	...	...	pΔ0.19	p0.26	....	0.40	9 Mo Sep	0.17	0.31	36
37	....	None Since Public			...	Nil	....	20.8	60.8	21.9	p6-30-95	....	...	11352	Sp	...	...	...	p0.21	P0.45	0.45				37
38◆	1988	S0.10	1-22-96	12-27	0.18	0.20	0.14	14.1	52.1	47.2	9-30-95	....	...	18385	Dc	0.53	0.59	0.78	0.96	....	0.96	9 Mo Sep	0.69	0.69	38
39◆	....	s0.02½	7-8-92	6-10	...	Nil	....	Equity per shr $12.68			9-30-95	[67]35.6	...	9340	Dc	1.14	Δ0.76	0.92	□[68]1.23	....	1.29	9 Mo Sep	□0.80	0.86	39
40	1990	Q0.06	12-28-95	12-6	0.23	0.24	0.20½	5.55	37.8	19.2	9-30-95	9.92	...	3460	Dc	1.41	□d0.43	0.42	0.90	....	0.58	9 Mo Sep	0.75	0.43	40
41	1930	Q0.28	12-1-95	11-13	1.12	1.12	1.12	Equity per shr $27.15			9-30-95	111	...	14342	Dc	2.07	Δ2.06	1.66	[69]2.76	....	3.56	9 Mo Sep	1.92	2.72	41
42	....	Wrrt	2-18-94	2-22	...	Nil	Wrrt	5.00	13.4	4.34	9-30-95	1.90	...	5815	Dc	d0.47	*0.03	Δ0.15	0.21	....	0.48	9 Mo Sep	0.09	0.36	42
43◆	....	None Since Public			...	Nil	....	5.13	52.4	19.8	6-30-95	4.34	...	13012	Sp	...	...	...	p0.39	Pp1.20	1.20				43
44	....	3%Stk	4-22-83	3-14	...	Nil	....	4.02	18.2	4.74	7-30-95	0.55	...	5004	Ja	0.16	0.10	0.02	[70]0.25	....	0.91	9 Mo Oct	0.12	0.78	44
45	....	None Paid			...	Nil	....	8.22	8.64	0.56	12-31-94	....	...	39906	Dc	d0.14	d0.12	d0.07	d0.09	....	d0.09				45
46◆	1978	Q0.05½	11-17-95	11-1	0.22	0.22	0.22	Equity per shr $6.30			9-30-95	423	...	73332	Je	□0.65	[72]0.73	0.96	1.16	1.02	0.96	3 Mo Sep	0.29	0.23	46
47	....	None Since Public			...	Nil	....	29.5	41.5	20.8	3-31-95	8.69	...	★22689	Dc	d1.02	d0.59	d1.16	d1.09	....	d1.44	9 Mo Sep	d0.93	d1.28	47
48	1987	0.15	7-1-93	6-9	...	Nil	....	30.7	590	335	9-30-95	564	797	±9867	Dc	±d1.02	±Δd0.73	□±d6.07	±□d2.87	....	d2.21	9 Mo Sep	□±d1.51	±d0.85	48
49	1987	0.12½	7-1-93	6-9	...	Nil	....	Cv into 1 Cl'A'				....	...	3331	Dc	±d1.02	±Δd0.73	±□d6.07	±□d2.87	....	d2.21	9 Mo Sep	□±d1.51	±d0.85	49
50	1987	Q1.25	2-1-96	1-9	5.00	5.00	a6.25	Cv into 1.3219 com,$75.65				....	634	...	Dc	b1.14	b1.19	b0.38	b0.58	....	....				50
51	....	None Since Public			...	Nil	....	64.1	335	133	9-30-95	9.10	...	33041	Dc	d2.10	0.55	d0.26	1.03	E1.15↓	1.11	9 Mo Sep	0.65	0.73	51
52	....	None Since Public			...	Nil	....	13.5	48.8	17.0	10-01-95	0.02	...	15312	Je	0.78	d0.48	d3.63	0.87	0.34	0.40	3 Mo Sep	0.05	0.11	52

◆**Stock Splits & Divs By Line Reference Index** [3]6-for-5,'94. [11]2-for-1,'91. [19]4-for-1,'92. [20]2-for-1,'93. [21]No adj for spl $20 dstr,'89:2-for-1,'92,'95. [24]No adj for stk dstr of Dean Witter,Discover,'93:No adj for stk dstr Allstate Corp,'95. [25]2-for-1,'94:3-for-2,'93,'95. [27]10%,'91,'92. [28]3-for-2,'92,'95. [36]2-for-1,'95. [38]2-for-1,'93. [39]Adj to 1%,Jun'92. [43]3-for-2,'95. [46]3-for-2,'93.

¶ S&P 500 # MidCap 400 ✣ SmallCap 600 • Options

Index	Ticker	Name of Issue (Call Price of Pfd. Stocks)	Market	Com. Rank. & Pfd. Rating	Inst. Hold Cos	Inst. Hold Shs. (000)	Principal Business	Price Range 1971-93 High	1971-93 Low	1994 High	1994 Low	1995 High	1995 Low	Dec. Sales in 100s	December, 1995 Last Sale Or Bid High	Low	Last	%Div Yield	P-E Ratio	Total Return % Annualized 12 Mo	36 Mo	60 Mo
✣1•[1]	SEQU	✓SEQUUS Pharmaceuticals	NNM	C	58	10239	Liposomes for pharmac'ls	25¾	⅞	12½	4½	15⅛	5½	71441	14¼	10⅝	14¼	...	d	119	12.5	43.1
2	SRI	✓Serenpet Inc	AS,To,Ch,Ph	NR	13	5574	Oil & gas explor dvlp prod'n	8¾	5¼	6¾	2¼	3¼	2	198	2½	2 1/16	2⅛B	...	d	–15.0	...	...
3	SERO	✓Serologicals Inc	NNM	NR	26	1631	Biomedical pr:human antibodies	....	....	....	....	18¼	10½	5622	17½	13	16½	...	41	...	...	...
¶4•[2]	SRV	✓Service Corp Intl	NY,B,Ch	A–	458	84276	Funeral service:cemetery	26⅜	¼	28	22½	44	26¼	49947	44	39⅜	44	1.0	26	60.7	36.0	25.9
#5•[3]	SME	✓Service Merchandise	NY,Ch	↓B–	138	51687	Catalog/showroom mdsr	15⅜	1/16	10	4¼	7⅞	4⅛	64405	6⅛	4½	4⅞	...	9	8.3	–29.9	11.6
6	SVM	✓ServiceMaster L.P.	NY,B,Ch,Ph	A+	140	10134	Health care sv: cleaning svs	31	¼	28⅜	21½	30⅜	21½	13171	30⅜	28¼	30¼	3.2	14	31.5	24.2	29.7
7	SER	✓Servico Inc	AS	NR	15	1546	Own/oper hotels in U.S.	6¾	2⅜	10½	6⅜	16	9⅛	8310	13⅝	10⅛	10½	...	25	3.7	37.9	...
8	SVT	✓Servotronics, Inc	AS,B	↓B–	9	102	Mfr advanced electr products	13	1/16	5⅜	3⅝	6	3½	79	4½	4⅛	4¼B	...	13	23.2	–6.0	15.0
9	SEVL	✓7th Level Inc	NNM	NR	21	2364	Dvlp entertainment softwr	....	....	11	4¾	22⅝	5	33586	19¾	13¾	14	...	d	180	...	...
10	SFFD	✓SFFed Corp[55]	NNM	NR	59	4248	Savings & loan, California	21¾	3¾	23¼	11⅝	31¾	11⅞	5796	31¾	31⅛	31⅝	0.6	62	167	48.7	41.1
11•[4]	STM	✓SGS-THOMSON N.V.	NY,Ch,Ph	NR	79	12879	Mfr,dstr semiconductors	....	....	22¾	21⅝	57½	22½	99660	41½	27⅞	40¼	...	11	79.9	...	...
12	SHMN	✓Shaman Pharmaceuticals	NNM	NR	35	3477	Dvlp stge:pharmaceut'l R&D	16¾	8½	12¾	2⅝	8	3	8328	7⅛	5¾	6⅝	...	d	82.8	...	...
13•[5]	SH	Shandong Huaneng Pwr ADS[56]	[6]NY,Ch	NR	63	17885	Electric generating, China	....	....	14½	8⅝	9⅞	6¼	7627	8	6⅜	6¾	6.7	..	–24.8	...	...
14•[7]	SHI	✓Shanghai Petrochemical ADS[57]	NY	NR	31	821	Integrated petroleum process'g	49¼	18¼	43	22	34¼	22⅛	2978	29⅝	25⅜	28½	5.3	11	4.3	...	...
¶15•[8]	SMED	✓Shared Medical Sys	NNM	B+	264	14984	Fin'l/admin hosp computer sv	53	2 7/16	34½	22⅛	57⅝	30⅞	103250	57⅝	42¾	54⅜	1.5	32	67.9	40.2	34.5
16	STCH	✓Shared Technologies	NNM	NR	19	2833	Telecommun/office auto'n svcs	29	1½	5⅜	2½	5¾	3⅛	4310	4⅝	3½	3⅞	...	15	–9.4	–11.2	...
17	SHRP	✓Sharper Image	NNM	B–	12	984	Catalog mdsr/retail stores	11	15/16	8⅛	3½	7⅞	5⅜	1455	6⅝	5¾	5¾	...	25	–14.8	24.2	38.6
18	SHAW	✓Shaw Group	NNM	NR	26	1620	Fabricator of piping systems	19½	14½	26½	2¾	10¾	3⅞	4718	10¾	8¾	8⅞	...	18	74.2	...	...
#19•[5]	SHX	✓Shaw Indus	NY,Ch,P	A	207	85590	Carpet manufacturer	25½	⅛	25	12⅞	17⅜	12	61166	16⅜	14¼	14¾	2.0	26	1.1	–2.5	26.1
20	SHE.EC	✓Sheffield Exploration	ECM	NR	..	...	Oil & gas ,explor dvlp, prod'n	3¼	1½	3⅝	1⅜	1 13/16	1 3/16	241	1⅝	1½	1⅜B	...	d	0.0	...	...
21	SHM	✓Sheffield Medl Tech	AS,Ph	NR	9	90	Dvlp stge: biomedical R&D	5¾	1⅝	9⅞	3⅛	5¾	3	15755	4⅛	3	3½	...	d	0.0	...	...
22	SY	✓Shelby Williams Ind	NY,Ph	B	38	3282	Mfrs restr/hotel seat'g prod	28¼	5¼	14⅝	7½	13¾	7⅝	1656	12¾	11⅜	11¾	2.4	42	41.9	7.3	17.1
23	SHEL	✓Sheldahl, Inc	NNM	B–	34	2765	Flexible printed circuits	13¾	11/16	14¾	8¾	21¼	10½	12843	19¾	17	18⅛	...	37	42.2	32.7	27.5
24•[9]	SHC	Shell Canada'A'vtg	To,Mo	B	22	4450	Canad'n integrated oil unit	52¾	9¾	46	37¼	46¼	39¼	7159	43½	41⅝	42⅞	4.0	9	4.5	10.4	...
25•[5]	SC	✓Shell Transp/Trad ADR[62]	NY,B,Ch,P,Ph	A–	149	6183	Owns 40% Royal Dutch/Shell	65⅛	2⅞	71¾	56⅞	82	64¼	14546	82	75¼	81½	3.5	17	30.8	22.1	14.3
26	SST	✓Shelter Components Corp	AS	B	40	2913	Dstr mfrd housing parts	11⅞	¾	16⅜	10⅛	17⅛	10¼	2759	17⅛	15¾	16⅜	0.4	10	43.4	23.1	66.7
27	SHCR	Sheridan Healthcare	NNM	NR	..	...	Physician mgmt services	....	....	....	....	13⅝	8¼	8974	13⅝	10⅝	12⅛	...	..	...	...	...
28•[10]	SE	Sherritt Inc	To	B–	41	16611	Metal min'g,ref'g,fab'g:chem	21¾	4	15⅜	10½	20¾	11⅝	141861	18	16⅜	17⅝	...	7	30.6	40.3	...
¶29•[7]	SHW	✓Sherwin-Williams	NY,B,Ch,Ph,P	A	430	53427	Large paint & varnish mfr	37½	1¼	35¾	29½	41½	32	26148	41½	38⅞	40¾	1.6	18	27.6	10.9	19.1
30	SHD	✓Sherwood Group	NY,Ch	B–	16	1024	Hldg co:securities brokerage	9½	⅜	8⅞	5¼	10¾	5⅛	2096	9½	8¼	8⅝	...	7	56.8	30.6	76.7
31•[5]	SHVA	✓Shiva Corp	NNM	NR	101	4567	Computer hardware/software	....	....	43	15	77½	27	41361	77½	54	72¾	...	d	69.2	...	...
✣32	SCVL	✓Shoe Carnival	NNM	NR	33	3452	Operates shoe store chain	19¼	8⅝	13⅜	4¾	7½	3⅜	5491	4¼	3⅝	3¾	...	..	–21.1	...	...
¶33•[8]	SHN	✓Shoney's Inc	NY,Ch,Ph	B	207	19449	Restaurant chain	33⅝	½	25⅝	12⅝	13½	8⅞	34114	11⅜	9⅜	10¼	...	16	–20.4	–23.6	–1.8
34	LSC	✓Shopco Laurel Centre L.P.	AS	NR	2	15	Shopping Mall, Maryland	10½	2¾	4¼	2¼	3⅛	1 11/16	2018	2 1/16	1 11/16	1 11/16	29.6	d	–21.9	–1.6	–6.1
✣35•[11]	SKO	✓Shopko Stores	NY,Ph	NR	98	11360	Genl merchandise discount strs	17¼	9¾	12⅛	8¾	14	8⅝	10078	11¾	11	11¼	3.9	10	26.6	–5.3	...
✣36•[12]	SHOR	✓Shorewood Packaging	NNM	B	93	12215	Print/mfr paperboard packag'g	19	2⅞	22¾	13¼	20½	13¾	29630	15	13¾	14¼	...	13	–29.6	6.6	39.3
✣37•[12]	SHBZ	✓ShowBiz Pizza Time	NNM	NR	50	5410	Family restr/enter'nt ctrs	35½	2¼	15¼	7¼	13⅝	7¼	13834	12⅞	11	12⅛	...	d	57.7	–28.4	6.3
✣38•[7]	SBO	✓Showboat, Inc	NY,B,Ch	↑B	82	7813	Intl Casinos/Hotels	24⅝	1 1/16	22⅞	11½	29⅜	13½	11426	29⅜	23⅝	26⅜	0.4	26	93.0	17.0	48.0
39	SHU	✓Shurgard Storage Centers	NY	NR	102	7297	Real estate investment trust	....	....	24¼	17¾	27⅞	19½	6988	27⅞	25	27	e6.8	..	48.0	...	...
40	SIDT	✓SI Diamond Technology	NSC	NR	4	141	Diamond coatings/technolog's	9¼	5⅛	7⅞	3⅞	10⅜	4½	10747	7⅜	6¼	6⅝	...	d	51.4	...	...
✣41•[11]	SIE	✓Sierra Health Services	NY,Ch,Ph	B–	145	8444	Owns/operates HMO in Nev	22⅝	⅝	33½	21¼	33⅝	22⅛	9076	32⅞	30½	31¾	...	17	1.2	17.1	37.1
42•[13]	SIER	✓Sierra On-Line	NNM	C	127	16790	Dvlp entertain't softwr prod	13⅞	2⅞	18⅛	7⅛	48¾	14⅝	102108	37½	25½	28¾	...	58	69.1	54.0	31.5
✣43	SRP	✓Sierra Pacific Resources[71]	NY,B,Ch,P	B	121	9592	Utility hldg:elec,gas,water	29	7⅝	20⅜	17¼	24⅛	18⅜	15124	24⅛	22⅞	23⅜	4.8	12	34.9	10.5	7.0
44•[14]	SERA	✓Sierra Semiconductor	NNM	NR	100	18475	Supplies integrated circuits	13½	3¼	8⅛	3⅜	28¾	7⅝	135284	18⅝	11½	13⅞	...	18	82.2	33.2	...
45	STBS	✓Sierra Tahoe Bancorp	NNM	B	8	73	Commercial banking, California	10⅝	2⅞	11	6¾	12	7½	931	11⅝	10⅝	10⅝	2.3	11	32.0	34.3	...
46	SIF	✓SIFCO Indus	AS	↑B–	23	973	Precision forg'gs:mach'd parts	12½	1	4¾	2½	5½	2⅞	3490	5⅜	3¾	5⅜	...	10	38.7	8.7	–4.0
¶47•[4]	SIAL	✓Sigma-Aldrich	NNM	A+	429	30558	Specialty chem prod	59¼	15/16	55¼	30	51¾	32½	38270	50½	48¼	49½	0.9	19	53.7	–4.0	11.8
48	SIGA	✓Sigma Circuits	NNM	NR	3	106	Mfr electronic interconnects	....	....	5¾	3⅜	20¾	3⅝	10040	20¾	15¼	20¼	...	36	440	...	...
49	SIGM	✓Sigma Designs	NNM	C	12	590	Mfr IBM compatible products	22¼	2⅝	15½	4⅜	8	3⅝	24913	7⅞	5½	7¾	...	d	31.9	5.4	8.6
50	SGMA	✓Sigmatron International	NNM	NR	4	10	Mfr electronic components	....	....	9½	6	8½	6	2209	7⅞	6¾	7	...	10	–16.4	...	...
51	SIA	✓Signal Apparel	NY,Ch	C	13	354	Hosiery,knitwear,apparel	24⅜	1 7/16	8⅛	4	8⅛	5¼	1001	7¾	6¼	7¼	...	d	–6.5	–20.9	–7.6
52	STZ	✓Signal Technology	AS	NR	15	1539	Mfr electronic components/sys	10	5½	6¾	2¾	6	3⅛	1854	5¾	4⅝	5⅛	...	85	15.5	...	...

Uniform Footnote Explanations-See Page 4. Other: [1]ASE:Cycle 1. [2]Ph:Cycle 2. [3]Ph:Cycle 1. [4]CBOE:Cycle 1. [5]CBOE:Cycle 2. [6]Ph [7]CBOE:Cycle 3. [8]P:Cycle 1. [9]To:Cycle 2. [10]To:Cycle 3. [11]Ph:Cycle 3. [12]P:Cycle 3. [13]CBOE,Ph:Cycle 1. [14]P,Ph:Cycle 2. [51]Excl subsid pfd. [52]®$1.43,'94. [53]8 Mo Dec'92. [54]®$0.33,'94. [55]First Nationwide Bank plan acq,$32. [56]Ea ADS rep 50 Ord'N' shrs,par RMB 1.00. [57]Ea ADS rep 100 Cl'H' shrs,RMB 1 par. [58]Approx. [59]Fiscal Oct,'91 & prior. [60]12 Mo Aug,'92. [61]Fiscal Jun'93 & prior. [62]Each N.Y. shr rep 6 ord shrs. [63]Proportionate shr of group B/S. [64]®$1.07,'94. [65]Fiscal Dec'94 & prior. [66]Special $4 deb dstr. [67]Spec divd. [68]Accum on pfd. [69]10 Mo Dec,'94. [70]®$0.71,'95. [71]Apprv comb w/Wash Wtr Pwr form Altus Corp,1.44 com. [72]Subsid pfd in $M. [73]®$0.96,'94.

Splits ◆ Index	Cash Divs. Ea.Yr. Since	Dividends: Latest Payment Period $	Date	Ex. Div.	Total $ So Far 1995	Ind. Rate	Paid 1994	Financial Position Mil-$ Cash& Equiv.	Curr. Assets	Curr. Liab.	Balance Sheet Date	Capitalization Lg Trm Debt Mil-$	Shs. 000 Pfd.	Com.	Earnings $ Per Shr. Years End	1991	1992	1993	1994	1995	Last 12 Mos.	Interim Earnings Period	$ per Shr. 1994	1995	Index
1	....	None Since Public			...	Nil	....	12.7	14.4	4.92	9-30-95	....	480	★25626	Dc	d0.37	d0.84	d1.05	d1.54	....	d1.55	9 Mo Sep	d1.16	d1.17	1
2	....	None Since Public			...	Nil	....	....	15.7	20.1	j12-31-94	41.0	...	22789	Dc	Nil	0.28	0.34	d1.03	....	jd1.20	6 Mo Jun	0.17	Nil	2
3	....	None Since Public			...	Nil	....	2.59	13.1	5.67	10-01-95	6.79	...	8042	Dc	...	...	...	□p0.44	....	0.40	9 Mo Sep	p□0.44	□0.40	3
4◆	1973	Q0.11	1-31-96	1-11	0.43½	0.44	0.42	170	763	454	9-30-95	p1986	[51]...	★122128	Dc	1.03	1.13	□1.24	[52]1.51	E1.70↓	1.70	9 Mo Sep	1.12	1.31	4
5◆	....	5.333	7-25-89	6-26	...	Nil	....	18.9	1461	1170	10-01-95	623	...	99673	Dc	0.76	0.83	Δ□0.80	□0.61	....	0.55	9 Mo Sep	□d0.24	d0.30	5
6◆	1962	Q0.24	1-31-96	1-10	0.95	0.96	0.92	53.7	424	346	9-30-95	440	...	77683	Dc	1.19	□1.71	1.90	1.81	E2.20	2.08	9 Mo Sep	1.33	1.60	6
7	....	None Since Public			...	Nil	....	11.1	31.3	67.3	9-30-95	173	...	8846	Dc	...	[53]0.20	0.25	Δ[54]0.34	....	0.42	9 Mo Sep	0.34	0.42	7
8◆	....	6%Stk	8-11-95	7-19	6%Stk	Stk	....	0.34	12.0	3.06	9-30-95	6.60	...	2183	Dc	0.75	0.66	Δ0.49	0.31	....	0.32	9 Mo Sep	0.30	0.31	8
9	....	None Since Public			...	Nil	....	8.38	12.0	4.93	9-30-95	0.33	...	12971	Dc	...	...	pd0.90	d0.85	....	d1.15	9 Mo Sep	d0.78	d1.08	9
10	1993	Q0.05	12-1-95	11-13	0.26	0.20	0.28	Book Value $24.28			9-30-95	268	...	7873	Dc	1.89	Δ1.62	1.24	d0.60	....	0.51	9 Mo Sep	d0.63	0.48	10
11	....	None Since Public			...	Nil	....	347	1813	1514	9-30-95	243	...	★136784	Dc	d1.93	0.06	1.92	3.04	....	3.69	9 Mo Sep	2.13	2.78	11
12	....	None Since Public			...	Nil	....	29.0	30.0	4.72	9-30-95	3.34	...	13221	Dc	pd1.32	pd0.85	d1.30	d1.50	....	d1.43	9 Mo Sep	d1.04	d0.97	12
13	1995	0.24	10-20-95	10-3	0.451	0.45	....	284	339	106	12-31-94	7.52	...	±4304716	Dc	...	...	...	0.74	....	....	6 Mo Jun	n/a	0.47	13
14	1994	[58]0.478	10-16-95	9-19	[58]1.497	1.50	1.042	236	606	525	12-31-94	252	...	±6550000	Dc	...	p1.92	1.99	2.70	....	2.70				14
15	1977	Q0.21	1-15-96	12-27	0.84	0.84	0.84	21.8	210	145	9-30-95	3.41	...	23235	Dc	1.11	1.24	1.35	1.51	E1.70	1.63	9 Mo Sep	1.12	1.24	15
16◆	....	None Paid			...	Nil	....	1.41	14.9	17.0	9-30-95	4.01	1364	8505	Dc	d1.60	Δd0.33	□0.01	0.27	....	0.26	9 Mo Sep	0.21	0.20	16
17	....	None Since Public			...	Nil	....	0.80	59.4	39.0	10-31-95	7.52	...	8261	Ja	d0.41	0.04	0.20	0.41	....	0.23	9 Mo Oct	d0.18	d0.36	17
18	....	None Since Public			...	Nil	....	0.77	80.6	40.6	8-31-95	9.61	...	8552	Au	[59]0.29	[60]0.44	0.63	Δ0.39	0.50	0.50				18
19◆	1972	Q0.075	11-21-95	11-7	0.30	0.30	0.22	42.9	988	337	9-30-95	658	...	135893	Dc	0.29	0.47	[61]0.71	□0.91	E0.57	0.53	9 Mo Sep	□0.71	□0.33	19
20	....	None Since Public			...	Nil	....	0.32	6.16	1.86	9-30-95	1.37	...	3391	Je	d0.02	0.06	0.23	0.02	d0.38	d0.37	3 Mo Sep	0.01	0.02	20
21	....	None Since Public			...	Nil	....	3.02	3.18	0.36	9-30-95	....	...	9320	Dc	d0.03	d0.65	d0.75	d0.96	....	d1.08	9 Mo Sep	d0.58	d0.70	21
22	1984	Q0.07	11-15-95	10-30	0.28	0.28	0.28	2.13	61.3	30.0	9-30-95	8.86	...	8956	Dc	d0.34	0.40	0.46	0.04	....	0.28	9 Mo Sep	0.31	0.55	22
23	....	h....	4-12-78	3-27	...	Nil	....	1.05	32.8	16.4	9-01-95	p23.3	...	★8584	Au	Δd1.50	0.04	0.29	Δ□0.42	0.45	0.49	3 Mo Nov	0.08	0.12	23
24	1965	gS0.85	12-19-95	12-6	g1.50	1.70	g1.00	256	1674	1211	j12-31-94	849	.1	p112208	Dc	d1.12	0.72	0.16	2.85	....	j4.91	9 Mo Sep	1.93	3.99	24
25	1898	1.298	11-8-95	9-27	2.889	2.89	2.48	2974	9202	7206	[63]j12-31-94	1526	12000	3314504	Dc	2.66	3.42	2.94	4.60	E4.89	5.96	9 Mo Sep	2.43	3.79	25
26◆	1993	S0.03	12-22-95	12-6	0.06	0.06	0.06	0.02	8.16	42.4	9-30-95	19.8	...	6079	Dc	0.21	0.77	1.13	1.49	....	1.71	9 Mo Sep	1.08	1.30	26
27	....	None Since Public			...	Nil	....	1.62	13.0	15.3	6-30-95	p25.7	p...	★6066	Dc	...	...	...	p0.40	....	....	9 Mo Sep	n/a	pd1.02	27
28	....	g0.14	12-31-91	12-12	...	Nil	....	129	591	187	j12-31-94	533	...	p67705	Dc	0.04	0.06	d0.97	[64]1.30	....	j2.39	9 Mo Sep	0.84	1.93	28
29◆	1979	Q0.16	12-1-95	11-15	0.64	0.64	0.56	216	1282	618	9-30-95	22.7	...	84958	Dc	1.45	□1.63	1.85	2.15	E2.30	2.31	9 Mo Sep	1.79	1.95	29
30	....	None Since Public			...	Nil	....	Equity per shr $5.37			8-31-95	....	...	12560	My	*0.01	*0.45	*0.64	1.20	1.07	1.18	3 Mo Aug	0.22	0.33	30
31	....	None Since Public			...	Nil	....	22.3	51.8	23.4	9-30-95	0.47	...	★14818	Dc	d0.23	d0.99	0.03	0.28	....	d0.48	9 Mo Sep	0.20	d0.56	31
32◆	....	None Since Public			...	Nil	....	1.34	81.1	24.6	7-29-95	15.9	...	13019	Ja	...	p0.55	p0.55	[65]0.09	....	....	9 Mo Oct	0.18	0.12	32
33◆	....	[66]....	8-3-88	8-4	...	Nil	....	5.65	91.7	154	8-06-95	437	...	41497	Oc	0.94	d0.65	1.44	□Δ[52]1.52	E0.66	1.06	40 Wk Aug	Δ□1.17	0.71	33
34	1987	Q0.12½	2-15-96	12-27	0.50	0.50	0.50	Equity per shr $3.18			9-30-95	54.2	...	4660	Dc	d0.08	d0.10	d0.05	d0.10	....	d0.02	9 Mo Sep	d0.12	d0.04	34
35	1992	Q0.11	12-15-95	11-29	0.44	0.44	0.44	28.1	472	278	9-09-95	413	...	32005	Fb	p1.55	1.56	1.00	1.18	....	1.13	40 Wk Nov	0.59	0.54	35
36	....	[67]3.25	7-2-91	7-3	...	Nil	....	6.20	105	69.2	10-28-95	116	...	18989	Ap	0.67	0.52	Δ0.78	□0.52	1.17	1.12	6 Mo Oct	0.66	0.61	36
37◆	....	None Since Public			...	[68]Nil	....	3.37	14.0	26.7	9-29-95	31.0	50	12215	Dc	1.28	1.11	0.86	0.03	....	d0.32	9 Mo Sep	0.45	0.10	37
38	1970	Q0.02½	1-10-96	12-13	0.10	0.10	0.10	126	152	56.4	9-30-95	392	...	15528	Dc	Δ0.53	□1.37	□Δ0.89	1.02	....	1.00	9 Mo Sep	0.96	0.94	38
39	1994	Q0.46	1-26-96	12-21	†1.92	1.84	1.02	Net Asset Val $19.40			9-30-95	132	...	±23194	Dc	...	...	...	□[69]1.12	....	....	9 Mo Sep	p□0.81	1.07	39
40	....	None Since Public			...	Nil	....	1.66	3.38	1.99	9-30-95	1.06	...	10301	Dc	d0.05	d0.52	d1.60	d1.07	....	d1.11	9 Mo Sep	d0.85	d0.89	40
41◆	....	None Since Public			...	Nil	....	117	134	73.6	9-30-95	12.7	...	p17480	Dc	0.91	1.14	1.42	1.71	....	1.90	9 Mo Sep	1.26	1.45	41
42◆	....	None Since Public			...	Nil	....	79.3	127	19.9	9-30-95	23.3	...	18635	Mr	0.33	d0.58	d0.59	[70]0.74	E0.50	1.22	6 Mo Sep	d0.31	0.17	42
43	1916	Q0.28	2-1-96	1-12	1.12	1.12	1.12	17.6	150	172	9-30-95	575	[72]87	30035	Dc	1.75	1.09	1.67	1.79	....	1.93	12 Mo Sep	1.74	1.93	43
44◆	....	None Since Public			...	Nil	....	22.6	79.0	43.8	10-01-95	6.93	...	★25728	Dc	0.65	0.54	d0.64	d0.39	E0.78↓	0.39	9 Mo Sep	d0.55	0.23	44
45◆	1995	S0.12	9-22-95	9-13	0.24	0.24	....	Equity per shr $11.30			9-30-95	10.0	...	2588	Dc	0.76	0.73	1.04	[73]1.12	....	0.97	9 Mo Sep	0.74	0.59	45
46	....	0.03	11-24-92	11-4	...	Nil	....	1.47	30.6	17.9	9-30-95	6.68	...	5092	Sp	0.57	d0.09	d1.80	0.01	0.55	0.55				46
47◆	1970	Q0.11	1-2-96	12-13	0.36	0.44	0.33	57.5	591	102	9-30-95	14.1	...	49863	Dc	1.60	1.92	□2.15	2.21	E2.65	2.52	9 Mo Sep	1.68	1.99	47
48	....	21.30			...	Nil	....	1.38	21.3	13.7	9-30-95	19.3	...	1942	Je	2.60	d5.73	0.58	0.74	0.12	0.56	3 Mo Sep	d0.17	0.27	48
49	....	None Since Public			...	Nil	....	8.10	14.8	8.91	7-31-95	....	...	7535	Ja	d0.67	d1.37	d5.15	d1.20	....	d2.83	9 Mo Oct	d0.22	d1.85	49
50	....	None Since Public			...	Nil	....	....	20.9	6.86	7-31-95	11.9	...	2738	Ap	...	...	p0.39	p0.59	0.69	0.71	6 Mo Oct	0.36	0.38	50
51	....	0.03	1-4-88	12-15	...	Nil	....	1.01	37.7	23.0	9-30-95	52.1	833	10078	Dc	±d6.56	±d2.45	±d4.06	±d6.88	....	d6.45	9 Mo Sep	±d2.12	±d1.69	51
52	....	None Since Public			...	Nil	....	1.22	46.7	16.9	9-30-95	16.8	...	6938	Dc	0.40	0.61	0.70	0.48	....	0.06	9 Mo Sep	0.42	Nil	52

◆**Stock Splits & Divs By Line Reference Index** [4]3-for-2,'92. [5]No adj for spl $10 dstr,'89:5-for-4,'91:3-for-2,'92. [6]3-for-2,'92,'93. [8]Adj for 6%,'95. [16]1-for-4 REVERSE,'92. [19]2-for-1,'92,'93. [26]5-for-4,'92:3-for-2,'94. [29]2-for-1,'91. [32]3-for-2,'93. [33]No adj for spl dstr,'88. [37]3-for-2,'91,'92. [41]2-for-1,'93. [42]3-for-2,'91:2-for-1,'95. [44]2-for-1, '95. [45]10%,'92. [47]2-for-1,'91.

¶ S&P 500 # MidCap 400 ✤ SmallCap 600 • Options Index	Ticker	Name of Issue (Call Price of Pfd. Stocks)	Market	Com. Rank. & Pfd. Rating	Inst. Hold Cos	Inst. Hold Shs. (000)	Principal Business	Price Range 1971-93 High	1971-93 Low	1994 High	1994 Low	1995 High	1995 Low	Dec. Sales in 100s	December, 1995 Last Sale Or Bid High	Low	Last	%Div Yield	P-E Ratio	Total Return % Annualized 12 Mo	36 Mo	60 Mo
1•[1]	SBK	✔Signet Banking	NY,B,Ch,Ph	B	222	34078	Commercial bkg,Virginia	36⅞	2 3/16	43⅞	27¼	36⅝	16½	44200	24⅞	22	23¾	3.4	12	...	...	...
2	SIGGY	✔Signet Group ADR	NNM	NR	..	...	Retail jewelry in U.K.&U.S.	14⅞	⅜	2 3/16	13/16	1¼	7/16	7228	13/16	9/16	11/16	...	d	−31.3	0.0	−41.2
¶3•[2]	SGI	✔Silicon Graphics	NY,Ch,Ph	↑B	588	103713	Mfr/svc CAE workstations	24¾	2¾	33⅛	18¾	45⅝	26⅞	439389	38¾	26⅞	27⅝	...	21	−11.2	24.9	32.2
4	SSTI	Silicon Storage Tech	NNM	NR	..	...	Flash memory components	...	...	...	...	18¼	9	48276	18¼	11¾	13¼	...	..	...	...	...
5•[3]	SVGI	✔Silicon Valley Group	NNM	B−	176	21343	Mfr equip for semicond'r ind	15¾	4	21¼	9¼	49⅜	18⅜	137626	27¾	21⅜	25¼	...	16	21.7	58.2	32.2
6	SILI	✔Siliconix Inc	NNM	B−	28	874	Semiconductors & circuits	130⅛	2	13½	6¼	40½	11½	2535	40½	32½	37	...	21	222	70.2	77.1
7	SLV	✔Silverado Foods	AS	NR	8	788	Mfr gourmet, snack foods	...	...	7⅛	3⅜	5	2½	3124	3⅜	2¾	2¾	...	d	−33.3	...	...
8	GOLDF	Silverado Mines	NSC,Vc	C	3	103	Mining & oil:gold,Alaska	8¼	1/16	2 7/16	⅝	1 1/16	⅜	69622	⅝	⅜	7/16	...	d	−41.7	2.5	47.3
9•[2]	SPG	✔Simon Property Group	NY,Ph	NR	167	28755	Real estate investment trust	22⅝	22¼	28	22½	26	22½	24929	25¼	22⅞	24⅜	8.1	21	9.0	...	...
10	SIMN	Simon Transportation Svcs'A'	NNM	NR	..	...	Trucking:temp-controlled svcs	...	...	...	...	10	8½	7815	9⅜	8½	9¼	...	14	...	...	...
✤11	SMPS	✔Simpson Indus	NNM	B+	80	11547	Machined metal auto parts	14⅝	9/16	15⅝	7⅞	12⅛	8	13740	9⅝	8⅝	9	4.4	11	4.3	0.3	14.9
12	SMCO	✔Simpson Manufacturing	NNM	NR	23	1855	Building:hardware,materials	...	...	12¾	9¾	15⅜	9⅜	1178	15⅛	12⅞	13½	...	11	27.1	...	...
13	SMU	✔Simula Inc	AS,Ch	NR	31	1825	Mfr crashworthy aircraft prd	4⅝	2¾	17	3½	25¼	12¼	4574	20⅝	16¼	18¾	...	44	25.9	82.6	...
14	SIMWF	Simware Inc	NNM	NR	22	666	Dvp/mkt software pds	...	...	...	...	11¼	5¾	7767	7⅜	5¾	6¼	...	..	...	...	...
15	SBGI	✔Sinclair Broadcast Group'A'	NNM	NR	68	4809	Own/oper T.V. stations	...	...	...	...	31	16	16085	22½	16¼	17¼	...	..	...	...	...
16•[4]	SEW	✔Singer Co N.V.	NY,Ch,Ph	NR	132	16179	Mfr sewing machines/electr prd	39¼	13½	38⅝	26½	30⅜	22	28969	27⅞	25⅜	27⅞	0.7	17	−2.7	0.4	...
17	SING	Singing Machine	NNM	NR	..	...	Mfr karaoke machine prd	...	...	4¾	2⅞	3¼	¾	3382	1⅛	¾	¾	...	d	−68.5	...	...
18	SNM	✔Sinter Metals 'A'	NY,Ph	NR	15	2223	Mfr precision metal components	...	...	10½	8⅞	12⅜	8½	779	12⅜	10⅝	12⅜	...	16	35.6	...	...
19	SROM	✔Sirrom Capital	NNM	NR	34	3109	Closed end invest co, SBIC	...	...	...	...	20	10¾	8344	20	17⅜	18⅞	...	..	...	...	...
20	SISK	✔Siskon Gold 'A'	NNM	NR	13	278	Explr,dvlp mineral properties	11⅞	1⅞	7⅛	3¾	4⅝	1⅞	6073	2⅝	1⅞	2	...	d	−48.4	−4.7	...
21	SITL	✔SITEL Corp	NNM	NR	44	2753	Telemarketing Services	...	...	...	...	33	13½	8491	33	25¾	30⅝	...	d	...	...	...
22	SYT	✔Sithe Energies	NY,Ph	NR	54	7881	Independent elec pwr producer	13¾	10⅜	14⅝	9¾	10½	5½	6793	7	5½	6	...	9	−42.9	...	...
23	SIZ	✔Sizeler Property Inv	NY,Ch,Ph	NR	58	4592	Real estate investment trust	22	8	13⅞	10½	11⅜	8½	3674	9	8½	8⅞	12.6	25	−6.5	1.4	9.9
#24	SZ	✔Sizzler International	NY	NR	86	16641	Chicken/steak franch'd restr	18⅞	7	9⅜	5	7⅛	3⅛	12078	4¼	3½	4¼	...	53	−18.7	−22.4	...
25	SJW	✔SJW Corp	AS	B+	37	399	Water service in California	41	6¾	42½	31¾	37⅞	31¼	196	37¾	34¼	37¾	5.7	11	25.0	8.1	15.4
26	SKII	✔S-K-I Ltd	NNM	↓B	28	1573	Ski vacations/services	22	6½	16½	9½	17½	11	1964	15¼	13¼	15¼	0.9	d	13.1	10.1	8.7
✤27•[5]	SKY	✔Skyline Corp	NY,B,Ch,P,Ph	B+	140	4561	Mobile homes,recreatn'l veh	74	8½	24⅛	16⅜	21⅞	16½	6007	21⅞	18¼	20¾	2.3	13	19.2	2.0	9.1
28	SL	✔SL Industries	NY,B,Ph	B−	16	920	Specialty ind'l prod & svs	10⅝	7/16	5	3½	9⅜	4⅜	2503	7⅞	6¾	7¼	0.8	11	62.5	30.8	14.5
29	SLO	✔Sloan's Supermarkets	AS,B	B−	8	208	Operates supermkt chain N.Y.	23¾	9/16	9⅞	3⅛	5¾	3⅜	1159	4	3⅜	3½	...	8	−28.4	7.9	25.2
30	SMF	✔Smart & Final Inc	NY,Ch,Ph	NR	59	7282	Oper food svc warehouse strs	20⅛	10⅛	16⅞	12¾	21¼	13¾	921	21¼	19⅜	21¼	0.9	26	56.4	4.9	...
31	SMOD	SMART Modular Tech	NNM	NR	..	...	Mfr/dgn memory modules	...	...	...	...	12¾	9½	27408	12⅜	9½	10⅝	...	15	...	...	...
32	SFLX	✔Smartflex Systems	NNM	NR	24	1876	Designs interconn't assemblies	...	...	...	...	20¼	12	6972	19	14	17¾	...	19	...	...	...
33	SMEI	SME[57]	ML,Ro	NR	..	...	Food process'g:retail dstr	6790	1474	4190	3461	4140	2720	....	3405	3100	3253	...	..	...	...	...
✤34	AOS	✔Smith (A.O.)	NY,Ph	B	134	10360	Auto chassis frames/elec mtrs	35¾	1⅝	40	21⅛	28⅝	19⅛	11777	23⅝	20	20¾	e2.9	7	−4.4	6.3	25.9
35	SMC.A	Cl'A'[59]	AS,Ch	B	20	296		35⅞	2 1/16	39¼	21½	28⅞	19⅝	110	23¾	20⅛	20⅜	2.9	7	−6.1	5.5	23.9
36	SRW	✔Smith(Charles E.)Res Rlty	NY,Ch,Ph	NR	63	6844	Real estate investment trust	...	...	26½	23⅜	25½	21¾	7453	23¾	22½	23⅝	8.1	17	2.1	...	...
37•[6]	SCO	✔Smith Corona Corp	NY,Ch,Ph	D	37	4146	Mfr typewriters/office prod	23⅜	3	6½	2⅜	3⅞	.01	26399	⅛	⅛	⅛	...	d	−95.8	−74.1	−53.0
38	SMTH	✔Smith Environmental Tech	NNM	B−	21	1515	Hazardous waste mgmt svcs	35½	2⅜	7⅝	2¾	7¼	3⅜	2184	4½	3⅜	4⅛	...	12	−21.4	−3.7	−14.9
#39•[7]	SII	✔Smith Intl	NY,B,Ch,P,Ph	B−	228	33058	Varied line drill,boring eq	70¼	1¼	17⅝	8⅜	23⅞	11	63713	23⅞	16⅞	23½	...	21	89.9	41.0	9.8
40	SMSI	✔Smith Micro Software	NNM	NR	33	1355	Communication software	...	...	...	...	15¼	5¼	40416	10¼	5¼	6¾	...	31	...	...	...
✤41•[7]	SFDS	✔Smithfield Foods	NNM	B	86	4514	Fresh pork,processed meats	25¼	1/16	34	17¾	34¼	19½	23179	32¼	30¾	31¾	...	32	−5.4	19.2	25.7
42•[8]	SBH	✔SmithKline Beecham ADS[63]	NY,Ch	NR	65	13283	Ethical drugs:healthcare prod	48	18⅞	36⅞	26⅜	55⅜	35¼	8674	55¼	51	55¼	2.1	21	59.4	18.2	16.2
43•[9]	SBE	✔ ADR Unit[65]	NY	NR	426	115902		43	16⅞	34⅝	23⅞	55½	33½	101465	55½	50¾	55½	2.4	21	69.7	24.5	19.9
44•[6]	SFD	✔Smith's Food & Drug'B'	NY,Ch,Ph	B+	115	7587	Food/drug supermarket chain	43¾	19	26¾	18⅛	27¾	18⅛	24728	27¾	24⅛	25¼	2.4	15	4.3	−7.9	−0.9
#45	SJM.A	✔Smucker (J.M.) Cl'A'	NY,Ch,Ph	A	104	4663	Preserves: jellies & fillings	39	½	26	20½	24½	17¼	7494	22	17¼	22	2.4	19	−5.2	−9.9	−12.2
46	SJM.B	✔ Cl'B' non-vtg	NY	A	59	5976		35⅛	19⅜	22⅞	20⅛	22¾	15¼	8334	19¼	15⅞	19¼	2.7	17	−9.2	−10.2	...
¶47•[10]	SNA	✔Snap-On Inc	NY,B,Ch,P,Ph	B+	307	29553	Hand tools: auto/ind'l maint	46½	3⅝	44⅜	29	47¼	31	16202	47¼	42¾	45¼	2.4	17	40.6	16.5	11.6
✤48•[10]	SNY	✔Snyder Oil Corp	NY	NR	102	16290	Oil&gas explor,dev,prod'n	23	4¾	21⅜	13⅞	15⅜	10	15714	12¾	11	12	2.2	d	−12.6	8.4	19.3
49	Pr A	Dep [66]cm Cv Ex[67]Pfd([68]26.05)	NY,Ch	B+	31	2183		31¾	25	29⅝	19¼	22⅜	18¼	2221	20¾	19	19¾	7.6	..	...	...	...
50	SQM	✔Sociedad Quimica Y Minera ADS[69]	[11]NY	NR	46	2311	Produce natural nitrates	30¾	23¼	38	25⅜	50	23	17375	47⅜	41½	47	1.2	25	64.3	...	...
51	SODK	✔Sodak Gaming	NNM	NR	53	2495	Mfr electr slot/video mach	39½	16	30¼	10	23¾	10½	5728	21½	19	20⅝	...	18	37.5	...	...
52•[12]	SDG	✔Sofamor/Danek Group	NY,Ph	NR	137	13223	Mfr spinal implant devices	45	7½	37⅛	10⅜	29⅞	12¾	26730	28⅝	21¾	28⅜	...	..	116	−12.3	...

Uniform Footnote Explanations-See Page 4. Other: [1]P:Cycle 3. [2]ASE:Cycle 2. [3]NY:Cycle 3. [4]ASE,NY:Cycle 1. [5]CBOE:Cycle 2. [6]NY:Cycle 1. [7]Ph:Cycle 1. [8]CBOE:Cycle 1. [9]P:Cycle 1. [10]ASE:Cycle 3. [11]Ch [12]CBOE:Cycle 3. [51]Stk dstr of Capital One Finl,'95. [52]Accum on pfd. [53]?0.36,'94. [54]51% owned by Semi-Tech Ltd. [55]Incl $0.38 non-taxable,'94. [56]Incl redemption of stk purch rt. [57]All data reported in Italian Lire. [58]All balance sheet data in blns of Italian Lire. [59]Cv into common shr for shr. [60]100% non-taxable,'94. [61]Incl current amts. [62]Liabs subj to compromise. [63]Each ADS rep 5 Ord A, 25p. [64]Approx. [65]Ea ADR Unit rep 5 Equity Units. [66]Dep for 0.25 shrs $6.00 Cv Exch Pfd. [67]Fr 3-31-96,scale to $25 in 2003. [68]Co opt fr 3-31-94 exch for $100 amt 6% Cv 2008. [69]Ea ADS rep 10 Sr'B',no-par. [70]Proceeds from sale of Rts.

Common and Convertible Preferred Stocks

Index (Splits ◆)	Cash Divs. Ea.Yr. Since	Dividends – Latest Payment – Period $	Date	Ex. Div.	Total $ – So Far 1995	Ind. Rate	Paid 1994	Financial Position Mil-$ – Cash& Equiv.	Curr. Assets	Curr. Liab.	Balance Sheet Date	Capitalization – Lg Trm Debt Mil-$	Shs. 000 – Pfd.	Com.	Earnings $ Per Shr. – Years End	1991	1992	1993	1994	1995	Last 12 Mos.	Interim Earnings – Period	$ per Shr. 1994	1995	Index
1◆	1963	Q0.20	11-21-95	10-27	h[51]0.79	0.80	1.00	Book Value $14.27			9-30-95	253	...	59065	Dc	d0.48	1.96	3.06	2.59	E2.00↓	2.44	9 Mo Sep	1.86	1.71	1
2	....	0.144	11-27-91	10-9	...	[52]Nil	....	141	711	593	j1-28-95	4.08	49890	295059	Ja	d2.71	d0.79	d1.72	d0.43	....	d0.50	6 Mo Jul	d0.47	d0.54	2
3◆	....	None Since Public			...	Nil	....	501	1524	554	9-30-95	278	18	161515	Je	Δ0.30	d1.09	Δ0.60	0.91	1.28	1.35	3 Mo Sep	0.26	0.33	3
4	....	None Since Public			...	Nil	....	3.80	11.3	8.59	p9-30-95	....	p...	★21922	Dc	...	...	...	pd0.23	....	....	9 Mo Sep	n/a	p0.10	4
5	....	None Since Public			...	Nil	....	181	466	142	9-30-95	0.65	...	★29268	Sp	0.12	d0.03	0.22	0.84	1.57	1.57				5
6◆	....	0.084	12-1-80	11-3	...	Nil	....	24.3	101	58.6	10-01-95	41.1	...	9960	Dc	Δd0.44	0.46	Δ0.64	1.07	....	1.77	9 Mo Sep	0.74	1.44	6
7	....	None Since Public			...	Nil	....	0.49	8.97	8.44	9-30-95	6.34	...	5922	Dc	...	...	p0.14	d0.78	....	d0.24	9 Mo Sep	d1.01	d0.47	7
8	....	None Paid			...	Nil	....	0.16	1.54	1.87	8-31-95	2.03	...	36351	Nv	d0.03	d0.07	Δd0.04	d0.09	....	d0.11	9 Mo Aug	d0.05	d0.07	8
9	1994	Q0.49¼	1-26-96	1-10	1.95¼	1.97	1.42½	Equity per shr $2.48			9-30-95	1986	...	±58239	Dc	...	±p0.69	±p0.80	□±0.71	E1.15	0.80	9 Mo Sep	□±0.70	±□0.79	9
10	....	None Since Public			...	Nil	....	0.35	8.74	25.5	9-30-95	p19.8	...	★±4600	Sp	p0.37	p0.85	p0.63	p0.83	p0.67	0.67				10
11◆	1947	Q0.10	12-21-95	11-28	0.40	0.40	0.387	8.16	77.6	37.3	9-30-95	62.4	...	17981	Dc	0.31	0.47	□0.53	0.80	E0.85	0.85	9 Mo Sep	0.61	0.66	11
12	....	None Since Public			...	Nil	....	4.36	67.0	16.2	9-30-95	....	...	11355	Dc	...	...	p0.76	0.51	....	1.23	9 Mo Sep	0.25	0.97	12
13◆	....	None Since Public			...	Nil	....	9.00	38.0	14.7	9-30-95	11.1	...	8831	Dc	p0.31	p0.29	0.23	[53]0.37	....	0.43	9 Mo Sep	0.27	0.33	13
14	....	None Since Public			...	Nil	....	0.49	7.87	6.42	j7-31-95	....	...	★6545	Ap	0.12	0.17	d0.25	d0.66	0.11	j0.31	6 Mo Oct	d0.18	0.02	14
15	....	None Since Public			...	Nil	....	105	177	48.5	9-30-95	416	...	±34750	Dc	...	...	...	p±d0.32	....	....	9 Mo Sep	n/a	□±0.02	15
16	1992	Q0.05	1-15-96	12-27	0.20	0.20	0.20	241	911	514	12-31-94	184	...	[54]50278	Dc	1.36	Δ1.57	1.75	1.92	....	1.66	9 Mo Sep	1.23	0.97	16
17◆	....	None Since Public			...	Nil	....	0.05	4.33	4.67	9-30-95	0.27	...	2812	Mr	...	...	p0.33	d1.09	....	d1.63	6 Mo Sep	0.03	d0.51	17
18	....	None Since Public			...	Nil	....	0.89	24.3	15.6	9-30-95	9.86	...	±7548	Dc	...	0.47	0.01	□0.72	....	0.77	9 Mo Sep	0.73	0.78	18
19	1995	0.23	11-8-95	10-13	0.62½	Nil	....	Net Asset Val $9.43			9-30-95	73.3	...	9195	Dc	...	...	...	§7.52	....	....				19
20◆	....	None Since Public			...	Nil	....	0.73	0.92	0.58	9-30-95	5.76	...	±p10539	Dc	d0.56	±d0.53	□±d0.56	±d0.10	....	d0.10	9 Mo Sep	±d0.06	±d0.06	20
21	....	None Since Public			...	Nil	....	7.22	36.7	9.21	8-31-95	0.15	...	7523	My	0.09	Δ0.10	0.15	0.33	d2.10	d2.04	3 Mo Aug	0.13	0.19	21
22	....	None Since Public			...	Nil	....	32.3	144	116	9-30-95	1212	...	55185	Dc	...	pΔ0.04	d0.02	0.17	....	0.66	9 Mo Sep	0.16	0.65	22
23	1987	Q0.28	12-6-95	11-20	1.12	1.12	[55]1.10	Equity per shr $11.42			9-30-95	114	...	8502	Dc	0.52	0.44	□0.59	Δ0.58	....	0.35	9 Mo Sep	0.46	0.23	23
24	1991	0.04	10-12-95	9-26	0.16	Nil	0.16	0.60	25.1	28.3	10-15-95	22.7	...	27775	Ap	...	0.75	d0.33	d3.26	0.24	0.08	24 Wk Oct	0.18	0.02	24
25	1932	Q0.54	12-1-95	10-30	2.16	2.16	2.10	3.75	17.0	17.3	9-30-95	62.5	...	3251	Dc	2.98	3.60	3.64	3.05	....	3.38	12 Mo Sep	3.45	3.38	25
26	1986	A0.13	1-17-96	12-6	0.12	0.13	0.11	2.79	11.0	14.2	7-31-95	50.2	...	5786	Jl	0.60	0.65	0.77	0.81	0.18	d0.36	3 Mo Oct	d0.86	d1.40	26
27	1960	Q0.12	1-2-96	12-13	0.48	0.48	0.48	45.0	113	43.4	8-31-95	....	...	10664	My	0.47	0.52	□0.92	1.34	1.38	1.62	6 Mo Nov	0.72	0.96	27
28	1973	Q0.03	11-30-95	11-13	0.06	0.06	[56]0.068	0.58	37.0	15.1	7-31-95	3.32	...	5661	Jl	□d1.32	*0.23	*0.15	Δ0.32	0.62	0.66	3 Mo Oct	0.09	0.13	28
29◆	....	None Since Public			...	Nil	....	0.18	5.22	7.14	9-03-95	1.47	...	3132	Fb	d0.41	d0.25	0.05	0.12	....	0.45	27 Wk Sep	Nil	0.33	29
30◆	1991	Q0.05	1-26-96	1-3	0.20	0.20	0.20	14.7	173	118	10-08-95	18.7	...	20252	Dc	0.17	0.71	□0.73	0.85	....	0.83	40 Wk oct	0.66	0.64	30
31	....	None Since Public			...	Nil	....	2.27	72.3	54.5	7-31-95	1.07	p...	★17653	Oc	0.08	0.02	0.23	0.37	P0.72	0.72				31
32	....	None Since Public			...	Nil	....	24.9	54.1	18.5	9-30-95	1.07	...	6219	Dc	p0.14	p0.23	p0.47	0.60	....	0.92	9 Mo Sep	0.43	0.75	32
33	1985	110.00	8-17-90	8-17	...	110.00	....	685	...	...	[58]12-31-89	128	...	436125	Dc	...	...	...	....	....	j224.00				33
34◆	1983	Q0.15	11-15-95	10-27	0.58	0.60	0.50	5.37	347	228	9-30-95	164	...	±20913	Dc	±0.10	□±1.40	±2.08	±2.75	....	2.84	9 Mo Sep	±2.10	±2.19	34
35◆	1940	Q0.15	11-15-95	10-27	0.58	0.60	0.50	....	...	...		....	...	5885	Dc	±0.10	□±1.40	±2.08	±2.75	....	2.84	9 Mo Sep	±2.10	±2.19	35
36	1994	0.49	11-13-95	11-1	1.91½	1.92	[60]0.48	Equity per shr $0.74			9-30-95	[61]465	...	9652	Dc	...	...	p1.05	p1.34	....	1.40	9 Mo Sep	p0.99	1.05	36
37	1990	0.02½	4-6-95	3-16	0.05	Nil	0.20	File bankruptcy Chapt 11				[62]67.7	...	30250	Je	0.65	0.73	d0.30	0.17	Δd2.03	d2.25	3 Mo Sep	0.04	d0.18	37
38	....	None Since Public			...	Nil	....	0.21	56.9	40.2	8-31-95	36.3	76	5857	Fb	0.14	d1.74	d1.75	0.44	....	0.34	6 Mo Aug	0.24	0.14	38
39	....	0.08	2-21-86	2-10	...	Nil	....	3.45	460	175	9-30-95	115	...	39778	Dc	d0.38	d0.10	□1.82	0.92	E1.12	1.10	9 Mo Sep	0.65	0.83	39
40	....	None Since Public			...	Nil	....	19.7	22.8	4.13	9-30-95	....	...	13700	Dc	...	...	...	p0.13	....	0.22	9 Mo Sep	p0.12	p0.21	40
41◆	....	None Paid			...	Nil	....	11.8	315	244	10-29-95	181	...	16438	Ap	1.99	1.37	Δ0.15	1.13	1.59	1.00	6 Mo Oct	0.58	d0.01	41
42◆	1990	[64]0.269	1-22-96	11-24	1.12	1.14	0.962	640	3479	4830	j12-31-94	1138	132300	±2689000	Dc	2.25	2.39	2.25	0.21	E2.70	0.28	9 Mo Sep	1.88	1.95	42
43◆	1990	0.316	1-15-96	11-24	1.33	1.34	1.113	....	...	...		....	...	2681067	Dc	...	...	...	....	E2.70	....	9 Mo Sep	1.88	1.95	43
44	1989	Q0.15	12-15-95	11-13	0.60	0.60	0.52	12.3	451	373	9-30-95	721	16282	±25071	Dc	±1.65	±1.79	±1.52	±1.73	....	1.70	9 Mo Sep	±1.20	±1.17	44
45◆	1949	Q0.13	12-1-95	11-15	0.51½	0.52	0.49	14.5	232	120	7-31-95	67.1	...	±29164	Ap	1.07	1.16	□1.27	±1.05	±1.25	1.16	6 Mo Oct	±0.74	±0.65	45
46	1991	Q0.13	12-1-95	11-15	0.51½	0.52	0.49	....	...	...		....	...	14781	Ap	1.07	1.16	□1.27	±1.05	±1.25	1.16	6 Mo Oct	±0.74	±0.65	46
47	1939	Q0.27	12-11-95	11-16	1.08	1.08	1.08	14.3	986	401	9-30-95	114	...	40450	Dc	□1.75	1.56	2.02	2.30	E2.75	2.62	9 Mo Sep	1.68	2.00	47
48	1990	Q0.06½	12-29-95	12-13	0.26	0.26	0.25	23.7	80.0	64.6	9-30-95	265	1035	30196	Dc	0.37	Δ0.53	□0.80	0.07	....	d0.68	9 Mo Sep	0.10	d0.65	48
49	1993	Q0.37½	12-29-95	12-13	1.50	1.50	1.50	Cv into 1.1905 com, $21				....	3600	...	Dc	...	...	...	....	....	....				49
50	1994	[70]0.002	11-30-95	11-13	[70]0.579	0.58	0.352	109	397	182	9-30-95	72.2	...	±★220412	Dc	0.29	1.22	1.12	1.10	....	1.86	9 Mo Sep	0.89	1.65	50
51	....	None Since Public			...	Nil	....	0.99	63.2	32.3	9-30-95	0.56	...	11361	Dc	p0.39	p0.31	p0.73	0.87	....	1.12	9 Mo Sep	0.47	0.72	51
52◆	....	None Since Public			...	Nil	....	9.67	104	36.2	9-30-95	28.2	...	23921	Dc	0.40	0.74	0.83	0.97	....	0.12	9 Mo Sep	0.66	d0.19	52

◆Stock Splits & Divs By Line Reference Index [1]2-for-1,'93:No adj for stk dstr Capital One Finl,'95. [3]2-for-1,'92,'93. [6]Reorg,1-for-6.7586 REVERSE,'90. [11]3-for-2,'94. [13]3-for-2,'95. [17]6-for-5,'95. [20]1-for-10 REVERSE'92. [29]10%,'94. [30]3-for-2,'93. [34]2-for-1,'93. [35]2-for-1,'93. [41]2-for-1,'91. [42]2-for-1,'92. [43]2-for-1,'92. [45]2-for-1 in Cl'B','91. [52]2-for-1,'92.

¶ S&P 500 # MidCap 400 ✣ SmallCap 600 • Options

Index	Ticker	Name of Issue (Call Price of Pfd. Stocks)	Market	Com. Rank. & Pfd. Rating	Inst. Hold Cos	Inst. Hold Shs. (000)	Principal Business	Price Range 1971-93 High	1971-93 Low	1994 High	1994 Low	1995 High	1995 Low	Dec. Sales in 100s	December, 1995 Last Sale Or Bid High	Low	Last	%Div Yield	P-E Ratio	Total Return % Annualized 12 Mo	36 Mo	60 Mo
1	SDSK	✔Softdesk Inc	NNM	NR	48	2960	Dvlp architecture softwr prd	...	...	23¾	10¾	28½	16	6124	23	18¾	19¾	...	25	−1.9	...	...
2	SOFT	✔SofTech Inc	NNM	B−	12	662	Devel software svcs & prod	25⅛	1	9⅞	3⅞	6¼	3¼	4054	4⅛	3¼	3¾	...	d	−18.9	12.6	24.0
3•[1]	SKEY	✔Softkey International	NNM	NR	226	24820	Dvlp,mkt software products	...	...	27¼	9¾	51¾	20⅜	189232	32¾	20⅜	23⅛	...	21	−10.0	...	...
4	SOF	✔Softnet Systems	AS	C	5	147	Hlth care cost mgmt svcs	14⅞	¾	9	5⅛	16⅜	5¾	1171	10⅜	8¾	10⅜	...	d	48.2	58.1	49.8
5	SWRT	✔Software Artistry	NNM	NR	32	1800	Design,dvlp software products	...	...	...	...	28	12½	8298	18½	14¼	15	...	38	...	...	...
6	SFWR	Software 2000	NNM	NR	..	...	Dvp business software sys	...	...	...	...	11¼	7	17243	10	7	7¾	...	19	...	...	...
7	SOI	✔S.O.I. Industries(New)	AS,Ph	C	7	23	Mfr cabinets/lamps&tape duplicat'n	32½	2½	31	13	24	1⅜	1971	3	1⅜	1 7/16	...	d	...	...	...
8	SOL	✔Sola International	NY,Ch	NR	79	10414	Mfr plastic eyeglass lenses	...	...	...	...	27¾	16⅜	10759	27¾	24⅝	25¼	...	20	...	...	...
#9•[2]	SLR	✔Solectron Corp	NY,Ph	B+	205	39248	Mfr computer prod/subsys	29¾	1½	34	23⅜	45⅛	22⅛	26928	45⅛	38	44⅛	...	23	62.7	34.0	81.4
10	SGT.EC	✔Soligen Technologies	ECM	NR	4	78	Dvlp stg: metal fabricat'g sys	...	...	2	½	1½	9/16	1264	¾	⅝	11/16	...	d	22.2	...	...
11	SOMA	✔Somatix Therapy	NNM	C	35	10703	Cellular medical technology	79	1½	9	2⅞	7⅝	2⅞	33419	6½	4¾	6	...	d	92.0	−14.2	14.9
12•[2]	SMTG	✔Somatogen Inc	NNM	NR	65	5452	Dvlp stge:human blood subst	50½	6¾	10½	5⅞	26⅛	6⅜	48710	21¼	12¾	18⅞	...	d	175	−0.7	...
13	SOMR	✔Somerset Group	NNM	B−	14	154	Construction prd/sv,banking	18	5	14¼	9¾	18¼	12½	83	18¼	17¼	17½B	1.1	8	41.9	38.4	25.5
¶14•[3]	SNT	✔Sonat, Inc	NY,B,C,Ch,P,Ph	B	498	54920	Nat'l gas P.L.: drill'g o&g	36½	3⅜	34⅞	26	36¼	26	81071	36¼	32¼	35⅝	3.0	14	32.2	19.9	13.3
✣15•[4]	RIG	✔Sonat Offshore Drilling	NY	NR	141	26014	Offshore oil&gas drilling svcs	23½	15¼	21½	15⅝	49¼	17¾	52302	49¼	34½	44¾	0.5	32	151	...	...
✣16	SONC	✔Sonic Corp	NNM	NR	80	7927	Oper fast food drive-in restr	22	8⅛	17⅝	11⅛	24⅜	13⅛	11608	22	18½	19	...	18	43.8	−0.9	...
#17•[2]	SON	✔Sonoco Products	NY,Ch,Ph	A−	266	32351	Mfr paper packaging products	24	9/16	24½	18¾	28¾	19⅛	20161	27¼	24⅜	26¼	2.3	15	40.2	9.8	14.9
18	Pr A	$2.25 Sr'A'cm Cv Pfd([56]51.575)	NY	A	45	2097		52¼	50¾	56½	46⅜	61	48	2822	58½	54⅞	57⅛	3.9	..	...	...	...
19•[5]	SNE	✔Sony Corp[57] ADR	[6]NY,To,B,C,Ch,P,Ph	NR	104	7298	Color TV sets,tape rec,radio	59¾	2⅝	63¼	49⅜	61½	42½	8960	61½	54⅛	61⅜	0.7	..	10.4	22.8	12.5
#20•[7]	BID	✔Sotheby's Hldgs Cl'A'	NY,Ch	NR	137	32920	Worlds largest art auctioneer	37	7¾	19¾	10⅝	15⅜	10⅜	10628	14½	13¼	14¼	1.7	35	29.0	8.0	9.9
21	SMQ	Source One Mtg 9.375%'QUICS'	NY	....[58]	..	...	Quarterly Income Capital Sec	...	...	...	...	26⅛	25⅛	536	26⅛	25⅛	26B	9.0	..	...	...	...
22	SJI	✔South Jersey Indus	NY,B,Ch,Ph	B+	54	1582	Hldg co: gas, fuel oil, sand	27½	4½	24	16⅝	23½	17⅞	1735	23½	21	23⅛	6.2	18	38.0	8.8	12.8
23	SWP	✔South West Prop Tr	NY,Ch	NR	87	13719	Real estate investment trust	77½	2½	14	11	13½	11⅜	10725	13½	12⅜	13½	7.4	19	20.8	12.7	24.9
#24	SDW	✔Southdown, Inc	NY,Ch,Ph	C	134	12470	Cement:concrete:environ'l svc	31½	1⅜	30¼	14¼	21¾	11½	7878	19¾	18⅜	19½	...	29	35.7	26.5	11.1
25	PrD	$2.875cm Cv Sr'D'Pfd([61]50)	NY	B	19	586		...	...	56¾	30¾	46½	29¾	1023	46½	44	44¼	6.5	..	...	...	...
26	SMGS	✔Southeastern Mich Gas Ent	NNM	A	31	749	Integrated natural gas sys	23⅜	2 3/16	20⅝	16¼	20¼	16¼	1409	18½	17½	18	s4.4	24	15.0	12.5	19.4
27	SRN	Southern Banc(AL)	AS,Ph	NR	..	...	Savings & loan Gadsen, AL	...	...	...	...	13⅛	10	542	12⅞	12⅜	12⅞	2.7	..	...	...	...
28	SCE.Q	So Cal Edison 8.375%'QUIDS'	AS	....[64]	1	.4	Qtly Income Debt Securities	...	...	...	...	26⅞	24¾	1530	26⅞	25½	26B	8.0	..	...	...	...
✣29	SCW	✔Southern Cal Water	NY	B+	55	1837	Water supply, some elec	24⅜	4¼	22	15¼	21	15¾	1744	21	18¾	20¼	6.0	13	22.7	7.5	14.5
¶30•[8]	SO	✔Southern Co	NY,B,C,Ch,P,Ph	A−	592	185695	Elec util hldg:Southeast	23⅝	4	22⅛	17	25	19⅜	150550	25	22⅞	24⅝	5.0	15	30.2	16.3	19.9
31	SECX	✔Southern Electronics	NNM	NR	23	2142	Dstr computers/eqp so'estn US	18½	⅞	12½	4¾	7½	4½	3713	5⅜	4¾	4¾	...	7	−5.0	−29.0	9.9
✣32	SEHI	✔Southern Energy Homes	NNM	NR	52	4988	Producer of manufactured homes	17	10⅜	15¼	8¼	18¾	8⅜	10719	18¾	15¼	17½	...	15	104	...	...
33	SIG	✔Southern Indiana G&E[67]	NY,Ch,Ph	A	105	3863	Utility:elec/gas,Evansville	35½	4⅛	33⅞	24	36⅜	26⅜	2008	36⅜	33⅜	34¾	4.9	15	36.9	6.7	13.0
34•[9]	SNB	✔Southern National	NY,Ph	A	153	19118	Comm'l bkg,North&So.Carolina	23½	2¾	22	16⅞	28	18¾	17907	27	25⅝	26¼	3.5	15	41.6	14.6	29.0
35	Pr A	6.75% cm Cv[69]Dep Pfd([70]26.0125)	NY	BB+	18	1211		37⅜	25	33¼	26⅛	40½	28¾	114	39⅞	37⅞	38¾	4.4	..	...	...	...
#36•[10]	SNG	✔Southern New Eng Telecom	[11]NY,B,Ch	A−	287	21867	Supplies telecommunic svcs	46½	6⅜	36¼	28¼	40¼	31¾	17544	40¼	36⅛	39¾	4.4	15	28.3	10.2	9.9
37•[8]	RSP	✔Southern Pacific Rail[71]	NY,Ch	NR	196	64805	Railroad freight transport'n	21⅜	13½	24⅜	16⅝	25¼	14½	71856	24½	22⅝	24	...	...	36.2	...	...
38	SUG	✔Southern Union	NY,B,Ch	NR	51	2343	Natural gas dstr: oil & gas	19⅛	7¼	22¼	15⅝	26½	14¾	6094	26½	24	25¼	...	18	63.8	60.6	35.3
39	SZB	✔SouthFirst Bancshares	AS	NR	3	68	Savings & loan, Alabama	...	...	...	...	16	10	275	16	14⅛	15½	e3.2	21	...	...	...
40	SLCM	Southland Corp	NNM	NR	52	29545	Oper 7-Eleven convenience strs	7⅝	½	6¾	3¾	4¾	2⅞	31710	3⅞	3	3¼	...	12	−25.4	2.3	...
#41•[12]	SOTR	✔SouthTrust Corp	NNM	A	201	31248	Commercial bkg,Alabama	22⅛	⅞	22⅛	17	27¼	18	37737	26	25	25⅝	3.1	11	47.5	19.8	34.4
42	SWTX	✔Southwall Technologies	NNM	C	15	925	Produces thin film coatings	12	2¼	5⅝	2⅛	4⅞	2⅝	2184	4½	4	4¼	...	d	54.5	−10.9	1.2
¶43•[5]	LUV	✔Southwest Airlines	NY,B,Ch,P,Ph	B+	407	72038	Airline svc mid-so'west U.S.	37⅝	1/32	39	15½	29⅞	16⅜	102414	26⅛	22⅛	23	0.2	19	39.7	6.1	32.1
44	OKSB	✔Southwest Bancorp	NNM	NR	5	323	Commercial banking,Oklahoma	12½	11¾	15	11	18½	12¾	202	18½	17	18½	1.3	13	44.6	...	...
✣45	SWX	✔Southwest Gas	NY,B,Ch,P,Ph	B	99	7601	Natural gas,banking,R.E. dvlp	26¾	6⅛	19⅜	13¾	18⅜	13⅝	11661	18⅛	17¼	17⅝	4.7	24	31.4	13.6	12.0
46	SWST	✔Southwest Securities Grp	NNM	NR	24	1247	Securities/brokerage svcs	14¼	5⅝	12¾	5¾	11¼	6	2464	11¼	10	11⅛	1.4	13	84.9	11.7	...
47	SWWC	✔Southwest Water Co	NNM	B	17	393	Water utility:serves CA,NM,TX	22⅞	2 7/16	11⅝	7⅛	10	7⅛	832	10	8½	9⅝	s3.9	22	22.9	−7.5	−3.3
✣48	SWN	✔Southwestern Energy	NY,Ch,Ph	A−	130	13871	Hldg gas utility,Ark: o & g	21⅞	⅝	18⅞	14	15½	11¾	8610	13¾	12⅝	12¾	1.9	28	−11.9	1.3	6.1
#49	SPS	✔Southwestern Pub[75]Sv[76]	NY,B,Ch,P,Ph	A−	170	11137	Electric util:Texas,Okl,N.M.	37⅞	8⅛	30⅞	23¾	33⅞	26½	14046	33⅜	32⅛	32¾	6.7	12	31.6	8.9	10.5
✣50•[13]	SVRN	✔Sovereign Bancorp	NNM	NR	69	9987	Savings bank,Wyomissing, PA	11⅝	1⅛	11⅝	7⅜	10⅞	7⅜	24505	10⅞	10	10⅛	s0.9	10	42.0	23.4	66.4
51	SSS	✔Sovran Self Storage	NY	NR	44	3908	Real estate investment trust	...	...	...	...	26¾	22⅜	3886	26¾	24¾	26½	7.6	15	...	...	...
52	SWH	✔Spaghetti Warehouse	NY,Ph	B	27	3133	Family-style Italian rest'ts	30¾	1¼	9⅜	4⅝	6½	4⅝	4323	5¼	4⅝	5	...	24	0.0	−36.2	−15.1

Uniform Footnote Explanations-See Page 4. Other: [1]AS,CBOE,NY:Cycle 1. [2]CBOE:Cycle 1. [3]ASE:Cycle 1. [4]Ph:Cycle 2. [5]CBOE:Cycle 3. [6]Mo [7]ASE,CBOE,P:Cycle 1. [8]CBOE:Cycle 2. [9]NY,Ph:cycle 3. [10]NY:Cycle 1. [11]Ph [12]P:Cycle 3. [13]Ph:Cycle 1. [51]Fiscal Jun'93 & prior. [52]Fiscal Aug'93 & prior. [53]12 Mo Sep'94. [54]Stk dstr of Newcare Health Corp. [55]®$1.62,'95. [56]Fr 11-8-96,scale to $50 in 2003. [57]ADR equal 1 ord shr, 50y. [58]Rated BBB by S&P. [59]Subsid Pfd. [60]Incl $0.117 non-taxable,'94. [61]Fr 1-27-2001. [62]If com exceeds 130% Cv price-20 trad.days. [63]Excl subsid pfd. [64]Rated A by S&P. [65]Excl $1432 subsid Pfd. [66]12 Mo Dec'92. [67]Approve hldg co, SIGCORP, 1 com. [68]®$2.27,'94. [69]Dep for 0.25 shr 6.75% cm Cv Series'A'Pfd. [70]Fr 3-1-96,scale to $25 in 2002. [71]Approve Union Pacific Corp acq, $25. [72]Fiscal Dec'93 & prior. [73]Incl curr amts. [74]®$0.40,'94. [75]Public Svc Colo plan mgr,0.95 com new Co. [76]Plan form new hldg co,New Century Energies.

Index	Cash Divs. Ea. Yr. Since	Dividends: Latest Payment: Period $	Date	Ex. Div.	Total $: So Far 1995	Ind. Rate	Paid 1994	Financial Position Mil-$: Cash & Equiv.	Curr. Assets	Curr. Liab.	Balance Sheet Date	Capitalization: Lg Trm Debt Mil-$	Shs. 000: Pfd.	Com.	Earnings $ Per Shr.: Years End	1991	1992	1993	1994	1995	Last 12 Mos.	Interim Earnings: Period	$ per Shr. 1994	1995	Index
1	....	None Since Public			...	Nil	....	9.45	21.3	5.54	9-30-95	....	...	5724	Dc	...	...	p0.17	p0.50	....	0.79	9 Mo Sep	p0.28	0.57	1
2	....	None Since Public			...	Nil	....	2.99	18.2	5.44	8-31-95	....	...	4062	My	d1.58	0.12	0.45	Δ0.64	d0.60	d0.97	3 Mo Aug	0.08	d0.29	2
3	....	None Since Public			...	Nil	....	87.1	141	38.4	9-30-95	4.38	...	25153	Dc	pd0.80	pd0.50	p[51]d3.90	1.04	....	1.13	9 Mo Sep	0.74	0.83	3
4	....	None Paid			...	Nil	....	0.36	3.36	5.62	6-30-95	4.10	...	★5300	Sp	d1.99	d0.17	d0.37	d0.75	Pd2.21	d2.21				4
5	....	None Since Public			...	Nil	....	19.0	27.0	6.63	9-30-95	0.06	...	6763	Dc	...	...	...	p0.27	....	0.40	9 Mo Sep	0.15	0.28	5
6	....	None Since Public			...	Nil	....	16.2	33.0	37.7	9-30-95	....	p...	★9592	Sp	d0.54	0.08	[52]0.05	Δ[53]0.07	0.40	0.40				6
7◆	....	h[54]....	12-5-94	11-23	...	Nil	h[54]....	0.32	8.86	10.1	9-30-95	1.65	...	1791	Je	0.16	Nil	0.32	1.28	d1.52	d2.08	3 Mo Sep	0.16	d0.40	7
8	....	None Since Public			...	Nil	....	18.2	197	109	9-30-95	105	...	21785	Mr	...	...	p0.42	p1.05	....	1.29	6 Mo Sep	p0.47	□0.71	8
9◆	....	None Since Public			...	Nil	....	149	726	371	8-31-95	30.0	...	49584	Au	0.35	0.44	0.80	1.32	[55]1.82	1.93	3 Mo Nov	0.43	0.54	9
10	....	None Since Public			...	Nil	....	2.19	2.86	1.55	9-30-95	0.36	...	28913	Mr	...	...	d0.11	d0.09	....	d0.07	6 Mo Sep	d0.05	d0.03	10
11◆	....	None Since Public			...	Nil	....	20.7	21.5	4.56	9-30-95	1.61	...	22690	Je	d7.92	d4.43	d1.19	d0.95	d2.34	d2.44	3 Mo Sep	d0.21	d0.31	11
12	....	None Since Public			...	Nil	....	37.3	38.5	4.34	9-30-95	0.10	...	★20565	Je	d1.21	d1.37	d2.37	d3.64	d0.94	d0.88	3 Mo Sep	d0.25	d0.19	12
13	1994	S0.10	9-15-95	8-30	0.20	0.20	0.10	8.30	9.94	1.04	9-30-95	2.50	...	1633	Dc	0.07	0.03	1.37	1.57	....	2.18	9 Mo Sep	1.15	1.76	13
14◆	1936	Q0.27	12-14-95	11-28	1.08	1.08	1.08	58.1	404	462	9-30-95	771	...	86057	Dc	0.77	2.47	□3.05	1.62	E2.62	2.40	9 Mo Sep	1.37	2.15	14
15	1993	Q0.06	11-28-95	11-10	0.24	0.24	0.24	115	189	66.8	9-30-95	30.0	...	28366	Dc	...	pΔ0.38	□1.00	0.45	....	1.41	9 Mo Sep	0.30	1.26	15
16◆	....	None Since Public			...	Nil	....	3.77	12.7	8.46	8-31-95	30.6	...	p13331	Au	□0.39	0.58	0.72	0.64	1.05	1.05				16
17◆	1925	Q0.15	12-8-95	11-15	0.283	0.60	0.529	79.6	699	393	10-01-95	588	3450	91098	Dc	1.05	□0.89	1.29	1.33	E1.75↑	1.65	9 Mo Sep	0.96	1.28	17
18	1994	Q0.56¼	2-1-96	1-10	2.25	2.25	2.23¾	Cv into 1.9753 com, $25.31				....	3450	...	Dc	...	...	...	....	....	....				18
19◆	1947	0.208	12-12-95	9-27	0.458	0.46	0.426	6092	24120	18078	3-31-95	10185	...	373911	Mr	2.20	0.79	0.41	d7.83	....	0.12	6 Mo Sep	d7.53	0.42	19
20	1988	Q0.06	12-15-95	11-17	0.24	0.24	0.24	17.4	317	188	9-30-95	....	...	±55995	Dc	±0.25	±0.07	±0.35	±0.36	....	0.41	9 Mo Sep	±0.04	±0.09	20
21	....	Plan qtly div			...	2.34	....	Co option redm fr 5-1-99 at $25				56.0	...	...	Dc	...	...	...	....	....	....	Mature 12-31-2025			21
22◆	1952	Q0.36	1-2-96	12-7	1.44	1.44	1.44	1.54	71.4	119	9-30-95	174	[59]24	10722	Dc	1.27	1.61	Δ1.55	1.21	....	1.30	12 Mo Sep	1.43	1.30	22
23◆	1993	Q0.25	1-17-96	12-28	0.98	1.00	[60]0.90	Equity per shr $9.08			9-30-95	174	...	20299	Dc	Δpd1.93	Δd3.31	0.39	0.64	....	0.73	9 Mo Sep	0.45	0.54	23
24	....	0.12½	3-1-91	2-11	...	Nil	....	10.5	186	95.6	9-30-95	200	4633	17300	Dc	□d2.86	d2.69	□d0.30	d0.40	....	0.67	9 Mo Sep	0.46	1.53	24
25	1994	Q0.71⅞	1-2-96	12-13	2.87½	2.875	1.949	Cv into 1.511 com,$33.092				....	1500	...	Dc	...	...	...	....	....	....	Co opt 1-27-97 to 1-27-2001 exch for com[62]			25
26◆	1956	sQ0.20	11-15-95	11-1	s0.781	0.80	s0.743	2.79	79.5	70.6	9-30-95	104	[63]7	11806	Dc	0.73	□0.90	□0.92	□0.97	....	0.75	12 Mo Sep	□1.06	0.75	26
27	1995	0.08¾	12-15-95	11-28	0.08¾	0.35	....	Book Value $14.72			3-31-95	....	...	★1455	Je	...	...	...	p0.68	....	....	9 Mo Mar	n/a	p0.20	27
28	1995	Q0.523	12-31-95	12-28	1.25	2.09	....	Co option redm fr 5-25-2000 at $25				100	...	...	Dc	...	...	...	....	....	....	Mature 6-30-2044			28
29◆	1931	Q0.30½	12-1-95	11-9	1.205	1.22	1.20	1.85	43.6	44.4	9-30-95	107	88	7845	Dc	2.34	1.82	1.66	1.43	....	1.53	12 Mo Sep	1.50	1.53	29
30◆	1948	Q0.30½	12-6-95	11-2	1.22	1.22	1.18	332	3103	3778	9-30-95	8484	[65]...	666157	Dc	1.39	1.51	1.57	1.52	E1.67	1.70	12 Mo Nov	1.47	1.70	30
31◆	....	None Paid			...	Nil	....	0.20	85.4	39.6	9-30-95	14.9	...	6993	Je	0.65	0.71	1.13	0.81	0.74	0.70	3 Mo Sep	0.18	0.14	31
32◆	....	None Since Public			...	Nil	....	13.2	45.6	19.2	9-30-95	0.04	...	★9941	Dc	...	p[66]0.55	p0.86	0.94	....	1.15	9 Mo Sep	0.70	0.91	32
33◆	1944	Q0.42¼	12-20-95	11-15	1.69	1.69	1.65	5.84	116	142	9-30-95	258	195	15755	Dc	2.37	2.26	2.45	2.53	....	2.37	12 Mo Sep	2.45	Δ2.37	33
34	1934	Q0.23	2-1-96	1-10	0.86	0.92	0.74	Book Value $15.52			9-30-95	1305	740	103300	Dc	1.36	1.84	□2.28	[68]2.38	....	1.71	9 Mo Sep	1.67	1.00	34
35	1992	Q0.422	11-15-95	10-30	1.68¾	1.69	1.68¾	Cv into 1.4767 com,$16.93				....	3080	...	Dc	...	...	...	....	....	....				35
36	1891	Q0.44	1-16-96	12-21	1.76	1.76	1.76	25.7	515	638	9-30-95	1183	...	65094	Dc	□2.06	□2.48	□d0.84	2.77	E2.60	2.63	9 Mo Sep	2.12	1.98	36
37	....	None Since Public			...	Nil	....	137	564	969	9-30-95	1655	...	156138	Dc	...	p0.31	□d0.54	□1.63	E0.20↓	0.94	9 Mo Sep	□0.65	d0.04	37
38◆	....	5%Stk	11-27-95	11-13	5%Stk	Stk	5%Stk	....	92.3	74.3	9-30-95	442	...	11533	Je	0.12	0.16	[72]0.78	0.44	1.33	1.38	12 Mo Sep	0.30	1.38	38
39	1995	†2.00	1-22-96	1-4	0.42½	0.50	....	Book Value $17.71			6-30-95	4.74	...	830	Sp	...	...	...	p0.63	P0.74	0.74				39
40	....	None Since Public			...	Nil	....	20.2	256	680	9-30-95	2120	...	409923	Dc	Δd0.22	d0.32	Δd0.03	0.22	....	0.27	9 Mo Sep	0.16	0.21	40
41◆	1944	Q0.20	1-1-96	11-21	0.77	0.80	0.66	Book Value $15.83			9-30-95	891	...	87624	Dc	1.42	1.66	1.94	2.15	....	2.31	9 Mo Sep	1.59	1.75	41
42	....	None Since Public			...	Nil	....	3.66	14.2	6.60	4-02-95	2.65	...	5847	Dc	d0.90	0.01	d0.23	d0.67	....	d0.43	9 Mo Sep	d0.20	0.04	42
43◆	1976	Q0.01	1-2-96	12-4	0.04	0.04	0.03	366	564	647	9-30-95	671	...	143932	Dc	0.21	Δ0.65	Δ1.05	1.22	E1.20	1.08	9 Mo Sep	1.08	0.94	43
44	1981	Q0.06	1-2-96	12-14	0.23	0.24	0.186	Book Value $10.82			9-30-95	....	690	3755	Dc	0.86	1.23	1.44	1.37	....	1.41	9 Mo Sep	1.01	1.05	44
45	1956	Q0.20½	12-1-95	11-13	0.82	0.82	0.80	Book Value $12.57			9-30-95	[73]858	40	24320	Dc	d0.76	0.81	Δ0.56	1.22	....	0.74	12 Mo Sep	0.95	0.74	45
46◆	1991	Q0.04	1-3-96	12-13	0.14½	0.16	0.12½	Equity per shr $8.43			9-30-95	....	...	8793	Je	0.75	1.03	1.51	0.99	0.69	0.87	3 Mo Sep	0.12	0.30	46
47◆	1960	5%Stk	1-20-96	12-28	0.381	0.38	0.381	0.51	11.2	16.7	9-30-95	19.6	p11	2576	Dc	0.08	0.92	0.04	[74]0.41	....	0.44	9 Mo Sep	0.30	0.33	47
48◆	1939	Q0.06	11-3-95	10-18	0.24	0.24	0.24	1.04	44.0	42.0	9-30-95	★188	...	24692	Dc	0.78	0.87	Δ1.05	0.98	....	0.46	12 Mo Sep	1.19	0.46	48
49	1942	Q0.55	12-1-95	11-13	2.20	2.20	2.20	36.9	171	170	8-31-95	582	1675	40918	Au	2.63	2.34	2.43	2.38	2.80	2.80				49
50◆	1987	5%Stk	2-15-96	1-30	s0.087	0.09	0.087	Book Value $4.15			9-30-95	932	2000	45498	Dc	0.40	0.54	Δ0.74	0.95	....	1.01	9 Mo Sep	0.71	0.77	50
51	1995	0.505	1-20-96	1-3	0.53	2.02	....	Equity per shr $19.84			9-30-95	....	...	7542	Dc	...	...	...	p1.66	....	1.75	9 Mo Sep	p1.09	p1.18	51
52◆	....	None Since Public			...	Nil	....	1.41	3.33	5.70	10-01-95	15.2	...	5597	Je	□0.80	0.88	0.62	0.28	0.22	0.21	3 Mo Sep	0.08	0.07	52

◆**Stock Splits & Divs By Line Reference Index** [7]1-for-8 REVERSE,'95. [9]2-for-1,'92,'93. [11]1-for-4 REVERSE,'91. [14]2-for-1,'93. [16]3-for-2,'95. [17]2-for-1,'93:Adj for 5%,'95. [19]10%,'91. [22]Adj for 2%,'93. [23]1-for-5 REVERSE,'92. [26]Adj to 5%,'95. [29]2-for-1,'93. [30]2-for-1,'94. [31]3-for-2,'92,'93. [32]5-for-4,'95. [33]4-for-3,'92. [38]3-for-2,'94:Adj to 5%,'95. [41]3-for-2,'92,'93. [43]2-for-1,'92:3-for-2,'93. [46]3-for-2,'93. [47]Adj for 5%,'95. [48]3-for-1,'93. [50]5-for-4,'91(3 times):6-for-5,'91,'92,'93(twice):10%,92(3 times),'94:Adj to 5%,'95. [52]3-for-2,'91.

¶ S&P 500 # MidCap 400 ✣ SmallCap 600 • Options

Index	Ticker	Name of Issue (Call Price of Pfd. Stocks)	Market	Com. Rank. & Pfd. Rating	Inst. Hold Cos	Inst. Hold Shs. (000)	Principal Business	Price Range 1971-93 High	1971-93 Low	1994 High	1994 Low	1995 High	1995 Low	Dec. Sales in 100s	December, 1995 Last Sale Or Bid High	Low	Last	%Div Yield	P-E Ratio	Total Return % Annualized 12 Mo	36 Mo	60 Mo
1	SPAN	Span-America Med Sys	NNM	B+	13	410	Foam pads for health care ind	16	1½	6¼	4¼	6⅜	4	1198	6⅜	5⅝	6	1.7	20	35.9	−10.2	14.9
2	SPTA	✔Sparta Pharmaceuticals	NSC	NR	3	82	Dvlp stge:pharmac'l R&D	...	...	6	4¼	5½	1⅜	3639	2¾	1⅜	2	...	d	−60.0	...	...
✣3•[1]	SPAR	✔Spartan Motors	NNM	B+	49	3581	Mfg heavy truck chassis	25¼	⅜	21¾	12⅜	14⅝	8⅝	12675	11¼	9¼	11	0.5	48	−17.3	−10.3	44.7
4	SEH	✔Spartech Corp	NY,Ch,Ph	B−	27	10539	PVC compounds,plastic sheet	22⅝	11/16	6¼	3¾	7¾	5	6937	7⅜	6½	7	e...	12	38.5	33.3	32.3
5	SPA	✔Sparton Corp	NY,Ch,Ph	↓C	23	1568	Sonobuoys: conveyors,auto eq	24	1	7¼	4¼	5⅜	3⅜	1068	4⅞	4⅛	4⅜	...	d	0.0	−10.6	7.0
6	CHM	✔Specialty Chemical Res	AS,Ph	NR	14	1258	Dvlp/pkg auto,ind'l chem prd	12⅛	5	7¼	2⅞	4⅞	1 13/16	5735	2¾	1 13/16	2	...	d	−33.3	−29.2	...
7	SPEQ	Specialty Equipment	NNM	NR	40	8311	Mfr food service equipment	7¼	4½	11	5	14	9¼	20170	12¾	9½	11½	...	d	12.9	...	...
8	DIAGF	✔Spectral Diagnostics	NNM,To	NR	12	698	Dvlp stge:diagnostic test prod	33½	3¾	33	13¼	28¼	7½	1321	16	7½	8¼	...	d	−45.0	−1.9	...
9	SPTR	✔SpecTran Corp	NNM	B−	19	854	Mfrs optical fibers	28¼	¼	12¼	4	7¼	4⅝	5446	5⅝	5	5½	...	..	14.3	−21.2	8.0
10	SVN	✔SpectraVision Inc 'B'[53]	AS,Ch	D	23	2095	Pay-per view hotel movie sys	15⅜	2⅜	9⅞	3/16	11/16	1/64	12121	1/16	1/64	1/64	...	d	−94.9	−86.2	...
11	SPCT	✔Spectrian Corp	NNM	NR	88	5125	Supply linear pwr amplifiers	...	...	29½	12½	51¼	15¾	20356	25¾	20¾	22¼	...	23	−19.8	...	...
12•[2]	SBYT	✔Spectrum HoloByte	NNM	NR	124	18496	Dvlp entertainment software	17	4½	17¼	6¼	21⅜	6	59363	9½	6	6½	...	d	−50.0	−6.7	...
13	SFAM	✔Speedfam Intl	NNM	NR	..	...	Mfr semiconductor mfg eq	...	...	...	...	19⅛	10	22239	16¾	10	11¼	...	..	...	...	...
14	TRK	✔Speedway Motorsports	NY,Ch,Ph	NR	41	3325	Own,oper motor speedways	...	...	...	...	31	17⅝	3069	30¼	27⅛	30	...	..	...	...	...
15	SPZN	✔Speizman Ind	NNM	NR	18	879	Sells knitting/hosiery mach's	20	2¾	17½	3¼	6¾	2⅝	4661	3⅛	2⅝	2⅞	...	11	−22.0	1.5	...
16•[3]	SP	✔Spelling Entertainment Grp	[4]NY,B,Ch,P	B−	77	8619	TV & motion picture distrib'n	50	1	12¼	8⅜	14	9¼	24538	13¼	12¼	12½	...	60	17.6	25.1	26.3
17	SD	✔Sphere Drake Holdings	NY,Ch	NR	..	...	Property & casualty insurance	21⅝	15½	18¼	10¾	19⅛	12⅞	3064	15⅛	13¾	14	1.1	6	1.9	...	...
18•[5]	SPGLA	✔Spiegel Cl'A'[56]	NNM	B	46	5305	Catalog:apparel,gen'l mdse	23⅜	3⅛	26¾	8¾	13⅞	6⅞	26570	9	6⅞	6⅞	...	d	−31.6	−4.8	2.3
19	SPK	✔Spieker Properties	NY	NR	112	23505	Real estate investment trust	20½	18½	23¼	18⅝	25⅞	19⅜	9889	25⅞	24¼	25⅛	6.7	35	36.5	...	...
20	SPYN	✔Spine-Tech Inc	NNM	NR	22	2264	Dvlp/mfr spinal implants&instr	...	...	...	...	23¼	9	18233	23¼	19	23¼	...	..	...	...	...
21	GYM	✔Sport Supply Group	NY,Ch,Ph	NR	38	2879	Mfr/dstr sports equipment	16⅜	4⅜	18	9¼	14¾	6¼	8045	8⅜	6¾	8⅜	1.4	16	−14.2	6.4	...
22	WS	Wrrt (Pur1.25com at$20)	AS	....	8	85		5⅛	2⅛	5½	1½	3⅛	⅜	974	1 1/16	⅝	¾	...	..	...	...	...
23•[6]	TSA	✔Sports Authority[57]	NY,Ch,Ph	NR	112	11956	Sporting goods superstores	...	...	25	19	30¼	16¼	17539	24⅜	19½	20⅜	...	19	1.9	...	...
24	SCY	✔Sports Club	AS	NR	16	1685	Dvp/oper sports&fitness clubs	...	...	9⅛	6½	8	2⅝	9398	3⅞	2⅝	3⅛	...	15	−54.5	...	...
✣25•[7]	WON	✔Sports & Recreation Inc	NY,Ch,Ph	NR	104	13084	Oper sporting equip superstrs	25	11⅝	29½	18¾	25½	6¼	24308	9	6¾	7⅛	...	11	−71.9	−29.7	...
26	SISB	✔Springfield Instit'n for Svgs	NNM	NR	23	2296	General banking, MA	...	...	...	...	17⅛	8	3158	17⅛	16	16⅜	...	..	...	...	...
¶27	SMI	✔Springs Industries'A'	NY,Ch,Ph	B+	271	8478	Finished fabrics:hm furn'gs	49	4⅛	41	29¼	44¾	35¼	4796	44½	41	41⅜	3.2	11	14.7	8.6	16.3
¶28•[8]	FON	✔Sprint Corp	NY,B,C,Ch,P,Ph	B	747	212109	Diversified telecommun sys	46⅜	5⅜	40⅛	26⅛	41⅛	25⅞	120032	41⅛	38½	39⅝	2.5	14	49.0	19.3	14.3
29	Pr	$1.50 cm Cv Ser 1 Pfd(42 1/2)vtg	NY	BBB−	4	18	Serves 19 states providing	130¾	16	117	102	104¼	90¼	...	...	...	118⅞B	1.3	..	...	...	...
30	Pr A	$1.50 cm Cv Ser 2 Pfd(50)vtg	NY	BBB−	4	2	local & long distance svc	111¼	14	96½	69	100	66½	8	100	98	99⅛B	1.5	..	...	...	...
31	FXN	Sprint Corp 8.25%'DECS' 2000	NY	....[59]	52	3731	Exch Notes For Com Stock	...	...	...	...	38	32⅜	8529	38	35¾	38	6.9	..	...	...	...
✣32	ST	✔SPS Technologies	NY,B,Ch,Ph	C	66	3030	Ind'l fasteners:mtls hldg	60⅛	3⅝	27⅜	18¾	53¾	25⅜	2255	53¾	45¼	53⅜	...	24	112	40.3	24.2
33	PAY	✔SPS Transaction Services	NY,Ph	NR	84	5787	Transaction process'g svcs	35⅝	8	32⅜	24	35½	24¾	4624	30⅛	27⅛	29⅝	...	19	9.7	11.9	...
34	SPSS	✔SPSS Inc	NNM	NR	58	4567	Dvlp, mkt software prd	10⅛	6⅝	15⅛	8¼	19⅞	11⅜	6589	19⅞	18¼	19½	...	22	64.2	...	...
✣35•[9]	SPW	✔SPX Corp	NY,Ch,P	B−	161	8966	Engine parts: piston rings	44⅝	2½	18½	13⅞	17⅜	10¾	6457	16⅝	14⅞	15⅞	2.5	27	−0.4	−0.2	5.2
36	SPYG	✔Spyglass Inc	NNM	NR	53	4144	Internet connectivity provider	...	...	...	...	61	8½	97410	61	43	57	...	..	...	...	...
37	SQAX	SQA Inc	NNM	NR	..	...	Dvp/mkt software pds	...	...	...	...	24	16	40339	24	16	19¼	...	d	...	...	...
38•[10]	STAA	✔STAAR Surgical	NNM	B−	34	1903	Mfr eye/surgery products	79	¼	10¾	4⅛	13⅛	7½	8097	12	9⅞	10¾	...	15	21.1	36.3	24.7
39	SBLI	✔Staff Builders 'A'	NNM	B−	42	12080	Staffing/health care svcs	12⅛	⅝	5	2⅝	5⅝	2½	39824	4	2⅝	2⅞	...	13	−1.1	5.5	33.7
40	SA	✔Stage II Apparel	AS	B−	7	256	Mkts sports/casual apparel	10⅝	1⅛	5⅜	2¾	4⅝	2½	1299	3	2½	3	...	d	−22.6	−20.8	12.7
41	SBP	✔Standard Br Paint	NY,Ch,P	D	14	11591	Paint & hm decorating ctrs	318¾	8¾	23¾	3⅛	9⅜	9/16	6410	1¼	9/16	11/16	...	..	−85.0	−57.8	−57.4
42	STW	✔Standard Commercial	NY,Ph	C	46	3419	Leaf tobacco,world mkt	33⅛	⅛	18¼	10¾	14⅝	9¼	1926	12¼	9¼	9⅞	s...	d	−10.1	−28.6	2.4
43•[5]	SFB	✔Standard Fedl Bancorp'n	NY,Ch,Ph,P	NR	170	23026	Savings bank,Michigan	32¼	4⅝	29¾	22¼	40⅞	23¾	17832	40⅜	38	39⅜	1.8	11	71.8	19.8	39.7
44	STND	✔Standard Financial	NNM	NR	44	5133	Savings bank, Chicago	...	...	11¾	9	14⅞	9½	13813	14⅞	13⅜	14⅝	...	15	51.0	...	...
✣45•[11]	SMSC	✔Standard Microsystems	NNM	B−	73	3224	Local area network equip	30¾	1/16	30⅜	13⅜	31⅝	12½	55122	21⅛	15⅞	16½	...	d	−45.5	−12.5	28.3
✣46	SMP	✔Standard Motor Prod	NY,Ch	B	71	5847	Ignition & fuel sys parts	26⅞	13/16	26⅞	14¾	20⅝	14½	2838	15⅝	14¾	15	2.1	10	−20.2	6.0	17.8
✣47	SPF	✔Standard Pacific	NY,B,Ch,P,Ph	NR	71	11470	Single family home builder	19⅞	⅛	12⅞	4⅞	8⅜	5⅛	17030	6⅞	5⅝	6⅜	1.9	49	15.4	−0.3	3.3
48	SPY	Standard & Poor's Dep Receipts	AS	NR	58	3134	'SPDRs' Stock Price Index Secs	47⅛	42¾	48¼	43⅜	62¾	45⅝	98168	62¾	60⅝	61½	2.1	..	36.6	...	...
49	MDY	Standard & Poor's MidCap Dep Rc	AS	NR	3	29	'SPDRs'Stock Price Index Sec	...	...	...	...	44½	37	4271	44½	41⅝	43½	1.3	..	...	...	...
✣50	SPD	✔Standard Products	NY,Ch,Ph	B−	93	10125	Rubber/plastic transp equip	36⅝	11/16	38¾	21⅜	24⅛	13½	8512	18¾	15¼	17⅝	3.9	39	−23.2	−9.2	15.0
#51	SREG	✔Standard Register	NNM	A	142	14500	Business forms & handl'g eq	28½	13/16	23¾	14½	23⅜	15¼	14039	22¾	20⅛	20⅛	3.8	12	26.5	9.0	18.3
✣52	SXI	✔Standex Intl	NY,B,Ch,Ph	A	94	6989	Diversified manufacturing	27¾	15/16	32⅝	24⅝	36¾	29	3590	36½	32⅛	32¾	2.2	13	7.9	22.8	27.8

Uniform Footnote Explanations-See Page 4. Other: [1]P:Cycle 3. [2]P:Cycle 2. [3]CBOE:Cycle 3. [4]Ph [5]CBOE:Cycle 2. [6]ASE,CBOE,NY,Ph:Cycle 1. [7]ASE,CBOE,NY:Cycle 2. [8]Ph:Cycle 2. [9]NY:Cycle 3. [10]CBOE,NY:Cycle 3. [11]ASE:Cycle 2. [51]To be determined. [52]8 Mo Mar'92. [53]ASE trading halted 5-1-95. [54]Incl liabs subs to compromise. [55]Incl current amts. [56]Non-vtg. [57]Plan SmallCap 600 listing:eff Jan 5. [58]Pfd in $M. [59]Rated BBBr by S&P. [60]Stock or cash re-specified cond.. [61]Excl. 1.3M ESOP Shares. [62]Stk dstr of Vision Sciences. [63]®$0.62,'94. [64]6 Mo Jan'94.

Splits ◆ Index	Cash Divs. Ea.Yr. Since	Dividends: Latest Payment Period $	Date	Ex. Div.	Total $ So Far 1995	Ind. Rate	Paid 1994	Financial Position Mil-$ Cash& Equiv.	Curr. Assets	Curr. Liab.	Balance Sheet Date	Capitalization Lg Trm Debt Mil-$	Shs. 000 Pfd.	Com.	Earnings $ Per Shr. Years End	1991	1992	1993	1994	1995	Last 12 Mos.	Interim Earnings Period	$ per Shr. 1994	1995	Index
1	1990	Q0.02½	12-4-95	11-13	0.10	0.10	0.10	4.67	11.3	2.53	7-01-95	0.30	...	3175	Sp	0.51	0.61	0.31	0.49	P0.30	0.30				1
2	....	None Since Public			...	Nil	....	1.08	1.33	0.12	9-30-95	....	...	6186	Dc	...	...	pd0.54	d0.70	....	d0.46	9 Mo Sep	d0.59	d0.35	2
3◆	1988	0.05	7-8-95	6-2	0.05	0.05	0.05	9.97	61.5	11.1	9-30-95	5.87	...	12711	Dc	0.58	0.72	0.80	0.80	....	0.23	9 Mo Sep	0.74	0.17	3
4	1995	Q0.03	1-5-96	12-20	†0.09	[51]....	....	1.70	88.1	51.7	7-29-95	p44.0	...	p24429	Oc	d5.02	0.42	0.54	0.97	P0.60	0.60				4
5	....	0.13	1-15-90	12-11	...	Nil	....	0.99	78.9	49.6	9-30-95	0.37	...	7811	Je	0.53	1.02	0.85	d0.63	d0.83	d1.01	3 Mo Sep	d0.16	d0.34	5
6	....	None Since Public			...	Nil	....	0.03	17.5	8.90	9-30-95	9.23	...	3933	Dc	p*0.47	*0.07	□0.44	Δd0.42	....	d0.64	9 Mo Sep	Δd0.14	d0.36	6
7	....	None Since Public			...	Nil	....	8.79	118	96.6	7-31-95	193	...	17011	Ja	...	pd4.60	pd3.56	d3.29	....	d0.93	9 Mo Oct	d2.32	□0.04	7
8	....	None Since Public			...	Nil	....	32.2	33.5	1.56	j3-31-95	0.13	...	7034	Mr	‡[52]d0.39	d0.79	d0.64	d1.34	....	jd1.74	6 Mo Sep	d0.64	d1.04	8
9	....	None Since Public			...	Nil	....	4.85	20.2	4.31	9-30-95	10.0	...	5353	Dc	0.57	0.66	0.67	d0.09	....	0.01	9 Mo Sep	d0.05	0.05	9
10	....	None Since Public			...	Nil	....	File bankruptcy Chapt 11				[54]599	...	±23984	Dc	±pd1.91	□d166.31	□d2.37	d10.60	....	d10.98	9 Mo Sep	d2.17	□d2.55	10
11	....	None Since Public			...	Nil	....	14.9	31.1	8.58	9-30-95	....	...	7746	Mr	...	...	pd0.11	0.74	....	0.97	6 Mo Sep	0.34	0.57	11
12	....	None Since Public			...	Nil	....	11.2	35.6	29.2	9-30-95	0.54	4000	24224	Mr	0.70	d0.78	d5.54	d0.91	....	d1.65	6 Mo Sep	d0.18	d0.92	12
13	....	None Since Public			...	Nil	....	0.31	36.9	25.6	8-31-95	p3.16	...	★9968	My	...	...	...	....	p0.18	....	6 Mo Nov	n/a	p0.26	13
14	....	None Since Public			...	Nil	....	22.3	43.3	37.2	9-30-95	1.64	...	19000	Dc	...	...	...	p0.67	....	....	9 Mo Sep	n/a	□0.49	14
15	....	None Paid			...	Nil	....	0.41	26.1	9.07	9-30-95	0.13	...	3209	Je	0.33	0.32	1.03	1.12	0.40	0.27	3 Mo Sep	0.01	d0.12	15
16	1988	0.02	9-6-94	8-15	...	Nil	0.06	Equity per shr $1.65			9-30-95	264	...	88748	Dc	Δ0.16	*0.11	□0.35	0.32	....	0.21	9 Mo Sep	0.21	0.10	16
17	1994	Q0.04	11-29-95	11-13	0.16	0.16	0.13	Equity per shr $16.02			9-30-95	[55]26.0	...	18350	Dc	pd0.95	p0.62	p□2.64	1.97	....	2.34	9 Mo Sep	1.37	1.74	17
18◆	1988	0.05	11-7-95	10-27	0.20	Nil	0.20	32.1	1782	804	9-30-95	1151	...	±107746	Dc	±0.17	Δ±0.37	±0.47	±0.23	....	d0.35	9 Mo Sep	±0.15	±d0.43	18
19	1994	Q0.42	1-18-96	12-27	1.66	1.68	1.39	Equity per shr $11.53			9-30-95	462	★5000	28722	Dc	...	p0.31	p1.62	0.46	....	0.72	9 Mo Sep	0.33	0.59	19
20	....	None Since Public			...	Nil	....	2.43	4.83	0.89	3-31-95	....	p...	★8970	Dc	d0.27	d0.30	pNil	pd0.06	....	....	9 Mo Sep	n/a	Nil	20
21◆	1991	Q0.03	11-27-95	11-16	0.12	0.12	0.122	1.50	57.6	14.3	9-30-95	27.8	...	6722	Dc	p0.46	0.64	0.74	0.70	....	0.53	9 Mo Sep	0.75	0.58	21
22	....	Terms&trad. basis should be checked in detail						Wrrts expire 12-15-98				....	...	921	Dc	...	...	...	....	....	....				22
23	....	None Since Public			...	Nil	....	14.4	302	222	10-22-95	....	...	20841	Ja	...	...	p0.62	p0.81	E1.07	0.95	9 Mo Oct	p0.30	0.44	23
24	....	None Since Public			...	Nil	....	1.77	5.78	10.5	9-30-95	30.5	...	11353	Dc	...	...	p0.25	p0.23	....	0.21	9 Mo Sep	p0.15	p0.13	24
25◆	....	None Since Public			...	Nil	....	4.64	248	59.8	7-30-95	217	...	19750	Ja	p□0.36	□0.39	0.63	□0.84	....	0.65	9 Mo Oct	0.49	0.30	25
26	....	None Since Public			...	Nil	....	Book Value $12.22			3-31-95	5.86	...	5563	Dc	...	...	pd2.56	n/a	....	....	9 Mo Sep	d5.00	0.76	26
27	1898	Q0.33	1-2-96	12-19	1.23	1.32	1.20	1.48	819	295	9-30-95	357	...	±20136	Dc	±1.53	±2.50	□2.65	3.50	E3.75	3.75	9 Mo Sep	±2.16	±2.41	27
28	1939	Q0.25	12-28-95	12-4	1.00	1.00	1.00	364	2578	3263	9-30-95	5474	[58]33	348791	Dc	1.68	pΔ□1.46	□1.35	2.55	E2.75	2.71	9 Mo Sep	1.94	2.10	28
29	1967	Q0.37½	12-28-95	12-4	1.50	1.50	1.50	Cv into 3 common				....	96	...	Dc	...	...	...	....	....	....				29
30	1969	Q0.37½	12-28-95	12-4	1.50	1.50	1.50	Cv into 2.5 common				....	652	...	Dc	...	...	...	....	....	....				30
31	1995	Q0.657	1-2-96	11-28	1.337	2.63	....	Amt pay maturity based on So.New Eng Tel stk[60]				....	...	3900	Dc	...	...	...	....	....	....	Due 3-31-2000			31
32	1972	0.32	10-4-93	9-14	...	Nil	....	5.51	184	82.2	9-30-95	64.8	...	5823	Dc	1.30	□d1.37	d6.07	0.62	....	2.22	9 Mo Sep	0.30	1.90	32
33◆	....	None Since Public			...	Nil	....	Equity per shr $6.90			9-30-95	41.7	...	27076	Dc	p0.42	□0.81	1.14	1.40	....	1.54	9 Mo Sep	1.03	1.17	33
34	....	None Since Public			...	Nil	....	9.57	22.5	18.8	9-30-95	....	...	7132	Dc	...	pd0.36	0.67	0.55	....	0.87	9 Mo Sep	0.24	0.56	34
35◆	1939	Q0.10	3-8-96	2-14	0.40	0.40	0.40	20.8	381	225	9-30-95	319	...	[61]12873	Dc	d1.40	□1.59	□1.20	1.10	E0.60	0.46	9 Mo Sep	1.03	□0.39	35
36◆	....	None Since Public			...	Nil	....	34.6	37.4	2.72	6-30-95	....	...	10572	Sp	...	...	...	Δp0.07	P0.25	0.25				36
37	....	None Since Public			...	Nil	....	6.92	9.62	4.01	9-30-95	....	p...	★7649	Dc	...	...	...	pd0.46	....	d0.19	9 Mo Sep	pd0.30	pd0.03	37
38◆	....	h[62]....	4-19-87	1-7	...	Nil	....	4.10	23.3	7.00	9-29-95	1.09	...	12746	Dc	d1.60	d0.50	0.20	[63]0.63	....	0.72	9 Mo Sep	0.32	0.41	38
39	....	None Paid			...	Nil	....	6.85	58.6	43.1	8-31-95	....	1	23687	Fb	Δd0.09	0.14	0.20	0.20	....	0.23	6 Mo Aug	0.09	0.12	39
40	1992	0.03	12-23-94	12-9	...	Nil	0.12	0.04	22.1	20.5	9-30-95	1.39	...	4196	Dc	0.21	0.55	Δ0.20	d0.21	....	d0.38	9 Mo Sep	d0.06	d0.23	40
41◆	....	1.50	9-18-87	8-11	...	Nil	....	File bankruptcy Chapt 11				21.0	184	31771	Ja	Δd38.40	d72.50	‡[64]d9.10	d2.15	....	2.38	9 Mo Oct	d5.33	d0.80	41
42◆	1967	1%Stk	3-15-96	2-28	4%Stk	Stk	s0.285	40.7	522	458	9-30-95	97.4	91	9038	Mr	*2.49	*2.28	d4.04	d3.52	....	d4.05	6 Mo Sep	d0.64	d1.17	42
43	1988	Q0.18	12-1-95	11-15	0.53	0.72	0.62	Book Value $23.51			9-30-95	1862	...	31422	Dc	2.11	3.00	3.60	3.70	E3.70	3.67	9 Mo Sep	2.76	2.73	43
44	....	None Since Public			...	Nil	....	Book Value $15.45			9-30-95	150	...	17855	Dc	...	...	...	0.37	....	0.95	9 Mo Sep	0.15	0.73	44
45	....	None Since Public			...	Nil	....	11.9	127	33.6	8-31-95	16.0	...	13367	Fb	0.05	1.27	1.52	□1.89	....	d0.56	9 Mo Nov	1.34	d1.11	45
46	1960	Q0.08	12-1-95	11-13	0.32	0.32	0.32	21.0	401	212	9-30-95	105	...	13128	Dc	0.51	0.68	□1.41	1.80	....	1.55	9 Mo Sep	1.42	1.17	46
47	1976	Q0.03	11-30-95	11-13	0.12	0.12	0.12	Equity per shr $9.52			9-30-95	327	...	30119	Dc	0.40	0.15	Δ0.06	0.19	....	0.13	9 Mo Sep	0.12	0.06	47
48	1993	0.382	1-31-96	12-15	1.259	1.29	1.182	Int based on S&P 500,as defined				....	...	9200	Dc	...	...	§46.62	§45.93	....	....	Mand termination 1-22-2018			48
49	1995	0.184	1-31-96	12-28	0.249	0.56	....	Int based on S&P MidCap 400,as defined				....	...	375	Dc	...	...	...	....	....	....	Mand termination 4-27-2020			49
50◆	1949	Q0.17	1-26-96	1-10	0.68	0.68	0.66	8.01	262	185	9-30-95	165	...	16755	Je	d3.59	1.79	□2.21	1.99	1.20	0.45	3 Mo Sep	0.17	d0.58	50
51	1927	Q0.19	3-8-96	2-21	0.72	0.76	0.68	29.2	322	84.9	10-01-95	7.84	...	±28665	Dc	±1.14	±1.37	±1.47	±1.53	....	1.66	9 Mo Sep	±1.08	±1.21	51
52◆	1964	Q0.18	11-25-95	11-8	0.68	0.72	0.57	5.97	229	75.3	9-30-95	126	...	13926	Je	1.05	1.23	1.47	1.78	2.64	2.50	3 Mo Sep	0.80	0.66	52

◆**Stock Splits & Divs By Line Reference Index** [3]3-for-2,'91,'93. [18]2-for-1,'93. [21]5-for-4,'94. [25]3-for-2,'94. [33]2-for-1,'94. [35]No adj for spl $13 dstr,'89. [36]2-for-1,'95. [38]1-for-2 REVERSE,'92. [41]1-for-10 REVERSE,'95. [42]Adj to 1% Nov,'95. [50]5-for-4,'93. [52]2-for-1,'93.

¶ S&P 500 # MidCap 400 ✣ SmallCap 600 • Options Index	Ticker	Name of Issue (Call Price of Pfd. Stocks)	Market	Com. Rank. & Pfd. Rating	Inst. Hold Cos	Inst. Hold Shs. (000)	Principal Business	Price Range 1971-93 High	1971-93 Low	1994 High	1994 Low	1995 High	1995 Low	Dec. Sales in 100s	December, 1995 Last Sale Or Bid High	Low	Last	%Div Yield	P-E Ratio	Total Return % Annualized 12 Mo	36 Mo	60 Mo
1	STII	✔Stanford Telecommun	NNM	B	26	3107	Mfrs sys for earth stations	27½	3½	21½	11	25¾	12½	3071	23⅜	16	22¼	...	..	45.9	37.8	25.1
#2•[1]	STH	✔Stanhome Inc	NY,B,Ch,P,Ph	A–	165	13824	Consumer prd/household items	44¾	1	37	28¾	33⅜	26⅞	13297	30¼	28½	29⅛	3.6	14	–2.4	–2.7	–0.5
¶3•[2]	SWK	✔Stanley Works	NY,B,Ch,P,Ph	B+	333	30062	Mfr full line hardware prod	48⅛	2¾	44⅞	34⅞	53⅜	35⅝	20981	53⅜	49⅜	51½	2.8	25	46.3	11.2	15.4
4	STNT	✔Stant Corp	NNM	NR	54	5724	Mfr automotive parts/tools	20¼	14¾	21¼	10½	16¼	8½	4160	10½	8½	9¾	0.8	13	–23.1	...	...
#5•[3]	SPLS	✔Staples Inc	NNM,Ph	NR	322	82007	Office product superstores	12½	2⅝	16½	9¾	29⅛	14⅜	285829	25⅞	20⅜	24⅜	...	41	50.0	27.6	48.7
6•[4]	STB	✔Star Banc Corp	NY,Ph	A+	158	9739	Comm'l bkg,Cincinnati, Ohio	39½	2⅞	44¾	33½	62¼	36¼	5379	62¼	59⅛	59½	2.7	13	68.6	21.1	33.6
7	SGASZ	Star Gas Ptnrs L.P.	NNM	NR	..	...	Retail dstr propane gas	....	....	....	....	22½	22	7954	22½	22	22	10.0	d	...	...	...
8•[5]	SBUX	✔Starbucks Corp	NNM	NR	186	43959	Retails high-quality coffees	14⅛	4¼	16¼	9½	23½	11⅛	187099	23½	19⅛	21	...	58	52.7	33.3	...
9	SHO	✔Starrett Corp	AS	B–	18	849	Dev/constr multi-unit hous'g	24	2⅛	10¼	6¼	10⅝	6⅝	1572	8¼	7¼	8¼	3.0	8	20.3	30.7	21.0
10	SCX	✔Starrett (L.S.)'A'	NY,B,Ch	B+	54	2123	Mechanics' measuring tools	29⅛	3⅜	25½	20	25⅞	21½	788	25⅞	22½	25⅞	2.8	13	20.0	2.8	7.3
11	SGHT	✔StarSight Telecast	NNM	NR	43	1881	Dvlp stg:TV prgrm/VCR ctrl sv	27¼	15	19¼	7¾	9¾	2¼	43423	6⅞	2¾	4⅞	...	..	–39.1	...	...
12•[6]	STA	✔Starter Corp	NY,Ph	NR	28	1689	Mkt,mfr'sports team'activewear	27	17⅛	17⅝	6¼	11½	6⅜	13223	7⅞	6⅝	6⅞	...	d	3.8	...	...
13	HOT	✔Starwood Lodging Tr[55]	NY,Ch,P	NR	82	10585	Real est inv tr:hotel mgmt	151½	2⅝	20¼	9	30⅛	15	9234	30⅛	27⅛	29¾	...	d	68.0	64.9	29.7
14	WS.B	Wrrt(Pur.167Unit at$101.70)	AS	....	6	501		8½	....	¼	1/16	⅛	1/32	1153	1/16	1/16	1/16	...	..	...	...	...
#15•[7]	STT	✔State Str Boston	NY,Ch,Ph	A+	382	63101	Comml bkg,Boston,Mass	49⅛	½	43⅛	27⅝	46¼	28	36460	46¼	43⅜	45	1.6	15	59.5	2.2	23.0
16	SFIN	Statewide Financial	NNM	NR	1	20	Savings & loan,New Jersey	....	....	....	....	13¾	12½	4864	13⅛	12½	13	...	12	...	...	...
17•[8]	STCI	✔Station Casinos	NNM	NR	118	17849	Own/oper gaming enterprises	24½	13¼	22¾	10	20	10¼	33729	15½	13½	14⅝	...	26	14.7	...	...
18	STBI	✔STB Systems	NNM	....	14	778	Dvlp/mfr graphic adapters	....	....	....	....	15½	6¾	6900	12¼	8⅞	9½	...	21	...	...	...
19	STEK	✔Steck-Vaughn Publishing	NNM	NR	24	2853	Publish educational materials	16	8¾	10¾	4¾	8¾	5	1097	7⅝	7	7⅜	...	16	34.1	...	...
✣20	STTX	✔Steel Technologies	NNM	B+	47	4354	Processes flat rolled steel	23½	3⅛	21¾	10⅛	13¾	6¼	10923	10	8⅜	8⅝	0.9	14	–31.8	–1.4	3.9
✣21	SMRT	✔Stein Mart	NNM	NR	69	5447	Off-price retail store chain	24¼	7⅜	21½	12¼	15	9¼	12829	12¾	10½	11	...	15	–12.0	–14.9	...
22•[9]	STE.A	Stelco Inc'A'	To,Mo	C	32	16818	Leader in Canadian steel	41	⅞	9⅞	7⅛	8½	5¼	35317	6⅛	5½	5⅝	...	4	–30.8	59.0	...
23	SCL	✔Stepan Co	AS,Ch	A–	33	2553	Basic/intermediate chemicals	22⅞	1¼	17¾	12⅜	20⅞	14¾	1059	16⅞	15⅛	16⅝	2.8	12	15.7	1.8	12.1
24	TSC	✔Stephan Co	AS,B	B+	16	459	Mfr hair & skin care prod	22	1/32	21¾	11	19⅜	12	6131	15⅞	14	15⅝	0.5	14	21.7	0.1	54.8
25	SYS	✔Sterile Concepts	NY,Ch,Ph	NR	47	4655	Mfr surgical procedure trays	....	....	17⅜	15⅛	17⅝	10¾	1945	15	12⅞	14½	1.1	10	–6.9	...	...
✣26•[10]	STRL	✔STERIS Corp	NNM	NR	136	13481	Mfr sterile processing sys	10⅝	3½	20	8⅜	45	14⅞	166877	45	28¾	32¼	...	60	61.4	58.4	...
27	STL	✔Sterling Bancorp	NY,Ch	B–	17	897	Commercial bkg,New York	16⅞	4¾	7¾	6⅜	12½	6¼	1847	12½	10¾	12½	2.2	15	98.3	19.9	14.7
28	SBIB	✔Sterling Bancshares	NNM	NR	17	1018	Commercial banking,Houston,TX	12⅞	8	12⅛	10½	18¼	11⅜	1006	18¼	16⅝	17½	1.8	11	53.2	24.4	...
#29•[11]	STX	✔Sterling Chemicals	NY	NR	141	20836	Mfr of petrominerals	18¾	3⅛	13⅞	3⅞	14⅛	7⅜	40732	9⅜	7⅞	8⅛	...	3	–35.6	29.8	9.9
30	SEC	✔Sterling Electronics	NY,Ch,Ph	↑B	36	2743	Distr electronic equip	15⅜	½	14¾	9¾	20¼	11¼	3364	17⅞	15¾	17⅛	s...	14	50.5	39.0	62.7
31	STER	✔Sterling Healthcare Group	NNM	NR	12	361	Physician contract mgmt svcs	....	....	13¾	9⅛	16½	8⅜	12723	13⅜	10	10⅝	...	17	14.9	...	...
32	SGH	✔Sterling House	AS	NR	..	...	Long-term care provider	....	....	....	....	13	9⅜	4449	11⅛	9⅜	9⅝	...	..	...	...	...
✣33•[3]	SSW	✔Sterling Software	NY,B,Ch,P,Ph	B–	234	19888	Mkts computer software prod	33⅝	5	36⅞	25	62⅜	32⅞	43241	62⅜	53	62⅜	...	..	71.5	44.6	51.8
34	STE	STET-Societa Fin Tel Ord ADS[59]	NY	NR	33	10524	Telecommunication svcs,Italy	....	....	....	....	33⅛	25⅝	5498	28⅛	25⅝	27⅞	1.7	21	...	...	...
35	STE.A	Savings ADS[60]	NY	NR	1	2500		....	....	....	....	27	18⅞	10	19¾	18⅞	19½B	...	15	...	...	...
36	SVG.A	✔Stevens Intl[61] Cl'A'	AS,Ch,Ph	NR	28	3608	Mfr print production systems	19¾	2¾	8½	5	8⅜	3¾	7219	6⅞	3¾	4⅜	...	7	–47.0	–3.5	3.8
37	SVG.B	✔ Class B(1 vote)[62]	AS	NR	6	116	Comm'l presses: collators	19¼	3¼	9	6⅜	8⅜	4⅛	149	5	4⅛	4¼	...	7	–50.7	–1.9	–2.7
#38•[4]	SSSS	✔Stewart & Stevenson	NNM	B	214	22753	Diesel/turbine eng pwr sys	52½	1 3/16	53¾	28	41¼	21½	119200	26⅝	21⅞	25¼	1.3	14	–24.5	–8.8	6.3
39	STEI	✔Stewart Enterprises'A'	NNM	B	149	16347	Funeral/cemetery services	28½	10¾	28¼	19¾	37⅜	23½	19154	37	32½	37	0.2	34	56.0	32.0	...
40	STC	✔Stewart Information Sv	NY	B	45	3902	Title insurance	22⅜	1	21⅜	14⅜	22½	15⅛	1239	22½	20½	21½	1.1	27	43.7	17.6	38.5
41	SF	✔Stifel Financial	NY,Ch	B–	22	939	Securities broker/fin'l svcs	13⅞	2⅞	9⅞	5¼	7⅛	5⅜	2000	6¾	5¾	6⅝	1.8	d	29.5	6.2	22.6
42	PGMS	✔Stillwater Mining	NNM	NR	61	9369	Platinum/palladium mining	....	....	13⅝	13	28¾	13¼	14969	20⅛	16¾	19¼	...	..	42.6	...	...
43	STIM	✔Stimsonite Corp	NNM	NR	47	3912	Mfr reflective hiway safety pd	11	9	14¼	9½	14½	6⅞	8154	9½	6⅞	9½	...	22	–9.5	...	...
44	SCSWF	Stolt Comex Seaway	NNM	NR	..	...	O&G engineering,constr'n svcs	19¾	11¾	14½	6⅝	11¾	5¾	2351	10	8½	8½	...	d	17.2	...	...
¶45•[4]	STO	✔Stone Container	NY,Ch,P	B–	321	74329	Paperboard packaging prod	39	13/16	21⅛	9⅝	24⅝	12½	152974	15⅝	12½	14⅜	4.2	3	–15.8	–5.8	7.2
46	Pr E	$1.75Ser'E'cmCv[65]ExPfd([66]26.05)	[12]NY	C	16	547		26¾	8¾	20⅞	15¼	24⅞	16⅞	9143	19⅞	17⅛	18½	9.5	..	...	...	...
47	SGY	✔Stone Energy	NY	NR	40	3427	Oil & gas explor dvlp prod'n	16⅝	11½	19¼	9⅞	19	11	5285	15¾	13½	15⅜	...	38	–11.5	...	...
✣48	SW	✔Stone & Webster	NY,B,Ch,P,Ph	B–	71	4184	Engineer'g,constr,consulting	45¾	7⅞	34	27¼	40	27¼	6259	37	34½	35⅞	1.7	24	10.3	15.2	5.1
49•[13]	SHP	✔Stop & Shop Cos	NY,Ph	NR	130	16693	Oper food supermkts	28¼	10⅞	27¾	19	28½	19⅜	25328	23⅛	20½	23⅛	...	15	–8.4	9.2	...
50	SOS	✔Storage Computer	AS	NR	5	58	Mfr data storage systems	....	....	....	....	13¾	6½	939	10⅛	8⅝	9	...	45	...	...	...
51	STG	✔Storage Properties Inc	AS,Ch	NR	3	121	Real estate investment trust	8⅛	4½	5½	4⅜	6⅜	4¾	447	6⅜	6⅛	6⅛	e5.2	14	36.0	17.8	14.7
#52•[10]	STK	✔Storage Technology	NY,B,Ch,Ph	C	169	26900	Data storage equip:printers	403¾	9¼	41½	25	33¼	17⅞	79174	26⅝	23¼	23⅞	...	24	–18.7	6.5	2.4

Uniform Footnote Explanations-See Page 4. Other: [1]ASE:Cycle 2. [2]P:Cycle 1. [3]Ph:Cycle 3. [4]P:Cycle 3. [5]CBOE:Cycle 1. [6]ASE,CBOE,Ph:Cycle 2. [7]Ph:Cycle 2. [8]ASE:Cycle 1. [9]To:Cycle 2. [10]CBOE:Cycle 3. [11]CBOE,Ph:Cycle 1. [12]Ch [13]NY:Cycle 2. [51]®$2.25,'94. [52]®$3.86,'94. [53]Fiscal Jun'93 & prior. [54]6 Mo Dec'94. [55]Trades with 1 shr of Hotel Inv Corp. [56]®$2.68,'94. [57]®$1.26,'94. [58]®$0.57,'94. [59]Ea ADS rep 10 ord shrs,Lit 1,000. [60]Ea ADS rep 10 svgs shrs,Lit 1,000. [61]1/10 vtg. [62]Formerly Stevens Graphics Cl'B'. [63]Fiscal Jul'92 & prior. [64]12 Mo Dec'93. [65]Co opt exch for$25amt 7%Cv2007 on div pmt dates. [66]Fr2-16-96scale to $25 in 2002.

Splits ◆ Index	Cash Divs. Ea.Yr. Since	Dividends: Latest Payment Period $	Date	Ex. Div.	Total $ So Far 1995	Ind. Rate	Paid 1994	Financial Position Mil-$: Cash& Equiv.	Curr. Assets	Curr. Liab.	Balance Sheet Date	Capitalization: Lg Trm Debt Mil-$	Shs. 000 Pfd.	Com.	Earnings $ Per Shr. Years End	1991	1992	1993	1994	1995	Last 12 Mos.	Interim Earnings Period	$ per Shr. 1994	1995	Index
1	. . . .	None Since Public			. . .	Nil	. . . .	11.4	74.4	23.8	9-30-95	0.12	. . .	6287	Mr	0.63	0.24	Δ0.54	0.02	. . . .	0.15	6 Mo Sep	0.27	0.40	1
2	1943	Q0.26½	1-1-96	12-15	1.06	1.06	1.015	22.9	385	286	9-30-95	. . . . .	. . .	18591	Dc	2.22	2.32	1.68	[51]2.26	. . . .	2.14	9 Mo Sep	1.68	1.56	2
3	1877	Q0.36	12-29-95	11-29	1.42	1.44	1.38	48.5	929	414	9-30-95	396	. . .	44332	Dc	□2.31	2.15	□2.06	2.80	E2.10	2.08	9 Mo Sep	2.04	1.32	3
4	1993	Q0.02	12-29-95	12-13	0.08	0.08	0.08	1.41	243	110	9-30-95	243	. . .	16227	Dc	. . .	p0.76	p0.93	□0.97	. . . .	0.75	9 Mo Sep	□0.77	0.55	4
5◆	. . . .	None Since Public			. . .	Nil	. . . .	92.3	960	485	10-28-95	348	. . .	104932	Ja	*0.14	0.22	0.31	0.43	. . . .	0.59	9 Mo Oct	0.20	0.36	5
6	1863	Q0.40	1-12-96	12-27	1.55	1.60	1.34	Book Value $18.22			12-31-94	p161	p4	p29851	Dc	2.24	2.57	3.36	[52]3.89	E4.50	4.36	9 Mo Sep	2.88	3.35	6
7	. . . .	Plan qtly div			. . .	2.20	. . . .	0.73	14.3	8.43	p9-30-95	p85.0	p. . .	★2600	Sp	. . .	. . .	. . .	. . . .	pd0.58	d0.58				7
8◆	. . . .	None Since Public			. . .	Nil	. . . .	105	211	62.5	7-02-95	★230	. . .	70722	Sp	p0.06	0.08	0.15	0.17	P0.37	0.37				8
9	1994	Q0.06¼	1-4-96	12-13	0.25	0.25	0.06¼	Equity per shr $7.96			9-30-95	23.1	. . .	6261	Dc	0.21	Δ0.04	0.34	0.98	. . . .	1.09	9 Mo Sep	0.51	0.62	9
10	1934	Q0.18	1-4-96	12-14	0.70	0.72	0.68	26.8	127	23.6	9-23-95	8.70	. . .	±7061	Je	±1.74	Δ±1.52	±1.25	±1.28	±1.91	1.97	3 Mo Sep	±0.30	±0.36	10
11	. . . .	None Since Public			. . .	Nil	. . . .	5.04	8.29	5.62	9-30-95	0.15	. . .	21151	Dc	d0.14	d0.29	[53]d0.70	□[54]d1.03	. . . .	. . . .	9 Mo Sep	□d0.99	d1.21	11
12	. . . .	None Since Public			. . .	Nil	. . . .	6.14	197	123	9-30-95	8.42	408	26422	Dc	. . .	p0.93	p1.00	d0.18	. . . .	d0.44	9 Mo Sep	0.41	0.15	12
13◆	. . . .	0.47	1-29-96	12-27	0.47	Nil	. . . .	Equity per shr $2.56			9-30-95	64.7	. . .	13810	Dc	d10.92	d9.78	d3.48	d2.28	. . . .	d0.42	9 Mo Sep	d1.05	0.81	13
14	. . . .	Terms&trad. basis should	be checked in detail					Wrrts expire 9-16-96				. . . . .	. . .	1660	Dc	. . .	. . .	. . .	. . . .	. . . .	. . . .				14
15◆	1910	Q0.18	1-15-96	12-28	0.66	0.72	0.58	Book Value $18.65			9-30-95	258	. . .	82540	Dc	1.86	2.10	2.36	[56]2.70	E2.95	2.92	9 Mo Sep	1.97	2.19	15
16	. . . .	None Since Public			. . .	Nil	. . . .	Book Value $12.68			3-31-95	41.5	. . .	★5200	Mr	. . .	. . .	. . .	p1.08	. . . .	1.08				16
17	. . . .	None Since Public			. . .	Nil	. . . .	27.1	50.4	77.0	9-30-95	329	. . .	35307	Mr	. . .	p0.44	p0.42	d0.26	. . . .	0.56	6 Mo Sep	d0.49	0.33	17
18	. . . .	None Since Public			. . .	Nil	. . . .	7.48	40.1	19.8	7-31-95	2.09	. . .	4500	Oc	. . .	. . .	. . .	p0.98	P0.45	0.45				18
19	. . . .	None Since Public			. . .	Nil	. . . .	11.5	53.1	12.1	9-30-95	1.11	. . .	14318	Dc	. . .	p0.58	p0.61	0.42	. . . .	0.45	9 Mo Sep	0.41	0.44	19
20◆	1985	S0.04	12-8-95	11-22	0.08	0.08	0.08	2.70	80.3	26.9	9-30-95	68.6	. . .	11990	Sp	0.29	0.50	0.83	0.87	0.61	0.61				20
21◆	. . . .	None Since Public			. . .	Nil	. . . .	6.03	137	56.8	9-30-95	28.7	. . .	22411	Dc	p0.43	p0.61	0.70	0.78	. . . .	0.72	9 Mo Sep	0.30	0.24	21
22	. . . .	g0.12½	2-1-91	12-24	. . .	Nil	. . . .	262	1174	672	j12-31-94	528	7133	±p104912	Dc	±d3.06	±d1.76	±d0.62	±1.01	. . . .	j1.50	9 Mo Sep	±0.57	±1.06	22
23◆	1967	Q0.11¾	12-15-95	11-29	0.44¾	0.47	0.42½	1.07	138	81.0	9-30-95	97.2	797	10011	Dc	1.15	Δ0.96	0.98	[57]1.29	. . . .	1.36	9 Mo Sep	0.95	1.02	23
24◆	1995	Q0.02	11-20-95	11-2	0.04	0.08	. . . .	7.24	20.2	2.39	9-30-95	0.69	. . .	4122	Dc	0.53	0.75	0.84	1.00	. . . .	1.12	9 Mo Sep	0.76	0.88	24
25	1995	Q0.04	1-10-96	12-27	0.16	0.16	. . . .	0.56	46.1	19.1	6-30-95	6.32	. . .	5526	Sp	. . .	. . .	p1.51	pΔ1.73	P1.48	1.48				25
26◆	. . . .	None Since Public			. . .	Nil	. . . .	16.6	43.7	8.94	9-30-95	. . . . .	. . .	17851	Mr	p. . .	0.16	Δ0.28	0.46	. . . .	0.54	6 Mo Sep	0.20	0.28	26
27	1946	Q0.07	12-31-95	12-13	0.25	0.28	0.21	Equity per shr $5.53			9-30-95	43.6	251	6347	Dc	d0.74	0.41	0.50	[58]0.63	. . . .	0.81	9 Mo Sep	0.45	0.63	27
28◆	1993	Q0.08	11-10-95	10-31	0.32	0.32	0.27	Book Value $8.51			9-30-95	6.40	. . .	5236	Dc	®0.92	®1.09	®1.00	®1.35	. . . .	1.57	9 Mo Sep	®0.98	®1.20	28
29	1989	0.20	4-28-93	4-7	. . .	Nil	. . . .	30.9	220	146	9-30-95	104	. . .	55674	Sp	0.67	□0.08	d0.10	0.34	□2.76	2.76				29
30	. . . .	5%Stk	2-1-96	1-9	. . .	Stk	. . . .	3.14	101	34.0	9-30-95	31.6	. . .	6589	Mr	Δ0.29	0.52	□1.00	1.17	. . . .	1.26	6 Mo Sep	0.54	0.63	30
31	. . . .	None Since Public			. . .	Nil	. . . .	. . . .	34.4	11.4	9-30-95	p4.47	. . .	★7850	Dc	. . .	. . .	p0.28	p0.48	. . . .	0.63	9 Mo Sep	p0.34	0.49	31
32	. . . .	None Since Public			. . .	Nil	. . . .	17.8	19.0	2.44	p6-30-95	15.1	. . .	★5035	Dc	. . .	. . .	. . .	pd0.17	. . . .	. . . .	6 Mo Jun	n/a	pd0.10	32
33	. . . .	0.05	6-30-85	6-12	. . .	Nil	. . . .	241	444	222	9-30-95	117	. . .	26675	Sp	Δ1.09	1.23	□d2.00	2.54	0.39	0.39				33
34	1995	0.458	7-12-95	6-12	0.458	0.46	. . . .	1365	10257	13518	12-31-94	10115	. . .	±5281212	Dc	±1.78	±1.38	±1.25	±1.31	. . . .	1.31				34
35	1995	. . . .			. . .	Nil	. . . .	. . . .	. . .	. . .		. . . . .	. . .	1446900	Dc	±1.78	±1.38	±1.25	±1.31	. . . .	1.31				35
36	. . . .	None Since Public			. . .	Nil	. . . .	0.59	57.2	30.5	3-31-95	23.7	. . .	±9402	Dc	±d1.50	±Δd0.36	Δ±0.08	□±0.26	. . . .	0.63	9 Mo Sep	±□0.13	±0.50	36
37	. . . .	None Since Public			. . .	Nil	. . . .	. . . .	. . .	. . .		. . . . .	. . .	2235	Dc	±d1.50	±Δd0.36	Δ±0.08	□±0.26	. . . .	0.63	9 Mo Sep	±□0.13	±0.50	37
38◆	1988	Q0.08	2-13-96	1-29	0.30	0.32	0.26	5.11	829	384	10-31-95	117	. . .	33050	Ja	1.18	□1.35	1.73	2.05	E1.85↓	2.01	9 Mo Oct	1.49	1.45	38
39◆	1992	Q0.02	1-26-96	1-10	0.05	0.08	0.04	9.90	120	53.0	7-31-95	287	. . .	±26486	Oc	0.89	0.96	1.30	1.28	P1.08	1.08				39
40◆	1967	Q0.06	1-31-96	12-27	0.20	0.24	0.193	Equity per shr $26.56			9-30-95	15.9	. . .	±6372	Dc	±0.27	±2.40	±3.87	±1.56	. . . .	0.80	9 Mo Sep	±1.36	±0.60	40
41◆	1992	Q0.03	11-21-95	11-3	0.12	0.12	0.086	Equity per shr $7.40			9-30-95	11.6	. . .	4168	Dc	d0.71	*[63]1.43	[64]1.46	d1.29	. . . .	d0.92	9 Mo Sep	d0.23	0.14	41
42	. . . .	None Since Public			. . .	Nil	. . . .	31.9	50.3	9.10	9-30-95	1.68	. . .	20070	Dc	. . .	. . .	p0.09	□p0.11	. . . .	0.06	9 Mo Sep	0.04	d0.01	42
43	. . . .	None Since Public			. . .	Nil	. . . .	0.35	41.5	32.1	10-01-95	13.5	. . .	8920	Dc	. . .	p0.33	□0.33	□0.69	. . . .	0.43	12 Mo Sep	□0.62	0.43	43
44	. . . .	None Since Public			. . .	Nil	. . . .	1.82	138	119	11-30-93	55.3	. . .	±17000	Nv	. . .	*pd0.44	Δ0.47	Pd2.11	. . . .	d0.25	9 Mo Aug	Δd1.22	0.64	44
45◆	1995	Q0.15	12-13-95	11-20	0.30	0.60	. . . .	102	2118	873	9-30-95	4379	4600	99134	Dc	d0.77	d2.50	□d4.59	□d1.60	E4.50↓	4.08	9 Mo Sep	□d1.89	□3.79	45
46	1992	Q0.43¾	11-15-95	10-30	0.87½	1.75	a1.75	Cv into 0.722 com,$34.62				. . . .	4600	. . .	Dc	. . .	. . .	. . .	. . . .	. . . .	. . . .				46
47	. . . .	None Since Public			. . .	Nil	. . . .	14.2	21.6	18.6	9-30-95	38.3	. . .	11792	Dc	p0.01	p0.45	0.88	0.34	. . . .	0.41	9 Mo Sep	0.27	0.34	47
48	1939	Q0.15	2-15-96	12-28	0.60	0.60	0.60	95.6	320	181	9-30-95	102	. . .	14227	Dc	*1.08	Δ*0.62	d0.03	d0.52	. . . .	1.48	9 Mo Sep	d0.78	1.22	48
49	. . . .	None Since Public			. . .	Nil	. . . .	11.6	363	524	1-28-95	760	. . .	49712	Ja	□0.86	□d2.99	□1.23	□1.59	E1.55	1.56	40 Wk Nov	□1.16	1.13	49
50	. . . .	None Since Public			. . .	Nil	. . . .	1.40	12.4	4.14	9-30-95	0.92	. . .	10516	Dc	. . .	pd0.26	p0.08	0.11	. . . .	0.20	9 Mo Sep	0.05	0.14	50
51	1990	†0.28	1-12-96	12-27	†0.64	0.32	†0.33	Equity per shr $8.27			9-30-95	. . . .	. . .	3348	Dc	0.91	0.92	0.71	0.53	. . . .	0.46	9 Mo Sep	0.39	0.32	51
52	. . . .	6%Stk	5-20-77	4-18	. . .	Nil	. . . .	201	899	450	9-29-95	174	3450	53156	Dc	2.33	0.37	Δd2.98	0.66	E1.00	0.25	9 Mo Sep	0.16	d0.25	52

◆**Stock Splits & Divs By Line Reference Index** [5]3-for-2,'91,'93,'94,'95. [8]2-for-1,'93,'95. [13]1-for-6 REVERSE,'95. [15]2-for-1,'92. [20]3-for-2,'93. [21]3-for-2,'93. [23]2-for-1,'94. [24]3-for-2(twice),'91,(once),'92,'93. [26]2-for-1,'95. [28]3-for-2,'95. [38]2-for-1,'92. [39]3-for-2,'93. [40]3-for-2,'94. [41]Adj to 5%,'95. [45]Adj for 2%,'92.

¶ S&P 500 # MidCap 400 ✣ SmallCap 600 • Options

Index	Ticker	Name of Issue (Call Price of Pfd. Stocks)	Market	Com. Rank. & Pfd. Rating	Inst. Hold Cos	Inst. Hold Shs. (000)	Principal Business	Price Range 1971-93 High	1971-93 Low	1994 High	1994 Low	1995 High	1995 Low	Dec. Sales in 100s	December, 1995 Last Sale Or Bid High	Low	Last	%Div Yield	P-E Ratio	Total Return % Annualized 12 Mo	36 Mo	60 Mo
1	SEA	✔Storage Trust Realty	NY	NR	81	7114	Real estate investment trust	...	...	17⅞	15½	22¾	17¼	3569	22¾	19⅝	22¾	6.8	..	40.2	...	...
2	SUS	✔Storage USA	NY,Ch,Ph	NR	144	14401	Real estate investment trust	...	...	28	21¾	32¾	26½	8849	32¾	30	32⅝	6.3	..	32.6	...	...
3	STMD	✔Storemedia 'A'	NNM	NR	70	10302	Mfr thin film computer disks	...	...	...	...	55¼	16	19959	42	33	36½	...	24	...	...	...
✣4•[1]	STRM	✔StrataCom Inc	NNM	NR	231	29811	Mfr wide area ntwk computer sys	9⅞	3½	37¼	6½	82	32	195899	77¼	61¾	73½	...	57	98.6	132	...
#5•[2]	SRA	✔Stratus Computer	NY,Ch,Ph	B+	194	19152	Fault tolerant computer sys	54¼	7¾	39⅞	22⅞	39⅞	23	21483	35	30½	34⅝	...	63	−8.6	1.1	8.3
✣6	STRWA	✔Strawbridge/Clothier'A'	NNM	B+	81	3826	Dept strs in Phila & environs	41⅜	1 9/16	23½	19½	25	14⅛	14330	25	22	24	4.6	d	15.3	7.4	13.6
¶7•[2]	SRR	✔Stride Rite	NY,Ch,Ph	A–	267	35260	Mfr/retail children's shoes	31⅞	⅜	18⅞	10½	13¼	7	75136	8⅞	7	7⅜	2.7	35	−30.9	−29.2	−10.4
8	STRB	Strober Organization	NNM	B–	16	709	Dstr bldg mat'ls:NY,NJ,Conn	15¼	⅞	5¼	2½	5⅞	3	593	4	3½	3½	...	6	5.5	21.2	28.9
9	STRO	✔Strouds Inc	NNM	NR	22	2575	Retail home textile products	...	...	16¼	9	9⅝	3¾	25550	5	4	4⅛	...	15	−54.8	...	...
#10•[3]	SDRC	✔Structural Dynamics Res	NNM	C	126	15730	Computer-aid engineer'g svc	30	1⅜	17⅛	3⅝	30½	5⅛	227899	30½	19⅞	29⅜	...	65	473	40.4	18.2
11	SIR	✔Struthers[53] Industries[54]	AS	↓C	9	554	Oil&gas explor,dvlp/dye mfg	8¾	2¾	11¼	1½	2¾	9/16	11968	2⅛	1 9/16	1 9/16	...	d	−16.7	−23.1	...
#12•[4]	STRY	✔Stryker Corp	NNM	A–	226	18841	Specialty medical devices	52¼	9/16	37½	23¾	58½	36⅛	74102	58½	48⅝	52½	0.2	29	43.6	11.8	28.2
13	STUA	Stuart Entertainment	NNM	B–	14	279	Mfr & dstr bingo cards & eq	16	1½	6¼	3¾	8¼	2¼	6661	8¼	6½	7¼	...	d	61.1	−1.1	26.4
14	STU	✔Student Loan Corp	NY	NR	55	3131	Orignates,svcs student loans	30½	14¼	20⅞	18⅛	35½	18⅜	685	35⅜	33¾	34	0.7	11	86.6	20.1	...
15•[5]	SLM	✔Student Loan Mktg	NY,B,Ch,P	A	314	58849	Student loan fin'g program	76	8⅜	49⅞	31¼	70⅞	32⅞	71770	70⅞	64⅜	66	2.4	14	108	1.7	9.8
16	SPHI	✔Studio Plus Hotels	NNM	NR	45	2930	Own/oper Studio Plus hotels	...	...	...	...	28¼	15	3683	28¼	21¼	25¾	...	..	...	...	...
✣17	RGR	✔Sturm Ruger	NY,Ch	A–	110	6778	Pistols, revolvers & rifles	32	⅝	33¼	23⅞	35⅝	25⅞	3750	31	27¼	27⅜	5.1	14	1.3	17.5	25.7
18	SOV	✔Styles on Video[56]	AS	NR	13	318	Mkt hairstyling image system	17¾	4⅞	17⅝	2½	...	...	...	...	...	...	...	..	−68.9	...	...
19	SUDS	✔Sudbury Inc	NNM	NR	32	4737	Mfr,dstr industrial products	7¼	5⅛	8	5⅜	9⅝	5⅛	9615	8	7	8	...	7	39.1	...	...
20•[6]	SUL	✔Sulcus Computer	AS,Ph	C	13	447	Info/document retrieval sys	14⅛	¾	8⅜	2 1/16	3¾	1⅞	14922	2 3/16	1 15/16	2⅛	...	d	−2.8	−37.0	−4.6
21	SUMA	✔Summa Four	NNM	NR	60	5267	Dstr telecom switching sys	39¾	17	42¼	10¼	33	11⅞	23889	15⅜	11⅞	13⅜	...	16	−53.1	...	...
22	SUMX	✔Summa Industries	NNM	B–	7	128	Mfrs ind'l process mchy	16⅜	¼	6¾	3½	5¾	3¾	377	4¾	4	4½	...	12	−21.7	15.8	62.7
✣23•[7]	SUBN	✔Summit Bancorp'n[59]	NNM	A–	128	10412	Commercial bkg,New Jersey	27¼	1⅞	21¾	17¼	31½	18¾	37148	31½	28⅞	31½	2.7	15	71.8	27.7	38.1
24	SMFR	✔Summit Family Restaurants[60]	NNM	↓C	20	2444	Family type restaurants	15¾	1	8¼	3⅝	6¼	3⅝	10344	6	5⅜	5½	...	d	29.4	−11.3	−0.4
25	SUMT	✔Summit Medical System	NNM	NR	36	2184	Healthcare industry software	...	...	...	...	25½	9	2466	22⅝	18¾	21½	...	d	...	...	...
26	SMT	✔Summit Properties	NY,Ch,Ph	NR	92	12247	Real estate investment trust	...	...	22⅜	15½	20	15¾	6504	20	18¾	19⅞	7.6	25	13.7	...	...
✣27•[8]	BEAM	✔Summit Technology	NNM	NR	82	5255	Dvlp medl laser surgery prod	25⅝	¼	26⅝	13⅝	38¾	18⅜	93243	38¾	31	33¾	...	d	77.3	19.8	32.2
28	SNI	✔Sun City Indus	AS	C	8	167	Produces & mkts shell eggs	7⅜	¾	6⅞	2¾	6	2	391	2⅝	2	2	...	d	−64.4	−13.8	2.8
¶29•[3]	SUN	✔Sun Co	NY,B,Ch,Ph	NR	374	41764	Petroleum refining&mktg	73⅛	12¾	35¼	25⅛	32⅞	24¾	38102	28⅜	26⅛	27⅜	3.7	11	−0.1	5.8	6.0
30	SN	✔Sun Coast Indus	NY	B–	27	1680	Mfr plastic caps for cont'nrs	40⅝	¾	17	8¼	15⅝	6⅝	1254	8½	6⅝	6¾	...	..	−54.6	−5.0	40.1
31	SUI	✔Sun Communities	NY,Ch,Ph	NR	93	7176	Real estate investment trust	21⅛	20	24⅜	19¾	26⅜	20⅞	4352	26⅜	25	26⅜	6.7	22	26.5	...	...
32	SDP.B	✔Sun Dstr L.P.'B'[62]	NY	NR	14	6058	Whsle dstr of industrial prod	4⅞	2⅛	6⅛	4	5⅛	3⅞	4006	5⅛	4⅝	5	e4.8	3	32.6	20.2	19.3
33	SDP	✔ Cl 'A'[64]	NY	NR	14	522		11⅞	7⅛	11	10⅛	11½	10¼	2051	11⅜	10⅞	11¼	9.8	10	20.0	14.7	18.8
34	SLP	✔Sun Energy Ptnrs L.P.[65]	NY,Ch,Ph	NR	14	222	Oil & gas explor,dev,prod'n	25⅛	6	7⅜	3¾	4¾	3⅝	6864	4¼	3⅝	3¾	12.3	15	7.5	−15.2	−7.3
35•[9]	SHG	✔Sun Healthcare Group	NY	NR	182	35690	Oper long-term care facilities	16¾	11	25⅞	16	28⅛	9⅛	62221	14¾	12⅛	13½	...	11	−46.0	...	...
¶36•[2]	SUNW	✔Sun Microsystems	NNM,Ch,Ph	B	599	153228	Mkt networked workstations	20½	2⅞	18⅞	9⅛	51½	15	1606580	51½	39¼	45⅝	...	23	150	40.1	33.1
37•[10]	SNTV	✔Sun Television & Appliances	NNM	NR	73	5720	Retail consumer electronics	27	4⅞	21¾	7¾	11⅜	3⅝	31875	5¾	3⅝	4⅛	0.8	7	−49.0	−38.3	...
38	SNR	✔Sunair Electronics	AS	B–	9	355	Mfr communications equip	14⅞	⅝	3⅛	1⅝	2¾	1⅝	200	2½	2¼	2⅜	...	59	31.1	−16.0	4.8
#39•[4]	SAI	✔SunAmerica Inc	NY,B,Ch,P,Ph	↑A–	240	33712	Life insurance/fin'l svcs	31	11/16	30⅞	22⅜	49¾	24	36819	48⅜	42½	47½	0.8	17	96.5	39.5	69.7
40•[5]	SOC	✔Sunbeam Corp	NY	NR	218	42568	Consumer prd:outdoor,househld	22⅝	11	26	17⅝	25½	12½	20690	16⅜	14⅝	15¼	0.3	16	−39.5	−3.4	...
41	SBN	✔Sunbelt Nursery Group	AS,Ph	NR	14	631	Retail lawn/garden products	8⅞	3	3¾	1¼	3½	1⅜	2477	3	2¼	2 5/16	...	d	12.1	−27.2	...
42	SU	✔Suncor Inc	AS,To,Mo	NR	54	5448	Integrated oil & gas oper,Cdn	24⅛	22¼	25⅛	20⅜	32	22	505	32	30¾	31⅞	...	..	44.9	...	...
#43•[11]	SNS	✔Sundstrand Corp	NY,B,Ch,P,Ph	B	248	25029	Aerospace parts: pwr transm	47¼	2½	52	41	70¾	44½	21047	70¾	62½	70⅜	1.7	31	58.7	24.2	22.8
✣44•[12]	SNDT	✔SunGard Data Systems	NNM	B+	173	29390	Provides data process'g svcs	21⅜	4¾	20½	15¾	32½	17¾	32109	32½	27¾	28½	...	23	53.1	23.2	38.4
45•[9]	RAYS	✔Sunglass Hut Intl	NNM	NR	186	51313	Sell nonprescript'n sunglasses	8½	5	12⅛	5⅞	29	10½	178981	25⅝	18½	23¾	...	66	110	...	...
✣46•[13]	SMD	✔Sunrise Medical	NY	B	155	10543	Mfrs home health care prod	31¾	1 13/16	33¼	20	36¾	14⅛	28716	19¾	15	18½	...	11	−33.3	−11.4	11.1
✣47	SSC	✔Sunshine Mining & Refining	[14]NY,B,Ch	C	79	14715	Silver & gold mining	26¼	⅛	3⅛	1½	2⅜	1¼	87353	1¾	1¼	1¼	...	d	−23.1	38.6	−1.9
48	SSHI	✔Sunstone Hotel Investors	NNM	....	27	4055	Real estate investment trust	...	...	...	...	10½	7⅞	13733	10½	9	10¼	9.0	13	...	...	...
¶49•[2]	STI	✔SunTrust Banks	NY,B,Ph	A+	406	56637	Comm'l bkg,Georgia,FL,Tenn	49⅝	4⅝	51⅜	43½	70⅞	47¼	19685	70⅞	66½	68½	2.3	14	45.0	18.3	28.0
✣50	SFS	✔Super Food Services	NY,Ph	B+	66	5380	Wholesaler to IGA, others	22	⅝	14⅝	10	14¾	10⅛	3417	13½	12½	13	3.1	15	31.0	15.6	−1.3
51	CUTS	✔Supercuts Inc	NNM	NR	48	4726	Franchisor of haircare strs	18¼	7⅜	17½	7¾	11½	6½	10246	8⅝	7¾	8	...	15	−7.2	−18.4	...
#52•[6]	SUP	✔Superior Indus Intl	NY,Ph	A	163	11428	Custom auto accessories	49⅜	⅛	46¼	24¼	35¾	23⅞	18978	27¾	24½	26⅜	0.8	15	1.2	12.1	36.7

Uniform Footnote Explanations-See Page 4. Other: [1]ASE:Cycle 2. [2]P:Cycle 1. [3]Ph:Cycle 2. [4]Ph:Cycle 3. [5]ASE,CBOE:Cycle 1. [6]CBOE:Cycle 2. [7]NY:Cycle 3. [8]ASE,NY,P:Cycle 3. [9]CBOE:Cycle 3. [10]NY:Cycle 1. [11]NY,P:Cycle 3. [12]Ph:Cycle 1. [13]P:Cycle 2. [14]Ph,Vc [51]Restated from $0.63. [52]Restated from $0.48. [53]Plan name chg, WIN Entertainment Inc. [54]Plan spin-off Rose Intl. [55]82% owned by Citibank. [56]ASE trading halted 12-28-94. [57]®$0.51,'93. [58]9 Mo May,'93. [59]Vote Jan 12,UJB Financial plan acq,0.90 com. [60]CKE Restaurants plan acq,cash & com. [61]Incl $0.568 non-taxable,'94. [62]Earnings after priority return Cl'A'. [63]Incl 6M shrs held by Lehman/SDI. [64]Entitles to $1.10 priority return earnings. [65]Hldrs have contingent put,co has Ltd call rts. [66]100% non-taxable,'94. [67]98% owned by Oryx Energy Co.. [68]®$1.10,'94. [69]Accum on Pfd. [70]Incl curr amts.

Splits ◆ Index	Cash Divs. Ea.Yr. Since	Dividends: Latest Payment Period $	Date	Ex. Div.	Total $ So Far 1995	Ind. Rate	Paid 1994	Financial Position Mil-$ Cash& Equiv.	Curr. Assets	Curr. Liab.	Balance Sheet Date	Capitalization Lg Trm Debt Mil-$	Shs. 000 Pfd.	Com.	Earnings $ Per Shr. Years End	1991	1992	1993	1994	1995	Last 12 Mos.	Interim Earnings Period	$ per Shr. 1994	1995	Index
1	1995	0.41	1-2-96	12-19	1.357	1.55	....	Equity per shr $16.02			9-30-95	3.37	...	8734	Dc	...	...	p1.12	p1.38	....	....	9 Mo Sep	n/a	1.03	1
2	1994	Q0.51	12-28-95	12-13	2.04	2.04	1.41	Book Value $20.71			9-30-95	6.88	...	17561	Dc	...	p1.02	p1.36	p1.61	....	....	9 Mo Sep	n/a	1.40	2
3	....	None Since Public			...	Nil	....	72.8	111	22.8	9-30-95	0.06	...	★±11327	Dc	...	...	...	p0.52	....	1.54	9 Mo Sep	p0.32	1.34	3
4◆	....	None Since Public			...	Nil	....	126	197	48.2	9-30-95	....	...	36742	Dc	Nil	0.15	0.23	0.55	E1.30	1.17	9 Mo Sep	0.33	0.95	4
5	....	None Since Public			...	Nil	....	156	395	113	10-01-95	5.94	...	25459	Dc	2.22	2.43	0.70	2.47	E0.55↓	0.68	9 Mo Sep	1.93	0.14	5
6◆	1947	Q0.27½	2-1-96	12-28	1.10	1.10	1.10	3.96	364	223	10-28-95	198	...	±10572	Ja	1.34	□1.71	1.71	1.92	....	d0.19	9 Mo Oct	d0.02	d2.13	6
7◆	1955	Q0.05	12-15-95	11-27	0.33½	0.20	0.38	48.5	305	78.0	9-01-95	1.67	...	49370	Nv	1.28	1.19	□1.19	0.40	E0.21	0.23	9 Mo Aug	0.42	0.25	7
8	....	None Since Public			...	Nil	....	5.24	36.1	12.5	9-30-95	1.09	...	5066	Dc	d0.41	d0.15	0.33	0.50	....	0.63	9 Mo Sep	0.32	0.45	8
9	....	None Since Public			...	Nil	....	0.48	58.6	25.4	8-26-95	2.94	...	8423	Fb	...	...	p0.45	0.47	....	0.28	9 Mo Nov	0.32	0.13	9
10◆	....	None Since Public			...	Nil	....	50.9	111	69.6	9-30-95	....	...	30289	Dc	[51]0.33	[52]0.29	[52]d0.39	d0.31	E0.45	0.08	9 Mo Sep	□d0.09	0.30	10
11	....	None Paid			...	Nil	....	0.83	11.4	2.73	9-30-95	0.34	...	11296	Dc	*0.14	*0.15	Δ0.19	d0.80	....	d1.20	9 Mo Sep	d0.01	d0.41	11
12◆	1992	A0.09	1-31-96	12-27	0.08	0.09	0.07	236	590	160	9-30-95	104	...	48519	Dc	0.70	1.00	1.25	1.50	E1.80	1.71	9 Mo Sep	1.06	1.27	12
13	....	0.05	3-16-82	2-23	...	Nil	....	1.18	44.0	25.0	9-30-95	40.1	...	6695	Dc	0.55	0.49	Δ0.15	d0.45	....	d0.75	9 Mo Sep	0.34	0.04	13
14	1993	Q0.06	12-1-95	11-13	0.24	0.24	0.24	Equity per shr $14.42			9-30-95	2900	...	[55]20000	Dc	p1.25	2.55	3.14	□2.77	....	2.97	9 Mo Sep	□2.04	2.24	14
15	1983	Q0.40	12-21-95	12-4	1.51	1.60	1.42	Book Value $17.01			6-30-95	37833	4278	p62900	Dc	±3.55	□±5.24	□±6.41	±□5.03	E4.65↑	4.54	9 Mo Sep	3.92	3.43	15
16	....	None Since Public			...	Nil	....	5.03	5.67	2.16	9-30-95	32.4	...	5115	Dc	...	...	...	p0.47	....	....	9 Mo Sep	n/a	p□0.66	16
17◆	1955	Q0.35	12-15-95	11-29	1.40	1.40	1.20	38.0	109	24.2	9-30-95	....	...	13455	Dc	1.09	1.64	□2.47	2.53	....	1.92	9 Mo Sep	1.88	1.27	17
18◆	....	None Since Public			...	Nil	....	7.43	16.1	0.71	9-30-94	....	...	4495	Dc	...	...	[57]0.54	....	....	0.90	9 Mo SepΔ	0.39	0.75	18
19	....	None Paid			...	Nil	....	0.09	65.5	48.4	8-31-95	16.3	...	10512	My	...	...	‡[58]0.24	0.55	1.07	1.15	6 Mo Nov	0.45	0.53	19
20	....	None Paid			...	Nil	....	13.8	25.4	17.2	9-30-95	0.04	...	14225	Dc	Δ0.24	Δ0.30	d0.22	d0.84	....	d0.31	9 Mo Sep	d0.41	0.12	20
21	....	None Since Public			...	Nil	....	18.4	34.3	6.33	9-30-95	....	...	6359	Mr	0.20	0.08	0.92	0.82	....	0.85	6 Mo Sep	0.30	0.33	21
22◆	....	0.32	11-30-84	7-11	...	Nil	....	0.04	7.18	3.43	11-30-95	1.13	...	1542	Au	*0.12	*0.40	Δ0.40	Δ0.40	0.42	0.38	3 Mo Nov	0.10	0.06	22
23◆	1911	Q0.21	12-15-95	11-20	0.84	0.84	0.783	Book Value $13.92			9-30-95	270	504	33898	Dc	0.91	1.11	1.50	0.70	E2.10	2.05	9 Mo Sep	0.21	1.56	23
24	....	0.04	2-28-86	2-10	...	Nil	....	2.09	5.87	17.2	9-25-95	10.2	947	4801	Sp	d0.22	Δd0.12	d0.49	□0.72	d1.05	d1.05				24
25	....	None Since Public			...	Nil	....	24.8	29.4	3.27	9-30-95	....	...	7154	Dc	d0.24	d0.03	0.05	Nil	....	d0.01	9 Mo Sep	d0.15	d0.16	25
26	1994	Q0.37¾	2-14-96	1-8	1.50	1.51	0.919	Equity per shr $10.97			6-30-95	p227	...	p16439	Dc	...	...	...	Δ0.64	....	0.81	9 Mo Sep	Δ0.44	□0.61	26
27◆	....	None Since Public			...	Nil	....	107	133	13.1	p9-30-95	1.10	...	★28571	Dc	*0.03	d0.02	d0.39	d0.63	....	d0.31	9 Mo Sep	d0.47	d0.15	27
28◆	....	0.018	12-15-80	11-21	...	Nil	....	0.31	13.1	7.89	10-28-95	8.52	...	1439	Ja	0.24	d0.23	0.15	d0.06	....	d1.33	9 Mo Oct	0.17	d1.10	28
29◆	1904	Q0.25	12-8-95	11-8	1.40	1.00	1.80	18.0	1316	1482	9-30-95	888	★12500	75038	Dc	■d3.65	□d2.80	Δ2.65	□0.91	E2.41	1.77	9 Mo Sep	□0.88	1.74	29
30◆	....	None Since Public			...	Nil	....	0.21	24.5	11.6	9-30-95	26.4	...	4012	Je	*□0.15	*0.46	0.89	0.85	0.26	0.02	3 Mo Sep	0.26	0.02	30
31	1994	Q0.44½	10-20-95	10-4	1.78	1.78	[61]1.412	Equity per shr $17.13			9-30-95	95.4	...	9916	Dc	...	p0.73	0.05	1.05	....	1.18	9 Mo Sep	0.78	0.91	31
32	1991	0.02	1-31-96	12-27	†0.39	0.24	0.208	9.25	187	81.0	9-30-95	70.5	...	[63]±32775	Dc	0.13	□1.10	0.28	0.79	....	1.54	9 Mo Sep	0.48	□1.23	32
33	1987	M0.091	1-31-96	12-27	1.10	1.10	1.10	....	...	...		....	...	11100	Dc	1.10	□1.10	1.10	1.10	....	1.10	9 Mo Sep	0.82	□0.82	33
34	1986	0.02	12-11-95	11-15	0.46	0.46	[66]0.27	4.00	78.0	177	9-30-95	65.0	...	[67]421171	Dc	0.28	0.29	0.11	□0.24	....	0.25	9 Mo Sep	□0.16	0.17	34
35	....	None Since Public			...	Nil	....	13.8	339	77.1	9-30-95	348	...	47758	Dc	...	p0.31	p0.81	[68]1.19	....	1.21	9 Mo Sep	p0.72	□p0.74	35
36◆	....	None Since Public			...	Nil	....	749	2417	1213	9-30-95	50.4	...	189954	Je	0.93	0.86	0.74	1.01	1.80	2.02	3 Mo Sep	0.20	0.42	36
37◆	1992	Q0.00⅞	12-5-95	11-28	0.03½	0.035	0.03½	11.6	171	83.3	8-26-95	44.9	...	17283	Fb	0.49	0.77	0.96	1.00	....	0.59	9 Mo Nov	0.63	0.22	37
38	....	†1.75	6-20-88	5-10	...	Nil	....	0.25	8.86	0.41	6-30-95	0.06	...	3932	Sp	Δd0.08	*0.29	0.21	Nil	P0.04	0.04				38
39◆	1962	Q0.10	11-24-95	11-15	0.40	0.40	0.30	Equity per shr $15.52			9-30-95	525	★9458	±54418	Sp	0.88	1.20	1.83	□2.39	2.84	2.84				39
40	1992	Q0.01	12-15-95	11-30	0.04	0.04	0.04	25.3	563	173	10-01-95	156	...	81851	Dc	0.61	□0.79	1.01	1.30	....	0.97	9 Mo Sep	0.94	0.61	40
41	....	None Since Public			...	Nil	....	2.04	31.6	24.5	7-31-95	9.99	...	8500	Ja	*0.43	d0.85	□d0.99	d0.59	....	d0.51	9 Mo Oct	0.07	0.15	41
42	1990	gQ0.30	12-22-95	12-13	g1.14	1.20	g1.06	4.00	392	364	j3-31-95	243	...	54584	Dc	1.42	d4.19	1.38	2.22	....	j2.81	9 Mo Sep	1.62	2.21	42
43	1940	Q0.30	12-19-95	12-1	1.20	1.20	1.20	75.0	760	426	9-30-95	238	...	30747	Dc	3.02	□2.31	□4.11	2.92	E2.30	2.44	9 Mo Sep	1.84	1.36	43
44◆	....	None Since Public			...	Nil	....	84.5	223	110	9-30-95	5.38	...	38149	Dc	0.70	0.83	1.07	1.12	....	1.24	9 Mo Sep	0.79	0.91	44
45◆	....	None Since Public			...	Nil	....	4.35	108	41.8	7-29-95	29.7	...	52758	Ja	...	p0.03	p0.21	0.36	....	0.36	9 Mo Oct	0.29	p0.29	45
46◆	....	None Since Public			...	Nil	....	1.74	253	117	6-30-95	182	...	18597	Je	0.78	0.94	1.21	1.41	1.63	1.63				46
47	....	0.10	9-29-81	9-9	...	[69]Nil	....	19.0	33.2	2.52	9-30-95	1.52	7166	193072	Dc	d0.47	□Δd0.44	□d0.25	d0.08	....	d0.13	9 Mo Sep	d0.05	d0.10	47
48	1995	0.23	1-31-96	12-27	0.11½	0.92	....	Equity per shr $6.04			3-31-95	....	...	★7255	Dc	...	...	...	p0.69	....	0.77	9 Mo Sep	p0.54	p0.62	48
49	1985	Q0.40	12-15-95	11-29	1.48	1.60	1.32	Book Value $33.67			9-30-95	1002	...	113160	Dc	2.90	3.28	3.77	4.37	E4.95	4.79	9 Mo Sep	3.24	3.66	49
50	1971	Q0.10	3-15-96	2-15	0.38½	0.40	0.36½	12.4	157	57.3	8-26-95	60.4	...	10949	Au	1.13	d0.51	0.85	0.81	0.83	0.86	3 Mo Nov	0.22	0.25	50
51◆	....	None Since Public			...	Nil	....	1.79	11.7	12.6	9-30-95	[70]25.3	...	11175	Dc	□0.48	0.69	0.63	0.66	....	0.53	9 Mo Sep	0.51	0.38	51
52◆	1985	Q0.05	1-26-96	1-10	0.19	0.20	0.15	11.2	169	84.2	9-30-95	19.4	...	29353	Dc	0.63	0.95	1.47	1.85	E1.75	1.88	9 Mo Sep	1.33	1.36	52

◆Stock Splits & Divs By Line Reference Index [4]2-for-1,'94. [6]Adj to 3%,'93. [7]2-for-1,'91. [10]2-for-1,'91. [12]2-for-1,'91. [17]2-for-1,'93. [18]3-for-2,'93. [22]1-for-100 REVERSE then 25-for-1,'93. [23]10%,'94. [27]3-for-2,'95. [28]3-for-2,'91. [29]No adj for Sun Expl&Prod spinoff'88. [30]1-for-5 REVERSE,'92. [36]2-for-1,'95. [37]2-for-1,'93. [39]No adj for spinoff,'89:3-for-2,'95. [44]2-for-1,'95. [45]2-for-1,'94,'95. [46]2-for-1,'92. [51]3-for-2,'92. [52]10%,'91:2-for-1,'92:3-for-2,'93.

¶ S&P 500 # MidCap 400 ✤ SmallCap 600 • Options Index	Ticker	Name of Issue (Call Price of Pfd. Stocks)	Market	Com. Rank. & Pfd. Rating	Inst. Hold Cos	Inst. Hold Shs. (000)	Principal Business	Price Range 1971-93 High	1971-93 Low	1994 High	1994 Low	1995 High	1995 Low	Dec. Sales in 100s	December, 1995 Last Sale Or Bid High	Low	Last	%Div Yield	P-E Ratio	Total Return % Annualized 12 Mo	36 Mo	60 Mo
1	SGC	✔**Superior Surgical**	AS,Ch	B+	45	3584	Hospital & ind'l uniforms, etc	22¾	⅜	16	11¾	14¾	8¾	3676	9¾	8¾	9⅝	3.7	9	–22.7	–20.7	1.3
¶2•[1]	SVU	✔**Supervalu Inc**	NY,B,Ch,P,Ph	↓A–	336	47076	Large food wholesaler:retail	37⅞	¾	40⅛	22	32⅞	22½	31656	32⅞	30⅞	31½	3.1	13	30.2	3.0	8.5
3	STS	✔**Supreme Industries'A'**	AS	B–	27	2329	Mfrs specialized truck bodies	9⅞	7/16	6¼	4⅛	9	4¾	1593	8½	7⅛	8⅜	...	10	93.0	...	...
4	WS	**2Wrrts(Pur1 Cl'A' at$6)**	AS	....	..	...		....	....	....	....	1⅞	1⅜	479	1⅞	1⅜	1⅞	...	..	...	...	...
5	SUPI	✔**Supreme International**	NNM	NR	26	1241	Designs, mkt men's sportswear	12	8½	13	8½	22½	9½	4221	17¾	14¾	16	...	11	64.1	...	...
6	HOOP	**Sure Shot Intl Inc**	NSC	NR	2	3	Mfr basketball eqp	....	....	....	....	3⅝	2¼	2954	3⅜	2¾	2⅞	...	26	...	...	...
7	SRY	✔**Surety Capital**	AS	NR	10	1070	Consumer loan/bkg svcs	22½	1 9/16	6⅝	2⅞	6¾	3	882	4⅛	3½	3½	...	13	16.7	–20.2	4.5
#8•[2]	SCA	✔**Surgical Care Affil**[54]	NY	B	174	21335	Outpatient surgical centers	46	13/16	20⅞	11⅞	34	17⅞	60802	34	31⅞	34	0.6	38	72.5	...	...
9	SLTI	✔**Surgical Laser Tech**	NNM	C	13	1333	Dvlp,mfr laser surgery sys	21¾	1¾	4⅝	1⅝	2⅞	1	15776	1 11/16	1	1¼	...	d	–41.2	–38.0	–41.2
10	SGTI	**Surgical Technologies**	NNM	NR	7	93	Specialized surgical products	10¼	2¼	5⅜	2¾	3⅜	1¼	1964	1 11/16	1¼	1 11/16	...	d	–41.3	–33.6	–10.1
11	STIQ	✔**Survival Technology**	NNM	B–	6	149	Medical injection technology	67	3	13¾	6½	10¼	6½	1940	10¼	8¼	8¾	...	46	9.4	–10.0	–8.0
12	SUSQ	✔**Susquehanna Bancshares**	NNM	A–	60	2098	Comm'l bkg,Pennsylvania	28¾	4⅜	28	21¼	30¼	21½	12752	29¼	26	26½	4.4	12	27.1	11.1	22.7
13	SNKI	✔**Swank Inc**	NSC	B–	6	187	Leather goods:jewelry	3½	5/16	1½	⅞	2 1/16	¾	1972	15/16	¾	¾	...	d	–29.4	–12.6	–1.6
14	SFY	✔**Swift Energy**	NY,Ch,P	B	52	7492	Oil & gas explor,dev,prod'n	16⅞	1	11⅜	8½	12⅝	7¾	13277	12⅝	10¼	12	...	33	18.5	19.0	7.5
15	SWG	**Swing-N-Slide Corp**	AS	NR	27	1516	Mfr wooden playground equip	17¾	9¼	13	7¾	8⅞	3¼	1463	4¼	3½	4	...	10	–49.2	–30.7	...
16•[3]	SYBS	✔**Sybase Inc**	NNM	NR	255	42094	Dvlp database mgmt software	43½	6¾	57	35¼	55	19⅞	265254	38⅜	34⅛	36	...	d	–32.1	13.5	...
✤17	SYB	✔**Sybron Intl**	NY,Ph	NR	171	35929	Mfr orthodontic/dental lab prd	16	7	18⅛	13¾	24⅛	16⅛	14293	24⅛	21⅜	23⅝	...	22	38.0	25.3	...
18	SLVN	✔**Sylvan Learning Systems**	NNM	NR	41	2201	Tutorial educational services	14	11	21¾	10¾	32¾	16¼	31629	29¾	23½	29¾	...	88	54.5	...	...
#19•[4]	SYMC	✔**Symantec Corp**	NNM	C	216	40553	Microcomputer softwr prod	51	5¼	19⅝	9⅞	33¼	16⅛	280110	28¾	21	23¼	...	52	31.5	19.1	12.3
#20•[5]	SBL	✔**Symbol Technologies**	NY,Ch,Ph	↑B	160	22967	Bar code laser scanners	29⅜	1 11/16	34⅜	15⅝	40⅝	24⅜	18737	40	35¾	39½	...	23	27.9	43.0	26.9
✤21•[6]	SYMM	✔**Symmetricom Inc**	NNM	B	59	4397	Electronic parts mfr	18¼	1/16	13⅝	6½	26⅝	12⅞	42789	17⅞	12⅞	13¾	...	20	4.8	11.7	43.6
22	SYM	✔**Syms Corp**	NY,B,Ch	B	39	3675	Off-price apparel stores	18⅝	6½	10¼	6⅜	9½	6⅝	1800	8	7⅜	7½	...	16	7.1	–7.4	–0.6
23	SBIO	✔**Synbiotics Corp**	NNM	C	15	1793	Dvlp/mfr biological products	15¾	2¼	5⅛	1⅝	5¼	1½	3765	2⅞	1⅞	2⅜	...	d	46.2	–9.9	0.0
24	SYNX	**Sync Research**	NNM	NR	..	...	Dvlp spcl networking prod	....	....	....	....	56	20	30373	56	39½	45¼	...	..	...	...	...
25	SNTC	✔**Synetic Inc**	NNM	B	29	3544	Mfr porous plastic products	23½	5¼	20¼	8¼	29⅝	19	4811	29⅝	25¼	29⅛	...	30	49.4	10.7	26.5
26•[7]	SNPS	✔**Synopsys Inc**	NNM	NR	182	33789	Dvlp elec sys design softwr	26⅜	9	24⅜	16½	38½	21⅜	53973	38¼	32½	38	...	51	77.0	31.1	...
27	SNV	✔**Synovus Financial**	NY,Ch,Ph	A+	88	19477	Commercial bkg,Georgia	20⅜	¾	19⅞	16⅝	30¼	17¾	5413	29	28	28½	1.9	19	58.9	25.6	27.3
28	NZYM	✔**Synthetech Inc**	NSC	B–	9	634	Produce pharmaceutical prod	4⅜	¼	3½	1 11/16	5½	1 11/16	5374	5⅛	3⅞	4¾	...	28	182	54.8	66.2
29•[6]	SYQT	✔**SyQuest Technology**	NNM	NR	52	3661	Mfr Winchester disk cartridges	28½	8¾	19½	8½	19⅝	8⅞	40500	12⅛	9⅞	10	...	d	–43.7	–26.3	...
30	SYR	✔**Syratech Corp**	NY	NR	50	3636	Mfr giftwr prd/resin furniture	22¾	13	19¼	15⅛	23	15	1750	21	20	20⅛	...	5	13.4	0.6	...
¶31•[8]	SYY	✔**Sysco Corp**	NY,B,Ch	A+	561	107261	Food distr & service systems	31	¼	29¼	21⅛	32⅝	24⅞	77690	32⅝	30⅛	32½	1.6	23	28.2	9.0	15.9
✤32•[6]	SSAX	✔**System Software**	NNM,Ch	B	155	26835	IBM mainframe softw prod	17	15/16	12	7⅛	30½	10¼	124608	25⅞	21	21¾	0.5	27	113	14.9	24.9
33•[7]	SYSM	✔**SysteMed Inc**	NNM	C	41	7906	Mail service prescriptions	30	⅝	9¼	3⅞	8	3⅞	25575	6⅛	3⅞	4⅝	...	23	–31.5	–12.4	10.5
34	STMX	✔**SyStemix Inc**	NNM	NR	29	2605	Human cell research/prod dvlp	60½	15	20¾	11¾	18½	11¾	562	16⅜	14¼	15	...	d	–13.7	–13.0	...
35•[9]	SCTC	✔**Systems & Computer Tech**	NNM	B–	85	10965	Comput'g sys/softw for educ	38½	1¾	23⅞	13¾	29⅝	15¾	28040	22½	18	19⅞	...	90	–4.2	36.2	47.2
36	TCEL	✔**T Cell Sciences**	NNM	C	26	3237	Dvlp diagnostic/therap'tc prd	14⅛	1 15/16	8⅝	2	5½	2⅜	32452	3½	2½	3⅛	...	d	31.6	–24.0	1.2
✤37•[3]	TJCO	✔**T J International**	NNM	B	88	7259	Prefab joists for constrn	33	⅝	32¼	14¼	21½	15¼	10392	19½	17½	18½	1.2	..	5.5	18.2	16.0
38	ROSE	✔**T R Financial**	NNM	NR	48	5241	Savings bank,New York	13½	9⅝	17⅛	11¼	27½	13	13235	26⅜	24¾	25½	1.9	14	99.7	...	...
39	TBP	✔**Tab Products**	AS,B	B–	28	2987	Office/computer access eq	20⅝	7/16	11⅛	6⅞	7¼	5¼	2054	7¼	6¼	6½	3.1	22	–5.9	–16.8	–8.4
✤40•[3]	TACO	✔**Taco Cabana'A'**	NNM,Ph	NR	57	10530	Mexican style restaurant chain	22¼	9	20	7¼	9⅛	4⅜	10642	5⅝	4⅝	5	...	d	–44.4	–27.5	...
41•[7]	TAD	✔**Tadiran Limited**	NY,Ph	NR	..	...	Telecomn,defense consumer prd	39⅝	14⅛	26½	14½	25⅛	15	4860	24½	22⅜	24	0.8	22	14.1	–3.4	...
42•[6]	TLB	✔**Talbots Inc**	NY,Ph	NR	166	11465	Retail women's apparel	27¾	21⅞	36½	23¼	43	23½	16259	30⅛	26	28¾	1.0	16	–4.6	...	...
43	TAL	✔**Talley Indus**	NY,B,Ch,Ph	C	29	3487	Aerospace,indl,consumer prod	24⅜	2¼	9½	5⅜	11	7⅜	11310	9	7⅜	8⅝	...	33	13.1	38.4	8.6
44	Pr B	**$1.00 cm Cv B Pfd(52 1/2)vtg**[10]	NY,B,Ch	NR	7	582	real estate,Arizona	32	5	16¼	10	17⅛	12½	631	16½	12⅞	16¼	...	..	...	...	...
#45•[2]	TMB	✔**Tambrands Inc**	NY,B,Ch,P	B+	286	24689	Mfr feminine hygiene prod	70½	5½	44½	34¾	53	37⅞	19610	53	46¼	47¾	3.9	20	28.2	–5.7	5.2
¶46•[5]	TDM	✔**Tandem Computers**	NY,Ch,Ph	↑B–	369	81043	Multi processor computer sys	37⅝	15/16	19⅛	10½	19¾	10	122958	12⅝	10⅝	10⅝	...	12	–39.3	–10.9	–2.2
47	TBAC	✔**Tandy Brands Accessories**	NNM	NR	22	1193	Mfr leather goods/accesssories	22½	2⅛	20½	11¾	15¼	6¼	2699	7⅝	6¼	6¼	...	69	–54.5	–23.6	...
¶48•[11]	TAN	✔**Tandy Corp**	NY,B,Ch,C,P	B	461	42282	Retails consumer electronics	64½	⅝	50⅝	30¾	64⅜	36½	92119	48	36½	41½	1.9	12	–16.0	14.4	9.5
49	TAC	✔**Tandycrafts, Inc**[66]	NY,B,Ch	B	31	2473	Leather crafts,picture frames	27⅝	15/16	19¼	10⅜	11½	6⅝	5579	9⅜	7¼	7⅞	...	28	–27.6	–17.6	15.5
50	SKT	✔**Tanger Factory Outlet Ctrs**	NY	NR	86	4470	Real estate investment trust	30	22½	34¾	20¼	27¾	22⅝	3000	26	23⅛	25	8.0	18	18.7	...	...
51	Pr A	**Cm Cv[69]Dep Pfd([70]25)**	NY	BB–	13	1146		25⅝	23¼	30⅞	18¾	24⅝	19¾	114	23⅜	20⅛	22⅝B	8.0	..	...	...	...

Uniform Footnote Explanations-See Page 4. Other: [1]Ph:Cycle 1. [2]NY:Cycle 1. [3]Ph:Cycle 3. [4]P:Cycle 1. [5]ASE:Cycle 1. [6]P:Cycle 2. [7]CBOE:Cycle 3. [8]NY:Cycle 2. [9]ASE:Cycle 2. [10]Ph [11]ASE,CBOE:Cycle 1. [51]Stk dstr of Contempri Homes Inc. [52]®$0.64,'94. [53]If com exceeds $8 15 consec trad days. [54]Health South Corp plan acq, 1.22 com. [55]®$0.28,'94. [56]®$0.71,'94. [57]®$1.33,'94. [58]Mar '94 & prior. [59]12 Mo Dec'94. [60]®$0.21,'95. [61]Fiscal Apr'92 & prior:12 Mo Dec'92 $d0.40. [62]®$0.44,'94. [63]Accum on pfd. [64]Fiscal Jun'91 & prior. [65]12 Mo Dec'92:Fiscal Jun'92 earned $2.24. [66]Plan name chge AMTAC Inc. [67]Stk of Color Tile. [68]Incl $0.342 non-taxable,'94. [69]Dep for 0.10 shr Sr'A'cm Cv Redm Pfd. [70]Fr 12-15-98. [71]Re-specified cond..

Splits ◆ Index	Cash Divs. Ea.Yr. Since	Dividends Latest Payment Period $	Date	Ex. Div.	Total $ So Far 1995	Ind. Rate	Paid 1994	Financial Position Mil-$ Cash& Equiv.	Curr. Assets	Curr. Liab.	Balance Sheet Date	Capitalization Lg Trm Debt Mil-$	Shs. 000 Pfd.	Com.	Earnings $ Per Shr. Years End	1991	1992	1993	1994	1995	Last 12 Mos.	Interim Earnings Period	$ per Shr. 1994	1995	Index
1◆	1977	Q0.09	11-30-95	11-16	0.36	0.36	0.32	9.07	78.0	12.8	9-30-95	18.3	...	8134	Dc	0.94	1.15	0.89	1.17	....	1.08	9 Mo Sep	0.84	0.75	1
2	1936	Q0.24½	3-15-96	2-28	0.96	0.98	0.91	5.47	1565	1330	9-09-95	1208	6	67963	Fb	□2.78	2.31	2.58	0.61	E2.35↓	2.33	40 Wk Nov	Nil	1.72	2
3◆	....	h[51]....	6-9-93	6-10	...	Nil	....	0.11	37.9	15.5	9-30-95	18.7	...	±8177	Dc	±d0.37	±...	±0.56	±[52]0.67	....	0.88	9 Mo Sep	±0.46	±0.67	3
4	....	Terms&trad. basis should			be checked in detail			Wrrts expire 6-9-96				....	...	1498	Dc	...	...	...	....	....	....	Callable at $0.10[53]			4
5	....	None Since Public			...	Nil	....	0.28	54.7	6.52	7-31-95	26.3	...	★4533	Ja	0.26	0.77	0.81	1.10	....	1.45	9 Mo Oct	0.77	1.12	5
6	....	None Paid			...	Nil	....	0.21	8.19	4.39	9-30-95	0.13	...	3331	Dc	...	...	0.08	0.15	....	0.11	9 Mo Sep	0.14	0.10	6
7◆	....	None Paid			...	Nil	....	Book Value $2.13			9-30-95	0.38	...	3506	Dc	d0.50	*Nil	0.19	0.20	....	0.27	9 Mo Sep	0.13	0.20	7
8◆	1989	Q0.05	12-8-95	11-22	0.19	0.20	0.16	39.1	86.4	43.8	9-30-95	65.1	...	38994	Dc	0.57	0.78	0.96	□0.80	....	0.90	9 Mo Sep	0.74	0.84	8
9	....	None Since Public			...	Nil	....	1.55	10.1	4.07	10-01-95	6.80	...	9853	Dc	d0.44	□d0.81	d0.33	0.10	....	d0.40	9 Mo Sep	0.10	d0.40	9
10	....	None Since Public			...	Nil	....	0.67	4.71	1.19	9-30-95	....	...	4219	Mr	d0.06	d0.03	d0.27	d0.73	....	d0.58	6 Mo Sep	d0.17	d0.02	10
11	....	None Since Public			...	Nil	....	0.01	11.5	8.12	10-31-95	1.26	...	3088	Jl	*0.60	*0.55	*0.60	0.68	0.15	0.19	3 Mo Oct	0.01	0.05	11
12◆	1982	Q0.29	11-20-95	10-27	1.10	1.16	1.02	Book Value $20.12			9-30-95	92.0	...	★12941	Dc	1.97	2.03	Δ2.04	□2.11	....	2.26	9 Mo Sep	□1.47	1.62	12
13	....	0.006	7-21-86	6-30	...	Nil	....	0.88	61.8	43.7	9-30-95	4.41	...	15924	Dc	0.08	0.24	Δ0.16	0.34	....	d0.05	9 Mo Sep	0.04	d0.35	13
14◆	....	None Since Public			...	Nil	....	12.2	44.8	25.5	9-30-95	28.8	...	12507	Dc	0.47	0.51	0.75	□0.56	....	0.36	9 Mo Sep	□0.52	0.32	14
15	....	None Since Public			...	Nil	....	0.01	10.8	7.40	9-30-95	37.0	...	6000	Dc	p0.32	p0.69	0.83	0.48	....	0.42	9 Mo Sep	0.78	0.72	15
16◆	....	None Since Public			...	Nil	....	177	404	261	9-30-95	....	...	72376	Dc	*0.19	0.48	0.86	1.38	Ed0.20	0.28	9 Mo Sep	0.74	d0.36	16
17◆	....	None Since Public			...	Nil	....	9.24	248	138	9-30-95	407	...	46530	Sp	p□0.12	0.31	□0.57	□0.92	□1.10	1.10				17
18	....	None Since Public			...	Nil	....	5.31	33.1	26.4	9-30-95	p3.06	...	★9111	Dc	...	pd0.53	pd0.04	[55]0.29	....	0.34	9 Mo Sep	0.27	0.32	18
19◆	....	None Since Public			...	Nil	....	114	181	70.6	6-30-95	15.0	...	p51741	Mr	0.77	d0.49	d0.37	[56]0.77	E0.45	1.12	6 Mo Sep	0.25	0.60	19
20	....	None Since Public			...	Nil	....	59.8	308	90.8	9-30-95	63.9	...	25811	Dc	0.91	□d0.65	0.50	[57]1.34	E1.70	1.62	9 Mo Sep	0.98	1.26	20
21	....	None Since Public			...	Nil	....	33.9	69.7	15.5	9-30-95	5.75	...	15403	Je	*0.11	*0.10	0.40	0.43	0.66	0.70	3 Mo Sep	0.13	0.17	21
22	1994	0.05	8-1-94	6-27	...	Nil	0.15	0.32	132	66.1	8-26-95	1.48	...	17694	Dc	0.81	0.86	0.61	0.48	....	0.46	6 Mo Aug	0.12	0.10	22
23	....	None Since Public			...	Nil	....	1.94	6.20	1.87	9-30-95	....	...	5816	Dc	d0.36	d0.32	[58]0.06	[59]d0.11	....	d0.02	9 Mo Sep	0.06	0.15	23
24	....	None Since Public			...	Nil	....	3.60	9.82	3.90	9-30-95	0.01	p...	★13077	Dc	...	...	...	pd0.12	....	....	9 Mo Sep	n/a	p0.02	24
25◆	....	None Since Public			...	Nil	....	105	122	16.4	6-30-95	....	...	16648	Je	0.22	0.33	0.35	0.14	0.93	0.98	3 Mo Sep	0.06	0.11	25
26◆	....	None Since Public			...	Nil	....	196	244	110	6-30-95	....	...	39034	Sp	0.14	0.24	0.42	0.42	P0.75	0.75				26
27◆	1930	Q0.135	1-2-96	12-19	0.51¾	0.54	0.431	Book Value $8.40			9-30-95	122	...	77202	Dc	0.75	0.92	□1.11	1.29	E1.48	1.45	9 Mo Sep	0.90	1.06	27
28	....	None Paid			...	Nil	....	2.62	5.57	0.55	9-30-95	....	...	12279	Mr	*0.03	Δ0.06	0.09	0.11	....	0.17	6 Mo Sep	0.03	0.09	28
29	....	None Since Public			...	Nil	....	21.8	120	40.6	6-30-95	....	...	11112	Sp	*0.30	*1.14	1.23	Δ0.43	Pd1.07	d1.07				29
30	....	None Since Public			...	Nil	....	97.6	191	23.2	9-30-95	....	...	11726	Dc	Δ1.08	1.65	1.52	1.69	....	3.89	9 Mo Sep	1.29	3.49	30
31◆	1970	Q0.13	2-16-96	1-24	0.44	0.52	0.36	90.3	1915	1077	9-30-95	p446	...	p186000	Je	0.83	0.93	1.08	1.18	1.38	1.42	3 Mo Sep	0.32	0.36	31
32◆	1991	A0.10	1-10-96	12-26	0.08	0.10	0.08	48.5	231	141	7-31-95	34.6	...	41189	Oc	0.42	0.66	0.57	0.38	P0.81	0.81				32
33	....	None Since Public			...	Nil	....	13.8	39.1	11.7	9-30-95	6.30	161	22144	Dc	0.10	□d0.07	d0.28	0.14	....	0.20	9 Mo Sep	0.09	0.15	33
34	....	None Since Public			...	Nil	....	65.9	68.5	6.27	9-30-95	5.99	...	14463	Dc	d1.35	d1.70	d1.89	d4.54	....	d4.13	9 Mo Sep	d2.95	d2.54	34
35	....	None Since Public			...	Nil	....	15.3	95.6	32.0	9-30-95	31.9	...	14058	Sp	*□0.24	*d0.21	*0.53	0.86	[60]0.22	0.22				35
36	....	None Paid			...	Nil	....	10.5	12.0	2.15	6-30-95	....	...	17069	Dc	d0.34	[61]d0.35	d0.56	d0.68	....	d0.73	9 Mo Sep	d0.42	d0.47	36
37◆	1977	Q0.05½	1-10-96	12-27	0.22	0.22	0.22	23.3	135	61.1	9-30-95	94.9	1189	17104	Dc	d0.32	Δ0.38	0.82	[62]0.46	....	0.06	9 Mo Sep	0.68	0.28	37
38	1994	Q0.12	12-1-95	11-13	0.37	0.48	0.05	Book Value $19.96			9-30-95	....	...	9620	Dc	...	p0.83	0.46	1.24	....	1.88	9 Mo Sep	0.89	1.53	38
39	1971	Q0.05	12-15-95	11-20	0.20	0.20	0.20	8.71	51.5	20.9	8-31-95	18.7	...	4852	My	0.11	0.26	□0.39	0.45	0.25	0.29	6 Mo Nov	0.25	0.29	39
40◆	....	None Since Public			...	Nil	....	4.39	13.1	15.6	10-01-95	16.3	...	15681	Dc	±p0.57	±0.41	±0.55	±0.55	....	d0.16	9 Mo Sep	±0.44	±d0.27	40
41	1993	0.204	6-30-95	6-6	0.204	0.20	0.08	98.4	559	429	9-30-95	36.3	...	19614	Dc	*1.37	*2.15	Δ2.56	2.01	....	1.11	9 Mo Sep	1.75	0.85	41
42	1994	Q0.07	12-18-95	11-30	0.26	0.28	0.18	3.48	296	154	10-28-95	35.0	...	33911	Ja	...	p0.84	p1.20	1.56	E1.80	1.69	9 Mo Oct	1.30	1.43	42
43	....	0.05	4-8-91	3-5	...	[63]Nil	....	8.90	156	75.9	9-30-95	229	1739	10051	Dc	d5.15	Δd1.95	□d0.85	0.13	....	0.26	9 Mo Sep	d0.04	Δ0.09	43
44	....	0.25	4-8-91	3-5	...	Nil	....	Cv into 1.3125 common				....	1548	...	Dc	bd0.23	b0.93	b0.71	b1.04	....	....	Accum $4.50 to 10-8-95			44
45	1943	Q0.46	12-15-95	11-29	1.78	1.84	1.70	17.6	220	229	9-30-95	71.3	...	36686	Dc	1.92	□3.09	□1.91	2.43	E2.35	2.33	9 Mo Sep	1.81	1.71	45
46	....	None Since Public			...	Nil	....	121	970	670	9-30-95	75.9	...	117004	Sp	0.33	d0.38	d4.72	1.50	0.91	0.91				46
47◆	....	None Since Public			...	Nil	....	0.05	48.5	11.9	9-30-95	18.2	...	5300	Je	0.41	0.64	0.80	0.97	0.18	0.09	3 Mo Sep	0.25	0.16	47
48	1987	Q0.20	1-23-96	12-27	0.72	0.80	0.60	103	2324	1147	9-30-95	138	100	63516	Dc	□[64]2.58	p[65]0.78	Δ1.01	2.91	E3.55	3.10	9 Mo Sep	1.56	1.75	48
49◆	....	h[67]....	4-9-79	4-10	...	Nil	....	2.07	104	27.6	9-30-95	59.0	...	11879	Je	0.18	0.04	0.69	0.79	0.46	0.28	3 Mo Sep	0.18	Nil	49
50	1993	Q0.50	11-15-95	10-25	1.96	2.00	[68]1.80	Equity per shr $11.07			12-31-94	p147	p145	p6266	Dc	...	pΔ0.67	□p1.39	1.32	....	1.39	9 Mo Sep	0.91	0.98	50
51	1994	Q0.451	11-15-95	10-25	1.766	[71]1.802	1.506	Cv into 0.901 com, $27.75				....	2294	...	Dc	...	...	...	....	....	....				51

◆**Stock Splits & Divs By Line Reference Index** [1]4-for-1,'92. [3]10%,'95. [7]1-for-10 REVERSE,'93. [8]3-for-2,'91. [12]5-for-4,'93. [14]10%,'94. [16]2-for-1,'93. [17]2-for-1,'95. [19]2-for-1,'91. [25]2-for-1,'93. [26]2-for-1,'95. [27]3-for-2,'93. [31]2-for-1,'92. [32]3-for-2,'91,'92,'95. [37]2-for-1,'93. [40]3-for-2,'93. [47]3-for-2,'91,'92,'93. [49]2-for-1,'92,'93.

Index	Ticker	Name of Issue (Call Price of Pfd. Stocks)	Market	Com. Rank. & Pfd. Rating	Inst. Hold Cos	Inst. Hold Shs. (000)	Principal Business	Price Range 1971-93 High	1971-93 Low	1994 High	1994 Low	1995 High	1995 Low	Dec. Sales in 100s	December, 1995 Last Sale Or Bid High	Low	Last	%Div Yield	P-E Ratio	Total Return % Annualized 12 Mo	36 Mo	60 Mo
1	TANK	✓**Tanknology Environmental**	NNM	NR	14	2253	Storage tank enviro svcs	13½	3½	6¼	2⅛	2⅞	1½	9918	2 5/16	1½	1 13/16	...	d	−19.5	−22.4	...
2	TGET	✓**Target Therapeutics**	NNM	NR	107	10970	Mfr disposable medical prod	16⅝	7	16⅛	8¼	43	13⅝	43483	43	33⅜	42¾	...	71	198	46.0	...
3	TAROF	**Taro Pharmaceutical Ind**	NNM	NR	2	33	Hldg co: pharmaceutical prod	12¾	⅝	8⅝	4½	8½	6	5776	7¼	6	6¾	...	23	−6.9	−6.9	...
4	TBC	✓**Tasty Baking**	AS,B,Ph	↓B+	38	2310	Small cakes/pies:graphic eq	27	2⅝	15½	12	15¼	11⅞	1479	13½	11⅞	12⅛	4.6	14	−2.8	...	...
5	TOFF	**Tatham Offshore**	NNM	NR	29	1430	Oil&gas explor,dvlp,prod'n	...	...	20	8⅞	13	⅞	24859	1⅞	1	1⅛	...	d	−91.2	...	...
6•[1]	TCO	✓**Taubman Centers**	NY,Ph	NR	98	23644	Real estate investment trust	15½	10½	13½	9⅜	10⅜	8⅞	16189	10⅛	9¼	10	8.8	26	12.4	2.8	...
✤7•[1]	TBCC	✓**TBC Corp**	NNM	B+	100	17275	Automotive replacement parts	18¼	1 1/16	13⅞	8½	11¾	6⅝	11430	8⅝	7	8⅝	...	13	−6.8	−18.2	10.3
#8•[2]	TCAT	✓**TCA Cable TV**	NNM	A−	136	11864	CATV sys in Tex,La & Ark	30⅛	2⅞	28⅜	17½	32½	20⅞	16458	28⅜	26¼	27⅝	2.0	22	31.7	10.3	15.2
✤9•[3]	TBY	✓**TCBY Enterprises**	NY,Ph	B	47	4114	Franchises frozen yogurt strs	29	¼	6⅞	5	6½	3⅞	17008	4½	3⅞	4	5.0	50	−27.6	−7.5	−4.0
10	TEL	✓**TCC Industries**	NY,Ch	B−	14	438	Mfr spec conveying/processing	18	9/16	4⅛	2	3	1¾	702	2⅝	1⅞	2	...	d	−30.4	17.0	21.7
✤11	TCB	✓**TCF Financial**	NY,Ch	B	188	20023	Savings Banks,Minnesota	20	2¾	21⅝	14¼	33⅜	18⅝	14436	33⅜	29¼	33⅛	1.9	23	68.3	36.7	58.0
12	TCSI	✓**TCSI Corp**	NNM	NR	38	3222	Dvlp telecomm software	10¼	2	11¾	4½	20¾	9⅞	22769	20¾	16¼	18½	...	32	85.0	83.4	...
13	TDK	✓**TDK Corp[52] ADS**	NY,B,Ch	NR	23	1160	Ferrite, ceramics, mag tapes	51¼	2½	49½	34¼	54½	39	462	53½	47½	52½	0.9	47	10.0	23.4	12.6
14	TMI	✓**Team, Inc**	AS,Ch	C	21	1342	Environmental services	35¾	1⅝	5⅛	1⅞	3	1½	874	2½	2	2	...	d	0.0	−27.4	−31.1
✤15•[3]	TECD	✓**Tech Data Corp**	NNM	B	124	24498	Dstr computer hardware prod	18⅜	1	22⅛	14	17⅞	8¼	76355	17⅞	15	15	...	32	−7.7	3.6	51.1
16	TO	✓**Tech/Ops Sevcon**	AS	B+	14	474	Mfr vehicle speed controllers	9	1 5/16	8⅝	4½	15⅞	7⅛	436	11¾	10⅜	10⅝	4.7	13	54.7	20.8	18.4
17	TSY	✓**Tech-Sym**	NY,Ch,P,Ph	B	82	4335	Electronic components/sys	27½	⅜	24⅜	17⅝	31⅞	21⅛	2516	31⅞	29¼	31⅝	...	13	39.0	32.8	27.9
18	TSH	✓**Teche Holding**	AS	NR	7	686	Savings & loan, Louisiana	...	...	...	...	14⅝	10	2460	14⅜	13½	13¾	3.6	17	...	...	...
19	TFRC	**TechForce Corp**	NNM	NR	..	...	Computer network svcs	...	...	...	...	11½	8¼	45360	11½	8¼	8¾	...	46	...	...	...
20	TECN	✓**Technalysis Corp**	NNM	B+	12	368	Sys design & analysis,prog svc	15¾	1/16	12½	10¼	12¾	10¼	340	12¾	12	12	4.8	39	23.1	9.9	12.4
21	TNL	✓**Technitrol Inc**	AS,Ph	B+	35	1844	Electronic/mechanical prod	14¼	3/16	16	9⅞	23¾	13¼	6339	23¾	18⅝	22¾	1.8	19	71.4	43.1	59.8
22	TRCI	**Technology Research**	NNM	B−	10	1379	Design electronic control dev	11¼	¾	8⅞	3½	6⅛	3	4501	4¼	3¾	4	6.0	13	2.8	1.7	16.6
23	TSCC	✓**Technology Solutions**	NNM	NR	40	5413	Computer sys consult'g/svcs	30¾	6¾	9¼	4¾	23⅞	7¼	48398	23⅞	16⅞	19½	...	67	140	10.4	...
24•[4]	TEK.A	**Teck Corp Cl'A'**	To,Mo	B	1	556	Mining & petroleum	28	7/16	26¾	21½	28	21¾	31	26	25	25½	0.8	26	4.9	16.1	...
✤25	TCNL	✓**Tecnol Medical Products**	NNM	NR	100	7462	Mfr disposable medical prod	21	9½	17½	12¼	23	14¼	11661	20	17½	18	...	25	24.1	0.1	...
26	TCNOF	**Tecnomatix Technologies Ltd**	NNM	NR	..	...	Computer-aided prod'n softwr	19	8	12¾	3⅝	13⅞	3⅝	10317	13⅞	10⅞	12½	...	26	144	...	...
#27	TE	✓**TECO Energy**	NY,B,C,Ch,P,Ph	A	297	46067	Hldg co:Tampa Electric	25⅞	2 3/16	22⅝	18⅛	25¾	20	23424	25¾	23⅞	25⅝	4.1	16	31.9	12.6	14.1
28	TSN	✓**TecSyn International**	To	B−	8	3016	Synthetic Fibers/pwdr metal pd	8	1/32	3½	1⅝	2⅞	1 5/16	16005	1¾	1 5/16	1¾	...	12	−15.5	...	...
#29•[5]	TECUA	✓**Tecumseh Products Cl'A'**	NNM	B+	186	14539	Refrigeration prod:motors	47¼	24	55½	40⅜	54	43¼	16143	54	49½	51¾	e2.0	9	18.7	29.4	...
30	TECUB	✓ **Cl'B'**	NNM	B+	59	4288		47½	4⅜	62¾	39	53	42½	3261	53	46	52¼	e2.0	10	22.0	26.4	24.8
31	TK	**Teekay Shipping**	NY,Ch	NR	..	...	Transp'n svc to oil industry	...	...	...	...	25⅝	22⅝	2768	25⅛	23¼	23⅝	3.6	28	...	...	...
32	TGAL	✓**Tegal Corp**	NNM	NR	..	...	Dgn/mfr plasma etch sys	...	...	...	...	14¼	9⅛	10768	11	9⅛	10¼	...	26	...	...	...
33	TEJ	✓**Tejas Gas Corp**	NY	B	97	6123	Oper natural gas pipeline	55½	8⅜	51⅝	37¼	54	36⅞	1763	54	49¾	52⅞	...	26	34.3	43.4	32.1
34	PrA	**5.25% cmCv[58]Dep Pfd([59]51.8375)**	NY	↑BB−	15	556		51½	45¾	53¾	40	50	39¾	230	49¾	46⅞	47½	5.5	..	...	...	...
35	TPC	✓**Tejas Power Corp**	AS	NR	45	4379	Natural gas gather'g/transm'n	10⅞	3½	12⅜	8	10¼	7¾	3784	9½	7¾	9⅛	...	..	−1.4	6.8	...
36	TRC	✓**Tejon Ranch**	AS([10]),Ch,P	B	36	2761	Seed:cattle:farm'g:oil:land	63¼	1 5/16	15½	11½	17¾	11⅝	1082	14⅞	13¾	14½	0.3	..	22.5	−3.1	−9.2
37	TKLC	✓**Tekelec**	NNM	B	63	6102	Telecommun'ns test eqp	12⅝	1½	17⅝	2⅞	26¾	8	64043	16½	8	10½	...	15	−29.9	26.5	8.9
¶38•[6]	TEK	✓**Tektronix Inc**	NY,B,Ch,P,Ph	B−	312	23194	Mfrs electronic equipment	43⅜	4½	40½	23⅝	61⅞	31⅜	40334	57⅜	48¼	49⅛	1.2	19	43.8	38.4	25.0
39•[7]	TEO	**Tel Argentina-France Tel'B'ADS[61]**	[8]NY	NR	65	7971	Telecommun svcs - Argentina	...	...	54	44¾	57¼	25¾	21180	49¼	41⅜	47½	4.5	18	−3.9	...	...
40	TALK	✓**Tel-Save Holdings**	NNM	NR	21	1188	Long distance telecom svcs	...	...	...	...	16½	12	3376	14¾	12	13⅞	...	15	...	...	...
41	TELC	✓**Telco Systems**	NNM	B	39	7168	Voice freq/fiber optics prod	22	1⅝	18⅛	7⅞	17	9¼	12302	11⅜	9¼	10⅝	...	d	−38.8	12.9	−4.0
42	TLCM	✓**TelCom Semiconductor**	NNM	NR	26	5338	Mfr high performance circuits	...	...	...	...	16	6¼	15579	9⅜	6⅞	7¼	...	45	...	...	...
¶43•[9]	TCOMA	✓**Tele-Communic'A'TCI Group**	NNM	NR	698	409678	CATV sys: microwave serv	33¼	1/16	30¼	18¼	26¼	16⅝	498756	21¼	18½	19⅞	...	..	...	...	...
44•[10]	TINTA	✓**Tele-Communications Intl**	NNM	NR	66	13732	Oper intl cable TV systems	...	...	...	...	26¼	14¾	32132	26¼	21⅞	22¾	...	..	...	...	...
45•[11]	TLD	✓**Tele Danmark A/S ADS[64]**	NY,Ph	NR	186	35640	Domestic/intl phone sv Denmark	...	...	29⅝	23⅛	29¼	24¼	48894	28⅛	24¼	27⅝	3.2	13	15.5	...	...
46•[6]	NZT	✓**Telecom Corp New Zealand ADS[65]**	[12]NY	NR	131	4537	Provides telecommun svcs	52¼	21⅛	56⅝	42	69⅜	51⅜	3434	69⅜	65½	69⅜	5.1	17	40.8	51.7	...
47•[7]	TBR	✓**Telecomun Brasil-Telebras ADS[67]**	NY	NR	132	10236	Telecommun svcs, Brasil	...	...	...	...	49⅜	37	166993	48⅞	43	47⅜	0.6	16	...	...	...
48	TLDCF	**Teledata Communication**	NNM	NR	..	...	Telephone services/equipment	25¼	9	18	4⅝	10⅛	4⅛	6350	6⅝	5¼	6¼	...	d	31.6	−26.1	...
¶49•[11]	TDY	✓**Teledyne Inc**	NY,B,C,Ch,P,Ph	NR	272	23643	Electronics/avionics equip	78	⅝	26⅝	14¼	27⅝	20	24611	26⅜	23⅛	25⅝	s1.6	9	31.7	12.8	...
#50•[13]	TFX	✓**Teleflex Inc**	NY,B,Ch,Ph	A+	175	9621	Auto,med'l,aerospace,marine prd	39½	¼	40¼	31¾	45¾	34⅜	5117	44⅞	39	41	1.5	15	18.0	11.7	15.3
51•[14]	TAR	✓**Telefonica De Argentina ADS[70]**	[12]NY,Ch	NR	102	19486	Telecommun svcs Argentina	...	...	41¼	23	30⅛	14⅝	127488	28	23⅜	27¼	3.8	16	10.1	...	...
52•[5]	TEF	✓**Telefonica de Espana ADS[71]**	NY,P,Ph	NR	235	32323	Domestic/intl tel sv in Spain	40⅛	16	46⅛	33½	44	33¼	28292	42¾	40½	41⅞	2.9	13	25.1	16.2	15.0

¶ S&P 500 # MidCap 400 ✤ SmallCap 600 • Options

Uniform Footnote Explanations-See Page 4. Other: [1]NY:Cycle 3. [2]CBOE:Cycle 3. [3]P:Cycle 3. [4]Vc:Cycle 2. [5]ASE:Cycle 3. [6]ASE,P:Cycle 3. [7]CBOE,NY:Cycle 1. [8]Ch [9]ASE:Cycle 1. [10]ASE,CBOE,Ph:Cycle 1. [11]CBOE:Cycle 1. [12]Ph [13]Ph:Cycle 2. [14]ASE,CBOE,P:Cycle 1. [51]Incl $0.08624 non-taxable,'94. [52]ADS equal to 1 com shr,par 50 yen. [53]?0.74,'95. [54]Subsid Pfd in $M. [55]®$0.15,'94. [56]Fiscal Apr'92 & prior. [57]11 Mo Mar'94. [58]Dep for 0.20 shr 5.25% Cv Pfd. [59]Fr 11-10-96,scale to $50 in 2003. [60]®$0.43,'94. [61]Ea ADS rep 10 Cl'B'Ord,Ps1.00. [62]Approx. [63]Stk dstr of Liberty Media Gr'A'. [64]Ea ADS rep 0.5 Cl'B',DKK10. [65]Each ADS rep 16 ord, NZ$1.00. [66]Incl share cap reduction,'94. [67]Ea ADS rep 1000 Pfd shrs,no par. [68]Shrs in millions,incl 178M pfd shrs. [69]In cash & stk,'95. [70]Ea ADS rep 10'B'ord shrs, p$1.00. [71]Each ADS rep 3 shrs par 500 pesetas.

Splits ◆ Index	Cash Divs. Ea.Yr. Since	Dividends: Latest Payment Period $	Date	Ex. Div.	Total $ So Far 1995	Ind. Rate	Paid 1994	Financial Position Mil-$ Cash& Equiv.	Curr. Assets	Curr. Liab.	Balance Sheet Date	Capitalization Lg Trm Debt Mil-$	Shs. 000 Pfd.	Com.	Earnings $ Per Shr. Years End	1991	1992	1993	1994	1995	Last 12 Mos.	Interim Earnings Period	$ per Shr. 1994	1995	Index
1	....	None Since Public			...	Nil	....	16.3	29.1	2.57	6-30-95	....	...	14230	Dc	0.40	0.24	0.33	0.11	....	d0.31	9 Mo Sep	0.07	d0.35	1
2◆	....	None Since Public			...	Nil	....	38.1	57.4	12.4	3-31-95	0.12	...	14198	Mr	*p0.25	0.26	Δ0.31	0.51	....	0.60	6 Mo Sep	0.23	0.32	2
3	....	None Since Public			...	Nil	....	2.95	25.0	18.9	12-31-94	1.81	...	±9888	Dc	Δ0.11	*0.04	±0.02	±0.34	....	0.29	9 Mo Sep	±0.23	±0.18	3
4◆	1915	Q0.14	12-1-95	11-1	0.56	0.56	0.53	0.24	26.8	12.0	9-30-95	7.33	...	6181	Dc	1.30	1.41	□1.04	0.94	....	0.86	9 Mo Sep	0.64	0.56	4
5	....	None Since Public			...	Nil	....	1.25	3.27	11.4	9-30-95	60.0	...	25000	Je	...	...	pd0.31	d0.45	d1.39	d1.09	3 Mo Sep	d0.20	0.10	5
6	1993	Q0.22	1-19-96	12-27	0.88	0.88	[51]0.88	Equity per shr $6.83			9-30-95	....	...	44170	Dc	p0.26	0.04	□0.34	□0.38	....	0.39	9 Mo Sep	□0.27	□0.28	6
7◆	....	None Since Public			...	Nil	....	....	174	99.9	9-30-95	....	...	23784	Dc	0.59	0.76	0.74	0.71	E0.67↓	0.69	9 Mo Sep	0.51	0.49	7
8	1982	Q0.14	1-10-96	12-22	0.48	0.56	0.44	Equity per shr Neg			7-31-95	251	...	24567	Oc	0.35	0.61	0.83	□0.93	E1.25	1.19	9 Mo Jul	□0.68	0.94	8
9	1988	Q0.05	1-15-96	12-27	0.20	0.20	0.20	9.86	48.8	11.8	8-31-95	13.4	...	25675	Nv	0.31	0.20	0.25	0.30	....	0.08	9 Mo Aug	0.29	0.07	9
10	....	0.17½	4-10-81	3-9	...	Nil	....	1.85	12.2	3.98	9-30-95	1.57	...	2759	Dc	Δd0.38	0.10	0.62	d0.03	....	d0.18	9 Mo Sep	0.05	d0.10	10
11◆	1988	Q0.15⅝	11-30-95	11-8	0.59⅜	0.62	0.50	Book Value $13.10			9-30-95	899	...	35569	Dc	*0.76	1.99	1.52	1.95	....	1.45	9 Mo Sep	1.49	□0.99	11
12	....	None Since Public			...	Nil	....	24.8	40.0	11.7	9-30-95	....	...	12268	Dc	p0.70	p0.19	0.22	0.45	....	0.58	9 Mo Sep	0.32	0.45	12
13	1976	0.209	12-26-95	9-27	0.457	0.46	0.427	1213	3713	1456	3-31-95	361	...	131498	Mr	1.23	1.20	Δ0.39	1.11	....	1.11				13
14	1989	0.02	3-1-93	2-3	...	Nil	....	2.29	18.8	4.80	8-31-95	51.6	...	5160	My	0.42	d2.33	0.37	d0.06	d1.16	d1.10	3 Mo Aug	d0.05	0.01	14
15◆	....	None Since Public			...	Nil	....	0.87	822	633	10-31-95	9.21	227	37901	Ja	0.44	0.63	0.83	0.91	....	0.47	9 Mo Oct	0.76	0.32	15
16◆	1990	Q0.12½	1-11-96	12-27	0.42½	0.50	0.28¾	2.69	10.1	4.68	9-30-95	....	...	3048	Sp	0.48	0.48	0.34	0.44	0.81	0.81				16
17	....	5%Stk	12-18-59		...	Nil	....	16.0	164	70.2	9-30-95	18.9	...	6546	Dc	1.50	1.13	1.80	2.12	....	2.36	9 Mo Sep	1.34	1.58	17
18	1995	Q0.12½	1-31-96	1-12	0.25	0.50	....	Book Value $14.43			6-30-95	14.2	...	4232	Sp	...	...	...	p1.00	P[53]0.80	0.80				18
19	....	None Since Public			...	Nil	....	1.03	17.6	14.0	9-30-95	p3.38	p...	★7906	Dc	...	...	...	p0.13	....	0.19	9 Mo Sep	p0.02	p0.08	19
20	1973	S0.29	8-1-95	7-14	0.58	0.58	0.56	3.50	8.08	0.61	9-30-95	....	...	2201	Dc	0.87	0.56	0.68	0.56	....	0.31	9 Mo Sep	0.47	0.22	20
21◆	1975	Q0.10	1-26-96	1-10	0.39	0.40	0.375	30.1	102	57.0	9-30-95	20.0	...	7833	Dc	0.47	0.48	Δ0.56	1.15	....	1.21	9 Mo Sep	0.83	0.89	21
22◆	1995	Q0.06	1-16-96	12-27	0.12	0.24	....	4.81	12.5	2.06	9-30-95	0.32	...	5284	Mr	Δ0.03	0.42	0.45	0.36	....	0.32	6 Mo Sep	0.24	0.20	22
23	....	None Since Public			...	Nil	....	18.7	42.6	12.5	8-31-95	....	...	9051	My	0.81	1.01	0.46	Nil	0.35	0.29	6 Mo Nov	0.19	0.13	23
24	1977	gS0.10	12-29-95	12-13	g0.20	0.20	g0.20	132	227	87.8	j12-31-94	476	...	±p91163	Dc	0.45	±0.30	±0.35	±0.77	....	j0.97	9 Mo Sep	±0.48	±0.68	24
25◆	....	None Since Public			...	Nil	....	0.80	55.5	14.7	9-02-95	13.1	...	19931	Nv	0.50	0.61	0.68	0.85	....	0.73	9 Mo Aug	0.60	0.48	25
26	....	None Since Public			...	Nil	....	2.22	11.2	5.47	12-31-92	0.02	...	★7805	Dc	d0.01	0.27	P0.34	Pd0.14	....	0.49	9 Mo Sep	d0.29	0.34	26
27◆	1900	Q0.26½	11-15-95	10-30	1.048	1.06	0.99¾	45.1	345	599	9-30-95	996	[54]55	116619	Dc	1.28	1.30	Δ1.30	1.32	E1.60	1.59	12 Mo Sep	1.43	1.59	27
28	....	None Paid			...	Nil	....	4.03	25.8	15.6	j8-31-94	10.7	...	p53289	Au	d8.19	0.14	0.64	[55]0.21	P0.15	j0.15				28
29◆	1992	†0.86	12-22-95	12-6	†1.61	1.04	†1.35	300	819	291	9-30-95	9.00	...	±21881	Dc	±1.94	±□2.39	±3.72	±5.50	E5.70	5.66	9 Mo Sep	±4.19	±4.35	29
30◆	1940	†0.86	12-22-95	12-6	†1.61	1.04	†1.35	....	...	...		....	...	5470	Dc	1.94	±□2.39	±3.72	±5.50	E5.50	5.66	9 Mo Sep	±4.19	±4.35	30
31	1995	0.21½	10-30-95	10-12	0.21½	0.86	....	109	150	84.7	9-30-95	694	...	27691	Mr	3.50	[56]6.27	[57]1.68	Δ0.29	....	0.86	6 Mo Sep	d0.11	0.46	31
32	....	None Since Public			...	Nil	....	2.17	30.2	18.4	6-30-95	p....	p...	★9527	Mr	...	...	...	p0.11	....	0.39	6 Mo Sep	pNil	p0.28	32
33◆	....	None Since Public			...	Nil	....	7.91	187	142	9-30-95	367	460	11603	Dc	Δ0.74	1.03	1.44	1.87	....	2.04	9 Mo Sep	1.27	1.44	33
34	1994	Q0.656	11-1-95	10-16	2.62½	2.625	2.574	Cv into 0.714 com,$70				....	1300	...	Dc	...	...	...	....	....	....				34
35	....	None Since Public			...	Nil	....	7.43	65.1	53.5	9-30-95	190	1	★±17559	Dc	d0.08	0.23	0.31	□0.22	....	0.03	9 Mo Sep	□0.19	Nil	35
36	1982	S0.02½	12-8-95	11-21	0.05	0.05	0.05	20.6	30.2	5.41	9-30-95	1.75	...	12682	Dc	0.12	0.12	0.23	0.12	....	0.11	9 Mo Sep	Nil	d0.01	36
37◆	....	None Since Public			...	Nil	....	44.9	73.5	15.9	9-30-95	0.44	...	11561	Dc	0.54	d1.02	d2.23	[60]0.47	....	0.72	9 Mo Sep	0.27	0.52	37
38	1972	Q0.15	2-5-96	1-17	0.60	0.60	0.60	49.9	690	355	8-26-95	154	...	p33478	My	1.66	0.67	□d1.95	2.00	2.63	2.63	6 Mo Nov	0.30	0.30	38
39	1995	[62]2.15	1-16-96	12-22	1.849	2.15	....	24.7	469	677	6-30-94	875	...	±984381	Sp	0.56	1.53	1.99	....	....	2.66	9 Mo JunΔ	1.36	2.03	39
40	....	None Since Public			...	Nil	....	30.6	55.9	20.2	p9-30-95	3.00	...	13000	Dc	p0.02	p0.09	p0.20	p0.55	....	0.94	9 Mo Sep	p0.38	p0.77	40
41	....	None Since Public			...	Nil	....	29.1	61.5	11.5	8-27-95	....	...	10265	Au	1.08	0.62	d1.75	0.48	0.06	d0.35	3 Mo Nov	0.15	d0.26	41
42	....	None Since Public			...	Nil	....	25.3	37.7	8.21	9-30-95	2.83	...	15480	Dc	...	...	...	Δ0.04	....	0.16	9 Mo Sep	Δ0.04	0.16	42
43◆	....	h[63]....	8-10-95	8-11	h[63]...	Nil	....	Equity per shr Neg			12-31-94	11162	...	±652806	Dc	d0.28	d0.12	d0.02	0.09	E0.05	d0.12	9 Mo Sep	±0.12	±d0.09	43
44	....	None Since Public			...	Nil	....	Equity per shr $5.55			3-31-95	★228	...	★±117500	Dc	...	...	...	p0.24	....	0.14	9 Mo Sep	pd0.52	pd0.62	44
45	1995	0.946	5-5-95	4-18	0.946	0.88	....	2275	3612	1325	6-30-95	530	...	±70007	Dc	0.42	0.56	0.88	1.61	....	2.18	6 Mo Jun	0.67	1.24	45
46	1992	1.79	12-6-95	11-14	3.527	3.53	[66]5.07	40.7	494	890	3-31-95	704	...	1889600	Mr	1.80	0.48	2.03	3.44	E4.00	3.44				46
47	1993	0.275	7-10-95	5-1	0.275	0.28	....	626	2458	2654	j6-30-95	1590	...	[68]±298698	Dc	...	...	...	2.47	....	2.89	6 Mo Jun	0.66	1.08	47
48	....	None Since Public			...	Nil	....	29.7	46.6	7.58	12-31-93	....	...	10375	Dc	0.54	0.71	0.96	P0.06	....	d0.57	9 Mo Sep	0.45	d0.18	48
49◆	1995	[69]0.25	11-21-95	11-2	[69]1.00	0.40	....	85.6	787	403	9-30-95	372	1656	55775	Dc	■d0.46	□0.83	□1.32	d0.15	E2.90↑	2.65	9 Mo Sep	d0.45	2.35	49
50◆	1977	Q0.15½	12-15-95	11-21	0.60	0.62	0.52	43.2	433	190	9-24-95	186	...	17486	Dc	1.77	Δ1.87	1.95	2.35	E2.70	2.63	9 Mo Sep	1.63	1.91	50
51◆	1994	0.516	1-5-96	12-19	0.991	1.03	0.409	201	604	880	9-30-94	495	...	±2357515	Sp	0.52	0.93	1.28	1.66	....	1.66				51
52	1947	0.735	8-17-95	7-25	1.202	1.20	1.037	Equity per shr $27.59			12-31-94	p14.7	...	939471	Dc	3.52	2.28	2.15	2.73	E3.25	3.06	6 Mo Jun	1.26	1.59	52

◆**Stock Splits & Divs By Line Reference Index** [2]2-for-1,'95. [4]No adj for stk dstr of Phillips & Jacobs,'93. [7]3-for-2,'91,'92. [11]2-for-1,'95. [15]2-for-1,'92,'94. [16]2-for-1,'95. [21]3-for-1,'94. [22]1-for-3 REVERSE,'95. [25]3-for-2,'93. [27]2-for-1,'93. [29]2-for-1,'93. [30]2-for-1 in Cl'A','92,'93. [33]3-for-2,'93:10%,'95. [37]2-for-1,'95. [43]No adj for dstr of Liberty Media G'A','95. [49]No adj for stk dstr of Unitrin Inc,'90. [50]3-for-2,'91. [51]2-for-1,'95.

¶ S&P 500 # MidCap 400 ✣ SmallCap 600 • Options Index	Ticker	Name of Issue (Call Price of Pfd. Stocks)	Market	Com. Rank. & Pfd. Rating	Inst. Hold Cos	Inst. Hold Shs. (000)	Principal Business	Price Range 1971-93 High	1971-93 Low	1994 High	1994 Low	1995 High	1995 Low	Dec. Sales in 100s	December, 1995 Last Sale Or Bid High	Low	Last	%Div Yield	P-E Ratio	Total Return % Annualized 12 Mo	36 Mo	60 Mo
1	TFONY	✓Telefonos de Mexico'A'ADR[51]	NSC	NR	43	19930	Telephone service in Mexico	3½	1/16	4	1⅞	2 1/16	1	139425	1 11/16	1¼	1 9/16	1.9	10	−24.4	−16.0	10.1
2•[1]	TMX	✓Telefonos de Mexico'L'ADS[52]	NY,Ch,Ph	NR	633	172205	Telephone service in Mexico	67⅞	24¼	76⅛	37	41½	23	662790	33⅞	29⅝	31⅞	2.7	10	−22.6	−15.3	...
3	TLSIF	✓Telepanel Systems	NSC,To	NR	8	795	Electr shelf pricing/info sys	8¾	⅝	6¼	1	2⅝	1⅛	7594	2	1¼	1 9/16	...	d	5.3	−27.2	...
#4•[2]	TDS	✓Telephone & Data Sys	AS,Ch	B+	252	38610	Telecommunications 29 states	57	1 9/16	51½	35½	46⅜	35⅝	38149	39¾	35⅝	39½	1.0	22	−14.7	0.7	3.9
5	TWSTY	TeleWest PLC[54] ADS	NNM	NR	50	4248	Cable T.V/telephone svcs	....	....	30¼	26¼	30¾	23⅜	4295	26½	23⅞	24⅛	...	..	−9.2	...	...
¶6•[3]	TLAB	✓Tellabs, Inc	NNM	B	397	57942	Voice,data commun'ns eqp	13⅝	1 5/16	28	11	52¾	23½	244356	41¾	33	37	...	31	36.1	110	72.1
7	TLTN	✓Teltrend Inc	NNM	NR	45	3286	Dgn/dvp network svcs tel equip	....	....	....	....	47½	16	29704	47½	36	46¾	...	34	...	...	...
8	TELT	Teltronics Inc	NSC	NR	3	133	Mfr telecommunications eq	39	6¼	25¾	3	6¾	1 7/16	955	5½	4½	5¼	...	d	58.5	−37.9	−12.4
9	WRLS	✓Telular Corp	NNM	NR	33	2270	Mfr wireless telecommun eqp	....	....	24½	6	20½	6½	11486	11	8	8⅝	...	d	38.0	...	...
✣10•[4]	TLXN	✓Telxon Corp	NNM	B	86	9656	Hand-held microcomputer sys	28½	3½	18¼	10	26½	12	40308	26	22½	22⅝	0.0	32	75.8	25.4	9.4
¶11•[5]	TIN	✓Temple-Inland	NY,B,P	B+	379	43853	Containers,paper,finl svcs	57½	10⅛	56¾	43	55¾	41½	34507	46⅜	42¼	43⅞	2.7	9	−1.2	−2.8	9.8
12	TMTX	✓Temtex Indus	NSC	B−	14	717	Fabricated metal prod	11⅝	5/16	13⅝	8⅛	9⅝	3⅝	3976	5¼	3⅝	3¾	...	27	−53.8	39.7	30.3
13•[6]	TNCR	✓Tencor Instruments	NNM	NR	186	22779	Mfr integrated circuits mfg eq	7	3¾	23⅞	5⅞	48¾	17¾	132097	38¼	24	24⅜	...	13	23.1	...	...
14	TNR	✓TENERA Inc	AS	NR	2	2	Svcs/softw to utility&mfg	39½	1 1/16	1 11/16	½	1⅞	½	2302	1⅛	⅞	15/16	...	..	36.4	−13.3	−33.8
¶15•[5]	THC	✓Tenet Healthcare	NY,B,Ch,P,Ph	NR	422	136324	Specialty & gen'l hospitals	25⅞	3/16	19½	12½	20¾	13⅜	166128	20¾	17⅞	20⅝	...	17	47.3	19.0	...
16	TANT	✓Tennant Co	NNM	A−	65	6919	Ind'l floor maintenance eq	24⅜	2½	24¼	20½	29	22¼	2395	25¾	22¼	23⅞	2.8	13	6.2	7.2	9.7
¶17•[5]	TEN	✓Tenneco Inc	NY,To,B,C,Ch,P,Ph	B−	680	124809	Nat gas,farm/construct'n eqp	71	16¾	58¾	37	50⅜	41⅞	95866	50⅜	46⅝	49⅝	3.6	12	22.2	10.5	5.2
18	TVA	Tenn Val Auth 8.00%'QUIDS'	NY	NR	4	25	Qtly Income Debt Securities	....	....	....	....	27¼	24	7580	27¼	26⅜	26⅝	7.5	..	...	...	...
19	TPP	✓Teppco Ptnrs L.P.	NY	NR	35	802	Refined petrol prod pipeline	29½	15¾	30	25⅛	37¼	25¼	2713	37¼	35⅝	36⅜	7.7	12	53.9	29.0	28.5
#20•[7]	TER	✓Teradyne Inc	NY,B,Ch	B−	308	62417	Mfr electronic sys/software	19¾	⅝	17⅛	10¼	42⅞	16⅛	172127	26¾	20⅛	25⅛	...	13	49.5	49.2	49.6
21	TEX	✓Terex Corp	NY,Ch	C	24	1834	Mfr truck trailers, heavy eqp	27¼	⅜	9⅞	4⅛	7⅛	3⅛	15181	4⅞	4	4¾	...	d	−26.9	−22.0	−13.8
22•[8]	TRA	✓Terra Industries	NY,To,B,Ch,Mo,P,Ph	B−	146	28241	Base mtls,agribus,lsg,coal	33⅞	2½	13⅛	5⅞	14⅞	9¾	30073	14⅛	13⅛	14⅛	0.8	7	44.2	44.8	31.8
23	TNH	✓Terra Nitrogen[58] L.P.[59]	NY	NR	27	911	Produce nitrogen fertilizers	27⅜	20⅝	31	22⅛	38⅞	24⅛	5265	38⅞	34½	37½	13.3	6	76.8	29.4	...
24	TSMAF	Tesma Intl 'A'	NNM	NR	..	...	Distrib orig eqp auto parts	....	....	....	....	8	4¾	308	6¾	4¾	6¾	...	7	...	...	...
25•[9]	TSO	✓Tesoro Petroleum	NY,B,Ch,P,Ph	B−	95	11542	Integrated oil company	32¼	2½	12⅜	5¼	12	7¼	19746	9½	8⅛	8⅝	...	4	−9.2	44.2	5.8
26	TESS	✓TESSCO Technologies	NNM	NR	34	2330	Wireless communication svc	....	....	19¾	12	28¾	14¾	1752	28¾	25½	28½	...	39	72.7	...	...
✣27	TTRA	✓TETRA Technologies	NNM	B−	72	11465	Waste recycl'g&treatm't svcs	21¾	5¾	12¼	6⅝	17⅞	10¼	10633	17⅞	16¼	17⅜	...	25	47.9	26.9	4.8
28•[4]	TEVIY	✓Teva Pharm Indus ADR[63]	NNM	NR	200	23409	Pharmac'ls,veterinary prod	33½	½	34½	22¼	47⅜	21⅜	88060	47⅜	41½	46⅜	0.4	30	95.7	29.9	46.4
¶29•[10]	TX	✓Texaco Inc	NY,To,B,C,Ch,P,Ph	B	958	149857	Major international oil co	70	20	68⅛	58⅛	80½	59¾	181771	80½	73½	78½	4.1	19	35.6	15.2	10.8
30	FTF	Texarkana First Financial	AS	NR	4	370	Savings & loan, Arkansas	....	....	....	....	15⅛	10	769	14⅛	13⅜	14⅛	1.3	..	...	...	...
31	TXB	✓Texas Biotechnology	AS	NR	8	968	Dvlp stge:biotechnology R&D	....	....	2 1/16	1⅛	3¾	1 3/16	7863	2⅜	1 11/16	2 1/16	...	d	50.0	...	...
32	WS	Wrrt(Pur 1 com at$8.44)	AS	....	3	428		....	....	5/16	⅛	⅜	⅛	1797	¼	⅛	3/16	...	..	...	...	...
✣33	TXI	✓Texas Indus	NY,B,Ch,Ph	↑B	138	6724	Cement,aggregate,concrete pd	41⅛	2 5/16	39¾	29½	55¼	30⅛	6596	53¼	50¼	53	0.8	10	68.6	36.4	30.0
¶34•[8]	TXN	✓Texas Instruments	NY,B,C,Ch,P	B	785	140169	Semiconductors:el'tronic eqp	42⅛	6⅝	44¾	30½	83¾	34⅜	589060	57⅜	46	51½	1.3	9	36.8	31.7	23.2
35•[5]	TMR	✓Texas Meridian Resources	AS,Ch	C	61	8027	Oil & gas explor,dev,prod'n	38¾	5/16	16⅛	8	14	9⅛	16035	14	10¾	13⅝	...	..	34.6	40.3	85.2
36	TPL	✓Texas Pac Ld Tr[66]	NY,B,Ch,Ph	B	21	672	Holds surface rights:royalties	71	2 7/16	22⅛	18	28¾	17	885	26½	22⅜	26¼	1.5	21	44.0	18.0	6.8
¶37•[7]	TXU	✓Texas Utilities	NY,B,C,Ch,P,Ph	B+	573	111219	Electric utility holding co.	49¾	14⅞	43⅛	29⅝	41¼	30⅛	140194	41¼	38⅛	41	4.9	d	40.9	7.0	10.6
38	TXF	✓Texfi Indus	NY,Ch	C	16	2323	Fabrics for apparel indus	50¾	1 1/16	4⅜	2½	3⅜	2⅜	4252	3¼	2¾	2¾	...	d	4.8	−25.9	−8.3
¶39•[11]	TXT	✓Textron, Inc	NY,B,C,Ch,P,Ph	A	528	55068	Aerospace/coml prod/finl svcs	58⅞	5¾	60⅝	46½	77⅜	48⅝	37446	77	67½	67½	2.3	12	37.2	18.3	23.0
40	Pr A	$2.08 cm Cv A Pfd(50)vtg	NY,B	BBB−	6	7	Mfrs commercial products	128	19	130⅜	101½	166⅝	109½	9	166⅝	157¾	150B	1.4	..	...	...	...
41	Pr B	$1.40 cm Cv B Pfd(45)vtg	NY,B	BBB−	3	.7	Financial & insurance svcs	103	14	106½	86	135¾	86¾	1	135¾	135¾	122B	1.1	..	...	...	...
42	TFCE	✓TFC Enterprises	NNM	NR	26	1437	Pur/sv auto installm't contr't	13¾	11½	14¾	6¾	15½	4½	18641	7	5¼	5⅝	...	8	−22.4	...	...
43	TGVI	✓TGV Software	NNM	NR	37	2120	Dvlp internetworking software	....	....	....	....	24	7½	7111	9¾	7⅞	9½	...	16	...	...	...
44	THK	✓Thackeray Corp	NY,Ch	NR	10	1824	Builder's hardware:Real est	22⅝	½	4¾	3¾	5⅝	3⅝	310	4¾	4⅜	4¾	...	d	11.8	0.9	−1.0
45	THRX	✓Theragenics Corp	NNM	B−	17	886	Dvlp/mfr medical devices	8	¼	4¾	2¼	12½	2¼	53938	12½	5½	11⅞	...	99	375	29.2	73.7
✣46	THRT	✓TheraTech Inc	NNM	NR	52	4956	Dvlp drug delivery systems	18¼	5	15½	8¾	20½	8¾	9677	19½	15	18	...	d	94.6	5.7	...
47	THTX	✓TheraTx Inc	NNM	NR	62	7840	Manage subacute rehab programs	....	....	23¾	10¾	23⅛	10¾	18594	13⅞	11¼	12	...	12	−38.9	...	...
48•[5]	TMD	✓Thermedics Inc	AS,Ch,P,Ph	B	94	9244	Mfrs biomedical prod & sys	19	2	16⅛	11¾	28	12½	15599	28	20⅞	27½	...	64	116	51.0	33.8
49	TCA	✓Thermo Cardiosystems	AS,Ph	NR	80	5041	Heart ventricle assist device	22½	1 15/16	23⅜	15	77¼	15⅝	13885	77¼	53½	77¼	...	..	387	108	62.0
50	TCK	✓Thermo Ecotek	AS	NR	22	1069	Oper non-utility elec pwr fac	....	....	....	....	17⅜	11	1085	16¾	15¼	16¾	...	20	...	...	...
#51•[6]	TMO	✓Thermo Electron	NY,B,Ch,Ph	B+	404	53513	Eng'd ind'l pr: environ instr	28⅞	9/16	31⅞	24	52	29¼	45333	52	47⅝	52	...	32	73.6	35.5	32.5
52	TFT	✓Thermo Fibertek	AS	NR	59	6123	Mfr paper produc'g/recycl'g eq	10⅝	5⅜	10¾	9⅛	22¾	10¼	4124	22¾	19¾	22½	...	51	121	54.8	...

Uniform Footnote Explanations-See Page 4. Other: [1]ASE,CBOE,NY,Ph:Cycle 1. [2]P:Cycle 2. [3]P:Cycle 3. [4]CBOE:Cycle 3. [5]ASE:Cycle 2. [6]NY:Cycle 3. [7]P:Cycle 1. [8]CBOE:Cycle 1. [9]Ph:Cycle 2. [10]ASE:Cycle 1. [11]Ph:Cycle 3. [51]Each ADR rep 1 'A' ord. [52]Each ADS rep 20 'L' ord. [53]Fr1-1-2001,prv'd'A'&'AA'shr less than51%outstg. [54]Ea ADS rep 10 com, L.1 par. [55]6 Wk Dec'94. [56]9 Mo Sep'93. [57]100% non-taxable,'94. [58]Convertible & redeemable re specified cond. [59]Sr Pref Units. [60]Incl 7.6M pref units & 6M Jr Pref units. [61]Accum on pfd. [62]Fiscal Sep'91 &prior. [63]ADR's represent 10 Ord par ISI. [64]Excl shrs held by subsid. [65]If com exceed 140% exercise price-30 con days. [66]Sub-share ctfs. [67]Subsid Pfd in $M. [68]Incl current amts. [69]®$0.55,'94. [70]®$1.23,'95.

Splits ◆ Index	Cash Divs. Ea.Yr. Since	Dividends: Latest Payment Period $	Date	Ex. Div.	Total $ So Far 1995	Ind. Rate	Paid 1994	Financial Position Mil-$ Cash& Equiv.	Curr. Assets	Curr. Liab.	Balance Sheet Date	Capitalization Lg Trm Debt Mil-$	Shs. 000 Pfd.	Com.	Earnings $ Per Shr. Years End	1991	1992	1993	1994	1995	Last 12 Mos.	Interim Earnings Period	$ per Shr. 1994	1995	Index
1◆	1951	0.016	12-1-95	11-17	0.035	0.03	0.062	1238	3005	1059	12-31-94	1777	...	±10499000	Dc	0.24	0.24	0.27	0.15	....	0.15				1
2	1991	0.39	12-1-95	11-17	0.87	0.87	1.466	Exch for'AA'shrs[53]				....	...	7934000	Dc	4.73	4.84	5.47	2.98	E3.15	2.98				2
3◆	....	None Since Public			...	Nil	....	3.23	6.21	2.42	j1-31-95	....	...	14968	Ja	d0.17	d1.09	d0.21	d0.22	....	jd0.26	9 Mo Oct	d0.15	d0.19	3
4	1974	Q0.09½	12-29-95	12-13	0.38	0.38	0.36	74.5	255	373	9-30-95	874	548	±57980	Dc	□0.59	□0.91	0.67	□1.07	E1.83↑	1.81	9 Mo Sep	□0.75	1.49	4
5	....	None Since Public			...	Nil	....	Equity per shr $12.79			9-30-95	50.4	153000	848245	Dc	...	...	...	†[55]d1.72	....	....	9 Mo Sep	n/a	d1.30	5
6◆	....	None Since Public			...	Nil	....	140	317	89.7	9-29-95	2.85	...	88548	Dc	0.09	0.20	Δ0.35	0.80	E1.20	1.14	9 Mo Sep	0.51	0.85	6
7	....	None Since Public			...	Nil	....	4.42	23.5	13.3	7-29-95	....	...	★6327	Jl	...	...	...	p0.64	p1.19	1.38	3 Mo Oct	p0.28	p0.47	7
8◆	....	None Since Public			...	Nil	....	0.58	6.09	5.40	9-30-95	1.06	...	2550	Dc	0.50	Δ0.50	Δ0.25	■d11.08	....	d9.69	9 Mo Sep	d1.10	0.29	8
9	....	None Since Public			...	Nil	....	20.4	41.6	7.03	6-30-95	....	...	22892	Sp	...	...	p†[56]d0.57	d1.25	Pd0.84	d0.84				9
10	1988	A0.01	3-30-95	3-17	0.01	0.01	0.01	22.8	247	141	9-30-95	31.0	...	15919	Mr	*1.13	□d0.79	d0.18	0.57	....	0.70	6 Mo Sep	0.18	0.31	10
11	1984	Q0.30	12-15-95	11-29	1.14	1.20	1.02	Equity per shr $34.78			9-30-95	1543	...	56096	Dc	2.51	2.65	Δ1.21	2.35	E5.15↑	4.72	9 Mo Sep	1.48	3.85	11
12	....	None Since Public			...	Nil	....	0.74	17.7	8.70	8-31-95	3.10	...	3464	Au	Nil	d0.15	*0.42	1.25	0.14	0.14				12
13◆	....	None Since Public			...	Nil	....	173	321	81.0	9-30-95	0.65	...	30670	Dc	0.55	0.22	0.33	0.89	....	1.85	9 Mo Sep	0.54	1.50	13
14	....	0.10	7-10-91	7-1	...	Nil	....	0.07	8.86	3.24	9-30-95	....	...	10417	Dc	d0.66	0.08	d0.03	d0.13	....	....	9 Mo Sep	n/a	p0.05	14
15◆	1973	0.12	9-10-93	8-16	...	Nil	....	242	1442	1257	8-31-95	3226	...	199921	My	□1.73	□0.77	0.96	Δd2.90	□1.04	1.25	3 Mo Aug	0.38	0.59	15
16◆	1933	Q0.17	12-29-95	12-13	0.68	0.68	0.65	1.83	113	57.6	9-30-95	22.1	...	9935	Dc	1.21	Δ□1.34	0.93	1.60	....	1.89	9 Mo Sep	1.10	1.39	16
17	1948	Q0.45	3-12-96	2-21	1.60	1.80	1.60	712	3665	2875	9-30-95	3310	1587	177325	Dc	■d6.09	□d4.35	□2.59	□2.45	E4.00	3.27	9 Mo Sep	□2.29	3.11	17
18	1995	Q0.50	12-29-95	12-26	1.444	2.00	....	Co option redm fr 3-30-2000 at $25				600	...	...	Sp	...	...	...	....	....	....				18
19	1990	Q0.70	11-10-95	10-27	2.65	2.80	[57]2.37	34.3	75.4	32.5	9-30-95	340	...	14500	Dc	1.36	1.70	□2.54	3.13	....	3.08	9 Mo Sep	2.21	2.16	19
20◆	....	None Paid			...	Nil	....	254	615	180	10-01-95	8.48	...	p82581	Dc	0.29	0.34	□0.50	0.95	E1.97↑	1.76	9 Mo Sep	0.66	1.47	20
21	....	0.06	6-5-91	5-14	...	Nil	....	16.2	430	303	9-30-95	337	...	10359	Dc	d3.37	d6.14	□d6.15	□d0.46	....	d3.12	9 Mo Sep	□d0.36	□d3.02	21
22	1993	Q0.03	12-12-95	11-22	0.10	0.12	0.08	93.4	949	520	9-30-95	504	...	81178	Dc	Δd2.33	Δ0.13	0.33	□Δ0.77	E2.00	1.98	9 Mo Sep	□Δ0.60	□1.81	22
23	1992	1.47	11-29-95	11-1	5.00	5.00	2.64	43.0	115	26.7	9-30-95	8.10	...	[60]18809	Dc	p2.82	p2.79	2.59	□4.57	....	6.66	9 Mo Sep	3.05	5.14	23
24	1996	g0.05	1-15-96	12-27	...	0.32	....	6.42	109	65.8	j4-30-95	20.5	700	±★17563	Jl	...	...	...	p0.90	P1.05	1.04	3 Mo Oct	0.26	0.25	24
25	....	0.10	8-25-86	8-5	...	[61]Nil	....	59.4	201	96.4	9-30-95	188	...	24567	Dc	[62]d0.37	□d3.87	0.54	□0.77	....	2.49	9 Mo Sep	□0.11	1.83	25
26	....	None Since Public			...	Nil	....	8.45	25.8	7.78	3-31-95	0.20	...	4103	Mr	Δ0.27	0.22	0.32	0.64	....	0.73	6 Mo Sep	0.31	0.40	26
27	....	None Since Public			...	Nil	....	10.3	55.8	22.9	9-30-95	1.11	...	12803	Dc	0.70	d0.31	0.07	0.48	....	0.69	9 Mo Sep	0.28	0.49	27
28◆	1984	0.049	12-7-95	11-20	0.20	0.20	0.246	50.6	400	240	12-31-94	80.8	...	[64]553062	Dc	0.49	0.61	1.07	1.32	E1.55	1.45	9 Mo Sep	0.97	1.10	28
29	1903	Q0.80	12-8-95	11-3	3.20	3.20	3.20	384	5544	4299	9-30-95	5605	844	264110	Dc	4.61	□3.53	3.74	3.17	E4.10	4.59	9 Mo Sep	1.68	3.10	29
30	1996	0.11¼	1-15-96	1-8	...	0.18	....	Book Value $15.27			12-31-94	....	...	★1984	Sp	...	...	...	p1.62	....	....	3 Mo DecΔ	n/a	p0.25	30
31	....	None Since Public			...	Nil	....	17.0	18.1	2.59	9-30-95	....	...	17439	Dc	d0.41	d0.52	d1.05	d0.97	....	d0.44	9 Mo Sep	d1.10	d0.57	31
32	....	Terms&trad. basis should			be checked in detail			Wrrts expire 12-14-98				....	...	3550	Dc	...	...	...	....	....	....	Callable at 5¢[65]			32
33	1962	Q0.10	11-30-95	11-1	0.40	0.40	0.20	12.0	298	104	8-31-95	171	6	11050	My	1.97	0.19	0.11	2.29	3.88	5.49	6 Mo Nov	1.81	3.42	33
34◆	1962	Q0.17	1-29-96	12-27	0.59	0.68	0.43	1603	5283	2894	9-30-95	822	...	188812	Dc	d2.70	1.25	□2.54	3.64	E5.67	5.12	9 Mo Sep	2.64	4.13	34
35◆	....	1.60	3-5-86	1-27	...	Nil	....	34.5	39.2	9.41	9-30-95	....	...	p14430	Dc	d0.44	d0.21	d0.51	0.12	....	0.10	9 Mo Sep	0.09	0.07	35
36	1956	A0.40	3-15-95	3-6	0.40	0.40	0.40	Equity per shr $3.53			9-30-95	....	...	3045	Dc	0.66	0.60	□0.77	1.58	....	1.23	9 Mo Sep	1.18	0.83	36
37	1917	Q0.50	1-2-96	12-5	3.08	2.00	3.08	14.0	794	1431	9-30-95	7885	[67]1132	225841	Dc	d1.98	Δ2.88	1.66	2.40	Ed0.75	d0.81	12 Mo Sep	2.26	d0.81	37
38	....	None Paid			...	Nil	....	0.12	45.3	42.2	7-28-95	56.1	...	8651	Oc	d2.13	1.62	d1.18	d1.03	Pd1.96	d1.96				38
39	1942	Q0.39	1-1-96	12-13	1.52	1.56	1.36	Equity per shr $20.41			9-30-95	10205	423	84821	Dc	3.42	□3.66	4.21	4.80	E5.45	5.31	9 Mo Sep	3.54	4.05	39
40	1968	Q0.52	1-1-96	12-13	2.08	2.08	2.08	Cv into 2.2 common				....	321	...	Dc	b1.39	b1.43	b1.57	....	....	....				40
41	1968	Q0.35	1-1-96	12-13	1.40	1.40	1.40	Cv into 1.8 common				....	138	...	Dc	b1.39	b1.43	b1.57	....	....	....				41
42	....	None Since Public			...	Nil	....	Equity per shr $3.03			9-30-95	[68]148	...	11283	Dc	...	Δp0.22	pd0.11	0.64	....	0.68	9 Mo Sep	0.48	0.52	42
43	....	None Since Public			...	Nil	....	39.6	43.9	10.1	9-30-95	....	...	5651	Je	0.66	0.61	0.66	0.49	0.72	0.59	3 Mo Sep	0.14	0.01	43
44	....	0.30	6-5-74	5-6	...	Nil	....	Book Value $1.96			9-30-95	....	...	5107	Dc	d0.68	d0.12	0.11	0.03	....	d0.35	9 Mo Sep	0.05	d0.33	44
45	....	None Paid			...	Nil	....	3.50	4.96	1.04	9-30-95	1.14	...	11201	Dc	*0.04	*0.08	Δ0.04	0.06	....	0.12	9 Mo Sep	0.04	0.10	45
46	....	None Since Public			...	Nil	....	11.6	19.7	6.19	9-30-95	10.7	...	13284	Dc	d0.25	d0.70	d0.75	d0.92	....	d0.71	9 Mo Sep	d0.76	d0.55	46
47	....	None Since Public			...	Nil	....	6.57	92.5	28.2	9-30-95	146	...	18832	Dc	...	...	p0.07	p0.74	E0.97	0.75	9 Mo Sep	p0.65	□0.66	47
48◆	....	None Since Public			...	Nil	....	108	186	49.1	9-30-95	60.8	...	33957	Dc	0.06	0.09	0.22	0.33	....	0.43	9 Mo Sep	0.23	0.33	48
49◆	....	None Since Public			...	Nil	....	40.2	51.0	3.47	9-30-95	22.1	...	23660	Dc	d0.05	Nil	0.02	0.08	....	0.23	9 Mo Sep	0.04	0.19	49
50	....	None Since Public			...	Nil	....	43.6	91.2	36.5	7-01-95	202	...	15505	Dc	d0.05	0.17	0.29	[69]0.72	....	0.85	9 Mo Sep	0.55	0.68	50
51◆	....	None Paid			...	Nil	....	999	1897	628	9-30-95	1077	...	86455	Dc	0.88	□1.01	1.17	[70]1.40	E1.65	1.63	9 Mo Sep	0.98	1.21	51
52◆	....	None Since Public			...	Nil	....	54.4	131	69.9	9-30-95	15.0	...	40551	Dc	0.23	0.23	0.19	0.27	....	0.44	9 Mo Sep	0.18	0.35	52

◆**Stock Splits & Divs By Line Reference Index** [1]No adj for stk dstr,'91. [3]1993 & prior pricing in Cdn$. [6]3-for-2,'93:2-for-1,'94,'95. [8]1-for-25 REVERSE,'94. [13]2-for-1,'95. [15]2-for-1,'91. [16]2-for-1,'95. [20]2-for-1,'95. [28]2-for-1,'93. [34]2-for-1,'95. [35]Reorg & 1-for-5 REVERSE,'90. [48]3-for-2,'93. [49]2-for-1,'93. [51]3-for-2,'93,'95. [52]3-for-2,'95.

¶ S&P 500 # MidCap 400 ✜ SmallCap 600 • Options

Index	Ticker	Name of Issue (Call Price of Pfd. Stocks)	Market	Com. Rank. & Pfd. Rating	Inst. Hold Cos	Inst. Hold Shs. (000)	Principal Business	Price Range 1971-93 High	1971-93 Low	1994 High	1994 Low	1995 High	1995 Low	Dec. Sales in 100s	December, 1995 Last Sale Or Bid High	Low	Last	%Div Yield	P-E Ratio	Total Return % Annualized 12 Mo	36 Mo	60 Mo
1•[1]	THI	✔Thermo Instrument Sys	AS,Ch	NR	84	4509	Mfrs analytical instruments	23¼	1$^{11}/_{16}$	23⅛	18⅛	33⅞	19⅞	7154	33⅞	30¾	33¾	...	32	78.9	33.1	41.4
2	THP	✔Thermo Power	AS,Ch	B–	30	2160	Mfr cogeneration systems	14½	3⅛	9⅞	7	19½	8⅞	2136	14⅝	12¼	12⅞	...	38	37.3	16.0	10.3
3	THN	✔Thermo Remediation	AS	NR	28	2031	Oper soil-remediation centers	9¼	8⅜	11¼	8⅜	17⅜	10¾	1339	15½	13⅛	13¼	1.5	32	27.9	...	...
4	TTT	✔Thermo Terratech[51]	AS,Ch	B	25	1964	Thermal process furnace sys	17¼	1$^{1}/_{16}$	9¼	7¾	13⅛	7¾	542	13	11¼	11⅜	...	95	44.4	7.1	–2.8
5	TVL	✔Thermo Voltek	AS,Ch	B–	20	441	Electrical components	20½	⅛	10⅜	7	17⅛	7⅞	1653	16⅝	14½	15¼	...	31	90.6	53.2	30.8
6	TLZ	✔ThermoLase Corp	AS,Ch,Ph	NR	57	7992	Dvlp hair removal system	....	....	5⅜	3⅝	27⅝	3⅝	12161	27	22½	25⅞	...	d	579	...	...
7	THS	✔ThermoSpectra Corp	AS	NR	21	539	Imaging,inspect'n,measure't sy	....	....	....	....	19½	14	3692	17¼	14⅞	15⅝	...	d	...	...	...
8	TKN	✔Thermotrex Corp	AS,Ch,Ph	NR	63	3868	Optics,electro-optic sys R&D	16½	7⅝	16⅝	12	50⅝	12	7981	50⅝	41	50	...	26	277	65.3	...
9	THM	✔Thermwood Corp	AS,B,P	B–	6	431	Mfr,svcs ind'l robots & sys	3¼	⅜	1⅜	$^{7}/_{16}$	2¾	⅞	13759	2½	2$^{1}/_{16}$	2⅜	...	6	138	39.5	44.7
#10•[2]	TKC	✔Thiokol Corp	NY,B,Ch,P,Ph	NR	187	15409	Aerospace propulsion sys	136⅞	8⅜	29	22¾	37⅛	25⅜	10903	35⅞	33⅝	33⅞	2.0	12	27.0	30.6	22.0
¶11	TNB	✔Thomas & Betts	NY,B,Ch,P	B+	306	14532	Elec connectors,components	72	8⅞	71¼	58⅛	76¼	62	7889	76¼	70¾	73¾	3.0	18	13.3	7.3	13.9
12	TGIS	✔Thomas Group	NNM	NR	22	2022	Provides management svcs	20	12⅝	18¾	5	16	6¼	2434	16	12¾	13½	...	42	135	...	...
✜13	TII	✔Thomas Indus	NY,Ch	B	69	5389	Light'g/compressors,vac pumps	23⅜	1¾	16½	12¾	24⅛	13⅝	2812	24⅛	20⅝	23½	1.7	20	68.9	41.2	23.8
✜14	TNM	✔Thomas Nelson	NY,Ch	B	110	10178	Book publ:prod'r,mktr-Bible	20¾	$^{3}/_{16}$	20¼	14¼	26½	12½	30839	17⅛	12½	13	1.2	18	–27.9	–1.8	21.1
15	TNM.B	Cl'B'	NY	B	9	88		20⅜	2½	20¾	14⅝	26	16¼	6	19	18⅜	18B	0.9	25	–5.4	7.7	28.3
16	TMSTA	✔Thomaston Mills'A'[54]	NNM	B	38	1619	Mfr textile fabrics&yarns	22½	6⅝	20½	13¾	15¾	12	1056	13½	12¼	12⅝	2.3	23	–11.1	–14.2	15.6
17	THOM	✔Thompson PBE	NNM	NR	38	5612	Distr auto paint/supplies	....	....	13⅜	10¾	20½	12⅞	12489	15¾	13½	14	...	15	5.7	...	...
18•[3]	TOC	Thomson Corp[55]	To,Mo	B+	72	22132	Publishing:info,travel svcs	20⅛	2$^{3}/_{16}$	19	14¾	19½	16⅜	70016	19¼	17½	19	2.9	28	13.3	...	...
✜19	THO	✔Thor Industries	NY,Ph	B	67	4057	Mfr travel trailers,mtr hms	28⅝	3⅜	30⅜	18¾	21¾	15¾	2463	20¼	16¾	19⅜	0.6	14	3.3	–8.1	25.0
20	TAVI	✔Thorn Apple Valley	NNM	B–	50	2957	Slaughtering hogs/meat prod	29¼	⅝	30¼	21	30	15⅛	5290	17¾	16	16¾	...	d	–42.1	–11.8	35.1
21	TMA	✔Thornburg Mortgage Asset	NY	NR	31	1533	Real estate investment trust	17¾	14½	17⅜	6¾	15⅞	7⅜	7367	15⅞	14½	15¾	9.7	25	123	...	...
22	TDD.B	✔Three D Depts Cv Cl'B'[57]	AS	B–	7	99	Spec'lty stores:domestics mdse	11⅜	$^{1}/_{16}$	1⅞	1¼	3⅞	1$^{7}/_{16}$	63	2⅛	1⅝	1⅝	1.8	d	20.0	1.8	–10.4
23	TDD.A	Class'A' (1/10 vtg)	AS	B–	4	60		9½	1¼	1⅞	1$^{1}/_{16}$	3⅜	1$^{3}/_{16}$	21	2	1⅞	1¾B	2.9	d	37.2	3.4	–7.6
✜24	TFS	✔Three-Five Systems	NY,Ch	NR	58	3012	Mfr opto-electr components	17⅝	⅜	50	16⅝	38⅞	16	11900	21½	16	16⅞	...	12	–55.7	110	102
25	THR	Three Rivers Finl	AS	NR	4	128	Savings & loan, Michigan	....	....	....	....	12¾	10	219	12¾	12⅛	12¼	2.4	..	...	...	...
26•[4]	COMS	✔3Com Corp[58]	NNM	B–	414	112461	Mfr computer commun'n sys	12⅛	1⅜	26⅝	10⅛	53⅝	22¼	1319563	46¾	35½	46⅝	...	45	76.5	86.0	86.4
27•[5]	THDO	✔3DO Company	NNM	NR	69	6195	Entertainment indus software	48¼	18½	27½	9	17¾	8⅝	104980	13⅜	9⅛	10	...	d	5.3	...	...
28	TIDE	Tide West Oil	NNM	NR	45	2865	Oil&gas explor,devel,prod'n	34⅜	3¾	15½	9¼	14	8¼	1978	14	12½	13⅜	...	33	33.8	21.3	–9.9
29	TIRTZ	✔Tidelands Rlty Tr B SBI	NSC	NR	9	91	Royalty interests-oil & gas	45	1¾	12¾	7¾	8½	6	30	7	6	6¼	11.0	9	–10.6	–4.0	–0.1
#30•[6]	TDW	✔Tidewater Inc	NY,B,Ch,P,Ph	↑B	221	43508	Offshore service vessels	54⅜	3	25	18	31⅝	16½	64965	31⅝	28⅝	31½	1.6	25	74.8	21.4	18.7
#31•[7]	TIF	✔Tiffany & Co	NY,P,Ph	NR	158	11470	Retailer:jewelry,gift items	61¼	9⅝	43⅝	28½	54⅞	29	12920	54⅞	50	50⅜	0.6	24	30.2	16.0	8.3
32•[8]	TIG	✔TIG Holdings	NY	NR	175	55590	Ins:property,casualty,comm'l	28	20¼	23¼	17	29	18⅝	34138	29	26¾	28½	0.7	17	60.8	...	...
✜33	TBL	✔Timberland Co Cl'A'	NY,Ch,P	NR	54	1315	Mfrs men/women footwear	85⅜	5	61	19⅞	36⅝	17½	15726	22⅞	18⅜	19⅞	...	d	–11.7	0.4	28.2
34	TMBS	✔Timberline Software	NNM	B–	10	283	Devel,dstr computer software	13	$^{15}/_{16}$	7⅝	3⅞	12⅝	5½	1684	9	7⅞	8⅞	1.4	21	36.0	20.7	17.4
¶35•[9]	TWX	✔Time Warner Inc	NY,B,Ch,P,Ph	B–	773	221253	Publish'g,entertainment,video	46⅞	1$^{9}/_{16}$	44¼	31½	45⅝	33⅝	165991	41¼	36¾	37⅞	1.0	d	8.4	10.6	13.0
¶36•[10]	TMC	✔Times Mirror 'A'	NY,B,Ch,P	B–	335	46766	Newspaper:books info svc	53	2$^{3}/_{16}$	37⅛	28¾	35¼	17¼	88152	35¼	32⅛	33⅞	0.7	d	10.8	3.3	5.6
¶37•[10]	TKR	✔Timken Co	NY,B,Ch,Ph	B	298	23022	Bearings, alloy steels	41⅜	12⅛	39¼	31¼	48	32½	11936	40¾	37⅛	38¼	3.1	11	11.6	16.0	17.1
38	TPY	✔Tipperary Corp	AS	↓C	24	1805	Oil & gas explor,dev,prod'n	754⅞	$^{3}/_{16}$	4⅛	2⅛	7⅝	3⅜	3433	5¼	4⅛	4⅞	...	d	53.0	21.0	19.5
39	TIS	✔TIS Mtge Investment	NY,Ch,Ph	NR	8	278	Real estate investment trust	10⅛	1½	2¼	1½	2½	1⅜	6110	1¾	1½	1½	...	d	–13.3	–19.6	–19.7
40	TTN	✔Titan Corp	NY,B,Ch,P,Ph	C	24	4429	Information systems/svcs	17½	1	8	2⅞	10⅜	5⅜	7380	7⅝	6⅝	7⅛	...	32	16.3	25.3	28.9
41	Pr	$1 cm Cv Pfd(20)vtg 1/3	NY,B,Ch,P	NR	3	73		15½	4⅛	13⅛	10½	13⅜	10⅞	31	12⅜	12	12¼	8.2	..	...	...	...
42	TH	✔Titan Holdings	NY,Ch	NR	34	1615	Property & casualty insurance	12¾	8⅞	11¼	7⅜	15¾	8⅞	4731	14⅞	13⅝	14⅜	2.1	11	68.7	...	...
43•[1]	TWI	✔Titan Wheel Intl	NY,Ph	NR	97	14194	Mfr off-highway eqp wheels	11½	6⅝	13⅝	9⅝	21⅛	11⅝	19461	17¾	14⅝	16¼	0.4	9	35.4	...	...
44	TIVS	✔Tivoli Systems	NNM	NR	56	6270	Dvlp systems softwr	....	....	....	....	45	14	20263	35	29¼	33¾	...	..	...	...	...
¶45•[11]	TJX	✔TJX Companies	NY,B,Ch,P,Ph	B	285	61612	Off-price specialty stores	43⅞	⅜	29⅜	14¼	19⅛	11⅛	82873	19⅛	15⅞	18⅞	1.5	20	29.0	–9.3	14.7
46	Pr C	$3.125cmCv'C'Pfd([66]52.1875)	NY	↓BBB–	23	1365		75½	50	68¾	37½	45¾	36¼	5349	45½	43	44¾	7.0	..	...	...	...
✜47	TNP	✔TNP Enterprises	NY,Ch,Ph	B	86	5404	Electric sv:Texas & New Mex	24	6¾	18⅞	13⅛	19⅛	14⅝	3820	19⅛	18½	18¾	4.7	6	36.9	6.9	7.3
✜48•[10]	TNTF	✔TNT Freightways	NNM	NR	155	21822	Trucking-gen'l commodities	27½	9⅜	29¾	19¼	28⅝	16¼	28371	20¾	18¾	20⅛	1.9	13	–18.1	15.1	...
49	TM	✔Toastmaster Inc	NY,Ph	NR	18	1924	Mfr elec consumer appliances	15⅜	5⅛	8½	6	7¾	3⅝	3216	4⅜	3⅝	4	2.0	25	–44.1	–22.8	...
50	TOD	✔Todd Shipyards	NY,Ch	B–	31	3052	Major shipbldg & repair co	41¾	1⅝	5⅞	4	7⅛	5	1411	6¼	5⅞	5⅞	...	15	11.9	11.4	6.1
51	TOF	✔Tofutti Brands	AS,Ph	B–	5	151	Non-dairy frozen desserts	18	$^{3}/_{16}$	1⅝	$^{13}/_{16}$	1½	$^{9}/_{16}$	1600	$^{13}/_{16}$	⅝	¾	...	75	–14.3	3.0	31.9
52	TOK	✔Tokheim Corp	NY,B,Ch,Ph	C	31	3308	Design/mfr gas station equip	35¼	⅞	15⅛	8⅛	9⅜	6⅛	5772	6⅞	6⅛	6⅝	...	d	–27.4	–4.6	–10.3

Uniform Footnote Explanations-See Page 4. Other: [1]ASE:Cycle 3. [2]Ph:Cycle 1. [3]To:Cycle 2. [4]P:Cycle 1. [5]ASE,CBOE,P,Ph:Cycle 1. [6]NY,Ph:Cycle 1. [7]Ph:Cycle 2. [8]NY,P:Cycle 3. [9]Ph:Cycle 3. [10]NY:Cycle 3. [11]CBOE:Cycle 1. [51]Formerly Thermo Process Sys. [52]®$0.26,'94. [53]®$0.83,'95. [54]Non-vtg. [55]All divd,finl pos'n and earnings amts in $U.S.. [56]6 Mo Dec,'93. [57]Cv into 1 Cl'A'. [58]Plan S&P 500 listing:eff Dec 30. [59]®$0.85,'95. [60]Fiscal/data of Tide West Oil(old)Feb'92 & prior. [61]®$2.20,'94. [62]Spl div. [63]Collateralized Mtge Obligations. [64]®$0.89,'94. [65]Incl redemption of stk purch rt. [66]To 9-1-96,scale to $50 in 2002. [67]Fiscal Jun'91 & prior,12 Mo Dec'91,$0.89.

Index	Cash Divs. Ea.Yr. Since	Dividends: Latest Payment Period $	Date	Ex. Div.	Total $ So Far 1995	Ind. Rate	Paid 1994	Financial Position Mil-$ Cash& Equiv.	Curr. Assets	Curr. Liab.	Balance Sheet Date	Capitalization Lg Trm Debt Mil-$	Shs. 000 Pfd.	Com.	Earnings $ Per Shr. Years End	1991	1992	1993	1994	1995	Last 12 Mos.	Interim Earnings Period	$ per Shr. 1994	1995	Index
1◆	....	None Since Public			...	Nil	....	315	692	280	9-30-95	329	...	73106	Dc	0.41	0.51	0.67	0.85	....	1.05	9 Mo Sep	0.60	0.80	1
2	....	None Since Public			...	Nil	....	23.5	84.8	24.7	9-30-95	0.36	...	12428	Sp	0.03	0.04	0.18	0.26	0.34	0.34				2
3◆	1994	S0.10	9-15-95	8-28	0.20	0.20	0.20	49.7	65.4	9.03	9-30-95	40.6	...	12350	Mr	...	p0.27	0.29	0.36	....	0.41	6 Mo Sep	0.16	0.21	3
4	....	None Since Public			...	Nil	....	65.0	136	39.3	9-30-95	170	...	17391	Mr	0.06	0.19	Δ0.20	0.24	....	0.12	6 Mo Sep	0.11	d0.01	4
5◆	....	None Paid			...	Nil	....	33.9	51.0	10.2	9-30-95	40.2	...	4870	Dc	d0.08	0.10	0.12	[52]0.28	....	0.50	9 Mo Sep	0.20	0.42	5
6◆	....	None Since Public			...	Nil	....	7.38	21.4	3.73	7-01-95	....	...	★40073	Dc	...	...	p0.01	ΔNil	....	d0.04	9 Mo Sep	ΔNil	d0.04	6
7	....	None Since Public			...	Nil	....	15.8	63.7	32.4	9-30-95	7.30	...	12432	Dc	...	...	...	pd0.76	....	d0.29	9 Mo Sep	pd0.21	p0.26	7
8◆	....	None Since Public			...	Nil	....	66.1	108	21.0	7-01-95	....	...	18999	Dc	0.02	0.02	0.03	0.50	....	1.93	9 Mo Sep	0.49	1.92	8
9	....	None Paid			...	Nil	....	0.01	5.03	2.22	7-31-95	1.87	1000	5851	Jl	d0.03	d0.40	d0.22	Nil	0.38	0.38	3 Mo Oct	0.03	0.03	9
10◆	1925	Q0.17	12-14-95	11-28	0.68	0.68	0.68	74.1	400	161	9-30-95	2.39	...	18285	Je	2.75	3.12	3.13	□3.02	□2.78	2.73	3 Mo Sep	0.76	0.71	10
11	1934	Q0.56	1-2-96	12-13	2.24	2.24	2.24	106	550	254	10-01-95	344	...	20000	Dc	2.84	2.72	Δ2.91	3.51	E4.15↑	3.89	9 Mo Sep	2.51	2.89	11
12	....	None Since Public			...	Nil	....	11.5	25.6	5.49	9-30-95	1.02	...	±6036	Dc	...	±p0.82	p1.00	±0.01	....	0.32	9 Mo Sep	±0.44	±0.75	12
13	1955	Q0.10	1-1-96	11-29	0.40	0.40	0.40	3.90	161	81.7	9-30-95	71.2	...	10095	Dc	0.38	d0.20	0.38	1.05	....	1.17	9 Mo Sep	0.88	1.00	13
14◆	1989	Q0.04	2-19-96	2-1	0.152	0.16	0.128	0.77	218	53.1	9-30-95	103	...	±16415	Mr	0.48	0.49	±Δ0.66	±[53]0.88	....	0.71	6 Mo Sep	±0.38	±0.21	14
15◆	1989	Q0.04	2-19-96	2-1	0.152	0.16	0.128	....	...	...		....	...	1110	Mr	±0.48	±0.48	±Δ0.66	±[53]0.88	....	0.71	6 Mo Sep	±0.38	±0.21	15
16◆	1939	Q0.07¼	1-1-96	12-14	0.285	0.29	0.27	1.33	90.9	20.9	9-30-95	41.3	...	±6538	Je	Nil	2.17	2.37	1.63	0.52	0.54	3 Mo Sep	0.07	0.09	16
17	....	None Since Public			...	Nil	....	0.91	40.8	21.4	6-30-95	p14.9	...	★8392	Sp	...	...	□pd0.37	p□0.24	P□p0.96	0.96				17
18	1980	tQ0.13¾	12-15-95	11-14	0.51¼	0.55	t0.464	514	1945	2006	12-31-94	2998	6000	p587263	Dc	0.53	0.30	0.48	0.74	....	j0.69	6 Mo Jun	0.07	0.02	18
19◆	1987	Q0.03	1-2-96	12-20	0.12	0.12	0.12	5.68	114	44.6	10-31-95	....	...	8896	Jl	0.08	1.15	Δ1.27	1.80	1.55	1.40	3 Mo Oct	0.65	0.50	19
20◆	1992	0.07	8-25-95	5-15	0.21	Nil	0.28	6.47	143	76.2	9-15-95	146	...	5774	My	*2.82	3.75	2.36	2.40	0.91	d0.43	16 Wk Sep	0.45	d0.89	20
21	1993	Q0.38	1-10-96	12-27	0.70	1.52	0.99	Equity per shr $13.16			9-30-95	....	...	12061	Dc	...	...	‡[56]0.36	1.02	....	0.63	9 Mo Sep	0.89	0.50	21
22	1978	Q0.00¾	11-8-95	10-27	0.03	0.03	0.03	0.32	17.8	5.90	7-29-95	9.78	...	±2428	Jl	±0.19	±d0.13	±d0.05	□±d0.27	±d0.21	d0.21				22
23	1984	Q0.01¼	11-8-95	10-27	0.05	0.05	0.05	....	...	...		....	...	1151	Jl	±0.19	±d0.13	±d0.05	□±d0.27	±d0.21	d0.21				23
24◆	....	None Paid			...	Nil	....	2.13	32.0	11.3	9-30-95	....	...	7725	Dc	0.03	0.14	Δ0.59	1.59	....	1.39	9 Mo Sep	1.13	0.93	24
25	1996	0.075	1-2-96	12-13	...	0.30	....	Book Value $14.81			9-30-95	5.21	...	860	Je	...	...	...	....	n/a	....	3 Mo Sep	n/a	0.10	25
26◆	....	None Since Public			...	Nil	....	338	781	272	8-31-95	110	...	p162193	My	d0.25	0.04	0.31	d0.23	[59]0.87	1.03	6 Mo Nov	0.25	0.42	26
27	....	None Since Public			...	Nil	....	13.7	24.1	13.9	9-30-95	1.73	...	25669	Mr	...	pd1.02	d2.60	d2.04	....	d1.39	6 Mo Sep	d1.32	d0.67	27
28◆	....	None Since Public			...	Nil	....	4.24	25.0	15.9	9-30-95	46.3	...	9839	Dc	[60]0.30	p0.30	□0.47	0.52	....	0.40	9 Mo Sep	0.48	0.36	28
29	1977	0.167	1-12-96	12-27	0.695	0.69	2.418	1.68	1.84	1.20	9-30-95	....	...	1386	Dc	0.71	0.66	2.83	1.08	....	0.68	9 Mo Sep	0.89	0.49	29
30	1992	Q0.12½	11-14-95	10-30	0.45	0.50	0.40	13.8	195	84.6	9-30-95	48.0	...	53332	Mr	0.50	0.59	□0.67	0.80	E1.25	1.02	6 Mo Sep	0.48	0.70	30
31	1988	Q0.07	1-10-96	12-18	0.28	0.28	0.28	30.7	407	160	7-31-95	102	...	15746	Ja	□2.01	1.00	d0.65	1.85	....	2.08	9 Mo Oct	0.63	0.86	31
32	1993	Q0.05	11-15-95	10-27	0.20	0.20	0.20	Equity per shr $19.98			9-30-95	98.0	...	±64115	Dc	...	p□d3.09	d2.04	0.79	....	1.69	9 Mo Sep	0.45	1.35	32
33	....	None Since Public			...	Nil	....	3.71	411	143	9-29-95	207	...	±11034	Dc	±0.75	±1.18	±2.01	±1.58	....	d0.85	9 Mo Sep	±1.32	±d1.11	33
34◆	1994	Q0.03	11-17-95	11-1	0.11	0.12	0.02	6.42	10.2	7.24	9-30-95	....	...	3459	Dc	0.01	0.09	0.18	0.34	....	0.42	9 Mo Sep	0.15	0.23	34
35◆	1930	Q0.09	12-15-95	11-29	0.36	0.36	0.35	378	3133	2837	9-30-95	9931	29700	387467	Dc	d2.40	d1.46	□d0.75	d0.27	Ed0.55	d0.44	9 Mo Sep	d0.30	□d0.47	35
36	1892	Q0.06	3-10-96	2-21	0.45	0.24	1.08	478	1355	877	9-30-95	248	13344	±108622	Dc	±0.64	□±0.44	p±0.19	±□1.44	Ed3.39↓	11.99	9 Mo Sep	±0.93	±□11.48	36
37	1921	Q0.30	12-4-95	11-15	1.11	1.20	1.00	9.51	731	517	9-30-95	151	...	31288	Dc	d1.21	0.15	□d0.57	[61]2.21	E3.40↓	3.54	9 Mo Sep	1.38	2.71	37
38	....	5%Stk	3-12-84	2-6	...	Nil	....	4.19	6.94	1.48	9-30-95	15.7	...	11210	Sp	*0.09	*1.05	*0.20	d0.17	d0.11	d0.11				38
39	1989	[62]0.02	12-30-94	12-9	...	Nil	[62]0.02	Equity per shr $1.29			9-30-95	[63]160	...	8106	Dc	1.13	d2.64	□d1.92	0.31	....	d0.09	9 Mo Sep	0.27	d0.13	39
40	....	None Paid			...	Nil	....	2.68	57.0	35.3	9-30-95	0.32	695	13823	Dc	0.25	0.26	Δd0.87	0.40	....	0.22	9 Mo Sep	0.27	0.09	40
41	1973	Q0.25	3-10-96	2-1	1.00	1.00	1.00	Cv into 0.666 common				....	695	...	Dc	b1.88	b2.53	bd3.20	b4.25	....	....				41
42◆	1993	Q0.075	11-30-95	11-16	s0.283	0.30	0.252	Equity per shr $7.95			9-30-95	p10.9	...	★8875	Dc	...	p0.90	□1.20	1.22	....	1.37	9 Mo Sep	0.88	1.03	42
43◆	1993	Q0.01½	1-15-96	12-27	0.042	0.06	0.027	11.0	287	134	9-30-95	142	...	22548	Dc	...	p□0.41	0.46	[64]1.14	....	1.84	9 Mo Sep	0.81	1.51	43
44	....	None Since Public			...	Nil	....	30.4	44.5	13.3	9-30-95	0.01	...	14795	Dc	...	...	...	p0.10	....	0.24	9 Mo Sep	p0.07	0.21	44
45◆	1980	Q0.07	2-29-96	2-7	0.56	0.28	[65]0.555	26.9	1306	870	10-28-95	411	1900	72430	Ja	0.29	□1.40	□1.62	1.03	E0.95	0.30	9 Mo Oct	0.89	0.16	45
46	1992	Q0.781	1-2-96	12-18	3.12½	3.125	3.12½	Cv into 1.9277 com, $25.9375				....	1650	...	Ja	...	b4.31	...	....	....	....				46
47	1936	Q0.22	12-15-95	11-28	0.82	0.88	1.21½	17.5	62.1	79.1	6-30-95	667	76	10908	Dc	2.23	1.17	1.01	d1.70	....	3.08	12 Mo Sep	d1.23	3.08	47
48◆	1992	Q0.093	1-5-96	12-20	0.373	0.373	0.373	3.04	169	139	9-30-95	126	...	21887	Dc	[67]0.63	□0.79	1.20	1.45	....	1.61	9 Mo Sep	1.04	1.20	48
49	1994	Q0.02	12-30-95	12-13	0.08	0.08	0.08	0.02	110	33.9	9-30-95	57.3	...	7553	Dc	1.11	□0.93	0.45	0.47	....	0.16	9 Mo Sep	0.21	d0.10	49
50	....	0.33	2-1-87	1-9	...	Nil	....	43.9	65.8	17.4	10-01-95	....	...	9939	Mr	Δ1.64	d0.99	d0.24	Δ0.32	....	0.39	6 Mo Sep	Δ0.01	0.08	50
51	....	None Since Public			...	Nil	....	0.01	1.15	0.40	9-30-95	0.08	...	6054	Dc	Nil	0.01	Δ0.03	0.02	....	0.01	9 Mo Sep	0.02	0.01	51
52	....	0.14	8-30-91	8-5	...	Nil	....	1.71	79.9	37.5	8-31-95	35.5	830	7934	Nv	d3.74	d4.23	d1.09	□0.03	....	d0.17	9 Mo Aug	□d0.18	d0.38	52

◆**Stock Splits & Divs By Line Reference Index** [1]3-for-2,'93,'95:To split 5-for-4,ex Jan 2. [3]3-for-2,'95. [5]1-for-3 REVERSE,'92:3-for-2,'93. [6]2-for-1,'95. [8]3-for-2,'93. [10]No adj for stk dstr of Morton Int'l '89. [14]3-for-2,'92:5-for-4,'95. [15]3-for-2,'92:5-for-4,'95. [16]2-for-1,'92. [19]3-for-2,'92. [20]3-for-2,'91,'92. [24]2-for-1,'94. [26]2-for-1,'94,'95. [28]1-for-10 REVERSE,'93. [34]3-for-2,'95. [35]4-for-1,'92. [42]Adj for 5%,'95. [43]3-for-2,'95(twice). [45]No adj for dstr of Waban, Inc,'89. [48]3-for-2,'93.

¶ S&P 500
# MidCap 400
✣ SmallCap 600
• Options

Index	Ticker	Name of Issue (Call Price of Pfd. Stocks)	Market	Com. Rank. & Pfd. Rating	Inst. Hold Cos	Inst. Hold Shs. (000)	Principal Business	Price Range 1971-93 High	1971-93 Low	1994 High	1994 Low	1995 High	1995 Low	Dec. Sales in 100s	December, 1995 Last Sale Or Bid High	Low	Last	%Div Yield	P-E Ratio	Total Return % Annualized 12 Mo	36 Mo	60 Mo
1•[1]	TKOS	✓Tokos Medical Corp[51]	NNM,Ph	C	41	5441	Special home hlth care svcs	46¼	4½	8	3¼	12⅞	4⅜	22447	9½	7¾	9⅛	...	d	46.0	−18.7	−6.8
✣2•[2]	TOL	✓Toll Brothers	NY,Ch,Ph	B	116	14055	Luxury single family homes	17¾	2¼	19¾	9⅛	23	10	39396	23	17⅞	23	...	16	133	18.7	55.9
3	TBK	✓Tolland Bank	AS	NR	6	21	Savings bank, Connecticut	18	2¾	9⅝	7¼	10⅜	7⅛	135	9¾	9	9½	...	d	22.6	10.7	18.2
4	TKS	✓Tomkins plc ADS[54]	NY	NR	22	4344	Industrial & consumer pd/mgmt co	19⅛	7¼	17¼	12⅞	17⅞	13½	3034	17⅞	16	17⅞	3.2	16	33.2	8.3	21.9
5•[3]	TOM	✓Tommy Hilfiger	NY,Ph	NR	..	...	Design,mkt men's sportswear	17	7½	22¾	14¾	47⅜	18½	26244	47⅜	39½	42⅜	...	31	89.6	49.6	...
6	TR	✓Tootsie Roll Indus	NY,Ch,Ph	A	88	4911	'Tootsie' line of candies	39¼	⅜	36⅜	26¼	41	28⅞	3186	40	34¾	39⅝	s0.6	22	37.6	5.1	20.7
7•[4]	TPS	✓Top Source Technol	AS	C	47	5874	Transportation related tech	5½	⅛	9	4¼	9⅛	5⅛	23640	8¼	6⅜	6⅞	...	d	3.8	47.9	85.5
#8•[5]	TOPP	✓Topps Co	NNM,Ph	B+	111	30176	Mkts collectible picture prod	20¼	2⅞	8	4⅛	7⅛	4¼	52776	5⅜	4¼	5⅛	...	30	−3.5	−25.7	−19.6
9	TRU	✓Torch Energy Royalty Trust	NY,Ch,Ph	NR	13	159	Royalty interest o&g prop	23⅜	21	24	15	19	12⅛	16513	13½	12⅛	12¾	19.8	5	−2.9	...	...
¶10•[6]	TMK	✓Torchmark Corp	NY,B,Ch,P	A+	389	39880	Insurance:fin'l services	64¾	2½	49½	32⅜	45¼	34¼	22609	45¼	42⅜	45¼	2.6	11	33.0	−4.7	9.8
11	TRGL	Toreador Royalty	NNM	NR	17	1433	Oil & gas explor & devel	14¾	9/16	4⅝	2¾	4⅛	2¼	1873	2¾	2⅜	2⅝	...	d	−19.2	7.3	2.0
✣12	TTC	✓Toro Co	NY,Ch,Ph	↑B	135	7161	Power mowers, sprinklers, etc	30	2 5/16	30½	20⅞	32⅞	25⅝	4831	32⅞	30⅝	32⅞	1.5	13	21.5	27.4	21.6
13•[7]	TD	Toronto-Dominion Bk	To,Mo,Vc	B	85	33703	General Banking,Canada	23⅛	1 9/16	23⅝	18⅞	25	19½	118116	24½	23⅜	24	4.2	10	17.7	17.9	...
14	TTL	✓Torotel, Inc	AS	C	5	133	Mfr magnetic components	16⅞	1/16	1 9/16	⅞	2½	1	371	1⅝	1⅜	1⅜	...	d	22.2	−5.4	6.6
#15•[8]	TOS	✓Tosco Corp	NY,B,Ch,P,Ph	B	233	32297	Refining & dstr petroleum prod	225⅝	5	35	26¾	38½	27½	14117	38¼	36½	38⅛	1.7	20	36.5	25.0	23.7
16•[9]	TOT	✓TOTAL 'B' ADS[63]	NY	NR	175	50560	Intl o&g explor,dev,prod'n	28⅝	19½	33	25⅜	34	25½	47079	34	30¼	34	1.8	19	18.8	21.5	...
17	TPN	✓Total Petrol'm NA	AS,To,Ch,P,Ph,Mo	B−	70	13079	Petroleum refining/mktg	31⅞	3⅝	18½	10⅜	13¼	9¼	10035	10¼	9¼	9¾	3.1	d	−18.3	22.7	−10.8
18	TRL	Total Renal Care Hldgs	NY,Ph	NR	..	...	Provides dialysis services	...	...	...	...	30	17⅜	13949	30	25⅝	30	...	81	...	...	...
19	TSS	✓Total System Svcs	NY,Ch,Ph	A−	41	2047	Bankcard data process'g svc	16½	13/16	19¾	9⅝	31⅝	13⅜	1481	31⅝	26⅝	30½	0.3	78	76.5	63.0	31.3
20	TOWR	✓Tower Air	NNM	NR	27	1621	Scheduled/charter air svcs	16	13	17¾	6¾	9⅛	6¼	6769	7⅞	6½	6¾	2.4	10	−15.2	...	...
21	TWER	✓Tower Automotive	NNM	NR	41	4034	Engineered metal stampings	...	...	14⅛	7⅜	17½	7⅜	10841	17½	12¾	17½	...	16	97.2	...	...
22	TSEMF	Tower Semiconductor	NNM	NR	..	...	Mfr integrated circuits	...	...	15	10	36	10¼	15533	26¼	20¾	22⅛	...	14	106	...	...
23	TNC	✓Town & Country Cl'A'	AS,Ch	C	16	4440	Mfr/wholesaler of jewelry	11¾	1¼	3⅜	9/16	1⅛	9/16	15011	¾	9/16	⅝	...	4	−28.6	−37.0	−17.4
24	TCT	✓Town & Country Trust	NY,Ch	NR	62	8111	Real estate investment trust	23⅛	19	22¼	12¾	15⅛	12	11614	13⅝	12	13	12.3	46	7.3	...	...
25	TBZ	✓Toy Biz'A'	NY,Ch,Ph	NR	40	2767	Design,mkt,dstr spcl toys	...	...	...	...	26¼	16⅜	5869	23	20⅞	21¾	...	22	...	...	...
26	TOYOY	Toyota Motor Corp ADR[68]	NSC	NR	48	5589	Autos,forklifts,prefab homes	35⅜	13/16	45⅛	31¾	42⅞	34¾	2431	42½	39⅝	42¼	1.0	..	1.8	23.0	16.5
¶27•[10]	TOY	✓Toys R Us	NY,B,Ch,P,Ph	B+	728	165014	Disc toy supermarts:dept str	42⅞	5/16	40⅞	29⅝	30⅞	21⅝	292084	23⅞	21⅝	21¾	...	12	−28.7	−18.2	−0.1
✣28•[11]	TPIE	✓TPI Enterprises[72]	NNM	C	44	8855	Restaurants/movie theatres	16	3/16	10⅝	3⅜	6⅝	2½	68777	3⅝	2½	3⅛	...	d	−15.2	−27.3	−8.0
29	TTRR	✓Tracor Inc	NNM	NR	86	9029	U.S.gvt electr hrdwr/sftwr pd	9¼	2⅝	12⅝	6⅞	18½	9⅝	17675	16⅛	14⅛	14½	...	12	20.8	64.6	...
30	TSCO	✓Tractor Supply	NNM	NR	47	4390	Farm supplies:retail stores	...	...	28½	19	24½	14⅝	2535	20½	19¼	19¾	...	15	−3.7	...	...
31	TRNI	Trans-Industries Inc	NNM	C	4	6	Electronic info display sys	13	11/16	2⅛	¾	3¼	⅞	316	3¼	2⅜	3	...	d	200	26.0	13.0
32	TLX	✓Trans-Lux	AS,B,Ph	B−	13	356	LED info display/facsimile eq	15½	13/16	10⅛	7¼	10⅜	7¾	254	8⅞	8	8	1.8	10	−10.9	2.7	16.4
33•[12]	TWA	Trans World Airlines	AS	NR	26	6933	Domestic,intl air service	...	...	...	...	14⅝	4	109028	14⅝	10	10⅜	...	..	...	...	...
34	WS	Wrrt(Pur 1com at$14.40)	AS	....	8	11		...	...	...	...	9⅞	1 15/16	9582	9⅞	6⅛	7	...	..	...	...	...
35	TNSI	✓Transaction Network Svcs	NNM	NR	64	3830	Data svcs communic ntwk	...	...	15	8½	27½	13½	7120	27½	23¾	25	...	42	66.7	...	...
36	TSAI	✓Transaction Sys Architects'A'	NNM	NR	70	6948	Dvlp financial software	...	...	...	...	33¾	15	5783	33¾	27¼	33¾	...	59	...	...	...
37	TA	Transalta Corp	To,Mo	B+	27	12573	Electric service in Alberta	15¾	2¾	16¼	13⅛	14⅞	13	32714	14⅞	14⅜	14⅝	6.7	3	8.9	9.2	...
¶38•[5]	TA	✓Transamerica Corp	NY,B,C,Ch,P,Ph	B	410	40261	Insurance/financial svcs	62⅜	5⅜	57⅝	46¼	77½	49½	25337	77⅜	72¼	72⅞	2.7	13	51.2	18.9	22.5
39	WSTE	✓TransAmerican Waste Indus	NSC	NR	8	186	Non-hazardous waste svcs	6¼	3½	4¾	¾	2¾	½	25830	1⅞	1 3/16	1½	...	d	41.2	−37.4	...
#40	TRH	✓Transatlantic Holdings	NY,Ch,Ph	B+	160	20057	Reinsur: property/casualty	61½	18⅞	57⅜	45⅜	73⅞	52¼	4960	73⅞	68⅝	73⅜	0.7	14	31.8	9.6	22.9
41•[13]	TRP	✓TransCanada P.L.	NY,To,Mo,Ch,Ph	B	179	67785	Nat gas pipeline/o&g explr	29	3¾	15⅞	11⅝	14	11⅝	46729	14	13⅜	13¾	...	..	21.1	5.9	5.0
42	TNI	✓Transcisco Indus	AS	NR	8	144	Railcare maintenance/leasing	9	1/16	2⅜	15/16	3⅝	1	2263	3⅛	2⅝	3⅛	...	11	155	194	...
43	TCI	✓Transcontinental Rlty	NY,Ch	NR	6	60	Real estate investment trust	81	2½	15	12½	16½	14½	530	16	14½	15	...	d	0.0	31.3	35.7
44	TRCW	✓Transcor Waste Services	NNM	NR	3	204	Solid waste mgmt services	6⅜	4⅜	5⅞	1⅛	12⅝	1¾	700	7½	5¼	5⅞	...	20	370	...	...
45•[14]	TMN	✓Transmedia Network	NY,Ch,Ph	B	34	1650	Restaurant charge cards	11	3/16	16⅜	8¼	13¼	8	4648	11	8¾	9⅜	0.4	20	3.1	15.5	91.7
46	TREX	✓Transnational Re'A'	NNM	NR	67	4697	Catastrophe retroces'1/reinsur	27	20	26½	17¼	27¼	18¾	3854	26⅞	24½	24½	...	7	9.1	...	...
47	TCAM	✓Transport Corp Amer	NNM	NR	18	2945	Trucking-gen'l commodities	...	...	11¾	9⅛	14⅜	9½	1773	13	10⅞	11½	...	13	21.1	...	...
48•[15]	TMM	✓Transportacion Maritima ADS[78]	NY,Ph	NR	33	4327	Maritime Shipping, Mexico	12⅞	6¾	12	5⅛	9⅝	3⅝	16096	9	7⅝	8⅜	...	d	4.7	−7.9	...
49•[15]	TMM.A	CPO ADS[79]	NY,Ph	NR	19	2213		11⅝	6⅝	10⅞	4½	8⅜	2⅞	11549	8⅛	6¾	7½	...	d	11.1	−10.1	...
50	TGS	Transportadora De Gas ADS[80]	NY,Ch	NR	34	6228	Natural gas transp'n-Argentina	...	...	11¼	8¾	12⅞	6½	17299	12⅞	10⅞	12⅞	7.5	14	52.5	...	...
51	TPR	✓TransPro Inc	NY,Ch	NR	3	164	Auto/truck radiator,metal pd	...	...	...	...	17¾	8½	17249	10⅞	8½	10⅝	...	8	...	...	...
52	TT	✓TransTechnology	NY,B,Ch	B	26	1531	Ind fastener/aerospace defense	30⅞	⅞	17⅞	10½	15⅛	10	1210	13½	11⅞	13⅜	1.9	17	20.2	14.4	24.2

Uniform Footnote Explanations-See Page 4. Other: [1]Ph:Cycle 3. [2]ASE:Cycle 3. [3]CBOE:Cycle 2. [4]NY:Cycle 3. [5]Ph:Cycle 2. [6]ASE:Cycle 2. [7]To:Cycle 3. [8]ASE:Cycle 1. [9]ASE,CBOE,NY:Cycle 1. [10]CBOE:Cycle 3. [11]P:Cycle 3. [12]CBOE:Cycle 1. [13]NY:Cycle 3,Vc:Cycle 2. [14]P:Cycle 1. [15]CBOE,Ph:Cycle 1. [51]Plan form new co w/Healthdyne Inc,1 new com. [52]®$1.41,'95. [53]Incl curr amts. [54]Each ADS rep 4 ord, 5p. [55]®$0.54,'93. [56]Dec'91 & prior. [57]9 Mo Sep'92. [58]5 Wks Dec'93. [59]Stk of Southland Royalty. [60]Fiscal Jul'94 & prior. [61]Fiscal Jul'95 earn $2.81. [62]®$2.24,'94. [63]Each ADS rep 0.50 ord'B'FF50. [64]Excl subsid pfd. [65]10 Mo Dec. [66]Incl $0.416 non-taxable,'94. [67]18 Wks Dec'93. [68]Each ADR rep 2 ord, y50. [69]Approx. [70]Fiscal Jun '93 & prior. [71]9 Mo Mar '95. [72]Shoney's Inc plan acq,0.28 com. [73]®$0.93,'94. [74]®$0.94,'94. [75]Fiscal Dec'93 & prior:12 Mo Mar'94 earned$d1.02. [76]To be determined. [77]2 Mo Dec'93 earned $0.05. [78]Ea ADS rep 1 'L'shr,no par. [79]Ea ADS rep 1 ord Part'n ctf(rep 1ser'A'shr int). [80]Ea ADS rep 5 Cl'B'shrs, Ps1.

Index	Splits ◆ Cash Divs. Ea.Yr. Since	Dividends: Latest Payment Period $	Date	Ex. Div.	Total $ So Far 1995	Ind. Rate	Paid 1994	Financial Position Mil-$ Cash& Equiv.	Curr. Assets	Curr. Liab.	Balance Sheet Date	Capitalization Lg Trm Debt Mil-$	Shs. 000 Pfd.	Com.	Earnings $ Per Shr. Years End	1991	1992	1993	1994	1995	Last 12 Mos.	Interim Earnings Period	$ per Shr. 1994	1995	Index
1	....	None Since Public			...	Nil	....	9.23	29.6	13.9	9-30-95	2.37	...	17489	Dc	0.44	0.37	d1.53	d0.34	....	d0.70	9 Mo Sep	d0.20	d0.56	1
2	....	None Paid			...	Nil	....	Equity per shr $7.10			7-31-95	292	...	33593	Oc	Δ0.12	□0.52	Δ0.82	1.08	P[52]1.47	1.47				2
3	....	0.04	11-13-90	10-25	...	Nil	....	Book Value $11.18			12-31-94	[53]6.89	...	1158	Dc	d0.93	0.16	Δ0.21	0.38	....	d1.16	9 Mo Sep	0.26	d1.28	3
4◆	1988	0.418	10-19-95	8-18	0.584	0.58	0.487	744	2398	1656	4-29-95	23.8	...	1182800	Ap	1.08	1.09	0.88	0.94	1.15	1.15				4
5◆	....	None Since Public			...	Nil	....	98.4	255	65.1	9-30-95	1.93	...	35623	Mr	0.40	[55]0.56	0.77	1.12	....	1.38	6 Mo Sep	0.44	0.70	5
6◆	1943	Q0.06¼	1-11-96	12-20	s0.232	0.25	s0.196	66.9	167	66.4	9-30-95	7.50	...	±22343	Dc	□1.18	1.43	1.59	1.70	....	1.78	9 Mo Sep	1.35	1.43	6
7	....	None Paid			...	Nil	....	1.15	5.68	2.51	6-30-95	2.06	...	27422	Sp	[56]d0.09	‡[57]d0.12	d0.18	0.07	Pd0.12	d0.12				7
8	1987	0.07	11-1-94	10-12	...	Nil	0.28	27.0	121	83.7	8-26-95	42.5	...	47048	Fb	1.15	0.40	0.57	0.33	....	0.17	9 Mo Nov	0.31	0.15	8
9	1994	0.559	12-11-95	11-29	2.529	2.53	3.407	Equity per shr $16.63			9-30-95	....	...	8600	Dc	...	...	‡[58]0.02	3.40	....	2.74	9 Mo Sep	2.64	1.98	9
10◆	1933	Q0.29	2-1-96	1-3	1.13	1.16	1.12	Book Value $14.44			9-30-95	793	...	71656	Dc	3.13	3.58	Δ3.76	3.72	E4.00	3.68	9 Mo Sep	2.83	2.79	10
11	....	h[59]....	11-16-81	10-8	...	Nil	....	3.81	4.14	0.10	6-30-95	....	...	5343	Dc	0.01	0.01	0.07	0.02	....	d0.11	9 Mo Sep	0.04	d0.09	11
12	1984	Q0.12	1-12-96	12-26	0.48	0.48	0.48	11.9	382	213	7-31-95	64.9	...	12161	Oc	0.81	■d1.98	1.05	[60]1.71	P[61]2.50	2.50				12
13	1857	gQ0.25	1-31-96	12-12	g0.88	1.00	g0.79	Book Value $18.31			j10-31-95	2404	16000	301403	Oc	1.51	1.25	0.82	2.14	2.51	j2.51				13
14	....	5%Stk	5-15-85	4-24	...	Nil	....	0.06	6.43	2.68	7-31-95	2.55	...	2767	Ap	Δ0.11	0.32	0.10	Δd0.09	d0.14	d0.09	6 Mo Oct	0.03	0.08	14
15	1989	Q0.16	1-2-96	12-20	0.48	0.64	0.62	39.0	802	555	9-30-95	634	...	37065	Dc	2.39	Δd3.40	2.38	[62]2.27	E1.95	1.72	9 Mo Sep	1.71	1.16	15
16	1992	0.616	7-21-95	5-31	0.616	0.62	0.514	24513	63215	41358	12-31-94	j22141	[64]...	±227294	Dc	±2.65	±1.23	1.14	1.32	E1.75	1.32				16
17◆	1994	tQ0.075	1-19-96	1-3	t0.30	0.30	t0.20	11.0	427	352	9-30-95	409	...	38632	Dc	d0.45	0.03	0.71	0.63	....	d0.07	9 Mo Sep	0.75	0.05	17
18	....	None Since Public			...	Nil	....	1.38	37.7	16.2	8-31-95	p53.0	...	★21388	My	...	...	...	....	p0.22	0.37	3 Mo Aug	pNil	0.15	18
19◆	1990	Q0.02¼	1-2-96	12-19	0.09	0.09	0.075	22.3	77.2	36.4	9-30-95	0.77	...	64631	Dc	0.24	0.27	0.31	0.35	....	0.39	9 Mo Sep	0.24	0.28	19
20	1994	Q0.04	12-15-95	12-6	0.16	0.16	0.16	13.0	48.5	84.9	6-30-95	28.0	...	15290	Dc	0.57	0.10	0.78	0.04	....	0.66	9 Mo Sep	0.14	0.76	20
21	....	None Since Public			...	Nil	....	3.90	68.2	37.4	9-30-95	71.4	...	10826	Dc	...	...	p0.87	0.97	....	1.11	9 Mo Sep	0.61	0.75	21
22	....	None Since Public			...	Nil	....	31.1	57.3	14.7	3-31-95	12.1	...	★13000	Dc	...	...	‡[65]0.55	1.03	....	1.62	9 Mo Sep	0.68	1.27	22
23	....	None Since Public			...	Nil	....	4.40	142	47.9	8-27-95	94.1	2266	±23784	Fb	Δd1.64	d3.80	0.08	d0.05	....	0.18	6 Mo Aug	d0.45	d0.22	23
24	1993	Q0.40	12-11-95	11-15	1.60	1.60	[66]1.60	Equity per shr $6.03			9-30-95	287	...	15662	Dc	...	...	‡[67]0.18	0.34	....	0.28	9 Mo Sep	0.24	0.18	24
25	....	None Since Public			...	Nil	....	39.0	111	38.3	9-30-95	....	...	±27020	Dc	...	...	...	p0.71	....	0.97	9 Mo Sep	p0.36	0.62	25
26◆	1970	[69]0.14	12-13-95	9-26	[69]0.408	0.41	0.297	19232	56404	34556	3-31-95	21350	...	3738135	Mr	1.78	0.99	[70]0.86	‡[71]0.77	....	....		[70]	[71]	26
27	....	None since reorg.			...	Nil	....	220	4083	4058	10-28-95	782	...	273086	Ja	1.15	1.47	1.63	1.85	E1.75	1.63	9 Mo Oct	0.42	0.20	27
28	....	None Paid			...	Nil	....	6.15	29.4	70.2	10-01-95	83.4	...	20496	Dc	0.55	□0.04	d1.55	d0.18	....	d0.34	40 Wk Oct	Nil	d0.16	28
29	....	None Paid			...	Nil	....	24.2	192	97.0	12-31-94	195	...	±★13280	Dc	...	±0.32	±0.56	±[73]0.96	....	1.20	9 Mo Sep	±0.67	±0.91	29
30	....	None Since Public			...	Nil	....	9.85	140	81.3	9-30-95	11.3	...	8718	Dc	...	...	p1.01	1.28	E1.35	1.32	9 Mo Sep	0.96	1.00	30
31	....	0.017	6-29-82	6-15	...	Nil	....	0.10	13.8	8.27	9-30-95	5.22	...	2927	Dc	d0.44	0.04	Δd0.20	d0.16	....	d0.02	9 Mo Sep	d0.03	0.11	31
32	1986	Q0.03½	1-5-96	12-13	0.14	0.14	0.14	1.07	7.32	9.41	9-30-95	22.9	...	±1254	Dc	±0.25	±0.28	±0.39	±[74]1.04	....	0.82	9 Mo Sep	±0.80	±0.58	32
33	....	None Since Public			...	Nil	....	251	769	933	9-30-95	1028	6425	42900	Dc	...	...	...	....	....	....				33
34	....	Terms&trad. basis should	be checked in detail					Wrrts expire 8-23-2002				....	...	1967	Dc	...	...	...	....	....	....				34
35	....	None Since Public			...	Nil	....	22.7	31.2	6.64	9-30-95	0.02	...	8071	Dc	...	...	p0.34	p0.49	....	0.60	9 Mo Sep	p0.33	0.44	35
36	....	None Since Public			...	Nil	....	14.1	47.4	32.4	6-30-95	0.43	...	★±12577	Sp	...	...	...	pd2.53	P□0.57	0.57				36
37	1956	gQ0.24½	1-1-96	11-29	g0.98	0.98	g0.98	58.0	328	381	j12-31-94	1570	15985	p158842	Dc	1.12	1.18	1.16	1.18	E5.70	j1.16	9 Mo Sep	0.84	0.82	37
38	1934	Q0.50	1-31-96	12-27	2.00	2.00	2.00	Equity per shr $53.96			9-30-95	10173	406	68370	Dc	□1.14	2.83	□4.80	5.45	E5.70	6.47	9 Mo Sep	4.02	5.04	38
39	....	None Paid			...	Nil	....	2.39	6.97	6.21	8-31-95	25.1	...	29647	Au	0.15	0.18	Nil	d0.75	d0.34	d0.22	3 Mo Nov	d0.10	0.02	39
40	1990	Q0.12	3-19-96	3-1	0.40	0.48	0.36	Equity per shr $40.74			9-30-95	....	...	22947	Dc	3.09	3.13	Δ3.79	4.44	E5.30	5.51	9 Mo Sep	3.18	4.25	40
41	1964	gQ0.27	1-31-96	12-27	g1.00	1.08	g0.92	113	861	1321	j12-31-94	4402	22253	184811	Dc	1.34	1.56	1.62	1.60	E1.75	j1.71	9 Mo Sep	1.20	1.31	41
42	....	0.075	1-22-91	12-21	...	Nil	....	0.81	12.2	8.62	9-30-95	6.50	...	5223	Mr	±d5.18	±d1.99	Δ[75]d1.02	0.11	....	0.28	6 Mo Sep	0.02	Δ0.19	42
43	....	0.10	12-31-95	12-13	0.10	[76]....	....	Equity per shr $32.80			9-30-95	[53]174	...	2675	Dc	d5.73	Δd1.98	Δd3.78	Δd1.73	....	d3.17	9 Mo Sep	Δd1.10	Δd2.54	43
44	....	None Since Public			...	Nil	....	3.16	11.9	11.4	9-30-95	12.9	...	3990	Dc	d0.17	0.10	0.40	0.04	....	0.29	9 Mo Sep	0.03	0.28	44
45◆	1993	S0.02	10-19-95	10-3	0.04	0.04	0.04	0.87	27.7	5.38	6-30-95	1.50	...	9840	Sp	0.13	0.21	0.29	0.44	P0.46	0.46				45
46	1995	0.05	12-15-95	11-4	0.05	[76]....	....	Equity per shr $22.41			9-30-95	....	...	±7016	Dc	...	...	[77]n/a	2.70	....	3.55	9 Mo Sep	2.03	2.88	46
47	....	None Since Public			...	Nil	....	0.15	19.1	26.1	9-30-95	20.3	...	6421	Dc	0.01	0.36	0.47	0.78	....	0.89	9 Mo Sep	0.60	0.71	47
48	1993	0.177	5-20-94	5-6	...	Nil	0.177	205	325	218	12-31-94	463	...	±54725	Dc	1.08	0.75	0.71	d1.19	....	d0.51	9 Mo Sep	d0.10	0.58	48
49	1993	0.177	5-20-94	5-6	...	Nil	0.177	....	...	...		....	...	41030	Dc	1.08	0.75	0.71	d1.19	....	d0.52	9 Mo Sep	d0.09	0.58	49
50	1995	0.473	9-8-95	8-28	0.971	0.97	....	46.2	90.2	152	6-30-94	366	...	±794495	Dc	...	...	0.92	....	....	0.92	6 Mo JunΔ	0.52	0.52	50
51	1996	0.05	1-8-96	12-13	...	[76]....	....	4.00	96.3	35.6	9-30-95	45.7	...	6615	Dc	...	...	...	p1.45	....	1.38	9 Mo Sep	p1.17	p1.10	51
52	1992	Q0.06½	12-1-95	11-13	0.26	0.26	0.25	2.98	96.8	38.5	10-01-95	74.3	...	5281	Mr	d1.85	1.01	1.34	0.50	....	0.79	6 Mo Sep	0.25	0.54	52

◆**Stock Splits & Divs By Line Reference Index** [4]2-for-1,'92. [5]2-for-1,'95. [6]Adj to 3%,'95:2-for-1,'95. [10]3-for-2,'92. [17]No adj for stk dstr,'91. [19]2-for-1,'93,'94. [26]10%,'91. [45]3-for-2,'92,'93,'94.

¶ S&P 500 # MidCap 400 ✣ SmallCap 600 • Options Index	Ticker	Name of Issue (Call Price of Pfd. Stocks)	Market	Com. Rank. & Pfd. Rating	Inst. Hold Cos	Inst. Hold Shs. (000)	Principal Business	Price Range 1971-93 High	1971-93 Low	1994 High	1994 Low	1995 High	1995 Low	Dec. Sales in 100s	December, 1995 Last Sale Or Bid High	Low	Last	%Div Yield	P-E Ratio	Total Return % Annualized 12 Mo	36 Mo	60 Mo
1	TTXG	✓TransTexas Gas	NNM	NR	50	8052	Nat'l gas explor,dev,prod'n	....	....	14⅛	10	21	9⅜	11701	16	12	13½	...	d	20.0	...	...
2	TXCC	✓TranSwitch Corp	NNM	NR	22	2796	Mfr eqp for semicond'r ind	....	....	....	....	14¼	8⅝	16361	13⅜	8⅝	11⅛	...	d	...	...	...
3	TNZ.A	✓Tranzonic Cos 'A'[51]	AS	↓B	17	465	Personal care disposable prod	21	15/16	22½	10⅞	17⅝	13½	207	14¾	13½	13¾	1.5	11	−18.1	−6.8	15.1
4	TNZ.B	Cl'B'(1/10 vtg)	AS	↓B	18	335		17¼	6½	20⅜	10½	17	13	214	14½	13½	13⅞	2.6	11	−15.2	−0.9	17.5
¶5•[1]	TRV	✓Travelers Group	NY,B,Ch,P,Ph	B+	775	223517	Diversified financial svcs	49½	8½	43⅛	30⅜	63⅞	32⅜	179481	63⅞	56¾	62⅝	1.3	14	...	...	...
6	Pr B	5.50% cm Cv'B'Pfd[53](51.925)	NY,Ch	A	46	1949		....	....	62½	49¾	87¼	51⅜	1088	87¼	78⅞	87¼	3.2	..	...	...	...
7	WS	Wrrt(Pur 1 com at $39)	NY,Ch	....	9	643		....	....	10⅞	6⅜	28⅝	7¼	9689	28⅝	23⅜	27⅝	...	..	...	...	...
8	TRR	✓TRC Cos	NY,Ch	B−	35	3850	Environment consult/research	17	1/32	13¼	7¾	9⅛	5½	4717	6⅝	5½	6⅝	...	21	−17.2	−7.5	−1.1
9	TRED	✓Treadco Inc	NNM	NR	34	2607	Truck tire retreader/dealer	22¾	10⅞	19	12½	16¼	5¼	7923	6¼	5¼	5¾	2.8	6	−63.0	−25.4	...
✣10	TG	✓Tredegar Indus	NY	NR	69	2270	Plastics, aluminum & energy	19	6⅜	18⅝	13⅞	35¼	17⅜	1491	35¼	31½	32¼	1.1	14	86.3	28.8	37.7
11	TRE	✓Tremont Corp	NY,Ph	NR	49	2910	Titanium prd/bentonite min'g	25	5⅞	13⅛	5¾	21¼	11	614	17½	16½	16⅝	...	d	38.5	27.0	3.6
12	TRND	✓Trend-Lines 'A' Inc	NNM	NR	30	3120	Retail woodworking tools	....	....	9¼	7⅛	14⅞	7⅝	15061	12	9	10	...	18	21.5	...	...
13	TSBS	Trenton Savings Bank	NNM	NR	7	657	Savings bank,New Jersey	....	....	....	....	14⅛	11	2116	13¾	12⅞	13	...	14	...	...	...
✣14	TREN	✓Trenwick Group	NNM	B	84	6127	Reinsurance:prop,casualty	49¾	8⅞	43⅞	33¼	57½	40¾	10357	57½	49¾	56¼	2.0	13	36.8	13.6	22.2
15	NRG	✓Tri-Lite Inc	AS,Ch,Ph	NR	7	10	Light'g fixt'rs/elc energy mgt	7⅛	4½	6⅝	1¼	2⅜	½	1366	13/16	½	9/16	...	d	−59.1	...	...
16	WS	Wrrt(Pur 1 com at $6)	AS	....	..	...		2⅝	1	2⅜	5/16	½	1/32	637	⅛	1/16	1/16	...	..	...	...	...
17	TGIC	✓Triad Guaranty	NNM	NR	29	1632	Mortgage insurance coverage	19	15½	19	11½	27½	12¾	2173	27¼	26½	26½	...	16	104	...	...
18	TRSC	✓Triad Systems	NNM	B	46	9319	Computer sys: business mgmt	54¼	1 13/16	5⅝	4⅛	7⅝	5	9826	6⅜	5⅜	6⅛	...	13	25.6	−0.7	22.2
19	TRIP	✓Triangle Pacific	NNM	NR	58	13373	Mfr wood flooring & cabinets	15⅞	10	17¼	11¼	19⅛	11⅞	3661	18¾	15⅝	17⅛	...	12	42.7	...	...
✣20•[2]	TRY	✓Triarc Cos Cl'A'	NY,B,Ch,P,Ph	C	57	4703	Textiles,softdr,fast fd,LP gas	33	⅜	26⅛	9½	16¾	9½	14597	11⅜	9⅞	11	...	22	−2.2	−9.3	30.8
¶21•[3]	TRB	✓Tribune Co.	NY,B,Ch,P	B+	437	35185	Newspaper pub,brdcg,CATV	63⅛	12	64½	48⅞	68⅞	50¾	44150	66¾	59⅝	61⅛	1.8	16	13.5	10.2	14.1
✣22•[4]	TRCD	✓Tricord Systems	NNM	NR	30	1496	Mfr network superservers	30	10⅝	26¾	3⅞	6½	2½	25060	3¼	2½	3	...	d	−44.2	...	...
23•[5]	TRID	✓Trident Microsystems	NNM	NR	55	3738	Dvlp computer graphics prod	20½	4½	11⅞	4¾	37¾	9¼	73498	37¾	23¼	23½	...	26	102	16.1	...
24	TRDX	✓Tridex Corp	NNM,Ch	↑B	14	315	Mfr electronic comp: relays	19⅞	½	10⅛	5	10¼	5½	5380	8⅛	6¾	7	...	11	24.4	−6.7	62.1
25	TGN	✓Trigen Energy	NY,Ch,Ph	NR	41	4183	Oper community energy sys	....	....	21	15¾	22½	16¾	578	19⅝	19	19½	0.7	19	3.4	...	...
26	TMS	✓TriMas Corp	NY,Ch	NR	113	13073	Mfr steel/alloy fasteners	24⅝	6	28½	18⅜	25½	18⅜	8607	20¼	18⅜	18¾	1.1	13	−4.3	9.9	24.7
27•[6]	TRMB	✓Trimble Navigation Ltd	NNM	B−	88	8551	Mfr electr navigat'n instr	19¼	5¾	16¾	8⅝	35⅜	14½	98288	22	14½	18⅝	...	28	14.6	28.6	16.3
28	TRI	✓TriNet Corporate Rlty Tr	NY	NR	64	6978	Real estate investment trust	30½	21¼	33⅛	24¾	29½	24¼	9020	27¾	26⅝	27¼	9.1	16	3.1	...	...
29	TSI	✓Trinitech Systems	AS,Ch	NR	4	88	Mfr securities account'g sys	3⅞	2⅜	3⅛	2	8¾	2¼	5646	7⅛	5	5⅛	...	d	116	...	...
#30•[2]	TRN	✓Trinity Indus	NY,B,Ch	B+	269	31311	Railcars: containers, steel	44⅛	¾	47⅜	30⅜	40⅜	28⅛	28283	32¾	29¼	31½	2.2	13	3.7	8.1	23.2
¶31•[7]	TNV	✓TRINOVA Corp	NY,B,Ch,P,Ph	B−	276	20759	Fluid pwr equip/plastic prod	44¼	4⅛	40	28½	38¾	23½	23728	31⅜	28⅛	28⅝	2.5	9	1.4	13.3	12.2
32	TRON	✓Trion Inc	NNM	B−	12	846	Mfr electronic air cleaners	10	⅛	7⅛	4⅝	6⅝	4⅝	813	5⅜	4⅞	5⅛	1.6	17	6.2	15.3	14.8
33	TPPPF	Triple P N.V.[64]	NNM	NR	..	...	Network application softwr	....	....	....	....	10¾	9½	53909	10¾	9½	10	...	d	...	...	...
34•[4]	TQNT	✓TriQuint Semiconductor	NNM	NR	68	4046	Mfr,mkt integrated circuits	13	11	18	4½	28⅝	10⅝	47386	17	10⅝	13½	...	84	120	...	...
35•[8]	OIL	✓Triton Energy	NY,B,Ph	C	208	27355	Oil & gas explor'n,devel't	52½	1⅛	37⅝	24¾	57⅞	30¾	33797	57⅞	50¼	57⅜	...	..	66.9	21.0	53.4
36	TGL	✓Triton Group Ltd	AS	NR	32	13993	Broadly diversified holding co	2⅞	1 1/16	2½	1 3/16	3¼	5/16	32904	3⅛	5/16	½	...	d	...	...	...
37	WS	Wrrt(Pur1.84com at$3.75)	AS	....	4	.9		9/16	3/16	15/16	5/16	⅝	1/16	1163	⅜	⅛	3/16	...	..	...	...	...
38	TZC	Trizec Corp Ltd	NY	NR	..	...	Real estate hldg/mgmt	....	....	....	....	7	7	118	7	7	7	...	..	...	...	...
39•[4]	TROW	✓T.Rowe Price Assoc	NNM	A−	152	13088	Advisor to mutual funds,dstr	32⅞	4⅜	38¼	24⅝	56¾	27	29992	55¾	46½	49¼	1.7	20	68.1	33.0	35.1
✣40	TNO	✓True North Communicns	NY,B,Ch	B+	86	10946	Int'l advertising agency	24	1 5/16	24	20	21⅞	15¾	5100	20¼	18	18½	3.2	21	−10.3	6.6	14.4
41	DJT	✓Trump Hotels & Casino Resorts [9]	NY,Ch	NR	44	8184	Own,operate gaming operations	....	....	....	....	21⅝	11⅜	13038	21⅝	19	21½	...	..	...	...	...
42	TCNJ	Trust Co of New Jersey	NNM	B+	32	853	Commercial bkg,New Jersey	16⅜	5/16	15¼	11¼	15	12¼	2353	13½	12⅞	13¼	2.4	30	8.6	2.3	19.3
¶43•[2]	TRW	✓TRW Inc	NY,B,Ch,P,Ph	B+	483	37559	Car & truck:elec/space:ind'l	70¼	5⅛	77½	61	82⅝	61¾	29726	78⅝	73¾	77½	2.8	12	20.9	13.3	19.5
44	Pr B	$4.40 cm Cv II Pref (104)vtg	NY,B	A	8	3	& energy: computer svs	294	36	326	275	....	....	2	325⅝	325⅝	341B	1.3	..	...	...	...
45	Pr D	$4.50cmCv II Pref 3 (100)	NY,B	A	9	5	spacecraft,tools,pumps	248	37⅜	272	232	....	....	5	290	280	288⅝B	1.6	..	...	...	...
✣46•[10]	TSNG	✓Tseng Labs	NNM	B	40	2278	IBM compatible softwr/hardwr	23⅜	1/32	11⅞	5⅞	11¼	5⅝	28458	11	8⅞	9⅜	...	45	57.1	−12.0	16.1
47	TCM	✓T/SF Communications	AS,Ch	NR	10	334	Newspaper publish'g/info svc	12⅜	1¼	6¼	4⅛	13½	5¾	186	13½	12¼	13½	...	4	125	35.9	41.6
48	TSII	✓TSI Inc	NNM	B+	26	1521	Flow measurement instr	9¼	1/32	9⅜	7	14¾	7¾	2998	14¾	11⅝	14	0.9	25	66.7	30.0	19.5
49	TSXX	✓TSX Corp	NNM,Ch	C	33	3013	Mfr cable television prod	68¾	1/32	24	2⅜	29¼	14¼	7386	24	19¾	21½	...	18	16.2	142	68.5
✣50	TUBO	✓Tuboscope Vetco Intl	NNM	NR	58	6919	Oil & gas ind services/prod	11½	4½	8	4½	8½	5⅝	18829	6½	5⅝	5⅝	...	14	−9.0	−1.8	−5.7
51	TAM	TubosDeAceroMex ADR[73]	AS,B,Ch,P,Ph	NR	36	13066	Mfr seamless steel pipe, tub'g	25	11/16	6⅝	4	7¾	2½	19419	7¾	6½	7	...	d	40.0	8.4	0.4
52	TUCK	✓Tucker Drilling	NNM	B−	15	529	Contract drilling:oil/gas	21⅝	⅞	6¾	4⅜	8¾	5	798	8½	7⅛	8¼	...	9	61.0	20.2	6.6

Uniform Footnote Explanations-See Page 4. Other: [1]Ph:Cycle 3. [2]ASE:Cycle 1. [3]CBOE:Cycle 2. [4]CBOE:Cycle 1. [5]P:Cycle 1. [6]P:Cycle 3. [7]Ph:Cycle 2. [8]ASE,CBOE,NY,Ph:Cycle 1. [9]Ph [10]ASE:Cycle 2. [51]Cv into 1 Cl'B'. [52]Stk dstr of Transport Holdings. [53]Fr 7-30-96,scale to $50 in 2003. [54]To be determined. [55]®$2.78,'94. [56]If com at least $9 re-specified cond.. [57]Spl dstr,ex-div'89. [58]Fiscal Apr'92 & prior. [59]8 Mo Dec'93:Fiscal Apr'93 earned $d1.82. [60]®$3.07,'94. [61]®$1.28,'94. [62]Fiscal Mar'92. [63]9 Mo Dec'92. [64]Par Nf1 0.20. [65]Spl div. [66]Fiscal May'93 & prior. [67]7 Mo Dec'94:fiscal May'94 earned d$0.27. [68]Stk dstr of Metromedia Intl Group. [69]9 Mo Mar. [70]Incl 25M non-vtg spcl stk. [71]5 Mo Dec.'94. [72]®$5.01,'94. [73]ADR equal 1 ord shr.

Index (Splits ◆)	Cash Divs. Ea.Yr. Since	Dividends: Latest Payment Period $	Date	Ex. Div.	Total $ So Far 1995	Ind. Rate	Paid 1994	Financial Position Mil-$: Cash& Equiv.	Curr. Assets	Curr. Liab.	Balance Sheet Date	Capitalization: Lg Trm Debt Mil-$	Shs. 000 Pfd.	Com.	Earnings $ Per Shr.: Years End	1991	1992	1993	1994	1995	Last 12 Mos.	Interim Earnings: Period	$ per Shr. 1994	1995	Index
1	....	None Since Public			...	Nil	....	81.4	171	64.3	7-31-95	800	...	74000	Jl	...	...	p0.75	0.33	d0.16	d0.25	3 Mo Oct	Nil	d0.09	1
2	....	None Since Public			...	Nil	....	21.1	27.8	3.46	9-30-95	....	...	11296	Dc	...	...	...	pd0.48	....	d0.26	9 Mo Sep	pd0.42	d0.20	2
3	1962	Q0.05	1-16-96	12-26	0.19	0.20	0.18	3.92	50.0	14.5	8-31-95	12.0	...	±3503	Fb	±1.29	±1.19	±0.80	±1.51	....	1.25	9 Mo Nov	±1.15	±0.89	3
4	1989	Q0.09	1-16-96	12-26	0.35	0.36	0.34	....	...	...		....	...	1317	Fb	±1.29	±1.19	±0.80	±1.51	....	1.25	9 Mo Nov	±1.15	±0.89	4
5◆	1986	h[52]....	10-2-95	10-3	h[52]0.60	0.80	0.57½	Equity per shr $25.59			9-30-95	★8963	11200	316340	Dc	2.14	□3.34	□3.88	3.86	E4.50	4.65	9 Mo Sep	2.88	3.67	5
6	1994	Q0.68¾	12-1-95	11-13	2.75	2.75	2.06¼	Cv into 1.36 com,$36.75				....	2500	...	Dc	...	...	...	b1.91	....	....				6
7	....	Terms&trad. basis should			be checked in detail			Wrrts expire 7-31-98				....	...	3749	Dc	...	...	...	....	....	....				7
8	....	None Since Public			...	Nil	....	1.48	35.6	13.0	9-30-95	10.4	...	7091	Je	0.60	0.63	d0.54	0.32	0.61	0.31	3 Mo Sep	0.15	d0.15	8
9	1992	Q0.04	11-21-95	11-3	0.16	0.16	0.16	0.38	61.7	19.4	9-30-95	8.00	...	5072	Dc	□0.77	1.05	1.16	1.28	....	0.92	9 Mo Sep	0.91	0.55	9
10◆	1989	Q0.09	1-1-96	12-6	0.24	0.36	0.24	11.4	135	73.0	9-30-95	35.0	...	8440	Dc	0.52	1.41	□0.97	3.73	....	2.38	9 Mo Sep	3.26	1.91	10
11◆	....	0.20	9-30-92	9-10	...	Nil	....	3.87	112	62.9	9-30-95	70.8	...	7355	Dc	d0.21	□d4.58	□d7.16	□d5.83	....	d2.58	9 Mo Sep	□d3.17	0.08	11
12◆	....	None Since Public			...	Nil	....	0.42	70.6	23.7	8-26-95	31.8	...	p±9265	Fb	...	...	p0.39	p±0.57	....	0.57	6 Mo Aug	p±0.16	±0.16	12
13	1995	0.05¾	12-8-95	11-13	0.05¾	[54]....	....	Book Value $9.39			12-31-94	p2.49	...	★3117	Dc	...	...	...	p0.96	....	0.96				13
14	1988	Q0.28	12-29-95	12-7	1.12	1.12	1.00	Equity per shr $34.85			9-30-95	104	...	6495	Dc	2.79	Δ2.50	3.48	[55]3.04	....	4.26	9 Mo Sep	2.04	3.26	14
15	....	None Since Public			...	Nil	....	6.75	13.7	9.53	9-30-95	0.42	...	6039	Dc	d0.37	0.11	0.12	d1.06	....	d0.83	9 Mo Sep	d0.34	d0.11	15
16	....	Terms&trad. basis should			be checked in detail			Wrrts expire 10-20-96				....	...	500	Dc	...	...	...	....	....	....	Callable at 10¢[56]			16
17	....	None Since Public			...	Nil	....	Equity per shr $15.87			12-31-94	....	...	4419	Dc	0.43	0.98	1.53	1.30	....	1.66	9 Mo Sep	0.92	1.28	17
18◆	....	[57]15.00			...	Nil	....	7.26	34.8	33.3	9-30-95	52.6	...	17393	Sp	0.18	□0.27	0.35	□0.43	□0.48	0.48				18
19	....	None Since Public			...	Nil	....	17.4	155	42.8	9-29-95	166	...	14663	Dc	...	pΔ0.06	p□0.53	1.28	....	1.49	9 Mo Sep	0.90	1.11	19
20	....	5%Stk	4-25-86	3-25	...	Nil	....	46.6	363	200	9-30-95	754	...	±29908	Dc	Δd0.68	[58]d0.29	□[59]d2.02	□d0.51	E0.50	d0.44	9 Mo Sep	Nil	0.07	20
21	1902	Q0.28	12-14-95	11-28	1.12	1.12	1.04	36.9	617	568	9-24-95	494	103	63617	Dc	1.94	□1.82	2.56	[60]3.32	E3.95↓	3.90	9 Mo Sep	2.36	2.94	21
22	....	None Since Public			...	Nil	....	13.2	36.6	11.8	9-30-95	....	...	13269	Dc	...	pd0.37	0.71	0.13	....	d2.40	9 Mo Sep	0.11	d2.42	22
23	....	None Since Public			...	Nil	....	46.6	74.2	24.6	9-30-95	....	...	11977	Je	0.24	0.98	0.86	0.12	0.61	0.92	3 Mo Sep	0.03	0.34	23
24	....	0.03	11-27-81	11-9	...	Nil	....	0.35	19.6	13.6	4-01-95	6.19	...	3680	Mr	d0.23	0.46	0.44	0.69	....	0.66	6 Mo Sep	0.28	0.25	24
25	1994	Q0.03½	1-15-96	12-27	0.14	0.14	0.03½	13.9	39.5	37.8	9-30-95	227	...	11407	Dc	...	...	p□0.85	0.89	....	1.01	9 Mo Sep	0.61	0.73	25
26◆	1992	Q0.05	2-20-96	1-17	0.18	0.20	0.14	80.9	243	57.0	9-30-95	187	...	36644	Dc	□0.67	□0.87	1.05	[61]1.35	....	1.49	9 Mo Sep	1.03	1.17	26
27	....	None Since Public			...	Nil	....	98.9	174	38.5	9-30-95	30.0	...	21451	Dc	0.40	□d1.37	0.19	0.53	....	0.66	9 Mo Sep	0.38	0.51	27
28	1993	Q0.62	1-12-96	12-27	2.44	2.48	2.33	Equity per shr $20.45			9-30-95	p217	...	★13842	Dc	...	p1.61	p1.75	1.84	....	1.76	9 Mo Sep	1.41	1.33	28
29	....	None Since Public			...	Nil	....	0.95	4.70	0.87	9-30-95	0.03	...	7270	Dc	[62]d0.06	[63]d0.01	d0.09	d0.04	....	d0.03	9 Mo Sep	d0.01	Nil	29
30◆	1964	Q0.17	1-31-96	1-10	0.68	0.68	0.68	Equity per shr $16.86			9-30-95	230	...	41551	Mr	0.69	1.27	Δ1.69	2.20	....	2.52	6 Mo Sep	1.00	1.32	30
31	1933	Q0.18	12-15-95	11-13	0.72	0.72	0.68	14.4	602	318	9-30-95	228	...	28994	Dc	d6.52	0.51	□0.37	2.26	E3.20	3.14	9 Mo Sep	1.64	2.52	31
32	1995	Q0.02	1-2-96	11-29	0.06	0.08	....	0.86	22.1	6.91	9-30-95	10.3	...	6451	Dc	d0.33	d0.04	0.25	0.28	....	0.31	9 Mo Sep	0.21	0.24	32
33	....	None Since Public			...	Nil	....	6.20	71.6	100	9-30-95	....	...	★23115	Dc	d0.06	d0.01	d0.14	d2.17	....	d1.67	9 Mo Sep	d0.34	0.16	33
34	....	None Since Public			...	Nil	....	62.2	79.8	14.4	9-30-95	5.43	...	7905	Dc	...	*0.10	0.19	d1.82	....	0.16	9 Mo Sep	d1.59	0.39	34
35	....	[65]0.01	6-16-95	5-26	[65]0.01	Nil	....	133	172	36.6	9-30-95	405	522	35859	Dc	*d0.04	d3.19	Δ[66]d2.73	[67]d0.81	....	....	9 Mo Sep	d1.04	0.04	35
36◆	1995	h[68]1.57	12-8-95	12-11	h[68]1.57	Nil	....	6.10	6.63	7.78	9-30-95	13.0	...	19978	Mr	...	...	†[69]d0.76	d1.21	....	d1.26	6 Mo Sep	d0.30	d0.35	36
37	....	Terms&trad. basis should			be checked in detail			Wrrts expire 6-25-98				....	...	813	Mr	...	...	...	....	....	....				37
38	....	None Paid			...	Nil	....	Equity per shr $8.91			12-31-94	★2545	...	[70]±108357	Dc	...	...	...	±†[71]0.17	....	....	9 Mo Sep	n/a	0.27	38
39◆	1986	Q0.21	1-12-96	12-26	0.64	0.84	0.52	Equity per shr $9.15			9-30-95	13.4	...	28630	Dc	1.02	1.18	Δ□1.60	2.00	E2.50↑	2.33	9 Mo Sep	1.47	□1.80	39
40◆	1963	Q0.15	1-2-96	12-14	0.60	0.60	0.60	46.1	425	464	9-30-95	5.26	...	23328	Dc	d0.91	Δ0.83	1.15	1.34	E0.90	0.82	9 Mo Sep	0.72	0.20	40
41	....	None Since Public			...	Nil	....	23.4	68.8	52.2	9-30-95	487	...	±10067	Dc	...	...	...	□pd3.40	....	....	16 Wk Sep	n/a	p±d0.13	41
42◆	1983	Q0.08	12-1-95	11-8	0.32	0.32	0.32	Book Value $7.19			12-31-94	....	60	19528	Dc	Δ1.13	1.00	Δd0.17	0.17	....	0.44	9 Mo Sep	0.17	0.44	42
43	1936	Q0.55	3-15-96	2-7	2.05	2.20	1.94	81.0	2356	1974	9-30-95	568	200	65572	Dc	d2.30	□3.09	□3.39	[72]5.05	E6.50↓	6.46	9 Mo Sep	3.56	4.97	43
44	1968	Q1.10	3-15-96	2-7	4.40	4.40	4.40	Cv into 4.40 common				....	100	...	Dc	b0.26	b2.17	...	....	....	....				44
45	1968	Q1.12½	3-15-96	2-7	4.50	4.50	4.50	Cv into 3.724 common				....	100	...	Dc	b0.26	b2.17	...	....	....	....				45
46	1993	0.05	6-15-95	5-24	0.10	Nil	0.20	36.3	50.4	2.48	9-30-95	....	...	18944	Dc	0.52	0.73	0.56	0.49	....	0.21	9 Mo Sep	0.36	0.08	46
47	....	None Since Public			...	Nil	....	14.9	29.8	18.3	9-30-95	4.89	...	3378	Dc	d0.25	2.66	Δd1.23	0.75	....	3.87	9 Mo Sep	d0.14	2.98	47
48◆	1975	Q0.03	11-30-95	11-16	0.12	0.12	0.113	1.09	20.6	6.40	9-30-95	....	...	5420	Mr	Δ0.33	0.44	0.62	0.65	....	0.57	6 Mo Sep	0.36	0.28	48
49◆	....	Wrrt	4-30-93	5-3	...	Nil	....	13.1	42.9	8.12	10-28-95	....	...	10211	Ap	0.04	d0.19	d1.38	Δd0.02	0.83	1.18	6 Mo Oct	0.30	0.65	49
50	....	None Since Public			...	Nil	....	8.37	79.7	37.7	9-30-95	121	100	18546	Dc	0.35	0.15	□d0.49	□0.41	....	0.42	9 Mo Sep	□0.23	0.24	50
51	....	0.015	1-17-77	12-27	...	Nil	....	89.0	279	269	12-31-94	231	...	69176	Dc	*0.79	Δd0.55	Δd0.27	Δd1.95	....	d1.06	9 Mo Sep	d0.28	0.61	51
52	....	None Since Public			...	Nil	....	8.24	10.6	1.55	9-30-95	....	...	2092	Mr	d0.39	d0.47	d0.13	1.25	....	0.97	6 Mo Sep	0.61	0.33	52

◆**Stock Splits & Divs By Line Reference Index** [5]3-for-2,'93:4-for-3,'93. [10]To split 3-for-2,ex Jan 3,'96. [11]1-for-10 REVERSE,'91. [12]3-for-2,'95. [18]No adj for spl $15 dstr,'89. [26]2-for-1,'93. [30]3-for-2,'93. [36]No adj for stk dstr Metromedia Intl,'95. [39]2-for-1,'93. [40]2-for-1,'95. [42]2-for-1,'93. [48]3-for-2,'91,'94. [49]2-for-1,'94.

¶ S&P 500 # MidCap 400 ✣ SmallCap 600 • Options Index	Ticker	Name of Issue (Call Price of Pfd. Stocks)	Market	Com. Rank. & Pfd. Rating	Inst. Hold Cos	Inst. Hold Shs. (000)	Principal Business	Price Range 1971-93 High	1971-93 Low	1994 High	1994 Low	1995 High	1995 Low	Dec. Sales in 100s	December, 1995 Last Sale Or Bid High	Low	Last	%Div Yield	P-E Ratio	Total Return % Annualized 12 Mo	36 Mo	60 Mo
1	TUC	✔Tucker Properties[51]	NY,Ch	NR	53	7642	Real estate investment trust	18⅝	16⅜	18½	11	13⅝	8⅝	4739	9¼	8⅝	8¾	11.4	42	−22.4	...	...
2	TEP	✔Tucson Elec Power[52]	NY,B,Ch,P,Ph	C	90	21576	Electric service, Arizona	65	1	4⅛	2⅞	3¾	2⅝	103488	3¼	3	3¼	...	14	4.0	9.1	−10.8
✣3	TTX	✔Tultex Corp	NY,Ch,P,Ph	C	73	10458	Mfr,mkt sports apparel	16	¼	7⅞	4⅛	6½	4	19370	4¾	4	4⅛	...	13	−10.8	−20.0	−10.5
4•[1]	TBS.A	✔Turner Broadcast'A'[53]	AS,B,Ch,Ph	B−	48	3826	Cable news:TV brdcstg:sports	29¾	1/16	27¾	14½	33½	16	7047	27¼	24⅝	25⅞	0.3	58	59.7	5.9	18.2
5•[1]	TBS.B	✔ Class 'B'(1/5 vtg)	AS,Ph	B−	117	38941		29⅜	2½	27¾	14½	31⅞	16⅛	24867	27⅝	24¾	26	0.3	65	59.3	6.5	18.0
6	TUR	✔Turner Corp	AS	B−	23	1170	Diversified builder,real est	31⅜	2½	9⅝	7¼	11⅞	7¾	1134	9⅜	7¾	8⅜	...	20	−5.6	4.3	−4.5
7•[1]	TVX	✔TVX Gold	NY,To,Ch,Ph,Mo	NR	124	61178	Acq,dvlp precious metals prop	7	1¾	7⅞	5⅛	8¼	5⅝	17873	7⅛	6½	7⅛	...	89	5.6	52.7	...
8•[2]	TW	✔20th Century Indus	NY,Ch,Ph	C	101	19779	Ins hldg:auto/homeowners,Cal	34	1/16	28⅛	8¾	21¼	10⅜	16510	21¼	18	19⅞	...	23	82.8	−9.0	8.6
9	TDI	✔Twin Disc	NY,Ch	B	25	965	Indust'l pwr transmission eqp	35	6	24¼	17	25¼	18⅜	327	23	22	22¾	3.1	11	28.5	8.6	10.1
10	IIVI	✔II-VI Inc	NNM	B−	24	1365	Mfr optical laser components	4½	13/16	4⅝	1½	24	3⅝	10315	13	9⅝	10¾	...	20	174	98.6	47.1
¶11•[3]	TYC	✔Tyco International	NY,B,Ch,P,Ph	B+	495	130602	Fire prot'n sys:cable:solar	32⅞	5/16	27⅝	21¼	35⅝	23¼	66711	35⅝	31⅜	35⅝	0.6	24	52.9	20.4	12.5
✣12•[4]	TTI	✔Tyco Toys	NY,Ph	C	63	16131	Mfr toys:telephones	23⅜	2½	10	5¼	7½	4¼	56372	5½	4¼	4½	...	d	−20.0	−28.2	−2.3
13	TYL	✔Tyler Corp	NY,B,Ch,Ph	C	39	5507	Mfr pipe/sell auto pd/finl svcs	18⅛	1 7/16	6½	3⅛	3⅞	2⅝	4209	3½	2¾	2¾	...	d	−15.4	−15.1	−2.5
#14•[5]	TYSNA	✔Tyson Foods Cl'A'	NNM	A	182	32590	Integrated poultry business	27⅛	1/32	25	18¾	27½	20¾	54076	26½	23¾	26⅛	0.5	17	24.1	2.1	11.4
15•[6]	UAL	✔UAL Corp	NY,B,C,Ch,P,Ph	C	179	11685	Holding:United Airlines	588	26	300	83⅛	211⅞	87⅝	31840	209½	172¾	178½	...	7	104	−10.1	...
16	UCR	✔UCAR International	NY	NR	70	13808	Mfr graphite/carbon electrodes	....	....	....	....	33¾	23¾	9218	33¾	29¾	33¾	...	..	...	...	...
17	UGI	✔UGI Corp	NY,Ph,B,Ch	↓B	132	17539	Holding co:natural gas,Pa	25⅝	4⅝	24½	17⅜	22⅛	18⅞	12485	21½	19¾	20¾	6.7	87	11.0	1.4	8.7
#18•[2]	UJB	✔UJB Financial[57]	NY,B,Ch	A−	211	22707	Comm'l bks,New Jersey,Penn	33½	3⅝	29¼	22½	37¼	24⅛	48894	35¾	33	35⅝	3.6	12	51.0	18.2	42.0
19	ULTK	✔Ultrak Inc	NNM	NR	15	773	Mfr CCTV security equipment	13⅞	15/16	8⅞	4⅜	9⅝	4¾	4064	6¾	4¾	6⅜	...	22	−8.0	2.4	41.7
20•[7]	ULR	✔Ultramar Corp	NY,Ph	NR	204	37163	Refiner/mkt petroleum prod	28½	14⅞	31½	22	28⅝	22½	28799	26⅝	24⅞	25¾	4.3	21	15.6	17.9	...
21•[6]	UTEK	✔Ultratech Stepper	NNM	NR	142	15069	Mfg photolithography eq	10⅛	6¼	20⅞	8¼	47½	17	69983	40	24⅜	25¾	...	22	32.9	...	...
22	UPX	Unapix Entertainment	AS	NR	11	715	Licensor films,TV programs	3⅝	1¾	4¼	2⅝	6	3⅛	3319	6	5⅛	5½	...	26	66.1	...	...
23	WS.B	Wrrt'B'(Pur1 com at$4.50)	AS	....	3	27		¾	¼	⅞	⅜	1¾	⅝	859	1¾	1¼	1 5/16	...	..	...	...	...
✣24	UNC	✔UNC Inc	NY,B,Ch,P,Ph	B−	71	10263	Aviation components,parts,svcs	34¼	2¾	11¾	4⅞	6⅞	4⅝	9602	6	5⅜	6	...	d	2.1	2.9	13.0
25	UNI	✔Uni-Marts Inc	AS	B+	17	717	Operates convenience stores	7¾	2¼	6½	4¾	9⅝	5⅛	1651	9⅛	7⅞	8¼	1.3	13	43.0	43.0	23.4
26	UNAM	✔Unico American	NNM	B	16	1453	Ins co & ins agcy hldg co	8¾	⅝	7⅝	4	6⅝	4⅛	1863	6¼	5⅞	6¼	1.1	8	53.3	18.8	17.7
¶27•[6]	UCM	✔Unicom Corp	NY,B,C,Ch,P,Ph	B	507	128575	Hldg co:Commonwealth Ed	43⅞	16¼	28¾	20⅝	33⅞	23¼	100842	33¼	30¾	32¾	4.9	11	46.8	16.0	0.0
#28•[1]	UFI	✔Unifi, Inc	NY,Ch,Ph	B+	207	45693	Texturizing polyester yarns	38⅜	1/32	27	20½	29⅛	21⅞	26303	24¼	22⅛	22¼	2.3	15	−11.6	−7.2	21.2
29	UNF	✔Unifirst Corp	NY	↑A	57	5875	Operates garment rental svcs	17¼	3¼	17½	11¼	18	11	1646	18	15⅞	18	0.6	18	48.1	11.6	17.5
30	UFX	✔Uniflex Inc	AS	B−	4	12	Mfr plastic bags/pkg prod	7⅞	5/16	7	4⅜	10½	5	335	9¼	8¾	8¾	...	17	52.2	45.1	64.2
31	UGNE	Unigene Laboratories	NNM	C	15	806	Hlth-care oriented biotech R&D	7⅛	7/16	3⅝	2¼	2⅞	1	29422	1¾	1 3/16	1 5/16	...	d	−44.0	−30.3	−3.4
32	ULAB	✔Unilab Corp	NNM	B−	58	17162	Oper clinical testing labs	16⅝	⅝	6⅜	3⅝	5⅞	2¼	63558	3⅛	2¼	2⅝	...	d	−30.7	−25.5	−14.7
33	UL	✔Unilever ADR[61]	NY,B,Ch,P,Ph	NR	41	968	Sister co to Unilver NV	75¼	2¾	74½	58⅜	85¼	71	1999	85¼	79¼	84½	2.2	16	20.2	10.8	12.8
¶34•[8]	UN	✔Unilever N.V.[62]	NY,B,Ch,Ph	A	375	23959	Controls vast int'l enterprise	119¼	5¼	120⅝	100⅛	142⅛	114¼	50425	142⅛	133⅞	140¾	2.4	15	24.4	13.7	12.7
35	UMR	✔Unimar Indonesian Ptc Units	AS,B,Ch	NR	12	407	Indonesian oil venture	11⅝	3½	10	8⅜	10	3⅝	11220	4	3⅝	3⅞	...	..	−45.6	1.9	24.5
36	UMED	✔Unimed Pharmaceuticals	NNM	C	11	856	Ethical drugs/pharmac'l R&D	22¼	5/16	5¼	2	7⅝	2⅜	3787	7⅝	6⅜	6⅝	...	55	179	−12.8	37.0
37	UACA	✔Union Acceptance'A'	NNM	NR	27	2268	Auto loan financing svcs	....	....	....	....	21¼	14	4510	16¾	14	14	...	..	...	...	...
38	UBNK	✔Union Bank[66]	NNM	A−	86	30902	Comm'l bkg,affil Bk of Tokyo	39½	5¾	31½	24¼	57¾	26¾	8438	54⅜	51	54¼	2.6	10	110	27.4	30.1
¶39•[1]	UCC	✔Union Camp	NY,B,Ch,P,Ph	B	496	55808	Paper,pkg,chem,bldg pr,dstr	55⅛	6½	50⅞	42¼	61¼	45¾	51391	49⅞	45¾	47⅝	3.8	7	2.4	4.8	9.4
¶40•[9]	UK	✔Union Carbide	NY,B,C,Ch,P,Ph	NR	511	88212	Chemicals & plastics: gases	33¼	9¾	35⅞	21½	42¾	25½	93573	41⅜	37	37½	2.0	6	28.4	...	...
41	UCO	✔Union Corp	NY,B,Ch,Ph	B	37	3751	A/C rec'v mgt/collect'n svc	27	1 9/16	14⅞	8¾	18¾	12½	1288	18¾	16⅞	18½	...	..	37.0	8.1	−3.7
¶42	UEP	✔Union Electric[68]	NY,B,C,Ch,P,Ph	A−	332	28979	Electricity in Mo,Ill&Iowa	44⅝	8⅞	39½	30¾	42	34⅝	44957	42	39⅞	41¾	6.0	14	27.6	11.4	14.1
¶43•[4]	UNP	✔Union Pacific	NY,B,C,Ch,P,Ph	A−	858	138649	RR,oil/gas,truck'g,RE,min'g	67	5⅞	67⅛	43¾	70⅛	45⅝	131487	70⅛	64½	66	2.6	22	47.2	6.3	16.9
44	UPR	✔Union Pacific Resources Group [10]	NY,Ch	NR	1	2	Oil&gas explor,dvlp,prod'n	....	....	....	....	26¼	21	55751	26¼	23½	25⅜	0.8	..	...	...	...
✣45•[4]	UPC	✔Union Planters	NY,Ch,Ph	B	151	12582	Comml bkg,Memphis, Tenn	30	2½	28⅞	19½	32½	20½	10262	32½	30⅝	31⅞	3.1	11	59.3	13.7	39.6
46	UNSW	✔Union Switch & Signal	NNM	NR	49	2798	Mfr railway signal,ctrl sys	16¼	14¾	22½	12⅞	17	6	3216	7¼	6½	6½	...	10	−50.0	...	...
47•[4]	UTH	✔Union Texas Petroleum	NY,Ch,P	↑B	249	64805	Oil & gas explor,prod'tn	27½	5¾	22	16¼	23⅞	17⅛	68368	19⅞	18	19⅜	1.0	17	−2.2	2.6	6.2
48	UA	Unionamerica Hldgs ADS[70]	NY	NR	..	...	Casualty & property reinsurer	....	....	....	....	17½	16½	26230	17½	16½	17	0.3	..	...	...	...
49	UQM	✔Unique Mobility	AS	C	10	229	R&D electric motor tech	9⅛	2⅝	8⅝	4¾	5⅞	3⅛	3599	4¼	3⅛	3½	...	d	−30.0	−23.7	...
50	UCHM	✔Uniroyal Chemical	NNM	NR	43	11746	Specialty chemicals,elastomers	....	....	....	....	12¼	7¼	27976	8½	7½	8¼	...	2	...	...	...
51	UNSN	✔Unison Software	NNM	NR	21	2108	Dvp/mkt system mgmt software	....	....	....	....	17¾	9	4594	17¾	11¾	17¼	...	43	...	...	...

Uniform Footnote Explanations-See Page 4. Other: [1]CBOE:Cycle 3. [2]CBOE:Cycle 1. [3]Ph:Cycle 1. [4]Ph:Cycle 2. [5]P:Cycle 1. [6]CBOE:Cycle 2. [7]Ph:Cycle 3. [8]ASE:Cycle 2. [9]ASE:Cycle 1. [10]Ph
[51]Bradley Real Estate plan acq. [52]Approve formation of hldg co. [53]Time Warner Inc propose acq, 0.70-0.80 com. [54]®$0.30,'94. [55]Spl dstr & 1-for-2 REVERSE in recap,'94. [56]Fiscal Dec'92 & prior.
[57]Plan name chg,Summit Bank. [58]If com price 133.33% of wrrt - 20 con trad day. [59]Redemption of Pfd Stk Pur Rt. [60]Subsid Pfd. [61]Each Am shr rep 4 ord, 25p. [62]NY Shrs. [63]Approx. [64]To be determined.
[65]Fiscal Sep'92 & prior, 12 Mo Dec $0.67d. [66]Plan mgr,name chge/Union Bank of Cal. [67]®$2.27,'94. [68]Approve mgr w/CIPSCO Inc form Ameren Cp,1 com. [69]84.82% owned by Union Pacific Corp.
[70]Ea ADS rep 1 Ord, $0.0448 par.

Splits ◆	Cash Divs.	Dividends: Latest Payment			Dividends: Total $			Financial Position: Mil-$				Capitalization	Shs. 000		Earnings $ Per Shr.: Years							Interim Earnings	$ per Shr.		
Index	Ea.Yr. Since	Period $	Date	Ex. Div.	So Far 1995	Ind. Rate	Paid 1994	Cash& Equiv.	Curr. Assets	Curr. Liab.	Balance Sheet Date	Lg Trm Debt Mil-$	Pfd.	Com.	End	1991	1992	1993	1994	1995	Last 12 Mos.	Period	1994	1995	Index
1	1994	Q0.25	12-29-95	12-7	1.47	1.00	1.42	Equity per shr $11.76			9-30-95	177	...	10828	Dc	...	p0.44	□0.17	0.73	....	0.21	9 Mo Sep	0.66	0.14	1
2	....	0.40	12-26-89	12-5	...	Nil	....	58.3	209	177	9-30-95	2105	...	160724	Dc	d18.10	d3.86	d0.16	0.13	....	0.24	12 Mo Sep	d0.06	0.24	2
3	1970	0.05	4-1-94	2-28	...	Nil	0.10	4.98	373	52.6	9-30-95	276	152	29824	Dc	Δ0.26	0.56	0.16	0.26	....	0.33	9 Mo Sep	d0.05	□0.02	3
4	1992	Q0.01¾	12-15-95	11-28	0.07	0.07	0.07	84.8	1233	744	9-30-95	2336	12397	±206272	Dc	*±0.06	±*0.13	□±0.27	±□0.16	E0.45	0.38	9 Mo Sep	±□0.07	±0.29	4
5	1992	Q0.01¾	12-15-95	11-28	0.07	0.07	0.07	....	...	...		....	...	137667	Dc	*±0.06	*±0.13	□±0.27	±□0.16	E0.40	0.38	9 Mo Sep	±□0.07	±0.29	5
6	....	0.25	6-6-91	5-20	...	Nil	....	Equity per shr $11.99			9-30-95	95.2	858	5214	Dc	2.06	Δ0.15	d1.55	[54]0.35	....	0.42	9 Mo Sep	0.30	0.37	6
7	....	None Paid			...	Nil	....	122	183	63.9	12-31-94	47.8	...	160023	Dc	0.05	0.08	0.12	0.14	....	0.08	9 Mo Sep	0.12	0.06	7
8◆	1978	0.16	6-5-94	5-13	...	Nil	0.32	Equity per shr $3.93			9-30-95	170	225	51493	Dc	2.02	1.90	Δ2.11	d9.69	E0.85	d0.43	9 Mo Sep	d8.74	0.52	8
9	1934	Q0.17½	12-1-95	11-8	0.70	0.70	0.70	3.76	91.3	39.0	9-30-95	14.0	...	2777	Je	d0.85	0.37	□0.95	1.57	2.03	2.04	3 Mo Sep	0.07	0.08	9
10◆	....	None Paid			...	Nil	....	1.15	11.7	4.05	9-30-95	0.97	...	6115	Je	0.08	0.14	0.02	0.22	0.47	0.54	3 Mo Sep	0.08	0.15	10
11◆	1975	Q0.05	2-1-96	1-2	0.20	0.20	0.20	57.1	1524	1118	9-30-95	507	...	152781	Je	1.29	1.03	□0.79	1.35	□1.44	1.51	3 Mo Sep	0.36	0.43	11
12◆	1992	0.02½	10-1-93	9-9	...	Nil	....	14.0	427	306	9-30-95	147	51	34818	Dc	□1.14	0.60	d2.08	d1.01	Ed0.51↓	d0.74	9 Mo Sep	d0.62	d0.35	12
13◆	....	0.02	2-20-90	1-31	...	Nil	....	1.85	98.3	44.0	9-30-95	72.5	...	19872	Dc	0.06	0.16	□0.07	d0.24	....	d0.23	9 Mo Sep	d0.21	d0.20	13
14◆	1976	Q0.03	3-15-96	2-28	0.09	0.12	0.08	33.1	1520	866	9-30-95	1621	...	±144790	Sp	±1.05	±1.16	±1.22	±d0.01	±1.51	1.51				14
15◆	....	[55]167.62	7-11-94	7-12	...	Nil	[55]167.62	1629	3536	4921	9-30-95	4009	p1981	12667	Dc	d28.62	□d34.68	□d5.28	□0.76	E27.00↓	25.40	9 Mo Sep	□1.25	25.89	15
16	....	None Since Public			...	Nil	....	102	445	185	9-30-95	726	...	45960	Dc	...	...	...	p1.09	....	....	9 Mo Sep	n/a	p1.11	16
17	1885	Q0.35	1-1-96	11-28	1.39	1.40	1.36	142	352	289	6-30-95	820	359	32894	Sp	1.01	[56]1.28	0.94	1.40	P□0.24	0.24				17
18	1935	Q0.32	2-1-96	1-2	1.13	1.28	0.89	Book Value $21.40			9-30-95	204	600	57667	Dc	0.45	1.09	Δ1.42	□2.38	E3.00	2.82	9 Mo Sep	□1.76	2.20	18
19◆	....	None Paid			...	Nil	....	....	42.0	32.4	9-30-95	....	195	7164	Dc	*0.06	*0.12	0.10	0.36	....	0.30	9 Mo Sep	0.32	0.26	19
20	1992	Q0.27½	12-14-95	11-16	1.10	1.10	1.10	79.1	603	361	9-30-95	654	...	★44394	Dc	p2.57	p1.47	2.23	1.56	E1.22	0.72	9 Mo Sep	1.52	Δ0.68	20
21◆	....	None Since Public			...	Nil	....	153	211	40.5	9-30-95	....	...	19675	Dc	...	...	p0.36	0.65	E1.17	1.01	9 Mo Sep	0.46	0.82	21
22	....	None Since Public			...	Nil	....	Equity per shr $1.75			9-30-95	3.13	1	4901	Dc	Nil	d0.57	d0.75	0.13	....	0.21	9 Mo Sep	0.09	0.17	22
23	....	Terms&trad. basis should			be checked in detail			Wrrts expire 6-22-98				....	...	1093	Dc	...	...	...	....	....	....	Callable at 10¢[58]			23
24	....	[59]0.01	10-26-87	10-13	...	Nil	....	1.27	221	92.9	9-30-95	192	...	18394	Dc	□0.50	0.66	□0.67	d3.89	....	d0.80	9 Mo Sep	d2.99	0.10	24
25	1987	Q0.02¾	1-18-96	12-22	0.11	0.11	0.10	6.15	27.7	27.7	6-29-95	33.2	...	6307	Sp	±0.36	±0.24	±0.45	±0.54	P±0.66	0.66				25
26	1991	A0.07	8-14-95	7-27	0.07	0.07	0.07	Equity per shr $4.91			9-30-95	3.67	...	5958	Mr	0.90	d1.17	0.58	0.63	....	0.83	6 Mo Sep	0.25	0.45	26
27	1890	Q0.40	2-1-96	12-27	1.60	1.60	1.60	0.61	1977	2105	9-30-95	7026	[60]24568	214821	Dc	0.08	2.08	Δ0.17	1.66	E3.10↑	3.19	12 Mo Sep	d0.31	3.19	27
28◆	1990	Q0.13	11-10-95	11-1	0.46	0.52	0.48	160	515	204	9-24-95	230	...	66296	Je	1.08	1.04	1.87	1.08	1.67	1.45	3 Mo Sep	0.32	0.10	28
29◆	1979	Q0.02½	1-3-96	12-13	0.10	0.10	0.10	5.89	88.6	57.1	8-26-95	32.4	...	±20511	Au	0.65	□0.70	0.87	0.92	1.01	1.01				29
30◆	....	0.01¼	5-11-90	4-25	...	Nil	....	0.77	8.98	2.51	10-31-95	3.00	...	2396	Ja	0.04	0.25	□0.36	0.43	....	0.53	9 Mo Oct	0.34	0.44	30
31	....	None Paid			...	Nil	....	0.01	0.52	5.23	6-30-95	1.76	...	23092	Dc	d0.17	d0.16	d0.19	d0.32	....	d0.47	9 Mo Sep	d0.19	d0.34	31
32	....	None Paid			...	Nil	....	3.40	64.2	48.8	9-30-95	82.5	...	±35974	Dc	*d0.10	□d2.59	0.15	±0.12	....	d0.98	9 Mo Sep	±0.12	±□d0.98	32
33	1937	0.461	12-29-95	11-24	1.816	1.82	2.027	1488	9806	7052	j12-31-94	2065	...	814480	Dc	Δ4.34	4.90	4.18	5.28	E5.40↓	5.69	9 Mo Sep	3.65	4.06	33
34	1955	[63]0.796	12-20-95	11-15	[63]3.396	3.40	[63]2.752	1626	10657	7959	12-31-94	2541	940	160041	Dc	Δ7.23	8.16	6.62	8.92	E9.30↓	9.59	9 Mo Sep	6.09	6.76	34
35	1985	0.40	11-29-95	11-10	1.82	[64]....	1.72	7.18	36.5	33.8	6-30-95	....	...	10779	Ptc units terminate Sept 25'99										35
36	....	None Since Public			...	Nil	....	7.87	13.8	5.52	9-30-95	....	...	6244	Dc	d0.13	[65]d0.79	d0.14	0.01	....	0.12	9 Mo Sep	d0.05	0.06	36
37	....	None Since Public			...	Nil	....	Book Value $4.73			9-30-95	110	...	±13206	Je	...	...	...	p0.53	n/a	....	3 Mo Sep	n/a	0.39	37
38	1957	Q0.35	1-5-96	12-6	1.40	1.40	1.40	Book Value $33.84			9-30-95	415	5400	36523	Dc	2.64	2.87	2.11	1.80	E5.30	4.82	9 Mo Sep	0.82	3.84	38
39	1940	Q0.45	12-13-95	11-30	1.66	1.80	1.56	43.3	1084	622	9-30-95	1203	...	70217	Dc	1.80	□Δ0.61	0.72	□1.67	E6.55↓	6.08	9 Mo Sep	□0.84	5.25	39
40◆	1918	Q0.18¾	12-1-95	11-14	0.75	0.75	0.75	109	1614	1285	12-31-94	899	16400	137261	Dc	d0.22	□1.27	□1.00	[67]2.44	E6.30	6.11	9 Mo Sep	1.44	5.11	40
41	....	7½%Stk	12-16-83	11-14	...	Nil	....	37.6	49.0	21.8	9-30-95	20.7	...	5581	Je	1.21	0.28	0.71	Δ0.72	0.09	0.11	3 Mo Sep	0.17	0.19	41
42	1906	Q0.62½	12-28-95	12-4	2.45½	2.50	2.395	75.0	589	544	9-30-95	1775	3435	102124	Dc	3.01	2.83	2.77	3.01	E2.91	2.86	12 Mo Sep	2.88	2.86	42
43◆	1900	Q0.43	1-2-96	12-20	1.72	1.72	1.63	91.0	1095	2557	9-30-95	6546	...	205581	Dc	■0.31	3.57	□3.43	2.66	E3.05↓	4.42	9 Mo Sep	1.41	3.17	43
44	....	Plan qtly div			...	0.20	....	19.7	357	1059	p6-30-95	216	...	[69]★243692	Dc	...	...	...	p1.33	....	....	6 Mo Jun	n/a	p0.43	44
45	1987	Q0.25	11-17-95	11-2	0.98	1.00	0.88	Book Value $17.72			9-30-95	409	p3152	41329	Dc	1.59	2.10	Δ□2.69	1.25	E3.02	1.90	9 Mo Sep	1.72	2.37	45
46	....	None Since Public			...	Nil	....	2.52	119	51.0	9-29-95	52.0	...	9738	Dc	...	p0.42	Δp0.60	0.93	....	0.66	9 Mo Sep	0.60	0.33	46
47	1988	Q0.05	11-15-95	10-27	0.20	0.20	0.20	21.7	169	315	9-30-95	614	...	87611	Dc	Δ2.59	□0.86	□0.35	0.76	E1.15	1.08	9 Mo Sep	0.57	0.89	47
48	....	Plan qtly div			...	0.05	....	Equity per shr $8.54			9-30-95	p40.0	p...	★8292	Dc	...	...	...	pd0.76	....	....	9 Mo Sep	n/a	□p0.81	48
49	....	None Since Public			...	Nil	....	1.76	3.59	1.02	7-31-95	0.83	...	10587	Oc	d0.13	d0.33	d0.28	d0.35	....	d0.19	9 Mo Jul	d0.23	d0.07	49
50	....	None Since Public			...	Nil	....	29.5	406	246	10-01-95	910	42	24150	Sp	...	...	...	pd7.78	□5.32	5.32				50
51	....	None Since Public			...	Nil	....	20.0	23.2	6.53	8-31-95	1.27	...	7458	My	0.06	0.07	d0.29	0.11	0.29	0.40	6 Mo Nov	0.07	0.18	51

◆**Stock Splits & Divs By Line Reference Index** [8]2-for-1,'91. [10]2-for-1,'95. [11]2-for-1,'95. [12]2-for-1,'92. [13]No adj for dstr of Akzo Corp,'89:Imperial Chem Indus,'90. [14]2-for-1,'91. [15]1-for-2 REVERSE,'94:No adj for cash dstr:$167.62,'94. [19]1-for-6 REVERSE,'93. [21]2-for-1,'95. [28]5-for-4,'92:3-for-2,'93. [29]2-for-1,'94. [30]2-for-1,'92,'93. [40]No Adj for:spl div'86,stk dstr'92. [43]2-for-1,'91.

¶ S&P 500 # MidCap 400 ✣ SmallCap 600 • Options Index	Ticker	Name of Issue (Call Price of Pfd. Stocks)	Market	Com. Rank. & Pfd. Rating	Inst. Hold Cos	Inst. Hold Shs. (000)	Principal Business	Price Range 1971-93 High	1971-93 Low	1994 High	1994 Low	1995 High	1995 Low	Dec. Sales in 100s	December, 1995 Last Sale Or Bid High	Low	Last	%Div Yield	P-E Ratio	Total Return % Annualized 12 Mo	36 Mo	60 Mo
¶1•[1]	UIS	✓Unisys Corp	NY,B,C,Ch,P,Ph	B–	281	66955	Mfrs business info systems	48⅜	1¾	16½	8¼	11¾	5½	214107	6⅝	5½	5½	...	d	–37.1	–18.4	15.9
2	Pr A	$3.75 cm Cv A Pfd([51]50.375)	NY	B–	106	8615	data process,aerospace prod	81⅝	6	51¼	31¼	43½	24⅛	24176	30½	26⅝	26⅞	14.0	..	...	...	...
3	UNT	✓Unit Corp	NY,Ch	B–	47	8151	Onshore contract drilling,o&g	34	1	3⅞	2⅝	4⅞	2½	9397	4⅞	3⅝	4¾	...	40	65.2	36.3	8.7
4	UAH	✓United Amer Healthcare	NY,Ch,Ph	B	62	2338	Manage HMO's Michigan & Ohio	17⅜	4¾	29½	12½	28½	9⅛	5910	11⅛	9¾	10	...	12	–60.0	4.2	...
5•[2]	UAM	✓United Asset Mgmt	NY,Ch	A	149	19311	Hldg co:instit'l inv mgmt svcvs	47¾	8⅞	41¾	29¾	41½	34¾	17086	39⅝	37¼	38⅜	3.1	18	8.6	12.6	22.3
6	AFP	✓United Capital Corp	AS	↓B–	11	400	Antenna sys/wire prd/R.E.	11½	1¼	12⅝	8⅜	9⅞	6⅝	216	7	6⅝	6⅞	...	d	–19.1	30.9	26.5
7	UCAR	✓United Carolina Bancsh	NNM	A–	52	1760	Comm'l bkg,No Carolina	25¾	2¾	27¾	20½	39	24¼	5579	39	33¾	33¾	3.0	14	45.1	23.7	23.9
✣8	UCIT	✓United Cities Gas	NNM	B+	46	1862	Utility:dstr nat'l & LP gas	21	2⅛	19	15	19¾	14¼	5689	19¾	16¼	18¾	5.4	24	28.9	11.3	14.5
9•[3]	UCFC	✓United Cos Financial	NNM	B+	108	11274	Insurance: consumer loans	18½	11/16	21⅞	11	37⅜	11⅜	25499	34½	25½	26⅜	0.8	14	106	92.5	56.9
10	UDCI	✓United Dental Care	NNM	NR	36	2064	Dental healthcare svcs	....	....	....	....	41¾	22	13553	41¾	34¼	41¼	...	62	...	...	...
11	UDI	✓United Dominion Indus	NY,To,B,Mo	B	87	10800	Ind'l engin'g,mfg & constr	115⅜	6¾	22¾	17⅛	25⅛	17⅜	1564	23	21¼	21⅝	0.9	12	14.9	40.3	23.8
12	UDR	✓United Dominion Rlty Tr	NY,Ch	NR	140	24442	Real estate investment trust	16⅞	1 7/16	15⅞	12¼	15⅜	13	19183	15	14	15	6.0	29	13.0	13.7	23.0
13	UFCS	✓United Fire & Casualty	NNM	B+	33	1253	Fire/casualty insur:life	28⅝	⅞	29⅞	24	43¾	26¾	561	43¾	35¾	42	2.1	10	55.3	18.4	26.1
14	UFD.B	✓United Foods Cv[53] Cl'B'	AS,B,P	B–	11	890	Frozen vegetables & fruits	5⅝	½	2 7/16	1 9/16	2¾	1⅝	1550	2⅛	1⅝	1 13/16	...	36	–14.7	3.7	2.2
15	UFD.A	Class'A'(1/4 vtg)	AS,B	B–	9	1197		4⅜	9/16	2 7/16	1 9/16	2⅝	1⅝	896	1 15/16	1⅝	1 15/16	...	39	–18.4	4.7	3.6
16	UG	✓United-Guardian Inc	AS,Ch	B–	10	370	Fine chem:pharmac'tls:R&D	14⅞	1¼	5½	1 7/16	2½	1½	1457	2¼	1½	1⅝	...	20	–7.1	–37.4	–20.1
¶17•[4]	UNH	✓United Healthcare	NY,Ph	B	770	157953	Manages health maint svcs	39⅜	11/16	55⅜	37¼	65⅝	34⅛	180235	65⅝	58⅝	65⅜	0.0	30	42.2	32.9	62.7
✣18	UIL	✓United Illuminating	NY,B,Ch,P,Ph	B	119	4960	Elec serv to parts of Conn	45⅞	9	40	28¾	38⅝	29⅜	16319	38⅝	36⅝	37⅜	7.5	11	37.5	3.8	12.1
19	UIC	✓United Industrial	NY,B,Ch	B–	42	4044	Defense:energy sys:plastic pd	24⅞	½	6⅝	4⅛	7¼	4⅜	5271	6⅛	4¾	5¾	3.5	17	23.3	–9.5	–0.1
20	UICI	✓United Insurance	NNM	B	45	4953	Hldg:accident,hlth,life ins	7⅜	⅞	8¾	6¼	19	8½	6398	19	16⅞	18⅞	...	15	123	55.8	53.2
21	UIHIA	✓United Intl Hldgs'A'	NNM	NR	103	13660	Intl multi-channel TV svcs	19⅛	9½	19	12	20¾	12½	24829	15	13	14¾	...	d	–15.7	...	...
22	UMM	✓United Merchants/Mfr	NY,Ch,P,Ph	C	13	939	Mfr/dstr apparel&textiles	32	1/16	½	⅛	⅜	1/16	3797	⅛	1/16	⅛	...	d	–42.9	–34.1	14.7
✣23	UMC	✓United Meridian	NY	NR	91	15972	Oil & gas explor,dvlp,prod'n	19⅞	12⅛	15⅞	11	18¾	10¼	8174	17⅞	16⅝	17⅜	...	d	41.8	...	...
24	UMH	✓United Mobile Homes	AS,Ch	B–	14	206	Own/oper mobile home parks	8¼	1	8½	6¾	10½	7⅛	319	10½	9⅝	9¾	6.2	23	40.3	35.5	40.6
25	UNEWY	✓United News & Media ADR[55]	NNM	NR	5	206	Newspaper,magazine publish	22½	9⅞	21⅝	14½	17¾	14½	53	17½	16⅜	17B	4.5	14	22.7	9.0	15.1
26	UPK	✓United Park City Mns	NY,B,Ch,P	C	3	7	Real estate development	140	3¾	10	5⅝	22½	6⅞	463	14⅞	11⅜	14⅞	...	..	138	16.6	21.5
27	URGI	✓United Retail Group	NNM	NR	39	3815	Sell large-size womens apparel	29¾	9	12½	6½	11⅛	4⅛	9520	5½	4¼	4⅜	...	55	–47.0	–44.6	...
28	AAA	✓U.S.Alcohol Testing of Amer	AS,Ph	NR	20	1368	Mfr breath analyzer products	11	½	6	1 11/16	4	1½	21944	2¼	1 13/16	1⅞	...	d	–51.6	7.7	...
29	Pr	14% Cl'A'cm Cv Pfd(NC)	AS	NR	..	...		48¼	3¼	25	9	17	8½	6	9½	8⅝	8½B	8.2	..	...	...	...
¶30•[5]	USBC	✓U.S. Bancorp	NNM,Ph	A	336	59127	Comml bkg,Oregon,Wash	28⅞	1⅞	28⅝	22⅛	36	22	134771	36	31½	33⅝	3.3	12	56.5	13.5	24.4
✣31	UBS	✓U.S. Bioscience	AS,Ch,Ph	NR	67	6362	Dvlp stge:anti-cancer drugs	44	3¼	10⅜	1⅝	5¾	2	83793	5½	3⅝	4¾	...	d	49.0	–24.7	–13.3
32	WS	Wrrt(Pur 1 com at$9.20)	AS	....	14	60		....	....	....	....	2 1/16	⅜	2405	2 1/16	¾	1⅝	...	..	...	...	...
33	USC	✓U.S. Can	NY,Ch,Ph	NR	94	9521	Mfr steel packaging containers	17⅛	11¼	19½	15	23¼	11	5546	14¼	12⅜	13½	...	15	–30.8	...	...
34	USM	✓U.S. Cellular	AS,Ch,Ph	NR	100	13936	Oper cellular telephone sys	41⅜	12¾	35¼	22⅜	36½	27¾	7088	35	32⅞	33¾	...	35	3.1	16.7	11.6
35	DLV	✓U.S. Delivery Systems	NY,Ch	NR	61	3692	Same-day delivery, dstr svcs	....	....	17⅝	10	31½	13⅝	17083	29½	23¼	29	...	..	111	...	...
✣36•[6]	USF	✓U.S. Filter	NY,Ph	B–	96	11349	Wastewater treatment equip	125⅜	1 9/16	16⅛	12⅛	27	14⅞	39272	27	21¾	26⅝	...	39	67.7	16.5	53.6
¶37•[1]	USHC	✓U.S. HealthCare	NNM,Ph	B+	636	105141	Health maintenance programs	40⅜	½	49	33¾	47½	26½	225240	46½	42¾	46½	2.4	19	14.7	...	...
38	UH	✓U.S. Home	NY	NR	81	8401	Builder-developer	29	19	29½	14	29¼	14¾	12680	29¼	26	29⅛	...	10	80.6	...	...
39	Pr	Cv non-cm Pfd (25)	NY	NR	3	166		28¾	19½	29	14⅜	26⅞	15⅜	5	26½	26½	29⅛B	...	..	...	...	...
40	WS	Wrrt(Pur 1 com at $20)	NY	....	12	104		16	6½	14⅞	4¼	11½	4¾	2323	11½	9½	11	...	..	...	...	...
41•[6]	USN	✓U.S. Industries	NY	NR	196	28253	Mfr consumer/industrial prd	....	....	....	....	18⅜	12⅝	31442	18⅜	15⅞	18⅜	...	d	...	...	...
42	USLM	✓U.S. Lime & Minerals	NNM	B–	10	469	Mine,sell limestone/lime prd	10¾	1 7/16	6¼	4¼	8¾	5½	329	8¾	8	8¾	1.1	9	60.8	39.6	17.9
43•[2]	USLD	✓U.S. Long Distance	NNM	NR	101	5158	Long distance services	22⅛	1 9/16	14⅝	8⅝	17⅞	10⅞	41309	14⅞	12¾	14	...	17	14.3	–9.5	41.8
44	OFIS	✓U.S. Office Products	NNM	NR	53	6098	Office products supplier	....	....	....	....	24⅞	10	73345	24⅞	16¼	22¾	...	..	...	...	...
45	USV	✓U.S. Restaurant[60] Properties	NY,B,Ch	NR	14	143	Leases prpty to Burger King	24⅜	10⅛	17½	13	20¼	14¼	1243	20⅛	19⅜	19¾	8.6	19	45.0	17.2	16.3
#46•[7]	USRX	✓U.S. Robotics	NNM	B+	302	32009	Mfr data communic prod/sys	17⅝	6⅛	23	12	110½	19⅝	159588	110½	73	87¾	...	57	322	102	...
¶47•[1]	USS	✓U.S. Surgical	NY,Ch,Ph	B+	276	29786	Surgical stapling devices	134½	⅜	32½	15⅞	27¾	18¾	69641	25¼	21¼	21¼	0.4	20	10.8	–31.7	–8.9
48	Pr A	$2.20'A'[63]Dep[64]'DECS'([65]20.50)	[8]NY,Ch	NR	35	7826		....	....	30¾	22	30⅜	22¾	3904	28⅝	25	25¼	8.7	..	...	...	...
✣49	USTC	✓U.S. Trust[66]	NNM	A–	69	4639	Banking/financial svcs	59¾	4¾	66	49½	81⅜	42	5049	49¾	47¼	49¾	...	16	...	...	...
¶50•[1]	USW	✓U S West Communic Grp	NY,B,Ch,P,Ph	B+	849	211030	Tel svc:Mtn St,NW,Pac NW	50¾	13¾	46¼	34⅝	48⅜	28⅜	212862	36⅜	31⅛	35⅝	6.0	15	...	...	...
¶51	UMG	✓U S West Media Group	NY,P	NR	..	...	Cable/telecommunic svcs	....	....	....	....	20	17⅜	283800	19¾	17⅞	19	...	95	...	...	...
52	XPRSA	✓U.S. Xpress Enterprises'A'	NNM	NR	26	1975	Transport'n svcs/trucking	....	....	15¾	10⅛	13⅞	6¾	6354	9⅛	7	7¼	...	19	–37.0	...	...

Uniform Footnote Explanations-See Page 4. Other: [1]ASE:Cycle 1. [2]P:Cycle 2. [3]Ph:Cycle 2. [4]ASE,CBOE,NY,Ph:Cycle 1. [5]ASE,P:Cycle 1. [6]CBOE:Cycle 1. [7]ASE,CBOE:Cycle 2. [8]Ph
[51]Thru 6-1-96,scale to $50 in '96. [52]Incl $0.1278 non-taxable:©$0.0035,'94. [53]Cv into 1 Cl'A'. [54]10 Mo Dec'91. [55]Each ADR rep 2 ord shrs,25p. [56]Telephone Data Sys own 79.9% of com. [57]®$2.50,'94.
[58]Divd restr'n to 6-21-95,re-specified cond. [59]Auto cv if com price greater $30-20 trd'g days. [60]L.P. Dep Units. [61]Redemption of Stk Purch Rt. [62]®$1.02,'94. [63]Dep for 0.02 shr Sr'A'Cv Pfd.
[64]Fr 4-1-97:$20.50 in com & $0.55 div,re-spec cond. [65]Divd Enhanced Cv Stock. [66]No adj for stk dstr of Chase Manhattan Bk. [67]Stk dstr of Chase Manhattan Bk. [68]To be determined. [69]®$2.09,'94.
[70]Dstr of 1 com-Media Group sh of US West,'95. [71]Pfd in $M.

Splits ◆	Dividends							Financial Position				Capitalization			Earnings $ Per Shr.							Interim Earnings			
	Cash Divs.	Latest Payment			Total $			Mil-$			Balance	Lg Trm	Shs. 000		Years						Last		$ per Shr.		
Index	Ea.Yr. Since	Period $	Date	Ex. Div.	So Far 1995	Ind. Rate	Paid 1994	Cash& Equiv.	Curr. Assets	Curr. Liab.	Sheet Date	Debt Mil-$	Pfd.	Com.	End	1991	1992	1993	1994	1995	12 Mos.	Period	1994	1995	Index
1	....	0.25	8-7-90	6-18	...	Nil	....	820	2952	2243	9-30-95	1534	28405	171397	Dc	d9.37	*1.06	Δ□1.46	□d0.07	Ed0.45	d0.69	9 Mo Sep	□0.40	d0.22	1
2	1986	Q0.93¾	1-15-96	12-22	3.75	3.75	a7.03⅛	Cv into 1.67 com,$29.97				....	28405	...	Dc	b0.41	b1.38	b1.66	b0.96	....	....				2
3	....	None Since Public			...	Nil	....	1.08	13.8	10.7	9-30-95	40.4	...	20976	Dc	*0.14	0.05	0.19	0.23	....	0.12	9 Mo Sep	0.20	0.09	3
4◆	....	None Since Public			...	Nil	....	12.0	20.8	5.77	9-30-95	8.72	...	6561	Je	0.83	0.73	0.73	1.13	1.01	0.84	3 Mo Sep	0.39	0.22	4
5	1986	Q0.30	1-12-96	12-27	1.12	1.20	0.96	96.4	225	156	9-30-95	674	...	30329	Dc	1.30	1.56	1.85	2.00	E2.15	2.08	9 Mo Sep	1.49	1.57	5
6	....	None Paid			...	Nil	....	1.51	27.5	34.5	9-30-95	45.6	...	5606	Dc	0.40	0.44	0.70	0.48	....	d0.51	9 Mo Sep	0.65	d0.34	6
7	1971	Q0.25	11-8-95	10-27	0.97	1.00	0.84	Book Value $19.79			9-30-95	2.98	...	14769	Dc	1.65	2.01	Δ2.27	□2.05	....	2.45	9 Mo Sep	□1.85	2.25	7
8	1955	Q0.255	12-15-95	11-28	1.02	1.02	1.00½	1.49	67.2	101	9-30-95	137	...	12665	Dc	0.97	1.07	1.19	1.16	....	0.79	12 Mo Sep	1.24	0.79	8
9◆	1974	Q0.05	1-2-96	12-13	0.19½	0.20	0.181	Equity per shr $12.37			9-30-95	233	...	28142	Dc	0.58	0.51	0.50	1.74	....	1.89	9 Mo Sep	1.53	1.68	9
10	....	None Since Public			...	Nil	....	47.5	50.7	10.1	9-30-95	2.47	...	6898	Dc	...	...	...	p0.44	E0.67	....	9 Mo Sep	n/a	p□0.45	10
11◆	1987	tQ0.05	12-29-95	11-29	0.20	0.20	t0.20	66.1	656	330	9-30-95	451	...	39618	Dc	0.79	0.61	0.97	1.55	....	1.77	9 Mo Sep	1.14	1.36	11
12◆	1973	Q0.22½	1-31-96	1-10	0.87	0.90	[52]0.76	Equity per shr $7.39			9-30-95	527	4200	★56346	Dc	□0.14	□0.19	0.29	□0.41	....	0.52	9 Mo Sep	0.30	0.41	12
13◆	1968	Q0.22½	1-5-96	12-14	0.80	0.90	0.72	Equity per shr $27.17			9-30-95	....	...	7220	Dc	□2.17	0.23	2.58	3.12	....	4.11	9 Mo Sep	1.79	2.78	13
14	....	0.20	5-30-90	5-15	...	Nil	....	0.75	76.8	30.1	8-31-95	40.7	...	±11797	Fb	±Nil	□±d0.02	±0.01	±0.19	....	0.05	6 Mo Aug	±0.12	±d0.02	14
15	....	0.22½	5-30-90	5-15	...	Nil	....	....	...	...		....	...	5915	Fb	±Nil	□±d0.02	±0.01	±0.19	....	0.05	6 Mo Aug	±0.12	±d0.02	15
16	....	5%Stk	5-22-84	4-17	...	Nil	....	0.20	3.81	0.86	9-30-95	0.76	...	4763	Dc	*[54]0.06	Δ0.08	0.10	0.03	....	0.08	9 Mo Sep	0.01	0.06	16
17◆	1990	A0.03	4-15-95	3-28	0.03	0.03	0.03	1584	1894	736	9-30-95	....	...	174696	Dc	0.60	0.82	1.24	Δ1.64	E2.15	2.03	9 Mo Sep	Δ1.16	1.55	17
18	1900	Q0.70½	1-1-96	12-5	2.80½	2.82	2.73½	42.6	186	235	9-30-95	848	110	14097	Dc	Δ3.14	3.76	2.57	□3.18	....	3.32	9 Mo Sep	□3.04	3.18	18
19	1968	Q0.05	11-30-95	10-30	0.26	0.20	0.28	8.62	78.9	44.7	9-30-95	18.7	...	12171	Dc	0.77	0.52	□Δd0.98	0.43	....	0.34	9 Mo Sep	0.33	0.24	19
20◆	....	None Since Public			...	Nil	....	Equity per shr $5.92			9-30-95	27.7	...	38057	Dc	0.63	0.92	0.88	0.96	....	1.29	9 Mo Sep	0.69	1.02	20
21◆	....	None Since Public			...	Nil	....	Equity per shr $4.48			8-31-95	★303	...	±★38327	Fb	...	pd0.79	pd0.68	±d1.10	....	d2.03	6 Mo Aug	±d0.29	±d1.22	21
22	....	0.10	12-29-76	12-2	...	Nil	....	0.81	27.4	16.6	9-30-95	84.6	450	17845	Je	d6.25	Δd2.23	d1.67	Δ□d1.30	d1.82	d1.10	3 Mo Sep	d0.29	0.43	22
23	....	None Since Public			...	Nil	....	21.9	91.3	102	9-30-95	★366	833	28093	Dc	...	□p1.22	pd0.25	d3.47	....	d3.20	9 Mo Sep	d0.22	0.05	23
24	1990	Q0.15	3-15-96	2-13	0.525	0.60	0.42½	Equity per shr $1.62			9-30-95	....	...	5757	Dc	0.14	0.21	0.26	0.40	....	0.42	9 Mo Sep	0.29	0.31	24
25	1987	0.251	12-11-95	10-13	0.767	0.77	0.728	69.8	267	246	j12-31-94	160	...	244444	Dc	Δ1.01	1.21	1.34	1.21	....	1.21				25
26◆	....	None Paid			...	Nil	....	Equity per shr $5.74			9-30-95	....	...	2700	Dc	d1.00	d1.00	d0.60	d0.20	....	0.07	9 Mo Sep	d0.19	0.08	26
27	....	None Since Public			...	Nil	....	10.8	75.9	38.8	10-28-95	12.6	...	12190	Ja	p0.66	d0.04	0.12	0.22	....	0.08	9 Mo Oct	0.06	d0.08	27
28◆	....	None Since Public			...	Nil	....	2.06	5.88	2.16	9-30-95	0.07	41	30314	Mr	d0.66	d0.68	d0.46	d0.28	....	d0.29	6 Mo Sep	d0.12	d0.13	28
29	1991	S0.35	1-5-96	12-19	0.70	0.70	0.70	Cv into 4.5 com				....	374	...	Mr	...	...	...	....	....	....				29
30◆	1899	Q0.28	1-2-96	12-6	1.03	1.12	0.91	Book Value $18.49			9-30-95	★1122	6000	97499	Dc	2.01	□2.05	2.47	1.40	E2.80	2.75	9 Mo Sep	0.77	2.12	30
31◆	....	None Since Public			...	Nil	....	15.3	19.4	8.08	9-30-95	★19.3	...	★42037	Dc	d0.18	d0.51	d1.03	d0.60	....	d0.45	9 Mo Sep	d0.46	d0.31	31
32	....	Terms&trad. basis should			be checked in detail			Wrrts expire 4-24-98				....	...	...	Dc	...	...	...	....	....	....				32
33	....	None Since Public			...	Nil	....	0.16	144	91.4	10-01-95	229	...	12738	Dc	...	□p0.54	□1.16	1.73	....	0.93	9 Mo Sep	1.41	0.61	33
34	....	None Since Public			...	Nil	....	59.0	148	116	9-30-95	344	...	[56]±82991	Dc	□d0.63	0.11	d0.45	0.21	....	0.97	9 Mo Sep	0.19	0.95	34
35	....	None Since Public			...	Nil	....	3.27	48.8	23.4	9-30-95	31.9	...	12597	Dc	...	...	p0.45	p0.71	....	....	9 Mo Sep	n/a	0.69	35
36◆	....	None Paid			...	Nil	....	88.8	305	117	9-30-95	209	1020	25516	Mr	d0.71	Δ0.33	0.41	0.51	....	0.68	6 Mo Sep	0.18	0.35	36
37◆	1985	Q0.27½	12-21-95	12-5	1.02½	1.10	0.723	1173	1355	645	9-30-95	....	...	±153531	Dc	±0.92	±1.23	±1.84	±2.42	E2.40	2.44	9 Mo Sep	±1.75	±1.77	37
38	....	None Since Public			...	Nil	....	Equity per shr $27.56			9-30-95	289	328	11234	Dc	...	p1.29	6.16	[57]2.89	E3.07	3.06	9 Mo Sep	2.05	2.22	38
39	....	None Since Public			...	[58]Nil	....	Cv into 1 com[59]				....	891	...	Dc	...	...	...	....	....	....				39
40	....	Terms&trad. basis should			be checked in detail			Wrrts expire 6-21-98				....	...	1905	Dc	...	...	...	....	....	....				40
41	....	None Since Public			...	Nil	....	51.0	981	535	9-30-95	834	...	53671	Sp	...	...	...	p1.60	pd1.84	d1.84				41
42	1995	0.02½	12-11-95	11-29	0.075	0.10	....	0.26	11.9	6.69	9-30-95	4.67	...	3836	Dc	d0.25	2.47	0.01	0.50	....	0.99	9 Mo Sep	0.40	0.89	42
43◆	....	None Since Public			...	Nil	....	23.6	127	105	6-30-95	15.2	...	13578	Sp	*0.06	*0.21	□0.43	0.43	P0.83	0.83				43
44	....	None Since Public			...	Nil	....	26.5	116	71.5	p7-31-95	15.4	...	p15581	Ap	...	...	...	p0.31	p0.34	....	6 Mo Oct	n/a	d0.16	44
45	1986	0.43	12-14-95	12-4	1.69	1.69	1.56	Equity per shr $9.81			9-30-95	5.35	...	4659	Dc	0.85	0.53	0.96	1.04	....	1.07	9 Mo Sep	0.81	0.84	45
46◆	1995	[61]0.00½	3-14-95		[61]0.00½	Nil	....	95.0	297	93.9	4-02-95	65.2	...	40498	Sp	0.39	0.50	0.71	Δ[62]1.03	P1.55	1.55				46
47◆	1985	Q0.02	12-8-95	11-29	0.08	0.08	0.08	10.3	493	244	9-30-95	211	177	57079	Dc	1.58	2.32	d2.48	0.08	E1.05↑	0.81	9 Mo Sep	0.06	0.79	47
48	1994	Q0.55	1-2-96	11-29	2.20	2.20	0.55	Cv into 0.953 com,$21.50				....	...	8870	Dc	...	...	...	....	....	....	Mandatory conversion into one com 4-1-98			48
49◆	1854	Q0.25	1-25-96	1-8	h[67]1.50	[68]....	1.97	Book Value $25.91			6-30-95	57.2	...	9661	Dc	3.32	□3.76	4.26	[69]2.12	E3.20	d7.77	9 Mo Sep	3.68	d6.21	49
50	1984	Q0.53½	2-1-96	1-18	h[70]2.14	2.14	2.14	43.0	2214	4968	p6-30-95	4252	50	470810	Dc	1.38	□2.86	□0.94	p2.53	E2.35	2.52	6 Mo Jun	p1.30	□p1.29	50
51	....	None Since Public			...	Nil	....	44.0	697	2662	6-30-95	374	[71]51	471395	Dc	...	...	...	p0.61	E0.20	0.43	6 Mo Jun	p0.26	p0.08	51
52	....	None Since Public			...	Nil	....	6.37	46.1	35.4	3-31-95	46.2	...	±11982	Mr	Δ0.20	0.19	0.63	0.76	....	0.38	6 Mo Sep	0.40	0.02	52

◆**Stock Splits & Divs By Line Reference Index** [4]5-for-4,'93. [9]15%,'91:10%,'94:2-for-1,'93,'95. [11]Adj for 2.9%,'91. [12]2-for-1,'93. [13]3-for-2,'92,'95:To split 3-for-2,ex Jan 8. [17]2-for-1,'92,'94. [20]2-for-1,'92:4-for-1,'95. [21]2-for-1,'94. [26]1-for-20 REVERSE,'95. [28]3-for-2,'91,'92. [30]3-for-2,'91. [31]2-for-1,'92. [36]1-for-75 REVERSE,'91:3-for-2,'94. [37]3-for-2,'91,'92,'94. [43]1-for-3 REVERSE,'91. [46]2-for-1,'95. [47]2-for-1,'91. [49]No adj for stk dstr of Chase Manhattan Bk.

¶ S&P 500 # MidCap 400 ✣ SmallCap 600 • Options Index	Ticker	Name of Issue (Call Price of Pfd. Stocks)	Market	Com. Rank. & Pfd. Rating	Inst. Hold Cos	Inst. Hold Shs. (000)	Principal Business	Price Range 1971-93 High	1971-93 Low	1994 High	1994 Low	1995 High	1995 Low	Dec. Sales in 100s	December, 1995 Last Sale Or Bid High	Low	Last	%Div Yield	P-E Ratio	Total Return % Annualized 12 Mo	36 Mo	60 Mo
1	USTR	✔United Stationers	NNM	B+	41	1993	Wholesaler of office prod	14⅜	2 1/16	7⅞	4⅜	27¾	6¼	2940	27¾	22¼	27¾	...	..	360	53.6	49.4
¶2•[1]	UTX	✔United Technologies	NY,B,C,Ch,P,Ph	B	725	91121	Aerospace,climate ctrl sys	66⅛	5¼	72	55	97¾	62¼	60712	97¾	91¼	94⅞	2.3	17	53.9	29.6	18.5
3	UT	United TransNet	NY	NR	..	...	Ground courier services	....	....	....	....	15⅜	14½	20670	15⅜	14½	15⅛	...	..	...	...	...
4	UVSGA	✔United Video Satellite Gp'A'	NNM	NR	70	3454	Satellite deliver'd prgm svc	17	12¼	25	10½	35⅞	20½	4276	30¾	26¾	27	...	23	17.4	...	...
5	UWR	✔United Water Res	NY,Ch,Ph	B+	76	4613	Hldg co:water util in N.J.	23	2⅜	14¾	12¼	14⅛	11¾	8025	12⅞	11¾	12	7.7	14	0.0	−0.3	7.9
6	UWZ	✔United Wisconsin Svcs	NY,Ch,Ph	NR	71	3154	Group hlth insur/care svcs	43¼	9⅝	39¾	27⅜	44⅜	18½	5931	25⅝	20½	22	2.2	20	−36.6	−7.9	...
7	UNV	✔Unitel Video	AS	↓C	19	975	Videotape rec'g,post-prod svcs	18¾	3¾	9⅜	4⅞	8½	4⅞	1190	6	5⅛	5⅝	...	d	13.7	−27.4	−0.2
8	UTL	✔UNITIL Corp	AS	B+	28	634	Hldg co: elec utility in N.H.	22⅝	6	19⅝	15⅞	21⅜	16	349	21⅜	20¼	20⅞	6.1	11	39.1	12.2	16.1
9•[2]	UNIT	✔Unitrin Inc	NNM	NR	129	11002	Ins hldg:life,accid&hlth,prop	46¾	24½	51½	38½	50½	43	6417	49	46½	48	4.2	13	15.7	8.2	12.8
10	UTR	✔Unitrode Corp	NY,B,Ch,Ph	B−	72	6118	Mfr semiconductor devices	36⅞	¾	21	13½	32½	17⅝	3300	29⅝	26½	28¼	...	21	52.7	36.4	54.1
11	UVX	✔Univar Corp	NY,B,Ch,P	B−	51	3621	Dstr ind'l chemicals	17⅞	1 11/16	14½	9¾	16¼	9⅝	5230	14	9⅝	10⅞	2.8	18	−13.6	0.7	2.7
#12	UVV	✔Univl Corp	NY,B,Ch,Ph	↓B	171	23157	Leaf tobacco/building prod	34¼	1⅜	26¼	17½	24⅝	18⅞	6038	24⅝	23⅜	24⅜	4.2	27	27.6	−6.7	...
#13•[3]	UFC	✔Univl Foods	NY,Ch,P	A	193	18083	Yeast, cheese: spec food prod	40⅜	1 5/16	34⅜	26⅛	41¼	27¼	22790	41¼	34¾	40⅛	2.5	16	50.3	8.9	7.5
✣14	UFPI	✔Univl Forest Products	NNM	NR	32	2112	Mfr,dstr lumber products	11	7	11	5⅞	10⅜	6	4434	9½	8¾	9¼	e0.6	12	38.6	...	...
15	UHT	✔Univl Health Realty	NY,Ch	NR	45	2288	Real estate investment trust	19⅛	8¼	18	15¾	17⅞	15¾	2787	17⅞	16½	17⅞	9.4	12	19.9	16.4	21.7
✣16•[4]	UHS	✔Univl Health Svs Cl'B'[57]	NY,Ph	B	125	9898	Acute care hospitals	29½	3	29⅝	19⅛	44½	22½	4739	44½	39⅝	44⅜	...	19	86.8	44.8	37.2
17	UNO	✔Uno Restaurant Corp	NY	B	53	4863	Operates pizza restaurants	13½	3¼	11⅛	6½	12¾	6⅜	8011	7⅛	6⅜	6⅞	...	12	−28.8	1.1	−3.7
¶18•[5]	UCL	✔Unocal Corp	NY,B,C,Ch,P,Ph	B	648	157459	Oil & gas explor,dvlp,prod'n	34½	3⅜	30¾	24⅜	30½	24¾	163991	29⅞	26⅞	29⅛	2.7	26	10.5	8.2	4.8
19	UNRI	✔UNR Industries	NNM,Ch	↑B	74	10974	Telecom equip/metal fab	15⅞	13/16	7⅛	5⅛	9¾	5¼	26372	9⅜	7⅜	8⅝	2.9	11	94.1	38.2	49.8
¶20•[6]	UNM	✔UNUM Corp	NY,B,Ch,P,Ph	NR	405	51515	Disability ins/emp ben/pens'n	60⅛	7¾	58	35⅛	56½	37⅝	36683	56½	53	55	1.9	14	45.7	3.0	21.1
21	UND	UNUM Corp 8.80% 'MIDS'[59]	NY	....[60]	3	5	Monthly Income Debt Sec	....	....	....	....	27⅛	25	2852	27	26⅛	26⅞	8.2	..	...	...	...
22	UPEN	✔Upper Peninsula Energy	NNM	B+	21	348	Electricity in upper Mich	20¾	5⅛	20¼	15	20½	15¼	699	19½	18	18½	6.8	10	29.8	6.8	14.1
23	URIX	✔Uranium Resources	NNM	B−	22	2737	Uranium exploration & mining	11½	1⅞	7⅝	2⅞	8⅝	2¾	5421	5⅝	5⅛	5½	...	d	−24.1	17.7	1.4
24	URBN	✔Urban Outfitters	NNM	NR	49	2603	Retail/wholesale apparel,gifts	31¾	21	31¼	19¼	28½	18	7507	24½	20¾	23¼	...	18	−18.4	...	...
25	URB	✔Urban Shopping Centers	NY,Ch	NR	61	5432	Real estate investment trust	24⅜	19¾	23⅞	18¾	22½	19¾	2900	21⅞	20⅜	21⅜	9.1	18	14.9	...	...
26•[7]	URO	✔UROHEALTH Systems'A'	AS	NR	12	227	Mfr,mkt medical products	13¾	2⅜	7¾	1⅞	4⅝	1½	12729	3⅛	2 1/16	2⅝	...	d	35.5	−25.6	...
27	WS	Wrrt(Pur 1 Cl'A' com at $5)	AS	....	1	18		8¾	15/16	4	½	1⅞	5/16	1714	15/16	5/16	5/16	...	..	...	...	...
28	URMD	✔UroMed Corp	NNM	NR	62	9067	Dvp stg:mfr urological prod	....	....	8¾	3	13¼	5⅛	24170	13¼	10	12⅞	...	d	140	...	...
29	URS	✔URS Corp	NY,B,Ch,P,Ph	B−	26	3851	Engin'g & architectural svcs	230	2¼	8	4¾	7⅜	5⅛	1616	7⅜	6¾	7	...	10	33.3	−8.0	17.5
30	USRE	✔US Facilities Corp	NNM	B−	50	2661	Insurance holding co	19	1¼	14⅝	8¼	23⅜	9¾	9839	23⅜	20⅜	21⅜	0.9	9	119	33.9	42.9
31	USO	✔US 1 Indus	NY,B,Ch,P	C	9	825	Trucking gen'l commodities	25⅜	⅛	1⅝	⅝	1⅛	¼	3818	11/16	⅜	11/16	...	d	−21.5	22.4	37.3
32	USOR	✔US Order Inc	NNM	NR	41	3891	Mfr network commun products	....	....	....	....	26½	13¼	19596	23¼	18¾	22⅜	...	d	...	...	...
33	USRV	US SerVis	NNM	C	15	291	Hlth mgmt sys softwr/hardwr	25⅝	⅞	6¼	2⅝	5¾	2¾	4395	4⅝	3⅝	3⅝	...	d	16.0	−38.4	−19.7
34	USAD	✔USA Detergents	NNM	NR	29	1545	Mfr laundry/hshld cleaning prd	....	....	....	....	28½	14½	5748	26¼	21⅜	23½	...	46	...	...	...
35	USAK	✔USA Truck	NNM	NR	31	2060	General commodities truck'g	19	6¼	20¼	14½	17¾	10½	4444	11¾	10¾	10¾	...	16	−25.9	1.1	...
✣36•[2]	UW	✔USA Waste Service	NY,Ch,Ph	NR	128	18615	Non-hazard solid waste mgmt	18½	1⅜	15⅛	10⅜	22½	10	102695	21½	17	18⅞	...	11	64.1	10.5	28.3
¶37•[8]	U	✔USAir Group	NY,B,C,Ch,Ph	C	213	27855	Hldg:major airline carrier	54¾	3¼	15⅜	3⅞	15⅞	4¼	122952	13⅞	11¾	13¼	...	27	231	1.6	−3.6
38	PrB	$4.375 'B' cm Cv[64]DepPfd[65]	NY,Ch,Ph	C	21	2840		70	27½	55	12¾	46½	15⅜	3035	41¾	37⅛	41⅛	...	..	...	...	...
¶39•[9]	FG	✔USF&G Corp	NY,B,C,Ch,P,Ph	B−	347	61796	Hldg co:multiline insurer	48¾	5⅝	16⅛	11⅝	19½	13⅜	71387	17⅞	16⅝	16⅞	1.2	13	25.4	14.8	21.4
40	Pr A	$4.10cmCv[68]ExchAPfd([69]50.82)	NY,Ch	BB−	32	526		62	26⅜	51¾	41⅞	52⅞	43⅝	361	52⅞	50½	51¼	8.0	..	...	...	...
41•[10]	USG	✔USG Corp	NY	NR	174	29056	Gypsum base bldg products	30½	9⅝	36	17¼	31⅜	19¼	43154	31⅜	27	30	...	d	57.9	...	...
42	WS	Wrrt(Pur 1com at$16.14)	NY	....	20	218		17⅜	3	21¼	7¾	17⅛	8	2891	17⅛	13	15¼	...	..	...	...	...
¶43	USH	✔USLIFE Corp	NY,B,C,Ch,P,Ph	B+	278	21785	Hldg:life insur	30½	3¼	27⅝	20⅝	32	22⅝	15831	32	28⅛	29⅞	3.1	10	34.8	10.3	23.3
44	USMX	✔USMX Inc	NNM	B−	22	3338	Mineral exploration,mining	10⅜	½	4¾	2⅜	2⅞	1¾	6004	2	1¾	2	...	d	−23.1	−9.8	7.4
45	USTB	✔UST Corp	NNM	B−	69	4976	Comm'l bkg,Massachusetts	28⅝	2¼	14⅜	8¾	15½	9¾	18264	15½	14	14½	...	22	53.2	14.8	19.1
¶46•[1]	UST	✔UST Inc	NY,B,Ch,P	A+	570	115338	Snuff,tobacco,wine,spirits	35⅜	7/16	31½	23⅝	36	26½	106577	36	32¼	33⅜	4.4	16	26.0	5.3	17.6
47•[7]	DGP	✔USX-Delhi Group	NY,Ph	NR	66	5262	Natural gas gathering svcs	24¾	13½	17⅞	9⅝	13⅛	8	15987	10⅝	9½	10¼	2.0	..	5.8	−13.0	...
¶48•[7]	MRO	✔USX-Marathon Grp	NY,B,C,Ch,P,Ph,Mo	NR	510	192621	Oil&gas explor,devel,prod'n	50	14½	19⅛	15⅝	21½	15¾	153618	20⅛	18⅜	19½	3.5	16	21.5	7.9	−4.6
¶49•[7]	X	✔USX-U.S. Steel Group	NY,Ch,Ph	NR	375	53709	Integrated steel producer	46	20	45⅝	30¼	39⅛	29⅛	74415	33½	30	30¾	3.3	8	−11.0	−0.2	...
50	Pr A	6.50% cm Cv Pfd([74]52.275)	NY	BB−	40	1867		61½	46⅞	59⅞	44	50⅛	43¼	3692	48½	46¼	47⅝	6.8	..	...	...	...
51•[7]	UTMD	✔Utah Medical Products	NNM	B	42	3351	Mfr medical devices/supplies	16½	⅝	10	6⅜	21⅜	8½	30374	21⅜	13¾	19¾	...	25	133	18.2	21.4
52	UTI	✔UTI Energy	AS,Ch	NR	8	461	Contract drilling/o&g svcs	8¼	7⅜	7⅝	3	5⅞	3⅜	786	5⅞	4⅞	5⅜B	...	d	59.3	...	...

Uniform Footnote Explanations-See Page 4. Other: [1]CBOE:Cycle 2. [2]CBOE:Cycle 1. [3]Ph:Cycle 3. [4]Ph:Cycle 2. [5]P:Cycle 1. [6]ASE:Cycle 3. [7]ASE:Cycle 1. [8]P:Cycle 3. [9]Ph:Cycle 1. [10]NY:Cycle 2.
[51]Pfd in $M. [52]Fiscal Aug'94 & prior. [53]Sr A ESOP Cv Pfd. [54]Excl subsid Pfd. [55]Excl subsid pfd. [56]Incl $0.136743 non-taxable,'94. [57]Ltd vtg. [58]Incl $1.30 return of cap,'95. [59]Jr Sub Deferrable Int Debs Sr'A'.
[60]Rated 'A' by S&P. [61]Incl $0.725452 non-taxable,'94. [62]Excl 0.3M Unit vtg stk. [63]If com'A'price exceeds $7.50for30trad days. [64]Dep for1/100 shr $437.50 Ser'B'cm cv Pfd.
[65]Callable:$53.0625 fr 5-15-94,scale to $50in2001. [66]Incl curr amts. [67]®$1.86,'94. [68]Co opt exch for $50 amt 8.20%Cv 2011. [69]Thru 10-30-95,scale to $50 in'95. [70]34 Wk Dec'93. [71]To be determined.
[72]Pfd in $M,incl subsid pfd. [73]®$2.33,'94. [74]Fr 4-1-1996,scale to $50 in 2003. [75]Cv into 1.084 com,$46.125.

Splits ◆ Index	Cash Divs. Ea.Yr. Since	Dividends: Latest Payment Period $	Date	Ex. Div.	Total $ So Far 1995	Ind. Rate	Paid 1994	Financial Position Mil-$ Cash& Equiv.	Curr. Assets	Curr. Liab.	Balance Sheet Date	Capitalization Lg Trm Debt Mil-$	Shs. 000 Pfd.	Com.	Earnings $ Per Shr. Years End	1991	1992	1993	1994	1995	Last 12 Mos.	Interim Earnings Period	$ per Shr. 1994	1995	Index
1◆	1972	0.05	3-28-95	3-9	0.10	Nil	0.20	10.6	635	375	9-30-95	468	[51]18	±12174	Dc	0.32	0.36	0.58	[52]0.43	....	....	9 Mo Sep	±0.14	□±d0.01	1
2	1936	Q0.55	12-10-95	11-15	2.05	2.20	1.90	904	8636	6358	9-30-95	1707	[53]13619	122008	Dc	■d8.91	□d0.05	3.53	4.40	E5.70	5.54	9 Mo Sep	3.14	4.28	2
3	....	None Since Public			...	Nil	....	1.63	25.6	29.8	p9-30-95	16.4	...	★8675	Dc	...	...	...	p0.39	....	....	9 Mo Sep	n/a	p0.39	3
4	....	None Since Public			...	Nil	....	60.0	92.7	30.8	9-30-95	24.8	...	±17905	Dc	...	p±0.21	p±0.31	±0.91	....	1.20	9 Mo Sep	±0.64	±0.93	4
5	1886	Q0.23	12-1-95	11-13	0.92	0.92	0.92	7.30	150	135	9-30-95	559	[54]3978	32515	Dc	0.96	0.87	1.03	1.01	....	0.84	12 Mo Sep	1.14	0.84	5
6◆	1992	Q0.12	12-27-95	12-11	0.48	0.48	0.48	Equity per shr $16.57			9-30-95	45.0	...	12600	Dc	1.41	2.34	Δ2.42	2.81	....	1.11	9 Mo Sep	2.07	0.37	6
7	....	None Since Public			...	Nil	....	0.16	15.9	19.4	8-31-95	19.9	...	2626	Au	0.67	1.07	Δ0.18	0.33	d2.53	d2.53				7
8◆	1908	Q0.32	11-15-95	10-30	1.28	1.28	1.24	3.64	22.3	21.6	9-30-95	63.5	[55]...	4302	Dc	p0.50	1.50	1.75	1.83	....	1.83	12 Mo Sep	1.88	1.83	8
9	1990	Q0.50	11-30-95	11-10	2.00	2.00	1.50	Equity per shr $33.11			12-31-94	246	...	39841	Dc	2.58	□3.15	1.83	2.96	....	3.70	9 Mo Sep	2.02	2.76	9
10	....	0.50	10-1-87	9-4	...	Nil	....	29.8	66.1	23.5	10-28-95	....	...	11441	Ja	d1.24	*0.48	Δ0.64	0.75	....	1.36	9 Mo Oct	0.44	1.05	10
11◆	1935	Q0.075	3-5-96	2-9	0.30	0.30	0.30	14.6	476	375	8-31-95	131	...	21672	Fb	d0.29	0.26	0.28	d0.76	....	0.59	9 Mo Nov	d0.79	0.56	11
12◆	1927	Q0.255	2-5-96	1-4	1.00	1.02	0.96	80.1	1406	1162	9-30-95	261	...	35032	Je	□0.73	2.15	2.39	□1.09	0.73	0.91	3 Mo Sep	0.11	0.29	12
13	1934	Q0.25	12-1-95	11-1	0.97	1.00	0.93	16.9	334	187	6-30-95	156	...	26083	Sp	2.18	2.02	□2.15	1.95	P2.54	2.54				13
14	1993	†0.08	12-15-95	11-29	†0.10½	0.06	0.05	28.4	125	45.5	9-30-95	54.0	...	17041	Dc	...	p0.35	0.68	0.61	....	0.80	9 Mo Sep	0.49	0.68	14
15	1987	Q0.42	12-29-95	12-13	1.68	1.68	[56]1.66½	Equity per shr $11.78			9-30-95	25.0	...	8947	Dc	1.53	d0.25	1.45	1.60	....	1.50	9 Mo Sep	1.24	1.14	15
16	....	0.20	10-20-89	9-26	...	Nil	....	0.16	136	128	9-30-95	245	...	±13849	Dc	±1.45	±1.43	±1.71	±2.02	....	2.36	9 Mo Sep	±1.70	±2.04	16
17◆	....	None Since Public			...	Nil	....	1.31	8.30	15.9	10-01-95	22.5	...	13189	Sp	0.30	0.15	0.37	0.50	0.58	0.58				17
18	1916	Q0.20	2-9-96	1-8	0.80	0.80	0.80	168	1541	1129	9-30-95	3895	10250	247141	Dc	0.31	Δ0.75	□1.27	□0.36	E1.13	0.43	9 Mo Sep	□0.68	0.75	18
19◆	1991	†1.00	12-28-95	12-14	†[58]2.55	0.25	0.20	83.9	239	139	3-31-95	21.7	...	51865	Dc	0.37	2.74	0.40	0.64	....	0.81	9 Mo Sep	0.27	0.44	19
20◆	1987	Q0.26½	11-17-95	10-26	1.03½	1.06	0.92	Equity per shr $28.85			9-30-95	588	...	72780	Dc	3.07	3.70	Δ□3.96	2.09	E3.90	3.76	9 Mo Sep	1.35	3.02	20
21	1995	0.183	12-29-95	12-26	1.399	2.20	....	Co option redm fr 5-11-2000 at $25				150	...	...	Dc	...	...	...	....	....	....	Mature 5-31-2025			21
22◆	1950	Q0.31¼	11-1-95	10-11	1.22½	1.25	1.18½	2.67	16.6	14.8	9-30-95	43.6	5	2969	Dc	1.48	1.21	2.24	1.82	....	1.93	12 Mo Sep	1.88	1.93	22
23	....	None Since Public			...	Nil	....	1.73	9.03	5.43	9-30-95	7.29	...	8146	Dc	0.59	0.36	d0.05	0.17	....	d0.21	9 Mo Sep	0.27	d0.11	23
24	....	None Since Public			...	Nil	....	19.9	41.7	8.96	7-31-95	....	...	8513	Ja	0.30	0.52	0.97	1.23	....	1.28	9 Mo Oct	0.94	0.99	24
25	1994	Q0.48½	12-6-95	11-16	1.94	1.94	[61]1.82	Equity per shr $9.71			9-30-95	241	...	[62]13441	Dc	...	p0.74	p0.93	1.26	....	1.17	9 Mo Sep	0.89	□0.80	25
26	....	None Since Public			...	Nil	....	0.48	8.24	8.40	9-30-95	1.81	[51]3	19127	Je	d0.15	d0.34	d0.52	d0.57	d0.57	d0.60	3 Mo Sep	d0.11	d0.14	26
27	....	Terms&trad. basis should			be checked in detail			Wrrts expire 3-20-97				....	...	140	Je	...	...	...	....	....	....	Callable at 25¢[63]			27
28	....	None Since Public			...	Nil	....	39.8	41.4	4.44	9-30-95	....	...	★23554	Dc	...	...	pd0.23	pd0.41	....	d0.44	9 Mo Sep	pd0.31	pd0.34	28
29	....	5%Stk	9-11-87	8-26	...	Nil	....	6.40	55.1	21.3	7-31-95	9.83	...	7142	Oc	0.40	0.55	0.18	0.60	P0.67	0.67				29
30	1995	Q0.05	12-27-95	12-13	0.20	0.20	....	Equity per shr $14.19			9-30-95	25.0	...	5723	Dc	*1.48	0.78	1.14	1.04	....	2.27	9 Mo Sep	0.58	1.81	30
31	....	0.02½	1-4-82	12-11	...	Nil	....	0.05	2.39	5.40	9-30-95	0.53	1094	9544	Dc	d0.25	d0.16	Δd1.16	Δ0.06	....	d0.04	9 Mo Sep	Δ0.05	d0.05	31
32	....	None Since Public			...	Nil	....	29.1	30.0	1.27	6-30-95	0.05	...	★14899	Dc	d0.30	d1.18	d2.01	0.28	....	d0.59	9 Mo Sep	0.43	d0.44	32
33◆	....	None Paid			...	Nil	....	2.12	9.90	4.59	6-30-95	....	...	6241	Mr	0.70	0.92	Δd0.21	d1.34	....	d1.40	6 Mo Sep	d0.18	d0.24	33
34	....	None Since Public			...	Nil	....	0.08	19.0	15.5	p3-31-95	p2.08	...	★8643	Dc	...	p0.03	p0.02	p0.34	....	0.51	9 Mo Sep	p0.29	p0.46	34
35◆	....	None Since Public			...	Nil	....	1.27	13.6	11.6	9-30-95	8.35	...	9693	Dc	0.28	0.44	0.56	0.80	....	0.69	9 Mo Sep	0.60	0.49	35
36	....	None Since Public			...	Nil	....	12.0	104	97.5	9-30-95	p394	...	★60659	Dc	0.32	0.65	p0.36	0.61	....	1.78	9 Mo Sep	d1.34	d0.17	36
37	....	0.03	7-31-90	7-10	...	Nil	....	865	1692	2560	9-30-95	2874	4661	62472	Dc	d7.62	□d13.88	□d7.68	d12.73	E0.50↑	d5.73	9 Mo Sep	d7.06	d0.06	37
38	1991	1.09⅜	8-15-94	8-1	...	Nil	3.28⅛	Cv into 2.4925 com,$20.06				....	4263	...	Dc	...	bd1.17	bd0.31	bd1.11	....	....	Accum $5.46875 to 11-15-95			38
39	1939	Q0.05	1-31-96	1-4	0.20	0.20	0.20	Equity per shr $13.36			9-30-95	[66]623	5110	p112358	Dc	d2.53	d0.24	Δ0.93	[67]2.14	E1.35	1.79	9 Mo Sep	1.45	1.10	39
40	1986	Q1.02½	1-31-96	1-4	4.10	4.10	4.10	Cv into 1.192 common,$41.95				....	4000	...	Dc	bd0.46	b0.85	...	....	....	....				40
41	....	None Since Public			...	Nil	....	64.0	535	366	9-30-95	923	...	45171	Dc	pd3.82	d3.42	□[70]d2.90	d2.14	Ed0.15	d0.96	9 Mo Sep	d1.34	d0.16	41
42	....	Terms&trad. basis should			be checked in detail			Wrrts expire 5-6-98				....	...	2602	Dc	...	...	...	....	....	....				42
43◆	1951	Q0.233	12-1-95	11-13	0.907	0.93	0.84	Equity per shr $34.80			9-30-95	595	6	34442	Dc	2.15	□2.03	2.83	2.78	E2.93	2.88	9 Mo Sep	2.12	2.22	43
44	....	None Since Public			...	Nil	....	6.04	8.81	1.44	9-30-95	....	...	14644	Dc	*0.13	Nil	Δ0.12	0.01	....	d0.32	9 Mo Sep	0.02	d0.31	44
45◆	....	0.05	12-15-95	11-29	0.05	[71]....	....	Book Value $9.06			9-30-95	4.32	...	17704	Dc	d0.58	d0.34	Δd1.36	0.27	....	0.66	9 Mo Sep	0.19	0.58	45
46◆	1912	Q0.37	3-15-96	3-1	1.30	1.48	1.12	54.7	418	156	9-30-95	125	...	193300	Dc	1.18	1.41	□1.71	1.87	E2.15	2.08	9 Mo Sep	1.38	1.59	46
47	1992	Q0.05	12-9-95	11-14	0.20	0.20	0.20	0.10	53.7	123	9-30-95	162	[72]4	9447	Dc	p0.06	p0.98	0.86	d2.22	....	0.08	9 Mo Sep	d2.32	□d0.02	47
48	1991	Q0.17	12-9-95	11-14	0.68	0.68	0.68	61.0	1866	1933	9-30-95	3502	[72]182	287398	Dc	d0.31	□0.37	□d0.04	1.10	E1.21	1.09	9 Mo Sep	0.98	□0.97	48
49	1991	Q0.25	12-9-95	11-14	1.00	1.00	1.00	62.0	1621	1509	9-30-95	1090	[72]71	82741	Dc	d10.00	□d4.92	□d2.96	[73]2.35	E3.70	3.98	9 Mo Sep	1.23	□2.86	49
50	1993	Q0.81¼	12-29-95	11-29	3.25	3.25	3.25	Cv USX-U.S.Steel Gp[75]				....	6900	...	Dc	...	...	...	....	....	....				50
51◆	1993	0.02	8-30-93	8-25	...	Nil	....	12.4	23.0	3.68	9-30-95	....	...	9821	Dc	0.46	0.58	0.60	0.68	....	0.78	9 Mo Sep	0.50	0.60	51
52	....	None Since Public			...	Nil	....	4.46	14.1	6.31	9-30-95	2.16	...	3466	Dc	...	pd2.53	d1.75	0.34	....	d0.04	9 Mo Sep	0.18	d0.20	52

◆**Stock Splits & Divs By Line Reference Index** [1]2-for-1,'95. [6]3-for-2,'92. [8]11%,'92:2-for-1,'92. [11]No adj for spinoff'85. [12]No adj for stk dstr,'91:2-for-1,'92. [17]5-for-4,'95. [19]No adj for spl $2 dstr,'93. [20]2-for-1,'92. [22]2-for-1,'92. [33]2-for-1,'91. [35]2-for-1,'93. [43]3-for-2,'92,'95. [45]Adj for 5%,'91. [46]2-for-1,'92. [51]3-for-2,'93.

¶ S&P 500 # MidCap 400 ✤ SmallCap 600 • Options Index	Ticker	Name of Issue (Call Price of Pfd. Stocks)	Market	Com. Rank. & Pfd. Rating	Inst. Hold Cos	Inst. Hold Shs. (000)	Principal Business	Price Range 1971-93 High	1971-93 Low	1994 High	1994 Low	1995 High	1995 Low	Dec. Sales in 100s	December, 1995 Last Sale Or Bid High	Low	Last	%Div Yield	P-E Ratio	Total Return % Annualized 12 Mo	36 Mo	60 Mo
#1	UCU	✔UtiliCorp United	NY,B,Ch,P,Ph	A–	160	10775	Utility: electric & gas	34	2⅞	31⅞	25⅛	29⅝	26⅜	13246	29⅝	27½	29⅜	5.9	15	16.7	7.9	14.1
2•[1]	UUNT	✔UUNET Technologies	NNM	NR	87	4137	Provides Internet svcs	....	....	....	....	98¾	14	100990	79¾	52¾	63	...	..	...	...	...
3	VAALY	✔Vaal Reefs Ex&Mng ADR[53]	NSC	NR	52	15475	South Africa gold mining	15¼	13/16	11¾	7⅛	9	5¼	25287	7⅛	6⅜	6⅜	3.1	18	–27.1	36.7	6.9
4	VDRY	✔Vacu-dry Co	NNM	B–	7	208	Dvlp,mkt fruit products	12½	2	11	7¾	8½	4¼	623	5½	4⅝	4⅝	...	..	–41.8	–25.6	3.4
✤5•[2]	VCI	✔Valassis Communications	NY,Ph	NR	106	19183	Prints consumer promotion prd	25⅛	9⅜	19¾	10½	18⅝	13⅝	9092	17⅞	15	17½	...	38	18.6	–7.0	...
✤6•[3]	VLNC	✔Valence Technology	NNM	NR	32	2340	Dvlp stg:R&D rech'ble batteries	27	7¼	20½	2⅛	6½	1 9/16	23019	5	3¾	4½	...	d	80.0	–43.3	...
#7•[4]	VLO	✔Valero Energy	NY,B,Ch,P,Ph	B	200	34372	Gas systems operations, Texas	43⅞	4½	24⅛	16½	25⅞	16	10870	25⅞	24⅛	24½	2.1	28	48.8	6.1	11.8
8	Pr	$3.125cm Cv Pfd([56]52.188)	NY	NR	61	2822		....	....	52	41¾	53¾	39½	909	53¾	51½	51½	6.1	..	...	...	...
9	VHI	✔Valhi Inc	NY,Ph	B–	30	2810	Multi-industrial mgmt co	22¾	1	8⅛	4¾	8⅝	5¾	1911	6⅜	5¾	6⅜	1.9	15	...	...	...
10	VALN	✔Vallen Corp	NNM	B+	38	1925	Ind'l safety health pr dstr	27	2 1/16	16	10	23	12½	652	22¼	18¾	19⅝	...	18	48.1	4.4	–1.5
11	VF	✔Valley Forge	AS	B+	13	260	Marine prod & mfg indus prod	24	1/16	19	12⅛	21⅜	16½	224	18½	17⅜	17¼B	2.0	10	–3.0	14.4	22.8
12	VLY	✔Valley Natl Bancorp	NY,Ph	A	53	2509	Commercial bkg,New Jersey	24¼	11/16	30⅛	20¼	27⅞	22⅞	4357	25½	24¼	25	s4.0	14	8.6	17.8	35.2
13	VR	✔Valley Resources	AS,B	A–	10	747	Supplies gas serv in R.I.	18⅞	1 1/16	15¼	10⅝	11⅞	10¼	406	11⅛	10½	10⅞B	6.6	18	–6.2	–6.8	6.7
14	VALY	✔ValliCorp Holdings	NNM	NR	32	2524	Commercial bkg,California	15¼	1¾	16½	12	18¾	12	7954	14¼	12	13⅞	2.9	20	–5.3	18.2	29.9
✤15	VALM	✔Valmont Indus	NNM	B	69	4319	Self prop irrig sys:steel tubg	25	7/16	20½	13½	26	16¼	1593	25¾	23⅞	24¾	1.2	15	52.2	12.6	19.2
16	VAL	✔Valspar Corp	NY,Ch,Ph	A+	110	11137	Mfr paints & coatings	41½	⅜	45⅞	30½	44⅝	33⅜	2822	44⅝	40½	44⅝	1.5	21	...	...	...
17	VCD	✔Value City Dept Stores	NY,Ph	NR	65	6807	Oper off-price dept str chain	25	9	17½	8¼	9⅜	5¾	9645	7⅝	6½	6¾	...	19	–21.7	–30.9	...
#18•[5]	VH	✔Value Health Inc	NY	NR	267	31334	Hlth care management svcs	41	8	52	30⅛	40¾	21¼	49552	29	24⅞	27½	...	16	–26.2	–9.5	...
19	VALU	✔Value Line	NNM	A–	40	1551	Investment advisory services	42	12½	40	29	39¼	26	626	39¼	34	38½	2.1	12	27.5	16.7	21.7
20	VLP	✔Value Property Trust	NY,B,Ch,P	NR	1		Real estate investment trust	991⅝	11½	27⅛	4⅛	12½	4⅛	749	10¾	10⅜	10⅝	...	..	126	–34.3	–33.8
21•[6]	VVTV	✔ValueVision Intl'A'	NNM	NR	71	8666	Oper TV home shopping ntwrk	15⅝	½	15⅝	3¾	7¼	3⅞	35357	6⅛	5	5½	...	20	18.7	50.7	...
22•[5]	VJET	✔ValuJet Airlines	NNM	NR	72	14562	Oper low fare airline	....	....	6⅜	3⅛	34¾	4¾	185735	31	20	24¾	...	21	380	...	...
#23•[3]	VCELA	✔Vanguard Cellular Sys	NNM	C	151	25861	Operates cellular tel system	27⅞	8	29⅛	18⅛	29⅝	19¾	38953	23¼	19¾	20¼	...	d	–20.6	5.7	4.8
24	VRO	✔Vanguard Real Estate Fd I[59]	AS,Ch	LIQ	1	.2	Real estate investment trust	10	6¼	8	3⅜	4¼	2½	512	3½	2⅞	2⅞	7.0	3	108	15.4	11.6
25	VRT	✔Vanguard Real Estate Fd II[62]	AS,Ch	NR	2	3	Real estate investment trust	8¾	5¼	6⅞	3⅞	4⅝	2½	660	3¾	2½	2½	e11.7	d	62.4	10.5	4.8
26	VNTV	✔Vantive Corp	NNM	NR	23	1635	Customer interaction software	....	....	....	....	29¼	12	3687	29¼	20¾	22½	...	..	...	...	...
#27•[7]	VRC	✔Varco Int'l	NY,Ch,P	B–	117	15312	Oil & gas drill'g tools	36	1⅞	7⅜	5⅛	12⅞	6	46986	12⅞	9	12¼	...	25	100	43.7	7.6
#28•[8]	VAR	✔Varian Associates	NY,B,Ch,P,Ph	B+	253	20776	Electron devices:instr'l:ind'l	31¾	1⅜	39¼	28¼	57⅜	34½	55746	48⅛	42½	47⅞	0.6	12	39.6	30.3	26.5
¶29•[6]	VAT	✔Varity Corp	NY,To,B,Ch,P,Ph,Mo	B–	350	30405	Farm & ind'l mchy:engines	322½	10½	50⅛	33	50¾	33½	41244	40½	35⅜	37⅛	...	11	2.1	13.3	11.8
30	VRLN	✔Varlen Corp	NNM	B+	92	4301	Transtn:mfr metal pd,lab eq	25¼	7/16	26⅜	16⅜	28½	18⅞	14849	26½	21¼	21½	1.9	6	2.9	13.2	31.1
31	VRI	✔Vastar Resources	NY,Ch,Ph	NR	86	17936	Oil&gas explor,dvlp,prod'n	....	....	30⅜	24¼	33	21⅞	6903	31⅞	28⅝	31¾	0.9	30	29.6	...	...
32	VCAR	Vector Aeromotive	NSC	NR	6	39	Mfr exotic sports cars	12½	⅛	1 1/16	7/16	1¼	⅜	16287	1	½	¾	...	d	71.6	58.6	–20.6
33	VECO	✔Veeco Instruments	NNM	NR	49	3526	Microelectronic prod mfg eqp	....	....	11½	8½	30	7¾	20989	18¾	13	14½	...	10	45.0	...	...
34	VELCF	Velcro Indus NV	NSC,Mo	B+	27	468	Mfr fastening tapes:other	43¾	4⅜	73	39	69	54½	36	62	60	61¼	e3.3	13	–7.6	29.0	30.6
✤35•[9]	VC	✔Vencor Inc	NY	B	235	33264	Acute/L-T care hospitals	26⅝	2⅜	30⅝	19⅛	38	26	45032	33¾	29¾	32½	...	22	20.4	11.2	42.6
36•[6]	VNTX	✔Ventritex Inc	NNM	NR	150	16961	Mfr implantable defibrillators	44½	14¼	46	15⅝	31¾	13	195542	22⅜	16⅞	17⅜	...	d	–33.8	–20.2	...
✤37	VEN	✔Venture Stores	NY	NR	103	9018	Retail dept stores-Midwest	33¾	4	24¾	10¾	14¾	3	28147	4	3	3⅜	...	d	–69.1	–48.7	–13.9
38	Pr	$3.25 cmCv[67]Dep Pfd([68]52.275)	NY	B–	7	129		52¾	41⅞	48½	31½	33¼	8¼	2209	16⅛	8¼	10	32.5	..	...	...	...
39	VENT	✔Venturian Corp	NNM	↓C	10	95	Computer sys,softwr/defense pd	26¼	5¼	9¾	5¾	9¼	4	292	6¼	5	5B	...	d	–16.7	–16.6	–9.3
#40•[5]	VFI	✔VeriFone Inc	NY,Ch,Ph	B	159	12832	Mfr transaction automat'n sys	30	5¾	24¼	14½	31⅜	19¾	15042	29¾	27⅛	28⅝	...	21	28.7	11.3	26.0
41	VRTY	✔Verity Inc	NNM	NR	..	...	Mfr,mkt software products	....	....	....	....	57½	12	12118	57½	40¾	44¼	...	..	...	...	...
42	VRSA	✔Versa Technologies	NNM	B+	44	3992	Silicone rubber,fluid pwr	17½	3/16	15¼	12¼	18	11½	2951	18	13½	15¼	†4.9	14	25.9	11.3	13.2
43	VSR	✔Versar Inc	AS	C	10	310	Technical environmental svcs	18	1⅞	4⅛	2½	5	2	332	3⅞	3¼	3⅝	...	28	...	...	...
44	VTA	✔Vesta Insurance Group	NY,Ch,Ph	NR	131	11465	Property & casualty insurance	25⅛	19⅝	32⅝	20¾	55½	27⅝	10660	55½	44	54½	0.4	16	94.9	...	...
¶45•[10]	VFC	✔V.F. Corp	NY,B,P	A–	464	54636	Apparel mfr:intimate,leisure	57½	1⅛	53¾	44¼	57⅛	46¾	33484	53⅝	51	52¾	2.7	22	12.6	3.3	26.7
¶46•[5]	VIA.B	✔Viacom Inc Cl'B'[71]	AS,Ph	NR	735	171325	Diverse entmt/commun'ns co	61¼	14⅛	45	21¾	54¼	40¼	286294	48⅝	44⅝	47⅜	...	79	17.0	5.4	14.2
47•[11]	VIA	✔ Cl'A'	AS,B	NR	290	15285		67½	5	49¾	24½	54⅛	41	24143	48⅜	44	46¼	...	..	11.4	2.3	12.5
48	WS.C	Wrrt(Pur 1 Cl'B'at $60)	AS,Ch	....	56	6089		....	....	3⅜	¾	6¾	2⅜	58956	4	2½	2⅞	...	..	...	...	...
49	WS.E	Wrrt(Pur 1 Cl'B'at $70)	AS,Ch	....	48	10484		....	....	5⅝	3	8¾	4¼	30904	6⅛	4½	5½	...	..	...	...	...
50	VIAS	✔VIASOFT Inc	NNM	NR	23	2238	Dvlp/svcs system software	....	....	....	....	17	7¾	7980	15⅝	11½	11⅞	...	16	...	...	...
51	VII	✔Vicon Indus	AS	C	7	219	Closed circ TV security sys	12⅝	1/16	2 3/16	1½	2⅞	1 3/16	710	1¾	1 3/16	1¼	...	d	–23.1	–21.9	–13.8
✤52•[3]	VICR	✔Vicor Corp	NNM	NR	95	8191	Mfr modular pwr converters	22⅞	1¼	15⅛	9	26	12¼	42973	20½	17⅝	20	...	31	60.0	31.5	37.0

Uniform Footnote Explanations-See Page 4. Other: [1]CBOE,NY:Cycle 1. [2]NY:Cycle 1. [3]CBOE:Cycle 1. [4]ASE:Cycle 3. [5]CBOE:Cycle 3. [6]CBOE:Cycle 2. [7]Ph:Cycle 3. [8]ASE:Cycle 2. [9]Ph:Cycle 1. [10]NY:Cycle 2. [11]CBOE:Cycle 3,Ph:Cycle 2. [51]Excl subsid pfd. [52]®$2.06,'94. [53]ADR equal 0.1 ord shr. [54]Fiscal June'93 & prior. [55]12 Mo Dec'94, June'94 earned $0.12. [56]Fr 6-1-97, scale to $50 in 2004. [57]Stk dstr of Tremont Corp,'95. [58]Stk dstr of McWhorter Technologies,'94. [59]Plan liquidation. [60]Liq div. [61]Incl liq div. [62]Co plan liquidation. [63]Incl $1.85 return of capital. [64]®$2.32,'94. [65]Fiscal Sep'94&prior:12 Mo Dec'94 d$0.19. [66]®$1.13,'94. [67]Dep for 0.10 shr cm Cv Pfd. [68]Thru 4-30-96,scale to $50 in 2002. [69]Stk dstr of Sarnia Corp,'94. [70]®$4.10,'94. [71]Non-vtg.

Splits ◆ Index	Cash Divs. Ea.Yr. Since	Dividends: Latest Payment: Period $	Date	Ex. Div.	Total $: So Far 1995	Ind. Rate	Paid 1994	Financial Position Mil-$: Cash& Equiv.	Curr. Assets	Curr. Liab.	Balance Sheet Date	Capitalization: Lg Trm Debt Mil-$	Shs. 000: Pfd.	Com.	Earnings $ Per Shr. Years: End	1991	1992	1993	1994	1995	Last 12 Mos.	Interim Earnings: Period	$ per Shr.: 1994	1995	Index
1	1939	Q0.43	12-12-95	11-20	1.72	1.72	1.70	157	558	784	9-30-95	1236	[51]1000	★45756	Dc	2.00	1.32	1.95	[52]2.08	....	1.96	12 Mo Sep	2.07	1.96	1
2	....	None Since Public			...	Nil	....	70.1	79.4	15.2	9-30-95	7.12	...	28434	Dc	...	...	...	pd0.35	....	....	9 Mo Sep	n/a	pd0.03	2
3	1968	0.082	10-2-95	8-2	0.19½	0.20	0.326	49.8	547	489	j12-31-94	115	2314	19115	Dc	0.99	0.96	0.40	0.35	....	0.35	No interim reporting			3
4	1994	0.05	1-20-95	1-5	0.05	Nil	0.15	0.22	9.08	5.20	9-30-95	1.99	...	1702	Je	0.40	0.50	0.65	0.70	0.11	0.02	3 Mo Sep	0.12	0.03	4
5	1992	0.14	4-26-93	3-30	...	Nil	....	29.4	149	150	9-30-95	418	...	43303	Dc	p0.75	1.62	[54]1.89	[55]0.08	....	0.46	9 Mo Sep	0.06	0.44	5
6	....	None Since Public			...	Nil	....	49.6	52.0	13.8	9-24-95	7.45	...	21659	Mr	pd0.17	d0.63	d1.08	d1.68	....	d0.97	6 Mo Sep	d1.30	d0.59	6
7	1989	Q0.13	12-8-95	11-6	0.52	0.52	0.52	23.3	486	394	9-30-95	993	3577	43694	Dc	2.28	1.94	0.82	0.40	....	0.89	9 Mo Sep	0.38	0.87	7
8	1994	Q0.78⅛	12-1-95	10-30	3.12½	3.125	2.153	Cv into 1.8498 com, $27.03				....	3000	...	Dc	...	...	...	....	....	....				8
9	1987	Q0.03	12-29-95	12-15	h[57]0.12	0.12	0.08	171	808	507	9-30-95	1083	...	113971	Dc	Δ0.18	□d0.19	□d0.56	0.10	....	0.42	9 Mo Sep	0.06	0.38	9
10◆	....	None Since Public			...	Nil	....	5.02	71.2	19.7	8-31-95	10.7	...	7251	My	0.98	0.92	0.89	0.65	1.00	1.07	6 Mo Nov	0.44	0.51	10
11	1984	Q0.08½	12-12-95	11-29	0.34	0.34	0.30	....	28.4	8.49	9-30-95	11.5	...	1778	Dc	0.40	1.05	1.21	1.57	....	1.78	9 Mo Sep	1.26	1.47	11
12◆	1936	Q0.25	1-2-96	12-6	s0.976	1.00	0.883	Book Value $10.91			9-30-95	0.63	...	35718	Dc	1.09	1.50	□1.96	1.96	....	1.77	9 Mo Sep	1.48	1.29	12
13	1962	Q0.18	1-15-96	12-27	0.71½	0.72	0.69½	0.45	18.4	23.9	8-31-95	24.6	...	4261	Au	0.56	0.74	0.89	0.91	0.61	0.61				13
14	1991	Q0.10	2-26-96	1-30	0.36	0.40	0.32	Book Value $9.83			9-30-95	26.0	...	10279	Dc	0.94	1.10	1.19	0.75	....	0.71	9 Mo Sep	0.72	0.68	14
15	1980	Q0.075	1-16-96	12-27	0.30	0.30	0.30	16.9	186	102	9-30-95	32.6	...	13512	Dc	d0.69	1.14	□0.85	1.38	....	1.71	9 Mo Sep	0.96	1.29	15
16◆	1964	Q0.16½	1-15-96	12-27	0.60	0.66	h[58]0.52	3.58	241	156	7-28-95	25.1	...	21977	Oc	1.26	1.57	1.85	2.08	P2.15	2.15				16
17◆	....	None Since Public			...	Nil	....	9.04	282	144	10-28-95	10.6	...	31682	Jl	p0.80	0.98	1.25	1.21	0.43	0.35	3 Mo Oct	0.16	0.08	17
18◆	....	None Since Public			...	Nil	....	124	520	278	9-30-95	2.70	...	p53457	Dc	Δ0.40	0.61	0.21	1.19	E1.75	0.14	9 Mo Sep	0.72	d0.33	18
19	1983	Q0.20	10-5-95	10-3	0.80	0.80	0.80	88.7	148	50.4	10-31-95	....	...	9976	Ap	1.97	2.64	2.78	2.90	2.32	3.13	6 Mo Oct	1.04	1.85	19
20◆	....	15.00	2-20-90	1-23	...	Nil	....	Equity per shr $9.37			p6-30-95	p110	...	11227	Sp	d107.33	d112.67	d162.33	p0.18	....	....	6 Mo Mar	n/a	p0.08	20
21	....	None Since Public			...	Nil	....	26.4	40.0	11.0	7-31-95	0.45	...	29309	Ja	±d0.35	±d0.23	±□d0.09	d0.22	....	0.28	9 Mo Oct	d0.23	0.27	21
22◆	....	None Since Public			...	Nil	....	137	157	85.7	6-30-95	56.3	...	54490	Dc	...	...	d0.03	0.44	E1.20↑	0.95	9 Mo Sep	0.31	0.82	22
23◆	....	None Since Public			...	Nil	....	8.71	46.1	56.2	9-30-95	495	...	41312	Dc	d0.96	d0.72	□d0.40	□d0.36	Ed0.21	□d0.37	9 Mo Sep	d0.12	d0.13	23
24	1989	[60]0.50	12-28-95	12-21	[60]0.65	0.20	[61]4.14	Equity per shr $3.70			9-30-95	2.40	...	11020	Dc	0.03	0.12	0.30	1.12	....	1.05	9 Mo Sep	0.25	0.18	24
25	1990	Q0.075	10-31-95	9-27	0.22½	0.30	[63]2.45	Equity per shr $4.02			9-30-95	17.1	...	6433	Dc	0.26	d0.82	0.05	d0.71	....	d0.84	9 Mo Sep	0.37	0.24	25
26	....	None Since Public			...	Nil	....	15.6	30.2	5.85	9-30-95	0.50	...	11945	Dc	...	...	...	pd0.06	....	0.10	9 Mo Sep	pd0.06	p0.10	26
27	....	0.06	8-13-82	7-26	...	Nil	....	7.65	146	57.2	9-30-95	29.5	...	30364	Dc	0.45	Δ0.01	0.21	0.36	....	0.49	9 Mo Sep	0.25	0.38	27
28◆	1973	Q0.07	1-2-96	12-6	0.27	0.28	0.23	123	758	501	9-29-95	89.4	...	31420	Sp	1.48	1.02	1.26	2.22	3.96	3.96				28
29◆	....	g2.50	12-20-77	11-18	...	Nil	....	151	698	498	7-31-95	164	2001	40972	Ja	d7.87	□0.56	□1.80	3.24	E3.30↓	2.92	9 Mo Oct	2.40	2.08	29
30◆	1971	Q0.10	1-31-96	1-10	0.282	0.40	0.364	21.3	117	48.2	10-28-95	73.1	...	5404	Ja	0.44	□1.05	1.98	[64]2.68	....	3.49	9 Mo Oct	2.11	2.92	30
31	1994	Q0.075	12-4-95	11-7	0.30	0.30	0.075	6.30	204	243	9-30-95	749	...	97250	Dc	...	...	p1.13	p1.54	....	1.07	9 Mo Sep	p1.13	0.66	31
32	....	None Paid			...	Nil	....	2.54	3.08	1.00	6-30-95	....	...	42380	Dc	d1.11	d0.39	d0.28	[65]d0.21	....	d0.12	9 Mo Sep	d0.21	d0.12	32
33	....	None Since Public			...	Nil	....	18.5	48.7	13.3	9-30-95	....	...	5782	Dc	...	...	p0.25	p□0.87	....	1.39	9 Mo Sep	0.32	0.84	33
34	1992	A2.00	1-3-96	11-30	2.00	2.00	†2.00	12.4	56.4	33.5	9-30-94	36.0	...	3004	Sp	Δ2.36	■3.06	4.14	6.02	P4.66	4.66				34
35◆	....	None Since Public			...	Nil	....	76.9	508	275	9-30-95	p732	...	p72115	Dc	0.42	0.63	0.85	[66]1.20	E1.45	d0.01	9 Mo Sep	0.94	□d0.27	35
36	....	None Since Public			...	Nil	....	65.3	88.9	19.5	9-30-95	....	...	20699	Je	d0.57	d0.48	d1.85	0.44	0.43	d0.48	3 Mo Sep	0.12	d0.79	36
37	1990	0.07	6-15-95	5-25	0.21½	Nil	0.58	17.5	448	406	10-28-95	145	77	17316	Ja	2.48	□2.82	Δ2.43	1.53	....	d0.64	9 Mo Oct	0.15	d2.02	37
38	1992	Q0.81¼	12-15-95	11-29	3.25	3.25	3.25	Cv into 1.3158 com, $38				....	770	...	Ja	...	...	...	....	....	....				38
39	1991	0.07	12-31-93	12-9	...	Nil	....	1.25	13.3	6.56	9-30-95	0.22	...	748	Dc	d0.56	0.91	□d1.55	d3.97	....	d5.53	9 Mo Sep	d0.09	d1.65	39
40	....	None Since Public			...	Nil	....	50.4	257	72.2	9-29-95	4.15	...	23660	Dc	0.82	1.02	0.90	1.18	....	1.35	9 Mo Sep	0.83	1.00	40
41	....	None Since Public			...	Nil	....	1.47	7.72	6.06	8-31-95	0.95	p...	★9500	My	...	...	...	....	pd0.80	....	6 Mo Nov	n/a	d0.27	41
42	1976	Q0.10	11-10-95	10-27	†0.73	0.75	†0.67	14.2	34.6	6.31	9-30-95	....	...	5984	Mr	0.86	0.90	Δ0.99	1.13	....	1.09	6 Mo Sep	0.55	0.51	42
43	....	h[69]....	6-27-94	6-28	...	Nil	h[69]....	0.06	14.8	9.35	9-30-95	....	...	4867	Je	d0.67	d0.25	Δd0.34	Δd0.74	0.10	0.13	3 Mo Sep	Nil	0.03	43
44◆	1994	Q0.05⅝	1-22-96	1-3	0.20	0.23	0.15	Equity per shr $21.60			9-30-95	98.5	...	12570	Dc	0.81	1.00	Δ1.36	2.33	....	3.32	9 Mo Sep	1.81	2.80	44
45	1941	Q0.36	12-18-95	12-6	1.38	1.44	1.30	64.1	1920	1055	9-30-95	615	2025	63755	Dc	2.75	3.97	3.80	[70]4.20	E2.40↓	4.13	9 Mo Sep	3.05	2.98	45
46	....	None Since Public			...	Nil	....	549	5550	4318	9-30-95	10892	24000	±368503	Dc	±□d0.41	□±0.55	±Δ□1.30	□±0.16	E0.60	0.01	9 Mo Sep	±□0.61	±0.46	46
47	....	None Since Public			...	Nil	....	....	...	...		....	...	74958	Dc	±□d0.41	±□0.55	±Δ□1.30	□±0.16	....	0.01	9 Mo Sep	±□0.61	±0.46	47
48	....	Terms&trad. basis should			be checked in detail			Wrrts expire 7-7-97				....	...	30568	Dc	...	...	...	....	....	....				48
49	....	Terms&trad. basis should			be checked in detail			Wrrts expire 7-7-99				....	...	18341	Dc	...	...	...	....	....	....				49
50	....	None Since Public			...	Nil	....	22.2	31.4	11.9	9-30-95	0.04	...	8087	Je	pd0.35	pd0.12	pd0.55	p0.56	0.71	0.73	3 Mo Sep	0.09	0.11	50
51	....	None Paid			...	Nil	....	1.83	22.4	14.6	6-30-95	2.13	...	2763	Sp	d0.14	d1.42	d0.68	0.02	Pd0.49	d0.49				51
52◆	....	None Since Public			...	Nil	....	64.3	109	14.0	9-30-95	....	...	±42604	Dc	±0.29	±0.28	±0.35	±0.52	....	0.65	9 Mo Sep	±0.37	±0.51	52

◆**Stock Splits & Divs By Line Reference Index** [10]3-for-2,'91. [12]3-for-2,'92:5-for-4,'93:10%,'94:Adj for 5%,'95. [16]No adj for stk dstr of McWhorter Tech, '94:2-for-1,'92. [17]2-for-1,'91. [18]3-for-2,'92. [20]1-for-33.33 REVERSE,'95. [22]2-for-1,'95(twice). [23]3-for-2,'94. [28]2-for-1,'94. [29]1-for-10 REVERSE,'91. [30]3-for-2,'93:10%,'95. [35]5-for-4,'92:3-for-2,'91,'94. [44]To split 3-for-2,ex Jan 23. [52]2-for-1,'91,'95.

¶ S&P 500 # MidCap 400 ✣ SmallCap 600 • Options

Index	Ticker	Name of Issue (Call Price of Pfd. Stocks)	Market	Com. Rank. & Pfd. Rating	Inst. Hold Cos	Inst. Hold Shs. (000)	Principal Business	Price Range 1971-93 High	1971-93 Low	1994 High	1994 Low	1995 High	1995 Low	Dec. Sales in 100s	December, 1995 Last Sale Or Bid High	Low	Last	%Div Yield	P-E Ratio	Total Return % Annualized 12 Mo	36 Mo	60 Mo
1	VRES	✓VICORP Restaurants	NNM	↓C	60	5935	Family style restr:franch'g	31½	5	21½	13¼	18	9½	10228	12	9½	9¾	...	d	−41.8	−24.3	−7.6
2	VICT	✓Victoria Bankshares[51]	NNM	B−	47	1226	Commercial bkg,Texas	29	5½	29	21¾	37	21¾	5421	34¾	32½	34½	e1.9	18	61.1	15.3	44.1
3	VIDA	✓Vidamed Inc	NNM	NR	12	2154	Mfr/dvlp prostate treatment eqp	...	...	...	...	10¾	5¾	8794	10¾	7½	9½	...	..	...	...	...
✣4•[1]	VLTS	✓Video Lottery Tech	NNM	NR	42	1584	Mfr video gaming equipment	39¾	9	23	7½	9⅞	3½	25388	6½	3⅞	4¾	...	d	−47.9	−31.1	...
5	VDNX	✓Videonics Inc	NNM	NR	28	1766	Post-prod video equip	...	...	13	11	24	10¾	6768	14¾	11¾	11¾	...	15	−2.1	...	...
6	VSVR	✓VideoServer Inc	NNM	NR	61	3803	Supplies data commun ntwk prd	...	...	...	...	49½	17	32183	34½	26½	31½	...	..	...	...	...
7	VRON	Videotron Hldgs Plc 'ADS'	NNM	NR	45	5561	Cable TV/telecommun U.K.	...	...	...	...	17¾	11⅜	15536	15⅜	12¾	12¾	...	..	...	...	...
✣8•[2]	VIEW	✓Viewlogic Systems	NNM	NR	59	5068	Dvlp engineering softwr prd	26½	9⅛	30	11¾	15⅛	7⅞	29010	11⅞	10	10	...	32	−44.8	−17.4	...
9•[3]	VGR	✓Vigoro Corp[54]	NY,Ph	NR	133	10704	Produce potash/fertilizer prd	30¾	13⅝	36½	25½	62	29¾	26623	62	53¾	61¾	1.5	17	113	45.2	...
10•[4]	VKNG	✓Viking Office Products	NNM	NR	281	33797	Direct mkt of office supplies	24⅝	2 3/16	32½	21	48⅝	25	50513	48⅝	42⅜	46½	...	40	52.5	55.4	73.6
11	VCO	Vina Concha y Toro ADS	NY,Ph	NR	32	1271	Chilean wine producer/exporter	...	...	19⅝	14½	22⅛	14¾	25359	18½	17⅛	18	2.1	33	13.0	...	...
✣12	VPI	✓Vintage Petroleum	NY	NR	81	8444	Oil & gas explor,dev,prod'n	26⅛	5½	22¾	14¾	22½	16	10133	22½	19¾	22½	0.4	44	34.9	21.7	25.7
13	VIR	✓Virco Mfg	AS	B	20	1070	Chairs,tables,contract seating	10⅛	3/16	9¾	5⅞	10⅝	7¼	232	10¼	9⅛	9⅛	0.4	10	19.8	36.8	29.2
#14	VSH	✓Vishay Intertechnology	NY,B,Ch,Ph	B+	253	33978	Electronic resistive systems	17⅛	⅛	25	14⅞	44⅜	23	110698	35	24⅞	31½	s. . .	19	40.0	34.4	46.4
15	VSIO	Visio Corp	NNM	NR	..	...	Dvlp drawing/diagramm'g softwr	...	...	...	...	31	16	16298	31	22½	28¼	...	..	...	...	...
16	VSNR	Visioneer Inc	NNM	NR	..	...	Dvp paper input systems	...	...	...	...	23	12	80972	23	12	22¼	...	d	...	...	...
17	VIST	✓Vista 2000 Inc	NSC	NR	4	111	Personal safety/hme secu'ty prd	...	...	4	2½	11⅛	3	64375	11⅛	8¾	9⅞	...	22	...	...	...
✣18•[5]	VISX	✓VISX Inc	NNM,Ch	NR	48	2790	Mfr vision correct'n sys	27¾	4¼	28¾	10	40⅛	10	70595	40⅛	30⅛	39	...	d	255	51.3	55.8
19	VTLK	✓Vitalink Pharmacy	NNM	NR	34	2057	Oper institutional pharmacies	18	7½	15½	8½	25⅜	11¾	2765	25⅜	18⅝	23¼	...	25	75.5	23.0	...
20•[6]	VTO	✓Vitro,Sociedad Anonima ADS[59]	NY,Ph	NR	39	5997	Mfr flat glass/glass products	26⅞	12½	23⅛	9⅜	11⅝	4⅜	94815	6⅛	4⅜	4¾	6.1	d	−57.4	−28.9	...
21	VTC	✓Vitronics Corp	AS	C	8	576	Mfr thermal solder'g equip	6⅞	⅜	1 13/16	⅝	3⅜	1 3/16	8857	2¾	2 3/16	2⅝	...	13	115	62.6	10.6
✣22•[7]	V	✓Vivra Inc	NY	NR	173	29706	Dialysis/Health care ctrs	17	4½	19⅞	13½	25⅝	17¾	18678	25⅝	22⅝	25⅛	...	23	38.5	26.3	27.1
23	VVUS	✓Vivus Inc	NNM	NR	59	5027	Dvlp stge:pharmac'l R&D	...	...	16	13	31½	11¼	21190	31½	23½	31¼	...	d	105	...	...
✣24•[8]	VLSI	✓VLSI Technology	NNM	B−	230	35741	Design/mfr integr'd circuits	23	3	16⅜	10¼	39⅛	11⅝	373416	23¾	15⅞	18⅛	...	18	53.4	30.7	33.7
25	VMRK	✓VMARK Software	NNM	NR	69	5636	Dvlp softwr for UNIX oper sys	19¼	5¼	23¼	12¼	21½	5¾	47525	10	5¾	9⅜	...	d	−44.9	6.6	...
26•[9]	VOD	✓Vodafone Group[61] ADR	NY,Ch,Ph	NR	374	114547	Mobile telecom svcs in U.K.	30⅜	9⅞	35¼	24⅜	45	27¼	543346	36¼	31¼	35¼	1.7	29	8.0	21.2	19.5
27	VPS.EC	✓Voice Control Systems	ECM	C	7	81	Speech recognit'n hardwr/softr	245	2⅝	8½	1½	12½	2½	4786	10¾	6⅞	7	...	d	107	−11.2	...
28	VPTI	✓Voice Powered Tech Intl	NSC	NR	11	572	Voice recognition tech R&D	11⅞	2⅛	5¼	1 9/16	4	1½	26348	2⅛	1½	1⅝	...	16	−16.1	−40.3	...
29	VOLT	✓Volt Info Sciences[62]	NNM	B−	32	2195	Tech svs: mfr typesetters	17⅛	1/16	15	7¾	27¼	13½	2114	27¼	25½	27¼	...	18	99.4	73.5	50.9
30	VCC	✓Volunteer Capital	NY,Ch	B−	18	1409	Fast food restaurant:Franch'g	18¾	3/16	14	5⅝	12½	6⅛	3055	10¼	8⅜	9½	...	10	58.3	10.7	50.0
31	VOLVY	✓Volvo AB 'B' ADR[63]	NNM	NR	60	14569	Swedish auto,truck,bus mfg	16¼	4¾	20½	13	25⅜	16½	60176	21⅛	19	20⅝	1.9	5	12.8	32.6	27.6
#32•[10]	VON	✓Vons Cos	NY,B,Ch,P,Ph	B−	170	22119	Food supermkt chain	34⅛	1/16	21½	15⅛	28¼	17⅝	21050	28¼	26⅛	28¼	...	22	54.8	3.0	5.2
33	VNO	✓Vornado Realty Trust	NY,B,Ch,Ph	B	100	12503	Real estate investment trust	42	⅜	37¾	30¼	39	32⅝	2663	37⅞	35¼	37½	6.0	18	12.1	21.9	...
34	VSEC	VSE Corp	NNM	↑B	7	11	Engin'g,dev,test,mgmt svc	21	1 9/16	14¾	11½	29	13¾	136	27	20	27	1.3	15	99.9	49.0	31.2
35	VUL	✓Vulcan Int'l Corp	AS,Ch	B	12	192	Shoe lasts,heels:bowl pins	33	1½	22½	17⅜	21¾	17¼	69	21¾	21½	21⅝B	3.7	98	26.6	9.0	14.5
#36	VMC	✓Vulcan Materials	NY,B,Ch,Ph	A−	190	19842	Constr'n materials/chemicals	56⅛	2⅝	56½	44	60⅜	48⅛	5258	58¾	55⅝	57⅝	2.5	12	16.6	8.9	15.1
37	VWRX	✓VWR Scientific Products	NNM	B−	38	3158	Dstr lab supplies,chem & eqp	17¼	4	12¼	6½	15	7¾	7480	13½	10¾	13⅜	...	..	63.9	1.8	...
✣38	WDFC	✓W D-40 Co	NNM	B+	93	2678	Aerosol lubricant/rust prev	50	1 3/16	48	37¾	45½	38¾	5489	41	38¾	41	6.0	16	−1.3	3.3	15.8
#39•[11]	WBN	✓Waban Inc	NY	NR	222	27683	Cash/carry mdse warehouses	26½	4⅝	20⅛	13	20⅜	13½	19682	19½	18½	18⅝	...	9	11.2	2.1	11.4
✣40•[6]	WNC	✓Wabash National	NY,Ph	NR	175	16864	Mfr/mkt truck trailers	23⅜	8⅝	43½	22⅝	40½	19⅜	86124	28	19⅜	22⅜	0.5	16	−42.8	10.7	...
¶41•[7]	WB	✓Wachovia Corp	NY,B,Ph	A−	472	92869	Comml bkg, N.&S.Carolina, GA	40½	2 1/16	35⅜	30⅛	48¼	32	42864	47⅛	44⅜	45¾	3.1	13	44.7	14.5	21.3
42	WAK	✓Wackenhut Corp Cl'A'	NY,Ch	B	46	1185	Investigative/security sv/sys	16	1 1/16	13	9¼	19	10½	912	18⅛	16¾	18	1.7	95	94.0	26.8	20.9
43	WAK B	✓ Cl'B'	NY,Ch	B	32	1514		11¾	7⅝	11¼	7½	16	9⅞	876	16	14¾	15½	1.9	82	76.6	...	...
44	WAL	✓Wahlco Enviro Systems	NY,Ch,Ph	NR	14	1133	Flue gas pollution ctrl sys	16⅝	4⅛	5¾	1¾	3¼	1	2880	2	1⅜	1⅜	...	d	−26.7	−42.9	−30.7
45	WOL	✓Wainoco Oil	NY,B,Ch	C	52	17257	Oil & gas expl,dev,prod	43⅜	½	5⅞	3⅞	5	2⅝	16291	3⅜	2⅞	3¼	...	d	−33.3	−4.7	−13.6
¶46•[11]	WMT	✓Wal-Mart Stores	NY,B,Ch,P	A+	1107	741912	Operates discount stores	34⅛	1/32	29¼	21	27⅝	20½	639149	24½	22⅛	22¼	0.9	17	3.1	−11.0	8.6
✣47	WALB	✓Walbro Corp	NNM	B	77	4845	Mfr carburetors,fuel pumps	38½	½	31¼	16½	23½	17¼	7945	19⅞	17¼	18	2.2	11	−3.3	−14.4	17.3
48	WDN	✓Walden Residential Prop	NY	NR	69	7865	Real estate investment trust	...	...	22⅝	16¼	21	17⅜	11141	21	17¾	20⅞	8.7	..	28.6	...	...
¶49•[8]	WAG	✓Walgreen Co	NY,B,Ch,P	A+	571	126426	Major retail drug chain	22⅜	5/16	22¾	16⅞	31⅜	21⅝	99557	30⅞	28⅜	29⅞	1.5	23	38.5	13.0	20.4
50	WALK	✓Walker Interactive Sys	NNM	NR	42	7541	Dvlp financial & ctrl softwr	23¾	5½	13¼	5½	9¾	4⅝	20714	8⅛	6¼	7⅜	...	d	14.4	−29.3	...
✣51•[12]	WALL	✓Wall Data	NNM	NR	67	4970	Dvlp/mkt software products	42½	12¾	60	29¼	55½	14½	29664	18¾	15¼	16½	...	14	−58.8	...	...
52	WSDI	✓Wall Street Deli	NNM	B	13	375	Operates fast food restaurants	14½	1⅛	14½	9¼	10	5¼	4079	7¼	5¾	6¼	...	d	−35.9	−18.9	9.1

Uniform Footnote Explanations-See Page 4. Other: [1]ASE,CBOE:Cycle 2. [2]CBOE,P:Cycle 2. [3]P:Cycle 2. [4]P:Cycle 3. [5]ASE:Cycle 3. [6]CBOE:Cycle 2. [7]P:Cycle 1. [8]ASE:Cycle 1. [9]ASE,CBOE:Cycle 1. [10]NY,P:Cycle 3. [11]CBOE:Cycle 3. [12]CBOE:Cycle 1. [51]Norwest Corp plan acq, 1.05 com. [52]Fiscal June'94 & prior. [53]6 Mo Dec'94. [54]IMC Global plan acq,com. [55]11 Mos Jun'91. [56]Approx. [57]12 Mo Dec'94. [58]82.3% owned by Manor Care Inc. [59]Ea ADS rep 3 ord. [60]®$0.07,'94. [61]Each ADR rep 10 ord shr,5p. [62]Plan name chge, Autologic Info Intl. [63]Each ADR rep 1 Cl'B' shr 25 SEK. [64]®$4.07,'94. [65]Incl $0.0802 non-taxable,'94. [66]®$1.83,'95. [67]®$3.12,'94. [68]Redemption of stkhldrs value rt. [69]Incl $0.0545 non-taxable,'94.

Splits ◆ Index	Cash Divs. Ea.Yr. Since	Dividends: Latest Payment Period $	Date	Ex. Div.	Total $ So Far 1995	Ind. Rate	Paid 1994	Financial Position Mil-$ Cash& Equiv.	Curr. Assets	Curr. Liab.	Balance Sheet Date	Capitalization Lg Trm Debt Mil-$	Shs. 000 Pfd.	Com.	Earnings $ Per Shr. Years End	1991	1992	1993	1994	1995	Last 12 Mos.	Interim Earnings Period	$ per Shr. 1994	1995	Index
1	....	0.03	8-1-86	7-9	...	Nil	....	6.28	25.4	43.7	8-06-95	39.3	...	9014	Oc	□0.73	□1.48	1.60	d0.69	Pd0.49	d0.49				1
2	1992	Q0.16	11-15-95	10-30	†0.73	0.64	0.52	Book Value $18.67			9-30-95	....	...	8275	Dc	□1.86	□2.70	Δ1.85	2.09	....	1.93	9 Mo Sep	1.53	1.37	2
3	....	None Since Public			...	Nil	....	17.3	20.0	9.69	9-30-95	1.79	...	9165	Dc	...	...	p[52]d2.64	p[53]d1.27	....	....	9 Mo Sep	n/a	pd2.38	3
4	....	None Since Public			...	Nil	....	2.24	58.4	37.1	9-30-95	5.16	1913	10584	Dc	p0.42	0.74	0.35	d1.54	....	d2.91	9 Mo Sep	0.57	d0.80	4
5	....	None Since Public			...	Nil	....	11.1	22.9	3.57	9-30-95	....	...	5507	Dc	...	...	p0.16	p0.79	....	0.79	9 Mo Sep	p0.50	0.50	5
6	....	None Since Public			...	Nil	....	43.6	49.1	6.80	9-30-95	0.54	...	12377	Dc	...	...	...	p0.10	....	0.28	9 Mo Sep	p0.06	p0.24	6
7	....	None Since Public			...	Nil	....	70.6	88.5	27.5	j11-30-94	189	p...	★272835	Au	...	...	...	pd0.15		....	3 Mo NovΔ	n/a	pd0.10	7
8	....	None Since Public			...	Nil	....	54.2	92.0	39.7	12-31-94	0.13	...	16700	Dc	0.27	Δ0.50	0.78	d0.36	....	0.31	9 Mo Sep	d0.37	0.30	8
9	1991	Q0.23	1-25-96	12-28	0.84	0.92	0.76	2.48	309	203	9-30-95	226	3	19880	Dc	Δ[55]1.86	2.10	□2.12	p2.64	E3.65	3.33	9 Mo Sep	2.20	2.89	9
10◆	....	None Since Public			...	Nil	....	4.20	250	117	9-30-95	....	...	41158	Je	0.23	0.33	0.42	0.76	1.08	1.15	3 Mo Sep	0.24	0.31	10
11	1995	[56]0.093	1-16-96	12-20	0.383	0.38	....	3.98	87.6	17.3	12-31-94	3.00	...	573301	Dc	...	...	p0.85	0.54	....	0.54				11
12	1992	Q0.02½	1-4-96	12-20	0.08½	0.10	0.06½	1.54	45.5	62.0	9-30-95	★306	...	★23661	Dc	0.41	0.51	Δ0.81	0.66	....	0.51	9 Mo Sep	0.51	0.36	12
13◆	1975	A0.04	12-6-95	11-2	0.04	0.04	0.036	0.44	74.2	25.1	10-31-95	34.2	...	5369	Ja	0.57	0.58	□0.80	0.93	....	0.92	9 Mo Oct	0.55	0.54	13
14◆	....	5%Stk	3-31-95	3-13	5%Stk	Stk	5%Stk	33.3	635	234	9-30-95	226	...	±58472	Dc	0.57	0.78	±Δ0.91	±1.20	....	1.64	9 Mo Sep	±0.87	±1.31	14
15	....	None Since Public			...	Nil	....	7.06	16.8	13.3	9-30-95	0.45	p...	★12875	Sp	...	...	...	....	p0.20	0.20				15
16	....	None Since Public			...	Nil	....	7.83	13.2	11.7	9-30-95	0.07	p...	★18131	Dc	...	...	...	pd0.76	....	d1.00	9 Mo Sep	pd0.56	pd0.80	16
17	....	None Paid			...	Nil	....	14.8	72.1	30.6	9-30-95	27.8	23	6881	Dc	...	...	...	[57]0.05	....	0.45	9 Mo Sep	d0.04	0.36	17
18	....	None Since Public			...	Nil	....	12.3	23.2	6.48	9-30-95	....	...	★14743	Dc	d0.22	d0.98	0.02	d0.60	....	d1.23	9 Mo Sep	d0.27	d0.90	18
19	....	None Since Public			...	Nil	....	0.30	24.6	7.00	8-31-95	....	...	[58]13975	My	p0.31	0.46	0.53	0.66	0.84	0.92	6 Mo Nov	0.39	0.47	19
20◆	1992	0.139	10-16-95	9-26	0.291	0.29	0.747	98.0	941	700	12-31-94	1683	...	360000	Dc	□1.55	1.61	0.53	d1.88	....	d1.88				20
21	....	None Paid			...	Nil	....	1.63	8.40	3.98	9-30-95	0.11	...	10235	Dc	d0.57	d0.70	d0.18	[60]0.08	....	0.21	9 Mo Sep	0.04	0.17	21
22◆	....	None Since Public			...	Nil	....	103	180	40.1	8-31-95	1.55	...	36500	Nv	0.55	0.65	0.81	0.99	....	1.09	9 Mo Aug	0.73	0.83	22
23	....	None Since Public			...	Nil	....	23.3	24.1	2.96	9-30-95	....	...	13448	Dc	...	...	pd0.79	d1.27	....	d1.80	9 Mo Sep	d0.73	d1.26	23
24	....	None Since Public			...	Nil	....	400	589	170	9-30-95	217	...	46902	Dc	±0.37	±d1.12	±0.45	±0.85	E1.01	0.92	9 Mo Sep	±0.59	±0.66	24
25	....	None Since Public			...	Nil	....	8.43	33.3	15.0	10-01-95	9.28	...	8100	Dc	*p0.33	*0.46	Δ0.72	pd0.03	....	d0.36	9 Mo Sep	d0.19	d0.52	25
26◆	1989	[56]0.325	2-22-96	12-1	0.548	0.60	0.443	15.9	308	443	j3-31-95	140	...	3047268	Mr	1.07	1.11	1.23	1.22	....	1.22				26
27◆	....	None Paid			...	Nil	....	1.48	3.81	0.72	9-30-95	1.16	...	4226	Dc	*0.04	d0.52	d1.20	d2.29	....	d0.61	9 Mo Sep	d1.57	0.11	27
28	....	None Since Public			...	Nil	....	2.08	10.3	5.93	9-30-95	....	...	12485	Dc	d0.74	d1.14	d1.14	0.03	....	0.10	9 Mo Sep	d0.03	0.04	28
29◆	....	0.004	11-15-67	10-10	...	Nil	....	19.9	156	103	7-28-95	29.3	...	9626	Oc	Δ0.04	0.12	□d0.39	□1.26	....	1.49	9 Mo Jul	□0.64	□0.88	29
30	....	None Paid			...	Nil	....	7.93	9.91	7.31	10-01-95	18.6	...	5269	Dc	Δ*0.20	0.48	0.93	0.90	....	1.00	9 Mo Sep	0.38	0.48	30
31◆	1984	0.395	5-23-95	4-18	0.395	0.39	0.169	24449	78374	72212	j12-31-94	11996	...	±444041	Dc	0.32	d1.20	d1.07	[64]4.13	....	4.13				31
32	....	0.15	1-6-70	12-4	...	Nil	....	6.30	436	574	10-08-95	689	...	43512	Dc	*1.56	□1.89	□0.76	0.61	....	1.28	9 Mo Sep	0.40	1.07	32
33◆	1990	Q0.56	11-14-95	11-2	2.24	2.24	[65]2.00	Equity per shr $8.00			9-30-95	290	...	24239	Dc	0.62	0.07	□1.57	1.89	....	2.14	9 Mo Sep	1.41	1.66	33
34	1973	Q0.08½	2-15-96	1-30	0.32½	0.34	0.30½	0.51	19.9	11.1	9-30-95	3.65	...	869	Dc	d2.78	1.35	Δ1.34	1.80	....	1.85	9 Mo Sep	1.30	1.35	34
35◆	1976	Q0.20	12-15-95	11-29	0.80	0.80	0.80	16.3	21.7	7.83	9-30-95	....	...	1220	Dc	2.00	□1.30	2.18	0.76	....	0.22	9 Mo Sep	0.61	0.07	35
36	1934	Q0.36½	12-8-95	11-20	1.46	1.46	1.32	9.32	401	267	9-30-95	91.8	...	35189	Dc	1.38	Δ2.41	2.39	2.67	E4.95	4.27	9 Mo Sep	1.80	3.40	36
37◆	1986	0.04	9-8-95	8-21	0.12	Nil	0.40	....	139	56.6	6-30-95	67.5	...	12899	Dc	0.70	0.85	□0.35	0.18	....	0.13	9 Mo Sep	0.25	0.20	37
38	1973	Q0.62	1-30-96	1-8	2.44	2.48	†2.40	24.3	49.6	11.1	8-31-95	3.13	...	7703	Au	2.02	2.38	2.52	1.65	2.66	2.62	3 Mo Nov	0.72	0.68	38
39	....	None Since Public			...	Nil	....	63.7	774	517	10-28-95	245	...	32822	Ja	1.01	1.33	Δd0.56	[66]1.95	E2.20	2.06	9 Mo Oct	1.31	1.42	39
40◆	1993	Q0.03	1-26-96	1-10	0.10	0.12	0.08	2.80	233	114	9-30-95	83.6	...	18961	Dc	p0.52	0.54	0.90	1.32	E1.40	1.45	9 Mo Sep	0.97	1.10	40
41◆	1936	Q0.36	12-1-95	11-3	1.38	1.44	1.23	Book Value $21.24			9-30-95	5010	...	170326	Dc	1.34	2.51	2.83	[67]3.13	E3.55	3.47	9 Mo Sep	2.30	2.64	41
42◆	1966	Q0.075	1-2-96	12-13	0.297	0.30	0.288	5.10	111	70.6	10-01-95	6.01	...	±9688	Dc	0.80	±Δ0.12	□±0.38	□±0.24	....	0.19	9 Mo Sep	±0.60	±0.55	42
43◆	1993	Q0.075	1-2-96	12-13	0.297	0.30	0.288	....	...	...		....	...	5830	Dc	0.80	±Δ0.12	□±0.38	□±0.24	....	0.19	9 Mo Sep	±0.60	±0.55	43
44	....	None Since Public			...	Nil	....	2.70	40.6	20.8	9-30-95	8.80	...	17649	Dc	0.66	d0.72	d0.62	d3.75	....	d0.33	9 Mo Sep	d3.60	d0.18	44
45	....	[68]0.10	6-1-87	4-21	...	Nil	....	1.83	49.6	44.4	9-30-95	167	...	27256	Dc	d0.90	d0.04	0.10	d0.46	....	d1.12	9 Mo Sep	0.22	d0.44	45
46◆	1973	Q0.05	1-5-96	11-29	0.19¼	0.20	0.16	13.0	20213	14825	10-31-95	10216	...	2294545	Ja	0.70	0.87	1.02	1.17	E1.30	1.23	9 Mo Oct	0.72	0.78	46
47	1967	Q0.10	1-31-96	12-27	0.40	0.40	0.40	20.3	211	103	9-30-95	247	...	8580	Dc	0.98	1.63	□1.47	1.70	....	1.61	9 Mo Sep	1.39	1.30	47
48	1994	Q0.45½	12-1-95	11-13	1.82	1.82	[69]1.09	Equity per shr $16.94			9-30-95	243	...	14113	Dc	...	...	p0.74	p0.61	....	....	9 Mo Sep	n/a	□0.57	48
49◆	1933	Q0.11	12-12-95	11-9	0.40¼	0.44	0.35¼	22.0	1813	1078	8-31-95	....	...	246141	Au	0.79	0.89	□0.99	1.14	1.30	1.30				49
50	....	None Since Public			...	Nil	....	35.0	47.0	28.2	9-30-95	....	...	13153	Dc	0.32	0.86	0.30	d1.01	....	d0.61	9 Mo Sep	d1.13	d0.73	50
51	....	None Since Public			...	Nil	....	58.2	83.5	21.2	9-30-95	....	...	9213	Dc	*Δ0.19	*0.58	1.00	1.40	....	1.16	9 Mo Sep	0.71	0.47	51
52◆	....	None Since Public			...	Nil	....	1.26	6.53	8.06	9-30-95	....	...	3550	Je	0.32	0.40	0.53	0.58	d0.27	d0.40	3 Mo Sep	0.14	0.01	52

◆**Stock Splits & Divs By Line Reference Index** [10]2-for-1,'92,'94. [13]10%,'91,'92,'93,'94,/95. [14]2-for-1,'95. [20]6-for-5,'95. [22]3-for-2,'91,'93,'95. [26]3-for-1,'94. [27]1-for-7 REVERSE,'91:1-for-4 REVERSE,'94. [29]2-for-1,'95. [31]5-for-1,'94. [33]5-for-1,'91:3-for-2,'93. [35]No adj for stk dstr of Eagle-Picher,'88. [37]2-for-1,'92. [40]3-for-2,'94. [41]2-for-1,'93. [42]2-for-1 in Cl'B','93:5-for-4 inCl'B','95:To split 5-for-4 in Cl'B',ex Jan 10. [43]5-for-4,'95:To split 5-for-4,ex Jan 10. [46]2-for-1,'93. [49]2-for-1,'91,'95. [52]3-for-2,'93.

¶ S&P 500
# MidCap 400
✣ SmallCap 600
• Options

Index	Ticker	Name of Issue (Call Price of Pfd. Stocks)	Market	Com. Rank. & Pfd. Rating	Inst. Hold Cos	Inst. Hold Shs. (000)	Principal Business	Price Range 1971-93 High	1971-93 Low	1994 High	1994 Low	1995 High	1995 Low	Dec. Sales in 100s	December, 1995 Last Sale Or Bid High	Low	Last	%Div Yield	P-E Ratio	Total Return % Annualized 12 Mo	36 Mo	60 Mo
#1•[1]	WCS	✓Wallace Computer Svc[51]	NY,Ch,Ph	A	207	14195	Business forms:comm'l print	33⅞	1¾	36¼	25⅞	60	27½	56361	59⅜	53⅝	54⅝	1.6	20	97.7	29.7	25.0
2	WNUT	Walnut Financial Services	NNM	NR	. .	. . .	Financial svcs/consulting	. . . .	. . . .	. . . .	. . . .	3⅝	2	2628	2⅞	2⅛	2¼	. . .	. .	. . .	. . .	. . .
3•[2]	WANG	✓Wang Laboratories	NNM	NR	111	24487	Dvlp software/office sys	19	14	21⅞	9⅛	19½	9⅞	30182	18	15⅞	16⅝	. . .	d	66.3	. . .	. . .
4	WAC	✓Warnaco Group'A'	NY,Ph	NR	176	38678	Mfr women's intimate apparel	20½	10½	19¼	13⅛	26⅞	14⅞	32388	26⅞	24	25	0.6	17	50.2	9.6	. . .
5	WCP	✓Warner Insurance Svcs	NY	C	12	799	Provides svcs to auto insur ind	11¼	7/16	5¼	2	3	15/16	4442	1⅝	1⅛	1½	. . .	d	−36.8	−43.8	−7.1
¶6•[3]	WLA	✓Warner-Lambert	NY,B,C,Ch,P,Ph	A−	880	99913	Drugs:toiletries:food:gum	82¼	8½	86¾	60	98	73⅜	66307	97⅛	89⅜	97⅛	2.7	18	30.0	16.0	11.1
7	WTEC	Warrantech Corp	NNM	B−	15	973	Warranty program services	16⅝	15/16	7⅝	3⅝	6⅜	4⅛	14503	5⅛	4⅛	4½	. . .	24	−11.0	10.6	15.2
✣8	WEG	✓Washington Energy[56]	NY	B	90	5108	Hldg:nat'l gas,Puget Sd area	26⅜	4¼	18⅞	12½	19⅛	13	9101	19	18¼	18⅝	5.4	d	53.9	1.3	4.6
9	WFSL	✓Washington Federal	NNM	A	109	19030	Svgs & In,Wash,Oregon,Idaho	26⅜	⅞	23⅞	16½	26⅛	17¼	18865	26⅛	23⅞	25⅝	3.7	13	52.7	7.5	13.9
#10	WGL	✓Washington Gas Lt	NY,B,Ch,Ph	A	142	9401	Natural gas:D.C.,Md,Va	22⅞	2½	21¼	16	22⅜	16⅛	6805	22⅜	20½	20½	5.5	14	30.7	8.3	13.9
11	WHI	✓Washington Homes	NY	NR	15	1013	Builds single-family homes	9⅞	7½	10⅜	3¼	6¼	3¼	2821	6¼	5	5½	. . .	9	57.1	. . .	. . .
12•[3]	WAMU	✓Washington Mutual	NNM	B	171	41429	Savings bank, Pacific,NW	28⅜	1½	25	15¾	29½	16⅝	54860	29½	27½	28⅞	2.8	11	78.3	11.0	40.6
✣13	WNT	✓Washington National	NY,Ch	B−	110	7884	Insur hldg co: life insur	39⅝	5	25⅜	18⅜	29¼	17¾	6350	29¼	23⅞	27⅝	3.9	11	56.4	12.6	28.7
14	Pr	$2.50 cm Cv Pfd (55)vtg	NY	NR	5	5	accident, health: annuities	69⅜	21¼	51	40	54¼	36¼	24	54¼	45¾	53B	4.7	. .	. . .	. . .	. . .
#15	WPO	✓Washington Post'B'	NY,B,P,Ph	B+	191	5562	Newspaper, magazine, TV	311	3¾	284	221¾	315	237½	1632	306½	279½	282	1.6	16	18.4	9.0	9.0
16	WRE	✓Washington REIT SBI	AS,Ch,Ph	NR	69	3024	Real estate investm't trust	24¾	1	21¼	14¾	16⅝	13⅞	11241	15⅞	14½	15⅞	6.3	19	13.5	−1.4	13.5
17	WSB	✓Washington Savings Bank	AS	B−	8	242	Savings bank,Waldorf, Maryland	6⅞	¼	6⅜	3⅝	6½	3	227	5⅜	4⅞	5	1.6	10	31.3	34.6	70.4
18	WWP	✓Washington Water Pwr[61]	NY,B,Ch,P,Ph	B+	110	9550	Hydroelectric pwr, nat'l gas	21	7⅝	18⅞	13⅝	18⅛	13½	22757	18⅛	17¼	17½	7.1	13	37.6	8.1	11.8
19•[4]	WME	✓Waste Mgmt Intl plc ADS[62]	NY,Ph	NR	86	21972	Waste collet'n/disposal svcs	24¾	15⅝	21⅛	10¾	13⅛	8	20791	11	10⅛	10¾	. . .	13	−2.3	−20.6	. . .
✣20	WHO	✓Waterhouse Investor Svc	NY,Ph	B+	47	2607	Discount securities broker	29¼	⅝	19⅝	9¼	26¾	9⅞	10484	24¾	19¾	24¾	0.8	13	156	43.0	102
21	WAT	Waters Corp	NY	NR	. .	. . .	Mfr liquid chromatography inst	. . . .	. . . .	. . . .	. . . .	18¼	13¼	30543	18¼	14	18¼	. . .	. .	. . .	. . .	. . .
✣22	WJ	✓Watkins-Johnson	NY,B,Ch,P,Ph	B	155	6924	Defense-electronics prod/sys	42½	3¾	36⅝	19⅝	57	29¾	5280	46	40½	43¾	1.1	13	52.7	49.5	29.8
23	WSO.B	✓Watsco Inc Cv Cl'B'[65]	AS	B+	11	253	Refrig & air cond controls	11⅛	½	11¼	8⅞	17½	10⅝	5	17½	16⅝	17⅜B	1.2	17	66.2	31.9	21.6
24	WSO	✓ Com(Ltd Vtg)	NY,Ch	B+	30	2465	personnel services	11⅜	15/16	11⅜	8⅝	17⅞	10½	908	17⅞	16½	17⅞	1.1	17	68.3	32.3	32.7
25	WGEN	✓Watson General Corp	NSC	C	2	178	Enviro test'g/storage tanks	5⅜	¼	6⅜	3	4⅝	1⅝	4712	2⅝	2	2¼	. . .	d	−30.8	6.3	17.6
#26•[5]	WATS	✓Watson Pharmaceuticals	NNM	NR	203	23185	Mfr off-patent medications	38½	12	29½	12¾	50½	20	75896	50½	39½	49	. . .	40	88.5	. . .	. . .
#27	WTS	✓Watts Industries'A'	NY,Ph	A−	162	17762	Mkts water & steam valves	29	6¼	29	18¼	25⅝	19¾	9042	23⅞	20½	23¼	1.1	15	12.6	−1.1	5.5
#28	WSAU	✓Wausau Paper Mills	NNM	A−	128	16014	Print,write,specialty papers	29¼	3/16	31⅞	19¾	28½	20¼	9131	28¼	24	27¼	1.0	27	32.5	14.5	30.7
29	WAVR	✓Waverly Inc	NNM	B	21	788	Medical/scientific public'n	34¼	1¼	27	16½	46¾	26¼	712	46¾	41	45¾B	1.0	33	73.3	27.8	23.8
30	WAX	✓Waxman Indus	NY,Ch,Ph	C	17	1940	Home elec/plumb'g mfr/dstr	12⅞	3/16	3¼	1⅛	1⅝	½	6299	⅞	½	13/16	. . .	d	−27.8	−39.1	−24.5
31	WRN	✓WCI Steel	NY,Ch,Ph	NR	26	1522	Integrated steel producer	. . . .	. . . .	12⅝	6½	9¾	3⅝	8376	5	3⅝	4⅜	. . .	10	−50.7	. . .	. . .
#32•[6]	WII	✓Weatherford Enterra	NY,Ch,Ph	B−	188	24741	Oil field eq,svs,rental:mfg	77⅝	1¼	29½	16	30	16½	34449	29½	25⅛	29	. . .	67	56.8	37.1	14.9
33•[7]	WBB	✓Webb (Del) Corp	NY,B,Ch,P,Ph	↑B	120	14060	Real estate development	38	2	18⅜	13⅝	25	16⅝	8670	20¾	18¾	20⅛	1.0	11	19.6	6.8	31.3
34	WEB	✓Webco Industries	AS	NR	25	1561	Mfr steel tubing/pipe	. . . .	. . . .	17¼	6	9⅝	5⅜	2667	6⅝	5½	5¾	. . .	d	−30.3	. . .	. . .
35	WKS	✓Weeks Corp	NY,Ch,Ph	NR	67	6252	Real estate investment trust	. . . .	. . . .	22⅜	18½	25⅞	20¾	7572	25⅛	22¾	25⅛	6.0	24	23.5	. . .	. . .
36	WGNR	✓Wegener Corp	NSC	C	13	786	Provides cable TV prod/svces	16⅛	5/16	3	1½	12⅜	2⅜	9930	12⅛	8⅜	12⅛	. . .	. .	373	140	108
37	WRI	✓Weingarten Rlty SBI	NY,Ch,Ph	NR	133	11493	Real estate investment trust	45¼	¼	40½	32¾	38½	33⅜	9975	38½	34½	38	6.3	22	7.8	7.5	16.1
38•[1]	WS	✓Weirton Steel	NY,Ch,Ph	NR	61	13218	Major integrated steelmaker	15⅜	3¼	11	6¼	9⅜	3¾	41969	4⅜	3¾	4⅛	. . .	2	−51.5	2.1	−9.4
39	WMK	✓Weis Markets	NY,B,Ch,Ph	A−	75	20392	Food supermkts,PA,MD,NY,WV,VA	41⅝	1⅝	28	23⅞	29	24	1576	28¾	27¾	28¼	3.0	15	19.4	6.1	1.4
40	WLD	✓Weldotron Corp	AS	C	6	146	Pack'g mchy:electr ctr sys	14	½	2⅝	1⅝	1¾	7/16	2138	1¼	⅝	1⅛	. . .	d	−35.7	−23.4	−16.4
41	WELL	✓WellCare Management Group	NNM	NR	42	1323	Provides health care svcs	24½	11¾	30	14¾	38	19	16710	24	20¾	21½	. . .	18	−8.5	. . .	. . .
42	WLC	✓Wellco Enterprises	AS	B	10	74	Footwear mfr: shoe mchy	34⅞	1⅛	18	14	17½	14⅞	18	15⅝	15	15	1.7	20	−4.7	11.4	11.5
#43•[8]	WLM	✓Wellman Inc	NY	B+	232	29661	Mfr/recycles textile fibers	43	6	34⅝	17⅛	30	21½	32864	26⅛	21½	22¾	1.2	9	−19.0	4.7	5.7
44•[9]	WLP	✓Wellpoint Hlth Networks'A'[68]	NY,Ch	NR	117	15408	Hlth care svcs,California	39¾	23	37	24¼	37	27	16131	33⅜	30¾	32⅛	. . .	14	11.7	. . .	. . .
¶45•[3]	WFC	✓Wells Fargo	NY,B,C,Ch,P,Ph	B+	481	28606	Commercial bkg,California	133½	4¾	160¾	127⅛	230¼	141	31285	221⅜	211	216	2.1	11	52.2	45.7	34.1
46	WRP	✓Wellsford Residential Prop Tr	NY	NR	112	9700	Real estate investment trust	30⅞	21¾	27⅜	18⅛	23⅛	18⅝	12982	23⅛	20¾	23	8.3	51	21.9	7.6	. . .
47	Pr	Sr'A'cm CvPfd([69]25.875)	NY	BB+	19	732		25	21⅜	24⅜	16½	21	17¾	2687	21	19	19⅝	8.9	. .	. . .	. . .	. . .
48	WGA	✓Wells-Gardner Electr	AS	C	14	543	Video monitors:TV receivers	21⅛	¼	4⅝	2½	6½	2½	2810	3⅞	2⅞	3⅛	. . .	d	24.4	−17.9	4.0
49	WMD	✓Wendt-Bristol Health Svcs	AS	B−	6	182	Nursing homes/medical svcs	7⅞	7/16	15/16	⅜	¾	5/16	1877	9/16	⅜	9/16	. . .	19	28.6	−15.7	−10.9
50	WS	Wrrt(Pur2.75com&1SerIIWr-$3.75)	AS	NR	. .	. . .		3¼	⅛	⅞	3/16	½	1/64	10	1/16	1/16	1/16B	. . .	. .	. . .	. . .	. . .
¶51•[10]	WEN	✓Wendy's Intl	NY,B,Ch,Ph	B+	381	60795	Fast food restaurant:franch'g	17¾	1 1/16	18½	13¼	22¾	14⅜	82330	21⅜	19¼	21¼	1.1	19	49.8	20.3	29.5
✣52	WERN	✓Werner Enterprises	NNM	A	131	12547	Motor carrier,gen'l freight	30½	5⅛	33¾	21¼	25¾	17½	12064	21¼	19¾	20¼	0.6	13	−12.4	−2.3	19.2

Uniform Footnote Explanations-See Page 4. Other: [1]Ph:Cycle 3. [2]CBOE:Cycle 1. [3]ASE:Cycle 1. [4]CBOE,NY:Cycle 3. [5]CBOE:Cycle 2. [6]ASE,CBOE:Cycle 3. [7]Ph:Cycle 2. [8]NY:Cycle 3. [9]ASE,CBOE:Cycle 1. [10]P:Cycle 3. [51]Moore Corp offer, $60 to Dec 20: co rejects. [52]9 Mo Jun'94. [53]Fiscal Oct'92 & prior. [54]Fiscal Oct'93:2 Mo Dec $0.04. [55]®$0.17,'95. [56]Plan mgr w/Puget Sound P&L form 0.86 new co. [57]Incl $0.75 non-taxable,'94. [58]®$2.46,'94. [59]®$2.50,'94. [60]Incl $0.087 non-taxable,'94. [61]Aprv comb w/Sierra Pac Res form Altus Corp,1com. [62]Ea ADS rep 2 ord,10p. [63]Special divd. [64]Pfd in $M. [65]Cv into 1 Cl'A'. [66]®$0.87,'94. [67]Incl $0.1148 non-taxable:©$0.0228,'94. [68]Health Systems Intl plan mgr to Jan 15. [69]Fr 11-1-98,scale to $25 in 2003. [70]If com 150% Cv price-20 trad.days. [71]®$0.91,'94. [72]Fiscal Feb'94 & prior. [73]12 Mo Dec'94.

Splits ◆ Index	Cash Divs. Ea.Yr. Since	Dividends: Latest Payment Period $	Date	Ex. Div.	Total $ So Far 1995	Ind. Rate	Paid 1994	Financial Position Mil-$ Cash& Equiv.	Curr. Assets	Curr. Liab.	Balance Sheet Date	Capitalization Lg Trm Debt Mil-$	Shs. 000 Pfd.	Com.	Earnings $ Per Shr. Years End	1991	1992	1993	1994	1995	Last 12 Mos.	Interim Earnings Period	$ per Shr. 1994	1995	Index
1	1933	Q0.21½	12-20-95	11-29	0.77	0.86	0.66½	34.7	276	75.7	10-31-95	25.6	...	22715	Jl	1.63	1.76	1.84	Δ□2.13	2.46	2.68	3 Mo Oct	0.52	0.74	1
2	....	None Paid			...	Nil	....	0.55	2.96	11.6	9-30-95	8.01	...	13749	Dc	...	...	...	p0.12	....	....	9 Mo Sep	n/a	d0.02	2
3	....	None Since Public			...	Nil	....	154	416	367	9-30-95	22.8	3004	34037	Je	...	...	...	‡[52]0.20	d2.02	d2.72	3 Mo Sep	0.02	d0.68	3
4◆	1995	0.07	1-8-96	11-29	0.14	0.14	....	2.93	578	226	10-07-95	198	...	51777	Dc	□d1.63	□0.98	□1.34	1.53	....	1.46	9 Mo Sep	0.96	0.89	4
5◆	1993	0.01	7-29-94	7-11	...	Nil	0.03	4.09	25.8	20.6	9-30-95	....	...	8561	Dc	0.19	[53]0.36	[54]0.40	d1.60	....	d2.25	9 Mo Sep	d0.33	d0.98	5
6	1926	Q0.65	12-8-95	11-1	2.60	2.60	2.44	507	2825	2609	9-30-95	430	...	135386	Dc	□■1.05	4.78	Δ2.11	5.17	E5.55	5.59	9 Mo Sep	4.15	4.57	6
7	....	None Paid			...	Nil	....	7.14	32.8	19.9	9-30-95	0.23	3235	13046	Mr	□*0.11	0.08	0.05	[55]0.19	....	0.19	6 Mo Sep	0.08	0.08	7
8	1960	Q0.25	3-11-96	2-8	1.00	1.00	[57]1.00	8.45	50.8	294	6-30-95	265	3600	24015	Sp	1.55	0.58	0.42	d1.97	Pd1.72	d1.72				8
9◆	1983	Q0.24	1-26-96	1-8	0.90	0.96	0.82	Book Value $14.02			9-30-95	527	...	38874	Sp	1.75	2.05	□2.33	2.32	1.97	1.97				9
10◆	1852	Q0.28	2-1-96	1-8	1.11¾	1.12	1.105	13.9	159	222	9-30-95	329	284	43065	Sp	1.33	1.27	1.31	1.42	1.45	1.45				10
11	1993	0.05	10-7-94	9-20	...	Nil	0.20	Equity per shr $5.91			7-31-95	72.6	...	±7943	Jl	...	p±0.93	p±0.91	±0.56	±0.64	0.65	3 Mo Oct	±0.08	±0.09	11
12◆	1986	Q0.20	11-15-95	10-27	0.77	0.80	0.70	Equity per shr $20.26			9-30-95	2055	6200	65903	Dc	1.68	□2.17	Δ2.74	[58]2.54	E2.60	2.58	9 Mo Sep	1.89	1.93	12
13	1923	Q0.27	1-2-96	12-8	1.08	1.08	1.08	Equity per shr $31.71			9-30-95	1.45	145	12211	Dc	d0.33	□1.65	□2.59	[59]2.53	....	2.52	9 Mo Sep	1.99	1.98	13
14	1969	Q0.62½	1-2-96	12-8	2.50	2.50	2.50	Cv into 1.875 common				....	145	...	Dc	n/a	n/a	n/a	....	....	....				14
15	1956	Q1.10	11-10-95	10-4	4.40	4.40	4.20	114	386	354	10-01-95	....	...	±11004	Dc	±□10.00	±10.80	±Δ13.10	±14.65	E17.65	16.89	9 Mo Sep	±10.11	±12.35	15
16◆	1962	Q0.25	12-29-95	12-13	0.99	1.00	[60]0.92	Equity per shr $6.32			9-30-95	....	...	31743	Dc	0.74	0.76	0.82	0.82	....	0.86	9 Mo Sep	0.62	0.66	16
17◆	1993	S0.04	9-14-95	8-29	0.08	0.08	0.08	Book Value $4.52			7-31-95	0.03	...	4220	Jl	0.11	0.17	0.50	Δ0.58	0.50	0.50	3 Mo Oct	0.11	0.11	17
18◆	1899	Q0.31	12-15-95	11-20	1.24	1.24	1.24	31.1	131	138	9-30-95	688	851	55696	Dc	1.34	1.37	1.44	1.28	....	1.32	12 Mo Sep	1.24	1.32	18
19	....	None Since Public			...	Nil	....	38.5	603	504	j12-31-94	528	...	375084	Dc	0.71	0.83	0.79	0.85	....	0.81	9 Mo Sep	0.63	0.59	19
20◆	1989	[63]A0.20	9-7-95	8-15	0.20	0.20	0.16	Equity per shr $5.83			8-31-95	48.5	...	11452	Au	0.30	0.74	1.26	1.37	1.68	1.90	3 Mo Nov	0.32	0.54	20
21	....	None Since Public			...	Nil	....	22.8	149	69.8	p9-30-95	186	[64]6	★28796	Dc	...	...	...	p0.47	....	....	9 Mo Sep	n/a	p0.67	21
22	1974	Q0.12	1-2-96	12-7	0.48	0.48	0.48	37.2	205	67.6	9-30-95	23.6	...	8092	Dc	d2.98	Δ0.66	1.45	2.56	E3.40	3.25	9 Mo Sep	1.79	2.48	22
23◆	1975	Q0.05	10-31-95	10-12	0.186	0.20	0.17	4.47	119	73.7	9-30-95	7.87	...	±6261	Dc	±0.50	±0.70	±0.84	±[66]0.89	....	1.03	9 Mo Sep	±0.77	±0.91	23
24◆	1984	Q0.05	10-31-95	10-12	0.186	0.20	0.17	....	...	...		....	...	4778	Dc	±0.50	±0.70	±0.84	±[66]0.89	....	1.03	9 Mo Sep	±0.77	±0.91	24
25	....	None Paid			...	Nil	....	0.79	1.46	0.50	6-30-95	0.35	...	9118	Sp	d0.21	d0.25	d0.12	d0.24	Pd0.12	d0.12				25
26	....	None Since Public			...	Nil	....	120	193	26.6	9-30-95	4.58	...	36060	Dc	0.12	0.26	0.74	1.05	....	1.23	9 Mo Sep	0.66	0.84	26
27◆	1986	Q0.06¼	12-15-95	11-29	0.25	0.25	0.22	....	368	127	9-30-95	134	...	±29636	Je	±1.22	±1.30	±□1.01	±1.38	±1.54	1.57	3 Mo Sep	±0.38	±0.41	27
28◆	1960	Q0.06⅞	1-17-96	12-28	0.25	0.28	0.218	2.35	120	52.8	8-31-95	68.6	...	29466	Au	1.03	1.35	□1.30	Δ1.42	1.06	1.02	3 Mo Nov	0.29	0.25	28
29	1925	Q0.12	12-12-95	11-22	0.47	0.48	0.44	38.0	73.5	48.8	9-30-95	5.08	...	4432	Dc	0.78	□1.10	d0.46	1.07	....	1.39	9 Mo Sep	0.47	0.79	29
30	1966	0.02	6-25-93	6-7	...	Nil	....	0.38	116	63.2	9-30-95	157	...	±11737	Je	0.23	□d0.33	□d2.33	□d3.86	d1.97	d2.08	3 Mo Sep	d0.05	d0.16	30
31	....	None Since Public			...	Nil	....	133	304	128	7-31-95	212	...	36578	Oc	...	...	p0.32	Δ□0.94	P0.42	0.42				31
32◆	....	0.20	12-17-82	11-29	...	Nil	....	31.5	455	181	p9-30-95	171	...	p50900	Dc	d0.42	0.62	0.82	p0.69	....	0.43	9 Mo Sep	p0.74	p0.48	32
33	1990	Q0.05	12-8-95	11-1	0.20	0.20	0.20	Equity per shr $16.14			9-30-95	493	...	17395	Je	Δd0.04	Δ1.09	Δ0.25	1.13	1.87	1.91	3 Mo Sep	0.35	0.39	33
34	....	None Since Public			...	Nil	....	1.66	36.5	19.6	7-31-95	18.0	...	6339	Jl	...	...	p0.45	□p0.02	d0.07	d0.01	3 Mo Oct	d0.04	0.02	34
35	1994	Q0.37½	10-31-95	10-18	1.50	1.50	0.15	Equity per shr $9.23			9-30-95	187	...	★11151	Dc	...	...	p0.72	p0.82	....	1.05	9 Mo Sep	p0.56	0.79	35
36	....	None Since Public			...	Nil	....	4.91	16.8	8.83	9-01-95	1.96	...	★8681	Au	d0.11	d0.41	d0.07	d0.01	0.05	0.05				36
37	1958	Q0.60	12-15-95	11-29	2.40	2.40	[67]2.28	Equity per shr $14.98			9-30-95	293	...	26530	Dc	1.08	□1.21	1.50	1.67	E1.70	1.69	9 Mo Sep	1.25	1.27	37
38	....	0.16	12-15-90	11-26	...	Nil	....	111	583	228	9-30-95	486	[64]16	42024	Dc	d3.49	Δd1.57	□d1.74	□Δ1.06	....	1.77	9 Mo Sep	0.48	□1.19	38
39	1940	Q0.21	11-24-95	11-8	0.80	0.84	0.74	459	613	108	9-30-95	....	...	43042	Dc	1.81	Δ1.63	1.66	1.75	....	1.83	9 Mo Sep	1.23	1.31	39
40	....	None Paid			...	Nil	....	0.07	12.3	8.33	8-31-95	0.01	...	2300	Fb	d1.27	d1.64	d1.04	d1.49	....	d1.34	6 Mo Aug	d0.39	d0.24	40
41	....	None Since Public			...	Nil	....	6.37	30.5	14.9	9-30-95	16.7	...	±6287	Dc	±d0.71	±*0.32	±Δ0.72	±1.00	....	1.18	9 Mo Sep	±0.69	±0.87	41
42	1986	S0.12½	1-26-96	1-3	0.25	0.25	0.25	3.34	11.3	3.06	9-30-95	....	...	885	Je	2.33	2.70	Δ1.98	1.75	1.10	0.77	3 Mo Sep	0.25	d0.08	42
43	1988	Q0.07	12-15-95	11-29	0.27	0.28	0.23	29.7	330	109	9-30-95	224	...	33389	Dc	1.39	1.60	□1.23	1.94	E2.44↓	2.54	9 Mo Sep	1.34	1.94	43
44	....	None Since Public			...	Nil	....	2166	2421	916	9-30-95	....	...	±99500	Dc	*p±1.45	±p1.76	±□1.88	±2.14	E2.25	2.20	9 Mo Sep	±1.62	±1.68	44
45	1936	Q1.15	11-20-95	10-27	4.60	4.60	4.00	Book Value $63.08			9-30-95	3020	2328	46967	Dc	0.04	4.44	10.10	14.78	E19.00	18.09	9 Mo Sep	10.83	14.14	45
46	1993	Q0.48	1-12-96	12-21	1.89	1.92	1.77	Equity per shr $14.61			9-30-95	286	6300	16990	Dc	p0.48	d0.34	0.91	0.25	....	0.45	9 Mo Sep	0.18	□0.38	46
47	1994	Q0.43¾	1-2-96	12-21	1.75	1.75	1.556	Cv into 0.8122 com,$30.78				....	3000	...	Dc	...	...	...	....	....	....	Red opt 11-1-96 to 11-1-98[70]			47
48	....	0.07	12-27-88	12-6	...	Nil	....	0.69	14.1	4.33	9-30-95	2.23	...	4053	Dc	d0.39	*0.26	Δd0.49	d0.45	....	d0.09	9 Mo Sep	d0.47	d0.11	48
49	....	None Since Public			...	Nil	....	0.07	4.08	8.31	9-30-95	7.45	...	6220	Dc	d0.62	0.04	d0.03	0.03	....	0.03	9 Mo Sep	0.01	0.01	49
50	....	Terms&trad. basis should			be checked in detail			Wrrts expire 5-1-96				....	...	416	Dc	...	...	...	....	....	....	Wrrts extended from 10-16-92			50
51	1976	Q0.06	11-28-95	11-9	0.24	0.24	0.24	66.3	138	146	10-01-95	★339	...	103417	Dc	□0.52	0.64	0.77	[71]0.93	E1.12	1.08	9 Mo Sep	0.72	0.87	51
52◆	1987	Q0.03	10-17-95	9-28	0.11½	0.12	0.10½	15.5	98.5	63.6	9-30-95	40.0	...	25161	Dc	□0.86	1.05	[72]1.31	[73]1.45	E1.60	1.43	9 Mo Sep	1.06	1.04	52

◆**Stock Splits & Divs By Line Reference Index** [4]2-for-1,'94. [5]Adj to 5%,'91:5-for-4,'93. [9]3-for-2,'92:10%,'93,'94. [10]2-for-1,'95. [12]3-for-2,'92,'93. [16]3-for-2,'92. [17]3-for-2,'93. [18]2-for-1,'93. [20]3-for-2,'92,'93:5-for-4,'91,'93,'95. [23]Adj for 5%,'92:3-for-2,'95. [24]Adj for 5%,'92:3-for-2,'95. [27]2-for-1,'94. [28]5-for-4,'91:2-for-1,'92:4-for-3,'93,'94:10%,'94:To split 5-for-4,ex Jan 18. [32]1-for-2 REVERSE,'95. [52]2-for-1,'92.

¶ S&P 500
\# MidCap 400
✣ SmallCap 600
• Options

Index	Ticker	Name of Issue (Call Price of Pfd. Stocks)	Market	Com. Rank. & Pfd. Rating	Inst. Hold Cos	Inst. Hold Shs. (000)	Principal Business	Price Range 1971-93 High	1971-93 Low	1994 High	1994 Low	1995 High	1995 Low	Dec. Sales in 100s	December, 1995 Last Sale Or Bid High	Low	Last	%Div Yield	P-E Ratio	Total Return % Annualized 12 Mo	36 Mo	60 Mo
1	WCSTF	✓Wescast Industries 'A'	NNM	NR	17	1148	Mfg exaust manifolds	....	....	12	7¾	11¾	7½	2183	10⅝	9⅜	9⅝	0.8	..	4.7	...	...
2	WSC	✓Wesco Financial	AS,B,P	B	43	6206	Prop & casualty insur/metal sv	149¾	2⅟16	136	112½	192	113½	106	192	162	182	0.6	45	56.7	31.0	31.5
3	WST	✓West Co	NY,Ph	B	99	8900	Pharmaceutical packaging	25¼	1⁵⁄16	29⅛	21¼	30⅝	22⅝	14300	24⅝	22⅝	23½	2.2	14	−12.6	4.9	15.7
4	WMAR	✓West Marine	NNM	NR	59	2258	Oper retail boat'g supply strs	15¼	13½	24	14	36¼	17¼	3397	36¼	31	31¼	...	27	65.6	...	...
5	WQP	West Penn Pwr 8.00% 'QUIDS'	NY	....[51]	1	4	Qtly Income Debt Securities	....	....	....	....	26½	24	1580	26½	25½	25⅞	7.7	..	...	...	...
6	WABC	✓Westamerica Bancorporation	NNM,Ch	B+	62	2503	Commercial bkg,California	30¼	3¾	33¼	25⅞	43¼	29	4565	43¼	40½	43¼	1.8	13	49.7	25.4	...
7	WBC	✓Westbridge Capital	NY	B−	16	1095	Ins hldg: life,accid,health	18¼	1⅟16	9⅝	6⅝	8⅛	5½	2063	6⅝	6	6⅝	...	9	−11.7	3.4	32.5
8	WE	✓Westcoast Energy	[1]NY,To,B,Ch,P,Ph,Mo	B	145	25326	Gas pipeline oper, Canada	19⅝	5	18⅝	14⅜	16⅜	13⅞	24178	15	14⅜	14⅝	...	..	−3.7	7.9	0.5
9	WES	✓Westcorp, Inc	NY,Ph	B	54	6189	Svgs&loan,California	14⅛	3⅝	11¼	7⅜	23½	7⅞	5655	20¼	17⅝	18½	s1.9	16	129	47.1	36.8
✣10•[2]	WCTV	✓Westcott Communications	NNM	NR	111	12185	Prod train'g/educ'l programs	22⅛	1⅞	24¾	6¾	18¼	11½	14655	15⅛	13⅛	13¾	...	19	10.0	7.1	43.8
11	WSTL	Westell Technologies'A'	NNM	NR	..	...	Dvlp telecommunication prd	....	....	....	....	27⅝	13	73145	27⅝	19½	25⅛	...	..	...	...	...
¶12•	WAI	✓Western Atlas	NY	NR	352	40506	Oilfield info sv/automat'n sys	....	....	50	36¾	52⅛	35⅝	31850	52⅛	47½	50½	...	27	35.1	...	...
13	WSBK	✓Western Bank	NNM	B+	22	882	General banking,Oregon	15½	⅞	16⅛	11¼	19¼	11½	1060	19¼	18½	18½	s2.0	16	64.3	38.7	60.1
14	BEEF	✓Western Beef Inc	NNM	B	16	561	Whsle/retails meat,groceries	14½	⅜	11⅛	5¼	7¼	4⅜	1033	6	5⅛	5¼	...	6	−10.6	3.8	...
15	WDEPY	✓Western Deep Levels ADR[55]	NSC	NR	36	3283	Gold mine in South Africa	84½	6⅛	58¼	30⅛	40¼	27¼	3406	36½	31¼	32¾	2.4	23	−16.6	56.8	6.2
16•[3]	WDC	✓Western Digital	NY,B,Ch,P,Ph	↑B−	177	28897	Computer controller mfr	32⅝	¼	20⅜	8⅝	22⅛	13⅛	106453	18⅞	15⅜	17⅞	...	9	5.1	28.1	31.0
17	WGR	✓Western Gas Resources	NY	NR	84	9177	Oper nat'l gas process'g ctrs	45⅛	8⅝	35⅜	17⅞	24¼	15	7065	17⅝	15¾	16⅛	1.2	d	−11.8	−12.4	8.6
18	Pr A	$2.625 cm Cv Pfd([57]51.838)	NY	BB	45	1919		....	....	51	30¼	38¾	30½	1401	35⅞	34⅝	35	7.5	..	...	...	...
19	WIR	✓Western Inv RE Tr SBI	AS,Ch	NR	53	6578	Real estate investment trust	21	9⅞	15⅛	11⅜	13	10⅜	6459	10⅞	10⅜	10¾	10.4	18	−4.4	4.7	2.9
20	WSTM	✓Western Micro Techn'gy	NNM	C	13	416	Dstr semiconductor parts	14	1⅞	11¼	4½	7⅝	2⅛	5895	6⅜	4¾	5¼	...	d	−22.2	7.3	14.9
21	WMC	✓Western Mining Hldg ADS[59]	NY	NR	34	4092	Expl/dvlp mineral&petro prod	21⅝	10¼	25½	18¾	27¾	19	1125	27¾	25⅞	26⅛	2.3	32	15.7	33.2	20.3
22•[2]	WNH	✓Western National	NY,Ch,Ph	NR	114	54153	Life insurance, annuity prd	....	....	16	9⅝	16¼	10⅞	16231	16¼	13½	16⅛	1.0	30	30.6	...	...
23	WPAC	Western Pacific Airlines	NNM	NR	..	...	Oper low fare airline	....	....	....	....	24¾	16½	55902	24¾	16½	16¾	...	..	...	...	...
#24	WPGI	✓Western Publishing	NNM	C	93	13039	Publisher of children's books	24¾	8½	20⅞	9¼	15⅛	7¾	19896	9⅞	7¾	7⅞	...	d	−16.0	−27.9	−4.7
25	WR	✓Western Resources	NY,B,Ch,P,Ph	A−	221	21821	Electric & gas utility	37¼	7¼	34⅞	26⅛	34	28⅝	41096	33⅞	31	33⅜	6.1	13	24.3	8.8	15.4
✣26	WW	✓Western Waste Ind[62]	NY	B−	75	6972	Waste management services	23½	3⅜	20⅝	13⅜	27½	14⅞	59858	27½	18¼	27⅜	...	24	88.8	33.5	8.2
27	WAB	✓Westinghouse Air Brake	NY,Ch,Ph	NR	37	14866	Mfr train air brakes	....	....	....	....	19	8⅝	18301	10¾	8⅝	10⅝	0.4	..	...	...	...
¶28•[3]	WX	✓Westinghouse Elec	NY,B,C,Ch,P,Ph	B	424	141054	Mfr electric equipment	39⅜	2	15¼	10⅞	17⅞	12⅛	324336	17⅞	15⅜	16⅜	1.2	82	35.5	11.1	−7.6
29	WGHI	Westmark Group Hldgs	NSC	NR	1	2	Real estate broker/finl svcs	161¼	19⅝	36⅝	11¼	14⅛	1½	2264	4¾	1½	1¹³⁄16	...	d	−86.2	−67.0	...
30	WCX	✓Westmoreland Coal	NY,Ph	C	31	2791	Metallurgical & steam coal	65¼	5	7⅛	3¾	6¾	2½	5109	3¼	2½	2⅝	...	d	−62.5	−38.4	−32.8
31	Pr A	Ser'A'cm[64]Cv[65]ExPfd([66]26.28)	NY	C	11	247		29	17¼	20½	13½	19	6	2079	7¾	6	6⅜	...	..	...	...	...
32	WN	Weston (George) Ltd	To,Mo,Vc	A−	15	1182	Food prd,dstr,retail: paper	46½	2⅝	44	35	50¼	39½	1616	50¼	47	50¼	1.6	13	20.8	12.9	...
33	WSTNA	✓Weston(Roy F)'A'	NNM	B−	26	2572	Environmental consult'g svcs	23	4¾	10¼	5⅛	6¼	4¼	3858	6¼	5⅛	5⅛	...	30	−6.8	−27.1	−4.3
34	WBK	Westpac Banking ADS[67]	NY,Ch,Ph	NR	43	3485	Commercial banking,Australia	23¼	8⅜	20⅛	14⅞	22½	16⅜	1944	22½	20⅜	22½	4.2	12	37.5	31.5	17.8
35	WPSN	✓Westpoint Stevens	NNM	NR	111	14662	Hshld prod,apparel,txtls	19¼	11¼	19½	12¾	23½	13⅛	30015	21	17⅞	20	...	d	39.6	...	...
¶36•[4]	W	✓Westvaco Corp	NY,B,Ch,P,Ph	B	381	66606	Printing & converting paper	27½	1¹⁵⁄16	26½	19¾	31⅞	24⅛	49312	27¾	24½	27¾	3.2	10	8.6	8.9	13.0
37	WNMP	Westwood Corp	NSC	NR	5	474	Marine elec dstr prod	2⅞	1⅛	3¼	1¾	3⅜	1⁹⁄16	1287	3¼	2¾	2⅞	1.4	10	57.3	39.1	...
¶38•[2]	WY	✓Weyerhaeuser Co	NY,B,C,Ch,P,Ph	B+	723	118886	Timber products: cartons	46½	13¾	51¼	35¾	50⅜	36⅞	116658	45¾	40⅞	43¼	3.7	9	17.3	7.7	18.6
39	WFSI	✓WFS Financial	NNM	NR	44	3058	Auto loan financing svcs	....	....	....	....	24½	13½	36970	20	13½	19½	...	..	...	...	...
40•[3]	WTI	✓Wheelabrator Tech	NY	NR	212	59293	Refuse-to-energy	23½	7⅝	21¼	13¼	17½	12½	53929	16¾	14¾	16¾	0.7	15	10.6	−3.2	12.2
¶41•[5]	WHR	✓Whirlpool Corp	NY,B,C,Ch,P,Ph	B	469	57062	Major household appliances	68	5½	73½	44⅝	60⅞	49¼	52980	57⅜	51⅞	53¼	2.6	18	7.2	8.2	21.0
42	WHRC	White River	NNM	NR	52	2690	Money mgmt,insur,finl svc	34½	29	37¾	29	39	29½	1059	38½	34½	38½	...	10	26.2	...	...
43	WHT	✓Whitehall Corp	NY,B,Ch	C	24	1570	Svc military & commer aircraft	65⅜	⅝	24¾	10¾	40½	20⅛	696	36	32¾	33½	...	41	47.3	23.3	20.6
¶44•[5]	WH	✓Whitman Corp	NY,B,Ch,P,Ph	B	349	76232	Pepsi bottlers/consumer prd	41¼	2⅝	18	14¾	23⅜	15⅝	35159	23⅜	21⅞	23¼	1.6	18	43.6	18.3	...
45	WIX	✓Whitman Medical	AS	↓C	5	174	Oper spcl medl training school	15	¾	8½	3¼	9¼	4⅞	1432	7⅜	5¾	7⅛	...	d	1.8	−0.6	21.0
✣46	WKR	✓Whittaker Corp	NY,B,Ch,P,Ph	NR	85	5978	Aerospace:Fluid ctrl/elec sys	53¼	1⅛	20¼	13½	24⅝	16⅞	5524	22	16⅞	21¾	...	27	13.7	21.1	...
✣47•[6]	WFMI	✓Whole Foods Market	NNM	NR	93	6920	Natural food supermkt chain	23⅜	7¼	25¾	9½	16¼	10⅛	14038	14⅝	12⅛	13⅞	...	24	42.3	−1.4	...
48	WHFI	✓Wholesome & Hearty Foods	NNM	NR	38	2490	Mfr frozen meatless burgers	14	1¹¹⁄16	30¾	9½	14½	7	21071	10⅛	7	7⅝	...	25	−35.8	48.9	...
✣49•[5]	WHX	✓WHX Corp	NY	NR	103	14282	Large U.S. steel producer	40⅛	2⅜	22⅝	12⅞	14⅝	9⅝	26806	11½	10	10⅞	...	5	−16.3	23.7	25.5
50	WS	Wrrts(Purch 1 com)	NY	....	7	51		12	⅞	16⅝	7⅛	8⅝	3⅜	4727	5⅜	3⅝	4⅛	...	..	...	...	...
51	Pr	Sr 'A'cm Cv Pfd([74]52.275)	NY,Ch	↓B	34	1362		67¼	48	77¾	47	51¼	39¾	3434	46¾	42¼	44	7.4	..	...	...	...
52	Pr B	Sr 'B'cm Cv Pfd([75]52.625)	NY	↓B	33	1271		....	....	51¼	41¾	47	37¾	3429	45	41	42½	8.8	..	...	...	...

Uniform Footnote Explanations-See Page 4. Other: [1]Vc [2]CBOE:Cycle 1. [3]ASE:Cycle 1. [4]P:Cycle 1. [5]CBOE:Cycle 3. [6]ASE:Cycle 2. [51]Rated'A' by S&P. [52]®$1.03,'94. [53]Fiscal Jul'93 & prior. [54]Stk dstr of Monorex Inc. [55]ADR equals 1 ord shr. [56]®$2.47,'95. [57]Fr 2-16-97,scale to $50 in 2004. [58]Incl $0.212 non-taxable:©$0.10,'94. [59]Each ADS rep 4 ord shr,$A0.50. [60]Incl proceeds from sale of rts. [61]31 Wks Dec'94. [62]USA Waste Svcs plan acq,1.5 com. [63]Fiscal Jun'93 & prior. [64]Dep for 0.25 shr Ser'A'Cv Exch Pfd. [65]Co opt fr 7-1-96 exch for $100 amt 8.50%Cv 2012. [66]Fr 7-1-96,scale to $25 in 2002. [67]Each ADS rep 5 Ord shrs,A$1.00. [68]Approx. [69]As reported, 12-25-94. [70]®$2.09,'94. [71]14 Wk Dec'93. [72]Stk dstr of BioWhittaker Inc,'91. [73]®$2.14,'94. [74]Fr 7-1-96,scale to $50 in 2003. [75]Fr 10-1-97,scale to $50 in 2004.

Splits ◆ Index	Cash Divs. Ea.Yr. Since	Dividends Latest Payment Period $	Date	Ex. Div.	Total $ So Far 1995	Ind. Rate	Paid 1994	Financial Position Mil-$ Cash& Equiv.	Curr. Assets	Curr. Liab.	Balance Sheet Date	Capitalization Lg Trm Debt Mil-$	Shs. 000 Pfd.	Com.	Earnings $ Per Shr. Years End	1991	1992	1993	1994	1995	Last 12 Mos.	Interim Earnings Period	$ per Shr. 1994	1995	Index
1	....	Plan qtly div			...	0.08	....	....	44.1	26.6	j1-01-95	15.6	...	±10741	Dc	...	...	p0.51	1.40	....	j1.20	9 Mo Sep	1.24	1.04	1
2	1973	Q0.255	12-6-95	11-6	1.02	1.02	0.98	Book Value $121.07			9-30-95	37.4	...	7120	Dc	4.15	0.70	Δ2.63	2.66	....	4.06	9 Mo Sep	2.63	4.03	2
3	1950	Q0.13	2-7-96	1-22	0.49	0.52	0.45	17.3	155	62.2	9-30-95	106	...	16620	Dc	□d0.55	1.26	Δ1.42	1.70	....	1.70	9 Mo Sep	1.26	1.26	3
4	....	None Since Public			...	Nil	....	0.48	74.4	17.0	9-30-95	6.49	...	7453	Dc	...	p0.53	p0.60	0.91	....	1.18	9 Mo Sep	0.84	1.11	4
5	1995	Q0.50	12-29-95	12-26	1.10	2.00	....	Co option redm fr 6-12-2000 at $25				70.0	...	...	Dc	...	...	...	....	....	....	Mature 6-30-2025			5
6	1935	Q0.20	2-14-96	1-17	0.74	0.80	0.62	Book Value $22.18			9-30-95	20.0	...	9830	Dc	2.18	2.40	1.17	3.06	....	3.26	9 Mo Sep	2.07	2.27	6
7	....	None Paid			...	Nil	....	Equity per shr $6.60			9-30-95	19.2	20	5986	Dc	0.20	Δ0.40	0.78	[52]1.13	....	0.77	9 Mo Sep	0.83	□0.47	7
8	1967	gQ0.24	12-31-95	12-6	g0.93	0.96	g0.89	....	816	1428	j3-31-95	3658	11295	86722	Dc	1.36	d1.31	1.82	1.83	....	j1.71	9 Mo Sep	1.35	1.23	8
9◆	1989	Q0.09	11-24-95	11-7	s0.356	0.36	s0.282	Book Value $11.72			9-30-95	176	...	26540	Dc	1.09	0.11	□0.65	0.77	....	1.19	9 Mo Sep	0.54	0.96	9
10◆	....	None Since Public			...	Nil	....	12.9	47.1	23.5	9-30-95	0.02	...	19747	Dc	0.12	0.30	0.47	0.61	....	0.73	9 Mo Sep	0.43	0.55	10
11	....	None Since Public			...	Nil	....	1.47	35.7	34.7	9-30-95	3.36	...	★±17234	Mr	...	...	...	pd0.01	....	....	6 Mo Sep	n/a	pd0.04	11
12	....	None Since Public			...	Nil	....	79.6	960	504	9-30-95	535	...	53193	Dc	...	...	p[53]0.77	1.60	E1.85	1.75	9 Mo Sep	1.20	1.35	12
13◆	1994	Q0.10	11-15-95	10-27	s0.393	0.37	s0.367	Book Value $7.40			3-31-95	0.84	...	8487	Dc	0.90	0.95	1.06	1.06	....	1.18	9 Mo Sep	0.79	0.91	13
14◆	....	h[54]....	4-10-84	4-11	...	Nil	....	1.09	26.9	17.9	9-30-95	7.16	...	5463	Dc	0.46	0.79	0.81	0.87	....	0.86	9 Mo Sep	0.62	0.61	14
15	1967	0.257	10-2-95	8-2	0.766	0.77	1.367	27.4	300	293	j12-31-94	....	...	27713	Dc	4.97	3.52	1.65	1.42	....	1.42	No interim reporting			15
16	....	None Since Public			...	Nil	....	242	729	385	9-30-95	....	...	47514	Je	d4.59	d2.49	d0.79	1.77	[56]2.56	1.99	3 Mo Sep	0.73	0.16	16
17	1991	Q0.05	2-14-96	12-27	0.20	0.20	0.20	6.87	175	246	6-30-95	432	4160	25761	Dc	0.94	1.43	1.25	d0.19	....	d0.42	9 Mo Sep	d0.19	d0.42	17
18	1994	Q0.65⅝	2-14-96	12-27	2.62½	2.625	1.889	Cv into 1.2579 com,$39.75				....	2400	...	Dc	...	...	...	....	....	....				18
19	1965	Q0.28	12-15-95	11-21	1.12	1.12	[58]1.12	Book Value $11.70			9-30-95	142	...	16969	Dc	0.91	0.69	0.70	0.92	....	0.59	9 Mo Sep	0.77	0.44	19
20	....	None Since Public			...	Nil	....	0.08	23.2	15.3	9-30-95	0.07	...	3709	Dc	d1.00	0.02	d0.19	d0.17	....	d1.61	9 Mo Sep	d0.02	d1.46	20
21	1990	0.365	11-10-95	10-2	0.597	0.60	[60]0.692	43.0	1372	914	j6-30-95	724	...	1117581	Je	□1.21	□0.51	□0.47	0.38	Δ0.82	0.82				21
22	1994	Q0.04	12-1-95	11-8	0.16	0.16	0.12	Equity per shr $11.74			9-30-95	148	...	62345	Dc	...	Δp1.37	p1.91	p1.18	....	0.53	9 Mo Sep	p1.11	0.46	22
23	....	None Since Public			...	Nil	....	3.05	19.8	18.1	9-30-95	....	p...	★13066	Dc	...	...	...	p[61]d0.17	....	....	9 Mo Sep	n/a	pd0.72	23
24	....	None Since Public			...	Nil	....	22.2	238	61.1	10-28-95	150	20	21067	Ja	0.62	0.80	□d1.99	d0.88	Ed3.30↓	d2.89	9 Mo Oct	d0.58	d2.59	24
25	1924	Q0.505	1-2-96	12-1	2.01	2.02	1.97	1.68	400	682	9-30-95	1342	1749	62675	Dc	Δ1.91	2.20	2.76	2.82	E2.65↑	2.51	12 Mo Sep	2.85	2.51	25
26	....	None Since Public			...	Nil	....	8.37	51.5	34.0	9-30-95	78.8	...	14658	Je	0.81	0.17	d0.73	Δ0.83	1.10	1.12	3 Mo Sep	0.26	0.28	26
27	1995	0.01	11-30-95	11-13	0.01	0.04	....	1.19	110	60.0	9-30-95	288	...	28558	Dc	...	...	...	p0.99	....	....	9 Mo Sep	n/a	p□1.05	27
28	1935	Q0.05	12-1-95	11-1	0.20	0.20	0.20	167	4313	3381	9-30-95	1746	4000	p415261	Dc	d3.46	□d2.83	□d0.91	0.07	E0.20	d0.34	9 Mo Sep	0.38	d0.03	28
29◆	....	None Since Public			...	Nil	....	0.53	17.8	19.6	9-30-95	0.01	...	1351	Dc	d3.60	d5.40	[63]d22.50	Δd7.50	....	d7.42	9 Mo Sep	d2.79	d2.71	29
30	....	0.08	12-10-92	11-12	...	Nil	....	30.0	37.9	40.2	9-30-95	2.34	575	6961	Dc	d1.62	d5.68	d14.74	2.19	....	d9.98	9 Mo Sep	d1.39	d13.56	30
31	1992	aQ0.53⅛	7-1-95	6-16	a1.06¼	Nil	1.06¼	Cv into 1.708 com,$14.64				....	2300	...	Dc	...	...	...	....	....	....	Accum on pfd $1.0625 to 7-1-95			31
32	1930	gQ0.20	1-1-96	12-13	g0.70	0.80	g0.70	251	1754	1753	j12-31-94	1008	41	47061	Dc	1.81	0.85	1.21	2.48	....	j3.74	9 Mo Sep	1.52	2.78	32
33	....	None Paid			...	Nil	....	19.1	125	56.2	9-30-95	25.2	...	±9517	Dc	±0.58	±0.79	±0.28	±d0.12	....	0.17	9 Mo Sep	±d0.05	±0.24	33
34	1817	[68]0.54¾	2-9-96	1-4	0.393	0.94	0.427	Book Value $14.36			9-30-94	2173	211200	1821240	Sp	1.58	d4.36	0.03	1.33	P1.89	1.89				34
35	....	None Since Public			...	Nil	....	2.36	453	300	9-30-95	1035	...	32232	Dc	...	...	□d10.03	d6.02	....	d5.89	9 Mo Sep	d4.56	d4.43	35
36◆	1892	Q0.22	1-2-96	12-6	0.77	0.88	0.733	152	787	429	10-31-95	1147	...	100613	Oc	1.40	1.37	Δ0.57	1.03	□2.80	2.80				36
37◆	1992	Q0.009	12-22-95	11-29	0.036	0.04	0.033	1.58	16.0	9.13	9-30-95	0.09	...	5582	Mr	0.32	0.30	0.38	0.29	....	0.29	6 Mo Sep	0.15	0.15	37
38	1933	Q0.40	11-27-95	10-25	1.50	1.60	1.20	Book Value $22.10			9-24-95	[69]★5382	...	201710	Dc	□d0.50	1.83	Δ2.58	2.86	E5.00	3.59	9 Mo Sep	1.95	2.68	38
39	....	None Since Public			...	Nil	....	Book Value $3.31			3-31-95	p571	...	★22749	Dc	...	...	...	p0.99	....	....	6 Mo Sep	n/a	p1.05	39
40◆	1992	A0.11	7-6-95	6-19	0.11	0.11	0.10	65.5	458	439	9-30-95	724	...	182781	Dc	0.73	□0.94	0.86	0.97	E1.10	1.04	9 Mo Sep	0.73	0.80	40
41	1929	Q0.34	12-31-95	11-29	1.36	1.36	1.22	144	3551	3608	9-30-95	978	...	74007	Dc	2.45	2.90	□3.19	[70]2.10	E3.00↓	1.35	9 Mo Sep	3.30	2.55	41
42	....	None Since Public			...	Nil	....	Equity per shr $27.22			12-31-94	85.7	7	6370	Dc	...	...	[71]d1.45	4.47	....	3.98	9 Mo Sep	3.20	2.71	42
43	....	None Paid			...	Nil	....	9.14	30.7	10.4	9-30-95	....	...	2718	Dc	d3.06	d0.49	d0.67	d0.45	....	0.81	9 Mo Sep	d0.52	0.74	43
44◆	1950	Q0.09½	1-1-96	12-6	0.36	0.38	0.32	83.5	820	531	9-30-95	850	...	105150	Dc	0.92	0.56	□0.99	0.97	E1.30	1.21	9 Mo Sep	0.70	0.94	44
45	....	None Paid			...	Nil	....	0.72	13.4	18.0	9-30-95	2.17	...	3806	Mr	0.22	d0.08	0.06	d0.10	....	d0.44	6 Mo Sep	d0.02	d0.36	45
46◆	....	h[72]....	12-2-91	12-3	...	Nil	....	0.68	127	49.4	7-31-95	77.0	1	8563	Oc	2.53	1.66	Δ0.60	1.06	P0.82	0.82				46
47◆	....	None Since Public			...	Nil	....	2.55	34.9	32.0	7-02-95	42.0	...	p14801	Sp	0.45	0.43	0.29	0.61	P0.58	0.58				47
48◆	....	None Since Public			...	Nil	....	8.09	15.4	2.56	9-30-95	....	...	7678	Dc	0.12	0.10	0.18	0.28	....	0.30	9 Mo Sep	0.24	0.26	48
49	....	None Paid			...	Nil	....	370	786	256	9-30-95	286	6949	25971	Dc	0.27	d1.85	□1.02	□[73]2.54	....	2.17	9 Mo Sep	□2.10	1.73	49
50	....	Terms&trad. basis should			be checked in detail			Wrrts expire 1-4-96				....	...	p2000	Dc	...	...	...	....	....	....				50
51	1993	Q0.81¼	1-2-96	12-13	3.25	3.25	3.25	Cv into 3.1686 com, $15.78				....	2700	...	Dc	...	...	...	....	....	....				51
52	1995	Q0.93¾	1-2-96	12-13	3.792	3.75	....	Cv into 2.451 com, $20.40				....	3500	...	Dc	...	...	...	....	....	....				52

◆**Stock Splits & Divs By Line Reference Index** [9]Adj to 5%,'95. [10]2-for-1,'93. [13]10%,'91,'92,'93:2-for-1,'93:Adj for 7%,'95. [14]10%,'93. [29]1-for-150 REVERSE,'91:1-for-30 REVERSE,'95. [36]3-for-2,'95. [37]1-for-3 REVERSE,'92:10%,'93,'94,'95. [40]2-for-1,'91,'93. [44]No adj for stk dstr,'91. [46]No adj for spl $40 dstr,'89:No adj for stk dstr of BioWhittaker,'91. [47]2-for-1,'93. [48]2-for-1,'93:3-for-2,'94.

¶ S&P 500 # MidCap 400 ✚ SmallCap 600 • Options

Index	Ticker	Name of Issue (Call Price of Pfd. Stocks)	Market	Com. Rank. & Pfd. Rating	Inst. Hold Cos	Inst. Hold Shs. (000)	Principal Business	Price Range 1971-93 High	1971-93 Low	1994 High	1994 Low	1995 High	1995 Low	Dec. Sales in 100s	December, 1995 Last Sale Or Bid High	Low	Last	%Div Yield	P-E Ratio	Total Return % Annualized 12 Mo	36 Mo	60 Mo
1	WRO	✓Wichita River Oil[51]	AS	NR	4	456	Oil & gas explor,dev,prod'n	711¼	¾	1 15/16	¾	1⅛	¼	....	....	....	....	...	..	−64.3	−33.5	−41.0
2	WIKS	✓Wickes Lumber	NNM	NR	27	2172	Retail,dstr building materials	18¼	12¼	24¾	10	16½	5	11698	6¼	5	5	...	2	−50.0	...	...
✚3	WIC	✓WICOR, Inc	NY,Ch	B	126	5098	Util hldg:Wisconsin Gas	32⅞	7¾	32⅝	25½	32⅞	26⅝	7244	32⅞	30⅝	32¼	5.1	16	24.5	13.2	17.0
4	JW.A	✓Wiley(John)Sons 'A'[52]	NY,Ch	B+	62	7748	College text,reference books	18½	4⅝	23	17½	35	21⅞	5499	35	31½	32¾	1.1	26	50.6	41.2	37.8
5	JW.B	Cl 'B'[54]	NY,Ch	B+	13	754		18½	9/16	23¼	17⅝	34¾	21⅞	236	34¾	31½	32½	1.0	26	49.3	39.1	36.8
¶6•[1]	WMTT	✓Willamette Indus	NNM	B+	370	35234	Mfr wood and paper products	50	2 7/16	59½	39½	72¾	46¾	52671	61	53¾	56¼	2.1	6	20.2	15.3	24.1
7	WTU	✓Williams Coal Seam Gas Rlty[55]	NY,Ch	NR	15	571	Natural gas royalty interests	29¼	20	27¼	15¾	20⅞	16⅛	3405	19¾	18½	19¾	13.6	8	33.4	...	...
8	WMCO	✓Williams Controls	NNM	NR	23	2426	Mfr electr/transportation pd	2½	¼	4	2 5/16	3¾	2 3/16	14912	3	2¼	2⅜	...	9	−30.0	68.8	40.6
¶9•[2]	WMB	✓Williams Cos	NY,B,Ch,P,Ph	↑B+	517	66190	Gas PL,petrol prod,telecomm	31⅞	6⅜	33⅜	22⅛	44½	24½	43253	44½	41¾	43⅞	2.5	17	81.7	35.2	32.3
10	WMZ	Williams Cos 9.60%'QUICS'	NY	....[56]	1	52	Quarterly Income Capital Sec	....	....	....	....	26⅝	25½	635	26⅝	25¾	26⅛	9.2	..	...	...	...
✚11•[3]	WSGC	✓Williams-Sonoma	NNM	B	118	9812	Retails cook'g/serv'g equip	18¾	1⅛	35¼	15¾	30⅜	15⅝	52092	20¼	16⅝	18½	...	58	−41.7	54.7	16.2
12	WCG	✓Willis Corroon Group ADS[57]	NY,Ph	NR	48	5713	Insurance brokerage	29⅝	12⅝	18⅛	10⅛	13⅝	9⅝	8017	11¾	10	11⅝	4.8	42	18.5	−2.8	−9.7
#13	WILM	✓Wilmington Trust Corp	NNM	A+	161	11589	Commercial bkg,Delaware	31	1 1/16	28½	22	32½	22¾	11831	32½	30¾	30⅞	3.9	12	41.7	10.5	12.8
14	WOC	✓Wilshire Oil Texas	NY,To,B,Ch,Ph,Vc	B–	24	1143	Oil & gas expl & prod'n	13	2⅝	7¼	6	7	5½	973	6⅛	5½	5¾	1.2	19	−15.5	−2.9	11.9
15	WIL	✓Wilshire Technologies	AS	NR	9	116	Mfr disposable medical prod	21⅝	6¼	15½	1⅛	2¼	⅜	6060	⅞	⅜	⅝	...	d	−50.0	−57.3	...
16•[4]	WND	✓Windmere Corp	NY,Ch,Ph	B–	62	7845	Mfr small electr appliances	29	1/16	12	6¾	10⅛	5¾	11021	7¼	5⅞	7⅛	2.8	20	−4.1	10.5	23.1
¶17•[5]	WIN	✓Winn-Dixie Stores	NY,B,Ch,Ph	A+	261	23938	Food supermarkets in south	39⅞	2⅝	29¼	21⅜	37⅝	25⅝	28053	37⅝	32⅛	36⅞	2.4	23	44.8	0.8	21.1
✚18•[5]	WGO	✓Winnebago Indus	NY,B,Ch,P,Ph	B–	65	5612	Mfr mtr homes: recr vehicles	48¼	1¾	13⅞	7⅝	10¾	7⅜	7634	8¼	7½	7¾	5.2	8	−14.6	−1.1	27.8
19•[6]	WCII	Winstar Communications	NNM	NR	45	8360	Telecommun,informat'n svcs	4	⅞	9¾	2¾	23⅛	4⅝	65221	18	13¾	17⅛	...	d	87.7	114	...
20	WINN	Winston Hotels	NNM	NR	51	5691	Real estate investment trust	....	....	12½	8¾	12	9	11876	12	11⅛	11⅞	e8.1	13	36.1	...	...
21	WRS	✓Winston Resources	AS	B–	4	287	Personnel recruit'g/placem't	6⅝	¼	2¾	1¼	2½	1⅛	686	1 5/16	1⅛	1 5/16	...	7	−16.0	61.4	24.5
22	WIRL	Wireless One	NNM	NR	..	...	Own/oper cable T.V. sys	....	....	....	....	18⅛	10½	10084	18⅛	14⅝	16½	...	..	...	...	...
23	WTT	✓Wireless Telecom	AS,Ch,Ph	NR	25	1757	Mfr communic sys test'g eqp	1⅞	11/16	9⅞	1 3/16	21⅝	5⅛	10586	18⅞	15⅞	16¾	1.4	31	119	196	...
24•[5]	WCLX	✓Wisconsin Central Trans	NNM	NR	176	13322	Oper regional railroad sys	30	8¼	48¼	29	68¾	39½	26097	67½	59	65¾	...	26	61.3	53.4	...
#25	WEC	✓Wisconsin Energy[60] Corp[61]	[7]NY,B,C,Ch	A	326	40664	Hdlg:El & gas utility	29⅜	3½	27½	23⅛	30⅞	25¾	23006	30⅞	29⅛	30⅝	4.8	14	24.0	10.8	13.7
26	FHC	✓Wisconsin Pharmacal[63]	AS,Ph	NR	13	815	Mfr special chem/consumer pd	28	3⅜	15	3¼	6¾	2⅜	3461	4⅛	2½	2⅞	...	d	−36.5	−41.1	−4.8
✚27	WZR	✓Wiser Oil	NY,Ch,Ph	B	67	4228	Oil/gas explor,devel,prod'n	33⅛	2	18⅞	13⅛	15	10⅞	4194	12⅞	11⅞	12	3.3	11	−14.7	−1.6	−1.5
#28•[8]	WIT	✓Witco Corp	NY,B,Ch,Ph	B	246	44872	Petroleum & spec chemicals	32¼	2 3/16	35	24⅜	35⅝	24¼	22369	30⅝	28⅜	29¼	3.8	12	22.1	10.4	19.2
29	WIZ.EC	✓Wiz Technology	ECM	NR	2	15	Markets computer software	6⅛	2	5¾	2	5½	2	4344	4¼	3⅜	4⅛	...	d	26.9	...	...
30	WLRF	✓WLR Foods Inc	NNM	B	60	3372	Major turkey/chicken producer	16⅞	5¾	21⅝	12⅛	18⅛	12	4806	17½	16	16½	1.5	21	−3.4	6.5	13.3
✚31•[9]	WMS	✓WMS Industries	NY,B,Ch,Ph	B–	97	11779	Coin-op games:casino hotels	34	1	29⅞	15⅞	24¼	16	13391	18⅞	16	16⅜	...	19	−3.7	−10.2	53.3
¶32•[9]	WMX	✓WMX Technologies	NY,B,C,Ch,P	A–	900	302798	Solid/chem waste mgmt serv	46⅝	3/16	30¾	22⅝	32½	25¾	255283	30⅞	28⅜	29¾	2.0	19	13.1	−7.6	−2.1
33	HBW	✓Wolf (Howard B)	AS	B	7	62	Women's fashion apparel	18¼	1⅜	8⅜	6	7¾	5⅝	187	7⅜	6½	7¼	4.4	8	12.7	1.8	30.6
34	WLHN	✓Wolohan Lumber	NNM	A–	54	2615	Building supply centers	25¼	⅞	18½	13¾	16¼	8¾	3186	10¼	8⅞	9¾	2.9	11	−31.3	−23.8	−0.7
35	WOSIN	Wolters Kluwer Nv[65]	Am	NR	..	...	Int'l publishing services	129	22¼	133½	101¼	151⅞	117½	....	151⅞	141¼	151¾	...	..	...	...	...
✚36•[10]	WLV	✓Wolverine Tube	NY,Ch,Ph	NR	138	10071	Mfr copper,copper-alloy tube	19¾	15½	26⅝	18⅞	43½	23¼	10146	37½	33½	37½	...	18	59.6	...	...
✚37	WWW	✓Wolverine World Wide	NY,B,Ch,Ph,P	B	146	12563	Mfr branded footwear	14⅞	7/16	18⅛	12⅜	34⅛	15⅜	12624	34⅛	31¼	31½	0.4	23	93.1	71.5	57.3
38•[11]	WNDR	✓Wonderware Corp	NNM	NR	103	10051	Dstr windows-based softwr prd	29¼	14	35½	12	42¾	12¾	145782	27	12¾	17⅛	...	d	−50.7	...	...
39	WDHD	✓Woodhead Indus	NNM	B+	60	6651	Electrical specialty prod	10⅝	13/16	12¼	8⅞	16¾	10½	4792	16	13⅞	14¼	1.8	17	36.0	23.0	28.4
¶40•[9]	Z	✓Woolworth Corp	NY,B,C,Ch,P,Ph	B–	361	67543	Variety,discount,shoe stores	36⅝	2	26¼	12⅞	19⅜	12¼	120221	15⅛	12¼	13	...	33	−9.5	−23.0	−12.4
41	Pr A	$2.20 cm Cv A Pfd(45)vtg	NY,Ch	NR	2	.3		205	18¾	145	79	106	76	1	80¼	80¼	73⅞B	3.0	..	...	...	...
42	WRLD	✓World Acceptance	NNM	NR	75	15935	Small-loan consumer finance	7⅝	2 3/16	8	5½	16¼	7	15827	12½	10	11¼	...	24	42.3	36.2	...
43	WLDA	✓World Airways	NNM	NR	..	...	Passenger/cargo air trans't sv	....	....	....	....	12¾	9	14872	11⅝	9¾	11¼	...	12	...	...	...
44	INT	✓World Fuel Services	NY,Ch,Ph,P	B	47	3151	Aviat'n fuel'g svc/oil recy'g	17⅜	1 1/16	10⅞	7¾	16	9¾	4830	15⅞	13⅝	15⅞	e1.3	13	59.3	23.3	11.1
#45•[12]	WCOM	✓WorldCom Inc	NNM	B	450	108884	Long distance telephone svcs	26⅜	....	29½	14	35⅞	19⅛	263196	35⅞	30¼	35¼	...	26	81.9	33.6	55.0
46•[12]	WOA	✓WorldCorp Inc	NY,B,Ch,P,Ph	C	59	11103	Hldg co:charter air services	15½	1½	10	3⅝	13⅝	7¼	27304	11½	9	10	...	4	40.4	16.2	20.1
47	WTX	✓Worldtex Inc	NY	NR	46	9236	Mfr covered elastic yarn	8⅞	4⅞	5⅞	3½	6⅝	3⅝	4692	6¼	5½	5¾	...	13	58.6	−8.0	...
¶48•[13]	WTHG	✓Worthington Indus	NNM,Ph	A–	306	49920	Steel process'g, plastics	21⅝	1/16	23½	17½	23¼	16⅝	55352	21⅜	18½	20¾	2.1	17	6.3	13.9	18.7
#49	WPH	✓WPL Holdings[68]	NY,B,Ch,P	A	117	5243	Utility hldg:Wisconsin Pwr/Lt	36¾	6¾	32⅞	26⅜	31¾	27¼	6583	31½	30⅜	30⅝	6.3	16	17.3	2.8	11.5
50	WPPGY	WPP Group ADS[69]	NNM	NR	32	1783	Intl mktg/advertising svcs	130⅝	5	19⅝	12¾	26⅞	15⅝	4527	25½	22¾	25⅜	0.8	20	56.2	52.3	15.2
51	WPS	✓WPS Resources	NY,B,Ch,P	↓A–	133	4764	Electric & natural gas	36½	5⅜	33⅝	26¼	34¼	26¾	5073	34¼	31⅝	34	5.5	16	33.8	4.8	8.7
¶52•[10]	WWY	✓Wrigley, (Wm) Jr	NY,Ch,Ph	A+	370	30653	Major chewing gum producer	46⅛	1 1/16	53⅞	38⅛	54	42⅞	38122	54	46⅞	52½	e1.3	27	9.7	18.2	27.7

Uniform Footnote Explanations-See Page 4. Other: [1]NY:Cycle 2. [2]CBOE:Cycle 2. [3]ASE,CBOE,P:Cycle 2. [4]P:Cycle 3. [5]CBOE:Cycle 1. [6]ASE,CBOE,NY:Cycle 1. [7]P,Ph [8]NY:Cycle 1. [9]Ph:Cycle 2. [10]ASE:Cycle 3. [11]CBOE,P:Cycle 1. [12]P:Cycle 1. [13]Ph:Cycle 3. [51]ASE trading halted 10-2-95. [52]1/10 vtg. [53]®$1.11,'95. [54]Cv into 1 Cl 'A'. [55]Trust Units. [56]Rated BB+ by S&P. [57]Ea ADS rep 5 ord shrs, 12.5p. [58]Approx. [59]®$0.26,'94. [60]Approve hldg co,Primergy Corp,1 com. [61]Approve mgr, Northern States Power. [62]Subsid pfd. [63]Plan name chg, Female Health Co. [64]®$1.91,'94. [65]All data reported in Dutch guilders. [66]Co est. $1.80 pymt for Fiscal'94. [67]®$0.53,'94. [68]Plan mgr w/IES Indus&Interstate Pwr,1 new co. [69]1-for-5 REVERSE,'95.

Index (Splits ◆)	Cash Divs. Ea. Yr. Since	Dividends: Latest Payment Period $	Date	Ex. Div.	Total $ So Far 1995	Ind. Rate	Paid 1994	Financial Position Mil-$ Cash& Equiv.	Curr. Assets	Curr. Liab.	Balance Sheet Date	Capitalization Lg Trm Debt Mil-$	Shs. 000 Pfd.	Com.	Earnings $ Per Shr. Years End	1991	1992	1993	1994	1995	Last 12 Mos.	Interim Earnings Period	$ per Shr. 1994	1995	Index
1	....	None Since Public			...	Nil	....	0.05	0.98	10.6	9-30-95	15.4	...	7974	Dc	Δd0.51	0.01	□0.02	d1.60	....	d1.63	9 Mo Sep	d0.12	d0.15	1
2	....	None Since Public			...	Nil	....	4.49	254	88.6	9-30-95	221	...	±6143	Dc	...	±p1.26	p±1.38	±4.59	....	3.03	9 Mo Sep	±1.53	±d0.03	2
3	1960	Q0.41	11-30-95	11-8	1.62	1.64	1.58	21.5	240	218	9-30-95	168	...	★18067	Dc	1.54	□1.40	1.82	1.99	....	2.05	9 Mo Sep	1.27	1.33	3
4◆	1982	Q0.08¾	1-18-96	12-26	0.33	0.35	0.293	2.08	121	102	10-31-95	....	...	±16088	Ap	±0.23	□±0.23	±0.50	±0.76	±[53]1.13	1.25	6 Mo Oct	±0.56	±0.69	4
5◆	1904	Q0.07¾	1-18-96	12-26	0.293	0.31	0.26	....	...	...		....	...	3291	Ap	±0.23	±□0.23	±0.50	±0.76	±[53]1.13	1.25	6 Mo Oct	±0.56	±0.69	5
6◆	1962	Q0.30	12-14-95	11-22	1.14	1.20	0.96	14.0	807	390	9-30-95	916	...	55274	Dc	0.90	1.52	Δ2.02	3.23	E9.60↓	8.38	9 Mo Sep	1.82	6.97	6
7	1993	0.695	11-29-95	11-10	2.691	2.69	2.237	5.13	5.13	0.06	9-30-95	....	...	9700	Dc	p0.48	p1.21	1.95	2.24	....	2.46	9 Mo Sep	1.77	1.99	7
8	....	None Paid			...	Nil	....	1.65	25.8	7.88	9-30-95	18.1	...	17265	Sp	□d0.10	Δ0.07	0.14	0.22	0.26	0.26				8
9◆	1974	Q0.27	12-26-95	11-29	1.08	1.08	0.84	63.6	1262	1945	9-30-95	2908	3369	101561	Dc	1.18	Δ1.25	2.20	□2.44	E2.60	13.00	9 Mo Sep	□1.68	12.24	9
10	1995	0.87½	2-1-96	1-17	0.80	2.40	....	Co option redm fr 9-1-97 at $25				69.0	...	...	Dc	...	...	...	....	....	....	Mature 9-30-2025			10
11◆	....	None Since Public			...	Nil	....	5.23	161	135	7-30-95	6.72	...	25379	Ja	0.06	0.09	0.44	0.75	....	0.32	9 Mo Oct	0.24	d0.19	11
12	1991	[58]0.136	1-9-96	11-28	0.556	0.56	0.53	702	2004	1783	j12-31-94	117	...	418938	Dc	□1.48	0.48	0.84	Nil	....	0.28	9 Mo Sep	0.60	0.88	12
13◆	1914	Q0.30	11-15-95	10-30	1.17	1.20	1.06	Book Value $12.72			9-30-95	....	...	35257	Dc	2.03	□2.09	2.24	2.37	E2.65	2.50	9 Mo Sep	1.77	1.90	13
14◆	1993	A0.07	8-18-95	7-26	0.07	0.07	s0.058	1.20	36.3	6.30	9-30-95	48.2	...	9588	Dc	d0.34	0.35	0.45	0.36	....	0.31	9 Mo Sep	0.35	0.30	14
15	....	None Since Public			...	Nil	....	0.05	2.19	2.66	8-31-95	7.30	...	4490	Nv	d2.54	d3.34	d1.38	d2.05	....	d1.29	9 Mo Aug	d1.35	d0.59	15
16	1994	0.05	12-15-95	11-29	0.20	0.20	0.15	5.60	148	21.4	9-30-95	3.06	...	16779	Dc	d0.59	Δ0.27	Δ0.60	1.17	....	0.36	9 Mo Sep	0.93	0.12	16
17◆	1934	M0.075	1-2-96	12-13	0.81½	0.90	0.74½	25.8	1425	1014	9-20-95	75.4	...	150610	Je	1.10	□1.41	1.56	1.45	1.56	1.58	12 Wk Sep	0.27	0.30	17
18	1995	Q0.10	12-4-95	11-1	0.40	0.40	....	11.0	121	51.2	8-26-95	12.7	...	25341	Au	d1.18	□d0.11	0.37	□0.69	1.10	0.92	14 Wk Nov	0.30	0.12	18
19	....	None Paid			...	Nil	....	8.97	21.5	8.12	8-31-95	12.6	933	24139	Fb	d1.26	d0.93	Δd1.09	d0.42	....	d0.50	6 Mo Aug	d0.14	d0.22	19
20	1994	†0.27	1-16-96	12-27	0.87	0.96	0.27	Equity per shr $8.31			9-30-95	34.4	...	9880	Dc	...	...	p0.63	p0.77	....	0.94	9 Mo Sep	p0.64	0.81	20
21	....	None Since Public			...	Nil	....	0.12	5.73	3.19	9-30-95	0.54	...	2919	Dc	d0.47	d0.16	0.07	0.20	....	0.18	9 Mo Sep	0.14	0.12	21
22	....	None Since Public			...	Nil	....	118	136	0.90	6-30-95	★148	p...	★13000	Dc	...	....	...	pd0.29	....	....	6 Mo Jun	n/a	pd0.20	22
23◆	1992	Q0.06	1-2-96	12-20	0.093	0.24	0.075	5.22	11.2	0.96	9-30-95	....	...	8621	Dc	p0.11	0.10	0.16	[59]0.27	....	0.54	9 Mo Sep	0.17	0.44	23
24◆	....	None Since Public			...	Nil	....	3.29	71.1	86.9	9-30-95	110	...	16815	Dc	□0.79	0.84	□1.14	□2.31	....	2.56	9 Mo Sep	1.73	□1.98	24
25◆	1939	Q0.36¾	12-1-95	11-6	1.45½	1.47	1.396	15.6	470	455	9-30-95	1250	[62]305	110454	Dc	1.87	1.67	1.81	1.67	E2.15↓	2.15	12 Mo Sep	1.61	2.15	25
26	....	None Paid			...	Nil	....	0.47	10.8	6.20	6-30-95	0.11	...	6393	Sp	d0.45	d1.24	d0.96	d0.62	Pd1.39	d1.39				26
27	1941	Q0.10	12-8-95	11-27	0.40	0.40	0.40	1.23	11.5	9.50	9-30-95	78.0	...	8939	Dc	0.28	0.05	0.11	1.01	....	1.10	9 Mo Sep	0.18	0.27	27
28◆	1950	Q0.28	1-2-96	12-14	1.12	1.12	1.03	307	938	308	9-30-95	345	7	56434	Dc	1.61	□1.19	0.46	[64]1.92	E2.45	2.67	9 Mo Sep	1.46	2.21	28
29	....	None Since Public			...	Nil	....	0.57	3.60	1.80	10-31-95	0.10	...	8069	Jl	...	0.02	0.01	d0.36	d0.07	d0.03	3 Mo Oct	0.01	0.05	29
30◆	1984	Q0.06	2-2-96	1-10	0.233	0.24	0.213	0.38	199	92.4	9-30-95	97.3	...	17584	Je	0.68	0.35	0.95	1.01	0.90	0.77	3 Mo Sep	0.38	0.25	30
31◆	....	0.075	11-21-83	10-25	...	Nil	....	66.4	222	82.6	9-30-95	83.3	...	24124	Je	*0.47	1.21	1.31	1.19	0.80	0.85	3 Mo Sep	d0.04	0.01	31
32	1976	Q0.15	1-4-96	12-18	0.60	0.60	0.60	287	3361	3374	9-30-95	6459	...	486568	Dc	1.23	□1.86	0.93	1.62	E1.60	1.56	9 Mo Sep	1.20	1.14	32
33	1988	Q0.08	2-8-96	1-4	0.32	0.32	0.28	0.97	7.24	1.43	8-31-95	....	...	1056	My	0.34	□0.44	0.67	0.74	0.75	0.86	6 Mo Nov	0.41	0.52	33
34◆	1983	Q0.07	1-1-96	11-29	0.28	0.28	0.28	17.0	100	36.4	9-30-95	25.9	...	7087	Dc	1.31	1.48	Δ1.12	1.55	....	0.91	9 Mo Sep	1.16	0.52	34
35	....	....			...	[66]....	....	48.9	497	990	j12-31-93	1.90	344	65674	Dc	3.35	3.89	4.93	....	....	j4.93				35
36	....	None Since Public			...	Nil	....	0.32	143	55.4	9-30-95	101	20	13663	Dc	p0.19	□0.98	□1.39	1.82	....	2.14	9 Mo Sep	1.44	1.76	36
37◆	1988	0.03½	2-1-96	12-28	0.13	0.14	0.098	1.95	213	39.5	9-09-95	p37.1	...	★17994	Dc	0.22	□d0.69	0.73	1.01	E1.40	1.25	36 Wk Sep	0.45	0.69	37
38	....	None Since Public			...	Nil	....	66.9	77.8	6.90	9-30-95	....	...	13128	Dc	...	p0.17	p0.36	0.58	....	d1.07	9 Mo Sep	0.40	d1.25	38
39◆	1961	Q0.06½	11-20-95	11-2	0.128	0.26	0.233	2.45	36.0	18.4	7-01-95	....	...	10357	Sp	0.29	0.47	0.55	0.68	P0.85	0.85				39
40	1912	0.15	3-1-95	1-26	0.15	Nil	0.88	105	2299	1771	7-29-95	568	101	133041	Ja	□d0.41	2.14	d3.76	0.36	E0.40	0.26	9 Mo Oct	d0.33	d0.43	40
41	1969	Q0.55	12-1-95	10-30	2.20	2.20	2.20	Cv into 5.68 common				....	109	...	Ja	b4.87	b4.22	...	....	....	....				41
42◆	....	None Since Public			...	Nil	....	Equity per shr $1.69			9-30-95	41.6	...	20833	Mr	□0.09	0.21	0.28	0.41	....	0.47	6 Mo Sep	0.16	0.22	42
43	....	None Since Public			...	Nil	....	4.45	25.4	55.9	6-30-95	14.5	...	★12000	Dc	2.28	□0.94	d1.01	d0.91	....	0.91	9 Mo Sep	d0.78	1.04	43
44◆	1994	Q0.05	1-7-96	12-20	†0.217	0.20	0.067	17.0	70.0	36.7	9-30-95	4.10	...	7923	Mr	0.82	0.22	0.73	1.10	....	1.23	6 Mo Sep	0.52	0.65	44
45◆	....	None Paid			...	Nil	....	10.9	652	873	9-30-95	3392	1244	193128	Dc	±0.43	□d0.03	0.85	d0.95	E1.38	0.40	9 Mo Sep	d0.46	0.89	45
46	....	None Paid			...	Nil	....	62.6	86.1	70.6	9-30-95	91.2	...	16271	Dc	Δ0.46	□d3.02	d2.12	[67]0.54	....	2.32	9 Mo Sep	0.89	2.67	46
47	....	None Since Public			...	Nil	....	3.04	77.7	28.0	9-30-95	69.0	...	14476	Dc	p0.38	0.50	0.50	0.40	....	0.44	9 Mo Sep	0.30	0.34	47
48◆	1968	Q0.11	12-29-95	12-4	0.43	0.44	0.39	12.1	425	136	8-31-95	83.1	...	90747	My	0.50	0.63	0.74	0.94	1.29	1.23	6 Mo Nov	0.59	0.53	48
49	1946	Q0.48½	11-15-95	10-27	1.94	1.94	1.92	5.41	150	281	9-30-95	427	1009	30774	Dc	2.43	2.11	2.11	2.13	....	1.97	12 Mo Sep	2.43	1.97	49
50	1993	[58]0.075	12-7-95	10-27	[58]0.201	0.20	0.174	317	1152	1328	j12-31-94	291	10536	720462	Dc	4.90	0.40	0.70	1.25	....	1.25				50
51	1940	Q0.46½	12-20-95	11-28	1.84	1.86	1.80	15.3	147	82.9	9-30-95	309	512	23897	Dc	2.23	2.35	2.47	2.21	....	2.20	12 Mo Sep	2.26	2.20	51
52◆	1913	Q0.17	2-1-96	1-10	†0.96	0.68	†0.90	290	757	255	9-30-95	....	...	±116151	Dc	±1.09	□±1.27	±1.50	±1.98	E1.92	1.83	9 Mo Sep	±1.68	±1.53	52

◆**Stock Splits & Divs By Line Reference Index** [4]2-for-1,'94,'95. [5]2-for-1,'94,'95. [6]2-for-1,'92. [9]2-for-1,'93. [11]3-for-2,'94(twice). [13]2-for-1,'92. [14]Adj to 3%,'94. [17]2-for-1,'95. [23]2-for-1,'94:3-for-2,'95. [24]2-for-1,'94. [25]3-for-2,'92. [28]2-for-1,'93. [30]3-for-2,'95. [31]2-for-1,'92. [34]10%,'91. [37]3-for-2,'94,'95. [39]2-for-1,'93:3-for-2,'95. [42]3-for-1,'95. [44]3-for-2,'95. [45]No adj for mgr/reorg,'89:3-for-2,'91,'93:2-for-1,'94. [48]3-for-2,'91,'93. [52]3-for-1,'92.

¶ S&P 500 # MidCap 400 ✤ SmallCap 600 • Options Index	Ticker	Name of Issue (Call Price of Pfd. Stocks)	Market	Com. Rank. & Pfd. Rating	Inst. Hold Cos	Inst. Hold Shs. (000)	Principal Business	Price Range 1971-93 High	1971-93 Low	1994 High	1994 Low	1995 High	1995 Low	Dec. Sales in 100s	December, 1995 Last Sale Or Bid High	Low	Last	%Div Yield	P-E Ratio	Total Return % Annualized 12 Mo	36 Mo	60 Mo
1	WRTE	✔WRT Energy	NNM	NR	21	1146	Oil & gas dvlp,production	12½	5½	12½	6⅞	8½	⅜	38151	1	⅜	13/16	...	d	−89.5	...	...
2	WTDI	✔WTD Industries	NNM	NR	14	1975	Mfr/sale of lumber products	68¾	7/16	4¾	1⅝	2¼	½	20176	13/16	½	⅝	...	d	−64.3	−16.2	−24.2
✤3•[1]	WYL	✔Wyle Electronics	NY,B,Ch,Ph	B+	132	7865	Mkts hi-tech electronic prd	21⅛	1⅜	20¾	16¼	46½	19⅜	8380	40	33½	35⅛	0.8	15	85.6	22.6	25.3
4	WYMN	✔Wyman-Gordon	NNM	C	60	7741	Forged metal components	37¼	1⅛	7⅛	4½	15⅛	5¼	13247	15	13	13¾	...	28	134	41.3	18.2
✤5	WN	✔Wynn's Intl	NY,Ch,Ph	B	67	4217	Automotive parts:petrochem	23¾	2 1/16	24	18¼	30¼	19½	2358	30¼	28⅝	29⅝	1.8	12	39.2	21.2	26.6
✤6	XRIT	✔X-Rite Inc	NNM	B+	74	3878	Quality control instruments	16⅝	⅞	21	10½	24	13¾	17837	15	13¾	14⅛	0.7	25	−29.0	2.9	39.1
7	XNET	✔XcelleNet Inc	NNM	NR	41	3291	Dvlp remote/mobile comput'g sys	....	....	17⅝	6¾	33¼	13¼	12923	22	14¼	14⅞	...	32	−11.2	...	...
8	XCL	✔XCL Ltd	AS,Ch	C	49	19413	Oil & gas explor'n,prod'n	4⅝	5/16	1 15/16	7/16	1 1/16	5/16	146187	7/16	5/16	5/16	...	d	−50.1	−34.8	−29.2
¶9•[2]	XRX	✔Xerox Corp	NY,B,C,Ch,P,Ph	B−	865	91669	Copiers & duplicators: svs	171⅞	27⅛	112¾	87¾	144⅝	96½	56544	144⅝	133⅝	137	2.2	16	41.7	24.1	36.4
10•[3]	XICO	✔Xicor Inc	NNM	C	21	2527	Dev-reprogrammable semicon	29	⅝	3⅛	1½	9	2	40112	7⅞	6¼	7¼	...	20	255	94.1	45.4
#11•[4]	XLNX	✔Xilinx Inc	NNM	B	314	63378	Supplier of semiconductors	18⅛	3⅛	20⅝	9⅝	55½	18⅛	398769	34½	23¼	30½	...	24	50.7	56.3	46.6
✤12•[3]	XIRC	✔Xircom Inc	NNM	NR	53	5451	Mfr computer network'g prd	22	7	28¼	12¾	19	8⅞	56477	13⅝	9¾	12⅜	...	d	−32.2	14.5	...
13	XOMA	✔XOMA Corp	NNM,Ch	C	41	2623	Biotech:protein therapeutics	38⅝	5	6¼	2 3/16	4¼	1⅛	110717	4⅛	1⅞	3½	...	d	30.3	−28.3	−29.9
14	XPED	✔Xpedite Systems	NNM	NR	40	2232	Fax communic svcs	....	....	22¾	12	23½	12½	7983	16¾	14¼	15½	...	17	−21.5	...	...
15•[5]	XTR	✔XTRA Corp	NY,B,Ch	↑B+	124	16050	Leases transportation equip	53	1 11/16	53¼	40	52½	41⅝	7002	43½	41⅝	42½	1.5	13	−5.6	11.8	44.6
16	XYX	✔Xytronyx Inc	AS,Ch	C	11	245	Dvlp stge:biotech/hlth prod	28¼	2¾	9¼	2½	4⅛	1¼	6134	2⅛	1¼	1 9/16	...	d	−54.6	−39.0	−33.6
17	YES	✔Yankee Energy System	NY	B	64	1876	Hldg co: gas utility,Conn	29¼	11⅞	25½	20	25½	19½	1967	25½	23	25¼	5.0	21	24.2	14.2	19.5
¶18•[3]	YELL	✔Yellow Corp	NNM	B−	207	21077	Hldg:motor freight carrier	42½	3⅞	30¼	16¾	24⅜	11⅞	26994	13	11⅞	12⅜	...	d	−46.7	−20.7	−12.2
19	YSCO	✔Yes Clothing	NSC	NR	7	36	Design/mkt womens apparel	13¼	1½	4⅛	1⅛	10½	1	1416	2⅜	1	1½	...	d	−62.5	−18.3	−17.8
20	YFED	York Financial	NNM	B+	21	792	Savings & loan,Pennsylvania	19¼	1 11/16	18¾	14	18⅞	13⅛	936	17	16¼	16⅞	3.2	14	32.2	22.9	42.8
#21•[6]	YRK	✔York International	NY,Ch,Ph	NR	317	35115	Mfr climate control systems	41½	22⅝	42½	33⅞	48½	34⅛	21990	47⅛	44⅛	47	0.5	17	28.4	15.0	...
22	YORK	✔York Research	NNM	C	21	2091	Oper cogeneration facilities	22½	1¼	6⅝	2⅞	7¾	4	16049	6	5⅛	5⅜	...	27	34.4	−9.0	−9.3
23	YBTVA	✔Young Broadcasting'A'	NNM	NR	67	5358	Own/oper T.V. stations	....	....	22	13½	35¾	17½	4811	28¼	25⅛	28¼	...	d	59.2	...	...
24	YONK	✔Younkers Inc[58]	NNM	NR	61	4885	Oper fashion dept str chain	36	9	22½	12¼	27⅛	15⅞	9066	26⅞	23¼	25⅜	...	15	47.1	−1.1	...
25•[7]	YPF	✔YPF Sociedad Anonima ADS[59]	NY	NR	367	110345	O&G expl,dvlp,prd-Argentina	29	18⅞	29⅝	20⅜	22¼	14⅜	209407	21⅞	19¼	21⅝	3.7	9	6.1	...	...
26	ZOS	✔Zapata Corp	NY,To,B,Ch,P	B−	35	6290	O&G explor,prdn svc/fish'g	198⅛	1 9/16	8¾	3¼	4⅝	2½	11799	3¾	3	3⅛	...	22	−7.4	−5.4	6.3
✤27•[8]	ZBRA	✔Zebra Technologies'A'	NNM	NR	127	14681	Mfr bar code labeling sys	30⅜	7¼	28⅝	11¾	35¼	18	32543	35¼	31½	34	...	40	75.0	43.1	...
28	ZEI	✔Zeigler Coal Holding	NY,Ph	NR	62	8524	Coal producing U.S.	....	....	15¾	10½	14¼	9¾	17730	14¼	11¼	13⅞	1.4	8	20.2	...	...
29	ZMX	✔Zemex Corp	NY	B−	26	1696	Ind'l min'ls,metal powders	22½	2⅝	11¾	5⅞	10⅝	8¼	4694	10	8⅝	10	s...	9	18.9	27.9	27.4
30•[9]	ZEN	✔Zeneca Group ADR[61]	NY	NR	79	8528	R&D ethical pharmaceuticals	37⅜	26⅞	42⅛	30¼	62⅛	40¼	4454	62⅛	55⅝	58⅜	2.5	25	48.1	...	...
31•[10]	ZE	✔Zenith Electronics	NY,B,C,Ch,P,Ph	C	175	15371	Consumer electr/related prod	56⅝	4	14⅛	7	12⅛	6⅝	37679	7¾	6⅝	6⅞	...	d	−40.2	4.6	1.5
✤32	ZNT	✔Zenith Natl Insurance	NY,Ch	↓B	65	10286	Workmen's compens'n insur	30½	⅛	27⅜	20⅝	24⅝	19⅜	3066	22⅜	20	21⅜	4.7	29	2.8	6.9	16.1
✤33	ZRO	✔Zero Corp	NY,B,Ch,P,Ph	A−	93	10230	Electronics enclosures	18½	¼	16⅛	11⅜	17⅞	12⅝	5289	17⅞	15¾	17¾	2.5	18	44.8	12.1	13.1
34	ZCO	✔Ziegler Cos	AS,Ch	↓B	11	206	Investment banking,financ'g	26	1¾	19	15	17	14¾	215	17	16⅜	17	†e4.2	23	18.7	9.2	16.0
35	ZILA	Zila Inc	NSC	C	18	1218	Mkt non-prescription medl prod	4	⅛	4⅝	2 7/16	6	2¾	18595	5½	4⅜	5⅛	...	d	67.4	26.0	19.3
✤36•[5]	ZLG	✔Zilog Inc	NY,Ph	NR	154	11597	Mfr/mkt integrated circuits	40¾	6⅝	37¾	24¾	54⅛	28¼	14142	36¾	32¼	36⅝	...	18	27.4	19.9	...
✤37	ZION	✔Zions Bancorp	NNM	B+	118	5194	Commercial bkg,Utah	49¼	2⅛	42	33½	81½	35½	16668	81½	69¾	80¼	2.0	15	132	31.5	42.9
38	ZITL	✔Zitel Corp	NNM	C	24	1138	Mfr semicond'r memory sys	11½	1¼	13⅞	1⅞	21	7⅞	22477	12⅞	10¾	12	...	11	−6.8	24.3	25.4
39	ZRC	✔Zurich Reinsurance Centre	NY,Ph	NR	59	10787	Prop & casualty reinsurance	36⅜	26¼	28⅞	24¼	30⅞	27⅞	2649	30½	28½	30⅜	...	35	6.6	...	...
40•[11]	ZRN	✔Zurn Indus	NY,B,Ch,P,Ph	B+	180	9105	Environment,energy,leisure	51⅛	1 15/16	29¾	16¾	26	16⅞	20307	25¼	20¼	21⅜	1.9	18	26.9	−14.9	−6.0
41	ZCON	✔Zycon Corp	NNM	NR	23	911	Mfrs circuit boards	....	....	....	....	15	10	7702	13¼	10	11¼	...	17	...	...	...
42	ZIGO	Zygo Corp	NNM	B−	27	931	Mfrs measur'g instr/sys	9½	2½	5⅝	3¾	35½	4⅝	20615	33¼	24	25⅛	...	30	439	84.6	53.9

Uniform Footnote Explanations-See Page 4. Other: [1]P, Cycle 3. [2]CBOE,P:Cycle 1. [3]CBOE:Cycle 3. [4]CBOE,P:Cycle 3. [5]ASE:Cycle 3. [6]CBOE:Cycle 2. [7]ASE,CBOE,NY:Cycle 1. [8]NY,P:Cycle 3. [9]CBOE,NY:Cycle 1. [10]ASE:Cycle 2. [11]ASE:Cycle 1. [51]Fiscal Jan'93 & prior. [52]11 Mo Dec'93. [53]Fiscal Dec'93 & prior. [54]®$1.99,'94. [55]Fiscal June'93 & prior. [56]As reported, incl Xerox Credit. [57]®$6.44,'94. [58]Approve Proffitt's Inc acq, 0.98 com. [59]Ea ADS rep 1 Cl'D' shr PS.1. [60]Accum on Pfd. [61]Ea ADS rep 3 ord shrs. [62]To be determined.

Splits ◆ Index	Cash Divs. Ea.Yr. Since	Dividends: Latest Payment Period $	Date	Ex. Div.	Total $ So Far 1995	Ind. Rate	Paid 1994	Financial Position Mil-$ Cash& Equiv.	Curr. Assets	Curr. Liab.	Balance Sheet Date	Capitalization Lg Trm Debt Mil-$	Shs. 000 Pfd.	Com.	Earnings $ Per Shr. Years End	1991	1992	1993	1994	1995	Last 12 Mos.	Interim Earnings Period	$ per Shr. 1994	1995	Index
1	....	None Since Public			...	Nil	....	2.15	14.2	12.4	9-30-95	108	1265	9818	Dc	d1.01	0.13	d0.54	0.18	....	d1.44	9 Mo Sep	0.26	d1.36	1
2◆	....	None Since Public			...	Nil	....	4.19	46.0	17.7	10-31-95	51.0	276	11077	Ap	d34.18	*0.73	Δ0.29	0.41	0.14	d0.34	6 Mo Oct	0.15	d0.33	2
3	1974	Q0.07	12-29-95	12-13	0.28	0.28	0.28	11.8	345	110	9-30-95	73.4	...	12373	Dc	0.95	[51]1.45	□[52]0.92	d0.03	....	2.28	9 Mo Sep	d0.28	2.03	3
4	....	0.10	9-10-91	8-27	...	Nil	....	21.4	193	89.1	9-02-95	90.3	...	35117	My	d5.59	1.21	□[53]d0.95	d4.02	0.03	0.49	6 Mo Nov	d0.15	0.31	4
5◆	1975	Q0.13	1-3-96	12-13	0.50	0.52	0.44	20.6	128	62.7	9-30-95	0.75	...	6029	Dc	■d2.06	1.35	1.62	[54]2.08	....	2.39	9 Mo Sep	1.60	1.91	5
6◆	1986	Q0.02½	2-12-96	1-10	0.10	0.10	0.08	5.45	32.8	2.74	9-30-95	....	...	21008	Dc	0.23	0.34	0.36	0.60	....	0.57	9 Mo Sep	0.43	0.40	6
7	....	None Since Public			...	Nil	....	25.8	33.8	2.60	9-30-95	....	...	7538	Dc	d0.59	0.16	[55]0.30	0.45	....	0.47	9 Mo Sep	0.29	0.31	7
8	....	None Since Public			...	Nil	....	0.56	1.51	14.2	9-30-95	35.5	647	249080	Dc	d0.32	d0.28	d0.17	□d0.20	....	d0.18	9 Mo Sep	□d0.13	d0.11	8
9	1930	Q0.75	1-1-96	11-29	3.00	3.00	3.00	Equity per shr $45.82			9-30-95	[56]9225	11200	107852	Dc	3.91	□d3.32	d1.84	[57]6.73	E8.80	8.09	9 Mo Sep	3.97	5.33	9
10	....	None Since Public			...	Nil	....	30.6	60.1	32.5	9-10-95	3.11	...	18299	Dc	d0.87	d1.64	d0.32	0.13	....	0.36	36 Wk Sep	0.09	0.32	10
11◆	....	None Since Public			...	Nil	....	112	262	92.1	9-30-95	0.47	...	70993	Mr	0.30	0.38	0.57	0.80	E1.27	0.92	6 Mo Sep	0.33	0.45	11
12	....	None Since Public			...	Nil	....	13.7	63.3	34.8	9-30-95	0.83	...	18926	Sp	0.19	0.41	0.59	0.95	d3.44	d3.44				12
13	....	None Since Public			...	Nil	....	25.3	26.2	6.01	9-30-95	....	16	24555	Dc	d1.77	d2.20	d1.46	d1.58	....	d1.24	9 Mo Sep	d1.08	d0.74	13
14	....	None Since Public			...	Nil	....	15.8	25.5	6.97	9-30-95	0.11	...	6448	Dc	...	p0.01	0.34	0.71	....	0.89	9 Mo Sep	0.50	0.68	14
15◆	1977	Q0.16	12-15-95	11-28	0.64	0.64	0.56	Equity per shr $21.66			9-30-95	898	...	16324	Sp	1.00	1.88	2.16	3.38	3.39	3.39				15
16	....	None Paid			...	Nil	....	0.32	0.73	0.72	9-30-95	....	...	5263	Mr	d0.92	d1.01	d1.10	d0.74	....	d0.72	6 Mo Sep	d0.32	d0.30	16
17◆	1989	Q0.315	12-28-95	12-15	1.25	1.26	1.205	10.8	52.5	50.0	6-30-95	144	...	10369	Sp	1.28	Δ1.44	1.70	1.81	P1.20	1.20				17
18	1958	0.23½	5-15-95	4-25	0.47	Nil	0.94	24.6	481	387	9-30-95	338	...	28106	Dc	0.95	□1.46	0.67	□d0.14	Ed0.40	0.14	9 Mo Sep	□d0.54	d0.26	18
19	....	None Since Public			...	Nil	....	0.07	4.46	2.71	9-30-95	0.13	...	7036	Mr	d0.19	d0.26	d0.77	d1.22	....	d1.43	6 Mo Sep	d0.29	d0.50	19
20◆	1984	Q0.136	11-15-95	11-1	0.545	0.54	0.496	Book Value $14.52			9-30-95	76.5	...	5989	Je	0.93	1.37	1.52	Δ1.21	1.25	1.25	3 Mo Sep	0.34	0.35	20
21	1991	Q0.06	12-29-95	12-15	0.24	0.24	0.16	5.92	851	614	12-31-94	p267	...	★41919	Dc	□0.56	□1.90	□2.01	2.40	E2.79	2.68	9 Mo Sep	1.83	2.11	21
22	....	0.20	3-22-78	2-23	...	Nil	....	1.66	3.28	3.26	8-31-95	....	...	12830	Fb	d0.97	d0.17	d0.03	0.02	....	0.20	6 Mo Aug	d0.06	0.12	22
23	....	None Since Public			...	Nil	....	5.04	38.8	32.1	9-30-95	293	...	±10857	Dc	...	...	□pd0.02	□d3.62	....	d0.38	9 Mo Sep	d3.19	□0.05	23
24	....	None Since Public			...	Nil	....	33.2	252	75.7	7-29-95	74.6	...	8986	Ja	pΔ1.14	□3.11	□1.55	1.47	....	1.68	9 Mo Oct	0.40	0.61	24
25	1993	0.20	11-30-95	11-24	0.80	0.80	0.80	81.0	1131	1503	12-31-94	692	...	353000	Dc	...	p■0.73	2.00	1.52	E2.35	2.27	9 Mo Sep	1.14	1.89	25
26◆	1994	0.03½	10-14-94	9-26	...	[60]Nil	0.07	2.49	151	37.1	9-30-95	37.5	3	29549	Sp	0.05	0.10	0.35	d0.28	0.14	0.14				26
27◆	....	None Since Public			...	Nil	....	68.0	112	17.8	9-30-95	0.19	...	±24162	Dc	p±0.38	0.50	0.76	0.87	....	0.86	9 Mo Sep	0.62	0.61	27
28	1995	Q0.05	1-3-96	12-13	0.20	0.20	....	22.3	177	130	9-30-95	358	...	28356	Dc	1.61	3.26	□d1.47	□1.35	E1.85	1.95	9 Mo Sep	0.80	1.40	28
29◆	....	2%Stk	12-8-95	11-21	2%Stk	Stk	2%Stk	2.82	35.5	13.5	9-30-95	7.50	...	8552	Dc	d1.32	0.06	0.42	1.12	....	1.12	9 Mo Sep	0.67	0.67	29
30	1993	0.566	11-13-95	9-22	1.463	1.46	1.361	735	2909	1896	j12-31-94	526	...	945484	Dc	...	p1.05	2.30	2.15	....	2.34	6 Mo Jun	□1.52	1.71	30
31	....	0.075	6-30-82	6-7	...	Nil	....	....	489	300	9-30-95	216	...	63434	Dc	d1.79	d3.59	d3.01	d0.34	Ed1.65	d1.53	9 Mo Sep	d0.27	d1.46	31
32	1978	Q0.25	2-15-96	1-29	1.00	1.00	1.00	Equity per shr $7.87			9-30-95	74.2	...	17774	Dc	*2.28	Δ□1.02	2.76	1.99	....	0.75	9 Mo Sep	1.53	0.29	32
33	1974	Q0.11	12-5-95	11-8	0.44	0.44	0.40	34.5	101	18.5	9-30-95	....	...	16057	Mr	0.62	0.74	0.81	0.93	....	0.98	6 Mo Sep	0.46	0.51	33
34	1954	†0.48	1-19-96	1-4	†0.72	0.72	†1.07	Equity per shr $20.92			9-30-95	64.2	...	2436	Dc	1.45	2.01	1.90	0.84	....	0.74	9 Mo Sep	0.75	0.65	34
35	....	None Paid			...	Nil	....	1.16	2.49	0.58	10-31-95	0.41	...	24482	Jl	d0.20	d0.01	0.02	d0.04	Δd0.04	d0.04	3 Mo Oct	ΔNil	Nil	35
36◆	....	None Since Public			...	Nil	....	91.3	168	68.4	10-01-95	....	...	19442	Dc	±0.76	±0.95	±1.43	1.80	....	2.03	9 Mo Sep	1.31	1.54	36
37◆	1966	Q0.41	1-26-96	12-29	1.30	1.64	1.14	Book Value $28.20			9-30-95	148	...	14540	Dc	2.39	3.52	Δ4.02	4.37	E5.42↑	5.18	9 Mo Sep	3.19	4.00	37
38	....	None Paid			...	Nil	....	11.3	23.2	3.25	9-30-95	....	...	7297	Sp	0.58	0.25	d1.34	d1.10	1.12	1.12				38
39	1996	0.10	1-15-96	12-13	...	[62]....	....	Equity per shr $24.33			9-30-95	200	...	26348	Dc	...	...	0.77	d1.19	....	0.86	9 Mo Sep	d1.07	0.98	39
40	1964	Q0.10	1-15-96	12-13	0.64	0.40	0.88	49.7	296	138	9-30-95	9.00	...	12341	Mr	□0.91	2.20	d1.12	0.76	E1.20	1.11	6 Mo Sep	0.36	0.71	40
41	....	None Since Public			...	Nil	....	5.01	33.3	30.3	9-30-95	20.5	...	★11000	Dc	...	...	...	p0.39	....	0.65	9 Mo Sep	p0.28	p0.54	41
42◆	....	None Since Public			...	Nil	....	8.87	24.7	6.66	9-30-95	....	...	★4779	Je	0.33	0.16	0.12	0.23	0.65	0.84	3 Mo Sep	0.04	0.23	42

◆**Stock Splits & Divs By Line Reference Index** [2]4-for-10 REVERSE,'92. [5]3-for-2,'93:To split 3-for-2,ex Jan 8. [6]2-for-1,'92,'94. [11]3-for-1,'95. [15]2-for-1,'93. [17]3-for-2,'93. [20]Adj to 5%,'91:10%,'91,'92,'93,'94,'95. [26]1-for-5 REVERSE,'94. [27]2-for-1,'95. [29]Adj to 2%,'95. [36]3-for-2,'93. [37]2-for-1,'93. [42]3-for-2,'95.

RATINGS OF UTILITY PREFERRED STOCKS

Because of space limitations, it is not possible to cover all utility preferred stocks in the Stock Guide. Standard & Poor's ratings are listed below for various utility companies arranged by the ratings assigned to their preferred issues.

AA+
Wisconsin Elec. Pwr.

AA
Central Ill. Pub.Sv.
Gen'l. Tel. of Michigan
GTE North
Tampa Electric
Wisconsin Public Sv.

AA–
Dayton Pwr. & Lt.
GTE California
GTE Florida
GTE Northwest
Kentucky Utilities
Louisville Gas & Elec.
Oklahoma Gas & Elec.
South'n Indiana Gas &El.
Southwest'n Public Sv.
Washington Gas Light
Wisconsin Pwr. & Lt.

A+
ALLTEL Corp
Central Illinois Light
Duke Power
Florida Pwr. & Lt.
Florida Power Corp
GTE South
GTE Southwest
Indianapolis Pwr. & Lt.
Iowa-Ill. Gas & Elec.
Mountain Fuel Supply
NICOR, Inc
NICOR, Inc. (Pref)
Northern States Power
Otter Tail Power
Southern California Gas
Southwest'n Elec. Pwr.
Union Electric

A
Alabama Power
Baltimore Gas & Elec.
Baltimore Gas & Elec.(Pref)
Bay State Gas
Brooklyn Union Gas
Consol. Edison N.Y.
Duke Power(Pref)
Georgia Power
Gulf Power
Interstate Power
Iowa-Ill. Gas & Elec. (Pref)
KN Energy
Massachusetts Electric
MDU Resources Group
Michigan Consol. Gas
Mississippi Power
Monongahela Power
Narragansett Electric
New England Power
Pacific Enterprises
Potomac Edison
Public Sv. of Oklahoma
Rochester Telephone
San Diego Gas & Elec.
San Diego Gas & Elec (Pref)
Savannah Elec. & Pwr.
Southern California Edison
West Penn Power
West Texas Utilities

A–
Atlanta Gas Light
Carolina Pwr. & Lt.
Central Louisiana Elec.
Central Pwr. & Lt.
Consol. Edison N.Y.(Pref)
Delmarva Pwr. & Lt.
Houston Ltg. & Pwr.
Idaho Power
Interstate Power(Pref)
Iowa Elec. Lt. & Pwr.
Kansas City Pwr. & Lt.
North'n Indiana Pub. Sv.
Northwest Natural Gas
ONEOK, Inc
Pacific Gas & Elec.
PacifiCorp
Potomac Electric Pwr.
South Carolina Elec & Gas
Virginia Elec. & Pwr.

BBB+
Appalachian Power
Atlantic City Electric
Central Hudson Gas & Elec.
Columbus Southern Power
Empire District Elec.
GTE Corp
Kansas Pwr. & Lt.
Minnesota Pwr. & Lt.
NIPSCO Industries
Northwest Natural Gas(Pref)
Ohio Power
Orange & Rockland Util.
Pennsylvania Electric
Pennsylvania Pwr & Lt
Pennsylvania Pwr & Lt(Pref.)
Portland Gen'l Elec
Public Sv. Elec. & Gas
Puget Sound Pwr. & Lt.
Sierra Pacific Power
Washington Water Pwr.

BBB
Cincinnati Gas & Elec.
Connecticut Lt. & Pwr.
Detroit Edison
Duquesne Light
Hawaiian Electric
Indiana & Michigan Elec
Jersey Central Pwr. & Lt.
Metropolitan Edison
Montana Power
Natural Gas Pipeline
N.Y. State Elec. & Gas
Philadelphia Electric
PSI Energy
Public Sv. Colorado
Rochester Gas & Elec.
Southern Union
Texas Utilities Elec.
UGI Corp

BBB–
Arizona Public Service
Arkansas Pwr. & Lt.
Boston Edison
Central Vermont Pub. Sv
Commonwealth Edison
Commonwealth Edison (Pref)
Duquesne Light(Pref)
Eastern Edison
Enron Corp
ENSERCH Corp
Illinois Power
Louisiana Pwr. & Lt.
Maine Yankee Atomic Pwr.
Mississippi Pwr. & Lt.
Nevada Power
New Orleans Pub Svc.
Northwest Pipeline
Sprint Corp
Tenneco Inc
Tenneco Inc(Pref)
Transcont'l Gas Pipe Line
UtiliCorp United(Pref)
Washington Nat'l Gas
West'n Massachusetts Elec.
Williams Natl Gas

BB+
ANR Pipeline
Centel Corp
Colorado Interstate Gas
Consumers Power
Gulf States Utilities
Long Island Lighting
Ohio Edison
Panhandle Eastern P.L.
Pennsylvania Power
Transco Energy
United Illuminating
Williams Companies Inc.

BB
Coastal Corp
Gulf States Utilities (Pref)
Pennsylvania Gas & Wtr.

BB–
Arkla Inc.
Public Sv. New Hampshire

B+
Central Maine Power

B
Cleveland Elec. Illum.
Niagara Mohawk Pwr.
Toledo Edison

B–
Public Sv. New Mexico

D
El Paso Electric
New Valley Corp

STANDARD & POOR'S

PREFERRED STOCK SUMMARY

Exchange / Ticker	Cm Divd	Issue	Rating	Reg. Call Price (Begins) Thru [see footnotes for Sink'g Fd]	Dividends Latest Payments Period $	Date	Ex Div.	Ind. Rate	Last Sale or Bid(B)	% Div. Yld.
N SEPPr		AB Svensk Exp Exch[1]7.375%	NR	25(8/03)	Q0.46	12-1-95	11-13	1.84	24⅛	7.6
N EKPPr		A/S Eksportfinans 8.70%	AA	25(3/03)	Q0.54	6-20-95	5-30	2.17	26⅞B	8.1
A AMAPr	*	Advanced Medical 10%[2]Vtg[3]	NR	10[4]	0.50	4-8-93	3-26	Nil	9½	....
N AETPrA	*	Aetna Capital 9.50%[5]'MIPS'	BBB+	25(11/99)	M0.20	12-29-95	12-26	2.37	27¾	8.5
N AHMPrB	*	Ahmanson(H F) 9.60% Dep[6]	BBB–	25(8/96)	Q0.60	12-1-95	11-8	2.40	25¾	9.3
N AHMPrC	*	Ahmanson(H F) 8.40% Dep[7]	BBB–	25(2/98)	Q0.52	12-1-95	11-8	2.10	26⅛	8.0
N ALPPrD	*	Ala Pwr Adj [8]Rt'A"93[9]	A	26.25 11/98	0.33	1-1-96	12-1	[10]1.30	20⅝	6.3
N AIBPr		Allied Irish Bk Pref[11]ADS[12]	BBB+	NC	0.59	1-31-96	1-11	2.29	27¾	8.3
A AAPr	*	Alum Co Amer $3.75	A+	100	Q0.94	1-1-96	12-13	3.75	72½	5.2
N AOPrA	*	AMERCO 8.50% Sr'A'	BBB–	25(11/00)	Q0.53	12-1-95	11-15	2.13	24	8.9
N AGCPrM	*	Amer Genl 8.45%'A'[5]'MIPS'	A+	25(6/00)	M0.18	12-29-95	12-26	2.11	26¾	7.9
N AGCPrN		Amer Genl 8.125%'B"MIPS'	A+	25(8/00)	M0.17	12-29-95	12-26	2.03	25⅞	7.8
N ARNPrA	*	Amer Re Cap 8.50%[13] 'QUIPS'	BBB+	25(9/00)	Q0.53	12-29-95	12-26	2.13	26⅜	8.1
N ACPPr	*	Amer R.E.Ptnrs 5%[14]'PIK'	NR	[15]10(3/00)	0.18	10-2-95	9-27	0.50	5¾B	8.7
N AWKPrA	*	Amer Water Wks 5% Pref	NR	25	Q0.31	12-1-95	11-8	1.25	19	6.6
N AOCPrA	*	Aon Corp 8% Perpetual	AA–	25(10/97)	Q0.50	2-1-96	1-16	2.00	26	7.7
N AEWPrC	*	Appal Pwr 7.40% Vtg	BBB+	102.11	Q1.85	2-1-96	1-8	7.40	101½B	7.3
N ACAPrA	*	Arcadian Corp Mand Cv[16]	NR	[17]	0.21	11-13-95	11-1	1.47	18	8.2
N ARPPrW	*	Arizona Pub Sv $1.8125	BBB–	25(11/98)	Q0.45	12-1-95	10-30	1.81	25	7.3
N AKPPr	*	Arkansas Pwr & Lt $2.40	BBB–	25(6/96)	Q0.60	1-1-96	12-13	2.40	25⅝	9.4
A ARMPr	*	ARM Fin'l 9.50%	BBB–	25(12/98)	Q0.59	12-15-95	11-28	2.38	26B	9.1
N AECPrA	*	Assoc Estates Rlty 9.75%[18]Dep	BB+	25(7/00)	Q0.61	12-15-95	12-1	2.44	24¾	9.8
N ATGPr	*	Atlanta Gas Lt 7.70% Dep	A–	25(11/97)	Q0.48	12-1-95	11-15	1.92	25⅝	7.5
N ANZPr	*	Austr&N.Zealand Bk 9.125%	A–	25(2/03)	Q0.57	12-31-95	12-13	2.28	27¼	8.4
N BLYPrP	*	Bally Enter 8.00%[19]'PRIDES'[20]	BB–	[21]11.348(10/98)	Q0.22	1-3-96	12-13	0.89	13⅝	6.5
N BGEPrB	*	Baltimore G&E 4.50% B	A	110	Q1.13	1-2-96	12-7	4.50	70	6.4
N BVGPr	*	BancoBilbaoVizcaya[22]9.75%[23]	A	25(11/01)	0.61	1-2-96	12-13	2.44	27⅞	8.8
N BVGPrC		Banco Bilbao Vizcaya 8%[24]	A	26(6/98)	0.50	1-2-96	12-13	2.00	25⅞	7.7
N BTGAPr	*	Banco Ganadero Cl'C'[25]	NR	NC	[26]0.23		12-23	[27]0.23	13	1.8
N CIB	*	Banco Indl Colombiano Pref ADS	NR	NC	0.06	12-11-95	11-21	0.92	16⅜	5.6
N BKBPrC	*	Bk of Boston Adj[28]Rt C	NR	100	1.37	12-15-95	11-13	5.48	82	6.7
N BKBPrE	*	Bank of Boston 8.60%'E'[29]Dep	BBB–	25(9/97)	Q0.54	12-15-95	11-13	2.15	26	8.3
N BKPrB	*	Bk of N.Y. 8.60%[30]Dep	BBB+	25(11/97)	Q0.54	12-1-95	11-13	2.15	26¼	8.2
N BKUPrB		Bank United Texas FSB 9.60%	BB+	26.25(9/00)	Q0.60	12-29-95	12-13	2.40	26½	9.1
N BACPrA	*	BankAmer Adj[31]A	A–	50	Q0.81	11-30-95	11-14	3.25	48¾	6.7
N BACPrB	*	BankAmer Adj[32]B	A–	100	Q1.50	11-30-95	11-14	6.00	90½	6.6
N BACPrF	*	BankAmer 9.625% Series'F'	A–	25(4/96)	Q0.60	11-30-95	11-14	2.41	25½	9.5
N BACPrH	*	BankAmer 9% Series'H'	A–	25(1/97)	Q0.56	11-30-95	11-14	2.25	25⅞	8.7
N BACPrJ	*	BankAmer 11%[33]Dep'J'	A–	26.375(3/96)	Q0.69	12-31-95	12-13	2.75	26⅞	10.2
N BACPrK	*	BankAmer 8.375% Ser'K'	A–	25(2/97)	Q0.52	11-30-95	11-14	2.09	25⅞	8.1
N BACPrL	*	BankAmer 8.16% Dep'L'[34]	A–	25(7/97)	Q0.51	11-30-95	11-14	2.04	25⅝	8.0
N BACPrM	*	BankAmer 7.875% Dep'M'[35]	A–	25(9/97)	Q0.49	11-30-95	11-14	1.97	25⅝	7.7
N BACPrN	*	BankAmer 8.50% Dep'N'[36]	A–	25(12/97)	Q0.53	11-30-95	11-14	2.13	26	8.2
A BPB	*	Bankers Tr N.Y. 7.50%[38]DepRec'P'	NR	30 8/98	Q0.47	11-15-95	10-27	1.88	25⅛	7.5
A BPR	*	Bankers Tr N.Y.7.625%[40]DepRec'O'	A	30 6/98	Q0.48	12-1-95	11-13	1.91	25¼	7.6
N BTPrI	*	Bankers Tr N.Y.[41]Dep'I'	A–	25(2/97)	Q0.53	12-1-95	11-13	2.14	25⅝	8.3
N BTPrR	*	Bankers Tr N.Y.[42]Adj[43]Dep'R'	A–	25(8/99)	0.37	12-1-95	11-13	1.33	21¼	6.2
N BTPrQ	*	Bankers Tr N.Y.[44]Adj[45]Dep'Q'	A–	25(2/99)	0.37	12-1-95	11-13	1.33	21⅛	6.3
N BTPrS	*	Bankers Tr N.Y.7.75%[46]Dep'S'	A–	25(5/00)	Q0.48	12-1-95	11-13	1.94	26	7.5
N BCBPr	*	Barclays Bk[47]E1/E2[48]Unit ADS[49]	A+	25(4/03)	0.50	12-1-95	11-28	2.00	25½	7.8
N BCBPrC		BarclaysBk[50]C1/C2[51]Unit ADS	A+	[52]25(6/00)	0.60	12-1-95	10-24	2.39	28⅝	8.3
N BCBPrD		BarclaysBk[53]D1/D2[54]Unit ADS	A+	[55]25(3/01)	0.61	12-1-95	10-24	2.44	28⅞	8.5
N BSCPrB	*	Bear Stearns 7.88%'B'[56]Dep	BBB	25(4/98)	Q0.49	1-15-96	12-27	1.97	25¼	7.8
N BSCPrZ	*	Bear Stearns LLC 8%'EPICS'[57]	NR	25(2/99)	M0.17	12-29-95	12-19	2.00	25⅛	8.0
N BNLPrB	*	Beneficial Corp $4.30 Vtg	A–	100	S2.15	9-30-95	8-30	4.30	65¾	6.5
N GRPrA		BFGoodrich Cap 8.30%[58]'QUIPS'	BBB–	[59]25(7/00)	Q0.52	12-29-95	12-26	2.08	25⅞	8.0
N BCCPrF	*	Boise Cascade 9.40%[60]Dep	BB+	25(2/98)	Q0.59	1-15-96	12-27	2.35	26¼	9.0
N BSEPrA	*	Boston Edison 8.25% Dep	BBB–	25(5/97)	Q0.51	2-1-96	1-8	2.06	26⅛	7.9
N BOWPrC	*	Bowater Inc'C'8.40%[61]Dep	BBB–	25(2/99)	Q0.52	1-16-96	12-7	2.10	25⅝B	8.2
N BFPr	*	Brown-Forman 4%	A+	10.25	Q0.10	1-1-96	11-30	0.40	7⅝	5.2
N CSDPrA	*	Cadbury Sch LP 8.625%[13]'QUIPS'	A–	25(4/02)	Q0.54	12-15-95	12-12	2.16	26½	8.2
N CALPrB		Calif Fed'l Bk[62]10.625%'B'	B	105.313(3/99)	Q2.66	11-15-95	10-30	10.63	108½B	9.8
N KREPrL	*	Capital Re LLC 7.65%'MIPS'[63]	A–	25(1/99)	M0.16	12-29-95	12-26	1.91	24⅞	7.7
A CPLPr	*	Carol P&L $5 Vtg	A–	110	Q1.25	4-1-96	3-18	5.00	71⅛	7.0

Footnotes and Sinking Fund: [1] Co opt exch for 7.375% non-cm Pfd. [2] Mand redm 25% each Mar 27 at $10. [3] Accum $2.50 to 9/30/95. [4] SF 10. [5] Monthly Income Preferred Shrs. [6] Dep for 0.5 shr 9.60% cm Ser'B'Pfd. [7] Dep for 0.1 shr 8.40% cm Ser'C'Pfd. [8] Div 5.21% to 12/31/95. [9] Red restr(5.09%)to 11-1-98. [10] $1.205 fr 1-1-96(rate 4.82%). [11] Each ADS rep 1 non-cm pref shr. [12] Opt redemption from 8-8-99,re certain cond.$25. [13] Quarterly Income Preferred Securities. [14] Pay in kind. [15] Pay in cash or Dep Units. [16] Mand Cv into 1 com, 8-10-98. [17] Cash or com re-spec cond. [18] Dep for 0.10 shr 9.75% Cl'A'cm Red Pfd. [19] Pfd Redeemable Increased Div Equity Sec. [20] Mandatory conversion into one com 10-3-99. [21] In com stock. [22] Ea ADS rep 1 non-cm Ser'A'Pref. [23] Callable at $25 fr 11-19-2001. [24] Ea ADS rep 1 non-cm Ser'C' Pref. [25] Ea ADS rep 100 Cl 'C' Cm Ptcp Pref,Ps.10. [26] Approx. [27] Subject to minimum div based on'B'shrs. [28] Div 5.5% to 12/15/95. [29] Dep for 0.10 shr 8.60% Ser'E'Pfd. [30] Dep for 0.04 shr 8.60% cm Pfd. [31] Div 6.50% to 2/29/96. [32] Div 6% to 2/29/96. [33] Dep for 1/20 11% J Pfd. [34] Dep for 0.05 shr 8.16% cm Ser'L'Pfd. [35] Dep for 0.05 shr 7.875%cmSer'M'Pfd. [36] Dep for 0.05 shr 8.50% cm Ser'N'Pfd. [37] Dep for 0.025 shr 7.50% Sr'P'Pfd. [38] Dep for 0.025 shr 7.50% Sr'P'Pfd. [39] Dep for 0.10 shr 7.625% Sr'O'Pfd. [40] Dep for 0.10 shr 7.625% Sr'O'Pfd. [41] Dep for 0.25 shr Sr'I'Pfd. [42] Div 5.306% to 2/29/96. [43] Dep for 0.01 shr Adj Rt cm Pfd Sr'R'. [44] Div 5.338% to 2/29/96. [45] Dep for 0.01 shr Adj Rt cm Pfd Sr'Q'. [46] Dep for 0.01 shr 7.75% cm Pfd Sr'S'. [47] Ea El ADS rep 1 8% note $20 amt. [48] Ea E2 ADS rep 1 8% note $5 amt. [49] Ea E1 note cv into El pref, E2 into E2 pref. [50] Ea C1 ADS rep 1 non-cm $-denominated Pref. [51] Ea C2 ADS rep 1non-cm$-denominated non-vtg Pref. [52] Pref redeem:Ser Cl1 $20, Ser C2 $5. [53] Ea D1 ADS rep 1 non-cm $-denominated Pref. [54] Ea D2 ADS rep1non-cm$-denominated non-vtg Pref. [55] Pref redeem:Ser D1 $20, Ser D2 $5. [56] Dep for 0.125 shr7.88%cm Pfd stk Ser'B'. [57] Exchangeable Pfd Income Cm Shrs. [58] Qtly Income Pfd Securities. [59] Mand redem repymt of 8.30% Jr Debs. [60] Dep for 0.025 shr 9.40%cm Pfd,Ser'F'. [61] Dep for 0.25 8.40% cm Pfd. [62] Spl Red:Fr4-1-96chge of ctrl re-specified cond. [63] Monthly income Preferred shrs.

Exchange	Ticker	Cm Divd	Issue	Rating	Reg. Call Price (Begins) Thru [see footnotes for Sink'g Fd]	Dividends – Latest Payments – Period $	Date	Ex Div.	Ind. Rate	Last Sale or Bid(B)	% Div. Yld.
N	HCLPr		Central Hispano Cap 10.50% 'A'	BBB	[1]26.3125(11/99)	Q0.66	1-2-96	12-13	2.63	27⅞	9.6
N	HCLPrB		Central Hispano Cap 9.43%'B'	BBB	[2]25(7/05)	Q0.59	1-2-96	12-13	2.36	25⅝	9.2
N	HPNPr		Central Hispano Int'A'[3]'MIPS'	BBB	[1]26.25(11/99)	0.21	12-29-95	12-22	2.47	26⅞	9.2
N	CERPr	*	Central Ill Lt 4.50% Vtg	A+	100	Q1.13	1-2-96	12-6	4.50	63½	7.1
N	CTPPrA	*	Central Maine Pwr 7.875%	B+	100(8/97)	Q1.97	1-1-96	12-6	7.88	97	8.1
N	CMBPrI	*	Chase Mhtn 10.84% I	BBB+	25(6/01)	Q0.68	12-31-95	12-14	2.71	30⅜	8.9
N	CMBPrJ	*	Chase Mhtn 9.08% J	BBB+	25(3/97)	Q0.57	12-31-95	12-14	2.27	26	8.7
N	CMBPrK	*	Chase Mhtn 8.50% K	BBB+	25(6/97)	Q0.53	12-31-95	12-14	2.13	25¾	8.3
N	CMBPrL	*	Chase Mhtn 8.32% L	BBB+	25(9/97)	Q0.52	12-31-95	12-14	2.08	25½	8.2
N	CMBPrM	*	Chase Mhtn 8.40% M	BBB+	25(3/98)	Q0.52	12-31-95	12-14	2.10	26	8.1
N	CMBPrN	*	Chase Mhtn Adj[4]Rt N	BBB+	25(6/99)	0.35	12-31-95	12-14	[5]1.39	21¼	6.5
N	CHLPrH	*	Chem Bkg 8.375%	BBB+	25(5/97)	Q0.52	12-31-95	12-13	2.09	25⅝	8.2
N	CHLPrI	*	Chem Bkg 7.92%[6]Dep	BBB+	25(9/97)	Q0.50	12-31-95	12-13	1.98	25½	7.8
N	CHLPrJ	*	Chem Bkg 7.58%[7]Dep	BBB+	25(3/98)	Q0.47	12-31-95	12-13	1.89	25¼	7.5
N	CHLPrK	*	Chem Bkg 7.50%[8]Dep	BBB+	25(5/98)	Q0.47	12-31-95	12-13	1.88	25¼	7.4
N	CHLPrL	*	Chem Bkg Adj Rt[9] 'L'	BBB+	100(6/99)	1.38	12-31-95	12-13	[10]5.50	88¼	6.2
N	CCNPrA	*	Chris-Craft Ind $1 Vtg	NR	25	Q0.25	12-29-95	12-13	1.00	16¼B	6.2
N	CCIPr	*	Citicorp Adj[11]Rt 2nd	A–	100	Q1.50	2-28-96	2-13	6.00	90	6.7
N	CCIPrA	*	Citicorp Adj[12]Rt 3rd	A–	100	Q1.75	2-28-96	2-13	7.00	97½B	7.2
N	CCIPrD	*	Citicorp 9.08%[13]Dep	A–	25(3/97)	Q0.57	11-15-95	10-27	2.27	26⅜	8.6
N	CCIPrE		Citicorp 8.00%[14]Dep	A–	25(5/98)	Q0.50	11-15-95	10-27	2.00	26	7.7
N	CCIPrF		Citicorp 7.50% Dep[15]	A–	25(8/98)	Q0.47	11-15-95	10-27	1.88	25½	7.4
N	CCIPrG	*	Citicorp Adj [16]Rt [17]Dep	A–	25(5/99)	0.33	2-28-96	2-13	1.32	21⅜	6.2
N	CCIPrH	*	Citicorp Adj[16]Rt[18]Dep'H'	A–	25(8/99)	0.33	2-28-96	2-13	1.32	21⅜	6.2
N	CCIPrI		Citicorp 8.30% Dep[19]	A–	25(11/99)	Q0.52	11-15-95	10-27	2.08	26½	7.8
N	CCIPrJ		Citicorp 8.50% Dep[20]	A–	25(2/00)	Q0.53	11-15-95	10-27	2.13	27	7.9
N	CCIPrK	*	Citicorp 7.75%[21]Dep Ser 22	A–	25(5/00)	Plan qtly div			1.94	26	7.5
N	CVXPrT	*	Cleveland El Ill'93'A'[22]Dep	B	25(5/98)	Q0.53	5-1-96	4-10	2.12	23¼	9.1
N	CPMPrA		CL&P Capital L.P.9.30%[3]'MIPS'	NR	25(1/00)	Q0.19	12-29-95	12-26	2.32	27⅛	8.6
N	CGPPrH	*	Coastal Corp Sr'H' $2.125	NR	25(4/98)	Q0.53	12-15-95	11-28	2.13	25⅝	8.3
N	CLPr	*	Colgate-Palmolive$4.25Vtg	A	100	Q1.06	12-29-95	12-13	4.25	71B	6.0
N	CDOPrA	*	Comdisco 8.75% Ser'A'	BBB–	25(9/97)	Q0.55	12-15-95	11-28	2.19	25¾B	8.5
N	CWEPrT	*	ComEd Fin 1 8.48%[23]'TOPrS'	BBB–	[24]25(9/00)	Q0.53	12-29-95	12-26	2.12	25¾	8.2
N	CWEPrK	*	CommonwlthEd $2.425 Pref Vtg	BBB–	25(7/99)	Q0.61	2-1-96	12-27	2.42	27¼	8.9
N	CQPrA	*	COMSAT Cap I 8.125%[25]'MIPS'	A–	[26]25(7/00)	M0.17	12-29-95	12-26	2.03	25¾	7.9
N	CAGPrA	*	ConAgra Cap L.C. 9%'A'[27]	BBB–	25(5/99)	0.19	12-29-95	12-26	2.25	26¾B	8.4
N	CAGPrB	*	ConAgra Cap L.C.Adj[28]Rt'B'	BBB–	25(6/99)	0.12	12-29-95	12-26	1.50	21⅜	7.0
N	CAGPrC	*	ConAgra Cap L.C.9.35%[29]	BBB–	25(2/00)	M0.19	12-29-95	12-26	2.34	27½	8.5
N	EDPrA	*	Consol Ed N.Y. $5 Vtg	A	105	Q1.25	2-1-96	1-8	5.00	70	7.1
N	CMSPrI	*	Consumers Pwr $2.08'A'	BB+	25	Q0.52	1-1-96	12-7	2.08	25¾	8.1
N	CNVPr	*	Convert Hldgs Inc Shrs[30]	NR	9.30	0.31	1-12-96	12-27	1.19	10	11.9
N	DPTPrA	*	Datapoint $1	NR	NC	0.25	7-15-94	7-5	Nil	2⅛	....
N	DTEPrI	*	Detroit Ed 7.75% Dep[31]	BBB	25(4/98)	Q0.48	1-15-96	12-13	1.94	25¾	7.5
N	DDRPrA	*	Develp Div Rlty 9.50%[32]Dep	BBB–	25(11/00)	Plan qtly div			2.38	25	9.5
N	DLPr	*	Dial Corp $4.75	BBB–	101[33]	Q1.19	1-15-96	12-13	4.75	67	7.1
N	DECPrA	*	Digital Equip 8.875% Dep	BB–	25(3/99)	Q0.55	1-16-96	12-27	2.22	26⅜	8.4
N	DUKPrA	*	Duke Pwr 6.375% A	A+	25.80(12/03)	Q0.40	12-18-95	11-15	1.59	24½	6.5
N	DDPrB	*	du Pont(E.I.) $4.50	AA–	120	Q1.13	1-25-96	1-8	4.50	75	6.0
N	EOLPrA	*	Elf Overseas Ltd 8.50% 'A'	A+	26.06(1/98)	Q0.53	12-29-95	12-13	2.13	26⅝	8.0
N	EOLPrB	*	Elf Overseas Ltd 7.625%'B'	NR	25.95(6/98)	Q0.48	12-29-95	12-13	1.91	24¾	7.7
N	EDEPrA	*	Empire Dist El 4.75%	BBB+	10.20	Q0.12	12-1-95	11-13	0.47	6B	7.9
N	ENEPrA	*	Enron Cap Res L.P.9%'A'	BBB–	25(8/99)	0.19	12-29-95	12-26	2.25	26½	8.5
N	ENEPrC	*	Enron Cap LLC 8% 'MIPS'[34]	BBB–	25(11/98)	M0.17	12-29-95	12-26	2.00	25½	7.8
N	ENSPrE	*	ENSERCH Adj[35]E[36]Dep	BBB–	100	Q1.75	2-1-96	1-17	7.00	93¾B	7.5
N	ENSPrF	*	ENSERCH Adj[37]F[38]Dep	BBB–	25(4/99)	0.35	2-1-96	1-17	1.40	21⅛	6.6
N	ETPPr	*	Enterprise Oil'A'Pref ADS[39]	A–	26.25(6/97)	Q0.56	12-15-95	11-29	2.23	26⅜	8.5
N	EQRPrA	*	Equity Res Prop Tr 9.375%	BBB–	25(5/00)	Q0.59	1-15-96	12-27	2.34	25⅞	9.0
N	EQRPrB	*	Equity Res Prop Tr 9.125% [40]Dep	BBB–	25(10/05)	Plan qtly div			2.28	25⅝	8.9
N	ESBPrA		Esprito Santo Overseas 8.50%	BBB	25(11/03)	Q0.53	12-31-95	12-13	2.13	24⅞	8.5
N	EVRPrA	*	Everen Cap 13.50%'A'[41]Exch	NR	28.50 9/96	0.86	12-15-95	11-21	[42]3.38	24½	13.8
N	BEXPr		Extecapital Ltd Ser'A'Pref	A	26.14(12/97)	Q0.57	1-2-96	12-13	2.28	26⅜B	8.6
N	FENPrC	*	Fairchild Indus Ser'C'	NR	45	Q1.06	1-17-96	12-29	[43]4.25	41B	10.4
N	FIGPrA	*	Farmers Grp Cap 8.45%[44]'QUIPS'	A–	25(9/00)	Plan qtly div			2.11	26	8.1
N	FIGPrB	*	Farmers Gp Cp II 8.25[44]'QUIPS'	NR	25(9/00)	Plan qtly div			2.06	25¾	8.0
N	FREPr		Fed'l Home Loan Mtge 7.90%	NR	25(6/97)	Q0.49	12-29-95	12-7	1.98	25⅞	7.6
N	FREPrA		Fed'l Home Loan Mtge 6.72%	NR	25(9/98)	Q0.42	12-29-95	12-7	1.68	25⅝B	6.6
N	FIAPr		Fiat SpA Pref ADR[45]	NR	NC	0.11	8-16-95	7-12	0.10	8⅞	1.1
N	FCNPrC	*	First Chi NBD[46]Adj[47]Div C	BBB+	100	Q1.63	11-30-95	11-1	6.50	100	6.5
N	FCNPrE	*	First Chi NBD[48]8.45% [47]Dep	BBB+	25(11/97)	Q0.53	1-1-96	12-6	2.11	25⅞	8.2
N	FCNPrU	*	FirstChiNBD[49]7.5%Pf[50]Pch[51]Uts	A+	[52]25(5/98)	Q0.47	11-10-95	11-7	1.88	25	7.5
N	FFBPrF	*	First Fidelity Banc Dep[53]	NR	25(6/96)	Q0.66	1-1-96	11-22	2.66	25⅞	10.3
N	FRPrA	*	First Indl Rlty Tr 9.50%	NR	25(11/00)	Plan qtly div			2.38	24⅞	9.5

Footnotes and Sinking Fund: [1] Red fr 11-22-99 at $25 re-spec cond. [2] Red fr 7-12-2000 at $25 re spec cond. [3] Monthly Income Preferred Shrs. [4] Div 5.567% to 12/31/95. [5] $1.285 fr 1-1-96(rate 5.1425%). [6] Dep for 0.25 shr 7.92% cm Pfd stk. [7] Dep for 0.25 shr 7.58% cm Pfd stk. [8] Dep for 0.25 shr 7.50% cm Pfd stk. [9] Div 5.502% to 12/31/95. [10] $5.082 fr 1-1-96(rate 5.082%). [11] Div 6% to 2/29/96. [12] Div 7% to 2/29/96. [13] Dep for 0.10 shr 9.08% Pfd Series 14. [14] Dep for 0.10 shr 8.00% non-cm Pfd Series 16. [15] Dep for 0.10 shr 7.50% non-cm Pfd Series 17. [16] Div 5.292% to 2/29/96. [17] Dep for 0.10 shr Adj Rt cm Pfd Series 18. [18] Dep for 0.10 shr Adj Rt cm Pfd Series 19. [19] Dep for 0.10 shr 8.30% non-cm Pfd Series 20. [20] Dep for 0.10 shr 8.50% non-cm Pfd Series 21. [21] Dep for 0.10 shr 7.75% Ser 22 Pfd. [22] Dep for 0.05 shr Serial Pfd,$42.40 Sr T. [23] Trust Originated Preferred Securities. [24] or anytime upon'Tax Event're-spec cond. [25] Monthly Income Preferred Shs. [26] Or earlier re spec cond. [27] Exch for Sr'A'Debs re-spec.cond. [28] Div 5.985% to 2/29/96. [29] Exch for Sr'C'Debs re-spec. cond. [30] To redm 7/31/97@$9.30. [31] Dep for 0.25 shr cm Pfd 7.75% Series. [32] Dep for 0.10 shr 9.50% Sr'A'CmRedPfd. [33] SF 100. [34] Monthly income preferred shrs. [35] Div 7% to 1/31/96. [36] Dep for 0.10 shr of Adj 'E' Pfd. [37] Div 5.594% to 1/31/96. [38] Dep for 0.025 shr of Adj'F'Pfd. [39] Ea ADS rep 1 cm Dollar Pref Series'A'. [40] Dep for 0.10 shr 9.125% Sr'B'Redm Pfd. [41] Co opt exch for $25amt 13.50%JrSubDebs2007. [42] In cash(or Pfd to 9-15-2000). [43] Thru 7-2-99,then $7.00. [44] Quarterly Income Preferred Securities. [45] Each ADR rep 5 preference shrs, lit.1000. [46] Div 6.50% to 2/29/96. [47] Formerly First Chicago. [48] Dep for 0.04 shr 8.45% Ser'E'cm Pfd. [49] Units:$25amt7.49%SubDeb2023 & 1.10%PurContract. [50] Req pur 1 dep(rep 0.25 shr) 7 1/2% cm Pfd by 5-10-2023. [51] Formerly NBD Bcp:pays int qtly fr 8-10-93. [52] On int pymt dates re-specified cond. [53] Dep for 0.025 shr 10.64% Ser'F'Pfd.

Preferred Stock Summary

Exchange / Ticker	Cm Divd / Issue	Rating	Reg. Call Price (Begins) Thru [see footnotes for Sink'g Fd]	Dividends – Latest Payments: Period $	Date	Ex Div.	Ind. Rate	Last Sale or Bid(B)	% Div. Yld.
N IPrF	* First Interstate 9.875% Dep[1]	BBB	25(11/96)	Q0.62	12-31-95	12-13	2.47	25⅞	9.5
N IPrG	* First Interstate 9% Dep[2]	BBB	25(5/97)	Q0.56	12-31-95	12-13	2.25	25⅞B	8.7
N FMBPr	First Maryland Banc 7.875%	BBB+	25(12/98)	Q0.49	1-31-96	1-11	1.97	25½	7.7
N FNWPr	First Nationwide Bk 11.50%	BB	105.75(8/99)	Q2.88	12-1-95	11-14	11.50	111½B	10.3
N FLTPrB	* Fleet Fin'l 10.12%Dep	BBB	26.265(5/96)	Q0.63	12-1-95	11-13	2.53	26¾	9.5
N FLTPrD	* Fleet[3]Fin'l 9.30[4]Dep	BB+	25(10/97)	Q0.58	1-15-96	12-27	2.33	26⅛	8.9
N FLTPrE	* Fleet[5]Fin'l 9.35%[4]Dep	BB+	25(1/00)	Q0.58	1-15-96	12-27	2.34	27¼	8.6
N FPLPrA	* Fla Pwr & Lt $2	A+	27 2/97	Q0.50	12-1-95	11-9	2.00	27¼	7.3
N FHIPr	* Ford Hldgs'A'[6]Dep	A	NC	Q0.50	12-1-95	11-16	2.00	25⅛	8.0
N FHIPrB	* Ford Hldgs'B'[7]Dep	A	NC	Q0.50	12-1-95	11-16	2.00	25⅛	8.0
N FHIPrC	* Ford Hldgs'C'[8]Dep	A	NC	Q0.44	12-1-95	11-16	1.78	25⅛	7.1
N FHIPrD	* Ford Hldgs'D'[9]Dep	A	NC	Q0.51	12-1-95	11-16	2.03	25¼	8.0
N FPrB	* Ford MotorDep'B'	A	25(11/02)	Q0.51	12-1-95	10-30	2.06	27¾	7.4
N FPrT	* Ford Mtr Cap Tr I 9.00%[10]'TOPrS'	A	[11]25(11/02)	Plan qtly div			2.25	27⅝	8.1
N FCXPrC	* Freept-McMo Cp/Gld'C'[12]Dep[13]	BB	[14]NC	0.31	11-1-95	10-12	[15]....	30⅜	....
N FOXPrA	* Foxmeyer Hlth[16]$4.20[17]Ex'A'	NR	40(10/98)	[18]....	1-15-96	1-4	[19]Stk	37¼	s....
N FCXPrB	* Freept-McMo Cp/Gld'B'[20]Dep[21]	BB	[14]NC	0.34	11-1-95	10-12	[22]....	33	....
N FCXPrD	Freept-McMo Cp Silver'D'[23]Dep[24]	BB–	[14]NC	0.22	11-1-95	10-12	[25]....	21⅛	....
N GMIPr	* Gemini II Inc Shrs Vtg[26]	NR	NC	0.40	1-31-96	12-27	1.83	10⅛	18.1
N GMPrD	* General Motors 7.92%[27]Dep[28]	BBB+	25(7/99)	Q0.50	2-1-96	12-28	1.98	26⅛	7.6
N GMPrG	* General Motors 9.12%[29]Dep[30]	BBB+	25(12/00)	Q0.57	2-1-96	12-28	2.28	28¼	8.1
N GMPrQ	* General Motors 9.125%[31]Dep[32]	BBB+	25(12/98)	Q0.57	2-1-96	12-28	2.28	27	8.4
N GPEPrK	* Georgia Pwr Adj[33]Cl'A'	A	27.50 5/98	0.36	1-1-96	12-13	[34]1.42	22	6.5
N GPEPrL	* Georgia Pwr Adj[35]Cl'A'(2nd'93Sr)	A	27.50 10/98	0.33	1-1-96	12-13	[36]1.32	20⅝	6.4
N GPEPrM	* Georgia Pwr Cap 9%[37]'MIPS'	A	25(12/99)	0.19	12-29-95	12-26	2.25	28½	7.9
N GRMPrA	* Grand Met Del L.P. 9.42%	A+	25(11/04)	Q0.59	10-31-95	10-26	2.35	29¼	8.0
N GWFPrA	* Great West'n Fin'l 8.30% Dep[38]	BBB–	25(10/97)	Q0.52	2-1-96	1-10	2.08	26⅛	7.9
N GWFPrT	* Great Westn Finl I 8.25%[10]'TOPrS'	BBB–	[39]25(12/00)	Plan qtly div			2.06	25⅜	8.1
N GTEPrY	* GTE Delaware 8.75%'B'[37]'MIPS'	BBB+	25(3/00)	M0.18	12-29-95	12-26	2.19	26⅞	8.1
N GTEPrZ	* GTE Delaware 9.25%'A'[37]'MIPS'	BBB+	25(10/99)	0.19	12-29-95	12-26	2.31	27¾	8.3
N GLFPrC	* GTE Fla 8.16%	AA–	102.04	Q2.04	2-15-96	1-24	8.16	102¼B	8.0
A GOUPr	* Gulf Cda Res[40]AdjSer1 Pref	NR	5	[41]g0.03	1-12-96	12-27	Nil	2¾B	....
N GSUPr	* Gulf States Util $1.75	BB	25(6/00)	Q0.44	12-15-95	11-28	1.75	24½B	7.1
N GSUPrD	* Gulf States Util Dep[42]Adj[43]B	BBB–	50[44]	0.94	12-15-95	11-28	3.50	48	7.3
N GSUPrK	* Gulf States Util $8.80	BB+	100[45]	Q2.20	12-15-95	11-28	8.80	101½	8.7
N HSAPrA	* HSBC Americas[46]Adj[47]Rt'A'	NR	50	Q0.75	1-2-96	12-6	3.00	45¼B	6.6
N HLFPrA	* Heller Finl 8.125% Ser'A'	BBB	25(9/00)	Q0.51	11-15-95	10-30	2.03	25⅞	7.8
N HIPrJ	* Household 7.35% Dep[48]	A–	25(10/98)	Q0.46	1-15-96	12-27	1.84	25⅛	7.3
N HIPrZ	* Household 8.25%'92 Dep[49]	A–	25(10/02)	Q0.52	1-15-96	12-27	2.06	26½B	7.8
N HIPrT	* Househld Cap Tr 8.25%'TOPrS'	A–	25(6/00)	Q0.52	12-29-95	12-26	2.06	25⅞	8.0
N IPCPrN	* Illinois Pwr Adj[50]Rt B	BBB–	50	Q0.88	2-1-96	1-8	3.50	46½B	7.5
N IPCPrM	* IllinoisPwrCap9.45%'A'[37]'MIPS'	BBB–	25(10/99)	0.20	12-29-95	12-26	2.36	27⅞	8.5
N IBMPrA	* Int Bus Mach 7 1/2% [51]Dep	A–	25(6/01)	Q0.47	1-2-96	12-14	1.88	26	7.2
A ITBPrA	Intl ThoroughBred 'A'	NR	NC	....			Nil	5⅞	....
N JRPrO	* James River 8.25%[52]Dep	BB+	25(9/97)	Q0.51	1-2-96	12-15	2.06	25⅛	8.2
N JYPPrZ	* JCP&L Cap L.P.8.56%'MIPS'[37]	BBB	25(5/00)	M0.18	12-29-95	12-26	2.14	26⅛	8.2
N JYPPrE	* Jersey Cent P&L 7.88%	BBB	103.65	Q1.97	2-1-96	1-11	7.88	100B	7.9
N KCCPr	* K-III Commun$2.875SrEx[53]	B	26.45(4/97)[54]	Q0.72	11-1-95	10-18	2.88	27¼	10.6
N KABPrA	* Kaneb Svcs Adj Rt A[55]	NR	11.33 6/96	0.22	12-29-95	12-13	[56]0.87	8¾B	9.9
N KSUPr	Kansas City So.Ind 4% Vtg	NR	NC	Q0.25	1-16-96	12-27	1.00	16	6.3
N KLTPrA	* Kansas City P&L 3.80%	A–	103.70	Q0.95	3-1-96	2-6	3.80	55	6.9
N KBHrB	* Kaufman & Broad$1.52 Dep[57]'B'[58]	NR	[59]	Q0.38	10-2-95	9-12	1.52	14⅞	10.2
N KEYPrA	* KeyCorp 10% Dep[60]	BBB	25(6/96)	Q0.63	12-29-95	12-13	2.50	25¾	9.7
N KIMPrB	* Kimco Rlty 8.50% Sr'B'Dep[61]	BBB+	25(7/00)	Q0.53	1-16-96	12-28	2.13	25⅜	8.4
N LSOPrA	* LASMO plc Sr'A'ADS[62]	BBB–	[63]25(6/98)	0.53	1-17-96	12-28	2.13	24⅛	8.8
N LITPrB	* Litton Indus $2 B Vtg	BBB+	80	Q0.50	1-1-96	12-13	2.00	26½B	7.5
N LWNPr	* Loewen Grp Cap 9.45%'A'[37]'MIPS'	BBB–	25(8/04)	0.20	12-29-95	12-26	2.36	23⅜	10.1
N LILPrA	* Long Island Ltg 7.95% AA	BB+	25(5/00)	Q0.50	12-1-95	11-15	1.99	24⅜	8.2
N LPLPrA	* Louisiana P&L 9.68%	BBB–	25 7/96	Q0.60	2-1-96	1-11	2.42	26⅜	9.2
N MKGPr	* Mallinckrodt Gr 4% Vtg[64]	BBB+	110	Q1.00	12-29-95	12-13	4.00	60	6.7
N MVLPr	* Manville Corp $2.70 Pref B	B	25	Q0.68	12-1-95	11-16	2.70	25⅛	10.7
N MXSPrA	* Maxus Energy $2.50	NR	25(11/98)	Q0.63	12-15-95	11-13	2.50	25⅞	9.7
N KRBPrA	* MBNA Corp 7.50% Sr'A'	NR	25(1/01)	Plan qtly div			1.88	25⅛	7.5
N MDRPrB	* McDermott $2.60 Vtg	BB+	31.25[65]	Q0.65	1-1-96	12-13	2.60	30	8.7
N MCDPrE	* McDonald's Cp 7.72%[66]Dep	AA	25(12/97)	Q0.48	12-1-95	11-9	1.93	26¼	7.4
N MCNPrT	* MCN Mich L.P. 9.375%	BBB+	25(11/99)	0.20	12-29-95	12-26	2.34	27½	8.5
N MELPrI	* Mellon Bk 9.60% 'I'	BBB+	25(8/96)	Q0.60	11-15-95	10-27	2.40	25⅞	9.3
N MELPrk	* Mellon Bk 8.20% 'K'	BBB+	25(2/98)	Q0.51	11-15-95	10-27	2.05	26⅛	7.8
N MUKPrA	* MEPC Intl Cap 9.125%[67]'QUIPS'	A	25(9/05)	Q0.57	12-29-95	12-26	2.28	25⅝	8.9
A MPFPr	MeridianPointRlty VI Vtg[68]	NR	NC	0.03	9-30-92	9-15	Nil	4⅛	....
A MPGPr	MeridianPointRlty VII Vtg[69]	NR	NC	0.10	12-30-93	12-14	Nil	4	....
A MPHPr	MeridianPointRlty VIII Vtg	NR	NC	0.07	12-29-95	12-15	0.28	5½	5.1

Footnotes and Sinking Fund: [1] Dep for 0.125 Series'F'cm Pfd. [2] Dep for 0.125 Series 'G'cm Pfd. [3] Dep for 0.10 shr 9.30% cm pfd stk. [4] Formerly Shawmut Natl. [5] Dep for 0.10 shr 9.35% cm Pfd stk. [6] Dep for 0.00025 shr Ser'A'cm Pfd. [7] Dep for 0.00025 shr Ser'B'cm Pfd. [8] Dep for 0.00025 shr Ser'C'cm Pfd. [9] Dep for 0.00025 shr Ser'D'cm Pfd. [10] Trust Originated Preferred Securities. [11] or anytime upon'Spcl Event're-spec cond. [12] Dep for 0.05 shr Gold-Denominated Pfd Sr II. [13] Mand red 2-1-2006 for value 0.10 oz gold. [14] Re-specified cond. [15] Based on curr val 0.000812502 gold on div date. [16] Co opt fr 10-15-96 exch for $40 amt Exchange Nts. [17] Mand redm 11-30-2003,$40. [18] In stk,cash eq $1.05. [19] Payable in $4.20 pfd to 10-15-96. [20] Dep for 0.05 shr Gold Denominated Pfd. [21] Mand red 8-1-2003 for value 0.10 once gold. [22] Based on curr val of.000875 oz gold on div date. [23] Dep for 0.025 shr Silver-Denominated Pfd. [24] Fr 8-1-99 redeem pfd with value 0.05 in slvr. [25] Based on Dollar Equivalent value of oz silver. [26] To redm 1/31/97@$9.30. [27] Dep for 0.25 shr Series'D'Pref. [28] Co offer for pfd $26.375 to May 22. [29] Dep for 0.25 shr Series 'G' Pref. [30] Co offer for pfd $28.25 to May 22. [31] Dep for 0.25 shr series'B'9.125% pref. [32] Co offer for pfd $27.50 to May 22. [33] Div 5.70% to 12/31/95. [34] $1.317 fr 1-1-96(rate 5.27%). [35] Div 5.24% to 12/31/95. [36] $1.212 fr 1-1-96(rate 4.85%). [37] Monthly Income Preferred Shrs. [38] Dep for 0.10 shr 8.30% cm Pfd stk. [39] or anytime upon 'Tax Event're-spec cond. [40] Adj mthly, 80% Cdn Prime. [41] Approx. [42] Dep for 1/2'B'. [43] Div 7.00% to 3/15/96. [44] SF 50. [45] SF 100. [46] Div 6% to 3/31/96. [47] Formerly Marine Midland. [48] Dep for 0.025 shr 7.35% cm Pfd Sr 1993-A. [49] Dep for 0.025 shr 8.25% cm '92'A'Pfd. [50] Div 7% to 1/31/96. [51] Dep for 0.25 shr Ser'A' 7 1/2% Pfd stk. [52] Dep for 0.05 shr Ser'O' 8.25% cm Pfd stk. [53] Co opt 5-1-94 or on IPO com,exch11.5%Subdebs'04. [54] SF 100(5/03). [55] Div 8.65% to 12/31/95. [56] $0.81 fr 1-1-96(rate 8.10%). [57] Dep for 0.20 shr Ser'B'Mand Cv Prem Divd Pfd. [58] Mand Cv into 1 com 4-1-96. [59] Callable fr $27.12 to $23.46 pd in com stk. [60] Dep for 0.2 shr 10% Ser'A'Pfd. [61] Dep for 0.10 shr 8.50% Sr'B'cm Red Pfd. [62] Ea ADS rep 1 cm Dollar Pref shr Series'A'. [63] Plus $1.25 special div. [64] Formerly IMCERA Group 4% Pfd. [65] SF 31.25. [66] Dep for 0.0005 shr 7.72% cm Pfd Ser'E'. [67] Qtly Income Pfd Securities. [68] Accum $0.4173 to 12/31/95. [69] Accum $0.2672 to 12/31/95.

Exchange Ticker	Cm Divd Issue	Rating	Reg. Call Price (Begins) Thru [see footnotes for Sink'g Fd]	Dividends Latest Payments Period $	Date	Ex Div.	Ind. Rate	Last Sale or Bid(B)	% Div. Yld.
N MERPrA	* Merrill Lynch 9%'A'[1]Dep	A–	25(12/04)	Q0.56	1-2-96	12-13	2.25	28⅝	7.9
N MTTPrZ	* Met-Ed Capital L.P.9%'MIPS'[2]	BBB	25(8/99)	0.19	12-29-95	12-26	2.25	26½	8.5
N MCNPr	* Mich Consol[3]Gas $2.05	CALL	25.205 1/96[4]	0.51	1-31-96		2.05	25⅝B	8.0
N MECPr	* MidAmer Energy[5]$1.7375[6]	A	26.0425 11/96	Q0.43	12-1-95	11-6	1.74	24½B	7.1
N MIBPrA	Midland Bank [7]A1/A2[8]Unit ADS	NR	[9]26.109(10/98)	0.47	12-15-95	11-28	1.89	24⅞	7.6
N MIBPrB	Midland Bank[10]B1/B2[11]Unit ADS	NR	[12]26.281(2/00)	0.54	12-15-95	11-28	2.18	26½	8.2
N MIBPrC	Midland Bank[13]C1/C2 [14]Unit ADS	NR	[15]26.141	Plan qtly div			1.94	25	7.8
A MPLPrB	* Minn P&L $7.36 Vtg	BBB+	103.34	Q1.84	1-1-96	12-13	7.36	99½B	7.4
N MEPrA	* Mission Capital 9.875%[2]'MIPS'	BBB	25(11/99)	M0.21	12-29-95	12-26	2.47	27½	9.0
N MEPrB	* Mission Capital 8.50%[2]'MIPS'	NR	25(8/00)	M0.18	12-29-95	12-26	2.13	25½	8.3
N MPPrA	* Mississippi Pwr 7.25%[16]Dep[17]	A	26.813 8/97	Q0.45	1-2-96	12-13	1.81	24⅝B	7.4
A MPNPrC	* Monongahela Pwr 4.50% C	A	103.50	Q1.13	2-1-96	1-10	4.50	64⅝	7.0
N JPMPrA	* Morgan(JP) Adj[18]Rt A	AA–	100	Q1.25	12-31-95	12-21	5.00	80	6.3
N MSPrB	* Morgan Stanley 8.88% Dep[19]	A–	25(11/96)	Q0.55	11-30-95	10-30	2.22	25⅞	8.6
N MSPrD	* Morgan Stanley 7.375% Dep[20]	A–	25 8/98	Q0.46	11-30-95	10-30	1.84	25⅛	7.3
N NWXPrA	* Natl Westm'tr Bk[21]Ex Cap Sec'A'	A+	25(11/03)	Q0.49	10-16-95	10-11	1.97	25⅜	7.8
N NWPrA	Natl Westminster Pref'A' ADS	A+	26.50(9/96)	Q0.57	1-17-96	12-1	2.26	27	8.4
N NWPrB	Natl Westminster Pref'B' ADS	A+	26.50(6/98)	0.46	1-17-96	12-1	1.86	25¾	7.2
N NGEPrD	* N.Y. State E&G Adj[22]Rt[23]B	BBB	27.50 11/98	0.34	1-1-96	12-4	[24]1.36	20¼	6.7
N NWSPr	News Corp Ltd Vtg ADS[25]	BBB–	NC	0.10	10-17-95	9-19	0.40	19¼	2.1
N NOPPrA	* Newscorp Overseas[26]8.625%	BBB–	25(7/98)	Q0.54	12-31-95	12-13	2.16	25⅝	8.4
N NOPPrB	* Newscorp Overseas[26]Adj Rt[27]'B'	BBB	25(6/99)	0.44	12-31-95	12-13	1.77	22¼	7.9
N NMKPrM	* Niag Moh Pwr 9.50%	B	25(9/99)	Q0.59	12-31-95	11-2	2.38	23⅝	10.1
N NOK.A	* Nokia CP[28]ADS[29]	NR	NC	0.49	4-17-95	3-30	0.22	39	0.6
N NSRPr	* Norfolk So'n Ry $2.60 A Vtg	AA	50	Q0.65	12-15-95	11-1	2.60	41	6.3
N NIPrA	* No'n Ind Pub Sv Adj[30]Rt	A–	50	Q0.75	1-12-96	12-13	3.00	46½B	6.5
N NOBPr	* Norwest 10.24%[31]Dep[32]	CALL	25	0.64	10-1-95	9-13	Call	24⅞	....
N NPSPrA	* NWPS Cap Fin 8.125% Tr Sec 1	A–	25(9/00)	Q0.51	12-29-95	12-26	2.03	26	7.8
N OECPrM	* Ohio Ed 7.75%'A'	BB+	25(3/98)	Q0.48	1-1-96	12-13	1.94	24⅝	7.9
N OECPrT	* Ohio Ed Fin Tr 9.00%CapSec	BB+	25(12/00)	Plan qtly div			2.25	26⅛	8.6
N OGEPrA	* Oklahoma G&E 4% Vtg	AA–	20	Q0.20	1-12-96	12-27	0.80	14	5.7
N ORIPrH	* Old Republic Int 8.75%'H'	A+	25(12/96)	Q0.55	12-29-95	12-15	2.19	26	8.4
A PETPrB	* Pac Ent $4.40	A	101.50	Q1.10	1-16-96	12-18	4.40	67⅝	6.5
A PCGPrU	* Pac G&E 7.04% Red 1st Vtg	A–	25.88(1/03)	Q0.44	11-15-95	10-12	1.76	25⅛B	7.0
N PPWPrE	* PacifiCorp $1.98	A–	25(5/97)	Q0.50	2-15-96	1-18	1.98	26⅛	7.6
N PEPrF	* PECO Energy[33] Dep	BBB	25	Q0.50	2-1-96	12-22	1.99	25⅜	7.8
N PEPrZ	* PECO Energy 9% [2]MIPS'A'	BBB	25(7/99)	0.19	12-29-95	12-26	2.25	26⅝	8.5
N PEPrY	* Peco En Cap Tr I 8.72%[34]'TOPrS'	NR	[35]25(9/97)	Plan monthly div			2.18	26	8.4
N PECPrZ	* Penelec Capital 8.75%[2] 'MIPS'	BBB+	25(7/99)	0.18	12-29-95	12-26	2.19	26¼	8.3
N PPLPrA	* Penn Pwr & Lt 4.40%	BBB+	102	Q1.10	1-1-96	12-6	4.40	63	7.0
A PCGPrCA	* PG&E Cap I 7.90%[36]'QUIPS'	A–	[37]25(11/00)	Plan qtly div			1.98	25⅞	7.6
N PGCPr	* Phillips Gas 9.32%	BBB–	25(12/97)	Q0.58	11-15-95	10-25	2.33	26½	8.8
N PLPrM	* PLC Capital LLC 9%'A'MIPS[2]	A–	25(6/99)	0.19	12-29-95	12-26	2.25	26½	8.5
N POMPrH	* Potomac El Pwr $3.37 '87	A–	52.25 7/97[38]	Q0.84	12-1-95	11-2	3.37	46B	7.3
N PGRPrA	* Progressive Cp 9.375%	A	25(5/96)	Q0.59	12-31-95	12-6	2.34	25½	9.2
N PVTPr	* Provident Cos[39] 8.10%Dep[40]	BBB	25(2/98)	Q0.51	2-1-96	1-10	2.02	26	7.8
N PVNPrM	Providian [2]LLC'MIPS'	AA–	25(5/99)	M0.18	12-29-95	12-26	2.22	27⅛	8.2
N PINPrK	* PSI Energy 7.44% Vtg	BBB	25(2/98)	Q0.46	12-1-95	11-9	1.86	25⅛	7.4
N PSRPrB	* Pub Sv Colo 8.40%	BBB	25.25	Q0.52	3-1-96	2-7	2.10	25⅜	8.3
N PEGPrI	* Pub Sv E&G 7.40%	BBB+	101	Q1.85	12-29-95	12-5	7.40	96¾B	7.6
N PEGPrX	* Pub Sv E&G Cap 8.00%'MIPS'	BBB+	25(9/00)	0.17	12-29-95	12-26	2.00	25¾	7.8
N PEGPrZ	* Public Sv E&G Cap 9.375%[2]'MIPS'	BBB+	25(11/99)	0.20	12-29-95	12-26	2.34	27¼	8.6
N PSAPrE	* Public Storage10%'E'	BBB+	25(1/05)	Q0.63	12-29-95	12-13	2.50	27½	9.1
N PSAPrF	* Public Storage[41]9.75% 'F'	BBB	25(4/05)	Q0.61	12-29-95	12-13	2.44	27¼	8.9
N PSAPrG	* Public Storage 8.875% Dep[42]	BBB+	25(12/00)	Plan qtly div			2.22	25⅜	8.7
N PSDPrB	* Puget Sound P&L Adj[43]Rt'B'	BBB+	27.50 2/99	0.36	11-15-95	10-19	1.32	22⅛	5.9
N KFVPr	* Quest For Value IncShrVtg[44]	NR	NC	†0.19	1-12-96	12-27	1.20	12	e10.0
N RLRPr	* ReliaStar Finl[45]10% Dep[46]	BBB	25(6/96)	Q0.63	12-31-95	12-13	2.50	25⅜	9.9
N RNBPrD	* Republic NY Adj [47]Rt [48]Dep	NR	25(6/99)	0.33	1-1-96	12-13	[49]1.33	22	6.0
N RNBPrE	* Republic NY $1.8125	A+	25(6/00)	Q0.45	1-1-96	12-13	1.81	25¼B	7.2
N RPOPrA	* Rhone-Poul Overseas 8.125%	BB+	25(7/03)	Q0.51	12-31-95	12-13	2.03	24⅜	8.3
N RNPrB	* RJR Nabisco Sr'B'[50]Dep	BB+	25(8/98)	Q0.58	12-1-95	11-14	2.31	25¾	9.0
N RNPrC	* RJR Nabisco[51]Sr'C'[52]PERCS[53]	BB+	[54]	Q0.15	11-15-95	10-27	0.60	6⅜	9.4
N RNPrT	* RJR Nabisco 10%'TOPrS'[34]	BB+	25(8/98)	Q0.63	12-31-95	12-13	2.50	26	9.6
N RSEPrZ	* Rouse Cap 9.25%[55]'QUIPS'	BBB–	[56]25(11/99)	0.22	12-29-95	12-26	2.31	24¾	9.3
N RBSPr	Royal Bk Scotland Ser'A'ADS[57]	A	25.84 9/97	Q0.60	12-29-95	12-13	2.39	26½	9.0
N RBSPrC	Royal Bk Scotland Ser'C'ADS[58]	A	26.18(8/97)	Q0.50	12-29-95	12-13	2.02	27⅛	7.4
N RBSPrD	Royal Bk Scotland Ser'D' ADS[59]	A	25(9/05)	0.48	12-29-95	12-13	1.94	25½	7.6
N RBSPrX	* Royal Bk Scotland[60]Ex Cap'A'	A	25(6/04)	Q0.53	12-29-95	12-26	2.13	25¾	8.3
A SGMPr	* Sahara Gaming [61]8% [62]Ex	NR	[63]	S[64]....	9-29-95	9-13	[65]....	¾	....
N SBPrC	* Salomon Inc 9.50% Dep[66]	BB+	25(6/96)	0.60	12-31-95	12-14	2.40	25⅝	9.4
N SBPrD	* Salomon Inc 8.08% Dep[67]	BB+	25(3/98)	Q0.51	12-31-95	12-14	2.02	25¼	8.0

Footnotes and Sinking Fund: [1] Dep for .0025 shr 9% Sr'A'cm Pfd. [2] Monthly Income Preferred Shrs. [3] Called Jan 31 at $25.00. [4] SF 25. [5] Red restr(7.15%)to 12-1-98. [6] Formerly Midwest Pwr Sys. [7] Ea A1 ADS rep 1 non-cm $-denominated Pref. [8] Ea A2 ADS rep 1 non-cm $-denominated Pref. [9] Pref redeem:Ser A1$20,Ser A2$5. [10] Ea B1 ADS rep 1 non-cm $ denominated Pref. [11] Ea B2 ADS rep 1 non-cm $ denominated Pref. [12] Pref redeem: Ser B1 $20, Ser B2 $5. [13] Ea C1 ADS rep 1 non-cm $ denominated Pref. [14] Ea C2 ADS rep 1 non-cm $ denominated Pref. [15] Pref redeem:Sr C1$20,Ser C2 $5. [16] Dep for 0.25 shr 7.25% Series cm Pfd stk. [17] Red rstr(7.66%)to 8-1-97. [18] Div 5% to 3/31/96. [19] Dep for 0.125 shr 8.88% cm Pfd. [20] Dep for 0.125 shr 7.375% cm Pfd. [21] Co Opt fr 10-16-96 exch for$25 amt non-cm$Pref. [22] Div 5.44% to 12/31/95. [23] Red rstr(5.24%)to 12-1-98. [24] $1.257 fr 1-1-96(rate 5.03%). [25] Ea ADS rep 4 Pfd Ltd Vtg Ord Shrs. [26] Gtd by News Corp Ltd. [27] Div 7.06% to 12/31/95. [28] Shr hldr purchase agreement,re-specifield cond. [29] Ea ADS rep 1 'A' shr,FIM 20. [30] Div 6% to 1/13/96. [31] Dep for 0.25 shr 10.24% cm Series'A'pfd. [32] Called Jan 2 at $25. [33] Dep for 0.25 shr $7.96 cm Pfd stk. [34] Trust Originated Preferred Securities. [35] or anytime upon 'Tax Event're-spec cond. [36] Quarterly Income Preferred Securities. [37] or earlier upon'Special Event'. [38] SF 50. [39] Dep for 0.167 shr 8.10% cm Pfd. [40] Formerly Provident Life & Accident. [41] Formerly Storage Equities. [42] Dep for 0.001 shr 8.875% cm Sr'G'Pfd. [43] Div 5.26% to 2/15/96. [44] To redm 1/31/97@$11.60. [45] Dep for 0.25 shr 10% Sr cm Pfd. [46] Formerly NWNL Cos. [47] Dep for 0.25 shr Adj Rt cm Pfd Series'D'. [48] Div 5.31% to 12/31/95. [49] $1.365 fr 1-1-96(rate 5.4625%). [50] Dep for 0.001 shr Sr'B'cm Pfd. [51] Dep for 0.10 shr Ser'C'CvPfd. [52] Preferred Equity Redempt'n Cumulative Stk. [53] Mand Cv 1 com,5-15-97. [54] Callable fr $11.2286 to $9.425 com or cash. [55] Mand 12-31-2025. [56] or earlier upon 'Tax Event'. [57] Ea ADS rep 1 non-cm Dollar Pref Series'A'. [58] Ea ADS rep 1 non-cm Dollar Pref Series'C'. [59] Ea ADS rep 1 non-cm Dollar Pref Series'D'. [60] Co opt exch for $25 amt non-cm $ Pref. [61] To10-1-98 then 11%of$2.14,then0.5%ea6 Mo to16%. [62] Co opt 10-1-98 exch for Jr Sub Nts at Liq Pref & divds. [63] At Liq Pref($2.14 plus accrued & unpaid divds). [64] Pd in pfd stk,cash equiv $0.085. [65] Co option pay $0.17 in pfd stk to 10-1-96. [66] Dep for 0.05 shr 9.50% cm Pfd'C'. [67] Dep for 0.05 shr 8.08% cm Pfd'D'.

Preferred Stock Summary

Exchange	Ticker	Cm Divd	Issue	Rating	Reg. Call Price (Begins) Thru [see footnotes for Sink'g Fd]	Dividends — Latest Payments: Period $	Date	Ex Div.	Ind. Rate	Last Sale or Bid(B)	% Div. Yld.
A	SDOPrH	*	San Diego G&E $1.82	A	26(11/98)	Q0.46	1-15-96	12-6	1.82	25⅛	7.2
N	BSFPrA		Santander Finance Sr'A'	NR	25.92(12/98)	Q0.46	12-31-95	12-13	1.84	23⅝	7.8
N	BSFPrB		Santander Finance Sr'B'	NR	25.99(3/99)	Q0.49	12-31-95	12-13	1.98	24⅝	8.0
N	BSFPrC		Santander Finance Sr'C'	A–	26.02(12/00)	0.38	12-31-95	12-13	2.03	25⅝	7.9
N	OPRPr		Santander Overseas Bk Ser'A'	A–	26.33(9/96)	Q0.66	1-2-96	12-13	2.66	27	9.9
N	OPRPrB		Santander Overseas Bk Ser'B'	A–	26.09(3/97)	Q0.54	1-2-96	12-13	2.17	26⅜	8.2
N	OPRPrC		Santander Overseas Bk Ser'C'	A–	26.12(12/97)	Q0.56	1-2-96	12-13	2.24	26½B	8.5
N	OPRPrD		Santander Overseas Bk Ser'D'	A–	26(6/98)	Q0.50	1-2-96	12-13	2.00	25⅞	7.7
N	SAVPrB	*	Savannah El & Pwr 6.64%[1]	A	26.66 11/98	Q0.42	1-15-96	12-27	1.66	24½	6.8
N	SCRPrC	*	Sea Cont Ltd $2.10 '82	B+	15.28 10/96[2]	Q0.52	1-16-96	12-27	2.10	18¾	11.2
N	SPrA	*	Sears, Roebuck 8.88% Dep[3]	BBB	25(9/96)	Q0.55	2-1-96	12-27	2.22	25¾	8.6
N	SCNPrA	*	Security Cap Ind Tr 9.40%'A'	BBB	25(6/00)	Plan qtly div			2.35	25⅜	9.3
N	PTRPrB	*	Security Cap Pac Tr 9% Sr'B'	BBB+	25(5/00)	Plan qtly div			2.25	25⅝	8.8
N	SORPr	*	Source Capital $2.40 Vtg	NR	27.50	Q0.60	12-15-95	11-21	2.40	28½	8.4
N	SOMPrA		Source One Mtg 8.42%'A'	BBB+	25(4/99)	Q0.53	2-1-96	1-17	2.10	26B	8.1
N	SACPr	*	So.Carolina E&G 5%	A–	52.50	Q0.63	1-1-96	12-6	2.50	34¾	7.2
N	SWXPrA	*	So.W.Gas Cp I 9.125%'TOPrS'	NR	[4]25(12/00)	Plan qtly div			2.28	26¼	8.7
A	SCEPrP	*	South'n Cal Ed 7.36%	A	25(1/97)	Q0.46	1-31-96	1-3	1.84	25½	7.2
P	SOUPr	*	South'n Cal Gas 6% A	A+	NC	Q0.38	1-16-96	12-18	1.50	21⅝B	6.9
N	SUGPrA	*	So Union Financ'g 9.48%[5]'TOPrS'	BBB–	25(5/00)	Q0.59	12-29-95	12-26	2.37	26¼	9.0
N	SPKPrB	*	Spieker Prop 9.45% Sr'B'	BBB–	25(12/00)	Plan qtly div			2.36	25⅛	9.4
N	SVCPr		Stokely-Van Camp 5% Pref	A	NC	Q0.25	1-3-96	12-14	1.00	14B	7.1
N	SLMPrA	*	Student Ln Mktg Adj[6]Rt A	NR	51.50	Q0.63	12-29-95	12-13	2.50	40B	6.3
N	SUNPrD	*	Sun Co'A'[7]Dep[8]'TARGETS'	NR	[9]	Q0.45	12-13-95	11-8	1.80	27¾	6.5
N	SAIPrB	*	SunAmerica 9 1/4%'B'[10]	NR	25(6/97)	Q0.58	12-15-95	12-1	2.31	26B	8.9
N	SAIPrD	*	SunAmerica[11] $2.78 [12]Dep'D'[13]	CALL	[14]	0.25	1-2-96		Call	47⅞	....
N	SAIPrE	*	SunAmerica $3.10 [15]Dep'E'[16]	A–	[17]	0.38	12-15-95	11-29	3.10	65½	4.7
N	SAIPrT	*	SunAmer Cap 9.95%'TOPrS'[5]	A–	[18]25	Q0.62	12-30-95	12-13	2.49	27¼	9.1
N	SAIPrV	*	SunAmer Cap II 8.35%[5]'TOPrS'	A–	[19]25(9/00)	Plan qtly div			2.09	25¾	8.1
N	SSCPr	*	Sunshine Min&Ref[20]10%[21]	NR	11.94[22]	[23]0.30	12-31-90	12-17	[24]Nil	10⅜	....
N	TEJPr	*	Tejas Gas Cp 9.96%[25]Dep	BB–	25(2/98)	Q0.62	11-1-95	10-16	2.49	26¼	9.5
N	TDYPrE	*	Teledyne Inc Sr'E'	NR	15	S0.60	9-1-95	8-11	1.20	14⅜	8.3
N	TXCPrA	*	Texaco Cap LLC 6.875%'MIPS'[26]	A+	25(10/98)	M0.14	12-29-95	12-26	1.72	24½	7.0
N	TXCPrB	*	Texaco Cap LLC'B'AdjRt[27]MIPS[28]	A+	25(6/99)	0.12	12-29-95	12-26	[29]1.44	21	6.8
N	TUEPr	*	Texas Util Elec[30]Dep	BBB	25(12/97)	Q0.51	1-1-96	12-15	2.05	26½	7.7
N	TUEPrA	*	Texas Util Elec'A'[31]Dep	BBB	25(7/01)	0.47	1-1-96	12-15	1.87	26¼	7.1
N	TUEPrB	*	Texas Util'B'[32]Dep	BBB	25(10/01)	0.45	1-1-96	12-15	1.81	25¼	7.2
N	TWXPrT	*	Time Warn Cp I 8.78% Tr Sec	BB+	[33]25(12/00)	0.15	12-29-95	12-26	2.22	25½	8.7
N	THA	*	TimeWarn[34]FinTr[35]$1.24'PERCS'[36]	BB+	[37]	Q0.31	12-29-95	12-13	1.24	31¼	4.0
N	TMCPrP	*	Times[38]Mirror'B'[39]PERCS[40]		[41]	Q0.34	3-15-96	2-21	1.37	25⅝B	5.4
N	TEDPrK	*	Toledo Ed Adj[42]A	B	25	0.46	12-1-95	11-8	1.75	19	9.2
N	TMKPrM	*	Torchmark Cap 9.18%[28]'MIPS'	A	25(9/99)	M0.19	12-29-95	12-26	2.29	27⅛	8.4
A	TWAPr	*	Trans World Air[43]12%[44]Exch	NR	[45]75 5/97	Plan qtly div			[46]12.00	68	17.6
N	TAPrD	*	Transamerica 8.50% Dep[47]	A–	26.0625(2/97)	Q0.53	11-15-95	10-30	2.13	26½	8.0
N	TAPrA	*	Transamer Del 9.125%'A''MIPS'[28]	A–	25(10/99)	0.19	12-29-95	12-26	2.28	27½	8.3
N	TRVPrA	*	Travelers[48]Grp[49] 8.125%'A'Dep	A	25(7/97)	Q0.51	12-1-95	11-13	2.03	25¾	7.9
N	TRVPrD	*	Travelers Grp[50](.25% Sr'D'Dep	A	25(6/97)	Q0.58	1-2-96	11-29	2.31	26⅛	8.8
N	TYPr	*	Tri-Continental $2.50 Vtg	NR	55	Q0.63	1-2-96	12-13	2.50	34½B	7.2
N	TUEPrM	*	TU Elec Cap I 8.25%[5]'TOPrS'	BBB	[51]25(10/01)	Plan qtly div			2.06	25½	8.1
N	TUEPrN	*	TU Elec Cap II 9.00%'TOPrS'	BBB	[51]25(12/97)	Plan qtly div			2.25	26⅝	8.5
N	TUEPrO	*	TU Elec Cap III 8.00%[52]'QUIPS'	BBB	[53]25(12/00)	Plan qtly div			2.00	25⅜	7.9
N	UALPrB	*	UAL Corp 12.25%[54]Dep'B'	B+	25(7/04)	Q0.77	2-1-96	1-11	3.06	33⅛	9.2
N	UJBPrB	*	UJB Adj[55]B	BBB–	50	Q0.75	2-1-96	1-2	3.00	47B	6.4
N	UEPPrI	*	Union El $7.44 Vtg	A+	101	Q1.86	2-15-96	1-17	7.44	100	7.4
N	UILPrA	*	Utd Cap Fd L.P.9.625%CapSec'A'	BB+	25(4/00)	M0.20	12-29-95	12-26	2.41	26½	9.1
N	UDRPrA	*	Utd Dominion Rlty 9.25% 'A'	BBB	25(4/00)	Q0.58	1-15-96	12-28	2.31	25⅞	8.9
N	UMMPr	*	United Merch/Mfr 10%	NR	NC	None paid			Nil	1¼	....
N	USWPrA	*	U.S. West Fin 7.96%[5]TOPrS	A+	[56]25(9/00)	Q0.50	12-29-95	12-26	1.99	26½	7.5
N	XLCPr	*	USX Capital LLC 8.75%[57]'MIPS'	BB–	25(3/99)	M0.18	12-29-95	12-26	2.19	25½	8.6
N	UCUPrC	*	UtiliCorp Capital 8.875%[28]'MIPS'	BBB–	25(6/00)	0.18	12-29-95	12-26	2.22	26¼	8.5
N	UCUPrA	*	UtiliCorp United $2.05	BBB–	25(2/97)	Q0.51	12-1-95	11-20	2.05	26B	7.9
N	VELPrT	*	Va Pwr Cap Tr 1 [58]8.05%	A–	[59]25(8/00)	Plan qtly div			2.01	26	7.7
N	WNGPrA		Wash Nat'l Gas 8.50% Sr III	BBB–	25(8/99)	Q0.53	4-1-96	3-14	2.13	25¾B	8.3
N	WFCPrC	*	Wells Fargo 9% Dep[60]	BBB	25(10/96)	Q0.56	4-1-96	3-13	2.25	26⅛	8.6
N	WFCPrD	*	Wells Fargo 8.875% Dep[61]	BBB	25(3/97)	Q0.55	4-1-96	3-13	2.22	26	8.5
N	WRPPrB	*	Wellsford Res Prop Tr 9.65%'B'	BBB–	25(8/00)	Q0.60	1-16-96	12-21	2.41	25¾	9.4
N	WSPPr	*	West Penn Pwr 4.50%	A	110	Q1.13	1-15-96	12-19	4.50	67	6.7
N	WGRPr	*	Western Gas Res $2.28	BB	25(11/97)	Q0.57	2-14-96	12-27	2.28	25⅝	8.9
N	WRPrA	*	Western Res Cap 7.875%[62]'QUIPS'	BBB+	[63]25(12/00)	Plan qtly div			1.97	25½	7.7
N	WMBPrA	*	Williams Cos $2.21	NR	25(8/97)	Q0.55	12-1-95	11-8	2.21	26¾	8.3
A	WISPr	*	Wis P&L 4.50 Vtg	AA–	107	Q1.13	12-15-95	11-28	4.50	67¾B	6.6
N	XRXPrA	*	Xerox Corp $3.6875 10 Yr	A–	[64]	Q0.92	1-1-96	11-29	3.69	52B	7.1

Footnotes and Sinking Fund: [1] Red rstr(6.85%)to 11-1-98. [2] SF 15. [3] Dep for 0.25 shr 8.88% Perpetual Pfd. [4] Or anytime upon 'Tax Event' re-spec cond. [5] Trust Originated Preferred Securities. [6] Div 5% to 3/31/96. [7] Dep for 0.50 shr Sr'A'cm Pref stk. [8] Targeted Growth Enhanced Terms Securities. [9] Callable fr $42.39976to$40 to6-12-98 then,1 com. [10] Co offer exch for9.95%Tr Orig Pfd Sec to May25. [11] Dep for 0.02 shr Ser'D'Mand Cv Prem Divd Pfd Stk. [12] Mand Cv into 1 com 3-1-96. [13] Called Jan 2 at $49.95. [14] Callable fr$57.45 to $49.95 in com stk. [15] Mand Cv into 1 com 11-1-98. [16] Dep for 0.02 shr Ser'E'Mand Cv Prem Divd Pfd St. [17] Callable fr $81.00 to $74.40 in com stk. [18] Upon mat(12/30/94)or earlier redem of JrSubDebs. [19] or anytime upon Tax Event re-spec cond. [20] Accum $4.165 to 6/30/94. [21] Formerly Sunshine Mining. [22] SF 11.94. [23] In com stk. [24] Co opt div in cash or com stk. [25] Dep for 0.10 shr 9.96% cm Pfd. [26] Monthly Income Preferred shrs. [27] Div 5.75% to 12/31/95. [28] Monthly Income Preferred Shrs. [29] $1.337 fr 1-1-96(rate 5.35%). [30] Dep for 0.25 shr $8.20 cm Pfd. [31] Dep for 0.25 shr $7.50 cm Pfd. [32] Dep for 0.25 shr $7.22 cm Pfd. [33] Or anytime upon'Special Event're-spec cond. [34] Preferred Exch Redemption Cumulative Sec. [35] Mand Cv 12-23-97(max $54.41)Hasbro com/cash. [36] Co option on Redm exch for Hasbro com or other'Exch Prop'. [37] Callable fr $56.71 to $54.41. [38] Preferred equity redempt'n cumulative stk. [39] Mand cv into 1 com Cl'A'3-31-98. [40] Rated 'Atr' by S&P. [41] Callable fr $31.92885 to $28.52685 in com. [42] Div 7.00% to 2/29/96. [43] Co opt fr 8-10-97ex for $100amt 11%Sub Nts2005. [44] Can accelerate redm to 11-1-2002 re-spec cond. [45] 'Non-cash Match div'arrears red$100re-spec cond. [46] In cash(or com re-spec cond). [47] Dep for 0.05 shr 8.50% Series'D'Pfd. [48] Dep for 0.10 shr 8.125% Ser'A'Pfd. [49] Formerly Travelers Inc. [50] Dep for 0.5 shr 9.25% Pfd Sr 'D'. [51] or anytime upon 'Tax Event're-spec cond. [52] Quarterly Income Preferred Securities. [53] or earlier upon 'Tax Event'. [54] Dep for 0.001 shr 12.25% Sr'B'Pfd. [55] Div 6.00% to 10/31/95. [56] or earlier on 'Tax Event' respec cond. [57] Monthly income preferred shrs. [58] Trust Preferred Sec. [59] or earlier for 'Special Event'. [60] Dep for 0.05 shr Ser'C' Pfd. [61] Dep for 0.05 shr Ser'D'Pfd. [62] Quarterly Income Preferred Securities. [63] or earlier upon'Special Event'. [64] SF 50.

STANDARD & POOR'S
CLOSED–END FUND SUMMARY

EXPLANATION OF ABBREVIATIONS

BD	Bond Fund–Corporate	FT	Finite Trust	GVT	Long Term Govt., GNMA	MU	Tax Free Income, General
C	Common Stock	GB	Global Bond–Long Term	ICA	Income & Capital Appreciation	MUS	Tax Free Income–State Specific
CA	Capital Appreciation	GE	Global Equity	ICF	Income–Global Corp. & Govt.	P	Income From Preferred Stock
CV	Convertible Bond & Pfd Stk	GEA	Global Equity–Asia	INTL	International	PM	Precious Metals
EG	Emerging Growth Com Stk	GEC	Global Equity–Country Specific	IRE	Income–Real Estate	SB	Small Business Investments
FL	Flexible–Short selling, hedge, etc	GSB	Global Short–Term Bond	MI	Income from Mortgages	ST	Short Term Investments

Footnoted amounts for cash or stock refer to Investment Income & Capital Gain for the calendar year stated.
Net Asset Values (NAV) are reported on a weekly basis. The premium or discount at which an issue trades (price percentage over or under the current NAV) is a tool used to compare and evaluate current market trends.

					Dividends									Price Range					Net Assets			
					Latest Payment			So Far 1995				1994				December, 1995			% NAV			
Ticker Symbol	Fund	Rating	Exc.	Type	Period $	Date	Ex. Div.	Invest. Income	Cap. Gain	Ind. Rate	Div. Yld. %	Invest. Income	Cap. Gain	1994 - 1995 High	1994 - 1995 Low	Last Sale or Bid High	Last Sale or Bid Low	Last	Prem. Disc.	Latest NAV	Latest Date	Com. Shs. 000
ACG	ACM Gvt Income Fund	NR	NY	GVT	0.035	1-19-96	1-3	0.932	....	0.90	9.9	†1.207	0.53	12⅝	9	9¾	9⅛	9⅛	-5.3	9.64	12-22-95	56617
AOF	ACM Gvt Opportunity Fd	NR	NY	GVT	0.055	1-19-96	1-3	0.682	....	0.66	8.9	0.795	....	10¼	6⅞	7½	7¼	7⅜	-12.7	8.45	12-22-95	13072
GSF	ACM Gvt Securities	NR	NY	GVT	0.055	1-19-96	1-3	0.932	....	0.90	10.9	1.22	0.615	12¼	7⅝	8¾	8⅛	8¼	-10.6	9.23	12-22-95	77550
SI	ACM Gvt Spectrum Fund	NR	NY	GVT	0.063	1-19-96	1-3	0.785	....	0.75	11.3	1.065	0.35	10⅝	6¼	7	6½	6⅝	-10.2	7.38	12-22-95	36939
ADF	ACM Managed Dollar Income	NR	NY	ICA	0.105	1-19-96	1-3	1.294	....	1.26	12.9	1.463	....	15⅛	9½	10	9⅝	9¾	-10.1	10.84	12-22-95	27794
AMF	ACM Managed Income Fund	NR	NY	ICA	0.075	1-19-96	1-3	1.035	....	0.90	10.0	1.13	....	12⅜	7⅜	9	8¾	9	2.7	8.76	12-22-95	20405
AMU	ACM Muni Securities Income	NR	NY	MU	0.075	1-19-96	1-3	0.90	....	0.90	7.1	0.90	....	15⅛	9⅛	12¾	12⅛	12¾	-0.5	12.81	12-22-95	10507
ADX	Adams Express	NR	NY	ICA	[1]1.30	12-27-95	11-16	0.55	1.11	0.50	⊙©2.7	[2]0.50	1.10	22¼	15⅜	18¾	18⅜	18½	-12.9	21.25	12-21-95	42498
AST	AIM Strategic Income Fd	NR	AS	CV	0.05	1-23-96	1-10	0.60	....	0.60	7.2	0.458	0.132	9¾	7⅞	8⅜	8⅛	8⅜	-13.2	9.65	12-22-95	6977
AJP	AJL Peps Trust[3,4]	NR	NY	C	Plan qtly div			....	....	1.44	7.4	....	....	....	....	19¾	18⅝	19½	....	....	....	15658
AAT	All-American Term Trust	NR	NY	BD	0.09	12-29-95	12-19	1.125	....	1.08	8.5	1.223	....	15¼	11⅛	12⅞	12¼	12¾	-10.0	14.17	12-21-95	13707
FUND	All Seasons Global Fund	NR	NNM	GE	0.07	1-16-95	12-23	0.07	....	0.11	2.6	0.04	....	4⅝	3⅜	4⅜	3⅝	4⅛	-20.1	5.24	12-22-95	8743
AMO	Alliance All-Mkt Adv Fd	NR	NY	CA	†1.631	1-12-96	12-27	1.476	....	1.90	e9.7	....	....	20	15¾	21⅝	19⅜	19⅝	-15.7	23.29	12-22-95	2505
AEF	Alliance Global Enviro Fd	NR	NY	GE	0.02	1-12-96	12-27	....	....	Nil	....	....	....	10½	8⅝	10⅜	9⅝	10⅛	-22.1	12.99	12-22-95	6907
AWG	Alliance World Dollar Gvt Fd	NR	NY	GB	0.108	1-19-96	1-3	1.355	....	1.29	e10.8	†1.80	....	22½	11⅜	12⅜	11¾	12	-6.0	12.77	12-22-95	8440
AWF	Alliance World Dollar Gvt Fd II	NR	NY	GB	0.119	1-19-96	1-3	1.423	0.225	1.42	⊙12.5	†1.463	....	16¼	9⅞	11⅝	10⅞	11⅜	-4.8	11.95	12-22-95	69932
ALM	Allmerica Sec Tr	NR	NY	BD	0.23	12-29-95	11-28	†0.86	....	0.84	e8.0	0.85	....	12¼	8¾	10½	10⅛	10½	-9.5	11.60	12-22-95	8592
ACB	Amer Cap Bond Fd[5]	NR	NY	BD	Q0.385	12-29-95	12-6	1.54	....	1.54	7.8	1.54	....	21⅞	16	20¼	19½	19⅝	-6.8	21.05	12-22-95	11362
ACS	Amer Cap Cv Sec[6]	NR	NY	ICA	1.063	12-29-95	12-6	1.18	1.055	1.36	⊙6.3	1.08	1.158	24	18	21¾	20¼	21⅝	-10.9	24.26	12-22-95	3251
ACD	Amer Capital Income Tr[7]	NR	NY	BD	0.054	12-29-95	12-13	0.645	....	0.65	9.0	†0.662	....	8⅜	6¼	7⅜	7⅛	7¼	-8.2	7.90	12-22-95	15290
AGF	Amer Gvt Income Fd	AAf	NY	GVT	0.064	1-11-96	12-27	0.768	....	0.77	14.0	†0.968	....	9⅞	5½	5¾	5⅜	5½	-6.3	5.87	12-21-95	21602
AAF	Amer Gvt Income Portfolio	AAf	NY	GVT	†0.105	1-11-96	12-27	†1.035	....	0.96	e14.8	†1.065	0.145	12¼	7	7	6½	6½	-6.6	6.96	12-21-95	24458

Uniform Footnote Explanations-See page 4. Other: [1] In cash or stk'95. [2] Incl $1.24 in cash or stk,'94. [3] $1.44 Prem Exch Ptcp Shrs. [4] Ex for Amway Japan ADS shrs 2-15-99 re-spec cond. [5] Plan name chge,Van Kampen Amer Cap Bond Fd. [6] Plan name chg,Van Kampen Amer Cap Cv Sec. [7] Plan name chg,Van Kampen Amer Cap Inc Tr.

Ticker Symbol	Fund	Rating	Exc.	Type	Dividends: Latest Payment Period $	Date	Ex. Div.	So Far 1995 Invest. Income	So Far 1995 Cap. Gain	Ind. Rate	Div. Yld. %	1994 Invest. Income	1994 Cap. Gain	Price Range 1994 - 1995 High	1994 - 1995 Low	December, 1995 Last Sale or Bid High	Low	Last	Net Assets % NAV Prem. Disc.	Latest NAV	Latest Date	Com. Shs. 000
XAA	Amer Muni Income Portfolio	Af	NY	MU	0.063	1-11-96	12-27	0.86	....	0.75	6.3	0.87	0.023	15⅝	10⅛	12¾	11⅞	12	-14.7	14.07	12-21-95	5756
AXT	Amer Muni Term Trust	AAf	NY	MU	0.054	1-11-96	12-27	0.65	....	0.65	5.9	0.65	....	11¾	9⅜	11	10¾	11	-6.5	11.76	12-21-95	8455
BXT	Amer Muni Term Trust II	AAf	NY	MU	0.058	1-11-96	12-27	0.62	....	0.62	⊙5.8	0.62	....	11¼	9	10¾	10¼	10⅝	-8.6	11.62	12-21-95	7356
CXT	Amer Muni Term Trust III	AAf	NY	MU	0.048	1-11-96	12-27	0.57	....	0.57	5.6	0.57	....	10⅝	8⅛	10¼	9¾	10⅛	-7.8	10.98	12-21-95	5300
OIF	Amer Opportunity Income	AAf	NY	GVT	0.07	1-11-96	12-27	0.92	....	0.84	14.6	†1.05	0.08	12¼	6¾	6⅜	5¾	5¾	-13.5	6.65	12-21-95	22765
SLA	Amer Select Portfolio	BBBf	NY	C	0.094	1-11-96	12-27	1.125	....	1.13	10.4	1.125	....	15⅛	9⅝	11	10⅝	10⅞	-15.2	12.83	12-21-95	13547
ASP	Amer Strategic Inc Portfolio	Af	NY	MI	†0.225	1-11-96	12-27	†1.80	....	1.50	e13.2	1.362	....	16⅞	11⅜	12⅛	11⅜	11⅜	-12.3	12.97	12-21-95	5328
BSP	Amer Strategic Inc Portfolio II	Af	NY	MI	0.103	1-11-96	12-27	1.29	....	1.23	11.3	1.35	....	16⅛	10⅝	11¼	10⅞	10⅞	-16.7	13.05	12-21-95	20399
CSP	Amer Strategic Inc Portfol III	Af	NY	MI	0.106	1-11-96	12-27	1.275	....	1.28	11.9	1.275	....	15⅝	10¼	11	10½	10¾	-13.6	12.44	12-21-95	27335
XUS	Americas Income Trust	NR	NY	ICA	[1]0.053	1-11-96	12-27	[2]0.774	....	0.63	9.3	1.063	....	15⅛	7⅞	7	6¾	6¾	-17.6	8.19	12-21-95	6432
APX	Apex Muni Fund	NR	NY	MU	0.053	12-28-95	12-20	0.693	....	0.63	7.3	0.73	....	11⅛	7⅞	9⅜	8⅝	8⅝	-14.6	10.10	12-22-95	19545
AF	Argentina Fund	NR	NY	GEC	0.33	1-16-96	12-27	0.27	0.455	0.33	⊙2.9	0.135	0.015	19⅝	9⅝	12⅛	11⅛	11½	-4.5	12.04	12-22-95	9203
ASA	ASA Ltd	NR	NY	PM	tQ0.50	11-24-95	11-14	t2.00	....	2.00	5.4	t2.00	....	56⅛	29¾	40½	36⅝	37⅛	0.0	37.13	12-21-95	9600
APB	Asia Pacific Fund	NR	NY	GEA	0.04	1-12-96	12-27	0.023	0.725	0.04	⊙0.3	....	2.59	25¾	12⅝	14¼	12¾	13⅞	-1.7	14.12	12-22-95	18900
GRR	Asia Tigers Fund	NR	NY	GEA	[3]0.081	1-12-96	12-27	0.227	....	0.10	0.9	0.015	....	16⅞	9¼	11½	10	11⅛	-10.2	12.39	12-22-95	20515
OST	Austria Fund	NR	NY	GEC	0.025	1-13-95	12-23	0.025	....	0.03	0.4	0.095	....	12⅜	6⅝	8⅜	8	8⅜	-17.7	10.18	12-22-95	8259
BKF	Baker,Fentress & Co	NR	NY	CA	[4]1.35	12-7-95	11-13	[4]0.35	1.20	0.35	⊙2.1	[5]0.35	1.46	19⅞	13⅜	17	16¼	16¾	-21.9	21.46	12-22-95	26442
BCV	Bancroft Convertible Fd	NR	AS	CV	[6]0.92	12-28-95	11-28	[6]1.197	0.593	1.16	⊙©5.1	[7]1.204	0.536	23¾	18½	24	21⅜	22¾	-9.2	25.05	12-22-95	2793
FBF	BEA Income Fd	NR	NY	SB	0.06	12-15-95	11-29	0.76	....	0.72	9.1	0.72	....	9⅝	6⅝	8⅛	7¾	7⅞	-8.4	8.60	12-22-95	24385
FBI	BEA Strategic Income Fd	NR	NY	ICF	0.068	1-15-96	1-2	0.81	....	0.81	9.1	0.81	....	10⅞	7⅞	8⅞	8⅝	8⅞	-10.9	9.96	12-22-95	8454
BEM	Bergstrom Capital	NR	AS	ICA	5.00	12-4-95	11-14	0.98	4.02	0.98	⊙©0.9	1.23	2.77	134	80½	112	104	109½	-14.6	128.25	12-22-95	1213
BAT	Blackrock Advantage Term	AAAf	NY	MI	0.052	1-31-96	12-21	0.619	....	0.62	7.2	0.742	....	11	7⅜	8⅞	8½	8⅝	-16.4	10.32	12-21-95	9511
BCT	Blackrock Broad Inv Gr 2009	NR	AS	FT	0.075	1-31-96	1-11	0.975	....	0.90	8.0	[8]1.056	....	15⅛	9⅞	11¾	11¼	11¼	-17.2	13.59	12-21-95	2957
BFC	Blackrock CA Ins Muni 2008 Tr	AAAf	NY	MUS	0.064	1-31-96	1-11	0.855	....	0.77	5.7	0.855	....	15⅞	11⅜	14⅞	13⅝	13⅝	-13.9	15.83	12-22-95	10407
RAA	Blackrock CA Inv Qual Muni	NR	AS	MUS	0.066	12-29-95	12-13	0.787	....	0.79	6.2	0.787	....	15⅛	9⅞	12⅞	12½	12¾	-10.7	14.28	12-22-95	1007
BRF	Blackrock FL Ins Muni 2008 Tr	AAAf	NY	MUS	0.072	12-29-95	12-13	0.863	....	0.86	5.7	0.863	....	15¾	11½	15⅛	14¾	15	-5.8	15.92	12-22-95	8707
RFA	Blackrock FL Inv Qual Muni	NR	AS	MUS	0.066	12-29-95	12-13	0.787	....	0.79	6.4	0.787	....	15⅛	9⅝	13¼	12⅛	12¼	-14.9	14.39	12-22-95	1127
BKT	Blackrock Income Trust	NR	NY	GVT	0.047	1-31-96	1-11	0.75	....	0.56	8.8	0.767	....	9½	5⅝	7	6¼	6⅜	-17.5	7.73	12-21-95	62850
BRM	Blackrock Ins Muni 2008 Tr	AAAf	NY	MU	0.968	1-31-96	12-27	0.833	....	0.90	⊙6.7	0.885	....	15⅝	11¼	14¼	13⅜	13½	-15.4	15.95	12-22-95	27207
BMT	Blackrock Ins Muni Term	AAAf	NY	MU	0.052	12-29-95	12-13	0.625	....	0.62	6.2	0.625	0.024	11	8⅛	10⅜	10	10	-8.7	10.95	12-22-95	25886
BKN	Blackrock Inv Qual Muni Tr	NR	NY	MU	†0.014	1-31-96	12-27	0.806	....	0.79	e6.5	0.90	....	15⅛	9⅝	12½	11⅞	12⅛	-16.8	14.58	12-22-95	16707
BQT	Blackrock Inv Qual Term Tr	NR	NY	BD	0.05	12-29-95	12-13	0.625	....	0.60	7.6	0.718	....	10⅛	6⅝	8¼	7¾	7⅞	-16.0	9.37	12-21-95	36811
BMN	Blackrock Muni Target Term	AAAf	NY	MUS	0.029	1-31-96	12-27	0.615	0.004	0.62	e⊙6.1	0.615	....	10⅞	8¼	10⅝	10⅛	10⅛	-8.9	11.12	12-22-95	45411
RNJ	Blackrock NJ Inv Qual Muni	NR	AS	MUS	0.064	12-29-95	12-13	0.769	....	0.77	6.3	0.769	....	15	9⅞	12½	11⅝	12¼	-11.0	13.76	12-22-95	1007
BLN	Blackrock NY Ins Muni 2008 Tr	AAAf	NY	MUS	0.071	12-29-95	12-13	0.855	....	0.86	5.9	0.855	0.002	15⅞	11⅝	15	14½	14⅝	-8.4	15.97	12-22-95	11257
RNY	Blackrock NY Inv Qual Muni	NR	AS	MUS	0.066	12-29-95	12-13	0.787	....	0.79	6.4	0.787	....	15⅛	9⅜	12⅞	12⅛	12⅜	-12.6	14.16	12-22-95	1307
BBT	Blackrock 1998 Term Tr	AAAf	NY	FT	0.042	1-31-96	12-21	0.537	....	0.50	5.6	0.642	....	10¾	8	9⅛	8¾	8⅞	-8.7	9.72	12-21-95	58661
BNN	Blackrock 1999 Term Tr	AAAf	NY	FT	0.038	1-31-96	12-21	0.512	....	0.45	5.5	0.63	....	10⅛	7⅛	8⅜	8	8⅛	-11.6	9.19	12-21-95	21611
BNA	Blackrock No Amer Gvt Inc	NR	NY	GVT	[9]0.078	12-29-95	12-13	[10]0.956	....	0.94	9.9	[11]1.063	....	13⅞	8⅛	10	9⅜	9½	-16.2	11.33	12-21-95	36207
BGT	Blackrock Strategic Term	AAAf	NY	FT	0.042	12-29-95	12-13	0.562	....	0.50	6.6	0.696	....	10¼	6⅝	7⅞	7½	7⅝	-16.9	9.18	12-21-95	57511
BTT	Blackrock Target Term	AAAf	NY	MI	0.048	1-31-96	12-21	0.65	0.003	0.58	6.6	0.717	....	10⅝	7⅞	9⅜	8⅝	8¾	-11.8	9.92	12-21-95	95461
BLK	Blackrock 2001 Term Trust	AAAf	NY	MI	0.038	12-29-95	12-13	0.512	....	0.45	5.9	0.683	....	9¾	7	7⅞	7⅜	7⅝	-14.5	8.92	12-21-95	14201
BLU	Blue Chip Value Fund	NR	NY	ICA	0.99	1-19-96	12-27	0.75	....	[12]0.76	⊙10.0	0.29	....	8⅝	6	8⅝	7½	7⅝	-18.7	9.38	12-22-95	10961
BZF	Brazil Fund	NR	NY	GEC	0.14	1-16-96	12-27	†0.16	3.165	0.14	⊙e0.7	0.08	0.93	36⅞	13⅜	21⅝	19¼	21⅛	1.3	20.85	12-21-95	16168
BZL	Brazilian Equity Fund	NR	NY	GEC	©2.22	1-11-96	1-12	0.03	3.83	0.03	⊙0.2	0.075	....	27½	9	15⅛	13⅛	14⅜	-0.5	14.44	12-21-95	4619
CSWC	Capital Southwest	NR	NNM	SB	0.40	11-30-95	11-13	[13]h0.60	....	0.60	1.2	0.60	....	40¾	34	51½	48¼	50	11.4	44.89	9-30-95	3767

Uniform Footnote Explanations-See page 4. Other: [1] Return of cap. [2] Incl return of cap. [3] Approx. [4] Incl $1.20 in cash or stk,'95. [5] Incl $1.46 in cash or stk,'94. [6] Incl $0.593 in cash or stk,'95. [7] Incl $0.84 in cash or stk,'94. [8] Incl $0.085358 non-taxable,'94. [9] Return of cap,'95. [10] Incl $0.078125 return of cap,'95. [11] Incl $0.0431 non-taxable,'94. [12] Plan cash payment of 10% of NAV. [13] Stk dstr of Palm Harbor Homes.

Ticker Symbol	Fund	Rating	Exc.	Type	Dividends: Latest Payment: Period $	Date	Ex. Div.	So Far 1995: Invest. Income	Cap. Gain	Ind. Rate	Div. Yld. %	1994: Invest. Income	Cap. Gain	Price Range 1994 - 1995: High	Low	December, 1995 Last Sale or Bid: High	Low	Last	Net Assets: % NAV Prem. Disc.	Latest: NAV	Date	Com. Shs. 000
CVF	Castle Convert Fund	NR	AS	CV	0.79	12-26-95	12-20	1.68	0.71	1.60	⊙6.0	1.60	0.81	28	22⅛	27	24⅛	26½	-3.8	27.56	12-22-95	2220
CEE	Central European Eq Fd	NR	NY	GEC	[1]0.38	1-16-96	12-22	[1]0.20	....	0.38	2.3	[1]0.08	....	16¾	11¼	16⅝	16¼	16⅜	-21.3	20.81	12-22-95	12147
CEF	Central Fund,Cda'A'	NR	AS	PM	gA0.01	11-14-95	10-27	g0.01	....	0.01	◆....	g0.01	....	6	3⅜	4¾	4½	4½	-6.6	4.82	12-21-95	18139
CET	Central Securities	NR	AS	CA	[2]Stk	12-27-95	11-8	s0.15	....	0.15	0.7	[3]0.224	1.386	18	11⅝	21¼	20¾	20⅞	2.1	20.44	12-22-95	12325
CH	Chile Fund Inc	NR	NY	GEC	0.81	1-12-96	12-27	0.495	0.095	0.60	⊙2.3	0.351	0.374	28¼	14⅝	26⅜	23¼	26	-5.6	27.54	12-22-95	13978
CHN	China Fund	NR	NY	GEC	0.191	1-17-96	1-2	0.009	0.601	0.19	⊙1.6	0.085	0.825	28¾	12¼	13	11¾	11¾	-3.4	12.16	12-22-95	10823
HIS	CIGNA High Income Shs	NR	NY	BD	†0.098	1-10-96	12-26	0.818	....	0.81	e10.3	†1.00	....	9¼	6⅞	8⅛	7¾	7⅞	8.5	7.26	12-22-95	35425
CIM	CIM High Yield Sec	NR	AS	BD	0.065	1-9-96	12-27	0.785	....	0.78	9.9	0.84	....	8¾	6⅞	8	7¾	7⅞	7.3	7.34	12-22-95	5439
CLM	Clemente Global Gr	NR	NY	GE	0.50	1-10-96	12-18	0.36	0.60	0.50	⊙6.0	....	0.65	11⅞	7¾	8¾	8⅛	8⅜	-20.8	10.57	12-21-95	5892
CNN	CNA Income Shares	NR	NY	BD	Q0.25	1-12-96	12-27	1.06	....	1.00	9.8	1.10	....	13	9⅛	10⅝	10¼	10¼	6.0	9.67	12-21-95	8278
RIF	Cohen & Steers Rlty Inc Fd	NR	AS	IRE	Q0.17	1-12-96	12-27	0.68	0.06	0.68	⊙7.5	0.68	....	10⅛	7⅞	9⅛	8¾	9⅛	5.4	8.66	12-22-95	2839
RFI	Cohen & Steers Total Rt Rty Fd	NR	NY	IRE	0.08	12-29-95	12-13	0.96	....	0.96	7.2	0.96	....	15⅛	11½	13½	12	13⅜	0.6	13.30	12-22-95	7399
CXE	Colonial High Income Muni	NR	NY	MU	0.049	1-5-96	12-27	0.592	....	0.58	7.9	0.613	....	9½	6⅜	8	7⅜	7⅜	-13.4	8.52	12-22-95	30919
CIF	Colonial Interm Hi Income	NR	NY	BD	0.058	1-5-96	12-27	0.696	....	0.70	10.2	0.696	0.05	7¼	5⅜	7⅛	6¾	6⅞	3.4	6.65	12-22-95	13938
CMK	Colonial InterMkt Inc Tr I	NR	NY	ICF	[4]0.115	1-2-96	12-13	0.948	....	0.96	9.1	1.309	....	12½	9	11⅛	10½	10½	-6.7	11.26	12-22-95	11009
CXH	Colonial Inv Grade Muni	NR	NY	MU	0.053	1-2-96	12-13	0.636	....	0.63	6.4	0.676	....	12⅝	8⅝	10⅛	9⅝	9⅞	-10.1	10.99	12-22-95	11509
CMU	Colonial Muni Inc Tr[5]	NR	NY	MU	0.043	1-5-96	12-27	0.552	....	0.51	7.6	0.582	....	8¾	6	6⅞	6½	6¾	-10.1	7.51	12-22-95	27346
CNV	Convertible Hldgs	NR	NY	CV	©0.036	1-12-96	12-27	....	....	Nil	⊙....	....	1.166	11¾	8¾	12⅛	11½	11¾	-16.5	14.07	12-22-95	11674
COY	Corporate High Yield Fund	NR	NY	BD	0.134	1-12-96	12-27	1.601	....	1.61	11.9	1.501	....	15¾	10⅞	13⅝	13	13½	-0.2	13.53	12-22-95	18950
KYT	Corporate High Yield Fd II	NR	NY	BD	0.17	1-12-96	12-27	1.381	....	2.04	16.8	1.419	....	15	10¼	12⅜	11⅞	12⅛	-2.8	12.47	12-22-95	7837
CTF	Counsellors Tandem	NR	NY	ICA	0.695	1-5-96	12-27	....	....	[6]....	⊙....	....	....	16⅞	11½	17⅝	17	17⅛	-12.3	19.52	12-22-95	2789
CUR	Current Inc Shares	NR	NY	C	©0.592	12-31-95	11-28	0.884	0.592	0.84	⊙7.1	0.94	....	13⅞	10¾	11⅞	11½	11⅞	-12.0	13.50	12-22-95	3673
CRF	Czech Republic Fund	NR	NY	GEC	[7]0.195	1-12-96	12-27	0.10	....	[6]0.20	1.5	....	....	15⅛	11	13⅞	12⅝	13½	2.1	13.22	12-22-95	4407
GVT	Dean Witter Gvt Income SBI	NR	NY	GVT	0.05	12-22-95	12-6	0.60	....	0.60	7.3	0.63	....	9¼	7¼	8⅜	8¼	8¼	-11.0	9.27	12-22-95	55986
DDF	Delaware Grp Dividend Income	NR	NY	ICA	0.125	12-29-95	12-13	1.181	....	1.50	10.4	1.10	0.50	15⅛	11⅜	14½	13¾	14⅜	1.4	14.18	12-22-95	14307
DGF	Delaware Grp Global Div & Inc	NR	NY	ICF	0.125	12-29-95	12-13	†1.353	....	1.50	e10.6	0.792	....	15⅛	11½	14⅛	13⅜	14⅛	-0.6	14.21	12-22-95	6707
DCM	Dreyfus Cal Muni Income	NR	AS	MUS	0.041	1-29-96	1-10	0.522	....	0.49	6.2	0.567	0.048	10½	7¼	8¼	7⅞	7⅞	-15.9	9.44	12-22-95	4502
DMF	Dreyfus Muni Income	NR	AS	MU	0.052	1-29-96	1-10	0.652	....	0.62	6.7	0.693	....	11⅜	7⅝	9⅝	9	9¼	-6.3	9.87	12-22-95	20058
DNM	Dreyfus N.Y. Muni Income	NR	AS	MUS	0.05	1-29-96	1-10	0.60	0.051	0.60	⊙5.9	0.60	0.007	11⅞	8⅜	10¼	9½	10⅛	0.2	10.10	12-22-95	3733
DSI	Dreyfus Strategic Gvts[8]	NR	NY	GVT	0.063	1-29-96	1-10	0.78	....	0.75	8.2	0.87	....	12⅛	8¼	9⅜	9⅛	9⅛	-14.6	10.68	12-22-95	11727
DSM	Dreyfus Strategic Muni Bd Fd	NR	NY	MU	0.052	1-29-96	1-10	0.639	....	0.62	6.8	0.664	....	11	7½	9⅜	9	9⅛	-5.1	9.62	12-22-95	45655
LEO	Dreyfus Strategic Municipals	NR	NY	MU	0.056	1-29-96	1-10	0.697	....	0.67	7.1	0.732	....	11½	8¼	9¾	9½	9½	-6.0	10.11	12-22-95	55629
DUC	Duff/Phelps Util & Cp Bd Tr	NR	NY	BD	0.098	1-5-96	12-27	1.176	....	1.18	8.5	†1.321	....	15⅝	10¼	14⅛	13⅝	13⅞	-5.4	14.67	12-22-95	26015
DNP	Duff/Phelps Util Income	NR	NY	ICA	0.07	1-10-96	12-27	0.72	....	0.84	9.3	0.74	0.097	11¼	7⅞	9	8¾	9	2.2	8.81	12-22-95	19322
DTF	Duff/Phelps Util Tax-Free Inc	NR	NY	MU	0.11	1-26-96	12-27	0.96	....	0.96	⊙6.2	0.96	....	17⅛	11¾	15⅝	15⅛	15½	-5.8	16.46	12-22-95	8372
BDF	1838 Bond-Deb Trad'g	NR	NY	BD	Q0.41	1-22-96	12-21	1.70	....	1.64	7.8	1.72	....	25⅛	18⅜	21⅝	20¾	21	-4.1	21.90	12-22-95	3653
ECF	Ellsworth Cv Growth/Income	NR	AS	CV	[9]0.40	11-29-95	11-1	[10]0.513	0.262	0.51	⊙5.4	[11]0.515	0.226	9⅞	7⅜	10¼	9	9½	-11.0	10.67	12-22-95	6305
FRG	Emerging Germany Fund	NR	NY	GEC	0.12	1-17-95	1-13	0.12	....	0.12	1.7	....	0.12	9⅜	6¼	7⅜	6⅞	7¼	-21.4	9.22	12-22-95	14008
EFL	Emerging Mkts Fltg Rt Fd	NR	NY	P	†0.223	12-29-95	12-21	†1.65	....	1.59	e12.5	†0.94	....	15⅛	11¼	13	12½	12¾	-3.3	13.19	12-22-95	3607
EMD	Emerging Mkts Income Fund	NR	NY	GE	0.443	12-29-95	12-21	1.65	0.03	1.65	⊙12.1	1.365	1.215	19⅝	11⅜	14⅜	13⅛	13⅝	-5.3	14.39	12-22-95	3512
EDF	Emerging Mkts Income Fund II	NR	NY	GB	Q0.413	12-29-95	12-21	1.65	....	1.65	13.8	1.65	....	16⅛	9⅞	12⅝	11¾	12	1.1	11.87	12-22-95	19007
EMG	Emerging Mkts Infrastructure	NR	NY	GE	0.09	1-12-96	12-27	0.05	....	0.09	0.9	....	....	16⅞	9⅞	10¾	9¾	10½	-11.7	11.89	12-22-95	16107
ETF	Emerging Mkts Telecommun Fd	NR	NY	GE	0.44	1-12-96	12-27	0.18	1.64	0.18	⊙1.1	0.147	1.063	29¾	13⅛	16¾	15¼	15⅞	-15.1	18.70	12-22-95	8435
MEF	Emerging Mexico Fund	NR	NY	GEC	2.44	1-19-95	12-23	0.27	2.17	Nil	⊙....	0.21	2.18	28⅛	11	6½	5¾	6⅛	-14.6	7.17	12-21-95	9115
TGF	Emerging Tigers Fund	NR	NY	GEA	0.036	1-12-96	12-27	0.124	0.024	[6]0.04	⊙0.3	....	....	15⅛	10⅞	13⅛	11⅝	13	-7.9	14.12	12-22-95	22007
EGX	Engex Inc	NR	AS	CA	1.36	12-27-89	11-28	....	....	Nil	....	....	....	13⅞	6⅜	13	10⅞	12⅛	-22.4	15.63	12-22-95	977

Uniform Footnote Explanations-See page 4. Other: [1] In cash or stk. [2] In stk or $1.78 cash,'95. [3] Incl $1.46 in cash & stk. [4] Incl $0.035 foreign currency gains. [5] Unit Benef. Int. [6] To be determined. [7] Approx. [8] Plan conversion to open-end fund. [9] In cash or stk,'95. [10] Incl $0.40 in cash or stk,'95. [11] Incl $0.366 in cash or stk,'94.

Ticker Symbol	Fund	Rating	Exc.	Type	Dividends: Latest Payment Period $	Date	Ex. Div.	So Far 1995 Invest. Income	So Far 1995 Cap. Gain	Ind. Rate	Div. Yld. %	1994 Invest. Income	1994 Cap. Gain	Price Range: 1994 - 1995 High	1994 - 1995 Low	December, 1995 Last Sale or Bid High	Low	Last	Net Assets: % NAV Prem. Disc.	Latest NAV	Latest Date	Com. Shs. 000
ATF	Equity Income Fund[1]	NR	AS	ICA	0.233	1-1-96	12-13	2.77	....	2.77	3.2	2.731	....	75⅝	61¼	87½	84	87¼	23.8	70.46	6-30-95	17702
EQS	Equus II Inc	NR	AS	CA	[2]2.00	12-28-95	11-13	[2]0.02	1.98	0.02	⊙0.2	[3]0.25	0.68	18¼	9	13½	13	13¼	-33.0	19.79	12-22-95	2908
EF	Europe Fund	NR	NY	GE	0.88	12-29-95	12-19	0.88	....	0.88	6.9	0.147	0.813	14¼	9⅞	13⅜	12¼	12¾	-9.6	14.10	12-22-95	10066
EWF	European Warrant Fund	NR	NY	GE	©1.903	12-30-94	12-19	....	....	Nil	....	....	1.903	18⅛	6⅝	8¾	7¾	8½	-15.6	10.07	12-21-95	8154
EIS	Excelsior Inc Shares	NR	NY	BD	0.33	1-26-96	12-20	1.07	....	1.32	8.3	1.05	0.43	19	13⅞	16¼	15¾	16	-14.8	18.78	12-21-95	2188
FAE	Fidelity Advisor Emer'g Asia	NR	NY	GEA	0.06	1-12-96	12-26	0.12	0.13	[4]0.06	0.5	....	....	16	11½	13¼	11½	13	-9.2	14.32	12-22-95	8447
FAK	Fidelity Advisor Korea Fund	NR	NY	CA	Plan annual div			....	....	....	....	....	....	15⅛	14	11⅝	10½	10⅝	-11.3	11.98	12-22-95	4407
IAF	First Australia Fund	NR	AS	GEC	[5]©0.191	1-31-96	12-27	[6]0.223	0.937	0.22	⊙2.7	0.103	0.107	14⅜	7½	8½	8	8¼	-19.5	10.25	12-22-95	15894
FAX	First Australia Prime	NR	AS	GB	0.075	1-12-96	12-27	[7]0.90	0.075	0.96	⊙10.4	0.825	0.173	11⅜	8	9½	9	9¼	0.2	9.23	12-22-95	15419
FCO	First Commonwealth Fund	NR	NY	GB	0.088	1-12-96	12-27	1.05	0.013	1.05	⊙9.2	1.05	....	13⅝	9⅝	11½	11¼	11⅜	-13.4	13.13	12-22-95	9266
FF	First Financial Fund	NR	NY	ICA	[5]2.46	1-16-96	11-28	[2]2.095	2.31	0.15	⊙1.2	[8]0.05	6.625	19¾	11¼	13⅛	12⅛	12¼	-4.6	12.84	12-22-95	14323
IBF	First Iberian Fund	NR	AS	GEC	0.07	1-16-96	12-27	....	....	[4]....	....	....	....	10⅝	5⅞	7⅞	7½	7¾	-23.7	10.16	12-22-95	6511
ISL	First Israel Fund	NR	NY	GEC	0.54	1-14-94	11-30	....	....	Nil	....	0.12	0.42	20¼	9½	12	10¾	11⅝	-11.3	13.11	12-22-95	5012
FPF	First Philippine Fund	NR	NY	GEC	1.02	1-10-96	12-18	1.25	0.85	1.25	⊙9.0	....	0.76	24½	10	15⅝	13⅞	13⅞	-19.0	17.13	12-22-95	8980
EME	Foreign/Colon'l Emg MidEast Fd	NR	NY	CA	Plan annual div			....	....	....	....	....	....	15⅛	12⅜	11	10	10⅝	-18.8	13.09	12-21-95	2807
FTD	Fort Dearborn Inc Sec	NR	NY	BD	†0.04	12-15-95	12-19	†1.16	....	1.12	e7.3	1.12	....	18¼	12⅝	15⅜	14⅞	15¼	-10.5	17.03	12-22-95	8872
FOR	Fortis Securities	NR	NY	BD	0.067	1-15-96	12-21	0.85	....	0.80	9.6	0.915	....	11⅞	8	8¾	8¼	8⅜	-9.4	9.24	12-22-95	12366
FRF	France Growth Fund	NR	NY	GEC	0.664	1-12-96	12-27	0.033	0.68	0.41	⊙4.2	....	....	14⅜	9⅛	10⅜	9⅜	9⅞	-18.2	12.07	12-22-95	15345
FKL	Franklin Hldg Corp	NR	AS	CA	[9]1.00	12-15-95	12-6	[9]1.00	....	Nil	....	....	....	10½	8	11½	9⅞	10⅛	-34.3	15.40	12-31-94	867
FMI	Franklin Multi-Income Tr	NR	NY	ICA	0.064	1-15-96	12-27	0.768	0.108	0.77	⊙©8.2	0.808	0.605	11	7¾	9⅞	9⅛	9⅜	-12.9	10.76	12-21-95	5858
FPT	Franklin Principal Maturity	NR	NY	BD	0.045	1-15-96	12-27	†0.591	....	0.54	e7.0	0.59	0.104	9	6⅜	8	7⅜	7¾	-9.8	8.59	12-21-95	20463
FT	Franklin Universal Tr	NR	NY	C	0.067	1-31-96	1-10	†0.846	....	0.80	e8.9	†0.81	....	9⅝	7⅛	9½	9	9	-6.8	9.66	12-21-95	26779
GCV	Gabelli Conv Securities Fd	NR	NY	CA	0.75	12-27-95	12-20	1.15	....	0.80	7.4	0.573	0.327	13	10⅝	11⅛	10¼	10¾	-2.5	11.03	12-22-95	8093
GAB	Gabelli Equity Trust	NR	NY	CA	0.50	12-21-95	12-13	1.00	....	1.00	10.7	[10]h1.08	....	12⅝	9⅛	9⅞	8¾	9⅜	-5.0	9.87	12-22-95	87224
GGT	Gabelli Global Multimedia Tr	NR	NY	CA	Plan qtly div			....	....	....	....	....	....	8⅜	6⅞	6⅞	6⅜	6¾	-13.2	7.78	12-22-95	8607
GMI	Gemini II	NR	NY	ICA	0.11	1-31-96	12-27	....	....	[4]Nil	....	....	....	20¾	14½	26⅞	25⅛	25¾	-6.6	27.58	12-22-95	10921
GAM	Genl Amer Investors	NR	NY	CA	[2]©2.58	12-21-95	11-9	[2]0.09	2.90	0.09	⊙0.5	[11]0.06	1.49	30	18¾	20⅝	20	20	-15.7	23.72	12-22-95	23291
GER	Germany Fund	NR	NY	GEC	0.83	1-16-96	12-22	[2]0.48	0.36	[4]....	⊙e....	[8]0.09	0.27	13¾	10⅛	12	11⅛	11⅜	-16.0	13.54	12-22-95	13494
GOV	Global Gvt Plus Fund[12]	NR	NY	GB	†0.36	1-5-96	12-19	0.435	....	0.48	6.5	0.47	0.325	7⅞	5½	8¼	7¼	7⅜	-3.2	7.62	12-22-95	45643
GHS	Global Health Sciences Fd	NR	NY	CA	0.20	1-14-94	12-23	....	....	Nil	....	0.20	....	12¼	9⅜	16⅞	15	16⅝	-17.9	20.26	12-22-95	20507
GHI	Global High Inc Dollar Fd	NR	NY	GB	0.106	12-29-95	12-21	1.29	....	1.27	11.0	[13]1.38	....	15¾	10¼	11¾	11¼	11½	-14.8	13.49	12-22-95	22737
GDF	Global Partners Income Fd	NR	NY	GB	†0.18	12-29-95	12-21	†1.486	....	1.43	e12.6	1.425	....	15⅛	9½	11¾	11¼	11⅜	-5.0	11.97	12-22-95	14507
GSG	Global Small Cap Fund	NR	AS	GE	0.014	12-18-95	12-12	0.014	....	0.01	0.1	....	0.797	17⅝	9⅝	9⅛	8⅝	8⅞	-20.8	11.20	12-22-95	3802
PGY	Global Total Return Fd[12]	NR	NY	GB	†0.43	12-29-95	12-14	†0.81	....	0.58	7.0	0.47	0.135	8⅞	6	8½	8	8¼	-1.6	8.38	12-22-95	66208
GCH	Greater China Fund	NR	NY	CA	0.055	1-12-96	12-27	0.155	....	0.29	2.1	0.06	0.62	28	11¾	14⅝	13¾	14⅛	-2.8	14.53	12-22-95	9584
GCM	Greenwich Street CA Muni Fd	NR	AS	GVT	0.024	12-29-95	12-21	0.696	0.024	0.70	⊙5.8	0.058	....	11⅞	10	12⅛	11⅝	12	-12.8	13.76	12-22-95	3658
GSI	Greenwich Street Muni Fund	NR	NY	MU	0.06	2-23-96	2-15	0.812	....	0.72	5.9	0.24	....	12⅛	9¾	12⅛	11⅝	12⅛	-6.2	12.92	12-22-95	17000
GSP	Growth Fund of Spain	NR	NY	GEC	0.71	12-29-95	12-12	0.42	0.29	0.42	⊙3.9	0.45	....	12½	7⅜	11⅛	10¼	10¾	-17.6	13.04	12-22-95	17259
GTD	G.T. Global Dvlp Mkt Fund	NR	NY	GE	0.722	12-29-95	12-20	1.172	....	0.72	7.5	....	....	15¼	9½	10⅛	9⅛	9⅝	-16.5	11.53	12-22-95	36417
GTF	G.T. Greater Europe Fd	NR	NY	GEC	0.18	12-29-95	12-20	0.186	0.342	[4]....	⊙e....	....	....	17¼	8⅞	13⅜	12⅛	12½	-15.1	14.73	12-22-95	16045
HQH	H&Q Healthcare Inv	NR	NY	CA	©1.22	12-15-95	11-21	....	1.22	Nil	©....	....	....	20⅛	12¾	20½	17	20⅜	-10.8	22.85	12-22-95	5549
HQL	H&Q Life Sciences Investors	NR	NY	CA	Plan annual div			....	....	....	....	....	....	15	8	15⅜	12½	15	-9.5	16.58	12-22-95	6676
HAT	Hatteras Income Sec	NR	NY	BD	0.11	12-29-95	12-13	1.37	....	1.32	8.2	†1.445	....	19½	14½	16¾	15⅞	16⅛	-3.1	16.64	12-22-95	3305
HHGP	Harris & Harris Group	NR	NNM	CA	0.01	12-14-90	11-26	....	....	Nil	....	....	....	8⅞	2⅞	8⅛	5¼	7⅞	129.6	3.43	12-31-94	10212
HGA	Heritage U.S.Govt Income Fd	AAf	NY	GVT	0.087	1-25-96	1-17	1.164	....	1.04	9.5	1.164	....	15¼	10⅛	11½	10⅞	11	-13.3	12.69	12-21-95	3115
YLD	High Income Advantage	NR	NY	BD	0.05	1-26-96	12-27	0.60	....	0.60	10.7	†0.642	....	6⅜	4¾	5⅞	5⅝	5⅝	7.3	5.24	12-22-95	30017

Uniform Footnote Explanations-See page 4. Other: [1] Unit Invest't Tr. [2] In cash or stk,'95. [3] Incl $0.68 in cash or stk,'94. [4] To be determined. [5] In cash or stk,'96. [6] Incl $0.937 in cash or stk,'95. [7] Incl $0.075 in cash or stk,'95. [8] In cash or stk,'94. [9] Spl div. [10] Stk dstr Gabelli Global Multimedia Tr,'94. [11] Incl $1.18 in cash or stk,'94. [12] Approve conversion to open-end fund. [13] Incl $0.074 non-taxable,'94.

Ticker Symbol	Fund	Rating	Exc.	Type	Dividends: Latest Payment Period $	Date	Ex. Div.	So Far 1995 Invest. Income	So Far 1995 Cap. Gain	Ind. Rate	Div. Yld. %	1994 Invest. Income	1994 Cap. Gain	Price Range 1994 - 1995 High	1994 - 1995 Low	December, 1995 Last Sale or Bid High	Low	Last	Net Assets % NAV Prem. Disc.	Latest NAV	Latest Date	Com. Shs. 000
YLT	**High Income Advantage II**	**NR**	**NY**	**BD**	†0.053	1-26-96	12-27	†0.667	....	0.63	e10.3	†0.717	....	7	5⅛	6¼	6	6⅛	3.8	5.90	12-22-95	35611
YLH	**High Income Advantage III**	**NR**	**NY**	**BD**	0.06	1-26-96	12-27	0.72	....	0.72	10.7	†0.766	....	7⅞	5⅞	7	6¾	6¾	7.0	6.31	12-22-95	12877
HIO	**High Income Opp Fd**	**NR**	**NY**	**BD**	0.093	12-29-95	12-21	1.134	....	1.12	10.7	1.152	....	12⅞	9½	10⅞	10½	10½	-9.0	11.54	12-22-95	69858
HYI	**High Yield Income Fd**	**NR**	**NY**	**BD**	0.073	12-29-95	12-8	0.87	....	0.87	11.2	0.90	....	9⅛	6⅞	8⅛	7¾	7¾	9.0	7.11	12-22-95	10989
HYP	**High Yield Plus Fund**	**NR**	**NY**	**BD**	0.07	1-12-96	12-27	†0.85	....	0.84	e9.7	0.863	....	9⅜	7¼	8¾	8½	8⅝	1.1	8.53	12-22-95	11039
HLA	**Highlander Income Fund**	**NR**	**AS**	**BD**	0.094	1-11-96	12-27	1.23	....	1.13	9.2	0.928	....	15¼	11	12⅜	12	12¼	-12.2	13.95	12-21-95	2000
HTA	**Hyperion 1997 Term Trust**	**AAAf**	**NY**	**BD**	0.04	12-28-95	12-14	0.512	....	0.47	6.6	0.60	....	10⅛	6⅞	7⅜	7⅛	7⅛	-9.9	7.91	12-21-95	60555
HTT	**Hyperion 1999 Term Trust**	**AAAf**	**NY**	**GVT**	0.04	12-28-95	12-14	0.512	....	0.47	7.1	0.563	....	10	6¼	6⅝	6⅜	6⅝	-12.8	7.60	12-21-95	63113
HTR	**Hyperion Total Return Fd**	**NR**	**NY**	**MI**	†0.035	1-11-96	12-27	0.87	....	0.84	e9.3	†1.11	....	12	7⅝	9¼	9	9	-15.0	10.59	12-21-95	24809
HTB	**Hyperion 2002 Term Trust**	**AAAf**	**NY**	**BD**	0.044	12-28-95	12-14	0.563	....	0.53	7.2	0.654	....	10⅛	6¼	7½	7⅛	7⅜	-14.8	8.66	12-21-95	36127
HTO	**Hyperion 2005 Inv Grd Oppt Tr**	**AAf**	**NY**	**MI**	0.054	12-28-95	12-14	0.675	....	0.65	8.5	0.75	....	10⅛	6¾	7⅞	7⅛	7⅝	-16.8	9.17	12-21-95	21405
IIS	**INA Investment Sec**	**NR**	**NY**	**BD**	Q0.33	12-8-95	11-24	†1.35	....	1.32	e⊙7.6	†1.425	0.20	18⅞	14¾	18	17	17⅜	-10.2	19.34	12-22-95	4792
IOF	**Income Opportunities Fd 1999**	**NR**	**NY**	**BD**	0.042	1-12-96	12-28	0.506	....	0.50	6.1	0.591	0.013	10	6⅞	8⅜	8⅛	8¼	-13.1	9.49	12-22-95	55511
IFT	**Income Opportunities Fd 2000**	**NR**	**NY**	**GVT**	0.046	1-12-96	12-28	0.555	....	0.55	6.3	0.631	0.001	10⅛	7	8¾	8⅜	8¾	-11.0	9.83	12-22-95	12913
IFN	**India Fund**	**NR**	**NY**	**GEC**	0.132	1-13-95	12-23	0.132	....	Nil	....	....	....	15¼	10¼	9½	8	8⅞	-0.6	8.93	12-22-95	34007
IGF	**India Growth Fund**	**NR**	**NY**	**GEC**	©0.348	1-17-96	12-27	....	0.918	Nil	⊙....	....	0.25	30¾	12½	14	12⅝	12⅞	6.2	12.12	12-20-95	8910
IF	**Indonesia Fund**	**NR**	**NY**	**GEC**	0.005	1-3-92	12-18	....	....	Nil	....	....	....	23⅝	8⅝	11	10⅛	10⅛	8.2	9.36	12-22-95	4609
IMF	**Inefficient-Mkt Fund**	**NR**	**AS**	**CA**	©0.106	12-29-95	12-21	0.106	1.936	Nil	⊙....	0.052	0.085	11⅛	9	11½	9½	9¾	-17.9	11.95	12-22-95	4384
PIF	**Insured Muni Income Fd**	**NR**	**NY**	**MU**	0.064	12-29-95	12-19	0.691	....	0.77	6.3	0.844	....	15⅜	9⅜	12⅝	11¾	12¼	-17.2	14.79	12-22-95	15932
IIC	**InterCapital Cal Ins Muni Inc**	**NR**	**NY**	**MUS**	0.06	12-22-95	12-6	0.745	....	0.72	6.3	0.87	....	16⅛	9⅛	12	11½	11½	-16.8	13.82	12-22-95	14083
IQC	**InterCapital Cal Qual Muni Sec**	**NR**	**NY**	**MUS**	0.058	12-22-95	12-6	0.715	....	0.69	6.3	0.81	....	15⅛	8½	11⅜	10⅞	10⅞	-17.9	13.25	12-22-95	12370
ICB	**InterCapital Inc Sec**	**NR**	**NY**	**P**	0.12	12-22-95	12-6	1.47	....	1.44	8.8	1.59	....	22	15⅛	16⅝	16¼	16⅜	-9.6	18.12	12-22-95	12201
ICS	**InterCapital Ins Cal Muni Sec**	**NR**	**NY**	**MUS**	0.071	12-22-95	12-6	0.665	0.009	0.75	⊙5.9	0.48	....	15⅛	10¼	13⅝	12¾	12¾	-16.2	15.22	12-22-95	4474
IMB	**InterCapital Ins Muni Bd Fd**	**NR**	**NY**	**MU**	0.075	12-22-95	12-6	1.00	....	0.90	6.6	1.11	....	18	11⅝	14¼	13⅝	13⅝	-12.5	15.57	12-22-95	5257
IIM	**InterCapital Ins Muni Income**	**NR**	**NY**	**MU**	0.063	12-22-95	12-6	0.775	....	0.75	6.5	0.90	....	15⅞	9⅜	11⅞	11½	11⅝	-17.6	14.10	12-22-95	34865
IMS	**InterCapital Ins Muni Sec**	**NR**	**NY**	**MU**	0.068	12-22-95	12-6	0.76	....	0.81	6.3	0.50	....	15⅜	10⅝	13⅜	12¾	12⅞	-15.8	15.30	12-22-95	10025
IMT	**InterCapital Ins Muni Tr**	**NR**	**NY**	**MU**	0.165	12-22-95	12-6	1.02	0.08	1.02	⊙6.9	1.02	0.018	16⅞	11⅜	15⅛	14⅝	14⅞	-7.1	16.01	12-22-95	23507
IQN	**InterCapital N.Y.Qual Muni Sec**	**NR**	**NY**	**MUS**	0.06	12-22-95	12-6	0.72	....	0.72	6.4	0.78	....	15¾	8¾	11½	11	11¼	-15.3	13.28	12-22-95	5645
IQI	**InterCapital Qual Muni Income**	**NR**	**NY**	**MU**	0.118	12-22-95	12-6	0.99	0.035	0.99	⊙7.1	0.99	....	16	10½	14⅛	13¾	13⅞	-11.2	15.63	12-22-95	37563
IQT	**InterCapital Qual Muni Inv**	**NR**	**NY**	**MU**	0.251	12-22-95	12-6	1.07	0.166	1.02	⊙7.1	1.08	....	16¾	11⅜	14¾	14⅛	14⅜	-6.8	15.42	12-22-95	18607
IQM	**InterCapital Qual Muni Sec**	**NR**	**NY**	**MU**	0.06	12-22-95	12-6	0.72	....	0.72	6.5	0.84	....	15⅛	8½	11½	11	11⅛	-17.8	13.54	12-22-95	23807
PPM	**Investment Grade Muni Inc**	**NR**	**NY**	**MU**	0.075	12-29-95	12-19	0.881	....	0.90	6.5	0.976	0.018	16⅜	10¾	14¼	13⅜	13¾	-15.7	16.32	12-22-95	10357
IRL	**Irish Investment Fund**	**NR**	**NY**	**GEC**	0.27	12-29-95	12-19	0.141	0.129	0.14	⊙1.2	0.105	....	11¼	6⅜	12⅝	11½	11¾	-13.5	13.59	12-22-95	5009
ITA	**Italy Fund**	**NR**	**NY**	**GEC**	0.02	12-29-95	12-21	0.02	....	0.02	0.3	0.172	....	12½	7¼	7¾	7½	7⅝	-14.8	8.95	12-22-95	9503
JGF	**Jakarta Growth Fund**	**NR**	**NY**	**GEC**	0.11	12-29-95	12-14	0.11	....	0.11	1.2	0.02	....	14⅞	6¼	9¼	8	8⅞	2.6	8.65	12-22-95	5013
JEQ	**Japan Equity Fund**	**NR**	**NY**	**GEC**	0.67	12-29-95	12-14	0.105	0.565	0.11	⊙0.8	0.089	1.386	18	8¼	13⅜	11⅝	13⅜	19.3	11.21	12-22-95	10780
JOF	**Japan OTC Equity Fund**	**NR**	**NY**	**GEC**	0.17	12-30-91	12-10	....	....	Nil	....	....	....	14½	7⅜	9	7¾	8¾	12.5	7.78	12-22-95	11384
JFC	**Jardine Fleming China Reg Fd**	**NR**	**NY**	**GEA**	0.07	12-29-95	12-4	0.118	....	0.09	0.9	0.11	3.03	26¾	11	10¼	9½	10	-8.9	10.98	12-22-95	9101
JFI	**Jardine Fleming India Fund**	**NR**	**NY**	**GEC**	©0.012	9-14-95	8-22	....	0.19	[1]....	⊙....	....	....	16⅝	11⅛	10	8⅞	9⅛	8.4	8.42	12-21-95	11307
BTO	**John Hancock Bk/Thrift Opp**	**NR**	**NY**	**CA**	0.803	12-28-95	12-20	0.478	0.325	0.48	⊙1.9	0.225	....	20¼	15⅝	24⅝	22	24⅝	-9.7	27.28	12-22-95	23005
JHS	**John Hancock Inc Sec[2]**	**NR**	**NY**	**P**	Q0.31	12-28-95	12-20	1.255	....	1.24	7.9	†1.277	0.078	18⅜	13⅛	16½	15¼	15¾	-5.2	16.61	12-22-95	10205
JHI	**John Hancock Inv Tr[2]**	**NR**	**NY**	**BD**	Q0.42	12-28-95	12-20	1.68	....	1.68	8.2	†1.683	0.033	25¼	17⅝	22¼	20⅜	20½	-5.9	21.78	12-22-95	7478
PGD	**John Hancock Patr Gl Div Fd**	**NR**	**NY**	**P**	0.088	1-25-96	1-9	1.081	....	1.05	7.9	1.237	....	15¾	9⅞	13⅜	12⅞	13¼	-4.3	13.85	12-22-95	8345
PPF	**John Hancock Patr Pfd Div Fd**	**NR**	**NY**	**P**	0.096	1-25-96	1-9	1.155	....	1.16	9.0	1.155	....	15⅛	9¾	13	12½	12⅞	-3.5	13.34	12-22-95	7257
PDF	**John Hancock Patr Prem Dv Fd**	**NR**	**NY**	**P**	0.067	1-4-96	12-15	0.80	....	0.80	8.5	†1.25	....	11¼	7⅜	9½	8¾	9⅜	-2.3	9.60	12-22-95	14645
PDT	**John Hancock Patr Prem Dv II**	**NR**	**NY**	**P**	0.075	1-16-96	12-28	0.90	....	0.90	8.1	0.90	....	13¼	8¼	11⅜	10⅝	11⅛	-8.4	12.15	12-22-95	15003

Uniform Footnote Explanations-See page 4. Other: [1] To be determined. [2] Shrs Ben Int.

Ticker Symbol	Fund	Rating	Exc.	Type	Dividends: Latest Payment Period $	Latest Payment Date	Ex. Div.	So Far 1995 Invest. Income	So Far 1995 Cap. Gain	Ind. Rate	Div. Yld. %	1994 Invest. Income	1994 Cap. Gain	Price Range 1994 - 1995 High	1994 - 1995 Low	December, 1995 Last Sale or Bid High	Low	Last	Net Assets % NAV Prem. Disc.	Latest NAV	Latest Date	Com. Shs. 000
DIV	John Hancock Patr Sel Div Tr	NR	NY	P	0.103	1-26-96	1-10	1.134	....	1.24	8.8	1.237	....	19½	11	14¾	13⅞	14⅛	-9.2	15.56	12-22-95	9840
KHI	Kemper High Income	NR	NY	BD	0.075	12-29-95	12-11	0.90	....	0.90	9.7	0.90	....	10½	7⅞	9½	9⅛	9¼	5.6	8.76	12-22-95	22610
KGT	Kemper Interm Gvt Tr[1]	NR	NY	GVT	0.048	12-29-95	12-11	0.591	....	0.57	7.9	0.678	....	9¼	6¾	7⅜	7⅛	7¼	-12.8	8.31	12-22-95	33996
KMM	Kemper Multi-Mkt Income	NR	NY	ICF	†0.16	1-12-96	12-21	†1.015	....	0.99	⊙e9.1	0.83	0.09	11⅝	8⅞	10⅞	10⅝	10⅞	1.0	10.77	12-22-95	19933
KTF	Kemper Muni Income	NR	NY	MU	0.073	12-29-95	12-11	0.87	....	0.87	6.8	0.87	....	13¾	9⅝	12⅞	12½	12⅞	3.9	12.39	12-22-95	37317
KST	Kemper Strategic Income	NR	AS	BD	†0.175	1-12-96	12-21	†1.72	....	1.74	e11.8	0.765	....	15⅛	11⅞	14⅞	14¼	14¾	9.9	13.42	12-22-95	3365
KSM	Kemper Strategic Muni Tr	NR	NY	MU	0.068	12-29-95	12-11	0.816	....	0.82	6.6	0.816	....	13¾	10⅜	12⅜	11⅞	12⅜	1.9	12.15	12-22-95	10460
KBA	Kleinwort Benson Aus	NR	NY	GB	†0.175	1-15-96	12-22	†0.898	0.002	0.78	e8.7	0.778	0.022	10¼	8½	9⅛	8⅝	9	-8.5	9.84	12-22-95	9564
KEF	Korea Equity Fund	NR	NY	GEC	0.02	12-29-95	12-21	0.02	....	0.02	0.2	....	0.28	15⅛	8¼	8⅞	8⅛	8¼	-9.2	9.09	12-22-95	8409
KF	Korea Fund	NR	NY	GEC	©0.055	1-16-96	12-27	....	0.313	0.01	⊙....	0.011	0.135	27⅝	12⅛	22½	20⅜	22	8.3	20.31	12-22-95	36931
KIF	Korean Investment Fund	NR	NY	GEC	0.293	1-12-96	12-27	....	....	[2]....	....	....	....	18½	10⅛	11⅛	9⅞	10⅛	-9.8	11.23	12-22-95	5963
LBF	Latin America Dollar Inc Fd	NR	NY	GB	Q0.375	1-16-96	12-27	†1.525	0.15	1.50	e12.8	†1.743	0.124	17⅛	10⅜	12⅜	11⅝	11¾	-4.5	12.31	12-22-95	5922
LAQ	Latin America Equity Fd	NR	NY	GEC	©0.24	9-29-95	9-13	....	3.34	0.17	⊙1.3	0.171	0.578	31⅝	13½	13½	12½	12⅞	-13.8	14.94	12-22-95	8547
LLF	Latin America Growth Fd	NR	NY	CA	Plan annual div			....	....	....	....	....	....	15⅛	11⅝	9⅞	9¼	9⅝	-13.5	11.13	12-22-95	4007
LAM	Latin America Inv Fd	NR	NY	GEC	©0.19	9-29-95	9-13	....	4.52	0.07	⊙0.5	0.069	2.032	35⅞	17⅛	15½	14⅛	14¾	-13.7	17.10	12-22-95	7762
LDF	Latin American Discovery Fd	NR	NY	GEC	©0.446	7-17-95	7-3	....	4.617	Nil	⊙....	0.001	1.569	30¼	13¼	10⅛	9⅛	9⅞	-11.8	11.19	12-22-95	11618
USA	Liberty ALL-STAR Eqty[3]	NR	NY	CA	[4]©0.28	1-8-96	11-29	0.49	0.51	1.00	⊙9.2	[5]0.76	0.27	11⅜	8¼	10⅞	10⅜	10⅞	-0.5	10.93	12-22-95	76742
ASG	Liberty ALL-STAR Growth Fd	NR	NY	CA	0.50	1-5-96	12-20	0.376	0.353	0.22	⊙2.3	0.003	0.003	10¾	8¼	10	9⅛	9⅜	-10.5	10.48	12-22-95	11339
LTT	Liberty Term Trust-1999	AAAf	NY	MI	0.054	12-29-95	12-19	0.44	....	0.65	8.8	0.598	....	10½	6⅞	7⅝	7⅜	7⅜	-13.2	8.50	12-22-95	5625
LNV	Lincoln Natl Cv Sec	NR	NY	CV	0.92	1-16-96	12-27	†1.08	....	0.96	e⊙5.7	†2.92	....	21¼	15⅛	18¼	16¾	16¾	-14.1	19.49	12-21-94	6364
LND	Lincoln Natl Income Fd	NR	NY	C	†0.48	1-16-96	12-27	†1.20	....	1.20	†⊙8.8	†1.73	....	17⅜	10¾	14¼	13⅜	13⅝	-6.1	14.51	12-21-95	6832
MF	Malaysia Fund	NR	NY	GEC	©0.766	1-9-96	12-27	....	1.978	Nil	⊙e....	0.019	1.696	29⅞	14¾	18⅜	16⅝	17	-12.3	19.38	12-22-95	9722
MHY	Managed High Inc Portfolio	NR	NY	BD	0.093	1-26-96	1-19	1.116	0.188	1.12	e⊙10.7	†1.148	....	12¾	9⅜	10⅞	10⅜	10½	-7.2	11.32	12-22-95	41982
PHT	Managed High Yield Fd	NR	NY	BD	0.116	12-29-95	12-19	1.392	....	1.39	11.6	1.285	....	15⅜	11⅛	12⅝	12	12	-6.8	12.88	12-22-95	6032
MMU	Managed Muni Portfolio	NR	NY	MU	0.064	2-23-96	2-15	0.753	0.112	0.77	⊙6.4	0.671	0.14	13⅛	9¾	12¼	11⅞	12⅛	-4.3	12.67	12-22-95	34153
MTU	Managed Muni Portfolio II	NR	NY	MU	0.063	2-23-96	2-15	0.746	0.036	0.76	⊙6.2	0.671	0.124	13⅛	9⅞	12¼	11¾	12¼	-3.5	12.70	12-8-95	11217
MHE	Mass Hlth & Edu Tax-Exempt Tr	NR	AS	MU	0.058	12-29-95	12-20	0.706	....	0.70	6.3	0.81	....	15⅞	9⅝	11⅝	10⅞	11⅛	-15.2	13.12	12-22-95	2307
MCI	MassMutual Corp Inv	NR	NY	ICA	1.62	1-18-96	12-27	2.316	0.484	2.80	⊙7.8	2.641	0.159	34⅝	25¾	36½	34⅝	35¾	8.5	32.94	12-31-94	4257
MPV	MassMutual Part'n Inv	NR	NY	ICA	Q0.19	1-18-96	12-27	0.70	....	0.76	8.3	[6]0.66	....	8¾	6⅝	9⅜	8⅞	9⅛	3.2	8.84	12-31-94	9217
MRF	Mentor Income Fund	NR	NY	MI	0.07	1-31-96	1-10	0.87	....	0.84	9.6	0.96	....	12⅛	7⅞	9⅛	8¾	8¾	-15.0	10.30	12-21-95	11818
MXE	Mexico Eqty & Income Fd	NR	NY	GEC	0.087	1-12-96	12-27	....	3.93	0.08	⊙0.9	0.42	1.67	27⅛	13¼	10⅜	8⅝	8⅝	-16.8	10.37	12-21-95	9356
MXF	Mexico Fund	NR	NY	GEC	t©0.029	1-31-96	12-26	....	0.067	Nil	⊙....	t0.355	0.153	40⅜	19⅝	14	12	12¾	-11.0	14.32	12-7-95	37282
MCR	MFS Charter Income Tr	NR	NY	BD	0.064	12-29-95	12-13	0.774	....	0.77	8.7	[7]0.623	0.141	10⅞	8	9¼	8⅞	8⅞	-15.4	10.49	12-22-95	83786
MGF	MFS Gvt Mkts Income Tr	NR	NY	ICF	0.04	12-29-95	12-13	0.488	....	0.48	7.5	0.519	....	7¾	5⅝	6¾	6⅜	6⅜	-16.6	7.64	12-22-95	89552
MIN	MFS Interm Income SBI	NR	NY	ICF	0.043	12-29-95	12-13	0.525	....	0.52	7.8	[8]0.517	0.047	8	5⅞	6⅞	6½	6⅝	-16.4	7.92	12-22-95	19249
MMT	MFS Multimkt Income	NR	NY	BD	0.045	12-29-95	12-13	0.565	....	0.54	8.3	[9]0.505	0.062	8	5⅝	6⅝	6¼	6½	-15.0	7.65	12-22-95	11754
MFM	MFS Municipal Inc Tr	NR	NY	MU	0.058	12-29-95	12-13	0.696	....	0.70	7.3	0.696	....	10	8⅜	9¾	9⅜	9⅝	8.6	8.86	12-22-95	37480
MFV	MFS Special Value Trust	NR	NY	ICA	0.138	12-29-95	12-13	1.512	0.344	1.65	⊙10.0	1.399	2.223	18¾	13	16¾	16⅜	16½	16.0	14.23	12-22-95	5968
MWK	Milwaukee Land	NR	AS	IRE	None Since Public			....	....	Nil	....	....	....	8	6	7⅜	6⅛	7⅜	-46.4	13.76	12-31-94	1671
MXA	Minnesota Muni Inc Portfolio	Af	AS	MUS	0.063	1-11-96	12-27	0.763	....	0.76	6.2	0.833	....	15¾	9⅞	12½	12⅛	12¼	-12.9	14.07	12-21-95	3607
MNA	Minnesota Muni Term Trust	Af	NY	MUS	0.054	1-11-96	12-27	0.611	....	0.61	⊙5.7	0.611	....	12¼	8⅝	11	10½	10⅝	-5.6	11.25	12-21-95	5733
MNB	Minnesota Muni Term Tr-II	Af	AS	MUS	0.058	1-11-96	12-27	0.59	....	0.59	⊙5.7	0.59	....	11¾	8⅜	10⅝	10	10⅜	-4.1	10.82	12-21-95	3460
MTS	Montgomery St Inc Sec	NR	NY	BD	Q0.36	12-29-95	12-14	1.40	....	1.44	8.0	1.36	....	22⅜	15¼	19⅛	17¾	18	-9.2	19.83	12-22-95	10025
MGC	Morgan Grenfell Smallcap	NR	NY	CA	©0.995	1-25-96	1-29	[10]....	1.227	1.14	⊙9.0	....	1.137	12½	8¼	12⅝	11⅞	12⅝	-10.5	14.11	12-22-95	5786
AFF	Morgan Stanley Africa Inv Fd	NR	NY	GEC	0.974	1-9-96	12-27	0.544	....	0.96	⊙7.5	....	....	15⅛	9⅞	13¾	12⅝	12⅞	-27.7	17.80	12-22-95	15448
APF	Morgan Stanley Asia-Pac Fund	NR	NY	GEA	0.051	1-9-96	12-27	0.045	0.03	0.05	⊙0.4	....	....	15⅛	10½	13½	11¾	13⅜	-6.7	14.34	12-22-95	53655

Uniform Footnote Explanations-See page 4. Other: [1] Plan to convert to open end fund. [2] To be determined. [3] Shrs Ben Int. [4] In cash or stk,'96. [5] Incl $0.27 in cash or stk,'94. [6] Incl return of cap,'94. [7] Incl $0.325787 non-taxable,'94. [8] Incl $0.340157 non-taxable,'94. [9] Incl $0.346548 non-taxable,'94. [10] In cash or stk,'95.

Ticker Symbol	Fund	Rating	Exc.	Type	Dividends: Latest Payment Period $	Date	Ex. Div.	So Far 1995 Invest. Income	So Far 1995 Cap. Gain	Ind. Rate	Div. Yld. %	1994 Invest. Income	1994 Cap. Gain	Price Range 1994 - 1995 High	1994 - 1995 Low	December, 1995 Last Sale or Bid High	Low	Last	Net Assets % NAV Prem. Disc.	Latest NAV	Date	Com. Shs. 000
MSF	**Morgan Stanley Emerging Mkt**	**NR**	**NY**	**GE**	©0.529	1-9-96	12-27	....	4.662	Nil	⊙....	....	2.596	32½	16½	16⅝	14⅜	15½	1.6	15.25	12-22-95	21481
MSD	**Morgan Stanley Emer'g Mkt Debt**	**NR**	**NY**	**GB**	0.476	1-9-96	12-27	†1.666	....	1.90	e15.2	1.055	0.414	18⅜	10½	13⅛	12	12½	-1.0	12.62	12-22-95	16056
MGB	**Morgan Stan Global Opt Bd Fd**	**NR**	**NY**	**GB**	0.376	1-9-96	12-27	1.763	....	1.50	12.0	0.36	....	15⅛	11¼	13¼	12⅜	12½	-5.2	13.19	12-22-95	4123
MSY	**Morgan Stanley Hi Yld Fd**	**NR**	**NY**	**BD**	0.154	1-9-96	12-27	†1.248	....	1.85	e14.4	1.24	....	15⅜	11⅛	13	12⅛	12⅞	-6.2	13.72	12-22-95	8718
IIF	**Morgan Stanley India Inv Fd**	**NR**	**NY**	**GEC**	0.167	1-10-95	12-23	....	0.167	[1]....	⊙....	....	....	15⅛	11⅛	10	8⅞	9⅛	2.3	8.92	12-22-95	35700
MUA	**Muniassets Fund**	**NR**	**NY**	**MU**	0.073	12-28-95	12-20	0.868	....	0.87	7.0	0.874	....	15	10	13	12¼	12⅜	-12.0	14.07	12-22-95	11308
MAF	**Municipal Advantage Fund**	**NR**	**NY**	**MU**	0.065	12-29-95	12-13	0.78	....	0.78	6.6	0.84	....	15⅛	8⅞	12⅛	11¾	11⅞	-16.3	14.19	12-22-95	7257
MHF	**Municipal High Income Fd**	**NR**	**NY**	**MU**	0.051	2-23-96	2-15	0.645	....	0.61	7.2	0.648	....	10⅛	7⅝	9	8¼	8½	-11.2	9.57	12-22-95	19371
OIA	**Municipal Income Opp Tr**	**NR**	**NY**	**MU**	0.055	12-22-95	12-6	0.635	....	0.66	7.8	0.63	....	8¾	6⅞	8¾	8⅜	8½	0.4	8.47	12-22-95	21730
OIB	**Municipal Income Opp Tr II**	**NR**	**NY**	**MU**	0.055	12-22-95	12-6	0.56	....	0.66	7.8	0.60	....	8⅞	6¾	8⅝	8⅜	8½	-4.2	8.87	12-22-95	20738
OIC	**Municipal Income Opp Tr III**	**NR**	**NY**	**MU**	0.055	12-22-95	12-6	0.585	....	0.66	7.5	0.608	0.073	10¼	7¼	9⅛	8⅝	8¾	-11.1	9.84	12-22-95	10969
TFA	**Municipal Income Trust**	**NR**	**NY**	**MU**	0.137	12-22-95	12-6	0.60	0.087	0.60	⊙6.6	0.61	0.343	11¾	8	9¼	8¾	9⅛	-8.8	10.01	12-22-95	31623
TFB	**Municipal Income Trust II**	**NR**	**NY**	**MU**	0.169	12-22-95	12-6	0.63	0.117	0.63	⊙6.3	0.635	0.14	11¼	8¼	10	9⅝	10	-2.6	10.27	12-22-95	27975
TFC	**Municipal Income Trust III**	**NR**	**NY**	**MU**	0.085	12-22-95	12-6	0.55	0.035	0.60	⊙6.2	0.545	0.074	10½	7½	9¾	9⅜	9⅝	-4.6	10.09	12-22-95	6632
MNP	**Municipal Partners Fund**	**NR**	**NY**	**MU**	0.065	12-29-95	12-7	0.798	....	0.78	e6.7	0.887	....	15⅜	9	12	11½	11⅝	-17.4	14.07	12-22-95	5757
MPT	**Municipal Partners Fund II**	**NR**	**NY**	**MU**	0.059	12-29-95	12-7	0.735	....	0.71	6.2	0.851	....	15⅛	8⅝	11½	11	11⅜	-16.4	13.60	12-22-95	6007
PIA	**Municipal Prem Income Tr**	**NR**	**NY**	**MU**	0.167	12-22-95	12-6	0.70	0.117	0.60	⊙6.6	0.725	0.096	11⅝	7⅞	9⅜	9⅛	9⅛	-12.7	10.45	12-22-95	25894
MEN	**MuniEnhanced Fund**	**NR**	**NY**	**MU**	0.059	12-28-95	12-20	0.728	....	0.71	6.6	0.796	0.115	13⅝	8⅝	11¼	10⅝	10¾	-12.7	12.31	12-22-95	29008
MIF	**MuniInsured Fund**	**NR**	**AS**	**MU**	0.041	12-28-95	12-20	0.517	....	0.50	5.8	0.557	0.193	11⅛	8	8⅞	8⅜	8½	-14.2	9.98	12-22-95	8070
MVC	**MuniVest CA Insured Fund**	**NR**	**NY**	**MUS**	0.066	12-28-95	12-20	0.775	....	0.79	6.4	0.808	....	15½	9¼	13⅜	12⅜	12⅜	-10.8	13.87	12-22-95	5961
MVS	**MuniVest Florida Fund**	**NR**	**NY**	**MUS**	0.062	12-28-95	12-20	0.744	....	0.74	6.0	0.833	....	16¼	8⅞	12½	11⅞	12¼	-9.1	13.48	12-22-94	5774
MVF	**MuniVest Fund**	**NR**	**AS**	**MU**	0.052	12-28-95	12-20	0.623	....	0.62	7.1	0.679	0.164	11½	7	9⅜	8½	8⅝	-11.7	9.84	12-22-95	61123
MVT	**MuniVest Fund II**	**NR**	**NY**	**MU**	0.069	12-28-95	12-20	0.841	....	0.83	6.7	0.863	....	15⅛	9½	12¾	12	12⅜	-13.5	14.30	12-22-95	19907
MVM	**MuniVest MI Insured Fund**	**NR**	**NY**	**MUS**	0.064	12-28-95	12-20	0.759	....	0.75	6.3	0.827	....	15⅝	9⅛	12½	11¾	12	-14.7	14.07	12-22-95	7296
MVJ	**MuniVest NJ Fund**	**NR**	**NY**	**MUS**	0.063	12-28-95	12-20	0.758	....	0.75	6.3	0.807	....	15⅜	9¼	12½	11⅞	12	-15.3	14.16	12-22-95	5483
MVY	**MuniVest NY Insured Fund**	**NR**	**NY**	**MUS**	0.06	12-28-95	12-20	0.745	....	0.71	6.1	0.845	....	15⅜	9⅛	12⅝	11½	11⅝	-14.3	13.57	12-22-95	7132
MVP	**MuniVest PA Insured Fund**	**NR**	**NY**	**MUS**	0.062	12-28-95	12-20	0.746	....	0.74	6.4	0.839	....	15½	9⅝	12⅛	11¼	11½	-13.0	13.22	12-22-95	4019
MZA	**MuniYield Arizona Fund**	**NR**	**AS**	**MUS**	0.065	12-28-95	12-20	0.777	....	0.78	6.4	0.881	....	15	9¼	12⅞	11⅞	12⅛	-10.7	13.58	12-22-95	4657
MYC	**MuniYield California Fund**	**NR**	**NY**	**MUS**	0.073	12-28-95	12-20	0.889	....	0.88	6.6	0.993	0.246	16⅜	11⅛	14	13¼	13¼	-14.4	15.47	12-22-95	16782
MIC	**MuniYield CA Insured Fund**	**NR**	**NY**	**MUS**	0.069	12-28-95	12-20	0.829	....	0.83	6.4	0.89	....	15¾	10⅛	13¾	12¾	12⅞	-13.9	14.96	12-22-95	16329
MCA	**MuniYield CA Insured Fund II**	**NR**	**NY**	**MUS**	0.07	12-28-95	12-20	0.861	....	0.84	6.3	0.928	0.071	16	10½	14¼	13⅛	13¼	-14.2	15.45	12-22-95	12679
MYF	**MuniYield Florida Fund**	**NR**	**NY**	**MUS**	0.072	12-28-95	12-20	0.868	....	0.87	6.3	0.935	....	17	10¼	14½	13½	13¾	-10.8	15.42	12-22-95	7859
MFT	**MuniYield FL Insured Fund**	**NR**	**NY**	**MUS**	0.069	12-28-95	12-20	0.838	0.065	0.82	⊙6.0	0.889	....	17	10⅜	14⅝	13⅜	13⅝	-12.3	15.54	12-22-95	8329
MYD	**MuniYield Fund**	**NR**	**NY**	**MU**	0.083	12-28-95	12-20	0.997	....	1.00	6.9	1.058	0.219	17	11⅛	15	14⅛	14½	-8.3	15.82	12-22-95	37061
MYI	**MuniYield Insured Fund**	**NR**	**NY**	**MU**	0.161	12-28-95	12-20	0.914	0.086	0.91	⊙6.6	0.975	0.04	16¾	10¾	14⅜	13⅜	13¾	-13.0	15.81	12-22-95	45187
MTI	**MuniYield Insured Fund II**	**NR**	**NY**	**MU**	0.102	12-28-95	12-20	0.889	0.029	0.89	⊙6.5	0.952	0.07	16⅝	10⅜	14¼	13⅜	13⅝	-13.2	15.69	12-22-95	16391
MYM	**MuniYield Michigan Fund**	**NR**	**NY**	**MUS**	0.114	12-28-95	12-20	0.906	0.041	0.88	⊙6.3	0.952	0.266	17⅛	11½	14¾	13⅝	13⅞	-10.9	15.58	12-22-95	7719
MIY	**MuniYield MI Insured Fund**	**NR**	**NY**	**MU**	0.07	12-28-95	12-20	0.856	....	0.84	6.1	0.894	0.264	17	10½	14¾	13⅝	13¾	-11.7	15.57	12-22-95	7374
MYJ	**MuniYield New Jersey Fund**	**NR**	**NY**	**MUS**	0.073	12-28-95	12-20	0.894	....	0.87	6.3	0.929	....	16½	10½	14¼	13⅜	13⅞	-11.2	15.63	12-22-95	8830
MJI	**MuniYield NJ Insured Fund**	**NR**	**NY**	**MUS**	0.071	12-28-95	12-20	0.871	....	0.85	6.2	0.921	....	17	10½	14¼	13½	13⅝	-12.2	15.51	12-22-95	8195
MYN	**MuniYield NY Insured Fund**	**NR**	**NY**	**MUS**	0.177	12-28-95	12-20	0.91	0.102	0.89	⊙6.1	0.968	0.104	17¼	11¼	15	14⅛	14⅝	-8.4	15.96	12-22-95	12047
MYT	**MuniYield NY Insured Fund II**	**NR**	**NY**	**MUS**	0.067	12-28-95	12-20	0.832	....	0.81	6.1	0.868	....	15⅞	10⅛	13⅞	13	13¼	-11.8	15.02	12-22-95	11115
MYY	**MuniYield NY Insured Fund III**	**NR**	**NY**	**MUS**	0.064	12-28-95	12-20	0.754	....	0.77	6.1	0.839	....	16⅛	9⅞	13⅜	12½	12⅝	-14.1	14.69	12-22-95	3674
MPA	**MuniYield Pennsylvania Fund**	**NR**	**NY**	**MUS**	0.074	12-28-95	12-20	0.892	....	0.89	6.5	0.895	0.049	16⅞	10½	14¼	13¼	13⅝	-13.4	15.73	12-22-95	5661
MQY	**MuniYield Quality Fund**	**NR**	**NY**	**MU**	0.074	12-28-95	12-20	0.884	....	0.89	7.0	0.96	0.019	15¾	10	13¼	12¼	12⅝	-15.7	14.97	12-22-95	30426
MQT	**MuniYield Quality Fund II**	**NR**	**NY**	**MU**	0.074	12-28-95	12-20	0.883	....	0.89	6.8	0.964	0.098	15⅞	10⅛	13⅜	12¾	13	-13.4	15.02	12-22-95	22071

Uniform Footnote Explanations-See page 4. Other: [1] To be determined.

Ticker Symbol	Fund	Rating	Exc.	Type	Dividends: Latest Payment Period $	Date	Ex. Div.	So Far 1995 Invest. Income	So Far 1995 Cap. Gain	Ind. Rate	Div. Yld. %	1994 Invest. Income	1994 Cap. Gain	Price Range 1994 - 1995 High	1994 - 1995 Low	December, 1995 Last Sale or Bid High	Low	Last	Net Assets % NAV Prem. Disc.	Latest NAV	Latest Date	Com. Shs. 000
NBM	Nations Bal Target Mat Fd	NR	NY	GVT	0.584	12-28-95	12-13	0.40	0.499	0.34	⊙3.4	0.195	0.04	10⅛	7⅝	9⅞	9	9⅞	-8.5	10.79	12-22-95	12511
NGI	Nations Gvt Inc Term Tr 2003	AAAf	NY	GVT	0.051	12-28-95	12-13	0.617	....	0.62	7.9	0.703	....	10⅜	5⅞	8¼	7⅜	7⅞	-8.3	8.59	12-22-95	25011
NGF	Nations Gvt Inc Term Tr 2004	NR	NY	GVT	0.054	12-28-95	12-13	0.646	....	0.65	8.1	0.553	....	10⅛	6½	8½	7¾	8	-9.0	8.79	12-22-95	25011
NAF	New Age Media Fund	NR	NY	CA	1.20	12-29-95	12-13	0.07	1.13	0.07	⊙0.5	0.007	....	16⅛	9⅞	15⅞	14⅛	14⅞	-16.0	17.71	12-22-95	14957
HYB	New Amer Hi Income Fd	NR	NY	ICA	†0.055	1-31-96	12-27	†0.52	....	0.48	e10.1	†0.645	....	5⅜	3⅞	5	4¾	4¾	0.2	4.74	12-22-95	34272
GF	New Germany Fund	NR	NY	GEC	0.41	1-16-96	12-22	[1]0.16	....	0.41	3.5	[2]0.06	....	14	9½	12¼	11½	11⅝	-23.3	15.15	12-22-95	32501
NSA	New South Africa Fund	NR	NY	GEC	0.68	1-12-96	12-27	0.83	0.06	[3]....	⊙....	....	....	15⅛	11⅛	15¾	14⅞	15	-26.4	20.39	12-22-95	3807
XTX	New York Tax Exempt Income	NR	AS	MUS	0.053	12-29-95	12-13	0.636	....	0.64	6.2	0.636	....	12¾	8⅞	10⅝	10⅛	10⅜	4.9	9.89	12-22-95	2408
NAZ	Nuveen AZ Prem Inc Muni Fd	NR	NY	MUS	0.065	12-29-95	12-13	0.78	....	0.78	5.8	0.78	....	16	9⅞	13⅞	13¼	13½	-10.3	15.05	12-22-95	4281
NQC	Nuveen CA Inv Qual Muni	NR	NY	MUS	0.086	12-29-95	12-13	1.028	....	1.03	6.5	†1.084	....	17¼	12⅞	16¼	15⅝	15⅞	0.4	15.81	12-22-95	13037
NCM	Nuveen CA Muni Income[4]	NR	NY	MUS	0.059	12-29-95	12-13	0.726	....	0.71	6.0	0.764	....	13⅝	10¼	12	11⅝	11⅞	-0.2	11.90	12-22-95	5210
NCO	Nuveen CA Muni Mkt Oppt	NR	NY	MUS	0.112	12-29-95	12-13	1.035	0.026	1.03	⊙6.5	1.063	....	18½	13	16⅛	15½	15¾	-3.0	16.23	12-22-95	7871
NCA	Nuveen CA Muni Val Fd	NR	NY	MUS	0.116	12-29-95	12-13	0.654	0.063	0.64	⊙6.1	0.672	0.008	12¼	9¼	10¾	10	10½	2.5	10.24	12-22-95	18972
NCP	Nuveen CA Perf Plus Muni	NR	NY	MUS	0.086	12-29-95	12-13	1.032	....	1.03	6.7	†1.042	0.019	17⅝	12⅝	16¼	15¼	15⅜	-2.9	15.84	12-22-95	12415
NCU	Nuveen CA Prem Inc Muni	NR	AS	MUS	0.062	12-29-95	12-13	0.752	....	0.74	6.5	†0.815	....	15¼	8⅞	11⅞	11¼	11⅜	-14.7	13.33	12-22-95	5736
NUC	Nuveen CA Qual Income Muni	NR	NY	MUS	0.098	12-29-95	12-13	0.96	0.018	0.96	⊙6.4	†0.982	....	16¼	11⅝	15¼	14¾	15	-4.1	15.64	12-22-95	21330
NVC	Nuveen CA Select Qual Muni	NR	NY	MUS	0.181	12-29-95	12-13	0.985	0.099	0.98	⊙6.4	†1.035	0.035	17⅛	12¼	15⅝	15	15¼	-2.8	15.69	12-22-95	22322
NTC	Nuveen CT Prem Inc Muni	NR	NY	MUS	0.062	12-29-95	12-13	0.726	....	0.74	5.7	0.736	....	16⅛	10⅛	13⅜	12⅞	12⅞	-6.2	13.72	12-22-95	4837
NQF	Nuveen FL Inv Qual Muni	NR	NY	MUS	0.086	12-29-95	12-13	0.99	0.004	0.99	⊙6.2	†1.005	0.017	17⅞	11⅞	16¼	15½	15⅞	0.6	15.78	12-22-95	16024
NUF	Nuveen FL Qual Income Muni	NR	NY	MUS	0.077	12-29-95	12-13	0.935	....	0.92	6.1	†0.937	....	16½	11¼	15½	14⅞	15	-4.6	15.73	12-22-95	14020
NPG	Nuveen GA Prem Inc Muni	NR	AS	MUS	0.061	12-29-95	12-13	0.706	....	0.73	5.8	0.744	....	15⅜	9¾	12¾	12	12⅝	-8.9	13.86	12-22-95	3525
NPC	Nuveen Ins CA Prem Inc Muni	NR	NY	MUS	0.066	12-29-95	12-13	0.804	....	0.79	6.0	0.851	....	15¾	11¼	13⅝	13	13¼	-14.5	15.49	12-22-95	6405
NCL	Nuveen Ins CA Prem Inc Muni 2	NR	NY	MUS	0.062	12-29-95	12-13	0.767	....	0.74	6.0	†0.829	....	15⅛	10	12⅝	12	12⅜	-10.9	13.89	12-22-95	12578
NXC	Nuveen Ins CA Sel Tax-Free Inc	NR	NY	MUS	0.067	12-29-95	12-13	0.815	....	0.80	6.0	0.817	....	15⅝	12¼	14¼	13¼	13⅜	-9.8	14.83	12-22-95	6257
NFL	Nuveen Ins FL Prem Inc Muni	NR	NY	MUS	0.065	12-29-95	12-13	0.78	....	0.78	6.0	†0.82	....	15⅞	9¾	13⅞	12⅞	13	-13.0	14.94	12-22-95	14319
NIO	Nuveen Ins Muni Oppt Fd	NR	NY	MU	0.139	12-29-95	12-13	0.984	0.057	0.98	⊙6.5	†1.00	....	16¼	11¾	15⅛	14⅝	15	-5.3	15.84	12-22-95	79586
NNF	Nuveen Ins NY Prem Inc Muni	NR	NY	MUS	0.067	12-29-95	12-13	0.798	....	0.80	6.2	†0.85	....	15¼	10⅛	13⅝	13	13	-11.6	14.71	12-22-95	4215
NXN	Nuveen Ins NY Sel Tax-Free Inc	NR	NY	MUS	0.108	12-29-95	12-13	0.78	0.043	0.78	⊙5.9	0.78	....	15¼	11¼	13¾	13	13¼	-9.5	14.64	12-22-95	3907
NPE	Nuveen Ins Prem Inc Muni	NR	NY	MU	0.067	12-29-95	12-13	0.828	....	0.80	6.2	†0.936	....	15¾	9⅞	13	12½	12⅞	-12.8	14.76	12-22-95	15128
NPX	Nuveen Ins Prem Inc Muni 2	NR	NY	MU	0.06	12-29-95	12-13	0.737	....	0.71	6.0	†0.777	....	15⅛	8½	11⅞	11¼	11¾	-12.5	13.43	12-22-95	20642
NQI	Nuveen Ins Quality Muni	NR	NY	MU	0.224	12-29-95	12-13	1.009	0.142	0.98	⊙6.5	†1.028	....	17¾	12	15½	14¾	15	-5.5	15.88	12-22-95	37340
NQM	Nuveen Inv Quality Muni	NR	NY	MU	0.087	12-29-95	12-13	1.072	....	1.04	6.9	1.108	....	17¾	12½	15¼	14¾	15⅛	-4.5	15.83	12-22-95	35196
NMY	Nuveen MD Prem Inc Muni Fd	NR	NY	MUS	0.062	12-29-95	12-13	0.738	....	0.74	6.0	0.739	....	15⅞	9½	12⅞	12	12⅜	-11.3	13.95	12-22-95	9823
NMT	Nuveen MA Prem Inc Muni Fd	NR	NY	MUS	0.066	12-29-95	12-13	0.792	....	0.79	5.7	0.75	....	15¼	10¼	14	13⅛	13¾	-3.4	14.24	12-22-95	4572
NMP	Nuveen MI Prem Inc Muni	NR	NY	MUS	0.065	12-29-95	12-13	0.786	....	0.77	6.2	0.81	....	15⅞	10¼	12¾	12¼	12½	-14.7	14.66	12-22-95	7678
NUM	Nuveen MI Qual Income Muni	NR	NY	MUS	0.148	12-29-95	12-13	0.969	0.068	0.95	⊙6.2	†1.024	0.049	16⅞	12⅞	16	14⅞	15⅜	-2.6	15.78	12-22-95	11121
NOM	Nuveen MO Prem Inc Muni	NR	AS	MUS	0.055	12-29-95	12-13	0.672	....	0.66	5.4	0.702	....	15¼	10⅛	12¼	11⅝	12⅛	-12.6	13.87	12-22-95	2107
NMA	Nuveen Muni Advantage Fd	NR	NY	MU	0.09	12-29-95	12-13	1.083	....	1.08	6.8	1.119	....	17½	12⅜	15⅞	15¼	15⅞	0.9	15.74	12-22-95	42012
NMI	Nuveen Muni Income Fd	NR	NY	MU	0.064	12-29-95	12-13	0.777	....	0.76	6.3	0.818	....	14	10½	12⅛	11⅝	12⅛	0.6	12.05	12-22-95	7618
NMO	Nuveen Muni Mkt Oppt	NR	NY	MU	0.09	12-29-95	12-13	1.083	....	1.08	6.8	1.119	....	17⅜	12½	15⅞	15¼	15⅞	-0.3	15.92	12-22-95	44762
NUV	Nuveen Muni Value Fd	NR	NY	MU	0.132	12-29-95	12-13	0.645	0.08	0.63	⊙6.4	0.662	0.029	12	8⅝	10	9⅝	9⅞	-4.2	10.31	12-22-95	16637
NQJ	Nuveen NJ Inv Qual Muni	NR	NY	MUS	0.079	12-29-95	12-13	0.959	....	0.94	6.0	†1.057	0.02	17⅞	11½	15⅝	15	15⅝	0.4	15.56	12-22-95	19325
NNJ	Nuveen NJ Prem Inc Muni	NR	NY	MUS	0.068	12-29-95	12-13	0.807	....	0.81	6.1	†0.787	0.013	16	10⅛	13¾	13⅛	13¼	-10.5	14.81	12-22-95	11858
NQN	Nuveen NY Inv Qual Muni	NR	NY	MUS	0.11	12-29-95	12-13	1.05	0.023	1.05	⊙6.3	†1.063	....	18	12⅝	17⅝	16⅜	16⅝	1.6	16.37	12-22-95	16941
NNM	Nuveen NY Muni Income[5]	NR	AS	MUS	0.057	12-29-95	12-13	0.69	....	0.68	5.9	0.731	....	13¼	9¾	11⅞	11⅛	11½	-0.2	11.52	12-22-95	2488
NNY	Nuveen NY Muni Val Fd	NR	NY	MUS	0.096	12-29-95	12-13	0.672	0.04	0.67	⊙6.0	0.672	0.001	12⅛	9¾	11¼	10⅝	11¼	7.6	10.46	12-22-95	11643

Uniform Footnote Explanations-See page 4. Other: [1] In cash or stk. [2] In cash or stk,'94. [3] To be determined. [4] Nuveen CA Mun Val Fund plan acq. [5] Nuveen NY Mun Val Fund plan acq.

Ticker Symbol	Fund	Rating	Exc.	Type	Dividends: Latest Payment Period $	Date	Ex. Div.	So Far 1995 Invest. Income	So Far 1995 Cap. Gain	Ind. Rate	Div. Yld. %	1994 Invest. Income	1994 Cap. Gain	Price Range: 1994 - 1995 High	1994 - 1995 Low	December, 1995 Last Sale or Bid High	Low	Last	Net Assets: % NAV Prem. Disc.	Latest NAV	Latest Date	Com. Shs. 000
NNP	**Nuveen NY Perform Plus Muni**	**NR**	**NY**	**MUS**	0.094	12-29-95	12-13	1.126	....	1.13	6.6	1.10	....	18¾	13¼	17½	16¾	17⅛	3.2	16.60	12-22-95	14097
NUN	**Nuveen NY Qual Income Muni**	**NR**	**NY**	**MUS**	0.098	12-29-95	12-13	0.936	0.02	0.94	⊙6.1	†0.947	0.015	16¼	11⅛	15⅝	14⅝	15½	-1.3	15.70	12-22-95	23388
NVN	**Nuveen NY Select Qual Muni**	**NR**	**NY**	**MUS**	0.109	12-29-95	12-13	1.007	0.025	1.01	⊙6.2	†1.039	....	17	12⅜	16⅝	15¾	16⅜	1.0	16.22	12-22-95	22347
NNC	**Nuveen NC Prem Inc Muni**	**NR**	**NY**	**MUS**	0.058	12-29-95	12-13	0.695	....	0.69	5.9	0.732	....	15¾	10⅜	12½	11⅝	11¾	-13.4	13.57	12-22-95	5887
NUO	**Nuveen OH Qual Income Muni**	**NR**	**NY**	**MUS**	0.08	12-29-95	12-13	0.935	....	0.96	6.2	†0.999	....	16⅞	12	16½	15⅜	15½	-4.3	16.19	12-22-95	10044
NQP	**Nuveen PA Inv Qual Muni**	**NR**	**NY**	**MUS**	0.119	12-29-95	12-13	1.056	0.031	1.06	⊙6.2	†1.108	....	18¾	13⅜	17⅛	16½	17⅛	5.5	16.23	12-22-95	15502
NPY	**Nuveen PA Prem Inc Muni 2**	**NR**	**NY**	**MUS**	0.066	12-29-95	12-13	0.802	....	0.79	6.4	†0.802	....	15½	9⅝	12¾	12	12⅜	-12.2	14.09	12-22-95	15747
NPP	**Nuveen Perform Plus Muni**	**NR**	**NY**	**MU**	0.09	12-29-95	12-13	1.08	....	1.08	6.9	†1.096	....	17	12¼	16⅛	15¼	15⅝	2.2	15.29	12-22-95	58392
NPI	**Nuveen Prem Income Muni**	**NR**	**NY**	**MU**	0.133	12-29-95	12-13	1.04	0.05	1.00	⊙7.0	1.127	....	18⅛	12	14¾	14	14⅜	-5.7	15.24	12-22-95	52947
NPM	**Nuveen Prem Income Muni 2**	**NR**	**NY**	**MU**	0.077	12-29-95	12-13	0.918	....	0.92	6.7	†0.942	....	15⅛	10⅜	14⅛	13⅜	13¾	-10.0	15.27	12-22-95	40731
NPT	**Nuveen Prem Income Muni 4**	**NR**	**NY**	**MU**	0.068	12-29-95	12-13	0.832	....	0.82	6.6	0.841	....	15⅛	9¾	12¾	12	12⅜	-12.9	14.20	12-22-95	40808
NIF	**Nuveen Prem Insured Muni Inc**	**NR**	**NY**	**MU**	0.078	12-29-95	12-13	0.936	....	0.94	6.4	†0.952	....	16⅛	11⅝	14⅞	14½	14⅝	-7.7	15.84	12-22-95	19123
NPF	**Nuveen Prem Muni Income**	**NR**	**NY**	**MU**	0.145	12-29-95	12-13	1.01	0.06	1.01	⊙6.7	†1.022	0.056	16	11⅞	15¼	14⅜	15⅛	-2.4	15.50	12-22-95	19647
NQU	**Nuveen Qual Income Muni Fd**	**NR**	**NY**	**MUS**	0.086	12-29-95	12-13	1.028	....	1.03	6.9	†1.082	....	16¾	12	15¼	14⅞	15	-4.1	15.64	12-22-95	53019
NIM	**Nuveen Select Maturities Muni**	**NR**	**NY**	**MU**	0.097	12-29-95	12-13	0.594	0.043	0.65	⊙5.7	0.648	0.022	12¾	9¾	11⅞	10⅞	11½	-3.3	11.89	12-22-95	12365
NQS	**Nuveen Select Qual Muni**	**NR**	**NY**	**MU**	0.085	12-29-95	12-13	1.035	....	1.01	6.9	1.081	....	16⅞	12	15⅛	14½	14⅝	-4.9	15.44	12-22-95	33067
NXP	**Nuveen Select Tax-Free Inc**	**NR**	**NY**	**MU**	0.077	12-29-95	12-13	0.943	....	0.92	6.0	0.948	0.044	16¼	12⅞	15¼	14⅞	15¼	-0.7	15.36	12-22-95	16378
NXQ	**Nuveen Select Tax-Free Inc 2**	**NR**	**NY**	**MU**	0.076	12-29-95	12-13	0.907	....	0.91	6.0	0.907	....	16	12	15⅛	14¾	15⅛	-0.4	15.19	12-22-95	17607
NXR	**Nuveen Select Tax-Free Inc 3**	**NR**	**NY**	**MU**	0.07	12-29-95	12-13	0.84	....	0.84	6.2	0.84	....	15	11⅜	14	13½	13⅝	-6.2	14.53	12-22-95	12964
NTX	**Nuveen TX Qual Income Muni**	**NR**	**NY**	**MUS**	0.117	12-29-95	12-13	0.96	0.037	0.96	⊙6.6	†1.025	....	16¼	11⅜	15⅜	14¼	14½	-6.8	15.55	12-22-95	9386
NPV	**Nuveen VA Prem Inc Muni Fd**	**NR**	**NY**	**MUS**	0.065	12-29-95	12-13	0.78	....	0.78	5.9	†0.81	....	15⅞	10⅛	13½	12¾	13¼	-6.1	14.11	12-22-95	8099
NPW	**Nuveen WA Prem Inc Muni Fd**	**NR**	**AS**	**MUS**	0.062	12-29-95	12-13	0.747	....	0.74	6.1	0.769	....	16⅛	9¾	12⅜	11⅞	12⅛	-14.8	14.23	12-22-95	2317
OGT	**Oppenheimer Multi-Gvt Tr**	**NR**	**NY**	**GVT**	0.056	12-22-95	12-6	0.684	....	0.67	9.9	0.681	....	9⅛	6⅝	7¼	6¾	6¾	-15.1	7.95	12-22-95	6616
OMS	**Oppenheimer Multi-Sector[1]**	**NR**	**NY**	**BD**	0.078	12-22-95	12-6	0.936	....	0.94	9.9	0.961	....	11⅜	8¾	10	9¼	9½	-6.7	10.18	12-22-95	29065
PAI	**Pacific Am'n Inc Shrs**	**NR**	**NY**	**ICA**	Q0.30	12-15-95	11-21	1.20	....	1.20	7.9	1.20	0.08	16⅞	12¾	15¼	14⅝	15¼	-5.6	16.16	12-22-95	9319
PKF	**Pakistan Investment Fd**	**NR**	**NY**	**GEC**	0.005	7-17-95	7-3	0.029	0.002	0.03	0.6	....	....	16¼	8½	5⅝	5	5¼	-17.1	6.33	12-22-95	11605
PEO	**Petroleum & Resources**	**NR**	**NY**	**ICA**	[2]1.49	12-27-95	11-16	[2]0.91	1.18	0.91	⊙©3.2	[3]0.92	1.18	30⅝	24⅝	28⅞	27⅜	28¼	-9.2	31.11	12-21-95	12380
PPR	**Pilgrim Prime Rate Trust**	**NR**	**NY**	**BD**	0.071	1-15-96	12-27	0.857	....	0.85	9.2	0.69	....	10	8⅞	9¾	9	9¼	-3.9	9.63	12-22-95	89794
PBS	**Pilgrim Regl Bk Shr**	**NR**	**NY**	**CA**	0.53	1-15-96	12-27	0.215	0.461	0.34	⊙2.6	[4]0.322	0.651	14	8¾	13	12½	12⅞	-14.6	15.08	12-22-95	14141
PCM	**PIMCO Comml Mtg Sec Tr**	**NR**	**NY**	**ICA**	0.094	1-11-96	12-27	1.312	....	1.13	9.0	1.094	....	15⅛	10¾	12½	12⅛	12½	-9.6	13.82	12-21-95	11007
MUO	**Pioneer Interest Shs**	**NR**	**NY**	**BD**	0.28	12-29-95	12-12	1.08	....	1.12	8.3	1.13	....	15⅞	11¼	13¾	13	13½	-0.4	13.55	12-22-95	7290
PGF	**Portugal Fund**	**NR**	**NY**	**GEC**	0.18	1-12-96	12-27	0.05	....	0.18	1.6	0.01	....	17⅛	7¾	12⅛	11	11⅛	-16.3	13.29	12-22-95	5299
PFD	**Preferred Income Fund**	**NR**	**NY**	**P**	0.087	12-29-95	12-19	1.132	....	1.04	7.7	1.428	0.832	19⅞	12½	14⅜	13¼	13½	-12.6	15.44	12-22-95	9624
PFM	**Preferred Income Mgmt Fund**	**NR**	**NY**	**P**	0.082	12-29-95	12-19	1.075	....	0.98	7.9	1.13	....	15⅛	10¾	13¼	12⅛	12⅜	-12.6	14.16	12-22-95	9417
PFO	**Preferred Income Oppt Fd**	**NR**	**NY**	**P**	0.07	12-29-95	12-19	0.903	....	0.83	8.0	1.124	0.17	14	9½	11¼	10¼	10⅜	-13.7	12.02	12-22-95	11130
PHY	**Prospect Street Hi Income**	**NR**	**NY**	**BD**	0.035	12-29-95	12-20	0.42	....	0.42	10.8	0.435	....	4⅝	3¼	4	3⅞	3⅞	5.6	3.67	12-22-95	24965
PCA	**Putnam Cal Inv Grade Muni**	**NR**	**AS**	**MUS**	0.078	1-2-96	12-18	0.93	0.162	0.93	⊙6.4	0.93	0.18	16⅛	11½	14⅞	14¼	14⅝	-4.2	15.26	12-22-95	4607
PCV	**Putnam Cv Opp Inc Tr**	**NR**	**NY**	**CA**	†0.538	1-2-96	12-18	0.408	....	....	....	....	....	....	....	22½	21⅞	22	-13.9	25.56	12-22-95	3704
PDI	**Putnam Dividend Income**	**NR**	**NY**	**P**	0.06	1-2-96	12-18	0.735	0.26	0.72	⊙7.7	†0.994	0.383	12⅞	8½	9¾	9¼	9⅜	-12.3	10.69	12-22-95	10821
PCF	**Putnam Hi Income Cv/Bd Fd**	**NR**	**NY**	**CV**	0.071	1-2-96	12-18	0.852	....	0.85	8.6	†0.871	....	10¼	8	10¼	9¾	9⅞	4.9	9.41	12-22-95	13159
PYM	**Putnam Hi Yield Muni**	**NR**	**NY**	**MU**	0.058	1-2-96	12-18	0.735	....	0.69	7.0	0.75	....	11⅜	8	9⅞	9½	9⅞	6.1	9.31	12-22-95	21199
PGT	**Putnam Interm Gvt Income[5]**	**NR**	**NY**	**ICF**	0.05	1-2-96	12-18	0.60	....	0.60	7.9	0.591	0.112	9⅜	6½	7¾	7½	7⅝	-12.6	8.72	12-22-95	65098
PGM	**Putnam Inv Grade Muni Tr**	**NR**	**NY**	**MU**	0.08	1-2-96	12-18	0.96	....	0.96	7.0	0.96	0.24	15	11⅛	13⅞	13⅜	13⅝	2.1	13.35	12-22-95	20039
PMG	**Putnam Inv Grade Muni Tr II**	**NR**	**NY**	**MU**	0.08	1-2-96	12-18	0.96	0.204	0.96	⊙6.9	0.96	0.077	15½	11	14¼	13¾	14	-3.4	14.49	12-22-95	13357
PML	**Putnam Inv Grade Muni Tr III**	**NR**	**AS**	**MU**	0.067	1-2-96	12-18	0.80	....	0.80	6.7	0.734	....	15	9⅝	11⅞	11½	11⅞	-11.8	13.47	12-22-95	11092
PTM	**Putnam Managed Hi Yield Tr**	**NR**	**NY**	**BD**	0.11	1-2-96	12-18	1.32	....	1.32	9.7	†1.472	....	15⅛	11¼	13⅞	13⅝	13⅝	1.5	13.42	12-22-95	7507

Uniform Footnote Explanations-See page 4. Other: [1] Shrs Beneficial Int. [2] In cash or stk'95. [3] Incl $1.50 in cash or stk,'94. [4] Incl $0.054 return of cap,'94. [5] Plan change to open end Inv co.

Ticker Symbol	Fund	Rating	Exc.	Type	Dividends: Latest Payment Period $	Date	Ex. Div.	So Far 1995 Invest. Income	So Far 1995 Cap. Gain	Ind. Rate	Div. Yld. %	1994 Invest. Income	1994 Cap. Gain	Price Range 1994 - 1995 High	1994 - 1995 Low	December, 1995 Last Sale or Bid High	Low	Last	Net Assets % NAV Prem. Disc.	Latest NAV	Latest Date	Com. Shs. 000
PMM	**Putnam Managed Muni Income**	**NR**	**NY**	**MU**	0.064	1-2-96	12-18	0.762	....	0.76	7.0	0.762	0.093	11⅝	8¾	11	10¾	10⅞	6.3	10.23	12-22-95	44450
PMT	**Putnam Master Income Tr**	**NR**	**NY**	**ICF**	0.058	1-2-96	12-18	0.69	....	0.69	8.6	0.745	0.096	9½	7	8⅜	7⅞	8	-12.8	9.17	12-22-95	53376
PIM	**Putnam Master Interm Income[1]**	**NR**	**NY**	**BD**	0.052	1-2-96	12-18	0.624	....	0.62	8.3	0.684	....	9¼	6⅝	7⅞	7⅜	7½	-12.2	8.54	12-22-95	39005
PMO	**Putnam Muni Opport Tr**	**NR**	**NY**	**MU**	0.083	1-2-96	12-18	0.99	0.123	0.99	⊙7.4	0.965	0.048	15¼	10⅛	13¾	13⅛	13⅜	-4.5	14.01	12-22-95	15007
PMN	**Putnam NY Inv Grade Muni**	**NR**	**AS**	**MUS**	0.068	1-2-96	12-18	0.93	0.089	0.81	⊙6.2	0.93	0.154	15½	10⅞	14¼	13	13	-8.0	14.13	12-22-95	2847
PPT	**Putnam Premier Income Tr**	**NR**	**NY**	**BD**	0.055	1-2-96	12-18	0.66	....	0.66	8.7	0.715	....	8¾	6¾	7⅞	7⅛	7⅝	-11.8	8.65	12-22-95	14071
PMH	**Putnam Tax-Free Hlth Care Fd**	**NR**	**NY**	**MU**	0.075	1-2-96	12-18	0.985	0.138	0.90	⊙7.1	1.013	0.185	15⅝	11½	13	12½	12⅝	-12.0	14.34	12-22-95	13807
KFV	**Quest For Value Dual Fd**	**NR**	**NY**	**CA**	©†0.19	1-12-96	12-27	....	0.353	Nil	⊙e....	....	0.285	26⅝	21⅜	32⅞	31¼	31⅞	-7.9	34.61	12-22-95	18004
RCS	**RCM Strategic Global Gvt Fund**	**NR**	**NY**	**GB**	0.074	1-25-96	1-9	0.894	....	0.89	8.9	†0.672	....	12½	9⅛	10¼	9⅞	10	-13.5	11.56	12-22-95	30516
ROC	**R.O.C. Taiwan Fund SBI**	**NR**	**NY**	**GEC**	0.39	1-15-96	12-27	....	....	0.39	3.7	0.15	....	15	7⅞	10⅝	9⅛	10½	15.6	9.08	12-22-95	35118
RVT	**Royce Value Trust**	**NR**	**NY**	**CA**	[2]1.29	12-26-95	12-5	[2]0.03	1.26	0.03	⊙0.3	[3]0.10	2.10	14¼	10⅞	13½	11⅞	11⅞	-12.6	13.58	12-15-95	23114
SBF	**Salomon Bros Fund**	**NR**	**NY**	**CA**	©1.45	12-29-95	12-20	0.39	1.45	0.36	⊙2.7	[4]0.335	1.39	14⅜	10½	14⅛	12¼	13⅜	-11.8	15.16	12-22-95	79031
HIF	**Salomon Bros High Income Fd**	**NR**	**NY**	**ICF**	†0.155	12-29-95	12-14	1.529	0.068	1.50	⊙e10.6	1.385	0.385	16¾	12⅞	14½	14	14⅛	5.3	13.41	12-22-95	4650
SBG	**Salomon Bros 2008 WW Dlr Gvt**	**NR**	**NY**	**GVT**	0.073	12-29-95	12-14	0.876	....	0.88	11.2	0.866	0.01	10⅛	6⅜	8¼	7¾	7⅞	-5.6	8.34	12-22-95	34511
SBW	**Salomon Bros W W Income Fd**	**NR**	**NY**	**C**	0.119	11-30-95	11-9	1.306	....	1.43	12.7	1.188	....	15⅛	9¼	11⅝	10⅞	11¼	-1.9	11.47	12-22-95	12567
SHF	**Schroder Asian Growth Fd**	**NR**	**NY**	**GEA**	Plan annual div			....	....	....	....	....	....	16⅛	9⅝	12⅜	10⅝	12	-6.8	12.88	12-22-95	19607
SAF	**Scudder New Asia Fd**	**NR**	**NY**	**GEA**	©0.81	1-16-96	12-27	4.22	0.86	0.23	⊙1.6	0.48	....	28⅝	14¼	15⅝	14⅛	14½	-9.2	15.97	12-22-95	8423
NEF	**Scudder New Europe Fund**	**NR**	**NY**	**GE**	0.05	1-16-96	12-27	....	....	Nil	....	....	....	12⅝	7½	11½	11	11¼	-13.6	13.02	12-22-95	16045
SWI	**Scudder World Inc Oppt Fd**	**NR**	**NY**	**GE**	†0.39	1-16-96	12-27	†1.677	0.321	1.36	e11.3	0.64	....	15	11⅝	12⅞	11¾	12	-13.7	13.90	12-22-95	3407
SQF	**Seligman Quality Muni Fd**	**NR**	**NY**	**MU**	0.181	12-27-95	12-13	0.938	0.103	0.94	⊙6.7	0.938	0.067	15⅞	10⅝	14¾	13⅞	14⅛	-8.9	15.50	12-22-95	4644
SEL	**Seligman Select Muni Fund**	**NR**	**NY**	**MU**	0.166	12-27-95	12-13	0.84	0.096	0.84	⊙6.7	0.84	0.027	13⅞	9¾	12⅞	12⅛	12½	0.6	12.42	12-22-95	13007
ARK	**Senior High Income Portfolio**	**NR**	**NY**	**BD**	0.079	1-12-96	12-27	0.91	0.07	0.94	⊙10.3	0.865	0.018	10¼	7⅝	9¼	8¾	9⅛	0.3	9.10	12-22-95	25388
SAL	**Senior High Inc Portfolio II**	**NR**	**NY**	**BD**	0.131	1-12-96	12-27	0.91	....	1.58	17.8	0.857	....	10	7⅞	9¼	8⅝	8⅞	-3.5	9.20	12-22-95	16611
SSN	**Senior Strategic Income Fd**	**NR**	**NY**	**C**	0.104	1-12-96	12-27	0.94	0.018	1.25	⊙14.1	0.55	....	9⅞	7¾	9⅜	8⅝	8⅞	-3.6	9.21	12-22-95	7740
SGF	**Singapore Fund**	**NR**	**NY**	**GEC**	[5]0.968	12-28-95	12-14	[5]0.296	0.672	0.30	⊙2.2	0.559	2.333	25½	10	14	12½	13⅜	2.3	13.08	12-21-95	6819
SBI	**Smith Barney Inter Muni Fd**	**NR**	**AS**	**MU**	0.05	3-29-96	3-22	0.60	....	0.60	5.8	0.60	....	11⅝	8½	10⅜	10	10⅜	-2.3	10.62	12-22-95	8289
SBT	**Smith Barney Muni Fund**	**NR**	**AS**	**MU**	0.071	3-29-96	3-22	0.852	....	0.85	6.2	0.781	....	15¾	12¼	14⅜	13¾	13¾	-12.4	15.69	12-22-95	4021
SOR	**Source Capital[6]**	**NR**	**NY**	**CA**	Q0.90	12-15-95	11-21	3.60	....	3.60	8.6	3.60	....	49⅛	36¾	42	39⅞	41⅞	-0.5	42.07	12-22-95	7145
SOA	**Southern Africa Fund**	**NR**	**NY**	**GEC**	©0.91	1-13-96	12-27	0.515	0.77	0.59	⊙3.6	....	....	15¼	10¾	18	16⅛	16⅜	-27.6	22.62	12-22-95	6007
SNF	**Spain Fund**	**NR**	**NY**	**GEC**	0.03	1-12-96	12-27	....	....	Nil	....	0.46	....	12¾	7¾	8⅝	8⅜	8⅝	-19.3	10.69	12-22-95	10027
SPR	**Sterling Capital**	**NR**	**AS**	**CA**	0.65	1-18-96	12-21	0.108	....	0.68	10.6	0.75	....	8⅝	4⅞	7⅛	6⅛	6⅜	-6.3	6.87	12-31-94	2500
SGL	**Strategic Global Income Fd**	**NR**	**NY**	**ICF**	0.095	11-30-95	11-21	0.87	....	1.14	10.0	[7]0.984	0.041	14⅝	10⅜	11⅞	11⅛	11⅜	-15.7	13.49	12-22-95	21407
SUA	**Summit Tax Exempt Bond[8]**	**NR**	**AS**	**MU**	Q0.21	2-15-96	12-27	0.84	....	0.84	8.7	0.84	....	14¼	8¼	10	9⅜	9⅝	-38.9	15.74	9-30-95	7906
SWZ	**Swiss Helvetia Fund**	**NR**	**NY**	**GEC**	0.59	12-29-95	12-20	0.378	0.273	0.38	⊙1.8	[3]0.27	0.99	24	13⅝	21½	20½	21¼	-12.5	24.29	12-22-95	12262
TYW	**Taiwan Equity Fd**	**NR**	**NY**	**GEC**	0.306	1-19-95	1-12	0.306	....	Nil	....	....	....	15¼	11½	10¾	9½	10⅝	12.3	9.46	12-21-95	4507
TWN	**Taiwan Fund**	**NR**	**NY**	**GEC**	©6.09	1-30-95	1-31	....	6.09	0.02	⊙0.1	0.15	....	39¾	17⅛	21⅜	19⅝	20½	9.7	18.68	12-21-95	14826
MCF	**Taurus MuniCalif Hldgs**	**NR**	**NY**	**MUS**	0.055	12-28-95	12-20	0.651	....	0.66	6.5	0.708	....	13½	7⅞	10½	9⅞	10⅛	-13.9	11.76	12-22-95	5176
MNY	**Taurus MuniNewYork Hldgs**	**NR**	**NY**	**MUS**	0.141	12-28-95	12-20	0.704	0.084	0.68	⊙6.3	0.763	0.051	15⅞	9	11⅜	10⅝	10⅞	-11.0	12.22	12-22-95	6715
CVT	**TCW Conv Sec Fund**	**NR**	**NY**	**ICA**	Q0.21	1-12-96	12-27	0.84	....	0.84	9.0	†0.961	0.249	10¾	7¾	9½	9	9⅜	9.9	8.53	12-22-95	31400
EMO	**TCW/DW Emerg Mkt Opp Tr**	**NR**	**NY**	**GE**	0.02	1-26-96	12-27	0.088	0.012	0.02	⊙0.2	....	....	15⅜	10⅛	10⅜	9⅜	10⅛	-15.8	12.02	12-22-95	22758
TDT	**TCW/DW Term Trust 2000**	**AAAf**	**NY**	**GVT**	0.038	1-26-96	12-27	0.438	....	0.45	5.8	0.64	....	10½	7⅛	8	7⅝	7¾	-13.9	9.00	12-22-95	56511
TRM	**TCW/DW Term Trust 2002**	**AAAf**	**NY**	**BD**	0.048	1-26-96	12-27	†0.607	0.009	0.57	e⊙7.1	0.84	....	10½	7⅛	8¼	8	8	-15.9	9.51	12-22-95	50011
TMT	**TCW/DW Term Trust 2003**	**AAAf**	**NY**	**BD**	0.045	1-26-96	12-27	0.55	....	0.54	7.1	0.72	....	10⅜	6	8	7½	7⅝	-17.8	9.28	12-22-95	11083
TCH	**Templeton China World Fd**	**NR**	**NY**	**GEC**	0.085	1-11-96	12-27	0.335	0.015	0.33	⊙3.1	0.16	1.065	20⅜	9⅞	10¾	10⅛	10⅝	-9.7	11.77	12-21-95	20384
TDF	**Templeton Dragon Fd**	**NR**	**NY**	**GEA**	0.395	1-11-96	12-27	0.22	0.005	0.47	⊙3.5	....	....	15⅛	11	13⅜	12	13⅜	-8.8	14.66	12-22-95	54007
EMF	**Templeton Emerg Mkts**	**NR**	**NY**	**GE**	0.11	1-11-96	12-27	0.235	2.105	0.27	⊙1.5	0.10	3.20	30⅝	14⅜	18⅞	17⅞	18½	24.2	14.90	12-22-95	16184

Uniform Footnote Explanations-See page 4. Other: [1] Prop conversion to open end. [2] In cash or stk,'95. [3] In cash or stk,'94. [4] Incl $1.135 in cash or stk,'94. [5] Approx. [6] Co plan offer for pfd .66 com. [7] Incl $0.1647 non-taxable,'94. [8] L.P.Ben Unit Ctf.

Ticker Symbol	Fund	Rating	Exc.	Type	Dividends: Latest Payment Period $	Date	Ex. Div.	So Far 1995 Invest. Income	So Far 1995 Cap. Gain	Ind. Rate	Div. Yld. %	1994 Invest. Income	1994 Cap. Gain	Price Range 1994 - 1995 High	1994 - 1995 Low	December, 1995 Last Sale or Bid High	Low	Last	Net Assets % NAV Prem. Disc.	Latest NAV	Latest Date	Com. Shs. 000
TEA	**Templeton Emerg Mkts Apprec**	**NR**	**NY**	**GE**	0.72	1-11-96	12-27	0.485	0.175	0.89	⊙6.7	....	....	15¼	12⅛	13¾	12⅛	13⅜	1.9	13.13	12-21-95	4233
TEI	**Templeton Emerg Mkts Income**	**NR**	**NY**	**GE**	Q0.31	1-15-96	12-27	1.24	....	1.30	11.7	1.315	0.045	15⅛	9⅝	11⅞	11	11⅛	-7.9	12.08	12-22-95	47606
TGG	**Templeton Global Gvts**	**NR**	**NY**	**GB**	0.05	1-12-96	12-27	†0.635	....	0.60	e8.1	0.56	0.05	9⅛	6¼	7⅝	7⅛	7⅜	-8.2	8.03	12-22-95	22843
GIM	**Templeton Global Income**	**NR**	**NY**	**ICF**	0.05	12-29-95	12-12	†0.635	....	0.60	e8.6	0.55	0.05	9	6¼	7⅛	6¾	7	-15.5	8.28	12-22-95	12045
TGU	**Templeton Global Utilities**[1]	**NR**	**AS**	**GE**	0.365	1-11-96	12-27	0.48	0.445	0.78	⊙5.9	0.56	1.225	18	12¼	13⅜	12⅝	13⅛	-6.8	14.08	12-22-95	3154
TRF	**Templeton Russia Fund**	**NR**	**NY**	**CA**	Plan semi annual div			....	....	....	....	....	....	....	....	14⅜	12	13¾	13.0	12.17	12-21-95	4607
TVF	**Templeton Vietnam Opport Fd**	**NR**	**NY**	**GEC**	0.375	1-11-96	12-27	0.125	....	0.38	⊙3.4	....	....	15½	11	12	11	11¼	-17.2	13.59	12-22-95	8047
TC	**Thai Capital Fund**	**NR**	**NY**	**GEC**	©0.10	10-6-95	9-18	....	2.002	Nil	⊙....	0.347	0.304	24¼	10⅝	15¾	14⅞	15¾	-10.9	17.68	12-22-95	6172
TTF	**Thai Fund**	**NR**	**NY**	**GEC**	©2.777	1-11-96	12-27	....	3.353	0.11	⊙0.5	0.28	2.051	37¾	18⅛	25⅜	22⅜	22⅜	-19.4	27.75	12-22-95	12152
TAI	**Transamerica Inc Shrs**	**NR**	**NY**	**P**	†0.17	1-15-96	12-27	1.92	....	1.92	⊙e7.8	1.931	0.059	26¾	20½	25¾	24½	24¾	-2.9	25.48	12-22-95	6319
TY	**Tri-Continental**	**NR**	**NY**	**ICA**	[2]©2.01	12-27-95	12-13	0.73	2.01	0.72	⊙3.2	[3]0.79	1.90	26¼	19¾	25	22¼	22⅝	-17.1	27.28	12-22-95	84144
TGB	**Triple A and Gvt Ser'97(New)**	**AAAf**	**AS**	**GVT**	0.042	12-29-95	12-19	0.48	....	0.50	5.0	0.507	....	10⅝	8¼	9⅞	9	9⅞	1.6	9.78	12-21-95	4246
TKF	**Turkish Investment Fund**	**NR**	**NY**	**GEC**	0.12	1-9-96	12-27	....	....	Nil	....	0.116	....	14⅝	5⅛	5⅞	5¼	5⅜	8.1	4.97	12-22-95	7040
TTR	**2002 Target Term Trust**	**AAAf**	**NY**	**ICA**	0.072	12-29-95	12-19	0.893	....	0.86	6.7	0.951	....	15½	10⅜	13	12⅜	12⅞	-10.3	14.35	12-21-95	10757
UKM	**United Kingdom Fund**	**NR**	**NY**	**GEC**	0.32	1-12-96	12-27	0.505	....	0.39	3.2	0.10	....	13⅞	8⅞	13	11⅝	12⅛	-17.9	14.76	12-22-95	4012
PHF	**USF&G Pacholder Fd**	**NR**	**AS**	**BD**	Q0.475	1-5-96	12-27	1.915	....	1.90	10.9	†2.09	0.21	23	16⅜	18	17⅛	17⅜	5.4	16.48	12-21-95	3496
UIF	**USLIFE Income Fund**	**NR**	**NY**	**BD**	Q0.20	12-1-95	11-17	0.80	....	0.80	8.2	0.81	....	11⅛	8⅛	9⅞	9½	9¾	-4.8	10.24	12-22-95	5644
VKA	**Van Kampen Merr Adv Muni**	**NR**	**NY**	**MU**	0.085	12-29-95	12-13	1.02	....	1.02	7.0	1.02	....	16¼	11½	15	14½	14⅝	-8.5	15.99	12-15-95	19107
VKI	**Van Kampen Merr Adv Muni II**	**NR**	**AS**	**MU**	0.065	12-29-95	12-13	0.829	....	0.78	6.9	0.834	....	14⅞	9¼	12	11⅜	11⅜	-16.6	13.64	12-15-95	8168
VAP	**Van Kampen Merr Adv PA Muni**	**NR**	**NY**	**MUS**	0.078	12-29-95	12-13	0.894	....	0.93	6.0	0.876	....	16¼	11⅜	15⅜	14⅝	15⅜	-9.5	16.98	12-15-95	4362
VKC	**Van Kampen Merritt CA Muni**	**NR**	**AS**	**MUS**	0.063	1-15-96	12-27	0.738	0.05	0.75	⊙6.6	0.72	0.006	12	8⅝	11½	11	11⅜	5.5	10.78	12-15-95	3175
VQC	**Van Kampen Merr CA Qual Muni**	**NR**	**NY**	**MUS**	0.088	12-29-95	12-13	1.05	....	1.05	6.8	1.05	0.002	17½	11⅞	16¼	15¼	15⅜	-7.7	16.65	12-15-95	9623
VCV	**Van Kampen Merr CA Val Muni**	**NR**	**NY**	**MUS**	0.06	12-29-95	12-13	0.756	....	0.72	5.9	0.828	....	15	10⅛	12½	12	12¼	-19.2	15.17	12-15-95	6030
VOF	**Van Kampen Merr FL Muni Opp**	**NR**	**AS**	**MUS**	0.061	12-29-95	12-13	0.732	....	0.73	6.1	0.778	....	15	9⅛	12⅝	12	12	-16.4	14.35	12-15-95	1682
VFM	**Van Kampen Merr FL Qual Muni**	**NR**	**NY**	**MUS**	0.088	12-29-95	12-13	1.05	....	1.05	6.2	1.05	0.068	17⅞	13	17⅛	16¾	17	-0.2	17.04	12-15-95	6432
VLT	**Van Kampen Merr Hi Income**	**NR**	**NY**	**BD**	0.08	12-29-95	12-13	0.96	....	0.96	11.0	1.18	....	10¾	7¼	9¼	8⅝	8¾	8.6	8.06	12-15-95	8109
VIM	**Van Kampen Merritt Ins Muni**	**NR**	**NY**	**MU**	0.088	12-29-95	12-13	1.05	....	1.05	6.6	1.05	....	17¾	12⅝	16⅛	15⅝	16	-5.4	16.92	12-15-95	9619
VIT	**Van Kampen Merritt Interm**	**NR**	**NY**	**FT**	0.059	12-29-95	12-13	0.702	....	0.70	11.0	0.954	....	8¾	5¼	6¾	6¼	6⅜	3.7	6.15	12-15-95	13711
VIG	**Van Kampen Merritt Inv Grade**	**NR**	**NY**	**MU**	0.065	1-15-96	12-27	0.818	....	0.78	7.4	0.925	....	14⅛	9¾	11	10½	10½	-37.9	16.90	12-15-95	4839
VIC	**Van Kampen Merr Inv Gr CA Muni**	**NR**	**NY**	**MUS**	0.08	12-29-95	12-13	0.92	....	0.96	6.1	0.924	....	16½	11¼	15¾	14⅞	15⅝	-7.6	16.91	12-15-95	4619
VTF	**Van Kampen Merr Inv Gr FL Muni**	**NR**	**NY**	**MUS**	0.08	12-29-95	12-13	0.952	....	0.96	6.2	0.936	....	17	11¾	16⅜	15½	15½	-11.7	17.56	12-15-95	4137
VGM	**Van Kampen Merr Inv Gr Muni**	**NR**	**NY**	**MU**	0.095	12-29-95	12-13	1.14	....	1.14	7.2	1.14	....	17¾	12⅞	16	15⅝	15¾	43.6	10.97	12-15-95	27013
VTJ	**Van Kampen Merr Inv Gr NJ Muni**	**NR**	**NY**	**MUS**	0.077	12-29-95	12-13	0.924	....	0.92	5.9	0.924	....	17⅛	11¾	15⅝	15	15½	-10.6	17.34	12-15-95	3925
VTN	**Van Kampen Merr Inv Gr NY Muni**	**NR**	**NY**	**MUS**	0.075	12-29-95	12-13	0.98	....	0.90	6.2	1.02	0.013	17¼	11⅞	15¼	14⅜	14½	-13.8	16.83	12-15-95	6201
VTP	**Van Kampen Merr Inv Gr PA Muni**	**NR**	**NY**	**MUS**	0.083	12-29-95	12-13	0.996	....	1.00	6.6	0.996	....	17⅜	12	15¾	14⅞	15¼	-11.5	17.23	12-15-95	7421
VMV	**Van Kampen Merr MA Value Muni**	**NR**	**AS**	**MUS**	0.06	12-29-95	12-13	0.756	....	0.72	5.9	0.828	....	15⅝	10½	12⅝	12	12⅛	-16.8	14.57	12-15-95	2655
VMT	**Van Kampen Merr Muni Income**	**NR**	**NY**	**MU**	0.065	12-29-95	12-13	0.82	....	0.78	7.4	0.84	....	12⅞	9	10⅝	10⅜	10½	3.8	10.12	12-15-95	27776
VMO	**Van Kampen Merr Muni Opp**	**NR**	**NY**	**MU**	0.075	12-29-95	12-13	0.998	....	0.90	6.7	1.02	....	16¾	11¾	14⅛	13½	13½	-17.3	16.32	12-15-95	15353
VOT	**Van Kampen Merr Muni Opp II**	**NR**	**NY**	**MU**	0.063	12-29-95	12-13	0.78	....	0.75	6.5	0.89	....	15	9⅜	12	11½	11½	-18.1	14.05	12-15-95	11681
VKQ	**Van Kampen Merr Muni Trust**	**NR**	**NY**	**MU**	0.085	12-29-95	12-13	1.052	....	1.02	7.2	1.116	....	17	12⅛	15	14⅛	14⅛	-13.4	16.32	12-15-95	36270
VJV	**Van Kampen Merr NJ Value Muni**	**NR**	**AS**	**MUS**	0.058	12-29-95	12-13	0.728	....	0.70	5.9	0.774	....	15	9⅜	12½	11¾	11⅞	-18.2	14.51	12-15-95	2500
VNM	**Van Kampen Merr NY Qual Muni**	**NR**	**NY**	**MU**	0.088	12-29-95	12-13	1.05	....	1.05	6.5	1.05	0.216	18⅛	12¾	17	16	16¼	-4.2	16.97	12-15-95	5643
VNV	**Van Kampen Merr NY Val Muni**	**NR**	**NY**	**MUS**	0.055	12-29-95	12-13	0.70	....	0.66	5.6	0.826	....	15¼	9⅝	12⅛	11⅝	11¾	-19.4	14.57	12-15-95	4291
VOQ	**Van Kampen Merr OH Qual Muni**	**NR**	**NY**	**MUS**	0.084	12-29-95	12-13	1.00	....	1.01	6.1	0.984	....	17¾	13⅞	17	16⅛	16½	-3.3	17.06	12-15-95	4188
VOV	**Van Kampen Merr OH Value Muni**	**NR**	**AS**	**MUS**	0.055	12-29-95	12-13	0.696	....	0.66	5.6	0.768	....	15¼	10	12⅜	11⅞	11⅞	-18.4	14.55	12-15-95	1681
VPQ	**Van Kampen Merr PA Qual Muni**	**NR**	**NY**	**MUS**	0.091	12-29-95	12-13	1.092	....	1.09	6.4	1.092	0.002	18½	13⅜	17½	16¾	17⅛	0.2	17.09	12-15-95	8061

Uniform Footnote Explanations-See page 4. Other: [1] Propose convert to open-end fund. [2] In cash or stk,'95. [3] Incl $1.90 in cash or stk,'94.

Ticker Symbol	Fund	Rating	Exc.	Type	Dividends: Latest Payment Period $	Date	Ex. Div.	So Far 1995 Invest. Income	So Far 1995 Cap. Gain	Ind. Rate	Div. Yld. %	1994 Invest. Income	1994 Cap. Gain	Price Range 1994 - 1995 High	1994 - 1995 Low	December, 1995 Last Sale or Bid High	Low	Last	Net Assets % NAV Prem. Disc.	Latest NAV	Latest Date	Com. Shs. 000
VPV	**Van Kampen Merr PA Val Muni**	**NR**	**NY**	**MUS**	0.063	12-29-95	12-13	0.806	....	0.75	6.1	0.822	....	15¼	10¼	13	12⅜	12⅜	-16.9	14.90	12-15-95	4469
VKL	**Van Kampen Merr Sel Sec Muni**	**NR**	**AS**	**MU**	0.058	12-29-95	12-13	0.754	....	0.69	6.3	0.759	....	15⅛	9	11⅛	10¾	11	-16.4	13.16	12-22-95	10807
VKS	**Van Kampen Merr Strat Sec Muni**	**NR**	**NY**	**MU**	0.068	12-29-95	12-13	0.853	....	0.81	6.8	0.938	....	15⅛	9⅞	12⅜	11¾	12	-14.2	13.99	12-15-95	10807
VKV	**Van Kampen Merr Value Muni**	**NR**	**NY**	**MU**	0.071	12-29-95	12-13	0.907	....	0.85	6.8	0.912	....	15⅜	10¼	12⅞	12⅜	12½	-14.9	14.69	12-15-95	23555
VES	**Vestaur Securities**	**NR**	**NY**	**BD**	†0.33	1-18-96	12-27	1.08	0.051	1.08	⊙8.0	1.10	0.156	15⅞	11½	14	13⅜	13½	-11.4	15.23	12-21-95	6652
VAZ	**Voyageur Arizona Muni Income**	**NR**	**AS**	**MUS**	0.061	12-29-95	12-15	0.739	....	0.73	5.9	0.794	0.047	15⅝	10	12¾	12⅛	12⅜	-14.2	14.42	12-22-95	2982
VCF	**Voyageur CO Ins Muni Income**	**NR**	**AS**	**MUS**	0.058	12-29-95	12-15	0.711	....	0.70	5.8	0.766	0.027	15¾	9⅞	12¾	12⅛	12⅛	-15.0	14.27	12-22-95	4837
VFL	**Voyageur FL Insured Muni Inc**	**NR**	**AS**	**MUS**	0.06	12-29-95	12-15	0.731	....	0.72	5.9	0.784	....	15½	9⅞	12¾	12	12⅛	-16.5	14.52	12-22-95	2422
VMN	**Voyageur Minn Muni Income**	**NR**	**AS**	**MUS**	0.078	12-29-95	12-15	0.93	....	0.93	6.4	0.93	0.024	17	12	14⅞	14¼	14⅝	-2.9	15.06	12-22-95	2595
VMM	**Voyageur Minn Muni Income II**	**NR**	**AS**	**MUS**	0.066	12-29-95	12-15	0.803	....	0.80	6.3	0.825	....	15⅝	9¾	13	12⅜	12¾	-10.0	14.16	12-22-95	7252
VYM	**Voyageur Minn Muni Income III**	**NR**	**AS**	**MUS**	0.06	12-29-95	12-15	0.72	....	0.72	6.1	0.732	....	15⅛	8⅝	12⅛	11⅛	11¾	-10.4	13.11	12-22-95	1837
WDV	**Worldwide Dollarvest Fund**	**NR**	**NY**	**GB**	M0.213	1-12-96	12-27	1.259	....	2.56	21.8	0.966	....	15⅛	9½	12⅛	10⅞	11¾	-9.3	12.95	12-22-95	6393
VLU	**Worldwide Value Fund**	**NR**	**NY**	**GE**	0.06	1-15-96	12-27	....	....	Nil	....	0.10	....	18½	11¾	17	16¼	16⅞	-19.2	20.88	12-22-95	3005
ZSEV	**Z Seven Fund**	**NR**	**NNM**	**GE**	[1]3.04	1-10-96	12-27	....	....	[2]....	....	....	....	18¾	15¼	25¾	19½	22¼	11.1	20.03	12-22-95	1516
ZIF	**Zenix Income Fund**	**NR**	**NY**	**BD**	0.06	2-23-96	2-15	0.741	....	0.72	10.9	†0.878	....	8	6	6¾	6⅜	6⅝	5.5	6.28	12-22-95	13279
ZF	**Zweig Fund**	**NR**	**NY**	**CA**	0.28	10-26-95	10-10	1.07	....	[3]1.12	10.0	0.83	0.31	13⅞	10⅛	11½	11	11¼	2.6	10.97	12-22-95	47622
ZTR	**Zweig Total Return Fd**	**NR**	**NY**	**ICA**	0.07	12-26-95	12-7	0.84	....	0.84	9.9	0.835	0.025	10⅞	7¾	8⅞	8½	8½	-0.7	8.56	12-22-95	72936

Uniform Footnote Explanations-See page 4. Other: [1] Approx. [2] To be determined. [3] Rate:2 1/2% of NAV each quarter.

STANDARD & POOR'S

MUTUAL FUND SUMMARY

PERFORMANCE OF THE S&P 500, S&P MIDCAP 400 AND THE SMALLCAP 600

Performance measures of the Standard & Poor's Indices are: S&P 500 with daily reinvestment of dividends; MIDCAP 400 with daily reinvestments (monthly prior to July, 1991); SmallCap 600 with daily reinvestments (monthly prior to January, 1994).

	% Change From Previous Dec. 31 — At Dec. 31					% Change From Previous Dec. 31	Dividends		$10,000 Invested	1995 Range		
	1990	1991	1992	1993	1994	Dec 29 1995	paid 1994	paid 1995	12-31-89 Now Worth	High	Low	Close 12-29-95
S&P 500	–3.1	+30.5	+7.62	+10.08	+1.32	+37.58	13.18	13.79	20,877	622.88	457.20	615.93
MIDCAP 400	–5.1	+50.1	+11.91	+13.96	–3.58	+30.95	3.55	3.60	22,929	220.73	167.93	217.84
SMALLCAP 600	–23.7	+48.5	+21.04	+18.78	–4.77	+29.96	1.06	1.13	20,163	122.69	92.45	121.10

EXPLANATION OF COLUMN HEADINGS AND FOOTNOTES

Fund-Year Formed: Title of fund and year originated or * initially offered to public.

Principal Objective: CA—Capital Appreciation; E—Objectives treated equally; EG—Emerging Growth; G—Growth; I—Income; P—Preservation of Capital; R—Return on Capital; S—Stability; VA—Value Oriented; in order of importance.

Type: B—Balanced; BD—Bond; C—Com; CV—Cv Bond & Pfd; FL—Flexible; GB—Lg term gov't, GNMA, etc; GL—Global (may incl. U.S. secs.); H—Hedge; INTL—Int'l; L—Leverage; P—Pfd; PM—Precious Metals; O—Options; SP—Specialized; TF—Tax Free; ST—Short term invests.

Total Net Assets: Total assets at market value less current liabilities (includes cash/equiv.).

Cash & Equivalent: Cash and receivables plus U.S. Govt securs., short term commercial paper and short-term municipal and corporate bonds and notes, less current liabilities.

IRA & Keogh: All funds have plans available except where noted as follows: ∫—No IRA plan available †—No Keogh plan available.

Net Assets per share % Change: Represents NAV (net asset value) at end of period plus capital gains and dividends distributed during the period, less NAV at beginning of period; divided by NAV at beginning of period, all on a per share basis & excl. sales charge.

Minimum Unit: Minimum initial purchase of shares (exclusive of contractual plans); usually lower for retirement plans.

Maximum Sales Charge %: A charge, covering costs and commissions added to net asset value in computing the offering price. Represents a percentage of the offering price (E.R.F.—Early Redemption Fee).

Distributions: Dividends from net investment income and distributions from security profits to record holders in year indicated.

$10,000 Invested 12-31-89 Now Worth: Shows the results of a $10,000 investment assuming that all dividends and capital gains are reinvested at year end. Calculations are based on NAV and exclude any sales charge. Mutual funds formed during 1990 are included from the date of formation.

Price Record: Ranges are based on net asset value per share.

% Yield From Investment Income: Dividends from investment income in 1994 divided by current offering price.

§—Fund not presently offered. ★—Rated AAAf by S&P n/a: Not available

#—1995 prices and NAV % change at end of month or latest available.

Ticker Symbol	Fund	Year Offered	Prin. Obj.	Type	Sept. 29, 1995 Total Net Assets (MIL.$)	Sept. 29, 1995 Cash & Equiv (MIL.$)	See Foot-notes	Net Assets per Share % Change from Previous Dec. 31 — At: Dec. 31 1991	1992	1993	1994	Dec. 29, 1995	Min. Unit	Max. Sales Chg. %	Distributions Per Share from Invest. Income 1994	Invest. Income 1995	Security Profits 1994	Security Profits 1995	$10,000 Invested 12-31-89 Now Worth	PRICE RECORD NAV Per Sh — 1995 — High	1995 Low	#12-29-95 NAV Per Shr.	#12-29-95 Offer Price	% Yield From Inv. Inc.
AGNMX	AARP GNMA & U.S.Treasury	*'84	I	GB	5235.8	n/a	....	+ 13.8	+ 6.3	+ 5.8	− 1.6	+ 11.9	$500	None	0.944	0.931	....	...	15,389	15.36	14.53	15.36	15.36	6.1
AGIFX	AARP Growth & Income Fund	*'84	GI	C	3006.3	n/a	....	+ 26.1	+ 9.1	+ 15.6	+ 3.0	+ 31.4	$500	None	0.97	1.10	1.225	0.84	21,051	40.68	31.68	39.77	39.77	2.4
ACRNX	Acorn Fund	'70	G	C	2400.9	180.0	[1]§	+ 47.0	+ 23.9	+ 55.7	− 8.0	+ 21.5	$1,000	None	0.11	0.09	0.56	1.08	26,151	14.69	12.00	13.60	13.60	0.8
ACINX	Acorn International Fund	*'92	G	INTL	1314.2	34.8	....	....	....	+ 49.1	− 3.8	+ 8.9	$1,000	None	....	....	....	0.01	.....	16.71	14.35	16.59	16.59	....
AAGFX	AIM Aggressive Growth Fund	*'84	G	C	2306.0	262.2	....	+ 61.2	+ 21.0	+ 32.0	+ 17.2	+ 41.4	$500	5.5	....	....	....	0.97	39,894	42.39	27.78	39.55	41.85	....
AMBLX	AIM Balanced Fund Cl.A	'78	GI	FL	63.0	n/a	....	+ 42.4	+ 9.4	+ 15.4	− 6.0	+ 33.0	$500	4.75	0.30	0.222	0.222	...	21,599	19.40	14.48	19.22	20.18	1.5
CHTRX	AIM Charter Fund	'67	GI	C	1975.0	n/a	....	+ 37.3	+ 1.1	+ 9.3	− 4.3	+ 35.3	$500	5.5	0.20	0.16	0.325	0.901	21,236	11.02	8.10	9.95	10.53	1.9
CSTGX	AIM Constellation Fund	'66	G	C	6999.0	390.5	....	+ 70.2	+ 15.0	+ 17.3	+ 1.2	+ 35.3	$500	5.5	....	....	0.52	0.752	30,148	24.94	16.81	22.51	23.82	....
AUTLX	AIM Global Utilities Cl.A	*'88	IG	C	159.0	n/a	[2]	+ 22.7	+ 7.3	+ 12.2	− 11.4	+ 26.5	$1,000	5.5	0.63	0.40	....	...	16,026	14.59	11.77	14.59	15.44	4.1
AGOVX	AIM Govt. Securities Cl.A	*'87	IP	GB	162.0	n/a	★	+ 12.4	+ 6.0	+ 7.8	− 3.4	+ 14.5	$500	4.75	0.72	0.59	....	...	15,470	9.70	8.98	9.70	10.18	7.1
AGWFX	AIM Growth Cl.A	*'67	G	C	174.0	n/a	....	+ 35.9	+ 0.1	+ 3.4	− 5.1	+ 34.1	$500	5.5	....	....	0.425	0.793	17,006	14.62	10.18	13.05	13.81	....
AMHYX	AIM High Yield Fund Cl.A	*'78	I	BD	781.0	n/a	[3]	+ 40.1	+ 17.9	+ 17.7	− 1.5	+ 14.4	$500	4.75	0.963	0.79	....	...	20,067	9.48	8.90	9.43	9.90	9.7
AMIFX	AIM Income Cl.A	*'68	I	BD	230.0	n/a	[4]	+ 17.2	+ 7.1	+ 15.1	− 7.5	+ 20.4	$500	4.75	0.60	0.50	0.013	...	16,621	8.17	7.16	8.17	8.58	7.0
AIIEX	AIM Intl. Equity Cl.A	*'92	GP		651.0	n/a	....	....	....	+ 45.8	− 3.4	+ 16.3	$500	5.5	0.042	0.006	0.443	0.375	.....	13.97	11.87	13.72	14.52	0.3
SHTIX	AIM Limited Maturity Treas. Shs.	*'87	I	GB	290.0	n/a	★	+ 10.1	+ 5.5	+ 4.3	+ 1.3	+ 8.2	$500	1.0	0.468	0.491	....	...	14,408	10.09	9.78	10.09	10.19	4.6
AMBDX	AIM Municipal Bond Cl.A	*'77	I	TF	277.0	n/a	[5]∫†	+ 18.3	+ 12.6	+ 11.4	− 3.7	+ 11.8	$500	4.75	0.48	0.386	0.028	...	16,775	8.33	7.77	8.31	8.72	5.5
AVLFX	AIM Value Cl.A	*'84	GI	C	3039.0	n/a	....	+ 42.6	+ 16.0	+ 18.5	+ 3.2	+ 34.7	$500	5.5	0.156	0.089	0.198	1.587	27,766	29.33	20.99	26.81	28.37	0.5
WEINX	AIM Weingarten Cl.A	*'66	G	C	4685.0	n/a		+ 46.7	− 1.4	+ 1.5	− 0.5	+ 34.4	$500	5.5	0.068	....	1.778	2.706	20,713	21.19	15.01	17.73	18.76	0.4
ALSCX	Alger Small Cap.Portfolio	*'86	G	C	498.3	15.0	[6]	+ 54.5	+ 4.0	+ 12.2	− 4.6	+ 48.8	None	ERF	....	....	0.004	0.596	27,307	12.27	7.23	10.53	10.53	....
CABNX	Alliance Balanced Shs:Cl A	'32	RS	B	123.7	n/a		+ 20.2	+ 6.7	+ 9.0	− 5.9	+ 26.6	$250	4.25	0.384	0.405	0.024	1.48	16,271	16.12	12.89	14.44	15.08	2.5
CBFAX	Alliance Bond:Corporate Bond Cl.A	'74	I	BD	241.8	n/a	[7]	+ 17.0	+ 12.6	+ 30.0	− 12.3	+ 24.2	$250	4.25	1.14	0.855	....	...	19,569	13.90	10.96	13.90	14.52	7.9
ABUSX	Alliance Bond:U.S.Govt.Cl.A	*'85	I	GB	450.4	n/a	....	+ 14.8	+ 5.7	+ 9.5	− 4.3	+ 14.0	$250	4.25	0.653	0.466	....	...	15,554	8.11	7.50	8.11	8.47	7.7
ALCPX	Alliance Counterpoint Cl.A	*'85	GI	C	40.8	n/a	....	+ 32.3	+ 4.6	+ 7.2	− 2.6	+ 33.0	$250	4.25	....	....	2.62	2.525	18,257	19.79	14.70	17.09	17.85	....
CHCLX	Alliance Fund:Cl A	'38	G	C	925.2	n/a	....	+ 45.7	+ 5.7	+ 16.5	− 12.6	+ 34.8	$250	4.25	0.014	0.02	1.00	1.065	20,440	7.83	5.61	6.52	6.81	0.2
GSCAX	Alliance Global:Small Cap.Cl.A	'66	G	C	61.7	n/a	....	+ 25.3	− 4.9	+ 20.0	− 5.1	+ 27.0	$250	4.25	....	....	2.113	0.525	12,943	11.09	8.70	10.79	11.27	....
AGBBX	Alliance Growth Fund Cl.B	*'87	G	C	1494.8	n/a	[8]	+ 62.4	+ 9.8	+ 27.7	− 1.9	+ 28.6	$250	ERF	0.01	....	0.41	0.628	26,429	26.19	20.10	25.37	25.37	....
CABDX	Alliance Growth & Income:Cl A	'32	IG	C	464.0	n/a		+ 26.1	+ 4.4	+ 9.7	− 4.2	+ 42.7	$250	4.25	0.053	0.163	0.116	0.207	19,309	2.89	2.12	2.67	2.79	1.9
ALIFX	Alliance International Cl.A	*'81	G	INTL	167.2	n/a	[9]	+ 7.7	− 5.9	+ 27.4	+ 5.5	+ 10.0	$250	4.25	....	....	1.619	1.05	11,852	17.77	15.41	17.04	17.80	....
ALMSX	Alliance Mtge.Secs.Inc.Cl.A	'83	I	GB	511.7	n/a	....	+ 14.6	+ 7.4	+ 9.9	− 6.0	+ 13.1	$250	4.25	0.598	0.443	....	...	15,847	8.75	8.10	8.75	9.14	6.5
ALCAX	Alliance Muni Income:Cal.Cl.A	*'86	I	TF	471.9	n/a	∫†	+ 10.6	+ 9.1	+ 12.6	− 9.9	+ 21.8	$250	4.25	0.594	0.439	....	...	15,969	10.81	9.18	10.79	11.27	5.3
BUICX	Alliance Muni Income:Insur.Cal.Cl.A	*'86	I	TF	102.8	n/a	∫†	+ 10.2	+ 9.3	+ 12.8	− 10.8	+ 22.2	$250	4.25	0.69	0.518	....	...	15,906	13.86	11.68	13.79	14.40	4.8
ALNYX	Alliance Muni Income:N.Y.Cl.A	*'86	I	TF	182.1	n/a	∫†	+ 11.9	+ 10.3	+ 12.5	− 9.9	+ 19.1	$250	4.25	0.556	0.411	....	...	15,779	9.88	8.61	9.87	10.31	5.4
CABTX	Alliance Muni Bond:Insur.Natl.Cl.A	*'77	I	TF	164.1	n/a	∫†	+ 11.8	+ 8.9	+ 12.7	− 9.1	+ 20.5	$250	4.25	0.536	0.396	....	...	16,006	10.40	8.93	10.39	10.85	4.9
ALTHX	Alliance Muni Bond:Natl. Cl.A	*'86	I	TF	334.2	n/a	∫†	+ 11.9	+ 9.7	+ 13.4	− 9.5	+ 20.2	$250	4.25	0.596	0.435	....	...	16,203	10.76	9.26	10.73	11.21	5.3
QUASX	Alliance Quasar Associates Cl.A	'68	G	C	147.9	n/a		+ 34.2	+ 2.8	+ 16.1	− 8.1	+ 46.5	$250	4.25	....	....	3.86	4.81	16,518	25.58	17.65	21.60	22.56	....
ASTTX	Alliance Short-Term Multi Mkt Tr.A	*'89	I	INTL,ST	330.5	n/a	[10]	+ 9.2	+ 0.4	+ 7.6	− 8.2	+ 2.6	$250	4.25	0.631	0.541	....	...	12,400	7.79	7.24	7.49	7.82	8.1
ASCBX	Alliance Short-Term Multi Mkt.Tr.B	*'90	I	INTL,ST	543.4	n/a	[10]	+ 8.5	− 0.4	+ 13.1	− 8.9	+ 2.0	$250	ERF	0.567	0.495	....	...	12,470	7.79	7.25	7.49	7.49	7.6
ALTFX	Alliance Technology Cl.A	'82	G	C	381.0	n/a	....	+ 72.2	+ 9.2	+ 13.1	+ 27.9	+ 45.7	$250	4.25	....	....	3.17	2.382	38,562	49.44	29.34	41.65	43.50	....
	Amer.Funds Group:																							
AMCPX	AMCAP	*'67	G	C	3462.4	563.1	....	+ 36.1	+ 7.0	+ 10.2	− 0.3	+ 18.6	$1,000	5.75	0.13	0.05	0.95	0.17	18,217	14.77	11.64	13.67	14.50	0.9
ABALX	Amer.Balanced	'32	IS	B	2748.2	581.3	....	+ 24.0	+ 9.1	+ 11.0	+ 0.3	+ 26.5	$500	5.75	0.56	0.56	0.05	0.47	18,729	14.74	12.01	14.15	15.01	3.7
AHITX	Amer.High-Income Trust	*'88	I	BD	1111.0	81.8	....	+ 31.0	+ 13.7	+ 16.6	− 4.9	+ 18.6	$1,000	4.75	1.285	1.143	0.075	...	19,608	14.45	12.99	14.43	15.15	8.5
AMRMX	Amer. Mutual	'49	ISG	C	6563.1	1443.9	....	+ 21.0	+ 7.6	+ 14.1	+ 0.2	+ 24.1	$250	5.75	0.84	0.63	0.87	...	18,158	25.54	20.15	24.33	25.81	3.3
ABNDX	Bond Fund of Amer.	*'74	I	BD	5920.8	579.1	....	+ 20.1	+ 10.9	+ 13.7	− 4.9	+ 17.7	$1,000	4.75	1.05	1.05	....	...	17,493	13.88	12.62	13.88	14.57	7.2
CAIBX	Capital Income Builder	*'87	IG	C,BD	4499.1	949.8	....	+ 25.1	+ 9.7	+ 15.0	− 2.4	+ 24.5	$1,000	5.75	1.67	1.75	0.10	0.50	19,867	37.44	31.61	37.23	39.50	4.2
CWBFX	Capital World Bond	*'87	I	BD,GL	652.8	64.0	....	+ 14.6	+ 1.1	+ 16.4	− 1.5	+ 20.9	$1,000	4.75	0.96	1.20	....	...	17,843	17.49	14.99	17.08	17.93	5.4

Uniform Footnote Explanations-See page 234. Stock Splits & Divs. (figures adjusted): [1] 2% redemption under 60 days. 5-for-1 split,Dec.'93.. [2] Was Utilities Fund(5/95). [3] Incl.High Yield Secs.(10/93). Rated Bf. [4] Rated BBBf. [5] Rated Af. [6] 5% E.R.F.reducing 1% per yr.over 6 yrs.. 3-for-1 split, Sept.'95. [7] Was Monthly Inc.Includes Hi Yld.(1/93). [8] 4% E.R.F. reducing 1% per year.. [9] Incls. Global Can. (3/94). [10] Maturities limited to 3 yrs.

Ticker Symbol	Fund	Year Offered	Prin. Obj.	Type	Sept. 29, 1995 Total Net Assets (MIL.$)	Cash & Equiv (MIL.$)	See Foot-notes	Net Assets per Share % Change from Previous Dec. 31 — At: Dec. 31 1991	1992	1993	1994	Dec. 29, 1995	Min. Unit	Max. Sales Chg. %	Distributions Per Share from Invest. Income 1994	Invest. Income 1995	Security Profits 1994	Security Profits 1995	$10,000 Invested 12-31-89 Now Worth	PRICE RECORD NAV Per Sh — 1995 — High	Low	#12-29-95 NAV Per Shr.	Offer Price	% Yield From Inv. Inc.
	Amer.Funds Group:																							
CWGIX	Capital World Growth & Inc.	*'93	GI		3520.4	294.1	....	....	....	....	+ 1.2	+ 21.1	$1,000	5.75	0.52	0.62	0.29	0.27	.....	20.43	17.26	20.26	21.50	2.4
AEPGX	Europacific Growth	*'84	G	INTL	10352.0	1544.7	[1]	+ 18.5	+ 2.3	+ 35.5	+ 1.1	+ 12.8	$250	5.75	0.32	0.49	0.90	0.21	18,732	23.53	20.31	23.13	24.54	1.3
ANCFX	Fundamental Investors	'32	GI	C	4160.8	262.8	....	+ 29.5	+ 9.8	+ 17.6	+ 1.3	+ 33.5	$250	5.75	0.44	0.40	0.45	0.68	21,189	22.72	17.48	22.29	23.65	1.9
AGTHX	Growth Fund of Amer.	'58	G	C	7665.6	1577.1	....	+ 35.1	+ 7.4	+ 14.4	....	+ 29.7	$1,000	5.75	0.17	0.29	1.04	2.27	20,625	33.91	25.39	30.54	32.40	0.5
AMECX	Income Fund Amer.	'70	I	FL	12916.6	985.8	....	+ 23.2	+ 11.8	+ 13.8	− 2.5	+ 28.5	$1,000	5.75	0.83	0.83	0.06	0.18	19,049	16.19	13.15	15.87	16.84	4.9
AIBAX	Intermed.Bond Fund of Amer.	*'88	IP	BD	1501.1	38.1	....	+ 13.6	+ 6.2	+ 9.0	− 2.9	+ 13.5	$1,000	4.75	0.94	0.91	....	...	15,550	13.75	12.89	13.75	14.44	6.5
AIVSX	Investment Co. Amer.	'33	GI	C	24215.4	2490.2	....	+ 26.0	+ 6.9	+ 11.5	+ 0.2	+ 30.3	$250	5.75	0.48	0.50	0.60	0.91	19,726	22.69	17.66	21.61	22.93	2.1
ANEFX	New Economy Fund	*'83	G	C	3370.9	491.0	[2]	+ 28.9	+ 16.6	+ 30.6	− 8.2	+ 24.2	$1,000	5.75	0.17	0.19	0.68	0.69	20,231	17.12	13.60	16.18	17.17	1.0
ANWPX	New Perspective	*'73	G	GL	8817.0	1468.5	....	+ 22.5	+ 4.0	+ 26.7	+ 2.9	+ 20.3	$250	5.75	0.23	0.31	0.84	0.60	19,582	17.26	14.19	16.38	17.38	1.3
SMCWX	SMALLCAP World Fund	*'90	G	C	4625.4	939.7	....	+ 32.9	+ 6.4	+ 29.9	− 3.0	+ 22.3	$1,000	5.75	0.11	0.23	1.35	2.45	21,072	26.36	20.85	23.50	24.93	0.4
AFTEX	Tax-Exempt Fund of Amer.	*'79	I	TF	1442.2	65.2	....	+ 10.4	+ 8.5	+ 11.5	− 4.2	+ 16.9	$1,000	4.75	0.729	0.671	....	0.085	15,750	12.26	11.08	12.23	12.84	5.7
TAFTX	Tax Exempt Fund of Calif.	*'86	I	TF	234.1	6.4	∫†	+ 9.6	+ 8.2	+ 12.6	− 5.0	+ 17.2	$1,000	4.75	0.839	0.863	....	...	15,655	16.28	14.57	16.25	17.06	4.9
TMMDX	Tax Exempt Fund of Maryland	*'86	I	TF	74.8	2.0	∫†	+ 9.5	+ 8.3	+ 10.1	− 4.7	+ 16.1	$1,000	4.75	0.764	0.815	....	...	15,255	15.86	14.31	15.83	16.62	4.6
TFVAX	Tax Exempt Fund of Virginia	*'86	I	TF	92.0	1.5	∫†	+ 10.6	+ 7.9	+ 11.1	− 4.7	+ 15.5	$1,000	4.75	0.808	0.83	....	0.055	15,396	16.26	14.77	16.21	17.02	4.7
AMUSX	U.S.Govt.Securities	*'85	I,P	GB	1346.8	241.0	....	+ 13.4	+ 7.2	+ 10.2	− 4.6	+ 14.9	$1,000	4.75	1.02	1.005	....	...	16,035	13.58	12.66	13.58	14.26	7.2
AWSHX	Washington Mutual Investors	'52	IG	C	17085.0	603.7	....	+ 23.0	+ 8.9	+ 13.0	+ 0.5	+ 40.6	$250	5.75	0.62	0.62	0.41	1.09	20,554	23.18	16.90	21.97	23.31	2.7
AMRGX	Amer. Growth Fund	'58	G	C,CV	102.0	15.0	....	+ 23.6	+ 12.6	+ 24.1	− 4.0	+ 21.1	$500	5.75	0.12	...	1.56	...	18,694	9.46	7.25	8.85	9.39	1.3
CAAPX	Ariel Appreciation Fund	*'90	G	C	143.3	8.2	[3]	+ 34.5	+ 13.2	+ 7.8	− 8.4	+ 24.1	$1,000	None	0.062	0.20	1.397	1.766	18,378	23.89	19.29	22.24	22.24	0.3
ARGFX	Ariel Growth Fund	*'86	GR	C	120.9	0.8	[3]	+ 32.4	+ 11.4	+ 8.3	− 4.2	+ 18.4	$1,000	None	0.234	0.437	1.70	4.182	15,219	31.58	26.48	27.32	27.32	0.9
PAAUX	Astra Strategic Inv.:Adjust.Rate IA	*'92	I	GB	18.6	0.1	[4]	....	....	+ 6.8	− 19.0	− 35.1	$5,000	ERF	0.438	0.37	....	...	.....	5.35	3.11	3.12	3.12	14.0
PAUSX	Astra Strategic Inv.Adjust.U.S.Govt.Tr.I.	*'91	I	GB	101.7	0.1	[5]	....	+ 6.0	+ 2.8	− 11.7	− 0.6	$5,000	ERF	0.359	0.317	....	...	.....	5.90	5.54	5.55	5.55	6.5
PAUAX	Astra Strategic Inv.:Adjust.U.S.Govt.IA	*'92	I	GB	69.9	0.1	[5]	....	....	+ 2.8	− 12.1	− 0.3	$5,000	ERF	0.355	0.314	....	...	.....	5.90	5.56	5.57	5.57	6.4
PAIIX	Astra Strategic Inv.:Adjust. U.S.Govt.II	*'91	I	GB	5.6	n/a	[6]	....	+ 7.1	+ 3.5	− 11.7	− 0.5	$5,000	3.0	0.359	0.329	....	...	.....	5.99	5.63	5.63	5.80	6.2
BCHYX	Benham Cal.TF High Yld	*'87	I	TF	120.3	n/a	∫†	+ 10.6	+ 8.9	+ 12.8	− 5.2	+ 17.3	$1,000	None	0.561	0.516	....	...	15,954	9.50	8.52	9.50	9.50	5.9
BCINX	Benham Cal.TF Insured	*'87	I	TF	180.2	n/a	∫†★	+ 10.9	+ 8.9	+ 13.1	− 6.4	+ 18.1	$1,000	None	0.529	0.491	....	...	16,096	10.42	9.21	10.41	10.41	5.1
BCITX	Benham Cal.TF Intermed	*'83	I	TF	420.4	n/a	∫†	+ 10.1	+ 6.9	+ 10.5	− 3.6	+ 12.8	$1,000	None	0.537	0.50	....	...	15,104	11.32	10.42	11.27	11.27	4.8
BCLTX	Benham Cal.TF Long Term	*'83	I	TF	274.9	n/a	∫†	+ 11.4	+ 7.9	+ 13.4	− 6.3	+ 18.8	$1,000	None	0.625	0.571	0.058	...	16,159	11.56	10.19	11.56	11.56	5.4
BGNMX	Benham GNMA Income	*'85	I	GB	1064.6	n/a	★	+ 14.9	+ 7.3	+ 6.4	− 1.5	+ 14.8	$1,000	None	0.697	0.689	....	...	16,213	10.68	9.88	10.68	10.68	6.5
BNTIX	Benham Natl.TF Intermed	*'84	I	TF	63.2	n/a	∫†	+ 11.3	+ 7.0	+ 9.9	− 3.4	+ 12.1	$1,000	None	0.503	0.469	0.037	...	15,123	10.99	10.18	10.95	10.95	4.6
BTFLX	Benham Natl.TF Long Term	*'84	I	TF	49.6	n/a	∫†	+ 12.4	+ 8.9	+ 14.0	− 6.0	+ 16.8	$1,000	None	0.615	0.569	0.055	...	16,332	11.94	10.67	11.93	11.93	5.2
BTMFX	Benham Target Mat.1995	*'85	R	SPBD	64.7	n/a	★	+ 16.2	+ 7.3	+ 6.9	+ 0.8	+ 6.8	$1,000	None	....	....	....	...	15,669	101.74	95.31	101.74	101.74	....
BTMTX	Benham Target Mat.2000	*'85	R	SPBD	294.7	n/a	★	+ 20.7	+ 8.5	+ 15.5	− 6.9	+ 20.7	$1,000	None	....	....	....	...	18,068	80.41	66.45	80.41	80.41	....
BTFIX	Benham Target Mat.2005	*'85	R	SPBD	182.5	n/a	★	+ 21.5	+ 9.6	+ 21.6	− 8.9	+ 32.6	$1,000	None	....	....	....	...	20,265	61.11	45.82	61.11	61.11	....
BTTNX	Benham Target Mat.2010	*'85	R	SPBD	94.8	n/a	★	+ 21.1	+ 9.8	+ 26.3	− 11.6	+ 42.1	$1,000	None	....	....	....	...	21,159	46.86	32.71	46.86	46.86	....
BTFTX	Benham Target Mat.2015	*'86	R	SPBD	114.5	n/a	★	+ 22.5	+ 7.8	+ 30.5	− 14.1	+ 52.7	$1,000	None	....	....	....	...	21,836	36.82	23.84	36.82	36.82	....
BTTTX	Benham Target Mat.2020	*'90	R	SP,BD	564.8	n/a	★	+ 17.4	+ 8.3	+ 35.6	− 17.7	+ 61.3	$1,000	None	....	....	....	...	21,857	26.25	16.01	26.25	26.25	....
CPTNX	Benham Treas.Note Fund	*'80	IP	ST	307.9	n/a	★	+ 13.2	+ 6.3	+ 0.9	− 7.1	+ 7.4	$1,000	None	....	....	....	...	13,180	10.48	9.75	10.48	10.48	....
BEONX	Berger One Hundred	*'66	G	C	2205.6	165.4	....	+ 86.0	+ 8.5	+ 21.2	− 6.7	+ 15.4	$250	None	....	....	....	...	24,623	19.21	15.12	18.10	18.10	....
BRWIX	Brandywine Fund	*'85	G	C	4137.5	49.6	....	+ 47.7	+ 15.5	+ 22.4	+ 0.1	+ 35.9	$25,000	None	....	....	1.453	3.845	28,490	34.98	22.93	28.08	28.08	....
BBGIX	Bull & Bear Gold Investors	*'59	GI	PM	28.6	n/a	....	− 1.1	− 17.2	+ 87.6	− 13.9	− 5.4	$1,000	None	....	....	1.45	1.61	9,798	14.28	11.38	12.10	12.10	....
BBGLX	Bull & Bear Global Income	*'83	I	BD	38.2	n/a	[7]	+ 17.2	+ 12.7	+ 24.1	− 13.2	+ 9.7	$1,000	None	0.66	0.55	....	...	15,155	8.19	7.53	8.19	8.19	8.1
BBSEX	Bull & Bear Special Equities	*'86	R	FL,O,L	63.1	n/a	[8]	+ 40.5	+ 28.4	+ 15.6	− 16.5	+ 40.3	$1,000	None	....	....	0.192	1.39	15,538	28.36	18.48	25.42	25.42	....
BBMIX	Bull & Bear Municipal Income	*'84	I	TF	15.9	n/a	[9]∫†	+ 13.4	+ 5.8	+ 10.4	− 9.7	+ 15.9	$1,000	None	0.677	0.642	....	...	14,375	17.04	15.19	17.04	17.04	4.0
BBUSX	Bull & Bear U.S.Govt.Secs.	*'86	I	GB	15.3	n/a	....	+ 14.6	+ 5.1	+ 10.2	− 4.6	+ 14.9	$1,000	None	0.658	0.712	....	...	15,626	15.63	14.18	15.63	15.63	4.2
BBOSX	Bull & Bear U.S. & Overseas	*'87	GI	INTL	11.9	n/a	[10]	+ 21.9	− 1.7	+ 26.6	− 13.1	+ 25.0	$1,000	None	....	....	0.485	0.49	14,930	9.43	6.65	8.36	8.36	....

Uniform Footnote Explanations-See page 234. Stock Splits & Divs. (figures adjusted): [1] 2-for-1 split,June'93. [2] 2-for-1 split May'94. [3] Was under Calvert Mgmt(9/94). [4] 4%E.R.F.reducing over 4 yrs.. Was Pilgrim Adj.Rate(4/95). [5] 4%E.R.F.reducing over 4 yrs.. Was Pilgrim Adj.US Govt.(4/95). [6] Was Pilgrim Adj.US Govt.(4/95). [7] Was High Yld(10/92). [8] Incl.Cap.Growth(6/92). [9] Was Tax Free Inc.. [10] 2-for-1 split Feb'92. Incl.Equity Inc.(3/92).

Ticker Symbol	Fund	Year Offered	Prin. Obj.	Type	Sept. 29, 1995 Total Net Assets (MIL.$)	Sept. 29, 1995 Cash & Equiv (MIL.$)	See Foot-notes	Net Assets per Share % Change from Previous Dec. 31 At: Dec. 31 1991	1992	1993	1994	Dec. 29, 1995	Min. Unit	Max. Sales Chg. %	Distributions Per Share from Invest. Income 1994	Invest. Income 1995	Security Profits 1994	Security Profits 1995	$10,000 Invested 12-31-89 Now Worth	PRICE RECORD NAV Per Sh 1995 High	1995 Low	#12-29-95 NAV Per Shr.	Offer Price	% Yield From Inv. Inc.
BURHX	Burnham Fund Cl.A	'61	GI	C	109.8	5.1	....	+ 15.2	+ 7.1	+ 8.7	+ 1.9	+ 26.8	$1,000	3.0	0.875	0.60	0.705	0.51	17,346	23.19	19.16	23.19	24.41	3.6
CSIEX	Calvert Social Inv.Equity Ptfl	*'87	GR	C	90.9	n/a	....	+ 21.8	+ 8.2	+ 2.9	− 12.0	+ 20.2	$1,000	4.75	0.042	....	1.248	1.814	13,641	21.64	17.11	19.65	20.63	0.2
CSIFX	Calvert Social Inv.Mgd.Growth	*'82	GI	B	560.8	n/a	....	+ 17.9	+ 7.2	+ 5.9	− 4.7	+ 24.7	$1,000	4.75	0.915	0.656	0.209	3.751	16,145	33.43	27.74	30.34	31.85	2.9
CTFLX	Calvert TF Reserve Ltd.Term Ptfl	*'81	I	TF	480.8	n/a	∫†	+ 6.3	+ 4.9	+ 4.0	+ 2.4	+ 5.1	$2,000	2.0	0.39	0.409	....	...	13,255	10.75	10.59	10.72	10.94	3.6
CGVIX	Capstone:Govt.Income Fund	*'68	IP	GB	86.4	11.8	....	+ 6.5	+ 3.6	+ 3.3	+ 1.3	− 0.4	$10,000	None	0.13	....	....	...	11,373	5.00	4.71	4.71	4.71	2.8
TRDFX	Capstone:Growth Fund	*'52	G	C	87.4	5.5	1	+ 33.4	+ 0.7	+ 5.6	− 7.7	+ 10.8	$200	None	0.11	....	0.17	...	13,971	14.22	12.42	13.81	13.81	0.8
MRIFX	Capstone:Medical Research Invest.	*'85	G	GL	17.6	0.2	....	+ 41.7	+ 2.0	+ 16.9	− 6.3	+ 58.9	$200	None	....	....	1.36	2.80	26,465	24.22	16.76	24.05	24.05	....
CNJFX	Capstone:Nikko Japan	*'89	G	C,SP	3.7	0.1	....	− 0.3	− 28.7	+ 25.3	+ 24.3	− 3.9	$200	None	....	....	....	...	7,437	7.59	6.31	7.33	7.33	....
CDFIX	Cardinal Fund	*'75	GI	C	226.2	3.2	....	+ 31.5	+ 9.6	+ 5.8	− 3.2	+ 26.1	$1,000	6.0	0.35	0.27	0.825	1.084	17,459	13.95	11.27	12.86	13.47	2.6
CGOGX	Cardinal Govt.Obligations	*'86	I	GB	151.7	(2.9)	....	+ 12.6	+ 6.1	+ 4.3	− 0.9	+ 12.9	$1,000	4.5	0.644	0.58	....	...	15,280	8.25	7.79	8.25	8.64	7.5
	Colonial Group:																							
CLMPX	Calif.Tax Exempt Trust:Cl.A	*'86	I	TF	295.6	n/a	∫†	+ 10.8	+ 7.6	+ 10.3	− 7.2	+ 18.6	$1,000	4.75	0.413	0.359	....	...	15,298	7.57	6.65	7.54	7.92	5.2
COLHX	Colonial Tr.:High Yield Secs.:Cl.A	'71	I	BD	447.3	n/a	2	+ 41.3	+ 20.5	+ 18.9	− 0.3	+ 16.1	$1,000	4.75	0.627	0.567	....	...	20,247	6.75	6.29	6.75	7.09	8.8
CUSGX	Colonial Tr.:U.S.Govt.Fund:Cl.A	*'87	I	GB	1152.2	n/a	3	+ 10.5	+ 4.8	+ 5.5	− 1.8	+ 14.0	$1,000	4.75	0.41	0.382	....	...	14,922	6.73	6.23	6.73	7.07	5.8
COLFX	Colonial Tr.:Colonial Fund:Cl.A	*'54	GI	FL	685.0	n/a	4	+ 25.8	+ 12.8	+ 14.4	− 2.1	+ 28.3	$1,000	5.75	0.18	0.20	0.50	0.636	18,800	9.36	7.32	8.58	9.10	2.0
COLGX	Colonial Tr.:Growth Shares Fund:Cl.A	'49	G	C	197.2	n/a	....	+ 33.9	+ 10.4	+ 9.7	− 2.8	+ 26.3	$1,000	5.75	0.118	....	1.21	...	17,877	16.70	12.03	15.30	16.23	0.7
CEXIX	Colonial Tr.:Tax Exempt Insured:Cl.A	*'85	I	TF	236.3	n/a	∫†	+ 11.3	+ 7.2	+ 10.7	− 6.1	+ 16.6	$1,000	4.75	0.43	0.387	....	...	15,343	8.49	7.58	8.46	8.88	4.8
COLTX	Colonial Tr.:Tax Exempt Fund:Cl.A	'78	I	TF	3051.6	n/a	5∫†	+ 11.3	+ 8.0	+ 10.5	− 6.9	+ 16.7	$1,000	4.75	0.69	0.702	....	...	15,326	13.88	12.43	13.82	14.51	4.8
CFSAX	Federal Securities:Cl.A	*'84	I	GB	1207.7	n/a	6	+ 14.3	+ 5.8	+ 11.9	− 5.5	+ 19.2	$1,000	4.75	0.77	0.668	....	...	16,158	11.09	9.73	11.09	11.64	6.6
COLIX	Income Fund:Cl.A	'69	I	BD	145.7	n/a	....	+ 18.2	+ 8.3	+ 11.8	− 4.0	+ 19.0	$1,000	4.75	0.50	0.44	....	...	16,693	6.64	5.93	6.64	6.97	7.2
COMAX	Mass.Tax Exempt Trust:Cl.A	*'87	I	TF	202.5	n/a	∫†	+ 12.6	+ 9.3	+ 11.6	− 5.6	+ 17.5	$1,000	4.75	0.45	0.394	....	...	16,164	8.06	7.16	8.03	8.43	5.3
CXMIX	Michigan Tax Exempt Trust:Cl.A	*'86	I	TF	41.8	n/a	∫†	+ 11.5	+ 8.5	+ 10.8	− 5.9	+ 15.7	$1,000	4.75	0.40	0.354	....	...	15,250	7.16	6.46	7.12	7.48	5.3
CLMNX	Minnesota Tax Exempt Trust:Cl.A	*'86	I	TF	35.9	n/a	∫†	+ 8.9	+ 7.1	+ 10.4	− 4.8	+ 15.3	$1,000	4.75	0.41	0.361	....	...	15,123	7.34	6.67	7.33	7.70	5.3
COLNX	New York Tax Exempt Trust:Cl.A	*'86	I	TF	55.0	n/a	∫†	+ 12.3	+ 8.2	+ 11.9	− 7.8	+ 17.7	$1,000	4.75	0.41	0.376	....	...	15,508	7.29	6.47	7.24	7.60	5.4
CTOHX	Ohio Tax Exempt Trust:Cl.A	*'86	I	TF	72.2	n/a	∫†	+ 10.6	+ 8.4	+ 10.2	− 6.2	+ 15.7	$1,000	4.75	0.40	0.318	....	...	15,328	7.53	6.74	7.49	7.86	5.1
CSMIX	Small Stock Fund:Cl.A	*'86	G	C	59.7	n/a	....	+ 18.9	+ 20.6	+ 18.8	+ 6.4	+ 37.6	$1,000	5.75	....	....	....	1.295	19,055	26.21	18.15	24.00	25.46	....
COSIX	Strategic Income Fund:Cl.A	'77	R	BD	689.0	n/a	7	+ 27.1	+ 9.5	+ 14.4	− 3.7	+ 18.7	$1,000	4.75	0.59	0.533	....	...	17,017	7.22	6.49	7.22	7.58	7.8
CUTLX	Utilities Fund:Cl.A	*'81	I	P,O	397.3	n/a	8	+ 25.2	+ 20.6	+ 9.3	− 10.2	+ 33.5	$1,000	4.75	0.68	0.578	....	...	18,795	15.01	11.71	15.01	15.76	4.3
CSGWX	Common Sense Trust:Growth Ptfl.	*'87	G	C	2664.3	n/a	....	+ 38.6	+ 7.1	+ 9.0	− 2.3	+ 14.0	$250	8.5	0.155	....	1.035	...	17,408	18.35	13.64	15.64	17.09	0.9
CMPBX	Composite Bond & Stock Cl.A	'39	IPG	B,P	208.2	6.1	....	+ 21.1	+ 9.7	+ 9.0	− 2.2	+ 30.7	$1,000	4.5	0.47	0.499	0.08	0.316	18,528	14.17	11.17	13.80	14.45	3.3
CMPFX	Composite Growth & Income Cl.A	'49	GI	C	130.4	0.3	9	+ 26.6	+ 10.8	+ 6.7	+ 2.4	+ 32.9	$1,000	4.5	0.19	0.217	0.40	0.536	19,167	15.62	11.90	15.09	15.80	1.2
CMPIX	Composite Income Cl.A	*'75	I,P	CV,BD	94.2	6.1	....	+ 16.6	+ 7.1	+ 10.6	− 4.8	+ 20.4	$1,000	4.0	0.595	0.538	....	...	17,050	9.44	8.27	9.44	9.83	6.1
CMNWX	Composite Northwest Fund Cl.A	*'86	G	C	161.8	1.9	10	+ 43.7	+ 4.1	+ 2.0	− 1.4	+ 26.5	$1,000	4.5	0.077	0.064	....	0.183	18,841	18.09	14.02	17.60	18.43	0.4
CMTEX	Composite Tax Exempt Bond Cl.A	*'76	I	TF	221.8	12.6	....	+ 11.0	+ 8.7	+ 12.3	− 6.5	+ 17.4	$1,000	4.0	0.391	0.352	....	...	15,825	8.03	7.11	8.02	8.35	4.7
CMPGX	Composite U.S.Govt.Secs.Cl.A	*'82	I	GB	180.0	2.3	....	+ 14.0	+ 5.9	+ 8.0	− 4.9	+ 18.4	$1,000	4.0	0.626	0.575	....	...	15,973	10.84	9.61	10.84	11.29	5.5
COIGX	Cowen Income + Growth Cl.A	*'86	IG	C	57.2	0.4	11	+ 25.9	+ 12.0	+ 9.1	− 6.0	+ 36.0	$1,000	4.75	0.51	0.49	....	0.494	17,995	13.63	10.46	13.19	13.85	3.7
CWNOX	Cowen Opportunity Cl.A	*'88	G	C	68.8	15.0	....	+ 44.2	+ 4.4	+ 30.4	+ 3.8	+ 15.4	$1,000	4.75	....	....	0.78	0.31	24,950	13.70	11.85	13.47	14.14	....
NYVTX	Davis New York Venture Cl.A	*'69	G	C	n/a	n/a	12	+ 39.1	+ 11.9	+ 15.8	− 2.0	+ 40.5	$1,000	4.75	0.12	0.15	0.45	1.01	24,049	15.57	11.20	14.52	15.24	0.8
DWIVX	Dean Witter Amer.Value	'79	G	C	2189.4	85.9	13	+ 55.2	+ 3.6	+ 18.4	− 6.8	+ 28.1	$1,000	ERF	....	....	0.318	...	22,569	30.49	20.95	27.16	27.16	....
DWCTX	Dean Witter Cal.TF Inc.	*'84	I	TF	1031.7	57.0	∫†	+ 9.8	+ 7.6	+ 10.8	− 5.8	+ 13.6	$1,000	ERF	0.64	0.562	0.023	...	14,779	13.02	11.85	12.92	12.92	5.0
DWCGX	Dean Witter Cap.Growth Secs	*'90	G	C	488.3	0.6	....	+ 47.9	− 0.5	− 9.1	− 3.0	+ 31.3	$1,000	ERF	....	....	....	...	17,633	15.70	11.80	15.57	15.57	....
DWSCX	Dean Witter Convert.Secs.	*'85	RI	CV	185.4	23.5	....	+ 24.4	+ 8.0	+ 15.5	− 2.8	+ 20.3	$1,000	ERF	0.406	0.564	....	...	16,077	11.83	10.08	11.61	11.61	3.5
DWDGX	Dean Witter Developing Growth	*'83	G	C	536.0	66.0	....	+ 48.2	− 2.5	+ 30.5	− 4.6	+ 36.3	$1,000	ERF	....	....	0.16	...	23,588	26.21	16.68	23.75	23.75	....
DWDIX	Dean Witter Diversified Income	*'92	I	BD	529.9	45.0	14	....	....	+ 9.4	− 1.3	+ 11.7	$1,000	ERF	0.72	0.66	....	...	.....	9.76	9.25	9.69	9.69	7.4
DWDVX	Dean Witter Dividend Growth	*'81	IGE	C	8584.9	436.2	....	+ 30.3	+ 5.7	+ 14.1	− 2.9	+ 34.7	$1,000	ERF	0.663	0.677	....	0.092	19,074	39.06	29.29	38.59	38.59	1.7
DWEGX	Dean Witter European Growth	*'90	G	GL	866.9	19.2	....	+ 5.8	− 0.8	+ 38.3	+ 6.8	+ 20.7	$1,000	ERF	....	0.30	1.057	...	16,896	14.73	11.73	14.00	14.00	....

Uniform Footnote Explanations-See page 234. **Stock Splits & Divs.** (figures adjusted): [1] Was U.S.Trend(10/94). [2] Incl.VIP High Inc.(6/92). [3] Incl.Liberty Fin'l US Govt.(3/95). [4] 3-for-1 split,12/93. [5] Incl.Liberty Fin'l Tax Free Bond(3/95). [6] Divds.incl.ret.of cap.. Was Govt.Secs.+(6/92). [7] Was Diversified(9/91). [8] 4-for-1 split,(2/92). Was Corporate Cash Trust I(3/92). [9] Was Composite Fund. Was Growth(1995). [10] 2-for-1 split,Dec.'92.. [11] ERF removed.. [12] Was NY Venture (9/95). [13] All DW Funds listed"ERF". have 5% ERF reducing over 6 yrs. [14] 5% ERF reducing over 6 yrs.

Ticker Symbol	Fund	Year Offered	Prin. Obj.	Type	Sept. 29, 1995 Total Net Assets (MIL.$)	Sept. 29, 1995 Cash & Equiv (MIL.$)	See Foot-notes	Net Assets per Share % Change from Previous Dec. 31 — At: Dec. 31 1991	1992	1993	1994	Dec. 29, 1995	Min. Unit	Max. Sales Chg. %	Distributions Per Share from Invest. Income 1994	Invest. Income 1995	Security Profits 1994	Security Profits 1995	$10,000 Invested 12-31-89 Now Worth	PRICE RECORD NAV Per Sh — 1995 — High	1995 Low	#12-29-95 NAV Per Shr.	#12-29-95 Offer Price	% Yield From Inv. Inc.
DGVPX	Dean Witter Federal Securities Trust	*'87	I	GB	824.7	9.9	[1]★	+ 13.6	+ 6.2	+ 9.0	− 5.0	+ 17.6	$1,000	ERF	0.61	0.534	....	...	15,661	9.71	8.69	9.71	9.71	6.3
DWGAX	Dean Witter Global Asset Allocation	*'95	G	GL	34.8	n/a	[2]	....	....	....	....	+ 8.5	$1,000	ERF	....	....	....	...	.....	11.93	10.53	11.46	11.46	....
DWGDX	Dean Witter Global Dividend Growth Secs.	*'93	G	GL	2118.5	8.7	[3]	....	....	....	+ 7.1	+ 17.3	$1,000	ERF	0.127	0.12	0.267	0.282	.....	12.48	10.60	12.36	12.36	1.0
DWGSX	Dean Witter Global Short-Term Income	*'90	I	GL,ST	110.2	9.2	[4]	+ 7.2	+ 2.2	+ 5.9	+ 0.2	+ 10.3	$1,000	ERF	0.545	0.495	....	...	.....	9.01	8.54	9.00	9.00	6.1
DWGUX	Dean Witter Global Utilities	*'94	GI	GL	359.8	n/a	[3]	....	....	....	....	+ 12.5	$1,000	ERF	0.115	0.12	....	...	.....	11.21	9.68	11.04	11.04	1.0
DWHSX	Dean Witter Health Sciences	*'92	G	C	292.0	0.9	[3]	....	....	+ 5.6	− 6.5	+ 51.1	$1,000	ERF	....	....	....	...	.....	15.64	10.16	15.64	15.64	....
DWHIX	Dean Witter High Income Securities	*'94	I	BD	331.1	n/a	[5]	....	....	....	....	+ 9.1	$1,000	ERF	0.492	0.71	....	...	.....	10.15	9.59	9.80	9.80	5.0
DWHYX	Dean Witter High Yield Secs.	*'79	IG	BD	456.5	52.8	[6]	+ 64.1	+ 23.9	+ 30.4	− 6.7	+ 16.4	$1,000	5.5	0.802	0.767	....	...	18,428	6.85	6.38	6.65	7.04	11.4
DWIIX	Dean Witter Interm.Inc.Secs	*'89	I	FL	236.0	33.1	....	+ 15.9	+ 6.1	+ 8.6	− 3.0	+ 12.8	$1,000	ERF	0.569	0.538	0.013	...	14,904	9.83	9.17	9.83	9.83	5.8
DWISX	Dean Witter Intl. SmallCap	*'94	G	INTL	107.3	n/a	[7]	....	....	....	....	+ 2.9	$1,000	ERF	....	....	....	...	.....	9.64	8.11	9.24	9.24	....
DWLTX	Dean Witter Limited Term Municipal	*'93	I	TF	80.1	4.3	....	....	....	....	− 7.8	+ 16.1	$1,000	None	0.417	0.375	....	...	.....	10.17	9.03	10.13	10.13	4.1
DWAZX	Dean Witter MSMS Arizona	*'91	I	TF	49.8	2.4	....	....	+ 9.7	+ 12.0	− 6.5	+ 16.5	$1,000	4.0	0.542	0.497	....	...	.....	10.73	9.61	10.73	11.18	4.8
DWCAX	Dean Witter MSMS California	*'91	I	TF	114.6	5.7	....	....	+ 8.9	+ 13.5	− 8.4	+ 18.3	$1,000	4.0	0.571	0.512	....	...	.....	10.80	9.54	10.80	11.25	5.1
DWFLX	Dean Witter MSMS Florida	*'91	I	TF	72.2	4.3	....	....	+ 9.7	+ 12.8	− 6.1	+ 16.5	$1,000	4.0	0.556	0.509	....	...	.....	10.99	9.84	10.99	11.45	4.9
DWNJX	Dean Witter MSMS New Jersey	*'91	I	TF	47.2	1.6	....	....	+ 9.7	+ 12.5	− 7.0	+ 16.2	$1,000	4.0	0.554	0.467	....	...	.....	10.83	9.68	10.82	11.27	4.9
DWOHX	Dean Witter MSMS Ohio	*'91	I	TF	22.4	1.1	....	....	+ 9.5	+ 13.8	− 7.2	+ 17.5	$1,000	4.0	0.553	0.511	0.009	...	.....	10.89	9.67	10.89	11.34	4.9
DWPAX	Dean Witter MSMS Pennsylvania	*'91	I	TF	51.1	2.6	....	....	+ 10.1	+ 12.9	− 6.8	+ 16.8	$1,000	4.0	0.554	0.503	....	...	.....	10.96	9.78	10.94	11.40	4.9
DMATX	Dean Witter Managed Assets	*'88	G	SP	370.6	265.1	....	+ 26.0	+ 5.4	+ 9.2	+ 2.6	+ 4.7	$1,000	ERF	0.251	0.32	0.549	...	15,423	10.68	10.34	10.51	10.51	2.4
DWMGX	Dean Witter Mid-Cap Growth	*'94	G	C	173.7	n/a	[3]	....	....	....	....	+ 29.1	$1,000	ERF	0.015	....	....	...	.....	14.24	9.66	13.01	13.01	0.1
DWNMX	Dean Witter National Municipal Trust	*'94	I	TF	64.0	n/a	[4]	....	....	....	....	+ 15.2	$1,000	ERF	0.197	0.382	....	...	.....	10.84	9.38	10.83	10.83	1.8
DWNAX	Dean Witter Natural Resources	*'81	G	C	137.4	3.1	....	+ 6.2	+ 6.6	+ 17.2	− 0.8	+ 17.5	$1,000	ERF	0.079	0.049	0.82	...	14,120	12.82	10.29	12.36	12.36	0.6
DWNYX	Dean Witter N.Y. Tax Free Income	'85	I	TF	213.9	9.0	∫†	+ 12.5	+ 8.5	+ 10.0	− 7.6	+ 15.1	$1,000	ERF	0.57	0.496	0.16	...	14,822	12.05	10.81	11.96	11.96	4.8
DWPGX	Dean Witter Pacific Growth	*'90	G	GL	1479.0	9.4	[3]	+ 20.4	+ 4.5	+ 94.6	− 17.5	+ 3.9	$1,000	ERF	....	0.434	0.967	...	.....	20.10	15.88	18.68	18.68	....
DWPMX	Dean Witter Precious Metals & Minerals	*'90	G	PM	63.0	2.4	[3]	− 4.4	− 10.0	+ 55.9	− 11.6	+ 3.1	$1,000	ERF	....	0.001	0.218	0.001	.....	11.43	9.13	10.56	10.56	....
DWPIX	Dean Witter Premier Income	*'91	I	BD	31.7	(5.0)	....	....	+ 3.9	− 0.1	+ 1.5	+ 8.5	$1,000	3.0	0.572	0.459	....	...	.....	8.84	8.55	8.82	9.09	6.3
DWSBX	Dean Witter Short Term Bond Fund	*'94	I	BD	30.2	5.1	....	....	....	....	− 1.7	+ 11.0	$1,000	None	0.588	0.547	....	...	.....	9.71	9.23	9.71	9.71	6.1
DWSHX	Dean Witter Short-Term U.S.Treasury	*'91	I	ST	272.5	81.3	....	....	+ 5.1	+ 4.9	− 1.2	+ 9.1	$1,000	None	0.475	0.478	....	...	.....	10.07	9.67	10.07	10.07	4.7
DWSTX	Dean Witter Strategist	*'88	GI	FL	902.8	30.7	....	+ 31.9	+ 7.3	+ 7.9	− 1.9	+ 14.0	$1,000	ERF	0.293	0.195	0.471	...	17,505	16.99	13.70	15.48	15.48	1.9
TCBLX	DW TCW/DW Balanced Fund	*'93	IG	B	106.7	3.9	....	....	....	....	− 9.6	+ 21.7	$1,000	None	0.10	0.075	....	...	.....	10.83	8.73	10.76	10.76	0.9
TCCEX	DW TCW/DW Core Equity Trust	*'92	G	C	781.3	3.1	[3]	....	....	....	− 7.8	+ 24.5	$1,000	ERF	....	....	....	...	.....	14.79	11.19	14.26	14.26	....
TCIGX	DW TCW/DW Income & Growth	*'93	IG	C	56.8	3.3	....	....	....	....	− 3.7	+ 17.0	$1,000	None	0.55	0.45	0.052	...	.....	11.11	9.70	10.91	10.91	5.0
TCLAX	DW TCW/DW Latin America Growth	*'92	G	GL	268.4	3.1	[3]	....	....	+ 46.8	− 23.6	− 20.3	$1,000	ERF	....	....	0.318	...	.....	10.36	6.34	8.58	8.58	....
TCGIX	DW TCW/DW North Amer.Govt.Income	*'92	I	GL,B	691.2	158.0	....	....	....	+ 7.9	− 14.2	+ 15.4	$1,000	None	0.731	0.642	....	...	.....	8.46	7.77	8.44	8.44	8.7
TCSCX	DW TCW/DW Small Cap.Growth	*'93	G	C	110.8	9.0	[3]	....	....	....	− 4.6	+ 60.2	$1,000	ERF	....	....	....	...	.....	15.60	9.31	15.54	15.54	....
TCTTX	DW TCW/DW Total Return	*'94	GI	C	39.4	n/a	....	....	....	....	....	+ 27.5	$1,000	None	0.04	0.256	....	0.492	.....	12.66	10.72	11.94	11.94	0.3
DWTEX	Dean Witter Tax Exempt	*'80	IP	TF	1304.4	30.6	∫†	+ 12.2	+ 8.8	+ 11.0	− 5.6	+ 16.4	$1,000	4.0	0.698	0.618	....	0.113	15,723	12.22	10.99	12.09	12.59	5.5
DWUSX	Dean Witter U.S.Govt.Secs	*'84	I	GB	8054.8	715.9	★	+ 10.7	+ 5.5	+ 7.0	− 3.5	+ 15.7	$1,000	ERF	0.576	0.524	....	...	15,068	9.21	8.39	9.21	9.21	6.3
DWUTX	Dean Witter Utilities	*'88	I	C	3145.9	38.8	....	+ 18.3	+ 8.4	+ 12.7	− 9.8	+ 27.9	$1,000	ERF	0.611	0.58	0.017	...	16,590	15.15	12.32	15.15	15.15	4.0
DWVAX	Dean Witter Value Added Equities	*'87	G	C	731.1	30.0	....	+ 32.0	+ 12.6	+ 12.5	+ 0.1	+ 28.9	$1,000	ERF	0.092	0.258	0.153	0.119	19,072	25.52	19.68	24.96	24.96	0.4
DWITX	Dean Witter Worldwide Income Tr	*'89	I	GL	141.4	(15.2)	[8]	+ 0.8	+ 3.0	+ 9.7	− 4.4	+ 17.7	$1,000	ERF	0.455	0.803	....	...	14,853	9.25	8.33	9.05	9.05	5.0
DWWWX	Dean Witter Worldwide Invest.Tr	*'83	G	GL	516.3	26.2	....	+ 18.7	− 7.4	+ 40.7	− 7.1	+ 4.6	$1,000	ERF	0.02	....	0.62	0.024	13,540	17.51	15.26	17.48	17.48	0.1
DELDX	Delaware:Decatur Income Cl.A	*'57	GI	C	1355.9	23.0	[9]	+ 21.5	+ 8.6	+ 15.2	− 0.8	+ 32.2	$1,000	5.75	0.69	0.694	0.42	1.34	17,522	19.51	15.32	18.18	19.09	3.6
DEDTX	Delaware:Decatur Total Return Cl.A	*'86	GI	C	514.4	23.1	[10]	+ 20.2	+ 8.0	+ 14.8	− 0.5	+ 36.1	$1,000	5.75	0.40	0.37	0.42	1.285	18,527	16.02	12.01	14.65	15.38	2.6
DELFX	Delaware:Delaware Fund Cl.A	*'38	GI	C	493.6	34.5	....	+ 20.6	+ 12.5	+ 9.3	− 1.4	+ 25.5	$1,000	5.75	0.63	0.655	0.25	1.08	18,258	20.97	17.16	19.89	20.88	3.0
DFCIX	Delaware:Delcap Fund Cl.A	*'86	G	C	889.0	19.5	....	+ 42.3	+ 1.9	+ 11.9	− 5.3	+ 29.8	$1,000	5.75	....	....	1.83	3.54	19,247	29.83	22.27	25.88	27.17	....
DETWX	Delaware:Delchester Hi Yld Bond Cl.A	*'87	I	BD	1015.4	n/a	....	+ 41.5	+ 16.6	+ 15.8	− 4.3	+ 13.5	$1,000	4.75	0.734	0.638	....	...	18,387	6.30	6.03	6.23	6.54	11.2

Uniform Footnote Explanations-See page 234. **Stock Splits & Divs.** (figures adjusted): [1] Was Govt.Secs.Plus(8/24/92). [2] % return from 4/95. 5% ERF reducing over 6 yrs. [3] 5% ERF reducing over 6 yrs. [4] 3% ERF reducing over 3 yrs. [5] 4% ERF reducing over 5 yrs. [6] Rated'BBB' or lower. [7] 5%ERF reducing over 6 yrs. [8] 1989 % change fr 4/89. [9] Was Series I(6/94). [10] Was Series II(6/94).

Ticker Symbol	Fund	Year Offered	Prin. Obj.	Type	Sept. 29, 1995 Total Net Assets (MIL.$)	Sept. 29, 1995 Cash & Equiv (MIL.$)	See Foot-notes	Net Assets per Share % Change from Previous Dec. 31 — At: Dec. 31 1991	1992	1993	1994	Dec. 29, 1995	Min. Unit	Max. Sales Chg. %	Distributions Per Share from Invest. Income 1994	Invest. Income 1995	Security Profits 1994	Security Profits 1995	$10,000 Invested 12-31-89 Now Worth	PRICE RECORD NAV Per Sh — 1995 — High	1995 Low	#12-29-95 NAV Per Shr.	Offer Price	% Yield From Inv. Inc.
DEGIX	Delaware:Intl.Equity Fund Cl.A	*'91	I	INTL	63.9	4.4	....	....	....	+ 28.3	+ 1.9	+ 11.5	$1,000	5.75	0.22	0.28	0.47	0.145	.....	12.56	11.06	12.26	12.87	1.7
DEGGX	Delaware:U.S.Govt.Fund Cl.A	*'85	I	GB	14.4	0.1	1	+ 14.4	+ 6.1	+ 7.6	− 5.7	+ 13.3	$1,000	4.75	0.676	0.646	....	...	15,098	8.03	7.62	8.03	8.43	8.0
DMFIX	Delaware:Tax Free Insur.Fund Cl.A	*'85	I	TF	86.7	n/a	2	+ 10.9	+ 7.6	+ 9.1	− 2.0	+ 13.5	$1,000	4.75	0.724	0.629	....	0.03	15,407	11.42	10.62	11.40	11.97	6.0
DMTFX	Delaware:Tax Free USA Fund Cl.A	*'84	I	TF	751.9	n/a	3	+ 12.0	+ 9.4	+ 11.3	− 3.2	+ 13.4	$1,000	4.75	0.724	0.735	....	0.06	15,509	12.33	11.56	12.31	12.92	5.6
DMUSX	Delaware:Tax Free USA Intermed.Fund	*'93	I	TF	20.4	n/a	....	....	....	+ 11.7	− 2.6	+ 11.9	$1,000	3.0	0.526	0.551	....	...	.....	10.58	9.90	10.54	10.87	4.8
DTRIX	Delaware:Limited-Term Govt.Cl.A	*'85	I	GB	693.2	n/a	4	+ 12.5	+ 5.5	+ 5.2	− 1.9	+ 8.6	$1,000	3.0	0.66	0.709	....	...	14,459	9.18	8.98	9.05	9.33	7.1
DELTX	Delaware:Trend Fund Cl.A	'68	G	C	374.9	25.1	5	+ 74.5	+ 20.9	+ 21.0	− 10.0	+ 45.0	$1,000	5.75	....	....	0.79	1.25	25,585	16.16	11.62	15.79	16.58	....
DELIX	Delaware:Tax Free DMC Pa Fund Cl.A	*'77	IS	TF	993.7	n/a	∫†	+ 12.5	+ 8.8	+ 10.7	− 3.9	+ 14.4	$1,000	4.75	0.492	0.482	....	0.05	15,537	8.57	7.93	8.55	8.98	5.5
DEVLX	Delaware:Value Fund Cl.A	*'87	G	C	175.5	28.6	....	+ 51.0	+ 14.8	+ 18.8	− 6.0	+ 23.5	$1,000	5.75	0.195	0.24	0.42	0.89	20,775	23.10	18.49	22.17	23.28	0.8
DRLEX	Dreyfus Capital Growth Cl.A	'68	G	L	572.1	1.9	6	+ 31.7	+ 6.2	+ 14.3	− 7.0	+ 13.0	$2,500	3.0	0.44	0.278	0.23	1.39	16,548	16.76	14.21	14.78	15.24	2.9
DRCVX	Dreyfus Capital Value Cl.A	*'85	RI	L	271.0	47.5	....	+ 4.1	− 10.4	+ 12.7	− 3.9	− 3.2	$2,500	4.5	0.26	0.455	....	...	9,896	11.42	10.11	10.30	10.79	2.4
DREVX	Dreyfus Fund	'47	GI	C	2786.7	111.7	....	+ 27.5	+ 5.4	+ 6.1	− 4.2	− 9.4	$2,500	None	0.22	0.165	0.395	0.229	11,979	14.30	10.36	10.42	10.42	2.1
DRGMX	Dreyfus GNMA	'85	I	GB	1440.1	75.1	....	+ 13.8	+ 6.0	+ 7.5	− 2.7	+ 14.1	$2,500	None	0.944	0.897	....	...	15,721	14.88	13.76	14.84	14.84	6.4
DREQX	Dreyfus Growth Opport.	*'72	GIS	C	408.4	7.9	....	+ 51.3	− 4.1	+ 1.5	− 5.8	+ 29.5	$2,500	None	0.087	0.12	1.85	1.386	16,780	10.44	8.17	9.09	9.09	1.0
DCVIX	Dreyfus/Laurel Core Value Inv.	'47	GI	C	392.2	11.2	7	+ 22.7	+ 3.9	+ 16.4	+ 0.4	+ 35.6	$1,000	None	0.399	0.451	2.969	2.708	17,516	35.29	24.54	30.13	30.13	1.3
DRTAX	Dreyfus Municipal Bond	'76	IS	TF	3800.0	262.4	8∫†	+ 11.6	+ 8.1	+ 12.4	− 6.9	+ 14.9	$2,500	None	0.74	0.649	0.07	...	15,318	12.72	11.61	12.71	12.71	5.8
EVCAX	EV Marathon Cal.Municipal Fund	'85	I	TF	401.8	48.2	9∫†	+ 9.1	+ 5.9	+ 11.2	− 8.9	+ 18.0	$1,000	ERF	0.546	0.479	0.117	...	14,460	9.87	8.73	9.85	9.85	5.5
EVFLX	EV Marathon Fla. Tax Free Fund	*'90	I	TF	701.8	16.8	10∫†	+ 12.9	+ 7.8	+ 12.6	− 8.8	+ 18.1	$1,000	ERF	0.59	0.521	....	...	14,760	11.22	9.90	11.19	11.19	5.3
EVGOX	EV Traditional Govt. Obligs.	*'84	I	GB	368.4	--	....	+ 13.5	+ 5.0	+ 9.0	− 2.0	+ 13.5	$1,000	3.75	0.832	0.809	....	...	15,648	11.03	10.41	11.02	11.45	7.3
EVHMX	EV Marathon Natl.Municipal Fund	*'85	I	TF	2182.5	--	11∫†	+ 11.3	+ 9.7	+ 14.2	− 7.9	+ 19.3	$1,000	ERF	0.62	0.569	....	...	15,811	10.61	9.04	10.24	10.24	6.1
EVNYX	EV Marathon N.Y. Tax Free Fund	*'90	I	TF	640.8	11.5	10∫†	+ 14.0	+ 8.9	+ 13.2	− 9.1	+ 17.5	$1,000	ERF	0.61	0.537	....	...	15,010	11.30	10.00	11.24	11.24	5.4
EVSGX	EV Marathon Strategic Income Fund	*'90	I	GL	154.9	1.1	....	+ 8.1	− 0.7	+ 10.5	− 5.2	+ 12.3	$1,000	ERF	0.63	0.568	....	...	12,628	8.70	7.67	8.70	8.70	7.2
EVTMX	EV Traditional Total Return	*'81	R	C	448.6	32.4		+ 22.2	+ 6.2	+ 9.6	− 12.1	+ 23.7	$1,000	4.75	0.388	0.319	....	...	15,435	9.29	7.53	9.13	9.59	4.0
EAMRX	Evergreen Amer.Retire.Cl.Y	*'88	PG	C	39.2	1.1	....	+ 18.2	+ 11.5	+ 10.7	− 2.8	+ 23.7	$2,000	None	0.60	0.365	....	...	17,437	12.90	10.64	12.83	12.83	4.7
EFONX	Evergreen Foundation Cl.Y	*'90	GI	C	523.6	105.2	....	+ 35.6	+ 19.5	+ 22.2	− 1.1	+ 27.2	$500	None	0.418	0.352	0.277	0.126	24,910	15.31	12.24	15.13	15.13	2.8
EVGRX	Evergreen Fund Cl.Y	'71	GR	C	614.9	97.7	....	+ 39.3	+ 8.7	+ 6.2	+ 0.4	+ 37.1	$2,000	None	0.073	0.089	2.155	0.576	19,545	16.38	11.97	15.83	15.83	0.5
EGLRX	Evergreen Global RE Equity Cl.Y	*'89	GI	GL	67.7	1.8	....	+ 13.1	+ 9.7	+ 52.0	− 14.1	+ 1.7	$2,000	None	0.097	....	0.515	...	13,328	12.72	10.58	12.26	12.26	0.8
EVVTX	Evergreen Growth & Income Cl.Y	*'86	G	C	127.2	21.1	12	+ 25.8	+ 13.8	+ 14.4	+ 1.8	+ 28.8	$2,000	None	0.14	0.064	1.01	...	20,529	19.02	14.48	18.64	18.64	0.8
EVLMX	Evergreen Limited Market Cl.Y	*'83	G	C	64.8	2.0	13	+ 50.6	+ 9.9	+ 9.4	− 10.7	+ 10.4	$5,000	None	....	....	3.683	0.558	15,994	18.90	15.68	16.78	16.78	....
EMUNX	Evergreen Short-Intermed.Minic.Cl.Y	*'91	IP	TF	39.8	6.3	14	....	+ 7.2	+ 7.4	− 1.0	+ 6.4	$2,000	None	0.50	0.381	....	...	.....	10.25	9.97	10.23	10.23	4.9
EVTRX	Evergreen Total Return Cl.Y	*'78	IG	C	953.3	40.9	....	+ 22.4	+ 9.6	+ 12.7	− 6.4	+ 20.1	$2,000	None	1.08	0.54	0.252	...	15,942	20.19	17.09	19.92	19.92	5.4
FAIMX	Fairmont Fund	*'81	G	C	27.7	1.4	....	+ 40.6	+ 14.0	+ 15.6	+ 7.3	+ 12.3	$1,000	None	....	....	....	...	16,968	31.63	23.86	27.02	27.02	....
FGMAX	Federated GNMA Trust	*'82	I	GB	1400.5	5.6	★	+ 14.6	+ 6.2	+ 6.4	− 2.5	+ 15.0	$25,000	None	0.81	0.722	....	...	15,942	11.33	10.46	11.33	11.33	7.1
FICMX	Federated Income Trust	*'82	I	GB	1021.8	29.6	★	+ 13.3	+ 5.4	+ 5.8	− 1.6	+ 14.4	$25,000	None	0.702	0.622	....	...	15,631	10.36	9.59	10.36	10.36	6.8
FIGTX	Federated US Govt.Secs. 2-5 yrs.	*'83	I	GB	820.6	18.8	15★	+ 12.9	+ 6.5	+ 7.0	− 1.9	+ 8.4	$25,000	None	0.517	0.165	....	...	14,899	10.69	10.00	10.69	10.69	4.8
FSGVX	Federated US Govt.Secs. 1-3 yrs.	*'84	I	GB	690.5	26.9	16★	+ 10.0	+ 5.1	+ 4.4	+ 0.6	+ 4.3	$25,000	None	0.478	0.115	....	...	13,766	10.43	10.11	10.43	10.43	4.6
FAEGX	Fidelity Advisor Equity Growth Ptfl.	*'92	G	C	1843.8	n/a	....	....	....	+ 14.7	− 9.0	+ 39.1	$2,500	3.5	0.08	0.06	0.32	1.88	.....	40.15	27.34	37.51	39.38	0.2
FAGNX	Fidelity Advisor:Global Resources Cl.A	*'87	GP	SP	277.4	n/a	17	+ 14.0	+ 13.1	+ 37.8	− 2.3	+ 28.6	$2,500	3.5	....	....	0.26	0.69	21,140	20.69	15.93	20.26	21.27	....
FAGVX	Fidelity Advisor:Govt.Invest.Cl.A	*'87	I	GB	188.8	n/a	17	+ 13.0	+ 6.3	+ 9.2	− 3.1	+ 17.2	$2,500	3.5	0.60	0.579	....	...	15,984	9.85	8.88	9.85	10.34	5.8
FAGOX	Fidelity Advisor:Growth Opport. Cl.A	*'87	G	C	9309.7	n/a	17	+ 41.5	+ 14.9	+ 22.1	+ 2.8	+ 33.0	$2,500	3.5	0.27	0.41	1.16	0.40	26,680	32.14	24.36	31.64	33.22	0.8
FAHIX	Fidelity Advisor:High Income Munic. Cl.A	*'87	I	TF	559.6	n/a	17	+ 11.8	+ 10.8	+ 13.5	− 7.8	+ 16.3	$2,500	3.5	0.71	0.695	....	...	16,463	12.15	11.00	12.10	12.70	5.6
FAHYX	Fidelity Advisor:High Yield Fund Cl.A	*'87	IR	CV	1100.5	n/a	18	+ 33.3	+ 22.5	+ 19.8	− 1.4	+ 18.1	$2,500	3.5	0.82	0.934	....	...	24,055	12.00	10.83	11.87	12.46	6.6
FAIGX	Fidelity Advisor:Inc. & Growth Cl.A	*'87	IG	CV,C	3534.9	n/a	17	+ 33.8	+ 9.1	+ 19.4	− 5.0	+ 13.9	$2,500	3.5	0.33	0.61	....	0.03	18,294	15.92	14.29	15.71	16.49	2.0
FAERX	Fidelity Advisor:Overseas Cl.A	*'90	G	INTL	752.1	n/a	19	+ 6.7	− 4.9	+ 41.8	+ 2.0	+ 8.6	$2,500	3.5	....	0.09	0.10	0.01	15,923	14.55	12.67	14.38	15.10	....
FASFX	Fidelity Advisor:Short Fxd.-Income Cl.A	*'87	IS	ST	560.5	n/a	17	+ 12.8	+ 7.6	+ 9.3	− 3.3	+ 9.6	$2,500	1.5	0.58	0.562	....	...	14,721	9.52	9.18	9.52	9.66	6.0
FASPX	Fidelity Advisor:Strategic Opport.Cl.A	*'83	G	C	553.2	n/a	20	+ 22.1	+ 12.7	+ 20.4	− 7.1	+ 38.0	$2,500	3.5	0.35	0.39	0.26	0.55	19,711	25.55	18.69	24.88	26.12	1.3

Uniform Footnote Explanations-See page 234. Stock Splits & Divs. (figures adjusted): [1] GNMA & US Govt.now combined. [2] 'USA'dropped(4/30/91). Long Term Bond. [3] Long Term Bond. [4] Was Treasury Res.Intermed.(8/95). Was Treas. Reserves(9/95). [5] Was Delta Trend. [6] Was Leverage(6/92). [7] Was Laurel Capital Apprec.(10/94). [8] Was Tax Exempt Bond(6/92). [9] 6% E.R.F.reducing 1% per yr.over 6 yrs. [10] 6%E.R.F.reducing 1% per yr. [11] 6%E.R.F.reducing 1% per yr. Was Hi Yld Muni. [12] Was Value Timing(9/94). [13] Closed to new investors. [14] 1991 divds.fr.Nov.'91. 1-for-5 reverse split(Aug.'92). [15] Was Intermed.Govt.Trust(5/95). [16] Was Short-Intermed Govt(5/95). [17] Was Plymouth Series. [18] Was Plymouth Aggressive Inc.Ptfl. [19] Was European Invmt. [20] Was Special Situations(9/93).

Ticker Symbol	Fund	Year Offered	Prin. Obj.	Type	Sept. 29, 1995 Total Net Assets (MIL.$)	Sept. 29, 1995 Cash & Equiv (MIL.$)	See Foot-notes	Net Assets per Share % Change from Previous Dec. 31 At: Dec. 31 1991	1992	1993	1994	Dec. 29, 1995	Min. Unit	Max. Sales Chg. %	Distributions Per Share from Invest. Income 1994	Invest. Income 1995	Security Profits 1994	Security Profits 1995	$10,000 Invested 12-31-89 Now Worth	PRICE RECORD NAV Per Sh 1995 High	1995 Low	#12-29-95 NAV Per Shr.	Offer Price	% Yield From Inv. Inc.
FASGX	Fidelity Asset Manager Growth	*'91	GI	C	2849.2	156.7	....	....	+ 19.0	+ 26.2	− 7.4	+ 19.9	$2,500	None	0.19	0.23	0.17	...	.....	15.32	12.45	15.17	15.17	1.3
FBALX	Fidelity Balanced	*'86	IG	B	4971.4	39.8	....	+ 26.1	+ 7.8	+ 19.0	− 5.2	+ 14.6	$2,500	None	0.40	0.57	....	...	17,486	13.62	12.26	13.52	13.52	3.0
FBGRX	Fidelity Blue Chip Growth	*'87	G	C	7062.8	388.4	....	+ 54.7	+ 6.0	+ 24.0	+ 9.8	+ 28.6	$2,500	3.0	....	0.12	0.58	2.47	29,717	33.92	24.72	30.77	31.72	....
FAGIX	Fidelity Capital & Income	'77	IR	BD	2367.8	n/a	[1]	+ 27.6	+ 27.6	+ 23.2	− 3.7	+ 16.3	$2,500	None	0.865	0.874	....	...	21,904	9.39	8.62	9.16	9.16	9.4
FTHRX	Fidelity Comw'th Trust:Intermed.Bond	*'75	IS	BD	2684.8	n/a		+ 13.9	− 1.4	+ 11.7	− 2.0	+ 12.4	$1,000	None	0.616	0.639	0.12	...	14,799	10.41	9.82	10.41	10.41	5.9
FCNTX	Fidelity Contrafund	'67	G	C	13785.5	n/a	[2]	+ 54.3	+ 15.6	+ 21.1	− 1.1	+ 36.2	$2,500	3.0	....	0.09	0.22	3.13	30,202	41.67	29.70	38.02	39.20	....
FHIGX	Fidelity Court St:High Yld.TaxFree	'77	I	TF,BD	1756.1	n/a	[3]∫†	+ 9.9	+ 8.1	+ 10.9	− 7.3	+ 15.9	$2,500	None	0.755	0.677	....	...	15,217	12.42	11.24	12.36	12.36	6.1
FDESX	Fidelity Destiny Plan I	'69	G	C	4053.9	n/a	[4]	+ 38.0	+ 14.2	+ 25.5	− 3.7	+ 36.8	$3,000	8.67	1.473	0.43	0.075	0.81	25,248	19.80	14.59	18.74	18.31	8.0
FDETX	Fidelity Destiny Plan II	*'85	G	C	2031.9	n/a	[4]	+ 40.2	+ 14.7	+ 26.2	+ 4.2	+ 35.8	$3,000	8.67	0.50	0.67	2.96	0.94	27,970	33.40	24.78	32.10	30.95	1.6
FEMKX	Fidelity Emerging Markets	*'90	G	INTL	1212.6	n/a	....	+ 6.7	+ 5.8	+ 81.7	− 17.9	− 3.2	$2,500	3.0	0.04	0.27	....	...	.....	20.16	13.16	15.34	15.81	0.3
FEQIX	Fidelity Equity Income	'66	IG	C	9631.3	443.0	[5]	+ 28.9	+ 14.4	+ 21.0	+ 0.9	+ 31.1	$2,500	None	0.98	0.96	2.48	1.36	20,345	39.07	30.58	37.93	37.93	2.6
FFIDX	Fidelity Fund	'30	GI	C	2915.8	148.7	....	+ 23.4	+ 8.3	+ 17.5	+ 2.5	+ 32.2	$2,500	None	0.33	0.42	0.94	1.40	20,214	23.49	18.37	22.61	22.61	1.5
FGOVX	Fidelity Govt. Secs.	'79	IS	GB	893.6	n/a	....	+ 14.5	+ 7.6	+ 9.1	− 5.1	+ 17.5	$2,500	None	0.624	0.609	0.02	...	16,322	10.17	9.15	10.17	10.17	6.1
FDGRX	Fidelity Growth Company	*'83	G	C	5841.8	940.5	....	+ 47.4	+ 7.8	+ 16.0	− 2.3	+ 39.5	$2,500	None	0.22	0.16	0.92	1.57	26,026	38.75	26.76	36.29	36.29	0.6
FGRIX	Fidelity Growth & Income	*'85	GI	C,CV	12948.4	725.1	[5]	+ 41.3	+ 10.7	+ 16.7	+ 2.3	+ 34.8	$2,500	3.0	0.40	0.48	1.24	0.90	23,486	27.36	21.05	27.05	27.05	1.5
FLPSX	Fidelity Low Priced Stock	*'89	G	C	3243.2	687.5	....	+ 45.7	+ 28.4	+ 19.5	+ 4.9	+ 24.8	$2,500	3.0	0.09	0.23	2.05	1.24	29,209	19.73	15.42	18.50	19.07	0.5
FMAGX	Fidelity Magellan Fund	'65	G	C	53038.2	1166.8	....	+ 39.7	+ 6.5	+ 17.1	− 1.8	+ 36.6	$2,500	3.0	0.13	0.59	2.64	4.69	22,319	95.13	66.01	85.98	83.72	0.2
FMBDX	Fidelity Munic. Bond	'76	I	TF,BD	1054.8	n/a	∫†	+ 11.5	+ 8.6	+ 12.7	− 8.9	+ 19.8	$2,500	None	0.417	0.542	0.14	0.004	15,877	8.31	7.35	8.27	8.27	5.0
FOCPX	Fidelity O-T-C	*'84	G	C	2245.9	145.9	[5]	+ 47.8	+ 13.6	− 5.9	− 2.7	+ 38.2	$2,500	3.0	0.21	0.02	....	1.80	20,226	32.49	23.00	30.33	31.27	0.7
FOSFX	Fidelity Overseas	*'84	G	GL	2343.4	229.6	[5]	+ 8.4	− 11.4	+ 37.8	+ 1.2	+ 9.0	$2,500	3.0	....	0.34	0.47	0.35	13,635	29.82	25.85	29.07	29.07	....
FPURX	Fidelity Puritan	'47	IP	FL	14782.6	458.2	....	+ 24.0	+ 14.9	+ 17.4	+ 2.0	+ 21.1	$2,500	None	0.54	0.49	0.71	0.44	19,380	17.30	14.69	17.01	17.01	3.2
FDFFX	Fidelity Retirement Growth	*'83	IG	C	3921.1	392.1	[6]	+ 44.8	+ 10.4	+ 10.3	....	+ 23.9	$2,500	None	0.22	0.35	1.68	1.58	19,706	19.88	15.99	18.19	18.19	1.2
FBIOX	Fidelity Select Ptfl:Biotechnology	*'85	G	C	639.0	....	....	+ 95.2	− 11.3	+ 0.7	− 18.2	+ 49.1	$2,500	3.0	....	0.07	....	...	30,643	34.83	22.96	34.83	35.91	....
FDCPX	Fidelity Select Ptfl:Computers	*'85	G	C	654.0	n/a	....	+ 30.7	+ 22.0	+ 27.9	+ 20.5	+ 52.1	$2,500	3.0	....	....	....	5.61	44,256	52.14	27.83	38.99	40.20	....
FSELX	Fidelity Select Ptfl:Electronics	*'85	G	C	1253.0	n/a	....	+ 35.3	+ 27.4	+ 31.2	+ 17.2	+ 67.6	$2,500	3.0	....	....	....	5.25	46,999	38.09	17.47	25.74	26.54	....
FSPHX	Fidelity Select Ptfl:Health Care	*'81	G	C	1159.0	....	....	+ 80.0	− 17.6	+ 2.4	+ 21.3	+ 44.9	$2,500	3.0	0.62	0.104	5.74	4.92	33,022	101.45	70.26	97.57	100.59	0.6
FTRNX	Fidelity Trend	'58	G	C	1362.9	102.2	....	+ 35.7	+ 16.6	+ 19.1	− 6.8	+ 21.9	$2,500	None	0.16	0.39	3.89	9.29	18,712	63.61	50.56	52.48	52.48	0.3
FIUIX	Fidelity Utilities Fund	*'87	I	C	1315.5	44.7	....	+ 20.4	+ 10.4	+ 15.4	− 5.1	+ 30.0	$2,500	None	0.54	0.54	0.80	0.28	19,189	16.44	12.89	16.16	16.16	3.3
FIFIX	First Investors Fund for Income	'70	I	BD	422.6	32.4	....	+ 41.3	+ 16.2	+ 17.4	+ 0.7	+ 17.8	$1,000	6.25	0.39	0.36	....	...	19,230	4.13	3.81	4.13	4.41	8.8
FIISX	First Investors Global Fund	'81	G	C	223.7	18.7		+ 16.8	− 4.8	+ 22.7	− 3.8	+ 12.5	$1,000	6.25	0.028	....	0.165	...	12,964	6.88	5.60	6.57	7.01	0.4
FITAX	First Investors Insured Tax Exempt	'76	IS	TF	1339.5	47.1	∫†★	+ 9.9	+ 7.8	+ 9.7	− 4.1	+ 15.7	$1,000	6.25	0.708	0.528	....	...	15,242	10.41	9.40	10.37	11.06	6.4
FICAX	First Investors MSITF Calif.Cl.A	'87	I	TF	16.9	0.3	∫†★	+ 11.0	+ 9.6	+ 13.0	− 4.6	+ 16.3	$1,000	6.25	0.79	0.565	....	...	16,229	12.16	10.76	11.96	12.76	6.2
FIMAX	First Investors MSITF Mass. Cl.A	'86	I	TF	22.4	0.3	∫†★	+ 11.1	+ 9.6	+ 11.7	− 4.1	+ 16.1	$1,000	6.25	0.771	0.566	....	...	16,128	12.26	11.00	12.22	13.03	5.9
FTMIX	First Investors MSITF Michigan	'86	I	TF	34.7	1.0	∫†★	+ 11.0	+ 10.3	+ 14.2	− 5.7	+ 16.7	$1,000	6.25	0.683	0.586	....	...	16,387	12.85	11.45	12.80	13.65	5.0
FINJX	First Investors MSITF New Jersey	*'88	I	TF	57.4	1.2	∫†★	+ 11.2	+ 9.4	+ 12.8	− 5.2	+ 15.0	$1,000	6.25	0.762	0.605	....	...	15,977	13.38	12.04	13.25	14.13	5.4
FIOHX	First Investors MSITF Ohio Cl.A	'86	I	TF	19.7	1.1	∫†★	+ 11.2	+ 9.7	+ 12.9	− 5.0	+ 15.7	$1,000	6.25	0.725	0.567	....	...	16,061	12.64	11.29	12.51	13.34	5.4
FTPAX	First Investors MSITF Pennsylvania	*'90	I	TF	37.8	2.3	∫†★	+ 9.9	+ 9.5	+ 6.1	− 5.1	+ 17.2	$1,000	6.25	0.781	0.583	....	...	14,201	13.20	11.69	13.14	14.02	5.6
FNYFX	First Investors N.Y.Insured Tax Free	'83	I	TF	209.7	9.7	∫†★	+ 10.7	+ 8.5	+ 9.6	− 4.0	+ 14.3	$1,000	6.25	0.908	0.682	....	...	15,239	15.06	13.64	14.93	15.93	5.7
FLEGX	Flag Investors Emerging Growth	*'88	G	C	39.5	n/a	[7]	+ 49.6	− 9.2	− 11.9	+ 5.0	+ 30.1	$2,000	4.5	....	....	0.04	...	12,898	17.72	12.50	16.58	17.36	....
FLINX	Flag Investors Intermed.Term Inc.	*'91	IS	GB	70.1	n/a	[8]	+ 9.6	+ 4.5	+ 8.9	− 2.8	+ 14.0	$2,000	1.5	0.652	0.50	....	...	13,821	10.50	9.60	10.47	10.63	6.1
FLITX	Flag Investors Intl.Trust	*'86	G	C	13.0	n/a	....	+ 8.2	− 10.3	+ 41.2	− 7.4	+ 5.3	$2,000	4.5	....	....	....	...	10,690	13.36	11.47	13.30	13.93	....
FLMMX	Flag Investors Managed Munic.	*'90	I	TF	46.4	n/a	∫†	+ 11.2	+ 6.0	+ 11.2	− 6.7	+ 16.9	$2,000	4.5	0.45	0.495	0.125	...	14,296	10.89	9.65	10.82	11.33	4.0
TISHX	Flag Investors Tel. Income Cl.A	*'84	I,G	C	490.7	n/a	....	+ 22.7	+ 11.7	+ 18.1	− 6.0	+ 22.9	$2,000	4.5	0.425	0.245	0.15	...	17,278	15.72	12.24	14.87	15.57	2.7
FLTSX	Flag Invest.Total Return US Treasury	*'88	I	GB	162.4	n/a	....	+ 15.6	+ 3.6	+ 13.5	− 3.4	+ 19.2	$2,000	4.45	0.696	0.469	....	...	16,528	10.44	9.12	10.43	10.92	6.4
FECLX	Fortis Equity:Capital Fund Cl.A	'49	GI	C	295.2	17.4	[9]	+ 48.9	+ 6.4	+ 2.7	+ 2.4	+ 21.4	$500	4.75	0.059	0.055	0.764	...	18,325	21.83	16.66	20.52	21.54	0.3
FGRWX	Fortis Growth Fund Cl.A	'59	G	C	691.3	64.2	[10]	+ 66.8	+ 0.9	+ 10.3	− 8.3	+ 25.3	$500	4.75	....	....	0.495	1.706	20,007	34.96	24.98	30.30	31.81	....

Uniform Footnote Explanations-See page 234. Stock Splits & Divs. (figures adjusted): [1] Closed to new investors. Was High Inc. [2] Was Contrafund. Sales charges waived for retirement accts. [3] Was High Yield Muni(5/93). [4] Contractual Plan. [5] Sales charges waived for retirement accts. [6] Was Freedom(2/91). [7] Min.invmt.for Flag investors is $500. [8] 1991 % change fr 5/91. [9] Was AMEV Capital(2/92). [10] Was AMEV Growth(2/92).

Ticker Symbol	Fund	Year Offered	Prin. Obj.	Type	Sept. 29, 1995 Total Net Assets (MIL.$)	Cash & Equiv (MIL.$)	See Foot-notes	Net Assets per Share — % Change from Previous Dec. 31 — At: Dec. 31 1991	1992	1993	1994	Dec. 29, 1995	Min. Unit	Max. Sales Chg. %	Distributions Per Share from Invest. Income 1994	1995	Security Profits 1994	1995	$10,000 Invested 12-31-89 Now Worth	PRICE RECORD NAV Per Sh — 1995 — High	Low	#12-29-95 NAV Per Shr.	Offer Price	% Yield From Inv. Inc.
FIUGX	Fortis Inc:U.S.Govt.Secs.Cl.E	*'73	I	GB	478.9	22.5	1	+ 13.2	+ 5.3	+ 8.1	− 5.5	+ 14.9	$500	4.5	0.70	0.593	....	...	15,362	9.31	8.60	9.31	9.75	7.2
	Fortress Inv. Program:																							
FHTFX	Fortress Municipal Income	*'87	I	TF	423.6	8.9	2∫†	+ 10.5	+ 7.7	+ 10.8	− 6.1	+ 15.4	$1,500	1%+ERF	0.552	0.638	....	...	15,174	10.93	10.00	10.93	11.04	5.0
FEUTX	Fortress Utility Fund	*'87	IG	SP	780.4	24.2	3†	+ 25.0	+ 8.5	+ 14.9	− 7.0	+ 24.5	$1,500	1%+ERF	0.629	0.496	....	...	18,097	14.09	11.68	14.09	14.23	4.4
FGOIX	Govt.Income Secs.	'86	I	GB	2401.1	9.6	4★	+ 12.4	+ 5.9	+ 4.6	− 1.9	+ 13.7	$1,500	1.0	0.627	0.57	....	...	15,137	8.89	8.32	8.89	8.98	7.0
FPPTX	FPA Capital Fund	*'68	G	C	364.0	66.0	....	+ 62.1	+ 19.7	+ 15.5	+ 9.6	+ 37.7	$1,500	6.5	0.04	0.14	1.34	0.73	29,662	28.72	20.13	27.50	29.41	0.1
FPNIX	FPA New Income	*'69	I	BD	207.0	45.0	....	+ 17.7	+ 10.6	+ 14.0	+ 0.1	+ 13.8	$1,500	4.5	0.71	0.67	0.27	...	18,223	11.17	10.22	11.17	11.70	6.1
FPRAX	FPA Paramount Fund	*'58	G	C	596.0	182.0	5	+ 22.2	+ 8.8	+ 17.9	+ 8.4	+ 11.6	$1,500	6.5	0.25	0.29	1.52	1.01	19,247	15.05	13.18	14.78	15.81	1.6
FPPFX	FPA Perennial Fund	*'84	GI	C	48.0	6.0	....	+ 20.3	+ 12.4	+ 4.4	− 0.1	+ 14.9	$1,500	6.5	0.46	0.44	1.31	2.48	16,366	22.42	19.21	22.36	23.91	1.9
	Franklin Funds:																							
FISAX	Adjust.U.S.Govt.Secs.	*'87	I	SP	520.7	n/a	6★	+ 8.3	+ 3.9	+ 1.3	− 1.9	+ 8.9	$100	2.25	0.336	0.553	....	...	13,273	9.43	9.10	9.36	9.58	3.5
AGEFX	AGE High Income	*'69	I	BD	1994.8	n/a	....	+ 46.4	+ 15.0	+ 16.8	− 1.6	+ 17.8	$100	4.25	0.264	0.264	....	...	19,808	2.80	2.57	2.80	2.92	9.0
FKCIX	Calif.Intermed-Term Tax Free Inc.	*'92	I	TF	94.3	n/a	∫†	....	....	+ 11.3	− 4.2	+ 15.6	$100	2.25	0.528	0.528	....	...	.....	10.93	9.83	10.86	11.11	4.8
FKTFX	Calif. Tax-Free Income Cl.I	*'77	I	TF	13126.7	n/a	....	+ 11.1	+ 8.3	+ 9.7	− 3.3	+ 14.6	$100	4.25	0.407	0.444	....	...	15,549	7.36	6.78	7.36	7.69	5.3
FKDNX	Dynatech Series	'67	G	C	92.9	n/a	7	+ 35.3	+ 4.2	− 0.1	+ 5.2	+ 26.2	$100	4.5	0.049	0.118	0.13	0.228	19,372	13.39	9.81	12.16	12.73	0.4
FKREX	Equity Fund	*'33	G	C	340.6	n/a	....	+ 26.0	+ 3.6	+ 8.5	− 1.5	+ 32.6	$100	4.5	0.07	0.07	0.62	0.462	17,000	7.97	5.99	7.48	7.83	0.9
FISEX	Equity Income	*'88	IR	SP	163.7	n/a	8	+ 27.4	+ 12.8	+ 17.4	− 0.3	+ 25.1	$100	4.5	0.63	0.629	0.24	0.399	19,233	16.11	13.47	15.79	16.53	3.8
FKTIX	Federal Tax Free Income	*'83	I	TF	7010.2	n/a	....	+ 13.3	+ 8.6	+ 11.4	− 4.7	+ 14.6	$100	4.25	0.65	0.753	....	...	15,748	12.19	11.23	12.19	12.73	5.1
FISCX	FI:Convert.Secs	*'87	GI	CV	84.1	n/a	....	+ 32.6	+ 15.6	+ 19.9	− 1.6	+ 17.5	$100	4.5	0.58	0.60	0.697	...	20,187	13.21	10.99	12.51	13.10	4.4
FRGVX	FI:US Govts:Short-Interm	*'87	P,I	ST	208.7	n/a	★	+ 11.5	+ 6.8	+ 7.6	− 3.0	+ 10.9	$100	2.25	0.394	0.555	....	...	15,038	10.42	9.89	10.42	10.66	3.7
FRGLX	Global Govt.Income Fund	*'88	I	GL	169.6	n/a	9	+ 13.2	− 0.3	+ 17.9	− 7.6	+ 17.2	$100	4.25	0.726	0.69	0.03	...	15,418	8.52	7.68	8.52	8.90	8.2
FRGUX	Global Utilities	*'92	GI	C,GL	122.4	n/a	....	....	....	+ 31.1	− 8.8	+ 27.0	$100	4.5	0.365	0.391	0.358	0.324	.....	13.87	11.22	13.80	14.45	2.5
FKRCX	Gold Fund	*'69	GI	PM	372.8	n/a	10	+ 6.0	− 20.1	+ 73.4	− 4.8	− 5.1	$100	4.5	0.149	0.191	....	...	10,760	15.58	12.77	14.05	14.71	1.0
FKGRX	Growth Series	*'48	G	C	712.9	n/a	7	+ 26.3	+ 2.9	+ 4.4	+ 2.9	+ 38.4	$100	4.5	0.135	0.164	0.042	0.154	19,806	20.66	14.95	20.44	21.40	0.6
FKINX	Income Series	*'48	I	C,BD	5885.8	n/a	....	+ 39.2	+ 14.8	+ 21.4	− 6.2	+ 20.3	$100	4.25	0.18	0.18	0.028	0.027	20,184	2.32	2.06	2.32	2.42	7.4
FIGPX	Mgd.Tr-Invest.Grade Inc.	*'87	I	SP	29.8	n/a	....	+ 16.5	+ 5.3	+ 9.2	− 1.2	+ 10.7	$100	4.25	0.443	0.442	....	...	15,618	9.16	8.64	9.16	9.57	4.6
FCCPX	Mgd.Tr-Corporate Qual.Divd.	*'87	I	SP	27.8	n/a	11	+ 23.1	+ 15.7	+ 6.9	+ 0.1	+ 6.1	$100	1.5	0.97	1.187	....	...	16,186	23.76	23.31	23.65	24.01	4.0
FRDPX	Mgd.Tr-Rising Divds.	*'87	I	C	260.9	n/a	....	+ 35.7	+ 10.3	− 3.5	− 5.2	+ 30.0	$100	4.5	0.278	0.329	....	...	17,818	18.31	14.31	18.25	19.11	1.5
FKBRX	Premier Return	*'51	I,G	O	31.8	n/a	12	+ 21.9	+ 13.1	+ 18.3	+ 0.5	+ 20.7	$100	4.5	0.14	0.125	....	...	18,241	7.33	6.11	7.25	7.59	1.8
FRHIX	Tax Free:Hi Yld.TF Inc	*'86	I	TF	3528.4	n/a	∫†	+ 11.9	+ 8.7	+ 12.9	− 2.5	+ 15.9	$100	4.25	0.746	0.732	....	...	16,279	11.27	10.34	11.26	11.76	6.3
FTFIX	Tax Free:Insur.TF Inc.	*'85	I	TF	1679.5	n/a	∫†★	+ 11.0	+ 8.9	+ 11.5	− 3.5	+ 13.3	$100	4.25	0.71	0.706	....	...	15,650	12.40	11.52	12.37	12.92	5.5
FRALX	Tax Free:Alabama TF Inc	*'87	I	TF	179.1	n/a	∫†	+ 12.0	+ 8.3	+ 12.0	− 4.3	+ 14.9	$100	4.25	0.65	0.65	....	...	15,685	11.85	10.84	11.82	12.34	5.3
FTAZX	Tax Free:Arizona TF Inc	*'87	I	TF	735.7	n/a	∫†	+ 11.8	+ 9.5	+ 10.9	− 4.0	+ 13.1	$100	4.25	0.64	0.646	....	...	15,552	11.62	10.70	11.47	11.98	5.3
FRCIX	Tax Free:Cal.Insur.TF Inc.	*'85	I	TF	1501.2	n/a	∫†★	+ 10.4	+ 8.3	+ 12.7	− 5.2	+ 16.0	$100	4.25	0.67	0.672	....	...	15,707	12.45	11.27	12.42	12.97	5.2
FRCOX	Tax Free:Colo. TF Inc	*'87	I	TF	203.8	n/a	∫†	+ 11.9	+ 9.5	+ 12.4	− 5.3	+ 15.7	$100	4.25	0.66	0.66	....	...	15,920	11.96	10.85	11.92	12.45	5.3
FXCTX	Tax Free:Connecticut TF Inc.	*'88	I	TF	163.2	n/a	....	+ 10.4	+ 7.9	+ 12.0	− 5.3	+ 14.0	$100	4.25	0.61	0.614	....	...	15,080	11.09	10.24	11.07	11.56	5.3
FRFLX	Tax Free:Florida TF Inc	*'87	I	TF	1307.4	n/a	∫†	+ 12.1	+ 8.3	+ 11.7	− 3.2	+ 14.3	$100	4.25	0.668	0.684	....	...	15,874	11.82	10.90	11.79	12.31	5.4
FTGAX	Tax Free:Georgia TF Inc	*'87	I	TF	122.9	n/a	∫†	+ 11.8	+ 8.4	+ 11.6	− 3.7	+ 13.8	$100	4.25	0.66	0.66	....	...	15,622	12.00	11.10	11.98	12.51	5.3
FXINX	Tax Free:Indiana TF Inc	*'87	I	TF	47.9	n/a	∫†	+ 11.8	+ 9.3	+ 12.5	− 4.9	+ 13.8	$100	4.25	0.66	0.66	....	...	15,726	11.87	10.99	11.86	12.39	5.3
FKLAX	Tax Free:Louisiana TF Inc.	*'87	I	TF	104.6	n/a	∫†	+ 11.8	+ 8.5	+ 10.9	− 4.7	+ 14.3	$100	4.25	0.637	0.648	....	...	15,562	11.47	10.57	11.44	11.95	5.3
FMDTX	Tax Free:Maryland TF Inc.	*'88	I	TF	165.7	n/a	....	+ 11.6	+ 8.4	+ 11.9	− 5.0	+ 16.9	$100	4.25	0.613	0.624	....	...	15,815	11.53	10.36	11.51	12.02	5.1
FMISX	Tax Free:Mass.Insur.TF Inc.	*'85	I	TF	239.6	n/a	∫†★	+ 11.1	+ 8.5	+ 11.5	− 3.6	+ 13.8	$100	4.25	0.663	0.66	....	...	15,453	11.75	10.89	11.74	12.26	5.4
FTTMX	Tax Free:Michigan Insur.TF Inc.	*'85	I	TF	1077.8	n/a	∫†★	+ 10.6	+ 9.0	+ 11.8	− 3.8	+ 13.5	$100	4.25	0.687	0.684	....	...	15,570	12.21	11.31	12.18	12.72	5.4
FMINX	Tax Free:Minn.Insur.TF Inc.	*'85	I	TF	479.9	n/a	∫†★	+ 10.5	+ 8.2	+ 10.7	− 3.2	+ 13.0	$100	4.25	0.728	0.672	....	...	15,274	12.27	11.42	12.26	12.80	5.7
FRMOX	Tax Free:Missouri TF Inc	*'87	I	TF	236.5	n/a	∫†	+ 11.6	+ 8.6	+ 12.9	− 5.0	+ 14.8	$100	4.25	0.652	0.584	....	...	15,863	11.99	10.93	11.98	12.51	5.2
FRNJX	Tax Free:N.J. TF Inc	*'88	I	TF	554.8	n/a	∫†	+ 12.1	+ 8.7	+ 10.7	− 5.1	+ 15.2	$100	4.25	0.655	0.636	....	...	15,661	11.83	10.79	11.81	12.33	5.3

Uniform Footnote Explanations-See page 234. Stock Splits & Divs. (figures adjusted): [1] Was AMEV U.S.Govt.Secs(2/92). [2] 1% E.R.F.reducing over 4 yrs. [3] 1% E.R.F. reducing over 4 yrs. [4] Incl.Total Perform.U.S.Treas(2/92). 1% E.R.F.reducing over 4 yrs. [5] Closed to new investors. [6] Was Adjust.Rate Mtge. [7] 2-for-1 split,June'92. [8] Was Special Equity Income(9/93). [9] Was Global Opportunity(12/93). [10] Was Research Capital. [11] Was Corporate Cash(6/91). [12] Was Option Fund(5/91).

Ticker Symbol	Fund	Year Offered	Prin. Obj.	Type	Sept. 29, 1995 Total Net Assets (MIL.$)	Sept. 29, 1995 Cash & Equiv (MIL.$)	See Foot-notes	Net Assets per Share % Change from Previous Dec. 31 At: Dec. 31 1991	1992	1993	1994	Dec. 29, 1995	Min. Unit	Max. Sales Chg. %	Distributions Per Share from Invest. Income 1994	Invest. Income 1995	Security Profits 1994	Security Profits 1995	$10,000 Invested 12-31-89 Now Worth	PRICE RECORD 1995 High	1995 Low	NAV Per Sh #12-29-95 NAV Per Shr.	Offer Price	% Yield From Inv. Inc.
	Franklin Funds:																							
FNYTX	Tax Free:N.Y. TF Inc	*'82	I	TF	4739.2	n/a	....	+13.7	+10.1	+11.0	−3.0	+13.2	$100	4.25	0.756	0.736	....	...	15,960	11.91	11.11	11.91	12.44	6.1
FRNYX	Tax Free:N.Y.Insur. TF Inc.	*'91	I	TF	246.1	n/a	★	....	+9.3	+13.7	−8.0	+18.1	$100	4.25	0.588	0.588	....	...	.....	11.45	10.14	11.41	11.92	4.9
FXNCX	Tax Free:N.C. TF Inc.	*'87	I	TF	230.5	n/a	∫†	+11.1	+8.7	+11.4	−5.6	+15.8	$100	4.25	0.648	0.648	....	...	15,574	11.92	10.81	11.89	12.42	5.2
FTOIX	Tax Free:Ohio Insur.TF Inc.	*'85	I	TF	662.7	n/a	∫†★	+10.6	+8.5	+12.2	−4.4	+13.5	$100	4.25	0.692	0.627	....	...	15,530	12.37	11.41	12.34	12.89	5.4
FRORX	Tax Free:Oregon TF Inc	*'87	I	TF	361.7	n/a	∫†	+12.2	+8.2	+10.7	−4.8	+14.8	$100	4.25	0.613	0.624	....	...	15,466	11.74	10.71	11.69	12.21	5.0
FRPAX	Tax Free:Penn.TF Inc	*'86	I	TF	614.1	n/a	∫†	+13.0	+9.3	+11.4	−3.2	+14.0	$100	4.25	0.612	0.622	....	...	15,730	10.56	9.78	10.54	11.01	5.6
FPRTX	Tax Free:P.R. TF Inc.	*'85	I	TF	185.2	n/a	∫†	+11.9	+8.1	+10.7	−4.2	+14.1	$100	4.25	0.684	0.67	....	...	15,384	11.76	10.84	11.71	12.23	5.6
FTXTX	Tax Free:Texas TF Inc	*'87	I	TF	129.1	n/a	∫†	+11.7	+8.1	+11.3	−2.7	+13.0	$100	4.25	0.666	0.67	....	...	15,619	11.70	10.91	11.67	12.19	5.5
FRVAX	Tax Free:Virginia TF Inc	*'87	I	TF	261.6	n/a	∫†	+12.1	+8.5	+12.1	−4.5	+15.1	$100	4.25	0.654	0.648	....	...	15,826	11.85	10.82	11.83	12.36	5.3
FKUSX	U.S. Govt. Secs.	*'70	I	BD	11101.8	n/a	★	+13.7	+6.3	+7.3	−2.7	+16.2	$100	4.25	0.50	0.488	....	...	16,144	6.97	6.37	6.97	7.28	6.9
FKUTX	Utilities Series	*'48	GI	C	2766.1	n/a	....	+23.1	+8.6	+9.7	−11.7	+29.7	$100	4.25	0.524	0.524	0.007	0.072	16,863	10.39	8.48	10.39	10.85	4.8
....	Frontier Funds:Equity Ptfl.	'92	G	C	1.5	n/a	[1]	....	+3.8	−24.5	−13.7	−1.3	$1,000	8.0	....	....	....	...	.....	8.47	5.43	6.27	6.82	....
GTAGX	G.T.Global:America Growth Cl.A	*'87	G	C	435.4	n/a	....	+19.3	+31.4	+7.9	+15.0	+23.6	$500	4.75	0.02	0.209	2.05	2.58	22,263	24.06	17.62	19.07	20.02	0.1
GPSAX	G.T.Global:Consumer Products Cl.A	*'95	G	GL	3.1	n/a	....	....	....	....	....	+34.7	$500	4.75	....	....	....	0.517	.....	14.99	11.27	14.88	15.62	....
GTEMX	G.T.Global:Emerging Markets Cl.A	*'92	G	INTL,C	273.2	n/a	[2]	....	−5.2	+64.3	−3.6	−13.9	$500	4.75	....	....	0.77	...	.....	15.69	12.43	13.80	14.49	....
GTGEX	G.T.Global:Europe Growth Cl.A	*'85	G	INTL	543.3	n/a	....	+4.2	−11.3	+28.3	−5.8	+9.8	$500	4.75	0.048	0.097	0.128	0.04	10,462	11.19	9.33	10.88	11.42	0.4
GFSAX	G.T.Global:Financial Services Cl.A	*'94	G	GL	5.7	n/a	....	....	....	....	....	+19.0	$500	4.75	....	0.119	....	0.005	.....	12.84	9.67	12.84	13.48	....
GGINX	G.T.Global:Govt.Inc.Cl.A	*'88	I	GL,BD	399.3	n/a	[3]	+12.8	+1.8	+24.4	−13.7	+15.2	$500	4.75	0.67	0.581	....	0.099	15,352	9.10	8.26	8.89	9.33	7.2
GAGIX	G.T.Global:Growth & Inc.Cl.A	*'90	GI	GL,FL	288.3	n/a	....	+18.7	+2.5	+26.8	−3.6	+15.0	$500	4.75	0.22	0.232	0.04	0.049	17,103	6.59	5.83	6.55	6.88	3.2
GGHCX	G.T.Global:Health Care Cl.A	*'89	G	GL,C	436.7	n/a	....	+57.8	−13.5	+2.6	+1.2	+36.5	$500	4.75	....	....	1.34	2.86	21,880	23.54	17.29	21.28	22.34	....
GHIAX	G.T.Global High Income Cl.A	*'92	I	GL	141.8	n/a	....	....	....	....	−16.3	+18.6	$500	4.75	1.11	1.114	0.09	...	.....	12.45	9.11	12.45	13.07	8.5
GIFAX	G.T.Global:Infrastructure Fund Cl.A	*'94	G	GL	37.4	n/a	....	....	....	....	....	+6.1	$500	4.75	....	....	....	...	.....	13.04	10.57	12.50	13.12	....
GINGX	G.T.Global:International Growth Cl.A	*'87	G	INTL	322.4	n/a	....	+13.2	−5.8	+34.2	−7.8	+6.0	$500	4.75	....	0.20	0.986	0.442	11,986	9.48	8.04	9.08	9.53	....
GJGRX	G.T.Global:Japan Growth Cl.A	*'85	G	INTL	98.8	n/a	....	−2.8	−21.5	+33.4	+6.5	+1.8	$500	4.75	....	....	0.214	1.37	7,901	12.33	10.34	11.00	11.55	....
GTLAX	G.T.Global:Latin Amer.Growth Cl.A	*'91	G	INTL	228.5	n/a	[4]	+19.9	−2.5	+52.8	−5.6	−21.4	$500	4.75	....	0.106	1.60	...	13,254	19.38	12.14	15.82	16.61	....
GTNAX	G.T.Global:Natural Resources Cl.A	*'94	G	GL	15.1	n/a	....	....	....	....	....	+7.0	$500	4.75	0.029	0.039	....	0.008	.....	12.37	10.53	12.37	12.99	0.2
GTPAX	G.T.Global:Pacific Growth Cl.A	*'77	G	INTL	406.3	n/a		+12.9	−8.0	+60.1	−19.7	+7.4	$500	4.75	0.006	0.102	0.622	0.425	12,778	13.53	10.54	12.47	13.09	....
GSIAX	G.T.Global:Strategic Inc.Cl.A	*'88	I	GL,BD	190.4	n/a	[5]	+14.6	+1.0	+41.7	−20.3	+16.1	$500	4.75	0.94	0.84	....	...	16,360	10.78	9.20	10.78	11.32	8.3
GTWGX	G.T.Global:Worlwide Growth Cl.A	*'87	G	GL	156.9	n/a	....	+20.2	+3.3	+27.4	−6.6	+11.2	$500	4.75	....	....	0.779	0.45	14,376	17.44	14.12	16.82	17.66	....
GTTCX	G.T.Global:Telecommunications Cl.A	*'92	G	GL,C	1527.8	n/a	[6]	....	+4.8	+47.5	−4.3	+8.4	$500	4.75	....	....	0.86	0.815	.....	18.17	13.85	16.08	16.88	....
GABVX	Gabelli Value Fund	*'89	G	C	514.0	n/a	†	+15.3	+12.7	+39.4	+0.1	+22.5	$1,000	5.5	0.091	0.05	1.509	1.18	20,990	12.94	10.44	11.62	12.30	0.7
GIEMX	Govett Emerging Markets	*'92	G	INTL	79.5	n/a	....	....	+7.2	+77.5	−11.5	−8.0	$500	4.95	....	....	2.367	...	.....	13.34	10.94	12.23	12.87	....
GSCGX	Goldman Sachs Capital Growth	'90	G	C	928.9	46.4	....	+25.5	+22.5	+14.0	+0.9	+26.1	$1,500	5.5	0.011	0.208	1.621	2.691	.....	17.60	13.58	14.53	15.38	0.1
GSIFX	Goldman Sachs Intl. Equity Fund	*'92	G	INTL	279.2	12.6	....	....	....	+20.7	−6.9	+18.8	$1,500	5.5	....	0.584	0.593	0.867	.....	18.18	14.38	16.97	17.96	....
GSGRX	Goldman Sachs Growth & Income	*'93	GI	C	371.0	3.7	....	....	....	....	+5.9	+33.3	$1,500	5.5	0.272	0.302	0.328	0.594	.....	20.22	15.41	19.55	20.69	1.3
GSSQX	Goldman Sachs Select Equity Cl.A	*'91	G	C	101.9	2.0	....	....	+0.1	+12.6	+1.3	+35.2	$1,500	5.5	0.196	0.158	0.936	0.407	.....	19.63	14.40	18.93	20.03	1.0
GGGIX	Govett Global Income Fund	*'92	I	GL,BD	42.5	n/a	[7]	....	+8.6	+16.9	−9.0	+5.7	$500	4.95	0.77	....	....	...	.....	9.02	8.46	8.96	9.43	8.2
GIEQX	Govett Intl.Equity	*'92	G	INTL	30.3	n/a	....	....	−5.3	+53.5	−8.0	+10.9	$500	4.95	0.64	....	1.372	...	.....	11.30	9.51	11.27	11.86	5.4
GPSQX	Govett Pacific Strategy	*'94	G	INTL	11.1	n/a	....	....	....	....	−12.1	−2.8	$500	4.95	....	....	....	...	.....	8.82	7.57	8.54	8.98	....
GSCQX	Govett Smaller Companies	*'93	G	GL	563.5	n/a	....	....	....	....	+27.6	+57.1	$500	4.95	....	....	1.159	...	.....	31.39	18.42	29.96	31.52	....
GPAFX	Guardian Park Ave.	*'72	GR	FL	931.2	n/a	....	+34.8	+20.3	+20.1	−1.4	+34.2	$1,000	4.5	0.31	0.329	1.02	1.789	22,653	36.38	26.79	33.97	35.57	0.9
TACAX	Hancock(J) Cal.Tax Free Inc.Cl.A	*'89	I	TF	297.4	n/a	[8]∫†	+11.1	+8.8	+12.8	−9.1	+20.4	$1,000	4.75	0.583	0.479	....	...	15,878	10.69	9.28	10.69	11.19	5.2
TSEGX	Hancock(J) Emerg.Growth Cl.B	*'87	G	C	397.7	n/a	[9]	+58.8	+12.1	+11.8	−1.5	+42.1	$1,000	ERF	....	....	....	...	27,522	36.64	24.82	35.76	35.76	....
TSNRX	Hancock(J) Global Resources Cl.B	*'87	G	SP	30.6	n/a	[10]	+14.1	+7.8	+8.2	−9.6	+1.4	$1,000	ERF	....	....	....	...	10,357	15.69	12.97	14.46	14.46	....
TSGIX	Hancock(J) Govt.Inc. Cl.B	*'88	IP	GB	226.2	n/a	[11]	+13.3	+5.0	+6.9	−5.2	+16.6	$1,000	ERF	0.658	0.591	....	...	15,055	9.52	8.67	9.52	9.52	6.9

Uniform Footnote Explanations-See page 234. Stock Splits & Divs. (figures adjusted): [1] 1992 % change fr.4/92. [2] 1992 change fr.May'92.. [3] Was GT Global Govt. Inc.(10/92). [4] Temp.suspended sales. [5] Was GT Global Bond(10/92). [6] 1992 change fr.Jan.'92.. [7] Was Global Govt. Inc.(6/95). Includes Develop. Markets Bond(6/95). [8] Formerly Transamerica Group. [9] Formerly Transamerica Group. 5% E.R.F.. [10] 5% ERF reducing over 6 yrs. Formerly Transamerica Group. [11] Formerly Transamerica Group. Incl. Govt. Secs. Tr.(9/95). 5% E.R.F..

Ticker Symbol	Fund	Year Offered	Prin. Obj.	Type	Sept. 29, 1995 Total Net Assets (MIL.$)	Sept. 29, 1995 Cash & Equiv (MIL.$)	See Foot-notes	Net Assets per Share % Change from Previous Dec. 31 At: Dec. 31 1991	1992	1993	1994	Dec. 29, 1995	Min. Unit	Max. Sales Chg. %	Distributions Per Share from Invest. Income 1994	Invest. Income 1995	Security Profits 1994	Security Profits 1995	$10,000 Invested 12-31-89 Now Worth	PRICE RECORD 1995 High	1995 Low	NAV Per Sh #12-29-95 NAV Per Shr.	Offer Price	% Yield From Inv. Inc.
TAGRX	Hancock(J) Growth & Inc.Cl.A	*'49	GI	FL	132.7	n/a	1	+ 31.9	+ 5.8	+ 9.6	− 8.4	+ 34.6	$1,000	5.75	0.247	0.171	....	...	18,782	14.51	10.68	14.20	14.95	1.7
TSHYX	Hancock(J) High Yld. Bond Cl.B	*'87	I	BD	178.7	n/a	2	+ 31.6	+ 12.9	+ 20.7	− 5.6	+ 13.2	$1,000	ERF	0.726	0.611	....	...	17,995	7.31	6.88	7.30	7.30	9.9
TSHTX	Hancock(J) High Yld.Tax Free Cl.B	*'86	I	TF	153.6	n/a	2∫†	+ 11.7	+ 8.1	+ 11.2	− 5.6	+ 17.9	$1,000	ERF	0.612	0.489	....	...	15,497	9.76	8.69	9.76	9.76	6.3
JHNLX	Hancock(J)Limited Term Govt.Cl.A	*'69	IG	B	198.7	n/a	3	+ 12.0	+ 4.0	+ 4.1	− 1.3	+ 10.5	$1,000	3.0	0.38	0.455	....	...	14,203	8.73	8.31	8.73	9.00	4.2
NTTFX	Hancock(J) Global Technology	*'83	GI	C	167.2	n/a	4	+ 33.7	+ 5.4	+ 31.5	+ 9.5	+ 37.4	$1,000	5.0	....	....	1.26	...	22,723	29.41	17.09	24.51	25.80	....
SOVIX	Hancock(J.)Sovereign Investors Cl.A	'36	GI	FL	1218.9	n/a	5	+ 29.9	+ 7.1	+ 5.6	− 1.9	+ 27.6	$1,000	5.0	0.458	0.307	0.111	...	19,162	18.14	14.25	17.87	18.81	2.4
FEQVX	Hancock(J)Sovereign Achiev.Cl.B	*'87	GI	SP	89.8	n/a	6	+ 30.4	+ 6.0	+ 8.8	− 6.0	+ 23.1	$1,000	ERF	0.03	0.011	0.52	...	15,836	13.70	10.98	13.54	13.54	0.2
JHNBX	Hancock(J)Sovereign Bond Cl.A	*'73	I	BD	1493.2	n/a	7	+ 15.8	+ 7.8	+ 11.5	− 2.8	+ 18.2	$1,000	4.5	1.12	1.027	0.08	...	16,999	15.40	13.87	15.40	16.13	6.9
JHTAX	Hancock Tax Exempt Inc	*'77	I	TF	476.2	n/a	∫†	+ 11.8	+ 8.1	+ 11.2	− 5.9	+ 15.8	$1,000	4.5	0.56	0.531	0.029	...	15,596	11.00	9.94	11.00	11.52	4.9
TAMBX	Hancock(J) Tax Free Bond Cl.A	*'90	I	TF	115.2	n/a	1∫†	+ 14.2	+ 10.6	+ 14.8	− 9.1	+ 19.2	$1,000	4.75	0.573	0.525	....	...	16,528	10.67	9.39	10.67	11.17	5.1
HULAX	Hawaiian Tax Free Trust	*'85	I	TF	661.0	10.0	∫†	+ 4.8	+ 7.7	+ 9.9	− 4.6	+ 14.6	$1,000	4.0	0.625	0.562	0.053	...	14,335	11.64	10.60	11.61	12.09	5.2
HRTVX	Heartland Value Fund	*'84	G	C	1170.2	n/a	8	+ 49.4	+ 42.5	+ 18.8	+ 1.6	+ 29.8	$1,000	None	0.658	0.13	0.218	1.40	27,651	29.91	22.59	27.95	27.95	2.4
HRCPX	Heritage Capital Apprec.Trust	*'85	G	C	73.6	9.1	....	+ 34.9	+ 9.6	+ 18.3	− 2.5	+ 20.1	$1,000	4.0	0.06	0.045	1.16	1.721	17,860	16.16	13.35	14.43	15.15	0.4
HRCVX	Heritage Income-Growth Trust	*'86	IG	FL	34.4	2.6	....	+ 33.5	+ 11.5	+ 2.9	− 0.9	+ 27.5	$1,000	4.0	0.31	0.344	0.49	0.247	17,244	13.10	10.44	12.84	13.48	2.3
IDEFX	IDEX Fund	*'85	G	C	328.2	37.1	....	+ 60.8	+ 0.1	+ 4.0	− 7.6	+ 47.2	$500	8.5	0.095	0.05	0.216	3.503	22,541	25.15	16.68	21.29	23.27	0.4
IDITX	IDEX II:Flexible Income Ptfl.Cl.A	*'87	I	FL	19.7	0.8	9	+ 23.9	+ 10.6	+ 13.4	− 4.1	+ 18.2	$500	4.75	0.631	0.615	....	...	16,646	9.47	8.34	9.47	9.94	6.3
IGLBX	IDEX II:Global Ptfl.Cl.A	*'92	G	GL	89.4	3.3	....	....	....	+ 30.9	− 1.0	+ 20.0	$500	5.5	....	....	0.59	0.625	.....	17.99	14.53	17.50	18.52	....
IDETX	IDEX II:Growth Ptfl.Cl.A	*'86	G	C	485.8	36.9	10	+ 57.9	+ 1.1	+ 3.6	− 8.3	+ 47.3	$500	5.5	....	....	0.07	3.16	22,205	24.33	16.10	20.83	22.04	....
IHIYX	IDEX II:Income Plus Cl.A	*'85	I	BD	68.7	11.1	11	+ 21.2	+ 12.1	+ 13.0	− 4.0	+ 18.0	$500	4.75	0.769	0.729	0.102	...	17,844	10.47	9.43	10.42	10.94	7.0
IGTEX	IDEX II:Tax Exempt Ptfl.Cl.A	*'85	I	TF	27.3	0.1	....	+ 10.6	+ 5.9	+ 8.4	− 2.3	+ 12.6	$500	4.75	0.532	0.565	0.035	0.068	14,037	11.65	10.79	11.54	12.12	4.4
INBNX	IDS Bond Cl.A	*'74	IS	BD	3279.0	181.5	12	+ 19.8	+ 10.2	+ 15.0	− 4.2	+ 20.6	$2,000	5.0	0.395	0.337	0.098	...	18,277	5.26	4.62	5.26	5.53	7.1
INVPX	IDS Equity Select Cl.A	'57	G	C	651.8	33.9	13	+ 31.4	+ 10.4	+ 14.5	− 7.9	+ 18.2	$2,000	5.0	0.10	0.087	0.494	...	17,503	12.49	9.80	11.61	12.22	0.8
INIDX	IDS Growth	*'72	G	C	1550.2	100.9	14§	+ 46.9	+ 8.1	+ 8.6	+ 3.0	+ 34.2	$2,000	5.0	0.04	....	1.51	...	24,195	23.51	16.39	22.28	23.45	0.2
INHYX	IDS High Yield Tax Exempt Cl.A	'78	I	TF	6186.0	174.5	∫†	+ 11.5	+ 8.4	+ 9.4	− 5.0	+ 16.8	$2,000	5.0	0.293	0.273	....	...	15,376	4.69	4.24	4.69	4.94	5.9
INMUX	IDS Mutual Cl.A	'40	GIS	B	2595.7	314.8	....	+ 22.9	+ 9.5	+ 14.2	− 2.9	+ 24.6	$2,000	5.0	0.568	0.525	0.506	0.128	18,017	13.26	11.05	13.08	13.77	4.1
INNDX	IDS New Dimensions	'68	G	C	6516.3	683.9	....	+ 50.7	+ 5.3	+ 14.0	− 3.0	+ 29.9	$2,000	5.0	0.118	....	0.505	...	24,002	18.25	13.16	17.27	18.18	0.6
INSEX	IDS Selective Cl.A	'45	IS	BD	1636.0	120.8	....	+ 16.3	+ 8.6	+ 12.8	− 4.3	+ 20.6	$2,000	5.0	0.59	0.596	0.123	0.029	17,446	9.60	8.46	9.60	10.11	5.8
INSTX	IDS Stock Cl.A	'45	IS	C	2025.7	92.9	....	+ 26.7	+ 6.6	+ 16.5	− 2.8	+ 25.4	$2,000	5.0	0.61	0.439	1.51	0.676	19,486	21.14	16.99	20.26	21.33	2.9
INTAX	IDS Tax Exempt Bond Cl.A	'76	I	TF	1135.5	117.0	∫†	+ 9.7	+ 6.6	+ 12.7	− 7.3	+ 17.9	$2,000	5.0	0.226	0.193	....	...	15,297	4.11	3.63	4.11	4.32	5.2
FIIIX	Invesco Industrial Income	'60	IG	C	4104.0	241.7	15	+ 44.8	+ 0.1	+ 17.0	− 3.8	+ 26.0	$1,000	None	0.412	0.30	0.54	0.236	20,885	13.06	10.54	12.72	12.72	3.2
FLRFX	Invesco Growth Fund	'35	GI	C	518.2	48.9	16	+ 40.8	+ 2.0	+ 16.4	− 8.8	+ 29.3	$1,000	None	0.034	0.053	0.50	0.842	19,476	5.81	4.48	4.95	4.95	0.7
INREX	Investors Research	*'59	G	L	32.0	1.6	....	+ 42.1	− 9.7	+ 6.3	− 0.6	+ 15.8	None	5.75	0.08	0.068	0.878	0.272	15,620	4.31	3.74	3.98	4.22	1.9
TRUSX	ISI Total Return U.S.Treas.	*'88	I	GB	n/a	n/a	....	+ 15.6	+ 4.2	+ 13.6	− 3.9	+ 20.5	$5,000	4.45	0.636	0.583	....	...	16,733	10.44	9.12	10.43	10.92	5.8
MCFIX	Ivy Bond Fund Cl.A	*'85	I	BD	108.6	n/a	17	+ 13.6	+ 7.6	+ 14.9	− 4.0	+ 16.0	$1,000	4.75	0.64	0.674	0.20	...	16,203	9.80	8.91	9.78	10.27	6.2
MCCNX	Ivy Canada Fund Cl.A	*'87	G	INTL	16.5	n/a	18	− 8.4	− 11.1	+ 59.3	− 14.1	+ 5.7	$1,000	5.75	0.021	0.003	....	0.198	9,694	9.87	7.61	9.21	9.77	0.2
MCGLX	Ivy Global Fund Cl.A	*'91	G	GL	21.3	n/a	19	....	+ 2.8	+ 29.2	− 5.0	+ 11.3	$1,000	5.75	0.01	0.006	0.696	0.512	.....	12.63	10.52	11.97	12.70	0.1
JANSX	Janus Fund	*'70	G	C	12058.0	892.2	....	+ 42.8	+ 5.3	+ 10.9	− 1.1	+ 29.3	$1,000	None	0.008	0.75	0.388	0.50	21,303	24.58	18.76	23.04	23.04	....
JAVLX	Janus Twenty Fund	*'85	G	C	3068.3	208.6	....	+ 69.3	+ 1.9	+ 3.4	− 6.7	+ 36.2	$1,000	None	0.067	2.25	....	3.00	22,804	31.46	22.52	25.67	25.67	0.3
JAVTX	Janus Venture Fund	*'85	G	C	1871.6	29.9	....	+ 47.6	+ 5.9	+ 9.0	+ 5.5	+ 26.4	$1,000	None	0.03	3.60	2.84	3.85	22,652	63.89	48.14	54.10	54.10	0.1
KAUFX	Kaufmann Fund	*'86	G	C	2915.0	n/a	20	+ 79.1	+ 11.3	+ 18.3	+ 9.0	+ 36.8	$1,500	None	....	0.095	....	...	33,018	5.16	3.64	5.05	5.05	....
KGRAX	Kemper Growth Cl.A	'66	G	C	1684.6	n/a	....	+ 65.9	− 1.6	+ 1.5	− 5.9	+ 31.6	$1,000	5.75	....	0.035	0.18	1.68	21,237	16.82	12.55	14.97	15.88	....
KGRBX	Kemper Growth Cl.B	*'94	G	C	781.0	n/a	21	....	....	....	− 2.4	+ 16.9	$1,000	ERF	....	....	0.18	...	11,409	16.56	12.48	14.74	14.74	....
KHYAX	Kemper High Yield Cl.A	*'78	I	BD	2492.9	n/a	22	+ 44.4	+ 16.6	+ 19.4	− 1.0	+ 14.2	$1,000	4.5	0.832	0.635	....	...	20,047	8.08	7.54	8.00	8.38	9.9
KHYBX	Kemper High Yield Cl.B	*'94	IG	BD	992.6	n/a	23	....	....	....	+ 0.2	+ 13.5	$1,000	ERF	0.403	0.577	....	...	11,373	8.07	7.53	8.00	8.00	5.0
KICAX	Kemper Inc. Cap. Pres. Cl.A	'72	I	BD	529.5	n/a	....	+ 17.0	+ 7.5	+ 11.4	− 3.3	+ 19.3	$1,000	4.5	0.618	0.515	....	...	17,134	8.86	7.84	8.86	9.28	6.7
KMBAX	Kemper Municipal Bond Cl.A	*'76	ISG	TF	3477.2	n/a	∫†	+ 12.3	+ 8.4	+ 12.9	− 5.5	+ 17.2	$1,000	4.5	0.613	0.504	0.035	...	16,181	10.59	9.38	10.54	11.04	5.6

Uniform Footnote Explanations-See page 234. Stock Splits & Divs. (figures adjusted): [1] Formerly Transamerica Group. [2] 5% ERF reducing over 6 yrs. Formerly Transamerica Group. [3] Was J.Hancock Balanced. [4] Was under AFA Group.. Was Natl.Tele.& Tech. [5] Was Sovereign Investors. [6] 3% ERF reducing over 3 yrs. Was Freedom Equity Value(10/92). [7] Was Hancock(J)Bond(5/92). Incl. Invest. Quality Bond(9/95). [8] 3% E.R.F.. [9] Was Total Income(10/93). [10] Was IDEX II Fund(10/93). [11] Was High Yield(10/93). [12] $2.50 redemption charge. [13] Was IDS Variable Pymt. Was Equity Plus (3/95). [14] Also custodian fee. [15] Was Financial Indust.Income(10/93). [16] Was Financial Industrial(10/93). [17] Incl.ret.of cap.. Was Mackenzie Fxd Inc Trust(10/94). [18] Was Mackenzie Canada Fund(10/94). [19] Was Mackenzie Global(10/94). [20] exit fee 0.2%. [21] Incls. Inv.Ptfl.Growth(6/94). 4% E.R.F.. % change fr.5/27/94. [22] 1994 adjusted for 1.22(5/94)merger ratio.. [23] Incls.Inv.Ptfl.Hi Yld(6/94). 4% E.R.F.. % change fr.5/27/94.

Ticker Symbol	Fund	Year Offered	Prin. Obj.	Type	Sept. 29, 1995 Total Net Assets (MIL.$)	Cash & Equiv (MIL.$)	See Foot-notes	Net Assets per Share % Change from Previous Dec. 31 — At: Dec. 31 1991	1992	1993	1994	Dec. 29, 1995	Min. Unit	Max. Sales Chg. %	Distributions Per Share from Invest. Income 1994	1995	Security Profits 1994	1995	$10,000 Invested 12-31-89 Now Worth	PRICE RECORD NAV Per Sh — 1995 — High	Low	#12-29-95 NAV Per Shr.	Offer Price	% Yield From Inv. Inc.
KSCAX	Kemper Small Cap.Equity Cl.A	'69	G	C	589.6	n/a	1	+67.5	....	+16.6	−3.5	+30.1	$1,000	5.75	....	....	0.34	1.05	23,073	7.23	5.34	6.00	6.37	....
KCTAX	Kemper State TF Inc.Ser:Cal.Cl.A	*'83	I	TF	1076.5	n/a	∫†	+11.0	+8.1	+12.3	−5.3	+16.8	$1,000	4.5	0.395	0.329	0.035	...	16,216	7.75	6.81	7.65	8.01	4.9
KTCAX	Kemper Technology Cl.A	'48	GI	C	952.8	n/a	....	+41.1	−1.3	+11.5	+10.9	+40.9	$1,000	5.75	....	....	1.50	2.13	24,337	15.19	9.59	11.66	12.37	....
KTRAX	Kemper Total Return Cl.A	*'64	B	C	1771.4	n/a	....	+39.2	+2.4	+11.3	−9.5	+18.2	$1,000	5.75	0.185	0.185	....	...	17,633	10.98	8.77	10.24	10.86	1.7
KTRBX	Kemper Total Return Cl.B	*'94	GI	C,FL	1139.8	n/a	2	....	....	....	+0.8	+24.3	$1,000	ERF	0.093	0.232	0.40	0.50	12,529	10.96	8.77	10.23	10.23	0.9
KUSAX	Kemper U.S.Govt. Secs. Cl.A	*'77	IP	BD	4680.3	n/a	★	+16.3	+4.4	+6.2	−3.0	+15.9	$1,000	4.5	0.694	0.491	....	...	15,801	9.06	8.20	9.04	9.47	7.3
KUMBX	Kemper U.S.Mtge Cl.B	*'94	I	GB	1455.4	n/a	3	....	....	....	+1.6	+14.7	$1,000	ERF	0.45	0.351	....	...	11,654	7.29	6.64	7.29	7.29	6.2
	Keystone America:																							
CPIFX	Capital Preserv. & Income Cl.B	*'91	IS	BD	19.2	0.3	4	....	+2.2	+3.4	+0.7	+7.4	$1,000	ERF	0.362	0.504	....	...	.....	9.75	9.50	9.71	9.71	3.7
KFAAX	Fund of the Americas Cl.A	*'93	GI	GL	15.6	0.5	....	....	....	....	−8.7	+9.5	$1,000	5.75	0.24	0.32	....	...	.....	10.47	8.12	10.14	10.76	2.2
KAGOX	Global Opport. Cl.A	*'88	G	GL	94.6	3.0	....	+30.2	+11.4	+37.7	+2.7	+23.7	$1,000	5.75	....	....	....	...	23,571	23.82	17.93	23.47	24.90	....
HRTLX	Hartwell Emerging Growth Cl.A	*'68	G	C	111.7	3.3	....	+70.2	+1.0	+4.6	−1.1	+21.7	$1,000	5.75	....	....	0.12	3.02	22,226	28.91	21.44	25.98	27.56	....
KAIAX	Intermed. Term Bond Cl.A	*'87	I	BD	14.2	0.5	5	+16.0	+7.8	+9.1	−2.7	+14.0	$1,000	4.75	0.65	0.622	....	...	15,859	9.10	8.52	9.09	9.54	6.8
OMGAX	Omega Fund Cl.A	*'68	C	C	120.3	6.8	....	+51.4	+2.2	+18.9	−5.6	+35.9	$1,000	5.75	....	....	0.61	1.56	23,201	19.56	15.22	19.56	20.75	....
KASAX	Strategic Income Fund Cl.A	*'87	I,G	BD	83.6	4.1	6	+41.4	+18.8	+30.5	−8.5	+10.4	$1,000	4.75	0.712	0.628	....	...	16,786	6.94	6.36	6.88	7.22	9.9
KATIX	Tax Free Income Cl.A	*'87	I	TF	94.1	0.3	∫†	+11.0	+8.4	+10.3	−7.5	+16.9	$1,000	4.75	0.548	0.516	....	...	15,011	10.15	9.07	10.10	10.60	5.2
	Keystone Funds:																							
KKONX	Balance Fund(K1)	'35	IS	B	1371.3	47.0	7	+23.4	+3.3	+10.1	−4.6	+26.6	$1,000	ERF	0.36	0.33	0.105	0.14	16,629	10.91	8.99	10.91	10.91	3.3
KBTWX	Diversified Bond(B2)	'35	I	BD	739.4	61.9	....	+17.9	+9.5	+15.9	−6.8	+15.1	$1,000	ERF	1.12	1.27	....	...	15,281	15.61	14.40	15.35	15.35	7.3
KBFOX	High Income Fund(B4)	'35	I	BD	760.5	12.0	8	+39.0	+17.6	+25.1	−11.6	+8.8	$1,000	ERF	0.42	0.412	....	...	15,813	4.44	4.15	4.18	4.18	10.0
KESTX	International	'54	G	GL	132.9	26.5	9	+14.1	+2.4	+30.4	−6.1	+11.4	$1,000	ERF	0.065	0.10	0.74	0.05	12,128	7.33	6.10	7.17	7.17	0.9
KSPMX	Precious Metals Holdings	*'74	GI	PM	195.5	1.4	10	+8.2	−13.5	+101.9	−14.3	−0.4	$1,000	ERF	0.12	....	....	...	11,936	24.31	18.95	22.65	22.65	0.5
KBONX	Quality Bond(B1)	'35	I	BD	302.5	17.4	11	+14.1	+3.7	+8.6	−4.9	+16.1	$1,000	ERF	0.946	0.936	....	...	15,067	15.72	14.33	15.72	15.72	6.0
KSFOX	Small Co. Growth(S4)	'35	G	C	1816.9	53.0	....	+68.0	+5.6	+23.8	−1.0	+46.6	$1,000	ERF	....	....	0.63	1.80	31,079	10.61	7.33	9.36	9.36	....
KKTWX	Strategic Growth(K2)	'35	G	C	503.2	13.5	12	+39.3	+8.2	+12.7	−2.8	+27.0	$1,000	ERF	....	0.02	0.93	0.92	19,459	8.48	7.03	8.14	8.14	....
KSTEX	Tax Exempt Trust	*'85	I,P	TF	675.9	5.6	∫†	+10.0	+7.2	+9.7	−7.0	+16.2	$1,000	ERF	0.584	0.553	....	...	14,720	10.98	9.87	10.93	10.93	5.3
KSTFX	Tax Free Fund	*'78	IP	TF	1192.9	11.6	13∫†	+9.8	+7.2	+10.4	−7.2	+16.2	$1,000	ERF	0.435	0.391	....	...	14,895	7.88	7.09	7.86	7.86	5.5
....	Laurel European Fund Cl.R	*'87	G	C	n/a	n/a	14	+11.6	−3.0	+20.6	−4.9	+15.7	$25	None	0.102	0.114	1.607	0.651	14,537	12.02	10.13	11.07	11.07	0.9
LMVTX	Legg Mason Value Trust	*'82	G	C	1315.5	42.8	15	+34.5	+11.3	+11.1	+1.4	+39.7	$1,000	None	0.05	0.172	0.04	1.24	19,484	25.64	18.98	25.19	25.19	0.2
	Liberty Funds:																							
FALDX	American Leaders Cl.A	'68	IG	C	363.1	14.5	....	+30.3	+11.1	+9.5	....	+33.3	$500	4.5	0.243	0.149	0.353	0.20	20,792	19.35	14.39	18.83	19.93	1.2
FTITX	F.T.Series:Intl.Equity Cl.A	*'84	GR	INTL	208.2	1.4	†	+7.5	−5.9	+30.8	+0.4	+6.3	$500	4.5	0.003	0.087	0.896	1.89	12,497	18.78	15.94	16.49	17.45	....
FUSGX	Fund for U.S.Govt.Secs.Cl.A	'69	I	BD	1371.1	26.0	★	+12.8	+5.0	+4.2	−1.9	+13.4	$500	4.5	0.562	0.522	....	...	14,979	7.98	7.49	7.98	8.36	6.7
LEIFX	Liberty Equity Income Cl.A	*'86	IR	CV	158.3	6.3	16	+40.8	+9.5	+20.0	−4.2	+30.5	$500	4.5	0.44	0.376	....	...	20,401	13.95	10.72	13.65	14.44	3.0
LMSFX	Liberty Municipal Securities Cl.A	'76	I	TF	676.3	15.5	17∫†	+12.1	+8.1	+10.1	−3.8	+6.2	$500	4.5	0.67	....	0.23	...	14,408	11.16	10.49	11.16	11.69	5.7
LBUTX	Liberty Utility Cl.A	*'87	IG	C	783.7	40.7	†	+24.9	+8.6	+14.9	−7.8	+24.9	$500	4.5	0.58	0.485	0.539	...	18,235	12.68	10.50	12.68	13.42	4.3
LDDVX	Lindner Dividend	*'76	IG	C	1990.3	114.0	18	+26.7	+20.6	+10.5	−3.2	+18.4	$2,000	ERF	1.90	1.41	0.573	...	18,132	27.68	23.92	26.96	26.96	7.0
LDNRX	Lindner Growth Fund	'54	GI	C	1438.9	112.5	18†	+23.3	+12.7	+19.7	−0.6	+15.0	$2,000	ERF	0.339	0.267	1.84	0.526	16,979	25.29	20.36	23.23	23.23	1.5
LAFFX	Lord Abbett:Affiliated	'34	GI	C	5052.1	200.0	....	+21.3	+11.9	+13.2	+3.5	+30.5	$250	5.75	0.315	0.26	0.77	1.19	19,612	12.34	9.97	11.59	12.30	2.6
LBNDX	Lord Abbett:Bond Debenture	*'71	IR	BD,CV	1235.5	166.6	....	+35.9	+15.2	+15.3	−3.6	+15.9	$1,000	4.75	0.877	0.803	....	...	18,756	9.29	8.64	9.29	9.75	9.0
LCFIX	Lord Abbett Calif.Tax-Free Inc.	*'85	I	TF	296.4	4.3	∫†	+12.9	+8.7	+13.6	−10.3	+15.7	$1,000	4.75	0.608	0.452	....	...	15,481	10.79	9.67	10.75	11.29	5.4
LAGWX	Lord Abbett:Developing Growth	'73	G	C,SP	196.3	4.1	....	+56.2	−3.1	+12.3	+6.2	+45.1	$1,000	5.75	....	0.125	0.808	2.74	24,516	14.71	9.55	11.56	12.27	....
LDFVX	Lord Abbett:Fundamental Value	*'86	G,I	C,CV	39.8	2.5	....	+18.8	+11.4	+12.6	−1.0	+25.8	$1,000	5.75	0.19	0.09	1.033	0.53	18,559	14.52	11.72	14.11	14.97	1.3
LAGIX	Lord Abbett:Global Income	*'88	IR	GL	240.7	3.9	....	+13.2	+6.1	+12.9	−3.3	+14.4	$1,000	4.75	0.74	0.55	....	...	16,636	8.90	7.90	8.58	9.01	8.2
LAGEX	Lord Abbett:Global Equity	*'88	G	GL	85.2	5.6	....	+14.7	−1.8	+26.0	−0.1	+8.2	$1,000	5.75	0.10	0.06	0.778	0.48	13,484	12.59	10.98	11.96	12.69	0.8
LANSX	Lord Abbett:Tax Free Inc.:National	*'84	I,P	TF	650.7	n/a	∫†	+12.1	+8.4	+12.7	−8.1	+15.5	$1,000	4.75	0.647	0.431	....	...	15,539	11.38	10.20	11.37	11.94	5.4

Uniform Footnote Explanations-See page 234. **Stock Splits & Divs.** (figures adjusted): [1] Was Summit. [2] Incls. Inv.Ptfl.Total Return (6/94). 4% E.R.F.. % change fr.5/27/94. [3] Incls.Inv.Ptfl.Govt.(6/94). 4% E.R.F.. [4] 3% ERF reducing over 4 yrs.. [5] Was Invest.Grade(4/93). [6] E.R.F.2% within 4 yrs. Was High Yield Bond(4/93). [7] Now incl.Mass.Fund. [8] Was B4 Hi Inc.Bond. [9] Was Polaris. [10] Was Precious Metals Hldgs. [11] Was B1 Hi Grade. All Keystone Custodian 4% ERF reducing 1% per yr.. [12] Incl.Travelers Equities. [13] Closed to public. [14] Was Capstone European Plus(11/93). [15] 2-for-1 split,Aug'91. [16] Was Convert.Secs. & Inc.. [17] Was Federated Tax Free Inc.(1/93). [18] 2% E.R.F..

Ticker Symbol	Fund	Year Offered	Prin. Obj.	Type	Sept. 29, 1995 Total Net Assets (MIL.$)	Cash & Equiv (MIL.$)	See Foot-notes	Net Assets per Share % Change from Previous Dec. 31 At: Dec. 31 1991	1992	1993	1994	Dec. 29, 1995	Min. Unit	Max. Sales Chg. %	Distributions Per Share from Invest. Income 1994	1995	Security Profits 1994	1995	$10,000 Invested 12-31-89 Now Worth	PRICE RECORD 1995 High	Low	NAV Per Sh #12-29-95 NAV Per Shr.	Offer Price	% Yield From Inv. Inc.
LANYX	Lord Abbett:Tax Free Inc:New York..	*'84	I	TF	331.6	4.8	....	+ 13.2	+ 8.6	+ 12.4	− 9.1	+ 14.3	$1,000	4.75	0.636	0.474	....	...	15,218	11.12	10.09	11.08	11.63	5.5
LATIX	Lord Abbett:Tax Free Inc:Texas	*'87	I	TF	100.3	0.4	∫†	+ 12.7	+ 8.4	+ 12.5	− 6.8	+ 16.2	$1,000	4.75	0.593	0.434	....	...	15,971	10.42	9.30	10.40	10.92	5.4
LAGVX	Lord Abbett:U.S.Govt.Secs	'32	IS	BD	3260.5	62.1	[1]	+ 15.9	+ 6.7	+ 9.0	− 4.2	+ 13.1	$500	4.75	0.245	0.178	....	...	15,861	2.75	2.58	2.75	2.89	8.5
LAVLX	Lord Abbett:Value Appreciation	'83	G	C	219.5	11.1	....	+ 25.8	+ 12.8	+ 12.5	− 2.8	+ 22.6	$1,000	5.75	0.16	0.17	0.875	1.45	18,149	12.18	9.65	12.18	12.92	1.2
LUBIX	Lutheran Bro Income	*'72	I	BD	936.5	121.8	....	+ 16.4	+ 7.7	+ 9.9	− 4.8	+ 17.1	$500	5.0	0.568	0.506	....	...	16,158	8.87	7.97	8.85	9.32	6.1
MCCAX	Mackenzie Funds:Calif.Municipal	*'88	I	TF	38.5	n/a	[2]∫†	+ 10.5	+ 5.2	+ 11.3	− 4.5	+ 15.5	$1,000	4.75	0.58	0.449	0.014	0.099	15,156	10.46	9.52	10.46	10.98	5.3
IVYFX	Mackenzie Funds:Ivy Growth Cl.A	'60	G	C	285.1	n/a	[3]	+ 30.5	+ 5.2	+ 12.2	− 3.3	+ 26.1	$1,000	5.75	0.095	....	0.646	0.79	18,069	17.58	13.73	16.75	17.77	0.5
IVYIX	Mackenzie Funds:Ivy Growth with Inc.Cl.A .	*'84	G	C	60.9	n/a	....	+ 36.1	+ 2.5	+ 14.9	− 5.1	+ 22.8	$1,000	5.75	0.135	....	....	0.166	18,642	11.28	8.91	10.98	11.65	1.2
IVINX	Mackenzie Funds:Ivy Intl.Cl.A............	*'86	G	INTL	414.6	n/a	....	+ 16.9	+ 1.0	+ 48.4	+ 3.3	+ 11.6	$1,000	5.75	0.091	0.039	0.924	0.099	17,594	30.67	26.09	30.67	32.54	0.3
MCTMX	Mackenzie Funds:Limited Term Municipal ..	*'91	I	TF	101.7	n/a	....	....	....	+ 7.3	− 2.0	+ 10.5	$1,000	3.0	0.601	0.413	....	...	.....	10.35	9.70	10.33	10.65	5.6
MCNMX	Mackenzie Funds:Natl.Municipal	*'88	I	TF	26.3	n/a	[4]∫†	+ 10.2	+ 6.1	+ 11.3	− 5.0	+ 14.9	$1,000	4.75	0.521	0.453	0.026	...	15,014	10.13	9.20	10.13	10.64	4.9
MCNYX	Mackenzie Funds:N.Y.Municipal	*'88	I	TF	39.6	n/a	[4]∫†	+ 11.6	+ 7.6	+ 10.0	− 3.9	+ 14.5	$1,000	4.75	0.522	0.457	0.049	...	15,232	10.04	9.16	10.04	10.54	5.0
MCSGX	Mainstay Government Fund	*'86	I	GB	988.5	n/a	[5]	+ 11.8	+ 3.6	+ 5.7	− 2.8	+ 13.9	$500	ERF	0.435	0.43	....	...	14,394	8.46	7.75	8.41	8.41	5.2
	Mass.Finl.Services:																							
MFBFX	MFS Bond Fund Cl.A	'74	I	BD	527.4	n/a	....	+ 17.1	+ 6.1	+ 13.6	− 4.4	+ 20.7	$1,000	4.75	0.896	0.96	....	...	17,377	13.68	12.03	13.68	14.36	6.2
MCGBX	MFS Capital Growth Cl.B	*'86	G	C	419.6	n/a	[6]	+ 29.9	+ 8.2	+ 4.4	− 0.9	+ 39.3	$1,000	ERF	0.053	....	0.621	2.507	19,872	17.99	12.97	15.59	15.59	0.3
MFEGX	MFS Emerging Growth Fund Cl.A..	*'93	GR	C	1154.2	n/a	....	....	....	....	+ 4.8	+ 41.2	$1,000	5.75	....	....	0.388	...	14,798	26.96	18.55	26.71	28.34	....
MEGBX	MFS Emerging Growth Cl.B...........	*'86	G	C	1774.6	n/a	....	+ 87.3	+ 11.7	+ 24.0	+ 4.0	+ 40.1	$1,000	ERF	....	....	0.245	...	37,270	26.74	18.52	26.46	26.46	....
MGMTX	MFS Govt.Mortgage Fund Cl.A.........	'86	I	GB	557.6	n/a	[7]	+ 12.3	+ 5.4	+ 7.0	− 2.2	+ 15.4	$1,000	4.75	0.47	0.36	....	...	14,551	6.84	6.23	6.84	7.18	6.5
MGTBX	MFS Govt.Mortgage Fund Cl.B.......	*'93	I	GB	757.1	n/a	[8]	....	....	....	− 2.8	+ 15.2	$1,000	ERF	0.42	0.351	....	...	11,197	6.84	6.23	6.84	6.84	6.1
MFGSX	MFS Govt.Securities Cl.A................	'84	I	GB	324.4	n/a	....	+ 13.5	+ 6.8	+ 9.9	− 3.2	+ 18.9	$1,000	4.75	0.716	0.609	....	...	16,452	10.01	8.91	10.01	10.51	6.8
MGOFX	MFS Growth Opportunities Cl.A.....	*'71	G	C	716.4	n/a	[9]	+ 21.9	+ 7.6	+ 16.1	− 4.1	+ 34.3	$1,000	5.75	0.032	....	0.879	1.718	18,770	13.63	10.04	11.94	12.67	0.3
MHITX	MFS High Income Fund Cl.A	*'78	I	BD	602.0	n/a	....	+ 46.7	+ 16.5	+ 18.7	− 2.0	+ 15.8	$1,000	4.75	0.442	0.403	....	...	19,477	5.20	4.82	5.18	5.44	8.1
MHIBX	MFS High Income Fund Cl.B	*'93	I	BD	289.9	n/a	....	....	....	....	− 3.3	+ 15.0	$1,000	ERF	0.399	0.362	....	...	11,121	5.20	4.82	5.18	5.18	7.7
MMNSX	MFS Managed Sectors Fund Cl.A..	*'93	G	SP	188.4	n/a	....	....	....	....	− 3.7	+ 33.0	$1,000	5.75	0.399	....	1.031	2.887	12,808	16.30	11.70	12.75	13.53	2.9
MSEBX	MFS Managed Sectors Fund Cl.B..	*'86	G	SP	189.9	n/a	....	+ 59.6	+ 3.9	+ 3.7	− 3.5	+ 32.0	$1,000	ERF	....	....	0.954	2.719	18,903	16.21	11.69	12.80	12.80	....
MMBFX	MFS Municipal Bond Fund Cl.A.......	'76	I	TF	1898.0	n/a	∫†	+ 12.3	+ 9.0	+ 20.5	− 6.4	+ 16.5	$1,000	4.75	0.602	0.548	0.001	...	16,953	11.36	10.16	11.30	11.86	5.1
MMIBX	MFS Municipal Income Fund Cl.B..	*'86	I	TF	346.8	n/a	....	+ 11.0	+ 7.6	+ 10.6	− 5.2	+ 13.1	$1,000	ERF	0.425	0.396	....	...	14,574	8.91	8.20	8.88	8.88	4.8
MFRFX	MFS Research Fund Cl.A..................	'74	GI	C,BD	506.2	n/a	[10]	+ 31.9	+ 11.0	+ 24.4	+ 0.4	+ 38.5	$1,000	5.75	0.018	0.051	1.28	0.973	23,452	16.57	11.94	15.64	16.59	0.1
MSFRX	MFS Total Return Cl.A......................	'70	IG	C,BD	2240.2	n/a	[11]	+ 21.1	+ 9.8	+ 13.9	− 2.9	+ 25.4	$1,000	4.75	0.498	0.526	0.059	0.665	17,759	14.83	12.42	14.41	15.13	3.3
MVLFX	MFS Value Fund Cl.A	*'83	G	C	210.5	n/a	[12]	+ 23.7	+ 17.9	+ 25.2	− 2.5	+ 31.1	$1,000	5.75	....	....	0.697	...	20,656	12.67	8.81	11.54	12.24	....
MWEBX	MFS World Equity Fund Cl.B..........	*'86	G	GL	52.6	n/a	....	+ 5.7	+ 1.6	+ 29.0	− 3.7	+ 17.3	$1,000	ERF	....	....	1.546	0.707	15,132	16.98	14.28	16.35	16.35	....
MWGTX	MFS World Govts.Fund Cl.A...........	*'81	P,I	BD,INTL	162.9	n/a	[13]	+ 13.4	+ 12.7	+ 6.0	− 6.4	+ 15.4	$1,000	4.75	0.155	....	0.452	1.575	17,252	12.58	10.85	11.02	11.57	1.3
MIGFX	Mass.Invest.Growth Stock Cl.A........	'32	G	C	1169.4	n/a	....	+ 47.3	+ 6.4	+ 14.4	− 6.8	+ 28.2	$1,000	5.75	....	....	1.08	1.614	20,394	12.73	9.40	10.63	11.28	....
MITTX	Mass.Invest.Trust Cl.A	'24	IR	C	1945.3	n/a	....	+ 27.1	+ 7.9	+ 10.1	− 1.0	+ 38.9	$1,000	5.75	0.246	0.251	1.069	1.03	20,722	13.87	10.05	12.71	13.49	1.8
MRYRX	Merrill Lynch:Bal.Fund for Inv.& Retire.Cl.B..	*'85	GI	C,BD	152.1	n/a	[14]	+ 23.1	+ 3.0	+ 14.3	− 7.4	+ 18.1	$1,000	ERF	0.174	0.205	0.973	0.44	15,342	12.12	10.25	11.60	11.60	1.5
MABAX	Merrill Lynch:Basic Value Cl.A	*'77	GI	C	3026.0	n/a	....	+ 26.8	+ 10.3	+ 21.9	+ 2.0	+ 32.1	$1,000	6.5	0.692	0.644	0.784	0.575	20,009	29.09	22.42	28.31	29.88	2.3
MLCPX	Merrill Lynch:Capital Fund Cl.A.........	*'73	GI	B	2915.0	n/a	....	+ 24.0	+ 4.8	+ 13.4	+ 0.8	+ 32.3	$1,000	6.5	0.937	1.156	1.56	2.299	19,869	32.84	25.73	30.55	32.24	2.9
MLHIX	Merrill Lynch:Corp.Bond:Hi Inc.Cl.A ...	*'78	I	BD	902.0	n/a	[15]	+ 37.9	+ 19.9	+ 16.7	− 2.5	+ 16.1	$1,000	4.0	0.798	0.666	....	...	20,968	7.84	7.31	7.82	8.15	9.8
MAFSX	Merrill Lynch:Federal Secs.Trust Cl.A...	'84	I	GB	218.0	n/a	....	+ 13.0	+ 5.5	+ 7.1	− 3.7	+ 14.0	$1,000	4.0	0.53	0.591	....	...	15,489	9.76	9.05	9.76	10.17	5.2
MLHYX	Merrill Lynch:Muni Bond National Cl.A..	*'79	I	TF	1041.0	n/a	[16]∫†	+ 12.1	+ 9.4	+ 12.2	− 6.4	+ 16.7	$1,000	4.0	0.598	0.527	0.209	...	15,872	10.45	9.37	10.44	10.88	5.5
MLMBX	Merrill Lynch:Muni Bond:Insured Cl.A...	*'77	I	TF	1687.0	n/a	∫†	+ 11.7	+ 8.7	+ 12.6	− 6.7	+ 16.4	$1,000	4.0	0.454	0.395	0.141	...	15,842	8.26	7.41	8.25	8.59	5.3
MLNYX	Merrill Lynch:N.Y.Muni Bond Cl.B.....	*'85	I	TF	564.0	n/a	[17]∫†	+ 12.4	+ 9.6	+ 11.1	− 9.0	+ 14.3	$1,000	ERF	0.573	0.446	....	...	14,819	11.50	10.41	11.48	11.48	5.0
BEGRX	Mutual Beacon Fund........................	*'62	GI	C	3435.3	618.3	....	+ 17.8	+ 22.7	+ 22.8	+ 5.6	+ 25.7	$5,000	None	0.44	0.84	1.36	2.21	21,652	38.38	31.08	35.94	35.94	1.2
MQIFX	Mutual Qualified Fund......................	*'80	GI	C,BD	2812.6	604.7	[18]	+ 21.0	+ 22.5	+ 22.5	+ 5.7	+ 26.2	$1,000	None	0.43	0.65	1.43	3.27	21,799	32.87	26.72	29.74	29.74	1.4
MUTHX	Mutual Shares Fund..........................	'49	G	SP	5123.7	958.1	[18]	+ 20.8	+ 21.1	+ 20.8	+ 4.5	+ 28.6	$5,000	None	1.34	1.93	4.56	12.81	21,445	98.62	78.73	86.45	86.45	1.6

Uniform Footnote Explanations-See page 234. Stock Splits & Divs. (figures adjusted): [1] Was Lord Abbett Inc. [2] Incl.ret.of cap.. [3] Incl. Amer. Fund(4/95). Was Ivy Fund. [4] Incl.ret.of cap. [5] 5% E.R.F.reducing over 7 yrs. Was Mackay-Shields Govt.Plus. [6] All Cl.B funds have 4% ERF reducing over 6 years. [7] Was Govt Plus(3/93). [8] Was Inc.Plus(3/93). [9] Was Capital Dvlpmt.(9/93). [10] Was Fin'l Dvlpmt(6/92). [11] Was Mass.Inc.Dvlpmt. [12] Was Special Fund(9/93). [13] Was Mass.Fin'l Intl.Tr.Bond. [14] 4% E.R.F.reducing over 5 yrs. Was ML Retire Ben Inv.Prog. [15] Rated "BBB" or lower. [16] Was High Yld.. [17] 4% E.R.F.reducing over 5 yrs. [18] Closed to new investors.

Ticker Symbol	Fund	Year Offered	Prin. Obj.	Type	Sept. 29, 1995 Total Net Assets (MIL.$)	Cash & Equiv (MIL.$)	See Foot-notes	Net Assets per Share % Change from Previous Dec. 31 At: Dec. 31 1991	1992	1993	1994	Dec. 29, 1995	Min. Unit	Max. Sales Chg. %	Distributions Per Share from Invest. Income 1994	Invest. Income 1995	Security Profits 1994	Security Profits 1995	$10,000 Invested 12-31-89 Now Worth	PRICE RECORD 1995 High	1995 Low	NAV Per Sh #12-29-95 NAV Per Shr.	Offer Price	% Yield From Inv. Inc.
MUIFX	Nationwide Fund	'33	I	C	800.1	21.8	[1]	+29.9	+2.9	+6.7	+0.5	+29.2	$250	4.5	0.298	0.23	1.26	...	18,556	18.76	14.47	18.55	19.42	1.5
NBSSX	Neub. & Berman Focus Fund	'52	G	SP	1009.5	32.3	[2]	+24.3	+19.7	+16.3	+0.9	+36.2	$1,000	None	0.20	0.11	1.48	1.35	22,353	30.09	21.47	27.93	27.93	0.7
NGUAX	Neub. & Berman Guardian Fund	'50	G	FL	298.4	55.5	[3]	+34.1	+13.8	+14.4	+0.6	+32.0	$1,000	None	0.25	0.28	0.23	0.76	22,093	24.49	18.14	23.03	23.03	1.1
NLMBX	Neub.& Berman Ltd. Maturity Bond Fund.	*'86	I	BD	296.6	1.2	....	+11.4	+5.0	+6.7	-0.4	+4.0	$2,000	None	0.56	....	....	...	14,001	10.15	9.69	10.15	10.15	5.5
NMANX	Neub. & Berman Manhattan Fund	*'79	G	C	634.3	10.1	....	+30.9	+17.8	+10.0	-3.6	+31.0	$1,000	None	0.01	....	0.70	0.96	19,707	13.89	9.88	12.14	12.14	0.1
NBMUX	Neub. & Berman Munic. Secs. Trust	*'87	I	TF	44.4	0.2	....	+8.7	+6.7	+3.8	-3.9	+7.9	$2,000	None	0.46	....	....	...	13,245	10.96	10.11	10.92	10.92	4.2
NPRTX	Neub. & Berman Partners	*'75	G	FL	1599.2	35.1		+22.1	+17.5	+16.5	-1.9	+35.2	$1,000	None	0.11	0.20	1.90	2.70	20,993	25.03	18.42	22.14	22.14	0.5
NEFGX	New England Growth	'68	G	C	1208.5	n/a	[4]	+56.7	-6.7	+12.2	-7.0	+34.6	$2,500	6.5	0.113	0.007	0.726	1.383	21,581	12.40	8.63	10.55	11.28	1.0
NICSX	Nicholas Fund	'69	G	C	3281.6	150.9	....	+41.7	+12.2	+5.8	-3.0	+34.7	$500	None	0.707	0.624	3.32	4.035	20,945	63.47	47.79	60.03	60.03	1.2
NCTWX	Nicholas II Fund	*'83	G,R	C	682.2	26.6	....	+39.4	+9.3	+6.3	+0.9	+28.4	$1,000	None	0.206	0.272	1.89	2.401	19,682	31.34	24.24	28.73	28.73	0.7
NCIBX	Nuveen Cal.TF:Insur.Bond	*'86	I	TF	210.2	4.9	∫†	+11.1	+9.1	+12.1	-6.8	+18.3	$1,000	None	0.556	0.509	0.027	...	15,940	10.91	9.60	10.88	10.88	5.1
NCSPX	Nuveen Cal.TF:Spl.Bond	*'86	I	TF	219.8	3.7	∫†	+10.7	+9.0	+11.1	-6.4	+17.4	$1,000	None	0.589	0.576	0.074	...	15,600	10.73	9.60	10.72	10.72	5.5
NITNX	Nuveen Ins.TF Bond:Natl	*'86	I	TF	780.0	16.2	∫	+12.4	+9.3	+13.2	-6.3	+18.7	$1,000	None	0.578	0.573	0.016	...	16,458	11.08	9.77	11.06	11.06	5.2
NIMAX	Nuveen Ins.TF Bond:Mass.	*'86	I	TF	63.4	1.2	∫†	+11.4	+8.9	+11.7	-4.7	+15.5	$1,000	None	0.546	0.545	....	...	15,840	10.60	9.60	10.57	10.57	5.2
NINYX	Nuveen Ins.TF Bond:NY Ptfl.	*'86	I	TF	358.2	7.7	∫†	+13.0	+9.4	+12.8	-6.1	+17.2	$1,000	None	0.57	0.584	0.019	...	16,129	10.74	9.62	10.71	10.71	5.3
NUVBX	Nuveen Municipal Bond Cl.R	'76	I	TF	2813.0	131.3	∫†	+11.0	+8.2	+8.4	-1.9	+14.9	$1,000	4.75	0.536	0.515	0.049	0.027	15,555	9.42	8.64	9.40	9.40	5.7
NBMAX	Nuveen TF Bond:Mass.Ptfl.	*'86	I	TF	78.0	2.8	∫†	+12.1	+9.6	+11.8	-5.0	+15.5	$1,000	None	0.536	0.546	....	...	15,855	10.03	9.11	9.99	9.99	5.4
NTNYX	Nuveen TF Bond:N.Y.Ptfl	*'86	I	TF	160.4	6.1	∫†	+13.4	+10.0	+12.7	-5.9	+17.5	$1,000	4.75	0.571	0.582	0.047	...	16,150	10.81	9.64	10.76	10.76	5.3
NXOHX	Nuveen TF Bond:Ohio Ptfl	*'86	I	TF	172.8	2.3	∫†	+11.6	+9.1	+12.7	-5.2	+16.5	$1,000	None	0.568	0.567	0.04	...	16,049	10.74	9.67	10.72	10.72	5.3
OAKMX	Oakmark Fund	*'91	G	C	2797.0	227.2	....	....	+48.8	+25.1	+3.1	+34.4	$2,500	None	0.231	0.284	1.469	0.841	.....	30.74	22.87	29.75	29.75	0.8
OAKIX	Oakmark International Fund	*'92	G	INTL	907.9	41.7	....	....	....	+53.4	-8.9	+8.2	$2,500	None	....	....	1.06	1.043	.....	14.10	11.38	12.38	12.38	....
OPOCX	Oppenheimer Discovery	*'85	G	C	799.4	n/a	....	+71.5	+16.6	+17.8	-11.3	+36.3	$1,000	5.75	....	....	1.617	3.592	24,179	44.83	32.57	41.90	44.46	....
OPPEX	Oppenheimer Equity Inc.Cl.A	'68	I	B	2008.8	n/a		+16.9	+6.8	+14.4	-2.7	+23.4	$1,000	5.75	0.48	0.36	0.127	...	16,909	11.41	9.15	10.92	11.59	4.1
OPPAX	Oppenheimer Global Cl.A	'69	G	GL	2186.0	n/a	....	+27.2	-14.2	+41.3	-3.2	+16.4	$1,000	5.75	....	0.238	3.749	2.051	17,237	37.20	30.92	34.89	37.02	....
OPGSX	Oppenheimer Gold & Spl.Minerals	*'83	G	PM	167.9	n/a	....	+2.5	-10.1	+61.8	-6.0	-1.5	$1,000	5.75	0.067	0.059	....	...	10,105	14.47	11.81	13.08	13.88	0.5
OPPHX	Oppenheimer High Yield Cl.A	'78	I	BD	1085.2	n/a	....	+27.1	+13.4	+19.6	-2.2	+13.6	$1,000	4.75	1.35	1.166	....	...	18,596	13.41	12.77	13.41	14.08	9.6
OPPSX	Oppenheimer Growth Cl.A	'72	G	SP	948.7	n/a	[5]	+43.8	+13.3	+2.7	+2.4	+21.1	$1,000	5.75	0.239	....	2.80	...	20,231	34.70	25.22	30.64	32.51	0.7
MSIGX	Oppenheimer Main Street Inc. & Growth	*'88	GI	C	2221.8	n/a	....	+62.5	+29.5	+33.6	-1.6	+29.6	$1,000	5.75	0.44	0.30	....	...	32,591	27.18	20.85	26.89	28.53	1.5
QFVFX	Oppenheimer Quest for Value Cl.A	*'80	G	C	290.9	n/a	[6]	+32.3	+17.8	+6.4	+0.8	+37.0	$1,000	5.5	0.083	0.103	0.828	0.977	21,320	15.08	11.17	14.26	15.13	0.5
OPSIX	Oppenheimer Strategic Inc.Cl.A	*'88	I	CV,GB	3220.2	n/a	....	+19.2	+7.0	+18.7	-4.3	+13.8	$1,000	4.75	0.43	0.409	0.014	...	17,708	4.77	4.46	4.77	5.01	8.6
OPTAX	Oppenheimer Tax Free Bond Cl.A	'76	IS	TF	546.9	n/a	∫†	+11.7	+9.8	+13.1	-9.1	+17.9	$1,000	4.75	0.56	0.547	0.004	...	15,699	10.00	8.92	9.98	10.48	5.3
OPTRX	Oppenheimer Total Return Cl.A	'44	GI	B	1486.8	n/a	....	+34.9	+12.3	+20.8	-7.8	+21.8	$1,000	5.75	0.212	0.15	....	...	19,791	9.96	7.77	9.35	9.92	2.1
PDGAX	PaineWebber Amer. Growth & Inc. Cl.A	*'83	GI	C	190.7	n/a	[7]	+35.1	+3.8	-2.6	-5.9	+23.2	$1,000	4.5	0.242	....	1.21	...	16,183	23.40	18.06	22.39	23.45	1.0
PASBX	PaineWebber Asset Alloc.Cl.B	*'86	RS	FL	49.6	n/a	[8]	+18.3	+4.4	+7.0	-14.7	+12.4	$1,000	ERF	0.119	0.034	0.701	...	12,974	11.55	9.39	10.57	10.57	1.1
PCIAX	PaineWebber Cal.Tax Free Income Cl.A	*'85	I	TF	165.9	n/a	∫†	+12.9	+7.3	+11.4	-8.3	+15.6	$1,000	4.0	0.544	0.487	0.097	...	15,207	11.20	10.07	11.18	11.65	4.7
PGBBX	PaineWebber Global Income Cl.B	*'87	IG	GL	495.8	n/a	[8]†	+10.1	+0.4	+8.8	-4.8	+11.4	$1,000	ERF	0.566	0.586	....	...	14,923	10.42	9.84	10.41	10.41	5.4
PGRAX	PaineWebber Olympus Growth Cl.A	*'85	GP	C	188.5	n/a	....	+47.5	+4.0	+13.3	-10.9	+22.9	$1,000	4.5	....	....	0.03	...	17,490	24.73	18.55	23.12	24.21	....
PHIAX	PaineWebber High Income Cl.A	*'84	IP	SP,L	264.3	n/a	[9]	+44.7	+23.1	+21.2	-11.3	+9.4	$1,000	4.0	0.819	0.696	....	...	19,127	7.32	6.92	6.92	7.21	11.4
PIGAX	PaineWebber Invstmt.Grade Income Cl.A	*'84	IP	BD	258.6	n/a	....	+17.8	+8.5	+5.8	-5.9	+18.0	$1,000	4.0	0.73	0.659	....	...	15,871	10.79	9.65	10.79	11.24	6.5
PMHAX	PaineWebber Municipal High Inc.Cl.A	*'87	I	TF	59.4	n/a	[10]∫†	+12.8	+8.2	+11.9	-8.0	+13.7	$1,000	4.0	0.547	0.466	0.026	...	15,043	10.37	9.50	10.36	10.79	5.1
PTFAX	PaineWebber Natl.Tax Free Income Cl.A	*'84	I	TF	321.1	n/a	[11]∫†	+10.8	+7.5	+12.1	-7.0	+14.1	$1,000	4.0	0.63	0.427	0.014	...	15,019	11.84	10.73	11.84	12.33	5.1
PNYAX	PaineWebber N.Y.Tax Free Inc.Cl.A	*'88	I	TF	29.8	n/a	∫†	+11.9	+9.5	+12.4	-8.3	+15.9	$1,000	4.0	0.544	0.412	0.102	...	15,399	10.83	9.66	10.81	11.26	4.8
PREAX	PaineWebber Regional Finl.Growth Cl.A	*'86	IP	C	63.9	n/a	....	+65.0	+38.7	-0.4	-0.8	+31.2	$1,000	4.5	0.135	....	1.27	...	26,047	22.82	15.73	20.57	21.54	0.6
PUGAX	PaineWebber U.S.Govt.Income Cl.A	*'84	I	GB	383.1	n/a	....	+13.9	+5.7	+3.5	-9.6	+15.7	$1,000	4.0	0.67	0.508	....	...	14,180	9.21	8.38	9.21	9.59	7.0
PGSGX	Paragon Gulf South Growth	*'91	G	C	96.4	n/a	[12]	+32.7	+20.9	+7.7	-8.4	+22.0	$250	4.5	....	....	0.266	0.435	19,309	18.58	14.72	17.70	18.53	....
PAITX	Paragon Intermed.Term Bond	*'90	I	GB	308.1	n/a	[13]	+14.7	+6.3	+9.6	-4.4	+16.4	$250	4.5	0.663	0.615	....	...	16,030	10.51	9.53	10.51	11.01	6.0

Uniform Footnote Explanations-See page 234. Stock Splits & Divs. (figures adjusted): [1] Was MIF Nat'wide Fund. [2] Was Selected Sectors(3/95). [3] 3-for-1 split(1/93). [4] Was TNE Growth(4/94). [5] Was Special(11/94). [6] 3-for-1 split,June'91. Was Quest for Value(11/95). [7] Was Divd. Growth (5/95). [8] 5% E.R.F.reducing over 6 yrs. [9] Was Hi Yld Bond Ptfl. Was Master Growth. [10] Was Classic Hi Yld Muni. [11] Was Tax Exempt Inc.. [12] 1991 % change fr.7/91. [13] 5-10 yr.category.

Ticker Symbol	Fund	Year Offered	Prin. Obj.	Type	Sept. 29, 1995 Total Net Assets (MIL.$)	Sept. 29, 1995 Cash & Equiv (MIL.$)	See Foot-notes	Net Assets per Share % Change from Previous Dec. 31 — At: Dec. 31 1991	1992	1993	1994	Dec. 29, 1995	Min. Unit	Max. Sales Chg. %	Distributions Per Share from Invest. Income 1994	Invest. Income 1995	Security Profits 1994	Security Profits 1995	$10,000 Invested 12-31-89 Now Worth	PRICE RECORD NAV Per Sh — 1995 — High	1995 Low	#12-29-95 NAV Per Shr.	#12-29-95 Offer Price	% Yield From Inv. Inc.
PGLAX	Paragon Louisiana Tax Free	*'90	I	TF	202.2	n/a	∫†	+ 9.5	+ 7.9	+ 10.5	− 3.2	+ 11.2	$250	4.5	0.523	0.487	....	...	14,053	10.82	10.10	10.76	11.27	4.6
PSTGX	Paragon Short-Term Govt.	*'90	I	ST	129.2	n/a	....	+ 10.7	+ 5.4	+ 5.9	− 0.1	+ 9.3	$250	4.5	0.494	0.497	....	...	14,639	10.25	9.82	10.25	10.73	4.6
PVEIX	Paragon Value Equity Income	*'90	I	C	129.3	n/a	....	+ 29.2	+ 9.1	+ 7.0	− 2.7	+ 42.2	$250	4.5	0.32	0.313	1.025	1.27	20,868	14.99	11.24	14.42	15.10	2.1
PAVGX	Paragon Value Growth	*'90	G	C	212.8	n/a	....	+ 37.7	+ 14.2	+ 9.8	− 8.3	+ 28.3	$250	4.5	0.20	0.325	0.436	1.373	20,761	17.21	13.40	15.63	16.37	1.2
PABRX	Pasadena Balanced Return Fund	*'87	GI	B	55.9	2.9	....	+ 38.8	+ 4.5	+ 1.0	− 4.4	+ 23.6	$1,500	5.5	0.46	....	....	...	17,241	26.47	20.44	25.39	26.87	1.7
PASGX	Pasadena Growth Fund	*'86	G	C	483.4	14.4	[1]	+ 67.8	+ 2.2	− 5.9	− 3.8	+ 25.2	$1,000	5.5	....	....	....	...	18,562	19.95	15.29	19.28	20.40	....
PANFX	Pasadena Nifty Fifty	*'91	G	C	159.4	7.9	....	+ 67.5	+ 3.7	− 0.5	+ 1.1	+ 28.2	$1,000	5.5	....	....	....	...	22,400	22.86	17.20	22.18	23.47	....
PAXWX	Pax World Fund	*'71	IGE	B	438.6	57.2	....	+ 20.2	+ 0.5	− 1.1	+ 2.5	+ 28.9	$250	None	0.50	0.79	....	0.14	17,490	17.12	13.37	16.33	16.33	3.1
PBHGX	PBHG Growth Fund	*'85	G	C	1700.0	n/a	[2]	+ 48.3	+ 23.1	+ 46.4	+ 4.7	+ 50.3	$1,000	None	....	....	0.011	...	37,431	23.92	15.01	23.92	23.92	....
PENNX	Pennsylvania Mutual	'62	G	C	696.2	n/a	[3]	+ 31.8	+ 16.2	+ 3.9	− 0.7	+ 18.6	$2,000	ERF	0.11	0.11	0.73	0.97	16,585	8.79	7.35	7.71	7.71	1.4
PHBLX	Phoenix Balanced	*'70	IG	C,BD	2375.0	324.0	....	+ 25.1	+ 6.6	+ 6.4	− 4.5	+ 23.0	$500	4.75	0.476	0.523	....	0.916	17,851	17.83	14.81	16.80	17.64	2.7
CTESX	Phoenix Cal.Tax Exempt Bonds	*'84	I	TF	120.0	6.0	[4]∫†	+ 10.7	+ 6.7	+ 9.5	− 5.1	+ 18.2	$500	4.75	0.756	0.693	0.395	...	15,524	13.39	11.88	13.37	14.04	5.4
PHCVX	Phoenix Convert.Fund	*'82	IR	C,CV	228.0	8.0	....	+ 12.3	+ 12.7	+ 9.8	− 3.7	+ 21.1	$500	4.75	0.799	0.986	0.19	0.567	16,854	19.10	16.52	18.49	19.41	4.1
NASTX	Phoenix Equity Opportunities Cl.A	'44	IGE	C	204.0	6.0	[5]	+ 22.8	+ 16.6	+ 13.1	− 5.1	+ 32.9	$500	4.75	0.087	....	0.46	0.886	19,097	9.31	6.76	8.15	8.56	1.0
PHGRX	Phoenix Growth	'58	G	C	2379.0	234.0	[6]	+ 26.8	+ 4.2	+ 4.3	− 1.6	+ 33.7	$500	4.75	0.289	0.238	0.813	1.633	19,218	26.45	19.50	24.34	25.55	1.1
PHCHX	Phoenix High Yield	*'80	IR	BD	506.0	8.0	[7]	+ 23.6	+ 16.4	+ 20.7	− 7.6	+ 16.8	$500	4.75	0.78	0.78	....	...	18,516	8.25	7.36	8.25	8.66	9.0
NAINX	Phoenix Inc.& Growth Cl.A	'40	I	FL	504.0	n/a	[8]	+ 22.8	+ 11.6	+ 14.3	− 6.1	+ 23.0	$500	4.75	0.484	0.43	0.462	0.035	17,802	9.87	8.33	9.78	10.27	4.7
NAMFX	Phoenix Multi Sector Fxd.Inc.Cl.A	*'89	IP	INTL,BD	169.0	n/a	[9]	+ 27.1	+ 11.7	+ 15.1	− 6.5	+ 19.1	$2,500	4.75	0.948	0.948	....	...	18,197	12.78	11.13	12.78	13.42	7.1
PHSKX	Phoenix Stock	*'81	G	C	177.0	3.0	....	+ 28.3	+ 7.6	+ 11.5	− 3.9	+ 50.1	$500	4.75	0.221	0.048	0.914	2.159	20,960	17.87	11.88	15.64	16.42	1.3
PHTBX	Phoenix Tax Exempt Bond	*'88	IP	TF	146.0	1.0	∫†	+ 10.5	+ 10.3	+ 13.2	− 7.3	+ 17.3	$500	4.75	0.642	0.55	0.044	...	15,453	11.48	10.19	11.43	12.00	5.3
PTRFX	Phoenix Total Return	*'82	G,I	FL	365.0	72.0	[10]	+ 28.4	+ 10.2	+ 10.4	− 2.3	+ 18.0	$500	4.75	0.309	0.516	0.001	0.987	18,802	17.19	14.79	15.98	16.78	1.8
NWWOX	Phoenix Worldwide Opportunities	'56	G	C	134.0	11.0	[11]	+ 24.5	+ 3.2	+ 37.8	+ 0.1	+ 14.8	$250	4.75	0.028	....	1.70	0.595	15,768	10.00	8.12	9.27	9.73	0.3
PGMAX	Pilgrim Govt. Secs. Income	*'84	I	GB	42.1	n/a	[12]★	+ 11.3	+ 7.0	+ 4.6	− 3.6	+ 14.0	$1,000	3.0	0.835	0.85	....	...	14,716	13.20	12.23	13.20	13.86	6.0
PMCFX	Pilgrim America Magna Cap Fund	*'70	GP	C	208.4	n/a		+ 24.9	+ 7.9	+ 4.0	+ 4.1	+ 35.6	$1,000	5.0	0.152	0.126	0.703	...	19,152	16.07	11.96	16.07	17.05	0.9
PQNCX	PIMCO Advisors Funds:Equity Inc. Cl.C	*'88	G	CV	174.3	n/a	[13]	+ 32.7	+ 7.7	+ 21.0	− 5.0	+ 26.8	$1,000	ERF	0.24	0.165	....	0.779	17,686	14.82	11.77	14.12	14.12	1.7
PGWCX	PIMCO Advisors Funds:Growth Cl.C	*'84	G	C	1290.0	n/a	[13]	+ 41.1	+ 2.1	+ 9.1	− 0.7	+ 27.6	$1,000	ERF	....	....	1.189	2.934	19,975	25.63	19.78	22.60	22.60	....
PHNCX	PIMCO Advisors High Inc.Cl.C	'84	I	GB	157.5	n/a	[13]	+ 11.3	+ 7.0	+ 7.1	− 6.9	+ 18.7	$1,000	ERF	0.57	0.553	....	...	14,278	8.02	7.22	8.02	8.02	7.1
PILCX	PIMCO Advisors Funds:Intl.Cl.C	*'86	G	INTL	215.3	n/a	[13]	+ 19.8	− 5.8	+ 33.3	− 8.1	+ 5.8	$1,000	ERF	....	....	0.244	...	12,374	11.95	10.28	11.87	11.87	....
POPCX	PIMCO Advisors Funds:Opportunity Cl.C.	*'84	G	C	715.2	n/a	[13]	+ 66.4	+ 28.4	+ 35.8	− 4.8	+ 42.4	$1,000	ERF	....	....	0.875	7.999	36,423	38.51	26.35	31.12	31.12	....
PPMCX	PIMCO Advisors Funds:Precious Metals Cl.C.	*'88	G	C	42.3	n/a	[13]	− 5.3	− 12.3	+ 89.5	− 9.7	− 4.2	$1,000	ERF	....	....	....	...	10,211	12.22	9.94	11.20	11.20	....
PTECX	PIMCO Advisors Funds:Tax Exempt Cl.C.	*'85	I	TF	54.2	n/a	[13]∫†	+ 9.7	+ 7.2	+ 10.4	− 9.4	+ 16.6	$1,000	ERF	0.49	0.449	....	...	13,962	12.29	10.86	12.23	12.23	4.0
PUSCX	PIMCO Advisors Funds:U.S.Govt. Cl.C	*'85	I	GB	287.1	n/a	[13]	+ 15.1	+ 2.3	+ 7.0	− 5.2	+ 16.1	$1,000	ERF	0.53	0.462	....	...	14,491	9.38	8.45	9.37	9.37	5.7
PUSGX	Pioneer Amer.Income Cl.A	*'88	I	GB	162.7	n/a	[14]	+ 11.3	+ 6.4	+ 8.9	− 3.9	+ 15.0	$1,000	4.5	0.659	0.622	....	...	15,464	10.20	9.38	10.20	10.68	6.2
PIOBX	Pioneer Bond Fund	*'78	I	BD	104.8	n/a	....	+ 14.8	+ 7.5	+ 11.2	− 4.1	+ 17.0	$1,000	4.5	0.674	0.602	....	...	16,445	9.62	8.72	9.62	10.07	6.7
PCGRX	Pioneer Capital Growth Cl.A	*'90	G	C	875.4	n/a	....	+ 36.8	+ 28.8	+ 16.5	+ 14.8	+ 24.2	$1,000	5.75	....	0.088	0.947	0.874	29,268	20.62	15.78	18.70	19.84	....
PEQIX	Pioneer Equity-Income	*'90	IR	C	246.6	n/a	....	+ 25.9	+ 20.4	+ 12.8	− 1.2	+ 31.6	$1,000	5.75	0.55	0.517	0.40	0.142	22,232	19.47	15.17	19.29	20.47	2.7
PEURX	Pioneer Europe	*'91	G	INTL	81.7	n/a	[15]	+ 3.7	− 3.3	+ 25.0	+ 5.9	+ 21.3	$1,000	5.75	0.056	....	1.399	1.425	16,102	22.04	17.25	19.79	21.00	0.3
PIODX	Pioneer Fund	'28	GI	C	2411.0	n/a	....	+ 21.8	+ 13.4	+ 14.1	− 0.6	+ 26.3	$50	5.75	0.49	0.486	1.30	2.089	17,727	26.80	21.28	24.36	25.85	1.9
PIGDX	Pioneer Gold Shares	*'90	G	PM	27.6	n/a	....	− 9.9	− 3.6	+ 70.8	− 11.7	+ 2.5	$1,000	5.75	....	....	....	...	13,427	8.07	6.35	7.40	7.85	....
PMBFX	Pioneer Intermed.Tax Free Fund	*'86	I	TF	79.4	n/a	[16]∫†	+ 10.8	+ 8.4	+ 10.8	− 5.9	+ 13.1	$1,000	3.5	0.50	0.444	0.002	...	15,027	10.48	9.60	10.44	10.82	4.6
PSTTX	Pioneer Short Term Income	*'92	IS	ST	53.4	n/a	[17]	....	+ 1.6	+ 5.7	− 0.1	+ 9.3	$5,000	2.5	0.217	0.239	....	...	.....	3.87	3.73	3.85	3.95	5.5
PIOTX	Pioneer II	*'69	GI	C	5115.5	n/a	....	+ 25.2	+ 9.1	+ 18.4	− 1.8	+ 27.0	$50	5.75	0.28	0.282	1.81	1.732	17,790	21.59	16.87	19.46	20.65	1.4
PITHX	Pioneer Three	'82	GI	C	1082.4	n/a	....	+ 36.1	+ 19.8	+ 15.9	− 5.8	+ 19.1	$1,000	5.75	0.24	0.229	1.145	1.709	18,466	21.87	17.95	19.53	20.72	1.2
PBALX	Piper Balanced Fund	*'87	ICA	C,BD	173.3	0.7	....	+ 26.9	+ 10.5	+ 7.1	− 0.3	+ 21.4	$250	4.0	0.398	0.33	0.121	...	17,668	14.28	11.63	13.81	14.39	2.8
PJEGX	Piper Emerging Growth	*'90	EG	C	252.7	18.4	....	+ 64.8	+ 7.8	+ 18.5	− 4.9	+ 26.4	$250	4.0	....	....	....	...	.....	26.44	18.65	24.05	25.05	....
SEPFX	Piper Equity Strategy Fund	*'87	CA	C,CV	48.5	1.8	[18]	+ 40.6	+ 11.5	+ 11.0	− 2.5	+ 10.3	$250	4.0	0.087	....	....	...	18,620	19.79	16.37	18.36	19.13	0.5

Uniform Footnote Explanations-See page 234. Stock Splits & Divs. (figures adjusted): [1] 2-for-1 split,9/91. [2] Was Capstone PBHG. [3] 1% E.R.F.. [4] Was Natl.Cal.T.E.(12/93). [5] Was Natl.Stock Fund(12/93). [6] Was Chase Fd. of Boston. [7] Includes Natl.Bond(12/93). [8] Was Total Inc.(5/92). Was Natl.Inc.& Gr.(12/93). [9] Was Natl.Multi S.Fxd.Inc.(12/93). [10] Includes Natl.Total Return(12/93). [11] Was Natl.WW Opport.(12/93). [12] Was Pilgrim GNMA(8/95). [13] Were Thomson Funds(11/94). [14] Was U.S.Govt.(7/94). [15] 1991 % change fr.4/91. [16] Was Muni Bond(3/94). [17] 1992 % change fr.8/92.. [18] Was Sector Performance(12/94).

Ticker Symbol	Fund	Year Offered	Prin. Obj.	Type	Sept. 29, 1995 Total Net Assets (MIL.$)	Sept. 29, 1995 Cash & Equiv (MIL.$)	See Foot-notes	Net Assets per Share % Change from Previous Dec. 31 At: Dec. 31 1991	1992	1993	1994	Dec. 29, 1995	Min. Unit	Max. Sales Chg. %	Distributions Per Share from Invest. Income 1994	Invest. Income 1995	Security Profits 1994	Security Profits 1995	$10,000 Invested 12-31-89 Now Worth	PRICE RECORD 1995 High	1995 Low	NAV Per Sh #12-29-95 NAV Per Shr.	Offer Price	% Yield From Inv. Inc.
PGPEX	Piper Global Pacific Europ.Growth	*'90	G	GL	161.5	0.9	....	+11.1	−0.9	+51.3	−3.8	−1.1	$250	4.0	....	....	1.052	...	.....	14.23	12.56	13.56	14.13	....
PJGIX	Piper Govt.Income Fund	*'87	IP	GB	105.9	0.5	....	+18.0	+4.0	+9.9	−8.9	+19.4	$250	4.0	0.699	0.614	....	...	15,858	9.20	8.19	9.20	9.58	7.3
PJGRX	Piper Growth & Income	*'92	V	GB,C	73.4	0.8	....	....	....	+6.1	+1.1	+34.9	$250	4.0	0.238	0.145	0.037	...	.....	13.83	10.21	13.66	14.23	1.7
PJIGX	Piper Institutional Govt.Income	*'88	IP	GB,ST	319.9	39.8	★	+16.9	+11.7	+15.4	−27.7	+22.3	$25,000	1.5	0.90	1.235	....	...	14,643	8.20	7.42	7.91	8.03	11.2
PJMNX	Piper Minnesota Tax Exempt	*'88	IP	TF	133.9	1.1	∫†	+10.6	+7.9	+12.6	−5.4	+18.4	$250	4.0	0.607	0.55	....	...	15,969	11.32	9.98	11.29	11.76	5.2
PJNTX	Piper National Tax Exempt	*'88	IP	TF	57.1	1.1	∫†	+11.6	+8.3	+15.9	−8.3	+17.6	$250	4.0	0.568	0.499	....	...	16,148	11.19	9.88	11.16	11.63	4.9
PJVLX	Piper Value Fund	*'87	G	C	173.3	0.4	....	+47.1	+2.8	+5.1	−3.5	+13.8	$250	4.0	0.072	0.07	0.097	2.00	17,663	21.07	18.28	18.98	19.77	0.4
PRGFX	Price T.Rowe:Growth Stock	'50	G	C	2626.9	145.1	....	+33.4	+6.0	+15.5	+0.8	+30.9	$2,500	None	0.18	0.23	1.66	0.97	.....	24.41	18.55	23.35	23.35	0.8
PRGIX	Price T.Rowe:Growth & Income	*'82	GIE	C	1623.9	250.4	....	+31.2	+15.0	+12.8	−0.2	+30.3	$2,500	None	0.49	0.59	0.42	0.60	.....	19.76	15.68	19.18	19.18	2.6
PRHYX	Price T.Rowe:High Yield	'84	I	BD	1218.0	113.0	....	+29.4	+14.2	+21.1	−7.8	+14.0	$2,500	None	0.751	0.647	....	...	16,891	8.24	7.74	8.19	8.19	9.2
PRITX	Price T.Rowe:Intl.Stock	*'80	G	INTL	6145.0	460.9	....	+15.6	−3.5	+40.0	−0.8	+11.4	$2,500	None	0.12	0.18	0.62	0.20	.....	12.57	10.56	12.23	12.23	1.0
PRNEX	Price T.Rowe:New Era	'69	G	C	1087.3	152.0	....	+14.4	+2.1	+15.3	+5.2	+20.7	$2,500	None	0.38	0.48	0.87	1.20	.....	24.22	19.95	22.65	22.65	1.7
PRNHX	Price T.Rowe:New Horizons	'60	G	C	2107.5	122.9	....	+51.9	+10.3	+21.4	+0.2	+55.2	$2,500	None	....	....	1.43	2.41	.....	22.52	14.56	20.50	20.50	....
PRCIX	Price T.Rowe:New Income	*'73	IP	BD	1572.0	50.9	....	+14.8	+4.7	+9.4	−2.2	+17.2	$2,500	None	0.576	0.553	0.07	...	16,293	9.28	8.37	9.28	9.28	6.2
OTCFX	Price T.Rowe:OTC Fund	*'56	G	C	274.4	36.6	1	+38.6	+13.2	+18.1	....	+33.7	$2,500	None	0.03	0.12	1.56	2.01	.....	18.22	13.67	16.32	16.32	0.2
PRTAX	Price T.Rowe:Tax-Free Income	'76	I	TF	1336.0	101.0	∫†	+11.8	+9.1	+12.5	−5.4	+16.8	$2,500	None	0.525	0.476	0.04	...	16,011	9.81	8.78	9.80	9.80	5.4
PRBDX	Princor Bond Cl.A	*'88	I	BD	104.8	3.1	....	+16.7	+8.2	+12.5	−4.5	+21.6	$1,000	4.75	0.78	0.779	0.01	...	17,206	11.60	10.15	11.59	12.17	6.4
PCACX	Princor Cap. Accum. Cl.A	'69	GI	C	344.5	5.7		+37.0	+7.9	+7.4	−0.8	+29.4	$300	4.75	0.204	....	0.344	1.467	18,240	25.21	19.53	23.83	25.02	0.8
PEMGX	Princor Emerging Growth Cl.A	*'88	G	C	148.2	15.0	2	+52.4	+14.8	+12.3	+3.0	+33.6	$300	4.75	0.015	....	0.144	0.749	25,360	32.30	24.18	31.84	33.43	....
PRGVX	Princor Govt. Secs. Income Cl.A	*'85	I	GB	258.2	2.6	....	+16.1	+5.8	+9.0	−4.9	+18.7	$1,000	4.75	0.681	0.706	....	...	16,474	11.47	10.20	11.45	12.02	5.7
PRGWX	Princor Growth Cl.A	*'69	G	C	172.3	12.3	....	+55.9	+9.4	+7.3	+2.7	+32.1	$300	4.75	0.129	....	0.627	1.177	24,505	38.60	29.39	37.78	39.66	0.3
PRMGX	Princor Balanced Fund Cl.A	*'88	R	BD	57.3	5.4	3	+31.4	+8.7	+8.9	−4.1	+21.1	$300	4.75	0.233	0.175	0.055	0.673	17,161	14.24	11.94	13.61	14.29	1.6
PTBDX	Princor Tax Exempt Bond Cl.A	*'86	I	TF	177.8	3.4	∫†	+11.7	+9.3	+12.1	−9.3	+20.3	$1,000	4.75	0.635	0.644	....	...	15,650	12.24	10.64	12.18	12.79	5.0
PRWLX	Princor World Fund Cl.A	*'82	G	GL	128.8	2.0	†	+15.2	+0.8	+46.3	−5.7	+10.3	$300	4.75	....	....	0.185	0.329	14,525	7.45	6.31	7.04	7.39	....
PBQFX	Prudential:Equity Cl.B	*'82	G	C	2046.1	245.5	4	+23.0	+12.6	+21.0	+1.5	+30.4	$1,000	ERF	0.12	0.16	0.647	0.678	21,249	16.72	13.20	16.43	16.43	0.7
PRGLX	Prudential:Global Cl.B	*'84	G	GL	275.4	13.4	5	+12.3	−5.3	+47.9	−5.5	+14.1	$1,000	ERF	....	....	0.185	0.715	14,161	15.53	12.20	14.26	14.26	....
PBGPX	Prudential:Govt.Income Cl.B	*'85	I	GB	619.1	4.9	6	+13.5	+5.4	+6.7	−4.6	+18.0	$1,000	ERF	0.532	0.494	....	...	15,203	9.32	8.30	9.32	9.32	5.7
PBHYX	Prudential:High Yield Cl.B	'79	R	BD	2680.6	179.6	7	+32.0	+14.9	+15.9	−2.8	+16.1	$1,000	ERF	0.777	0.725	....	...	18,032	8.18	7.66	8.18	8.18	9.5
PBHMX	Prudential:Natl.Muni.Cl.B	'80	I	TF	189.9	17.0	8∫†	+12.0	+8.2	+11.8	−6.3	+15.7	$1,000	ERF	0.75	0.705	0.10	...	15,510	16.07	14.42	16.02	16.02	4.7
PRUTX	Prudential:Utility Cl.B	*'81	I	C	2351.7	5.4	9	+18.6	+8.8	+16.9	−8.4	+24.4	$1,000	ERF	0.24	0.22	0.375	0.189	16,071	9.87	8.15	9.87	9.87	2.4
PAGVX	Putnam Amer.Govt.Income	'85	I	GB	2185.7	78.7	10★	+8.7	+5.7	+5.9	−2.9	+17.7	$500	4.75	0.622	0.609	....	...	14,824	8.91	8.03	8.91	9.35	6.7
PMITX	Putnam Balanced Retirement Fund Cl.A	*'85	R	O	473.3	9.9	11	+23.0	+10.7	+12.1	−1.2	+26.3	$500	5.75	0.52	0.45	....	0.182	17,866	10.08	8.48	10.08	10.69	4.9
PCTEX	Putnam Cal.Tax Ex.Inc. Cl.A	'83	I	TF	3169.9	31.0	∫†	+11.0	+8.7	+12.7	−7.0	+18.3	$500	4.75	0.44	0.435	0.025	...	15,948	8.76	7.75	8.73	9.17	4.8
PCONX	Putnam Cvt.Inc-Gwth Tr.	*'72	IG	CV	780.2	61.6	....	+28.8	+20.7	+16.6	−1.9	+22.0	$500	5.75	0.96	0.762	1.16	0.714	19,590	20.35	17.13	19.43	20.62	4.7
EBERX	Putnam Energy Resources	*'80	G	C	136.9	3.3	....	+7.2	+6.6	+12.7	−4.4	+21.6	$500	5.75	....	....	....	...	14,253	17.18	13.64	16.79	17.81	....
PFITX	Putnam Federal Income Trust	*'86	I	GB	425.4	2.6	12	+14.5	+5.6	+4.9	−3.1	+18.4	$500	4.75	0.652	0.588	....	...	15,672	10.41	9.25	10.41	10.93	6.0
PGEOX	Putnam(George) Cl.A	'37	GIS	B	1100.4	39.3	....	+22.2	+7.6	+10.6	−0.4	+29.4	$500	5.75	0.57	0.577	0.321	0.628	18,518	15.81	12.93	15.50	16.45	3.5
PGGIX	Putnam Global.Govt.Income	*'87	I	GL	367.9	23.5	....	+14.1	+4.1	+12.7	−9.8	+14.6	$500	4.75	0.90	0.75	....	...	15,941	14.05	12.65	14.05	14.75	6.1
PEQUX	Putnam Global Growth Cl.A	'67	G	GL	1724.2	122.4		+17.8	+0.1	+31.8	−0.9	+14.7	$500	5.75	....	0.176	0.313	0.406	16,023	10.40	8.77	9.99	10.60	....
PGRWX	Putnam Growth & Income Cl.A	'57	GI	C	7888.2	489.8	....	+18.6	+11.5	+14.2	−0.3	+36.1	$500	5.75	0.40	0.40	0.439	0.72	20,963	16.86	12.74	16.19	17.18	2.3
PHSTX	Putnam Health Sciences Cl.A	*'82	G	C	995.5	37.3	....	+47.9	−10.5	−0.1	+15.1	+46.8	$500	5.75	0.257	0.27	0.516	0.922	25,807	43.21	29.44	42.61	45.21	0.6
PHIGX	Putnam High Yield Cl.A	*'78	I	BD	3055.8	85.0	....	+36.8	+18.7	+17.6	−4.4	+17.2	$500	4.75	1.26	1.235	....	...	20,219	12.19	11.34	12.19	12.80	9.8
PHYIX	Putnam High Yld.Advantage	*'86	I	BD	843.1	48.8	....	+42.9	+18.0	+20.0	−4.8	+17.9	$500	4.75	1.02	0.99	....	...	20,985	9.62	8.92	9.62	10.10	10.1
PINCX	Putnam Income Cl.A	'54	IS	B	906.7	1.6	....	+17.4	+9.4	+11.6	−3.2	+19.1	$500	4.75	0.516	0.479	....	...	17,169	7.23	6.45	7.23	7.59	6.8
PINVX	Putnam Investors Cl.A	'25	GIS	C	994.1	44.1	....	+27.3	+7.8	+17.3	−3.5	+37.5	$500	5.75	....	0.085	0.734	1.123	20,761	9.84	7.08	8.61	9.14	....
PTFLX	Putnam Florida Tax Exempt Inc.Cl.A	*'90	I	TF	258.4	8.3	∫†	+11.7	+9.3	+10.5	−6.1	+16.5	$500	4.75	0.50	0.452	....	...	15,289	9.41	8.43	9.38	9.85	5.1

Uniform Footnote Explanations-See page 234. Stock Splits & Divs. (figures adjusted): [1] Was USF&G OTC Secs.9/3/92. [2] Was Aggressive Growth(2/92). [3] Was Managed(12/94). [4] 5%E.R.F.reducing 1% per yr. [5] 5% E.R.F.reducing 1% per yr. [6] 5%E.R.F.,reducing 1% per yr. [7] 5% E.R.F.,reducing 1% per yr. [8] 4% E.R.F.,reducing over 5 yrs. [9] 5% E.R.F.reducing over 5yrs. 2-for-1 split,July '93. [10] Incl.ret.of cap.. Was Hi Inc.Govt.Tr.(11/92). [11] Incl.ret.of cap.. Was Option Inc.Tr II. Was Managed Income(6/95). [12] Was Putnam GNMA Plus.

Ticker Symbol	Fund	Year Offered	Prin. Obj.	Type	Sept. 29, 1995 Total Net Assets (MIL.$)	Sept. 29, 1995 Cash & Equiv (MIL.$)	See Foot-notes	Net Assets per Share % Change from Previous Dec. 31 — At: Dec. 31 1991	1992	1993	1994	Dec. 29, 1995	Min. Unit	Max. Sales Chg. %	Distributions Per Share from Invest. Income 1994	Invest. Income 1995	Security Profits 1994	Security Profits 1995	$10,000 Invested 12-31-89 Now Worth	PRICE RECORD NAV Per Sh — 1995 — High	1995 Low	#12-29-95 NAV Per Shr.	Offer Price	% Yield From Inv. Inc.
PXMAX	Putnam Mass.Tax Exempt Inc.II	*'89	I	TF	251.8	2.9	∫†	+ 13.2	+ 10.4	+ 11.9	− 6.0	+ 16.2	$500	4.75	0.54	0.412	0.02	...	16,314	9.55	8.54	9.52	9.99	5.4
PXMIX	Putnam Mich.Tax Exempt Inc.II	*'89	I	TF	136.7	4.0	∫†	+ 12.7	+ 7.9	+ 11.3	− 5.3	+ 14.9	$500	4.75	0.518	0.417	....	...	15,522	9.32	8.42	9.27	9.73	5.3
PXMNX	Putnam Minn.Tax Exempt Inc.II Cl.A	*'89	I	TF	95.9	2.6	∫†	+ 9.9	+ 7.6	+ 11.3	− 5.3	+ 15.6	$500	4.75	0.504	0.449	....	...	15,215	9.21	8.32	9.18	9.64	5.2
PTNJX	Putnam N.J.Tax Exempt Inc.	*'90	I	TF	236.8	n/a	∫†	+ 11.5	+ 8.4	+ 12.2	− 6.2	+ 15.4	$500	4.75	0.504	0.449	....	...	15,678	9.22	8.34	9.19	9.65	5.2
PTEIX	Putnam N.Y.Tax Exempt Inc.Cl.A	'83	I	TF	1972.0	28.5	∫†	+ 13.9	+ 10.1	+ 13.0	− 7.2	+ 14.6	$500	4.75	0.505	0.45	....	...	15,628	9.07	8.25	9.02	9.47	5.3
PXOHX	Putnam Ohio Tax Exempt Inc.II	*'89	I	TF	190.0	2.9	∫†	+ 10.9	+ 9.1	+ 10.8	− 5.2	+ 14.3	$500	4.75	0.476	0.411	0.012	...	15,412	9.21	8.36	9.16	9.62	4.9
PTFHX	Putnam Municipal Income Cl.A	*'89	I	TF	821.4	13.4	[1]∫†	+ 11.8	+ 10.9	+ 11.7	− 6.3	+ 17.7	$500	4.75	0.533	0.484	....	...	16,251	9.27	8.24	9.23	9.69	5.5
POEGX	Putnam OTC Emerging Growth Cl.A	*'82	G	C	845.2	45.6	....	+ 40.7	+ 12.4	+ 31.8	+ 1.8	+ 54.9	$500	5.75	....	....	0.857	1.709	29,581	17.15	10.57	15.02	15.94	....
PTEPX	Putnam Penn.Tax Exempt Income	*'89	I	TF	179.3	3.0	∫†	+ 12.3	+ 9.3	+ 12.2	− 5.7	+ 15.9	$500	4.75	0.434	0.48	0.013	...	16,136	9.52	8.58	9.48	9.95	4.4
PTAEX	Putnam Tax Exempt Inc.Cl.A	'76	I	TF	179.3	3.0	∫†	+ 12.3	+ 9.5	+ 13.2	− 7.7	+ 16.6	$500	4.75	0.53	0.465	....	...	15,685	9.16	8.21	9.12	9.57	5.5
PTHYX	Putnam Tax Free High Yield	*'85	I	TF	486.3	9.3	[2]∫†	+ 11.3	+ 10.2	+ 12.2	− 5.8	+ 15.1	$500	ERF	0.862	0.758	....	...	15,458	14.76	13.41	14.70	14.70	5.9
PTFIX	Putnam Tax Free Inc.Insured	*'85	I	TF	186.5	3.0	[2]∫†★	+ 10.7	+ 6.9	+ 11.0	− 6.3	+ 16.2	$500	ERF	0.745	0.657	....	...	15,017	15.63	13.94	15.57	15.57	4.8
PGSIX	Putnam U.S.Govt.Income Fund Cl.A	*'84	I	GB	2904.0	n/a	[3]★	+ 11.2	+ 6.3	+ 6.1	− 2.5	+ 15.7	$500	4.75	0.928	0.909	....	...	15,464	13.19	12.09	13.19	13.85	6.7
PVISX	Putnam Vista Basic Value Cl.A	*'68	G	C	926.9	51.4	....	+ 36.4	+ 17.3	+ 17.1	− 3.8	+ 26.7	$500	5.75	....	....	0.055	...	21,260	9.90	7.04	9.10	9.66	....
PVOYX	Putnam Voyager Cl.A	*'69	G	C	5329.2	123.1	....	+ 49.6	+ 9.6	+ 18.3	+ 0.3	+ 39.8	$500	5.75	....	0.22	0.508	0.64	26,409	16.12	11.37	15.25	16.18	....
REAGX	Rea-Graham Fund	*'82	G	C	13.6	6.2	....	+ 14.6	+ 4.2	+ 0.2	− 5.3	+ 15.6	$1,000	4.75	0.098	0.31	....	...	12,326	14.61	12.71	14.38	15.10	0.6
RCVGX	Rochester Bond Fund for Growth	*'86	GI	CV	223.6	n/a	[4]	+ 27.7	+ 30.3	+ 20.8	− 2.1	+ 25.1	$2,000	3.25	0.685	0.867	....	0.491	22,673	14.69	12.20	13.90	14.37	4.8
RMUNX	Rochester Fund Municipals	*'86	IP	TF	2059.5	n/a	∫†	+ 12.3	+ 10.9	+ 14.2	− 8.2	+ 18.1	$2,000	4.0	1.14	1.089	....	...	16,499	18.21	16.28	18.18	18.94	6.0
LTNYX	Rochester Limited Term N.Y.Municipal	*'91	I	TF	542.1	n/a	∫†	....	+ 9.3	+ 9.9	− 0.5	+ 14.3	$5,000	2.0	0.163	0.32	....	...	.....	3.28	3.15	3.28	3.35	4.9
RYEQX	Royce Fund:Equity Income	*'90	GI	C,CV	61.6	n/a	[5]	+ 30.0	+ 19.1	+ 5.5	+ 0.8	+ 29.3	$2,000	ERF	0.18	0.18	0.10	0.74	21,290	5.87	5.08	5.70	5.70	3.2
RYVFX	Royce Fund:Value Series	*'82	G	C	172.6	n/a	[6]	+ 30.7	+ 16.0	+ 2.3	+ 7.2	+ 11.3	$2,000	None	0.05	0.08	0.41	0.04	15,989	10.83	9.04	10.02	10.02	0.5
SACPX	Salomon Bros.Capital Fund	*'76	GI	C	99.7	2.8	....	+ 32.9	+ 4.9	+ 16.7	− 13.8	+ 34.6	$1,000	None	0.03	0.14	2.31	2.21	17,178	20.81	15.53	18.67	18.67	0.2
SAIFX	Salomon Bros. Investors Cl.O	'58	GI	C	415.6	15.9		+ 28.3	+ 7.0	+ 14.6	− 1.3	+ 40.1	$500	None	0.27	1.055	1.49	1.41	20,362	17.94	13.61	16.63	16.63	1.6
SCDUX	Scudder Fds:Cap.Growth	'56	G	C	1491.6	n/a	[7]	+ 42.2	+ 7.0	+ 19.9	− 9.9	+ 31.6	$1,000	None	....	0.08	0.725	3.50	17,954	24.42	18.02	20.67	20.67	....
SCDGX	Scudder Fds:Growth & Inc	'29	GI	C	2806.4	n/a		+ 27.7	+ 9.3	+ 15.4	+ 2.6	+ 31.5	$1,000	None	0.505	0.68	0.905	0.48	21,188	20.65	16.25	20.23	20.23	2.5
SCINX	Scudder Fds:International	'53	G	INTL	2392.6	n/a	....	+ 11.8	− 2.6	+ 36.3	− 3.0	+ 12.2	$1,000	None	....	0.40	2.42	1.18	14,748	45.62	38.23	43.72	43.72	....
SCMBX	Scudder Fds:Man.Mun.Bds	'76	IR	TF	753.6	n/a	∫†	+ 11.8	+ 8.6	+ 12.9	− 5.9	+ 16.2	$1,000	None	0.457	0.44	0.02	...	15,948	8.98	8.04	8.94	8.94	5.1
SECEX	Security Equity	'62	G	C	460.0	4.0	....	+ 34.6	+ 10.7	+ 14.5	− 2.6	+ 38.3	$100	5.75	....	0.06	0.407	0.482	21,901	6.98	5.02	6.43	6.82	....
SBDFX	Security Inc.Corp.Bond	*'70	I,P	GB	97.0	2.0	....	+ 15.3	+ 8.5	+ 13.5	− 8.2	+ 17.6	$100	4.75	0.493	0.468	....	...	16,264	7.39	6.66	7.39	7.76	6.4
SECIX	Security Growth & Income Cl.A	'44	IG	FL	69.0	1.0	[8]	+ 21.4	+ 4.6	+ 8.2	− 7.8	+ 27.4	$100	5.75	0.091	0.158	0.215	0.275	15,639	8.24	6.52	7.94	8.42	1.1
SECUX	Security Ultra	'69	G	C	71.0	(3.0)	....	+ 59.6	+ 7.6	+ 9.7	− 6.6	+ 19.0	$100	5.75	....	....	0.135	0.996	15,180	8.44	6.56	6.95	7.37	....
SLASX	Selected Amer. Shares	'33	GI	B	861.7	0.9	....	+ 61.4	+ 5.9	+ 5.1	− 3.2	+ 37.4	$1,000	None	0.22	0.16	0.82	0.15	22,937	18.07	13.10	17.68	17.68	1.2
SCFIX	Seligman Capital	'69	G	C,L	201.0	n/a	....	+ 53.7	+ 11.5	+ 4.8	− 7.4	+ 35.8	$1,000	4.75	....	....	1.60	2.298	22,901	16.95	13.02	15.59	16.37	....
SCSFX	Seligman Com. Stock	'29	IG	C,FL	652.0	n/a	....	+ 29.4	+ 10.7	+ 14.7	− 1.9	+ 27.8	$1,000	4.75	0.37	0.36	0.72	0.944	19,796	15.26	12.10	14.19	14.90	2.5
SLMCX	Seligman Commun & Info	*'83	G,R	C,SP	3012.0	n/a	....	+ 53.6	+ 17.0	+ 34.4	+ 34.8	+ 43.6	$1,000	4.75	....	....	1.46	1.905	41,611	29.67	15.65	21.99	23.09	....
SGRFX	Seligman Growth	'37	G	C	603.0	n/a	[9]	+ 38.5	+ 11.3	+ 6.0	− 4.0	+ 28.4	$1,000	4.75	0.01	0.01	0.50	0.598	19,114	5.87	4.49	5.22	5.48	0.2
SINFX	Seligman Income Cl.A	'47	I	B	399.0	n/a	....	+ 29.3	+ 17.1	+ 15.7	− 5.3	+ 20.2	$1,000	4.75	0.75	0.78	....	0.276	18,346	14.99	13.03	14.63	15.36	4.9
SENCX	Sentinel Group:Com.Stk	*'33	GI	C	1020.3	58.4	....	+ 30.2	+ 5.7	+ 9.1	− 1.2	+ 23.2	$500	5.0	0.834	0.526	1.11	...	17,782	36.45	27.36	33.21	34.96	2.4
SEQUX	Sequoia Fund	'69	G	C	2017.0	n/a	§†	+ 38.9	+ 9.9	+ 9.9	+ 1.7	+ 41.5	$1,000	None	0.037	0.456	0.163	0.08	23,225	79.01	55.59	78.13	78.13	....
SHAPX	SMBS Appreciation Cl.A	'70	G	C	1879.6	n/a	....	+ 26.9	+ 6.2	+ 8.1	− 0.7	+ 27.1	$1,000	5.0	0.179	....	0.596	0.999	18,332	12.83	10.17	11.90	12.53	1.4
SHRCX	SMBS Calif.Munic.Cl.A	*'84	IP	TF	410.4	n/a	?∫	+ 11.1	+ 7.7	+ 12.3	− 6.5	+ 21.5	$1,000	4.0	0.888	0.879	0.189	...	16,257	16.50	14.22	16.44	17.13	5.2
SLDSX	SMBS Diversified Strategic Inc.Cl.B	*'89	I	FL	2358.9	n/a	....	+ 18.0	+ 5.9	+ 12.2	− 3.5	+ 13.8	$1,000	ERF	0.612	0.572	....	...	16,537	7.98	7.46	7.96	7.96	7.7
HGVSX	SMBS Govt.Securities Cl.B	*'84	I	GB	164.2	n/a	[10]	+ 15.4	+ 5.2	+ 10.2	− 3.1	+ 12.4	$1,000	ERF	0.526	0.473	....	...	15,518	9.90	9.11	9.83	9.83	5.4
HBDIX	SMBS Investment Grade Bond Cl.B	*'82	I	BD	266.9	n/a	....	+ 21.7	+ 8.2	+ 17.7	− 9.7	+ 33.0	$1,000	ERF	0.767	0.759	0.307	0.159	19,098	13.27	10.60	13.27	13.27	5.8
SHMGX	SMBS Managed Govt.Cl.A	*'84	I	GB	520.7	n/a	....	+ 15.3	+ 5.8	+ 8.9	− 1.8	+ 12.9	$1,000	4.5	0.782	0.715	....	...	16,127	12.91	12.01	12.91	13.52	5.8
SHMMX	SMBS Managed Municipals Cl.A	*'81	I	TF	1814.4	n/a	....	+ 13.7	+ 9.0	+ 15.6	− 4.4	+ 19.8	$1,000	4.0	0.948	0.939	0.287	0.05	17,212	16.31	14.36	16.25	16.93	5.6

Uniform Footnote Explanations-See page 234. **Stock Splits & Divs.** (figures adjusted): [1] Was Tax Free Hi Inc.(5/92). [2] 5% ERF reducing over 7 yrs. [3] "Gtd"dropped fr name(1/91). [4] Was Convert. Growth(5/93). [5] 2% E.R.F.before 6 yrs. Incl.Tot.Return & Inc.Funds(6/28/91). [6] 1% E.R.F.within 5 yrs.. [7] Incl.Scudder Special:. Each Special hldr.rec'd 4.5785 Cap.Growth shs. [8] Was Investment(10/93). [9] Was Natl. Investors. [10] Was Hutton Govt.Secs.

Ticker Symbol	Fund	Year Offered	Prin. Obj.	Type	Sept. 29, 1995 Total Net Assets (MIL.$)	Sept. 29, 1995 Cash & Equiv (MIL.$)	See Foot-notes	Net Assets per Share % Change from Previous Dec. 31 — At: Dec. 31 1991	1992	1993	1994	Dec. 29, 1995	Min. Unit	Max. Sales Chg. %	Distributions Per Share from Invest. Income 1994	Invest. Income 1995	Security Profits 1994	Security Profits 1995	$10,000 Invested 12-31-89 Now Worth	PRICE RECORD NAV Per Sh — 1995 — High	1995 Low	#12-29-95 NAV Per Shr.	#12-29-95 Offer Price	% Yield From Inv. Inc.
SHNYX	**SMBS New York Municipals Cl.A**		IP	TF	490.2	n/a	?∫	+ 12.5	+ 8.9	+ 9.5	− 7.9	+ 16.7	$1,000	4.5	0.994	0.984	0.098	...	15,168	17.14	15.41	17.04	17.75	5.6
SOPTX	**SMBS Premium Total Return Cl.B**	*'85	GI	C	1737.9	n/a	....	+ 27.9	+ 12.1	+ 10.8	+ 2.0	+ 20.4	$1,000	ERF	1.065	1.10	....	...	19,841	17.14	15.16	17.12	17.12	6.2
HSPEX	**SMBS Special Equities Cl.B**	*'82	G	C	126.9	n/a	....	+ 44.0	+ 9.1	+ 31.9	− 6.3	+ 58.1	$1,000	ERF	....	....	....	...	23,207	31.29	17.62	29.76	29.76	....
SXMTX	**SMBS Tax Exempt Cl.B**	*'85	I	TF	726.9	n/a	?∫	+ 10.8	+ 8.5	+ 11.5	− 6.4	+ 15.0	$1,000	ERF	0.973	0.897	....	0.02	15,741	17.93	16.30	17.87	17.87	5.4
SLSUX	**SMBS Utilities Fund Cl.B**		IG	C	1606.0	n/a	....	+ 20.7	+ 6.9	+ 11.9	− 10.0	+ 30.0	$1,000	ERF	0.799	0.78	....	0.084	17,383	15.75	12.77	15.75	15.75	5.1
SBCIX	**Smith Barney Income & Growth Cl.A**	*'66	IG	C	592.0	n/a	....	+ 26.1	+ 7.0	+ 10.3	− 5.2	+ 22.3	$1,000	5.0	0.437	0.31	....	...	15,616	15.89	12.20	14.59	15.36	2.8
SGENX	**SoGen Intl.Fund**	'70	G	GL	2463.7	n/a	†	+ 17.8	+ 8.4	+ 26.1	+ 2.5	+ 15.2	$1,000	3.75	0.15	0.81	0.56	0.73	18,747	25.90	22.40	24.58	25.54	0.6
SFAAX	**Stagecoach Asset Allocation Fund**	*'92	SG	FL	1042.0	304.5	....	....	+ 8.6	+ 12.8	− 2.9	+ 26.7	$250	4.5	0.767	0.386	0.761	0.056	.....	20.95	16.68	20.75	21.73	3.5
MSSCX	**State St. Research Capital Apprec. Cl.A**	'86	G	C	594.2	n/a	1	+ 74.5	+ 7.6	+ 22.0	− 2.7	+ 30.7	$2,500	4.5	....	....	0.445	1.286	25,169	13.31	9.34	11.20	11.73	....
MSEIX	**State St. Research Equity Income Cl.A**	*'86	IG	C	96.3	n/a	....	+ 16.6	+ 12.5	+ 22.4	− 4.7	+ 28.4	$2,500	4.5	0.28	0.28	0.542	0.158	17,662	12.78	10.23	12.76	13.36	2.1
MSSIX	**State St. Research Equity Invest. Cl.A**	*'86	G	C	95.7	n/a	....	+ 34.8	+ 8.8	+ 12.3	− 4.9	+ 32.7	$2,500	4.5	....	0.02	0.327	0.631	18,852	15.97	12.10	15.49	16.22	....
SMEGX	**State St. Research Global Energy Cl.A**	*'90	G	SP	37.5	n/a	....	− 17.8	+ 6.8	+ 32.1	− 4.4	+ 22.6	$2,500	4.5	....	....	....	...	13,592	13.17	9.95	13.17	13.79	....
MSHIX	**State St. Research High Income Cl.A**	*'86	I	BD	632.7	n/a	....	+ 34.8	+ 20.1	+ 22.1	− 1.6	+ 11.1	$2,500	4.5	0.656	0.535	0.058	0.008	18,325	5.92	5.67	5.77	6.04	10.9
MSMAX	**State St. Research Managed Assets Cl.A**	*'88	G	FL	411.5	n/a	....	+ 20.5	+ 7.6	+ 21.0	− 5.8	+ 21.2	$2,500	4.5	0.17	0.15	0.138	0.156	17,356	10.15	8.34	9.84	10.30	1.7
SSGIX	**State St. Research Govt. Income Cl.A**	*'87	I	GB	654.3	n/a	2	+ 15.1	+ 6.6	+ 10.4	− 2.9	+ 17.1	$2,500	4.5	0.785	0.808	....	...	16,680	12.80	11.59	12.80	13.40	5.9
MSHTX	**State St. Research Tax Exempt Cl.A**	*'86	I	TF	229.1	n/a	....	+ 11.5	+ 9.1	+ 11.9	− 6.8	+ 16.2	$2,500	4.5	0.383	0.406	0.012	...	15,420	8.29	7.45	8.26	8.65	4.4
STSTX	**State St. Research Invest. Cl.C**	'24	GI	C	749.4	n/a	3	+ 27.9	+ 6.3	+ 10.2	− 3.5	+ 32.1	$2,500	None	0.14	0.09	0.498	0.984	18,927	10.23	7.72	9.18	9.18	1.5
SRFCX	**SteinRoe Capital Opport.**	*'69	G	C	242.3	39.9	4	+ 62.7	+ 2.4	+ 27.5	− 0.1	+ 51.1	$2,500	None	....	0.115	....	0.994	22,734	23.78	10.24	23.35	23.35	....
SRSPX	**SteinRoe Special**	*'68	G	C	1201.3	61.8	....	+ 33.7	+ 13.9	+ 20.1	− 3.4	+ 18.5	$2,500	None	0.145	0.108	1.312	1.912	19,701	25.63	21.34	23.72	23.72	0.6
SRFSX	**SteinRoe Growth Stock**	'58	G	C	362.3	22.4	....	+ 45.3	+ 8.5	+ 2.7	− 3.8	+ 35.4	$2,500	None	0.147	0.099	3.016	2.333	21,279	27.56	19.96	25.05	25.05	0.6
SRFBX	**SteinRoe Total Return**	'49	GI	FL	228.5	6.6	5	+ 28.9	+ 7.7	+ 12.1	− 4.1	+ 22.1	$2,500	None	1.186	1.171	0.276	0.702	17,895	28.50	24.31	27.80	27.80	4.3
SRPEX	**SteinRoe Prime Equities**	*'87	G	C	139.5	31.7	....	+ 31.9	+ 9.9	+ 12.7	− 0.1	+ 29.8	$2,500	None	0.181	0.282	0.594	1.432	20,803	17.71	13.73	16.17	16.17	1.1
STRFX	**Strong Total Return**	*'81	GI	FL	687.0	48.0	....	+ 33.4	+ 0.5	+ 22.4	− 1.4	+ 21.3	$250	None	0.345	0.269	....	...	18,253	29.56	23.33	28.38	28.38	1.2
SBABX	**SunAmerica Balanced Assets Cl.B**	*'85	GI	C,BD,P	161.0	8.5	....	+ 27.3	+ 5.3	+ 13.9	− 2.6	+ 26.7	$500	ERF	0.316	0.219	0.578	0.989	18,408	17.04	13.60	16.07	16.07	2.0
SEGAX	**Sunamerica Small Co. Growth Cl.A**	*'86	G	C	90.7	24.0	6	+ 43.8	+ 16.1	+ 2.0	+ 4.7	+ 49.5	$500	5.75	....	....	0.414	4.525	23,057	26.29	17.21	21.81	23.14	....
SGTBX	**SunAmerica U.S.Govt.Secs.Cl.B**	*'86	IP	GB	517.3	3.6	7	+ 9.5	+ 5.1	+ 4.3	− 1.3	+ 14.2	$2,500	ERF	0.415	0.448	....	...	14,585	8.76	8.06	8.76	8.76	4.7
TEDMX	**Templeton Developing Markets**	*'91	G	INTL	2247.6	417.7	....	....	− 9.8	+ 74.2	− 8.5	− 2.5	$100	5.75	0.12	0.005	0.425	0.065	.....	14.38	12.00	13.01	13.80	0.9
TEMFX	**Templeton Foreign**	'82	G	INTL	7173.1	1338.6	8	+ 17.9	− 0.1	+ 43.9	+ 0.6	+ 11.0	$100	5.75	0.155	0.25	0.515	0.36	18,377	9.92	8.61	9.18	9.74	1.6
TEGO	**Templeton Global Opportunities**	*'90		INTL	535.6	11.4	....	+ 33.2	+ 6.9	+ 38.0	− 3.7	+ 12.5	$100	5.75	0.06	0.195	2.015	0.565	.....	13.80	11.39	12.57	13.34	0.4
TEPLX	**Templeton Growth**	'54	G	GL	7214.9	1424.5	9	+ 30.5	+ 3.7	+ 32.2	+ 1.1	+ 19.5	$100	5.75	0.29	0.435	1.29	1.61	19,647	19.52	16.06	17.35	18.41	1.6
TEMGX	**Templeton Smaller Cos.Growth**	*'81	G	GL	1464.4	358.5	10	+ 39.4	+ 2.8	+ 31.8	− 4.6	+ 17.5	$100	5.75	0.105	0.12	0.09	0.98	17,763	8.99	7.21	7.63	8.10	1.3
TEMWX	**Templeton World**	'77	G	GL	6020.6	729.0	....	+ 28.8	+ 2.7	+ 32.8	+ 1.2	+ 21.1	$100	5.75	0.28	0.365	1.45	1.88	18,084	17.29	14.03	14.91	15.82	1.8
LTMFX	**Thornburg Ltd. Term Munic:Natl. Cl.A**	*'84	I	TF	931.0	n/a	....	+ 8.3	+ 7.5	+ 8.6	− 1.5	+ 9.4	$5,000	2.5	0.63	0.582	....	...	14,483	13.59	12.81	13.55	13.90	4.5
TWRSX	**Tower Funds:Capital Apprec.**	*'88	G	C	150.1	2.3	....	+ 30.5	+ 0.1	+ 14.2	− 3.0	+ 37.4	$1,000	4.5	0.177	0.199	0.264	0.838	19,505	17.16	12.89	16.71	17.23	1.0
TLMIX	**Tower Funds:La.Munic.Income**	*'88	I	TF	66.1	0.5	∫†	+ 10.9	+ 9.2	+ 11.2	− 5.0	+ 15.6	$1,000	4.5	0.537	0.591	0.084	...	15,558	11.31	10.24	11.28	11.63	4.6
TWRGX	**Tower Funds:U.S.Govt.Income**	*'88	I	GB	42.3	1.0	....	+ 14.0	+ 4.7	+ 7.6	− 3.3	+ 15.1	$1,000	4.5	0.684	0.70	....	...	15,309	10.32	9.54	10.30	10.62	6.4
TWCGX	**20th Century Growth**	'58	G	C	5262.3	67.6	....	+ 69.0	− 4.3	+ 3.5	− 1.7	+ 20.1	None	None	0.051	0.069	3.222	3.056	18,991	25.12	18.39	19.39	19.39	0.3
TWCIX	**20th Century Select**	*'58	G	C	4185.8	150.3	....	+ 31.4	− 4.4	+ 14.6	− 8.1	+ 22.5	None	None	0.281	0.269	2.874	4.659	16,125	41.02	32.63	35.62	35.62	0.8
TWCUX	**20th Century Ultra**	*'81	G	C	14046.4	153.1	11	+ 86.5	+ 1.3	+ 21.8	− 3.7	+ 37.4	None	None	....	....	0.645	1.299	33,188	29.13	19.28	26.11	26.11	....
TWUSX	**20th Century U.S.Govts.**	*'82	I	GB	389.0	n/a	12	+ 6.9	+ 0.3	+ 3.7	− 0.5	+ 9.7	$2,500	None	0.442	0.471	....	...	12,925	9.58	9.16	9.58	9.58	4.6
UNACX	**United Accumulative**	'40	G	C	1179.0	65.0	....	+ 23.3	+ 14.1	− 3.3	− 0.1	+ 33.8	$500	5.75	0.125	0.107	0.483	0.92	16,366	8.77	6.56	7.78	8.25	1.5
UNHIX	**United High Inc.**	*'79	IG	B	969.0	93.0	....	+ 35.1	+ 16.0	+ 16.9	− 3.5	+ 17.1	$1,000	5.75	0.791	0.801	....	...	17,866	9.16	8.45	9.14	9.70	8.2
UNCMX	**United Income**	'40	IS	C	3993.0	109.0	....	+ 29.2	+ 12.0	+ 13.2	− 1.8	+ 29.5	$500	5.75	0.355	0.348	0.632	0.915	19,727	30.61	23.26	28.96	30.73	1.2
UNMBX	**United Munic.Bond**	'76	IS	TF	971.0	1.0	∫†	+ 12.9	+ 9.2	+ 14.0	− 7.0	+ 19.7	$500	4.25	0.378	0.386	0.038	0.052	16,475	7.60	6.63	7.51	7.84	4.8
UNVGX	**United Vanguard**	'69	G	C	1287.0	168.0	....	+ 26.9	+ 3.4	+ 14.2	+ 6.1	+ 24.6	$500	5.75	0.015	0.047	0.616	0.45	19,136	9.20	6.93	8.30	8.81	0.2
USTEX	**USAA Tax Exempt Long Term Fund**	*'82	I	TF,BD	1790.0	n/a	∫†	+ 11.9	+ 8.3	+ 12.1	− 7.8	+ 17.6	$3,000	None	0.775	0.743	0.086	...	15,643	13.66	12.21	13.63	13.63	5.7

Uniform Footnote Explanations-**See page 234.** **Stock Splits & Divs.** (figures adjusted): [1] 2-for-1 split Oct.'92.. [2] Was Metlife State St.Govt Inc.. [3] 2-for-1 split,Oct.'92. Changed fr. trust to Cl. A on Feb. '93. [4] 2-for-1 split, Aug. '95. [5] Was Stein Roe Balanced. [6] Was Emerging Growth(6/94). [7] 4% E.R.F.. [8] 3-for-1 split,Feb.'94. [9] In Can. Curr.. Spun-off Can.assets. [10] Now incls.Global II assts.. Was Global. [11] 0.5% redempt.fee. [12] 10-for-1 split,Nov.'93.

Ticker Symbol	Fund	Year Offered	Prin. Obj.	Type	Sept. 29, 1995 Total Net Assets (MIL.$)	Sept. 29, 1995 Cash & Equiv (MIL.$)	See Foot-notes	Net Assets per Share % Change from Previous Dec. 31 — At: Dec. 31 1991	1992	1993	1994	Dec. 29, 1995	Min. Unit	Max. Sales Chg. %	Distributions Per Share from Invest. Income 1994	Invest. Income 1995	Security Profits 1994	Security Profits 1995	$10,000 Invested 12-31-89 Now Worth	PRICE RECORD 1995 High	1995 Low	NAV Per Sh #12-29-95 NAV Per Shr.	Offer Price	% Yield From Inv. Inc.
INIVX	Van Eck Funds:Intl.Investors	*'55	G	PM	581.0	4.3	....	+4.9	−29.0	+113.2	−1.0	−11.6	$1,000	5.75	0.18	0.10	0.52	...	10,158	14.84	12.37	13.35	14.16	1.3
ACSTX	Van Kampen Amer.Cap.Comstock Cl.A	'68	G	FL	1049.1	45.6	[1]	+31.2	+6.4	+8.7	−3.5	+35.2	$500	5.75	0.375	0.27	3.04	1.96	19,144	16.33	12.40	14.54	15.43	2.4
ACEGX	Van Kampen Amer.Cap.Emerging Growth Cl.A	*'70	G	FL	1080.7	89.7		+59.2	+9.4	+23.5	−7.2	+44.1	$500	5.75	....	....	0.62	3.19	29,310	33.54	22.84	30.49	32.35	...
ACENX	Van Kampen Amer.Cap.Enterprise Cl.A	'53	G	FL	1052.6	96.8	....	+38.3	+7.8	+10.4	−0.3	+33.4	$500	5.75	0.085	0.072	0.673	2.10	21,300	15.42	11.30	13.07	13.87	0.6
ACEIX	Van Kampen Amer.Cap.Equity Income Cl.A	*'60	IP	C	317.7	21.9	....	+26.1	+10.5	+15.7	−1.6	+32.5	$500	5.75	0.203	0.208	0.098	0.32	20,074	6.67	5.15	6.31	6.69	3.0
ACFMX	Van Kampen Amer.Cap.Ltd.Mat.Govt.Cl.A		IP	GB	44.7	(10.3)	....	+9.4	+3.1	+3.1	+0.1	+9.7	$500	2.25	0.538	0.649	....	...	13,906	12.41	11.89	12.41	12.83	4.2
ACGVX	Van Kampen Amer.Cap.Govt.Secs.Cl.A	*'84	I	GB	2552.1	(876.0)	....	+15.4	+6.2	+8.5	−4.3	+16.2	$500	4.75	0.666	0.688	....	...	15,970	10.55	9.59	10.55	11.08	6.0
ACGIX	Van Kampen Amer.Cap.Growth & Inc.Cl.A	'46	GS	C	351.5	24.2	[2]	+29.8	+9.3	+15.8	−1.4	+35.3	$500	5.75	0.315	0.27	1.13	0.90	20,799	15.17	11.36	14.21	15.08	2.1
ACHBX	Van Kampen Amer.Cap.Harbor Cl.A	'56	ISG	CV,BD	394.2	22.0	....	+22.4	+9.3	+13.1	−6.1	+22.8	$500	5.75	0.645	0.805	0.327	0.417	17,255	15.67	13.22	15.04	15.96	4.0
ACPAX	Van Kampen Amer.Cap.Pace Cl.A	*'69	G	FL	2450.2	163.8		+31.4	+4.2	+10.5	−3.9	+32.6	$500	5.75	0.123	0.15	1.298	1.76	18,142	13.08	9.73	11.07	11.75	1.0
VKCIX	Van Kamp.M.Cal.Ins.T.F.Cl.A	*'85	IP	TF	141.3	n/a	∫†★	+9.7	+9.8	+14.2	−8.5	+17.8	$1,000	3.0	0.912	0.888	....	...	15,879	17.79	15.77	17.74	18.34	5.0
VKHYX	Van Kamp.M.Corp.Hi Yld Cl.A	*'86	I	SP	263.4	n/a	[3]	+33.3	+16.4	+17.0	−3.2	+16.8	$1,000	4.65	1.032	0.96	....	...	18,329	9.55	8.99	9.55	10.03	10.3
VKMTX	Van Kamp.M.Ins.Tax Free Cl.A	*'84	I	TF	1277.7	n/a	∫†★	+10.3	+9.2	+12.1	−6.2	+17.1	$1,000	4.65	1.056	1.03	....	...	16,240	19.57	17.53	19.55	20.52	5.1
VKMPX	Van Kampen M.Penn TF Inc.Cl.A	*'87	I	TF	217.2	n/a	∫†	+11.3	+9.8	+13.0	−5.6	+16.2	$1,000	4.65	0.961	0.95	....	...	16,208	17.77	16.04	17.74	18.62	5.2
VKMHX	Van Kampen M.TF Hi Inc	*'85	I	TF	638.5	n/a	∫†	+14.5	+0.1	+15.1	−4.8	+15.2	$1,000	4.65	1.02	0.96	....	...	14,916	15.00	13.82	14.99	15.74	6.5
VKMGX	Van Kampen M.U.S.Govt.Cl.A	'84	I	GB	2955.5	n/a	★	+15.0	+5.9	+7.8	−5.0	+17.1	$1,000	4.65	1.176	1.09	....	...	15,919	14.95	13.62	14.95	15.70	7.5
VFIIX	Vanguard FIS:GNMA	*'80	I	G	6567.0	220.0	....	+16.0	+6.6	+5.8	−1.0	+16.6	$3,000	None	0.68	0.742	0.007	...	16,567	10.43	9.54	10.43	10.43	6.5
VWESX	Vanguard FIS:Long-Term Corp.	*'73	I	BD	3145.0	135.0	[4]	+19.9	+9.3	+11.8	−5.1	+25.5	$3,000	None	0.624	0.626	0.072	...	18,444	9.48	8.02	9.48	9.48	6.6
VWAHX	Vanguard High Yield Muni Bond	*'79	I	TF	1881.0	188.0	∫†	+42.1	+9.5	+12.9	−5.0	+19.5	$3,000	None	0.625	0.788	0.173	...	21,040	10.78	9.63	10.76	10.76	5.8
VFINX	Vanguard Index Trust 500 Ptfl.	'76	GI	SP	15106.0	166.0	....	+29.9	+7.3	+8.7	+1.2	+35.6	$3,000	None	1.17	0.66	0.20	...	20,084	58.78	42.96	57.60	57.60	2.0
VWIGX	Vanguard Intl.Growth Ptfl.	'85	G	INTL	3475.0	91.0		+4.7	−5.8	+43.6	+0.7	+14.9	$3,000	None	0.18	0.20	....	0.21	14,421	15.34	12.60	15.02	15.02	1.2
VMRGX	Vanguard Morgan Growth	'68	G	C	1407.0	126.0	....	+28.4	+9.4	+7.0	−1.7	+24.7	$3,000	None	0.14	....	0.31	0.08	18,148	15.63	11.27	14.09	14.09	1.0
VWSTX	Vanguard Mun.Short Term	'76	I	TF	1429.0	854.0	[5]∫†	+7.1	+4.7	+4.1	+2.0	+5.9	$3,000	None	0.612	0.611	0.001	...	13,416	15.63	15.33	15.62	15.62	3.9
VWITX	Vanguard Mun.Intermed	'76	I	TF	5511.0	811.0	[6]∫†	+11.8	+8.6	+11.8	−1.1	+14.6	$3,000	None	0.821	0.838	0.158	...	16,446	13.42	12.36	13.36	13.36	6.1
VWLTX	Vanguard Mun.Long Term	'76	I	TF	1057.0	94.0	[7]∫†	+12.9	+9.0	+13.2	−3.4	+19.9	$3,000	None	0.868	0.757	0.156	...	17,167	11.12	9.85	11.09	11.09	7.8
VTRIX	Vanguard:Trustees'Equity:Intl.Ptfl.	*'83	G	INTL	996.0	45.0	....	+9.5	−8.6	+31.5	+5.2	+1.4	$10,000	None	0.56	0.63	0.63	0.165	12,368	33.75	29.60	31.11	31.11	1.8
VWINX	Vanguard:Wellesley Income	'68	I	FL	6725.0	141.0	....	+20.7	+8.4	+14.4	−4.3	+24.8	$3,000	None	1.11	0.84	0.24	...	18,502	20.78	17.04	20.44	20.44	5.4
VWELX	Vanguard:Wellington Fund	'28	GIR	B	11670.0	232.0	....	+23.0	+7.7	+13.3	−0.4	+32.4	$3,000	None	0.88	0.97	0.03	0.28	19,218	25.03	19.39	24.43	24.43	3.6
VWNDX	Vanguard:Windsor Fund	'58	GI	C	13542.0	2366.0	[8]	+27.5	+16.1	+19.1	−0.1	+30.0	$3,000	None	0.44	0.46	0.86	1.38	19,393	16.55	12.69	14.53	14.53	3.0
VWNFX	Vanguard:Windsor II Fund	*'85	GI	C	10369.0	594.0	....	+27.9	+11.8	+13.4	−1.1	+38.6	$3,000	None	0.55	0.58	0.47	0.69	20,004	21.70	15.89	20.66	20.66	2.7
VCAGX	Vista Capital Growth	*'87	G	C	790.4	n/a	....	+70.7	+12.9	+20.1	−1.6	+17.6	$2,500	4.75	0.088	0.114	0.676	...	25,230	37.73	30.16	35.78	37.56	0.2
VGRIX	Vista Growth & Income	*'87	GI	C	1558.4	n/a	....	+58.9	+15.0	+12.2	−3.4	+20.8	$2,500	4.75	0.517	0.455	....	...	23,973	36.88	29.07	34.68	36.41	1.4
WFAGX	Winthrop Focus:Aggressive Growth	*'67	G	C	206.7	6.9	[9]	+50.3	+4.9	+13.1	−0.6	+20.1	$1,000	ERF	....	0.037	0.696	0.409	18,499	17.32	14.49	17.10	17.10	....
WFFIX	Winthrop Focus:Fxd.Inc	*'86	I	BD	50.2	2.4	[10]	+13.8	+7.0	+3.7	−3.6	+8.2	$1,000	ERF	0.57	....	....	...	14,303	10.35	9.55	10.35	10.35	5.5
WIGRX	Winthrop Focus:Growth	*'86	G	C	55.7	1.9	[11]	+27.9	+1.9	+13.7	−4.0	+23.3	$1,000	ERF	0.012	0.038	0.685	0.782	16,277	11.59	9.57	11.08	11.08	0.1
WFGIX	Winthrop Focus:Growth & Income	'49	GI	C	87.0	2.4	[12]	+23.9	+2.8	+15.5	−2.2	+29.1	$1,000	ERF	0.245	0.247	0.567	0.35	17,924	15.21	12.18	15.17	15.17	1.6
VNEPX	World Fds:Vontobel Europacific	*'84	G	INTL	n/a	n/a	[13]	+27.0	−2.3	+40.2	−4.9	+5.5	$1,000	None	0.08	....	....	...	14,294	17.91	14.77	17.13	17.13	0.5
VUSVX	World Fds:Vontobel U.S.Value	*'90	GI	C	n/a	n/a	....	+37.2	+15.8	+5.0	+0.4	+29.1	$1,000	None	0.18	....	2.21	...	21,623	14.48	10.29	13.25	13.25	1.4
ZAPAX	Zweig Appreciation Cl.A	*'91	GS	C	272.8	54.5	[14]	+6.3	+9.5	+14.7	−1.9	+23.7	$1,000	5.5	0.06	0.331	0.46	0.507	.....	16.59	13.34	15.91	16.84	0.4
ZAPCX	Zweig Appreciation Cl.C	*'92	GS	C	186.5	37.3	[15]	....	+5.5	+13.8	−2.6	+23.1	$1,000	ERF	....	0.108	0.46	0.507	.....	16.40	13.26	15.83	15.83	....
ZGVAX	Zweig Govt.Securities Cl.A	*'85	IP	GB	42.3	3.8	....	+14.4	+4.5	+10.3	−2.8	+13.4	$1,000	4.75	0.507	0.533	....	...	15,421	10.39	9.57	10.39	10.91	4.6
ZGVCX	Zweig Govt.Securities Cl.C	*'92	IP	GB	20.5	1.8	[15]	....	+6.3	+9.5	−3.2	+13.4	$1,000	ERF	0.45	0.482	....	...	.....	10.38	9.57	10.38	10.38	4.3
ZMAAX	Zweig Managed Assets Cl.A	*'93	G	C	148.5	32.6	....	....	....	....	−2.9	+15.9	$1,000	5.5	0.26	0.748	....	0.40	.....	13.18	11.62	12.48	13.21	2.0
ZMACX	Zweig Managed Assets Cl.C	*'93	GS	GL	533.4	117.3	[16]	....	....	....	−3.5	+14.5	$1,000	ERF	0.18	0.549	....	0.40	.....	13.14	11.62	12.49	12.49	1.4
ZSTAX	Zweig Strategy Fund Cl.A	*'89	GS	C	544.6	136.1	....	+23.4	+7.6	+15.0	+1.1	+24.8	$1,000	5.5	0.20	0.375	0.10	0.545	18,861	15.56	12.29	14.51	15.35	1.3
ZSTCX	Zweig Strategy Fund Cl.C	*'92	GS	C	486.0	121.5	[15]	....	+6.0	+14.2	+0.4	+25.3	$1,000	ERF	0.11	0.315	0.10	0.545	.....	15.56	12.31	14.56	14.56	0.8

Uniform Footnote Explanations-See page 234. Stock Splits & Divs. (figures adjusted): [1] Formerly Amer. Cap. Group(10/95). [2] Incl.Van Kamp.Growth & Inc.(10/95). [3] Sec.pfts incl.return of capital. [4] Was Westminster Bd. Inv. Gr.. [5] Was Warwick Municipal. [6] Was Warwick Intermediate. [7] Was Warwick Long Term. [8] Closed to new investors. [9] Was Neuwirth Fund(11/92). 4%E.R.F.. [10] 4%E.R.F.. [11] 4% E.R.F.. [12] Was Pine Street(11/92). 4% E.R.F.. [13] Was T.V.Europacific(3/91). [14] 1991 % change from 10/91.. [15] 1.25% ERF within 12 mos.. 1992 % change fr.Feb.'92.. [16] 1.25% ERF within 12 mos..

STANDARD & POOR'S
VARIABLE ANNUITY/LIFE INVESTMENT SUMMARY

EXPLANATION OF ABBREVIATIONS

AG	Aggr. Growth	GB	Global Bond	HYB	High Yield Bond	MI	Mortgage Income
B	Balanced	GE	Global Equity	IB	Income—Bond	MM	Money Market
CA	Capital Appreciation	GM	Global Mixed	IE	Income—Equity	NR	Natural Resources
CB	Corporate Bond	G+I	Growth and Income	IM	Income—Mixed	PM	Precious Metals
FP	Flexible Portfolio	GNMA	Ginnie Mae	IX	Index	RE	Real Estate
G	Growth	GV	Government	INT	International	SC	Small Capitalization

PERFORMANCE OF THE S&P 500[1]

% Change from Previous Dec. 31			
At Dec. 31			
1992	1993	1994	Dec. 27, 1995
+7.6	+10.1	+1.3	+37.3

Company Name (Contract Name)	Investment Vehicle	Investment Manager/ Sub Manager	Inv. Obj.	Date First Offered	6/30/95 Tot. Assets ($ Mil)	Fees & Expenses % Sep. Acct.	% Fund Chge.	Admin./ Surrender/ Sales Charge	–% Change in Unit Value– from Previous Dec. 31 1992	1993	1994	YTD	Unit Value Dec. 27 1995
AEtna Life Ins. & Annuity	AEtna Var III-Inc./Grwth.	AEtna Life Ins. & Annuity	G+I	5/75	4,990.0	1.50	0.30	ADMIN: $20 annual contract fee.	+5.4	+5.4	-2.2	+30.2	137.45
(Var.Annuity Acct.C-Qual)	AEtna Encore III-MM	AEtna Life Ins. & Annuity	MM	8/75	495.5	1.50	0.36	SUR: 5% yrs. 1-5, scale to 0%	+2.4	+1.9	+2.8	+4.7	37.966
1-800-525-4225	AEtna Inc.Shrs. III-Inc.Bd.	AEtna Life Ins. & Annuity	IB	11/77	628.8	1.50	0.31	through yr. 10.	+6.1	+8.3	-5.0	+16.3	46.712
	AEtna Advisors Fund-FP	AEtna Life Ins. & Annuity	FP	9/89	1,070.0	1.50	0.33		+5.1	+8.5	-1.6	+25.2	17.888
Allianz Life Ins. Co.	High Income	Franklin Advisers Inc.	IM	1/89	345.6	1.40	0.64	ADMIN: $30 annual contract fee.	+14.7	+14.2	-4.3	+18.7	17.220
(Franklin ValuemarkII-VA)	Invest.Grade Intermed. Bd.	Franklin Advisers Inc.	CB	1/89	164.1	1.40	0.66	SUR: 6% yr. 1, 5% yr. 2, 4% yr. 3	+4.3	+7.0	-0.8	+8.2	15.430
1-800-782-VALU	Global Income	Franklin Advisers Inc.	GM	1/89	246.7	1.40	0.73	3% yr. 4, 1.5% yr. 5.	-1.8	+15.1	-6.3	+13.0	15.510
	U.S. Gov't Securities	Franklin Advisers Inc.	GV	3/89	623.8	1.40	0.54	*Note: 5% yrs. 1&2, 4% yr. 3,	+6.2	+8.2	-5.9	+17.5	16.250
	Growth & Income	Franklin Advisers Inc.	G	1/89	660.8	1.40	0.58	3% yr. 4, 1.5% yr. 5 in NY.	+5.2	+8.8	-3.4	+30.7	17.270
	Precious Metals	Franklin Advisers Inc.	PM	1/89	117.7	1.40	0.68		-11.4	+53.5	-3.3	+1.1	14.140
	Real Estate Securities	Franklin Advisers Inc.	RE	1/89	208.9	1.40	0.67		+10.5	+17.3	+1.4	+15.0	17.930
	Income Securities	Franklin Advisers Inc.	IM	1/89	1,158.8	1.40	0.56		+11.6	+17.0	-7.6	+20.4	19.740
	Utility Equity	Franklin Advisers Inc.	G	1/89	1,332.4	1.40	0.51		+7.2	+9.0	-12.8	+28.9	19.470
	Adjustable U.S. Gov't	Franklin Advisers Inc.	MI	12/90	195.7	1.40	0.58		+3.0	+2.1	-1.5	+7.9	11.950
(cont'd)	Rising Dividends	Franklin Advisers Inc.	G+I	1/92	417.8	1.40	0.79		NA	-4.8	-5.4	+27.7	12.480

DEFINITION: **Unit Value** is the value of a separate account after deducting all investment charges and mortality and expense fees.

[1] Assumes daily reinvestment of dividends. VA–Variable Annuity.

Company Name (Contract Name)	Investment Vehicle	Investment Manager/ Sub Manager	Inv. Obj.	Date First Of-fered	6/30/95 Tot. Assets ($ Mil)	% Sep. Acct.	% Fund Chge.	Fees & Expenses Admin./ Surrender/ Sales Charge	–% Change in Unit Value– from Previous Dec. 31 1992	1993	1994	YTD	Unit Value Dec. 27 1995
Allianz Life Ins. Co.	International Equity	FAI/Templeton Inv. Coun'l	INT	1/92	867.9	1.40	1.12		NA	+26.8	-0.5	+9.1	13.270
(Franklin ValuemarkII-VA)	Pacific Growth	FAI/Templeton Inv. Coun'l	INT	1/92	342.8	1.40	1.14		NA	+45.8	-10.0	+6.4	13.620
1-800-782-VALU	Developing Mkt. Portfolio	FAI/Templeton Inv. Coun'l	INT	3/94	154.7	1.40	1.75		NA	NA	NA	+1.5	9.590
	Global Growth	FAI/Templeton Inv. Coun'l	GE	3/94	302.8	1.40	1.25		NA	NA	NA	+0.7	11.280
American Capital	Money Market	AmeriCapital Asset Mgt.	MM	5/88	23.2	1.30	0.60	ADMIN: $30 annual contract fee.	+2.0	+1.3	+2.4	+4.0	13.717
(The Invest. Annuity-VA)	Common Stock	AmeriCapital Asset Mgt.	G	5/88	74.1	1.30	0.60	SUR: 7% yr. 1, scale down 1% per	+6.7	+7.3	-4.6	+34.6	25.657
1-800-421-5666	Multiple Strategy	AmeriCapital Asset Mgt.	FP	5/88	62.8	1.30	0.60	yr. through yr. 7.	+6.4	+6.0	-4.9	+29.0	21.164
	Domestic Strategy	AmeriCapital Asset Mgt.	HYB	5/88	26.1	1.30	0.60		+11.6	+14.8	-5.6	+19.2	15.778
	Government	AmeriCapital Asset Mgt.	GV	1/90	66.9	1.30	0.60		+4.8	+6.4	-5.9	+15.1	14.753
Anchor Nat'l Life Ins.	Cash Management	Capital Research & Mgt.	MM	2/84	110.3	1.30	0.64	ADMIN: $30 annual contract fee.	+1.8	+1.3	+2.4	+4.1	17.288
(American Pathway II-VA)	High Yield Bond	Capital Research & Mgt.	HYB	2/84	143.7	1.30	0.69	SUR: 5% yrs. 1 through 5.	+11.7	+14.5	-6.2	+18.1	36.017
1-800-445-7862	Growth-Income	Capital Research & Mgt.	G+I	2/84	866.1	1.30	0.59		+5.9	+11.7	-0.5	+31.5	47.355
	Growth	Capital Research & Mgt.	G	2/84	908.8	1.30	0.62		+10.9	+17.4	-0.8	+32.6	55.675
	U.S. Government	Capital Research & Mgt.	IB	11/85	140.0	1.30	0.66		+6.1	+9.8	-5.1	+14.7	20.911
	Asset Allocation	Capital Research & Mgt.	FP	4/89	152.9	1.30	0.77		+7.1	+9.1	-1.8	+28.7	19.455
	International	Capital Research & Mgt.	INT	8/90	232.9	1.30	1.40		-2.8	+32.7	-2.0	+11.9	14.691
Anchor Nat'l Life Ins.	Strat. Multi Asset	Wellington	FP	3/87	63.7	1.40	1.30	ADMIN: $30 annual contract fee.	+2.5	+13.7	-3.9	+20.7	18.295
(ICAP II-VA)	Growth	Wellington	G	9/84	299.1	1.40	0.90	SUR: 5% yr. 1, scale down 1% per	+3.9	+6.3	-6.0	+23.9	33.907
1-800-445-7862	Capital Appreciation	Wellington	AG	3/87	342.6	1.40	1.00	yr. through yr. 5.	+24.3	+19.4	-5.1	+31.3	28.388
	Foreign Securities	Wellington	INT	3/87	53.6	1.40	1.40		-14.3	+28.4	-4.5	+11.2	13.157
	Convertible Secs.	Wellington	G+I	3/87	32.7	1.40	1.10		+18.5	+20.3	-10.9	+14.9	19.156
	Gov't & Qual. Bd.	Wellington	IB	9/84	210.3	1.40	0.80		+5.4	+6.8	-4.4	+17.2	26.484
	Fixed Income	Wellington	IB	9/84	27.4	1.40	0.90		+5.1	+6.4	-4.6	+17.0	25.360
	High Yield	Wellington	HYB	12/85	49.1	1.40	1.00		+12.4	+17.4	-5.8	+16.9	20.994
	Natural Resources	Wellington	NR	12/87	27.9	1.40	1.20		+1.0	+34.3	-0.4	+15.0	17.315
	Multi Asset	Wellington	FP	3/87	166.9	1.40	1.20		+6.7	+5.8	-3.0	+22.6	20.100
	Money Market	Wellington	MM	9/84	105.3	1.40	0.70		+1.9	+1.3	+2.4	+4.1	16.759
	Target '98	Wellington	G	5/88	13.3	1.40	1.00		+5.7	+9.7	-5.4	+12.8	18.684
Fidelity Invt. Life Ins.	Fidelity VIPF-Money Mkt.	Fidelity Mgt. & Research	MM	1/88	794.0	1.00	0.38	ADMIN: $30 annual contract fee.	+2.9	+2.2	+3.2	+4.8	14.657
(Fid. Retirement Res-VA)	Fidelity VIPF-Invt. Grade	Fidelity Mgt. & Research	IB	12/88	159.4	1.00	0.80	SUR: 5% yr. 1, scale down 1% per	+5.6	+9.9	-4.8	+15.8	16.925
1-800-544-6666	Fidelity VIPF-High Income	Fidelity Mgt. & Research	HYB	2/88	929.6	1.00	0.97	yr. through yr. 5.	+21.8	+19.3	-2.6	+19.1	21.994
(Ext. 2327)	Fidelity VIPF-Eq. Income	Fidelity Mgt. & Research	G+I	2/94	4,085.1	1.00	0.74		+15.8	+17.0	+6.0	+33.1	27.303
	Fidelity VIPF-Growth	Fidelity Mgt. & Research	G	2/88	4,028.6	1.00	0.84		+8.2	+18.2	-1.1	+33.6	30.681
	Fidelity VIPF-Overseas	Fidelity Mgt. & Research	GE	2/88	1,286.2	1.00	1.26		-11.6	+35.9	+0.7	+8.8	19.031
	Fidelity VIPF-Asset Mgr.	Fidelity Mgt. & Research	FP	8/89	3,271.8	1.00	1.08		+10.8	+19.8	-7.1	+15.6	18.248
Fortis Benefits Ins. Co.	Divers. Income Port.	Fortis Investors	IB	5/88	105.9	1.35	0.75	ADMIN: $35 annual contract fee.	+5.6	+11.3	-6.5	+15.2	1.746
(Opportunity-VA)	Growth Stock Port.	Fortis Investors	G	5/88	516.4	1.35	0.82	SUR: 5% yrs. 1 through 5.	+1.5	+7.3	-4.1	+25.7	2.583
1-800-800-AMEV	Asset Alloc. Port.	Fortis Investors	FP	5/88	328.6	1.35	0.70		+5.5	+7.9	-1.3	+19.8	2.124
	Money Market Port.	Fortis Investors	MM	5/88	41.6	1.35	0.55		+1.9	+1.4	+2.5	+4.2	1.366
(cont'd)	U.S. Gov't Port.	Fortis Investors	GV	5/89	178.7	1.35	0.64		+4.7	+8.0	-7.7	+16.6	15.728

DEFINITION: **Unit Value** is the value of a separate account after deducting all investment charges and mortality and expense fees.

VA–Variable Annuity.

Company Name (Contract Name)	Investment Vehicle	Investment Manager/ Sub Manager	Inv. Obj.	Date First Offered	6/30/95 Tot. Assets ($ Mil)	% Sep. Acct.	% Fund Chge.	Fees & Expenses: Admin./ Surrender/ Sales Charge	% Change in Unit Value from Previous Dec. 31: 1992	1993	1994	YTD	Unit Value Dec. 27 1995
Fortis Benefits Ins. Co.	Divers. Income Port.	Fortis Investors	IB	1/90	105.9	0.90	0.75	ADMIN: No annual contract fee.	+5.8	+11.4	-6.3	+15.4	15.602
(Wall St. Ser. 220-VUL)	Growth Stock Port.	Fortis Investors	G	1/90	516.4	0.90	0.81	SUR: varies	+1.8	+7.5	-3.9	+26.0	19.253
1-800-800-AMEV	Asset Alloc. Port.	Fortis Investors	FP	1/90	328.6	0.90	0.70	SALES: 9.8% prem. tax&sales chrg.	+5.7	+8.5	-1.5	+20.0	17.271
	Money Market Port.	Fortis Investors	MM	1/90	41.6	0.90	0.55		+2.2	+1.6	+2.7	+4.4	12.468
	U.S. Gov't Port.	Fortis Investors	GV	1/90	105.9	0.90	0.64		+4.9	+8.2	-7.5	+16.8	14.810
General American Life	S&P 500 Index	General American	IX	5/88	20.1	1.00	0.30	ADMIN: No annual contract fee.	+6.4	+8.7	+0.1	+35.1	27.190
(Var. Annuity Contract)	Money Market	General American	MM	5/88	13.8	1.00	0.21	SUR: 9% yr. 1, scale down 1% per	+2.7	+2.1	+3.2	+4.8	14.487
1-314-525-5935	Bond Index	General American	IB	5/88	15.0	1.00	0.43	yr. through yr. 9	+5.5	+9.3	-5.0	+17.2	17.563
	Managed Equity	General American	G	5/88	19.6	1.00	0.60		+5.6	+7.8	-4.5	+46.2	28.597
	Asset Allocation	General American	FP	5/88	16.5	1.00	0.60		+5.6	+8.5	-4.9	+26.7	20.924
G.T. Global/Gen. Amer. Life	Growth & Income	G.T. Global Mgt.	GM	2/93	29.4	1.40	1.25	ADMIN: $30 annual contract fee.	NA	NA	-4.2	+13.9	15.230
(GT Global Allocator-VA)	U.S. Gov't Income	G.T. Global Mgt.	GV	2/93	4.9	1.40	1.00	SUR: 6% yr. 1, scale down 1% per	NA	NA	-7.6	+12.9	13.151
1-800-548-9994	Global Gov't Income	G.T. Global Mgt.	GB	2/93	11.1	1.40	1.00	yr. through yr. 6.	NA	NA	-9.9	+14.2	13.317
	Strategic Income	G.T. Global Mgt.	GB	2/93	23.6	1.40	1.00		NA	NA	-18.2	+17.5	14.516
	America	G.T. Global Mgt.	SC	2/93	41.4	1.40	1.00		NA	NA	+17.2	+25.8	20.038
	New Pacific	G.T. Global Mgt.	INT	2/93	20.5	1.40	1.25		NA	NA	-13.7	-1.6	13.484
	Europe	G.T. Global Mgt.	INT	2/93	15.8	1.40	1.25		NA	NA	-2.0	+7.4	15.937
	Latin America	G.T. Global Mgt.	INT	2/93	20.3	1.40	1.25		NA	NA	+7.6	-24.8	14.132
	Telecommunications	G.T. Global Mgt.	GE	10/93	52.7	1.40	1.25		NA	NA	+5.7	+21.5	16.726
	Money Market	G.T. Global Mgt.	MM	2/93	15.0	1.40	0.75		NA	NA	+2.1	+3.7	12.865
	Emerging Markets	G.T. Global Mgt.	INT	7/94	8.6	1.40	1.25		NA	NA	NA	-9.2	10.831
	International	G.T. Global Mgt.	INT	7/94	3.5	1.40	1.25		NA	NA	NA	-2.3	10.959
Guardian Ins. & Annuity	Value LineStrat.AssetMgt.	Value Line, Inc.	G+I	10/87	836.2	1.15	0.58	ADMIN: $35 annual contract fee.	+13.8	+10.5	-5.9	+26.0	21.520
(Guardian Investor-VA)	Value Line Centurion	Value Line, Inc.	G	11/83	519.5	1.15	0.53	SUR: Sin. prem.: 6% yr. 1 & 2, scale	+4.7	+7.9	-3.3	+37.7	24.100
1-800-221-3253	Guardian Stock Fund	Guardian Investor Svs.	G	4/83	1,546.3	1.15	0.56	down 1% per yr. through yr. 7.	+18.7	+18.5	-2.4	+33.1	21.780
	Guardian Bond Fund	Guardian Investor Svs.	IB	5/83	353.5	1.15	0.57	Flex: Lessor of: 6% prem. paid	+6.5	+8.6	-4.6	+15.8	15.630
	Guardian Cash Fund	Guardian Investor Svs.	MM	11/81	358.2	1.15	0.55	past 7 yrs. or 6% withdrawl.	+2.0	+1.5	+2.6	+4.2	12.310
	Guardian Real Estate	The O'Conner Group	RE	10/88	15.8	1.15	1.00		-16.6	-9.9	-5.1	+10.8	8.520
	Baillie Gifford Int'l Fund	Guardian/Baillie Gifford	INT	2/91	309.9	1.15	1.67		-10.1	+32.6	-0.2	+10.1	14.060
	Baillie Gifford Emer. Mkt.Fd.	Guardian/Baillie Gifford	INT	10/94	33.0	1.15	1.90		NA	NA	NA	-2.3	8.580
	Gabelli Capital Asset Fund	Gabelli Funds, Inc.	G	6/95	23.2	1.15	1.20		NA	NA	NA	NA	10.710
Hartford Life Ins.	Bond Fund	Hartford Investment Mgt.	IB	8/77	296.0	1.25	0.57	ADMIN: $30 annual contract fee.	+4.2	+8.9	-5.2	+16.4	1.870
(The Director II-VA)	Stock Fund	Hartford/Wellington	G	8/77	1,668.0	1.25	0.53	SUR: 6% yr. 1, scale down 1% per	+8.7	+12.9	-3.1	+32.0	2.878
1-800-862-6668	Money Market	Hartford Investment Mgt.	MM	6/80	329.6	1.25	0.48	yr. through yr. 7.	+2.3	+1.6	+2.7	+4.3	1.526
	Advisers	Hartford/Wellington	FP	3/83	3,863.0	1.25	0.70		+6.8	+11.0	-3.9	+26.3	2.514
	Int'l Opportunities	Hartford/Wellington	INT	7/90	623.0	1.25	1.00		-5.6	+31.9	-3.1	+12.6	1.330
	Capital Appreciation	Hartford/Wellington	AG	4/84	1,914.0	1.25	0.76		+15.5	+19.4	+1.3	+27.5	3.335
	Mortgage Securities	Hartford Investment Mgt.	GNMA	1/85	317.9	1.25	0.50		+3.4	+5.0	-2.9	+14.3	1.871
	Index	Hartford Investment Mgt.	IX	5/87	258.0	1.25	0.49		+5.5	+7.7	-0.3	+34.5	2.354
	Dividend and Growth	Hartford/Wellington	G+I	2/94	177.0	1.25	1.00		NA	NA	NA	+33.9	1.351
Kemper Investors Life Ins.	Money Market	Kemper Financial Services	MM	4/82	12.1	1.25	0.56	ADMIN: $30 annual contract fee.	+4.5	+3.8	+2.7	+8.9	1.160
(Passport-VA) *(cont'd)*	Total Return	Kemper Financial Services	FP	4/82	80.6	1.25	0.61	SUR: 4% yr. 1, 3% yrs. 2&3,	+36.0	+11.2	-10.6	+24.0	1.230

DEFINITION: **Unit Value** is the value of a separate account after deducting all investment charges and mortality and expense fees.

VA–Variable Annuity. VUL–Variable Universal Life.

Company Name (Contract Name)	Investment Vehicle	Investment Manager/ Sub Manager	Inv. Obj.	Date First Of-fered	6/30/95 Tot. Assets ($ Mil)	% Sep. Acct.	% Fund Chge.	Fees & Expenses Admin./ Surrender/ Sales Charge	–% Change in Unit Value– from Previous Dec. 31 1992	1993	1994	YTD	Unit Value Dec. 27 1995
Kemper Investors Life Ins.	High Yield	Kemper Financial Services	HYB	4/82	50.1	1.25	0.67	2% yrs. 4&5, 1% yr. 6.	+49.8	+37.7	-3.4	+15.5	1.510
(Passport-VA)	Equity	Kemper Financial Services	CA	12/83	73.5	1.25	0.67		+57.6	+15.8	-5.2	+29.9	1.420
1-800-621-5001	Gov't Securities	Kemper Financial Services	GV	11/89	29.3	1.25	0.63		+13.8	+10.0	-3.9	+16.9	1.240
	International	Kemper Financial Services	INT	1/92	28.1	1.25	1.00		NA	+31.2	-4.8	+11.0	1.360
Keyport Life Ins.	Cash Income Fund	Stein Roe & Farnham	MM	5/85	68.7	1.40	0.65	ADMIN: $25 annual contract fee.	+2.1	+1.3	+2.4	+4.1	12.824
(Preferred Advisor-VA)	Mtg. Sec. Income Fd.	Stein Roe & Farnham	MI	10/86	74.2	1.40	0.70	SUR: 7% yr. 1, scale down 1% per	+4.5	+4.8	-2.9	+13.8	16.054
1-800-437-4466	Managed Assets Fund	Stein Roe & Farnham	FP	5/85	216.8	1.40	0.75	yr. through yr. 7.	+6.0	+7.8	-4.5	+23.0	18.544
	Managed Growth Stock Fd.	Stein Roe & Farnham	G	5/87	117.7	1.40	0.80		+5.2	+3.5	-7.6	+35.4	22.714
	Capital Appreciation Fd.	Stein Roe & Farnham	AG	5/85	131.1	1.40	0.80		+12.9	+33.8	-0.2	+8.9	23.071
	Utilities Fund	Colonial-Keyport	G+I	7/93	43.8	1.40	1.00		NA	NA	-11.5	+32.8	11.472
	Growth & Income Fund	Colonial-Keyport	G+I	7/93	58.9	1.40	1.00		NA	NA	-2.1	+28.0	13.068
	Strategic Income Fund	Colonial-Keyport	IB	7/94	21.5	1.40	1.10		NA	NA	NA	+16.3	11.642
	U.S. Fund for Growth	Colonial-Keyport	G	7/94	30.9	1.40	1.40		NA	NA	NA	+27.9	13.264
	Int'l Fund for Growth	Colonial-Keyport	INT	5/94	20.2	1.40	1.60		NA	NA	NA	+4.4	9.723
Lincoln National Life Ins.	Growth Fund	Capital Research & Mgt.	G	8/89	3,024.2	1.35	0.56	ADMIN: $35 annual contract fee.	+9.3	+14.8	-0.8	+31.2	2.043
(Ameri Legacy II-VA)	Growth-Income Fund	Capital Research & Mgt.	G+I	8/89	3,730.0	1.35	0.56	SUR: 6% yr. 1, scale down 1% per	+6.5	+10.8	+0.7	+30.8	1.868
1-800-443-8137	Asset Allocation Fund	Capital Research & Mgt.	FP	8/89	819.7	1.35	0.59	yr. through yr. 7.	+7.0	+9.0	-1.6	+27.3	1.752
	High Yield Bond Fund	Capital Research & Mgt.	HYB	8/89	510.0	1.35	0.63		+11.0	+14.8	-7.8	+19.6	1.810
	U.S. Gov't/AAA Bd. Fd.	Capital Research & Mgt.	GV	8/89	521.4	1.35	0.58		+6.2	+9.7	-5.6	+13.4	1.553
	Cash Management Fund	Capital Research & Mgt.	MM	8/89	187.1	1.35	0.58		+1.8	+1.4	+2.4	+4.0	1.254
	International	Capital Research & Mgt.	INT	5/90	1,663.0	1.35	0.96		-2.2	+32.5	+0.6	+11.1	1.512
MFS/Sun Life (U.S.)	Money Market	MFS	MM	12/84	16.0	1.30	0.59	ADMIN: $30 annual contract fee.	+2.0	+1.3	+2.4	+11.2	16.513
(Compass 2-NY-VA)	High Yield	MFS	HYB	12/84	13.6	1.30	1.05	SUR: 5% yrs. 1 through 5.	+13.5	+16.2	-3.5	+28.4	26.089
1-800-343-2829	Capital Appreciation	MFS	AG	12/84	41.3	1.30	0.85		+12.2	+16.5	-4.8	+22.3	37.412
(Ext. 3052)	Government Securities	MFS	GV	12/84	36.2	1.30	0.64		+5.4	+7.3	-3.4	+31.9	25.483
	World Government	MFS	GB	5/88	8.3	1.30	1.12		-0.6	+17.4	-5.7	+15.3	18.090
	Total Return	MFS	B	5/88	35.8	1.30	0.85		+7.2	+12.0	-3.5	+28.9	22.160
	Managed Sectors	MFS	AG	5/88	7.2	1.30	1.03		+5.2	+2.8	-3.1	+41.7	31.345
MFS/Sun Life (U.S.)	Capital Appreciation	MFS	G	11/91	734.4	1.40	0.83	ADMIN: $30 annual contract fee.	+11.6	+16.4	-4.9	+31.5	18.686
(Regatta Gold-VA)	Conservative Growth	MFS	G+I	11/91	245.5	1.40	0.66	SUR: 6% yrs. 1&2, 5% yrs. 3&4, 4%	NA	+6.9	-2.5	+35.0	16.076
1-800-343-2829	Managed Sectors	MFS	AG	11/91	78.0	1.40	0.84	yrs. 5&6, 3% yr. 7.	+5.0	+2.6	-0.5	+26.6	15.970
	World Growth	MFS	GE	11/93	129.0	1.40	1.22		NA	NA	+1.5	+22.8	13.234
	Total Return	MFS	B	11/91	1,020.0	1.40	0.78		+6.9	+11.8	-3.6	+24.5	14.774
	Utilities	MFS	G+I	11/93	33.7	1.40	0.70		NA	NA	-5.9	+30.3	12.214
	Government Securities	MFS	GV	11/91	343.0	1.40	0.63		+5.3	+7.2	-3.5	+15.6	13.045
	World Government	MFS	GB	11/91	97.0	1.40	0.95		-0.9	+17.3	-5.8	+13.9	13.234
	High Yield	MFS	HYB	11/91	59.0	1.40	0.88		+13.4	+16.1	-3.6	+15.1	14.678
	Money Market	MFS	MM	11/91	156.0	1.40	0.58		+1.9	+1.2	+2.3	+3.9	11.006
North American Sec. Life	Equity	Fidelity Mgt.	G	6/85	748.0	1.40	0.89	ADMIN: $30 annual contract fee.	+6.4	+14.7	-1.9	+40.5	20.783
(Venture-VA)	U.S. Gov't Securities	Salomon Bros.	GV	3/88	189.0	1.40	0.87	SUR: 6% yrs. 1&2, 5% yr. 3, 4%	+4.7	+6.2	-2.6	+13.6	16.037
1-800-334-4437	Money Market	Wellington Mgt.	MM	6/85	274.0	1.40	0.60	yr. 4, 3% yr. 5, 2% yr. 6.	+1.9	+1.3	+2.4	+4.1	14.184
(cont'd)	Global Equity	Oechsle Int'l	GE	3/88	586.0	1.40	1.23		-2.1	+31.0	+0.3	+6.4	16.491

DEFINITION: **Unit Value** is the value of a separate account after deducting all investment charges and mortality and expense fees.

VA–Variable Annuity.

Company Name (Contract Name)	Investment Vehicle	Investment Manager/ Sub Manager	Inv. Obj.	Date First Offered	6/30/95 Tot. Assets ($ Mil)	% Sep. Acct.	% Fund Chge.	Fees & Expenses Admin./ Surrender/ Sales Charge	–% Change in Unit Value– from Previous Dec. 31 1992	1993	1994	YTD	Unit Value Dec. 27 1995
North American Sec. Life	Global Gov't Bond	Fidelity Mgt.	GB	3/88	218.0	1.40	1.14		+0.9	+17.3	-7.1	+21.1	17.713
(Venture-VA)	Conser. Asset Allocat'n	Fidelity Mgt.	FB	4/87	221.0	1.40	0.88		+5.9	+7.5	-3.2	+16.1	14.285
1-800-334-4437	Moderate Asset Allocat'n	Fidelity Mgt.	FB	4/87	626.0	1.40	0.86		+6.8	+8.5	-3.0	+18.7	14.718
	Aggressive Asset Allocat'n	Fidelity Mgt.	FB	4/87	191.0	1.40	0.88		+6.7	+8.8	-2.1	+20.8	14.957
Northbrook Life Ins.	Money Market	Dean Witter InterCapital	MM	10/90	245.4	1.35	0.59	ADMIN: $30 annual contract fee.	+2.0	+1.4	+2.4	+4.2	11.650
(Dean Witter VA-II)	High Yield	Dean Witter InterCapital	HYB	10/90	147.6	1.35	0.74	SUR: 6% yr. 1, scale down 1% per	+16.8	+22.6	-3.8	+13.1	21.780
1-800-869-3863	Equity	Dean Witter InterCapital	G	10/90	328.1	1.35	0.62	yr. through yr. 6.	-1.2	+18.1	-6.2	+39.4	25.640
	Quality Income Plus	Dean Witter InterCapital	IB	10/90	495.8	1.35	0.58		+6.9	+11.5	-7.9	+22.0	16.280
	Strategist Fund	Dean Witter InterCapital	FP	10/90	392.4	1.35	0.58		+5.8	+8.9	+2.5	+7.8	16.890
	Dividend Growth	Dean Witter InterCapital	IE	10/90	785.4	1.35	0.69		+6.7	+12.8	-4.6	+34.0	21.420
	Utilities	Dean Witter InterCapital	IM	10/90	449.3	1.35	0.73		+11.1	+14.1	-10.2	+26.2	17.900
	European Growth	Dean Witter InterCapital	INT	3/91	182.2	1.35	1.73		+2.6	+39.0	+6.9	+23.8	18.910
	Capital Growth	Dean Witter InterCapital	G	3/91	60.5	1.35	0.86		NA	-8.2	-2.6	+30.7	14.870
	Global Dividend Growth	Dean Witter InterCapital	GE	2/94	185.6	1.35	0.90		NA	NA	NA	+20.0	11.890
	Pacific Growth	Dean Witter InterCapital	INT	2/94	89.6	1.35	1.33		NA	NA	NA	+3.9	9.580
Phoenix Mutual Life	Bond Series	Phoenix Invest. Counsel	HYB	1/83	71.9	1.25	0.65	ADMIN: $35 annual contract fee.	+8.7	+14.5	-6.6	+21.5	3.293
(Big Edge Plus -VA)	Money Market Series	Phoenix Invest. Counsel	MM	1/83	74.7	1.25	0.55	SUR: 6% yr. 1, scale down 1% per	+2.4	+1.6	+2.6	+4.4	2.000
1-800-243-4840	Growth Series	Phoenix Invest. Counsel	G	1/83	533.2	1.25	0.79	yr. through yr. 6.	+8.9	+18.2	+0.2	+28.8	8.061
	Total Return Series	Phoenix Invest. Counsel	FP	1/83	216.3	1.25	0.74		+9.3	+9.6	-2.6	+16.4	3.431
Phoenix Mutual Life	Bond Series	Phoenix Invest. Counsel	HYB	9/88	6.2	0.80	0.65	ADMIN: $60 annual contract fee.	+9.1	+15.0	-6.2	+22.1	1.864
(Flex Edge-VUL)	Money Market Series	Phoenix Invest. Counsel	MM	9/88	12.6	0.80	0.55	SUR: Varies yrs. 1 through 10.	+2.6	+2.1	+3.0	+4.8	1.325
1-800-243-4840	Growth Series	Phoenix Invest. Counsel	G	9/88	103.5	0.80	0.79		+9.3	+18.9	+0.5	+29.3	3.120
	Total Return Series	Phoenix Invest. Counsel	FP	9/88	18.8	0.80	0.74		+9.7	+10.1	-2.2	+16.9	2.140
Putnam/Hartford Life Ins.	Growth & Income Fund	Putnam Mgt. Co.	G+I	2/88	2,800.0	1.40	0.72	ADMIN: $25 annual contract fee.	+8.2	+12.7	-1.0	+34.1	27.066
(Putnam Capital Mgr-VA)	High Yield Fund	Putnam Mgt. Co.	HYB	2/88	429.5	1.40	0.92	SUR: 7% yr. 1, scale down 1% per	+17.3	+17.8	-2.3	+16.3	20.327
1-800-862-6668	Money Market Fund	Putnam Mgt. Co.	MM	2/88	251.6	1.40	0.50	yr. through yr. 7.	+3.0	+1.3	+2.4	+4.0	1.378
	Global Asset Alloc.	Putnam Mgt. Co.	FP	2/88	460.6	1.40	0.87		+4.8	+15.8	-3.8	+22.5	20.002
	U.S. Gov't/High Qual. Bd.	Putnam Mgt. Co.	GV	2/88	684.7	1.40	0.74		+6.0	+9.7	-4.6	+18.2	18.356
	Voyager Fund	Putnam Mgt. Co.	G	2/88	1,680.0	1.40	0.81		+8.8	+17.1	-0.4	+37.4	32.205
	Global Growth	Putnam Mgt. Co.	GE	5/90	707.1	1.40	0.99		-1.7	+30.5	-2.3	+13.7	14.916
Security Benefit Life	Growth Series	Security Management	G	6/84	478.9	1.20	0.87	ADMIN: $30 annual contract fee.	+9.8	+12.3	-2.8	+34.2	37.490
(Variflex-VA)	Income/Growth Series	Security Management	G+I	6/84	756.5	1.20	0.86	SUR: 8% yr. 1, scale down 1% per	+5.0	+8.3	-4.1	+27.8	39.670
1-800-888-2461	Money Market Series	Security Management	MM	6/84	105.9	1.20	0.61	yr. through yr. 8	+2.0	+1.4	+2.5	+4.1	17.590
	High Grade Series	Security Management	IB	5/85	127.8	1.20	0.86		+6.2	+11.3	-8.0	+16.5	21.980
Union Central Life	Equity Portfolio	Carillon Advisers	G	6/85	54.2	1.45	0.75	ADMIN: $30 annual contract fee.	+10.2	+12.5	+1.9	+24.0	33.664
(Carillon Account-VA)	Bond Portfolio	Carillon Advisers	IB	6/85	10.4	1.45	0.73	SUR: 7% yrs. 1&2, scale down 1%	+6.1	+10.3	-3.0	+16.8	23.759
1-800-999-1840	Money Market	Scudder	MM	6/85	4.2	1.45	0.69	per yr. through yr. 8.	+1.7	+1.1	+2.2	+4.1	15.464
	Capital Portfolio	Carillon Advisers	FP	5/90	32.8	1.45	0.95		+6.4	+11.1	-0.5	+12.5	16.192
	Scudder Cap. Growth	Scudder	G	5/92	10.3	1.45	0.71		NA	+19.1	-11.0	+26.9	14.405
	Scudder Int'l	Scudder	INT	5/92	14.2	1.45	1.39		NA	+35.9	-2.3	+9.3	14.169

DEFINITION: **Unit Value** is the value of a separate account after deducting all investment charges and mortality and expense fees.

VA–Variable Annuity. VUL–Variable Universal Life.

THE BOND GUIDE

HOW TO USE STANDARD & POOR'S BOND GUIDE

The Bond Guide in a one-page format employs two sets of column headings in the corporate bond section.

1—One set of headings, in italics explained below, relates to the company title, industry code, fixed charge coverage, balance sheet figures, long-term debt outstanding, capitalization and total debt-to-capital ratio.

2—The second set of headings, in lightface type, explained on page 259, relates to the individual issues of the debtor companies, ie., the exchange where traded, description of issue, interest dates, recent rating history (present rating, prior rating and date of change), redemption provisions, and additional statistics.

It is necessary to read these instructions along with those on pages 260 and 261 to correctly interpret data and abbreviations used in the Bond Guide.

EXPLANATION OF COLUMN HEADINGS RELATING TO DEBTOR COMPANIES

Title-Industry Code & Co. Finances (in Italics)	*Industry*	*Fixed Charge Coverage*				*Million $*			*Balance Sheet Date*	*L. Term Debt (Mil. $)*	*Capitalization (Mil. $)*	*Total Debt % Capital*
		19—	*19—*	*19—*	*Year End*	*Cash & Equiv.*	*Curr. Assets*	*Curr. Liabs.*				
The name of the issuer. Pertinent information as to control; name change; subsidiary, etc., footnoted to reference on respective pages. For explanation of standard abbreviations see page 261.	Industry code—Company's principal business is indicated by numerical reference to directory.	Represents number of times available earnings (*before income taxes* and extraordinary charges or credits) cover fixed charges. Charges include interest on funded debt, other interest, amortization of debt discount and expense and similar charges.			Represents month fiscal year ends. For fiscal years ending March 31 or earlier, figures are shown under columns of preceding calendar year.	Figures are reported in millions of dollars (000,000 omitted) as: 1275—$1,275,200,000; 17.5—$17,500,000. Data is updated from annual and interim reports, date of which is shown. Utilities with a reasonable debt to property ratio may often report current liabilities in excess of current assets. In many instances this is of no real significance as utilities have constant tax deferrals, high current debt maturity and the ability to forecast revenues.				Debts and certain obligations due after one year, including bonds, debentures, mortgages, and capitalized lease obligations. Increased debt resulting from new financing and offered subsequent to latest balance sheet date is indicated by symbol ★.	The sum of the stated values of common shareholders' equity, preferred and preference stock, total debt, and minority interest.	Total debt (including short-term debt) of company divided by total capital. Provides a measurement of a company's degree of leverage.

HOW TO USE STANDARD & POOR'S BOND GUIDE (continued)

EXPLANATION OF COLUMN HEADINGS RELATING TO INDIVIDUAL ISSUES

Exchange	Individual Issue Statistics	Interest Dates	S&P Debt Rating	Eligibility	Bond Form	Redemption Provisions: Regular (Begins) Price Thru	Redemption Provisions: Sinking Fund (Begins) Price Thru	Redemption Provisions: Refund/Other Restriction (Begins) Price Thru	Outst'g (Mil. $)	Underwriting Firm Year	Price Range 19xx High Low	Mo. End Price Sale(s) or Bid	Curr. Yield—Yield to Mat.
Traded: ● New York Stock Exchange; ◆ American Stock Exchange	Descriptions of individual issues—For abbreviations see page 261.	Interest dates are indicated by first letter of alternate six months in which interest is payable. (An) or (Q) precedes dates on which interest is payable either annually or quarterly. Unless otherwise noted, dates are the first day of the month. Month of maturity is indicated by a capital letter. Symbols following interest dates note foreign issues payable in U.S. funds or currency of issuing country, and issues in default. See page 260 for explanation.	Standard & Poor's Debt Rating definitions appear in the front section of the Bond Guide. Please see the Table of Contents for specific location each month.	Eligible for bank purchase. See page 260.		Regular call price with beginning or ending date. See page 260 for additional information.	Sinking fund, if any, is reported together with applicable price and date.	Refund restrictions are denoted by the symbol ®, giving date at which restriction expires. Redemption provision may include the symbol NC, which means non-callable, and others (‡, Z, ∗), which are explained on page 260.	Amount of issue outstanding, in millions of dollars, as of the latest available complete balance sheet.	Indicates by key to Directory of Underwriters (see Table of Contents), the original underwriter, usually the head of the syndicate, and the year the issue was originally offered.	Price ranges for current calendar year to date. An explanation of pricing methodology for listed and over-the-counter bonds appears on page 260.	Last sale price is shown for listed issues, and latest bid price or S&P valuation for over-the-counter issues or listed issues not traded last day of the month. "Flat" indicates issue is traded "without accrued interest". A—Ask price.	Yields both current and to maturity, are computed on month-end price shown in preceding column.

UNIFORM FOOTNOTE EXPLANATIONS

To provide for consistency, eliminate repetition, and allow space for situations requiring further explanation, items recurring frequently that demand footnote explanation have been designated with specific symbols, which are explained on this page. Additional explanations appear at the bottom of respective pages.

ISSUE DESCRIPTION & YIELD—See how to use explanation on pages 258 & 259. Other situations require uniform footnotes, as follows:

- ● — Listed on New York Stock Exch.
- ◆ — Listed on American Stock Exch.
- $ — Prin. & int. pay. in U.S. funds; tax status not determined.
- § — Int. and/or prin. in default
- A — Ask price.
- © — Prin. & int. pay. in Canadian funds.
- ‡ — Price in Canadian funds

BOND FORM—BE—Book-Entry; C—Coupon; R—Registered; CR—Coupon & Registered.

EARNINGS—Explanation of earnings per share for the company into which bonds are convertible.

ELIGIBILITY—Under regulations of the Comptroller of the Currency, only certain bonds are eligible for bank investment as indicated by the following symbols:

- **X** — Issues eligible as bank investments on the basis of confirmatory ratings.
- **Y** — Issues ineligible on the basis of confirmatory ratings, but not in default.
- **Z** — Bonds with default status.
- **Q** — Foreign bonds, eligibility not determined by rating agencies.

OTHER FOOTNOTES:

- ★ — Giving effect to new financing.
- c — Company only.
- d — Deficit.
- p — Pro-forma.
- △ — Times Earned 1993, 1994, 1995

REDEMPTION PROVISIONS

Regular Call Price—The Bond Guide reports the present call price and, if not currently callable, designates the date when company may normally redeem bonds. Bonds may be called by the company in whole or in part at the regular call price usually on a sliding scale to par at maturity.

Special Redemptions—Some indentures contain special redemption provisions with requirements for retirement under terms of sinking, improvement, maintenance and replacement funds, etc. Details should be checked carefully.

Sinking Fund Call Price—A sinking fund makes possible the retirement of a substantial portion of the issue prior to maturity. Included in the indenture are terms covering amounts to be called, years of call and a sliding scale of call prices. Bonds to be retired are determined by lot, or provision is often made for purchase of bonds in the open market or by tender if cost is below the sinking fund call price. Also reported is the date when sinking fund starts, if not currently in operation.

Applicable footnotes are:

- ✲ — On interest dates.
- ‡ — On int. dates; price decline within 12 mos.
- ± — Price decline within 12 mos.
- □ — Debt retirement & improve fund.
- ■ — In whole only.
- **Z** — Callable re specified conditions.
- ▲ — Through application of trust moneys or proceeds of eminent domain.

Refund/Other Restrictions—Some indentures include a restrictive clause for a period of five to ten years after issue, to assure holders that their investment is not disturbed during that period. Reported is the earliest call price preceded by symbol ® and date when company may normally call bonds for refunding purposes. Column is also used to denote special call features.

PRICING METHODOLOGY

Listed Bonds—Ranges represent actual high and low trades as recorded on an exchange; they do not include bid prices or valuations. However, for the period between date of offering and date of listing, they include high and low over-the-counter bid prices.

Over-the-Counter Bonds—Ranges are based on best available information as to high and low bid prices during the period. Due to lack of complete data from an official centralized source, they should be viewed as reasonable approximations. Ranges for over-the-counter utility bonds on which quotations are unavailable, or unrealistic, are based on valuations made by Standard & Poor's. Included in the various factors used are: prevailing yields; market conditions; S&P Debt Ratings; call features; etc. Subscribers are alerted to the fact that these valuations may differ somewhat from actual trading prices.

ABBREVIATIONS USED

Accr—Accrue(s)
adj—Adjustment
Asmd—Assumed
Astd—Assented
C/D—Ctfs of Deposit
Chge—Change
CT—Collateral Trust
Coll—Collateral
Con—Consolidated
Ctfs—Certificates
Ctrl—Control
Curr—Current
Cv—Convertible
Deb—Debenture
Def—Default
Dev—Development
Dfrd—Deferred
Disc—Discount
Excl—Excludes
Ext—External
Extd—Extended
1st—First Mortgage
F/R—Floating Rate
Fdg—Funding
Fr—From
Fxd—Fixed
Gen—General
Gtd—Guaranteed
HRO—Holder's repayment option
Imp—Improvement
Inc—Income
Incl—Includes
IPO—Initial Public Offering
Ln—Lien
Lshld—Leasehold
Mand—Mandatory
M–T—Medium Term
Mtg—Mortgage
NC—Non – Callable
non-cm—Non – Cumulative
NR—Not Rated
Nts—Notes
OID—Original Issue Discount
PF—Purchase Fund
PIK—Pay – In – Kind
Perp—Perpetual
Pr—Prior
Pr Ln—Prior Lien
Ptc—Participating
RE—Real Estate
Rdj—Readjustment
Red—Redemption
Ref—Refunding
Reg—Registered
Rest'n—Restriction
s—Sale
SF—Sinking fund
Sec—Secured
Ser—Serial; Series
Spl—Special
Sr—Senior
Stpd—Stamped
Sub—Subordinated
Subj—Subject
Tr—Trustees or Trustee
Unif—Unified
V/R—Variable Rat
Var—Various; variable
vtg—Voting
ws—With stock
ww—With warrants
xs—Without stock
xw—Without warrants

DIRECTORY OF UNDERWRITERS

Security underwriters listed below are keyed by the symbols to the column in the Corporate and Foreign bond sections headed Underwriting, which shows the principal underwriter and year in which bonds were offered originally. Home offices only are shown, plus telephone number for that office; many of the firms have extensive branch operations in other cities.

Symbols		Telephone
0	Out of Business	
A1	Advest Inc., Hartford, Conn.	(203) 525-1421
A2	Allen & Co., Inc., N.Y.	(212) 832-8000
A3	Asiel & Co., N.Y.	(212) 747-1000
B1	Bache Halsey Stuart Shields, Inc (Now Prudential Securities)	
B2	Baird (Robert W.), Milwaukee	(414) 765-3500
B3	Bank of America, San Fran.	(415) 622-2201
B4	Bankers Trust Co., N.Y.	(212) 250-2500
B5	Bear, Stearns & Co., N.Y.	(212) 272-2000
B6	Blyth Eastman Dillon, N.Y. (Mgr w/PaineWebber Inc)	
B7	Bradford (J. C.), Nashville	(615) 748-9000
B8	Brown (Alex.) & Sons, Baltimore	(410) 727-1700
B9	BT Securities, N.Y.	(212) 250-5000
C1	Chase Securities, N.Y.	(212) 552-7416
C2	Chemical Securities, N.Y.	(212) 834-4500
C3	Chicago Corp., Chicago	(312) 855-7600
C4	Citicorp Securities Inc. N.Y.	(212) 291-1000
C5	CS First Boston, N.Y.	(212) 909-2000
C6	Cutter & Dixon, N.Y.	(212) 344-3590
D1	Dain Bosworth, Minneapolis	(612) 371-2811
D2	Daiwa Securities Amer., N.Y.	(212) 945-0100
D3	Dean Witter Capital Mkts, N.Y.	(212) 392-2222
D4	Dillon, Read & Co., Inc., N.Y.	(212) 906-7000
D5	Discount Corp of N.Y.	(212) 248-8900
D6	Donaldson, Lufkin & Jenrette, N.Y.	(212) 504-3000
D7	Drexel, Burnham, Lambert, N.Y.	(ob)
D8	duPont, Walston, Inc., N.Y.	(ob)
E1	Eastman Dillon, Union Securities (Mgr w/Blyth Eastman,Paine Webber)	
E2	Edwards (A. G.) & Sons, St. Louis	(314) 289-3000
E3	Equitable Secur., Nashville, TN.	(615) 780-9300
E4	Ernst & Co., N.Y.	(212) 898-6200
F1	First Boston Corp., N.Y. (Now CS First Boston)	
F2	First Chicago Capital Mkts, Chi	(312) 732-5600
F3	Freeman Secur., Jersey City, N.J.	(201) 434-7400
F4	Furman Selz Inc., N.Y.	(212) 309-8200
G1	Goldman, Sachs Inc., N.Y.	(212) 902-1000
H1	Halsey, Stuart Colk Inc., Chicago (Now Prudential Securities)	
H2	Hambrecht & Quist, San Fran	(415) 576-3300
H3	Herzig (P. R.) & Co., N.Y.	(212) 797-2900
H4	Hutton (E. F.) & Co., N.Y. (Now Lehman Bros)	
I1	Interstate/Johnson Lane, Charlotte, N.C.	(704) 379-9000
J1	Jeffries & Co., Los Angeles	(310) 445-1199
J2	Jones (Edward D.) & Co., St. Louis	(314) 851-2000
K1	Kemper Securities Inc., Chi	(312) 574-6000
K2	Kidder, Peabody & Co., N.Y.	(212) 510-3000
K3	Kuhn, Loeb & Co., N.Y. (Now Lehman Bros)	
L1	Lazard Freres & Co., N.Y.	(212) 632-6000
L2	Legg Mason Wood Walker, Balt.	(410) 539-0000
L3	Lehman Bros., N.Y.	(212) 891-2300
M1	McDonald & Co. Secur., Cleve.	(216) 443-2300
M2	Merrill Lynch Capital Mkts, N.Y.	(212) 449-1000
M3	Montgomery Secur., San Fran	(415) 627-2000
M4	Morgan, Keegan & Co., Memphis	(901) 524-4100
M5	Morgan (J. P.) Securities, N.Y.	(212) 483-2323
M6	Morgan Stanley & Co., Inc., N.Y.	(212) 703-4000
M7	Moseley Int'l., Inc., N.Y.	(ob)
N1	NatWest Secur. Ltd, N.Y.	(212) 602-4800
N2	Nomura Securities Int'l., N.Y.	(212) 667-9300
O1	Offerman & Co., Minneapolis	(612) 541-8999
O2	Ohio (The) Co., Columbus	(614) 464-6811
O3	Oppenheimer & Co., N.Y.	(212) 667-7000
P1	PaineWebber Inc., N.Y.	(212) 713-2000
P2	Piper Jaffray Inc., Minneapolis	(612) 342-6000
P3	Principal Fin'l Secur., Dallas	(214) 880-9000
P4	Prudential Securities, N.Y.	(212) 214-1000
R1	Raymond, James & Assoc. St. Petersburg, Fla.	(813) 573-3800
R2	RBC Dominion Sec., Toronto	(416) 864-4000
R3	Robertson, Stephens, San Fran	(415) 781-9700
R4	Robinson-Humphrey, Atlanta	(404) 266-6000
R5	Rothschild Inc., N.Y.	(212) 757-6000
R6	Rothschild (L.F.) & Co., Inc., N.Y.	(ob)
S1	Salomon Bros. Inc., N.Y.	(212) 783-7000
S2	Schroder Wertheim, N.Y.	(212) 492-6000
S3	ScotiaMcLeod Inc., Toronto	(416) 863-7411
S4	Shearson Lehman Hutton, N.Y. (Now Lehman Bros)	
S5	Smith Barney, N.Y.	(212) 399-6000
S6	Smithers (F. S.) Inc., N.Y.	(ob)
S7	Stephens Inc, Little Rock, AR	(501) 374-4361
S8	Stern Bros. & Co., Kansas City, MO	(816) 471-6460
S9	Stifel, Nicolaus & Co., St. Louis	(314) 342-2000
S10	Stone & Webster Securities, N.Y.	(ob)
T1	Thomson McKinnon Secur., N.Y.	(212) 742-0700
U1	UBS Securities Inc., N.Y.	(212) 821-6353
W1	Warburg Paribas Becker, N.Y. (Acq by Merrill Lynch)	
W2	Wedbush Morgan Sec., L.A.	(213) 688-8000
W3	Wertheim Schroder, N.Y. (Now Schroder Wertheim)	
W4	Wheat First Butcher & Singer, Richmond VA.	(804) 649-2311
W5	White, Weld & Co. Inc., N.Y. (Acq by Merrill Lynch)	
W6	Wood, Gundy & Co., N.Y.	(212) 856-6777

ob—Out of business.

INDUSTRY CODE CLASSIFICATIONS

0– Not specific
1– Advertising/Communications
2– Aerospace
a– Major Contractor
b– Subsystems/components
c– Research/develop.
3– Aircraft manufacturing/components
a– Services
4– Air Transport
a– Cargo/charter
5– Aluminum
6– Arms/Ammunition
7– Auto rental/service
8– Auto parts/equipment
9– Auto/Truck mfrs.
a– Trucks, trailers
b– Motor homes
10– Banking
a– Savings Banks
b– Savings and Loan
11– Beverages
a– Beer and Ale
b– Distillers
c– Wines and Liquors
e– Soft drink syrup
f– Bottlers
12– Broadcasting
a– CATV
b– Radio
c– TV
d– Equipment
e– Programming/Entertainment
13– Building
a– Brick, cement
b– Climate controls
c– Contracting, engineering, construction
d– Forest products
e– Hardware/hand tool
f– Plumbing
g– Roofing, Wallboard
h– Homebuilding
14– Chemicals
a– Agricultural
b– Industrial gases
c– Sulphur
15– Coatings, paint, varnishes
16– Containers
a– Glass
b– Metal
c– Paper
d– Plastic
17– Conglomerate/Diversified
a– Diversified
18– Cosmetics/Toiletries
19– Cosmetics– Toiletries– Drugs
20– Data Processing
a– Leasing/distributor
b– Computer systems
c– Computer services
d– Software
e– Peripherals
f– Components
21– Drugs– Generic and OTC
a– Ethical
b– Biotechnology
c– Research
d– Drug Wholesalers
22– Education
23– Electronics/Electric
a– Industry leaders
b– Component, controls
c– Motors
d– Household appliances
e– Information svcs, communication sys
f– Radio, TV, tape
g– Electronic equipment
h– Semiconductors
i– Defense electronics
24– Filmed Entertainment
a– Distributor
b– Theaters
c– Services/technology/equipment
25– Finance
a– Consumer loan
b– Agency
c– Leasing
d– Receivables
e– Services
f– S.B.I.C.
g– Diversified/Misc.
h– Mortgage Banking/Brokers
i– Pawnshops
26– Food
a– Bakery, mill, sugar
b– Canned
c– Corn refiners
d– Dairy products
e– Meat/poultry
f– Pkgd./snacks
g– Distributors
h– Candy, gum
i– Seafood
j– Frozen
27– Food serving
a– Food Servicing
b– Fast foods
c– Restaurants
28– Glass/products
29– Graphic Arts
a– Printing
b– Supplies, equipment
30– Health Care Centers
a– Health Care Services
31– Home Furnishings
a– Carpets, floor cov.
b– Furniture
32– Hotels/Motels/Inns
33– Household Products
34– Housewares
35– Insurance
a– Life/Health
b– Broker/agency
c– Property/Casualty
d– Multiline
36– Investment
37– Jewelry, silverware, time pieces, china
38– Land dev./Real Estate
39– Leather/Shoes
a– Shoe producer
b– Shoe mfr./dstr.
d– Leather
40– Leisure/Amusement
a– Boating
b– Bowling/billiard
c– Musical instr.
d– Photo equipment/finishing
e– Records/homevideo
f– Sports/Outdoor equipment
g– Tourism/resorts
h– Toys, games
i– Casinos/gaming
j– Gambling/Amusement equipment
k– Sports collectibles
l– Racetracks
m–Misc.
41– Machinery
a– Agriculture
b– Construction material handling
c– Industrial
d– Machine tools
e– Specialties
f– Steam generator
g– Components (General Industrial)
h– Flow Control Filtration Components
i– Bearings
42– Manufacturing/Distr
a– Consumer
b– Industrial
43– Medical equipment/supply
a– Laboratory/research
44– Metal
a– Precious fabricating
d– Other fabricating
45– Mining/Diversified
a– Coal
b– Copper
c– Lead, Zinc
d– Uranium
e– Gold
f– South African Gold
g– Silver
h– Exploration/development
i– Industrial Minerals
j– Junior Gold
46– Mobile/Modular Homes
a– Components
47– Mutual Fund
48– Office Equipment
a– Furniture
b– Forms, supplies
49– Oil and Gas
a– Crude producer
b– Domestic
c– International
d– Retailer
e– Well supply, service, drilling
f– Canadian
g– Refiner
h– Foreign
50– Paper/Products
51– Pet and Supplies
52– Plastic/Products
53– Pollution Control
54– Publishing
a– Books
b– Periodicals
c– Newspapers
d– Textbooks
e– Electronic
55– Railroads
56– Rail Equipment
a– Car leasing
b– Parts, accessories
57– Real Estate Investment Trust
58– Rendering
59– Retail Stores
a– Apparel
b– Convenience foods
c– Food supermarkets
d– Variety
e– Drugs
f– Department
g– Discount
h– Mail order/catalogs
i– Showroom/catalog
j– Furniture
k– Fabric
l– Specialty
m–Warehouse clubs
60– Retail merchandiser
61– Rubber
a– Fabricating
62– Securities
63– Services
64– Shipping/Shipbuilding
65– Specialty Instruments
66– Steel– Iron
a– Major integrated
b– Other integrated
c– Stainless
d– Other specialties
e– Ore producer
f– Steel mill machinery
g– Steel Converter/Processor
h– Steel Minimill
67– Telecommunications
a– Local
b– Long Distance
c– Foreign
d– Telegraph
e– Satellite
f– Equipment/Services
g– Mobile, cellular
68– Textiles
a– Producer
b– Synthetic fibers
c– Apparel manufacturer
69– Tobacco
a– Cigarettes
c– Leaf/snuff
70– Transportation
a– Bus
b– Freight forwarding
71– Trucking
72– Utilities– Electric
a– Operating
b– Holding
73– Utilities– Gas
a– Pipeline cos.
b– Distributors
c– Producer, gatherer
d– LP gas
e– Integrated
74– Utilities– Water
75– Util.– Diversified

Title-Industry Code & Co. Finances (In Italics) / Exchange – Individual Issue Statistics	Ind / Interest Dates	Fixed Charge Coverage 1992 / S&P Debt Rating	1993 / Date of Last Rating Change	1994 / Prior Rating	Year End / Eligible	Bond Form	Million $ Cash & Equiv. / Redemption Provisions: Regular Price	Curr. Assets / Regular (Begins) Thru	Curr. Liab. / Sinking Fund Price	Balance Sheet Date / Sinking Fund (Begins) Thru	L. Term Debt (Mil $) / Refund/Other Restriction Price	Refund/Other Restriction (Begins) Thru	Capital-ization (Mil $) / Outst'g (Mil $)	Total Debt % Capital / Underwriting Firm	Underwriting Year	Price Range 1995 High	Low	Mo. End Price Sale(s) or Bid	Curr. Yield	Yield to Mat.
A I M Management Gr	62	2.45	6.67	2.78	Dc		62.60			9-30-95	192.0		153.0	125.0						
Sr[1]Sec[2]Nts 9s 2003	mN15	BB			Y	R	104.50	(11-15-98)	....	....	[3]Z108.50	11-14-96	110	M2	'93	105	87	105	8.57	8.13
A+ Network	67g	n/a	n/a	n/a	Dc		41.90	72.80	14.30	p6-30-95	★124.0		22.00	58.4						
◆Sr Sub Nts[2] 11⅞s 2005	mN	CCC+		CCC+	Y	R	104.50	(11-1-00)	....	....	....	....	125	P4	'95	101½	99¼	s101½	11.70	11.61
Aames Financial	25h	Δ40.60	Δ28.90	Δ6.35	Je					9-30-95	23.10		108.0	21.4						
• Sr Nts 10½s 2002	[4]Feb	NR				R	■100	(2-1-00)	100	(2-1-99)	....	....	23.0	P2	'95	105	99	104½	10.05	9.51
AAR Corp	3a	Δ2.12	Δ2.43	Δ2.35	My		28.60	311.0	59.50	8-31-95	119.0		319.0	37.9						
Nts[5] 9½s 2001	mN	BBB–	1/95	BBB	X	R	NC	....	....	....	....	....	65.0	G1	'89	112⅜	98⅜	112⅜	8.45	6.89
Nts 7¼s 2003	aO15	BBB–	1/95	BBB	X	R	NC	....	....	....	....	....	50.0	G1	'93	101¼	85	101¼	7.16	7.04
[6]***Abbey Healthcare Group***	30a	4.04	3.53	1.55	Dc		19.60	393.0	216.0	9-30-95	468.0		742.0	64.4						
Sr[7]Sub Nts 9½s 2002	mN	BB+	7/95	B–	Y	R	104.75	(11-1-98)	....	....	....	....	200	D6	'93	106½	90¼	106	8.96	8.33
Abbott Laboratories	21a	28.70	35.69	44.34	Dc		415.0	4077	3567	9-30-95	435.0		5649	24.3						
Nts 5.60s 2003	aO	AAA			X	BE	NC	....	....	....	....	....	200	G1	'93	98⅜	84½	98⅜	5.69	5.86
Nts 6.80s 2005	Mn15	AAA			X	BE	NC	....	....	....	....	....	150	G1	'95	106¼	98½	106¼	6.40	5.92
ACF Indus	56	0.91	2.81	1.48	Dc		394.0	574.0	383.0	12-31-94	638.0		1222	67.2						
Eq Tr Ctf 14½s '96	jD	B+	4/86	BBB	Y	R	NC	....	100	....	....	....	12.0	B1	'81	104	102	102	14.22	12.11
Eq Tr Ctf 11.60s 2000	Mn15	B+	4/86	BBB	Y	R	NC	....	100	....	....	....	15.0	B1	'80	103⅝	98½	103⅝	11.19	10.54
Acme Metals	66b	0.49	3.07	3.72	Dc		204.0	336.0	117.0	6-26-95	271.0		512.0	52.9						
Sr Sec[8]Disc Nts[9] 13½s 2004	fA	B			Y	R	106.75	(8-1-99)	....	....	....	....	[10]118	L3	'94	80	68	80	....	Flat
Sr Sec Nts[2] 12½s 2002	fA	B			Y	R	106.25	(8-1-98)	....	....	....	....	125	L3	'94	103½	96½	99½	12.56	12.61
Act III Broadcasting	12c	0.24	0.85	1.42	Dc		3.10	28.90	21.50	3-31-95	162.0		78.80	208.0						
Sr[2]Sub Nts[11] 9⅝s 2003	jD15	B–	12/95	B	Y	R	103.61	(12-15-98)	....	....	[12]Z108.625	12-15-96	100	D6	'93	104	90¾	100¼	9.60	9.58
Act III Theatres	24b	n/a	1.23	1.20	Dc		10.00	13.60	20.00	9-30-95	230.0		205.0	113.0						
Sr Sub Nts[2] 11⅞s 2003	Fa	B–			Y	R	105.938	(2-1-98)	100	(2-1-02)	....	....	85.0	K2	'93	110⅛	94¼	108¼	10.97	10.21
[13]***Actava Group***	42a	2.34	0.62	0.21	Dc		38.90	307.0	155.0	6-30-95	157.0		335.0	67.8						
• Su Sub SF Deb[14] 9⅞s '97	Ms15	B	5/91	B+	Y	R	100.515	3-14-96	....	....	....	....	[10]21.2	L3	'77	101⅜	95¼	99¾	9.90	10.07
• Sub SF Deb 10s '99	aO	B	5/91	B+	Y	R	100	....	....	....	....	....	6.70	Exch.	'74	102	93½	98	10.20	10.65
• Sub Deb 9½s '98	fA	B	5/91	B+	Y	R	100	....	....	....	....	....	59.5	Exch.	'93	100¾	87	s96⅞	9.81	10.91
Adelphia Communications	12a	0.68	0.65	0.66	Mr		60.40			9-30-95	2091		1026	204.0						
Sr Deb 11⅞s 2004	mS15	B			Y	R	104.50	(9-15-99)	....	....	....	....	125	S1	'92	100½	87¾	94½	12.57	12.94
Sr Nts 12½s 2002	Mn15	B			Y	R	106	(5-15-97)	....	....	....	....	400	S1	'92	104	90½	97½	12.82	13.08
[15]***ADT Operations***	63	2.89	3.26	2.82	Dc		228.0	567.0	522.0	6-30-95	838.0		2159	45.7						
Sr Nts[2] 8¼s 2000	fA	BBB–	8/95	BB+	X	R	NC	....	....	....	....	....	250	M2	'93	106	92	105¾	7.80	6.77
Sr[2]Sub Nts[16] 9¼s 2003	fA	BB+	4/95	BB–	Y	R	103.75	(8-1-98)	....	....	....	....	350	M2	'93	107	92¼	107	8.64	8.00
Advanced Medical Inc	21c	1.35	0.99	1.87	Dc		6.87	49.20	22.30	9-30-95	63.20									
◆Sub[17]Deb[18] 15s '99	jJ15	NR				R	110	(3-31-96)	....	....	....	....	21.9	Exch.	'95	96	92	96	....	Flat
ADVANTA Corp	25e	6.09	5.76	4.16	Dc					9-30-95	1104		1739	63.5						
Nts 5⅛s '96	mN15	BBB–			X	BE	NC	....	....	....	....	....	150	C5	'93	99⅝	94⅜	99⅝	5.14	5.56
AES Corp	63	1.65	1.79	2.19	Dc		285.0	429.0	187.0	6-30-95	1136		1732	69.8						
Sr Sub Nts[2] 9¾s 2000	Jd15	B+			Y	R	103.25	(6-15-97)	....	....	....	....	75.0	M5	'93	102⅞	94⅞	102¾	9.49	8.99
Aetna Life & Casual	35d	1.27	6.56	7.66	Dc		2581			9-30-95	1121		8092	14.7						
Deb 6¾s 2013	mS15	A–	7/95	A+	X	BE	NC	....	....	....	....	....	200	G1	'93	96½	79¾	96½	6.99	7.10
Deb 8s 2017	Jj15	A–	7/95	A+	X	R	104	(1-15-97)	100	(1-15-97)	....	....	200	M2	'87	105⅝	90⅝	105⅝	7.57	7.47
Deb 7¼s 2023	fA15	A–	7/95	A+	X	BE	NC	....	....	....	....	....	200	G1	'93	98½	80⅛	98½	7.36	7.38
Nts 8⅝s '98	Ms	A–	7/95	A+	X	R	NC	....	....	....	....	....	100	M6	'88	105¾	100⅝	105¾	8.16	5.76
Nts 6⅝s 2003	fA15	A–	7/95	A+	X	BE	NC	....	....	....	....	....	200	G1	'93	100	85¼	100	6.38	6.37
Affiliated Newspapers Investments	54c	Δ0.43	Δd0.09	Δ0.58	Je		5.83	43.00	34.40	9-30-95	347.0		225.0	156.0						
xw Sr[19]Disc Deb[2] 13¼s 2006	jJ	B+			Y	R	106.75	(7-1-99)	....	....	[20]Z112.25	6-30-96	[10]174	B9	'94	59	47½	A59	....	Flat

Uniform Footnote Explanations-See Page 260. Other: [1] Gtd by AIM Advisors Inc. [2] (HRO)On Chge of Ctrl at 101. [3] Max $35M red w/proceeds of Pub Equity Off'g. [4] Int pd monthly. [5] (HRO)For Trigger Event at 100. [6] Now Apria Healthcare Group. [7] Co must offer repurch at 101 on Chge of Ctrl. [8] Int accrues at 13.5% fr 8-1-97. [9] (HRO)On Chge of Ctrl at 101(Accreted Val). [10] Incl disc. [11] Purch offer, $1040 to Nov 28. [12] Max $33.3M red w/proceeds of Pub Eq Off'g. [13] Now Metromedia Intl Gr. [14] Was Fuqua Indus. [15] Gtd by & data of ADT Ltd. [16] Gtd by ADT Ltd. [17] Issued in min denom $500. [18] (HRO)On Chge of Ctrl at 100. [19] Int accr at 13.25% fr 7-1-99(1st pymt 1-1-00). [20] Max $60.8M red w/proceeds Pub Equity Off'g.

Title-Industry Code & Co. Finances (In Italics) / Individual Issue Statistics — Exchange	Ind / Interest Dates	Fixed Charge Coverage 1992 / S&P Debt Rating	1993 / Date of Last Rating Change	Prior Rating	1994 / Eligible	Year End / Bond Form	Million $ Cash & Equiv. / Redemption Provisions Regular Price	Curr. Assets / Regular (Begins) Thru	Curr. Liab. / Sinking Fund Price	Balance Sheet Date / Sinking Fund (Begins) Thru	L. Term Debt (Mil $) / Refund/Other Restriction Price	Refund/Other Restriction (Begins) Thru	Capital-ization (Mil $) / Outst'g (Mil $)	Total Debt % Capital / Underwriting Firm	Year	Price Range 1995 High	Low	Mo. End Price Sale(s) or Bid	Curr. Yield	Yield to Mat.
Affinity Group	***23e***	***0.47***	***0.95***		***1.49***	***Dc***		***25.60***	***25.80***	***9-30-95***	***151.0***		***75.50***	***207.0***						
Sr[1]Sub Nts 11½s 2003	aO15	**B**			Y	R	104.313	(10-15-98)	....	....	[2]Z108.625	10-14-96	120	C4	'93	102	94¼	101	11.39	11.30
[3]***Agricultural Min & Chem***	***14a***	***2.71***	***3.28***		***5.04***	***Dc***	***93.40***	***949.0***	***520.0***	***9-30-95***	***504.0***		***1354***	***45.1***						
Sr Nts[1] 10¾s 2003	mS30	**B+**	10/94	B	Y	R	105.375	(9-30-98)	....	....	[4]Z110	9-29-96	175	M6	'93	106½	101	105	10.24	9.81
Ahmanson (H.F.)& Co	***10b***	***1.87***	***0.40***		***1.81***	***Dc***				***9-30-95***	***6270***		***9341***	***67.1***						
Nts 8¼s 2002	aO	**BBB+**			X	R	[5]Z100	....	....	....	....	....	250	G1	'92	110⅜	96⅝	110¼	7.48	6.36
Sub Nts[6] 7⅞s 2004	mS	**BBB**			X	BE	NC	....	....	....	....	....	125	L3	'94	110	93¾	110	7.16	6.36
Air Products & Chemicals	***14b***	***△5.66***	***△5.44***		***△5.01***	***Sp***	***87.00***	***1332***	***1311***	***9-30-95***	***1194***		***4079***	***41.2***						
Deb 8½s 2006	Ao	**A+**			X	R	100	(4-1-04)	....	....	....	....	100	G1	'86	114⅞	100½	114⅞	7.40	6.49
• Deb 8¾s 2021	Ao15	**A+**			X	R	NC	....	....	....	....	....	100	S4	'91	No Sale		103½	8.45	8.41
Nts 8⅞s 2001	fA	**A+**			X	R	NC	....	....	....	....	....	100	S4	'89	113⅝	103⅛	113⅝	7.81	5.97
Nts 8.35s 2002	Jj15	**A+**			X	BE	NC	....	....	....	....	....	100	G1	'95	111⅝	99⅞	111⅝	7.48	6.03
Nts 6¼s 2003	Jd15	**A+**			X	R	NC	....	....	....	....	....	100	L3	'93	100¾	87⅝	100½	6.22	6.16
Nts 7⅜s 2005	Mn	**A+**			X	BE	NC	....	....	....	....	....	150	L3	'95	108⅝	99¼	107¾	6.84	6.26
Airborne Freight	***4a***	***0.43***	***3.17***		***3.61***	***Dc***	***14.10***	***321.0***	***236.0***	***9-30-95***	***476.0***		***882.0***	***54.8***						
Nts 8⅞s 2002	jD15	**BBB**	8/95	BBB+	X	R	NC	....	....	....	....	....	100	G1	'92	113¾	100⅜	112⅞	7.86	6.54
Nts 7.35s 2005	mS15	**BBB**			X	BE	NC	....	....	....	....	....	100	G1	'95	104⅜	99¼	104⅜	7.04	6.73
[7]***AK Steel Corp***	***66a***	***n/a***	***p0.49***		***4.15***	***Dc***	***347.0***	***878.0***	***375.0***	***9-30-95***	***325.0***		***980.0***	***33.2***						
Sr[8]Nts[1] 10¾s 2004	Ao	**BB−**	7/95	B+	Y	R	104.031	(4-1-99)	....	....	....	....	325	C5	'94	110	99	108⅝	9.90	9.23
Alabama Bancorporation	***10***	***Now AmSouth Bancorp, see***																		
• [9]F/R[10]Nts 6½s '99	mS	**A−**	6/95	A	X	R	100	....	....	....	....	....	7.47	F1	'74	99	98⅞	98⅞	6.57	....
Alabama Power Co.[11]	***72a***	***3.38***	***3.50***		***3.73***	***Dc***	***12.90***	***864.0***	***824.0***	***6-30-95***	***2397***		***5525***	***44.5***						
1st 4½s '96	Ms	**A+**	3/95	A	X	R	NC	....	....	....	....	....	60.0	S1	'93	99⅞	96½	99⅞	4.51	5.16
1st 5½s '98	Fa	**A+**	2/95	A	X	R	NC	....	....	....	....	....	50.0	M5	'93	99¾	92¾	99¾	5.51	5.63
1st 6⅜s '99	fA	**A+**	3/95	A	X	R	NC	....	....	....	....	....	170	S1	'92	101¾	92⅝	101¾	6.27	5.83
1st 6s 2000	Ms	**A+**	3/95	A	X	R	NC	....	....	....	....	....	100	M5	'93	100½	90¼	100½	5.97	5.86
1st 6.85s 2002	fA	**A+**	3/95	A	X	R	101.53	(8-1-97)	Z100	....	....	....	100	S1	'92	102⅛	90¾	102⅛	6.71	6.45
1st 7s 2003	Jj	**A+**	3/95	A	X	R	101.64	(1-1-98)	Z100	(1-1-98)	....	....	125	M6	'93	102⅝	90⅞	102⅝	6.82	6.53
1st 6¾s 2003	Fa	**A+**	3/95	A	X	R	101.60	(2-1-98)	Z100	(2-1-98)	....	....	175	M6	'93	101¾	89⅛	101¾	6.63	6.44
1st 7¼s 2007	fA	**A+**	3/95	A	X	R	103.45	(8-1-97)	Z100	....	....	....	175	M6	'92	104	89⅛	104	6.97	6.75
• 1st 9¼s 2021	Mn	**A+**	3/95	A	X	R	106.44	4-30-96	Z100	....	®106.03	4-30-96	[12]75.3	F1	'91	106¼	101	104	8.89	8.85
1st 8¾s 2021	jD	**A+**	3/95	A	X	R	106.60	11-30-96	Z100	....	®106.19	11-30-96	149	S1	'91	108⅝	97¼	106¾	8.20	8.12
1st 8½s 2022	Mn	**A+**	3/95	A	X	R	106.30	4-30-97	Z100	....	®105.91	4-30-97	198	K2	'92	107¾	95⅝	107½	7.91	7.82
1st 8.30s 2022	jJ	**A+**	3/95	A	X	R	106.06	6-30-96	Z100	....	®105	6-30-97	99.6	L3	'92	106¾	94⅛	106¾	7.78	7.70
1st 7¾s 2023	Fa	**A+**	3/95	A	X	R	105.63	1-31-96	Z100	....	®104.69	1-31-98	100	S1	'93	104½	89	104½	7.42	7.36
1st 7.45s 2023	jJ	**A+**	3/95	A	X	R	105.57	6-30-96	Z100	....	®104.65	6-30-98	150	L3	'93	102	86¼	102	7.30	7.28
1st 7.30s 2023	mN	**A+**	3/95	A	X	R	105.46	10-31-96	Z100	....	®104.55	10-31-98	100	P1	'93	97¾	84⅝	97¾	7.47	7.49
1st 9s 2024	jD	**A+**	3/95	A	X	R	106.32	(12-1-99)	Z100	(12-1-99)	....	....	150	D6	'94	113¼	102¼	113¼	7.95	7.83
Alaska Housing Finance Cp	***25b***	***△1.35***	***△1.35***		***△1.58***	***Je***	***1768***			***9-30-95***	***2244***		***3932***	***57.1***						
Sec Bonds '86B 9.30s 2001	Jd	**AAA**			X	R	NC	....	*100	(12-1-96)	[13]*Z100	(6-1-96)	26.0	S1	'86	110½	100½	100½	9.25	9.18
Sec Bonds '86D 8⅝s 2001	mN15	**AAA**			X	R	NC	....	*100	(3-15-97)	[14]*Z100	(9-15-96)	35.3	S1	'86	107½	103⅜	107½	8.02	7.01
Sec Bonds '86E 8¾s 2001	aO15	**AAA**			X	R	NC	....	*100	(4-15-97)	[14]*Z100	(9-15-96)	31.1	S1	'86	108½	104	108½	8.06	6.94
Albertson's, Inc	***59c***	***12.43***	***11.51***		***11.20***	***Ja***	***53.40***	***1252***	***1087***	***11-2-95***	***719.0***		***2668***	***30.1***						
Nts 6⅜s 2000	Jd	**A+**			X	BE	NC	....	....	....	....	....	200	G1	'95	102	98½	102	6.25	5.85
[15]***Alco Health Distribution***[16]	***21d***	***0.89***	***1.02***		***1.24***	***Sp***	***25.30***	***652.0***	***518.0***	***9-30-94***	***488.0***		***187.0***	***261.0***						
Sr Deb[1] 11¼s 2005	jJ15	**B−**			Y	R	105.62	(7-15-98)	....	....	[17]Z110	7-26-96	127	D6	'93	107	98	107	10.51	10.09
Alco Capital Resources	***25***	***1.53***	***1.69***		***1.85***	***Sp***				***6-30-95***	***682.0***		***797.0***	***85.6***						
M-T Nts 'A 6.60s '96	[18]jd15	**A**			X	BE	NC	....	....	....	....	....	30.0	G1	'94	100½	99½	100¼	6.58	5.50

Uniform Footnote Explanations-See Page 260. Other:[1] (HRO)On Chge of Ctrl at 101. [2] Max $36M red w/proceeds of Pub Eq off'g. [3] Now Terra Indus Inc. [4] Max $61.3M red w/proceeds of Pub Equity Off'g. [5] Plus Make-Whole Premium. [6] Issued in min denom $100T. [7] Gtd by & data of AK Steel Holding. [8] Gtd by AK Steel Holding. [9] (HRO)On int dates at 100. [10] Int thru 2-26-96,adj semi-anly aft. [11] Subsid of Southern Co. [12] Called $23.8M for SF on 1-2-96. [13] Fr 6-1-96 for spl mand red(fr surplus rev). [14] Fr 9-15-96 for spl mand red(fr surplus rev). [15] Now AmeriSource Distribution Co. [16] Subsid of AmeriSource Corp. [17] Max $63.25M red w/proceeds Pub Equity Off'g. [18] Due 3-29-96.

Title-Industry Code & Co. Finances (In Italics)	Ind	Fixed Charge Coverage 1992	1993	1994		Year End	Million $ Cash & Equiv.	Curr. Assets	Curr. Liab.	Balance Sheet Date	L. Term Debt (Mil $)		Capital-ization (Mil $)	Total Debt % Capital						
Individual Issue Statistics Exchange ↓	**Interest Dates**	**S&P Debt Rating**	**Date of Last Rating Change**	**Prior Rating**	**Eligible ↓**	**Bond Form**	**Redemption Provisions: Regular Price**	**Regular (Begins) Thru**	**Sinking Fund Price**	**Sinking Fund (Begins) Thru**	**Refund/Other Restriction Price**	**Refund/Other Restriction (Begins) Thru**	**Outst'g (Mil $)**	**Underwriting Firm**	**Underwriting Year**	**Price Range 1995 High**	**Low**	**Mo. End Price Sale(s) or Bid**	**Curr. Yield**	**Yield to Mat.**
Alco Capital Resources *(Cont.)*																				
M-T Nts 'A' 7.13s '97	[1]jd15	A			X	BE	NC	....	....	....	....	....	35.0	M2	'95	101⅞	100	101⅞	7.00	5.54
M-T Nts 'A' 6.14s '97	[2]jd15	A			X	BE	NC	....	....	....	....	....	48.0	L3	'95	100¾	99¼	100¾	6.09	5.61
M-T Nts 'A' 6.95s '97	[3]jd15	A			X	BE	NC	....	....	....	....	....	35.0	L3	'94	102	98⅞	102	6.81	5.61
M-T Nts 'A' 7.02s '97	[3]jd15	A			X	BE	NC	....	....	....	....	....	25.0	L3	'94	102⅛	99	102⅛	6.87	5.60
M-T Nts 'A' 8s '97	[4]jd15	A			X	BE	NC	....	....	....	....	....	45.0	L3	'94	104¼	101⅛	104¼	7.67	5.61
M-T Nts 'B' 5.85s '97	[5]jd15	A			X	BE	NC	....	....	....	....	....	30.0	G1	'95	100⅜	100	100⅜	5.83	5.64
M-T Nts 'A' 7.89s '98	[6]jd15	A			X	BE	NC	....	....	....	....	....	30.0	L3	'95	104⅜	100	104⅜	7.56	5.68
M-T Nts 'A' 7.33s '98	[7]jd15	A			X	BE	NC	....	....	....	....	....	35.0	C1	'95	103½	100	103½	7.08	5.64
M-T Nts 'A' 7.10s '98	[8]jd15	A			X	BE	NC	....	....	....	....	....	25.0	G1	'95	103	100	103	6.89	5.70
M-T Nts 'A' 6.45s '99	[9]jd15	A			X	BE	NC	....	....	....	....	....	35.0	M2	'95	101⅞	98⅜	101⅞	6.33	5.85
M-T Nts 'A' 6¾s 2000	jd15	A			X	BE	NC	....	....	....	....	....	25.0	L3	'95	103⅛	100	103⅛	6.55	5.96
M-T Nts 'B' 6.10s '97	jd15	A			X	BE	NC	....	....	....	....	....	50.0	L3	'95	100⅞	100	100⅞	6.05	5.56
Alex. Brown	***62***	***10.01***	***10.94***	***6.40***		***Dc***	***23.80***			***6-30-95***	***★190.0***		***596.0***	***28.2***						
• Sr Nts 7⅝s 2005	fA15	BBB			X	BE	NC	....	....	....	....	....	110	B8	'95	99⅜	99⅜	97	7.86	8.08
Alco Standard	***50***	***Δ3.36***	***Δ4.82***	***Δ3.78***		***Sp***	***90.10***	***2161***	***1390***	***9-30-95***	***★1438***		***3319***	***43.7***						
Bonds 6¾s 2025	jD	A			X	BE	[10]Z100	....	....	....	....	....	300	M6	'95	99	97⅝	99	6.82	6.83
Nts 8⅞s 2001	Ao15	A			X	R	NC	....	....	....	....	....	150	G1	'91	113⅛	101¼	113⅛	7.85	5.95
Allbritton Communications Co	***12c***	***1.30***	***n/a***	***n/a***		***Sp***	***2.35***	***35.50***	***30.50***	***6-30-95***	***187.0***		***55.80***	***353.0***						
Sr Sub Deb[11] 11½s 2004	fA15	B–			Y	R	104.75	(8-15-97)	100	(8-15-03)	....	....	125	M2	'92	106½	99½	105⅛	10.94	10.57
Allegheny Generating[12]	***72***	***3.01***	***2.87***	***3.50***		***Dc***		***5.48***	***6.07***	***9-30-95***	***257.0***		***477.0***	***54.5***						
Deb 5⅝s 2003	mS	A			X	R	NC	....	[13]Z100	....	....	....	50.0	P4	'93	96⅞	83¼	96⅞	5.81	6.14
Deb 6⅞s 2023	mS	A			X	R	103.28	(9-1-03)	[13]Z100	....	....	....	100	G1	'93	100	80¾	100	6.88	6.87
Allegheny Ludlum	***66c***	***9.75***	***12.91***	***5.17***		***Dc***	***59.40***	***432.0***	***189.0***	***10-1-95***	***★182.0***		***518.0***	***25.8***						
Deb 6.95s 2025	jD15	A			X	BE	NC	....	....	....	....	....	150	G1	'95	101⅝	99⅞	101⅝	6.84	6.82
Allegheny & Western Ry	***55***	***Issue gtd by Buffalo,Roch&Pitts Ry.Rental B&O***																		
• 1st 4s '98	aO	NR			X	CR	NC	....	....	....	....	....	1.97		1899	94¼	88¼	s91½	4.37	7.47
Allied Corp[14]	***14***	***Gtd by Allied Signal,see***																		
• Bonds Zero Cpn '97	[15]	A	12/92	A–	X	CR	100	....	....	....	....	....	[16]28.5	S1	'84	91	80⅝	90¾	....	6.20
• Bonds Zero Cpn '99	[15]	A	12/92	A–	X	CR	100	....	....	....	....	....	[16]28.5	S1	'84	80⅜	68⅝	80⅛	....	6.27
• Bonds Zero Cpn 2001	[15]	A	12/92	A–	X	CR	100	....	....	....	....	....	[16]28.5	S1	'84	71	58¼	s70	....	6.48
• Bonds Zero Cpn 2003	[15]	A	12/92	A–	X	CR	100	....	....	....	....	....	[16]28.5	S1	'84	62⅝	49¾	60¾	....	6.68
• Bonds Zero Cpn 2005	[15]	A	12/92	A–	X	CR	100	....	....	....	....	....	[16]28.5	S1	'84	53⅞	43	52¾	....	6.78
• Bonds Zero Cpn 2007	[15]	A	12/92	A–	X	CR	100	....	....	....	....	....	[16]28.5	S1	'84	47¼	35¼	45⅛	....	6.99
• Bonds Zero Cpn 2009	[15]	A	12/92	A–	X	CR	100	....	....	....	....	....	[16]128	S1	'84	40	29⅛	s39⅜	....	6.98
• Nts Zero Cpn '96	[17]	A	12/92	A–	X	C	NC	....	....	....	....	....	[16]90.0	S1	'82	99½	92¼	s99⅝	....	Mat.
• Nts Zero Cpn '98	[18]	A	12/92	A–	X	C	NC	....	....	....	....	....	[16]90.0	S1	'82	85	73⅛	84⅜	....	6.37
• Nts Zero Cpn 2000	[19]	A	12/92	A–	X	C	NC	....	....	....	....	....	[16]90.0	S1	'82	75⅜	62¼	s75	....	6.31
AlliedSignal Inc[20]	***17***	***3.32***	***4.99***	***6.78***		***Dc***	***545.0***	***4985***	***3630***	***9-30-95***	***1377***		***5577***	***38.4***						
• Deb 9⅞s 2002	Jd	A	12/92	A–	X	R	NC	....	....	....	....	....	250	G1	'87	113⅞	109	113¾	8.68	7.16
• Deb 9.20s 2003	Fa15	A	12/92	A–	X	BE	NC	....	....	....	....	....	100	G1	'91	No Sale		107	8.60	7.89
• Deb 9½s 2016	Jd	A	12/92	A–	X	R	NC	....	....	....	....	....	100		'86	109	109	107⅜	8.85	8.72
Nts 6¾s 2000	fA15	A			X	BE	NC	....	....	....	....	....	100	G1	'95	103⅞	99⅞	103⅞	6.50	5.78
Allied Supermarkets	***59c***	***Merged into Vons Cos,see***																		
Sr Sub Deb 6⅝s '98	Mn15	BB–	3/92	B+	Y	R	100	....	100	....	....	....	[16]87.5	D7	'86	98¼	90⅝	97¾	6.78	7.67
Allied Waste Industries	***53***	***1.55***	***1.55***	***1.66***		***Dc***	***9.47***	***49.20***	***56.40***	***9-30-95***	***177.0***		***335.0***	***63.3***						
Sr[21]Sub[22]Nts 12s 2004	Fa	B			Y	R	106	(2-1-99)	....	....	....	....	100	J1	'94	108½	97	108½	11.06	10.42

Uniform Footnote Explanations-See Page 260. Other: [1] Due 3-27-97. [2] Due 6-30-97. [3] Due 7-30-97. [4] Due 11-24-97. [5] Due 12-1-97. [6] Due 2-16-98. [7] Due 3-27-98. [8] Due 4-27-98. [9] Due 6-29-99. [10] Co may red at greater of 100 or amt based on formula. [11] Co must offer repurch at 101 on Chge in Ctrl. [12] Affil with Allegheny Pwr Sys. [13] Conditional SF. [14] Was Allied Chemical. [15] Due Aug 1. [16] Incl disc. [17] Due 1-15-96. [18] Due 9-15-98. [19] Due 8-15-00. [20] See Allied Corp. [21] (HRO)On Chge of Ctrl at 101. [22] Int incr fr 10.75% eff Jan 30.

Title-Industry Code & Co. Finances (In Italics) / Individual Issue Statistics (Exchange ↓)	Ind / Interest Dates	Fixed Charge Coverage 1992 / S&P Debt Rating	1993 / Date of Last Rating Change	Prior Rating	1994 / Eligible ↓	Year End / Bond Form	Million $ Cash & Equiv. / Regular Price	Curr. Assets / Regular (Begins) Thru	Curr. Liab. / Sinking Fund Price	Balance Sheet Date / Sinking Fund (Begins) Thru	L. Term Debt (Mil $) / Refund/Other Restriction Price	Refund/Other Restriction (Begins) Thru	Capital-ization (Mil $) / Outst'g (Mil $)	Total Debt % Capital / Underwriting Firm	Underwriting Year	Price Range 1995 High	Price Range 1995 Low	Mo. End Price Sale(s) or Bid	Curr. Yield	Yield to Mat.
Allmerica Financial Corp	***35c***	***n/a***	***n/a***		***n/a***	***Dc***				***p6-30-95***	***★200.0***		***2340***	***9.7***						
• Sr Deb 7⅝s 2025	aO15	**A–**			X	BE	NC	....	....	....	....	....	200	M2	'95	99⅝	99⅝	102⅜	7.45	7.42
Allnet Communication Services	***67b***	***2.40***	***6.56***		***19.64***	***Dc***	***8.13***	***163.0***	***206.0***	***9-30-95***	***9.40***		***260.0***	***32.6***						
◆Sr Sub[1]Nts[2] 9s 2003	Mn15	**A–**	8/95	B	X	R	103	(5-15-98)	....	....	....	....	4.25	P1	'93	109½	92½	103	8.74	8.44
Allstate Corp	***35***	***n/a***	***17.86***		***7.42***	***Dc***				***9-30-95***	***1225***		***12813***	***9.6***						
Deb 7½s 2013	Jd15	**A**			X	BE	NC	....	....	....	....	....	250	G1	'93	106¾	87⅜	106¾	7.03	6.83
Nts 5⅞s '98	Jd15	**A**			X	BE	NC	....	....	....	....	....	300	G1	'93	100½	92⅜	100½	5.85	5.65
Nts 6¾s 2003	Jd15	**A**			X	BE	NC	....	....	....	....	....	300	G1	'93	103⅜	88¼	103⅜	6.53	6.18
ALLTEL Corp[3]	***67a***	***4.79***	***5.25***		***4.47***	***Dc***	***34.10***	***714.0***	***559.0***	***9-30-95***	***1853***		***3760***	***50.3***						
Deb 7¼s 2004	Ao	**A+**			X	BE	NC	....	....	....	....	....	250	S7	'94	106⅞	92	106⅞	6.78	6.17
Deb 6¾s 2005	mS15	**A+**			X	BE	NC	....	....	....	....	....	200	S7	'95	103¾	99¾	103¾	6.51	6.23
Deb 6½s 2013	mN	**A+**			X	R	NC	....	....	....	....	....	200	S7	'93	97½	81⅜	97½	6.67	6.74
Deb 9½s 2021	Ms	**A+**			X	R	107.125	(3-1-96)	....	....	....	....	200	S7	'91	109⅜	103½	107⅝	8.83	8.74
Aluminum Co. of Amer	***5***	***5.61***	***4.73***		***5.64***	***Dc***	***996.0***	***5068***	***2430***	***9-30-95***	***1432***		***7620***	***20.9***						
Nts 4⅝s '96	Fa15	**A+**			X	BE	NC	....	....	....	....	....	175	F1	'93	99⅞	96⅞	99⅞	4.63	5.52
Nts 5¾s 2001	Fa	**A+**			X	BE	NC	....	....	....	....	....	250	C5	'94	99¼	87¾	99¼	5.79	5.92
Amax, Inc	***5***	***See Cyprus Amax Minerals***																		
• Nts 9⅞s 2001	Jd13	**BBB–**			X	R	NC	....	....	....	....	....	300	M2	'91	111	108	105½	9.36	8.59
AMBAC Inc	***35c***	***12.99***	***16.67***		***10.58***	***Dc***				***9-30-95***	***224.0***		***1529***	***14.7***						
Deb 7½s 2023	Mn	**AA**	8/95	AA+	X	R	NC	....	....	....	....	....	75.0	M6	'93	108⅞	86⅝	108⅞	6.89	6.78
AMC Entertainment	***24b***	***1.41***	***1.70***		***1.70***	***Mr***	***153.0***	***173.0***	***85.40***	***6-29-95***	***264.0***		***428.0***	***62.4***						
Sr Nts[4] 11⅞s 2000	fA	**BB–**	2/94	B+	Y	R	103.40	(8-1-97)	....	....	Z100	....	100	C4	'92	112	105	112	10.60	8.65
Sr Sub Nts[4] 12⅝s 2002	[5]fa	**B**	2/94	B–	Y	R	105.60	(8-1-97)	....	....	Z100	....	100	C4	'92	114½	106	114½	11.03	9.59
American Airlines[6]	***4***	***d0.03***	***1.06***		***0.95***	***Dc***	***1166***	***3728***	***5966***	***9-30-95***	***5141***		***9025***	***59.0***						
• Sub Deb 6¼s '96	Ms	**BB–**	3/93	BBB–	Y	R	100	....	....	....	....	....	[7]5.50	M6	'86	100	98⅛	99¾	6.27	7.57
• Sub Deb[8] 5¼s '98	jJ	**NR**				R	100	....	100	....	....	....	2.30		'80	97	86⅜	95¾	5.48	7.13
American Annuity Group	***35***	***0.42***	***1.42***		***3.95***	***Dc***	***10.30***			***6-30-95***	***168.0***		***463.0***	***36.3***						
• Sr Nts[9] 9½s 2001	fA15	**BB**	6/95	B+	Y	R	104.071	(8-16-97)	....	....	....	....	100	D6	'93	No Sale		100	9.50	9.50
• Sr Sub Nts[9] 11⅛s 2003	Fa	**B+**	6/95	B–	Y	R	103.179	(2-1-98)	100	(2-1-01)	....	....	125	D6	'93	No Sale		105½	10.55	10.02
Amer Bankers Insur Grp	***35d***	***7.21***	***10.70***		***8.15***	***Dc***				***9-30-95***	***236.0***		***719.0***	***32.8***						
M-T Nts 7.60s '99	[10]mn15	**BBB+**			X	BE	NC	....	....	....	....	....	75.0	P1	'94	104¾	96¼	104¾	7.26	6.01
American Brands	***69a***	***6.18***	***5.41***		***5.80***	***Dc***	***393.0***	***3316***	***2348***	***9-30-95***	***1383***		***5497***	***28.7***						
• Deb 9⅛s 2016	Ms	**A**	2/92	A–	X	R	104.4375	(3-1-96)	100	(3-1-97)	....	....	150	M6	'86	106¼	102	104¾	8.71	8.62
• Deb 7⅞s 2023	Jj15	**A**			X	R	NC	....	....	....	....	....	150	G1	'93	104	91	100	7.88	7.87
• Nts 7½s '99	Mn15	**A**			X	R	NC	....	....	....	....	....	150	M6	'92	104¾	96⅛	102	7.35	6.82
• Nts 9s '99	Jd15	**A**	2/92	A–	X	R	NC	....	....	....	....	....	100	M6	'89	108½	102	108	8.33	6.39
• Nts 8½s 2003	aO	**A**	2/92	A–	X	R	NC	....	....	....	....	....	200	M5	'91	111½	100	s111½	7.62	6.58
• Deb 8⅝s 2021	mN15	**A**	2/92	A–	X	R	NC	....	....	....	....	....	150	M6	'91	111	98½	108	7.99	7.89
Amer Express	***25e***	***1.10***	***0.43***		***2.87***	***Dc***	***4577***			***9-30-95***	***6284***		***30889***	***75.9***						
Nts 8¾s '96	Jd15	**A+**	3/93	AA–	X	R	NC	....	....	....	....	....	200	S4	'89	102¾	101	101⅜	8.63	5.67
Nts 8½s 2001	fA15	**A+**	3/93	AA–	X	R	NC	....	....	....	....	....	300	L3	'91	112½	100⅝	112½	7.56	5.86
Deb 8⅝s 2022	Mn15	**A+**	3/93	AA–	X	R	103.861	(5-15-02)	....	....	....	....	200	S1	'92	113⅞	96¾	113⅞	7.57	7.42
Amer Express Credit	***25d***	***1.29***	***1.34***		***1.30***	***Dc***	***1493***			***9-30-95***	***2616***		***18207***	***89.7***						
Sr Nts[11] 9.45s '96	Fa15	**A+**	3/93	AA–	X	R	NC	....	....	....	....	....	100	S4	'86	102⅜	100½	100½	9.40	5.32
Sr Nts 7⅞s '96	jD	**A+**	3/93	AA–	X	R	NC	....	....	....	....	....	250	S4	'86	102½	99⅝	102⅛	7.71	5.47
Sr Nts 7¾s '97	Ms	**A+**	3/93	AA–	X	R	NC	....	....	....	....	....	200	S4	'87	102⅝	99⅛	102½	7.56	5.51
Sr Nts 7⅜s '99	Fa	**A+**	3/93	AA–	X	R	NC	....	....	....	....	....	200	L3	'92	104⅞	96⅛	104⅞	7.03	5.63

Uniform Footnote Explanations-See Page 260. Other: [1] (HRO)On Chge of Ctrl at 101. [2] Gtd by ALC Communications. [3] See Mid-Penn Tel. [4] Co must offer repurch at 101 on Chge of Ctrl. [5] Due 7-15-02. [6] Subsid of AMR Corp. [7] Incl disc. [8] Conversion priv exp 7-1-82. [9] (HRO)On Chge in Ctrl at 101. [10] Due 5-3-99. [11] Int incr fr 8.45% on 2-15-91.

Individual Issue Statistics / Exchange	Interest Dates	S&P Debt Rating	Date of Last Rating Change	Prior Rating	Eligible	Bond Form	Redemption Provisions: Regular Price	Regular (Begins) Thru	Sinking Fund Price	Sinking Fund (Begins) Thru	Refund/Other Restriction Price	Refund/Other Restriction (Begins) Thru	Outst'g (Mil $)	Underwriting Firm	Underwriting Year	Price Range 1995 High	Price Range 1995 Low	Mo. End Price Sale(s) or Bid	Curr. Yield	Yield to Mat.
Title-Industry Code & Co. Finances (In Italics)	*Ind*	*Fixed Charge Coverage 1992*		*1993*	*1994*	*Year End*	*Million $ Cash & Equiv.*	*Curr. Assets*	*Curr. Liab.*	*Balance Sheet Date*	*L. Term Debt (Mil $)*		*Capital-ization (Mil $)*	*Total Debt % Capital*						
***Amer Express Credit** (Cont.)*																				
Sr Nts 8½s '99	Jd15	A+	3/93	AA−	X	R	NC	....	....	....	....	....	150	S4	'89	108⅜	100½	108⅜	7.84	5.79
• Sr Nts 6⅛s 2000	Jd15	A+			X	R	NC	....	....	....	....	....	300	L3	'93	101½	90⅝	100¼	6.11	6.06
Sr Nts 6½s 2000	fA	A+			X	BE	NC	....	....	....	....	....	250	L3	'95	102⅞	98⅝	102⅞	6.32	5.78
Sr Nts 6¾s 2001	Jd	A+			X	BE	NC	....	....	....	....	....	250	G1	'95	104¼	99⅛	104¼	6.47	5.82
Sr Nts 6⅛s 2001	mN15	A+			X	BE	NC	....	....	....	....	....	300	G1	'95	101⅛	99⅝	101⅛	6.06	5.89
Step-Up(Reset)[1]Sr Nts 6¼s 2005	fA10	A+			X	R	100	(8-10-00)	....	....	....	....	100	L3	'93	102½	85½	102½	6.10	....
American Financial	***35d***	***0.60***		***0.69***	***1.22***	***Dc***	***260.0***			***9-30-95***	***1140***		***2240***	***50.9***						
Deb 9¾s 2004	Ao20	BB	6/95	B+	Y	R	104.75	(4-20-99)	....	....	....	....	204	Exch.	'94	103¼	91⅜	103¼	9.44	9.18
Amer & Foreign Pwr	***13d***	***Now Boise Cascade Corp,see***																		
• Deb 5s 2030	Ms	BBB−	11/95	BB+	X	CR	107.50	2-28-10	....	....	....	....	32.8	D4	'30	66	54¼	64	7.81	8.13
Amer Gen'l Corp[2]	***25g***	***2.53***		***2.78***	***2.44***	***Dc***				***9-30-95***	***6147***		***15737***	***60.3***						
SF Deb 9⅝s 2018	Fa	AA−	11/94	AA	X	R	104.638	(2-1-98)	100	(2-1-99)	....	....	137	F1	'88	111½	104¼	111	8.67	8.51
Nts 7.70s '99	aO15	AA−	11/94	AA	X	R	NC	....	....	....	....	....	100	S1	'94	106⅜	97¼	106⅜	7.24	5.80
Nts 9⅝s 2000	jJ15	AA−	11/94	AA	X	R	NC	....	....	....	....	....	200	M2	'88	114½	104⅞	114½	8.41	5.94
Nts 6¼s 2003	Ms15	AA−	11/94	AA	X	R	NC	....	....	....	....	....	100	F1	'93	100¼	87¼	100¼	6.23	6.20
Nts 7¾s 2005	Ao	AA−			X	R	NC	....	....	....	....	....	150	S1	'95	109	99⅝	109	7.11	6.44
Nts 6¾s 2005	Jd15	AA−			X	BE	NC	....	....	....	....	....	150	M2	'95	103¼	96⅜	103¼	6.54	6.29
Nts 7½s 2025	jJ15	AA−			X	BE	NC	....	....	....	....	....	150	M5	'95	108	94½	108	6.94	6.86
American Gen'l[3]Finance[4]	***25a***	***0.68***		***1.89***	***1.94***	***Dc***	***963.0***			***9-30-95***	***4933***		***8811***	***83.6***						
Sr Nts 8⅞s '96	Ms15	A+			X	R	NC	....	....	....	....	....	100	S1	'91	102	100⅝	100⅝	8.82	5.73
Sr Nts 5s '96	Jd15	A+			X	BE	NC	....	....	....	....	....	150	G1	'93	99¾	95⅞	99¾	5.01	5.55
Sr Nts 7⅜s '96	mN15	A+			X	R	NC	....	....	....	....	....	100	S1	'91	101⅞	99	101⅝	7.26	5.44
Sr Nts 7¾s '97	Jj15	A+			X	R	NC	....	....	....	....	....	100	M2	'87	102⅝	99	102¼	7.58	5.50
Sr Nts 5.80s '97	Ao	A+			X	BE	NC	....	....	....	....	....	150	S1	'94	100⅜	94⅞	100⅜	5.78	5.48
Sr Nts 7.15s '97	Mn15	A+			X	R	NC	....	....	....	....	....	150	G1	'92	102⅛	97¾	102⅛	7.00	5.52
Sr Nts 6⅝s '97	Jd	A+			X	BE	NC	....	....	....	....	....	150	L3	'94	101½	96¼	101½	6.53	5.51
Sr Nts 7s '97	aO	A+			X	BE	NC	....	....	....	....	....	150	M5	'94	102⅜	96⅝	102⅜	6.84	5.55
Sr Nts 7.70s '97	mN15	A+			X	R	NC	....	....	....	....	....	200	S1	'94	103¾	98	103¾	7.42	5.56
Sr Nts 7¼s '98	Ms	A+			X	BE	NC	....	....	....	....	....	200	F1	'95	103⅜	99¾	103⅜	7.01	5.57
Sr Nts 8¼s '98	Jj15	A+			X	BE	NC	....	....	....	....	....	200	S1	'95	105⅛	100	105⅛	7.85	5.56
Sr Nts 8½s '98	fA15	A+			X	R	NC	....	....	....	....	....	100	S1	'91	106⅞	100	106⅞	7.95	5.64
Sr Nts 8½s '99	Jd15	A+			X	R	NC	....	....	....	....	....	150	M6	'89	108	100¾	108	7.87	5.91
Sr Nts 6⅞s '99	jJ	A+			X	BE	NC	....	....	....	....	....	150	F1	'94	103⅜	94⅜	103⅜	6.65	5.80
Sr Nts 7⅛s '99	jD	A+			X	R	NC	....	....	....	....	....	150	S1	'92	104½	94⅛	104½	6.82	5.82
Sr Nts 6⅞s 2000	Jj15	A+			X	R	NC	....	....	....	....	....	150	M5	'93	103¾	93	103¾	6.63	5.82
Sr Nts 8s 2000	Fa15	A+			X	BE	NC	....	....	....	....	....	200	L3	'95	107⅝	100	107⅝	7.43	5.89
Sr Nts 7¼s 2000	Ao15	A+			X	BE	NC	....	....	....	....	....	200	G1	'95	105¼	99⅜	105¼	6.89	5.85
Sr Nts 5⅞s 2000	jJ	A+			X	BE	NC	....	....	....	....	....	150	M5	'93	100⅛	88⅞	100⅛	5.87	5.84
Sr Nts 7.45s 2002	jJ	A+			X	R	NC	....	....	....	....	....	150	G1	'92	107⅜	93⅞	107⅜	6.94	6.06
• Sr Nts 6⅜s 2003	Ms	A+			X	BE	NC	....	....	....	....	....	150	S1	'93	99	95	99¼	6.42	6.51
Sr Nts 7¼s 2005	Mn15	A+			X	BE	NC	....	....	....	....	....	200	C1	'95	107	99⅝	107	6.78	6.25
Sr Nts[5] 8⅛s 2009	fA15	A+			X	R	NC	....	....	....	....	....	150	S1	'89	114¾	100¼	114¾	7.08	6.48
• Sr Nts[6] 8.45s 2009	aO15	A+			X	R	NC	....	....	....	....	....	150	B5	'89	No Sale		103½	8.16	8.02
M-T Nts 'C'[7] 5.62s '96	[8]ao	A+			X	BE	NC	....	....	....	....	....	10.0	G1	'93	100⅛	98	100	5.62	Mat.
M-T Nts 'C'[7] 4.98s '96	[9]ao	A+			X	BE	NC	....	....	....	....	....	5.00	G1	'93	99⅞	96¾	99⅞	4.99	5.44
M-T Nts 'C'[7] 4.65s '96	[10]ao	A+			X	BE	NC	....	....	....	....	....	6.00	G1	'93	99¾	96⅛	99¾	4.66	5.41

Uniform Footnote Explanations-See Page 260. Other: [1] Int 6.25% to 8-9-00,7.45% aft. [2] Was Amer Gen'l Insur. [3] Sub Credithrift Fin'l Inc(Amer Gen'l). [4] Was Credithrift Fin'l Corp. [5] (HRO)On 8-15-96 at 100. [6] (HRO)On 10-15-99 at 100. [7] Issued in min denom $100T. [8] Due 1-8-96. [9] Due 3-25-96. [10] Due 4-22-96.

Title-Industry Code & Co. Finances (In Italics)	Ind	Fixed Charge Coverage 1992	1993	1994	Year End		Million $ Cash & Equiv.	Curr. Assets	Curr. Liab.	Balance Sheet Date	L. Term Debt (Mil $)	Capital-ization (Mil $)	Total Debt % Capital							
Exchange ↓ Individual Issue Statistics	**Interest Dates**	**S&P Debt Rating**	**Date of Last Rating Change**	**Prior Rating**	**Eligible ↓**	**Bond Form**	**Redemption Provisions: Regular Price**	**Regular (Begins) Thru**	**Sinking Fund Price**	**Sinking Fund (Begins) Thru**	**Refund/Other Restriction Price**	**Refund/Other Restriction (Begins) Thru**	**Outst'g (Mil $)**	**Underwriting Firm**	**Underwriting Year**	**Price Range 1995 High**	**Price Range 1995 Low**	**Mo. End Price Sale(s) or Bid**	**Curr. Yield**	**Yield to Mat.**
***American Gen'l Finance** (Cont.)*																				
M-T Nts 'C'[1] 4.63s '96	[2]ao	A+			X	BE	NC	....	....	....	....	....	12.8	G1	'93	99⅜	94⅞	99⅜	4.66	5.57
M-T Nts 'C'[1] 4.47s '96	[3]ao	A+			X	BE	NC	....	....	....	....	....	5.00	G1	'93	99⅛	94¼	99⅛	4.51	5.59
M-T Nts 'C'[1] 4.85s '96	[4]ao	A+			X	BE	NC	....	....	....	....	....	5.00	G1	'93	99½	94⅝	99½	4.87	5.43
M-T Nts 'C'[1] 4.90s '96	[5]ao	A+			X	BE	NC	....	....	....	....	....	5.00	G1	'93	99½	94½	99½	4.92	5.45
M-T Nts 'C'[1] 4.85s '96	[6]ao	A+			X	BE	NC	....	....	....	....	....	5.00	G1	'93	99½	94¼	99½	4.87	5.39
M-T Nts 'C'[1] 4.86s '96	[7]ao	A+			X	BE	NC	....	....	....	....	....	5.00	G1	'93	99⅜	94⅛	99⅜	4.89	5.51
M-T Nts 'C'[1] 4.90s '97	[8]ao	A+			X	BE	NC	....	....	....	....	....	5.00	G1	'94	99½	94⅛	99½	4.92	5.40
M-T Nts 'C'[1] 4.70s '97	[9]ao	A+			X	BE	NC	....	....	....	....	....	5.00	G1	'94	99¼	93¾	99¼	4.74	5.43
M-T Nts 'C'[1] 5.65s '97	[10]ao	A+			X	BE	NC	....	....	....	....	....	5.00	G1	'94	100¼	95⅛	100¼	5.64	5.43
M-T Nts 'C'[1] 5.67s '97	[11]ao	A+			X	BE	NC	....	....	....	....	....	5.00	G1	'94	100¼	95⅛	100¼	5.66	5.45
M-T Nts 'C'[1] 5.78s '97	[12]ao	A+			X	BE	NC	....	....	....	....	....	10.0	G1	'94	100⅜	95⅜	100⅜	5.76	5.45
M-T Nts 'C'[1] 6.73s '97	[13]ao	A+			X	BE	NC	....	....	....	....	....	10.0	G1	'94	101⅝	97	101⅝	6.62	5.52
M-T Nts 'C'[1] 6.70s '97	[14]ao	A+			X	BE	NC	....	....	....	....	....	10.0	G1	'94	101⅝	96⅞	101⅝	6.59	5.53
M-T Nts 'C'[1] 6.96s '97	[15]ao	A+			X	BE	NC	....	....	....	....	....	5.00	G1	'94	102⅛	97¼	102⅛	6.82	5.50
M-T Nts 'C'[1] 6.09s '98	[16]ao	A+			X	BE	NC	....	....	....	....	....	5.00	G1	'93	101⅛	94¼	101⅛	6.02	5.52
M-T Nts 'C'[1] 5.81s '98	[17]ao	A+			X	BE	NC	....	....	....	....	....	5.00	G1	'93	100½	93⅜	100½	5.78	5.56
M-T Nts 'C'[1] 5.63s '98	[18]ao	A+			X	BE	NC	....	....	....	....	....	5.00	G1	'93	100⅛	92¾	100⅛	5.62	5.56
M-T Nts 'C'[1] 5.65s '98	[19]ao	A+			X	BE	NC	....	....	....	....	....	5.00	G1	'93	100⅛	92¾	100⅛	5.64	5.59
M-T Nts 'C'[1] 5.65s '98	[20]ao	A+			X	BE	NC	....	....	....	....	....	5.00	G1	'93	100⅛	92⅝	100⅛	5.64	5.59
M-T Nts 'C'[1] 5.55s '98	[21]ao	A+			X	BE	NC	....	....	....	....	....	5.00	G1	'93	100	92¼	100	5.55	5.55
M-T Nts 'C'[1] 5¾s '98	[22]ao	A+			X	BE	NC	....	....	....	....	....	5.00	G1	'93	100⅜	92⅝	100⅜	5.73	5.58
M-T Nts 'C'[1] 6.71s '97	[23]ao	A+			X	BE	NC	....	....	....	....	....	6.00	G1	'94	101¾	96⅝	101¾	6.59	5.53
M-T Nts 'C'[1] 5.70s '98	[24]ao	A+			X	BE	NC	....	....	....	....	....	5.00	G1	'93	100¼	92¼	100¼	5.69	5.59
M-T Nts 'C'[1] 5.45s '98	[25]ao	A+			X	BE	NC	....	....	....	....	....	5.00	G1	'93	99⅝	91⅜	99⅝	5.47	5.61
M-T Nts 'C'[1] 5.45s '98	[26]ao	A+			X	BE	NC	....	....	....	....	....	5.00	G1	'93	99⅝	91⅜	99⅝	5.47	5.61
M-T Nts 'C'[1] 5.15s '98	[27]ao	A+			X	BE	NC	....	....	....	....	....	5.00	G1	'93	98⅞	90⅛	98⅞	5.21	5.60
M-T Nts 'C'[1] 5.10s '98	[28]ao	A+			X	BE	NC	....	....	....	....	....	5.00	G1	'93	98⅝	89⅝	98⅝	5.17	5.63
M-T Nts 'C'[1] 5.43s '99	[29]ao	A+			X	BE	NC	....	....	....	....	....	5.00	G1	'94	99⅜	90	99⅜	5.46	5.65
M-T Nts 'C'[1] 6.44s '99	[30]ao	A+			X	BE	NC	....	....	....	....	....	10.0	G1	'94	102¼	93¼	102¼	6.30	5.67
M-T Nts 'C'[1] 7s '99	[31]ao	A+			X	BE	NC	....	....	....	....	....	5.00	G1	'94	103⅞	95	103⅞	6.74	5.75
M-T Nts 'C'[1] 7s '99	[32]ao	A+			X	BE	NC	....	....	....	....	....	5.00	G1	'93	104½	94¾	104½	6.70	5.72
M-T Nts 'C'[1] 7s '99	[33]ao	A+			X	BE	NC	....	....	....	....	....	10.0	G1	'92	104⅛	94⅜	104⅛	6.72	5.83
M-T Nts 'C'[1] 6¾s 2000	[34]ao	A+			X	BE	NC	....	....	....	....	....	5.00	G1	'93	103¼	93¼	103¼	6.54	5.84
M-T Nts 'C'[1] 5.48s 2000	[35]ao	A+			X	BE	NC	....	....	....	....	....	5.00	G1	'93	98⅜	86¾	98⅜	5.57	5.87
M-T Nts 'C'[1] 6.45s 2003	[36]ao	A+			X	BE	NC	....	....	....	....	....	5.00	G1	'93	101⅞	88	101⅞	6.33	6.12
M-T Nts 'C'[1] 7.33s '99	[37]ao	A+			X	BE	NC	....	....	....	....	....	5.00	G1	'94	105	96⅛	105	6.98	5.76
M-T Nts 'D' 6.65s 2000	[38]ms15	A+			X	BE	NC	....	....	....	....	....	29.0		'95	103⅛	100	103⅛	6.45	5.87
M-T Nts 'D' 6.89s 2002	[39]ms15	A+			X	BE	NC	....	....	....	....	....	25.0		'95	104⅜	100	104⅜	6.60	6.07
Amer Home Products	***21a***	***55.76***	***43.38***	***19.47***	***Dc***		***2080***	***8038***	***4626***	***9-30-95***	***8492***	***14100***	***60.8***							
Deb 7¼s 2023	Ms	A−	9/94	AAA	X	BE	NC	....	....	....	....	....	250	F1	'93	107⅜	85⅝	107⅜	6.75	6.66
• Nts 6⅞s '97	Ao15	A−	9/94	AAA	X	BE	NC	....	....	....	....	....	250	M6	'92	102	97⅛	100⅝	6.83	6.35
Nts 7.70s 2000	Fa15	A−			X	BE	NC	....	....	....	....	....	1000	G1	'95	107	99¾	107	7.20	5.77
Nts 6½s 2002	aO15	A−	9/94	AAA	X	BE	NC	....	....	....	....	....	250	F1	'92	102¾	89⅛	102¾	6.33	6.00
Nts 7.90s 2005	Fa15	A−			X	BE	NC	....	....	....	....	....	1000	G1	'95	112½	99¾	112½	7.02	6.09
American Life Holding	***35***	***n/a***	***n/a***	***1.13***	***Dc***					***3-31-95***	***291.0***	***569.0***	***51.1***							
Sr Sub Nts[40] 11¼s 2004	mS15	BB−			Y	R	105.625	(9-15-99)	....	....	....	....	150	M6	'94	105¾	97¾	104	10.82	10.53

Uniform Footnote Explanations-See Page 260. Other: [1] Issued in min denom $100T. [2] Due 9-3-96. [3] Due 10-18-96. [4] Due 11-15-96. [5] Due 12-9-96. [6] Due 12-16-96. [7] Due 12-30-96. [8] Due 1-13-97. [9] Due 1-21-97. [10] Due 3-14-97. [11] Due 3-17-97. [12] Due 3-24-97. [13] Due 6-2-97. [14] Due 6-16-97. [15] Due 7-15-97. [16] Due 2-12-98. [17] Due 2-26-98. [18] Due 3-9-98. [19] Due 3-30-98. [20] Due 4-16-98. [21] Due 4-27-98. [22] Due 6-10-98. [23] Due 7-28-97. [24] Due 6-30-98. [25] Due 7-22-98. [26] Due 7-27-98. [27] Due 9-17-98. [28] Due 10-21-98. [29] Due 2-4-99. [30] Due 3-29-99. [31] Due 6-15-99. [32] Due 12-23-99. [33] Due 12-30-99. [34] Due 1-31-00. [35] Due 10-4-00. [36] Due 3-3-03. [37] Due 7-21-99. [38] Due 8-30-00. [39] Due 7-31-02. [40] (HRO)On Chge of Ctrl at 101.

Title-Industry Code & Co. Finances (In Italics) / Individual Issue Statistics (Exchange)	Ind / Interest Dates	Fixed Charge Coverage 1992 / S&P Debt Rating	1993 / Date of Last Rating Change	1994 / Prior Rating	Eligible	Year End / Bond Form	Cash & Equiv. / Regular Price	Curr. Assets / Regular (Begins) Thru	Curr. Liab. / Sinking Fund Price	Balance Sheet Date / Sinking Fund (Begins) Thru	L. Term Debt (Mil $) / Refund/Other Restriction Price	Refund/Other Restriction (Begins) Thru	Capital-ization (Mil $) / Outst'g (Mil $)	Total Debt % Capital / Underwriting Firm	Underwriting Year	Price Range 1995 High	Price Range 1995 Low	Mo. End Price Sale(s) or Bid	Curr. Yield	Yield to Mat.
Amer Media[1] Operations[2]	***54b***	***2.20***	***2.87***	***2.33***		***Mr***	***4.64***	***25.00***	***96.80***	***6-26-95***	***560.0***		***618.0***	***94.2***						
• Sr Sub Nts[3] 11⅝s 2004	mN15	B			Y	R	104.359	(11-15-99)	....	....	....	....	200	C5	'94	108¾	98⅜	100⅛	11.61	11.60
Amer Medical Int'l	***30***	***Merged into Nat'l Medical Entpr,see***																		
Sr Nts[3] 11s 2000	aO15	BB	2/95	BB−	Y	R	103.14	(10-15-96)	....	....	....	....	2.00	F1	'91	106¾	104½	106⅜	10.34	9.31
Sr Sub[3]Nts[4] 13½s 2001	fA15	B+	2/95	B	Y	R	103.86	(8-15-96)	....	....	....	....	13.0	F1	'91	111	104½	106⅞	12.63	11.79
Amer President Cos Ltd	***64***	***3.94***	***7.88***	***4.80***		***Dc***	***166.0***	***537.0***	***443.0***	***9-22-95***	***498.0***		***1027***	***49.9***						
Sr Deb 8s 2024	Jj15	BBB−			X	BE	NC	....	....	....	....	....	150	S1	'94	104⅝	84¼	104⅝	7.65	7.60
Sr Nts 7⅛s 2003	mN15	BBB−			X	BE	NC	....	....	....	....	....	150	M6	'93	102	88¼	102	6.99	6.79
American Re Corp	***35c***	***n/a***	***3.18***	***3.01***		***Dc***				***9-30-95***	***450.0***		***1687***	***26.7***						
Sub Deb[5] 10⅞s 2004	mS15	A−	8/95	BBB+	X	R	104.75	(9-15-97)	100	(9-15-01)	[6]Z100	....	450	M2	'92	112⅛	107⅛	112⅛	9.70	8.84
American Shared Hosp Svcs	***30a***	***0.14***	***d0.47***	***d0.25***		***Dc***	***0.59***	***7.39***	***15.60***	***9-30-95***	***25.40***		***24.70***	***138.0***						
◆Sr Sub[7]Nts[8] 16½s '96	aO15	NR	10/91	C		R	100	....	100	....	....	....	18.8	D7	'88	No Sale		A10	....	Flat
American Standard[9]	***13b***	***0.83***	***0.71***	***0.94***		***Dc***	***92.70***	***1065***	***1079***	***12-31-94***	***2152***		***1566***	***151.0***						
SF Deb 9¼s 2016	jD	BB−	9/95	B+	Y	R	105.088	11-30-96	100	(12-1-97)	®104.625	11-30-96	150	F1	'86	104	90½	104	8.89	8.83
Sr Deb[3] 11⅜s 2004	Mn15	BB−	9/95	B+	Y	R	105.69	(5-15-97)	....	....	....	....	250	F1	'92	111	102½	111	10.25	9.44
Sr Nts[3] 10⅞s '99	Mn15	BB−	9/95	B+	Y	R	NC	....	....	....	....	....	150	F1	'92	109½	101¼	109¼	9.95	7.71
Sr Sub Nts[3] 9⅞s 2001	Jd	B+	9/95	B	Y	R	102.82	(6-1-98)	....	....	....	....	200	B9	'93	108	96⅜	107¼	9.21	8.19
Sr Sub Disc[10]Deb[3] 10½s 2005	Jd	B+	9/95	B	Y	R	104.66	(6-1-98)	100	(6-1-03)	[11]Z108.16	5-31-96	751	B9	'93	85½	63½	85½	....	Flat
American Stores	***59c***	***2.80***	***3.35***	***4.55***		***Ja***	***3.09***	***3059***	***1951***	***10-28-95***	***2074***		***4437***	***49.4***						
Deb 7.40s 2005	Mn15	BBB+	7/95	BBB	X	R	NC	....	....	....	....	....	200	M5	'95	106½	99⅜	106½	6.95	6.46
Nts 9⅛s 2002	Ao	BBB+	7/95	BBB	X	R	NC	....	....	....	....	....	250	L3	'92	114⅝	100⅞	114⅝	7.96	6.26
[12]Ameritech Capital Funding	***25***	***4.92***	***5.79***	***6.28***		***Dc***	***266.0***	***3420***	***4987***	***9-30-95***	***4547***		***13312***	***47.7***						
[13]Gtd Deb 7½s 2005	Ao	AA+			X	BE	NC	....	....	....	....	....	192	L3	'95	109⅞	99⅞	109⅞	6.83	6.09
[13]Gtd([14]Amort[15])Deb 8.85s 2005	Jd	AA+	7/91	AAA	X	BE	NC	....	....	....	....	....	53.7	G1	'91	114	103½	114	7.76	....
[13]Gtd([16]Amort) Deb 9.10s 2016	Jd	AA+	7/91	AAA	X	BE	NC	....	....	....	....	....	96.3	G1	'91	113¾	103⅜	113¾	8.00	....
F/R[17]Nts[13] 5⅞s '97	QMay2	AA+			X	BE	NC	....	....	....	....	....	225	G1	'94	100	99	100	5.88	....
F/R[18]Nts 5.925s '98	QMay12	AA+			X	BE	NC	....	....	....	....	....	225	G1	'94	100¼	99½	100	5.93	....
AmeriTrust Corp	***10***	***Merged into Society Corp, now KeyCorp, see***																		
Nts 8⅝s '96	Jd31	A−	3/92	BBB−	X	R	100	....	....	....	....	....	100	S4	'86	101¼	99	100	8.63	8.62
AMETEK, Inc	***41e***	***4.38***	***2.93***	***3.86***		***Dc***	***10.70***	***259.0***	***238.0***	***9-30-95***	***150.0***		***299.0***	***72.9***						
• Sr Nts[19] 9¾s 2004	Ms15	BB+	8/95	BB	Y	R	104.875	(3-15-99)	....	....	....	....	150	G1	'94	111	101	109	8.94	8.22
[20]Amoco Co[21]	***49c***	***5.70***	***8.38***	***8.83***		***Dc***	***1127***	***6129***	***5451***	***9-30-95***	***3775***		***19907***	***24.4***						
SF Deb 9⅞s 2016	Fa	AAA			X	R	104.3875	(2-1-96)	100	(2-1-97)	....	....	25.0	M6	'86	107⅛	104⅝	104⅝	9.44	9.36
• SF Deb 8⅝s 2016	jD15	AAA			X	R	104.3125	(12-15-96)	100	(12-15-97)	....	....	52.0	M6	'86	108⅞	103	106⅛	8.13	8.02
Amphenol Corp	***23b***	***1.50***	***1.94***	***3.29***		***Dc***	***3.55***	***215.0***	***111.0***	***9-30-95***	***195.0***		***533.0***	***38.3***						
Sr Sub Nts[3] 12¾s 2002	jD15	BB+	8/94	B+	Y	R	104.80	(12-15-97)	....	....	....	....	95.0	M2	'92	114¼	109	109	11.70	10.87
AMR Corp	***4***	***0.07***	***1.05***	***1.98***		***Dc***	***899.0***	***3492***	***5550***	***6-30-95***	***7391***		***11902***	***69.7***						
SF Deb 8⅝s 2017	Ms	BB+	3/93	BBB	Y	R	105.18	2-29-96	100	(3-1-97)	®104.31	2-28-97	93.5	S1	'87	105¼	86⅛	105¼	8.19	8.10
Deb 9s 2012	fA	BB+	3/93	BBB	Y	R	NC	....	....	....	....	....	350	G1	'92	112½	88¾	112½	8.00	7.66
• Deb 9s 2016	mS15	BB+	3/93	BBB	Y	R	NC	....	....	....	....	....	100	D7	'86	112⅜	92	s111	8.11	7.91
Deb[22] 10.20s 2020	Ms15	BB+	3/93	BBB	Y	R	NC	....	....	....	....	....	125	M6	'90	124⅝	40⅛	124⅝	8.18	7.90
Deb[23] 9.88s 2020	Jd15	BB+	3/93	BBB	Y	R	NC	....	....	....	....	....	100	M6	'90	122⅝	95⅝	122⅝	8.06	7.79
Deb 10s 2021	Ao15	BB+	3/93	BBB	Y	R	NC	....	....	....	....	....	350	G1	'91	124⅛	95⅞	124⅛	8.06	7.80
Deb 9¾s 2021	fA15	BB+	3/93	BBB	Y	R	NC	....	....	....	....	....	200	M2	'91	121½	93¼	121½	8.02	7.80
Deb 9.80s 2021	aO	BB+	3/93	BBB	Y	R	NC	....	....	....	....	....	100	G1	'91	121⅛	95	121⅛	8.09	7.87
Amortizing[24]Nts 6½s '97	Ms15	BB+	3/93	BBB	Y	R	NC	....	....	....	....	....	100	M2	'92	100⅞	94⅝	100⅞	6.44	....
Nts 7¾s '97	jD	BB+	3/93	BBB	Y	R	NC	....	....	....	....	....	200	M6	'92	103¼	96⅛	103¼	7.51	5.93

Uniform Footnote Explanations-See Page 260. Other: [1] Was Enquirer/Star Inc,see. [2] Subsid of American Media Inc. [3] (HRO)On Chge of Ctrl at 101. [4] Purch offer,100 to May 1. [5] (HRO)On Chge in Ctrl at 101. [6] On Chge in Ctrl,plus premium. [7] Int incr fr 14% on 10-15-89. [8] Int of 4-91 pd 5-91, 10-92 to 4-95 pd 5-17-95. [9] Subsid of Amer Stand Cos Inc. [10] Int accr at 10.5% fr 6-1-98. [11] Max $263M w/proceeds of com sold. [12] Gtd by & data of Ameritech Corp. [13] Gtd by Ameritech Corp. [14] Prin pyts due ea 6-1:97-8,$74.49,99-01,$102.42. [15] Prin pyts due ea 6-1:02-05,$135.94. [16] Prin pyts due ea 6-1:06-15,$75.80,16,$242.00. [17] Int to 2-1-96,adj qtrly to equal to 3 Mo LIBOR. [18] Int to 2-12-96,adj qtrly aft(3 Mo LIBOR&0.05%). [19] Co must offer repurch at 101 on Chge of Ctrl. [20] Gtd by & data of Amoco Corp. [21] Was Standard Oil(Ind). [22] Int may be adj for Designated Event&Rat'g Chge. [23] Int sub to adj for Designated Event&Rat'g Chge. [24] Princ pyts due on int dates to 3-15-97.

Title-Industry Code & Co. Finances (In Italics) / Individual Issue Statistics	Ind / Interest Dates	1992 / S&P Debt Rating	1993 / Date of Last Rating Change	Prior Rating	1994 / Eligible	Year End / Bond Form	Cash & Equiv. / Regular Price	Curr. Assets / Regular (Begins) Thru	Curr. Liab. / Sinking Fund Price	Balance Sheet Date / Sinking Fund (Begins) Thru	L. Term Debt (Mil $) / Refund/Other Restriction Price	Refund/Other Restriction (Begins) Thru	Capitalization (Mil $) / Outst'g (Mil $)	Total Debt % Capital / Underwriting Firm	Underwriting Year	Price Range 1995 High	Price Range 1995 Low	Mo. End Price Sale(s) or Bid	Curr. Yield	Yield to Mat.
***AMR Corp** (Cont.)*																				
Nts 9½s '98	jJ15	**BB+**	3/93	BBB	Y	R	NC	....	....	....	....	....	150	G1	'91	108⅛	100¼	108⅛	8.79	6.01
• Nts 8.10s '98	[1]Nov	**BB+**	3/93	BBB	Y	R	NC	....	....	....	....	....	150	L3	'91	105½	96	s104½	7.75	6.34
Nts[2] 9¾s 2000	Ms15	**BB+**	3/93	BBB	Y	R	NC	....	....	....	....	....	200	M6	'90	111⅜	100	111⅜	8.75	6.61
Nts 10s 2001	Fa	**BB+**	3/93	BBB	Y	R	NC	....	....	....	....	....	100	M6	'91	114	100¾	114	8.77	6.70
Nts 9½s 2001	Mn15	**BB+**	3/93	BBB	Y	R	NC	....	....	....	....	....	200	S1	'91	112⅜	98¾	112⅜	8.45	6.72
M-T Nts 'D'[3] 7.67s '97	[4]mn15	**BB+**			Y	BE	NC	....	....	....	....	....	5.00	S1	'92	102	97¾	102	7.52	5.88
M-T Nts 'D'[3] 7.71s '97	[4]mn15	**BB+**			Y	BE	NC	....	....	....	....	....	25.0	M6	'92	102⅛	97¾	102⅛	7.55	5.81
M-T Nts 'D'[3] 8.47s 2002	[5]mn15	**BB+**			Y	BE	NC	....	....	....	....	....	28.0	M6	'92	109½	94⅛	109½	7.74	6.56
M-T Nts 'D'[3] 8.60s 2002	[6]mn15	**BB+**			Y	BE	NC	....	....	....	....	....	10.0	M2	'92	110⅛	94¾	110⅛	7.81	6.58
***AmSouth Bancorp**[7]*	*10*	*4.25*	*4.87*		*3.41*	*Dc*				*9-30-95*	*313.0*		*1700*	*18.4*						
Sub Deb[8] 6¾s 2025	mN	**BBB+**			X	BE	NC	....	....	....	....	....	150	M6	'95	103⅜	99¼	103⅜	6.53	6.49
Sub Cap[9]Nts 9⅜s '99	Mn	**BBB+**	6/95	A–	X	R	NC	....	....	....	....	....	100	M2	'87	110⅛	102⅝	110⅛	8.51	5.98
Sub Nts 7¾s 2004	Mn15	**BBB+**	6/95	A–	X	BE	NC	....	....	....	....	....	150	S1	'94	108½	94¼	108½	7.14	6.42
***Anadarko Petroleum Corp**[10]*	*49*	*1.87*	*2.81*		*3.47*	*Dc*	*7.76*	*110.0*	*91.80*	*9-30-95*	*669.0*		*1575*	*42.5*						
Deb[11] 7¼s 2025	Ms15	**BBB+**			X	BE	NC	....	....	....	....	....	100	M5	'95	108¼	95½	108¼	6.70	6.61
Nts 8⅜s '98	Fa15	**BBB+**	1/92	A–	X	R	NC	....	....	....	....	....	100	K2	'91	106⅜	101⅝	106⅜	8.23	5.53
Nts 8¼s 2001	mN15	**BBB+**	1/92	A–	X	R	NC	....	....	....	....	....	100	M5	'91	111¼	98¾	111¼	7.42	5.95
Nts 6¾s 2003	Ms15	**BBB+**			X	R	NC	....	....	....	....	....	100	K2	'93	103¾	89⅝	103¾	6.51	6.10
Nts 5⅞s 2003	aO15	**BBB+**			X	R	NC	....	....	....	....	....	100	K2	'93	98⅜	84⅛	98⅜	5.97	6.14
Analog Devices	*23h*	*4.17*	*8.73*		*14.56*	*Oc*	*129.0*	*486.0*	*202.0*	*7-29-95*	*★280.0*		*702.0*	*11.7*						
Nts 6⅝s 2000	Ms	**BBB+**	11/95	BBB	X	R	NC	....	....	....	....	....	80.0	G1	'93	101	90⅞	101	6.56	6.35
Anchor Bancorp	*10b*	*2.09*	*2.49*		*1.29*	*Je*				*9-30-94*	*378.0*		*3076*	*86.0*						
Sr Nts 8.9375s 2003	jj1	**BB**			Y	R	102.55	(7-9-98)	....	....	....	....	100	S5	'93	101	90	101	8.85	8.75
Anchor Glass Container	*16a*	*1.21*	*0.75*		*0.67*	*Dc*	*15.60*	*319.0*	*210.0*	*9-30-95*	*528.0*		*897.0*	*61.9*						
Sr[12]Sub Deb 9⅞s 2008	jD15	**CCC+**	11/95	B	Y	R	104.9375	(12-16-00)	....	....	....	....	200	D6	'93	91	50	59	16.74	18.21
Anheuser-Busch	*11a*	*8.85*	*8.58*		*8.61*	*Dc*	*91.60*	*2038*	*1600*	*9-30-95*	*3157*		*7937*	*39.8*						
• SF Deb 8⅝s 2016	jD	**AA–**			X	R	104.744	11-30-96	100	(12-1-97)	®104.313	11-30-96	150	D4	'86	106	100⅛	104¼	8.27	8.20
SF Deb 8½s 2017	Ms	**AA–**			X	R	104.50	2-29-96	100	(3-1-98)	®103.75	2-28-97	150	D4	'87	107⅛	96½	104½	8.13	8.05
SF Deb 10s 2018	jJ	**AA–**			X	R	106.50	6-30-96	100	(7-1-99)	®105	6-30-98	68.0	D4	'88	108	106¾	108	9.26	9.15
[13]Deb[14] 9s 2009	jD	**AA–**			X	R	NC	....	....	....	....	....	350	D4	'89	125⅝	103½	125⅝	7.16	6.22
Deb 7¼s 2015	mS15	**AA–**			X	BE	103.57	(9-15-05)	....	....	....	....	150	D4	'95	105⅜	99	105⅜	6.88	6.75
Deb 7⅜s 2023	jJ	**AA–**			X	R	103.28	(7-1-03)	....	....	....	....	200	D4	'93	105⅝	87⅜	105⅛	7.02	6.95
Deb 7s 2025	jD	**AA–**			X	BE	103.34	(12-1-05)	....	....	....	....	200	D4	'95	101⅞	99⅝	101⅞	6.87	6.85
[13]Nts[14] 8¾s '99	jD	**AA–**			X	R	NC	....	....	....	....	....	250	D4	'89	110¾	102	110¾	7.90	5.65
Nts 6.90s 2002	aO	**AA–**			X	R	100	(10-1-99)	....	....	....	....	200	D4	'92	103¾	91½	103¾	6.65	6.21
Nts 6¾s 2005	Jd	**AA–**			X	BE	100	(6-1-02)	....	....	....	....	200	D4	'95	103½	97½	103¼	6.54	6.29
Nts 7s 2005	mS	**AA–**			X	BE	100	(9-1-02)	....	....	....	....	100	D4	'95	105	99¾	105	6.67	6.30
***AnnTaylor, Inc**[15]*	*59a*	*1.99*	*2.78*		*5.42*	*Ja*	*1.25*	*214.0*	*88.80*	*10-28-95*	*268.0*		*595.0*	*45.0*						
• Sub Nts[16] 8¾s 2000	Jd15	**B–**	12/95	B+	Y	R	102.75	(6-15-98)	....	....	....	....	110	M2	'93	101⅝	75½	s82½	10.61	14.17
Sr Sub[17]Disc Nts 14⅜s '99	jJ15	**B–**	12/95	B+	Y	R	103.594	7-14-96	....	....	....	....	[18]50.3	M2	'89	105	105	105	....	Flat
***ANR** [19]**Pipeline**[20]*	*73a*	*4.92*	*5.67*		*5.38*	*Dc*	*23.20*	*586.0*	*322.0*	*9-30-95*	*510.0*		*1445*	*39.5*						
• Deb 9⅝s 2021	mN	**BBB–**			X	R	NC	....	....	....	....	....	300	L3	'91	No Sale		125½	7.67	7.40
• Deb 7⅜s 2024	Fa15	**BBB–**			X	BE	NC	....	....	....	....	....	125	C4	'94	97¼	82⅜	82	8.99	9.17
• Deb[21] 7s 2025	Jd	**BBB–**			X	BE	NC	....	....	....	....	....	75.0		'95	100	95	78	8.97	9.17
Aon Corp	*35d*	*7.93*	*12.33*		*12.59*	*Dc*				*9-30-95*	*553.0*		*3447*	*25.4*						
• Nts 6⅞s '99	aO	**AA**			X	R	NC	....	....	....	....	....	100	M6	'92	102½	95⅝	100⅛	6.87	6.83

Uniform Footnote Explanations-See Page 260. Other: [1] Int pd monthly. [2] Int subj to adj for Designated Event&Rat'g Chge. [3] Issued in min denom $100T. [4] Due 3-5-97. [5] Due 2-20-02. [6] Due 3-4-02. [7] See Alabama Bancorporation. [8] (HRO)On 11-1-05 at 100. [9] To be exch for Cap Sec when due. [10] Was Anadarko Production. [11] (HRO)On 3-15-00 at 100. [12] Co must offer repurch at 101 on Chge of Ctrl. [13] (HRO)At 100 for Rat'g Decline. [14] Co may red at 100 if 80% outstg put. [15] Subsid of AnnTaylor Stores Corp. [16] (HRO)On Chge of Ctrl at 101. [17] Int accrues at 14.375% fr 1-15-94. [18] Incl disc. [19] Subsid of Amer Natural Resources(Coastal Corp). [20] Was Mich Wisc PL. [21] (HRO)On 6-1-05 at 100.

Title-Industry Code & Co. Finances (In Italics)	Ind	Fixed Charge Coverage 1992	1993	1994		Year End	Million $ Cash & Equiv.	Curr. Assets	Curr. Liab.	Balance Sheet Date	L. Term Debt (Mil $)		Capital-ization (Mil $)	Total Debt % Capital						
Individual Issue Statistics Exchange ↓	Interest Dates	S&P Debt Rating	Date of Last Rating Change	Prior Rating	Eligible ↓	Bond Form	Redemption Provisions: Regular Price	Regular (Begins) Thru	Sinking Fund Price	Sinking Fund (Begins) Thru	Refund/Other Restriction Price	Refund/Other Restriction (Begins) Thru	Outst'g (Mil $)	Underwriting Firm	Underwriting Year	Price Range 1995 High	Price Range 1995 Low	Mo. End Price Sale(s) or Bid	Curr. Yield	Yield to Mat.
***Aon Corp** (Cont.)*																				
• Nts 7.40s 2002	aO	**AA**			X	R	NC	....	....	....	....	....	100	M2	'92	No Sale		97½	7.59	7.88
Nts 6.70s 2003	Jd15	**AA**			X	R	NC	....	....	....	....	....	150	M6	'93	102⅞	88½	102⅞	6.51	6.21
Nts 6.30s 2004	Jj15	**AA**			X	R	NC	....	....	....	....	....	100	M6	'94	100¼	85⅝	100¼	6.28	6.26
Apache Corp	***49a***	***1.85***	***2.64***	***2.64***		***Dc***	***16.50***	***202.0***	***207.0***	***9-30-95***	***1058***		***2166***	***49.6***						
• Nts 9¼s 2002	Jd	**BBB**	12/93	BBB–	X	R	NC	....	....	....	....	....	100	G1	'92	112¼	106	112	8.26	6.90
APL Corp	***42a***	***n/a***	....	....		***Sp***	***Bankruptcy Chapt 11***						***2.90***	***NM***						
Sub SF Deb[1] 10¾s '97	§fA	**NR**	5/87	CCC–	Z	R			Default 8-1-91 int				24.3	B6	'77	45	5	5	....	Flat
Appalachian Power[2]	***72a***	***2.68***	***2.75***	***2.51***		***Dc***	***6.79***	***303.0***	***315.0***	***9-30-95***	***1278***		***2574***	***52.5***						
1st 7½s '98	jD	**A–**	12/84	BBB	X	R	100.60	11-30-96	Z100.27	11-30-96	....	....	45.0	F1	'68	101¼	97⅛	100¾	7.44	7.21
1st 7⅝s 2002	Fa	**A–**	12/84	BBB	X	R	100.73	1-31-96	Z100.73	1-31-96	....	....	43.4	K3	'72	101¼	95⅜	100½	7.59	7.52
1st 7½s 2002	jD	**A–**	12/84	BBB	X	R	100.71	11-30-96	Z100.71	11-30-96	....	....	59.8	S1	'72	101⅛	94⅝	100¾	7.44	7.36
1st 9⅞s 2020	jD	**A–**			X	R	106.87	11-30-96	Z100	....	....	....	46.8	D6	'90	107⅞	104⅝	106	9.32	9.25
Sec M-T Nts 7s '99	jD	**A–**			X	BE	NC	....	....	....	....	....	30.0	S1	'92	103⅝	94½	103⅝	6.76	5.95
Sec M-T Nts[3] 7.95s 2002	Ms	**A–**			X	BE	102.28	(3-1-97)	Z100	....	....	....	60.0	S1	'92	105⅛	96¾	104¾	7.59	6.99
Sec M-T Nts 7.38s 2002	[4]jd	**A–**			X	BE	102.11	(8-15-97)	Z100	....	....	....	50.0	S1	'92	104⅝	93½	104⅝	7.05	6.51
Sec M-T Nts 7.40s 2002	jD	**A–**			X	BE	NC	....	....	....	....	....	30.0	S1	'92	106⅜	93¾	106⅜	6.96	6.25
Sec M-T Nts 6.65s 2003	Mn	**A–**			X	BE	101.90	(5-1-98)	Z100	(5-1-98)	....	....	40.0	S1	'93	101⅜	88⅝	101⅜	6.56	6.41
Sec M-T Nts 6.85s 2003	Jd	**A–**			X	BE	101.96	(6-1-98)	Z100	(6-1-98)	....	....	30.0	S1	'93	102½	89¾	102½	6.68	6.42
Sec M-T Nts 6s 2003	mN	**A–**			X	BE	101.72	(11-1-98)	Z100	(11-1-98)	....	....	30.0	S1	'93	97⅞	84½	97⅞	6.13	6.35
Sec M-T Nts 8s 2005	Mn	**A–**			X	BE	NC	....	....	....	....	....	50.0	S1	'95	110⅞	100	110⅞	7.22	6.43
Sec M-T Nts 6.89s 2005	[5]ms	**A–**			X	BE	NC	....	....	....	....	....	30.0	S1	'95	103¼	96⅝	103¼	6.67	6.43
Sec M-T Nts[3] 9.35s 2021	fA	**A–**			X	BE	107.02	(8-1-96)	Z100	....	....	....	50.0	S1	'91	110¼	104⅛	109	8.58	8.48
Sec M-T Nts[3] 8¾s 2022	[6]jd	**A–**			X	BE	106.57	(2-20-97)	Z100	(2-20-97)	....	....	50.0	S1	'92	110¼	98⅜	109⅝	7.98	7.87
Sec M-T Nts[3] 8.70s 2022	Mn22	**A–**			X	BE	106.53	(6-1-97)	Z100	....	....	....	40.0	S1	'92	110⅝	97⅞	110⅛	7.90	7.79
Sec M-T Nts 8.43s 2022	Jd	**A–**			X	BE	106.33	(8-14-97)	Z100	(8-14-97)	....	....	50.0	S1	'92	110	95¼	110	7.66	7.55
Sec M-T Nts 8½s 2022	jD	**A–**			X	BE	104.25	(12-4-02)	Z100	(12-4-02)	....	....	70.0	S1	'92	115⅛	96⅝	115⅛	7.38	7.22
Sec M-T Nts 7.80s 2023	Mn	**A–**			X	BE	105.85	(5-1-98)	Z100	(5-1-98)	....	....	40.0	S1	'93	106⅞	88⅞	106⅞	7.30	7.22
Sec M-T Nts 7.90s 2023	[7]mn	**A–**			X	BE	105.93	(6-1-98)	Z100	(6-1-98)	....	....	30.0	S1	'93	108	89⅞	108	7.31	7.22
Sec M-T Nts 7.15s 2023	mN	**A–**			X	BE	105.37	(11-1-98)	Z100	(11-1-98)	....	....	30.0	S1	'93	99½	82¼	99½	7.19	7.19
Sec M-T Nts 7⅛s 2024	Mn	**A–**			X	BE	103.57	(5-1-04)	Z100	(5-1-04)	....	....	50.0	S1	'93	100¼	82½	100¼	7.11	7.10
SF Deb 6s '96	Ms	**BBB+**	12/84	BBB–	X	R	100	....	Z100	....	....	....	7.25	D4	'66	100	98⅛	100	6.00	5.88
Apple Computer Inc	***20b***	***△n/a***	***△10.35***	***△14.56***		***Sp***	***952.0***	***5224***	***2325***	***9-30-95***	***303.0***		***3665***	***20.8***						
Nts 6½s 2004	Fa15	**BBB**	8/94	A–	X	BE	[8]Z100	....	....	....	....	....	300	G1	'94	98⅜	86⅜	98⅜	6.61	6.76
Applied Materials	***23g***	***4.88***	***11.81***	***21.96***		***Oc***	***700.0***	***2058***	***760.0***	***7-30-95***	***231.0***		***1937***	***17.0***						
Sr Nts 8s 2004	mS	**BBB**	7/95	BBB–	X	BE	NC	....	....	....	....	....	100	M6	'94	110¼	95¾	109⅜	7.31	6.56
ARA Group, Inc	***27a***	***Now ARAMARK Corp, see ARAMARK Services***																		
Sub Nts 8½s 2003	Jd	**BB+**	7/94	BB–	Y	R	104.25	(6-1-98)	....	....	....	....	100	M5	'93	105	93	104¾	8.11	7.65
ARA Services	***27a***	***Gtd by ARAMARK Corp, see ARAMARK Services***																		
Gtd[9]Nts[10] 10⅝s 2000	fA	**BBB–**	7/94	BB	X	R	NC	....	100	(8-1-99)	....	....	100	G1	'91	115⅛	104¾	114⅞	9.25	6.79
[11]ARAMARK Services, Inc[12]	***27a***	***1.90***	***2.13***	***2.48***		***Sp***	***18.30***	***857.0***	***762.0***	***12-30-94***	***★1168***		***1392***	***84.2***						
Gtd[13]Nts 8.15s 2005	Mn	**BBB–**			X	BE	NC	....	....	....	....	....	150	G1	'95	108⅞	99⅞	108⅝	7.50	6.88
Archer-Daniels-Midland	***26c***	***△5.16***	***△4.58***	***△6.67***		***Je***	***1141***	***3912***	***1412***	***9-30-95***	***2070***		***8128***	***26.3***						
Deb 10¼s 2006	Jj15	**AA–**	10/89	A	X	R	NC	....	....	....	....	....	100	G1	'86	130¾	113⅜	130¾	7.84	6.11
Deb 8⅞s 2011	Ao15	**AA–**			X	BE	NC	....	....	....	....	....	300	S1	'91	124¾	104⅜	124¾	7.11	6.32
Deb 7s 2011	Mn15	**AA–**	10/89	A	X	R	100	....	....	....	....	....	[14]250	G1	'81	105¾	86⅝	105¾	6.62	6.41
Deb 8⅛s 2012	Jd	**AA–**			X	BE	NC	....	....	....	....	....	300	S7	'92	115¼	96⅝	115¼	7.05	6.59

Uniform Footnote Explanations-See Page 260. Other: [1] Int of 8-1-90 pd 10-18-90, 2-1-91 pd 3-25-91. [2] Subsid of Amer Elec Pwr. [3] Issued in min denom $100T. [4] Due 8-15-02. [5] Due 6-22-05. [6] Due 2-1-22. [7] Due 6-1-23. [8] Plus Make-Whole Premium. [9] Gtd by ARA Group Inc. [10] (HRO)Under certain conditions. [11] Gtd by & data of ARAMARK Corp. [12] See ARA Group & ARA Services. [13] Gtd by ARAMARK Corp. [14] Incl disc.

Title-Industry Code & Co. Finances (In Italics) / Exchange · Individual Issue Statistics	I n d / Interest Dates	Fixed Charge Coverage 1992 / S&P Debt Rating	1993 / Date of Last Rating Change	1994 / Prior Rating	Eligible	Year End / Bond Form	Million $ Cash & Equiv. / Redemption Provisions — Regular Price	Curr. Assets / Regular (Begins) Thru	Curr. Liab. / Sinking Fund Price	Balance Sheet Date / Sinking Fund (Begins) Thru	L. Term Debt (Mil $) / Refund/Other Restriction Price	Capital-ization (Mil $) / Refund/Other Restriction (Begins) Thru	Outst'g (Mil $)	Total Debt % Capital / Underwriting Firm	Underwriting Year	Price Range 1995 High	Price Range 1995 Low	Mo. End Price Sale(s) or Bid	Curr. Yield	Yield to Mat.
***Archer-Daniels-Midland** (Cont.)*																				
Deb 7⅛s 2013	Ms	AA–			X	BE	NC	....	....	....	....	....	250	S1	'93	105⅛	87⅜	105⅛	6.78	6.62
Deb 8⅜s 2017	Ao15	AA–			X	BE	NC	....	....	....	....	....	300	S1	'92	119⅞	99¼	119⅞	6.99	6.62
Deb Zero Cpn 2002	[1]	AA–	10/89	A	X	R	100	....	....	....	....	....	[2]400	G1	'82	69⅛	54⅞	69⅛	....	5.91
Nts 6¼s 2003	Mn15	AA–			X	BE	NC	....	....	....	....	....	250	S7	'93	101½	88⅛	101½	6.16	5.99
ARCO Chemical	*14*	*3.94*	*3.96*	*6.25*		*Dc*	*152.0*	*1340*	*578.0*	*9-30-95*	*897.0*	*2977*		*31.1*						
Deb 9.90s 2000	mN	A			X	R	NC	....	....	....	....	....	200	M2	'90	117⅜	106⅞	117⅜	8.43	5.73
Deb 9⅜s 2005	jD15	A			X	R	NC	....	....	....	....	....	100	S1	'90	124	106	124	7.56	6.12
Deb 10¼s 2010	mN	A			X	R	NC	....	....	....	....	....	100	M2	'90	138¾	112⅞	138¾	7.39	6.21
Deb 9.80s 2020	Fa	A			X	R	NC	....	....	....	....	....	225	M2	'90	138⅛	109⅝	138⅛	7.10	6.61
Argyle Television, Inc	*12c*	*n/a*	*n/a*	*n/a*		*Dc*	*15.00*	*30.50*	*17.50*	*6-30-95*	*★157.0*	*193.0*		*63.3*						
Sr Sub Nts[3] 9¾s 2005	mN	B–			Y	BE	[4]Z100	11-1-00	....	....	[5]Z109.75	10-31-98	150	C1	'95	100	100	A100	9.75	9.75
Aristar Inc[6]	*25a*	*1.85*	*1.92*	*2.05*		*Dc*	*10.80*			*9-30-95*	*1017*	*1644*		*74.8*						
Sr Nts[7] 6¼s '96	jJ15	A–	2/93	A	X	BE	NC	....	....	....	....	....	100	M2	'92	100⅜	97⅜	100⅜	6.23	5.53
Sr Nts[7] 7⅜s '97	Fa15	A–	2/93	A	X	R	NC	....	....	....	....	....	100	F1	'92	102¼	98⅛	102	7.23	5.51
Sr Nts[7] 8⅛s '97	[8]jd15	A–			X	BE	NC	....	....	....	....	....	100	M2	'94	104⅜	99¼	104⅜	7.78	5.69
Sr Nts 5¾s '98	jJ15	A–			X	BE	NC	....	....	....	....	....	150	L3	'93	100⅛	92	100⅛	5.74	5.70
Sr Nts[7] 7⅞s '99	Fa15	A–	2/93	A	X	R	NC	....	....	....	....	....	100	F1	'92	106	98	106	7.43	5.75
Sr Nts[7] 6.30s 2000	jJ15	A–			X	BE	NC	....	....	....	....	....	100	G1	'95	101½	97⅜	101½	6.21	5.92
• Sr Nts[7] 7¾s 2001	Jd15	A–			X	BE	NC	....	....	....	....	....	150	M2	'94	No Sale		95	8.16	8.93
Sr Sub Nts[7] 8⅞s '98	fA15	BBB+	2/93	A–	X	R	NC	....	....	....	....	....	100	M2	'91	107⅝	101	107⅝	8.25	5.70
• Sr Sub Nts[7] 7½s '99	jJ	BBB+	2/93	A–	X	BE	NC	....	....	....	....	....	100	M2	'92	No Sale		95	7.89	9.20
Arizona Public Service[9]	*75*	*3.12*	*3.40*	*3.16*		*Dc*	*23.20*	*403.0*	*456.0*	*9-30-95*	*2153*	*4074*		*52.9*						
1st 7⅛s '97	Jj15	BBB			X	R	NC	....	....	....	[10]Z101.40	1-14-97	150	F1	'92	101⅜	97⅞	101⅜	7.03	5.75
1st 7⅝s '98	Ms15	BBB			X	R	NC	....	....	....	[10]Z103.63	3-14-96	100	S1	'92	103½	97½	103½	7.37	5.91
1st 7⅝s '99	Jd15	BBB			X	R	NC	....	....	....	[10]Z104.204	6-14-96	100	G1	'92	104⅞	96½	104⅞	7.27	6.04
1st 5¾s 2000	mS15	BBB			X	R	NC	....	....	....	[10]Z104.02	9-14-96	100	S1	'93	98¼	87⅜	98¼	5.85	6.18
1st 8⅛s 2002	Ms15	BBB			X	R	NC	....	....	....	[10]Z105.25	3-14-96	125	S1	'92	108¾	96⅝	108¾	7.47	6.39
1st 6⅝s 2004	Ms	BBB			X	R	NC	....	....	....	[10]Z105.54	2-29-96	100	S1	'94	100⅛	87¼	100⅛	6.62	6.60
1st 10¼s 2020	Mn15	BBB	11/91	BBB–	X	R	104.63	(5-15-00)	Z100	....	[10]Z106.48	5-14-97	124	S1	'90	117⅛	106⅛	108½	9.45	9.36
1st 9½s 2021	Ao15	BBB	11/91	BBB–	X	R	103.78	(4-15-01)	Z100	....	[10]Z106.04	4-14-96	100	F1	'91	115¼	101¾	111¾	8.50	8.37
1st 9s 2021	jD15	BBB			X	R	103.94	(12-15-01)	Z100	....	[10]Z106.30	12-14-96	150	S1	'91	110⅞	98⅛	110⅞	8.12	8.00
1st 7¼s 2023	fA	BBB			X	R	102.72	(8-1-03)	....	....	[10]Z104.90	7-31-96	100	F1	'93	98⅞	82⅛	98⅞	7.33	7.34
1st 8¾s 2024	Jj15	BBB			X	R	104.31	(1-15-02)	....	....	[10]Z106.46	1-14-97	175	F1	'92	110	96¼	110	7.95	7.86
1st 8s 2025	Fa	BBB			X	R	103.38	(2-1-03)	Z100	(2-1-03)	[10]Z106.08	1-31-96	150	S1	'93	105½	88¾	104¾	7.64	7.59
Arkansas Power & Light[11]	*72a*	*2.40*	*2.13*	*1.51*		*Dc*	*28.70*	*544.0*	*495.0*	*6-30-95*	*1384*	*2734*		*51.6*						
1st 5¾s '96	Ms	BBB	4/90	BBB–	X	CR	100	....	100	....	....	....	25.0	B6	'66	100	97⅝	100	5.75	5.64
1st 5⅞s '97	Ms	BBB	4/90	BBB–	X	CR	100.27	2-29-96	100.24	2-29-96	....	....	30.0	H1	'67	100	95¼	100	5.88	5.87
1st 7⅜s '98	Jd	BBB	4/90	BBB–	X	R	100.66	5-31-96	100.47	5-31-96	....	....	15.0	E1	'68	100¾	96⅝	100¾	7.32	7.03
1st 7.90s 2002	mN	BBB			X	R	102.71	(11-1-97)	Z100	....	....	....	25.0	B5	'92	106¼	94¼	106¼	7.44	6.74
1st 6s 2003	aO	BBB			X	BE	101.78	(10-1-98)	Z100	....	....	....	155	K2	'93	96⅝	83¼	96⅝	6.21	6.56
1st 6.65s 2005	fA	BBB			X	BE	102.55	(8-1-98)	Z100	....	....	....	115	K2	'93	99⅝	85⅜	99⅝	6.68	6.70
1st 7½s 2007	fA	BBB			X	R	104.18	(8-1-97)	100	....	....	....	100	B5	'92	104⅝	90⅝	104⅝	7.17	6.91
1st 9¾s 2019	[12]fa	BBB	4/90	BBB–	X	R	106.11	6-30-96	100	....	....	....	75.0	M6	'89	106⅝	102¼	105⅛	9.27	9.21
1st 10s 2020	[13]ms	BBB	4/90	BBB–	X	R	107.68	1-31-96	100	....	....	....	20.0	F1	'90	108	103¾	107⅞	9.27	9.18
1st 10⅜s 2020	aO	BBB			X	R	104.82	9-30-96	100	....	....	....	154	M6	'90	108¼	104⅜	105⅝	9.82	9.77
1st 8.70s 2022	mN	BBB			X	R	106.28	(11-1-97)	Z100	....	....	....	25.0	B5	'92	107¾	94⅛	107¾	8.07	7.99

Uniform Footnote Explanations-See Page 260. Other: [1] Due May 1. [2] Incl disc. [3] (HRO)On Chge of Ctrl at 101. [4] Thru 11-1-00,plus Applicable Prem:On Chge of Ctrl. [5] Max $45M red w/proceeds of Pub Eq Off'gs. [6] Subsid of Great Western Fin'l. [7] Issued in min denom $100T. [8] Due 12-1-97. [9] Subsid of Pinnacle West Capital Corp. [10] In whole. [11] Subsid of Entergy Corp. [12] Due 7-1-19. [13] Due 2-1-20.

Title-Industry Code & Co. Finances (In Italics) / Individual Issue Statistics (Exchange)	Ind / Interest Dates	S&P Debt Rating / Fixed Charge Coverage 1992	Date of Last Rating Change / 1993	Prior Rating	Eligible / 1994	Bond Form / Year End	Redemption Provisions: Regular Price / Cash & Equiv. (Million $)	Regular (Begins) Thru / Curr. Assets	Sinking Fund Price / Curr. Liab.	Sinking Fund (Begins) Thru / Balance Sheet Date	Refund/Other Restriction Price / L. Term Debt (Mil $)	Refund/Other Restriction (Begins) Thru	Outst'g (Mil $) / Capital-ization (Mil $)	Underwriting Firm / Total Debt % Capital	Underwriting Year	Price Range 1995 High	Price Range 1995 Low	Mo. End Price Sale(s) or Bid	Curr. Yield	Yield to Mat.
***Arkansas Power & Light** (Cont.)*																				
1st 7s 2023	aO	**BBB**			X	BE	104.23	(10-1-98)	Z100	....	....	....	175	G1	'93	96¼	79⅝	96¼	7.27	7.32
[1]Arkla Inc	***73e***	***1.04***	***1.69***		***1.56***	***Dc***	***18.40***	***299.0***	***814.0***	***3-31-95***	***1324***		***2333***	***67.1***						
Deb 8.90s 2006	jD15	**BB+**	4/92	BBB	Y	R	NC	....	....	....	....	....	145	F1	'86	111⅜	94⅜	111⅜	7.99	7.37
Deb 9⅞s 2018	Fa15	**BB+**	4/92	BBB	Y	R	106.42	2-14-96	100	(2-15-99)	®104.94	2-14-98	122	F1	'88	108⅛	98¼	106⅛	9.31	9.22
Deb 10s 2019	mN15	**BB+**	4/92	BBB	Y	R	105	(11-15-99)	100	(11-15-05)	....	....	159	F1	'89	114¼	99⅜	114¼	8.75	8.58
Nts 9⅞s '97	Ao15	**BB+**			Y	BE	NC	....	....	....	....	....	225	F1	'92	105⅜	101⅜	104⅜	9.46	6.29
Nts 8⅞s '99	jJ15	**BB+**			Y	R	NC	....	....	....	....	....	200	F1	'92	107⅛	98⅛	107⅛	8.28	6.59
Armco Inc	***66a***	***d3.05***	***d0.27***		***3.03***	***Dc***	***126.0***	***662.0***	***420.0***	***9-30-95***	***361.0***		***167.0***	***230.0***						
• SF Deb[2] 9.20s 2000	jJ15	**B**	4/93	BB−	Y	R	100	7-14-96	100	....	....	....	35.0	S5	'75	101⅞	93¼	99½	9.25	9.34
• SF Deb[2] 8½s 2001	mS	**B**	4/93	BB−	Y	R	100.41	8-31-96	100	....	....	....	48.0	S5	'76	98¾	85	99	8.59	8.72
• Sr Nts[3] 11⅜s '99	aO15	**B**	4/93	BB−	Y	R	102	(10-15-97)	....	....	....	....	100	S1	'92	109	99¾	104	10.94	10.07
Sr Nts[3] 9⅜s 2000	mN	**B**			Y	R	101.75	(11-1-98)	....	....	....	....	125	S1	'93	99⅝	90½	99	9.47	9.63
Armstrong World Indus	***31a***	***d0.51***	***5.81***		***11.76***	***Dc***	***18.40***	***787.0***	***511.0***	***9-30-95***	***438.0***		***1344***	***41.7***						
• Deb 9¾s 2008	Ao15	**A+**	1/91	AA−	X	R	NC	....	....	....	....	....	125	S5	'88	122	108⅛	120½	8.09	7.21
Arvin Industries	***8***	***2.63***	***1.08***		***2.49***	***Dc***	***56.20***	***547.0***	***445.0***	***10-1-95***	***324.0***		***889.0***	***51.9***						
SF Deb 9⅛s 2017	Ms	**BBB−**	5/90	BBB	X	R	105.199	2-29-96	100	(3-1-98)	®104.333	2-28-97	46.7	M2	'87	105½	94¾	105¼	8.67	8.58
Nts 10s 2000	fA	**BBB−**			X	BE	NC	....	....	....	....	....	50.0	M2	'90	112¾	102⅛	112¾	8.87	6.72
Nts 6⅞s 2001	Fa15	**BBB−**			X	BE	NC	....	....	....	....	....	75.0	M2	'94	100¾	88⅝	100¾	6.82	6.70
ASARCO Inc	***45b***	***1.47***	***d1.00***		***1.28***	***Dc***	***229.0***	***1196***	***584.0***	***9-30-95***	***1120***		***3316***	***35.0***						
Deb 7⅞s 2013	Ao15	**BBB**			X	R	NC	....	....	....	....	....	100	F1	'93	106⅝	90¾	106⅝	7.39	7.20
Deb 8½s 2025	Mn	**BBB**			X	R	NC	....	....	....	....	....	150	C5	'95	114⅜	98⅜	114⅜	7.43	7.30
Nts 7⅜s 2003	Fa	**BBB**			X	R	NC	....	....	....	....	....	100	F1	'93	105⅜	92¾	105⅜	7.00	6.42
[4]Ashland Oil Inc	***49d***	***△2.41***	***△2.98***		***△1.16***	***Sp***	***52.00***	***2575***	***2094***	***9-30-95***	***1828***		***3934***	***53.4***						
SF Deb 11⅛s 2017	aO15	**BBB**	2/91	A−	X	R	105.562	(10-15-97)	100	(10-15-98)	....	....	200	S1	'87	115⅛	110⅛	114	9.76	9.58
Deb 8.80s 2012	mN15	**BBB**			X	BE	NC	....	....	....	....	....	250	S1	'92	118⅛	99¾	118⅛	7.45	6.96
M-T Nts 'F' 7.91s 2004	[5]jd15	**BBB**			X	BE	NC	....	....	....	....	....	15.0	C5	'94	109⅞	95	109⅞	7.20	6.39
M-T Nts 'F' 7.98s 2004	[5]jd15	**BBB**			X	BE	NC	....	....	....	....	....	10.0	C4	'94	110¼	95⅜	110¼	7.24	6.40
M-T Nts 'F' 7.85s 2004	[6]jd15	**BBB**			X	BE	NC	....	....	....	....	....	25.0	C5	'94	109⅝	94⅜	109⅝	7.16	6.41
M-T Nts 'F' 7.82s 2005	[7]jd15	**BBB**			X	BE	NC	....	....	....	....	....	30.0	B5	'95	109⅝	99¼	109⅝	7.13	6.42
M-T Nts 'F' 7.90s 2006	[8]jd15	**BBB**			X	BE	NC	....	....	....	....	....	10.0	C5	'94	110⅞	94	110⅞	7.13	6.47
M-T Nts 'F' 7.79s 2006	[9]jd15	**BBB**			X	BE	NC	....	....	....	....	....	15.0	C5	'94	110⅛	93⅛	110⅛	7.07	6.46
Associated Dry Goods	***59f***	***Subsid of May Dept Stores,see***																		
Deb 8.85s 2006	Ms	**A**	10/90	A+	X	R	NC	....	....	....	....	....	100	S4	'86	119⅝	101⅛	119⅝	7.40	6.22
Associated Estates Realty	***57***	***n/a***	***n/a***		***3.10***	***Dc***				***9-30-95***	***162.0***		***310.0***	***52.3***						
Sr Nts 8⅜s 2000	Ao15	**BBB−**			X	BE	NC	....	....	....	....	....	75.0	D3	'95	106⅛	99½	106⅛	7.89	6.71
Sr Nts 7.10s 2002	mN15	**BBB−**			X	BE	NC	....	....	....	....	....	10.0	D3	'95	101⅝	100	101⅝	6.99	6.80
Associated Materials	***42***	***2.20***	***2.49***		***2.23***	***Dc***	***2.81***	***121.0***	***72.80***	***9-30-95***	***82.60***		***107.0***	***78.8***						
Sr Sub Nts[10] 11½s 2003	fA15	**B−**			Y	R	104.313	(8-15-98)	....	....	[11]Z110	8-14-96	75.0	B5	'93	102½	80¾	102½	11.22	11.00
Associates Corp of N.A.[12]	***25g***	***1.56***	***1.65***		***1.64***	***Dc***	***1201***			***6-30-95***	***16884***		***33607***	***87.7***						
• Sr Deb 6s 2001	Jd15	**AA−**	6/85	A+	X	R	100	....	....	....	....	....	[13]150	K2	'81	97¼	93⅛	91¼	6.58	8.01
Sr Deb([14]'99) 8.55s 2009	jJ15	**AA−**			X	R	NC	....	....	....	....	....	200	M6	'89	119¼	102⅛	119¼	7.17	6.40
Sr Nts 8¾s '96	Fa	**AA−**			X	R	NC	....	....	....	....	....	300	M6	'91	101⅝	100¼	100¼	8.73	5.72
Sr Nts 4½s '96	Fa15	**AA−**			X	R	NC	....	....	....	....	....	300	L3	'93	99⅞	96⅝	99⅞	4.51	5.39
Sr Nts 8.80s '96	Ms	**AA−**			X	R	NC	....	....	....	....	....	300	M6	'91	101⅞	100½	100½	8.76	5.70
Sr Nts 8⅜s '96	Jd	**AA−**			X	R	NC	....	....	....	....	....	67.0	S1	'87	102¼	100⅝	101⅛	8.28	5.61
Sr Nts 4¾s '96	fA	**AA−**			X	R	NC	....	....	....	....	....	300	M2	'93	99⅝	95⅜	99⅝	4.77	5.40

Uniform Footnote Explanations-See Page 260. Other: [1] Now Noram Energy. [2] Was Armco Steel. [3] (HRO)On Chge of Ctrl at 101. [4] Now Ashland Inc. [5] Due 7-21-04. [6] Due 11-30-04. [7] Due 3-21-05. [8] Due 8-5-06. [9] Due 8-9-06. [10] Co must offer repurch at 101 on Chge of Ctrl. [11] Max $18.8M red w/proceeds of Pub Eq Off'g. [12] Subsid of Ford Motor Co. [13] Incl disc. [14] (HRO)On 7-15-99 at 100.

Title-Industry Code & Co. Finances (In Italics)	Ind	Fixed Charge Coverage 1992	1993	1994	Year End	Million $ Cash & Equiv.	Curr. Assets	Curr. Liab.	Balance Sheet Date	L. Term Debt (Mil $)	Capital-ization (Mil $)	Total Debt % Capital

Exchange ↓ Individual Issue Statistics	Interest Dates	S&P Debt Rating	Date of Last Rating Change	Prior Rating	Eligible ↓	Bond Form	Redemption Provisions: Regular Price	Regular (Begins) Thru	Sinking Fund Price	Sinking Fund (Begins) Thru	Refund/Other Restriction Price	Refund/Other Restriction (Begins) Thru	Outst'g (Mil $)	Underwriting Firm	Underwriting Year	Price Range 1995 High	Low	Mo. End Price Sale(s) or Bid	Curr. Yield	Yield to Mat.
Associates Corp of N.A. *(Cont.)*																				
Sr Nts 7½s '96	aO15	**AA–**			X	R	NC	....	....	....	....	....	300	M5	'91	101¾	99⅛	101⅝	7.38	5.37
Sr Nts 4⅝s '96	mN30	**AA–**			X	R	NC	....	....	....	....	....	300	M6	'94	99⅜	93¾	99⅜	4.65	5.33
Sr Nts 8.70s '97	Jj	**AA–**			X	R	NC	....	....	....	....	....	250	F1	'89	103¾	101	103⅛	8.44	5.46
Sr Nts 6⅞s '97	Jj15	**AA–**			X	R	NC	....	....	....	....	....	300	K2	'92	101⅜	97⅝	101⅜	6.78	5.50
Sr Nts 9.70s '97	Mn	**AA–**			X	R	NC	....	....	....	....	....	250	G1	'89	106⅛	103⅛	105⅜	9.21	5.47
Sr Nts 8⅝s '97	Jd15	**AA–**			X	R	NC	....	....	....	....	....	300	S1	'91	104¾	100¼	104⅜	8.26	5.47
Sr Nts 6¾s '97	jJ15	**AA–**			X	R	NC	....	....	....	....	....	300	M5	'94	101⅞	96⅜	101⅞	6.63	5.46
Sr Nts 5⅞s '97	fA15	**AA–**			X	R	NC	....	....	....	....	....	300	K2	'92	100⅝	94⅜	100⅝	5.84	5.46
Sr Nts 7¾s '97	mN	**AA–**			X	R	NC	....	....	....	....	....	300	U1	'94	103⅞	98⅝	103⅞	7.46	5.50
Sr Nts 6⅝s '97	mN15	**AA–**			X	R	NC	....	....	....	....	....	300	F1	'92	102	95¾	102	6.50	5.48
Sr Nts 8⅜s '98	Jj15	**AA–**			X	R	NC	....	....	....	....	....	200	S1	'88	105½	100	105⅜	7.95	5.56
Sr Nts 8⅛s '98	Jj15	**AA–**			X	R	NC	....	....	....	....	....	300	U1	'95	104⅞	99⅝	104⅞	7.75	5.57
Sr Nts 6⅛s '98	Fa	**AA–**			X	R	NC	....	....	....	....	....	150	K2	'93	101¼	93⅞	101¼	6.05	5.48
Sr Nts 7.30s '98	Ms15	**AA–**			X	R	NC	....	....	....	....	....	300	L3	'95	103½	99⅞	103½	7.05	5.59
Sr Nts 7¼s '98	Mn15	**AA–**			X	R	NC	....	....	....	....	....	300	M6	'94	103⅝	96¼	103⅝	7.00	5.60
Sr Nts 6⅝s '98	Mn15	**AA–**			X	R	NC	....	....	....	....	....	300	C5	'95	102⅜	99¾	102⅜	6.47	5.54
Sr Nts 8.80s '98	fA	**AA–**			X	R	NC	....	....	....	....	....	300	M6	'91	107⅝	101⅛	107⅝	8.18	5.59
Sr Nts 6⅜s '98	fA15	**AA–**			X	R	NC	....	....	....	....	....	300	C5	'95	101⅞	99⅞	101⅞	6.26	5.59
Sr Nts 5¼s '98	mS	**AA–**			X	BE	NC	....	....	....	....	....	300	F1	'93	99¼	90⅛	99¼	5.29	5.55
Sr Nts 5¾s '98	mN15	**AA–**			X	R	NC	....	....	....	....	....	200	C5	'95	100⅜	99¾	100⅜	5.73	5.60
Sr Nts 6¼s '99	Ms15	**AA–**			X	R	NC	....	....	....	....	....	300	S5	'94	101⅝	91⅞	101⅝	6.15	5.69
Sr Nts 7½s '99	Mn15	**AA–**			X	R	NC	....	....	....	....	....	300	S1	'92	105½	96	105½	7.11	5.68
Sr Nts 7¼s '99	mS	**AA–**			X	R	NC	....	....	....	....	....	300	C5	'94	104⅞	95¼	104⅞	6.91	5.75
Sr Nts 6¾s '99	aO15	**AA–**			X	R	NC	....	....	....	....	....	300	G1	'92	103⅜	93⅝	103⅜	6.53	5.74
Sr Nts 8¼s '99	jD	**AA–**			X	R	NC	....	....	....	....	....	300	C5	'94	108½	99	108½	7.60	5.79
Sr Nts 6s 2000	Ms15	**AA–**			X	R	NC	....	....	....	....	....	300	S1	'93	100⅞	89⅝	100⅞	5.95	5.76
Sr Nts 5¼s 2000	Ms30	**AA–**			X	R	NC	....	....	....	....	....	300	S1	'93	97⅞	86½	97⅞	5.36	5.82
Sr Nts 9⅛s 2000	Ao	**AA–**			X	R	NC	....	....	....	....	....	250	S1	'90	112¾	102⅝	112¾	8.09	5.70
Sr Nts 6s 2000	Jd15	**AA–**			X	R	NC	....	....	....	....	....	300	M2	'93	100¾	89¼	100¾	5.96	5.81
Sr Nts 6¼s 2000	mS15	**AA–**			X	R	NC	....	....	....	....	....	300		'95	101¾	98⅞	101¾	6.14	5.82
Sr Nts 7⅞s 2001	mS30	**AA–**			X	R	NC	....	....	....	....	....	300	U1	'94	109⅛	99⅞	109⅛	7.22	5.97
Sr Nts 7½s 2002	Ao15	**AA–**			X	R	NC	....	....	....	....	....	300	M5	'95	107⅝	99⅞	107⅝	6.97	6.02
Sr Nts 6⅜s 2002	jJ15	**AA–**			X	R	NC	....	....	....	....	....	300	C5	'95	101⅞	96⅛	101⅞	6.26	6.02
Sr Nts 6⅜s 2002	aO15	**AA–**			X	R	NC	....	....	....	....	....	300	M6	'95	101⅞	99¾	101⅞	6.26	6.03
Sr Nts 6s 2002	jD	**AA–**			X	R	NC	....	....	....	....	....	300	S1	'95	100	98¾	99¾	6.02	6.04
Sr Nts 6⅞s 2003	Fa	**AA–**			X	R	NC	....	....	....	....	....	150	K2	'93	104¾	90⅜	104¾	6.56	6.04
Sr Nts 5¾s 2003	aO15	**AA–**			X	R	NC	....	....	....	....	....	300	L3	'93	97⅞	82⅞	97⅞	5.87	6.09
Sr Nts[1] 7¾s 2005	Fa15	**AA–**			X	R	NC	....	....	....	....	....	300	L3	'95	112¾	99⅝	112¾	6.87	5.92
Sr Nts 6⅝s 2005	Jd15	**AA–**			X	BE	NC	....	....	....	....	....	300		'95	103¼	95⅝	103¼	6.42	6.17
Sr Nts 6⅜s 2005	mN15	**AA–**			X	R	NC	....	....	....	....	....	200	C5	'95	101½	99⅜	101½	6.28	6.17
M-T Sr Nts 'G'[2] 5.475s '96	[3]mn	**AA–**			X	BE	NC	....	....	....	....	....	7.00	P1	'94	100	97⅛	100	5.48	5.41
M-T Sr Nts 'G'[2] 6.82s '97	[4]mn	**AA–**			X	BE	NC	....	....	....	....	....	11.5	S1	'94	101¾	96⅞	101¾	6.70	5.47
M-T Sr Nts 'G'[2] 6.82s '97	[4]mn	**AA–**			X	BE	NC	....	....	....	....	....	5.00	M2	'94	101¾	96⅞	101¾	6.70	5.47
M-T Sr Nts 'G'[2] 7.05s '97	[5]mn	**AA–**			X	BE	NC	....	....	....	....	....	20.0	M6	'94	102	97⅜	102	6.91	5.52
M-T Sr Nts 'G'[2] 7s '97	[6]mn	**AA–**			X	BE	NC	....	....	....	....	....	5.00	S1	'94	102	97¼	102	6.86	5.46
M-T Sr Nts 'G'[2] 6.78s '97	[7]mn	**AA–**			X	BE	NC	....	....	....	....	....	5.00	M2	'94	101¾	96¾	101¾	6.66	5.48

Uniform Footnote Explanations-See Page 260. Other: [1] (HRO)On 2-15-00 at 100. [2] Issued in min denom $100T. [3] Due 4-4-96. [4] Due 5-12-97. [5] Due 5-15-97. [6] Due 5-13-97. [7] Due 6-2-97.

Title-Industry Code & Co. Finances (In Italics)	Ind	Fixed Charge Coverage 1992	1993	1994	Year End	Million $ Cash & Equiv.	Curr. Assets	Curr. Liab.	Balance Sheet Date	L. Term Debt (Mil $)	Capital-ization (Mil $)	Total Debt % Capital

Individual Issue Statistics / Exchange ↓	Interest Dates	S&P Debt Rating	Date of Last Rating Change	Prior Rating	Eligible ↓	Bond Form	Redemption Provisions: Regular Price	Regular (Begins) Thru	Sinking Fund Price	Sinking Fund (Begins) Thru	Refund/Other Restriction Price	Refund/Other Restriction (Begins) Thru	Outst'g (Mil $)	Underwriting Firm	Underwriting Year	Price Range 1995 High	Price Range 1995 Low	Mo. End Price Sale(s) or Bid	Curr. Yield	Yield to Mat.
Associates Corp of N.A. *(Cont.)*																				
M-T Sr Nts 'G'[1] 7s '97	[2]mn	**AA–**			X	BE	NC	....	....	....	....	....	20.0	C5	'94	102	97¼	102	6.86	5.47
M-T Sr Nts 'G'[1] 6¾s '97	[3]mn	**AA–**			X	BE	NC	....	....	....	....	....	10.0	L3	'94	101¾	96⅝	101¾	6.63	5.45
M-T Sr Nts 'G'[1] 6.78s '97	[3]mn	**AA–**			X	BE	NC	....	....	....	....	....	5.00	M2	'94	101¾	96¾	101¾	6.66	5.48
M-T Sr Nts 'G'[1] 6.80s '97	[3]mn	**AA–**			X	BE	NC	....	....	....	....	....	25.0	S1	'94	101¾	96¾	101¾	6.68	5.50
M-T Sr Nts 'G'[1] 6.81s '97	[3]mn	**AA–**			X	BE	NC	....	....	....	....	....	10.0	M2	'94	101¾	96¾	101¾	6.69	5.51
M-T Sr Nts 'G'[1] 6.70s '97	[4]mn	**AA–**			X	BE	NC	....	....	....	....	....	5.00	P4	'94	101¾	96½	101¾	6.58	5.41
M-T Sr Nts 'G'[1] 6.77s '97	[5]mn	**AA–**			X	BE	NC	....	....	....	....	....	10.0	C5	'94	101¾	96¾	101¾	6.65	5.49
M-T Sr Nts 'G'[1] 6¾s '97	[6]mn	**AA–**			X	BE	NC	....	....	....	....	....	20.0	M6	'94	101¾	96⅝	101¾	6.63	5.48
M-T Sr Nts 'G'[1] 6.55s '97	[6]mn	**AA–**			X	BE	NC	....	....	....	....	....	5.00	L3	'94	101½	96¼	101½	6.45	5.46
M-T Sr Nts 'G'[1] 6.65s '97	[7]mn	**AA–**			X	BE	NC	....	....	....	....	....	18.0	L3	'94	101⅝	96⅝	101⅝	6.54	5.48
M-T Sr Nts 'G'[1] 6.61s '97	[7]mn	**AA–**			X	BE	NC	....	....	....	....	....	5.00	U1	'94	101½	96⅜	101½	6.51	5.53
M-T Sr Nts 'G'[1] 6.74s '97	[8]mn	**AA–**			X	BE	NC	....	....	....	....	....	10.0	D6	'94	101¾	96⅝	101¾	6.62	5.49
M-T Sr Nts 'G'[1] 6.71s '97	[8]mn	**AA–**			X	BE	NC	....	....	....	....	....	9.60	D6	'94	101¾	96½	101¾	6.59	5.46
M-T Sr Nts 'G'[1] 6.77s '97	[9]mn	**AA–**			X	BE	NC	....	....	....	....	....	5.00	P4	'94	101¾	96⅝	101¾	6.65	5.54
M-T Sr Nts 'G'[1] 7.01s '97	[10]mn	**AA–**			X	BE	NC	....	....	....	....	....	10.0		'94	102¼	97	102¼	6.86	5.48
M-T Sr Nts 'G'[1] 5.03s '97	[11]mn	**AA–**			X	BE	NC	....	....	....	....	....	15.0	L3	'94	99⅛	91⅜	99⅛	5.07	5.51
M-T Sr Nts 'G'[1] 5.57s '98	[12]mn	**AA–**			X	BE	NC	....	....	....	....	....	12.0	S5	'94	99¾	90¼	99¾	5.58	5.66
M-T Sr Nts 'G'[1] 7.06s '98	[13]mn	**AA–**			X	BE	NC	....	....	....	....	....	10.0	S1	'94	103⅜	95⅞	103⅜	6.83	5.62
M-T Sr Nts 'G'[1] 5.49s '99	[14]mn	**AA–**			X	BE	NC	....	....	....	....	....	13.7	S1	'94	99½	89¾	99½	5.52	5.67
M-T Sr Nts 'G'[1] 5.47s '99	[14]mn	**AA–**			X	BE	NC	....	....	....	....	....	5.00	S5	'94	99½	89¾	99½	5.50	5.65
M-T Sr Nts 'G'[1] 5½s '99	[15]mn	**AA–**			X	BE	NC	....	....	....	....	....	5.00	S5	'94	99½	89¾	99½	5.53	5.68
M-T Sr Nts 'G'[16] 5¾s '99	[17]mn	**AA–**			X	BE	NC	....	....	....	....	....	10.0	P1	'94	100¼	90⅝	100¼	5.74	5.66
M-T Sr Nts 'G'[1] 5.77s '99	[18]mn	**AA–**			X	BE	NC	....	....	....	....	....	10.0	K2	'94	100¼	90⅝	100¼	5.76	5.68
M-T Sr Nts 'G'[1] 7¼s '99	[19]mn	**AA–**			X	BE	NC	....	....	....	....	....	20.0	M6	'94	104⅝	95½	104⅝	6.93	5.72
M-T Sr Nts 'G'[1] 7.22s '99	[20]mn	**AA–**			X	BE	NC	....	....	....	....	....	19.0		'94	104⅝	95¼	104⅝	6.90	5.71
M-T Sr Nts 'G'[1] 7.328s '99	[20]mn	**AA–**			X	BE	NC	....	....	....	....	....	20.0	M2	'94	104⅞	95⅝	104⅞	6.99	5.74
M-T Sr Nts 'G'[1] 7.20s '99	[21]mn	**AA–**			X	BE	NC	....	....	....	....	....	5.00	L3	'94	104½	95⅛	104½	6.89	5.75
M-T Sr Nts 'G'[1] 7.30s '99	[22]mn	**AA–**			X	BE	NC	....	....	....	....	....	15.0	S1	'94	104⅞	95½	104⅞	6.96	5.74
M-T Sr Nts 'G'[1] 7.38s '99	[23]mn	**AA–**			X	BE	NC	....	....	....	....	....	7.00	L3	'94	105⅛	95¾	105⅛	7.02	5.74
M-T Sr Nts 'G'[1] 7.35s '99	[24]mn	**AA–**			X	BE	NC	....	....	....	....	....	10.0	P4	'94	105⅛	95⅝	105⅛	6.99	5.72
M-T Sr Nts 'G'[1] 7.40s '99	[25]mn	**AA–**			X	BE	NC	....	....	....	....	....	20.0	D6	'94	105¼	95⅞	105¼	7.03	5.73
M-T Sr Nts 'G'[1] 7.43s '99	[26]mn	**AA–**			X	BE	NC	....	....	....	....	....	5.00	B5	'94	105¼	96	105¼	7.06	5.77
M-T Sr Nts 'G'[1] 7.55s '99	[27]mn	**AA–**			X	BE	NC	....	....	....	....	....	5.00	U1	'94	105⅝	96⅜	105⅝	7.15	5.77
M-T Sr Nts 'G'[1] 7.46s 2000	[28]ao	**AA–**			X	BE	NC	....	....	....	....	....	25.0	B5	'95	106	99¼	106	7.04	5.84
M-T Sr Nts 'G'[1] 7.45s 2000	[29]mn	**AA–**			X	BE	NC	....	....	....	....	....	32.0	B5	'95	106	99⅞	106	7.03	5.83
M-T Sr Nts 'G'[1] 7.62s 2002	[30]mn	**AA–**			X	BE	NC	....	....	....	....	....	25.0	M6	'95	108	100	108	7.06	6.06
M-T Sr Nts 'G'[1] 6.32s 2004	[31]mn	**AA–**			X	BE	NC	....	....	....	....	....	5.30	M2	'94	100⅝	85½	100⅝	6.28	6.22
M-T Sr Nts 'G'[1] 6.44s 2004	[32]mn	**AA–**			X	BE	NC	....	....	....	....	....	26.0	K2	'94	101⅜	86⅛	101⅜	6.35	6.22
M-T Sr Nts 'G'[1] 6.20s 2004	[33]mn	**AA–**			X	BE	NC	....	....	....	....	....	20.0	M6	'94	99⅞	84⅝	99⅞	6.21	6.22
M-T Sr Nts 'G'[1] 6.39s 2004	[34]mn	**AA–**			X	BE	NC	....	....	....	....	....	5.00	F4	'94	101⅛	85¾	101⅛	6.32	6.21
M-T Sr Nts 'G'[1] 6.41s 2004	[34]mn	**AA–**			X	BE	NC	....	....	....	....	....	5.00	D4	'94	101¼	85⅞	101¼	6.33	6.21
M-T Sr Nts 'G'[1] 7.08s 2004	[35]mn	**AA–**			X	BE	NC	....	....	....	....	....	7.00	P1	'94	105½	89⅞	105½	6.71	6.22
M-T Sr Nts 'G'[1] 7.64s 2004	[36]mn	**AA–**			X	BE	NC	....	....	....	....	....	10.0	C5	'94	109	93⅜	109	7.01	6.25
M-T Sr Nts 'G'[1] 7.55s 2004	[37]mn	**AA–**			X	BE	NC	....	....	....	....	....	30.0	M6	'94	108½	92¾	108½	6.96	6.24
M-T Sr Nts 'G'[1] 7⅝s 2004	[38]mn	**AA–**			X	BE	NC	....	....	....	....	....	10.0	M6	'94	109	93¼	109	7.00	6.23
M-T Sr Nts 'G'[1] 7.88s 2004	[39]mn	**AA–**			X	BE	NC	....	....	....	....	....	10.0	U1	'94	110⅝	94⅞	110⅝	7.12	6.24

Uniform Footnote Explanations-See Page 260. Other: [1] Issued in min denom $100T. [2] Due 5-15-97. [3] Due 6-2-97. [4] Due 6-3-97. [5] Due 6-9-97. [6] Due 6-13-97. [7] Due 6-16-97. [8] Due 6-23-97. [9] Due 6-30-97. [10] Due 7-21-97. [11] Due 12-15-97. [12] Due 12-31-98. [13] Due 7-15-98. [14] Due 1-28-99. [15] Due 2-9-99. [16] Issued in min demon $100T. [17] Due 2-12-99. [18] Due 2-15-99. [19] Due 5-10-99. [20] Due 6-1-99. [21] Due 6-15-99. [22] Due 6-29-99. [23] Due 7-1-99. [24] Due 7-6-99. [25] Due 7-7-99. [26] Due 7-12-99. [27] Due 7-15-99. [28] Due 3-28-00. [29] Due 3-30-00. [30] Due 3-27-02. [31] Due 1-13-04. [32] Due 1-15-04. [33] Due 1-26-04. [34] Due 2-17-04. [35] Due 4-1-04. [36] Due 5-26-04. [37] Due 6-01-04. [38] Due 6-1-04. [39] Due 6-2-04.

Title-Industry Code & Co. Finances (In Italics)	Ind	Fixed Charge Coverage 1992	1993	1994	Year End	Million $ Cash & Equiv.	Curr. Assets	Curr. Liab.	Balance Sheet Date		L. Term Debt (Mil $)		Capital-ization (Mil $)	Total Debt % Capital						
Individual Issue Statistics Exchange ↓	Interest Dates	S&P Debt Rating	Date of Last Rating Change	Prior Rating	Eligible ↓ Bond Form	Redemption Provisions: Regular Price	Regular (Begins) Thru	Sinking Fund Price	Sinking Fund (Begins) Thru	Refund/Other Restriction Price	Refund/Other Restriction (Begins) Thru	Outst'g (Mil $)	Underwriting Firm	Underwriting Year	Price Range 1995 High	Price Range 1995 Low	Mo. End Price Sale(s) or Bid	Curr. Yield	Yield to Mat.	
***Associates Corp of N.A.** (Cont.)*																				
M-T Sr Nts 'G'[1] 7.70s 2004	[2]mn	**AA–**			X BE	NC	....	....	....	....	....	10.0	B5	'94	109½	93¾	109½	7.03	6.24	
M-T Sr Nts 'G'[1] 7.81s 2004	[3]mn	**AA–**			X BE	NC	....	....	....	....	....	5.00	W3	'94	110⅛	94⅜	110⅛	7.09	6.26	
M-T Sr Nts 'G'[1] 7.92s 2004	[4]mn	**AA–**			X BE	NC	....	....	....	....	....	10.0	B5	'94	110⅞	95	110⅞	7.14	6.26	
M-T Sr Nts 'G'[1] 7.95s 2004	[4]mn	**AA–**			X BE	NC	....	....	....	....	....	10.0	D6	'94	111⅛	95¼	111⅛	7.15	6.25	
M-T Sr Nts 'G'[1] 8.02s 2004	[5]mn	**AA–**			X BE	NC	....	....	....	....	....	15.0	D6	'94	111⅝	95⅝	111⅝	7.18	6.24	
M-T Sr Nts 'G'[1] 7.97s 2004	[6]mn	**AA–**			X BE	NC	....	....	....	....	....	5.00	P1	'94	111¼	95⅜	111¼	7.16	6.25	
M-T Sr Nts 'G'[1] 7.70s 2005	[7]mn	**AA–**			X BE	NC	....	....	....	....	....	31.5	S1	'95	109⅞	99¾	109⅞	7.01	6.28	
M-T Sr Nts 'H'[1] 6.998s '98	[8]mn	**AA–**			X BE	NC	....	....	....	....	....	25.0		'95	103⅛	100	103⅛	6.79	5.57	
M-T Sr Nts 'H'[1] 6.04s '98	[9]mn	**AA–**			X BE	NC	....	....	....	....	....	40.0	P1	'95	101⅛	99⅞	101⅛	5.97	5.59	
M-T Sr Nts 'H'[1] 6.84s 2000	[10]mn	**AA–**			X BE	NC	....	....	....	....	....	25.0		'95	103¾	100	103¾	6.59	5.86	
M-T Sr Nts 'H'[1] 6.33s 2000	[11]mn	**AA–**			X BE	NC	....	....	....	....	....	50.0		'95	101⅞	97⅞	101⅞	6.21	5.84	
M-T Sr Nts 'H'[1] 6.45s 2000	[12]mn	**AA–**			X BE	NC	....	....	....	....	....	30.0	M6	'95	102⅜	98⅜	102⅜	6.30	5.84	
M-T Sr Nts 'H'[1] 6.68s 2000	[13]mn	**AA–**			X BE	NC	....	....	....	....	....	25.0	B5	'95	103¼	99¼	103¼	6.47	5.86	
M-T Sr Nts 'H'[1] 6.78s 2001	[14]mn	**AA–**			X BE	NC	....	....	....	....	....	25.0	L3	'95	103¾	99	103¾	6.53	5.98	
M-T Sr Nts 'H'[1] 6.93s 2002	[15]mn	**AA–**			X BE	NC	....	....	....	....	....	25.0	L3	'95	104⅝	99⅛	104⅝	6.62	6.07	
M-T Sr Nts 'H'[1] 6.52s 2002	[16]mn	**AA–**			X BE	NC	....	....	....	....	....	25.0	U1	'95	102⅜	99⅞	102⅜	6.37	6.09	
M-T Sr Nts 'H'[1] 7⅝s 2005	[17]mn	**AA–**			X BE	NC	....	....	....	....	....	60.0	D6	'95	109⅜	100	109⅜	6.97	6.28	
Sub Deb 7⅝s '98	Ao15	**A+**			X R	100	(4-15-96)	....	....	....	....	100	S1	'86	102⅝	97⅝	100⅜	7.60	7.44	
• Sub Deb([18]'96) 8.15s 2009	fA	**A+**			X R	NC	....	....	....	....	....	125	M6	'89	No Sale		103	7.91	7.79	
***AT&T Corp**[19]*	***67b***	***9.22***	***11.42***	***10.48***	***Dc***	***4082***	***42197***	***34652***	***9-30-95***		***13073***	***50500***	***57.6***							
• Deb 4⅜s '96	aO	**AA**	8/84	AAA	X CR	100	....	....	....	....	....	250	F1	'62	99⅜	94	99⅛	4.41	5.56	
• Deb 4¾s '98	Jd	**AA**	8/84	AAA	X CR	100	....	....	....	....	....	250	M6	'61	98¼	90¼	s98	4.85	5.64	
• Deb 4⅜s '99	Mn	**AA**	8/84	AAA	X CR	100	....	....	....	....	....	250	M6	'63	97	86¼	95⅜	4.59	5.92	
• Deb 6s 2000	fA	**AA**	8/84	AAA	X R	100	....	....	....	....	....	250	H1	'67	100⅞	90⅜	s100	6.00	6.00	
• Deb 5⅛s 2001	Ao	**AA**	8/84	AAA	X R	100.17	3-31-96	....	....	....	....	250	F1	'66	96½	84¼	s96⅛	5.33	5.99	
• Deb 8⅛s 2022	Jj15	**AA**			X BE	103.21	(1-15-02)	....	....	....	....	500	L3	'92	108⅜	95⅛	s108¼	7.51	7.41	
• Deb 8⅛s 2024	jJ15	**AA**			X BE	103.971	(7-15-02)	....	....	....	....	500	M6	'92	109	94¾	s108¾	7.47	7.38	
• Deb 8.35s 2025	Jj15	**AA**			X BE	103.288	(1-15-05)	....	....	....	....	300	S1	'95	112¼	96¼	112¼	7.44	7.33	
• Deb 8⅝s 2031	jD	**AA**			X BE	105.56	(12-1-01)	....	....	....	....	676	M6	'91	113¾	98	112⅜	7.68	7.61	
• Nts 4½s '96	Fa15	**AA**			X BE	NC	....	....	....	....	....	400	M6	'93	100	96⅝	99⅝	4.52	7.34	
• Nts 7⅛s 2002	Jj15	**AA**			X BE	NC	....	....	....	....	....	500	L3	'92	106¼	93⅞	s106¼	6.71	5.88	
• Nts 6¾s 2004	Ao	**AA**			X BE	NC	....	....	....	....	....	400	S1	'94	105	90	104¾	6.44	6.01	
• Nts 7s 2005	Mn15	**AA**			X BE	NC	....	....	....	....	....	300	M5	'95	107	99⅛	104	6.73	6.42	
• Nts 7½s 2006	Jd	**AA**			X BE	NC	....	....	....	....	....	500	M6	'94	110¼	93¾	110⅛	6.81	6.17	
Nts 7¾s 2007	Ms	**AA**			X BE	NC	....	....	....	....	....	500	L3	'95	111¾	99⅞	111¾	6.94	6.27	
M-T([20]Reset[21])Nts[22] 'A' 8⅛s 2002	Fa	**AA**			X BE	*100	(2-1-96)	....	....	....	....	25.0	M6	'95	101½	100	100⅞	8.05	....	
M-T Nts 'A' 7⅝s 2002	[23]Mar15	**AA**			X BE	*100	(3-15-96)	....	....	....	....	35.0	M6	'95	102⅜	100	100½	7.59	7.52	
M-T([24]Reset[25])Nts[26] 'A' 8.15s 2005	Fa9	**AA**			X BE	*100	(2-9-97)	....	....	....	....	25.0	D3	'95	104	100	103⅛	7.90	....	
• M-T Nts 'A' 8.20s 2005	Fa15	**AA**			X BE	*100	(2-15-00)	....	....	....	....	100	C1	'95	107	99¾	107⅛	7.65	7.12	
M-T([27]Reset[28])Nts[29]'A' 7.35s 2005	Ao28	**AA**			X BE	*100	(4-28-96)	....	....	....	....	25.0	S5	'95	101¼	100	101¼	7.26	....	
M-T Nts 'A' 7.35s 2005	[23]May11	**AA**			X BE	*100	(5-11-96)	....	....	....	....	25.0	L3	'95	103¼	99¼	100¾	7.30	7.24	
M-T([30]Reset[31])Nts 'A' 7½s 2005	[23]May16	**AA**			X BE	*100	(5-16-96)	....	....	....	....	35.0	M6	'95	102⅜	100	101⅜	7.40	....	
M-T([32]Reset[33])Nts[34] 'A' 6¼s 2005	jJ15	**AA**			X BE	*100	(7-5-96)	....	....	....	....	25.4	D3	'95	101	95	101	6.19	....	
M-T Nts 'A' 8s 2025	Mn15	**AA**			X BE	104.062	(5-15-05)	....	....	....	....	50.0	M6	'95	112	100¼	112	7.14	7.03	
M-T Nts 'A' 7¾s 2025	Mn15	**AA**			X BE	103.713	(5-15-05)	....	....	....	....	25.0	B5	'95	109	98¼	109	7.11	7.02	
Atlanta Gas Light	***73b***	***△2.85***	***△3.07***	***△3.45***	***Sp***	***3.70***	***220.0***	***231.0***	***9-30-95***		***555.0***	***1222***	***49.6***							
M-T Nts 'C' 5.90s 2003	[35]mn	**A–**			X BE	NC	....	....	....	....	....	29.0	M2	'93	97⅝	83½	97⅝	6.04	6.29	

Uniform Footnote Explanations-See Page 260. Other:[1] Issued in min denom $100T. [2] Due 6-10-04. [3] Due 7-1-04. [4] Due 7-13-04. [5] Due 7-19-04. [6] Due 7-20-04. [7] Due 4-1-05. [8] Due 5-15-98. [9] Due 10-13-98. [10] Due 5-22-00. [11] Due 6-9-00. [12] Due 6-15-00. [13] Due 7-25-00. [14] Due 7-31-01. [15] Due 7-25-02. [16] Due 10-11-02. [17] Due 4-27-05. [18] (HRO)On 8-1-96 at 100. [19] Was American Tel & Tel. [20] Int thru 1-31-96, 8.15% aft thru 1-31-97. [21] Int incr ea 2-1:8.20%'97, 8.25%'98, 8.30%'99. [22] Int incr ea 2-1:8.40%'00, 8.50% aft. [23] Int pd monthly. [24] Int thru 2-8-97,8.30% aft thru 2-8-98. [25] Int incr ea 2-9:8.5%'99,8.75%'00,8.875%'01. [26] Int incr ea 2-9:9%'02,9.25%'03,9.50%'04,10% aft. [27] Int thru 4-27-96,7.45% aft thru 4-27-97. [28] Int incr ea 4-28:7.55%'97,7.65%'98,8%'99,8.25%'00. [29] Int incr ea 4-28:8.5%'01,9%'02,9.75%'03,10.5% aft. [30] Int thru 5-15-01, 7.625% aft thru 5-15-03. [31] Int incr ea 5-16:7.75% '03, 8% aft. [32] Int thru 7-4-96,6.45% aft thru 7-4-97. [33] Int incr ea 7-5:6.65% '97, 6.85% '99, 7.05% '00. [34] Int 7-5:7.25%'01,7.5%'02,7.75%'03,8%'04,8.5% aft. [35] Due 10-6-03.

Title-Industry Code & Co. Finances (In Italics) / Exchange ↓ Individual Issue Statistics	Ind / Interest Dates	Fixed Charge Coverage 1992 / S&P Debt Rating	1993 / Date of Last Rating Change	1994 / Prior Rating	Eligible ↓	Year End / Bond Form	Million $ Cash & Equiv. / Redemption Provisions: Regular Price	Curr. Assets / Regular (Begins) Thru	Curr. Liab. / Sinking Fund Price	Balance Sheet Date / Sinking Fund (Begins) Thru	L. Term Debt (Mil $) / Refund/Other Restriction Price	Refund/Other Restriction (Begins) Thru	Capital-ization (Mil $) / Outst'g (Mil $)	Total Debt % Capital / Underwriting Firm	Underwriting Year	Price Range 1995 High	Price Range 1995 Low	Mo. End Price Sale(s) or Bid	Curr. Yield	Yield to Mat.
Atlanta Gas Light (Cont.)																				
M-T Nts 'C' 6.55s 2005	[1]mn	**A–**			X	BE	100	(12-7-03)	....	....	....	....	42.0	F1	'93	100⅞	85⅛	100⅞	6.49	6.43
M-T Nts 'C' 6s 2006	[2]mn	**A–**			X	BE	100	(10-23-03)	....	....	....	....	10.0	M2	'93	96⅞	80⅜	96⅞	6.19	6.40
M-T Nts 'C' 7.05s 2013	[3]mn	**A–**			X	BE	102.35	(12-1-03)	....	....	....	....	16.5	M2	'93	100¾	83⅝	100¾	7.00	6.98
M-T Nts 'C' 7.20s 2013	[4]mn	**A–**			X	BE	102.35	(12-7-03)	....	....	....	....	5.25	S1	'93	102⅜	85	102⅜	7.03	6.97
M-T Nts 'C' 7.20s 2013	[5]mn	**A–**			X	BE	102.35	(12-15-03)	....	....	....	....	20.0	F1	'93	102⅜	85	102⅜	7.03	6.97
M-T Nts 'C' 7s 2014	[6]mn	**A–**			X	BE	102.33	(1-20-04)	....	....	....	....	5.00	M2	'94	100¼	83⅛	100¼	6.98	6.97
M-T Nts 'C' 7s 2015	[7]mn	**A–**			X	BE	100	(1-27-07)	....	....	....	....	11.3	M2	'94	100½	82⅞	100½	6.97	6.95
M-T Nts 'C' 7s 2019	[8]mn	**A–**			X	BE	103.50	(1-18-19)	....	....	....	....	5.00	M2	'94	99¾	81⅜	99¾	7.02	7.02
M-T Nts 'C' 7.10s 2019	[8]mn	**A–**			X	BE	103.55	(1-20-04)	....	....	....	....	38.5	F1	'94	101	82⅜	101	7.03	7.01
M-T Nts 'C' 6.85s 2023	[9]mn	**A–**			X	BE	103.425	(10-26-03)	....	....	....	....	2.00	M2	'93	97⅝	78⅞	97⅝	7.02	7.04
Atlantic City Electric[10]	***72a***	***3.35***		***3.51***	***3.27***	***Dc***	***66.50***	***321.0***	***188.0***	***9-30-95***	***894.0***		***1916***	***48.0***						
1st 5⅛s '96	Fa	**A–**	10/93	A	X	R	100	....	100	....	....	....	9.98	H1	'66	100	97½	100	5.13	5.02
1st 7½s 2002	Ao	**A–**	10/93	A	X	R	101.80	3-31-96	Z100.54	3-31-96	....	....	20.0	H1	'72	102¾	94½	102¾	7.30	6.95
1st 7¾s 2003	Jd	**A–**	10/93	A	X	R	102.06	5-31-96	Z100.42	5-31-96	....	....	30.0	B6	'73	102⅝	95¼	102⅝	7.55	7.28
1st 7s 2023	mS	**A–**	10/93	A	X	R	102.88	(9-1-03)	Z100	(9-1-03)	....	....	75.0	K2	'93	97½	80⅞	97½	7.18	7.21
1st 6⅝s 2013	fA	**A–**	10/93	A	X	R	NC	....	....	....	....	....	75.0	G1	'93	97½	80½	97½	6.79	6.87
1st 7s 2028	fA	**A–**	10/93	A	X	R	105.24	7-31-96	Z100	....	®102.91	7-31-03	75.0	B5	'93	97½	81⅝	97½	7.18	7.20
Sec M-T Nts 'A' 7.52s '99	[11]mn	**A–**	10/93	A	X	BE	NC	....	....	....	....	....	26.0	F1	'92	105⅛	96⅝	105⅛	7.15	5.83
Sec M-T Nts 'A' 7.98s 2004	[12]mn	**A–**	10/93	A	X	BE	100	(5-19-02)	....	....	....	....	19.5	F1	'92	110½	95¾	110½	7.22	6.34
Sec M-T Nts 'A' 7.97s 2004	[13]mn	**A–**	10/93	A	X	BE	100	(5-19-02)	....	....	....	....	10.5	F1	'92	110½	95¾	110½	7.21	6.34
Sec M-T Nts 'B' 6.37s '98	jj	**A–**	10/93	A	X	BE	NC	....	....	....	....	....	46.0	F1	'93	101⅜	94¾	101⅜	6.28	5.66
Sec M-T Nts 'B' 6.84s 2000	[14]jj	**A–**	10/93	A	X	BE	NC	....	....	....	....	....	18.0	F1	'93	103¼	93¼	103¼	6.62	5.93
Sec M-T Nts 'B' 6.82s 2000	[14]jj	**A–**	10/93	A	X	BE	NC	....	....	....	....	....	13.0	F1	'93	103⅛	93¼	103⅛	6.61	5.94
Sec M-T Nts 'B' 6.81s 2000	[14]jj	**A–**	10/93	A	X	BE	NC	....	....	....	....	....	5.00	F1	'93	103⅛	93⅛	103⅛	6.60	5.93
Sec M-T Nts 'B' 6.81s 2000	[15]jj	**A–**	10/93	A	X	BE	NC	....	....	....	....	....	5.00	F1	'93	103⅛	93⅛	103⅛	6.60	5.93
Sec M-T Nts 'B' 7.16s 2003	[16]jj	**A–**	10/93	A	X	BE	NC	....	....	....	....	....	10.0	F1	'93	105¼	91¾	105¼	6.80	6.23
Sec M-T Nts 'B' 7.19s 2003	[16]jj	**A–**	10/93	A	X	BE	NC	....	....	....	....	....	8.00	F1	'93	105⅜	91⅞	105⅜	6.82	6.24
Sec M-T Nts 'B' 7⅛s 2004	[17]jj	**A–**	10/93	A	X	BE	100	(2-2-03)	....	....	....	....	28.0	F1	'93	105	90⅝	105	6.79	6.32
Sec M-T Nts 'B' 6.67s 2005	[18]jj	**A–**	10/93	A	X	BE	NC	....	....	....	....	....	10.0	F1	'93	102⅛	86¾	102⅛	6.53	6.36
Sec M-T Nts 'B' 6.40s 2005	[19]jj	**A–**	10/93	A	X	BE	NC	....	....	....	....	....	11.0	F1	'93	100⅛	84½	100⅛	6.39	6.38
Sec M-T Nts 'B' 6.78s 2008	[20]jj	**A–**	10/93	A	X	BE	NC	....	....	....	....	....	10.0	F1	'93	103	85	103	6.58	6.42
Sec M-T Nts 'B' 6¾s 2008	[21]jj	**A–**	10/93	A	X	BE	NC	....	....	....	....	....	10.0	F1	'93	102¾	84¾	102¾	6.57	6.42
Sec M-T Nts 'B' 6¾s 2008	[21]jj	**A–**	10/93	A	X	BE	NC	....	....	....	....	....	11.0	F1	'93	102¾	84¾	102¾	6.57	6.42
SF Deb 5¼s '96	Fa	**BBB+**	10/93	A–	X	R	100	1-31-96	Z100	....	....	....	2.27	E1	'66	100	97½	100	5.25	5.14
SF Deb 7¼s '98	Mn	**BBB+**	10/93	A–	X	R	100.61	4-30-96	Z100.35	4-30-96	....	....	2.62	E1	'68	100¾	96¾	100¾	7.20	6.89
Atlantic Richfield	***49b***	***2.73***		***2.55***	***2.36***	***Dc***	***2789***	***5387***	***3574***	***9-30-95***	***6724***		***15188***	***52.9***						
•SF Deb 5⅝s '97	Mn15	**A**	4/94	A+	X	R	100	....	100	....	....	....	14.0	S5	'67	99¾	95	99⅛	5.67	6.29
•Deb 10⅞s 2005	jJ15	**A**	4/94	A+	X	R	NC	....	....	....	....	....	500	S1	'85	131⅞	116⅞	131	8.30	6.47
•Deb 9⅛s 2011	Ms	**A**	4/94	A+	X	R	NC	....	....	....	....	....	300	S1	'86	123	104	121½	7.51	6.83
Deb 8½s 2012	Ao	**A**	4/94	A+	X	BE	NC	....	....	....	....	....	194	G1	'92	117⅞	98⅝	117⅞	7.21	6.68
•Deb 9⅞s 2016	Ms	**A**	4/94	A+	X	R	NC	....	....	....	....	....	450	S1	'86	129	114¼	127⅞	7.72	7.23
Deb 9s 2021	Ao	**A**	4/94	A+	X	BE	NC	....	....	....	....	....	286	S1	'91	127¼	102¾	127¼	7.07	6.74
Deb 8¼s 2022	Fa	**A**	4/94	A+	X	BE	NC	....	....	....	....	....	250	S1	'92	118⅜	95⅛	118⅜	6.97	6.74
Deb 9s 2031	Mn	**A**	4/94	A+	X	BE	NC	....	....	....	....	....	136	S1	'91	130½	101⅝	130½	6.90	6.73
Deb 9⅛s 2031	fA	**A**	4/94	A+	X	BE	NC	....	....	....	....	....	350	S1	'91	131⅞	103	131⅞	6.92	6.75
Deb 8¾s 2032	Ms	**A**	4/94	A+	X	BE	NC	....	....	....	....	....	203	G1	'92	127⅜	99⅛	127⅜	6.87	6.72

Uniform Footnote Explanations-See Page 260. Other: [1] Due 12-7-05. [2] Due 10-23-06. [3] Due 12-2-13. [4] Due 12-9-13. [5] Due 12-13-13. [6] Due 1-21-14. [7] Due 1-27-15. [8] Due 1-18-19. [9] Due 10-26-23. [10] Subsid of Atlantic Energy. [11] Due 5-19-99. [12] Due 5-19-04. [13] Due 5-15-04. [14] Due 1-26-00. [15] Due 1-27-00. [16] Due 1-27-03. [17] Due 2-2-04. [18] Due 3-23-05. [19] Due 7-18-05. [20] Due 3-26-08. [21] Due 5-12-08.

Title-Industry Code & Co. Finances (In Italics) / Individual Issue Statistics (Exchange)	Ind / Interest Dates	1992 / S&P Debt Rating	1993 / Date of Last Rating Change	1994 / Prior Rating	Eligible	Year End / Bond Form	Cash & Equiv. / Regular Price	Curr. Assets / Regular (Begins) Thru	Curr. Liab. / Sinking Fund Price	Balance Sheet Date / Sinking Fund (Begins) Thru	L. Term Debt (Mil $) / Refund/Other Restriction Price	Refund/Other Restriction (Begins) Thru	Capitalization (Mil $) / Outst'g (Mil $)	Total Debt % Capital / Underwriting Firm	Underwriting Year	Price Range 1995 High	Price Range 1995 Low	Mo. End Price Sale(s) or Bid	Curr. Yield	Yield to Mat.
[1]Atlantis Group	***52***	*1.27*	*1.53*	*1.70*		*Dc*	*3.69*	*60.20*	*28.30*	*9-30-95*	*120.0*		*161.0*	*75.8*						
Sr Nts[2] 11s 2003	Fa15	B	5/95	B–	Y	R	104.125	(2-15-98)	100	(2-15-01)	....	....	100	B5	'93	103	87½	87½	12.57	13.80
Auburn Hills Trust	***25c***	***Gtd by Chrysler Corp,see***																		
•[3]Gtd[4]Exch[5]Ctfs 12s 2020	[6]Mn	A–	1/95	BBB+	X	BE	NC	....	....	....	....	....	1100	S1	'90	151½	129	149⅝	....	Flat
Aurora Electronics[7]	***23h***	*1.35*	*3.06*	*0.07*		*Sp*	*0.01*	*24.70*	*22.70*	*7-2-95*	*44.90*		*61.90*	*81.4*						
◆Sr Sub Nts 'A' 9¼s '96	mN15	NR				R	100	....	....	....	....	....	3.37	Exch.	'89	95	83¾	88½	10.45	24.53
◆Sr Sub Nts 'B' 9¼s '96	mN15	NR				R	100	....	....	....	....	....	[8]5.76	Exch.	'89	95	83¾	88½	10.45	24.53
Avalon Properties	***57***	*0.74*	*[9]0.76*	*5.93*		*Dc*				*9-30-95*	*310.0*		*729.0*	*42.5*						
Nts 7⅜s 2002	mS15	BBB–			X	BE	[10]Z100	(9-15-00)	....	....	....	....	100	M5	'95	102½	99⅛	102½	7.20	6.90
Avatar Hldgs	***38***	*0.74*	*2.16*	*d0.27*		*Dc*				*9-30-95*	*162.0*		*325.0*	*49.8*						
Sr Deb 9s 2000	aO	NR				R	100	....	....	....	....	....	26.8	Exch.	'92	112	95	111⅞	8.04	6.08
Avco Financial Svcs[11]	***25a***	*1.55*	*1.70*	*1.77*		*Dc*	*12.90*			*9-30-95*	*6252*		*7257*	*86.2*						
Sr Nts 8.85s '96	Fa	A			X	R	NC	....	....	....	....	....	150	M6	'91	101⅝	100¼	100¼	8.83	5.81
Sr Nts 7½s '96	mN15	A			X	R	NC	....	....	....	....	....	200	S1	'91	102	98⅞	101¾	7.37	5.42
Sr Nts 5⅞s '97	aO15	A			X	R	NC	....	....	....	....	....	200	M2	'92	100⅝	94¼	100⅝	5.84	5.50
Sr Nts 5½s '98	Mn	A			X	R	NC	....	....	....	....	....	200	S1	'93	99⅞	92	99⅞	5.51	5.55
Sr Nts 7¼s '99	jJ15	A			X	R	NC	....	....	....	....	....	200	M2	'94	104¾	95½	104¾	6.92	5.75
Sr Nts 8½s '99	aO15	A			X	R	NC	....	....	....	....	....	100	M6	'89	108¼	100	108¼	7.85	6.03
Sr Nts 5½s 2000	Ao	A			X	R	NC	....	....	....	....	....	200	M6	'93	98¾	87⅝	98¾	5.57	5.83
Sr Nts 6.35s 2000	mS15	A			X	R	NC	....	....	....	....	....	200	M6	'95	101⅜	99½	101⅜	6.26	6.01
Sr Nts 7⅜s 2001	fA15	A			X	R	NC	....	....	....	....	....	200	S1	'94	106¾	94½	106¾	6.91	5.94
Sr Nts 6s 2002	fA15	A			X	R	NC	....	....	....	....	....	200	M2	'95	99⅝	98¾	99½	6.03	6.09
Zero Cpn M-T Nts 'E' '98	jD16	A			X	BE	NC	....	....	....	....	....	30.0	C4	'93	102⅝	83⅝	84½	....	5.76
F/R[12]M-T Nts 'E' 6.0875s '99	QJan11	A			X	BE	NC	....	....	....	....	....	50.0	L3	'94	100⅛	99½	100	6.09	....
F/R[13]M-T Nts 'E' 6.1125s '99	QJan14	A			X	BE	NC	....	....	....	....	....	50.0	M2	'94	100	98	98½	6.21	....
M-T Nts 'E' 5.40s '99	Jj15	A			X	BE	NC	....	....	....	....	....	50.0	M5	'94	99	89¾	99	5.45	5.76
Avery Dennison	***48b***	*3.84*	*3.85*	*4.87*		*Dc*	*3.90*	*763.0*	*549.0*	*9-30-95*	*438.0*		*1291*	*39.3*						
M-T Nts 'B'[14] 7.67s 2004	[15]jJ15	A			X	BE	NC	....	....	....	....	....	10.0	G1	'94	109⅝	94⅛	109⅝	7.00	6.18
M-T Nts 'B'[14] 7.67s 2004	[15]jJ15	A			X	BE	NC	....	....	....	....	....	10.0	G1	'94	109⅝	94⅛	109⅝	7.00	6.18
M-T Nts 'B'[14] 7.63s 2004	[16]jJ15	A			X	BE	NC	....	....	....	....	....	8.50	G1	'94	109⅜	93⅞	109⅜	6.98	6.19
M-T Nts 'B'[14] 7.57s 2004	[17]jJ15	A			X	BE	NC	....	....	....	....	....	5.00	G1	'94	109	93½	109	6.94	6.19
Avnet, Inc	***23h***	*△13.72*	*△6.04*	*△11.50*		*Je*	*58.90*	*1687*	*530.0*	*9-29-95*	*438.0*		*1822*	*24.0*						
Nts 6⅞s 2004	Ms15	A			X	R	NC	....	....	....	....	....	100	D4	'94	103⅞	90¼	103⅞	6.62	6.26
Aztar Corp[18]	***40i***	*1.90*	*1.36*	*1.39*		*Dc*	*48.90*	*92.00*	*95.70*	*9-28-95*	*455.0*		*828.0*	*55.1*						
Sr[19]Sub Nts[20] 11s 2002	aO	B			Y	R	103.143	(10-1-97)	....	....	[21]Z106.286	9-30-96	200	S1	'92	101⅛	91	99¾	11.03	11.05
Sr[20]Sub Nts[19] 13¾s 2004	aO	B			Y	R	106.875	(10-1-99)	....	....	....	....	180	S1	'94	113⅞	101½	110¾	12.42	11.74
Aztar Mortgage Funding	***25***	***Gtd by Aztar Corp,see***																		
[20]1st Mtg[19]Nts[22] 13½s '96	mS15	BB–			Y	R	100	....	100	....	....	....	170	S1	'89	106⅛	100	A100	13.50	13.42
Baker Hughes[23]	***49e***	*△3.20*	*△3.29*	*△4.69*		*Sp*	*6.82*	*1565*	*580.0*	*9-30-95*	*798.0*		*2315*	*34.6*						
Nts 7⅝s '99	Fa15	A–			X	R	NC	....	....	....	....	....	150	F1	'92	105⅜	97⅞	105⅜	7.24	5.72
Nts 8s 2004	Mn15	A–			X	R	NC	....	....	....	....	....	100	L3	'92	111⅛	96½	111⅛	7.20	6.27
Baker Int'l	***49e***	***Now Baker Hughes, see***																		
Deb 6s 2002	Ms15	A–	3/87	A	X	R	100	....	....	....	....	....	[8]225	G1	'82	99⅜	87⅛	99⅜	6.04	6.12
[24]Bally's Grand,Inc	***40i***	*0.88*	*0.83*	*1.06*		*Dc*	*158.0*	*210.0*	*159.0*	*6-30-95*	*1289*		*1643*	*78.9*						
1st Mtg Nts[25]'B' 10⅜s 2003	jD15	BB	8/95	B+	Y	R	105.19	(12-15-98)	....	....	[26]109.375	12-15-96	315	M2	'93	101½	87	101½	10.22	10.09
Bally's Health&Tennis[27]	***40***	*0.76*	*0.02*	*d0.97*		*Dc*	*59.60*	*235.0*	*219.0*	*6-30-95*	*369.0*		*600.0*	*62.0*						
Sr Sub[28]Nts[25] 13s 2003	Jj15	B+	2/94	B	Y	R	106.50	(1-15-98)	....	....	....	....	200	M2	'93	90	74	83	15.66	17.26

Uniform Footnote Explanations-See Page 260. Other: [1] Now Atlantis Plastics. [2] (HRO)On Chge of Ctrl or Fundamental Chge at 101. [3] Co may exch in whole for Deb'20. [4] Gtd by Chrysler Corp. [5] Int decr fr 14.875 on 10-5-93. [6] Int(11.125%-16.875%)may adj for rat'g chge. [7] Was BSN Corp. [8] Incl disc. [9] 11 mo Nov'93. [10] Plus Make-Whole Amt. [11] Subsid of Avco Corp(Textron). [12] Int to 1-11-96,adj qtrly(3 Mo LIBOR&0.15%). [13] Int to 1-14-96,adj qtrly aft. [14] Issued in min denom $100T. [15] Due 5-25-04. [16] Due 6-9-04. [17] Due 6-10-04. [18] See Aztar Mtg Funding. [19] (HRO)On Chge of Ctrl at 100. [20] State gaming laws may req hldr's sale/Co red. [21] In whole,on Chge of Ctrl. [22] Gtd by Aztar Corp. [23] See Baker Int'l. [24] Subsid & data of Bally Entertainment. [25] (HRO)On Chge of Ctrl at 101. [26] Max $105M red w/proceeds of Pub Eq Off'g. [27] Subsid of Bally Mfg. [28] Co must offer repurch at 100 for certain events.

Title-Industry Code & Co. Finances (In Italics) / Exchange – Individual Issue Statistics	Ind / Interest Dates	Fixed Charge Coverage 1992 / S&P Debt Rating	1993 / Date of Last Rating Change	Prior Rating	1994 / Eligible	Year End / Bond Form	Million $ Cash & Equiv. / Redemption Provisions Regular Price	Curr. Assets / Regular (Begins) Thru	Curr. Liab. / Sinking Fund Price	Balance Sheet Date / Sinking Fund (Begins) Thru	L. Term Debt (Mil $) / Refund/Other Restriction Price	Refund/Other Restriction (Begins) Thru	Capital-ization (Mil $) / Outst'g (Mil $)	Total Debt % Capital / Underwriting Firm	Underwriting Year	Price Range 1995 High	Price Range 1995 Low	Mo. End Price Sale(s) or Bid	Curr. Yield	Yield to Mat.
[1]Bally's Park Pl Fnd'g	***25***	***1.31***	***1.91***		***2.09***	***Dc***	***15.60***	***38.80***	***37.00***	***9-30-95***	***428.0***		***450.0***	***95.1***						
1st[2]Mtg Nts[3] 9¼s 2004	Ms15	**BB**			Y	R	104.50	(3-15-99)	....	....	[4]Z109.25	3-14-97	425	M2	'94	101	85½	101	9.16	9.07
Baltimore Gas & Elec	***75***	***2.55***	***2.90***		***2.96***	***Dc***	***28.10***	***725.0***	***807.0***	***9-30-95***	***2509***		***6257***	***46.8***						
1st Ref 5⅛s '96	Ao15	**A+**	4/90	AA−	X	R	100	....	100	....	....	....	26.6	W5	'66	99⅞	96¾	99⅞	5.13	5.50
1st Ref 6⅛s '97	fA	**A+**	4/90	AA−	X	R	100.28	7-31-96	100.24	7-31-96	....	....	25.0	H1	'67	100¼	95½	100¼	6.11	5.95
1st Ref[5]F/R 6.0875s '99	QApr15	**A+**			X	BE	100	(4-15-96)	100	(8-1-96)	....	....	125	K1	'94	100⅛	99	99¾	6.10	....
1st Ref 8.40s '99	aO15	**A+**	4/90	AA−	X	R	NC	....	....	....	....	....	100	S4	'89	108½	99⅞	108½	7.74	5.86
1st Ref 5½s 2000	jJ15	**A+**			X	R	NC	....	....	....	....	....	125	C4	'93	98¾	87¼	98¾	5.57	5.82
1st Ref 8⅜s 2001	fA15	**A+**			X	R	NC	....	....	....	....	....	125	S1	'91	110⅞	99½	110⅞	7.55	6.06
1st Ref 7⅛s 2002	Jj	**A+**	4/90	AA−	X	R	101.23	12-31-96	100	....	....	....	50.0	F1	'72	102⅛	92⅞	101½	7.02	6.82
1st Ref 7¼s 2002	jJ	**A+**			X	R	NC	....	....	....	....	....	125	S1	'92	103⅞	93⅛	103⅞	6.98	6.51
1st Ref 6½s 2003	Fa15	**A+**			X	R	NC	....	....	....	....	....	125	G1	'93	102⅝	88¾	102⅝	6.33	6.04
1st Ref 6⅛s 2003	jJ	**A+**			X	BE	NC	....	....	....	....	....	125	C4	'93	100⅜	86½	100⅜	6.10	6.06
1st Ref 5½s 2004	aO15	**A+**			X	R	NC	....	....	....	....	....	125	K2	'93	95¾	81¾	95¾	5.74	6.16
1st Ref 7½s 2007	Jj15	**A+**			X	R	NC	....	....	....	....	....	125	L3	'92	109⅞	92½	109⅞	6.83	6.25
1st Ref 6⅝s 2008	Ms15	**A+**			X	R	NC	....	....	....	....	....	125	M6	'93	103¾	84⅞	103¾	6.39	6.18
1st Ref 7½s 2023	Ms	**A+**			X	R	104.98	(3-1-98)	100	(8-1-98)	....	....	125	F1	'93	103¼	87	103¼	7.26	7.22
1st Ref 7½s 2023	Ao15	**A+**			X	R	105.30	(4-15-98)	100	(7-15-98)	....	....	100	L3	'93	102¾	86⅞	102¾	7.30	7.27
Banc One Corp[6]	***10***	***6.11***	***7.03***		***3.64***	***Dc***				***9-30-95***	***2677***		***10679***	***25.1***						
Sub Deb 7¾s 2025	jJ15	**A+**			X	BE	NC	....	....	....	....	....	300	S1	'95	111⅛	97⅝	111⅛	6.97	6.87
Sub Nts 7¼s 2002	fA	**A+**			X	BE	NC	....	....	....	....	....	350	F1	'92	106⅜	92¾	106⅜	6.82	6.06
Sub Nts 8.74s 2003	mS15	**A+**			X	R	NC	....	....	....	....	....	170	S1	'91	115½	100⅝	115½	7.57	6.18
Sub Nts 7s 2005	jJ15	**A+**			X	BE	NC	....	....	....	....	....	300	S1	'95	105½	97⅝	105½	6.64	6.23
Sub Nts 9⅞s 2009	Ms	**A+**	3/91	AA−	X	R	NC	....	....	....	....	....	200	M2	'89	129⅝	108⅛	129⅝	7.62	6.49
Sub Nts 10s 2010	fA15	**A+**	3/91	AA−	X	R	NC	....	....	....	....	....	200	S1	'90	132½	109⅛	132½	7.55	6.52
[7]Bancorp of Mississippi	***10***	***7.06***	***10.02***		***8.34***	***Dc***				***9-30-95***	***45.60***		***295.0***	***15.5***						
Sub Cap Deb[8] 9s '99	QNov	**BBB−**			X	R	101.50	10-31-96	....	....	....	....	25.0	B7	'89	103½	95	103½	8.70	7.92
Bank of Boston[3]	***10***	***1.32***	***1.43***		***1.38***	***Dc***				***6-30-95***	***2110***		***5575***	***37.8***						
F/R[9]Nts 6.0825s '96	QJun20	**BBB+**			X	BE	NC	....	....	....	....	....	100	M2	'94	100⅛	97	100⅛	6.07	....
Sub[10]Cap Nts 9½s '97	fA15	**BBB**	11/93	BBB−	X	R	NC	....	....	....	Z100	....	129	G1	'87	106⅛	102⅝	104⅞	9.06	6.29
Sub Nts 6⅞s 2003	jJ15	**BBB**	11/93	BBB−	X	BE	NC	....	....	....	....	....	100	M2	'93	103½	88⅛	103½	6.64	6.28
Sub Nts 6⅝s 2004	Fa	**BBB**			X	BE	NC	....	....	....	....	....	300	M2	'93	101⅝	85½	101⅝	6.52	6.36
Sub Nts 6⅝s 2005	jD	**BBB**			X	BE	NC	....	....	....	....	....	350	M2	'93	101⅞	84⅛	101⅞	6.50	6.37
Bank of New York[11]	***10***	***2.79***	***3.90***		***3.97***	***Dc***				***9-30-95***	***1836***		***6936***	***26.5***						
Sub Nts 7⅝s 2002	jJ15	**A−**	6/93	BBB+	X	BE	NC	....	....	....	....	....	350	L3	'92	108⅛	94⅛	108⅛	7.05	6.10
Sub Nts 7⅞s 2002	mN15	**A−**	6/93	BBB+	X	BE	NC	....	....	....	....	....	250	S1	'92	109¾	95⅝	109¾	7.18	6.12
Sub Nts 6⅝s 2003	Jd15	**A−**			X	BE	NC	....	....	....	....	....	300	D6	'93	102¾	87⅝	102¾	6.45	6.16
Sub Nts 6½s 2003	jD	**A−**			X	BE	NC	....	....	....	....	....	250	G1	'93	101⅞	86⅜	101⅞	6.38	6.20
Sub Nts 8½s 2004	jD15	**A−**			X	BE	NC	....	....	....	....	....	300	U1	'94	115½	99⅛	115½	7.36	6.22
Bank South Corp	***10***	***2.52***	***5.25***		***2.84***	***Dc***				***9-30-95***	***189.0***		***864.0***	***21.9***						
Sub Nts 10.20s '99	Jd	**BB+**	11/93	BB−	Y	R	NC	....	....	....	....	....	13.0	P4	'87	107	94	107	9.53	7.82
Bank of Virginia	***10***	***Now Signet Banking, see***																		
F/R[12]Sub Nts 6s '97	QMay15	**BB+**	1/93	BB−	Y	R	100	....	....	....	....	....	50.0	G1	'85	99⅞	98½	99⅞	6.01	....
BankAmerica Corp[13]	***10***	***3.38***	***3.74***		***3.47***	***Dc***				***9-30-95***	***15882***		***35743***	***44.4***						
Nts 7½s '97	Ms15	**A+**	10/95	A	X	BE	NC	....	....	....	....	....	350	L3	'92	102⅜	98⅝	102⅜	7.33	5.44
Nts 6s '97	jJ15	**A+**	10/95	A	X	BE	NC	....	....	....	....	....	350	F1	'92	100¾	95	100¾	5.96	5.48
Sr M-T Nts 'G'[14] 4.86s '96	[15]ao15	**A+**	10/95	A	X	BE	NC	....	....	....	....	....	5.00	C5	'93	99⅞	96¾	99⅞	4.87	5.46
Sr M-T Nts 'G'[14] 4.55s '96	[16]ao15	**A+**	10/95	A	X	BE	NC	....	....	....	....	....	5.00	C5	'93	99¾	96⅜	99¾	4.56	5.74

Uniform Footnote Explanations-See Page 260. Other: [1] Gtd by & data of Bally's Park Place. [2] Gtd by Bally's Park Place, Inc. [3] (HRO)On Chge of Ctrl at 101. [4] Max $142M red w/proceeds Pub Equity Off'g. [5] Int to 1-15-96,adj qtrly aft(3 Mo LIBOR&0.15). [6] See Liberty Nat'l Bancorp,Valley Nat'l Corp. [7] Now BancorpSouth. [8] Death redemption benefit,ltd as defined. [9] Int thru 12-20-95,adj qtrly aft(3 Mo LIBOR&0.27%). [10] Co may exch for Cap Sec when due. [11] See Irving Bank Corp. [12] Int to 2-15-96,adj qtrly aft. [13] See Security Pacific. [14] Issued in min denom $100T. [15] Due 3-5-96. [16] Due 3-11-96.

Title-Industry Code & Co. Finances (In Italics)	Ind	Fixed Charge Coverage 1992	1993	1994	Year End	Million $ Cash & Equiv.	Curr. Assets	Curr. Liab.	Balance Sheet Date	L. Term Debt (Mil $)	Capital-ization (Mil $)	Total Debt % Capital

Exchange ↓ Individual Issue Statistics	Interest Dates	S&P Debt Rating	Date of Last Rating Change	Prior Rating	Eligible ↓	Bond Form	Redemption Provisions: Regular Price	Regular (Begins) Thru	Sinking Fund Price	Sinking Fund (Begins) Thru	Refund/Other Restriction Price	Refund/Other Restriction (Begins) Thru	Outst'g (Mil $)	Underwriting Firm	Underwriting Year	Price Range 1995 High	Low	Mo. End Price Sale(s) or Bid	Curr. Yield	Yield to Mat.
BankAmerica Corp *(Cont.)*																				
Sr M-T Nts 'G'[1] 4.95s '96	[2]ao15	**A+**	10/95	A	X	BE	NC	....	....	....	....	....	25.0	S1	'93	99⅞	96¾	99⅞	4.96	5.45
Sr M-T Nts 'G'[1] 5¾s '98	[3]ao15	**A+**	10/95	A	X	BE	NC	....	....	....	....	....	25.0	S1	'93	100⅛	92⅜	100⅛	5.74	5.68
Sr M-T Nts 'H' 5s '96	Jd	**A+**	10/95	A	X	BE	NC	....	....	....	....	....	100	D6	'93	99¾	96⅛	99¾	5.01	5.58
Sr M-T Nts 'H'[1] 4⅞s '96	[4]ao15	**A+**	10/95	A	X	BE	NC	....	....	....	....	....	2.00	S1	'93	99¾	96	99¾	4.89	5.45
F/R[5]Sr M-T Nts 'H'[1] 6.0125s '96	[6]	**A+**	10/95	A	X	BE	NC	....	....	....	....	....	20.0		'93	100	99	100	6.01	....
F/R[5]Sr M-T Nts 'H'[1] 5.8625s '97	[7]	**A+**	10/95	A	X	BE	*100	....	....	....	....	....	50.0	M2	'94	100	99	100	5.86	....
F/R[5]Sr M-T Nts 'H'[1] 5.8925s '97	[7]	**A+**	10/95	A	X	BE	NC	....	....	....	....	....	50.0		'94	100	99	99⅞	5.90	....
F/R[5]Sr M-T Nts 'H'[1] 5.8925s '97	[8]	**A+**	10/95	A	X	BE	*100	....	....	....	....	....	5.70	L3	'94	100	99	100	5.89	....
F/R[5]Sr M-T Nts 'H'[1] 5.8925s '97	[8]	**A+**	10/95	A	X	BE	NC	....	....	....	....	....	50.0	S5	'94	100	99	100	5.89	....
F/R[9]Sr M-T Nts 'H'[1] '97	[10]	**A+**	10/95	A	X	BE	*100	....	....	....	....	....	75.0	M2	'94	100	99	100	....	....
F/R[9]Sr M-T Nts 'H'[1] '97	[11]	**A+**	10/95	A	X	BE	*100	....	....	....	....	....	25.0	S1	'94	100	99	100	....	....
F/R[9]Sr M-T Nts 'H'[1] '97	[12]	**A+**	10/95	A	X	BE	*100	....	....	....	....	....	50.0	S1	'94	100	99	100	....	....
F/R[5]Sr M-T Nts 'H'[1] 6.0625s '97	[13]	**A+**	10/95	A	X	BE	NC	....	....	....	....	....	20.0		'93	100	99	100	6.06	....
F/R[5]Sr M-T Nts 'H'[1] 6.0925s '98	[14]	**A+**	10/95	A	X	BE	*100	....	....	....	....	....	50.0	C5	'93	100	98½	100	6.09	....
F/R[5]Sr M-T Nts 'H'[1] 6.0625s '98	[15]	**A+**	10/95	A	X	BE	*100	(9-18-96)	....	....	....	....	50.0	L3	'93	100	98½	100	6.06	....
F/R[5]Sr M-T Nts 'H'[1] 6.0625s '98	[16]	**A+**	10/95	A	X	BE	*100	(9-18-96)	....	....	....	....	40.0	S1	'93	100¼	98½	100¼	6.05	....
Sr M-T Nts 'H'[1] 5.80s '98	mS15	**A+**	10/95	A	X	BE	[17]100	(9-16-96)	....	....	....	....	50.0	L3	'93	100	98½	100	5.80	5.80
F/R[5]Sr M-T Nts 'H'[1] 6.0125s '98	[18]	**A+**	10/95	A	X	BE	*100	(12-18-96)	....	....	....	....	52.0	M2	'93	100	98½	100	6.01	....
F/R[9]Sr M-T Nts 'I' '97	[19]	**A+**	10/95	A	X	BE	NC	....	....	....	....	....	10.0	L3	'94	100	99	100	....	....
F/R[9]Sr M-T Nts 'I' '97	[19]	**A+**	10/95	A	X	BE	*100	(3-20-96)	....	....	....	....	50.0	C5	'94	100	99	100	....	....
F/R[20]Sr M-T Nts 'I' '97	[19]	**A+**	10/95	A	X	BE	*100	(3-20-96)	....	....	....	....	50.0	M2	'94	100	99	99⅞	....	....
F/R[21]Sr M-T Nts 'I' 5.9125s '97	[22]	**A+**	10/95	A	X	BE	*100	(3-20-96)	....	....	....	....	25.0		'94	100	99	100	5.91	....
F/R[21]Sr M-T Nts 'I' 6.0625s '97	QSep19	**A+**	10/95	A	X	BE	NC	....	....	....	....	....	25.0		'94	100	99	99⅞	6.07	....
Sr M-T Nts 'I' 7⅛s 2005	Mn12	**A+**	10/95	A	X	BE	NC	....	....	....	....	....	150	M2	'95	103	98¼	99	7.20	7.27
Sub Nts 9¾s 2000	jJ	**A**	10/95	A–	X	R	NC	....	....	....	....	....	100	S1	'90	115⅛	105⅛	115⅛	8.47	5.88
Sub Nts 9.70s 2000	fA	**A**	10/95	A–	X	R	NC	....	....	....	....	....	125	M2	'90	115⅛	104	115⅛	8.43	5.89
Sub Nts 9⅝s 2001	Fa13	**A**	10/95	A–	X	R	NC	....	....	....	....	....	125	S1	'91	116	104½	116	8.30	5.95
Sub Nts 9⅜s 2001	Ms	**A**	10/95	A–	X	BE	NC	....	....	....	....	....	100	L3	'91	114⅞	102½	114⅞	8.16	5.98
Sub Nts 9½s 2001	Ao	**A**	10/95	A–	X	BE	NC	....	....	....	....	....	200	S1	'91	115⅝	103⅞	115⅝	8.22	5.99
Sub Nts 8⅛s 2002	Fa	**A**	10/95	A–	X	BE	NC	....	....	....	....	....	300	F1	'92	110⅛	97⅛	110⅛	7.38	6.11
Sub Nts 8⅜s 2002	Ms15	**A**	10/95	A–	X	BE	NC	....	....	....	....	....	250	S1	'92	111½	97⅞	111½	7.51	6.12
Sub Nts 7¾s 2002	jJ15	**A**	10/95	A–	X	BE	NC	....	....	....	....	....	500	S1	'92	108⅝	94½	108⅝	7.13	6.13
Sub Nts 7.20s 2002	mS15	**A**	10/95	A–	X	BE	NC	....	....	....	....	....	250	G1	'92	105¾	91⅞	105¾	6.81	6.14
Sub Nts 7½s 2002	aO15	**A**	10/95	A–	X	BE	NC	....	....	....	....	....	300	S1	'92	107⅜	93	107⅜	6.98	6.15
Sub Nts 7⅞s 2002	jD	**A**	10/95	A–	X	BE	NC	....	....	....	....	....	250	M2	'92	109⅝	95	109⅝	7.18	6.15
Sub Nts 10s 2003	Fa	**A**	10/95	A–	X	R	NC	....	....	....	....	....	100	M2	'91	121¾	106½	121¾	8.21	6.16
Sub Nts 6.85s 2003	Ms	**A**	10/95	A–	X	BE	NC	....	....	....	....	....	250	G1	'93	103¾	89	103¾	6.60	6.19
Sub Nts 9.20s 2003	Mn15	**A**	10/95	A–	X	BE	NC	....	....	....	....	....	100	G1	'91	117¼	102⅞	117¼	7.85	6.24
Sub Nts 6⅞s 2003	Jd	**A**	10/95	A–	X	BE	NC	....	....	....	....	....	350	M5	'93	103⅞	88⅞	103⅞	6.62	6.21
Sub Nts 7⅝s 2004	Jd15	**A**	10/95	A–	X	BE	NC	....	....	....	....	....	250	S1	'94	108¾	92¾	108¾	7.01	6.28
Sub Nts 8⅛s 2004	fA15	**A**	10/95	A–	X	BE	100	(8-15-99)	....	....	....	....	150	C5	'94	107⅛	94⅛	107⅛	7.58	7.01
Sub Nts 8.95s 2004	mN15	**A**	10/95	A–	X	BE	*100	(11-15-99)	....	....	....	....	200	S5	'94	109⅜	99	109⅜	8.18	7.48
Sub Nts 6¾s 2005	mS15	**A**	10/95	A–	X	BE	NC	....	....	....	....	....	200	S5	'95	103⅜	98⅜	103⅜	6.53	6.28
Sub Nts 7.20s 2006	Ao15	**A**	10/95	A–	X	BE	NC	....	....	....	....	....	300	L3	'94	106½	89	106½	6.76	6.33
F/R[23]Sub Nts 5.925s 2003	QAug15	**A**	10/95	A–	X	BE	NC	....	....	....	....	....	150	F1	'93	99¾	98	99¾	5.94	....
F/R[5]Sub M-T Nts 'H'[1] 6.1125s '98	[24]	**A**	10/95	A–	X	BE	100	....	....	....	....	....	60.0	L3	'93	100⅛	99	100⅛	6.10	....

Uniform Footnote Explanations-See Page 260. Other: [1] Issued in min denom $100T. [2] Due 3-18-96. [3] Due 3-18-98. [4] Due 6-4-96. [5] Int thru 3-20-96,adj qtrly aft. [6] Due 10-7-96:Int pd qtrly,apx ea 20th,Mar,etc. [7] Due 3-31-97:Int pd qtrly,apx ea 20th,Mar,etc. [8] Due 4-7-97:Int pd qtrly,apx ea 20th,Mar,etc. [9] Int adj daily. [10] Due 5-27-97:Int pd qtrly,apx ea 20th, Mar, etc. [11] Due 6-9-97:Int pd qtrly,apx ea 20th, Mar, etc. [12] Due 6-24-97:Int pd qtrly,apx ea 20th, Mar, etc. [13] Due 9-15-97:Int pd qtrly,apx ea 20th,Mar,etc. [14] Due 5-27-98:Int pd qtrly,apx ea 20th,Mar,etc. [15] Due 8-25-98:Int pd qtrly,apx ea 20th,Mar,etc. [16] Due 9-8-98:Int pd qtrly,apx ea 20th,Mar,etc. [17] On 9-16-96. [18] Due 11-23-98:Int pd qtrly,apx ea 20th,Mar,etc. [19] Due 9-2-97:Int pd qtrly,apx ea 20th day,Dec,etc. [20] Int adj weekly. [21] Int to 3-20-96,adj qtrly aft. [22] Due 9-2-97:Int pd qtrly,apx ea 20th day,Dec, etc. [23] Int to 2-15-96,adj qtrly aft. [24] Due 10-1-98:Int pd qtrly,apx ea 20th,Mar,etc.

Title-Industry Code & Co. Finances (In Italics)	Ind	Fixed Charge Coverage 1992	1993	1994		Year End	Million $ Cash & Equiv.	Curr. Assets	Curr. Liab.	Balance Sheet Date	L. Term Debt (Mil $)		Capital-ization (Mil $)	Total Debt % Capital						
Individual Issue Statistics Exchange ↓	Interest Dates	S&P Debt Rating	Date of Last Rating Change	Prior Rating	Eligible ↓	Bond Form	Redemption Provisions: Regular Price	Regular (Begins) Thru	Sinking Fund Price	Sinking Fund (Begins) Thru	Refund/Other Restriction Price	Refund/Other Restriction (Begins) Thru	Outst'g (Mil $)	Underwriting Firm	Underwriting Year	Price Range 1995 High	Price Range 1995 Low	Mo. End Price Sale(s) or Bid	Curr. Yield	Yield to Mat.
BankAmerica Corp *(Cont.)*																				
F/R[1]Sub M-T Nts 'H[2] 6.1425s '98	[3]	**A**	10/95	A–	X	BE	*100	....	....	....	....	....	10.0	M2	'93	100	99	100	6.14	....
Bankers Life Holding	***35a***	***n/a***	***6.34***	***6.44***		***Dc***				***9-30-95***	***273.0***		***1256***	***21.7***						
• Sr Sub[4]Nts 'B' 13s 2002	mN	**BB–**	8/95	BB+	Y	R	106.50	(11-1-97)	....	....	....	....	113	Exch.	'93	115	108½	112	11.61	10.49
Bankers Trust NY	***10***	***1.46***	***1.73***	***1.30***		***Dc***				***9-30-95***	***8354***		***13415***	***62.3***						
Deb 7¼s '96	mN	**A+**	1/95	AA–	X	BE	NC	....	....	....	....	....	298	L3	'91	101¼	98⅜	101¼	7.16	5.69
Nts 4.70s '96	jJ	**A+**	1/95	AA–	X	BE	NC	....	....	....	....	....	300	G1	'93	99½	95⅜	99½	4.72	5.72
Sub Deb 8¼s '96	jJ2	**A**	1/95	A+	X	R	100	(7-1-96)	....	....	....	....	149	S4	'86	102	100¼	101⅛	8.16	5.97
Sub Deb 8s '97	Ms15	**A**	1/95	A+	X	R	NC	....	....	....	....	....	199	S4	'87	102¾	99⅜	102¾	7.79	5.61
Sub Deb 9½s 2000	Jd14	**A**	1/95	A+	X	R	NC	....	....	....	....	....	198	S4	'90	113⅛	102¾	113⅛	8.40	6.09
Sub Deb 9.40s 2001	Ms	**A**	1/95	A+	X	BE	NC	....	....	....	....	....	99.0	M2	'91	114	102⅜	114	8.25	6.19
Sub Deb 9s 2001	fA	**A**	1/95	A+	X	BE	NC	....	....	....	....	....	99.0	L3	'91	113	100⅝	113	7.96	6.21
Sub Deb 7½s 2002	Jj15	**A**	1/95	A+	X	BE	NC	....	....	....	....	....	200	G1	'92	106¼	92⅛	106¼	7.06	6.24
Sub Deb 8⅛s 2002	Mn15	**A**	1/95	A+	X	BE	NC	....	....	....	....	....	150	L3	'92	109¾	95½	109¾	7.40	6.25
Sub Deb 7⅛s 2002	jJ31	**A**	1/95	A+	X	BE	NC	....	....	....	....	....	100	M2	'92	104⅝	89¾	104⅝	6.81	6.26
Sub Deb 7¼s 2003	Jj15	**A**	1/95	A+	X	BE	NC	....	....	....	....	....	100	L3	'93	105⅜	89¾	105⅜	6.88	6.29
Sub Nts 8⅛s 2002	Ao	**A**			X	BE	NC	....	....	....	....	....	150	S5	'95	109⅝	99	109⅝	7.41	6.24
Sub Nts 8¼s 2005	Mn	**A**			X	BE	NC	....	....	....	....	....	150	S5	'95	112¼	100	112¼	7.35	6.48
Sub Nts 6s 2008	aO15	**A**	1/95	A+	X	BE	NC	....	....	....	....	....	150	K2	'93	93⅞	75⅝	93⅞	6.39	6.72
Sub Nts 7½s 2010	Jd15	**A**			X	BE	■100	(6-15-00)	....	....	....	....	75.0	M2	'95	103¾	94½	103¾	7.23	7.08
Sub Nts 7⅛s 2010	[5]Nov22	**A**			X	BE	*■100	(11-22-00)	....	....	....	....	50.0	S5	'95	103¼	98	103¼	6.90	6.77
Sub Nts 7½s 2015	mN15	**A**			X	BE	NC	....	....	....	....	....	150	G1	'95	103¾	99¼	103¾	7.23	7.14
Sub[6]Cap Nts 9.20s '99	jJ15	**A**	1/95	A+	X	R	NC	....	....	....	....	....	100	P4	'87	110⅛	102⅛	110⅛	8.35	5.99
Sub[7]F/R[8]Nts 6s 2003	QMar19	**A**	1/95	A+	X	BE	NC	....	....	....	....	....	100	L3	'93	99	83	97	6.19	....
BanPonce Corp	***10***	***3.12***	***3.16***	***2.68***		***Dc***				***9-30-95***	***★869.0***		***1846***	***40.3***						
Sub Nts 6¾s 2005	jD15	**BBB**			X	BE	NC	....	....	....	....	....	125	C5	'95	100½	99¼	100½	6.72	6.68
BarclaysAmerCorp[9]	***25***	***Subsid of Barclays Bank Int'l***																		
Nts 9⅛s '97	jD	**AA**	6/92	AA+	X	R	NC	....	....	....	....	....	100	G1	'87	106⅝	101⅝	106⅛	8.60	5.71
Sub Nts 7⅞s '98	fA15	**AA**	6/92	AA+	X	R	NC	....	....	....	....	....	100	G1	'86	104⅝	98½	104⅝	7.53	5.94
Barnett Bks, Inc[10]	***10***	***4.92***	***7.91***	***5.62***		***Dc***				***9-30-95***	***1151***		***4479***	***25.7***						
F/R[11]Nts[2] 6.105s '96	QJun	**A–**			X	BE	100	....	....	....	....	....	150	G1	'93	100⅛	99¾	100⅛	6.10	....
• Sub Nts 9⅞s 2001	Jd	**BBB+**			X	BE	NC	....	....	....	....	....	100	F1	'91	112¾	107	111⅜	8.87	7.29
• Sub Nts 10⅞s 2003	Ms15	**BBB+**			X	BE	NC	....	....	....	....	....	55.0	F1	'91	123	112	118¼	9.20	7.54
Sub Nts 6.90s 2005	mS	**BBB+**			X	BE	NC	....	....	....	....	....	150	M6	'95	104¼	99	104¼	6.62	6.30
• Sub Nts 8½s 2007	Jj15	**BBB+**			X	BE	NC	....	....	....	....	....	100	L3	'92	111	97	110⅛	7.72	7.16
• Sub Cap Nts[6] 8½s '99	Ms	**BBB+**	11/90	A–	X	R	NC	....	....	....	....	....	200	F1	'87	106⅞	100¼	106⅜	7.99	6.25
Baroid Corp	***49e***	***Merged into Dresser Indus, see***																		
• Sr[12]Nts 8s 2003	Ao15	**A**	12/94	A–	X	R	NC	....	....	....	....	....	150	S1	'93	106	97	99	8.08	8.18
Baxter Int'l[13]	***43***	***4.66***	***3.97***	***4.27***		***Dc***	***468.0***	***4304***	***2797***	***9-30-95***	***2358***		***6169***	***42.4***						
Deb 8⅞s 2018	Jd15	**A–**	7/91	BBB+	X	R	104.37	(6-15-98)	....	....	....	....	100	F1	'88	110⅜	97¼	109⅞	8.08	7.93
Amortizing[14]Nts 6¼s '97	Ms11	**A–**			X	R	NC	....	....	....	....	....	100	M2	'92	100⅞	96⅛	100⅞	6.20	....
Nts 9¼s '96	mS15	**A–**	7/91	BBB+	X	R	NC	....	....	....	....	....	150	M2	'89	103⅞	101¾	102½	9.02	5.59
Nts 7½s '97	Mn	**A–**			X	R	NC	....	....	....	....	....	200	G1	'92	102¾	98⅜	102½	7.32	5.53
Nts 9¼s '99	jD15	**A–**	7/91	BBB+	X	R	NC	....	....	....	....	....	100	G1	'89	111¾	103⅛	111¾	8.28	5.88
Nts 8⅛s 2001	mN15	**A–**			X	R	NC	....	....	....	....	....	150	M2	'91	110⅛	98⅜	110⅛	7.38	6.05
Nts 7⅝s 2002	mN15	**A–**			X	R	NC	....	....	....	....	....	150	F1	'92	108⅛	93¾	108⅛	7.05	6.16
Nts[15] 9½s 2008	Jd15	**A–**	7/91	BBB+	X	R	NC	....	....	....	....	....	100	G1	'88	129⅝	106⅞	129⅝	7.33	6.08

Uniform Footnote Explanations-See Page 260. Other: [1] Int thru 3-20-96,adj qtrly aft. [2] Issued in min denom $100T. [3] Due 10-1-98:Int pd qtrly,apx ea 20th,Mar,etc. [4] (HRO)On Chge of Ctrl,lesser 101/curr red price. [5] Int pd monthly. [6] Co may exch for Cap Sec when due. [7] Issued in min denom $250T. [8] Int(min 6%)to 3-18-96,adj qtrly aft. [9] Was American Credit. [10] Was Barnett Bks of Fla. [11] Int thru 2-28-96,adj qtrly aft. [12] (HRO)On Chge of Ctrl at 101. [13] Was Baxter Travenol Labs, see. [14] Princ pyts due on int pyt dates to 3-11-97. [15] (HRO)On 6-15-98 at 100.

Title-Industry Code & Co. Finances (In Italics) / Exchange, Individual Issue Statistics	Ind / Interest Dates	Fixed Charge Coverage 1992 / S&P Debt Rating	1993 / Date of Last Rating Change	1994 / Prior Rating	Eligible	Year End / Bond Form	Cash & Equiv. (Million $) / Regular Price	Curr. Assets (Million $) / Regular (Begins) Thru	Curr. Liab. (Million $) / Sinking Fund Price	Balance Sheet Date / Sinking Fund (Begins) Thru	L. Term Debt (Mil $) / Refund/Other Restriction Price	Refund/Other Restriction (Begins) Thru	Capitalization (Mil $) / Outst'g (Mil $)	Total Debt % Capital / Underwriting Firm	Underwriting Year	Price Range 1995 High	Price Range 1995 Low	Mo. End Price Sale(s) or Bid	Curr. Yield	Yield to Mat.
***Baxter Int'l** (Cont.)*																				
Nts 7¼s 2008	Fa15	A–			X	BE	NC	....	....	....	....	....	200	F1	'93	107¼	88⅝	107¼	6.76	6.38
Baxter Travenol Labs	***43***	***Now Baxter Int'l,see***																		
Ext'd[1]Nts[2] 9¾s 2000	[3]Jj	A–	7/91	BBB+	X	R	[4]100	....	....	....	....	....	6.00	F1	'85	112	104	112	8.71	6.63
Bay State Gas	***73b***	***△3.83***	***△3.69***	***△3.16***		***Sp***	***2.76***	***66.90***	***118.0***	***9-30-95***	***199.0***		***456.0***	***50.7***						
SF Nts[5] 7.95s '97	Jd15	A	6/85	A–	X	R	100.34	5-14-96	100	....	....	....	3.44	M2	'72	100⅞	98⅞	100½	7.91	7.58
M-T Nts[6] 6s 2000	[7]fa	A			X	BE	NC	....	....	....	....	....	10.0	S5	'93	99¾	89⅛	99¾	6.02	6.06
M-T Nts[6] 6s 2001	[8]fa	A			X	BE	NC	....	....	....	....	....	5.00	S5	'93	99½	88⅛	99½	6.03	6.11
M-T Nts[6] 7.42s 2001	[9]fa	A			X	BE	NC	....	....	....	....	....	10.0	S5	'94	105⅞	94¼	105⅞	7.01	6.18
M-T Nts[6] 7¼s 2002	[10]mn	A			X	BE	NC	....	....	....	....	....	20.0	M2	'92	105⅛	92⅝	105⅛	6.90	6.29
M-T Nts[6] 7⅜s 2002	mN	A			X	BE	NC	....	....	....	....	....	7.00	M2	'92	105⅞	93⅛	105⅞	6.97	6.30
M-T Nts[6] 7.45s 2002	[11]mn	A			X	BE	NC	....	....	....	....	....	5.00	M2	'92	106¼	93⅜	106¼	7.01	6.33
M-T Nts[6] 7.37s 2002	[12]mn	A			X	BE	NC	....	....	....	....	....	5.00	M2	'92	105⅞	92⅞	105⅞	6.96	6.32
M-T Nts[6] 7.38s 2002	[12]mn	A			X	BE	NC	....	....	....	....	....	5.00	M2	'92	105⅞	93	105⅞	6.97	6.33
M-T Nts[6] 6s 2003	[13]fa	A			X	BE	NC	....	....	....	....	....	15.0	S5	'93	97⅝	84⅛	97⅝	6.15	6.39
M-T Nts[6] 9.20s 2011	[14]mn	A			X	BE	NC	....	....	....	....	....	10.0	M2	'91	123⅛	103¾	123⅛	7.47	6.76
M-T Nts 9.28s 2021	[15]mn	A			X	BE	NC	....	....	....	....	....	5.00	M2	'91	127	104⅞	127	7.31	7.00
M-T Nts[6] 8.15s 2022	[16]mn	A			X	BE	104.075	(5-1-02)	....	....	....	....	12.0	M2	'92	113¾	93¼	113¾	7.16	7.00
BayBanks, Inc	***10***	***15.13***	***19.48***	***5.51***		***Dc***				***9-30-95***	***64.80***		***971.0***	***6.7***						
F/R[17]Nts 5.9375s '97	QSep30	BBB	5/94	BBB–	X	R	100	....	....	....	....	....	50.0	S4	'85	100	97	99¾	5.95	....
Bayou Steel	***66h***	***0.84***	***0.56***	***1.70***		***Sp***	***11.10***	***98.20***	***22.60***	***6-30-95***	***85.20***		***171.0***	***50.2***						
1st[18] 10¼s 2001	Ms	B			Y	BE	103.33	(3-1-98)	....	....	....	....	75.0		'94	102¼	88½	102¼	10.02	9.68
BE Aerospace	***3***	***5.76***	***1.70***	***d0.26***		***Fb***	***7.49***	***157.0***	***65.00***	***8-26-95***	***188.0***		***320.0***	***60.6***						
Sr Nts[18] 9¾s 2003	Ms	BB–			Y	R	104.875	(3-1-98)	....	....	....	....	125	M2	'93	101	93¼	100¼	9.73	9.70
Bear Stearns Cos	***62***	***△1.87***	***△1.63***	***△1.23***		***Je***				***9-30-95***	***4205***		***6763***	***62.2***						
Sr Nts 5⅞s '96	Jj15	A	4/93	A–	X	BE	NC	....	....	....	....	....	150	B5	'93	100	98	100	5.88	Mat.
• Sr Nts[19] 9⅛s '98	Ao15	A	4/93	A–	X	BE	NC	....	....	....	....	....	150	B5	'91	102	101⅝	100⅜	9.09	8.93
Sr Nts 7⅝s '99	mS15	A			X	BE	NC	....	....	....	....	....	200	B5	'94	105⅝	98⅜	105⅝	7.22	5.91
Sr Nts 7⅝s 2000	Ms15	A			X	BE	NC	....	....	....	....	....	150	B5	'95	106⅛	99½	106⅛	7.18	5.96
Sr Nts 6½s 2000	Jd15	A			X	BE	NC	....	....	....	....	....	200	B5	'93	102	90	102	6.37	5.98
Sr Nts 6¾s 2000	fA15	A			X	BE	NC	....	....	....	....	....	200	B5	'95	102⅞	98¾	102⅞	6.56	6.03
• Sr Nts[19] 9⅜s 2001	Jd	A	4/93	A–	X	BE	NC	....	....	....	....	....	150	B5	'91	110	110	95⅛	9.86	10.58
Sr Nts 8¼s 2002	Fa	A	4/93	A–	X	BE	NC	....	....	....	....	....	150	B5	'92	110⅝	95⅞	110⅝	7.46	6.13
Sr Nts 6¾s 2003	Ao15	A			X	BE	NC	....	....	....	....	....	200	B5	'93	102½	86⅞	102½	6.59	6.31
Sr Nts 6.70s 2003	fA	A			X	BE	NC	....	....	....	....	....	200	B5	'93	102¼	86⅞	102¼	6.55	6.32
Sr Nts 6⅝s 2004	Jj15	A			X	BE	NC	....	....	....	....	....	250	B5	'93	101	84¾	101	6.56	6.46
Sr Nts 8¾s 2004	Ms15	A	4/93	A–	X	BE	NC	....	....	....	....	....	150	B5	'92	114¾	98⅛	114¾	7.63	6.41
Sr Nts 6⅞s 2005	aO	A			X	BE	NC	....	....	....	....	....	150	B5	'95	103	99¼	103	6.67	6.45
F/R[20]Nts 6.2875s '98	QMay15	A			X	BE	NC	....	....	....	....	....	100	B5	'95	100½	99⅞	100¼	6.27	....
M-T Nts 'B' 7.07s '96	[21]ao15	A			X	BE	NC	....	....	....	....	....	30.0	B5	'95	100⅝	100	100¼	7.05	5.26
M-T Nts 'B'[6] 6s '96	[22]ao15	A			X	BE	NC	....	....	....	....	....	5.00	B5	'94	100⅛	97⅞	100⅛	5.99	5.31
F/R[23]M-T Nts 'B'[6] '96	QApr15	A			X	BE	NC	....	....	....	....	....	8.00	B5	'94	100	99¾	100	....	....
F/R[24]M-T Nts 'B'[6] '96	[25]May24	A			X	BE	NC	....	....	....	....	....	12.0	B5	'94	100	99¾	100	....	....
F/R[26]M-T Nts 'B'[6] 5.02s '96	QMay24	A			X	BE	NC	....	....	....	....	....	50.0	B5	'94	100	99⅜	99⅞	5.03	....
F/R[23]M-T Nts 'B'[6] '96	QMay31	A			X	BE	NC	....	....	....	....	....	75.0	B5	'94	100⅛	99¾	100	....	....
F/R[27]M-T Nts 'B'[6] 6.1375s '96	QAug12	A			X	BE	NC	....	....	....	....	....	25.0	B5	'94	100⅛	99¾	100⅛	6.13	....
F/R[24]M-T Nts 'B'[6] '97	[25]Feb25	A			X	BE	NC	....	....	....	....	....	100	B5	'94	100¼	99¾	100¼	....	....

Uniform Footnote Explanations-See Page 260. Other: [1] Int to 7-1-00,adj aft as defined. [2] (HRO)On 7-1-00,aft as defined. [3] Due 1-1-01. [4] On 7-1-00,aft as defined. [5] Was Springfield Gas Lt. [6] Issued in min denom $100T. [7] Due 7-6-00. [8] Due 1-30-01. [9] Due 9-10-01. [10] Due 8-5-02. [11] Due 12-16-02. [12] Due 12-31-02. [13] Due 9-29-03. [14] Due 6-6-11. [15] Due 8-12-21. [16] Due 8-26-22. [17] Int to 12-25-95,adj qtrly aft. [18] (HRO)On Chge of Ctrl at 101. [19] Issued in min denom $25T. [20] Int to 11-15-95,adj qtrly(3 Mo LIBOR&0.35%). [21] Due 2-23-96. [22] Due 3-15-96. [23] Int adj weekly. [24] Int adj monthly. [25] Int pd monthly. [26] Int thru 2-24-96,adj qtrly aft. [27] Int thru 2-13-96,adj qtrly aft.

Title-Industry Code & Co. Finances (In Italics) / Individual Issue Statistics (Exchange)	Ind / Interest Dates	Fixed Charge Coverage 1992 / S&P Debt Rating	Date of Last Rating Change	1993 / Prior Rating	1994 / Eligible	Year End / Bond Form	Cash & Equiv. (Million $) / Regular Price	Curr. Assets / Regular (Begins) Thru	Curr. Liab. / Sinking Fund Price	Balance Sheet Date / Sinking Fund (Begins) Thru	L. Term Debt (Mil $) / Refund/Other Restriction Price	Capital-ization (Mil $) / Refund/Other Restriction (Begins) Thru	Outst'g (Mil $)	Total Debt % Capital / Underwriting Firm	Underwriting Year	Price Range 1995 High	Price Range 1995 Low	Mo. End Price Sale(s) or Bid	Curr. Yield	Yield to Mat.
***Bear Stearns Cos** (Cont.)*																				
F/R[1]M-T Nts 'B'[2] '97	[3]	**A**			X	BE	NC	....	....	....	....	....	5.00	B5	'94	100¼	99¾	100⅛	....	....
F/R[4]M-T Nts 'B'[2] 5.47s '97	QAug26	**A**			X	BE	NC	....	....	....	....	....	15.0	B5	'94	99⅞	99	99⅝	5.49	....
F/R[5]M-T Nts 'B'[2] 5.82s 2000	QFeb4	**A**			X	BE	NC	....	....	....	....	....	10.0	B5	'94	99⅞	98¼	99⅛	5.87	....
F/R[6]M-T Nts 'B'[2] 5.58s 2000	QMar	**A**			X	BE	NC	....	....	....	....	....	10.0	B5	'94	99¾	98⅝	99	5.64	....
Beazer Homes USA	***13h***	***n/a***		***n/a***	***3.67***	***Sp***	***4.59***			***6-30-95***	***160.0***	***299.0***		***53.5***						
Sr Nts[7] 9s 2004	Ms	**B+**			Y	R	102.571	(3-1-99)	....	....	[8]Z108	3-1-97	115	D4	'94	97	83	96⅝	9.31	9.60
Becton,Dickinson	***43***	***△4.06***		***△6.32***	***△6.43***	***Sp***	***240.0***	***1328***	***720.0***	***9-30-95***	***558.0***	***2162***		***35.3***						
SF Deb 9¼s 2016	Jd	**A+**			X	R	104.813	5-30-96	100	(6-1-97)	®104.375	5-31-96	81.4	G1	'86	106½	102⅝	105¾	8.75	8.64
Deb 8.70s 2025	Jj15	**A+**			X	BE	103.949	(1-15-05)	....	....	....	....	100	G1	'95	116⅝	98⅝	116⅝	7.46	7.31
Nts 8⅜s '96	Jd	**A+**			X	R	NC	....	....	....	....	....	50.0	G1	'86	102¼	100¾	101⅛	8.28	5.61
Nts 7⅞s '96	jD15	**A+**			X	R	NC	....	....	....	....	....	100	G1	'86	102¾	99⅝	102¼	7.70	5.44
Nts[9] 9.95s '99	Ms15	**A+**			X	R	NC	....	....	....	....	....	100	G1	'89	112⅜	105⅛	112¼	8.86	5.71
Nts 8.80s 2001	Ms	**A+**			X	R	NC	....	....	....	....	....	100	G1	'91	112⅝	101¾	112⅝	7.81	5.93
Bell & Howell	***54***	***1.29***		***1.56***	***2.05***	***Dc***	***8.90***	***280.0***	***335.0***	***9-30-95***	***468.0***	***291.0***		***170.0***						
Sr Nts[7] 9¼s 2000	jJ15	**BB−**	5/95	B+	Y	R	104.625	(7-15-97)	....	....	[10]Z108	7-14-97	80.0	D6	'93	103⅛	92½	102½	9.02	8.57
Bell Atlantic Fin'l Services	***25***	***Issued under support agreement w/Bell Atlantic Corp***																		
Nts 6⅝s '97	mN30	**A+**	4/94	A	X	BE	NC	....	....	....	....	....	130	M2	'92	101⅞	95¾	101⅞	6.50	5.58
Bell[11] Atlantic-N.J.[12]	***67a***	***6.39***		***7.18***	***7.30***	***Dc***	***10.70***	***920.0***	***1066***	***9-30-95***	***1298***	***3110***		***49.6***						
Deb 5⅞s 2004	Fa	**AA+**			X	BE	NC	....	....	....	....	....	250	M6	'94	99⅛	84⅞	99⅛	5.93	6.01
[12]Bell Tel. of Penna[13]	***67a***	***4.82***		***5.46***	***5.96***	***Dc***	***32.80***	***807.0***	***939.0***	***3-31-95***	***1632***	***3143***		***55.4***						
Deb 3¼s '96	Ms	**AA**	10/87	AA+	X	CR	100	....	....	....	....	....	35.0	H1	'56	99⅝	95¼	99⅝	3.26	5.39
Deb 4¾s 2001	Mn	**AA**	10/87	AA+	X	CR	100.19	4-30-96	....	....	....	....	50.0	F1	'61	95	83⅜	95	5.00	5.85
Deb 6⅝s 2002	mS15	**AA**			X	BE	NC	....	....	....	....	....	100	S1	'92	103¾	90½	103¾	6.39	5.94
Deb 4⅜s 2003	Fa	**AA**	10/87	AA+	X	CR	100.51	1-31-96	....	....	....	....	50.0	F1	'63	91	77⅝	91	4.81	5.95
Deb 6⅛s 2003	Ms15	**AA**			X	BE	NC	....	....	....	....	....	150	S1	'93	100⅞	87	100⅞	6.07	5.97
Deb 7⅜s 2007	jJ15	**AA**			X	BE	NC	....	....	....	....	....	150	F1	'92	110¼	92⅜	110¼	6.69	6.12
Deb 6¾s 2008	Mn	**AA**	10/87	AA+	X	R	101.20	4-30-96	....	....	....	....	100	M6	'68	101⅛	86⅛	101⅛	6.67	6.61
•Deb 7⅛s 2012	Jj	**AA**	10/87	AA+	X	R	101.93	12-31-96	....	....	....	....	75.0	M6	'72	101½	86	s100¾	7.07	7.05
•Deb 7½s 2013	Mn	**AA**	10/87	AA+	X	R	102.65	4-30-96	....	....	....	....	125	M6	'73	102¾	89	102⅛	7.34	7.28
Deb 7.70s 2023	Jj15	**AA**			X	BE	103.234	(1-15-03)	....	....	....	....	100	M2	'93	108⅛	89⅜	108⅛	7.12	7.02
Deb[14] 8.35s 2030	jD15	**AA**			X	BE	NC	....	....	....	....	....	175	L3	'90	126¾	103⅜	126¾	6.59	6.42
Deb 8¾s 2031	fA15	**AA**			X	BE	NC	....	....	....	....	....	125	M2	'91	125⅝	102⅜	125⅝	6.97	6.82
Deb 7⅜s 2033	Ms15	**AA**			X	BE	104.28	(3-15-03)	....	....	....	....	225	F1	'93	105⅝	84⅞	105⅝	6.98	6.95
BellSouth Capital Funding	***25***	***Issued under support agreement w/BellSouth***																		
•Nts 9¼s '98	Jj15	**AAA**	6/88	AA	X	R	NC	....	....	....	....	....	115	M6	'88	107½	102½	106¼	8.71	5.95
BellSouth[15]Telecommunications[16]	***67***	***3.74***		***5.59***	***6.57***	***Dc***	***91.60***	***3306***	***4068***	***9-30-95***	***6805***	***16169***		***47.3***						
•Deb 5⅞s 2009	Jj15	**AAA**			X	R	NC	....	....	....	....	....	350	M6	'93	97¼	79	96¾	6.07	6.24
•Amortizing Deb[17] 6.30s 2015	jD15	**AAA**			X	BE	NC	....	....	....	....	....	375	S1	'95	99⅝	99⅝	99⅝	6.32	....
•Deb 7s 2025	aO	**AAA**			X	BE	NC	....	....	....	....	....	300	M6	'95	104¾	99¼	99¾	7.02	7.02
•Deb 8¼s 2032	jJ	**AAA**			X	R	104.83	(7-1-02)	....	....	....	....	250	G1	'92	111⅜	94⅜	110⅜	7.47	7.42
•Deb 7⅞s 2032	fA	**AAA**			X	R	104.29	(8-1-02)	....	....	....	....	300	M6	'92	108⅜	90½	s107⅞	7.30	7.26
•Deb 7½s 2033	Jd15	**AAA**			X	R	104.75	(6-15-03)	....	....	....	....	300	G1	'93	105	86½	104⅛	7.20	7.18
•Deb 6¾s 2033	aO15	**AAA**			X	R	103.50	(10-15-03)	....	....	....	....	400	M6	'93	98⅝	79	s97⅝	6.91	6.93
•Deb 7⅝s 2035	Mn15	**AAA**			X	R	103.66	(5-15-05)	....	....	....	....	300	M6	'95	107	95½	95⅜	7.99	8.01
•Deb[18] 5.85s 2045	mN15	**AAA**			X	BE	NC	....	....	....	....	....	300	M6	'95	99⅞	99⅞	90	6.50	6.53
•Deb 7s 2095	jD	**AAA**			X	BE	NC	....	....	....	....	....	500	M6	'95	99⅝	99⅝	100	7.00	7.00

Uniform Footnote Explanations-See Page 260. Other: [1] Int adj monthly. [2] Issued in min denom $100T. [3] Due 8-4-97:Int pd monthly,ea 1st Thur. [4] Int thru 2-27-96,adj qtrly aft. [5] Int thru 2-6-96,adj qtrly aft. [6] Int thru 3-1-96,adj qtrly aft. [7] (HRO)On Chge of Ctrl at 101. [8] Max $23M red w/proceeds of Com Stk Off'g. [9] (HRO)At 100,for Designated Event&Rat'g Decline. [10] Max $26.7M red w/proceeds Equity Off'g. [11] Was New Jersey Bell Tel, see. [12] Subsid of Bell Atlantic Corp. [13] Now Bell Atlantic-Pennsylvania. [14] (HRO)On 12-15-97('00 &'02)at 100. [15] Subsid of BellSouth Corp. [16] See So'n Bell T.&T. & South Cen Bell Tel. [17] Princ pyts due on int dates. [18] (HRO)On 11-15-00 at 100.

Title-Industry Code & Co. Finances (In Italics) / Individual Issue Statistics, Exchange	Ind / Interest Dates	Fixed Charge Coverage 1992 / S&P Debt Rating	1993 / Date of Last Rating Change	1994 / Prior Rating	Eligible	Year End / Bond Form	Cash & Equiv. (Million $) / Redemption Provisions Regular Price	Curr. Assets (Million $) / Regular (Begins) Thru	Curr. Liab. (Million $) / Sinking Fund Price	Balance Sheet Date / Sinking Fund (Begins) Thru	L. Term Debt (Mil $) / Refund/Other Restriction Price	Refund/Other Restriction (Begins) Thru	Capital-ization (Mil $) / Outst'g (Mil $)	Total Debt % Capital / Underwriting Firm	Underwriting Year	Price Range 1995 High	Price Range 1995 Low	Mo. End Price Sale(s) or Bid	Curr. Yield	Yield to Mat.
BellSouth Telecommunications (Cont.)																				
• ([1]Deferred) Deb 6.65s 2095	jD15	**AAA**			X	BE	NC	....	....	....	....	....	[2]500	S1	'95	25⅛	25⅛	25⅛	....	....
• Nts 6½s 2000	Fa	**AAA**			X	R	NC	....	....	....	....	....	275	M6	'93	102⅞	92	103	6.31	5.67
• Nts 6¼s 2003	Mn15	**AAA**			X	R	NC	....	....	....	....	....	450	M6	'93	102⅛	87¾	s102	6.13	5.91
• Nts 6⅜s 2004	Jd15	**AAA**			X	R	NC	....	....	....	....	....	200	G1	'93	103	87½	s102¼	6.23	6.03
• Nts 7s 2005	Fa	**AAA**			X	R	NC	....	....	....	....	....	150	M6	'93	106⅜	91½	s106⅜	6.58	6.08
• Nts 6½s 2005	Jd15	**AAA**			X	BE	NC	....	....	....	....	....	300	M6	'95	103⅜	96¾	103⅛	6.30	6.06
Bemis Co	***16d***	***13.42***	***11.66***	***15.47***		***Dc***	***23.10***	***431.0***	***215.0***	***9-30-95***	***158.0***		***619.0***	***25.8***						
Nts 6.70s 2005	jJ	**A**			X	BE	NC	....	....	....	....	....	100	G1	'95	102⅝	95⅞	102⅝	6.53	6.33
Beneficial Corp	***25a***	***1.39***	***1.50***	***1.48***		***Dc***	***197.0***			***9-30-95***	***6964***		***12120***	***87.6***						
• Deb 8s 2001	[3]Jd15	**A**	1/89	A–	X	R	NC	....	....	....	....	....	0.46	B6	'76	No Sale		100	8.00	8.00
• Deb('08[4]) 8.40s 2008	Mn15	**A**	1/89	A–	X	R	NC	....	....	....	....	....	47.7	B6	'78	114⅞	100½	106⅛	7.92	7.62
• Deb 12⅞s 2013	fA	**A**	1/89	A–	X	R	105.15	(8-1-98)	....	....	Z103.348	7-31-96	42.8	M2	'83	117¾	115	118	10.91	10.59
Nts 9⅛s '98	Fa15	**A**			X	R	NC	....	....	....	....	....	300	M2	'91	106⅞	102⅛	106⅞	8.54	5.64
Bergen Brunswig	***21d***	***12.86***	***[5]4.58***	***6.48***		***Sp***	***50.90***	***1667***	***1247***	***6-30-95***	***440.0***		***949.0***	***46.5***						
• Sr Nts 5⅝s '96	Jj15	**A–**			X	R	NC	....	....	....	....	....	100	M2	'93	100⅛	97⅛	99¾	5.64	Mat.
• Sr Nts 7⅜s 2003	Jj15	**A–**			X	R	NC	....	....	....	....	....	150	M2	'93	No Sale		95⅛	7.75	8.30
Sr Nts 7¼s 2005	Jd	**A–**			X	R	NC	....	....	....	....	....	100	M2	'95	105⅜	98½	105⅜	6.88	6.48
Berkeley Fed'l Bank & Tr FSB	***10a***	***9.29***	***12.91***	***19.98***		***Dc***				***3-31-95***	***★105.0***		***108.0***	***5.0***						
Sub Deb 12s 2005	Jd15	**B+**			Y	BE	105.333	(6-15-00)	....	....	[6]Z112	6-14-98	100	D4	'95	103	98¾	103	11.65	11.47
Berkley(W.R.)Corp	***35c***	***3.83***	***3.71***	***2.11***		***Dc***				***9-30-95***	***322.0***		***1080***	***29.8***						
Deb 9⅞s 2008	Mn15	**A+**	1/95	AA–	X	R	NC	....	....	....	....	....	100	M2	'88	125½	108⅜	125½	7.87	6.79
Deb 8.70s 2022	Jj	**A+**	1/95	AA–	X	R	NC	....	....	....	....	....	100	M6	'92	117¼	97⅜	117¼	7.42	7.22
Nts[7] 6.31s 2000	[8]jd15	**A+**	1/95	AA–	X	BE	NC	....	....	....	....	....	25.0	M2	'93	101⅜	91	101⅜	6.22	5.93
Nts[7] 6.71s 2003	[9]jd15	**A+**	1/95	AA–	X	BE	NC	....	....	....	....	....	25.0	M2	'93	102¾	89	102¾	6.53	6.23
Berkshire Hathaway[10]	***35c***	***5.42***	***15.73***	***16.48***		***Dc***	***1879***			***9-30-95***	***807.0***		***17230***	***4.7***						
Deb 9¾s 2018	Jj15	**AAA**	2/89	AA+	X	R	105.85	1-14-97	100	(1-15-99)	®104.875	1-14-98	10.0	S1	'88	111¼	105¼	106	9.20	9.11
Best Buy Co	***59l***	***9.25***	***8.77***	***4.37***		***Fb***	***43.70***	***1601***	***1017***	***8-26-95***	***442.0***		***1030***	***61.9***						
• Sr Sub Nts[11] 8⅝s 2000	aO	**B+**			Y	R	102.50	(10-1-98)	....	....	....	....	150	G1	'93	101¼	89¼	s99½	8.67	8.75
• Sub Nts 9s '97	Jd15	**NR**	3/92	B–		R	NC	....	....	....	....	....	3.90	P2	'87	101⅛	100	101⅛	8.90	8.16
Bethlehem Steel Corp.	***66a***	***d3.18***	***0.86***	***1.83***		***Dc***	***102.0***	***1551***	***1009***	***9-30-95***	***585.0***		***1960***	***34.6***						
• SF Deb 6⅞s '99	Ms	**B+**	6/93	BB–	Y	R	100	....	100	....	....	....	16.0	K3	'69	100	90⅜	98⅛	7.01	7.55
• SF Deb 8⅜s 2001	Ms	**B+**	6/93	BB–	Y	R	100.21	2-29-96	100	....	....	....	41.6	K3	'76	100	91⅛	s98⅞	8.47	8.64
• SF Deb 8.45s 2005	Ms	**B+**	6/93	BB–	Y	R	100.95	2-29-96	100	....	....	....	90.7	K3	'75	101	90¼	s99¼	8.51	8.57
Sr[12]Nts 10⅜s 2003	mS	**B+**			Y	R	NC	....	....	....	....	....	105	S1	'93	106¼	98	106¼	9.76	9.22
Beverly Enterprises	***30***	***2.04***	***2.44***	***2.77***		***Dc***	***55.70***	***691.0***	***446.0***	***9-30-95***	***897.0***		***1987***	***48.1***						
[13]Nts[14] 8¾s 2003	[15]feb	**B+**			Y	R	100	(12-31-96)	....	....	....	....	25.0	D1	'93	98½	88	98½	8.88	9.02
Bibb Co.[16]	***68***	***0.61***	***1.07***	***....***		***Dc***	***0.14***	***114.0***	***54.00***	***10-1-94***	***215.0***		***199.0***	***109.0***						
Sr Sub Nts[17] 14s '99	§aO	**D**	4/95	CCC–	Z	R			Default 4-3-95 int				127	M2	'89	59	29	39	....	Flat
Big Flower Press Inc	***1***	***△1.97***	***[18]△1.09***	***△1.42***		***Je***	***1.32***	***162.0***	***130.0***	***6-30-95***	***227.0***		***336.0***	***73.4***						
Sr[12]Sub Nts 10¾s 2003	fA	**B–**			Y	R	104.031	(8-1-98)	....	....	[19]Z108	7-31-98	150	B9	'93	106¾	92	106	10.14	9.61
BJ Services[20]	***49e***	***1.36***	***1.49***	***....***		***Dc***	***3.40***	***99.70***	***47.80***	***9-30-94***	***90.90***		***294.0***	***30.9***						
• Sr[11]Nts[20] 12⅞s 2002	jD	**NR**	9/94	B+		R	105.25	(12-1-97)	....	....	....	....	2.20	S1	'92	No Sale		104	12.38	12.00
Black & Decker Corp	***13e***	***0.87***	***1.83***	***1.98***		***Dc***	***112.0***	***2097***	***2010***	***10-1-95***	***1677***		***3747***	***65.5***						
Nts 6⅝s 2000	mN15	**BBB–**			X	R	NC	....	....	....	....	....	250	G1	'93	101⅝	89½	101⅝	6.52	6.23
Nts 7½s 2003	Ao	**BBB–**			X	R	NC	....	....	....	....	....	500	L3	'93	107	90⅜	107	7.01	6.28
Nts 7s 2006	Fa	**BBB–**			X	R	NC	....	....	....	....	....	250	L3	'94	103⅛	84¼	103⅛	6.79	6.57

Uniform Footnote Explanations-See Page 260. Other: [1] Int accrues at 6.65% fr 12-15-15. [2] Incl disc. [3] Due 6-15-01. [4] (HRO)On ea Dec 15 to 2008 at 100. [5] Fiscal Aug'93 & prior. [6] Max $35M red w/proceeds of Pub Eq Off'g. [7] Issued in min denom $100T. [8] Due 3-6-00. [9] Due 3-4-00. [10] See World Book Finance. [11] Co must offer repurch at 101 on Chge of Ctrl. [12] (HRO)On Chge of Ctrl at 101. [13] (HRO)On Fundamental Chge at 100. [14] Death redemp benefit(ltd). [15] Due 12-31-03:int pd 1st day ea month. [16] See NTC Group. [17] (HRO)On Chge of Ctrl at 100. [18] 11 Mo Jun,'94. [19] Max $50M w/proceeds of Equity Off'g. [20] Was Western Co of No Amer.

Title-Industry Code & Co. Finances (In Italics) / Individual Issue Statistics (Exchange ↓)	Ind / Interest Dates	Fixed Charge Coverage 1992 / S&P Debt Rating	1993 / Date of Last Rating Change	1994 / Prior Rating	Eligible ↓	Year End / Bond Form	Million $ Cash & Equiv. / Redemption Provisions Regular Price	Million $ Curr. Assets / Regular (Begins) Thru	Million $ Curr. Liab. / Sinking Fund Price	Balance Sheet Date / Sinking Fund (Begins) Thru	L. Term Debt (Mil $) / Refund/Other Restriction Price	Refund/Other Restriction (Begins) Thru	Capital-ization (Mil $) / Outst'g (Mil $)	Total Debt % Capital / Underwriting Firm	Underwriting Year	Price Range 1995 High	Price Range 1995 Low	Mo. End Price Sale(s) or Bid	Curr. Yield	Yield to Mat.
Black Hills Corp	***72a***	***4.60***	***4.60***	***4.31***		***Dc***	***16.40***	***41.00***	***30.50***	***9-30-95***	***166.0***		***348.0***	***48.3***						
1st 'AB' 8.30s 2024	mS	A			X	R	104.04	(9-1-04)	....	....	....	....	45.0	M2	'94	112	95¾	112	7.41	7.29
1st[1]'AC' 8.06s 2010	Fa	A			X	R	NC	....	....	....	....	....	30.0	M2	'95	115⅞	97⅛	115⅞	6.96	6.34
1st 'AD' 6½s 2002	jJ15	A			X	R	NC	....	....	....	....	....	15.0	P1	'95	101⅞	97¾	101⅞	6.38	6.15
Blockbuster Entertainment	***40e***	***Acquired by Viacom Inc,see***																		
Sr Nts 6⅝s '98	Fa15	BB+	5/95	BBB–	Y	R	NC	....	....	....	....	....	150	M2	'93	100¾	92¾	100¼	6.61	6.49
Blount, Inc.	***13c***	***2.14***	***4.27***	***6.89***		***Fb***	***62.90***	***278.0***	***124.0***	***8-31-95***	***96.70***		***330.0***	***30.9***						
Sr Sub Nts[2] 9s 2003	Jd15	BB–	6/94	B+	Y	R	103.375	(6-15-98)	....	....	....	....	80.0	M5	'93	106⅝	95½	105⅝	8.52	7.98
Boatmen's Bancshares	***10***	***3.91***	***5.50***	***3.58***		***Dc***				***6-30-95***	***562.0***		***3344***	***16.8***						
Sub Nts 9¼s 2001	mN	A–			X	R	NC	....	....	....	....	....	150	M6	'89	115⅜	103¼	115⅜	8.02	6.08
Sub Nts 6¾s 2003	Ms15	A–			X	BE	NC	....	....	....	....	....	100	G1	'93	103⅜	89	103⅜	6.53	6.16
Sub Nts 8⅝s 2003	mN15	A–			X	R	NC	....	....	....	....	....	50.0	M6	'91	114⅞	100¼	114⅞	7.51	6.21
Sub Nts 7⅝s 2004	aO	A–			X	BE	NC	....	....	....	....	....	100	G1	'92	109¼	92⅝	109¼	6.98	6.24
Boeing Co	***2a***	***28.38***	***13.38***	***9.79***		***Dc***	***4201***	***12305***	***7148***	***9-30-95***	***2355***		***12419***	***21.1***						
Deb 8.10s 2006	mN15	AA			X	R	NC	....	....	....	....	....	175	F1	'91	116	97⅝	116	6.98	6.07
Deb 8¾s 2021	fA15	AA			X	R	NC	....	....	....	....	....	400	F1	'91	126⅝	101⅛	126⅝	6.91	6.58
Deb[3] 7.95s 2024	fA15	AA			X	R	NC	....	....	....	....	....	300	F1	'92	119½	95	119½	6.65	6.45
Deb 7¼s 2025	Jd15	AA			X	R	NC	....	....	....	....	....	250	F1	'93	108⅛	85⅛	108⅛	6.71	6.62
Deb 8¾s 2031	mS15	AA			X	R	NC	....	....	....	....	....	250	F1	'91	129¾	100⅞	129¾	6.74	6.58
Deb 8⅝s 2031	Mn15	AA			X	R	NC	....	....	....	....	....	175	F1	'91	128⅛	99⅝	128⅛	6.73	6.57
Deb 7⅞s 2043	Ao15	AA			X	R	NC	....	....	....	....	....	175	S1	'93	121¼	90⅜	121¼	6.49	6.43
Deb 6⅞s 2043	aO15	AA			X	R	NC	....	....	....	....	....	125	F1	'93	106¾	79½	106¾	6.44	6.42
• Nts 8⅜s '96	Ms	AA	4/90	AA–	X	R	NC	....	....	....	....	....	250	F1	'86	102⅞	100⅜	100⅜	8.34	6.01
Nts 6.35s 2003	Jd15	AA			X	R	NC	....	....	....	....	....	300	G1	'93	102½	87¾	102½	6.20	5.93
Boise Cascade[4]	***50***	***d0.65***	***0.06***	***0.79***		***Dc***	***74.40***	***1163***	***859.0***	***9-30-95***	***1497***		***3385***	***49.6***						
Deb[5] 9.45s 2009	mN	BBB–	11/95	BB+	X	R	NC	....	....	....	....	....	150	G1	'89	125	98	122⅞	7.69	6.86
Nts 7⅜s '97	fA	BBB–	11/95	BB+	X	BE	NC	....	....	....	....	....	100	S1	'92	102¼	96⅛	102¼	7.21	5.87
[5]Nts[6] 10⅛s '97	jD15	BBB–	11/95	BB+	X	R	NC	....	....	....	....	....	120	F1	'90	108½	102⅝	107⅝	9.41	5.95
Nts[5] 9.90s 2000	Ms15	BBB–	11/95	BB+	X	R	NC	....	....	....	....	....	100	G1	'90	113⅜	102½	113⅜	8.73	6.23
Nts 9⅞s 2001	Fa15	BBB–	11/95	BBB+	X	R	100	(2-15-99)	....	....	....	....	100	S1	'89	111½	102¼	111	8.90	7.26
[5]Nts[6] 9.85s 2002	Jd15	BBB–	11/95	BB+	X	R	NC	....	....	....	....	....	125	F1	'90	117⅝	103	117⅝	8.37	6.47
Boomtown Inc	***40i***	***n/a***	***n/a***	***n/a***		***Sp***	***17.70***	***29.50***	***20.30***	***6-30-95***	***107.0***		***217.0***	***50.7***						
1st Mtg Nts[7] 11½s 2003	mN	B+			Y	BE	104.25	(11-1-98)	....	....	[8]Z108.50	10-31-96	104		'93	93¾	79	82½	13.94	15.41
Borden Chem & Plastics/BCP Fin...	***14***	***2.81***	***0.91***	***11.32***		***Dc***	***82.90***	***242.0***	***196.0***	***6-30-95***	***200.0***		***442.0***	***45.2***						
Nts[9] 9½s 2005	Mn	BB+			Y	R	104	(5-1-00)	....	....	....	....	200	C5	'95	103¼	99¾	103⅛	9.21	8.99
Borden (Co.) Inc.	***26***	***3.43***	***1.44***	***1.72***		***Dc***	***130.0***	***1515***	***1293***	***9-30-95***	***1228***		***2236***	***60.7***						
• SF Deb 8⅜s 2016	Ao15	BBB–	3/95	BBB	X	R	100	(4-15-06)	100	(4-15-07)	....	....	78.5	S1	'86	103¾	84½	s99⅝	8.41	8.41
SF Deb[5] 9¼s 2019	Jd15	BBB–	3/95	BBB	X	R	103.75	(6-15-99)	100	(6-15-00)	....	....	48.7	F1	'89	111⅞	90⅜	111⅞	8.27	8.11
Deb 9.20s 2021	Ms15	BBB–	3/95	BBB	X	R	NC	....	....	....	....	....	117	F1	'91	118½	89	118½	7.76	7.55
Deb 7⅞s 2023	Fa15	BBB–	3/95	BBB	X	BE	NC	....	....	....	....	....	250	F1	'93	103⅛	77⅛	103⅛	7.64	7.60
Nts[10] 9⅞s '97	mN	BBB–	3/95	BBB–	X	R	NC	....	....	....	....	....	78.1	F1	'87	107¼	100⅞	106½	9.27	6.08
Borg-Warner Corp	***8***	***Now Borg-Warner Security,see***																		
Nts 8s '96	Ao	B+	5/95	BB–	Y	R	100	....	....	....	....	....	100	G1	'86	100⅛	97¼	99¾	8.02	8.83
Borg-Warner Security Corp[11]	***63***	***p1.95***	***p2.11***	***1.20***		***Dc***	***17.40***	***184.0***	***190.0***	***9-30-95***	***476.0***		***532.0***	***90.8***						
• Sr Sub Nts[9] 9⅛s 2003	Mn	B–	5/95	B	Y	R	104.562	(5-1-98)	....	....	....	....	150	M2	'93	93¼	76	s92¼	9.89	10.67
Boston Edison	***72a***	***1.93***	***2.29***	***2.49***		***Dc***	***29.00***	***386.0***	***545.0***	***9-30-95***	***1160***		***2598***	***52.5***						
Deb 5⅛s '96	Ms15	BBB	5/95	BBB–	X	R	NC	....	....	....	....	....	100	G1	'93	99⅞	96⅝	99⅞	5.13	5.64

Uniform Footnote Explanations-See Page 260. Other: [1] (HRO)On 2-1-02 at 100. [2] Co must offer repurch at 101 on Chge in Ctrl. [3] (HRO)At 100 on 8-15-2012. [4] See Amer & Foreign Pwr. [5] (HRO)At 100 for Designated Event&Rat'g Decline. [6] Co may red in whole at 100 if 80% outstg put. [7] Co must offer repurch at 101 on Chge of Ctrl. [8] Max $25.9 M red w/proceeds of Cap Stk Off'g. [9] (HRO)On Chge of Ctrl at 101. [10] (HRO)On Chge of Ctrl,as defined,at 100. [11] See Borg-Warner Corp.

Title-Industry Code & Co. Finances (In Italics)	Ind	Fixed Charge Coverage 1992	1993	1994		Year End	Million $ Cash & Equiv.	Curr. Assets	Curr. Liab.	Balance Sheet Date	L. Term Debt (Mil $)		Capital-ization (Mil $)	Total Debt % Capital						
Individual Issue Statistics Exchange ↓	Interest Dates	S&P Debt Rating	Date of Last Rating Change	Prior Rating	Eligible ↓	Bond Form	Redemption Provisions Regular Price	(Begins) Thru	Sinking Fund Price	(Begins) Thru	Refund/Other Restriction Price	(Begins) Thru	Outst'g (Mil $)	Underwriting Firm	Year	Price Range 1995 High	Low	Mo. End Price Sale(s) or Bid	Curr. Yield	Yield to Mat.
***Boston Edison** (Cont.)*																				
Deb 5.70s '97	Ms15	**BBB**	5/95	BBB–	X	R	NC	....	....	....	....	....	100	G1	'93	99⅝	94¼	99⅝	5.72	6.02
Deb 5.95s '98	Ms15	**BBB**	5/95	BBB–	X	R	NC	....	....	....	....	....	100	G1	'93	99½	92⅛	99½	5.98	6.19
Deb 6.80s 2000	Fa	**BBB**	5/95	BBB–	X	R	NC	....	....	....	....	....	65.0	G1	'93	101⅜	91⅞	101⅜	6.71	6.41
Deb 6.05s 2000	fA15	**BBB**	5/95	BBB–	X	R	NC	....	....	....	....	....	100	G1	'93	98⅝	87½	98⅝	6.13	6.40
Deb 6.80s 2003	Ms15	**BBB**	5/95	BBB–	X	R	NC	....	....	....	....	....	150	G1	'93	100½	87⅜	100½	6.77	6.71
Deb 7.80s 2010	Mn15	**BBB**	5/95	BBB–	X	R	NC	....	....	....	....	....	125	G1	'95	107⅞	98⅜	107⅞	7.23	6.93
Deb 9⅞s 2020	Jd	**BBB**	5/95	BBB–	X	R	104.483	(6-1-00)	....	....	....	....	100	G1	'90	114⅞	100⅝	114⅞	8.60	8.43
Deb 9⅜s 2021	fA15	**BBB**	5/95	BBB–	X	R	104.612	(8-15-01)	....	....	....	....	125	G1	'91	112⅝	98⅛	112⅝	8.32	8.19
Deb 8¼s 2022	mS15	**BBB**	5/95	BBB–	X	R	103.78	(9-15-02)	....	....	....	....	60.0	G1	'92	103½	87¾	103½	7.97	7.93
Deb 7.80s 2023	Ms15	**BBB**	5/95	BBB–	X	R	103.73	(3-16-03)	....	....	....	....	200	G1	'93	100⅜	83⅞	100⅜	7.77	7.77
Boston Gas[1]	***73b***	***3.45***	***2.68***	***3.01***		***Dc***	***1.14***	***148.0***	***82.20***	***9-30-95***	***213.0***		***452.0***	***47.3***						
SF Deb 9s 2001	Mn15	**A**	12/90	A+	X	R	102.46	5-14-96	100	(5-15-97)	®101.85	5-14-96	30.0	F1	'86	103⅝	101⅜	102⅝	8.77	8.38
SF Deb 8¾s 2001	jD15	**A**	12/90	A+	X	R	102.69	12-14-96	100	(12-15-97)	®102.02	12-14-96	30.0	F1	'86	104	100⅛	102⅞	8.51	8.13
M-T Nts A[2] 9.05s 2021	ao	**A**			X	BE	NC	....	....	....	....	....	15.0	F1	'91	125⅝	102½	125⅝	7.20	6.90
M-T Nts A[2] 8.33s 2022	[3]ao	**A**			X	BE	NC	....	....	....	....	....	10.0	F1	'92	117¼	95⅛	117¼	7.10	6.90
M-T Nts A[2] 8.33s 2018	[4]ao	**A**			X	BE	NC	....	....	....	....	....	10.0	F1	'92	116½	95⅜	116½	7.15	6.88
M-T Nts A[2] 8.33s 2017	[5]ao	**A**			X	BE	NC	....	....	....	....	....	8.00		'92	116⅛	95⅜	116⅛	7.17	6.88
M-T Nts B[2] 6.93s 2014	[6]ao	**A**			X	BE	NC	....	....	....	....	....	5.00	F1	'94	100¾	83	100¾	6.88	6.86
M-T Nts B[2] 6.93s 2016	[7]ao	**A**			X	BE	NC	....	....	....	....	....	5.00	F1	'94	100¾	82¼	100¾	6.88	6.86
M-T Nts B[2] 6.93s 2016	Ao	**A**			X	BE	NC	....	....	....	....	....	10.0	F1	'94	100¾	82¼	100¾	6.88	6.86
M-T Nts B[2] 6.93s 2019	[8]ao	**A**			X	BE	NC	....	....	....	....	....	10.0	F1	'94	100⅝	81⅜	100⅝	6.89	6.88
M-T Nts B[2] 6.93s 2024	[9]ao	**A**			X	BE	NC	....	....	....	....	....	6.00	F1	'94	100½	80⅜	100½	6.90	6.89
Bowater,Inc	***50***	***d0.98***	***d0.63***	***0.49***		***Dc***	***207.0***	***619.0***	***286.0***	***9-30-95***	***817.0***		***2120***	***38.6***						
Deb[10] 9s 2009	fA	**BBB**	10/95	BBB–	X	R	NC	....	....	....	[11]Z100	....	300	F1	'89	121⅞	97¾	121⅞	7.38	6.54
Deb 9½s 2012	aO15	**BBB**	10/95	BBB–	X	R	NC	....	....	....	....	....	125	F1	'92	125⅜	102⅛	125⅜	7.58	6.92
Deb 9⅜s 2021	jD15	**BBB**	10/95	BBB–	X	R	NC	....	....	....	....	....	200	F1	'91	128⅜	100	128⅜	7.30	6.99
Nts 8¼s '99	aO15	**BBB**	10/95	BBB–	X	R	NC	....	....	....	....	....	8.00	F1	'92	107½	98⅛	107½	7.67	6.01
Nts 8½s 2001	jD15	**BBB**	10/95	BBB–	X	R	NC	....	....	....	....	....	18.0	F1	'91	111¼	99	111¼	7.64	6.21
Bradlees, Inc	***59g***	***n/a***	***1.83***	***1.33***		***Ja***	***Bankruptcy Chapt 11***				***[12]379.0***		***482.0***	***79.9***						
Sr Sub Nts[13] 11s 2002	§fA	**D**	6/95	B–	Z	R				Default 8-1-95 int			125	M2	'92	91⅜	18⅞	23	....	Flat
Brewer (C.) & Co Ltd	***26***	....	....	....		***Dc***	***No Recent Fin'ls***													
Sub[14]Disc Nts 16s '96	jD15	**NR**	4/90	B–		R	100	....	....	....	....	....	[15]75.0	D3	'86	88	88	A88	....	Flat
Bridge Oil(USA)	***49a***	***Acquired by Parker & Parsley Pet,see***																		
• Sr Nts[16] 9½s 2000	fA15	**NR**	8/94	BB	Y	R	101.583	(8-15-98)	....	....	[17]Z109.50	8-23-96	5.00	D6	'93	100	97½	100⅛	9.49	9.46
Bristol-Myers Squibb	***21a***	***47.19***	***44.06***	***40.64***		***Dc***	***2184***	***6610***	***4211***	***9-30-95***	***632.0***		***7648***	***17.4***						
Deb 7.15s 2023	Jd15	**AAA**			X	BE	NC	....	....	....	....	....	350	S1	'93	109¾	86½	109¾	6.51	6.39
Brown Group	***39b***	***1.30***	***0.33***	***4.80***		***Ja***	***28.70***	***527.0***	***319.0***	***10-28-95***	***107.0***		***447.0***	***48.5***						
• SF Deb 7⅜s '98	Jj15	**BB+**	10/95	BBB	Y	R	100	....	100	....	....	....	5.99	G1	'73	101¼	97¼	100¼	7.36	7.24
Browning-Ferris Ind	***53***	***△5.00***	***△5.96***	***△4.99***		***Sp***	***198.0***	***1422***	***1414***	***9-30-95***	***2411***		***5215***	***47.4***						
Deb 9¼s 2021	Mn	**A**	1/94	A+	X	BE	NC	....	....	....	....	....	100	S5	'91	130⅜	103⅞	130⅜	7.09	6.73
Deb 7.40s 2035	mS15	**A**			X	BE	[18]Z100	....	....	....	....	....	400	M6	'95	107⅞	97⅝	107⅞	6.86	6.82
Sr Nts 7⅞s 2005	Ms15	**A**			X	BE	NC	....	....	....	....	....	300	L3	'95	112¼	99⅝	112¼	7.02	6.11
Bruno's, Inc	***59c***	***△n/a***	***△4.36***	***[19]△3.56***		***Ja***	***19.10***	***299.0***	***209.0***	***9-23-95***	***868.0***		***665.0***	***134.0***						
Sr Sub Nts[20] 10½s 2005	fA	**B–**			Y	R	105.25	(8-1-00)	....	....	[21]Z110.50	7-31-98	400	B9	'95	100	95¾	98¾	10.63	10.71
Brunswick Corp	***40a***	***3.07***	***4.18***	***7.96***		***Dc***	***260.0***	***1233***	***650.0***	***9-30-95***	***316.0***		***1316***	***24.5***						
Deb 7⅜s 2023	mS	**BBB+**			X	R	NC	....	....	....	....	....	125	M2	'93	104⅜	83⅛	104⅜	7.07	7.01

Uniform Footnote Explanations-See Page 260. Other: [1] Contr by East'n Gas & Fuel Assoc. [2] Issued in min denom $100T. [3] Due 7-5-22. [4] Due 7-10-18. [5] Due 7-10-17. [6] Due 1-15-14. [7] Due 1-15-16. [8] Due 1-15-19. [9] Due 1-15-24. [10] (HRO)At 100 for Designated Event&Rat'g Decline. [11] Co may red in whole if 90% outstg put. [12] Incl liabs subj to reorg. [13] (HRO)At 101 for a Chge in Ctrl Event. [14] Int accrues at 16% fr 12-16-91. [15] Incl disc. [16] Co must offer repurch at 101 on Chge of Ctrl. [17] Max $25M red w/proceeds of com off'g. [18] Red at greater of par & certain int pyts,etc. [19] Fiscal Jun'95 & prior. [20] (HRO)On Chge of Ctrl at 101. [21] Max $160M red w/proceeds of Pub Eq Off'gs.

Title-Industry Code & Co. Finances (In Italics) / Individual Issue Statistics (Exchange)	Ind / Interest Dates	Fixed Charge Coverage 1992 / S&P Debt Rating	1993 / Date of Last Rating Change	1994 / Prior Rating	Eligible	Year End / Bond Form	Cash & Equiv. (Million $) / Regular Price	Curr. Assets (Million $) / Regular (Begins) Thru	Curr. Liab. (Million $) / Sinking Fund Price	Balance Sheet Date / Sinking Fund (Begins) Thru	L. Term Debt (Mil $) / Refund/Other Restriction Price	Refund/Other Restriction (Begins) Thru	Capitalization (Mil $) / Outst'g (Mil $)	Total Debt % Capital / Underwriting Firm	Underwriting Year	Price Range 1995 High	Price Range 1995 Low	Mo. End Price Sale(s) or Bid	Curr. Yield	Yield to Mat.
Brunswick Corp *(Cont.)*																				
Nts 8⅛s '97	Ao	BBB+	10/89	A−	X	R	NC	....	....	....	....	....	100	S4	'87	103⅛	98⅞	102⅞	7.90	5.71
Buckeye Cellulose	*50*	*△2.01*	*△2.06*	*△3.58*		*Je*	*18.60*	*145.0*	*55.00*	*9-30-95*	*★215.0*		*319.0*	*51.4*						
Sr Nts[1] 10¼s 2001	Mn15	BB+	11/95	B+	Y	R	103.875	(5-15-97)	100	(5-15-99)	[2]Z106	5-20-96	15.8	M2	'93	106	94½	106	9.67	8.82
SrSub[3]Nts 8½s 2005	jD15	BB−			Y	R	104.25	(12-15-00)	....	....	[4]108.50	12-14-98	150	M2	'95	99⅝	96⅝	96⅝	8.80	9.02
Burlington Industries	*68a*	*1.30*	*1.74*	*4.29*		*Sp*	*30.40*	*766.0*	*320.0*	*7-1-95*	*★894.0*		*1565*	*61.7*						
Nts 7¼s 2005	mS15	BBB−		BBB−	X	BE	NC	....	....	....	....	....	150	M6	'95	103¾	99⅜	103¾	6.99	6.72
Burlington Motor Holdings	*71*	*n/a*	*0.03*	*0.15*		*Dc*	*Bankruptcy Chapt 11*				*[5]281.0*		*294.0*	*112.0*						
Sr[3]Sub Nts 11½s 2003	mN	D	12/95	CCC−		R	105.75	(11-1-98)	....	....	[6]Z110	11-1-96	100	M2	'93	92½	17	17	....	Flat
Burlington Northern[7]	*55*	*3.43*	*4.54*	*5.45*		*Dc*	*29.00*	*1111*	*1483*	*9-30-95*	*2423*		*5027*	*48.8*						
• Deb 9s 2016	Ao	BBB	6/88	A−	X	R	104.95	3-31-96	100	(4-1-97)	®104.50	3-31-96	156	M6	'86	105½	100⅜	104⅝	8.60	8.51
Deb 8¾s 2022	Fa25	BBB			X	BE	NC	....	....	....	....	....	200	M2	'92	120⅞	99⅝	120⅞	7.24	7.00
Deb 7½s 2023	jJ15	BBB			X	BE	103.02	(7-15-03)	....	....	....	....	150	M2	'93	103	85⅜	103	7.28	7.25
Nts 7.40s '99	Mn15	BBB			X	BE	NC	....	....	....	....	....	150	M6	'94	104½	96⅛	104½	7.08	5.91
Nts 7s 2002	fA	BBB			X	BE	NC	....	....	....	....	....	150	M2	'92	103⅞	91½	103⅞	6.74	6.27
Burlington[7]***Northern***[8]***R.R.***	*55*	*5.81*	*7.58*	*10.63*		*Dc*	*29.00*	*1108*	*1401*	*9-30-95*	*1320*		*4704*	*28.6*						
• Con Mtg H 9¼s 2006	aO	BBB	7/95	BBB+	X	R	NC	....	....	....	....	....	275	M6	'86	112⅜	102	109⅛	8.48	7.97
• Con Mtg K 6.55s 2020	Jj	BBB	7/95	BBB+	X	R	NC	....	....	....	....	....	3.98	Exch.	'90	87½	75½	87	7.53	7.75
• Con Mtg L 3.80s 2020	Jj	BBB	7/95	BBB+	X	R	NC	....	....	....	....	....	6.20	Exch.	'90	58⅞	50	56¾	6.70	7.82
• Con Mtg M 3.20s 2045	QJan	BBB	7/95	BBB+	X	R	NC	....	....	....	....	....	13.0	Exch.	'90	47¾	37½	43⅛	7.42	7.68
• Con Mtg N 8.15s 2020	QJan	BBB	7/95	BBB+	X	R	NC	....	....	....	....	....	2.51	Exch.	'91	105	97	s103⅛	7.90	7.86
• Con Mtg O 6.55s 2020	Jj	BBB	7/95	BBB+	X	R	NC	....	....	....	....	....	15.4	Exch.	'91	90⅞	77	87⅞	7.45	7.66
• Con Mtg P 8.15s 2020	Jj	BBB	7/95	BBB+	X	R	NC	....	....	....	....	....	5.57	Exch.	'91	103	92	105	7.76	7.69
Burlington Northern Santa Fe[9]	*55*	*n/a*	*n/a*	*n/a*		*Dc*	*62.00*	*1414*	*2286*	*9-30-95*	*4164*		*9676*	*44.6*						
Deb 7s 2025	jD15	BBB			X	BE	[10]Z100	....	....	....	....	....	350	G1	'95	99⅜	98⅛	98¾	7.09	7.10
Nts 6⅜s 2005	jD15	BBB			X	BE	[11]Z100	....	....	....	....	....	300	G1	'95	100½	99	100½	6.34	6.31
Burlington Resources	*73e*	*3.12*	*3.48*	*2.00*		*Dc*	*19.80*	*234.0*	*315.0*	*9-30-95*	*1278*		*3494*	*36.6*						
Deb 9⅞s 2010	Jd15	A−			X	R	NC	....	....	....	....	....	150	L3	'90	132⅜	109	132⅜	7.46	6.41
Deb 9⅛s 2021	aO	A−			X	R	NC	....	....	....	....	....	150	L3	'91	127½	103⅛	127½	7.16	6.84
Deb 8.20s 2025	Ms15	A−			X	R	NC	....	....	....	....	....	150	M6	'95	116¾	99⅜	116¾	7.02	6.86
Nts 6⅞s '99	fA	A−			X	R	NC	....	....	....	....	....	150	M6	'92	103⅜	93⅞	103⅜	6.65	5.82
Nts 7.15s '99	Mn	A−			X	R	NC	....	....	....	....	....	300	M6	'94	104¼	95½	104¼	6.86	5.73
Nts 9⅝s 2000	Jd15	A−			X	R	NC	....	....	....	....	....	150	L3	'90	114⅜	104¾	114⅜	8.42	5.91
Nts 8½s 2001	aO	A−			X	R	NC	....	....	....	....	....	150	L3	'91	111⅞	100½	111⅞	7.60	6.02
Cablevision Industries	*12a*	*0.26*	*0.13*	*0.37*		*Dc*	*7.99*			*9-30-95*	*1490*		*852.0*	*175.0*						
Sr Nts 10¾s 2002	Jj30	BB−	11/93	B+	Y	R	105.375	(1-30-97)	....	....	....	....	300	M6	'92	109⅝	99½	109	9.86	8.80
Cablevision Systems Corp	*12a*	*0.38*	*0.25*	*0.24*		*Dc*	*22.00*			*9-30-95*	*3226*		*1157*	*279.0*						
Sr Sub Deb 10¾s 2004	Ao	B			Y	R	103.071	(4-1-97)	100	(4-1-02)	....	....	275	M2	'92	107½	100	105¾	10.17	9.72
Sr Sub Deb 9⅞s 2013	Fa15	B			Y	R	104.80	(2-15-03)	....	....	....	....	200	M2	'93	110	91	106½	9.27	9.12
Sr Sub Nts 9¼s 2005	mN	B			Y	R	104.625	(11-1-00)	....	....	....	....	300	M2	'95	101¼	100	101¼	9.14	9.05
Cabot Corp	*14*	*3.47*	*3.30*	*3.50*		*Sp*	*34.50*	*681.0*	*441.0*	*6-30-95*	*314.0*		*1148*	*39.4*						
Nts 10¼s '97	jD15	BBB+			X	R	NC	....	....	....	....	....	100	M2	'87	109¼	104⅞	108¼	9.47	5.74
Caesars World	*40i*	*3.69*	*5.98*	*7.66*		*Jl*	*156.0*	*291.0*	*174.0*	*10-31-94*	*199.0*		*808.0*	*28.0*						
Sr Sub Nts 8⅞s 2002	fA15	BBB−	10/95	BB+	X	R	103.266	(8-15-97)	....	....	....	....	150	M2	'92	106¼	97	106¼	8.35	7.65
CAI Wireless Systems	*12a*	*[12]d0.31*	*[13]d1.24*	*d7.65*		*Mr*	*143.0*			*9-30-95*	*316.0*		*627.0*	*50.4*						
Sr[3]Nts 12¼s 2002	mS15	BB−			Y	R	106.125	(9-15-99)	....	....	[14]Z111	9-14-98	275	S5	'95	107	100	106⅝	11.49	10.83
California Energy	*41f*	*3.21*	*2.80*	*1.73*		*Dc*				*9-30-95*	*1958*		*2485*	*78.8*						
• Ltd Recourse Sr Sec[3]Nts[15] 9⅞s 2003	Jd30	BB−			Y	BE	104.9375	(6-30-00)	....	....	[16]Z109.875	6-29-98	200	C5	'95	104	100	103½	9.54	9.22

Uniform Footnote Explanations-See Page 260. Other: [1] Co must offer repurch at 101 on Chge of Ctrl. [2] Max $14M w/proceeds of equity offerings. [3] (HRO)On Chge of Ctrl at 101. [4] Max $50M red w/proceeds of Pub Eq Off'g. [5] Incl Chapt 11 liabs. [6] Max $25M w/proceeds of Pub Eq Off'g. [7] Subsid of Burlington No'n Santa Fe. [8] See Gr Nor'n Ry,Nor'n Pac Ry,St Louis-SF Ry. [9] See Burlington No'n, Santa Fe Pacific. [10] Greater of 100 of amt based on formula. [11] Greater of 100 or amt based on formula. [12] 8 Mos Aug '93. [13] 7 Mos Mar '94. [14] Max $96.2M red w/proceeds of Pub Equity Off'gs. [15] Secured by an assignment & pledge of stk in subsid. [16] Max $70M red w/proceeds of Com Equity Off'gs.

Title-Industry Code & Co. Finances (In Italics) / Individual Issue Statistics (Exchange)	Ind / Interest Dates	Fixed Charge Coverage 1992 / S&P Debt Rating	1993 / Date of Last Rating Change	1994 / Prior Rating	Eligible	Year End / Bond Form	Cash & Equiv. (Million $) / Regular Price	Curr. Assets / Regular (Begins) Thru	Curr. Liab. / Sinking Fund Price	Balance Sheet Date / Sinking Fund (Begins) Thru	L. Term Debt (Mil $) / Refund/Other Restriction Price	Refund/Other Restriction (Begins) Thru	Capital-ization (Mil $) / Outst'g (Mil $)	Total Debt % Capital / Underwriting Firm	Underwriting Year	Price Range 1995 High	Price Range 1995 Low	Mo. End Price Sale(s) or Bid	Curr. Yield	Yield to Mat.
***California Energy** (Cont.)*																				
• Sr[1]Disc Nts[2] 10¼s 2004	Jj15	BB–			Y	BE	105.125	(1-15-99)	....	....	....	....	[3]530	L3	'94	96⅞	71	s94⅞	....	Flat
[4]California Hotel Finance	***25***	*Δ1.93*	*Δ1.95*	*Δ1.47*		*Je*	*21.80*	*44.50*	*85.10*	*6-30-95*	*369.0*		*500.0*	*79.1*						
Sr[5]Sub[6]Nts[7] 11s 2002	jD	BB–	5/95	B+	Y	R	104.125	(12-1-97)	....	....	....	....	185	S1	'92	106	91	106	10.38	9.78
Calmar Spraying Systems,Inc	***16d***	....	....	....		*Dc*	*No Recent Fin'ls*													
Sr Sub[8]Disc Nts 14s '99	Fa15	NR	11/95	CCC+		R	102	2-14-96	100	(2-15-97)	....	....	[3]150	D7	'89	103	99	A103	13.59	12.79
Calpine Corp	***72a***	*7.54*	*1.13*	*1.41*		*Dc*	*22.40*	*56.10*	*101.0*	*9-30-95*	*320.0*		*430.0*	*94.2*						
Sr Nts[9] 9¼s 2004	Fa	B			Y	BE	104.625	(3-1-99)	....	....	[10]Z109.25	1-31-97	105	M6	'94	96½	82	96½	9.59	9.89
Cambridge Electric Lt[11]	***72a***	*0.84*	*2.12*	*4.28*		*Dc*	*0.33*	*18.40*	*41.10*	*9-30-95*	*21.90*		*110.0*	*38.5*						
SF Nts C 6¼s '97	Jd	BBB	3/91	BBB+	X	R	100.37	5-31-96	100.37	6-1-96	....	....	4.38	H1	'67	100¼	95⅛	100¼	6.23	6.06
SF Nts D 7¾s 2002	Jd	BBB	3/91	BBB+	X	R	101.97	5-31-96	100.80	6-1-96	....	....	2.80	M2	'72	102½	93¾	102½	7.56	7.25
Campbell Soup	***26***	*Δ10.06*	*Δ12.62*	*Δ9.71*		*Jl*	*69.00*	*1969*	*2514*	*10-29-95*	*852.0*		*4519*	*42.8*						
Deb 8⅞s 2021	Mn	AA			X	BE	NC	....	....	....	....	....	200	G1	'91	128	104	128	6.93	6.59
Nts 9s '97	mN	AA			X	R	NC	....	....	....	....	....	100	M6	'90	106⅜	101⅞	106¼	8.47	5.38
Nts[12] 8.58s 2001	[13]jd15	AA			X	BE	NC	....	....	....	....	....	50.0	G1	'91	112⅛	101⅛	112⅛	7.65	5.84
Nts 5⅝s 2003	mS15	AA			X	BE	100	(9-15-00)	....	....	....	....	100	G1	'93	97⅜	83¾	97⅜	5.78	6.05
Canal Electric[11]	***72***	*3.66*	*3.34*	*4.29*		*Dc*	*0.01*	*20.10*	*51.70*	*9-30-95*	*100.0*		*216.0*	*54.2*						
1st A 7s '96	aO	BBB+	2/89	BBB	X	R	100	....	‡100	....	....	....	4.18	F1	'68	100⅜	98⅛	100	7.00	6.98
1st & Gen B 8.85s 2006	mS	BBB+	2/89	BBB	X	R	103.42	8-31-96	100.70	8-31-96	....	....	34.7	F1	'76	103⅞	99¼	103⅝	8.54	8.33
Canandaigua Wine Co	***11c***	*Δ5.03*	*Δ3.34*	*Δ3.75*		*Au*	*4.18*	*402.0*	*175.0*	*8-31-95*	*199.0*		*551.0*	*36.1*						
Sr[14]Sub Nts 8¾s 2003	jD15	B+			Y	R	104.375	(12-15-98)	....	....	....	....	130	C1	'93	100	91	99½	8.79	8.84
Capital Cities/ABC Inc	***12***	*6.75*	*14.80*	*22.89*		*Dc*	*1310*	*2962*	*1290*	*10-1-95*	*514.0*		*5462*	*11.1*						
Nts 8⅞s 2000	jD15	AA–	9/94	A+	X	R	NC	....	....	....	....	....	250	S1	'90	112⅞	103	112⅞	7.86	5.85
Deb 8¾s 2021	fA15	AA–	9/94	A+	X	R	NC	....	....	....	....	....	250	S1	'91	124⅜	100¾	124⅜	7.04	6.74
Capital Gaming Intl	***40i***	*Δn/a*	*Δd0.43*	*Δd0.52*		*Je*	*1.73*	*6.56*	*148.0*	*9-30-95*	*20.70*		*49.50*	*299.0*						
Sr Sec Nts[14]'B' 11½s 2001	§Fa	NR			Z	R	Default 8-1-95 int						135	Exch.	'94	82	38½	50	....	Flat
[15]Capital Holding	***35d***	*6.84*	*7.82*	*6.08*		*Dc*				*9-30-95*	*699.0*		*3558*	*19.7*						
SF Deb 8¾s 2017	Jj15	AA			X	R	104.8125	1-14-97	100	(1-15-98)	®104.375	1-14-97	95.0	G1	'87	107	97¼	105¾	8.27	8.17
Capital Re	***35***	*70.47*	*9.04*	*9.12*		*Dc*				*9-30-95*	*90.70*		*472.0*	*19.2*						
Deb 7¾s 2002	mN	A	12/93	A+	X	R	NC	....	....	....	....	....	75.0	G1	'92	108¾	95⅛	108¾	7.13	6.16
Carbide/Graphite Group	***42b***	*Δ3.31*	*Δ1.36*	*Δ2.57*		*Jl*	*42.70*	*149.0*	*42.40*	*7-31-95*	*110.0*		*153.0*	*71.9*						
Sr[14]Nts 11½s 2003	mS	B+			Y	R	105.75	(9-1-98)	....	....	[16]Z110	8-31-96	105	B5	'93	109	101	108	10.65	9.98
Cardinal Distribution	***21d***	**Now Cardinal Health Inc, see**																		
Nts 8s '97	Ms	BBB+	11/94	BBB	X	R	NC	....	....	....	....	....	100	G1	'92	103	98⅞	102¾	7.79	5.53
Cardinal Health Inc[17]	***21d***	*Δn/a*	*Δ6.88*	*Δ8.74*		*Je*	*62.20*	*1776*	*1159*	*9-30-95*	*208.0*		*799.0*	*28.8*						
Nts 6½s 2004	Fa15	A–	11/95	BBB+	X	R	NC	....	....	....	....	....	100	S5	'94	101⅛	86⅛	101⅛	6.43	6.32
Caremark Int'l	***30a***	*n/a*	*n/a*	*n/a*		*Dc*	*26.00*	*616.0*	*498.0*	*9-30-95*	*330.0*		*821.0*	*55.8*						
Nts 6⅞s 2003	fA15	BBB–			X	R	NC	....	....	....	....	....	100	L1	'93	99	85⅝	99	6.94	7.04
Carlisle Plastics, Inc	***52***	*0.88*	*1.41*	*1.28*		*Dc*	*3.83*	*129.0*	*66.00*	*9-30-95*	*190.0*		*271.0*	*73.8*						
Sr Nts[18] 10¼s '97	Jd15	B+	5/95	BB–	Y	R	102.56	6-14-96	....	....	....	....	90.0	F1	'92	101½	96¾	99	10.35	11.00
Carnival Corp[19]	***40g***	*4.56*	*6.08*	*6.05*		*Nv*	*148.0*	*289.0*	*663.0*	*8-31-95*	*1072*		*3428*	*33.4*						
• Deb[20] 7.20s 2023	aO	A–			X	BE	NC	....	....	....	....	....	125	G1	'93	96⅛	82⅜	103⅜	6.96	6.92
• Nts[20] 5¾s '98	Ms15	A–	10/93	BBB+	X	BE	NC	....	....	....	....	....	200	S1	'93	99¾	96½	98⅝	5.83	6.42
• Nts[20] 6.15s 2003	aO	A–			X	BE	NC	....	....	....	....	....	125	G1	'93	96	85½	94½	6.51	7.08
• Nts[20] 7.70s 2004	jJ15	A–			X	BE	NC	....	....	....	....	....	100	G1	'94	105¼	94⅜	95⅛	8.09	8.51
• Nts[20] 7.05s 2005	Mn15	A–			X	BE	NC	....	....	....	....	....	100	M2	'95	100⅞	97¼	92½	7.62	8.21
Carolina Power & Light	***72a***	*3.43*	*3.45*	*3.46*		*Dc*	*14.90*	*635.0*	*558.0*	*9-30-95*	*2684*		*5515*	*49.6*						
1st 5⅛s '96	Ao	A	1/87	A–	X	R	100	3-31-96	□100	....	....	....	30.0	L3	'66	99⅞	97⅛	99⅞	5.13	5.55

Uniform Footnote Explanations-See Page 260. Other: [1] Int accr at 10.25% fr 1-15-97. [2] (HRO)On Chge of Ctrl at 101(Accreted Val). [3] Incl disc. [4] Subsid&data of Calif Hotel&Casino(Boyd Gaming). [5] Gtd by Calif Hotel & Casino. [6] Gaming laws may req disposition/red by a hldr. [7] (HRO)On Chge in Ctrl at 101. [8] Int accr at 14% fr 2-15-92. [9] Co must offer repurch at 101 on Chge of Ctrl. [10] Max $36.8M red w/proceeds of Pub Equity Off'gs. [11] Subsid of Commonwealth Energy Sys. [12] Issued in min denom $100T. [13] Due 3-15-01. [14] (HRO)On Chge of Ctrl at 101. [15] Now Providian Corp. [16] Max $40M red w/proceeds of com stk off'g. [17] Was Cardinal Distribution, see. [18] (HRO)At 101 for Chge of Ctrl/Fundamental Chge. [19] Was Carnival Cruise Lines. [20] Co may red in whole at 100 for certain tax chge.

Title-Industry Code & Co. Finances (In Italics) / Individual Issue Statistics (Exchange)	Ind / Interest Dates	1992 / S&P Debt Rating	1993 / Date of Last Rating Change	1994 / Prior Rating	Eligible	Year End / Bond Form	Cash & Equiv. / Regular Price	Curr. Assets / Regular (Begins) Thru	Curr. Liab. / Sinking Fund Price	Balance Sheet Date / Sinking Fund (Begins) Thru	L. Term Debt (Mil $) / Refund/Other Restriction Price	Refund/Other Restriction (Begins) Thru	Capitalization (Mil $) / Outst'g (Mil $)	Total Debt % Capital / Underwriting Firm	Underwriting Year	Price Range 1995 High	Price Range 1995 Low	Mo. End Price Sale(s) or Bid	Curr. Yield	Yield to Mat.
***Carolina Power & Light** (Cont.)*																				
1st 6⅜s '97	aO	**A**	1/87	A–	X	R	100.22	9-30-96	□100	....	....	....	40.0	K2	'67	100⅜	95½	100⅜	6.35	6.14
1st 5⅜s '98	jJ	**A**			X	R	NC	....	....	....	....	....	100	M2	'93	99⅜	91⅜	99⅜	5.41	5.65
1st 6⅞s '98	aO	**A**	1/87	A–	X	R	100.54	9-30-96	□100.21	9-30-96	....	....	40.0	K2	'68	101¼	96¼	100⅝	6.83	6.62
1st 6⅛s 2000	Fa	**A**			X	R	NC	....	....	....	....	....	150	L3	'93	100⅞	90⅞	100⅞	6.07	5.88
1st 6¾s 2002	aO	**A**			X	R	NC	....	....	....	....	....	100	P4	'92	103½	90⅞	103½	6.52	6.11
1st 7¾s 2003	Mn	**A**	1/87	A–	X	R	101.96	4-30-96	□100.18	4-30-96	....	....	100	L3	'73	102⅝	95¾	102½	7.56	7.30
1st 8⅛s 2003	mN	**A**	1/87	A–	X	R	102.21	10-31-96	□100.52	10-31-96	....	....	22.6	K2	'73	103	97¾	102¼	7.95	7.73
1st 5⅞s 2004	Jj15	**A**			X	R	NC	....	....	....	....	....	150	P4	'94	98⅛	84⅛	98⅛	5.99	6.17
1st 7⅞s 2004	Ao15	**A**			X	R	NC	....	....	....	....	....	150	P4	'92	110¼	96	110¼	7.14	6.27
1st 8⅞s 2021	Fa15	**A**			X	R	105.69	(2-15-96)	Z105.69	(2-15-96)	....	....	125	M2	'91	107	98⅝	106¼	8.35	8.28
1st 8⅝s 2021	mS15	**A**			X	R	NC	....	....	....	....	....	100	K2	'91	122⅜	98	122⅜	7.05	6.77
1st 9s 2022	Ao	**A**			X	R	105.89	(4-1-96)	Z105.89	(4-1-96)	....	....	100	M6	'91	107¾	99¾	106⅞	8.42	8.35
1st 8.20s 2022	jJ	**A**			X	R	103.55	(7-1-02)	Z103.55	(7-1-02)	....	....	150	P4	'92	111⅛	94¼	111⅛	7.38	7.25
1st 7½s 2023	Ms	**A**			X	R	103.22	(3-1-03)	Z103.22	(3-1-03)	....	....	150	P4	'93	105¼	87¼	105¼	7.13	7.06
1st 6⅞s 2023	fA15	**A**			X	R	102.84	(8-15-03)	Z102.84	(8-15-03)	....	....	100	K2	'93	100⅛	80¾	100⅛	6.87	6.86
Carolina Tel. & Tel.[1]	***67a***	***6.08***	***4.47***	***7.25***		***Dc***	***0.06***	***130.0***	***192.0***	***9-30-95***	***248.0***		***846.0***	***37.6***						
Deb 5¾s 2000	fA15	**A**			X	BE	NC	....	....	....	....	....	50.0	G1	'93	99⅜	88⅞	99⅜	5.79	5.90
Deb 6⅛s 2003	Mn	**A**			X	BE	NC	....	....	....	....	....	50.0	S1	'93	99½	86⅛	99½	6.16	6.21
Deb 7¼s 2004	jD15	**A**			X	R	NC	....	....	....	....	....	50.0	C4	'92	107	91½	107	6.78	6.22
Deb 6¾s 2013	fA15	**A**			X	BE	NC	....	....	....	....	....	50.0	M2	'93	100¼	83⅞	100¼	6.73	6.72
Deb 9s 2016	Mn15	**A**	12/92	A–	X	R	104.48	5-14-96	....	....	....	....	50.0	K2	'86	104⅞	100⅛	104⅝	8.60	8.52
Carpenter Technology	***66c***	***△3.08***	***△4.03***	***△5.16***		***Je***	***10.60***	***241.0***	***123.0***	***9-30-95***	***195.0***		***487.0***	***44.4***						
SF Deb 9s 2022	Ms15	**A–**			X	R	104.24	(3-15-02)	100	(3-15-03)	....	....	100	F1	'92	117⅝	102⅜	117⅝	7.65	7.46
M-T Nts 'A'[2] 7¾s '98	[3]jj15	**A–**			X	BE	NC	....	....	....	....	....	10.0	M5	'94	105⅛	97⅞	105⅛	7.37	5.73
M-T Nts 'A'[2] 7.43s '99	[4]jj15	**A–**			X	BE	NC	....	....	....	....	....	7.50	C5	'94	105⅛	96⅛	105⅛	7.07	5.84
M-T Nts 'A'[2] 7.44s '99	[4]jj15	**A–**			X	BE	NC	....	....	....	....	....	7.50	M5	'94	105⅛	96⅛	105⅛	7.08	5.85
M-T Nts 'A'[2] 7.80s 2000	[5]jj15	**A–**			X	BE	NC	....	....	....	....	....	10.0	C5	'94	107⅜	96¾	107⅜	7.26	5.99
M-T Nts 'A'[2] 7.79s 2001	[6]jj15	**A–**			X	BE	NC	....	....	....	....	....	7.50	M5	'94	108⅛	96⅛	108⅛	7.20	6.08
M-T Nts 'A'[2] 7.80s 2001	[6]jj15	**A–**			X	BE	NC	....	....	....	....	....	7.50	C5	'94	108⅛	96¼	108⅛	7.21	6.09
Carrols Corp	***27b***	***0.89***	***0.65***	***1.01***		***Dc***	***2.09***	***8.44***	***14.10***	***9-30-95***	***128.0***		***102.0***	***127.0***						
Sr Nts[7] 11½s 2003	fA15	**B+**			Y	R	104.31	(8-15-98)	....	....	[8]Z111.50	8-10-96	110	C4	'93	101	92	101	11.39	11.29
Case Corp	***41***	***d5.12***	***1.11***	***2.51***		***Dc***	***59.00***	***3053***	***2176***	***9-30-95***	***1112***		***3360***	***54.8***						
Nts 7¼s 2005	fA	**BBB–**			X	BE	NC	....	....	....	....	....	300	C5	'95	105½	97⅝	105½	6.87	6.47
Caterpillar Financial Svcs	***25***	***1.30***	***1.34***	***1.24***		***Dc***				***9-30-95***	***1767***		***5333***	***88.9***						
M-T Nts 'E' 4½s '96	[9]ao	**A**	4/95	A–	X	BE	NC	....	....	....	....	....	10.0	G1	'93	99¾	96⅛	99¾	4.51	5.45
M-T Nts 'E' 6.31s '96	[10]ao	**A**	4/95	A–	X	BE	NC	....	....	....	....	....	15.0	G1	'94	100½	97½	100⅜	6.29	5.64
M-T Nts 'E' 6.32s '96	[10]ao	**A**	4/95	A–	X	BE	NC	....	....	....	....	....	10.0	G1	'94	100½	97½	99¾	6.34	6.75
M-T Nts 'E' 4.64s '96	[11]ao	**A**	4/95	A–	X	BE	NC	....	....	....	....	....	20.0	G1	'94	99⅜	94½	99⅜	4.67	5.49
M-T Nts 'E' 5.01s '97	[12]ao	**A**	4/95	A–	X	BE	NC	....	....	....	....	....	10.0	G1	'93	99½	94¼	99½	5.04	5.52
M-T Nts 'E' 5.05s '97	[13]ao	**A**	4/95	A–	X	BE	NC	....	....	....	....	....	15.0	G1	'93	99½	94¼	99½	5.08	5.55
M-T Nts 'E' 5.05s '97	[14]ao	**A**	4/95	A–	X	BE	NC	....	....	....	....	....	10.0	G1	'93	99½	94	99½	5.08	5.50
M-T Nts 'E' 4¾s '97	[15]ao	**A**	4/95	A–	X	BE	NC	....	....	....	....	....	6.00	G1	'93	99⅛	93⅜	99⅛	4.79	5.54
M-T Nts 'E' 6.58s '97	[16]ao	**A**	4/95	A–	X	BE	NC	....	....	....	....	....	25.0	G1	'94	101¼	96⅝	101¼	6.50	5.53
M-T Nts 'E' 5.16s '97	[17]ao	**A**	4/95	A–	X	BE	NC	....	....	....	....	....	10.0	G1	'93	99½	94	98⅞	5.22	6.04
M-T Nts 'E' 5.22s '97	[18]ao	**A**	4/95	A–	X	BE	NC	....	....	....	....	....	15.0	G1	'93	99½	92¾	99½	5.25	5.52
M-T Nts 'E' 5.38s '98	[19]ao	**A**	4/95	A–	X	BE	NC	....	....	....	....	....	10.0	G1	'94	99⅜	90⅞	99⅜	5.41	5.65

Uniform Footnote Explanations-See Page 260. Other: [1] Subsid of Sprint Corp. [2] Issued in min denom $100T. [3] Due 10-13-98. [4] Due 8-16-99. [5] Due 9-28-00. [6] Due 9-19-01. [7] (HRO)On Chge of Ctrl at 101. [8] Max $33M red w/proceeds of pub com off'g. [9] Due 3-29-96. [10] Due 8-1-96. [11] Due 9-30-96. [12] Due 1-6-97. [13] Due 1-15-97. [14] Due 12-17-97. [15] Due 2-21-97. [16] Due 4-4-97. [17] Due 5-1-97. [18] Due 9-15-97. [19] Due 7-15-98.

Title-Industry Code & Co. Finances (In Italics) / Individual Issue Statistics, Exchange	Ind / Interest Dates	Fixed Charge Coverage 1992 / S&P Debt Rating	1993 / Date of Last Rating Change	Prior Rating	1994 / Eligible	Year End / Bond Form	Million $ Cash & Equiv. / Redemption Provisions: Regular Price	Curr. Assets / Regular (Begins) Thru	Curr. Liab. / Sinking Fund Price	Balance Sheet Date / Sinking Fund (Begins) Thru	L. Term Debt (Mil $) / Refund/Other Restriction Price	Refund/Other Restriction (Begins) Thru	Capitalization (Mil $) / Outst'g (Mil $)	Total Debt % Capital / Underwriting Firm	Underwriting Year	Price Range 1995 High	Price Range 1995 Low	Mo. End Price Sale(s) or Bid	Curr. Yield	Yield to Mat.
***Caterpillar Financial Svcs** (Cont.)*																				
M-T Nts 'E' 5.34s '98	[1]ao	**A**	4/95	A–	X	BE	NC	....	....	....	....	....	5.00	G1	'93	99¼	90⅝	99¼	5.38	5.65
M-T Nts 'E' 5.52s '98	[2]ao	**A**	4/95	A–	X	BE	NC	....	....	....	....	....	15.0	G1	'93	99⅝	90⅞	99⅝	5.54	5.67
M-T Nts 'E' 5.18s '98	aO	**A**	4/95	A–	X	BE	NC	....	....	....	....	....	20.0	G1	'93	98¾	89¾	98¾	5.25	5.67
M-T Nts 'E' 5.35s '98	[3]ao	**A**	4/95	A–	X	BE	NC	....	....	....	....	....	5.00	G1	'93	99⅛	90	99⅛	5.40	5.68
M-T Nts 'E' 5.47s '98	[4]ao	**A**	4/95	A–	X	BE	NC	....	....	....	....	....	15.0	G1	'94	99⅜	90⅛	99⅜	5.50	5.70
M-T([5]Reset)Nts 'E'[6] 4.44s 2003	[7]ao	**A**	4/95	A–	X	BE	NC	....	....	....	....	....	54.0	G1	'93	98½	91	92	4.83	....
F/R[8]M-T Nts 'E' '96	[9]Qjan	**A**	4/95	A–	X	BE	NC	....	....	....	....	....	12.0	G1	'94	100¼	98	100	....	Mat.
F/R[10]M-T Nts 'E' '96	QFeb	**A**	4/95	A–	X	BE	NC	....	....	....	....	....	25.0	G1	'94	100¼	99¼	100	....	....
F/R[11]M-T Nts 'E' 6.0638s '96	QSep6	**A**	4/95	A–	X	BE	NC	....	....	....	....	....	10.0	G1	'93	100¼	99¼	100	6.06	....
F/R[10]M-T Nts 'E' '96	QMay6	**A**	4/95	A–	X	BE	NC	....	....	....	....	....	5.50	G1	'94	100⅛	99¼	100	....	....
F/R[12]M-T Nts 'E' 6.1106s '96	[13]Qnov24	**A**	4/95	A–	X	BE	NC	....	....	....	....	....	5.00	G1	'93	100¼	99	100	6.11	....
F/R[14]M-T Nts 'E' 6.1531s '97	QMay9	**A**	4/95	A–	X	BE	NC	....	....	....	....	....	38.0	G1	'94	100¼	99	100⅛	6.15	....
F/R[15]M-T Nts 'E' 5.335s '98	QNov24	**A**	4/95	A–	X	BE	NC	....	....	....	....	....	25.0	G1	'93	100	99	100	5.34	....
F/R[16]M-T Nts 'E' 7.455s '98	QDec7	**A**	4/95	A–	X	BE	NC	....	....	....	....	....	25.0	G1	'93	99¾	98¼	98¾	7.55	....
F/R[17]M-T Nts 'E' 5.67s '99	QApr	**A**	4/95	A–	X	BE	NC	....	....	....	....	....	20.0	G1	'94	99¼	97½	98¼	5.77	....
F/R[17]M-T Nts 'E' 5.67s '99	QApr	**A**	4/95	A–	X	BE	NC	....	....	....	....	....	20.0	G1	'94	99¼	97½	98¼	5.77	....
F/R[17]M-T Nts 'E' 5.67s '99	[18]QApr	**A**	4/95	A–	X	BE	NC	....	....	....	....	....	20.0	G1	'94	99¼	97½	98¼	5.77	....
Caterpillar Inc[19]	***41b***	***0.25***	***2.64***		***4.10***	***Dc***	***897.0***	***8304***	***5874***	***9-30-95***	***4589***		***10256***	***65.9***						
• SF[20]Deb 9¾s 2019	Jd	**A**	4/95	A–	X	BE	104.875	(6-1-99)	100	(6-1-00)	....	....	300	S4	'89	116½	103	114	8.55	8.38
• Deb 9s 2006	Ao15	**A**	4/95	A–	X	BE	NC	....	....	....	....	....	250	L3	'91	118⅜	102½	117¼	7.68	6.66
• Deb 6s 2007	Mn	**A**	4/95	A–	X	R	100	....	....	....	....	....	[21]250	G1	'82	97½	78¾	97	6.19	6.37
• Deb 9⅜s 2011	fA15	**A**	4/95	A–	X	BE	NC	....	....	....	....	....	150	G1	'91	120¾	108⅛	119⅛	7.87	7.30
• Deb 9⅜s 2021	Ms15	**A**	4/95	A–	X	BE	NC	....	....	....	....	....	250	G1	'91	107⅞	107⅞	110⅝	8.47	8.36
• Deb 8s 2023	Fa15	**A**	4/95	A–	X	BE	NC	....	....	....	....	....	200	L3	'93	107¼	107¼	106	7.55	7.48
• Nts 9⅛s '96	jD15	**A**	4/95	A–	X	BE	NC	....	....	....	....	....	150	M2	'90	105	101½	103	8.86	5.86
• Nts 9⅜s 2000	jJ15	**A**	4/95	A–	X	BE	NC	....	....	....	....	....	150	M2	'90	112½	105	111⅛	8.44	6.51
• Nts 9⅜s 2001	jJ15	**A**	4/95	A–	X	BE	NC	....	....	....	....	....	200	M2	'91	114⅜	104	113¼	8.28	6.49
CBI Indus	***14b***	***8.00***	***4.15***		***3.86***	***Dc***	***35.70***	***541.0***	***352.0***	***9-30-95***	***716.0***		***1540***	***52.0***						
Nts 6¼s 2000	Jd30	**BBB**			X	BE	NC	....	....	....	....	....	75.0	M2	'93	100⅝	90⅜	100⅜	6.23	6.15
Nts 6⅝s 2003	Ms15	**BBB**			X	BE	NC	....	....	....	....	....	75.0	L3	'93	101¾	88⅝	101	6.56	6.45
CBS,[22]Inc[23]	***12***	***4.06***	***8.87***		***8.16***	***Dc***	***49.50***	***850.0***	***646.0***	***6-30-95***	***507.0***		***955.0***	***56.3***						
Sr Deb 8⅞s 2022	Jd	**BB**	11/95	A	Y	BE	104.14	(6-1-02)	....	....	....	....	91.6	S1	'92	111¼	94¾	102½	8.66	8.63
Sr Nts 7¾s '99	Jd	**BB**	11/95	A	Y	BE	NC	....	....	....	....	....	125	S1	'92	104¾	95½	101⅜	7.64	7.29
Sr Nts 7⅝s 2002	Jj	**BB**	11/95	A	Y	BE	NC	....	....	....	....	....	150	S1	'92	105⅜	93⅛	100⅛	7.62	7.60
Sr Nts 7⅛s 2023	mN	**BB**	11/95	A	Y	BE	NC	....	....	....	....	....	97.3	B5	'93	96¾	77¾	86⅞	8.20	8.34
CCP Insurance	***35a***	***1.33***	***1.42***		***1.45***	***Dc***				***6-30-95***	***197.0***		***694.0***	***28.4***						
Sr Nts 10½s 2004	jD15	**BB+**	8/95	BBB	Y	BE	NC	....	....	....	....	....	200	M6	'94	108¼	107⅜	108¼	9.70	9.13
Cellular Inc	***67g***	***Now CommNet Cellular,see***																		
Sr Sub[24]Disc Nts[25] 11¾s 2003	mS	**CCC**			Y	R	105.87	(9-1-98)	....	....	....	....	[21]177	B9	'93	79⅝	65½	79⅝	....	Flat
[26]CenCall Communications	***67g***	***d3.76***	***d7.99***		***d2.44***	***Dc***	***98.60***	***112.0***	***95.20***	***3-31-95***	***285.0***		***318.0***	***89.9***						
Sr Redeem[27]Disc Nts[28] 10⅛s 2004	Jj15	**CCC–**	2/94	NR	Y	R	104.80	(1-15-99)	....	....	....	....	[21]410	M2	'94	56	28½	56	....	Flat
Centel Capital	***25***	***Gtd by Sprint Corp,see***																		
Deb[29] 9s 2019	aO15	**BBB**	2/94	BBB–	X	R	NC	....	....	....	....	....	150	M6	'89	124¾	105½	124¾	7.21	6.87
Centennial Cellular	***67***	***Δd1.57***	***Δd1.07***		***Δd1.22***	***My***	***95.40***	***115.0***	***30.70***	***8-31-95***	***350.0***		***712.0***	***49.2***						
Sr Nts[30] 8⅞s 2001	mN	**B**			Y	R	105.25	(5-1-99)	....	....	....	....	250	M2	'93	98¼	87½	98¼	9.03	9.26
Sr Nts[30] 10⅛s 2005	Mn15	**B**			Y	R	NC	....	....	....	....	....	100	M2	'95	105	97¾	104¾	9.67	9.35

Uniform Footnote Explanations-See Page 260. Other: [1] Due 8-14-98. [2] Due 9-16-98. [3] Due 11-10-98. [4] Due 12-15-98. [5] Int at 4.44% to 10-21-96,6.38% aft. [6] (HRO)On 10-22-96 at 100. [7] Due 10-22-03. [8] Int at 0% thru maturity. [9] Due 1-8-96. [10] Int adj weekly. [11] Int thru 3-5-96,adj qtrly aft. [12] Int thru 2-23-96,adj qtrly aft. [13] Due 11-29-96. [14] Int thru 2-8-96,adj qtrly aft. [15] Int thru 2-24-96,adj qtrly aft. [16] Int thru 3-6-96,adj qtrly aft. [17] Int thru 12-31-95,adj qtrly aft. [18] Due 4-5-99. [19] Was Caterpillar Tractor. [20] (HRO)To 6-1-99 at 100,for a Risk Event. [21] Incl disc. [22] Was Columbia Broadcasting. [23] Acq by Westinghouse Elec. [24] Int accr at 11.75% fr 9-1-98. [25] (HRO)On Chge of Ctrl at 101(Accreted Val). [26] Now OneComm Corp. [27] Int accrues at 10.125% fr 1-15-99. [28] Co must offer 101(Accreted Val),on Chge of Ctrl. [29] (HRO)On 10-15-99 at 100. [30] (HRO)On Chge of Ctrl at 101.

Title-Industry Code & Co. Finances (In Italics) / Individual Issue Statistics, Exchange	Ind / Interest Dates	Fixed Charge Coverage 1992 / S&P Debt Rating	1993 / Date of Last Rating Change	1994 / Prior Rating	Eligible	Year End / Bond Form	Cash & Equiv. (Million $) / Redemption Provisions: Regular Price	Curr. Assets (Million $) / Regular (Begins) Thru	Curr. Liab. (Million $) / Sinking Fund Price	Balance Sheet Date / Sinking Fund (Begins) Thru	L. Term Debt (Mil $) / Refund/Other Restriction Price	Refund/Other Restriction (Begins) Thru	Capitalization (Mil $) / Outst'g (Mil $)	Total Debt % Capital / Underwriting Firm	Underwriting Year	Price Range 1995 High	Price Range 1995 Low	Mo. End Price Sale(s) or Bid	Curr. Yield	Yield to Mat.
Centex Corp	***13h***	***5.15***	***5.55***	***3.12***		***Mr***				***9-30-95***	***322.0***		***1692***	***59.2***						
Sr Nts 9.05s '96	Mn	**BBB**			X	BE	NC	....	....	....	....	....	100	D6	'91	101⅞	101	101	8.96	5.95
Sub Deb 7⅜s 2005	Jd	**BBB–**			X	BE	NC	....	....	....	....	....	100		'95	102¾	94⅜	102¾	7.18	6.97
Central Bancshrs South[1]	***10***	***3.70***	***4.69***	***3.97***		***Dc***				***9-30-95***	***660.0***		***1332***	***49.5***						
Sub Nts 7s 2003	Mn	**BBB**			X	BE	NC	....	....	....	....	....	75.0	F1	'93	103¾	89¾	103¾	6.75	6.35
Central Fidelity Banks	***10***	***29.86***	***8.83***	***4.01***		***Dc***				***9-30-95***	***754.0***		***1538***	***49.0***						
Sub Nts 8.15s 2002	mN15	**BBB**			X	BE	NC	....	....	....	....	....	150	S1	'92	110⅛	96½	110⅛	7.40	6.31
Central Hudson Gas & Elec	***75***	***3.97***	***3.35***	***3.58***		***Dc***	***41.80***	***147.0***	***89.20***	***9-30-95***	***389.0***		***917.0***	***43.0***						
1st 8¾s 2001	Mn	**A–**	6/91	BBB+	X	R	102.07	(5-1-96)	▲100	....	....	....	30.0	K2	'91	104	100	103	8.50	8.04
1st 9¼s 2021	Mn	**A–**	6/91	BBB+	X	R	104.08	(5-1-01)	▲100	....	....	....	70.0	K2	'91	114¾	101	114¾	8.06	7.89
Central Illinois Light[2]	***75***	***3.24***	***3.58***	***3.76***		***Dc***	***0.65***	***106.0***	***79.70***	***9-30-95***	***286.0***		***712.0***	***44.5***						
1st 5⅛s '96	Fa	**AA–**	7/94	AA	X	R	100	....	▲100	....	....	....	16.0	F1	'66	100	97⅜	100	5.13	5.02
1st 5½s '97	Ms	**AA–**	7/94	AA	X	R	100.23	2-29-96	▲100.14	2-29-96	....	....	20.0	S1	'67	99⅞	94¾	99⅞	5.51	5.60
1st 5.70s '98	Jd8	**AA–**	7/94	AA	X	BE	NC	....	....	....	....	....	10.7	K2	'93	100⅜	92⅝	100⅜	5.68	5.53
1st 6.40s 2000	Fa9	**AA–**	7/94	AA	X	BE	NC	....	....	....	....	....	30.0	K2	'93	102¼	92	102¼	6.26	5.78
1st 6.82s 2003	Fa10	**AA–**	7/94	AA	X	BE	NC	....	....	....	....	....	25.4	K2	'93	104¼	90½	104¼	6.54	6.07
1st 7½s 2007	Jj15	**AA–**	7/94	AA	X	BE	NC	....	....	....	....	....	50.0	S5	'92	109¾	92⅞	109¾	6.83	6.26
1st 8.20s 2022	Jj15	**AA–**	7/94	AA	X	BE	103.66	(1-15-02)	▲100	(1-15-02)	....	....	65.0	S5	'92	110⅞	94	110⅞	7.40	7.26
1st 7.80s 2023	Fa9	**AA–**	7/94	AA	X	BE	103.90	(2-9-03)	▲100	....	....	....	8.00	K2	'93	113	91⅛	113	6.90	6.75
1st 7.80s 2023	Fa9	**AA–**	7/94	AA	X	BE	103.90	(2-9-03)	▲100	....	....	....	2.00	K2	'93	113	91⅛	113	6.90	6.75
Central Illinois Pub Serv[3]	***75***	***4.03***	***4.76***	***4.90***		***Dc***	***6.60***	***207.0***	***143.0***	***9-30-95***	***479.0***		***1145***	***41.8***						
1st L 5⅞s '97	Mn	**AA+**	10/84	AA	X	R	100.31	4-30-96	100.31	4-30-96	....	....	15.0	S1	'67	100¼	95½	100¼	5.86	5.67
1st W 7⅛s '99	Mn15	**AA+**			X	R	NC	....	....	....	....	....	50.0	M6	'92	104¼	96	104¼	6.83	5.72
1st W 8½s 2022	Mn15	**AA+**			X	R	106.37	(5-15-97)	....	....	....	....	33.0	M6	'92	108⅞	99½	108⅞	7.81	7.71
1st X 6⅛s '97	jJ	**AA+**			X	R	NC	....	....	....	....	....	43.0	M6	'92	100⅞	95¾	100⅞	6.07	5.51
1st X 7½s 2007	jJ	**AA+**			X	R	100	(7-1-02)	....	....	....	....	50.0	M6	'92	108⅝	93	108⅝	6.90	6.43
1st Y 6¾s 2002	mS15	**AA+**			X	R	NC	....	....	....	....	....	23.0	M6	'92	104½	90¾	104½	6.46	5.93
1st Z 6s 2000	Ao	**AA+**			X	R	NC	....	....	....	....	....	25.0	M6	'93	100¾	90⅜	100¾	5.96	5.80
1st Z 6⅜s 2003	Ao	**AA+**			X	R	NC	....	....	....	....	....	40.0	M6	'93	102½	88⅛	102½	6.22	5.94
Central La Elec	***72a***	***3.18***	***3.64***	***3.32***		***Dc***	***18.50***	***72.20***	***113.0***	***9-30-95***	***361.0***		***788.0***	***49.9***						
1st X 9½s 2005	Ms15	**A**	12/91	A–	X	R	NC	....	....	....	....	....	60.0	S1	'90	119¼	104⅝	119¼	7.97	6.67
1st Y 9⅝s 2021	jJ15	**A**	12/91	A–	X	R	107.70	7-14-96	Z100	....	®107.22	7-14-96	50.0	F1	'91	109¼	106⅞	106⅞	9.01	8.94
Central Maine Power	***72a***	***2.32***	***2.54***	***2.08***		***Dc***	***61.70***	***231.0***	***159.0***	***9-30-95***	***628.0***		***1261***	***50.0***						
Gen & Ref N 8½s 2001	mS15	**BB+**	1/94	BBB–	Y	R	NC	....	Z100	....	....	....	22.5	L3	'91	105¼	94	105¼	8.08	7.35
Gen & Ref O 7⅜s '99	Jj	**BB+**	1/94	BBB–	Y	R	NC	....	Z100	....	....	....	50.0	K2	'91	100⅞	92⅝	100⅞	7.31	7.05
Gen & Ref Q 7.05s 2008	Ms	**BB+**	1/94	BBB–	Y	R	102.80	(3-1-99)	....	....	....	....	75.0	K2	'93	94⅝	80¼	94⅝	7.45	7.74
Gen & Ref R 7⅞s 2023	Jd	**BB+**	1/94	BBB–	Y	R	103.30	(6-1-03)	Z100	....	....	....	50.0	L3	'93	101⅞	85⅞	101⅞	7.73	7.71
Gen & Ref T 6¼s '98	mN	**BB+**	1/94	BBB–	Y	R	NC	....	Z100	....	....	....	75.0	K2	'93	98⅛	89⅝	98⅛	6.37	6.98
Central Power & Light[4]	***72a***	***2.60***	***2.32***	***2.75***		***Dc***	***1.47***	***162.0***	***340.0***	***9-30-95***	***1518***		***3228***	***47.0***						
1st J 6⅝s '98	Jj	**A**	6/92	A–	X	CR	100.58	12-31-96	100.34	12-31-96	....	....	28.0	F1	'68	101	95⅝	100⅝	6.58	6.29
1st L 7s 2001	Fa	**A**	6/92	A–	X	R	101.32	1-31-96	100.25	1-31-96	....	....	36.0	F1	'71	101⅞	93⅜	101⅝	6.89	6.62
1st BB 6s '97	aO	**A**			X	R	NC	....	....	....	....	....	200	M2	'92	100½	94⅝	100½	5.97	5.69
1st CC 7¼s 2004	aO	**A**			X	R	NC	....	....	....	....	....	100	M2	'92	106⅞	92	106⅞	6.78	6.22
1st DD 7⅛s '99	jD	**A**			X	R	NC	....	....	....	....	....	25.0	M6	'92	104⅛	95	104⅛	6.84	5.93
1st EE 7½s 2002	jD	**A**			X	R	NC	....	....	....	....	....	115	M6	'92	107½	94½	107½	6.98	6.15
1st FF 6⅞s 2003	Fa	**A**			X	R	NC	....	....	....	....	....	50.0	M6	'93	104⅛	91	104⅛	6.60	6.15
1st GG 7⅛s 2008	Fa	**A**			X	R	NC	....	....	....	....	....	75.0	M6	'93	106½	87⅞	106½	6.69	6.35

Uniform Footnote Explanations-See Page 260. Other: [1] Now Compass Bancshares. [2] Subsid of CILCORP Inc. [3] Subsid of CIPSCO Inc. [4] Subsid of Central & South West.

Title-Industry Code & Co. Finances (In Italics) / Individual Issue Statistics — Exchange	Ind / Interest Dates	Fixed Charge Coverage 1992 / S&P Debt Rating	1993 / Date of Last Rating Change	Prior Rating	1994 / Eligible	Year End / Bond Form	Million $ Cash & Equiv. / Redemption Provisions — Regular Price	Curr. Assets / Regular (Begins) Thru	Curr. Liab. / Sinking Fund Price	Balance Sheet Date / Sinking Fund (Begins) Thru	L. Term Debt (Mil $) / Refund/Other Restriction Price	Refund/Other Restriction (Begins) Thru	Capital-ization (Mil $) / Outst'g (Mil $)	Total Debt % Capital / Underwriting Firm	Underwriting Year	Price Range 1995 High	Price Range 1995 Low	Mo. End Price Sale(s) or Bid	Curr. Yield	Yield to Mat.
***Central Power & Light** (Cont.)*																				
1st II 7½s 2023	Ao	**A**			X	R	103.32	(4-1-03)	....	....	....	....	100	M6	'93	103¼	86½	103¼	7.26	7.22
1st HH 6s 2000	Ao	**A**			X	R	NC	....	....	....	....	....	100	M6	'93	100⅜	90⅛	100⅜	5.98	5.90
1st JJ 7½s '99	Mn	**A**			X	R	NC	....	....	....	....	....	100	M2	'94	105⅛	96¾	105⅛	7.13	5.79
1st KK 6⅝s 2005	jJ	**A**			X	R	NC	....	....	....	....	....	200	M6	'95	102⅞	95⅜	102⅞	6.44	6.22
Century Communications	***12a***	***Δ0.42***	***Δ0.47***		***Δ0.20***	***My***	***168.0***	***212.0***	***115.0***	***8-31-95***	***1751***		***1430***	***126.0***						
Sr Nts 9½s 2000	fA15	**BB−**	1/94	B+	Y	R	NC	....	....	....	....	....	150	B9	'92	103⅛	95½	103	9.22	8.69
Sr Nts 9¾s 2002	Fa15	**BB−**	1/94	B+	Y	R	NC	....	....	....	....	....	200	D6	'92	104	95¾	104	9.38	8.89
Zero[1]Cpn Sr Disc Nts 2003	[2]	**BB−**	1/94	B+	Y	R	NC	....	....	....	....	....	[3]444	L3	'93	53½	40½	53½	....	8.86
Sr Nts 9½s 2005	Ms	**BB−**			Y	R	NC	....	....	....	....	....	250	M2	'95	103⅛	96½	103⅛	9.21	8.99
Sr Sub Deb 11⅞s 2003	aO15	**B+**	1/94	B	Y	R	105	(4-15-97)	100	(10-15-01)	....	....	204	D6	'91	107¾	103½	107¾	11.02	10.39
Century Telephone Enterprises	***67a***	***4.12***	***4.24***		***4.43***	***Dc***	***10.00***	***94.00***	***183.0***	***9-30-95***	***570.0***		***1487***	***42.2***						
Sr Nts 'A' 7¾s 2004	Mn	**BBB+**			X	R	NC	....	....	....	....	....	50.0	P1	'94	109	94	109	7.11	6.34
Sr Nts 'B' 8¼s 2024	Mn	**BBB+**			X	R	103.62	(5-1-04)	....	....	....	....	100	P1	'94	109¾	93½	109¾	7.52	7.42
Sr Nts 'C' 6.55s 2005	jD	**BBB+**		BBB+	X	R	NC	....	....	....	....	....	50.0	P1	'95	101⅛	99⅞	101⅛	6.48	6.39
Sr Nts 'D' 7.20s 2025	jD	**BBB+**			X	R	[4]Z100	....	....	....	....	....	100	P1	'95	102⅜	99¾	102⅜	7.03	7.01
Champion Int'l	***50***	***0.46***	***0.22***		***1.35***	***Dc***	***343.0***	***1554***	***1162***	***9-30-95***	***2777***		***6636***	***47.3***						
Deb 7⅝s 2023	mS	**BBB**			X	BE	103.451	(9-1-03)	....	....	....	....	100	G1	'93	103⅜	85⅛	103⅜	7.38	7.34
Deb 7¾s 2025	mS	**BBB**			X	BE	NC	....	....	....	....	....	150	G1	'95	107⅝	99½	107	7.24	7.18
Deb 7.35s 2025	mN	**BBB**			X	BE	[4]Z100	(11-1-96)	....	....	....	....	200	S1	'95	102⅝	99¼	102⅝	7.16	7.14
Nts 9.80s '98	Fa	**BBB**			X	R	NC	....	....	....	....	....	225	G1	'91	108½	103⅜	108	9.07	5.68
Nts 7.70s '99	jD15	**BBB**			X	BE	NC	....	....	....	....	....	200	G1	'93	106¼	96½	106¼	7.25	5.91
Nts 9⅞s 2000	Jd	**BBB**			X	R	NC	....	....	....	....	....	200	G1	'90	115	105½	115	8.59	5.96
Nts 9.70s 2001	Mn	**BBB**			X	R	NC	....	....	....	....	....	200	G1	'91	116½	105⅝	116½	8.33	6.04
Nts 7.10s 2005	mS	**BBB**			X	BE	NC	....	....	....	....	....	150	G1	'95	104⅞	99⅞	104⅞	6.77	6.41
Chancellor Broadcast'g Co	***23f***	***n/a***	***n/a***		***1.37***	***Dc***	***1.25***	***15.60***	***13.20***	***9-30-95***	***167.0***		***226.0***	***75.2***						
Sr Sub Nts[5] 12½s 2004	aO	**B−**			Y	R	105.556	(10-1-99)	....	....	[6]Z111.111	9-30-96	80.0	B9	'94	107	97	107	11.68	11.22
Chartwell Re	***35c***	***d2.90***	***2.43***		***0.31***	***Dc***				***3-31-95***	***75.00***		***137.0***	***54.7***						
Sr Nts[7] 10¼s 2004	Ms	**BB**	12/95	BB−	Y	R	103.84	(3-1-99)	....	....	[8]Z108.97	2-29-96	75.0	S1	'94	100	100	A100	10.25	10.24
Chase Manhattan Corp	***10***	***1.37***	***1.28***		***1.84***	***Dc***				***9-30-95***	***5518***		***14496***	***38.1***						
Nts 7⅞s '97	Jj15	**A**	4/94	A−	X	R	NC	....	....	....	....	....	227	F1	'87	102½	99⅛	102⅜	7.69	5.50
• F/R[9]Nts[10] 6.35s '99	Jd15	**NR**				R	100	....	....	....	....	....	11.0	L3	'74	100⅛	99	99	6.41	....
• F/R[11]Sub Nts 5.9375s 2003	QAug	**A−**	4/94	BBB+	X	BE	NC	....	....	....	....	....	100	S1	'93	No Sale		100	5.94	....
• F/R[12]Sub Nts 6.0625s 2003	QJul15	**A−**	4/94	BBB+	X	BE	NC	....	....	....	....	....	150	B5	'93	No Sale		100	6.06	....
• Sub Nts 7½s '97	jD	**A−**	4/94	BBB+	X	BE	NC	....	....	....	....	....	200	M2	'92	102⅞	97⅞	102⅛	7.34	6.30
Sub Nts 10s '99	Jd15	**A−**	4/94	BBB+	X	R	NC	....	....	....	....	....	275	S1	'87	112¾	105	112¾	8.87	5.87
• Sub Nts 8s '99	Jd15	**A−**	4/94	BBB+	X	BE	NC	....	....	....	....	....	200	S1	'92	105½	98	s104½	7.66	6.52
• Sub Nts 7¾s '99	mN	**A−**	4/94	BBB+	X	BE	NC	....	....	....	....	....	200	G1	'92	106	96⅝	104½	7.42	6.41
• Sub Nts 8.80s 2000	Fa	**A−**			X	BE	100	(2-1-97)	....	....	....	....	150	D6	'95	104⅞	100	102¼	8.61	8.14
Sub Nts 9⅜s 2001	jJ	**A−**	4/94	BBB+	X	R	NC	....	....	....	....	....	200	M2	'89	115⅜	102⅞	115⅜	8.13	6.05
Sub Nts 9¾s 2001	mN	**A−**	4/94	BBB+	X	BE	NC	....	....	....	....	....	150	M2	'91	117⅞	104⅞	117⅞	8.27	6.07
• Sub Nts 9.05s 2002	Fa	**A−**			X	BE	100	(2-1-97)	....	....	....	....	100	S5	'95	102¼	100	100¾	8.98	8.88
• Sub Nts 8s 2002	Ao15	**A−**			X	BE	*100	(4-15-97)	....	....	....	....	150	C1	'95	103	99¼	100½	7.96	7.89
• Sub Nts 7½s 2003	Fa	**A−**	4/94	BBB+	X	BE	NC	....	....	....	....	....	200	S1	'93	106¾	93¾	106½	7.04	6.35
• Sub Nts 8s 2004	Mn15	**A−**			X	BE	100	(5-15-99)	....	....	....	....	150	D6	'94	106½	94⅛	102⅝	7.80	7.57
• Sub Nts 7⅞s 2004	fA	**A−**			X	BE	100	(8-1-99)	....	....	....	....	150	B5	'94	104	93¼	103⅛	7.64	7.38
• Sub Nts 8s 2005	Mn	**A−**			X	R	*100	(5-1-98)	....	....	....	....	150	C1	'95	104¼	99¾	102⅞	7.78	7.56

Uniform Footnote Explanations-See Page 260. Other: [1] (HRO)For a Triggering Event at 101. [2] Due 3-15-03. [3] Incl disc. [4] Greater of 100 or amt based on formula. [5] (HRO)On Chge of Ctrl at 101. [6] Max $20M red w/proceeds of Pub Eq Off'g. [7] (HRO)On Chge of Ctrl & Ratings Decline,at 101. [8] Max $26.3M red w/proceeds Pub Equity Off'g. [9] (HRO)On int pyt dates at 100. [10] Int thru 6-14-96,adj for T-Bill Rte,etc. [11] Int thru 2-1-96,adj qtrly aft. [12] Int(min 4.35%)to 1-16-96,adj qtrly aft.

Title-Industry Code & Co. Finances (In Italics) / Exchange ↓ Individual Issue Statistics	Ind / Interest Dates	Fixed Charge Coverage 1992 / S&P Debt Rating	1993 / Date of Last Rating Change	Prior Rating	1994 / Eligible ↓	Year End / Bond Form	Million $ Cash & Equiv. / Regular Price	Curr. Assets / Regular (Begins) Thru	Curr. Liab. / Sinking Fund Price	Balance Sheet Date / Sinking Fund (Begins) Thru	L. Term Debt (Mil $) / Refund/Other Restriction Price	Refund/Other Restriction (Begins) Thru	Capital-ization (Mil $) / Outst'g (Mil $)	Total Debt % Capital / Underwriting Firm	Underwriting Year	Price Range 1995 High	Low	Mo. End Price Sale(s) or Bid	Curr. Yield	Yield to Mat.
***Chase Manhattan Corp** (Cont.)*																				
• Sub Nts 6½s 2005	fA	**A–**	4/94	BBB+	X	BE	NC	....	....	....	....	....	200	C1	'93	101¾	85	99	6.57	6.64
• Sub Nts 6¾s 2008	fA15	**A–**	4/94	BBB+	X	BE	NC	....	....	....	....	....	200	L3	'93	98⅝	85	98	6.89	6.99
• Sub Nts 6⅛s 2008	aO15	**A–**	4/94	BBB+	X	BE	NC	....	....	....	....	....	100	C1	'93	98	84	94⅛	6.51	6.82
• Sub Nts 6½s 2009	Jj15	**A–**	4/94	BBB+	X	BE	NC	....	....	....	....	....	150	G1	'94	99¾	86¾	95	6.84	7.09
Chemical Bank	***10***	***Subsid of Chemical Banking Corp, see***																		
F/R[1]Sub Nts 6s 2003	QJul29	**A**			X	BE	NC	....	....	....	....	....	150	B5	'93	99½	96⅜	98½	6.09	....
Sub Nts 7¼s 2002	mS15	**A**	3/93	A–	X	R	NC	....	....	....	....	....	300	G1	'92	106⅜	91⅜	106⅜	6.82	6.08
Sub Nts 7s 2005	Jd	**A**			X	BE	NC	....	....	....	....	....	200	G1	'93	105¼	88	105¼	6.65	6.25
Sub Nts 6⅝s 2005	fA15	**A**			X	BE	NC	....	....	....	....	....	150	S1	'93	102⅞	85	102⅞	6.44	6.22
Sub Nts 6⅛s 2008	mN	**A**			X	BE	NC	....	....	....	....	....	150	M2	'93	97⅞	78	97⅞	6.26	6.37
Sub Nts 6.70s 2008	fA15	**A**			X	BE	NC	....	....	....	....	....	150	M6	'93	102¾	82⅛	102¾	6.52	6.38
***Chemical Banking Corp**[2]*	***10***	***1.79***	***2.48***		***2.24***	***Dc***				***9-30-95***	***7537***		***19368***	***38.9***						
Sr Nts 7⅜s '97	Jd15	**A**	3/93	A–	X	R	NC	....	....	....	....	....	100	M2	'92	102½	98	102½	7.20	5.57
Sr Nts 6⅝s '98	Jj15	**A**	3/93	A–	X	R	NC	....	....	....	....	....	300	M2	'93	102	95¼	102	6.50	5.57
F/R[3]Sr Nts 6.31s '96	QMar11	**A**	3/93	A–	X	R	NC	....	....	....	....	....	100	K2	'93	100	100	100	6.31	....
Sub Deb 8⅝s 2002	Mn	**A–**	3/93	BBB+	X	R	NC	....	....	....	....	....	150	F1	'92	113⅛	99⅜	113⅛	7.62	6.10
Sub Deb 7⅛s 2005	Ms	**A–**	3/93	BBB+	X	R	NC	....	....	....	....	....	200	F1	'93	105⅞	89⅛	105⅞	6.73	6.27
Sub Deb 7⅞s 2006	jJ15	**A–**			X	BE	NC	....	....	....	....	....	150		'94	111¾	95½	111¾	7.05	6.33
Sub Deb 6½s 2009	Jj15	**A–**			X	BE	NC	....	....	....	....	....	200	C5	'94	100½	80¾	100½	6.47	6.44
Sub Nts 10⅜s '99	Ms15	**A–**	3/93	BBB+	X	R	NC	....	....	....	....	....	100	M2	'89	113¼	106⅛	113¼	9.16	5.79
Sub Nts 8½s 2002	Fa15	**A–**	3/93	BBB+	X	R	NC	....	....	....	....	....	200	M2	'92	112⅛	98½	112⅛	7.58	6.10
Sub Nts 8⅛s 2002	Jd15	**A–**	3/93	BBB+	X	R	NC	....	....	....	....	....	100	G1	'92	110⅝	96¾	110⅝	7.34	6.11
Sub Nts 7⅝s 2003	Jj15	**A–**	3/93	BBB+	X	R	NC	....	....	....	....	....	200	L3	'93	108¼	93⅜	108¼	7.04	6.16
Sub Cap[4]Nts 10⅛s 2000	mN	**A–**	3/93	BBB+	X	R	NC	....	....	....	....	....	150	S1	'88	116	106⅝	115⅞	8.74	6.27
Chemical N.Y. Corp.	***10***	***Now Chemical Banking, see***																		
Sub Cap[4]Nts 9¾s '99	Jd15	**A–**	3/93	BBB+	X	R	NC	....	....	....	....	....	300	F1	'87	112¼	104⅛	112¼	8.69	5.79
*[5]**Chesapeake[6]Pot.Tel Md***	***67a***	***4.94***	***5.91***		***5.99***	***Dc***		***491.0***	***560.0***	***12-31-94***	***976.0***		***1973***	***51.8***						
Deb 5⅞s '99	mS15	**AA**			X	BE	NC	....	....	....	....	....	100	S1	'92	100⅜	91	100⅜	5.85	5.76
Deb 4⅜s 2002	Jj	**AA**	3/91	AA–	X	CR	100.24	12-31-96	....	....	....	....	50.0	M6	'63	92¼	79⅜	92¼	4.74	5.93
Deb 6s 2003	Mn	**AA**			X	BE	NC	....	....	....	....	....	200	S1	'93	99⅝	85⅞	99⅝	6.02	6.06
Deb 5⅞s 2004	Jd	**AA**	3/91	AA–	X	R	100.84	5-31-96	....	....	....	....	60.0	M2	'67	97⅜	84¼	97⅜	6.03	6.28
Deb 6⅝s 2008	aO	**AA**	3/91	AA–	X	R	101.29	9-30-96	....	....	....	....	75.0	M6	'68	100⅛	85⅜	100⅛	6.62	6.61
• Deb 7¼s 2012	Fa	**AA**	3/91	AA–	X	R	102.26	1-31-96	....	....	....	....	50.0	M6	'72	101	87¼	101¼	7.16	7.12
Deb 7.15s 2023	Mn	**AA**			X	BE	100	(5-1-13)	....	....	....	....	250	G1	'93	104⅞	85¾	104⅞	6.82	6.76
Deb[7] 8s 2029	a015	**AA**	3/91	AA–	X	R	NC	....	....	....	....	....	50.0	M6	'89	118½	100⅞	118½	6.75	6.62
Deb[8] 8.30s 2031	fA	**AA**			X	BE	NC	....	....	....	....	....	100	L3	'91	122¾	101	122¾	6.76	6.63
*[5]**Chesapeake&Pot.Tel Va**[9]*	***67a***	***5.90***	***6.28***		***6.99***	***Dc***		***449.0***	***541.0***	***12-31-94***	***937.0***		***1989***	***48.2***						
Deb 7⅛s 2002	Jj15	**AA+**			X	BE	NC	....	....	....	....	....	100	S1	'92	105¾	93½	105¾	6.74	5.98
Deb 5¼s 2005	Mn	**AA+**	4/87	AAA	X	R	100.95	4-30-96	....	....	....	....	50.0	F1	'66	93½	79¼	93½	5.61	6.18
Deb 6⅛s 2005	jJ15	**AA+**			X	BE	NC	....	....	....	....	....	100	L3	'93	100⅜	84⅝	100⅜	6.10	6.07
Deb 5⅝s 2007	Ms	**AA+**	4/87	AAA	X	R	101.33	2-29-96	....	....	....	....	65.0	F1	'67	94¾	79½	94¾	5.94	6.28
Deb 6¾s 2008	Mn	**AA+**	4/87	AAA	X	R	101.27	4-30-96	....	....	....	....	70.0	M6	'68	101⅛	86⅛	101⅛	6.67	6.61
• Deb 7¼s 2012	Jd	**AA+**	4/87	AAA	X	R	102.10	5-31-96	....	....	....	....	50.0	F1	'72	101¼	86⅛	s101¼	7.16	7.12
Deb 7⅝s 2012	jD	**AA+**			X	BE	NC	....	....	....	....	....	100	F1	'92	110	92	110	6.93	6.63
Deb 7⅞s 2022	Jj15	**AA+**			X	BE	NC	....	....	....	....	....	100	S1	'92	114	93⅜	114	6.91	6.73
Deb 7¼s 2024	Ao15	**AA+**			X	BE	103.17	(4-15-03)	....	....	....	....	75.0	L3	'93	104¾	85¾	104¾	6.92	6.87

Uniform Footnote Explanations-See Page 260. Other: [1] Int(min 4.20%)to 1-29-96,adj qtrly aft. [2] See Chemical Bank,Mfrs Hanover,Margaretten Finl. [3] Int(max 7%)to 3-11-96,adj qtrly aft. [4] To be exch for Cap Sec when due. [5] Subsid of Bell Atlantic Corp. [6] Now Bell Atlantic-Maryland. [7] (HRO)On 10-15-96 at 100. [8] (HRO)On 8-1-96 at 100. [9] Now Bell Atlantic-Virginia.

Title-Industry Code & Co. Finances (In Italics) / Individual Issue Statistics (Exchange)	Ind / Interest Dates	Fixed Charge Coverage 1992 / S&P Debt Rating	1993 / Date of Last Rating Change	Prior Rating	1994 / Eligible	Year End / Bond Form	Million $ Cash & Equiv. / Redemption Provisions: Regular Price	Million $ Curr. Assets / Regular (Begins) Thru	Million $ Curr. Liab. / Sinking Fund Price	Balance Sheet Date / Sinking Fund (Begins) Thru	L. Term Debt (Mil $) / Refund/Other Restriction Price	Refund/Other Restriction (Begins) Thru	Capital-ization (Mil $) / Outst'g (Mil $)	Total Debt % Capital / Underwriting Firm	Underwriting Year	Price Range 1995 High	Price Range 1995 Low	Mo. End Price Sale(s) or Bid	Curr. Yield	Yield to Mat.
Chesapeake&Pot.Tel Va (Cont.)																				
Deb 7s 2025	jJ15	**AA+**			X	BE	102.93	(7-15-03)	....	....	....	....	125	C4	'93	102½	82⅝	102½	6.83	6.80
Deb[1] 8⅜s 2029	aO	**AA+**			X	R	NC	....	....	....	....	....	100	M2	'89	125⅛	103	125⅛	6.69	6.52
[2]Chesapeake[3]Pot.TelWashDC	***67a***	***3.50***	***3.66***		***4.70***	***Dc***		***213.0***	***169.0***	***12-31-94***	***249.0***		***468.0***	***55.1***						
Deb 4⅜s '98	Fa	**AA**	3/83	AAA	X	CR	100	....	....	....	....	....	20.0	H1	'61	97½	89¾	97½	4.49	5.66
Deb 5⅝s 2006	jJ	**AA**	3/83	AAA	X	R	101.04	6-30-96	....	....	....	....	25.0	H1	'66	94¼	79¼	94¼	5.97	6.38
Deb 7s 2009	Fa	**AA**	3/83	AAA	X	R	101.35	1-31-96	....	....	....	....	50.0	F1	'69	101⅛	88⅜	101⅛	6.92	6.87
• Deb 7¾s 2013	mN	**AA**	3/83	AAA	X	R	102.46	10-31-96	....	....	....	....	60.0	W5	'73	102	90	101⅛	7.66	7.63
Deb 7¾s 2023	Fa	**AA**			X	BE	103.512	(2-1-03)	....	....	....	....	90.0	F1	'93	108⅛	89¼	108⅛	7.17	7.07
[2]Chesapeake&Pot.TelWVa[4]	***67a***	***6.09***	***7.22***		***8.64***	***Dc***		***127.0***	***133.0***	***12-31-94***	***264.0***		***581.0***	***45.4***						
Deb 5s 2000	Ms	**AA+**	3/93	AA	X	CR	100	2-29-96	....	....	....	....	25.0	H1	'60	96¾	86½	96¾	5.17	5.89
Deb 6.05s 2003	Mn15	**AA+**			X	BE	NC	....	....	....	....	....	50.0	M2	'93	100	86⅜	100	6.05	6.05
Deb 7s 2004	fA15	**AA+**	3/93	AA	X	BE	NC	....	....	....	....	....	50.0	G1	'92	106¼	91⅛	106¼	6.59	6.06
Deb 7¼s 2009	Mn	**AA+**	3/93	AA	X	R	101.55	4-30-96	....	....	....	....	40.0	W5	'69	102⅝	90	102¼	7.09	6.99
• Deb 7¼s 2013	Fa	**AA+**	3/93	AA	X	R	102.45	1-31-96	....	....	....	....	50.0	F1	'73	103⅞	85¼	s103⅞	6.98	6.86
Chesapeake Corp	***50***	***1.72***	***1.63***		***2.87***	***Dc***	***0.30***	***301.0***	***144.0***	***9-30-95***	***371.0***		***823.0***	***45.2***						
Deb[5] 9⅞s 2003	Mn	**BBB**	2/95	BBB–	X	R	NC	....	....	....	....	....	60.0	G1	'91	120¾	106½	120¾	8.18	6.30
Deb[5] 7.20s 2005	Ms15	**BBB**	2/95	BBB–	X	R	NC	....	....	....	[6]Z100	....	50.0	S1	'93	105¼	89⅝	105¼	6.84	6.43
Nts[5] 10⅜s 2000	aO	**BBB**	2/95	BBB–	X	R	NC	....	....	....	[6]Z100	....	55.0	S1	'90	117¾	106⅞	117¾	8.81	6.02
Chevron Capital U.S.A.	***25***	***Gtd by Chevron Corp,see***																		
• Gtd[7]Deb 9¾s 2017	jJ15	**AA**			X	R	104.875	(7-15-97)	100	(7-15-98)	....	....	190	M2	'87	110½	103	108⅝	8.98	8.85
Gtd[7]Nts 7.45s 2004	fA15	**AA**			X	BE	100	(8-15-01)	....	....	....	....	350	G1	'94	107½	93⅞	107½	6.93	6.31
Chevron[8]Corp[9]	***49c***	***5.95***	***7.27***		***6.49***	***Dc***	***1317***	***7587***	***8798***	***9-30-95***	***4472***		***23361***	***35.2***						
• SF Deb 9⅜s 2016	Jd	**AA**	7/87	AA–	X	R	104	(6-1-96)	100	(6-1-97)	....	....	278	S1	'86	107	103½	s105	8.93	8.84
Chiquita Brands Int'l[10]	***26***	***d0.01***	***0.74***		***0.79***	***Dc***	***224.0***	***995.0***	***634.0***	***9-30-95***	***1320***		***2215***	***68.6***						
Sr Nts[11] 9⅝s 2004	Jj15	**B+**	3/95	BB–	Y	R	NC	....	....	....	....	....	250	L3	'91	102½	89½	101	9.53	9.44
Sr Nts[11] 9⅛s 2004	Ms	**B+**	3/95	BB–	Y	R	NC	....	....	....	....	....	175	L3	'94	100¾	86¾	99½	9.17	9.21
• Sub SF Deb 10½s 2004	fA	**B**	3/95	B+	Y	R	100	....	100	(8-1-99)	....	....	60.0	Exch.	'87	105¾	99⅝	s102½	10.24	10.06
Sub Nts 11½s 2001	Jd	**B**	3/95	B+	Y	R	105.70	(6-1-96)	....	....	....	....	220	M2	'91	105¾	97	104	11.06	10.51
Chrysler Corp[12]	***9***	***1.45***	***4.24***		***7.22***	***Dc***	***7611***			***9-30-95***	***[13]9105***		***23632***	***55.5***						
• SF Deb 10.95s 2017	fA	**A–**	1/95	BBB+	X	R	105.475	(8-1-97)	100	(8-1-98)	....	....	267	F1	'87	113⅞	105¾	s111⅝	9.81	9.66
• Nts 10.40s '99	fA	**A–**	1/95	BBB+	X	R	100	(8-1-97)	....	....	....	....	245	M6	'87	108⅞	102½	106⅝	9.75	8.23
Chrysler Financial	***25g***	***1.29***	***1.34***		***1.42***	***Dc***	***1207***			***9-30-95***	***11133***		***14436***	***77.1***						
• Nts 6s '96	Ao15	**A–**	1/95	BBB+	X	BE	NC	....	....	....	....	....	250	S1	'93	100¼	97¼	99⅜	6.04	8.07
Nts 8⅛s '96	jD15	**A–**	1/95	BBB+	X	BE	NC	....	....	....	....	....	200	S1	'94	102¾	99⅝	102¼	7.95	5.68
• Nts 6½s '98	Jd15	**A–**	1/95	BBB+	X	BE	NC	....	....	....	....	....	250	M2	'93	101½	94⅜	99½	6.53	6.72
Nts 5⅜s '98	aO15	**A–**	1/95	BBB+	X	BE	NC	....	....	....	....	....	250	S1	'93	98⅞	89⅞	98⅞	5.44	5.81
Nts 5⅝s '99	Jj15	**A–**	1/95	BBB+	X	BE	NC	....	....	....	....	....	250	B5	'94	99⅜	90⅝	99⅜	5.66	5.85
• Nts 13¼s '99	aO15	**A–**	1/95	BBB+	X	R	NC	....	....	....	....	....	200	S1	'84	124¾	117	122⅛	10.85	6.56
• Nts 12¾s '99	mN	**A–**	1/95	BBB+	X	R	NC	....	....	....	....	....	200	M2	'84	123⅜	116	121⅛	10.53	6.44
• Sr Nts 9½s '99	jD15	**A–**	1/95	BBB+	X	BE	NC	....	....	....	....	....	400	M2	'92	111½	103⅜	110½	8.60	6.45
• Nts 6⅝s 2000	fA15	**A–**	1/95	BBB+	X	BE	NC	....	....	....	....	....	300	S1	'93	103	91¼	101⅝	6.52	6.21
F/R[14]Nts 6¼s '96	QNov15	**A–**	1/95	BBB+	X	BE	NC	....	....	....	....	....	250	M5	'93	100⅜	99¾	100¼	6.23	....
• Put-Ext'd[15]Nts[16] 8½s '96	[17]Fa	**A–**	1/95	BBB+	X	R	[18]100	....	....	....	....	....	200	M2	'88	106⅞	102½	105	8.10	....
Remkt Reset Nts[19] 10.34s '96	[20]Mn15	**A–**	1/95	BBB+	X	R	[21]100	....	....	....	....	....	300	M2	'88	103⅜	101⅝	101⅝	10.17	....
M-T Nts 'M' 4.57s '96	[22]jj15	**A–**	1/95	BBB+	X	BE	NC	....	....	....	....	....	15.0	M2	'94	100	96⅝	100	4.57	Mat.
M-T Nts 'M' 4.54s '96	[23]jj1	**A–**	1/95	BBB+	X	BE	NC	....	....	....	....	....	20.0	M2	'94	100	96½	100	4.54	Mat.

Uniform Footnote Explanations-See Page 260. Other: [1] (HRO)On 10-1-99 at 100. [2] Subsid of Bell Atlantic Corp. [3] Now Bell Atlantic-Washington D.C. [4] Now Bell Atlantic-West Virginia. [5] (HRO)On Chge of Ctrl at 100. [6] In whole,if 80% outstg put. [7] Gtd by Chevron Corp. [8] Was Standard Oil(Calif). [9] See Chevron Capital U.S.A. [10] Was United Brands. [11] (HRO)On Chge of Ctrl Triggering Event at 101. [12] See Auburn Hills Trust. [13] As reported,incl Chrysler Financial. [14] Int to 11-15-95,adj qtrly aft. [15] (HRO)On 2-1-96(2000)at 100,aft as defined. [16] Int to 2-1-2000,adj aft as defined. [17] Due 2-1-2018. [18] On 2-1-2000,aft as defined. [19] Int thru 5-15-96,aft as defined. [20] Due 5-15-08(unless extended to5-15-16on5-1-96). [21] On 5-15-96,aft as defined. [22] Due 1-22-96. [23] Due 1-29-96.

Title-Industry Code & *Co. Finances (In Italics)*	Ind	*Fixed Charge Coverage* 1992	1993	1994	Year End	*Million $* Cash & Equiv.	Curr. Assets	Curr. Liab.	Balance Sheet Date	L. Term Debt (Mil $)	Capital-ization (Mil $)	Total Debt % Capital

Individual Issue Statistics Exchange	Interest Dates	S&P Debt Rating	Date of Last Rating Change	Prior Rating	Eligible	Bond Form	Redemption Provisions: Regular Price	Regular (Begins) Thru	Sinking Fund Price	Sinking Fund (Begins) Thru	Refund/Other Restriction Price	Refund/Other Restriction (Begins) Thru	Outst'g (Mil $)	Underwriting Firm	Underwriting Year	Price Range 1995 High	Price Range 1995 Low	Mo. End Price Sale(s) or Bid	Curr. Yield	Yield to Mat.
***Chrysler Financial** (Cont.)*																				
M-T Nts 'M' 5.08s '97	[1]jj15	A–	1/95	BBB+	X	BE	NC	....	....	....	....	....	17.0	B5	'94	99⅜	94	99⅜	5.11	5.69
M-T Nts 'M' 5⅛s '97	[1]jj15	A–	1/95	BBB+	X	BE	NC	....	....	....	....	....	10.0	S1	'94	99½	94	99½	5.15	5.61
M-T Nts 'M' 5.01s '97	[2]jj15	A–	1/95	BBB+	X	BE	NC	....	....	....	....	....	50.0	M6	'94	99⅜	93¾	99⅜	5.04	5.61
M-T Nts 'M' 5.02s '97	[2]jj15	A–	1/95	BBB+	X	BE	NC	....	....	....	....	....	21.5	S1	'94	99⅜	93⅞	99⅜	5.05	5.62
M-T Nts 'M' 5.08s '97	[2]jj15	A–	1/95	BBB+	X	BE	NC	....	....	....	....	....	10.0	S1	'94	99⅜	94	99⅜	5.11	5.68
M-T Nts 'M' 4.92s '97	[3]jj15	A–	1/95	BBB+	X	BE	NC	....	....	....	....	....	14.0	M2	'94	99¼	93⅝	99¼	4.96	5.63
M-T Nts 'M' 5.28s '97	[4]jj15	A–	1/95	BBB+	X	BE	NC	....	....	....	....	....	6.00	S1	'94	99⅝	94⅛	99⅝	5.30	5.62
M-T Nts 'M' 6.56s '97	[4]jj15	A–	1/95	BBB+	X	BE	NC	....	....	....	....	....	25.0	S1	'94	101	96⅝	101	6.50	5.62
M-T Nts 'N' 7.08s '97	[5]ms15	A–			X	BE	NC	....	....	....	....	....	25.0	S1	'95	101⅝	99⅝	101⅝	6.97	5.72
M-T Nts 'M' 6.70s '97	[6]jj15	A–	1/95	BBB+	X	BE	NC	....	....	....	....	....	25.0	S1	'94	101¼	96⅝	101¼	6.62	5.69
M-T Nts 'M' 6.65s '97	[7]jj15	A–	1/95	BBB+	X	BE	NC	....	....	....	....	....	16.0	S1	'94	101¼	96½	101¼	6.57	5.65
M-T Nts 'M' 6.62s '97	[8]jj15	A–	1/95	BBB+	X	BE	NC	....	....	....	....	....	10.0	G1	'94	101⅛	96⅜	101⅛	6.55	5.72
M-T Nts 'M' 7.13s '97	[9]jj15	A–	1/95	BBB+	X	BE	NC	....	....	....	....	....	10.0	S1	'94	101⅞	97⅜	101⅞	7.00	5.70
M-T Nts 'M' 5.64s '98	[10]jj15	A–	1/95	BBB+	X	BE	NC	....	....	....	....	....	5.00	S1	'94	99⅞	92⅝	99⅞	5.65	5.70
M-T Nts 'M' 5.41s '98	[11]jj15	A–	1/95	BBB+	X	BE	NC	....	....	....	....	....	15.0	M2	'94	99⅜	91⅞	99⅜	5.44	5.73
M-T Nts 'M' 5.41s '98	[12]jj15	A–	1/95	BBB+	X	BE	NC	....	....	....	....	....	10.0	S1	'94	99⅜	91⅞	99⅜	5.44	5.73
M-T Nts 'M' 5.34s '98	[13]jj15	A–	1/95	BBB+	X	BE	NC	....	....	....	....	....	7.00	S1	'94	99¼	91⅝	99¼	5.38	5.72
M-T Nts 'M' 7s '98	[14]jj15	A–	1/95	BBB+	X	BE	NC	....	....	....	....	....	10.0	M2	'94	102⅝	95¾	102⅝	6.82	5.76
M-T Nts 'M' 7.20s '98	[15]jj15	A–	1/95	BBB+	X	BE	NC	....	....	....	....	....	10.0	M2	'94	103	96⅜	103	6.99	5.80
M-T Nts 'M' 7.05s '98	[16]jj15	A–	1/95	BBB+	X	BE	NC	....	....	....	....	....	15.0	M2	'94	102¾	95⅞	102¾	6.86	5.77
M-T Nts 'M' 7.14s '98	[17]jj15	A–	1/95	BBB+	X	BE	NC	....	....	....	....	....	15.0	M2	'94	103	96	103	6.93	5.78
M-T Nts 'M' 7.19s '98	[17]jj15	A–	1/95	BBB+	X	BE	NC	....	....	....	....	....	25.0	M2	'94	103⅛	96¼	103⅛	6.97	5.78
M-T Nts 'M' 7.26s '98	[18]jj15	A–	1/95	BBB+	X	BE	NC	....	....	....	....	....	20.0	S1	'94	103⅜	96¼	103⅜	7.02	5.79
M-T Nts 'M' 7.29s '98	[19]jj15	A–	1/95	BBB+	X	BE	NC	....	....	....	....	....	25.0	M2	'94	103½	96⅜	103½	7.04	5.78
M-T Nts 'M' 5.83s '99	Jj15	A–	1/95	BBB+	X	BE	NC	....	....	....	....	....	15.0	D6	'94	100	90¾	100	5.83	5.83
M-T Nts 'M' 5.60s '99	[20]jj15	A–	1/95	BBB+	X	BE	NC	....	....	....	....	....	15.0	B5	'94	99¼	90	99¼	5.64	5.87
M-T Nts 'M' 5.65s '99	[20]jj15	A–	1/95	BBB+	X	BE	NC	....	....	....	....	....	5.00	M2	'94	99½	90⅛	99½	5.68	5.83
M-T Nts 'M' 5.72s '99	[21]jj15	A–	1/95	BBB+	X	BE	NC	....	....	....	....	....	23.7	S1	'94	99⅝	90⅜	99⅝	5.74	5.85
M-T Nts 'M' 5.61s '99	[22]jj15	A–	1/95	BBB+	X	BE	NC	....	....	....	....	....	5.00	S1	'94	99¼	90	99¼	5.65	5.88
M-T Nts 'M' 5.55s '99	[23]jj15	A–	1/95	BBB+	X	BE	NC	....	....	....	....	....	10.0	M2	'94	99⅛	89¾	99⅛	5.60	5.86
M-T Nts 'M' 5.86s '99	[24]jj15	A–	1/95	BBB+	X	BE	NC	....	....	....	....	....	10.0	B5	'94	100	90⅝	100	5.86	5.86
M-T Nts 'M' 6.70s '99	[25]jj15	A–	1/95	BBB+	X	BE	NC	....	....	....	....	....	7.00	M2	'94	102⅜	93⅜	102⅜	6.54	5.88
F/R[26]M-T Nts 'M' 5.73s '99	QFeb4	A–	1/95	BBB+	X	BE	NC	....	....	....	....	....	61.4	C5	'94	99½	98⅝	99¼	5.77	....
M-T Nts 'N' 7.60s '97	[27]ms15	A–			X	BE	NC	....	....	....	....	....	50.0	S1	'95	102¼	100	102⅛	7.44	5.66
M-T Nts 'N' 7.63s '97	[27]ms15	A–			X	BE	NC	....	....	....	....	....	45.0	M2	'95	102¼	100	102⅛	7.47	5.69
M-T Nts 'N' 7.56s '97	[28]ms15	A–			X	BE	NC	....	....	....	....	....	55.5	S1	'95	102⅛	100	102⅛	7.40	5.66
M-T Nts 'N' 7.57s '97	[29]ms15	A–			X	BE	NC	....	....	....	....	....	25.0	S1	'95	102¼	100	102⅛	7.41	5.73
M-T Nts 'N' 7.23s '97	[29]ms15	A–			X	BE	NC	....	....	....	....	....	25.0	M2	'95	101¾	99½	101¾	7.11	5.71
F/R[30]M-T Nts 'N' 6.1875s '97	[31]	A–			X	BE	NC	....	....	....	....	....	50.0	M2	'95	100	99¾	100	6.19	....
M-T Nts 'N' 7.35s '98	[32]ms15	A–			X	BE	NC	....	....	....	....	....	25.0	M2	'95	103¼	99⅛	103¼	7.12	5.78
M-T([33]Reset[34])Nts 'N' 8s 2002	Ms16	A–			X	BE	*100	(3-16-96)	....	....	....	....	25.0	S1	'95	103	99	101⅛	7.91	....
M-T Nts 'P' 6.15s '97	[35]ms15	A–			X	BE	NC	....	....	....	....	....	25.0	M2	'95	100⅝	99⅛	100⅝	6.11	5.71
M-T Nts 'P' 6.38s '97	[36]ms15	A–			X	BE	NC	....	....	....	....	....	26.0	S1	'95	101	99½	101	6.32	5.70
M-T Nts 'P' 6.33s '97	[37]ms15	A–			X	BE	NC	....	....	....	....	....	50.0	S1	'95	101	99⅜	101	6.27	5.66
M-T Nts 'P' 6.41s '97	[37]ms15	A–			X	BE	NC	....	....	....	....	....	25.0	D6	'95	101⅛	99⅝	101⅛	6.34	5.65
M-T Nts 'P' 6.32s '97	[38]ms15	A–			X	BE	NC	....	....	....	....	....	25.0	S1	'95	100⅞	99⅞	100⅞	6.27	5.73

Uniform Footnote Explanations-See Page 260. Other: [1] Due 1-24-97. [2] Due 1-27-97. [3] Due 2-4-97. [4] Due 2-14-97. [5] Due 4-4-97. [6] Due 4-22-97. [7] Due 4-28-97. [8] Due 4-29-97. [9] Due 5-19-97. [10] Due 1-13-98. [11] Due 1-26-98. [12] Due 1-27-98. [13] Due 1-28-98. [14] Due 4-15-98. [15] Due 4-27-98. [16] Due 4-29-98. [17] Due 5-26-98. [18] Due 7-1-98. [19] Due 7-7-98. [20] Due 1-21-99. [21] Due 1-25-99. [22] Due 1-28-99. [23] Due 2-3-99. [24] Due 2-22-99. [25] Due 3-31-99. [26] Int thru 2-6-96,adj qtrly aft. [27] Due 2-24-97. [28] Due 3-3-97. [29] Due 3-17-97. [30] Int thru 9-19-95,adj qtrly(3 Mo LIBOR & 0.125%). [31] Due 4-1-97: Int pd qtrly 3rd Wed ea Mar, etc. [32] Due 3-30-98. [33] Int to 3-16-96,incr 0.10% anly aft to 3-16-01. [34] Int at 8.75% fr 3-16-01. [35] Due 6-30-97. [36] Due 7-25-97. [37] Due 7-28-97. [38] Due 8-4-97.

Title-Industry Code & Co. Finances (In Italics) / Individual Issue Statistics / Exchange	Ind / Interest Dates	Fixed Charge Coverage 1992 / S&P Debt Rating	Date of Last Rating Change	1993 / Prior Rating	1994 / Eligible	Year End / Bond Form	Cash & Equiv. (Million $) / Regular Price	Curr. Assets (Million $) / Regular (Begins) Thru	Curr. Liab. (Million $) / Sinking Fund Price	Balance Sheet Date / Sinking Fund (Begins) Thru	L. Term Debt (Mil $) / Refund/Other Restriction Price	Refund/Other Restriction (Begins) Thru	Capital-ization (Mil $) / Outst'g (Mil $)	Total Debt % Capital / Underwriting Firm	Underwriting Year	Price Range 1995 High	Price Range 1995 Low	Mo. End Price Sale(s) or Bid	Curr. Yield	Yield to Mat.
***Chrysler Financial** (Cont.)*																				
M-T Nts 'P' 6½s '97	[1]ms15	**A–**			X	BE	NC	....	....	....	....	....	31.9	M2	'95	101¼	100	101¼	6.42	5.69
M-T Nts 'P' 6.23s '97	[2]ms15	**A–**			X	BE	NC	....	....	....	....	....	50.0	M2	'95	100⅞	99¾	100⅞	6.18	5.67
M-T Nts 'P' 5.99s '97	[3]ms15	**A–**			X	BE	NC	....	....	....	....	....	55.0	S1	'95	100½	100	100½	5.96	5.70
M-T Nts 'P' 5.98s '97	[4]ms15	**A–**			X	BE	NC	....	....	....	....	....	30.0	S1	'95	100½	100	100½	5.95	5.70
M-T Nts 'P' 5⅞s '97	[5]ms15	**A–**			X	BE	NC	....	....	....	....	....	50.0	C2	'95	100¼	99¾	100¼	5.86	5.73
M-T Nts 'P' 6.23s '98	[6]ms15	**A–**			X	BE	NC	....	....	....	....	....	25.0	M2	'95	101	98½	101	6.17	5.80
M-T Nts 'P' 6.36s '98	[7]ms15	**A–**			X	BE	NC	....	....	....	....	....	25.0	S1	'95	101¼	98⅞	101¼	6.28	5.83
M-T Nts 'P' 6.60s '98	[8]ms15	**A–**			X	BE	NC	....	....	....	....	....	45.0	S1	'95	101⅞	99½	101⅞	6.48	5.81
M-T Nts 'P' 6.12s '98	[9]ms15	**A–**			X	BE	NC	....	....	....	....	....	40.0	S1	'95	100¾	100	100¾	6.07	5.83
M-T Nts 'P' 6.24s '98	[10]ms15	**A–**			X	BE	NC	....	....	....	....	....	25.0	S1	'95	101⅛	100	101⅛	6.17	5.80
M-T Nts 'P' 6.20s 2000	[11]ms15	**A–**			X	BE	NC	....	....	....	....	....	30.0	M2	'95	100½	99⅞	100½	6.17	6.08
Chubb Capital Corp	***25***	***Gtd by Chubb Corp,see***																		
Gtd[12]Nts 6s '98	Fa	**AA+**			X	R	NC	....	....	....	....	....	150	M5	'93	100⅞	94	100⅞	5.95	5.55
Gtd[12]Nts 6⅞s 2003	Fa	**AA+**			X	R	NC	....	....	....	....	....	100	M5	'93	105⅛	91⅛	105⅛	6.54	5.98
Chubb Corp[13]	***35c***	***8.47***		***4.40***	***7.26***	***Dc***	***4.80***			***9-30-95***	***1165***		***6371***	***21.5***						
Nts 8¾s '99	mN15	**AA+**			X	R	NC	....	100	....	....	....	150	G1	'89	106½	100½	105⅝	8.28	7.06
CIGNA Corp	***35d***	***2.79***		***1.69***	***7.65***	***Dc***	***1775***			***9-30-95***	***1068***		***8033***	***20.4***						
Nts 8s '96	mS	**BBB+**	12/94	A	X	R	NC	....	....	....	....	....	150	G1	'86	101⅞	99⅝	101½	7.88	5.67
Nts 8¾s 2001	aO	**BBB+**	12/94	A	X	BE	NC	....	....	....	....	....	100	F1	'91	111½	100	111½	7.85	6.33
Nts 7.40s 2003	Jj15	**BBB+**	12/94	A	X	BE	NC	....	....	....	....	....	100	M2	'93	105⅝	91⅞	105⅝	7.01	6.39
Nts 6⅜s 2006	Jj15	**BBB+**	12/94	A	X	BE	NC	....	....	....	....	....	100	C5	'94	98¼	81⅞	98¼	6.49	6.62
Nts 8¼s 2007	Jj	**BBB+**	12/94	A	X	BE	NC	....	....	....	....	....	100	G1	'92	111¾	95⅝	111¾	7.38	6.72
Nts 8.30s 2023	Jj15	**BBB+**	12/94	A	X	BE	NC	....	....	....	....	....	100	M2	'93	108	91⅛	108	7.69	7.60
Nts 7.65s 2023	Ms	**BBB+**	12/94	A	X	BE	NC	....	....	....	....	....	100	G1	'93	101⅞	84⅞	101⅞	7.51	7.49
Cincinnati Bell[14]	***67a***	***2.21***		***2.02***	***3.37***	***Dc***	***136.0***	***449.0***	***410.0***	***9-30-95***	***491.0***		***1122***	***53.9***						
[15]Deb[16] 4⅜s 2002	fA	**AA–**	8/92	AA+	X	CR	100.32	7-31-96	....	....	....	....	20.0	H1	'62	91	77⅞	91	4.81	6.05
[16]Deb 7⅜s 2011	fA	**AA–**	8/92	AA+	X	R	102.22	7-31-96	....	....	....	....	50.0	M2	'71	102¾	89	102¾	7.18	7.08
Nts 6.70s '97	jD15	**A–**	9/94	A	X	R	NC	....	....	....	....	....	100	M6	'92	101⅞	95¾	101⅞	6.58	5.67
Nts[17] 9.10s 2000	Jd15	**A–**	9/94	A	X	R	NC	....	....	....	....	....	75.0	M6	'90	111⅞	102⅞	111⅞	8.13	6.02
Nts 7¼s 2023	dJ15	**A–**	9/94	A	X	R	NC	....	....	....	....	....	50.0	M6	'93	105⅞	84¼	105⅞	6.85	6.78
Cincinnati Bell Tel	***67a***	***Gtd by Cin Bell Inc, see***																		
Nts[18] 7.30s '96	Ao31	**CALL**	12/95	AA–		R			Called 1-18-96 at 100				40.0	S1	'86	100⅜	99¼	100	7.30	Call
Nts[18] 8⅝s '99	jD15	**CALL**	12/95	AA–		R			Called 1-18-96 at 100				40.0	M6	'89	102¼	99⅝	100⅛	8.61	Call
Cincinnati Gas & Elec[19,20]	***75***	***1.93***		***2.53***	***2.14***	***Dc***	***66.50***	***650.0***	***514.0***	***9-30-95***	***1866***		***3689***	***52.9***						
1st 5⅞s '97	jJ	**A–**	7/95	BBB+	X	R	100.22	6-30-96	100.18	6-30-96	....	....	30.0	M6	'67	100¼	94⅞	100¼	5.86	5.70
1st 6¼s '97	mS	**A–**	7/95	BBB+	X	R	NC	....	....	....	....	....	100	M6	'92	101	95⅜	101	6.19	5.61
1st 5.80s '99	Fa15	**A–**	7/95	BBB+	X	R	NC	....	....	....	....	....	110	M6	'94	99⅞	91	99⅞	5.81	5.84
1st 7⅜s '99	Mn	**A–**	7/95	BBB+	X	R	100.99	4-30-96	100.60	4-30-96	....	....	50.0	B6	'69	101¼	96	101⅛	7.29	6.99
1st 7⅜s 2001	mN	**A–**	7/95	BBB+	X	R	101.45	10-31-96	100.41	10-31-96	....	....	60.0	B6	'71	102	94	101⅝	7.26	7.03
1st 7¼s 2002	mS	**A–**	7/95	BBB+	X	R	NC	....	....	....	....	....	100	M6	'92	106	92¾	106	6.84	6.14
1st 8⅛s 2003	fA	**A–**	7/95	BBB+	X	R	102.31	7-31-96	100.79	7-31-96	....	....	60.0	H1	'73	102⅝	97¼	102½	7.93	7.68
1st 6.45s 2004	Fa15	**A–**	7/95	BBB+	X	R	NC	....	....	....	....	....	110	M6	'94	101½	87⅛	101½	6.35	6.21
1st 10.20s 2020	jD	**A–**	7/95	BBB+	X	R	107.44	11-30-96	Z100	....	....	....	150	M6	'90	109⅞	98⅝	107⅛	9.52	9.45
1st 8.95s 2021	jD15	**A–**	7/95	BBB+	X	R	106.33	(12-15-96)	Z100	....	....	....	100	S1	'91	110½	98⅛	109⅝	8.16	8.06
1st 8½s 2022	mS	**A–**	7/95	BBB+	X	R	106.21	(9-1-97)	Z100	....	....	....	100	M6	'92	108¼	95	108¼	7.85	7.76
1st 7.20s 2023	aO	**A–**	7/95	BBB+	X	R	103.54	(10-1-03)	Z100	(10-1-03)	....	....	300	M6	'93	99¾	83⅞	99¾	7.22	7.22

Uniform Footnote Explanations-See Page 260. Other: [1] Due 8-21-97. [2] Due 9-2-97. [3] Due 11-20-97. [4] Due 11-24-97. [5] Due 11-28-97. [6] Due 7-17-98. [7] Due 7-20-98. [8] Due 8-3-98. [9] Due 11-30-98. [10] Due 11-2-98. [11] Due 12-6-00. [12] Gtd by Chubb Corp. [13] See Chubb Capital. [14] See Cin. Bell Tel. [15] Was Cincinnati & Suburban Bell Tel. [16] Oblig of Cinn Bell Tel. [17] Purch offer to Dec 22. [18] Gtd on subord basis by Cincinnati Bell Inc. [19] See Public Serv, Ind. [20] Subsid of CINergy Corp.

Title-Industry Code & Co. Finances (In Italics) / Individual Issue Statistics (Exchange)	Ind / Interest Dates	Fixed Charge Coverage 1992 / S&P Debt Rating	1993 / Date of Last Rating Change	1994 / Prior Rating	Eligible	Year End / Bond Form	Cash & Equiv. (Million $) / Redemption Provisions: Regular Price	Curr. Assets (Million $) / Regular (Begins) Thru	Curr. Liab. (Million $) / Sinking Fund Price	Balance Sheet Date / Sinking Fund (Begins) Thru	L. Term Debt (Mil $) / Refund/Other Restriction Price	Refund/Other Restriction (Begins) Thru	Capitalization (Mil $) / Outst'g (Mil $)	Total Debt % Capital / Underwriting Firm	Underwriting Year	Price Range 1995 High	Price Range 1995 Low	Mo. End Price Sale(s) or Bid	Curr. Yield	Yield to Mat.
***Cincinnati Gas & Elec** (Cont.)*																				
Deb[1] 6.90s 2025	Jd	**BBB+**	7/95	BBB	X	BE	NC	....	....	....	....	....	150	M6	'95	106¼	97½	106¼	6.49	6.42
Cincinnati Milacron	***41d***	***2.41***	***3.08***	***3.73***		***Dc***	***43.70***	***688.0***	***373.0***	***10-7-95***	***329.0***		***533.0***	***61.7***						
SF Deb 12s 2010	jJ15	**BB**	9/91	BBB–	Y	R	106	7-14-96	100	(7-15-96)	....	....	10.0	G1	'85	116	106	106⅝	11.25	11.07
Nts 8⅜s 2004	Ms15	**BB**			Y	BE	NC	....	....	....	....	....	115	C5	'94	104	90⅞	99⅝	8.41	8.44
Cinemark USA	***24b***	***1.73***	***1.96***	***1.77***		***Dc***	***17.30***	***24.60***	***28.60***	***6-30-95***	***175.0***		***180.0***	***97.2***						
Sr Nts[2] 12s 2002	Jd	**BB–**	2/95	B+	Y	R	106	(6-1-97)	100	(6-1-00)	....	....	125	B5	'92	109	102¼	107½	11.16	10.37
Circus Circus Enterpr	***40i***	***8.97***	***5.52***	***5.48***		***Ja***	***74.70***	***133.0***	***113.0***	***10-31-95***	***740.0***		***1945***	***38.1***						
Sr Sub Deb[3] 7⅝s 2013	jJ15	**BBB**	1/95	BBB+	X	R	NC	....	....	....	....	....	150	S1	'93	102⅞	82¼	102⅞	7.41	7.33
Sr Sub Nts[4] 10⅝s '97	Jd15	**BBB**	1/95	BBB+	X	R	NC	....	....	....	....	....	100	M2	'90	107½	103¾	106½	9.98	5.91
Sr Sub Nts[3] 6¾s 2003	jJ15	**BBB**	1/95	BBB+	X	R	NC	....	....	....	....	....	150	S1	'93	101	86¾	101	6.68	6.58
CIT[5] Group Holdings[6]	***25***	***1.47***	***1.61***	***1.49***		***Dc***				***9-30-95***	***13352***		***15229***	***87.7***						
Amortizing[7]Nts 6s '97	Fa15	**A+**			X	BE	NC	....	....	....	....	....	90.0	C1	'92	100½	96⅜	100½	5.97	....
Nts 8¾s '96	Fa15	**A+**			X	BE	NC	....	....	....	....	....	250	K2	'91	101¾	100⅜	100⅜	8.72	5.61
Nts 4¾s '96	Ms15	**A+**			X	BE	NC	....	....	....	....	....	150	S1	'93	99⅞	96½	99⅞	4.76	5.28
Nts 8⅞s '96	Jd15	**A+**	1/90	A	X	R	NC	....	....	....	....	....	150	M2	'89	102⅝	101⅜	101½	8.74	5.52
Nts 5¾s '97	Ms21	**A+**			X	BE	NC	....	....	....	....	....	100	M6	'94	100⅜	95⅛	100⅜	5.73	5.42
Nts 8¾s '97	jJ	**A+**			X	BE	NC	....	....	....	....	....	150	G1	'91	104⅞	101⅛	104⅝	8.36	5.51
• Nts 8¾s '98	Ao15	**A+**			X	BE	NC	....	....	....	....	....	150	S1	'91	103½	100¼	104⅞	8.34	6.42
Nts 5⅝s '98	Ao	**A+**			X	BE	NC	....	....	....	....	....	100	L3	'93	100⅛	92⅜	100⅛	5.62	5.56
Nts 6¾s '98	Ao30	**A+**			X	BE	NC	....	....	....	....	....	200	C5	'95	102⅝	99¾	102⅝	6.58	5.53
Nts 6⅝s 2005	Jd15	**A+**			X	BE	NC	....	....	....	....	....	250	U1	'95	103¼	95⅝	103¼	6.42	6.17
• Nts 5⅞s 2008	aO15	**A+**			X	BE	NC	....	....	....	....	....	200	M6	'93	No Sale		88⅜	6.65	7.29
F/R[8]Nts 6.0625s '99	QJan15	**A+**			X	BE	NC	....	....	....	....	....	250	S1	'94	100¼	99¼	100	6.06	....
M-T[9]F/R Sr Nts '97	[10]Feb28	**A+**			X	BE	NC	....	....	....	....	....	50.0	U1	'94	100⅛	99⅝	100⅛	....	....
M-T[11]F/R Sr Nts 6.1375s '97	[12]QApr29	**A+**			X	BE	NC	....	....	....	....	....	50.0	G1	'94	100	99⅝	100	6.14	....
M-T[13]F/R Sr Nts 5.0042s '97	QMay21	**A+**			X	BE	NC	....	....	....	....	....	50.0	S1	'94	99⅞	98⅞	99½	5.03	....
M-T[14]F/R Sr Nts '97	[15]Mn2	**A+**			X	BE	NC	....	....	....	....	....	150	U1	'94	100⅛	99⅝	100	....	....
M-T[16]F/R Sr Nts '97	QMay19	**A+**			X	BE	NC	....	....	....	....	....	200	M2	'94	99⅞	99⅜	99⅞	....	....
Sr M-T Nts 6.35s '98	jJ31	**A+**			X	BE	NC	....	....	....	....	....	150	M6	'95	101⅝	99⅛	101⅝	6.25	5.66
M-T[17]F/R Sr Nts 5.73s '99	QMar29	**A+**			X	BE	NC	....	....	....	....	....	55.0	U1	'94	99⅞	97⅞	99¼	5.77	....
M-T[18]F/R Sr Nts[8] 5.665s '99	QApr14	**A+**			X	BE	NC	....	....	....	....	....	75.0	S1	'94	99⅞	98⅝	99¼	5.71	....
M-T Sr Nts 5½s '97	Fa28	**A+**			X	BE	NC	....	....	....	....	....	100	U1	'94	100	94⅞	100	5.50	5.49
M-T Sr Nts 6⅛s '98	mS	**A+**			X	BE	NC	....	....	....	....	....	100	S1	'95	101⅛	99¼	101⅛	6.06	5.66
M-T Sr Sub Cap Nts[3] 9¼s 2001	Ms15	**A**			X	BE	NC	....	....	....	....	....	100	M2	'91	114⅜	103½	114⅜	8.09	5.99
M-T Sr Sub Cap Nts 6.98s 2004	Ms	**A**			X	BE	100	(3-1-98)	....	....	....	....	100	C1	'94	104½	90	104½	6.68	6.27
Sr Sub Cap Nts 8⅜s 2001	mN	**A**			X	R	NC	....	....	....	....	....	100	S1	'91	111¾	99	111¾	7.49	5.96
CitFed Bancorp	***10a***	***2.32***	***1.93***	....		***Mr***				***12-31-94***	***477.0***		***601.0***	***79.4***						
Sub[19]Nts[20] 8¼s 2003	[21]sep15	**B**	6/95	B–	Y	BE	100	(9-1-96)	....	....	....	....	40.3	M1	'93	100½	87	100½	8.21	8.16
Citicorp	***10***	***1.28***	***1.52***	***1.78***		***Dc***				***9-30-95***	***18956***		***38451***	***49.3***						
• F/R[22]Nts 6.21s '98	Mn15	**A+**	7/95	A	X	R	NC	....	....	....	....	....	16.2	S1	'83	No Sale		100	6.21	....
• F/R[23]Nts 6½s 2004	Mn	**A+**	7/95	A	X	R	102.21	4-30-96	100	....	....	....	346	F1	'79	103	99	s99⅝	6.52	....
Nts 8¾s '96	mN	**A+**	7/95	A	X	R	NC	....	....	....	....	....	200	S1	'89	102⅝	100¼	102⅝	8.53	5.49
Sub Nts 7⅛s 2004	Ms15	**A**	7/95	A–	X	BE	NC	....	....	....	....	....	200	S1	'94	105¾	90¼	105¾	6.74	6.22
Sub Nts 7⅝s 2005	Mn	**A**	7/95	A–	X	BE	NC	....	....	....	....	....	150	G1	'95	109½	99¼	109½	6.96	6.26
Sub Nts 6¾s 2005	fA	**A**	7/95	A–	X	BE	NC	....	....	....	....	....	350	G1	'93	103½	86½	103½	6.52	6.26
Sub Nts 7¾s 2006	Jd15	**A**	7/95	A–	X	BE	NC	....	....	....	....	....	250	C4	'94	110⅞	92⅞	110⅞	6.99	6.31

Uniform Footnote Explanations-See Page 260. Other: [1] (HRO)On 6-1-05 at 100. [2] (HRO)On Chge of Ctrl at 101. [3] Issued in min denom $100T. [4] (HRO)At 100 for Desginated Event&Rat'g Decline. [5] Owned by Dai-Ichi Kangyo Bank & Mfrs Hanover. [6] Was C.I.T. Financial. [7] Princ pyts due on int dates to 2-15-97. [8] Int thru 1-16-96,adj qtrly aft. [9] Int adj monthly. [10] Due 2-28-97. [11] Int thru 1-17-96,adj qtrly aft. [12] Due 6-29-97:Int pd qtrly,ea 3rd Wed in Jul, etc. [13] Int thru 3-31-96,adj qtrly aft. [14] Int adj monthly for certain Treas rates. [15] Int due 1st Tues in ea May & Nov. [16] Int adj weekly. [17] Int thru 12-29-95,adj qtrly aft. [18] Int at lesser of 9% or 3 Mo LIBOR & 0.20%. [19] Death red benefit(ltd)at 100. [20] Issued in min denom $5T. [21] Due Sep 1:Int pd mthly on 15th. [22] Int tnru 5-14-96,adj semi-anly aft. [23] Int thru 4-30-96,adj semi-anly as defined.

Title-Industry Code & Co. Finances (In Italics)	*Ind*	*Fixed Charge Coverage 1992*	*1993*		*1994*	*Year End*	*Million $ Cash & Equiv.*	*Curr. Assets*	*Curr. Liab.*	*Balance Sheet Date*	*L. Term Debt (Mil $)*		*Capital-ization (Mil $)*	*Total Debt % Capital*						
Individual Issue Statistics / Exchange ↓	Interest Dates	S&P Debt Rating	Date of Last Rating Change	Prior Rating	Eligible ↓	Bond Form	Redemption Provisions: Regular Price	Regular (Begins) Thru	Sinking Fund Price	Sinking Fund (Begins) Thru	Refund/Other Restriction Price	Refund/Other Restriction (Begins) Thru	Outst'g (Mil $)	Underwriting Firm	Underwriting Year	Price Range 1995 High	Price Range 1995 Low	Mo. End Price Sale(s) or Bid	Curr. Yield	Yield to Mat.
***Citicorp** (Cont.)*																				
Sub Nts 10¾s 2015	jD15	**A**	7/95	A–	X	R	104.928	12-14-96	100	....	....	....	150	M2	'85	107¼	102⅛	102⅜	10.50	10.46
Sub Nts 10½s 2016	Fa	**A**	7/95	A–	X	R	104.50	(2-1-96)	100	....	....	....	150	S1	'86	106¾	104¾	104¾	10.02	9.95
Sub Nts 9⅜s 2016	Ms	**A**	7/95	A–	X	R	104.062	(3-1-96)	100	....	....	....	190	S1	'86	105¾	102	104½	8.97	8.89
Sub Nts 8½s 2017	Fa	**A**	7/95	A–	X	R	102.625	(2-1-97)	100	....	....	....	177	F1	'87	106½	94¾	105⅛	8.09	7.99
Sub[1]Cap Nts 9s '99	Ao15	**A**	7/95	A–	X	R	NC	....	....	....	....	....	300	S1	'87	109⅝	101⅜	109⅝	8.21	5.75
Sub[1]Cap Nts 9¾s '99	fA	**A**	7/95	A–	X	R	NC	....	....	....	....	....	300	F1	'87	112⅝	104½	112⅝	8.66	5.80
Sub Securities 9½s 2002	Fa	**A**	7/95	A–	X	BE	NC	....	....	....	....	....	150	G1	'92	116½	103⅞	116½	8.15	6.20
Sub Securities 8⅝s 2002	jD	**A**	7/95	A–	X	BE	NC	....	....	....	....	....	150	L3	'92	112	92	112	7.70	6.45
Sub Securities 8s 2003	Fa	**A**	7/95	A–	X	BE	NC	....	....	....	....	....	400	C4	'93	110⅜	96	110⅜	7.25	6.17
Sub Securities 7⅛s 2003	Jd	**A**	7/95	A–	X	BE	NC	....	....	....	....	....	250	S1	'93	105½	90½	105½	6.75	6.19
M-T Sub Nts 'E' 7½s 2001	Jun15	**A**	7/95	A–	X	BE	100	(6-15-96)	....	....	....	....	10.8	S5	'94	106½	94⅜	106½	7.04	6.08
M-T Sub Nts 'E' 7.55s 2001	[2]Jul	**A**	7/95	A–	X	BE	100	(7-15-96)	....	....	....	....	10.0	S3	'94	106⅝	94½	106⅝	7.08	6.11
M-T Sub Nts 'E' 7.85s 2001	[2]Jul15	**A**	7/95	A–	X	BE	100	(7-15-96)	....	....	....	....	7.50	S5	'94	108	96	108	7.27	6.13
M-T Sub Nts 'E' 7.60s 2001	[2]Aug15	**A**	7/95	A–	X	BE	100	(8-15-96)	....	....	....	....	5.18	S5	'94	106⅞	94¾	106⅞	7.11	6.13
M-T Sub Nts 'E' 7.70s 2001	[2]Aug15	**A**	7/95	A–	X	BE	100	(8-15-96)	....	....	....	....	4.90	S5	'94	107½	95⅛	107½	7.16	6.10
M-T Sub Nts 'E' 7¾s 2001	[2]Aug15	**A**	7/95	A–	X	BE	100	(8-15-96)	....	....	....	....	8.50	S5	'94	102⅝	95	102¼	7.58	7.25
M-T Sub Nts 'E' 8s 2004	[2]Jul15	**A**	7/95	A–	X	BE	100	(7-15-99)	....	....	....	....	8.60	S5	'94	110⅜	95	110⅜	7.25	6.40
M-T Sub Nts 'E' 8.05s 2004	[2]Oct15	**A**	7/95	A–	X	BE	100	(10-15-99)	....	....	....	....	5.00	S5	'94	111	95⅛	111	7.25	6.39
Citizens Utilities	***75***	***5.07***	***5.75***		***3.86***	***Dc***	***17.90***	***225.0***	***426.0***	***9-30-95***	***1072***		***2780***	***44.2***						
Deb 8.45s 2001	mS	**AA+**	10/95	AAA	X	BE	NC	....	....	....	....	....	50.0	M6	'91	112¼	100⅝	112¼	7.53	5.88
Deb 7.45s 2004	Jj15	**AA+**	10/95	AAA	X	BE	NC	....	....	....	....	....	100	L3	'92	108¾	94⅝	108¾	6.85	6.06
Deb 7.60s 2006	Jd	**AA+**	10/95	AAA	X	BE	NC	....	....	....	....	....	175	L3	'94	111	94⅛	111	6.85	6.15
Deb 7s 2025	mN	**AA+**	10/95	AAA	X	BE	NC	....	....	....	....	....	150	M6	'95	103⅜	98¼	103⅜	6.77	6.74
Deb[3] 7.68s 2034	aO	**AA+**	10/95	AAA	X	BE	NC	....	....	....	....	....	100	M6	'94	117⅞	90¾	117⅞	6.52	6.42
Deb 7.45s 2035	jJ	**AA+**	10/95	AAA	X	BE	NC	....	....	....	....	....	125	M6	'95	107½	95⅛	107½	6.93	6.89
Claridge Hotel & Casino	***40i***	***3.39***	***3.05***		***0.07***	***Dc***	***38.00***	***57.90***	***37.40***	***9-30-95***	***85.00***		***95.90***	***92.4***						
• [4]1st[5] 11¾s 2002	Fa	**B**			Y	R	105.036	(2-1-98)	....	....	[6]....	....	85.0	D6	'94	85	65	s84¼	13.95	15.87
Clark Equipment Co.	***41b***	***Acquired by Ingersoll-Rand,see***																		
Nts 9¾s 2001	Ms	**A**	5/95	BBB	X	R	NC	....	....	....	....	....	100	F1	'91	116⅜	104¾	116⅜	8.38	6.02
[7]Clark Oil & Refining	***49***	***0.68***	***1.28***		***2.26***	***Dc***	***394.0***	***856.0***	***417.0***	***6-30-95***	***1199***		***2000***	***60.0***						
Sr Nts[5] 10½s 2001	jD	**BB**	2/93	BB+	Y	R	105.25	(12-1-96)	....	....	....	....	225	G1	'91	106	100½	105½	9.95	9.27
• Sr Nts[5] 9½s 2004	mS15	**BB**	2/93	BB+	Y	R	104.75	(9-15-97)	100	(9-15-03)	....	....	175	G1	'92	106⅝	95⅜	s104½	9.09	8.75
Clean Harbors	***53***	***2.11***	***1.80***		***1.45***	***Dc***	***0.11***	***59.40***	***40.70***	***9-30-95***	***73.50***		***143.0***	***53.9***						
Sr Nts[5] 12½s 2001	Mn15	**B**			Y	R	106.25	(5-15-99)	....	....	....	....	50.0	C5	'94	100	58	58	21.55	....
Cleveland Elec. Illum[8]	***72a***	***1.84***	***1.09***		***1.84***	***Dc***	***92.90***	***528.0***	***653.0***	***9-30-95***	***2710***		***4536***	***64.5***						
1st 7⅝s 2002	fA	**BB**	12/93	BBB–	Y	R	NC	....	....	....	....	....	245	M6	'92	96¾	86¼	96¾	7.88	8.27
1st 7⅜s 2003	Jd	**BB**	12/93	BBB–	Y	R	NC	....	....	....	....	....	100	M6	'93	94½	83½	94½	7.80	8.38
1st B 9½s 2005	Mn15	**BB**			Y	BE	100	(5-15-02)	....	....	....	....	300	M6	'95	104⅛	98½	104⅛	9.12	8.84
• 1st 8¾s 2005	mN15	**BB**	12/93	BBB–	Y	R	101.36	11-14-96	....	....	....	....	75.0	F1	'70	101⅞	87¾	s101	8.66	8.60
• 1st 9¼s 2009	Mn	**BB**	12/93	BBB–	Y	R	102.92	4-30-96	....	....	....	....	50.0	B6	'74	102¾	90	s101	9.16	9.12
• 1st 8⅜s 2011	jD	**BB**	12/93	BBB–	Y	R	103.38	11-30-96	....	....	....	....	125	M6	'76	98⅞	82⅛	s95½	8.77	8.91
• 1st 8⅜s 2012	fA	**BB**	12/93	BBB–	Y	R	103.61	7-31-96	....	....	....	....	75.0	M2	'77	98¾	81¾	s95	8.82	8.96
1st A 9⅜s 2017	Ms	**BB**	12/93	BBB–	Y	R	105.25	2-29-96	....	....	....	....	300	M6	'87	99¾	83¾	99¾	9.40	9.40
1st E 10s 2020	Jd	**BB**	12/93	BBB–	Y	R	106.62	5-31-96	....	....	....	....	100	M6	'90	102¼	86⅝	102¼	9.78	9.76
1st ('23E) 9s 2023	jJ	**BB**	12/93	BBB–	Y	R	104.13	(7-1-03)	....	....	....	....	150	M6	'93	95¼	80½	95¼	9.45	9.49
Clorox Co	***33***	***△15.59***	***△17.64***		***△14.27***	***Je***	***128.0***	***503.0***	***426.0***	***9-30-95***	***253.0***		***1287***	***25.6***						
Nts 8.80s 2001	jJ15	**AA–**			X	R	NC	....	....	....	....	....	200	M5	'91	113⅜	102½	113¼	7.77	5.96

Uniform Footnote Explanations-See Page 260. Other: [1] To be exch for Cap Sec when due. [2] Int pd monthly. [3] (HRO)On 10-1-01 at 100. [4] Gtd by Claridge, at Park Place Inc. [5] (HRO)On Chge of Ctrl at 101. [6] May redeem under certain conditions & prices. [7] Subsid & data of Horsham Corp. [8] Subsid of Centerior Energy.

Title-Industry Code & Co. Finances (In Italics) / Individual Issue Statistics — Exchange	Ind / Interest Dates	Fixed Charge Coverage 1992 / S&P Debt Rating	1993 / Date of Last Rating Change	Prior Rating	1994 / Eligible	Year End / Bond Form	Million $ Cash & Equiv. / Redemption Provisions: Regular Price	Curr. Assets / Regular (Begins) Thru	Curr. Liab. / Sinking Fund Price	Balance Sheet Date / Sinking Fund (Begins) Thru	L. Term Debt (Mil $) / Refund/Other Restriction Price	Refund/Other Restriction (Begins) Thru	Capital-ization (Mil $) / Outst'g (Mil $)	Total Debt % Capital / Underwriting Firm	Underwriting Year	Price Range 1995 High	Price Range 1995 Low	Mo. End Price Sale(s) or Bid	Curr. Yield	Yield to Mat.
CMI Industries	***68***	***3.12***	***2.05***		***1.15***	***Dc***	***2.46***	***152.0***	***49.50***	***9-30-95***	***166.0***		***221.0***	***75.1***						
Sr Sub[1]Nts[2] 9½s 2003	aO	**B+**			Y	R	104.75	(10-1-98)	....	....	[3]Z108.50	10-28-96	125	M2	'93	93⅞	80	80	11.88	13.77
CMS Energy	***75***	***d0.29***	***2.08***		***2.13***	***Dc***	***37.00***	***742.0***	***1380***	***9-30-95***	***2864***		***4984***	***71.1***						
Sr Deferred Cpn Nts'A'[4] 9½s '97	aO	**BB**	6/94	BB+	Y	R	NC	....	....	....	....	....	[5]172	D6	'92	103¾	92⅜	103¾	....	Flat
Sr Deferred Cpn Nts'B'[4] 9⅞s '99	aO	**BB**	6/94	BB+	Y	R	101.646	(10-1-97)	....	....	....	....	[5]268	D6	'92	103⅝	93	103⅝	....	Flat
CNA Financial	***35d***	***d36.47***	***7.55***		***d0.90***	***Dc***				***6-30-95***	***2995***		***9009***	***33.3***						
Deb 7¼s 2023	mN15	**A–**	5/95	A+	X	BE	NC	....	....	....	....	....	250	G1	'93	99¼	78⅜	99¼	7.30	7.31
Sr Nts 8⅝s '96	Ms	**A–**	5/95	A+	X	R	NC	....	....	....	....	....	250	L3	'91	101½	100⅜	100⅜	8.59	6.25
Sr Nts 8⅞s '98	Ms	**A–**	5/95	A+	X	R	NC	....	....	....	....	....	150	L3	'91	105⅞	100¾	105⅞	8.38	5.94
Nts 6¼s 2003	mN15	**A–**	5/95	A+	X	BE	NC	....	....	....	....	....	250	G1	'93	99⅛	83¼	99⅛	6.31	6.39
[6]***Coast Fed'l Bank***	***10a***	***1.28***	***1.05***		***0.82***	***Dc***				***6-30-95***	***690.0***		***1080***	***63.9***						
(Sub)Cap Nts[7] 13s 2002	QDec31	**BB–**	11/95	B+	Y	R	105.5714	(12-31-97)	....	....	....	....	57.5	K1	'92	113¾	108½	113¾	11.43	10.20
Coastal Corp	***73a***	***0.46***	***1.43***		***1.54***	***Dc***	***64.60***	***2278***	***2298***	***9-30-95***	***3516***		***6629***	***61.1***						
• Sr Deb 9¾s 2003	fA	**BB+**	4/92	BBB–	Y	R	NC	....	....	....	....	....	300	L3	'91	112⅞	103⅛	113⅛	8.62	7.45
• Sr Deb[8] 10¼s 2004	aO15	**BB+**	4/92	BBB–	Y	R	NC	....	....	....	....	....	200	D7	'89	117½	108	118⅛	8.68	7.41
• Sr Deb 11¾s 2006	Jd15	**BB+**	4/92	BBB–	Y	R	103.917	(6-15-96)	100	(6-15-96)	....	....	400	D7	'86	109⅛	104⅛	s105¾	11.11	10.82
• Sr Deb 10¾s 2010	aO	**BB+**	4/92	BBB–	Y	R	NC	....	....	....	....	....	150	L3	'90	120	107	118⅛	9.10	8.56
• Sr Deb 9⅝s 2012	Mn15	**BB+**			Y	R	NC	....	....	....	....	....	150	L3	'92	108⅞	106	108	8.91	8.70
• Sr Deb 7¾s 2035	aO15	**BB+**			Y	BE	NC	....	....	....	....	....	150	L3	'95	99⅞	98⅞	102⅝	7.55	7.54
• Sr Nts 8¾s '99	Mn15	**BB+**			Y	R	NC	....	....	....	....	....	150	L3	'92	104	101⅛	104	8.41	7.39
• Sr Nts 10⅜s 2000	aO	**BB+**	4/92	BBB–	Y	R	NC	....	....	....	....	....	250	L3	'90	111½	109¼	112⅝	9.21	7.19
• Sr Nts 10s 2001	Fa	**BB+**	4/92	BBB–	Y	R	NC	....	....	....	....	....	300	L3	'91	111¾	111¾	111¾	8.95	7.20
• Sr Nts 8⅛s 2002	mS15	**BB+**			Y	R	NC	....	....	....	....	....	250	L3	'92	108½	95¼	109	7.45	6.45
Coca-Cola Bott Consol	***11f***	***1.13***	***1.77***		***1.78***	***Dc***	***2.72***	***65.30***	***64.80***	***10-1-95***	***420.0***		***462.0***	***90.9***						
Deb 6.85s 2007	mN	**BBB**			X	BE	NC	....	....	....	....	....	100	C4	'95	103½	99⅝	103½	6.62	6.42
Coca-Cola Bottling Gr(SW)[9]	***11f***	***0.77***	***0.96***		***1.04***	***Dc***	***3.59***	***40.80***	***37.10***	***9-30-95***	***254.0***		***190.0***	***139.0***						
Sr[1]Sub Nts 9s 2003	mN15	**B+**	7/95	B	Y	R	104.50	(11-15-98)	....	....	....	....	140	C4	'93	100¾	87	100¾	8.93	8.86
Coca-Cola Co	***11e***	***16.65***	***18.84***		***19.73***	***Dc***	***1925***	***6112***	***7815***	***9-30-95***	***880.0***		***9022***	***41.6***						
Deb 7⅜s 2093	jJ29	**AA**			X	BE	NC	....	....	....	....	....	150	M2	'93	110⅝	86⅜	110⅝	6.67	6.67
Nts 7¾s '96	Fa15	**AA**			X	R	NC	....	....	....	....	....	250	G1	'91	101⅛	100¼	100¼	7.73	5.62
Nts 7⅞s '98	mS15	**AA**			X	R	NC	....	....	....	....	....	250	M2	'91	106	99⅛	106	7.43	5.46
Nts 6⅝s 2002	aO	**AA**			X	R	NC	....	....	....	....	....	150	G1	'92	104⅜	90⅞	104⅜	6.35	5.83
Nts 6s 2003	jJ15	**AA**			X	R	NC	....	....	....	....	....	150	M2	'93	100⅜	86⅞	100⅜	5.98	5.94
Coca-Cola Enterprises[10]	***11f***	***0.96***	***1.16***		***1.39***	***Dc***		***1009***	***844.0***	***9-29-95***	***4251***		***5717***	***75.2***						
Deb 8½s 2012	Fa	**AA–**			X	BE	NC	....	....	....	....	....	250	S1	'92	118⅜	100½	118⅜	7.18	6.62
Deb 8¾s 2017	Ao	**AA–**			X	R	104.89	3-31-96	100	(4-1-98)	®104.08	3-31-97	154	A2	'87	105¼	97⅞	105¼	8.31	8.22
Deb 8½s 2022	Fa	**AA–**			X	BE	NC	....	....	....	....	....	750	S1	'92	122⅛	98¼	122⅛	6.96	6.69
Deb 8s 2022	mS15	**AA–**			X	BE	NC	....	....	....	....	....	250	S1	'92	116	93½	116	6.90	6.70
Deb 6¾s 2023	mS15	**AA–**			X	BE	NC	....	....	....	....	....	250	S1	'93	100½	80¾	100⅜	6.72	6.72
Nts 6½s '97	mN	**AA–**			X	BE	NC	....	....	....	....	....	300	L3	'92	101⅞	95⅞	101⅞	6.38	5.43
Nts 7s '99	mN15	**AA–**			X	BE	NC	....	....	....	....	....	200	L3	'92	104½	94⅞	104½	6.70	5.69
Nts 7⅞s 2002	Fa	**AA–**			X	BE	NC	....	....	....	....	....	500	S1	'92	109⅞	97⅝	109⅞	7.17	5.92
Nts[11] 8s 2005	Jj4	**AA–**			X	BE	NC	....	....	....	....	....	250	M2	'92	114	101⅝	114	7.02	5.97
Cogentrix Energy	***72b***	***△1.65***	***△1.54***		***△1.50***	***Je***	***47.60***	***151.0***	***78.90***	***9-30-95***	***704.0***		***840.0***	***89.3***						
Sr Nts[12] 8.10s 2004	Ms15	**BBB–**			X	R	Z100	(3-15-01)	100	(3-15-01)	....	....	100	S1	'94	107¼	93	107¼	7.55	6.92
Cole Nat'l Group	***59l***	***n/a***	***2.09***		***1.97***	***Ja***	***18.10***	***137.0***	***88.70***	***7-29-95***	***184.0***		***190.0***	***97.4***						
Sr[12]Nts 11¼s 2001	aO	**B+**			Y	R	105.625	(10-1-98)	....	....	[13]Z112.50	9-30-96	190	M2	'93	102½	93	100¼	11.22	11.18

Uniform Footnote Explanations-See Page 260. Other: [1] Co must offer repurch at 101 on Chge of Ctrl. [2] Co may red at 100 plus Premium on Chge of Ctrl. [3] Max $43.8M red w/proceeds of Com Off'g. [4] (HRO)On Chge in Ctrl as defined. [5] Incl disc. [6] Subsid & data of Coast Savings Fin'l. [7] Death redemp benefit,ltd,as defined. [8] On Chge of Ctrl Co may be req to repurch at 100. [9] Subsid of Texas Bottling Gr. [10] See Johnston Coca-Cola Bottling. [11] (HRO)On ea Jan 4 fr 1994 at 100. [12] (HRO)On Chge of Ctrl at 101. [13] Max $50M red w/proceeds of Pub Eq Off'g.

Title-Industry Code & Co. Finances (In Italics) / Exchange ↓ Individual Issue Statistics	Ind / Interest Dates	Fixed Charge Coverage 1992 / S&P Debt Rating	1993 / Date of Last Rating Change	Prior Rating	1994 / Eligible ↓	Year End / Bond Form	Million $ Cash & Equiv. / Redemption Provisions: Regular Price	Curr. Assets / Regular (Begins) Thru	Curr. Liab. / Sinking Fund Price	Balance Sheet Date / Sinking Fund (Begins) Thru	L. Term Debt (Mil $) / Refund/Other Restriction Price	Refund/Other Restriction (Begins) Thru	Capital-ization (Mil $) / Outst'g (Mil $)	Total Debt % Capital / Underwriting Firm	Underwriting Year	Price Range 1995 High	Price Range 1995 Low	Mo. End Price Sale(s) or Bid	Curr. Yield	Yield to Mat.
Cole Taylor Fin'l Group	***10***	***2.66***	***2.62***		***2.71***	***Dc***				***9-30-95***	***116.0***		***264.0***	***43.9***						
Sub Nts 9s 2001	[1]Jun15	**NR**				R	100	(6-15-97)	....	....	....	....	25.0	C3	'94	104⅞	91	104⅞	8.58	7.88
Colgate-Palmolive Co	***33***	***9.12***	***11.30***		***8.28***	***Dc***	***277.0***	***2579***	***1842***	***9-30-95***	***3011***		***4977***	***66.7***						
Deb 9⅝s 2017	jJ15	**A**	11/95	A+	X	R	105.775	7-14-96	100	(7-15-98)	®104.8125	7-14-97	30.0	G1	'87	116½	102¼	A116½	8.26	8.00
M-T Nts 'B' 6.67s '97	[2]jd	**A**	11/95	A+	X	BE	NC	....	....	....	....	....	10.0	C4	'94	101¾	96¾	101¾	6.56	5.35
M-T Nts 'B' 6.88s '97	[3]jd	**A**	11/95	A+	X	BE	NC	....	....	....	....	....	6.00	G1	'94	102¾	96⅜	102¾	6.70	5.40
M-T Nts 'B' 6.98s '98	[4]jd	**A**	11/95	A+	X	BE	NC	....	....	....	....	....	15.0	M2	'94	103½	96⅛	103½	6.74	5.41
M-T Nts 'B' 7.18s '99	[5]jd	**A**	11/95	A+	X	BE	NC	....	....	....	....	....	25.0	M2	'94	105	95½	105	6.84	5.54
M-T Nts 'B' 7.18s '99	[6]	**A**	11/95	A+	X	BE	NC	....	....	....	....	....	20.0	M5	'94	105	95½	105	6.84	5.55
M-T Nts 'B' 7.21s '99	[5]jd	**A**	11/95	A+	X	BE	NC	....	....	....	....	....	10.0	C4	'94	105⅛	95⅝	105⅛	6.86	5.54
M-T Nts 'B' 7.44s 2001	[7]jd	**A**	11/95	A+	X	BE	NC	....	....	....	....	....	10.0	M5	'94	107¾	94⅞	107¾	6.90	5.75
M-T Nts 'B' 7.54s 2002	[8]jd	**A**	11/95	A+	X	BE	NC	....	....	....	....	....	10.0	C4	'94	108¾	94⅝	108¾	6.93	5.88
M-T Nts 'B' 7.60s 2004	[9]jd	**A**	11/95	A+	X	BE	NC	....	....	....	....	....	22.0	G1	'94	110⅛	93¾	110⅛	6.90	6.04
M-T Nts 'B' 7.63s 2004	[9]jd	**A**	11/95	A+	X	BE	NC	....	....	....	....	....	5.00	M2	'94	110⅜	93⅞	110⅜	6.91	6.04
M-T Nts 'B' 7.64s 2004	[9]jd	**A**	11/95	A+	X	BE	NC	....	....	....	....	....	20.0	M2	'94	110⅜	94	110⅜	6.92	6.05
F/R[10]M-T Nts 'B' '97	QMay23	**A**	11/95	A+	X	BE	NC	....	....	....	....	....	50.0	M2	'94	100	99½	100	....	....
Colonial Nat'l Bank USA	***10***	***n/a***	....		....	***Dc***				***3-31-93***	***★50.00***		***109.0***	***NM***						
Sub Nts[11] 7s 2003	fA	**BBB–**			X	BE	NC	....	....	....	....	....	50.0	F1	'93	102⅞	89¼	102⅞	6.80	6.51
Color Tile Inc	***60***	***1.23***	***1.40***		***1.02***	***Ja***	***26.60***	***101.0***	***328.0***	***10-1-95***	***198.0***		***425.0***	***98.6***						
Sr[12]Nts[13] 10¾s 2001	jD15	**D**	12/95	C		R	104.61	(12-15-97)	....	....	[14]Z110	12-15-96	200	B5	'93	87	8	11¼	....	Flat
Colorado Interstate Gas[15]	***73c***	***7.21***	***6.50***		***7.40***	***Dc***	***0.74***	***307.0***	***134.0***	***9-30-95***	***179.0***		***633.0***	***28.3***						
• Sr Deb[16] 10s 2005	Jd15	**BBB–**			X	R	NC	....	....	....	....	....	180	S4	'90	116¾	109	107	9.35	8.89
Colt Indus.	***2b***	***Now Coltec Indus, see***																		
Deb 11¼s 2015	jD	**BB**	4/92	B	Y	R	105.625	11-30-96	100	(12-1-96)	....	....	142	F1	'85	106½	103¾	105⅝	10.65	10.57
Coltec Industries[17]	***2b***	***1.78***	***1.24***		***2.64***	***Dc***	***10.80***	***485.0***	***254.0***	***10-1-95***	***977.0***		***506.0***	***194.0***						
Sr Nts 9¾s '99	mN	**BB–**	5/95	B+	Y	R	NC	....	....	....	....	....	150	M6	'92	104¼	97⅞	102½	9.51	8.96
Sr Nts 9¾s 2000	Ao	**BB–**	5/95	B+	Y	R	NC	....	....	....	....	....	200	M6	'92	104⅞	70¾	103	9.47	8.88
Sr Sub Nts 10¼s 2002	Ao	**B+**			Y	R	105.125	(4-1-97)	....	....	....	....	231	M6	'92	103	98½	103	9.95	9.59
Columbia/HCA Healthcare[18]	***30***	***3.45***	***4.52***		***6.72***	***Dc***	***113.0***	***2867***	***1959***	***3-31-95***	***4263***		***10127***	***43.8***						
Deb[19] 8.36s 2024	Ao15	**BBB+**			X	R	NC	....	....	....	....	....	150	M6	'94	121⅝	97⅜	121⅝	6.87	6.65
Deb 7.19s 2015	mN15	**BBB+**			X	BE	[20]Z100	....	....	....	....	....	150	M6	'95	102½	100	102½	7.01	6.95
Deb 7.05s 2027	jD	**BBB+**			X	BE	NC	....	....	....	....	....	150	S1	'95	102⅜	100	102⅜	6.89	6.86
Deb 7½s 2095	mN15	**BBB+**			X	BE	NC	....	....	....	....	....	200	M6	'95	107¼	100	107¼	6.99	6.99
Nts 6½s '99	Ms15	**BBB+**			X	BE	NC	....	....	....	....	....	175	L3	'94	102⅛	93½	102⅛	6.36	5.76
Nts 7.15s 2004	Ms30	**BBB+**			X	BE	NC	....	....	....	....	....	150	S1	'94	105⅝	90⅛	105⅝	6.77	6.26
M-T Nts 6.87s 2003	mS15	**BBB+**			X	BE	NC	....	....	....	....	....	125	L3	'95	103⅞	100	103⅞	6.61	6.23
M-T Nts 8.85s 2007	[21]jd15	**BBB+**			X	BE	NC	....	....	....	....	....	150	M6	'94	119	99⅝	119	7.44	6.42
M-T Nts 9s 2014	jD15	**BBB+**			X	BE	NC	....	....	....	....	....	150	L3	'95	122¼	99¼	122¼	7.36	6.88
M-T Nts 7⅝s 2025	mS15	**BBB+**			X	BE	NC	....	....	....	....	....	125	L3	'95	108½	99⅞	108½	7.03	6.94
Columbia Healthcare	***30***	***Now Columbia/HCA Healthcare,see***																		
Deb 7½s 2023	jD15	**BBB+**			X	R	NC	....	....	....	....	....	150	M6	'93	107¾	85⅛	107¾	6.96	6.87
Nts 6⅛s 2000	jD15	**BBB+**			X	R	NC	....	....	....	....	....	150	M6	'93	100¾	89⅜	100¾	6.08	5.95
Columbia Pictures Ent	***24***	***Acquired by Sony Corp***																		
Sr Sub Nts 9⅞s '98	Fa	**A–**	6/93	A	X	R	NC	....	....	....	....	....	325	A2	'88	108¼	102⅛	108¼	9.12	5.63
Columbus&So. Ohio Elec	***72a***	***Now Columbus So'n Pwr,see***																		
1st 6¼s '97	aO	**A–**	8/95	BBB+	X	R	100.24	9-30-96	100.10	9-30-96	....	....	14.6		'67	100½	95	100½	6.22	5.94
1st 7s '98	Jd	**A–**	8/95	BBB+	X	R	100.62	5-31-96	100.41	6-1-96	....	....	24.8	L3	'68	101	95¾	100⅝	6.96	6.71

Uniform Footnote Explanations-See Page 260. Other: [1] Int pd monthly. [2] Due 5-23-97. [3] Due 12-23-97. [4] Due 5-26-98. [5] Due 5-24-99. [6] Due 5-25-99. [7] Due 5-25-01. [8] Due 5-23-02. [9] Due 5-24-04. [10] Int adj weekly. [11] Issued in min denom $100T. [12] (HRO)On Chge of Ctrl at 101. [13] Int of 12-15-95 not pd when due. [14] Max $70M red w/proceeds of Pub Eq Off'g. [15] Subsid of Coastal Corp. [16] On Chge of Ctrl Co must offer to repurch at 100. [17] See Colt Indus. [18] See Columbia Healthcare,Hospital Corp of Amer. [19] (HRO)On Chge of Ctrl at 90.95 on 4-15-04. [20] Greater of 100 & amt based on formula. [21] Due 1-1-07.

Exchange / Individual Issue Statistics	Interest Dates	S&P Debt Rating	Date of Last Rating Change	Prior Rating	Eligible	Bond Form	Regular Price	Regular (Begins) Thru	Sinking Fund Price	Sinking Fund (Begins) Thru	Refund/Other Restriction Price	Refund/Other Restriction (Begins) Thru	Outst'g (Mil $)	Underwriting Firm	Underwriting Year	Price Range 1995 High	Price Range 1995 Low	Mo. End Price Sale(s) or Bid	Curr. Yield	Yield to Mat.
Title-Industry Code & Co. Finances (In Italics)	***Ind***	***Fixed Charge Coverage 1992***	***1993***	***1994***		***Year End***	***Million $ Cash & Equiv.***	***Curr. Assets***	***Curr. Liab.***	***Balance Sheet Date***	***L. Term Debt (Mil $)***		***Capital-ization (Mil $)***	***Total Debt % Capital***						
Columbus Southern Power[1]	***72a***	***1.45***	***2.28***	***2.24***		***Dc***	***59.20***	***237.0***	***272.0***	***9-30-95***	***993.0***		***1854***	***59.2***						
1st 7¼s 2002	aO	A–	8/95	BBB+	X	BE	NC	....	....	....	....	....	75.0	L3	'92	105⅜	92¼	105⅜	6.88	6.26
1st 6.60s 2003	[2]mn	A–	8/95	BBB+	X	BE	101.89	(8-1-98)	Z100	....	....	....	40.0	S1	'93	101⅛	87⅜	101⅛	6.53	6.41
1st 6.55s 2004	[3]mn	A–	8/95	BBB+	X	BE	101.88	(3-1-99)	....	....	....	....	50.0	S1	'94	100½	86⅜	100½	6.52	6.47
1st 8.40s 2022	fA15	A–	8/95	BBB+	X	BE	104.20	(8-15-02)	Z100	....	....	....	40.0	L3	'92	114⅝	94⅛	114¼	7.35	7.19
1st 7¾s 2023	[2]mn	A–	8/95	BBB+	X	BE	105.82	(8-1-98)	Z100	....	....	....	40.0	S1	'93	106⅜	87⅜	106⅜	7.29	7.21
1st 7.45s 2024	[3]mn	A–	8/95	BBB+	X	BE	103.73	(3-1-04)	....	....	....	....	50.0	S1	'94	104⅛	84½	104⅛	7.15	7.11
Comcast Corp	***12a***	***0.93***	***0.85***	***0.84***		***Dc***	***828.0***	***1492***	***1146***	***9-30-95***	***6619***		***6116***	***112.0***						
Sr Sub Deb 10¼s 2001	aO15	B+	9/93	B	Y	R	NC	....	....	....	....	....	125	G1	'91	109¼	97½	109¼	9.38	8.21
Sr Sub Deb 9⅜s 2005	Mn15	B+			Y	R	104.688	(5-15-00)	....	....	....	....	250	L3	'95	104½	98⅝	104¼	8.99	8.70
Sr Sub Deb 9⅛s 2006	aO15	B+			Y	R	104.562	(10-15-00)	....	....	....	....	250	G1	'95	104	98⅝	104	8.77	8.55
Sr Sub Deb 9½s 2008	Jj15	B+	9/93	B	Y	R	103	(1-15-00)	....	....	....	....	200	F1	'93	105½	90	105½	9.00	8.75
Sr Sub Deb 10⅝s 2012	jJ15	B+	9/93	B	Y	R	NC	....	....	....	....	....	300	M2	'92	112⅞	97½	112⅞	9.41	9.10
Comdisco, Inc.	***20a***	***△1.49***	***△1.64***	***△1.61***		***Sp***	***85.00***			***9-30-95***	***2457***		***3233***	***76.0***						
Nts 9¾s '97	Jj15	BBB	3/92	BBB+	X	R	NC	....	....	....	....	....	200	M2	'90	105¼	102¼	104	9.38	5.74
Nts 7¼s '98	Ao15	BBB			X	BE	NC	....	....	....	....	....	200	S5	'95	102⅞	99¾	102⅞	7.05	5.89
Nts 7¾s '99	mS	BBB			X	R	NC	....	....	....	....	....	100	S5	'92	105½	96¼	105½	7.35	6.05
Nts 6½s 2000	Jd15	BBB			X	BE	NC	....	....	....	....	....	200	M2	'95	101¼	97⅜	101¼	6.42	6.17
M-T Nts 'C' 6.38s '96	[4]ms	BBB			X	BE	NC	....	....	....	....	....	18.0	M2	'93	100¼	98¼	100⅛	6.37	5.57
M-T Nts 'C' 6.20s '96	[5]ms	BBB			X	BE	NC	....	....	....	....	....	8.00	M2	'93	100⅛	98	100⅛	6.19	5.41
M-T Nts 'C' 7.41s '96	[6]ms	BBB			X	BE	NC	....	....	....	....	....	20.6	M2	'93	101¼	99	100⅞	7.35	5.44
M-T Nts 'C' 6⅜s '96	[7]ms	BBB			X	BE	NC	....	....	....	....	....	15.0	M2	'94	100⅜	97⅝	100⅜	6.35	5.57
M-T Nts 'C' 6.84s '96	[8]ms	BBB			X	BE	NC	....	....	....	....	....	10.0	M2	'94	100⅞	97⅞	100¾	6.79	5.67
M-T Nts 'C' 6.89s '96	[8]ms	BBB			X	BE	NC	....	....	....	....	....	15.0	M2	'94	101	98	100¾	6.84	5.72
M-T Nts 'C' 6.72s '96	[9]ms	BBB			X	BE	NC	....	....	....	....	....	20.0	M2	'94	100¾	97⅝	100⅝	6.68	5.74
M-T Nts 'C' 6.72s '96	[10]ms	BBB			X	BE	NC	....	....	....	....	....	25.0	M2	'94	100¾	97⅝	100¾	6.67	5.59
M-T Nts 'C' 6.87s '96	[11]ms	BBB			X	BE	NC	....	....	....	....	....	25.0	M2	'94	101	98¼	100⅞	6.81	5.62
M-T Nts'C' 7.73s '97	[12]ms	BBB			X	BE	NC	....	....	....	....	....	40.0	M2	'95	102⅜	100	102⅜	7.55	5.53
M-T Nt 'C' 6.78s '97	[13]ms	BBB			X	BE	NC	....	....	....	....	....	15.0	M2	'94	101⅝	96⅜	101⅝	6.67	5.61
M-T Nt 'C' 6.08s '97	[14]ms	BBB			X	BE	NC	....	....	....	....	....	10.0	M2	'94	100⅛	98⅜	100	6.08	6.08
M-T Nts'D' 6.689s '98	[15]ms	BBB			X	BE	NC	....	....	....	....	....	25.0	M2	'95	102¼	100	102¼	6.54	5.67
Comerica Inc	***10***	***4.08***	***5.08***	***2.82***		***Dc***				***9-30-95***	***4949***		***7502***	***66.0***						
Sub Deb 10⅛s '98	Jd	A–	6/92	BBB+	X	R	NC	....	....	....	....	....	75.0	F1	'88	109½	104⅜	109⅜	9.26	5.91
Sub Cap[16]Nts 9¾s '99	Mn	A–	6/92	BBB+	X	R	NC	....	....	....	Z100	....	75.0	F1	'87	111	104⅝	111	8.78	6.06
Sub Nts 7¼s 2007	fA	A–			X	R	NC	....	....	....	....	....	150	L3	'95	106⅝	99⅝	106⅝	6.80	6.43
Commerce Bancorp	***10***	***n/a***	***6.91***	***3.00***		***Dc***				***9-30-95***	***23.00***		***179.0***	***12.8***						
Sub Nts 8⅜s 2003	jJ15	NR				R	102	(7-15-00)	....	....	....	....	23.0	W4	'93	108½	93⅞	108½	7.72	6.91
Commercial Credit Co[17]	***25a***	***2.13***	***2.18***	***1.90***		***Dc***	***13.50***			***9-30-95***	***5150***		***7706***	***84.5***						
Deb 10s 2009	Mn15	A+	10/93	A	X	R	NC	....	....	....	....	....	100	S5	'89	131⅜	109¾	131⅜	7.61	6.46
Deb[18] 8.70s 2009	Jd15	A+	10/93	A	X	R	NC	....	....	....	....	....	150	M6	'89	120⅞	103⅞	120⅞	7.20	6.37
Deb[19] 8.70s 2010	Jd15	A+	10/93	A	X	R	NC	....	....	....	....	....	100	B5	'90	124⅛	104⅛	124⅛	7.01	6.16
Nts 6⅜s '96	Jj	A+	10/93	A	X	R	NC	....	....	....	....	....	200	L3	'91	100¼	98⅝	100	6.38	Mat.
• Nts 8s '96	mS	A+	10/93	A	X	R	NC	....	....	....	....	....	100	L3	'91	102	98⅞	101¼	7.90	6.05
Nts 7⅜s '96	mN15	A+	10/93	A	X	R	NC	....	....	....	....	....	150	L3	'91	101¾	98¾	101⅝	7.26	5.44
Nts 6¾s '97	Jj15	A+	10/93	A	X	R	NC	....	....	....	....	....	200	M5	'92	101¼	97½	101¼	6.67	5.50
Nts 8⅛s '97	Ms	A+	10/93	A	X	R	NC	....	....	....	....	....	150	M6	'87	103¼	99¾	102⅞	7.90	5.55
Nts 8½s '98	Fa15	A+	10/93	A	X	R	NC	....	....	....	....	....	100	F1	'88	105½	100½	105⅛	8.09	5.90

Uniform Footnote Explanations-See Page 260. Other: [1] See Columbus & So'n Ohio Elec. [2] Due Aug 1. [3] Due Mar 1. [4] Due 3-4-96. [5] Due 3-5-96. [6] Due 6-14-96. [7] Due 6-22-96. [8] Due 8-30-96. [9] Due 9-1-96. [10] Due 9-9-96. [11] Due 9-23-96. [12] Due 2-18-97. [13] Due 6-16-97. [14] Due 12-14-97. [15] Due 5-22-98. [16] To be exch for Cap Sec when due. [17] Subsid of Primerica Corp. [18] (HRO)On 6-15-99 at 100. [19] (HRO)On 6-15-96('99,'02 or '05)at 100.

Title-Industry Code & Co. Finances (In Italics)	Ind	Fixed Charge Coverage 1992	1993	1994		Year End	Million $ Cash & Equiv.	Curr. Assets	Curr. Liab.	Balance Sheet Date		L. Term Debt (Mil $)	Capital-ization (Mil $)		Total Debt % Capital					
Individual Issue Statistics Exchange ↓	Interest Dates	S&P Debt Rating	Date of Last Rating Change	Prior Rating	Eligible ↓	Bond Form	Redemption Provisions: Regular Price	Regular (Begins) Thru	Sinking Fund Price	Sinking Fund (Begins) Thru	Refund/Other Restriction Price	Refund/Other Restriction (Begins) Thru	Outst'g (Mil $)	Underwriting Firm	Underwriting Year	Price Range 1995 High	Price Range 1995 Low	Mo. End Price Sale(s) or Bid	Curr. Yield	Yield to Mat.
***Commercial Credit Co** (Cont.)*																				
Nts 5.70s '98	Ms	**A+**	10/93	A	X	R	NC	....	....	....	....	....	100	S1	'93	100¼	92⅞	100¼	5.69	5.57
Nts 5½s '98	Mn15	**A+**	10/93	A	X	BE	NC	....	....	....	....	....	100	L3	'93	99⅞	91⅞	99⅞	5.51	5.55
Nts 10s '99	Mn	**A+**	10/93	A	X	R	NC	....	....	....	....	....	100	M6	'89	112⅝	105⅝	112⅝	8.88	5.78
Nts 9.60s '99	Mn15	**A+**	10/93	A	X	R	NC	....	....	....	....	....	100	S5	'89	111½	104⅛	111½	8.61	5.80
Nts 6.70s '99	fA	**A+**	10/93	A	X	BE	NC	....	....	....	....	....	150	S1	'92	103	93¼	103	6.50	5.76
Nts 6⅛s 2000	Ms	**A+**	10/93	A	X	R	NC	....	....	....	....	....	100	S1	'93	101	90⅝	101	6.06	5.85
Nts 6s 2000	Ao15	**A+**	10/93	A	X	BE	NC	....	....	....	....	....	150	S1	'93	100½	89½	100½	5.97	5.86
Nts 6¾s 2000	Mn15	**A+**			X	BE	NC	....	....	....	....	....	200	C5	'95	103⅜	99½	103⅜	6.53	5.86
Nts 6½s 2005	Jd	**A+**			X	BE	NC	....	....	....	....	....	200	C5	'95	101⅞	94¼	101⅞	6.38	6.23
Nts 6s 2000	Jd15	**A+**	10/93	A	X	BE	NC	....	....	....	....	....	100	L3	'93	100½	89¼	100½	5.97	5.87
Nts 5¾s 2000	jJ15	**A+**	10/93	A	X	BE	NC	....	....	....	....	....	200	S1	'93	99½	88⅛	99½	5.78	5.88
Nts 8¼s 2001	mN	**A+**			X	BE	NC	....	....	....	....	....	300	C5	'94	110⅞	98⅝	110⅞	7.44	6.01
Nts 7⅜s 2002	Ms15	**A+**			X	BE	NC	....	....	....	....	....	200	C5	'95	107	98¼	107	6.89	6.01
Nts 6⅞s 2002	Mn	**A+**			X	BE	NC	....	....	....	....	....	200	B5	'95	104⅜	98¾	104⅜	6.59	6.03
Nts 6⅜s 2002	Ms15	**A+**			X	BE	NC	....	....	....	....	....	200	M5	'95	101¾	98	101¾	6.27	6.05
Nts 5.90s 2003	mS	**A+**	10/93	A	X	BE	NC	....	....	....	....	....	200	S5	'93	98⅜	84¼	98⅜	6.00	6.17
Nts 7⅞s 2004	jJ15	**A+**			X	BE	NC	....	....	....	....	....	200	L3	'94	110¾	95⅝	110¾	7.11	6.23
Nts 7¾s 2005	Ms	**A+**			X	BE	NC	....	....	....	....	....	200	M6	'95	110⅜	99¾	110⅜	7.02	6.25
Nts 6⅛s 2005	jD	**A+**			X	BE	NC	....	....	....	....	....	200	L3	'95	99⅛	97⅞	99	6.19	6.26
Nts 7⅜s 2005	Ao15	**A+**			X	BE	NC	....	....	....	....	....	200	S1	'95	107⅞	98⅛	107⅞	6.84	6.24
Nts 10s 2008	jD	**A+**	10/93	A	X	R	NC	....	....	....	....	....	150	S5	'88	130¾	109⅞	130¾	7.65	6.45
Nts[1] 6⅝s 2015	Jd	**A+**			X	BE	NC	....	....	....	....	....	200	C5	'95	104¼	97¾	104¼	6.35	6.24
Nts[2] 7⅞s 2025	Fa	**A+**			X	BE	NC	....	....	....	....	....	200	S5	'95	113⅞	99⅞	113⅞	6.92	6.78
Commercial Federal Corp	***10a***	***△1.37***	***△1.42***	***△1.43***		***Je***				***9-30-95***	***1629***	***1951***		***83.4***						
Sub Nts[3] 10¼s '99	jD15	**B+**	4/95	B	Y	R	100	....	....	....	....	....	40.3	P2	'92	100	96	99	10.35	10.56
Commercial Metals	***44***	***△4.73***	***△5.41***	***△4.80***		***Au***	***21.00***	***534.0***	***268.0***	***8-31-95***	***158.0***	***480.0***		***36.9***						
Nts 7.20s 2005	jJ15	**BBB+**			X	BE	NC	....	....	....	....	....	100	G1	'95	105⅝	98	105⅝	6.82	6.40
CommNet Cellular[4]	***67g***	***△d0.29***	***△0.48***	***△0.58***		***Sp***	***41.00***	***57.60***	***17.70***	***9-30-95***	***246.0***	***308.0***		***80.2***						
Sub Nts[5] 11¼s 2005	jJ	**CCC+**			Y	R	106	(7-1-00)	....	....	....	....	80.0	M2	'95	100	99	A99	11.36	11.42
[6]Commonwealth Edison	***72a***	***2.22***	***0.63***	***2.08***		***Dc***	***584.0***	***1952***	***2111***	***9-30-95***	***6990***	***14714***		***54.3***						
1st V 5¼s '96	Ao	**BBB**	1/93	BBB+	X	CR	100	3-31-96	....	....	....	....	50.0	H1	'66	99¾	96½	99¾	5.26	6.16
1st X 5¾s '96	jD	**BBB**	1/93	BBB+	X	R	100	11-30-96	....	....	....	....	50.0		'66	99¾	95¼	99¾	5.76	6.03
1st Y 5⅜s '97	Ao	**BBB**	1/93	BBB+	X	R	100.22	3-31-96	....	....	....	....	50.0	F1	'67	99¼	93½	99¼	5.42	6.00
1st Z 6¼s '98	Fa	**BBB**	1/93	BBB+	X	R	100.48	1-31-96	....	....	....	....	50.0		'68	100	93¼	100	6.25	6.25
1st Ser 15 6¾s '98	jJ	**BBB**	1/93	BBB+	X	R	100.51	6-30-96	....	....	....	....	50.0	F1	'68	100⅞	93¾	100⅞	6.69	6.37
1st Ser 16 6⅜s '98	aO	**BBB**	1/93	BBB+	X	R	100.48	9-30-96	....	....	....	....	75.0	H1	'68	100	92¼	100	6.38	6.37
1st Ser 22 7½s 2001	Jj	**BBB**	1/93	BBB+	X	R	101.12	12-31-96	....	....	....	....	100	F1	'71	102½	93⅜	101⅛	7.42	7.23
• 1st Ser 25 7⅝s 2003	Jd	**BBB**	1/93	BBB+	X	R	101.91	5-31-96	....	....	....	....	100	H1	'73	102	91¼	100⅝	7.58	7.51
• 1st Ser 26 8s 2003	aO15	**BBB**	1/93	BBB+	X	R	102.17	10-14-96	....	....	....	....	125	K2	'73	103¼	94½	s102⅛	7.83	7.63
• 1st Ser 35 8⅛s 2007	Jj15	**BBB**	1/93	BBB+	X	R	102.63	1-14-97	....	....	....	....	180	M6	'77	103¾	92	s102	7.97	7.85
1st Ser 57 9½s 2016	Mn	**BBB**	1/93	BBB+	X	R	104.75	(5-1-96)	....	....	....	....	200	M6	'86	106¾	97⅝	105¾	8.98	8.88
1st Ser 73 9⅜s 2000	Fa15	**BBB**	1/93	BBB+	X	R	NC	....	....	....	....	....	125	S1	'90	111⅜	102	111⅜	8.42	6.21
1st Ser 74 9¾s 2020	Fa15	**BBB**	1/93	BBB+	X	R	103.97	(2-15-00)	....	....	....	....	225	S1	'90	114⅛	100⅛	114⅛	8.54	8.38
1st Ser 75 9⅞s 2020	Jd15	**BBB**	1/93	BBB+	X	R	102.27	(6-15-05)	....	....	....	....	260	M6	'90	118⅝	101⅜	118⅝	8.32	8.11
1st Ser 76 8¼s 2006	aO	**BBB**	1/93	BBB+	X	R	NC	....	....	....	....	....	100	M6	'91	113⅞	93⅞	113⅞	7.24	6.44
1st Ser 77 8⅞s 2021	aO	**BBB**	1/93	BBB+	X	R	105.99	(10-1-96)	....	....	....	....	100	M6	'91	109⅛	92¾	109⅛	8.13	8.03

Uniform Footnote Explanations-See Page 260. Other: [1] (HRO)On 6-1-02 at 100. [2] (HRO)On 2-1-05 at 100. [3] Death red benefit,ltd,as defined. [4] See Cellular Inc. [5] (HRO)On Chge of Ctrl at 101.
[6] Subsid of Unicom Corp.

Title-Industry Code & Co. Finances (In Italics)	*Ind*	*Fixed Charge Coverage 1992*		*1993*	*1994*	*Year End*	*Million $ Cash & Equiv.*	*Curr. Assets*	*Curr. Liab.*	*Balance Sheet Date*	*L. Term Debt (Mil $)*	*Capital-ization (Mil $)*		*Total Debt % Capital*						
Individual Issue Statistics Exchange ↓	Interest Dates	S&P Debt Rating	Date of Last Rating Change	Prior Rating	Eligible ↓	Bond Form	Redemption Provisions: Regular Price	Regular (Begins) Thru	Sinking Fund Price	Sinking Fund (Begins) Thru	Refund/Other Restriction Price	Refund/Other Restriction (Begins) Thru	Outst'g (Mil $)	Underwriting Firm	Underwriting Year	Price Range 1995 High	Price Range 1995 Low	Mo. End Price Sale(s) or Bid	Curr. Yield	Yield to Mat.
***Commonwealth Edison** (Cont.)*																				
1st Ser 78 8⅜s 2006	aO15	**BBB**	1/93	BBB+	X	R	NC	....	....	....	....	....	125	M2	'91	114⅞	95⅜	114⅞	7.29	6.44
1st Ser 79 9⅛s 2021	aO15	**BBB**	1/93	BBB+	X	R	106.63	(10-15-96)	....	....	....	....	125	M2	'91	109⅜	94⅜	109⅜	8.34	8.24
1st Ser 80 7s '97	Fa	**BBB**	1/93	BBB+	X	R	NC	....	....	....	....	....	150	S1	'92	101¼	96⅝	101¼	6.91	5.79
1st Ser 81 8⅝s 2022	Fa	**BBB**	1/93	BBB+	X	R	103.84	(2-1-02)	....	....	....	....	200	S1	'92	110	92	110	7.84	7.73
1st Ser 83 8s 2008	Mn15	**BBB**	1/93	BBB+	X	R	NC	....	....	....	....	....	140	S1	'92	112⅜	91¼	112⅜	7.12	6.53
1st Ser 84 8½s 2022	jJ15	**BBB**	1/93	BBB+	X	BE	103.915	(7-15-02)	....	....	....	....	200	M2	'92	108⅞	91⅜	108⅞	7.81	7.71
1st Ser 85 7⅜s 2002	mS15	**BBB**	1/93	BBB+	X	R	NC	....	....	....	....	....	200	P1	'92	105⅞	91¼	105⅞	6.97	6.29
1st Ser 86 8⅜s 2022	mS15	**BBB**	1/93	BBB+	X	R	103.425	(9-15-02)	....	....	....	....	200	P1	'92	108⅝	90⅛	108⅝	7.71	7.61
1st Ser 87 6¼s '97	aO	**BBB**	1/93	BBB+	X	BE	NC	....	....	....	....	....	60.0	0	'92	100¾	94	100¾	6.20	5.79
1st Ser 88 8⅜s 2023	Fa15	**BBB**			X	BE	103.863	(2-15-03)	....	....	....	....	250		'93	108¾	90	108¾	7.70	7.61
1st Ser 89 6s '98	Ms15	**BBB**			X	BE	NC	....	....	....	....	....	130	P1	'93	100¼	92¾	100¼	5.99	5.87
1st Ser 90 6½s 2000	Ao15	**BBB**			X	BE	NC	....	....	....	....	....	230	M2	'93	101½	90½	101½	6.40	6.09
1st Ser 91 8s 2023	Ao15	**BBB**			X	BE	103.664	(4-15-03)	....	....	....	....	160	M2	'93	104¾	86⅜	104¾	7.64	7.58
1st Ser 92 7⅝s 2013	Ao15	**BBB**			X	BE	NC	....	....	....	....	....	220	S1	'93	104⅞	86¼	104⅞	7.27	7.13
1st Ser 93 7s 2005	jJ	**BBB**			X	BE	NC	....	....	....	....	....	225	P1	'93	103¾	86⅞	103¾	6.75	6.47
1st Ser 94 7½s 2013	jJ	**BBB**			X	BE	NC	....	....	....	....	....	150	P1	'93	103¾	85½	103¾	7.23	7.12
1st Ser 95 6⅜s 2000	jJ15	**BBB**			X	BE	NC	....	....	....	....	....	100	S1	'93	101½	89⅜	101½	6.28	5.99
1st Ser 96 6⅝s 2003	jJ15	**BBB**			X	BE	NC	....	....	....	....	....	100	M2	'93	101⅝	85¾	101⅝	6.52	6.35
1st Ser 97 7¾s 2023	jJ15	**BBB**			X	BE	103.765	(7-15-03)	....	....	....	....	150	M2	'93	103	84⅛	103	7.52	7.49
• SF Deb 3s '99	Ao	**BBB−**	1/93	BBB	X	CR	100.35	3-31-96	100.15	11-30-96	....	....	9.66	F1	'49	88⅝	75⅛	88⅝	3.39	6.96
• SF Deb 2¾s '99	Ao	**BBB−**	1/93	BBB	X	CR	100.07	3-31-96	100.03	11-30-96	....	....	11.6	H1	'50	86	82	87¾	3.13	7.02
• SF Deb 2⅞s 2001	Ao	**BBB−**	1/93	BBB	X	CR	100.53	3-31-96	100.24	11-30-96	....	....	18.6	H1	'51	80	80	82¼	3.50	6.96
• SF Deb 7⅝s 2003	Fa15	**BBB−**	1/93	BBB	X	R	102.27	2-14-96	100.44	2-14-96	....	....	80.5	H1	'73	102	90½	100½	7.59	7.53
SF Deb 3⅛s 2004	aO	**BBB−**	1/93	BBB	X	CR	100.60	3-31-96	100.01	4-1-04	....	....	14.9		'55	78½	64¼	78½	3.98	6.37
SF Deb 3⅞s 2008	Jj	**BBB−**	1/93	BBB	X	CR	101.27	6-30-96	100.43	6-30-96	....	....	17.0	F1	'58	85⅝	62⅜	85⅝	4.53	5.53
SF Deb 4⅝s 2009	Jj	**BBB−**	1/93	BBB	X	CR	101.71	6-30-96	100.71	6-30-96	....	....	7.67	F1	'59	88¼	66¼	88¼	5.24	5.93
SF Deb 4¾s 2011	jD	**BBB−**	1/93	BBB	X	CR	102.04	5-31-96	100.72	5-31-96	....	....	17.2	F1	'61	86¾	64⅝	86¾	5.48	6.06
Nts 7s '97	Fa15	**BBB−**			X	BE	NC	....	....	....	....	....	150	S1	'94	101	96⅝	101	6.93	6.06
Nts 6½s '97	jJ15	**BBB−**	1/93	BBB	X	BE	NC	....	....	....	....	....	100	M2	'92	100½	95	100½	6.47	6.15
Nts 6.40s 2005	aO15	**BBB−**			X	BE	NC	....	....	....	....	....	235	P1	'93	97	80⅛	97	6.60	6.82
Community Health Sys	*30*	*3.99*		*3.17*	*2.39*	*Dc*	*11.20*	*148.0*	*78.80*	*9-30-95*	*209.0*	*455.0*		*47.0*						
Sr[1]Sub Deb 10¼s 2003	mN30	**B**	12/94	B−	Y	R	102.929	(11-30-98)	....	....	....	....	100	L3	'93	108	98¾	108	9.49	8.82
[2]***Compact Video***	*12*	*0.71*		*0.88*	*0.95*	*Dc*	*176.0*	*678.0*	*467.0*	*12-31-94*	*2303*	*2721*		*88.3*						
Sub Deb 12¾s '96	jJ	**NR**				R	100	....	....	....	....	....	13.6	D7	'86	80	65	80	15.94	....
Compaq Computer Corp	*20b*	*7.18*		*10.97*	*17.50*	*Dc*	*1120*	*6578*	*2764*	*9-30-95*	*300.0*	*4745*		*6.3*						
Sr Nts 6½s '99	Ms15	**BBB+**			X	R	NC	....	....	....	....	....	150	M2	'94	102	93⅛	102	6.37	5.80
Sr Nts 7¼s 2004	Ms15	**BBB+**			X	R	NC	....	....	....	....	....	150	M2	'94	105¾	91¾	105¾	6.86	6.34
CompUSA Inc	*59*	*△9.91*		*△0.24*	*△3.53*	*Je*	*95.30*	*498.0*	*322.0*	*6-24-95*	*115.0*	*291.0*		*41.2*						
• Sr Sub Nts[3] 9½s 2000	Jd15	**B−**	11/95	CCC+	Y	R	102.714	(6-15-98)	....	....	....	....	110	K2	'93	101½	84¼	s100¾	9.43	9.29
Computervision Corp	*20d*	*0.26*		*d0.12*	*1.20*	*Dc*	*31.90*	*162.0*	*277.0*	*10-1-95*	*p219.0*	*d147.0*		*NM*						
Sr Sub Nts[4] 11⅜s '99	fA15	**B−**	11/95	CCC+	Y	R	101.896	(8-15-97)	....	....	....	....	175	L3	'92	105½	81½	105½	10.78	9.54
COMSAT Corp[5]	*67e*	*2.85*		*3.27*	*3.27*	*Dc*	*16.50*	*306.0*	*202.0*	*9-30-95*	*594.0*	*1674*		*36.4*						
• Deb 8⅛s 2004	Ao	**A**			X	R	NC	....	....	....	....	....	160	F1	'92	107	107	112⅛	7.25	6.22
• Nts 8.95s 2001	Mn15	**A**			X	R	NC	....	....	....	....	....	75.0	F1	'91	No Sale		117⅛	7.64	5.25
ConAgra Inc.	*26*	*△3.23*		*△3.46*	*△3.63*	*My*	*92.20*	*6476*	*5828*	*8-27-95*	*2414*	*8713*		*64.1*						
Sr Nts 9¾s '97	mN	**BBB**			X	BE	NC	....	....	....	....	....	300	M2	'90	107⅞	103⅛	106⅞	9.12	5.75

Uniform Footnote Explanations-See Page 260. Other: [1] (HRO)For Chge in Ctrl Triggering Event at 101. [2] Now Andrews Group(subsid of Mafco Hldgs). [3] (HRO)On Chge of Ctrl at 101. [4] Co must offer repurch at 100 on Chge in Ctrl. [5] Was Communications Satellite.

Title-Industry Code & Co. Finances (In Italics)	Ind	Fixed Charge Coverage 1992	1993	1994		Year End	Million $ Cash & Equiv.	Curr. Assets	Curr. Liab.	Balance Sheet Date	L. Term Debt (Mil $)		Capital-ization (Mil $)	Total Debt % Capital						
Individual Issue Statistics — Exchange	**Interest Dates**	**S&P Debt Rating**	**Date of Last Rating Change**	**Prior Rating**	**Eligible**	**Bond Form**	**Redemption Provisions — Regular Price**	**Regular (Begins) Thru**	**Sinking Fund Price**	**Sinking Fund (Begins) Thru**	**Refund/Other Restriction Price**	**Refund/Other Restriction (Begins) Thru**	**Outst'g (Mil $)**	**Underwriting Firm**	**Underwriting Year**	**Price Range 1995 High**	**Price Range 1995 Low**	**Mo. End Price Sale(s) or Bid**	**Curr. Yield**	**Yield to Mat.**
***ConAgra Inc** (Cont.)*																				
Sr Nts 9⅞s 2005	mN15	**BBB**			X	BE	NC	....	....	....	....	....	100	M2	'90	125⅛	108⅝	124⅝	7.92	6.46
Sub Nts 9¾s 2021	Ms	**BBB–**			X	BE	NC	....	....	....	....	....	400	M2	'91	131⅞	106⅞	129¾	7.51	7.18
Sub Nts 7.40s 2004	mS15	**BBB–**			X	BE	NC	....	....	....	....	....	300	F1	'92	106⅝	92⅝	105⅝	7.01	6.54
Cone Mills	***68a***	***7.42***	***12.44***	***8.01***		***Dc***	***0.75***	***240.0***	***128.0***	***10-1-95***	***162.0***		***417.0***	***43.9***						
Deb 8⅛s 2005	Ms15	**BBB**			X	BE	NC	....	....	....	....	....	100	M6	'95	112⅛	99¾	112⅛	7.25	6.36
Congoleum Corp[1]	***31a***	***n/a***	***n/a***	***5.11***		***Dc***	***24.60***	***110.0***	***54.00***	***6-30-95***	***90.00***		***111.0***	***81.1***						
Sr Nts[2] 9s 2001	Fa	**BB–**			Y	R	103	(2-1-98)	....	....	[3]Z108	1-31-97	90.0	D6	'94	101	91½	101	8.91	8.75
Connecticut Lt & Pwr[4]	***72a***	***3.20***	***2.67***	***3.78***		***Dc***	***3.26***	***504.0***	***393.0***	***9-30-95***	***1924***		***4012***	***52.0***						
1st & Ref T 6½s '98	Jj	**BBB+**	6/84	BBB–	X	R	100	....	Z100	....	....	....	20.0	M2	'67	100	95½	100	6.50	6.50
1st & Ref UU 7⅝s '97	Ao	**BBB+**			X	R	101.91	3-31-96	Z100	....	®100	3-31-97	200	S1	'92	101⅝	98⅛	101⅝	7.50	6.25
1st & Ref VV 7¼s '99	jJ	**BBB+**			X	R	102.48	6-30-96	Z100	....	®100	6-30-97	100	M6	'92	102¾	94¾	102¾	7.06	6.36
1st & Ref XX 5¾s 2000	jJ	**BBB+**			X	R	100	(7-1-98)	Z100	(7-1-98)	....	....	200	M2	'93	98⅞	88⅛	98⅞	5.82	6.04
1st & Ref YY 7½s 2023	jJ	**BBB+**			X	R	105.27	(7-1-98)	Z100	....	....	....	100	S1	'93	100⅛	85⅛	100⅛	7.49	7.49
1st & Ref ZZ 7⅜s 2025	jD	**BBB+**			X	BE	104.47	(12-1-98)	Z100	(12-1-98)	....	....	125	L3	'93	99½	83⅛	99½	7.41	7.42
1st & Ref '94A 5½s '99	Fa	**BBB+**			X	BE	NC	....	....	....	....	....	140	G1	'94	99⅛	90	99⅛	5.55	5.81
1st & Ref '94B 6⅛s 2004	Fa	**BBB+**			X	BE	101.68	(2-1-99)	Z100	(2-1-99)	....	....	140	S1	'94	97⅞	84	97⅞	6.26	6.47
1st & Ref '94C 8½s 2024	Jd	**BBB+**			X	BE	103.87	(6-1-04)	Z100	(6-1-04)	....	....	115	M6	'94	110¾	95⅛	110¾	7.67	7.57
Conn.Yankee Atom.Pwr.	***72***	***3.05***	***2.54***	***2.82***		***Dc***	***4.78***	***47.70***	***62.40***	***12-31-94***	***177.0***		***292.0***	***65.4***						
Gen & Ref A[5] 12s 2000	Jd	**BBB–**	5/90	BB+	X	R	102.40	(6-1-97)	Z100	....	Z103.60	5-31-96	86.0	S1	'88	105⅛	103⅜	104¾	11.46	10.62
Conseco Inc	***35a***	***1.44***	***1.99***	***2.29***		***Dc***				***9-30-95***	***921.0***		***2283***	***40.3***						
• Sr Nts 8⅛s 2003	Fa15	**BB+**	8/95	BBB–	Y	BE	NC	....	....	....	....	....	200	M2	'93	99⅜	83½	s99⅛	8.20	8.29
Consolidated Cigar[6]	***69***	***1.88***	***[7]1.36***	***1.75***		***Dc***	***1.20***	***59.10***	***19.10***	***9-30-95***	***120.0***		***165.0***	***72.7***						
Sr Sub Nts[8] 10½s 2003	Ms	**B**			Y	R	103	(3-1-98)	....	....	[9]Z107.50	2-29-96	90.0	F1	'93	104	90	104	10.10	9.71
Consolidated Edison	***75***	***4.08***	***4.36***	***4.80***		***Dc***	***430.0***	***1469***	***1072***	***9-30-95***	***4066***		***10353***	***40.3***						
1st & Ref CC 5s '96	Jj	**A+**	5/95	AA–	X	R	100	....	▲100	....	....	....	100	M2	'65	100	97½	100	5.00	Mat.
1st & Ref DD 5.90s '96	jD15	**A+**	5/95	AA–	X	R	100	12-14-96	▲100	....	....	....	75.0	M6	'66	100	96¼	100	5.90	5.90
Deb '90A 9.70s 2025	jD	**A+**	2/94	AA–	X	R	107.56	11-30-96	....	....	....	....	27.4	M2	'90	110⅛	107⅛	107⅞	8.99	8.94
Deb'91A 9⅜s 2026	Jd	**A+**	2/94	AA–	X	R	106.88	(6-1-96)	....	....	....	....	95.3	G1	'91	110⅛	103⅜	108⅜	8.65	8.59
Deb '92A 7⅜s 2000	mS15	**A+**	2/94	AA–	X	R	NC	....	....	....	....	....	150	G1	'92	106	95⅜	106	6.96	5.89
Deb '92B 7⅝s 2004	Ms	**A+**	2/94	AA–	X	R	NC	....	....	....	....	....	150	G1	'92	109½	94⅜	109½	6.96	6.13
Deb '92C 7.60s 2000	Jj15	**A+**	2/94	AA–	X	R	NC	....	....	....	....	....	125	G1	'92	106⅛	96¾	106⅛	7.16	5.88
Deb '92D 6½s '99	mS	**A+**	2/94	AA–	X	R	NC	....	....	....	....	....	75.0	G1	'92	102¼	93	102¼	6.36	5.81
Deb '92E 7⅜s 2005	mS	**A+**	2/94	AA–	X	R	103.133	(9-1-97)	....	....	....	....	75.0	G1	'92	105½	91¾	105½	6.99	6.59
Deb '92F 8.05s 2027	jD15	**A+**	2/94	AA–	X	R	105.3336	(12-15-97)	....	....	....	....	100	G1	'92	105¼	90¾	105¼	7.65	7.61
Deb '93A 6¼s '98	Ao	**A+**	2/94	AA–	X	R	NC	....	....	....	....	....	100	M2	'93	101¼	94¼	101¼	6.17	5.65
Deb '93B 6½s 2001	Fa	**A+**	2/94	AA–	X	R	NC	....	....	....	....	....	150	L3	'93	102½	91⅛	102½	6.34	5.92
Deb '93C 6⅝s 2002	Fa	**A+**	2/94	AA–	X	R	NC	....	....	....	....	....	150	L3	'93	103⅛	90⅛	103⅛	6.42	6.00
Deb '93D 6⅜s 2003	Ao	**A+**	2/94	AA–	X	R	NC	....	....	....	....	....	150	L3	'93	101½	87⅜	101½	6.28	6.11
Deb '93E 5.30s '97	fA	**A+**	2/94	AA–	X	R	NC	....	....	....	....	....	100	G1	'93	99½	93⅜	99½	5.33	5.63
Deb '93F 5.70s '98	aO	**A+**	2/94	AA–	X	R	NC	....	....	....	....	....	100	G1	'93	100	91¾	100	5.70	5.70
Deb '93G 7½s 2023	Jd15	**A+**	2/94	AA–	X	R	103.2725	(6-15-03)	....	....	....	....	380	L3	'93	102⅝	86⅜	102⅝	7.31	7.28
Deb '94A 7⅛s 2029	Fa15	**A+**			X	R	103.642	(2-15-04)	....	....	....	....	150	G1	'94	98⅞	81⅝	98⅞	7.21	7.21
F/R[10]Deb '94B 6.1562s '99	QJul	**A+**			X	BE	*100	(7-1-96)	....	....	....	....	150	L3	'94	100⅛	99⅝	99⅞	6.16	....
Deb '95A 6⅝s 2005	jJ	**A+**			X	BE	NC	....	....	....	....	....	100	M2	'95	103⅝	96	103⅝	6.39	6.12
Consolidated Freightways	***71***	***0.72***	***3.86***	***5.01***		***Dc***	***102.0***	***1188***	***1082***	***9-30-95***	***496.0***		***1305***	***44.4***						
Nts[11] 9⅛s '99	fA15	**BBB–**	3/95	BB	X	R	NC	....	....	....	....	....	118	F1	'89	109½	96½	109½	8.33	6.16

Uniform Footnote Explanations-See Page 260. Other: [1] Subsid of Resilient Hldgs. [2] Co must offer repurch at 101 on Chge of Ctrl. [3] Max $22.5M red w/proceeds of Initial Pub Off'g. [4] Contr by Northeast Utilities. [5] Red in whole for plant closure at prices,as def. [6] Subsid of Mafco Hldgs. [7] 10 mos Dec'93. [8] (HRO)On Chge of Ctrl at 101. [9] On Chge of Ctrl. [10] Int to 1-1-96,adj qtrly(3 Mo LIBOR&0.1875%). [11] (HRO)At100for Designated Event&Rat'g Decline.

Title-Industry Code & Co. Finances (In Italics) / Individual Issue Statistics: Exchange	Ind / Interest Dates	Fixed Charge Coverage 1992 / S&P Debt Rating	1993 / Date of Last Rating Change	Prior Rating	1994 / Eligible	Year End / Bond Form	Million $ Cash & Equiv. / Regular Price	Curr. Assets / Regular (Begins) Thru	Curr. Liab. / Sinking Fund Price	Balance Sheet Date / Sinking Fund (Begins) Thru	L. Term Debt (Mil $) / Refund/Other Restriction Price	Refund/Other Restriction (Begins) Thru	Capital-ization (Mil $) / Outst'g (Mil $)	Total Debt % Capital / Underwriting Firm	Underwriting Year	Price Range 1995 High	Price Range 1995 Low	Mo. End Price Sale(s) or Bid	Curr. Yield	Yield to Mat.
***Consolidated Freightways** (Cont.)*																				
Nts[1] 7.35s 2005	Jd	**BBB−**			X	R	NC	....	....	....	....	....	100	M2	'95	104⅞	98¾	104⅞	7.01	6.64
Consolidated Nat Gas	***73e***	***3.44***	***4.08***		***3.74***	***Dc***	***26.40***	***851.0***	***936.0***	***9-30-95***	***1298***		***3436***	***41.9***						
• SF Deb 8⅝s 2011	jD	**AA−**	2/90	AA	X	R	105.40	11-30-96	100	(12-1-96)	®105.04	11-30-96	100	M6	'86	105⅛	102¼	103⅞	8.30	8.18
• SF Deb 8¾s 2019	aO	**AA−**	2/90	AA	X	R	103.80	(10-1-99)	100	(10-1-99)	....	....	150	D7	'89	No Sale		107	8.18	8.08
• Deb 9⅜s '97	Fa	**AA−**	2/90	AA	X	R	NC	....	....	....	....	....	100	S1	'89	104½	101⅜	104½	8.97	5.07
• Deb 5⅞s '98	aO	**AA−**			X	R	NC	....	....	....	....	....	150	S1	'92	100¼	92¼	99⅞	5.88	5.92
• Deb 8¾s '99	Jd	**AA−**	2/90	AA	X	R	NC	....	....	....	....	....	100	S4	'89	108	102½	107	8.18	6.44
• Deb 5¾s 2003	fA	**AA−**			X	R	NC	....	....	....	....	....	150	S1	'93	96¾	82	94	6.12	6.77
• Deb 7⅜s 2005	Ao	**AA−**			X	BE	NC	....	....	....	....	....	150	M2	'95	104½	98⅜	106¼	6.94	6.47
• Deb 6⅝s 2013	jD	**AA−**			X	R	NC	....	....	....	....	....	150	G1	'93	100	81½	96⅝	6.86	6.96
[2]***Consolidated Rail***	***55***	***3.67***	***3.81***		***4.31***	***Dc***	***81.00***	***1187***	***1238***	***9-30-95***	***2037***		***5405***	***43.0***						
Deb 9¾s 2020	Jd15	**A**			X	BE	NC	....	....	....	....	....	544	M6	'90	134½	111¼	134½	7.25	6.83
Deb 7⅞s 2043	Mn15	**A**			X	BE	NC	....	....	....	....	....	250	M6	'93	117	90⅜	117	6.73	6.68
Nts 9¾s 2000	Jd	**A**			X	BE	NC	....	....	....	....	....	250	M6	'90	114¾	105¾	114¾	8.50	5.91
Consumer Portfolio Svcs	***25e***	***d57.66***	***d1.89***		***4.27***	***Mr***				***9-30-95***	***★23.00***		***61.30***	***44.4***						
• Incr Rt[3]Sub[4]Nts[5] 10s 2006	[6]Jan	**NR**				BE	102	(1-1-98)	100	(1-1-00)	....	....	20.0		'95	No Sale		98	10.20	10.33
Consumers Power Co[7]	***75***	***3.96***	***2.66***		***3.18***	***Dc***	***5.00***	***618.0***	***1134***	***9-30-95***	***2022***		***4011***	***52.6***						
• 1st 5⅞s '96	jJ	**BBB−**	6/94	BBB	X	R	100	....	Z100	....	....	....	35.8	M2	'66	99⅝	96⅛	99⅝	5.90	6.64
1st 6s '97	jJ	**BBB−**	6/94	BBB	X	R	100.27	6-30-96	Z100.25	6-30-96	....	....	50.3	M6	'67	99⅞	94⅛	99⅞	6.01	6.09
1st 8¾s '98	Fa15	**BBB−**	6/94	BBB	X	R	NC	....	....	....	....	....	248	F1	'88	105¼	100⅛	105	8.33	6.20
• 1st 6⅞s '98	Mn	**BBB−**	6/94	BBB	X	R	100.63	4-30-96	Z100.47	4-30-96	....	....	43.1	W5	'68	101	95	99⅞	6.88	6.93
• 1st 6⅝s '98	aO	**BBB−**	6/94	BBB	X	R	100.53	9-30-96	Z100.21	6-30-96	....	....	45.2	B6	'68	99⅞	93	99⅝	6.65	6.77
1st 8⅞s '99	mN15	**BBB−**	6/94	BBB	X	R	NC	....	....	....	....	....	200	M2	'89	108¾	101	108¾	8.16	6.29
• 1st 7½s 2001	mN	**BBB−**	6/94	BBB	X	R	101.61	10-31-96	Z100.77	10-31-96	....	....	57.2	M6	'71	101½	92⅝	s100¼	7.48	7.44
• 1st 7½s 2002	Jd	**BBB−**	6/94	BBB	X	R	101.87	5-31-96	Z100.71	5-31-96	....	....	62.2	M6	'72	102	93¼	s100	7.50	7.50
1st 6⅜s 2003	mS15	**BBB−**	6/94	BBB	X	R	102.391	(9-15-98)	....	....	....	....	300	G1	'93	97⅞	85	97⅞	6.51	6.73
1st 7⅜s 2023	mS15	**BBB−**	6/94	BBB	X	R	103.688	(9-15-03)	....	....	....	....	300	M6	'93	99⅝	81¾	99⅝	7.40	7.41
[8]***Container Corp of Amer***	***59h***	***0.91***	***d0.03***		***1.09***	***Dc***	***15.20***	***719.0***	***655.0***	***9-30-95***	***2244***		***1752***	***131.0***						
Sr[9]Nts[10] 9¾s 2003	Ao15	**B+**			Y	R	NC	....	....	....	....	....	500	M6	'93	101⅞	94½	98	9.95	10.14
Sr[10]Nts[9]'A' 11¼s 2004	Mn	**B+**			Y	R	105.625	(5-1-99)	....	....	[11]Z110	4-30-97	300	M6	'94	108½	101⅝	102	11.03	10.87
Sr[10]Nts[9]'B' 10¾s 2002	Mn	**B+**			Y	R	NC	....	....	....	....	....	100	M6	'94	106⅝	100	101	10.64	10.52
[12]***Continental Bank, NA***	***10***	***Subsid of Continental Bank Corp, see***																		
Sub Nts[13] 11¼s 2001	jJ	**A+**	10/95	A	Y	R	100	(7-1-98)	....	....	....	....	100	L3	'91	113	107¼	111¼	10.11	8.64
Sub Nts[14] 7⅞s 2003	Fa	**A+**	10/95	A	Y	BE	NC	....	....	....	....	....	100		'93	109⅝	95	109⅝	7.18	6.18
Continental Bank Corp[15]	***10***	***1.37***	***1.90***		....	***Dc***				***6-30-94***	***1189***		***3169***	***37.5***						
Nts 9⅞s '96	Jd15	**A+**	10/95	A	X	R	NC	....	....	....	....	....	150	L3	'91	103	101⅝	101⅝	9.72	6.23
F/R[16]Nts 6.2969s 2000	QMay18	**A+**	10/95	A	X	BE	NC	....	....	....	....	....	150	G1	'93	101⅛	99½	100½	6.27	....
[17]***Cont'l Broadcast'g Ltd/Capital***	***12c***	***n/a***	***d0.32***		....	***Dc***	***2.66***	***25.00***	***24.50***	***6-30-94***	***140.0***		***152.0***	***92.1***						
Sr Sub Nts[10] 10⅝s 2003	jJ	**B−**			Y	R	105.25	(7-1-98)	....	....	[18]Z108	6-30-96	120	M2	'93	102⅝	97¼	101	10.52	10.43
Continental Cablevision, Inc	***12a***	***0.68***	***0.93***		***0.65***	***Dc***				***9-30-95***	***4084***		***2609***	***157.0***						
Sr[19]Deb[13] 8⅞s 2005	mS15	**BB+**	5/95	BB	Y	R	NC	....	....	....	....	....	275	M6	'93	105¼	90	104½	8.49	8.19
Sr Deb[19] 9s 2008	mS	**BB+**	5/95	BB	Y	R	NC	....	....	....	....	....	300	M6	'93	104¾	85½	104½	8.61	8.41
Sr[19]Deb[13] 9½s 2013	fA	**BB+**	5/95	BB	Y	R	104.75	(8-1-05)	....	....	....	....	525	M6	'93	106	89¾	106	8.96	8.82
Sr[13]Nts[19] 8½s 2001	mS15	**BB+**	5/95	BB	Y	R	NC	....	....	....	....	....	200	M6	'93	103½	91½	103	8.25	7.83
Sr Nts[19] 8⅝s 2003	fA15	**BB+**	5/95	BB	Y	R	NC	....	....	....	....	....	100	M6	'93	103⅜	89¼	103⅜	8.34	8.02
Sr Sub[19]Deb[13] 11s 2007	Jd	**BB−**	11/93	B+	Y	R	105.50	(6-1-99)	....	....	....	....	300	M6	'92	111¾	100¾	111½	9.87	9.34

Uniform Footnote Explanations-See Page 260. Other: [1] Issued in min denom $250T. [2] Now Conrail Inc. [3] Int thru 12-31-96,incr 0.25% anly aft to 1-1-04,12.5% aft. [4] Death red benefit,ltd,as defined. [5] (HRO)For a Special Red Event at 100. [6] Int pd monthly. [7] Subsid of CMS Energy. [8] Subsid & data of Jefferson Smurfit. [9] Gtd by Jefferson Smurfit. [10] (HRO)On Chge of Ctrl at 101. [11] Max $100M red w/proceeds Cap Stk Off'g. [12] Now Bank of America Illinois. [13] Issued in min denom $100T. [14] Issued in min denom $200T. [15] See Continental Bank N.A. [16] Int(min 4.50%)to 2-20-96,adj qtrly aft. [17] Subsid & data of Cont'l Broadcasting Group. [18] Max $42M red w/proceeds of Pub Eq Off'g. [19] (HRO)For Certain Events at declining prices.

Title-Industry Code & Co. Finances (In Italics) / Individual Issue Statistics (Exchange)	Ind / Interest Dates	Fixed Charge Coverage 1992 / S&P Debt Rating	Date of Last Rating Change	1993 / Prior Rating	1994 / Eligible	Year End / Bond Form	Million $ Cash & Equiv. / Redemption Provisions: Regular Price	Curr. Assets / Regular (Begins) Thru	Curr. Liab. / Sinking Fund Price	Balance Sheet Date / Sinking Fund (Begins) Thru	L. Term Debt (Mil $) / Refund/Other Restriction Price	Refund/Other Restriction (Begins) Thru	Capital-ization (Mil $) / Outst'g (Mil $)	Total Debt % Capital / Underwriting Firm	Underwriting Year	Price Range 1995 High	Price Range 1995 Low	Mo. End Price Sale(s) or Bid	Curr. Yield	Yield to Mat.
***Continental Cablevision, Inc** (Cont.)*																				
Sr Sub[1]Nts[2] 10⅝s 2002	Jd15	BB–	11/93	B+	Y	R	105.313	(6-15-97)	....	....	....	....	100	M6	'92	108	100	108	9.84	8.97
Continental Corp	***35c***	*4.12*		*4.66*	....	*Dc*				*9-30-94*	*778.0*		*2344*	*41.3*						
Nts 8¼s '99	Ao15	BBB–	10/94	A–	X	R	NC	....	....	....	....	....	100	G1	'92	106	96⅞	106	7.78	6.20
Nts 7¼s 2003	Ms	BBB–	10/94	A–	X	R	NC	....	....	....	....	....	150	G1	'93	103⅝	88⅛	103⅝	7.00	6.60
Nts 8⅜s 2012	fA15	BBB–	10/94	A–	X	R	NC	....	....	....	....	....	100	G1	'92	109⅞	86⅞	109⅞	7.62	7.34
Continental Homes Hldg	***13h***	*△1.55*		*△2.95*	*△1.52*	*My*				*8-31-95*	*★199.0*		*336.0*	*65.8*						
Sr Nts[3] 12s '99	fA	B			Y	R	104	(8-1-97)	....	....	....	....	110	K2	'92	108	94	108	11.11	9.32
Continental Med Sys	***30***	*8.78*		*3.70*	*1.98*	*Je*	*23.10*	*284.0*	*145.0*	*3-31-95*	*311.0*		*571.0*	*55.0*						
Sr Sub Nts[4] 10⅞s 2002	fA15	NR	10/95	B		R	104.10	(8-15-97)	....	....	....	....	200	M2	'92	109¾	80	109	9.98	9.04
Sr Sub[4]Nts[5] 10⅜s 2003	Ao	NR	10/95	B		R	104.50	(4-1-98)	....	....	....	....	150	M2	'93	109	78	109	9.52	8.67
[6]Continental Tel of Cal[7]	***67a***	*12.51*		*12.69*	*10.27*	*Dc*	*2.24*	*87.00*	*163.0*	*12-31-94*	*90.00*		*374.0*	*42.2*						
1st J 7⅝s '97	[8]jj	AA–	3/91	A+	X	R	100	12-31-96	100	....	....	....	10.0	H1	'73	100⅞	98⅛	100⅜	7.60	7.42
[9]CoreStates Capital	***25***	*4.06*		*4.76*	*3.24*	*Dc*				*9-30-95*	*1862*		*4178*	*44.6*						
Gtd[10]F/R[11]Sr M-T Nts '96	QMay15	A			X	BE	NC	....	....	....	....	....	17.5	M2	'93	100¼	99¾	100⅛	....	....
Gtd[10]F/R[11]Sr M-T Nts '96	QJun19	A			X	BE	NC	....	....	....	....	....	20.0	M2	'93	100	99⅝	100	....	....
Gtd[10]F/R[12]Sr M-T Nts '96	[13]	A			X	BE	NC	....	....	....	....	....	25.0	M2	'93	100	99⅝	100	....	....
Gtd[10]F/R[12]Sr M-T Nts '96	[14]	A			X	BE	NC	....	....	....	....	....	35.0	M2	'93	100	99⅝	100	....	....
Gtd[10]F/R[12]Sr M-T Nts '96	[15]	A			X	BE	NC	....	....	....	....	....	25.0	M2	'93	100	99⅝	100	....	....
Gtd[10]F/R[16]Sr M-T Nts '96	[17]	A			X	BE	NC	....	....	....	....	....	25.0	M2	'93	100	99⅝	100	....	....
Gtd[10]F/R[18]Sr M-T Nts '96	[19]	A			X	BE	NC	....	....	....	....	....	25.0	M2	'94	100	99⅝	99⅞	....	....
Gtd[10]F/R[18]Sr M-T Nts '97	[20]	A			X	BE	NC	....	....	....	....	....	50.0	M2	'94	100	99⅝	100	....	....
Gtd[10]F/R[12]Sr M-T Nts '99	[21]	A			X	BE	NC	....	....	....	....	....	50.0	M2	'94	100	99½	99¾	....	....
Gtd[10]Sub Nts 9⅝s 2001	Fa15	A–			X	R	NC	....	....	....	....	....	150	L3	'91	115	104¾	115	8.37	6.17
Gtd[10]Sub Nts 9⅜s 2003	Ao15	A–			X	R	NC	....	....	....	....	....	100	L3	'91	118¼	103⅝	118¼	7.93	6.22
Gtd[22]Sub Nts 5⅞s 2003	aO15	A–			X	BE	NC	....	....	....	....	....	200	L3	'93	98	83¼	98	5.99	6.20
Gtd[10]Sub Nts 6⅝s 2005	Ms15	A–			X	R	NC	....	....	....	....	....	175	M5	'93	102⅜	86	102⅜	6.47	6.28
Corning Glass Works	***28***	***Now Corning Inc, see***																		
Deb 8¼s 2002	Ms15	A+	3/91	A	X	R	NC	....	....	....	....	....	75.0	L1	'87	111	98⅝	111	7.43	6.09
Deb 7s 2007	Ms15	A+	3/91	A	X	R	100	....	....	....	....	....	[23]100	L1	'82	104⅞	88	104⅞	6.67	6.38
Deb 8⅞s 2016	Ms15	A+	3/91	A	X	R	NC	....	....	....	....	....	74.4	L1	'86	122½	102¼	122½	7.24	6.81
Nts 8⅜s '96	mN	A+	3/91	A	X	R	NC	....	....	....	....	....	74.9	G1	'86	103	100¾	102¼	8.19	5.58
Corning Inc[24]	***28***	*6.05*		*4.39*	*4.98*	*Dc*	*109.0*	*1818*	*1035*	*10-8-95*	*1473*		*4340*	*33.8*						
• SF Deb 7¾s '98	mN15	A+	3/91	A	X	R	100	....	100	....	....	....	17.3	L1	'73	103	97¾	102	7.60	6.97
Deb 6¾s 2013	mS15	A+			X	R	NC	....	....	....	....	....	100	G1	'93	99⅛	83¾	99⅛	6.81	6.83
Deb 8⅞s 2021	fA15	A+			X	R	NC	....	....	....	....	....	75.0	L1	'91	124⅜	102⅛	124⅜	7.14	6.84
Deb[25] 7⅝s 2024	fA	A+			X	R	NC	....	....	....	....	....	100	L1	'94	111¾	88¼	111¾	6.82	6.70
Nts[26] 8¾s '99	jJ15	A+	3/91	A	X	R	NC	....	....	....	....	....	100	G1	'89	109⅜	101¼	109⅜	8.00	5.79
Nts 6s 2003	fA15	A+			X	R	NC	....	....	....	....	....	100	G1	'93	98⅝	85⅜	98⅝	6.08	6.23
Cort Furniture Rental	***75***	*p0.65*		*[27]1.75*	*n/a*	*Dc*	*4.42*			*9-30-95*	*108.0*		*136.0*	*79.4*						
Sr Nts[3] 12s 2000	mS	B	5/95	B–	Y	R	107	(9-1-98)	....	....	[28]Z110	9-1-96	[29]100	D6	'93	107	94	107	11.21	10.08
Coty Inc	***18***	*n/a*		*2.80*	*2.77*	*Dc*	*5.70*	*275.0*	*175.0*	*9-30-95*	*271.0*		*367.0*	*77.9*						
• Sr Sub Nts[3] 10¼s 2005	Mn	B+			Y	R	105.10	(5-1-00)	....	....	[30]Z110	4-30-98	135	P1	'95	107¼	100	105⅛	9.75	9.41
[31]Countrywide Funding	***25h***	*2.57*		*2.08*	*1.55*	*Fb*	*5.47*			*8-31-95*	*5479*		*6698*	*82.1*						
Sub Nts[32] 8¼s 2002	jJ15	A–			X	R	NC	....	....	....	....	....	200	S1	'92	110	95⅞	110	7.50	6.36
[32]Nts[2] 6⅞s 2005	mS15	A			X	BE	NC	....	....	....	....	....	150	L3	'95	107½	99⅝	104	6.61	6.32
Cox Communications[33]	***54c***	*n/a*		*p6.68*	*3.09*	*Dc*				*9-30-95*	*★2388*		*4542*	*52.5*						
Deb[33] 7⅛s 2013	Ms	A–	2/95	A+	X	R	NC	....	....	....	....	....	8.88	M6	'93	103	87¼	103	6.92	6.82

Uniform Footnote Explanations-See Page 260. Other: [1] (HRO)For Certain Events at declining prices. [2] Issued in min denom $100T. [3] (HRO)On Chge of Ctrl at 101. [4] (HRO)On Chge of Ctrl at 100. [5] Tender offer, $1092.50, to Sep 25. [6] Now Contel of California. [7] Subsid of Contel Corp. [8] Due Dec 31. [9] Gtd by & data of CoreStates Fin'l. [10] Gtd by CoreStates Fin'l. [11] Int adj daily. [12] Int adj monthly. [13] Due 7-17-96:Int pd monthly,ea 3rd Wed. [14] Due 8-21-96:Int pd monthly,ea 3rd Wed. [15] Due 9-18-96:Int pd monthly,ea 3rd Wed. [16] Int(max 6.05%)adj monthly. [17] Due 11-29-96:Int pd monthly,ea 29th. [18] Int adj weekly. [19] Due 10-16-96:Int pd monthly,ea 3rd Wed. [20] Due 5-27-97:Int pd monthly,ea 3rd Wed. [21] Due 2-2-99:Int pd monthly,ea 3rd Wed. [22] Gtd by Corestates Fin'l. [23] Incl disc. [24] See Corning Glass Works. [25] (HRO)On 8-1-04 at 100. [26] (HRO)At 100 for Designated Event&Rat'g Decline. [27] 9 Mo Dec'93. [28] Max $50M red w/proceeds of Pub Eq Off'g. [29] Called $30M on 12-22-95 at 110. [30] Max $47.3M red w/proceed of Pub Eq Off'g. [31] Subsid & data of Countrywide Credit Indus. [32] Gtd by Countrywide Credit Indus. [33] Was Times Mirror(Old).

Title-Industry Code & Co. Finances (In Italics) / Individual Issue Statistics / Exchange	Ind / Interest Dates	Fixed Charge Coverage 1992 / S&P Debt Rating	1993 / Date of Last Rating Change	Prior Rating	1994 / Eligible	Year End / Bond Form	Million $ Cash & Equiv. / Redemption Provisions Regular Price	Million $ Curr. Assets / Regular (Begins) Thru	Million $ Curr. Liab. / Sinking Fund Price	Balance Sheet Date / Sinking Fund (Begins) Thru	L. Term Debt (Mil $) / Refund/Other Restriction Price	Refund/Other Restriction (Begins) Thru	Capital-ization (Mil $) / Outst'g (Mil $)	Total Debt % Capital / Underwriting Firm	Underwriting Year	Price Range 1995 High	Price Range 1995 Low	Mo. End Price Sale(s) or Bid	Curr. Yield	Yield to Mat.
***Cox Communications** (Cont.)*																				
Deb 7¼s 2015	mN15	**A–**			X	R	[1]Z100	....	....	....	....	....	100	C5	'95	103¾	99	103¾	6.99	6.90
Deb[2] 7⅜s 2023	jJ	**A–**	2/95	A+	X	R	NC	....	....	....	....	....	1.20	G1	'93	106¼	86⅞	106¼	6.94	6.87
Deb 7⅝s 2025	Jd15	**A–**			X	R	NC	....	....	....	....	....	150	C5	'95	109½	93⅛	109½	6.96	6.87
Nts[2] 8.70s '99	Jd15	**A–**	2/95	A+	X	R	NC	....	....	....	....	....	21.9	G1	'89	109	101⅜	109	7.98	5.79
Nts[2] 8.55s 2000	Jd	**A–**	2/95	A+	X	R	NC	....	....	....	....	....	6.25	M6	'90	110⅛	100½	110⅛	7.76	5.91
Nts 6⅜s 2000	Jd15	**A–**			X	R	NC	....	....	....	....	....	425	C5	'95	101⅞	97⅝	101⅞	6.26	5.89
Nts[2] 8⅞s 2001	Ms	**A–**	2/95	A+	X	R	NC	....	....	....	....	....	13.9	G1	'91	112¾	103⅝	112¾	7.87	5.97
Nts 6½s 2002	mN15	**A–**			X	R	[1]Z100	....	....	....	....	....	200	C5	'95	101¾	99⅝	101¾	6.39	6.18
Nts 6⅞s 2005	Jd15	**A–**			X	R	NC	....	....	....	....	....	375	C5	'95	103¾	96⅛	103¾	6.63	6.34
CP Ltd Partnership	***38***	***n/a***	***p1.78***		....	***Dc***				***p9-30-94***	***★132.0***		***200.0***	***66.2***						
Sr Nts 8¾s 2000	Ms2	**BBB–**			X	BE	[3]Z100	....	....	....	....	....	75.0	M2	'95	100½	98⅞	A100	8.75	8.74
CPC Int'l	***26***	***7.29***	***8.19***		***6.61***	***Dc***	***183.0***	***2414***	***2099***	***9-30-95***	***972.0***		***3517***	***43.9***						
• Deb 8½s 2016	Ao15	**A+**	2/93	A	X	R	104.675	4-14-96	100	(4-15-97)	®104.25	4-14-96	100	S1	'86	No Sale		98⅛	8.66	8.70
Crane Co	***17***	***6.06***	***8.00***		***4.77***	***Dc***	***0.42***	***531.0***	***255.0***	***9-30-95***	***306.0***		***690.0***	***46.5***						
Nts 7¼s '99	Jd15	**BBB**			X	BE	NC	....	....	....	....	....	150	M5	'94	103¾	95	103¾	6.99	6.03
Nts 8½s 2004	Ms15	**BBB**	5/94	A–	X	R	NC	....	....	....	....	....	100	M5	'92	113⅛	98½	112½	7.56	6.51
Crestar Financial	***10***	***2.80***	***4.32***		***3.76***	***Dc***				***9-30-95***	***380.0***		***1639***	***23.2***						
Sub Nts 8¼s 2002	jJ15	**BBB+**	10/94	BBB	X	BE	NC	....	....	....	....	....	125	M6	'92	110⅞	97⅝	110⅞	7.44	6.20
Sub Nts 8¾s 2004	mN15	**BBB+**			X	BE	NC	....	....	....	....	....	150	M6	'94	116⅛	99⅝	116⅛	7.53	6.34
Crown Central Petroleum	***49g***	***d1.31***	***1.07***		***d5.60***	***Dc***	***47.60***	***234.0***	***158.0***	***9-30-95***	***129.0***		***389.0***	***33.7***						
Sr Nts[4] 10⅞s 2005	Fa	**BB–**			Y	R	105.438	(2-1-00)	....	....	[5]Z110.875	2-1-98	125	S1	'95	106¾	100⅛	105	10.36	10.02
Crown Cork & Seal	***16b***	***4.29***	***4.12***		***4.01***	***Dc***	***58.00***	***1954***	***1754***	***9-30-95***	***1163***		***3790***	***58.7***						
Deb 8s 2023	Ao15	**BBB+**			X	BE	103.813	(4-15-03)	....	....	....	....	200	S1	'93	108¼	90⅞	108¼	7.39	7.30
Nts 5⅞s '98	Ao15	**BBB+**			X	BE	NC	....	....	....	....	....	100	S1	'93	100⅜	93	100⅜	5.85	5.69
Nts 7s '99	Jd15	**BBB+**			X	R	NC	....	....	....	....	....	100	S1	'94	103⅝	94⅞	103⅝	6.76	5.83
Nts 6¾s 2003	Ao15	**BBB+**			X	BE	NC	....	....	....	....	....	200	S1	'93	102¾	89⅞	102¾	6.57	6.27
Nts 8⅜s 2005	Jj15	**BBB+**			X	R	NC	....	....	....	....	....	300	S1	'95	113¾	99¾	113¾	7.36	6.35
CSX Corp	***55***	***3.56***	***3.51***		***4.58***	***Dc***	***563.0***	***1810***	***2644***	***9-30-95***	***2564***		***7095***	***43.8***						
Deb 9s 2006	fA15	**BBB+**	5/95	BBB	X	R	NC	....	....	....	....	....	300	F1	'86	120¾	102	120¾	7.45	6.29
Deb 8⅝s 2022	Mn15	**BBB+**	5/95	BBB	X	BE	NC	....	....	....	....	....	200	L3	'92	122¼	98½	122¼	7.06	6.80
Deb 8.10s 2022	mS15	**BBB+**	5/95	BBB	X	BE	NC	....	....	....	....	....	150	F1	'92	115⅞	93¼	115⅞	6.99	6.80
Nts 8.40s '96	fA	**BBB+**	5/95	BBB	X	R	NC	....	....	....	....	....	200	F1	'86	102⅝	100½	101⅝	8.27	5.54
Nts 8¼s '96	mN	**BBB+**	5/95	BBB	X	R	NC	....	....	....	....	....	100	F1	'86	102¾	100⅛	102¼	8.07	5.45
Nts 9½s 2000	fA	**BBB+**	5/95	BBB	X	BE	NC	....	....	....	....	....	250	F1	'90	114⅜	103⅞	114⅜	8.31	5.88
Nts 7s 2002	mS15	**BBB+**	5/95	BBB	X	BE	NC	....	....	....	....	....	100	F1	'92	104⅞	91¼	104⅞	6.67	6.10
CVD Financial	***25***	***Δn/a***	***Δ0.13***		***Δd2.71***	***Je***				***6-30-95***	***42.30***		***38.10***	***111.0***						
V/R Sub[6]Nts[7]'A' 2008	[8]jj25	**NR**				R	NC	....	100	(7-31-04)	Z100	....	42.3		'93	63	39½	60	....	Flat
Cyprus Amax Minerals[9]	***45b***	***6.85***	***4.74***		***3.24***	***Dc***	***163.0***	***1139***	***822.0***	***9-30-95***	***1638***		***4267***	***42.3***						
Nts 7⅜s 2007	Mn15	**BBB–**			X	BE	NC	....	....	....	....	....	250	S5	'95	106⅞	98¼	106⅞	6.90	6.51
Cyprus Minerals	***45b***	***Now Cyprus Amax Minerals,see***																		
Deb 8⅜s 2023	Fa	**BBB–**	11/93	BBB	X	R	103.73	(2-1-03)	....	....	....	....	150	F1	'93	110⅝	91½	110⅝	7.57	7.46
Nts[10] 10⅛s 2002	Ao	**BBB–**	11/93	BBB	X	R	NC	....	....	....	[11]Z100	....	150	F1	'90	119⅞	105½	119⅞	8.45	6.24
Nts 6⅝s 2005	aO15	**BBB–**	11/93	BBB	X	R	NC	....	....	....	....	....	250	K2	'93	101⅛	84⅛	101⅛	6.55	6.47
Dairy Mart Convenience Strs	***59b***	***1.05***	***1.41***		***0.74***	***Ja***	***17.80***	***53.20***	***43.90***	***10-28-95***	***87.90***		***114.0***	***78.6***						
Sr Sub Nts[4] 10¼s 2004	Ms15	**CCC+**	1/95	B	Y	R	104.75	(3-2-99)	....	....	[12]Z110	3-2-97	75.0	B5	'94	86	72	85	12.06	13.30
Dal-Tile Int'l	***13***	***1.11***	***0.93***		***1.33***	***Dc***	***9.41***	***191.0***	***94.20***	***9-30-95***	***480.0***		***416.0***	***126.0***						
Sr Sec Zero Cpn Nts[13] '98	[14]	**CCC+**			Y	R	NC	....	....	....	[15]Z106	7-14-96	[16]133	G1	'93	60	60	A60	....	21.12

Uniform Footnote Explanations-See Page 260. Other: [1] Greater of 100 & amt based on formula. [2] Was Times Mirror(Old). [3] Plus Make-Whole Amt. [4] (HRO)On Chge of Ctrl at 101. [5] Max $33.5M red w/proceeds of Pub Equity Off'gs. [6] Exch offer,472 com & wrrts to Dec 19. [7] Int of 7-25-95 pd 8-22-95. [8] Due 7-31-08. [9] See Amax Inc & Cyprus Minerals. [10] (HRO)At 100 for Designated Event&Rat'g Decline. [11] Co may red in whole if min 90% amt outstg put. [12] Max $20M red w/proceeds Pub Equity Off'g. [13] Co must offer repurch at 101 on Chge of Ctrl. [14] Due 7-15-98. [15] To 7-15-96, max $44.4M red w/proceeds of Cap Stk Off'g. [16] Incl disc.

Individual Issue Statistics / Exchange ↓	Interest Dates	S&P Debt Rating	Date of Last Rating Change	Prior Rating	Eligible ↓	Bond Form	Redemption Provisions: Regular Price	Regular (Begins) Thru	Sinking Fund Price	Sinking Fund (Begins) Thru	Refund/Other Restriction Price	Refund/Other Restriction (Begins) Thru	Outst'g (Mil $)	Underwriting Firm	Underwriting Year	Price Range 1995 High	Price Range 1995 Low	Mo. End Price Sale(s) or Bid	Curr. Yield	Yield to Mat.
Title-Industry Code & Co. Finances (In Italics)	*Ind*	*Fixed Charge Coverage 1992*	*1993*	*1994*		*Year End*	*Million $ Cash & Equiv.*	*Curr. Assets*	*Curr. Liab.*	*Balance Sheet Date*	*L. Term Debt (Mil $)*		*Capital-ization (Mil $)*	*Total Debt % Capital*						
Dan River Inc	***68***	***2.01***	***1.50***	***n/a***		***Dc***	***1.62***	***173.0***	***51.80***	***9-30-95***	***182.0***		***273.0***	***68.5***						
Sr[1]Sub Nts 10⅛s 2003	jD15	B			Y	R	105.10	(12-15-98)	....	....	[2]Z109.125	12-15-96	120	M2	'93	100⅞	89½	92	11.01	11.69
Data General	***20b***	***0.21***	***d1.04***	***d2.60***		***Sp***	***182.0***	***599.0***	***379.0***	***7-1-95***	***155.0***		***431.0***	***36.6***						
• SF Deb 8⅜s 2002	mS15	NR	10/87	BBB+		R	100.763	9-14-96	100	....	....	....	32.6	B1	'77	98½	86	97⅛	8.62	8.95
Dauphin Deposit	***10***	***4.24***	***4.25***	***3.39***		***Dc***				***9-30-95***	***40.60***		***572.0***	***7.1***						
Sr Nts 8.70s '96	mN15	A–			X	R	NC	....	....	....	....	....	35.0	B5	'86	103½	97	102¾	8.47	5.44
Dayton Hudson Corp	***59g***	***2.36***	***2.33***	***2.68***		***Ja***	***177.0***	***5720***	***4329***	***10-28-95***	***4968***		***8848***	***63.2***						
SF Deb 9⅞s 2017	Jd	BBB+	12/95	A	X	R	105.925	5-31-96	100	(6-1-98)	®104.9375	5-31-97	150	G1	'87	110⅛	105⅜	107	9.23	9.12
SF Deb 9½s 2016	aO15	BBB+	12/95	A	X	R	104.675	10-14-96	100	(10-15-97)	®104.25	10-14-96	200	G1	'86	107¼	101⅞	104⅞	9.06	8.98
SF Deb 9¼s 2016	mN15	BBB+	12/95	A	X	R	104.8125	11-14-96	100	(11-15-97)	®104.375	11-14-96	250	G1	'86	105½	99⅞	105	8.81	8.72
Deb 9¼s 2006	Ms	BBB+	12/95	A	X	R	100	(3-1-01)	....	....	....	....	100	G1	'86	114	102⅝	113⅞	8.12	7.29
Deb 9⅝s 2008	Fa	BBB+	12/95	A	X	R	NC	....	....	....	....	....	100	G1	'88	125¾	107⅝	125¾	7.65	6.51
Deb 9¼s 2011	fA15	BBB+	12/95	A	X	R	NC	....	....	....	....	....	100	G1	'91	123½	105	123½	7.49	6.79
Deb 8.60s 2012	Jj15	BBB+	12/95	A	X	R	NC	....	....	....	....	....	200	G1	'92	116	98⅝	116	7.41	6.93
Deb 9⅞s 2020	jJ	BBB+	12/95	A	X	R	NC	....	....	....	....	....	200	G1	'90	133⅞	110⅞	133⅞	7.38	6.97
Deb 9.70s 2021	Jd15	BBB+	12/95	A	X	R	NC	....	....	....	....	....	200	G1	'91	132⅛	109⅜	132⅛	7.34	6.98
Deb 9s 2021	aO	BBB+	12/95	A	X	R	NC	....	....	....	....	....	125	G1	'91	123⅞	100⅞	123⅞	7.27	6.99
Deb 8⅞s 2022	Ao	BBB+	12/95	A	X	R	NC	....	....	....	....	....	100	G1	'92	122½	100¾	122½	7.24	6.99
Deb 8.80s 2022	Mn15	BBB+	12/95	A	X	R	NC	....	....	....	....	....	100	G1	'92	121⅝	100⅜	121⅝	7.24	6.99
Deb 8½s 2022	jD	BBB+	12/95	A	X	BE	103.75	(12-1-02)	....	....	....	....	200	G1	'92	108⅝	95⅜	108⅝	7.83	7.73
Deb 7⅞s 2023	Jd15	BBB+	12/95	A	X	BE	103.551	(6-15-03)	....	....	....	....	200	G1	'93	105⅜	89⅜	104¾	7.52	7.47
Deb 7.65s 2023	fA	BBB+	12/95	A	X	BE	103.825	(8-1-03)	....	....	....	....	100	G1	'93	104½	87⅛	104½	7.32	7.27
Nts 9¾s '98	mN	BBB+	12/95	A	X	R	NC	....	....	....	....	....	100	G1	'88	110⅜	104⅝	110⅛	8.85	5.82
Nts 7½s '99	Ms	BBB+	12/95	A	X	BE	NC	....	....	....	....	....	150	G1	'95	105⅛	99⅜	105⅛	7.13	5.71
Nts 10s 2000	jD	BBB+	12/95	A	X	R	NC	....	....	....	....	....	250	G1	'90	116¼	107⅜	116¼	8.60	6.12
Nts 9.40s 2001	Fa15	BBB+	12/95	A	X	R	NC	....	....	....	....	....	100	G1	'91	114⅛	104	114⅛	8.24	6.14
Nts 9¾s 2002	jJ	BBB+	12/95	A	X	R	NC	....	....	....	....	....	200	G1	'90	118⅜	106¾	118⅜	8.24	6.27
Nts 6⅝s 2003	Ms	BBB+	12/95	A	X	BE	NC	....	....	....	....	....	150	G1	'93	101⅝	89	101½	6.53	6.36
Nts 7¼s 2004	mS	BBB+	12/95	A	X	R	NC	....	....	....	....	....	100	G1	'92	105⅜	91⅞	105¼	6.89	6.45
Nts 10s 2011	Jj	BBB+	12/95	A	X	R	NC	....	....	....	....	....	175	G1	'91	132⅜	110½	132⅜	7.55	6.57
Dayton Power & Light[3]	***75***	***2.56***	***3.25***	***3.66***		***Dc***	***70.60***	***302.0***	***216.0***	***9-30-95***	***999.0***		***2183***	***45.8***						
1st 5⅝s '97	Mn	AA–	3/94	A	X	R	100.25	4-30-96	100.05	4-30-97	....	....	40.0	M6	'67	100⅛	95	100⅛	5.62	5.52
1st 6¾s '98	Jd15	AA–	3/94	A	X	R	100.50	6-14-96	100	....	....	....	25.0	H1	'68	100⅝	95¾	100⅝	6.71	6.47
• 1st 8s 2003	mN	AA–	3/94	A	X	R	101.95	10-31-96	100	....	....	....	40.0	B6	'73	103	98	101½	7.88	7.74
1st 8.40s 2022	jD	AA–	3/94	A	X	BE	105.918	(12-1-97)	....	....	....	....	225	M6	'92	109⅜	96	109⅜	7.68	7.58
1st 7⅞s 2024	Fa15	AA–	3/94	A	X	BE	103.765	(2-15-03)	....	....	....	....	220	F1	'93	108⅛	91¾	108⅛	7.28	7.20
1st 8.15s 2026	Jj15	AA–	3/94	A	X	BE	104.075	(1-15-03)	Z100	....	....	....	226	M6	'93	111	93⅞	111	7.34	7.25
Dean Foods	***26d***	***△8.71***	***△8.65***	***△7.09***		***My***	***388.0***	***598.0***	***388.0***	***8-27-95***	***227.0***		***900.0***	***33.9***						
Sr Nts 6¾s 2005	Jd15	A			X	BE	NC	....	....	....	....	....	100	M6	'95	102⅝	95⅞	102⅝	6.58	6.38
Dean Witter, Discover & Co	***25e***	***n/a***	***2.22***	***2.16***		***Dc***				***9-30-95***	***6873***		***11597***	***59.3***						
Fed Funds[4]F/R Nts '96	QNov15	A			X	BE	NC	....	....	....	....	....	150	D3	'94	100⅜	99¾	100⅛	....	....
LIBOR[5]F/R Nts 6.1375s '96	QNov15	A			X	BE	NC	....	....	....	....	....	350	D3	'94	100⅛	99¾	100⅛	6.13	....
LIBOR[6]F/R Nts 6.4375s 2000	QMar	A			X	BE	NC	....	....	....	....	....	150	D3	'95	101⅛	99½	100½	6.41	....
Nts 5s '96	Ao	A			X	BE	NC	....	....	....	....	....	350	D3	'93	99⅞	96½	99⅞	5.01	5.43
Nts 6s '98	Ms	A			X	BE	NC	....	....	....	....	....	750	D3	'93	100⅞	93¼	100⅞	5.95	5.56
Nts 6¼s 2000	Ms15	A			X	BE	NC	....	....	....	....	....	400	D3	'93	101½	90¼	101½	6.16	5.84
Nts 6¾s 2000	fA15	A			X	BE	NC	....	....	....	....	....	200	D3	'95	103½	99½	103½	6.52	5.87

Uniform Footnote Explanations-See Page 260. Other: [1] (HRO)On Chge of Ctrl at 101. [2] Max $36M red w/proceeds of Pub Eq Off'g. [3] Subsid of DPL Inc. [4] Int reset daily. [5] Int to 11-15-95,adj qtrly(3 Mo LIBOR&0.20%). [6] Int to 9-1-95,adj qtrly(3 Mo LIBOR&0.375%).

Title-Industry Code & Co. Finances (In Italics)	Ind	Fixed Charge Coverage 1992	1993	1994	Year End	Million $ Cash & Equiv.	Curr. Assets	Curr. Liab.	Balance Sheet Date	L. Term Debt (Mil $)	Capital-ization (Mil $)	Total Debt % Capital

Individual Issue Statistics Exchange ↓	Interest Dates	S&P Debt Rating	Date of Last Rating Change	Prior Rating	Eligible ↓	Bond Form	Redemption Provisions: Regular Price	Regular (Begins) Thru	Sinking Fund Price	Sinking Fund (Begins) Thru	Refund/Other Restriction Price	Refund/Other Restriction (Begins) Thru	Outst'g (Mil $)	Underwriting Firm	Underwriting Year	Price Range 1995 High	Price Range 1995 Low	Mo. End Price Sale(s) or Bid	Curr. Yield	Yield to Mat.
***Dean Witter, Discover & Co** (Cont.)*																				
Nts 6⅞s 2003	Ms	A			X	BE	NC	....	....	....	....	....	750	D3	'93	104	89⅞	104	6.61	6.17
Nts 6½s 2005	mN	A			X	BE	NC	....	....	....	....	....	250	D3	'93	101⅝	84½	101⅝	6.40	6.27
Deb 6¾s 2013	aO15	A			X	BE	NC	....	....	....	....	....	250	D3	'93	99¾	80½	99¾	6.77	6.77
M-T Nts 'I' 7.40s '99	[1]ao	A			X	BE	NC	....	....	....	....	....	5.00	D3	'94	104⅝	96⅛	104⅝	7.07	5.89
M-T Nts 'I' 7.44s '99	[2]ao	A			X	BE	NC	....	....	....	....	....	6.00	D3	'94	104¾	96¼	104¾	7.10	5.89
M-T Nts 'I' 7.26s '99	[3]ao	A			X	BE	NC	....	....	....	....	....	20.0	D3	'94	104⅜	95⅜	104⅜	6.96	5.91
M-T Nts 'I' 5.88s 2001	[4]ao	A			X	BE	NC	....	....	....	....	....	10.0	D3	'94	99¼	87⅝	99¼	5.92	6.05
M-T Nts 'I' 6s 2001	[5]ao	A			X	BE	NC	....	....	....	....	....	10.0	D3	'94	99¾	88⅛	99¾	6.02	6.06
M-T Nts 'I' 7.55s 2001	[6]ao	A			X	BE	NC	....	....	....	....	....	10.0	D3	'94	106	95	106	7.12	6.21
M-T Nts 'I' 7¾s 2001	[7]ao	A			X	BE	NC	....	....	....	....	....	5.00	D3	'94	107½	96⅛	107½	7.21	6.10
M-T Nts 'I' 7.53s 2001	[8]ao	A			X	BE	NC	....	....	....	....	....	10.0	D3	'94	106½	95	106½	7.07	6.11
M-T Nts 'I' 7.58s 2001	[8]ao	A			X	BE	NC	....	....	....	....	....	50.0	D3	'94	106¾	95¼	106¾	7.10	6.10
M-T Nts 'I' 7¾s 2001	[9]ao	A			X	BE	NC	....	....	....	....	....	19.0	D3	'94	107½	96	107½	7.21	6.13
M-T Nts 'I' 7.62s 2001	[10]ao	A			X	BE	NC	....	....	....	....	....	15.0	D3	'94	107	95⅜	107	7.12	6.12
M-T Nts 'I' 7.78s 2001	[11]ao	A			X	BE	NC	....	....	....	....	....	10.0	D3	'94	107¾	96⅛	107¾	7.22	6.12
M-T Nts 'I' 7.62s 2002	[12]ao	A			X	BE	NC	....	....	....	....	....	10.0	D3	'94	107⅜	94⅞	107⅜	7.10	6.20
M-T Nts 'I' 8.05s 2004	[13]ao	A			X	BE	NC	....	....	....	....	....	5.00	D3	'94	110¾	96¼	110¾	7.27	6.38
M-T Nts 'I' 7.81s 2004	[14]ao	A			X	BE	NC	....	....	....	....	....	10.0	D3	'94	109⅛	94¾	109⅛	7.16	6.39
M-T Nts 'I' 7.82s 2004	[14]ao	A			X	BE	NC	....	....	....	....	....	10.0	D3	'94	109¼	94¾	109¼	7.16	6.39
M-T Nts 'I' 7.76s 2004	[15]ao	A			X	BE	NC	....	....	....	....	....	10.0	D3	'94	108⅞	94⅜	108⅞	7.13	6.39
M-T Nts 'I' 8.02s 2004	[16]ao	A			X	BE	NC	....	....	....	....	....	10.0	D3	'94	110½	96	110½	7.26	6.40
M-T Nts 'I' 7.94s 2004	[17]ao	A			X	BE	NC	....	....	....	....	....	13.0	D3	'94	110	95½	110	7.22	6.40
M-T Nts 'I' 7.85s 2004	[18]ao	A			X	BE	NC	....	....	....	....	....	10.0	D3	'94	109	96	109	7.20	6.46
M-T Nts 'I' 7.97s 2004	[19]ao	A			X	BE	NC	....	....	....	....	....	10.0	D3	'94	110⅛	95⅝	110⅛	7.24	6.41
M-T Nts 'I' 8.09s 2004	[19]ao	A			X	BE	NC	....	....	....	....	....	10.0	D3	'94	111	96⅜	111	7.29	6.40
M-T Nts 'I' 8.14s 2004	[20]ao	A			X	BE	NC	....	....	....	....	....	8.00	D3	'94	111⅜	96¾	111⅜	7.31	6.39
M-T Nts 'I' 8.06s 2004	[21]ao	A			X	BE	NC	....	....	....	....	....	15.0	D3	'94	110¾	96¼	110¾	7.28	6.41
M-T Nts 'I' 7.86s 2004	[22]ao	A			X	BE	NC	....	....	....	....	....	5.00	D3	'94	109½	94⅞	109½	7.18	6.41
M-T Nts 'I' 7.07s 2014	[23]ao	A			X	BE	NC	....	....	....	....	....	40.0	D3	'94	101¾	84¼	101¾	6.95	6.90
F/R[24]M-T Nts 'I' '96	[25]	A			X	BE	NC	....	....	....	....	....	10.0	D3	'94	100	96½	100	....	Mat.
F/R[24]M-T Nts 'I' '96	[26]	A			X	BE	NC	....	....	....	....	....	20.0	D3	'94	100	99½	100	....	....
F/R[24]M-T Nts 'I' '96	[27]	A			X	BE	NC	....	....	....	....	....	10.0	D3	'94	100	99½	100	....	....
F/R[24]M-T Nts 'I' '96	[28]	A			X	BE	NC	....	....	....	....	....	10.0	D3	'94	100	99½	100	....	....
F/R[24]M-T Nts 'I' '96	[28]	A			X	BE	NC	....	....	....	....	....	15.0	D3	'94	100	99½	100	....	....
F/R[24]M-T Nts 'I' '96	[29]	A			X	BE	NC	....	....	....	....	....	10.0	D3	'94	100	99½	100	....	....
F/R[24]M-T Nts 'I' '96	[30]	A			X	BE	NC	....	....	....	....	....	25.0	D3	'94	100	99½	100	....	....
F/R[24]M-T Nts 'I' '96	[31]	A			X	BE	NC	....	....	....	....	....	10.0	D3	'94	100	99½	100	....	....
F/R[32]M-T Nts 'I' 5.8925s '96	[33]	A			X	BE	NC	....	....	....	....	....	15.0	D3	'94	100	99½	100	5.89	....
F/R[24]M-T Nts 'I' '97	[34]	A			X	BE	NC	....	....	....	....	....	20.0	D3	'94	100⅛	99¼	100⅛	....	....
F/R[24]M-T Nts 'I' '97	[34]	A			X	BE	NC	....	....	....	....	....	20.0	D3	'94	100⅛	99⅛	100⅛	....	....
F/R[24]M-T Nts 'I' '97	[35]	A			X	BE	NC	....	....	....	....	....	8.00	D3	'94	100⅛	99⅛	100⅛	....	....
F/R[24]M-T Nts 'I' '97	[36]	A			X	BE	NC	....	....	....	....	....	50.0	D3	'94	100	99⅛	100	....	....
F/R[24]M-T Nts 'I' '97	[37]	A			X	BE	NC	....	....	....	....	....	30.0	D3	'94	100	99⅛	99⅞	....	....
F/R[38]M-T Nts 'I' '97	QMar17	A			X	BE	NC	....	....	....	....	....	50.0	D3	'94	100	99⅛	99⅞	....	....
F/R[24]M-T Nts 'I' '97	[39]	A			X	BE	NC	....	....	....	....	....	50.0	D3	'94	100	99⅛	100	....	....
F/R[24]M-T Nts 'I' '97	[40]	A			X	BE	NC	....	....	....	....	....	25.0	D3	'94	100⅛	74¼	99⅞	....	....

Uniform Footnote Explanations-See Page 260. Other: [1] Due 6-1-99. [2] Due 6-8-99. [3] Due 8-24-99. [4] Due 2-7-01. [5] Due 2-8-01. [6] Due 5-1-01. [7] Due 6-1-01. [8] Due 6-11-01. [9] Due 7-9-01. [10] Due 7-23-01. [11] Due 8-1-01. [12] Due 5-15-02. [13] Due 6-8-04. [14] Due 6-10-04. [15] Due 6-22-04. [16] Due 7-6-04. [17] Due 6-28-04. [18] Due 7-1-04. [19] Due 7-8-04. [20] Due 7-20-04. [21] Due 7-21-04. [22] Due 9-8-04. [23] Due 2-10-14. [24] Int adj monthly. [25] Due 1-29-96:Int pd monthly,ea 3rd Wed. [26] Due 1-30-96:Int pd monthly,ea 3rd Wed. [27] Due 2-1-96:Int pd monthly,ea 3rd Wed. [28] Due 2-12-96:Int pd monthly,ea 3rd Wed. [29] Due 2-16-96:Int pd monthly,ea 3rd Wed. [30] Due 2-20-96:Int pd monthly,ea 3rd Wed. [31] Due 2-22-96:Int pd monthly,ea 3rd Wed. [32] Int thru 3-19-96,adj qtrly aft. [33] Due 3-4-96:Int pd qtrly,ea 3rd Wed, Mar, etc. [34] Due 1-27-97:Int pd monthly,ea 3rd Wed. [35] Due 1-28-97:Int pd monthly,ea 3rd Wed. [36] Due 2-3-97:Int pd monthly,ea 3rd Wed. [37] Due 3-3-97:Int pd monthly,ea 3rd Wed. [38] Int adj weekly. [39] Due 6-2-97:Int pd monthly,ea 3rd Wed. [40] Due 8-4-97:Int pd monthly,ea 3rd Wed.

Title-Industry Code & Co. Finances (In Italics) / Individual Issue Statistics (Exchange)	Ind / Interest Dates	Fixed Charge Coverage 1992 / S&P Debt Rating	1993 / Date of Last Rating Change	1994 / Prior Rating	Eligible	Year End / Bond Form	Cash & Equiv. / Redemption Provisions Regular Price	Curr. Assets (Million $) / Regular (Begins) Thru	Curr. Liab. / Sinking Fund Price	Balance Sheet Date / Sinking Fund (Begins) Thru	L. Term Debt (Mil $) / Refund/Other Restriction Price	Refund/Other Restriction (Begins) Thru	Capital-ization (Mil $) / Outst'g (Mil $)	Total Debt % Capital / Underwriting Firm	Underwriting Year	Price Range 1995 High	Price Range 1995 Low	Mo. End Price Sale(s) or Bid	Curr. Yield	Yield to Mat.
***Dean Witter, Discover & Co** (Cont.)*																				
F/R[1]M-T Nts 'I' '99	QMar2	**A**			X	BE	NC	....	....	....	....	....	125	D3	'94	100	99	100	....	....
F/R[2]M-T Nts 'I' 5.17s '99	QMar10	**A**			X	BE	NC	....	....	....	....	....	50.0	D3	'94	99¼	97⅝	98⅜	5.26	....
F/R[3]M-T Nts 'I' '99	[4]	**A**			X	BE	NC	....	....	....	....	....	5.00	D3	'94	100¾	99	100⅜	....	....
F/R[1]M-T Nts 'I' '99	[5]	**A**			X	BE	NC	....	....	....	....	....	27.5	D3	'94	100⅜	99	100	....	....
DeepTech International	***49***	*Δd0.19*	*Δ0.17*	*Δ1.22*		*Je*	*16.40*	*26.00*	*22.30*	*9-30-95*	*91.40*		*106.0*	*92.8*						
Sr Sec Nts[6] 12s 2000	jD15	**CCC+**			Y	R	106	6-14-99	....	....	[7]111.50	3-21-97	82.0	D6	'94	94½	74½	90	13.33	14.92
Deere & Co.	***41a***	*1.11*	*1.74*	*4.04*		*Oc*	*1658*			*7-31-95*	*2377*		*8658*	*65.0*						
• Deb[8] 8.95s 2019	Jd15	**A**	11/93	A–	X	R	100	(6-15-09)	....	....	....	....	200	M2	'89	113⅝	109	s112½	7.96	7.78
• Deb 8½s 2022	Jj9	**A**	11/93	A–	X	R	NC	....	....	....	....	....	200	M2	'92	117	98½	113¼	7.51	7.35
• Nts 8¼s '96	Jd	**A**	11/93	A–	X	R	NC	....	....	....	....	....	150	M2	'91	102⅞	100⅛	100½	8.21	6.99
• Nts 9⅛s '96	jJ	**A**	11/93	A–	X	R	NC	....	....	....	....	....	100	M2	'86	104⅛	101	101⅛	9.02	6.82
Deere (John) Capital[9]	***25d***	*1.75*	*2.01*	*1.97*		*Oc*	*154.0*			*7-31-95*	*1414*		*2426*	*71.7*						
Nts 4⅝s '96	mS2	**A**	11/93	A–	X	R	NC	....	....	....	....	....	200	M2	'93	99⅜	94⅞	99⅜	4.65	5.57
• Nts 7.20s '97	Mn15	**A**	11/93	A–	X	R	NC	....	....	....	....	....	100	G1	'92	105	98⅜	101¼	7.11	6.23
F/R[10]Nts '98	QMar20	**A**			X	BE	NC	....	....	....	....	....	150	S1	'95	100⅝	99½	100⅛	....	....
• Sub Deb[11] 8⅝s 2019	fA	**A–**	11/93	BBB+	X	R	100	(8-1-04)	....	....	....	....	150	G1	'89	100⅛	98¼	108½	7.95	7.83
• Sub Nts 9⅝s '98	mN	**A–**	11/93	BBB+	X	R	NC	....	....	....	....	....	150	M2	'88	No Sale		104¾	9.19	7.72
DEKALB Energy[12]	***49a***	*d3.75*	*2.58*	*3.74*		*Dc*	*15.20*	*24.90*	*15.20*	*3-31-95*	*67.00*		*164.0*	*40.9*						
Nts 10s '98	Ao15	**BBB**	6/95	BB–	X	R	100	....	....	....	....	....	38.6	M2	'88	102	95	100½	9.95	9.74
Nts 9⅞s 2000	jJ15	**BBB**	6/95	BB–	X	R	NC	....	....	....	....	....	31.1	M2	'90	101	97⅝	100	9.88	9.87
Delmarva Pwr. & Light	***75***	*3.14*	*3.65*	*3.75*		*Dc*	*37.40*	*243.0*	*288.0*	*9-30-95*	*876.0*		*2098*	*48.0*						
• 1st & CT 6⅜s '97	mS	**A**	11/93	A+	X	CR	100.26	8-31-96	100.14	8-31-96	....	....	25.0	F1	'67	100	95¼	100	6.38	6.37
1st 6.95s 2002	aO	**A**	11/93	A+	X	BE	NC	....	....	....	....	....	30.0	M6	'92	104⅜	90¾	104⅜	6.66	6.15
1st 6.40s 2003	jJ	**A**	11/93	A+	X	BE	NC	....	....	....	....	....	90.0	M6	'93	100¾	87	100¾	6.35	6.27
1st 8.15s 2015	aO	**A**	11/93	A+	X	BE	104.058	(10-1-02)	Z100	....	....	....	66.0	M6	'92	109¼	93	109¼	7.46	7.26
1st[13] 8½s 2022	Fa	**A**	11/93	A+	X	BE	104.003	(2-1-02)	Z100	....	....	....	50.0	M6	'92	111¾	95⅛	111¾	7.61	7.47
1st 'I' 7.71s 2025	Jd	**A**			X	BE	103.855	(6-1-05)	....	....	....	....	100	M2	'95	106½	96⅞	106½	7.24	7.18
1st([14]Amortizing) 'I' 6.95s 2008	Jd	**A**			X	BE	NC	....	....	....	....	....	25.8	M2	'95	105⅞	97	105⅞	6.56	....
Delphi Fin'l Group[15]	***35a***	*2.86*	*5.11*	*4.06*		*Dc*				*9-30-95*	*351.0*		*553.0*	*63.5*						
Sr Nts[16] 8s 2003	aO	**BBB–**	10/93	BB+	X	R	NC	....	....	....	....	....	85.0	M2	'93	97⅞	83¼	97⅞	8.17	8.37
Delta Air Lines	***4***	*Δd1.64*	*Δ0.44*	*Δ2.59*		*Je*	*1632*	*3141*	*3575*	*9-30-95*	*3048*		*5278*	*61.7*						
Deb[13] 10⅛s 2010	Mn15	**BB**	3/93	BBB–	Y	R	NC	....	....	....	....	....	113	G1	'90	126	96⅛	126	8.04	7.19
Deb[13] 10⅜s 2011	Fa	**BB**	3/93	BBB–	Y	R	NC	....	....	....	....	....	176	G1	'91	128⅜	97¾	128⅜	8.08	7.25
Deb 9s 2016	Mn15	**BB**	3/93	BBB–	Y	R	NC	....	....	....	....	....	135	G1	'86	113⅞	86⅛	113⅞	7.90	7.64
Deb[13] 9¾s 2021	Mn15	**BB**	3/93	BBB–	Y	R	NC	....	....	....	....	....	350	G1	'91	122⅞	90¾	122⅞	7.93	7.69
Nts[13] 8½s 2002	Ms15	**BB**	3/93	BBB–	Y	R	NC	....	....	....	....	....	96.0	G1	'92	108⅝	92⅛	108⅝	7.83	6.77
Nts 8¼s '96	Mn15	**BB**	3/93	BBB–	Y	R	NC	....	....	....	....	....	150	G1	'86	101½	99⅛	100¾	8.19	6.16
Nts[13] 9⅞s '98	Jj	**BB**	3/93	BBB–	Y	R	NC	....	....	....	....	....	225	G1	'91	107⅝	100⅝	106¾	9.25	6.24
Nts[13] 9⅞s 2000	Mn15	**BB**	3/93	BBB–	Y	R	NC	....	....	....	....	....	165	G1	'90	112¼	99⅛	112¼	8.80	6.60
M-T[17]Nts'B' 7.79s '98	jD	**BB**			Y	BE	NC	....	....	....	....	....	100	G1	'93	103⅛	95	103⅛	7.55	6.59
Delta Natural Gas	***73b***	*Δ2.18*	*Δ2.89*	*Δ2.24*		*Je*	*0.10*	*2.17*	*14.90*	*9-30-95*	*23.60*		*46.10*	*53.6*						
Deb[18] 9s 2011	Ao31	**NR**				R	105	(4-30-96)	....	....	....	....	10.0	J2	'91	105⅝	94⅜	105⅝	8.52	8.34
Deb[19] 6⅝s 2023	aO	**NR**				BE	105	(10-1-98)	....	....	....	....	15.0	J2	'93	96	74⅜	91½	7.24	7.35
Deluxe Corp	***29a***	*22.13*	*28.73*	*21.42*		*Dc*	*51.90*	*430.0*	*370.0*	*9-30-95*	*114.0*		*1028*	*20.0*						
Nts 8.55s 2001	Fa15	**AA–**			X	R	NC	....	....	....	....	....	100	G1	'91	111½	100⅝	111½	7.67	5.91
Detroit Edison Co.	***72a***	*3.25*	*3.51*	*3.35*		*Dc*	*12.30*	*817.0*	*814.0*	*9-30-95*	*3974*		*7929*	*52.5*						
• Gen Ref R 6s '96	jD	**BBB+**	2/90	BBB	X	R	100	11-30-96	....	....	....	....	100	F1	'66	99⅞	95½	s99¾	6.02	6.28

Uniform Footnote Explanations-See Page 260. Other: [1] Int adj weekly. [2] Int thru 3-10-96,adj qtrly aft. [3] Int adj monthly. [4] Due 6-14-99:Int pd monthly,ea 3rd Wed. [5] Due 8-2-99:Int pd monthly,ea 3rd Wed. [6] (HRO)On Chge of Ctrl at 101. [7] Max 30% of Sr Nts w/proceeds IPO. [8] (HRO)On 6-15-99 at 100. [9] Was Deere(John)Credit. [10] Int adj daily. [11] (HRO)On 8-1-97 at 100. [12] Was DEKALB AgResearch, then DEKALB Corp. [13] Issued in min denom $100T. [14] Princ pyts due ea 6/1/97-08. [15] Was Hyponex Corp. [16] (HRO)On Chge of Ctrl & Rat'g Decline at 101. [17] Issued in min denom of $10T. [18] (HRO)Ea Apr 30 at 100,ltd,as defined. [19] (HRO)Ea Oct 1 at 100,ltd,as defined.

Title-Industry Code & Co. Finances (In Italics) / Individual Issue Statistics — Exchange	Ind / Interest Dates	Fixed Charge Coverage 1992 / S&P Debt Rating	1993 / Date of Last Rating Change	1994 / Prior Rating	Eligible	Year End / Bond Form	Cash & Equiv. / Redemption Provisions — Regular Price	Million $ Curr. Assets / Regular (Begins) Thru	Curr. Liab. / Sinking Fund Price	Balance Sheet Date / Sinking Fund (Begins) Thru	L. Term Debt (Mil $) / Refund/Other Restriction Price	Refund/Other Restriction (Begins) Thru	Capital-ization (Mil $) / Outst'g (Mil $)	Total Debt % Capital / Underwriting Firm	Underwriting Year	Price Range 1995 High	Price Range 1995 Low	Mo. End Price Sale(s) or Bid	Curr. Yield	Yield to Mat.
***Detroit Edison Co.** (Cont.)*																				
• Gen Ref S 6.40s '98	aO	**BBB+**	2/90	BBB	X	R	100	....	....	....	....	....	150	M6	'68	100¼	93¾	100	6.40	6.39
Sec M-T Nts 'G' 5.41s '97	Mn	**BBB+**			X	BE	NC	....	....	....	....	....	125	M6	'93	99¾	94	99¾	5.42	5.60
Sec M-T Nts 'G' 6.56s 2001	Mn	**BBB+**			X	BE	NC	....	....	....	....	....	100	M6	'93	102⅛	90¼	102⅛	6.42	6.09
Developers Diversified Rlty	***57***	***0.86***	***1.81***	***2.01***		***Dc***				***9-30-95***	***424.0***		***691.0***	***61.4***						
Sr Nts 7⅝s 2000	Mn15	**BBB**			X	BE	NC	....	....	....	....	....	100	D3	'95	102½	98	102½	7.44	6.95
Dexter Corp	***14***	***4.89***	***4.44***	***4.40***		***Dc***	***61.60***	***456.0***	***202.0***	***9-30-95***	***224.0***		***685.0***	***35.3***						
SF Deb 9¼s 2016	jD15	**A**			X	R	105.088	12-14-96	100	(12-15-97)	®104.625	12-14-96	50.0	G1	'86	108	103⅛	105¼	8.79	8.70
Di Giorgio Corp	***26g***	***n/a***	***1.26***	***1.03***		***Dc***	***0.42***	***122.0***	***119.0***	***9-30-95***	***146.0***		***225.0***	***84.9***						
Sr Nts[1] 12s 2003	Fa15	**B**			Y	R	104.50	(2-15-98)	....	....	....	....	100	B9	'93	99⅝	72	76	15.79	18.12
Dial Corp[2]	***17a***	***1.98***	***4.51***	***4.68***		***Dc***	***17.50***	***1127***	***2152***	***9-30-95***	***731.0***		***1356***	***59.7***						
Sr Nts 6⅝s 2003	Jd15	**BBB**			X	BE	NC	....	....	....	....	....	100	S1	'93	101⅞	87⅞	101	6.56	6.45
Dial Page, Inc.	***67f***	***0.10***	***0.14***	***d2.99***		***Dc***	***122.0***	***127.0***	***40.00***	***9-30-95***	***431.0***		***700.0***	***61.7***						
Sr Nts[1] 12¼s 2000	Fa15	**B**	6/95	CCC−	Y	R	102.04	(2-15-98)	....	....	....	....	1.57	B8	'93	109	94	A108	11.34	9.84
Diamond Shamrock	***49g***	***2.09***	***2.10***	***3.91***		***Dc***	***24.40***	***485.0***	***298.0***	***9-30-95***	***607.0***		***1229***	***49.7***						
Deb 8¾s 2015	Jd15	**BBB**			X	BE	NC	....	....	....	....	....	75.0	L3	'95	116⅝	100	116⅝	7.50	7.15
Deb 8s 2023	Ao	**BBB**			X	BE	103.803	(4-1-03)	....	....	....	....	100	L3	'93	105⅞	89¼	105⅞	7.56	7.49
Nts 9⅜s 2001	Ms	**BBB**			X	BE	NC	....	....	....	....	....	75.0	M2	'91	113¾	101½	113¾	8.24	6.22
[3]Diamond State Telephone[4]	***67a***	***7.32***	***8.45***	....		***Dc***		***55.20***	***87.60***	***6-30-94***	***99.00***		***296.0***	***41.2***						
Deb 6⅛s 2003	jD	**AA+**			X	BE	NC	....	....	....	....	....	20.0	S1	'93	100⅝	88	100⅝	6.09	6.02
Deb 4⅝s 2005	mS	**AA+**	10/93	AAA	X	R	100.63	8-31-96	....	....	....	....	7.00	D8	'65	89¾	74⅜	89¾	5.15	6.04
• Deb 7s 2008	jD	**AA+**	10/93	AAA	X	R	101.56	11-30-96	....	....	....	....	10.0	D8	'68	99⅝	87	98⅞	7.08	7.13
Deb 7¾s 2013	jD	**AA+**	10/93	AAA	X	R	102.69	11-30-96	....	....	....	....	15.0	M2	'73	103⅞	91⅞	103⅜	7.50	7.41
Deb[5] 8⅜s 2019	Ms15	**AA+**	10/93	AAA	X	R	NC	....	....	....	....	....	15.0	S1	'89	123⅝	102¾	123⅝	6.77	6.42
Deb 7s 2023	jD	**AA+**			X	BE	100	(12-1-13)	....	....	....	....	20.0	S1	'93	103	88	103	6.80	6.76
Deb 8⅝s 2031	aO15	**AA+**	10/93	AAA	X	BE	NC	....	....	....	....	....	15.0	F1	'91	125⅝	101	125⅝	6.87	6.72
Dictaphone Corp	***42***	***n/a***	***n/a***	***0.27***		***Dc***	***14.00***	***167.0***	***95.40***	***9-30-95***	***360.0***		***469.0***	***77.8***						
Sr Sub Nts[1] 11¾s 2005	fA	**B−**			Y	R	105.875	(8-1-00)	....	....	[6]Z110	7-31-98	200	M6	'95	100	99¾	99¾	11.78	11.79
Digital Equipment	***20b***	***Δd3.41***	***Δd10.10***	***Δ1.84***		***Je***	***1501***	***7102***	***3921***	***9-30-95***	***1013***		***4622***	***22.2***						
Deb 8⅝s 2012	mN	**BB+**	9/95	BB−	Y	BE	NC	....	....	....	....	....	250	L3	'92	108⅞	84¼	108⅞	7.92	7.68
Deb 7¾s 2023	Ao	**BB+**	9/95	BB−	Y	BE	NC	....	....	....	....	....	250	L3	'93	98⅜	74½	98⅜	7.88	7.89
Nts 7s '97	mN15	**BB+**	9/95	BB−	Y	BE	NC	....	....	....	....	....	250	F1	'92	101⅜	94½	101⅜	6.91	6.21
Nts 7⅛s 2002	aO15	**BB+**	9/95	BB−	Y	BE	NC	....	....	....	....	....	250	M2	'92	101	83⅛	101	7.05	6.94
Dillard Dept Stores[7]	***59f***	***4.08***	***4.05***	***4.27***		***Ja***	***59.40***	***2990***	***1253***	***10-28-95***	***1172***		***3950***	***37.9***						
Deb 9½s 2001	aO15	**A+**	6/91	A	X	R	NC	....	....	....	....	....	50.0	G1	'89	117½	105¼	117½	8.09	5.89
Deb 9½s 2009	mS	**A+**	6/91	A	X	R	NC	....	....	....	....	....	50.0	G1	'89	129⅝	107⅜	129⅝	7.33	6.24
Deb 7⅞s 2023	Jj	**A+**			X	BE	NC	....	....	....	....	....	100	M6	'93	114½	91½	114½	6.88	6.71
Nts 8½s '96	Jd15	**A+**			X	BE	NC	....	....	....	....	....	50.0	S7	'91	102⅜	100½	101⅜	8.38	5.43
Nts 9⅝s '97	mS15	**A+**	6/91	A	X	BE	NC	....	....	....	....	....	50.0	M6	'90	107½	103	106¾	9.02	5.43
Nts 9½s '98	Jj15	**A+**	6/91	A	X	R	NC	....	....	....	....	....	50.0	G1	'88	107¾	102⅝	107¾	8.82	5.44
Nts 8¾s '98	Jd15	**A+**			X	BE	NC	....	....	....	....	....	50.0	S7	'91	107⅜	100¾	107⅜	8.15	5.50
Nts 8s '99	Jj15	**A+**	6/91	A	X	R	NC	....	....	....	....	....	50.0	G1	'87	106¾	98⅝	106¾	7.49	5.56
Nts 7⅜s '99	Jd15	**A+**			X	BE	NC	....	....	....	....	....	100	M6	'92	105⅜	96⅜	105⅜	7.00	5.64
Nts 7.15s 2002	mS	**A+**			X	BE	NC	....	....	....	....	....	100	G1	'92	106¼	92⅜	106¼	6.73	6.00
Nts 6⅞s 2005	Jd	**A+**			X	BE	NC	....	....	....	....	....	100	M6	'95	105	97⅛	105	6.55	6.17
Nts 9⅛s 2011	fA	**A+**			X	BE	NC	....	....	....	....	....	100	M6	'91	125¾	104⅝	125¾	7.26	6.48
Nts 7.85s 2012	aO	**A+**			X	BE	NC	....	....	....	....	....	100	G1	'92	112	92⅛	112	7.01	6.65

Uniform Footnote Explanations-See Page 260. Other: [1] (HRO)On Chge of Ctrl at 101. [2] See Greyhound Corp. [3] Subsid of Bell Atlantic Corp. [4] Now Bell Atlantic-Delaware. [5] (HRO)On 9-15-99 at 100. [6] Max $70M red w/proceeds of Pub Eq Off'gs. [7] See Dillard Investment Co.

Title-Industry Code & Co. Finances (In Italics) / Individual Issue Statistics (Exchange)	Ind / Interest Dates	S&P Debt Rating	Date of Last Rating Change	Prior Rating	Eligible	Bond Form	Redemption Provisions: Regular Price	Regular (Begins) Thru	Sinking Fund Price	Sinking Fund (Begins) Thru	Refund/Other Restriction Price	Refund/Other Restriction (Begins) Thru	Outst'g (Mil $)	Underwriting Firm	Underwriting Year	Price Range 1995 High	Price Range 1995 Low	Mo. End Price Sale(s) or Bid	Curr. Yield	Yield to Mat.
Co. Finances:	*Ind*	*Fixed Charge Coverage 1992*	*1993*		*1994*	*Year End*	*Cash & Equiv. (Million $)*	*Curr. Assets*	*Curr. Liab.*	*Balance Sheet Date*	*L. Term Debt (Mil $)*		*Capitalization (Mil $)*	*Total Debt % Capital*						
Dillard Investment Co	***25d***	***Subsid of Dillard Dept Stores,see***																		
Nts 9¼s '97	Mn	**A+**	6/91	A	X	R	NC	....	....	....	....	....	75.0	G1	'87	105⅝	102	104¾	8.83	5.51
Nts 9¼s 2001	Fa	**A+**	6/91	A	X	BE	NC	....	....	....	....	....	100	M6	'91	114¼	104⅞	114¼	8.10	5.96
Disney (Walt) Co	***40g***	*△7.81*	*△16.12*		*△9.87*	*Sp*	*1943*			*9-30-95*	*2984*		*9635*	*31.0*						
Sr Deb[1] 7.55s 2093	jJ15	**AA–**			X	BE	103.02	(7-15-23)	....	....	....	....	300	M6	'93	108	84½	108	6.99	6.99
Dr Pepper Bottling Co of Texas	***11e***	*n/a*	*1.46*		*1.53*	*Dc*	*14.80*	*64.10*	*67.80*	*9-30-95*	*283.0*		*195.0*	*153.0*						
Sr Nts[2] 10¼s 2000	Fa15	**B–**			Y	R	101.708	(2-16-98)	....	....	....	....	117	D6	'93	106	99½	105½	9.72	8.63
Dr Pepper Bottling Hldgs	***11e***	*n/a*	*1.46*		*1.09*	*Dc*	*14.80*	*65.20*	*71.20*	*6-30-95*	*285.0*		*159.0*	*189.0*						
Sr Disc[3]Nts[4] 11⅝s 2003	Fa15	**CCC+**			Y	R	104.359	(2-16-98)	....	....	....	....	[5]117	D6	'93	82	67½	79½	....	Flat
Dr Pepper/Seven-Up Cos	***11e***	*0.99*	*2.10*		*2.50*	*Dc*		*134.0*	*231.0*	*6-30-95*	*666.0*		*410.0*	*187.0*						
◆Sr Sub[6]Disc[7]Nts 11½s 2002	mN	**A–**	3/95	B–	X	R	104.3125	(11-1-97)	100	(11-1-00)	....	....	[5]472	B9	'92	94	79	s93½	....	Flat
Doehler-Jarvis, Inc	***5***	*n/a*	*n/a*		*0.86*	*Dc*		*90.40*	*56.90*	*3-31-95*	*126.0*		*112.0*	*113.0*						
Sr[2]Nts[8] 11⅞s 2002	Jd	**NR**	8/95	B		R	105.089	(6-1-98)	....	....	[9]Z110	6-1-97	87.0	B9	'94	105¾	98	A105	11.31	10.77
Dole Food Co[10]	***26***	*2.61*	*2.38*		*1.99*	*Dc*	*31.20*	*1060*	*666.0*	*10-7-95*	*1098*		*2207*	*50.5*						
• Deb 7⅞s 2013	jJ15	**BBB–**			X	BE	NC	....	....	....	....	....	175	G1	'93	106	90¼	102	7.72	7.67
• Nts 6¾s 2000	jJ15	**BBB–**			X	BE	NC	....	....	....	....	....	225	G1	'93	102¼	91⅛	99⅝	6.78	6.85
• Nts 7s 2003	Mn15	**BBB–**			X	BE	NC	....	....	....	....	....	300	B9	'93	102	87½	s102	6.86	6.65
Dominion Bankshares	***10***	***Mgr into FirstUnion Corp, see***																		
Sub[11]Cap Nts 9⅝s '99	Jd15	**A–**	9/93	BBB+	Y	R	NC	....	....	....	....	....	74.9	S4	'87	110¾	104⅛	110¾	8.69	6.13
Donald,Lufkin & Jenrette	***62***	*2.15*	*1.79*		*1.41*	*Dc*	*130.0*			*6-30-95*	*★868.0*		*3474*	*68.4*						
Sr Nts 6⅞s 2005	mN	**A–**			X	BE	NC	....	....	....	....	....	500	D6	'95	102½	99¼	102½	6.71	6.53
Donnelley(RR) & Sons	***29a***	*9.11*	*7.93*		*8.38*	*Dc*	*19.20*	*1867*	*1066*	*9-30-95*	*1629*		*3774*	*44.0*						
Deb 8⅞s 2021	Ao15	**AA–**			X	R	NC	....	....	....	....	....	150	M2	'91	127¼	105⅛	125¾	7.06	6.74
Nts 9⅛s 2000	jD	**AA–**			X	R	NC	....	....	....	....	....	200	L3	'90	113⅞	103½	113⅞	8.01	5.84
Nts 7s 2003	Jj	**AA–**			X	BE	NC	....	....	....	....	....	110	S1	'93	103	93	103	6.80	6.46
[12]***Doskocil Cos***	***26e***	*1.48*	*1.24*		*0.35*	*Dc*	*4.93*	*95.30*	*63.90*	*9-30-95*	*164.0*		*209.0*	*79.9*						
Sr Sub Red Nts[2] 9¾s 2000	jJ15	**B**			Y	R	103	(7-15-98)	....	....	[13]Z100	....	110	M2	'93	99	85	98¼	9.92	10.24
Dover Corp	***42***	*11.06*	*12.10*		*9.32*	*Dc*	*160.0*	*1314*	*1068*	*9-30-95*	*★502.0*		*1925*	*39.0*						
Nts 6.45s 2005	mN15	**A+**			X	BE	NC	....	....	....	....	....	250	G1	'95	102⅝	99¾	102⅝	6.29	6.09
Dow Capital B.V.	***25***	***Subsid of & gtd by Dow Chemical,see***																		
[14]Gtd[15]Deb 9s 2010	$Mn15	**A**			Q	R	NC	....	....	....	....	....	150	G1	'90	121⅞	101½	121¼	7.42	6.68
[14]Gtd[15]Deb 9.20s 2010	$Jd	**A**			Q	R	NC	....	....	....	....	....	200	S1	'90	122	103⅞	122	7.54	6.78
[14]Gtd[15]SF Deb 8.70s 2022	$Mn15	**A**			Q	R	103.13	(5-15-02)	100	(5-15-03)	....	....	150	M2	'92	114	96¾	112	7.77	7.64
[14]Gtd[15]Nts 8¼s '96	$Fa15	**A**			Q	R	NC	....	....	....	....	....	150	G1	'91	101¼	100¼	100¼	8.23	6.09
[14]Gtd[15]Nts 5¾s '97	$mS15	**A**			Q	BE	NC	....	....	....	....	....	200	G1	'92	99⅞	94	99⅞	5.76	5.82
[14]Gtd[15]Nts 7⅜s 2002	$jJ15	**A**			Q	BE	NC	....	....	....	....	....	150	S1	'92	106	94⅜	104¼	7.07	6.56
[14]Gtd[15]Nts 7⅛s 2003	$Jj	**A**			Q	BE	NC	....	....	....	....	....	150	G1	'93	104⅜	92⅝	102¾	6.93	6.63
Dow Chemical Co.	***14***	*2.50*	*2.74*		*4.29*	*Dc*	*4638*	*12149*	*6078*	*9-30-95*	*5026*		*14343*	*45.1*						
Deb 8⅝s 2006	Ao	**A**	5/88	A–	X	R	NC	....	....	....	....	....	200	S5	'86	117½	100⅛	115½	7.47	6.53
• Deb 6.85s 2013	fA15	**A**			X	BE	NC	....	....	....	....	....	150	M2	'93	93⅞	83	91½	7.49	7.74
Deb 9s 2021	Ao	**A**			X	R	NC	....	....	....	....	....	300	M2	'91	123¾	101⅞	123⅝	7.28	6.99
Deb 8.85s 2021	mS15	**A**			X	R	NC	....	....	....	....	....	200	L3	'91	122⅞	100⅝	122	7.25	6.99
Deb 7⅜s 2023	Ms	**A**			X	BE	NC	....	....	....	....	....	150	M2	'93	104⅜	85	104⅜	7.07	7.01
Nts 9.35s 2002	Ms15	**A**			X	R	100	(3-15-00)	....	....	....	....	200	M2	'90	113	102⅞	112½	8.31	6.84
Nts[16] 8.55s 2009	aO15	**A**			X	R	[17]NC	....	....	....	....	....	150	M2	'89	117¾	101	117¾	7.26	6.57
Dow Corning Corp[18]	***14***	*5.29*	*5.55*		*3.85*	*Dc*	***Bankruptcy Chapt 11***				*378.0*		*1719*	*49.2*						
Deb 9⅜s 2008	§Fa	**D**	5/95	B–	Z	R			Default 8-1-95 int				75.0	M6	'88	75⅝	51	64¼	....	Flat

Uniform Footnote Explanations-See Page 260. Other: [1] Issued in min denom $25T. [2] (HRO)On Chge of Ctrl at 101. [3] Int accrues at 11.625% fr 2-16-98. [4] (HRO)On Chge of Ctrl at 101(Accreted Val). [5] Incl disc. [6] (HRO)On Chge of Ctrl at 101(Accreted Amt). [7] Int accr fr 11-1-97. [8] Harvard Indus purch offer,$1055,Jul 28. [9] Max $29M red w/proceeds of IPO. [10] Was Castle & Cooke. [11] To be exch for Cap Sec when due. [12] Now Foodbrands America. [13] On Chge of Ctrl,plus Applicable Premium. [14] Gtd by Dow Chemical. [15] Co may red in whole at 100 if add'l pyt due. [16] (HRO)On 10-15-99 at 100. [17] Red fr 10-15-99 at 100 if $15M or less outstg. [18] Affil. with Dow Chemical.

Title-Industry Code & Co. Finances (In Italics) / Exchange ↓ Individual Issue Statistics	Ind / Interest Dates	Fixed Charge Coverage 1992 / S&P Debt Rating	1993 / Date of Last Rating Change	1994 / Prior Rating	Eligible ↓	Year End / Bond Form	Million $ Cash & Equiv. / Redemption Provisions Regular Price	Curr. Assets / Regular (Begins) Thru	Curr. Liab. / Sinking Fund Price	Balance Sheet Date / Sinking Fund (Begins) Thru	L. Term Debt (Mil $) / Refund/Other Restriction Price	Refund/Other Restriction (Begins) Thru	Capital-ization (Mil $) / Outst'g (Mil $)	Total Debt % Capital / Underwriting Firm	Underwriting Year	Price Range 1995 High	Low	Mo. End Price Sale(s) or Bid	Curr. Yield	Yield to Mat.
***Dow Corning Corp** (Cont.)*																				
Deb[1] 8.15s 2029	§aO15	**D**	5/95	B−	Z	R			Default 10-15-95 int				50.0	M6	'89	95⅞	70½	86⅛	....	Flat
Dow Jones & Co	***54c***	*9.30*	*14.05*	*20.78*		*Dc*	*4.76*	*326.0*	*538.0*	*9-30-95*	*279.0*		*1843*	*15.4*						
Nts 5¾s 2000	jD	**AA**			X	BE	NC	....	....	....	....	....	150	C2	'95	100¼	99⅜	100¼	5.74	5.69
Dresser Industries[2]	***49e***	*4.52*	*7.95*	*8.12*		*Oc*	*515.0*	*2197*	*1367*	*10-31-94*	*461.0*		*2130*	*23.4*						
Nts 6¼s 2000	Jd15	**A**	12/94	A−	X	BE	NC	....	....	....	....	....	300	M2	'93	101½	90⅞	101½	6.16	5.86
Dual Drilling Co	***49e***	*d0.48*	*1.10*	*d0.35*		*Dc*	*45.40*	*73.60*	*19.50*	*9-30-95*	*139.0*		*285.0*	*50.9*						
Sr[3]Sub Nts 9⅞s 2004	Jj15	**B−**			Y	R	104.94	(1-15-99)	....	....	....	....	100	M2	'94	95½	77	94½	10.45	10.92
Duke Power Co.	***72a***	*3.57*	*4.75*	*4.42*		*Dc*	*136.0*	*1098*	*653.0*	*9-30-95*	*3695*		*9296*	*40.9*						
1st & Ref[4] 5⅝s '97	[5]ao	**AA−**			X	BE	NC	....	Z100	....	....	....	100	M2	'92	100⅛	94¼	100⅛	5.62	5.54
• 1st & Ref 5⅜s '97	Ao	**AA−**	10/83	A+	X	R	100.22	3-31-96	Z100.11	3-31-96	....	....	72.6	M6	'67	99¼	94¾	98⅞	5.44	6.31
1st & Ref[4] 6¼s '99	[6]ao	**AA−**			X	BE	NC	....	Z100	....	....	....	65.0	M2	'92	101⅝	92⅜	101⅝	6.15	5.74
1st & Ref 7½s '99	Ao	**AA−**			X	R	NC	....	Z100	....	....	....	100	M2	'92	105¼	97¼	105¼	7.13	5.71
• 1st & Ref B 8s '99	mN	**AA−**			X	R	NC	....	Z100	....	....	....	200	M2	'94	108	98⅞	105⅛	7.61	6.47
• 1st & Ref 7s 2000	Jd	**AA−**			X	R	NC	....	Z100	....	....	....	100	L3	'92	103⅝	94⅛	103½	6.76	6.08
• 1st & Ref B 7s 2000	jJ	**AA−**			X	R	NC	....	Z100	....	....	....	100	G1	'92	103	94¼	102½	6.83	6.35
• 1st & Ref 5⅞s 2001	Jd	**AA−**			X	R	NC	....	Z100	....	....	....	150	M2	'93	100½	87¾	98¾	5.95	6.15
• 1st & Ref B 6⅝s 2003	Fa	**AA−**			X	R	NC	....	Z100	....	....	....	100	G1	'93	103½	89¾	102⅜	6.47	6.20
• 1st & Ref C 5⅞s 2003	Ms	**AA−**			X	R	100.517	(3-1-98)	Z100	....	....	....	75.0	K2	'93	100	84⅞	97	6.06	6.40
• 1st & Ref 8s 2004	Ms	**AA−**			X	R	103.687	(3-1-97)	Z100	....	....	....	75.0	M2	'92	106¼	97	102⅜	7.81	7.60
• 1st & Ref B 6¼s 2004	Mn	**AA−**			X	R	101.891	(5-1-98)	Z100	....	....	....	100	M6	'93	100	86¼	s97	6.44	6.72
• 1st & Ref 7s 2005	mS	**AA−**			X	R	103.13	(9-1-97)	Z100	....	....	....	200	F1	'92	102¾	89⅝	101⅝	6.89	6.77
• 1st & Ref 6⅜s 2008	Ms	**AA−**			X	R	101.66	(3-1-98)	Z100	....	....	....	125	F1	'93	99	83	96⅜	6.61	6.82
• 1st & Ref 8¾s 2021	Ms	**AA−**			X	R	104.17	2-28-96	Z100	....	....	....	150	M2	'91	106	97½	103⅝	8.44	8.40
• 1st & Ref B 8⅜s 2021	jD	**AA−**			X	R	103.80	11-30-96	Z100	....	®103.563	11-30-96	150	G1	'91	106¼	93⅞	102⅞	8.14	8.11
• 1st & Ref 8⅝s 2022	Ms	**AA−**			X	R	106.188	(3-1-97)	Z100	....	....	....	100	M2	'92	109	96¼	105	8.21	8.16
• 1st & Ref 7⅜s 2023	Ms	**AA−**			X	R	103.37	(3-1-98)	Z100	....	....	....	200	M2	'93	102	85⅝	101	7.30	7.29
• 1st & Ref B 6⅞s 2023	fA	**AA−**			X	R	103	(8-1-98)	Z100	....	....	....	200	K2	'93	96⅜	81⅛	95	7.24	7.30
• 1st & Ref 7⅞s 2024	Mn	**AA−**			X	R	103.592	(5-1-99)	Z100	....	....	....	150	D6	'94	104⅞	90⅞	s104½	7.54	7.49
• 1st & Ref 6¾s 2025	fA	**AA−**			X	R	102.677	(8-1-98)	Z100	....	....	....	150	S1	'93	98⅜	79¾	s97¾	6.91	6.93
• 1st & Ref B 7½s 2025	fA	**AA−**			X	R	103.355	(8-1-00)	Z100	....	....	....	100	D6	'95	102¼	96⅞	101	7.43	7.42
• 1st & Ref 7s 2033	jJ	**AA−**			X	R	102.35	(7-1-03)	Z100	....	....	....	150	L3	'93	99	82¼	96⅛	7.28	7.30
Duke Realty L.P.	***57***	*0.91*	*1.65*	*2.74*		*Dc*				*6-30-95*	*★411.0*		*831.0*	*36.1*						
Nts 7¼s 2002	mS22	**BBB**			X	BE	NC	....	....	....	....	....	50.0	M2	'95	103	99	103	7.04	6.69
Nts 7⅜s 2005		**BBB**					[7]Z100	(9-22-02)	....	....	....	....	100	M2	'95	103⅞	98⅝	103⅞	7.10	6.82
du Pont(E.I.) de Nemours	***14***	*2.63*	*4.15*	*6.32*		*Dc*	*1541*	*11604*	*13476*	*9-30-95*	*5971*		*21349*	*61.2*						
• Deb 6s 2001	jD	**AA−**	4/95	AA	X	R	100	....	....	....	....	....	[8]660	M6	'81	100	87⅞	s99⅜	6.04	6.13
Deb 8¼s 2022	Jj15	**AA−**	4/95	AA	X	BE	103.94	(1-15-02)	....	....	....	....	400	F1	'92	112⅜	96	112⅜	7.34	7.19
Deb 7.95s 2023	Jj15	**AA−**	4/95	AA	X	BE	103.86	(1-15-03)	....	....	....	....	300	F1	'93	110½	92½	110½	7.19	7.07
Nts 8.45s '96	aO15	**AA−**	4/95	AA	X	R	NC	....	....	....	....	....	300	S4	'89	103⅛	100¾	102⅜	8.25	5.34
Nts 8.65s '97	jD	**AA−**	4/95	AA	X	BE	NC	....	....	....	....	....	300	M6	'90	105⅞	101⅛	105⅞	8.17	5.39
Nts[9] 9.15s 2000	Ao15	**AA−**	4/95	AA	X	R	NC	....	....	....	....	....	300	F1	'90	113¼	103½	113¼	8.08	5.63
Nts 6¾s 2002	aO15	**AA−**	4/95	AA	X	BE	NC	....	....	....	....	....	300	M6	'92	104⅝	90¾	104⅝	6.45	5.91
Nts 8½s 2003	Fa15	**AA−**	4/95	AA	X	BE	100	(2-15-01)	....	....	....	....	300	G1	'91	112⅞	101	112⅞	7.53	6.23
Nts 8⅛s 2004	Ms15	**AA−**	4/95	AA	X	BE	NC	....	....	....	....	....	350	G1	'92	113⅝	98½	113⅝	7.15	6.00
Nts 8¼s 2006	mS15	**AA−**	4/95	AA	X	BE	NC	....	....	....	....	....	300	M2	'91	117¼	98⅞	117¼	7.04	6.04
Duquesne Light Co.[10]	***72a***	*3.01*	*3.17*	*3.28*		*Dc*	*23.00*	*229.0*	*250.0*	*6-30-95*	*1319*		*2742*	*51.3*						
1st CT 6⅝s 2004	Jd15	**BBB+**			X	BE	101.614	(6-15-98)	....	....	....	....	100	M2	'93	99⅞	86¾	99⅞	6.63	6.64

Uniform Footnote Explanations-See Page 260. Other: [1] (HRO)On 10-15-96 at 100. [2] See Baroid Corp. [3] (HRO)On Chge of Ctrl at 101. [4] Issued in min denom $100T. [5] Due 8-12-97. [6] Due 8-12-99. [7] Plus Make-Whole Amt. [8] Incl disc. [9] Issued in min denom $25T. [10] Subsid of DQE, Inc.

Title-Industry Code & Co. Finances (In Italics)	Ind	Fixed Charge Coverage 1992	1993		1994	Year End	Million $ Cash & Equiv.	Curr. Assets	Curr. Liab.	Balance Sheet Date	L. Term Debt (Mil $)		Capital-ization (Mil $)	Total Debt % Capital						
Exchange ↓ Individual Issue Statistics	**Interest Dates**	**S&P Debt Rating**	**Date of Last Rating Change**	**Prior Rating**	**Eligible ↓**	**Bond Form**	**Redemption Provisions: Regular Price**	**Regular (Begins) Thru**	**Sinking Fund Price**	**Sinking Fund (Begins) Thru**	**Refund/Other Restriction Price**	**Refund/Other Restriction (Begins) Thru**	**Outst'g (Mil $)**	**Underwriting Firm**	**Underwriting Year**	**Price Range 1995 High**	**Low**	**Mo. End Price Sale(s) or Bid**	**Curr. Yield**	**Yield to Mat.**
***Duquesne Light Co.** (Cont.)*																				
1st CT 8¾s 2022	Mn15	**BBB+**			X	BE	106.5625	(5-15-97)	....	....	....	....	100	S1	'92	109¼	97	109¼	8.01	7.91
1st CT 7⅝s 2023	Ao15	**BBB+**			X	BE	105.381	(4-15-98)	....	....	....	....	100	G1	'93	102⅛	87¾	102⅛	7.47	7.44
1st CT 8⅜s 2024	Mn15	**BBB+**			X	BE	105.3992	(5-15-97)	....	....	....	....	100	G1	'92	105⅞	93¼	105⅞	7.91	7.85
1st CT 7.55s 2025	Jd15	**BBB+**			X	BE	103.8662	(6-15-00)	....	....	....	....	100	M2	'93	101¼	86	101¼	7.46	7.44
• SF Deb 5s 2010	Ms	**BBB**	6/90	BBB–	X	CR	101.78	8-31-96	100.52	8-31-96	....	....	6.04	F1	'60	74	69¼	73	6.85	8.27
Duty Free Intl	***59l***	***52.89***	***29.82***		***3.53***	***Ja***	***45.60***	***193.0***	***73.20***	***7-30-95***	***118.0***		***327.0***	***37.3***						
Nts 7s 2004	Jj15	**BBB–**	3/95	BBB	X	R	NC	....	....	....	....	....	115	M6	'94	97¾	76⅞	97¼	7.20	7.46
Eagle Food Centers, Inc	***59c***	***n/a***	***1.50***		***d0.64***	***Ja***	***2.07***	***114.0***	***123.0***	***10-28-95***	***115.0***		***171.0***	***82.5***						
Sr Nts[1] 8⅝s 2000	Ao15	**B+**	10/94	BB–	Y	R	103.50	(4-15-98)	....	....	....	....	100	G1	'93	67	32	67	12.87	20.54
Eagle Industries	***42b***	***[2]0.99***	***0.88***		***1.57***	***Dc***	***32.40***	***280.0***	***173.0***	***9-30-95***	***318.0***		***529.0***	***64.8***						
Sr[3]Deferred Cpn Nts[4] 10½s 2003	jJ15	**B–**			Y	R	100	(7-15-98)	....	....	[5]Z100	7-14-96	259	M2	'93	81	63	81	12.96	14.75
Eastern[6]Edison Co.[7]	***72a***	***2.73***	***2.75***		***3.04***	***Dc***	***17.90***	***95.60***	***82.10***	***9-30-95***	***222.0***		***529.0***	***49.9***						
1st & CT 5⅞s '98	Mn	**BBB**	8/94	BBB+	X	R	102.734	4-30-96	Z100	....	....	....	20.0	S1	'93	99¾	91	99¾	5.89	5.99
1st & CT 6⅞s 2003	Mn	**BBB**	8/94	BBB+	X	R	104.554	4-30-96	Z100	....	....	....	40.0	S1	'93	101¾	88¾	101¾	6.76	6.57
1st & CT 8s 2023	Mn	**BBB**	8/94	BBB+	X	R	106.192	4-30-96	....	....	®103.44	4-30-03	40.0	S1	'93	105⅜	89½	105⅜	7.59	7.53
Eastman Chemical Co	***14a***	***n/a***	***n/a***		***7.32***	***Dc***	***66.00***	***1442***	***866.0***	***9-30-95***	***1205***		***2675***	***45.0***						
Deb 7¼s 2024	Jj15	**BBB+**	9/95	BBB	X	BE	NC	....	....	....	....	....	500	G1	'94	106	82¼	106	6.84	6.77
Deb[8] 7⅝s 2024	Jd15	**BBB+**	9/95	BBB	X	BE	NC	....	....	....	....	....	200	G1	'94	113⅛	93⅜	113⅛	6.74	6.60
Nts 6⅜s 2004	Jj15	**BBB+**	9/95	BBB	X	BE	NC	....	....	....	....	....	500	G1	'94	101¼	86½	101¼	6.30	6.17
Eastman Kodak	***40d***	***3.23***	***2.81***		***8.06***	***Dc***	***1333***	***7069***	***4422***	***9-30-95***	***653.0***		***5825***	***18.3***						
Deb 9.95s 2018	jJ	**A+**	9/94	BBB+	X	R	[9]....	....	....	....	....	....	3.10	M6	'88	136¾	111	136¾	7.28	6.75
Deb 9.20s 2021	Jd	**A+**	9/94	BBB+	X	R	NC	....	....	....	....	....	10.3	M2	'91	131¼	106¼	131¼	7.01	6.64
Nts 7¼s '97	Ao15	**A+**	9/94	BBB+	X	R	NC	....	....	....	....	....	8.20	M6	'87	102⅜	97⅞	102⅜	7.08	5.32
Nts 8.55s '97	Mn	**A+**	9/94	BBB+	X	R	NC	....	....	....	....	....	102	F1	'87	104¼	101	104⅛	8.21	5.31
Nts 7¼s '99	jJ	**A+**	9/94	BBB+	X	R	NC	....	....	....	....	....	77.8	M2	'92	105¼	96¾	105¼	6.89	5.58
Nts[10] 10s 2001	Jd15	**A+**	9/94	BBB+	X	R	100	(6-15-96)	....	....	....	....	122	F1	'88	103¾	101⅞	101⅞	9.82	9.55
Nts 9⅜s 2003	Ms15	**A+**	9/94	BBB+	X	R	NC	....	....	....	....	....	144	G1	'88	119⅝	106⅜	119⅝	7.84	5.98
Nts[11] 9⅞s 2004	mN	**A+**	9/94	BBB+	X	R	100	(11-1-98)	....	....	....	....	104	F1	'88	111⅜	104⅜	110⅝	8.93	8.16
Nts 9¾s 2004	aO	**A+**	9/94	BBB+	X	R	NC	....	....	....	....	....	91.0	F1	'89	125	109⅜	125	7.80	6.03
Eaton Corp	***8***	***2.90***	***5.23***		***6.36***	***Dc***	***39.00***	***2067***	***1111***	***9-30-95***	***1147***		***3097***	***38.3***						
Deb[12] 8s 2006	fA15	**A**			X	R	NC	....	....	....	....	....	86.0	M2	'86	115¾	99⅞	115¾	6.91	5.98
Deb 8.90s 2006	fA15	**A**			X	R	NC	....	....	....	....	....	100	G1	'91	121⅛	103	121⅛	7.35	6.16
• Deb 7s 2011	Ao	**A**	1/85	A–	X	R	100	....	....	....	....	....	[13]200	M2	'81	99⅝	86⅞	97½	7.18	7.27
Deb[14] 8⅞s 2019	Jd15	**A**			X	R	NC	....	....	....	....	....	38.0	S4	'89	128⅜	105¾	128⅜	6.91	6.50
Deb 8.10s 2022	fA15	**A**			X	R	NC	....	....	....	....	....	100	G1	'92	118	94¼	118	6.86	6.65
Deb 7⅝s 2024	Ao	**A**			X	R	NC	....	....	....	....	....	100	L3	'94	112⅛	70⅛	112⅛	6.80	6.67
Deb[15] 6½s 2025	Jd	**A**			X	R	NC	....	....	....	....	....	150	L3	'95	99⅝	92⅞	97	6.70	6.74
Nts 6⅜s '99	Ao	**A**			X	R	NC	....	....	....	....	....	100	L3	'94	102⅜	93¼	102⅜	6.23	5.56
Eaton ETN Offshore Ltd	***8***	***Gtd by & subsid of Eaton Corp,see***																		
Gtd[16]Nts 9s 2001	Fa15	**A**			X	R	NC	....	....	....	[17]Z100	....	100	G1	'91	113¼	102¾	113¼	7.95	5.96
Eckerd(Jack)Corp[18]	***59e***	***0.94***	***1.39***		***1.93***	***Ja***	***9.37***	***964.0***	***580.0***	***10-28-95***	***814.0***		***819.0***	***99.5***						
• Sr[1]Sub Nts 9¼s 2004	fA15	**B**			Y	R	104.625	(2-15-99)	....	....	[19]Z100	....	200	M2	'93	108	96½	s106⅜	8.70	8.16
EG&G Inc	***65***	***10.21***	***15.13***		***10.89***	***Dc***	***64.30***	***443.0***	***355.0***	***10-1-95***	***★115.0***		***548.0***	***34.5***						
Nts 6.80s 2005	aO15	**A**			X	BE	NC	....	....	....	....	....	115	G1	'95	102⅛	99	102⅛	6.66	6.50
El Paso Electric (Texas)	***72a***	***1.03***	***0.75***		***0.62***	***Dc***	***Bankruptcy Chapt 11***				***[20]1587***		***1268***	***125.0***						
1st 4⅝s '92	§Fa	**D**	2/92	CCC	Z	CR			Default 2-1-92 P&I[21]				10.4	S1	'62	101	87	A101	....	Flat

Uniform Footnote Explanations-See Page 260. Other: [1] (HRO)On Chge of Ctrl at 101. [2] Fiscal Jul'92 & prior. [3] (HRO)On Chge of Ctrl at 101(Accretal Amt). [4] Int accr at 10.5% fr 7-15-98. [5] Accr Amt:Max $110.25M w/proceeds Equity Off'g. [6] Subsid of Eastern Util Assoc. [7] Was Brocton Edison. [8] (HRO)On 6-15-06 at 100. [9] Fr7-1-03,greater of 100 or amt based on formula. [10] Plan call on 6-16-96 at 100. [11] Plan call on 11-1-98 at 100. [12] (HRO)On 8-15-96 at 100. [13] Incl disc. [14] (HRO)For a Risk Event & on 6-15-04 at 100. [15] (HRO)On 6-1-05 at 100. [16] Gtd by Eaton Corp. [17] Co may red in whole for UK tax law chge. [18] Was Eckerd Hldgs. [19] Plus Applicable Premium,on Chge of Ctrl. [20] Liabs subj to compromise. [21] Co has made some partial int pyts.

Title-Industry Code & Co. Finances (In Italics) | *Ind* | *Fixed Charge Coverage: 1992, 1993, 1994, Year End* | *Million $: Cash & Equiv., Curr. Assets, Curr. Liab.* | *Balance Sheet Date* | *L. Term Debt (Mil $)* | *Capitalization (Mil $)* | *Total Debt % Capital*

Individual Issue Statistics / Exchange	Interest Dates	S&P Debt Rating	Date of Last Rating Change	Prior Rating	Eligible	Bond Form	Redemption Provisions: Regular Price	Regular (Begins) Thru	Sinking Fund Price	Sinking Fund (Begins) Thru	Refund/Other Restriction Price	Refund/Other Restriction (Begins) Thru	Outst'g (Mil $)	Underwriting Firm	Underwriting Year	Price Range 1995 High	Price Range 1995 Low	Mo. End Price Sale(s) or Bid	Curr. Yield	Yield to Mat.
El Paso Electric (Texas) *(Cont.)*																				
1st 6¾s '98	§Mn	**D**	5/92	CCC	Z	R			Default 5-1-92 int[1]				24.8	E3	'68	103	90⅝	103	....	Flat
1st 7¾s 2001	§Ao	**D**	4/92	CCC	Z	R			Default 4-1-92 int[1]				15.8	S10	'71	103½	90⅝	103½	....	Flat
1st 9s 2004	§mN	**D**	5/92	CCC	Z	R			Default 5-1-92 int[1]				20.0	K2	'74	104	96⅛	104	....	Flat
1st 10½s 2005	§mN	**D**	5/92	CCC	Z	R			Default 5-1-92 int[1]				15.0	H4	'75	103	97	A103	....	Flat
1st 8½s 2007	§Ao	**D**	4/92	CCC	Z	R			Default 4-1-92 int[1]				25.0	M2	'77	103	90	A103	....	Flat
El Paso Natural Gas	***73a***	***2.71***	***2.93***		***2.87***	***Dc***	***24.50***	***324.0***	***540.0***	***9-30-95***	***768.0***		***1702***	***58.9***						
• SF Deb 8⅝s 2012	Ms	**A–**	5/90	A	X	R	NC	....	100	(3-1-98)	....	....	16.8	M6	'87	108½	102	104¾	8.23	8.09
Deb 8⅝s 2022	Jj15	**A–**			X	R	NC	....	....	....	....	....	258	M6	'92	119⅛	98⅜	119⅛	7.24	7.02
Nts 6.90s '97	Jj15	**A–**			X	R	NC	....	....	....	....	....	100	M6	'92	101¼	97½	101¼	6.81	5.65
Nts 7¾s 2002	Jj15	**A–**			X	R	NC	....	....	....	....	....	215	M6	'92	107¾	95¾	107¾	7.19	6.19
• Nts 9.45s '99	mS	**A–**	5/90	A	X	R	NC	....	....	....	....	....	47.0	M6	'89	109⅛	104¼	109	8.67	6.64
Elizabethtown Water[2]	***74***	***2.04***	***2.84***		***3.12***	***Dc***	***1.12***	***29.80***	***82.30***	***9-30-95***	***142.0***		***384.0***	***51.3***						
Deb 8¾s 2021	aO	**A**			X	BE	106.92	9-30-96	Z100	....	®106.46	9-30-96	27.5		'91	108½	98⅜	107	8.18	8.10
Deb 8s 2022	mS	**A**			X	BE	106.80	8-31-96	Z100	....	®106	8-31-97	15.0	S1	'92	105	90¾	105	7.62	7.56
Deb 7¼s 2028	mN	**A**			X	BE	105.44	(11-1-98)	Z100	(11-1-98)	....	....	50.0	S1	'93	99¼	82	99¼	7.30	7.31
Emerson Electric	***23c***	***12.47***	***10.34***		***14.88***	***Sp***	***213.0***	***4080***	***3489***	***6-30-95***	***★526.0***		***6791***	***29.4***						
Nts 6.30s 2005	mN	**AA+**			X	R	NC	....	....	....	....	....	250	G1	'95	102⅝	99¼	102⅝	6.14	5.94
Empire District Electric	***72a***	***2.92***	***2.74***		***3.06***	***Dc***	***4.32***	***42.10***	***30.10***	***9-30-95***	***195.0***		***422.0***	***46.2***						
1st 5.70s '98	Mn	**A–**	5/94	A	X	R	NC	....	....	....	....	....	23.0	S1	'93	100	92⅝	100	5.70	5.70
1st[3] 8⅛s 2009	mN	**A–**			X	R	NC	....	....	....	....	....	20.0	S1	'94	116⅝	96⅛	116⅝	6.97	6.31
1st 7.60s 2005	Ao	**A–**			X	R	NC	....	....	....	....	....	10.0	S1	'95	108⅝	98⅝	108⅝	7.00	6.35
1st 7½s 2002	jJ	**A–**	5/94	A	X	R	NC	....	....	....	....	....	37.5	S1	'92	107¾	94⅜	107¾	6.96	6.04
1st 7s 2023	aO	**A–**	5/94	A	X	R	103.26	(10-1-03)	....	....	....	....	45.0	S1	'93	99⅜	80¾	99⅜	7.04	7.05
1st 7¾s 2025	Jd	**A–**			X	BE	103.875	(6-1-05)	....	....	....	....	30.0	S1	'95	105⅞	97¾	105⅞	7.32	7.26
1st[4] 7¼s 2028	Jd	**A–**	5/94	A	X	R	104	(6-1-98)	....	....	....	....	14.5	J2	'93	99⅜	82	99⅜	7.30	7.30
Empire Gas Corp[5]	***49***	***△1.58***	***△1.05***		***△d0.24***	***Je***	***0.98***	***18.10***	***14.90***	***9-30-95***	***119.0***		***79.10***	***150.0***						
Sub SF Deb 9s 2007	jD31	**NR**	3/94	CC		R	100	....	100	....	....	....	[6]9.75	Mgr	'83	72	65	65	13.85	15.51
[7]***Empress River Casino Finance***	***25***	***44.00***	***28.96***		***5.84***	***Dc***	***62.20***	***65.30***	***16.10***	***12-31-94***	***151.0***		***187.0***	***81.3***						
[8]Sr[9]Nts[10] 10¾s 2002	Ao	**BB**			Y	R	[11]105.38	(4-1-99)	....	....	[12]Z110	4-1-97	150	D6	'94	103½	86	102	10.54	10.30
Energen Corp	***73b***	***△3.03***	***△3.49***		***△2.95***	***Sp***	***36.70***	***119.0***	***138.0***	***9-30-95***	***132.0***		***307.0***	***43.3***						
Deb[13] 8s 2007	Fa	**A**			X	BE	105	(2-1-97)	....	....	....	....	20.0	J2	'92	107½	92⅜	106⅞	7.49	7.09
Energy Ventures	***49e***	***1.06***	***2.69***		***1.34***	***Dc***	***9.37***	***233.0***	***77.70***	***9-30-95***	***129.0***		***355.0***	***39.2***						
Sr Nts[9]'B' 10¼s 2004	Ms15	**BB–**			Y	BE	103.844	(3-15-99)	....	....	....	....	119	L3	'94	104¾	94	103⅞	9.87	9.55
Engelhard Corp	***14***	***7.33***	***8.11***		***7.44***	***Dc***	***45.00***	***563.0***	***391.0***	***9-30-95***	***212.0***		***1027***	***30.2***						
Nts 10s 2000	jJ15	**A**			X	R	100	(7-15-96)	....	....	....	....	100	G1	'88	104⅛	102⅛	102½	9.76	9.31
Enhance Financial Svcs Grp	***35***	***65.86***	***10.55***		***6.63***	***Dc***				***9-30-95***	***79.80***		***498.0***	***18.4***						
• Deb 6¾s 2003	Ms	**A+**			X	BE	NC	....	....	....	....	....	75.0	S1	'93	No Sale		102⅞	6.56	6.24
Enquirer/Star, Inc[14]	***54b***	***Now Amer Media Operations,see***																		
• Sr Sub Nts[15]Zero Cpn '97	[16]	**B**	9/94	BB–	Y	R	NC	....	....	....	....	....	[6]22.0	S1	'92	No Sale		80	....	16.87
Enron Corp[17]	***73e***	***2.01***	***2.40***		***2.84***	***Dc***	***106.0***	***2017***	***1862***	***9-30-95***	***3425***		***7244***	***47.3***						
Sr Deb 7s 2023	fA15	**BBB+**	12/95	BBB	X	R	102.575	(8-15-03)	....	....	....	....	100	M2	'93	99½	80¾	99½	7.04	7.04
Nts 8.10s '96	jD15	**BBB+**	12/95	BBB	X	R	NC	....	....	....	....	....	150	G1	'94	102⅞	100	102⅜	7.91	5.52
Sr Nts 10s '98	Jd	**BBB+**	12/95	BBB	X	R	NC	....	....	....	....	....	100	D7	'88	110⅛	104	109¾	9.11	5.63
Nts 8½s 2000	Fa	**BBB+**	12/95	BBB	X	BE	100	(2-1-97)	....	....	....	....	150	L3	'95	104	99⅝	103⅜	8.22	7.52
Sr Nts[18] 9.65s 2001	Mn15	**BBB+**	12/95	BBB	X	R	NC	....	....	....	....	....	100	P4	'89	117⅝	105½	117⅝	8.20	5.79
Nts 9⅛s 2003	Ao	**BBB+**	12/95	BBB	X	R	NC	....	....	....	....	....	200	M6	'91	117	102¾	117	7.80	6.18

Uniform Footnote Explanations-See Page 260. Other: [1] Co has made some partial int pyts. [2] Subsid of E'town Corp. [3] (HRO)On 11-1-01 at 100. [4] Death red benefit,ltd,as defined. [5] Was Empire Inc. [6] Incl disc. [7] Gtd by & data of Empress River Casino Corp. [8] Co may red at 100 for Requred Regulatory Redemp. [9] (HRO)On Chge of Ctrl at 101. [10] Gtd by Empress River Casino,et al. [11] 4-1-99. [12] Max $50 red w/proceeds of IPO. [13] (HRO)At 100,ltd as defined. [14] Subsid of American Media Inc. [15] (HRO)On Chge of Ctrl at Default Amt. [16] Due 5-15-97. [17] See InterNorth. [18] (HRO)On 5-15-96 at 100.

Title-Industry Code & Co. Finances (In Italics) / Individual Issue Statistics, Exchange	Ind / Interest Dates	*Fixed Charge Coverage 1992* / S&P Debt Rating	*1993* / Date of Last Rating Change	Prior Rating	*1994* / Eligible	*Year End* / Bond Form	*Cash & Equiv. (Million $)* / Redemption Provisions: Regular Price	*Curr. Assets (Million $)* / Regular (Begins) Thru	*Curr. Liab. (Million $)* / Sinking Fund Price	*Balance Sheet Date* / Sinking Fund (Begins) Thru	*L. Term Debt (Mil $)* / Refund/Other Restriction Price	Refund/Other Restriction (Begins) Thru	*Capital-ization (Mil $)* / Outst'g (Mil $)	*Total Debt % Capital* / Underwriting Firm	Underwriting Year	Price Range 1995 High	Price Range 1995 Low	Mo. End Price Sale(s) or Bid	Curr. Yield	Yield to Mat.
***Enron Corp** (Cont.)*																				
Nts 9⅞s 2003	Jd15	**BBB+**	12/95	BBB	X	R	NC	....	....	....	....	....	100	F1	'88	121¾	108⅛	121¾	8.11	6.19
Nts 7⅝s 2004	mS10	**BBB+**	12/95	BBB	X	R	NC	....	....	....	....	....	200	M2	'92	109⅛	93½	109⅛	6.99	6.25
Nts 6¾s 2004	mS15	**BBB+**	12/95	BBB	X	R	NC	....	....	....	....	....	50.0	S1	'95	103	97⅞	103	6.55	6.30
Nts 7⅛s 2007	Mn15	**BBB+**	12/95	BBB	X	R	NC	....	....	....	....	....	150	G1	'95	106	96⅝	106	6.72	6.37
Nts 6⅞s 2007	aO15	**BBB+**	12/95	BBB	X	R	NC	....	....	....	....	....	100	M2	'95	104⅛	99¾	104⅛	6.60	6.37
Sr Sub Deb 6¾s 2005	jJ	**BBB**	12/95	BBB−	X	R	NC	....	....	....	....	....	200	L3	'93	103	86¾	103	6.55	6.33
Sr Sub Deb 8¼s 2012	mS15	**BBB**	12/95	BBB−	X	R	NC	....	....	....	....	....	150	B5	'92	114⅜	95⅛	114⅜	7.21	6.80
ENSERCH Corp	***73b***	***0.94***	***0.86***		***1.19***	***Dc***	***8.74***	***431.0***	***616.0***	***9-30-95***	***948.0***		***2375***	***49.7***						
Nts 8s '97	Ms15	**BBB**			X	BE	NC	....	....	....	....	....	100	K2	'92	103⅛	99⅜	102⅝	7.80	5.71
Nts 7s '99	fA15	**BBB**			X	BE	NC	....	....	....	....	....	150	F1	'92	103⅜	94¼	103⅜	6.77	5.95
Nts 8⅞s 2001	Ms15	**BBB**			X	BE	103.906	3-14-96	....	....	®101.302	3-14-97	100	K2	'92	105	100⅞	104⅛	8.52	7.89
Nts 6⅜s 2004	Fa	**BBB**			X	BE	NC	....	....	....	....	....	150	L3	'94	99¾	85⅜	99¾	6.39	6.41
Nts 7⅛s 2005	Jd15	**BBB**			X	BE	NC	....	....	....	....	....	150	S5	'95	104⅜	97⅜	104⅜	6.83	6.50
Envirodyne Industries	***52***	***0.56***	***1.62***		***1.03***	***Dc***	***19.40***	***255.0***	***130.0***	***9-28-95***	***530.0***		***663.0***	***81.7***						
Sr Nts 10¼s 2001	jD	**B−**	4/94	NR	Y	R	104	12-31-96	....	....	....	....	219	Reorg	'93	82	72	73½	13.95	17.63
EnviroSource, Inc	***44***	***0.80***	***0.98***		***1.60***	***Dc***	***3.31***	***49.40***	***87.50***	***9-30-95***	***257.0***		***293.0***	***89.4***						
Sr[1]Nts 9¾s 2003	Jd15	**B**	5/95	B−	Y	R	104.875	(6-15-98)	....	....	....	....	220	M6	'93	91½	86½	88½	11.02	12.13
Envirotest Systems	***53***	***1.38***	***1.72***		***1.17***	***Sp***	***25.50***	***40.00***	***29.20***	***6-30-95***	***388.0***		***437.0***	***88.8***						
Sr Nts[2] 9⅛s 2001	Ms15	**B**	9/95	B+	Y	R	103.083	(3-15-98)	....	....	....	....	200	D6	'94	85	54¼	83	10.99	13.80
Sr Sub Nts[2] 9⅝s 2003	Ao	**B−**	8/95	B	Y	R	103.609	(4-1-98)	....	....	....	....	125	D6	'93	79¾	55	72	13.37	16.34
Equifax Inc	***63***	***36.94***	***15.69***		***14.28***	***Dc***	***75.50***	***384.0***	***297.0***	***9-30-95***	***258.0***		***724.0***	***47.4***						
Sr Nts[3] 6½s 2003	Jd15	**A−**			X	R	NC	....	....	....	....	....	200	F1	'93	101½	88⅜	101½	6.40	6.24
Equitable Cos	***35a***	***0.99***	***1.26***		***1.40***	***Dc***				***9-30-95***	***[4]4627***		***8156***	***56.7***						
Sr Nts 9s 2004	jD15	**A+**	10/95	BBB+	X	BE	100	(12-15-99)	....	....	....	....	300	D6	'94	115	99¾	114½	7.86	6.81
Equitable of Iowa	***35a***	***9.58***	***15.18***		***20.19***	***Dc***				***9-30-95***	***281.0***		***994.0***	***28.3***						
Nts 8½s 2005	Fa15	**A**			X	BE	NC	....	....	....	....	....	100	S1	'95	114	99⅝	114	7.46	6.45
Equitable Resources	***73e***	***3.11***	***2.27***		***2.58***	***Dc***	***29.70***	***291.0***	***458.0***	***9-30-95***	***415.0***		***1453***	***48.2***						
Deb 8¼s '96	jJ	**A**	10/94	A+	X	R	NC	....	....	....	....	....	75.0	F1	'86	102¼	100¾	101¼	8.15	5.71
• Deb 7½s '99	jJ	**A**	10/94	A+	X	R	NC	....	....	....	....	....	[5]75.0	F1	'87	100⅝	100⅝	101	7.43	7.17
Deb 9.90s 2013	Ao15	**A**	10/94	A+	X	R	103.65	(4-15-98)	100	(4-15-99)	....	....	75.0	F1	'88	112⅝	107⅞	110¾	8.94	8.68
ERP Operating L.P.	***57***	***n/a***	***n/a***		***2.24***	***Dc***				***12-31-94***	***★1022***		***1782***	***55.8***						
Nts 7.95s 2002	Ao15	**BBB**			X	BE	[6]Z100	....	....	....	....	....	125	M2	'95	106¼	98	106¼	7.48	6.71
F/R[7]Nts[8] 6⅝s '97	QDec22	**BBB**			X	BE	NC	....	....	....	....	....	100	M2	'94	100⅜	97	100¼	6.61	....
Essex Group, Inc[9]	***42b***	***n/a***	***1.89***		***3.15***	***Dc***	***2.38***	***338.0***	***159.0***	***9-30-95***	***402.0***		***543.0***	***79.6***						
Sr Nts[2] 10s 2003	Mn	**B+**			Y	R	103.75	(5-1-98)	....	....	[10]Z109	5-7-96	200	D6	'93	98½	93	98	10.20	10.39
[11]Ethan Allen Inc	***31b***	***△0.91***	***△4.23***		***△4.34***	***Je***	***7.55***	***176.0***	***53.50***	***6-30-95***	***127.0***		***323.0***	***40.3***						
• Sr Nts[1] 8¾s 2001	Ms15	**BB+**	2/95	BB	Y	R	101.458	(3-15-98)	....	....	....	....	75.0	K2	'93	104½	96	s104	8.41	7.80
Exide Corp	***8***	***1.30***	***1.84***		***1.20***	***Mr***	***52.90***	***1384***	***788.0***	***7-2-95***	***1134***		***1729***	***73.8***						
Sr Nts[12] 10¾s 2002	jD15	**BB−**	12/93	B	Y	R	105.375	(12-15-97)	....	....	....	....	150	M6	'92	99	99	105⅝	10.18	9.62
Sr Sub Dfrd[13] Cpn Deb[12] 12¼s 2004	jD15	**B+**	1/95	B	Y	R	100	....	....	....	....	....	[5]110	M6	'92	84	71	84	14.58	15.62
[14]Exxon[15]Capital	***25***	***7.25***	***7.65***		***6.68***		***2537***	***17498***	***18583***	***9-30-95***	***8362***		***50947***	***21.4***						
Gtd[16]Nts 7¾s '96	Fa14	**AAA**			X	R	NC	....	....	....	....	....	250	S1	'91	101⅛	100¼	100¼	7.73	5.57
Gtd[16]Nts 7⅞s '96	Ao15	**AAA**			X	R	NC	....	....	....	....	....	250	B5	'91	101¾	100¼	100⅝	7.83	5.63
Gtd[16]Nts 7⅞s '97	fA15	**AAA**			X	R	NC	....	....	....	....	....	250	M6	'91	104⅛	99½	103¾	7.59	5.43
Gtd[16]Nts 6½s '99	jJ15	**AAA**			X	R	NC	....	....	....	....	....	250	M2	'92	102⅞	93¾	102⅞	6.32	5.59
Gtd[16]Nts 8¼s '99	mN	**AAA**			X	R	NC	....	....	....	....	....	200	S1	'89	108⅞	99⅞	108⅞	7.58	5.64

Uniform Footnote Explanations-See Page 260. Other: [1] Co must offer repurch at 101 on Chge of Ctrl. [2] (HRO)On Chge of Ctrl at 101. [3] (HRO)For a Put Event at 100. [4] Incl current amts. [5] Incl disc. [6] Plus Make-Whole Amt. [7] Int reset qtrly on 3rd Wed of ea Feb,etc. [8] Int to 2-17-96,adj qtrly(3 Mo LIBOR&0.75%). [9] Subsid of BCP/Essex Holdings. [10] Max $67M w/proceeds of Equity Off'g. [11] Gtd by & data of Ethan Allen Interiors. [12] (HRO)On Chge of Ctrl Triggering Event at 101. [13] Int accrues at 12.25% fr 12-15-97. [14] Gtd by & data of Exxon Corp. [15] See Seariver Maritime. [16] Gtd by Exxon Corp.

Title-Industry Code & Co. Finances (In Italics) / Exchange, Individual Issue Statistics	Ind / Interest Dates	Fixed Charge Coverage 1992 / S&P Debt Rating	1993 / Date of Last Rating Change	1994 / Prior Rating	Eligible	Year End / Bond Form	Million $ Cash & Equiv. / Regular Price	Curr. Assets / Regular (Begins) Thru	Curr. Liab. / Sinking Fund Price	Balance Sheet Date / Sinking Fund (Begins) Thru	L. Term Debt (Mil $) / Refund/Other Restriction Price	Refund/Other Restriction (Begins) Thru	Capitalization (Mil $) / Outst'g (Mil $)	Total Debt % Capital / Underwriting Firm	Underwriting Year	Price Range 1995 High	Price Range 1995 Low	Mo. End Price Sale(s) or Bid	Curr. Yield	Yield to Mat.
***Exxon Capital** (Cont.)*																				
Gtd[1]Nts 7.45s 2001	jD15	**AAA**			X	R	NC	....	....	....	....	....	250	U1	'91	108⅜	95⅞	108⅜	6.87	5.77
Gtd[1]Nts 6⅝s 2002	fA15	**AAA**			X	R	NC	....	....	....	....	....	250	U1	'92	104⅜	90⅞	104⅜	6.35	5.82
• Gtd[1]Nts 6s 2005	jJ	**AAA**			X	BE	NC	....	....	....	....	....	250	L3	'93	100¾	85	s100¾	5.96	5.90
EZ Communication	***12b***	*[2]1.07*	*[3]3.08*	*2.76*		*Dc*	*1.53*	*22.90*	*7.55*	*6-30-95*	*115.0*		*155.0*	*74.3*						
Sr Sub Nts[4] 9¾s 2005	jD	**B–**			Y	R	104.875	(12-1-00)	....	....	[5]Z109.75	11-30-98	150	C5	'95	99⅛	93½	93½	10.43	10.83
Fairchild Corp[6]	***2b***	*△0.33*	*△0.35*	*△0.27*		*Je*	*56.60*	*280.0*	*179.0*	*9-30-95*	*503.0*		*630.0*	*87.5*						
• Sr Sub Nts 12¼s '96	Ms15	**B–**			Y	R	100	....	....	....	....	....	57.0	D7	'86	102	96	99⅜	12.33	14.78
• Sub Deb[7] 12s 2001	aO15	**B–**	11/87	NR	Y	R	100	....	100	(10-15-97)	....	....	[8]128	Co.	'87	100½	83	97⅞	12.26	12.52
• Sub Deb 13⅛s 2006	Ms15	**B–**			Y	R	101.31	3-14-96	100	(3-15-97)	....	....	38.0	D7	'86	98	75	s97¼	13.50	13.62
• Jr Sub Deb 13s 2007	Ms	**B–**	11/87	NR	Y	R	102.20	2-29-96	100	(3-1-98)	....	....	24.7	Co.	'87	99⅞	75⅛	s98	13.27	13.34
Fairchild Indus[9]	***3***	*△1.12*	*△0.92*	*△0.69*		*Je*	*2.41*	*191.0*	*134.0*	*6-30-95*	*249.0*		*418.0*	*63.3*						
Sr Sec Nts[4] 12¼s '99	fA	**B**			Y	R	102	(8-1-97)	....	....	....	....	125	C4	'92	106	98	104	11.78	10.69
• Sub SF Deb 9¾s '98	Ao	**B–**	6/89	B	Y	R	100	....	100	....	....	....	3.00	Exch.	'78	98	90	97	10.05	11.28
Fairfield Manufacturing	***41g***	*n/a*	*0.74*	*0.93*		*Dc*	*0.17*	*57.10*	*43.30*	*9-30-95*	*114.0*		*122.0*	*95.1*						
Sr Sub Nts[10] 11⅜s 2001	jJ	**CCC+**			Y	R	104.25	(7-1-98)	....	....	[11]Z100	....	85.0	M2	'93	97⅜	93	97⅜	11.68	12.04
Family Restaurants Inc	***27b***	*n/a*	*0.29*	*[12]0.72*		*Dc*	*9.55*	*38.50*	*295.0*	*9-24-95*	*480.0*		*473.0*	*123.0*						
Sr[10]Nts 9¾s 2002	Fa	**CCC**	8/95	CCC+	Y	R	102.786	(2-1-99)	....	....	[13]Z109	2-1-97	300	D6	'94	77¾	46	55	17.73	24.25
Sr Sub[14]Disc Nts[15] 10⅞s 2004	Fa	**CCC–**	8/95	CCC	Y	R	104.078	(2-1-99)	....	....	[16]Z110	2-1-97	[8]150	D6	'94	58½	8	10½	....	Flat
Farm Fresh Inc	***59c***	*0.96*	*0.36*	*0.45*		*Dc*	*1.16*	*72.40*	*69.30*	*9-9-95*	*263.0*		*161.0*	*165.0*						
Sr Nts[17] 12¼s 2000	aO	**B–**	9/94	B+	Y	R	103.50	(10-1-97)	100	(10-1-99)	....	....	165	B9	'92	97½	82	82	14.94	18.02
[18]Farmers Group	***35b***	*n/a*	*n/a*	*n/a*		*Dc*				*12-31-94*	*613.0*									
Nts 8¼s '96	jJ15	**A**	9/95	A+	X	R	NC	....	....	....	....	....	200	M6	'86	102	100	101¼	8.15	5.87
Federal Express	***70b***	*△1.81*	*△3.03*	*△4.49*		*My*	*207.0*	*1730*	*1737*	*8-31-95*	*1319*		*3900*	*40.4*						
SF Deb[19] 9⅝s 2019	aO15	**BBB**	4/91	BBB+	X	R	103.7805	(10-15-99)	100	(10-15-00)	....	....	100	K2	'89	116⅛	101	114⅞	8.38	8.19
Sr Nts 9¾s '96	Mn15	**BBB**	4/91	BBB+	X	R	NC	....	....	....	....	....	150	K2	'89	103¼	101½	101½	9.61	5.63
Sr Nts[20] 10s '99	Ao15	**BBB**	4/91	BBB+	X	R	NC	....	....	....	....	....	100	K2	'89	112⅛	104⅞	112⅛	8.92	5.89
Nts 6¼s '98	Ao15	**BBB**			X	BE	NC	....	....	....	....	....	100	M2	'93	101	93⅝	101	6.19	5.77
Nts 9⅞s 2002	Ao	**BBB**			X	BE	NC	....	....	....	....	....	175	M2	'92	118⅜	106⅜	118⅜	8.34	6.27
Nts 9.65s 2012	Jd15	**BBB**			X	BE	NC	....	....	....	....	....	300	M2	'92	126¾	105⅛	126¾	7.61	6.90
Fed'l Home Loan Mtg	***25b***	....	....	....		*Dc*	*207.0*	*1730*	*1737*	*8-31-95*	*1319*		*3900*	*40.4*						
Nts[21] 7¾s '97	Jj27	**NR**			X	BE	NC	....	....	....	....	....	500	N2	'95	102⅞	99⅞	102⅝	7.56	5.30
Nts[22] 7⅛s '99	jJ21	**AAA**			X	BE	NC	....	....	....	....	....	1500	G1	'94	105¼	96⅛	105⅜	6.77	5.47
Nts[22] 6.93s 2000	mS5	**NR**			X	BE	■100	(9-5-97)	....	....	....	....	500	G1	'95	102½	100	102⅝	6.75	6.28
Nts[23] 6.10s 2000	mN27	**NR**			X	BE	[24]100	(11-27-98)	....	....	....	....	100	G1	'95	101⅛	100	101⅛	6.03	5.83
F/R[25]Deb[26] '96	QMar24	**NR**			X	BE	NC	....	....	....	....	....	50.0	S1	'94	99⅞	99½	99⅞	....	....
F/R[27]Deb[22] 3.71s '96	QMar25	**NR**			X	BE	NC	....	....	....	....	....	200	L3	'93	100	98¼	99⅝	3.72	....
F/R[28]Deb[22] 5.9375s '96	[29]Qjan6	**NR**			X	BE	NC	....	....	....	....	....	34.0	M2	'94	100	99¾	100	5.94	....
F/R[25]Deb[21] '96	QMay6	**NR**			X	BE	NC	....	....	....	....	....	100	G1	'93	100¼	99¾	100⅛	....	....
[30]F/R[31]Deb[22] 5.623s '96	QJun6	**NR**			X	BE	NC	....	....	....	....	....	200	M2	'94	100	99¾	100	5.62	....
F/R[32]Deb[22] '96	QJun7	**NR**			X	BE	NC	....	....	....	....	....	100	M2	'94	100⅜	99¾	100¼	....	....
F/R[25]Deb[21] '96	QJun20	**NR**			X	BE	NC	....	....	....	....	....	100	S1	'94	100	99¼	99⅝	....	....
F/R[33]Deb[21] '96	QOct4	**NR**			X	BE	NC	....	....	....	....	....	263	M2	'94	100	99⅛	99½	....	....
F/R[34]Deb[21] '96	Oct28	**NR**			X	BE	NC	....	....	....	....	....	100	M2	'93	100	98⅜	99⅛	....	....
F/R[35]Deb[21] '96	[36]Nov4	**NR**			X	BE	NC	....	....	....	....	....	100	M2	'93	100	96½	99⅜	....	....
F/R[37]Deb[26] '97	QJan14	**NR**			X	BE	NC	....	....	....	....	....	100	S1	'94	100⅝	99⅝	100⅜	....	....
F/R[38]Deb[21] 4.1502s '97	QAug26	**NR**			X	BE	■100	....	....	....	....	....	100	M2	'93	100	94⅝	98½	4.21	....

Uniform Footnote Explanations-See Page 260. Other: [1] Gtd by Exxon Corp. [2] Fiscal Mar'93. [3] 9 Mo Dec,'93. [4] (HRO)On Chge of Ctrl at 101. [5] Max $50M red w/proceeds of Pub Eq Off'gs. [6] Was Banner Indus. [7] Indenture has Consol Net Worth requirements. [8] Incl disc. [9] Controlled by Fairchild Corp. [10] Co must offer repurch at 101 on Chge of Ctrl. [11] On Chge of Ctrl,plus Applicable Premium. [12] 11 Mo Dec'94. [13] Max $105M red w/proceeds of Pub Eq Off'g. [14] Co must offer repur at 101(Accreted Val)Chge of Ctrl. [15] Int accrues at 10.875% fr 2-1-97. [16] Max $52.5M red w/proceeds of Pub Eq Off'g. [17] (HRO)On Chge in Ctrl at 101. [18] Subsid & data of B.A.T. Indus p.l.c. [19] (HRO)At 100 for Restructuring Event,as defined. [20] (HRO)Under certain circumstances at 100. [21] Issued in min denom $10T. [22] Issued in min denom $5T. [23] issued in min denom $5T. [24] Red in whole or in part. [25] Int adj weekly. [26] Issued in min denom $100T. [27] Int 3-25-96,adj qtrly aft. [28] Int to 1-6-96,adj qtrly aft(3 Mo LIBOR&0.20%). [29] Due 3-25-96. [30] Int(max 24%)to 3-1-96,adj qtrly aft. [31] Int to be 3 Mo LIBOR minus 0.25%. [32] Int(max 24%)adj daily. [33] Int(max 24%)adj weekly. [34] Int(min 3%,max 24%)adj & paid monthly. [35] Int(min 3%,max 24%)adj monthly. [36] Int paid monthly. [37] Int add weekly. [38] Int(max 10%)to 1-26-96,adj mthly aft.

Title-Industry Code & Co. Finances (In Italics)	I n d	Fixed Charge Coverage 1992	1993	1994	Year End	Million $ Cash & Equiv.	Curr. Assets	Curr. Liab.	Balance Sheet Date	L. Term Debt (Mil $)	Capital-ization (Mil $)	Total Debt % Capital

Exchange ↓ Individual Issue Statistics	Interest Dates	S&P Debt Rating	Date of Last Rating Change	Prior Rating	Eligible ↓	Bond Form	Redemption Provisions: Regular Price	Regular (Begins) Thru	Sinking Fund Price	Sinking Fund (Begins) Thru	Refund/Other Restriction Price	Refund/Other Restriction (Begins) Thru	Outst'g (Mil $)	Underwriting Firm	Underwriting Year	Price Range 1995 High	Price Range 1995 Low	Mo. End Price Sale(s) or Bid	Curr. Yield	Yield to Mat.
Fed'l Home Loan Mtg *(Cont.)*																				
F/R[1]Deb[2] 4.65s '98	QMar11	**NR**			X	BE	NC	....	....	....	....	....	100	M2	'93	99⅞	93¾	98¼	4.73	....
F/R[3]Deb[2] 4.60s '98	QApr8	**NR**			X	BE	NC	....	....	....	....	....	100	L3	'93	99⅞	93½	98⅛	4.69	....
F/R[2]Deb[4] 6¼s '98	QMay13	**NR**			X	BE	NC	....	....	....	....	....	100	L3	'93	101⅛	99½	101	6.19	....
F/R[5]Deb[2] '98	[6]Qmay24	**NR**			X	BE	NC	....	....	....	....	....	100	M2	'93	100⅞	99½	100⅜	....	....
F/R[7]Deb[2] '98	QJun30	**NR**			X	BE	NC	....	....	....	....	....	75.0	L3	'93	101	99½	100¾	....	....
F/R[8]Deb[9] 3.93s '98	fA18	**NR**			X	BE	NC	....	....	....	....	....	50.0	M2	'93	99⅝	95¾	97⅝	4.03	....
F/R[10]Deb[11] 4.0271s '98	QSep	**NR**			X	BE	■100	....	....	....	....	....	100	M2	'93	100	96⅛	99½	4.05	....
F/R[12]Deb[13] '98	[14]Nov9	**NR**			X	BE	NC	....	....	....	....	....	150	M1	'93	100	96⅞	98⅛	....	....
F/R[15]Deb[11] 4.77s '99	QMar2	**NR**			X	BE	NC	....	....	....	....	....	85.0	M1	'94	100	99¼	100	4.77	....
F/R[16]Deb[2] 4.08s '99	Mn21	**NR**			X	BE	NC	....	....	....	....	....	100	M2	'92	99⅞	95¼	97¼	4.20	....
F/R[17]Deb[2] 5s 2000	QMar10	**NR**			X	BE	NC	....	....	....	....	....	200	M2	'93	99¾	89⅝	97⅜	5.13	....
F/R[18]Deb[2] 5s 2000	QMar18	**NR**			X	BE	NC	....	....	....	....	....	100	M2	'93	100	96⅜	97⅜	5.13	....
F/R[19]Deb[9] 5⅜s 2000	Ao13	**NR**			X	BE	*■100	....	....	....	....	....	100	M2	'93	99¾	91⅞	98¾	5.44	....
F/R[20]Deb[2] 5s 2003	[21]mn18	**NR**			X	BE	NC	....	....	....	....	....	50.0	M2	'93	99⅞	88⅜	94⅞	5.27	....
Step-Up Deb[2] 5.17s '96	Fa16	**NR**			X	BE	■100	....	....	....	....	....	100	G1	'93	100	98⅜	100	5.17	5.07
Step-Up([22]Reset)Deb[11] 6.70s '96	QMar22	**NR**			X	BE	■100	....	....	....	....	....	250	M2	'95	101	99¾	100	6.70	....
Step-Up([23]Reset[11])Deb 6.55s '96	QApr26	**NR**			X	BE	■100	....	....	....	....	....	100	D3	'95	101	99⅞	100	6.55	....
Step-Up Deb[9] 4.70s '96	jJ26	**NR**			X	BE	■100	....	....	....	....	....	100	M2	'93	99¾	98⅜	99¾	4.71	5.14
Step-Up Deb[2] 5s '96	fA5	**NR**			X	BE	■100	....	....	....	....	....	100	U1	'93	100	97⅞	99⅞	5.01	5.26
Step-Up Deb[2] 5.10s '96	fA23	**NR**			X	BE	■100	....	....	....	....	....	250	G1	'93	99⅝	95¾	99⅝	5.12	5.68
Step-Up Deb[2] 4¾s '96	fA26	**NR**			X	BE	■100	....	....	....	....	....	200	L3	'93	99⅞	99½	99⅝	4.77	5.33
Step-Up Deb[2] 4.45s '96	aO25	**NR**			X	BE	■100	....	....	....	....	....	100	G1	'93	99⅜	94	99⅜	4.48	5.23
Step-Up Deb[2] 4.53s '96	mN	**NR**			X	BE	■100	....	....	....	....	....	50.0	L3	'93	99⅜	94	99⅜	4.56	5.29
Step-Up Deb[2] 5.10s '97	Jj13	**NR**			X	BE	■100	....	....	....	....	....	100		'94	99½	93¼	99½	5.13	5.60
Step-Up Deb[2] 4.82s '97	Jj20	**NR**			X	BE	■100	....	....	....	....	....	100	L3	'94	99½	93	99½	4.84	5.31
Step-Up Deb[2] 4.80s '97	Jj20	**NR**			X	BE	■100	....	....	....	....	....	100	L3	'94	99⅜	92¾	99⅜	4.83	5.41
Step-Up Deb[2] 5¼s '97	Fa14	**NR**			X	BE	■100	....	....	....	....	....	100	M2	'94	100	94⅛	100	5.25	5.24
Step-Up Deb[2] 5.03s '97	Fa24	**NR**			X	BE	■100	....	....	....	....	....	100	G1	'94	99½	93⅝	99½	5.06	5.48
Step-Up Deb[2] 5¼s '97	jJ21	**NR**			X	BE	■100	....	....	....	....	....	100		'93	99⅜	93⅞	99⅜	5.28	5.67
Step-Up Deb[9] 5.20s '97	fA4	**NR**			X	BE	■100	....	....	....	....	....	150	M2	'93	99½	93½	99⅝	5.22	5.51
Step-Up Deb[9] 6.10s '98	Jd23	**CALL**	12/95	NR		BE			Called 1-12-96 at 100				100	M2	'93	100¾	98¼	100	6.10	Call
Step-Up Deb[2] 6.05s '98	Jd30	**CALL**	12/95	NR		BE			Called 1-12-96 at 100				200	K2	'93	100⅛	92½	100	6.05	Call
Step-Up Deb[2] 5.80s '98	jJ7	**NR**			X	BE	■100	....	....	....	....	....	300	G1	'93	100¾	98⅛	100¾	5.76	5.48
Step-Up Deb[2] 5.76s '98	jJ13	**NR**			X	BE	■100	....	....	....	....	....	200	L3	'93	99⅞	89½	99⅞	5.77	5.81
Step-Up Deb[2] 5.825s '98	fA11	**NR**			X	BE	■100	....	....	....	....	....	100		'93	99⅞	98⅞	99⅞	5.83	5.87
Step-Up Deb[2] 5.55s '98	mS7	**NR**			X	BE	■100	....	....	....	....	....	100	L3	'93	99¼	90⅛	99¼	5.59	5.85
Step-Up Deb[2] 5.55s '98	mS8	**NR**			X	BE	■100	....	....	....	....	....	100	G1	'93	99¼	90¼	99¼	5.59	5.85
Step-Up Deb[9] 5½s '98	mS22	**NR**			X	BE	■100	....	....	....	....	....	250	M2	'93	100¼	90¾	100¼	5.49	5.40
Step-Up Deb[9] 5½s '98	aO6	**NR**			X	BE	■100	....	....	....	....	....	50.0	M2	'93	100⅛	88½	100⅛	5.49	5.45
Step-Up Deb 5.30s '98	aO26	**NR**			X	BE	■100	....	....	....	....	....	150	L3	'93	99¾	89⅞	99¾	5.31	5.39
Step-Up Deb[2] 5½s '98	aO30	**NR**			X	BE	■100	....	....	....	....	....	50.0	S1	'93	100⅛	89¾	100⅛	5.49	5.45
Step-Up Deb[2] 5¾s '98	mN16	**NR**			X	BE	■100	....	....	....	....	....	200		'93	100⅞	89	100⅞	5.70	5.42
Step-Up Deb[11] 5.63s '99	Jj5	**NR**			X	BE	■100	....	....	....	....	....	100	D3	'94	100½	90⅜	100½	5.60	5.45
Step-Up([24]Reset)Deb[9] 5s '99	Jj12	**NR**			X	BE	■100	....	....	....	....	....	125	M2	'94	100¼	90¼	100¼	4.99	....
Step-Up([25]Reset)Deb[2] 4.65s '99	Jj18	**NR**			X	BE	■100	....	....	....	....	....	50.0	M6	'94	100⅝	88¼	100⅝	4.62	....
Step-Up([26]Reset)Deb[2] 4¾s '99	Fa2	**NR**			X	BE	■100	(2-2-96)	....	....	....	....	125	M2	'94	100⅝	90¼	100⅝	4.72	....

Uniform Footnote Explanations-See Page 260. Other: [1] Int(min 4.65%,max 24%)to 3-10-96,adj qtrly aft. [2] Issued in min denom $5T. [3] Int(min 4.60%,max24%)to 1-8-96,adj qtrly aft. [4] Int(max 24%)to 2-13-96,adj qtrly aft. [5] Int(max 24%)adj daily. [6] Due 5-26-98. [7] Int adj daily. [8] Int(max 24%)to 1-18-96,adj mthly aft. [9] Issued in min denom $10T. [10] Int(min 3.5%)thru 2-28-96,adj qtrly aft. [11] Issued in min denom $100T. [12] Int adj on 9th day of ea month. [13] Issued in min denom $500T. [14] Int pd monthly. [15] Int(min 4%)to 1-2-96,adj mthly aft. [16] Int(max 24%)to 1-21-96,adj mthly adj. [17] Int(min 5%,max24%)to 3-9-96,adj qtrly aft. [18] Int(min5%,max24%)to 3-18-96,adj qtrly aft. [19] Int(5.375%-24%)to 4-12-96,adj semi-anly aft. [20] Int(min 5%,max 24%)to 5-17-96,adj semi-anly aft. [21] Due 5-19-03. [22] Int to 12-22-95,6.95% aft. [23] Int to 1-26-96, 7.05% aft. [24] Int to 1-12-96,5.85% aft. [25] Int to 1-18-96,5.70% aft. [26] Int at 4.75% to 2-2-96,5.70% aft.

Title-Industry Code & Co. Finances (In Italics)	Ind	Fixed Charge Coverage 1992	1993	1994	Year End	Million $ Cash & Equiv.	Curr. Assets	Curr. Liab.	Balance Sheet Date	L. Term Debt (Mil $)	Capital-ization (Mil $)	Total Debt % Capital

Individual Issue Statistics Exchange ↓	Interest Dates	S&P Debt Rating	Date of Last Rating Change	Prior Rating	Eligible ↓	Bond Form	Redemption Provisions: Regular Price	Regular (Begins) Thru	Sinking Fund Price	Sinking Fund (Begins) Thru	Refund/Other Restriction Price	Refund/Other Restriction (Begins) Thru	Outst'g (Mil $)	Underwriting Firm	Underwriting Year	Price Range 1995 High	Price Range 1995 Low	Mo. End Price Sale(s) or Bid	Curr. Yield	Yield to Mat.
***Fed'l Home Loan Mtg** (Cont.)*																				
Step-Up([1]Reset)Deb[2] 5.08s '99	Fa15	**NR**			X	BE	■100	(2-15-96)	....	....	....	....	150	L3	'94	100⅝	90½	100⅝	5.05	....
Step-Up([3]Reset)Deb[2] 4.95s '99	Fa23	**NR**			X	BE	■100	(2-23-96)	....	....	....	....	100	G1	'94	100¾	89	100¾	4.91	....
Step-Up Deb[2] 5.60s '99	AnMar	**NR**			X	BE	■100	....	....	....	....	....	100	S1	'94	99	89⅞	99	5.66	5.95
Step-Up([4]Reset[5])Deb 5.70s '99	Ms24	**NR**			X	BE	■100	....	....	....	....	....	100	S1	'94	100¾	93⅞	100¾	5.66	....
Step-Up([6]Reset[7])Deb[2] 6.72s '99	Ao28	**NR**			X	BE	[8]*100	....	....	....	....	....	75.0	S1	'94	100⅜	99½	100	6.72	....
[9]Step-Up([10]Reset[11])Deb 6.18s '99	Ao28	**NR**			X	BE	[8]*100	....	....	....	....	....	50.0	S1	'94	101	95¼	100	6.18	....
Step-Up([12]Reset)Deb[2] 6¾s '99	Mn6	**NR**			X	BE	■100	(5-6-96)	....	....	....	....	50.0	M2	'94	101⅛	95	101⅛	6.67	....
Step-Up Deb[2] 6.55s 2000	Jd30	**NR**			X	BE	■100	....	....	....	....	....	50.0		'93	100⅞	90⅝	100⅞	6.49	6.32
Step-Up([13]Reset)Deb[14] 5⅛s 2000	fA4	**NR**			X	BE	■100	....	....	....	....	....	150	M2	'93	100⅛	88¾	100⅛	5.12	....
Step-Up([2]Reset)Deb[15] 5½s 2000	mS20	**NR**			X	BE	■100	....	....	....	....	....	100		'93	100¾	86⅝	100¾	5.46	....
Step-Up Deb[2] 6⅜s 2000	mN22	**NR**			X	BE	■100	....	....	....	....	....	50.0		'93	101¼	84⅞	101¼	6.30	6.07
[16]Step-Up([17]Reset[18])Deb [2] 7s 2003	[19]jj13	**CALL**	12/95	NR		BE			Called 1-13-96 at 100				25.0	S1	'94	100⅞	94⅝	100	7.00	Call
[16]Step-Up([20]Reset[21])Deb [2] 7s 2003	[19]jj13	**CALL**	12/95	NR		BE			Called on 1-13-96 at 100				25.0	S1	'94	100⅞	95¾	100	7.00	Call
Step-Up([13]Reset)Deb[22] 4.90s 2003	mS3	**NR**			X	BE	■100	(9-3-96)	....	....	....	....	150	G1	'93	100⅝	84⅞	100⅝	4.87	....
Step-Up([23]Reset)Deb[11] 6.58s 2004	Ao6	**NR**			X	BE	[8]*100	(4-6-96)	....	....	....	....	75.0	S1	'94	101	95¾	101	6.51	....
Step-Up([23]Reset)Deb[2] 6.60s 2004	Ao6	**NR**			X	BE	[8]*100	(4-6-96)	....	....	....	....	25.0	S1	'94	101	95¾	101	6.53	....
(Amort[24])Deb[11] 4.692s '97	[25]Dec29	**NR**			X	BE	NC	....	....	....	....	....	50.0	M2	'92	98⅝	91¼	98¾	4.76	....
Deb[2] 6.65s '96	Jan2	**NR**			X	BE	NC	....	....	....	....	....	17.0		'94	100⅜	99⅛	100	6.65	Mat.
Deb[2] 4.10s '96	Jj18	**NR**			X	BE	■100	....	....	....	....	....	100	G1	'94	99⅞	96⅝	100	4.10	Mat.
Deb[2] 7.24s '96	[26]Feb5	**NR**			X	BE	NC	....	....	....	....	....	185	M6	'95	100⅞	99⅝	100¼	7.23	5.21
Deb[2] 6.79s '96	Fa20	**NR**			X	BE	NC	....	....	....	....	....	400	S1	'95	100½	100	100¼	6.78	5.33
Deb[2] 6.84s '96	Fa28	**NR**			X	BE	NC	....	....	....	....	....	1000	M6	'95	100⅝	100	100¼	6.83	5.37
Deb 4.44s '96	Ms8	**NR**			X	BE	■100	....	....	....	....	....	100	M2	'93	99¾	96¼	99⅞	4.45	5.52
Deb[2] 4.40s '96	Ms11	**NR**			X	BE	■100	....	....	....	....	....	125	P4	'93	99¾	96⅛	99¾	4.41	5.59
Deb 4.87s '96	Ms11	**NR**			X	BE	NC	....	....	....	....	....	300		'94	99⅞	96⅞	99⅞	4.88	5.42
Deb[2] 4.675s '96	Ms25	**NR**			X	BE	■100	....	....	....	....	....	100	G1	'93	99¾	96⅜	99⅞	4.69	5.54
Deb[2] 4.58s '96	Ms29	**NR**			X	BE	■100	....	....	....	....	....	200	G1	'93	100	96½	99¾	4.59	Call
Deb 4.55s '96	Ao	**NR**			X	BE	■100	....	....	....	....	....	200	M2	'93	99⅝	96½	99¾	4.56	5.60
Deb[2] 6.45s '96	Ao8	**NR**			X	BE	NC	....	....	....	....	....	250	L3	'95	100½	100	100⅜	6.43	5.34
Deb[2] 5.72s '96	Ao25	**NR**			X	BE	■100	(4-25-96)	....	....	....	....	100	L3	'94	100	97¾	100⅛	5.72	5.57
Deb[2] 4.35s '96	Ao29	**NR**			X	BE	■100	....	....	....	....	....	250	P4	'93	99½	96¾	99⅝	4.37	5.55
Deb[2] 5.98s '96	Mn10	**NR**			X	BE	NC	....	....	....	....	....	50.0	L3	'94	100⅛	97⅞	100¼	5.97	5.32
Deb[2] 6.21s '96	Mn13	**NR**			X	BE	NC	....	....	....	....	....	250	M6	'95	100⅜	100	100⅜	6.19	5.31
Deb[2] 6.005s '96	[27]Mn13	**NR**			X	BE	NC	....	....	....	....	....	250	M5	'95	100¼	100	100¼	5.99	5.28
Deb[2] 4.60s '96	Jd28	**NR**			X	BE	■100	....	....	....	....	....	200	L3	'93	99½	95¾	99⅝	4.62	5.44
Deb[2] 6.06s '96	jJ	**NR**			X	BE	NC	....	....	....	....	....	75.0	C5	'94	100¼	97¾	100¼	6.04	5.55
Deb[2] 13½s '96	jJ24	**NR**			X	BE	NC	....	....	....	....	....	110		'95	107⅝	104½	104½	12.92	5.35
Deb[2] 4.37s '96	jJ26	**NR**			X	BE	■100	....	....	....	....	....	100	P4	'93	99⅜	95⅛	99½	4.39	5.37
Deb[2] 5.73s '96	QAug1	**NR**			X	BE	■100	....	....	....	....	....	70.0	M2	'95	101	100	100	5.73	5.72
Deb[2] 4.65s '96	fA9	**NR**			X	BE	■100	....	....	....	....	....	100	G1	'93	99⅞	99⅜	99⅝	4.67	5.38
Deb[2] 5.645s '96	fA15	**NR**			X	BE	NC	....	....	....	....	....	200	M6	'95	101	99⅞	100¼	5.63	5.27
Deb[2] 6.27s '96	fA16	**NR**			X	BE	NC	....	....	....	....	....	15.0	M6	'94	100½	97¾	100⅝	6.23	5.29
Deb[2] 13½s '96	fA28	**NR**			X	BE	NC	....	....	....	....	....	140		'95	107¼	105¼	105¼	12.83	5.32
Deb[13] 4.20s '96	mS9	**NR**			X	BE	■100	....	....	....	....	....	100	M2	'93	99⅛	94⅜	99¼	4.23	5.35
Deb[2] 6.185s '96	mS9	**NR**			X	BE	NC	....	....	....	....	....	55.0	C5	'94	100½	97½	100⅝	6.15	5.29
Deb[2] 4.22s '96	mS13	**NR**			X	BE	■100	....	....	....	....	....	100	S1	'93	99⅛	94⅜	99¼	4.25	5.40

Uniform Footnote Explanations-See Page 260. Other: [1] Int at 5.08% to 2-15-96,6% aft. [2] Issued in min denom $5T. [3] Int at 4.95% to 2-23-96,6.15% aft. [4] Int at 5.70% to 3/24/96. [5] Int 6.35% 3/24/96-97,7.35% 3/24/97-98,8.35% aft. [6] Int to 4-28-96,adj anly aft. [7] Int adj ea 4-28: '96,6.97%, '97,7.97%, '98,8.97%. [8] Red in whole or in part. [9] Int to 4-28-96,6.43% aft to 4-28-97. [10] Int at 6.68% fr 4-28-97,incr 1% anly aft. [11] Issued in min denom $100T. [12] Int to 5-6-96,7.375% aft. [13] Issued in min denom $10T. [14] Int to 8-3-96,6.20% aft to 8-3-98,6.60% aft. [15] Int thru 9-19-98,6.50% aft. [16] Int to 7-13-96,adj ea 7-13 aft. [17] Int adj ea 7-13:7.25%'96,7.65%'97,8.05%'98. [18] Int adj 8.45%'00,9.20%'01,9.95%'02,10.70% aft. [19] Due 7-14-03. [20] Int adj ea 7-13:7.35%'96, 7.70%'97, 8.05%'98. [21] Int adj 8.30%'00, 8.55%'01, 8.80%'02, 9.35% aft. [22] Int to 9-2-96,6.70% aft. [23] Int to 4-6-96,incr 0.50% ea 4-6 aft. [24] Princ pyts due 29th day of ea month. [25] Due 12-29-97:int pd mthly ea 29th day. [26] Due 2-5-96:int pd 8-3-95 & 2-5-96. [27] Int pd 11-12-95 & 5-15-96.

Title-Industry Code & Co. Finances (In Italics)	*Ind*	*Fixed Charge Coverage 1992*	*1993*	*1994*	*Year End*	*Million $ Cash & Equiv.*	*Curr. Assets*	*Curr. Liab.*	*Balance Sheet Date*	*L. Term Debt (Mil $)*	*Capital-ization (Mil $)*	*Total Debt % Capital*

Exchange ↓ Individual Issue Statistics	Interest Dates	S&P Debt Rating	Date of Last Rating Change	Prior Rating	Eligible ↓	Bond Form	Redemption Provisions: Regular Price	Regular (Begins) Thru	Sinking Fund Price	Sinking Fund (Begins) Thru	Refund/Other Restriction Price	Refund/Other Restriction (Begins) Thru	Outst'g (Mil $)	Underwriting Firm	Underwriting Year	Price Range 1995 High	Price Range 1995 Low	Mo. End Price Sale(s) or Bid	Curr. Yield	Yield to Mat.
***Fed'l Home Loan Mtg** (Cont.)*																				
Deb[1] 4.20s '96	mS20	**NR**			X	BE	■100	....	....	....	....	....	200	G1	'93	99⅛	94¼	99¼	4.24	5.39
Deb[1] 4.26s '96	mS27	**NR**			X	BE	■100	....	....	....	....	....	150	M6	'93	99⅛	94¼	99¼	4.29	5.33
Deb[1] 4.29s '96	aO7	**NR**			X	BE	■100	....	....	....	....	....	100	G1	'93	99⅛	94¼	99¼	4.32	5.33
Deb[1] 6.715s '96	aO11	**NR**			X	BE	NC	....	....	....	....	....	30.0		'94	101⅛	98¼	101⅛	6.64	5.26
Deb[1] 6.755s '96	aO14	**NR**			X	BE	NC	....	....	....	....	....	10.0	M5	'94	101⅛	98⅛	101⅛	6.68	5.35
Deb[1] 4⅛s '96	aO21	**NR**			X	BE	NC	....	....	....	....	....	250		'93	99	94	99⅛	4.16	5.31
Deb[1] 6.71s '96	aO25	**NR**			X	BE	NC	....	....	....	....	....	15.0	P1	'94	101⅛	98⅛	101⅛	6.64	5.28
Deb[1] 6.78s '96	aO28	**NR**			X	BE	NC	....	....	....	....	....	10.0	C5	'94	101⅜	98¼	101¼	6.70	5.25
Deb[1] 5.53s '96	mN	**NR**			X	BE	NC	....	....	....	....	....	100	S1	'95	100¼	100	100¼	5.52	5.21
Deb[2] 7.01s '96	mN12	**NR**			X	BE	NC	....	....	....	....	....	100	M2	'94	101⅝	98½	101½	6.91	5.29
Deb[1] 4⅝s '96	mN15	**NR**			X	BE	■100	....	....	....	....	....	300	M6	'93	99¼	94½	99⅜	4.66	5.39
Deb[2] 4.64s '96	jD9	**NR**			X	BE	■100	....	....	....	....	....	300	M2	'93	99⅜	94¼	99⅜	4.67	5.32
Deb[1] 7.69s '96	jD16	**NR**			X	BE	NC	....	....	....	....	....	250	M6	'94	102⅝	99⅞	102¼	7.52	5.29
Deb[1] 7.88s '96	jD20	**NR**			X	BE	NC	....	....	....	....	....	350	G1	'94	102⅞	99⅞	102½	7.69	5.28
Deb[1] 7.73s '97	[3]jj4	**NR**			X	BE	NC	....	....	....	....	....	200	G1	'94	102½	99¾	102½	7.55	5.27
Deb[1] 7.815s '97	[4]jj11	**NR**			X	BE	NC	....	....	....	....	....	50.0	D6	'95	102½	99	102⅝	7.62	5.21
Deb[1] 7.91s '97	[4]jj12	**NR**			X	BE	NC	....	....	....	....	....	150	M2	'95	102⅝	99	102¾	7.71	5.25
Deb[1] 7.86s '97	[5]jj12	**NR**			X	BE	NC	....	....	....	....	....	125	M2	'95	103	99	102⅝	7.66	5.27
Deb[1] 7.81s '97	jj18	**NR**			X	BE	NC	....	....	....	....	....	50.0	M6	'95	103	99	102⅝	7.62	5.30
Deb[1] 7.86s '97	[6]jj19	**NR**			X	BE	NC	....	....	....	....	....	400	S5	'95	102⅝	102¼	102¾	7.66	5.25
Deb[1] 7.82s '97	Jj24	**NR**			X	BE	NC	....	....	....	....	....	165	M6	'95	103	99	102⅝	7.62	5.29
Deb[1] 4.525s '97	Jj27	**NR**			X	BE	■100	....	....	....	....	....	200	L3	'94	99	93⅝	99⅛	4.57	5.46
Deb[1] 8.05s '97	[3]jj5	**CALL**	12/95	NR		BE			Called 1-5-96 at 100				200	G1	'94	101⅛	99⅞	100⅛	8.05	Call
Deb 4.78s '97	Fa10	**NR**			X	BE	■100		....	....	....	....	300	0	'94	99⅛	98⅛	99¼	4.82	5.51
Deb[1] 5.19s '97	Ms3	**NR**			X	BE	■100	....	....	....	....	....	100	G1	'94	99⅝	94⅜	99¾	5.20	5.43
Deb[1] 5.515s '97	Ms17	**NR**			X	BE	■100	....	....	....	....	....	300	S5	'94	100	95⅛	100⅛	5.51	5.48
Deb[1] 5.47s '97	Ms21	**NR**			X	BE	NC	....	....	....	....	....	200	M6	'94	100⅛	95⅛	100¼	5.46	5.28
Deb[1] 5.17s '97	Ms24	**NR**			X	BE	■100	....	....	....	....	....	200	G1	'93	99⅝	94½	99¾	5.19	5.43
Deb[1] 6.10s '97	Ao11	**NR**			X	BE	■100	....	....	....	....	....	250	M2	'94	100⅝	94¼	100⅝	6.07	5.66
Deb[1] 6.10s '97	Ao11	**CALL**	12/95	NR		BE			Called 1-2-96 at 100				250	M2	'94	100	96	100	6.10	Call
Deb[1] 6.20s '97	Ao28	**NR**			X	BE	NC	....	....	....	....	....	100		'94	101⅛	96¼	101¼	6.13	5.28
Deb[1] 7.175s '97	Mn15	**NR**			X	BE	NC	....	....	....	....	....	25.0	M5	'94	102⅛	98⅛	102¼	7.02	5.47
Deb[1] 6.51s '97	Jd8	**NR**			X	BE	NC	....	....	....	....	....	50.0	M6	'94	101⅝	96⅞	101¾	6.40	5.30
Deb[1] 6.47s '97	jJ7	**NR**			X	BE	NC	....	....	....	....	....	125	L3	'94	101⅝	96¾	101¾	6.36	5.28
Deb[1] 6.275s '97	fA18	**NR**			X	BE	■100	(2-19-96)	....	....	....	....	116	M2	'95	101	100	100⅛	6.27	6.23
Deb[1] 5.57s '97	fA20	**NR**			X	BE	NC	....	....	....	....	....	100	G1	'92	100⅜	94½	100½	5.55	5.30
Deb[1] 6.425s '97	fA26	**NR**			X	BE	■100	(2-26-96)	....	....	....	....	100	M2	'95	100⅜	100	100¼	6.41	6.28
Deb[1] 6.505s '97	mS8	**NR**			X	BE	NC	....	....	....	....	....	20.0	M5	'94	101¾	96½	101⅞	6.39	5.36
Deb[1] 6.83s '97	mS29	**NR**			X	BE	NC	....	....	....	....	....	150	C5	'94	102⅜	97¼	102½	6.67	5.36
Deb[1] 7.11s '97	aO13	**NR**			X	BE	NC	....	....	....	....	....	13.0	M6	'94	102⅞	97¾	102⅞	6.91	5.40
Deb[1] 7.37s '97	aO17	**NR**			X	BE	■100	....	....	....	....	....	25.0	P4	'94	101	98½	100	7.37	7.36
Deb[1] 8.42s '98	[7]jj10	**CALL**	12/95	NR		BE			Call 1-12-96 at 100				146	S1	'94	105	99	100⅛	8.41	Call
Deb[1] 8.20s '98	Jj16	**NR**			X	BE	■100	(1-17-97)	....	....	....	....	250	M2	'94	103¼	99⅞	102¾	7.99	6.77
Deb[1] 8.08s '98	[8]fa7	**NR**			X	BE	■100	(2-7-96)	....	....	....	....	200	B5	'95	106	99½	100½	8.04	7.81
Deb[1] 7.44s '98	Ms16	**NR**			X	BE	■100	(3-6-96)	....	....	....	....	100	M2	'95	101	100	100⅜	7.42	7.28
Deb[1] 7.36s '98	Ms5	**NR**			X	BE	■100	(3-5-96)	....	....	....	....	200	L3	'95	100⅞	100	100¼	7.35	7.26

Uniform Footnote Explanations-See Page 260. Other:[1] Issued in min denom $5T. [2] Issued in min denom $10T. [3] Due 1-6-97. [4] Due 1-13-97. [5] Due 1-15-97. [6] Due 1-21-97. [7] Due 1-12-98. [8] Due 2-9-98.

Title-Industry Code & Co. Finances (In Italics)	Ind	Fixed Charge Coverage 1992	1993	1994	Year End	Million $ Cash & Equiv.	Curr. Assets	Curr. Liab.	Balance Sheet Date	L. Term Debt (Mil $)	Capital-ization (Mil $)	Total Debt % Capital

Exchange ↓ Individual Issue Statistics	Interest Dates	S&P Debt Rating	Date of Last Rating Change	Prior Rating	Eligible ↓	Bond Form	Redemption Provisions: Regular Price	Regular (Begins) Thru	Sinking Fund Price	Sinking Fund (Begins) Thru	Refund/Other Restriction Price	Refund/Other Restriction (Begins) Thru	Outst'g (Mil $)	Underwriting Firm	Underwriting Year	Price Range 1995 High	Price Range 1995 Low	Mo. End Price Sale(s) or Bid	Curr. Yield	Yield to Mat.
***Fed'l Home Loan Mtg** (Cont.)*																				
Deb[1] 7.35s '98	Ms9	**NR**			X	BE	■100	(3-9-96)	....	....	....	....	125	F2	'95	100⅞	99⅞	100⅜	7.33	7.20
Deb[1] 5.19s '98	Ms11	**NR**			X	BE	■100	....	....	....	....	....	200	S1	'93	99⅛	91⅞	99¼	5.23	5.58
Deb 5.275s '98	Ms11	**NR**			X	BE	■100	....	....	....	....	....	100	M2	'93	99	93⅞	99⅛	5.33	5.75
Deb 5.40s '98	Ms16	**NR**			X	BE	■100	....	....	....	....	....	200	M2	'93	99¼	92½	99⅜	5.44	5.73
Deb 5.39s '98	Ao8	**NR**			X	BE	■100	(4-8-96)	....	....	....	....	70.0	M2	'93	99⅜	92	99½	5.42	5.65
Deb[1] 6.905s '98	Ao13	**NR**			X	BE	NC	....	....	....	....	....	125	U1	'95	103¼	100	103⅜	6.68	5.34
Deb[1] 5.31s '98	Ao29	**NR**			X	BE	■100	....	....	....	....	....	200	L3	'93	99¼	92	99⅜	5.35	5.62
Deb 5.23s '98	Mn18	**NR**			X	BE	■100	....	....	....	....	....	100	M2	'93	98⅝	91⅝	98¾	5.30	5.81
Deb[1] 6.77s '98	Mn20	**NR**			X	BE	■100	(5-20-96)	....	....	....	....	100	M2	'95	101	100	100¾	6.73	6.47
Deb[1] 5.18s '98	fA26	**NR**			X	BE	■100	....	....	....	....	....	100	M6	'93	98⅝	90¾	98¾	5.25	5.70
Deb[1] 4.95s '98	mS9	**NR**			X	BE	■100	....	....	....	....	....	150	L3	'93	98⅛	89¾	98⅛	5.04	5.71
Deb[1] 4.77s '98	mS14	**NR**			X	BE	■100	....	....	....	....	....	200	S1	'93	98	89½	98⅛	4.86	5.53
Deb[2] 4¾s '98	mS17	**NR**			X	BE	■100	(9-17-96)	....	....	....	....	200	M2	'93	97¾	89½	97¾	4.86	5.65
Deb[1] 6.29s '98	mS18	**NR**			X	BE	■100	(9-18-96)	....	....	....	....	150	L3	'95	100¾	99⅞	100⅞	6.24	5.94
Deb[1] 6.23s '98	mS25	**NR**			X	BE	■100	(9-25-96)	....	....	....	....	100	M6	'95	100⅝	100	100⅝	6.19	5.99
Deb[1] 6.28s '98	aO2	**NR**			X	BE	■100	(10-2-96)	....	....	....	....	100	G1	'95	100¾	99⅞	100⅞	6.23	5.94
Deb[1] 6.035s '98	mN6	**NR**			X	BE	■100	(11-6-96)	....	....	....	....	130	M2	'95	100⅝	100	100¾	6.00	5.78
Deb[1] 5.18s '98	mN18	**NR**			X	BE	■100	(11-18-96)	....	....	....	....	300		'93	98⅝	90⅜	98¾	5.25	5.68
Deb[1] 6.07s '98	mN20	**NR**			X	BE	■100	(11-20-96)	....	....	....	....	500	G1	'95	100½	99⅞	100⅝	6.03	5.84
Deb[1] 5.37s '98	jD7	**NR**			X	BE	■100	....	....	....	....	....	200	G1	'93	99⅛	90⅝	99¼	5.42	5.68
Deb[1] 5s '98	jD15	**NR**			X	BE	NC	....	....	....	....	....	125	S1	'93	98¾	90	98⅞	5.06	5.44
Deb[1] 5.39s '98	jD23	**NR**			X	BE	■100	(12-23-96)	....	....	....	....	200	G1	'93	99⅜	90⅞	99½	5.42	5.61
Deb 5.19s '99	Jj20	**NR**			X	BE	■100	(1-20-97)	....	....	....	....	300		'94	98½	90	98⅝	5.27	5.72
Deb[2] 5.34s '99	Jj25	**NR**			X	BE	■100	....	....	....	....	....	150	M2	'94	99	90⅜	99⅛	5.39	5.68
Deb[1] 5.57s '99	Fa22	**NR**			X	BE	■100	....	....	....	....	....	100	S1	'94	99½	90⅞	99½	5.60	5.74
Deb[1] 5.94s '99	Ms8	**NR**			X	BE	■100	....	....	....	....	....	150	G1	'94	100½	92	100⅝	5.91	5.74
Deb[1] 7.70s '99	Ms16	**NR**			X	BE	■100	(3-16-96)	....	....	....	....	100	S5	'95	101	100	100⅜	7.67	7.56
Deb[1] 6.06s '99	Ms15	**NR**			X	BE	■100	....	....	....	....	....	100	S1	'94	100½	92⅜	100⅛	6.06	6.05
Deb[1] 6.07s '99	Ms15	**NR**			X	BE	■100	....	....	....	....	....	200	L3	'94	100½	92¾	100⅛	6.07	6.06
Deb[1] 6.14s '99	Ms18	**NR**			X	BE	■100	(3-18-96)	....	....	....	....	200	L3	'94	100¼	92⅜	100⅛	6.13	6.10
Deb[1] 6.19s '99	Ms23	**NR**			X	BE	■100	....	....	....	....	....	200	G1	'94	99¾	94¼	99⅞	6.20	6.25
Deb[1] 6.39s '99	Ao5	**NR**			X	BE	■100	(4-5-96)	....	....	....	....	200	G1	'94	100¾	93⅜	100¼	6.38	6.31
Deb 6.55s '99	Ao19	**NR**			X	BE	NC	....	....	....	....	....	250		'94	103¼	94⅜	103⅜	6.34	5.43
Deb[1] 7.14s '99	Jd28	**NR**			X	BE	■100	(6-28-96)	....	....	....	....	100	S1	'94	101⅛	95⅞	100⅞	7.08	6.88
Deb[1] 6.46s '99	fA3	**NR**			X	BE	■100	....	....	....	....	....	200	M2	'92	100	95⅜	100⅛	6.46	6.44
Deb[1] 6.52s '99	fA10	**NR**			X	BE	■100	....	....	....	....	....	150	F1	'92	100¾	98¼	100⅛	6.51	6.48
Deb[1] 7.33s '99	fA23	**NR**			X	BE	■100	(8-23-96)	....	....	....	....	65.0	M2	'94	101½	96¼	101⅛	7.25	6.97
Deb[1] 6.30s '99	fA25	**NR**			X	R	■100	....	....	....	....	....	200	G1	'92	100¼	92⅞	100⅜	6.28	6.21
Deb[2] 7.31s '99	mS3	**NR**			X	BE	■100	(9-3-96)	....	....	....	....	100	M2	'94	101¼	96⅛	101⅛	7.23	6.97
Deb[1] 7.188s '99	mS15	**NR**			X	BE	■100	(9-15-97)	....	....	....	....	300	M2	'94	103	95¾	102½	7.01	6.43
Deb[1] 7.42s '99	mS23	**NR**			X	BE	■100	(9-23-97)	....	....	....	....	125	G1	'94	103	96½	103	7.20	6.50
Deb 5.94s '99	mS21	**NR**			X	BE	NC	....	....	....	....	....	100	G1	'92	101¼	91⅝	101¼	5.87	5.56
Deb[1] 7½s '99	aO6	**NR**			X	BE	■100	(10-6-97)	....	....	....	....	100	M6	'94	103⅛	96⅞	103¼	7.27	6.53
Deb 6.18s '99	aO13	**NR**			X	BE	■100	....	....	....	....	....	100	M6	'92	100⅝	91⅞	100⅛	6.18	6.17
Deb[1] 7.61s '99	aO20	**NR**			X	BE	■100	(10-20-97)	....	....	....	....	75.0	M2	'94	104½	97½	104½	7.28	6.27
Deb 6.55s 2000	Jj4	**NR**			X	BE	NC	....	....	....	....	....	150	M2	'92	103⅛	93⅜	103¼	6.35	5.64

Uniform Footnote Explanations-See Page 260. Other: [1] Issued in min denom $5T. [2] Issued in min denom $10T.

Title-Industry Code & Co. Finances (In Italics)	Ind	Fixed Charge Coverage 1992	1993	1994	Year End	Million $ Cash & Equiv.	Curr. Assets	Curr. Liab.	Balance Sheet Date	L. Term Debt (Mil $)	Capital-ization (Mil $)	Total Debt % Capital

Individual Issue Statistics Exchange	Interest Dates	S&P Debt Rating	Date of Last Rating Change	Prior Rating	Eligible	Bond Form	Redemption Provisions: Regular Price	Regular (Begins) Thru	Sinking Fund Price	Sinking Fund (Begins) Thru	Refund/Other Restriction Price	Refund/Other Restriction (Begins) Thru	Outst'g (Mil $)	Underwriting Firm	Underwriting Year	Price Range 1995 High	Price Range 1995 Low	Mo. End Price Sale(s) or Bid	Curr. Yield	Yield to Mat.
***Fed'l Home Loan Mtg** (Cont.)*																				
Deb[1] 8.60s 2000	Jj26	NR			X	BE	■100	(1-26-97)	....	....	....	....	250	M2	'95	104	99	103½	8.31	7.59
Deb[1] 6.44s 2000	Jj28	NR			X	BE	NC	....	....	....	....	....	150	G1	'93	102⅞	93¼	102⅞	6.26	5.64
Deb[1] 6.33s 2000	Fa16	NR			X	BE	■100	(2-16-96)	....	....	....	....	250	L3	'93	100	92½	100⅛	6.33	6.31
Deb[1] 6.09s 2000	Ms	NR			X	BE	■100	(3-1-96)	....	....	....	....	100	S1	'93	100	91½	100⅛	6.08	6.06
Deb[1] 5⅞s 2000	Ms15	NR			X	BE	■100	(3-15-96)	....	....	....	....	100	L3	'93	100	90⅜	100⅛	5.87	5.86
Deb[1] 5⅞s 2000	Ms22	NR			X	BE	NC	....	....	....	....	....	150	L3	'93	100⅞	90⅝	101	5.82	5.62
Deb[1] 6.09s 2000	Ms22	NR			X	BE	■100	(3-22-96)	....	....	....	....	100	G1	'93	100¾	91	100⅞	6.04	5.87
Deb[1] 6.16s 2000	Ms29	NR			X	BE	■100	(3-29-96)	....	....	....	....	100	S1	'93	100½	91¼	100⅛	6.15	6.12
Deb[1] 6.02s 2000	Ao5	NR			X	BE	■100	(4-5-96)	....	....	....	....	100	G1	'93	100½	90⅝	100⅝	5.98	5.86
Deb[1] 5.90s 2000	Ao21	NR			X	BE	■100	(4-21-97)	....	....	....	....	200		'93	100⅛	89⅞	100¼	5.89	5.86
Zero Cpn Deb[1] 2000	[2]	NR			X	BE	NC	....	....	....	....	....	100	G1	'93	65	65	A65	....	10.09
Deb[1] 6.395s 2000	Mn16	NR			X	BE	NC	....	....	....	....	....	175	G1	'95	102⅞	99	103	6.21	5.63
Deb[1] 7.19s 2000	Mn17	NR			X	BE	■100	(5-17-96)	....	....	....	....	150	M2	'95	101	99⅞	100⅝	7.15	7.03
Deb[1] 6.54s 2000	Mn19	NR			X	BE	NC	....	....	....	....	....	125	G1	'95	103¾	100	103⅞	6.30	5.55
Deb[1] 5.76s 2000	Jd9	NR			X	BE	NC	....	....	....	....	....	100	M6	'95	100¾	96⅝	100⅞	5.71	5.54
Deb[1] 6.385s 2000	Jd13	NR			X	BE	■100	(6-13-97)	....	....	....	....	100		'95	101	98⅛	101	6.32	6.12
Deb[1] 5.905s 2000	Jd13	NR			X	BE	NC	....	....	....	....	....	150	G1	'95	101	97⅛	101⅛	5.84	5.63
Deb[1] 7.13s 2000	jJ24	NR			X	BE	■100	....	....	....	....	....	25.0	D6	'95	100⅛	99	99⅞	7.14	7.16
Deb[1] 5.55s 2000	mS7	NR			X	BE	■100	....	....	....	....	....	100	M6	'93	98⅜	87⅜	98½	5.64	5.94
Deb[1] 5.27s 2000	mS20	NR			X	BE	■100	(9-20-96)	....	....	....	....	200	S5	'93	98⅛	86⅝	98¼	5.37	5.71
Deb[1] 5.40s 2000	mN	NR			X	BE	■100	(11-1-96)	....	....	....	....	350	M6	'93	98⅜	87⅛	98⅜	5.49	5.79
Deb[1] 5.69s 2000	mN29	NR			X	BE	■100	(11-29-96)	....	....	....	....	80.0	S1	'93	99¼	88	99⅜	5.73	5.85
Deb[3] 5⅞s 2000	jD13	NR			X	BE	■100	(12-13-96)	....	....	....	....	100	M2	'93	100⅜	89¼	100½	5.85	5.77
Deb[1] 5.69s 2001	Jj24	NR			X	BE	■100	(1-24-97)	....	....	....	....	100	L3	'94	99⅛	87¾	99¼	5.73	5.87
Deb[1] 6.095s 2001	Fa23	NR			X	BE	■100	....	....	....	....	....	150	S1	'94	100⅛	88¾	100¼	6.09	6.06
Deb[3] 6.35s 2001	Ms7	NR			X	BE	■100	....	....	....	....	....	150	M2	'94	100½	89⅞	100⅛	6.35	6.34
Deb[1] 6.54s 2001	Ms21	NR			X	BE	■100	(3-21-97)	....	....	....	....	200	M6	'94	101⅛	91	101⅛	6.47	6.28
Deb[1] 6.73s 2001	Ms21	NR			X	BE	■100	....	....	....	....	....	100	S1	'94	100¾	91⅝	100⅛	6.73	6.71
Deb[1] 6.78s 2001	Ms28	NR			X	BE	■100	(3-28-96)	....	....	....	....	150	L3	'94	100½	92	100¼	6.76	6.72
Deb[1] 7.68s 2001	Mn23	NR			X	BE	■100	(5-23-97)	....	....	....	....	75.0	M2	'94	102⅝	95¾	102⅝	7.49	7.09
Deb[1] 7.265s 2001	Jd22	NR			X	BE	■100	(6-22-98)	....	....	....	....	75.0	G1	'94	103½	94⅞	103⅝	7.02	6.48
Deb[1] 7s 2001	fA2	NR			X	BE	■100	(2-2-96)	....	....	....	....	100		'95	100¼	99⅛	100¼	6.99	6.96
Deb[1] 7.66s 2001	fA15	NR			X	BE	■100	(8-15-97)	....	....	....	....	40.0	L3	'94	102⅞	95⅝	103	7.44	7.02
Deb[1] 7.525s 2001	mS12	NR			X	BE	■100	(9-12-97)	....	....	....	....	100	M5	'94	103	95⅝	103⅛	7.30	6.86
Deb[1] 8.18s 2001	aO17	NR			X	BE	■100	(10-17-97)	....	....	....	....	25.0	L3	'94	104⅛	98	104¼	7.85	7.28
Deb[1] 8.10s 2001	aO29	NR			X	BE	■100	(10-29-97)	....	....	....	....	25.0		'94	103⅞	97¼	104	7.79	7.25
Deb[1] 8.12s 2001	aO29	NR			X	BE	■100	(10-29-97)	....	....	....	....	10.0		'94	104	97⅜	104	7.81	7.26
Deb[1] 8.33s 2001	mN16	NR			X	BE	■100	(11-16-97)	....	....	....	....	25.0		'94	105	99¾	105	7.94	7.29
Deb[1] 8.40s 2001	mN30	NR			X	BE	■100	(11-30-98)	....	....	....	....	35.0		'94	107¼	100⅜	107⅜	7.83	6.87
Deb[1] 8.45s 2001	jD7	NR			X	BE	■100	(12-7-98)	....	....	....	....	45.0	M6	'94	108⅜	99⅞	108½	7.79	6.70
Deb[1] 8.41s 2001	jD7	NR			X	BE	■100	(12-7-98)	....	....	....	....	30.0	M6	'94	106⅞	100	107	7.86	6.96
Deb[1] 8.515s 2002	[4]jj13	NR			X	BE	■100	(1-13-98)	....	....	....	....	50.0	D6	'95	105½	100	105⅝	8.06	7.35
Deb[1] 7.05s 2002	Mn15	NR			X	BE	■100	(5-15-98)	....	....	....	....	200	M2	'95	102¾	99⅛	102⅞	6.86	6.50
Deb[1] 7.24s 2002	Mn15	NR			X	BE	■100	(5-15-98)	....	....	....	....	110	M2	'95	103¾	100	103⅞	6.98	6.50
Deb[1] 6.99s 2002	Mn24	NR			X	BE	■100	(5-24-99)	....	....	....	....	100	U1	'95	103⅛	99¾	103¼	6.78	6.38
Deb[1] 6.825s 2002	mS18	NR			X	BE	■100	(9-18-98)	....	....	....	....	100	M2	'95	102⅞	100	103	6.63	6.28

Uniform Footnote Explanations-See Page 260. Other: [1] Issued in min denom $5T. [2] Due 5-15-00. [3] Issued in min denom $10T. [4] Due 1-14-02.

Title-Industry Code & Co. Finances (In Italics)	Ind	Fixed Charge Coverage 1992	1993	1994	Year End	Million $ Cash & Equiv.	Curr. Assets	Curr. Liab.	Balance Sheet Date	L. Term Debt (Mil $)	Capital-ization (Mil $)	Total Debt % Capital

Exchange ↓ Individual Issue Statistics	Interest Dates	S&P Debt Rating	Date of Last Rating Change	Prior Rating	Eligible ↓	Bond Form	Redemption Provisions — Regular Price	Regular (Begins) Thru	Sinking Fund Price	Sinking Fund (Begins) Thru	Refund/Other Restriction Price	Refund/Other Restriction (Begins) Thru	Outst'g (Mil $)	Underwriting Firm	Underwriting Year	Price Range 1995 High	Price Range 1995 Low	Mo. End Price Sale(s) or Bid	Curr. Yield	Yield to Mat.
***Fed'l Home Loan Mtg** (Cont.)*																				
Deb 7.12s 2003	Jj22	**NR**			X	BE	■100	....	....	....	....	....	100	B5	'93	100½	91½	100⅛	7.11	7.10
Deb[1] 7.05s 2003	Jj29	**NR**			X	BE	■100	....	....	....	....	....	250	L3	'93	100⅝	91¾	100¾	7.00	6.93
Deb 6.78s 2003	Fa12	**NR**			X	BE	■100	(2-12-96)	....	....	....	....	100	S1	'93	100¾	90½	100⅛	6.77	6.76
Deb[1] 6.61s 2003	Ms4	**NR**			X	BE	■100	(3-4-96)	....	....	....	....	100	S1	'93	100¾	89½	100¼	6.60	6.58
Deb[1] 6.44s 2003	Ms10	**NR**			X	BE	■100	(3-10-96)	....	....	....	....	100	L3	'93	100⅞	88½	100¼	6.43	6.41
Deb 6⅜s 2003	Ms11	**NR**			X	BE	■100	(3-11-96)	....	....	....	....	100	M2	'93	100⅜	87¾	100⅛	6.37	6.35
Deb[1] 6.30s 2003	Ms15	**NR**			X	BE	■100	(3-15-96)	....	....	....	....	100	L3	'93	99	88½	99⅛	6.36	6.46
Deb 6.22s 2003	Ms24	**NR**			X	BE	NC	....	....	....	....	....	200	M2	'93	102	88¾	102⅛	6.10	5.87
Deb[1] 6.60s 2003	Ms25	**NR**			X	BE	■100	(3-25-96)	....	....	....	....	100	S1	'93	100½	89	100¼	6.59	6.56
Deb 6.55s 2003	Ao2	**NR**			X	BE	■100	(4-2-98)	....	....	....	....	400		'93	100¾	88¾	100⅞	6.50	6.41
Deb 6.20s 2003	Ao15	**NR**			X	BE	NC	....	....	....	....	....	150	P1	'93	102	88½	102⅛	6.07	5.84
[2]Deb[3] 5.035s 2003	Ao28	**NR**			X	BE	NC	....	....	....	....	....	100	M2	'93	95⅛	81¼	95¼	5.29	5.84
Deb[1] 6.59s 2003	Jd4	**NR**			X	BE	■100	(6-4-96)	....	....	....	....	150	G1	'93	101¼	89⅝	100½	6.56	6.51
Deb[1] 6½s 2003	Jd10	**NR**			X	BE	■100	(6-10-96)	....	....	....	....	100	G1	'93	99¾	87¾	99⅞	6.51	6.54
Deb[1] 6.39s 2003	jJ12	**NR**			X	BE	■100	(7-2-96)	....	....	....	....	200	L3	'93	100⅞	88⅜	100½	6.36	6.32
Deb[1] 6.30s 2003	jJ9	**NR**			X	BE	■100	(7-9-96)	....	....	....	....	150	M2	'93	101½	86¾	101⅝	6.20	6.04
Deb[1] 6.28s 2003	jJ15	**NR**			X	BE	■100	(7-15-96)	....	....	....	....	100	S1	'93	99¼	88	99⅜	6.33	6.40
Deb[3] 6.39s 2003	fA6	**NR**			X	BE	■100	(8-6-96)	....	....	....	....	100	M2	'93	100⅜	87¼	100½	6.36	6.32
Deb[1] 5.74s 2003	mS17	**NR**			X	BE	■100	(9-17-96)	....	....	....	....	200	L3	'93	97⅞	84⅜	98	5.86	6.07
Deb[1] 5.78s 2003	aO22	**NR**			X	BE	■100	(10-22-96)	....	....	....	....	200	G1	'93	97	84	97	5.96	6.27
Deb[1] 6.35s 2003	mN10	**NR**			X	BE	■100	....	....	....	....	....	150	L3	'93	99⅝	87⅜	99¾	6.37	6.40
Deb[1] 6.185s 2003	mN26	**NR**			X	BE	■100	(11-26-96)	....	....	....	....	200	M6	'93	100⅛	86⅝	100¼	6.18	6.16
Deb[1] 5.99s 2003	jD	**NR**			X	BE	NC	....	....	....	....	....	100	L3	'93	101¼	86⅞	101⅜	5.91	5.78
Deb[1] 6.24s 2003	jD16	**NR**			X	BE	■100	(12-16-96)	....	....	....	....	125	M6	'93	100⅞	87	101	6.18	6.09
Deb[1] 6⅜s 2003	jD23	**NR**			X	BE	■100	(12-23-96)	....	....	....	....	200	P1	'93	100⅞	88	99¾	6.40	6.43
Deb[1] 6.19s 2004	Jj21	**NR**			X	BE	■100	(1-21-97)	....	....	....	....	200	S1	'94	98⅝	86¾	98⅝	6.28	6.41
Deb[1] 6.27s 2004	Jj27	**NR**			X	BE	■100	(1-27-97)	....	....	....	....	250	G1	'94	100⅞	86⅞	101	6.21	6.13
Deb[1] 6.485s 2004	Fa18	**NR**			X	BE	■100	(2-18-97)	....	....	....	....	200	G1	'94	101	87⅝	101⅛	6.42	6.32
Deb[1] 6.31s 2004	Fa23	**NR**			X	BE	■100	(2-23-99)	....	....	....	....	200	S1	'94	99⅞	87	100	6.32	6.32
Deb[1] 6.615s 2004	Ms3	**NR**			X	BE	■100	(3-3-97)	....	....	....	....	150	M6	'94	101¼	88¾	101¼	6.53	6.41
Deb[1] 6.81s 2004	Ms11	**NR**			X	BE	■100	(3-11-99)	....	....	....	....	100	L3	'94	103⅛	90	103¼	6.60	6.31
Deb[1] 6.78s 2004	Ms15	**NR**			X	BE	■100	(3-15-99)	....	....	....	....	200	G1	'94	103	89⅞	103⅛	6.58	6.29
Deb[1] 6.93s 2004	Ms17	**NR**			X	BE	■100	(3-17-99)	....	....	....	....	100	G1	'94	103½	90¾	103½	6.70	6.37
Deb[1] 7.05s 2004	Ms24	**NR**			X	BE	■100	(3-24-97)	....	....	....	....	250	G1	'94	101⅝	90⅞	101¾	6.93	6.78
Deb[1] 6.95s 2004	Ms25	**NR**			X	BE	■100	(3-25-99)	....	....	....	....	100	G1	'94	102⅛	90⅞	102⅛	6.81	6.61
Deb[1] 7.03s 2004	Ao5	**NR**			X	BE	■100	(4-5-99)	....	....	....	....	100	M6	'94	103⅜	91⅜	103½	6.79	6.48
Deb[1] 7.29s 2004	Ao7	**NR**			X	BE	■100	(4-7-97)	....	....	....	....	200	L3	'94	101⅞	92¾	102	7.15	6.97
Deb[1] 7.445s 2004	Ao14	**NR**			X	BE	■100	(4-14-99)	....	....	....	....	100		'94	104¾	93⅜	104⅞	7.10	6.68
Deb[1] 7.88s 2004	Ao28	**NR**			X	BE	■100	(4-28-97)	....	....	....	....	200	L3	'94	102⅞	95¼	103	7.65	7.39
Deb[1] 7¼s 2004	Ao28	**NR**			X	BE	NC	....	....	....	....	....	12.0		'94	108⅝	93⅞	108¾	6.67	5.91
Deb[1] 7.54s 2004	Mn3	**NR**			X	BE	■100	(5-3-99)	....	....	....	....	150	G1	'94	104⅞	93⅝	105	7.18	6.75
Deb[1] 7.89s 2004	Mn12	**NR**			X	BE	■100	(5-12-97)	....	....	....	....	100	G1	'94	102⅞	95⅛	102⅞	7.67	7.43
Deb[3] 8.05s 2004	Mn19	**NR**			X	BE	■100	(5-19-97)	....	....	....	....	100	M2	'94	103¼	96	103¼	7.80	7.52
Deb[1] 8.14s 2004	Mn20	**NR**			X	BE	■100	(5-20-97)	....	....	....	....	200	L3	'94	103¼	96½	103⅛	7.89	7.63
Deb[1] 7.74s 2004	Jd	**NR**			X	BE	■100	(6-1-99)	....	....	....	....	200	G1	'94	105⅜	95	105½	7.34	6.87
Deb[1] 7.71s 2004	Jd21	**NR**			X	BE	■100	(6-21-99)	....	....	....	....	100	M5	'94	105⅝	94¾	105¾	7.30	6.82

Uniform Footnote Explanations-See Page 260. Other: [1] Issued in min denom $5T. [2] (HRO)On 4-28-97(99)at 75(100). [3] Issued in min denom $10T.

Title-Industry Code & Co. Finances (In Italics)	Ind	Fixed Charge Coverage 1992	1993	1994	Year End	Million $ Cash & Equiv.	Curr. Assets	Curr. Liab.	Balance Sheet Date	L. Term Debt (Mil $)	Capital-ization (Mil $)	Total Debt % Capital

Exchange ↓ Individual Issue Statistics	Interest Dates	S&P Debt Rating	Date of Last Rating Change	Prior Rating	Eligible ↓	Bond Form	Redemption Provisions: Regular Price	Regular (Begins) Thru	Sinking Fund Price	Sinking Fund (Begins) Thru	Refund/Other Restriction Price	Refund/Other Restriction (Begins) Thru	Outst'g (Mil $)	Underwriting Firm	Underwriting Year	Price Range 1995 High	Price Range 1995 Low	Mo. End Price Sale(s) or Bid	Curr. Yield	Yield to Mat.
***Fed'l Home Loan Mtg** (Cont.)*																				
Deb[1] 7.81s 2004	Jd23	**NR**			X	BE	■100	(6-23-97)	....	....	....	....	50.0	M5	'94	102¾	94½	102⅞	7.60	7.36
Deb[1] 7.97s 2004	jJ7	**NR**			X	BE	■100	(7-7-97)	....	....	....	....	100	M6	'94	104⅜	95½	104¼	7.65	7.30
Deb[1] 7.81s 2004	jJ27	**NR**			X	BE	■100	(7-27-99)	....	....	....	....	125	C5	'94	106	95⅜	106⅛	7.36	6.86
Deb[1] 7.95s 2004	jJ28	**NR**			X	BE	■100	(7-28-97)	....	....	....	....	100	M6	'94	103¼	95⅜	103⅜	7.69	7.41
Deb[1] 7.88s 2004	fA5	**NR**			X	BE	■100	(8-5-97)	....	....	....	....	100	M6	'94	103¼	94⅝	103⅜	7.63	7.35
Deb[1] 7.73s 2004	fA10	**NR**			X	BE	■100	(8-10-99)	....	....	....	....	100	C5	'94	105⅝	94⅝	105¾	7.32	6.85
Deb[1] 7.83s 2004	fA11	**NR**			X	BE	■100	(8-11-97)	....	....	....	....	150	L3	'94	104⅜	94½	104½	7.50	7.13
Deb[1] 8.08s 2004	fA19	**NR**			X	BE	■100	(8-19-97)	....	....	....	....	150	G1	'94	103⅞	95⅝	103½	7.81	7.52
Deb[1] 7.61s 2004	mS	**NR**			X	BE	■100	(9-1-97)	....	....	....	....	235	S1	'94	102⅞	93½	103	7.39	7.14
Deb[1] 7.98s 2004	mS8	**NR**			X	BE	■100	(9-8-97)	....	....	....	....	100	L3	'94	104⅜	94⅞	104½	7.64	7.28
Deb[1] 8.24s 2004	mS23	**NR**			X	BE	■100	(9-23-97)	....	....	....	....	100	L3	'94	104½	97	104¼	7.90	7.56
Deb[1] 8.14s 2004	mS29	**NR**			X	BE	■100	(9-29-99)	....	....	....	....	200	M2	'94	108⅛	97	108⅛	7.53	6.89
Deb[1] 8.19s 2004	aO6	**NR**			X	BE	■100	(10-6-99)	....	....	....	....	250	M5	'94	108⅛	97	108⅛	7.57	6.94
Deb[1] 8.35s 2004	aO6	**NR**			X	BE	■100	(10-6-97)	....	....	....	....	250	L3	'94	104½	97⅛	104½	8.00	7.65
Deb[1] 8.52s 2004	aO14	**NR**			X	BE	■100	(10-14-97)	....	....	....	....	30.0	D3	'94	104¼	97½	104⅜	8.17	7.82
Deb[1] 8.385s 2004	aO20	**NR**			X	BE	■100	(10-20-97)	....	....	....	....	30.0	D3	'94	104½	98¼	104⅝	8.02	7.66
Deb[1] 8.45s 2004	aO20	**NR**			X	BE	■100	(10-20-97)	....	....	....	....	25.0		'94	104⅝	98½	104¾	8.07	7.71
Deb[1] 8.44s 2004	aO27	**NR**			X	BE	■100	(10-27-97)	....	....	....	....	100	G1	'94	104⅝	98⅜	104⅝	8.07	7.71
Deb[1] 8.47s 2004	aO27	**NR**			X	BE	■100	(10-27-97)	....	....	....	....	50.0	M6	'94	104⅝	98½	104⅝	8.10	7.74
Deb[1] 8.80s 2004	mN17	**NR**			X	BE	■100	(11-17-97)	....	....	....	....	100	M2	'94	106¼	101¾	105⅞	8.31	7.87
Deb[1] 8.53s 2004	mN18	**NR**			X	BE	■100	(11-18-99)	....	....	....	....	50.0	M6	'94	108⅞	99	109	7.83	7.15
Deb[1] 8.82s 2004	mN29	**NR**			X	BE	■100	(11-29-97)	....	....	....	....	50.0	D3	'94	106	101⅜	105⅞	8.34	7.90
Deb[1] 8⅝s 2004	mN29	**NR**			X	BE	■100	(11-29-99)	....	....	....	....	50.0	M2	'94	109¼	99¾	109⅜	7.89	7.19
Deb[1] 8.74s 2004	jD8	**NR**			X	BE	■100	(12-8-97)	....	....	....	....	100	L3	'94	106¼	99⅞	106¼	8.23	7.76
Deb[1] 8.61s 2004	jD13	**NR**			X	BE	■100	(12-13-97)	....	....	....	....	100	L3	'94	105¾	99⅞	105⅞	8.14	7.70
Deb[1] 8.115s 2005	Jj31	**NR**			X	BE	NC	....	....	....	....	....	100	M6	'95	115	100	115	7.06	5.95
Deb[1] 7.974s 2005	Ao20	**NR**			X	BE	■100	(4-20-98)	....	....	....	....	100	D3	'95	105⅛	100	105¼	7.58	7.20
Deb[1] 7.90s 2005	Ao27	**NR**			X	BE	■100	(4-27-98)	....	....	....	....	100	L3	'95	105	100	105⅛	7.52	7.14
Deb[1] 7.65s 2005	Mn10	**NR**			X	BE	■100	(5-10-00)	....	....	....	....	100	M6	'95	106	100	106	7.22	6.77
Deb[1] 7.60s 2005	Mn12	**NR**			X	BE	■100	(5-12-98)	....	....	....	....	125	M6	'95	104	99⅞	104⅛	7.31	7.00
Deb[1] 7.225s 2005	Mn17	**NR**			X	BE	■100	(5-17-00)	....	....	....	....	125	L3	'95	105¼	99¾	105¼	6.86	6.47
Deb[1] 7.41s 2005	Mn18	**NR**			X	BE	■100	(5-18-98)	....	....	....	....	100	M2	'95	103¾	99½	103⅞	7.14	6.85
Deb[1] 7.49s 2005	Mn25	**NR**			X	BE	■100	(5-25-98)	....	....	....	....	150	M6	'95	104⅜	100	104½	7.17	6.84
Deb[1] 7.09s 2005	Jd	**NR**			X	BE	■100	(6-1-00)	....	....	....	....	100	L3	'95	104	98⅜	104	6.82	6.51
Deb[1] 7.05s 2005	Jd8	**NR**			X	BE	■100	(6-8-00)	....	....	....	....	100	B5	'95	104¼	98⅝	104⅜	6.76	6.43
Deb[1] 7¼s 2005	Jd8	**NR**			X	BE	■100	(6-8-98)	....	....	....	....	100	G1	'95	102⅝	98¼	102¾	7.06	6.85
Deb[1] 6.83s 2005	Jd15	**NR**			X	BE	■100	(6-15-00)	....	....	....	....	45.0		'95	102½	96⅞	102⅝	6.66	6.46
Deb[1] 7.35s 2005	Jd	**NR**			X	BE	■100	(6-1-98)	....	....	....	....	100	G1	'95	103⅝	99¼	103¾	7.09	6.82
Deb[1] 7.23s 2005	Jd23	**NR**			X	BE	■100	(6-23-98)	....	....	....	....	100	L3	'95	103	98½	103⅛	7.02	6.79
Deb[1] 7.13s 2005	Jd30	**NR**			X	BE	■100	(6-30-98)	....	....	....	....	100	M6	'95	102½	97⅜	102⅝	6.95	6.76
Deb[1] 7.52s 2005	mS	**NR**			X	BE	■100	(9-1-98)	....	....	....	....	100	L3	'95	105⅛	100	105¼	7.15	6.78
Deb[1] 7.01s 2005	jJ13	**NR**			X	BE	■100	(7-13-98)	....	....	....	....	45.0		'95	101⅝	96½	101¾	6.90	6.77
Deb[1] 7.13s 2005	mS15	**NR**			X	BE	■100	(9-15-98)	....	....	....	....	150	G1	'95	103¼	99¾	103⅜	6.90	6.65
Deb[1] 7.155s 2005	mS15	**NR**			X	BE	■100	(9-15-98)	....	....	....	....	100	L3	'95	103¼	100	103⅜	6.93	6.69
Deb[1] 6.785s 2005	mS21	**NR**			X	BE	■100	(9-21-00)	....	....	....	....	100		'95	102⅜	100	102½	6.62	6.44
Deb[1] 7.12s 2005	mS30	**NR**			X	BE	■100	(9-30-98)	....	....	....	....	100	G1	'95	102⅞	99¾	103	6.92	6.71

Uniform Footnote Explanations-See Page 260. Other: [1] Issued in min denom $5T.

Title-Industry Code & Co. Finances (In Italics) / Individual Issue Statistics (Exchange ↓)	Ind / Interest Dates	Fixed Charge Coverage 1992 / S&P Debt Rating	1993 / Date of Last Rating Change	1994 / Prior Rating	Eligible ↓	Year End / Bond Form	Million $ Cash & Equiv. / Redemption Provisions: Regular Price	Curr. Assets / Regular (Begins) Thru	Curr. Liab. / Sinking Fund Price	Balance Sheet Date / Sinking Fund (Begins) Thru	L. Term Debt (Mil $) / Refund/Other Restriction Price	Refund/Other Restriction (Begins) Thru	Capital-ization (Mil $) / Outst'g (Mil $)	Total Debt % Capital / Underwriting Firm	Underwriting Year	Price Range 1995 High	Price Range 1995 Low	Mo. End Price Sale(s) or Bid	Curr. Yield	Yield to Mat.
Fed'l Home Loan Mtg *(Cont.)*																				
Deb[1] 6.89s 2005	aO3	NR			X	BE	■100	(10-3-00)	....	....	....	....	100	M6	'95	103⅝	100	103¾	6.64	6.37
Deb[1] 6.97s 2005	aO3	NR			X	BE	■100	(10-3-00)	....	....	....	....	100	M6	'95	104	100	104⅛	6.70	6.41
Deb[1] 7.06s 2005	aO4	NR			X	BE	■100	(10-4-00)	....	....	....	....	100	M2	'95	104⅞	100	105	6.73	6.38
Deb[1] 7.033s 2005	aO19	NR			X	BE	■100	(10-19-98)	....	....	....	....	120		'95	102⅛	100	102¼	6.88	6.72
Deb[1] 6.66s 2005	jD5	NR			X	BE	■100	(12-5-00)	....	....	....	....	100	G1	'95	101	99¾	101	6.59	6.52
Deb[1] 6.67s 2005	jD14	NR			X	BE	■100	(12-14-98)	....	....	....	....	120	L3	'95	100½	99⅝	100½	6.64	6.60
Deb[1] 6.78s 2005	jD7	NR			X	BE	■100	(12-7-98)	....	....	....	....	100	G1	'95	100⅛	100	100⅛	6.77	6.76
Deb[2] 8s 2007	Ms	NR			X	BE	■101.50	(3-1-99)	....	....	....	....	25.0	C4	'94	108¼	94½	108⅜	7.39	6.92
Deb[1] 7.55s 2007	mN27	NR			X	BE	■100	(11-27-97)	....	....	....	....	100	F1	'92	103⅛	92	103⅛	7.32	7.15
Deb[1] 6.62s 2008	Ms17	NR			X	BE	■100	(3-17-98)	....	....	....	....	100	G1	'93	101¾	84⅜	101⅞	6.50	6.40
Deb[3] 6.20s 2008	mS8	NR			X	BE	■100	(9-8-98)	....	....	....	....	100	M2	'93	98⅞	81⅛	99	6.27	6.32
Deb[1] 6.13s 2008	aO	NR			X	BE	■100	(10-1-98)	....	....	....	....	25.0		'93	99⅝	81⅝	99⅝	6.15	6.17
Deb[1] 6.08s 2008	aO29	NR			X	BE	■100	(10-29-98)	....	....	....	....	100	L3	'93	99½	81⅜	99⅝	6.11	6.13
Deb[1] 6.59s 2008	jD9	NR			X	BE	■100	(12-9-98)	....	....	....	....	100	L3	'93	102⅝	85	102⅝	6.42	6.29
Deb[1] 6.63s 2009	Jj12	NR			X	BE	■100	(1-12-99)	....	....	....	....	100	L3	'94	102⅝	84⅞	102⅝	6.46	6.33
Deb[1] 6.84s 2009	Ms2	NR			X	BE	■100	(3-2-99)	....	....	....	....	100	L3	'94	103	86	103⅛	6.63	6.49
Deb[1] 7.81s 2009	Ao13	NR			X	BE	■100	(4-13-99)	....	....	....	....	50.0	L3	'94	105½	92⅜	105½	7.40	7.16
Deb[1] 8.268s 2009	jJ8	NR			X	BE	■100	(7-8-99)	....	....	....	....	50.0	C5	'94	108⅝	96	108¾	7.61	7.25
Deb[1] 8.325s 2009	jJ15	NR			X	BE	■100	(7-15-99)	....	....	....	....	75.0	C5	'94	108⅛	96⅜	108¼	7.70	7.36
Deb[1] 8s 2009	fA5	NR			X	BE	■100	(8-5-99)	....	....	....	....	50.0	C5	'94	107¼	93¾	107⅜	7.46	7.15
Deb[1] 8.02s 2009	fA24	NR			X	BE	■100	(8-24-99)	....	....	....	....	100	C5	'94	107¾	94⅛	107⅞	7.44	7.11
Deb[1] 8.33s 2009	mS16	NR			X	BE	■100	(9-16-99)	....	....	....	....	50.0	M6	'94	108⅞	95⅝	109	7.65	7.29
Deb[1] 8.28s 2009	mS21	NR			X	BE	■100	(9-21-99)	....	....	....	....	40.0	G1	'94	108⅞	94⅞	109	7.60	7.24
Deb[1] 8.36s 2009	mS23	NR			X	BE	■100	(9-23-99)	....	....	....	....	50.0	L3	'94	108¼	95¾	108⅜	7.72	7.38
Deb[1] 8.29s 2009	mS30	NR			X	BE	■100	(9-30-01)	....	....	....	....	25.0	M2	'94	111⅝	96½	111⅝	7.43	6.96
Deb[1] 8.64s 2009	aO14	NR			X	BE	■100	(10-14-99)	....	....	....	....	20.0	C5	'94	110½	97⅜	110⅝	7.81	7.40
Deb[1] 8.57s 2009	aO26	NR			X	BE	■100	(10-26-99)	....	....	....	....	25.0	C5	'94	109⅜	98⅛	109½	7.83	7.46
Deb[1] 8.60s 2009	aO27	NR			X	BE	■100	(10-27-99)	....	....	....	....	15.0	C4	'94	110⅜	97¾	110½	7.79	7.38
Deb[1] 8.80s 2009	jD7	NR			X	BE	■100	(12-7-99)	....	....	....	....	20.0	S5	'94	110⅝	99⅞	110¾	7.95	7.54
M-T Nts 5.59s '96	Ao5	NR			X	BE	NC	....	....	....	....	....	50.0	M6	'94	100⅛	97⅝	100⅛	5.58	5.05
F/R[4]M-T Nts[1] '96	QJun15	NR			X	BE	NC	....	....	....	....	....	30.0	M5	'94	100⅜	99¾	100⅛	....	....
M-T Nts[1] 7.27s 2007	mS15	NR			X	BE	■100	(9-15-97)	....	....	....	....	67.2	P4	'92	102	89⅜	102	7.13	7.01
M-T Nts[1] 7.14s 2007	jD15	NR			X	BE	NC	....	....	....	....	....	15.0	P4	'92	110⅜	91½	110⅜	6.47	5.92
M-T Nts[1] 6.54s 2008	Jd30	NR			X	BE	■100	(6-30-98)	....	....	....	....	25.0	F1	'93	107	98	100	6.54	6.54
M-T Nts[1] 6½s 2008	fA11	NR			X	BE	■100	(8-11-98)	....	....	....	....	25.0	F1	'93	96⅞	83½	96⅞	6.71	6.87
M-T Nts[1] 7.69s 2022	mS15	NR			X	BE	NC	....	....	....	....	....	5.50	P4	'92	117⅞	93⅞	117⅞	6.52	6.30
Federal Mogul	***8***	***1.85***	***3.22***	***5.82***		***Dc***	***22.20***	***904.0***	***427.0***	***9-30-95***	***467.0***		***1208***	***48.6***						
•SF Deb 7½s '98	Jj15	BBB–	3/94	BB+	X	R	100	....	100	....	....	....	5.29	G1	'73	100	98	98⅛	7.64	8.52
Federal Nat'l Mtg Assoc'n	***25b***	***1.21***	***1.24***	***1.22***		***Dc***				***12-31-94***	***14462***		***266771***	***96.4***						
Deb 6.85s 2000	Mn26	NR				BE	100	(5-26-98)	....	....	....	....	500	M2	'95	102⅝	⅞	102¾	6.67	6.14
Deb[3] 7.40s 2004	jJ	NR				BE	NC	....	....	....	....	....	1500	M2	'94	110¼	94⅞	110⅜	6.71	5.85
Federal Paper Board	***16c***	***2.34***	***1.48***	***1.82***		***Dc***	***0.29***	***438.0***	***337.0***	***9-9-95***	***816.0***		***1961***	***46.1***						
Deb 8⅛s 2002	jJ	BBB–			X	R	NC	....	....	....	....	....	50.0	M5	'92	108⅝	96	108⅝	7.48	6.48
Deb 10s 2011	Ao15	BBB–			X	R	NC	....	....	....	....	....	200	M5	'91	127¾	106¾	127¾	7.83	7.01
Deb 8⅞s 2012	jJ	BBB–			X	R	NC	....	....	....	....	....	125	M5	'92	115⅛	97	115⅛	7.71	7.29
Federal Realty Inv Tr	***57***	***1.20***	***1.51***	***1.66***		***Dc***	***7.18***			***9-30-95***	***469.0***		***803.0***	***58.4***						
Nts 8⅞s 2000	Jj15	BBB+			X	BE	NC	....	....	....	....	....	100	G1	'95	108	99¾	108	8.22	6.59

Uniform Footnote Explanations-See Page 260. Other: [1] Issued in min denom $5T. [2] Issued in min denom $100T. [3] Issued in min denom $10T. [4] Int adj daily.

Title-Industry Code & Co. Finances (In Italics)	*Ind*	*Fixed Charge Coverage 1992*	*1993*	*1994*		*Year End*	*Million $ Cash & Equiv.*	*Curr. Assets*	*Curr. Liab.*	*Balance Sheet Date*	*L. Term Debt (Mil $)*		*Capital-ization (Mil $)*	*Total Debt % Capital*						
Individual Issue Statistics Exchange ↓	Interest Dates	S&P Debt Rating	Date of Last Rating Change	Prior Rating	Eligible ↓	Bond Form	Redemption Provisions Regular Price	Regular (Begins) Thru	Sinking Fund Price	Sinking Fund (Begins) Thru	Refund/Other Restriction Price	Refund/Other Restriction (Begins) Thru	Outst'g (Mil $)	Underwriting Firm	Underwriting Year	Price Range 1995 High	Price Range 1995 Low	Mo. End Price Sale(s) or Bid	Curr. Yield	Yield to Mat.
***Federal Realty Inv Tr** (Cont.)*																				
Nts 6⅝s 2005	jD	**BBB+**			X	BE	NC	....	....	....	....	....	40.0	B8	'95	100¼	100	100¼	6.61	6.59
Federated Dept Stores	***59f***	***n/a***	***n/a***	***2.26***		***Ja***	***158.0***	***7142***	***3882***	***10-28-95***	***5943***		***10909***	***63.1***						
• Sr Nts[1] 10s 2001	Fa15	**BB–**	5/95	BB	Y	BE	NC	....	....	....	....	....	450	G1	'95	110¾	100	s108⅜	9.23	7.97
• Sr Nts[1] 8⅛s 2002	aO15	**BB–**			Y	BE	NC	....	....	....	....	....	400	G1	'95	102⅛	98	100½	8.08	8.02
[2]Ferrellgas,L.P./Finance	***49d***	***△1.03***	***△2.48***	***△1.79***		***Jl***	***14.60***	***154.0***	***136.0***	***10-31-95***	***347.0***		***446.0***	***77.8***						
Sr Nts[3] 10s 2001	fA	**BB–**			Y	R	105	(8-1-98)	....	....	....	....	200	D6	'94	106½	97¾	106	9.43	8.62
F/R[4]Sr Nts[3] 9.0312s 2001	QAug	**BB–**			Y	R	*100	....	100	(8-1-99)	....	....	50.0	D6	'94	100	97½	100	9.03	....
Ferro Corp	***14***	***10.44***	***9.08***	***7.90***		***Dc***	***90.80***	***509.0***	***257.0***	***9-30-95***	***163.0***		***575.0***	***32.5***						
Deb 7⅝s 2013	Mn	**BBB+**			X	R	NC	....	....	....	....	....	25.0	F1	'93	106⅝	89¾	106⅝	7.15	6.96
Deb 7⅜s 2015	mN	**BBB+**			X	R	NC	....	....	....	....	....	25.0	C5	'95	102¾	98¾	102¾	7.18	7.11
Deb 8s 2025	Jd15	**BBB+**			X	R	103.31	(6-15-05)	....	....	....	....	50.0	C5	'95	108¼	96⅛	108¼	7.39	7.31
FHP Int'l Corp	***30***	***△24.92***	***△15.75***	***△6.86***		***Je***	***455.0***	***676.0***	***743.0***	***9-30-95***	***320.0***		***1499***	***23.3***						
Sr Nts 7s 2003	mS15	**BBB–**			X	R	NC	....	....	....	....	....	100	S5	'93	98⅞	85¾	98⅞	7.08	7.19
Fieldcrest Cannon	***68a***	***1.86***	***2.33***	***2.99***		***Dc***	***5.87***	***446.0***	***155.0***	***9-30-95***	***365.0***		***599.0***	***61.1***						
Sr Sub Deb 11¼s 2004	Jd15	**B+**	4/95	B	Y	R	105.625	(6-15-97)	100	(6-15-02)	....	....	85.0	K2	'92	102¾	98	98	11.48	11.63
Figgie Int'l (Hldgs)[5]	***42b***	***2.01***	***d4.62***	***d0.26***		***Dc***	***29.10***	***235.0***	***150.0***	***9-30-95***	***211.0***		***313.0***	***82.7***						
Sr Nts 9⅞s '99	aO	**BB**	2/95	BB+	Y	R	NC	....	....	....	....	....	174	D7	'89	100	81	99¾	9.90	9.95
Sub SF Deb 10⅜s '98	Ao	**B+**	2/95	BB–	Y	R	100	....	100	(4-1-98)	....	....	11.2	H4	'78	99½	82	99½	10.43	10.61
Finlay Enterprises Inc	***37***	***n/a***	***1.33***	....		***Ja***	***2.42***	***216.0***	***205.0***	***10-29-94***	***199.0***		***243.0***	***119.0***						
xsSr[6]Disc Deb[7] 12s 2005	Mn	**B–**			Y	R	103.429	(5-1-98)	....	....	[8]110	4-30-96	[9]98.0	D6	'93	69	56½	66	....	Flat
Finlay Fine Jewelry[10]	***37***	***1.47***	***1.75***	***2.04***		***Ja***	***2.38***	***217.0***	***165.0***	***7-29-95***	***135.0***		***265.0***	***78.9***						
Sr Nts[3] 10⅝s 2003	Mn	**B**			Y	R	103.984	(5-1-98)	....	....	[11]Z110	4-30-96	135	D6	'93	99	91	97½	10.90	11.13
FINOVA Capital[12]	***25***	***1.37***	***1.67***	***1.56***		***Dc***	***20.40***			***9-30-95***	***5403***		***6240***	***86.6***						
F/R[13]Nts 6⅛s '98	QMar6	**BBB+**			X	BE	NC	....	....	....	....	....	150	M2	'95	100	99½	100	6.13	....
Nts 8s 2000	Fa	**BBB+**			X	BE	NC	....	....	....	....	....	100	S1	'95	107¼	99½	107¼	7.46	5.97
Nts 6⅜s 2000	aO15	**BBB+**			X	BE	NC	....	....	....	....	....	147	L3	'95	101⅜	99½	101⅜	6.29	6.04
Nts 6.45s 2000	Jd	**BBB+**			X	BE	NC	....	....	....	....	....	125	M6	'95	101¾	98	101¾	6.34	5.99
Nts 6⅝s 2001	mS15	**BBB+**			X	BE	NC	....	....	....	....	....	100	G1	'95	102⅜	99½	102⅜	6.47	6.12
• Nts 9⅛s 2002	Fa27	**BBB+**	1/95	BBB	X	BE	NC	....	....	....	....	....	175	M2	'92	No Sale		98¼	9.29	9.50
[14]Fireman's Fund Mtg	***25***	***2.07***	***2.37***	***1.53***		***Dc***	***0.40***			***9-30-95***	***456.0***		***1431***	***54.4***						
Deb 8¼s '96	mN	**BBB+**	4/95	A–	X	R	NC	....	....	....	....	....	125	S4	'86	102⅝	100⅛	101⅞	8.10	5.91
Nts 8⅞s 2001	aO15	**BBB+**	4/95	A–	X	R	NC	....	....	....	....	....	160	L3	'91	110⅜	101	110⅜	8.04	6.68
First Amer (Tenn)	***10***	***4.20***	***8.60***	***5.16***		***Dc***				***9-30-95***	***260.0***		***898.0***	***29.0***						
Sub Nts 6⅞s 2003	Ao15	**BBB–**			X	R	NC	....	....	....	....	....	50.0	M2	'93	101⅞	87¾	101⅞	6.75	6.55
Sub Nts 6⅝s 2005	jD18	**BBB–**			X	BE	NC	....	....	....	....	....	50.0	M2	'95	99¾	99⅝	99¾	6.64	6.66
First of America Bank	***10***	***8.79***	***10.00***	***4.43***		***Dc***				***9-30-95***	***490.0***		***2255***	***21.7***						
Sub Nts 8½s 2004	Fa	**BBB+**			X	R	NC	....	....	....	....	....	150	M2	'92	113⅝	98⅞	113⅝	7.48	6.32
Sub Nts 7¾s 2004	jJ15	**BBB+**			X	BE	NC	....	....	....	....	....	200	B5	'94	109⅜	93	109⅜	7.09	6.31
First Bank Nat'l Assn	***10***	***Subsid of First Bank System,see***																		
Sub[15]Step-Up Nts[16] 6¼s 2005	fA15	**A**				BE	[17]100	8-15-00	....	....	....	....	100	L3	'93	98¼	86½	98¼	6.36	6.50
First Bank System[18]	***10***	***3.39***	***5.53***	***4.78***		***Dc***				***9-30-95***	***3127***		***5863***	***53.3***						
Sub Nts 6⅝s 2003	Mn	**A–**	8/93	BBB+	X	BE	NC	....	....	....	....	....	100	M6	'93	102¾	88	102¾	6.45	6.15
Sub Nts 8s 2004	jJ2	**A–**	8/93	BBB+	X	BE	NC	....	....	....	....	....	125	M5	'92	111½	95¾	111½	7.17	6.24
Sub Nts 7⅝s 2005	Mn	**A–**			X	BE	NC	....	....	....	....	....	150	D6	'95	109½	98¾	109½	6.96	6.26
Sub Nts 6⅞s 2007	mS15	**A–**			X	BE	NC	....	....	....	....	....	250	M6	'95	104¼	98⅝	104¼	6.59	6.35
First Brands Corp	***42a***	***△4.81***	***△5.37***	***△4.98***		***Je***	***9.52***	***296.0***	***189.0***	***9-30-95***	***197.0***		***575.0***	***36.7***						
Sr Sub Nts 9⅛s '99	Ao	**BB+**	10/94	BB–	Y	R	100	(4-1-97)	....	....	....	....	100	F1	'92	105	98⅝	103	8.86	8.05

Uniform Footnote Explanations-See Page 260. Other: [1] Co must offer repurch at 101 on Chge of Ctrl. [2] Subsid & data of Ferrellgas Ptnrs L.P. [3] (HRO)On Chge of Ctrl at 101.
[4] Int to 1-31-96,adj qtrly(3 Mo LIBOR&3.125%). [5] Was A-T-O Inc. [6] Int accr at 12% fr 5-1-98. [7] (HRO)On Chge of Ctrl at 101(Accreted Val). [8] Max $49M red w/proceeds of public Cap Stk off'g. [9] Incl disc.
[10] Subsid of Finlay Enterprises, Inc. [11] Max $67.5M w/net proceeds of Cap Stk off'g. [12] Was Greyhound Fin'l,see. [13] Int to 9-6-95,adj aft(3 Mo LIBOR&0.25%). [14] Subsid & data of Fund Amer Enterprises Hldg.
[15] Int to 8-14-00, 7.30% aft. [16] Issued in min denom $250T. [17] On 8-15-00. [18] See First Bank N.A.

Title-Industry Code & Co. Finances (In Italics) / Individual Issue Statistics, Exchange	Ind / Interest Dates	Fixed Charge Coverage 1992 / S&P Debt Rating	1993 / Date of Last Rating Change	1994 / Prior Rating	Eligible	Year End / Bond Form	Million $ Cash & Equiv. / Redemption Provisions Regular Price	Curr. Assets / Regular (Begins) Thru	Curr. Liab. / Sinking Fund Price	Balance Sheet Date / Sinking Fund (Begins) Thru	L. Term Debt (Mil $) / Refund/Other Restriction Price	Refund/Other Restriction (Begins) Thru	Capital-ization (Mil $) / Outst'g (Mil $)	Total Debt % Capital / Underwriting Firm	Underwriting Year	Price Range 1995 High	Price Range 1995 Low	Mo. End Price Sale(s) or Bid	Curr. Yield	Yield to Mat.
First Chicago Corp.	***10***	***Now First Chicago NBD,see***																		
F/R[1]Sub Nts 6.0625s 2003	QJul28	**A**	12/95	A–	X	BE	NC	....	....	....	....	....	150	F1	'93	99½	97⅛	98⅝	6.15	....
Sub Nts 9s '99	Jd15	**A**	12/95	A–	X	R	NC	....	....	....	....	....	198	S1	'89	110	101½	110	8.18	5.77
Sub Nts 9⅞s '99	jJ	**A**	12/95	A–	X	R	NC	....	....	....	....	....	200	S1	'87	112¾	104¾	112¾	8.76	5.80
Sub Nts 9⅞s 2000	fA15	**A**	12/95	A–	X	BE	NC	....	....	....	....	....	99.0	S1	'90	115¾	105⅝	115¾	8.53	5.93
Sub Nts 11¼s 2001	Fa20	**A**	12/95	A–	X	BE	NC	....	....	....	....	....	100	S1	'91	123	111½	123	9.15	5.98
Sub Nts 10¼s 2001	Mn	**A**	12/95	A–	X	BE	NC	....	....	....	....	....	100	S1	'91	119¼	107⅞	119¼	8.60	5.98
Sub Nts 9¼s 2001	mN15	**A**	12/95	A–	X	BE	NC	....	....	....	....	....	100	S1	'91	115¾	102¾	115¾	7.99	6.03
Sub Nts 8⅞s 2002	Ms15	**A**	12/95	A–	X	BE	NC	....	....	....	....	....	100	S1	'92	114¼	100½	114¼	7.77	6.08
Sub Nts 8¼s 2002	Jd15	**A**	12/95	A–	X	BE	NC	....	....	....	....	....	100	S1	'92	111½	97⅛	111½	7.40	6.07
Sub Nts 7⅝s 2003	Jj15	**A**	12/95	A–	X	BE	NC	....	....	....	....	....	200	S1	'93	108⅜	93⅜	108⅜	7.04	6.14
Sub Nts 6⅞s 2003	Jd15	**A**	12/95	A–	X	BE	NC	....	....	....	....	....	200	S1	'93	104⅛	88⅞	104⅛	6.60	6.18
Sub Nts 6⅜s 2009	Jj30	**A**	12/95	A–	X	BE	NC	....	....	....	....	....	200	C5	'94	99⅝	79⅜	99⅝	6.40	6.42
First Chicago NBD[2]	***10***	***1.29***	***3.01***	***2.23***		***Dc***				***p6-30-95***	***5283***		***44888***	***81.7***						
• Nts[3] 8½s '98	[4]Jd	**A+**	12/95	A	X	R	NC	....	....	....	....	....	99.0	S1	'86	104	104	102⅛	8.32	7.52
• Sub Nts[5] 8.10s 2002	Ms	**A**	12/95	A+	X	BE	NC	....	....	....	....	....	200	G1	'92	106¾	100¼	100⅝	8.05	7.97
• Sub Deb[5] 7¼s 2004	fA15	**A**	12/95	A+	X	BE	NC	....	....	....	....	....	200	M6	'92	103⅝	89⅜	103¾	6.99	6.67
First Colony	***35a***	***n/a***	***29.88***	***14.67***		***Dc***				***9-30-95***	***175.0***		***1515***	***11.6***						
Sr Nts 6⅝s 2003	fA	**A+**			X	R	NC	....	....	....	....	....	175	F1	'93	102	88	102	6.50	6.29
First Data	***25e***	***7.82***	***8.02***	***9.63***		***Dc***				***9-30-95***	***633.0***		***2723***	***33.5***						
• Nts[6] 6⅝s 2003	Ao	**A**			X	BE	NC	....	....	....	....	....	200	L3	'93	102	84½	100⅛	6.62	6.60
Nts 6¾s 2005	jJ15	**A**			X	BE	NC	....	....	....	....	....	200	L3	'95	104⅛	97⅛	104⅛	6.48	6.17
First Fidelity[7] Bancorp[8]	***10***	***5.11***	***9.12***	***4.54***		***Dc***				***9-30-95***	***677.0***		***3748***	***18.1***						
F/R[9]Sr Nts 6.0375s '96	QAug2	**A–**			X	BE	NC	....	....	....	....	....	200	G1	'94	100	99½	100	6.04	....
Sub Nts 9⅝s '99	fA15	**BBB+**	1/94	BBB	X	R	NC	....	....	....	....	....	150	G1	'89	112¼	103⅞	112¼	8.57	5.83
Sub Nts 6.80s 2003	Jd15	**BBB+**	1/94	BBB	X	R	NC	....	....	....	....	....	150	G1	'93	101⅝	88⅝	101⅝	6.69	6.52
Sub Cap Nts[10] 8½s '98	Ao	**BBB+**	1/94	BBB	X	R	NC	....	....	....	....	....	149	G1	'86	105⅜	100⅛	105⅜	8.07	5.91
First Finl Corp Wis	***10b***	***6.68***	***4.61***	***3.82***		***Dc***				***9-30-85***	***528.0***		***893.0***	***59.1***						
Sub Nts[11] 8s '99	[12]Nov	**CALL**	12/96	BB+		R			Called 1-15-96 at 100				55.0	B2	'92	100	91	100	8.00	Call
First Fin'l Hldgs	***10b***	***△2.69***	***△4.20***	***△2.77***		***Sp***				***9-30-95***	***128.0***		***219.0***	***58.4***						
Sr[13]Nts[14] 9⅜s 2002	QSep	**NR**				R	104	8-31-96	....	....	....	....	19.8	B7	'92	118⅜	99	118⅜	7.92	5.99
First Hawaiian	***10***	***5.13***	***4.52***	***2.88***		***Dc***				***9-30-95***	***225.0***		***873.0***	***25.8***						
Sub Nts 6¼s 2000	fA15	**BBB+**			X	BE	NC	....	....	....	....	....	100	G1	'93	100¼	89⅛	100¼	6.23	6.18
First Interstate Bancorp[15]	***10***	***2.67***	***6.79***	***10.43***		***Dc***				***9-30-95***	***1368***		***5349***	***25.6***						
Nts 10½s '96	Ms	**A–**	12/93	BBB+	X	R	NC	....	....	....	....	....	65.7	M2	'91	103	100¾	100¾	10.42	5.90
Nts 11s '98	Ms5	**A–**	12/93	BBB+	X	R	NC	....	....	....	....	....	54.4	M6	'91	111¼	106⅞	110	10.00	6.03
Nts 9⅜s '98	mN15	**A–**	12/93	BBB+	X	R	NC	....	....	....	....	....	100	K2	'92	108⅝	102	108¼	8.66	6.20
Sub Cap[10]Nts 8⅝s '99	Ao	**BBB+**	12/93	BBB	X	R	NC	....	....	....	....	....	182	G1	'87	107¼	100⅛	107¼	8.04	6.13
F/R[16]Sub Nts 6.1875s '97	QJun30	**BBB+**	12/93	BBB	X	R	NC	....	....	....	....	....	82.7	S1	'85	100⅜	99½	100¼	6.17	....
Sub Nts 12¾s '97	Mn	**BBB+**	12/93	BBB	X	R	NC	....	....	....	....	....	68.5	S1	'90	110⅝	108⅜	108⅜	11.76	6.12
Sub Nts 10⅞s 2001	Ao15	**BBB+**	12/93	BBB	X	BE	NC	....	....	....	....	....	100	S1	'91	120⅞	109⅞	120⅞	9.00	6.19
Sub Nts 9.90s 2001	mN15	**BBB+**	12/93	BBB	X	R	NC	....	....	....	....	....	150	M6	'91	117½	105⅞	117½	8.43	6.29
Sub Nts 8.15s 2002	Ms15	**BBB+**			X	BE	100	(3-15-98)	....	....	....	....	100	L3	'95	104⅝	99⅛	104⅝	7.79	7.21
Sub Nts 9⅛s 2004	Fa	**BBB+**	12/93	BBB	X	R	NC	....	....	....	....	....	133	M6	'92	118⅛	102⅛	118⅛	7.72	6.24
Sub Nts 9s 2004	mN15	**BBB+**			X	BE	*100	(11-15-99)	....	....	....	....	125	M6	'94	110	99	110	8.18	7.44
First Kentucky Nat'l	***10***	***Subsid of National City Corp,see***																		
• F/R Nts[17] 6.0625s '97	[18]Qoct17	**A**	3/91	A+	X	R	100	....	....	....	....	....	50.0	S4	'85	No Sale		92	6.59	....

Uniform Footnote Explanations-See Page 260. Other: [1] Int(min 4.25%)to 1-28-96,adj qtrly. [2] See First Chicago Corp, NBD Bancorp. [3] Was First Chicago Corp. [4] Due 6-1-98. [5] Was NBD Bancorp. [6] (HRO)For a Put Event at 100. [7] Was First Natl State Bancorp. [8] See Baltimore Bancorp. [9] Int to 2-1-96,adj qtrly aft(3 Mo LIBOR&0.10%). [10] To be exch for Cap Sec when due. [11] Death red benefit,ltd,as defined. [12] Int pd monthly, Nov 1, etc. [13] Issued in min denom $2T. [14] (HRO)At 100,ltd,as defined. [15] Was Western Bancorp. [16] Int(max 12.75%)to 12-29-95,adj qtrly aft. [17] Int thru 1-25-96,adj qtrly aft. [18] Due 10-31-97.

Title-Industry Code & Co. Finances (In Italics)	Ind	Fixed Charge Coverage 1992	1993	1994		Year End	Million $ Cash & Equiv.	Million $ Curr. Assets	Million $ Curr. Liab.	Balance Sheet Date	L. Term Debt (Mil $)		Capital-ization (Mil $)	Total Debt % Capital						
Individual Issue Statistics Exchange ↓	Interest Dates	S&P Debt Rating	Date of Last Rating Change	Prior Rating	Eligible ↓	Bond Form	Redemption Provisions: Regular Price	Regular (Begins) Thru	Sinking Fund Price	Sinking Fund (Begins) Thru	Refund/Other Restriction Price	Refund/Other Restriction (Begins) Thru	Outst'g (Mil $)	Underwriting Firm	Underwriting Year	Price Range 1995 High	Price Range 1995 Low	Mo. End Price Sale(s) or Bid	Curr. Yield	Yield to Mat.
First Maryland Bancorp[1]	***10***	***3.48***	***3.81***	***3.37***		***Dc***				***9-30-95***	***190.0***		***1328***	***14.3***						
Sub[2]Cap Nts 10⅜s '99	fA	**A–**	3/89	BBB+	X	R	NC	....	....	....	....	....	60.0	B8	'87	114	106⅜	114	9.10	5.98
Sub Nts 8⅜s 2002	Mn15	**A–**			X	R	NC	....	....	....	....	....	100	L3	'92	111	98⅜	111	7.55	6.25
First Nationwide Bank[3]	***10a***	....	***10.78***	***2.34***						***12-31-94***	***2606***		***3447***	***75.6***						
Sub Deb 10s 2006	aO	**BBB–**	10/94	BBB	X	R	NC	....	....	....	....	....	100	F1	'86	108	99½	102	9.80	9.69
First Republic Bancorp	***10b***	***2.02***	***1.99***	***1.40***		***Dc***				***9-30-95***	***621.0***		***728.0***	***85.3***						
• Sub[4]Deb[5] 8½s 2008	Mn15	**NR**				R	101	(5-16-98)	....	....	....	....	13.0		'93	95	83⅛	92	9.24	9.62
• Sub[6]Deb[5] 8s 2009	QJan15	**NR**				R	104	1-14-97	....	....	....	....	5.44	O1	'93	89	80	82⅞	9.65	10.43
First Security	***10***	***4.20***	***4.62***	***3.02***		***Dc***				***9-30-95***	***857.0***		***1876***	***45.7***						
• F/R[7]Nts[8] 7.15s '99	mS	**BBB+**	8/92	BBB	X	R	100	....	....	....	....	....	7.48	F1	'74	98⅞	98¾	99	7.22	....
Sr Nts 7⅞s '99	aO15	**BBB+**			X	BE	NC	....	....	....	....	....	100	M5	'94	106¼	97⅜	106¼	7.41	6.00
Sub Nts 7½s 2002	fa15	**BBB**			X	BE	NC	....	....	....	....	....	75.0	F1	'92	106⅝	92⅝	106⅝	7.03	6.27
Sub Nts 7s 2005	jJ15	**BBB**			X	BE	NC	....	....	....	....	....	125	C5	'95	104¼	95⅞	104¼	6.71	6.40
First Tenn Nat'l	***10***	***4.47***	***4.69***	***3.79***		***Dc***				***9-30-95***	***★263.0***		***1026***	***19.6***						
Sub[2]Cap Nts 10⅜s '99	Jd	**BBB+**			X	R	NC	....	....	....	Z100	....	75.0	G1	'87	113⅜	106⅛	113⅜	9.15	5.99
Sub Nts 6¾s 2005	mN15	**BBB+**			X	BE	NC	....	....	....	....	....	75.0	D6	'95	102⅜	99⅜	102⅜	6.59	6.42
First Union[9] Corp[10]	***10***	***3.18***	***3.43***	***3.28***		***Dc***				***9-30-95***	***6041***		***11726***	***51.5***						
SF Deb 7½s 2002	jD	**NR**			X	R	100	....	100	....	....	....	15.6	G1	'72	101	94⅛	100⅝	7.45	7.38
Nts 6¾s '98	Jj15	**A**	9/93	A–	X	R	NC	....	....	....	....	....	250	G1	'93	102	95¾	102	6.62	5.70
F/R Ext'd[11]Nts 5.9625s 2000	[12]QJun15	**A**	9/93	A–	X	R	100	....	....	....	....	....	9.00	S4	'85	100	99	100	5.96	....
Sub Deb[13] 6.55s 2035	aO15	**A–**			X	R	NC	....	....	....	....	....	250	G1	'95	103¼	98¾	103¼	6.34	6.32
F/R[14]Sub Nts 6.0625s 2003	QJul22	**A–**	9/93	BBB+	X	R	NC	....	....	....	....	....	150	G1	'93	100	97⅛	98⅝	6.15	....
Sub Nts 8⅛s '96	jD15	**A–**	9/93	BBB+	X	R	NC	....	....	....	....	....	100	S4	'87	102⅞	99⅞	102¼	7.95	5.68
Sub Nts 9.45s '99	Jd15	**A–**	9/93	BBB+	X	R	NC	....	....	....	....	....	250	G1	'89	111⅜	103½	111⅜	8.48	5.78
Sub Nts 9.45s 2001	fA15	**A–**	9/93	BBB+	X	R	NC	....	....	....	....	....	150	G1	'91	116	104⅛	116	8.15	6.05
Sub Nts 8⅛s 2002	Jd24	**A–**	9/93	BBB+	X	R	NC	....	....	....	....	....	248	F1	'92	110½	96⅞	110½	7.35	6.14
Sub Nts 8s 2002	mN15	**A–**	9/93	BBB+	X	R	NC	....	....	....	....	....	223	G1	'92	110¼	96⅛	110¼	7.26	6.15
Sub Nts 7¼s 2003	Fa15	**A–**	9/93	BBB+	X	R	NC	....	....	....	....	....	150	G1	'93	105⅞	91½	105⅞	6.85	6.22
Sub Nts 8.77s 2004	mN15	**A–**			X	R	100	(11-15-99)	....	....	....	....	150	D6	'94	109¼	98¾	109¼	8.03	7.33
Sub Nts 6⅝s 2005	jJ15	**A–**	9/93	BBB+	X	BE	NC	....	....	....	....	....	250	G1	'93	102⅜	84⅞	102⅜	6.47	6.29
Sub Nts 7.05s 2005	fA	**A–**			X	R	NC	....	....	....	....	....	250	G1	'95	105¼	98⅛	105¼	6.70	6.31
Sub Nts 6⅞s 2005	mS15	**A–**			X	R	NC	....	....	....	....	....	250		'95	104⅛	99⅞	104⅛	6.60	6.30
Sub Nts 6s 2008	aO30	**A–**			X	R	NC	....	....	....	....	....	200	C1	'93	96¼	77¼	96¼	6.23	6.43
Sub Nts 6⅜s 2009	Jj15	**A–**			X	R	NC	....	....	....	....	....	150	G1	'94	99	79⅞	99	6.44	6.49
Sub Nts 8s 2009	fA15	**A–**			X	R	[15]■100	....	....	....	....	....	150	G1	'94	112⅜	95¼	112⅜	7.12	6.61
Sub Nts[16] 7½s 2035	Ao15	**A–**			X	R	NC	....	....	....	....	....	250	G1	'95	110⅜	98¾	110⅜	6.80	6.74
First Union RE Eq SBI	***57***	***1.67***	***1.55***	***1.30***		***Dc***	***0.80***			***9-30-95***	***248.0***		***378.0***	***65.6***						
• Sr[17]Nts 8⅞s 2003	aO	**BB+**	8/94	BBB–	Y	R	NC	....	....	....	....	....	100	S1	'93	102¼	92	101½	8.74	8.60
Firstar Corp	***10***	***7.26***	***9.00***	***4.97***		***Dc***				***9-30-95***	***776.0***		***2290***	***33.9***						
• Nts 10s '96	Jd	**A–**	4/88	BBB+	X	R	NC	....	....	....	....	....	44.2	M2	'86	108	101½	99	10.10	12.40
Sub Nts 10¼s '98	Mn	**BBB+**			X	R	NC	....	....	....	....	....	78.7	M2	'88	109⅝	104⅜	109⅝	9.35	5.78
Sub Nts 7.15s 2000	mS	**BBB+**			X	BE	100	(9-1-98)	....	....	....	....	100	M2	'95	103½	100	103½	6.91	6.27
Fisher Scientific Intl	***43***	***25.95***	***8.32***	***7.96***		***Dc***	***15.20***	***388.0***	***234.0***	***9-30-95***	***★466.0***		***363.0***	***38.7***						
Sr Nts 7⅛s 2005	jD15	**BBB**			X	BE	[18]Z100	....	....	....	....	....	150	C5	'95	100½	99⅛	100½	7.09	7.05
Flagstar Corp[19]	***27c***	***0.81***	***0.76***	***0.83***		***Dc***	***86.60***	***241.0***	***342.0***	***9-30-95***	***2162***		***945.0***	***232.0***						
Sr Nts 10¾s 2001	mS15	**B–**	5/95	B	Y	R	NC	....	....	....	[20]Z110	9-14-96	275	M6	'93	97½	91½	91¾	11.72	12.82
Sr Nts 10⅞s 2002	jD	**B–**	5/95	B	Y	R	105.4375	(12-1-97)	....	....	....	....	300	M6	'92	97⅜	90	90	12.08	13.11

Uniform Footnote Explanations-See Page 260. Other: [1] Subsid of Allied Irish Bank plc. [2] To be exch for Cap Sec when due. [3] Subsid of Ford Motor. [4] Death redemp benefit,ltd,as defined. [5] Issued in min denom \$2T. [6] Death redemp benefit,ltd as defined. [7] Int thru 8-31-95,adj semi-anly aft. [8] (HRO)On int dates at 100. [9] Was Cameron Fin'l. [10] See Dominion Bankshares,Florida Nat'l Banks. [11] Int to 3-15-96,adj qtrly aft. [12] Due 6-15-05. [13] (HRO)On 10-15-05 at 100. [14] Int(min 4.125%)to 1-22-96,adj qtrly aft. [15] On 8-15-04. [16] (HRO)On Chge of Ctrl at 100. [17] (HRO)For Chge in Ctrl Triggering Event at 101. [18] Greater of 100 or amt based of formula. [19] Was TW Services. [20] Max \$96M red w/proceeds of Public Com Stk Off'g.

Title-Industry Code & Co. Finances (In Italics) / Individual Issue Statistics (Exchange)	Ind / Interest Dates	Fixed Charge Coverage 1992 / S&P Debt Rating	1993 / Date of Last Rating Change	1994 / Prior Rating	Eligible	Year End / Bond Form	Cash & Equiv. (Million $) / Regular Price	Curr. Assets / Regular (Begins) Thru	Curr. Liab. / Sinking Fund Price	Balance Sheet Date / Sinking Fund (Begins) Thru	L. Term Debt (Mil $) / Refund/Other Restriction Price	Capital-ization (Mil $) / Refund/Other (Begins) Thru	Outst'g (Mil $)	Total Debt % Capital / Underwriting Firm	Underwriting Year	Price Range 1995 High	Price Range 1995 Low	Mo. End Price Sale(s) or Bid	Curr. Yield	Yield to Mat.
***Flagstar Corp** (Cont.)*																				
Sr Sub Deb 11⅜s 2003	mS15	CCC+	4/94	B−	Y	R	105.688	(9-15-98)	....	....	[1]Z110	9-14-96	125	M6	'93	86	72¼	72¼	15.74	18.19
Sr Sub Deb 11¼s 2004	mN	CCC+	4/94	B−	Y	R	105.625	(11-1-97)	100	(11-1-03)	....	....	722	Exch.	'92	85½	70½	71	15.85	17.89
Fleet Fin'l Group[3]	***10***	***2.34***	***2.97***	***2.94***		***Dc***				***9-30-95***	***p6734***	***8128***		***46.3***						
Sr Nts 7¼s '97	aO15	A−			X	BE	NC	....	....	....	....	....	200	G1	'94	102¾	97⅜	102¾	7.06	5.61
Nts 7¼s '99	mS	A−			X	BE	NC	....	....	....	....	....	200	M2	'94	104¾	94¾	104¾	6.92	5.79
Sr Nts 7⅛s 2000	Mn	A−			X	BE	NC	....	....	....	....	....	250	C5	'95	104⅝	99½	104⅝	6.81	5.90
Sr Nts 6s '98	aO26	A−			X	BE	NC	....	....	....	....	....	250	G1	'95	101	99¾	101	5.94	5.61
Sub Nts 7⅝s '99	jD	BBB+	4/93	BBB	X	BE	NC	....	....	....	....	....	150	S1	'92	106	96⅝	106	7.19	5.89
Sub Nts 6⅞s 2003	Ms	BBB+	4/93	BBB	X	BE	NC	....	....	....	....	....	150	S1	'93	103⅞	89¼	103⅞	6.62	6.20
Sub Nts 8⅛s 2004	jJ	BBB+	4/93	BBB	X	BE	NC	....	....	....	....	....	250	S1	'92	111¾	95⅝	111¾	7.27	6.32
Fleet Mortgage Group	***25h***	***n/a***	***1.50***	***2.60***		***Dc***	***104.0***			***9-30-95***	***901.0***	***3722***		***83.4***						
Nts 6⅛s '97	fA15	A	5/93	A−	X	BE	NC	....	....	....	....	....	150	G1	'92	100⅞	94¾	100⅞	6.07	5.55
Nts 6½s '99	mS15	A	5/93	A−	X	BE	NC	....	....	....	....	....	150	M2	'92	102¼	92¼	102¼	6.36	5.81
Nts 6½s 2000	Jd15	A			X	BE	NC	....	....	....	....	....	200	M5	'95	102⅜	98¼	102⅜	6.35	5.89
Fleet/Norstar Fin'lGroup	***10***	***Now Fleet Fin'l Group,see***																		
Nts 7.65s '97	Ms	A−	4/93	BBB+	X	BE	NC	....	....	....	....	....	100	M2	'92	102⅛	98⅝	102⅛	7.49	5.74
Sub Nts 9.90s 2001	Jd15	BBB+	4/93	BBB	X	R	NC	....	....	....	....	....	175	M2	'91	117⅝	105¾	117⅝	8.42	6.06
Sub Nts 9s 2001	jD	BBB+	4/93	BBB	X	R	NC	....	....	....	....	....	150	S1	'91	114¼	101⅝	114¼	7.88	6.10
Sub Nts 8⅝s 2007	Jj15	BBB+	4/93	BBB	X	R	NC	....	....	....	....	....	107	S1	'92	117¼	98½	117¼	7.36	6.42
Fleming Cos.	***26g***	***3.53***	***3.46***	***2.05***		***Dc***	***4.75***	***1597***	***1316***	***10-7-95***	***1636***	***2838***		***61.6***						
Sr Nts[4] 10⅝s 2001	jD15	BB−	6/95	BB+	Y	R	103	(12-15-99)	....	....	[5]Z110	12-14-97	300	M2	'94	106¾	99	99	10.73	10.85
F/R[6]Sr Nts[4] 8¼s 2001	QDec15	BB−	6/95	BB+	Y	R	100.50	12-14-99	100	(12-15-99)	....	....	200	M2	'94	100	99¾	100	8.25	....
• SF Deb 9½s 2016	Ao	NR	7/94	BB+		R	105.225	3-31-96	100	(4-1-97)	®104.75	3-31-96	7.00	M2	'86	102	95	100¾	9.43	9.41
[7]Flexi-Van Leasing	***25c***	***1.60***	....	....		***Dc***	***No Recent Fin'ls***													
Gtd Nts 9¾s '96	jJ15	B+	5/88	BBB	Y	R	NC	....	....	....	....	....	65.8	G1	'86	101	99	101	9.65	7.82
Flores & Rucks	***49a***	***n/a***	***3.11***	***0.46***		***Dc***		***15.20***	***34.50***	***9-30-95***	***165.0***	***176.0***		***93.8***						
Sr Nts[4] 13½s 2004	jD	B			Y	BE	106.75	(12-1-99)	....	....	....	....	125	M2	'94	114	100	A113	11.95	11.16
[8]Florida East Coast Ry	***55***	***Coverage not meaningful***																		
• Coll Tr[9] 5s 2001	[10]jj	NR	8/93	A	X	R	105	....	*100	....	....	....	[11]12.9	Reorg	'61	91	83¾	s91	5.49	6.89
Florida Nat'l Banks	***10***	***Merged into First Union Corp,see***																		
Sub Cap[12]Nts 9⅞s '99	Mn15	A−	9/93	BBB+	X	R	NC	....	....	....	Z100	....	74.0	S1	'87	112⅜	98	112⅜	8.79	5.78
Florida Power Corp.[13]	***72a***	***3.65***	***3.68***	***3.81***		***Dc***	***4.70***	***436.0***	***382.0***	***9-30-95***	***1257***	***3181***		***41.1***						
1st 6⅛s '97	fA	AA−	6/90	A+	X	CR	100.28	7-31-96	100.24	7-31-96	....	....	16.7	H1	'67	100⅝	95⅝	100⅝	6.09	5.70
1st 6½s '99	jD	AA−			X	R	NC	....	....	....	[14]Z100	....	75.0	K2	'92	102⅜	93	102⅜	6.35	5.81
1st 7⅜s 2002	Jd	AA−	6/90	A+	X	R	101.85	5-31-96	100.68	5-31-96	....	....	50.0	M6	'72	102	94⅛	102	7.23	6.98
1st A 7¼s 2002	mN	AA−	6/90	A+	X	R	101.71	10-31-96	100.49	10-31-96	....	....	50.0	B6	'72	102⅞	93	102⅞	7.05	6.72
1st 6⅛s 2003	Ms	AA−			X	R	NC	....	....	....	[14]Z100	....	70.0	G1	'93	100⅛	86⅞	100⅛	6.12	6.10
1st 6s 2003	jJ	AA−			X	R	NC	....	....	....	[14]Z100	....	110	M5	'93	99⅜	85¾	99⅜	6.04	6.10
1st 6⅞s 2008	Fa	AA−			X	R	NC	....	....	....	[14]Z100	....	80.0	M5	'93	105½	88½	105½	6.52	6.22
1st 8⅝s 2021	mN	AA−			X	R	105.54	(11-1-96)	....	....	....	....	150	S1	'91	110¼	97¾	110¼	7.82	7.70
1st 8s 2022	jD	AA−			X	R	103.75	(12-1-02)	100	....	Z100	....	150	S1	'92	109¼	91⅞	109¼	7.32	7.22
1st 7s 2023	jD	AA−			X	R	103.19	(12-1-03)	[14]Z100	....	....	....	100	M5	'93	100¾	81⅝	100¾	6.95	6.94
Florida Power & Light[15]	***72a***	***3.28***	***3.39***	***3.96***		***Dc***	***2.75***	***1003***	***1488***	***9-30-95***	***3056***	***8211***		***39.8***						
1st[16] 4.90s '96	[17]jj	AA−	7/95	A+	X	BE	NC	....	....	....	....	....	60.0	G1	'93	99¾	96¼	99¾	4.91	5.48
1st[16] 4.85s '96	[18]jj	AA−	7/95	A+	X	BE	NC	....	....	....	....	....	40.0	G1	'93	99¾	96	99¾	4.86	5.37
1st 5½s '99	jJ	AA−	7/95	A+	X	R	NC	....	....	....	....	....	230	M2	'93	99¼	89⅝	99¼	5.54	5.74

Uniform Footnote Explanations-See Page 260. Other: [1] Max $44M red w/proceeds of Public Com Stk Off'g. [2] Was Industrial Nat'l. [3] See Fleet/Norstar Fin'l Corp. [4] (HRO)On Chge of Ctrl at 101. [5] Max $60M red w/proceeds Pub Equity Off'g. [6] Int thru 9-14-95,adj qtrly(3 Mo LIBOR&2.25%). [7] Gtd by & data of Flexi-Van Corp. [8] Subsid & data of Fla East Coast Indus. [9] Formerly 1st Mtg 'A',5s,2011. [10] Due 11-15-01. [11] Defeased,funds deposited with trustee. [12] To be exch for Cap Sec when due. [13] Subsid of Florida Progress. [14] In whole. [15] Subsid of FPL Group. [16] Issued in min denom $100T. [17] Due 6-04-96. [18] Due 6-24-96.

Title-Industry Code & Co. Finances (In Italics) / Individual Issue Statistics (Exchange)	Ind / Interest Dates	S&P Debt Rating	Date of Last Rating Change	Prior Rating	Eligible	Bond Form	Regular Price	Regular (Begins) Thru	Sinking Fund Price	Sinking Fund (Begins) Thru	Refund/Other Restriction Price	Refund/Other Restriction (Begins) Thru	Outst'g (Mil $)	Underwriting Firm	Underwriting Year	Price Range 1995 High	Price Range 1995 Low	Mo. End Price Sale(s) or Bid	Curr. Yield	Yield to Mat.
Fixed Charge Coverage / Million $ / Balance Sheet		*1992*	*1993*		*1994*	*Year End*	*Cash & Equiv.*	*Curr. Assets*	*Curr. Liab.*	*Balance Sheet Date*	*L. Term Debt (Mil $)*		*Capital-ization (Mil $)*	*Total Debt % Capital*						
Florida Power & Light (Cont.)																				
1st 5⅜s 2000	Ao	**AA−**	7/95	A+	X	R	NC	....	....	....	....	....	125	M6	'93	98¼	87¼	98¼	5.47	5.84
1st 9⅝s 2000	mN	**AA−**	7/95	A+	X	R	102.66	10-31-96	....	....	....	....	125	S1	'90	104½	102⅝	103⅛	9.33	8.81
1st 6⅝s 2003	Fa	**AA−**	7/95	A+	X	R	101.27	(2-1-98)	....	....	....	....	100	M2	'93	101⅝	89¼	101⅝	6.52	6.34
1st[1] 5.79s 2003	[2]jj	**AA−**	7/95	A+	X	BE	NC	....	....	....	....	....	70.0	G1	'93	97⅝	84	97⅝	5.93	6.18
1st 6⅞s 2004	Ao	**AA−**	7/95	A+	X	R	102.37	(4-1-98)	....	....	....	....	125	S1	'93	102⅝	89⅞	102⅝	6.70	6.46
1st 7⅞s 2007	Jj	**AA−**	7/95	A+	X	R	104.66	12-31-96	....	....	®103.88	12-31-96	75.0	S1	'92	106⅝	94¾	104⅝	7.53	7.26
1st 7⅞s 2012	jD	**AA−**	7/95	A+	X	R	104.96	11-30-96	....	....	®104.13	11-30-97	150	S1	'92	105⅝	92½	105⅝	7.46	7.29
1st 7⅞s 2013	Jj	**AA−**	7/95	A+	X	R	105.39	12-31-96	....	....	®104.49	12-31-97	250	S1	'93	105½	91¾	105	7.50	7.35
1st 7.30s 2016	Ao	**AA−**	7/95	A+	X	R	103.74	(4-1-98)	....	....	....	....	225	L3	'93	102	86	102	7.16	7.11
1st 8½s 2022	Jj	**AA−**	7/95	A+	X	R	106.80	12-31-96	....	....	®106.37	12-31-96	100	S1	'92	107⅝	95½	106¾	7.96	7.89
1st 8½s 2022	jJ	**AA−**	7/95	A+	X	R	106.84	6-30-96	....	....	®106.04	6-30-98	150	S1	'92	108¼	96¾	107⅜	7.92	7.84
1st 8s 2022	[3]jj	**AA−**	7/95	A+	X	BE	105.10	8-24-96	....	....	®104.50	8-24-97	100	K2	'92	105⅜	90¾	105⅜	7.59	7.53
1st 7¾s 2023	Fa	**AA−**	7/95	A+	X	R	104.78	(2-1-98)	....	....	....	....	150	K2	'93	105⅞	89¼	105⅞	7.32	7.25
1st 7⅝s 2024	Jd	**AA−**	7/95	A+	X	R	104.41	(6-1-98)	....	....	....	....	175	K2	'93	104⅞	87⅝	104⅞	7.27	7.22
1st 7s 2025	mS	**AA−**	7/95	A+	X	R	103.50	(9-1-03)	....	....	....	....	125	G1	'93	100	81¼	100	7.00	7.00
1st 7.05s 2026	jD	**AA−**	7/95	A+	X	R	102.73	(12-1-03)	....	....	....	....	135	G1	'93	100⅜	82⅜	100⅜	7.02	7.02
Florida Steel Corp[4]	***66h***	*[5]0.24*	*d0.56*		*1.85*	*Mr*	*1.59*	*210.0*	*89.80*	*9-30-95*	*230.0*		*390.0*	*64.4*						
[6]1st[7] 11½s 2000	jD15	**BB−**			Y	R	103.833	(12-15-96)	....	....	....	....	100	B9	'92	104	98¼	98¼	11.70	11.97
Florsheim Shoe	***59l***	*n/a*	*n/a*		*1.92*	*Dc*	*2.89*	*152.0*	*24.30*	*9-30-95*	*93.80*		*152.0*	*61.8*						
• Sr Nts[7] 12¾s 2002	mS	**B**	8/95	B+	Y	R	106.375	(9-1-98)	....	....	[8]Z112.75	8-31-97	85.0	S5	'94	100¾	71⅜	s82½	15.45	17.25
FMC Corp	***42b***	*3.78*	*3.76*		*4.71*	*Dc*	*101.0*	*1749*	*1684*	*9-30-95*	*995.0*		*2108*	*63.7*						
Sr Nts 8¾s '99	Ao	**BBB**	5/94	BBB−	X	R	NC	....	....	....	....	....	250	M6	'92	108	100⅜	108	8.10	6.00
Sr Nts 6⅜s 2003	mS	**BBB**	5/94	BBB−	X	BE	NC	....	....	....	....	....	200	M6	'93	100	85⅝	99⅜	6.42	6.48
[9]***Foamex L.P./Foamex Capital***	***42b***	*2.25*	*1.00*		*1.71*	*Dc*	*25.60*	*405.0*	*213.0*	*10-1-95*	*713.0*		*830.0*	*87.7*						
Sr Sec Nts[7] 9½s 2000	Jd	**B+**	6/94	BB−	Y	R	101.583	(6-1-98)	....	....	[10]Z109	5-31-96	160	D6	'93	100½	91	97	9.79	10.36
Sr Nts[11] 11¼s 2002	aO	**B**	6/94	B+	Y	R	104.219	(10-1-97)	....	....	....	....	150	D6	'92	103¼	94½	96	11.72	12.13
Sr Sub Deb[11] 11⅞s 2004	aO	**B−**	6/94	B	Y	R	105.938	(10-1-97)	....	....	....	....	126	D6	'92	101	94	96	12.37	12.63
Food 4 Less Supermarkets	***59c***	*△0.59*	*[12]△0.98*		*[13]△0.84*	*Ja*	*19.60*	*290.0*	*365.0*	*1-29-95*	*507.0*		*592.0*	*90.2*						
Sr Nts[14] 10.45s 2000	Ao15	**NR**	6/95	B	Y	R	104.48	(4-15-96)	100	(4-15-99)	....	....	4.67	B9	'92	101	96½	101	10.35	10.15
Foodmaker, Inc.	***27c***	*1.52*	*d0.15*		*0.44*	*Sp*	*14.30*	*77.80*	*133.0*	*7-9-95*	*440.0*		*469.0*	*94.0*						
Sr Nts 9¼s '99	Ms	**B−**	7/95	B+	Y	R	104.875	(6-1-97)	....	....	....	....	175	M6	'92	96	80¼	96	9.64	10.76
Sr Sub Nts 14¼s '98	Mn15	**CCC+**	7/95	B−	Y	R	103.17	5-14-96	100	(5-15-96)	....	....	42.8	Exch.	'88	102⅞	99½	101¼	14.07	13.60
Sr Sub Nts 9¾s 2002	Jd	**CCC+**	7/95	B−	Y	R	102.643	(3-1-97)	....	....	....	....	125	M6	'92	90½	70	90½	10.77	11.90
Ford Capital B.V.	***25***	***Subsid of & gtd by Ford Motor Co,see***																		
Gtd[15]Deb[16] 9½s 2010	$Jd	**A+**	1/95	A	Q	BE	NC	....	....	....	....	....	500	M2	'90	127	105⅞	127	7.48	6.57
Gtd[15]Nts[16] 9s '96	$Jd	**A+**	1/95	A	Q	BE	NC	....	....	....	....	....	300	M5	'91	102⅝	101¼	101⅜	8.88	5.63
Gtd[15]Nts[16] 9⅜s '98	$Jj	**A+**	1/95	A	Q	BE	NC	....	....	....	....	....	500	G1	'91	107¾	102⅛	107⅛	8.75	5.57
Gtd[15]Nts[16] 9⅛s '98	$Mn	**A+**	1/95	A	Q	BE	NC	....	....	....	....	....	400	S1	'91	107⅝	101½	107⅝	8.48	5.60
Gtd[15]Nts[16] 9s '98	$fA15	**A+**	1/95	A	Q	BE	NC	....	....	....	....	....	500	M2	'91	108¼	101⅛	108⅛	8.32	5.63
Gtd[15]Nts[16] 10⅛s 2000	$mN15	**A+**	1/95	A	Q	BE	NC	....	....	....	....	....	500	G1	'90	117½	106¼	117½	8.62	5.94
Gtd[15]Nts[16] 9⅜s 2001	$Mn15	**A+**	1/95	A	Q	BE	NC	....	....	....	....	....	250	G1	'91	115½	103	115½	8.12	5.96
Gtd[15]Nts[16] 9½s 2001	$jJ	**A+**	1/95	A	Q	BE	NC	....	....	....	....	....	300	F1	'91	116⅜	104⅞	116⅜	8.16	5.97
Gtd[15]Nts 9⅞s 2002	$Mn15	**A+**	1/95	A	Q	BE	NC	....	....	....	....	....	400	F1	'90	119⅞	106	119⅞	8.24	6.07
Ford Holdings, Inc	***25***	***Subsid of & Gtd by Ford Motor Co, see***																		
Gtd Deb 9⅜s 2020	Ms	**A+**	1/95	A	X	BE	NC	....	....	....	....	....	500	G1	'90	127⅞	106⅝	127⅞	7.33	6.97
Gtd Nts 9¼s '97	jJ15	**A+**	1/95	A	X	BE	NC	....	....	....	....	....	552	G1	'90	106⅛	101¾	105⅜	8.78	5.57

Uniform Footnote Explanations-See Page 260. Other: [1] Issued in min denom $100T. [2] Due 9-15-03. [3] Due 8-25-22. [4] Subsid of FLS Hldgs. [5] Fiscal Sep'92 & prior. [6] Co must offer repurch at 100 for asset sales. [7] (HRO)On Chge of Ctrl at 101. [8] Max $28.3M red w/proceeds of Equity Off'g. [9] Subsid & data of Foamex Intl. [10] Max $53.3M red w/proceeds of com off'g. [11] Co must offer repurch at 101 on Chge in Ctrl. [12] Fiscal Jun'94 & prior. [13] 7 Mos Jan'95. [14] (HRO)On Chge in Ctrl at 101. [15] Gtd by Ford Motor Co. [16] Co may red in whole at 100 if certain taxes due.

Title-Industry Code & Co. Finances (In Italics)	Ind	Fixed Charge Coverage 1992	1993		1994	Year End	Million $ Cash & Equiv.	Curr. Assets	Curr. Liab.		Balance Sheet Date	L. Term Debt (Mil $)		Capital-ization (Mil $)	Total Debt % Capital					
Individual Issue Statistics Exchange	Interest Dates	S&P Debt Rating	Date of Last Rating Change	Prior Rating	Eligible	Bond Form	Redemption Provisions: Regular Price	Regular (Begins) Thru	Sinking Fund Price	Sinking Fund (Begins) Thru	Refund/Other Restriction Price	Refund/Other Restriction (Begins) Thru	Outst'g (Mil $)	Underwriting Firm	Underwriting Year	Price Range 1995 High	Price Range 1995 Low	Mo. End Price Sale(s) or Bid	Curr. Yield	Yield to Mat.
***Ford Holdings, Inc** (Cont.)*																				
Gtd Nts 9¼s 2000	Ms	**A+**	1/95	A	X	BE	NC	....	....	....	....	....	500	G1	'90	112¼	102⅝	112¼	8.24	5.89
Ford Motor Co[1]	***9***	***0.98***	***1.53***		***2.16***	***Dc***	***14184***			***9-30-95***	***[2]65207***		***169672***	***84.1***						
Deb 9½s 2011	mS15	**A+**	1/95	A	X	BE	NC	....	....	....	....	....	350	G1	'91	127⅜	106¾	127⅜	7.46	6.66
Deb 8⅞s 2022	Jj15	**A+**	1/95	A	X	BE	NC	....	....	....	....	....	700	B5	'92	124½	100⅞	124½	7.13	6.85
Deb 8⅞s 2022	mN15	**A+**	1/95	A	X	BE	104.153	(11-15-02)	....	....	....	....	250	M5	'92	115½	99¾	115½	7.68	7.52
Deb 7⅛s 2025	mN15	**A+**			X	BE	NC	....	....	....	....	....	300	L3	'95	103⅛	99	103⅛	6.91	6.88
Deb[3] 9.95s 2032	Fa15	**A+**	1/95	A	X	BE	NC	....	....	....	[4]Z100	....	300	G1	'92	141¾	112¾	141¾	7.02	6.82
Deb 7¾s 2043	Jd15	**A+**	1/95	A	X	BE	NC	....	....	....	....	....	200	G1	'93	112⅞	85⅞	112⅞	6.87	6.83
Nts 7⅞s '96	aO15	**A+**	1/95	A	X	BE	NC	....	....	....	....	....	300	L3	'91	102¼	99⅝	101¾	7.74	5.58
Nts 7½s '99	mN15	**A+**	1/95	A	X	BE	NC	....	....	....	....	....	250	M5	'92	105⅝	95⅞	105⅝	7.10	5.85
Nts 9s 2001	mS15	**A+**	1/95	A	X	BE	NC	....	....	....	....	....	350	G1	'91	114⅛	101¾	114⅛	7.89	6.04
Ford Motor Credit	***25d***	***1.38***	***1.57***		***1.50***	***Dc***	***2325***			***9-30-95***	***75512***		***83571***	***90.4***						
Nts 8⅞s '96	Ms15	**A+**	1/95	A	X	BE	NC	....	....	....	....	....	200	S1	'91	102	100⅝	100⅝	8.82	5.73
Nts 8⅝s '96	Ao15	**A+**	1/95	A	X	BE	NC	....	....	....	....	....	250	G1	'91	102	100⅞	100⅞	8.55	5.51
Nts[3] 8¼s '96	Mn15	**A+**	1/95	A	X	R	NC	....	....	....	....	....	300	G1	'86	101⅞	100½	101	8.17	5.49
Nts[3] 8⅞s '96	fA	**A+**	1/95	A	X	R	NC	....	....	....	....	....	300	G1	'91	103	101¼	101⅞	8.71	5.58
Nts 8s '96	aO	**A+**	1/95	A	X	BE	NC	....	....	....	....	....	300	B5	'91	102⅜	100	101¾	7.86	5.58
Nts 8s '96	jD	**A+**	1/95	A	X	BE	NC	....	....	....	....	....	200	S1	'86	102⅝	99⅞	102⅛	7.83	5.60
Nts 7⅞s '97	Jj15	**A+**	1/95	A	X	BE	NC	....	....	....	....	....	200	G1	'87	102⅝	99⅜	102¼	7.70	5.62
Nts[3] 5⅝s '97	Ms3	**A+**	1/95	A	X	BE	NC	....	....	....	....	....	500	C5	'94	100⅛	94⅞	100⅛	5.62	5.51
Nts[3] 6.80s '97	fA15	**A+**	1/95	A	X	BE	NC	....	....	....	....	....	500	G1	'94	101⅞	100⅝	101⅞	6.67	5.57
Nts 7⅛s '97	jD	**A+**	1/95	A	X	BE	NC	....	....	....	....	....	500	G1	'92	102⅞	97⅛	102⅞	6.93	5.52
Nts 8s '97	jD	**A+**	1/95	A	X	BE	NC	....	....	....	....	....	500	B5	'94	104½	99	104½	7.66	5.50
Nts 9⅜s '97	jD15	**A+**	1/95	A	X	BE	NC	....	....	....	....	....	200	M2	'90	107¼	102¾	106¾	8.78	5.69
Nts 6¼s '98	Fa26	**A+**	1/95	A	X	BE	NC	....	....	....	....	....	1500	G1	'93	101¼	94⅛	101¼	6.17	5.62
Nts[3] 9¼s '98	Jd15	**A+**	1/95	A	X	BE	NC	....	....	....	....	....	250	G1	'91	108¼	102⅝	108⅛	8.55	5.66
Nts 5⅝s '98	jD15	**A+**	1/95	A	X	BE	NC	....	....	....	....	....	500	L3	'93	99⅞	90¾	99⅞	5.63	5.67
Nts[3] 8s '99	Jj15	**A+**	1/95	A	X	BE	NC	....	....	....	....	....	400	G1	'92	106⅛	98⅝	106⅛	7.54	5.78
Nts 5⅝s '99	Jj15	**A+**	1/95	A	X	BE	NC	....	....	....	....	....	500	S1	'93	99¾	90¼	99¾	5.64	5.71
Nts 7¼s '99	Mn15	**A+**	1/95	A	X	BE	NC	....	....	....	....	....	500	G1	'94	104⅜	95⅜	104⅜	6.95	5.80
Nts 8⅞s '99	Jd15	**A+**	1/95	A	X	BE	NC	....	....	....	....	....	200	G1	'89	109½	101⅛	109½	8.11	5.80
Nts 6⅜s '99	mS15	**A+**	1/95	A	X	BE	NC	....	....	....	....	....	400	B5	'92	101⅞	91¾	101⅞	6.26	5.80
Nts 7¾s '99	aO	**A+**	1/95	A	X	BE	NC	....	....	....	....	....	500	L3	'94	106⅝	96⅞	106⅝	7.27	5.76
Nts 8⅜s 2000	Jj15	**A+**	1/95	A	X	BE	NC	....	....	....	....	....	500	C5	'95	109	99¾	109	7.68	5.84
Nts 9½s 2000	Ao15	**A+**	1/95	A	X	BE	NC	....	....	....	....	....	200	G1	'90	113⅜	104¼	113⅜	8.38	5.92
Nts 6⅜s 2000	Ao15	**A+**	1/95	A	X	BE	NC	....	....	....	....	....	500	G1	'93	101¾	90⅞	101¾	6.27	5.90
Nts 6.85s 2000	fA15	**A+**			X	BE	NC	....	....	....	....	....	500	G1	'95	103⅝	99½	103⅝	6.61	5.94
Nts 6⅜s 2000	aO6	**A+**			X	BE	NC	....	....	....	....	....	500	S1	'95	101¾	99¾	101¾	6.27	5.95
Nts[3] 7½s 2000	mN	**A+**	1/95	A	X	R	NC	....	....	....	....	....	15.0	G1	'85	100⅝	100	100⅝	7.45	7.34
Nts[5] 6¼s 2000	mN8	**A+**			X	BE	NC	....	....	....	....	....	1000	G1	'95	101⅜	99⅝	101⅜	6.17	5.92
Nts 8.20s 2002	Fa15	**A+**			X	BE	NC	....	....	....	....	....	500	G1	'95	110⅞	99⅞	110⅞	7.40	6.05
Nts 8s 2002	Jd15	**A+**	1/95	A	X	BE	NC	....	....	....	....	....	400	M5	'92	110	97⅛	110	7.27	6.10
Nts 7¾s 2002	mN15	**A+**	1/95	A	X	BE	NC	....	....	....	....	....	400	F1	'92	109⅛	95⅝	109⅛	7.10	6.10
Nts 7½s 2003	Jj15	**A+**	1/95	A	X	BE	NC	....	....	....	....	....	500	S1	'93	108	93⅜	108	6.94	6.09
Nts 6⅝s 2003	Jd30	**A+**	1/95	A	X	BE	NC	....	....	....	....	....	500	L3	'93	102¾	88	102¾	6.45	6.16
Nts 7½s 2004	Jd15	**A+**	1/95	A	X	BE	NC	....	....	....	....	....	500	M6	'94	108	92⅞	108	6.94	6.27

Uniform Footnote Explanations-See Page 260. Other: [1] See First Nationwide Bank. [2] L-T-D as of 12-31-94. [3] Issued in min denom $5T. [4] Co may red in whole if 95% outstg put.
[5] Co may red in whole,at 100,for tax law chge.

Title-Industry Code & Co. Finances (In Italics)	Ind	Fixed Charge Coverage 1992	1993		1994	Year End	Million $ Cash & Equiv.	Curr. Assets	Curr. Liab.	Balance Sheet Date	L. Term Debt (Mil $)		Capital-ization (Mil $)	Total Debt % Capital						
Individual Issue Statistics Exchange ↓	Interest Dates	S&P Debt Rating	Date of Last Rating Change	Prior Rating	Eligible ↓	Bond Form	Redemption Provisions: Regular Price	Regular (Begins) Thru	Sinking Fund Price	Sinking Fund (Begins) Thru	Refund/Other Restriction Price	Refund/Other Restriction (Begins) Thru	Outst'g (Mil $)	Underwriting Firm	Underwriting Year	Price Range 1995 High	Price Range 1995 Low	Mo. End Price Sale(s) or Bid	Curr. Yield	Yield to Mat.
***Ford Motor Credit** (Cont.)*																				
Nts 7¾s 2005	Ms15	**A+**			X	BE	NC	....	....	....	....	....	500	M5	'95	110⅜	98¾	110⅜	7.02	6.25
Nts 6¾s 2005	Mn15	**A+**	1/95	A	X	BE	NC	....	....	....	....	....	500	M2	'93	103½	98¾	103½	6.52	6.25
Nts 6¼s 2005	jD8	**A+**			X	BE	NC	....	....	....	....	....	500	M2	'95	100	98½	100	6.25	6.25
Nts 6⅜s 2005	jD15	**A+**	1/95	A	X	BE	NC	....	....	....	....	....	300	L3	'93	101	84	101	6.31	6.24
Nts 6½s 2006	Fa15	**A+**	1/95	A	X	BE	NC	....	....	....	....	....	300	L3	'94	101¾	84⅜	101¾	6.39	6.26
Nts 6¾s 2008	fA15	**A+**	1/95	A	X	BE	NC	....	....	....	....	....	300	M5	'93	103	84⅝	103	6.55	6.40
• Nts 6⅜s 2008	mN5	**A+**	1/95	A	X	BE	NC	....	....	....	....	....	300	G1	'93	99	80½	98½	6.47	6.55
Ext'd Nts[1] 5¼s 2000	Ao15	**A+**	1/95	A	X	R	100	....	....	....	....	....	1.72	G1	'85	100¼	99½	100	5.25	5.25
[2]Ext'd[3]Nts[4] 6¾s '97	[5]jJ15	**A+**	1/95	A	X	R	100	....	....	....	....	....	39.1	G1	'86	100	100	100	6.75	6.75
Forest Oil	***49a***	***1.41***	***0.55***		***0.63***	***Dc***	***3.42***	***22.20***	***31.00***	***9-30-95***	***182.0***		***226.0***	***80.5***						
Sr[6]Sub Nts 11¼s 2003	mS	**B–**			Y	R	105.688	(9-1-98)	....	....	[7]Z110	8-31-96	100	L3	'93	95	84	94	11.97	12.48
Fort Howard Corp[8]	***50***	***0.79***	***0.78***		***0.87***	***Dc***	***44.00***	***299.0***	***277.0***	***9-30-95***	***3011***		***1208***	***254.0***						
Sr Nts 9¼s 2001	Ms15	**B+**			Y	R	NC	....	....	....	....	....	450	M6	'93	101¾	92¼	101¼	9.14	8.94
Sr Nts 8¼s 2002	Fa	**B+**			Y	R	NC	....	....	....	....	....	100	M6	'94	97¼	88¼	97	8.51	8.90
Sr Sub Nts 9s 2006	Fa	**B**			Y	R	104.50	(2-1-99)	....	....	[9]Z109	1-31-97	650	M6	'94	98½	83¾	98¼	9.16	9.27
Sub Nts 10s 2003	Ms15	**B**			Y	R	105	(3-15-98)	....	....	....	....	300	M6	'93	103½	91½	103½	9.66	9.32
Foster Wheeler	***13c***	***2.91***	***3.94***		***4.14***	***Dc***	***519.0***	***1486***	***1089***	***9-29-95***	***★655.0***		***1147***	***57.4***						
Nts 6¾s 2005	mN15	**BBB**			X	BE	NC	....	....	....	....	....	200	L3	'95	102⅜	99⅝	102⅜	6.59	6.42
Foundation Health	***30a***	***△52.61***	***△13.61***		***△18.60***	***Je***				***9-30-95***	***224.0***		***1008***	***22.2***						
Sr Nts[6] 7¾s 2003	Jd	**BBB–**			X	R	NC	....	....	....	....	....	125	S1	'93	105¼	90⅛	105¼	7.36	6.83
FPA Corp	***38***	***△d1.71***	***△0.20***		***△0.56***	***Je***	***1.26***			***9-30-95***	***44.60***		***57.00***	***78.2***						
◆Sub SF[10]Deb[11] 14½s 2000	mS	**NR**	8/87	CCC		R	100	....	100	....	....	....	[12]4.34	D7	'80	89	88	88	....	Flat
FPL Group Capital[13]	***25***	***1.00***	***1.80***		....	***Dc***	***29.60***	***96.40***	***314.0***	***12-31-93***	***286.0***		***897.0***	***62.9***						
Deb 6½s '97	jJ	**A+**	7/95	A	X	R	NC	....	....	....	....	....	150	S1	'92	101⅛	95¾	101⅛	6.43	5.71
Deb 7⅝s 2013	Mn	**A+**	7/95	A	X	R	103.84	(5-1-98)	....	....	....	....	125	S1	'93	103⅜	88	103⅜	7.38	7.28
Franchise Finance Corp Amer	***57***	***108.24***	***170.97***		***22.84***	***Dc***				***9-30-95***	***★244.0***		***744.0***	***32.7***						
Sr Nts 7s 2000	mN30	**BBB–**			X	BE	NC	....	....	....	....	....	150	M2	'95	100½	99⅛	100½	6.97	6.88
Sr Nts 7⅞s 2005	mN30	**BBB–**			X	BE	NC	....	....	....	....	....	50.0	M2	'95	108	99¾	108	7.29	6.75
Franklin Universal Tr	***47***	***n/a***	***n/a***		***n/a***	***Au***				***8-31-94***	***74.90***		***308.0***	***24.3***						
Sr Nts 5⅝s '98	mS	**AAA**			X	R	Z100	....	....	....	....	....	75.0	P1	'93	99⅝	91⅝	99⅝	5.65	5.77
Freeport-McMoRan	***45***	***1.86***	***0.28***		***1.36***	***Dc***	***28.70***	***219.0***	***205.0***	***9-30-95***	***301.0***		***635.0***	***47.4***						
• Sr Sub Deb 10⅞s 2001	Mn15	**NR**	7/95	BB–	Y	R	100	(5-15-96)	100	(5-15-96)	....	....	[14]45.3	K2	'86	105¼	101½	101½	10.71	10.50
Freeport-McMoRan Res LP	***14a***	***1.06***	***d2.54***		***3.51***	***Dc***	***23.90***	***200.0***	***117.0***	***9-30-95***	***347.0***		***752.0***	***46.1***						
• Sr Sub Nts[15] 8¾s 2004	Fa15	**BB+**	9/95	BB–	Y	R	104.375	(2-15-99)	....	....	....	....	150	G1	'94	103½	92	101	8.66	8.57
Fruit of the Loom[16]	***68c***	***4.90***	***5.12***		***2.40***	***Dc***	***14.40***	***1262***	***306.0***	***9-30-95***	***1499***		***2726***	***55.5***						
◆([17]Sec)Deb 7s 2011	Ms15	**BBB+**	7/93	BBB	X	R	100	....	....	....	....	....	[12]125	G1	'81	95	79½	s94½	7.41	7.61
Deb 7⅜s 2023	mN	**BBB+**			X	R	NC	....	....	....	....	....	150	C5	'93	101¾	83⅛	101¾	7.25	7.23
Sr Nts[6] 7⅞s '99	aO15	**BBB+**	8/93	BBB	X	R	NC	....	....	....	....	....	250	F1	'92	106⅛	96⅞	106	7.43	6.08
Nts 6½s 2003	mN15	**BBB+**			X	R	NC	....	....	....	....	....	150	C5	'93	100¾	86¾	100	6.50	6.50
Galaxy Telecom LP/Cap	***12a***	***n/a***	***n/a***		***n/a***	***Dc***				***6-30-95***	***★150.0***		***99.30***	***67.2***						
Sr[6]Sub Nts 12⅜s 2005	aO	**B–**			Y	R	106.15	(10-1-00)	....	....	[18]Z112.375	9-30-98	120	M2	'95	107⅜	99½	107⅜	11.53	11.11
Gannett Co	***54c***	***12.30***	***14.04***		***18.14***	***Dc***	***35.50***	***676.0***	***595.0***	***9-24-95***	***542.0***		***2621***	***22.9***						
Nts 8½s '96	Fa	**A+**	10/95	AA–	X	R	NC	....	....	....	....	....	17.3	S4	'86	102⅜	100¼	100¼	8.48	5.48
• Nts 5¼s '98	Ms	**A+**	10/95	AA–	X	BE	NC	....	....	....	....	....	275	L3	'93	99¾	91⅜	98⅞	5.31	5.80
• Nts 5.85s 2000	Mn	**A+**	10/95	AA–	X	BE	NC	....	....	....	....	....	250	G1	'93	99⅝	91	98½	5.94	6.25
Garden St. Newspapers, Inc	***54c***	***△0.45***	***△0.12***		***△0.87***	***Je***	***5.63***	***42.90***	***43.40***	***9-30-95***	***233.0***		***222.0***	***112.0***						
Sr Sub Sec Nts[6] 12s 2004	jJ	**B+**			Y	R	107.50	(7-1-99)	....	....	....	....	100	B9	'94	100¼	95	100	12.00	12.00

Uniform Footnote Explanations-See Page 260. Other: [1] Int adj to maturity. [2] (HRO)On 7-15-97 at 100,aft as defined. [3] Int to 7-15-97. [4] Issued in min $5T denom. [5] Due 7-15-06. [6] (HRO)On Chge of Ctrl at 101. [7] Max $30M red w/proceeds of Com Stk Off'g. [8] Was Fort Howard Paper. [9] Max $228M red w/proceeds Pub Eq Off'g. [10] Int:'90,3-1 pd 4-3-90,9-1 pd 11-9-90. [11] Int:'91,3-1 & 9-1 pd 10-2-91. [12] Incl disc. [13] Subsid of FPL Group,Inc. [14] Defeased,fds deposited w/trustee. [15] Co must offer repurch at 101 on Specified Chge of Ctrl. [16] Was Northwest Ind,then Farley/Northwest Ind. [17] Classified Sr Secured Debt. [18] Max $42M red w/proceeds of Pub Eq Off'g.

Title-Industry Code & Co. Finances (In Italics) / Individual Issue Statistics (Exchange)	Ind / Interest Dates	1992 / S&P Debt Rating	1993 / Date of Last Rating Change	Prior Rating	1994 / Eligible	Year End / Bond Form	Cash & Equiv. / Redemption Provisions: Regular Price	Curr. Assets / Regular (Begins) Thru	Curr. Liab. / Sinking Fund Price	Balance Sheet Date / Sinking Fund (Begins) Thru	L. Term Debt (Mil $) / Refund/Other Restriction Price	Refund/Other Restriction (Begins) Thru	Capitalization (Mil $) / Outst'g (Mil $)	Total Debt % Capital / Underwriting Firm	Underwriting Year	Price Range 1995 High	Price Range 1995 Low	Mo. End Price Sale(s) or Bid	Curr. Yield	Yield to Mat.
[1]GATX Leasing	***25c***	*1.06*	*1.66*		*1.70*	*Dc*	*5.23*			*3-31-95*	*597.0*		*905.0*	*65.9*						
Nts 10s '96	Jj	BBB+	5/86	A−	X	R	NC	....	....	....	....	....	50.0	M6	'85	102⅛	100	100	10.00	Mat.
Nts 9⅜s '97	Jj	BBB+			X	R	NC	....	....	....	....	....	50.0	M6	'86	104⅛	101⅛	103¼	9.08	6.00
Gaylord Container	***16c***	*0.34*	*0.09*		*0.15*	*Sp*	*7.20*	*263.0*	*169.0*	*6-30-95*	*689.0*		*778.0*	*92.7*						
Sr Nts[2] 11½s 2001	Mn15	B			Y	R	104.93	(5-15-97)	....	....	....	....	225	B9	'93	104⅜	101½	103	11.17	10.74
Sr Sub[3]Disc Deb[4] 12¾s 2005	Mn15	B−			Y	R	106.38	(5-15-98)	....	....	....	....	[5]434	B9	'93	101¼	88¼	98	....	Flat
GB Property Funding[6]	***25***	*n/a*	*n/a*		*1.00*	*Dc*		*4.25*	*4.25*	*9-30-95*	*185.0*		*185.0*	*100.0*						
◆1st[2] 10⅞s 2004	Jj15	B+			Y	R	104.08	(1-15-99)	*100	(7-15-99)	....	....	185	S1	'94	90	82½	85	12.79	14.04
GEICO Corp	***35c***	*8.80*	*18.71*		*10.00*	*Dc*				*9-30-95*	*433.0*		*2172*	*19.9*						
Deb 9.15s 2021	mS15	AA			X	R	104.575	(9-15-01)	....	....	....	....	100	S1	'91	115¼	101⅜	115¼	7.94	7.77
Deb 7.35s 2023	jJ15	AA			X	R	NC	....	....	....	....	....	150	S1	'93	106⅛	85¼	106⅛	6.93	6.85
Nts 7½s 2005	Ao15	AA			X	R	NC	....	....	....	....	....	100	S1	'95	109½	99¾	109½	6.85	6.14
General American Trans[7]	***56a***	*1.92*	*2.33*		*2.44*	*Dc*	*13.20*			*9-30-95*	*1067*		*1883*	*61.2*						
Deb[8] 10⅛s 2002	Ms15	BBB+	5/95	A−	X	BE	NC	....	....	....	....	....	115	S1	'90	119¾	108	119¾	8.46	6.24
Nts 8⅝s 2004	jD	BBB+	5/95	A−	X	BE	NC	....	....	....	....	....	100	M6	'94	114⅝	99⅞	114⅝	7.52	6.44
General Chemical Corp	***14***	*2.55*	*2.55*		*2.78*	*Dc*	*18.80*	*141.0*	*122.0*	*9-30-95*	*260.0*		*98.60*	*277.0*						
Sr Sub Nts[9] 9¼s 2003	fA15	B+			Y	R	103.469	(8-15-98)	....	....	[10]Z109.25	8-14-96	100	F1	'93	99	93½	99	9.34	9.43
General Dynamics	***2a***	*6.40*	*22.74*		*68.20*	*Dc*	*993.0*	*1970*	*858.0*	*10-1-95*	*186.0*		*1666*	*11.2*						
•Deb 9.95s 2018	Ao	A	5/92	A−	X	R	104.45	(4-1-98)	100	(4-1-99)	....	....	39.0	M6	'88	114	107	111½	8.92	8.76
General Electric Co.[11]	***23a***	*1.92*	*1.95*		*2.75*	*Dc*	*3159*			*9-30-95*	*49853*		*140937*	*78.1*						
Nts 7⅞s '96	Mn	AAA			X	BE	NC	....	....	....	....	....	500	K2	'91	101⅝	100⅜	100¾	7.82	5.55
Nts 7⅞s '98	mS15	AAA			X	BE	NC	....	....	....	....	....	500	K2	'91	106	99	106	7.43	5.46
General Electric[12]Capital	***25***	*1.45*	*1.65*		*1.85*	*Dc*				*9-30-95*	*47474*		*114147*	*87.8*						
Deb 5½s 2001	mN	AAA			X	R	100	....	....	....	....	....	[5]385	M6	'81	97½	85⅜	97½	5.64	6.01
Amortizing[13]Nts 6.20s '97	Ms15	AAA			X	R	NC	....	....	....	....	....	200	G1	'92	100¾	96⅜	100¾	6.15	....
Nts 7.85s '96	jJ17	AAA			X	BE	NC	....	....	....	....	....	200	M2	'95	101⅞	100	101¼	7.75	5.50
Nts 8¾s '96	mN26	AAA			X	BE	NC	....	....	....	....	....	250	K2	'90	103⅞	101¼	102⅞	8.51	5.45
Nts 8s '97	Fa	AAA			X	BE	NC	....	....	....	....	....	250	L3	'91	103⅜	99⅞	102⅝	7.80	5.48
Nts 8s '98	Jj15	AAA			X	BE	NC	....	....	....	....	....	200	U1	'95	104¾	99¾	104¾	7.64	5.51
Nts 8⅜s 2001	Ms	AAA			X	BE	NC	....	....	....	....	....	250	L3	'91	111¼	100⅜	111¼	7.53	5.82
Nts 8.70s 2003	Fa15	AAA			X	R	NC	....	....	....	....	....	250	S4	'90	115⅛	101⅞	115⅛	7.56	6.05
Nts 7⅞s 2004	mN22	AAA			X	R	NC	....	....	....	....	....	200	S1	'89	113¼	96¾	113¼	6.95	5.94
Nts 8.85s 2005	Ao	AAA			X	R	NC	....	....	....	....	....	300	G1	'90	119¼	103¼	119¼	7.42	6.10
Nts 8¾s 2007	Mn21	AAA			X	R	NC	....	....	....	....	....	250	K2	'90	121⅜	102¾	121⅜	7.21	6.12
Nts[14] 8⅝s 2008	Jd15	AAA			X	R	NC	....	....	....	....	....	250	K2	'90	121¼	101⅝	121¼	7.11	6.16
Nts 8½s 2008	jJ24	AAA			X	R	NC	....	....	....	....	....	250	M2	'90	119⅝	101⅞	119⅝	7.11	6.23
Nts[15] 8.30s 2009	mS20	AAA			X	R	NC	....	....	....	....	....	250	K2	'89	120⅜	101⅛	120⅜	6.90	6.09
[16]Reset[17]Nts[18] 7.98s '96	[19]jD15	AAA			X	BE	[20]100	....	....	....	....	....	500	M2	'87	109½	97½	103	7.75	....
F/R[21]Nts 5.61s 2018	Ms15	AAA	9/88	NR	X	R	[22]100	....	....	....	....	....	25.0	S1	'88	100	95⅛	100	5.61	....
F/R[23]Nts[24] 2049	mN	AAA			X	R	105	(11-1-19)	....	....	....	....	50.0	K2	'89	100	98½	100	....	....
[25]F/R[26]Nts[27] 2050	[28]Fa	AAA			X	R	105	(2-1-20)	....	....	....	....	25.0	G1	'90	100	98½	100	....	....
[29]F/R[30]Nts[25] 2050	[28]Mn	AAA			X	R	105	(5-1-20)	....	....	....	....	250	K2	'90	100	98½	100	....	....
[25]F/R[31]Nts[32] 2051	[28]Mn	AAA			X	BE	105	(5-31-21)	....	....	....	....	25.0	K2	'91	100	98½	100	....	....
•Gtd[33]Sub Nts 7⅞s 2006	jD	AAA			X	BE	NC	....	....	....	....	....	250	K2	'91	113	96	s112¼	7.02	6.31
Gtd[33]Sub Nts 8⅛s 2012	Mn15	AAA			X	BE	NC	....	....	....	....	....	450	K2	'92	116⅛	97¾	116⅛	7.00	6.51
F/R[34]Global M-T Nts 'A' '96	QFeb15	AAA			X	BE	NC	....	....	....	....	....	100	G1	'95	100⅛	100	100	....	....
F/R[35]Global M-T Nts 'A' '96	QFeb16	AAA			X	BE	NC	....	....	....	....	....	100	M2	'95	100	100	100	....	....

Uniform Footnote Explanations-See Page 260. Other: [1] Now GATX Capital. [2] (HRO)On Chge of Ctrl at 101. [3] (HRO)On Chge of Ctrl at 101(Accreted Val). [4] Int accrues at 12.75% fr 5-15-96. [5] Incl disc. [6] Subsid of Pratt Hotel Corp. [7] Subsid of GATX Corp. [8] Int sub to adj for Designated Event&Rat'g Chge. [9] (HRO)On Chge in Ctrl at 101. [10] Max $30M red w/proceeds of Pub Eq Off'g. [11] See Gen'l Electric Capital Services. [12] Was General Electric Credit. [13] Princ pyts due on int dates thru 3-15-97. [14] (HRO)On 6-15-96 at 100. [15] (HRO)On 9-1-98 at 100. [16] (HRO)On 12-15-96 at 100,aft as defined. [17] Issued in min denom $100T. [18] Int to 12-15-96,reset aft as defined. [19] Due 12-15-07. [20] On 12-15-96,aft as defined. [21] Int reset 3-15-97,adj ea 3rd 3-15 aft. [22] On 3-15-97,aft as defined. [23] (HRO)Ea Nov 1:'99,99.39,'02,99.6,'05,99.87. [24] (HRO)Ea 3rd Nov 1 fr '08 to maturity at 100. [25] Int adj mthly,as defined. [26] (HRO)On Feb 1,2000 at 99.39. [27] (HRO)On Feb 1:2003,99.60,2006,99.87,2009-50,100. [28] Co may pay int monthly or semi-anly. [29] (HRO)On May 1:2003,99.60,2006,99.87,2009-50,100. [30] (HRO)On May 1,2000 at 99.39. [31] (HRO)On May 1,2001 at 99.39. [32] (HRO)On May 1:2004,99.60,2007,99.87,2010-51,100. [33] Gtd by Gen'l Elec Co on Sr Basis. [34] Int reset daily(Prime minus 2.65%). [35] Int reset daily(Fed Fds Rt & 0.125%).

Title-Industry Code & Co. Finances (In Italics)	Ind	Fixed Charge Coverage 1992	1993		1994	Year End	Million $ Cash & Equiv.	Curr. Assets	Curr. Liab.	Balance Sheet Date	L. Term Debt (Mil $)		Capital-ization (Mil $)	Total Debt % Capital						
Exchange ↓ Individual Issue Statistics	Interest Dates	S&P Debt Rating	Date of Last Rating Change	Prior Rating	Eligible ↓	Bond Form	Redemption Provisions: Regular Price	Regular (Begins) Thru	Sinking Fund Price	Sinking Fund (Begins) Thru	Refund/Other Restriction Price	Refund/Other Restriction (Begins) Thru	Outst'g (Mil $)	Underwriting Firm	Underwriting Year	Price Range 1995 High	Price Range 1995 Low	Mo. End Price Sale(s) or Bid	Curr. Yield	Yield to Mat.
***General Electric Capital** (Cont.)*																				
Global M-T Nts 'A' 6.95s '96	Ms	**AAA**			X	BE	NC	....	....	....	....	....	100	L3	'95	100¾	100	100¼	6.93	5.36
F/R[1]Global M-T Nts 'A' '96	QMar22	**AAA**			X	BE	NC	....	....	....	....	....	100		'95	100	100	100	....	....
F/R[1]Global M-T Nts 'A' '96	QMar25	**AAA**			X	BE	NC	....	....	....	....	....	50.0		'95	100	100	100	....	....
Global M-T Nts 'A' 6.55s '96	[2]ms15	**AAA**			X	BE	NC	....	....	....	....	....	200	M2	'95	100⅝	100	100¼	6.53	5.40
Global M-T Nts 'A' 6.55s '96	[3]ms15	**AAA**			X	BE	NC	....	....	....	....	....	100	M2	'95	100⅝	100	100¼	6.53	5.44
Global M-T Nts 'A' 6.39s '96	Mn6	**AAA**			X	BE	NC	....	....	....	....	....	200	M5	'95	100½	100	100⅜	6.37	5.26
Global M-T Nts 'A' 6.09s '96	[4]ms15	**AAA**			X	BE	NC	....	....	....	....	....	25.0	S5	'95	100¼	100	100¼	6.07	5.42
Global M-T Nts 'A' 5.78s '96	[5]ms15	**AAA**			X	BE	NC	....	....	....	....	....	25.0	G1	'95	100¼	99¾	100¼	5.77	5.23
Global M-T Nts 'A' 5.85s '96	[6]ms15	**AAA**			X	BE	NC	....	....	....	....	....	50.0	G1	'95	100¼	99⅞	100¼	5.84	5.45
Global M-T Nts 'A' 5.68s '96	[7]ms15	**AAA**			X	BE	NC	....	....	....	....	....	50.0	G1	'95	100⅛	99¾	100⅛	5.67	5.48
Global M-T Nts 'A' 5.715s '96	aO16	**AAA**			X	BE	NC	....	....	....	....	....	50.0	M5	'95	100¼	100	100¼	5.70	5.38
Global M-T Nts 'A' 7s '97	[8]ms15	**AAA**			X	BE	NC	....	....	....	....	....	25.0	M5	'95	101⅞	100	101⅞	6.87	5.33
Global M-T Nts 'A' 6.043s '97	[9]ms15	**AAA**			X	BE	NC	....	....	....	....	....	25.0	C5	'95	101	99⅝	101	5.98	5.31
Global M-T Nts 'A' 5.84s '97	[10]ms15	**AAA**			X	BE	NC	....	....	....	....	....	25.0	M5	'95	100¾	99¾	100¾	5.80	5.38
Global M-T Nts'A' 5.77s '97	[11]ms15	**AAA**			X	BE	NC	....	....	....	....	....	25.0	B5	'95	100¾	100	100¾	5.73	5.33
Global M-T Nts 'A' 7.65s '98	[12]ms15	**AAA**			X	BE	NC	....	....	....	....	....	50.0	G1	'95	104½	100	104½	7.32	5.38
Global M-T Nts 'A' 7.65s '98	[13]ms15	**AAA**			X	BE	NC	....	....	....	....	....	25.0	G1	'95	104½	100	104½	7.32	5.40
Global M-T Nts 'A' 7½s '98	[14]ms15	**AAA**			X	BE	NC	....	....	....	....	....	25.0	G1	'95	104¼	100	104¼	7.19	5.39
Global M-T Nts 'A' 7s '98	[15]ms15	**AAA**			X	BE	NC	....	....	....	....	....	50.0	M5	'95	103¼	99⅞	103¼	6.78	5.43
Global M-T Nts 'A' 7.05s '98	[16]ms15	**AAA**			X	BE	NC	....	....	....	....	....	50.0	G1	'95	103⅜	100	103⅜	6.82	5.43
Global M-T Nts 'A' 7.08s '98	[17]ms15	**AAA**			X	BE	NC	....	....	....	....	....	25.0	P1	'95	103½	100	103½	6.84	5.40
Global M-T Nts 'A' 7⅛s '98	Ao6	**AAA**			X	BE	NC	....	....	....	....	....	50.0	M5	'95	103⅝	99⅞	103⅝	6.88	5.40
Global M-T Nts 'A' 6.844s '98	Ao23	**AAA**			X	BE	NC	....	....	....	....	....	50.0	M5	'95	103	100	103	6.64	5.44
Global M-T Nts 'A' 6.84s '98	[18]ms15	**AAA**			X	BE	NC	....	....	....	....	....	25.0	S5	'95	103	100	103	6.64	5.44
Global M-T Nts 'A' 7.34s '99	[19]ms15	**AAA**			X	BE	NC	....	....	....	....	....	50.0	G1	'95	105⅛	100	105⅛	6.98	5.55
Global M-T Nts 'A' 7.01s '99	[20]ms15	**AAA**			X	BE	NC	....	....	....	....	....	25.0	M6	'95	104⅜	100	104⅜	6.72	5.56
Global M-T Nts 'A' 7.02s 2000	[21]ms15	**AAA**			X	BE	NC	....	....	....	....	....	25.0	S5	'95	105	100	105	6.69	5.70
Global M-T Nts 'A' 7s 2005	[22]Jul28	**AAA**			X	BE	*■100	(7-28-96)	....	....	....	....	25.0	L3	'95	100⅞	100⅛	100⅞	6.94	6.87
Global M-T Nts 'A' 7¼s 2007	[22]Aug29	**AAA**			X	BE	100	(8-29-96)	....	....	....	....	25.0	L3	'95	104	100	101⅛	7.17	7.10
Global M-T Nts 'A' 7.10s 2007	[22]Sep5	**AAA**			X	BE	*100	(9-5-96)	....	....	....	....	25.0	L3	'95	103⅛	100⅛	101⅛	7.02	6.96
Global M-T Nts 'A' 7s 2010	[22]Jul14	**AAA**			X	BE	■*100	(8-1-97)	....	....	....	....	25.0	L3	'95	102⅝	100	102⅝	6.82	6.71
Global M-T Nts 'A' 7s 2010	[22]Aug22	**AAA**			X	BE	100	(8-22-97)	....	....	....	....	25.0	B5	'95	104⅛	99⅛	102⅝	6.82	6.71
Global M-T Nts 'A' 7.15s 2010	[22]Sep27	**AAA**			X	BE	*100	(9-27-96)	....	....	....	....	25.0	L3	'95	103⅞	100	101⅛	7.07	7.02
Global M-T Nts 'A' 7.10s 2010	[22]Oct6	**AAA**			X	BE	*100	(10-6-96)	....	....	....	....	25.0	L3	'95	104	100	101¼	7.01	6.96
Global M-T Nts 'A' 7.10s 2010	[22]Oct26	**AAA**			X	BE	*100	(10-26-96)	....	....	....	....	25.0	L3	'95	104½	100	104½	6.79	6.62
Gen'l Electric Capital Svcs	***25***	***Gtd by Gen'l Electric Co,see***																		
• Gtd[23]Sub Nts 7½s 2035	fA21	**AAA**			X	BE	NC	....	....	....	....	....	300	M2	'95	99⅜	99⅜	110¾	6.77	6.72
General Foods Corp	***26f***	***Subsid of Kraft Gen'l Foods, see Philip Morris Cos***																		
Deb 6s 2001	Jd15	**A**	10/85	AA	X	R	100	....	....	....	....	....	[24]150	G1	'81	100	87⅜	100	6.00	6.00
Deb 7s 2011	Jd15	**A**	10/85	AA	X	R	100	....	....	....	....	....	[24]200	G1	'81	100¼	84¾	100¼	6.98	6.97
General Host	***59l***	***1.04***	***d0.33***		***1.34***	***Ja***	***26.40***	***186.0***	***156.0***	***11-5-95***	***176.0***		***345.0***	***67.8***						
• Sr Nts[25] 11½s 2002	Fa15	**B–**	6/94	B	Y	R	109	2-14-96	....	....	®105.40	2-14-97	78.0	S5	'92	103	87⅞	s95	12.11	12.69
General Mills	***26***	***△10.69***	***△7.14***		***△5.63***	***My***	***16.70***	***1001***	***1305***	***8-27-95***	***1335***		***1815***	***88.4***						
Amort[26]Med-Term Nts 6.235s '97	Ms15	**A+**			X	BE	NC	....	....	....	....	....	100	G1	'92	100¾	99¼	A100	6.24	....
General Motors Acceptance	***25a***	***1.36***	***1.33***		***1.34***	***Dc***				***9-30-95***	***31856***		***77723***	***89.3***						
Deb 5½s 2001	jD15	**A–**	10/95	BBB+	X	R	100	....	....	....	....	....	[24]400	M6	'81	96⅜	82½	96⅜	5.71	6.24

Uniform Footnote Explanations-See Page 260. Other: [1] Int reset daily(Prime minus 2.65%). [2] Due 3-25-96. [3] Due 3-28-96. [4] Due 5-24-96. [5] Due 6-19-96. [6] Due 8-29-96. [7] Due 9-9-96. [8] Due 3-3-97. [9] Due 6-6-97. [10] Due 9-25-97. [11] Due 10-30-97. [12] Due 2-16-98. [13] Due 2-23-98. [14] Due 2-27-98. [15] Due 3-24-98. [16] Due 3-27-98. [17] Due 3-30-98. [18] Due 4-26-98. [19] Due 3-2-99. [20] Due 5-5-99. [21] Due 4-25-00. [22] Int pd monthly. [23] Gtd on Sr basis by Gen'l Elec Co. [24] Incl disc. [25] (HRO)On Chge of Ctrl at 101. [26] Princ pyts due on int pyt dates 3-15-97.

Individual Issue Statistics (Exchange ↓)	Interest Dates	S&P Debt Rating	Date of Last Rating Change	Prior Rating	Eligible ↓	Bond Form	Redemption Provisions: Regular Price	Regular (Begins) Thru	Sinking Fund Price	Sinking Fund (Begins) Thru	Refund/Other Restriction Price	Refund/Other Restriction (Begins) Thru	Outst'g (Mil $)	Underwriting Firm	Underwriting Year	Price Range 1995 High	Price Range 1995 Low	Mo. End Price Sale(s) or Bid	Curr. Yield	Yield to Mat.
Title-Industry Code & Co. Finances (In Italics)	*Ind*	*Fixed Charge Coverage 1992*	*1993*	*1994*		*Year End*	*Million $ Cash & Equiv.*	*Curr. Assets*	*Curr. Liab.*	*Balance Sheet Date*	*L. Term Debt (Mil $)*		*Capital-ization (Mil $)*	*Total Debt % Capital*						
***General Motors Acceptance** (Cont.)*																				
• Deb 6s 2011	Ao	**A–**	10/95	BBB+	X	R	100	....	....	....	....	....	[1]400	M6	'81	92⅛	74½	s91⅝	6.55	6.89
• Deb 8¼s 2016	Ao	**A–**	10/95	BBB+	X	R	103.60	(4-1-96)	....	....	....	....	300	S1	'86	104¾	92	103	8.01	7.95
• Dfrd Int Deb[2] 2012	[3]	**A–**	10/95	BBB+	X	R	100	....	....	....	....	....	[1]1214	M6	'82	320	217	s320	....	....
• Dfrd Int Deb[2] 2015	[4]	**A–**	10/95	BBB+	X	R	100	....	....	....	....	....	[1]1625	M6	'82	271	178	s271	....	....
Nts 8¾s '96	Fa	**A–**	10/95	BBB+	X	BE	NC	....	....	....	....	....	300	M6	'91	101½	100¼	100¼	8.73	5.72
Nts 8⅝s '96	jJ15	**A–**	10/95	BBB+	X	BE	NC	....	....	....	....	....	300	L3	'91	102½	100½	101½	8.50	5.78
Nts 8¼s '96	fA	**A–**	10/95	BBB+	X	BE	NC	....	....	....	....	....	300	M2	'89	102⅛	100⅛	101½	8.13	5.61
Nts 8s '96	aO	**A–**	10/95	BBB+	X	R	NC	....	....	....	....	....	300	F1	'91	102⅜	99⅝	101¾	7.86	5.58
• Nts 8⅜s '97	Mn	**A–**	10/95	BBB+	X	R	NC	....	....	....	....	....	200	M2	'87	104¾	100	103⅜	8.10	5.71
Nts 7¾s '97	Ao15	**A–**	10/95	BBB+	X	BE	NC	....	....	....	....	....	500	M6	'92	102½	98⅜	101⅞	7.61	6.21
F/R[5]Nts 6⅛s '98	QFeb2	**A–**	10/95	BBB+	X	BE	NC	....	....	....	....	....	350	L3	'95	100¼	99¾	100⅛	6.12	....
Nts 5⅝s '99	Fa	**A–**	10/95	BBB+	X	BE	NC	....	....	....	....	....	300	M5	'94	99¾	89⅜	99¾	5.64	5.71
Nts 7¾s '99	Jj15	**A–**	10/95	BBB+	X	BE	NC	....	....	....	....	....	500	M2	'92	105½	96¾	105½	7.35	5.75
Nts 7⅛s '99	Jd	**A–**	10/95	BBB+	X	BE	NC	....	....	....	....	....	300	B5	'94	104	94	104	6.85	5.82
Nts 8⅝s '99	Jd15	**A–**	10/95	BBB+	X	R	NC	....	....	....	....	....	400	M2	'89	107½	100⅛	107½	8.02	6.18
Nts 8.40s '99	aO15	**A–**	10/95	BBB+	X	BE	NC	....	....	....	....	....	400	S4	'89	107½	98⅞	107	7.85	6.29
Nts 7s 2000	Ms	**A–**	10/95	BBB+	X	BE	NC	....	....	....	....	....	500	M6	'93	104	92⅞	104	6.73	5.90
Nts 9⅜s 2000	Ao	**A–**	10/95	BBB+	X	BE	NC	....	....	....	....	....	300	F1	'90	112½	102⅞	112½	8.33	6.00
Nts 9⅝s 2000	Mn15	**A–**	10/95	BBB+	X	BE	NC	....	....	....	....	....	250	M6	'90	113⅝	103⅜	113⅝	8.47	6.03
Nts 9⅝s 2001	jD15	**A–**	10/95	BBB+	X	BE	NC	....	....	....	....	....	500	M2	'91	116⅜	104⅛	116⅜	8.27	6.29
Nts 7s 2002	mS15	**A–**	10/95	BBB+	X	BE	NC	....	....	....	....	....	500	L3	'92	104¾	90	104¾	6.68	6.12
Nts 6⅝s 2002	aO	**A–**	10/95	BBB+	X	BE	NC	....	....	....	....	....	500	M6	'95	102⅞	99¾	102⅞	6.44	6.10
Nts 8½s 2003	Jj	**A–**	10/95	BBB+	X	BE	NC	....	....	....	....	....	500	M2	'93	113⅛	98¼	113⅛	7.51	6.16
Nts[6] 8¾s 2005	jJ15	**A–**	10/95	BBB+	X	R	NC	....	....	....	....	....	200	M2	'90	117¼	102¼	117¼	7.46	6.32
Nts 6⅝s 2005	aO15	**A–**	10/95	BBB+	X	BE	NC	....	....	....	....	....	500	M2	'95	102⅜	98¾	102⅜	6.47	6.29
Nts[7] 8⅞s 2010	Jd	**A–**	10/95	BBB+	X	BE	NC	....	....	....	....	....	500	M2	'90	121¾	103⅜	121¾	7.29	6.52
F/R[8]M-T Nts 6.025s '97	QJun2	**A–**	10/95	BBB+	X	BE	NC	....	....	....	....	....	100	M2	'95	100	100	100	6.03	....
General Motors Corp.	***9***	***0.87***	***1.69***	***2.49***		***Dc***	***13890***			***9-30-95***	***[9]37490***		***100744***	***77.3***						
Deb 8⅛s 2016	Ao15	**A–**	10/95	BBB+	X	R	104.01	4-14-96	....	....	®103.65	4-14-96	500	S1	'86	107⅞	89½	103⅛	7.88	7.81
Deb 9.40s 2021	jJ15	**A–**	10/95	BBB+	X	BE	NC	....	....	....	....	....	300	M2	'91	130	105½	130	7.23	6.89
Deb 7.40s 2025	mS	**A–**	10/95	BBB+	X	BE	NC	....	....	....	....	....	500	S1	'95	106	97⅞	106	6.98	6.92
Nts 7⅝s '97	Fa15	**A–**	10/95	BBB+	X	BE	NC	....	....	....	....	....	400	M6	'92	102⅜	98⅜	102¼	7.46	5.53
Nts 9¾s '99	Mn15	**A–**	10/95	BBB+	X	R	100	(5-15-96)	....	....	....	....	200	S1	'89	103¼	101⅝	101¾	9.58	9.13
Nts 9⅝s 2000	jD	**A–**	10/95	BBB+	X	BE	NC	....	....	....	....	....	700	S1	'90	115¼	103⅞	115¼	8.35	6.00
Nts 9⅛s 2001	jJ15	**A–**	10/95	BBB+	X	BE	NC	....	....	....	....	....	400	M2	'91	114¼	102⅛	114¼	7.99	6.06
Nts 8⅞s 2003	Mn15	**A–**	10/95	BBB+	X	BE	NC	....	....	....	....	....	100	S1	'91	115¼	100⅞	115¼	7.70	6.26
Nts 7s 2003	Jd15	**A–**	10/95	BBB+	X	BE	NC	....	....	....	....	....	300	S1	'93	104⅜	89⅝	104⅜	6.71	6.26
Nts[10] 8.80s 2021	Ms	**A–**	10/95	BBB+	X	BE	NC	....	....	....	....	....	600	M2	'91	125⅜	103⅛	125⅜	7.02	6.70
General Nutrition, Inc	***59l***	***1.78***	***3.25***	***4.97***		***Ja***		***197.0***	***123.0***	***2-4-95***	***298.0***		***519.0***	***61.1***						
Sr Sub Nts[11] 11⅜s 2000	Ms	**NR**	3/95	B		R	102.843	(3-1-97)	....	....	....	....	[12]13.9	D6	'92	110	106⅜	108⅜	10.50	8.92
General Physics	***63***	***n/a***	***n/a***	***2.44***		***Dc***	***0.53***	***35.90***	***18.90***	***9-30-95***	***12.30***		***37.20***	***47.3***						
• Sr Sub Deb 6s 2004	QJun30	**NR**				R	NC	....	....	....	....	....	15.0	Mgr	'94	66	25	63¼	9.49	13.36
General Re Corp	***35c***	***25.96***	***27.03***	***32.76***		***Dc***				***6-30-95***	***156.0***		***5865***	***2.7***						
Deb 9s 2009	mS12	**AAA**			X	R	NC	....	....	....	....	....	150	F1	'89	124⅜	102⅝	124⅜	7.24	6.31
General Tel. California	***67a***	***Now GTE California,see***																		
1st S 6s '96	aO	**AA–**	9/86	A+	X	R	100	....	....	....	....	....	45.0	F1	'66	100⅛	96¾	100	6.00	5.98

Uniform Footnote Explanations-See Page 260. Other: [1] Incl disc. [2] Pays $10,000 at maturity. [3] Due Dec 1. [4] Due Jun 15. [5] Int to 11-2-95,adj qtrly(3 Mo LIBOR&0.25%). [6] (HRO)On 7-15-97 at 100. [7] (HRO)On 6-1-00 & '05 at 100. [8] Int to 3-2-96,adj qtrly aft(3 Mo LIBOR&0.15%). [9] L-T-D as of 12-31-94. [10] (HRO)On 3-1-98 at 100. [11] (HRO)On Chge of Ctrl at 101. [12] Defeased, fds deposited w/trustee.

Title-Industry Code & Co. Finances (In Italics)	Ind	Fixed Charge Coverage 1992	1993	1994	Year End	Million $ Cash & Equiv.	Curr. Assets	Curr. Liab.	Balance Sheet Date	L. Term Debt (Mil $)	Capital-ization (Mil $)	Total Debt % Capital

Individual Issue Statistics / Exchange	Interest Dates	S&P Debt Rating	Date of Last Rating Change	Prior Rating	Eligible	Bond Form	Redemption Provisions: Regular Price	Regular (Begins) Thru	Sinking Fund Price	Sinking Fund (Begins) Thru	Refund/Other Restriction Price	Refund/Other Restriction (Begins) Thru	Outst'g (Mil $)	Underwriting Firm	Underwriting Year	Price Range 1995 High	Price Range 1995 Low	Mo. End Price Sale(s) or Bid	Curr. Yield	Yield to Mat.
General Tel. California *(Cont.)*																				
1st T 6¾s '97	jD	**AA–**	9/86	A+	X	R	100.23	11-30-96	....	....	....	....	55.0	F1	'67	101	96⅛	100¼	6.73	6.61
1st U 7⅛s '98	jD	**AA–**	9/86	A+	X	R	100.49	11-30-96	....	....	....	....	60.0	P1	'68	101¼	96	100½	7.09	6.93
1st X 7⅝s 2001	jD	**AA–**	9/86	A+	X	R	101.31	11-30-96	....	....	....	....	50.0	M2	'71	102⅛	95½	101⅜	7.52	7.33
General Tel Florida	***67a***	***Now GTE Florida,see***																		
1st L 6½s '97	mN	**AA–**	4/86	A+	X	R	100.22	11-1-96	□100	....	....	....	20.0	P1	'67	100⅜	95¾	100⅜	6.48	6.27
1st N 8s 2001	Ms	**AA–**	4/86	A+	X	R	101.64	2-29-96	100.66	2-29-96	....	....	45.0	P1	'71	101¾	97¼	101½	7.88	7.64
◆1st O 7½s 2002	fA	**AA–**	4/86	A+	X	R	101.36	7-31-96	□100	....	....	....	50.0	F1	'72	102	96	100½	7.46	7.40
1st BB 8⅜s 2027	Ms	**AA–**			X	R	104.53	2-29-96	....	....	....	....	75.0	K2	'87	105¾	95¼	105	7.98	7.94
General Tel. Illinois	***67a***	***Now GTE North,see***																		
1st 8½s 2000	jD	**AA**	4/87	AA+	X	R	101.21	11-30-96	....	....	....	....	26.0	P1	'70	102⅞	99⅜	101¼	8.40	8.18
1st 7½s 2002	Fa	**AA**	4/87	AA+	X	R	101.68	1-31-96	....	....	....	....	20.0	D8	'72	102¼	94⅞	102	7.35	7.09
1st 8¼s 2003	jJ	**AA**	4/87	AA+	X	R	102.13	6-30-96	....	....	....	....	16.7	P1	'73	102⅝	98⅝	102⅛	8.08	7.87
General Tel. Indiana	***67a***	***Now GTE North,see***																		
1st 6⅜s '98	fA	**AA**	9/75	A	X	R	100.40	7-31-96	....	....	....	....	17.0	P1	'68	100¾	94⅜	100¾	6.33	6.05
1st 7½s 2001	jD	**AA**	9/75	A	X	R	101.40	11-30-96	....	....	....	....	17.9	P1	'71	102¼	94⅞	101½	7.39	7.18
1st 8s 2003	jD	**AA**	9/75	A	X	R	101.93	11-30-96	....	....	....	....	24.6	M2	'73	102⅞	96⅞	101¾	7.86	7.70
General Tel. Kentucky	***67a***	***Merged w/GTE South,see***																		
1st 7¾s 2003	Jd	A+	10/83	A	X	R	101.75	5-31-96	....	....	....	....	10.9	S6	'73	102	101¾	101¾	7.62	7.44
General Tel. Michigan	***67a***	***Now GTE North,see***																		
1st 7½s 2001	mN	**AA**	4/87	A+	X	R	101.29	10-31-96	....	....	....	....	18.0	F1	'71	102⅛	94⅞	101⅜	7.40	7.20
1st 7⅝s 2003	Mn	**AA**	4/87	A+	X	R	101.91	4-30-96	....	....	....	....	20.0	P1	'73	102¾	94½	102⅝	7.43	7.16
1st 8½s 2006	mS	**AA**	4/87	A+	X	R	102.93	8-31-96	....	....	....	....	25.0	B1	'76	104½	99⅝	102⅞	8.26	8.09
General Tel. Midwest	***67a***	***Now GTE North,see***																		
1st F 7½s 2001	Fa	**NR**	10/93	AA	X	R	101.16	1-31-96	....	....	....	....	11.0	P1	'71	102	95¾	101¼	7.41	7.20
1st G 7⅝s 2003	Jj	**NR**	10/93	AA	X	R	101.84	12-31-96	....	....	....	....	13.0	B6	'73	102⅝	94⅞	102¼	7.46	7.21
1st I 8⅛s 2007	jJ	**NR**	10/93	AA	X	R	102.98	6-30-96	....	....	....	....	20.0	P1	'77	103½	96⅞	103¼	7.87	7.69
General Tel. Northwest	***67a***	***Now GTE Northwest,see***																		
1st U 7⅞s 2002	Mn	**A+**	4/94	AA–	X	R	101.69	4-30-96	100.14	4-30-96	....	....	20.0	H1	'72	102⅛	96⅝	101¾	7.74	7.52
1st W 8¼s 2007	Fa	**A+**	4/94	AA–	X	R	103.13	1-31-96	100	....	....	....	48.0	P1	'77	103⅞	97¾	103¼	7.99	7.81
1st BB 8¾s 2016	Ao15	A+	4/94	AA–	X	R	103.99	4-14-96	100	....	....	....	125	M6	'86	104¼	99¼	104⅛	8.40	8.32
General Tel. Ohio	***67a***	***Now GTE North,see***																		
1st 7⅝s 2001	Ao	**AA**	6/84	A+	X	R	101.16	1-31-96	....	....	....	....	20.0	L3	'71	101⅝	95⅞	101¼	7.53	7.33
1st 7⅝s 2002	mS	**AA**	6/84	A+	X	R	101.52	8-31-96	....	....	....	....	19.9	P1	'72	102½	94⅞	101⅞	7.48	7.26
General Tel. Pennsylvania	***67a***	***Now GTE North,see***																		
1st I 8s 2003	mS	**AA**	4/87	A+	X	R	101.69	8-31-96	....	....	....	....	24.8	S1	'73	102⅜	97	101¾	7.86	7.69
1st O 8⅞s 2026	jD	**AA**	4/87	A+	X	R	104.04	11-30-96	....	....	....	....	75.0	M6	'86	104⅞	99⅞	104	8.53	8.51
General Tel. South[1]	***67a***	***Now GTE South Inc,see***																		
1st S 8¾s 2001	Mn	A+	3/82	A	X	R	101.44	4-30-96	100	....	....	....	20.7	P1	'71	105½	100⅝	105	8.33	7.59
1st T 8s 2001	jD	A+	3/82	A	X	R	101.58	11-30-96	100.48	11-30-96	....	....	20.8	E1	'71	102½	97	101¾	7.86	7.63
1st U 7⅝s 2002	jJ	A+	3/82	A	X	R	101.58	6-30-96	100	....	....	....	21.0	P1	'72	102¼	95⅛	102	7.48	7.23
General Tel. Wisconsin	***67a***	***Now GTE North,see***																		
1st 5s '96	Fa	**AA**	4/87	AA–	X	R	100	....	100	....	....	....	4.57	D8	'66	100	97¼	100	5.00	4.90
1st 7⅛s '99	Fa	**AA**	4/87	AA–	X	R	100.71	1-31-96	....	....	....	....	12.9	S1	'69	101½	95⅞	100¾	7.07	6.85
1st 7⅛s 2001	Fa	**AA**	4/87	AA–	X	R	101.28	1-31-96	....	....	....	....	15.0	S1	'71	102	93⅞	101⅜	7.03	6.80
1st 7½s 2002	Ms	**AA**	4/87	AA–	X	R	101.50	2-29-96	....	....	....	....	24.5	P1	'72	102¼	94⅝	101⅝	7.38	7.17
1st 7¾s 2003	Jd	**AA**	4/87	AA–	X	R	101.81	5-31-96	....	....	....	....	25.0	F1	'73	102⅝	95⅜	102	7.60	7.39

Uniform Footnote Explanations-See Page 260. Other: [1] Was Gen'l Tel Southeast.

Title-Industry Code & Co. Finances (In Italics) / Individual Issue Statistics (Exchange)	Ind / Interest Dates	Fixed Charge Coverage 1992 / S&P Debt Rating	1993 / Date of Last Rating Change	1994 / Prior Rating	Eligible	Year End / Bond Form	Cash & Equiv. (Million $) / Regular Price	Curr. Assets (Million $) / Regular (Begins) Thru	Curr. Liab. (Million $) / Sinking Fund Price	Balance Sheet Date / Sinking Fund (Begins) Thru	L. Term Debt (Mil $) / Refund/Other Restriction Price	Refund/Other Restriction (Begins) Thru	Capital-ization (Mil $) / Outst'g (Mil $)	Total Debt % Capital / Underwriting Firm	Underwriting Year	Price Range 1995 High	Price Range 1995 Low	Mo. End Price Sale(s) or Bid	Curr. Yield	Yield to Mat.
General Tel. Wisconsin *(Cont.)*																				
1st 8¾s 2026	jD15	**AA**	4/87	AA–	X	R	105.74	12-14-96	....	....	....	....	45.0	F1	'86	106⅞	98⅝	105⅞	8.26	8.22
Genesco, Inc.	***59l***	***3.43***	***d1.03***	***0.95***		***Ja***	***22.60***	***163.0***	***57.60***	***10-31-95***	***76.70***		***112.0***	***69.7***						
• Sr Nts 10⅜s 2003	Fa	**B**	11/94	B+	Y	R	102.96	(2-1-98)	....	....	....	....	75.0	D6	'93	95	70⅛	s92¼	11.25	12.03
Genesis Health Ventures	***30***	***2.41***	***4.75***	***2.81***		***Sp***	***7.60***	***149.0***	***43.70***	***6-30-95***	***298.0***		***513.0***	***58.7***						
1st[1]A[2] 9¼s 2007	QSep	**BB–**	6/95	B+	Y	R	106	(9-1-97)	....	....	....	....	25.0	B7	'92	103⅝	95½	100¼	9.23	9.21
• Sr Sub Nts[3] 9¾s 2005	Jd15	**B**			Y	R	104.05	(6-15-00)	....	....	....	....	120	M2	'95	107	99¾	105¼	9.26	8.92
Geneva Steel Co.	***66b***	***d0.10***	***0.12***	***d0.24***		***Sp***	***6.79***	***136.0***	***112.0***	***6-30-95***	***333.0***		***488.0***	***68.2***						
Sr[4]Nts[5] 11⅛s 2001	Ms15	**B**	7/95	B+	Y	R	103.18	(3-15-98)	....	....	....	....	135	C4	'93	95⅞	75	83	13.40	16.05
Sr[5]Nts 9½s 2004	Jj15	**B**	7/95	B+	Y	R	105	(1-15-99)	....	....	[6]Z109.50	1-14-97	190	C4	'94	85⅞	65	77¾	12.22	14.23
Georgia Gulf Corp	***14***	***2.11***	***2.47***	***6.13***		***Dc***	***3.33***	***196.0***	***121.0***	***9-30-95***	***276.0***		***321.0***	***86.0***						
Nts 7⅝s 2005	mN15	**BBB–**			X	BE	NC	....	....	....	....	....	100	G1	'95	102⅛	99⅝	102⅛	7.47	7.32
Georgia-Pacific Corp[7]	***50***	***0.87***	***1.04***	***2.26***		***Dc***	***375.0***	***2950***	***2308***	***9-30-95***	***4268***		***8497***	***59.5***						
SF Deb 9¼s 2016	Ms15	**BBB–**	11/92	BB+	X	R	105.088	3-14-96	100	(3-15-97)	®105.088	3-14-96	150	F1	'86	105¼	96¾	105⅛	8.80	8.70
SF Deb 9¾s 2018	Jj15	**BBB–**	11/92	BB+	X	R	104.50	1-14-97	100	(1-15-99)	®103.75	1-14-98	200	M6	'88	106¼	100⅝	104¾	9.31	9.24
[8]Deb[9] [10]9.95s 2002	Jd15	**BBB–**	11/92	BB+	X	R	NC	....	....	....	....	....	300	B5	'90	118¾	106½	118¾	8.38	6.36
Deb 9½s 2011	jD	**BBB–**	11/92	BB+	X	R	NC	....	....	....	....	....	250	S1	'91	123	104	122⅞	7.73	7.08
Deb 7.70s 2015	Jd15	**BBB–**			X	BE	NC	....	....	....	....	....	250	G1	'95	105⅜	95⅝	105⅜	7.31	7.18
Deb 9½s 2018	Fa15	**BBB–**	11/92	BB+	X	R	104.973	2-14-96	....	....	®104.208	2-14-98	200	S1	'88	108⅛	99⅞	105⅛	9.04	8.96
Deb 9⅞s 2021	mN	**BBB–**	11/92	BB+	X	R	104.696	(11-1-01)	....	....	....	....	250	G1	'91	119⅛	103	119⅛	8.29	8.10
Deb 9⅝s 2022	Ms15	**BBB–**	11/92	BB+	X	R	104.348	(3-15-02)	....	....	....	....	250	B5	'92	118	102½	118	8.16	7.98
Deb 9½s 2022	Mn15	**BBB–**	11/92	BB+	X	R	104.325	(5-15-02)	....	....	....	....	250	G1	'92	117⅛	101	117⅛	8.11	7.94
Deb 9⅛s 2022	jJ	**BBB–**	11/92	BB+	X	R	103.563	(7-1-02)	....	....	....	....	250	S1	'92	114⅝	98⅝	114⅝	7.96	7.81
Deb 8¼s 2023	Ms	**BBB–**			X	BE	103.75	(3-1-03)	....	....	....	....	250	S1	'93	108	91	108	7.64	7.55
Deb 8⅛s 2023	Jd15	**BBB–**			X	BE	103.376	(6-15-03)	....	....	....	....	250	G1	'93	106⅞	89½	106⅞	7.60	7.53
Deb 8⅝s 2025	Ao30	**BBB–**			X	R	104.205	(4-30-05)	....	....	....	....	250	S1	'95	110⅜	99¾	110⅜	7.81	7.72
Deb 7⅜s 2025	jD	**BBB–**			X	BE	NC	....	....	....	....	....	250	S1	'95	101	98½	101	7.30	7.29
[11]Nts[9] [12]9.85s '97	Jd15	**BBB–**	11/92	BB+	X	R	NC	....	....	....	....	....	300	B5	'90	106½	103⅛	105⅝	9.33	5.78
Nts 10⅛s 2000	Mn15	**BBB–**	11/92	BB+	X	R	100	....	....	....	....	....	200	S4	'88	107	100¼	A106	9.55	8.45
Georgia Power Co.[13]	***72a***	***3.12***	***3.44***	***3.61***		***Dc***	***15.40***	***1208***	***1661***	***6-30-95***	***3309***		***9024***	***44.9***						
1st 4¾s '96	Ms	**A+**	3/95	A	X	R	NC	....	....	....	....	....	150	B5	'93	99⅞	96⅝	99⅞	4.76	5.40
1st 5½s '98	Ao	**A+**	3/95	A	X	R	NC	....	....	....	....	....	100	M2	'93	99¾	92⅛	99¾	5.51	5.61
• 1st 6⅛s '99	mS	**A+**	3/95	A	X	R	NC	....	....	....	....	....	195	K2	'92	102	91¼	99¼	6.17	6.35
1st 6s 2000	Ms	**A+**	3/95	A	X	R	NC	....	....	....	....	....	100	M6	'93	100⅜	90¼	100⅜	5.98	5.89
1st 7s 2000	aO	**A+**	3/95	A	X	R	100	(10-1-97)	Z100	....	....	....	100	M6	'92	102⅞	92¾	102⅞	6.80	6.29
• 1st 6⅞s 2002	mS	**A+**	3/95	A	X	R	101.71	(9-1-97)	Z100	....	....	....	150	M2	'92	99¾	94	100¼	6.86	6.83
1st 6⅝s 2003	Ao	**A+**	3/95	A	X	R	101.79	(4-1-98)	Z100	....	....	....	200	M6	'93	101½	88⅝	101½	6.53	6.36
1st 6.35s 2003	fA	**A+**	3/95	A	X	R	101.45	(8-1-98)	Z100	....	....	....	75.0	P4	'93	100⅛	86½	100⅛	6.34	6.33
1st 6⅞s 2008	Ao	**A+**	3/95	A	X	R	103.50	(4-1-98)	Z100	(4-1-98)	....	....	50.0	F1	'93	102¼	85⅞	102¼	6.72	6.60
1st 8⅝s 2022	Jd	**A+**	3/95	A	X	R	106.83	5-31-96	Z100	....	®106.03	5-31-97	64.0	M6	'92	107⅝	96⅛	103	8.37	8.34
1st 7.95s 2023	Fa	**A+**	3/95	A	X	R	105.82	1-31-96	Z100	....	®104.85	1-31-98	160	M6	'93	107¼	91	107	7.43	7.35
1st 7⅝s 2023	Ms	**A+**	3/95	A	X	R	106.15	2-29-96	Z100	....	®105.12	2-28-98	100	M5	'93	103	88⅜	103	7.40	7.37
1st 7¾s 2023	Ao	**A+**	3/95	A	X	R	106.15	3-31-96	Z100	....	®105.13	3-31-98	75.0	G1	'93	103¾	88½	103¾	7.47	7.43
1st 7.55s 2023	fA	**A+**	3/95	A	X	R	105.75	7-31-96	Z100	....	®104.79	7-31-98	125	P4	'93	102⅝	86¾	102⅝	7.36	7.33
1st 7.70s 2025	Mn	**A+**			X	R	105.19	(5-1-00)	Z100	(5-1-00)	....	....	75.0	M5	'95	104	96¼	104	7.40	7.36
Gerrity Oil & Gas	***49***	***4.59***	***2.80***	***1.12***		***Dc***	***0.16***	***12.70***	***14.60***	***9-30-95***	***136.0***		***302.0***	***45.0***						
• Sr Sub Nts[3] 11¾s 2004	jJ15	**B**			Y	R	105.875	(7-15-99)	....	....	....	....	100	M6	'94	100	77	94¾	12.40	12.77

Uniform Footnote Explanations-See Page 260. Other: [1] (HRO)For Fundamental Structural Chge at 100. [2] Death Red Benefit,ltd,as defined. [3] (HRO)On Chge of Ctrl at 101. [4] Co must offer 100 for some asset sales. [5] Co must offer repurch at 101 on Chge of Ctrl. [6] Max $50M red w/proceeds of Pub Eq Off'g. [7] See Great No'n Nekoosa. [8] Credit Sensitive Deb. [9] Int subj to adj for rating chge. [10] Int 10.10% thru 11-2-92. [11] Credit Sensitive Nts. [12] Int 10% thru 11-2-92. [13] Subsid of Southern Co.

Title-Industry Code & Co. Finances (In Italics) / Individual Issue Statistics — Exchange ↓	Ind / Interest Dates	Fixed Charge Coverage 1992 / S&P Debt Rating	1993 / Date of Last Rating Change	Prior Rating	1994 / Eligible ↓	Year End / Bond Form	Million $ Cash & Equiv. / Redemption Provisions — Regular Price	Curr. Assets / Regular (Begins) Thru	Curr. Liab. / Sinking Fund Price	Balance Sheet Date / Sinking Fund (Begins) Thru	L. Term Debt (Mil $) / Refund/Other Restriction Price	Refund/Other Restriction (Begins) Thru	Capital-ization (Mil $) / Outst'g (Mil $)	Total Debt % Capital / Underwriting Firm Year	Price Range 1995 High	Low	Mo. End Price Sale(s) or Bid	Curr. Yield	Yield to Mat.
Giant Industries	***49g***	***0.22***	***2.74***		***0.75***	***Dc***	***34.50***	***89.90***	***42.70***	***9-30-95***	***112.0***		***223.0***	***52.0***					
Sr[1]Sub Nts 9¾s 2003	mN15	B+			Y	R	104.875	(11-15-98)	....	....	....	....	100	K2 '93	101½	88	101	9.65	9.56
Giddings & Lewis	***41d***	***6.01***	***17.89***		***29.16***	***Dc***	***6.86***	***509.0***	***217.0***	***10-1-95***	***100.0***		***700.0***	***26.9***					
Nts 7½s 2005	aO	BBB			X	BE	NC	....	....	....	....	....	100	F1 '95	104¾	100	104¾	7.16	6.82
Gillette Co	***18***	***10.99***	***16.77***		***19.10***	***Dc***	***68.50***	***2863***	***1801***	***9-30-95***	***550.0***		***3552***	***31.5***					
Nts 4¾s '96	fA15	AA–	11/94	A+	X	BE	NC	....	....	....	....	....	150	M5 '93	99⅝	95⅜	99⅝	4.77	5.36
Nts 6¼s 2003	fA15	AA–	11/94	A+	X	BE	NC	....	....	....	....	....	150	M5 '93	101¾	88⅛	101¾	6.14	5.96
Nts 5¾s 2005	aO15	AA–	11/94	A+	X	BE	NC	....	....	....	....	....	200	M5 '93	97⅞	81⅝	97⅞	5.87	6.04
Glatfelter (P.H.) Co	***50***	***n/a***	***7.39***		***2.39***	***Dc***	***6.04***	***152.0***	***86.50***	***9-30-95***	***150.0***		***464.0***	***32.5***					
Nts 5⅞s '98	Ms	BBB+	2/95	A–	X	BE	NC	....	....	....	....	....	150	B5 '93	100⅛	93⅜	100	5.88	5.87
Global Marine	***49e***	***0.44***	***0.18***		***1.06***	***Dc***	***88.30***	***174.0***	***63.50***	***9-30-95***	***225.0***		***478.0***	***47.1***					
Sr Sec Nts[1] 12¾s '99	jD15	B+			Y	R	102	(12-15-97)	....	....	....	....	225	S1 '92	111	106	110¼	11.56	9.58
Golden West Fin'l	***10b***	***2.10***	***2.06***		***1.89***	***Dc***				***9-30-95***	***9163***		***11359***	***80.7***					
Sub Nts[2] 10¼s '97	Mn15	A–			X	R	NC	....	....	....	....	....	115	M2 '90	107	104	105⅞	9.68	5.74
Sub Nts[2] 9.15s '98	Mn23	A–			X	R	NC	....	....	....	....	....	100	M2 '91	107½	102	107⅜	8.52	5.81
Sub Nts[2] 8⅝s '98	fA30	A–			X	R	NC	....	....	....	....	....	100	L3 '91	107	100¼	106¾	8.08	5.85
Sub Nts[2] 7s 2000	Jj15	A–			X	R	NC	....	....	....	....	....	100	G1 '93	103⅝	93⅝	103⅝	6.76	5.98
Sub Nts 10¼s 2000	jD	A–			X	R	NC	....	....	....	....	....	114	M2 '88	117⅝	107¼	117⅝	8.71	6.05
Sub Nts[2] 7⅞s 2002	Jj15	A–			X	R	NC	....	....	....	....	....	100	L3 '92	108⅝	95⅞	108⅝	7.25	6.14
Sub Nts[2] 8⅜s 2002	Ao15	A–			X	R	NC	....	....	....	....	....	100	L3 '92	111½	98⅜	111½	7.51	6.14
Sub Nts[2] 6.70s 2002	jJ	A–				BE	NC	....	....	....	....	....	100	G1 '95	102⅞	96⅜	102⅞	6.51	6.16
Sub Nts[2] 7¼s 2002	fA15	A–			X	R	NC	....	....	....	....	....	100	G1 '92	105⅞	92¼	105⅞	6.85	6.16
Sub Nts[2] 6s 2003	aO	A–			X	R	NC	....	....	....	....	....	200	G1 '93	98¼	84⅜	98¼	6.11	6.29
Goodrich (B.F.) Co.	***14***	***1.21***	***1.88***		***3.16***	***Dc***	***53.90***	***960.0***	***657.0***	***9-30-95***	***386.0***		***1420***	***38.5***					
Nts 9⅝s 2001	jJ	BBB			X	BE	NC	....	....	....	....	....	175	G1 '91	115½	104¾	115½	8.33	6.25
•Sub Deb 7s '97	fA15	BBB–	10/88	BB+	X	R	100	....	100	....	....	....	[3]9.10	G1 '72	No Sale		100⅛	6.99	6.91
[4]Grace(W.R.) & Co-Conn	***14***	***2.98***	***3.71***		***2.27***	***Dc***	***80.90***	***1764***	***1947***	***9-30-95***	***1256***		***3616***	***53.3***					
Nts 7.40s 2000	Fa	BBB–			X	BE	NC	....	....	....	....	....	300	S1 '93	104⅞	94¼	104⅞	7.06	6.03
•Nts[5] 7¾s 2002	aO	BBB–			X	BE	NC	....	....	....	....	....	150	S1 '92	106	98⅛	98⅜	7.88	8.06
Nts[5] 8s 2004	fA15	BBB–			X	BE	NC	....	....	....	....	....	300	M5 '94	110⅜	94¼	110⅜	7.25	6.41
M-T Nts 'A' 7.09s '97	[6]mn15	BBB–			X	BE	NC	....	....	....	....	....	15.0	S1 '94	101½	97	101½	6.99	5.93
M-T Nts 'A' 7.09s '97	Mn15	BBB–			X	BE	NC	....	....	....	....	....	15.0	U1 '94	101½	97	101½	6.99	5.93
M-T Nts 'A' 7.24s '97	[7]mn15	BBB–			X	BE	NC	....	....	....	....	....	20.0	M5 '94	101¾	97¼	101¾	7.12	5.90
GranCare, Inc.	***30***	***4.23***	***2.34***		***3.14***	***Dc***	***29.00***	***218.0***	***103.0***	***9-30-95***	***320.0***		***487.0***	***66.5***					
•Sr Sub Nts[8] 9⅜s 2005	mS15	B			Y	BE	104.688	(9-15-00)	....	....	....	....	100	S5 '95	103	99	s103	9.10	8.90
Grand Casinos	***40i***	***28.51***	***3.24***		***4.20***	***Dc***	***66.70***	***101.0***	***111.0***	***10-1-95***	***327.0***		***707.0***	***51.7***					
•1st[1] 10⅛s 2003	jD	BB			Y	R	105.0625	(12-1-99)	....	....	....	....	450	D6 '95	103	100	104⅛	9.72	9.37
Great Atlantic & Pacific Tea	***59c***	***1.78***	***1.10***		***d0.77***	***Fb***	***132.0***	***1192***	***1119***	***9-9-95***	***700.0***		***1589***	***49.9***					
Nts[9] 9⅛s '98	Jj15	BB+	5/95	BBB–	Y	BE	NC	....	....	....	....	....	200	D4 '91	105	97¼	105	8.69	6.47
Sr[9]Nts 7.70s 2004	Jj15	BB+	5/95	BBB–	Y	BE	NC	....	....	....	....	....	200	M2 '94	100⅞	84¼	100⅞	7.63	7.55
Great Dane Holdings[10]	***9a***	***0.84***	***1.40***		***2.09***	***Dc***	***38.30***	***296.0***	***190.0***	***9-30-95***	***320.0***		***239.0***	***141.0***					
◆Sr Sub Deb 12¾s 2001	fA	CCC	3/94	CC	Y	R	101.06	7-31-96	100	(8-1-96)	....	....	132	B5 '86	102	86	s91	14.01	15.19
◆Sub Disc[11]Deb 14½s 2006	Jj	CCC	3/94	CC	Y	R	100	....	100	(1-1-97)	....	....	[3]61.3	Mgr '85	101	89¾	s92	15.76	16.14
Great Lakes Carbon[12]	***14***	***n/a***	***n/a***		***n/a***	***Dc***	***1.46***	***50.90***	***25.40***	***9-30-95***	***★73.20***		***87.80***	***12.3***					
Sr Sec Nts[1] 10s 2006	Jj	BB–			Y	R	105	(1-1-01)	....	....	[13]Z109	12-31-98	65.0	D6 '95	100	100	100	10.00	10.00
Great Northern Nekoosa	***13d***	***Merged into Georgia Pacific,see***																	
Nts 9⅛s '98	Fa	BBB–	11/92	BB+	X	R	NC	....	....	....	....	....	100	G1 '88	106⅞	101⅜	106⅜	8.58	5.83

Uniform Footnote Explanations-See Page 260. Other: [1] (HRO)On Chge of Ctrl at 101. [2] Issued in min denom $100T. [3] Incl disc. [4] Subsid & data of Grace(W.R.)& Co. [5] Gtd by Grace(W.R.) & Co. [6] Due 5-12-97. [7] Due 5-19-97. [8] Co must offer repurch at 101 on Chge of Ctrl. [9] Issued in min denom $10T. [10] Was Int'l Controls. [11] Int accrues fr 12-27-90. [12] Subsid of Horsehead Indus. [13] Max $16M red w/proceeds of Pub Eq Off'g.

Title-Industry Code & Co. Finances (In Italics)	Ind	Fixed Charge Coverage 1992	1993	1994		Year End	Million $ Cash & Equiv.	Curr. Assets	Curr. Liab.	Balance Sheet Date	L. Term Debt (Mil $)		Capital-ization (Mil $)	Total Debt % Capital						
Individual Issue Statistics Exchange ↓	Interest Dates	S&P Debt Rating	Date of Last Rating Change	Prior Rating	Eligible ↓	Bond Form	Redemption Provisions: Regular Price	Regular (Begins) Thru	Sinking Fund Price	Sinking Fund (Begins) Thru	Refund/Other Restriction Price	Refund/Other Restriction (Begins) Thru	Outst'g (Mil $)	Underwriting Firm	Underwriting Year	Price Range 1995 High	Price Range 1995 Low	Mo. End Price Sale(s) or Bid	Curr. Yield	Yield to Mat.
Great Northern Railway	***55***	***Now Burlington Northern RR,see***																		
•Gen Mtg O 3⅛s 2000	Jj	**BBB**	7/95	BBB+	X	CR	100.375	1-1-97	100.125	1-1-97	....	....	33.5	H1	'45	85½	82	87	3.59	6.89
•Gen Mtg Q 2⅝s 2010	Jj	**BBB**	7/95	BBB+	X	CR	100.25	1-1-01	100	....	....	....	28.8	M6	'46	58½	53¼	57	4.61	7.69
Great Western Bank,F.S.B.	***10a***	***Subsid of Great West'n Fin'l,see***																		
Sub Nts[1] 10½s 2000	Mn30	**BBB+**	2/93	A–	Y	R	100	(2-26-99)	....	....	....	....	130	M2	'90	112½	105⅜	112⅛	9.36	7.24
Sub Nts[1] 10¼s 2000	Jd15	**BBB+**	2/93	A–	Y	R	100	(3-15-99)	....	....	....	....	150	S4	'90	112⅛	105¼	111¾	9.17	7.13
Sub Nts[1] 9⅞s 2001	Jd15	**BBB+**	2/93	A–	Y	R	NC	....	....	....	....	....	150	F1	'91	117¾	104½	117¾	8.39	6.01
Great West'n Fin'l	***10b***	***1.28***	***1.26***	***2.14***		***Dc***				***9-30-95***	***2434***		***5088***	***47.8***						
Nts[1] 6⅛s '98	Jd15	**BBB+**			X	R	NC	....	....	....	....	....	150	M2	'93	100⅞	92⅞	100⅞	6.07	5.74
Nts[1] 8⅝s '98	jD	**BBB+**	2/93	A–	X	R	NC	....	....	....	....	....	100	M2	'91	106	99⅝	106	8.14	6.34
Nts[1] 6⅜s 2000	jJ	**BBB+**			X	R	NC	....	....	....	....	....	225	M2	'93	101⅝	89⅞	101⅝	6.27	5.96
Nts[1] 8.60s 2002	Fa	**BBB+**	2/93	A–	X	R	NC	....	....	....	....	....	200	M2	'92	112⅛	99⅛	112⅛	7.67	6.18
Green Tree Financial[2]	***25g***	***3.65***	***4.92***	***8.26***		***Dc***	***262.0***			***9-30-95***	***638.0***		***1553***	***41.1***						
•Sr Sub Nts 10¼s 2002	Jd	**BBB+**	8/95	BBB–	X	R	NC	....	....	....	....	....	267	Exch.	'92	115¾	104½	115	8.91	7.28
Greyhound Corp	***17a***	***Now Dial Corp,see***																		
Sub Deb 10½s 2006	Mn15	**BBB–**			X	R	NC	....	....	....	....	....	150	G1	'86	129⅛	109⅞	129⅛	8.13	6.58
Greyhound Financial	***25***	***Now FINOVA Capital,see***																		
F/R[3]Nts 6.1875s '96	QFeb15	**BBB+**	1/95	BBB	X	BE	NC	....	....	....	....	....	100	C4	'94	100⅛	99⅝	100	6.19	....
Nts 8s '97	Jj15	**BBB+**			X	BE	NC	....	....	....	....	....	125	C5	'95	102⅝	99⅞	102⅜	7.81	5.62
Nts 8¼s '97	Ms11	**BBB+**	1/95	BBB	X	BE	NC	....	....	....	....	....	150	M2	'92	103¼	99¾	103	8.01	5.62
Nts 8½s '98	Mn	**BBB+**	1/95	BBB	X	BE	NC	....	....	....	....	....	100	C4	'92	106⅛	100	106⅛	8.01	5.66
Nts 8½s '99	Fa15	**BBB+**	1/95	BBB	X	BE	NC	....	....	....	....	....	125	M2	'92	107⅝	99⅞	107⅝	7.90	5.80
Nts 7¼s 2001	Ao	**BBB+**	1/95	BBB	X	BE	NC	....	....	....	....	....	100	C4	'94	105½	93⅜	105½	6.87	6.01
Nts[4] 6¾s '99	Ms25	**BBB+**	1/95	BBB	X	BE	NC	....	....	....	....	....	150	M2	'94	102⅞	93½	102⅞	6.56	5.76
F/R[5]M-T Nts 'B' '98	QJun	**BBB+**	1/95	BBB	X	BE	NC	....	....	....	....	....	77.6	L3	'94	100	99	99¾	....	....
Greyhound Lines, Inc	***70a***	***1.57***	***1.29***	***d1.96***		***Dc***	***0.81***	***62.40***	***113.0***	***9-30-95***	***176.0***		***330.0***	***57.3***						
◆Sr Nts 10s 2001	jJ31	**CCC**	11/95	CCC–	Y	R	106	7-30-96	100	(7-31-96)	....	....	[6]163	Exch.	'91	94	65	s92	10.87	12.00
Griffin Gaming & Entmt[7]	***40i***	***d0.27***	***0.07***	***0.91***		***Dc***	***47.50***	***68.80***	***39.10***	***9-30-95***	***216.0***		***243.0***	***89.3***						
◆1st[8]Pass-Thru Nts[9] 2000	[10]jj15	**CCC–**	4/93	CCC+	Y	R	100	....	....	....	....	....	[6]105	Reorg	'90	93	77	91½	....	Flat
Grumman Corp	***2a***	***Now Northrop Grumman, see***																		
Nts[11] 10⅜s '99	Jj	**CALL**	11/95	BBB		R			Called 1-3-96 at 100.00				153	D4	'89	102⅝	100	100	10.38	Call
[12]***GS Technologies Oper***	***66d***	***n/a***	***n/a***	***3.55***		***Dc***	***11.70***	***147.0***	***97.40***	***9-30-95***	***176.0***		***162.0***	***113.0***						
Sr[13]Nts[14] 12s 2004	mS	**B**			Y	R	106	(9-1-99)	....	....	[15]Z111	8-31-97	125	G1	'94	102⅞	97¾	98⅞	12.14	12.21
[13]Sr[14]Nts 12¼s 2005	aO	**B**			Y	R	106.125	(10-1-00)	....	....	[15]Z110	9-30-98	125	G1	'95	111⅞	99¼	111¾	10.96	10.31
GTE California[16]	***67a***	***6.07***	***6.03***	***8.07***		***Dc***	***35.00***	***680.0***	***976.0***	***9-30-95***	***1281***		***3830***	***38.6***						
1st TT 6¼s '98	Jj15	**AA–**			X	R	NC	....	....	....	....	....	150	S1	'93	101⅜	94½	101⅜	6.17	5.53
Deb 'A' 5⅝s 2001	Fa	**AA–**	5/95	A+	X	R	NC	....	....	....	....	....	300	M6	'94	98⅞	87⅜	98⅞	5.69	5.88
Deb 'B' 6¾s 2004	Ms15	**AA–**	5/95	A+	X	R	NC	....	....	....	....	....	250	G1	'94	103¾	89½	103¾	6.51	6.16
Deb 'C' 8.07s 2024	Ao15	**AA–**	5/95	A+	X	R	104.04	(4-15-04)	....	....	....	....	250	S1	'94	111¾	92⅝	111¾	7.22	7.10
GTE Corp[17]	***67a***	***2.87***	***3.50***	***4.84***		***Dc***	***487.0***	***5649***	***8476***	***9-30-95***	***12157***		***28067***	***52.3***						
SF Deb 10¾s 2017	mS15	**BBB+**	7/92	A–	X	R	105.13	(9-15-97)	100	(9-15-98)	....	....	200	M2	'87	113⅛	108	112¾	9.53	9.36
Deb 8.85s '98	Ms	**BBB+**	7/92	A–	X	R	NC	....	....	....	....	....	700	P1	'91	106¼	101⅛	106	8.35	5.86
Deb 9⅜s 2000	jD	**BBB+**	7/92	A–	X	R	NC	....	....	....	....	....	500	S1	'90	113¾	103¾	113⅜	8.27	6.18
Deb 9.10s 2003	Jd	**BBB+**	7/92	A–	X	R	NC	....	....	....	....	....	500	P1	'91	116½	102½	115¾	7.86	6.40
Deb 8½s 2017	Ao	**BBB+**	7/92	A–	X	R	103	(4-1-97)	....	....	....	....	250	U1	'87	106½	93⅞	105⅝	8.05	7.95
Deb 10.30s 2017	mN15	**BBB+**	7/92	A–	X	R	105.15	(11-15-97)	....	....	....	....	200	P1	'87	114	111⅛	112¾	9.14	8.96
Deb 10¼s 2020	mN	**BBB+**	7/92	A–	X	R	104.62	(11-1-00)	....	....	....	....	400	P1	'90	121⅛	107⅝	121⅛	8.46	8.24

Uniform Footnote Explanations-See Page 260. Other: [1] Issued in min denom $100T. [2] Was Green Tree Acceptance. [3] Int to 11-15-95,adj qtrly aft(3 Mo LIBOR&0.25%). [4] (HRO)At 100 for Rating Decline. [5] Int adj daily. [6] Incl disc. [7] See Resorts Int'l Hotel Finance. [8] Int consists of pass-thru of certain lease pyts rec'd. [9] State gaming laws may req hldr's sale/Co red. [10] Due 6-30-00. [11] (HRO)For certain events at 100. [12] Gtd by & data of GS Technologies Corp. [13] Gtd by GS Technologies Corp. [14] Co must offer repurch at 101 on Chge of Ctrl. [15] Max $40M red w/proceeds of Com Off'g. [16] See Gen'l Tel Calif. [17] See Cont'l Tel CA.

Title-Industry Code & Co. Finances (In Italics) / Individual Issue Statistics, Exchange	Ind / Interest Dates	S&P Debt Rating / Fixed Charge Coverage 1992	Date of Last Rating Change / 1993	Prior Rating / 1994	Eligible	Bond Form / Year End	Regular Price / Cash & Equiv. (Million $)	Regular (Begins) Thru / Curr. Assets (Million $)	Sinking Fund Price / Curr. Liab. (Million $)	Sinking Fund (Begins) Thru / Balance Sheet Date	Refund/Other Restriction Price / L. Term Debt (Mil $)	Refund/Other Restriction (Begins) Thru	Outst'g (Mil $) / Capitalization (Mil $)	Underwriting Firm / Total Debt % Capital	Underwriting Year	Price Range 1995 High	Price Range 1995 Low	Mo. End Price Sale(s) or Bid	Curr. Yield	Yield to Mat.
***GTE Corp** (Cont.)*																				
Deb 8¾s 2021	mN	**BBB+**	7/92	A–	X	R	NC	....	....	....	....	....	300	M2	'91	122¼	98½	122¼	7.16	6.89
Deb 7.83s 2023	mN	**BBB+**			X	R	103.92	(5-1-03)	....	....	....	....	500	G1	'93	106⅞	87¼	106⅞	7.33	7.25
***GTE Florida*[1]**	***67a***	***4.56***	***3.33***	***4.70***		***Dc***	***10.00***	***318.0***	***399.0***	***9-30-95***	***724.0***		***2062***	***38.6***						
Deb 'A' 6.31s 2002	jD15	**AA–**	10/95	A+	X	R	NC	....	....	....	....	....	200	M2	'93	101	87¼	101	6.25	6.13
Deb 'B' 7.41s 2023	jD15	**AA–**	10/95	A+	X	R	103.71	(12-15-03)	....	....	....	....	200	M2	'93	104⅜	84⅞	104⅜	7.10	7.05
Deb 'C' 7¼s 2025	aO15	**AA–**			X	R	103.23	(10-15-05)	....	....	....	....	100	C5	'95	102½	98¾	102½	7.07	7.05
Deb 'D' 6¼s 2005	mN15	**AA–**			X	R	NC	....	....	....	....	....	100	U1	'95	100⅛	98⅛	100⅛	6.24	6.23
***GTE Hawaiian Tel*[2]**	***67a***	***3.35***	***3.00***	***2.18***		***Dc***	***3.86***	***181.0***	***210.0***	***9-30-95***	***520.0***		***1103***	***50.8***						
1st AA 9s 2000	jD	**BBB+**	6/95	A	X	R	‡101.50	11-30-96	Z100	....	....	....	75.0	K2	'90	103⅜	101⅝	103⅜	8.71	8.15
1st BB 6¾s 2005	Fa15	**BBB+**	6/95	A	X	R	NC	....	Z100	....	....	....	125	F1	'93	102⅝	88¼	102⅝	6.58	6.36
Deb 'A' 7s 2006	Fa	**BBB**			X	R	NC	....	....	....	....	....	150	M2	'95	104⅞	99	104⅞	6.67	6.34
***GTE North Inc*[3]**	***67a***	***5.57***	***5.17***	***7.68***		***Dc***	***39.90***	***797.0***	***1103***	***9-30-95***	***1319***		***4120***	***39.7***						
1st 8½s 2031	jD15	**AA**			X	R	104.88	(12-15-01)	....	....	....	....	250	F1	'91	112⅜	96⅛	112⅜	7.56	7.50
Deb'A' 6s 2004	Jj15	**AA–**			X	R	NC	....	....	....	....	....	250	D4	'94	99	85½	99	6.06	6.16
Deb'B' 5½s '99	Fa15	**AA–**			X	R	NC	....	....	....	....	....	200	K2	'94	99⅝	90⅜	99⅝	5.52	5.63
***GTE Northwest*[4]**	***67a***	***4.51***	***3.15***	***3.49***		***Dc***	***22.60***	***234.0***	***350.0***	***9-30-95***	***658.0***		***1625***	***41.0***						
1st FF 6⅛s '99	Fa15	**A+**	4/94	AA–	X	R	NC	....	100	....	....	....	125	M6	'93	101¼	92½	101¼	6.05	5.68
Deb A 7⅜s 2001	Mn	**A**			X	R	NC	....	....	....	....	....	200	M6	'94	106¼	94¾	106¼	6.94	5.99
***GTE South Inc*[5]**	***67a***	***4.22***	***4.07***	***4.44***		***Dc***	***16.60***	***251.0***	***484.0***	***9-30-95***	***593.0***		***1775***	***39.5***						
1st FF 9s 2029	mS15	**A+**			X	R	105.20	9-14-96	....	....	....	....	100	S1	'89	108½	99⅜	105¼	8.55	8.52
1st GG 9⅜s 2030	Jd15	**A+**			X	R	105.18	6-14-96	....	....	....	....	125		'90	106⅞	101⅛	105⅛	8.92	8.89
Deb 6¼s '97	mN15	**A**			X	R	NC	....	....	....	....	....	75.0	K2	'92	101	94⅞	101	6.19	5.68
Deb 7¼s 2002	fA	**A**			X	R	NC	....	....	....	....	....	150	S1	'94	106⅛	93	106⅛	6.83	6.11
***GTE Southwest*[6]**	***67a***	***3.95***	***3.08***	***3.86***		***Dc***	***24.50***	***302.0***	***516.0***	***9-30-95***	***665.0***		***1829***	***39.7***						
1st 6⅞s '98	Ms	**A+**	7/92	AA–	X	R	100.45	2-29-96	....	....	....	....	25.0	P1	'68	100¾	95⅞	100⅝	6.83	6.56
◆1st 7½s 2002	aO	**A+**	7/92	AA–	X	R	101.31	9-30-96	....	....	....	....	40.0	L3	'72	101	97	99	7.58	7.69
1st 8½s 2031	mN15	**A+**	7/92	AA–	X	R	NC	....	....	....	....	....	100	L3	'91	121⅝	97⅛	121⅝	6.99	6.87
Deb 'A' 5.82s '99	jD	**A+**	5/95	A	X	R	NC	....	....	....	....	....	250	P1	'93	99⅝	90	99⅝	5.84	5.93
Deb 'B' 6.54s 2005	jD	**A+**	5/95	A	X	R	NC	....	....	....	....	....	250	P1	'93	101⅝	86	101⅝	6.44	6.32
Guess? Inc	***68***	***96.72***	***9.68***	***6.79***		***Dc***	***2.47***	***134.0***	***58.50***	***10-1-95***	***151.0***		***153.0***	***101.0***						
Sr Sub[7]Nts'B' 9½s 2003	fA15	**BB–**	10/93	NR	Y	R	104.75	(8-15-98)	....	....	....	....	130	M2	'93	103⅜	94¾	103⅜	9.19	8.88
Gulf Mobile & Ohio	***55***	***Now Illinois Central Gulf,see***																		
• Inc Deb A 5s 2056	jD	**NR**	7/94	BBB–		CR	100	....	....	....	....	....	7.60		'58	62½	55	59	....	Flat
***Gulf Power Co.*[8]**	***72a***	***3.32***	***3.51***	***3.85***		***Dc***	***0.91***	***165.0***	***158.0***	***9-30-95***	***328.0***		***915.0***	***41.7***						
1st 5⅞s '97	fA	**A+**	3/95	A	X	R	NC	....	....	....	....	....	25.0	M6	'92	100½	94⅝	100½	5.85	5.54
1st 5s '98	jJ	**A+**	3/95	A	X	R	NC	....	....	....	....	....	30.0	C4	'93	98½	90	98½	5.08	5.65
1st 6⅛s 2003	jJ	**A+**	3/95	A	X	R	101.31	(7-1-98)	Z100	....	....	....	30.0	M2	'93	99¼	85⅞	99⅛	6.18	6.27
1st 8¾s 2021	jD	**A+**	3/95	A	X	R	106.22	11-30-96	Z100	....	®105.83	11-30-96	50.0	L3	'91	108	98½	106⅜	8.23	8.15
***Gulf States Utilities*[9]**	***72a***	***1.70***	***1.60***	***0.70***		***Dc***	***137.0***	***747.0***	***525.0***	***6-30-95***	***2406***		***4455***	***56.4***						
1st 5s '96	Jj	**BBB–**	3/95	BBB	X	R	100	....	Z100	....	....	....	20.0	S1	'66	100	97⅜	100	5.00	Mat.
1st A 6.67s '96	mN	**BBB–**	3/95	BBB	X	R	NC	....	Z100	....	....	....	75.0	G1	'92	100⅝	97⅜	100⅝	6.63	5.88
1st 5⅜s '97	Fa	**BBB–**	3/95	BBB	X	R	100.30	1-31-96	Z100.30	1-31-96	....	....	35.0	L3	'67	99¼	94⅜	99⅛	5.42	6.21
1st A 6.99s '97	mN	**BBB–**	3/95	BBB	X	R	NC	....	Z100	....	....	....	75.0	G1	'92	101¾	96⅜	101¾	6.87	5.96
1st 6⅝s '98	Fa	**BBB–**	3/95	BBB	X	R	100.65	1-31-96	Z100.50	1-31-96	....	....	25.0	S10	'68	100½	95	100½	6.59	6.36
1st A 6¾s '98	aO	**BBB–**	3/95	BBB	X	R	100.60	9-30-96	Z100.30	9-30-96	....	....	40.0	F1	'68	101	93⅞	101	6.68	6.34
1st B 7.35s '98	mN	**BBB–**	3/95	BBB	X	R	NC	....	Z100	....	....	....	75.0	G1	'92	103½	96⅛	103½	7.10	5.99

Uniform Footnote Explanations-See Page 260. Other: [1] See General Tel Florida. [2] See Hawaiian Tel [3] See Gen'l Tel's of IL,MI,MW,OH,PA,WI. [4] Was Gen'l Tel. Northwest,see. [5] See Gen'l Tel Kentucky & Gen'l Tel South. [6] Was Gen'l Tel Southwest. [7] (HRO)On Chge in Ctrl at 101. [8] Subsid of Southern Co. [9] Subsid of Entergy Corp.

Exchange / Individual Issue Statistics	Interest Dates	S&P Debt Rating	Date of Last Rating Change	Prior Rating	Eligible	Bond Form	Regular Price	Regular (Begins) Thru	Sinking Fund Price	Sinking Fund (Begins) Thru	Refund/Other Restriction Price	Refund/Other Restriction (Begins) Thru	Outst'g (Mil $)	Underwriting Firm	Underwriting Year	Price Range 1995 High	Price Range 1995 Low	Mo. End Price Sale(s) or Bid	Curr. Yield	Yield to Mat.
Title-Industry Code & Co. Finances (In Italics)	*Ind*	*Fixed Charge Coverage 1992*	*1993*	*1994*		*Year End*	*Million $ Cash & Equiv.*	*Curr. Assets*	*Curr. Liab.*	*Balance Sheet Date*	*L. Term Debt (Mil $)*		*Capital-ization (Mil $)*	*Total Debt % Capital*						
***Gulf States Utilities** (Cont.)*																				
1st 7¼s '99	Ms	**BBB–**	3/95	BBB	X	R	100.88	2-29-96	Z100.35	2-29-96	....	....	25.0	F1	'69	102⅛	95	102⅛	7.10	6.49
1st B 7.46s '99	mN	**BBB–**	3/95	BBB	X	R	NC	....	Z100	....	....	....	75.0	G1	'92	104¼	95⅜	104¼	7.16	6.20
1st A 6.41s 2001	fA	**BBB–**	3/95	BBB	X	R	NC	....	....	....	....	....	170	G1	'93	100½	88⅜	100½	6.38	6.30
1st 8.21s 2002	Jj	**BBB–**	3/95	BBB	X	R	104.926	12-31-96	Z100	....	®100	12-31-01	150	G1	'92	105½	96⅜	105½	7.78	7.07
1st A 6¾s 2003	Ms	**BBB–**	3/95	BBB	X	R	NC	....	Z100	....	....	....	50.0	F1	'93	101⅝	87¾	101⅝	6.64	6.46
1st A 8¼s 2004	Ao	**BBB–**	3/95	BBB	X	R	NC	....	....	....	....	....	300	G1	'92	110¾	96⅞	110¾	7.45	6.54
1st B 6.77s 2005	fA	**BBB–**	3/95	BBB	X	R	NC	....	....	....	....	....	120	G1	'93	101⅛	86½	101⅛	6.69	6.61
1st 8.94s 2022	Jj	**BBB–**	3/95	BBB	X	R	107.152	12-31-96	Z100	....	®104.47	12-31-01	150	G1	'92	111¾	94⅞	111¾	8.00	7.87
1st 8.70s 2024	Ao	**BBB–**	3/95	BBB	X	R	103.765	(4-1-02)	Z100	(4-1-02)	....	....	300	G1	'92	107⅝	94⅜	107⅝	8.08	8.01
Deb 9.72s '98	jJ	**BB+**	3/95	BBB–	Y	BE	NC	....	100	....	....	....	200	G1	'91	106½	101⅝	104⅝	9.29	7.66
[1]Hacienda Resorts[2]	***40i***	***0.76***	***0.97***	***0.76***		***Sp***	***28.50***	***46.40***	***73.90***	***6-30-95***	***355.0***		***416.0***	***96.6***						
Sub SF Deb 10¼s '98	Jd15	**NR**	11/87	CC		R	100	....	100	....	....	....	[3]15.4	M2	'83	92	90	92	11.14	14.21
Halliburton Co.	***49e***	***d2.21***	***d2.78***	***5.01***		***Dc***	***70.80***	***1894***	***1002***	***9-30-95***	***232.0***		***2245***	***12.3***						
Deb 8¾s 2021	Fa15	**A**	1/93	AA–	X	R	NC	....	....	....	....	....	200	L3	'91	123⅜	100⅜	123⅜	7.09	6.80
Hallmark Healthcare	***30***	***1.96***	***2.81***	***2.76***		***Je***	***23.40***	***59.20***	***26.00***	***9-30-94***	***87.60***		***122.0***	***71.9***						
Sr Sub Nts[4] 10⅝s 2003	mN15	**NR**	11/94	B–		R	105.3125	(11-15-98)	....	....	....	....	7.30	S5	'93	102⅞	94⅜	102⅞	10.33	10.08
Hallwood Group	***36***	***△1.53***	***△0.62***	***△0.04***		***Jl***				***7-31-95***	***48.60***		***51.90***	***93.6***						
• Sub Deb 13½s 2009	[5]Anaug15	**NR**				R	100	....	....	....	....	....	18.2	Reorg	'89	68	33¼	s45⅜	....	Flat
Hammons(J.Q.)Hotels LP/Fin	***32***	***1.46***	***1.80***	***1.47***		***Dc***	***96.40***	***103.0***	***50.80***	***12-30-94***	***371.0***		***402.0***	***94.8***						
1st[6] 8⅞s 2004	Fa15	**BB–**			Y	R	104.438	(2-15-99)	....	....	[7]Z108.875	2-14-97	300	K2	'94	98⅛	86½	98⅛	9.04	9.20
Hanna(M.A.)Co[8]	***14***	***2.28***	***2.65***	***3.32***		***Dc***	***119.0***	***607.0***	***361.0***	***9-30-95***	***232.0***		***729.0***	***32.2***						
• Sr Nts 9s '98	mS15	**BBB–**			X	R	NC	....	....	....	....	....	118	S1	'91	97	97	98¾	9.11	9.52
• Sr Nts 9⅜s 2003	mS15	**BBB–**			X	R	NC	....	....	....	....	....	118	S1	'91	No Sale		98	9.57	9.74
Harcourt General[9]	***17a***	***3.04***	***4.10***	***3.33***		***Oc***	***493.0***	***1626***	***781.0***	***7-31-95***	***824.0***		***1747***	***47.9***						
Sr Deb 8⅞s 2022	Jd	**BBB+**			X	BE	NC	....	....	....	....	....	150	S1	'92	121⅛	98¾	121⅛	7.33	7.09
Sr Nts 8¼s 2002	Jd	**BBB+**			X	BE	NC	....	....	....	....	....	150	S1	'92	110½	97¾	110½	7.47	6.24
Sub Nts 9⅜s '97	jJ	**BBB**			X	R	NC	....	....	....	....	....	124	F1	'87	105⅞	102¼	105⅛	8.92	5.77
Sub Nts 9½s 2000	Ms15	**BBB**			X	R	NC	....	....	....	....	....	125	F1	'88	112¾	103⅞	112¾	8.43	6.02
Harleysville Group	***35c***	***n/a***	***23.08***	***3.60***		***Dc***				***6-30-95***	***98.00***		***411.0***	***23.8***						
Nts 6¾s 2003	mN15	**BBB+**			X	R	NC	....	....	....	....	....	75.0	P4	'93	100½	84⅞	100½	6.72	6.67
Harman Int'l Indus	***23f***	***△1.79***	***△2.93***	***△3.42***		***Je***	***8.80***	***606.0***	***291.0***	***9-30-95***	***314.0***		***660.0***	***54.5***						
Sr Sub Nts[10] 12s 2002	fA	**B+**	9/94	B–	Y	R	106	(8-1-97)	....	....	....	....	64.5	L3	'92	110½	108	110	10.91	9.89
Harnischfeger Indus	***41c***	***6.23***	***1.97***	***2.32***		***Oc***	***182.0***	***1112***	***615.0***	***7-31-95***	***467.0***		***114.0***	***43.4***						
Deb 8.90s 2022	Ms	**BBB**	12/94	A–	X	BE	NC	....	....	....	....	....	75.0	M2	'92	121	99⅝	120½	7.39	7.15
Deb 7⅛s 2025	jD15	**BBB**			X	BE	NC	....	....	....	....	....	150	L3	'95	100¼	99⅛	100¼	7.11	7.10
Harrah's Jazz Co./Finance	***40i***	***n/a***	***n/a***	***n/a***		***Ap***	***Bankruptcy Chapt 11***				***★573.0***		***615.0***	***94.3***						
1st[11]Mtg[12]Nts[6] 14¼s 2001	mN15	**D**	11/95	B+		R			Plan default 11-15-95 int				435	D6	'94	111	27	28	....	Flat
Harrah's Operating Co[13]	***40i***	***1.71***	***2.59***	***2.78***		***Dc***	***Bankruptcy Chapt 11***				***727.0***		***1370***	***53.2***						
Nts[14] 8⅜s '96	Ao15	**BBB–**	10/95	BB+	X	R	100	....	....	....	....	....	0.23	S5	'86	101¼	98	100⅝	8.32	6.11
• Sr Sub[14]Nts[6] 10⅞s 2002	Ao15	**BBB–**	10/95	BB+	X	R	104.833	(4-15-97)	....	....	[15]Z107.25	4-14-96	200	D6	'92	109⅜	102¼	s107¾	10.09	9.22
Harris Bankcorp[16]	***10***	***2.10***	***2.57***	***1.95***		***Dc***				***9-30-95***	***988.0***		***2618***	***57.3***						
Sub Nts 9⅜s 2001	Jd	**A+**			X	R	NC	....	....	....	....	....	100	F1	'89	115⅛	104½	115⅛	8.14	6.06
Harris Chemical No. Amer	***14***	***1.64***	***d0.33***	***0.67***		***Mr***		***197.0***	***109.0***	***9-24-95***	***740.0***		***500.0***	***149.0***						
Sr Sec[17]Disc Nts[18] 10¼s 2001	jJ15	**B+**			Y	R	103	(10-15-98)	....	....	[19]Z110	10-14-96	[19,3]250	C1	'93	96	82	96	....	Flat
Sr SubNts 10¾s 2003	aO15	**B**			Y	R	104.05	(10-15-98)	....	....	....	....	335	C1	'93	98½	81	90	11.94	12.81
Harris Corp	***23e***	***△3.83***	***△4.62***	***△4.63***		***Je***	***64.30***	***1758***	***1012***	***9-30-95***	***476.0***		***1889***	***32.2***						
• SF Deb 7¾s 2001	jD15	**BBB+**	1/95	BBB	X	R	100.35	12-14-96	100	....	....	....	16.1	K2	'76	100⅛	99	95	8.16	8.85

Uniform Footnote Explanations-See Page 260. Other: [1] Subsid & data of Sahara Gaming Corp. [2] See Pioneer Finance, Santa Fe Hotel. [3] Incl disc. [4] Co must offer repurch at 101 on Chge of Ctrl. [5] Due 7-31-09:int pd ea 8-15 to '08 & 7-31-09. [6] (HRO)On Chge of Ctrl at 101. [7] Max $75M red w/proceeds of Pub Eq Off'g. [8] Was Hanna Mining. [9] Was Gen'l Cinema. [10] (HRO)At 101 for a Chge of Ctrl Triggering Event. [11] State gaming laws may red hldr's sale/Co red. [12] Contingent int is payable,as defined. [13] Was Holiday Inns,then Embassy Suites. [14] Gtd on a subordinated basis by Promus Co's Inc. [15] For Chge of Ctrl Triggering Event. [16] Subsid of Bankmont Fin'l(Bank of Montreal). [17] Co must offer repurch at 101(Accreted Vallon Chge of Ctrl. [18] Int accr at 10.25% fr 1-15-96. [19] Percent Accreted Val:Max $87.5M w/proceeds Com Off'g.

Title-Industry Code & Co. Finances (In Italics)	Ind	Fixed Charge Coverage 1992	1993		1994	Year End	Million $ Cash & Equiv.	Curr. Assets	Curr. Liab.	Balance Sheet Date	L. Term Debt (Mil $)		Capital-ization (Mil $)	Total Debt % Capital						
Individual Issue Statistics / Exchange	Interest Dates	S&P Debt Rating	Date of Last Rating Change	Prior Rating	Eligible	Bond Form	Redemption Provisions: Regular Price	Regular (Begins) Thru	Sinking Fund Price	Sinking Fund (Begins) Thru	Refund/Other Restriction Price	Refund/Other Restriction (Begins) Thru	Outst'g (Mil $)	Underwriting Firm	Underwriting Year	Price Range 1995 High	Price Range 1995 Low	Mo. End Price Sale(s) or Bid	Curr. Yield	Yield to Mat.
Harris Corp *(Cont.)*																				
Deb[1] 10⅜s 2018	jD	**BBB+**	1/95	BBB	X	R	105.138	(12-1-98)	....	....	....	....	150	S1	'88	117½	106¾	116¾	8.89	8.68
Harrow Industries, Inc	*13*	*1.07*	*1.03*		*1.41*	*Nv*	*0.92*	*31.20*	*14.80*	*11-27-94*	*45.00*		*42.00*	*107.0*						
◆Sr Sub Deb 12⅜s 2002	Ao15	**CCC**	5/94	NR	Y	R	100	....	100	....	....	....	38.0	B5	'87	No Sale		91	13.60	14.60
Harsco Corp	*17a*	*8.25*	*6.99*		*3.82*	*Dc*	*58.30*	*515.0*	*406.0*	*9-30-95*	*182.0*		*928.0*	*32.2*						
Nts[2] 8¾s '96	Mn15	**A**	10/92	A–	X	R	NC	....	....	....	Z®100	....	100	G1	'91	102¼	101⅛	101⅛	8.65	5.65
Nts 6s 2003	mS15	**A**			X	BE	NC	....	....	....	....	....	150	M5	'93	98⅝	84⅝	98⅝	6.08	6.23
Hartford Electric Lt	*72a*	***Merged into Conn L&P,see***																		
1st 5⅝s '97	Ao	**BBB+**			X	R	100	....	100	....	....	....	20.0	L3	'67	99½	94¾	98⅞	5.69	6.56
1st 6½s '98	Fa	**BBB+**			X	R	100	....	100	....	....	....	10.0	L3	'68	100½	95¼	99½	6.53	6.76
1st 7⅛s '98	mN	**BBB+**			X	R	100	....	100	....	....	....	25.0	L3	'68	102¼	95⅜	100¼	7.11	7.02
1st 7⅝s 2001	jD	**BBB+**			X	R	100.95	11-30-96	100.36	11-30-96	....	....	30.0	F1	'71	106¼	95¾	101¼	7.53	7.36
1st 7½s 2002	Jd	**BBB+**			X	R	101.21	5-31-96	100.27	5-31-96	....	....	35.0	F1	'72	105⅞	94	103⅜	7.26	6.84
1st 7½s 2003	Mn	**BBB+**			X	R	101.51	4-30-96	100.30	4-30-96	....	....	40.0	F1	'73	106⅛	93⅞	101¾	7.37	7.19
Hartford National[3]	*10*	***Now Shawmut National***																		
Sub Cap[4]Nts 9.85s '99	Jd	**BBB+**	12/95	BBB–	X	R	NC	....	....	....	Z100	....	150	F1	'87	110⅞	103⅞	110⅞	8.88	6.27
Hartmarx Corp	*59a*	*d0.71*	*1.28*		*1.50*	*Nv*	*1.42*	*304.0*	*81.50*	*8-31-95*	*186.0*		*318.0*	*64.8*						
Sr Sub Nts[5] 10⅞s 2002	Jj15	**B**			Y	R	103.107	(1-15-99)	....	....	[6]Z110	1-14-97	100	C5	'94	99½	87½	87½	12.43	14.00
Harvard Industries	*8*	*n/a*	*d0.57*		*3.14*	*Sp*	*64.60*	*177.0*	*131.0*	*6-30-95*	*107.0*		*149.0*	*72.5*						
Sr Nts[5] 12s 2004	jJ15	**B+**	8/95	B	Y	R	106	(7-15-99)	....	....	[7]Z111	7-14-99	100	F1	'94	106	100½	105	11.43	11.08
Hawaiian Electric Co.	*72a*	*2.95*	*3.20*		*3.41*	*Dc*	*0.29*	*156.0*	*288.0*	*9-30-95*	*517.0*		*1283*	*41.1*						
1st O 5¾s '97	Ms	**BBB+**	2/93	A–	X	CR	‡100	....	....	....	....	....	13.0	D4	'67	100	95⅛	100	5.75	5.74
• 1st S 7⅝s 2002	jD	**BBB+**	2/93	A–	X	R	‡101.51	6-1-96	....	....	....	....	10.0	D4	'72	101½	94⅝	101⅜	7.52	7.37
Nts 5.15s '96	jD	**BBB+**	5/95	BBB	X	BE	NC	....	....	....	....	....	20.0	S5	'93	99½	94⅝	99½	5.18	5.71
Nts 5.83s '98	jD	**BBB+**	5/95	BBB	X	BE	NC	....	....	....	....	....	30.0	S5	'93	99⅞	91	99⅞	5.84	5.88
Hawaiian Telephone Co.	*67a*	***Now GTE Hawaiian Tel,see***																		
1st R 5⅝s '97	Ao15	**BBB+**	6/95	A	X	R	‡100	....	Z100	....	....	....	16.0	K2	'67	99⅞	94⅞	99⅞	5.63	5.72
1st S 6¾s '98	Ao	**BBB+**	6/95	A	X	R	‡100.21	10-1-96	Z100	....	....	....	20.0	P1	'68	100¾	95½	100⅝	6.71	6.44
1st T 8¾s 2000	mS	**BBB+**	6/95	A	X	R	‡101.10	9-1-96	Z100	....	....	....	35.0	P1	'70	102⅛	100	101½	8.62	8.35
1st U 8s 2001	mS	**BBB+**	6/95	A	X	R	‡101.26	9-1-96	Z100.41	8-31-96	....	....	20.0	D8	'71	103¼	96¼	101¾	7.86	7.61
1st V 8½s 2006	Ao	**BBB+**	6/95	A	X	R	‡102.59	3-31-96	Z100	....	....	....	35.0	P1	'76	102¾	97⅜	102¾	8.27	8.10
Hayes Wheels Int'l[8]	*8*	*1.23*	*4.10*		....	*Ja*	*2.00*	*151.0*	*107.0*	*10-31-94*	*140.0*		*353.0*	*41.4*						
Sr Nts[9] 9¼s 2002	mN15	**BBB–**	5/95	BB+	X	R	104.625	(11-15-97)	100	(11-15-99)	....	....	100	S5	'92	108⅝	95¾	108⅝	8.52	7.61
Health & Retirement Prop Tr[10]	*57*	*3.88*	*7.07*		*7.46*	*Dc*				*9-30-95*	*p273.0*		*982.0*	*37.2*						
• F/R[11]Sr Nts 'A' 6.9875s '99	QJul13	**BBB–**	11/95	BBB	X	BE	*100	....	....	....	....	....	75.0	M2	'94	No Sale		100	6.99	....
• F/R[12]Sr Nts 'B' 6.6575s '99	QJul13	**BBB–**	11/95	BBB	X	BE	*100	(7-13-96)	....	....	....	....	125	M2	'94	No Sale		100	6.66	....
HEALTHSOUTH Corp[13]	*30*	*4.76*	*4.87*		*2.75*	*Dc*	*93.20*	*494.0*	*195.0*	*9-30-95*	*1386*		*1961*	*71.6*						
• Sr Sub Nts[5] 9½s 2001	Ao	**B**			Y	R	104.75	(4-1-98)	....	....	....	....	250	S5	'94	107½	96½	s105½	9.00	8.19
Healthtrust,Inc-The Hospital Co	*30*	*2.51*	*3.38*		*3.63*	*Au*	*94.80*	*890.0*	*526.0*	*11-30-94*	*1742*		*2818*	*61.8*						
Sub Deb[14] 8¾s 2005	Ms15	**BBB**	4/95	B	X	R	104.375	(3-15-98)	....	....	....	....	14.0	D6	'93	116⅞	95⅜	109	8.03	7.38
Sub Nts[14] 10¾s 2002	Mn	**BBB**	4/95	B	X	R	104	(5-1-97)	....	....	....	....	31.0	M2	'92	112½	106⅛	109⅞	9.78	8.69
Sub Nts[15] 10¼s 2004	Ao15	**NR**	7/95	BBB		R	103.844	(4-15-99)	....	....	....	....	4.00	D6	'94	126⅞	105⅝	116	8.84	7.61
Hechinger Co	*59l*	*3.30*	*2.53*		*2.56*	*Ja*	*62.00*	*604.0*	*363.0*	*10-28-95*	*401.0*		*887.0*	*45.7*						
Sr Deb 9.45s 2012	mN15	**BB–**	9/95	BB+	Y	BE	NC	....	....	....	....	....	100	M6	'92	115⅞	66⅞	68	13.90	14.59
Sr Nts 6.95s 2003	aO15	**BB–**	9/95	BB+	Y	BE	NC	....	....	....	....	....	100	M6	'93	99	62⅞	66	10.53	14.32
[16]***Heileman Acquisition Co***	*11a*	*n/a*	*2.13*		*d0.13*	*Dc*	*12.10*	*97.40*	*131.0*	*12-31-94*	*324.0*		*362.0*	*90.9*						
Sr[17]Sub Nts[18] 9⅝s 2004	Jj31	**CC**	9/95	CCC	Y	R	104.813	(1-31-98)	....	....	[17]108.422	1-30-96	160	B9	'94	70⅞	17	28	....	Flat

Uniform Footnote Explanations-See Page 260. Other: [1] (HRO)At 100 to 12-1-98 for Put Events. [2] (HRO)At 100 for a Trigger Event. [3] See Shawmut (Assoc'n) Corp. [4] To be exch for Cap Sec when due. [5] (HRO)On Chge of Ctrl at 101. [6] Max $25M red w/proceeds of Pub Equity Off'g. [7] Max $25M red w/proceeds of Pub Eq Off'gs. [8] Subsid of Varity Corp. [9] Co must offer repurch at 101 on Chge in Ctrl. [10] Was Health & Rehabilitation Properties Trust. [11] Int to 1-13-96,adj qtrly aft(3 Mo LIBOR&1.05%). [12] Int to 1-13-96,adj qtrly aft(3 Mo LIBOR&0.72%). [13] Was HEALTHSOUTH Rehab. [14] (HRO)On Chge of Ctrl at 100. [15] (HRO)On Chge of Ctrl Triggering Event at 100. [16] Now Heileman G. Brewing. [17] Max $56M red w/proceeds of Initial Pub Off'g. [18] Plan default 1-31-96 int.

Title-Industry Code & Co. Finances (In Italics) / Individual Issue Statistics (Exchange)	Ind / Interest Dates	Fixed Charge Coverage 1992 / S&P Debt Rating	1993 / Date of Last Rating Change	1994 / Prior Rating	Eligible	Year End / Bond Form	Million $ Cash & Equiv. / Redemption Provisions: Regular Price	Curr. Assets / Regular (Begins) Thru	Curr. Liab. / Sinking Fund Price	Balance Sheet Date / Sinking Fund (Begins) Thru	L. Term Debt (Mil $) / Refund/Other Restriction Price	Refund/Other Restriction (Begins) Thru	Capitalization (Mil $) / Outst'g (Mil $)	Total Debt % Capital / Underwriting Firm	Underwriting Year	Price Range 1995 High	Price Range 1995 Low	Mo. End Price Sale(s) or Bid	Curr. Yield	Yield to Mat.
Heinz (H.J.) Co.	***26***	***Δ5.89***	***Δ6.33***	***Δ5.45***		***Ap***	***190.0***	***3265***	***2778***	***11-1-95***	***2330***		***6285***	***57.5***						
Nts 5½s '97	mS15	**A+**	3/95	AA–	X	R	NC	....	....	....	....	....	250	D4	'92	100⅛	94	100⅛	5.49	5.42
Nts 6¾s '99	aO15	**A+**	3/95	AA–	X	R	NC	....	....	....	....	....	300	D4	'92	103¾	94⅛	103¾	6.51	5.64
Nts 6⅞s 2003	Jj15	**A+**	3/95	AA–	X	R	NC	....	....	....	....	....	200	D4	'93	105⅛	91⅞	105⅛	6.54	5.97
Heller Financial[1]	***25***	***1.14***	***1.49***	***1.46***		***Dc***	***222.0***			***9-30-95***	***7126***		***8555***	***83.3***						
F/R[2]Nts 6.1875s '99	QApr27	**BBB+**	12/95	A	X	BE	NC	....	....	....	....	....	200	L3	'94	100⅝	99⅜	100⅛	6.18	....
Sr Amortizing[3]Nts 6.45s '97	Fa15	**BBB+**	12/95	A	X	R	NC	....	....	....	....	....	100	M2	'92	100	95¼	100	6.45	....
Nts 8.85s '96	Ao15	**BBB+**	12/95	A	X	R	NC	....	....	....	....	....	100	M2	'91	102⅛	100⅞	100⅞	8.77	5.72
Nts 7¾s '97	Mn15	**BBB+**	12/95	A	X	BE	NC	....	....	....	....	....	200	L3	'92	102⅞	98⅞	102⅞	7.53	5.55
Nts 9⅜s '98	Ms15	**BBB+**	12/95	A	X	R	NC	....	....	....	....	....	500	G1	'91	107⅞	102⅝	107½	8.72	5.71
Nts 8s '98	jD15	**BBB+**	12/95	A	X	R	NC	....	....	....	....	....	200	G1	'91	106	98¼	106	7.55	5.77
Nts 9⅛s '99	fA	**BBB+**	12/95	A	X	R	NC	....	....	....	....	....	200	M2	'91	110¼	102	110¼	8.28	5.91
Nts 7⅞s '99	mN	**BBB+**	12/95	A	X	BE	NC	....	....	....	....	....	200	M2	'94	106½	97⅜	106½	7.39	5.95
Nts 5⅝s 2000	Ms15	**BBB+**	12/95	A	X	BE	NC	....	....	....	....	....	200	G1	'93	98⅜	87⅞	98⅜	5.72	6.07
Nts 6½s 2000	Mn15	**BBB+**	12/95	A	X	BE	NC	....	....	....	....	....	200	M2	'93	101⅝	91⅛	101⅝	6.40	6.07
Nts 7s 2002	Mn15	**BBB+**	12/95	A	X	BE	NC	....	....	....	....	....	150	M5	'95	104⅛	98⅞	104⅛	6.72	6.21
Hercules, Inc	***14***	***6.27***	***11.31***	***11.40***		***Dc***	***82.60***	***960.0***	***722.0***	***9-30-95***	***248.0***		***1627***	***32.1***						
Nts 6⅝s 2003	Jd	**A**			X	BE	NC	....	....	....	....	....	125	M5	'93	103⅜	89½	103⅜	6.41	6.05
[4]Heritage Media Services	***1***	***0.64***	***1.10***	***1.99***		***Dc***	***2.59***	***80.10***	***65.70***	***6-30-95***	***362.0***		***464.0***	***78.4***						
Sr Sec Nts 11s 2002	Jd15	**BB–**			Y	R	105.50	(6-15-97)	....	....	....	....	150	G1	'92	106⅝	101½	106⅝	10.32	9.60
Hershey Foods	***26h***	***14.41***	***13.21***	***11.83***		***Dc***	***27.30***	***1054***	***1307***	***10-1-95***	***154.0***		***2028***	***49.6***						
Deb 8.80s 2021	Fa15	**AA–**			X	R	NC	....	....	....	....	....	100	G1	'91	126	102¾	126	6.98	6.65
Nts 6.70s 2005	aO	**AA–**			X	BE	NC	....	....	....	....	....	200	G1	'95	105¼	99¾	105¼	6.37	5.98
Hertz Corp[5]	***7***	***1.10***	***1.40***	***1.94***		***Dc***	***134.0***			***9-30-95***	***4824***		***5667***	***85.1***						
Sr Nts[6] 9.30s '96	Ms	**A**	1/95	A–	X	R	NC	....	....	....	....	....	100	S4	'86	102	100½	100½	9.25	6.18
Sr Nts 9⅝s '96	Jd15	**A**	1/95	A–	X	R	NC	....	....	....	....	....	50.0	M2	'88	103¼	101¾	101¾	9.46	5.71
Sr Nts 9.70s '97	mS15	**A**	1/95	A–	X	R	NC	....	....	....	....	....	75.0	F1	'88	107¼	103¼	106½	9.11	5.65
Sr Nts 9¾s '98	Fa	**A**	1/95	A–	X	R	NC	....	....	....	....	....	100	L3	'91	108	103⅜	108	9.03	5.63
Sr Nts 8.30s '98	Fa2	**A**			X	BE	NC	....	....	....	....	....	150	M2	'95	105⅜	99⅞	105⅜	7.88	5.54
Sr Nts 9½s '98	Ms15	**A**	1/95	A–	X	R	100	....	....	....	....	....	100	M2	'88	107⅛	100	100½	9.45	9.23
Sr Nts 8⅛s '99	Ms11	**A**	1/95	A–	X	R	NC	....	....	....	....	....	100	M2	'92	106⅞	98¼	106⅞	7.60	5.74
Sr Nts 6½s 2000	Ao	**A**	1/95	A–	X	R	NC	....	....	....	....	....	100	M5	'93	102	91⅜	102	6.37	5.96
Sr Nts 6s 2001	Fa	**A**	1/95	A–	X	BE	NC	....	....	....	....	....	150	M5	'94	99⅞	87⅞	99⅞	6.01	6.03
Sr Nts 7s 2001	Ao15	**A**	1/95	A–	X	BE	NC	....	....	....	....	....	150	L3	'94	104⅜	92⅜	104⅜	6.71	6.02
Sr Nts 7⅜s 2001	Jd15	**A**	1/95	A–	X	BE	NC	....	....	....	....	....	100	L3	'94	106⅛	94⅛	106⅛	6.95	6.04
Sr Nts 6.70s 2002	Jd15	**A**			X	BE	NC	....	....	....	....	....	150	M5	'95	103⅜	96⅞	103⅜	6.48	6.06
Sr Nts 7⅝s 2002	fA	**A**	1/95	A–	X	R	NC	....	....	....	....	....	100	M2	'92	108	94⅞	108	7.06	6.13
Sr Nts 6⅜s 2005	aO15	**A**	1/95	A–	X	R	NC	....	....	....	....	....	100	L3	'93	100⅜	85	100⅜	6.35	6.32
Sr Nts[7] 9s 2009	mN	**A**	1/95	A–	X	R	[8]NC	....	....	....	....	....	100	M2	'89	125	104¾	125	7.20	6.27
Sr Sub Nts 9⅛s '96	fA	**A–**	1/95	BBB+	X	R	NC	....	....	....	....	....	100	S4	'89	103⅛	101⅝	102	8.95	5.61
Sr Sub Nts 10⅛s '97	Ms	**A–**	1/95	BBB+	X	R	NC	....	....	....	....	....	50.0	S4	'90	106¼	103⅜	105	9.64	5.64
Sr Sub Nts 9½s '98	Mn15	**A–**	1/95	BBB+	X	R	NC	....	....	....	....	....	100	L3	'91	108¼	102¾	108¼	8.78	5.73
•Jr Sub Nts 6⅝s 2000	jJ15	**A–**	1/95	BBB+	X	R	NC	....	....	....	....	....	150	M5	'93	100	90⅝	99½	6.66	6.75
•Jr Sub Nts 7s 2003	jJ15	**A–**	1/95	BBB+	X	R	NC	....	....	....	....	....	250	M5	'93	100½	92⅝	102	6.86	6.66
HFS Inc[9]	***32***	***2.14***	***4.00***	***5.85***		***Dc***	***41.20***	***205.0***	***148.0***	***9-30-95***	***302.0***		***863.0***	***38.6***						
•Sr Nts 5⅞s '98	jD15	**A–**	12/95	BBB+	X	R	NC	....	....	....	....	....	150	M2	'93	No Sale		87	6.75	11.15
Hills Stores	***59g***	***n/a***	***n/a***	....		***Ja***	***8.99***	***552.0***	***366.0***	***10-29-94***	***287.0***		***629.0***	***46.4***						
•Sr[10]Gtd Nts[11] 10¼s 2003	Ms31	**NR**				R	104	9-30-96	100	(3-31-02)	....	....	136	Reorg	'93	100½	84	s88⅛	11.63	12.69

Uniform Footnote Explanations-See Page 260. Other: [1] Subsid of Fuji Bank Ltd. [2] Int to 1-27-96,adj qtrly aft(3 Mo LIBOR&0.25%). [3] Prin pyts due on int dates thru 2-15-97. [4] Gtd by & data of Heritage Media Corp. [5] Subsid of Park Ridge Corp. [6] Int adj fr 8.5% on 2-28-91. [7] (HRO)On 11-1-99 at 100. [8] Red fr 11-1-99 at 100 if $10M or less outstg. [9] Was Hospitality Franchise Sys. [10] Gtd by Hills Dept Strs. [11] Co must offer repurch at 101 on Chge of Ctrl.

Title-Industry Code & Co. Finances (In Italics) / Exchange, Individual Issue Statistics	Ind / Interest Dates	Fixed Charge Coverage 1992 / S&P Debt Rating	1993 / Date of Last Rating Change	1994 / Prior Rating	Eligible	Year End / Bond Form	Million $ Cash & Equiv. / Redemption Provisions Regular Price	Curr. Assets / Regular (Begins) Thru	Curr. Liab. / Sinking Fund Price	Balance Sheet Date / Sinking Fund (Begins) Thru	L. Term Debt (Mil $) / Refund/Other Restriction Price	Refund/Other Restriction (Begins) Thru	Capitalization (Mil $) / Outst'g (Mil $)	Total Debt % Capital / Underwriting Firm	Underwriting Year	Price Range 1995 High	Low	Mo. End Price Sale(s) or Bid	Curr. Yield	Yield to Mat.
Hillenbrand Indus	***43***	***9.07***	***11.39***	***10.77***		***Nv***	***164.0***	***605.0***	***260.0***	***9-2-95***	***209.0***		***991.0***	***25.4***						
Deb 8½s 2011	jD	**A+**			X	R	NC	....	....	....	....	....	100	L3	'91	116½	98⅛	116½	7.30	6.79
Deb 7s 2024	Fa15	**A+**			X	R	NC	....	....	....	....	....	100	L3	'94	100⅛	83⅛	100⅛	6.99	6.99
[1]Hillhaven Corp	***30***	***4.86***	***7.02***	***8.74***		***Dc***	***76.90***	***508.0***	***275.0***	***9-30-95***	***p732.0***		***1523***	***61.2***						
Sr Sub Nts[2] 10⅛s 2001	mS	**B+**	10/95	B–	Y	R	103.75	(9-1-98)	....	....	[3]Z109	9-1-96	3.00	M2	'93	108¾	99¾	108¾	9.31	8.16
Hilton Hotels	***32***	***3.03***	***2.32***	***3.05***		***Dc***	***378.0***	***634.0***	***465.0***	***9-30-95***	***1098***		***2475***	***51.3***						
Nts 7.70s 2002	jJ15	**A**			X	BE	NC	....	....	....	....	....	300	M2	'92	104⅞	95⅛	104⅞	7.34	6.76
Hocking Valley Ry	***55***	***Asmd by CSX Transportation,see Seaborad Coast Ln***																		
• 1st Con 4½s '99	jJ	**BBB+**	3/91	A–	X	CR	NC	....	....	....	....	....	15.8		1899	99¾	89	93¾	4.80	6.52
Hoechst Celanese	***14***	***6.04***	***4.55***	***3.64***		***Dc***	***552.0***	***3705***	***2396***	***9-30-95***	***1050***		***4897***	***22.4***						
Nts 9⅝s '99	mS	**A+**	6/95	AA–	X	R	100	(9-1-97)	....	....	....	....	250	F1	'87	107⅜	103	106⅝	9.03	7.52
Nts 6⅛s 2004	Fa	**A+**	6/95	AA–	X	BE	NC	....	....	....	....	....	250	C5	'94	100	86½	100	6.13	6.12
M-T Nts 'B' 7½s 2004	mN25	**A+**	6/95	AA–	X	BE	NC	....	....	....	....	....	30.0	C5	'94	108¼	93	108¼	6.93	6.28
M-T Nts 'B' 7⅛s 2009	Ms15	**A+**	6/95	AA–	X	BE	NC	....	....	....	....	....	100	C5	'94	107	87⅞	107	6.66	6.33
Home Holdings Inc	***35c***	***2.81***	***d1.10***	***d8.84***		***Dc***				***9-30-95***	***[4]895.0***		***522.0***	***172.0***						
[5]Sr[6]Nts 7¾s '98	jD15	**B–**	1/95	BB–	Y	R	NC	....	....	....	....	....	100	L3	'93	90¾	53	89¾	8.64	11.96
[5]Sr[7]Nts[8] 8⅝s 2003	jD15	**B–**	1/95	BB–	Y	R	NC	....	....	....	....	....	180	L3	'93	81	49	80	10.78	12.69
Home Savings of America	***10a***	***2.07***	***0.71***	....		***Dc***				***9-30-94***	***6208***		***9342***	***66.5***						
Sub Nts[9] 6s 2000	mN	**BBB+**				BE	NC	....	....	....	....	....	250	L3	'93	99⅞	87⅝	99⅞	6.01	6.03
Honeywell Inc.	***23***	***6.10***	***8.04***	***6.59***		***Dc***	***229.0***	***2707***	***1967***	***10-1-95***	***565.0***		***2901***	***30.5***						
Deb 8⅝s 2006	Ao15	**A**	5/91	A–	X	R	NC	....	....	....	....	....	100	M6	'86	118½	100¼	118½	7.28	6.17
Hook-SupeRx, Inc	***59e***	***Merged into Revco D.S.,see***																		
Sr Nts[2] 10⅛s 2002	Jd	**BBB–**	7/94	BB–	X	R	105	(6-1-97)	....	....	....	....	145	G1	'92	109½	101¾	109½	9.25	8.19
Horsehead Indus, Inc.	***44***	....	....	....		***Dc***	***No Recent Fin'ls***				***297.0***		***543.0***	***70.3***						
Sub Nts 14s '99	Jd	**CCC–**	4/93	CCC+	Y	R	104.667	5-31-96	100	(6-1-98)	....	....	125	D7	'89	104¼	99	104	13.46	12.52
Hospital Corp of Amer	***30***	***Merged into Columbia/HCA Healthcare,see***																		
SF Deb 9s 2016	Ms15	**NR**	6/95	BBB+		R	104.54	3-14-96	100	(3-15-97)	®104.13	3-14-96	[10]24.5	S1	'86	105⅞	97⅛	104⅝	8.60	8.51
SF Deb 8½s 2017	Ms	**NR**	6/95	BBB+		R	105.10	2-29-96	100	(3-1-98)	®104.25	2-28-97	[10]8.70	S1	'87	105⅜	94¾	105⅜	8.07	7.97
Nts 8s '96	Ao15	**BBB+**	2/94	B+	X	R	NC	....	....	....	....	....	140	S1	'86	101⅝	100⅜	100⅝	7.95	5.75
Houghtin Mifflin	***54d***	***10.51***	***17.77***	***7.92***		***Dc***	***110.0***	***449.0***	***156.0***	***9-30-95***	***226.0***		***514.0***	***44.0***						
Nts 7⅛s 2004	Ao	**BBB+**	10/95	A	X	BE	NC	....	....	....	....	....	100	C5	'94	103⅝	91¾	103⅝	6.88	6.55
Household Bank, f.s.b.	***10b***	***Subsid of Household Int'l,see***																		
Sub Nts 8.45s 2002	jD10	**A–**			X	R	NC	....	....	....	....	....	100	M2	'92	112¾	99⅛	112¾	7.49	6.16
Sub Nts 6½s 2003	jJ15	**A–**				R	NC	....	....	....	....	....	100	L3	'93	101⅝	87¼	101⅝	6.40	6.23
Household Finance[11]	***25a***	***1.52***	***1.64***	***1.49***		***Dc***				***9-30-95***	***8397***		***14682***	***85.4***						
Nts 9⅜s '96	Fa15	**A**	4/92	A+	X	R	NC	....	....	....	....	....	150	G1	'91	102¼	100⅜	100⅜	9.34	6.20
Nts 7.80s '96	mN	**A**	4/92	A+	X	R	NC	....	....	....	....	....	150	L3	'91	102¼	99⅝	101⅞	7.66	5.47
Nts 7⅝s '96	jD15	**A**	4/92	A+	X	R	NC	....	....	....	....	....	150	M2	'91	102⅜	98⅞	102	7.48	5.46
Nts 7½s '97	Ms15	**A**	4/92	A+	X	R	NC	....	....	....	....	....	150	M6	'92	102⅜	98¼	102¼	7.33	5.54
Nts 7¾s '97	Jd15	**A**	4/92	A+	X	R	NC	....	....	....	....	....	95.0	M6	'86	103	98⅞	103	7.52	5.58
Nts 6¼s '97	aO15	**A**			X	R	NC	....	....	....	....	....	300	S1	'92	101¼	95⅛	101¼	6.17	5.50
Nts 7¾s '99	Jd	**A**			X	R	NC	....	....	....	....	....	150	M2	'92	106⅛	97¾	106⅛	7.30	5.75
Nts 7⅝s '99	Jd15	**A**			X	R	NC	....	....	....	....	....	150	G1	'92	105⅞	97	105⅞	7.20	5.73
Nts 8⅞s '99	jJ5	**A**	4/92	A+	X	R	100	(7-5-96)	....	....	....	....	150	S4	'89	104⅞	101	101⅜	8.75	8.41
Nts 8.95s '99	mS15	**A**	4/92	A+	X	R	NC	....	....	....	....	....	150	G1	'89	110½	101⅝	110½	8.10	5.76
Nts 6¾s 2000	Jd	**A**			X	BE	NC	....	....	....	....	....	200	M5	'95	103⅜	99⅛	103⅜	6.53	5.87
Nts 8⅜s 2001	mN15	**A**			X	R	NC	....	....	....	....	....	250	M6	'94	111⅝	99½	111⅝	7.50	6.00

Uniform Footnote Explanations-See Page 260. Other: [1] Merged into & data of Vencor Inc. [2] (HRO)On Chge of Ctrl at 101. [3] Max $50M red w/proceeds of Pub Equity Off'g. [4] Incl current amts. [5] Co must offer repurch,at 101,on Chge of Ctrl. [6] Int incr fr 7% eff 11-7-94. [7] Int incr fr 7.875% eff 11-7-94. [8] Exch offer,new 7.875% Notes,to Aug 4. [9] Issued in min denom $100T. [10] Defeased,fds deposited w/trustee. [11] Subsid of Household Int'l.

Title-Industry Code & Co. Finances (In Italics) / Individual Issue Statistics (Exchange)	Ind / Interest Dates	Fixed Charge Coverage 1992 / S&P Debt Rating	1993 / Date of Last Rating Change	Prior Rating	1994 / Eligible	Year End / Bond Form	Cash & Equiv. (Million $) / Redemption Provisions: Regular Price	Curr. Assets (Million $) / Regular (Begins) Thru	Curr. Liab. (Million $) / Sinking Fund Price	Balance Sheet Date / Sinking Fund (Begins) Thru	L. Term Debt (Mil $) / Refund/Other Restriction Price	Refund/Other Restriction (Begins) Thru	Capital-ization (Mil $) / Outst'g (Mil $)	Total Debt % Capital / Underwriting Firm	Underwriting Year	Price Range 1995 High	Price Range 1995 Low	Mo. End Price Sale(s) or Bid	Curr. Yield	Yield to Mat.
***Household Finance** (Cont.)*																				
Nts 6.70s 2002	Jd15	**A**			X	R	NC	....	....	....	....	....	200	M6	'95	103⅜	97¾	103⅜	6.48	6.06
Nts 7⅝s 2003	Jj15	**A**			X	R	NC	....	....	....	....	....	300	M6	'93	108⅜	94½	108⅜	7.04	6.14
Nts 6⅞s 2003	Ms	**A**			X	R	NC	....	....	....	....	....	300	M6	'93	104	90¼	104	6.61	6.17
Nts 8s 2004	fA	**A**			X	R	NC	....	....	....	....	....	250	M6	'94	111½	95⅞	111½	7.17	6.25
Nts 8¼s 2005	Fa15	**A**			X	R	NC	....	....	....	....	....	200	L3	'95	113½	99⅜	113½	7.27	6.28
Nts 7⅛s 2005	mS	**A**			X	BE	NC	....	....	....	....	....	150	M5	'95	106¼	99⅝	106¼	6.71	6.25
Nts 7.65s 2007	Mn15	**A**			X	BE	NC	....	....	....	....	....	250	M6	'95	110½	99¾	110½	6.92	6.34
Nts 6.45s 2009	Fa	**A**			X	R	NC	....	....	....	....	....	200	S1	'94	100¼	81¼	100¼	6.43	6.42
Sr Sub Nts 10⅛s '96	Jd15	**A–**	4/92	A	X	R	NC	....	....	....	....	....	100	M6	'85	103¾	101⅞	101⅞	9.94	5.92
Sr Sub Nts 9.55s 2000	Ao	**A–**	4/92	A	X	R	NC	....	....	....	....	....	150	G1	'90	113¼	103¾	113¼	8.43	5.97
• Sr Sub Nts 9⅝s 2000	jJ15	**A–**	4/92	A	X	R	NC	....	....	....	....	....	150	L3	'90	106½	105	106⅞	9.01	7.80
• Sr Sub Nts 9s 2001	mS28	**A–**	4/92	A	X	R	NC	....	....	....	....	....	100	M6	'89	110⅝	102⅜	107½	8.37	7.37
***Household Int'l**[1]*	***25a***	***1.20***	***1.39***		***1.42***	***Dc***				***9-30-95***	***[2]11154***		***13990***	***79.7***						
F/R[3]Nts 6s '96	QOct20	**A**			X	R	NC	....	....	....	....	....	150	M6	'94	100⅛	99½	100	6.00	....
F/R[4]Nts 6.0627s '97	[5]Qmay26	**A**			X	R	NC	....	....	....	....	....	100	L3	'94	100¼	99⅝	100⅛	6.06	....
Household Int'l Neth B.V.	***25***	***Gtd by Household Int'l,see***																		
Sr Nts[6] 5¼s '98	aO15	**A**			Q	R	NC	....	....	....	....	....	125	M6	'93	98⅝	90⅛	98⅝	5.32	5.79
***Houston Indus**[7]*	***72b***	***2.03***	***2.42***		***2.45***	***Dc***	***64.50***	***446.0***	***873.0***	***9-30-95***	***3558***		***8466***	***45.5***						
Deb 7¼s '96	jD	**BBB**			X	R	NC	....	....	....	....	....	200	F1	'91	101⅝	98⅜	101⅜	7.15	5.69
Deb 9⅜s 2001	Jd	**BBB**			X	R	NC	....	....	....	....	....	250	F1	'91	114¾	103⅝	114¾	8.17	6.13
Deb 7⅞s 2002	jJ	**BBB**			X	R	NC	....	....	....	....	....	100	F1	'92	108¾	96¼	108¾	7.24	6.22
***Houston Lighting & Pwr.**[8]*	***72a***	***2.95***	***3.47***		***3.90***	***Dc***	***94.40***	***371.0***	***677.0***	***6-30-95***	***3015***		***7034***	***45.4***						
1st 5¼s '96	Ao	**A**	5/91	A–	X	R	100	....	100	....	....	....	40.0	K2	'66	99⅞	97⅜	99⅞	5.26	5.67
1st 5¼s '97	Jj	**A**	5/91	A–	X	R	100	....	100	....	....	....	40.0	L3	'67	99¾	95⅜	99¾	5.26	5.51
1st 7⅝s '97	Ms	**A**			X	R	NC	....	....	....	....	....	150	F1	'92	102¼	98¾	102¼	7.46	5.60
1st 6¾s '97	mN	**A**	5/91	A–	X	R	100.29	10-31-96	100.24	10-31-96	....	....	35.0	L3	'67	100¾	96⅜	100½	6.72	6.45
1st 6¾s '98	Ao	**A**	5/91	A–	X	R	100.54	3-31-96	100.22	3-31-96	....	....	35.0	L3	'68	100⅞	96¼	100⅝	6.71	6.44
1st 7¼s 2001	Fa	**A**	5/91	A–	X	R	101.47	1-31-96	100.49	1-31-96	....	....	50.0	L3	'71	102¼	94⅝	101⅝	7.13	6.86
1st 9.15s 2021	Ms15	**A**	5/91	A–	X	R	NC	....	....	....	....	....	160	F1	'91	123⅝	104	123⅝	7.40	7.12
1st 8¾s 2022	Ms	**A**			X	R	103.95	(3-1-02)	Z100	....	....	....	100	F1	'92	114	98⅛	114	7.68	7.52
1st 7¾s 2023	Ms15	**A**			X	R	103.77	(3-15-03)	Z100	....	....	....	250	G1	'93	105⅞	88½	105⅞	7.32	7.25
1st 7½s 2023	jJ	**A**			X	R	103.51	(7-1-03)	Z100	....	....	....	200	F1	'93	103¾	85¾	103¾	7.23	7.19
*[9]**Hovnanian(K.)Enterprises***	***38***	***0.81***	***[10]1.09***		***1.73***	***Oc***	***11.30***			***7-31-95***	***382.0***		***548.0***	***69.7***						
Sub Nts[11] 9¾s 2005	Jd	**B**			Y	R	104.875	(6-1-99)	....	....	....	....	100	G1	'93	87½	73½	87½	11.14	12.00
HS Resources, Inc	***49b***	***2.87***	***6.21***		***2.34***	***Dc***	***1.08***	***9.64***	***15.60***	***9-30-95***	***124.0***		***243.0***	***51.0***						
Sr[12]Sub Nts 9⅞s 2003	jD	**B**			Y	R	103.75	(12-1-98)	....	....	....	....	75.0	L3	'93	98¾	92½	98	10.08	10.25
Hubbell Inc	***23g***	***187.15***	***39.83***		***25.03***	***Dc***				***6-30-95***	***★103.0***		***762.0***	***16.3***						
Nts 6⅝s 2005	aO	**AA–**			X	BE	NC	....	....	....	....	....	100	M6	'95	104⅝	99⅜	104⅝	6.33	5.99
Hunt (JB) Transport	***71***	***6.33***	***5.70***		***4.30***	***Dc***	***4.37***	***193.0***	***216.0***	***9-30-95***	***294.0***		***743.0***	***49.7***						
Nts 6¼s 2003	mS	**A–**	3/95	A	X	R	NC	....	....	....	....	....	100	M2	'93	101⅛	87¼	101⅛	6.18	6.06
***Huntington Bancshares**[13]*	***10***	***3.59***	***3.97***		***3.17***	***Dc***				***9-30-95***	***1622***		***3105***	***52.2***						
Sub Nts 7⅞s 2002	mN15	**BBB+**			X	BE	NC	....	....	....	....	....	150	L3	'92	108⅝	94⅝	108⅝	7.25	6.31
Huntington Nat'l Bank	***10***	***Subsid of Huntington Bancshares,see***																		
Sub Nts[14] 7⅝s 2003	Jj15	**A–**			X	BE	NC	....	....	....	....	....	50.0	L3	'93	107½	94	107½	7.09	6.29
Sub Nts[14] 6¾s 2003	Jd15	**A–**			X	BE	NC	....	....	....	....	....	100	L3	'93	102½	88½	102½	6.59	6.32
Huntsman Corp	***14***	***n/a***	***n/a***		***[15]2.43***	***Dc***	***89.00***	***445.0***	***211.0***	***9-30-95***	***633.0***		***891.0***	***71.0***						
[12]1st[16] 10⅝s 2001	Ao15	**BB–**			Y	R	101.771	(4-15-99)	....	....	[17]Z108.854	4-15-96	200	B9	'94	112¼	101¾	112	9.49	7.81

Uniform Footnote Explanations-See Page 260. Other: [1] See Household Bank, Household Int'l Neth B.V. [2] Incl curr amts. [3] Int to 1-20-96,adj qtrly(3 Mo LIBOR&0.0625%). [4] Int 2-26-96,adj qtrly(3 Mo LIBOR&0.1877%). [5] Due 5-27-97. [6] Red in whole at 100 if add'l taxes due. [7] See Houston Lighting & Power. [8] Subsid of Houston Indus. [9] Gtd by & data of Hovnanian Enterprises. [10] Fiscal Feb'94 & prior. [11] Gtd by Hovnanian Enterprises. [12] (HRO)On Chge of Ctrl at 101. [13] See Huntington Nat'l Bank. [14] Issued in min denom $250T. [15] 9 Mo Dec'94. [16] Purch offer, $1,117.36 to Jan 2. [17] Max $50M red w/proceeds of com IPO.

Title-Industry Code & Co. Finances (In Italics)	Ind		Fixed Charge Coverage 1992	1993	1994	Year End	Million $ Cash & Equiv.	Curr. Assets	Curr. Liab.	Balance Sheet Date	L. Term Debt (Mil $)	Capital-ization (Mil $)		Total Debt % Capital						
Exchange ↓ Individual Issue Statistics	Interest Dates	S&P Debt Rating	Date of Last Rating Change	Prior Rating	Eligible ↓	Bond Form	Redemption Provisions: Regular Price	Regular (Begins) Thru	Sinking Fund Price	Sinking Fund (Begins) Thru	Refund/Other Restriction Price	Refund/Other Restriction (Begins) Thru	Outst'g (Mil $)	Underwriting Firm	Underwriting Year	Price Range 1995 High	Price Range 1995 Low	Mo. End Price Sale(s) or Bid	Curr. Yield	Yield to Mat.
Huntsman Corp *(Cont.)*																				
[1]1st[2] 11s 2004	Ao15	**BB–**			Y	R	104.125	(4-15-99)	....	....	[3]Z109.625	4-15-96	318	B9	'94	115¼	103½	115	9.57	8.44
Hutton (E.F.) Group	***62***	***See Shearson Lehman Bros***																		
Nts 8⅞s '96	Mn	**A**	5/88	BBB–	X	R	NC	....	....	....	....	....	125	H4	'86	101⅞	100¾	101	8.79	5.78
IBM Credit Corp[4]	***25d***		***1.79***	***2.08***	....	***Dc***	***345.0***			***9-30-95***	***1201***	***8284***		***86.1***						
M-T Nts[5] 5.17s '96	[6]fa15	**A**			X	BE	NC	....	....	....	....	....	5.00	C5	'94	100	97	100	5.17	5.09
M-T Nts[5] 4.64s '96	[7]fa15	**A**			X	BE	NC	....	....	....	....	....	6.75	C5	'93	99¾	96¼	99¾	4.65	5.59
M-T Nts[5] 5½s '96	[7]fa15	**A**			X	BE	NC	....	....	....	....	....	10.0	C5	'94	100	97¼	100	5.50	5.43
M-T Nts[5] 5.84s '96	[7]fa15	**A**			X	BE	NC	....	....	....	....	....	10.0	C5	'94	100⅛	97⅝	100⅛	5.83	5.26
M-T Nts[5] 5⅞s '96	[8]fa15	**A**			X	BE	NC	....	....	....	....	....	25.0	C5	'94	100⅛	97⅝	100⅛	5.87	5.30
M-T Nts[5] 5.95s '96	[9]fa15	**A**			X	BE	NC	....	....	....	....	....	25.0	C5	'94	100⅛	97¾	100⅛	5.94	5.44
M-T Nts[5] 5.96s '96	[9]fa15	**A**			X	BE	NC	....	....	....	....	....	25.0	C5	'94	100⅛	97¾	100⅛	5.95	5.45
M-T Nts 5.85s '96	[10]fa15	**A**			X	BE	NC	....	....	....	....	....	25.0	C5	'94	100⅛	97½	100⅛	5.84	5.37
M-T Nts 6.40s '96	[11]ms	**A**			X	BE	NC	....	....	....	....	....	32.0	C5	'95	100⅜	99⅞	100¼	6.38	5.54
M-T Nts[5] 6.085s '96	[12]fa15	**A**			X	BE	NC	....	....	....	....	....	25.0	C5	'94	100¼	97¾	100¼	6.07	5.32
M-T Nts 6.24s '96	[13]fa15	**A**			X	BE	NC	....	....	....	....	....	10.0	C5	'94	100⅜	97⅞	100¼	6.22	5.51
M-T Nts 6.15s '96	[14]ms	**A**			X	BE	NC	....	....	....	....	....	25.0	C5	'95	100¼	99⅞	100¼	6.13	5.47
M-T Nts 6.15s '96	[15]ms	**A**			X	BE	NC	....	....	....	....	....	50.0	C5	'95	100¼	99⅞	100¼	6.13	5.52
M-T Nts 15s '96	Jd13	**A**			X	BE	NC	....	....	....	....	....	50.0	C5	'95	108¾	104⅛	104⅛	14.41	5.67
M-T Nts 6s '96	[16]ms	**A**			X	BE	NC	....	....	....	....	....	25.0	C5	'95	100¼	99⅞	100¼	5.99	5.43
M-T Nts 6.05s '96	[16]ms	**A**			X	BE	NC	....	....	....	....	....	25.0	C5	'95	100¼	99⅞	100¼	6.03	5.48
M-T Nts 6.16s '96	[13]fa15	**A**			X	BE	NC	....	....	....	....	....	5.00	C5	'94	100¼	97¾	100¼	6.14	5.43
M-T Nts[5] 4½s '96	[17]fa15	**A**			X	BE	NC	....	....	....	....	....	10.0	C5	'93	99⅛	94	99⅛	4.54	5.61
M-T Nts[5] 5.12s '96	[18]fa15	**A**			X	BE	NC	....	....	....	....	....	15.0	C5	'93	99⅝	94⅞	99⅝	5.14	5.56
M-T Nts[5] 5.07s '96	[19]fa15	**A**			X	BE	NC	....	....	....	....	....	5.00	C5	'93	99⅝	94¾	99⅝	5.09	5.51
M-T Nts[5] 5.14s '96	[19]fa15	**A**			X	BE	NC	....	....	....	....	....	5.00	C5	'93	99⅝	94⅞	99⅝	5.16	5.58
F/R[20]M-T Nts '97	[21]Mar27	**A**			X	BE	NC	....	....	....	....	....	25.0	C5	'95	100¼	99⅞	100⅛	....	....
M-T Nts[5] 5.45s '97	[22]fa15	**A**			X	BE	NC	....	....	....	....	....	10.0	C5	'93	99¾	92⅞	99¾	5.46	5.59
M-T Nts[5] 5.43s '97	[23]fa15	**A**			X	BE	NC	....	....	....	....	....	5.00	C5	'93	99⅝	92¾	99⅝	5.45	5.64
M-T Nts[5] 5.17s '97	[24]fa15	**A**			X	BE	NC	....	....	....	....	....	5.00	C5	'94	99⅛	91¾	99⅛	5.22	5.64
• M-T Nts[5] 5.36s '98	[25]fa15	**A**			X	BE	NC	....	....	....	....	....	5.00	C5	'93	93⅛	90⅛	98⅞	5.42	5.79
M-T([26]Reset)Nts[27] 7s '99	fA26	**A**			X	BE	*■100	....	....	....	....	....	25.0	S5	'94	103⅞	96¾	103⅞	6.74	....
M-T Nts 7½s 2000	Mn16	**A**			X	BE	*100	(5-16-96)	....	....	....	....	25.0	C5	'95	102	100	100¾	7.44	7.29
ICF Kaiser Int'l	***53***		***2.32***	***d0.96***	***0.81***	***Fb***	***29.30***	***227.0***	***145.0***	***8-31-95***	***121.0***	***170.0***		***71.8***						
xwSr[1]Sub Nts 12s 2003	jD31	**B–**			Y	R	108	(12-31-98)	....	....	....	....	125	D4	'93	106	87	106	11.32	10.86
[28]I.C.H. Corp	***35a***		***d0.71***	***0.60***	***d1.65***	***Dc***	***Bankruptcy Chapt 11***				***310.0***	***405.0***		***91.3***						
Sr Sub Nts 11¼s '96	jD	**D**	10/95	C		R			Plan default 12-1-95 int				256	K2	'86	83½	44	60	....	Flat
ICN Pharmaceuticals(New)	***21a***		***d0.24***	***d0.68***	***d17.24***	***Dc***	***32.30***	***310.0***	***112.0***	***9-30-95***	***170.0***	***346.0***		***58.1***						
Idaho Power Co.	***72a***		***2.41***	***3.04***	***2.94***	***Dc***	***7.65***	***139.0***	***169.0***	***9-30-95***	***673.0***	***1485***		***46.7***						
1st 5¼s '96	Ao	**A**	10/92	A+	X	R	100	3-31-96	100	....	....	....	20.0	B6	'66	99⅞	97⅜	99⅞	5.26	5.67
1st 5.33s '98	[29]mn	**A**			X	BE	NC	....	....	....	....	....	30.0	G1	'93	99⅛	90¾	99⅛	5.38	5.68
1st 8.65s 2000	Jj	**A**	10/92	A+	X	R	NC	....	....	....	....	....	80.0	G1	'89	109½	101⅛	109½	7.90	5.95
1st 6.40s 2003	Mn	**A**			X	BE	NC	....	....	....	....	....	80.0	S1	'93	100⅞	87½	100⅞	6.34	6.25
1st 8s 2004	Ms15	**A**	10/92	A+	X	R	NC	....	....	....	....	....	50.0	G1	'92	111	96⅝	111	7.21	6.26
1st 9½s 2021	Jj	**A**	10/92	A+	X	R	104.50	(1-1-01)	....	....	....	....	75.0	G1	'91	119⅝	102⅞	119⅝	7.94	7.72
1st 7½s 2023	Mn	**A**			X	BE	103.366	(5-1-02)	....	....	....	....	80.0	S1	'93	103¾	86	103¾	7.23	7.18
1st 8¾s 2027	Ms15	**A**	10/92	A+	X	R	104.188	(3-15-02)	....	....	....	....	50.0	G1	'92	112¾	96⅝	112¾	7.76	7.67

Uniform Footnote Explanations-See Page 260. Other: [1] (HRO)On Chge of Ctrl at 101. [2] Purch offer, $1,146.94 to Jun 2. [3] Max $50M red w/proceeds of com IPO. [4] Subsid of Int'l Bus. Mach. [5] Issued in min denom $100T. [6] Due 3-8-96. [7] Due 3-29-96. [8] Due 4-1-96. [9] Due 4-12-96. [10] Due 4-19-96. [11] Due 4-24-96. [12] Due 5-6-96. [13] Due 5-13-96. [14] Due 5-22-96. [15] Due 5-31-96. [16] Due 6-14-96. [17] Due 10-22-96. [18] Due 11-12-96. [19] Due 11-15-96. [20] Int adj monthly(one month LIBOR&0.20%). [21] Int pd monthly. [22] Due 11-10-97. [23] Due 11-19-97. [24] Due 12-30-97. [25] Due 10-27-98. [26] Int adj ea 8-26:7.25%,'96,7.5%,'97,8%,'98,9%,aft. [27] Issued in min denom $5T. [28] Now Southwestern Life. [29] Due 9-1-98.

Title-Industry Code & Co. Finances (In Italics)	Ind	Fixed Charge Coverage 1992	1993	1994		Year End	Million $ Cash & Equiv.	Curr. Assets	Curr. Liab.	Balance Sheet Date	L. Term Debt (Mil $)		Capital-ization (Mil $)	Total Debt % Capital						
Individual Issue Statistics Exchange ↓	Interest Dates	S&P Debt Rating	Date of Last Rating Change	Prior Rating	Eligible ↓	Bond Form	Redemption Provisions: Regular Price	Regular (Begins) Thru	Sinking Fund Price	Sinking Fund (Begins) Thru	Refund/Other Restriction Price	Refund/Other Restriction (Begins) Thru	Outst'g (Mil $)	Underwriting Firm	Underwriting Year	Price Range 1995 High	Price Range 1995 Low	Mo. End Price Sale(s) or Bid	Curr. Yield	Yield to Mat.
IDEX Corp	***41h***	*3.54*	*4.48*	*4.87*		*Dc*	*3.28*	*168.0*	*72.70*	*9-30-95*	*179.0*		*322.0*	*55.6*						
Sr Sub Nts[1] 9¾s 2002	mS15	BB–	11/95	B+	Y	R	103.75	(9-15-97)	100	(9-15-00)	[2]Z100	....	75.0	M2	'92	106	97½	106	9.20	8.55
Illinois Bell Telephone[3]	***67a***	*6.38*	*6.32*	*7.90*		*Dc*	*0.10*	*821.0*	*1285*	*9-30-95*	*1335*		*3204*	*60.3*						
1st G 4⅞s '97	jJ	AAA			X	CR	100	....	....	....	....	....	50.0	H1	'60	99⅛	93	99⅛	4.92	5.49
1st H 4⅜s 2003	jJ	AAA			X	CR	100.38	6-30-96	....	....	....	....	50.0	S1	'63	91⅛	77⅛	91⅛	4.80	5.85
• 1st K 7⅝s 2006	Ao	AAA			X	R	101.59	3-31-96	....	....	....	....	200	S1	'71	103¾	94⅛	101⅞	7.48	7.36
Deb 7⅛s 2023	jJ	AAA			X	BE	102.982	(7-1-03)	....	....	....	....	100	L3	'93	104⅜	84⅜	104⅜	6.83	6.77
Deb 7¼s 2024	Ms15	AAA			X	BE	103.191	(3-15-03)	....	....	....	....	200	G1	'93	105½	85⅝	105½	6.87	6.81
Deb 6⅝s 2025	Fa	AAA			X	BE	101.904	(2-1-04)	....	....	....	....	100	L3	'94	99⅛	79¼	99⅛	6.68	6.69
Deb 8½s 2026	Ao22	AAA			X	R	104.55	4-21-96	....	....	....	....	275	F1	'86	106	96⅜	104⅞	8.10	8.07
Nts 5.80s 2004	Fa	AAA			X	BE	NC	....	....	....	....	....	100	G1	'94	98⅞	84⅛	98⅞	5.87	5.98
Illinois Central[4]RR Co[5]	***55***	*3.63*	*5.67*	*6.84*		*Dc*	*9.10*	*104.0*	*213.0*	*6-30-95*	*342.0*		*784.0*	*46.6*						
Nts 6¾s 2003	Mn15	BBB			X	BE	NC	....	....	....	....	....	100	L3	'93	104⅝	85⅝	104⅝	6.45	5.96
Nts 7¾s 2005	Mn	BBB			X	BE	NC	....	....	....	....	....	100	L3	'95	111⅞	99⅞	111⅞	6.93	6.06
Illinois Power Co[6]	***75***	*2.21*	*2.48*	*3.01*		*Dc*	*11.20*	*407.0*	*551.0*	*9-30-95*	*1803*		*3679*	*68.8*						
1st 5.85s '96	aO	BBB	4/94	BBB+	X	R	100	....	100	....	....	....	40.0	F1	'66	100	96⅜	100	5.85	5.84
• 1st 6½s '99	mS	BBB	4/94	BBB+	X	R	NC	....	....	....	....	....	72.0	S1	'92	No Sale		99⅝	6.52	6.61
• 1st 7.95s 2004	jJ	BBB	4/94	BBB+	X	R	NC	....	....	....	....	....	72.0	M2	'92	No Sale		104⅞	7.58	7.17
• 1st 8¾s 2021	jJ	BBB	4/94	BBB+	X	R	106.491	(7-1-97)	....	....	....	....	125	M2	'92	103¾	103¾	104⅛	8.40	8.36
• New Mtg 6⅛s 2000	Ms15	BBB	4/94	BBB+	X	BE	NC	....	....	....	....	....	40.0	M2	'93	No Sale		97⅝	6.27	6.78
• New Mts 5⅝s 2000	Ao15	BBB	4/94	BBB+	X	BE	NC	....	....	....	....	....	110	M2	'93	No Sale		98⅝	5.70	5.99
• New Mtg 6½s 2003	fA	BBB	4/94	BBB+	X	BE	NC	....	....	....	....	....	100	B5	'93	No Sale		97⅛	6.69	6.99
• New Mtg 6¾s 2005	Ms15	BBB	4/94	BBB+	X	BE	NC	....	....	....	....	....	70.0	M2	'93	No Sale		96½	6.99	7.28
• New Mtg 8s 2023	Fa15	BBB	4/94	BBB+	X	BE	105.25	(2-15-98)	....	....	....	....	235	B5	'93	104⅜	93⅞	103¾	7.71	7.67
• New Mtg 7½s 2025	jJ15	BBB	4/94	BBB+	X	BE	103.45	(7-15-03)	....	....	....	....	200	M2	'93	96⅝	96½	98	7.65	7.67
Illinois Tool Works	***13e***	*8.23*	*11.11*	*17.71*		*Dc*	*102.0*	*1495*	*794.0*	*9-30-95*	*282.0*		*2255*	*19.0*						
Nts 7½s '98	jD	AA–			X	R	NC	....	....	....	....	....	125	F1	'91	105⅛	97⅝	105⅛	7.13	5.57
Nts 5⅞s 2000	Ms	AA–			X	BE	NC	....	....	....	....	....	125	F1	'93	100¼	89⅞	100¼	5.86	5.80
IMC Global Inc[7]	***14a***	*△0.97*	*△1.74*	*△7.35*		*Je*	*218.0*	*591.0*	*291.0*	*9-30-95*	*516.0*		*1832*	*30.3*						
Sr Deb 9.45s 2011	jD15	BB–	4/95	B	Y	R	NC	....	....	....	....	....	100	M5	'91	108	89½	107	8.83	8.63
Sr[1]Nts 9¼s 2000	aO	BB–	4/95	B	Y	R	NC	....	....	....	....	....	61.6	L3	'93	106½	98⅛	106½	8.69	7.59
[8]IMCERA Group[9]	***14***	*d2.57*	*6.10*	*7.20*		*Je*	*87.90*	*932.0*	*671.0*	*6-30-94*	*522.0*		*1686*	*39.7*						
Deb 7s 2013	jD15	BBB+			X	BE	NC	....	....	....	....	....	100	G1	'93	102¼	84⅛	102¼	6.85	6.78
Nts 6s 2003	aO15	BBB+			X	BE	NC	....	....	....	....	....	100	G1	'93	98⅞	84¾	98⅞	6.07	6.18
Imo (Delaval) Indus	***23***	*d0.45*	*0.81*	*1.19*		*Dc*	*2.31*	*194.0*	*116.0*	*9-30-95*	*231.0*		*256.0*	*94.1*						
Sr Sub Deb 12¼s '97	fA15	B–	5/93	B+	Y	R	100	....	....	....	....	....	150	M6	'87	101	100	100¼	12.22	12.05
Sr Sub Deb 12s 2001	mN	B–	5/93	B+	Y	R	102.50	10-31-96	100	(11-1-99)	....	....	150	M6	'89	103½	100¼	102	11.76	11.51
Imperial Holly Corp	***26a***	*0.97*	*d0.03*	*0.03*		*Mr*	*38.80*	*189.0*	*102.0*	*9-30-95*	*95.30*		*236.0*	*53.0*						
Sr Nts 8⅜s '99	aO15	BB–	8/95	BB+	Y	R	NC	....	....	....	....	....	100	S5	'92	102	91	102	8.21	7.75
Indiana Bell Telephone[10]	***67a***	*8.01*	*10.27*	*12.81*		*Dc*		*305.0*	*476.0*	*9-30-95*	*94.10*		*869.0*	*27.6*						
Deb 4⅜s 2003	Jd	AAA			X	CR	100.55	5-31-96	....	....	....	....	20.0	H1	'63	90¼	76⅝	90¼	4.85	6.02
Deb 4¾s 2005	aO	AAA			X	R	100.92	9-30-96	....	....	....	....	25.0	M2	'65	90⅝	74⅞	90⅝	5.24	6.03
Deb 5½s 2007	Ao	AAA			X	R	101.24	3-31-96	....	....	....	....	40.0	S1	'67	93¾	78¼	93¾	5.87	6.28
Indiana Gas[11]	***73b***	*△3.63*	*△4.26*	*△4.47*		*Sp*	*0.20*	*84.10*	*120.0*	*9-30-95*	*174.0*		*442.0*	*39.4*						
1st M 9⅜s 2016	jJ15	AA–			X	R	104.613	(7-15-96)	100	(7-15-97)	....	....	19.0	G1	'86	107¼	103⅞	106⅜	8.81	8.70
Nts A 9⅛s 2021	Fa15	AA–			X	R	105.475	(2-15-01)	100	(2-15-02)	....	....	40.0	G1	'91	119¼	100⅜	119¼	7.65	7.42
Deb[12]B 8½s 2021	mS15	AA–			X	BE	105	(9-15-96)	....	....	....	....	25.0	J2	'91	108	96⅞	108	7.87	7.77

Uniform Footnote Explanations-See Page 260. Other: [1] (HRO)On Chge of Ctrl at 101. [2] On Chge of Ctrl,plus premium. [3] Subsid of Ameritech Corp. [4] Subsid of Illinois Central Corp. [5] See Gulf,Mobile & Ohio. [6] Subsid of Illinova Corp. [7] Was IMC Fertilizer Group. [8] Now Mallinckrodt Group. [9] See Int'l Minerals & Chem. [10] Subsid of Ameritech. [11] Subsid of Indiana Energy. [12] Death red benefit(ltd) at 100.

Title-Industry Code & Co. Finances (In Italics)	Ind	Fixed Charge Coverage 1992		1993	1994	Year End	Million $ Cash & Equiv.	Curr. Assets	Curr. Liab.	Balance Sheet Date	L. Term Debt (Mil $)		Capital-ization (Mil $)	Total Debt % Capital						
Individual Issue Statistics / Exchange ↓	Interest Dates	S&P Debt Rating	Date of Last Rating Change	Prior Rating	Eligible ↓	Bond Form	Redemption Provisions: Regular Price	Regular (Begins) Thru	Sinking Fund Price	Sinking Fund (Begins) Thru	Refund/Other Restriction Price	Refund/Other Restriction (Begins) Thru	Outst'g (Mil $)	Underwriting Firm	Underwriting Year	Price Range 1995 High	Price Range 1995 Low	Mo. End Price Sale(s) or Bid	Curr. Yield	Yield to Mat.
***Indiana Gas** (Cont.)*																				
Nts D 6⅝s '97	jD	**AA–**			X	R	NC		....		....	....	35.0	G1	'92	101⅞	96	101⅞	6.50	5.58
[1]***Indiana & Mich Elec***	***72a***	***2.81***		***3.13***	***3.64***	***Dc***	***6.21***	***271.0***	***311.0***	***9-30-95***	***1038***		***2341***	***48.4***						
1st 7s '98	Mn	**BBB+**	12/84	BBB	X	R	100.57	4-30-96	□100.27	4-30-96	....	....	35.0	F1	'68	100⅞	96⅜	100⅝	6.96	6.70
SF Deb 7¼s '98	Mn	**BBB**			X	R	100.63	4-30-96	100.40	4-30-96	....	....	6.05	B6	'68	100⅝	96⅞	100½	7.21	7.01
Indianapolis Pwr & Lt[2]	***72a***	***4.20***		***4.52***	***4.10***	***Dc***	***4.59***	***157.0***	***256.0***	***9-30-95***	***639.0***		***1535***	***47.8***						
1st 5⅛s '96	Ao	**AA–**	9/93	AA	X	CR	100	....	100	....	....	....	15.0	L3	'66	99⅞	97¼	99⅞	5.13	5.55
1st 5⅝s '97	Mn	**AA–**	9/93	AA	X	CR	100.25	4-30-96	100.18	4-30-96	....	....	[3]11.5	E1	'67	100⅛	95¼	100⅛	5.62	5.52
1st 6.05s 2004	Fa	**AA–**			X	R	NC	....	▲100	....	....	....	80.0	D4	'94	99⅝	85¾	99⅝	6.07	6.11
1st 8s 2006	aO15	**AA–**	9/93	AA	X	R	NC	....	▲100	....	....	....	58.8	L3	'91	113⅞	96⅜	113⅞	7.03	6.21
1st 7⅜s 2007	fA	**AA–**	9/93	AA	X	R	NC	....	▲100	....	....	....	80.0	D4	'92	109⅝	91¾	109⅝	6.73	6.20
1st 9⅝s 2019	Jd	**AA–**	9/93	AA	X	R	106.738	5-31-96	▲100	....	....	....	50.0	S4	'89	107⅜	104¾	105¾	9.10	9.03
1st 7.05s 2024	Fa	**AA–**			X	R	103.31	(2-1-04)	▲100	....	....	....	100	D4	'94	100½	83¼	100½	7.01	7.01
Infinity Broadcasting	***12b***	***0.76***		***1.41***	***1.76***	***Dc***	***9.21***	***94.30***	***48.90***	***9-30-95***	***553.0***		***541.0***	***102.0***						
• Sr Sub Nts[4] 10⅜s 2002	Ms15	**BB–**	7/94	B+	Y	R	105.19	(3-15-97)	....	....	....	....	200	L3	'92	107½	101	107	9.70	8.88
Ingersoll-Rand Co.[5]	***41c***	***4.42***		***6.10***	***6.86***	***Dc***	***197.0***	***2450***	***1423***	***9-30-95***	***1384***		***3368***	***48.7***						
Deb 9s 2021	fA15	**A**			X	BE	NC	....	....	....	....	....	125	S1	'91	124½	103⅝	124½	7.23	6.94
Deb[6] 6.48s 2025	Jd	**A**			X	BE	NC	....	....	....	....	....	150	M2	'95	102⅝	94	102⅝	6.31	6.28
Deb 7.20s 2025	Jd	**A**			X	BE	NC	....	100	(6-1-06)	....	....	150	S1	'95	104¼	99½	104¼	6.91	6.86
Nts 8¼s '96	mN	**A**	6/90	A–	X	R	NC	....	....	....	....	....	75.0	S1	'86	102⅞	100½	102⅛	8.08	5.61
Nts 6⅞s 2003	Fa	**A**			X	BE	NC	....	....	....	....	....	100	S1	'93	104⅛	91½	104⅛	6.60	6.15
M-T Nts 'A' 6.24s '97	[7]jj15	**A**			X	BE	NC	....	....	....	....	....	25.0	S1	'95	101⅛	100	101⅛	6.17	5.49
M-T Nts 'A' 6.37s '97	[8]jj15	**A**			X	BE	NC	....	....	....	....	....	25.0	G1	'95	101⅜	100	101⅜	6.28	5.49
M-T Nts 'A' 6.57s '99	[9]jj15	**A**			X	BE	NC	....	....	....	....	....	25.0	S1	'95	102¾	100	102¾	6.39	5.71
M-T Nts 'A' 6.62s '99	[10]jj15	**A**			X	BE	NC	....	....	....	....	....	25.0	C1	'95	103	100	103	6.43	5.70
M-T Nts 'A' 6.60s 2000	[11]jj15	**A**			X	BE	NC	....	....	....	....	....	25.0	S1	'95	103⅛	100	103⅛	6.40	5.81
M-T Nts 'A' 6.60s 2000	[12]jj15	**A**			X	BE	NC	....	....	....	....	....	25.0	S1	'95	103⅛	100	103⅛	6.40	5.81
M-T Nts 'A' 6.86s 2002	[13]jj15	**A**			X	BE	NC	....	....	....	....	....	25.0	S1	'95	104½	100	104½	6.56	6.02
Inland Steel Co.[14]	***66a***	***d4.11***		***d0.74***	***2.67***	***Dc***		***512.0***	***593.0***	***9-30-95***	***410.0***		***665.0***	***62.9***						
• 1st R 7.90s 2007	Jj15	**BB–**	11/92	BB	Y	R	101.56	1-14-97	100	....	....	....	87.9	K3	'77	96	84	95	8.32	8.61
1st T[4] 12s '98	jD	**BB–**	11/92	BB	Y	R	NC	....	....	....	....	....	125	G1	'91	110⅝	106	109¼	10.98	8.36
Inland Steel Indus	***66a***	***d3.47***		***0.34***	***3.37***	***Dc***	***182.0***	***1272***	***584.0***	***9-30-95***	***870.0***		***1618***	***55.1***						
Nts[4] 12¾s 2002	jD15	**B+**			Y	R	106.375	(12-15-97)	....	....	....	....	150	G1	'92	112¾	107	112½	11.33	10.20
Insight Comm/Insight Fin	***12a***	***d0.28***		***0.22***	***0.67***	***Dc***	***0.66***			***12-31-94***	***170.0***		***49.90***	***341.0***						
Sr Sub([15]Reset)Nts[16] 8¼s 2000	Ms	**B–**			Y	R	103	(3-1-97)	....	....	....	....	[17]108	L1	'93	101½	93½	100½	8.21	....
Integon Corp	***35c***	***6.79***		***4.36***	***2.22***	***Dc***				***9-30-95***	***151.0***		***392.0***	***42.9***						
Sr Nts 8s '99	fA15	**BBB–**	8/94	BBB	X	R	NC	....	....	....	....	....	75.0	S5	'92	103¼	93⅛	103¼	7.75	6.97
Sr Nts 9½s 2001	aO15	**BBB–**			X	R	NC	....	....	....	....	....	75.0	S5	'94	108	97½	108	8.80	7.76
Integra Fin'l Corp	***10***	***3.40***		***3.44***	***3.12***	***Dc***				***9-30-95***	***1263***		***2341***	***54.0***						
• Sub Deb 8½s 2002	Mn15	**BBB**			X	BE	NC	....	....	....	....	....	100	L3	'92	No Sale		109¼	7.78	6.69
• Sub Nts 6½s 2000	Ao15	**BBB**			X	R	NC	....	....	....	....	....	100	F1	'93	No Sale		88¼	7.37	9.92
Integrated Health Svcs	***30***	***5.95***		***3.83***	***3.49***	***Dc***	***35.70***	***268.0***	***165.0***	***9-30-95***	***692.0***		***1204***	***58.1***						
• Sr Sub Nts[4] 10¾s 2004	jJ15	**B**	5/95	B–	Y	R	105.375	7-14-99	....	....	....	....	100	S5	'94	101½	101½	100¼	10.72	10.70
• Sr Sub Nts 'A'[4] 9⅝s 2002	Mn31	**B**			Y	R	NC	....	....	....	....	....	115	S5	'95	100	100	A100	9.63	9.62
Inter-City Products (USA)	***13b***	***1.86***		***0.31***	***0.60***	***Dc***	***2.33***	***207.0***	***74.60***	***6-30-95***	***166.0***		***236.0***	***70.3***						
Sr Sec[18]Nts[19] 9¾s 2000	Ms	**B**			Y	R	101.625	(3-1-98)	....	....	....	....	140	C4	'93	92½	62	70	13.93	20.84
INTERCO Inc	***31b***	***n/a***		***2.35***	***1.43***	***Dc***	***61.40***	***438.0***	***125.0***	***9-30-95***	***381.0***		***695.0***	***57.8***						
Sec Nts 'A' 10s 2001	Jd	**NR**	12/94	B+		R	100	....	100	(6-1-96)	....	....	[20]114	Reorg	'92	101⅛	92	A98	10.20	10.49

Uniform Footnote Explanations-See Page 260. Other: [1] Now Indiana Michigan Pwr,sub of Amer Elec Pwr. [2] Subsid of IPALCO Enterprises. [3] Called $0.15M on 5-1-95. [4] (HRO)On Chge of Ctrl at 101. [5] See Clark Equipment. [6] (HRO)On 6-1-05 at 100. [7] Due 8-1-97. [8] Due 8-28-97. [9] Due 8-2-99. [10] Due 8-30-99. [11] Due 7-28-00. [12] Due 8-1-00. [13] Due 8-5-02. [14] Subsid of Inland Steel Industries. [15] Int at 8.25% to 3-1-96,11.25% aft. [16] Co must offer 101(Accreted Val)on Chge of Ctrl. [17] Incl disc. [18] Co must offer 100 for some asset sales. [19] Co must offer repurch at 101 on Chge of Ctrl. [20] Defeased,fds deposited w/trustee.

Title-Industry Code & Co. Finances (In Italics) / Individual Issue Statistics — Exchange ↓	Ind / Interest Dates	Fixed Charge Coverage 1992 / S&P Debt Rating	1993 / Date of Last Rating Change	1994 / Prior Rating	Eligible ↓	Year End / Bond Form	Million $ Cash & Equiv. / Redemption Provisions — Regular Price	Million $ Curr. Assets / Regular (Begins) Thru	Million $ Curr. Liab. / Sinking Fund Price	Balance Sheet Date / Sinking Fund (Begins) Thru	L. Term Debt (Mil $) / Refund/Other Restriction Price	Capital-ization (Mil $) / Refund/Other Restriction (Begins) Thru	Total Debt % Capital / Outst'g (Mil $)	Underwriting Firm	Underwriting Year	Price Range 1995 High	Price Range 1995 Low	Mo. End Price Sale(s) or Bid	Curr. Yield	Yield to Mat.
Interlake Corp	***17***	***1.02***	***0.56***	***0.51***		***Dc***	***23.90***	***253.0***	***153.0***	***10-1-95***	***441.0***	***190.0***	***234.0***							
Sr Nts[1] 12s 2001	mN15	B−			Y	R	106	(5-15-99)	....	....	[2]Z111	11-14-98	100	D6	'95	100⅜	96	100	12.00	11.99
Sr Sub Deb[1] 12⅛s 2002	Ms	CCC+	2/94	B−	Y	R	104.547	(3-1-97)	100	(3-1-01)	....	....	220	D6	'92	103	93	95	12.76	13.33
Int'l Business Machines	***20b***	***2.72***	***1.08***	***5.12***		***Dc***	***6951***	***37642***	***29016***	***9-30-95***	***★11186***	***43176***	***49.8***							
• Deb 7½s 2013	Jd15	A	7/93	AA−	X	BE	NC	....	....	....	....	....	550	M6	'93	109	88¼	s108⅜	6.92	6.68
• Deb 8⅜s 2019	mN	A	7/93	AA−	X	BE	NC	....	....	....	....	....	750	S1	'89	119½	95⅞	s118	7.10	6.83
• Deb 7s 2025	aO30	A			X	BE	[3]....	....	....	....	....	....	600	M2	'95	103	99½	s103	6.80	6.76
• Deb 7s 2045	aO30	A			X	BE	[3]....	....	....	....	....	....	150	M2	'95	98⅛	98⅛	95⅝	7.32	7.33
• Nts 6⅜s '97	mN	A	7/93	AA−	X	BE	NC	....	....	....	....	....	900	F1	'92	101¾	95⅜	s101¼	6.30	5.64
• Nts 6⅜s 2000	Jd15	A	7/93	AA−	X	BE	NC	....	....	....	....	....	1250	M6	'93	102¼	91⅛	s102	6.25	5.86
• Nts 7¼s 2002	mN	A	7/93	AA−	X	BE	NC	....	....	....	....	....	750	F1	'92	107½	93¼	s107	6.78	5.99
Int'l CableTel Inc	***67***	***n/a***	***d2.54***	....		***Dc***	***374.0***	***381.0***	***26.40***	***9-30-94***	***149.0***	***624.0***	***25.2***							
Sr[4]Dfrd Cpn Nts[5] 10⅞s 2003	aO15	NR				R	103.107	(10-15-98)	....	....	....	....	[6]212	D6	'93	71¼	52½	71¼	15.26	17.83
Int'l Lease Finance	***25c***	***2.01***	***1.92***	***1.83***		***Dc***	***47.80***			***9-30-95***	***9414***	***11281***	***83.5***							
Nts 5¾s '96	Jj15	A+			X	BE	NC	....	....	....	....	....	150	L3	'93	100	98⅛	100	5.75	Mat.
Nts 4¾s '96	jJ15	A+			X	BE	NC	....	....	....	....	....	100	S1	'93	99⅝	95½	99⅝	4.77	5.45
Nts 5½s '97	Ao	A+			X	R	NC	....	....	....	....	....	100	M2	'93	99⅞	94½	99⅞	5.51	5.60
Nts 6⅝s '96	Jd	A+			X	R	NC	....	....	....	....	....	100	L3	'92	100⅜	98⅛	100⅜	6.60	5.69
Nts 7.90s '96	aO	A+			X	R	NC	....	....	....	....	....	100	L3	'91	102⅛	99⅞	101⅝	7.77	5.65
Nts 6⅜s '96	mN	A+			X	R	NC	....	....	....	....	....	150	M6	'92	100⅝	97	100⅝	6.34	5.59
Nts 4¾s '97	Jj15	A+			X	R	NC	....	....	....	....	....	100	L3	'94	99¼	93⅝	99¼	4.79	5.50
Nts 5⅞s '97	Fa	A+			X	R	NC	....	....	....	....	....	100	L3	'93	100⅜	95⅜	100⅜	5.85	5.51
Nts 6½s '97	jJ15	A+			X	R	NC	....	....	....	....	....	150	S1	'92	101⅜	95⅞	101⅜	6.41	5.56
Nts 6¾s '97	fA	A+			X	R	NC	....	....	....	....	....	100	L3	'94	101⅞	96⅝	101⅞	6.63	5.50
Nts 8⅛s '98	Jj15	A+			X	R	NC	....	....	....	....	....	150	M6	'95	104¾	99½	104¾	7.76	5.63
Nts 5⅝s '98	Ms	A+			X	R	NC	....	....	....	....	....	100	L3	'94	100	92⅜	100	5.63	5.62
Nts 5¾s '98	Ms15	A+			X	R	NC	....	....	....	....	....	100	M2	'93	100¼	92½	100¼	5.74	5.62
Nts 7s '98	Jd	A+			X	BE	NC	....	....	....	....	....	100	S1	'94	103	95⅞	103	6.80	5.65
Nts 6¼s '98	Jd15	A+			X	R	NC	....	....	....	....	....	100	M6	'95	101⅜	99	101⅜	6.17	5.64
Nts 5¾s '98	jJ	A+			X	R	NC	....	....	....	....	....	100	M2	'93	100¼	92	100¼	5.74	5.64
Nts 8.35s '98	aO	A+			X	R	NC	....	....	....	....	....	100	M2	'91	106⅝	99⅝	106⅝	7.83	5.71
Nts 5¾s '99	Jj15	A+			X	R	NC	....	....	....	....	....	150	S1	'94	100	90⅞	100	5.75	5.75
Nts 7½s '99	Ms	A+			X	R	NC	....	....	....	....	....	100	S1	'95	105	99⅞	105	7.14	5.75
Nts 6⅝s '99	Ao	A+			X	R	NC	....	....	....	....	....	100	M6	'94	102½	93½	102½	6.46	5.77
Nts 6½s '99	fA15	A+			X	R	NC	....	....	....	....	....	100	M2	'92	102¼	92⅝	102¼	6.36	5.80
Nts 6⅛s '99	mN	A+			X	BE	NC	....	....	....	....	....	100	M2	'95	101	99⅜	101	6.06	5.83
Nts 5¾s '99	jD15	A+			X	BE	NC	....	....	....	....	....	150	M2	'95	99⅝	99⅜	99⅜	5.79	5.93
Nts 8¼s 2000	Jj15	A+			X	R	NC	....	....	....	....	....	100	S1	'95	108⅜	99	108⅜	7.61	5.89
Nts 6.20s 2000	Mn	A+			X	R	NC	....	....	....	....	....	100	M6	'93	101¼	90¼	101¼	6.12	5.87
Nts 7s 2000	Mn15	A+			X	R	NC	....	....	....	....	....	100	S1	'95	104¼	99½	104¼	6.71	5.88
Nts 6¼s 2000	aO15	A+			X	BE	NC	....	....	....	....	....	100	S1	'95	101½	99½	101½	6.16	5.88
Nts 8⅞s 2001	Ao15	A+			X	R	NC	....	....	....	....	....	150	M2	'91	112¾	101½	112¾	7.87	6.02
Nts 8⅜s 2004	jD15	A+			X	R	NC	....	....	....	....	....	100	S1	'94	114	98½	114	7.35	6.31
F/R[7]Nts 6⅜s '97	[8]	A+			X	R	NC	....	....	....	....	....	100	L3	'93	100⅝	99½	100⅜	6.35	....
F/R[9]Nts 6.075s '99	QJun2	A+			X	R	NC	....	....	....	....	....	100	L3	'95	100½	99⅞	100	6.08	....
F/R[10]Nts 6.1375s '99	QJul15	A+			X	BE	NC	....	....	....	....	....	100	L3	'95	100¼	99⅝	100⅛	6.13	....
M-T Nts 'F' 6.35s '96	[11]ao15	A+			X	BE	NC	....	....	....	....	....	5.00	L3	'94	100⅜	98⅛	100⅜	6.33	5.30

Uniform Footnote Explanations-See Page 260. Other: [1] Co must offer repurch at 101 on Chge of Ctrl. [2] Max $35M red w/proceeds of Equity Sales. [3] Red at greater of 100 or amt based on formula. [4] (HRO)On Chge of Ctrl at 101(Accreted Val). [5] Int accr at 10.875% fr 10-15-98. [6] Incl disc. [7] Int to 1-17-96,adj qtrly aft. [8] Due 10-15-97:Int pd qtrly on 3rd Wed Jan,etc. [9] Int to 3-2-96,adj qtrly aft(3 Mo LIBOR&0.20%). [10] Int to 1-14-96,adj qtrlyy(3 Mo LIBOR&0.20%). [11] Due 5-15-96.

Title-Industry Code & Co. Finances (In Italics)	Ind	Fixed Charge Coverage 1992		1993	1994	Year End	Million $ Cash & Equiv.	Curr. Assets	Curr. Liab.	Balance Sheet Date	L. Term Debt (Mil $)		Capital-ization (Mil $)	Total Debt % Capital						
Individual Issue Statistics Exchange ↓	Interest Dates	S&P Debt Rating	Date of Last Rating Change	Prior Rating	Eligible	Bond Form	Redemption Provisions: Regular Price	Regular (Begins) Thru	Sinking Fund Price	Sinking Fund (Begins) Thru	Refund/Other Restriction Price	Refund/Other Restriction (Begins) Thru	Outst'g (Mil $)	Underwriting Firm	Underwriting Year	Price Range 1995 High	Price Range 1995 Low	Mo. End Price Sale(s) or Bid	Curr. Yield	Yield to Mat.
***Int'l Lease Finance** (Cont.)*																				
M-T Nts 'F' 6s '97	[1]ao15	**A+**			X	BE	NC	....	....	....	....	....	5.00	L3	'94	100⅝	95	100⅝	5.96	5.58
M-T Nts 'F' 5.60s '98	[2]ao15	**A+**			X	BE	NC	....	....	....	....	....	5.00	L3	'94	99¾	91	99¾	5.61	5.69
M-T Nts 'F' 7.20s '98	[3]ao15	**A+**			X	BE	NC	....	....	....	....	....	5.00	L3	'94	103½	96¾	103½	6.96	5.60
M-T Nts 'F' 5.68s '99	[4]ao15	**A+**			X	BE	NC	....	....	....	....	....	7.25	L3	'94	99½	89⅜	99½	5.71	5.83
F/R[5]M-T Nts 'F' '99	QMar24	**A+**			X	BE	NC	....	....	....	....	....	50.0	L3	'94	100	99	100	....	....
M-T Nts 'G' 6½s '96	[6]ao15	**A+**			X	BE	NC	....	....	....	....	....	5.00	L3	'94	100⅝	98	100½	6.47	5.47
M-T Nts 'G' 6¼s '96	[7]ao15	**A+**			X	BE	NC	....	....	....	....	....	5.00	L3	'94	100⅜	97½	100⅜	6.23	5.62
M-T Nts 'G' 6.626s '96	[8]ao15	**A+**			X	BE	NC	....	....	....	....	....	70.0	L3	'94	100⅞	97⅞	100⅝	6.58	5.66
M-T Nts 'G' 6.55s '96	[9]ao15	**A+**			X	BE	NC	....	....	....	....	....	6.00	L3	'94	100¾	97¾	100⅝	6.51	5.60
M-T Nts 'G' 6.80s '96	[10]ao15	**A+**			X	BE	NC	....	....	....	....	....	20.0	L3	'94	101	98	100⅞	6.74	5.58
M-T Nts 'G' 6.65s '97	[11]ao15	**A+**			X	BE	NC	....	....	....	....	....	5.00	L3	'94	101½	96⅝	101½	6.55	5.56
M-T Nts 'G' 7.37s '97	[12]ao15	**A+**			X	BE	NC	....	....	....	....	....	10.1	L3	'94	103	97⅞	103	7.16	5.58
M-T Nts 'G' 6.92s '97	[13]ao15	**A+**			X	BE	NC	....	....	....	....	....	30.0	L3	'94	102⅜	96⅝	102⅜	6.76	5.54
M-T Nts 'G' 6.93s '97	[14]ao15	**A+**			X	BE	NC	....	....	....	....	....	10.0	L3	'94	102⅜	96⅝	102⅜	6.77	5.61
M-T Nts 'G' 7½s '98	[15]ao15	**A+**			X	BE	NC	....	....	....	....	....	5.00	L3	'94	103⅝	98	103⅝	7.24	5.60
M-T Nts 'G' 7.52s '98	[16]ao15	**A+**			X	BE	NC	....	....	....	....	....	5.00	L3	'94	103¾	98	103¾	7.25	5.59
M-T Nts 'G' 7⅛s '98	[17]ao15	**A+**			X	BE	NC	....	....	....	....	....	54.0	L3	'94	103½	96⅛	103½	6.88	5.69
M-T Nts 'G' 7.30s '98	[18]ao15	**A+**			X	BE	NC	....	....	....	....	....	10.0	L3	'94	104	96⅝	104	7.02	5.69
M-T Nts 'G' 7.68s '98	[19]ao15	**A+**			X	BE	NC	....	....	....	....	....	16.0	L3	'94	105⅛	97¾	105⅛	7.31	5.70
M-T Nts 'G' 7.74s '98	[19]ao15	**A+**			X	BE	NC	....	....	....	....	....	5.00	L3	'94	105¼	97⅞	105¼	7.35	5.71
M-T Nts 'G' 7.95s '98	[20]ao15	**A+**			X	BE	NC	....	....	....	....	....	5.00	L3	'94	105⅞	98⅝	105⅞	7.51	5.68
M-T Nts 'G' 7.10s '99	[21]ao15	**A+**			X	BE	NC	....	....	....	....	....	5.00	L3	'94	104⅛	95⅛	104⅛	6.82	5.77
M-T Nts 'G' 7.41s '99	[22]ao15	**A+**			X	BE	NC	....	....	....	....	....	50.0	L3	'94	105⅛	96⅛	105⅛	7.05	5.84
M-T Nts 'G' 7.83s '99	[23]ao15	**A+**			X	BE	NC	....	....	....	....	....	25.0	L3	'94	106⅝	97⅝	106⅝	7.34	5.85
M-T Nts 'G' 8.32s '99	[24]ao15	**A+**			X	BE	NC	....	....	....	....	....	7.00	L3	'94	108½	99½	108½	7.67	5.86
M-T Nts 'G' 8.15s 2004	aO	**A+**			X	BE	NC	....	....	....	....	....	100	G1	'94	112⅛	97	112⅛	7.27	6.32
Int'l Minerals & Chem	***14***	***Now IMCERA Group, see***																		
SF Deb 9⅞s 2011	Ms15	**BBB+**	11/92	BBB	X	R	100	(3-15-01)	100	(3-15-02)	....	....	134	L1	'86	118	105⅝	116¼	8.49	8.01
International Paper	***50***	***2.94***		***2.52***	***2.76***	***Dc***	***372.0***	***6102***	***5365***	***9-30-95***	***5474***		***21781***	***38.0***						
• Deb 5⅛s 2012	mN15	**A–**	10/86	A+	X	R	100	....	....	....	....	....	[25]149	G1	'82	83½	69	s82½	6.21	6.89
Deb[26] 7⅝s 2023	Ms	**A–**			X	BE	103.43	(3-1-03)	....	....	....	....	200	F1	'93	106	88⅜	106	7.19	7.12
Deb 6⅞s 2023	mN	**A–**			X	R	NC	....	....	....	....	....	200	K2	'93	102¼	81¼	102¼	6.72	6.69
Nts[27] 9.70s 2000	Ms15	**A–**			X	R	NC	....	....	....	....	....	150	F1	'90	114¼	105½	114¼	8.49	5.83
Nts[27] 9.40s 2002	Jd	**A–**			X	R	NC	....	....	....	....	....	100	F1	'90	117⅞	105⅛	117⅞	7.97	6.00
Nts[26] 6⅛s 2003	mN	**A–**			X	BE	NC	....	....	....	....	....	200	C5	'93	100	86⅛	100	6.13	6.12
Nts[26] 7½s 2004	Mn15	**A–**			X	BE	NC	....	....	....	....	....	150	K2	'94	109	94⅛	109	6.88	6.11
Nts[26] 7⅝s 2004	fA	**A–**			X	R	NC	....	....	....	....	....	150	M6	'94	109⅝	94⅞	109⅝	6.96	6.16
Nts[26] 7⅞s 2006	fA	**A–**			X	R	NC	....	....	....	....	....	150	C5	'94	112⅜	95¼	112⅜	7.01	6.26
Nts[27] 7⅝s 2007	Jj15	**A–**			X	R	NC	....	....	....	....	....	200	K2	'92	110½	93¾	110½	6.90	6.29
M-T Nts 'E' 8s 2006	[28]ao	**A–**			X	BE	NC	....	....	....	....	....	10.0	M6	'94	112¼	94⅞	112¼	7.13	6.42
M-T Nts 'E' 8.10s 2009	[29]ao	**A–**			X	BE	NC	....	....	....	....	....	10.0	M6	'94	114⅝	95	114⅝	7.07	6.45
M-T Nts 'E' 8.10s 2009	[30]ao	**A–**			X	BE	NC	....	....	....	....	....	7.00	C5	'94	114⅝	95	114⅝	7.07	6.45
M-T Nts 'E' 8.10s 2009	[30]ao	**A–**			X	BE	NC	....	....	....	....	....	7.00	K2	'94	114⅝	95	114⅝	7.07	6.45
International Shipholding	***64***	***1.94***		***1.78***	***1.92***	***Dc***	***42.50***	***100.0***	***82.60***	***9-30-95***	***324.0***		***519.0***	***69.2***						
• Sr Nts[31] 9s 2003	jJ	**BB–**			Y	R	103.375	(7-1-98)	....	....	....	....	95.0	B8	'93	100⅞	91	99¾	9.02	9.05
Int'l Telephone & Tel	***17***	***Now ITT Corp,see***																		
Deb 6½s 2001	jJ	**BBB**	10/95	A+	X	R	100	....	....	....	....	....	[25]150	L3	'81	101⅜	89⅜	99⅝	6.52	6.58

Uniform Footnote Explanations-See Page 260. Other: [1] Due 8-1-97. [2] Due 11-16-98. [3] Due 5-15-98. [4] Due 10-1-99. [5] Int adj monthly. [6] Due 6-28-96. [7] Due 8-15-96. [8] Due 9-3-96. [9] Due 9-9-96. [10] Due 9-30-96. [11] Due 6-13-97. [12] Due 10-14-97. [13] Due 11-3-97. [14] Due 12-1-97. [15] Due 1-15-98. [16] Due 2-2-98. [17] Due 9-1-98. [18] Due 9-21-98. [19] Due 11-2-98. [20] Due 11-3-98. [21] Due 6-15-99. [22] Due 9-1-99. [23] Due 10-12-99. [24] Due 12-2-99. [25] Incl disc. [26] (HRO)On Chge of Ctrl at 100. [27] (HRO)At 100 for certain events. [28] Due 11-15-06. [29] Due 5-20-09. [30] Due 5-18-09. [31] (HRO)On Chge of Ctrl at 101.

Title-Industry Code & Co. Finances (In Italics) / Individual Issue Statistics — Exchange	Ind / Interest Dates	Fixed Charge Coverage 1992 / S&P Debt Rating	1993 / Date of Last Rating Change	1994 / Prior Rating	Eligible	Year End / Bond Form	Cash & Equiv. (Million $) / Regular Price	Curr. Assets / Regular (Begins) Thru	Curr. Liab. / Sinking Fund Price	Balance Sheet Date / Sinking Fund (Begins) Thru	L. Term Debt (Mil $) / Refund/Other Restriction Price	Refund/Other Restriction (Begins) Thru	Capitalization (Mil $) / Outst'g (Mil $)	Total Debt % Capital / Underwriting Firm	Underwriting Year	Price Range 1995 High	Price Range 1995 Low	Mo. End Price Sale(s) or Bid	Curr. Yield	Yield to Mat.
***Int'l Telephone & Tel** (Cont.)*																				
Deb 7½s 2011	jJ	**BBB**	10/95	A+	X	R	100	....	....	....	....	....	[1]150	L3	'81	105⅜	86¾	100⅛	7.49	7.49
InterNorth,Inc	***73e***	***Now Enron Corp,see***																		
Nts 9⅝s 2006	Ms15	**BBB+**	12/95	BBB	X	R	NC	....	....	....	....	....	192	G1	'86	124	106⅛	124	7.76	6.39
Interstate Power	***75***	***2.69***	***2.68***	***2.71***		***Dc***	***1.56***	***67.60***	***87.20***	***9-30-95***	***189.0***		***423.0***	***44.7***						
1st 6⅛s '97	Mn	**A+**	10/82	A	X	CR	100.23	4-30-96	100.05	4-30-96	....	....	17.0	H1	'67	100¼	96	100¼	6.11	5.92
1st 8s 2007	Fa15	**A+**			X	R	NC	....	100	....	....	....	25.0	S1	'92	113¼	96¾	113¼	7.06	6.32
1st 8⅝s 2021	mS15	**A+**			X	R	107.44	9-14-96	100	....	®105.65	9-14-01	25.0	S1	'91	109⅜	98	108⅛	7.98	7.88
1st 7⅝s 2023	Mn15	**A+**			X	R	105.18	5-14-96	Z100	....	®104.31	5-14-03	94.0	S1	'93	106⅛	88¼	106⅛	7.18	7.11
[2]Iowa Elec Lt & Pwr[3]	***75***	***2.37***	***3.59***	***3.29***		***Dc***	***2.14***	***119.0***	***336.0***	***12-31-94***	***416.0***		***1095***	***51.8***						
1st J 6¼s '96	mS	**A**	8/77	A–	X	R	100	....	Z100	....	....	....	15.0	M2	'66	100⅛	97⅝	100	6.25	6.23
1st L 7⅞s 2000	jD	**A**	8/77	A–	X	R	101.09	11-30-96	Z100	....	....	....	15.0	S1	'70	101½	98¼	101¼	7.78	7.56
1st M 7⅝s 2002	Mn	**A**	8/77	A–	X	R	101.58	4-30-96	Z100	....	....	....	30.0	E3	'72	102	95⅝	102	7.48	7.22
1st Y 8⅝s 2001	Mn15	**A**			X	R	NC	....	Z100	....	....	....	60.0	M2	'91	112⅛	100½	112⅛	7.69	5.95
1st Z 7.60s '99	Ms	**A**			X	R	NC	....	Z100	....	....	....	50.0	M6	'92	105	96⅞	105	7.24	5.85
CT Bonds 6s 2008	aO	**A**			X	R	NC	....	Z100	....	....	....	50.0	M6	'93	97⅛	80¼	97⅛	6.18	6.33
CT Bonds 7s 2023	aO	**A**			X	R	102.75	(10-1-03)	Z100	....	....	....	50.0	M6	'93	100	86	100	7.00	7.00
Iowa-Illinois Gas & Elec	***75***	***3.13***	***4.14***	***4.42***		***Dc***	***33.40***	***137.0***	***236.0***	***3-31-95***	***603.0***		***1272***	***55.6***						
1st 5⅞s '97	jJ15	**A+**	7/95	AA–	X	R	100.22	7-14-96	100.05	7-14-96	....	....	22.0	M2	'67	100⅜	95¼	100⅜	5.85	5.62
1st 5.05s '98	aO15	**A+**	7/95	AA–	X	R	NC	....	....	....	....	....	50.0	S5	'93	98½	89¾	98½	5.13	5.63
1st 6s 2000	Ms15	**A+**	7/95	AA–	X	R	NC	....	....	....	....	....	35.0	S5	'93	100⅛	90	100⅛	5.99	5.96
1st 7.70s 2004	Mn15	**A+**	7/95	AA–	X	R	NC	....	....	....	....	....	60.0	S5	'92	109¼	94⅞	109¼	7.05	6.26
1st 7.45s 2023	Ms15	**A+**	7/95	AA–	X	R	103.97	(3-15-03)	Z103.97	(3-15-03)	....	....	30.0	S5	'93	103¾	86⅞	103¾	7.18	7.13
1st 6.95s 2025	aO15	**A+**	7/95	AA–	X	R	103.48	(10-15-03)	Z103.48	(10-15-03)	....	....	50.0	S5	'93	99¼	80⅝	99¼	7.00	7.01
Iowa Southern Utilities	***75***	***Merged w/Iowa Elec Lt & Pwr,see***																		
1st 6⅛s '97	Jd	**A**	6/93	AA–	X	R	100.22	5-31-96	100	....	....	....	8.00	D8	'67	100¼	95⅞	100¼	6.11	5.93
1st 7⅜s 2003	Fa	**A**	6/93	AA–	X	R	101.79	1-31-96	100	....	....	....	10.0	H1	'73	102⅝	94¼	102⅝	7.19	6.90
1st 7¼s 2007	mS	**A**	6/93	AA–	X	R	101.70	(9-1-02)	Z100	....	....	....	30.0	G1	'92	106¾	89¾	106¾	6.79	6.42
Irving Bank Corp[4]	***10***	***Now Bank of N.Y.,see***																		
SF Deb 8½s 2002	Jd	**A**	6/93	A–	X	R	100.85	5-31-96	100	....	....	....	39.4	S1	'77	102¾	97¾	101	8.42	8.29
F/R Nts[5] 6.159s 2004	Mn	**A**	6/93	A–	X	R	101.80	4-30-96	100	....	....	....	60.1	S1	'79	100	98	100	6.16	....
[6]ISP Chemicals/ISP Tech	***14***	***3.61***	***2.95***	***3.46***		***Dc***	***134.0***	***340.0***	***197.0***	***10-1-95***	***354.0***		***1035***	***38.9***						
Sr Nts[7] 9s '99	Ms	**BB+**			Y	R	NC	....	....	....	....	....	200	M2	'92	107⅛	96½	107⅛	8.40	6.47
Ithaca Industries	***68c***	***1.90***	***1.20***	***1.55***		***Ja***	***1.40***	***162.0***	***74.10***	***10-27-95***	***220.0***		***186.0***	***131.0***						
Sr Sub[8]Nts[9] 11⅛s 2002	jD15	**D**	12/95	CCC+		R	105.50	(12-15-97)	....	....	[10]Z100	....	125	M2	'92	98	37	37	....	Flat
ITT Corp(Old)	***17***	***Now ITT Industries***																		
Deb 8¼s 2001	fA	**BBB**	10/95	A+	X	R	NC	....	....	....	....	....	100	M2	'89	110⅞	98⅝	109¾	7.52	6.16
Deb[11] 8⅞s 2008	Fa	**BBB**	10/95	A+	X	R	NC	....	....	....	....	....	100	M6	'88	120	101	118⅛	7.51	6.67
Deb 9¾s 2021	Fa15	**BBB**	10/95	A+	X	R	104.875	(2-15-01)	....	....	....	....	250	G1	'91	120¾	104¼	118¾	8.21	8.00
Deb 9½s 2021	Ao15	**BBB**	10/95	A+	X	R	104.75	(4-15-01)	....	....	....	....	150	S1	'91	119¾	101⅞	117⅛	8.11	7.92
Deb 7.40s 2025	mN15	**BBB**			X	BE	[12]....	....	....	....	....	....	250	L1	'95	104⅜	99⅞	104⅜	7.09	7.05
[13]Sr SF Deb 8⅜s 2007	Ms	**BBB**	10/95	A	X	R	NC	....	100	(3-1-98)	....	....	27.7	M6	'87	116⅝	97¼	114¾	7.30	6.50
[13]Sr Deb 8½s '98	Jj15	**BBB**	10/95	A	X	R	NC	....	....	....	....	....	56.9	G1	'88	106⅜	100⅛	105¼	8.08	5.74
[13]Sr Deb 10⅛s '99	Ao5	**BBB**	10/95	A	X	R	NC	....	....	....	....	....	225	M2	'89	113⅞	105	112⅜	9.01	5.90
[13]Sr Deb 9¼s 2001	jJ15	**BBB**	10/95	A	X	R	100	(7-15-98)	....	....	....	....	97.5	M2	'91	109⅝	102⅛	108⅜	8.54	7.38
[13]Sr Deb 8½s 2001	aO15	**BBB**	10/95	A	X	R	[14]Z100	....	....	....	....	....	100	M2	'89	112½	101⅛	111⅛	7.65	6.18
[13]Sr Deb 9⅜s 2001	jD15	**BBB**	10/95	A	X	R	NC	....	....	....	[15]Z100	....	125	M2	'91	117¼	103¾	115½	8.12	6.22

Uniform Footnote Explanations-See Page 260. Other: [1] Incl disc. [2] Now IES Utilities,subsid of IES Indus. [3] See Iowa Southern Util. [4] Was Charter NY Corp. [5] Int thru 4-30-96,adj semi-annly aft. [6] Subsid & data of Int'l Specialty Prod. [7] Gtd by Int'l Specialty Prod. [8] (HRO)On Chge of Ctrl at 101. [9] Int of 12-15-95 not pd when due. [10] On Chge in Ctrl,plus Applicable Premium. [11] (HRO)On 2-1-98 at 100. [12] Co may red at greater of 100 or amt based on formula. [13] Was ITT Fin'l. [14] In whole if $10M or less outstg. [15] In whole,if less than $12.5M outstg.

Title-Industry Code & Co. Finances (In Italics) / Individual Issue Statistics (Exchange)	Ind / Interest Dates	Fixed Charge Coverage 1992 / S&P Debt Rating	1993 / Date of Last Rating Change	Prior Rating	1994 / Eligible	Year End / Bond Form	Million $ Cash & Equiv. / Redemption Provisions: Regular Price	Curr. Assets / Regular (Begins) Thru	Curr. Liab. / Sinking Fund Price	Balance Sheet Date / Sinking Fund (Begins) Thru	L. Term Debt (Mil $) / Refund/Other Restriction Price	Refund/Other Restriction (Begins) Thru	Capitalization (Mil $) / Outst'g (Mil $)	Total Debt % Capital / Underwriting Firm	Underwriting Year	Price Range 1995 High	Price Range 1995 Low	Mo. End Price Sale(s) or Bid	Curr. Yield	Yield to Mat.
ITT Corp(Old) *(Cont.)*																				
[1]Sr Deb 8⅝s 2005	Fa15	**BBB**	10/95	A	X	R	NC	....	....	....	....	....	90.4	G1	'90	115⅞	98⅞	114⅞	7.51	6.44
[1]Sr Deb 8¾s 2006	Ms	**BBB**	10/95	A	X	R	103.059	(3-1-96)	....	....	....	....	64.7	G1	'86	104⅞	99½	103¾	8.43	8.20
[1]Sr Deb[2] 8.55s 2009	Jd15	**BBB**	10/95	A	X	R	NC	....	....	....	....	....	100	G1	'89	118⅞	102⅛	116½	7.34	6.67
[1]Sr Deb[3] 8⅞s 2010	Jd	**BBB**	10/95	A	X	R	[4]Z100	....	....	....	....	....	100	M2	'90	122⅜	100⅝	120¼	7.38	6.67
[1]Sr Deb 6½s 2011	Mn	**BBB**	10/95	A	X	R	100	....	....	....	....	....	[5]200	L3	'81	96	79⅜	95	6.84	7.04
Nts 5¼s '96	Fa15	**BBB**	10/95	A+	X	R	NC	....	....	....	....	....	200	S1	'93	100	97⅝	100	5.25	5.15
Nts 8⅜s '96	Ms15	**BBB**	10/95	A+	X	R	NC	....	....	....	....	....	150	S1	'86	101¾	100¼	100½	8.33	5.84
Nts 7¼s '96	mN15	**BBB**	10/95	A+	X	R	NC	....	....	....	....	....	125	L1	'91	102⅛	98⅜	101⅜	7.15	5.61
Sr Nts 8½s '96	Jd	**BBB**	10/95	A	X	R	NC	....	....	....	....	....	78.3	M6	'91	102½	100⅝	101⅛	8.41	5.73
Sr Nts 7s '97	Jj15	**BBB**	10/95	A	X	R	NC	....	....	....	....	....	176	F1	'92	102	97½	101⅜	6.91	5.62
[1]Sr Nts 7¼s '97	Mn15	**BBB**	10/95	A	X	R	NC	....	....	....	....	....	84.9	S1	'92	102¾	97½	102	7.11	5.71
[1]Sr Nts 8⅛s '98	mN15	**BBB**	10/95	A	X	R	NC	....	....	....	....	....	151	S1	'91	107⅛	98⅜	106	7.67	5.83
[1]Sub Deb[6] ('06) 8¾s '96	[7]Ms	**BBB–**	10/95	A–	X	R	100	(3-1-01)	....	....	....	....	75.0	M6	'86	118⅛	100	114	7.68	....
[8]Sub Deb 8.35s 2004	mN	**BBB–**	10/95	A–	X	R	[9]Z100	....	....	....	....	....	149	M2	'89	114	97¾	110¾	7.54	6.72
[1]Sub Deb[10] 8.85s 2005	jJ15	**BBB–**	10/95	A–	X	R	[11]Z100	....	....	....	....	....	200	M2	'90	118⅛	101⅞	117⅛	7.56	6.42
[1]Sub Nts 9⅞s '97	Ao15	**BBB–**	10/95	A–	X	R	NC	....	....	....	....	....	97.5	M6	'89	107	103	104⅞	9.42	5.89
ITT Corp(New)	***40i***	***1.51***	***3.53***		***1.98***		***470.0***	***1332***	***1275***	***9-30-95***	***663.0***		***7327***	***11.4***						
• Deb[12] 7⅜s 2015	mN15	**BBB**			X	BE	NC	....	....	....	....	....	450	B5	'95	100¼	99½	102⅛	7.22	7.17
• Deb[12] 7¾s 2025	mN15	**BBB**			X	BE	103.186	(11-15-05)	....	....	....	....	150	B5	'95	99⅜	98½	101⅛	7.66	7.65
• Nts[12] 6¾s 2005	mN15	**BBB**			X	BE	NC	....	....	....	....	....	450	B5	'95	100¼	99¾	97¼	6.94	7.14
• Nts[13] 6¼s 2000	mN15	**BBB**			X	BE	NC	....	....	....	....	....	700	B5	'95	99⅞	99⅝	95	6.58	7.49
ITT Industries[14]	***17***	***1.20***	***1.43***		***4.74***	***Dc***	***183.0***	***2624***	***3261***	***9-30-95***	***801.0***		***10225***	***22.2***						
• [1]Sr Deb([15]'97) 8⅞s 2003	Jd15	**BBB**	10/95	A	X	R	NC	....	....	....	....	....	110	L3	'78	110	101⅜	106	8.37	7.80
ITT Hartford Group	***35***	***n/a***	***12.00***		***10.40***	***Dc***				***9-30-95***	***597.0***		***6087***	***24.8***						
• Deb 7.30s 2015	mN	**A+**			X	R	[16]....	....	....	....	....	....	200	G1	'95	99⅝	99¾	101⅝	7.18	7.14
Nts 7¼s '96	jD	**A+**	3/95	AA	X	R	[16]....	....	....	....	....	....	100	G1	'91	101⅛	98½	101⅛	7.17	5.97
Nts 8.20s '98	ao15	**A+**	3/95	AA	X	R	[16]....	....	....	....	....	....	200	G1	'91	106	99¼	106	7.74	5.84
Nts 8.30s 2001	jD	**A+**	3/95	AA	X	R	[16]....	....	....	....	....	....	200	G1	'91	110½	98⅝	110½	7.51	6.16
• Nts 6⅜s 2002	mN	**A+**			X	R	[16]....	....	....	....	....	....	300	G1	'95	99¼	99¼	100½	6.34	6.28
[17]ITT Rayonier	***13d***	***4.79***	***5.51***		....	***Dc***	***10.80***	***400.0***	***198.0***	***9-30-95***	***483.0***		***1244***	***38.9***						
• Nts 7½s 2002	aO15	**BBB**	1/94	A+	X	BE	NC	....	....	....	....	....	110	M6	'92	No Sale		106⅛	7.07	6.37
IVAC Corp	***43***	***121.39***	***31.99***		***d5.43***	***Dc***	***17.90***	***122.0***	***154.0***	***9-30-95***	***★131.0***		***175.0***	***86.1***						
Sr Nts[18] 9¼s 2002	jD	**BB**			Y	R	106.25	(12-1-98)	....	....	[19]Z108.25	11-30-98	100	D6	'95	100½	100	100½	9.20	9.15
Ivex Packaging Corp	***16***	***0.50***	***0.96***		***1.06***	***Dc***	***3.36***	***107.0***	***63.00***	***6-30-95***	***341.0***		***221.0***	***158.0***						
Sr Sub Nts[18] 12½s 2002	jD15	**B–**			Y	R	106.25	(12-15-97)	....	....	....	....	158	L3	'92	108	99¼	107	11.68	11.03
James River Corp	***50***	***0.40***	***1.01***		***0.93***	***Dc***	***43.70***	***1898***	***1131***	***9-24-95***	***2457***		***4864***	***50.9***						
Deb 9¼s 2021	mN15	**BBB–**	6/94	BBB	X	R	NC	....	....	....	....	....	200	S1	'91	124¾	99½	124¾	7.41	7.14
Deb 7¾s 2023	mN15	**BBB–**	6/94	BBB	X	R	NC	....	....	....	....	....	150	S1	'93	107⅞	85¼	107⅞	7.18	7.10
Nts 6¾s '99	aO	**BBB–**	6/94	BBB	X	R	NC	....	....	....	....	....	200	S1	'92	102⅛	92⅞	102⅛	6.61	6.10
Nts 8⅜s 2001	mN15	**BBB–**	6/94	BBB	X	R	NC	....	....	....	....	....	200	S1	'91	110½	98¼	110½	7.58	6.21
Nts 6.70s 2003	mN15	**BBB–**	6/94	BBB	X	R	NC	....	....	....	....	....	250	S1	'93	101¼	87⅜	101¼	6.62	6.49
Jersey Cent'l Pwr.& Lt[20]	***72a***	***2.65***	***3.20***		***3.25***	***Dc***	***8.23***	***465.0***	***480.0***	***9-30-95***	***1193***		***3139***	***44.7***						
1st 6⅛s '96	fA	**BBB+**	6/94	A–	X	CR	100	....	100	....	....	....	25.7	E1	'66	100	97½	100	6.13	6.11
1st 6⅝s '97	mS	**BBB+**	6/94	A–	X	CR	100.33	8-31-96	100.33	8-31-96	....	....	25.9	E1	'67	100⅜	96	100⅜	6.60	6.38
1st 7¼s '98	aO	**BBB+**	6/94	A–	X	R	100.63	9-30-96	100.40	9-30-96	....	....	24.2	E1	'68	101⅛	96	100¾	7.20	6.94
• 1st 6⅜s 2003	Mn	**BBB+**	6/94	A–	X	R	NC	....	Z100	....	Z100	....	150	L3	'93	99¾	84⅞	97	6.57	6.90

Uniform Footnote Explanations-See Page 260. Other: [1] Was ITT Fin'l. [2] (HRO)On 6-15-98(&'04)at 100. [3] (HRO)On 6-1-00('05)at 100. [4] In whole if $10M or less outst'g. [5] Incl disc. [6] (HRO)On 3-1-96 at 100. [7] Due 3-1-06. [8] Was ITT Finl. [9] In whole if $15M or less outstg. [10] (HRO)On 7-15-97 at 100. [11] In whole if $20M or less outstg. [12] State gaming laws may req hldr's sale/co red. [13] State gaming laws req hldr's sale/co red. [14] See ITT Corp(Old),Int'l Tel & Tel. [15] (HRO)On 6-15-97 at 100. [16] Greater:100/Discounted Remaining Fixed Amt Pyts. [17] Now Rayonier Inc. [18] (HRO)On Chge of Ctrl at 101. [19] Max red $35M w/proceeds of Pub Com Off'gs. [20] Subsid of Gen'l Pub Utilities.

Exchange / Individual Issue Statistics	Interest Dates	S&P Debt Rating	Date of Last Rating Change	Prior Rating	Eligible	Bond Form	Regular Redemption Price	Regular (Begins) Thru	Sinking Fund Price	Sinking Fund (Begins) Thru	Refund/Other Restriction Price	Refund/Other Restriction (Begins) Thru	Outst'g (Mil $)	Underwriting Firm	Underwriting Year	Price Range 1995 High	Price Range 1995 Low	Mo. End Price Sale(s) or Bid	Curr. Yield	Yield to Mat.
Title-Industry Code & Co. Finances (In Italics)	*Ind*	*Fixed Charge Coverage 1992*	*1993*	*1994*		*Year End*	*Million $ Cash & Equiv.*	*Curr. Assets*	*Curr. Liab.*	*Balance Sheet Date*	*L. Term Debt (Mil $)*	*Capital-ization (Mil $)*		*Total Debt % Capital*						
***Jersey Cent'l Pwr.& Lt** (Cont.)*																				
• 1st 7⅛s 2004	aO	**BBB+**	6/94	A–	X	R	100	(10-1-02)	Z100	....	....	....	160	S5	'92	102⅜	96¾	101	7.05	6.97
• 1st 7½s 2023	Mn	**BBB+**	6/94	A–	X	R	103.33	(4-27-03)	Z100	....	....	....	125	M2	'93	99⅞	82½	95⅛	7.88	7.94
• 1st 6¾s 2025		**BBB+**	6/94	A–	X	BE	102.82	(10-27-03)	Z100	....	....	....	150	M6	'93	93	78¼	s93	7.26	7.33
Sec M-T Nts 'B'[1] 6.90s '97	[2]jj	**BBB+**	6/94	A–	X	BE	NC	....	Z100	....	....	....	30.0	M2	'92	101¼	97⅛	101⅛	6.82	5.81
Sec M-T Nts 'B'[1] 9s 2002	[3]jj	**BBB+**	6/94	A–	X	BE	100	(3-27-01)	Z100	....	....	....	50.0	M2	'91	113½	100⅞	113½	7.93	6.34
Sec M-T Nts 'B'[1] 8¼s 2006	[4]jj	**BBB+**	6/94	A–	X	BE	100	(11-19-01)	Z100	....	....	....	50.0	M2	'91	112⅜	94¾	112⅜	7.34	6.63
Sec M-T Nts 'B'[1] 7.90s 2007	[5]jj	**BBB+**	6/94	A–	X	BE	100	(1-23-02)	Z100	....	....	....	40.0	M2	'92	109⅞	92⅛	109⅞	7.19	6.63
Sec M-T Nts 'B'[1] 9.20s 2021	jJ	**BBB+**	6/94	A–	X	BE	104.60	(7-1-01)	Z100	....	....	....	50.0	M2	'91	123½	100	123½	7.45	7.18
Sec M-T Nts 'B'[1] 8.55s 2022	[6]jj	**BBB+**	6/94	A–	X	BE	104.28	(1-29-02)	Z100	....	....	....	30.0	M2	'92	116⅛	93½	116⅛	7.36	7.17
Sec M-T Nts 'C'[1] 6.70s '97	[7]ms	**BBB+**	6/94	A–	X	BE	NC	....	Z100	....	....	....	20.0	M2	'92	101⅝	95⅛	101⅝	6.59	5.81
Sec M-T Nts 'C'[1] 6.04s 2000	[8]ms	**BBB+**	6/94	A–	X	BE	NC	....	Z100	....	....	....	40.0	M2	'93	99⅝	88⅞	99⅝	6.06	6.14
Sec M-T Nts 'C'[1] 6.78s 2005	[9]ms	**BBB+**	6/94	A–	X	BE	100	(3-29-03)	Z100	....	....	....	50.0	M2	'93	101¼	86⅞	101¼	6.70	6.60
Sec M-T Nts 'C'[1] 8.82s 2022	[10]ms	**BBB+**	6/94	A–	X	BE	104.41	(3-27-02)	Z100	....	....	....	12.0	M2	'92	119⅜	96¼	119⅜	7.39	7.17
Sec M-T Nts 'C'[1] 8.85s 2022	[11]ms	**BBB+**	6/94	A–	X	BE	104.43	(3-27-02)	Z100	....	....	....	38.0	M2	'92	119¾	96½	119¾	7.39	7.17
Sec M-T Nts 'C'[1] 8.32s 2022	[12]ms	**BBB+**	6/94	A–	X	BE	104.16	(12-18-02)	Z100	....	....	....	40.0	M2	'92	112½	91½	112½	7.40	7.26
Sec M-T Nts 'C'[1] 7.98s 2023	[13]ms	**BBB+**	6/94	A–	X	BE	103.99	(2-16-03)	Z100	....	....	....	40.0	M2	'93	109⅝	90½	109⅝	7.28	7.17
Sec M-T Nts 'D'[1] 8.45s 2025	[14]jd	**BBB+**			X	BE	104.23	(3-23-05)	Z100	....	....	....	50.0	M6	'95	112⅞	99	112⅞	7.49	7.37
Johnson Controls	***13b***	***△6.58***	***△9.02***	***△6.54***		***Sp***	***104.0***	***2064***	***1910***	***9-30-95***	***630.0***	***2168***		***38.2***						
Deb[15] 7.70s 2015	Ms	**A**			X	BE	NC	....	....	....	....	....	125	S1	'95	115½	99¾	115½	6.67	6.30
Deb 8.20s 2024	Jd15	**A**			X	BE	104.10	(6-15-04)	....	....	....	....	125	S1	'94	110⅜	92	110⅜	7.43	7.33
Deb 6.95s 2045	jD	**A**			X	BE	NC	....	....	....	....	....	125	M5	'95	100¾	98¾	100¾	6.90	6.90
Johnson & Johnson	***43***	***13.17***	***14.13***	***15.18***		***Dc***	***1338***	***8084***	***4311***	***10-1-95***	***2108***	***11429***		***22.0***						
Deb 6.73s 2023	mN15	**AAA**			X	BE	NC	....	....	....	....	....	250	M6	'93	104⅝	81⅜	104⅝	6.43	6.37
Deb 8.72s 2024	mN	**AAA**			X	BE	104.36	(11-1-04)	....	....	....	....	300	M2	'94	119⅝	101¼	119⅝	7.29	7.11
Nts 8s '98	mS	**AAA**			X	BE	100	(9-1-96)	....	....	....	....	200	M6	'91	102½	99⅛	101⅞	7.85	7.21
Nts 7⅜s 2002	Jd29	**AAA**			X	BE	NC	....	....	....	....	....	200	M2	'92	108	95⅝	108	6.83	5.88
Johnston Coca-Cola Bott.	***11f***	***Subsid of Coca-Cola Enterprises,see***																		
Sub Nts 11½s 2001	mS15	**A+**	12/91	BB+	X	R	104	(9-15-96)	....	....	....	....	9.50	S1	'91	108¾	106¼	106¼	10.82	10.03
Johnstown America Indus	***56***	***0.82***	***4.19***	***36.30***		***Dc***	***10.90***	***156.0***	***125.0***	***9-30-95***	***306.0***	***389.0***		***82.0***						
Sr Sub Nts[16] 11¾s 2005	fA15	**B**			Y	BE	105.875	(8-15-00)	....	....	[17]Z111.75	8-14-98	100	C2	'95	104¼	100	104¼	11.27	11.02
Jones Intercable	***12a***	***△1.40***	***△0.43***	***△0.58***		***My***	***271.0***			***5-31-95***	***481.0***	***747.0***		***64.4***						
Sr Nts 9⅝s 2002	Ms15	**BB**			Y	R	NC	....	....	....	....	....	200	S1	'95	107⅜	99¾	107⅜	8.96	8.09
Sr Sub Deb 11½s 2004	jJ15	**B+**	4/94	B	Y	R	106.75	(7-15-97)	100	(7-15-02)	....	....	160	D6	'92	110¾	103	110½	10.41	9.66
Sr Sub Deb 10½s 2008	Ms	**B+**	4/94	B	Y	R	105.25	(3-1-00)	....	....	....	....	100	L3	'93	108¾	98	108¾	9.66	9.28
Jordan Industries,Inc	***17***	***0.64***	***0.93***	***1.09***		***Dc***	***14.10***	***198.0***	***93.20***	***9-30-95***	***494.0***	***459.0***		***115.0***						
Sr Nts[16] 10⅜s 2003	fA	**B+**			Y	R	105.1875	(8-1-98)	....	....	....	....	275	D6	'93	95½	82½	85	12.21	13.60
Sr Sub[18]Disc Deb 11¾s 2005	fA	**B–**			Y	R	105.875	(8-1-98)	....	....	....	....	[19]133	D6	'93	62	51½	57	....	Flat
Jorgensen (Earle M.)	***44***	***0.71***	***0.86***	***1.67***		***Mr***	***16.30***	***398.0***	***160.0***	***9-29-95***	***304.0***	***373.0***		***81.8***						
Sr Nts[16] 10¾s 2000	Ms	**B**			Y	R	103.107	(3-1-98)	....	....	[20]Z110	3-11-96	155	D6	'93	99⅜	91½	92	11.68	13.30
Joy Technologies	***41***	***0.84***	***[21]1.56***	***[22]0.43***		***Oc***	***4.98***	***331.0***	***136.0***	***7-31-95***	***215.0***	***247.0***		***91.5***						
Sr Nts[16] 10¼s 2003	mS	**BBB**	12/94	B	X	R	105.125	(9-1-98)	....	....	....	....	200	M6	'93	113	104½	113	9.07	7.95
JPS Automotive L.P.	***8***	***5.66***	***[23]7.83***	***[24]1.85***		***Dc***	***4.02***	***75.50***	***45.60***	***10-1-95***	***199.0***	***313.0***		***63.9***						
• Sr Nts[16] 11⅛s 2001	Jd15	**B**			Y	R	NC	....	....	....	[25]Z110	6-28-97	180	D6	'94	100	97½	101	11.01	10.87
K & F Industries, Inc	***3***	***0.60***	***0.39***	***0.78***		***Mr***	***10.70***	***112.0***	***60.30***	***9-30-95***	***310.0***	***277.0***		***112.0***						
Sr Sec Nts[16] 11⅞s 2003	jD	**B+**			Y	R	105.28	(6-1-97)	....	....	....	....	100	L3	'92	108	97	107¼	11.07	10.50
Sr Sub Deb[16] 13¾s 2001	fA	**B–**			Y	R	103.75	7-31-96	100	(8-1-99)	....	....	210	S4	'89	105	91	105	13.10	12.47

Uniform Footnote Explanations-See Page 260. Other: [1] Issued in min denom $100T. [2] Due 1-29-97. [3] Due 3-27-02. [4] Due 11-20-06. [5] Due 1-23-07. [6] Due 1-31-22.. [7] Due 12-19-97. [8] Due 3-15-00. [9] Due 3-29-05. [10] Due 3-28-22. [11] Due 3-29-22. [12] Due 12-19-22. [13] Due 2-16-23. [14] Due 3-24-25. [15] (HRO)On 3-1-05 at 100. [16] (HRO)On Chge of Ctrl at 101. [17] Max $33.3M red w/proceeds of Pub Eq Off'gs. [18] (HRO)On Chge of Ctrl at 101(Accreted Val). [19] Incl disc. [20] Max $54.3M to 3/96 w/com off'g proceeds. [21] Fiscal Feb'94 & prior. [22] 8 Mo Oct'94. [23] Fiscal Oct'93 & prior. [24] 6 Mo Dec, '94. [25] Max $60M red w/proceeds of Pub Com Off'g.

Title-Industry Code & Co. Finances (In Italics) / Individual Issue Statistics — Exchange ↓	Ind / Interest Dates	Fixed Charge Coverage 1992 / S&P Debt Rating	1993 / Date of Last Rating Change	Prior Rating	1994 / Eligible ↓	Year End / Bond Form	Million $ Cash & Equiv. / Redemption Provisions — Regular Price	Curr. Assets / Regular (Begins) Thru	Curr. Liab. / Sinking Fund Price	Balance Sheet Date / Sinking Fund (Begins) Thru	L. Term Debt (Mil $) / Refund/Other Restriction Price	Refund/Other Restriction (Begins) Thru	Capital-ization (Mil $) / Outst'g (Mil $)	Total Debt % Capital / Underwriting Firm	Underwriting Year	Price Range 1995 High	Price Range 1995 Low	Mo. End Price Sale(s) or Bid	Curr. Yield	Yield to Mat.
K-III Communications	***54***	***d0.90***	***d0.16***		***0.28***	***Dc***	***20.80***	***254.0***	***287.0***	***6-30-95***	***1210***		***1441***	***84.4***						
Sr Sec Nts[1] 10⅝s 2002	Mn	**BB–**	3/93	BB	Y	R	104	(5-1-97)	100	(5-1-01)	[2]Z100	....	250	D6	'92	107	97¼	107	9.93	9.14
Sr[1]Nts[3] 10¼s 2004	Jd	**BB–**			Y	R	104.95	(6-1-99)	....	....	[4]Z109.25	6-1-97	100	M2	'94	108½	94¼	107	9.58	9.04
Kaiser Alum & Chem[5]	***5***	***1.36***	***1.48***		***1.59***	***Dc***	***14.70***	***873.0***	***542.0***	***6-30-95***	***805.0***		***838.0***	***99.6***						
Sr Nts[6] 9⅞s 2002	Fa15	**B+**			Y	R	104.125	(2-15-98)	....	....	....	....	225	M2	'94	102⅞	91¼	102¾	9.61	9.27
Sr Sub Nts[6] 12¾s 2003	Fa	**B–**			Y	R	106.375	(2-1-98)	....	....	....	....	400	M2	'93	110¾	100¼	109¾	11.62	10.74
Kaiser Found'n Hosp/Hlth Plan[7]	***30***	....	....		....	***Dc***	***No Recent Fin'ls***													
Deb 9.55s 2005	jJ15	**AA**			X	R	NC	....	....	....	....	....	200	G1	'90	125½	108⅛	125½	7.61	6.00
Nts 9s 2001	mN	**AA**			X	R	NC	....	....	....	....	....	150	F1	'89	115½	103⅝	115½	7.79	5.83
Kansas City Power & Light	***72a***	***3.28***	***4.06***		***4.39***	***Dc***	***46.30***	***189.0***	***256.0***	***9-30-95***	***836.0***		***1879***	***47.3***						
Sec M-T Nts 4.70s '96	[8]ao	**A**			X	BE	NC	....	....	....	....	....	10.5	M2	'93	99¾	96⅛	99¾	4.71	5.46
Sec M-T Nts 4.70s '96	[8]ms	**A**			X	BE	NC	....	....	....	....	....	19.5	M2	'93	99¾	96⅛	99¾	4.71	5.46
Sec M-T Nts 8¼s '96	[9]ao	**A**			X	BE	NC	....	....	....	....	....	3.50	M2	'91	101⅞	100½	100⅞	8.18	5.38
Sec M-T Nts 8.30s '96	[10]ao	**A**			X	BE	NC	....	....	....	....	....	3.00	M2	'91	102	100½	101	8.22	5.37
Sec M-T Nts 7.78s '96	[11]ao	**A**			X	BE	NC	....	....	....	....	....	5.00	M2	'91	102¼	99½	101½	7.67	5.65
Sec M-T Nts 7.80s '96	[12]ao	**A**			X	BE	NC	....	....	....	....	....	5.00	M2	'91	102¼	99⅝	101½	7.68	5.68
Sec M-T Nts 6.10s '98	[13]fa	**A**			X	BE	NC	....	....	....	....	....	4.00	M2	'93	100⅞	93⅞	100⅞	6.05	5.66
Sec M-T Nts 5¾s '98	[14]ms	**A**			X	BE	NC	....	....	....	....	....	13.0	M2	'93	100¼	92⅞	100¼	5.74	5.62
Sec M-T Nts 5¾s '98	[15]ms	**A**			X	BE	NC	....	....	....	....	....	9.00	M2	'93	100¼	92⅞	100¼	5.74	5.62
Sec M-T Nts 5.60s '98	[16]ms	**A**			X	BE	NC	....	....	....	....	....	25.0	M2	'93	99⅞	92⅜	99⅞	5.61	5.66
Sec M-T Nts 8.17s '98	[17]ao	**A**			X	BE	NC	....	....	....	....	....	5.00	M2	'91	106⅛	99¼	106⅛	7.70	5.71
Sec M-T Nts 8.18s '98	[18]ao	**A**			X	BE	NC	....	....	....	....	....	5.00	M2	'91	106⅛	99¼	106⅛	7.71	5.73
Sec M-T Nts 7.55s 2000	[19]ao	**A**			X	BE	NC	....	....	....	....	....	15.0	M2	'91	105¾	96¼	105¾	7.14	5.92
Sec M-T Nts 6.51s 2000	[20]fa	**A**			X	BE	NC	....	....	....	....	....	9.00	M2	'93	102⅛	91⅞	102⅛	6.37	5.92
Sec M-T Nts 6½s 2000	[21]fa	**A**			X	BE	NC	....	....	....	....	....	17.0	M2	'93	102⅛	91⅞	102⅛	6.36	5.91
Sec M-T Nts 6½s 2001	[22]ms	**A**			X	BE	NC	....	....	....	....	....	10.0	M2	'93	102⅛	90⅝	102⅛	6.36	6.00
Sec M-T Nts 6.40s 2001	[23]ms	**A**			X	BE	NC	....	....	....	....	....	20.0	M2	'93	101¾	89⅞	101¾	6.29	6.00
Sec M-T Nts 6½s 2003	[24]ms	**A**			X	BE	NC	....	....	....	....	....	9.00	M2	'93	101½	87⅝	101½	6.40	6.24
Sec M-T Nts 6½s 2003	[25]ms	**A**			X	BE	NC	....	....	....	....	....	10.0	M2	'93	101½	87⅝	101½	6.40	6.24
Sec M-T Nts 7.85s 2004	[26]fa	**A**			X	BE	NC	....	....	....	....	....	14.5	M2	'92	109¾	95	109¾	7.15	6.35
Sec M-T Nts 7.35s 2004	[27]fa	**A**			X	BE	NC	....	....	....	....	....	12.0	M2	'92	106½	91⅝	106½	6.90	6.36
Sec M-T Nts 7.35s 2005	[28]fa	**A**			X	BE	103.68	(10-1-97)	....	....	....	....	40.0	S5	'92	106⅞	90⅞	106⅞	6.88	6.39
Sec M-T Nts 7½s 2007	[29]fa	**A**			X	BE	103.75	(2-1-98)	....	....	....	....	6.00	M2	'93	108½	91⅛	108½	6.91	6.42
Sec M-T Nts 6.99s 2007	[30]ms	**A**			X	BE	103.50	(3-5-98)	....	....	....	....	10.0	M2	'93	104⅝	87¼	104⅝	6.68	6.40
Sec M-T Nts 6.98s 2007	[30]ms	**A**			X	BE	103.49	(3-3-98)	....	....	....	....	5.00	M2	'93	104⅝	87¼	104⅝	6.67	6.39
Sec M-T Nts 6.98s 2007	[31]ms	**A**			X	BE	103.49	(3-9-98)	....	....	....	....	6.00	M2	'93	104⅝	87¼	104⅝	6.67	6.39
Kansas City So Ind	***55***	***3.80***	***4.07***		***3.78***	***Dc***	***14.60***	***428.0***	***392.0***	***9-30-95***	***1038***		***1843***	***61.6***						
Deb 8.80s 2022	jJ	**BBB+**			X	BE	104.04	6-30-03	....	....	....	....	100	M2	'92	115½	98½	115½	7.62	7.45
Deb 7s 2025	jD15	**BBB+**			X	BE	[32]Z100	....	....	....	....	....	100	S1	'95	99⅞	98½	99⅞	7.01	7.01
Nts 5¾s '98	jJ8	**BBB+**			X	BE	NC	....	....	....	....	....	100	M2	'93	100⅜	92⅝	100⅜	5.73	5.59
Nts 7⅞s 2002	jJ	**BBB+**			X	BE	NC	....	....	....	....	....	100	M2	'92	109⅞	96⅛	109⅞	7.17	6.02
Nts 6⅝s 2005	Ms	**BBB+**			X	BE	NC	....	....	....	....	....	100	F1	'93	103⅛	88¼	103⅛	6.42	6.17
Kansas Gas & Electric[33]	***72a***	***2.73***	***3.60***		***4.12***	***Dc***	***0.05***	***311.0***	***171.0***	***9-30-95***	***684.0***		***2044***	***35.7***						
1st 5⅝s '96	Mn	**A–**	2/92	BBB+	X	R	100	....	100	....	....	....	16.0	L3	'66	100	97½	100	5.63	5.57
1st 7.60s 2003	jD15	**A–**			X	R	NC	....	....	....	....	....	135	D4	'92	107⅝	94⅛	107⅝	7.06	6.36
1st 6½s 2005	fA	**A–**			X	R	NC	....	....	....	....	....	65.0	D4	'93	101	86⅛	101	6.44	6.36
1st 6.20s 2006	Jj15	**A–**			X	R	NC	....	....	....	....	....	100	D4	'94	98¾	83¾	98¾	6.28	6.37

Uniform Footnote Explanations-See Page 260. Other: [1] (HRO)On Chge of Ctrl at 101. [2] On Chge in Ctrl,plus Applicable Premium. [3] Red on Chge of Ctrl at 100,plus Applicable Prem. [4] Max $35M red w/proceeds of Pub Equity Off'g. [5] Subsid of Kaiser Aluminum Corp. [6] Co must offer repurch at 101 on Chge of Ctrl. [7] Part of Kaiser Permanente program. [8] Due 4-22-96. [9] Due 4-24-96. [10] Due 5-7-96. [11] Due 9-24-96. [12] Due 9-25-96. [13] Due 2-23-98. [14] Due 3-3-98. [15] Due 3-6-98. [16] Due 3-10-98. [17] Due 9-24-98. [18] Due 9-25-98. [19] Due 1-4-00. [20] Due 2-11-00. [21] Due 2-14-00. [22] Due 1-2-2001. [23] Due 3-2-01. [24] Due 4-21-2003. [25] Due 5-1-03. [26] Due 7-2-04. [27] Due 8-3-04. [28] Due 10-1-05. [29] Due 1-29-07. [30] Due 3-5-07. [31] Due 3-9-07. [32] Greater of 100 or amt based on formula. [33] Subsid of Western Resources.

Title-Industry Code & Co. Finances (In Italics) / Exchange, Individual Issue Statistics	Ind / Interest Dates	Fixed Charge Coverage 1992 / S&P Debt Rating	1993 / Date of Last Rating Change	1994 / Prior Rating	Eligible	Year End / Bond Form	Cash & Equiv. (Million $) / Regular Price	Curr. Assets / Regular (Begins) Thru	Curr. Liab. / Sinking Fund Price	Balance Sheet Date / Sinking Fund (Begins) Thru	Refund/Other Restriction Price	Refund/Other Restriction (Begins) Thru / L. Term Debt (Mil $)	Outst'g (Mil $) / Capitalization (Mil $)	Underwriting Firm / Total Debt % Capital	Underwriting Year	Price Range 1995 High	Price Range 1995 Low	Mo. End Price Sale(s) or Bid	Curr. Yield	Yield to Mat.
Kansas Power & Light	*75*	***Now Western Resources,see***																		
1st 8⅞s 2000	Ms	A–	2/92	AA–	X	R	NC	....	....	....	....	....	75.0	D4	'90	110	101¾	110	8.07	6.12
[1]***Katz Corp.***	*1*	*1.70*	*0.86*	*0.51*		*Dc*	*2.22*	*72.00*	*53.90*	*9-30-95*		*178.0*	*286.0*	*62.2*						
Sr Sub Nts[2] 12¾s 2002	mN15	B			Y	R	106.375	(11-15-97)	....	....	....	....	100	C4	'92	107	99	107	11.92	11.25
Kaufman & Broad Home	*13h*	*1.36*	*1.75*	*1.81*		*Nv*				*8-31-95*		*904.0*	*1309*	*69.1*						
• Sr [2]Nts[3] 10⅜s '99	mS	BB+			Y	BE	100	(9-1-97)	....	....	....	....	100	M2	'92	104½	100½	102⅛	10.16	9.66
• Sr Sub Nts[2] 9⅜s 2003	Mn	BB–			Y	R	100	(5-1-00)	....	....	....	....	175	M2	'93	100	86	s99¾	9.40	9.42
Kelley Oil & Gas	*49a*	*d1.25*	*d4.48*	*d5.95*		*Dc*	*6.31*	*20.10*	*33.60*	*9-30-95*		*142.0*	*276.0*	*51.4*						
Sr Nts[2] 13½s '99	Jd15	B+			Y	BE	NC	....	....	....	[4]Z112	6-14-97	100	S1	'95	100½	77	81	16.67	21.56
Kellogg Co	*26*	*37.66*	*32.05*	*22.47*		*Dc*	*464.0*	*1743*	*1441*	*9-30-95*		*718.0*	*2919*	*36.1*						
Nts 5.90s '97	jJ15	AAA			X	R	NC	....	....	....	....	....	300	G1	'92	100¾	94⅞	100¾	5.86	5.39
Kemmerer Bottling Group	*11f*	*d0.24*	*1.00*	*....*		*Dc*	*2.27*	*43.30*	*28.30*	*4-2-94*		*80.90*	*76.00*	*107.0*						
Sr Sec Nts[2] 10⅞s 2000	Jd	NR	9/95	B–		R	104	(6-1-97)	....	....	....	....	3.40	B9	'93	101⅜	98¼	101⅜	10.73	10.47
Kemper Corp	*35d*	*d2.65*	*d0.49*	*2.49*		*Dc*				*9-30-95*		*357.0*	*1937*	*18.4*						
Nts 8.80s '98	mN	BB+	4/95	BBB	Y	R	NC	....	....	....	....	....	111	G1	'91	106⅞	96½	106⅞	8.23	6.12
KENETECH Corp	*72*	*1.13*	*0.35*	*0.98*		*Dc*	*26.30*	*245.0*	*136.0*	*9-30-95*		*152.0*	*439.0*	*43.5*						
Sr Sec Nts 12¾s 2002	jD15	CCC	12/95	B–	Y	R	106.375	(12-15-97)	....	....	....	....	100	M2	'92	106⅛	37	37	....	....
Kentucky Power[5]	*72a*	*2.28*	*1.94*	*2.33*		*Dc*	*0.94*	*50.90*	*106.0*	*9-30-95*		*263.0*	*531.0*	*61.0*						
1st 5⅛s '96	Jj	BBB+	11/88	BBB	X	R	100	....	100	....	....	....	29.4		'65	100	97⅞	100	5.13	Mat.
1st 7⅞s 2002	mS	BBB+	11/88	BBB	X	R	100.67	8-31-96	100.67	8-31-96	....	....	45.0	W5	'72	100⅞	97	100¾	7.82	7.73
1st 6.65s 2003	Mn	BBB+			X	BE	101.90	(5-1-98)	Z100	....	....	....	15.0	S1	'93	100⅝	87⅝	100⅝	6.61	6.54
1st 6.70s 2003	[6]fa	BBB+			X	BE	101.92	(6-1-98)	Z100	....	....	....	15.0	S1	'93	100¾	87⅞	100¾	6.65	6.57
1st 6.70s 2003	[7]fa	BBB+			X	BE	101.92	(7-1-98)	Z100	....	....	....	15.0	S1	'93	101½	88⅛	101½	6.60	6.44
1st 7.90s 2023	[6]fa	BBB+			X	BE	105.93	(6-1-98)	Z100	....	....	....	15.0	S1	'93	105⅝	88⅛	105⅝	7.50	7.44
1st 7.90s 2023	[6]fa	BBB+			X	BE	105.93	(6-1-98)	Z100	....	....	....	25.0	S1	'93	105⅝	88⅛	105⅝	7.50	7.44
Kentucky Utilities[8]	*72a*	*3.88*	*4.84*	*4.51*		*Dc*	*4.09*	*158.0*	*134.0*	*6-30-95*		*546.0*	*1148*	*47.6*						
1st K 7⅜s 2002	jD	AA–	2/93	AA	X	R	101.89	9-30-96	□100.79	11-30-96	....	....	35.5	F1	'72	102⅝	95¼	102⅝	7.19	6.89
1st P 7.92s 2007	Mn15	AA–	2/93	AA	X	R	NC	....	....	....	....	....	53.0	G1	'92	113¾	96½	113¾	6.96	6.21
1st P 8.55s 2027	Mn15	AA–	2/93	AA	X	R	105.13	(5-15-02)	....	....	....	....	33.0	G1	'92	114¾	96⅝	114¾	7.45	7.34
1st Q 5.95s 2000	Jd15	AA–			X	R	NC	....	....	....	....	....	61.5	G1	'93	100⅛	90	100⅛	5.94	5.92
1st Q 6.32s 2003	Jd15	AA–			X	R	NC	....	....	....	....	....	62.0	G1	'93	101⅜	87⅞	101⅜	6.23	6.09
1st R 7.55s 2025	Jd	AA–			X	BE	103.775	(6-1-05)	....	....	....	....	50.0	G1	'95	102	98	100⅝	7.50	7.50
Kerr-McGee Corp	*49b*	*0.02*	*2.52*	*3.24*		*Dc*	*102.0*	*798.0*	*594.0*	*9-30-95*		*577.0*	*2027*	*28.5*						
• SF Deb 8½s 2006	Jd	A–	5/86	A	X	R	101.86	5-31-96	100	....	....	....	56.0	L3	'76	104⅜	95⅜	102	8.33	8.21
Deb 7s 2011	mN	A–	5/86	A	X	R	100	....	....	....	....	....	[9]250	L3	'81	98¼	83⅛	96¾	7.24	7.35
[10]***KeyCorp***[11]	*10*	*n/a*	*n/a*	*3.71*		*Dc*				*9-30-95*		*4048*	*9131*	*44.3*						
Sub Cap[12]Nts 8.40s '99	Ao	BBB+	10/90	A–	X	R	NC	....	....	....	Z100	....	75.0	F1	'87	107¼	99⅛	107¼	7.83	5.91
Sub Nts 8s 2004	jJ	BBB+			X	R	NC	....	....	....	....	....	125	M2	'92	111⅛	95⅛	111⅛	7.20	6.29
Keystone Group	*62*	*1.50*	*1.74*	*1.66*		*Dc*	*33.70*	*38.40*	*20.00*	*12-31-94*		*145.0*	*82.30*	*176.0*						
Sr[13]Sec[2]Nts 9¾s 2003	mS	BB–			Y	R	103.375	(9-1-98)	....	....	[14]Z109	10-31-96	145	M2	'93	102½	92	96½	10.10	10.42
KHE Finance, Inc	*25*	***Gtd by Hovnanian Enterprises,see***																		
Sub Nts[2] 11¼s 2002	Ao15	B			Y	R	105.625	(4-15-97)	100	(4-15-00)	....	....	100	K2	'92	101	82½	93⅝	12.02	12.74
[15]***Kidde,Inc***[16]	*17*	*n/a*	*n/a*	*n/a*		*Sp*	*6815*	*9933*	*6704*	*:9-30-94*		*5038*	*13674*	*66.4*						
Sr Nts 8⅛s '98	Fa	NR	5/88	BBB		R	NC	....	....	....	....	....	2.03	D7	'87	104⅝	96½	104⅝	8.12	6.10
Sub Nts 9.20s '96	jD	NR	5/88	BBB–		R	NC	....	....	....	....	....	5.75	D4	'86	103¾	95	102⅞	8.94	5.94
Kimberly-Clark[17]	*33*	*6.87*	*7.33*	*6.72*		*Dc*	*235.0*	*3692*	*3971*	*p6-30-95*		*2176*	*6516*	*47.6*						
SF Deb 9½s 2018	Fa	AA			X	R	105.85	1-31-96	100	(2-1-99)	®104.50	1-31-98	49.8	G1	'88	110½	104⅝	106	8.96	8.87

Uniform Footnote Explanations-See Page 260. Other: [1] Now Katz Media. [2] (HRO)On Chge of Ctrl at 101. [3] Issued in min denom $100T. [4] Max $25M red w/proceeds of Equity Off'g. [5] Subsid of Amer Elec Pwr. [6] Due Jun 1. [7] Due Jul 1. [8] Subsid of KU Energy. [9] Incl disc. [10] Was Key Banks,First Commercial Banks. [11] See Society Corp,AmeriTrust. [12] Co may exch for Cap Sec when due. [13] Gtd by Keystone Custodian Funds. [14] Max $50 red w/proceeds of Pub Eq Off'g. [15] Was Kidde(Walter)&Co. [16] Subsid & data of Hanson PLC. [17] See Scott Paper Co.

Title-Industry Code & Co. Finances (In Italics) / Individual Issue Statistics (Exchange)	Ind / Interest Dates	Fixed Charge Coverage 1992 / S&P Debt Rating	1993 / Date of Last Rating Change	1994 / Prior Rating	Eligible	Year End / Bond Form	Cash & Equiv. (Million $) / Redemption Provisions Regular Price	Curr. Assets (Million $) / Regular (Begins) Thru	Curr. Liab. / Sinking Fund Price	Balance Sheet Date / Sinking Fund (Begins) Thru	L. Term Debt (Mil $) / Refund/Other Restriction Price	Refund/Other Restriction (Begins) Thru	Capital-ization (Mil $) / Outst'g (Mil $)	Total Debt % Capital / Underwriting Firm	Underwriting Year	Price Range 1995 High	Price Range 1995 Low	Mo. End Price Sale(s) or Bid	Curr. Yield	Yield to Mat.
***Kimberly-Clark** (Cont.)*																				
Deb 6⅞s 2014	Fa15	**AA**			X	BE	NC	....	....	....	....	....	100	G1	'94	103	85⅞	103	6.67	6.59
Deb 7⅞s 2023	Fa	**AA**			X	BE	103.85	(2-1-03)	....	....	....	....	200	G1	'93	109⅝	91¾	109⅝	7.18	7.07
Nts 9⅛s '97	Jd	**AA**			X	R	NC	....	....	....	....	....	100	G1	'87	106	102⅛	105	8.69	5.42
Nts 9s 2000	fA	**AA**			X	R	NC	....	....	....	....	....	99.7	G1	'90	112⅞	103⅜	112⅞	7.97	5.76
Nts 8⅝s 2001	Mn	**AA**			X	R	NC	....	....	....	....	....	199	G1	'91	112⅞	101½	112⅞	7.64	5.78
Kimco Realty	***57***	***2.05***	***3.00***	***3.01***		***Dc***				***9-30-95***	***349.0***		***797.0***	***43.8***						
Sr Nts 6½s 2003	aO	**A–**			X	BE	NC	....	....	....	....	....	100	M2	'93	100⅛	86⅝	100⅛	6.49	6.48
M-T Nts 7.91s 2005	[1]ao	**A–**			X	BE	NC	....	....	....	....	....	20.0	M2	'95	109½	100	109½	7.22	6.53
F/R[2]Sr Nts 6⅜s '98	QMay11	**A–**			X	BE	100	(5-11-96)	....	....	....	....	50.0	M2	'94	100¼	95	100	6.38	....
F/R[3]Sr Nts 6⅜s '99	QFeb10	**A–**			X	BE	NC	....	....	....	....	....	100	M2	'94	101	99	100¾	6.33	....
KinderCare Learning Ctrs	***63***	***Δn/a***	***Δ2.85***	***Δ3.08***		***My***	***10.50***	***34.60***	***77.50***	***9-22-95***	***153.0***		***400.0***	***38.5***						
Sr Nts[4] 10⅜s 2001	Jd	**B**	5/95	BB–	Y	R	105.1875	(6-1-98)	....	....	....	....	100	M2	'94	105¼	100¼	105¼	9.86	9.12
Kings County El Lt & Pr	***75***	***Assmd by Consol Edison NY, see***																		
• PM Mtg 6s '97	aO	**NR**	6/80	A	X	C	NC	....	....	....	....	....	1.45	F3	1898	100	100	98½	6.09	6.91
K mart	***59g***	***4.10***	***2.39***	***1.21***		***Ja***	***470.0***	***10574***	***6509***	***10-25-95***	***3658***		***11329***	***49.5***						
Deb 12½s 2005	Ms	**BBB**	1/95	BBB+	X	R	NC	....	....	....	....	....	100	G1	'85	135	79¾	86⅛	14.51	15.36
Deb 7¾s 2012	aO	**BBB**	1/95	BBB+	X	BE	NC	....	....	....	....	....	200	M6	'92	96¼	71½	73	10.62	11.39
Deb[5] 8⅜s 2022	jJ	**BBB**	1/95	BBB+	X	BE	103.913	(7-1-02)	....	....	....	....	100	M6	'92	101⅜	70¾	72½	11.55	11.78
Deb 7.95s 2023	Fa	**BBB**	1/95	BBB+	X	BE	NC	....	....	....	....	....	300	G1	'93	98	62⅞	76¼	10.43	10.64
Nts 8⅛s 2006	jD	**BBB**	1/95	BBB+	X	BE	NC	....	....	....	....	....	200	M6	'91	104⅜	73¼	75¼	10.80	12.30
Nts 8¼s 2022	Jj	**BBB**	1/95	BBB+	X	BE	NC	....	....	....	....	....	100	M6	'92	100⅞	69½	72½	11.38	11.63
KN Energy[6]	***73b***	***2.62***	***2.82***	***2.61***		***Dc***	***22.90***	***234.0***	***239.0***	***9-30-95***	***320.0***		***801.0***	***47.6***						
SF Deb 9.95s 2020	Ao	**A**	2/92	A–	X	R	103.58	(4-1-00)	100	(4-1-01)	....	....	20.0	M2	'90	117⅞	98	117⅞	8.44	8.23
SF Deb 9⅝s 2021	fA	**A**	2/92	A–	X	R	104.81	(8-1-01)	100	(8-1-02)	....	....	45.0	D4	'91	120	104⅝	119½	8.05	7.85
SF Deb 8.35s 2022	mS15	**A**			X	BE	104.175	(9-15-02)	100	(9-15-03)	....	....	35.0	M2	'92	111⅛	90	111⅛	7.51	7.39
Deb 6½s 2013	mS	**A**			X	BE	NC	....	100	(9-1-04)	....	....	50.0	D4	'93	96	78⅝	96	6.77	6.89
Deb[7] 7.85s 2022	mS	**A**			X	BE	105	(9-1-98)	....	....	....	....	30.0	J2	'92	107¼	84½	107¼	7.32	7.23
Deb 8¾s 2024	aO15	**A**			X	BE	104	(10-15-04)	....	....	....	....	75.0	M2	'94	116	94	116	7.54	7.40
Knight-Ridder Inc[8]	***54c***	***5.30***	***6.45***	***7.55***		***Dc***	***17.70***	***479.0***	***428.0***	***9-24-95***	***593.0***		***1683***	***35.2***						
Deb[9] 9⅞s 2009	Ao15	**AA–**			X	R	NC	....	....	....	....	....	200	G1	'89	132⅛	110⅜	132⅛	7.47	6.27
Amortizing[10]Nts 8½s 2001	mS	**AA–**			X	R	NC	....	....	....	....	....	160	G1	'91	108⅝	100¼	108⅜	7.84	....
Sr Nts 6.30s 2005	jD15	**AA–**			X	BE	[11]Z100	....	....	....	....	....	100	G1	'95	99¾	99¾	99¾	6.32	6.33
Koppers Industries	***14***	***n/a***	***1.94***	***1.93***		***Dc***	***3.55***	***149.0***	***53.10***	***9-30-95***	***174.0***		***258.0***	***70.2***						
• Sr Nts[4] 8½s 2004	Fa	**BB–**			Y	R	104.25	(2-1-99)	....	....	[12]Z108.50	1-31-97	110	S5	'94	98	91	s95½	8.90	9.30
[13]Kraft Inc	***26***	***Subsid of Philip Morris Cos,see***																		
SF Deb 8½s 2017	Fa15	**A**	11/88	AA	X	R	104.50	2-14-96	100	(2-15-98)	®103.75	2-14-97	175	G1	'87	104⅝	92⅝	104⅝	8.12	8.04
Kroger Co.	***59c***	***1.36***	***1.78***	***2.29***		***Dc***	***43.90***	***2076***	***2479***	***10-7-95***	***3505***		***1800***	***196.0***						
Sr Sec Deb[14] 8½s 2003	Jd15	**BB+**	4/95	BB	Y	BE	104.25	(6-15-98)	....	....	[15]Z100	....	200	C4	'93	105¾	94½	105¾	8.04	7.48
Sr Sec Deb[14] 9¼s 2005	Jj	**BB+**	4/95	BB	Y	BE	104.625	(1-1-98)	....	....	[15]Z100	....	160	C4	'93	108⅜	98⅜	108⅜	8.54	7.93
Sr Sub Deb[14] 9⅞s 2002	fA	**BB–**	4/95	B+	Y	R	100	(8-1-99)	....	....	[15]Z100	7-31-99	211	G1	'92	109	100¾	109	9.06	8.08
Sr Sub Deb[14]'A' 9¾s 2004	Fa15	**BB–**	4/95	B+	Y	R	104.875	(2-15-97)	....	....	[15]Z100	2-14-97	127	G1	'92	108⅝	101	108	9.03	8.37
Sr Sub Deb[14]'B' 9¾s 2004	Fa15	**BB–**	4/95	B+	Y	R	104.875	(2-15-97)	....	....	[15]Z100	....	70.0	L3	'92	108¼	100⅞	108	9.03	8.37
Sr Sub Nts[14] 10s '99	Mn	**BB–**	4/95	B+	Y	R	NC	....	....	....	[15]Z100	....	223	G1	'92	109½	102⅜	109	9.17	6.93
• Sr Sub Nts 9s '99	fA15	**BB–**	4/95	B+	Y	R	100	(8-15-96)	....	....	[15]Z100	8-14-96	125	G1	'92	103¾	100⅛	s102⅛	8.81	8.30
La Petite Holdings	***22***	***Δn/a***	***Δ0.96***	***Δ0.45***		***Au***	***16.30***	***41.40***	***45.50***	***8-26-95***	***91.40***		***108.0***	***91.9***						
Sr Sec Nts[16] 9⅝s 2001	fA	**B**			Y	R	104.125	(8-1-97)	100	(8-1-00)	....	....	85.0	B9	'93	90	83	87¾	10.97	12.75

Uniform Footnote Explanations-See Page 260. Other: [1] Due 4-26-05. [2] Int thru 2-11-96,adj qtrly aft. [3] Int thru 2-10-96,adj qtrly aft. [4] (HRO)On Chge of Ctrl at 101. [5] Issued in min denom $100T. [6] Was Kansas-Nebraska Natural Gas. [7] (HRO)At 100,ltd,as defined. [8] Was Knight-Ridder Newspapers. [9] (HRO)To 4-15-99 at 100, for an Event, etc. [10] Mand amortiz,25% of ea note 9/1/98-01. [11] Greater of 100 or amt based on formula. [12] Max $30M red w/proceeds of Com Off'g. [13] Now Kraft Gen'l Foods. [14] (HRO)For a Redemp Event at 101. [15] For Redemp Event,in whole at 100 plus premium. [16] Co must offer repurch at 101 on Chge of Ctrl.

Title-Industry Code & Co. Finances (In Italics)	Ind	Fixed Charge Coverage 1992	1993	1994		Year End	Million $ Cash & Equiv.	Curr. Assets	Curr. Liab.	Balance Sheet Date	L. Term Debt (Mil $)		Capital-ization (Mil $)	Total Debt % Capital						
Exchange ↓ Individual Issue Statistics	**Interest Dates**	**S&P Debt Rating**	**Date of Last Rating Change**	**Prior Rating**	**Eligible ↓**	**Bond Form**	**Redemption Provisions: Regular Price**	**Regular (Begins) Thru**	**Sinking Fund Price**	**Sinking Fund (Begins) Thru**	**Refund/Other Restriction Price**	**Refund/Other Restriction (Begins) Thru**	**Outst'g (Mil $)**	**Underwriting Firm**	**Year**	**Price Range 1995 High**	**Low**	**Mo. End Price Sale(s) or Bid**	**Curr. Yield**	**Yield to Mat.**
La Quinta Inns	***32***	***2.32***	***2.43***	***2.89***		***Dc***	***3.69***	***35.30***	***83.80***	***9-30-95***	***486.0***		***835.0***	***59.9***						
Sr Nts 7.40s 2005	mS15	BBB–			X	BE	NC	....	....	....	....	....	100	M6	'95	103⅜	99¼	103⅜	7.16	6.91
Sr Sub Nts[1] 9¼s 2003	Mn15	BB+	5/95	BB–	Y	R	103.469	(5-15-98)	....	....	....	....	120	D6	'93	106	94	105	8.81	8.33
Laclede Gas Co.	***73b***	***△3.48***	***△3.12***	***△2.66***		***Sp***	***1.56***	***108.0***	***128.0***	***9-30-95***	***154.0***		***443.0***	***48.3***						
1st[2] 9⅝s '98	[3]Mn15	AA–	4/91	AA	X	R	100	(5-15-98)	Z100	....	....	....	25.0	M6	'88	108⅝	102½	108⅝	8.86	5.69
1st 6¼s 2003	Mn	AA–			X	R	NC	....	Z100	....	....	....	25.0	P1	'93	101⅜	87¾	101⅜	6.17	6.01
1st 8½s 2004	mN15	AA–	4/91	AA	X	R	NC	....	Z100	....	....	....	25.0	S1	'89	115¾	100⅞	115¾	7.34	6.17
1st 6½s 2010	mN15	AA–			X	R	NC	....	■100	....	....	....	25.0	C5	'95	102	99	102	6.37	6.29
Laidlaw Inc	***53***	***△2.06***	***△2.06***	***△2.25***		***Au***	***147.0***	***719.0***	***552.0***	***8-31-95***	***1669***		***3416***	***50.3***						
Deb 8¾s 2000	$Jj	BBB+			Q	BE	NC	....	....	....	....	....	200	G1	'94	109½	99⅝	109½	7.99	6.04
Deb 7.70s 2002	$fA15	BBB+			Q	BE	NC	....	....	....	....	....	200	G1	'92	107½	91¼	107½	7.16	6.30
Deb 7.05s 2003	Mn15	BBB+			Q	BE	NC	....	....	....	....	....	100	G1	'93	104⅝	89⅞	104⅝	6.74	6.26
Deb 7⅞s 2005	Ao15	BBB+			Q	BE	NC	....	....	....	....	....	150	G1	'95	110	99½	110	7.16	6.43
Deb 8¼s 2023	Mn15	BBB+			Q	BE	NC	....	....	....	....	....	100	G1	'93	114¼	90⅞	114¼	7.22	7.07
Deb 8¾s 2025	Ao15	BBB+			Q	BE	NC	....	....	....	....	....	150	G1	'95	120⅜	99⅜	120⅜	7.27	7.09
Lamar Advertising Co.	***1***	***1.13***	***1.15***	***1.38***		***Oc***	***1.97***	***17.00***	***16.90***	***7-31-95***	***141.0***		***119.0***	***125.0***						
Sr Sec Nts[4] 11s 2003	Mn15	B+	6/95	B	Y	R	105.50	(5-15-98)	....	....	....	....	100	G1	'93	103½	94¾	103½	10.63	10.31
LaRoche Indus	***14***	***3.80***	***3.30***	***2.96***		***Fb***	***22.00***	***138.0***	***67.40***	***8-31-95***	***115.0***		***174.0***	***71.3***						
Sr Sub Nts[1] 13s 2004	fA15	B			Y	R	106.50	(8-15-99)	....	....	....	....	100	C1	'94	106¾	92	106½	12.21	11.77
Lear Seating	***8***	***0.82***	***[5]1.56***	***3.45***		***Dc***	***15.20***	***1144***	***1146***	***9-30-95***	***1132***		***1702***	***68.3***						
Sr Sub[1]Nts[6] 11¼s 2000	jJ15	B	1/95	B–	Y	R	100	(7-15-97)	....	....	....	....	125	L3	'92	106¼	101¼	105	10.71	9.86
Sub Nts[7] 8¼s 2002	Fa	B	1/95	B–	Y	R	101.65	(2-1-98)	....	....	....	....	145	L3	'94	98¾	88⅛	98	8.42	8.68
Lehman Bros Hldgs[8]	***62***	***1.00***	***[9]1.13***	***[10]1.04***		***Nv***	***2101***			***8-31-95***	***12897***		***16528***	***78.0***						
Nts[8] 9¾s '96	Ao	A			X	R	NC	....	....	....	....	....	150	S4	'91	102½	100⅞	100⅞	9.67	6.13
Nts[8] 5½s '96	Jd15	A			X	R	NC	....	....	....	....	....	175	L3	'93	99⅞	95⅛	99⅞	5.51	5.77
Nts[8] 8⅜s '97	Ao	A			X	R	NC	....	....	....	....	....	200	L3	'92	103	98¼	103	8.13	5.85
Nts[8] 7⅝s '97	Jd15	A			X	R	NC	....	....	....	....	....	200	L3	'92	102⅜	97⅜	102⅜	7.45	5.90
Nts[8] 5¾s '98	Fa15	A			X	R	NC	....	....	....	....	....	200	L3	'93	99¾	90½	99¾	5.76	5.87
Nts[8] 6⅜s '98	Jd	A			X	R	NC	....	....	....	....	....	150	L3	'93	100⅞	91⅛	100⅞	6.32	5.98
Nts[8] 8⅞s '98	mN	A			X	R	NC	....	....	....	....	....	120	L3	'91	107⅜	99⅜	107⅜	8.27	6.01
Nts[8] 8⅜s '99	Fa15	A			X	R	NC	....	....	....	....	....	200	L3	'92	106¼	96	106¼	7.88	6.14
Nts[8] 7⅝s '99	jJ15	A			X	R	NC	....	....	....	....	....	200	L3	'92	104½	93⅞	104½	7.30	6.19
Nts 6⅝s 2000	mN15	A			X	BE	NC	....	....	....	....	....	200	L3	'95	101¼	99¾	101¼	6.54	6.32
Nts[8] 8⅞s 2002	Ms	A			X	R	NC	....	....	....	....	....	200	L3	'92	111¾	96½	111¾	7.94	6.53
• Nts[8] 8¾s 2002	Mn15	A			X	R	NC	....	....	....	....	....	200	L3	'92	111¾	97¼	109¼	8.01	6.93
Nts 7⅛s 2003	mS15	A			X	BE	NC	....	....	....	....	....	175	L3	'95	102⅝	99¼	102⅝	6.94	6.68
Nts 8¾s 2005	Ms15	A			X	R	NC	....	....	....	....	....	175	L3	'95	113½	98⅛	113½	7.71	6.75
Nts 8½s 2007	Mn	A			X	BE	NC	....	....	....	....	....	250	L3	'95	113	99¼	113	7.52	6.83
Nts 7⅜s 2007	Mn15	A			X	BE	NC	....	....	....	....	....	200	L3	'95	104⅜	96⅞	104⅜	7.07	6.81
Nts[11] 8.80s 2015	Ms	A			X	R	NC	....	....	....	....	....	300	L3	'95	114⅝	96⅛	114⅝	7.68	7.36
Nts 8½s 2015	fA	A			X	BE	NC	....	....	....	....	....	150	L3	'95	111	97½	111	7.66	7.42
M-T Nts 'E'[12] 7.40s '97	[13]fa15	A			X	BE	NC	....	....	....	....	....	5.00	L3	'94	101⅞	97⅛	101⅞	7.26	5.96
M-T[14]Nts 'E'[12] 8.05s 2019	Jj15	A			X	BE	NC	....	....	....	....	....	50.0	L3	'94	106¾	100	106	7.59	7.50
F/R[15]M-T Nts 'E'[12] 5.98s '96	QJan5	A			X	BE	NC	....	....	....	....	....	50.0	L3	'94	100	99⅝	100	5.98	Mat.
F/R[16]M-T Nts 'E'[12] '96	[17]Feb9	A			X	BE	NC	....	....	....	....	....	15.0	L3	'94	100	99⅝	100	....	....
F/R[16]M-T Nts 'E'[12] '96	[17]Feb10	A			X	BE	NC	....	....	....	....	....	100	L3	'94	100	99⅝	100	....	....
F/R[18]M-T Nts 'E'[12] 6.075s '96	QMar	A			X	BE	NC	....	....	....	....	....	5.00	L3	'94	100	99⅝	100	6.08	....

Uniform Footnote Explanations-See Page 260. Other: [1] (HRO)On Chge of Ctrl at 101. [2] (HRO)On 5-15-98 at 100. [3] Due 5-15-13. [4] Co must offer repurch at 101 on Chge of Ctrl. [5] Fiscal Jun'93 & prior. [6] Gtd by Lear Hldgs. [7] (HRO)On Chge of Ctrl Triggering Event at 101. [8] Was Shearson Lehman Bros Hldgs. [9] Fiscal Dec'93 & prior. [10] 11 Mo Nov'94. [11] (HRO)On 3-1-02 at 100. [12] Issued in min denom $100T. [13] Due 5-16-97. [14] (HRO)On 1-15-99 at 98. [15] Int thru 1-5-96,adj qtrly aft. [16] Int adj monthly. [17] Int pd monthly. [18] Int adj thru maturity.

Title-Industry Code & Co. Finances (In Italics) / Individual Issue Statistics (Exchange)	Ind / Interest Dates	Fixed Charge Coverage 1992 / S&P Debt Rating	1993 / Date of Last Rating Change	1994 / Prior Rating	Year End / Eligible	Bond Form	Million $ Cash & Equiv. / Redemption Provisions: Regular Price	Curr. Assets / Regular (Begins) Thru	Curr. Liab. / Sinking Fund Price	Balance Sheet Date / Sinking Fund (Begins) Thru	L. Term Debt (Mil $) / Refund/Other Restriction Price	Refund/Other Restriction (Begins) Thru	Capitalization (Mil $) / Outst'g (Mil $)	Total Debt % Capital / Underwriting Firm	Underwriting Year	Price Range 1995 High	Price Range 1995 Low	Mo. End Price Sale(s) or Bid	Curr. Yield	Yield to Mat.
Lehman Bros Hldgs *(Cont.)*																				
F/R[1]M-T Nts 'E'[2] 6.075s '96	QMar	**A**			X	BE	NC	....	....	....	....	....	12.6	L3	'94	100⅛	99⅝	100	6.08	....
F/R[2]M-T Nts 'E'[3] 6.2375s '96	[4]Mar18	**A**			X	BE	NC	....	....	....	....	....	25.0	L3	'95	100	100	100	6.24	....
F/R[5]M-T Nts 'E'[2] 5.868s '96	QMar22	**A**			X	BE	NC	....	....	....	....	....	10.0	L3	'94	100	99⅝	100	5.87	....
F/R[6]M-T Nts 'E'[2] '96	[4]Apr8	**A**			X	BE	NC	....	....	....	....	....	5.00	L3	'94	100	99¾	100	....	....
F/R[6]M-T Nts 'E'[2] '96	[4]Apr15	**A**			X	BE	NC	....	....	....	....	....	50.0	L3	'94	100⅛	99¾	100⅛	....	....
F/R[7]M-T Nts 'E'[2] 5.05s '96	QMay20	**A**			X	BE	NC	....	....	....	....	....	15.0	L3	'94	100	99¾	100	5.05	....
F/R[8]M-T Nts 'E'[2] 3.7875s '96	QJun14	**A**			X	BE	NC	....	....	....	....	....	10.0	L3	'94	100	99¾	100	3.79	....
F/R[6]M-T Nts 'E'[2] '96	[9]Jun19	**A**			X	BE	NC	....	....	....	....	....	80.0	L3	'94	100⅛	99¾	100⅛	....	....
F/R[6]M-T Nts 'E'[2] '96	[4]Aug16	**A**			X	BE	NC	....	....	....	....	....	20.0	L3	'94	100	99¾	100	....	....
F/R[7]M-T Nts 'E'[2] 6.185s '96	QAug19	**A**			X	BE	NC	....	....	....	....	....	10.0	L3	'94	100⅛	99¾	100	6.19	....
• F/R[10]M-T Nts 'E'[2] '96	[11]	**A**			X	BE	NC	....	....	....	....	....	100	L3	'95	100	100	100	....	....
F/R[12]M-T Nts'E'[2] 6.2125s '96	[13]	**A**			X	BE	NC	....	....	....	....	....	5.00	L3	'93	100¼	91¼	100¼	6.20	....
F/R[14]M-T Nts 'E'[2] 6.3625s '97	QJan21	**A**			X	BE	NC	....	....	....	....	....	50.0	L3	'94	100⅛	99¼	100	6.36	....
F/R[12]M-T Nts'E'[2] 6.3125s '97	[15]	**A**			X	BE	NC	....	....	....	....	....	50.0	L3	'93	100⅛	99¼	100	6.31	....
M-T Nts 'E'[2] 8.26s '97	[16]fa15	**A**			X	BE	NC	....	....	....	....	....	104	L3	'95	103⅝	99⅞	103⅝	7.97	5.93
F/R[6]M-T Nts 'E'[2] '97	[4]Sep2	**A**			X	BE	NC	....	....	....	....	....	5.00	L3	'94	100⅛	99¼	100	....	....
F/R[17]M-T Nts'E'[2] 6.4375s '97	QOct22	**A**			X	BE	NC	....	....	....	....	....	10.0	L3	'93	100⅛	99¼	100	6.44	....
F/R[18]M-T Nts'E'[2] 6.4063s '97	QNov5	**A**			X	BE	NC	....	....	....	....	....	5.00	L3	'93	100⅛	99¼	100	6.41	....
F/R[19]M-T Nts 'E'[2] 6⅜s '97	QNov10	**A**			X	BE	NC	....	....	....	....	....	5.00	L3	'93	100⅛	99¼	100	6.38	....
F/R[20]M-T Nts'E'[2] 6.4672s '97	QNov24	**A**			X	BE	NC	....	....	....	....	....	10.0	L3	'93	100⅛	99¼	100	6.47	....
M-T Nt 'E' 8.38s '98	[21]fa15	**A**			X	BE	NC	....	....	....	....	....	25.0	L3	'95	104¾	100	104¾	8.00	5.99
M-T Nts 'E'[2] 7.85s '98	[22]fa15	**A**			X	BE	NC	....	....	....	....	....	38.1	L3	'95	104	100	104	7.55	6.01
M-T Nts 'E'[2] 6⅞s '98	[23]fa15	**A**			X	BE	NC	....	....	....	....	....	25.0	L3	'95	101⅞	99¼	101⅞	6.75	6.04
F/R[24]M-T Nts 'E'[2] 5.98s '99	QJan12	**A**			X	BE	NC	....	....	....	....	....	100	L3	'94	99⅞	98⅝	99	6.04	....
M-T Nts 'E'[2] 8.23s '99	[25]fa15	**A**			X	BE	NC	....	....	....	....	....	30.0	L3	'95	106	100	106	7.76	6.13
F/R[7]M-T Nts 'E'[2] 6.425s '99	QMay19	**A**			X	BE	NC	....	....	....	....	....	15.0	L3	'94	100¼	98⅞	100¼	6.41	....
M-T Nts 'E'[2] 7.41s '99	[26]fa15	**A**			X	BE	NC	....	....	....	....	....	30.0	L3	'95	103¾	100	103¾	7.14	6.17
F/R[6]M-T Nts 'E'[2] '99	[27]	**A**			X	BE	NC	....	....	....	....	....	5.00	L3	'94	100¼	99	100	....	....
F/R[28]M-T Nts 'E'[2] 5.95s '99	QSep	**A**			X	BE	NC	....	....	....	....	....	18.0	L3	'94	99⅞	98⅝	98⅞	6.02	....
M-T Nts 'E'[2] 8⅞s 2000	Fa15	**A**			X	BE	NC	....	....	....	....	....	149	L3	'95	109¼	99¼	109¼	8.12	6.29
M-T[2]Nts[29]'E'[30] 6½s 2005	[31]fa15	**A**			X	BE	NC	....	....	....	....	....	42.0	L3	'95	106½	100	106½	6.10	5.61
Lehman[32]Bros[33]Inc	***62***	***1.05***	***[34]1.06***	***1.00***	***Nv***		***1170***			***8-31-95***	***3482***		***7315***	***70.5***						
Sr Sub Deb[35] 11⅝s 2005	Mn15	**A**	5/88	AA–	X	R	NC	....	....	....	....	....	100	S4	'85	132½	114½	132½	8.77	6.87
([36]Reset)Sr[37]Sub Nts 5.04s 2003	jD15	**A**			X	R	NC	....	....	....	....	....	200	L3	'93	103¾	92½	103¾	4.86	....
• Sr Sub Nts[35] 10¾s '96	[38]ms	**A**			X	R	NC	....	....	....	....	....	96.2	Mgr	'88	104	100¾	100¾	10.67	8.29
Sr Sub Nts 7s '97	Mn15	**A**			X	R	NC	....	....	....	....	....	200	L3	'94	101½	95⅞	101½	6.90	5.84
Sr Sub[2]Nts[35] 9½s '97	Jd15	**A**			X	R	NC	....	....	....	....	....	191	S4	'89	105⅛	100¾	105	9.05	5.88
Sr Sub Nts 7⅜s '97	fA15	**A**			X	R	NC	....	....	....	....	....	150	L3	'94	102¼	96	102¼	7.21	5.90
Sr Sub Nts 7⅝s '98	fA	**A**			X	R	NC	....	....	....	....	....	150	L3	'94	103⅞	98½	103⅞	7.34	5.98
Sr Sub Nts 5¾s '98	mN15	**A**			X	R	NC	....	....	....	....	....	200	L3	'93	99½	88¾	99½	5.78	5.94
Sr Sub[2]Nts[35] 10s '99	Mn15	**A**			X	R	NC	....	....	....	....	....	200	S4	'89	111¾	101⅞	111¾	8.95	6.09
Sr Sub[2]Nts[35] 9⅞s 2000	aO15	**A**			X	R	NC	....	....	....	....	....	192	S4	'88	113	101⅝	113	8.74	6.66
Sr Sub Nts 7⅛s 2002	jJ15	**A**			X	R	NC	....	....	....	....	....	250	L3	'95	102⅞	96⅜	102⅞	6.93	6.58
Lenfest Communications	***12a***	***0.69***	***0.82***	***0.57***	***Dc***		***3.83***			***6-30-95***	***★828.0***		***577.0***	***113.0***						
Sr Nts 8⅜s 2005	mN	**BB+**			Y	R	NC	....	....	....	....	....	700	S1	'95	99⅝	99⅛	99⅛	8.45	8.51
Leucadia Nat'l Corp[39]	***25g***	***5.34***	***5.54***	***3.31***	***Dc***		***428.0***			***9-30-95***	***[40]526.0***		***1584***	***33.2***						
• Sr Nts[41] 7¾s 2013	fA15	**BBB+**	5/94	BBB	X	R	NC	....	....	....	....	....	100		'93	100	88	99½	7.79	7.80

Uniform Footnote Explanations-See Page 260. Other: [1] Int adj thru maturity. [2] Issued in min denom $100T. [3] Int to 1-18-96,adj mthly(1 MO LIBOR&0.30%). [4] Int pd monthly. [5] Int thru 3-21-96,adj qtrly aft. [6] Int adj monthly. [7] Int thru 2-20-96,adj qtrly aft. [8] Int thru 3-14-96,adj qtrly aft. [9] Int pd monthly,ea 3rd Wed. [10] Int adj monthly(1 Mo LIBOR & 0.55). [11] Due 9-20-96:Int pd monthly. [12] Int thru 3-20-96,adj qtrly aft. [13] Due 11-1-96:Int pd qtrly,ea 3rd Wed, Mar etc. [14] Int thru 1-21-96,adj qtrly aft. [15] Due 3-17-97:Int pd qtrly,ea 3rd Wed,Mar etc. [16] Due 8-29-97. [17] Int thru 1-24-96,adj qtrly aft. [18] Int thru 2-4-96,adj qtrly aft. [19] Int thru 2-9-96,adj qtrly aft. [20] Int thru 2-23-96,adj qtrly aft. [21] Due 2-24-98. [22] Due 5-11-98. [23] Due 6-8-98. [24] Int thru 1-11-96,adj qtrly aft. [25] Due 3-8-99. [26] Due 5-25-99. [27] Due 8-9-99:Int pd monthly,ea 9th day. [28] Int thru 12-1-95,adj qtrly aft. [29] (HRO)On 1-7-98 at 100. [30] Int to incr to 7.80% on 1-7-98. [31] Due 7-7-05. [32] Was Shearson Lehman Bros Inc,see. [33] Subsid Lehman Bros Hldgs(Amer Express). [34] Fiscal Dec'93 & prior. [35] Was Shearson Lehman Hutton. [36] Int to 12-15-96,7.36% aft. [37] (HRO)On 12-15-96 at 100. [38] Due 4-29-96. [39] Was Talcott Nat'l. [40] Incl curr amts. [41] (HRO)On Chge of Ctrl at 101.

Title-Industry Code & Co. Finances (In Italics) / Individual Issue Statistics (Exchange)	Ind / Interest Dates	Fixed Charge Coverage 1992 / S&P Debt Rating	1993 / Date of Last Rating Change	1994 / Prior Rating	Eligible	Year End / Bond Form	Cash & Equiv. (Million $) / Regular Price	Curr. Assets / Regular (Begins) Thru	Curr. Liab. / Sinking Fund Price	Balance Sheet Date / Sinking Fund (Begins) Thru	L. Term Debt (Mil $) / Refund/Other Restriction Price	Refund/Other Restriction (Begins) Thru	Capitalization (Mil $) / Outst'g (Mil $)	Total Debt % Capital / Underwriting Firm	Underwriting Year	Price Range 1995 High	Price Range 1995 Low	Mo. End Price Sale(s) or Bid	Curr. Yield	Yield to Mat.
***Leucadia Nat'l Corp** (Cont.)*																				
• Sr Sub Nts 10⅜s 2002	Jd15	**BBB**	5/94	BBB−	X	R	104.50	(6-15-97)	100	(6-15-00)	....	....	125		'92	110⅛	104⅛	108⅜	9.57	8.65
• Sr Sub Nts[1] 8¼s 2005	Jd15	**BBB**			X	R	NC	....	....	....	....	....	100	J1	'95	103	100	100⅝	8.20	8.15
Levitz Furniture	***59j***	***1.22***	***1.50***	***1.13***		***Mr***	***8.28***	***206.0***	***180.0***	***9-30-95***	***410.0***		***374.0***	***114.0***						
Sr Nts[2] 12⅜s '97	Ao15	**CCC+**	10/95	B	Y	R	NC	....	....	....	....	....	97.6	D6	'92	103½	88	92	13.45	19.61
Sr Sub Nts[1] 9⅝s 2003	jJ15	**CCC**	10/95	B−	Y	R	102.75	(7-15-98)	....	....	....	....	100	D6	'93	80	47½	56	17.19	21.74
Liberty Nat'l Bancorp	***10***	***Merged into Banc One,see***																		
Sr Nts[3] 7¾s '99	Jj	**AA−**	8/94	A−	X	R	102	12-31-96	....	....	....	....	24.0		'91	105⅜	96⅞	105⅜	7.35	5.78
Liberty Nat'l Bank & Trust	***10***	***Subsid of Liberty Nat'l Bancorp,see***																		
Sub Nts[4] 6¾s 2003	Jd	**AA−**	8/94	A−	Y	BE	NC	....	....	....	....	....	55.0		'93	102½	89¼	102½	6.59	6.32
Life Partners Group	***35***	***2.75***	***4.15***	***3.82***		***Dc***				***9-30-95***	***221.0***		***640.0***	***36.9***						
Sr Sub Nts[2] 12¾s 2002	jJ15	**BB+**	10/94	BB−	Y	BE	103.643	(7-16-97)	....	....	....	....	95.1	F1	'92	106½	103	106½	11.97	11.31
Lilly (Eli)	***21a***	***25.38***	***27.33***	***17.36***		***Dc***	***1055***	***4110***	***5315***	***9-30-95***	***2118***		***10185***	***46.1***						
Nts 6¾s '99	mN15	**AA**	10/94	AAA	X	BE	NC	....	....	....	....	....	100	M6	'92	103¾	93⅞	103¾	6.51	5.66
• Nts 8⅛s 2001	jD	**AA**			X	BE	NC	....	....	....	....	....	150	M6	'94	111	99¼	109½	7.42	6.18
Nts 6¼s 2003	Ms15	**AA**	10/94	AAA	X	BE	NC	....	....	....	....	....	200	G1	'93	101⅞	88	101⅞	6.13	5.92
• Nts 8⅜s 2006	jD	**AA**			X	BE	NC	....	....	....	....	....	300	M6	'94	111⅞	100¼	116	7.22	6.32
• Nts 7⅛s 2025	Jd	**AA**			X	BE	NC	....	....	....	....	....	500	M6	'95	98⅞	98⅞	93	7.66	7.73
Limited, Inc	***59a***	***12.82***	***11.03***	***12.38***		***Ja***	***275.0***	***3017***	***800.0***	***10-28-95***	***650.0***		***4067***	***16.0***						
Deb 7½s 2023	Ms15	**BBB+**	12/95	A	X	BE	103.16	(3-15-03)	....	....	....	....	250	M5	'93	103⅜	84⅝	103⅜	7.26	7.21
Nts 8⅞s '99	fA15	**BBB+**	12/95	A	X	BE	NC	....	....	....	....	....	100	S1	'89	109½	101¾	109½	8.11	5.92
Nts 9⅛s 2001	Fa	**BBB+**	12/95	A	X	BE	NC	....	....	....	....	....	150	M6	'91	113¼	103	113¼	8.06	6.06
Nts 7.80s 2002	Mn15	**BBB+**	12/95	A	X	BE	NC	....	....	....	....	....	150	G1	'92	108½	96⅛	108½	7.19	6.17
Lincoln Nat'l	***35d***	***8.89***	***16.61***	***7.24***		***Dc***				***9-30-95***	***622.0***		***5295***	***17.8***						
Deb 7¼s 2005	Mn15	**A**			X	BE	NC	....	....	....	....	....	200	L3	'95	105⅞	99	105⅞	6.85	6.41
Deb 9⅛s 2024	aO	**A**	4/95	A+	X	BE	104.3325	(10-1-04)	....	....	....	....	200	M6	'94	118⅛	100¼	118⅛	7.72	7.57
Nts 7⅛s '99	jJ15	**A**	4/95	A+	X	BE	NC	....	....	....	....	....	100	M2	'92	103¾	94⅞	103¾	6.87	5.93
Nts 7⅝s 2002	jJ15	**A**	4/95	A+	X	BE	NC	....	....	....	....	....	100	M2	'92	107¾	94	107¾	7.08	6.17
Litchfield Financial	***25h***	***4.98***	***2.43***	***2.37***		***Dc***	***27.40***			***9-30-95***	***57.90***		***77.60***	***74.6***						
[5]Nts[6] 10s 2002	[7]Nov	**NR**				R	104	10-31-96	....	....	....	....	12.9	B7	'92	104⅜	96	104⅜	9.58	9.12
[5]Nts[6] 8⅞s 2003	[7]Nov	**NR**				R	104	(6-1-96)	....	....	....	....	17.0	B7	'93	105⅜	92	105⅜	8.42	7.94
[5]Nts[6] 10s 2004	[7]Nov	**NR**				R	104	(4-1-98)	....	....	....	....	16.0	M1	'95	113	98½	113	8.85	7.92
[8]Lockheed Corp[9]	***2a***	***6.68***	***5.84***	***7.00***		***Dc***	***122.0***	***8013***	***5969***	***9-30-95***	***2892***		***9862***	***36.6***						
Deb 7⅞s 2023	Ms15	**A+**	3/95	A−	X	BE	103.738	(3-15-03)	....	....	....	....	300	F1	'93	108⅞	89⅛	108⅞	7.23	7.13
Nts 4⅞s '96	Fa15	**A+**	3/95	A−	X	BE	NC	....	....	....	....	....	275	G1	'93	100	97⅛	100	4.88	4.79
Nts 5.65s '97	Ao	**A+**	3/95	A−	X	BE	NC	....	....	....	....	....	100	M5	'93	100⅛	94½	100⅛	5.64	5.54
Nts 5⅞s '98	Ms15	**A+**	3/95	A−	X	BE	NC	....	....	....	....	....	300	F1	'93	100¾	93⅛	100¾	5.83	5.51
Nts[10] 9⅜s '99	aO15	**A+**	3/95	A−	X	R	NC	....	....	....	....	....	300	G1	'89	112¼	103⅝	112¼	8.35	5.73
Nts 6¾s 2003	Ms15	**A+**	3/95	A−	X	BE	NC	....	....	....	....	....	300	F1	'93	104½	89⅝	104½	6.46	5.97
M-T Nts 'A' 5.68s '97	[11]jj	**A+**	3/95	A−	X	BE	NC	....	....	....	....	....	10.0	M2	'93	100¼	94⅝	100¼	5.67	5.46
M-T Nts 'A' 5¾s '97	[12]jj	**A+**	3/95	A−	X	BE	NC	....	....	....	....	....	10.0	G1	'94	100¼	94¾	100¼	5.74	5.54
Loehmann's Holdings,Inc	***59f***	***0.96***	***0.50***	***0.92***		***Ja***	***9.30***	***56.40***	***45.00***	***7-29-95***	***131.0***		***117.0***	***112.0***						
Sr Sub Nts 13¾s '99	Fa15	**CCC+**	4/92	B−	Y	R	102.50	2-14-96	100	(2-15-97)	....	....	77.6	M2	'89	101	89	89¾	15.32	18.16
Loews Corp	***35d***	***d2.48***	***5.25***	***2.52***		***Dc***				***9-30-95***	***4242***		***12640***	***33.6***						
Deb 8¼s 2007	Jj15	**AA−**			X	R	103.60	(1-15-97)	....	....	....	....	200	M2	'87	106½	95⅞	106½	7.75	7.38
Deb 8⅞s 2011	Ao15	**AA−**			X	R	NC	....	....	....	....	....	175	S1	'86	121¼	100½	121¼	7.32	6.64
Nts 8½s '98	Ao15	**AA−**			X	R	NC	....	....	....	....	....	118	S1	'86	105⅞	100	105⅞	8.03	5.72

Uniform Footnote Explanations-See Page 260. Other: [1] (HRO)On Chge of Ctrl at 101. [2] (HRO)On Chge in Ctrl at 101. [3] (HRO)On Chge of Ctrl at 100. [4] Issued in min denom $150T. [5] Ltd red,on death & at hldr's opt. [6] (HRO)For Certain Events at 100. [7] Int pd monthly. [8] Now Lockheed Martin. [9] See Martin Marietta & Martin Marietta Technol. [10] (HRO)At 100 for Designated Event&Rat'g Decline. [11] Due 4-1-97. [12] Due 4-7-97.

Title-Industry Code & Co. Finances (In Italics)	Ind	Fixed Charge Coverage 1992	1993	1994		Year End	Million $ Cash & Equiv.	Curr. Assets	Curr. Liab.	Balance Sheet Date	L. Term Debt (Mil $)	Capital-ization (Mil $)		Total Debt % Capital						
Exchange ↓ Individual Issue Statistics	Interest Dates	S&P Debt Rating	Date of Last Rating Change	Prior Rating	Eligible ↓	Bond Form	Redemption Provisions: Regular Price	Regular (Begins) Thru	Sinking Fund Price	Sinking Fund (Begins) Thru	Refund/Other Restriction Price	Refund/Other Restriction (Begins) Thru	Outst'g (Mil $)	Underwriting Firm	Underwriting Year	Price Range 1995 High	Price Range 1995 Low	Mo. End Price Sale(s) or Bid	Curr. Yield	Yield to Mat.
***Loews Corp** (Cont.)*																				
Sr Nts 7⅝s 2023	Jd	**AA–**			X	BE	103.8125	(6-1-03)	....	....	....	....	300	D6	'93	104⅜	84⅝	104⅜	7.31	7.25
Sr Nts 7s 2023	aO15	**AA–**			X	BE	102.387	(10-15-03)	....	....	....	....	400	M5	'93	97⅝	79	97⅝	7.17	7.20
***Lomas Mortgage USA, Inc*[1]**	***25h***	***n/a***	***1.63***	***d0.08***		***Je***	***Bankruptcy Chapt 11***				***[2]724.0***	***934.0***		***77.5***						
Sr Nts[3] 9¾s '97	§aO	**D**	10/95	CCC	Z	R			Default 10-1-95 int				150	G1	'92	90	46	49¼	....	Flat
Sr Nts[3] 10¼s 2002	§aO	**D**	10/95	CCC	Z	R			Default 10-1-95				190	G1	'92	81½	46½	49¼	....	Flat
Lone Star Indus (New)	***13a***	***n/a***	***n/a***	***4.08***		***Dc***	***46.90***	***152.0***	***61.70***	***9-30-95***	***78.00***	***237.0***		***32.9***						
• Sr Nts[4] 10s 2003	jJ31	**NR**				R	100	....	100	(7-31-00)	....	....	78.0	Reorg	'94	102	95	101½	9.85	9.71
Long Island Light'g	***75***	***1.89***	***1.87***	***1.94***		***Dc***	***245.0***	***1089***	***961.0***	***9-30-95***	***4723***	***8299***		***61.9***						
• Gen & Ref 8¾s '96	Mn	**BBB–**	12/93	BBB	X	R	NC	....	....	....	Z■100	....	415	L3	'91	101¾	100¼	100⅛	8.74	8.25
• Gen & Ref 8¾s '97	Fa15	**BBB–**	12/93	BBB	X	R	NC	....	....	....	Z■100	....	250	L3	'91	103	100	101¼	8.64	7.56
• Gen & Ref 7⅝s '98	Ao15	**BBB–**			X	R	NC	....	....	....	Z■100	....	100	L3	'94	101½	98	100	7.63	7.62
• Gen & Ref 7.85s '99	Mn15	**BBB–**	12/93	BBB	X	R	NC	....	....	....	Z■100	....	56.0	L3	'92	No Sale		98¾	7.95	8.28
• Gen & Ref 8⅝s 2004	Ao15	**BBB–**			X	R	NC	....	....	....	Z■100	....	185	L3	'94	105¾	93¾	102	8.46	8.28
• Gen & Ref 8½s 2006	Mn15	**BBB–**	12/93	BBB	X	R	104.25	(5-15-97)	....	....	Z■100	....	75.0	L3	'92	103	91½	100⅜	8.47	8.44
• Gen & Ref 7.90s 2008	jJ15	**BBB–**	12/93	BBB	X	R	104.26	(7-15-97)	....	....	Z■100	....	80.0	L3	'92	98¾	86	95⅝	8.26	8.47
• Gen & Ref 9¾s 2021	Mn	**BBB–**	12/93	BBB	X	R	106.77	(5-1-96)	Z100	....	Z■100	....	415	L3	'91	104¼	92½	s102¼	9.54	9.51
• Gen & Ref 9⅝s 2024	jJ	**BBB–**	12/93	BBB	X	R	106.33	(7-1-96)	Z100	....	Z■100	....	375	L3	'91	104	92	s102⅝	9.38	9.36
• Deb 7.30s '99	jJ15	**BB+**	12/93	BBB–	Y	R	NC	....	....	....	....	....	397	L3	'92	101	91	s99¾	7.32	7.38
• Deb 7.30s 2000	Jj15	**BB+**	12/93	BBB–	Y	R	NC	....	....	....	....	....	36.0	L3	'93	98	94	97	7.53	8.18
Deb 6¼s 2001	jJ15	**BB+**	12/93	BBB–	Y	R	NC	....	....	....	....	....	145	L3	'93	96⅛	82⅛	96⅛	6.50	7.11
• Deb 7.05s 2003	Ms15	**BB+**	12/93	BBB–	Y	R	NC	....	....	....	....	....	150	L3	'93	98⅜	81	s97	7.27	7.60
• Deb 7s 2004	Ms	**BB+**	12/93	BBB–	Y	R	NC	....	....	....	....	....	59.0	L3	'93	95½	83	94¼	7.43	7.97
Deb 7⅛s 2005	Jd	**BB+**	12/93	BBB–	Y	R	NC	....	....	....	....	....	200	L3	'93	96¼	79¼	96¼	7.40	7.69
• Deb 7½s 2007	Ms	**BB+**	12/93	BBB–	Y	R	103.54	(3-1-98)	....	....	....	....	142	L3	'93	96½	78½	s95⅝	7.84	8.10
• Deb 8.90s 2019	jJ15	**BB+**	12/93	BBB–	Y	R	106.37	(7-15-97)	....	....	....	....	420	L3	'92	102	81	s98⅝	9.02	9.04
• Deb 9s 2022	mN	**BB+**	12/93	BBB–	Y	R	104.19	(11-1-02)	....	....	....	....	451	L3	'92	104⅞	82	s100⅞	8.92	8.91
• Deb 8.20s 2023	Ms15	**BB+**	12/93	BBB–	Y	R	104	(3-15-03)	....	....	....	....	270	L3	'93	100	76¼	96½	8.50	8.53
Loral Corp	***23i***	***5.81***	***8.67***	***5.53***		***Mr***	***111.0***	***1859***	***1325***	***9-30-95***	***1832***	***3693***		***49.6***						
Sr Deb 9⅛s 2022	Fa	**BBB**	12/93	BBB+	X	R	NC	....	....	....	....	....	100	L3	'92	123⅜	100¾	123⅜	7.40	7.14
• Sr Deb 8⅜s 2023	Jj15	**BBB**	12/93	BBB+	X	BE	NC	....	....	....	....	....	100	L3	'93	97½	97½	95⅝	8.76	8.80
• Sr Deb 7s 2023	mS15	**BBB**	12/93	BBB+	X	BE	NC	....	....	....	....	....	200	L3	'93	96	88	89	7.87	7.99
• Sr Nts 7⅝s 2004	Jd15	**BBB**			X	BE	NC	....	....	....	....	....	250	L3	'94	98½	98½	96⅝	7.89	8.18
• Sr Deb 8⅜s 2024	Jd15	**BBB**			X	BE	NC	....	....	....	....	....	400	L3	'94	No Sale		95⅛	8.80	8.85
• Sr Deb 7⅝s 2025	Jd15	**BBB**			X	R	NC	....	....	....	....	....	150	B5	'95	99	99	97⅛	7.85	7.88
Louis Dreyfus Natural Gas	***73e***	***1.27***	***1.25***	***2.27***		***Dc***	***6.42***	***34.90***	***28.20***	***9-30-95***	***307.0***	***532.0***		***57.7***						
• Sr Sub Nts[5] 9¼s 2004	Jd15	**BB+**			Y	BE	NC	....	....	....	[6]Z109.25	6-14-97	100	D6	'94	No Sale		80	11.56	13.25
Louisiana Land/Exp	***49a***	***1.33***	***0.63***	***d0.37***		***Dc***	***7.60***	***155.0***	***154.0***	***9-30-95***	***712.0***	***1076***		***66.2***						
Deb 7⅝s 2013	Ao15	**BBB**	5/94	BBB+	X	R	NC	....	....	....	....	....	100	M5	'93	104	87½	104	7.33	7.21
Deb 7.65s 2023	jD	**BBB**	5/94	BBB+	X	R	NC	....	....	....	....	....	200	M6	'93	104¼	85⅝	104¼	7.34	7.29
• Nts 8¼s 2002	Jd15	**BBB**	5/94	BBB+	X	R	NC	....	....	....	....	....	100	M6	'92	No Sale		110⅛	7.49	6.32
***Louisiana Power & Light*[7]**	***72a***	***2.89***	***3.14***	***2.99***		***Dc***	***32.10***	***346.0***	***411.0***	***6-30-95***	***1411***	***3003***		***51.6***						
1st 5¾s '96	Ms	**BBB**	1/94	BBB+	X	CR	100	....	100	....	....	....	35.0	E1	'66	100	97¾	100	5.75	5.64
1st 5⅝s '97	Fa	**BBB**	1/94	BBB+	X	CR	100.37	1-31-96	100.37	1-31-96	....	....	16.0	M2	'67	99⅞	95¼	99⅞	5.63	5.74
1st 6½s '97	mS	**BBB**	1/94	BBB+	X	CR	100.30	8-31-96	100.28	8-31-96	....	....	18.0	F1	'67	100½	95⅞	100⅜	6.48	6.25
1st 7⅛s '98	Ms	**BBB**	1/94	BBB+	X	CR	100.60	2-29-96	100.34	2-29-96	....	....	35.0	F1	'68	100⅝	96⅝	100⅝	7.08	6.80
1st 6s 2000	Ms	**BBB**	1/94	BBB+	X	BE	NC	....	Z100	....	....	....	100	K2	'93	99⅜	89½	99⅜	6.04	6.17

Uniform Footnote Explanations-See Page 260. Other: [1] Subsid of Lomas Fin'l Corp. [2] Incl. curr amts. [3] (HRO)For a Redemp Event at 101. [4] Co must offer repurch at 100 on Chge of Ctrl. [5] Co must offer repurch at 101 on Chge of Ctrl. [6] Max $30M red w/proceeds of Cap Stk Off'g. [7] Subsid of Entergy Corp.

Exchange / Individual Issue Statistics / Interest Dates	S&P Debt Rating	Date of Last Rating Change	Prior Rating	Eligible	Bond Form	Regular Price	Regular (Begins) Thru	Sinking Fund Price	Sinking Fund (Begins) Thru	Refund/Other Restriction Price	Refund/Other Restriction (Begins) Thru	Outst'g (Mil $)	Underwriting Firm	Underwriting Year	Price Range 1995 High	Price Range 1995 Low	Mo. End Price Sale(s) or Bid	Curr. Yield	Yield to Mat.
Title-Industry Code & Co. Finances (In Italics) / Ind	***Fixed Charge Coverage 1992***	***1993***	***1994***		***Year End***	***Million $ Cash & Equiv.***	***Curr. Assets***	***Curr. Liab.***	***Balance Sheet Date***	***L. Term Debt (Mil $)***		***Capital-ization (Mil $)***	***Total Debt % Capital***						
***Louisiana Power & Light** (Cont.)*																			
1st 7⅞s 2001 ... Ao	**BBB**	1/94	BBB+	X	R	101.71	3-31-96	100.82	3-31-96	....	....	18.7	E1	'71	102	96¼	102	7.72	7.40
1st 7½s 2002 ... Jj	**BBB**	1/94	BBB+	X	R	101.56	12-31-96	100.60	12-31-96	....	....	23.0	M2	'72	102⅜	93⅞	101⅞	7.36	7.11
1st 7.74s 2002 ... jJ	**BBB**	1/94	BBB+	X	R	102.91	(7-1-97)	Z100	(7-1-97)	....	....	179	K2	'92	104⅝	94¼	104⅝	7.40	6.85
1st 7½s 2002 ... mN	**BBB**	1/94	BBB+	X	R	101.93	10-31-96	100.81	10-31-96	....	....	15.3	B6	'72	102⅝	93¼	102¼	7.33	7.08
1st 8s 2003 ... Jd	**BBB**	1/94	BBB+	X	R	102.27	5-31-96	100.71	5-31-96	....	....	25.6	M6	'73	102⅞	95⅝	102½	7.80	7.55
1st 8¾s 2006 ... jD	**BBB**	1/94	BBB+	X	R	103.50	11-30-96	100.91	11-30-96	....	....	21.9	S1	'76	108	99	103⅞	8.42	8.20
1st 10⅛s 2020 ... Ao	**BBB**	1/94	BBB+	X	R	106.53	3-31-96	100	....	....	....	95.0	S1	'90	106¾	104½	106¾	9.48	9.41
1st 8½s 2022 ... jJ	**BBB**	1/94	BBB+	X	R	106.48	6-30-96	Z100	....	®105.87	6-30-97	90.0	M6	'92	107¼	93¼	107¼	7.93	7.85
Louisville Gas & Electric[1] ... 75	***3.30***	***4.00***	***4.31***		***Dc***	***109.0***	***282.0***	***141.0***	***9-30-95***	***647.0***		***1403***	***47.3***						
1st 5⅝s '96 ... Jd	**AA**	2/75	AAA	X	CR	100	....	100	....	....	....	16.0	K2	'66	100	97	100	5.63	5.60
1st 6¾s '98 ... Jd	**AA**	2/75	AAA	X	R	100.54	5-31-96	100.22	5-31-96	....	....	20.0	F1	'68	100⅝	96	100⅝	6.71	6.46
• 1st 7½s 2002 ... jJ	**AA**	2/75	AAA	X	R	101.85	6-30-96	100.58	9-1-96	....	....	20.0	D4	'72	105	96½	101	7.43	7.30
1st 6s 2003 ... fA15	**AA**			X	R	NC	....	....	....	....	....	42.6	M6	'93	100	83¼	100	6.00	6.00
Louisville & Nash RR ... 55	***See Seaboard Coast Line RR***																		
• 1st Ref F 3⅜s 2003 ... Ao	**BBB+**	3/91	A–	X	CR	101.50	4-1-00	101.625	3-31-00	....	....	31.6	H1	'45	80	68	77¾	4.34	7.39
• 1st Ref G 2⅞s 2003 ... Ao	**BBB+**	3/91	A–	X	CR	100.375	4-1-00	100	....	....	....	29.2	M6	'45	74½	65¼	76	3.78	7.17
Lowe's Cos ... 59l	***7.38***	***8.31***	***8.57***		***Ja***	***143.0***	***1706***	***1082***	***10-31-95***	***★849.0***		***2389***	***31.9***						
Sr Nts 6⅜s 2005 ... jD15	**A–**			X	BE	NC	....	....	....	....	....	100	M2	'95	100⅞	99½	100⅞	6.32	6.26
Lubrizol Corp ... 14	***n/a***	***n/a***	***n/a***		***Dc***	***28.80***	***650.0***	***241.0***	***9-30-95***	***196.0***		***1075***	***19.5***						
Deb 7¼s 2025 ... Jd15	**AA**			X	BE	NC	....	....	....	....	....	100	M6	'95	109⅝	95	109⅝	6.61	6.51
Lukens Inc ... 66d	***4.98***	***2.89***	***3.05***		***Dc***	***5.76***	***309.0***	***168.0***	***7-1-95***	***229.0***		***529.0***	***45.0***						
Nts 7⅝s 2004 ... fA	**BBB+**			X	R	NC	....	....	....	....	....	150	F1	'92	108⅝	93	108⅝	7.02	6.31
Lyondell Petrochemical Co ... 49	***1.44***	***1.28***	***5.80***		***Dc***	***44.00***	***784.0***	***757.0***	***9-30-95***	***732.0***		***1854***	***57.0***						
Nts[2] 9.95s '96 ... Jd	**BBB–**	2/92	BBB	X	R	NC	....	....	....	....	....	150	S1	'89	103¼	101⅝	101⅝	9.79	5.96
Nts 8¼s '97 ... Ms15	**BBB–**			X	BE	NC	....	....	....	....	....	100	L3	'92	103⅛	98⅝	102¾	8.03	5.85
Nts[2] 10s '99 ... Jd	**BBB–**	2/92	BBB	X	R	NC	....	....	....	....	....	150	S1	'89	111½	103½	111½	8.97	6.21
Nts 9⅛s 2002 ... Ms15	**BBB–**			X	BE	NC	....	....	....	....	....	100	L3	'92	113⅞	99⅞	113⅞	8.01	6.38
MacAndrews & Forbes Group ... 26h	***Now Mafco Inc,see***																		
Sub Nts 12¼s '96 ... jJ	**NR**				R	100	....	....	....	....	....	[3]155	D7	'86	100½	99⅞	100¼	12.22	11.72
MacAndrews&Forbes Hldgs ... 26h	....	....	....		***Dc***	***No Recent Fin'ls***													
Sub SF Deb 13s '99 ... Ms	**NR**	7/89	CCC+		R	100	....	100	....	....	....	[3]110	D7	'84	102¼	100⅜	100⅜	12.95	12.83
Madison Gas & Electric ... 75	***3.71***	***4.30***	***4.54***		***Dc***	***0.32***	***51.10***	***44.30***	***9-30-95***	***128.0***		***330.0***	***41.2***						
1st 8½s 2022 ... Ao15	**AA**			X	R	104.25	(4-1-02)	....	....	....	....	40.0	F1	'92	113⅞	97⅜	113⅞	7.46	7.30
1st 7.70s 2028 ... Fa15	**AA**			X	R	104.26	(2-15-03)	....	....	....	....	25.0	F1	'93	107⅛	88½	107⅛	7.19	7.13
[4]Mafco Inc[5] ... 26	***1.56***	***1.73***	***1.98***		***Dc***	***10.70***	***72.50***	***21.10***	***4-2-95***	***114.0***		***75.00***	***163.0***						
Sr Sub Nts[6] 11⅞s 2002 ... mN15	**B**			Y	R	105.9375	(11-15-97)	....	....	....	....	85.0	B5	'92	104	93¾	101½	11.70	11.55
Magellan Health Svcs[7] ... 30	***n/a***	***n/a***	***1.31***		***Sp***	***130.0***	***325.0***	***215.0***	***9-30-94***	***533.0***		***590.0***	***90.3***						
◆Sr Sub Nts 'A'[8] 11¼s 2004 ... Ao15	**B**			Y	R	105.625	(4-15-99)	....	....	....	....	365	Exch.	'94	108	108	108	10.42	9.81
Magma Copper ... 45b	***2.79***	***1.60***	***3.15***		***Dc***	***62.00***	***396.0***	***241.0***	***9-30-95***	***582.0***		***1470***	***39.9***						
Sr Sub Nts 12s 2001 ... jD15	**BB+**	3/94	BB–	Y	R	106	(12-15-96)	....	....	....	....	200	G1	'91	111¼	107½	110⅞	10.82	9.56
Sr Sub Nts 11½s 2002 ... Jj15	**BB+**	3/94	BB–	Y	R	106	1-14-97	....	....	....	....	125	G1	'92	107¾	105¼	106¼	10.82	10.09
Sr Sub Nts 8.70s 2005 ... Mn15	**BB+**			Y	BE	NC	....	....	....	....	....	200	G1	'95	114	97¾	114	7.63	6.67
MagneTek, Inc ... 23	***△1.95***	***△0.24***	***△2.06***		***Je***	***0.31***	***490.0***	***215.0***	***6-30-95***	***431.0***		***566.0***	***79.2***						
Sr Sub Deb[6] 10¾s '98 ... mN15	**B**			Y	R	NC	....	....	....	....	....	125	F1	'91	106¼	99	104	10.34	9.13
Mallinckrodt Group ... 43	***△6.10***	***△7.20***	***△5.86***		***Je***	***88.20***	***1038***	***786.0***	***9-30-95***	***★602.0***		***1957***	***39.5***						
Nts 6¾s 2005 ... mS15	**A–**	11/95	BBB+	X	BE	NC	....	....	....	....	....	100	G1	'95	104	99	104	6.49	6.19

Uniform Footnote Explanations-See Page 260. Other: [1] Subsid of LG&E Energy. [2] (HRO)At 100 for Designated Event&Rat'g Decline. [3] Incl disc. [4] Was MacAndrews & Forbes Co,see. [5] Now Mafco Worldwide Corp. [6] (HRO)On Chge in Ctrl at 101. [7] Was Charter Medical. [8] (HRO)On Chge of Ctrl at 101.

Title-Industry Code & Co. Finances (In Italics) / Individual Issue Statistics — Exchange	Ind / Interest Dates	Fixed Charge Coverage 1992 / S&P Debt Rating	1993 / Date of Last Rating Change	1994 / Prior Rating	Eligible	Year End / Bond Form	Million $ Cash & Equiv. / Regular Price	Million $ Curr. Assets / Regular (Begins) Thru	Million $ Curr. Liab. / Sinking Fund Price	Balance Sheet Date / Sinking Fund (Begins) Thru	L. Term Debt (Mil $) / Refund/Other Restriction Price	Refund/Other Restriction (Begins) Thru	Capital-ization (Mil $) / Outst'g (Mil $)	Total Debt % Capital / Underwriting Firm	Underwriting Year	Price Range 1995 High	Price Range 1995 Low	Mo. End Price Sale(s) or Bid	Curr. Yield	Yield to Mat.
***Mallinckrodt Group** (Cont.)*																				
Nts 6½s 2007	mN15	**A–**			X	BE	NC	....	....	....	....	....	100	M5	'95	101⅝	99	101⅝	6.40	6.30
Manor Care	***30***	*△3.48*	*△5.38*	*△6.57*		*My*	*32.90*	*217.0*	*197.0*	*8-31-95*	*360.0*		*1021*	*35.9*						
Sr Sub Nts 9½s 2002	mN15	**BBB–**	10/94	BB+	X	R	103.56	(11-15-97)	....	....	....	....	150	D4	'92	108¼	102	108	8.80	7.96
[1]Manufacturers & Traders Trust Co	***10***	*5.18*	*3.69*	*3.43*		*Dc*				*9-30-95*	*196.0*		*1006*	*19.5*						
Sub Nts[2] 8⅛s 2002	jD	**BBB+**			X	BE	NC	....	....	....	....	....	75.0	L3	'92	110⅜	95⅜	110⅜	7.36	6.25
Sub Nts[2] 7s 2005	jJ	**BBB+**				BE	NC	....	....	....	....	....	100	M2	'95	104½	96⅝	104½	6.70	6.36
Manufacturers Hanover	***10***	***Merged into Chemical Bkg,see***																		
Nts 8⅛s '97	Jj15	**A**	3/93	A–	X	R	NC	....	....	....	....	....	139	S1	'87	102⅞	99⅝	102½	7.93	5.62
Sub Cap Nts 8½s '99	Fa15	**A–**	3/93	BBB+	X	R	NC	....	....	....	....	....	150	M2	'87	107⅜	99¾	107⅜	7.92	5.88
Manville Corp	***13g***	*1.60*	*1.25*	*1.87*		*Dc*	*410.0*	*1166*	*633.0*	*9-30-95*	*1453*		*2947*	*59.1*						
• Int Def SF Deb[3] 9s 2003	[4]jD31	**B**	11/94	B–	Y	R	100	....	100	....	....	....	[5]26.4	Reorg	'88	101	94	s99½	9.05	9.09
Marathon Oil Co.	***49b***	***Gtd by USX Corp, see***																		
• SF Deb 8½s 2006	mN	**BB+**	9/93	BBB–	Y	R	101.92	10-31-96	100	....	....	....	172	F1	'76	103½	94¼	s102	8.33	8.22
• Gtd[6]Nts[7] 9¾s '99	Ms	**BB+**	9/93	BBB–	Y	R	100	(3-1-96)	....	....	....	....	161	Exch.	'90	103⅛	100¾	s100⅞	9.67	9.42
• [8]Gtd[7]Nts[6] 7s 2002	[9]Jun	**BB+**	9/93	BBB–	Y	R	NC	....	....	....	....	....	134	Exch.	'93	102⅛	88	s100¾	6.95	6.85
Marcus Cable Co L.P./Cap	***12a***	*d0.59*	*d0.79*	*d0.22*		*Dc*	*5.33*	*9.88*	*9.49*	*12-31-94*	*327.0*		*306.0*	*107.0*						
Sr Deb[10] 11⅞s 2005	aO	**B**			Y	R	105.90	(10-1-98)	....	....	[11]Z110	10-1-96	100	G1	'93	107⅝	89½	107⅝	11.03	10.60
Marcus Cable Operating/Cap II	***12a***	***Gtd by Marcus Cable Co L.P.,see***																		
Sr Sub[12]Gtd[13]Disc Nts[14] 13½s 2004	fA	**B**	5/95	B+	Y	R	105	(8-1-99)	....	....	[15]Z110	7-29-97	[5]413	G1	'94	75	52¼	74⅛	....	Flat
Margaretten Financial	***25h***	***Merged into Chemical Banking,see***																		
Nts 6¾s 2000	Jd15	**A+**	7/94	BBB+	X	BE	NC	....	....	....	....	....	150	G1	'93	103	92⅞	103	6.55	5.97
Marine Midland Banks[16]	***10***	*2.44*	*2.51*	*4.74*		*Dc*				*6-30-95*	*711.0*		*2342*	*30.4*						
Sub Cap[17]Nts 8⅝s '97	Ms	**BBB+**	5/91	A–	X	R	NC	....	....	....	Z100	....	125	F1	'87	103¾	100¾	103⅛	8.36	5.82
Mark IV Industries	***8***	*2.24*	*2.63*	*3.05*		*Fb*	*0.90*	*830.0*	*406.0*	*8-31-95*	*638.0*		*1390*	*50.9*						
Sr Sub Nts[18] 8¾s 2003	Ao	**BB+**	1/95	B+	Y	R	104.375	(4-1-98)	....	....	....	....	258	B5	'93	104¾	90¾	104¾	8.35	7.87
Markel Corp	***35b***	*5.04*	*6.70*	*4.35*		*Dc*				*9-30-95*	*118.0*		*312.0*	*37.8*						
Nts 7¼s 2003	mN	**BBB**	9/95	BBB–	X	BE	NC	....	....	....	....	....	100	S5	'93	100⅜	85⅜	100⅜	7.22	7.18
Marriott Corp	***32***	***Now Host Marriott Corp,see***																		
Deb [19] 9⅜s 2007	Jd15	**B**	5/93	BBB	Y	R	NC	....	....	....	....	....	12.6	M2	'87	103	95	103	9.10	8.95
Sr Nts B 9⅝s '96	Fa	**B**	5/93	BBB	Y	R	100	....	....	....	....	....	10.1	F1	'86	100¼	98	100⅛	9.61	7.90
Sr Nts C 8⅛s '96	jD	**B**	5/93	BBB	Y	R	NC	....	....	....	....	....	54.6	S5	'86	99½	98	99½	8.17	8.69
Sr Nts D 8⅞s '97	Mn	**B**	5/93	BBB	Y	R	NC	....	....	....	....	....	16.8	M2	'87	100¼	98	100¼	8.85	8.66
Sr Nts E 9⅞s '97	mN	**B**	5/93	BBB	Y	R	100	....	....	....	....	....	16.5	M2	'87	101	98	100¼	9.85	9.71
Sr Nts K 10¼s 2001	jJ18	**B**	5/93	BBB	Y	R	NC	....	....	....	....	....	7.99	M2	'91	103½	97½	103½	9.90	9.42
Sr Nts L 10s 2012	Mn	**B**	5/93	BBB	Y	R	NC	....	....	....	....	....	10.9	S1	'92	102	96¾	100½	9.95	9.93
Sr Nts M 9½s 2002	Mn	**B**	5/93	BBB	Y	R	NC	....	....	....	....	....	14.0	S1	'92	101	95	100	9.50	9.49
Marriott Int'l	***32***	*10.48*	*6.17*	*11.69*		*Dc*	*269.0*	*1372*	*1500*	*9-8-95*	*687.0*		*1652*	*41.6*						
Sr Nts[20]'A' 6¾s 2003	jD15	**A–**			X	R	NC	....	....	....	....	....	150	L3	'93	102⅜	88½	101½	6.65	6.51
Sr Nts 'B' 7⅞s 2005	Ao15	**A–**			X	BE	NC	....	....	....	....	....	200	L3	'95	109⅜	99⅜	108⅝	7.25	6.62
Sr Nts 'C' 7⅛s 2007	Jd	**A–**			X	BE	NC	....	....	....	....	....	150	L3	'95	103⅞	96¾	103½	6.88	6.68
Sr Nts'D' 6¾s 2009	jD	**A–**			X	BE	NC	....	....	....	....	....	100	M2	'95	100¼	98½	100¼	6.73	6.72
Marshall & Ilsley	***10***	*6.18*	*7.02*	*4.46*		*Dc*				*9-30-95*	*495.0*		*1714*	*28.9*						
Sub Nts 6⅜s 2003	jJ15	**A**			X	BE	NC	....	....	....	....	....	99.0	G1	'93	100½	86¾	100½	6.34	6.29
Martin Marietta Corp	***2a***	***Merged w/Lockheed Corp,see***																		
Deb 7s 2011	Ms15	**A**	3/93	A+	X	R	100	....	....	....	....	....	[5]175	G1	'81	100½	86¼	100	7.00	7.00
Nts 8½s '96	Ms	**A**	3/93	A+	X	R	NC	....	....	....	....	....	100	G1	'91	101½	100½	100½	8.46	5.42

Uniform Footnote Explanations-See Page 260. Other: [1] Subsid & data of First Empire State Corp. [2] Issued in min denom $250T. [3] Int accrues at 9% fr 1-1-94. [4] Due 12-31-03. [5] Incl disc. [6] (HRO)On Chge of Ctrl at 100. [7] Gtd by USX Corp. [8] Int at 9.75% to 3-1-94,7% aft. [9] Int pd monthly. [10] Co must offer repurch at 101 on Chge of Ctrl. [11] Max 25% outstg w/proceeds of Cap Stk Off'g. [12] Gtd by Marcus Cable Co L.P. [13] Int accrues at 13.50% fr 8-1-99. [14] Co must offer repurch on Chge of Ctrl at 101(Accreted Val). [15] Accreted Val(%):Max $103M red w/proceeds Cap Off'g. [16] Acquired by Hongkong & Shanghai Banking. [17] Co may exch for Cap Sec when due. [18] (HRO)On Chge of Ctrl at 101. [19] (HRO)On 6-15-97 at 100. [20] (HRO)For a Put Event at 100.

Title-Industry Code & Co. Finances (In Italics)	Ind	Fixed Charge Coverage 1992	1993	1994		Year End	Million $ Cash & Equiv.	Curr. Assets	Curr. Liab.	Balance Sheet Date	L. Term Debt (Mil $)		Capital-ization (Mil $)	Total Debt % Capital						
Individual Issue Statistics Exchange ↓	Interest Dates	S&P Debt Rating	Date of Last Rating Change	Prior Rating	Eligible ↓	Bond Form	Redemption Provisions: Regular Price	Regular (Begins) Thru	Sinking Fund Price	Sinking Fund (Begins) Thru	Refund/Other Restriction Price	Refund/Other Restriction (Begins) Thru	Outst'g (Mil $)	Underwriting Firm	Underwriting Year	Price Range 1995 High	Price Range 1995 Low	Mo. End Price Sale(s) or Bid	Curr. Yield	Yield to Mat.
***Martin Marietta Corp** (Cont.)*																				
Nts 9s 2003	Ms	**A**	3/93	A+	X	R	NC	....	....	....	....	....	100	G1	'91	116⅛	102¼	116⅛	7.75	6.18
Martin Marietta Materials	***13a***	***55.27***	***23.90***	***14.17***		***Dc***		***279.0***	***200.0***	***9-30-95***	***★173.0***		***588.0***	***29.8***						
Deb 7s 2025	jD	**A**			X	BE	NC	....	....	....	....	....	125	G1	'95	102⅞	99¼	102⅞	6.80	6.77
Martin Marietta Technologies	***2a***	***Gtd by Lockheed Martin,see Lockheed Corp***																		
Deb[1] 7⅜s 2013	Ao15	**A+**	3/95	A	X	R	NC	....	....	....	....	....	150	G1	'93	105⅝	88½	105⅝	6.98	6.81
Deb[1] 7¾s 2023	Ao15	**A+**	3/95	A	X	R	103.735	(4-15-03)	....	....	....	....	150	G1	'93	106⅝	88⅛	106⅝	7.27	7.19
Nts[1] 6½s 2003	Ao15	**A+**	3/95	A	X	R	NC	....	....	....	....	....	400	G1	'93	101¾	88⅜	101¾	6.39	6.20
Marvel (Parent) Holdings	***54***	***n/a***	***n/a***	***1.38***		***Dc***	***24.70***	***498.0***	***282.0***	***9-30-95***	***1142***		***1196***	***95.9***						
Sr Sec Disc[2]Nts Zero Cpn '98	[3]	**B–**	7/95	B	Y	R	100	....	....	....	[4]....	....	[5]252	B5	'93	73¼	60¾	70	....	16.17
Maryland Cable Corp	***12a***	....	....	....		***Dc***	***No Recent Fin'ls***													
Sr[6]Sub[7]Disc Nts 15⅜s '98	[8]mN15	**NR**	12/94	D		R	100	....	....	....	....	....	[5]162	M2	'88	33	33	A33	....	Flat
Masco Corp	***13f***	***2.21***	***3.98***	***5.05***		***Dc***	***84.60***	***2033***	***635.0***	***9-30-95***	***1656***		***4038***	***42.4***						
Deb 7⅛s 2013	fA15	**BBB+**			X	R	NC	....	....	....	....	....	200	S1	'93	103⅜	85	103⅜	6.89	6.79
Nts 9s '96	Ao15	**BBB+**			X	R	NC	....	....	....	....	....	250	S1	'91	102¼	100⅞	100⅞	8.92	5.87
Nts 6⅝s '99	mS15	**BBB+**			X	R	NC	....	....	....	....	....	200	S1	'92	102¾	92¾	102¾	6.45	5.79
Nts 9s 2001	aO	**BBB+**			X	R	NC	....	....	....	....	....	175	S1	'91	114⅛	102⅛	114⅛	7.89	6.05
Nts 6⅛s 2003	mS15	**BBB+**			X	R	NC	....	....	....	....	....	200	S1	'93	99⅜	85¼	99⅜	6.16	6.23
Massachusetts Electric[9]	***72a***	***3.14***	***2.28***	***3.05***		***Dc***	***1.17***	***222.0***	***294.0***	***6-30-95***	***333.0***		***845.0***	***49.0***						
1st T(93-1) 8.15s 2023	[10]jj	**A+**			X	BE	106.11	(2-1-98)	Z100	(2-1-98)	....	....	10.0	C5	'93	110⅛	92⅞	110⅛	7.40	7.29
1st T(93-2) 7.09s 2003	[11]jj	**A+**			X	BE	NC	....	....	....	....	....	20.0	K2	'93	104⅜	92⅛	104⅜	6.79	6.31
1st T(93-3) 7.98s 2023	[12]jj	**A+**			X	BE	105.98	(2-1-98)	Z100	(2-1-98)	....	....	10.0	K2	'93	108⅜	91¼	108⅜	7.36	7.27
1st T(93-4) 7.69s 2023	[13]jj	**A+**			X	BE	103.84	(2-1-03)	Z100	(2-1-03)	....	....	10.0	C5	'93	106	88⅞	106	7.25	7.18
1st T(93-5) 6.40s 2003	[14]jj	**A+**			X	BE	NC	....	....	....	....	....	10.0	K2	'93	100¼	87⅝	100¼	6.38	6.36
1st T(93-7) 6.66s 2008	[15]jj	**A+**			X	BE	NC	....	....	....	....	....	5.00	K2	'93	101⅛	85	101⅛	6.59	6.53
1st T(93-8) 6.66s 2008	[16]jj	**A+**			X	BE	NC	....	....	....	....	....	5.00	C5	'93	101⅛	85	101⅛	6.59	6.53
1st T(93-9) 7½s 2023	[17]jj	**A+**			X	BE	103.75	(6-30-03)	Z100	(6-30-03)	....	....	7.00	K2	'93	104	86⅞	104	7.21	7.17
1st T(93-10) 6.11s 2008	[18]jj	**A+**			X	BE	NC	....	....	....	....	....	10.0	K2	'93	96⅜	80⅜	96⅜	6.34	6.53
1st T(93-11) 6⅜s 2008	[19]jj	**A+**			X	BE	NC	....	....	....	....	....	10.0	K2	'93	98⅝	82⅜	98⅝	6.46	6.53
1st U(93-1) 6.24s 2003	[20]ms	**A+**			X	BE	NC	....	....	....	....	....	5.00	C5	'93	99	86¼	99	6.30	6.40
1st U(93-2) 7.20s 2023	[21]ms	**A+**			X	BE	103.60	(11-1-03)	Z100	(11-1-03)	....	....	10.0	C5	'93	100½	83¾	100½	7.16	7.16
1st U(94-1) 7.05s 2024	[22]ms	**A+**			X	BE	103.53	(2-2-04)	Z100	(2-2-04)	....	....	10.0	C5	'94	100¾	83	100¾	7.00	6.99
1st U(94-2) 8.08s 2024	[23]ms	**A+**			X	BE	104.04	(5-2-04)	Z100	(5-2-04)	....	....	5.00	C5	'94	110⅞	92⅞	110⅞	7.29	7.18
1st U(94-3) 8.03s 2024	[24]ms	**A+**			X	BE	104.02	(6-14-04)	Z100	(6-14-04)	....	....	5.00	C5	'94	110⅜	92⅜	110⅜	7.28	7.17
1st U(94-4) 8.16s 2024	[25]ms	**A+**			X	BE	104.08	(8-9-04)	....	....	....	....	5.00	C5	'94	114¼	94⅝	114¼	7.14	7.00
Mattel,Inc	***40h***	***4.92***	***6.62***	***9.40***		***Dc***	***101.0***	***2079***	***1209***	***9-30-95***	***464.0***		***2023***	***36.6***						
• Sr Nts 6⅞s '97	fA	**A–**	4/95	BBB+	X	R	NC	....	....	....	....	....	100	M6	'92	No Sale		100⅛	6.87	6.79
Nts 6¾s 2000	Mn15	**A–**	4/95	BBB+	X	R	NC	....	....	....	....	....	100	M6	'93	102½	92⅛	102½	6.59	6.09
F/R[26]M-T Nts 'A' 6.0937s '96	[27]Qmar29	**A–**	4/95	BBB+	X	BE	NC	....	....	....	....	....	15.0	M6	'94	100	99⅞	100	6.09	Mat.
M-T Nts 'A' 8s '99	[28]mn15	**A–**	4/95	BBB+	X	BE	NC	....	....	....	....	....	15.0	M6	'94	107¼	97⅝	107¼	7.46	5.84
M-T Nts 'A' 8s '99	[29]mn15	**A–**	4/95	BBB+	X	BE	NC	....	....	....	....	....	15.0	M6	'94	107¼	97⅝	107¼	7.46	5.84
M-T Nts 'A' 8½s 2001	[30]mn15	**A–**	4/95	BBB+	X	BE	NC	....	....	....	....	....	20.5	M6	'94	111⅞	100	111⅞	7.60	6.09
M-T Nts 'A' 8.48s 2001	[31]mn15	**A–**	4/95	BBB+	X	BE	NC	....	....	....	....	....	10.0	M6	'94	111⅞	100	111⅞	7.58	6.07
M-T Nts 'A' 7.65s 2002	[32]mn15	**A–**	4/95	BBB+	X	BE	NC	....	....	....	....	....	30.0	M6	'95	108	100	108	7.08	6.09
M-T Nts 'A' 8.55s 2004	[33]mn15	**A–**	4/95	BBB+	X	BE	NC	....	....	....	....	....	20.0	M6	'94	113	100	113	7.57	6.60
M-T Nts 'A' 7.20s 2007	[34]mn15	**A–**			X	BE	NC	....	....	....	....	....	30.0	M6	'95	106¾	98⅜	106¾	6.74	6.36
Maui Electric Co Ltd	***72a***	***Gtd by Hawaiian Electric Co,see***																		
Nts 5.15s '96	jD	**BBB+**	5/95	BBB	X	BE	NC	....	....	....	....	....	10.0	S5	'93	99⅝	91	99½	5.18	5.71

Uniform Footnote Explanations-See Page 260. Other: [1] Gtd by Martin Marietta Corp. [2] (HRO)On Chge of Ctrl at a Put Amt. [3] Due 4-15-98. [4] On Chge of Ctrl in whole at price of Accreted Val&Premium. [5] Incl disc. [6] (HRO)On Chge of Ctrl,as defined. [7] Int accrues at 15.375% fr 11-15-93. [8] Due 11-15-98. [9] Contr by New Eng Elec Sys. [10] Due 1-20-23. [11] Due 1-27-03. [12] Due 1-27-23. [13] Due 2-24-23. [14] Due 6-24-03. [15] Due 6-23-08. [16] Due 6-30-08. [17] Due 6-29-23. [18] Due 9-8-08. [19] Due 11-17-08. [20] Due 11-17-03. [21] Due 11-15-23. [22] Due 2-2-24. [23] Due 5-2-24. [24] Due 6-14-24. [25] Due 8-9-24. [26] Int to 12-29-95,adj qtrly(3 Mo LIBOR&0.125%). [27] Due 1-29-96. [28] Due 10-14-99. [29] Due 10-17-99. [30] Due 12-10-01. [31] Due 12-12-01. [32] Due 4-4-02. [33] Due 12-13-04. [34] Due 5-24-07.

Title-Industry Code & Co. Finances (In Italics) / Individual Issue Statistics (Exchange)	Ind / Interest Dates	1992 / S&P Debt Rating	1993 / Date of Last Rating Change	Prior Rating	1994 / Eligible	Year End / Bond Form	Million $ Cash & Equiv. / Regular Price	Curr. Assets / Regular (Begins) Thru	Curr. Liab. / Sinking Fund Price	Balance Sheet Date / Sinking Fund (Begins) Thru	L. Term Debt (Mil $) / Refund/Other Restriction Price	Refund/Other Restriction (Begins) Thru	Capital-ization (Mil $) / Outst'g (Mil $)	Total Debt % Capital / Underwriting Firm	Underwriting Year	Price Range 1995 High	Price Range 1995 Low	Mo. End Price Sale(s) or Bid	Curr. Yield	Yield to Mat.
Maxus Energy	***49a***	***1.56***	***1.33***		***0.62***	***Dc***	***144.0***	***414.0***	***171.0***	***12-31-94***	***971.0***		***1192***	***81.9***						
• SF Deb 8½s 2008	Ao	**BB–**	6/94	BB	Y	R	101.76	3-31-96	100	....	....	....	97.7	L3	'78	97⅞	73¼	s96	8.85	9.04
SF Deb 11¼s 2013	Mn	**BB–**	6/94	BB	Y	R	104.145	4-30-96	100	....	....	....	20.5	L3	'83	102⅛	80½	101¾	11.06	11.02
SF Deb 11½s 2015	mN15	**BB–**	6/94	BB	Y	R	105.168	11-14-96	100	(11-15-96)	....	....	109	S4	'85	103¼	80	103¼	11.14	11.09
Nts 9⅞s 2002	aO15	**BB–**	6/94	BB	Y	BE	100	(10-15-99)	....	....	....	....	250	F1	'92	100⅝	79	100⅝	9.81	9.74
Nts 9½s 2003	Fa15	**BB–**	6/94	BB	Y	BE	100	(2-15-00)	....	....	....	....	100	M2	'93	98⅝	78	98⅝	9.63	9.77
Nts 9⅜s 2003	mN	**BB–**	6/94	BB	Y	BE	NC	....	....	....	....	....	200	F1	'93	98⅝	77½	98⅝	9.51	9.62
Nts'B' 9⅜s 2003	mN	**BB–**	6/94	BB	Y	BE	NC	....	....	....	....	....	60.0	C5	'94	101⅛	77½	101⅛	9.27	9.17
M-T Nts 'C' 10.83s 2004	[1]fa15	**BB–**			Y	BE	NC	....	....	....	....	....	40.0	L3	'94	107⅜	82⅛	107⅜	10.09	9.56
MAXXAM Group[2]	***5***	***1.01***	***0.78***		***d0.03***	***Dc***	***69.80***	***166.0***	***55.00***	***9-30-95***	***762.0***		***659.0***	***118.0***						
Sr Sec Nts[3] 11¼s 2003	fA	**B–**			Y	R	105.50	(8-1-98)	....	....	....	....	100	D6	'93	99½	92½	97½	11.54	11.75
Sr Disc Nts[4] 12¼s 2003	fA	**B–**			Y	R	106.125	(8-1-98)	....	....	[5]Z110	7-31-97	[6]127	D6	'93	78⅝	54½	78⅝	15.58	17.42
MAXXAM Inc[7]	***5***	***0.93***	***d0.04***		***d0.03***	***Dc***	***131.0***	***1146***	***587.0***	***9-30-95***	***1620***		***1546***	***107.0***						
◆Sr Sub Nts[8] 14s 2000	Mn20	**B–**	10/89	NR	Y	R	100	....	....	....	....	....	[6]25.0	Mgr	'88	108	101	s103½	13.53	12.92
◆Sub SF Deb 12½s '99	jD15	**NR**				R	100	....	100	....	....	....	22.6	Exch.	'79	105	100¾	s101½	12.32	12.01
May Department Stores[9]	***59f***	***4.13***	***5.44***		***5.98***	***Ja***	***28.00***	***5420***	***2109***	***10-28-95***	***3456***		***7816***	***44.9***						
Deb 9⅞s 2000	Jd15	**A**	10/90	A+	X	R	NC	....	....	....	....	....	200	M6	'88	115⅝	105¾	115⅝	8.54	5.84
Deb 9⅞s 2002	jD	**A**			X	R	NC	....	....	....	....	....	175	M6	'90	121⅜	107½	121⅜	8.14	6.05
Deb 10⅝s 2010	mN	**A**	12/90	NR	X	R	NC	....	....	....	....	....	150	M6	'90	139⅛	115⅛	139⅛	7.64	6.48
Deb 7⅝s 2013	fA15	**A**			X	R	NC	....	....	....	....	....	125	M6	'95	108¾	98⅞	108¾	7.01	6.77
Deb 7½s 2015	Jd	**A**			X	R	NC	....	....	....	....	....	100	M6	'95	107⅝	95⅞	107⅝	6.97	6.79
Deb 9¼s 2016	Ms	**A**	10/90	A+	X	R	105.09	2-29-96	100	(3-1-97)	®104.63	2-28-96	112	M6	'86	106⅛	102⅝	105⅜	8.78	8.68
Deb 9⅛s 2016	jD	**A**	10/90	A+	X	R	105.02	11-30-96	100	(12-1-97)	®104.56	11-30-96	150	M6	'86	107	99⅛	105¼	8.67	8.58
Deb 9⅞s 2017	Jd	**A**	10/90	A+	X	R	105.93	5-31-96	100	(6-1-98)	®104.94	5-31-97	100	M6	'87	110⅜	104⅞	106¼	9.29	9.20
Deb 10¾s 2018	Jd15	**A**	10/90	A+	X	R	106.988	6-14-96	100	(6-15-99)	®105.375	6-14-98	55.0	M6	'88	107¾	107¼	107⅜	10.01	9.92
Deb 10¼s 2021	Jj	**A**			X	R	NC	....	....	....	....	....	100	M6	'91	141	114¼	141	7.27	6.81
Deb 9⅞s 2021	Jd15	**A**			X	R	104.563	(6-15-01)	100	(6-15-02)	....	....	100	M6	'91	120⅝	108	120⅝	8.19	7.97
Deb 8⅜s 2022	aO	**A**			X	R	104.044	(10-1-02)	100	(10-1-03)	....	....	200	M6	'92	112	95⅝	112	7.48	7.34
Deb 8⅜s 2024	fA	**A**			X	R	104.188	(8-1-04)	[10]100	7-31-05	....	....	200	M6	'94	113½	95⅛	113½	7.38	7.25
Deb 8⅛s 2035	fA15	**A**			X	R	100	(8-15-15)	....	....	....	....	150	M6	'95	113	99⅞	113	7.19	7.13
Deb 7.60s 2025	Jd	**A**			X	R	NC	....	....	....	....	....	100	M6	'95	108⅞	96	108⅞	6.98	6.89
[11]Amortizing Deb 9¾s 2021	Fa15	**A**			X	R	NC	....	....	....	....	....	125	M6	'91	133¾	110⅝	133¾	7.29	....
[12]Amortizing Deb 9½s 2021	Ao15	**A**			X	R	NC	....	....	....	....	....	150	M6	'91	131⅞	107¼	131⅞	7.20	....
Nts 7.15s 2004	fA15	**A**			X	R	NC	....	....	....	....	....	125	M6	'95	106⅜	99⅝	106⅜	6.72	6.18
Mayfair Super Markets	***59c***	***0.92***	***0.62***		***0.06***	***Au***	***6.73***	***38.70***	***54.60***	***9-3-94***	***137.0***		***116.0***	***126.0***						
Sr Sub Nts[4] 11¾s 2003	Ms30	**NR**	9/95	B–		R	105.25	(3-30-98)	100	(3-30-01)	....	....	75.0	B5	'93	116	83	116	10.13	8.72
Maytag Corp	***23d***	***2.32***	***2.86***		***4.43***	***Dc***	***135.0***	***1005***	***359.0***	***9-30-95***	***537.0***		***1235***	***43.7***						
Nts 8⅞s '97	jJ	**BBB+**	4/92	A–	X	R	NC	....	....	....	....	....	100	G1	'87	104⅞	101⅛	104⅝	8.48	5.63
Nts[13] 8⅞s '99	jJ15	**BBB+**	4/92	A–	X	R	NC	....	....	....	....	....	175	G1	'89	109⅞	101⅛	109⅞	8.08	5.75
Nts 9¾s 2002	Mn15	**BBB+**	4/92	A–	X	R	NC	....	....	....	....	....	200	G1	'90	119⅜	106¼	119⅜	8.17	6.04
MBIA Inc	***35c***	***12.90***	***13.05***		***13.13***	***Dc***				***9-30-95***	***299.0***		***2412***	***13.3***						
Deb 8.20s 2022	aO	**AA**	8/95	AA+	X	BE	103.988	(10-1-02)	....	....	....	....	100	D6	'92	112⅛	94½	112⅛	7.31	7.17
Nts 9s 2001	Fa15	**AA**	8/95	AA+	X	R	NC	....	....	....	....	....	100	D6	'91	113⅛	102⅝	113⅛	7.96	5.99
Nts 9⅜s 2011	Fa15	**AA**	8/95	AA+	X	R	NC	....	....	....	....	....	100	D6	'91	129¼	105¾	129¼	7.25	6.34
MBNA America Bank,NA	***10***	***Subsid of MBNA Corp,see***																		
Sub Nts[14] 7¼s 2002	mS15	**BBB+**	9/93	BBB	X	BE	NC	....	....	....	....	....	200	M2	'92	105⅝	91⅝	105⅝	6.86	6.21
MBNA Corp[15]	***10***	***n/a***	***11.07***		***6.17***	***Dc***				***9-30-95***	***2509***		***3565***	***70.4***						
• Sr Nts 6⅞s '99	aO	**BBB+**	9/93	BBB	X	BE	NC	....	....	....	....	....	150	M2	'92	No Sale		84	8.18	12.32

Uniform Footnote Explanations-See Page 260. Other: [1] Due 9-1-04. [2] Subsid of MAXXAM Inc. [3] (HRO)On Chge of Ctrl at 100. [4] (HRO)On Chge of Ctrl at 101. [5] Accreted Val(%):max $44.4M w/proceeds Eq Off'g. [6] Incl disc. [7] Was McCulloch Oil,MCO Hldgs. [8] Int reset fr 13.5%,5-20-89,16%,11-15-91. [9] See Assoc Dry Goods. [10] Fr 8-1-05. [11] Deb prin will amortize ea F&A 15 fr 8-15-01. [12] Deb prin will amortize ea A&O 15 fr 10-15-01. [13] (HRO)At 100 for Designated Event&Rat'g Decline. [14] Issued in min denom $100T. [15] See MBNA America Bank,NA.

Title-Industry Code & Co. Finances (In Italics) / Individual Issue Statistics (Exchange)	Ind / Interest Dates	Fixed Charge Coverage 1992 / S&P Debt Rating	1993 / Date of Last Rating Change	1994 / Prior Rating	Eligible	Year End / Bond Form	Million $ Cash & Equiv. / Redemption Provisions: Regular Price	Curr. Assets / Regular (Begins) Thru	Curr. Liab. / Sinking Fund Price	Balance Sheet Date / Sinking Fund (Begins) Thru	L. Term Debt (Mil $) / Refund/Other Restriction Price	Refund/Other Restriction (Begins) Thru	Capitalization (Mil $) / Outst'g (Mil $)	Total Debt % Capital / Underwriting Firm	Underwriting Year	Price Range 1995 High	Price Range 1995 Low	Mo. End Price Sale(s) or Bid	Curr. Yield	Yield to Mat.
***MBNA Corp** (Cont.)*																				
Sr Nts 6⅞s 2005	Jd	BBB+			X	BE	NC	....	....	....	....	....	100	M2	'95	102⅝	97⅜	102⅝	6.70	6.50
M-T Sr Nts[1] 6.15s 2003	[2]fa15	BBB+			X	BE	NC	....	....	....	....	....	100	B5	'93	99½	85	99½	6.18	6.23
McCormick & Co	*26*	*5.45*	*5.82*	*5.07*		*Nv*	*30.50*	*695.0*	*702.0*	*8-31-95*	*350.0*		*1219*	*60.1*						
Nts 8.95s 2001	jJ	A			X	BE	NC	....	....	....	....	....	74.3	F1	'91	114⅝	100½	114⅝	7.81	5.81
McCrory Corp[3]	*59d*	*d2.69*	*d23.38*	*d5.78*		*Ja*	***Bankruptcy Chapt 11***				*[4]404.0*		*166.0*	*257.0*						
• Sub SF Deb[5] 7½s '94	§Mn15	NR			Z	R			Default 5-15-92 int				14.8	Exch.	'69	13	1¼	s3	....	Flat
• Sub SF Deb[5] 7¾s '95	§mS15	NR	3/95	D	Z	R			Default 3-15-92 int				[6]14.7	Exch.	'73	13	1½	s2½	....	Flat
• Sub SF Deb[7] 7⅝s '97	§jD15	NR	3/95	D	Z	R			Default 6-15-92 int				[6]11.8	Exch.	'72	17	2	s2	....	Flat
McDermott Inc[8]	*49e*	*0.48*	*0.53*	*d1.50*		*Mr*	*173.0*	*1023*	*846.0*	*6-30-95*	*423.0*		*1159*	*48.3*						
Nts 9⅜s 2002	Ms15	BBB–			X	BE	NC	....	....	....	....	....	225	G1	'92	113⅝	101⅜	113½	8.26	6.68
McDonald's Corp.	*27b*	*4.56*	*5.73*	*6.43*		*Dc*	*318.0*	*913.0*	*1938*	*9-30-95*	*3979*		*12999*	*37.1*						
• Deb 8⅞s 2011	Ao	AA			X	R	NC	....	....	....	....	....	100	M5	'91	119½	108	111⅛	7.99	7.63
• Deb 7.05s 2025	mN15	AA			X	BE	103.26	(11-15-05)	....	....	....	....	150	M5	'95	99⅜	99⅜	90	7.83	7.93
• Deb 7⅜s 2033	jJ15	AA			X	R	104.635	(7-15-03)	....	....	....	....	200	S1	'93	105⅜	87⅝	105⅛	7.02	6.99
• Nts 9¾s '99	Jj15	CALL	11/95	AA		R			Called 1-15-96 at 100				100	S1	'89	104⅝	100⅛	100⅛	9.74	Call
• Nts 7⅜s 2002	jJ15	AA			X	R	100	(7-15-99)	....	....	....	....	150	S1	'92	105¾	94⅛	104⅛	7.08	6.59
• Nts 6¾s 2003	Fa15	AA			X	R	100	(2-15-00)	....	....	....	....	125	M5	'93	104⅜	90⅝	s103	6.55	6.22
• Nts 6⅝s 2005	mS	AA			X	BE	100	(9-1-02)	....	....	....	....	150	M6	'95	102	98	99	6.69	6.77
McDonnell Douglas	*2a*	*3.20*	*2.81*	*4.69*		*Dc*	*660.0*			*9-30-95*	*2558*		*6644*	*38.5*						
• Deb 9¾s 2012	Ao	BBB			X	R	NC	....	....	....	....	....	350	M2	'92	127½	105½	127⅛	7.67	6.94
• Nts 8⅝s '97	Ao	BBB			X	R	NC	....	....	....	....	....	250	M2	'92	103⅞	100¼	103¼	8.35	5.89
• Nts 8¼s 2000	jJ	BBB			X	BE	NC	....	....	....	....	....	200	M2	'93	108⅛	98⅞	s107	7.71	6.44
• Nts 9¼s 2002	Ao	BBB			X	R	NC	....	....	....	....	....	350	M2	'92	116¼	102⅛	115⅛	8.03	6.28
McDonnell Douglas Finance	*25*	*1.33*	*1.35*	....		*Dc*	*10.90*			*9-30-95*	*1212*		*1513*	*82.1*						
F/R[9]M-T Nts 'IX'[1] 6.21s '96	QMay28	BBB			X	BE	NC	....	....	....	....	....	30.0	M2	'94	100	99⅝	100	6.21	....
Sr M-T Nts 'IX'[1] 6.90s '96	[10]ms15	BBB			X	BE	NC	....	....	....	....	....	30.0	P4	'95	100⅞	99⅞	100⅝	6.86	5.71
F/R[9]M-T Nts 'IX'[1] 6.29s '97	QMay27	BBB			X	BE	NC	....	....	....	....	....	30.0	M2	'94	100	99½	100	6.29	....
F/R[9]M-T Nts 'IX'[1] 6.58s '98	QMay28	BBB			X	BE	NC	....	....	....	....	....	30.0	M2	'94	100⅝	99¼	100½	6.55	....
F/R[9]M-T Nts 'IX'[1] 6.58s '99	QMay28	BBB			X	BE	NC	....	....	....	....	....	30.0	M2	'94	100¾	99	100⅝	6.54	....
Sub M-T Nts 'IX'[1] 8.31s 2004	[11]jj15	BBB–			X	BE	NC	....	....	....	....	....	20.0	C1	'94	112½	95½	112½	7.39	6.40
[12]McGaw, Inc	*43*	*n/a*	*n/a*	*6.70*		*Dc*	*29.50*	*607.0*	*188.0*	*9-30-95*	*290.0*		*1048*	*28.4*						
Sr[13]Nts 10⅜s '99	Ao	BB+	3/94	B+	Y	R	104.15	3-31-96	....	....	®100	3-31-97	91.0	D6	'92	103½	101⅛	103½	10.02	9.10
McGraw-Hill Companies	*54*	*7.72*	*8.37*	*7.62*		*Dc*	*4.92*	*1323*	*1084*	*9-30-95*	*657.0*		*1807*	*44.0*						
Nts[14] 9.43s 2000	mS	[15]...				R	NC	....	....	....	....	....	250	M6	'90	114⅞	104	114⅞	8.21	5.75
MCI Communications	*67b*	*5.42*	*5.12*	*9.37*		*Dc*	*1235*	*4477*	*3898*	*9-30-95*	*2905*		*12292*	*24.9*						
Sr Deb 8¼s 2023	Jj20	A–	10/93	BBB+	X	BE	103.74	(1-20-03)	....	....	....	....	200	M2	'93	111¾	92¾	111¾	7.38	7.25
Sr Deb 7¾s 2024	Ms15	A–	10/93	BBB+	X	BE	103.665	(3-15-03)	....	....	....	....	240	M2	'93	107½	88⅝	107½	7.21	7.13
Sr Deb 7¾s 2025	Ms23	A–			X	BE	103.469	(3-23-04)	....	....	....	....	450	M2	'94	108⅛	88⅝	108⅛	7.17	7.09
Sr Nts 7⅝s '96	mN7	A–	10/93	BBB+	X	BE	NC	....	....	....	....	....	250	M2	'91	102¼	99⅜	101¾	7.49	5.49
Sr Nts 6¼s '99	Ms23	A–			X	BE	NC	....	....	....	....	....	300	M2	'94	101¾	92⅝	101¾	6.14	5.65
Sr Nts 7⅛s 2000	Jj20	A–	10/93	BBB+	X	BE	NC	....	....	....	....	....	200	M2	'93	104¾	95	104¾	6.80	5.79
Sr Nts 7½s 2004	fA20	A–	10/93	BBB+	X	BE	NC	....	....	....	....	....	400	M2	'92	109⅝	94⅜	109⅝	6.84	6.05
Sr[16]F/R Nts 6.0337s '99	QMar16	A–			X	BE	NC	....	....	....	....	....	200	M2	'94	100¼	99	100	6.03	....
McKesson Corp	*19*	*4.28*	*4.15*	*d0.65*		*Mr*	*766.0*	*2769*	*1800*	*9-30-95*	*456.0*		*1676*	*33.7*						
Nts 8⅝s '98	Fa	A+			X	R	NC	....	....	....	....	....	49.0	M6	'91	106¼	100½	106¼	8.12	5.42
MDU Resources Group	*75*	*2.83*	*3.33*	*3.31*		*Dc*	*37.10*	*150.0*	*152.0*	*9-30-95*	*233.0*		*603.0*	*42.0*						
1st 9⅛s 2006	Mn15	A	3/92	A–	X	R	106.36	5-14-96	Z100	(11-15-97)	®105.73	5-14-96	50.0	K2	'91	107	93	107	8.53	8.11

Uniform Footnote Explanations-See Page 260. Other: [1] Issued in min denom $100T. [2] Due 10-1-03. [3] Subsid of Rapid-American. [4] Incl Chapt 11 liabs. [5] Prop exch for new 10.25% Sub Deb in reorg. [6] Incl disc. [7] Prop reinstatement under reorg plan. [8] Subsid of McDermott Int'l. [9] Int thru 11-30-95,adj qtrly aft. [10] Due 7-15-96. [11] Due 8-16-04. [12] Merged into & data of IVAX Corp. [13] On Chge in Ctrl,Co must offer repurch at 101. [14] Int subj to adj for Designated Event&Rat'g Chge. [15] S&P is a div of McGraw-Hill Cos, debt not rated. [16] Int to 3-14-96,adj qtrly aft(3 Mo LIBOR&0.19%).

Title-Industry Code & Co. Finances (In Italics) / Individual Issue Statistics — Exchange	Ind / Interest Dates	Fixed Charge Coverage 1992 / S&P Debt Rating	1993 / Date of Last Rating Change	1994 / Prior Rating	Eligible	Year End / Bond Form	Cash & Equiv. (Million $) / Regular Price	Curr. Assets / Regular (Begins) Thru	Curr. Liab. / Sinking Fund Price	Balance Sheet Date / Sinking Fund (Begins) Thru	L. Term Debt (Mil $) / Refund/Other Restriction Price	Refund/Other Restriction (Begins) Thru	Capital-ization (Mil $) / Outst'g (Mil $)	Total Debt % Capital / Underwriting Firm	Underwriting Year	Price Range 1995 High	Low	Mo. End Price Sale(s) or Bid	Curr. Yield	Yield to Mat.
***MDU Resources Group** (Cont.)*																				
1st 9⅛s 2016	aO	A	3/92	A–	X	R	106.69	9-30-96	Z100	(11-15-97)	®106.08	9-30-96	20.0	G1	'91	108⅜	99	106⅞	8.54	8.42
Mead Corp	***50***	*2.67*	*2.82*	*2.24*		*Dc*	*337.0*	*1470*	*825.0*	*10-1-95*	*704.0*		*2927*	*26.7*						
Deb 8⅛s 2023	Fa	A–	11/94	BBB+	X	BE	103.68	(2-1-03)	....	....	....	....	150	G1	'93	110½	92⅞	110½	7.35	7.23
Deb 7⅛s 2025	fA	A–	11/94	BBB+	X	BE	103	(8-1-03)	....	....	....	....	150	S5	'93	101⅜	82⅞	101⅜	7.03	7.01
Med-Term[1]Nts 'A' 8½s '96	[2]ms15	A–	11/94	BBB+	X	BE	NC	....	....	....	....	....	100	G1	'91	102⅛	100¾	101⅛	8.41	5.41
***Mediplex Group**[3]*	***30***	*4.56*	*3.84*	*[4]3.14*		*Dc*	*12.40*	*141.0*	*32.80*	*6-30-95*	*369.0*		*740.0*	*50.3*						
• Sr Sub Nts[5] 11¾s 2002	aO	NR	1/95	B–		R	103.357	(10-1-97)	....	....	....	....	6.18	S5	'92	108	94⅛	102	11.52	11.31
*[6]**MEDIQ/PRN Life Support Svcs***	***43***	*1.38*	*1.04*	*0.39*		*Sp*	*0.50*	*100.0*	*74.90*	*3-31-95*	*249.0*		*334.0*	*88.6*						
Sr Sec Nts[7] 11⅛s '99	jJ	B	9/94	B+	Y	R	103.50	(7-1-97)	....	....	....	....	100	D4	'92	106½	91	106½	10.45	8.92
Meditrust	***57***	*1.88*	*2.02*	*2.19*		*Dc*				*9-30-95*	*750.0*		*1778*	*42.8*						
• Nts 7⅜s 2000	jJ15	BBB–			X	BE	[8]Z100	....	....	....	....	....	125	G1	'95	99¾	98½	104⅜	7.07	6.25
• Nts 7.60s 2001	jJ15	BBB–			X	BE	[8]Z100	....	....	....	....	....	80.0	G1	'95	99⅞	98⅜	105⅝	7.20	6.38
Megafoods Stores	***59c***	*1.33*	*d8.34*	....		*Dc*	***Bankruptcy Chapt 11***				*145.0*		*173.0*	*91.2*						
Sr Nts 10¼s 2000	§aO15	D	8/94	C	Z	R				Default 10-15-94 int			100	P1	'93	29	15	15	....	Flat
*[9]**Mellon Fin'l***	***25***	*3.32*	*4.88*	*4.80*		*Dc*				*9-30-95*	*1642*		*5335*	*30.8*						
Sr[10]Nts 6½s '97	jD	A	8/94	A–	X	BE	NC	....	....	....	....	....	200	F1	'93	101½	95⅜	101½	6.40	5.66
Sr[10]Nts 7⅝s '99	mN15	A	8/94	A–	X	BE	NC	....	....	....	....	....	200	G1	'92	106	96⅝	106	7.19	5.87
Sr[10]Nts 6.30s 2000	Jd	A			X	BE	NC	....	....	....	....	....	200	L3	'95	101¾	97⅝	101¾	6.19	5.84
Sub[10]Deb 9¾s 2001	Jd15	A–	8/94	BBB+	X	BE	NC	....	....	....	....	....	100	L3	'91	115⅞	104½	115⅞	8.41	6.27
Sub[10]Deb 9¼s 2001	fA15	A–	8/94	BBB+	X	BE	NC	....	....	....	....	....	100	F1	'91	115	103⅛	115	8.04	6.06
Sub[10]Deb 6⅞s 2003	Ms	A–	8/94	BBB+	X	BE	NC	....	....	....	....	....	150	G1	'93	104	89⅞	104	6.61	6.17
Mercantile Bancorp	***10***	*4.22*	*5.68*	*4.76*		*Dc*				*9-30-95*	*304.0*		*1723*	*17.6*						
Sub Nts 7⅝s 2002	aO15	BBB	10/93	BBB–	X	BE	NC	....	....	....	....	....	150	S1	'92	106¼	93¼	106¼	7.18	6.47
Mercantile Stores	***59f***	*5.04*	*4.97*	*7.15*		*Ja*	*79.00*	*1314*	*356.0*	*10-28-95*	*257.0*		*1670*	*15.7*						
Deb 8.20s 2022	mS15	A+	8/94	AA–	X	BE	100	(9-15-02)	100	(9-15-03)	....	....	100	G1	'92	107⅛	91⅝	107⅛	7.65	7.57
Nts 6.70s 2002	mS15	A+	8/94	AA–	X	BE	100	(9-15-97)	100	(9-15-97)	....	....	95.0	G1	'92	100	91¼	99⅞	6.71	6.72
Merchants National Corp	***10***	***Merged into Nat'l City Corp,see***																		
• Sub Nts 9⅞s '99	aO	A–	5/92	BBB–	X	R	NC	....	....	....	....	....	65.0	S1	'89	111½	103¾	105⅛	9.39	8.25
Merck & Co	***21a***	*50.25*	*47.38*	*37.43*		*Dc*	*2917*	*7754*	*5661*	*9-30-95*	*1337*		*14520*	*11.9*						
Nts[1] 7¾s '96	Mn	AAA			X	R	NC	....	....	....	....	....	250	S1	'91	101½	100⅛	100¾	7.69	5.43
Med-Term[1]Nts'A' 6s '97	Jj15	AAA			X	BE	NC	....	....	....	....	....	100	G1	'92	100¾	96⅛	100¾	5.96	5.25
Meridian Bancorp	***10***	*5.59*	*4.46*	*3.61*		*Dc*				*9-30-95*	*515.0*		*1781*	*28.9*						
Nts 6⅝s 2000	Jd15	BBB+			X	BE	NC	....	....	....	....	....	150	C5	'95	102⅞	98½	102⅞	6.44	5.88
Sub Deb 7⅞s 2002	jJ15	BBB			X	BE	NC	....	....	....	....	....	100	F1	'92	109½	95⅛	109½	7.19	6.09
Merisel, Inc	***20a***	*3.19*	*3.86*	*1.69*		*Dc*	*1.47*	*1249*	*974.0*	*9-30-95*	*263.0*		*557.0*	*58.5*						
Sr Nts[7] 12½s 2004	jD31	B			Y	R	106.25	(12-31-99)	....	....	[11]Z110	12-30-97	125	C4	'94	112¼	100	112¼	11.14	10.37
Merrill Lynch	***62***	*1.34*	*1.40*	*1.20*		*Dc*				*9-29-95*	*16156*		*53996*	*88.7*						
Nts 4¾s '96	Jd26	A+			X	BE	NC	....	....	....	....	....	300	M2	'93	99⅝	95¾	99⅝	4.77	5.54
Nts 5s '96	jD15	A+			X	BE	NC	....	....	....	....	....	200	M2	'93	99½	94⅛	99½	5.03	5.54
Nts 7¼s '97	Mn15	A+			X	R	NC	....	....	....	....	....	150	M2	'92	102¼	97⅞	102¼	7.09	5.52
Nts 9s '98	Mn	A+	1/92	A	X	R	NC	....	....	....	....	....	250	M2	'91	107¼	101⅛	107¼	8.39	5.64
Nts 10⅜s '99	Fa	A+	1/92	A	X	R	NC	....	....	....	....	....	165	M2	'91	113	106¼	113	9.18	5.72
Nts 7¾s '99	Ms	A+			X	R	NC	....	....	....	....	....	175	M2	'92	105¾	96¾	105¾	7.33	5.74
Nts 6⅜s '99	Ms30	A+			X	BE	NC	....	....	....	....	....	200	M2	'94	101⅝	91⅞	101⅝	6.27	5.82
Nts 8¼s '99	mN15	A+	1/92	A	X	R	NC	....	....	....	....	....	300	M2	'91	108¼	98½	108¼	7.62	5.84
Nts 8⅜s 2000	Fa9	A+			X	BE	NC	....	....	....	....	....	150	M2	'95	109	100	109	7.68	5.88

Uniform Footnote Explanations-See Page 260. Other: [1] Issued in min denom $100T. [2] Due 5-15-96. [3] Subsid of Sun Healthcare Group. [4] 6 Mo Dec'94. [5] (HRO)On Chge of Ctrl at 100. [6] Subsid & data of MEDIQ Inc. [7] (HRO)On Chge of Ctrl at 101. [8] Plus Make-Whole Amt. [9] Subsid & data of Mellon Bank Corp. [10] Gtd by Mellon Bank Corp. [11] Max $43.8M red w/proceeds of Equity Off'g.

Title-Industry Code & Co. Finances (In Italics)	Ind	Fixed Charge Coverage 1992	1993	1994		Year End	Million $ Cash & Equiv.	Curr. Assets	Curr. Liab.	Balance Sheet Date	L. Term Debt (Mil $)	Capital-ization (Mil $)		Total Debt % Capital						
Individual Issue Statistics Exchange ↓	Interest Dates	S&P Debt Rating	Date of Last Rating Change	Prior Rating	Eligible ↓	Bond Form	Redemption Provisions: Regular Price	Regular (Begins) Thru	Sinking Fund Price	Sinking Fund (Begins) Thru	Refund/Other Restriction Price	Refund/Other Restriction (Begins) Thru	Outst'g (Mil $)	Underwriting Firm	Underwriting Year	Price Range 1995 High	Price Range 1995 Low	Mo. End Price Sale(s) or Bid	Curr. Yield	Yield to Mat.
***Merrill Lynch** (Cont.)*																				
Nts 6.70s 2000	fA	**A+**			X	BE	NC	....	....	....	....	....	150	M2	'95	103⅛	99⅛	103⅛	6.50	5.91
Nts 8s 2002	Fa	**A+**			X	R	NC	....	....	....	....	....	225	M2	'92	109¾	95½	109¾	7.29	6.06
Nts 7⅜s 2002	fA17	**A+**			X	BE	NC	....	....	....	....	....	150	M2	'92	106⅞	91⅞	106⅞	6.90	6.10
Nts 6.64s 2002	mS19	**A+**			X	BE	NC	....	....	....	....	....	250	M2	'95	102¾	98⅝	102¾	6.46	6.13
Nts 8.30s 2002	mN	**A+**			X	R	NC	....	....	....	....	....	150	M2	'92	112	97½	112	7.41	6.12
Nts 6⅞s 2003	Ms	**A+**			X	BE	NC	....	....	....	....	....	200	M2	'93	103⅞	89⅜	103⅞	6.62	6.20
Nts 7.05s 2003	Ao15	**A+**			X	BE	100	(4-15-98)	....	....	....	....	150	M2	'93	103¼	89⅝	103¼	6.83	6.48
Nts 6¼s 2006	Jj15	**A+**			X	BE	NC	....	....	....	....	....	200	M2	'94	98⅞	82	98⅞	6.32	6.40
Nts 6⅜s 2006	mS8	**A+**			X	BE	100	(9-8-03)	....	....	....	....	125	M2	'93	98⅝	82⅞	98⅝	6.46	6.55
Nts 8s 2007	Jd	**A+**			X	R	NC	....	....	....	....	....	150	M2	'92	112½	93	112½	7.11	6.44
Nts 7s 2008	Ao27	**A+**			X	BE	NC	....	....	....	....	....	250	M2	'93	104⅜	84⅜	104⅜	6.71	6.48
Nts 6¼s 2008	aO15	**A+**			X	BE	NC	....	....	....	....	....	150	M2	'93	98	78¼	98	6.38	6.48
Nts 8.40s 2019	mN	**A+**	1/92	A	X	R	NC	....	....	....	....	....	200	M2	'89	121½	98⅞	121½	6.91	6.60
• [1]CP([2]Reset)Nts '98	jD31	[3]**A+**			X	R	NC	....	....	....	....	....	25.0	M2	'93	95	87¾	98	....	....
• [4]SMART([5]Reset)Nts[6] '97	jD31	[3]**A+**			X	BE	NC	....	....	....	....	....	28.0	M2	'92	104¾	91½	s98¼	....	....
• [4]SMART([7]Reset)Nts[6] '99	jD31	[3]**A+**			X	BE	NC	....	....	....	....	....	50.0	M2	'93	103⅛	86⅝	96½	....	....
[8]Indexed([9]F/R)Nts 5.08s '97	QMar24	**A+**			X	BE	NC	....	....	....	....	....	100	M2	'94	100⅛	99⅜	100	5.08	....
◆[4]SMART([10]Reset)Nts[11] 2000	[12]jd31	[3]**A+**			X	BE	NC	....	....	....	....	....	25.0	M2	'94	104¾	88	105	....	....
Step-Up([13]Reset)Nts 6.14s 2000	Jj26	**A+**			X	BE	*100	....	....	....	....	....	50.0	M2	'93	100¾	98⅜	100¾	6.09	....
• F/R[14]Nts '98	jD31	**A+**			X	BE	NC	....	....	....	....	....	25.0	M2	'93	105	86	100	....	....
Merry Land & Invest	*57*	*2.50*	*4.20*	*4.40*		*Dc*				*9-30-95*	*304.0*	*1004*		*30.3*						
Nts 7¼s 2005	Jd15	**BBB+**			X	BE	Z100	(6-15-02)	....	....	....	....	120	M5	'95	103	96⅛	103	7.04	6.81
Nts 6⅞s 2003	mN	**BBB+**			X	BE	NC	....	....	....	....	....	40.0	M5	'95	101⅜	99⅛	101⅜	6.78	6.65
Nts 6⅞s 2004	mN	**BBB+**			X	BE	NC	....	....	....	....	....	40.0	M5	'95	101⅛	98½	101⅛	6.80	6.70
[15]***Mesa Capital***	*25*	*0.40*	*0.48*	*1.02*		*Dc*	*161.0*	*205.0*	*168.0*	*9-30-95*	*1135*	*1317*		*94.7*						
• Sub[16]Nts[17] 13½s '99	Mn	**NR**	8/93	D		R	103.375	4-30-96	....	....	Z103.375	4-30-96	7.39	0	'89	104¾	92	94	....	Flat
Metrocall Inc	*67g*	*2.16*	*3.36*	*0.67*		*Dc*	*3.45*	*23.50*	*18.10*	*6-30-95*	*★154.0*	*182.0*		*64.5*						
Sr Sub[18]Nts 10⅜s 2007	aO	**B–**			Y	R	105.188	(10-1-00)	....	....	....	....	150	L3	'95	100	95½	95½	10.86	11.06
Metropolitan Bancorp	*10b*	*2.18*	*1.93*	*1.35*		*Mr*				*9-30-95*	*244.0*	*294.0*		*83.0*						
Sub Nts 8½s 2003	[19]	**NR**				R	100	(7-31-96)	....	....	....	....	20.0	D1	'93	101¾	93	101¾	8.35	8.18
Metropolitan Edison[20]	*72a*	*3.66*	*3.45*	*0.80*		*Dc*	*5.40*	*188.0*	*238.0*	*6-30-95*	*603.0*	*1406*		*48.9*						
1st 5¾s '96	Jd	**BBB+**	8/94	A–	X	CR	100	....	100	....	....	....	15.0	M2	'66	100	97⅜	100	5.75	5.72
Sec M-T Nts 'A'[21] 7.47s '97	[22]jj	**BBB+**	8/94	A–	X	BE	NC	....	....	....	....	....	20.0	G1	'92	102½	98⅛	102¼	7.31	5.63
Sec M-T Nts 'A'[21] 9.20s '97	[23]jj	**BBB+**	8/94	A–	X	BE	NC	....	....	....	....	....	20.0	G1	'90	106⅜	101⅞	105⅝	8.71	5.67
Sec M-T Nts 'A'[21] 9.48s 2000	[24]jj	**BBB+**	9/94	A–	X	BE	NC	....	....	....	....	....	20.0	G1	'90	113¼	103⅜	113¼	8.37	6.00
Sec M-T Nts 'A'[21] 9.10s 2003	[25]jj	**BBB+**	8/94	A–	X	BE	100	(3-19-01)	....	....	....	....	30.0	G1	'91	116½	102	116½	7.81	6.36
Sec M-T Nts 'A'[21] 8.60s 2022	[26]jj	**BBB+**	8/94	A–	X	BE	104.30	(1-24-02)	100	....	....	....	30.0	G1	'92	119⅞	96	119⅞	7.17	6.94
Sec M-T Nts 'A'[21] 8.80s 2022	[27]jj	**BBB+**	8/94	A–	X	BE	104.40	(4-9-02)	....	....	....	....	30.0	G1	'92	122¼	98	122¼	7.20	6.95
Sec M-T Nts 'B'[21] 7.05s '99	[28]fa	**BBB+**	8/94	A–	X	BE	NC	....	....	....	....	....	30.0	M6	'92	103¾	93¾	103¾	6.80	5.96
Sec M-T Nts 'B'[21] 6.20s 2000	[29]fa	**BBB+**	8/94	A–	X	BE	NC	....	....	....	....	....	30.0	M6	'93	100¾	89½	100¾	6.15	6.01
Sec M-T Nts 'B'[21] 7.22s 2003	[30]fa	**BBB+**	8/94	A–	X	BE	NC	....	....	....	....	....	40.0	M6	'93	105¼	91¼	105¼	6.86	6.29
Sec M-T Nts 'B'[21] 6.60s 2003	[31]fa	**BBB+**	8/94	A–	X	BE	NC	....	....	....	....	....	20.0	M6	'93	101¾	87¼	101¾	6.49	6.30
Sec M-T Nts 'B'[21] 6.34s 2004	[32]fa	**BBB+**	8/94	A–	X	BE	NC	....	....	....	....	....	40.0	M6	'93	99⅝	84¼	99⅝	6.36	6.40
Sec M-T Nts 'B'[21] 7.35s 2005	Fa	**BBB+**	8/94	A–	X	BE	100	(1-29-03)	....	....	....	....	20.0	M6	'93	106⅜	90⅜	106⅜	6.91	6.41
Sec M-T Nts 'B'[21] 8.15s 2023	[33]fa	**BBB+**	8/94	A–	X	BE	104.08	(1-29-03)	....	....	....	....	60.0	M6	'93	110	90⅜	110	7.41	7.30
Sec M-T Nts 'B'[21] 7.65s 2023	[34]fa	**BBB+**	8/94	A–	X	BE	103.83	(6-18-03)	....	....	....	....	30.0	M6	'93	106⅜	85⅜	106⅜	7.19	7.12

Uniform Footnote Explanations-See Page 260. Other: [1] Currency Protected Nts. [2] Int(min 3%)set 7th business day bef int pyt. [3] Note:'r'added to derivative/hybrid secur ratings. [4] SMART-Stk Mkt Annual Reset Term. [5] Int(min 3%,max 10.5%)adj annually. [6] Int pd:3% in Jun,bal in Dec. [7] Int(min 3%,max 10%)adj annually. [8] Constant Maturity Treasury Rate Indexed Notes. [9] Int to 3-23-96,adj qtrly aft. [10] Int(min 2%)adj annually. [11] Int pd:50% min amt in Jul,bal Dec. [12] Due 12-29-00. [13] Int at 6.14% to 1-26-96,8.5% aft. [14] Int(min 3%)adj for Index Bund. [15] Gtd by & data of Mesa Inc. [16] Co must offer repurch at 100 on Chge of Ctrl. [17] Int of 5-1-93 pd 9-2-93. [18] (HRO)On Chge of Ctrl at 101. [19] Due 7-31-03,int pd mthly. [20] Subsid of Gen'l Public Util. [21] Issued in min denom $100T. [22] Due 4-15-97. [23] Due 9-11-97. [24] Due 5-22-00. [25] Due 9-18-03. [26] Due 1-24-22. [27] Due 4-15-22. [28] Due 11-29-99. [29] Due 6-19-00. [30] Due 1-30-03. [31] Due 6-18-03. [32] Due 8-27-04. [33] Due 1-30-23. [34] Due 6-19-03.

Individual Issue Statistics (Exchange ↓)	Interest Dates	S&P Debt Rating	Date of Last Rating Change	Prior Rating	Eligible ↓	Bond Form	Redemption Provisions: Regular Price	Regular (Begins) Thru	Sinking Fund Price	Sinking Fund (Begins) Thru	Refund/Other Restriction Price	Refund/Other Restriction (Begins) Thru	Outst'g (Mil $)	Underwriting Firm	Underwriting Year	Price Range 1995 High	Price Range 1995 Low	Mo. End Price Sale(s) or Bid	Curr. Yield	Yield to Mat.
Title-Industry Code & Co. Finances (In Italics)	***Ind***	***Fixed Charge Coverage 1992***	***1993***	***1994***		***Year End***	***Million $ Cash & Equiv.***	***Curr. Assets***	***Curr. Liab.***	***Balance Sheet Date***	***L. Term Debt (Mil $)***		***Capital-ization (Mil $)***	***Total Debt % Capital***						
***Metropolitan Edison** (Cont.)*																				
Sec M-T Nts 'B'[1] 6.97s 2023	[2]fa	BBB+	8/94	A–	X	BE	103.49	(10-19-03)	....	....	....	....	30.0	M6	'93	98⅜	78½	98⅜	7.09	7.10
Sec M-T Nts 'C'[1] 6.36s 2006	[3]mn	BBB+	8/94	A–	X	BE	100	(2-8-04)	....	....	....	....	17.0	M2	'94	99⅛	82⅝	99⅛	6.42	6.48
Sec M-T Nts 'C'[1] 6.40s 2006	[4]mn	BBB+	8/94	A–	X	BE	100	(2-8-04)	....	....	....	....	33.0	M2	'94	99½	82⅞	99½	6.43	6.47
MFS Communications	***67***	***n/a***	***n/a***	***d2.75***		***Dc***	***183.0***	***389.0***	***241.0***	***9-30-95***	***610.0***		***1512***	***40.5***						
Sr Disc[5]Nts[6] 9⅜s 2004	Jj15	B			Y	R	103.52	(1-15-99)	....	....	....	....	[7]788	S1	'94	80	59	80	....	Flat
MGM Grand Hotel Finance[8]	***25***	***0.79***	***0.48***	***2.02***		***Dc***				***9-30-95***	***473.0***		***480.0***	***98.5***						
• [9]1st[10] 11¾s '99	Mn	BB–	12/93	B+	Y	R	101.958	(5-1-97)	100	(5-1-97)	....	....	220	B5	'92	111⅞	105¼	106⅜	11.05	9.47
• [9]1st[10] 12s 2002	Mn	BB–	12/93	B+	Y	R	105.333	(5-1-97)	100	(5-1-00)	....	....	253	B5	'92	112¼	108⅜	s110⅜	10.87	9.76
Michigan Bell Telephone[11]	***67a***	***5.17***	***5.55***	***6.74***		***Dc***		***681.0***	***768.0***	***9-30-95***	***1115***		***2593***	***48.4***						
Deb 4⅝s '96	fA	AAA	8/88	AA+	X	CR	100	....	....	....	....	....	35.0	H1	'60	99½	95½	99½	4.65	5.49
Deb 6⅜s 2005	Fa	AAA	8/88	AA+	X	R	100.98	1-31-96	....	....	....	....	125	M2	'68	100⅜	87⅛	100⅜	6.35	6.32
• Deb 7¾s 2011	Jd	AAA	8/88	AA+	X	R	102.24	5-31-96	....	....	....	....	150	M2	'71	103¼	94⅛	102⅛	7.59	7.51
• Deb 7s 2012	mN	AAA	8/88	AA+	X	R	102.06	10-31-96	....	....	....	....	75.0	D4	'72	101	85¼	100	7.00	7.00
Deb 7.85s 2022	Jj15	AAA			X	BE	NC	....	....	....	....	....	200	G1	'92	115¾	93⅝	115¾	6.78	6.58
Deb 7½s 2023	Fa15	AAA			X	BE	103.483	(2-15-03)	....	....	....	....	200	G1	'93	108¼	88½	108¼	6.93	6.83
Nts 5⅞s '99	mS15	AAA			X	BE	NC	....	....	....	....	....	150	L3	'92	100¾	91¼	100¾	5.83	5.65
Nts 6⅜s 2002	mS15	AAA			X	BE	NC	....	....	....	....	....	100	L3	'92	102⅜	89⅛	102⅜	6.23	5.94
Michigan Consol Gas[12]	***73b***	***3.13***	***3.78***	***3.39***		***Dc***	***33.60***	***279.0***	***250.0***	***6-30-95***	***516.0***		***991.0***	***52.5***						
1st 6¼s '97	Mn	A			X	BE	NC	....	....	....	....	....	50.0	M2	'92	100¾	95⅞	100¾	6.20	5.65
1st 5¾s 2001	Mn	A			X	BE	NC	....	100	(5-1-99)	....	....	60.0	M2	'93	98⅞	87¼	98⅞	5.82	6.00
1st 8s 2002	Mn	A			X	BE	NC	....	....	....	....	....	70.0	M2	'92	109¼	98⅛	109¼	7.32	6.21
1st 8¼s 2014	Mn	A			X	BE	NC	....	....	....	....	....	80.0	M2	'94	114¾	96¾	114¾	7.19	6.83
1st 7s 2025	Mn	A			X	BE	102.88	(5-1-03)	....	....	....	....	40.0	M2	'93	98¾	82⅝	98⅜	7.12	7.13
Sec M-T Nts 'A'[13] 7½s 2020	Mn	A			X	BE	105	(5-1-00)	....	....	....	....	10.0	J2	'95	104⅝	98⅜	103¼	7.26	7.21
Sec M-T Nts 'B'[13] 7½s 2020	Mn	A			X	BE	105	(5-1-00)	....	....	....	....	20.0	J2	'95	104⅝	98¼	103¼	7.26	7.21
Mid-American Waste Sys	***52***	***1.71***	***0.16***	***1.06***		***Dc***	***14.90***	***43.90***	***42.90***	***9-30-95***	***307.0***		***617.0***	***54.0***						
Sr Sub Nts[10] 12¼s 2003	Fa15	B			Y	R	106.125	(5-15-99)	....	....	....	....	175	D6	'94	104½	93½	94	13.03	13.58
[14]Mid-Penn Telephone	***67a***	***Subsid of ALLTEL Corp, see***																		
SF Deb 7¾s 2002	Ms15	AA–	11/90	A+	X	R	101.50	3-14-96	100		....	....	5.80	M2	'72	101¾	96⅛	101¾	7.62	7.39
Midland American Capital	***25***	***Gtd by Midland Bank plc***																		
• Gtd Nts 12¾s 2003	mN15	A	3/95	A–	X	R	100	(11-15-98)	....	....	[15]Z100	....	150	G1	'83	115	114¼	118⅛	10.79	9.43
Midland Enterprises[16]	***64***	***2.57***	***1.42***	***n/a***		***Dc***	***16.30***	***126.0***	***50.20***	***9-30-95***	***146.0***		***304.0***	***49.3***						
1st Pfd Ship Mtg 9.90s 2008	Ao	A			X	R	102.42	(4-1-98)	100	(4-1-99)	....	....	50.0	F1	'88	111⅞	106	111⅝	8.87	8.36
Midland-Ross Corp[17]	***44***	....	....	....		***Dc***	***No Recent Fin'ls***													
Deb 6s 2007	Fa15	NR	9/88	B–		R	100	....	....	....	....	....	[7]125	S1	'82	74⅜	60	74⅜	8.07	9.84
Midlantic Corp	***10***	***1.17***	***1.42***	***6.47***		***Dc***				***9-30-95***	***369.0***		***1817***	***20.3***						
Nts 9¼s '99	mS	BBB	1/95	BB+	X	R	NC	....	....	....	....	....	100	M6	'89	110	101⅜	109⅞	8.42	6.20
Sub[18]Cap Nts 9.20s 2001	fA	BBB–	1/95	BB–	X	R	NC	....	....	....	[19]Z100	....	100	F1	'89	114	101	114	8.07	6.20
Sub[20]Cap Nts 9⅞s '99	jD	BBB–	1/95	BB–	X	R	NC	....	....	....	....	....	100	M6	'87	113	103⅝	113	8.74	6.10
Midwest Power Systems[21]	***75***	***2.14***	***3.32***	***3.03***		***Dc***	***2.88***	***183.0***	***239.0***	***12-31-94***	***736.0***		***1523***	***52.2***						
Gen Mtg 6¼s '98	Fa	A+			X	R	NC	....	....	....	....	....	75.0	P1	'93	101¼	94½	101¼	6.17	5.60
Gen Mtg 7⅞s '99	mN	A+			X	R	NC	....	....	....	....	....	60.0	P1	'94	106⅞	98⅛	106⅞	7.37	5.85
Gen Mtg 6¾s 2000	Fa	A+			X	R	NC	....	....	....	....	....	75.0	P1	'93	103	93⅝	103	6.55	5.91
Gen Mtg 7⅛s 2003	Fa	A+			X	R	NC	....	....	....	....	....	100	P1	'93	119⅝	92	105½	6.75	6.15
Gen Mtg 7s 2005	Fa15	A+			X	R	NC	....	....	....	....	....	100	P1	'93	105⅜	89¾	105⅜	6.64	6.22
Gen Mtg 7⅜s 2008	Fa	A+			X	R	101.55	(2-1-03)	....	....	....	....	75.0	P1	'93	106½	90⅞	106½	6.92	6.59

Uniform Footnote Explanations-See Page 260. Other: [1] Issued in min denom $100T. [2] Due 10-19-23. [3] Due 2-8-06. [4] Due 2-9-06. [5] Int accrues at 9.375% fr 1-15-99. [6] (HRO)On Chge of Ctrl at 101(Accreted Val). [7] Incl disc. [8] Subsid of MGM Grand Inc. [9] Gtd by MGM Grand Inc. [10] (HRO)On Chge of Ctrl at 101. [11] Subsid of Ameritech Corp. [12] Subsid of MCN Corp. [13] Death redemp benefit,ltd,as defined. [14] Now ALLTEL Penna. [15] Co may red in whole on UK tax law chge. [16] Subsid of East'n Enterprises. [17] Acquired by Forstmann Little. [18] Co may exch for Cap Sec when due. [19] For certain events relating to Fed Inc Tax. [20] Co may exch for Cap when due. [21] See Iowa Pwr & Iowa Pub Serv.

Company rows: Title-Industry Code & Co. Finances (In Italics) | Fixed Charge Coverage 1992, 1993, 1994 | Year End | Million $: Cash & Equiv., Curr. Assets, Curr. Liab. | Balance Sheet Date | L. Term Debt (Mil $) | Capital-ization (Mil $) | Total Debt % Capital

Individual Issue Statistics (Exchange)	Interest Dates	S&P Debt Rating	Date of Last Rating Change	Prior Rating	Eligible	Bond Form	Redemption Provisions: Regular Price	Regular (Begins) Thru	Sinking Fund Price	Sinking Fund (Begins) Thru	Refund/Other Restriction Price	Refund/Other Restriction (Begins) Thru	Outst'g (Mil $)	Underwriting Firm	Underwriting Year	Price Range 1995 High	Price Range 1995 Low	Mo. End Price Sale(s) or Bid	Curr. Yield	Yield to Mat.
***Midwest Power Systems** (Cont.)*																				
Gen Mtg 8s 2022	Fa15	A+			X	R	105.13	(2-15-98)	....	....	....	....	50.0	P1	'93	107½	91⅝	107½	7.44	7.35
Gen Mtg 8⅛s 2023	Fa	A+			X	R	106.28	1-31-96	....	....	®105.23	1-31-98	100	P1	'93	109⅝	91⅛	109⅝	7.41	7.30
Miles Homes Services, Inc	*13h*	*0.93*	*2.29*	*d0.63*		*Dc*				*12-31-94*	*73.90*		*107.0*	*69.1*						
Sr Nts[1] 12s 2001	Ao	CCC+			Y	R	103.50	(4-1-99)	....	....	....	....	50.0	B9	'94	82	63	A76	15.79	19.48
Minnesota Power & Light	*72a*	*3.01*	*3.06*	*2.59*		*Dc*	*96.40*	*278.0*	*284.0*	*9-30-95*	*622.0*		*1352*	*53.4*						
1st 6½s '98	Jj	A–	3/92	A	X	R	100.26	12-31-96	100.13	12-31-96	....	....	18.0	E1	'68	100⅜	95¾	100¼	6.48	6.36
1st 7⅜s '97	Ms	A–			X	R	NC	....	....	....	....	....	60.0	P1	'92	101⅞	98⅜	101⅞	7.24	5.69
1st 6¼s 2003	jJ	A–			X	R	NC	....	....	....	....	....	25.0	P1	'93	99⅞	86½	99⅞	6.26	6.27
1st 7¾s 2007	Jd	A–			X	R	101.31	(6-1-02)	....	....	....	....	55.0	P1	'92	108⅜	92⅝	107⅞	7.18	6.75
1st 7½s 2007	fA	A–			X	R	100	(8-1-05)	....	....	....	....	35.0	P1	'92	107½	91⅛	107½	6.98	6.56
1st 7s 2008	Ms	A–			X	R	100	(3-1-06)	....	....	....	....	50.0	P1	'93	103⅝	87	103⅝	6.76	6.56
Mississippi Power Co.[2]	*72a*	*3.41*	*4.38*	*4.62*		*Dc*	*1.40*	*110.0*	*163.0*	*6-30-95*	*286.0*		*809.0*	*45.6*						
1st 5⅜s '98	Ms	A+			X	R	NC	....	....	....	....	....	35.0	M5	'93	99½	92⅜	99½	5.40	5.62
1st 6⅝s 2000	fA	A+			X	R	101.98	7-31-96	Z100	....	®100	7-31-97	40.0	K2	'92	101⅝	92⅝	101⅝	6.52	6.21
1st 6.60s 2004	Ms	A+			X	R	101.40	(3-1-99)	100	(3-1-99)	....	....	35.0	C4	'94	101⅝	88⅜	101⅝	6.49	6.34
1st 9¼s 2021	Mn	A+			X	R	106.76	4-30-96	Z100	....	®106.34	4-30-96	47.1	L3	'91	108⅛	101⅛	106⅞	8.65	8.58
1st 7.45s 2023	Jd	A+			X	R	105.77	5-31-96	Z100	....	®104.81	5-31-98	35.0	G1	'93	102⅜	86¾	102⅜	7.28	7.25
1st 6⅞s 2025	jD	A+			X	R	102.97	(12-1-05)	Z100	(12-1-05)	....	....	30.0	S1	'95	99	99	99	6.94	6.95
Mississippi Power & Lt.[3]	*72a*	*2.36*	*2.86*	*2.11*		*Dc*	*37.50*	*321.0*	*272.0*	*9-30-95*	*505.0*		*1095*	*52.1*						
1st 5⅛s '96	Jj	BBB	4/91	BBB–	X	CR	100	....	100	....	....	....	25.0	E3	'66	100	97⅜	100	5.13	Mat.
1st 6⅜s '96	mN	BBB	4/91	BBB–	X	CR	100	....	100	....	....	....	10.0	E1	'66	100⅛	96¾	100	6.38	6.36
Gen & Ref 8¼s 2004	jJ	BBB			X	BE	102	(7-1-99)	Z100	(7-1-99)	....	....	25.0	B5	'94	108⅜	96⅞	108⅜	7.61	6.93
Gen & Ref 6⅝s 2003	mN	BBB			X	BE	101.87	(11-1-98)	Z100	....	....	....	65.0	K2	'93	101	88	101	6.56	6.46
Gen & Ref 8.80s 2005	Ao	BBB			X	BE	100	(4-1-98)	....	....	....	....	80.0	B5	'95	105⅜	100	105⅜	8.35	7.96
Gen & Ref 8.65s 2023	Jj15	BBB			X	BE	106.35	(1-15-98)	Z100	(1-15-98)	....	....	125	G1	'93	109¼	94½	105⅛	8.23	8.18
Missouri-Kan-Tex RR	*55*	***Subsid of Union Pacific Corp,see***																		
• Sub[4]Inc[5]Deb[6] 5½s 2033	Anapr	CI	5/89	C	Y	CR	100	....	100	....	....	....	27.1	Exch.	'58	61½	52¼	62	....	Flat
Missouri[7] Pacific RR.[8]	*55*	*3.71*	*4.31*	*5.09*		*Dc*	*6.83*	*282.0*	*1311*	*9-30-95*	*369.0*		*1824*	*21.8*						
• 1st C 4¼s 2005	Jj	A–	4/95	A+	X	CR	102	12-31-01	100	....	....	....	93.0	Reorg	'56	85⅜	69¼	85	5.00	6.47
• Gen[9]Inc[6]A 4¾s 2020	AnApr	A	5/89	AA–	X	R	100	....	100	....	....	....	33.1	Reorg	'56	64	52½	60½	....	Flat
• Gen[9]Inc[6]B 4¾s 2030	AnApr	A	5/89	AA–	X	R	100	....	100	....	....	....	34.7	Reorg	'56	63¼	49⅜	s60⅛	....	Flat
• Inc [10]Deb[6] 5s 2045	Anapr	A	5/89	AA–	X	R	100	....	....	....	....	....	100	Reorg	'56	62½	52¼	s62½	....	Flat
Missouri Power & Light	*72a*	***Merged into & Asmd by Union Elec,See***																		
1st 5⅝s '96	Ms	AA–	4/92	A+	X	CR	100	....	100	....	....	....	5.00	D8	'66	100	97⅞	100	5.63	5.52
1st 5⅝s '97	Ao	AA–	4/92	A+	X	CR	100.24	3-31-96	100.15	3-31-96	....	....	5.00	D8	'67	100⅛	95⅛	100⅛	5.62	5.51
Mitchell Energy & Devel	*49*	*1.15*	*1.16*	*1.60*		*Ja*	*13.10*	*240.0*	*206.0*	*7-31-95*	*787.0*		*1259*	*63.5*						
Sr Nts 5.10s '97	Fa15	BBB–			X	R	NC	....	....	....	....	....	100	M2	'94	99¼	93⅝	99¼	5.14	5.79
Sr Nts 8s '99	jJ15	BBB–			X	R	NC	....	....	....	....	....	100	F1	'92	106⅛	97⅛	106⅛	7.54	6.05
Sr Nts 9¼s 2002	Jj15	BBB–			X	R	NC	....	....	....	....	....	250	F1	'92	114½	101⅞	114½	8.08	6.32
Sr[11]Nts 6¾s 2004	Fa15	BBB–			X	R	NC	....	....	....	....	....	250	C5	'94	101¼	86⅞	101¼	6.67	6.55
MNC Financial	*10*	***Acquired by NationsBank,see***																		
Sub Cap Nts 9⅜s '97	Mn	A–	10/93	B–	Y	R	NC	....	....	....	....	....	75.0	G1	'87	105¼	101⅞	104⅛	9.00	6.11
Mobil Corp	*49c*	*5.70*	*13.40*	*8.98*		*Dc*	*597.0*	*11724*	*13698*	*9-30-95*	*4793*		*25655*	*30.3*						
• Deb 8⅝s 2021	fA15	AA			X	R	NC	....	....	....	....	....	250	M2	'91	119⅜	119⅜	106	8.14	8.07
• Deb 8s 2032	fA12	AA			X	R	105.007	(8-12-02)	....	....	....	....	250	M2	'92	105	92½	104	7.69	7.67
• Deb 7⅝s 2033	Fa23	AA			X	R	104.384	(2-23-03)	....	....	....	....	250	F1	'93	104½	104½	99	7.70	7.71

Uniform Footnote Explanations-See Page 260. Other: [1] (HRO)On Chge of Ctrl at 101. [2] Subsid of Southern Co. [3] Subsid of Entergy Corp. [4] Int non-cum contg. [5] Arrears 16.50% max. [6] Due Jan 1. [7] Contr by Missouri Pac Corp(Union Pac). [8] See Texas&Pac Ry. [9] Int contingent cum to 13.50%. [10] Int non-cum contingent. [11] (HRO)On Special Redemption Event at 100.

Title-Industry Code & Co. Finances (In Italics) / Exchange ↓ Individual Issue Statistics	Ind / Interest Dates	Fixed Charge Coverage 1992 / S&P Debt Rating	1993 / Date of Last Rating Change	1994 / Prior Rating	Eligible ↓	Year End / Bond Form	Million $ Cash & Equiv. / Redemption Provisions Regular Price	Curr. Assets / Regular (Begins) Thru	Curr. Liab. / Sinking Fund Price	Balance Sheet Date / Sinking Fund (Begins) Thru	L. Term Debt (Mil $) / Refund/Other Restriction Price	Refund/Other Restriction (Begins) Thru	Capital-ization (Mil $) / Outst'g (Mil $)	Total Debt % Capital / Underwriting Firm	Underwriting Year	Price Range 1995 High	Price Range 1995 Low	Mo. End Price Sale(s) or Bid	Curr. Yield	Yield to Mat.
***Mobil Corp** (Cont.)*																				
Nts 6½s '96	jD17	**AA**			X	R	NC	....	....	....	....	....	200	M6	'91	101⅛	97½	101⅛	6.43	5.29
Nts 6½s '97	Fa15	**AA**			X	R	NC	....	....	....	....	....	200	M6	'92	101⅜	96¾	101⅜	6.41	5.22
Nts 7¼s '99	Ms15	**AA**			X	R	NC	....	....	....	....	....	200	U1	'92	105⅛	96¾	105⅛	6.90	5.48
• Nts 8⅜s 2001	Fa12	**AA**			X	R	NC	....	....	....	....	....	200	S1	'91	111⅛	101	s110⅜	7.59	5.99
Mobile Telecommun Tech	***67g***	***1.05***	***2.29***	***3.65***		***Dc***	***29.20***	***91.70***	***76.40***	***9-30-95***	***269.0***		***760.0***	***35.5***						
Sr Nts[1] 13½s 2002	jD15	**BB–**			Y	R	106.75	(12-15-98)	....	....	[2]114.50	12-14-97	265	B5	'95	113⅞	100⅝	111	12.16	11.18
MobileMedia Communications[3]	***67g***	***d6.18***	***d1.11***	***d1.09***		***Dc***	***4.70***	***37.60***	***66.70***	***9-30-95***	***345.0***		***597.0***	***57.8***						
Sr Sub Defr[4]Cpn[5]Nts 10½s 2003	jD	**B–**	6/95	CCC+	Y	R	103	(12-1-98)	....	....	[6]Z111.50	12-1-96	[7]210	D6	'93	77⅝	53½	77⅝	....	Flat
Sr Sub Nts[1] 9⅜s 2007	mN	**B–**			Y	R	104.688	(11-1-00)	....	....	....	....	250	L3	'95	102½	100	102½	9.15	9.02
Monon R.R.	***55***	***See Seaboard Coast Line RR***																		
• Inc[8]SF[9]Deb[10] 6s 2007	Anapr	**NR**	7/94	BBB		CR	100	....	100	....	....	....	4.08	Exch.	'58	90	81⅜	92	....	Flat
Monongahela Power Co.[11]	***72a***	***3.56***	***3.38***	***3.30***		***Dc***	***0.12***	***140.0***	***143.0***	***6-30-95***	***489.0***		***1063***	***46.0***						
1st 5½s '96	Ms	**A+**	4/94	AA–	X	R	100	....	Z100	....	....	....	18.0	F1	'66	100	97¾	100	5.50	5.40
1st 6½s '97	fA	**A+**	4/94	AA–	X	R	100.30	7-31-96	Z100.28	7-31-96	....	....	15.0	M2	'67	100⅜	96½	100⅜	6.48	6.24
1st 5⅝s 2000	Ao	**A+**	4/94	AA–	X	R	NC	....	Z100	....	....	....	65.0	G1	'93	99¼	88⅝	99¼	5.67	5.82
1st 7⅜s 2002	jJ	**A+**	4/94	AA–	X	R	NC	....	Z100	....	....	....	25.0	M6	'92	107	94⅜	107	6.89	6.06
1st 7¼s 2007	mS	**A+**	4/94	AA–	X	R	100	(9-1-02)	Z100	....	....	....	25.0	M6	'92	104⅞	90⅜	104⅞	6.91	6.64
1st 8⅝s 2021	mN	**A+**	4/94	AA–	X	R	106.70	10-31-96	Z100	....	®104.19	10-31-01	50.0	S1	'91	110⅛	96¾	106⅞	8.07	7.99
1st 8½s 2022	Jd	**A+**	4/94	AA–	X	R	106.59	5-31-96	Z100	....	®105.82	5-31-97	65.0	M6	'92	108¼	96	106¾	7.96	7.89
1st 8⅜s 2022	jJ	**A+**	4/94	AA–	X	R	104.12	(7-1-02)	[12]Z100	....	....	....	40.0	M6	'92	112⅛	92¾	112⅛	7.47	7.33
1st 7⅝s 2025	Mn	**A+**			X	R	102.953	(5-1-05)	Z100	....	....	....	70.0	G1	'95	106¾	94⅛	106¾	7.14	7.07
Monsanto Co	***14***	***2.55***	***6.65***	***7.83***		***Dc***	***144.0***	***4179***	***2964***	***9-30-95***	***1685***		***6120***	***40.7***						
Deb[13] 8⅞s 2009	jD15	**A**			X	R	NC	....	....	....	....	....	100	M2	'89	124½	102½	124½	7.13	6.22
Deb 8.70s 2021	aO15	**A**			X	BE	NC	....	....	....	....	....	100	G1	'91	123⅜	100¼	123⅜	7.04	6.75
Deb 8.20s 2025	Ao15	**A**			X	BE	104.064	(4-15-05)	....	....	....	....	150	S1	'95	114⅞	99½	114⅞	7.14	7.00
Nts 6s 2000	jJ	**A**			X	BE	NC	....	....	....	....	....	150	M2	'93	100⅝	89¾	100⅝	5.96	5.84
Montana Power Co.	***75***	***4.09***	***6.45***	***4.66***		***Dc***	***17.00***	***236.0***	***284.0***	***9-30-95***	***618.0***		***1701***	***37.3***						
1st 7.70s '99	Fa	**BBB+**			X	R	NC	....	....	....	....	....	55.0	G1	'91	105⅜	97⅞	105⅜	7.31	5.77
1st 7½s 2001	Ao	**BBB+**	9/85	BBB–	X	R	101.30	3-31-96	100	....	....	....	25.0	K2	'71	101½	95⅛	101⅜	7.40	7.18
1st 7s 2005	Ms	**BBB+**			X	R	NC	....	....	....	....	....	50.0	G1	'93	104	88¼	104	6.73	6.41
1st 8¼s 2007	Fa	**BBB+**			X	R	NC	....	....	....	....	....	55.0	G1	'91	114⅜	97¾	114⅜	7.21	6.42
1st 8.95s 2022	Fa	**BBB+**			X	R	104.449	(2-1-02)	....	....	....	....	50.0	G1	'91	115	100⅛	115	7.78	7.62
SF Deb 7½s '98	Jj	**BBB**	9/85	BB+	X	R	100.34	12-31-96	100.09	12-31-96	....	....	16.5	K2	'73	100⅝	100⅜	100⅜	7.47	7.30
[14]Moran Energy	***49***	***1.18***	***2.03***	***2.20***		***Dc***	***28.20***	***73.80***	***46.30***	***9-30-95***	***126.0***		***282.0***	***46.1***						
Sub SF Deb[15] 11½s '98	Mn	**NR**	12/90	C		R	100	....	100	....	....	....	5.01	S5	'78	100	83	A100	....	Flat
Morgan (J.P.)& Co[16]	***10***	***1.54***	***1.72***	***1.38***		***Dc***				***9-30-95***	***9450***		***19563***	***48.3***						
Nts 6.20s '96	Mn13	**AA+**			X	BE	NC	....	....	....	....	....	500	M5	'95	100¼	99¾	100¼	6.18	5.47
F/R[17]Nts '97	QMar21	**AA+**			X	BE	NC	....	....	....	....	....	500	M5	'95	100¼	99¾	100	....	....
Sub Nts 7⅝s '98	mN15	**AA**	2/94	AA+	X	BE	NC	....	....	....	....	....	250	K2	'91	105⅜	97¾	105⅜	7.24	5.57
Sub Nts 9⅝s '98	jD15	**AA**	2/94	AA+	X	R	100	....	....	....	....	....	298	S4	'88	102⅛	100	100	9.63	9.62
Sub Nts Zero Cpn '98	[18]	**AA**	2/94	AA+	X	R	NC	....	....	....	....	....	400	L3	'91	88	76⅞	88	....	5.75
Sub Nts 7¼s 2002	Jj15	**AA**	2/94	AA+	X	BE	NC	....	....	....	....	....	200	F1	'92	106¼	93⅞	106¼	6.82	6.00
Sub Nts 8½s 2003	fA15	**AA**	2/94	AA+	X	BE	NC	....	....	....	....	....	150	F1	'91	114⅜	100⅛	114⅜	7.43	6.11
Sub Nts 7⅝s 2004	mS15	**AA**	2/94	AA+	X	BE	NC	....	....	....	....	....	500	M5	'94	110	94⅜	110	6.93	6.12
Sub Nts 8s 2005	Mn30	**AA**			X	BE	*100	(5-30-98)	....	....	....	....	100	M5	'95	105⅛	100	105⅛	7.61	7.24
Sub Nts 6¼s 2005	jD15	**AA**			X	BE	NC	....	....	....	....	....	300	M5	'95	100½	99½	100½	6.22	6.18

Uniform Footnote Explanations-See Page 260. Other: [1] (HRO)On Chge of Ctrl at 101. [2] Max $66.3M red w/proceeds of Cap Stk Off'g. [3] Subsid of MobileMedia Corp. [4] Int accrues at 10.5% fr 12-1-98(1st pyt 6-1-99). [5] Co must offer repurch at 101 on Chge of Ctrl(Accreted Val). [6] Max $70M red w/proceeds of Pub Eq Off'g. [7] Incl disc. [8] Int pay extent earned, cum to 12%. [9] Due 1-1-07. [10] Arrears cleared 10-1-65. [11] Contr by Allegheny Pwr Sys. [12] Fr 4-30-94 for Improv & SF. [13] (HRO)At 100 for DesignatedEvent&Rat'gDecline. [14] Now Kaneb Services,was Moran Bros. [15] Int arrears paid 3-31-89. [16] See Morgan Gty & Morgan(J.P.)Delaware. [17] Int adj daily. [18] Due 4-1-98.

Title-Industry Code & Co. Finances (In Italics) / Individual Issue Statistics, Exchange	Ind / Interest Dates	Fixed Charge Coverage 1992 / S&P Debt Rating	1993 / Date of Last Rating Change	1994 / Prior Rating	Eligible	Year End / Bond Form	Cash & Equiv. (Million $) / Redemption Provisions: Regular Price	Curr. Assets (Million $) / Regular (Begins) Thru	Curr. Liab. (Million $) / Sinking Fund Price	Balance Sheet Date / Sinking Fund (Begins) Thru	L. Term Debt (Mil $) / Refund/Other Restriction Price	Refund/Other Restriction (Begins) Thru	Capital-ization (Mil $) / Outst'g (Mil $)	Total Debt % Capital / Underwriting Firm	Underwriting Year	Price Range 1995 High	Price Range 1995 Low	Mo. End Price Sale(s) or Bid	Curr. Yield	Yield to Mat.
Morgan (J.P.)& Co *(Cont.)*																				
Sub Nts 5¾s 2008	aO15	**AA**	2/95	AA+	X	BE	NC	....	....	....	....	....	150	K2	'93	95¼	76⅞	95¼	6.04	6.29
Sub Nts 6¼s 2009	Jj15	**AA**	2/95	AA+	X	BE	NC	....	....	....	....	....	300	M5	'94	99⅜	80	99⅜	6.29	6.32
Sub[1]F/R[2]Nts 5.30s 2000	QMar13	**AA**	2/95	AA+	X	BE	NC	....	....	....	....	....	200	L3	'93	100	99¼	100	5.30	....
Morgan Guaranty Trust N.Y.	***10***	***Subsid of Morgan (J.P.) & Co,see***																		
Sub Nts[1] 8⅛s '96	Ms15	**AA+**			X	R	NC	....	....	....	....	....	100	L3	'91	101⅜	100½	100½	8.08	5.60
Sub Nts[1] 7⅜s 2002	Fa	**AA+**			X	R	NC	....	....	....	....	....	200	F1	'92	107¼	94⅛	107¼	6.88	5.94
Morgan Stanley Group	***62***	***1.18***	***1.24***	***[3]1.11***		***Nv***				***8-31-95***	***9111***		***21394***	***73.9***						
Deb 8.33s 2007	Jj15	**A+**			X	BE	NC	....	....	....	....	....	100	M6	'92	114⅝	95⅛	114⅝	7.27	6.46
Deb[4] 10s 2008	Jd15	**A+**			X	R	NC	....	....	....	....	....	100	M6	'88	129	106⅞	129	7.75	6.56
Deb 7s 2013	aO	**A+**			X	BE	NC	....	....	....	....	....	175	M6	'93	99	81⅞	99	7.07	7.10
Deb 7½s 2024	Fa	**A+**			X	BE	103.688	(2-1-04)	....	....	....	....	250	M6	'94	100⅝	82⅜	100⅝	7.45	7.45
Nts 8⅞s '96	Ao	**A+**			X	BE	NC	....	....	....	....	....	200	M6	'91	102	100¾	100¾	8.81	5.77
Nts 8s '96	aO15	**A+**			X	BE	NC	....	....	....	....	....	200	M6	'91	102¼	99⅝	101¾	7.86	5.70
Nts 7.32s '97	Jj15	**A+**			X	BE	NC	....	....	....	....	....	300	M6	'92	101¾	98¼	101¾	7.19	5.57
Nts 5.65s '97	jd15	**A+**			X	BE	NC	....	....	....	....	....	150	M6	'93	100	94⅛	100	5.65	5.65
Nts 9¼s '98	Ms	**A+**			X	R	NC	....	....	....	....	....	300	M6	'91	107	102⅛	107	8.64	5.77
Nts 7½s '99	mS	**A+**			X	BE	NC	....	....	....	....	....	200	M6	'94	105½	96½	105½	7.11	5.81
Nts 9⅜s 2001	Jd15	**A+**			X	BE	NC	....	....	....	....	....	125	M6	'91	114⅞	102⅞	114⅞	8.16	6.13
Nts 8⅞s 2001	aO15	**A+**			X	BE	NC	....	....	....	....	....	200	M6	'91	113⅜	100¼	113⅜	7.83	6.10
Nts 8.10s 2002	Jd24	**A+**			X	BE	NC	....	....	....	....	....	250	M6	'92	110¼	96¾	110¼	7.35	6.16
Nts 6¾s 2003	Ms4	**A+**			X	BE	NC	....	....	....	....	....	100	M6	'93	103¼	88¾	103¼	6.54	6.18
Nts 6⅛s 2003	aO	**A+**			X	BE	NC	....	....	....	....	....	150	M6	'93	99⅜	83½	99⅜	6.16	6.23
Nts 6⅜s 2003	jD15	**A+**			X	BE	NC	....	....	....	....	....	150	M6	'93	100⅞	85¼	100⅞	6.32	6.23
Morton International	***14***	***△7.82***	***△13.86***	***△17.57***		***Je***	***76.20***	***1240***	***568.0***	***9-30-95***	***219.0***		***1988***	***13.6***						
[5]Deb[6] 9¼s 2020	Jd	**AA–**			X	R	NC	....	....	....	....	....	200	G1	'90	132⅜	107	132⅜	6.99	6.57
Mosler Inc	***63***	***△0.79***	***△0.47***	***△0.81***		***Je***		***65.30***	***44.60***	***9-30-95***	***135.0***		***51.80***	***263.0***						
Sr Nts[7] 11s 2003	[8]jj15	**CCC–**	5/95	CC	Y	R	104.125	(7-15-98)	....	....	[9]108.25	7-14-96	115	F1	'93	80	67	76	14.47	16.82
Motorola, Inc.	***23a***	***4.89***	***9.38***	***13.69***		***Dc***	***994.0***	***1005***	***7384***	***9-30-95***	***1961***		***14434***	***25.6***						
Nts 7.60s 2007	Jj	**AA**	6/94	AA–	X	R	NC	....	....	....	....	....	300	G1	'92	113¼	94⅜	113¼	6.71	5.94
Nts 6½s 2008	Ms	**AA**	6/94	AA–	X	R	NC	....	....	....	....	....	200	M2	'93	103⅝	85⅛	103⅝	6.27	6.07
Deb 7½s 2025	Mn15	**AA**			X	R	NC	....	....	....	....	....	400	G1	'95	111⅞	98⅞	111⅞	6.70	6.58
Deb[10] 6½s 2025	mS	**AA**			X	BE	NC	....	....	....	....	....	400	G1	'95	104¾	99¼	104¾	6.21	6.15
Deb[11] 8.40s 2031	fA15	**AA**	6/94	AA–	X	R	NC	....	....	....	[12]Z100	....	200	G1	'91	126¼	102⅛	126¼	6.65	6.50
Mountain States Tel&Tel	***67a***	***Now U S WEST Commun,see***																		
Deb 5s 2000	Ao	**AA–**	4/90	AA	X	CR	100	....	....	....	....	....	40.0	H1	'60	97⅛	86⅞	97⅛	5.15	5.77
Deb 4½s 2002	Jd	**AA–**	4/90	AA	X	CR	100.39	5-31-96	....	....	....	....	50.0	F1	'62	92½	80⅛	92½	4.86	5.92
Deb 5½s 2005	Jd	**AA–**	4/90	AA	X	R	100.83	5-31-96	....	....	....	....	40.8	M2	'66	95⅜	81⅛	95⅜	5.77	6.15
Deb 6s 2007	fA	**AA–**	4/90	AA	X	R	101.05	7-31-96	....	....	....	....	70.2	F1	'67	97⅛	82¼	97⅛	6.18	6.35
Deb 7⅜s 2030	Mn	**AA–**			X	BE	NC	....	....	....	....	....	55.2	M6	'90	110	86½	110	6.70	6.63
Nts 9½s 2000	Mn	**AA–**			X	BE	NC	....	....	....	....	....	100	M6	'90	113¾	104½	113¾	8.35	5.86
Movie Star Inc[13]	***68c***	***△1.39***	***△0.02***	***△0.51***		***Je***	***0.10***	***48.70***	***26.00***	***6-30-95***	***22.50***		***47.00***	***81.5***						
◆Sub Deb 12⅞s 2001	aO	**CCC–**	10/95	B–	Y	R	104.44	9-30-96	100	(10-1-96)	....	....	22.4	B5	'86	92⅞	40	s50	....	....
[14]MS/Essex Holdings	***42b***	***n/a***	***0.84***	***1.28***		***Dc***	***16.90***	***328.0***	***106.0***	***12-31-94***	***459.0***		***525.0***	***87.4***						
Sr[15]Disc Deb 16s 2004	Mn15	**B**	4/93	B–	Y	R	100	....	100	(5-15-02)	....	....	[16]278	M6	'89	96⅝	96⅝	A96⅝	....	Flat
Multicare Cos.	***30a***	***1.32***	***1.78***	***3.09***		***Dc***	***49.30***	***134.0***	***33.90***	***9-30-95***	***233.0***		***350.0***	***66.9***						
Sr Sub Nts[7] 12½s 2002	jJ	**B–**			Y	R	105.778	(1-1-98)	....	....	....	....	68.6	D6	'92	116	111½	115	10.87	9.37

Uniform Footnote Explanations-See Page 260. Other: [1] Issued in min denom $250T. [2] Int(min 5.30%)to 3-13-96,adj qtrly aft. [3] Fiscal Jan'95 & prior. [4] Negative Pledge,as defined. [5] Credit Sensitive Deb. [6] Int subj to adj for rating chge. [7] (HRO)On Chge in Ctrl at 101. [8] Due 4-15-03. [9] Max $35M red w/proceeds Pub Eq Off'g. [10] (HRO)On 9-1-05 at 100. [11] (HRO)On 8-15-01 at 100. [12] On 8-15-01,if 95% or more put. [13] Was Sanmark-Stardust. [14] Now BCP/Essex Holdings. [15] Int accrues at 16% fr 5-15-95. [16] Incl disc.

Title-Industry Code & Co. Finances (In Italics) / Individual Issue Statistics / Exchange	Ind / Interest Dates	Fixed Charge Coverage 1992 / S&P Debt Rating	1993 / Date of Last Rating Change	1994 / Prior Rating	Eligible	Year End / Bond Form	Million $ Cash & Equiv. / Redemption Provisions Regular Price	Curr. Assets / Regular (Begins) Thru	Curr. Liab. / Sinking Fund Price	Balance Sheet Date / Sinking Fund (Begins) Thru	L. Term Debt (Mil $) / Refund/Other Restriction Price	Refund/Other Restriction (Begins) Thru	Capital-ization (Mil $) / Outst'g (Mil $)	Total Debt % Capital / Underwriting Firm	Underwriting Year	Price Range 1995 High	Price Range 1995 Low	Mo. End Price Sale(s) or Bid	Curr. Yield	Yield to Mat.
[1]Musicland Group Inc	***59l***	***2.86***	***3.86***	***2.76***		***Dc***	***1.30***	***701.0***	***460.0***	***9-30-95***	***446.0***		***634.0***	***72.9***						
Sr Sub[2]Nts[3] 9s 2003	Jd15	B+			Y	R	103.375	(6-15-98)	....	....	[4]Z110	6-15-96	110	D6	'93	90½	59	59	15.25	19.71
Nabisco, Inc[5]	***69a***	***0.88***	***0.98***	***1.86***		***Dc***	***133.0***	***1612***	***1227***	***9-30-95***	***4400***		***8658***	***51.7***						
• SF Deb 7¾s 2001	Mn	BBB	6/95	BBB–	X	R	100.31	4-30-96	100	....	....	....	22.5	L1	'71	101	92¼	101	7.67	7.52
• SF Deb 7¾s 2003	mN	BBB	6/95	BBB–	X	R	100.87	10-31-96	100	....	....	....	17.0	L1	'73	101¼	85⅞	100	7.75	7.75
Deb 7.55s 2015	Jd15	BBB			X	BE	NC	....	....	....	....	....	400	G1	'95	104¾	95½	104¾	7.21	7.10
• Nts 8.30s '99	Ao15	BBB			X	R	NC	....	....	....	....	....	538	Exch.	'95	106⅛	103	105¾	7.85	6.33
• Nts 8s 2000	Jj15	BBB			X	BE	NC	....	....	....	....	....	689	Exch.	'95	106½	103	s105⅞	7.56	6.33
[6]Nts[7] 6.80s 2001	mS	BBB			X	BE	NC	....	....	....	....	....	93.9	Exch.	'95	101½	98	101½	6.70	6.48
Nts 6.70s 2002	Jd15	BBB			X	BE	NC	....	....	....	....	....	400	G1	'95	102	96¾	102	6.57	6.32
Nts 6.85s 2005	Jd15	BBB			X	BE	NC	....	....	....	....	....	400	G1	'95	102	95½	102	6.72	6.56
Nts 7.05s 2007	jJ15	BBB			X	BE	NC	....	....	....	....	....	400	G1	'95	102⅞	95¾	102⅞	6.85	6.69
NAC Re Corp	***35c***	***1.78***	***4.64***	***3.93***		***Dc***				***9-30-95***	***★318.0***		***630.0***	***31.7***						
Nts 8s '99	Jd15	A–			X	R	NC	....	....	....	....	....	100	D4	'92	105⅝	96¾	105⅝	7.57	6.17
Nts 7.15s 2005	mN15	A–			X	BE	NC	....	....	....	....	....	100	D4	'95	101⅞	99⅞	101⅞	7.02	6.88
NACOLAH Holding Corp	***35***	***n/a***	***n/a***	***5.77***		***Dc***	***4.34***			***9-30-95***	***75.00***		***146.0***	***51.4***						
Sr[3]Nts 9½s 2003	jD	BB–			Y	R	104.75	(12-1-98)	....	....	[8]Z109.50	12-23-96	75.0	D6	'93	105	89	105	9.05	8.61
Narragansett Electric Co[9]	***72a***	***3.02***	***2.17***	***1.96***		***Dc***	***1.42***	***106.0***	***115.0***	***9-30-95***	***204.0***		***502.0***	***46.8***						
1st S 9⅛s 2021	Mn	A+			X	R	104.04	(5-1-01)	Z100	....	....	....	22.2	K2	'91	115⅜	100¾	115⅜	7.91	7.73
1st T 8⅞s 2021	fA	A+			X	R	103.79	(8-1-01)	100	....	....	....	40.0	M2	'91	117¼	98⅝	117¼	7.57	7.37
1st U(93-5) 7.05s 2023	[10]fa	A+			X	BE	103.52	(9-1-03)	Z100	(9-1-03)	....	....	5.00	C5	'93	99⅞	82⅝	99⅞	7.06	7.06
1st U(94-1) 7.05s 2024	[11]fa	A+			X	BE	103.53	(2-2-04)	Z100	(2-2-04)	....	....	5.00	K2	'94	102	83⅜	102	6.91	6.89
1st V(94-1) 8.08s 2024	[12]ms	A+			X	BE	104.04	(5-2-04)	Z100	(5-2-04)	....	....	5.00	C5	'94	112⅛	93⅜	112⅛	7.21	7.08
1st V(94-4) 7.42s 2004	[13]ms	A+			X	BE	NC	....	....	....	....	....	5.00	C5	'94	107	93½	107	6.93	6.34
1st V(94-5) 8.16s 2024	[14]ms	A+			X	BE	104.08	(8-9-04)	Z100	(8-9-04)	....	....	5.00	C5	'94	115⅝	95⅛	115⅝	7.06	6.90
National City Corp[15]	***10***	***3.96***	***4.86***	***3.91***		***Dc***				***9-30-95***	***1216***		***4085***	***29.8***						
• Nts 8⅜s '96	Ms15	A	3/91	A+	X	R	NC	....	....	....	....	....	100	S1	'86	100	100	98⅛	8.54	17.16
• F/R[16]Sub Nts 6.0625s '97	QJan31	A–	3/91	A	X	R	100	....	....	....	....	....	75.0	S1	'85	No Sale		100	6.06	....
Sub Nts 6⅝s 2004	Ms	A–			X	BE	NC	....	....	....	....	....	250	S1	'94	102⅜	87⅞	102⅜	6.47	6.25
Sub Nts 7.20s 2005	Mn15	A–			X	BE	NC	....	....	....	....	....	250	M2	'95	106½	99	106½	6.76	6.27
National Fuel Gas	***73b***	***△3.24***	***△3.76***	***△3.21***		***Sp***	***12.80***	***189.0***	***393.0***	***9-30-95***	***474.0***		***1364***	***41.3***						
Deb 7¾s 2004	Fa	A–	10/92	BBB+	X	R	NC	....	....	....	....	....	125	K2	'92	108⅝	94⅛	108⅝	7.13	6.37
Nat'l Medical Entpr	***30***	***Now Tenet Healthcare,see***																		
Nts[7] 7⅜s '97	mS	BB–	2/95	BB+	Y	BE	NC	....	....	....	....	....	58.0	M2	'92	101	95½	101	7.30	6.72
Natl Re Corp	***35c***	***3.38***	***6.54***	***3.28***		***Dc***				***9-30-95***	***211.0***		***570.0***	***37.0***						
Sr Nts 8.85s 2005	Jj15	A+			X	BE	NC	....	....	....	....	....	100	M2	'95	114⅝	99¾	114⅝	7.72	6.67
Sr Nts 7½s 2005	jJ31	A+			X	BE	NC	....	....	....	....	....	25.0	M2	'95	105¾	97⅛	105¾	7.09	6.68
Nat'l Rural Util.Co-opFin	***25***	***△1.16***	***△1.12***	***△1.13***		***My***	***53.30***			***8-31-95***	***3749***		***7348***	***79.8***						
• CT Bonds O 9s 2016	Ms15	AA	5/94	AA–	X	R	102.65	3-14-96	100	....	®102	3-14-96	83.2	S4	'86	105	99	102½	8.78	8.73
• CT Bonds T 9½s '97	Mn15	AA	5/94	AA–	X	R	NC	....	....	....	....	....	150	S4	'90	106¼	103½	103¼	9.20	6.97
• CT Bonds U 8½s '98	Fa15	AA	5/94	AA–	X	R	NC	....	....	....	....	....	150	L3	'91	105	101¾	103	8.25	6.95
• CT Bonds V 9s 2021	mS	AA	5/94	AA–	X	R	104	(9-1-01)	....	....	....	....	150	L3	'91	110	101⅞	116⅞	7.70	7.51
F/R[17]CT Bonds '94A' '96	[18]Sep15	AA			X	BE	NC	....	....	....	....	....	150	L3	'94	100⅛	99¾	100	....	....
CT Bonds 6½s 2002	mS15	AA			X	BE	NC	....	....	....	....	....	100	L3	'95	103⅛	99¼	103⅛	6.30	5.93
CT Bonds 6.65s 2005	aO	AA			X	BE	NC	....	....	....	....	....	50.0	L3	'95	103⅞	99½	103⅞	6.40	6.12
CT Bonds 7.20s 2015	aO	AA			X	BE	NC	....	....	....	....	....	50.0	L3	'95	104⅞	99⅝	104⅞	6.87	6.75
National Steel[19]Corp[20]	***66a***	***0.30***	***d1.55***	***1.11***		***Dc***	***162.0***	***823.0***	***598.0***	***12-31-94***	***p598.0***		***988.0***	***64.2***						
• 1st 8⅜s 2006	fA	BB–	9/93	BB	Y	R	102.01	7-31-96	100	....	....	....	75.0	M2	'76	95⅝	87⅛	s94⅞	8.83	9.14

Uniform Footnote Explanations-See Page 260. Other: [1] Subsid & data of Musicland Stores. [2] Gtd by Musicland Stores. [3] (HRO)On Chge of Ctrl at 101. [4] Max $25M red to 6-15-96 w/proceeds of com off'g. [5] Subsid of Nabisco Hldgs. [6] (HRO)On 9-2-97 at 100. [7] Issued in min denom $100T. [8] Max $25M red w/proceeds of Pub Eq Off'g. [9] Contr by New England Elec System. [10] Due 9-1-23. [11] Due 2-2-24. [12] Due 5-2-24. [13] Due 6-15-04. [14] Due 8-9-24. [15] See First Kentucky Nat'l,Merchants Nat'l. [16] Int to 1-31-96,adj qtrly aft. [17] Int adj monthly. [18] Int pd monthly. [19] Subsid of Nat'l Intergroup. [20] Was Granite City Steel.

Title-Industry Code & Co. Finances (In Italics) / Individual Issue Statistics / Exchange	Ind / Interest Dates	Fixed Charge Coverage 1992 / S&P Debt Rating	1993 / Date of Last Rating Change	1994 / Prior Rating	Eligible	Year End / Bond Form	Million $ Cash & Equiv. / Redemption Provisions: Regular Price	Million $ Curr. Assets / Regular (Begins) Thru	Million $ Curr. Liab. / Sinking Fund Price	Balance Sheet Date / Sinking Fund (Begins) Thru	L. Term Debt (Mil $) / Refund/Other Restriction Price	Refund/Other Restriction (Begins) Thru	Capital-ization (Mil $) / Outst'g (Mil $)	Total Debt % Capital / Underwriting Firm	Underwriting Year	Price Range 1995 High	Price Range 1995 Low	Mo. End Price Sale(s) or Bid	Curr. Yield	Yield to Mat.
***NationsBank Corp*[1]**	***10***	***2.53***	***2.42***	***1.88***		***Dc***				***9-30-95***	***15741***		***27682***	***56.9***						
Sr Nts 4¾s '96	fA15	**A**			X	R	NC	....	....	....	....	....	400	M2	'93	99½	95¼	99½	4.77	5.56
Sr Nts 7½s '97	Fa15	**A**			X	R	NC	....	....	....	....	....	250		'95	102⅜	99⅞	102⅛	7.34	5.52
Sr Nts 6⅝s '98	Jj	**A**			X	R	NC	....	....	....	....	....	400	M2	'93	102	95¼	102	6.50	5.57
Sr Nts 5⅛s '98	mS15	**A**			X	R	NC	....	....	....	....	....	300		'93	98¾	89½	98¾	5.19	5.63
Sr Nts 5⅜s 2000	aO15	**A**			X	R	NC	....	....	....	....	....	400		'93	98⅜	86½	98⅜	5.46	5.81
Sub Nts 8⅛s 2002	Jd15	**A–**			X	R	NC	....	....	....	....	....	350	M2	'92	110⅜	96⅞	110⅜	7.36	6.15
Sub Nts 6½s 2003	fA15	**A–**			X	R	NC	....	....	....	....	....	600	M2	'93	101⅝	86⅞	101⅝	6.40	6.23
Sub Nts 7¾s 2004	fA15	**A–**			X	R	NC	....	....	....	....	....	300		'94	109¾	96⅛	109¾	7.06	6.27
Sub Nts 6⅞s 2005	Fa15	**A–**			X	R	NC	....	....	....	....	....	400	M2	'93	104⅛	87	104⅛	6.60	6.27
Sub Nts 7⅝s 2005	Ao15	**A–**			X	BE	NC	....	....	....	....	....	300		'95	109½	98½	109½	6.96	6.26
Sub Nts 7¾s 2015	fA15	**A–**			X	BE	NC	....	....	....	....	....	350		'95	109½	100	109½	7.08	6.86
Sub Nts 7¼s 2025	aO15	**A–**			X	BE	NC	....	....	....	....	....	450		'95	103¾	97⅞	103¾	6.99	6.95
***Navistar*[2]*Fin'l Corp*[3]**	***25d***	***1.54***	***1.62***	***1.88***		***Oc***	***174.0***			***7-31-95***	***773.0***		***1066***	***76.6***						
Sr[4]Sub Nts 8⅞s '98	mN15	**B+**			Y	R	NC	....	....	....	....	....	100	M5	'93	101	93½	101	8.79	8.47
***Navistar*[5]*Intl Trans*[3]**	***9a***	***d0.53***	***d3.85***	***1.38***		***Oc***	***448.0***			***1-31-95***	***1743***		***458.0***	***425.0***						
• SF Deb 6¼s '98	Ms	**BB**	10/93	B–	Y	R	100	....	100	....	....	....	14.0	M6	'68	98¼	89½	94⅝	6.61	9.02
• SF Deb 9s 2004	Jd15	**BB**	10/93	B–	Y	R	101.32	6-14-96	100	....	....	....	84.0	M6	'74	101½	92⅛	101¼	8.89	8.79
NBD Bancorp	***10***	***Now First Chicago NBD,see***																		
Sub Nts 7⅛s 2007	Mn15	**A**	12/95	A+	X	BE	NC	....	....	....	....	....	200	L3	'95	106⅜	97⅞	106⅜	6.70	6.33
NBD Bank N.A. Detroit	***10***	***Subsid of NBD Bancorp,see***																		
M-T Bank Nts[6] 6.85s '98	[7]jj15	**A+**	12/95	AA	X	BE	NC	....	....	....	....	....	100		'95	102¾	99⅞	102¾	6.67	5.59
NCNB Corp	***10***	***Now NationsBank Corp,see***																		
◆Deb 7¾s 2002	fA	**A**	8/83	A–	X	R	100	....	....	....	....	....	[8]27.5	S1	'82	102½	95	100	7.75	7.75
• Nts 8½s '96	mN	**A**			X	R	NC	....	....	....	....	....	150	S1	'86	103⅝	100	102	8.33	6.00
Sub Nts 9⅛s 2001	aO15	**A–**			X	R	NC	....	....	....	....	....	300	M2	'91	114⅝	102⅝	114⅝	7.96	6.09
Sub Nts 9⅜s 2009	mS15	**A–**			X	R	NC	....	....	....	....	....	400	M2	'89	125½	103⅜	125½	7.47	6.53
Sub Nts 10.20s 2015	jJ15	**A–**			X	R	NC	....	....	....	....	....	200	M2	'90	135	110½	135	7.56	6.91
[9]*NCNB Texas Nat'l Bank*	***10***	***Subsid of NationsBank Corp,see***																		
Cap Nts Oblig 9½s 2004	Jd	**A**	1/93	A–	X	R	NC	....	....	....	....	....	300	S8	'89	120¼	106	120¼	7.90	6.36
Nevada Power	***72a***	***2.61***	***3.11***	***3.34***		***Dc***	***65.10***	***213.0***	***181.0***	***9-30-95***	***786.0***		***1619***	***49.8***						
1st I 7⅛s '98	Ao	**BBB**	8/93	BBB–	X	R	100.50	3-31-96	100	....	....	....	15.0	W5	'68	100⅝	96⅝	100½	7.09	6.87
1st L 7⅝s 2002	mN	**BBB**	8/93	BBB–	X	R	101.64	10-31-96	100.14	10-31-96	....	....	15.0	B6	'72	102⅛	94½	102⅛	7.47	7.22
1st Z 8½s 2023	Jj	**BBB**	8/93	BBB–	X	R	103.71	(1-1-03)	....	....	....	....	45.0	P1	'93	111¼	93⅝	111¼	7.64	7.52
1st 7.06s 2000	Mn	**BBB**			X	R	NC	....	....	....	....	....	85.0	P1	'95	103½	99¾	103½	6.82	6.13
***New England Power Co.*[10]**	***72a***	***4.31***	***5.40***	***6.54***		***Dc***	***2.48***	***370.0***	***373.0***	***9-30-95***	***735.0***		***1864***	***48.9***						
1st M 6⅞s '97	aO	**A+**	5/89	AA–	X	R	100.33	9-30-96	100.33	9-30-96	....	....	15.0	L3	'67	100⅝	97	100½	6.84	6.56
1st N 7⅛s '98	jJ	**A+**	5/89	AA–	X	R	100.63	6-30-96	100.44	6-30-96	....	....	20.0	L3	'68	101	96⅝	101	7.05	6.68
1st O 7⅜s '98	jD	**A+**	5/89	AA–	X	R	100.66	11-30-96	100.47	11-30-96	....	....	20.0	M2	'68	101¼	97	100⅞	7.31	7.04
1st R 7⅝s 2002	jJ	**A+**	5/89	AA–	X	R	101.77	6-30-96	100.41	6-30-96	....	....	25.0	F1	'72	102½	95⅜	102⅛	7.47	7.21
Gen & Ref U 8s 2022	fA	**A+**			X	R	103.61	(8-1-02)	Z100	(8-1-02)	....	....	170	G1	'92	109⅛	91⅜	108½	7.37	7.27
Gen & Ref W(93-1) 7s 2003	[11]mn	**A+**			X	BE	NC	....	....	....	....	....	25.0	C5	'93	104¾	91	104¾	6.68	6.16
Gen & Ref W(93-3) 5.12s '96	[12]mn	**A+**			X	BE	NC	....	....	....	....	....	5.00	C5	'93	100	97⅜	100	5.12	5.02
Gen & Ref W(93-5) 6.17s '98	[13]mn	**A+**			X	BE	NC	....	....	....	....	....	5.00	C5	'93	101⅛	94⅜	101⅛	6.10	5.59
Gen & Ref W(93-6) 6.58s 2000	[14]mn	**A+**			X	BE	NC	....	....	....	....	....	5.00	C5	'93	102½	92⅜	102½	6.42	5.88
Gen & Ref W(93-7) 6.10s '98	[15]mn	**A+**			X	BE	NC	....	....	....	....	....	10.0	C5	'93	101	94⅛	101	6.04	5.58
Gen & Ref W(93-8) 5.06s '96	[16]mn	**A+**			X	BE	NC	....	....	....	....	....	5.00	C5	'93	100	97¼	100	5.06	4.96

Uniform Footnote Explanations-See Page 260. Other: [1] See NCNB Corp, NCNB Tex Natl Bk. [2] Was Int'l Harvester Credit. [3] Subsid of Navistar Int'l. [4] (HRO)On Chge of Ctrl at 101. [5] Was Int'l Harvester/Navistar Intl. [6] Issued in min denom $250T. [7] Due 5-11-98. [8] Incl disc. [9] Now NationsBank of Texas N.A. [10] Subsid of New England Elec System. [11] Due 2-3-03. [12] Due 2-2-96. [13] Due 2-3-98. [14] Due 2-10-00. [15] Due 2-4-98. [16] Due 2-5-96.

Title-Industry Code & Co. Finances (In Italics)	Ind	Fixed Charge Coverage 1992	1993		1994	Year End	Cash & Equiv. (Million $)	Curr. Assets (Million $)	Curr. Liab. (Million $)	Balance Sheet Date	L. Term Debt (Mil $)		Capital-ization (Mil $)	Total Debt % Capital						
Individual Issue Statistics Exchange ↓	Interest Dates	S&P Debt Rating	Date of Last Rating Change	Prior Rating	Eligible ↓	Bond Form	Redemption Provisions: Regular Price	Regular (Begins) Thru	Sinking Fund Price	Sinking Fund (Begins) Thru	Refund/Other Restriction Price	Refund/Other Restriction (Begins) Thru	Outst'g (Mil $)	Underwriting Firm	Underwriting Year	Price Range 1995 High	Price Range 1995 Low	Mo. End Price Sale(s) or Bid	Curr. Yield	Yield to Mat.
New England Power Co. *(Cont.)*																				
Gen & Ref W(93-9) 6.04s '98	[1]mn	**A+**			X	BE	NC	....	....	....	....	....	29.4	C5	'93	100⅞	94	100⅞	5.99	5.59
Gen & Ref Y(94-1) 8.53s 2024	[2]mn	**A+**			X	BE	104.27	(9-23-04)	Z100	(9-23-04)	....	....	5.00	C5	'94	115⅞	97⅜	115⅞	7.36	7.21
New England Tel. & Tel.[3]	***67a***	***4.84***	***1.38***		***5.56***	***Dc***	***4.00***	***1149***	***1254***	***9-30-95***	***2172***		***4678***	***46.5***						
• Deb 4⅝s '99	Ao	**AA−**	6/91	AA	X	CR	100	....	....	....	....	....	45.0	F1	'61	98	87¼	96	4.82	5.99
• Deb 4½s 2002	jJ	**AA−**	6/91	AA	X	CR	100.30	6-30-96	....	....	....	....	50.0	F1	'62	92½	77⅝	s91⅛	4.94	6.18
• Deb 4⅝s 2005	jJ	**AA−**	6/91	AA	X	R	100.72	6-30-96	....	....	....	....	60.0	H1	'65	90½	73	90¼	5.12	5.98
• Deb 6⅛s 2006	aO	**AA−**	6/91	AA	X	R	101.13	9-30-96	....	....	....	....	100	L3	'67	99	81¼	98	6.25	6.38
• Deb 7⅜s 2007	aO15	**AA−**	6/91	AA	X	R	101.65	10-14-96	....	....	....	....	200	M6	'72	102	89¾	101½	7.27	7.18
• Deb 6⅜s 2008	mS	**AA−**	6/91	AA	X	R	101.30	8-31-96	....	....	....	....	125	F1	'68	100¾	81⅛	100	6.38	6.37
• Deb 7⅞s 2022	mS	**AA−**			X	BE	103.551	(9-1-02)	....	....	....	....	100	L3	'92	101¾	100	102⅜	7.69	7.66
• Deb 6⅞s 2023	aO	**AA−**			X	R	102.75	(10-1-03)	....	....	....	....	250	F1	'93	97	81½	97½	7.05	7.08
• Deb[4] 7⅞s 2029	mN15	**AA−**	6/91	AA	X	R	NC	....	....	....	....	....	350	S1	'89	109½	96¾	107⅛	7.35	7.30
• Deb 9s 2031	fA	**AA−**			X	BE	106	(8-1-01)	....	....	....	....	100	G1	'91	103	103	105⅝	8.52	8.49
• Nts 6¼s '97	jD15	**AA−**			X	BE	NC	....	....	....	....	....	175	F1	'92	101⅛	95	s101	6.19	5.70
• Nts 5.05s '98	aO	**AA−**			X	BE	NC	....	....	....	....	....	100	G1	'93	98¼	89⅝	97⅝	5.17	5.99
• Nts 6.15s '99	mS	**AA−**			X	BE	NC	....	....	....	....	....	100	M6	'92	102	92½	100½	6.12	5.99
• Nts 5¾s 2000	Mn	**AA−**			X	BE	NC	....	....	....	....	....	100	M5	'93	99½	88¼	99⅛	5.80	5.98
• Nts 8⅝s 2001	fA	**AA−**			X	BE	NC	....	....	....	....	....	100	G1	'91	112	101¾	111¼	7.75	6.21
• Nts 6¼s 2003	Ms15	**AA−**			X	BE	NC	....	....	....	....	....	225	M6	'93	101⅜	86½	100	6.25	6.25
New Jersey Bell Tel[5]	***67a***	***Now Bell Atlantic-N.J.,see***																		
Deb 4⅞s 2000	mN	**AA+**	10/93	AAA	X	CR	100	10-31-96	....	....	....	....	20.0	M6	'60	95¾	84⅝	95¾	5.09	5.90
Deb 7¼s 2002	Jd	**AA+**	10/93	AAA	X	BE	NC	....	....	....	....	....	100	S1	'92	107	94⅜	107	6.78	5.92
Deb 4⅝s 2005	Jd	**AA+**	10/93	AAA	X	R	100.81	5-31-96	....	....	....	....	40.0	W5	'65	89⅞	74⅝	89⅞	5.15	6.05
Deb 5⅞s 2006	jD	**AA+**	10/93	AAA	X	R	100.95	11-30-96	....	....	....	....	55.0	S1	'66	97⅜	81⅞	97⅜	6.03	6.21
Deb 6⅝s 2008	Ao	**AA+**	10/93	AAA	X	R	101.29	3-31-96	....	....	....	....	50.0	M2	'68	101⅝	86⅛	101⅜	6.54	6.46
• Deb 7¼s 2011	Ao	**AA+**	10/93	AAA	X	R	102.48	3-31-96	....	....	....	....	125	M6	'71	102¾	88⅜	101½	7.14	7.09
• Deb 7⅜s 2012	Jd	**AA+**	10/93	AAA	X	R	102.20	5-31-96	....	....	....	....	75.0	H1	'72	102⅜	89	101¾	7.25	7.19
Deb 8s 2022	Jd	**AA+**	10/93	AAA	X	BE	NC	....	....	....	....	....	200	G1	'92	117¾	95¾	117¾	6.79	6.57
Deb 7¼s 2023	Ms	**AA+**	10/93	AAA	X	BE	103.42	(3-1-03)	....	....	....	....	100	F1	'93	106⅛	85⅜	106⅛	6.83	6.75
Deb 6.80s 2024	jD15	**AA+**			X	BE	101.536	(12-15-08)	....	....	....	....	100	M6	'93	101⅜	81⅜	101⅜	6.71	6.69
Deb[6] 7.85s 2029	mN15	**AA+**	10/93	AAA	X	R	NC	....	....	....	....	....	150	M2	'89	118⅞	101⅜	118⅞	6.60	6.47
New Orleans Public Serv[7]	***75***	***2.68***	***3.98***		***1.94***	***Dc***	***53.10***	***170.0***	***138.0***	***9-30-95***	***156.0***		***381.0***	***50.9***						
1st 5⅝s '96	Ao	**BBB**	1/92	BBB−	X	CR	100	....	100	....	....	....	23.3	H1	'66	99⅞	97	99⅞	5.63	6.04
1st 5⅞s '97	Ao	**BBB**	1/92	BBB−	X	CR	100.24	3-31-96	100.14	3-31-96	....	....	12.0	H1	'67	99⅞	94⅝	99⅞	5.88	5.97
Gen & Ref[8] 7s 2003	Ms	**BBB**			X	BE	101.97	(3-1-98)	100	(3-1-99)	Z104.93	2-29-96	25.0	G1	'93	102¼	83	102¼	6.85	6.60
Gen & Ref[8] 8s 2023	Ms	**BBB**			X	BE	105.49	2-29-96	100	(3-1-99)	Z106.59	2-29-96	45.0	G1	'93	107⅜	83¾	107⅜	7.45	7.37
Gen & Ref[8] 8.67s 2005	Ao	**BBB**			X	BE	100	(4-1-98)	Z100	(4-1-98)	....	....	30.0	M6	'95	104¾	100	104¾	8.28	7.93
Gen & Ref[8] 7.55s 2023	mS	**BBB**			X	BE	105.57	(9-1-98)	Z100	(9-1-98)	Z106.68	8-31-96	30.0	K2	'93	100⅜	83¼	100⅜	7.52	7.52
New Plan Realty Tr	***57***	***Δ32.19***	***Δ23.86***		***Δ9.74***	***Jl***				***10-31-95***	***p244.0***		***779.0***	***26.6***						
Sr Nts 7¾s 2005	Ao6	**A+**			X	BE	NC	....	....	....	....	....	100	M2	'95	109⅛	98⅝	109⅛	7.10	6.43
Sr Nts 6.80s 2002	Mn15	**A+**			X	BE	NC	....	....	....	....	....	81.0	L3	'95	103	97⅜	103	6.60	6.22
New York St. Elec & Gas	***75***	***2.82***	***2.88***		***3.05***	***Dc***	***6.63***	***249.0***	***245.0***	***9-30-95***	***1617***		***3608***	***45.0***						
1st 5⅝s '97	Jj	**BBB+**	6/94	A−	X	R	100	....	100	....	....	....	25.0	F1	'67	99⅞	95¼	99⅞	5.63	5.75
1st 6¼s '97	mS	**BBB+**	6/94	A−	X	R	100.29	8-31-96	100.28	8-31-96	....	....	25.0	K2	'67	100⅜	95⅛	100⅜	6.23	6.00
1st 6½s '98	mS	**BBB+**	6/94	A−	X	R	100.54	8-31-96	100.27	8-31-96	....	....	30.0	F1	'68	100⅞	94¼	100⅞	6.44	6.14
• 1st 7⅝s 2001	mN	**BBB+**	6/94	A−	X	R	101.58	10-31-96	100.60	10-31-96	....	....	50.0	B6	'71	101	95¼	100⅞	7.56	7.43

Uniform Footnote Explanations-See Page 260. Other: [1] Due 2-4-98. [2] Due 9-23-24. [3] Subsid of NYNEX Corp. [4] (HRO)On 11-15-96 at 100. [5] Subsid of Bell Atlantic Corp. [6] (HRO)On 11-15-99 at 100. [7] Subsid of Entergy Corp. [8] (HRO)On Chge of Ctrl at prices,as defined.

Company header row: Title-Industry Code & Co. Finances (In Italics) | Ind | Fixed Charge Coverage 1992, 1993, 1994, Year End | Million $: Cash & Equiv., Curr. Assets, Curr. Liab. | Balance Sheet Date | L. Term Debt (Mil $) | Capital-ization (Mil $) | Total Debt % Capital

Individual Issue Statistics / Exchange	Interest Dates	S&P Debt Rating	Date of Last Rating Change	Prior Rating	Eligible	Bond Form	Redemption Provisions: Regular Price	Regular (Begins) Thru	Sinking Fund Price	Sinking Fund (Begins) Thru	Refund/Other Restriction Price	Refund/Other Restriction (Begins) Thru	Outst'g (Mil $)	Underwriting Firm	Underwriting Year	Price Range 1995 High	Price Range 1995 Low	Mo. End Price Sale(s) or Bid	Curr. Yield	Yield to Mat.
***New York St. Elec & Gas** (Cont.)*																				
1st 6¾s 2002	aO15	BBB+	6/94	A–	X	R	NC	....	....	....	Z100	....	150	M2	'92	102	88⅞	102	6.62	6.38
• 1st 8⅝s 2007	mN	BBB+	6/94	A–	X	R	102.88	10-31-96	100	....	....	....	14.0	B6	'77	105	100	102	8.46	8.35
1st 9⅞s 2020	Fa	BBB+	6/94	A–	X	R	106.52	1-31-96	Z100	....	Z100	....	100	S1	'90	108⅞	103¼	106⅝	9.26	9.19
1st 9⅞s 2020	Mn	BBB+	6/94	A–	X	R	104.18	(5-1-00)	Z100	....	....	....	100	S1	'90	118	104¼	115	8.59	8.41
1st 9⅞s 2020	mN	BBB+	6/94	A–	X	R	104.34	(11-1-00)	Z100	....	....	....	100	S1	'90	116	104⅝	116	8.51	8.34
1st 8⅞s 2021	mN	BBB+	6/94	A–	X	R	103.79	(11-1-01)	Z100	....	....	....	150	M2	'91	113¾	97	113¾	7.80	7.65
1st 8.30s 2022	jD15	BBB+	6/94	A–	X	R	103.43	(12-15-02)	Z100	(12-15-02)	Z100	....	100	M2	'92	108⅞	91⅞	108⅞	7.62	7.53
1st 7.55s 2023	Ao	BBB+	6/94	A–	X	R	102.78	(4-1-03)	Z100	....	....	....	50.0	M2	'93	102¼	85⅝	102¼	7.38	7.36
1st 7.45s 2023	jJ15	BBB+	6/94	A–	X	R	103.50	(7-15-03)	Z100	(7-15-03)	Z100	....	100	M2	'93	101½	84⅛	101½	7.34	7.32
New York Telephone Co[1]	***67a***	***4.30***	***1.04***		***2.54***	***Dc***	***27.80***	***1942***	***2656***	***9-30-95***	***3914***		***6812***	***63.2***						
• Ref I 3⅜s '96	Ao	A	12/89	AA	X	CR	100	....	....	....	....	....	55.0	M6	'56	99¼	94⅜	99⅛	3.40	6.80
• Ref L 4⅝s '97	aO	A	12/89	AA	X	CR	100	....	....	....	....	....	60.0	H1	'60	97¾	90⅛	97¾	4.73	5.99
• Ref M 4⅝s 2002	Jj	A	12/89	AA	X	CR	100.17	12-31-96	....	....	....	....	60.0	H1	'62	92¼	80¾	91¾	5.04	6.30
• Ref N 4¼s 2000	Jj	A	12/89	AA	X	CR	....	....	....	....	....	....	70.0	H1	'63	94¼	83¼	93½	4.55	6.10
• Ref O 4⅝s 2004	Jj	A	12/89	AA	X	CR	100.57	12-31-96	....	....	....	....	130	M6	'64	91	75¼	s91	5.08	6.06
• Ref P 4⅞s 2006	Jj	A	12/89	AA	X	R	100.75	12-31-96	....	....	....	....	100	M6	'66	90¾	73⅛	88¾	5.49	6.42
• Ref Q 6s 2007	mS	A	12/89	AA	X	R	101.23	8-31-96	....	....	....	....	75.0	H1	'67	98	77½	95¾	6.27	6.52
• Ref R 7½s 2009	Ms	A	12/89	AA	X	R	101.83	2-29-96	....	....	....	....	150	M6	'69	103¼	88⅝	101⅛	7.42	7.36
• Ref T 7¾s 2006	jD15	A	12/89	AA	X	R	101.86	12-14-96	....	....	....	....	200	M6	'70	103	93⅝	101¼	7.65	7.58
• Ref V 7⅜s 2011	jD15	A	12/89	AA	X	R	102.71	12-14-96	....	....	....	....	200	M6	'71	102⅜	86⅝	s101¼	7.28	7.24
• Deb 6½s 2005	Ms	A			X	BE	NC	....	....	....	....	....	200	S1	'93	101¾	86	100½	6.47	6.43
• Deb 8⅝s 2010	mN15	A	12/89	AA	X	R	NC	....	....	....	....	....	150	M6	'89	109⅛	103	111⅝	7.73	7.33
• Deb 7s 2013	Mn	A			X	BE	NC	....	....	....	....	....	100	S1	'93	96⅞	89	99⅛	7.06	7.09
• Deb 7s 2013	Jd15	A			X	BE	NC	....	....	....	....	....	100	S1	'93	100	91¼	100	7.00	7.00
• Deb 7⅞s 2017	Jd15	A	12/89	AA	X	R	103.83	6-14-96	....	....	....	....	200	S1	'77	104	89½	103⅛	7.64	7.58
• Deb 7⅝s 2023	Fa	A			X	BE	102.879	(2-1-03)	....	....	....	....	100	K2	'93	103½	87⅛	102¼	7.46	7.43
Deb 6.70s 2023	mN	A			X	BE	100	(11-1-13)	....	....	....	....	250	S1	'93	94¼	76	94	7.13	7.20
• Deb 7¼s 2024	Fa15	A			X	BE	103.061	(2-15-04)	....	....	....	....	450	M6	'94	100⅛	86¾	99½	7.29	7.29
• Deb 7s 2025	fA	A			X	BE	102.34	(8-15-03)	....	....	....	....	250	G1	'93	100	80⅝	s99¾	7.02	7.02
• Deb 9⅜s 2031	jJ15	A			X	BE	106.08	(7-15-01)	....	....	....	....	200	S1	'91	111½	106½	113¼	8.28	8.22
• Deb 7s 2033	jD	A			X	BE	100	(12-1-13)	....	....	....	....	200	K2	'93	98⅞	92	98⅝	7.10	7.10
• Nts 5¼s '98	mS	A			X	BE	NC	....	....	....	....	....	100	M6	'93	99¼	91⅛	98¼	5.34	5.96
• Nts 5⅞s 2003	mS	A			X	BE	NC	....	....	....	....	....	200	C4	'93	99	85½	98¾	5.95	6.08
Nts 5⅝s 2003	mN	A			X	BE	NC	....	....	....	....	....	150	M6	'93	95¼	82⅜	95	5.92	6.45
• Nts 6¼s 2004	Fa15	A			X	BE	NC	....	....	....	....	....	150	G1	'94	102	85	101½	6.16	6.01
New York Times	***54c***	***3.07***	***4.43***		***6.44***	***Dc***	***77.40***	***461.0***	***491.0***	***9-30-95***	***638.0***		***2348***	***33.5***						
Deb 8¼s 2025	Ms15	A+			X	R	103.76	(3-15-05)	....	....	....	....	150	C5	'95	113⅜	99¼	113⅜	7.28	7.15
Nts 7⅝s 2005	Ms15	A+			X	R	NC	....	....	....	....	....	250	C5	'95	110⅞	99⅝	110⅞	6.88	6.06
NewCity Commun	***23e***	***0.76***	***0.92***		***1.08***	***Dc***	***0.38***	***12.60***	***10.00***	***9-30-95***	***84.70***		***74.00***	***116.0***						
Sr Sub Nts[2] 11⅜s 2003	MN	B–			Y	R	104.266	(11-1-98)	....	....	[3]Z110	12-31-96	75.0	B5	'93	97¼	90	92½	12.30	12.92
Newmont Mining	***45e***	***8.13***	***6.34***		***1.64***	***Dc***	***123.0***	***335.0***	***194.0***	***9-30-95***	***604.0***		***1464***	***43.2***						
Nts 8⅝s 2002	Ao	BBB+			X	R	NC	....	....	....	....	....	150	L1	'92	110⅝	98¼	110⅝	7.80	6.53
NEXTEL Communic'ns	***67***	***d25.87***	***d1.73***		....	***Mr***	***507.0***	***577.0***	***353.0***	***9-30-95***	***1481***		***4505***	***32.9***						
Sr[4]Red[2]Disc Nts 11½s 2003	mS	CCC–	10/94	CCC+	Y	R	105.10	(9-1-98)	....	....	....	....	[5]526	M2	'93	61½	30½	61⅜	....	Flat
Sr Red[6]Disc Nts[7] 9¾s 2004	fA15	CCC–	10/94	CCC+	Y	R	104.875	(2-15-99)	....	....	[8]Z109.75	2-14-96	[5]1126	M2	'94	58	29	53¼	....	Flat
NGC Corp	***73e***	***1.53***	***1.52***		***1.22***	***Dc***	***27.60***	***542.0***	***478.0***	***9-30-95***	***★525.0***		***1058***	***49.5***						
Sr Nts 6¾s 2005	jD15	BBB–			X	BE	NC	....	....	....	....	....	150	L3	'95	99⅞	99⅞	99⅞	6.76	6.77

Uniform Footnote Explanations-See Page 260. Other: [1] Subsid of NYNEX Corp. [2] (HRO)On Chge of Ctrl at 101. [3] Max $25M red w/proceeds of Pub Eq Off'g. [4] Int acccr at 11.50% fr 9-1-98. [5] Incl disc. [6] (HRO)On Chge of Ctrl at 101(Accreted Val). [7] Int accr at 9.75% fr 2-15-99. [8] Accreted Val(%):Max 20% w/proceeds Cap Stk sale.

Title-Industry Code & Co. Finances (In Italics) / Individual Issue Statistics (Exchange)	Ind / Interest Dates	Fixed Charge Coverage 1992 / S&P Debt Rating	1993 / Date of Last Rating Change	1994 / Prior Rating	Eligible	Year End / Bond Form	Million $ Cash & Equiv. / Redemption Provisions: Regular Price	Curr. Assets / Regular (Begins) Thru	Curr. Liab. / Sinking Fund Price	Balance Sheet Date / Sinking Fund (Begins) Thru	L. Term Debt (Mil $) / Refund/Other Restriction Price	Refund/Other Restriction (Begins) Thru	Capital-ization (Mil $) / Outst'g (Mil $)	Total Debt % Capital / Underwriting Firm	Underwriting Year	Price Range 1995 High	Price Range 1995 Low	Mo. End Price Sale(s) or Bid	Curr. Yield	Yield to Mat.
Niagara Mohawk Power	*75*	*2.30*	*2.38*	*1.98*		*Dc*	*104.0*	*874.0*	*640.0*	*9-30-95*	*3457*		*6651*	*53.7*						
1st 5⅞s '96	mN	**BB**	10/95	BBB–	Y	CR	100	....	□100	....	....	....	45.0	M6	'66	99⅜	95¾	98¾	5.95	7.42
1st 6¼s '97	fA	**BB**	10/95	BBB–	Y	R	100.27	7-31-96	□100.23	7-31-96	....	....	40.0	M6	'67	99½	94½	98⅜	6.35	7.35
1st 6½s '98	fA	**BB**	10/95	BBB–	Y	R	100.57	7-31-96	□100.38	7-31-96	....	....	60.0	M6	'68	99⅜	92¾	97½	6.67	7.58
1st 9½s 2000	Jd	**BB**	10/95	BBB–	Y	R	NC	....	....	....	....	....	150	M2	'90	110⅛	100⅝	102⅝	9.26	8.77
1st 6⅞s 2001	Ms	**BB**	10/95	BBB–	Y	R	NC	....	....	....	....	....	210	M2	'94	99⅝	88⅝	95⅜	7.21	7.98
1st 9¼s 2001	aO	**BB**	10/95	BBB–	Y	R	NC	....	....	....	....	....	100	M2	'89	110½	99⅞	102¼	9.05	8.74
1st 5⅞s 2002	mS	**BB**	10/95	BBB–	Y	R	NC	....	....	....	....	....	230	M2	'93	93⅞	81⅜	88⅜	6.65	8.17
1st 6⅞s 2003	Ao	**BB**	10/95	BBB–	Y	R	NC	....	....	....	....	....	85.0	G1	'93	98¾	85¾	92¼	7.45	8.32
1st 7⅜s 2003	fA	**BB**	10/95	BBB–	Y	R	NC	....	....	....	....	....	220	M2	'92	101¾	87¾	94⅛	7.84	8.44
1st 8s 2004	Jd	**BB**	10/95	BBB–	Y	R	NC	....	....	....	....	....	300	M2	'92	105¼	91½	97	8.25	8.50
1st 6⅝s 2005	jJ	**BB**	10/95	BBB–	Y	R	NC	....	....	....	....	....	110	M2	'93	95⅞	81¾	88⅛	7.52	8.47
1st 9¾s 2005	mN	**BB**	10/95	BBB–	Y	R	NC	....	....	....	....	....	150	M2	'90	117⅛	100⅜	103¾	9.40	9.16
1st 7¾s 2006	Mn15	**BB**	10/95	BBB–	Y	R	NC	....	....	....	....	....	275	P1	19	103⅞	91⅜	94½	8.20	8.56
1st 9½s 2021	Ms	**BB**	10/95	BBB–	Y	R	106.91	(3-2-96)	□100	(3-1-96)	....	....	150	M2	'91	109⅝	92½	103¼	9.20	9.16
1st 8¾s 2022	Ao	**BB**	10/95	BBB–	Y	R	104	(4-1-02)	□100	(4-1-02)	....	....	150	M2	'92	103⅝	90	97¼	9.00	9.02
1st 8½s 2023	jJ	**BB**	10/95	BBB–	Y	R	103.894	(7-2-03)	□100	(7-2-02)	....	....	165	G1	'92	101½	87½	94¾	8.97	9.02
1st 7⅞s 2024	Ao	**BB**	10/95	BBB–	Y	R	102.999	(4-1-03)	□100	....	....	....	210	G1	'93	97⅛	82⅝	91¼	8.63	8.71
NIPSCO Capital Markets	*25*	*Issued under support agreement w/NIPSCO Indus*																		
Nts Zero Cpn '97	[1]	**A–**	2/94	BBB	X	R	NC	....	....	....	....	....	[2]72.5	G1	'92	89⅞	74	89⅞	....	5.63
NL Industries	*14*	*0.64*	*0.23*	*0.48*		*Dc*	*153.0*	*550.0*	*261.0*	*9-30-95*	*751.0*		*579.0*	*141.0*						
Sr Sec Nts[3] 11¾s 2003	aO15	**B**			Y	R	101.50	(10-15-00)	....	....	....	....	250	S1	'93	106¾	99⅜	106¾	11.01	10.46
Sr Sec[4]Disc Nts[5] 13s 2005	aO15	**B**			Y	R	106	(10-15-98)	....	....	[6]Z113	10-15-96	[2]188	S1	'93	76¾	61	76¾	....	Flat
Noble Affiliates	*49a*	*3.86*	*1.76*	*0.92*		*Dc*	*22.30*	*89.10*	*112.0*	*9-30-95*	*402.0*		*815.0*	*49.3*						
Nts 7¼s 2023	aO15	**BBB**			X	R	NC	....	....	....	....	....	100	K2	'93	101⅞	81⅞	101⅞	7.12	7.09
Noble Drilling Corp	*49e*	*0.26*	*5.00*	*3.84*		*Dc*	*86.00*	*190.0*	*74.40*	*9-30-95*	*126.0*		*647.0*	*19.6*						
Sr Nts 9¼s 2003	aO	**BB–**			Y	R	103.47	(10-1-98)	100	(10-1-01)	....	....	125	S1	'93	104¼	94¼	104¼	8.87	8.49
NorAm Energy Corp	*73*	*1.09*	*1.69*	*1.54*		*Dc*	*7.34*	*382.0*	*766.0*	*9-30-95*	*1475*		*2480*	*70.4*						
Nts 7½s 2000	fA	**BB+**			Y	BE	NC	....	....	....	....	....	200	M2	'95	103	98¾	103	7.28	6.73
Nordstrom Credit	*25d*	*1.87*	*2.10*	*2.03*		*Ja*	*0.44*			*1-31-95*	*487.0*		*657.0*	*74.1*						
SF Deb 9⅜s 2016	Fa15	**A+**	5/86	A	X	R	104.56	(2-15-96)	100	(2-15-97)	....	....	75.0	F1	'86	106½	103¼	104⅞	8.94	8.85
Nts 6.70s 2005	jJ	**A+**			X	BE	NC	....	....	....	....	....	100	G1	'95	103¼	95¾	103¼	6.49	6.24
Nordstrom,Inc	*59f*	*5.53*	*6.63*	*9.43*		*Ja*	*52.30*	*1812*	*1017*	*10-31-95*	*390.0*		*2135*	*35.0*						
Nts 8⅞s '98	Fa15	**A+**			X	BE	NC	....	....	....	....	....	50.0	G1	'91	106⅜	100¾	106⅜	8.34	5.65
Norfolk Southern[7]	*55*	*6.60*	*6.45*	*7.78*		*Dc*	*287.0*	*1340*	*1181*	*9-30-95*	*1691*		*6440*	*25.3*						
Nts 7⅞s 2004	Fa15	**AA**			X	R	NC	....	....	....	....	....	250	M5	'92	111¾	97⅛	111¾	7.05	6.02
Nts 9s 2021	Ms	**AA**			X	R	NC	....	....	....	....	....	250	G1	'91	129½	104⅞	129½	6.95	6.58
Norfolk & Western Ry	*55*	***Subsid of Norfolk Southern, see***																		
• 1st Con 4s '96	aO	**AA**			X	CR	NC	....	....	....	....	....	23.8		'10	98½	93⅝	98¼	4.07	6.40
• Sub Inc Deb 4.85s 2015	mN15	**AA–**	12/80	BBB+	X	CR	101.25	11-14-96	100.625	11-14-96	....	....	1.75	Exch.	'65	77	64⅛	75	6.47	7.24
Nortek, Inc.	*13*	*0.88*	*1.33*	*2.11*		*Dc*	*108.0*	*339.0*	*149.0*	*9-30-95*	*220.0*		*353.0*	*63.5*						
Sr Sub Nts[3] 9⅞s 2004	Ms	**CCC+**	5/95	CCC	Y	R	104.214	(3-1-99)	....	....	....	....	190	B5	'94	96	87	93	10.62	11.20
North Atlantic Energy[8]	*72a*	*n/a*	*0.64*	*0.88*		*Dc*	*24.90*	*54.40*	*42.70*	*9-30-95*	*520.0*		*760.0*	*71.1*						
1st 'A' 9.05s 2002	Jd	**BB**	3/94	BB+	Y	R	[9]Z106.335	5-31-96	100	....	....	....	355	M6	'92	104¾	93½	102⅛	8.86	8.61
North Shore Gas (Ill)[10]	*73b*	*3.81*	*2.96*	*3.27*		*Sp*	*17.60*	*44.70*	*42.40*	*6-30-95*	*72.70*		*167.0*	*45.9*						
1st[11]J 8s 2020	mN	**AA–**			X	R	Z105	(11-1-98)	▲100	....	....	....	24.9	J2	'90	117½	92	115⅝	6.92	6.70
Northeast Utilities	*72b*	*2.38*	*2.00*	*2.09*		*Dc*	*51.20*	*889.0*	*1070*	*9-30-95*	*3844*		*7265*	*59.1*						
Amortizing[12]Nts'A'[13] 8.58s 2006	jD	**BBB–**			X	BE	NC	....	....	....	....	....	175	M6	'91	111	94⅞	111	7.73	....

Uniform Footnote Explanations-See Page 260. Other: [1] Due 12-1-97. [2] Incl disc. [3] (HRO)On Chge of Ctrl at 101. [4] Int accr at 13% fr 10-15-98. [5] (HRO)On Chge of Ctrl at 101(Accreted Val). [6] Max $62.6M red w/proceeds of Com Stk Off'g. [7] See Norfolk & West'n Ry. [8] Subsid of Northeast Utilities. [9] Red w/proceeds of property sales. [10] Subsid of Peoples Energy. [11] (HRO)At 100, ltd as defined. [12] Fr 12-1-94,print pyts due on int dates. [13] Issued in min denom $100T.

Title-Industry Code & Co. Finances (In Italics) / Exchange ↓ Individual Issue Statistics	Ind / Interest Dates	S&P Debt Rating	Date of Last Rating Change	Prior Rating	Eligible ↓	Bond Form	Regular Price	Regular (Begins) Thru	Sinking Fund Price	Sinking Fund (Begins) Thru	Refund/Other Restriction Price	Refund/Other Restriction (Begins) Thru	Outst'g (Mil $)	Underwriting Firm	Underwriting Year	Price Range 1995 High	Price Range 1995 Low	Mo. End Price Sale(s) or Bid	Curr. Yield	Yield to Mat.
Company finances:		*Fixed Charge Coverage 1992*	*1993*	*1994*		*Year End*	*Million $ Cash & Equiv.*	*Curr. Assets*	*Curr. Liab.*	*Balance Sheet Date*	*L. Term Debt (Mil $)*		*Capital-ization (Mil $)*	*Total Debt % Capital*						
Northern Illinois Gas[1]	***73b***	***4.41***	***4.53***	***4.80***		***Dc***	***0.10***	***190.0***	***471.0***	***9-30-95***	***397.0***		***1128***	***39.6***						
1st 4½s '96	Ms15	**AA**			X	R	NC	....	....	....	....	....	50.0	S1	'93	99¾	96⅝	99¾	4.51	5.63
1st 5½s '97	Fa	**AA**			X	R	NC	....	....	....	....	....	25.0	M2	'93	100	95⅜	100	5.50	5.49
1st 5⅞s '98	Fa	**AA**			X	R	100	(2-1-97)	....	....	....	....	25.0	M2	'93	100⅜	94	100⅜	5.85	5.68
1st 6¼s '99	Fa	**AA**			X	R	100	(2-1-98)	....	....	....	....	25.0	M2	'93	101½	93⅜	101½	6.16	5.71
1st 5⅞s 2000	Mn	**AA**			X	R	100	(5-1-98)	....	....	....	....	50.0	F1	'93	100⅛	89⅞	100⅛	5.87	5.84
1st 9s 2019	jJ	**AA**			X	R	106.16	6-30-96	....	....	....	....	50.0	P1	'89	106¾	102⅛	106¼	8.47	8.39
1st 8⅞s 2021	fA15	**AA**			X	R	106.81	8-14-96	....	....	....	....	50.0	M6	'91	108⅞	99⅞	106⅞	8.30	8.23
1st 8¼s 2022	jJ15	**AA**			X	R	106	(7-15-97)	....	....	....	....	75.0	M2	'92	109⅞	94½	109⅞	7.51	7.39
1st 7⅜s 2023	jJ	**AA**			X	R	105.31	(7-1-98)	....	....	....	....	50.0	S1	'95	104⅛	94	104⅛	7.08	7.03
1st 8¼s 2024	fA15	**AA**			X	R	106.13	(8-15-99)	....	....	....	....	50.0	P1	'94	113	95	113	7.30	7.17
1st 7.26s 2025	aO15	**AA**			X	R	105.09	(10-15-00)	....	....	....	....	50.0	M6	'95	103½	98⅝	103½	7.01	6.98
Northern Ind Pub Svc[2]	***75***	***3.40***	***4.10***	***4.24***		***Dc***	***7.78***	***232.0***	***521.0***	***9-30-95***	***1059***		***2403***	***51.9***						
1st O 6⅜s '97	mS	**A**	2/94	A–	X	CR	100.32	8-31-96	100.40	2-29-96	....	....	25.7	F1	'67	100⅜	96	100⅜	6.35	6.13
1st P 6⅞s '98	aO	**A**	2/94	A–	X	R	100.62	9-30-96	100.51	3-31-96	....	....	14.5	F1	'68	100⅞	95⅝	100¾	6.82	6.57
1st T 7½s 2002	Ao	**A**	2/94	A–	X	R	101.82	3-31-96	100.56	9-30-96	....	....	40.5	F1	'72	102¼	94⅝	102¼	7.33	7.05
Northern Pac.Ry	***55***	***Merged into Burlington No'n RR see***																		
• Pr[3]Ln & Ld Gr[4] 4s '97	QJan	**BBB**	7/95	BBB+	X	CR	NC	....	....	....	....	....	[5]67.4		1896	102	101	100½	3.98	3.49
• Pr[4]Ln & Ld Gr-Stpd 4s '97	QJan	**BBB**	7/95	BBB+	X	R	NC	....	....	....	....	....	[6]69.9		1896	97¼	92	97¼	4.11	6.88
• Gen[3]Ln Mtg[7] 3s 2047	[8]Qfeb	**BBB**	7/95	BBB+	X	CR	NC	....	....	....	....	....	[5]34.5		1896	79¾	65	71½	4.20	4.41
• Gen Ln[7]Mtg-Stpd 3s 2047	[8]Qfeb	**BBB**	7/95	BBB+	X	R	NC	....	....	....	....	....	[6]35.0		1896	44	33	42	7.14	7.40
Northern Sts Pwr (Minn)	***75***	***3.07***	***3.88***	***3.78***		***Dc***	***46.00***	***625.0***	***859.0***	***9-30-95***	***1545***		***3957***	***43.3***						
1st 5⅞s '97	aO	**AA–**			X	R	NC	....	....	....	....	....	100	G1	'92	100⅝	94⅜	100⅝	5.84	5.49
1st 5½s '99	Fa	**AA–**			X	BE	NC	....	....	....	....	....	200	M6	'94	99½	90⅜	99½	5.53	5.68
1st 5¾s 2000	jD	**AA–**			X	R	NC	....	....	....	....	....	100	K2	'93	99½	88¼	99½	5.78	5.87
1st 7⅞s 2001	aO	**AA–**			X	BE	NC	....	....	....	....	....	150	K2	'94	109¼	97⅞	109¼	7.21	5.95
1st 7⅜s 2002	Ms	**AA–**	8/90	AA	X	R	101.60	2-29-96	100.14	12-1-96	....	....	50.0	M2	'72	101¾	94⅝	101¾	7.25	7.02
1st 7½s 2003	Fa	**AA–**	8/90	AA	X	R	102	1-31-96	100.42	12-1-96	....	....	50.0	B6	'73	102⅜	95⅝	102⅜	7.33	7.07
1st 6⅜s 2003	Ao	**AA–**			X	R	NC	....	....	....	....	....	80.0	K2	'93	101¾	88½	101¾	6.27	6.07
1st 6⅛s 2005	jD	**AA–**			X	R	NC	....	....	....	....	....	70.0	K2	'93	99¾	84¼	99¾	6.14	6.16
1st 7⅛s 2025	jJ	**AA–**			X	BE	NC	....	....	....	....	....	250	P1	'95	106⅝	93¼	106⅝	6.68	6.61
North'n Sts Pwr (Wisc)[9]	***75***	***4.23***	***4.27***	***4.13***		***Dc***	***0.08***	***73.70***	***61.50***	***3-31-95***	***214.0***		***554.0***	***41.5***						
1st 5¾s 2003	a0	**AA**			X	BE	NC	....	....	....	....	....	40.0	K2	'93	97⅞	83¾	97⅞	5.87	6.10
1st 9⅛s 2021	Ao	**AA**			X	BE	105.344	(4-1-96)	100	....	....	....	49.0	G1	'91	107⅛	101⅝	106⅛	8.60	8.53
1st 7¼s 2023	Ms	**AA**			X	R	102.84	(3-1-03)	100	....	....	....	110	G1	'93	98¼	84⅜	97⅛	7.46	7.50
Northrop Grumman[10]	***2a***	***n/a***	***p1.98***	***1.60***		***Dc***	***32.00***	***2371***	***1868***	***9-30-95***	***1433***		***3175***	***55.0***						
Deb 9⅜s 2024	aO15	**BBB**			X	BE	104.363	(10-15-04)	....	....	....	....	250	C5	'94	120⅛	100⅝	120⅛	7.80	7.64
Nts 8⅝s 2004	aO15	**BBB**			X	BE	NC	....	....	....	....	....	350	C5	'94	114⅝	99¾	114⅝	7.52	6.42
Northwest Natural Gas	***73b***	***1.85***	***3.36***	***3.20***		***Dc***	***2.91***	***55.50***	***98.60***	***9-30-95***	***271.0***		***641.0***	***45.6***						
1st 9⅛s 2019	aO	**A**			X	R	105.90	9-30-96	Z100	....	®106.32	9-30-96	25.0	S4	'89	107⅛	100¼	106	8.61	8.53
Sec M-T Nts A 4.80s '96	[11]jd	**A**			X	BE	NC	....	....	....	....	....	5.00	M2	'93	99¾	96	99¾	4.81	5.39
Sec M-T Nts A 7.38s '97	[12]jd	**A**			X	BE	NC	....	....	....	....	....	10.0	M2	'93	102½	98⅜	102⅜	7.21	5.56
Sec M-T Nts A 7.38s '97	[12]jd	**A**			X	BE	NC	....	....	....	....	....	10.0	M2	'92	102½	98⅜	102⅜	7.21	5.56
Sec M-T Nts A 7.69s '99	[13]jd	**A**			X	BE	NC	....	....	....	....	....	10.0	M2	'92	105⅝	97⅝	105⅝	7.28	5.79
Sec M-T Nts A 8.05s 2002	[14]jd	**A**			X	BE	NC	....	....	....	....	....	10.0	M2	'92	109⅝	97¾	109⅝	7.34	6.18
Sec M-T Nts A 9.05s 2021	[15]jd	**A**			X	BE	NC	....	....	....	....	....	10.0	M2	'91	125⅝	103⅝	125⅝	7.20	6.90
Sec M-T Nts B 5.96s 2000	[16]jd	**A**			X	BE	NC	....	....	....	....	....	5.00	M2	'93	99⅞	88⅝	99⅞	5.97	5.99

Uniform Footnote Explanations-See Page 260. Other: [1] Subsid of Nicor, Inc. [2] Subsid of NIPSCO Industries. [3] Unstpd. [4] Red thru purch fund 110(max). [5] Incl amt of stpd issue. [6] Incl amt of unstpd issue. [7] Red thru purch fund at 100. [8] Due 1-1-47. [9] Contr by No'n Sts Pwr (Minn). [10] See Grumman Corp. [11] Due 5-31-96. [12] Due 5-15-97. [13] Due 4-15-99. [14] Due 4-15-02. [15] Due 8-13-21. [16] Due 12-15-00.

Title-Industry Code & Co. Finances (In Italics) / Individual Issue Statistics (Exchange)	Ind / Interest Dates	Fixed Charge Coverage 1992 / S&P Debt Rating	1993 / Date of Last Rating Change	1994 / Prior Rating	Eligible	Year End / Bond Form	Million $ Cash & Equiv. / Redemption Provisions: Regular Price	Million $ Curr. Assets / Regular (Begins) Thru	Million $ Curr. Liab. / Sinking Fund Price	Balance Sheet Date / Sinking Fund (Begins) Thru	L. Term Debt (Mil $) / Refund/Other Restriction Price	Capitalization (Mil $) / Refund/Other Restriction (Begins) Thru	Outst'g (Mil $)	Total Debt % Capital / Underwriting Firm	Underwriting Year	Price Range 1995 High	Price Range 1995 Low	Mo. End Price Sale(s) or Bid	Curr. Yield	Yield to Mat.
***Northwest Natural Gas** (Cont.)*																				
Sec M-T Nts B 5.98s 2000	[1]jd	**A**			X	BE	NC	....	....	....	....	....	5.00	M2	'93	100	88⅝	100	5.98	5.98
Sec M-T Nts B 6.40s 2003	[2]jd	**A**			X	BE	NC	....	....	....	....	....	20.0	M2	'93	100¾	87¼	100¾	6.35	6.27
Sec M-T Nts B 6.34s 2005	[3]jd	**A**			X	BE	NC	....	....	....	....	....	5.00	M2	'93	99¾	84¾	99¾	6.36	6.37
Sec M-T Nts B 6.38s 2005	[4]jd	**A**			X	BE	NC	....	....	....	....	....	5.00	M2	'93	100	85	100	6.38	6.38
Sec M-T Nts B 6.45s 2005	[5]jd	**A**			X	BE	NC	....	....	....	....	....	5.00	M2	'93	100½	85½	100½	6.42	6.38
Sec M-T Nts B 6½s 2008	[6]jd	**A**			X	BE	NC	....	....	....	....	....	5.00	M2	'93	100⅝	83¼	100⅝	6.46	6.43
Sec M-T Nts B 8.26s 2014	[7]jd	**A**			X	BE	NC	....	....	....	....	....	10.0		'94	114½	96	114½	7.21	6.87
Sec M-T Nts B 8.31s 2019	[8]jd	**A**			X	BE	Z100	(9-21-97)	....	....	....	....	10.0		'94	116½	96	116½	7.13	6.89
Sec M-T Nts B 7½s 2023	[9]jd	**A**			X	BE	103.75	(7-1-03)	....	....	....	....	4.00	M2	'93	107½	87⅜	107½	6.98	6.89
Sec M-T Nts B 7.52s 2023	[9]jd	**A**			X	BE	103.76	(7-1-03)	....	....	....	....	11.0	M2	'93	107¾	87½	107¾	6.98	6.89
Sec M-T Nts B 7¼s 2023	[10]jd	**A**			X	BE	103.65	(8-18-03)	....	....	....	....	20.0	M2	'93	102¼	83⅞	102¼	7.09	7.06
Unsec M-T Nts A 4.90s '96	[11]jd	**A**			X	BE	NC	....	....	....	....	....	10.0	M2	'93	99¾	96	99¾	4.91	5.48
Unsec M-T Nts A 8.69s '96	[12]jd	**A**			X	BE	NC	....	....	....	....	....	5.00	M2	'91	102⅝	101	101½	8.56	5.65
Unsec M-T Nts A 7.40s '97	[13]jd	**A**			X	BE	NC	....	....	....	....	....	5.00	M2	'92	102¼	98⅜	102⅛	7.25	5.66
Unsec M-T Nts A 8.95s '98	[14]jd	**A**			X	BE	NC	....	....	....	....	....	10.0	M2	'91	107½	101¾	107⅜	8.34	5.75
Unsec M-T Nts A 8.93s '98	[14]jd	**A**			X	BE	NC	....	....	....	....	....	5.00	M2	'91	107½	101⅝	107¼	8.33	5.78
Unsec M-T Nts A 8.47s 2001	[15]jd	**A**			X	BE	NC	....	....	....	....	....	5.00	M2	'91	111	99½	111	7.63	6.15
Northwest Pipeline[16]	***73a***	***3.19***	***2.41***	***2.88***		***Dc***	***2.31***	***92.50***	***123.0***	***9-30-95***	***287.0***	***771.0***		***38.5***						
SF Deb[17] 10.65s 2018	mN15	**BBB**	2/95	BBB+	X	R	106.92	11-14-96	100	(11-15-99)	®105.33	11-14-98	100	F1	'88	107¾	107	107	9.95	9.87
Deb 9s 2022	fA	**BBB**	2/95	BBB+	X	R	104.24	(8-1-02)	100	(8-1-03)	....	....	150	F1	'92	113½	98⅝	113½	7.93	7.79
Deb 7⅛s 2025	jD	**BBB**			X	BE	NC	....	....	....	....	....	85.0	M2	'95	102¼	99½	102¼	6.97	6.94
Northwestern Bell Tel	***67a***	***Merged into U S WEST Commun***																		
• Deb 3¼s '96	Fa	**AA−**	4/90	AA	X	CR	100	....	....	....	....	....	[18]25.0	M6	'56	98⅝	97½	99½	3.27	8.80
Deb 4⅞s '98	Jd	**AA−**	4/90	AA	X	CR	100	....	....	....	....	....	35.4	H1	'60	98¼	90¾	98¼	4.96	5.66
Deb 6s 2001	mS	**AA−**	4/90	AA	X	R	100.19	8-31-96	....	....	....	....	50.0	B6	'66	99½	88¼	99½	6.03	6.10
Deb 4⅜s 2003	Ms	**AA−**	4/90	AA	X	CR	100.55	2-29-96	....	....	....	....	[18]40.0	F1	'63	90⅞	77⅛	90⅞	4.81	5.96
Deb 6¼s 2007	Jj	**AA−**	4/90	AA	X	R	100.93	12-31-96	....	....	....	....	89.7	H1	'68	99¼	84¼	99¼	6.30	6.35
Nts 9½s 2000	Mn	**AA−**			X	BE	NC	....	....	....	....	....	75.0	M6	'90	113¾	105	113¾	8.35	5.86
Northwestern Pub. Serv.	***75***	***3.97***	***3.52***	***3.41***		***Dc***	***8.90***	***58.30***	***45.30***	***9-30-95***	***190.0***	***379.0***		***50.4***						
Mtg Bonds 7.10s 2005	fA	**A**			X	BE	NC	....	....	....	....	....	60.0	M6	'95	106⅝	99¾	106⅝	6.66	6.17
New Mtg 7s 2023	fA15	**A**	7/95	A+	X	BE	103.163	(8-15-03)	....	....	....	....	55.0	M6	'93	99⅛	81⅜	99⅛	7.06	7.07
Northwestern Steel & Wire	***66h***	***△0.93***	***△1.56***	***△2.08***		***Jl***	***5.45***	***180.0***	***87.50***	***10-31-95***	***165.0***	***259.0***		***66.4***						
Sr Nts[19] 9½s 2001	Jd15	**B**			Y	R	103.208	(6-15-97)	....	....	....	....	115	L3	'93	104	90½	98¼	9.67	9.92
Norwest Corp[20]	***10***	***2.21***	***2.62***	***2.62***		***Dc***				***9-30-95***	***12686***	***17626***		***72.0***						
Sr Nts 5¾s '98	Ms15	**AA−**	1/94	A+	X	R	NC	....	....	....	....	....	100	M2	'93	100½	93⅛	100½	5.72	5.50
Sr Nts 6s 2000	Ms15	**AA−**	1/94	A+	X	R	NC	....	....	....	....	....	200	M2	'93	100¾	90	100¾	5.96	5.79
F/R[21]M-T Nts 'C' 5.9125s '96	[22]	**AA−**			X	BE	NC	....	....	....	....	....	10.0	M2	'93	100⅛	99⅞	100	5.91	....
F/R[21]M-T Nts 'C' 5.8625s '96	[22]	**AA−**			X	BE	NC	....	....	....	....	....	25.0	M6	'93	100	99⅞	100	5.86	....
M-T Nts 'C' 4.34s '96	[23]jj15	**AA−**	1/94	A+	X	BE	NC	....	....	....	....	....	20.0	D6	'93	99⅛	94⅛	99⅛	4.38	5.47
F/R[21]M-T Nts 'C' 5.8625s '96	[24]	**AA−**	1/94	A+	X	BE	NC	....	....	....	....	....	25.0	S1	'93	100	99⅞	100	5.86	....
F/R[21]M-T Nts 'C' 5.9625s '98	[25]	**AA−**	1/94	A+	X	BE	*100	....	....	....	....	....	50.0	M2	'93	100	99½	100	5.96	....
F/R[21]M-T Nts 'C' 5.9625s '98	[26]	**AA−**	1/94	A+	X	BE	NC	....	....	....	....	....	50.0	C5	'93	100⅛	99½	100	5.96	....
M-T Nts 'D' 7.20s '99	[27]jj15	**AA−**			X	BE	NC	....	....	....	....	....	100	G1	'94	105	95¾	105	6.86	5.66
M-T Nts 'D' 7⅛s '99	mS9	**AA−**			X	BE	NC	....	....	....	....	....	50.0	S5	'94	104¾	95⅜	104¾	6.80	5.68
M-T Nts 'D' 7.45s '99	mS15	**AA−**			X	BE	NC	....	....	....	....	....	25.0	C5	'94	105⅞	96⅝	105⅞	7.04	5.67
F/R[28]M-T Nts 'D' '96	[29]	**AA−**			X	BE	NC	....	....	....	....	....	200		'94	100	99½	100	....	....

Uniform Footnote Explanations-See Page 260. Other: [1] Due 12-15-00. [2] Due 6-30-03. [3] Due 7-25-05. [4] Due 7-27-05. [5] Due 7-29-05. [6] Due 7-30-08. [7] Due 9-21-14. [8] Due 9-21-19. [9] Due 6-30-23. [10] Due 8-18-23. [11] Due 5-31-96. [12] Due 7-2-96. [13] Due 4-15-97. [14] Due 7-1-98. [15] Due 9-17-01. [16] Subsid of Northwest Energy Co. [17] To11-15-98,events may cause red at100/int adj. [18] Defeased, fds deposited w/trustee. [19] (HRO)On Chge of Ctrl at 101. [20] Was Northwest Bancorp. [21] Int to 3-20-96,adj qtrly aft. [22] Due 9-18-96:Int pd qtrly, ea 3rd Wed, Mar,etc. [23] Due 10-15-96. [24] Due 10-15-96:Int pd qtrly, ea 3rd Wed, Mar,etc. [25] Due 9-15-98:Int pd qtrly, ea 3rd Wed, Mar,etc. [26] Due 9-26-98:Int pd qtrly, ea 3rd Wed, Mar,etc. [27] Due 8-25-99. [28] Int adj monthly. [29] Due 5-20-96:Int pd on 3rd Wed of ea month.

Title-Industry Code & Co. Finances (In Italics)	*Ind*	*Fixed Charge Coverage 1992*	*1993*	*1994*	*Year End*		*Million $ Cash & Equiv.*	*Curr. Assets*	*Curr. Liab.*	*Balance Sheet Date*	*L. Term Debt (Mil $)*	*Capital-ization (Mil $)*		*Total Debt % Capital*						
Individual Issue Statistics Exchange ↓	**Interest Dates**	**S&P Debt Rating**	**Date of Last Rating Change**	**Prior Rating**	**Eligible ↓**	**Bond Form**	**Redemption Provisions: Regular Price**	**Regular (Begins) Thru**	**Sinking Fund Price**	**Sinking Fund (Begins) Thru**	**Refund/Other Restriction Price**	**Refund/Other Restriction (Begins) Thru**	**Outst'g (Mil $)**	**Underwriting Firm**	**Underwriting Year**	**Price Range 1995 High**	**Price Range 1995 Low**	**Mo. End Price Sale(s) or Bid**	**Curr. Yield**	**Yield to Mat.**
Norwest Corp *(Cont.)*																				
F/R[1]M-T Nts 'D' '96	[2]	AA–			X	BE	NC	....	....	....	....	....	200	M2	'94	100	99½	100	....	....
F/R[3]M-T Nts 'D' 5.8625s '99	[4]	AA–			X	BE	NC	....	....	....	....	....	200	G1	'94	100	99	99⅞	5.87	....
M-T Nts 'D' 7⅝s '99	aO15	AA–			X	BE	NC	....	....	....	....	....	100	F1	'94	106½	98⅝	106½	7.16	5.69
M-T Nts 'D' 8.15s 2001	mN	AA–			X	BE	NC	....	....	....	....	....	100	M6	'94	110⅞	100½	110⅞	7.35	5.92
M-T Nts 'E' 7¾s '96	jD31	AA–			X	BE	NC	....	....	....	....	....	200	M6	'95	102¾	100	102¼	7.58	5.42
M-T Nts 'E' 7⅞s '97	Jj30	AA–			X	BE	NC	....	....	....	....	....	200	L3	'95	103⅛	100	102⅝	7.67	5.35
M-T Nts 'E' 7.70s '97	mN15	AA–			X	BE	NC	....	....	....	....	....	200	M6	'95	104	100	104	7.40	5.43
M-T Nts 'E' 8.67s 2000	Jj18	AA–			X	BE	*100	(1-21-97)	....	....	....	....	25.0	S5	'95	104¼	100	103⅜	8.39	7.68
M-T Nts 'E' 7¾s 2002	Ms	AA–			X	BE	NC	....	....	....	....	....	125	M5	'95	109⅛	99½	109⅛	7.10	5.96
M-T Nts 'F' 7⅛s 2000	Ao	AA–			X	BE	NC	....	....	....	....	....	200	B5	'95	105⅛	100	105⅛	6.78	5.75
M-T Nts 'F' 6¾s 2000	Mn12	AA–			X	BE	NC	....	....	....	....	....	200	M2	'95	103¾	100	103¾	6.51	5.76
M-T Nts 'F' 7.68s 2002	Mn10	AA–			X	BE	Z100	(5-10-98)	....	....	....	....	100	M6	'95	104¾	100	104¾	7.33	6.75
M-T Nts 'F' 6.80s 2002	Mn15	AA–			X	BE	NC	....	....	....	....	....	200	M6	'95	104½	98⅞	104½	6.51	5.94
M-T Nts 'F' 7.65s 2005	Ms15	AA–			X	BE	NC	....	....	....	....	....	100	M6	'95	110¼	100	110¼	6.94	6.17
M-T Nts 'F' 6½s 2005	Jd	AA–			X	BE	NC	....	....	....	....	....	200	S5	'95	102⅜	95	102⅜	6.35	6.16
M-T Nts 'G' 6s '98	aO13	AA–			X	BE	NC	....	....	....	....	....	250	S1	'95	101¼	100	101¼	5.93	5.51
M-T Nts 'G' 6⅛s 2000	aO15	AA–			X	BE	NC	....	....	....	....	....	200	S1	'95	101½	99½	101½	6.03	5.76
M-T Nts 'G' 5¾s '98	mN16	AA–			X	BE	NC	....	....	....	....	....	200	M5	'95	100⅝	100	100⅝	5.71	5.51
M-T Nts 'G' 6⅜s 2002	mS15	AA–			X	BE	NC	....	....	....	....	....	200	M6	'95	102⅛	98¼	102⅛	6.24	5.98
Sub Deb 6.65s 2023	aO15	A+	1/94	A	X	BE	NC	....	....	....	....	....	200	M6	'93	98½	78¾	98½	6.75	6.77
Sub[5]Cap Nts 9¼s '97	Mn	A+	1/94	A	X	R	NC	....	....	....	....	....	100	M2	'87	105¾	102⅛	104⅞	8.82	5.42
Sub Nts 6⅝s 2003	Ms15	A+	1/94	A	X	R	NC	....	....	....	....	....	200	M2	'93	102⅜	88⅞	102⅜	6.47	6.21
Norwest Fin'l	***25a***	***2.05***	***2.27***	***2.31***	***Dc***					***9-30-95***	***3987***		***4959***	***80.4***						
Sr Nts 8⅞s '96	jJ	AA–	3/93	A+	X	R	NC	....	....	....	....	....	100	M2	'89	102¾	101¼	101⅝	8.73	5.57
Sr Nts 7.10s '96	mN15	AA–	3/93	A+	X	R	NC	....	....	....	....	....	150	M2	'91	101⅜	98¼	101⅜	7.00	5.46
Sr Nts 6½s '97	Mn15	AA–			X	R	NC	....	....	....	....	....	150	M2	'94	101⅜	96½	101⅜	6.41	5.44
Sr Nts 6s '97	fA15	AA–	3/93	A+	X	R	NC	....	....	....	....	....	150	M2	'92	100⅝	94¾	100⅝	5.96	5.59
Sr Nts 6¼s '97	Fa15	AA–			X	R	NC	....	....	....	....	....	150	M2	'94	100⅞	96¼	100⅞	6.20	5.43
Sr Nts 6½s '97	mN15	AA–	3/93	A+	X	R	NC	....	....	....	....	....	150	M2	'92	101¾	95⅜	101¾	6.39	5.50
Sr Nts 5½s '98	Ao15	AA–			X	R	NC	....	....	....	....	....	150	M2	'93	99¾	92⅛	99¾	5.51	5.61
Sr Nts 8½s '98	fA15	AA–	3/93	A+	X	R	NC	....	....	....	....	....	100	M2	'91	107	100⅝	107	7.94	5.59
Sr Nts 6.23s '98	mS	AA–			X	R	NC	....	....	....	....	....	150	M2	'95	101¾	99⅞	101¾	6.12	5.51
Sr Nts 6¼s '99	Ms15	AA–			X	R	NC	....	....	....	....	....	150	M2	'94	101½	92¾	101½	6.16	5.73
Sr Nts 6.20s '99	mS15	AA–	3/93	A+	X	R	NC	....	....	....	....	....	75.0	M2	'92	101½	91⅞	101½	6.11	5.74
Sr Nts 6⅞s '99	jD15	AA–	3/93	A+	X	R	NC	....	....	....	....	....	100	M2	'92	103½	93¾	103½	6.64	5.87
Sr Nts 8⅜s 2000	Jj15	AA–			X	R	NC	....	....	....	....	....	150	M2	'95	108⅛	100	106⅞	7.84	6.42
Sr Nts 7¼s 2000	Ms15	AA–			X	R	NC	....	....	....	....	....	150	M2	'95	105½	99	105½	6.87	5.76
Sr Nts 5⅛s 2000	Ao15	AA–			X	R	NC	....	....	....	....	....	150	M2	'93	97½	86⅝	97½	5.26	5.79
Sr Nts 6⅞s 2000	Jd15	AA–			X	R	NC	....	....	....	....	....	150	M2	'94	104⅛	93½	104⅛	6.60	5.81
Sr Nts 7¾s 2001	fA15	AA–			X	R	NC	....	....	....	....	....	100	M2	'94	108⅝	96¾	108⅝	7.13	5.92
Sr Nts 7⅞s 2002	Fa15	AA–			X	R	NC	....	....	....	....	....	150	M2	'95	109¾	99⅝	109¾	7.18	5.95
Sr Nts 7.95s 2002	Mn15	AA–	3/93	A+	X	R	NC	....	....	....	....	....	100	M2	'92	109⅝	97½	109⅝	7.25	6.10
Sr Nts 6¼s 2002	mN	AA–			X	R	NC	....	....	....	....	....	200	M2	'95	101⅜	99⅜	101⅜	6.17	6.00
• Sr Nts 7s 2003	Jj15	AA–	3/93	A+	X	R	NC	....	....	....	....	....	150	M2	'93	104⅝	100¾	102¾	6.81	6.51
Sr Nts 6⅛s 2003	fA	AA–			X	R	NC	....	....	....	....	....	150	M2	'93	100⅜	86⅝	100⅜	6.10	6.06
Sr Nts 7½s 2005	Ao15	AA–			X	R	NC	....	....	....	....	....	150	M2	'95	109¼	99⅜	109¼	6.86	6.18

Uniform Footnote Explanations-See Page 260. Other: [1] Int adj monthly. [2] Due 5-23-96: Int pd on 3rd Wed of ea month. [3] Int to 12-29-95,adj qtrly aft. [4] Due 2-24-99:Int pd qtrly,ea 3rd Wed, Mar,etc.
[5] Co may exch for Cap Sec when due.

Title-Industry Code & Co. Finances (In Italics) / Individual Issue Statistics, Exchange	Ind / Interest Dates	Fixed Charge Coverage 1992 / S&P Debt Rating	1993 / Date of Last Rating Change	1994 / Prior Rating	Eligible	Year End / Bond Form	Million $ Cash & Equiv. / Redemption Provisions Regular Price	Million $ Curr. Assets / Regular (Begins) Thru	Million $ Curr. Liab. / Sinking Fund Price	Balance Sheet Date / Sinking Fund (Begins) Thru	L. Term Debt (Mil $) / Refund/Other Restriction Price	Capital-ization (Mil $) / Refund/Other Restriction (Begins) Thru	Total Debt % Capital / Outst'g (Mil $)	Underwriting Firm	Underwriting Year	Price Range 1995 High	Price Range 1995 Low	Mo. End Price Sale(s) or Bid	Curr. Yield	Yield to Mat.
***Norwest Fin'l** (Cont.)*																				
Sr Nts 6¾s 2005	Jd	**AA–**			X	R	NC	....	....	....	....	....	150	M2	'95	104⅛	96¾	104⅛	6.48	6.17
Sr Nts 6¼s 2007	jD15	**AA–**			X	R	NC	....	....	....	....	....	100	M2	'95	99⅛	99	99⅛	6.31	6.36
Sr Sub M-T Nts 'A'[1] 4.97s '96	[2]ao	**A+**			X	BE	NC	....	....	....	....	....	25.0	M2	'93	100	94	99½	4.99	5.58
Sr Sub M-T Nts 'A'[1] 4.85s '96	[3]ao	**A+**			X	BE	NC	....	....	....	....	....	10.0	S1	'93	99½	94⅝	99½	4.87	5.43
Sr Sub M-T Nts 'A'[1] 4.85s '96	[3]ao	**A+**			X	BE	NC	....	....	....	....	....	10.0	M2	'93	99½	94⅝	99½	4.87	5.43
Sr Sub M-T Nts 'A'[1] 4.89s '96	[3]ao	**A+**			X	BE	NC	....	....	....	....	....	10.0	S1	'93	99⅝	94¾	99⅝	4.91	5.33
Sr Sub M-T Nts 'A'[1] 4.93s '96	[3]ao	**A+**			X	BE	NC	....	....	....	....	....	20.0	S1	'93	99⅝	94¾	99⅝	4.95	5.37
Sr Sub M-T Nts 'A'[1] 6.40s '96	[3]ao	**A+**			X	BE	NC	....	....	....	....	....	25.0	S1	'94	100⅞	97¼	100⅞	6.34	5.36
Sr Sub M-T Nts 'A'[1] 5.58s '96	[3]ao	**A+**			X	BE	NC	....	....	....	....	....	20.0	S1	'94	100⅛	95⅞	100⅛	5.57	5.42
Sr Sub M-T Nts 'A'[1] 5.20s '97	[4]ao	**A+**			X	BE	NC	....	....	....	....	....	25.0	M2	'93	100⅛	94¾	99⅜	5.23	5.69
NTC Group	***68***	***Now Bibb Co.,see***																		
Sr Sub Nts 13⅞s '99	§fA	**D**	8/95	C	Z	R			Default 8-1-95 int				32.8	H4	'87	58½	27	33	....	Flat
Nuevo Energy Co	***49a***	*1.87*	*2.23*	*1.59*		***Dc***	*7.19*	*32.50*	*16.60*	*9-30-95*	*120.0*	*275.0*	*44.7*							
• Sr Sub Nts[5] 12½s 2002	Jd15	**B–**			Y	R	104	(6-16-97)	100	(6-15-00)	....	....	75.0	P1	'92	110¼	102⅛	108½	11.52	10.64
NVF Co.	***66b***	*d0.54*	*1.24*	*d0.82*		***Dc***	***Bankruptcy Chapt 11***				*[6]88.50*	*31.20*	*315.0*							
Sub SF Deb 10s 2003	§mN15	**NR**	5/87	C	Z	R			Default 11-15-93 int				[7]11.4	Exch.	'74	46	26	46	....	Flat
NVR Inc	***13h***	*n/a*	*n/a*	*1.60*		***Dc***	*33.40*			*9-30-95*	*349.0*	*490.0*	*71.2*							
Sr[8]Nts 11s 2003	[9]jd	**B**			Y	R	105.50	(12-1-98)	....	....	[10]Z110	11-30-96	135	B5	'93	100½	83¼	100½	10.95	10.89
NWA Inc	***4***	....	....	....		***Dc***	***No Recent Fin'ls***													
Nts 8⅝s '96	fA	**B+**	12/95	B	Y	R	NC	....	....	....	....	....	200	M2	'86	101	95½	100¼	8.60	8.16
NYNEX Capital Funding	***25***	***Subsid of & Gtd by NYNEX Corp,see***																		
(Gtd[11])M-T Nts 'B' 7.59s '99	[12]ms15	**A–**	8/95	A	X	BE	NC	....	....	....	....	....	7.00	M5	'94	105⅝	96⅝	105⅝	7.19	5.81
(Gtd[11])F/R[13]M-T Nts 'B' 6.0437s '97	QMay27	**A–**	8/95	A	X	BE	NC	....	....	....	....	....	5.00	L3	'94	102	98½	100	6.04	....
(Gtd[11])F/R[14]M-T Nts 'B' '97	QJun	**A–**	8/95	A	X	BE	NC	....	....	....	....	....	117	S1	'94	102	98½	100	....	....
(Gtd[11])M-T Nts 'B' 7.60s '99	[12]ms15	**A–**	8/95	A	X	BE	NC	....	....	....	....	....	30.7	L3	'94	105⅝	96¾	105⅝	7.20	5.82
(Gtd[11])M-T Nts 'B' 7.61s '99	[12]ms15	**A–**	8/95	A	X	BE	NC	....	....	....	....	....	28.0	L3	'94	105¾	96¾	105¾	7.20	5.80
(Gtd[11])M-T Nts 'B' 7.62s '99	[12]ms15	**A–**	8/95	A	X	BE	NC	....	....	....	....	....	21.0	M6	'94	105¾	96¾	105¾	7.21	5.81
(Gtd[11])M-T Nts 'B' 7.63s '99	[12]ms15	**A–**	8/95	A	X	BE	NC	....	....	....	....	....	10.0	S1	'94	105¾	96⅞	105¾	7.22	5.81
(Gtd[11])M-T Nts 'B' 7.66s '99	[12]ms15	**A–**	8/95	A	X	BE	NC	....	....	....	....	....	10.0	S1	'94	105⅞	97	105⅞	7.23	5.81
(Gtd[11])M-T Nts 'B' 7.64s '99	[12]ms15	**A–**	8/95	A	X	BE	NC	....	....	....	....	....	9.00	S1	'94	105¾	96⅞	105¾	7.22	5.82
(Gtd[11])F/R[15]M-T Nts[16] 'B' '99	QOct5	**A–**	8/95	A	X	BE	NC	....	....	....	....	....	10.0	S1	'94	100	98⅛	98⅝	....	....
(Gtd[11])M-T Nts 'B' 8.11s '99	[17]ms15	**A–**	8/95	A	X	BE	NC	....	....	....	....	....	20.5	M5	'94	107⅝	99	107⅝	7.54	5.86
(Gtd)M-T Nts 'B' 8.10s '99	[17]ms15	**A–**	8/95	A	X	BE	NC	....	....	....	....	....	42.0	S1	'94	107⅝	99⅜	107⅝	7.53	5.85
(Gtd[11])M-T Nts 'B 8.10s '99	[17]ms15	**A–**	8/95	A	X	BE	NC	....	....	....	....	....	15.0	M6	'94	107⅝	99	107⅝	7.53	5.85
(Gtd[11])M-T Nts 'B' 8.14s '99	[17]ms15	**A–**	8/95	A	X	BE	NC	....	....	....	....	....	10.0	M6	'94	107¾	99	107¾	7.55	5.85
(Gtd[11])M-T Nts 'B' 8.35s '99	jD15	**A–**	8/95	A	X	BE	NC	....	....	....	....	....	25.0	M5	'94	108⅝	99	108⅝	7.69	5.88
(Gtd[11])M-T Nts 'B' 8.06s 2001	[18]ms15	**A–**	8/95	A	X	BE	NC	....	....	....	....	....	10.0	S1	'94	109⅝	98⅞	109⅝	7.35	6.06
(Gtd[11])M-T Nts 'B' 8.22s 2001	[18]ms15	**A–**	8/95	A	X	BE	NC	....	....	....	....	....	65.0	M6	'94	110⅜	98⅞	110⅜	7.45	6.07
(Gtd[11])M-T Nts 'B' 8.40s 2001	jD13	**A–**	8/95	A	X	BE	NC	....	....	....	....	....	10.0	L3	'94	111⅜	98⅞	111⅜	7.54	6.09
(Gtd[11])M-T Nts 'B' 8.32s 2004	[19]ms15	**A–**	8/95	A	X	BE	NC	....	....	....	....	....	10.0	S1	'94	113⅜	99⅞	113⅜	7.34	6.31
• (Gtd[11])M-T Nts'B' 8¾s 2004	jD	**A–**	8/95	A	X	BE	NC	....	....	....	....	....	150	S1	'94	111⅛	100⅝	116½	7.51	6.30
(Gtd[11])M-T Nts 'B' 8.61s 2006	Mn15	**A–**	8/95	A	X	BE	NC	....	....	....	....	....	10.0	M6	'94	116⅞	100	116⅞	7.37	6.36
(Gtd[11])[20]Reset[21]M-T Nts 'B' 8s 2004	mS30	**A–**	8/95	A	X	BE	NC	....	....	....	....	....	25.0	S1	'94	105	98	103⅛	7.76	....
NYNEX Corp	***67a***	*3.75*	*0.33*	*2.63*		***Dc***	*130.0*	*3889*	*5577*	*9-30-95*	*7759*	*15881*	*62.3*							
• ([22]Amort) Deb 9.55s 2010	Mn	**A–**	8/95	A	X	BE	NC	....	....	....	....	....	369	F1	'90	101	101	101⅛	9.44	....
Oakwood Homes	***46***	*1.84*	*2.50*	*3.22*		***Sp***	*6.01*			*6-30-95*	*226.0*	*529.0*	*42.7*							
Reset[23]Deb[24]'A' 9⅛s 2007	QJun	**BB+**	9/95	BB	Y	R	[25]101	5-31-96	....	....	....	....	17.0	B7	'92	101¼	94⅛	101¼	9.01	....

Uniform Footnote Explanations-See Page 260. Other: [1] Issued in min denom $100T. [2] Due 10-29-96. [3] Due 11-15-96. [4] Due 4-29-97. [5] Co must offer repurch at 101 for Chge of Ctrl. [6] Incl liab subj to compromise. [7] Incl disc. [8] (HRO)On Chge of Ctrl at 101. [9] Due 4-15-03. [10] Max $56M red w/proceeds of Pub Eq Off'g. [11] Gtd by NYNEX Corp. [12] Due 7-19-99. [13] Int to 2-25-96,adj qtrly(3 Mo LIBOR&0.20%). [14] Int adj qtrly,Mar 1 etc. [15] Int adj qtrly,Jan 4 etc. [16] Issued in min denom $5T. [17] Due 11-1-99. [18] Due 10-17-01. [19] Due 10-19-04. [20] Int adj ea 9-30:8.125%'97,8.25%'98,8.375%'99. [21] Int adj 8.50%'00,8.625%'01,8.75%'02,9%'03,10% aft. [22] Princ pyts due ea May 1 fr 1991. [23] Int to be reset 6-1-97('02). [24] Death red benefit,ltd, as defined. [25] Min $10M.

Title-Industry Code & Co. Finances (In Italics) / Individual Issue Statistics (Exchange ↓)	Ind / Interest Dates	Fixed Charge Coverage 1992 / S&P Debt Rating	Date of Last Rating Change	1993 / Prior Rating	1994 / Eligible ↓	Year End / Bond Form	Million $ Cash & Equiv. / Redemption Provisions: Regular Price	Million $ Curr. Assets / Regular (Begins) Thru	Million $ Curr. Liab. / Sinking Fund Price	Balance Sheet Date / Sinking Fund (Begins) Thru	L. Term Debt (Mil $) / Refund/Other Restriction Price	Refund/Other Restriction (Begins) Thru	Capital-ization (Mil $) / Outst'g (Mil $)	Total Debt % Capital / Underwriting Firm	Underwriting Year	Price Range 1995 High	Price Range 1995 Low	Mo. End Price Sale(s) or Bid	Curr. Yield	Yield to Mat.
***Oakwood Homes** (Cont.)*																				
Reset[1]Deb[2]'B' 9s 2007	QJun	**BB+**	9/95	BB	Y	R	[3]101	5-31-96	....	....	....	....	23.0	B7	'92	101⅜	94	101⅜	8.88	....
***Occidental Petroleum**[4]*	***49b***	***1.42***		***1.33***	***1.06***	***Dc***	***118.0***	***2160***	***2033***	***9-30-95***	***5271***		***10019***	***53.1***						
• Sr Deb 10⅛s 2009	mS15	**BBB**	1/91	BBB–	X	R	NC	....	....	....	....	....	276	S4	'89	127⅝	106¾	s127⅝	7.93	6.96
• Sr Deb 11¾s 2011	Ms15	**BBB**	1/91	BBB–	X	R	104.838	(3-15-96)	100	(3-15-97)	....	....	955	D7	'86	110	105¼	s105¾	11.11	10.96
• Sr Deb 11⅛s 2019	Jd	**BBB**	1/91	BBB–	X	R	105.563	(6-1-99)	100	(6-1-00)	....	....	144	D7	'89	119½	108⅛	s118¾	9.37	9.16
• Sr Deb[5] 9¼s 2019	fA	**BBB**	1/91	BBB–	X	R	NC	....	....	....	....	....	300	M2	'89	123	102	121⅛	7.64	7.35
• Sr Nts 9⅝s '99	jJ	**BBB**	1/91	BBB–	X	R	100	(7-1-96)	....	....	....	....	300	S1	'89	104	101½	s102	9.44	8.95
Sr Nts 8½s 2001	mN9	**BBB**			X	BE	NC	....	....	....	....	....	150	M2	'94	109⅝	98	109⅝	7.75	6.50
• Sr Nts 10⅛s 2001	mN15	**BBB**	1/91	BBB–	X	R	NC	....	....	....	....	....	330	D6	'89	119⅛	107¼	s118	8.58	6.40
Sr Nts[6] 11⅛s 2010	fA	**BBB**	1/91	BBB–	X	BE	NC	....	....	....	....	....	150	D6	'90	139¼	115	139¼	7.99	6.83
Sr Nts 8¾s 2023	Jj15	**BBB**			X	BE	NC	....	....	....	....	....	100	M5	'93	119	94⅜	119	7.35	7.15
F/R[7]Sr Nts 6½s '99	QNov4	**BBB**			X	BE	*100	(11-4-96)	....	....	....	....	150	M5	'94	100¾	99	100¾	6.45	....
Ogden Corp	***17a***	***1.92***		***1.94***	***2.12***	***Dc***	***126.0***	***954.0***	***508.0***	***9-30-95***	***2055***		***2708***	***77.8***						
Deb 9¼s 2022	Ms	**BBB+**			X	BE	NC	....	....	....	....	....	100	G1	'92	126½	103	126½	7.31	7.02
***Ohio Bell Tel. Co.**[8]*	***67a***	***6.54***		***7.18***	***7.45***	***Dc***		***574.0***	***640.0***	***9-30-95***	***835.0***		***1704***	***49.0***						
Deb 5s 2006	Fa	**AAA**	8/88	AA	X	R	100.90	1-31-96	....	....	....	....	60.0	S1	'66	91⅝	76¾	91⅝	5.46	6.12
Deb 5⅜s 2007	Ms	**AAA**	8/88	AA	X	R	101.05	2-29-96	....	....	....	....	75.0	E1	'67	93¾	78⅛	93¾	5.73	6.16
Deb 6¾s 2008	jJ	**AAA**	8/88	AA	X	R	101.31	6-30-96	....	....	....	....	55.0	K2	'68	102	87¾	102	6.62	6.51
• Deb 7½s 2011	aO	**AAA**	8/88	AA	X	R	102.16	9-30-96	....	....	....	....	100	M6	'71	102¾	91⅛	101⅝	7.38	7.32
• Deb 7⅞s 2013	aO	**AAA**	8/88	AA	X	R	102.59	9-30-96	....	....	....	....	200	M6	'73	103⅝	93⅝	102⅜	7.69	7.63
Deb 7.85s 2022	jD15	**AAA**			X	BE	103.764	(12-15-02)	....	....	....	....	100	L3	'92	111¾	92¼	111¾	7.02	6.89
Nts 5¾s 2000	Mn	**AAA**			X	BE	NC	....	....	....	....	....	100	M2	'93	100⅛	90	100⅛	5.74	5.71
Nts 6⅛s 2003	Mn15	**AAA**			X	BE	NC	....	....	....	....	....	150	K2	'93	100⅞	87½	100⅞	6.07	5.98
Ohio Edison Co.	***72a***	***2.50***		***2.57***	***2.73***	***Dc***	***113.0***	***593.0***	***1021***	***9-30-95***	***2877***		***6170***	***55.3***						
1st ('91) 8½s '96	Mn	**BBB–**	12/93	BBB	X	BE	NC	....	....	....	....	....	150	M6	'91	101⅞	100⅝	100⅞	8.43	5.79
1st ('91) 8¾s '98	Fa15	**BBB–**	12/93	BBB	X	BE	NC	....	....	....	....	....	150	M5	'91	105⅛	100	105⅛	8.32	6.14
1st ('92) 6⅞s '99	mS15	**BBB–**	12/93	BBB	X	BE	NC	....	....	....	....	....	150	M6	'92	102⅛	92⅞	102⅛	6.73	6.22
1st('93) 6⅜s 2000	Ao	**BBB–**	12/93	BBB	X	BE	NC	....	....	....	....	....	80.0	M6	'93	100⅜	90⅛	100⅜	6.35	6.27
1st 8¼s 2002	Ao	**BBB–**	12/93	BBB	X	BE	NC	....	....	....	....	....	125	M6	'92	108½	96⅜	108½	7.60	6.57
1st 7½s 2002	fA	**BBB–**	12/93	BBB	X	R	101.26	7-31-96	Z100.49	7-31-96	....	....	34.3	F1	'72	102	92¼	101⅝	7.38	7.18
1st ('92) 7⅜s 2002	mS15	**BBB–**	12/93	BBB	X	BE	NC	....	....	....	....	....	120	M6	'92	104⅞	91	104⅞	7.03	6.47
1st ('91) 8⅝s 2003	mS15	**BBB–**	12/93	BBB	X	BE	NC	....	....	....	....	....	150	M6	'91	111½	97⅝	111½	7.74	6.69
1st('93) 6⅞s 2005	Ao	**BBB–**	12/93	BBB	X	BE	NC	....	....	....	....	....	80.0	M6	'93	101¾	85⅞	101¾	6.76	6.62
1st ('89) 9¾s 2019	jJ15	**CALL**	12/95	BBB–		R			Called 1-15-96 at 106.60				35.3	M6	'89	107⅛	101⅜	106⅝	9.14	Call
1st ('92) 8¾s 2022	Jd15	**BBB–**	12/93	BBB	X	BE	106.25	(6-15-97)	Z100	....	....	....	100	M6	'92	107¾	92⅝	107¾	8.12	8.04
1st ('93) 7⅞s 2023	Ao	**BBB–**	12/93	BBB	X	BE	103.38	(4-1-03)	Z100	(4-1-03)	....	....	100	M6	'93	102⅜	86⅜	102⅜	7.69	7.66
1st ('93) 7⅝s 2023	Jd15	**BBB–**	12/93	BBB	X	BE	103.34	(6-15-03)	Z100	(6-15-03)	....	....	75.0	M6	'93	100⅝	83⅞	100⅝	7.58	7.57
***Ohio Power Co.**[9]*	***72a***	***3.00***		***3.55***	***3.48***	***Dc***	***55.60***	***558.0***	***516.0***	***6-30-95***	***1089***		***2831***	***46.2***						
1st 5s '96	Jj	**A–**	12/84	BBB+	X	R	100	....	□100	....	....	....	38.8	F1	'67	100	97⅝	100	5.00	Mat.
1st 6½s '97	fA	**A–**	12/84	BBB+	X	R	100.32	7-31-96	□100.32	7-31-96	....	....	46.6	F1	'66	100⅜	96¼	100⅜	6.48	6.24
1st 6¾s '98	Ms	**A–**	12/84	BBB+	X	R	100.60	2-29-96	□100.41	2-29-96	....	....	55.7	F1	'68	100⅝	96	100⅝	6.71	6.43
1st[6] 8.10s 2002	Fa15	**A–**			X	BE	102.32	(2-10-97)	□100	(2-10-97)	....	....	50.0	S1	'92	105⅛	96½	104⅝	7.74	7.15
1st[6] 8¼s 2002	[10]jd	**A–**			X	BE	102.36	(3-1-97)	100	(3-4-97)	....	....	50.0	S1	'92	105½	97⅜	105	7.86	7.23
1st 7⅝s 2002	Ao	**A–**	12/84	BBB+	X	R	100.68	3-31-96	□100.68	3-31-96	....	....	16.9	F1	'72	101	95	100⅞	7.56	7.44
1st 7¾s 2002	aO	**A–**	12/84	BBB+	X	R	100.54	9-30-96	□100.54	9-30-96	....	....	24.0	H1	'72	101¾	94⅞	101⅜	7.64	7.48
1st 6¾s 2003	Ao	**A–**			X	BE	NC	....	....	....	....	....	40.0	S1	'93	101¾	88⅝	101¾	6.63	6.44

Uniform Footnote Explanations-See Page 260. Other:[1] Int to be reset 6-1-97('02). [2] Death red benefit,ltd,as defined. [3] Min $10M. [4] See OXY O&G USA. [5] (HRO)On 8-1-04 at 100. [6] Issued in min denom $100T. [7] Int to 2-4-96,adj qtrly(3 Mo LIBRO&0.625%). [8] Subsid of Ameritech Corp. [9] Contr. by Amer Elec Pwr. [10] Due 3-15-02.

Title-Industry Code & Co. Finances (In Italics) / Individual Issue Statistics (Exchange)	Ind / Interest Dates	Fixed Charge Coverage 1992 / S&P Debt Rating	1993 / Date of Last Rating Change	1994 / Prior Rating	Eligible	Year End / Bond Form	Million $ Cash & Equiv. / Redemption Provisions Regular Price	Curr. Assets / Regular (Begins) Thru	Curr. Liab. / Sinking Fund Price	Balance Sheet Date / Sinking Fund (Begins) Thru	L. Term Debt (Mil $) / Refund/Other Restriction Price	Refund/Other Restriction (Begins) Thru	Capitalization (Mil $) / Outst'g (Mil $)	Total Debt % Capital / Underwriting Firm	Underwriting Year	Price Range 1995 High	Price Range 1995 Low	Mo. End Price Sale(s) or Bid	Curr. Yield	Yield to Mat.
***Ohio Power Co.** (Cont.)*																				
1st 6s 2003	[1]ao	**A–**			X	BE	101.72	(11-1-98)	□100	(11-1-98)	....	....	25.0	S1	'93	96⅜	83⅛	96⅜	6.23	6.60
1st 6.15s 2003	[2]ao	**A–**			X	BE	101.76	(12-1-98)	□100	(12-1-98)	....	....	50.0	S1	'93	97⅞	84¼	97⅞	6.28	6.50
1st 9⅞s 2020	fA	**A–**			X	R	107.41	7-31-96	□100	....	....	....	[3]2.54	L3	'90	108⅜	101	101	9.78	9.77
1st[4] 8.80s 2022	[5]jd	**A–**			X	BE	104.40	(2-1-01)	100	(2-10-02)	....	....	50.0	S1	'92	115¼	97⅝	115¼	7.64	7.46
1st 7¾s 2023	Ao	**A–**			X	BE	103.88	(4-1-03)	100	....	....	....	40.0	S1	'93	104⅝	87¼	104⅝	7.41	7.35
1st 7.10s 2023	[6]ao	**A–**			X	BE	103.55	(11-1-03)	□100	(11-1-03)	....	....	25.0	S1	'93	97⅛	80½	97⅛	7.31	7.34
SF Deb 5⅛s '96	Jj	**BBB+**	4/77	BB	X	R	100	....	□100	....	....	....	8.69	B6	'66	100	97⅝	100	5.13	Mat.
SF Deb 6⅝s '97	fA	**BBB+**	4/77	BB	X	R	100.33	7-31-96	□100.33	7-31-96	....	....	4.25	H1	'67	100⅜	96⅜	100⅜	6.60	6.37
SF Deb 7⅞s '99	Ms	**BBB+**	4/77	BB	X	R	101.03	2-29-96	□100.60	2-29-96	....	....	4.91	E1	'69	101⅛	97¾	101⅛	7.79	7.46
Oklahoma Gas & Electric	***72a***	***3.05***	***3.32***	***3.58***		***Dc***	***4.53***	***347.0***	***304.0***	***9-30-95***	***845.0***		***1912***	***47.2***						
1st 5⅛s '97	Jj	**AA–**	3/93	AA	X	R	100	....	100	....	....	....	15.0	S1	'67	99⅝	94⅞	99⅝	5.14	5.51
1st 6⅜s '98	Jj	**AA–**	3/93	AA	X	R	100.22	12-31-96	100	....	....	....	25.0	H1	'68	100⅜	95⅝	100⅛	6.37	6.31
1st 7⅛s '99	Jj	**AA–**	3/93	AA	X	R	100.56	12-31-96	100.20	2-1-96	....	....	12.5	H1	'69	100⅞	96¼	100½	7.09	6.94
1st 7⅛s 2002	Jj	**AA–**	3/93	AA	X	R	101.39	12-31-96	100.37	2-1-96	....	....	40.0	S1	'72	101¾	93⅝	101⅜	7.03	6.84
1st 8⅜s 2007	Jj	**AA–**	3/93	AA	X	R	103.45	12-31-96	101.04	12-31-96	....	....	75.0	B6	'77	104	97½	103⅛	8.12	7.94
1st 8⅝s 2007	mN	**AA–**	3/93	AA	X	R	103.79	10-31-96	101.01	10-31-96	....	....	35.0	M2	'77	104¼	99⅝	103½	8.33	8.16
1st 8¼s 2016	fA15	**AA–**	3/93	AA	X	R	100.96	8-14-96	100	....	....	....	100	K2	'86	101½	95⅞	100¼	8.23	8.22
1st 8⅞s 2020	jD	**AA–**	3/93	AA	X	R	102.317	11-30-96	100	....	....	....	75.0	M2	'90	104⅛	98¾	103	8.62	8.58
Sr Nts 6¼s 2000	aO15	**AA–**			X	BE	NC	....	....	....	....	....	110	B5	'95	101¾	99¾	101¾	6.14	5.82
Sr Nts 7.30s 2025	aO15	**AA–**			X	BE	103.261	(10-15-05)	....	....	....	....	110	M2	'95	103⅝	99⅛	103⅝	7.04	7.01
Old Kent Fin'l	***10***	***7.83***	***9.88***	***6.34***		***Dc***				***9-30-95***	***★101.0***		***1000***	***NM***						
Sub Nts 6⅝s 2005	mN15	**A–**			X	BE	NC	....	....	....	....	....	100	C5	'95	101⅞	98¾	101⅞	6.50	6.37
Old Republic Int'l	***35c***	***11.85***	***10.81***	***10.69***		***Dc***				***9-30-95***	***309.0***		***1889***	***16.4***						
SF Deb 10s 2018	[7]jd	**AA–**			X	R	106.192	1-31-96	100	(2-1-99)	®104.763	1-31-98	74.0	M2	'88	107¼	106⅜	106⅜	9.40	9.31
Olin Corp	***14***	***2.95***	***d1.75***	***4.81***		***Dc***	***5.60***	***1054***	***789.0***	***9-30-95***	***426.0***		***1464***	***43.6***						
Nts 8s 2002	Jd15	**BBB**			X	R	NC	....	....	....	....	....	100	L3	'92	109½	95⅝	109½	7.31	6.19
Sub Nts 9½s '97	Jd15	**BBB–**			X	R	NC	....	....	....	....	....	125	M6	'87	106¼	102¼	105⅜	9.02	5.61
Olympic Financial Ltd	***25e***	***d0.81***	***1.80***	***2.15***		***Dc***				***9-30-95***	***157.0***		***322.0***	***48.8***						
Sr Nts[8] 13s 2000	Mn	**BB**	9/95	NR	Y	R	108.50	(5-1-98)	....	....	....	....	145	D6	'95	109½	100	109	11.93	10.36
OMI Corp	***64***	***0.58***	***0.37***	***d0.38***		***Dc***	***29.20***	***61.50***	***59.30***	***9-30-95***	***239.0***		***424.0***	***60.4***						
Sr Nts[8] 10¼s 2003	mN	**B–**	3/95	B	Y	R	105.125	(11-1-98)	....	....	....	....	161	G1	'93	98⅛	89⅝	97¼	10.54	10.77
ONEOK Inc	***73b***	***2.41***	***2.52***	***2.60***		***Au***	***12.50***	***194.0***	***174.0***	***8-31-95***	***351.0***		***817.0***	***51.3***						
Deb 9.70s 2019	jD	**A–**	11/90	BBB+	X	R	104.75	(12-1-99)	100	(6-1-00)	....	....	125	P1	'89	116⅜	106⅝	116⅜	8.34	8.13
Deb 9¾s 2020	jD	**A–**			X	R	104.35	(12-1-00)	100	(6-1-01)	....	....	75.0	P1	'90	118¼	107	118¼	8.25	8.04
[9]OPI Int'l	***49e***	***1.33***	***2.63***	***[10]3.14***		***Mr***	***68.00***	***602.0***	***571.0***	***9-30-95***	***336.0***		***1105***	***48.1***						
Gtd[11]Sr Nts[12] 12⅞s 2002	jJ15	**BB+**	6/95	B+	Y	R	106.40	(7-15-97)	100	(7-20-00)	....	....	70.0	B5	'92	114	108	113¼	11.37	10.06
Orange & Rockland Utils[13]	***75***	***2.96***	***3.13***	***2.98***		***Dc***	***5.08***	***221.0***	***208.0***	***9-30-95***	***360.0***		***791.0***	***45.5***						
1st I 6½s '97	aO	**A–**	6/94	A	X	R	100.27	9-30-96	100.19	9-30-96	....	....	23.0	F1	'67	100⅜	96¼	100⅜	6.48	6.26
Deb 'A' 9⅜s 2000	Ms15	**A–**	6/94	A	X	R	NC	....	....	....	....	....	80.0	G1	'90	112¼	102¾	112¼	8.35	6.03
Deb 'B' 6½s '97	aO15	**A–**	6/94	A	X	BE	NC	....	....	....	....	....	55.0	S5	'92	100¼	95¼	100¼	6.48	6.34
Deb 'C' 6.14s 2000	Ms	**A–**	6/94	A	X	BE	NC	....	....	....	....	....	20.0	S5	'93	100⅜	90	100⅜	6.12	6.03
Deb 'D' 6.56s 2003	Ms	**A–**	6/94	A	X	BE	NC	....	....	....	....	....	35.0	S5	'93	100⅞	87⅞	100⅞	6.50	6.40
[14]Orchard Supply Hardware Corp	***59l***	***1.24***	***1.88***	***1.18***		***Ja***	***15.90***	***156.0***	***79.20***	***10-29-95***	***133.0***		***228.0***	***59.6***						
Sr Nts[8] 9⅜s 2002	Fa15	**B**			Y	R	103.125	(2-15-98)	....	....	....	....	100	L3	'94	96¼	79	96¼	9.74	10.21
Orient Express Hotels[15]	***32***	***Acquired by Sea Containers Ltd,see***																		
• Sub SF Deb[16] 10¼s '98	mS	**BB–**	10/92	BB+	Y	R	100	....	100	....	....	....	27.8	W1	'78	102	97½	s101	10.15	9.80

Uniform Footnote Explanations-See Page 260. Other: [1] Due 11-1-03. [2] Due 12-1-03. [3] Called $43.6M on 8-1-95. [4] Issued in min denom $100T. [5] Due 2-10-22. [6] Due 11-1-23. [7] Due 2-1-18. [8] (HRO)On Chge of Ctrl at 101. [9] Now McDermott (J. Ray) Inc. [10] Fiscal Jul'94 & prior. [11] Gtd by Offshore Pipelines. [12] Co must offer repurch at 101 On Chge of Ctrl. [13] See Rockland Electric. [14] Gtd by&data of Orchard Supply Hardware Strs. [15] Was Sea Containers Inc,then SeaCo Inc. [16] Asmd by Sea Containers Ltd.

Title-Industry Code & Co. Finances (In Italics) / Individual Issue Statistics (Exchange)	Ind / Interest Dates	Fixed Charge Coverage 1992 / S&P Debt Rating	1993 / Date of Last Rating Change	1994 / Prior Rating	Eligible	Year End / Bond Form	Million $ Cash & Equiv. / Redemption Provisions: Regular Price	Curr. Assets / Regular (Begins) Thru	Curr. Liab. / Sinking Fund Price	Balance Sheet Date / Sinking Fund (Begins) Thru	L. Term Debt (Mil $) / Refund/Other Restriction Price	Refund/Other Restriction (Begins) Thru	Capital-ization (Mil $) / Outst'g (Mil $)	Total Debt % Capital / Underwriting Firm	Underwriting Year	Price Range 1995 High	Price Range 1995 Low	Mo. End Price Sale(s) or Bid	Curr. Yield	Yield to Mat.
Oriole Homes Corp	***13h***	***1.57***	***0.60***	***0.71***		***Dc***	***2.67***			***9-30-95***	***90.00***		***169.0***	***53.3***						
Sr Nts[1] 12½s 2003	Jj15	**B**			Y	R	105	(1-15-98)	100	(1-15-01)	....	....	70.0	B5	'93	92¼	81	82	15.24	16.97
Orion Capital	***35c***	***3.88***	***5.84***	***5.41***		***Dc***				***9-30-95***	***209.0***		***673.0***	***31.1***						
Sr Nts 9⅛s 2002	mS	**BBB**	9/93	BBB–	X	R	NC	....	....	....	....	....	110	M2	'92	113¾	98¼	113¾	8.02	6.55
Sr Nts 7¼s 2005	jJ15	**BBB**			X	BE	NC	....	....	....	....	....	100	L3	'95	103¾	98	103¾	6.99	6.71
OrNda HealthCorp[2]	***30***	***△1.29***	***△0.45***	***△1.79***		***Au***	***4.96***	***404.0***	***398.0***	***8-31-95***	***p1032***		***1467***	***73.2***						
Sr Sub Nts[3] 12¼s 2002	Mn15	**B–**			Y	R	104.594	5-14-97	....	....	....	....	400	D6	'92	109⅞	105	109½	11.19	10.18
Sr Sub Nts 11⅜s 2004	fA15	**B–**			Y	R	105.69	(8-15-99)	....	....	....	....	125	M2	'94	112½	102½	111¾	10.18	9.36
Oryx Energy Co[4]	***49a***	***1.16***	***0.10***	***0.88***		***Dc***	***12.00***	***298.0***	***627.0***	***9-30-95***	***978.0***		***1109***	***119.0***						
Nts 9.30s '96	Mn	**BB**	9/94	BBB–	Y	R	NC	....	....	....	....	....	100	M5	'91	101½	99⅛	100⅞	9.22	6.56
Nts 10s '99	Jd15	**BB**	9/94	BBB–	Y	R	NC	....	....	....	....	....	100	L3	'91	109⅛	98¼	109⅛	9.16	6.98
Nts 9½s '99	mN	**BB**	9/94	BBB–	Y	R	NC	....	....	....	....	....	100	F1	'91	108⅝	96⅛	108⅝	8.75	6.90
Nts 10s 2001	Ao	**BB**	9/94	BBB–	Y	R	NC	....	....	....	....	....	150	M2	'91	112¼	97⅜	112¼	8.91	7.16
Nts 8s 2003	aO15	**BB**			Y	BE	NC	....	....	....	....	....	100	C5	'95	102⅛	100	101⅜	7.89	7.76
Nts 8⅛s 2005	aO15	**BB**			Y	BE	NC	....	....	....	....	....	150	C5	'95	103	99⅞	101⅜	8.01	7.92
Otter Tail Power	***72a***	***4.04***	***3.99***	***4.21***		***Dc***	***1.40***	***67.30***	***71.00***	***9-30-95***	***166.0***		***415.0***	***46.7***						
1st 8¾s '97	jD15	**AA–**			X	R	NC	....	100	....	....	....	19.2	P2	'90	105¾	101	105¼	8.31	5.87
1st 7¼s 2002	fA	**AA–**			X	R	NC	....	100	....	....	....	19.6	S5	'92	104⅝	93⅜	104⅝	6.93	6.38
1st 7⅝s 2003	Fa	**AA–**	6/90	A+	X	R	101.91	1-31-96	100.15	1-31-96	....	....	9.48	W5	'73	102	96	102	7.48	7.26
1st 8¾s 2021	mS15	**AA–**			X	R	103.54	(9-15-01)	Z100	....	....	....	19.4	P2	'91	113⅛	99	113⅛	7.73	7.58
1st 8¼s 2022	fA	**AA–**			X	R	104.13	(8-1-02)	100	....	....	....	29.4	S5	'92	111¼	93⅞	111¼	7.42	7.29
Outboard Marine Corp	***40a***	***△d7.08***	***△4.54***	***△3.34***		***Sp***	***58.30***	***502.0***	***249.0***	***9-30-95***	***177.0***		***433.0***	***41.1***						
SF Deb 9⅛s 2017	Ao15	**BB**	6/92	BB+	Y	R	105.325	4-14-96	100	(4-15-98)	®104.438	4-14-97	65.7	S1	'87	100½	86	100½	9.08	9.07
Outdoor Systems	***1***	***0.89***	***1.03***	***0.92***		***Dc***	***1.77***	***16.50***	***5.05***	***9-30-95***	***151.0***		***134.0***	***113.0***						
Sr Nts[5] 10¾s 2003	fA15	**B**			Y	R	105.375	(8-15-98)	....	....	[6]Z110	8-15-01	115	B5	'93	97	92	97	11.08	11.34
Overhead Door Corp[7]	***42***	***0.57***	***1.40***	***1.99***		***Dc***	***2.07***	***188.0***	***112.0***	***9-30-95***	***227.0***		***348.0***	***72.4***						
Sr Nts[5] 12¼s 2000	Fa	**B–**	8/94	B	Y	R	102.04	(2-1-98)	....	....	....	....	85.0	F1	'93	102¾	95	97	12.63	13.21
Overseas Shipholding Gr	***64***	***1.16***	***1.25***	***0.65***		***Dc***	***193.0***	***259.0***	***78.40***	***9-30-95***	***1123***		***1922***	***59.2***						
Deb 8¾s 2013	jD	**BBB–**			X	BE	[8]Z100	....	....	....	....	....	100	G1	'93	107⅛	89¾	106⅝	8.21	8.04
Nts 8s 2003	jD	**BBB–**			X	BE	[8]Z100	....	....	....	....	....	100	G1	'93	104¾	88⅞	103⅛	7.76	7.47
Owens-Corning Fiberglas	***28***	***1.94***	***3.00***	***3.35***		***Dc***	***20.00***	***1030***	***1015***	***9-30-95***	***798.0***		***658.0***	***145.0***						
Deb 8⅞s 2002	Jd	**BBB–**			X	BE	NC	....	....	....	....	....	150	G1	'92	111⅞	98⅛	111⅞	7.93	6.58
Deb 9⅜s 2012	Jd	**BBB–**			X	BE	NC	....	....	....	....	....	150	G1	'92	120¼	101⅜	120¼	7.80	7.25
Ext'd[9]Nts[10] 5.79s '96	[11]jD15	**BBB–**	5/89	BB	X	R	100	....	....	....	....	....	8.00	G1	'85	100	97½	99⅞	5.80	5.92
Owens-Illinois	***16***	***1.60***	***d0.02***	***1.55***		***Dc***	***169.0***	***1214***	***920.0***	***9-30-95***	***2746***		***3356***	***84.6***						
• Sr([5]Amort)Deb[12] 11s 2003	jD	**BB**			Y	R	103	(12-1-99)	....	....	....	....	1000	M2	'91	113	103½	s113	9.73	....
• Sr Sub Nts 10¼s '99	Ao	**B+**			Y	R	100	(4-1-97)	....	....	....	....	250	M6	'92	104¾	98½	s104	9.86	8.80
• Sr Sub Nts 10½s 2002	Jd15	**B+**			Y	R	105.25	(6-15-97)	....	....	....	....	150	M6	'92	107¼	97⅞	107	9.81	9.04
• Sr Sub Nts 10s 2002	fA	**B+**			Y	R	105	(8-1-97)	....	....	....	....	250	G1	'92	No Sale		106	9.43	8.78
• Sr Sub Nts 9¾s 2004	fA15	**B+**			Y	R	104.875	(8-15-97)	....	....	....	....	200	M6	'92	106¼	94¼	s105⅜	9.25	8.84
• Sr Sub Nts 9.95s 2004	aO15	**B+**			Y	R	104.975	(10-15-97)	....	....	....	....	100	N2	'92	106	96¼	s106	9.39	8.95
OXY USA Inc[13]	***49a***	***Gtd by Occidental Petroleum, see***																		
• SF Deb[14] 6⅛s '97	mN	**BBB**	1/91	BBB–	X	R	100	....	100	....	....	....	15.2	F1	'67	100⅛	91⅝	99	6.19	6.71
• SF Deb[14] 6⅝s '99	fA	**BBB**	1/91	BBB–	X	R	100	....	100	....	....	....	[15]55.4	F1	'69	No Sale		98¾	6.71	7.02
Deb[16] 7s 2011	Ao15	**BBB**	1/91	BBB–	X	R	100	....	....	....	....	....	[15]274	F1	'81	96¼	82¼	96¼	7.27	7.41
P&C Food Markets	***59c***	***Subsid of Penn Traffic Co,see***																		
Sr Nts[1] 11½s 2001	aO15	**BB–**	4/93	B	Y	R	104.25	(10-15-96)	....	....	....	....	125	S1	'91	105¾	96¾	97	11.86	12.23

Uniform Footnote Explanations-See Page 260. Other: [1] (HRO)On Chge in Ctrl at 101. [2] Was Republic Health Corp. [3] (HRO)On Chge of Ctrl at 100. [4] Was Sun Explor'n & Prod'n. [5] (HRO)On Chge of Ctrl at 101. [6] Max $38M red w/proceeds of Pub Eq Off'g. [7] Subsid of DCO Hldgs. [8] Plus Make-Whole Premium. [9] (HRO)On 12-15-96 at 100,aft as defined. [10] Int to 12-15-96,adj aft as defined. [11] Due 12-15-05. [12] Prin pyts of $200 due ea Dec 1, 1999-03. [13] Was Cities Service Co,then OXY Oil&Gas USA. [14] Gtd by Occidental Petroleum. [15] Incl disc. [16] Not gtd by Occidental Petroleum.

Title-Industry Code & Co. Finances (In Italics) / Exchange, Individual Issue Statistics	Ind / Interest Dates	Fixed Charge Coverage 1992 / S&P Debt Rating	1993 / Date of Last Rating Change	1994 / Prior Rating	Eligible	Year End / Bond Form	Million $ Cash & Equiv. / Redemption Provisions: Regular Price	Curr. Assets / Regular (Begins) Thru	Curr. Liab. / Sinking Fund Price	Balance Sheet Date / Sinking Fund (Begins) Thru	L. Term Debt (Mil $) / Refund/Other Restriction Price	Capital-ization (Mil $) / Refund/Other Restriction (Begins) Thru	Outst'g (Mil $)	Total Debt % Capital / Underwriting Firm	Underwriting Year	Price Range 1995 High	Price Range 1995 Low	Mo. End Price Sale(s) or Bid	Curr. Yield	Yield to Mat.
PA Holdings Corp	***3***	....	....	....		***Dc***	***No Recent Fin'ls***													
Sr Sub Nts 13¾s '99	jJ15	B+	7/92	B–	Y	R	103.44	7-14-96	100	(7-15-97)	Z103.44	7-14-96	250	F1	'89	104¾	104⅛	104⅛	13.21	12.27
Pace Membership Warehouse	***59m***	....	....	....		***Ja***	***No Recent Fin'ls***													
Sub Nts 13s '96	Ao15	NR				R	100	....	....	....	....	....	25.5	K2	'86	102	98	102	12.75	5.93
PacifiCorp	***72b***	***1.71***	***2.57***	***2.95***		***Dc***	***16.00***	***734.0***	***1354***	***9-30-95***	***3707***	***8143***		***48.5***						
1st & CT 6¾s 2005	Ao	A	9/94	A–	X	R	NC	....	....	....	....	....	150	G1	'93	102⅞	87¾	102⅞	6.56	6.33
Pacific[1] Bell[2]	***67a***	***4.71***	***4.48***	***4.79***		***Dc***	***66.00***	***2443***	***2961***	***9-30-95***	***5103***	***8386***		***65.3***						
• Deb 6⅞s 2023	fA15	AA–			X	R	101.57	(8-15-03)	....	....	....	....	100	L3	'93	99½	80⅛	s99½	6.91	6.91
Deb 7⅜s 2025	Jd15	AA–			X	R	103.367	(6-15-03)	....	....	....	....	350	G1	'93	103¾	85⅝	103¾	7.11	7.07
• Deb 7⅛s 2026	Ms15	AA–			X	R	NC	....	....	....	....	....	625	L3	'93	106	84	105	6.79	6.73
Deb 8½s 2031	fA15	AA–			X	R	102.76	(8-15-01)	....	....	....	....	225	M2	'91	111⅝	95⅝	111⅝	7.61	7.55
Deb 7¾s 2032	mS15	AA–			X	R	103.92	(9-15-02)	....	....	....	....	300	M2	'92	107⅞	87⅞	107⅞	7.18	7.14
• Deb 7½s 2033	Fa	AA–			X	R	102.94	(2-1-03)	....	....	....	....	400	L3	'93	104½	85¾	s103½	7.25	7.23
• Deb 6⅝s 2034	aO15	AA–			X	R	101.12	(10-15-13)	....	....	....	....	550	L3	'93	95¼	78	94¼	7.03	7.06
Deb 7⅜s 2043	jJ15	AA–			X	R	102.89	(7-15-13)	....	....	....	....	300	S1	'93	104⅜	84	104⅜	7.07	7.05
Nts 8.70s 2001	Jd15	AA–			X	R	NC	....	....	....	....	....	200	L3	'91	112⅞	101⅞	112⅞	7.71	5.91
• Nts 7¼s 2002	jJ	AA–			X	R	NC	....	....	....	....	....	300	L3	'92	107	93⅞	s107	6.78	5.94
Nts 7s 2004	jJ15	AA–			X	R	NC	....	....	....	....	....	325	S1	'92	105	90¾	105	6.67	6.24
• Nts 6¼s 2005	Ms	AA–			X	R	NC	....	....	....	....	....	325	L3	'93	101½	84⅛	s101	6.19	6.10
Pacific Gas & Electric	***75***	***3.40***	***3.40***	***3.39***		***Dc***	***339.0***	***3386***	***3097***	***9-30-95***	***8207***	***18085***		***47.8***						
• 1st & Ref JJ 4½s '96	Jd	A	7/88	A+	X	CR	100	....	*100	....	....	....	12.0	H1	'63	99¾	96	99¼	4.53	6.30
• 1st & Ref KK 4½s '96	jD	A	7/88	A+	X	CR	100	....	*100	....	....	....	13.7	H1	'64	98⅝	96½	98⅝	4.56	6.05
1st & Ref LL 4⅝s '97	Jd	A	7/88	A+	X	CR	100.19	5-31-96	‡100.19	5-31-96	....	....	19.6	F1	'65	98⅞	92⅜	98⅞	4.68	5.45
1st & Ref MM 5⅜s '98	Jd	A	7/88	A+	X	CR	100.17	11-30-96	‡100.17	11-30-96	....	....	48.1	F1	'66	99¼	91⅜	99¼	5.42	5.71
1st & Ref NN 5¾s '98	jD	A	7/88	A+	X	CR	100.37	11-30-96	‡100.37	11-30-96	....	....	66.4	B6	'66	99⅝	91⅞	99⅝	5.77	5.89
1st & Ref OO 5½s '99	Jd	A	7/88	A+	X	CR	100.61	5-31-96	‡100.61	5-31-96	....	....	66.8	F1	'67	98⅞	89⅞	98⅞	5.56	5.87
1st & Ref PP 6⅞s '99	jD	A	7/88	A+	X	CR	100.76	11-30-96	‡100.76	11-30-96	....	....	79.9	F1	'67	100⅞	94	100¾	6.82	6.65
1st & Ref QQ 6⅝s 2000	Jd	A	7/88	A+	X	CR	100.85	5-31-96	‡100.85	5-31-96	....	....	49.9	F1	'68	100⅞	92⅞	100⅞	6.57	6.39
1st & Ref RR 6¾s 2000	jD	A	7/88	A+	X	CR	100.96	11-30-96	‡100.96	11-30-96	....	....	59.8	B6	'68	101	92¾	101	6.68	6.51
1st & Ref 90B 8¾s 2001	[3]jd	A			X	R	NC	....	....	....	....	....	100	F1	'90	111⅛	101¼	111⅛	7.87	6.13
1st & Ref 91A 8.80s 2024	[4]jd	A			X	R	NC	....	....	....	....	....	200	G1	'91	123⅞	102	123⅞	7.10	6.87
1st & Ref 91B 8⅞s 2024	[5]jd	A			X	R	103.42	(6-1-96)	‡103.42	(6-1-96)	....	....	67.2	F1	'91	105⅞	97⅛	104⅝	8.48	8.44
1st & Ref 92A 7⅞s 2002	[6]jd	A			X	R	NC	....	....	....	....	....	400	G1	'92	108⅞	96½	108⅞	7.23	6.12
1st & Ref 92B 8⅜s 2025	[4]jd	A			X	R	102.51	(6-1-02)	‡102.51	(6-1-02)	....	....	200	M6	'92	111⅜	94⅛	111⅜	7.52	7.42
1st & Ref 92C 8s 2025	[7]jd	A			X	R	104.82	(12-1-97)	‡104.82	(12-1-97)	....	....	250	G1	'92	107½	91¼	107½	7.44	7.37
1st & Ref 92D 8¼s 2022	[8]jd	A			X	R	103.14	(12-1-02)	‡103.14	(12-1-02)	....	....	400	F1	'92	109½	93¼	109½	7.53	7.43
1st & Ref 93A 7¼s 2026	[6]jd	A			X	R	102.02	(6-1-03)	‡102.02	(6-1-03)	....	....	300	F1	'93	100⅜	83⅛	100⅜	7.22	7.22
1st & Ref 93B 5⅜s '98	[9]jd	A			X	R	NC	....	....	....	....	....	400	G1	'93	99	90⅞	99	5.43	5.79
1st & Ref 93C 6¼s 2003	[9]jd	A			X	R	NC	....	....	....	....	....	400	G1	'93	99½	86⅜	99½	6.28	6.33
1st & Ref 93D 7¼s 2026	[9]jd	A			X	R	103.63	(6-1-03)	*103.63	(6-1-03)	....	....	450	G1	'93	100	83⅛	100	7.25	7.25
1st & Ref 93E 5⅞s 2005	jd	A			X	R	NC	....	....	....	....	....	300	F1	'93	96⅞	81¼	96⅞	6.06	6.31
1st & Ref 93F 6¾s 2023	[7]jd	A			X	R	102.74	(12-1-03)	‡102.74	(12-1-03)	....	....	400	F1	'93	96⅝	79½	96⅝	6.99	7.03
1st & Ref 93G 6¼s 2004	[6]jd	A			X	R	NC	....	....	....	....	....	350	M6	'93	99½	85⅛	99½	6.28	6.33
1st & Ref 93H 7.05s 2024	[6]jd	A			X	R	NC	....	....	....	....	....	350	M6	'93	101⅛	82¼	101⅛	6.97	6.96
Pacific Gas Transmission[10]	***73a***	***2.36***	***2.47***	***2.65***		***Dc***	***23.80***	***114.0***	***85.90***	***9-30-95***	***564.0***	***1002***		***56.3***						
• Sr Deb 7.80s 2025	Jd	A–			X	BE	103.036	(6-1-05)	....	....	....	....	150	M6	'95	98¼	98¼	100	7.80	7.80
• Sr Nts 7.10s 2005	Jd	A–			X	BE	NC	....	....	....	....	....	250	M6	'95	99⅞	99⅞	94⅛	7.54	8.00

Uniform Footnote Explanations-See Page 260. Other: [1] Subsid of Pacific Telesis Gr. [2] See Pacific Tel & Tel. [3] Due Jan 1. [4] Due May 1. [5] Due Jul 1. [6] Due Mar 1. [7] Due Oct 1. [8] Due Nov 1. [9] Due Aug 1. [10] Subsid of Pacific Gas & Elec.

Title-Industry Code & Co. Finances (In Italics) / Individual Issue Statistics, Exchange	Ind / Interest Dates	Fixed Charge Coverage 1992 / S&P Debt Rating	1993 / Date of Last Rating Change	1994 / Prior Rating	Eligible	Year End / Bond Form	Million $ Cash & Equiv. / Redemption Provisions: Regular Price	Curr. Assets / Regular (Begins) Thru	Curr. Liab. / Sinking Fund Price	Balance Sheet Date / Sinking Fund (Begins) Thru	L. Term Debt (Mil $) / Refund/Other Restriction Price	Capital-ization (Mil $) / Refund/Other Restriction (Begins) Thru	Total Debt % Capital / Outst'g (Mil $)	Underwriting Firm	Underwriting Year	Price Range 1995 High	Price Range 1995 Low	Mo. End Price Sale(s) or Bid	Curr. Yield	Yield to Mat.
Pacific Lumber[1]	***13d***	***0.87***	***0.93***	***1.47***		***Dc***	***16.80***	***111.0***	***51.30***	***9-30-95***	***572.0***	***583.0***	***101.0***							
Sr Nts[2] 10½s 2003	Ms	**B+**			Y	R	103	(3-1-98)	....	....	....	....	235	S1	'93	95	92¼	94⅜	11.13	11.67
Pacific NorthwestBellTel	***67a***	***Merged into U S WEST Commun,see***																		
Deb 4½s 2000	jD	**AA–**	4/90	AA	X	CR	100	11-30-96	....	....	....	....	50.0	M6	'63	94¼	82⅞	94¼	4.77	5.86
Deb 4⅜s 2002	mS	**AA–**	4/90	AA	X	CR	100.37	8-31-96	....	....	....	....	50.0	M6	'62	91¼	78⅛	91¼	4.79	5.98
Deb 4½s 2003	Ao	**AA–**	4/90	AA	X	CR	100.60	3-31-96	....	....	....	....	50.0	M6	'63	91	77⅝	91	4.95	6.05
Nts 7½s '96	jD	**AA–**	4/90	AA	X	R	NC	....	....	....	....	....	170	S1	'86	102	99⅛	101⅝	7.38	5.66
Pacific Telephone & Tel[3]	***67a***	***Now Pacific Bell,see***																		
Deb 4⅝s '99	Ao	**AA–**	2/90	A+	X	CR	100	....	....	....	....	....	100	L3	'64	96⅞	87⅝	96⅞	4.77	5.69
Deb 4⅝s 2000	Mn	**AA–**	2/90	A+	X	CR	100	4-30-96	....	....	....	....	125	M2	'65	95½	84¼	95½	4.84	5.81
Deb 6s 2002	mN	**AA–**	2/90	A+	X	R	100.36	10-31-96	....	....	....	....	130	L3	'66	99⅛	86⅜	99⅛	6.05	6.16
Deb 6½s 2003	jJ	**AA–**	2/90	A+	X	R	100.62	6-30-96	....	....	....	....	165	H1	'68	101⅝	88⅝	101⅝	6.40	6.23
• Deb 7¼s 2008	Fa	**AA–**	2/90	A+	X	R	101.94	1-31-96	....	....	....	....	175	S1	'72	101¾	88¾	s101½	7.14	7.06
Paging Network	***67g***	***0.71***	***0.39***	***0.67***		***Dc***	***256.0***	***307.0***	***108.0***	***9-30-95***	***1150***	***1080***	***106.0***							
Sr Sub Nts[4] 11¾s 2002	Mn15	**B**	1/94	B–	Y	R	105.875	(5-15-97)	....	....	....	....	200	G1	'92	110¾	98½	110⅝	10.62	9.49
Sr Sub Nts[4] 8⅞s 2006	Fa	**B**			Y	R	104.438	(2-1-99)	....	....	....	....	300	G1	'94	102⅜	78¾	102⅜	8.67	8.52
Sr Sub Nts[4] 10⅛s 2007	fA	**B**			Y	BE	105.0625	(8-1-07)	....	....	....	....	400	G1	'95	108⅞	100	108⅞	9.30	8.88
Paine Webber Group	***62***	***1.47***	***1.36***	***1.03***		***Dc***	***196.0***			***9-30-95***	***2423***	***5849***	***70.0***							
Nts 6¼s '98	Jd15	**BBB+**			X	R	NC	....	....	....	....	....	200	P1	'93	100⅝	91¾	100⅝	6.21	5.97
Nts 7s 2000	Ms	**BBB+**			X	R	NC	....	....	....	....	....	200	P1	'93	102⅜	90⅞	102⅜	6.84	6.34
Nts 9¼s 2001	jD15	**BBB+**			X	R	NC	....	....	....	....	....	150	P1	'91	113⅛	99⅝	113⅛	8.18	6.55
Nts 8¼s 2002	Mn	**BBB+**			X	R	NC	....	....	....	....	....	125	P1	'95	108½	100	108½	7.60	6.59
Nts 7⅞s 2003	Fa15	**BBB+**			X	R	NC	....	....	....	....	....	100	P1	'93	107	90¼	107	7.36	6.62
Nts 8⅞s 2005	Ms15	**BBB+**			X	R	NC	....	....	....	....	....	125	P1	'95	113¾	99	113¾	7.80	6.84
Nts 6½s 2005	mN	**BBB+**			X	R	NC	....	....	....	....	....	200	P1	'93	97¾	79¼	97¾	6.65	6.82
Nts 7⅝s 2014	Fa15	**BBB+**			X	R	NC	....	....	....	....	....	200	P1	'94	101¾	80¼	101¾	7.49	7.45
Sub Nts 7¾s 2002	mS	**BBB**			X	R	NC	....	....	....	....	....	175	P1	'92	106¼	90⅜	106¼	7.29	6.58
Pamida, Inc[5]	***59g***	***1.41***	***1.06***	***1.42***		***Ja***	***10.80***	***244.0***	***142.0***	***10-29-95***	***245.0***	***279.0***	***89.2***							
Sr Sub Nts[4] 11¾s 2003	Ms15	**B–**			Y	R	105.875	(3-15-98)	....	....	[6]Z111.75	3-14-96	140	C4	'93	98	78	78½	14.97	17.02
PanAmSat L.P./Capital	***67e***	***n/a***	***2.59***	***1.73***		***Dc***	***27.20***	***39.00***	***12.70***	***6-30-95***	***527.0***	***777.0***	***68.1***							
Sr[7]Sec Nts 9¾s 2000	fA	**BB–**	9/95	B+	Y	R	101.625	(8-1-98)	....	....	....	....	175	D6	'93	105¾	95	105¾	9.22	8.22
Sr Sub[8]Disc Nts[7] 11⅜s 2003	fA	**B**	9/95	B–	Y	R	104.266	(8-1-98)	100	(8-1-01)	[9]Z110	7-31-96	[10]460	D6	'93	82	62¼	82	....	Flat
Panhandle East'n Corp.	***73a***	***2.11***	***1.71***	***2.58***		***Dc***	***80.30***	***805.0***	***956.0***	***9-30-95***	***2251***	***4574***	***52.4***							
Deb 8⅝s 2025	Ao15	**BBB–**			X	R	104.03	(4-15-05)	....	....	....	....	100	M6	'95	113⅞	99⅜	113⅞	7.57	7.45
Nts 8⅝s '99	jD	**BBB–**			X	R	NC	....	....	....	....	....	100	M2	'94	108½	99⅞	108½	7.95	6.15
Nts 7¼s 2005	Mn15	**BBB–**			X	R	NC	....	....	....	....	....	100	M2	'95	106⅜	97¼	106⅜	6.82	6.34
Panhandle East'n P.L.[11]	***73a***	***2.33***	***4.05***	***4.79***		***Dc***	***0.20***	***184.0***	***198.0***	***6-30-95***	***424.0***	***1373***	***30.9***							
• Deb 7.95s 2023	Ms15	**BBB**	10/94	BBB–	X	R	103.975	(3-15-03)	....	....	....	....	100	K2	'93	No Sale		90	8.83	8.93
Deb 7.20s 2024	fA15	**BBB**	10/94	BBB–	X	R	103.225	(8-15-03)	....	....	....	....	100	K2	'93	100⅝	82	100⅝	7.16	7.15
Nts 7⅞s 2004	fA15	**BBB**	10/94	BBB–	X	R	NC	....	....	....	....	....	100	D4	'94	110⅝	93¼	110⅝	7.12	6.26
[12]***Pantry Pride***	***59c***	....	....	....		***Dc***	***No Recent Fin'ls***													
Sub Deb 14⅜s '97	jJ15	**NR**	7/89	CCC+		R	100	....	100	....	....	....	149	D7	'85	104½	101⅝	104½	13.76	11.11
Paracelsus Healthcare	***30***	***3.10***	***3.48***	***2.80***		***Sp***	***11.50***	***131.0***	***61.80***	***6-30-95***	***127.0***	***235.0***	***56.2***							
Sr Sub Nts[7] 9⅞s 2003	aO15	**B**			Y	R	104.94	(10-15-98)	....	....	....	....	75.0	D6	'93	103	94⅜	102	9.68	9.50
Paramount Communications Inc[13]	***24***	***Merged with Viacom Inc, see Viacom Int'l***																		
Sr Deb 8¼s 2022	fA	**BB+**	5/95	BB	Y	R	103.467	(8-1-02)	....	....	....	....	250	F1	'92	103¼	84	103¼	7.99	7.95
Sr Deb 7½s 2023	jJ15	**BB+**	5/95	BB	Y	R	103.564	(7-15-03)	....	....	....	....	150	S1	'93	100¼	76⅛	100¼	7.48	7.48

Uniform Footnote Explanations-See Page 260. Other: [1] Subsid of MAXXAM Group. [2] (HRO)On Chge of Ctrl at 100. [3] Subsid of Pacific Telesis Group. [4] Co must offer repurch at 101 on Chge of Ctrl. [5] Subsid of Pamida Hldgs. [6] Max $28M to 3-15-96 w/proceeds of Pub Offer'g. [7] (HRO)On Chge of Ctrl at 101. [8] Int accr at 11.375% fr 8-1-98. [9] Accreted Val:max $135M w/proceeds Cap Stk Off'g. [10] Incl disc. [11] Subsid of Panhandle Eastern Corp. [12] Now Revlon Group. [13] Was Gulf & Western.

Title-Industry Code & Co. Finances (In Italics) / Individual Issue Statistics, Exchange	Ind / Interest Dates	Fixed Charge Coverage 1992 / S&P Debt Rating	1993 / Date of Last Rating Change	Prior Rating	1994 / Eligible	Year End / Bond Form	Cash & Equiv. (Million $) / Regular Price	Curr. Assets / Regular (Begins) Thru	Curr. Liab. / Sinking Fund Price	Balance Sheet Date / Sinking Fund (Begins) Thru	L. Term Debt (Mil $) / Refund/Other Restriction Price	Refund/Other Restriction (Begins) Thru	Capital-ization (Mil $) / Outst'g (Mil $)	Total Debt % Capital / Underwriting Firm	Underwriting Year	Price Range 1995 High	Price Range 1995 Low	Mo. End Price Sale(s) or Bid	Curr. Yield	Yield to Mat.
Paramount Communications Inc (Cont.)																				
Sr Nts 5⅞s 2000	jJ15	BB+	5/95	BB	Y	R	NC	....	....	....	....	....	150	S1	'93	96⅜	84⅜	96¼	6.10	6.85
Sr Nts 7½s 2002	Jj15	BB+	5/95	BB	Y	R	NC	....	....	....	....	....	250	F1	'92	103	89¼	101½	7.39	7.19
• Sub Deb 'A' 7s 2003	jJ	BB−	5/95	B+	Y	R	100	....	....	....	....	....	150	Exch.	'73	97½	81½	97	7.22	7.53
• Sub Deb 'B' 7s 2003	jJ	BB−	5/95	B+	Y	R	100	....	....	....	....	....	81.4	Exch.	'73	97½	81⅛	s97	7.22	7.53
Parisian Inc	***59l***	***1.37***	***1.13***		***0.60***	***Ja***	***1.49***	***207.0***	***84.80***	***10-28-95***	***161.0***		***247.0***	***70.0***						
Sr Sub Nts 9⅞s 2003	jJ15	B−			Y	R	104.938	(7-15-98)	....	....	[1]Z110	7-15-96	125	L3	'93	85	68½	84	11.76	13.30
Parker & Parsley Petrol	***49a***	***2.63***	***2.08***		***0.59***	***Dc***	***17.80***	***126.0***	***125.0***	***9-30-95***	***571.0***		***1188***	***48.4***						
Sr Nts 8⅞s 2005	Ao15	BBB−			X	BE	NC	....	....	....	....	....	150	S1	'95	111½	100	111½	7.96	7.16
Sr Nts 8¼s 2007	fA15	BBB−			X	BE	NC	....	....	....	....	....	150	S1	'95	107⅝	99⅜	107⅝	7.67	7.27
Parker-Hannifin	***41h***	***△3.29***	***△5.93***		***△13.34***	***Je***	***47.00***	***1250***	***640.0***	***9-30-95***	***237.0***		***1579***	***21.9***						
Deb 10⅜s 2018	Jd	A			X	R	104.8875	(6-1-98)	100	(6-1-99)	....	....	100	K2	'88	114⅞	108⅝	114⅝	9.05	8.86
Deb 9¾s 2021	Fa15	A			X	R	104.585	(2-15-01)	100	(2-15-02)	....	....	100	K2	'91	119¼	106⅞	119¼	8.18	7.96
Pathmark Stores, Inc	***59c***	***0.96***	***0.95***		***0.93***	***Ja***	***3.89***	***203.0***	***444.0***	***7-29-95***	***1328***		***208.0***	***669.0***						
Sr Sub[2]Nts[3] 9⅝s 2003	Mn	B−	12/95	B	Y	R	104.82	(10-31-98)	....	....	[4]Z109	11-1-96	440	M2	'93	101	88	96¼	10.00	10.36
Sub Deb 12⅝s 2002	Jd15	B−	12/95	B	Y	R	112.625	6-14-97	....	....	....	....	95.8	Exch.	'93	108	101	102½	12.32	12.05
Sub Nts[3] 11⅝s 2002	Jd15	B−	12/95	B	Y	R	105.8125	(6-15-97)	100	(6-15-00)	....	....	200	Exch.	'93	107¼	95¾	100½	11.57	11.51
• Jr Sub[5]Dfr Cpn Nts[6] 10¾s 2003	mN	B−	12/95	B	Y	R	105	(10-31-99)	....	....	[7]Z110	11-1-96	225	M2	'93	67½	48⅝	s61½	....	Flat
Payless Cashways	***59***	***1.00***	***1.24***		***2.47***	***Nv***	***2.71***	***476.0***	***369.0***	***5-27-95***	***646.0***		***1130***	***61.5***						
• Sr Sub Nts[8] 9⅛s 2003	Ao15	B+			Y	R	104.5625	(4-15-98)	....	....	[9]Z100	....	174	G1	'93	93	73	s78¼	11.66	13.97
[10]Penn Central	***35c***	***2.55***	***4.69***		***1.85***	***Dc***				***6-30-95***	***p925.0***		***1281***	***96.4***						
Sub Nts[11] 9¾s '99	fA	BBB−			X	R	NC	....	....	....	....	....	200	S4	'89	105⅞	99	101⅝	9.59	9.20
Sub Nts[11] 10⅝s 2000	Ao15	BBB−			X	R	NC	....	....	....	....	....	150	S4	'90	110⅞	101	108⅛	9.83	8.33
Sub Nts[11] 10⅞s 2011	Mn	BBB−			X	BE	NC	....	....	....	....	....	150	D6	'91	117⅜	99⅝	110	9.89	9.61
Penn Traffic Co	***26g***	***1.13***	***1.25***		***1.32***	***Ja***	***41.30***	***523.0***	***379.0***	***10-28-95***	***1338***		***1333***	***101.0***						
Sr Nts[3] 10¼s 2002	Fa	BB−	4/93	B	Y	R	104	(2-15-97)	....	....	....	....	125	G1	'92	103⅛	92¼	95⅞	10.69	11.19
Sr[3]Nts 8⅝s 2003	jD15	BB−			Y	R	103.234	(12-15-98)	....	....	....	....	200	G1	'93	94⅜	83½	88⅝	9.73	10.79
Sr Nts[3] 10⅜s 2004	aO	BB−	4/93	B	Y	R	104	(10-1-97)	....	....	....	....	100	G1	'92	100¼	90	94¼	11.01	11.42
Sr Nts[3] 10.65s 2004	mN	BB−			Y	BE	104	(11-1-99)	....	....	....	....	100	G1	'94	105½	92⅜	95½	11.15	11.47
• Sr Sub Nts[3] 9⅝s 2005	Ao15	B			Y	R	104	(4-15-98)	....	....	....	....	400	G1	'93	98	69½	s78	12.34	13.91
PennCorp Financial Group	***35***	***2.63***	***7.80***		***4.21***	***Dc***				***9-30-95***	***199.0***		***469.0***	***42.4***						
Sr[12]Sub Nts 9¼s 2003	jD15	BB+	7/95	BB−	Y	R	104.625	(12-15-98)	....	....	....	....	150	S5	'93	103	87	102	9.07	8.89
Penney (J.C.) Co.	***59f***	***4.68***	***6.29***		***6.35***	***Ja***	***321.0***	***10419***	***5199***	***10-28-95***	***4023***		***12085***	***53.1***						
SF Deb 9¾s 2021	Jd15	A+			X	R	104.57	(6-15-01)	100	(6-15-02)	....	....	250	F1	'91	120⅞	106	120	8.13	7.91
SF Deb 8¼s 2022	fA15	A+			X	R	103.87	(8-15-02)	100	(8-15-03)	....	....	250	F1	'92	111¼	96⅛	111¼	7.42	7.29
Deb 6s 2006	Mn	A+			X	R	100	....	....	....	....	....	[13]200	F1	'81	98	82½	98	6.12	6.26
Deb 7⅛s 2023	mN15	A+			X	R	NC	....	....	....	....	....	275	C5	'93	105¾	84⅛	105¾	6.74	6.67
Nts 10s '97	aO15	A+	11/90	NR	X	R	NC	....	....	....	....	....	250	F1	'90	108	104⅜	107⅜	9.31	5.61
Nts 5⅜s '98	mN15	A+			X	R	NC	....	....	....	....	....	400	C5	'93	99⅜	90⅞	99⅜	5.41	5.61
Nts 6⅞s '99	Jd15	A+			X	R	NC	....	....	....	....	....	225	F1	'94	103½	94¾	103½	6.64	5.74
Nts 9.05s 2001	Ms	A+	3/91	NR	X	R	NC	....	....	....	....	....	250	F1	'91	113⅛	103⅝	113⅛	8.00	6.05
Nts 9.45s 2002	jJ15	A+			X	R	100	(7-15-00)	....	....	....	....	250	F1	'90	113⅞	104	113⅝	8.32	6.83
Nts 6⅛s 2003	mN15	A+			X	R	NC	....	....	....	....	....	325	C5	'93	100¼	86¼	100¼	6.11	6.08
Nts 7⅜s 2004	Jd15	A+			X	R	NC	....	....	....	....	....	275	F1	'94	108⅛	94	108⅛	6.82	6.13
M-T Nts 'A' 6⅜s 2000	mS15	A+			X	BE	NC	....	....	....	....	....	300	C5	'95	102	99⅝	102	6.25	5.88
Pennsylvania Electric[14]	***72a***	***4.44***	***4.26***		***1.67***	***Dc***	***4.63***	***193.0***	***208.0***	***9-30-95***	***677.0***		***1615***	***46.4***						
1st 6¼s '96	mN	A−	8/94	A	X	CR	100	....	□100	....	....	....	25.0	B6	'66	100⅛	97¼	100	6.25	6.24

Uniform Footnote Explanations-See Page 260. Other: [1] Max $25M red w/proceeds of Pub Com Off'g. [2] To 11-1-98 Co may red on Chge of Ctrl. [3] (HRO)On Chge of Ctrl at 101. [4] Max $154M red w/proceeds Cap Stk Off'g. [5] (HRO)On Chge of Ctrl at 101(Acrreted Val). [6] To 11-1-99 Co may red on Chge of Ctrl. [7] Percent Accreted Val:max $78.8M w/proceeds Cap Stk Off'g. [8] (HRO)For a Redemp Event at 101. [9] For Redemp Event,plus Applicable Premium. [10] Now Amer Fin'l Group. [11] (HRO)For Designated Event&Rat'g Decline at 100. [12] Co must offer repurch,at 101,on Chge of Ctrl. [13] Incl disc. [14] Subsid of Gen'l Public Util.

Title-Industry Code & Co. Finances (In Italics) / Individual Issue Statistics (Exchange ↓)	Ind / Interest Dates	Fixed Charge Coverage 1992 / S&P Debt Rating	1993 / Date of Last Rating Change	1994 / Prior Rating	Eligible ↓	Year End / Bond Form	Million $ Cash & Equiv. / Redemption Provisions: Regular Price	Curr. Assets / Regular (Begins) Thru	Curr. Liab. / Sinking Fund Price	Balance Sheet Date / Sinking Fund (Begins) Thru	L. Term Debt (Mil $) / Refund/Other Restriction Price	Capital-ization (Mil $) / Refund/Other Restriction (Begins) Thru	Outst'g (Mil $)	Total Debt % Capital / Underwriting Firm	Underwriting Year	Price Range 1995 High	Low	Mo. End Price Sale(s) or Bid	Curr. Yield	Yield to Mat.
***Pennsylvania Electric** (Cont.)*																				
1st 6¼s '97	Jd	**A–**	8/94	A	X	CR	100.38	3-31-96	□100.38	5-31-96	....	....	26.0	D7	'67	100⅜	96⅛	100⅜	6.23	5.97
Sec M-T Nts 'A'[1] 8.72s '99	[2]mn	**A–**	8/94	A	X	BE	100	....	□100	....	....	....	30.0	S5	'89	107⅞	100	107⅞	8.08	6.25
Sec M-T Nts 'B'[1] 7.45s '96	[3]fa	**A–**	8/94	A	X	BE	NC	....	□100	....	....	....	30.0	S5	'91	101⅞	99	101½	7.34	5.56
Sec M-T Nts 'B'[1] 6.80s '96	[4]fa	**A–**	8/94	A	X	BE	NC	....	□100	....	....	....	20.0	S5	'91	101¼	97⅝	101¼	6.72	5.46
Sec M-T Nts 'B'[1] 8.70s 2001	[5]fa	**A–**	8/94	A	X	BE	100	(4-19-01)	□100	....	....	....	30.0	S5	'91	112½	100⅞	112½	7.73	6.02
Sec M-T Nts 'B'[1] 7.92s 2002	[6]fa	**A–**	8/94	A	X	BE	100	(12-20-01)	□100	....	....	....	10.0	S5	'91	109¾	96⅜	109¾	7.22	6.18
Sec M-T Nts 'B'[1] 8.05s 2006	[7]fa	**A–**	8/94	A	X	BE	100	(12-20-01)	□100	....	....	....	10.0	S5	'91	113¼	95⅝	113¼	7.11	6.35
Sec M-T Nts 'C'[1] 6.15s 2000	[8]ms	**A–**	8/94	A	X	BE	NC	....	□100	....	....	....	30.0	S5	'93	101	90½	101	6.09	5.87
Sec M-T Nts 'C'[1] 7.43s 2002	[9]ms	**A–**	8/94	A	X	BE	NC	....	□100	....	....	....	30.0	S5	'92	106⅞	93⅞	106⅞	6.95	6.14
Sec M-T Nts 'C'[1] 7.40s 2002	[10]ms	**A–**	8/94	A	X	BE	NC	....	□100	....	....	....	10.0	S5	'92	106⅞	93½	106⅞	6.92	6.16
Sec M-T Nts 'C'[1] 7.40s 2003	Ms	**A–**	8/94	A	X	BE	NC	....	□100	....	....	....	10.0	S5	'92	106⅞	93¼	106⅞	6.92	6.20
Sec M-T Nts 'C'[1] 6.60s 2003	[11]ms	**A–**	8/94	A	X	BE	NC	....	□100	....	....	....	30.0	S5	'93	102⅜	88⅜	102⅜	6.45	6.20
Sec M-T Nts 'C'[1] 7.48s 2004	[12]ms	**A–**	8/94	A	X	BE	NC	....	□100	....	....	....	40.0	S5	'92	107¾	92¾	107¾	6.94	6.29
Sec M-T Nts 'C'[1] 8.33s 2022	[13]ms	**A–**	8/94	A	X	BE	104.17	(11-25-02)	□100	....	....	....	20.0	S5	'92	116	95⅝	116	7.18	7.00
Sec M-T Nts 'C'[1] 7.49s 2023	[14]ms	**A–**		A	X	BE	103.75	(6-30-03)	□100	....	....	....	30.0	S5	'93	103¾	85⅞	103¾	7.22	7.18
Sec M-T Nts 'D'[1] 8.38s 2024	[15]fa	**A–**	8/94	A	X	BE	104.19	(6-1-04)	□100	(6-1-04)	....	....	40.0	S5	'94	116⅞	96	116⅞	7.17	7.00
Sec M-T Nts 'D'[1] 6.10s 2004	[16]jj	**A–**	8/94	A	X	BE	NC	....	□100	....	....	....	30.0	S5	'93	98¾	83⅞	98¾	6.18	6.29
Sec M-T Nts 'D'[1] 6.35s 2006	[17]jj	**A–**	8/94	A	X	BE	100	(1-26-04)	□100	(1-26-04)	....	....	40.0	M2	'94	100⅛	84	100⅛	6.34	6.33
Sec M-T Nts 'D'[1] 6.55s 2009	[18]jj	**A–**	8/94	A	X	BE	100	(1-26-04)	□100	(1-26-04)	....	....	50.0	S5	'94	101⅜	83	101⅜	6.46	6.40
Penna Enterprises	***73b***	***1.65***	***1.45***	***2.07***		***Dc***	***0.76***	***42.60***	***87.00***	***9-30-95***	***155.0***	***413.0***		***52.5***						
Sr[19]Nts[20] 10⅛s '99	QJun15	**BB**			Y	R	100	(6-15-97)	....	....	....	....	30.0		'92	104⅛	97	104⅛	9.72	8.72
Pennsylvania Gas&Water[21]	***75***	***1.40***	***1.98***	***2.39***		***Dc***	***0.53***	***41.80***	***88.00***	***9-30-95***	***105.0***	***410.0***		***40.7***						
1st 8⅜s 2002	jD	**BBB–**			X	R	NC	....	....	....	....	....	30.0		'92	107⅞	95⅝	107⅞	7.76	6.92
Pennsylvania Power Co[22]	***72a***	***2.39***	***1.82***	***1.87***		***Dc***	***40.10***	***118.0***	***96.60***	***9-30-95***	***391.0***	***746.0***		***55.4***						
1st 9s '96	jD	**BBB–**	12/93	BBB	X	BE	NC	....	....	....	....	....	50.0	M6	'90	103⅜	101½	102⅝	8.77	6.02
1st 7½s 2003	fA	**BBB–**	12/93	BBB	X	BE	NC	....	....	....	....	....	40.0	M6	'92	103⅞	92⅞	103⅞	7.22	6.84
1st 6⅝s 2004	jJ	**BBB–**	12/93	BBB	X	BE	NC	....	....	....	....	....	20.0	M6	'93	100⅜	87⅜	100⅜	6.60	6.57
1st 6⅜s 2004	mS	**BBB–**	12/93	BBB	X	BE	NC	....	....	....	....	....	50.0	M6	'93	98¾	85⅛	98¾	6.46	6.56
1st 8½s 2022	jJ15	**BBB–**	12/93	BBB	X	BE	104.15	(7-15-02)	Z100	....	....	....	50.0	M6	'92	110⅜	93⅜	110	7.73	7.62
1st 7⅝s 2023	jJ	**BBB–**	12/93	BBB	X	BE	103.32	(7-1-03)	Z100	....	....	....	40.0	M6	'93	101¼	84¾	101¼	7.53	7.52
Pennsylvania Pwr & Light[23]	***72b***	***3.21***	***3.36***	***3.39***		***Dc***	***54.60***	***618.0***	***635.0***	***9-30-95***	***2978***	***6051***		***51.3***						
1st 5⅝s '96	Jd	**A–**	7/94	A	X	R	100	....	Z100	....	....	....	30.0	W5	'66	100	97¼	100	5.63	5.60
1st 6¾s '97	mN	**A–**	7/94	A	X	R	100.37	10-31-96	Z100.37	10-31-96	....	....	30.0	D7	'67	100⅝	96⅝	100⅜	6.72	6.52
1st 5½s '98	Ao	**A–**	7/94	A	X	R	NC	....	....	....	....	....	150	F1	'93	99⅜	92¼	99⅜	5.53	5.79
1st 7s '99	Jj	**A–**	7/94	A	X	R	100.54	12-31-96	Z100.16	12-31-96	....	....	40.0	F1	'69	100⅞	95¾	100⅝	6.96	6.77
1st 8⅛s '99	Jd	**A–**	7/94	A	X	R	100.99	5-31-96	Z100.43	5-31-96	....	....	40.0	H1	'69	101⅜	99	101⅛	8.03	7.74
1st 6s 2000	Jd	**A–**	7/94	A	X	R	NC	....	....	....	....	....	125	F1	'93	100	89⅞	100	6.00	6.00
1st 7¼s 2001	Fa	**A–**	7/94	A	X	R	101.47	1-31-96	Z100.49	1-31-96	....	....	60.0	W5	'71	101½	94¾	101½	7.14	6.89
1st 7⅝s 2002	Fa	**A–**	7/94	A	X	R	101.77	1-31-96	Z100.41	1-31-96	....	....	75.0	F1	'72	101⅞	95¾	101⅞	7.48	7.24
1st 7¾s 2002	Mn	**A–**	7/94	A	X	R	NC	....	....	....	....	....	150	F1	'92	107⅜	96⅝	107⅜	7.22	6.32
1st 7½s 2003	Jj	**A–**	7/94	A	X	R	101.73	12-31-96	Z100.38	12-31-96	....	....	80.0	W5	'73	102¾	94⅜	101⅞	7.36	7.15
1st 6⅞s 2003	Fa	**A–**	7/94	A	X	R	NC	....	....	....	....	....	100	F1	'93	103¾	91	103¾	6.63	6.21
1st 6⅞s 2004	Ms	**A–**	7/94	A	X	R	NC	....	....	....	....	....	150	C5	'94	103⅞	89¾	103⅞	6.62	6.26
1st 6½s 2005	Ao	**A–**	7/94	A	X	R	NC	....	....	....	....	....	125	F1	'93	101¼	86⅛	101¼	6.42	6.32
1st 6.55s 2006	Ms	**A–**	7/94	A	X	R	NC	....	....	....	....	....	150	C5	'94	101½	85¾	101½	6.45	6.35
1st[24] 7.70s 2009	aO	**A–**			X	R	NC	....	....	....	....	....	200	C5	'94	112⅝	100	112⅝	6.84	6.31

Uniform Footnote Explanations-See Page 260. Other: [1] Issued in min denom $100T. [2] Due 8-8-99. [3] Due 10-28-06. [4] Due 12-20-96. [5] Due 7-19-01. [6] Due 12-20-02. [7] Due 12-20-06. [8] Due 3-6-00. [9] Due 7-15-02. [10] Due 11-25-02. [11] Due 6-9-03. [12] Due 7-15-04. [13] Due 11-25-22. [14] Due 6-30-23. [15] Due 6-3-24. [16] Due 9-2-04. [17] Due 1-26-06. [18] Due 6-26-09. [19] (HRO)On Chge of Ctrl at 100. [20] Death redemp benefit,ltd, as defined. [21] Subsid of Penna. Enterprises. [22] Subsid of Ohio Edison. [23] Subsid of PP&L Resources. [24] (HRO)On 10-1-99 at 100.

Title-Industry Code & Co. Finances (In Italics) / Individual Issue Statistics, Exchange	Ind / Interest Dates	Fixed Charge Coverage 1992 / S&P Debt Rating	1993 / Date of Last Rating Change	1994 / Prior Rating	Year End / Eligible	Cash & Equiv. (Million $) / Bond Form	Curr. Assets (Million $) / Regular Price	Curr. Liab. (Million $) / Regular (Begins) Thru	Balance Sheet Date / Sinking Fund Price	L. Term Debt (Mil $) / Sinking Fund (Begins) Thru	Capitalization (Mil $) / Refund/Other Restriction Price	Total Debt % Capital / Refund/Other Restriction (Begins) Thru	Outst'g (Mil $)	Underwriting Firm	Underwriting Year	Price Range 1995 High	Price Range 1995 Low	Mo. End Price Sale(s) or Bid	Curr. Yield	Yield to Mat.
***Pennsylvania Pwr & Light** (Cont.)*																				
1st 7⅜s 2014	Ms	**A–**	7/94	A	X	R	NC	....	....	....	....	....	100	C5	'94	105¾	87⅝	105¾	6.97	6.82
1st 9¼s 2019	aO	**A–**	7/94	A	X	R	104.53	(10-1-99)	Z100	(10-1-99)	....	....	250	F1	'89	113⅝	100⅜	112⅜	8.23	8.07
1st 9⅜s 2021	jJ	**A–**	7/94	A	X	R	104.46	(7-1-01)	Z100	(7-1-01)	....	....	150	F1	'91	118⅜	102⅝	118⅜	7.92	7.72
1st 8½s 2022	Mn	**A–**	7/94	A	X	R	104.14	(5-1-02)	Z100	....	....	....	150	F1	'92	113⅜	94⅜	113⅜	7.50	7.34
1st 7⅞s 2023	Fa	**A–**	7/94	A	X	R	103.57	(2-1-03)	Z100	(2-1-03)	....	....	200	F1	'93	106¾	90⅛	106¾	7.38	7.30
1st 6¾s 2023	aO	**A–**	7/94	A	X	R	102.86	(10-1-03)	Z100	(10-1-03)	....	....	150	F1	'93	96¼	79⅜	96¼	7.01	7.06
1st 7.30s 2024	Ms	**A–**	7/94	A	X	R	103.41	(3-1-04)	Z100	(3-1-04)	....	....	150	C5	'94	102¼	84	102¼	7.14	7.11
Pennzoil Co.	***49b***	***0.96***	***2.09***	***d0.06***	***Dc***	***50.90***	***629.0***	***865.0***	***9-30-95***	***1987***	***3346***	***74.4***								
SF Deb 9s 2017	Ao	**BBB**	11/92	A–	X	R	104.95	3-31-96	100	(4-1-98)	®104.50	3-31-97	38.5	M2	'87	105½	95⅛	105½	8.53	8.44
Deb 10⅝s 2001	Jd	**BBB**	11/92	A–	X	R	100	(6-1-99)	....	....	....	....	150	M2	'89	114⅞	105	114⅜	9.29	7.36
Deb 10¼s 2005	mN	**BBB**	11/92	A–	X	R	NC	....	....	....	....	....	250	L3	'90	126⅜	109⅜	126⅜	8.11	6.57
Deb 10⅛s 2009	mN15	**BBB**	11/92	A–	X	R	NC	....	....	....	....	....	200	S4	'89	129⅜	108⅜	127¾	7.93	6.97
Nts 9⅝s '99	mN15	**BBB**	11/92	A–	X	R	NC	....	....	....	....	....	200	S4	'89	112	103¼	112	8.59	6.10
[1]Penske Truck Lsg/PTL Fin	***25c***	***1.39***	***1.69***	***1.83***	***Dc***				***6-30-95***	***1463***	***1874***	***78.1***								
Sr Nts[2] 7¾s '99	Mn15	**BBB–**			X	R	NC	....	....	....	....	....	150	K2	'94	105½	96½	105½	7.35	5.93
Sr Nts[2] 8¼s '99	mN	**BBB–**			X	R	NC	....	....	....	....	....	150	K2	'94	107⅝	98⅜	107⅝	7.67	5.99
Pep Boys-Manny,Mo,Ja	***59l***	***5.03***	***5.93***	***5.49***	***Ja***	***17.10***	***418.0***	***333.0***	***10-28-95***	***381.0***	***1134***	***43.1***								
Nts 8⅞s '96	Ao15	**BBB**	1/93	BBB–	X	R	NC	....	....	....	....	....	111	M6	'91	102⅛	100⅞	100⅞	8.80	5.75
Nts 6⅝s 2003	Mn15	**BBB**			X	R	NC	....	....	....	....	....	75.0	F1	'93	102⅛	88½	102⅛	6.49	6.26
Nts 7s 2005	Jd	**BBB**			X	BE	NC	....	....	....	....	....	100	C5	'95	104⅛	96⅛	104⅛	6.72	6.41
PepsiCo Capital Resources	***25***	***Gtd by PepsiCo Inc,see***																		
Gtd[3]Deb[4]Zero Cpn '96	[5]	**A**	7/84	A+	X	R	100	....	....	....	....	....	[6]15.0	F1	'82	98¾	91	98¾	....	4.95
Gtd[3]Deb[4]Zero Cpn '97	[5]	**A**	7/89	A+	X	R	100	....	....	....	....	....	[6]15.0	F1	'82	93⅝	83⅝	93⅝	....	5.32
Gtd[3]Deb[4]Zero Cpn '98	[5]	**A**	7/89	A+	X	R	100	....	....	....	....	....	[6]25.0	F1	'82	88½	77¼	88½	....	5.49
Gtd[3]Deb[4]Zero Cpn '99	[5]	**A**	7/89	A+	X	R	100	....	....	....	....	....	[6]25.0	F1	'82	83½	71¼	83½	....	5.62
Gtd[3]Deb[7]Zero Cpn 2000	[5]	**A**	7/89	A+	X	R	100	....	....	....	....	....	[6]25.0	F1	'82	78¾	65¾	78¾	....	5.69
Gtd[3]Deb[7]Zero Cpn 2001	[5]	**A**	7/89	A+	X	R	100	....	....	....	....	....	[6]25.0	F1	'82	74⅛	59⅝	74⅛	....	5.78
Gtd[3]Deb[7]Zero Cpn 2002	[5]	**A**	7/89	A+	X	R	100	....	....	....	....	....	[6]25.0	F1	'82	69⅞	55½	69⅞	....	5.81
Gtd[3]Deb[7]Zero Cpn 2003	[5]	**A**	7/89	A+	X	R	100	....	....	....	....	....	[6]25.0	F1	'82	65⅛	50¼	65⅛	....	6.00
Gtd[3]Deb[7]Zero Cpnb 2004	[5]	**A**	7/89	A+	X	R	100	....	....	....	....	....	[6]25.0	F1	'82	60¾	46⅞	60¾	....	6.13
Gtd[3]Deb[7]Zero Cpn 2005	[5]	**A**	7/89	A+	X	R	100	....	....	....	....	....	[6]25.0	F1	'82	56⅞	42⅜	56⅞	....	6.19
Gtd[3]Deb[7]Zero Cpn 2006	[5]	**A**	7/89	A+	X	R	100	....	....	....	....	....	[6]25.0	F1	'82	53⅛	39½	53⅛	....	6.26
Gtd[3]Deb[7]Zero Cpn 2007	[5]	**A**	7/89	A+	X	R	100	....	....	....	....	....	[6]25.0	F1	'82	49⅝	35⅜	49⅝	....	6.32
Gtd[3]Deb[7]Zero Cpn 2008	[5]	**A**	7/89	A+	X	R	100	....	....	....	....	....	[6]75.0	F1	'82	46¼	33⅜	46¼	....	6.39
Gtd[3]Deb[7]Zero Cpn 2009	[5]	**A**	7/89	A+	X	R	100	....	....	....	....	....	[6]75.0	F1	'82	42¾	29⅞	42¾	....	6.51
Gtd[3]Deb[7]Zero Cpn 2010	[5]	**A**	7/89	A+	X	R	100	....	....	....	....	....	[6]75.0	F1	'82	39¾	28	39¾	....	6.58
Gtd[3]Deb[7]Zero Cpn 2011	[5]	**A**	7/89	A+	X	R	100	....	....	....	....	....	[6]75.0	F1	'82	37	25⅝	37	....	6.62
Gtd[3]Deb[7]Zero Cpn 2012	[5]	**A**	7/89	A+	X	R	100	....	....	....	....	....	[6]75.0	F1	'82	34⅜	23⅝	34⅜	....	6.68
PepsiCo Inc[8]	***11e***	***4.24***	***5.23***	***5.10***	***Dc***	***1376***	***5547***	***5459***	***9-9-95***	***8691***	***17010***	***55.9***								
Nts 7⅞s '96	fA15	**A**			X	R	NC	....	....	....	....	....	350	L3	'91	102⅛	99¾	101½	7.76	5.40
Nts 7s '96	mN15	**A**			X	R	NC	....	....	....	....	....	200	M6	'91	101½	98¼	101⅜	6.91	5.37
Nts 6⅞s '97	Mn15	**A**			X	R	NC	....	....	....	....	....	250	F1	'92	102	97¼	102	6.74	5.34
Nts 6⅛s '98	Jj15	**A**			X	BE	NC	....	....	....	....	....	300	L3	'93	101⅜	94¾	101⅜	6.04	5.40
Nts 7¾s '98	aO	**A**			X	R	NC	....	....	....	....	....	250	M5	'91	105¾	98½	105¾	7.33	5.47
Nts 7⅝s '98	mN	**A**			X	R	NC	....	....	....	....	....	300	L3	'91	105⅝	98¼	105⅝	7.22	5.46
•Nts 7⅝s '98	jD18	**A**	7/89	A+	X	R	NC	....	....	....	....	....	165	M6	'86	106	98⅜	s106	7.19	5.41

Uniform Footnote Explanations-See Page 260. Other: [1] Data as Penske Truck Leasing Co., L.P. [2] (HRO)On Chge of Ctrl at 101. [3] Gtd by PepsiCo Inc. [4] Issued in min denom $5T. [5] Due Apr 1. [6] Incl disc. [7] Issued in min denom $10T. [8] See PepsiCo Capital Resources.

Title-Industry Code & Co. Finances (In Italics) / Individual Issue Statistics — Exchange, Interest Dates	Ind / S&P Debt Rating	Fixed Charge Coverage 1992 / Date of Last Rating Change	1993 / Prior Rating	1994 / Eligible	Year End / Bond Form	Million $ Cash & Equiv. / Redemption Provisions: Regular Price	Curr. Assets / Regular (Begins) Thru	Curr. Liab. / Sinking Fund Price	Balance Sheet Date / Sinking Fund (Begins) Thru	L. Term Debt (Mil $) / Refund/Other Restriction Price	Refund/Other Restriction (Begins) Thru	Capitalization (Mil $) / Outst'g (Mil $)	Total Debt % Capital / Underwriting Firm	Underwriting Year	Price Range 1995 High	Price Range 1995 Low	Mo. End Price Sale(s) or Bid	Curr. Yield	Yield to Mat.
***PepsiCo Inc** (Cont.)*																			
Nts 6¼s '99 ... mS	A			X	R	NC	....	....	....	....	....	200	M5	'92	102¼	92¼	102¼	6.11	5.56
Fixed Rate Debt Sec '1' 5s '97 ... Fa24	A			X	BE	NC	....	....	....	....	....	250	M2	'94	99⅝	93⅞	99⅝	5.02	5.33
Fixed Rate Debt Sec 5⅞s 2000 ... Jd	A			X	BE	NC	....	....	....	....	....	200	U1	'95	100¾	96⅝	100¾	5.83	5.68
Debt Securities 7.13s '96 ... Jj23	A			X	BE	NC	....	....	....	....	....	25.0	D6	'95	100¾	100	100⅛	7.12	Mat.
Debt Securities 7.24s '96 ... Jj30	A			X	BE	NC	....	....	....	....	....	75.0	C1	'95	100⅞	100	100⅛	7.23	5.61
Debt Securities 17s '96 ... Fa	A			X	BE	NC	....	....	....	....	....	50.0	M6	'95	109¼	101	101	16.83	5.32
Debt Securities 6.85s '96 ... Fa23	A			X	BE	NC	....	....	....	....	....	50.0	M2	'95	100⅝	100	100¼	6.83	5.05
Debt Securities[1] 8s 2000 ... Fa23	A			X	BE	*100	(2-23-96)	....	....	....	....	25.0	S5	'95	101⅜	100	100⅜	7.97	7.89
Debt Securities 6.80s 2000 ... Mn15	A			X	BE	NC	....	....	....	....	....	200	L3	'95	104¼	99¾	104¼	6.52	5.69
Debt Securities 6.65s 2000 ... Jd6	A			X	BE	■100	(6-6-97)	....	....	....	....	25.0	B5	'95	102	99½	101¾	6.54	6.19
Debt Securities 7½s 2002 ... [2]Apr24	A			X	BE	*100	(4-24-96)	....	....	....	....	35.0	L3	'95	102¼	99⅝	100⅝	7.45	7.37
Debt Securities 7½s 2002 ... [2]Apr26	A			X	BE	*100	(4-26-96)	....	....	....	....	25.0	L3	'95	102¼	99⅝	100¾	7.44	7.35
Debt Securities 7s 2005 ... [2]Jul26	A			X	BE	*100	(7-26-96)	....	....	....	....	25.0	L3	'95	102½	100	100⅞	6.94	6.87
Debt Securities 7.13s 2007 ... [2]Aug17	A			X	BE	100	(8-17-99)	....	....	....	....	25.0	M2	'95	105	100	105	6.79	6.51
Debt Securities 7.425s 2007 ... fA17	A			X	BE	*100	(8-17-99)	....	....	....	....	25.0	M2	'95	105⅞	100	105⅞	7.01	6.69
Debt Securities 7.15s 2007 ... [2]Aug22	A			X	BE	100	(8-22-97)	....	....	....	....	25.0	M6	'95	103¾	100	102¾	6.96	6.80
Debt Securities 7s 2007 ... aO2	A			X	BE	*100	(10-2-97)	....	....	....	....	25.0	M5	'95	104	99¾	102¾	6.81	6.66
Debt Securities 7s 2010 ... [2]Sep27	A			X	BE	■100	(9-27-97)	....	....	....	....	25.0	L3	'95	104½	96⅜	102¾	6.81	6.70
Step-Up[3]Nts[1] 7½s 2002 ... Ao	A			X	BE	NC	....	....	....	....	....	25.0	S5	'95	101⅜	100	101¼	7.41	7.24
[4]Step-Up[5]Nts 8s 2002 ... Fa22	A			X	BE	NC	....	....	....	....	....	25.0	M6	'95	102⅛	100	101	7.92	7.79
***Pet Inc** ... 26*		*3.81*	*4.46*	*7.67*	*Je*	*15.70*	*381.0*	*256.0*	*12-31-94*	*486.0*		*906.0*	*60.0*						
Nts 5¾s '98 ... jJ	A+	5/95	BBB+	X	R	NC	....	....	....	....	....	100	F1	'93	100⅛	89	100⅛	5.74	5.70
Nts 6½s 2003 ... jJ	A+	5/95	BBB+	X	R	NC	....	....	....	....	....	100	F1	'93	102	86¾	101¾	6.39	6.20
***Petroleum Heat & Power** ... 49d*		*0.80*	*0.68*	*0.94*	*Dc*	*16.20*	*102.0*	*94.20*	*9-30-95*	*362.0*		*273.0*	*134.0*						
Sub Deb[6] 12¼s 2005 ... Fa	B+			Y	R	104.594	(2-1-00)	....	....	[7]Z111	1-31-98	71.2	D6	'95	110¾	98½	110¾	11.06	10.39
Sub[6]Nts 10⅛s 2003 ... Ao	B+			Y	R	105.063	(4-1-98)	....	....	....	....	50.0	K2	'93	98	93	98	10.33	10.52
Sub[6]Nts 9⅜s 2006 ... Fa	B+			Y	R	104.688	(2-1-99)	....	....	[8]Z109	1-31-97	75.0	D6	'94	96	82½	95⅞	9.78	10.03
***Pfizer, Inc** ... 21a*		*13.29*	*14.19*	*15.67*	*Dc*	*1670*	*6137*	*5799*	*10-1-95*	*358.0*		*8686*	*39.2*						
Nts[9] 7⅛s '96 ... aO	AAA			X	BE	NC	....	....	....	....	....	250	L1	'91	101½	98¾	101¼	7.04	5.40
Nts 6½s '97 ... Fa	AAA			X	BE	NC	....	....	....	....	....	250	L1	'92	101¼	96⅞	101¼	6.42	5.30
***Phelps Dodge Corp.** ... 45b*		*8.73*	*6.07*	*9.90*	*Dc*	*530.0*	*1534*	*620.0*	*9-30-95*	*620.0*		*3288*	*21.8*						
Nts 7¾s 2002 ... Jj	A	7/93	A–	X	BE	NC	....	....	....	....	....	100	M6	'92	108¼	96	108¼	7.16	6.09
***PHH Corp** ... 63*		*△1.62*	*△1.79*	*△1.70*	*Ap*				*10-31-95*	*[10]4227*		*4800*	*88.1*						
Nts 6½s 2000 ... Fa	A+			X	BE	NC	....	....	....	....	....	100	F1	'93	102¼	92⅛	102¼	6.36	5.87
*[11]**Philadelphia Electric** ... 75*		*2.52*	*2.99*	*2.50*	*Dc*	*199.0*	*829.0*	*1271*	*9-30-95*	*4314*		*9969*	*48.8*						
• 1st & Ref 6⅛s '97 ... aO	BBB+	4/92	BBB	X	R	100.30	9-30-96	....	....	....	....	75.0	W5	'67	100⅛	94⅜	99⅞	6.13	6.19
• 1st & Ref 5⅜s '98 ... fA15	BBB+			X	R	NC	....	....	....	....	....	225	L3	'93	No Sale		96½	5.57	6.85
1st & Ref 7½s '99 ... Jj15	BBB+	4/92	BBB	X	R	NC	....	....	....	....	....	250	G1	'92	104¾	96½	104¾	7.16	5.77
1st & Ref 9¼s '99 ... aO	BBB+	4/92	BBB	X	R	NC	....	....	....	....	....	75.0	P1	'89	110½	102½	110½	8.37	6.08
• 1st & Ref 5⅝s 2001 ... mN	BBB+			X	R	NC	....	....	....	....	....	250	C4	'93	97	84⅞	95½	5.89	6.56
• 1st & Ref 7⅜s 2001 ... jD15	BBB+	4/92	BBB	X	R	101.50	12-14-96	....	....	....	....	80.0	M2	'71	102⅞	93⅛	s101½	7.27	7.06
1st & Ref 8s 2002 ... Ao	BBB+			X	R	NC	....	....	....	....	....	200	L3	'92	109	96⅞	109	7.34	6.24
1st & Ref 7½s 2002 ... jJ15	BBB+			X	R	NC	....	....	....	....	....	100	F1	'92	107¼	93⅞	107¼	6.99	6.14
1st & Ref 7⅛s 2002 ... mS	BBB+			X	R	NC	....	....	....	....	....	200	F1	'92	105¼	91¾	105¼	6.77	6.15
1st & Ref 6⅝s 2003 ... Ms	BBB+			X	R	NC	....	....	....	....	....	250	L3	'93	101⅞	88¼	101⅞	6.50	6.29
• 1st & Ref 6½s 2003 ... Mn	BBB+			X	R	NC	....	....	....	....	....	200	G1	'93	100¼	90⅜	100½	6.47	6.41

Uniform Footnote Explanations-See Page 260. Other: [1] Issued in min denom \$5T. [2] Int pd monthly. [3] Int to 3-31-96,incr 0.20% anly aft. [4] Int incr 0.20% anly aft 2-21-00. [5] Int to 2-21-96, incr 0.10% anly to 2-21-00. [6] (HRO)On Chge of Ctrl at 101. [7] Max \$81.3M red w/proceeds of certain Cap Stk sales. [8] Max \$25M red w/proceeds of Cap Stk Off'g. [9] Issued in min denom \$100T. [10] Incl liabs under mgmt programs. [11] Now PECO Energy.

Title-Industry Code & Co. Finances (In Italics) / Individual Issue Statistics — Exchange	Ind / Interest Dates	Fixed Charge Coverage 1992 / S&P Debt Rating	1993 / Date of Last Rating Change	1994 / Prior Rating	Eligible	Year End / Bond Form	Cash & Equiv. / Regular Price	Million $ Curr. Assets / Regular (Begins) Thru	Curr. Liab. / Sinking Fund Price	Balance Sheet Date / Sinking Fund (Begins) Thru	L. Term Debt (Mil $) / Refund/Other Restriction Price	Capital-ization (Mil $) / Refund/Other Restriction (Begins) Thru	Outst'g (Mil $)	Total Debt % Capital / Underwriting Firm	Underwriting Year	Price Range 1995 High	Low	Mo. End Price Sale(s) or Bid	Curr. Yield	Yield to Mat.
***Philadelphia Electric** (Cont.)*																				
• 1st & Ref 6⅜s 2005	fA15	**BBB+**			X	R	103.05	(8-15-98)	....	....	....	....	75.0	M6	'93	90¾	84¾	94⅝	6.74	7.16
1st & Ref 8¾s 2022	Ao	**BBB+**			X	R	106.16	(4-1-97)	....	....	....	....	150	L3	'92	109	96	108⅝	8.06	7.96
1st & Ref 8⅝s 2022	Jd	**BBB+**			X	R	105.57	(6-1-97)	....	....	....	....	125	F1	'92	108¼	95⅜	108¼	7.97	7.88
1st & Ref 8¼s 2022	mS	**BBB+**			X	R	105.20	(9-1-97)	....	....	....	....	250	L3	'92	105⅝	91¾	105⅝	7.81	7.75
1st & Ref 7¾s 2023	Ms	**BBB+**			X	R	104.95	(3-1-98)	....	....	....	....	100	G1	'93	104⅝	87⅛	104⅝	7.41	7.35
• 1st & Ref (Ser 2) 7¾s 2023	Mn	**BBB+**			X	R	105.29	(5-1-98)	....	....	....	....	250	G1	'93	103⅞	87	s103¾	7.47	7.43
• 1st & Ref 7⅛s 2023	fA15	**BBB+**			X	R	104.16	(8-15-98)	....	....	....	....	200	C4	'93	97¾	82	s97¾	7.29	7.31
• 1st & Ref 7¼s 2024	mN	**BBB+**			X	R	104.71	(10-31-98)	....	....	....	....	225	L3	'93	99½	81½	s99½	7.29	7.29
***Philip Morris Cos*[1]**	***69a***	***6.69***	***5.19***	***7.38***		***Dc***	***878.0***			***9-30-95***	***14247***	***30564***		***54.5***						
SF Deb 8⅜s 2017	Jj15	**A**			X	R	104.606	1-14-97	100	(1-15-98)	®104.188	1-14-97	200	F1	'87	104⅜	93⅝	104⅜	8.02	7.94
Nts 8⅞s '96	jJ	**A**			X	R	NC	....	....	....	....	....	500	S1	'89	102¾	101½	101½	8.74	5.82
Nts 8¾s '96	jD	**A**			X	R	NC	....	....	....	....	....	450	S1	'89	103⅝	100⅞	102¾	8.52	5.64
Nts 7½s '96	fA	**A**			X	R	NC	....	....	....	....	....	100	F1	'86	101½	98⅞	101	7.43	5.74
Nts 7½s '97	Ms15	**A**			X	BE	NC	....	....	....	....	....	350	M2	'92	102½	98⅜	102¼	7.33	5.54
Nts 9¾s '97	Mn	**A**			X	R	NC	....	....	....	....	....	300	F1	'90	106⅝	102¾	105⅜	9.25	5.52
Nts 8¾s '97	Jd15	**A**			X	BE	NC	....	....	....	....	....	300	G1	'91	104⅞	100⅝	104⅜	8.38	5.59
Nts 9¼s '97	jD	**A**			X	R	NC	....	....	....	....	....	500	M2	'90	107¼	101⅞	106⅝	8.68	5.56
Nts 6⅜s '98	Jj15	**A**			X	BE	NC	....	....	....	....	....	350	L3	'93	101¼	94½	101¼	6.30	5.72
Nts 9s '98	Mn15	**A**			X	R	NC	....	....	....	....	....	350	S1	'88	107½	101⅜	107	8.41	5.80
Nts 9.80s '98	jD15	**A**			X	R	100	....	....	....	....	....	500	M2	'88	109¼	100	100	9.80	9.80
Nts 7⅜s '99	Fa15	**A**			X	BE	NC	....	....	....	....	....	350	L3	'92	104⅛	96	104⅛	7.08	5.91
Nts 8⅝s '99	Ms	**A**			X	R	NC	....	....	....	....	....	350	M6	'91	107¾	100	107¾	8.00	5.91
Nts 7¾s '99	Mn	**A**			X	BE	NC	....	....	....	....	....	300	F1	'92	105⅞	97⅛	105⅞	7.32	5.79
Nts 7⅛s '99	jD	**A**			X	BE	NC	....	....	....	....	....	300	F1	'92	104⅜	94	104⅜	6.83	5.86
Nts 9¼s 2000	Fa15	**A**			X	R	NC	....	....	....	....	....	350	M2	'90	111¾	102⅜	111¾	8.28	5.99
Nts 9s 2001	Jj	**A**			X	R	NC	....	....	....	....	....	350	M2	'91	112⅜	101⅛	112⅜	8.01	6.09
Nts 8¾s 2001	Jd	**A**			X	BE	NC	....	....	....	....	....	300	S1	'91	112	99¾	112	7.81	6.11
Nts 7½s 2002	Jj15	**A**			X	BE	NC	....	....	....	....	....	500	L3	'92	106⅝	93⅝	106⅝	7.03	6.17
Nts 7⅝s 2002	Mn15	**A**			X	BE	NC	....	....	....	....	....	300	L3	'92	107¼	94⅛	107¼	7.11	6.23
Nts 7⅛s 2002	fA15	**A**			X	BE	NC	....	....	....	....	....	350	S1	'92	104¾	90¾	104¾	6.80	6.24
Nts 7¼s 2003	Jj15	**A**			X	BE	NC	....	....	....	....	....	350	L3	'93	105⅜	91⅜	105⅜	6.88	6.29
Nts 8¼s 2003	aO15	**A**			X	BE	NC	....	....	....	....	....	350	M2	'91	112⅛	96⅜	112⅛	7.36	6.26
Nts 7⅛s 2004	aO	**A**			X	BE	NC	....	....	....	....	....	250	M6	'92	105⅝	88⅝	105⅝	6.75	6.28
Philip Morris Inc.	***69a***	***Subsid Philip Morris Cos, see***																		
Deb 6s '99	mN15	**A**	10/85	A+	X	R	100	....	....	....	....	....	[2]200	G1	'81	99⅛	89⅞	99⅛	6.05	6.26
Deb 6s 2001	jJ15	**A**	10/85	A+	X	R	100	....	....	....	....	....	[2]250	L3	'81	98½	86½	98½	6.09	6.32
Phillips Petroleum	***49b***	***2.09***	***2.44***	***3.47***		***Dc***	***143.0***	***2442***	***2778***	***9-30-95***	***2876***	***6408***		***45.3***						
• Nts 9½s '97	mN15	**BBB**			X	R	NC	....	....	....	....	....	300	M6	'90	105	105	103¾	9.16	7.32
• Nts 9s 2001	Jd	**BBB**			X	R	NC	....	....	....	....	....	250	M6	'91	112	101½	108½	8.29	7.08
• Nts 6.65s 2003	Ms	**BBB**			X	R	NC	....	....	....	....	....	100	M2	'93	98⅝	91¾	98⅜	6.76	6.94
• Nts 9⅜s 2011	Fa15	**BBB**			X	R	NC	....	....	....	....	....	350	M6	'91	No Sale		106⅛	8.83	8.64
• Nts 9.18s 2021	mS15	**BBB**			X	R	104.59	(9-15-01)	....	....	....	....	300	G1	'91	109⅝	99⅝	110¼	8.33	8.21
• Nts 8.86s 2022	Mn15	**BBB**			X	R	104.43	(5-15-02)	....	....	....	....	250	G1	'92	109	99½	107⅛	8.27	8.19
• Nts 8.49s 2023	Jj	**BBB**			X	R	104.245	(1-1-03)	....	....	....	....	250	M6	'93	106¼	99⅞	106½	7.97	7.90
• Nts 7.92s 2023	Ao15	**BBB**			X	R	103.96	(4-15-03)	....	....	....	....	250	M6	'93	103	96½	102½	7.73	7.70
• Nts 7.20s 2023	mN	**BBB**			X	R	103.60	(11-1-03)	....	....	....	....	250	M2	'93	97	84	s95⅛	7.57	7.62

Uniform Footnote Explanations-See Page 260. Other: [1] See Gen'l Foods,Mallory(P.R.)Philip Morris Inc. [2] Incl disc.

Title-Industry Code & Co. Finances (In Italics) / Individual Issue Statistics — Exchange, Interest Dates	Fixed Charge Coverage 1992 / S&P Debt Rating	1993 / Date of Last Rating Change	1994 / Prior Rating	Eligible	Year End / Bond Form	Million $ Cash & Equiv. / Regular Price	Million $ Curr. Assets / Regular (Begins) Thru	Million $ Curr. Liab. / Sinking Fund Price	Balance Sheet Date / Sinking Fund (Begins) Thru	L. Term Debt (Mil $) / Refund/Other Restriction Price	Refund/Other Restriction (Begins) Thru	Capital-ization (Mil $) / Outst'g (Mil $)	Total Debt % Capital / Underwriting Firm	Underwriting Year	Price Range 1995 High	Price Range 1995 Low	Mo. End Price Sale(s) or Bid	Curr. Yield	Yield to Mat.
***Phillips-Van Heusen*....... 68c**	*4.24*	*4.82*	*3.61*		*Ja*	*15.60*	*509.0*	*229.0*	*7-31-95*	*240.0*		*627.0*	*56.3*						
Deb[1] 7¾s 2023 .... mN15	BBB			X	BE	NC	....	....	....	....	....	100	G1	'93	102½	84⅞	102½	7.56	7.53
***Phoenix Re*[2] 35c**	*d22.87*	*13.25*	*6.96*		*Dc*				*9-30-95*	*67.80*		*268.0*	*25.3*						
Sr[3]Nts 9¾s 2003 .... fA15	BB+			Y	R	103.656	(8-15-98)	....	....	....	....	75.0	D4	'93	108	100¾	106¾	9.13	8.52
***Pier 1 (Inc) Imports*....... 59l**	*3.40*	*1.50*	*4.06*		*Fb*	*37.60*	*374.0*	*120.0*	*8-26-95*	*140.0*		*386.0*	*40.9*						
• Sub Deb 11½s 2003 .... jJ15	NR	2/90	B		R	100	....	100	....	....	....	[4]22.5	B5	'83	104⅞	100	s102	11.27	11.10
***Pilgrim's Pride Corp*....... 26e**	*Δ2.28*	*Δ3.06*	*Δ1.08*		*Sp*	*11.90*	*193.0*	*105.0*	*9-30-95*	*183.0*		*353.0*	*56.9*						
Sr Sub Nts[5] 10⅞s 2003 .... fA	B–	3/94	CCC+	Y	R	104.078	(8-1-98)	....	....	....	....	100	D6	'93	96	90	91	11.95	12.76
***Pioneer Finance*....... 25**	*Acq by Sahara Gaming, see Hacienda Resorts*																		
[6]1st[3] 13½s '98 .... jD	B–	12/93	CCC+	Y	R	101.68	11-30-96	100	(12-1-96)	....	....	103	M2	'88	88	72	75	18.00	....
***Pitney Bowes Credit*....... 25**	*2.27*	*2.38*	*2.47*		*Dc*	*14.00*			*9-30-95*	*1153*		*4168*	*79.8*						
Nts 5⅝s '97 .... Fa15	AA			X	BE	NC	....	....	....	....	....	200	C5	'94	100¼	95¼	100¼	5.61	5.39
Nts 6¼s '98 .... Jd	AA			X	BE	NC	....	....	....	....	....	100	C5	'95	101⅝	99¼	101⅝	6.15	5.52
Nts 6⅝s 2002 .... Jd	AA			X	BE	NC	....	....	....	....	....	100	C5	'95	104	98⅛	104	6.37	5.87
Nts 8.80s 2003 .... Fa15	AA			X	R	NC	....	....	....	....	....	150	G1	'91	116⅜	101⅞	116⅜	7.56	5.95
Nts[7] 8⅝s 2008 .... Fa15	AA	8/88	AA–	X	R	NC	....	....	....	....	....	100	F1	'88	120⅝	102¼	120⅝	7.15	6.18
Nts[8] 9¼s 2008 .... Jd15	AA	8/88	AA–	X	R	NC	....	....	....	....	....	100	G1	'88	125⅛	109	125⅛	7.39	6.31
Nts[9] 8.55s 2009 .... mS15	AA			X	R	NC	....	....	....	....	....	150	G1	'89	120⅝	103½	120⅝	7.09	6.28
***Plains Resources*....... 49a**	*0.12*	*d1.28*	*1.05*		*Dc*	*5.07*	*46.40*	*52.70*	*9-30-95*	*150.0*		*222.0*	*68.5*						
◆Sr Sub Nts[10] 12s '99 .... aO	B–			Y	R	106	9-30-96	100	(10-1-98)	....	....	100		'92	106½	97	s106½	11.27	9.87
***Plantronics Inc*....... 67f**	*n/a*	*d0.68*	*5.42*		*Mr*	*17.20*	*70.80*	*35.50*	*9-30-95*	*65.10*		*52.40*	*124.0*						
Sr[11]Nts 10s 2001 .... Jj15	B			Y	R	102	(1-15-99)	....	....	....	....	65.1	C4	'94	105⅛	96	105⅛	9.51	8.72
***Plastic Containers, Inc*....... 16d**	*0.23*	*0.33*	*0.74*		*Dc*	*7.09*	*62.20*	*47.50*	*9-30-95*	*105.0*		*141.0*	*74.5*						
Sr Sec[12]Nts[3] 10¾s 2001 .... Ao	B+			Y	R	105	(4-1-97)	100	(4-1-97)	....	....	105	C4	'92	102	99¼	101⅞	10.55	10.27
***Plastic Specialities & Tech*....... 52**	*Δ1.30*	*Δ1.52*	*Δ0.66*		*Jl*	*4.74*	*88.50*	*62.90*	*7-31-95*	*126.0*		*145.0*	*106.0*						
Sr[11]Sec Nts 11¼s 2003 .... jD	B–			Y	R	105.625	(12-1-98)	....	....	[13]110	12-1-96	125	W3	'93	94½	88	90	12.50	13.33
[14]*Playtex Family Products*....... 18	*0.90*	*1.03*	*1.38*		*Dc*	*10.40*	*114.0*	*96.30*	*12-31-94*	*841.0*		*410.0*	*214.0*						
Sr[3]Sub Nts 9s 2003 .... jD15	B+	5/95	B	Y	R	[15]Z100	12-14-98	....	....	[16]Z108	12-15-96	360	M2	'94	98¾	86¼	88	10.23	11.33
[17]*PMI Acquisition Corp*[18] 26	*n/a*	*n/a*	*1.12*		*Dc*	*11.30*	*124.0*	*119.0*	*6-30-95*	*376.0*		*472.0*	*89.4*						
Sr[3]Sub Nts 10¼s 2003 .... mS	B			Y	R	104.556	(9-1-98)	....	....	[19]Z110	9-1-96	200	K2	'93	103¾	93½	102¼	10.02	9.82
[20]*PNC Funding*....... 25	*2.56*	*2.77*	*2.75*		*Dc*				*9-30-95*	*9616*		*14120*	*68.1*						
Sub Nts[21] 9⅞s 2001 .... Ms	BBB+	2/95	A–	X	BE	NC	....	....	....	....	....	100	S1	'91	116¾	105⅝	116¾	8.46	6.05
Sub Nts[21] 6⅞s 2003 .... Ms	BBB+	2/95	A–	X	BE	NC	....	....	....	....	....	200	S1	'93	103⅝	89⅛	103⅝	6.63	6.24
Sub Nts[21] 6⅛s 2003 .... mS	BBB+	2/95	A–	X	BE	NC	....	....	....	....	....	250	S5	'93	99⅛	84⅛	99⅛	6.18	6.27
Sub Nts[21] 7¾s 2004 .... Jd	BBB+	2/95	A–	X	BE	NC	....	....	....	....	....	200	S5	'94	109¼	93¼	109¼	7.09	6.32
***Poindexter(J.B.) & Co, Inc*....... 8**	*n/a*	*n/a*	*1.74*		*Dc*	*1.63*	*114.0*	*49.20*	*9-30-95*	*131.0*		*155.0*	*90.3*						
Sr Nts[3] 12½s 2004 .... Mn15	B+	5/95	B	Y	R	106.25	(5-15-99)	....	....	[22]Z110	5-14-97	100	M6	'94	97½	80	80¼	15.58	16.99
***Polaroid Corp*....... 40d**	*3.79*	*3.12*	*4.45*		*Dc*	*66.70*	*1420*	*615.0*	*10-1-95*	*547.0*		*1553*	*47.6*						
Nts 7¼s '97 .... Jj15	BBB	12/95	BBB+	X	R	NC	....	....	....	....	....	150	L3	'92	101½	98	101½	7.14	5.75
Nts 8s '99 .... Ms15	BBB	12/95	BBB+	X	R	NC	....	....	....	....	....	200	L3	'92	105⅜	96⅞	105⅜	7.59	6.13
***Pope & Talbot*....... 50**	*0.80*	*4.32*	*3.25*		*Dc*	*4.48*	*182.0*	*80.70*	*9-30-95*	*177.0*		*399.0*	*48.4*						
Deb 8⅜s 2013 .... Jd	BB+	8/95	BBB–	Y	R	NC	....	....	....	....	....	75.0	F1	'93	108⅜	94	94	8.91	9.07
***Portland General Elec*[23] 72a**	*3.57*	*3.67*	*3.63*		*Dc*	*4.44*	*292.0*	*334.0*	*9-30-95*	*874.0*		*1914*	*50.1*						
1st 6.60s '97 .... aO	A–	10/91	A	X	R	100.23	9-30-96	Z100	....	....	....	15.7	B6	'67	100⅜	96⅜	100¼	6.58	6.44
1st 7¾s 2002 .... mN	A–	10/91	A	X	R	101.61	10-31-96	Z100	....	....	....	19.9	B6	'72	102	94⅞	101¾	7.62	7.42
1st 7.95s 2003 .... Ao	A–	10/91	A	X	R	101.92	3-31-96	Z100	....	....	....	29.1	B6	'73	102⅛	95½	102	7.79	7.58
1st 7¾s 2023 .... Ao15	A–			X	R	103.751	(4-15-03)	Z100	....	....	....	150	G1	'93	105⅛	87⅞	105⅛	7.37	7.31

Uniform Footnote Explanations-See Page 260. Other: [1] (HRO)At 100 for a Designated Event. [2] Now PXRE Corp. [3] (HRO)On Chge of Ctrl at 101. [4] Incl disc. [5] Co must offer repurch at 101 on Chge in Ctrl. [6] Mand red at 100 in certain events,as defined. [7] (HRO)On 2-15-98 at 100. [8] (HRO)On 6-15-98 at 100. [9] (HRO)On 9-15-99 at 100. [10] (HRO)On Chge of Ctrl at 100. [11] Co must offer repurch at 101 on Chge of Ctrl. [12] Co must offer to repurch at 100 for Asset Sales. [13] Max $42.5M red w/proceeds of Com Stk Off'g. [14] Asmd by & data of Playtex Products. [15] On Chge of Ctrl,plus Applicable Prem. [16] Max $126M red w/proceeds of Com Stk Off'g. [17] Now Purina Mills Inc. [18] Subsid & data of PM Holdings. [19] Max $70M red w/proceeds Com Off'g. [20] Gtd by & data of PNC Bank Corp. [21] Gtd by PNC Bank Corp. [22] Max $35M red w/proceeds of IPO. [23] Subsid of Portland Gen'l Corp.

Title-Industry Code & Co. Finances (In Italics) / Individual Issue Statistics — Exchange	Ind / Interest Dates	1992 / S&P Debt Rating	1993 / Date of Last Rating Change	1994 / Prior Rating	Eligible	Year End / Bond Form	Cash & Equiv. (Million $) / Regular Price	Curr. Assets (Million $) / Regular (Begins) Thru	Curr. Liab. / Sinking Fund Price	Balance Sheet Date / Sinking Fund (Begins) Thru	L. Term Debt (Mil $) / Refund/Other Restriction Price	Refund/Other Restriction (Begins) Thru	Capital-ization (Mil $) / Outst'g (Mil $)	Total Debt % Capital / Underwriting Firm	Underwriting Year	Price Range 1995 High	Price Range 1995 Low	Mo. End Price Sale(s) or Bid	Curr. Yield	Yield to Mat.
***Portland General Elec** (Cont.)*																				
M-T Nts[1] 9s '96	[2]ao15	**A–**	10/91	A	X	BE	NC	....	....	....	....	....	10.0	M2	'90	104⅛	102	103	8.74	5.50
M-T Nts[1] 8.88s '99	[3]ao15	**A–**	10/91	A	X	BE	NC	....	....	....	....	....	13.0	M2	'91	109⅞	102	109⅞	8.08	5.81
M-T Nts[1] 9.07s 2005	[4]ao15	**A–**	10/91	A	X	BE	NC	....	....	....	....	....	18.0	M2	'91	119¼	103½	119¼	7.61	6.36
M-T Nts[1] 9.31s 2021	[5]ao15	**A–**	10/91	A	X	BE	NC	....	....	....	....	....	20.0	M2	'91	129½	105⅞	129½	7.19	6.85
M-T Nts[1] 9.46s 2021	[6]ao15	**A–**	10/91	A	X	BE	104.73	(8-12-01)	....	....	....	....	25.0	M2	'91	131¼	107⅜	131¼	7.21	6.85
M-T Nts 'I'[1] 6.76s '97	Jj15	**A–**			X	BE	NC	....	....	....	....	....	24.0	S1	'92	101⅜	98	101¼	6.68	5.51
M-T Nts 'I'[1] 6.60s '97	[7]jj15	**A–**			X	BE	NC	....	....	....	....	....	15.0	S1	'92	101½	96⅞	101½	6.50	5.58
M-T Nts 'I'[1] 5.65s '98	[8]jj15	**A–**			X	BE	NC	....	....	....	....	....	27.0	S1	'93	100⅛	92¾	100⅛	5.64	5.59
M-T Nts 'I'[1] 7.28s '99	[9]jj15	**A–**			X	BE	NC	....	....	....	....	....	24.0	S1	'92	104⅜	96⅝	104⅜	6.97	5.69
M-T Nts 'I'[1] 7.66s 2002	[10]jj15	**A–**			X	BE	NC	....	....	....	....	....	15.0	S1	'92	107⅞	95¾	107⅞	7.10	6.08
M-T Nts 'I'[1] 7.61s 2004	[11]jj15	**A–**			X	BE	NC	....	....	....	....	....	11.0	S1	'92	108½	94⅛	108½	7.01	6.31
M-T Nts 'I'[1] 7.61s 2004	[12]jj15	**A–**			X	BE	NC	....	....	....	....	....	26.0	S1	'92	108½	94⅛	108½	7.01	6.31
M-T Nts 'I'[1] 7.60s 2004	[13]jj15	**A–**			X	BE	NC	....	....	....	....	....	8.00	S1	'92	108½	94	108½	7.00	6.30
M-T Nts 'II'[1] 5.69s '98	fA15	**A–**			X	BE	NC	....	....	....	....	....	35.0	S1	'93	100⅛	92¼	100⅛	5.68	5.64
M-T Nts 'II'[1] 6.47s 2003	fA15	**A–**			X	BE	NC	....	....	....	....	....	40.0	S1	'93	101½	87¾	101½	6.37	6.22
M-T Nts 'III'[1] 6¾s '97	mS15	**A–**			X	BE	NC	....	....	....	....	....	30.0	U1	'94	101⅞	96½	101⅞	6.63	5.58
M-T Nts 'III'[1] 7.40s 2001	mS15	**A–**			X	BE	NC	....	....	....	....	....	45.0	U1	'94	106½	94⅜	106½	6.95	6.03
Portola Packaging, Inc	***16d***	***1.47***	***1.75***	***1.43***		***Au***	***1.51***	***31.50***	***16.70***	***5-31-95***	***★110.0***		***91.20***	***90.2***						
Sr[14]Nts 10¾s 2005	aO	**B**			Y	R	105.375	(10-1-00)	....	....	[15]Z110.75	9-30-98	110	C1	'95	104½	100	104½	10.29	10.01
Potlatch Corp	***50***	***3.10***	***2.11***	***2.36***		***Dc***	***42.60***	***397.0***	***272.0***	***9-30-95***	***601.0***		***1600***	***40.0***						
SF Deb[16] 9⅝s 2016	Ao15	**A–**	8/89	BBB+	X	R	105.29	4-14-96	100	(4-15-97)	®104.81	4-14-96	100	G1	'86	107	103⅝	105½	9.12	9.03
[17]Deb[18] 9⅛s 2009	jD	**A–**			X	R	NC	....	....	....	....	....	100	G1	'89	125¾	103½	125¾	7.26	6.32
Deb[1] 6.95s 2015	jD15	**A–**			X	BE	NC	....	....	....	....	....	100	G1	'95	101	99¾	101	6.88	6.86
Potomac Edison Co.[19]	***72a***	***3.30***	***3.21***	***3.35***		***Dc***	***41.70***	***173.0***	***153.0***	***6-30-95***	***629.0***		***1386***	***51.1***						
1st CT 5⅞s '96	Mn	**A+**	4/94	AA–	X	R	100	....	100	....	....	....	18.0	H1	'66	100	97¾	100	5.88	5.82
1st 5⅞s 2000	Ms	**A+**	4/94	AA–	X	R	NC	....	Z100	....	....	....	75.0	G1	'93	99½	90⅛	99½	5.90	6.01
1st 8s 2006	Jd	**A+**	4/94	AA–	X	R	104.76	11-30-96	Z100	....	®100	11-30-01	50.0	G1	'91	106⅜	97⅞	105⅜	7.59	7.25
1st 8⅞s 2021	fA	**A+**	4/94	AA–	X	R	106.54	7-31-96	Z100	....	....	....	50.0		'91	107⅞	99⅝	106⅝	8.32	8.25
1st 8s 2022	jD	**A+**	4/94	AA–	X	R	103.398	(12-1-02)	Z100	....	....	....	50.0		'92	109⅝	89⅞	109⅝	7.30	7.19
1st 7¾s 2023	Fa	**A+**	4/94	AA–	X	R	103.475	(2-1-03)	Z100	....	....	....	45.0	G1	'93	107⅜	87⅞	107⅜	7.22	7.13
1st 8s 2024	Jd	**A+**			X	R	103.597	(6-1-04)	Z100	....	....	....	75.0	G1	'94	107⅞	92⅜	107⅞	7.42	7.34
1st 7¾s 2025	Mn	**A+**			X	R	103.084	(5-1-05)	100	....	....	....	65.0	G1	'95	106⅛	98	106⅛	7.30	7.24
1st 7⅝s 2025	Mn	**A+**			X	R	103.263	(5-1-05)	Z100	....	....	....	80.0	P4	'95	106⅞	96⅞	106⅞	7.13	7.07
Potomac Electric Power	***72a***	***2.16***	***3.33***	***3.36***		***Dc***	***21.90***	***534.0***	***568.0***	***9-30-95***	***1983***		***4379***	***50.2***						
1st 4⅜s '98	Fa15	**A**	1/95	A+	X	CR	100.37	2-14-96	....	....	....	....	50.0	D4	'63	97⅜	89¾	97⅜	4.49	5.70
1st 4½s '99	Mn15	**A**	1/95	A+	X	CR	100.46	5-14-96	....	....	....	....	45.0	K2	'64	95⅞	86⅜	95⅞	4.69	5.86
1st 9s 2000	Ao15	**A**	1/95	A+	X	R	100	(4-15-99)	....	....	....	....	100	G1	'90	109	101⅝	109	8.26	6.56
1st 5⅛s 2001	Ao	**A**	1/95	A+	X	R	100.94	3-31-96	....	....	....	....	15.0	K2	'66	95¾	84½	95¾	5.35	6.08
1st 5⅞s 2002	Mn	**A**	1/95	A+	X	R	101.37	4-30-96	....	....	....	....	35.0	K2	'67	98	86	98	5.99	6.26
1st 6⅝s 2003	Fa15	**A**	1/95	A+	X	R	101.73	2-14-96	....	....	....	....	40.0	K2	'68	101½	89	101½	6.53	6.36
1st 5⅝s 2003	aO15	**A**	1/95	A+	X	R	NC	....	....	....	....	....	50.0	G1	'93	96⅛	83	96⅛	5.85	6.26
1st 6½s 2005	mS15	**A**			X	R	NC	....	....	....	....	....	100	S1	'95	102⅛	98¼	102⅛	6.36	6.20
1st 6½s 2008	Ms15	**A**	1/95	A+	X	R	NC	....	....	....	....	....	78.0	B5	'93	100⅞	84⅜	100⅞	6.44	6.39
1st 5⅞s 2008	aO15	**A**	1/95	A+	X	R	NC	....	....	....	....	....	50.0	M6	'93	95⅞	79½	95⅞	6.13	6.35
1st 9s 2021	Jd	**A–**	1/95	A+	X	R	103.61	(6-1-01)	....	....	....	....	100	M2	'91	117⅞	99½	117⅞	7.64	7.43
1st 7¼s 2023	jJ	**A**	1/95	A+	X	R	102.99	(6-30-03)	....	....	....	....	100	M2	'93	102⅝	84¾	102⅝	7.06	7.03

Uniform Footnote Explanations-See Page 260. Other: [1] Issued in min denom $100T. [2] Due 11-21-96. [3] Due 8-12-99. [4] Due 8-15-05. [5] Due 8-11-21. [6] Due 8-12-21. [7] Due 7-21-97. [8] Due 5-15-98. [9] Due 1-13-99. [10] Due 1-14-02. [11] Due 7-14-04. [12] Due 7-20-94. [13] Due 7-21-04. [14] (HRO)On Chge of Ctrl at 101. [15] Max $33M red w/proceeds of Pub Eq Off'gs. [16] Plan call. [17] Credit Sensitive Deb. [18] Int(min8.825%,max14%)subj to adj for Rat'g chge. [19] Subsid of Allegheny Power Systems.

Title-Industry Code & Co. Finances (In Italics) / Individual Issue Statistics — Exchange, Interest Dates	Ind / S&P Debt Rating	Fixed Charge Coverage 1992 / Date of Last Rating Change	1993 / Prior Rating	1994 / Eligible	Year End / Bond Form	Cash & Equiv. (Million $) / Redemption Provisions: Regular Price	Curr. Assets (Million $) / Regular (Begins) Thru	Curr. Liab. (Million $) / Sinking Fund Price	Balance Sheet Date / Sinking Fund (Begins) Thru	L. Term Debt (Mil $) / Refund/Other Restriction Price	Refund/Other Restriction (Begins) Thru	Capital-ization (Mil $) / Outst'g (Mil $)	Total Debt % Capital / Underwriting Firm	Underwriting Year	Price Range 1995 High	Price Range 1995 Low	Mo. End Price Sale(s) or Bid	Curr. Yield	Yield to Mat.
***Potomac Electric Power** (Cont.)*																			
1st 6⅞s 2023 ... mS	**A**	1/95	A+	X	R	102.66	(9-1-03)	....	....	....	....	100	F1	'93	98¾	81	98¾	6.96	6.98
1st 6⅞s 2024 ... aO15	**A**	1/95	A+	X	R	103.10	(10-15-03)	....	....	....	....	75.0	L3	'93	98¾	80⅞	98¾	6.96	6.98
1st 7⅜s 2025 ... mS15	**A**			X	R	103.38	(9-15-05)	....	....	....	....	75.0	C5	'95	103⅞	97⅞	103⅞	7.10	7.06
1st 8½s 2027 ... Mn15	**A**	1/95	A+	X	R	103.21	(5-15-02)	....	....	....	....	75.0	S1	'92	113⅜	95⅝	113⅜	7.50	7.40
1st 7½s 2028 ... Ms15	**A**	1/95	A+	X	R	103.45	(3-15-03)	....	....	....	....	40.0	S1	'93	105⅞	86¾	105⅞	7.08	7.04
PPG Indus ... 15	***4.55***	***6.68***	***10.76***		***Dc***	***118.0***	***2375***	***1580***	***9-30-95***	***745.0***		***3830***	***31.0***						
Deb 9s 2021 ... Mn	**A**			X	BE	NC	....	....	....	....	....	148	F1	'91	127¾	103⅝	127¾	7.05	6.71
Nts 6⅞s 2005 ... fA	**A**			X	BE	NC	....	....	....	....	....	100	C5	'95	106	98¼	106	6.49	6.04
Praxair, Inc ... 14b	***2.36***	***3.25***	***4.14***		***Dc***	***12.00***	***890.0***	***1016***	***9-30-95***	***936.0***		***2842***	***49.7***						
Deb 8.70s 2022 ... jJ15	**BBB+**	6/95	BBB	X	BE	104.35	(7-15-02)	....	....	....	....	300	G1	'92	114¼	95⅞	114¼	7.61	7.46
Nts 6¾s 2003 ... Ms	**BBB+**	6/95	BBB	X	BE	NC	....	....	....	....	....	300	M6	'93	103¼	89⅜	103¼	6.54	6.18
Nts 6.85s 2005 ... Jd15	**BBB+**			X	BE	NC	....	....	....	....	....	150	M6	'95	103¾	96¾	103¾	6.60	6.32
Premark Int'l ... 34	***5.86***	***8.16***	***13.51***		***Dc***	***88.80***	***1403***	***1013***	***9-30-95***	***198.0***		***1360***	***29.7***						
Nts 10½s 2000 ... mS15	**BBB+**	9/95	BBB	X	R	NC	....	....	....	....	....	100	G1	'90	115½	106	115½	9.09	6.61
Presley Cos ... 13h	***d0.41***	***d1.44***	***0.52***		***Dc***				***9-30-95***	***263.0***		***367.0***	***71.7***						
Sr Nts[1] 12½s 2001 ... jJ	**B–**			Y	R	106	(7-1-98)	....	....	[2]Z111.50	6-30-97	200	D6	'94	88¼	82	82½	15.15	17.59
Price/Costco Inc ... 59m	***Δ8.30***	***Δ7.41***	***Δ6.42***		***Au***	***45.70***	***1702***	***1693***	***9-3-95***	***1095***		***2752***	***42.5***						
Sr Nts 7⅛s 2005 ... Jd15	**BBB**			X	R	NC	....	....	....	....	....	300	D6	'95	105⅛	97	105⅛	6.78	6.39
PriCellular Wireless ... 67g	***n/a***	***n/a***	***n/a***		***Dc***	***21.80***	***26.50***	***14.10***	***6-30-95***	***★287.0***		***200.0***	***61.2***						
Sr Sub[3]Disc Nts[4] 12¼s 2003 ... aO	**CCC+**			Y	R	106.125	(10-1-99)	....	....	....	....	[5]205	D6	'95	77½	69⅞	77½	15.81	17.67
Primark Corp ... 17a	***3.74***	***2.45***	***2.65***		***Dc***	***11.80***	***172.0***	***198.0***	***9-30-95***	***267.0***		***589.0***	***55.7***						
• Sr Nts[1] 8¾s 2000 ... aO15	**BB–**	7/95	BB	Y	R	104.375	(10-15-97)	....	....	[6]Z109	10-14-97	112	P1	'93	103¾	93½	s102½	8.54	8.10
Private Export Funding ... 25	***Gtd by Export-Import Bank of U.S.***																		
Sec[7]Nts X 7.70s '97 ... Jj31	**AAA**			X	R	NC	....	....	....	....	....	88.0	S1	'86	102⅜	100¾	102½	7.51	5.33
Sec[7]Nts BB 9.10s '98 ... aO30	**AAA**			X	R	NC	....	....	....	....	....	100	C4	'88	109⅜	103½	109⅜	8.32	5.49
Sec[7]Nts CC 9½s '99 ... Ms31	**AAA**			X	R	NC	....	....	....	....	....	100	M5	'89	111¾	104⅞	111⅝	8.52	5.57
Sec[7]Nts DD 9.45s '99 ... jD31	**AAA**			X	R	NC	....	....	....	....	....	100		'89	114	105¼	113⅞	8.30	5.54
Sec[7]Nts FF 9s '96 ... Jj31	**AAA**			X	R	NC	....	....	....	....	....	178		'90	102	100⅜	100⅜	8.97	5.62
Sec[7]Nts GG 8.95s '97 ... aO31	**AAA**			X	R	NC	....	....	....	....	....	100	M6	'90	106½	102⅜	106	8.45	5.49
Sec[7]Nts HH 8.35s 2001 ... Jj31	**AAA**			X	R	NC	....	....	....	....	....	100		'91	111⅝	100¾	111¾	7.48	5.67
Sec[7]Nts II 8.40s 2001 ... jJ31	**AAA**			X	R	NC	....	....	....	....	....	200	B9	'91	112⅛	102⅞	112¼	7.49	5.81
Sec[7]Nts JJ 8.15s '97 ... Ao30	**AAA**			X	R	NC	....	....	....	....	....	100		'91	103⅞	100¼	103⅝	7.87	5.37
Sec[7]Nts KK 8¾s 2003 ... Jd30	**AAA**			X	R	NC	....	....	....	....	....	100	M5	'91	117½	103⅛	117½	7.45	5.84
Sec[7]Nts LL 7.90s 2000 ... Ms31	**AAA**			X	R	NC	....	....	....	....	....	150		'91	108⅜	99	108½	7.28	5.63
Sec[7]Nts MM 7⅛s '96 ... aO31	**AAA**			X	R	NC	....	....	....	....	....	95.0	D4	'91	101⅝	98⅞	101½	7.02	5.34
Sec[7]Nts NN 7.30s 2002 ... Jj31	**AAA**			X	R	NC	....	....	....	....	....	99.0	B9	'92	108	95¼	108⅛	6.76	5.72
Sec[7]Nts OO 5¾s '98 ... Ao31	**AAA**			X	BE	NC	....	....	....	....	....	150	C4	'92	100¾	93⅜	100⅞	5.70	5.36
Sec[7]Nts PP 6.90s 2003 ... Jj31	**AAA**			X	BE	NC	....	....	....	....	....	93.0	B3	'93	106⅜	92⅜	106½	6.48	5.78
Sec([8]Amort)[7]Nts QQ 5.65s 2003 ... Ms15	**AAA**			X	BE	NC	....	....	....	....	....	72.0	M5	'93	105¼	91⅝	100⅜	5.63	....
Sec([8]Amort)[7]Nts RR 5.48s 2003 ... mS15	**AAA**			X	BE	NC	....	....	....	....	....	98.0	B9	'93	103¼	89⅝	95⅜	5.75	....
Sec([9]Amort)[7]Nts SS 5.80s 2004 ... Fa	**AAA**			X	BE	NC	....	....	....	....	....	85.0	B9	'94	100	85¼	100	5.80	....
Sec([10]Amort)[7]Nts TT 6.86s 2004 ... Ao31	**AAA**			X	BE	NC	....	....	....	....	....	206	B9	'94	105⅝	93½	105⅝	6.50	....
Sec[7]Nts UU 7.95s 2006 ... mN	**AAA**			X	BE	100	(11-1-04)	....	....	....	....	94.0	B9	'94	113⅛	98⅛	113¼	7.02	6.25
Sec[7]Nts VV 6.24s 2002 ... Mn15	**AAA**			X	BE	NC	....	....	....	....	....	125	C2	'95	102½	97⅛	102⅝	6.09	5.76
Sec[7]Nts WW 6.62s 2005 ... aO	**AAA**			X	BE	NC	....	....	....	....	....	125	C2	'95	105⅛	100	105⅛	6.30	5.92
Procter & Gamble Co. ... 33	***Δ6.25***	***Δ7.64***	***Δ9.20***		***Je***	***1993***	***11386***	***8693***	***9-30-95***	***5018***		***17239***	***36.1***						
Deb 7⅜s 2023 ... Ms	**AA**			X	BE	103.608	(3-1-03)	....	....	....	....	175	G1	'93	105⅜	86⅜	105⅜	7.00	6.93

Uniform Footnote Explanations-See Page 260. Other: [1] (HRO)On Chge of Ctrl at 101. [2] Max $70M red w/proceeds of Public Off'g. [3] (HRO)On Chge of Ctrl at 101(Accreted Val). [4] Int accrues at 12.25% fr 10-1-98. [5] Incl disc. [6] Max $35M red w/proceeds of Capital Stk Off'g. [7] Gtd by Export-Import Bank of U.S. [8] Prin due in 20 equal pyts ea Mar & Sep 15. [9] Prin due in 10 equals pyts ea Feb & Aug 1. [10] Prin due in 20 equal pyts ea Apr 30 & Oct 31.

Exchange / Individual Issue Statistics	Interest Dates	S&P Debt Rating	Date of Last Rating Change	Prior Rating	Eligible	Bond Form	Redemption Provisions: Regular Price	Regular (Begins) Thru	Sinking Fund Price	Sinking Fund (Begins) Thru	Refund/Other Restriction Price	Refund/Other Restriction (Begins) Thru	Outst'g (Mil $)	Underwriting Firm	Underwriting Year	Price Range 1995 High	Price Range 1995 Low	Mo. End Price Sale(s) or Bid	Curr. Yield	Yield to Mat.
Title-Industry Code & Co. Finances (In Italics)	*Ind*	*Fixed Charge Coverage 1992*	*1993*	*1994*		*Year End*	*Million $ Cash & Equiv.*	*Curr. Assets*	*Curr. Liab.*	*Balance Sheet Date*	*L. Term Debt (Mil $)*		*Capital-ization (Mil $)*	*Total Debt % Capital*						
Procter & Gamble Co. *(Cont.)*																				
Deb[1] 8s 2029	aO26	**AA**	4/91	AA+	X	R	NC	....	....	....	....	....	100	M6	'89	119⅛	99⅞	119⅛	6.72	6.58
Nts 6.85s '97	Jd	**AA**			X	BE	NC	....	....	....	....	....	200	G1	'92	102	97⅜	102	6.72	5.37
Nts 8.70s 2001	fA	**AA**			X	BE	NC	....	....	....	....	....	175	M5	'91	113⅝	102	113⅝	7.66	5.81
Nts 8s 2003	mN15	**AA**			X	BE	NC	....	....	....	....	....	200	G1	'91	112⅝	97⅞	112⅝	7.10	5.97
Nts[2] 8½s 2009	fA10	**AA**	4/91	AA+	X	R	NC	....	....	....	....	....	150	M2	'89	121⅞	100¼	121⅞	6.97	6.11
Progressive Corp	***35c***	***6.47***	***10.40***	***7.87***		***Dc***				***9-30-95***	***676.0***		***2068***	***32.7***						
Nts 10s 2000	jD15	A+	2/95	A–	X	R	NC	....	....	....	....	....	150	B5	'88	117	105⅜	117	8.55	5.99
Nts 6.60s 2004	Jj15	A+	2/95	A–	X	BE	NC	....	....	....	....	....	200	M5	'94	101⅝	87	101⅝	6.49	6.34
Nts 7s 2013	aO	A+	2/95	A–	X	BE	NC	....	....	....	....	....	150	F1	'93	100½	81⅝	100½	6.97	6.95
Sub Nts 10⅛s 2000	jD15	**A**	2/95	BBB+	X	R	NC	....	....	....	....	....	150	B5	'88	117½	105⅝	117½	8.62	5.99
[3]***Property Trust of Amer***	***57***	***2.89***	***4.36***	***2.60***		***Dc***				***9-30-95***	***376.0***		***1676***	***22.4***						
Nts[4] 6⅞s 2008	Fa15	A–			X	BE	[5]Z100	....	....	....	....	....	100	M5	'94	100⅞	86¼	100⅞	6.82	6.77
[6]Nts[7] 7½s 2014	Fa15	A–			X	BE	[5]Z100	....	....	....	....	....	100	M5	'94	101¼	84⅞	101¼	7.41	7.37
Protective Life Corp	***35a***	***n/a***	***n/a***	***14.61***		***Dc***				***9-30-95***	***141.0***		***618.0***	***22.8***						
Sr Nts 7.95s 2004	jJ	**A**			X	BE	NC	....	....	....	....	....	75.0	G1	'94	109⅜	95⅝	109⅜	7.27	6.50
PRT Funding[8]	***25***	***n/a***	***n/a***	***1.00***		***Dc***	***1.10***	***5.90***	***5.90***	***9-30-95***	***100.0***		***100.0***	***100.0***						
◆Sr Nts[9] 11⅝s 2004	Ao15	B–			Y	R	104.36	(4-15-99)	....	....	....	....	85.0	S1	'94	85	85	A80	14.53	16.06
Prudential Rlty Secur	***25***	***0.62***	***0.58***	***0.70***		***Dc***	***1.47***			***12-31-94***	***16.30***		***25.30***	***64.4***						
• Zero Cpn Mtg-Bk '96	[10]	**AAA**			X	R	NC	....	....	....	Z100	....	[11]3.89	P4	'83	99⅞	90⅜	98¼	....	6.97
• Zero Cpn Mtg-Bk '97	[10]	**AAA**			X	R	NC	....	....	....	Z100	....	[11]1.93	P4	'83	90⅞	81¾	91⅛	....	7.54
Public Serv, Colorado	***75***	***2.64***	***2.65***	***2.55***		***Dc***	***6.29***	***456.0***	***829.0***	***9-30-95***	***1080***		***2984***	***49.6***						
1st 5⅜s '96	Mn	**BBB+**	11/86	A+	X	CR	100	4-30-96	100	....	....	....	35.0	D7	'66	99⅞	97⅛	99⅞	5.38	5.70
1st 5⅞s '97	jJ	**BBB+**	11/86	A+	X	R	100.21	6-30-96	100	....	....	....	35.0	H1	'67	100	95⅛	100	5.88	5.87
1st 6¾s '98	jJ	**BBB+**	11/86	A+	X	R	100.54	6-30-96	100.15	7-1-96	....	....	25.0	H1	'68	100⅝	95⅜	100⅝	6.71	6.48
1st 8⅛s 2004	Ms	**BBB+**			X	BE	NC	....	....	....	....	....	100	K2	'92	109⅞	96¾	109⅞	7.39	6.54
1st 9⅞s 2020	jJ	**BBB+**			X	R	104.61	(7-1-00)	....	....	....	....	75.0	M2	'90	117¾	106⅝	115⅜	8.56	8.39
1st 8¾s 2022	Ms	**BBB+**			X	BE	104.18	(3-1-02)	100	(3-1-02)	....	....	150	K2	'92	113½	96⅜	113½	7.71	7.56
1st Coll Tr Ser 1 6⅜s 2005	mN	**BBB+**			X	BE	NC	....	....	....	....	....	135	M2	'93	99⅛	84	99⅛	6.43	6.50
1st Coll Tr Ser 2 6s 2001	Jj	**BBB+**			X	BE	NC	....	....	....	....	....	103	M2	'94	99⅜	88⅜	99⅜	6.04	6.15
1st Coll Tr Ser 2 7¼s 2024	Jj	**BBB+**			X	BE	102.87	(1-1-04)	....	....	....	....	110	M2	'94	99¼	82½	99¼	7.30	7.31
[12]***Public Serv, Indiana***	***72a***	***Merged into CINergy Corp,see Cin Gas & El***																		
• 1st S 7s 2002	Jj	A–	7/95	BBB+	X	R	101.21	12-31-96	100	....	....	....	26.4	F1	'71	100⅝	90½	100⅛	6.99	6.97
• 1st Y 7⅝s 2007	Jj	A–	7/95	BBB+	X	R	102.63	12-31-96	100	....	....	....	24.1	M6	'77	102¼	90⅝	101	7.55	7.49
Public Serv, New Hamp.[13]	***72a***	[14]***2.07***	***2.28***	***2.88***		***Dc***	***0.61***	***280.0***	***447.0***	***9-30-95***	***1543***		***2525***	***72.4***						
1st[15]'A' 8⅞s '96	Mn15	BB+	3/94	BBB–	Y	R	NC	....	[16]Z100	....	[17]Z100	....	173	M6	'91	102¼	100¾	101	8.79	6.10
1st[15]'B' 9.17s '98	Mn15	BB+	3/94	BBB–	Y	R	NC	....	[16]Z100	....	[17]Z103.06	5-15-96	170	M6	'91	106⅛	99½	106⅛	8.64	6.35
Public Serv, New Mexico	***72a***	***1.34***	***1.70***	***2.71***		***Dc***	***98.00***	***258.0***	***172.0***	***9-30-95***	***729.0***		***1440***	***50.6***						
1st 5⅞s '97	Mn	**BB**	12/93	BB+	Y	R	100.26	4-30-96	100.20	4-30-96	....	....	14.7	F1	'67	99½	91⅞	99½	5.90	6.26
1st 7¼s '99	Ao	**BB**	12/93	BB+	Y	R	100.69	3-31-96	100	....	....	....	12.1	B6	'69	100¾	90⅝	100¾	7.20	6.98
1st 8⅛s 2001	mS15	**BB**	12/93	BB+	Y	R	101.36	9-14-96	100	....	....	....	16.7	B6	'71	102½	90⅞	102½	7.93	7.57
1st 7½s 2002	Jd15	**BB**	12/93	BB+	Y	R	101.51	6-14-96	100	....	....	....	16.7	H1	'72	99⅛	87⅝	99⅛	7.57	7.67
1st 9⅛s 2005	Ms15	**BB**	12/93	BB+	Y	R	102.84	3-14-96	100	....	....	....	21.8	K2	'75	105⅛	93¾	105⅛	8.68	8.31
1st 8⅛s 2007	Jd15	**BB**	12/93	BB+	Y	R	102.98	6-14-96	100	....	....	....	26.7	F1	'77	102⅝	85	102⅝	7.92	7.77
1st 9s 2008	Mn	**BB**	12/93	BB+	Y	R	103.32	4-30-96	100	....	....	....	54.4	M5	'78	105¼	90¾	105⅛	8.56	8.32
Public Serv, Oklahoma[18]	***72a***	***2.83***	***3.36***	***3.78***		***Dc***	***3.10***	***99.10***	***209.0***	***9-30-95***	***379.0***		***923.0***	***43.8***						
1st J 5¼s '96	Ms	A+	10/94	AA–	X	CR	100	....	□100	....	....	....	25.0	M2	'66	99⅞	97⅝	99⅞	5.26	5.88

Uniform Footnote Explanations-See Page 260. Other: [1] (HRO)On 10-26-96 at 100. [2] Min denom $10T. [3] Merged into&data of Security Cap Pacific Tr. [4] Prin pyts of $125 due ea 2-15,fr 2-15-01. [5] Plus Make-Whole Amt. [6] Prin pyts due ea 2-15:09,$100,10,$125,11,$150. [7] Prin pyts due ea 2-15:12,$175,13,$200,14,$250. [8] Subsid of Pratt Hotel Corp. [9] (HRO)On Chge of Ctrl at 101. [10] Due Apr 1. [11] Incl disc. [12] Now PSI Energy, subsid of CINERGY Corp. [13] Merged into Northeast Utilities. [14] 7 Mo Dec,'91 & '92. [15] Issued in min denom $5T. [16] Fr condemnation or insurance proceeds. [17] Fr proceeds of Asset Sales. [18] Contr by Central & South West Corp.

Individual Issue Statistics / Exchange	Interest Dates	S&P Debt Rating	Date of Last Rating Change	Prior Rating	Eligible	Bond Form	Redemption Provisions: Regular Price	Regular (Begins) Thru	Sinking Fund Price	Sinking Fund (Begins) Thru	Refund/Other Restriction Price	Refund/Other Restriction (Begins) Thru	Outst'g (Mil $)	Underwriting Firm	Underwriting Year	Price Range 1995 High	Price Range 1995 Low	Mo. End Price Sale(s) or Bid	Curr. Yield	Yield to Mat.
Title-Industry Code & Co. Finances (In Italics)	*Ind*	*Fixed Charge Coverage 1992*	*1993*	*1994*		*Year End*	*Million $ Cash & Equiv.*	*Curr. Assets*	*Curr. Liab.*	*Balance Sheet Date*	*L. Term Debt (Mil $)*	*Capital-ization (Mil $)*		*Total Debt % Capital*						
***Public Serv, Oklahoma** (Cont.)*																				
1st K 7¼s '99	Jj	**A+**	10/94	AA−	X	CR	100.55	12-31-96	□100.14	12-31-96	....	....	25.0	W5	'69	100⅞	96⅞	100⅝	7.20	7.02
1st L 7⅜s 2002	Ms	**A+**	10/94	AA−	X	CR	101.53	2-29-96	□100	....	....	....	30.0	B6	'72	101⅝	95⅛	101⅝	7.26	7.04
1st S 7¼s 2003	jJ	**A+**	10/94	AA−	X	R	NC	....	....	....	....	....	65.0	M2	'92	106½	92⅞	106½	6.81	6.16
1st T 7⅜s 2004	jD	**A+**	10/94	AA−	X	R	NC	....	□100	....	....	....	50.0	M6	'92	107⅝	93	107⅝	6.85	6.25
1st U 6¼s 2003	Ao	**A+**	10/94	AA−	X	R	NC	....	□100	....	....	....	35.0	M2	'93	100¾	87¾	100¾	6.20	6.12
1st V 7⅜s 2023	Ao	**A+**	10/94	AA−	X	R	102.97	(4-1-03)	□100	....	....	....	100	M2	'93	103	85⅝	103	7.16	7.12
1st W 6½s 2005	Jd	**A+**	10/94	AA−	X	R	NC	....	Z100	....	....	....	50.0	M6	'93	101⅝	86⅞	101⅝	6.40	6.27
***Public Serv Elec & Gas*[1]**	***75***	***2.52***	***3.30***	***3.32***		***Dc***	***27.50***	***1248***	***1474***	***12-31-94***	***4541***	***10328***		***50.9***						
• 1st & Ref Z 8¾s '99	jJ	**A−**	1/94	A	X	R	NC	....	....	....	Z100	....	100	S1	'89	106⅞	104½	105½	8.29	6.95
• 1st & Ref BB 9⅛s 2005	jJ	**A−**	1/94	A	X	R	NC	....	Z100	....	....	....	125	P1	'90	115	105	114	8.00	7.08
• 1st & Ref CC 9¼s 2021	Jd	**A−**	1/94	A	X	R	NC	....	Z100	....	....	....	150	F1	'91	No Sale		111⅛	8.32	8.20
• 1st & Ref DD 8⅞s 2003	Jd	**A−**	1/94	A	X	R	NC	....	Z100	....	....	....	150	M2	'91	No Sale		103⅛	8.61	8.30
• 1st & Ref EE 8¾s 2021	mN	**A−**	1/94	A	X	R	107.18	10-31-96	Z100	....	®106.89	10-31-99	200	L3	'91	108½	96¾	105½	8.29	8.23
• 1st & Ref FF 7⅞s 2001	mN	**A−**	1/94	A	X	R	NC	....	Z100	....	....	....	100	K2	'91	106¼	97½	105⅝	7.46	6.69
• 1st & Ref GG 7⅛s '97	mN	**A−**	1/94	A	X	R	NC	....	Z100	....	....	....	150	L3	'91	102	97⅜	101½	7.02	6.24
• 1st & Ref HH 8¾s 2022	Fa	**A−**	1/94	A	X	R	107.04	(2-1-97)	Z100	....	....	....	150	F1	'92	109⅞	96¾	106¾	8.20	8.12
• 1st & Ref II 7⅝s 2000	Fa	**A−**	1/94	A	X	R	NC	....	Z100	....	....	....	100	S1	'92	106½	96¼	s105¼	7.24	6.15
• 1st & Ref KK 6⅞s '97	Jd	**A−**	1/94	A	X	R	NC	....	Z100	....	....	....	150	M2	'92	100⅞	96¾	100¼	6.86	6.68
• 1st & Ref LL 8½s 2022	Jd	**A−**	1/94	A	X	R	‡105.97	(6-1-97)	Z100	....	....	....	200	M5	'92	105½	95	104	8.17	8.13
• 1st & Ref MM 6⅞s 2003	Jj	**A−**	1/94	A	X	R	NC	....	Z100	....	....	....	150	G1	'93	103	89	100½	6.84	6.78
• 1st & Ref NN 6s '98	jJ	**A−**	1/94	A	X	R	NC	....	Z100	....	....	....	100	M2	'93	100¼	93¼	99⅝	6.02	6.20
• 1st & Ref OO 7½s 2023	Ms	**A−**	1/94	A	X	R	‡105.38	(3-1-98)	Z100	....	....	....	250	M2	'93	101⅜	85⅛	s101	7.43	7.41
• 1st & Ref PP 6½s 2004	Mn	**A−**	1/94	A	X	R	NC	....	Z100	....	....	....	300	F1	'93	101	85¾	99½	6.53	6.58
• 1st & Ref QQ 6s 2000	Mn	**A−**	1/94	A	X	R	NC	....	Z100	....	....	....	300	M5	'93	100¾	88½	99	6.06	6.26
• 1st & Ref RR 6⅛s 2002	fA	**A−**	1/94	A	X	R	NC	....	Z100	....	....	....	300	M5	'93	100	87½	99	6.19	6.31
• 1st & Ref SS 7s 2024	mS	**A−**	1/94	A	X	R	102.74	(9-1-03)	Z100	....	....	....	300	G1	'93	98⅛	79½	97	7.22	7.25
• 1st & Ref TT 7⅜s 2014	Ms	**A−**			X	R	102.13	(3-1-04)	Z100	....	....	....	175	K2	'94	102⅛	86¾	100	7.38	7.37
• 1st & Ref UU 6¾s 2006	Ms	**A−**			X	R	NC	....	Z100	....	....	....	175	C5	'94	102	90	97	6.96	7.17
• 1st & Ref 5s 2037	jJ	**A−**	1/94	A	X	CR	NC	....	....	....	....	....	7.54	Exch.	'38	73	55⅝	71½	6.99	7.16
• 1st & Ref 8s 2037	Jd	**A−**	1/94	A	X	CR	NC	....	....	....	....	....	7.46	Exch.	'38	103½	88½	101½	7.88	7.88
Sec M-T Nts 'A' 8.16s 2009	[2]jj	**A−**			X	BE	NC	....	....	....	....	....	16.5	M2	'94	114¼	96¼	114¼	7.14	6.55
Sec M-T Nts 'A' 8.10s 2009	[2]jj	**A−**			X	BE	NC	....	....	....	....	....	43.5	M2	'94	113¾	95¾	113¾	7.12	6.54
◆ Deb 6s '98	jJ	**BBB+**	1/94	A−	X	CR	NC	....	....	....	....	....	18.2	Exch.	'48	99½	93	98	6.12	6.88
Pueblo Xtra Int'l	***59c***	***1.75***	***0.75***	***0.69***		***Ja***	***3.61***	***96.90***	***112.0***	***8-12-95***	***313.0***	***398.0***		***81.4***						
Sr Nts[3] 9½s 2003	fA	**B−**			Y	R	104.75	(8-1-98)	....	....	[4]Z109.50	7-31-96	180	M6	'93	96¼	83¼	93½	10.16	10.77
Puget Sound Power & Lt	***72a***	***3.04***	***3.44***	***3.18***		***Dc***	***11.10***	***288.0***	***303.0***	***9-30-95***	***928.0***	***2438***		***43.5***						
1st 5¼s '96	Jj	**A−**	3/86	BBB	X	CR	100	....	100	....	....	....	20.0	M2	'66	100	97¾	100	5.25	Mat.
Sec M-T Nts 'A'[5] 7⅞s '97	[6]ao15	**A−**			X	BE	NC	....	....	....	....	....	100	S1	'91	103¾	99	103⅝	7.60	5.67
Sec M-T Nts 'A'[5] 8.83s '98	[7]ao15	**A−**			X	BE	NC	....	....	....	....	....	25.0	S1	'91	107⅜	101⅜	107¼	8.23	5.76
Sec M-T Nts 'A'[5] 6½s '99	[8]ao15	**A−**			X	BE	NC	....	....	....	....	....	16.5	S1	'92	101⅞	92⅜	101⅞	6.38	5.93
Sec M-T Nts 'A'[5] 7.15s 2002	[9]ao15	**A−**			X	BE	NC	....	....	....	....	....	5.00	S1	'92	104⅞	92	104⅞	6.82	6.25
Sec M-T Nts 'A'[5] 6.65s '99	[10]ao15	**A−**			X	BE	NC	....	....	....	....	....	10.0	S1	'92	102⅜	93	102⅜	6.50	5.92
Sec M-T Nts 'A'[5] 6.41s '99	[11]ao15	**A−**			X	BE	NC	....	....	....	....	....	20.5	S1	'92	101⅝	92⅛	101⅝	6.31	5.91
Sec M-T Nts 'A'[5] 9.14s 2001	[12]ao15	**A−**			X	BE	100	(6-22-98)	....	....	....	....	30.0	S1	'91	113⅞	102⅞	113⅞	8.03	6.12
Sec M-T Nts 'A'[5] 7.85s 2002	[13]ao15	**A−**			X	BE	NC	....	....	....	....	....	30.0	S1	'92	108½	96	108½	7.24	6.22
Sec M-T Nts 'A'[5] 7.07s 2002	[14]ao15	**A−**			X	BE	NC	....	....	....	....	....	27.0	S1	'92	104½	91½	104½	6.77	6.23

Uniform Footnote Explanations-See Page 260. Other: [1] Subsid of Public Serv Enterprise Gr. [2] Due 5-26-09. [3] (HRO)On Chge of Ctrl at 101. [4] Max $63M red w/proceeds of Pub Equity Off'g. [5] Issued in min denom $100T. [6] Due 10-1-97. [7] Due 7-27-98. [8] Due 9-14-99. [9] Due 9-11-02. [10] Due 9-15-99. [11] Due 9-16-99. [12] Due 6-21-01. [13] Due 5-29-02. [14] Due 8-28-02.

Title-Industry Code & Co. Finances (In Italics) / Individual Issue Statistics (Exchange)	Ind / Interest Dates	Fixed Charge Coverage 1992 / S&P Debt Rating	1993 / Date of Last Rating Change	1994 / Prior Rating	Eligible	Year End / Bond Form	Million $ Cash & Equiv. / Regular Price	Curr. Assets / Regular (Begins) Thru	Curr. Liab. / Sinking Fund Price	Balance Sheet Date / Sinking Fund (Begins) Thru	L. Term Debt (Mil $) / Refund/Other Restriction Price	Capital-ization (Mil $) / Refund/Other Restriction (Begins) Thru	Total Debt % Capital / Outst'g (Mil $)	Underwriting Firm	Underwriting Year	Price Range 1995 High	Price Range 1995 Low	Mo. End Price Sale(s) or Bid	Curr. Yield	Yield to Mat.
***Puget Sound Power & Lt** (Cont.)*																				
Sec M-T Nts 'A'[1] 8.06s 2006	[2]ao15	**A–**			X	BE	NC	....	....	....	....	....	46.0	S1	'92	112⅛	95½	112⅛	7.19	6.45
Sec M-T Nts 'A'[1] 8.14s 2006	[3]ao15	**A–**			X	BE	NC	....	....	....	....	....	25.0	S1	'91	113	95⅞	113	7.20	6.46
Sec M-T Nts 'A'[1] 7¾s 2007	[4]ao15	**A–**			X	BE	NC	....	....	....	....	....	100	S1	'92	110⅛	92	110⅛	7.04	6.46
Sec M-T Nts 'A'[1] 8.40s 2007	[5]ao15	**A–**			X	BE	100	(5-1-02)	....	....	....	....	10.0	S1	'92	115¼	97¾	115¼	7.29	6.48
Sec M-T Nts 'A'[1] 8.59s 2012	[6]ao15	**A–**			X	BE	102.89	(4-9-02)	....	....	....	....	5.00	S1	'92	116¼	98⅜	116¼	7.39	6.91
Sec M-T Nts 'B'[1] 4.85s '96	[7]jj15	**A–**			X	BE	NC	....	....	....	....	....	15.0	K2	'93	99⅞	96¾	99⅞	4.86	5.45
Sec M-T Nts 'B'[1] 6.17s '98	[8]jj15	**A–**			X	BE	NC	....	....	....	....	....	10.0	K2	'93	101	94⅛	101	6.11	5.66
Sec M-T Nts 'B'[1] 5.70s '98	[9]jj15	**A–**			X	BE	NC	....	....	....	....	....	5.00	K2	'93	100	92¾	100	5.70	5.70
Sec M-T Nts 'B'[1] 7¼s '99	[10]jj15	**A–**			X	BE	NC	....	....	....	....	....	50.0	K2	'92	104½	95	104½	6.94	5.95
Sec M-T Nts 'B'[1] 6.61s 2000	[11]jj15	**A–**			X	BE	NC	....	....	....	....	....	10.0	K2	'93	102¼	92⅜	102¼	6.46	5.98
Sec M-T Nts 'B'[1] 7⅝s 2002	[12]jj15	**A–**			X	BE	NC	....	....	....	....	....	25.0	K2	'92	107½	94⅜	107½	7.09	6.28
Sec M-T Nts 'B'[1] 7.02s 2003	[13]jj15	**A–**			X	BE	NC	....	....	....	....	....	30.0	K2	'93	104¼	90⅞	104¼	6.73	6.27
Sec M-T Nts 'B'[1] 6.20s 2003	[14]jj15	**A–**			X	BE	NC	....	....	....	....	....	3.00	K2	'93	99⅛	85⅛	99⅛	6.25	6.34
Sec M-T Nts 'B'[1] 6.40s 2003	[15]jj15	**A–**			X	BE	NC	....	....	....	....	....	11.0	K2	'93	100¼	86⅜	100¼	6.38	6.36
Sec M-T Nts 'B'[1] 7.70s 2004	[16]jj15	**A–**			X	BE	NC	....	....	....	....	....	50.0	K2	'92	108⅝	93¾	108⅝	7.09	6.42
Sec M-T Nts 'B'[1] 8.20s 2012	[17]ao15	**A–**			X	BE	102.70	(12-21-02)	....	....	....	....	30.0	K2	'92	112¾	94¾	112¾	7.27	6.91
Sec M-T Nts 'B'[1] 7.35s 2024	[18]ao15	**A–**			X	BE	103.68	(2-1-04)	....	....	....	....	55.0	S1	'94	105	84¾	105	7.00	6.94
***Pulte Corp**[19]*	***13h***	***1.64***	***2.14***	***2.20***		***Dc***				***9-30-95***	***★655.0***	***1484***	***50.5***							
Sr Nts[20] 7s 2003	jD15	**BBB**			X	BE	NC	....	....	....	....	....	100	M2	'93	100⅜	87⅜	100⅜	6.97	6.94
Sr Nts[20] 8⅜s 2004	fA15	**BBB**			X	BE	NC	....	....	....	....	....	115	M2	'94	108⅞	94⅜	108⅞	7.69	6.99
Sr Nts 7.30s 2005	aO24	**BBB**			X	BE	NC	....	....	....	....	....	125	M2	'95	102⅜	99¼	102⅜	7.13	6.96
Pulte Home Corp	***13h***	***Subsid of Pulte Corp, see***																		
Sr Sub Deb 10⅛s '99	jJ15	**BBB–**	9/92	BB+	X	R	NC	....	....	....	....	....	23.2	F1	'87	111⅞	99⅞	111⅞	9.05	6.33
Quaker Oats	***26***	***△8.50***	***△5.86***	***△3.21***		***Je***	***174.0***	***1319***	***1845***	***9-30-95***	***1055***	***2840***	***58.6***							
M-T Nts 'D' 7.07s '98	ms15	**A**			X	BE	NC	....	....	....	....	....	38.3	B5	'95	103	100	103	6.86	5.69
M-T Nts 'D' 7½s 2005	[21]ms15	**A**			X	BE	NC	....	....	....	....	....	25.0	L3	'95	107¾	100	107¾	6.96	6.38
M-T Nts 'D' 7.77s 2025	ms15	**A**			X	BE	NC	....	....	....	....	....	30.0	L1	'95	111	100	111	7.00	6.89
***Quaker State Corp**[22]*	***49d***	***3.79***	***4.06***	***5.12***		***Dc***	***29.90***	***267.0***	***170.0***	***9-30-95***	***★171.0***	***355.0***	***21.2***							
• Nts 6⅝s 2005	aO15	**BBB**			X	BE	[23]....	....	....	....	....	....	100	C5	'95	99⅜	99⅜	99	6.69	6.76
Questar Pipeline Co	***73b***	***3.51***	***3.75***	***4.03***		***Dc***	***1.67***	***16.00***	***18.80***	***9-30-95***	***135.0***	***360.0***	***38.3***							
Deb[24] 9⅞s 2020	Jd	**A+**	9/93	A	X	R	104.67	(6-1-00)	100	(6-1-01)	[25]Z100	....	50.0	F1	'90	118⅝	108⅜	118⅝	8.32	8.11
Deb 9⅜s 2021	Jd	**A+**	9/93	A	X	R	104.51	(6-1-01)	100	(6-1-02)	....	....	85.0	M2	'91	117⅜	105½	117⅜	7.99	7.79
Quorum Health Group	***30a***	***△2.97***	***△3.51***	***△5.35***		***Je***	***27.60***	***248.0***	***103.0***	***9-30-95***	***★430.0***	***804.0***	***53.1***							
Sr Sub Nts[26] 11⅞s 2002	jD15	**B+**	5/95	B–	Y	R	105.875	(12-15-97)	....	....	....	....	100	G1	'92	112	105½	112	10.60	9.48
Sr Sub Nts[26] 8¾s 2005	mN	**B+**			Y	R	104.375	(11-1-00)	....	....	....	....	150	G1	'95	103⅜	100	103⅜	8.46	8.24
Ralcorp Holdings	***26***	***27.61***	***33.73***	***8.15***		***Sp***		***183.0***	***150.0***	***6-30-95***	***320.0***	***554.0***	***68.6***							
Nts 8¾s 2004	mS15	**BBB–**			X	BE	NC	....	....	....	....	....	150	L3	'94	112⅞	97⅜	112⅞	7.75	6.77
***Rally's Hamburgers**[27]*	***27b***	***11.17***	***0.86***	***0.28***		***Dc***	***15.60***	***23.80***	***27.80***	***10-1-95***	***96.10***	***130.0***	***75.7***							
• Sr Nts[28] 9⅞s 2000	Jd15	**B–**	3/95	B	Y	R	103	(6-15-96)	100	(6-15-99)	....	....	85.0	P1	'93	64	46	s51⅛	19.32	....
Ralphs Grocery Co	***59c***	***1.16***	***1.41***	***1.29***		***Ja***	***64.80***	***669.0***	***815.0***	***10-8-95***	***1915***	***2124***	***92.3***							
Sr Sub Nts[29] 10¼s 2002	jJ15	**NR**	6/95	B–	Y	R	105	(7-15-97)	....	....	....	....	3.04	M2	'92	101¾	96¾	101⅛	10.14	10.01
Ralston Purina Co	***26***	***3.23***	***3.44***	***3.37***		***Sp***	***73.90***	***1917***	***2092***	***6-30-95***	***1539***	***3538***	***73.3***							
• SF Deb 9½s 2016	Jd	**A–**			X	R	103.905	5-31-96	100	(6-2-96)	®103.55	5-31-96	42.0	F1	'86	106½	100½	s104⅜	9.10	9.03
• SF Deb 9⅜s 2016	jJ	**A–**			X	R	102.91	6-30-96	100	(7-2-96)	®102.64	6-30-96	46.7	S1	'86	106¾	101¾	103¼	9.08	9.02
• Deb[30] 9¼s 2009	aO15	**A–**			X	R	NC	....	....	....	....	....	181	S1	'89	118⅞	102¾	117¼	7.89	7.25
• Deb 7¾s 2015	aO	**A–**			X	BE	NC	....	....	....	....	....	175	M6	'95	103¼	99⅞	90	8.61	8.83

Uniform Footnote Explanations-See Page 260. Other: [1] Issued in min denom $100T. [2] Due 6-19-06. [3] Due 11-30-06. [4] Due 2-1-07. [5] Due 5-7-07. [6] Due 4-9-12. [7] Due 3-5-96. [8] Due 2-9-98. [9] Due 3-5-98. [10] Due 12-10-99. [11] Due 2-9-00. [12] Due 12-10-02. [13] Due 2-10-03. [14] Due 12-1-03. [15] Due 12-2-03. [16] Due 12-10-04. [17] Due 12-21-12. [18] Due 2-1-24. [19] See Pulte Home Corp. [20] (HRO)On Chge of Ctrl at 100. [21] Due 5-2-05. [22] Was Quaker St Oil Ref. [23] Co may red at greater of 100 or amt based on formula. [24] (HRO)To 6-1-00 at 100 for Rat'g Decline. [25] Co may redeem upon repurch of 80% deb. [26] Co must offer repurch at 101 on Chge in Ctrl. [27] Was Rally's Inc. [28] Co must offer repurch at 101 on Chge of Ctrl. [29] (HRO)On Chge in Ctrl Triggering Event at 101. [30] (HRO)At 100 for Designated Event&Rat'g Decline.

Title-Industry Code & Co. Finances (In Italics) / Individual Issue Statistics — Exchange, Interest Dates	S&P Debt Rating / Fixed Charge Coverage 1992	Date of Last Rating Change / 1993	Prior Rating	Eligible / 1994	Bond Form / Year End	Regular Price / Cash & Equiv. (Million $)	Regular (Begins) Thru / Curr. Assets (Million $)	Sinking Fund Price / Curr. Liab. (Million $)	Sinking Fund (Begins) Thru / Balance Sheet Date	Refund/Other Restriction Price / L. Term Debt (Mil $)	Refund/Other Restriction (Begins) Thru	Outst'g (Mil $) / Capitalization (Mil $)	Underwriting Firm / Total Debt % Capital	Underwriting Year	Price Range 1995 High	Price Range 1995 Low	Mo. End Price Sale(s) or Bid	Curr. Yield	Yield to Mat.
***Ralston Purina Co** (Cont.)*																			
• Deb[1] 9.30s 2021 Mn	**A–**			X	R	NC	....	....	....	....	....	200	G1	'91	118	118	114	8.16	8.00
• Deb[1] 8⅝s 2022 Fa15	**A–**			X	BE	NC	....	....	....	....	....	250	G1	'92	113½	96⅛	111⅝	7.73	7.59
• Deb[1] 8⅛s 2023 Fa	**A–**			X	BE	NC	....	....	....	....	....	175	M5	'93	107⅞	91½	95⅝	8.50	8.54
• Deb 7⅞s 2025 Jd15	**A–**			X	BE	NC	....	....	....	....	....	225	L3	'95	104¾	96½	90	8.75	8.83
• Nts 9s '96 Jd15	**A–**			X	R	NC	....	....	....	....	....	200	G1	'86	104½	100¾	s101⅛	8.90	6.53
***[2]Rapid-American Corp[3]** 17*	....	....		....	*Ja*	***Bankruptcy Chapt 11***				***580.0***		***d29.90***	***NM***						
Sub Deb[4]('69) 7s '94 §Mn15	**D**	5/91	C	Z	R			Default 5-15-91 int				50.3	Exch.	'69	1½	⅛	½	....	Flat
Sub Deb[4]('72) 7s '94 §Mn15	**D**	5/91	C	Z	R			Default 5-15-91 int				[5]60.7	Exch.	'72	1½	⅛	½	....	Flat
Sub SF Deb[4] 12s '99 §QJan15	**NR**			Z	R			Default 4-15-91 int				[5]13.8	Exch.	'78	1½	⅛	½	....	Flat
Sub SF Deb[4] 10¾s 2003 §QDec	**NR**			Z	R			Default 3-1-91 int				104	Exch.	'77	1½	⅛	½	....	Flat
Sub SF Deb[4] 10¾s 2004 §QOct	**NR**			Z	R			Default 4-1-91 int				5.66	Exch.	'78	1½	⅛	½	....	Flat
Sub SF Deb[4] 11s 2005 §QOct	**NR**			Z	R			Default 4-1-91 int				[5]11.4	Exch.	'78	1½	⅛	½	....	Flat
Sub SF Deb[4] 10s 2006 §fA	**NR**			Z	R			Default 2-1-91 int				[5]140	Exch.	'81	1	1	1	....	Flat
Sr Sub Nts[4] 14½s '94 §Ms	**D**	3/91	C	Z	R			Default 3-1-91 int				105	D7	'84	15	½	4	....	Flat
***Raytheon Co** 23i*	*20.84*	*33.72*		*24.43*	*Dc*	*207.0*	*5559*	*4266*	*10-1-95*	*1480*		*7736*	*45.8*						
Deb 7⅜s 2025 jJ15	**A+**			X	BE	102.881	(7-15-05)	....	....	....	....	375	C5	'95	104⅞	92¾	104⅞	7.03	6.98
Nts 6½s 2005 jJ15	**A+**			X	BE	NC	....	....	....	....	....	750	C5	195	103¼	95½	103¼	6.30	6.05
***Redwood Empire Bancorp** 10*	*10.65*	*9.36*		*0.15*	*Dc*				*9-30-95*	*12.00*		*42.50*	*28.2*						
Sub Nts 8½s 2004 [6]Jan15	**NR**				R	100	(1-15-97)	....	....	....	....	12.0	P2	'93	102⅞	97	102⅞	8.26	8.01
***Price REIT** 57*	*3.25*	*3.54*		*5.00*	*Dc*				*9-30-95*	*★93.80*		*316.0*	*29.7*						
Sr Nts 7¼s 2000 mN	**BBB–**			X	BE	NC	....	....	....	....	....	100	M2	'95	100⅝	99	100⅝	7.20	7.09
***Reebok Int'l** 39a*	*21.57*	*16.19*		*26.27*	*Dc*	*104.0*	*1562*	*628.0*	*9-30-95*	*255.0*		*1361*	*28.1*						
Deb 6¾s 2005 mS15	**A–**			X	BE	NC	....	....	....	....	....	100	C5	'95	102⅝	98⅝	102⅝	6.58	6.38
***Reeves Industries, Inc** 17*	*1.49*	*1.79*		*1.87*	*Dc*	*4.20*	*108.0*	*50.80*	*10-1-95*	*146.0*		*175.0*	*83.4*						
Sr Nts[7] 11s 2002 jJ15	**BB–**			Y	R	104.125	(7-15-97)	....	....	....	....	123	D6	'92	102⅛	87	87	12.64	14.10
***Regency Health Services** 30*	*3.46*	*4.24*		*3.22*	*Dc*	*27.50*	*98.20*	*62.10*	*9-30-95*	*★178.0*		*190.0*	*54.7*						
Sr Sub Nts[7] 9⅞s 2002 aO15	**B–**			Y	R	104.938	(10-15-99)	....	....	....	....	110	B5	'95	100	98½	99¼	9.95	10.02
***Regions Financial[8]** 10*	*16.93*	*11.81*		*4.99*	*Dc*				*9-30-95*	*574.0*		*1688*	*34.0*						
Sub Nts 7.65s 2001 fA15	**A**			X	BE	NC	....	....	....	....	....	25.0	B5	'94	106⅝	95⅝	106⅝	7.17	6.23
Sub Nts[8] 7.80s 2002 jD	**A**	10/93	A+	X	BE	NC	....	....	....	....	....	75.0	B5	'92	108¼	96	108¼	7.21	6.31
Sub Nts[9] 7¾s 2024 mS15	**A**			X	BE	NC	....	....	....	....	....	100	C5	'94	111¼	85	111¼	6.97	6.85
***Reliance Electric** 23c*	***Mgr into Rockwell Int'l, see***																		
Nts[10] 6.80s 2003 Ao15	**AA–**	11/94	BBB	X	R	NC	....	....	....	....	....	150	G1	'93	103½	89⅝	103½	6.57	6.19
***Reliance Financial Svcs.[11]** 25*	*5.52*	*13.59*		*9.89*	*Dc*	*45.90*			*9-30-95*	*40.30*		*1487*	*14.2*						
• Sr[12]Reset Nts 9.48s 2000 mN	**BBB**	11/93	BB+	X	R	100	....	100	....	....	....	50.0	D7	'85	No Sale		98¼	9.65	....
• Sr Nts[13] 7.866s 2000 jD	**BBB**	11/93	BB+	X	R	100	....	100	....	....	....	50.0	D7	'85	No Sale		101½	7.75	7.49
***Reliance Group Hldgs** 35d*	*0.30*	*1.83*		*1.57*	*Dc*				*9-30-95*	*690.0*		*1452*	*60.1*						
• Sr Nts 9s 2000 mN15	**BB+**			Y	BE	NC	....	....	....	....	....	400	D6	'93	104	91¾	s103½	8.70	8.11
• Sr Sub Deb[14] 9¾s 2003 mN15	**BB–**			Y	BE	103.656	(11-15-98)	....	....	....	....	250	D6	'93	103¾	88	s103	9.47	9.20
***ReliaStar Financial[15]** 35d*	*4.68*	*7.33*		*13.44*	*Dc*				*9-30-95*	*238.0*		*1707*	*25.4*						
• Nts 6⅝s 2003 mS15	**BBB+**			X	BE	NC	....	....	....	....	....	120	M2	'93	99	89	99¼	6.68	6.75
• Nts 8⅝s 2005 Fa15	**BBB+**			X	BE	NC	....	....	....	....	....	110	S1	'95	99¼	97	100⅛	8.61	8.60
***Repap Wisconsin Inc[16]** 50*	*d0.09*	*1.29*		*n/a*	*Dc*	*0.01*	*116.0*	*84.70*	*6-30-95*	*382.0*		*494.0*	*77.5*						
1st Pr Sr Sec Nts[7] 9¼s 2002 Fa	**BB–**	4/95	B+	Y	R	102.643	(2-1-99)	....	....	[17]Z109	1-31-97	250	C5	'94	100	88	95	9.74	10.37
2nd Pr Sr Sec Nts[7] 9⅞s 2006 Mn	**B+**	4/95	B	Y	R	104.389	(5-1-99)	....	....	[18]Z110	4-30-97	150	C5	'94	99¾	85⅝	95	10.39	10.68
***Republic Bancorp** 10*	*11.70*	*4.50*		....	*Dc*				*9-30-94*	*99.80*		*220.0*	*45.4*						
Sub Nts 9s 2003 [19]	**NR**				BE	100	(2-1-96)	....	....	....	....	17.3		'93	100¼	99	100¼	8.98	8.95

Uniform Footnote Explanations-See Page 260. Other: [1] Issued in min denom $100T. [2] Now McCrory Parent Corp. [3] Subsid of E-II Hldgs. [4] Asmd by McCrory Parent Corp. [5] Incl disc. [6] Int pd mthly. [7] (HRO)On Chge of Ctrl at 101. [8] Was First Alabama Bancshrs. [9] (HRO)On 9-15-04 at 100. [10] (HRO)For a Designated Event at 100. [11] Subsid of Reliance Group Hldgs. [12] Int thru 10-31-97,adj ea 3yrs aft as defined. [13] Int reset fr 10.36% on 12-1-95. [14] (HRO)On Chge of Ctrl at 100. [15] Was NWNL Cos. [16] Subsid of Repap Enterprises. [17] Max $87.5M red w/proceeds of Pub Eq Off'g. [18] Max $52.5M red w/proceeds of Pub Eq Off'g. [19] Due 2-1-03:Int pd monthly,Feb 1,etc.

Title-Industry Code & Co. Finances (In Italics) / Individual Issue Statistics (Exchange)	Ind / Interest Dates	Fixed Charge Coverage 1992 / S&P Debt Rating	1993 / Date of Last Rating Change	— / Prior Rating	1994 / Eligible	Year End / Bond Form	Cash & Equiv. (Million $) / Regular Price	Curr. Assets (Million $) / Regular (Begins) Thru	Curr. Liab. (Million $) / Sinking Fund Price	Balance Sheet Date / Sinking Fund (Begins) Thru	L. Term Debt (Mil $) / Refund/Other Restriction Price	Refund/Other Restriction (Begins) Thru	Capitalization (Mil $) / Outst'g (Mil $)	Total Debt % Capital / Underwriting Firm	Underwriting Year	Price Range 1995 High	Price Range 1995 Low	Mo. End Price Sale(s) or Bid	Curr. Yield	Yield to Mat.
Republic Engineered Steels	66d	Δ0.23	Δd0.35		Δ0.32	Je	4.61	266.0	124.0	6-30-95	243.0		332.0	73.2						
1st[1] 9⅞s 2001	jD15	B+	5/95	B	Y	R	104.23	(12-15-98)	....	....	[2]Z109.875	12-14-96	200	C4	'93	95¾	89¼	89¾	11.00	12.35
Republic N.Y. Corp	10	1.59	1.84		1.99	Dc				9-30-95	4159		7050	59.0						
• Deb 8⅜s 2007	Fa15	AA			X	R	NC	....	....	....	....	....	100	S1	'87	106	100¼	105⅝	7.93	7.61
• Nts 8⅜s '96	Mn	AA			X	R	NC	....	....	....	....	....	100	S1	'86	102⅝	99¾	100	8.38	8.26
Sub Deb 9½s 2014	Ao15	AA–			X	R	NC	....	....	....	....	....	150	S1	'89	128⅝	107¾	128⅝	7.39	6.75
Sub Nts 9½s 2000	jJ	AA–			X	R	NC	....	....	....	....	....	100	G1	'90	114¼	104¼	114¼	8.32	5.86
Sub Nts 9¾s 2000	jD	AA–			X	R	NC	....	....	....	....	....	100	G1	'90	116½	105⅝	116½	8.37	5.84
Sub Nts 8⅞s 2001	Fa15	AA–			X	R	NC	....	....	....	....	....	100	L3	'91	113	101½	113	7.85	5.90
Sub Nts 8¼s 2001	mN	AA–			X	R	NC	....	....	....	....	....	150	L3	'91	111⅜	98¼	111⅜	7.41	5.92
Sub Nts 7⅞s 2001	jD12	AA–			X	R	NC	....	....	....	....	....	100	M2	'91	109⅝	96⅞	109⅝	7.18	5.93
Sub Nts 7¾s 2002	Mn15	AA–			X	R	NC	....	....	....	....	....	150	S1	'92	109	95¼	109	7.11	6.03
Sub Nts 7¼s 2002	jJ15	AA–			X	BE	NC	....	....	....	....	....	250	L3	'92	106½	93⅛	106½	6.81	6.03
Sub Nts 5⅞s 2008	aO15	AA–			X	BE	NC	....	....	....	....	....	250	S1	'93	96⅜	77¾	96⅜	6.10	6.29
Sub Nts 9.70s 2009	Fa	AA–			X	R	NC	....	....	....	....	....	150	G1	'89	128¾	107⅞	128¾	7.53	6.42
Sub Nts 7¾s 2009	Mn15	AA–			X	BE	NC	....	....	....	....	....	200	L3	'94	112⅜	92⅜	112⅜	6.90	6.36
Sub Nts 9⅛s 2021	Mn15	AA–			X	R	NC	....	....	....	....	....	100	L3	'91	128⅝	103⅜	128⅝	7.09	6.75
Sub Nts 9.30s 2021	Jd	AA–			X	R	NC	....	....	....	....	....	100	M2	'91	130	105¼	130	7.15	6.80
F/R[3]Sub Nts 5.8953s 2002	QAug7	AA–			X	BE	NC	....	....	....	....	....	100	L3	'92	99⅝	97⅜	98⅝	5.98	....
F/R[4]Sub Nts 5.9713s 2002	QOct28	AA–			X	BE	NC	....	....	....	....	....	150	L3	'92	100⅛	98⅞	99⅛	6.02	....
Sub[5]F/R Yield Curve Nts 3.65s 2002	jD29	AA–			X	BE	NC	....	....	....	....	....	100	M2	'92	100	98⅞	100	3.65	....
Resorts Int'l Hotel Finance	40i	***See Resorts Int'l, Inc***																		
◆Mtg Nts[6] 11s 2003	mS15	NR				R	100	(5-3-99)	Z100	5-3-99	....	....	125		'94	94	68½	s92¼	11.92	12.59
◆Jr Mtg([7]PIK)Nts([8]Units)[6] 11⅜s 2004	jD15	NR				R	100	(5-3-99)	....	....	....	....	35.0	Reorg	'94	95	59	s92	....	Flat
Revco D.S.,Inc(New)[9]	59e	Δ1.79	Δ4.18		Δ3.09	My	8.30	1237	742.0	11-18-95	720.0		1552	48.6						
Sr Nts[10] 9⅛s 2000	Jj15	BBB–	1/94	BB	X	R	103	(1-15-98)	....	....	....	....	140	M2	'93	108	98⅝	108	8.45	6.83
Revlon Consumer Pr[11]	18	0.64	0.15		0.07	Dc	39.60	800.0	491.0	9-30-95	1536		850.0	182.0						
• SF Deb 10⅞s 2010	jJ15	B+	5/93	NR	Y	R	102.44	7-14-96	100	....	....	....	78.4	L1	'80	103⅞	91½	s102	10.66	10.60
• Sr Nts[10] 9½s '99	Jd	B			Y	R	NC	....	....	....	....	....	200	F1	'93	102⅛	91¾	s101⅞	9.33	8.85
Sr[10]Nts[12]'B' 9⅜s 2001	Ao	B			Y	R	104	(4-1-98)	....	....	[13]Z100	....	260	Exch.	'93	101	88½	100½	9.33	9.25
Sr Sub[10]Nts[14] 'B' 10½s 2003	Fa15	B–			Y	R	105.25	(2-15-98)	....	....	[15]Z100	....	555	Exch.	'93	103¼	88¼	102½	10.24	10.00
Revlon Worldwide	18	0.64	0.11		0.39	Dc	39.60	800.0	491.0	9-30-95	2394		907.0	268.0						
Sr[16]Sec Disc(Zero Cpn)Nts 'B' '98	[17]	B–			Y	R	100	....	....	....	....	....	[18]1116	Exch.	'93	74	55	73	....	14.75
Rexene Corp(New)	14	n/a	0.31		d0.30	Dc	44.40	197.0	82.80	9-30-95	175.0		308.0	56.8						
• Sr Nts[10] 11¾s 2004	jD	BB–	5/95	B+	Y	R	105.875	(12-1-99)	....	....	[19]Z110	11-30-97	175	S5	'94	112⅛	102	s106¾	11.01	10.56
Reynolds Metals Co	5	0.19	d2.39		1.65	Dc	248.0	2346	1268	9-30-95	1907		4508	42.6						
Deb[20] 9⅜s '99	Jd15	BBB+			X	R	NC	....	....	....	....	....	100	G1	'89	110⅞	102⅛	110⅞	8.46	5.86
Deb[20] 9s 2003	fA15	BBB+			X	BE	NC	....	....	....	....	....	100	G1	'91	117	100⅝	117	7.69	6.17
RHP[21] Holdings[22]	41c	1.35	0.78		0.79	Je	63.20	258.0	134.0	1-1-95	308.0		638.0	50.8						
• Sr Sub Deb[23] 11⅞s '99	Ms	B–	11/87	NR	Y	R	101.23	2-29-96	100	(3-1-97)	....	....	85.6	Co.	'87	No Sale		100	11.88	11.86
Riggs National Corp	10	d0.14	d3.21		2.15	Dc				9-30-95	218.0		579.0	37.7						
Sub Deb 9.65s 2009	Jd15	BB–	10/95	B	Y	R	NC	....	....	....	....	....	66.5	P4	'89	109	97	106	9.10	8.88
Sub Nts 8½s 2006	Fa	BB–	10/95	B	Y	BE	104.25	(2-1-99)	....	....	....	....	125	D4	'94	105½	90	105½	8.06	7.70
Rite Aid	59e	7.52	7.79		6.47	Fb	28.30	1535	688.0	12-2-95	971.0		2283	53.6						
Sr Deb 6⅞s 2013	fA15	A–	2/94	A	X	BE	NC	....	....	....	....	....	200	B5	'93	98½	81⅝	97¾	7.03	7.10
Sr Nts 7⅝s 2005	Ao15	A–			X	BE	NC	....	....	....	....	....	200	D6	'95	108¼	99¾	107¼	7.11	6.57
Riverwood Int'l[24]	16c	1.87	0.92		1.69	Dc	42.50	468.0	347.0	9-30-95	1018		1579	64.5						
• Sr Nts[25] 10¾s 2000	Jd15	B+	11/94	B	Y	R	103.072	(6-15-97)	....	....	....	....	150	M5	'92	109	101	104	10.34	9.62

Uniform Footnote Explanations-See Page 260. Other: [1] Co must offer repurch,at 101,on Chge of Ctrl. [2] Max $60M red w/proceeds of Pub Eq off'g. [3] Int(min 5%,max 10%)thru 2-7-96,adj qtrly aft. [4] Int(min 5%,max 9.50%)thru 1-28-96,adj qtrly aft. [5] Int to 12-28-95,adj aft as defined. [6] Gtd by Resorts Int'l Hotel Inc. [7] Co may pay int in cash or add'l units. [8] Incl one Cl B com of Resorts Int'l. [9] See Hook-SupeRx Inc. [10] (HRO)On Chge of Ctrl at 101. [11] Was Revlon, Inc. [12] Red in whole at 100 & prem on Chge of Ctrl. [13] In whole, plus premium. [14] Co may red at 100 & prem on Chge of Ctrl. [15] Plus Applicable Prem, on Chge of Ctrl. [16] Red in whole at 100(Accreted Val)& prem on Ctrl Chge. [17] Due 3-15-98. [18] Incl disc. [19] Max $58.3M red w/proceeds of Com Off'g. [20] (HRO)For Designated Event&Rat'g Decline at 100. [21] Subsid of Banner Indus. [22] Was Rexnord Inc. [23] Indenture has Consol Net Worth requirements. [24] Subsid of Manville Corp. [25] Co must offer repurch at 100 for Chge in Ctrl.

Exchange / Individual Issue Statistics	Interest Dates	S&P Debt Rating	Date of Last Rating Change	Prior Rating	Eligible	Bond Form	Regular Price	Regular (Begins) Thru	Sinking Fund Price	Sinking Fund (Begins) Thru	Refund/Other Restriction Price	Refund/Other Restriction (Begins) Thru	Outst'g (Mil $)	Underwriting Firm	Underwriting Year	Price Range 1995 High	Price Range 1995 Low	Mo. End Price Sale(s) or Bid	Curr. Yield	Yield to Mat.
Title-Industry Code & Co. Finances (In Italics)	*Ind*	*Fixed Charge Coverage 1992*	*1993*	*1994*	*Year End*		*Million $ Cash & Equiv.*	*Curr. Assets*	*Curr. Liab.*	*Balance Sheet Date*	*L. Term Debt (Mil $)*		*Capital-ization (Mil $)*	*Total Debt % Capital*						
Riverwood Int'l (Cont.)																				
• Sr Nts II 10¾s 2000	Jd15	B+	11/94	B	Y	R	103.072	(6-15-97)	....	....	....	....	37.5	G1	'93	No Sale		107¼	10.02	8.75
• Sr Sub Nts[1] 11¼s 2002	Jd15	B+	11/94	B	Y	R	104.218	(6-15-97)	....	....	....	....	250	M5	'92	110¾	103	106¼	10.59	9.91
• Sr Sub Nts II 11¼s 2002	Jd15	B+	11/94	B	Y	R	104.218	(6-15-97)	....	....	....	....	62.5	G1	'93	No Sale		101	11.14	11.03
• Sr Sub Nts[2] 10⅝s 2004	Jd31	B+	11/94	B	Y	R	104.611	(6-30-99)	....	....	[3]Z110.375	6-29-97	100	M5	'94	102	102	102	10.17	10.02
RJR[4] Nabisco[5] Inc[6]	*69a*	*2.09*	*1.09*	*2.29*	*Dc*		*353.0*	*4523*	*3357*	*9-30-95*	*9524*		*21942*	*44.8*						
• Deb 9¼s 2013	fA15	BBB–			X	BE	NC	....	....	....	....	....	500	L3	'93	104½	90⅝	s102⅝	9.01	8.95
SF Deb 8⅝s 2017	Ms15	BBB–	12/91	BB+	X	R	105.175	3-14-96	100	(3-15-98)	®104.313	3-14-97	32.1	S4	'87	105¼	84¼	105¼	8.19	8.10
• Sr Nts[7] 8.30s '99	Ao15	BBB–			X	R	NC	....	....	....	....	....	61.9	G1	'92	107¾	95¾	103½	8.02	7.08
• Nts 8s 2000	Jj15	BBB–			X	BE	NC	....	....	....	....	....	60.7	M2	'93	106⅛	93½	s103¼	7.75	7.06
Nts[8] 7⅝s 2000	mS	BBB–			X	BE	NC	....	....	....	....	....	100	D6	'92	105⅝	91½	105⅝	7.22	6.22
• Nts 8s 2001	jJ15	BBB–			X	BE	NC	....	....	....	....	....	400	M2	'95	102⅝	99½	101½	7.88	7.66
[9]Nts[8] 6.80s 2001	mS	BBB–			X	BE	NC	....	....	....	....	....	6.10	C4	'92	100⅞	93⅝	100⅞	6.74	6.61
• Nts 8⅝s 2002	jD	BBB–			X	BE	NC	....	....	....	....	....	875	M6	'92	104¼	92⅜	s104	8.29	7.86
• Nts 7⅝s 2003	mS15	BBB–			X	BE	NC	....	....	....	....	....	750	S1	'92	98¾	85¾	s98⅝	7.73	7.86
• Sr Nts[7] 8¾s 2004	Ao15	BBB–			X	R	NC	....	....	....	....	....	600	G1	'92	104	92	s102⅝	8.53	8.30
• Nts 8¾s 2005	fA15	BBB–			X	BE	NC	....	....	....	....	....	500	L3	'93	104	90½	s102⅝	8.53	8.35
• Nts 8¾s 2007	jJ15	BBB–			X	BE	NC	....	....	....	....	....	250	M2	'95	103¾	99¼	s102¾	8.52	8.37
RLC Corp	*25c*	***Now Rollins Truck Leasing,see***																		
CT Deb H 10.60s '99	Ms15	BBB+			X	R	100	(3-15-96)	....	....	....	....	75.0	G1	'89	104¼	101	101⅛	10.48	10.17
Roadmaster Industries	*40f*	*2.06*	*2.13*	*1.37*	*Dc*		*5.13*	*391.0*	*251.0*	*9-30-95*	*229.0*		*451.0*	*78.5*						
Sr[10]Sub Nts 11¾s 2002	jJ15	B–			Y	R	105.875	(12-15-98)	....	....	....	....	100	J1	'93	97	64	69	17.03	20.57
Rochester Gas & Electric	*75*	*2.70*	*3.00*	*3.51*	*Dc*		*26.10*	*253.0*	*171.0*	*9-30-95*	*717.0*		*1613*	*45.6*						
1st W 6¼s '97	mS15	BBB+	3/87	A–	X	R	100.29	9-14-96	Z100.28	9-14-96	....	....	20.0	S1	'67	100¼	95¼	100¼	6.23	6.09
1st Y 8s '99	fA15	BBB+	3/87	A–	X	R	100.88	8-14-96	Z100.17	8-14-96	....	....	30.0	F1	'69	101⅞	97⅝	101	7.92	7.67
• 1st CC 8⅜s 2007	mS15	BBB+	3/87	A–	X	R	103.18	9-14-96	Z100	....	....	....	50.0	M2	'77	105	96¼	102¼	8.19	8.07
1st PP 9⅜s 2021	Ao	BBB+			X	R	104.47	(4-1-01)	Z100	(4-1-01)	....	....	100	F1	'91	114¾	100⅝	114¾	8.17	8.00
1st QQ 8¼s 2002	Ms15	BBB+			X	R	NC	....	Z100	....	....	....	100	F1	'92	109½	97½	109½	7.53	6.37
[11]Rochester Telephone Corp.	*67a*	*3.21*	*3.73*	*4.89*	*Dc*		*45.10*	*505.0*	*533.0*	*9-30-95*	*633.0*		*1514*	*42.3*						
Deb 9s 2021	fA15	A			X	R	104.50	(8-15-01)	....	....	....	....	100	S1	'91	114⅞	100¾	114⅞	7.83	7.66
Rock-Tenn Co	*16c*	*15.75*	*14.34*	*22.57*	*Sp*		*7.04*	*174.0*	*66.10*	*6-30-95*	*★147.0*		*461.0*	*34.9*						
Nts 7¼s 2005	fA	BBB			X	BE	NC	....	....	....	....	....	100	M5	'95	106¼	99¾	106¼	6.82	6.37
Rockland Electric Co.	*72a*	***Subsid of Orange & Rockland Util,see***																		
1st I 6s 2000	jJ	A–	6/94	A	X	R	NC	....	▲100	....	....	....	20.0	D6	'93	100	89¾	100	6.00	6.00
Rockwell Int'l[12]	*23*	*△9.69*	*△11.57*	*△8.21*	*Sp*		*665.0*	*5805*	*4111*	*9-30-95*	*1776*		*6213*	*39.1*						
Nts 7⅝s '98	Fa17	AA–			X	R	NC	....	....	....	....	....	300	M6	'95	102¼	95	100¾	7.57	7.23
• Nts 8⅞s '99	mS15	AA–	11/94	AA	X	R	NC	....	....	....	....	....	300	M6	'89	111	102½	108¾	8.16	6.19
• Nts 8⅜s 2001	Fa15	AA–	11/94	AA	X	R	NC	....	....	....	....	....	200	G1	'91	110¾	100	109	7.68	6.29
• Nts 6¾s 2002	mS15	AA–	11/94	AA	X	R	NC	....	....	....	....	....	300	U1	'92	104½	90¼	102⅝	6.58	6.26
Nts 7⅞s 2005	Fa15	AA–			X	R	NC	....	....	....	....	....	200	M6	'95	110	94	109⅝	7.18	6.46
• Nts 6⅝s 2005	Jd	AA–			X	R	NC	....	....	....	....	....	300	M6	'95	99⅝	98½	100	6.63	6.62
Rogers Cablesystems Ltd[13]	*12a*	*0.77*	*0.93*	*1.14*	*Dc*					*:9-30-95*	*★2420*		*2430*	*91.8*						
Sr[14]Sec[15]2nd Pr'ty Deb[16] 10⅛s 2012	$mS	BB+			Q	R	104	(9-1-02)	....	....	....	....	200	M2	'92	105¾	95¼	105¾	9.57	9.43
Sr[14]Sec[15]2nd Pr'ty[16]Deb 9.65s 2014	[17]$Jj15	BB+			Q	R	104.825	(1-15-04)	....	....	....	....	[18]300	M2	'94	87½	63	63	15.32	15.94
Sr[14]Sec[15]2nd Pr'ty Deb[16] 10s 2007	jD	BB+			Q	R	105	(12-1-02)	....	....	....	....	150	M2	'95	100	100	100	10.00	10.00
Sr[16]Sec[14]2nd Pr'ty Nts[15] 9⅝s 2002	$fA	BB+			Q	R	NC	....	....	....	....	....	250	M2	'92	105	95¾	105	9.17	8.61
Sr[14]Sub[15]Gtd Deb[16] 11s 2015	jD	BB–			Q	R	105.50	(12-1-05)	....	....	....	....	125	M2	'95	100	100	100	11.00	11.00

Uniform Footnote Explanations-See Page 260. Other: [1] Co must offer repurch at 100 for Chge of Ctrl. [2] Co must offer repurch at 100 on Chge of Ctrl. [3] Max $35M red w/proceeds of Cap Stk Off'g. [4] See Nabisco,Standard Brands. [5] Was Reynold(RJ)Indus. [6] Subsid of RJR Nabisco Hldgs Corp. [7] Was RJR Nabisco Capital. [8] Issued in min denom $100T. [9] (HRO)On 9-2-97 at 100. [10] (HRO)On Chge of Ctrl at 101. [11] Now Frontier Corp. [12] See Reliance Electric. [13] Subsid of Rogers Communications Inc. [14] Co may offer repurch at 101 on Chge of Ctrl. [15] Co may red in whole,at 100,for tax law chge. [16] Gtd by Rogers Cable TV Ltd. [17] Int pd in U.S.$ unless pyt in Can$ elected. [18] Denom in Can$.

Title-Industry Code & Co. Finances (In Italics) / Individual Issue Statistics — Exchange	Ind / Interest Dates	Fixed Charge Coverage 1992 / S&P Debt Rating	1993 / Date of Last Rating Change	1994 / Prior Rating	Eligible	Year End / Bond Form	Cash & Equiv. (Million $) / Redemption Provisions: Regular Price	Curr. Assets (Million $) / Regular (Begins) Thru	Curr. Liab. (Million $) / Sinking Fund Price	Balance Sheet Date / Sinking Fund (Begins) Thru	L. Term Debt (Mil $) / Refund/Other Restriction Price	Refund/Other Restriction (Begins) Thru	Capitalization (Mil $) / Outst'g (Mil $)	Total Debt % Capital / Underwriting Firm	Underwriting Year	Price Range 1995 High	Price Range 1995 Low	Mo. End Price Sale(s) or Bid	Curr. Yield	Yield to Mat.
Rogers Cantel Mobile Inc[1]	***67f***	***d0.26***	***0.27***	***1.01***		***Dc***				***:12-31-94***	***956.0***		***1045***	***106.0***						
Sr Sec[2]Gtd[3]Nts 10¾s 2001	$mN	**BB+**	11/95	BB	Y	R	103	(11-1-96)	100	(11-1-99)	[4]Z100	....	460	M2	'91	105⅜	100½	105⅜	10.20	9.52
Sr Sub[2]Gtd[3]Nts 11⅛s 2002	$jJ15	**BB−**	5/93	B	Y	R	103.30	(7-15-97)	....	....	[4]Z100	....	200	M2	'92	107⅛	100¼	107⅛	10.39	9.63
Rogers Communications	***12a***	***0.21***	***0.58***	***0.96***		***Dc***				***:12-31-94***	***4175***		***4926***	***84.8***						
Sr Deb[5] 10⅞s 2004	$Ao15	**BB−**			Y	R	104.61	(4-15-97)	....	....	[4]Z100	....	250	M2	'92	104¾	98¼	103⅞	10.47	10.17
Rohm & Haas	***14***	***4.73***	***4.75***	***7.36***		***Dc***	***60.00***	***1422***	***774.0***	***9-30-95***	***619.0***		***2449***	***28.6***						
Deb[6] 9⅜s 2019	mN15	**A**			X	R	104.69	(11-15-99)	....	....	....	....	100	G1	'89	118	105⅛	115½	8.12	7.92
[7]**(Hldgs)**[6]Deb[8] 9.80s 2020	Ao15	**A**			X	R	NC	....	....	....	....	....	150	G1	'90	135¼	110⅛	135¼	7.25	6.81
Nts[9] 9⅞s 2000	mS	**A**			X	R	[10]Z100	....	....	....	....	....	100	G1	'90	116¼	106⅜	116¼	8.49	5.85
Rohr (Indus) Inc	***2b***	***Δd0.04***	***Δ1.27***	***Δ1.29***		***Jl***	***48.90***	***588.0***	***189.0***	***10-29-95***	***540.0***		***731.0***	***75.8***						
Sr Nts[11] 11⅝s 2003	Mn15	**BB−**			Y	R	105.81	(5-15-99)	....	....	....	....	100	S1	'94	108⅜	89	108⅜	10.73	9.99
Sub Deb 9¼s 2017	Ms	**B**	3/93	BB−	Y	R	105.55	2-29-96	100	(3-1-98)	®104.63	2-28-97	150	D4	'87	90	76½	90	10.28	10.43
Rollins Truck Leasing	***25c***	***Δ2.59***	***Δ2.80***	***Δ2.52***		***Sp***	***22.70***	***111.0***	***54.10***	***9-30-95***	***553.0***		***850.0***	***67.5***						
CT Deb I 10.35s 2000	Mn15	**BBB+**			X	R	NC	....	....	....	....	....	50.0	G1	'90	116¼	103½	116¼	8.90	6.06
CT Deb J 8⅝s '98	jD15	**BBB+**			X	R	NC	....	....	....	....	....	30.0	M2	'91	107⅜	100½	107⅜	8.03	5.87
CT Deb K 7¾s '97	Ao15	**BBB+**			X	R	NC	....	....	....	....	....	50.0	M2	'92	102¾	98⅞	102½	7.56	5.71
CT Deb L 7s 2003	Ms15	**BBB+**			X	R	NC	....	....	....	....	....	70.0	G1	'93	104¼	90¾	104¼	6.71	6.26
CT Deb M 7s 2001	Ms15	**BBB+**			X	R	NC	....	....	....	....	....	60.0	M2	'94	103¾	93½	103¾	6.75	6.15
CT Deb O 7¼s 2005	Ms15	**BBB+**			X	R	NC	....	....	....	....	....	50.0	M2	'95	106⅛	98½	106⅛	6.83	6.37
Roosevelt Fin'l Group	***10a***	***1.58***	***1.83***	***1.65***		***Dc***				***9-30-95***	***2345***		***2808***	***83.5***						
Sub Nts 9½s 2002	[12]sep15	**NR**				BE	100	....	....	....	....	....	27.7		'92	100½	99½	100½	9.45	9.39
Rouse Co	***38***	***0.90***	***1.01***	***1.06***		***Dc***	***26.20***			***9-30-95***	***2560***		***2614***	***97.9***						
Nts 8½s 2003	Jj15	**BBB**			X	R	[13]100	....	....	....	....	....	120	G1	'93	107½	97⅝	104⅜	8.14	7.68
Rowan Cos	***49e***	***d1.79***	***0.47***	***0.18***		***Dc***	***88.50***	***265.0***	***68.20***	***9-30-95***	***248.0***		***670.0***	***37.2***						
• Sr Nts 11⅞s 2001	jD	B+	4/94	BB−	Y	R	106	(12-1-96)	....	....	....	....	200	M2	'91	109	102⅝	s108	11.00	10.05
Royal Caribbean Cruises	***40g***	***1.74***	***2.96***	***4.28***		***Dc***	***34.80***	***109.0***	***313.0***	***6-30-95***	***★969.0***		***1889***	***51.6***						
Sr Nts 7⅛s 2002	mS18	**BBB−**			X	BE	NC	....	....	....	....	....	150	M2	'95	102¼	98¾	102¼	6.97	6.70
Sr Nts 8⅛s 2004	jJ28	**BBB−**			X	BE	NC	....	....	....	....	....	125	M2	'94	108⅛	95	108⅛	7.51	6.86
Sr Nts 8¼s 2005	Ao	**BBB−**			X	BE	NC	....	....	....	....	....	150	G1	'95	107⅞	98¾	107⅞	7.65	7.07
Sr Sub[11]Nts[14] 11⅜s 2002	$Mn15	**BB+**	3/94	BB−	Y	R	104.95	(5-15-97)	....	....	....	....	126	M2	'92	110½	105¾	109½	10.39	9.36
[15]Royal Crown Corp[16]	***11e***	***[17]0.90***	***[18]0.68***	***1.15***		***Dc***	***46.60***	***363.0***	***200.0***	***9-30-95***	***754.0***		***855.0***	***93.3***						
Sr Sec Nts[11] 9¾s 2000	fA	**B+**			Y	R	102.786	(8-1-98)	....	....	[19]Z110	7-31-96	275	D6	'93	98¼	80	80	12.19	16.07
Ryder System	***7***	***2.13***	***2.68***	***2.80***		***Dc***	***96.60***	***805.0***	***1114***	***9-30-95***	***2318***		***3684***	***67.5***						
Deb 6.95s 2025	jD	**A−**			X	BE	[20]Z100	....	....	....	....	....	150	M6	'95	99⅜	99¼	99⅜	6.99	7.00
• Ext'd[21]Nts[22]E 8¾s '96	[23]jJ	**A−**	1/90	A	X	R	[24]100	....	....	....	....	....	15.5	S1	'85	105	99½	100	8.75	8.75
• Bonds G 9s 2016	Mn15	**A−**	1/90	A	X	R	103	(5-15-06)	100	(5-15-07)	....	....	100	S1	'86	109⅞	99¾	110⅝	8.14	7.94
• Bonds H 8⅜s 2017	Fa15	**A−**	1/90	A	X	R	104.1875	(2-15-97)	100	(2-15-98)	....	....	125	S1	'87	105	94½	108¾	7.70	7.54
• Bonds J 8¾s 2017	Ms15	**A−**	1/90	A	X	R	104.175	(3-15-97)	100	(3-15-98)	....	....	100	S1	'87	106¼	96	104⅞	8.34	8.26
• Bonds K 9⅞s 2017	Mn15	**A−**	1/90	A	X	R	101.925	(5-15-07)	100	(5-15-08)	....	....	100	S1	'87	119	119	118⅛	8.36	8.08
Nts N 9¼s 2001	Mn15	**A−**			X	BE	NC	....	....	....	....	....	100	S1	'91	114⅝	104	114⅝	8.07	6.02
M-T Nts '9' 7.05s '98	[25]fa15	**A−**			X	BE	NC	....	....	....	....	....	100	S1	'94	103⅛	95⅞	103⅛	6.84	5.59
M-T Nts '9' 6.92s '98	[26]fa15	**A−**			X	BE	NC	....	....	....	....	....	36.9	M2	'94	102⅞	95½	102⅞	6.73	5.58
M-T Nts '9' 7.19s '98	[27]fa15	**A−**			X	BE	NC	....	....	....	....	....	10.0	S1	'94	103⅝	96¼	103⅝	6.94	5.57
M-T Nts '9' 7.19s '98	[28]fa15	**A−**			X	BE	NC	....	....	....	....	....	10.0	S1	'94	103⅝	96⅛	103⅝	6.94	5.57
M-T Nts '9' 7.19s '98	[28]fa15	**A−**			X	BE	NC	....	....	....	....	....	25.0	M2	'94	103⅝	96⅛	103⅝	6.94	5.57
M-T Nts '9' 7.03s '99	[29]fa15	**A−**			X	BE	NC	....	....	....	....	....	15.0	M2	'94	103⅞	94½	103⅞	6.77	5.72
M-T Nts '9' 7.33s '99	[30]fa15	**A−**			X	BE	NC	....	....	....	....	....	10.0	M5	'94	104⅞	95⅜	104⅞	6.99	5.74

Uniform Footnote Explanations-See Page 260. Other: [1] Subsid of Rogers Communications. [2] Gtd by Rogers Cantel Inc. [3] Co may be req to red at 101 for a Chge in Ctrl. [4] In whole for certain tax law chge. [5] Co must offer repurch at 101 on Chge of Ctrl. [6] (HRO)For Trigger Event at 100. [7] Mand pyt 2.5% of issued on int dates fr10-15-00. [8] Gtd by Rohm&Haas Co. [9] (HRO)At 100 for a Trigger Event. [10] Red in whole if 80% Nts put. [11] (HRO)On Chge of Ctrl at 101. [12] Due 8-1-02:int pd monthly. [13] Plus Make-Whole Premium. [14] Co may red in whole,spl red price,for tax chge. [15] Subsid & data of Triarc Cos. [16] Now RC/Arby's. [17] Fiscal Apr'92 & prior. [18] 8 Mo Dec'93. [19] Max $90.75M red w/proceeds of Pub Eq Off'g. [20] Greater of 100 or amt based on formula. [21] (HRO)On 7-1-96 at 100,aft as defined. [22] Int thru 6-30-96,adj aft as defined. [23] Due 7-1-2000. [24] On 7-1-96,aft as defined. [25] Due 4-27-98. [26] Due 4-29-98. [27] Due 6-1-98. [28] Due 6-2-98. [29] Due 4-19-99. [30] Due 6-1-99.

Title-Industry Code & Co. Finances (In Italics) / Individual Issue Statistics / Exchange	Ind / Interest Dates	*Fixed Charge Coverage 1992* / S&P Debt Rating	*1993* / Date of Last Rating Change	*1994* / Prior Rating	Eligible	*Year End* / Bond Form	*Million $ Cash & Equiv.* / Redemption Provisions: Regular Price	*Curr. Assets* / Regular (Begins) Thru	*Curr. Liab.* / Sinking Fund Price	*Balance Sheet Date* / Sinking Fund (Begins) Thru	*L. Term Debt (Mil $)* / Refund/Other Restriction Price	Refund/Other Restriction (Begins) Thru	*Capital-ization (Mil $)* / Outst'g (Mil $)	*Total Debt % Capital* / Underwriting Firm	Underwriting Year	Price Range 1995 High	Price Range 1995 Low	Mo. End Price Sale(s) or Bid	Curr. Yield	Yield to Mat.
***Ryder System** (Cont.)*																				
M-T Nts '9' 7.47s '99	[1]fa15	**A–**			X	BE	NC	....	....	....	....	....	6.00	S1	'94	105½	95¾	105½	7.08	5.75
M-T Nts '9' 7.47s '99	[1]fa15	**A–**			X	BE	NC	....	....	....	....	....	8.00		'94	105½	95¾	105½	7.08	5.75
M-T Nts '9' 7.49s '99	[1]fa15	**A–**			X	BE	NC	....	....	....	....	....	12.0	M2	'94	105½	95⅞	105½	7.10	5.77
M-T Nts '9 7.52s '99	[1]fa15	**A–**			X	BE	NC	....	....	....	....	....	6.00	S1	'94	105⅝	96	105⅝	7.12	5.76
M-T Nts '12' 7.30s 2000	Mn	**A–**			X	BE	NC	....	....	....	....	....	35.0	S1	'95	105½	100	105½	6.92	5.84
M-T Nts '12' 7.34s 2000	mN	**A–**			X	BE	NC	....	....	....	....	....	26.0	S1	'95	106	100	106	6.92	5.89
Rykoff-Sexton Inc.	***26g***	*Δ0.98*	*Δ1.80*	*Δ2.40*		***Ap***	*16.90*	*370.0*	*244.0*	*10-28-95*	*133.0*		*420.0*	*49.0*						
Sr[2]Sub Nts 8⅞s 2003	mN	**BB–**			Y	R	104.44	(11-1-98)	....	....	[3]Z100	11-1-98	130	M2	'93	101	91½	99½	8.92	8.96
Ryland Group	***13h***	*1.18*	*0.98*	*1.36*		***Dc***	*65.70*			*9-30-95*	*811.0*		*1512*	*78.5*						
Sr Sub Nts[4] 10½s 2002	jJ15	**BB–**	11/93	BB+	Y	R	105.25	(7-15-97)	....	....	....	....	100	K2	'92	100½	88	98½	10.66	10.82
Sr Sub Nts[2] 9⅝s 2004	jD	**BB–**			Y	R	100	(12-1-00)	....	....	....	....	100	D4	'93	98½	82	96¼	10.00	10.30
Rymer Foods	***26e***	*0.56*	*0.75*	*1.64*		***Oc***		*34.90*	*5.54*	*7-29-95*	*34.60*		*54.00*	*64.4*						
Sr([5]PIK)Nts 11s 2000	jD15	**NR**				R	100	....	....	....	....	....	20.4	Reorg	'93	94	75	75	14.67	19.00
SAFECO Corp.	***35c***	*7.06*	*10.20*	*6.39*		***Dc***				*9-30-95*	*1087*		*4698*	*23.1*						
Nts 7⅞s 2005	Ao	**AA**			X	BE	100	(4-1-03)	....	....	....	....	200	G1	'95	109⅝	99¼	109⅝	7.18	6.47
Safety-Kleen Corp	***53***	*6.91*	*6.45*	*6.58*		***Dc***	*37.60*	*218.0*	*175.0*	*9-9-95*	*298.0*		*720.0*	*41.5*						
Nts[6] 9¼s '99	mS15	**BBB+**	3/94	A	X	R	NC	....	....	....	....	....	100	A2	'89	110⅝	102⅛	110⅝	8.36	6.01
Safeway Inc.	***59c***	*1.55*	*1.69*	*2.79*		***Dc***	*48.70*	*1430*	*1800*	*9-9-95*	*1940*		*2864*	*73.5*						
• Sr Sec Deb[7] 9.30s 2007	Fa	**BBB–**	3/95	BB+	X	R	NC	....	....	....	[8]Z100	....	100	S1	'92	116¼	100⅛	111	8.38	7.80
• Sr Nts 10s 2002	mN	**BBB–**	5/95	BB+	X	BE	NC	....	....	....	....	....	74.0	S1	'92	117	108½	115	8.70	7.18
• Sr Sub Deb 9.65s 2004	Jj15	**BB+**	3/95	BB–	Y	R	NC	....	....	....	....	....	300	G1	'92	113⅞	100⅞	s113	8.54	7.47
• Sr Sub Deb 9⅞s 2007	Ms15	**BB+**	3/95	BB–	Y	R	NC	....	....	....	....	....	150	G1	'92	117	101¾	s116⅜	8.49	7.67
• Sr Sub Nts 9.35s '99	Ms15	**BB+**	3/95	BB–	Y	R	NC	....	....	....	....	....	250	G1	'92	108	101	107¼	8.72	6.79
• Sr Sub Nts 10s 2001	jD	**BB+**	3/95	BB–	Y	R	NC	....	....	....	....	....	300	G1	'91	114	103⅛	s113⅛	8.84	7.23
St Louis-San Fran Ry	***55***	***Merged into Burlington No'n RR,see***																		
• 1st A 4s '97	Jj	**BBB**	7/95	BBB+	X	CR	100	....	100	....	....	....	22.0	Reorg	'46	97⅛	92	97⅛	4.12	7.01
• Inc Deb A 5s 2006	[9]mn	**NR**	7/95	BBB		CR	100	....	100	....	....	....	8.00	E1	'56	81⅞	69½	80½	....	Flat
St Paul Cos	***35c***	*1.92*	*13.68*	*15.23*		***Dc***				*9-30-95*	*620.0*		*4116*	*15.1*						
Nts 9⅜s '97	Jd15	**AA**	4/95	AA–	X	R	NC	....	....	....	....	....	100	G1	'90	105⅞	102½	105¼	8.91	5.58
Salomon Inc	***62***	*1.24*	*1.32*	*0.83*		***Dc***				*9-30-95*	*15857*		*19856*	*79.9*						
• SF Deb[10] 11⅝s 2015	fA	**BBB**	8/95	BBB+	X	R	105.50	7-31-96	100	(8-1-96)	....	....	12.7	S1	'85	108	101	s106	10.97	10.88
Sr Nts 7s '98	Jj20	**BBB**	8/95	BBB+	X	BE	NC	....	....	....	....	....	150	S1	'93	101¼	94⅝	101¼	6.91	6.34
Sr Nts 9⅜s '98	Ao15	**BBB**	8/95	BBB+	X	BE	NC	....	....	....	....	....	126	S1	'91	106½	100⅝	106¼	8.82	6.39
Sr Nts 6.70s '98	jD	**BBB**			X	BE	NC	....	....	....	....	....	250	S1	'95	100⅝	100	100⅝	6.66	6.46
Sr Nts 7⅛s '99	fA	**BBB**	8/95	BBB+	X	BE	NC	....	....	....	....	....	250	S1	'92	101⅞	92⅜	101⅞	6.99	6.53
Sr Nts 7¼s 2000	Jj15	**BBB**	8/95	BBB+	X	BE	NC	....	....	....	....	....	150	S1	'93	102¼	92¼	102¼	7.09	6.61
Sr Nts 7¾s 2000	Mn15	**BBB**	8/95	BBB+	X	BE	NC	....	....	....	....	....	150	S1	'95	104¼	99⅝	104¼	7.43	6.61
Sr Nts 9¼s 2001	Mn	**BBB**	8/95	BBB+	X	BE	NC	....	....	....	....	....	61.6	S1	'91	111⅛	99⅝	111⅛	8.32	6.73
Sr Nts 7½s 2003	Fa	**BBB**	8/95	BBB+	X	BE	NC	....	....	....	....	....	200	S1	'93	102¾	89½	102¾	7.30	7.00
Sr Nts 7s 2003	Jd15	**BBB**	8/95	BBB+	X	BE	NC	....	....	....	....	....	150	S1	'93	99⅞	86¼	99⅞	7.01	7.02
Sr Nts 6¾s 2003	fA15	**BBB**	8/95	BBB+	X	BE	NC	....	....	....	....	....	200	S1	'93	98⅜	84½	98⅜	6.86	7.03
Sr Nts 6⅞s 2003	jD15	**BBB**	8/95	BBB+	X	BE	NC	....	....	....	....	....	150	S1	'93	98⅞	84⅝	98⅞	6.95	7.06
Sr Nts 6¾s 2006	Jj15	**BBB**	8/95	BBB+	X	BE	NC	....	....	....	....	....	150	S1	'94	97½	81½	97½	6.92	7.10
F/R[11]M-T Nts 'D' 6.975s '96	QFeb14	**BBB**	8/95	BBB+	X	BE	NC	....	....	....	....	....	63.5	S1	'95	100⅛	99⅞	100⅛	6.97	....
M-T Nts 'D' 7.40s '96	[12]ms15	**BBB**	8/95	BBB+	X	BE	NC	....	....	....	....	....	150	S1	'95	100½	100	100⅜	7.37	5.75
M-T Nts 'D' 6.22s '96	[13]ms15	**BBB**	8/95	BBB+	X	BE	NC	....	....	....	....	....	29.5	S1	'95	100	99¼	100	6.22	6.22

Uniform Footnote Explanations-See Page 260. Other: [1] Due 7-29-99. [2] (HRO)On Chge of Ctrl at 101. [3] On Chge of Ctrl. [4] Co must offer repurch at 101 on Chge of Ctrl. [5] Int may be pd in add'l notes to 6-15-97. [6] (HRO)At 100 for Designated Event&Rat'g Decline. [7] (HRO)At 100 for certain chge in collateral. [8] In whole,for certain chge in collateral. [9] Due 1-1-06. [10] Was Phibro-Salomon. [11] Int to 8-15-95,adj qtrly (3 Mo LIBOR&0.85%). [12] Due 3-28-96. [13] Due 7-3-96.

Title-Industry Code & Co. Finances (In Italics) / Individual Issue Statistics (Exchange)	Ind / Interest Dates	Fixed Charge Coverage 1992 / S&P Debt Rating	1993 / Date of Last Rating Change	1994 / Prior Rating	Eligible	Year End / Bond Form	Million $ Cash & Equiv. / Redemption Provisions Regular Price	Curr. Assets / Regular (Begins) Thru	Curr. Liab. / Sinking Fund Price	Balance Sheet Date / Sinking Fund (Begins) Thru	L. Term Debt (Mil $) / Refund/Other Restriction Price	Refund/Other Restriction (Begins) Thru	Capital-ization (Mil $) / Outst'g (Mil $)	Total Debt % Capital / Underwriting Firm	Underwriting Year	Price Range 1995 High	Price Range 1995 Low	Mo. End Price Sale(s) or Bid	Curr. Yield	Yield to Mat.
***Salomon Inc** (Cont.)*																				
F/R[1]M-T Nts 'D' 7s '97	[2]QFeb13	BBB	8/95	BBB+	X	BE	NC	....	....	....	....	....	10.0	S1	'95	100	99⅝	100	7.00	....
F/R[3]M-T Nts 'D' 6.90s '97	[4]	BBB	8/95	BBB+	X	BE	NC	....	....	....	....	....	25.0	S1	'95	100⅛	99½	100⅛	6.89	....
M-T Nts 'D' 8.55s '97	[5]ms15	BBB	8/95	BBB+	X	BE	NC	....	....	....	....	....	30.0	S1	'95	102¾	99⅞	102½	8.34	6.22
M-T Nts 'D' 8⅝s '97	[5]ms15	BBB	8/95	BBB+	X	BE	NC	....	....	....	....	....	26.5	S1	'95	102⅞	100	102⅝	8.40	6.18
F/R[6]M-T Nts 'D' 6.80s '97	[7]	BBB	8/95	BBB+	X	BE	NC	....	....	....	....	....	25.0	S1	'95	100⅛	99⅝	100⅛	6.79	....
M-T Nts 'D' 8.53s '97	[8]ms15	BBB	8/95	BBB+	X	BE	NC	....	....	....	....	....	35.0	S1	'95	102¾	100	102½	8.32	6.21
M-T Nts 'D' 8.36s '97	[9]ms15	BBB	8/95	BBB+	X	BE	NC	....	....	....	....	....	31.0	S1	'95	102½	100	102⅜	8.17	6.20
M-T Nts 'D' 8s '97	[10]ms15	BBB	8/95	BBB+	X	BE	NC	....	....	....	....	....	26.7	S1	'95	102⅛	100	102⅛	7.83	6.19
M-T Nts 'D' 7.73s '97	[11]ms15	BBB	8/95	BBB+	X	BE	NC	....	....	....	....	....	29.0	S1	'95	102⅝	100	102⅝	7.53	6.23
M-T Nts 'D' 8.91s '98	[12]ms15	BBB	8/95	BBB+	X	BE	NC	....	....	....	....	....	23.0	S1	'95	105¼	100	105¼	8.47	6.23
M-T Nts 'D' 8.64s '98	[13]ms15	BBB	8/95	BBB+	X	BE	NC	....	....	....	....	....	62.0	S1	'95	104¾	100	104¾	8.25	6.25
M-T Nts 'D' 8.69s '99	[14]ms15	BBB	8/95	BBB+	X	BE	NC	....	....	....	....	....	25.0	S1	'95	106½	100	106½	8.16	6.39
M-T Nts 'D' 7.76s '98	[15]ms15	BBB	8/95	BBB+	X	BE	NC	....	....	....	....	....	29.0	S1	'95	103¼	100	103¼	7.52	6.26
F/R[16]M-T Nts 'D' 6¾s '99	[17]Qjun15	BBB	8/95	BBB+	X	BE	NC	....	....	....	....	....	200	S1	'94	100⅛	99	100	6.75	....
M-T Nts 'D' 9.15s 2001	[18]ms15	BBB	8/95	BBB+	X	BE	NC	....	....	....	....	....	35.0	S1	'95	110½	100	110½	8.28	6.69
Nts[19]'G' 8s 2010	[20]Nov15	BBB			X	BE	*100	(11-15-96)	....	....	....	....	31.0	S1	'95	103⅛	100	103⅛	7.76	7.64
San Diego Gas & Electric	*75*	*4.20*	*4.27*	*4.23*		*Dc*	*140.0*	*470.0*	*691.0*	*9-30-95*	*1396*		*3181*	*48.9*						
1st I 5½s '97	Ms	A+	4/84	A–	X	R	100.25	2-29-96	....	....	Z100.25	2-29-96	25.0	F1	'67	99⅞	95	99⅞	5.51	5.60
1st JJ 9⅝s 2020	Ao15	A+			X	R	104.04	(4-15-00)	....	....	....	....	100	M2	'90	115⅞	103¼	114⅝	8.40	8.22
1st LL 8½s 2022	Ao	A+			X	BE	103.66	(4-1-02)	....	....	Z100	....	60.0	D6	'92	113⅛	96⅛	113⅛	7.51	7.36
1st MM 7⅝s 2002	Jd15	A+			X	BE	NC	....	....	....	....	....	80.0	S1	'92	107½	95¼	107½	7.09	6.20
Santa Fe Energy Res	*49a*	*0.90*	*d1.53*	....		*Dc*	*69.40*	*152.0*	*110.0*	*9-30-94*	*350.0*		*856.0*	*41.4*						
Sr Sub Deb[21] 11s 2004	Mn15	BB–	10/95	B	Y	R	104.13	(5-15-99)	....	....	....	....	100	S1	'94	109½	100¼	109½	10.05	9.34
Santa Fe Hotel	*40j*	*Mgr into Sahara Gaming,see Hacienda Res*																		
xw 1st[22] 11s 2000	jD15	B–			Y	R	106.23	(12-15-97)	....	....	[23]Z110	12-14-97	116	D6	'94	101	63	63	17.46	24.20
Santa Fe[24]Pacific Corp	*55*	*0.44*	*2.87*	*3.32*		*Dc*	*30.10*	*306.0*	*776.0*	*6-30-95*	*1885*		*2578*	*78.9*						
Nts 8⅜s 2001	mN	BBB			X	BE	NC	....	....	....	....	....	100	M5	'94	109¾	99⅛	109¾	7.63	6.35
Nts 8⅝s 2004	mN	BBB			X	BE	NC	....	....	....	....	....	100	M5	'94	114	100⅜	114	7.57	6.51
Santa Fe Pacific Gold	*45e*	*2.24*	*4.31*	*9.75*		*Dc*	*65.20*	*200.0*	*65.50*	*9-30-95*	*200.0*		*747.0*	*26.8*						
Sr Deb 8⅜s 2005	jJ	BB+			Y	BE	NC	....	....	....	....	....	200	M5	'95	103	99	103	8.13	7.92
Sara Lee[25]	*26*	*△7.68*	*△6.96*	*△6.02*		*Je*	*222.0*	*5287*	*4913*	*9-30-95*	*1873*		*7878*	*37.8*						
SF Deb 8¾s 2016	Mn15	AA–	12/88	AA	X	R	104.81	5-14-96	100	(5-15-97)	®104.38	5-14-96	150	M6	'86	107⅛	99⅝	105	8.33	8.24
Savannah Electric&Power[26]	*72a*	*4.01*	*4.07*	*3.76*		*Dc*	*2.76*	*53.10*	*38.50*	*6-30-95*	*165.0*		*361.0*	*46.0*						
1st 6⅜s 2003	jJ	A+	3/95	A	X	R	101.73	(7-1-98)	Z100	....	....	....	20.0	S1	'93	100	88¼	100	6.38	6.37
1st 9⅜s 2021	jJ	A+	3/95	A	X	R	107.10	6-30-96	Z100	....	®106.66	6-30-96	29.7	L3	'91	108⅞	101⅞	107¼	8.74	8.67
1st 8.30s 2022	jJ	A+	3/95	A	X	R	106	6-30-96	Z100	....	®105.29	6-30-97	30.0	G1	'92	106⅝	93⅞	106⅛	7.82	7.75
1st 7.40s 2023	jJ	A+	3/95	A	X	R	105.34	6-30-96	Z100	....	®104.45	6-30-98	25.0	L3	'93	100⅛	85⅞	100⅛	7.39	7.39
1st 7⅞s 2025	Mn	A+			X	R	105.43	(5-1-00)	Z100	(5-1-00)	....	....	15.0	D6	'95	107⅜	97⅜	107⅜	7.33	7.26
SC Int'l Services, Inc	*27a*	*n/a*	*n/a*	*p0.72*		*Dc*				*6-30-95*	*★402.0*		*462.0*	*87.1*						
Sr Sub[27]Nts 13s 2005	aO	B			Y	R	105.778	(10-1-00)	....	....	[28]Z113	9-30-96	125	B9	'95	110½	100	110½	11.76	11.20
SCE Capital Co	*25*	*Gtd by Southern Calif Edison,see*																		
Nts[29] 7⅜s 2003	jD15	A	11/92	AA–	X	R	101.36	(12-15-96)	....	....	....	....	[30]200	L3	'91	104¼	91⅛	103	7.16	6.88
Scherer (R.P.) Corp	*21*	*3.61*	*3.97*	*7.66*		*Mr*	*29.20*	*219.0*	*101.0*	*9-30-95*	*192.0*		*493.0*	*40.6*						
• Sr Nts 6¾s 2004	Fa	BBB–			X	BE	NC	....	....	....	....	....	100	L3	'94	No Sale		99⅛	6.81	6.89
Schuller Int'l Group[31]	*13g*	*10.00*	*11.67*	*8.34*		*Dc*	*125.0*	*452.0*	*277.0*	*9-30-95*	*409.0*		*631.0*	*68.8*						
• Sr Nts[32] 10⅞s 2004	jD15	BB–			Y	R	105.488	12-14-99	....	....	[33]Z110	12-11-97	400	G1	'94	109	102	105	10.36	10.02

Uniform Footnote Explanations-See Page 260. Other: [1] Int thru 9-15-95,adj qtrly(3 Mo LIBOR&1.0%). [2] Int pd qtrly, 3rd Wed ea Mar, etc. [3] Int to 9-15-95,adj qtrly(3 Mo LIBOR&0.90%). [4] Due 2-14-97:Int pd qtrly 3rd Wed ea Mar, etc. [5] Due 2-17-97. [6] Int to 9-15-95,adj qtrly(3 Mo LIBOR&0.80%). [7] Due 2-18-97:Int pd qtrly 3rd Wed ea Mar, etc. [8] Due 2-18-97. [9] Due 2-28-97. [10] Due 3-28-97. [11] Due 11-17-97. [12] Due 2-16-98. [13] Due 2-27-98. [14] Due 3-1-99. [15] Due 5-11-98. [16] Int thru 9-15-95,adj qtrly(3 Mo LIBOR&0.75%). [17] Due 5-18-99: Int pd qtrly 3rd Wed ea Jun, etc. [18] Due 2-13-01. [19] Death redemp benefit,ltd,as defined. [20] Int pd monthly. [21] (HRO)On Chge of Ctrl & Rat'g Decline at 101. [22] Co must offer repurch,at 101,on Chge of Ctrl. [23] Max $20M red w/proceeds of Pub Eq Off'g. [24] Subsid of Burlington No'n Santa Fe. [25] Was Consolidated Foods. [26] Subsid of Southern Co. [27] (HRO)On Chge of Ctrl at 101. [28] Max $43.75M red w/proceeds of Pub Eq Off'gs. [29] Gtd by Southern Calif Edison. [30] Incl disc. [31] Subsid of Manville Corp. [32] Co must offer repurch at 100 on Chge of Ctrl. [33] Max $132M red w/proceeds of Pub Equity Off'g.

Title-Industry Code & *Co. Finances (In Italics)* / Individual Issue Statistics (Exchange)	Ind / Interest Dates	*1992* / S&P Debt Rating	*1993* / Date of Last Rating Change	Prior Rating	*1994* / Eligible	*Year End* / Bond Form	*Cash & Equiv.* / Regular Price	*Curr. Assets* / Regular (Begins) Thru	*Curr. Liab.* / Sinking Fund Price	*Balance Sheet Date* / Sinking Fund (Begins) Thru	*L. Term Debt (Mil $)* / Refund/Other Restriction Price	Refund/Other Restriction (Begins) Thru	*Capital-ization (Mil $)* / Outst'g (Mil $)	*Total Debt % Capital* / Underwriting Firm	Underwriting Year	Price Range 1995 High	Price Range 1995 Low	Mo. End Price Sale(s) or Bid	Curr. Yield	Yield to Mat.
SCI Holdings	*12c*	*Merged into Storer Commun, See*																		
Scotia Pacific Holding Co[1]	*13d*	*n/a*	*[2]3.56*		*3.74*	*Dc*	*5.52*	*19.90*	*21.00*	*9-30-95*	*336.0*		*279.0*	*125.0*						
Timber Coll (Amort)[3]Nts[4] 7.95s 2015	jJ20	BBB			X	R	[5]Z100	....	....	....	....	....	364	S1	'93	101⅝	92¾	101⅜	7.84	....
Scotsman Group	*25c*	*n/a*	*0.99*		*1.14*	*Dc*	*0.72*			*9-30-95*	*222.0*		*283.0*	*78.4*						
Sr[6]Sec Nts[7] 9½s 2000	jD15	BB–			Y	R	103.167	(12-15-97)	Z107	12-14-96	[8]Z106.333	12-14-96	165	B8	'93	100	91½	100	9.50	9.50
Scott Cable Commun	*12a*	....	....		....	*Mr*	*No Recent Fin'ls*													
Sub Deb 12¼s 2001	Ao15	NR	4/89	CCC		R	100	4-14-96	100	(4-15-96)	....	....	50.0	R6	'86	75½	64½	65½	18.70	24.09
Scott Paper Co[9]	*33*	*1.98*	*d0.72*		*3.90*	*Dc*	*210.0*	*1546*	*954.0*	*7-1-95*	*1210*		*3190*	*39.5*						
Deb 8⅞s '98	Ms	A–	11/94	BBB	X	R	NC	....	....	....	....	....	[10]41.8	S1	'86	107	101⅞	106⅝	8.32	5.59
Deb 10s 2002	Ms	A–	11/94	BBB	X	R	NC	....	....	....	....	....	[10]52.8	G1	'90	120⅜	108¾	120⅜	8.31	6.00
Deb 8.30s 2004	Ms15	A–	11/94	BBB	X	R	NC	....	....	....	....	....	63.2	G1	'92	113¾	101⅞	113¾	7.30	6.14
Deb 10s 2005	Ms15	A–	11/94	BBB	X	R	NC	....	....	....	....	....	51.1	G1	'90	126¾	110⅞	126¾	7.89	6.15
Deb 8.80s 2022	Mn15	A–	11/94	BBB	X	R	104.106	(5-15-02)	....	....	....	....	11.4	G1	'92	115⅛	103⅝	115	7.65	7.49
Deb 7s 2023	fA15	A–	11/94	BBB	X	BE	102.116	(8-15-03)	....	....	....	....	200	S1	'93	99⅞	80¼	99⅞	7.01	7.01
Nts 9⅜s '97	aO	A–	11/94	BBB	X	R	NC	....	....	....	....	....	200	S1	'90	107⅞	103¾	107	9.11	5.50
Scotts Co[11]	*14*	*2.64*	*5.18*		*3.40*	*Sp*	*10.70*	*329.0*	*135.0*	*7-1-95*	*243.0*		*628.0*	*38.9*						
• Sr Sub[12]Nts 9⅞s 2004	fA	BB+			Y	BE	104.9375	(8-1-99)	....	....	....	....	100	G1	'94	108	102	106½	9.27	8.78
[13]Scripps Howard, Inc	*54c*	*4.40*	*7.00*		*13.42*	*Dc*	*52.60*	*354.0*	*262.0*	*9-30-95*	*63.50*		*1272*	*8.7*						
Nts 7⅜s '98	jD15	A			X	BE	NC	....	....	....	....	....	61.2	D4	'91	104¼	96⅛	104¼	7.07	5.79
Sea Containers Ltd[14]	*16b*	*1.74*	*1.65*		*1.40*	*Dc*	*61.90*			*9-30-95*	*553.0*		*952.0*	*58.1*						
• Sr[7]Nts[15] 9½s 2003	jJ	BB–			Y	R	104.75	(7-1-98)	....	....	....	....	100	Exch.	'93	102½	88⅞	100	9.50	9.50
• Sr Sub[16]Deb[15] 12½s 2004	jD	BB–			Y	R	106.25	(12-1-99)	....	....	....	....	100	L1	'92	112	101	107¾	11.60	11.11
• Sr Sub[15]Deb[12]'B' 12½s 2004	jD	BB–			Y	R	106.25	(12-1-99)	....	....	....	....	25.0	Exch.	'93	110	104	108¼	11.55	11.02
Seagram(Jos.E.)& Sons	*11b*	*Gtd by Seagram Co. Ltd,see*																		
Gtd[17]Deb 7s 2008	Ao15	A			X	BE	NC	....	....	....	....	....	200	G1	'93	104¾	87	104¾	6.68	6.43
Gtd[17]Deb 8⅜s 2007	Fa15	A	3/88	A+	X	R	NC	....	....	....	....	....	200	G1	'87	114⅞	98⅛	114⅞	7.29	6.48
Gtd[17]Deb 8⅞s 2011	mS15	A			X	R	NC	....	....	....	....	....	225	G1	'91	120¼	100¾	120¼	7.38	6.76
Gtd[17]Deb[18] 9.65s 2018	fA15	A			X	R	NC	....	....	....	....	....	250	G1	'88	134⅞	110⅞	134⅞	7.15	6.65
Gtd[17]Deb 9s 2021	fA15	A			X	R	NC	....	....	....	....	....	200	G1	'91	123⅜	101⅝	123⅜	7.29	7.02
Gtd[17]Nts 9¾s 2000	Jd15	A			X	R	100	(6-15-96)	....	....	....	....	250	G1	'88	103½	102	102	9.56	9.19
Seagram Co. Ltd[19]	*11b*	*3.21*	*3.09*		*2.63*	*Ja*	*231.0*	*5834*	*3538*	*7-31-95*	*2955*		*13545*	*30.1*						
Deb 6½s 2003	aO	A			X	BE	NC	....	....	....	....	....	200	G1	'93	101⅞	88	101⅞	6.38	6.17
Deb 8.35s 2006	mN15	A			X	BE	NC	....	....	....	....	....	200	G1	'91	115¼	98¼	115¼	7.25	6.38
Deb 8.35s 2022	Jj15	A			X	BE	NC	....	....	....	....	....	200	G1	'92	116¼	95⅝	116¼	7.18	6.99
Deb 6⅞s 2023	mS	A			X	BE	NC	....	....	....	....	....	200	G1	'93	98⅛	80	98⅛	7.01	7.03
Seagull Energy	*73a*	*1.33*	*2.10*		*1.02*	*Dc*	*12.50*	*93.40*	*87.00*	*9-30-95*	*538.0*		*983.0*	*54.9*						
Sr Nts[7] 7⅞s 2003	fA	BB+			Y	R	NC	....	....	....	....	....	100	D4	'93	100⅛	86¼	100⅛	7.87	7.85
Sr Sub Nts[7] 8⅝s 2005	fA	BB–			Y	R	102.59	(8-1-00)	....	....	....	....	150	D4	'93	100½	83¾	100½	8.58	8.55
Sealy Corp	*31b*	*n/a*	*n/a*		*2.68*	*Nv*	*2.26*	*151.0*	*104.0*	*8-31-95*	*292.0*		*632.0*	*47.9*						
Sr Sub Nts[7] 9½s 2003	Mn	B+			Y	R	104.75	(5-1-98)	....	....	[20]Z107.125	4-30-96	200	F1	'93	101½	94	101½	9.36	9.21
Seariver Maritime	*64*	*Subsid of Exxon Corp,see Exxon Capital*																		
• Gtd V/R[21]Debt[22]Sec[23] 2011	QOct	AAA			X	R	Z100	....	100	(10-1-97)	....	....	150	S1	'86	No Sale		90	....	Flat
Gtd[24]Defrd Int Deb 2012	[25]	AAA			X	R	[26]100	....	....	....	....	....	[27]771	Co.	'82	35⅞	23⅞	35⅞	....	Flat
Sears Roebuck Acceptance	*25*	*1.34*	*1.26*		*1.29*	*Dc*	*231.0*			*9-30-95*	*1909*		*3134*	*60.9*						
Nts 6½s 2000	Jd15	BBB			X	R	NC	....	....	....	....	....	250	M6	'95	102	97⅞	102	6.37	5.98
• Nts 6¾s 2005	mS15	BBB			X	R	NC	....	....	....	....	....	250	G1	'95	101¼	98⅝	100¾	6.70	6.64
M-T Nts 'I' 6.17s '99	[28]mn15	BBB			X	BE	NC	....	....	....	....	....	40.0	G1	'95	101¼	100	101¼	6.09	5.72

Uniform Footnote Explanations-See Page 260. Other: [1] Subsid of Pacific Lumber Co. [2] 9 Mos Dec,'93. [3] Rated maturity:7-20-15(all outstg princ must be pd). [4] Scheduled Maturity:7-20-09(if Amort pyts made on scheduled). [5] In whole,plus premium,etc. [6] To 12-15-96,Co may red in whole on Chge of Ctrl. [7] (HRO)On Chge of Ctrl at 101. [8] Max $49.5M red w/proceeds of Cap Stk Off'g. [9] Subsid of Kimberly-Clark. [10] Defeased,fds deposited w/trustee. [11] Was Scotts Co./Scott(O.M.)& Sons. [12] Co must offer repurch at 101 on Chge of Ctrl. [13] Gtd by & data of Scripps(E.W.)Co. [14] See Orient Express Hotels. [15] Co may red in whole at 100 for certain tax chge. [16] Co must offer repurch at 101 on Chge in Ctrl. [17] Gtd by Seagram Co Ltd. [18] (HRO)On 8-15-03 at 100. [19] See Seagram (Jos.E.)& Sons. [20] Max $60M w/proceeds of Pub Equity Off'gs. [21] (HRO)At 100, as defined. [22] Int adj monthly. [23] Issued in min denom $5T. [24] At mat:$270 prin&$730 defrd int to be pd. [25] Due 9-1-12. [26] Percent of Accreted Value. [27] Incl disc. [28] Due 1-29-99.

Title-Industry Code & Co. Finances (In Italics) / Individual Issue Statistics / Exchange	Ind / Interest Dates	Fixed Charge Coverage 1992 / S&P Debt Rating	1993 / Date of Last Rating Change	1994 / Prior Rating	Eligible	Year End / Bond Form	Cash & Equiv. / Regular Price	Curr. Assets / Regular (Begins) Thru	Curr. Liab. / Sinking Fund Price	Balance Sheet Date / Sinking Fund (Begins) Thru	L. Term Debt (Mil $) / Refund/Other Restriction Price	Refund/Other Restriction (Begins) Thru	Capitalization (Mil $) / Outst'g (Mil $)	Total Debt % Capital / Underwriting Firm	Underwriting Year	Price Range 1995 High	Price Range 1995 Low	Mo. End Price Sale(s) or Bid	Curr. Yield	Yield to Mat.
***Sears Roebuck Acceptance** (Cont.)*																				
M-T Nts 'I' 6.29s 2000	[1]mn15	BBB			X	BE	NC	....	....	....	....	....	25.0	G1	'95	101½	100	101½	6.20	5.92
M-T Nts 'I' 6.24s '99	mN15	BBB			X	BE	NC	....	....	....	....	....	28.0	G1	'95	101⅜	100	101⅜	6.16	5.84
M-T Nts 'I' 6.55s '98	[2]mn15	BBB			X	BE	NC	....	....	....	....	....	30.0	G1	'95	100	100	100	6.55	6.55
M-T Nts 'I'[3] 6.13s 2005	mN15	BBB			X	BE	NC	....	....	....	....	....	50.0	G1	'95	100	100	100	6.13	6.13
M-T Nts 'I'[3] 6.15s 2005	mN15	BBB			X	BE	NC	....	....	....	....	....	55.0	G1	'95	102¼	100	102¼	6.01	5.85
Sears, Roebuck & Co.	*59f*	*d0.11*	*2.49*	*2.39*		*Dc*	*469.0*	*25336*	*14392*	*9-30-95*	*9434*		*21069*	*79.6*						
Deb 6s 2000	Mn	BBB	11/94	BBB+	X	R	100	....	....	....	....	....	[4]300	G1	'82	99⅜	89¼	99⅜	6.04	6.16
Deb 9⅜s 2011	mN	BBB	11/94	BBB+	X	R	NC	....	....	....	Z100	....	300	D3	'91	126⅞	104⅞	126⅞	7.39	6.61
Nts 8.55s '96	fA	BBB	11/94	BBB+	X	R	NC	....	....	....	Z100	....	200	G1	'89	102⅝	100½	101¾	8.40	5.47
Nts 9s '96	mS15	BBB	11/94	BBB+	X	R	NC	....	....	....	Z100	....	200	D3	'89	103¾	101⅛	102⅜	8.79	5.53
Nts 9¼s '97	fA	BBB	11/94	BBB+	X	R	NC	....	....	....	Z100	....	300	D3	'90	106	101⅞	105½	8.77	5.58
Nts 9¼s '98	Ao15	BBB	11/94	BBB+	X	R	NC	....	....	....	Z100	....	500	D3	'91	108⅛	102⅛	107⅝	8.59	5.65
Nts 8.45s '98	mN	BBB	11/94	BBB+	X	R	NC	....	....	....	Z100	....	250	D3	'91	107⅛	99¾	107⅛	7.89	5.69
• Nts 9½s '99	Jd	BBB	11/94	BBB+	X	R	NC	....	....	....	Z100	....	200	G1	'89	112⅜	103¾	108⅝	8.75	6.64
• Ext'd Nts 8.20s '99	Ao15	BBB	11/94	BBB+	X	R	NC	....	....	....	....	....	30.6	G1	'84	105¾	98⅜	104	7.88	6.82
Nts 6¼s 2004	Jj15	BBB	11/94	BBB+	X	R	NC	....	....	....	Z100	....	300	M6	'94	100⅛	86½	100⅛	6.24	6.23
M-T Nts 'VII'[5] 4.89s '97	[6]ao	BBB	11/94	BBB+	X	BE	NC	....	....	....	....	....	5.00	D3	'94	99⅜	93⅝	99⅜	4.92	5.48
M-T Nts 'VII'[5] 4.85s '97	[7]ao	BBB	11/94	BBB+	X	BE	NC	....	....	....	....	....	5.00	D3	'94	99¼	93⅝	99¼	4.89	5.56
M-T Nts 'VII'[5] 5.21s '97	[8]ao	BBB	11/94	BBB+	X	BE	NC	....	....	....	....	....	36.0	D3	'94	99⅝	94⅛	99⅝	5.23	5.55
M-T Nts 'VII'[5] 5¼s '97	[9]ao	BBB	11/94	BBB+	X	BE	NC	....	....	....	....	....	50.0	D3	'94	99¾	94¼	99¾	5.26	5.47
M-T Nts 'VII'[5] 7.64s '97	[9]ao	BBB			X	BE	NC	....	....	....	....	....	35.0	D3	'95	102⅝	100	102⅜	7.46	5.48
M-T Nts 'VII'[5] 5.24s '97	[10]ao	BBB	11/94	BBB+	X	BE	NC	....	....	....	....	....	50.0	D3	'94	99¾	94⅛	99¾	5.25	5.46
M-T Nts 'VII'[5] 6.66s '97	[11]ao	BBB	11/94	BBB+	X	BE	NC	....	....	....	....	....	35.0	D3	'94	101½	96½	101½	6.56	5.52
M-T Nts 'VII'[5] 6¾s '97	[12]ao	BBB	11/94	BBB+	X	BE	NC	....	....	....	....	....	25.0	D3	'94	101⅝	96¾	101⅝	6.64	5.53
M-T Nts 'VII'[5] 7.83s '98	[13]ao	BBB			X	BE	NC	....	....	....	....	....	25.0	D3	'95	104⅜	100	104⅜	7.50	5.64
M-T Nts 'VII'[5] 7.69s '98	[14]ao	BBB			X	BE	NC	....	....	....	....	....	26.7	D3	'95	103⅝	100	103⅝	7.42	5.87
M-T Nts 'VII'[5] 7.40s '98	[15]ao	BBB			X	BE	NC	....	....	....	....	....	30.0	D3	'95	103⅝	100	103⅝	7.14	5.63
M-T Nts 'VII'[5] 7.42s '98	[15]ao	BBB			X	BE	NC	....	....	....	....	....	35.0	D3	'95	103¾	100	103¾	7.15	5.59
M-T Nts 'VII'[5] 7.32s '98	[16]ao	BBB			X	BE	NC	....	....	....	....	....	30.0	D3	'95	103½	99¾	103½	7.07	5.62
M-T Nts 'VII'[5] 6.05s '98	[17]ao	BBB	11/94	BBB+	X	BE	NC	....	....	....	....	....	5.00	D3	'93	101	92⅞	101	5.99	5.62
M-T Nts 'VII'[5] 5.90s '98	[18]ao	BBB	11/94	BBB+	X	BE	NC	....	....	....	....	....	7.00	D3	'93	100⅝	92⅜	100⅝	5.86	5.63
M-T Nts 'VII'[5] 5.83s '98	[19]ao	BBB	11/94	BBB+	X	BE	NC	....	....	....	....	....	20.0	D3	'93	100⅜	92⅛	100⅜	5.81	5.67
M-T Nts 'VII'[5] 5.49s '98	[20]ao	BBB	11/94	BBB+	X	BE	NC	....	....	....	....	....	10.0	D3	'93	99½	90⅝	99½	5.52	5.69
M-T Nts 'VII'[5] 5.86s '99	[21]ao	BBB	11/94	BBB+	X	BE	NC	....	....	....	....	....	30.0	D3	'93	100½	91⅛	100½	5.83	5.68
M-T Nts 'VII' 5.58s '99	[22]ao	BBB	11/94	BBB+	X	BE	NC	....	....	....	....	....	5.00	D3	'94	99⅝	90⅛	99⅝	5.60	5.71
M-T Nts 'VII'[5] 5.82s '99	[23]ao	BBB	11/94	BBB+	X	BE	NC	....	....	....	....	....	10.0	D3	'94	100¼	90¾	100¼	5.81	5.73
M-T Nts 'VII'[5] 5.82s '99	[24]ao	BBB	11/94	BBB+	X	BE	NC	....	....	....	....	....	10.0	D3	'94	100¼	90¾	100¼	5.81	5.73
M-T Nts 'VII'[5] 5.91s '99	[25]ao	BBB	11/94	BBB+	X	BE	NC	....	....	....	....	....	13.0	D3	'94	100½	91	100½	5.88	5.73
M-T Nts 'VII'[5] 5.99s '99	[26]ao	BBB	11/94	BBB+	X	BE	NC	....	....	....	....	....	12.0	D3	'94	100¾	91¼	100¾	5.95	5.72
M-T Nts 'VII'[5] 5.54s '99	[27]ao	BBB	11/94	BBB+	X	BE	NC	....	....	....	....	....	35.0	D3	'93	99¼	89	99¼	5.58	5.78
M-T Nts 'VII'[5] 6.24s '99	[28]ao	BBB	11/94	BBB+	X	BE	NC	....	....	....	....	....	20.0	D3	'93	101⅜	91½	101⅜	6.16	5.81
M-T Nts 'VII'[5] 6.58s 2000	[29]ao	BBB	11/94	BBB+	X	BE	NC	....	....	....	....	....	5.00	D3	'93	102⅝	91½	102⅝	6.41	5.90
M-T Nts 'VII'[5] 6.70s 2000	[29]ao	BBB	11/94	BBB+	X	BE	NC	....	....	....	....	....	5.00	D3	'93	103⅛	92	103⅛	6.50	5.89
M-T Nts 'VII'[5] 6¼s 2000	ao	BBB	11/94	BBB+	X	BE	NC	....	....	....	....	....	20.0	D3	'93	101⅜	90	101⅜	6.17	5.90
M-T Nts 'VII'[5] 6.27s 2000	[30]ao	BBB	11/94	BBB+	X	BE	NC	....	....	....	....	....	36.0	D3	'93	101½	90	101½	6.18	5.89
M-T Nts 'VII'[5] 6.28s 2000	[31]ao	BBB	11/94	BBB+	X	BE	NC	....	....	....	....	....	7.50	D3	'93	101½	90	101½	6.19	5.90

Uniform Footnote Explanations-See Page 260. Other: [1] Due 10-18-00. [2] Due 12-1-98. [3] (HRO)On 11-15-00 at 100. [4] Incl disc. [5] Issued in min denom $100T. [6] Due 2-3-97. [7] Due 2-4-97. [8] Due 2-18-97. [9] Due 2-24-97. [10] Due 2-25-97. [11] Due 5-20-97. [12] Due 5-27-97. [13] Due 2-23-98. [14] Due 2-27-98. [15] Due 3-16-98. [16] Due 3-20-98. [17] Due 6-29-98. [18] Due 7-8-98. [19] Due 7-27-98. [20] Due 9-28-98. [21] Due 1-22-99. [22] Due 2-1-99. [23] Due 2-22-99. [24] Due 2-23-99. [25] Due 2-25-99. [26] Due 3-2-99. [27] Due 7-15-99. [28] Due 8-3-99. [29] Due 6-15-00. [30] Due 7-20-00. [31] Due 8-09-00.

Title-Industry Code & Co. Finances (In Italics) / Individual Issue Statistics (Exchange ↓)	Ind / Interest Dates	Fixed Charge Coverage 1992 / S&P Debt Rating	1993 / Date of Last Rating Change	1994 / Prior Rating	Eligible ↓	Year End / Bond Form	Million $ Cash & Equiv. / Redemption Provisions: Regular Price	Curr. Assets / Regular (Begins) Thru	Curr. Liab. / Sinking Fund Price	Balance Sheet Date / Sinking Fund (Begins) Thru	L. Term Debt (Mil $) / Refund/Other Restriction Price	Capital-ization (Mil $) / Refund/Other Restriction (Begins) Thru	Outst'g (Mil $)	Total Debt % Capital / Underwriting Firm	Underwriting Year	Price Range 1995 High	Price Range 1995 Low	Mo. End Price Sale(s) or Bid	Curr. Yield	Yield to Mat.
Sears, Roebuck & Co. *(Cont.)*																				
M-T Nts 'VII'[1] 5.81s 2000	[2]ao	**BBB**	11/94	BBB+	X	BE	NC	....	....	....	....	....	10.0	D3	'93	99½	87½	99½	5.84	5.93
M-T Nts 'VII'[1] 6.56s 2003	[3]ao	**BBB**	11/94	BBB+	X	BE	NC	....	....	....	....	....	25.0	D3	'93	102⅛	87⅞	102⅛	6.42	6.19
M-T Nts 'VII'[1] 6.57s 2003	[4]ao	**BBB**	11/94	BBB+	X	BE	NC	....	....	....	....	....	5.00	D3	'93	102⅛	87⅜	102⅛	6.43	6.21
M-T Nts 'VII'[1] 6.67s 2003	[5]ao	**BBB**	11/94	BBB+	X	BE	NC	....	....	....	....	....	40.0	D3	'93	102¾	88⅛	102¾	6.49	6.21
M-T Nts 'VII'[1] 6.65s 2003	[6]ao	**BBB**	11/94	BBB+	X	BE	NC	....	....	....	....	....	10.0	D3	'93	102⅝	88⅜	102⅝	6.48	6.19
M-T Nts 'VII'[1] 6.76s 2003	[3]ao	**BBB**	11/94	BBB+	X	BE	NC	....	....	....	....	....	10.0	D3	'93	103¼	89⅛	103¼	6.55	6.19
M-T Nts 'VII'[1] 6.66s 2003	[7]ao	**BBB**	11/94	BBB+	X	BE	NC	....	....	....	....	....	25.0	D3	'93	102⅝	88	102⅝	6.49	6.22
M-T Nts 'VII'[1] 6.65s 2003	[8]ao	**BBB**	11/94	BBB+	X	BE	NC	....	....	....	....	....	5.00	D3	'93	102	87⅜	102	6.52	6.31
M-T Nts 'VII'[1] 6.34s 2004	[9]ao	**BBB**	11/94	BBB+	X	BE	NC	....	....	....	....	....	5.00	D3	'93	100⅜	85	100⅜	6.32	6.28
F/R[10]M-T Nts 'VII'[1] '96	[11]	**BBB**	11/94	BBB+	X	BE	NC	....	....	....	....	....	175	D3	'94	100¼	99⅞	100⅛	....	....
F/R[10]M-T Nts 'VII'[1] '97	[12]Feb3	**BBB**			X	BE	NC	....	....	....	....	....	50.0	D3	'95	100½	100	100	....	....
F/R[13]M-T Nts 'VII'[1] 5.7261s '99	QMar10	**BBB**	11/94	BBB+	X	BE	NC	....	....	....	....	....	30.0	D3	'94	100½	98⅛	98⅝	5.81	....
Security Capital Ind Tr	***57***	***0.88***	***15.12***	***4.71***		***Dc***				***6-30-95***	***324.0***	***1389***		***34.3***						
Nts 7⅛s '98	Mn15	**BBB+**			X	BE	[14]Z100	....	....	....	....	....	15.0	M5	'95	102⅛	99½	102⅛	6.98	6.15
Nts 7¼s 2000	Mn15	**BBB+**			X	BE	[14]Z100	....	....	....	....	....	17.5	M5	'95	103⅞	99⅛	103⅞	6.98	6.22
Nts 7.30s 2001	Mn15	**BBB+**			X	BE	[14]Z100	....	....	....	....	....	17.5	M5	'95	101½	98⅞	100⅞	7.24	7.10
([15]Amort)Nts 8.72s 2009	Ms	**BBB+**			X	BE	[14]Z100	....	....	....	....	....	150	M6	'95	109	100	A109	8.00	....
([16]Amort)Nts 7⅞s 2009	Mn15	**BBB+**			X	BE	[14]Z100	....	....	....	....	....	75.0	M5	'95	105⅜	99½	105⅜	7.47	....
([17]Amort)Nts 9.34s 2015	Ms	**BBB+**			X	BE	[14]Z100	....	....	....	....	....	50.0	M6	'95	110	100	A110	8.49	....
Security Pacific Corp	***10***	***Merged into BankAmer Corp,see***																		
Nts 7¾s '96	jD	**A+**	10/95	A	X	BE	NC	....	....	....	....	....	150	G1	'91	102⅛	99¼	101¾	7.62	5.77
• F/R[18]Sub[19]Cap Nts '96	QAug15	**A**	10/95	A–	X	R	[20]100	....	....	....	....	....	250	S1	'84	No Sale		100	....	....
Sub Nts 9¾s '99	Mn15	**A**	10/95	A–	X	R	NC	....	....	....	....	....	250	S4	'87	111¾	104¼	111¾	8.72	5.86
Sub Nts 11½s 2000	mN15	**A**	10/95	A–	X	R	NC	....	....	....	....	....	150	M2	'90	122⅞	113⅛	122⅞	9.36	6.02
Sub Nts 11s 2001	Ms	**A**	10/95	A–	X	R	NC	....	....	....	....	....	250	M2	'91	121½	111⅜	121½	9.05	6.09
Sequa Corp[21]	***2***	***1.60***	***0.25***	***0.53***		***Dc***	***30.70***	***590.0***	***335.0***	***9-30-95***	***564.0***	***1144***		***50.7***						
• Nts 9⅝s '99	aO15	**BB**	8/93	BB+	Y	R	NC	....	....	....	....	....	150	M2	'89	103⅛	93⅝	s103⅛	9.33	8.63
• Sr[22]Nts 8¾s 2001	jD15	**BB**			Y	R	104.375	(12-15-97)	....	....	[23]Z108.75	12-15-96	125	B5	'93	97	87	91¼	9.59	10.78
• Sr[24]Sub Nts 9⅜s 2003	jD15	**B+**			Y	R	104.6875	(12-15-98)	....	....	[25]Z109.375	12-15-96	175	B5	'93	98¼	84½	97⅛	9.65	9.90
Service Corp Int'l[26]	***63***	***3.55***	***3.91***	***3.73***		***Dc***	***170.0***	***763.0***	***454.0***	***9-30-95***	***p1986***	***3731***		***58.7***						
Deb 7⅞s 2013	Fa	**BBB+**			X	R	NC	....	....	....	....	....	150	M2	'93	111¼	92¼	111¼	7.08	6.75
Nts 6⅜s 2000	aO	**BBB+**			X	BE	NC	....	....	....	....	....	150	M5	'95	101¾	99¾	101¾	6.27	5.94
Nts 8⅜s 2004	jD15	**BBB+**			X	BE	NC	....	....	....	....	....	200	M5	'94	115⅛	98¼	115⅛	7.27	6.15
Nts 6⅞s 2007	aO	**BBB+**			X	BE	NC	....	....	....	....	....	150	M5	'95	104⅛	99⅝	104⅛	6.60	6.37
Nts[27] 7s 2015	Jd	**BBB+**			X	BE	NC	....	....	....	....	....	300	M5	'95	105⅝	95	105⅝	6.63	6.49
◆Sub SF Deb 10s 2000	fA15	**NR**				R	100	....	100	....	....	....	1.00	Exch.	'80	105	100	102⅛	9.79	9.42
Service Merchandise	***59i***	***2.49***	***2.87***	***2.35***		***Dc***	***18.90***	***1461***	***1170***	***10-1-95***	***623.0***	***1383***		***77.9***						
• Sr Nts[28] 8⅜s 2001	Jj15	**BB**	4/95	BB+	Y	R	NC	....	....	....	....	....	100	M2	'93	97⅞	84	s96½	8.68	9.26
• Sr Sub Deb[28] 9s 2004	jD15	**B+**	4/95	BB–	Y	R	104.50	(12-15-97)	100	(12-15-03)	....	....	300	M2	'93	87⅝	71½	s82	10.98	12.38
Seven-Up/RC Bottling So'n CA	***11f***	***0.41***	***0.32***	***0.27***		***Dc***	***4.36***	***94.90***	***257.0***	***9-30-95***		***143.0***		***136.0***						
Sr Sec Nts[29] 11½s '99	§fA	**D**	8/95	B–	Z	R			Default 8-1-95 int				140	C4	'92	91¼	45	60	....	Flat
SFX Broacasting	***12b***	***n/a***	***0.88***	***1.32***		***Dc***	***11.30***	***30.40***	***8.39***	***9-30-95***	***81.40***	***170.0***		***48.2***						
Sr Sub Nts[28] 11⅜s 2000	aO	**B**	9/94	B–	Y	R	101.896	(10-1-98)	....	....	....	....	80.0	K2	'93	105	98½	105	10.83	10.02
Shawmut (Assoc'n) Corp	***10***	***Now Shawmut Nat'l,see***																		
Nts 8⅞s '96	Ao	**A–**	12/95	BBB	X	R	NC	....	....	....	....	....	150	P1	'86	101⅞	100¾	100¾	8.81	5.77
Nts 8⅛s '97	Fa	**A–**	12/95	BBB	X	R	NC	....	....	....	....	....	100	P1	'87	102¾	99⅝	102¼	7.95	5.95

Uniform Footnote Explanations-See Page 260. Other: [1] Issued in min denom $100T. [2] Due 10-25-00. [3] Due 2-20-03. [4] Due 8-19-03. [5] Due 7-07-03. [6] Due 2-20-2003. [7] Due 7-29-03. [8] Due 8-06-03. [9] Due 6-15-04. [10] Int adj monthly. [11] Due 7-22-96:Int pd monthly,ea 3rd Wed. [12] Int pd monthly ea 3rd Wed. [13] Int to 9-10-95,adj qtrly aft. [14] Plus Make-Whole Amt. [15] Princ pyts of $125/bond due ea 3-1 (fr 3-1-02). [16] Princ pyts of $125/bond due ea 5-15(fr 5-15-02). [17] Princ pyts due ea 3-1:'10, $100, incr $25 anly aft. [18] Co may exch for Cap Sec when due. [19] Int:adj wkly for London interbk rts:min 5.25%. [20] Co may exch for Cap Sec. [21] Was Sun Chemical. [22] Co must offer repurch, at 101, on Chge of Ctrl. [23] Max $25M red w/proceeds of Pub Eq Off'g. [24] Co must offer repurch,at 101,on Chge of Ctrl. [25] Max $114M red w/proceeds of Pub Eq Off'g. [26] Was IFS Indus. [27] (HRO)On 6-1-02 at 100. [28] (HRO)On Chge of Ctrl at 101. [29] (HRO)On Chge in Ctrl at 101.

Title-Industry Code & Co. Finances (In Italics) / Exchange ↓ Individual Issue Statistics	Ind / Interest Dates	Fixed Charge Coverage 1992 / S&P Debt Rating	1993 / Date of Last Rating Change	Prior Rating	1994 / Eligible ↓	Year End / Bond Form	Million $ Cash & Equiv. / Regular Price	Million $ Curr. Assets / Regular (Begins) Thru	Million $ Curr. Liab. / Sinking Fund Price	Balance Sheet Date / Sinking Fund (Begins) Thru	L. Term Debt (Mil $) / Refund/Other Restriction Price	Refund/Other Restriction (Begins) Thru	Capital-ization (Mil $) / Outst'g (Mil $)	Total Debt % Capital / Underwriting Firm	Underwriting Year	Price Range 1995 High	Price Range 1995 Low	Mo. End Price Sale(s) or Bid	Curr. Yield	Yield to Mat.
Shawmut Nat'l[1]	*10*	*1.31*	*1.72*		*2.10*	*Dc*				*6-30-95*	*2339*		*4917*	*47.6*						
Sub Nts 8⅝s '99	jD15	**BBB+**	12/95	BBB−	X	BE	NC	....	....	....	....	....	150	M6	'92	109⅝	99¾	109⅝	7.87	5.87
Sub Nts 7.20s 2003	Ao15	**BBB+**	12/95	BBB−	X	BE	NC	....	....	....	....	....	150	M6	'93	104½	90⅝	104½	6.89	6.42
Shell Oil Co[2]	*49a*	*2.91*	*5.62*		*2.86*	*Dc*	*483.0*	*4354*	*5782*	*9-30-95*	*1295*		*17316*	*20.2*						
• SF Deb 7¼s 2002	Fa15	**AAA**	10/87	AA+	X	R	100.29	2-14-96	100	....	....	....	[3]12.0	M6	'72	103½	94⅞	101½	7.14	6.94
Nts 7.70s '96	Fa	**AAA**			X	BE	NC	....	....	....	....	....	250	M2	'91	101	100⅛	100⅛	7.69	6.09
Nts 6s '97	Jj15	**AAA**			X	BE	NC	....	....	....	....	....	250	M2	'92	100¾	96⅜	100¾	5.96	5.25
Nts 6.95s '98	jD15	**AAA**			X	BE	NC	....	....	....	....	....	250	U1	'92	104	95¾	104	6.68	5.47
Nts 6⅝s '99	jJ	**AAA**			X	BE	NC	....	....	....	....	....	250	M6	'92	103⅜	94	103⅜	6.41	5.55
Nts 6.70s 2002	fA15	**AAA**			X	BE	NC	....	....	....	....	....	250	M5	'92	104¾	90⅞	104¾	6.40	5.82
• **(PL)** SF Deb[4] 7½s '99	jJ	**AAA**	10/87	AA+	X	R	100	....	100	....	....	....	2.38	M6	'69	101½	96⅝	100⅜	7.47	7.38
[5]Sherwin-Williams Devel	*15*	*27.35*	*41.97*		*93.79*	*Dc*	*216.0*	*1282*	*618.0*	*9-30-95*	*22.70*		*1201*	*1.9*						
Gtd[6]Deb 9⅞s 2016	Jd15	**A**	12/91	A−	X	R	100	(6-15-06)	100	(6-15-07)	....	....	15.9	S1	'86	123⅜	106⅝	123⅜	8.00	7.60
ShopKo Stores	*59g*	*5.46*	*3.47*		*3.15*	*Fb*	*28.10*	*472.0*	*278.0*	*9-9-95*	*413.0*		*811.0*	*51.0*						
Sr Nts 8½s 2002	[7]jd15	**BBB**	8/94	BBB+	X	R	NC	....	....	....	....	....	100	G1	'92	108½	97⅜	108½	7.83	6.80
Sr Nts 6½s 2003	fA15	**BBB**	8/94	BBB+	X	BE	NC	....	....	....	....	....	100	G1	'93	97⅝	85	97⅝	6.66	6.90
Sr Nts 9s 2004	mN15	**BBB**			X	BE	NC	....	....	....	....	....	100	G1	'94	113⅞	98⅜	113⅞	7.90	6.88
Sr Nts 9¼s 2022	[7]jd15	**BBB**	8/94	BBB+	X	R	NC	....	....	....	....	....	100	G1	'92	113¾	96¾	113¾	8.13	7.99
Showboat, Inc	*40i*	*1.89*	*1.96*		*1.34*	*Dc*	*126.0*	*152.0*	*56.40*	*9-30-95*	*392.0*		*565.0*	*69.4*						
• [8]1st[9] 9¼s 2008	[10]Mn	**BB−**			Y	R	102.775	(5-1-00)	....	....	....	....	275	D6	'93	100¾	84¼	100	9.25	9.25
Sr Sub[11]Nts[9] 13s 2009	fA	**B**			Y	R	103.90	(8-1-01)	....	....	....	....	120	D6	'94	112½	95½	112½	11.56	11.19
Sierra Pacific Power[12]	*75*	*2.84*	*3.00*		*3.11*	*Dc*	*3.80*	*103.0*	*142.0*	*9-30-95*	*525.0*		*1213*	*46.8*						
1st 6½s '97	jJ	**A−**	6/86	BBB+	X	R	100.23	6-30-96	100	....	....	....	15.0	S10	'67	100⅜	96½	100¼	6.48	6.32
Signet Banking Corp[13]	*10*	*2.41*	*3.35*		*4.34*	*Dc*				*9-30-95*	*253.0*		*1096*	*23.1*						
Sub Nts 9⅝s '99	Jd	**BB+**	1/93	BB−	Y	R	NC	....	....	....	....	....	100	G1	'89	110¾	103⅜	110¾	8.69	6.09
Silgan Corp	*16b*	*1.32*	*1.52*		*2.10*	*Dc*	*3.85*	*490.0*	*377.0*	*9-30-95*	*578.0*		*667.0*	*87.7*						
Sr Sub Nts[9] 11¾s 2002	Jd15	**B−**			Y	R	105.875	(6-15-97)	....	....	....	....	135	M6	'92	106½	102	106½	11.03	10.34
Silgan Holdings	*16b*	*0.74*	*0.77*		*1.14*	*Dc*	*3.86*	*490.0*	*375.0*	*9-30-95*	*772.0*		*622.0*	*125.0*						
Sr[14]Disc Deb[15] 13¼s 2002	Jd15	**B−**			Y	R	100	....	....	....	....	....	[16]275	M6	'92	95⅞	82¾	95⅞	....	Flat
Simula, Inc	*3*	*n/a*	*4.53*		*2.98*	*Dc*	*9.00*	*38.00*	*14.70*	*9-30-95*	*11.10*		*58.10*	*21.2*						
◆Sr Sub Nts[9] 12s '98	mN15	**NR**				R	NC	....	....	....	....	....	5.70		'93	106	103	103⅛	11.64	10.70
Sinclair Broadcast Group	*12c*	*0.50*	*1.81*		*0.84*	*Dc*	*105.0*	*177.0*	*48.50*	*9-30-95*	*416.0*		*513.0*	*81.7*						
Sr Sub Nts[9] 10s 2003	jD15	**B+**			Y	R	105	(12-15-98)	....	....	[17]Z109	12-15-96	100	C1	'93	103¼	93	102	9.80	9.63
Sr Sub Nts[9] 10s 2005	mS30	**B+**			Y	R	105	(9-30-00)	....	....	[18]Z110	9-29-98	300	C1	'95	103⅛	100	102¼	9.78	9.63
Smith Barney Hldgs Inc	*62*	*n/a*	*3.33*		*1.88*	*Dc*				*6-30-95*	*1735*		*6422*	*62.1*						
• Nts 5⅜s '96	Jd	**A−**			X	BE	NC	....	....	....	....	....	150	Exch.	'93	No Sale		97	5.54	12.81
Nts 6s '97	Ms15	**A−**			X	BE	NC	....	....	....	....	....	200	S5	'94	100½	96¾	100½	5.97	5.56
Nts 5⅝s '98	mN15	**A−**			X	BE	NC	....	....	....	....	....	150	S5	'93	99¾	90¼	99¾	5.64	5.72
Nts 5½s '99	Jj15	**A−**			X	BE	NC	....	....	....	....	....	200	B5	'94	99¼	89¼	99¼	5.54	5.77
Nts 7⅞s '99	aO	**A−**			X	BE	NC	....	....	....	....	....	150	S5	'94	106½	96⅝	106½	7.39	5.92
Nts 7.98s 2000	Ms	**A−**			X	BE	NC	....	....	....	....	....	200	S5	'95	107¼	100	107¼	7.44	5.99
Nts 7s 2000	Mn15	**A−**			X	BE	NC	....	....	....	....	....	150	S5	'95	103⅞	99½	103⅞	6.74	5.98
• Nts 6⅝s 2000	Jd	**NR**				BE	NC	....	....	....	....	....	150	Exch.	'93	No Sale		102⅛	6.49	6.07
Nts 7½s 2002	Mn	**A−**			X	BE	NC	....	....	....	....	....	150	S5	'95	106½	99¼	106½	7.04	6.24
Nts 6½s 2002	aO15	**A−**			Y	BE	NC	....	....	....	....	....	150	S5	'95	101¼	99	101¼	6.42	6.27
Nts 6⅞s 2005	Jd15	**A−**			X	BE	NC	....	....	....	....	....	175	S5	'95	103	95	103	6.67	6.45
Snap-On Inc	*13e*	*n/a*	*13.19*		*15.22*	*Dc*	*14.30*	*986.0*	*401.0*	*9-30-95*	*★214.0*		*998.0*	*26.9*						
Nts 6⅝s 2005	aO	**AA**			X	BE	NC	....	....	....	....	....	100	M2	'95	104½	99⅝	104½	6.34	6.01

Uniform Footnote Explanations-See Page 260. Other: [1] See Shawmut(Assoc'n)Corp,Hartford Nat'l. [2] Subsid of SPNV Hldg. [3] Excl defeased amts. [4] Gtd by Shell Oil. [5] Gtd by & data of Sherwin Williams Co. [6] Gtd by Sherwin-Williams Co. [7] Due 3-15. [8] Gtd by Ocean Showboat. [9] (HRO)On Chge of Ctrl at 101. [10] State gaming laws may req hldr's sale/Co red. [11] State gaming laws may reg hldr's sale/Co red. [12] Subsid of Sierra Pacific Resources. [13] See Bank of Virginia. [14] Int accrues at 13.25% fr 6-15-96. [15] (HRO)On Chge of Ctrl at 100. [16] Incl disc. [17] Max $50M red w/proceeds of Pub Eq Off'g. [18] Max $75M red w/proceeds of Pub Eq Off'g.

Title-Industry Code & Co. Finances (In Italics) — Ind / Individual Issue Statistics: Exchange, Interest Dates	S&P Debt Rating	Date of Last Rating Change	Prior Rating	Eligible	Bond Form	Regular Price	Regular (Begins) Thru	Sinking Fund Price	Sinking Fund (Begins) Thru	Refund/Other Restriction Price	Refund/Other Restriction (Begins) Thru	Outst'g (Mil $)	Underwriting Firm	Underwriting Year	Price Range 1995 High	Price Range 1995 Low	Mo. End Price Sale(s) or Bid	Curr. Yield	Yield to Mat.
Co. Finances	*Fixed Charge Coverage 1992*	*1993*	*1994*		*Year End*	*Cash & Equiv. (Million $)*	*Curr. Assets (Million $)*	*Curr. Liab. (Million $)*	*Balance Sheet Date*	*L. Term Debt (Mil $)*		*Capitalization (Mil $)*	*Total Debt % Capital*						
SnyderGeneral Corp **13b**	....	....	....		***Dc***	***No Recent Fin'ls***													
Sr Sub Deb 14¼s 2000 mN15	**NR**	5/94	B–	Y	R	101.78	11-14-96	100	(11-15-97)	[1]Z101.78	11-14-96	225	F1	'88	100⅛	99⅞	A100	14.25	14.24
Society Corp **10**	***Merged with KeyCorp, see***																		
Nts 8⅞s '96 Mn15	**A–**	3/92	A	X	R	NC	....	....	....	....	....	75.0	F1	'86	102¼	101⅛	101⅛	8.78	5.77
Sub Nts 8⅛s 2002 Jd15	**BBB+**			X	BE	NC	....	....	....	....	....	200	G1	'92	110⅜	96⅞	110⅜	7.36	6.15
[2]Sola Group Ltd. **43**	***n/a***	***n/a***	***2.12***		***Mr***	***14.70***	***186.0***	***105.0***	***6-30-95***	***105.0***		***283.0***	***41.3***						
Sr[3]Sub([4]Reset)Nts 6s 2003 jD15	**BB–**	9/95	B	Y	R	104.813	(12-15-98)	....	....	[5]Z109.625	12-14-96	[6]117	M6	'93	96	75½	91¾	6.54	....
Sonat Inc **73a**	***2.08***	***3.15***	***2.22***		***Dc***	***58.10***	***404.0***	***462.0***	***9-30-95***	***771.0***		***2392***	***37.2***						
Nts 9½s '99 fA15	**BBB+**	9/95	BBB	X	R	NC	....	....	....	....	....	100	G1	'89	111⅜	103½	111⅜	8.53	5.96
Nts 9s 2001 Mn	**BBB+**	9/95	BBB	X	R	NC	....	....	....	....	....	100	G1	'91	112⅞	102	112⅞	7.97	6.13
Nts 6⅞s 2005 Jd	**BBB+**	9/95	BBB	X	BE	NC	....	....	....	....	....	200	G1	'95	104⅜	96⅝	104⅜	6.59	6.25
Sonoco Products **16c**	***6.70***	***7.01***	***4.88***		***Dc***	***79.60***	***699.0***	***393.0***	***10-1-95***	***588.0***		***1564***	***42.0***						
Deb 6¾s 2010 mN	**A+**			X	BE	NC	....	....	....	....	....	100	M5	'95	100	99¾	100	6.75	6.75
Deb 9.20s 2021 fA	**A+**			X	R	NC	....	....	....	....	....	100	M5	'91	129⅞	105¼	129⅞	7.08	6.73
Nts 5⅞s 2003 mN	**A+**			X	BE	NC	....	....	....	....	....	100	M5	'93	98⅝	84¾	98⅝	5.96	6.10
Source One Mortgage Svcs **25h**	***1.23***	***1.30***	***1.23***		***Dc***	***15.30***			***6-30-95***	***640.0***		***1023***	***62.6***						
Deb[7] 9s 2012 Jd	**BBB+**	4/95	A–	X	BE	NC	....	....	....	....	....	100	S1	'92	118⅝	99⅞	118⅝	7.59	7.06
South Carolina El. & Gas[8] **75**	***2.67***	***3.51***	***3.39***		***Dc***		***249.0***	***299.0***	***6-30-95***	***1348***		***2639***	***52.6***						
1st & Ref 6s '97 Jd	**A**	9/89	A+	X	CR	100.22	5-31-96	100.04	5-31-96	....	....	15.0	K2	'67	100⅛	95⅝	100⅛	5.99	5.90
1st & Ref 6½s '98 mS	**A**	9/89	A+	X	R	100.45	8-31-96	Z100	....	....	....	20.0	K2	'68	100½	94¾	100½	6.47	6.29
1st & Ref 7¼s 2002 Jj	**A**	9/89	A+	X	R	101.25	12-31-96	Z100	....	....	....	30.0	K2	'72	101⅝	94¼	101¼	7.16	6.99
1st & Ref 9s 2006 jJ15	**A**			X	R	NC	....	....	....	[9]Z100	....	145	S1	'91	119⅝	103⅞	119⅝	7.52	6.41
1st & Ref 8⅞s 2021 fA15	**A**			X	R	103.79	(8-15-01)	Z100	....	....	....	155	P1	'91	114⅜	99⅞	114⅜	7.76	7.59
1st 6s 2000 Jd15	**A**			X	R	NC	....	....	....	....	....	100	P1	'93	100⅜	90¼	100⅜	5.98	5.90
1st 6¼s 2003 jD15	**A**			X	R	NC	....	....	....	....	....	100	P1	'93	100⅜	86¾	100⅜	6.23	6.19
1st 7.70s 2004 jJ15	**A**			X	R	NC	....	....	....	....	....	100	P1	'94	109⅞	95¼	109⅞	7.01	6.19
1st 7⅛s 2013 Jd15	**A**			X	R	NC	....	....	....	....	....	150	P1	'93	104	87¼	104	6.85	6.73
1st 7⅝s 2023 Jd	**A**			X	R	103.66	(6-1-03)	....	....	....	....	100	P1	'93	108⅝	88⅞	108⅝	7.02	6.92
1st 7½s 2023 Jd15	**A**			X	R	103.44	(6-15-03)	....	....	....	....	150	P1	'93	105	87⅝	105	7.14	7.08
1st[10] 7⅝s 2025 Ao	**A**			X	R	102	(4-1-05)	....	....	....	....	100	P1	'95	111	96¾	111	6.87	6.76
South Central Bell Tel **67a**	***Now BellSouth Telecommunications, see***																		
• Deb 7⅜s 2012 fA	**AAA**			X	R	102.53	7-31-96	....	....	....	....	100	M6	'72	102⅞	88⅝	101	7.30	7.27
• Deb 8¼s 2017 Ms	**CALL**	12/95	AAA		R			Called 1-12-96 at 103.73				210	M2	'77	104⅜	95⅝	s103¾	7.95	Call
[11]Southeastern Mich Gas Co **73b**	***2.14***	***2.32***	***2.51***		***Dc***	***2.79***	***79.50***	***70.60***	***9-30-95***	***104.0***		***250.0***	***56.4***						
Deb[12] 8⅝s 2017 QApr15	**NR**				BE	105	(4-15-97)	....	....	....	....	25.0	J2	'92	108⅛	84	108⅛	7.98	7.83
Southeast'n Public Sv[13] **17a**	***[14]0.33***	***[15]0.74***	***1.08***		***Dc***	***17.60***	***23.40***	***47.70***	***9-30-95***			***172.0***	***24.9***						
Sr Sub Deb[16] 11⅞s '98 Fa	**B–**	7/93	C	Y	R	100	....	100	....	....	....	[17]36.0	D7	'83	101	97	99½	11.93	12.14
Southern Bell Tel. & Tel **67a**	***Now BellSouth Telecommunications, see***																		
• Deb[18] 5s '97 jD	**AAA**	6/88	AA+	X	CR	100	....	....	....	....	....	75.0	M6	'60	99½	92	98¾	5.06	5.69
• Deb 4⅜s '98 Ms	**AAA**	6/88	AA+	X	CR	100	....	....	....	....	....	70.0	M6	'61	97¾	89⅝	96⅝	4.53	6.05
• Deb[18] 4¾s 2000 mS	**AAA**	6/88	AA+	X	R	100	8-31-96	....	....	....	....	100	M6	'65	95½	84½	95	5.00	5.99
• Deb 4⅜s 2001 Ao	**AAA**	6/88	AA+	X	CR	100.22	3-31-96	....	....	....	....	75.0	M6	'62	93⅜	81¾	92¾	4.72	6.00
• Deb[18] 4⅜s 2003 fA	**AAA**	6/88	AA+	X	CR	100.47	7-31-96	....	....	....	....	70.0	L3	'63	90	76⅝	90½	4.83	5.95
• Deb 6s 2004 aO	**AAA**	6/88	AA+	X	R	100.68	3-30-96	....	....	....	....	100	H1	'66	99½	84⅝	s98⅛	6.11	6.28
• Deb 7⅜s 2010 jJ15	**AAA**	6/88	AA+	X	R	101.95	7-14-96	....	....	....	....	150	M6	'72	102⅞	88½	s102	7.23	7.15
• Deb 7⅝s 2013 Ms15	**AAA**	6/88	AA+	X	R	102.83	3-14-96	....	....	....	....	350	S1	'73	103	89½	s102½	7.44	7.36
• Deb 8⅛s 2017 Mn	**CALL**	12/95	AAA		R			Called 1-12-96 at 103.70				275	M6	'77	104½	94⅛	103⅝	7.84	Call

Uniform Footnote Explanations-See Page 260. Other: [1] On Chge of Ctrl. [2] Now Sola Int'l. [3] (HRO)On Chge of Ctrl at 101(Accreted Val). [4] Int 6% to 12-15-98,9.625% aft. [5] Percent Accret Val:Max $40.8M w/proceeds of Eq Off'g. [6] Incl disc. [7] Issued in min denom $100T. [8] Subsid of SCANA Corp. [9] Co may red for mgrs/consol. [10] (HRO)On 4-1-05 at 100. [11] Subsid & data of Southeastern Mich Gas Entpr. [12] (HRO)At 100,ltd as defined. [13] Subsid of Triarc Cos. [14] Fiscal Feb,'93 & prior. [15] 10 Mo Dec,'93. [16] Plan call on 2-22-96,at 100. [17] Called $9M for SF on 2-1-96. [18] Oblig of So Cent Bell Tel,contingently liable.

Title-Industry Code & Co. Finances (In Italics) / Individual Issue Statistics (Exchange ↓)	Ind / Interest Dates	Fixed Charge Coverage 1992 / S&P Debt Rating	1993 / Date of Last Rating Change	1994 / Prior Rating	Eligible ↓	Year End / Bond Form	Million $ Cash & Equiv. / Redemption Provisions: Regular Price	Million $ Curr. Assets / Regular (Begins) Thru	Million $ Curr. Liab. / Sinking Fund Price	Balance Sheet Date / Sinking Fund (Begins) Thru	L. Term Debt (Mil $) / Refund/Other Restriction Price	Refund/Other Restriction (Begins) Thru	Capital-ization (Mil $) / Outst'g (Mil $)	Total Debt % Capital / Underwriting Firm	Underwriting Year	Price Range 1995 High	Price Range 1995 Low	Mo. End Price Sale(s) or Bid	Curr. Yield	Yield to Mat.
Southern Calif Edison[1]	***72a***	***3.16***	***3.33***	***3.39***		***Dc***	***480.0***	***1981***	***2632***	***6-30-95***	***5393***		***11033***	***54.4***						
1st & Ref '86C 8⅝s 2019	Ao15	**A+**	11/92	AA	X	R	105.33	4-14-96	....	....	....	....	200	M6	'86	105½	95⅛	105½	8.18	8.09
1st & Ref '86K 8⅜s 2017	jD	**A+**	11/92	AA	X	R	102.48	11-30-96	....	....	....	....	125	M6	'86	103⅝	93⅜	102⅝	8.16	8.12
1st & Ref '90D 9¼s 2022	jD	**A+**	11/92	AA	X	R	104.06	11-30-96	....	....	....	....	200	G1	'90	105¼	100	104¼	8.87	8.83
1st & Ref '91B 8⅞s 2023	Mn	**A+**	11/92	AA	X	R	104.05	(5-1-96)	....	....	....	....	200	L3	'91	106½	98¼	104¾	8.47	8.43
1st & Ref '91C 8⅞s 2024	Jd	**A+**	11/92	AA	X	R	103.68	(6-1-96)	....	....	....	....	200	F1	'91	108¼	97¾	104⅞	8.46	8.42
1st & Ref '92B 7½s '99	Ao15	**A+**	11/92	AA	X	R	NC	....	....	....	....	....	150	G1	'92	104⅝	96¾	104⅝	7.17	5.93
1st & Ref '92D 6⅛s '97	jJ15	**A+**	11/92	AA	X	R	NC	....	....	....	....	....	300	L3	'92	100¾	95½	100¾	6.08	5.61
1st & Ref '93A 6¾s 2000	Jj15	**A+**			X	R	NC	....	....	....	....	....	225	S1	'93	103¼	93⅛	103¼	6.54	5.84
1st & Ref '93B 5.90s '97	Jj15	**A+**			X	R	NC	....	....	....	....	....	200	M2	'93	100¼	95⅞	100¼	5.89	5.65
1st & Ref '93C 7¼s 2026	Ms	**A+**			X	R	102.43	(3-1-03)	....	....	....	....	300	G1	'93	100¼	83⅝	100¼	7.23	7.23
1st & Ref '93E 5.45s '98	Jd15	**A+**			X	R	NC	....	....	....	....	....	150	M2	'93	99½	91⅞	99½	5.48	5.67
1st & Ref '93F 6¼s 2003	Jd15	**A+**			X	R	NC	....	....	....	....	....	125	S1	'93	100	86⅛	100	6.25	6.25
1st & Ref '93G 7⅛s 2025	jJ15	**A+**			X	R	102.09	(7-15-03)	....	....	....	....	225	L3	'93	98¾	82½	98¾	7.22	7.23
1st & Ref '93H 5⅞s 2004	mS	**A+**			X	R	NC	....	....	....	....	....	125	F1	'93	97¼	82¾	97¼	6.04	6.29
1st & Ref '93I 6.90s 2018	aO	**A+**			X	R	103.39	(10-1-98)	....	....	....	....	200	L3	'93	98⅛	81	98⅛	7.03	7.07
1st & Ref '93J 5⅝s 2002	aO	**A+**			X	R	NC	....	....	....	....	....	200	S1	'93	96⅞	83⅞	96⅞	5.81	6.20
Nts 5⅞s '98	Fa	**A**			X	R	NC	....	....	....	....	....	125	L3	'93	100¼	93⅜	100¼	5.86	5.74
Nts 5.60s '98	jD15	**A**			X	R	NC	....	....	....	....	....	170	M2	'93	99⅜	90⅝	99⅜	5.64	5.83
Nts 8¼s 2000	Fa	**A**			X	R	NC	....	....	....	....	....	100	M2	'95	107⅞	99¾	107⅞	7.65	6.04
Nts 6½s 2001	Jd	**A**			X	R	NC	....	....	....	....	....	200	S1	'95	102⅜	97⅜	102⅜	6.35	5.98
Southern California Gas[2]	***73b***	***4.34***	***4.00***	***4.11***		***Dc***	***153.0***	***655.0***	***823.0***	***6-30-95***	***1292***		***3110***	***48.4***						
• 1st Y 8¾s 2021	aO	**AA–**	4/95	A+	X	R	103.59	(10-1-01)	Z103.59	(10-1-01)	....	....	150	L3	'91	108½	101	105⅞	8.26	8.20
• 1st Z 6⅞s 2002	fA15	**AA–**	4/95	A+	X	R	NC	....	....	....	....	....	100	M5	'92	102¾	92¼	100⅞	6.82	6.71
• 1st AA 6½s '97	jD15	**AA–**	4/95	A+	X	R	NC	....	....	....	....	....	125	F1	'92	101	97¾	100⅜	6.48	6.29
• 1st BB 7⅜s 2023	Ms	**AA–**	4/95	A+	X	R	103.53	(3-1-03)	Z103.53	(3-1-03)	....	....	100	F1	'93	100¾	88⅛	100	7.38	7.37
• 1st CC 5¼s '98	Ms	**AA–**	4/95	A+	X	R	NC	....	....	....	....	....	100	M2	'93	98⅝	91¼	98¼	5.34	6.12
• 1st DD 7½s 2023	Jd15	**AA–**	4/95	A+	X	R	103.15	(6-15-03)	Z103.15	(6-15-03)	....	....	125	M6	'93	No Sale		97	7.73	7.77
• 1st EE 6⅞s 2025	mN	**AA–**	4/95	A+	X	R	101.96	(11-1-03)	Z101.96	(11-1-03)	....	....	175	C5	'93	96¾	82	94	7.31	7.37
• 1st FF 5¾s 2003	mN15	**AA–**	4/95	A+	X	R	NC	....	....	....	....	....	100	M2	'93	94¾	86	95	6.05	6.57
Southern Indiana Gas & El	***75***	***3.67***	***3.59***	***3.43***		***Dc***	***5.84***	***116.0***	***142.0***	***9-30-95***	***258.0***		***626.0***	***46.3***						
1st 6s '96	mS	**AA**			X	R	100	....	100	....	....	....	8.00	E1	'66	100⅛	97⅜	100⅛	5.99	5.79
1st 6⅜s '98	fA	**AA**			X	R	100.56	7-31-96	100.34	7-31-96	....	....	12.0	E1	'68	100⅝	94⅞	100⅝	6.34	6.11
1st 6s '99	Ao	**AA**			X	R	NC	....	....	....	....	....	45.0	G1	'93	100⅞	92½	100⅞	5.95	5.70
1st 8⅞s 2016	Jd	**AA**			X	R	NC	....	....	....	....	....	25.0	G1	'86	121¾	102½	121¾	7.29	6.88
1st 7.60s 2023	Ao	**AA**			X	R	103.745	(4-1-03)	Z100	(4-1-03)	....	....	45.0	G1	'93	107	89⅜	107	7.10	7.02
Southern Natural Gas[3]	***73a***	***3.88***	***3.26***	***2.59***		***Dc***	***4.20***	***315.0***	***108.0***	***9-30-95***	***318.0***		***897.0***	***36.2***						
Nts 8⅞s 2001	Fa15	**A–**			X	R	NC	....	....	....	....	....	100	G1	'91	112⅛	102	112⅛	7.92	6.08
• Nts 7.85s 2002	Jj15	**A–**			X	R	NC	....	....	....	....	....	100	G1	'92	107⅞	97¼	104⅛	7.54	7.00
Nts 8⅝s 2002	Mn	**A–**			X	R	NC	....	....	....	....	....	100	G1	'92	110⅞	99¼	110⅞	7.78	6.50
Southern New England Tel[4]	***67a***	***4.72***	***4.83***	***6.67***		***Dc***	***55.10***	***495.0***	***487.0***	***6-30-95***	***747.0***		***1964***	***38.0***						
Deb 4⅜s 2001	jD	**AA**	5/91	AA+	X	CR	100.15	11-30-96	....	....	....	....	45.0	F1	'66	92¼	79¾	92¼	4.74	5.95
Med-Term Nts[5]'A' 8.70s 2031	fA15	**AA**			X	BE	107.25	(2-15-97)	....	....	....	....	80.0	S1	'91	113	100½	109¾	7.93	7.88
Med-Term Nts[5]'C' 6⅛s 2003	jD15	**AA**			X	BE	NC	....	....	....	....	....	200	L3	'93	100⅜	86	100⅜	6.10	6.06
Med-Term Nts[5]'C' 7¼s 2033	jD15	**AA**			X	BE	104.37	(12-15-03)	....	....	....	....	245	L3	'93	105¼	84¼	105¼	6.89	6.86
Southern Pacific Rail	***55***	***0.56***	***0.52***	***2.58***		***Dc***	***137.0***	***564.0***	***969.0***	***9-30-95***	***1655***		***2770***	***61.8***						
Sr Nts[6] 9⅜s 2005	fA15	**BB–**	12/94	B+	Y	R	104.167	(8-15-98)	....	....	....	....	375	K2	'93	109	92¼	108¾	8.62	8.05

Uniform Footnote Explanations-See Page 260. Other: [1] Subsid of SCEcorp. [2] Subsid of Pacific Enterprises. [3] Subsid of Sonat Inc. [4] Subsid of Southern N.E.Telecommunications. [5] Issued in min denom $100T. [6] (HRO)On Chge in Ctrl Triggering Event at 101.

Title-Industry Code & Co. Finances (In Italics) / Ind	Fixed Charge Coverage 1992	1993	1994		Year End	Million $ Cash & Equiv.	Curr. Assets	Curr. Liab.	Balance Sheet Date		L. Term Debt (Mil $)	Capital-ization (Mil $)	Total Debt % Capital						
Individual Issue Statistics Exchange ↓ / Interest Dates	S&P Debt Rating	Date of Last Rating Change	Prior Rating	Eligible ↓	Bond Form	Redemption Provisions: Regular Price	Regular (Begins) Thru	Sinking Fund Price	Sinking Fund (Begins) Thru	Refund/Other Restriction Price	Refund/Other Restriction (Begins) Thru	Outst'g (Mil $)	Underwriting Firm	Underwriting Year	Price Range 1995 High	Price Range 1995 Low	Mo. End Price Sale(s) or Bid	Curr. Yield	Yield to Mat.
***Southern[1] PacificTransp* 55**	***2.99***	***d0.45***	***2.96***		***Dc***	***125.0***	***529.0***	***939.0***	***9-30-95***	***1289***		***3603***	***37.4***						
• 1st & Ref B 8.20s 2001 .... jD	BB+	12/94	BB	Y	R	101.71	11-30-96	100	....	....	....	46.7	S8	'76	101	95¾	100⅜	8.17	8.12
***[2]Southern Railway[3]* 55**	....	....	....		***Dc***	***No Recent Fin'ls***													
Eq Tr 'A' 8.35s '99 .... jD15	AAA			X	R	NC	....	....	....	....	....	70.8	M2	'89	109⅛	100¼	109⅛	7.65	5.74
• Memp Div 1st 5s '96 .... jJ	AA	3/80	A+	X	CR	NC	....	....	....	....	....	3.72		1898	98½	98½	99⅛	5.04	6.79
***Southern Union* 73b**	***[4]Δ1.84***	***Δ1.53***	***Δ1.66***		***Je***		***92.30***	***74.30***	***9-30-95***	***442.0***		***763.0***	***58.1***						
Sr Nts 7.60s 2024 .... Fa	BBB			X	R	NC	....	....	....	....	....	475	M2	'94	103⅜	83½	103⅜	7.35	7.31
***SouthTrust Corp* 10**	***4.66***	***4.62***	***3.12***		***Dc***				***9-30-95***	***891.0***		***2279***	***39.1***						
Sub Nts 7s 2003 .... Mn15	BBB+			X	BE	NC	....	....	....	....	....	100	F1	'93	104⅛	90	104⅛	6.72	6.29
Sub Nts 7⅝s 2004 .... Mn	BBB+			X	BE	NC	....	....	....	....	....	100	M2	'94	108¼	93⅛	108¼	7.04	6.33
Sub Nts 8⅝s 2004 .... Mn15	BBB+			X	BE	NC	....	....	....	....	....	100	F1	'92	114½	99	114½	7.53	6.36
Sub Cap[5]Nts 9.95s '99 .... Jd	BBB+	8/90	A–	X	R	NC	....	....	....	Z100	....	75.0	F1	'87	112	104⅝	112	8.88	6.01
***Southwest Airlines* 4**	***3.23***	***5.32***	***6.12***		***Dc***	***366.0***	***564.0***	***647.0***	***9-30-95***	***671.0***		***2067***	***33.1***						
Deb 7⅞s 2007 .... mS	A–			X	R	NC	....	....	....	....	....	100	L3	'92	110¾	93⅜	110¾	7.11	6.54
Nts 9¼s '98 .... Fa15	A–			X	R	NC	....	....	....	....	....	100	L3	'91	107⅛	101¾	106¾	8.67	5.82
Nts 9.40s 2001 .... jJ	A–			X	R	NC	....	....	....	....	....	100	M2	'91	114¼	102⅞	114¼	8.23	6.30
Nts 8¾s 2003 .... aO15	A–			X	R	NC	....	....	....	....	....	100	F1	'91	113⅞	100¾	113⅞	7.68	6.45
Nts 8s 2005 .... Ms	A–			X	BE	NC	....	....	....	....	....	100	S1	'95	110¼	99⅜	110¼	7.26	6.50
***Southwest Gas* 73b**	***1.71***	***1.46***	***1.75***		***Dc***	***127.0***			***9-30-95***	***858.0***		***1282***	***71.3***						
Deb[6]A[7] 9s 2011 .... QOct	BBB–	9/90	BBB	X	R	103	9-30-96	....	....	....	....	27.6	J2	'86	104⅝	95⅞	104⅜	8.62	8.49
Deb[8]B[7] 9s 2011 .... QNov	BBB–	9/90	BBB	X	R	103	10-31-96	....	....	....	....	31.9	J2	'86	104⅞	94⅞	104⅜	8.62	8.49
Deb[9]C[7] 8¾s 2011 .... QDec	BBB–	9/90	BBB	X	R	103	11-30-96	....	....	....	....	19.3	J2	'86	104⅞	92⅞	104¼	8.39	8.26
Deb D 9⅜s 2017 .... Fa	BBB–	9/90	BBB	X	R	105.25	1-31-96	100	(2-1-98)	....	....	120	P1	'87	106⅛	96⅛	104⅞	8.94	8.86
Deb[10]E[7] 10s 2013 .... QAug	BBB–	9/90	BBB	X	R	104	7-31-96	....	....	....	....	23.1	J2	'88	104¾	100½	104½	9.57	9.47
Deb F 9¾s 2002 .... Jd15	BBB–			X	BE	NC	....	....	....	....	....	100	S1	'92	116⅞	104	116⅞	8.34	6.51
***[11]Southwestern Bell Cap* 25**	***4.14***	***4.65***	***5.60***		***Dc***	***455.0***	***3790***	***5283***	***9-30-95***	***5660***		***13639***	***55.0***						
M-T Nts 'D' 6.45s '98 .... [12]ms	A+	6/95	A	X	BE	NC	....	....	....	....	....	5.00	C5	'93	101⅝	95	101⅝	6.35	5.60
M-T Nts 'D' 6.45s '98 .... [12]ms	A+	6/95	A	X	BE	NC	....	....	....	....	....	7.00	S1	'93	101⅝	95	101⅝	6.35	5.60
M-T Nts 'D' 6¼s '98 .... [13]ms	A+	6/95	A	X	BE	NC	....	....	....	....	....	10.0	S1	'93	101¼	94⅜	101¼	6.17	5.61
M-T Nts 'D' 7s '99 .... [14]ms	A+	6/95	A	X	BE	NC	....	....	....	....	....	8.00	S1	'92	103⅞	94¼	103⅞	6.74	5.86
M-T Nts 'D' 7s '99 .... [15]ms	A+	6/95	A	X	BE	NC	....	....	....	....	....	15.0	C5	'92	104	94⅛	104	6.73	5.84
• M-T Nts 'D' 8.48s '99 .... [16]ms	A+			X	BE	102	(12-8-97)	....	....	....	....	75.0	S1	'95	100	100	90	9.42	11.72
M-T Nts 'D' 6¾s 2000 .... [17]ms	A+	6/95	A	X	BE	NC	....	....	....	....	....	20.0	S1	'93	103⅛	92⅞	103⅛	6.55	5.88
M-T Nts 'D' 6¾s 2000 .... [18]ms	A+	6/95	A	X	BE	NC	....	....	....	....	....	15.0	M2	'93	101¼	94⅜	101¼	6.67	6.40
M-T Nts 'D' 7¼s 2003 .... [19]ms	A+	6/95	A	X	BE	NC	....	....	....	....	....	11.0	S1	'93	106⅛	92¼	106⅛	6.83	6.16
M-T Nts 'D' 7.30s 2003 .... [19]ms	A+	6/95	A	X	BE	NC	....	....	....	....	....	10.0	S1	'93	106⅜	92½	106⅜	6.86	6.17
M-T Nts 'D' 7.10s 2003 .... [20]ms	A+	6/95	A	X	BE	NC	....	....	....	....	....	5.00	C5	'93	105¼	91⅜	105¼	6.75	6.17
M-T Nts 'D' 7.30s 2003 .... [21]ms	A+	6/95	A	X	BE	NC	....	....	....	....	....	6.00	C5	'93	106⅜	92⅜	106⅜	6.86	6.18
M-T Nts 'D' 7.05s 2004 .... [22]ms	A+	6/95	A	X	BE	NC	....	....	....	....	....	10.0	S1	'93	105	89⅝	105	6.71	6.29
F/R[23]M-T Nts 'D'[24] 4.9351s '97 .... QMar14	A+	6/95	A	X	BE	NC	....	....	....	....	....	50.0	S1	'94	100	99	99½	4.96	....
F/R[25]M-T Nts 'D' '97 .... QMay19	A+	6/95	A	X	BE	NC	....	....	....	....	....	50.0	M2	'94	100	99¾	100	....	....
F/R[26]M-T Nts 'D'[24] 5.52s '99 .... QApr26	A+	6/95	A	X	BE	NC	....	....	....	....	....	50.0	S1	'94	100⅛	99½	100	5.52	....
***Southwest'n Bell Tel[27]* 67a**	***4.17***	***4.70***	***5.43***		***Dc***	***50.50***	***2062***	***3198***	***9-30-95***	***4218***		***7637***	***65.2***						
Deb 4½s '97 .... fA	AA	6/95	A+	X	CR	100	....	....	....	....	....	100	H1	'62	98½	92	98½	4.57	5.50
Deb 5⅞s 2003 .... Jd	AA	6/95	A+	X	R	100.61	5-31-96	....	....	....	....	150	S1	'67	98	85⅛	98	5.99	6.21
Deb 5⅜s 2006 .... Jd	AA	6/95	A+	X	R	100.80	5-31-96	....	....	....	....	150	M6	'66	93¼	78⅜	93¼	5.76	6.27
Deb 6¾s 2008 .... Jd	AA	6/95	A+	X	R	101.20	5-31-96	....	....	....	....	150	H1	'68	102¾	85⅞	102¾	6.57	6.42

Uniform Footnote Explanations-See Page 260. Other: [1] Subsid of SPTC Holding (Rio Grande Indus),see. [2] Now Norfolk So'n Ry. [3] See Va & So'w'n Ry. [4] Fiscal Dec'93 & prior. [5] To be exch for Cap Sec when due. [6] (HRO)On any Jan 1 at 100(ltd). [7] Death red benefit,qtrly,as defined. [8] (HRO)On any Feb 1 at 100(ltd). [9] (HRO)On any Mar 1 at 100(ltd). [10] (HRO)On any Aug 1 at 100(ltd). [11] Subsid & data of SBC Communications. [12] Due 1-20-98. [13] Due 2-2-98. [14] Due 11-4-99. [15] Due 11-22-99. [16] Due 12-8-99. [17] Due 2-1-00. [18] Due 2-2-00. [19] Due 1-13-03. [20] Due 2-3-03. [21] Due 3-1-03. [22] Due 9-22-04. [23] Int adj thru 3-15-96,adj qtrly aft. [24] Issued in min denom $5T. [25] Int adj weekly. [26] Int thru 1-26-96,adj qtrly aft. [27] Subsid of SBC Communications.

Title-Industry Code & Co. Finances (In Italics) / Individual Issue Statistics (Exchange)	Ind / Interest Dates	1992 / S&P Debt Rating	1993 / Date of Last Rating Change	Prior Rating	1994 / Eligible	Year End / Bond Form	Cash & Equiv. / Redemption Provisions: Regular Price	Curr. Assets / Regular (Begins) Thru	Curr. Liab. / Sinking Fund Price	Balance Sheet Date / Sinking Fund (Begins) Thru	L. Term Debt (Mil $) / Refund/Other Restriction Price	Refund/Other Restriction (Begins) Thru	Capital-ization (Mil $) / Outst'g (Mil $)	Total Debt % Capital / Underwriting Firm	Underwriting Year	Price Range 1995 High	Price Range 1995 Low	Mo. End Price Sale(s) or Bid	Curr. Yield	Yield to Mat.
***Southwest'n Bell Tel** (Cont.)*																				
◆Deb 7¾s 2009	mS	**AA**	6/95	A+	X	R	102.12	8-31-96	....	....	....	....	125	B6	'71	103	92⅜	s103	7.52	7.40
◆Deb 6⅞s 2011	Fa	**AA**	6/95	A+	X	R	102.48	1-31-96	....	....	....	....	200	H1	'71	100⅜	83½	s99¾	6.89	6.90
◆Deb 7⅜s 2012	Mn	**AA**	6/95	A+	X	R	102.42	4-30-96	....	....	....	....	175	M6	'72	102¾	87⅝	s102¾	7.18	7.09
◆Deb 7⅝s 2013	aO	**AA**	6/95	A+	X	R	102.65	9-30-96	....	....	....	....	300	M6	'73	103	90⅛	s102½	7.44	7.37
•Deb 7s 2015	jJ	**AA**	6/95	A+	X	BE	NC	....	....	....	....	....	250	G1	'93	106½	86	102	6.86	6.81
•Deb 7⅝s 2023	Ms	**AA**	6/95	A+	X	BE	103.735	(3-1-03)	....	....	....	....	200	S1	'93	105	85⅝	104	7.33	7.28
Deb 6⅝s 2024	mS	**AA**	6/95	A+	X	BE	102.188	(9-1-03)	....	....	....	....	200	S1	'93	98	79⅛	98	6.76	6.78
•Deb 7¼s 2025	jJ15	**AA**	6/95	A+	X	BE	102.8605	(7-15-03)	....	....	....	....	150	G1	'93	104	84⅛	100¼	7.23	7.23
Deb 7.20s 2026	aO15	**AA**			X	BE	103.5375	(10-15-05)	....	....	....	....	300	M2	'95	103¾	97	103¾	6.94	6.90
•Nts 8.30s '96	Jd	**AA**	6/95	A+	X	BE	NC	....	....	....	....	....	200	G1	'91	103⅜	100¼	100¾	8.24	6.43
•Nts 6⅛s 2000	Ms	**AA**	6/95	A+	X	BE	NC	....	....	....	....	....	150	S1	'93	102	90¼	s100	6.13	6.12
•Nts 6⅜s 2001	Ao	**AA**	6/95	A+	X	BE	NC	....	....	....	....	....	200	M2	'93	102	91¼	101	6.31	6.15
Nts 6¼s 2002	aO15	**AA**			X	BE	NC	....	....	....	....	....	150	M2	'95	101⅝	98⅝	101⅝	6.15	5.95
Nts 5¾s 2004	mS	**AA**	6/95	A+	X	BE	100.674	(9-1-00)	....	....	....	....	200	S1	'93	97	82⅝	97	5.93	6.20
•Nts 6⅝s 2005	Ao	**AA**	6/95	A+	X	BE	NC	....	....	....	....	....	150	M2	'93	102¼	84¼	102	6.50	6.33
Southwest'n Elec Power[1]	***72a***	***3.48***	***3.79***		***3.64***	***Dc***	***0.45***	***163.0***	***219.0***	***9-30-95***	***595.0***		***1355***	***44.4***						
1st V 7¾s 2004	Jd	**AA–**			X	R	NC	....	□100	....	....	....	40.0	M6	'92	111¼	96¾	111¼	6.97	6.03
1st W 6⅛s '99	mS	**AA–**			X	R	NC	....	□100	....	....	....	40.0	F1	'92	100	92¼	98¾	6.20	6.51
1st X 7s 2007	mS	**AA–**			X	R	NC	....	□100	....	....	....	90.0	F1	'92	106⅝	89	106⅝	6.57	6.19
1st Y 6⅝s 2003	Fa	**AA–**			X	R	NC	....	□100	....	....	....	55.0	M2	'93	103	90⅛	103	6.43	6.10
1st Z 7¼s 2023	jJ	**AA–**			X	R	103.06	(7-1-03)	□100	....	....	....	45.0	G1	'93	102¼	84¾	102¼	7.09	7.06
1st AA 5¼s 2000	Ao	**AA–**			X	R	NC	....	....	....	....	....	45.0	M6	'93	97½	87¼	97½	5.38	5.92
1st BB 6⅞s 2025	aO	**AA–**			X	R	103.08	(10-1-03)	....	....	....	....	80.0	M6	'93	97¾	80½	97¾	7.03	7.06
Southwestern Energy	***73b***	***3.97***	***5.29***		***4.75***	***Dc***	***1.04***	***44.00***	***42.00***	***9-30-95***	***★188.0***		***373.0***	***48.8***						
Str Nts 6.70s 2005	jD	**BBB+**			X	BE	NC	....	....	....	....	....	125	M6	'95	101¼	99¾	101¼	6.62	6.53
Southwestern Public Serv	***72a***	***△4.82***	***△4.83***		***△5.21***	***Au***	***36.90***	***171.0***	***170.0***	***8-31-95***	***582.0***		***1652***	***35.3***						
1st 5.70s '97	Fa	**AA**			X	R	100.20	1-31-96	□100	....	....	....	15.0	D4	'67	100⅛	96	100⅛	5.69	5.57
1st 6⅞s '99	jD	**AA**			X	BE	NC	....	....	....	....	....	90.0	D4	'92	103½	94⅛	103½	6.64	5.86
1st 7¼s 2004	jJ15	**AA**			X	R	NC	....	....	....	....	....	135	D4	'92	107⅜	92¾	107⅜	6.75	6.13
1st 8¼s 2022	jJ15	**AA**			X	R	103.575	(7-15-02)	▲100	....	....	....	40.0	D4	'92	112⅝	94⅞	112⅝	7.33	7.18
1st 8.20s 2022	jD	**AA**			X	BE	104.038	(12-1-02)	Z100	....	....	....	100	D4	'92	112⅞	94⅞	112⅞	7.26	7.12
1st 8½s 2025	Fa15	**AA**			X	BE	104.225	(2-15-05)	▲100	....	....	....	70.0	D4	'95	116⅜	99⅞	116⅜	7.30	7.15
Sovereign Bancorp	***10a***	***2.20***	***2.13***		***1.97***	***Dc***				***9-30-95***	***933.0***		***1348***	***69.2***						
Sr Nts 6¾s 2000	jJ	**BBB**			X	BE	NC	....	....	....	....	....	50.0	M2	'95	102	80	102	6.62	6.23
Sub Deb 6¾s 2000	mS	**BB+**			Y	BE	NC	....	....	....	....	....	50.0	B5	'93	99¼	80	98⅜	6.86	7.16
Sub Deb 8½s 2002	mS15	**NR**				R	101.70	(9-15-99)	....	....	....	....	20.0	W4	'92	103	90⅝	102	8.33	8.10
Sovran Financial[2]	***10***	***Now NationsBank Corp,see NCNB Corp***																		
Nts 9¼s 2006	Jd15	**A**	1/92	A–	X	R	NC	....	....	....	....	....	125	F1	'86	122	102¾	122	7.58	6.34
Sub Cap[3]Nts 9¾s '99	Jd15	**A–**	1/92	BBB+	X	R	NC	....	....	....	Z100	....	100	F1	'87	111⅞	104⅜	111⅞	8.72	5.90
Specialty Equipment Cos	***42b***	***n/a***	***d1.00***		***d0.80***	***Ja***	***3.24***	***118.0***	***96.60***	***7-31-95***	***193.0***		***70.60***	***273.0***						
Sr Sub Nts[4] 11⅜s 2003	jD	**B–**			Y	R	105.70	(12-1-98)	....	....	[5]Z110	12-1-96	185	M2	'93	104½	96½	103	11.04	10.80
SpectraVision Inc[6]	***24a***	***0.15***	***0.22***		***d0.38***	***Dc***	***Bankruptcy Chapt 11***				***[7]599.0***		***164.0***	***365.0***						
Sr Disc[8]Nts[9] 11½s 2001	§aO	**D**	6/95	CCC+	Z	R			Default 10-1-95 int				[10]210	D6	'93	47	8½	21	....	Flat
◆Sr Sub([11]PIK)Reset Nts[12] 11.65s 2002	§jD	**D**	6/95	CCC–	Z	R			Default 6-1-95 int				226	Exch.	'92	16⅞	3	6	....	Flat
Spieker Properties L.P.	***57***	***n/a***	***n/a***		***1.30***	***Dc***	***8.97***			***9-30-95***	***★463.0***		***931.0***	***49.7***						
Nts 6.65s 2000	jD15	**BBB**			X	BE	[13]Z100	....	....	....	....	....	100	G1	'95	99⅞	99	99⅞	6.66	6.68

Uniform Footnote Explanations-See Page 260. Other: [1] Contr by Central & South West Corp. [2] Was Virginia Nat'l Bankshrs. [3] To be exch for Cap Sec when due. [4] (HRO)On Chge of Ctrl at 101. [5] Max $55.5M red w/proceeds of Pub Off'g. [6] Was SPI Holdings. [7] Incl liabs subj to compromise. [8] (HRO)On Chge of Ctrl at 101(Accreted Val). [9] Int accr at 11.50% fr 10-1-96. [10] Incl disc. [11] Co to pay int in add'l nts for 6-1-95 pyt. [12] ASE trad'g halted 6-8-95, trad'g O-T-C. [13] Plus make-whole premium.

Title-Industry Code & Co. Finances (In Italics) / Individual Issue Statistics, Exchange	Ind / Interest Dates	Fixed Charge Coverage 1992 / S&P Debt Rating	1993 / Date of Last Rating Change	1994 / Prior Rating	Eligible	Year End / Bond Form	Million $ Cash & Equiv. / Redemption Provisions: Regular Price	Curr. Assets / Regular (Begins) Thru	Curr. Liab. / Sinking Fund Price	Balance Sheet Date / Sinking Fund (Begins) Thru	L. Term Debt (Mil $) / Refund/Other Restriction Price	Refund/Other Restriction (Begins) Thru	Capital-ization (Mil $) / Outst'g (Mil $)	Total Debt % Capital / Underwriting Firm	Underwriting Year	Price Range 1995 High	Low	Mo. End Price Sale(s) or Bid	Curr. Yield	Yield to Mat.
***Spieker Properties L.P.** (Cont.)*																				
Nts 6.80s 2001	jD15	**BBB**			X	BE	[1]Z100	....	....	....	....	....	50.0	G1	'95	101⅞	99⅞	101⅞	6.67	6.42
Nts 6.95s 2002	jD15	**BBB**			X	BE	[1]Z100	....	....	....	....	....	110	G1	'95	100	98⅝	99¼	7.00	7.09
Spreckels Indus	***26a***	*Δn/a*	*Δn/a*	*Δ0.53*		*Je*	*2.44*	*164.0*	*96.00*	*6-30-95*	*83.70*		*193.0*	*62.2*						
Sr[2]Sec Nts 11½s 2000	[3]mn	**B**			Y	R	100	(9-1-98)	....	....	....	....	70.0	Exch.	'93	107¼	95¼	106¼	10.82	9.79
Sprint[4]Corp[5]	***67b***	*2.52*	*3.31*	*4.37*		*Dc*	*364.0*	*2578*	*3263*	*9-30-95*	*5474*		*11119*	*54.3*						
Deb 9¼s 2022	Ao15	**BBB**	2/94	BBB–	X	R	NC	....	....	....	....	....	200	D6	'92	127¾	104	127¾	7.24	6.94
Nts 8⅛s 2002	jJ15	**BBB**	2/94	BBB–	X	R	NC	....	....	....	....	....	150	L3	'92	110⅝	97⅝	110⅝	7.34	6.13
SPX Corp	***8***	*3.34*	*1.78*	*1.46*		*Dc*	*20.80*	*381.0*	*225.0*	*9-30-95*	*319.0*		*489.0*	*65.8*						
• Sr Sub Nts[6] 11¾s 2002	Jd	**B**			Y	R	[7]Z100	5-31-98	....	....	[8]Z110.75	5-31-96	260	M2	'94	107⅞	101	106	11.08	10.44
Standard Brands	***69a***	***Now Nabisco Brands,see RJR Nabisco, Inc***																		
• SF Deb 7¾s 2001	Mn	**BBB**	6/95	BBB–	X	R	100.31	4-30-96	100	....	....	....	8.70	L3	'71	100	91	99⅞	7.76	7.78
[9]Standard[10]Oil(Ohio)[11]	***49c***	*n/a*	*n/a*	*n/a*		*Dc*	*188.0*	*8897*	*8589*	*:12-31-94*	*5705*		*17804*	*37.9*						
Gtd[12]Deb 9s 2019	Jd	**AA–**	6/92	AA	X	R	100	(6-1-99)	....	....	[13]Z100	....	158	Exch.	'89	109½	101	109½	8.22	8.09
Standard Pacific	***13h***	*0.40*	*0.32*	*0.67*		*Dc*				*9-30-95*	*327.0*		*617.0*	*53.0*						
• Sr Nts 10½s 2000	Ms	**BB**			Y	R	NC	....	100	(3-1-97)	....	....	100	L3	'93	104½	97½	s103⅛	10.18	9.57
Stanley Works	***13e***	*6.06*	*5.63*	*7.01*		*Dc*	*48.50*	*929.0*	*414.0*	*9-30-95*	*396.0*		*1158*	*35.2*						
Nts 9s '98	Fa	**A**			X	R	NC	....	....	....	....	....	34.8	S1	'88	106⅞	101	106¾	8.43	5.53
Nts 7⅜s 2002	jD15	**A**			X	BE	NC	....	....	....	....	....	100	F1	'92	107⅜	94⅜	107⅜	6.87	6.06
Star Cablevision Gr	***12a***	....	....	....		*Dc*	***No Recent Fin'ls***													
Sr Sub Deb 13½s 2002	§fA15	**NR**	6/90	CCC	Z	R			Default 2-15-91 int				50.0	M6	'87	21	21	A21	....	Flat
State St Boston	***10***	*2.40*	*2.55*	*2.22*		*Dc*				*9-30-95*	*656.0*		*2195*	*29.9*						
Nts 5.95s 2003	mS15	**AA–**			X	BE	NC	....	....	....	....	....	100	G1	'93	98	84¼	98	6.07	6.28
Stater Bros. Holdings	***59c***	*2.38*	*1.98*	*2.35*		*Sp*	*21.90*	*155.0*	*110.0*	*6-25-95*	*173.0*		*187.0*	*93.6*						
◆Sr Nts[14] 11s 2001	Ms	**B+**	7/94	NR	Y	BE	NC	....	....	....	....	....	165	Exch.	'94	No Sale		A95	11.58	12.33
Station Casinos	***40i***	*3.00*	*3.04*	*0.39*		*Mr*	*27.10*	*50.40*	*77.00*	*9-30-95*	*329.0*		*524.0*	*66.4*						
Sr[15]Sub[16]Nts 9⅝s 2003	Jd	**B+**	7/95	B	Y	R	103.61	(6-1-98)	....	....	....	....	110	S1	'93	98¼	84	98	9.82	10.01
Sr[16]Sub[15]Nts 9⅝s 2003	Jd	**B+**	7/95	B	Y	R	103.61	(5-4-98)	....	....	....	....	83.0	S1	'94	98¼	84	98	9.82	10.01
Stevens(JP)&Co	***68a***	***Now WestPoint Stevens,see***																		
SF Deb 9s 2017	Ms	**BB**	11/93	CCC–	Y	R	105.40	2-29-96	100	(3-1-98)	®104.50	2-28-97	75.0	G1	'87	100	85	100	9.00	9.00
Stone Container	***16c***	*0.48*	*d0.07*	*0.67*		*Dc*	*102.0*	*2118*	*873.0*	*9-30-95*	*4379*		*5753*	*77.1*						
• 1st Mtg Nts[15] 10¾s 2002	aO	**BB–**	6/95	B+	Y	R	103.07	(10-1-99)	....	....	....	....	500	S1	'94	108	99	104	10.34	9.92
• Sr Nts[15] 12⅝s '98	jJ15	**B+**	6/95	B	Y	R	NC	....	....	....	....	....	150	S1	'93	108½	105⅝	107½	11.74	9.24
• Sr Nts[15] 11⅞s '98	jD	**B+**	6/95	B	Y	R	NC	....	....	....	....	....	240	M2	'91	110	102⅝	s104⅞	11.32	9.91
• Sr Nts[15] 9⅞s 2001	Fa	**B+**	6/95	B	Y	R	101.646	(2-1-99)	....	....	....	....	710	S1	'94	102	93⅝	s98	10.08	10.39
• Sr Nts[15] 11½s 2004	aO	**B+**	6/95	B	Y	R	104.31	(10-1-99)	....	....	....	....	200	S1	'94	112	99⅛	s102⅜	11.23	11.06
• Sr Sub[17]Deb[15] 10¾s 2002	Ao	**B**	6/95	B–	Y	R	105.375	(4-1-97)	....	....	....	....	200	B5	'92	104½	94⅜	s98½	10.91	11.08
• Sr Sub Nts 10¾s '97	Jd15	**B**	6/95	B–	Y	R	104	6-14-96	....	....	....	....	150	S1	'92	104⅝	100⅝	s102⅛	10.53	9.16
• Sr Sub Nts[15] 11s '99	fA15	**B**	6/95	B–	Y	R	104	(8-15-97)	....	....	....	....	125	B9	'92	105⅝	97¼	s98½	11.17	11.51
• Sr Sub Nts[17] 11½s '99	mS	**B**	6/95	B–	Y	R	102.875	8-31-96	100	(9-1-97)	....	....	230	D7	'89	104⅜	98¼	s101⅜	11.34	11.02
Stop & Shop Cos	***59c***	*2.27*	*2.66*	*3.15*		*Ja*	*11.60*	*363.0*	*524.0*	*1-28-95*	*760.0*		*1063*	*74.5*						
Sr Sub Nts 9¾s 2002	Fa	**BB+**	4/94	BB–	Y	R	NC	....	....	....	....	....	195	B9	'92	110	100¾	109½	8.90	7.76
Storer[18]Communications[19]	***12***	*0.43*	*1.01*	*0.48*		*Dc*	*0.96*			*9-30-95*	*125.0*		*1259*	*9.9*						
◆Sub Deb 10s 2003	Mn15	**B+**	9/93	B	Y	R	100	....	100	....	....	....	[20]139	L3	'83	101½	95	101⅛	9.89	9.78
Strawbridge & Clothier	***59f***	*2.27*	*2.28*	*2.54*		*Ja*	*3.96*	*364.0*	*223.0*	*10-28-95*	*198.0*		*534.0*	*56.4*						
Nts 6⅝s 2003	aO15	**BBB–**	9/95	BBB	X	R	NC	....	....	....	....	....	50.0	K2	'93	98⅝	87⅝	93	7.12	7.84
Student Loan Mktg Assn	***25b***	*1.39*	*1.56*	*1.27*		*Dc*	*12697*			*12-31-94*	*34319*		*48806*	*97.0*						
Nts[21] 7.56s '96	jD9	**NR**				BE	NC	....	....	....	....	....	300	L3	'94	102½	99½	102⅛	7.40	5.25

Uniform Footnote Explanations-See Page 260. Other: [1] Plus make-whole premium. [2] (HRO)On Chge of Ctrl at 101 to 8-31-98,100 aft. [3] Due Sep 1. [4] See United Telecommun. [5] See Centel Cap, Central Tel Va. [6] Co must offer repurch at 101 on Chge of Ctrl. [7] On Chge of Ctrl,plus Applicable Prem to 6-1-98. [8] Max $78M red w/proceeds Pub Eq Off'g. [9] See Kennecott Copper. [10] Acquired by BP America. [11] Subsid & data of British Petroleum. [12] Gtd by British Petroleum Co plc. [13] May red for U.K. tax law chge. [14] Co must offer repurch at 101 or Chge of Ctrl. [15] (HRO)On Chge of Ctrl at 101. [16] State gaming laws may req hldr's sale/Co red. [17] Int may be reset if below min Net Worth levels. [18] See SCI Hldgs. [19] Subsid of Comcast Corp. [20] Incl disc. [21] Issued in min denom $10T.

Title-Industry Code & Co. Finances (In Italics)	Ind	Fixed Charge Coverage 1992	1993	1994	Year End	Million $ Cash & Equiv.	Curr. Assets	Curr. Liab.	Balance Sheet Date	L. Term Debt (Mil $)	Capital-ization (Mil $)	Total Debt % Capital

Exchange ↓ Individual Issue Statistics	Interest Dates	S&P Debt Rating	Date of Last Rating Change	Prior Rating	Eligible ↓ Bond Form	Redemption Provisions: Regular Price	Regular (Begins) Thru	Sinking Fund Price	Sinking Fund (Begins) Thru	Refund/Other Restriction Price	Refund/Other Restriction (Begins) Thru	Outst'g (Mil $)	Underwriting Firm	Underwriting Year	Price Range 1995 High	Price Range 1995 Low	Mo. End Price Sale(s) or Bid	Curr. Yield	Yield to Mat.
***Student Loan Mktg Assn** (Cont.)*																			
Nts[1] 7.82s '99	aO14	**NR**			BE	■100	(10-14-96)	....	....	....	....	500	C5	'94	102⅛	98¾	101⅝	7.70	7.33
Nts 9.80s 2000	mS20	**NR**			BE	100	....	....	....	....	....	200	S1	'88	103	100	100	9.80	9.79
Nts 7.30s 2012	fA	**NR**			BE	NC	....	....	....	....	....	131	L3	'92	109⅜	90⅞	109½	6.67	6.37
Global Nts[1] 7s '98	Ms3	**NR**			BE	NC	....	....	....	....	....	750	M2	'95	103⅜	99½	103½	6.77	5.30
Global Nts[2] 7.44s 2000	Ms28	**NR**			BE	■*100	(3-28-97)	....	....	....	....	300	L3	'95	102⅞	100	102¼	7.28	6.84
F/R[3]Nts 'BC' '96	QAug22	**NR**			BE	NC	....	....	....	....	....	200	M6	'91	100½	99½	100⅛	....	....
F/R[3]Nts 'BE' '96	QNov	**NR**			BE	NC	....	....	....	....	....	150	M6	'91	100¼	99½	100⅛	....	....
F/R[3]Nts 'BK' '97	QJan23	**NR**			BE	NC	....	....	....	....	....	500	M2	'92	100½	99½	100¼	....	....
F/R[3]Nts 'BM' '97	QFeb14	**NR**			BE	NC	....	....	....	....	....	400	G1	'92	100¼	99	100¼	....	....
F/R[4]Nts 'BP' '99	QApr16	**NR**			BE	NC	....	....	....	....	....	150	M2	'92	101⅝	99	101⅜	....	....
F/R[5]Nts[6]'BQ' 6.18s '97	QApr21	**NR**			BE	NC	....	....	....	....	....	300	M2	'92	100⅞	99	100½	6.15	....
F/R[7]Nts[8]'BR' '96	QMay	**NR**			BE	NC	....	....	....	....	....	300	L3	'92	100	99¾	100	....	....
F/R[3]Nts'BX' '97	QOct30	**NR**			BE	NC	....	....	....	....	....	500	M6	'92	100½	99½	100¼	....	....
F/R[3]Nts'BZ' '97	QNov20	**NR**			BE	NC	....	....	....	....	....	500	L3	'92	100½	99½	100¼	....	....
F/R[7]Nts 'CA' '98	QJan21	**NR**			BE	NC	....	....	....	....	....	500	G1	'93	100⅜	99¼	100¼	....	....
F/R[7]Nts 'CC' '97	QMar3	**NR**			BE	NC	....	....	....	....	....	500	M2	'93	100⅜	99½	100⅛	....	....
F/R[7]Nts 'CD' '96	QApr16	**NR**			BE	NC	....	....	....	....	....	600	L3	'93	100⅛	99⅞	100	....	....
F/R[7]Nts 'CE' '96	QMay14	**NR**			BE	NC	....	....	....	....	....	500	G1	'93	100⅛	99⅞	100	....	....
F/R[7]Nts 'CF' '96	QJul19	**NR**			BE	NC	....	....	....	....	....	600	M6	'93	100	99⅞	100	....	....
F/R[7]Nts 'CG' '98	QAug20	**NR**			BE	100	(8-20-98)	....	....	....	....	500	L3	'93	100	99⅛	99⅞	....	....
F/R[9]Nts 'CH' '98	QSep28	**NR**			BE	■100	....	....	....	....	....	600	M2	'93	100	99⅛	99⅞	....	....
F/R[9]Nts 'CJ' '97	QOct14	**NR**			BE	■100	....	....	....	....	....	700	G1	'93	100	99½	99⅞	....	....
F/R[9]Nts 'CK' '98	QNov10	**NR**			BE	■100	....	....	....	....	....	700	L3	'93	100	99⅛	99⅞	....	....
F/R[7]Nts 'CL' '97	QNov24	**NR**			BE	■100	....	....	....	....	....	700	M6	'93	100	99½	99⅞	....	....
F/R[7]Nts 'CM' '99	QJan13	**NR**			BE	■100	....	....	....	....	....	700	C5	'94	100	99	99⅞	....	....
F/R[10]Nts 'CN' '99	QFeb8	**NR**			BE	■100	....	....	....	....	....	700	G1	'94	100	99	99⅞	....	....
F/R[10]Nts 'CQ' 2001	QMar7	**NR**			BE	■100	(3-7-96)	....	....	....	....	500	M2	'94	99⅞	98½	99¾	....	....
F/R[9]Nts 'CS' '99	QAug2	**NR**			BE	■100	....	....	....	....	....	800	L3	'94	100	99	99⅞	....	....
F/R[7]Nts 'CT' '96	QSep23	**NR**			BE	■100	....	....	....	....	....	700	M5	'94	100	99¾	100	....	....
F/R[10]Nts 'CU' '97	QOct17	**NR**			BE	■100	....	....	....	....	....	500	C5	'94	100	99½	100	....	....
F/R[9]Nts 'CX' '96	QDec20	**NR**			BE	NC	....	....	....	....	....	700	L3	'95	100	99⅞	100	....	....
F/R[9]Nts 'DA' '98	QFeb17	**NR**			BE	NC	....	....	....	....	....	600	M6	'95	100¼	99¾	100⅛	....	....
F/R[7]Nts 'DF' '97	QAug4	**NR**			BE	NC	....	....	....	....	....	600	C5	'95	100⅛	100	100	....	....
F/R[11]Nts '10B' 4.85s '96	fA6	**NR**			BE	NC	....	....	....	....	....	100	M6	'91	100	99¾	100	4.85	....
F/R[12]Nts '10C' 4.07s '97	[13]fa6	**NR**			BE	NC	....	....	....	....	....	200	M2	'92	100	96⅝	98⅜	4.14	....
F/R[14]Nts '10D' 3.88s '97	[15]fa18	**NR**			BE	NC	....	....	....	....	....	100	M2	'92	99¾	96½	98⅛	3.95	....
F/R[16]Nts[2] '10J' 4⅝s '98	QJun	**NR**			BE	NC	....	....	....	....	....	150	M2	'93	100	95	98	4.72	....
Multi-Ind[17]F/R Nts'T' '96	mN15	**NR**			BE	NC	....	....	....	....	....	50.0	F1	'91	101	99⅞	100	....	....
Multi-Ind[18]F/R Nts'AM' 6.08s '96	[19]jd30	**NR**			BE	NC	....	....	....	....	....	1000	M2	'93	100⅜	99¼	100⅜	6.06	....
Multi-Ind[10]F/R Nts'AV'[1] '97	Jd30	**NR**			BE	NC	....	....	....	....	....	1250	M2	'94	101	99½	100	....	....
Prime Indexed[20]F/R Nts[2] '96	QMay15	**NR**			BE	NC	....	....	....	....	....	100	M2	'93	99⅞	98¾	99⅞	....	....
Prime Indexed[2]F/R[20]Nts '97	QJan21	**NR**			BE	NC	....	....	....	....	....	100	C4	'94	100⅝	99½	100⅜	....	....
F/R[21]Nts[22] 4.611s '96	QOct	**NR**			BE	NC	....	....	....	....	....	350	M2	'91	100¼	97½	99⅛	4.65	....
F/R[23]Nts 4.466s '96	QOct15	**NR**			R	NC	....	....	....	....	....	150	L3	'91	100	96⅝	99⅛	4.51	....
T-Bill[9]Inverse[24]F/R[2]Nts '97	QMay5	**NR**			BE	NC	....	....	....	....	....	100	L3	'92	101⅞	99½	101⅞	....	....
LIBOR Inverse[25]F/R Nts 7.6207s '97	Fa20	**NR**			BE	NC	....	....	....	....	....	100	M6	'92	101½	99½	101½	7.51	....

Uniform Footnote Explanations-See Page 260. Other: [1] Issued in min denom $10T. [2] Issued in min denom $100T. [3] Int(max 24%)adj weekly,as defined. [4] Int(max 9%)adj weekly,as defined. [5] Int thru 1-20-96,adj qtrly aft. [6] Int max 8.75% to 4-21-96,incr 1% ea 4-21 aft. [7] Int adj weekly,as defined. [8] Int max 5.80% to 5-1-93,incr 1% ea 5-1 aft. [9] Int adj weekly. [10] Int adj weekly, as defined. [11] Int(max 24%)to 2-5-96,adj qtrly aft. [12] Int(max 24%)to 1-5-96,adj mthly aft. [13] Due 11-6-97. [14] Int (max 24%)to 01-17-96,adj mthly aft. [15] Due 12-18-97. [16] Int(max 5.265%)to 2-28-96,adj qtrly aft. [17] Int(max 24%)at 0% to 5-15-96. [18] Int to 6-30-96,adj anly aft. [19] Due 7-1-96:int pd j&d 30 to 1995,then 7-1-96. [20] Int adj daily. [21] Int(max 24%)to 1-1-96,adj mthly aft. [22] Int adj mthly for 11 Dist Cost of Funds. [23] Int(max 25%)to 1-14-96,adj mthly aft. [24] Int min:4.25% to 5-5-94,incr 0.75% ea 5-5- aft. [25] Int(max 14.75%)to 2-19-96,adj semi-anly aft.

Title-Industry Code & Co. Finances (In Italics) / Individual Issue Statistics (Exchange)	Ind / Interest Dates	Fixed Charge Coverage 1992 / S&P Debt Rating	1993 / Date of Last Rating Change	1994 / Prior Rating	Eligible	Year End / Bond Form	Million $: Cash & Equiv. / Redemption Provisions: Regular Price	Curr. Assets / Regular (Begins) Thru	Curr. Liab. / Sinking Fund Price	Balance Sheet Date / Sinking Fund (Begins) Thru	L. Term Debt (Mil $) / Refund/Other Restriction Price	Refund/Other Restriction (Begins) Thru	Capitalization (Mil $) / Outst'g (Mil $)	Total Debt % Capital / Underwriting Firm	Underwriting Year	Price Range 1995 High	Price Range 1995 Low	Mo. End Price Sale(s) or Bid	Curr. Yield	Yield to Mat.
***Student Loan Mktg Assn** (Cont.)*																				
Inverse[1]F/R[2]Nts[3] '98	QNov16	**NR**				BE	*Z■100	....	....	....	....	....	50.0	G1	'93	100	83⅝	88½	....	....
Step-Up Nts[1] 6s '99	Fa24	**NR**				BE	■100	....	....	....	....	....	100	M6	'94	100⅛	94⅜	100⅛	5.99	5.95
LIBOR[4]F/R Nts 5½s '98	QFeb4	**NR**				BE	NC	....	....	....	....	....	100	M2	'93	100¾	99¼	100½	5.47	....
Summit Communications Group	***12***	***1.29***	***1.34***	***1.53***		***Dc***	***96.20***	***102.0***	***14.80***	***9-30-95***	***140.0***		***150.0***	***93.3***						
Sr Sub Deb[5] 10½s 2005	Ao15	**NR**	5/95	B–		R	102.62	(4-15-99)	....	....	....	....	140	D6	'93	111	101	111	9.46	8.74
Sun Co.	***49d***	***2.33***	***4.30***	***2.36***		***Dc***	***18.00***	***1316***	***1482***	***9-30-95***	***888.0***		***2704***	***33.5***						
• SF Deb 9⅜s 2016	Jd	**BBB+**	10/94	A–	X	R	100	(6-1-06)	100	(6-1-07)	....	....	200	F1	'86	114	100⅛	110⅛	8.51	8.33
Deb 9s 2024	mN	**BBB+**			X	R	NC	....	....	....	....	....	100	C5	'94	123½	99⅜	123½	7.29	7.08
Nts 8⅛s '99	mN	**BBB+**			X	R	NC	....	....	....	....	....	150	C5	'94	107¼	98½	107¼	7.58	5.98
• Nts 7.95s 2001	jD15	**BBB+**	10/94	A–	X	R	NC	....	....	....	....	....	150	L3	'91	106	93½	104½	7.61	7.01
Nts 7⅛s 2004	Ms15	**BBB+**	10/94	A–	X	R	NC	....	....	....	....	....	100	L3	'94	105⅜	91	105⅜	6.76	6.28
SunAmerica Inc[6]	***35a***	***△6.08***	***△5.77***	***△1.52***		***Sp***	***855.0***			***9-30-95***	***525.0***		***1791***	***29.3***						
Deb 9.95s 2012	Fa	**A**			X	R	NC	....	....	....	....	....	100	M2	'92	129	109⅝	129	7.71	6.93
Deb 8⅛s 2023	Ao28	**A**			X	R	NC	....	....	....	....	....	100	M2	'93	110⅞	88¼	110⅞	7.33	7.21
Nts 9s '99	Jj15	**A**			X	R	NC	....	....	....	....	....	125	M2	'92	108½	102	108⅛	8.32	6.04
SunTrust Banks Inc[7]	***10***	***5.16***	***5.42***	***4.44***		***Dc***				***9-30-95***	***1002***		***5069***	***19.8***						
Nts 8⅜s '96	Ms	**A+**	5/90	AA	X	R	NC	....	....	....	....	....	74.5	M2	'86	101½	100⅜	100⅜	8.34	6.01
Nts 8⅞s '98	Fa	**A+**	5/90	AA	X	R	NC	....	....	....	....	....	94.5	S1	'88	106½	101⅛	106¼	8.35	5.66
Nts 7⅜s 2002	jJ	**A+**			X	BE	NC	....	....	....	....	....	200	L3	'92	107⅛	93⅜	107⅛	6.88	6.03
F/R[8]Nts 6.2065s '99	QJun18	**A+**			X	BE	NC	....	....	....	....	....	200	S1	'94	100½	99	100	6.21	....
Sub Nts 6⅛s 2004	Fa15	**A**			X	BE	NC	....	....	....	....	....	200	L3	'94	99⅞	84¼	99⅞	6.13	6.14
[9]Super Rite Foods	***59c***	***0.98***	***1.71***	***2.87***		***Fb***	***7.47***	***135.0***	***106.0***	***9-2-95***	***92.60***		***155.0***	***65.2***						
Sr Sub[10]Nts[11] 10⅝s 2002	Ao	**BB+**	11/95	B	Y	R	105.31	(4-1-97)	....	....	....	....	75.0	B5	'92	109½	96½	109⅜	9.71	8.65
Super Value Stores	***26g***	***Now Supervalu Inc,see***																		
SF Deb[12] 8⅞s 2016	Ao	**BBB+**	6/95	A	X	R	104.736	3-31-96	100	(4-1-97)	®104.306	3-31-96	22.1	G1	'86	107⅛	98¾	104⅞	8.46	8.37
[13]Nts[12] 8⅞s '99	Jd15	**BBB+**	6/95	A	X	R	NC	....	....	....	....	....	45.0	F1	'89	109¾	101⅝	109¾	8.09	5.73
Supervalu Inc[14]	***26g***	***3.84***	***3.32***	***2.79***		***Fb***	***5.47***	***1565***	***1330***	***9-9-95***	***1208***		***2550***	***53.8***						
Nts 7¼s '99	jJ15	**BBB+**	6/95	A	X	BE	NC	....	....	....	....	....	150	G1	'94	104⅞	98⅜	104⅞	6.91	5.71
Nts 7.80s 2002	mN15	**BBB+**	6/95	A	X	BE	NC	....	....	....	....	....	300	G1	'92	109⅝	95⅞	109⅝	7.12	6.07
Nts 8⅞s 2022	mN15	**BBB+**	6/95	A	X	BE	104.396	(11-15-02)	....	....	....	....	100	G1	'92	115⅞	97⅛	115⅞	7.66	7.49
Surgical Health	***30a***	***3.75***	***3.53***	***1.93***		***Dc***	***5.86***	***33.10***	***14.10***	***3-31-95***	***95.90***		***176.0***	***55.6***						
• Sr Sub Nts[15] 11½s 2004	jJ15	**NR**	6/95	B–		R	105.75	(7-15-99)	....	....	[16]Z110	7-14-97	7.50	S5	'94	No Sale		115	10.00	8.95
Susquehanna Bancshares	***10***	***11.15***	***12.33***	***12.54***		***Dc***				***9-30-95***	***92.00***		***326.0***	***28.2***						
Sub Nts 9s 2005	Fa	**BBB–**			X	BE	NC	....	....	....	....	....	50.0		'95	105	96	105	8.57	8.21
[17]Sweetheart Cup Co	***50***	***[18]0.48***	***0.57***	***1.42***		***Sp***	***12.20***	***304.0***	***141.0***	***9-30-94***	***370.0***		***481.0***	***77.1***						
Sr Sec[5]Nts[19] 9⅝s 2000	mS	**B+**			Y	R	103.208	(9-1-97)	....	....	[20]109.625	8-30-96	190	D6	'93	101¼	93	101	9.53	9.35
Sr Sub[5]Nts[19] 10½s 2003	mS	**B–**			Y	R	103.938	(9-1-98)	....	....	[21]110.50	8-30-96	110	D6	'93	100	92	100	10.50	10.49
Synovus Financial	***10***	***6.36***	***8.44***	***8.52***		***Dc***				***9-30-95***	***122.0***		***813.0***	***15.0***						
Sr Nts 6⅛s 2003	aO15	**A**			X	BE	NC	....	....	....	....	....	75.0	S1	'93	99⅜	83	99⅜	6.16	6.23
Synthetic Indus	***68b***	***△1.37***	***△2.00***	***△1.24***		***Sp***	***0.11***	***108.0***	***39.30***	***9-30-95***	***192.0***		***250.0***	***76.8***						
Sr Sub Deb[5] 12¾s 2002	jD	**B–**			Y	R	106.375	(12-1-97)	....	....	....	....	140	M2	'92	101	88	98	13.01	13.19
Sysco Corp	***26g***	***△9.28***	***△10.92***	***△10.86***		***Je***	***90.30***	***1915***	***1077***	***9-30-95***	***p446.0***		***2004***	***28.2***						
Sr Nts 6½s 2005	Jd15	**AA–**			X	BE	NC	....	....	....	....	....	150	M2	'95	103½	95⅜	103½	6.28	6.01
System Energy Resources[22]	***72***	***2.07***	***1.86***	***1.23***		***Dc***	***51.70***	***202.0***	***488.0***	***9-30-95***	***1243***		***2502***	***65.0***						
1st 10½s '96	mS	**BBB–**	4/90	BB+	X	R	NC	....	Z100	....	....	....	250	M6	'86	104⅜	102⅝	102⅝	10.23	6.42
1st 6s '98	Ao	**BBB–**			X	BE	NC	....	Z100	....	....	....	60.0	M6	'93	98½	92	98½	6.09	6.72

Uniform Footnote Explanations-See Page 260. Other: [1] Issued in min denom $100T. [2] Int(max 14%,min 0%). [3] Int at 0% thru 11-15-96,adj ea 11-15 aft. [4] Int to 2-2-96,adj qtrly aft. [5] (HRO)On Chge of Ctrl at 101. [6] Was Broad Inc, see. [7] See Third Nat'l Corp. [8] Int to 9-17-95,adj qtrly aft(3 Mo LIBOR&0.18%). [9] Subsid & data of Super Rite Corp. [10] Co offer on Chge in Ctrl,101/Asset Sale,100. [11] Gtd by SRF Subsid Corp, Foodarama Inc, et al. [12] Issued in min denom $5T. [13] (HRO)At 100 for Designated Event&Rat'g Decline. [14] Was Super Valu Stores,see. [15] Co must offer repurch at 101 on Chge of Ctrl. [16] Max $18.75M red w/proceeds Com Off'g. [17] Subsid & data of Sweetheart Holdings. [18] Fiscal Dec,'92 & prior. [19] Gtd by Sweetheart Holdings. [20] Max $63.3M red w/proceeds of Com Off'g. [21] Max $36.7M red w/proceeds of Com Off'g. [22] Subsid of Entergy Corp.

Title-Industry Code & Co. Finances (In Italics) / Individual Issue Statistics, Exchange	Ind / Interest Dates	Fixed Charge Coverage 1992 / S&P Debt Rating	1993 / Date of Last Rating Change	1994 / Prior Rating	Eligible	Year End / Bond Form	Cash & Equiv. (Million $) / Regular Price	Curr. Assets (Million $) / Regular (Begins) Thru	Curr. Liab. (Million $) / Sinking Fund Price	Balance Sheet Date / Sinking Fund (Begins) Thru	L. Term Debt (Mil $) / Refund/Other Restriction Price	Refund/Other Restriction (Begins) Thru	Capital-ization (Mil $) / Outst'g (Mil $)	Total Debt % Capital / Underwriting Firm	Underwriting Year	Price Range 1995 High	Price Range 1995 Low	Mo. End Price Sale(s) or Bid	Curr. Yield	Yield to Mat.
***System Energy Resources** (Cont.)*																				
1st 8¼s 2002	aO	**BBB–**			X	R	103.07	(10-1-98)	Z100	....	....	....	70.0	M6	'92	106¾	94⅛	106¾	7.73	6.98
1st 11⅜s 2016	mS	**BBB–**	4/90	BB+	X	R	106.80	(9-1-96)	[1]Z100	(9-1-97)	Z107.16	8-31-96	90.3	M6	'86	109⅞	107⅜	109⅝	10.38	10.24
Talley Industries	*17a*	*1.07*	*0.87*	*0.97*		*Dc*	*8.90*	*156.0*	*75.90*	*9-30-95*	*229.0*		*291.0*	*80.8*						
Sr[2]Disc Deb 12¼s 2005	aO15	**B–**			Y	R	106.125	(10-15-98)	100	(10-15-00)	[3]Z110	10-14-96	127	B5	'93	75⅞	50½	75⅞	....	Flat
Talley Mfg & Tech	*17a*	*1.32*	*1.75*	*1.79*		*Dc*	*2.55*	*149.0*	*69.60*	*9-30-95*	*129.0*		*179.0*	*73.7*						
Sr Nts[4] 10¾s 2003	aO15	**B**			Y	R	105.375	(10-15-98)	100	(10-15-00)	[5]Z100	10-15-96	115	B5	'93	101	87	100¼	10.72	10.70
Tampa Electric Co.[6]	*72a*	*4.92*	*4.68*	*5.41*		*Dc*	*0.24*	*227.0*	*325.0*	*9-30-95*	*583.0*		*1776*	*38.4*						
1st 5½s '96	Ao	**AA**	4/76	AA–	X	R	100	....	100	....	....	....	24.8	G1	'66	99⅞	97½	99⅞	5.51	5.92
1st 5¾s 2000	Mn	**AA**			X	BE	NC	....	....	....	....	....	80.0	C1	'93	99⅞	89⅝	99⅞	5.76	5.78
1st 6⅛s 2003	Mn	**AA**			X	BE	NC	....	....	....	....	....	75.0	C1	'93	99⅞	86⅝	99⅞	6.13	6.14
1st 7¾s 2022	mN	**AA**			X	R	101.46	(11-1-02)	100	....	....	....	75.0	C1	'92	103½	90⅛	103⅜	7.50	7.46
Taubman Realty Group	*38*	*1.01*	*1.26*	*1.25*		*Dc*				*9-30-95*	*923.0*		*505.0*	*183.0*						
F/R[7]Nts 6.3437s '97	[8]	**BBB**	5/95	BBB+	X	BE	NC	....	....	....	....	....	100	M6	'94	100⅜	99	100	6.34	....
Nts 8s '99	Jd15	**BBB**	5/95	BBB+	X	R	NC	....	....	....	....	....	200	M6	'94	104⅜	96⅝	103⅝	7.72	6.81
TCI Communications[9]	*12a*	*1.36*	*1.29*	*1.29*		*Dc*				*9-30-95*	*12143*		*14272*	*85.1*						
Sr Deb[10] 8¾s 2015	fA	**BBB–**			X	R	NC	....	....	....	....	....	750	M2	'95	110⅛	99⅛	110⅛	7.95	7.74
Sr Nts[10] 8.65s 2004	mS15	**BBB–**			X	R	NC	....	....	....	....	....	300	M6	'94	111½	98⅝	111½	7.76	6.87
Sr Nts[10] 8s 2005	fA	**BBB–**			X	R	NC	....	....	....	....	....	350	M2	'95	106¾	99¼	106¾	7.49	7.02
Tektronix Inc	*65*	*△6.13*	*△9.57*	*△11.47*		*My*	*49.90*	*690.0*	*355.0*	*8-26-95*	*154.0*		*853.0*	*27.5*						
Nts 7½s 2003	fA	**BBB–**			X	BE	NC	....	....	....	....	....	100	M5	'93	104¾	89½	104¾	7.16	6.69
Nts 7⅝s 2002	fA15	**BBB–**			X	BE	NC	....	....	....	....	....	50.0	M5	'95	105⅝	99¾	105⅝	7.22	6.56
Tele-Communications(Old)	*12a*	***Now TCI Commmunications,see***																		
Sr Deb[10] 9.80s 2012	Fa	**BBB–**	10/92	BB	X	R	NC	....	....	....	....	....	600	M2	'92	119¼	97⅞	119¼	8.22	7.69
Sr Deb 7⅞s 2013	fA	**BBB–**			X	R	NC	....	....	....	....	....	550	M2	'93	103⅜	81⅞	103⅜	7.62	7.52
Sr Deb 10⅛s 2022	Ao15	**BBB–**	10/92	BB	X	R	NC	....	....	....	....	....	150	F1	'92	125	100⅝	124½	8.13	7.90
Sr Deb[10] 9⅞s 2022	Jd15	**BBB–**	10/92	BB	X	R	NC	....	....	....	....	....	100	F1	'92	123⅝	100⅜	123⅜	7.99	7.76
Sr Deb[10] 9¼s 2023	Jj15	**BBB–**			X	R	104.42	(1-15-03)	....	....	....	....	500	F1	'93	109⅜	91¼	109⅜	8.46	8.37
Sr Deb[10] 8¾s 2023	Fa15	**BBB–**			X	R	103.65	(2-15-03)	....	....	....	....	250	F1	'93	104½	86⅝	104½	8.37	8.33
Sr Nts 9⅞s '98	Ao	**BBB–**	10/92	BB	X	R	NC	....	....	....	....	....	100	M2	'91	108⅜	102⅝	108¼	9.12	5.91
Sr Nts[10] 7⅜s 2000	Fa15	**BBB–**			X	R	NC	....	....	....	....	....	300	F1	'93	103⅞	93	103⅞	7.10	6.29
Sr Nts[10] 10⅛s 2001	fA	**BBB–**	10/92	BB	X	R	NC	....	....	....	....	....	100	F1	'91	116½	104⅜	116½	8.69	6.55
Sr Nts 9¼s 2002	Ao15	**BBB–**	10/92	BB	X	R	NC	....	....	....	....	....	200	F1	'92	113¼	99⅞	113¼	8.17	6.64
Sr Nts[10] 8¼s 2003	Jj15	**BBB–**			X	R	NC	....	....	....	....	....	550	F1	'93	108¾	94⅛	108¾	7.59	6.67
Sr Nts 9.65s 2003	aO	**BBB–**	10/92	BB	X	R	NC	....	100	(10-1-99)	....	....	150	M2	'91	112⅞	101	112⅞	8.55	7.43
Sr Nts 7¼s 2005	fA	**BBB–**			X	R	NC	....	....	....	....	....	300	M2	'93	101¾	85⅝	101¾	7.13	7.00
Sr Sub SF Deb 11⅛s 2003	aO	**BB+**	10/92	B+	Y	R	103.46	9-30-96	100	(10-1-99)	....	....	10.8	P4	'88	113⅞	98	104¼	10.67	10.31
Teledyne Inc	*17*	*2.11*	*3.51*	*0.86*		*Dc*	*85.60*	*787.0*	*403.0*	*9-30-95*	*372.0*		*779.0*	*47.8*						
• Sub SF Deb[11] 7s '99	Jd	**BBB–**	6/94	BBB	X	R	100	....	100	....	....	....	23.9	Mgr	'69	100¼	88	100	7.00	7.00
• Sub SF Deb A 10s 2004	Jd	**BBB–**	6/94	BBB	X	R	100	....	100	....	....	....	[12]59.0	Exch.	'74	103⅜	97¾	s102¾	9.73	9.52
• Sub SF Deb C 10s 2004	Jd	**BBB–**	6/94	BBB	X	R	100	....	100	....	....	....	[12]386	Exch.	'80	103	98⅛	s103	9.71	9.47
Telex Communications, Inc	*67f*	*1.36*	*1.52*	*1.26*		*Mr*	*6.80*	*58.60*	*17.70*	*9-30-95*	*100.0*		*97.10*	*103.0*						
Sr Nts[4] 12s 2004	jJ15	**B**			Y	R	106	(7-15-99)	....	....	[13]Z110	7-14-97	100	M6	'94	109⅜	97½	109⅜	10.97	10.32
Temple-Inland	*16c*	*2.84*	*2.02*	*2.73*		*Dc*	*427.0*			*9-30-95*	*1543*		*3495*	*44.1*						
Deb[14] 8¼s 2022	mS15	**A**			X	BE	104.125	(9-15-02)	....	....	....	....	150	S1	'92	111¾	94	111¾	7.38	7.25
Med-Term Nts 8⅜s '96	aO	**A**			X	R	NC	....	....	....	....	....	70.0	S1	'86	103	100⅝	102⅛	8.20	5.45
Nts[14] 9s 2001	Mn	**A**			X	BE	NC	....	....	....	....	....	200	S1	'91	114⅛	102⅛	114⅛	7.89	5.88

Uniform Footnote Explanations-See Page 260. Other: [1] Also for SF fr 9-1-97. [2] Int accr at 12.25% fr 10-15-98. [3] Max $44.3M red w/proceeds of Cap Stk Off'g. [4] (HRO)On Chge of Ctrl at 101. [5] Max $40.3M red w/proceed of Cap Stk Off'g. [6] Subsid of TECO Energy, Inc. [7] Int to 3-15-96,adj qtrly(3 Mo LIBOR&0.50%). [8] Due 11-3-97:Int pd qtrly ea third Wed Feb,etc. [9] Subsid of Tele-Communications(New). [10] (HRO)On Chge of Ctrl at 100. [11] Formerly Cont'l Motors. [12] Incl disc. [13] Max $35M red w/proceeds of Pub Eq Off'gs. [14] Issued in min denom $100T.

Title-Industry Code & Co. Finances (In Italics)	Ind	Fixed Charge Coverage 1992	1993	1994		Year End	Million $ Cash & Equiv.	Curr. Assets	Curr. Liab.	Balance Sheet Date	L. Term Debt (Mil $)		Capital-ization (Mil $)	Total Debt % Capital						
Exchange ↓ Individual Issue Statistics	Interest Dates	S&P Debt Rating	Date of Last Rating Change	Prior Rating	Eligible ↓	Bond Form	Redemption Provisions: Regular Price	Regular (Begins) Thru	Sinking Fund Price	Sinking Fund (Begins) Thru	Refund/Other Restriction Price	Refund/Other Restriction (Begins) Thru	Outst'g (Mil $)	Underwriting Firm	Underwriting Year	Price Range 1995 High	Price Range 1995 Low	Mo. End Price Sale(s) or Bid	Curr. Yield	Yield to Mat.
***Temple-Inland** (Cont.)*																				
Nts[1] 7¼s 2004	mS15	**A**			X	BE	NC	....	....	....	....	....	100	S1	'92	107½	91⅛	107½	6.74	6.12
Tenet Healthcare[2]	***30***	***△4.80***	***△5.66***	***△3.30***		***My***	***242.0***	***1442***	***1257***	***8-31-95***	***3226***		***5611***	***62.5***						
• Sr Nts[3] 9⅝s 2002	mS	**BB–**	11/95	B+	Y	R	NC	....	....	....	....	....	300	D6	'95	111	100	s111	8.67	7.50
• Sr Nts[3] 8⅝s 2003	jD	**BB–**	11/95	B+	Y	R	NC	....	....	....	....	....	500	D6	'95	107	99⅝	s106½	8.10	7.52
• Sr Sub Nts[3] 10⅛s 2005	Ms	**B+**			Y	R	105.063	(3-1-00)	....	....	....	....	900	D6	'95	110¼	100	108⅜	9.34	8.77
Tenneco Credit	***25d***	***1.72***	***1.72***	***1.55***		***Dc***				***9-30-95***	***706.0***		***1019***	***79.5***						
• Nts 9¼s '96	mN	**BBB–**	11/91	BBB	X	R	NC	....	....	....	....	....	150	M2	'89	103⅞	100⅝	101¾	9.09	7.04
• Nts 10⅛s '97	jD	**BBB–**	11/91	BBB	X	R	NC	....	....	....	....	....	150	M6	'90	107⅞	103⅛	107	9.46	6.20
• Nts 9⅝s 2001	fA15	**BBB–**	11/91	BBB	X	R	NC	....	....	....	....	....	250	F1	'91	114¾	104⅜	111⅜	8.64	7.13
Tenneco Inc	***17***	***1.35***	***1.82***	***2.43***		***Dc***	***712.0***	***3665***	***2875***	***9-30-95***	***3310***		***7549***	***52.7***						
• Deb[4] 10s 2008	Ms15	**BBB–**	11/91	BBB	X	R	NC	....	....	....	....	....	250	M6	'88	124½	109½	122¾	8.15	7.17
• Deb 9s 2012	mN15	**BBB–**			X	R	NC	....	....	....	....	....	150	F1	'92	110	109	109⅛	8.25	8.00
Deb 7¼s 2025	jD15	**BBB–**			X	BE	NC	....	....	....	....	....	300	M6	'95	101½	100	101½	7.14	7.13
• Nts 10s '98	fA	**BBB–**	11/91	BBB	X	R	NC	....	....	....	....	....	500	M6	'91	108⅞	105⅞	108⅛	9.25	6.53
• Nts 8s '99	mN15	**BBB–**			X	R	NC	....	....	....	....	....	250	F1	'92	105⅝	96	103¾	7.71	6.88
• Nts 10⅜s 2000	mN15	**BBB–**	11/91	BBB	X	R	NC	....	....	....	....	....	175	M6	'90	117¾	107	114⅜	9.07	6.85
• Nts 9⅞s 2001	Fa	**BBB–**	11/91	BBB	X	R	NC	....	....	....	....	....	200	M6	'91	115	104	s112	8.82	7.03
• Nts 7⅞s 2002	aO	**BBB–**			X	R	NC	....	....	....	....	....	500	M6	'92	107¾	94⅝	104⅝	7.53	7.00
Nts 6½s 2005	jD15	**BBB–**			X	BE	[5]Z100	....	....	....	....	....	300	M6	'95	100¼	99⅜	100¼	6.48	6.47
Tennessee Gas[6] Pipeline[7]	***49***	***3.24***	***3.86***	***4.78***		***Dc***	***706.0***	***6152***	***2479***	***9-30-95***	***536.0***		***9164***	***10.5***						
• Deb 6s 2011	jD15	**BBB–**	11/91	BBB	X	R	100	....	....	....	....	....	[8]400	M6	'81	90⅝	74	s89⅜	6.71	7.12
• Nts 9¼s '96	Mn15	**BBB–**	11/91	BBB	X	R	NC	....	....	....	....	....	250	M6	'86	103	100⅝	101	9.16	6.47
• Nts 9s '97	Jj15	**BBB–**	11/91	BBB	X	R	NC	....	....	....	....	....	250	M6	'86	104	101	102⅝	8.77	6.36
Tennessee Valley[9] Auth[10]	***72***	***1.05***	***1.14***	***1.02***		***Sp***	***163.0***	***1285***	***4402***	***8-31-95***	***23458***		***30922***	***86.6***						
• Pwr Bonds '89D 8⅜s '99	aO	**AAA**			X	BE	NC	....	....	....	....	....	1000	F1	'89	107	100⅞	109⅛	7.67	5.64
Pwr Bonds '89F 8¼s '96	mN15	**AAA**			X	BE	NC	....	....	....	....	....	1500	M6	'89	103½	100⅝	102½	8.05	5.32
• Pwr Bonds '89G 8⅝s 2029	mN15	**AAA**			X	BE	■106.161	(11-15-99)	....	....	....	....	2500	M6	'89	108¼	98¼	111¼	7.75	7.69
• Pwr Bonds '91A 7.45s 2001	aO15	**NR**			X	BE	■105	10-14-96	....	....	....	....	500	L3	'91	102¾	95⅞	103⅞	7.18	6.64
• Pwr Bonds '92A 6s '97	Jj15	**NR**			X	BE	■100.984	7-14-96	....	....	....	....	1000	L3	'92	99½	96⅜	100⅝	5.96	5.40
• Pwr Bonds '92C 6⅞s 2002	Jj15	**NR**			X	BE	■103.102	7-14-96	....	....	....	....	500	L3	'92	93⅛	93	102⅞	6.68	6.29
• Pwr Bonds '92D 8¼s 2042	Ao15	**NR**			X	BE	■106	(4-15-12)	....	....	....	....	1000	G1	'92	96¼	96¼	117½	7.02	6.98
• Pwr Bonds '92E 6¼s '99	fA	**NR**			X	BE	■103	1-31-96	....	....	....	....	750	G1	'92	98½	92⅞	101⅝	6.15	5.74
• Pwr Bonds '92F 6⅞s 2002	fA	**NR**			X	BE	■104	1-31-96	....	....	....	....	500	G1	'92	92¾	92⅝	102¾	6.69	6.36
• Pwr Bonds '92G 7⅝s 2022	mS	**NR**			X	BE	■104	(9-1-97)	....	....	....	....	700	S1	'92	97⅞	88⅝	103⅞	7.34	7.29
• Pwr Bonds '92I 7¾s 2022	jD15	**NR**			X	BE	■104	(12-15-97)	....	....	....	....	1000	L3	'92	101½	92	104¾	7.41	7.35
• Pwr Bonds '93A 4⅜s '96	Ms4	**NR**			X	BE	■100	....	....	....	....	....	750	L3	'93	98½	96⅜	99⅞	4.38	5.52
• Pwr Bonds '93B 5⅛s '98	Ms4	**NR**			X	BE	■100	....	....	....	....	....	250	L3	'93	93¼	93¼	99	5.18	5.61
• Pwr Bonds '93C 6⅛s 2003	jJ15	**NR**			X	BE	■103.227	(7-15-96)	....	....	....	....	1250	L3	'93	95	86⅞	100¼	6.11	6.09
• Pwr Bonds '93D 7¼s 2043	jJ15	**NR**			X	BE	■105.438	(7-15-03)	....	....	....	....	750	F1	'93	94⅝	84⅛	103	7.04	7.03
• Pwr Bonds '93E 4.60s '96	jD15	**NR**			X	BE	■100	....	....	....	....	....	1000	S1	'93	97½	94⅛	99½	4.63	5.21
• Pwr Bonds '93F 6⅞s 2043	jD15	**NR**			X	BE	■104.50	(12-15-03)	....	....	....	....	500	S1	'93	88⅜	79¼	99¼	6.93	6.94
• Pwr Bonds '94A 7.85s 2044	Jd15	**NR**			X	BE	■106.729	(6-15-99)	....	....	....	....	850	M6	'94	100	89⅝	106¼	7.39	7.37
• Pwr Bonds '94B 8.05s 2024	jJ15	**NR**			X	BE	■100	(7-15-99)	....	....	....	....	500	F1	'94	103⅜	95⅝	105½	7.63	7.58
• Pwr Bonds '94C 8¼s 2034	mS15	**NR**			X	BE	■100	(9-15-99)	....	....	....	....	500	C5	'94	104	94⅜	106⅜	7.76	7.73
• Pwr Bonds '94D 7⅝s '99	mS15	**CALL**	11/95	NR	X	BE			Called 9-15-96 at 100				550	L3	'94	103⅛	97⅜	101½	7.51	Call
• Pwr Bonds '94E 7⅞s 2001	mS15	**NR**			X	BE	■100	(9-15-97)	....	....	....	....	250	L3	'94	98	97⅞	103⅝	7.60	7.09

Uniform Footnote Explanations-See Page 260. Other: [1] Issued in min denom $100T. [2] See Nat'l Med'l Entpr, Amer Med'l Int'l. [3] (HRO)On Chge of Ctrl at 101. [4] (HRO)On 3-15-98 at 100. [5] Greater of 100 or amt based on formula. [6] Was Tenneco Inc. [7] Subsid of Tenneco Inc. [8] Incl disc. [9] Gvt agency:Int exempt state,local tax. [10] Balance sheet data of Pwr program.

Title-Industry Code & Co. Finances (In Italics) / Individual Issue Statistics — Exchange, Interest Dates	Fixed Charge Coverage 1992 / S&P Debt Rating	1993 / Date of Last Rating Change	1994 / Prior Rating	Eligible	Year End / Bond Form	Cash & Equiv. / Regular Price	Curr. Assets / Regular (Begins) Thru	Curr. Liab. / Sinking Fund Price	Balance Sheet Date / Sinking Fund (Begins) Thru	L. Term Debt (Mil $) / Refund/Other Restriction Price	Refund/Other Restriction (Begins) Thru	Capital-ization (Mil $) / Outst'g (Mil $)	Total Debt % Capital / Underwriting Firm	Underwriting Year	Price Range 1995 High	Price Range 1995 Low	Mo. End Price Sale(s) or Bid	Curr. Yield	Yield to Mat.
***Tennessee Valley Auth** (Cont.)*																			
• Global Pwr Bonds '95A 6⅜s 2005 .... Jd15	**NR**			X	BE	NC	....	....	....	....	....	2000	L3	'95	99¼	99¼	103⅛	6.18	5.94
• Pwr[1]Bonds '95B 6.235s 2045 .... jJ15	**NR**			X	BE	■100	(7-15-20)	....	....	....	....	500	M2	'95	100	100	103⅛	6.05	6.04
• Pwr Bonds '95C 5.95s '98 .... mS15	**NR**			X	BE	NC	....	....	....	....	....	200		'95	100	100	101¼	5.88	5.44
• Global Pwr Bonds'95D 6s 2000 ..... mN	**NR**			X	BE	NC	....	....	....	....	....	1000	L3	'95	99⅞	99⅞	101¼	5.93	5.70
• Global Pwr Bonds'95E 6¾s 2025 .... mN	**NR**			X	BE	NC	....	....	....	....	....	600	L3	'95	99⅜	99⅜	101¼	6.67	6.65
Terminal RR Assn. St. L.* *55	***5.06***	***7.15***	***6.84***		***Dc***	***5.60***	***12.40***	***8.75***	***12-31-94***	***7.79***		***41.60***	***18.7***						
• Imp C 4s 2019 .... jJ	**NR**	6/87	AA		CR	[2]....	....	....	....	....	....	7.79	Exch.	'45	64	52	63½	6.30	7.26
Tesoro Petroleum* *49g	***d1.08***	***2.28***	***2.26***		***Dc***	***59.40***	***201.0***	***96.40***	***9-30-95***	***188.0***		***405.0***	***48.6***						
• Sub Deb 12¾s 2001 .... Ms15	**NR**	4/94	CCC+		R	100	....	100	....	....	....	[3]23.7	L1	'83	104⅜	99⅝	s104	12.26	11.69
• Exch Nts 13s 2000 .... jD	**B–**	4/94	NR	Y	R	100	....	....	....	....	....	44.1	Exch.	'94	104½	101	s104⅛	12.48	11.86
Texaco Capital*[4] *25	***3.19***	***3.24***	***3.42***		***Dc***	***384.0***	***5544***	***4299***	***9-30-95***	***5605***		***16542***	***36.0***						
Gtd[5]Deb 8¼s 2006 .... aO	**A+**			X	R	NC	....	....	....	....	....	150	F1	'91	116½	98½	116½	7.08	6.13
• Gtd[5]Deb 8⅝s 2010 .... Jd30	**A+**			X	R	NC	....	....	....	....	....	150	M6	'90	113	110	111⅛	7.76	7.36
• Gtd[5]Deb 9¾s 2020 .... Ms15	**A+**			X	R	NC	....	....	....	....	....	250	S1	'90	No Sale		122	7.99	7.73
Gtd[5]Deb 8⅞s 2021 .... mS	**A+**			X	R	NC	....	....	....	....	....	150	S1	'91	127¼	102⅛	127¼	6.97	6.65
Gtd[5]Deb 8⅜s 2022 .... jJ15	**A+**			X	R	103.672	(7-15-02)	....	....	....	....	200	F1	'92	113¼	95⅞	113¼	7.40	7.24
Gtd[5]Deb 6⅞s 2023 .... fA15	**A+**			X	R	102.109	(8-15-03)	....	....	....	....	200	F1	'93	99⅝	81½	99⅝	6.90	6.90
Gtd[5]Deb 8⅝s 2031 .... mN15	**A+**			X	R	NC	....	....	....	....	....	200	M6	'91	124¾	99	124¾	6.91	6.78
Gtd[5]Deb 8⅝s 2032 .... Ao	**A+**			X	R	NC	....	....	....	....	....	200	S1	'92	126	99	126	6.85	6.70
Gtd[5]Deb 8s 2032 .... fA	**A+**			X	R	NC	....	....	....	....	....	150	M6	'92	117⅜	93¼	117⅜	6.82	6.72
Gtd[5]Deb 7¾s 2033 .... Fa15	**A+**			X	R	104.635	(2-15-03)	....	....	....	....	200	F1	'93	109⅝	89½	109⅝	7.07	7.02
Gtd[5]Deb 7½s 2043 .... Ms	**A+**			X	R	102.717	(3-1-13)	....	....	....	....	200	S1	'93	108⅛	85⅝	108⅛	6.94	6.91
• Gtd[6]Ext'd[7]Nts[5] [8] 8½s '98 .... [9]Jd	**A+**	3/90	A	X	R	[10]100	....	....	....	....	....	4.97	S1	'84	105	101½	102⅛	8.32	7.52
• Gtd[8]Ext'd[5]Nts 8.95s 2000 .... Jj15	**A+**	3/90	A	X	R	100	(1-15-97)	....	....	....	....	21.7	F1	'84	104¾	101¼	102	8.77	8.35
• Gtd[8]Ext'd[5]Nts 9.45s 2000 .... Ms	**A+**	3/90	A	X	R	NC	....	....	....	....	....	50.8	S1	'85	112½	103⅜	112⅜	8.41	6.05
• Gtd[5]Nts 9s '96 .... mN15	**A+**	3/90	A	X	R	NC	....	....	....	....	....	400	M6	'89	104¼	101⅝	s102⅝	8.78	5.98
• Gtd[5]Nts 9s '97 .... mN15	**A+**			X	R	NC	....	....	....	....	....	200	S1	'90	108	101½	105¾	8.51	5.72
• Gtd[5]Nts 8.65s '98 .... Jj30	**A+**			X	R	NC	....	....	....	....	....	200	F1	'91	106	102	105½	8.20	5.81
Gtd[5]Nts 6⅞s '99 .... jJ15	**A+**			X	R	NC	....	....	....	....	....	200	F1	'92	103⅞	94⅝	103⅞	6.62	5.65
• Gtd[5]Nts 9s '99 .... jD15	**A+**	3/90	A	X	R	NC	....	....	....	....	....	200	M6	'89	110¼	102⅛	109¾	8.20	6.19
• Gtd[5]Nts 8½s 2003 .... Fa15	**A+**			X	R	NC	....	....	....	....	....	200	M6	'91	114	101⅝	111½	7.62	6.46
Texas Bottling Group* *11f	***n/a***	***1.16***	***1.11***		***Dc***	***8.91***	***40.20***	***36.90***	***9-30-95***	***220.0***		***223.0***	***103.0***						
Sr[11]Sub Nts 9s 2003 .... mN15	**B+**	7/95	B	Y	R	104.50	(11-15-98)	....	....	....	....	125	C4	'93	100	87¼	100	9.00	9.00
Texas Eastern Transm.*[12] *73a	***2.93***	***1.85***	***3.36***		***Dc***	***0.10***	***163.0***	***338.0***	***9-30-95***	***820.0***		***2802***	***29.3***						
• SF Deb 10⅛s 2011 .... mS	**BBB**	10/94	BBB–	X	R	105.569	8-31-96	100	(9-1-97)	®105.062	8-31-96	100	D4	'86	110	100	105⅜	9.61	9.46
SF Deb 10s 2011 .... aO	**BBB**	10/94	BBB–	X	R	105.50	9-30-96	100	(10-1-97)	®105	9-30-96	150	D4	'86	107¼	105	105⅞	9.45	9.28
Nts 10⅜s 2000 .... mN15	**BBB**	10/94	BBB–	X	R	NC	....	....	....	....	....	200	F1	'90	118¼	107⅞	118¼	8.77	6.00
Nts 10s 2001 .... fA15	**BBB**	10/94	BBB–	X	R	NC	....	....	....	....	....	100	D4	'91	118¼	106⅝	118¼	8.46	6.12
Nts 8s 2002 .... jJ15	**BBB**	10/94	BBB–	X	R	NC	....	....	....	....	....	100	K2	'92	110	95⅜	110	7.27	6.12
Nts 8¼s 2004 .... aO15	**BBB**			X	R	NC	....	....	....	....	....	100	M2	'94	113¼	95⅞	113¼	7.28	6.27
Texas Gas Transmission*[13] *73a	***3.26***	***3.57***	***3.02***		***Dc***	***0.35***	***165.0***	***138.0***	***9-30-95***	***252.0***		***992.0***	***25.4***						
Nts 9⅝s '97 .... jJ15	**BBB**	2/95	BB	X	R	NC	....	....	....	....	....	100	F1	'92	106¾	101⅝	105¾	9.10	5.68
Nts 8⅝s 2004 .... Ao	**BBB**	2/95	BB	X	R	NC	....	....	....	....	....	150	M2	'93	115⅛	97¼	115⅛	7.49	6.25
Texas Instruments* *23h	***8.24***	***15.81***	***22.27***		***Dc***	***1603***	***5283***	***2894***	***9-30-95***	***822.0***		***4735***	***18.7***						
Nts 9s '99 .... jJ15	**A**	3/91	A+	X	R	100	(7-15-96)	....	....	....	....	150	M6	'89	103¼	101½	102	8.82	8.33
Nts 9s 2001 .... Ms15	**A**			X	R	NC	....	....	....	....	....	150	M6	'91	113⅛	102⅝	113⅛	7.96	6.02

Uniform Footnote Explanations-See Page 260. Other:[1] (HRO)On 7-15-01 at 100. [2] At price to yield 3% at maturity. [3] Incl disc. [4] Gtd by & data of Texaco Inc. [5] Gtd by Texaco Inc. [6] Int thru 5-31-98,adj aft. [7] (HRO)On 6-1-98,aft as defined. [8] Int arrears pd 4-8-88. [9] Due 6-1-99. [10] On 6-1-98,aft as defined. [11] Co must offer repurch at 101 on Chge of Ctrl. [12] Subsid of Texas Eastern Corp. [13] Subsid of Texas Gas Co(Transco Energy).

Title-Industry Code & Co. Finances (In Italics)	Ind	Fixed Charge Coverage 1992	1993	1994		Year End	Million $ Cash & Equiv.	Curr. Assets	Curr. Liab.	Balance Sheet Date		L. Term Debt (Mil $)		Capital-ization (Mil $)	Total Debt % Capital					
Individual Issue Statistics Exchange	Interest Dates	S&P Debt Rating	Date of Last Rating Change	Prior Rating	Eligible	Bond Form	Redemption Provisions: Regular Price	Regular (Begins) Thru	Sinking Fund Price	Sinking Fund (Begins) Thru	Refund/Other Restriction Price	Refund/Other Restriction (Begins) Thru	Outst'g (Mil $)	Underwriting Firm	Underwriting Year	Price Range 1995 High	Price Range 1995 Low	Mo. End Price Sale(s) or Bid	Curr. Yield	Yield to Mat.
***Texas Instruments** (Cont.)*																				
Nts 9¼s 2003	Jd15	A			X	R	NC	....	....	....	....	....	150	M6	'91	118	104	118	7.84	6.20
Nts 8¾s 2007	Ao	A			X	R	NC	....	....	....	....	....	150	M6	'92	119¾	101⅛	119¾	7.31	6.27
Texas-New Mexico Pwr[1]	*72a*	*1.20*	*1.24*	*1.15*		*Dc*	*44.80*	*81.00*	*108.0*	*9-30-95*	*617.0*		*881.0*	*73.6*						
1st M 8.70s 2006	mS	BB–	11/93	BB	Y	R	103	8-31-96	100	....	....	....	8.28	S1	'76	106⅝	90⅛	96½	9.02	9.22
1st R 10s 2017	jJ	BB–	11/93	BB	Y	R	106	6-30-96	100	....	....	....	63.1	S4	'87	104	93¼	101⅝	9.84	9.82
1st S 9⅝s 2019	jJ	BB–	11/93	BB	Y	R	106.74	6-30-96	Z100	....	....	....	19.8	S4	'89	100½	90	98⅛	9.81	9.83
1st T[2] 11¼s '97	Jj15	BB–	11/93	BB	Y	R	NC	....	....	....	....	....	130	L3	'92	105¼	103⅛	104½	10.77	6.71
1st U[2] 9¼s 2000	mS15	BB–	11/93	BB	Y	R	NC	....	....	....	....	....	100	D4	'93	106⅞	96	106	8.73	7.70
Sec Deb[2] 12½s '99	Jj15	B	11/93	B+	Y	R	NC	....	....	....	....	....	130	L3	'92	112⅝	106⅜	109⅜	11.43	8.91
Sec Deb 10¾s 2003	mS15	B	11/93	B+	Y	R	100	(9-15-00)	....	....	....	....	140	D4	'93	107½	97	106⅛	10.13	9.60
Texas & Pacific Ry	*55*	***Merged into Missouri Pacific RR, see***																		
•1st 5s 2000	Jd	A–	4/95	A+	X	CR	NC	....	....	....	....	....	19.0	L3	1883	95½	87¼	s95½	5.24	6.18
Texas Utilities Electric[3]	*72a*	*1.92*	*2.19*	*2.48*		*Dc*	*13.00*	*739.0*	*1185*	*9-30-95*	*7234*		*14499*	*51.9*						
1st & CT 7⅛s '97	Jd	BBB+	7/95	BBB	X	R	NC	....	....	....	....	....	150	S1	'92	101⅞	97⅝	101⅞	6.99	5.73
1st & CT 6⅜s '97	fA	BBB+	7/95	BBB	X	R	NC	....	....	....	....	....	175	G1	'92	101	95½	101	6.31	5.70
1st & CT 5⅞s '98	Ao	BBB+	7/95	BBB	X	R	NC	....	....	....	....	....	175	M6	'93	100¼	92⅞	100¼	5.86	5.75
1st & CT 5¾s '98	jJ	BBB+	7/95	BBB	X	R	NC	....	....	....	....	....	150	S1	'93	100	91⅞	100	5.75	5.75
1st & CT 5½s '98	aO	BBB+	7/95	BBB	X	R	NC	....	....	....	....	....	125	M2	'93	99¼	90½	99¼	5.54	5.79
F/R[4]1st & CT 6.3125s '99	QMay	BBB+	7/95	BBB	X	BE	*100	(5-1-96)	....	....	....	....	300	L3	'94	100⅛	98¾	100	6.31	....
1st & CT 9½s '99	fA	BBB+	7/95	BBB	X	R	NC	....	....	....	....	....	200	M2	'89	111	104	111	8.56	6.04
1st & CT 7⅜s '99	mN	BBB+	7/95	BBB	X	R	NC	....	....	....	....	....	100	M6	'92	104⅝	94½	104⅝	7.05	6.00
1st & CT 7⅜s 2001	fA	BBB+	7/95	BBB	X	R	NC	....	....	....	....	....	150	G1	'92	105⅞	94⅛	105⅞	6.97	6.12
1st & CT 8⅛s 2002	Fa	BBB+	7/95	BBB	X	R	NC	....	....	....	....	....	150	M2	'92	109⅜	96⅞	109⅜	7.43	6.25
1st & CT 8s 2002	Jd	BBB+	7/95	BBB	X	R	NC	....	....	....	....	....	147	S1	'92	109⅞	96⅞	109⅞	7.28	6.12
1st & CT 6¾s 2003	Ms	BBB+	7/95	BBB	X	R	NC	....	....	....	....	....	200	G1	'93	102⅝	89	102⅝	6.58	6.29
1st & CT 6¾s 2003	Ao	BBB+	7/95	BBB	X	R	NC	....	....	....	....	....	100	M6	'93	102⅝	88⅞	102⅝	6.58	6.29
1st & CT 8¼s 2004	Ao	BBB+	7/95	BBB	X	R	NC	....	....	....	....	....	100	G1	'92	112	97	112	7.37	6.36
1st & CT 6¼s 2004	aO	BBB+	7/95	BBB	X	R	NC	....	....	....	....	....	125	M2	'93	99¼	84⅞	99¼	6.30	6.36
1st & CT 6¾s 2005	jJ	BBB+	7/95	BBB	X	R	NC	....	....	....	....	....	100	S1	'93	102	87	102	6.62	6.47
1st & CT 9¾s 2021	Mn	BBB+	7/95	BBB	X	R	104.87	(5-1-01)	....	....	....	....	300	S1	'91	119⅞	102⅝	119⅞	8.13	7.92
1st & CT 8⅞s 2022	Fa	BBB+	7/95	BBB	X	R	104.26	(2-1-02)	....	....	....	....	175	M2	'92	113⅞	96⅞	113⅞	7.79	7.64
1st & CT 9s 2022	Ao	BBB+	7/95	BBB	X	R	106.62	(4-1-97)	....	....	....	....	100	G1	'92	110⅛	98¼	109¼	8.24	8.14
1st & CT 7⅞s 2023	Ms	BBB+	7/95	BBB	X	R	103.84	(3-1-03)	....	....	....	....	300	G1	'93	107	88⅛	107	7.36	7.28
1st & CT 8¾s 2023	mN	BBB+	7/95	BBB	X	R	104.01	(11-1-02)	....	....	....	....	200	M6	'92	114¼	95⅞	114¼	7.66	7.52
1st & CT 8½s 2024	fA	BBB+	7/95	BBB	X	R	104.05	(8-1-02)	....	....	....	....	175	G1	'92	111¾	93½	111¾	7.61	7.50
1st & CT 7⅞s 2024	Ao	BBB+	7/95	BBB	X	R	103.85	(4-1-03)	....	....	....	....	225	M6	'93	107⅝	87⅝	107⅝	7.32	7.24
1st & CT 7⅝s 2025	jJ	BBB+	7/95	BBB	X	R	102.69	(7-1-03)	....	....	....	....	250	S1	'93	104½	85⅝	104½	7.30	7.25
1st & CT 7⅜s 2025	aO	BBB+	7/95	BBB	X	R	103.35	(10-1-03)	....	....	....	....	300	G1	'93	101⅜	82¾	101⅜	7.27	7.26
M-T Nts 'D' 6.27s 2000	[5]ms	BBB+			X	BE	NC	....	....	....	....	....	25.0	B5	'95	101⅛	100	101⅛	6.20	5.95
M-T Nts 'D' 6.27s 2000	[6]ms	BBB+			X	BE	NC	....	....	....	....	....	40.0	B5	'95	101	100	101	6.21	6.03
Texfi Indus	*68a*	*2.31*	*0.37*	*0.24*		*Oc*	*0.12*	*45.30*	*42.20*	*7-28-95*	*56.10*		*68.60*	*92.4*						
•Sr Sub[7]Deb[8] 8¾s '99	fA	NR				R	NC	....	....	....	....	....	30.0	I1	'93	85	73	82¼	10.64	15.36
•Sub[9]Ext[10]Deb'C'[11] 13s '96	[12]Ao	NR				R	100	....	....	....	....	....	7.15	I1	'90	100	98	98½	13.20	Mat.
Textron, Inc.	*17*	*1.71*	*1.92*	*2.13*		*Dc*				*9-30-95*	*10205*		*13431*	*76.0*						
•Deb 9¼s 2016	Ms15	BBB	9/86	BBB+	X	R	105.09	3-14-96	100	(3-15-97)	®104.63	3-14-96	54.0	S1	'86	107	99⅞	104¾	8.83	8.74
Deb 8¾s 2022	jJ	BBB			X	BE	104.07	(7-1-02)	....	....	....	....	200	M6	'92	113⅜	95¼	113⅜	7.72	7.57

Uniform Footnote Explanations-See Page 260. Other: [1] Subsid of TNP Enterprises. [2] (HRO)On Chge of Ctrl at 101. [3] Subsid of Texas Utilities. [4] Int to 2-1-96,adj qtrly(3 Mo LIBOR&0.375). [5] Due 2-1-00. [6] Due 11-13-00. [7] Death red benefit,ltd,as defined. [8] (HRO)On Chge of Ctrl at 100. [9] Int thru 3-31-96,adj anly aft,as defined. [10] (HRO)Ea Apr 1 fr 1995 at 100. [11] (HRO)At 100 for Chge of Ctrl & Rat'g Decline. [12] Due 4-1-00.

Title-Industry Code & Co. Finances (In Italics) / Individual Issue Statistics (Exchange)	Ind / Interest Dates	Fixed Charge Coverage 1992 / S&P Debt Rating	1993 / Date of Last Rating Change	1994 / Prior Rating	Eligible	Year End / Bond Form	Cash & Equiv. (Million $) / Regular Price	Curr. Assets (Million $) / Regular (Begins) Thru	Curr. Liab. (Million $) / Sinking Fund Price	Balance Sheet Date / Sinking Fund (Begins) Thru	L. Term Debt (Mil $) / Refund/Other Restriction Price	Refund/Other Restriction (Begins) Thru	Capital-ization (Mil $) / Outst'g (Mil $)	Total Debt % Capital / Underwriting Firm	Underwriting Year	Price Range 1995 High	Price Range 1995 Low	Mo. End Price Sale(s) or Bid	Curr. Yield	Yield to Mat.
Third Nat'l Corp.	10	Subsid of SunTrust Banks																		
SF Deb 7½s 2002	mN15	NR			X	R	100.54	11-14-96	100	....	....	....	13.0	F1	'72	103	92⅛	101⅝	7.38	7.19
Thomas & Betts	23b	3.09	3.59	3.47		Dc	106.0	550.0	254.0	10-1-95	344.0		949.0	38.7						
Nts 8¼s 2004	Jj15	BBB	12/95	BBB+	X	R	NC	....	....	....	....	....	125	M2	'92	112⅜	97½	112⅜	7.34	6.27
Thrifty PayLess, Inc	59e	n/a	n/a	1.32		Sp		1256	716.0	7-2-95	943.0		1281	75.3						
Sr Nts[1] 11¾s 2003	Ao15	B			Y	R	105.875	(4-15-99)	....	....	....	....	250	D6	'94	109	98	108¼	10.85	10.12
xc[2]Sr Sub Nts[1] 12¼s 2004	Ao15	B−			Y	R	106.125	(4-15-99)	....	....	[3]Z110	4-15-97	[4]300	D6	'94	108	94¾	107	11.45	10.94
TIG Holdings	35c	n/a	n/a	n/a		Dc				9-30-95	98.00		1379	7.1						
Nts 8⅛s 2005	Ao15	A−			X	BE	NC	....	....	....	....	....	100	S1	'95	109⅛	99	109⅛	7.45	6.78
Time Warner Entertainment	54	Subsid of Time Warner,see																		
• Sr Deb 7¼s 2008	Ms	BBB−	6/94	NR	X	R	NC	....	....	....	....	....	600	Exch.	'94	100¾	83¾	99⅜	7.30	7.32
Sr Deb 8⅜s 2023	Ms15	BBB−			X	R	NC	....	....	....	Z100	....	990	Exch.	'93	108¼	82	108¼	7.74	7.65
Time Warner Inc[5]	54	1.44	0.71	0.89		Dc	378.0	3133	2837	9-30-95	9931		14011	71.0						
• SF Deb 8¾s 2017	Ao	BBB−	6/92	BB	X	R	104.68	3-31-96	100	(4-1-98)	®103.90	3-31-97	500	S1	'87	104¾	84	s104⅛	8.40	8.33
• Deb 8.11s 2006	fA15	BBB−			X	R	NC	....	....	....	....	....	548	Exch.	'95	107	98⅜	s105½	7.69	7.35
• Deb 8.18s 2007	fA15	BBB−			X	R	NC	....	....	....	....	....	548	Exch.	'95	105¾	98¼	s104⅞	7.80	7.54
• Deb 9⅛s 2013	Jj15	BBB−			X	BE	NC	....	....	....	....	....	1000	M2	'93	112	88⅝	s111¾	8.17	7.86
• Deb 9.15s 2023	Fa	BBB−			X	BE	NC	....	....	....	....	....	1000	M2	'93	112½	86	s112½	8.13	8.01
F/R[6]Nts 6.8975s 2000	QAug15	BBB−			X	R	101	8-14-96	....	....	....	....	457	Exch.	'95	100½	100	100⅜	6.87	....
• Nts 7.45s '98	Fa	BBB−			X	BE	NC	....	....	....	....	....	500	S1	'93	102⅝	95½	s102½	7.27	6.15
• Nts 7.95s 2000	Fa	BBB−			X	BE	NC	....	....	....	....	....	500	S1	'93	105	93½	s104	7.64	6.81
• Nts 7.975s 2004	fA15	BBB−			X	R	NC	....	....	....	....	....	274	Exch.	'95	105¾	98⅛	s105¼	7.58	7.15
• Nts 7¾s 2005	Jd15	BBB−			X	BE	NC	....	....	....	....	....	500	M6	'95	105	98	104⅜	7.43	7.11
Times Mirror (New)	54c	n/a	p3.34	4.25		Dc	478.0	1355	877.0	9-30-95	248.0		2450	10.1						
Deb 7¼s 2013	Ms	A+			X	R	NC	....	....	....	....	....	141	Exch.	'95	105¼	87	105¼	6.89	6.73
Deb 7½s 2023	jJ	A+			X	R	NC	....	....	....	....	....	98.8	Exch.	'95	107⅞	84	107⅞	6.95	6.86
TJX Cos[7]	59g	7.49	11.96	6.48		Ja	26.90	1306	870.0	10-28-95	411.0		1152	49.0						
• SF Deb 9½s 2016	Mn	BBB	11/95	A−	X	R	105.225	4-30-96	100	(5-1-97)	®104.75	4-30-96	100	W3	'86	105⅜	100	104	9.13	9.06
Nts 6⅝s 2000	Jd15	BBB	11/95	A−	X	BE	NC	....	....	....	....	....	100	S1	'95	102⅝	97¾	102⅝	6.46	5.95
Nts 7s 2005	Jd15	BBB	11/95	A−	X	BE	NC	....	....	....	....	....	100	S1	'95	103½	96	103½	6.76	6.50
TKR Cable I	12a	Subsid of Tele-Communications,see																		
Sr Deb[8] 10½s 2007	aO30	BBB−			X	R	105.25	(10-30-99)	....	....	....	....	350	M2	'92	117⅛	101¼	117⅛	8.96	8.21
TLC Beatrice Int'l Hldgs	26g	2.80	2.13	2.87		Dc	78.60	461.0	464.0	6-30-95	★213.0		498.0	58.4						
Sr Sec[1]Nts 11½s 2005	aO	BB−			Y	R	105.75	(10-1-00)	....	....	[9]Z110	9-30-98	175	G1	'95	100	97	98¾	11.65	11.71
TNT Freightways	71	19.50	7.84	7.52		Dc	3.04	169.0	139.0	9-30-95	126.0		355.0	35.8						
Nts 6⅝s 2000	Mn	BBB+	3/94	BBB	X	BE	NC	....	....	....	....	....	100	M2	'93	101	89⅜	101	6.56	6.35
Toledo Edison Co.[10]	72a	1.84	d2.71	2.00		Dc	102.0	298.0	283.0	9-30-95	1082		2141	55.1						
1st 6⅛s '97	fA	BB	12/93	BBB−	Y	R	100.25	7-31-96	100.14	7-31-96	....	....	31.4	B6	'67	99⅜	92	99⅜	6.16	6.54
1st 7¼s '99	fA	BB	12/93	BBB−	Y	R	NC	....	....	....	....	....	100	M6	'92	100⅝	89¼	100⅝	7.20	7.05
• 1st 7½s 2002	fA	BB	12/93	BBB−	Y	R	101.50	7-31-96	100	....	....	....	26.0	B6	'72	98¼	82⅞	95⅜	7.86	8.43
• 1st 8s 2003	mN	BB	12/93	BBB−	Y	R	101.94	10-31-96	100	....	....	....	35.7	B6	'73	100	83½	98⅝	8.11	8.24
1st 7⅞s 2004	fA	BB	12/93	BBB−	Y	R	NC	....	....	....	....	....	145	M6	'92	95½	82¾	95½	8.25	8.63
Deb 8.70s 2002	mS	B+	12/93	BB+	Y	R	NC	....	....	....	....	....	135	M6	'92	95¾	86⅝	93¾	9.28	10.00
[11]Toll Corp	13h	3.04	2.92	4.12		Oc	19.90			7-31-95	292.0		531.0	55.0						
Sr Sub Nts[12] 10½s 2002	Ms15	B+	3/93	B	Y	R	[12]103	(3-15-97)	....	....	....	....	100	M2	'92	105½	91¾	105⅛	9.99	9.39
• Sr Sub Nts[12] 9½s 2003	Ms15	B+			Y	R	104	(3-15-98)	....	....	....	....	75.0	M2	'93	105¾	87⅞	s103¼	9.20	8.88
Torchmark Corp	35a	8.51	7.56	6.07		Dc				9-30-95	793.0		2751	35.0						
SF Deb 8⅝s 2017	Ms	A	6/95	A+	X	R	105.013	2-29-96	100	(3-1-98)	®104.178	2-28-97	200	F1	'87	108⅜	94½	105⅜	8.19	8.09

Uniform Footnote Explanations-See Page 260. Other: [1] (HRO)On Chge of Ctrl at 101. [2] Separately transferable 180 days fr 4-20-94. [3] Max $105M red w/proceeds of Pub Off'g. [4] Incl disc. [5] See Time Warner Entmt. [6] Int to 11-15-95,adj qtrly(3 Mo LIBOR&0.96%). [7] Was Zayre Corp. [8] (HRO)On Chge of Ctrl at 100. [9] Max $52.5M red w/proceeds of Pub Eq Off'gs. [10] Subsid of Centerior Energy. [11] Gtd by & data of Toll Bros. [12] Gtd by Toll Bros.

Title-Industry Code & Co. Finances (In Italics) / Exchange ↓ Individual Issue Statistics	Ind / Interest Dates	Fixed Charge Coverage 1992 / S&P Debt Rating	1993 / Date of Last Rating Change	1994 / Prior Rating	Eligible ↓	Year End / Bond Form	Million $ Cash & Equiv. / Redemption Provisions: Regular Price	Curr. Assets / Regular (Begins) Thru	Curr. Liab. / Sinking Fund Price	Balance Sheet Date / Sinking Fund (Begins) Thru	L. Term Debt (Mil $) / Refund/Other Restriction Price	Refund/Other Restriction (Begins) Thru	Capital-ization (Mil $) / Outst'g (Mil $)	Total Debt % Capital / Underwriting Firm	Underwriting Year	Price Range 1995 High	Price Range 1995 Low	Mo. End Price Sale(s) or Bid	Curr. Yield	Yield to Mat.
Torchmark Corp *(Cont.)*																				
Sr Nts 9⅝s '98	Mn	**A**	6/95	A+	X	R	NC	....	....	....	....	....	200	F1	'88	108⅝	103	108¼	8.89	5.80
Nts 7⅜s 2013	fA	**A**	6/95	A+	X	R	NC	....	....	....	....	....	100	M6	'93	104¾	86¾	104¾	7.04	6.90
Nts 7⅞s 2023	Mn15	**A**	6/95	A+	X	R	NC	....	....	....	....	....	200	M6	'93	107	88	107	7.36	7.28
Toro Co	***42a***	***△2.25***	***△3.73***	***△6.13***		***Jl***	***11.90***	***382.0***	***213.0***	***7-31-95***	***64.90***		***289.0***	***36.0***						
SF Deb 11s 2017	fA	**BBB–**	12/94	BB+	X	R	106.60	7-31-96	100	(8-1-98)	®105.50	7-31-97	50.0	G1	'87	109⅞	103⅝	106¾	10.30	10.22
Tosco Corp	***49d***	***3.13***	***4.06***	***2.99***		***Dc***	***39.00***	***802.0***	***555.0***	***9-30-95***	***634.0***		***1233***	***51.4***						
• 1st 'A' 9s '97	Ms15	**BBB–**	10/94	BB+	X	R	NC	....	....	....	....	....	100	L3	'92	102	100	100½	8.96	8.54
• 1st 'B' 9⅝s 2002	Ms15	**BBB–**	10/94	BB+	X	R	NC	....	....	....	....	....	200	L3	'92	110½	105	116½	8.26	6.36
Nts 7s 2000	jJ15	**BB+**			Y	BE	NC	....	....	....	....	....	125	M6	'95	101⅞	97⅜	101¾	6.88	6.55
Town & Country	***37***	***0.30***	***1.27***	***d0.21***		***Fb***	***4.40***	***142.0***	***47.90***	***8-27-95***	***94.10***		***174.0***	***64.4***						
Sr Sub([1]PIK)Nts[2] 13s '98	[3]nm15	**CCC**	11/95	CCC+	Y	R	106	(5-14-96)	....	....	....	....	57.0	Exch.	'93	67	34½	45	....	....
Toyota Motor Credit	***25d***	***1.39***	***1.56***	***1.60***		***Sp***				***6-30-95***	***13388***		***15050***	***89.0***						
• M-T Nts 7.55s '97	[4]mn15	**AAA**			X	BE	NC	....	....	....	....	....	50.0	M2	'95	100	100	100	7.55	7.54
Toys R Us	***59g***	***9.78***	***10.70***	***10.21***		***Ja***	***220.0***	***4083***	***4058***	***10-28-95***	***782.0***		***5637***	***40.4***						
Deb 8¼s 2017	Fa	**AA**			X	R	104.95	1-31-96	100	(2-1-98)	®104.125	1-31-97	87.9	S1	'87	105⅛	96⅝	105⅛	7.85	7.75
Deb 8¾s 2021	mS	**AA**			X	BE	NC	....	....	....	....	....	200	G1	'91	126⅜	102½	126⅜	6.92	6.60
Tracor Inc	***23i***	***2.97***	***2.87***	***1.85***		***Dc***	***24.20***	***192.0***	***97.00***	***12-31-94***	***195.0***		***357.0***	***74.5***						
Sr[5]Sub Nts 10⅞s 2001	FA15	**B**			Y	R	104.661	(8-15-97)	....	....	....	....	105	B9	'93	105¾	95	102¾	10.58	10.21
Trans Fin'l Bancorp[6]	***10***	***12.56***	***8.23***	***4.80***		***Dc***				***9-30-95***	***36.90***		***164.0***	***22.5***						
Sub[7]Nts 7¼s 2003	[8]Qoct	**NR**				BE	NC	....	....	....	....	....	30.0	M4	'93	100	78⅞	98	7.40	7.59
Trans Leasing Int'l	***43***	***△1.31***	***△1.08***	***△1.19***		***Je***	***2.92***			***9-30-95***	***197.0***		***223.0***	***88.3***						
Sub[9]Deb 10½s 2002	aO15	**NR**				R	104	(10-15-97)	....	....	....	....	13.0	I1	'92	100	92	100	10.50	10.49
Trans Ocean Container	***16b***	***2.75***	***2.37***	***1.60***		***Dc***				***9-30-95***	***269.0***		***303.0***	***88.8***						
Sr Sub Nts[5] 12¼s 2004	jJ	**B–**			Y	R	[10]Z100	6-30-99	....	....	[11]Z111.25	7-1-97	75.0	M2	'94	104	94	104	11.78	11.50
Trans-Resources,Inc	***14a***	***1.83***	***1.38***	***0.87***		***Dc***	***22.00***	***192.0***	***158.0***	***9-30-95***	***246.0***		***348.0***	***95.7***						
Sr Sub Nts[12] 14½s '96	mS	**B–**			Y	R	101	....	....	....	....	....	26.8	D7	'89	102½	100½	102½	14.15	10.49
Transamerica Corp	***25g***	***1.99***	***2.17***	***2.20***		***Dc***				***9-30-95***	***10173***		***14466***	***70.3***						
Deb 9⅜s 2008	Ms	**A**			X	R	NC	....	....	....	....	....	100	G1	'88	124⅝	103⅞	124⅝	7.52	6.43
Nts 9⅞s '98	Jj	**A**			X	R	NC	....	....	....	....	....	100	G1	'88	108¼	104	107¾	9.16	5.73
Transamerica Finance[13]Corp[14]	***25a***	***1.80***	***1.65***	***1.85***		***Dc***	***156.0***			***9-30-95***	***9589***		***11293***	***84.9***						
Deb[15] 6½s 2011	Ms15	**A+**			X	R	100	....	....	....	....	....	[16]102	G1	'81	97	80½	97	6.70	6.82
Nts 5.85s '96	jJ15	**A+**			X	BE	NC	....	....	....	....	....	150	F1	'92	100⅛	97	100⅛	5.84	5.61
Nts 8.55s '96	Jd15	**A+**			X	R	NC	....	....	....	....	....	100	S1	'89	101⅞	100½	101⅜	8.43	5.47
Nts[15] 7⅞s '97	Fa15	**A+**			X	R	NC	....	....	....	....	....	100	G1	'87	102⅞	99¼	102½	7.68	5.55
Sr Nts 6¾s '97	fA15	**A+**			X	BE	NC	....	....	....	....	....	150	U1	'94	101⅞	96⅜	101⅞	6.63	5.52
Sr Nts 6.80s '99	Ms15	**A+**			X	BE	NC	....	....	....	....	....	300	G1	'94	103¼	94⅜	103¼	6.59	5.67
Nts 8¾s '99	aO	**A+**			X	R	NC	....	....	....	....	....	100	M6	'89	109	100⅞	108⅛	8.09	6.28
• Nts[17] 8½s 2001	jJ	**A+**	7/78	A	X	R	NC	....	....	....	....	....	0.75	M2	'76	104	104	105½	8.06	7.27
Sr Nts 7½s 2004	Ms15	**A+**			X	BE	NC	....	....	....	....	....	200	G1	'94	108⅛	93¼	108⅛	6.94	6.22
M-T Nts 'D'[18] 7.18s '98	[19]ms	**A+**			X	BE	NC	....	....	....	....	....	20.0	M6	'94	103⅝	96½	103⅝	6.93	5.65
M-T Nts 'D'[18] 7.60s 2001	[20]ms	**A+**			X	BE	NC	....	....	....	....	....	25.0	S1	'94	107⅜	95½	107⅜	7.08	6.04
F/R[21]M-T Nts 'D'[18] '96	QMay16	**A+**			X	BE	NC	....	....	....	....	....	50.0	S1	'94	100	99⅞	100	....	....
F/R[22]M-T Nts 'D'[18] '96	[23]Jul26	**A+**			X	BE	NC	....	....	....	....	....	50.0	C5	'94	100	99⅞	100	....	....
F/R[18]M-T Nts 'D'[24] 6.0375s '97	QApr14	**A+**			X	BE	NC	....	....	....	....	....	50.0	S5	'94	100	99⅞	100	6.04	....
F/R[18]M-T Nts 'D'[25] '97	QMay27	**A+**			X	BE	NC	....	....	....	....	....	50.0	U1	'94	100	99⅞	100	....	....
Sub[15]Nts 8⅛s '96	aO15	**A**			X	R	NC	....	....	....	....	....	50.0	G1	'86	102⅝	99⅞	102	7.97	5.50

Uniform Footnote Explanations-See Page 260. Other: [1] Co may pay int in add'l Nts thru 5-15-95. [2] (HRO)On Chge of Ctrl at 100. [3] Due 5-31-98. [4] Due 1-30-97. [5] (HRO)On Chge of Ctrl at 101. [6] Now Trans Financial. [7] Death red benefit,ltd,as defined. [8] Due 9-15-03. [9] Death red benefit, ltd, as defined. [10] To 7-1-99,on Chge of Ctrl, plus premium. [11] Max $18.75M red w/proceeds of IPO. [12] Co must offer repurch at 100 on Chge of Ctrl. [13] Was Transmer Fin'l,then Transamer Finance Group. [14] Subsid of Transamerica Corp. [15] Trades as Transamer Fin'l. [16] Incl disc. [17] (HRO)Ea Jul 1 to 2000 at 100. [18] Issued in min denom $100T. [19] Due 7-29-98. [20] Due 8-23-01. [21] Int adj daily. [22] Int adj monthly. [23] Int pd 26th day ea month. [24] Int to 1-14-96,adj qtrly aft. [25] Int adj weekly.

Title-Industry Code & Co. Finances (In Italics) / Individual Issue Statistics (Exchange)	Ind / Interest Dates	Fixed Charge Coverage 1992 / S&P Debt Rating	1993 / Date of Last Rating Change	1994 / Prior Rating	Eligible	Year End / Bond Form	Million $ Cash & Equiv. / Redemption Provisions: Regular Price	Curr. Assets / Regular (Begins) Thru	Curr. Liab. / Sinking Fund Price	Balance Sheet Date / Sinking Fund (Begins) Thru	L. Term Debt (Mil $) / Refund/Other Restriction Price	Capital-ization (Mil $) / Refund/Other Restriction (Begins) Thru	Total Debt % Capital / Outst'g (Mil $)	Underwriting Firm	Underwriting Year	Price Range 1995 High	Price Range 1995 Low	Mo. End Price Sale(s) or Bid	Curr. Yield	Yield to Mat.
***Transamerica Finance Corp** (Cont.)*																				
Sub Nts 6¾s '98	Jj15	**A**			X	BE	NC	....	....	....	....	....	100	S1	'93	102¼	95⅞	102¼	6.60	5.57
Sub Nts 6¾s 2000	Jd	**A**			X	BE	NC	....	....	....	....	....	100	S1	'95	103¼	99⅛	103¼	6.54	5.90
Sub M-T Nts 'D'[1] 5.85s '96	[2]ms	**A**			X	BE	NC	....	....	....	....	....	20.0	C5	'94	100⅛	97½	100⅛	5.84	5.39
Sub M-T Nts 'D'[1] 5.62s '98	[3]ms	**A**			X	BE	NC	....	....	....	....	....	7.50	S1	'93	99¾	91⅛	99¾	5.63	5.72
Sub M-T Nts 'D'[1] 5.57s '98	[4]ms	**A**			X	BE	NC	....	....	....	....	....	6.00	C5	'93	99⅝	90⅝	99⅝	5.59	5.71
Sub M-T Nts 'D'[1] 5.59s '98	[5]ms	**A**			X	BE	NC	....	....	....	....	....	5.00	G1	'93	99⅝	90¾	99⅝	5.61	5.73
Sub M-T Nts 'D'[1] 5.60s '98	[5]ms	**A**			X	BE	NC	....	....	....	....	....	15.0	M6	'93	99⅝	90¾	99⅝	5.62	5.74
Sub M-T Nts 'D'[1] 5.71s '98	[6]ms	**A**			X	BE	NC	....	....	....	....	....	7.50	G1	'93	100	91	100	5.71	5.71
Sub M-T Nts 'D'[1] 5.74s '98	[7]ms	**A**			X	BE	NC	....	....	....	....	....	60.0	M5	'93	100	91⅛	100	5.74	5.74
Sub M-T Nts 'D'[1] 7.42s '99	[8]ms	**A**			X	BE	NC	....	....	....	....	....	10.0	C5	'94	104⅞	96⅛	104⅞	7.08	5.86
Sub M-T Nts 'D'[1] 5¾s '99	[9]ms	**A**			X	BE	NC	....	....	....	....	....	5.00	C5	'93	99⅝	89½	99⅝	5.77	5.86
Sub M-T Nts 'D'[1] 5.97s '99	[10]ms	**A**			X	BE	NC	....	....	....	....	....	5.00	G1	'93	100¼	90	100¼	5.96	5.90
Sub M-T Nts 'D'[1] 6.05s 2000	[11]ms	**A**			X	BE	NC	....	....	....	....	....	6.00	M5	'93	100¼	88⅝	100¼	6.03	5.99
Sub M-T Nts 'D'[1] 6.51s 2003	[12]ms	**A**			X	BE	NC	....	....	....	....	....	10.0	G1	'93	101¼	87	101¼	6.43	6.31
Sub M-T Nts 'D'[1] 6.49s 2003	[12]ms	**A**			X	BE	NC	....	....	....	....	....	5.00	M6	'93	101⅛	86⅞	101⅛	6.42	6.31
Sub F/R[1]M-T Nts 'D'[13] '96	QMay2	**A**			X	BE	NC	....	....	....	....	....	51.0	M6	'94	100	99⅞	100	....	....
Transco Energy Co	***73a***	***Merged into Williams Cos, see***																		
Deb 9⅞s 2020	Jd15	**BBB–**	2/95	B+	X	R	NC	....	....	....	....	....	125	M2	'90	133¾	102	133¾	7.38	6.98
Nts 9⅛s '98	Mn	**BBB–**	2/95	B+	X	BE	NC	....	....	....	....	....	200	M2	'91	107⅜	99⅞	107⅜	8.50	5.71
Nts[14] 11¼s '99	jJ	**NR**	5/95	BBB–		R	101.875	(7-1-97)	....	....	....	....	[15]13.6	F1	'92	111⅜	106	109¾	10.25	8.00
Nts 9⅝s 2000	Jd15	**BBB–**	2/95	B+	X	R	NC	....	....	....	....	....	125	M2	'90	113⅞	101⅞	113⅞	8.45	6.03
Nts 9⅜s 2001	fA15	**BBB–**	2/95	B+	X	BE	NC	....	....	....	....	....	150	M2	'91	115¼	99⅝	115¼	8.13	6.13
Transcont'l Gas PipeLine[16]	***73a***	***2.48***	***3.54***	***3.94***		***Dc***	***3.79***	***382.0***	***427.0***	***9-30-95***	***652.0***	***2327***	***28.0***							
SF Deb 9⅛s 2017	Fa	**BBB**	2/95	BB	X	R	105.14	1-31-96	100	(2-1-98)	®104.28	1-31-97	150	M2	'87	105¾	96	105⅜	8.66	8.57
Nts 9s '96	mN15	**BBB**	2/95	BB	X	R	NC	....	....	....	....	....	150	L1	'86	103⅞	100⅛	102¾	8.76	5.73
[17]Nts[18] 8⅛s '97	Jj15	**BBB**	2/95	BB	X	R	NC	....	....	....	....	....	100	M6	'87	103	98¾	102½	7.93	5.62
Nts 8⅞s 2002	mS15	**BBB**	2/95	BB	X	R	NC	....	....	....	....	....	125	F1	'92	114	97⅝	114	7.79	6.28
TransTexas Gas	***49***	***Δ38.01***	***Δ1.54***	***Δ0.79***		***Jl***	***81.40***	***171.0***	***64.30***	***7-31-95***	***800.0***	***625.0***	***128.0***							
• Sr[19]SecNts 10½s 2000	mS	**BB–**			Y	R	103	(9-1-98)	100	(9-1-97)	....	....	1.00		'93	107½	96	101⅛	10.38	10.18
Sr Sec Nts[19] 11½s 2002	Jd15	**BB–**			Y	R	105.75	(6-15-00)	....	....	[20]Z111.50	6-14-98	800	J1	'95	105	100	103¼	11.14	10.79
Travelers Group[21]	***35d***	***d8.09***	***3.14***	***2.48***		***Dc***				***9-30-95***	***★8963***	***21172***	***47.9***							
Deb 8⅝s 2007	Fa	**A+**	12/93	A	X	R	NC	....	....	....	....	....	100	M6	'87	117¾	99	117¾	7.32	6.37
Nts 8⅜s '96	jD15	**A+**	12/93	A	X	R	NC	....	....	....	....	....	100	S1	'86	103¼	100¼	102⅝	8.16	5.53
• Nts 7⅝s '97	Jj15	**A+**	12/93	A	X	R	NC	....	....	....	....	....	185	D4	'87	102½	99⅛	s101½	7.51	6.12
• Nts 7¾s '99	Jd15	**A+**	12/93	A	X	R	NC	....	....	....	....	....	100	L3	'92	104	98⅛	102⅜	7.57	6.96
Nts 6⅛s 2000	Jd15	**A+**	12/93	A	X	BE	NC	....	....	....	....	....	200	M2	'93	100⅞	89⅝	100⅞	6.07	5.90
Sr Nts[22] 9½s 2002	Ms	**A+**	12/93	A	X	R	NC	....	....	....	....	....	300	M2	'92	115½	102	115½	8.23	6.42
Nts 6⅝s 2005	mS15	**A+**			X	BE	NC	....	....	....	....	....	150	C5	'95	102½	98	102½	6.46	6.28
Nts 7⅞s 2025	Mn15	**A+**			X	BE	NC	....	....	....	....	....	200	S5	'95	111⅝	98½	111⅝	7.05	6.94
Nts[23] 6⅞s 2025	Jd	**A+**			X	BE	NC	....	....	....	....	....	150	S1	'95	104¾	96⅝	104¾	6.56	6.51
Triangle Pacific Corp	***42***	***[24]0.91***	***1.60***	....		***Dc***	***11.50***	***131.0***	***45.20***	***9-30-94***	***169.0***	***272.0***	***62.5***							
Sr[25]Nts 10½s 2003	fA	**B**			Y	R	103.938	(8-1-98)	....	....	....	....	160	D6	'93	105	94	105	10.00	9.56
[26]Trident NGL, Inc	***73c***	***1.82***	***1.52***	***1.22***		***Dc***	***1.59***	***118.0***	***102.0***	***12-31-94***	***372.0***	***622.0***	***62.2***							
Sub[27]Nts[28] 10¼s 2003	Ao15	**BB+**	6/95	B+	Y	R	104.556	(4-15-98)	....	....	[29]Z109.111	4-22-96	105	D6	'93	111½	97	110½	9.28	8.30
TRINOVA Corp	***41h***	***1.91***	***2.69***	***5.81***		***Dc***	***14.40***	***602.0***	***318.0***	***9-30-95***	***228.0***	***623.0***	***37.2***							
Sr SF Deb 9.55s 2018	Fa	**BBB**	2/92	A–	X	R	106.2075	1-31-96	100	(2-1-99)	®104.775	1-31-98	50.0	B5	'88	108⅞	103¼	106¾	8.95	8.85

Uniform Footnote Explanations-See Page 260. Other: [1] Issued in min denom $100T. [2] Due 4-22-96. [3] Due 10-1-98. [4] Due 11-23-98. [5] Due 11-30-98. [6] Due 12-1-98. [7] Due 12-9-98. [8] Due 6-28-99. [9] Due 10-1-99. [10] Due 12-9-99. [11] Due 11-22-00. [12] Due 12-9-03. [13] Int adj daily. [14] (HRO)On Chge in Ctrl at 101. [15] Defeased,fds deposited w/trustee. [16] Subsid of Transco Energy. [17] SPREADS-Spread Protected Debt Secur. [18] Issued in $10T denom & higher multiples of $1T. [19] (HRO)On Chge of Ctrl at 101. [20] Max $240M w/proceeds of Pub Equity Off'g. [21] Was Travelers Corp, then Travelers Inc. [22] Issued in min denom $250T. [23] (HRO)On 6-1-05 at 100. [24] 7 Mo Dec'92. [25] Co must offer repurch at 101 on Chge of Ctrl. [26] Subsid & data of Trident NGL Holding. [27] (HRO)On Chge of Ctrl at 101 to 4-15-02,100 aft. [28] Purch offer, 101, to Jun 12. [29] Max $35M may be red w/proceeds com off'g.

Title-Industry Code & Co. Finances (In Italics)	Ind	Fixed Charge Coverage 1992	1993	1994		Year End	Million $ Cash & Equiv.	Curr. Assets	Curr. Liab.	Balance Sheet Date	L. Term Debt (Mil $)	Capital-ization (Mil $)		Total Debt % Capital						
Individual Issue Statistics Exchange	Interest Dates	S&P Debt Rating	Date of Last Rating Change	Prior Rating	Eligible	Bond Form	Redemption Provisions: Regular Price	Regular (Begins) Thru	Sinking Fund Price	Sinking Fund (Begins) Thru	Refund/Other Restriction Price	Refund/Other Restriction (Begins) Thru	Outst'g (Mil $)	Underwriting Firm	Underwriting Year	Price Range 1995 High	Price Range 1995 Low	Mo. End Price Sale(s) or Bid	Curr. Yield	Yield to Mat.
TRINOVA Corp *(Cont.)*																				
Nts 7.95s '97	Mn	**BBB**			X	BE	NC	....	....	....	....	....	75.0	M5	'92	103	99	102⅞	7.73	5.68
TRISM Inc	***70b***	***0.34***	***1.21***	....		***Dc***	***1.09***	***64.00***	***35.60***	***9-30-94***	***128.0***	***168.0***		***81.5***						
Sr[1]Sub Nts 10¾s 2000	jD15	**B**			Y	R	105	(12-15-98)	....	....	[2]Z110.75	12-14-96	100	S5	'93	100	93½	96¾	11.11	11.63
Triton Energy	***49a***	***d2.91***	***[3]d2.71***	***[4]d0.60***		***Dc***	***133.0***	***172.0***	***36.60***	***9-30-95***	***405.0***	***649.0***		***62.6***						
Sr Sub Disc (Zero) Nts[5] '97	[6]	**B+**			Y	R	[7]....	....	....	....	....	....	[8]240	M2	'92	86¼	73½	86¼	....	8.21
Sr Sub Disc Nts[5] 9¾s 2000	jD15	**B+**			Y	R	104.875	(12-15-97)	....	....	....	....	[8]170	B5	'93	93¼	74¼	93¼	....	Flat
Truck Components	***8***	***n/a***	***n/a***	***[9]2.63***		***Dc***	***0.91***	***81.80***	***50.20***	***6-30-95***	***82.20***	***156.0***		***52.8***						
[10]Trump Plaza Funding	***25***	***p0.96***	***1.15***	***0.80***		***Dc***	***20.10***	***40.20***	***41.80***	***9-30-95***	***332.0***	***417.0***		***80.1***						
[11]Mtg[1]Nts[12] 10⅞s 2001	Jd15	**B+**	5/95	B	Y	R	105	(6-15-98)	....	....	Z100	....	330	M2	'93	103½	75½	103½	10.51	10.03
[13]Trump Taj Mahal Fdg	***25***	***0.56***	***0.79***	***0.68***		***Dc***	***109.0***	***137.0***	***73.00***	***9-30-95***	***688.0***	***742.0***		***92.9***						
◆wsMtg'A'([14]Units)[15] 11.35s '99	mN15	**NR**				R	100	....	....	....	....	....	765	Exch.	'91	96½	66	s96¼	....	Flat
TRW, Inc	***17***	***2.70***	***3.45***	***6.10***		***Dc***	***81.00***	***2356***	***1974***	***9-30-95***	***568.0***	***3065***		***28.1***						
M-T[16]Nts'A'[17] 9.35s 2020	[18]fa15	**A**	3/95	A–	X	R	NC	....	....	....	....	....	100	M2	'90	112	103⅞	A111	8.42	8.29
Nts[16] 9⅜s 2021	Ao15	**A**	3/95	A–	X	BE	NC	....	....	....	....	....	100	S1	'91	112⅛	103¾	A111	8.45	8.32
[19]Tuboscope Vetco Int'l Inc	***49e***	***1.36***	***1.29***	***2.12***		***Dc***	***8.37***	***79.70***	***37.70***	***9-30-95***	***121.0***	***252.0***		***49.6***						
Sr Sub[20]Nts[1] 10¾s 2003	Ao15	**B–**			Y	R	105.375	(4-15-98)	....	....	....	....	75.0	L3	'93	103½	98¼	99⅞	10.76	10.77
Tucson Elec Pwr[21]	***72a***	***0.58***	***0.84***	***1.13***		***Dc***	***58.30***	***209.0***	***177.0***	***9-30-95***	***2105***	***2156***		***99.7***						
1st 8½s '99	mN	**B+**	11/92	B	Y	R	100.88	10-31-96	100	....	....	....	15.0	B6	'69	102⅜	94⅜	102⅛	8.32	7.84
• 1st 8⅛s 2001	mS	**B+**	11/92	B	Y	R	101.41	8-31-96	100	....	....	....	25.0	B6	'71	102⅛	90	s100¼	8.10	8.07
• 1st 7.55s 2002	Ms	**B+**	11/92	B	Y	R	101.57	2-29-96	100	....	....	....	25.0	B6	'72	100	86½	99⅛	7.62	7.73
• 1st 7.65s 2003	Mn	**B+**	11/92	B	Y	R	101.85	4-30-96	100	....	....	....	40.0	B6	'73	100	86	98⅝	7.76	7.90
1st 8½s 2009	aO	**B+**	11/92	B	Y	R	103.56	9-30-96	100	....	....	....	60.0	M2	'77	105⅛	85½	105⅛	8.09	7.88
Tultex Corp	***68c***	***2.50***	***1.53***	***1.55***		***Dc***	***4.98***	***373.0***	***52.60***	***9-30-95***	***276.0***	***464.0***		***60.1***						
Sr Nts[22] 10⅝s 2005	[23]jd15	**BB–**			Y	R	104.722	(3-15-00)	....	....	[24]Z110.625	3-14-98	110	M5	'95	104⅝	100	101¾	10.44	10.32
Turner Broadcast'g Sys	***12e***	***1.58***	***1.72***	***1.32***		***Dc***	***84.80***	***1233***	***744.0***	***9-30-95***	***2336***	***2759***		***84.7***						
Sr Deb[25] 8.40s 2024	Fa	**BB+**			Y	R	104.161	(2-1-04)	....	....	....	....	200	G1	'94	95⅞	77⅜	95⅞	8.76	8.80
Sr Nts[25] 7.40s 2004	Fa	**BB+**			Y	R	NC	....	....	....	....	....	250	G1	'94	100½	83¼	100½	7.36	7.32
Sr Nts[26] 8⅜s 2013	jJ	**BB+**			Y	R	NC	....	....	....	....	....	300	F1	'93	102	81¼	102	8.21	8.16
Tyco International[27]	***13***	***Δ3.56***	***Δ5.47***	***Δ7.70***		***Je***	***57.10***	***1524***	***1118***	***9-30-95***	***507.0***	***2342***		***27.8***						
Deb 9½s 2022	Mn	**BBB+**	7/93	BBB	X	BE	NC	....	....	....	....	....	200	M5	'92	127¾	101⅞	127¾	7.44	7.15
Deb 8s 2023	Ms	**BBB+**	7/93	BBB	X	BE	NC	....	....	....	....	....	50.0	M5	'93	109⅞	88⅜	109⅞	7.28	7.17
Nts 8⅛s '99	mN	**BBB+**			X	BE	NC	....	....	....	....	....	145	L3	'94	106⅝	98⅝	106⅝	7.62	6.16
Nts 6⅜s 2004	Jj15	**BBB+**			X	R	NC	....	....	....	....	....	105	M5	'94	98⅞	85⅛	98⅞	6.45	6.56
Tyco Toys	***40h***	***3.33***	***d2.38***	***0.15***		***Dc***	***14.00***	***427.0***	***306.0***	***9-30-95***	***147.0***	***568.0***		***49.8***						
• Sr Sub Nts[1] 10⅛s 2002	fA15	**B–**	3/95	B	Y	R	103.797	(8-15-97)	....	....	....	....	127	K2	'92	95½	74	s90⅜	11.20	12.28
Tyson Foods	***26e***	***Δ5.25***	***Δ2.38***	***Δ3.99***		***Sp***	***33.10***	***1520***	***866.0***	***9-30-95***	***1621***	***3452***		***57.5***						
Nts 6¾s 2005	Jd	**A–**			X	BE	NC	....	....	....	....	....	150	M5	'95	103½	95⅞	103½	6.52	6.25
M-T Nts 6⅝s 2005	[28]jd	**A–**			X	BE	NC	....	....	....	....	....	150	M2	'95	102⅞	99½	102⅞	6.44	6.23
[29]UCC Investors Holdings	***14***	***0.76***	***0.85***	***0.89***		***Sp***	***56.20***	***362.0***	***176.0***	***9-30-94***	***1035***	***735.0***		***142.0***						
Sr Nts[1] 10½s 2002	Mn	**B–**			Y	R	NC	....	....	....	[30]Z110	2-1-96	300	M6	'93	106¾	98	103	10.19	9.85
Sr Sub Nts[1] 11s 2003	Mn	**B–**			Y	R	105.50	(5-1-98)	....	....	[31]Z110	1-31-96	325	M6	'93	103¼	98	101¾	10.81	10.64
Sub[32]Disc Nts[1] 12s 2005	Mn	**B–**			Y	R	100	(5-1-98)	....	....	[33]Z111	1-31-96	[8]230	M6	'93	77	65	74¾	....	Flat
[34]UGI Corp	***73b***	***[35]2.18***	***[36]3.19***	***3.47***		***Sp***	***20.70***	***117.0***	***147.0***	***3-31-95***	***160.0***	***426.0***		***48.1***						
1st 7.85s '96	mN	**A–**	10/92	BBB+	X	R	100	....	100	....	....	....	8.58	F1	'71	101¾	99¾	100	7.85	7.83
UJB Financial[37]	***10***	***2.52***	***2.88***	***3.23***		***Dc***				***9-30-95***	***204.0***	***1468***		***13.9***						
• Sub Nts 8⅝s 2002	jD10	**BBB–**			X	BE	NC	....	....	....	....	....	175	M2	'92	111	106	109⅛	7.90	6.95

Uniform Footnote Explanations-See Page 260. Other: [1] (HRO)On Chge of Ctrl at 101. [2] Max $30M red w/proceeds of Pub Eq Off'g. [3] Fiscal May '93 & prior. [4] 7 Mo Dec '94. [5] (HRO)On Chge of Ctrl at 101 of accreted amt. [6] Due 11-1-97. [7] Red 54.76 plus accr OID & Make-Whole Premium. [8] Incl disc. [9] 33 Wks Dec '94. [10] Gtd by & data of Trump Plaza Assoc. [11] Gtd by Trump Plaza Assoc. [12] State gaming laws may req hldr's sale/Co red. [13] Gtd by & data of Trump Taj Mahal Assoc LP. [14] Units incl one Cl B Red Com(not seperable). [15] Int in cash to 9.375%,add'l int in cash/kind. [16] Issued in min denom $100T. [17] (HRO)On 8-15-00 at 100. [18] Due 6-4-20. [19] Gtd by & data of Tuboscope Vetco Int'l Corp. [20] Gtd by Tuboscope Vetco Int'l Corp. [21] Was Tucson Gas & Elec. [22] Co must offer repurch at 101 on Chge of Ctrl. [23] Due 3-15-05. [24] Max $35.2M red w/proceeds of Cap Stk Off'g. [25] (HRO)For Triggering Event at 101. [26] (HRO)For a Triggering Event at 101. [27] Was Tyco Labs. [28] Due 10-17-05. [29] Now Uniroyal Chemical Corp. [30] Max $105M red w/proceeds of Pub Equity Off'g. [31] To 2-1-96,max $113.75 fr Pub Equity Offerings. [32] Int accr at 12% fr 5-1-98. [33] To 2-1-96,max 35% princ fr Pub Equity offerings. [34] Now UGI Utilities Inc, subsid of UGI Corp. [35] Fiscal Dec'92 & prior. [36] 9 Mo Sep,'93. [37] See United Jersey Banks.

Title-Industry Code & *Co. Finances (In Italics)* / Individual Issue Statistics	Ind / Interest Dates	*1992* / S&P Debt Rating	*1993* / Date of Last Rating Change	*1994* / Prior Rating	Eligible	*Year End* / Bond Form	*Cash & Equiv.* / Regular Price	*Curr. Assets* / Regular (Begins) Thru	*Curr. Liab.* / Sinking Fund Price	*Balance Sheet Date* / Sinking Fund (Begins) Thru	*L. Term Debt (Mil $)* / Refund/Other Restriction Price	Refund/Other Restriction (Begins) Thru	*Capital-ization (Mil $)* / Outst'g (Mil $)	*Total Debt % Capital* / Underwriting Firm	Underwriting Year	Price Range 1995 High	Price Range 1995 Low	Mo. End Price Sale(s) or Bid	Curr. Yield	Yield to Mat.
Ultramar Corp	***49g***	***1.92***	***3.66***	***3.16***		***Dc***	***79.10***	***603.0***	***361.0***	***9-30-95***	***654.0***		***1232***	***53.1***						
[1]Nts[2] 8¼s '99	jJ	**BBB**			X	BE	NC	....	....	....	....	....	175	G1	'92	107	98⅜	107	7.71	6.01
Ultramar Credit	***25***	***Gtd by Ultramar Corp,see***																		
Gtd[3]Nts[2] 8⅝s 2002	jJ	**BBB**			X	BE	NC	....	....	....	....	....	275	G1	'92	112½	99	112½	7.67	6.26
UNC Inc[4]	***3***	***2.05***	***1.52***	***d3.39***		***Dc***	***1.27***	***221.0***	***92.90***	***9-30-95***	***192.0***		***299.0***	***66.2***						
• Sr Nts 9⅛s 2003	jJ15	**BB–**	7/94	BB	Y	R	103.422	(7-15-98)	....	....	....	....	100	F1	'93	98½	85	s98	9.31	9.50
Union Bank	***10***	***2.63***	***2.67***	***2.34***		***Dc***				***9-30-95***	***415.0***		***1890***	***22.0***						
• Cap SF Nts 7.35s 2001	Fa	**NR**			X	R	100	....	100	....	....	....	17.9	L3	'71	100	91	98⅞	7.43	7.62
Union Camp Corp	***50***	***1.90***	***1.69***	***2.51***		***Dc***	***43.30***	***1084***	***622.0***	***9-30-95***	***1203***		***3335***	***36.1***						
• SF Deb 8⅝s 2016	Ao15	**A–**	9/93	A	X	R	104.744	4-14-96	100	(4-15-97)	®104.313	4-14-96	100	G1	'86	104⅞	102¾	103⅝	8.32	8.25
SF Deb[5] 10s 2019	Mn	**A–**	9/93	A	X	R	105	(5-1-99)	100	(5-1-00)	....	....	100	M6	'89	116⅞	108⅞	116⅞	8.56	8.34
SF Deb 9¼s 2021	fA15	**A–**	9/93	A	X	R	104.283	(8-16-01)	100	(8-15-02)	....	....	125	G1	'91	116⅞	101	116⅞	7.91	7.73
Deb 9½s 2002	Ms15	**A–**	9/93	A	X	R	NC	....	....	....	....	....	100	S1	'90	117⅜	105⅛	117⅜	8.09	6.09
Deb 9¼s 2011	Fa	**A–**	9/93	A	X	R	NC	....	....	....	....	....	125	F1	'91	126⅝	103¾	126⅝	7.31	6.46
Deb 8½s 2022	Mn15	**A–**	9/93	A	X	R	104.25	(5-15-02)	....	....	....	....	100	S1	'92	116	97⅜	112⅛	7.58	7.44
Nts 7⅜s '99	Mn15	**A–**	9/93	A	X	R	NC	....	....	....	....	....	50.0	S1	'92	104¾	96¼	104¾	7.04	5.80
Union Carbide[6]	***14***	***1.99***	***3.54***	***5.92***		***Dc***	***109.0***	***1614***	***1285***	***12-31-94***	***899.0***		***2627***	***36.0***						
Deb 7½s 2025	Jd	**BBB**			X	BE	NC	....	....	....	....	....	150	M6	'95	106	93½	106	7.08	7.01
Deb[7] 6.79s 2025	Jd	**BBB**			X	BE	NC	....	....	....	....	....	250	M6	'95	104	96⅝	104	6.53	6.48
Union Carbide Chem & Plastics	***14***	***Gtd by Union Carbide,see***																		
Deb[8] 8¾s 2022	fA	**BBB**			X	BE	104.337	(8-1-02)	....	....	....	....	125	M6	'92	114⅝	95⅝	114⅝	7.63	7.47
Deb 7⅞s 2023	Ao	**BBB**			X	BE	NC	....	....	....	....	....	175	M6	'93	111	89	111	7.09	6.97
Nts[8] 7s '99	fA	**BBB**			X	BE	NC	....	....	....	....	....	175	M6	'92	103⅝	93⅞	103⅝	6.76	5.86
Nts 6¾s 2003	Ao	**BBB**			X	BE	NC	....	....	....	....	....	125	M6	'93	103¼	88⅛	103¼	6.54	6.19
Union Electric Co[9]	***72a***	***4.37***	***4.59***	***4.66***		***Dc***	***75.00***	***589.0***	***544.0***	***9-30-95***	***1775***		***4421***	***41.7***						
1st 5½s '96	Mn	**AA–**	4/92	A+	X	R	100	....	□100	....	....	....	30.0	F1	'66	100	97⅜	100	5.50	5.45
1st 5½s '97	Ms	**AA–**	4/92	A+	X	R	100.25	2-29-96	□100.19	2-29-96	....	....	40.0	F1	'67	99⅞	95¼	99⅞	5.51	5.60
1st 6¾s '99	aO15	**AA–**			X	BE	NC	....	....	....	....	....	100	S1	'92	103⅛	93¾	103⅛	6.55	5.82
1st 7.65s 2003	Jj15	**AA–**	4/92	A+	X	BE	NC	....	....	....	....	....	100	S1	'92	109⅜	94¾	109⅜	6.99	6.08
1st 7⅜s 2004	jD15	**AA–**			X	BE	NC	....	....	....	....	....	85.0	S1	'92	108⅝	92¾	108⅝	6.79	6.11
1st 6⅞s 2004	fA	**AA–**			X	BE	NC	....	....	....	....	....	188	S1	'93	105⅜	90½	105⅜	6.52	6.06
1st 6¾s 2008	mN	**AA–**			X	BE	NC	....	....	....	....	....	148	S1	'93	104½	86½	104½	6.46	6.22
1st 8¾s 2021	jD	**AA–**	4/92	A+	X	BE	104.38	(12-1-01)	....	....	....	....	125	S1	'91	114⅝	98⅝	114⅝	7.63	7.47
1st 8¼s 2022	aO15	**AA–**			X	BE	103.61	(10-15-02)	....	....	....	....	104	S1	'92	113	94⅜	113	7.30	7.15
1st 8s 2022	jD15y	**AA–**			X	BE	103.38	(12-15-02)	....	....	....	....	85.0	S1	'92	111½	92⅜	111½	7.17	7.04
1st 7.15s 2023	fA	**AA–**			X	BE	103.01	(8-1-03)	....	....	....	....	75.0	S1	'93	102⅛	83⅞	102⅛	7.00	6.97
1st 7s 2024	Jj15	**AA–**			X	BE	103.41	(1-15-04)	....	....	....	....	100	S1	'94	100¼	82⅜	100¼	6.98	6.98
Union Light Heat & Pwr[10]	***72a***	***1.13***	***2.68***	***2.57***		***Dc***	***1.50***	***34.30***	***53.90***	***9-30-95***	***69.40***		***204.0***	***47.0***						
1st 6½s '99	fA	**A–**	7/95	BBB+	X	R	NC	....	....	....	....	....	20.0	M6	'92	101⅞	92⅞	101⅞	6.38	5.91
1st 8s 2003	aO	**A–**	7/95	BBB+	X	R	102.42	9-30-96	101.06	9-30-96	....	....	10.0	M2	'73	102⅞	96⅜	102½	7.80	7.56
1st 9½s 2008	jD	**A–**	7/95	BBB+	X	R	104.35	11-30-96	100.82	11-30-96	....	....	10.0	H4	'78	104⅞	103¼	104½	9.09	8.91
1st 10¼s 2020	mN15	**A–**	7/95	BBB+	X	R	107.20	11-14-96	Z100	....	....	....	15.0	M6	'90	108¾	107⅛	107⅜	9.55	9.47
Union Oil of California[11]	***49a***	***1.92***	***3.01***	***....***		***Dc***	***193.0***	***1526***	***1006***	***9-30-94***	***3445***		***6677***	***52.4***						
Deb[12] 9¼s 2003	Fa	**BBB**			X	R	NC	....	....	....	....	....	250	M2	'91	117½	104	117½	7.87	6.16
Deb[12] 9⅛s 2006	Fa15	**BBB**			X	R	NC	....	....	....	....	....	200	M2	'91	120¾	103⅞	120¾	7.56	6.32
Nts[12] 9¾s 2000	jD	**BBB**			X	R	NC	....	....	....	....	....	250	M2	'90	116	105⅝	116	8.41	5.95
Nts[12] 8¾s 2001	fA15	**BBB**			X	R	NC	....	....	....	....	....	200	F1	'91	112⅞	101	112⅞	7.75	6.02

Uniform Footnote Explanations-See Page 260. Other: [1] Co must repurch at 100 for certain asset sales. [2] Co may offer 101 on Chge of Ctrl Trigger'g Event. [3] Co must offer repurch at 100 for certain asset sales. [4] Was UNC Resources. [5] (HRO)At 100 to 5-1-99 for a Designated Event. [6] See Union Carbide Chem & Plastics. [7] (HRO)On 6-1-05 at 100. [8] Gtd by Union Carbide. [9] See Missouri Pwr & Lt. [10] Subsid of Cinn Gas & Elec. [11] Subsid of Unocal Corp. [12] Gtd by Unocal Corp.

Title-Industry Code & Co. Finances (In Italics) / Individual Issue Statistics — Exchange	Ind / Interest Dates	Fixed Charge Coverage 1992 / S&P Debt Rating	1993 / Date of Last Rating Change	1994 / Prior Rating	Eligible	Year End / Bond Form	Million $ Cash & Equiv. / Redemption Provisions — Regular Price	Curr. Assets / Regular (Begins) Thru	Curr. Liab. / Sinking Fund Price	Balance Sheet Date / Sinking Fund (Begins) Thru	L. Term Debt (Mil $) / Refund/Other Restriction Price	Refund/Other Restriction (Begins) Thru	Capitalization (Mil $) / Outst'g (Mil $)	Total Debt % Capital / Underwriting Firm	Underwriting Year	Price Range 1995 High	Price Range 1995 Low	Mo. End Price Sale(s) or Bid	Curr. Yield	Yield to Mat.
***Union Oil of California** (Cont.)*																				
Nts[1] 6⅜s 2004	Fa	**BBB**			X	R	NC	....	....	....	....	....	200	G1	'94	100⅝	87	100⅝	6.34	6.27
Nts[1] 7.20s 2005	Mn15	**BBB**			X	BE	NC	....	....	....	....	....	200	G1	'95	106⅛	99⅞	106⅛	6.78	6.32
M-T Nts 'C' 7.64s 2002	[2]jj31	**BBB**			X	BE	NC	....	....	....	....	....	30.0	S1	'95	107⅝	100	107⅝	7.10	6.16
M-T Nts 'C' 7.68s 2005	[3]jj31	**BBB**			X	BE	NC	....	....	....	....	....	26.0	C5	'95	109	100	109	7.05	6.38
M-T Nts 'C' 6.70s 2007	[4]jj31	**BBB**			X	BE	NC	....	....	....	....	....	100	U1	'95	102¼	98⅞	102¼	6.55	6.42
***Union Pacific Corp**[5]*	*55*	*4.06*	*4.45*	*4.58*		*Dc*	*91.00*	*1095*	*2557*	*9-30-95*	*6546*		*12684*	*56.5*						
SF Deb 8½s 2017	Jj15	**A–**	4/95	A	X	R	104.675	1-14-97	100	(1-15-97)	®104.25	1-14-97	200	F1	'87	105⅜	94⅞	104⅞	8.10	8.02
SF Deb 8⅝s 2022	Mn15	**A–**	4/95	A	X	BE	103.93	(5-15-02)	100	(5-15-03)	....	....	150	F1	'92	113	97½	113	7.63	7.49
SF Deb 8.35s 2025	Mn	**A–**			X	BE	104.12	(5-1-05)	100	(5-1-06)	....	....	275	C5	'95	112⅝	99½	112⅝	7.41	7.30
Deb 7⅞s 2023	Fa	**A–**	4/95	A	X	BE	103.37	(2-1-03)	....	....	....	....	150	F1	'93	107⅛	89⅞	107⅛	7.35	7.27
Nts 6¼s '99	Ms15	**A–**	4/95	A	X	BE	NC	....	....	....	....	....	150	C5	'94	101⅜	92⅝	101⅜	6.17	5.77
Nts 7s 2000	Jd15	**A–**	4/95	A	X	BE	NC	....	....	....	....	....	150	F1	'94	104¼	94	104¼	6.71	5.90
Nts 7⅜s 2001	Mn15	**A–**			X	BE	NC	....	....	....	....	....	150	G1	'95	106	100	106	6.96	6.05
Nts 7⅞s 2002	Fa15	**A–**	4/95	A	X	BE	NC	....	....	....	....	....	200	F1	'92	109	96¾	109	7.22	6.09
Nts 9⅝s 2002	jD15	**A–**	4/95	A	X	BE	NC	....	....	....	....	....	100	F1	'90	119⅜	106⅞	119⅜	8.06	6.16
Nts 6s 2003	mS	**A–**	4/95	A	X	BE	100	(9-1-00)	....	....	....	....	150	F1	'93	98⅛	83½	98⅛	6.11	6.31
Nts 6⅛s 2004	Jj15	**A–**	4/95	A	X	BE	100	(1-15-01)	....	....	....	....	150	C5	'94	98¾	84½	98¾	6.20	6.33
Nts 7.60s 2005	Mn	**A–**			X	BE	NC	....	....	....	....	....	425	C5	'95	109⅜	97⅝	109⅜	6.95	6.26
Union Pacific RR	*55*	***Subsid of Union Pacific,see***																		
Eq Tr Ctfs '87(1) 6.44s '98	Jj15	**AA–**	4/95	AA+	X	R	NC	....	....	....	....	....	101	M2	'93	101⅝	95	101⅝	6.34	5.59
Eq Tr Ctfs '88(1) 9½s '99	Fa15	**AA–**	4/95	AA+	X	R	100	(2-15-96)	....	....	....	....	102	M2	'89	109¼	100⅜	100⅜	9.46	9.35
Eq Tr Ctfs '88(2) 9s '99	Jd15	**AA–**	4/95	AA+	X	R	100	(6-15-96)	....	....	....	....	105	M2	'89	103	101⅜	101⅜	8.88	8.53
Eq Tr Ctfs (A) 9⅝s 2002	Ms15	**AA–**	4/95	AA+	X	R	100	(3-15-97)	....	....	....	....	60.8	M2	'90	118⅞	106½	118⅞	8.10	5.94
Union Planters	*10*	*5.50*	*5.80*	*2.99*		*Dc*				*9-30-95*	*★509.0*		*1384*	*36.8*						
Sub Cap Deb[6] 10⅛s '99	QApr	**BBB–**	9/93	BB+	Y	R	100	(4-1-96)	....	....	....	....	[7]34.0		'89	108¾	98	101	10.02	9.75
Sub Nts[8] 8½s 2002	QOct	**BBB–**	9/93	BB+	Y	BE	100	(10-1-97)	....	....	....	....	40.3		'92	104¼	96⅛	104¼	8.15	7.68
Sub Nts 6¼s 2003	mN	**BBB–**			X	R	NC	....	....	....	....	....	75.0	M2	'93	98⅜	85⅛	98⅜	6.35	6.52
Sub Nts 6¾s 2005	mN	**BBB–**			X	BE	NC	....	....	....	....	....	100	S1	'95	101⅜	98⅜	101⅜	6.66	6.56
***Union Tank Car**[9]*	*56a*	*1.77*	*1.94*	*2.13*		*Dc*	*34.50*			*9-30-95*	*859.0*		*1381*	*62.2*						
Eq Tr '14' 8.30s '96	jD	**A+**	8/89	A	X	R	NC	....	100	....	....	....	8.80	S1	'76	102¼	100⅜	102⅛	8.13	5.89
Eq Tr '15' 8.35s '97	jD	**A+**	8/89	A	X	R	NC	....	100	....	....	....	8.80	S1	'77	104⅝	99⅝	104½	7.99	5.84
Eq Tr '16' 9.80s '99	Jd	**A+**	8/89	A	X	R	NC	....	100	....	....	....	24.0	S1	'79	111	103½	111	8.83	6.18
Eq Tr '18' 14s 2001	Jj15	**A+**	8/89	A	X	R	NC	....	100	....	....	....	0.90	S1	'81	123	123	A123	11.38	8.32
Eq Tr '24' 6.60s 2009	Fa15	**A+**			X	BE	NC	....	....	....	....	....	100	S1	'94	108½	90½	108½	6.08	5.67
Union Texas Petrol Hldgs	*49a*	*9.74*	*2.19*	*17.80*		*Dc*	*21.70*	*169.0*	*315.0*	*9-30-95*	*614.0*		*1175*	*64.2*						
• Sr Nts 8¼s '99	mN15	**BBB–**	8/95	BBB	X	R	[10]Z100	....	....	....	....	....	100	G1	'92	105	101	104	7.93	7.05
Sr Nts 8⅜s 2005	Ms15	**BBB–**	8/95	BBB	X	BE	[10]Z100	....	....	....	....	....	125	G1	'95	112¼	99⅜	112¼	7.46	6.58
Sr Nts 8½s 2007	Ao15	**BBB–**	8/95	BBB	X	BE	[10]Z100	....	....	....	....	....	75.0	G1	'95	113½	99⅝	113½	7.49	6.77
***Uniroyal Chemical Co, Inc**[11]*	*14*	*0.76*	*0.85*	*d1.59*		*Sp*	*35.30*	*423.0*	*250.0*	*7-2-95*	*912.0*		*623.0*	*148.0*						
Sr[12]Nts 9s 2000	mS	**B+**			Y	R	NC	....	....	....	....	....	270	M6	'93	100¼	93	100	9.00	8.99
Uniroyal Technology	*52*	*d1.41*	*0.70*	*0.63*		*Sp*	*4.25*	*64.60*	*32.10*	*10-2-94*	*80.60*		*138.0*	*58.6*						
xwSr Sec Nts[13] 11¾s 2003	Jd	**B**			Y	R	104.41	(6-1-98)	....	....	....	....	80.0	S1	'93	107	80½	107	10.98	10.37
***Unisys Corp**[14]*	*20b*	*2.28*	*3.08*	*1.75*		*Dc*	*820.0*	*2952*	*2243*	*9-30-95*	*1534*		*4512*	*42.0*						
Sr SF Deb[15] 9¾s 2016	mS15	**BB–**	9/93	B+	Y	R	104.96	9-14-96	100	(9-15-97)	®104.51	9-14-96	190	S4	'86	99⅜	82	83	11.75	11.98
Sr Nts[16] 9¾s '96	mS15	**BB–**	9/93	B+	Y	BE	NC	....	....	....	....	....	238	L3	'92	102¾	96	97	10.05	14.27
• [17]Nts[18] 13½s '97	jJ	**BB–**	9/93	B+	Y	BE	NC	....	....	....	....	....	292	B5	'90	116½	94	s97¾	....	Flat

Uniform Footnote Explanations-See Page 260. Other: [1] Gtd by Unocal Corp. [2] Due 4-22-02. [3] Due 4-25-05. [4] Due 10-15-07. [5] See Union Pac RR. [6] Death red benefit,ltd, as defined. [7] Defeased,fds deposited w/trustee. [8] Death red benefit,ltd,as defined. [9] Subsid of Marmon Indus. [10] Plus Make-Whole Premium. [11] Subsid of Uniroyal Chem Corp(was UCC Inv Hldgs). [12] (HRO)On Chge of Ctrl at 101. [13] Co must offer repurch at 101 on Chge of Ctrl. [14] Was Sperry Rand Corp. [15] Was Burroughs Corp. [16] (HRO)On Chge in Ctrl at 101. [17] Credit Sensitive:int adj for rating chge. [18] Int(9.90%-15%)decr fr 15% on 9-9-93.

Title-Industry Code & Co. Finances (In Italics) / Individual Issue Statistics (Exchange ↓)	Ind / Interest Dates	Fixed Charge Coverage 1992 / S&P Debt Rating	1993 / Date of Last Rating Change	Prior Rating	1994 / Eligible ↓	Year End / Bond Form	Million $ Cash & Equiv. / Redemption Provisions: Regular Price	Curr. Assets / Regular (Begins) Thru	Curr. Liab. / Sinking Fund Price	Balance Sheet Date / Sinking Fund (Begins) Thru	L. Term Debt (Mil $) / Refund/Other Restriction Price	Refund/Other Restriction (Begins) Thru	Capital-ization (Mil $) / Outst'g (Mil $)	Total Debt % Capital / Underwriting Firm	Underwriting Year	Price Range 1995 High	Price Range 1995 Low	Mo. End Price Sale(s) or Bid	Curr. Yield	Yield to Mat.
Unisys Corp (Cont.)																				
Nts 8⅞s '97	jJ15	BB–	9/93	B+	Y	R	100	....	....	....	....	....	150	F1	'87	100⅛	89	89	9.97	17.28
Nts 9½s '98	jJ15	BB–	9/93	B+	Y	R	100	....	....	....	....	....	200	S4	'88	100¼	87½	87½	10.86	15.63
Sr Nts[1] 10⅝s '99	aO	BB–	9/93	B+	Y	BE	101.77	(10-1-97)	....	....	....	....	330	L3	'92	107⅝	88½	88½	12.01	14.70
United Air Lines[2]	*4*	*d1.33*	*0.86*		*1.42*	*Dc*	*1548*	*3450*	*5004*	*9-30-95*	*3423*		*4515*	*83.2*						
Eq Tr '91A 10.11s 2006	Jj5	BB+	3/93	BBB	Y	R	[3]Z100	....	100	....	....	....	36.2	M2	'91	116⅜	97⅛	116⅜	8.69	7.73
Eq Tr '91A 10.85s 2014	jJ5	BB+	3/93	BBB	Y	R	[4]Z100	....	100	(1-5-08)	....	....	62.1	M2	'91	127⅝	99¼	127⅝	8.50	7.97
Eq Tr '91B 10.11s 2006	Fa19	BB+	3/93	BBB	Y	R	[3]Z100	....	100	....	....	....	35.3	M2	'91	116⅝	97⅛	116⅝	8.67	7.71
Eq Tr '91B 10.85s 2015	Fa19	BB+	3/93	BBB	Y	R	[4]Z100	....	100	(2-19-07)	....	....	65.6	M2	'91	127¾	99⅛	127¾	8.49	7.99
Eq Tr '91C 9.76s 2006	Mn13	BB+	3/93	BBB	Y	R	[4]Z100	....	[5]100	....	....	....	25.4	M2	'91	116⅜	94⅞	116⅜	8.39	7.46
Eq Tr '91E 9.76s 2006	Mn27	BB+	3/93	BBB	Y	R	[4]Z100	....	[5]100	....	....	....	24.9	M2	'91	115⅛	94⅜	115⅛	8.48	7.63
Eq Tr '91E 10.36s 2012	mN27	BB+	3/93	BBB	Y	R	[4]Z100	....	[5]100	(5-27-07)	....	....	35.1	M2	'91	126¾	95⅜	126¾	8.17	7.53
• Deb 'A' 10.67s 2004	Mn	BB			Y	R	NC	....	....	....	....	....	370	M2	'94	121	101	117	9.12	7.85
Deb 9⅛s 2012	Jj15	BB	3/93	BBB–	Y	R	NC	....	....	....	....	....	200	M2	'92	112	86⅞	112	8.15	7.80
• Deb 'B' 11.21s 2014	Mn	BB			Y	R	NC	....	....	....	....	....	371	M2	'94	128	103	126⅛	8.89	8.39
Deb 10¼s 2021	jJ15	BB	3/93	BBB–	Y	R	NC	....	....	....	....	....	300	F1	'91	125¾	94¼	125¾	8.15	7.89
Deb 9¾s 2021	fA15	BB	3/93	BBB–	Y	R	NC	....	....	....	....	....	250	S1	'91	120¼	90	120¼	8.11	7.89
Nts 6¾s '97	[6]mn	BB			Y	BE	NC	....	....	....	....	....	100	M6	'93	101	92¾	100½	6.72	6.47
Nts 9s 2003	jD15	BB	3/93	BBB–	Y	R	NC	....	....	....	....	....	150	S1	'91	111	91⅛	111	8.11	7.16
United Cos Financial	*35a*	*1.52*	*1.39*		*6.24*	*Dc*				*9-30-95*	*233.0*		*581.0*	*40.1*						
Sr Nts 7s '98	jJ15	BBB–			X	BE	NC	....	....	....	....	....	100	S1	'95	101⅞	99¼	101⅞	6.87	6.19
Sr Nts 9.35s '99	mN	BBB–			X	BE	NC	....	....	....	....	....	125	M2	'94	107¾	98⅝	107¾	8.68	7.01
United Dominion Rlty Tr	*57*	*1.69*	*1.67*		*1.68*	*Dc*				*9-30-95*	*527.0*		*1046*	*50.4*						
Deb[7] 8½s 2024	mS15	BBB+			X	BE	NC	....	....	....	....	....	150	G1	'94	111⅜	97½	111⅜	7.63	7.53
Nts 7¼s '99	Ao	BBB+			X	BE	[8]Z100	....	....	....	....	....	75.0	G1	'94	100¾	94⅜	100⅛	7.24	7.20
United Illuminating	*72a*	*1.88*	*1.83*		*2.03*	*Dc*	*42.60*	*186.0*	*235.0*	*9-30-95*	*848.0*		*1457*	*65.5*						
Nts[9] 7s '97	[10]ms	BBB–			X	BE	NC	....	....	....	....	....	50.0	M6	'92	100⅞	97	100⅞	6.94	6.12
Nts[9] 7⅜s '98	[11]ms	BBB–			X	BE	NC	....	....	....	....	....	100	M6	'92	102¼	95⅞	102¼	7.21	6.18
Nts 6.20s '99	Jj15	BBB–			X	BE	NC	....	....	....	....	....	100	M6	'93	99½	90½	99½	6.23	6.38
United Int'l Hldgs	*12*	*n/a*	*n/a*		*n/a*	*Fb*	*38.70*			*8-31-95*	*★303.0*		*389.0*	*58.2*						
Sr Sec Disc Nts(Zero Cpn)[12] '99	[13]	B–			Y	R	NC	....	....	....	....	....	[14]130	D6	'95	68¼	67⅛	68¼	....	10.10
United Jersey Banks	*10*	*Now UJB Fin'l,see*																		
• SF Deb 7¾s '97	mN	NR			X	R	100	....	100	....	....	....	10.7	M2	'72	101	98	100⅛	7.74	7.67
United Merch & Mfrs	*68a*	*Δd1.12*	*Δd0.95*		*Δd0.67*	*Je*	*0.81*	*27.40*	*16.60*	*9-30-95*	*84.60*		*34.20*	*247.0*						
Sr Sub Sec Deb 3½s 2009	jJ	NR	7/95	C		R	100	....	....	....	....	....	[14]69.1		'90	6½	1	1	....	....
United Meridian	*49a*	*1.05*	*0.46*		*d2.07*	*Dc*	*21.90*	*91.30*	*102.0*	*9-30-95*	*★366.0*		*431.0*	*50.6*						
• Sr Sub Nts[15] 10⅜s 2005	aO15	B			Y	BE	105.19	(10-15-00)	....	....	....	....	150	M2	'95	99½	99½	102⅛	10.16	10.02
United Parcel Service of Amer	*70b*	*31.28*	*43.11*		*55.31*	*Dc*	*326.0*	*3334*	*2960*	*9-30-95*	*1409*		*6661*	*21.2*						
Deb 8⅜s 2020	Ao	AAA			X	R	NC	....	....	....	....	....	700	M2	'89	122⅝	99¾	122⅝	6.83	6.51
U.S. Bancorp	*10*	*2.65*	*3.75*		*2.24*	*Dc*				*9-30-95*	*★11222*		*2773*	*29.6*						
Sub Nts 8⅛s 2002	Mn15	A–			X	BE	NC	....	....	....	....	....	150	G1	'92	110½	97	110½	7.35	6.11
Sub Nts 7s 2003	Ms15	A–			X	R	NC	....	....	....	....	....	150	G1	'93	104¾	90½	104¾	6.68	6.17
Sub Nts 6¾s 2005	aO15	A–			X	BE	NC	....	....	....	....	....	300	C5	'95	103⅛	99⅜	103⅛	6.55	6.32
[16]U.S. Banknote[17]	*29a*	*1.94*	*2.24*		*0.62*	*Dc*	*19.10*	*95.20*	*40.70*	*9-30-95*	*191.0*		*261.0*	*73.2*						
Sr Nts[15] 10⅜s 2002	Jd	B+	6/95	BB–	Y	R	105.1875	(6-1-97)	100	(6-1-00)	....	....	127	B5	'92	85½	75	75	13.83	16.89
U.S. Can Co[18]	*16b*	*1.28*	*1.98*		*2.46*	*Dc*	*0.45*	*154.0*	*84.60*	*7-2-95*	*248.0*		*349.0*	*75.4*						
Sr Sub Nts[1] 13½s 2002	Jj15	B	11/94	B–	Y	R	104	(1-15-97)	....	....	....	....	100	S1	'91	111⅜	109	109¼	12.36	11.34

Uniform Footnote Explanations-See Page 260. Other: [1] (HRO)On Chge in Ctrl at 101. [2] Subsid of UAL Corp. [3] In whole, plus red premium:dates&circum.,as def. [4] In whole,plus red premium:dates&circum.,as def. [5] Prin pyts due,made pro rata among all hldrs. [6] Due 12-1-97. [7] (HRO)On 9-15-04 at 100. [8] Plus Make-Whole amt. [9] Issued in min denom $100T. [10] Due 1-15-97. [11] Due 1-15-98. [12] (HRO)On Chge of Ctrl at 101 (Accreted Val). [13] Due 11-15-99. [14] Incl disc. [15] (HRO)On Chge of Ctrl at 101. [16] Now Amer Banknote. [17] Was Intl Banknote. [18] Subsid of U.S. Can Corp.

Title-Industry Code & Co. Finances (In Italics)	Ind	Fixed Charge Coverage 1992	1993	1994		Year End	Million $ Cash & Equiv.	Curr. Assets	Curr. Liab.	Balance Sheet Date	L. Term Debt (Mil $)		Capital-ization (Mil $)	Total Debt % Capital						
Exchange ↓ Individual Issue Statistics	Interest Dates	S&P Debt Rating	Date of Last Rating Change	Prior Rating	Eligible ↓	Bond Form	Redemption Provisions: Regular Price	Regular (Begins) Thru	Sinking Fund Price	Sinking Fund (Begins) Thru	Refund/Other Restriction Price	Refund/Other Restriction (Begins) Thru	Outst'g (Mil $)	Underwriting Firm	Underwriting Year	Price Range 1995 High	Price Range 1995 Low	Mo. End Price Sale(s) or Bid	Curr. Yield	Yield to Mat.
U.S. Gypsum Co	***13g***	***Subsid of USG Corp,see***																		
• SF Deb 7⅞s 2004	Jj	**BB**	1/95	BB–	Y	R	100.89	12-31-96	100	....	....	....	44.1	K2	'74	98⅞	92	97½	8.08	8.31
U.S. Home Corp(New)	***13h***	***n/a***	***n/a***	***2.68***		***Dc***				***9-30-95***	***289.0***		***687.0***	***53.7***						
Sr Nts[1] 9¾s 2003	Jd15	**BB–**	9/95	B+	Y	R	103.656	(6-15-98)	....	....	....	....	200	D4	'93	102½	85¼	102½	9.51	9.28
U.S. Leasing Int'l	***25***	***Now USL Capital,see***																		
Sr Nts[2] 8¾s '96	Mn	**A+**	3/95	A	X	R	NC	....	....	....	....	....	250	G1	'91	102⅛	100⅞	101	8.66	5.66
Sr Nts 7s '97	mN	**A+**	3/95	A	X	BE	NC	....	....	....	....	....	150	L3	'92	102¼	96⅞	102¼	6.85	5.69
◆Sr Nts[2] 8¾s 2001	jD	**A+**	3/95	A	X	BE	NC	....	....	....	....	....	200	L3	'91	No Sale		80	10.94	13.80
Sr Nts 6⅝s 2003	Mn15	**A+**	3/95	A	X	BE	NC	....	....	....	....	....	150	L3	'93	101¼	85	101¼	6.54	6.41
Sr Nts 5.95s 2003	aO15	**A+**	3/95	A	X	BE	NC	....	....	....	....	....	150	G1	'93	97⅞	84	97⅞	6.08	6.30
U.S. Leather, Inc	***39d***	***1.16***	***1.30***	***1.51***		***Dc***	***2.01***	***131.0***	***70.50***	***9-30-95***	***130.0***		***250.0***	***68.0***						
Sr Nts[1] 10¼s 2003	jJ31	B–	11/95	B+	Y	R	104.354	(7-31-98)	....	....	[3]Z110	7-31-96	135	B5	'93	87	74	74	13.85	16.34
U.S. Shoe Corp.	***59a***	***1.45***	***d0.42***	....		***Ja***	***147.0***	***736.0***	***466.0***	***10-29-94***	***88.90***		***622.0***	***22.5***						
Nts 8⅝s 2002	aO	**NR**	7/95	BB+		R	NC	....	....	....	....	....	75.0	S1	'92	108	90	90	9.58	10.74
U.S.Trust Co N.Y.	***10***	***3.69***	***5.58***	***2.11***		***Dc***				***6-30-95***	***57.20***		***307.0***	***18.6***						
Nts 8s '96	Ao15	**A**	9/95	AA–	X	R	NC	....	....	....	....	....	30.0	F1	'86	101½	100⅛	100⅝	7.95	5.75
United Technologies	***17***	***1.70***	***4.14***	***4.60***		***Dc***	***904.0***	***8636***	***6358***	***9-30-95***	***1707***		***6136***	***29.3***						
Deb[4] 8⅞s 2019	mN15	**A+**	1/92	AA–	X	R	NC	....	....	....	....	....	300	B5	'89	126½	103¾	126½	7.02	6.65
Deb 8¾s 2021	Ms	**A+**	1/92	AA–	X	BE	NC	....	....	....	....	....	250	S1	'91	124¾	100⅞	124¾	7.01	6.70
Nts 9⅝s '99	Mn15	**A+**	1/92	AA–	X	R	100	(5-15-96)	....	....	....	....	100	S1	'89	103⅛	101⅝	101¾	9.46	9.01
United Telecommunications	***67b***	***Now Sprint Corp,see***																		
Nts 9¾s 2000	Ao	**BBB**	2/94	BBB–	X	R	NC	....	....	....	....	....	250	D4	'90	113½	104¼	113½	8.59	6.10
Nts 9½s 2003	Ao	**BBB**	2/94	BBB–	X	R	NC	....	....	....	....	....	200	D4	'91	118½	104¾	118½	8.02	6.28
United Tel Co(Florida)[5]	***67a***	***4.80***	***6.38***	....		***Dc***	***4.21***	***202.0***	***230.0***	***6-30-95***	***438.0***		***1133***	***38.8***						
1st CC 9¼s 2019	mS15	**A**	12/92	A–	X	R	106.189	9-14-96	Z100	....	....	....	135	M2	'89	106¾	101⅛	106⅜	8.70	8.61
1st DD 7¼s 2004	jD15	**A**	12/92	A–	X	R	NC	....	Z100	....	....	....	50.0	C4	'92	107¼	91⅞	107¼	6.76	6.18
1st EE 6¼s 2003	Mn15	**A**			X	R	NC	....	Z100	....	....	....	70.0	D6	'93	100⅜	87¼	100⅜	6.23	6.18
1st FF 6⅞s 2013	jJ15	**A**			X	BE	NC	....	Z100	....	....	....	60.0	L3	'93	101½	84⅞	101½	6.77	6.73
1st GG 7⅛s 2023	jJ15	**A**			X	BE	NC	....	Z100	....	....	....	75.0	M2	'93	103⅞	85⅛	103⅞	6.86	6.81
United Tel Co (Ohio)[5]	***67a***	***5.31***	***4.27***	***6.44***		***Dc***	***2.34***	***122.0***	***123.0***	***12-31-94***	***164.0***		***444.0***	***36.9***						
1st BB 6⅝s 2002	aO	**A**	12/92	A–	X	R	NC	....	Z100	....	....	....	60.0	K2	'92	100⅝	89⅝	100	6.63	6.62
1st DD 5⅞s 2000	Jd	**A**			X	BE	NC	....	Z100	....	....	....	30.0	L3	'93	99⅝	89⅜	99⅝	5.90	5.97
1st EE 6½s 2005	Jd	**A**			X	BE	NC	....	Z100	....	....	....	35.0	L3	'93	101½	86¾	101½	6.40	6.29
United Tel Co (Penna)[5]	***67a***	***4.89***	***5.04***	***5.45***		***Dc***	***0.98***	***59.40***	***41.30***	***9-30-95***	***116.0***		***299.0***	***39.8***						
1st Y 7⅜s 2002	jD	**A**	12/92	A–	X	R	NC	....	Z100	....	....	....	55.0	K2	'92	105⅝	93	105⅝	6.98	6.36
United Virginia Bankshrs	***10***	***Now Crestar Fin'l,see***																		
Sub Nts[6] 8⅝s '98	Ao15	**BBB**	10/93	BBB–	X	R	NC	....	....	....	....	....	50.0	S4	'86	105¾	99	105¾	8.16	5.90
Universal Corp	***69c***	***Δ3.57***	***Δ1.75***	***Δ2.05***		***Je***	***80.10***	***1406***	***1162***	***9-30-95***	***261.0***		***1383***	***69.8***						
Nts 9¼s 2001	Fa15	**A–**			X	BE	NC	....	....	....	....	....	100	G1	'91	114¼	103¼	114¼	8.10	5.98
Univl Health Svcs	***30***	***4.43***	***5.81***	***9.67***		***Dc***	***0.16***	***136.0***	***128.0***	***9-30-95***	***245.0***		***543.0***	***46.4***						
Sr Nts[7] 8¾s 2005	fA15	**B+**			Y	BE	102.265	(8-15-00)	....	....	....	....	135	D4	'95	102	97⅜	102	8.58	8.44
UNUM Corp	***35a***	***37.56***	***37.24***	***11.62***		***Dc***				***9-30-95***	***588.0***		***2688***	***21.9***						
M-T Nts 'B'[2] 6.16s '96	[8]mn15	**A+**	1/95	AA	X	BE	NC	....	....	....	....	....	15.0	M6	'94	100¼	98	100¼	6.14	5.36
M-T Nts 'B'[2] 6.56s '97	[9]mn15	**A+**	1/95	AA	X	BE	NC	....	....	....	....	....	5.00	M6	'94	101¼	96¾	101¼	6.48	5.62
M-T Nts 'B'[2] 7s '99	[10]mn15	**A+**	1/95	AA	X	BE	NC	....	....	....	....	....	5.00	M6	'94	103⅝	95⅛	103⅝	6.76	5.83
M-T Nts 'B'[2] 6.95s '99	[11]mn15	**A+**	1/95	AA	X	BE	NC	....	....	....	....	....	10.0	M6	'94	103½	95	103½	6.71	5.82
M-T Nts 'B'[2] 6½s '97	[12]mn15	**A+**	1/95	AA	X	BE	NC	....	....	....	....	....	10.0	M6	'94	101¼	96½	101¼	6.42	5.60
M-T Nts 'B'[2] 7.08s 2024	[13]mn15	**A+**	1/95	AA	X	BE	NC	....	....	....	....	....	10.0	M6	'94	102⅜	83¼	102⅜	6.92	6.89

Uniform Footnote Explanations-See Page 260. Other: [1] (HRO)On Chge of Ctrl at 101. [2] Issued in min denom $100T. [3] Max $33.8M red w/proceeds of Initial Pub Off'g. [4] Int(min 8.875%)may be adj for certain events. [5] Subsid of Sprint Corp. [6] To be exch for Cap Sec when due. [7] (HRO)On Chge of Ctrl at 100. [8] Due 5-1-96. [9] Due 5-27-97. [10] Due 6-14-99. [11] Due 6-15-99. [12] Due 6-16-97. [13] Due 2-1-24.

Title-Industry Code & Co. Finances (In Italics) / Exchange, Individual Issue Statistics	Ind / Interest Dates	Fixed Charge Coverage 1992 / S&P Debt Rating	1993 / Date of Last Rating Change	1994 / Prior Rating	Eligible	Year End / Bond Form	Cash & Equiv. (Million $) / Regular Price	Curr. Assets (Million $) / Regular (Begins) Thru	Curr. Liab. (Million $) / Sinking Fund Price	Balance Sheet Date / Sinking Fund (Begins) Thru	L. Term Debt (Mil $) / Refund/Other Restriction Price	Refund/Other Restriction (Begins) Thru	Capital-ization (Mil $) / Outst'g (Mil $)	Total Debt % Capital / Underwriting Firm	Underwriting Year	Price Range 1995 High	Price Range 1995 Low	Mo. End Price Sale(s) or Bid	Curr. Yield	Yield to Mat.
Upjohn Co	***21a***	***23.40***	***11.06***	***18.20***		***Dc***	***304.0***	***2142***	***1079***	***6-30-95***	***782.0***		***3345***	***25.2***						
Nts 5⅞s 2000	Ao15	**AA–**	4/95	AA	X	BE	NC	....	....	....	....	....	200	M6	'93	100½	89½	100½	5.85	5.74
URS Corp[1]	***63***	***4.91***	***2.17***	***4.93***		***Oc***	***6.45***	***55.10***	***21.30***	***7-31-95***	***9.83***		***47.20***	***20.8***						
• Sr Sub Deb[2] 8⅝s 2004	Jj15	**NR**				R	100	....	....	....	....	....	6.46	Exch.	'89	92¾	81	90	9.58	10.49
USA Mobile Communications II	***67g***	***0.63***	***0.62***	***0.33***		***Dc***	***0.78***	***25.80***	***31.40***	***6-30-95***	***235.0***		***219.0***	***107.0***						
Sr Nts[3] 9½s 2004	Fa	**CCC+**			Y	R	104.75	(2-1-99)	....	....	....	....	125	N2	'94	97¾	81	97¼	9.77	10.00
Sr[4]Nts[5] 14s 2004	mN	**CCC+**			Y	R	107	(11-1-99)	....	....	[6]Z112	10-31-97	100	M6	'94	117	100	117	11.97	10.94
USAir,[7]Inc[8]	***4***	***d1.69***	***d0.40***	***d1.51***		***Dc***	***865.0***	***1692***	***2560***	***9-30-95***	***2874***		***2128***	***139.0***						
Sr[9]Nts 9⅝s 2001	Fa	**CCC+**	9/94	B–	Y	BE	NC	....	....	....	....	....	175	L3	'94	91	53	87¼	11.03	13.13
Sr[9]Nts 10s 2003	jJ	**CCC+**	9/94	B–	Y	R	105	(7-1-98)	....	....	....	....	300	M6	'93	91	54	87	11.49	12.74
USF&G Corp	***35c***	***3.15***	***3.41***	***4.62***		***Dc***				***9-30-95***	***[10]623.0***		***2379***	***26.2***						
Sr Nts 7s '98	Mn15	**BBB–**			X	BE	NC	....	....	....	....	....	150	M5	'95	102¼	99½	102¼	6.85	5.97
Sr Nts 8⅜s 2001	Jd15	**BBB–**			X	BE	NC	....	....	....	....	....	149	M2	'94	109⅛	96½	109⅛	7.67	6.37
Sr Nts 7⅛s 2005	Jd	**BBB–**			X	BE	NC	....	....	....	....	....	80.0	M2	'95	103	95¾	103	6.92	6.69
USG Corp[11]	***13g***	***0.33***	***[12]0.14***	***0.75***		***Dc***	***64.00***	***535.0***	***366.0***	***9-30-95***	***9233***		***930.0***	***100.0***						
Deb 8¾s 2017	Ms	**BB**	7/95	B+	Y	R	105.12	2-29-96	100	(3-1-98)	®104.267	2-28-97	200	S1	'87	100¼	84½	100	8.75	8.75
Sr Nts 8s '96	jD15	**BB**	7/95	B+	Y	R	NC	....	....	....	....	....	74.0	S1	'86	101⅜	95	101⅜	7.89	6.50
Sr Nts 8s '97	Ms15	**BB**	7/95	B+	Y	R	NC	....	....	....	....	....	74.0	S1	'87	101	95	101	7.92	7.11
• Sr Nts[13] 8½s 2005	fA	**BB**			Y	R	NC	....	....	....	....	....	150	S1	'95	103¼	100	101	8.42	8.34
USL[14]Capital[15]Corp	***25***	***1.58***	***1.64***	***1.72***		***Dc***				***9-30-95***	***2692***		***5123***	***83.7***						
F/R[16]Sr Nts 6s '96	[17]Qfeb28	**A+**	3/95	A	X	BE	NC	....	....	....	....	....	125	C1	'94	100⅛	99¾	100⅛	5.99	....
Sr Nts 8⅛s 2000	Fa15	**A+**	3/95	A	X	BE	NC	....	....	....	....	....	125	L3	'95	108	99⅛	108	7.52	5.91
Sr Nts 6½s 2003	jD	**A+**	3/95	A	X	BE	NC	....	....	....	....	....	250	M2	'93	101⅝	87⅜	101⅝	6.40	6.24
USLIFE Corp	***35a***	***4.09***	***5.68***	***5.13***		***Dc***				***9-30-95***	***595.0***		***1793***	***33.2***						
Nts 6¾s '98	Jj15	**A+**			X	R	NC	....	....	....	....	....	150	B5	'93	101⅞	95½	101⅞	6.63	5.76
Nts 9.15s '99	Jd15	**A+**	10/92	AA–	X	R	100	(6-15-96)	....	....	....	....	50.0	B5	'89	102¾	101½	101½	9.01	8.64
Nts 6⅜s 2000	Jd15	**A+**			X	R	NC	....	....	....	....	....	150	B5	'93	101	90⅜	101	6.31	6.11
[18]U S WEST Cap Fndg	***25***	***3.32***	***4.76***	***5.73***		***Dc***	***87.00***	***2812***	***7531***	***6-30-95***	***★6176***		***16669***	***53.9***						
Gtd[19]Nts 8s '96	aO15	**A+**	4/90	AA–	X	R	NC	....	....	....	....	....	275	S1	'86	102⅝	100	102	7.84	5.38
Gtd[20]Nts 6¾s 2005	aO	**A+**			X	BE	NC	....	....	....	....	....	300	G1	'95	103	99¾	103	6.55	6.33
Nts 6.31s 2005	mN	**A+**			X	BE	NC	....	....	....	....	....	250	M2	'95	101¾	98	101¾	6.20	6.07
U S WEST[21]Communications[22]	***67a***	***4.39***	***5.19***	***5.80***		***Dc***	***65.00***	***2175***	***4392***	***9-30-95***	***4465***		***10160***	***63.7***						
Deb 7½s 2023	Jd15	**AA–**			X	BE	103.3605	(6-15-03)	....	....	....	....	484	S1	'93	106⅜	87	106⅜	7.05	6.98
Deb 7¼s 2025	mS15	**AA–**			X	BE	NC	....	....	....	....	....	250	S1	'95	106¾	98½	106¾	6.79	6.72
Deb 7.20s 2026	mN10	**AA–**			X	BE	103.038	(11-10-05)	....	....	....	....	250	M2	'95	102⅝	97⅞	102⅝	7.02	6.99
Deb 8⅞s 2031	Jd	**AA–**			X	BE	105.917	(6-1-01)	....	....	....	....	250	G1	'91	116¼	99½	116¼	7.63	7.55
Deb 6⅞s 2033	mS15	**AA–**			X	BE	101.951	(9-15-03)	....	....	....	....	1000	L3	'93	98⅛	78¾	98⅛	7.01	7.02
Deb 7¼s 2035	aO15	**AA–**			X	BE	101.94	(10-15-15)	....	....	....	....	250	L3	'95	104⅝	98½	104⅝	6.93	6.91
Deb 7⅛s 2043	mN15	**AA–**			X	BE	102.74	(11-15-13)	....	....	....	....	250	M2	'93	102⅝	81	102⅝	6.94	6.93
Nts 6⅜s 2002	aO15	**AA–**			X	BE	NC	....	....	....	....	....	250	L3	'95	102	99½	102	6.25	6.01
Nts 6⅝s 2005	mS15	**AA–**			X	BE	NC	....	....	....	....	....	250	S1	'95	103¾	99	103¾	6.39	6.11
Nts 6⅛s 2005	mN15	**AA–**			X	BE	NC	....	....	....	....	....	150	M2	'93	99⅞	84⅝	99⅞	6.13	6.14
USX Corp[23]	***49b***	***0.71***	***0.71***	***1.84***		***Dc***	***101.0***	***3351***	***3152***	***6-30-95***	***4975***		***10031***	***53.8***						
Deb 9⅜s 2012	Fa15	**BB+**	9/93	BBB–	Y	R	NC	....	....	....	....	....	200	F1	'92	117⅝	98⅝	117⅝	7.97	7.47
Deb 9⅛s 2013	Jj15	**BB+**	9/93	BBB–	Y	BE	NC	....	....	....	....	....	300	M5	'92	116	96¼	116	7.87	7.45
Deb 9⅜s 2022	Mn15	**BB+**	9/93	BBB–	Y	R	NC	....	....	....	....	....	150	S1	'92	120⅝	96¾	120⅝	7.77	7.56
Deb 8½s 2023	Ms	**BB+**	9/93	BBB–	Y	BE	NC	....	....	....	....	....	150	M6	'93	109¾	89⅛	109¾	7.74	7.64

Uniform Footnote Explanations-See Page 260. Other: [1] Was Thortec Int'l. [2] Mand offer:red(10%)at 100 when Net Worth low. [3] (HRO)On Chge of Ctrl at 101. [4] (HRO)On Chge of Ctrl at 102. [5] Purch offer, $1020 to Nov 6. [6] Max $35M red w/proceeds of Pub Equity Off'gs. [7] Was Allegheny Airlines. [8] Subsid of USAir Group. [9] Gtd by USAir Group. [10] Inc curr amts. [11] See U.S. Gypsum. [12] 8 Mo Dec,'93. [13] Co must offer repurch at 100 on Chge of Ctrl. [14] Formerly U.S. Leasing Int'l,see. [15] Subsid of Ford Holdings Inc. [16] Int to 2-28-96,adj qtrly(3 Mo LIBOR&0.125%). [17] Due 10-31-96. [18] Gtd by & data of U S WEST. [19] Gtd by US West, Inc. [20] Gtd by U S West, Inc. [21] Subsid of U S WEST Inc. [22] See Mountain St T&T,No'w'n Bell & Pac NW Bell. [23] Was U.S. Steel,See Marathon Oil.

Title-Industry Code & Co. Finances (In Italics) / Exchange, Individual Issue Statistics	Ind / Interest Dates	Fixed Charge Coverage 1992 / S&P Debt Rating	1993 / Date of Last Rating Change	1994 / Prior Rating	Eligible	Year End / Bond Form	Million $ Cash & Equiv. / Redemption Provisions Regular Price	Curr. Assets / Regular (Begins) Thru	Curr. Liab. / Sinking Fund Price	Balance Sheet Date / Sinking Fund (Begins) Thru	L. Term Debt (Mil $) / Refund/Other Restriction Price	Refund/Other Restriction (Begins) Thru	Capital-ization (Mil $) / Outst'g (Mil $)	Total Debt % Capital / Underwriting Firm	Underwriting Year	Price Range 1995 High	Price Range 1995 Low	Mo. End Price Sale(s) or Bid	Curr. Yield	Yield to Mat.
***USX Corp** (Cont.)*																				
Deb 8⅛s 2023	jJ15	**BB+**	9/93	BBB−	Y	BE	NC	....	....	....	....	....	250	F1	'93	105½	86⅜	105½	7.70	7.64
• Nts 8⅞s '97	mS15	**BB+**	9/93	BBB−	Y	R	NC	....	....	....	....	....	150	L3	'91	103½	100	102½	8.66	7.28
Nts 6⅜s '98	jJ15	**BB+**	9/93	BBB−	Y	BE	NC	....	....	....	....	....	350	F1	'93	101	93	101	6.31	5.94
Nts 9.80s 2001	jJ	**BB+**	9/93	BBB−	Y	R	NC	....	....	....	....	....	250	G1	'91	115⅜	103¼	115⅜	8.49	6.44
Nts 9⅝s 2003	fA15	**BB+**	9/93	BBB−	Y	R	NC	....	....	....	....	....	150	F1	'91	117½	102¼	117½	8.19	6.66
Nts 7.20s 2004	Fa15	**BB+**			Y	BE	NC	....	....	....	....	....	300	S1	'94	102⅞	87½	102⅞	7.00	6.73
• Sub SF Deb 4⅝s '96	Jj	**BB−**	9/93	BB+	Y	R	100	....	100	....	....	....	[1]125	Exch.	'65	100⅜	96⅞	99¾	4.64	Mat.
UtiliCorp United	***75***	***2.03***	***2.39***	***2.43***		***Dc***	***157.0***	***558.0***	***784.0***	***9-30-95***	***1236***		***2632***	***58.5***						
Sr Nts 6s '98	Ao	**BBB**			X	R	NC	....	....	....	....	....	70.0	S5	'93	100¼	92¾	100¼	5.99	5.87
Sr Nts 8.45s '99	mN15	**BBB**			X	R	NC	....	....	....	....	....	100	D6	'94	107¾	99½	107¾	7.84	6.17
Sr Nts[2] 6⅜s 2005	Jd	**BBB**			X	R	NC	....	....	....	....	....	100	D6	'95	100¼	96⅝	100¼	6.36	6.34
Sr Nts 8.20s 2007	Jj15	**BBB**			X	R	NC	....	....	....	....	....	130	S5	'92	112⅜	94⅝	112⅜	7.30	6.60
Sr Nts 10½s 2020	jD	**BBB**	10/91	BBB−	X	R	104.80	(12-1-00)	....	....	....	....	125	D6	'90	120⅞	110½	120⅞	8.69	8.47
Sr Nts 9s 2021	mN15	**BBB**			X	R	104.027	(11-15-01)	....	....	....	....	150	G1	'91	113⅛	96⅜	113⅛	7.96	7.81
Sr Nts 8s 2023	Ms	**BBB**			X	R	103.752	(3-1-03)	....	....	....	....	125	G1	'93	106⅛	86¾	106⅛	7.54	7.47
Valassis Communications[3]	***54***	***4.38***	***[4]4.39***	***[5]1.19***		***Dc***	***29.40***	***149.0***	***150.0***	***9-30-95***	***418.0***		***119.0***	***351.0***						
Sr Nts 9.55s 2003	jD	**BB+**	12/95	BBB−	Y	R	NC	....	....	....	....	....	255	S1	'94	112⅛	100½	102¾	9.29	9.05
Valassis Inserts, Inc	***54***	***Now Valassis Communications,see***																		
Sr Nts[6] 8⅜s '97	Ms15	**BB+**	12/95	BBB−	Y	R	NC	....	....	....	....	....	7.29	S1	'92	103¼	99¾	102	8.21	6.61
Sr Nts[6] 8⅞s '99	Ms15	**BB+**	12/95	BBB−	Y	R	NC	....	....	....	....	....	6.15	S1	'92	105⅜	100⅛	105⅜	8.42	6.97
Sr Sub Nts[6] 9⅜s '99	Ms15	**BB−**	12/95	BB+	Y	R	NC	....	....	....	....	....	150	S1	'92	106⅜	99⅝	102⅛	9.18	8.59
Valcor Inc	***17a***	***n/a***	***8.48***	....		***Dc***	***11.90***	***99.00***	***66.80***	***9-30-95***	***202.0***		***250.0***	***86.0***						
Sr[6]Nts 9⅝s 2003	mN	**B**			Y	R	104.813	(11-1-98)	....	....	[7]Z109.625	11-1-96	100	M6	'93	93	88⅜	91	10.58	11.39
Valley Nat'l Corp	***10***	***Subsid of Banc One Corp,see***																		
Deb 9⅞s 2016	Ms	**AA−**	3/93	BB	X	R	104.8125	(3-1-96)	100	(3-1-97)	....	....	79.5	M6	'86	121	105⅜	105⅜	9.37	9.28
Van Kampen Merritt Cos	***62***	***n/a***	***2.33***	....		***Dc***	***20.50***			***12-31-93***	***292.0***		***475.0***	***61.5***						
Sr Sec Nts[6] 9¾s 2003	Fa15	**BB−**			Y	R	103.60	(2-15-98)	....	....	....	....	150	M2	'93	106	93	103½	9.42	9.07
Varity Corp	***41a***	***1.33***	***2.52***	***5.51***		***Ja***	***151.0***	***698.0***	***498.0***	***7-31-95***	***164.0***		***999.0***	***16.9***						
• Sr[6]Nts[8] 11⅜s '98	mN15	**BBB+**	7/94	BBB−	X	R	100	(11-15-96)	....	....	....	....	150	D4	'91	No Sale		104½	10.89	9.54
Vastar Resources	***49b***	***n/a***	***n/a***	***3.33***		***Dc***	***6.30***	***204.0***	***243.0***	***9-30-95***	***749.0***		***820.0***	***91.3***						
Nts 8¾s 2005	Fa	**BBB**			X	BE	NC	....	....	....	....	....	150	G1	'95	115⅜	99	115⅜	7.58	6.48
Venture Holdings Trust	***8***	***1.49***	***2.27***	....		***Dc***	***27.90***	***108.0***	***24.30***	***9-30-94***	***150.0***		***200.0***	***76.5***						
Sr Sub[9]Nts[6] 9¾s 2004	Ao	**B**			Y	R	104.875	(4-1-99)	....	....	[10]Z109	3-31-97	100	B8	'94	89½	82	83	11.75	13.18
Vesta Insurance Group	***35c***	***n/a***	***n/a***	***25.63***		***Dc***				***9-30-95***	***98.50***		***385.0***	***29.6***						
Sr Deb 8¾s 2025	jJ15	**BBB+**		BBB+	X	BE	NC	....	....	....	....	....	100	M6	'95	111	99	111	7.88	7.79
V.F. Corp	***68c***	***6.29***	***6.50***	***6.68***		***Dc***	***64.10***	***1920***	***1055***	***9-30-95***	***615.0***		***2497***	***24.7***						
Nts[11] 9½s '99	aO15	**A−**	10/92	BBB+	X	R	100	(10-15-96)	....	....	....	....	100	G1	'89	104½	102¼	103¼	9.20	8.47
Nts 9½s 2001	Mn	**A−**	10/92	BBB+	X	R	NC	....	....	....	....	....	100	G1	'91	115⅛	105	115⅛	8.25	6.13
Nts 6⅝s 2003	Ms15	**A−**			X	R	100	(3-15-00)	....	....	....	....	100	G1	'93	101⅛	88⅞	101⅛	6.55	6.43
Nts 6¾s 2005	Jd	**A−**			X	BE	NC	....	....	....	....	....	100	G1	'95	102½	95¼	101⅞	6.63	6.48
Deb 9¼s 2022	Mn	**A−**	10/92	BBB+	X	R	104.52	(5-1-02)	....	....	....	....	100	G1	'92	117⅛	101⅜	117⅛	7.90	7.72
Viacom Inc[12]	***12***	***1.79***	***2.60***	***1.76***		***Dc***	***549.0***	***5550***	***4318***	***9-30-95***	***10892***		***22926***	***47.5***						
◆Sr Deb 7⅝s 2016	Jj15	**BB+**			Y	BE	NC	....	....	....	....	....	200	G1	'95	99¼	99¼	100½	7.59	7.58
◆Sr Nts 6¾s 2003	Jj15	**BB+**			Y	BE	NC	....	....	....	....	....	350	G1	'95	99⅞	99⅞	100	6.75	6.75
◆Sr Nts[13] 7¾s 2005	Jd	**BB+**			Y	BE	NC	....	....	....	....	....	1000	B5	'95	104½	99	102	7.60	7.45
◆Sub Deb[14] 8s 2006	jj15	**BB−**	5/95	B+	Y	R	103	(7-7-99)	....	....	....	....	1070	Mgr	'94	103	85⅜	s103	7.77	7.58

Uniform Footnote Explanations-See Page 260. Other: [1] Defeased,funds deposited with trustee. [2] (HRO)On 6-1-00 at 100. [3] Was Valassis Inserts,see. [4] Jun'93 & prior. [5] 6 Mo Dec'94. [6] (HRO)On Chge of Ctrl at 101. [7] Max $35M red w/proceeds of Pub Eq Off'g. [8] Co may repurch at 100 for certain asset sales. [9] Gtd by Venture Industries Canada. [10] Max $25M red w/proceeds of Pub Eq off'g. [11] (HRO)At 100 for Designated Event&Rat'g Decline. [12] See Blockbuster Entmt, Viacom Int'l Inc. [13] Gtd by Viacom Int'l. [14] Initial int pyt is 1-1-95,pays jj15 aft.

Individual Issue Statistics / Exchange	Interest Dates	S&P Debt Rating	Date of Last Rating Change	Prior Rating	Eligible	Bond Form	Redemption Provisions: Regular Price	Regular (Begins) Thru	Sinking Fund Price	Sinking Fund (Begins) Thru	Refund/Other Restriction Price	Refund/Other Restriction (Begins) Thru	Outst'g (Mil $)	Underwriting Firm	Underwriting Year	Price Range 1995 High	Price Range 1995 Low	Mo. End Price Sale(s) or Bid	Curr. Yield	Yield to Mat.
Title-Industry Code & Co. Finances (In Italics)	*Ind*	*Fixed Charge Coverage 1992*	*1993*	*1994*		*Year End*	*Million $ Cash & Equiv.*	*Curr. Assets*	*Curr. Liab.*	*Balance Sheet Date*	*L. Term Debt (Mil $)*		*Capital-ization (Mil $)*	*Total Debt % Capital*						
Viacom Int'l Inc	***12***	***Subsid of Viacom Inc,see***																		
◆Sr Sub Nts 9⅛s '99	fA15	**BB−**	5/95	B+	Y	R	102.607	(2-15-97)	....	....	....	....	150	M5	'92	105½	99	104	8.77	7.83
◆Sr Sub Nts[1] 10¼s 2001	mS15	**BB−**	5/95	B+	Y	R	NC	....	....	....	....	....	200	G1	'91	114	102¼	112	9.15	7.61
◆Sr Sub[2]Reset Nts[1] 8¾s 2001	Mn15	**BB−**	5/95	B+	Y	R	[3]101	5-15-98	....	....	....	....	100	G1	'92	103	100	101¾	8.60	....
Vintage Petroleum	***49a***	***3.29***	***3.99***	***2.29***		***Dc***	***1.54***	***45.50***	***62.00***	***9-30-95***	***★306.0***		***490.0***	***63.0***						
Sr Sub Nts[4] 9s 2005	jD15	**B+**			Y	BE	104.50	(12-15-00)	....	....	....	....	125	S1	'95	99⅝	97⅛	97⅛	9.27	9.45
Virginia Electric & Pwr[5]	***72a***	***3.03***	***3.37***	***3.23***		***Dc***	***204.0***	***1071***	***1180***	***9-30-95***	***3936***		***9265***	***46.9***						
1st & Ref U 5⅛s '97	Fa	**A**	11/91	A+	X	R	100.19	1-31-96	100.05	1-31-96	....	....	49.3	E1	'67	99⅝	94⅞	99⅝	5.14	5.48
1st & Ref '88A 9⅜s '98	Jd	**A**	11/91	A+	X	R	NC	....	....	....	....	....	150	S1	'88	108⅜	103⅛	107¾	8.70	5.89
1st & Ref '89B 8⅞s '99	Jd	**A**	11/91	A+	X	R	NC	....	....	....	....	....	100	F1	'89	109⅜	101½	109⅜	8.11	5.81
1st & Ref '90 A 9¾s 2020	Ms	**A**	11/91	A+	X	R	106.45	2-29-96	Z100	....	....	....	[6]119	M6	'90	108⅞	104¾	106⅝	9.14	9.07
1st & Ref '91A 8¾s 2021	Ao	**A**	11/91	A+	X	R	102.20	(4-1-01)	Z100	....	....	....	100	M2	'91	112⅝	99½	112⅝	7.77	7.62
1st & Ref '92B 7¼s '97	Ms	**A**			X	R	NC	....	....	....	....	....	250	M2	'92	101⅞	98	101⅞	7.12	5.57
1st & Ref '92C 8s 2004	Ms	**A**			X	R	NC	....	....	....	....	....	250	M2	'92	111⅝	97¼	111⅝	7.17	6.17
1st & Ref '92D 7⅝s 2007	jJ	**A**			X	R	NC	....	....	....	....	....	215	L3	'92	111	93⅜	111	6.87	6.27
1st & Ref '92E 7⅜s 2002	jJ	**A**			X	R	NC	....	....	....	....	....	155	L3	'92	107¼	94⅛	107¼	6.88	6.01
1st & Ref '92F 6¼s '98	fA	**A**			X	R	NC	....	....	....	....	....	75.0	G1	'92	101⅜	93⅞	101⅜	6.17	5.67
1st & Ref '93A 7¼s 2023	Fa	**A**			X	R	100.44	(2-1-03)	Z100	....	....	....	100	L3	'93	102⅛	84¾	102⅛	7.10	7.07
1st & Ref '93B 6⅝s 2003	Ao	**A**			X	R	NC	....	....	....	....	....	200	M6	'93	103⅜	89⅝	103⅜	6.41	6.04
1st & Ref '93C 5⅞s 2000	Ao	**A**			X	R	NC	....	....	....	....	....	135	F1	'93	100⅛	89⅝	100⅛	5.87	5.84
1st & Ref '93D 7½s 2023	Jd	**A**			X	R	103.16	(6-1-03)	Z100	5-31-03	....	....	200	G1	'93	105¼	87⅞	105¼	7.13	7.06
1st & Ref '93E 6s 2001	fA	**A**			X	R	NC	....	....	....	....	....	100	M2	'93	100½	87⅞	100½	5.97	5.89
1st & Ref '93F 6s 2002	fA	**A**			X	R	NC	....	....	....	....	....	100	M6	'93	100	86⅝	100	6.00	6.00
1st & Ref '93G 6¾s 2023	aO	**A**			X	R	102.77	(10-1-03)	Z100	(10-1-03)	....	....	200	F1	'93	97½	79⅞	97½	6.92	6.95
1st & Ref '94A 7s 2024	Jj	**A**			X	R	102.82	(1-1-04)	Z100	(1-1-04)	....	....	125	S1	'94	101½	82½	101½	6.90	6.88
1st & Ref '94B 8⅝s 2024	aO	**A**			X	R	103.86	(10-1-04)	Z100	(10-1-04)	....	....	200	L3	'94	116⅝	98½	116⅝	7.40	7.24
1st & Ref '95A 8¼s 2025	Ms	**A**			X	R	103.48	(3-1-05)	Z100	(3-1-05)	....	....	200	S1	'95	113⅜	98½	113⅜	7.28	7.15
M-T Nts 'E' 6.28s '96	[7]jj	**A−**			X	BE	NC	....	....	....	....	....	30.0	M2	'94	100⅜	98	100⅜	6.26	5.33
M-T Nts 'E' 6.35s '96	[8]jj	**A−**			X	BE	NC	....	....	....	....	....	15.0	M2	'94	100½	98⅛	100⅜	6.33	5.41
M-T Nts 'E' 6.35s '96	[9]jj	**A−**			X	BE	NC	....	....	....	....	....	15.0	M2	'94	100½	98	100⅜	6.33	5.43
M-T Nts 'E' 6.15s '96	[10]jj	**A−**			X	BE	NC	....	....	....	....	....	30.0	M2	'94	100⅜	97¾	100¼	6.13	5.60
M-T Nts 'E' 7.27s '99	[11]jj	**A−**			X	BE	NC	....	....	....	....	....	10.0	M2	'94	104⅜	96	104⅜	6.97	5.84
Virginia & Southwestn Ry	***55***	***Sub of Norfolk So'n Ry, see So'n Ry***																		
• 1st 5s 2003	Jj	**NR**			X	C	NC	....	....	....	....	....	1.48		'02	90	86⅜	91	5.49	6.63
Virginian Ry	***55***	***Asmd by Norfolk & Western Ry,see***																		
• Sub Inc Deb 6s 2008	fA	**AA−**	12/80	BBB+	X	CR	104	7-31-96	103	7-31-96	....	....	4.79	Exch.	'58	91¾	78	90⅝	6.62	7.14
[12]VIS Capital	***25***	***1.15***	***1.51***	***1.94***		***Oc***	***19.90***	***156.0***	***103.0***	***7-28-95***	***29.30***		***135.0***	***26.5***						
Sr Sub Deb 12⅜s '98	jJ	**NR**	11/93	B−		R	100	....	100	....	....	....	32.8	D7	'83	100	92	A100	12.38	12.37
Vons Companies,Inc[13]	***59c***	***3.03***	***2.92***	***2.24***		***Dc***	***6.30***	***436.0***	***574.0***	***10-8-95***	***689.0***		***1314***	***54.3***						
Sr Sub Nts 8⅜s '99	aO	**BB−**			Y	R	100	(10-1-97)	....	....	....	....	100	D6	'92	102	93¼	101½	8.25	7.90
Sr Sub Nts 9⅝s 2002	Ao	**BB−**			Y	R	103.609	(4-1-97)	....	....	....	....	150	D6	'92	106¼	97⅜	106	9.08	8.37
Waban Inc	***59m***	***5.89***	***4.84***	***5.61***		***Ja***	***63.70***	***774.0***	***517.0***	***10-28-95***	***245.0***		***790.0***	***32.8***						
Sr Sub Nts[4] 11s 2004	Mn15	**BB−**			Y	R	105.50	(5-15-99)	....	....	....	....	100	B5	'94	103½	96¾	102	10.78	10.63
Wachovia Corp	***10***	***3.67***	***3.41***	***2.53***		***Dc***				***9-30-95***	***5010***		***8628***	***58.1***						
Sub Nts 7s '99	jD15	**AA−**			X	R	NC	....	....	....	....	....	300	M2	'92	104⅜	94⅞	104⅜	6.71	5.75
Sub Nts 6⅜s 2003	Ao15	**AA−**			X	BE	NC	....	....	....	....	....	250	M2	'93	102	87⅛	102	6.25	6.03
Sub Nts 6.80s 2005	Jd	**AA−**			X	BE	NC	....	....	....	....	....	250	M2	'95	104½	97¼	104½	6.51	6.16

Uniform Footnote Explanations-See Page 260. Other: [1] Gtd by Viacom Inc. [2] Int(min 8.75%)thru 5-15-98,adj aft. [3] On 5-15-95('98). [4] (HRO)On Chge of Ctrl at 101. [5] Subsid of Dominion Resources. [6] Defeased,fds deposited w/trustee. [7] Due 5-28-96. [8] Due 5-30-96. [9] Due 6-3-96. [10] Due 6-19-96. [11] Due 6-1-99. [12] Gtd by & data of Volt Info Sciences. [13] Was Allied Supermarkets,see.

Title-Industry Code & Co. Finances (In Italics) / Exchange, Individual Issue Statistics	Ind / Interest Dates	Fixed Charge Coverage 1992 / S&P Debt Rating	1993 / Date of Last Rating Change	1994 / Prior Rating	Eligible	Year End / Bond Form	Million $ Cash & Equiv. / Redemption Provisions: Regular Price	Million $ Curr. Assets / Regular (Begins) Thru	Million $ Curr. Liab. / Sinking Fund Price	Balance Sheet Date / Sinking Fund (Begins) Thru	L. Term Debt (Mil $) / Refund/Other Restriction Price	Capitalization (Mil $) / Refund/Other Restriction (Begins) Thru	Total Debt % Capital / Outst'g (Mil $)	Underwriting Firm	Underwriting Year	Price Range 1995 High	Price Range 1995 Low	Mo. End Price Sale(s) or Bid	Curr. Yield	Yield to Mat.
***Wachovia Corp** (Cont.)*																				
Sub Nts 6.735s 2009	Fa	**AA–**			X	BE	NC	....	....	....	....	....	250	M2	'94	100⅝	81⅝	100⅝	6.69	6.66
Sub Nts[1] 6.605s 2025	Ao	**AA–**			X	BE	NC	....	....	....	....	....	250	C5	'95	103⅜	100	103⅜	6.37	6.33
Wainoco Oil	***49a***	***0.86***	***1.06***	***1.17***		***Dc***	***1.83***	***49.60***	***44.40***	***9-30-95***	***167.0***	***207.0***	***80.7***							
• Sr Nts[2] 12s 2002	fA	**B–**			Y	R	103.43	(8-1-97)	....	....	....	....	100	F1	'92	104¼	97	s98	12.24	12.45
◆Sub SF Deb 10¾s '98	aO	**CCC+**	10/91	B–	Y	R	100	....	100	....	....	....	[3]17.5	B6	'78	106	97	98	10.97	11.60
Wal-Mart Stores	***59g***	***8.66***	***7.23***	***6.40***		***Ja***	***13.00***	***20213***	***14825***	***10-31-95***	***10216***	***24307***	***42.0***							
Deb 7¼s 2013	Jd	**AA**			X	R	NC	....	....	....	....	....	500	G1	'93	107	87¾	107	6.78	6.57
Deb 6¾s 2023	aO15	**AA**			X	R	NC	....	....	....	....	....	250	G1	'93	101⅞	80⅝	101⅞	6.63	6.60
Deb 8½s 2024	mS15	**AA**			X	R	103.7655	(9-15-04)	....	....	....	....	250	G1	'94	114⅛	98⅛	114⅛	7.45	7.31
Nts 8s '96	Mn	**AA**			X	R	NC	....	....	....	....	....	250	G1	'91	101¾	100¾	100¾	7.94	5.67
Nts 5½s '97	mS15	**AA**			X	R	NC	....	....	....	....	....	500	G1	'92	100	93⅞	100	5.50	5.49
Nts 6½s 2003	Jd	**AA**			X	R	NC	....	....	....	....	....	500	G1	'93	102⅝	89⅝	102⅝	6.33	6.05
Nts 5½s '98	Ms	**AA**			X	R	NC	....	....	....	....	....	500	G1	'93	99⅞	92⅞	99⅞	5.51	5.56
Nts 6⅛s '99	aO	**AA**			X	R	NC	....	....	....	....	....	500	G1	'92	101⅝	91¾	101⅝	6.03	5.64
Nts 9.10s 2000	jJ15	**AA**			X	R	NC	....	....	....	....	....	500	G1	'90	113	103¼	113	8.05	5.80
Nts 8⅝s 2001	Ao	**AA**			X	R	NC	....	....	....	....	....	750	G1	'91	112⅜	101½	112⅜	7.68	5.85
Nts 6¾s 2002	Mn15	**AA**			X	R	NC	....	....	....	....	....	300	G1	'95	104⅝	100¾	104⅝	6.45	5.87
Nts 6⅜s 2003	Ms	**AA**			X	R	NC	....	....	....	....	....	250	G1	'93	101¾	88⅞	101¾	6.27	6.07
Nts 7½s 2004	Mn15	**AA**			X	R	NC	....	....	....	....	....	500	G1	'94	109⅛	95	109⅛	6.87	6.09
Nts 5⅞s 2005	aO15	**AA**			X	R	NC	....	....	....	....	....	750	G1	'93	98½	82½	98½	5.96	6.08
Nts 8s 2006	mS15	**AA**			X	R	NC	....	....	....	....	....	250	G1	'94	114⅝	97⅛	114⅝	6.98	6.12
• Sr Nts 'B'[4] 9⅞s 2005	jJ15	**NR**				R	104.938	(7-15-00)	....	....	[5]Z110	7-15-98	110	S5	'95	No Sale		97	10.18	10.38
Warner-Lambert	***21a***	***11.62***	***5.96***	***10.67***		***Dc***	***507.0***	***2825***	***2609***	***9-30-95***	***430.0***	***3285***	***31.9***							
Nts 8s '98	mS	**AA**			X	BE	NC	....	....	....	....	....	150	G1	'91	106¼	99⅛	106¼	7.53	5.45
Nts 6⅝s 2002	mS15	**AA**			X	BE	NC	....	....	....	....	....	200	G1	'92	104⅛	90	104⅛	6.36	5.87
Washington Gas Light	***73b***	***△4.17***	***△4.05***	***△4.13***		***Sp***	***13.90***	***159.0***	***222.0***	***9-30-95***	***329.0***	***923.0***	***41.4***							
1st[6] 7⅞s 2016	mS	**AA–**			X	R	100	(9-1-96)	....	....	....	....	50.0	G1	'86	103⅞	90¾	101½	7.76	7.73
1st 8⅝s 2017	Ms	**AA–**			X	R	105.17	(3-1-97)	100	(3-1-98)	....	....	35.5	G1	'87	108¼	99	107¾	8.00	7.87
[7]1st 9¼s 2018	Ao15	**AA–**			X	R	100	(4-15-98)	....	....	....	....	17.3	G1	'88	108⅛	102⅞	107¾	8.58	8.47
1st[8] 8¾s 2019	jJ	**AA–**			X	R	100	(7-1-99)	....	....	....	....	50.0	M2	'89	109¾	101⅞	109¾	7.97	7.84
Washington Mutual	***10a***	***2.24***	***2.62***	***1.98***		***Dc***				***9-30-95***	***2055***	***3558***	***57.8***							
Sr Nts 7¼s 2005	fA15	**BBB**			X	BE	NC	....	....	....	....	....	150	L3	'95	105¾	99⅛	105¾	6.86	6.44
Washington Water Power	***75***	***2.88***	***3.26***	***3.01***		***Dc***	***31.10***	***131.0***	***138.0***	***9-30-95***	***688.0***	***1522***	***45.2***							
Sec M-T Nts'A'[9] 4.72s '96	[10]mn	**A–**			X	BE	NC	....	....	....	....	....	20.0	G1	'93	99½	95¼	99½	4.74	5.59
Sec M-T Nts'A'[9] 6.13s 2000	[11]mn	**A–**			X	BE	NC	....	....	....	....	....	5.00	G1	'93	100⅞	90	100⅞	6.08	5.90
Sec M-T Nts'A'[9] 6.15s 2000	[11]mn	**A–**			X	BE	NC	....	....	....	....	....	15.0	G1	'93	101	90⅛	101	6.09	5.88
Sec M-T Nts'A'[9] 6.28s 2002	[12]mn	**A–**			X	BE	NC	....	....	....	....	....	5.00	G1	'93	100⅞	87½	100⅞	6.23	6.11
Sec M-T Nts'A'[9] 6.32s 2002	[13]mn	**A–**			X	BE	NC	....	....	....	....	....	15.0	G1	'93	101	87⅝	101	6.26	6.13
Sec M-T Nts'A'[9] 6.28s 2002	[14]mn	**A–**			X	BE	NC	....	....	....	....	....	5.00	G1	'93	100⅞	87⅜	100⅞	6.23	6.11
Sec M-T Nts'A'[9] 6¼s 2003	[15]mn	**A–**			X	BE	NC	....	....	....	....	....	5.00	G1	'93	100	85½	100	6.25	6.25
Sec M-T Nts'A'[9] 6¼s 2003	[16]mn	**A–**			X	BE	NC	....	....	....	....	....	10.0	G1	'93	100	85⅜	100	6.25	6.25
Sec M-T Nts'A'[9] 7.98s 2004	[17]mn	**A–**			X	BE	102.28	(5-19-99)	....	....	....	....	15.0	G1	'94	110⅞	95¾	110⅞	7.20	6.29
Sec M-T Nts'A'[9] 6s 2004	[18]mn	**A–**			X	BE	100	(10-13-98)	....	....	....	....	10.0	G1	'93	98	82¾	98	6.12	6.30
Sec M-T Nts'A'[9] 8.06s 2005	[19]mn	**A–**			X	BE	102.30	(5-19-99)	....	....	....	....	5.00	G1	'94	112⅛	95⅞	112⅛	7.19	6.33
Sec M-T Nts'A'[9] 6.40s 2005	[20]mn	**A–**			X	BE	102.40	(11-21-98)	....	....	....	....	10.0	G1	'93	100⅜	84¼	100⅜	6.38	6.35
Sec M-T Nts'A'[9] 6.95s 2008	[21]mn	**A–**			X	BE	NC	....	....	....	....	....	10.0	G1	'93	104⅞	86¼	104⅞	6.63	6.38

Uniform Footnote Explanations-See Page 260. Other: [1] (HRO)On 10-1-05 at 100. [2] (HRO)On Chge of Ctrl at 101. [3] Incl disc. [4] Co must offer repurch at 101 on Chge of Ctrl. [5] Max $33M red w/proceeds of Pub Eq Off'g. [6] (HRO)On 9-1-96 at 100. [7] (HRO)On 4-15-98 at 100. [8] (HRO)On 7-1-99 at 100. [9] Issued in min denom $100T. [10] Due 7-30-96. [11] Due 5-8-00. [12] Due 6-28-02. [13] Due 7-8-02. [14] Due 7-9-02. [15] Due 11-19-03. [16] Due 11-24-03. [17] Due 5-19-04. [18] Due 10-13-04. [19] Due 5-19-05. [20] Due 11-21-05. [21] Due 6-3-08.

Title-Industry Code & Co. Finances (In Italics) / Individual Issue Statistics (Exchange)	Ind / Interest Dates	1992 / S&P Debt Rating	1993 / Date of Last Rating Change	1994 / Prior Rating	Year End / Eligible	Bond Form	Cash & Equiv. (Million $) / Regular Price	Curr. Assets (Million $) / Regular (Begins) Thru	Curr. Liab. (Million $) / Sinking Fund Price	Balance Sheet Date / Sinking Fund (Begins) Thru	L. Term Debt (Mil $) / Refund/Other Restriction Price	Refund/Other Restriction (Begins) Thru	Capital-ization (Mil $) / Outst'g (Mil $)	Total Debt % Capital / Underwriting Firm	Underwriting Year	Price Range 1995 High	Price Range 1995 Low	Mo. End Price Sale(s) or Bid	Curr. Yield	Yield to Mat.
***Washington Water Power** (Cont.)*																				
Sec M-T Nts'A'[1] 6.89s 2008	[2]mn	A–			X	BE	NC	....	....	....	....	....	10.0	G1	'93	104⅜	85¾	104⅜	6.60	6.37
Sec M-T Nts'A'[1] 6.67s 2010	[3]mn	A–			X	BE	NC	....	....	....	....	....	5.00	G1	'93	102⅜	82½	102⅜	6.52	6.42
Sec M-T Nts'A'[1] 7.37s 2012	[4]mn	A–			X	BE	NC	....	....	....	....	....	7.00	G1	'93	105⅝	87⅝	105⅝	6.98	6.79
Sec M-T Nts'A'[1] 7.39s 2018	[5]mn	A–			X	BE	NC	....	....	....	....	....	7.00	G1	'93	106½	86⅛	106½	6.94	6.82
Sec M-T Nts'A'[1] 7.45s 2018	[6]mn	A–			X	BE	NC	....	....	....	....	....	15.5	G1	'93	107⅛	86⅝	107⅛	6.95	6.82
Sec M-T Nts'A'[1] 7.26s 2018	[7]mn	A–			X	BE	103.23	(7-22-03)	....	....	....	....	5.00	G1	'93	103⅛	84⅛	103⅛	7.04	6.98
Sec M-T Nts'A'[1] 7s 2019	[8]mn	A–			X	BE	103.11	(10-13-03)	....	....	....	....	10.0	G1	'93	102	82	102	6.86	6.83
Sec M-T Nts'A'[1] 7.53s 2023	[9]mn	A–			X	BE	NC	....	....	....	....	....	6.00	G1	'93	108½	86¾	108½	6.94	6.84
Sec M-T Nts'A'[1] 7.40s 2023	[10]mn	A–			X	BE	103.70	(8-2-03)	....	....	....	....	10.0	G1	'93	104⅝	84½	104⅝	7.07	7.02
Sec M-T Nts'A'[1] 7.18s 2023	[11]mn	A–			X	BE	NC	....	....	....	....	....	10.0	G1	'93	104⅛	83	104⅛	6.90	6.84
Sec M-T Nts'A'[1] 7.30s 2023	[11]mn	A–			X	BE	103.65	(8-12-03)	....	....	....	....	20.0	G1	'93	103⅜	83½	103⅜	7.06	7.02
Sec M-T Nts'A'[1] 7.06s 2023	[12]mn	A–			X	BE	103.53	(10-13-03)	....	....	....	....	5.00	G1	'93	102¾	81¾	102¾	6.87	6.84
Sec M-T Nts'B'[1] 8¼s '99	[13]fa	A–			X	BE	NC	....	....	....	....	....	20.0	G1	'94	108¼	100	108¼	7.62	5.88
Sec M-T Nts'B'[1] 7.95s 2005	[14]jj	A–			X	BE	102.27	(5-24-99)	....	....	....	....	5.00	G1	'94	111⅜	95¼	111⅜	7.14	6.33
Sec M-T Nts'B'[1] 7.89s 2006	[15]fa	A–			X	BE	NC	....	....	....	....	....	26.0	G1	'94	111¾	95⅞	111¾	7.06	6.35
Waste Management	***53***	***Now WMX Technologies, see***																		
• Deb 8¾s 2018	Mn	A+	4/95	AA–	X	R	100	(5-1-08)	....	....	....	....	250	M2	'88	112	97¾	112	7.81	7.62
Deb 7.65s 2011	Ms15	A+	4/95	AA–	X	BE	NC	....	....	....	....	....	150	M2	'91	113	92⅛	113	6.77	6.31
Nts 4⅝s '96	Ao14	A+	4/95	AA–	X	BE	NC	....	....	....	....	....	200	M2	'93	99¾	96⅜	99¾	4.64	5.44
Nts 7⅞s '96	fA15	A+	4/95	AA–	X	BE	NC	....	....	....	....	....	200	M2	'91	102⅛	99⅞	101½	7.76	5.40
Nts 6⅜s '97	jJ	A+	4/95	AA–	X	BE	NC	....	....	....	....	....	250	M2	'92	101¼	96	101¼	6.30	5.50
Step-Up Nts 4.10s 2002	aO	A+	4/95	AA–	X	BE	NC	....	....	....	....	....	300	M2	'92	109¼	95⅞	109¼	3.75	2.60
Watts Industries	***41h***	*Δ7.13*	*Δ8.67*	*Δ7.89*	*Je*			*368.0*	*127.0*	*9-30-95*	*134.0*		*569.0*	*25.5*						
Nts 8⅜s 2003	jD	A–			X	R	NC	....	....	....	....	....	75.0	D6	'91	113¼	98½	113¼	7.40	6.23
Waxman Indus	***13f***	*Δ0.30*	*Δ0.85*	*Δ0.58*	*Je*		*0.38*	*116.0*	*63.20*	*9-30-95*	*157.0*		*138.0*	*145.0*						
Sr Sub Nts[16] 13¾s '99	Jd	CCC+	3/94	B–	Y	R	103.438	5-31-96	100	(6-1-96)	....	....	38.8	D7	'89	94	74½	74½	18.46	....
Webb (Del) Corp	***38***	*Δ1.05*	*Δ0.78*	*Δ0.94*	*Je*		*29.90*			*9-30-95*	*493.0*		*773.0*	*63.8*						
• Sr Nts[17] 10⅞s 2000	Ms31	B+	2/94	BB–	Y	R	100	(3-31-97)	....	....	....	....	100	D4	'92	106	98	103	10.56	9.98
• Sr Sub Deb[17] 9¾s 2003	Ms	B–	2/94	B	Y	R	104.875	(3-1-98)	....	....	....	....	100	G1	'93	104	84	s102⅞	9.48	9.19
• Sr Sub Deb[18] 9s 2006	Fa15	B–			Y	R	104.50	(2-15-99)	....	....	....	....	100	G1	'94	97½	77⅝	s97	9.28	9.46
Webcraft Technologies	***1***	*0.37*	*0.66*	*0.37*	*Dc*		*6.84*	*88.20*	*43.90*	*9-30-95*	*95.00*		*136.0*	*70.6*						
Sr Sub[17]Nts[19] 9⅜s 2002	Fa15	B			Y	R	104	(2-15-98)	....	....	[20]109	2-15-97	90.0	S5	'94	95¼	85	95	9.87	10.50
Webster Fin'l Corp	***10a***	*2.88*	*2.85*	*1.95*	*Dc*					*6-30-95*	*445.0*		*595.0*	*74.8*						
Sr Nts 8¾s 2000	Jd30	BB+			Y	R	NC	....	....	....	....	....	40.0	M2	'93	102	98¼	102	8.58	8.21
Weingarten Rlty Inv	***57***	*1.89*	*4.05*	*4.30*	*Dc*					*3-31-95*	*253.0*		*672.0*	*37.6*						
M-T Nts'A' 6.82s 2000	[21]ms15	A+			X	BE	NC	....	....	....	....	....	25.0	G1	'95	103	99½	103	6.62	6.04
Weirton Steel Corp	***66a***	*Nil*	*0.26*	*1.09*	*Dc*		*111.0*	*583.0*	*228.0*	*9-30-95*	*486.0*		*681.0*	*71.4*						
Sr Nts[17] 11½s '98	Ms	B			Y	R	NC	....	....	....	....	....	140	L3	'93	105½	99	102	11.27	10.43
Sr Nts[16] 10⅞s '99	aO15	B	11/92	B+	Y	R	NC	....	....	....	Z100	....	300	B5	'89	104	97⅜	99¾	10.90	10.95
Wells Fargo & Co.	***10***	*2.86*	*5.30*	*5.83*	*Dc*					*9-30-95*	*3020*		*6894*	*43.8*						
Sub Nts 8¾s 2002	Mn	BBB+			X	BE	NC	....	....	....	....	....	200	G1	'92	113⅝	99⅝	113⅝	7.70	6.12
Sub Nts 8⅜s 2002	Mn15	BBB+			X	BE	NC	....	....	....	....	....	150	S1	'92	111⅞	97⅝	111⅞	7.49	6.10
Sub Nts 6⅞s 2003	Ao15	BBB+			X	BE	NC	....	....	....	....	....	150	M6	'93	103⅞	88⅝	103⅞	6.62	6.20
Sub Nts 6⅛s 2003	mN	BBB+			X	BE	NC	....	....	....	....	....	250	S1	'93	99⅝	83⅞	99⅝	6.15	6.18
F/R[22]Sub Nts '97	[23]Jun25	BBB+	6/91	A	X	R	100	....	....	....	....	....	100	S1	'85	100⅜	99⅝	100⅛	....	....
Wellsford Residential Prop Tr	***57***	*n/a*	*n/a*	*n/a*	*Dc*					*9-30-95*	*286.0*		*691.0*	*41.4*						
Nts 9⅜s 2002	Fa	BBB	8/95	BBB–	X	BE	Z100	(2-1-00)	....	....	....	....	100	M5	'95	113⅛	99⅜	113⅛	8.29	6.71

Uniform Footnote Explanations-See Page 260. Other: [1] Issued in min denom $100T. [2] Due 6-4-08. [3] Due 7-12-10. [4] Due 5-10-12. [5] Due 5-11-18. [6] Due 6-11-18. [7] Due 7-23-18. [8] Due 10-14-19. [9] Due 5-5-23. [10] Due 8-2-23. [11] Due 8-11-23. [12] Due 10-13-23. [13] Due 12-13-99. [14] Due 5-24-05. [15] Due 8-25-06. [16] (HRO)On Chge of Ctrl at 100. [17] (HRO)On Chge of Ctrl at 101. [18] Co must offer repurch at 101 on Chge of Ctrl. [19] Co may repurch at 100,plus prem,on Chge of Ctrl. [20] Max $29.7M red w/proceeds of Pub Eq Off'g. [21] Due 6-1-00. [22] Int(max 13%)adj monthly as defined. [23] Int pd monthly.

Exchange / Individual Issue Statistics	Interest Dates	S&P Debt Rating	Date of Last Rating Change	Prior Rating	Eligible	Bond Form	Redemption Provisions: Regular Price	Regular (Begins) Thru	Sinking Fund Price	Sinking Fund (Begins) Thru	Refund/Other Restriction Price	Refund/Other Restriction (Begins) Thru	Outst'g (Mil $)	Underwriting Firm	Underwriting Year	Price Range 1995 High	Price Range 1995 Low	Mo. End Price Sale(s) or Bid	Curr. Yield	Yield to Mat.
Title-Industry Code & Co. Finances (In Italics)	*Ind*	*Fixed Charge Coverage 1992*	*1993*	*1994*		*Year End*	*Million $ Cash & Equiv.*	*Curr. Assets*	*Curr. Liab.*	*Balance Sheet Date*	*L. Term Debt (Mil $)*		*Capital-ization (Mil $)*	*Total Debt % Capital*						
***Wellsford Residential Prop Tr** (Cont.)*																				
Sr Nts 7¼s 2000	fA15	**BBB**			X	BE	NC	....	....	....	....	....	55.0	M2	'95	103⅛	99⅜	103⅛	7.03	6.46
Sr Nts 7¾s 2005	fA15	**BBB**			X	BE	Z100	(8-24-02)	....	....	....	....	70.0	M2	'95	104⅞	98¾	104⅞	7.39	7.04
Wendy's Int'l	***27b***	***5.49***	***6.36***	***7.11***		***Dc***	***66.30***	***138.0***	***146.0***	***10-1-95***	***★339.0***		***924.0***	***15.9***						
Deb 7s 2025	jD15	**BBB+**			X	BE	NC	....	....	....	....	....	100	G1	'95	101⅜	99⅛	101⅜	6.91	6.89
Nts 6.35s 2005	jD15	**BBB+**			X	BE	NC	....	....	....	....	....	100	G1	'95	100⅞	99¾	100⅞	6.29	6.23
Wesco Fin'l Corp	***35c***	***6.31***	***6.74***	***10.63***		***Dc***				***9-30-95***	***37.40***		***899.0***	***4.2***						
Nts[1] 8⅞s '99	mN	**AAA**	5/94	AA+	X	R	NC	....	....	....	....	....	30.0	S1	'89	110⅛	101⅝	110⅛	8.06	5.89
West Penn Power Co.[2]	***72a***	***3.41***	***3.40***	***3.42***		***Dc***	***1.07***	***255.0***	***225.0***	***9-30-95***	***907.0***		***2018***	***48.0***						
1st FF 8⅞s 2021	Fa	**A+**	3/92	AA−	X	R	106.06	1-31-96	‡Z100	....	®103.79	1-31-01	100	K2	'91	106½	99⅞	106¼	8.35	8.28
1st GG 7⅞s 2004	jD	**A+**	3/92	AA−	X	R	104.52	11-30-96	Z‡100	....	®100	11-30-01	70.0	G1	'91	107¾	94½	104⅝	7.53	7.16
1st HH 7⅜s 2007	fA	**A+**			X	R	100	(8-1-02)	Z‡100	....	....	....	45.0	G1	'92	106	90	106	6.96	6.62
1st II 7⅞s 2022	mS	**A+**			X	R	103.51	(9-1-02)	Z*100	....	....	....	135	G1	'92	109	90⅜	109	7.22	7.12
1st JJ 5½s '98	Jd	**A+**			X	R	NC	....	Z100	....	....	....	102	M6	'93	99¾	92⅜	99¾	5.51	5.61
1st KK 6⅜s 2003	Jd	**A+**			X	R	NC	....	Z100	....	....	....	80.0	G1	'93	101⅛	87⅝	101⅛	6.30	6.18
1st MM 7¾s 2025	Mn	**A+**			X	R	103.073	(5-1-05)	Z100	....	....	....	30.0	P4	'95	108¼	98	108¼	7.16	7.08
West Texas Utilities[3]	***72a***	***3.16***	***2.79***	***3.26***		***Dc***	***3.78***	***75.80***	***87.90***	***9-30-95***	***250.0***		***538.0***	***46.7***						
1st P 7¾s 2007	Jd	**A+**	10/94	AA−	X	R	NC	....	....	....	....	....	25.0	M6	'92	111⅝	94⅛	111⅝	6.94	6.31
1st Q 6⅞s 2002	aO	**A+**	10/94	AA−	X	R	NC	....	....	....	....	....	35.0	F1	'92	104⅜	91⅛	104⅜	6.59	6.07
1st R 7s 2004	aO	**A+**	10/94	AA−	X	R	NC	....	....	....	....	....	40.0	F1	'92	104⅞	90⅛	104⅞	6.67	6.27
1st S 6⅛s 2004	Fa	**A+**	10/94	AA−	X	R	NC	....	....	....	....	....	40.0	S5	'94	99⅝	86	99⅝	6.15	6.18
1st U 6⅜s 2005	aO	**A+**			X	R	NC	....	....	....	....	....	80.0	M5	'95	101½	98¼	101½	6.28	6.17
1st T 7½s 2000	Ao	**A+**			X	R	NC	....	....	....	....	....	40.0	M6	'95	105¾	99⅜	105¾	7.09	5.95
Westbridge Capital	***35a***	***1.78***	***2.87***	***3.88***		***Dc***				***9-30-95***	***19.20***		***78.50***	***24.5***						
• Sr Sub Nts[4] 11s 2002	[5]Mar	**NR**				R	100	(3-1-98)	....	....	....	....	20.0	C3	'95	100½	99	100½	10.95	10.88
Western Atlas Inc	***49e***	***8.72***	***[6]9.46***	***3.23***		***Dc***	***79.60***	***960.0***	***504.0***	***9-30-95***	***535.0***		***1898***	***30.0***						
Deb 8.55s 2024	Jd15	**A−**	3/95	BBB	X	BE	NC	....	....	....	....	....	150	M2	'94	119¼	94½	119¼	7.17	6.98
Nts 7⅞s 2004	Jd15	**A−**	3/95	BBB	X	BE	NC	....	....	....	....	....	250	M2	'94	110¾	95⅛	110¾	7.11	6.22
[7]Western Fin'l Savings Bk	***10a***	***1.05***	***1.98***	***2.59***		***Dc***				***9-30-95***	***176.0***		***490.0***	***37.3***						
Sub Cap Deb 8½s 2003	jJ	**BB+**			Y	BE	100	(7-1-00)	....	....	....	....	104	D6	'93	102⅛	90⅜	96	8.85	9.25
Western Mass. Electric[8]	***72a***	***2.52***	***2.96***	***3.98***		***Dc***	***0.09***	***65.00***	***83.50***	***9-30-95***	***368.0***		***781.0***	***52.9***						
1st F 5¾s '97	Ms	**BBB**	2/95	BBB+	X	R	100	....	100	....	....	....	15.0	E3	'67	100	95⅝	100	5.75	5.74
1st G 6¾s '98	Ms	**BBB**	2/95	BBB+	X	R	100	2-29-96	100	....	....	....	10.0	E3	'68	100⅜	96⅛	100	6.75	6.74
1st V 7¾s 2002	jD	**BBB**	2/95	BBB+	X	R	102.88	(12-1-97)	100	....	....	....	85.0	M6	'92	104⅞	96½	104⅞	7.39	6.85
1st W 6⅞s 2000	Jj	**BBB**	2/95	BBB+	X	R	NC	....	Z100	....	....	....	60.0	S1	'93	102⅞	94¼	102⅞	6.68	6.06
1st X 6¼s '99	Ms	**BBB**	2/95	BBB+	X	BE	NC	....	....	....	....	....	40.0	M6	'94	100⅜	93⅛	100⅜	6.23	6.11
1st Y 7¾s 2024	Ms	**BBB**	2/95	BBB+	X	BE	104.65	(3-1-99)	Z100	(3-1-99)	....	....	50.0	M6	'94	102⅞	87⅛	102⅞	7.53	7.50
Western Natl Corp	***35a***	***n/a***	***n/a***	***12.89***		***Dc***				***9-30-95***	***148.0***		***880.0***	***16.8***						
• Sr Nts 7⅛s 2004	Fa15	**BBB+**	7/94	BBB	X	R	NC	....	....	....	....	....	150	M2	'94	99⅜	90	99⅜	7.17	7.23
Western Publishing Group	***54a***	***3.74***	***d1.16***	***d1.02***		***Ja***	***22.20***	***238.0***	***61.10***	***10-28-95***	***150.0***		***247.0***	***60.7***						
Sr Nts 7.65s 2002	mS15	**B**	10/95	BB−	Y	BE	NC	....	....	....	....	....	150	B5	'92	88	72	72	10.63	14.26
Western Resources, Inc[9]	***75***	***2.32***	***2.77***	***3.14***		***Dc***	***1.68***	***400.0***	***682.0***	***9-30-95***	***1342***		***3392***	***49.7***						
1st 7¼s '99	jJ	**A−**			X	R	NC	....	....	....	....	....	125	D4	'92	104⅜	96	104⅜	6.95	5.85
1st 7¼s 2002	fA15	**A−**			X	R	NC	....	....	....	....	....	100	D4	'92	105⅜	93	105⅜	6.88	6.25
1st 8½s 2022	jJ	**A−**			X	R	103.73	(7-1-02)	....	....	....	....	125	D4	'92	113⅛	95⅜	113⅛	7.51	7.37
1st 7.65s 2023	Ao15	**A−**			X	R	103.72	(4-15-03)	....	....	....	....	100	D4	'93	105½	87¾	105½	7.25	7.19
Westinghouse Air Brake	***56b***	***1.51***	***2.94***	***4.38***		***Dc***	***0.35***	***117.0***	***83.50***	***3-31-95***	***★310.0***		***105.0***	***316.0***						
Sr Nts[10] 9⅜s 2005	Jd15	**B+**			Y	R	104.688	(6-15-00)	....	....	....	....	100	M6	'95	104	98	101⅞	9.20	9.07

Uniform Footnote Explanations-See Page 260. Other: [1] (HRO)On Chge of Ctrl at 100. [2] Subsid of Allegheny Pwr System. [3] Contr by Central & South West Corp. [4] Death red benefit,ltd,as defined. [5] Due 3-1-02:Int pd mthly. [6] Fiscal Jul,'93 & prior. [7] Subsid & data of Westcorp, Inc. [8] Subsid of Northeast Util. [9] Was Kansas P&L,see. [10] (HRO)On Chge of Ctrl at 101.

Title-Industry Code & Co. Finances (In Italics) / Individual Issue Statistics (Exchange)	Ind / Interest Dates	Fixed Charge Coverage 1992 / S&P Debt Rating	1993 / Date of Last Rating Change	1994 / Prior Rating	Eligible	Year End / Bond Form	Cash & Equiv. / Regular Price	Curr. Assets / Regular (Begins) Thru	Curr. Liab. / Sinking Fund Price	Balance Sheet Date / Sinking Fund (Begins) Thru	L. Term Debt (Mil $) / Refund/Other Restriction Price	Refund/Other Restriction (Begins) Thru	Capitalization (Mil $) / Outst'g (Mil $)	Total Debt % Capital / Underwriting Firm	Underwriting Year	Price Range 1995 High	Price Range 1995 Low	Mo. End Price Sale(s) or Bid	Curr. Yield	Yield to Mat.
Westinghouse Credit	***25***	***Assmd by Westinghouse Elec,see***																		
[1]Nts[2] 8⅞s 2014	Jd14	B+	11/95	BBB–	Y	R	[3]NC	....	....	....	....	....	150	M2	'90	111½	99½	106½	8.33	8.19
Westinghouse Electric[4]	***23a***	***3.84***	***2.39***	***1.89***		***Dc***	***167.0***	***4313***	***3381***	***9-30-95***	***1746***		***4213***	***56.4***						
Deb 8⅝s 2012	fA	B+	11/95	BBB–	Y	BE	NC	....	....	....	....	....	275	G1	'92	105⅝	89¼	99⅞	8.64	8.64
Deb 7⅞s 2023	mS	B+	11/95	BBB–	Y	BE	NC	....	....	....	....	....	325	L3	'93	97⅜	81½	91	8.65	8.74
Nts 7¾s '96	Ao15	B+	11/95	BBB–	Y	R	NC	....	....	....	....	....	300	S4	'86	101	99⅛	100⅛	7.74	7.20
Nts 8⅞s 2001	Jd	B+	11/95	BBB–	Y	BE	NC	....	....	....	....	....	250	L3	'91	107⅝	96⅞	104⅜	8.50	7.87
Nts 8⅜s 2002	Jd15	B+	11/95	BBB–	Y	BE	NC	....	....	....	....	....	350	M6	'92	106½	93¼	102⅛	8.20	7.95
Nts 6⅞s 2003	mS	B+	11/95	BBB–	Y	BE	NC	....	....	....	....	....	275	L3	'93	97½	84	95⅛	7.23	7.73
WestPoint[5]Stevens	***68a***	***n/a***	***d3.20***	***d0.77***		***Dc***	***2.36***	***453.0***	***300.0***	***9-30-95***	***1035***		***592.0***	***186.0***						
Sr[6]Nts[7] 8¾s 2001	jD15	BB–			Y	R	104.375	(12-15-98)	....	....	[8]Z108	12-14-96	400	D6	'93	102	92¼	100¼	8.73	8.69
Sr[6]Sub[7]Deb 9⅜s 2005	jD15	B+			Y	R	104.688	(12-15-98)	....	....	[9]Z108	12-14-96	550	D6	'93	100¾	89⅜	98¾	9.49	9.57
Westvaco Corp	***50***	***△1.89***	***△2.36***	***△5.24***		***Oc***	***152.0***	***787.0***	***429.0***	***10-31-95***	***1147***		***3269***	***36.3***						
• SF Deb 8⅛s 2007	fA15	A			X	R	102.07	8-14-96	100	....	....	....	31.2	M2	'77	103⅞	100	100½	8.08	8.06
• SF Deb 12.30s 2015	Jj15	CALL	11/95	A		R			Called 1-15-96 for SF at 100				11.3	M2	'84	109⅞	100⅛	100	12.30	Call
• SF Deb 10¼s 2018	jJ	A			X	R	106.6635	6-30-96	100	(7-1-99)	®105.125	6-30-98	100	G1	'88	110	106	106⅞	9.59	9.50
SF Deb 10.30s 2019	Jj15	A			X	R	106.695	1-14-97	100	(1-15-00)	®105.15	1-14-99	100	M2	'89	107½	106¾	106¾	9.65	9.57
SF Deb 10⅛s 2019	Jd	A			X	R	105.0625	(6-1-99)	100	(6-1-00)	....	....	100	M2	'89	117⅞	103¾	117⅞	8.59	8.37
SF Deb 8.30s 2022	fA	A			X	R	104.15	(8-1-02)	100	(8-1-03)	....	....	125	M2	'92	111¾	96	111¾	7.43	7.29
SF Deb 7¾s 2023	Fa15	A			X	R	103.619	(2-15-03)	100	(2-15-04)	....	....	150	G1	'93	107¼	90⅜	107¼	7.23	7.14
SF Deb 7s 2023	fA15	A			X	R	103.025	(8-15-03)	100	(8-15-04)	....	....	150	M2	'93	100⅛	81¾	100⅛	6.99	6.99
Deb 9.65s 2002	Ms	A			X	R	NC	....	....	....	....	....	100	G1	'90	118⅝	105	118⅝	8.13	5.99
Deb 9¾s 2020	Jd15	A			X	R	NC	....	....	....	....	....	100	G1	'90	134¾	111⅞	134¾	7.24	6.81
Weyerhaeuser Co	***50***	***2.16***	***2.82***	***3.06***		***Dc***	***227.0***			***9-26-95***	***[10]★5382***		***9955***	***54.1***						
Deb 8⅜s 2007	Fa15	A	8/92	A+	X	R	NC	....	....	....	....	....	150	M6	'87	117¾	99¼	117¾	7.11	6.15
Deb 7½s 2013	Ms	A			X	R	NC	....	....	....	....	....	250	M6	'93	109⅛	91⅛	109⅛	6.87	6.60
Deb 7¼s 2013	jJ	A			X	R	NC	....	....	....	....	....	250	M6	'93	106½	88¼	106½	6.81	6.62
Deb 7⅛s 2023	jJ15	A			X	R	NC	....	....	....	....	....	250	M6	'93	105¾	85	105¾	6.74	6.67
Deb 8½s 2025	Jj15	A			X	R	NC	....	....	....	....	....	300	M6	'95	123½	98⅞	123½	6.88	6.66
Deb 7.95s 2025	Ms15	A			X	R	NC	....	....	....	....	....	250	M6	'95	116⅝	97½	116⅝	6.82	6.65
Nts 9.05s 2003	Fa	A	8/92	A+	X	R	NC	....	....	....	....	....	200	M6	'91	117⅝	103	117⅝	7.69	5.96
[11]Wheeling Pittsburgh	***66b***	***d0.16***	***2.20***	***5.90***		***Dc***	***370.0***	***786.0***	***256.0***	***9-30-95***	***286.0***		***1049***	***27.6***						
1st Mtg Nts[6] 12¼s 2000	mN15	BB–	11/95	BB	Y	R	106	(11-15-96)	100	(11-15-99)	....	....	9.00	C4	'91	113½	95	95	12.89	13.68
• Sr[6]Nts[12] 9⅜s 2003	mN15	BB–	11/95	BB	Y	R	102.50	(11-15-00)	....	....	....	....	325	M2	'93	97¼	86	s95½	9.82	10.22
Whirlpool Corp.	***23d***	***2.64***	***3.36***	***3.92***		***Dc***	***144.0***	***3551***	***3608***	***9-30-95***	***978.0***		***4946***	***58.7***						
Nts 9½s 2000	Jd15	A+			X	R	NC	....	....	....	....	....	200	G1	'90	114⅜	104⅜	114⅜	8.31	5.80
Nts 9s 2003	Ms	A+			X	R	NC	....	....	....	....	....	200	G1	'91	116¾	100⅝	116¾	7.71	6.08
Nts 9.10s 2008	Fa	A+	3/90	AA–	X	R	NC	....	....	....	....	....	125	G1	'88	124	101½	124	7.34	6.24
Whitman Corp.	***11f***	***2.75***	***3.07***	***4.33***		***Dc***	***83.50***	***820.0***	***531.0***	***9-30-95***	***850.0***		***1769***	***53.2***						
Nts 7½s 2001	fA15	BBB+	6/95	BBB	X	BE	NC	....	....	....	....	....	75.0	M2	'94	106	94⅞	106	7.08	6.22
Nts 7½s 2003	Fa	BBB+	6/95	BBB	X	BE	NC	....	....	....	....	....	125	F1	'93	106	94	106	7.08	6.43
Nts 6½s 2006	Fa	BBB+	6/95	BBB	X	BE	NC	....	....	....	....	....	100	M2	'94	100¼	84⅝	100¼	6.48	6.46
Nts 8¼s 2007	Fa15	BBB+	6/95	BBB	X	BE	NC	....	....	....	....	....	100	M2	'95	114⅝	99¼	114⅝	7.20	6.39
Wickes Lumber	***59l***	***1.33***	***1.50***	***1.71***		***Dc***	***4.49***	***254.0***	***88.60***	***9-30-95***	***221.0***		***256.0***	***86.7***						
Sr Sub Nts[6] 11⅝s 2003	jD15	B–			Y	R	105.8125	(12-15-00)	....	....	....	....	100	B9	'93	96½	69½	71	16.37	18.78
Willamette Indus.	***50***	***2.65***	***3.76***	***4.46***		***Dc***	***14.00***	***807.0***	***390.0***	***9-30-95***	***916.0***		***2693***	***35.5***						
Deb 9s 2021	aO	A			X	R	NC	....	....	....	....	....	150	G1	'91	124½	103¾	124½	7.23	6.94

Uniform Footnote Explanations-See Page 260. Other: [1] (HRO)On 6-14-99('04)at 100. [2] Assmd by Westinghouse Elec. [3] Red at 100 if less than $10M outstg. [4] See Westinghouse Credit. [5] See Stevens(JP) & Co. [6] (HRO)On Chge of Ctrl at 101. [7] Co may red in whole on Chge of Ctrl. [8] Max $140M red w/proceeds of Cap Stk Off'g. [9] Max $193M red w/proceeds of Cap Stk Off'g. [10] As reported, 12-25-94. [11] Now WHX Corp. [12] Co may offer repurch on Chge of Ctrl.

Title-Industry Code & Co. Finances (In Italics) / Individual Issue Statistics — Exchange	Ind / Interest Dates	Fixed Charge Coverage 1992 / S&P Debt Rating	1993 / Date of Last Rating Change	Prior Rating	1994 / Eligible	Year End / Bond Form	Cash & Equiv. / Redemption Provisions: Regular Price	Million $ Curr. Assets / Regular (Begins) Thru	Curr. Liab. / Sinking Fund Price	Balance Sheet Date / Sinking Fund (Begins) Thru	L. Term Debt (Mil $) / Refund/Other Restriction Price	Refund/Other Restriction (Begins) Thru	Capitalization (Mil $) / Outst'g (Mil $)	Total Debt % Capital / Underwriting Firm	Underwriting Year	Price Range 1995 High	Price Range 1995 Low	Mo. End Price Sale(s) or Bid	Curr. Yield	Yield to Mat.
***Willamette Indus** (Cont.)*																				
Nts 9⅝s 2000	fA15	**A**	9/91	A+	X	R	NC	....	....	....	....	....	150	S1	'90	114⅝	105⅞	114⅝	8.40	5.96
Nts 7¾s 2002	jJ15	**A**			X	R	NC	....	....	....	....	....	100	S1	'92	108⅝	96⅜	108⅝	7.13	6.13
***Williams Cos**[1]*	*73a*	*1.76*	*2.61*		*2.38*	*Dc*	*63.60*	*1262*	*1945*	*9-30-95*	*2908*		*6313*	*49.7*						
Deb 8⅞s 2012	mS15	**BBB–**	2/95	BBB	X	R	NC	....	....	....	....	....	150	F1	'92	119⅝	98½	119⅝	7.42	6.88
Deb 10¼s 2020	jJ15	**BBB–**	2/95	BBB	X	R	NC	....	....	....	....	....	150	F1	'90	138⅜	110⅛	138⅜	7.41	6.96
Deb 9⅜s 2021	mN15	**BBB–**	2/95	BBB	X	R	NC	....	....	....	....	....	100	L3	'91	128⅜	102⅝	128⅜	7.30	6.99
Nts 8¼s '98	mN15	**BBB–**	2/95	BBB	X	R	NC	....	....	....	....	....	100	L3	'91	106⅜	98½	106⅜	7.76	5.81
Nts 7½s '99	mS15	**BBB–**	2/95	BBB	X	R	NC	....	....	....	....	....	150	F1	'92	105¼	94¾	105¼	7.13	5.90
***Wisconsin Bell** [2]**Inc**[3]*	*67a*	*5.13*	*7.63*		*9.30*	*Dc*		*251.0*	*324.0*	*9-30-95*	*317.0*		*956.0*	*45.2*						
• Deb 7¼s 2007	Fa	**AAA**			X	R	101.93	1-31-96	....	....	....	....	90.0	M6	'71	103½	91	101¾	7.13	7.02
Deb 6¾s 2024	fA15	**AAA**			X	BE	102.274	(8-15-03)	....	....	....	....	150	F1	'93	100	81⅛	100	6.75	6.75
***Wisconsin Electric Power**[4]*	*75*	*3.69*	*3.61*		*4.11*	*Dc*	*13.00*	*394.0*	*347.0*	*9-30-95*	*1158*		*2929*	*46.6*						
1st 4½s '96	Ms15	**AA+**			X	BE	NC	....	....	....	....	....	30.0	K2	'93	99¾	96½	99¾	4.51	5.63
1st 5⅞s '97	aO	**AA+**			X	R	NC	....	....	....	....	....	130	S1	'92	100⅜	94⅝	100⅜	5.85	5.64
1st 5⅛s '98	mS15	**AA+**			X	BE	NC	....	....	....	....	....	60.0	S1	'93	98⅝	90⅜	98⅝	5.20	5.68
1st 6⅝s '99	fA	**AA+**			X	R	NC	....	....	....	....	....	51.0	S1	'92	102¾	94¼	102¾	6.45	5.76
1st 6½s '99	aO	**AA+**			X	R	NC	....	....	....	....	....	40.0	S1	'92	102¼	93⅜	102¼	6.36	5.82
1st 7¼s 2004	fA	**AA+**			X	R	NC	....	....	....	....	....	140	S1	'92	106⅞	93⅛	106⅞	6.78	6.20
1st 7⅛s 2016	Ms15	**AA+**			X	BE	102.76	(3-15-03)	....	....	....	....	100	K2	'93	102⅛	85⅜	102⅛	6.98	6.93
1st 7¾s 2023	Jj15	**AA+**			X	BE	102.72	(1-15-03)	....	....	....	....	100	G1	'93	108⅛	89¾	108⅛	7.17	7.07
1st 7.05s 2024	fA	**AA+**			X	BE	102.08	(8-1-03)	....	....	....	....	60.0	S1	'93	100½	82¾	100½	7.01	7.01
1st 9⅛s 2024	mS	**AA+**			X	R	106.65	8-31-96	....	....	....	....	3.44	S1	'89	107⅛	102⅝	106⅞	8.54	8.48
1st 8⅜s 2026	jD	**AA+**			X	R	102.92	(12-1-01)	....	....	....	....	100	G1	'91	112½	95¼	112½	7.44	7.35
1st 7.70s 2027	jD15	**AA+**			X	BE	102.10	(12-15-02)	....	....	....	....	200	M6	'92	108⅜	89⅞	108⅜	7.10	7.04
Deb 6⅞s 2095	jD	**AA**			X	BE	NC	....	....	....	....	....	100	M6	'95	99⅞	97⅝	99⅞	6.88	6.88
***Wisconsin Gas Co.**[5]*	*73b*	*2.90*	*3.11*		*3.08*	*Dc*	*8.89*	*102.0*	*103.0*	*9-30-95*	*142.0*		*329.0*	*43.8*						
Deb 6.60s 2013	mS15	**AA–**			X	BE	NC	....	....	....	....	....	45.0	D3	'93	102⅝	79¼	102⅝	6.43	6.35
Nts 7½s '98	mN15	**AA–**			X	R	NC	....	....	....	....	....	40.0	D3	'91	104¾	97¼	104¾	7.16	5.68
Nts 6⅜s 2005	mN	**AA–**			X	BE	NC	....	....	....	....	....	65.0	D3	'95	102¼	99½	102¼	6.23	6.07
***Wisconsin Natural Gas**[4]*	*73b*	*3.08*	*3.68*		*5.18*	*Dc*	*1.53*	*68.60*	*79.90*	*9-30-95*	*66.60*		*234.0*	*42.4*						
1st 6⅝s '97	Jj15	**AA**			X	R	NC	....	....	....	....	....	10.0	K2	'92	101	97⅜	101	6.56	5.62
Deb 6⅛s '97	mS	**AA**			X	BE	NC	....	....	....	....	....	25.0	K2	'92	100⅞	95⅜	100⅞	6.07	5.56
Deb 8¼s 2022	jD15	**AA**			X	BE	103.80	(12-15-02)	....	....	....	....	25.0	K2	'92	113¼	94⅝	113¼	7.28	7.14
***Wisconsin Power & Light**[6]*	*75*	*3.58*	*3.97*		*4.60*	*Dc*	*0.86*	*80.30*	*225.0*	*9-30-95*	*319.0*		*1043*	*41.2*						
1st L 6¼s '98	fA	**AA**	9/89	AA+	X	R	100.44	7-31-96	□100	....	....	....	8.90	F1	'68	100½	94¼	100½	6.22	6.04
1st V 9.30s 2025	jD	**AA**			X	R	105.82	11-30-96	....	....	®104.36	11-30-00	50.0	G1	'90	107¾	104¾	106	8.77	8.73
1st W 8.60s 2027	Ms15	**AA**			X	R	105.06	(3-15-02)	....	....	....	....	90.0	G1	'92	115⅞	97⅞	115⅝	7.44	7.32
1st X 7¾s 2004	Jd	**AA**			X	R	NC	....	....	....	....	....	62.0	G1	'92	110⅞	96⅞	110⅞	6.99	6.08
1st Y 7.60s 2005	jJ	**AA**			X	R	NC	....	....	....	....	....	72.0	G1	'92	109⅞	94⅞	109⅞	6.92	6.21
1st Z 6⅛s '97	jJ15	**AA**			X	R	NC	....	....	....	....	....	55.0	G1	'92	100⅞	95⅞	100⅞	6.07	5.52
*[7]**Wisconsin Public Service***	*75*	*4.14*	*4.63*		*4.38*	*Dc*	*15.30*	*147.0*	*82.90*	*9-30-95*	*309.0*		*827.0*	*38.6*						
1st 5¼s '98	jJ	**AA+**			X	R	NC	....	....	....	....	....	50.0	K2	'93	99⅛	91¼	99⅛	5.30	5.63
1st 7.30s 2002	aO	**AA+**			X	R	NC	....	....	....	....	....	50.0	K2	'92	106⅛	93⅝	106⅛	6.88	6.17
1st 8.80s 2021	mS	**AA+**			X	R	104.40	(9-1-01)	100	(9-1-01)	....	....	60.0	G1	'91	114¾	100	114¾	7.67	7.50
1st 7⅛s 2023	jJ	**AA+**			X	R	102.705	(7-1-03)	....	....	....	....	50.0	K2	'93	102¼	84⅛	102¼	6.97	6.94

Uniform Footnote Explanations-See Page 260. Other: [1] See Transco Energy. [2] Was Wisc Tel,see. [3] Subsid of Ameritech Corp. [4] Subsid of Wisc Energy. [5] Subsid of Wicor, Inc. [6] Subsid of WPL Holdings.
[7] Now WPS Resources.

Title-Industry Code & Co. Finances (In Italics) / Individual Issue Statistics, Exchange	Ind / Interest Dates	1992 / S&P Debt Rating	1993 / Date of Last Rating Change	1994 / Prior Rating	Eligible	Year End / Bond Form	Cash & Equiv. / Regular Price	Curr. Assets / Regular (Begins) Thru	Curr. Liab. / Sinking Fund Price	Balance Sheet Date / Sinking Fund (Begins) Thru	L. Term Debt (Mil $) / Refund/Other Restriction Price	Refund/Other Restriction (Begins) Thru	Capitalization (Mil $) / Outst'g (Mil $)	Total Debt % Capital / Underwriting Firm	Underwriting Year	Price Range 1995 High	Price Range 1995 Low	Mo. End Price Sale(s) or Bid	Curr. Yield	Yield to Mat.
Wisconsin Telephone Co	***67a***	***Now Wisconsin Bell,see***																		
Deb 4⅜s 2002	Mn	AAA			X	CR	100.35	4-30-96	....	....	....	....	20.0	H1	'62	91⅝	79⅜	91⅝	4.77	5.98
Deb 6¼s 2004	fA	AAA			X	R	100.69	7-31-96	....	....	....	....	50.0	M6	'68	100⅛	86¾	100⅛	6.24	6.23
Witco Corp[1]	***14***	***6.86***	***4.46***	***5.62***		***Dc***	***307.0***	***938.0***	***308.0***	***9-30-95***	***345.0***		***1401***	***25.1***						
Deb 7¾s 2023	Ao	A			X	R	103.776	(4-1-03)	....	....	....	....	110	G1	'93	105⅞	87⅝	105⅞	7.32	7.25
Nts 6.60s 2003	Ao	A			X	R	NC	....	....	....	....	....	165	G1	'93	102¼	89¼	102¼	6.45	6.21
WMX Technologies[2]	***53***	***5.07***	***4.24***	***4.19***		***Dc***	***287.0***	***3361***	***3374***	***9-30-95***	***6459***		***13988***	***54.0***						
Nts 4⅞s '96	Jd15	A+	4/95	AA–	X	BE	NC	....	....	....	....	....	300	K2	'93	99¾	96	99¾	4.89	5.42
Nts 5.84s '96	jJ3	A+			X	BE	NC	....	....	....	....	....	100	M2	'95	100¼	99⅞	100¼	5.83	5.34
Nts 7⅛s '97	Ms22	A+	4/95	AA–	X	BE	NC	....	....	....	....	....	200	M2	'95	102	99⅞	102	6.99	5.41
Nts 8⅛s '98	Fa	A+	4/95	AA–	X	BE	NC	....	....	....	....	....	250	D6	'95	105⅛	99⅞	104⅞	7.75	5.61
Nts 8¼s '99	mN15	A+	4/95	AA–	X	BE	NC	....	....	....	....	....	200	M2	'94	108½	99	108½	7.60	5.77
Nts 6¼s 2000	aO15	A+			X	BE	NC	....	....	....	....	....	250	D6	'95	101¾	99¾	101¾	6.14	5.82
Nts 6⅜s 2003	jD	A+	4/95	AA–	X	BE	NC	....	....	....	....	....	500	M2	'93	101⅝	87⅞	101⅝	6.27	6.11
Nts[3] 6.65s 2005	Mn15	A+			X	BE	NC	....	....	....	....	....	200	D6	'95	103⅜	99½	103⅜	6.43	6.17
Nts 7s 2005	Mn15	A+			X	BE	NC	....	....	....	....	....	100	D6	'95	106¼	98⅜	106¼	6.59	6.11
Step-Up([4]Reset)Nts[5] 6.22s 2004	Ao30	A+	4/95	AA–	X	BE	NC	....	....	....	....	....	150	M2	'94	110	96½	110	5.65	....
Wolverine Tube, Inc	***44d***	***3.41***	***3.98***	***6.35***		***Dc***	***0.32***	***143.0***	***55.40***	***9-30-95***	***101.0***		***260.0***	***38.7***						
Sr Sub Nts[6] 10⅛s 2002	mS	B+	10/93	B	Y	R	103.80	(9-1-97)	....	....	....	....	99.0	F1	'92	107	100½	107	9.46	8.71
Woolworth Corp[7]	***59l***	***6.02***	***0.14***	***2.15***		***Ja***	***105.0***	***2299***	***1711***	***7-29-95***	***68.00***		***2810***	***51.7***						
Deb 8½s 2022	Jj15	BBB–	3/95	BBB+	X	R	NC	....	....	....	....	....	200	M2	'92	112⅞	92	112⅞	7.53	7.38
Nts 7s 2000	Jd	BBB–			X	BE	NC	....	....	....	....	....	200	M5	'95	102⅜	97¾	102⅜	6.84	6.37
World Book Finance	***25d***	***Subsid of Berkshire Hathaway,see***																		
Nts 8⅛s '96	mS	AAA	2/89	AA+	X	R	NC	....	....	....	....	....	120	F1	'86	102¼	100¼	101¾	7.99	5.42
World Color Press	***29a***	***n/a***	***d2.31***	***2.66***		***Dc***	***9.60***	***456.0***	***249.0***	***10-1-95***	***503.0***		***901.0***	***58.7***						
• Sr Sub Nts 9⅛s 2003	Ms15	BB–			Y	R	104.56	(3-15-98)	....	....	[8]Z108	3-15-98	150	D6	'93	101	90	99⅛	9.21	9.29
World Savings & Loan Ass'n[9]	***10b***	***2.60***	***2.34***	***2.19***		***Dc***				***12-31-94***	***★8052***		***9942***	***79.0***						
M-T Nts[10] 5⅝s '96	Jj15	A+			X	BE	NC	....	....	....	....	....	100	L3	'93	100	98	100	5.63	Mat.
M-T Nts[10] 5¼s '96	Fa15	A+			X	BE	NC	....	....	....	....	....	100	L3	'93	100	97⅜	100	5.25	5.15
M-T Nts[10] 7⅝s '97	Fa18	A+			X	BE	NC	....	....	....	....	....	200	L3	'95	102⅝	100	102⅜	7.45	5.43
F/R[11]M-T Nts[10] 6.0625s '98	QFeb18	A+			X	BE	NC	....	....	....	....	....	100	L3	'95	100⅛	99½	100⅛	6.05	....
Sub[10]Nts[12] 10¼s '97	aO	A	5/91	A–	Y	R	NC	....	....	....	....	....	100	M2	'90	108⅜	104¾	107⅝	9.52	5.62
Sub Nts[10] 9.90s 2000	jJ	A	5/91	A–	Y	R	100	(4-1-99)	....	....	....	....	100	M2	'90	111⅛	104⅛	111⅛	8.91	6.98
WorldCorp, Inc	***4a***	***d2.98***	***d2.01***	***1.86***		***Dc***	***62.60***	***86.10***	***70.60***	***9-30-95***	***91.20***		***75.30***	***151.0***						
Sub Nts 13⅞s '97	fA15	CCC–	8/93	B–	Y	R	100	....	100	....	....	....	25.0	D7	'87	101	97	100¼	13.84	13.67
Wyman-Gordon Co	***41g***	***[13]Δd0.45***	***Δd4.74***	***Δ1.06***		***My***	***21.40***	***193.0***	***89.10***	***9-2-95***	***90.30***		***181.0***	***52.5***						
Sr Nts[6] 10¾s 2003	Ms15	BB–			Y	R	104.78	(3-15-98)	....	....	....	....	90.0	D6	'93	105	91	105	10.24	9.76
Wyndham Baking	***26f***	....	....	....		***Dc***	***No Recent Fin'ls***													
Sr Sub Nts 13⅝s '98	mS15	NR	8/90	CCC+		R	103.03	9-14-96	100	(9-15-96)	....	....	100	P1	'88	106	103½	103½	13.16	12.05
Xerox Corp	***48***	***1.76***	***2.74***	***2.94***		***Dc***	***137.0***			***9-30-95***	***9225***		***19011***	***64.7***						
Nts 9⅝s '97	mS	A			X	R	NC	....	....	....	....	....	200	S1	'90	107⅜	103½	106½	9.04	5.49
Nts 9.20s '99	jJ15	A	7/90	A+	X	R	100	(7-15-96)	....	....	....	....	250	S1	'89	105⅞	101½	102⅛	9.01	8.49
Nts 9¾s 2000	Ms15	A	7/90	A+	X	R	NC	....	....	....	....	....	200	S1	'90	114½	104⅞	114½	8.52	5.81
Nts 8⅛s 2002	Ao15	A			X	R	NC	....	....	....	....	....	200	M5	'92	110⅞	97⅜	110⅞	7.33	6.02
Nts 7.15s 2004	fA	A			X	R	NC	....	....	....	....	....	200	F1	'92	106⅜	91¾	106⅜	6.72	6.18
Xerox Credit	***25d***	***1.75***	***1.74***	***1.73***		***Dc***				***9-30-95***	***1769***		***2861***	***82.3***						
Nts 6¼s '96	Jj15	A			X	R	NC	....	....	....	....	....	200	G1	'92	100⅛	98½	100	6.25	Mat.

Uniform Footnote Explanations-See Page 260. Other: [1] Was Witco Chemical. [2] Was Waste Management,see. [3] (HRO)On 5-15-00 at 100. [4] Int to 4-30-97,8% aft. [5] (HRO)On 4-30-97 at 100. [6] (HRO)On Chge of Ctrl at 101. [7] Was Woolworth (F.W.) Co. [8] To 3-15-98 w/net proceeds of Equity Offering. [9] Subsid of Golden West Fin'l. [10] Issued in min denom $100T. [11] Int to 2-18-96,adj qtrly(3 Mo LIBOR&0.1875%). [12] Not available for purch by savings assoc. [13] Yr Dec'93 & prior.

Title-Industry Code & Co. Finances (In Italics) / Individual Issue Statistics, Exchange	Ind / Interest Dates	S&P Debt Rating	Date of Last Rating Change	Prior Rating	Eligible	Bond Form	Redemption Provisions: Regular Price	Regular (Begins) Thru	Sinking Fund Price	Sinking Fund (Begins) Thru	Refund/Other Restriction Price	Refund/Other Restriction (Begins) Thru	Outst'g (Mil $)	Underwriting Firm	Underwriting Year	Price Range 1995 High	Price Range 1995 Low	Mo. End Price Sale(s) or Bid	Curr. Yield	Yield to Mat.
Title-Industry Code & Co. Finances (In Italics)	*Ind*	*Fixed Charge Coverage 1992*	*1993*	*1994*		*Year End*	*Million $ Cash & Equiv.*	*Curr. Assets*	*Curr. Liab.*	*Balance Sheet Date*	*L. Term Debt (Mil $)*		*Capital-ization (Mil $)*	*Total Debt % Capital*						
***Xerox Credit** (Cont.)*																				
• Nts 10s '99	Ao	**A**	7/90	A+	X	R	NC	....	....	....	....	....	150	S1	'89	112	103⅛	s110	9.09	6.53
Nts 10⅛s '99	Ao15	**A**	7/90	A+	X	R	100	(4-15-96)	....	....	....	....	150	S1	'89	103⅜	101	101	10.02	9.75
F/R[1]Nts[2] 2048	fA15	**A**	7/90	A+	X	R	[3]Z100	....	....	....	....	....	61.0	G1	'88	100	98½	100	....	....
M-T Nts 'C'[4] 5.28s '96	[5]ao15	**A**			X	BE	NC	....	....	....	....	....	25.0	G1	'94	100	97¼	100	5.28	5.19
M-T Nts 'C'[4] 5.27s '96	[6]ao15	**A**			X	BE	NC	....	....	....	....	....	25.0	C5	'94	100	97¼	100	5.27	5.18
M-T Nts 'C'[4] 5.20s '96	[7]ao15	**A**			X	BE	NC	....	....	....	....	....	50.0	L3	'95	100	97⅛	100	5.20	5.11
M-T Nts 'C'[4] 5.69s '97	[8]ao15	**A**			X	BE	NC	....	....	....	....	....	25.0	C5	'94	100¼	95¼	100¼	5.68	5.46
M-T Nts 'C'[4] 5.79s '97	[9]ao15	**A**			X	BE	NC	....	....	....	....	....	25.0	M2	'94	100¼	95¼	100¼	5.78	5.57
M-T Nts 'C'[4] 5.76s '97	[9]ao15	**A**			X	BE	NC	....	....	....	....	....	31.4	M2	'94	100¼	95¼	100¼	5.75	5.54
M-T Nts 'C'[4] 5.82s '97	[9]ao15	**A**			X	BE	NC	....	....	....	....	....	25.0	L3	'94	100⅜	95⅜	100⅜	5.80	5.49
M-T Nts 'C'[4] 5.81s '97	[9]ao15	**A**			X	BE	NC	....	....	....	....	....	25.0	S1	'94	100⅜	95⅜	100⅜	5.79	5.48
F/R[4]M-T Nts 'C'[10] '96	QFeb7	**A**			X	BE	NC	....	....	....	....	....	50.0	L3	'94	100	98½	100	....	....
[10]F/R M-T Nts 'C'[4] '96	QMar29	**A**			X	BE	NC	....	....	....	....	....	25.0	M5	'94	100	99⅞	100	....	....
F/R M-T Nts 'C'[4] '96	[11]	**A**			X	BE	NC	....	....	....	....	....	50.0	C5	'93	100	98½	100	....	....
[10]F/R M-T Nts 'C'[4] '97	QMay13	**A**			X	BE	NC	....	....	....	....	....	50.0	M5	'94	100	99½	99⅞	....	....
[10]F/R M-T Nts 'C'[4] '97	QMay13	**A**			X	BE	NC	....	....	....	....	....	75.0	L3	'94	100	99½	99⅞	....	....
F/R[12]M-T Nts 'C'[4] '97	[13]May16	**A**			X	BE	NC	....	....	....	....	....	25.0	C5	'95	100⅛	99½	100	....	....
M-T Nts 'D' 6.84s 2000	Jd	**A**			X	BE	100	(6-1-98)	....	....	....	....	100	M2	19	103⅝	99¾	103⅝	6.60	5.90
[14]XTRA, Inc	***25c***	***3.10***	***2.86***	***3.90***		***Sp***				***9-30-95***	***898.0***		***1256***	***71.4***						
M-T[15]Nts 'C'[4] 6.68s 2001	[16]ao	**BBB+**			X	BE	NC	....	....	....	....	....	20.0	G1	'95	102½	97¾	102½	6.52	6.17
M-T Nts[4]'C'[15] 7.22s 2005	[17]ao	**BBB+**			X	BE	NC	....	....	....	....	....	25.0	G1	'95	105⅝	100	105⅝	6.84	6.43
M-T Nts[4]'C'[15] 7.42s 2007	[18]ao	**BBB+**			X	BE	NC	....	....	....	....	....	25.0	G1	'95	107⅝	100	107⅝	6.89	6.48
York International	***13b***	***3.93***	***6.11***	***5.23***		***Dc***	***5.92***	***851.0***	***614.0***	***12-31-94***	***p267.0***		***876.0***	***39.8***						
Sr Nts 6¾s 2003	Ms	**BBB+**	6/95	BBB	X	BE	NC	....	....	....	....	....	100	M6	'93	103⅜	89⅝	103⅜	6.53	6.16
Young Broadcasting Inc	***12c***	***n/a***	***n/a***	***n/a***		***Dc***	***5.04***	***38.80***	***32.10***	***9-30-95***	***293.0***		***293.0***	***104.0***						
Sr Sub Nts[19] 11¾s 2004	mN15	**B**			Y	R	104.406	(11-15-99)	....	....	[20]Z111.75	11-14-97	120	B9	'94	112¼	100½	112	10.49	9.70
Zapata Corp	***49***	***△d0.33***	***△d0.55***	***△0.71***		***Sp***	***2.49***	***151.0***	***37.10***	***9-30-95***	***37.50***		***199.0***	***26.9***						
• Sub SF Deb[21] 10¼s '97	Ms15	**NR**	1/91	D		R	100	....	100	....	....	....	[22]15.6	L3	'77	102	95½	100½	....	Flat
• Sub SF Deb[21] 10⅞s 2001	Mn	**NR**	1/91	D		R	100	....	100	....	....	....	10.2	Exch.	'76	103	92¾	93½	....	Flat
Zenith Nat'l Insurance	***35c***	***6.53***	***12.04***	***10.70***		***Dc***				***9-30-95***	***74.20***		***401.0***	***18.5***						
Sr Nts[23] 9s 2002	Mn	**A−**			X	R	NC	....	....	....	....	....	75.0	S1	'92	112⅝	101¾	112	8.04	6.65
Zions Bancorp	***10***	***1.98***	***4.71***	***2.47***		***Dc***				***9-30-95***	***148.0***		***573.0***	***28.4***						
Sub Nts 8⅝s 2002	aO15	**BBB−**	11/93	BB+	X	BE	NC	....	....	....	....	....	50.0	G1	'92	111½	97⅝	111½	7.74	6.50
Zurich Reinsurance Centre Hldgs	***35***	***n/a***	***6.84***	***d1.93***		***Dc***				***9-30-95***	***200.0***		***860.0***	***23.3***						
• Sr Nts 7⅛s 2023	aO15	**A−**			X	R	NC	....	....	....	....	....	200	F1	'93	88	86	A100	7.13	7.12

Uniform Footnote Explanations-See Page 260. Other: [1] (HRO)Min $0.1M ea Aug 15 to 2012. [2] Co may pay int mthly(15th day)/semi-anly fA15. [3] Red only if $5M or less outstdg. [4] Issued in min denom $100T. [5] Due 2-29-96. [6] Due 4-28-96. [7] Due 3-1-96. [8] Due 2-28-97. [9] Due 3-17-97. [10] Int adj weekly. [11] Due 8-9-96:Int pd mthly,ea 3rd Wed. [12] Int adj monthly. [13] Int pd monthly. [14] Gtd by & data of XTRA Corp. [15] Gtd by XTRA Corp. [16] Due 11-30-01. [17] Due 8-11-05. [18] Due 8-15-07. [19] (HRO)On Chge of Ctrl at 101. [20] Max $80M red w/proceeds of Pub Eq Off'g. [21] Arrears cleared 1-9-91. [22] Incl disc. [23] (HRO)At 100 for Designated Event&Rat'g Decline.

Exchange ↓ BONDS Description	Interest Rate	Due	Interest Dates	S&P Debt Rating	Redemption Provisions: Regular	For Sinking Fund	Refund Earliest/ Other	Underwriting: Firm	Price	Year	Out-standing Mil-$ This Issue	Price Range 1983-1994: High	Low	1995: High	Low	Month End Price Sale(s) or Bid	Yield to Matur-ity
Abbey Nat'l 1st Capital B.V. .... [1]Sub[2]Notes[3]	8.20s	2004	$aO15	AA–	NC	....	....	M2	99.77	'94	500	99¾	96¾	113⅜	97½	113⅜	6.20
AEGON N.V. .... Sub Notes[2]	8s	2006	$fA15	AA–	NC	....	....	M5	99.09	'94	400	99¾	94	112⅝	95⅛	112⅝	6.35
• African Development Bank .... Notes	10s	1997	$mN	AA+	NC	....	....	K2	100	'87	200	110½	99⅜	107¼	107¼	100	9.98
African Development Bank .... Notes	6¾s	2004	$aO	AA+	NC	....	....	G1	98.28	'92	300	108	88⅞	105⅝	90¼	105⅝	5.92
• African Development Bank .... Sub Notes ('88)	9¾s	2003	$jD15	AA–	NC	....	....	K2	100	'88	100	100	99¼	No Sale		123	6.06
African Development Bank .... Sub Notes ('90)	9.30s	2000	$jJ	AA–	NC	....	....	K2	99.55	'90	300	123½	95¼	113¾	104⅞	113¾	5.79
African Development Bank .... Sub Notes ('91)	7¾s	2001	$jD15	AA–	NC	....	....	G1	99.31	'91	200	115⅜	97	109⅜	97⅛	109⅜	5.86
African Development Bank .... Sub Notes ('95)	6⅞s	2015	$aO15	AA–	NC	....	....	M2	99.29	'95	400	....	....	103	99¼	102⅞	6.61
[4]Aktiebolaget SKF .... Sr[2]Notes	7⅝s	2003	$jJ15	BBB	NC	....	....	M2	99.60	'93	100	103⅜	86½	106⅝	87⅜	106⅝	6.50
Alberta(Province of) .... Notes	9.20s	1997	$mN	AA	NC	....	....	M2	99	'90	300	116	99	107⅛	102⅝	106⅝	5.36
Alberta(Province of) .... Notes	9¼s	2000	$Ao	AA	NC	....	....	M6	99⅞	'90	500	121¾	95⅞	113⅜	104½	113⅜	5.66
Alcan Aluminum Corp .... Gtd[5]Deb	6⅜s	1997	$mS	A–	NC	....	....	M6	99.54	'92	150	104⅛	95⅜	101¼	95½	101¼	5.58
Alcan Aluminum Corp .... Gtd[5]Deb	7¼s	1999	$jD15	A–	NC	....	....	F1	99.51	'92	100	108	95	104⅞	94⅞	104⅞	5.85
Alcan Aluminium Ltd .... Deb	8.20s	1996	$mS	A–	NC	....	....	M6	99.91	'91	150	108¾	99¾	102½	99⅞	101¾	5.49
Alcan Aluminium Ltd .... Deb	9.70s	1996	$aO15	A–	NC	....	....	M6	99.82	'90	125	113½	99⅞	104⅝	102⅛	103⅛	5.60
Alcan Aluminium Ltd .... Deb	9.10s	1998	$Jd15	A–	NC	....	....	F1	99.77	'91	125	114	100	113	101¾	113	3.54
Alcan Aluminium Ltd .... Deb	5⅞s	2000	$Ao	A–	NC	....	....	M6	99.38	'93	150	100	89	99⅞	89⅛	99⅞	5.91
Alcan Aluminium Ltd .... Deb	9.20s	2001	$Ms15	A–	[6]100	....	....	F1	99.93	'91	150	121	99⅛	107¾	101½	107¾	7.38
Alcan Aluminium[7]Ltd[8] .... [9]Deb	9½s	2010	$Jj15	A–	[10]103.494	....	....	M6	98.99	'89	100	121	92⅝	116¼	104¼	116¼	7.60
Alcan Aluminium Ltd .... Deb	8⅞s	2022	$Jj15	A–	[11]104.15	....	....	F1	99.42	'92	150	120¾	93⅝	115	96⅛	115	7.55
Alcan Aluminium Ltd[8] .... [12]SF[7]Deb[13]	9⅝s	2019	$jJ15	A–	[14]104.64	[15]100	....	F1	99.65	'89	150	121⅜	92	114⅛	103½	112⅛	8.43
Algoma Steel Inc .... 1st Mtg[2]Notes[16]	12⅜s	2005	$jJ15	B	NC	....	....	B9	90.15	'95	[17]306	....	....	95	87¼	89¾	14.38
Amoco Canada Petroleum Co Ltd .... Gtd[18]Deb	6¾s	2005	$Fa15	AAA	NC	....	....	G1	99.64	'93	300	108⅝	88⅜	105½	90¼	105½	5.96
Amoco Canada Petroleum Co Ltd .... Gtd[18]Deb	7.95s	2022	$aO	AAA	[19]103.294	....	....	G1	98.64	'92	300	118⅞	92¾	111⅜	93⅛	111⅜	7.00
Amoco Canada Petroleum Co Ltd .... Gtd[18]Deb	6¾s	2023	$mS	AAA	[20]102.742	....	....	G1	98.73	'93	300	101¼	78	99⅜	80⅜	99¼	6.81
Amoco Canada Petroleum Co Ltd .... Gtd[18]Notes	7¼s	2002	$jD	AAA	NC	....	....	G1	99.65	'92	300	111¾	94⅛	107¾	94½	107¾	5.87
• Asian Development Bank .... Bonds	10¾s	1997	$Jd	AAA	NC	....	....	S4	99.73	'85	100	105¾	99⅝	No Sale		107⅛	5.47
• Asian Development Bank .... Bonds	11⅛s	1998	$Mn	AAA	NC	....	....	F1	99.45	'83	76.2	100	99⅜	No Sale		111⅞	5.63
• Asian Development Bank .... Bonds	8s	2001	$Ao31	AAA	NC	....	....	M2	99.55	'86	56.2	100½	97½	No Sale		110⅜	5.71
Asian Development Bank .... Notes	9⅛s	2000	$Jd	AAA	NC	....	....	S4	99.20	'90	300	123	96¾	113½	103⅝	113½	5.63
Asian Development Bank .... Notes	8½s	2001	$Mn2	AAA	NC	....	....	S1	99.65	'91	300	119⅞	99	112⅛	101	112⅛	5.82
Asian Development Bank .... Notes[21]	6½s	2002	$mS21	AAA	NC	....	....	L3	98.99	'92	300	107⅛	90	103⅜	89⅞	103⅜	5.88
• Australia(Commonwealth) .... Bonds	9¼s	1996	$fA	AA	NC	....	....	M6	99.55	'86	65.0	108	98	103	100	100	9.22
Australia(Commonwealth) .... Bonds	7⅝s	1997	$mS15	AA	NC	....	....	M6	99¼	'87	99.8	109⅞	84⅝	101	98	100	7.61
• Australia(Commonwealth) .... Bonds	9⅝s	2006	$Fa	AA	NC	....	....	M6	99.20	'86	114	110¾	99⅛	No Sale		103	9.16
Australia(Commonwealth) .... Bonds	8⅜s	2017	$Ms15	AA	NC	....	....	M6	99.87	'87	68.0	119⅛	79⅞	118⅞	95½	118⅞	6.69
Australia & New Zealand Bkg .... Sub Notes[2]	6¼s	2004	$Fa	A	NC	....	....	G1	99.71	'94	250	99⅝	84⅝	99¾	85½	99¾	6.29
Austria (Republic of) .... Bonds	9⅛s	1999	$Ao25	AAA	NC	....	....	S1	99.27	'88	100	119⅝	94⅝	110½	103¼	110⅜	5.65
• Banco Nacional de Comercio .... Notes[2]	7¼s	2004	$Fa2	BB	NC	....	....	G1	99.52	'94	1000	99½	99½	No Sale		A68	13.97
Banco Rio de la Plata .... Neg[2]Obligs	8¾s	2003	$jD15	BB–	NC	....	....	G1	99.85	'93	250	102⅛	68⅜	70	58	A62	17.88
Bank of China .... [22]Bonds[23]	8¼s	2014	$Ms15	BBB	NC	....	....	M6	99.70	'94	100	99⅝	87¼	100½	89¾	100½	8.19
Bank of China .... [22]Notes[23]	6¾s	1999	$Ms15	BBB	NC	....	....	M6	99.71	'94	400	99⅝	92¾	101½	92¾	101½	6.22
Bank of Montreal[24] .... Sub[25]Notes[26]	6.10s	2005	$mS15	A+	NC	....	....	M2	99¾	'93	300	99¾	82¼	98⅜	83¾	98⅜	6.32
Bank of Montreal[24] .... Sub[27]Notes	7.80s	2007	$Ao	A+	[28]*Z100	....	....	G1	99.33	'95	300	....	....	111⅛	99⅛	111⅛	6.40
Bank of Nova Scotia .... Sub[3]Deb[2]	6⅞s	2003	$Mn	A+	NC	....	Z100	G1	....	'93	250	93¾	89⅝	104	90⅛	104	6.19
Bank of Nova Scotia .... Sub[2]Deb[29]	6¼s	2008	$mS15	A+	NC	....	....	S1	99.45	'93	250	102	78¾	98¾	79⅞	98¾	6.39
Banque Paribas .... Sub[2]Notes	8.35s	2007	$Jd15	A–	NC	....	....	M2	100	'92	250	117¾	93¾	113½	95½	113½	6.65
Banque Paribus .... Sub[2]Notes[30]	6⅞s	2009	$Ms	A–	NC	....	....	M2	99.21	'94	300	99⅛	81⅜	99⅞	82½	99⅞	6.89
• Barclays N. Amer Capital .... [31]Gtd Cap Notes[2]	11⅝s	2003	$Mn	AA–	[32]100	....	....	G1	99½	'83	400	125	80	114	109	102⅛	11.19
Barclays N. Amer Capital .... [31]Gtd Cap Notes[2]	10½s	2017	$jD15	AA–	[33]104.929	....	....	S4	99.35	'87	400	128	96¾	114⅛	109⅜	113	9.12
Barclays N. Amer Capital .... [31]Gtd Cap Notes[2]	9¾s	2021	$Ms15	AA–	[34]104.725	....	....	G1	99.70	'91	500	126⅝	96⅜	120½	105½	120½	7.87

Uniform Footnote Explanations-See Page 260. Other: [1] Gtd by Abbey Nat'l plc. [2] Co may red in whole,at 100,for tax law chge. [3] Issued in min denom U.S.$100T. [4] A/K/A SKF AB. [5] Gtd by Alcan Aluminium Ltd. [6] Fr 3-15-98. [7] Co may reset int for certain events. [8] Co may red in whole at 100 if 90% outstg put. [9] (HRO)To 1-15-00 at 100 for certain events. [10] Fr 1-15-00. [11] Fr 1-15-02. [12] Terms chge for Designated Event&Rat'g Decline. [13] (HRO)For certain events at 100. [14] Fr 7-15-99. [15] Fr 7-15-00. [16] (HRO)On Chge of Ctrl at 101. [17] Incl disc. [18] Gtd by Amoco Corp & Amoco Co. [19] Fr 10-1-02. [20] Fr 9-1-03. [21] Also issued as registered ctfs. [22] (HRO)For a Redemp Event at 100. [23] Issued in min denom $5T. [24] Chicago Branch. [25] Issued in min denom U.S. $125T. [26] May red at 100 on int dates fr 3-15-99 for tax chge. [27] Issued in min denom U.S.$125T. [28] Fr 4-7-00. [29] Issued in min denom U.S. $100T. [30] Issued in min denom $100T. [31] Gtd by Barclays Bank PLC. [32] Fr 5-1-98. [33] Fr 12-15-97. [34] Fr 5-15-01.

Exchange ↓ BONDS Description, Interest Rate, Due and Interest Dates				S&P Debt Rating	Redemption Provisions Regular	For Sinking Fund	Refund Earliest/ Other	Underwriting Firm	Price	Year	Out-standing Mil-$ This Issue	Price Range 1983-1994 High	Low	1995 High	Low	Month End Price Sale(s) or Bid	Yield to Matur-ity
Bass America, Inc .... Gtd[2]Notes[3]	6¾s	1999	[1]$ms31	A+	NC	....	....	M6	99.78	'92	250	106¾	94¼	103¼	94⅛	103¼	5.73
Bass America, Inc .... Gtd[2]Notes[3]	8⅛s	2002	$Ms31	A+	NC	....	....	M6	99⅞	'92	350	115⅝	98⅛	111⅜	99	111⅜	5.92
Bass America, Inc .... Gtd[2]Notes[3]	6⅝s	2003	$Ms31	A+	NC	....	....	M5	99.97	'93	300	106⅜	88¾	103⅜	89¼	103⅜	6.04
Bayerische Landesbank(N.Y. Branch) ... Sub[3]Notes[4]	7⅜s	2002	$jD14	AAA	NC	....	....	M2	99.73	'92	250	111¾	94⅝	108½	95⅛	108½	5.87
BBV Int'l Finance Ltd........ Sub[5]Gtd[4]Notes[6]	6⅞s	2005	$jJ	A+	NC	....	....	L3	99.32	'95	150	....	....	102⅞	95⅜	102⅞	6.47
BCH Cayman Islands Ltd .... Sub[7]Gtd[3]Deb	7½s	2005	$Jd15	A–	NC	....	....	M6	99.12	'95	100	....	....	105⅜	97⅜	105⅜	6.72
BCH Cayman Islands Ltd .... Sub[7]Gtd[3]Notes	8¼s	2004	$Jd15	A–	NC	....	....	M6	99.26	'94	225	99¼	93½	109¾	94⅝	109¾	6.72
Bell Cablemedia plc .... Sr[8]Disc[3]Notes[9]	11.95s	2004	$jJ15	BB–	[10]104.48	....	....	S1	56.10	'94	[11]490	56⅝	50½	70⅞	53½	70⅞	Flat
Bell Tel Canada[12] .... Deb EL	7¾s	2006	$Ao	A+	NC	....	....	G1	99.66	'92	200	112½	94⅛	111⅛	94¾	111⅛	6.26
BET Icecalm B.V. .... Gtd[13]Notes[3]	8⅝s	2001	$aO15	A–	NC	....	....	M2	99.60	'91	200	115⅞	99	111⅞	99¾	111⅞	6.15
BHP Finance(USA)Ltd .... Gtd[14]Notes[3]	7s	1997	$jD	A	NC	....	....	M6	99.69	'92	250	106¼	96½	102⅛	96½	102⅛	5.81
BHP Finance(USA)Ltd .... Gtd[14]Notes[3]	5⅝s	2000	$mN	A	NC	....	....	M6	99¾	'93	300	99¾	87	98⅜	87⅛	98⅜	6.01
BHP Finance(USA)Ltd .... Gtd[14]Notes[3]	7⅞s	2002	$jD	A	NC	....	....	M6	99.22	'92	250	112¾	95⅝	108⅞	95⅝	108⅞	6.27
BHP Finance(USA)Ltd .... Gtd[14]Notes[3]	8½s	2012	$jD	A	NC	....	....	M6	99.67	'92	250	117⅛	95	118⅜	97⅝	118⅜	6.67
BHP Finance(USA)Ltd .... Gtd[14]Deb[3]	6¾s	2013	$mN	A	NC	....	....	M6	99.55	'93	200	99½	79⅛	100⅛	81⅝	100⅛	6.74
BP America .... [15]Gtd Deb[3]	8¾s	2003	$Fa	AA–	NC	....	Z100	M2	99¾	'91	350	121⅛	98	116¼	101¾	116¼	5.91
BP America .... [15]Gtd Deb[3]	9⅞s	2004	$Ms15	AA–	NC	....	Z100	G1	100	'89	250	130	98⅛	125	109½	125	5.98
BP America .... [15]Gtd Deb[3]	10s	2018	$jJ	AA–	[16]104.66	....	....	G1	99.32	'88	200	121¼	95⅞	114¾	109¼	114¾	8.52
BP America .... [15]Gtd Notes[3]	10.15s	1996	$Ms15	AA–	NC	....	....	G1	99.80	'89	200	114⅝	99⅞	103¼	100⅞	100⅞	5.79
BP America .... [15]Gtd Notes[3]	8⅞s	1997	$jD	AA–	NC	....	....	M6	99.56	'90	300	113¾	99½	106⅝	101⅞	106¼	5.40
BP America .... [15]Gtd Notes[3]	9½s	1998	$Jj	AA–	NC	....	....	G1	99.30	'88	250	116⅛	96⅜	108⅛	103	107¾	5.37
BP America .... [15]Gtd Notes[3]	9⅝s	2000	$mN	AA–	NC	....	....	G1	99.30	'90	350	122⅝	99¼	115⅜	104¾	115⅜	5.69
BP America .... [15]Gtd Notes[3]	8½s	2001	$Ao15	AA–	NC	....	....	S4	99.14	'91	200	118	96⅝	112½	100⅞	112½	5.73
• BP America .... [15]Gtd[3]Notes	7⅞s	2002	$Mn15	AA–	NC	....	....	M2	99.44	'92	450	114	97¼	109	97⅛	107½	6.42
BP North Amer Inc[17] .... [15]Gtd[3]Notes	9⅜s	1997	$Jd	AA–	Z100	....	....	S1	99.20	'87	250	107⅜	93⅞	105¼	102	105¼	5.48
British Col Hydro Pwr........ Bonds[18]EK	8⅝s	2006	$jD	AA+	101.75	....	....	F1	100	'76	175	114	60⅝	102¼	100	A100	8.62
British Col Hydro Pwr........ Bonds[18]FG	15s	2011	$Ao15	AA+	[19]±105.20	....	....	S1	99⅜	'81	250	148¼	96⅛	113⅜	107⅝	107⅝	13.78
British Col Hydro Pwr........ Bonds[18]FH	15½s	2011	$jJ15	AA+	[20]±106.64	....	....	S1	99.30	'81	250	150¾	98⅞	116¾	111⅝	111⅝	13.67
British Col Hydro Pwr........ Bonds FJ[18]	15½s	2011	$mN15	AA+	[21]±106.64	....	....	F1	99.05	'81	300	150⅞	99¼	119	114⅝	114⅝	13.26
British Col Hydro Pwr........ Bonds[18]FN	12½s	2013	$mS	AA+	[22]104	....	....	F1	98.65	'83	250	135	90⅛	121½	115¾	120⅛	10.04
British Col Hydro Pwr........ Bonds[18]FP	12½s	2014	$Jj15	AA+	[23]104.08	....	....	L3	....	'84	200	136⅛	85½	123¼	116¾	122⅛	9.85
British Col Mun Fin Auth .... SF Deb	8¾s	2001	$aO15	AA+	101.625	100	....	K2	100	'76	45.4	109⅞	64½	103	101½	A102	8.30
British Columbia (Prov of) ... Bonds Ser BCUSD-1	7s	2003	$Jj15	AA+	NC	....	....	L3	99.26	'93	500	109⅞	92⅛	106½	93	106½	5.86
British Gas Finance .... [24]Gtd[3]Notes	8¾s	1998	$Ms15	AA–	NC	....	....	G1	99⅞	'88	200	113⅝	92¾	106⅝	101¼	106⅜	5.64
[25]British Telecom Fin........ Gtd[26]Notes[3]	9⅜s	1999	$Fa15	AAA	NC	....	....	G1	99.78	'89	300	119⅞	96½	110⅝	104	110¼	5.74
[25]British Telecom Fin........ Gtd[26]Deb[3]	9⅝s	2019	$Fa15	AAA	[27]104.7375	....	....	G1	99.85	'89	200	124⅜	94⅛	115	108¼	114¾	8.19
Canadian National Ry .... Deb	7⅝s	2023	$Mn15	BBB	NC	....	....	S1	98¾	'93	150	109⅜	84¾	109⅜	87¾	109⅜	6.86
Canadian National Ry .... Notes	6⅝s	2003	$Mn15	BBB	NC	....	....	S1	100	'93	150	105¼	87½	102	89	102	6.28
Canadian National Ry .... Notes	7s	2004	$Ms15	BBB	NC	....	....	S1	99.24	'94	300	99⅛	90	103¾	89¼	103¾	6.40
Canadian Pacific .... Deb	9.45s	2021	$fA	A–	NC	....	....	G1	99⅞	'91	250	122⅝	99⅞	130⅛	105⅜	130⅛	6.92
Canadian Pacific .... Deb	8.85s	2022	$Jd	A–	[28]104.335	....	....	G1	99.82	'92	250	116⅞	94⅛	118⅛	96¾	118⅛	7.29
Canadian Pacific .... Notes	6⅞s	2003	$Ao15	A–	NC	....	....	M2	100	'93	250	105¼	92	97⅛	90	97⅛	7.39
• Canadian Pacific .... Per Con Deb Stk	4s		$jj	A–	NC	....	....		....	'21	178	57¼	33	49¼	45	48⅛	....
Canadian Pacific Forest Prod........ Deb	10¼s	2003	$Jj15	BB	NC	....	....	G1	100	'93	75.0	110⅞	95½	107	95⅝	107	8.89
Canadian Reynolds Metals Co,Ltd[29] Gtd[30]Amort[31]Notes	6⅝s	2002	$jJ15	BBB+	NC	....	....	M2	99.48	'93	285	103⅝	87½	100½	88⅛	100½	....
Carter Holt Harvey Ltd........ Sr Deb[3]	8⅜s	2015	$Ao15	BBB+	NC	....	....	C5	99.85	'95	125	....	....	116⅛	99¾	116⅛	6.85
Carter Holt Harvey Ltd........ Sr Deb[3]	9½s	2024	$jD	BBB+	NC	....	....	C5	99.70	'94	150	102⅞	99⅝	132⅜	102¼	132⅜	6.90
Carter Holt Harvey Ltd........ Sr Notes[3]	7⅝s	2002	$Ao15	BBB+	NC	....	....	C5	99.54	'95	150	....	....	107⅝	99⅜	107⅝	6.14
Carter Holt Harvey Ltd........ Sr Notes[3]	8⅞s	2004	$jD	BBB+	NC	....	....	C5	99⅜	'94	350	101⅛	99⅜	117	100½	117	6.35
CF CABLE TV Inc........ Sr[3]Sec[9]1st Priority Notes	9⅛s	2007	$jJ15	BBB–	[32]100	....	....	M2	100	'95	100	....	....	102¾	97½	102¾	8.74
CF CABLE TV INC........ Sr[3]Sec[9]2nd Priority Notes	11⅝s	2005	$Fa15	BB+	[33]105.8125	....	....	M2	100	'95	110	....	....	110	97	110	9.93

Uniform Footnote Explanations-See Page 260. Other: [1] Due 8-1-99. [2] Gtd by Bass PLC. [3] Co may red in whole,at 100,for tax law chge. [4] Issued in min denom $100T.
[5] Gtd by Banco Bilbao Vizcaya,S.A.,N.Y. Branch. [6] Fr 7-1-00 Co may red in whole,at 100,for tax chge. [7] Gtd by Banco Central Hispanoamericano,S.A.(N.Y.). [8] Int accrues at 11.95% fr 1-15-00.
[9] (HRO)On Chge of Ctrl at 101. [10] Fr 7-15-99. [11] Incl disc. [12] Subsid of Bell Canada Enterprises. [13] Gtd by BET PLC. [14] Gtd by Broken Hill Proprietary Co Ltd. [15] Subsid of & gtd by British Petroleum Co plc.
[16] Fr 7-1-98. [17] Now BP America Inc. [18] Invested SF,fds set aside. [19] Fr 4-15-96. [20] Fr 7-15-96. [21] Fr 11-15-96. [22] Fr 9-1-98. [23] Fr 1-15-99. [24] Gtd by British Gas plc. [25] Now BT USA Capital Corp.
[26] Gtd by British Telecom plc. [27] Fr 2-15-99. [28] Fr 6-1-02. [29] A/K/A Societe Canadienne de Metaux Reynolds,Lte. [30] Subsid of & gtd by Reynolds Metals Co. [31] Princ pyts:$200 prin amt due ea 7-15 '98-'02.
[32] Fr 7-15-05. [33] Fr 2-15-00.

Exchange ↓	BONDS Description	Interest Rate	Due	Interest Dates	S&P Debt Rating	Redemption Provisions: Regular	For Sinking Fund	Refund Earliest/ Other	Underwriting: Firm	Price	Year	Out-standing Mil-$ This Issue	Price Range 1983-1994: High	Low	1995: High	Low	Month End Price Sale(s) or Bid	Yield to Matur-ity
	Chevron Canada Finance Ltd ..... Gtd[1]Notes	5.60s	1998	$Ao	AA	NC	....	....	G1	99.93	'93	190	102½	92⅝	99½	92½	99½	5.83
	China (People's Republic) ..... Bonds	6½s	2004	$Fa17	BBB	NC	....	....	M2	99.41	'94	1000	99⅜	84¼	98⅜	83⅝	98⅜	6.76
	China Int'l Trust & Investment ..... [2]Bonds	6⅞s	2003	$fA	BBB	NC	....	....	G1	99.71	'93	250	104¾	87⅞	96¾	87½	96¾	7.44
	China Int'l Trust&Investment ..... Bonds[3]	9s	2006	$aO15	BBB	NC	....	....	M5	99.50	'94	200	99½	97	111⅝	98⅜	111⅝	7.41
	Colombia (Republic of) ..... Notes	8¾s	1999	$aO6	BBB−	NC	....	....	M2	99¾	'94	175	99¾	99¾	101¾	99	101¾	8.19
	Colombia (Republic of) ..... Notes	7¼s	2004	$Fa23	BBB−	NC	....	....	M2	99.20	'94	250	99⅛	89	94½	88	94⅜	8.21
	Commun Urb de Montreal ..... Deb[4]	9⅛s	2001	$Ms15	A+	NC	....	....	M2	99.38	'91	135	120¼	98⅞	112½	103⅜	112½	6.27
	Corporacion Andina de Fomento ..... Bonds	7⅜s	2000	$jJ21	BBB	NC	....	....	M2	99.89	'95	250	....	....	102⅜	99½	102⅜	6.76
	CRA Finance(USA)Ltd ..... [5]Gtd[6]Nts	6½s	2003	$jD	A+	NC	....	....	M6	99.85	'93	200	101	85⅝	101⅞	87⅛	101⅞	6.20
	CRA Finance(USA)Ltd ..... [5]Gtd[6]Nts	7⅛s	2013	$jD	A+	NC	....	....	M6	99.42	'93	100	99⅞	82½	104⅛	84⅞	104⅛	6.72
	CSR America, Inc ..... [6]Notes	6⅞s	2005	$jJ21	A	NC	....	....	M2	99.42	'95	250	....	....	103⅞	96¼	103⅞	6.33
	CSR Finance Ltd ..... [6]Notes[7]	7.70s	2025	$jJ21	A	NC	....	....	M2	99.61	'95	150	....	....	110	97⅛	110	6.90
•	Cuba (Republic of) ..... External	4½s	1977	§Jd30	NR	Default 12-31-60 int			Exch.	....	'38	44.4	55	9¼	55	35	A54	Flat
	Denmark (Kingdom of) ..... Bonds	7¾s	1996	$jD15	AA+	NC	....	....	S1	100	'86	300	109¼	85⅛	102⅝	99¼	102⅛	5.45
	Diamond Cable Commun PLC ..... Sr[8]Disc[9]Notes[10]	13¼s	2004	$mS30	B−	[11]107.125	....	[12]Z113.25	G1	52.61	'94	[13]285	52½	52½	70¼	64	70¼	Flat
	Doman Industries Ltd ..... Sr Notes[14]	8¾s	2004	$Ms15	BB−	[15]104.375	....	....	B5	100	'94	425	100	88	100	89	99⅞	8.77
	Dominion Textile(USA) ..... Gtd[16]Sr Nts[14]	8⅞s	2003	$mN	BB	[17]104.375	....	....	G1	99.51	'93	150	100¾	89¼	100¼	90¼	98¾	9.10
	Domtar Inc ..... Deb	11¼s	2017	$mS15	BB	±106.23	[18]100	[19]105.19	M6	99⅛	'87	150	117⅛	87	108¾	92½	106	10.54
	Domtar Inc ..... [20]Notes[6]	11¾s	1999	$Ms15	BB	NC	....	....	S1	100	'92	175	111	87	111½	102½	111⅜	7.68
	Domtar Inc ..... [21]Notes[22]	12s	2001	$Ao15	BB	NC	....	....		100	'93	175	113½	100	117¾	103	117⅝	7.86
	English China Clays Del Inc ..... Gtd[23]Notes[6]	7⅜s	2002	$aO	A+	NC	....	....	M2	100	'92	250	109	93	106¾	93¼	106¾	6.14
•	European Invest Bank ..... Notes	10⅛s	2000	$aO	AAA	NC	....	....	S4	99¼	'87	200	124	99¼	115¼	110	110⅛	7.55
•	European Invest Bank ..... Notes	8⅞s	2001	$Ms	AAA	NC	....	....	S1	99.91	'90	300	99⅞	97⅝	No Sale		100	8.87
•	European Invest Bank ..... Notes	9⅛s	2002	$Jd	AAA	NC	....	....	F1	99.32	'90	300	102½	99¼	No Sale		102½	8.61
	Export Development Corp ..... Notes	7⅜s	1997	$Fa	AA+	NC	....	....	S1	99.54	'87	150	108⅜	85⅛	102¼	98¾	102⅛	5.33
	Export Development Corp ..... Notes	8⅛s	1999	$fA10	AA+	NC	....	....	M2	99⅝	'89	200	114⅝	92⅜	108¼	100¼	108¼	5.57
•	Export-Import Bank,Japan ..... [24]Gtd Notes	7½s	1997	$Ms9	AAA	NC	....	....	S1	99.80	'87	100	105	86	No Sale		98	9.29
	Export-Import Bank,Japan ..... [24]Gtd Notes	10⅛s	1997	$aO28	AAA	NC	....	....	G1	99.45	'87	250	119½	98¼	109⅜	104⅞	108	5.46
	Export-Import Bank,Japan ..... [24]Gtd Notes	9s	1998	$Ao15	AAA	NC	....	....	M6	99.07	'88	150	116⅜	94¼	107½	102⅜	107½	5.47
	Export-Import Bank,Japan ..... [24]Gtd Notes	8.35s	1999	$jD	AAA	NC	....	....	D7	100	'89	150	116⅝	93⅜	109¼	100⅜	109¼	5.68
	Export-Import Bank,Korea ..... Bonds	9s	1998	$Mn	AA−	NC	....	....	S1	99½	'91	200	115	98½	107¼	99⅛	106⅞	5.81
	Export-Import Bank,Korea ..... Bonds	6½s	2000	$Mn15	AA−	NC	....	....	F1	99.55	'93	200	105¼	89⅞	101⅝	90¼	101⅝	6.07
	Fairfax Financial Hldgs ..... Notes	7¾s	2003	$jD15	BBB+	NC	....	....	M5	99.81	'93	100	99¾	93⅝	95½	92¾	94	8.81
	Farm Credit Corp ..... Notes	7½s	1996	$jD24	AA+	NC	....	....	G1	99⅜	'87	100	110¼	85⅝	102⅜	99¼	102	5.39
	Federal Industries Ltd ..... Sr[25]Notes[6]	10¼s	2000	$Jd15	B−	[26]103.42	....	....	C4	100	'93	100	103¾	94	102	92¼	96	11.42
•	Finland (Republic of) ..... Bonds	7.80s	1996	$jD15	AA−	NC	....	....	F1	100	'86	100	106	88	102	102	100	7.79
	Finland (Republic of) ..... Bonds	9⅝s	2028	$Ao	AA−	[27]104.31	....	....	M6	99	'88	200	121⅛	94	115⅛	102⅝	110	8.69
	Finland (Republic of) ..... Notes	6¾s	1997	$mN24	AA−	NC	....	....	M2	99.55	'92	3000	106	96⅜	102⅜	96⅜	102⅜	5.42
	Finland (Republic of) ..... Notes	7⅞s	2004	$jJ28	AA−	NC	....	....	M2	99.27	'94	1500	101	95⅞	112⅝	96⅜	112⅝	5.97
	Gearbulk Holding Ltd ..... Sr[28]Notes[6]	11¼s	2004	$jD	BB	[29]105.625	....	....		100	'94	175	100	100	107¾	100	106¾	10.08
•	GPA Delaware Inc ..... Gtd[30]Notes[31]	8¾s	1998	$jD15	CCC+	NC	....	....	M2	99.63	'91	500	100	54	94⅞	72⅛	s93¼	11.50
	Grand Metropolitan Investment ... Zero Cpn[33]Bonds[34]		2004	[32]	A+	NC	....	....	G1	46.55	'94	[13]1224	47⅞	45⅛	61⅝	46⅜	61⅝	6.13
	Grand Metropolitan Investment ..... Gtd[33]Deb[6]	9s	2011	$fA15	A+	NC	....	....	M6	99.17	'91	300	125¾	99⅛	123⅝	103¾	123⅝	6.56
	Grand Metropolitan Investment ..... Gtd[33]Deb[6]	8s	2022	$mS15	A+	NC	....	....	G1	99½	'92	300	116⅛	90⅝	113⅞	93⅜	113⅞	6.86
	Grand Metropolitan Investment ..... Gtd[33]Notes[6]	8⅛s	1996	$fA15	A+	NC	....	....	M6	99.94	'91	300	109⅛	99⅞	102⅜	100¼	101⅝	5.44
	Grand Metropolitan Investment ..... Gtd[33]Notes[6]	6½s	1999	$mS15	A+	NC	....	....	G1	100	'92	300	105⅝	92⅞	102⅜	92¾	102⅜	5.78
	Grand Metropolitan Investment ..... Gtd[33]Notes[6]	8⅝s	2001	$fA15	A+	NC	....	....	M6	99.70	'91	300	117⅛	99⅝	112¾	100¼	112¾	5.93
	Grand Metropolitan Investment ..... Gtd[33]Notes[6]	7⅛s	2004	$mS15	A+	NC	....	....	G1	100	'92	200	109	90¼	106¾	91½	106¾	6.11
	Grand Metropolitan Investment .. Gtd[33]Sr[6]Notes[35]	7.45s	2035	$Ao15	A+	NC	....	....	L3	100	'95	400	....	....	111½	92	111½	6.62
	Great Lakes Power Inc ..... Notes[6]	8.90s	1999	$jD	BBB−	NC	....	....	G1	99.80	'94	125	99¾	99⅛	108	99	108	6.55
	Great Lakes Power Inc ..... Notes[6]	9s	2004	$fA	BBB−	NC	....	....	G1	99.53	'94	175	100⅜	95¼	112⅜	96⅞	112⅜	7.05

Uniform Footnote Explanations-See Page 260. Other: [1] Gtd by Chevron Corp. [2] Issued in min denom U.S. $5T. [3] Issued in min denom U.S.$5T. [4] A/K/A Montreal Urban Community. [5] Gtd by CRA Ltd. [6] Co may red in whole,at 100,for tax law chge. [7] Gtd by CSR Ltd. [8] Int accrues at 13.25% fr 9-30-98. [9] (HRO)On Chge of Ctrl at 101(Accreted Val). [10] Co may red in whole at 100(Accreted Val)for tax chge. [11] Fr 9-30-99. [12] Accreted Val(%):Max $71M red w/proceeds stk sales. [13] Incl disc. [14] (HRO)On Chge of Ctrl at 101. [15] Fr 3-15-99. [16] Subsid of & gtd by Dominion Textile Inc. [17] Fr 11-1-98. [18] Fr 9-15-98. [19] Red rest'n(11.35%)to 9-15-97. [20] (HRO)At 101 for a Triggering Event. [21] Co may red,in whole,at 100 for tax law chge. [22] Co must offer repurch at 102 on Chge of Ctrl. [23] Gtd by English China Clays plc. [24] Gtd by Japan. [25] Co must offer repurch at 101 on Chge of Ctrl. [26] Fr 6-15-98. [27] Fr 4-1-98. [28] Co may offer repurch at 101 on Chge of Ctrl. [29] Fr 12-1-99. [30] Gtd by GPA Group plc. [31] Co may red in whole,at 100,for tax chge. [32] Due 1-6-04:payable in U.S.$. [33] Gtd by Grand Metropolitan PLC. [34] Red in whole for certain tax chge. [35] (HRO)On Chge of Ctrl at 100.

Exchange ↓ BONDS Description, Interest Rate, Due and Interest Dates	S&P Debt Rating	Redemption Provisions: Regular	For Sinking Fund	Refund Earliest/ Other	Underwriting: Firm	Price	Year	Out-standing Mil-$ This Issue	Price Range 1983-1994: High	Low	1995: High	Low	Month End Price Sale(s) or Bid	Yield to Matur-ity
Gulf Canada Resources Ltd Deb 9s 1999 $fA15	BB	NC	....	....	S1	98½	'89	125	107¼	88	101	92⅞	101	8.67
Gulf Canada Resources Ltd Sr[1]Sub Deb 9¼s 2004 $Jj	B+	[2]103.47	....	....	S1	99.37	'94	300	101⅝	88¼	103⅝	90⅜	103⅝	8.61
Hanson Overseas B.V. Gtd[3]Sr[1]Notes[4] 5½s 1996 $Jj15	A+	NC	....	....	F1	99.75	'93	500	102⅜	97⅝	100	97⅝	100	Mat.
Hanson Overseas B.V. Gtd[3]Sr[1]Notes[4] 7⅜s 2003 $Jj15	A+	NC	....	....	F1	99.47	'93	750	110⅛	93⅛	107¼	93⅞	107¼	6.09
Household Fin'l Corp Ltd Sr[5]Notes 6s 1998 $Jd30	A	NC	....	....	S1	99.57	'93	75.0	103½	94	100⅜	93¾	100⅜	5.84
Household Fin'l Corp Ltd Sr[5]Notes 7⅛s 1999 $Ao30	A	NC	....	....	L3	99.63	'94	125	99⅝	95½	103⅞	95⅜	103⅞	5.83
Household Fin'l Corp Ltd Sr Notes[5] 7.45s 2000 $Ao	A	NC	....	....	M6	99.82	'95	100	....	....	105⅝	99¾	105⅝	5.93
Household Int'l Neth B.V. [1]Sr[6]Notes[4] 6s 1999 $Ms15	A	NC	....	....	M6	99.59	'94	175	99½	91⅝	100¼	91⅝	100¼	5.91
Hydro-Quebec Deb[7]'FG' 13⅜s 2013 $Fa15	A+	[8]104.75	[9]Z100	....	F1	100	'83	89.4	139⅜	89⅛	121	116¾	119	10.90
Hydro-Quebec Deb[7]'FL' 13¼s 2013 $jD15	A+	[10]104.75	[9]Z100	....	F1	100	'83	137	138¾	88½	125⅝	118⅞	123¾	10.32
Hydro-Quebec Deb[11]'FU'[7] 11¾s 2012 $Fa	A+	NC	....	....	F1	99.60	'85	200	152¾	93	146⅞	122⅞	146⅞	6.88
Hydro-Quebec [12]Deb[13]'GF'[7] 8⅞s 2026 $Ms	A+	NC	....	....	F1	99.73	'86	250	124⅞	83½	121¾	96⅜	121¾	7.11
Hydro-Quebec [12]Deb[14]'GH'[7] 8¼s 2026 $Ao15	A+	NC	....	....	M2	99⅜	'86	250	117¼	78⅞	114⅛	90⅛	114⅛	7.11
Hydro-Quebec Deb[15]'GQ'[7] 8¼s 2027 $Jj15	A+	NC	....	....	M2	99.55	'87	250	117⅜	78⅜	114¼	90	114¼	7.11
Hydro-Quebec Deb[15]'GV'[7] 10.70s 2007 $aO15	A+	[16]100	....	....	F1	99.10	'87	250	119⅝	99	109⅛	105⅜	108	9.55
Hydro-Quebec Deb[15]'GW'[7] 9¾s 2018 $Jj15	A+	[17]100	....	....	M2	100	'88	250	130⅞	94⅞	117	103	117	8.08
Hydro-Quebec Deb[15]'HH'[7] 8½s 2029 $jD	A+	NC	....	....	F1	99.70	'89	500	120⅞	86¼	117¼	92¼	117¼	7.14
Hydro-Quebec Deb[15]'HK'[7] 9⅜s 2030 $Ao15	A+	NC	....	....	M2	99.87	'90	500	131¼	94	128⅜	101	128⅜	7.15
Hydro-Quebec Deb[7]'HQ' 9½s 2030 $mN15	A+	NC	....	....	F1	99.43	'90	500	135½	99⅜	130	102¼	130	7.15
Hydro-Quebec Deb[7]'HS' 9.40s 2021 $Fa	A+	NC	....	....	M2	99.17	'91	900	130	99	126⅞	102	126⅞	7.09
Hydro-Quebec Deb[7]'HY' 8.40s 2022 $Jj15	A+	NC	....	....	F1	99.27	'92	1000	118¼	91⅞	115⅞	92⅜	115⅞	7.06
Hydro-Quebec [18]Deb[19]'IM' 7s 2004 ©Jd	A+	NC	....	....	M2	98.34	'94	1000	102	82	94½	69.02	70.44	12.84
Hydro-Quebec Deb[7]'IF' 7⅜s 2003 $Fa	A+	NC	....	....	M2	100	'93	500	110¼	92⅝	106½	92½	106½	6.23
Hydro-Quebec Deb[7]'IF' 8s 2013 $Fa	A+	NC	....	....	M2	99.49	'93	1000	113¾	90¼	111⅜	90⅞	111⅜	6.86
Hydro-Quebec Deb[7]'IO'[20] 8.05s 2024 $jJ7	A+	NC	....	....	F1	100	'94	1000	100⅞	94¾	114⅛	95⅞	114⅛	6.91
ICI Wilmington Inc Gtd[21]Notes[1] 7⅝s 1997 $Ms15	A+	NC	....	....	M2	99.81	'92	225	108⅜	98½	102¾	98⅝	102½	5.45
ICI Wilmington Inc[22] Gtd[21]Notes[1] 9½s 2000 $mN15	A+	NC	....	....	G1	99.82	'90	300	117½	99	115⅜	104⅜	115⅜	5.83
ICI Wilmington Inc Gtd[21]Notes[1] 8¾s 2001 $Mn	A+	NC	....	....	M2	99.91	'91	250	117	95⅛	112¾	101⅛	112¾	5.93
ICI Wilmington Inc Gtd[21]Notes[1] 7½s 2002 $J15	A+	NC	....	....	G1	99¾	'92	200	112⅜	95⅜	107¾	95½	107¾	5.95
ICI North Amer [23]Gtd Deb 8⅞s 2006 $mN15	A+	NC	....	....	G1	100	'86	250	124¼	85⅛	121¼	101⅞	121¼	6.16
Imperial Oil Ltd SF Deb 8¾s 2019 $aO15	AA+	[24]103.7755	[25]100	....	F1	98.80	'89	222	124	87¾	110⅞	102⅛	110⅞	7.74
Imperial Oil Ltd Notes 8.30s 2001 $fA20	AA+	NC	....	....	M5	99.80	'91	200	117⅞	98⅞	111½	98¾	111½	5.87
Inco Ltd SF Deb[26] 9⅞s 2019 $Jd15	BBB–	[27]103.638	[28]100	[29]Z100	M6	97.40	'89	150	119⅛	89⅝	112	104	112	8.67
Inco Ltd Deb 9.60s 2022 $Jd15	BBB–	[30]104.80	....	....	M6	100	'92	187	117¼	96⅜	115⅜	98¾	115⅜	8.17
Indah Kiat Int'l Fin Co B.V. Gtd[31]Sec[1]Notes[32] 11⅜s 1999 $Jd15	BB	NC	....	....	M6	100	'94	150	102	98	104⅝	96½	103¼	10.23
Indah Kiat Int'l Fin Co B.V. Gtd[31]Sec[1]Notes[32] 11⅞s 2002 $Jd15	BB	NC	....	....	M6	100	'94	200	101¾	97	103½	94	101⅛	11.62
Indah Kiat Int'l Fin Co B.V. Gtd[31]Sec[1]Notes[32] 12½s 2006 $Jd15	BB	[33]106.25	....	....	M6	100	'94	150	102¼	96½	103½	94	99¼	12.63
• Inter-Amer Devel Bank Bonds 12¼s 2008 $jD15	AAA	NC	....	....	S1	99.30	'83	200	162¼	95¼	152.31	130.44	154.22	6.13
Inter-Amer Devel Bank Bonds[34] 8⅞s 2009 $Jd	AAA	NC	....	....	S1	99.45	'89	300	130.94	96⅝	127.53	105¾	127.53	5.88
Inter-Amer Devel Bank Bonds[35] 8.40s 2009 $mS	AAA	NC	....	....	M2	99.57	'89	300	125⅝	93⅜	120½	101¾	120½	6.16
• Inter-Amer Devel Bank Bonds 8½s 2011 $Ms15	AAA	NC	....	....	S1	99	'86	300	124⅞	82	119⅞	100⅝	122.16	6.22
• Inter-Amer Devel Bank Notes 7½s 1996 $jD15	AAA	NC	....	....	M2	99.85	'86	200	108.97	86	102.16	99.47	101.97	5.37
Inter-Amer Devel Bank Notes 9½s 1997 $aO15	AAA	NC	....	....	G1	99.56	'87	199	117.06	97½	107.41	103.22	106.69	5.53
Inter-Amer Devel Bank Notes 9.45s 1998 $mS15	AAA	NC	....	....	K2	99.82	'88	200	118¾	97¼	109½	103.47	109.22	5.72
Inter-Amer Devel Bank Notes 8½s 2001 $Mn	AAA	NC	....	....	G1	99.93	'91	300	119.94	97⅞	112⅜	101.28	112⅜	5.77
• Int'l Bank for Reconstr[36] Bonds 8⅛s 2001 $Ms	AAA	NC	....	....	M2	98.83	'91	1500	107⅝	96⅜	No Sale		111½	5.53
• Int'l Bank for Reconstr[36] Bonds 6¾s 2002 $Jj16	AAA	NC	....	....	M2	99.07	'92	1500	111⅛	93¼	No Sale		107¾	5.24
• Int'l Bank for Reconstr[36] Bonds 7⅝s 2023 $Jj19	AAA	NC	....	....	G1	99.49	'93	1250	99⅜	99⅜	No Sale		115.44	6.42
[37]Int'l Semi-Tech Microelectr Sr Sec[38]Disc[1]Notes[39] 11½s 2003 $fA15	B+	[40]103.29	....	....	K2	45.86	'93	[41]654	49½	43⅛	53⅜	42¼	52½	....
Ireland Bonds 8⅝s 2001 $Ao15	AA	NC	....	....	G1	99⅜	'91	200	119⅛	97⅛	112⅜	101¼	112⅜	5.87
Ireland Bonds 7⅞s 2001 $jD	AA	NC	....	....	M2	99.15	'91	200	115⅜	97½	109⅞	97⅜	109⅞	5.88

Uniform Footnote Explanations-See Page 260. Other: [1] Co may red in whole,at 100,for tax law chge. [2] Fr 1-16-99. [3] Gtd by Hanson PLC. [4] Issued in min denom $100T. [5] Gtd by Household Int'l. [6] Gtd by Household Intl. [7] Gtd by Quebec(Prov). [8] Fr 2-15-98. [9] Fr gen'l fds. [10] Fr 12-15-98. [11] Invested SF fr gen'l fds to 2-1-95. [12] Issued in min denom U.S. $5T. [13] Invested SF,fr gen'l fds ea Mar 1 to 2006. [14] Invested SF,fr gen'l fds ea Apr 15 to 2006. [15] Issued in min denom U.S.$5T. [16] Fr 10-15-97. [17] Fr 1-15-03. [18] May red in whole,at 100,for tax law chge. [19] Gtd by Quebec (Prov). [20] (HRO)On 7-7-06 at 100. [21] Gtd by Imperial Chemical Indus PLC. [22] Was ICI Financial. [23] Subsid of & gtd by Imperial Chemical Indus. [24] Fr 10-15-99. [25] Fr 10-15-00. [26] Terms chge for Designated Event&Rat'g Decline. [27] Fr 6-15-99. [28] Fr 6-15-00. [29] Co may red in whole if 90% of outstg are put. [30] Fr 6-15-02. [31] Gtd by P.T. Indah Kiat Pulp & Paper Corp. [32] (HRO)On Chge of Ctrl at 100. [33] Fr 6-15-01. [34] (HRO)On 6-1-99 at 100. [35] (HRO)On 9-1-99('04) at 100. [36] A/K/A World Bank. [37] Now Semi-Tech Corp. [38] Co may repurch at 101(Accreted Amt)on Chge of Ctrl. [39] Int accrues fr 8-15-00. [40] Fr 8-15-98,percent accreted amt. [41] Incl disc.

Exchange ↓ BONDS Description	Interest Rate	Due	Interest Dates	S&P Debt Rating	Redemption Provisions Regular	For Sinking Fund	Refund Earliest/ Other	Underwriting Firm	Price	Year	Out-standing Mil-$ This Issue	Price Range 1983-1994 High	Low	1995 High	Low	Month End Price Sale(s) or Bid	Yield to Matur-ity
Ireland .... Bonds	**7⅛s**	**2002**	**$jJ15**	**AA**	NC	....	....	L3	99	'92	300	109½	93¼	106½	93⅛	106½	5.91
Japan Fin for Muni Ent .... Gtd Bonds[1]	**9¼s**	**1998**	**$mS21**	**AAA**	NC	....	....	G1	99.36	'88	150	118	96½	109½	103¼	109⅜	5.50
Japan Fin for Muni Ent .... Gtd Bonds[1]	**9⅛s**	**2000**	**$Ms13**	**AAA**	NC	....	....	F1	99.71	'90	150	118¾	97	113	103½	113	5.61
Japan Fin for Muni Ent .... Gtd Bonds[1]	**9⅛s**	**2000**	**$aO11**	**AAA**	NC	....	....	M6	99.52	'90	150	121⅜	97⅞	114	104	114	5.73
Japan Fin for Muni Ent .... Gtd Bonds[1]	**8.70s**	**2001**	**$jJ30**	**AAA**	NC	....	....	G1	99⅞	'91	150	121⅛	99⅞	113⅞	102⅜	113⅞	5.76
Japan Fin for Muni Ent .... Gtd[1]Bonds	**7⅜s**	**2005**	**$Ao27**	**AAA**	NC	....	....	M2	99.95	'95	300	....	....	110⅞	99⅞	110⅞	5.84
Kansallis-Osake-Parkki .... Sub Notes[2]	**10s**	**2002**	**$Mn**	**BBB−**	NC	....	....	M5	99⅜	'92	200	124¼	99⅜	118⅝	105⅝	118⅝	6.38
KFW Int'l Finance .... [3]Gtd[4]Deb[2]	**8s**	**2010**	**$Fa15**	**AAA**	NC	....	....	M2	99.87	'95	250	....	....	113¾	99¾	113¾	6.50
KfW Int'l Finance .... [3]Gtd[4]Deb[2]	**7.20s**	**2014**	**$Ms15**	**AAA**	NC	....	....	M2	99.53	'94	250	99½	85⅞	109¼	88⅞	109¼	6.34
• KfW Int'l Finance .... [3]Gtd[4]Notes[2]	**9⅜s**	**1998**	**$jJ15**	**AAA**	NC	....	....	F1	100	'88	300	113¾	97	107⅝	107⅝	A107	6.35
KfW Int'l Finance .... [3]Gtd[4]Notes[2]	**8.85s**	**1999**	**$Jd15**	**AAA**	NC	....	....	F1	99.89	'89	200	118	95	109¾	102⅛	109¾	5.70
KfW Int'l Finance .... [3]Gtd[4]Notes[2]	**9½s**	**2000**	**$jD15**	**AAA**	NC	....	....	F1	99¾	'88	200	124⅝	95¾	116⅜	106	116⅜	5.67
KfW Int'l Finance .... [3]Gtd[4]Notes[2]	**9⅛s**	**2001**	**$Mn15**	**AAA**	NC	....	....	M6	100	'90	200	123⅛	99⅞	115½	104¼	115½	5.73
KfW Int'l Finance .... [3]Gtd[4]Notes[2]	**7⅝s**	**2004**	**$Fa15**	**AAA**	NC	....	....	M6	99.34	'92	200	114¾	94⅞	110⅞	96	110⅞	5.92
KfW Int'l Finance .... [3]Gtd[2]Notes[4]	**7s**	**2013**	**$Ms**	**AAA**	NC	....	....	M2	98.89	'93	250	107½	84⅜	107	87¼	107	6.32
Korea Development Bank .... Bonds	**9¼s**	**1998**	**$Jd15**	**AA−**	NC	....	....	M2	100	'91	250	115⅞	100	108⅛	101⅛	107½	5.93
Korea Development Bank .... Bonds	**7s**	**1999**	**$jJ15**	**AA−**	NC	....	....	M2	98.54	'92	300	107⅜	93¼	103½	94⅛	103½	5.89
Korea Development Bank .... Bonds	**8.65s**	**2000**	**$Jj26**	**AA−**	NC	....	....	C5	99.94	'95	500	....	....	109¾	99⅞	109¾	5.92
Korea Development Bank .... Bonds	**6¼s**	**2000**	**$Mn**	**AA−**	NC	....	....	S1	99.33	'93	300	103¾	89⅛	101⅛	89⅜	101⅛	5.95
Korea Development Bank .... Bonds[5]	**9.60s**	**2000**	**$jD**	**AA−**	NC	....	....	G1	99.90	'90	300	122⅜	99¼	115¼	103¼	115¼	5.98
Korea Development Bank .... Bonds[5]	**7.90s**	**2002**	**$Fa**	**AA−**	NC	....	....	M2	98.61	'92	500	112⅜	94¼	108	94¾	108	6.30
Korea Development Bank .... Bonds	**6¾s**	**2005**	**$jD**	**AA−**	NC	....	....	M2	99.62	'93	200	104⅜	83¼	102⅞	84⅜	102⅞	6.35
Korea Development Bank .... Notes	**5⅞s**	**1998**	**$jD**	**AA−**	NC	....	....	M2	99.87	'93	200	99⅞	90⅝	100	90⅝	100	5.87
Korea Development Bank .... Notes[6]	**8.09s**	**2004**	**$aO6**	**AA−**	NC	....	....	C5	100	'94	500	103	96¾	112⅛	94	112⅛	6.27
Korea Electric Power .... Deb[7]	**7¾s**	**2013**	**$Ao**	**AA−**	NC	....	....	L3	99.35	'93	350	111¼	83½	108¼	86	108¼	6.92
Korea Electric Power .... Notes[7]	**8s**	**2002**	**$jJ**	**AA−**	NC	....	....	L3	99.26	'92	300	113⅝	93¾	109¼	94	109¼	6.25
Korea Electric Power .... Notes[7]	**6⅜s**	**2003**	**$jD**	**AA−**	NC	....	....	L3	98.55	'93	1350	98½	83¼	100¼	84⅜	100¼	6.33
Korea Telecom .... Notes[2]	**7.40s**	**1999**	**$jD**	**AA−**	NC	....	....	S1	100	'92	100	107	93⅝	105¼	93½	105¼	5.88
• Landeskreditbank Baden-Wurt .... [2]Notes[8]	**7⅞s**	**2001**	**$aO15**	**AAA**	NC	....	....	M5	99.23	'91	200	103½	99⅛	No Sale		100	7.87
Landeskreditbank Baden-Wurt .... Sub Notes[2]	**7⅝s**	**2023**	**$Fa**	**AAA**	NC	....	....	S1	99.05	'93	300	112¼	87¾	113¼	90⅞	113¼	6.57
• Landeskreditbank Baden-Wurt .... Sub Notes[2]	**7⅞s**	**2004**	**$Ao15**	**AAA**	NC	....	....	M5	99.27	'92	250	99¼	99¼	No Sale		100	7.87
LASMO(USA) Inc .... Gtd[9]Notes[2]	**8⅜s**	**2023**	**$Jd**	**BBB**	[10]*103.9375	....	....	M2	99½	'93	150	112	87	106⅜	89⅜	106⅜	7.81
LASMO(USA) Inc .... Gtd[9]Notes[2]	**7⅛s**	**2003**	**$Jd**	**BBB**	NC	....	....	M2	99.13	'93	200	105⅞	88½	101¾	89⅜	101¾	6.82
Legrand S.A. .... [11]Deb[2]	**8½s**	**2025**	**$Fa15**	**A**	NC	....	Z100	M5	99.15	'95	400	....	....	120	99	120	6.90
MacMillan Bloedel(Del) .... Gtd[12]Deb	**8½s**	**2004**	**$Jj15**	**BBB**	NC	....	....	G1	99.85	'92	150	112¼	90¾	112⅛	97⅜	112⅛	6.54
Malaysia .... Bonds[5]	**9⅞s**	**2000**	**$mS27**	**A+**	NC	....	....	S1	99	'90	200	123⅛	99	116½	106½	116½	5.84
Manitoba (Prov of) .... Ser AZ[5]Deb[13]	**7¾s**	**2016**	**$jJ17**	**A+**	NC	....	....	S1	99.65	'86	150	116¼	86¼	112⅝	99⅞	112⅝	6.62
Manitoba (Prov of) .... Ser BM[5] Deb[14]	**9⅛s**	**2018**	**$Jj15**	**A+**	NC	....	....	M2	99.32	'88	200	130⅝	93⅛	127¾	108⅛	127¾	6.70
Manitoba (Prov of) .... Ser BT Deb	**9½s**	**1998**	**$mS15**	**A+**	NC	....	....	F1	99.60	'88	200	118¾	95⅞	110¼	103¾	109⅞	5.52
Manitoba (Prov of) .... Ser BU[5]Deb	**9⅝s**	**2018**	**$jD**	**A+**	NC	....	....	S1	99.08	'88	300	134⅞	96	134½	108½	134½	6.67
Manitoba (Prov of) .... Ser BW[5]Deb	**9⅝s**	**1999**	**$Ms15**	**A+**	NC	....	....	M2	99½	'89	250	120¼	97½	112⅛	104¼	111⅝	5.61
Manitoba (Prov of) .... Ser CB[5]Deb	**8.80s**	**2020**	**$Jj15**	**A+**	NC	....	....	F1	99.68	'90	250	125	87¾	125⅝	100⅝	125⅝	6.65
Manitoba (Prov of) .... Ser CD Deb	**9¼s**	**2020**	**$Ao**	**A+**	NC	....	....	S1	99.40	'90	300	130⅛	93⅜	131	104⅞	131	6.66
Manitoba (Prov of) .... Ser CJ Deb	**9½s**	**2000**	**$aO**	**A+**	NC	....	....	M2	99.73	'90	350	122⅞	99⅝	115⅜	105	115⅜	5.75
Manitoba (Prov of) .... Ser CK Deb	**9s**	**2000**	**$jD15**	**A+**	NC	....	....	F1	99.42	'90	250	120¾	99⅜	113¾	102¾	113¾	5.77
Manitoba (Prov of) .... Ser CN Deb	**8¾s**	**2001**	**$Mn15**	**A+**	NC	....	....	S1	99.55	'91	300	119⅜	98	113¼	101⅝	113¼	6.04
Manitoba (Prov of) .... Ser CO Deb	**8⅞s**	**2021**	**$mS15**	**A+**	NC	....	....	M2	99.62	'91	300	126½	98¾	126⅝	101⅜	126⅝	6.69
Manitoba (Prov of) .... Ser CQ Deb	**8s**	**2002**	**$Ao15**	**A+**	NC	....	....	S1	99.53	'92	300	115	97¾	110⅞	97¾	110⅞	5.90
Manitoba (Prov of) .... Ser CP Deb	**7¾s**	**2002**	**$Fa**	**A+**	NC	....	....	F1	99.93	'92	500	113⅛	96½	109¼	96½	109¼	5.92
Manitoba (Prov of) .... Ser CT Deb	**6⅞s**	**2002**	**$mS15**	**A+**	NC	....	....	M2	99.29	'92	300	107¼	90⅞	105⅛	91¼	105⅛	5.94
Manitoba (Prov of) .... Ser CU Deb	**6s**	**1997**	**$aO15**	**A+**	NC	....	....	F1	99.60	'92	250	104½	94¾	101⅛	94⅞	101⅛	5.33

Uniform Footnote Explanations-See Page 260. Other: [1] Gtd by Japan. [2] Co may red in whole,at 100,for tax law chge. [3] Gtd by Kreditanstalt fur Wiederaufbau. [4] (HRO)On or aft a Redemption Event at 100. [5] Issued in min denom U.S. $5T. [6] (HRO)On 10-6-99 at 100. [7] Co may red,in whole,at 100 for tax law chge. [8] (HRO)At 100 for a Redemption Event. [9] Gtd by LASMO plc. [10] Fr 6-1-03. [11] (HRO)On Chge of Ctrl at 100. [12] Gtd by MacMillan Bloedel Ltd. [13] (HRO)On 7-15-96 at 100,as defined. [14] (HRO)On 1-15-98,at 100,as defined.

Exchange ↓ BONDS Description	Interest Rate	Due	Interest Dates	S&P Debt Rating	Redemption Provisions Regular	For Sinking Fund	Refund Earliest/ Other	Underwriting Firm	Price	Year	Outstanding Mil-$ This Issue	Price Range 1983-1994 High	Low	1995 High	Low	Month End Price Sale(s) or Bid	Yield to Maturity
Manitoba (Prov of) .... Ser CZ Deb	6¾s	2003	$Ms	A+	NC	....	....	S1	100	'93	300	106⅜	89⅝	104¾	90¼	104¾	5.93
Manitoba (Prov of) .... Ser DH Deb	6⅛s	2004	$Jj19	A+	NC	....	....	C5	99.90	'94	350	99⅞	84¾	100¾	85⅝	100¾	6.01
Matsushita Elec Industrial .... Bonds[1]	7¼s	2002	$fA	AA	NC	....	....	L3	99.32	'92	1000	110⅜	93½	106⅞	94¼	106⅞	5.97
Methanex Corp .... Sr Sec 2nd Priority[2]Notes[1]	8⅞s	2001	$mN15	BBB+	[3]103	....	....	C5	99.30	'93	[4]275	104¾	95	106½	97¼	106½	7.48
• Mexico(Un.Mex'n S.of) .... Ext SF	8⅛s	1997	$jD	NR	±100.25	100	....	M2	99	'72	27.4	104	45	97	85	97	9.87
Midland Bank plc .... Sub[5]Notes[1]	8⅝s	2004	$jD15	A	NC	....	....	M5	99⅝	'94	400	99½	98⅞	115	98⅞	115	6.40
Nat'l Bank of Canada(N.Y. Branch).. Sub[1]Notes 'B'[6]	8⅛s	2004	$fA15	BBB+	NC	....	....	G1	99.98	'94	250	99⅞	95¼	111	96¼	111	6.44
National Bank of Hungary .... Bonds	8.80s	2002	$aO	BB+	NC	....	....	S1	97.62	'92	200	105½	97½	103	100	A102	8.40
National Bank of Hungary .... Bonds	7.95s	2003	$mN	BB+	NC	....	....	S1	99.84	'93	200	102	95⅝	100¼	96	A98	8.30
National Bank of Hungary .... Bonds	8⅞s	2013	$mN	BB+	NC	....	....	M6	100	'93	200	103½	97¾	104	99¾	A103	8.54
Nat'l Westminster Bancorp[7] .... [8]Gtd Cap Notes[1]	9⅜s	2003	$mN15	AA–	NC	....	....	M2	99.48	'88	500	124½	94	119¾	104¾	119¾	6.17
Nat'l Westminster Bank[9]PLC .... Sub[1]Notes	9.45s	2001	$Mn	AA–	NC	....	....	G1	100	'91	750	122¾	98¼	115⅝	104⅜	115⅝	5.98
• [10]NatWest Capital .... [8]Gtd Cap Notes[1]	12⅛s	2002	mN15	AA–	[11]100	....	....	M6	99⅝	'82	100	122	97½	No Sale		A112	9.69
New Brunswick (Prov of) .... Ser DM Deb	9½s	2018	$Ms3	AA–	[12]100	....	....	F1	99.80	'88	150	129	92⅛	116¾	103⅞	116¾	7.89
New Brunswick (Prov of) .... Ser DU Deb	9¾s	2020	$Mn15	AA–	NC	....	....	S1	98.85	'90	200	136⅛	96¼	137	110	137	6.66
New Brunswick (Prov of) .... Deb	7⅛s	2002	$aO	AA–	NC	....	....	S1	99.68	'92	225	109⅝	92½	106½	92½	106½	5.94
New Brunswick (Prov of) .... Deb[13]	7⅝s	2004	$Jd29	AA–	NC	....	....	F1	99.35	'94	200	99½	94	110⅝	94¾	110⅝	6.01
New Brunswick (Prov of) .... Deb	7⅝s	2013	$Fa15	AA–	NC	....	....	F1	99.85	'93	200	112¼	89	111¼	91¼	111¼	6.52
New Brunswick (Prov of) .... Deb[13]	8¾s	2022	$Mn	AA–	NC	....	....	F1	99.70	'92	200	125¼	97¾	126⅛	100⅛	126⅛	6.64
New Zealand (Govt) .... Notes[14]	8¼s	1996	$mS25	AA	NC	....	....	G1	99½	'86	100	110¼	87⅞	102¾	100⅛	101⅞	5.60
• New Zealand (Govt) .... Notes	10⅝s	2005	$mN15	AA	NC	....	....	F1	99.06	'85	200	115½	99	No Sale		A96	11.30
New Zealand (Govt) .... Notes[14]	8¾s	2006	$jD15	AA	NC	....	....	F1	100	'86	300	125¾	84⅜	122¼	102⅛	122¼	5.96
• New Zealand (Govt) .... Notes	9⅞s	2011	$Jj15	AA	NC	....	....	K2	99¼	'86	150	107	98	No Sale		A96	10.41
New Zealand (Govt) .... Notes	8¾s	2016	$Ao	AA	NC	....	....	M2	99.57	'86	200	126⅝	82	125¾	102	125¾	6.45
New Zealand (Govt) .... Notes[14]	9⅛s	2016	$mS25	AA	NC	....	....	G1	99	'86	150	131⅜	85⅞	129¾	105⅝	129¾	6.49
Newfoundland (Prov) .... SF[13]Deb	8½s	1996	$aO15	BBB+	NC	....	....	M2	99½	'86	100	109⅝	90⅛	102⅞	100¼	102⅛	5.71
Newfoundland (Prov) .... SF[13]Deb	11⅝s	2007	$aO15	BBB+	NC	....	....	M2	100	'87	100	147¾	100	140⅝	119½	140⅝	6.61
Newfoundland (Prov) .... SF[13]Deb	9⅞s	2020	$Jd	BBB+	NC	....	....	M2	99.76	'90	150	134⅜	95¼	132⅞	105¾	132⅞	7.04
Newfoundland (Prov) .... SF[13]Deb	10s	2020	$jD	BBB+	NC	....	....	M2	99.74	'90	150	136	99¾	134½	107	134½	7.04
Newfoundland (Prov) .... SF Deb[13]	9s	2021	$aO15	BBB+	NC	....	....	G1	100	'91	200	118¾	96¼	122¾	97¼	122¾	7.07
Newfoundland (Prov) .... SF[13]Deb	8.65s	2022	$aO22	BBB+	NC	....	....	M2	100	'92	200	119⅜	91⅞	117½	95½	117½	7.17
Newfoundland(Prov) .... SF[13]Deb	7.32s	2023	$aO	BBB+	NC	....	....	M2	100	'93	200	106	79⅝	103⅞	81	103⅞	7.00
News Amer Holdings Inc .... [1]Sr[15]Deb[16]	10⅛s	2012	$aO5	BBB	[17]104.50	....	....	M2	100	'92	290	123½	98¾	121⅝	104⅝	121⅜	7.82
News Amer Holdings Inc .... [16]Sr[1]Deb[15]	9¼s	2013	$Fa	BBB	NC	....	....	M2	99.24	'93	484	116	95	118½	97½	118½	7.33
News Amer Holdings Inc .... [16]Sr[15]Deb[1]	8¼s	2018	$FA10	BBB	NC	....	....	M2	100	'93	242	110	85¾	109⅛	87½	109⅛	7.41
News Amer Holdings Inc .... [16]Sr[1]Deb[15]	8⅞s	2023	$Ao26	BBB	NC	....	....	M2	98.09	'93	242	113	90⅛	119	92⅞	119	7.26
News Amer Holdings Inc .... [1]Sr[15]Deb[16]	7¾s	2024	$Jj20	BBB	NC	....	....	M2	100	'94	194	100½	79⅞	103¾	81⅛	103¾	7.43
News Amer Holding Inc .... [15]Sr[1]Deb[16]	9½s	2024	$jJ15	BBB	NC	....	....	M2	99.90	'94	194	100	98⅝	122¾	98	122¾	7.55
News Amer Holdings[16]Inc .... [1]Sr[18]Deb[15]	8½s	2025	$Fa23	BBB	NC	....	....	M2	100	'95	194	....	....	115¾	99⅞	115¾	7.20
News Amer Holding Inc .... [1]Sr[15]Deb[16]	8.45s	2034	$fA	BBB	NC	....	....	G1	100	'94	194	100	91¼	116¼	93⅜	116¼	7.20
News Amer Holdings Inc .... [15]Sr[1]Notes[16]	9⅛s	1999	$aO15	BBB	NC	....	....	M2	100	'92	532	114¾	98¾	110⅛	100¾	110⅛	6.09
News Amer Holdings Inc .... [16]Sr[1]Notes[15]	7½s	2000	$Ms	BBB	NC	....	....	M2	100	'93	484	106¼	94¼	104⅞	94	104⅞	6.15
News Amer Holdings Inc .... [16]Sr[1]Notes[15]	7.45s	2000[19]	$ms15	BBB	NC	....	....	C4	100	'93	97.0	105⅝	93½	104⅞	93½	104⅞	6.17
News Amer Holdings Inc .... Sr[16]Notes[1]	12s	2001	$jD15	BBB	[20]±106	....	....	M6	100	'91	387	122	99¾	113⅞	111⅜	111¾	9.38
News Amer Holdings Inc .... [16]Sr[1]Notes[15]	8⅝s	2003	$Fa	BBB	NC	....	....	M2	99.85	'93	484	110⅞	96½	111⅞	97⅜	111⅞	6.51
News Amer Holdings Inc .... [16]Sr[1]Notes[15]	8½s	2005	$Fa15	BBB	NC	....	....	M5	100	'93	484	113	94⅝	112¾	95⅜	112¾	6.62
Nippon Tel & Tel .... Notes[1]	9½s	1998	$jJ27	AAA	NC	....	....	G1	99½	'88	500	116¾	96½	109⅛	103⅝	109⅛	5.64
Noranda Inc .... F/R[21]Deb	5s	2000	$QAug18	BBB	NC	....	....	U1	100	'93	100	100	99½	101¾	99	101¼	....
• Noranda Inc .... Deb	8⅝s	2002	$jJ15	BBB	NC	....	....	G1	99.66	'92	200	99⅝	99⅝	105	101	105	7.64
Noranda Inc .... Deb	8s	2003	$Jd	BBB	NC	....	....	G1	100	'93	200	108	94⅞	109⅝	95¾	109⅝	6.35
Noranda Inc .... Deb	8⅛s	2004	$Jd15	BBB	NC	....	....	F1	99.90	'94	300	100¼	94⅝	111	95⅞	111	6.42

Uniform Footnote Explanations-See Page 260. Other: [1] Co may red in whole,at 100,for tax law chge. [2] Co must offer repurch at 101 on Chge of Ctrl. [3] Fr 11-15-98. [4] Defeased,fds deposited w/trustee. [5] Issued in min denom $150T. [6] Issued in min denom $100T. [7] Was NatWest Capital. [8] Gtd by Nat'l Westminster Bank PLC. [9] N.Y. Branch. [10] Now Nat'l Westminster Bancorp. [11] Fr 11-15-97. [12] Fr 3-3-03. [13] Invested SF,fds set aside. [14] Issued in min denom U.S. $5T. [15] (HRO)On Chge of Ctrl Triggering Event at 101. [16] Gtd by News Corp Ltd. [17] Fr 10-15-02. [18] (HRO)On 2-23-07 at 100. [19] Due 6-1-00. [20] Fr 12-15-96. [21] Int(min 5%)thru 8-15-95,adj qtrly aft.

Exchange ↓ BONDS Description	Interest Rate	Due	Interest Dates	S&P Debt Rating	Redemption Provisions: Regular	Redemption Provisions: For Sinking Fund	Redemption Provisions: Refund Earliest/ Other	Underwriting: Firm	Underwriting: Price	Underwriting: Year	Out-standing Mil-$ This Issue	Price Range 1983-1994: High	Price Range 1983-1994: Low	1995: High	1995: Low	Month End Price Sale(s) or Bid	Yield to Matur-ity
Noranda Forest Inc .... Deb	8⅞s	1999	$aO15	BBB	NC	....	....	F1	99.66	'92	100	111½	99	109½	100⅛	109½	6.03
Noranda Forest Inc .... Deb	7½s	2003	$jJ15	BBB	NC	....	....	F1	99.24	'93	150	104⅞	90¾	107⅛	91⅝	107⅛	6.30
• Nordiska[1]Inv'bken[2] .... Vari-Spr F/R[3]Notes	5.7733s	2004	$QDec27	AAA	*100	....	....	S1	100	'84	100	100½	99¾	No Sale		A100	....
Norsk Hydro a.s .... Deb[4]	9s	2012	$Ao15	A–	NC	....	....	G1	100	'92	350	122¾	99½	123	101⅞	123	6.66
Norsk Hydro a.s .... Deb[4]	7¾s	2023	$Jd15	A–	NC	....	....	M6	99.54	'93	300	110	85½	112⅛	88½	112⅛	6.77
Northern Telecom Ltd .... Notes	8¼s	1996	[5]$jd12	A	NC	....	....	S1	99.52	'91	221	109⅛	98⅞	102⅛	100⅝	101⅛	5.70
Northern Telecom Ltd .... Notes	8¾s	2001	$Jd12	A	NC	....	....	S1	99.56	'91	221	118½	98⅜	112½	101⅝	112½	6.03
Northern Telecom Ltd .... Notes	6⅞s	2002	$aO	A	NC	....	....	G1	100	'92	300	109⅛	90⅞	103⅞	91¼	103⅞	6.16
Northern Telecom Ltd .... Notes	6s	2003	$mS	A	NC	....	....	G1	99.51	'93	200	100⅞	84¼	98⅝	85⅛	98⅝	6.23
Northern Telecom Ltd .... Notes	6⅞s	2023	$mS	A	NC	....	....	G1	98.71	'93	200	100¾	78⅜	98⅝	80⅝	98⅝	6.99
NOVA Gas Transmission[6] .... Deb	8½s	2012	$jD15	A–	NC	....	....	G1	99.22	'92	175	117⅝	94	117¾	97¼	117¾	6.73
• NOVA Gas Transmission[6] .... Deb	7⅞s	2023	$Ao	A–	NC	....	....	G1	99.36	'93	200	109½	97⅛	No Sale		A86	9.29
NOVA Gas Transmission .... Notes	7¼s	1999	[7]$jj	A–	NC	....	....	M2	99.94	'94	150	100	95¼	104¼	95¼	104¼	5.89
NOVA Gas Transmission[6] .... Notes	7⅞s	2002	$jD15	A–	NC	....	....	G1	99.85	'92	125	112½	94⅛	109⅝	95	109⅝	6.15
NOVA Gas Transmission .... Notes	8½s	2004	$jD8	A–	NC	....	....	M6	99.74	'94	125	99⅝	97½	115½	97½	115½	6.21
Nova Scotia Pwr .... SF Deb	9.40s	2021	$Ao	A–	NC	....	....	M2	99.90	'91	300	131	97⅞	130¾	105	130¾	6.83
Nova Scotia (Prov) .... SF[8]Deb '8L'	11½s	2013	$Mn15	A–	[9]104.60	....	....	M2	100	'83	150	128	76¼	117¼	111⅝	116¼	9.56
Nova Scotia (Prov) .... SF[8] Deb '8V'	8⅞s	2016	$Ms15	A–	NC	....	....	M2	99¼	'86	150	122⅝	83¾	121	98⅞	121	6.93
Nova Scotia (Prov) .... SF[8]Deb '9B'	9½s	2019	$Fa	A–	NC	....	....	M2	99.90	'89	200	130½	94⅜	128⅜	104½	128⅜	7.00
Nova Scotia (Prov) .... SF[10]Deb[8] '9D'	8¼s	2019	$mN15	A–	NC	....	....	M2	99.78	'89	250	117⅞	83⅝	117⅜	98⅛	117⅜	6.77
Nova Scotia (Prov) .... SF Deb[11] '9E'	9¼s	2020	$Ms	A–	NC	....	....	M2	99.07	'90	300	129	92½	126	102	126	7.00
Nova Scotia (Prov) .... Deb '9F'	9⅜s	2002	$jJ15	A–	NC	....	....	M2	99.36	'90	300	123⅛	95⅜	117⅛	103⅞	117⅛	6.16
Nova Scotia (Prov) .... Deb[11] '9J'	9⅛s	2021	$Mn	A–	NC	....	....	M2	98.82	'91	300	126½	95¼	125	100⅞	125	7.00
Nova Scotia (Prov) .... Deb[11]	7¼s	2013	$jJ27	A–	NC	....	....	M2	98.96	'93	300	105⅛	82¾	104⅜	85⅜	104⅜	6.82
Nova Scotia (Prov) .... Deb[11]	8¾s	2022	$Ao	A–	NC	....	....	M2	98.30	'92	300	122¼	95¼	121	97⅛	121	6.99
Nova Scotia (Prov) .... Deb[11]	8¼s	2022	$jJ30	A–	NC	....	....	M2	98.20	'92	300	116⅜	90⅜	115¼	92¼	115¼	6.98
• NZI Capital .... Gtd[12]Notes	8¼s	1997	$Ms15	A–	NC	....	....	K2	99.26	'87	150	99¼	88½	99⅜	99⅜	100¼	8.01
Ontario (Prov) .... Bonds[13]	5.70s	1997	$aO	AA–	NC	....	....	G1	99.57	'92	2000	103⅛	94⅛	100⅝	94¼	100⅝	5.32
Ontario (Prov) .... Bonds[14]	7¾s	2002	$Jd4	AA–	NC	....	....	M5	99.49	'92	2000	113⅛	96	109¾	96	109¾	5.90
Ontario (Prov) .... Bonds[14]	8s	2003	©Ms11	AA–	NC	....	....	M2	98.45	'93	1500	108⅜	89⅝	103	87½	103	7.46
Ontario (Prov) .... Bonds[14]	7¾s	2003	©jD8	AA–	NC	....	....	M2	98⅛	'93	1250	110	89⅜	101⅝	94⅝	101⅝	7.48
Ontario (Prov) .... Bonds[14]	7⅝s	2004	$Jd22	AA–	NC	....	....	G1	99.86	'94	1000	99¾	94	110¼	94⅝	110¼	6.06
Ontario (Prov) .... Deb	15⅛s	2011	$Mn	AA–	[15]±105.78	....	....	S1	99.31	'81	175	151⅜	99⅛	114⅛	108⅝	108⅝	13.75
Ontario (Prov) .... Deb	17s	2011	$mN5	AA–	[16]±106.61	....	....	S1	99.53	'81	150	161⅞	114⅜	120⅞	115½	115½	14.47
Ontario (Prov) .... Deb	15¾s	2012	$Ms15	AA–	[17]106.30	....	....	S1	100	'82	196	154⅛	103¼	121⅛	117⅜	117⅜	13.13
Ontario (Prov) .... Deb	15¼s	2012	$fA31	AA–	[18]105.95	....	....	S1	99⅝	'82	96.9	151⅛	100¼	123¼	120	120¼	12.35
Ontario (Prov) .... Deb	11½s	2013	$Ms10	AA–	[19]104.30	....	....	S1	99¼	'83	100	130⅞	81⅜	116½	111¾	115½	9.63
Ontario (Prov) .... Deb	11¾s	2013	$Ao25	AA–	[20]104.70	....	....	S1	....	'83	100	131½	82¾	118⅛	113	116⅞	9.71
Ontario (Prov) .... Notes	8¼s	1996	$Ao8	AA–	NC	....	....	S1	99.96	'91	500	109	99	101¾	100½	100¾	5.38
Ontario (Prov) .... F/R[14]Notes[21]	3.56s	1999	$QAug17	AA–	NC	....	....	L3	99.60	'94	2000	100	99¼	99⅞	98⅝	99⅝	....
Ontario (Prov) .... Notes	8s	2001	$aO17	AA–	NC	....	....	M6	99.93	'91	750	115⅜	97¾	110⅜	97¾	110⅜	5.86
Ontario Hydro .... [4]Bonds[22]	8⅝s	2002	Fa6	AA–	NC	....	....	G1	....	'92	1500	112.64	94⅛	106¾	77.57	79⅛	13.79
Ottawa-Carlton(RegMunic) .... SF Deb	9⅜s	1996	$Jj	AA+	NC	100	....	M2	99½	'75	30.0	108⅞	68⅞	101⅝	100	100	Mat.
Pacific Dunlop USA Inc .... ([23]Gtd) Notes[4]	9¾s	2000	$jD15	A	NC	....	....	M2	99.80	'90	100	125⅛	99¼	116⅝	104¼	116⅝	5.84
• PDV America, Inc .... Sr[24]Notes[25]	7¼s	1998	$fA	BB–	NC	....	....	S1	99.59	'93	250	99½	99½	No Sale		85	14.38
• PDV America, Inc .... Sr[24]Notes[25]	7¾s	2000	$fA	BB–	NC	....	....	S1	100	'93	250	100	100	No Sale		88¾	10.93
• PDV America, Inc .... Sr[24]Notes[25]	7⅞s	2003	$fA	BB–	NC	....	....	S1	99.19	'93	500	99⅛	91	No Sale		85	10.82
Petro-Canada .... Deb	9¼s	2021	$aO15	BBB	NC	....	....	M6	100	'91	300	126⅛	100	126⅝	103⅛	126⅝	7.00
Petro-Canada .... Notes	8.60s	2001	$aO15	BBB	NC	....	....	M6	100	'91	300	117⅛	97⅝	111⅜	100⅜	111⅜	6.23
Petro-Canada(Ltd) .... ([26]Gtd) Deb	9½s	2003	$Jd30	AA+	NC	....	....	M6	100	'88	[27]96.4	130	95⅝	121⅝	107⅜	121⅝	5.89
Petro-Canada(Ltd) .... ([26]Gtd) Deb	8.60s	2010	$Jj15	AA+	NC	....	....	M6	100	'90	[27]158	123	90¾	119½	101¾	119½	6.47

Uniform Footnote Explanations-See Page 260. Other: [1] A/K/A Nordic Investment Bank. [2] (HRO)On int dates at 100. [3] Int thru 9-27-95,adj qtrly aft. [4] Co may red in whole,at 100,for tax law chge. [5] Due 6-13-96. [6] Was NOVA Corp of Alberta. [7] Due 7-6-99. [8] Invested SF. [9] Fr 5-15-98. [10] (HRO)On 11-15-01 at 100. [11] Invested SF,fds set aside. [12] Gtd by NZI Corp Ltd. [13] Red in whole,at 100,for Canadian tax chge. [14] Red in whole,at 100,for tax law chge. [15] Fr 5-1-96. [16] Fr 11-5-96. [17] Fr 3-15-97. [18] Fr 8-31-97. [19] Fr 3-10-98. [20] Fr 4-25-98. [21] Int to 5-17-94, adj qtrly aft for 3 Mo LIBOR. [22] Gtd by Ontario(Prov). [23] Gtd by Pacific Dunlop Ltd. [24] Gtd by Properyn B.V. & Petroleos de Venezuela, S.A. [25] (HRO)On Chge of Ctrl at 101. [26] Gtd by Canada. [27] Defeased,fds deposited w/trustee.

Exchange ↓ BONDS Description	Interest Rate	Due	Interest Dates	S&P Debt Rating	Redemption Provisions: Regular	Redemption Provisions: For Sinking Fund	Redemption Provisions: Refund Earliest/ Other	Underwriting: Firm	Underwriting: Price	Underwriting: Year	Out-standing Mil-$ This Issue	Price Range 1983-1994: High	Price Range 1983-1994: Low	1995: High	1995: Low	Month End Price Sale(s) or Bid	Yield to Matur-ity
Petro-Canada(Ltd) ([1]Gtd) Deb	8¼s	2016	$jD15	AA+	NC	....	....	M6	98⅛	'86	[2]38.2	123⅜	79⅞	120¼	98¼	120¼	6.47
Petro-Canada(Ltd) ([1]Gtd) Deb	9.70s	2018	$Jd30	AA+	NC	....	....	M6	100	'88	[2]16.1	142	96⅛	138	113	138	6.47
Petro-Canada(Ltd) ([1]Gtd)[3]Deb	8.80s	2019	$Jd	AA+	NC	....	....	M2	100	'89	[2]3.50	126⅜	95¾	126¾	103⅝	126¾	6.55
Philippine Long Distance Tel Notes	10⅝s	2004	$Jd2	BB–	NC	....	....	B9	99.48	'94	250	....	....	110	97¼	110	8.91
Philips Electronics NV Deb[4]	7¼s	2013	$fA15	BBB+	NC	....	....	G1	99.15	'93	250	102¼	82¾	104⅞	85¾	104⅞	6.77
Philips Electronics NV Notes[4]	6¾s	2003	$fA15	BBB+	NC	....	....	G1	99.72	'93	250	103⅜	87⅞	103½	89	103½	6.17
Philips Electronics NV Notes[4]	7¾s	2004	$Ao15	BBB+	NC	....	....	M5	100	'94	250	100	93⅞	109¾	94½	109¾	6.23
Philips Electronics N.V. Notes[4]	8⅜s	2006	$mS15	BBB+	NC	....	....	M6	99.58	'94	400	99½	96⅜	116⅛	97⅝	116⅛	6.28
Placer Dome Inc Notes	7⅛s	2003	$Mn15	BBB	NC	....	....	M5	99.81	'93	200	106½	89⅞	103¾	90¾	103¾	6.48
Plitt Theatres, Inc[5] Sr[4]Sub[6]Notes[7]	10⅞s	2004	$Jd15	B	[8]105.438	....	Z110	M6	100	'94	200	100	92½	100	90	90	12.85
Pohang Iron & Steel Co. Ltd Notes[4]	7½s	2002	$fA	A+	NC	....	....	G1	99.37	'92	250	109⅛	91⅜	106½	91⅝	106½	6.28
Pohang Iron & Steel Co. Ltd Notes[4]	6⅝s	2003	$jJ	A+	NC	....	....	S1	99.20	'93	200	103½	84½	101¾	85¼	101¾	6.33
Portugal (Republic of) Bonds	5¾s	2003	$aO8	NR	NC	....	....	M2	99.35	'93	1000	100⅝	82⅞	98¾	83¾	98¾	5.95
• P.T. ALatieF Freeport Fin B.V. Sr[4]Notes[9]	9¾s	2001	$Ao15	BBB–	NC	....	....	C5	99.90	'94	120	....	....	No Sale		100	9.74
Quebec (Prov) Deb[10]	9⅜s	1999	$Ao	A+	NC	....	....	F1	99.80	'89	250	118⅜	95¼	110⅝	102⅝	110¼	5.86
Quebec (Prov) Deb[10]	9⅛s	2000	$Ms	A+	NC	....	....	M2	99.85	'90	500	119⅞	96⅜	111½	102⅛	111½	5.97
Quebec (Prov) Deb	7½s	2002	$jJ15	A+	NC	....	....	M2	99.77	'92	750	111½	93½	107	93¼	107	6.18
Quebec (Prov) Deb	8.80s	2003	$Ao15	A+	NC	....	....	F1	99.69	'91	500	121	96⅞	114¾	100⅜	114¾	6.25
Quebec (Prov) Deb[11]	13¼s	2014	$mS15	A+	[12]104.50	....	....	M2	99.33	'84	150	141⅝	97⅜	128⅛	120¾	127⅝	9.96
Quebec (Prov) [10]Deb[11]	11s	2015	$Jd15	A+	[13]103.75	....	....	M2	99¾	'85	200	132¼	95¼	120½	111⅝	120½	8.78
Quebec (Prov) Deb[14]NJ	7½s	2023	$jJ15	A+	NC	....	....	F1	99.69	'93	1000	107½	82½	105⅜	83	105⅜	7.05
Quebec(Prov) Deb[15]NN	7⅛s	2024	$Fa	A+	NC	....	....	M2	99.48	'94	1000	99⅞	78⅝	100¾	79⅛	100¾	7.06
Quebec (Prov) Deb NS	8⅝s	2005	$Jj19	A+	NC	....	....	C5	99.30	'95	500	....	....	115½	97½	115½	6.35
Quebec (Prov) Deb[11]	8⅝s	2026	$jD	A+	NC	....	....	F1	99.60	'86	300	121⅛	82	118⅜	93¾	118⅜	7.14
Rainy River Forest Products Inc... Sr Sec[16]Notes[4]	10¾s	2001	$aO15	BB+	[17]101.79	....	....	S1	99.76	'94	110	99¾	99¾	110½	99¾	109¾	8.57
RBSG Capital Corp [18]Gtd Cap[4]Notes	10⅛s	2004	$Ms	A+	NC	....	....	M2	99¼	'89	250	129	96¼	124	108⅞	124	6.32
Repap New Brunswick Inc.. 1st Priority Sr Sec[6]Notes[4]	9⅞s	2000	$jJ15	BB–	NC	....	....	C5	100	'95	150	....	....	102	100	102	9.32
Repap New Brunswick Inc. 2nd Priority Sr Sec[6]Notes[4]	10⅝s	2005	$Ao15	B+	[19]103.984	[20]100	[21]Z110.625	C5	100	'95	350	....	....	106	100	106	9.63
• Rhone-Poulenc Notes[4]	6¾s	1999	$aO15	BBB	NC	....	[22]Z100	L3	99.34	'92	500	105	92½	100⅝	96	98⅝	7.17
• Rhone-Poulenc Notes[4]	7¾s	2002	$Jj15	BBB	NC	....	[22]Z100	B5	99.31	'92	500	109⅜	94	101	93	101¼	7.49
Saga Petroleum a.s. Deb[4]	9⅛s	2014	$jJ15	BBB+	NC	....	....	G1	99.93	'94	100	102¼	95¾	119⅝	98	119⅝	7.19
Saga Petroleum a.s. Notes[4]	8.40s	2004	$jJ15	BBB+	NC	....	....	G1	99.74	'94	100	101¼	95¾	110⅞	97⅛	110⅞	6.71
Santander Fin'l Issuances Ltd.. Sub[23]Gtd[4]Notes[24]	7⅞s	2005	$Ao15	A+	NC	....	....	M2	99.59	'95	300	....	....	110⅛	99½	110⅛	6.41
Saskatchewan (Prov) Deb	9⅜s	2020	$jD15	BBB+	NC	....	....	S1	99.33	'90	300	128⅜	96⅛	130¼	105⅛	130¼	6.83
Saskatchewan (Prov) Deb	9⅛s	2021	$Fa15	BBB+	NC	....	....	S1	99.13	'91	200	125⅞	96⅜	127⅜	102½	127⅜	6.83
Saskatchewan (Prov) Deb	8s	2013	$Fa	BBB+	NC	....	....	S1	98.33	'93	400	112⅞	91¼	113⅝	93⅜	113⅝	6.65
Saskatchewan (Prov) Deb	7⅜s	2013	$jJ15	BBB+	NC	....	....	S1	99.10	'93	300	106⅜	84¾	107¾	87¾	107¾	6.62
Saskatchewan (Prov) Deb	8½s	2022	$jJ15	BBB+	NC	....	....	S1	99.84	'92	300	119	93¾	120⅝	96½	120⅝	6.81
Saskatchewan (Prov) Notes	6⅝s	2003	$jJ15	BBB+	NC	....	....	S1	99.83	'93	200	103¾	88	103⅜	88⅝	103⅜	6.06
Shell Canada Ltd Notes	7⅜s	1999	$Jd	AA	NC	....	....	M2	99.74	'92	250	110⅜	97¼	105⅜	97⅛	105⅜	5.62
Shell Canada Ltd Notes	8⅞s	2001	$Jj14	AA	NC	....	....	G1	99.92	'91	300	119⅛	99¼	113¼	102⅝	113¼	5.80
[25]Sherritt Gordon Ltd [4]Notes[6]	9¾s	2003	$Ao	BB–	[26]104.875	....	....	G1	100	'93	200	104⅜	94	105¾	94¼	105¾	8.66
Sherritt Inc [4]Deb[6]	10½s	2014	$Ms31	BB–	[27]105.25	....	....	G1	100	'94	100	100	95¼	108¼	95	108	9.56
Sherritt Inc [4]Notes[6]	11s	2004	©Ms31	BB–	[28]105.50	....	....	G1	99½	'94	135	103	97⅝	108	97⅝	108	9.57
Sifto Canada Inc Sr[6]Sec[4]Notes[29]	8½s	2000	$jJ15	BB–	NC	....	[30]Z110	C1	100	'93	100	100½	90½	98	95	96¾	9.39
Singer Co N.V. Notes[4]	7s	2003	$Ao	BB+	NC	....	....	M2	99.55	'93	150	102⅝	84¾	97¾	85½	97¾	7.40
Skandinaviska Enskilda Banken ...... Sub[31]Notes[4]	8.45s	2002	$Mn15	BBB+	NC	....	....	G1	99.84	'92	400	115⅝	98¾	110¾	99⅛	110¾	6.37
Societe Nat'l Elf Aquitaine Notes[4]	7¾s	1999	$Mn	AA	NC	....	....	M2	99.80	'92	250	111½	97¾	105½	97¾	105½	5.91
Societe Nat'l Elf Aquitaine Notes[4]	8s	2001	$aO15	AA	NC	....	....	G1	99.66	'91	300	114	97⅜	110⅜	98½	110⅜	5.86
Spain (Kingdom of) Notes	9⅛s	2000	$fA	AA	NC	....	....	M6	100	'90	300	120⅝	99⅞	113½	103¾	113½	5.73
Stone-Consolidated Corp Sr[16]Sec[4]Notes	10¼s	2000	$jD15	BB+	[32]101.71	....	....	S1	100	'93	225	100	95½	107¼	97½	107	8.49

Uniform Footnote Explanations-See Page 260. Other: [1] Gtd by Canada. [2] Defeased,fds deposited w/trustee. [3] (HRO)On 6-1-04 at 100. [4] Co may red in whole,at 100,for tax law chge. [5] Gtd by Cineplex Odeon Corp. [6] Co must offer repurch at 101 on Chge of Ctrl. [7] Max $70M red w/proceeds of Pub Equity Off'g. [8] Fr 6-15-99. [9] Gtd by Freeport-McMoRan Copper & Gold Inc. [10] Issued in min denom U.S. $5T. [11] Invested SF,fds set aside. [12] Fr 9-15-99. [13] Fr 6-15-2000. [14] Invest SF,fds set aside. [15] Invested SF, funds set aside. [16] (HRO)On Chge of Ctrl Triggering Event at 101. [17] Fr 10-15-99. [18] Gtd by Royal Bank of Scotland Group plc. [19] Fr 4-15-00. [20] Fr 7-15-98. [21] Max $125M red w/proceeds of Pub Equity Off'g. [22] Mandatory,in whole,as defined. [23] Gtd by Banco Santander, S.A., N.Y. Branch. [24] Issued in min denom U.S.$100T. [25] Now Sherritt Inc. [26] Fr 4-1-98. [27] Fr 3-31-04. [28] Fr 3-31-99. [29] Gtd by Harris Chemical No. Amer. [30] Max $35M red w/proceeds of com Off'g. [31] Issued in min denom U.S. $100T. [32] Fr 12-15-98.

Exchange ↓ BONDS Description, Interest Rate, Due and Interest Dates				S&P Debt Rating	Redemption Provisions: Regular	For Sinking Fund	Refund Earliest/ Other	Underwriting: Firm	Price	Year	Out-standing Mil-$ This Issue	Price Range 1983-1994: High	Low	1995: High	Low	Month End Price Sale(s) or Bid	Yield to Matur-ity
Sunclipse, Inc .... Gtd[1]Notes[2]	6¾s	2003	$Jd15	A	NC	....	....	M6	99.45	'93	125	104⅜	89¼	103⅞	90	103⅞	6.10
Svenska Handelsbanken[3] .... Sub[2]Notes[4]	8.35s	2004	$jJ15	A	NC	....	....	M2	100	'92	400	117⅝	96⅞	112⅛	97⅜	112⅛	6.48
Svenska Handelsbanken[3] .... Sub[2]Notes[4]	8⅛s	2007	$fA15	A	NC	....	....	M2	98.90	'92	100	117⅝	93½	113¼	94½	113¼	6.48
• Sweden (Kingdom of) .... Bonds	12¾s	1997	$aO15	AA+	NC	....	....	S1	99¼	'82	100	132⅝	93⅝	111½	111½	107	8.44
• Sweden (Kingdom of) .... Bonds	12s	2010	$Fa	AA+	NC	....	....	S1	99.60	'85	123	136	99½	133	133	110	10.61
Sweden (Kingdom of) .... Bonds	11⅛s	2015	$Jd	AA+	NC	....	....	M2	Unit	'85	331	153⅜	98⅝	149	123⅜	149	6.61
Sweden (Kingdom of) .... Bonds	10¼s	2015	$mN	AA+	[5]100	....	....	M6	99⅜	'85	135	142¾	99⅜	134⅛	114¾	134⅛	7.03
Swedish Export Cr .... Deb	8¼s	2003	$Jj15	AA+	[6]103.665	....	....	L3	99.08	'93	150	112⅜	91½	111½	93¾	111½	6.21
Swedish Export Cr .... Deb	9⅞s	2038	$Ms15	AA+	[7]104.94	....	....	M2	100	'88	150	125⅛	92¼	117½	104⅞	111	8.87
Teck Corp .... Deb	8.70s	2002	$Mn	BBB	NC	....	....	G1	99.87	'92	125	114⅜	98	110¾	98⅜	110¾	6.59
• Telefonica de Argentina S.A. .... Notes[2]	11⅞s	2004	$mN	BB–	NC	....	....	S1	98.01	'94	300	99	92	105½	73¼	s104¾	11.01
• Terra Nova Insurance(UK)Hldgs plc ..... [2]Sr[9]Notes[10]	[8]10¾s	2005	$jJ	BB	[11]104.03	....	[12]Z109.75	D6	100	'95	100	....	....	100	100	A100	10.75
Thailand (Kingdom of) .... Bonds	8.70s	1999	$fA	A	NC	....	....	S1	100	'89	200	114¾	89½	108⅞	100½	108⅞	5.92
Thailand (Kingdom of) .... Bonds	8¼s	2002	$Ms15	A	NC	....	....	S1	99.67	'92	300	113⅝	98¼	110¾	98⅛	110¾	6.14
Tiphook Finance Corp .... [13]Notes[2]	7⅛s	1998	$Mn	CC	NC	....	....	L3	99.69	'93	119	103	65¾	83	70½	74	21.89
Tiphook Finance Corp .... [2]Notes[13]	8s	2000	$Ms15	CC	NC	....	....	L3	99.91	'93	209	104	58½	81	70	74	16.86
Tiphook Finance Corp .... [13]Notes[2]	10¾s	2002	$mN	CC	NC	....	....	S1	100	'92	89.5	118	60	86	71½	74	17.38
• Tokyo (Metropolis) .... Gtd[14]Bonds	7½s	1997	$Ms18	AAA	NC	....	....	F1	99.51	'87	100	108⅜	93	No Sale		100	7.49
• Tokyo (Metropolis) .... Gtd[14]Bonds	10⅜s	1997	$aO20	AAA	NC	....	....	F1	100	'87	150	109¼	100	107	105⅛	100	10.36
Tokyo (Metropolis) .... Gtd[14]Bonds	9¼s	1998	$aO11	AAA	NC	....	....	G1	99.87	'88	175	116	95½	108	103	108	6.08
Tokyo (Metropolis) .... Gtd[14]Bonds	8.70s	1999	$aO5	AAA	NC	....	....	G1	99.90	'89	175	117⅛	94⅝	110¼	102	110¼	5.64
Tokyo (Metropolis) .... Gtd[14]Bonds	9¼s	2000	$mN8	AAA	NC	....	....	F1	99.78	'90	200	122⅞	99¾	115	104¾	115	5.67
Tokyo (Metropolis) .... Gtd[14]Bonds	8.65s	2001	$jJ18	AAA	NC	....	....	G1	99.70	'91	200	120⅛	99¼	113¾	102¼	113¾	5.72
TOLMEX S.A. de C.V. .... [15]Gtd[2]Notes[16]	8⅜s	2003	$mN	BB	NC	....	....	G1	99.77	'93	250	105¾	81	85	35	80	12.44
Toronto-Dominion Bank .... F/R[2]Sub[17]Notes	5.9063s	2003	QAug4	AA–	NC	....	....	M6	100	'93	150	100⅛	98	100½	98⅜	99	....
Toronto-Dominion Bank .... Sub[18]Notes[2]	7⅞s	2004	$fA15	AA–	[19]■100	....	....	K2	99.90	'94	150	99⅞	93⅜	109	94⅜	109	6.49
Toronto-Dominion Bank .... Sub[18]Notes[2]	6.45s	2009	$Jj15	AA–	NC	....	[20]Z100	U1	99.85	'94	150	99¾	80⅜	100½	81½	100½	6.39
Toronto-Dominion Bank .... [18]Sub[2]Notes	6½s	2008	$fA15	AA–	NC	....	....	K2	99.72	'93	150	99⅝	81	101	82½	101	6.38
Toronto-Dominion Bank .... [2]Sub[18]Notes	6.15s	2008	$aO15	AA–	NC	....	....	M6	99.64	'93	150	99⅝	78⅜	97⅞	79¼	97⅞	6.39
TransCanada P.L. .... Deb	8⅝s	2012	$Mn15	A–	NC	....	....	M6	99.44	'92	200	120⅛	96¼	116½	98⅝	116½	6.92
TransCanada P.L. .... Deb	9⅞s	2021	$Jj	A–	NC	....	....	M6	99⅞	'91	400	136⅝	99⅞	137¼	109	137¼	6.77
TransCanada P.L. .... Deb	8½s	2023	$Ms20	A–	[21]104.138	....	....	M6	99.78	'92	200	118⅞	93⅛	114¾	95⅜	114¾	7.25
TransCanada P.L. .... Sub Deb	9⅛s	2006	$Ao20	BBB+	NC	....	....	M6	99.07	'91	200	124	95⅝	120¼	103	120¼	6.41
• Transportacion Maritima Mex .... [16]Notes[2]	8½s	2000	$aO15	BB–	NC	....	....	B5	99.35	'93	150	101	85½	90⅞	62½	89	11.54
• Transportacion Maritima Mex .... [16]Notes[2]	9¼s	2003	$Mn15	BB–	[22]104.625	....	....	B5	99.77	'93	200	102	89	90	60	89½	11.39
• Trizec Finance Ltd .... Sr[23]Notes[2]	10⅞s	2005	$aO15	BB–	[24]105.438	....	[25]Z109	G1	99.25	'95	250	....	....	104½	99¼	s104¼	10.17
Twinpak Inc .... Gtd[1]Notes[2]	6⅜s	2000	$Jd15	A	NC	....	....	M6	99.71	'93	75.0	101⅛	85	94½	89	A94	8.00
Union Bank of Finland Ltd[26] .... [18]Notes[2]	5¼s	1996	$Jd15	BBB	NC	....	....	F1	99.74	'93	200	100¾	96⅛	99⅞	96⅛	99⅞	5.52
United Mexican States .... Notes	8½s	2002	$mS15	BB	NC	....	....	G1	99¾	'92	250	107¼	80	89	46	85¾	11.61
Victorian Pub Auth Fin Agy .... [27]Gtd[28]Bonds	9½s	1998	$jD	AA	NC	....	....	M6	99.70	'88	150	119	96⅜	110⅜	104⅛	109¾	5.82
Victorian Pub Auth Fin Agy .... [27]Gtd[28]Bonds[29]	9½s	1999	$Fa	AA	NC	....	....	S1	99⅞	'89	200	119¼	96¼	110¾	104⅛	110¼	5.82
Victorian Pub Auth Fin Agy .... [27]Gtd[28]Bonds[29]	8.45s	2001	$aO	AA	NC	....	....	S1	99.93	'91	350	117¾	99⅞	112⅞	100½	112⅞	5.78
Videotron Ltee .... Sr Sub[2]Notes[30]	10¼s	2002	$aO15	BB+	[31]105	....	....	C4	100	'92	150	111	97¼	106	97¾	105	9.24
Westpac Banking Corp .... Sub[4]Deb[2]	9⅛s	2001	$fA15	A	NC	....	....	F1	99.60	'89	400	119¼	86⅞	114	102	114	6.14
Westpac Banking Corp .... Sub[4]Deb[2]	7⅞s	2002	$aO15	A	NC	....	....	F1	99.26	'92	350	111¾	95⅛	109⅛	95	109⅛	6.21
Wharf Capital Int'l(1994)Ltd .... Gtd[32]Notes[2]	8⅞s	2004	$mN	A	NC	....	....	M6	98.16	'94	200	98⅛	98⅛	101	98⅛	A101	8.71
Wilrig AS .... Sr Sec[2]Notes[16]	11¼s	2004	$Ms15	B	[33]105.625	....	....	S1	100	'94	110	103	100	109¼	103	109¼	9.59
WMC Finance(USA)Ltd .... Gtd[34]Notes[2]	6½s	2003	$mN15	A	NC	....	....	G1	99.78	'93	250	99¾	87⅜	102	87⅜	102	6.17
WMC Finance(USA)Ltd .... Gtd[34]Deb[2]	7¼s	2013	$mN15	A	NC	....	....	G1	99.68	'93	150	99⅝	82⅝	104⅛	84⅛	104⅛	6.85
YPF Sociedad Anonima .... [35]Negotiable[2]Oblig[36]	8s	2004	$Fa15	BB–	NC	....	....	C5	99.77	'94	350	99¾	93	100	94	A100	8.00
Zeneca Wilmington Inc .... Gtd[2]Deb[37]	7s	2023	$mN15	A+	NC	....	....	G1	99.10	'93	300	99	80⅜	104⅛	82¾	104⅛	6.67

Uniform Footnote Explanations-See Page 260. Other: [1] Gtd by Amcor Ltd. [2] Co may red in whole,at 100,for tax law chge. [3] N.Y. Branch. [4] Issued in min denom U.S. $100T. [5] Fr 11-1-2010. [6] Fr 1-15-03. [7] Fr 3-15-98. [8] Int may incr to 11.25% fr 7-1-97 for certain events. [9] Co must offer repurch at 101 on Chge of Ctrl. [10] Gtd by Terra Nova(Bermuda)Hldgs Ltd. [11] Fr 7-1-00. [12] Max $35M red w/proceeds of Cap Stk Off'g. [13] Gtd by Tiphook plc. [14] Gtd by Japan. [15] Gtd by Empresas Tolteca & Cegusa SA. [16] (HRO)On Chge of Ctrl at 101. [17] Int(min 4.10%)to 2-4-96,adj qtrly aft. [18] Issued in min denom $100T. [19] Fr 8-15-99. [20] Fr 1-24-99,under certain conditions. [21] Fr 9-20-02. [22] Fr 5-15-98. [23] Gtd by Trizec Corp Ltd. [24] Fr 10-15-00. [25] Max $82.5M red w/proceeds of Pub Equity Off'g. [26] Subsid of Unitas Ltd. [27] Issued in min denom U.S. $5T. [28] Gtd by gov't of Victoria,Australia. [29] Red in whole,at 100,for tax law chge. [30] (HRO)On Chge of Ctrl Triggering Event at 101. [31] Fr 10-15-97. [32] Gtd by Wharf(Hldgs)Ltd. [33] Fr 3-15-99. [34] Gtd by Western Mining Corp Hldg Ltd. [35] Issued in min denom $10T. [36] (HRO)On Chge of Ctrl at 100. [37] Gtd by Zeneca Group.

Selected Municipal Ratings

Every month the S&P Bond Guide brings you a special section on Municipal Bond Ratings. This is merely a sampling of what can be found in STANDARD & POOR'S MUNICIPAL RATINGS HANDBOOK. The MUNICIPAL RATINGS HANDBOOK has over 1,100 pages of carefully compiled, researched and analyzed findings. You'll find Credit Ratings and supporting statistics on almost 50,000 bonds and notes rated by Standard & Poor's Municipal Finance department.

The Municipal Ratings Handbook is organized by state and by type of debt within each state, so you can go straight to the issuers, the issues, and the information you need in seconds. The Municipal Ratings Handbook also contains special sections to help you find the bond information necessary to help you to make your investment decisions:

— Rating Changes — all ratings changed since the last issue, complete with previous rating and date of rating change
— CreditWatch® Tables — all Municipal Bonds, Notes and IRB's placed on or removed from Standard & Poor's CreditWatch in the past two months
— Selected Issuer Index — providing quick rating information on the 200 most frequent issuers

For more information call (212)208-1527, or write Standard & Poor's 25 Broadway, P.O. Box 992, New York, NY, 10275

*Continuance of the rating contingent upon S&Ps receipt of an executed copy of the escrow agreement or closing documentation confirming investment and cash flows

ALABAMA .... **AA**

Alabama Hsg Fin Auth
Sin Fam Mtg Rev Bnds Ser 82 A .... **AA-**
Sin Fam Mtg Rev Bnds Ser 82 B .... **AA-**
Sin Fam Mtg Rev Bnds Ser 83 A .... **AA**
Sin Fam Mtg Rev Bnds Ser 83 B .... **AA**
Sin Fam Mtg Rev Bnds Ser 84 A .... **AA**
Sin Fam Mtg Ser 84 B ...... **AA**

ALASKA .... **AA**

Alaska Hsg Fin Corp
Collat Home Mtg Bnds Ser 86 A .... **AAA**
Collat Home Mtg Ser 85 B . **AAA**
Home Mtg Ser 83-2 .... **AA**
Hsg Mtg Ser 72 A 73 A B 75 A B .... **AA**
Secd Bnds Ser 86 A .... **AAA**
Secd Bnds Ser 86 B & Med-T Nts Ser 86-1 ...... **AAA**
Secd Bnds Ser 86 C & Med-T Nts Ser 86-2 ...... **AAA**
Secd Bnds Ser 86 D & Med-T Mts Taxable Ser 86-3 .. **AAA**
St Gtd Vet Mtg Prog Ser 83-1 .... **AA**
St Gtd Vet Mtg Prog Ser 83-2 .... **AA**
St Gtd Vet Mtg Prog Ser 83-3 .... **AA**
Alaska St Hsg Auth
(Chinook Apts) FHA Ins Mtg Ser 83 A .... **AAA**
(Coho Pk) FHA Ins Mtg Ser 82 A .... **AAA**
Alaska Hsg Fin Corp
Ins Mtg Prog .... **A+**
North Slope Boro .... **A-**

ARIZONA .... **AA**

Arizona Dept of Transp
(Hwy Imp Proj) Ser 80 82 86 87 90 93 .... **AAA**
Phoenix .... **AA+**
Phoenix Civ Plaza Bldg Corp Ser 86 87 89 91 94 ... **AA+**
Phoenix
Str & Hwy Sr Lien .... **AA**
Wtr Rfdg Ser 86 88 93 ...... **AA**
(Phoenix Aviation Dept) Arpt Imp Ser 65 79 84 94 A-D .... **A+**
Phoenix Civ Imp Corp (Phoenix) .... **AA+**
Salt River Elec Sys .... **AA**
Valley Hsg Dev Corp
FHA Ins Ser 79 .... **A-**

ARKANSAS .... **AA**

Arkansas Dev Fin Auth
(Pines & Terr Apt) Rehab Bnd Fund Ser 85 A .... **AA-**
Econ Dev (Taxable) Ser 87 A C 90 A NT 92 A NT 92 A B D 93 A .... **A-**
Multifam Mtg Purch Prog Bnd Fund Rfd Ser 82 ..... **AAA**
Sin Fam Mtg Purch Prog FHA/VA Bnd Fund Ser 78 A ..... **AA**
Sin Fam Mtg Replacement Bnd Fund Ser 87 A .... **A+**
Sin Fam Replacement Mtg Ser 87 B .... **A+/NR**
Sin Fam Resid Mtg Ser 84 A A-1 .... **A+/NR**
Arkansas Std Ln Auth Rfd Ser 78 .... **NR**

CALIFORNIA .... **A**

California Dept of Vet
Affairs Home Purch Ser 84 A 85 A 86 A 88 A 91 ...... **A+**
California Hsg Fin Agy
Homeownership & Home Imp Rev Bnds Ser 91 A ..... **A+**
Homeownership Mtg Bnds Ser 85 A5 A .... **AA**
Multi Unit Rent Hsg Rev Bnds Ser 79 A 80 A 92 A 93 A 94 A B .... **A+**
Multi-Unit Rent Hsg II Ser 84 A 85 A 92 A-C .... **A+**
Multifam Rev Bnds Ser 79 A B .... **AA**
Sin Fam Mtg Purch Prog Bnds Ser 76 A .... **AA**
California St Military Dept
Natl Guard Home Purch Ser 80 A 83 A .... **A+**
California Hsg Fin
Agy Home Mtg Fha .... **AA-**
Inglewood-Los Angeles Cnty Civ Ctr Hlth Fac Auth Rev 72 .. **BBB**
Los Angeles .... **AA**
Los Angeles Cnty .... **A-**
Los Angeles Cnty (Adams & Grand Complex Inc) ..... **BBB**
Los Angeles Cnty Martin Luther King Jr Gen Hosp
Auth (Psychiatric & Clin Sciences Fac) Ser 78..... **BBB**
Auth (Supplement III) ...... **BBB**
Los Angeles Cnty Pico Rivera Pub Fac Auth (Sheriffs Stn) .... **BBB**
Los Angeles Cnty-Frank G Bonelli Regl Cnty Pk & Recre Area Auth (North Shore & Phase III) .... **BBB**
Los Angeles Cnty-Frank G Bonelli Regl Cnty Pk & Recre Area Auth (Puddingstone Swimpk) .... **BBB**
Los Angeles Dept of Wtr & Pwr
Elec .... **AA-**
Ser 1964-1994 .... **AA**
Sacramento Mun Util Dist
Elec Ser P-S V-W 93 F .... **A-**
Rfdg Subord Elec Ser 85 .. **BBB+**
San Diego .... **AA+**
San Francisco Arpts
Com Ser B D E .... **NR**
San Francisco Port
Com Ser A-C .... **BBB+**
San Francisco Pub
Util Com Ser 87 91 .... **AA**
San Francisco St Bldg Auth
Cert of Part Dtd 5-1-86 .... **A-**
San Francisco Stad
Recre Ctr Inc Lse Ser A ...... **A-**
San Francisco Bay Area Rapid Transit Dist........... **AA-**
San Francisco City & Cnty ... **AA-**

COLORADO .... **NR**

Colorado Hsg Fin Auth
Sin Fam Mtg Rev Bnds Ser 83 B C .... **A+**
Sin Fam Mtg Ser 84 A Tender Opt Term Due 95 .... **A+**
Sin Fam Hsg Ser 78 A 80 A B 91 A 95 A .... **AA+**
Multifam FHA Ins Mtg .... **AA**

Colorado (Continued)
Denver City & Cnty .... **AA**
Arpt........................ **BBB**
Moffat Cnty (Tri-State Generating & Transmission Assn) Poll Ctl .... **A**
Platte River Pwr Auth Elec Ser D H .... **AA**

CONNECTICUT.............. **AA-**

Connecticut Hsg Comr FNMA Multifam Ser 85..... **AAA**
Connecticut Resource Recov Auth (Greater Bridgeport Sys)Rfd......... **AAA**
Connecticut Hsg Fin Auth Hsg Mtg Fin Prog........... **AA**

DELAWARE................. **AA+**

Delaware Dept of Comnty Affairs & Econ Dev
(Free Flow Packaging Corp)............ **AA+**
(Rodel Inc)...................... **AA+**
Delaware Econ Dev Auth (Valley Stream Apts) GNMA Multifam Ser 85 .... **AAA**
Delaware Econ Dev Com (Chestnut Crossing Apts) Multifam GNMA Collat Ser 85 Dtd 6-1-85 ... **AAA**
Delaware St Hsg Auth Multifam Mtg Ser 79 87 A..... **A+**
Delaware Dept of Comnty Affairs & Econ Dev (Delaware) .... **AA+**

DISTRICT OF COLUMBIA..... **B**

Hsg Fin Agy (Parcel 13 Apts) Pooled FHA Ins & Co-Ins Multifamser 85 C .. **AAA**
(Southern Hills Apts.) Pooled FHA Ins Ser 1985A....... **AAA**
National Rur Util Coop Fin Corp Collat TR.......... **AA**

FLORIDA.................... **AA**

Dade Cnty .... **A+**
Florida Brd of Ed Cap Outlay Ser 74 A 75 A B 76 A 77 A 78 A 79 A 80 A 86 A 88 A 90A 91 A ...... **AA+**
Florida Brd of Ed Pub Ed Ser A-1 A-2 Ser B-1 B-2 .... **AA**
Florida Div of Bnd Fin Madison Cnty Rd .... **AA**
Florida Hsg Fin Agy
FHA Ins Multifam Mtg Rfd Ser 82 B.......... **NR**
Resid Mtg Ser 83-1 Inclusive of 2002 & 2016 Maturities .. **AA**
Resid Mtg Ser 84-I Due 2016 .... **AA**
Sin Fam Mtg Ser 85 A 86 A 93 A-C 94 A B ...... **AAA**
Florida Mun Pwr Agy (St Lucie Proj) Ser 92 Dtd 7-15-92 Due 10-1-93-2007 2012 2016 2021 ..... **AAA**
Florida Dept of Nat Resources (Save Our Coast) Ser A C-J 93 A Due 2012..... **A**
Jacksonville Elec Auth
Rfd Ser 56 60 63 67 71 73 .... **AAA**
Rfd Ser 56 60 63 67 71 73.. **AA**
Miami
Pkg Sys Ser 92 A 93 A .... **A**
Pkg Sys Ser 92 A 93 A .... **A**
Orlando Utils Com Wtr & Elec Rfdg Ser 92 93 .... **AA**

GEORGIA .... **AA+**

Atlanta .... **AA**
Georgia Port Auth 61 66 68 74 .... **AA+**
Georgia Hsg & Fin Auth
Homeownership Mtg FHA Ins or VA Gtd .... **AA+**
Sin Fam Mtg Bnds Ser 1986A, 87A B, 88A-C, 93 A-C, 94 A-C, 95 A B .... **AA+**
Jekyll Island-St Pk Auth Ser 68A 71 72......... **AA+**
Metro Atlanta Rapid Transit Auth Sales Tax (1st Indenture) Ser A B F-O ..... **AA-**

HAWAII..................... **AA**

Hawaii Hsg Fin & Dev Corp Sin Fam Mtg Purch Ser 85 A 86 A B 88 A 89 A 90 A 91 A B 94 A B .... **A**
Honolulu .... **AA**

IDAHO...................... **NR**

Idaho Hsg Agy
FHA Ins (Breir Apts) Ser 86. **AA+**
FHA Ins Hsg Rev Bnds (Hillcrest Retirement Ctr) Ser 83 A .... **AAA**
Sin Fam Mtg Purch Ser 78 A 83 A B............ **AA**

ILLINOIS .... **AA-**

Chicago........................ **A**
Chicago Pub Bldg Com Ser 75 B .... **A**
Chicago Sch Fin Auth........ **AA-**
Chicago
Wastewtr Transmission Rfd Ser 89 90 .... **A-**
Wtr Ser 89.................... **A+**
O'Hare Intl Arpt Gen Arpt Ser 83 A B 84 A B 85 A 88 A Ser 90 A B 92 A 93 A ..... **A+**
Illinois Dev Fin Auth Infrastructure Assist Ser 86 A................... **NR**
Illinois Hsg Dev Auth Fix Rate Hsg Ser 84 A-D .... **A+**

INDIANA.................... **NR**

Indiana Bnd Bank Ser 85 A-C 86 A 87 A 91 B C 92 A .... **A**
Indiana Hsg Fin Auth Collat Mtg Oblig Ser 85 A 86 ..... **AAA**
Indiana Mun Pwr Agy Pwr Supp Sys Ser 83 85 89 93 C . **A**
Indianapolis Arpt Auth........ **AA+**
Spl Rev Ser 85 88 .... **A**
Indianapolis Flood Ctl Dist ... **AA+**
Indianapolis Metro Thoro Dist .... **AA+**
Indianapolis San Dist......... **AA+**
Indiana Bnd Bank (Greencastle Comnty Sch Corp) Ser 86 D .... **A**
Spl Prog .... **A**
Indianapolis Local Pub Imp Bnd Bank Ser 87 A Due 96-2001 .... **AA+**
Indianapolis Pub Transp Corp Ser 81........... **A+**

IOWA .... **NR**

Iowa Fin Auth
Sin Fam Hsg Ser 83 A ...... **AA**
Sin Fam Hsg Ser 85 A ... **A+/NR**
Sin Fam Mtg Ser 77 A ...... **AA**

KANSAS .... **NR**

Kansas Hsg Dev Corp (Hesston) FHA Ins Sect 8 Mtg Ser 80 B .... **AA**

KENTUCKY .... **NR**

Kentucky Poll Abatement Auth Rfd Ser 73 A 78 A 79 A 80 A 88 A .... **AAA**
Kentucky St Prop & Bldg Com
(Proj 16) Rfd............... **NR**
(Proj 17-Capital Plaza)........ **A+**
(Proj 19) .... **NR**
(Proj 21) Due 7-1-94-96....... **A+**
(Proj 28) .... **AAA**
(Proj 29) .... **AAA**
(Proj 30-2nd Ser) .... **NR**
(Proj 31) Rfd Due 12-1-94-95 .... **AAA**
(Proj 33) Rfd Dtd 4-1-86 Due 12-1-94-95 .... **AAA**
(Proj 34) .... **NR**
Kentucky Hsg Corp Sin Fam.............. **AAA**
Kentucky St Prop & Bldg Com (Proj 18-Univ of Kentucky Stad) .... **A**

LOUISIANA.................... **A-**

Louisiana Hsg Fin Auth Agy Multifam Taxable Ser 86 A.... **D**
Louisiana Office Bldg Corp Ser 67 .... **BBB-**
Louisiana Port of New Orleans Ser 61 62 66 .... **A-**
Louisiana Pub Fac Auth (Lake Shore Place Apts) Multifam GNMA Collat Mtg Ser 85 .. **AAA**
New Orleans .... **BBB+**

MAINE...................... **AA+**

Maine St Hsg Auth
Hsg Fin Rev Bnds Ser 88-1 92-I .... **A+**
Sin Fam Mtg Acquis Prog Ser 80-1 83-1 83-2 85-1 85-2 91-1 .... **AA-**
Mtg Purch .... **AA-**

MARYLAND .... **NR**

Baltimore .... **A**
Baltimore Cnty .... **AA+**
Washington Suburban San Dist
(Montgomery & Prince Georges Cntys)............. **AA**
(Montgomery Cnty) Storm Wtr Dr .... **AAA**
(Prince Georges Cnty) Storm Wtr Dr .... **AA**

MASSACHUSETTS............ **A+**

Boston Wtr & Swr Com Sr Lien Ser 86 89 91 92 93 ...... **A**
Boston .... **A+**
Connecticut Hsg Comr FNMA Multifam Ser 85..... **AAA**
Massachusetts Conv Ctr Auth .. **A+**
Massachusetts Hsg Fin Agy
Hsg Dev Rev Bnds Ser 86 A 87 A .... **A**
Multifam Hsg Bnds 1st Iss Sect 8 Asst Rfd Ser 79 A. **AAA**
Multifam Hsg Ins Mtg Bnds Rfd Ser 78 A .... **NR**
Multifam Jr Rev Bnds (Harbor PT Dev) Ser 86 .. **BBB+**
Multifam Mtg Rev (GNMA Collat) Ser 85 A .... **AAA**
Massachusetts Mun Wholesale El C Pwr Ser 76-87 A 92 A-F 93 A-C .... **BBB+**

Massachusetts (Continued)
Massachusetts
Pub Hsg Rfd 76 .... **AAA**
Massachusetts Hsg Fin Agy
Resid Hsg Rev 87
A C 88 A B 89 A .... **BBB+**
Sin Fam Hsg Ser 1-18
21-22 26-33 36-44........... **A+**

MICHIGAN.................... **NR**

Detroit .... **BBB**
Michigan St Bldg Auth (Univ
of Michigan Adult Gen Hosp)
Rfd Ser 82 III Dtd 12-1-
82Due 12-1-2008 .... **AAA**
Michigan St Hsg Dev Auth
FHA Ins Resid Mtg
Subord Term Ser 83 B ..... **AA**
FHA Ins Resid Mtg
Subord Term Ser 84
A Due 7-15-2016 .... **AA**
Sin Fam Ins Mtg Ser
77 A 78 A B 80 A .... **AA+**
FHA Ins Home Imp Prog
Ser 82A 88A 89A&b .... **A+**

MINNESOTA .... **AA+**

Brooklyn Ctr-Columbia Hgts-
Rubbinsdale & Moorhead
Sin Fam Mtg Ser 82 .... **NR**
Minneapolis .... **AAA**
Minnesota Hsg Fin Agy
Multifam Hsg Ser
76 A 77 A .... **AA**
Hsg Dev Ser 76 A B 77 A
78 A 79 A 80 A 83 B-C
85 A B 88 A 91 A 92 A ..... **AA**
Resid Mtg 85 A B........... **AA**
St Paul........................ **AA+**
St Paul Port Auth .... **AA+**
Indl Dev Resolution #876 .. **CCC**

MISSISSIPPI................. **AA-**

Mississippi Home Corp
Sin Fam Mtg Ser 84 ... **AA-/NR**
Mississippi St Aid Cnty Rd ..... **A**

MISSOURI .... **AAA**

Missouri Brd of Pub Bldg
Rfdg Rfd Ser 85 A .... **AAA**
Missouri Hsg Dev Com
(Grandview Heights) Multifam
FHA Ins Ser 86 F......... **AAA**
(Justin Place) Multifam
FHA Ins Ser 86 B .... **AAA**
(Lakeview II) Multifam
FHA Ins Ser 86 A .... **AAA**
(Lucas Heights) Multifam
FHA Ins Ser 86 E .... **AAA**
FHA Ins Sin Fam
Mtg Ser 9-1-86 .... **AA+**
Mtg Purch FHA-VA
Gtd Dtd 8-15-78 5-
15-79 1-15-79 9-1-91 .... **AA+**
Qual Mtg Purch Nts FHA
Ins - VA Gtd Dtd 3-15-83 ... **AA+**
Sin Fam Mtg Rev Bnds
GNMA Ser 86 A .... **AAA**
Sin Fam Mtg Rev
Nts Dtd 8-1-84.............. **AA+**
Sin Fam Resid GNMA
Collat Dtd 11-1-86 .... **AAA**
St Louis..................... **BBB+**

MONTANA .... **AA-**

(Communications Sys)
Cert of Part Rfd .... **NR**
Montana Brd of Hsg Sin Fam
Mtg Bnd Ser 77 A-B 78 A 87
A B-1 & B-2 88 A-1 & A-2... **AA+**
Montana Dept of Nat Resources
& Conserv (Wtr Dev Proj) Coal
Severance Tax Ser 87 C89 A
90 B 91 A 92 A B.......... **AA-**
Montana Brd of Hsg Sin Fam
Prog Ser 79A 83C 84A
85AB 92A 94 A-C 95A...... **AA+**

NEBRASKA .... **NR**

Lincoln Elec Sys
Distrib Ser 77 A 78 A 92 A.. **AA-**
Pwr Supp Ser 92 A .... **AA+**
Nebraska Invest Fin Auth
Sin Fam Mtg Ser 83 A ...... **AA-**
Sin Fam Mtg Ser 83 I .. **AA-/NR**
Nebraska Pub Pwr Dist
Nuclear Fac Ser 68 92 .... **A+**
Nuclear Fac Ser 68 92 .... **A+**
Elec Sys .... **A+**
Omaha Pub Pwr
Dist Ser 93 A-E .... **AA**

NEVADA .... **AA**

Nevada (Colorado
River Comm) .... **AA**
Nevada Hsg Div
Multi-Unit Hsg Loans to
Lenders Prog Ser 85 ..... **AAA**
Multi-Unit Prog
Ser 79 A B 82 B.......... **AAA**
Sin Fam Prog Mtg
Purch Ser 77 A .... **AA**
Sin Fam Prog Ser
1986A 1993R 1994E .... **AA**

NEW HAMPSHIRE .... **AA+**

New Hampshire Hsg Fin Auth
(Claremont-Gorham) Multifam
Hsg Proj (Sect 8 Asst) .... **A**
Sect 8 Asst Multifam Hsg
Purch Bnds Ser 79 I .... **A**
Sin Fam Resid Mtg 82 A
83 A B 84 A 85 A 86 A
87 A B 88 A 89 A B 90 A
91 A-D 93 A 94 A B D....... **A+**
New Hampshire Mun Bnd Bank
St Gtd .... **AA+**
(New Hampshire) Not St Gtd.. **A+**

NEW JERSEY .... **AA+**

New Jersey Econ Dev Auth
(Absecon Manor Nsg Home)
FHA Ins Mtg Ser 86 .... **A-**
(Hunterdon Convalescent
Ctr) FHA Ins Ser 84 A .... **A-**
New Jersey Hlth Care Fac
Fin Auth (St Josephs Hosp
& Med Ctr) FHA Ins Ser B . **AAA**
New Jersey Hsg & Mtg Fin Agy
(Corinthian Twrs) FHA
Ins Sect 8 Asst)
Multifam Hsg Ser 84 I .... **A+**
11 B (Chestnut St
Hsg) Mtg Ser 83 A .... **AAA**
11 B (Hampshire Hsg
Proj Mtg) Ser 83 A .... **AAA**
11 B (Highview Terrace Proj)
FHA Ins Mtg Ser 83 A .... **AAA**
Gen Hsg Ln Ser 70
A 71 A 72 A 72 B .... **A+**
Mtg Rev Issue 77
A (Sect 8 Asst) .... **A+**
Mtg Rev Issue 77 B
(Sect 236 Asst) .... **A+**
Sin Fam Mtg Purch
Rev Bnds Ser 1 .... **A+**
Spl Pledge Rev
Oblig Ser 75-1............... **A+**
South Jersey Port Corp Marine
Term Ser 85 87 89 93 .... **A+**

NEW MEXICO .... **AA+**

New Mexico Mtg Fin Auth
Multifam Hsg Rev FNMA Collat
Lns to Lenders 85 A...... **AAA**
Resid Rent Hsg Rev Bnds Lns
to Lenders FNMA Collat Dtd
12-1-85 Ser 85 A........... **NR**
Sin Fam Mtg Prog Ser 82 A... **A+**
Sin Fam Mtg Prog Ser 83 A... **A+**
Sin Fam Mtg Purch Rfd
Ser 78 A 79 A B 84 A .... **AAA**
New Mexico Severance Tax.. **AA**

NEW YORK ST .... **A-**

Metropolitan Transp Auth
Commuter Fac Ser B .... **NR**
Metropolitan Transp Auth
Commuter Fac Svc
Contract Ser C-E I J N
& Part of Ser A BF G H.... **BBB**
Metropolitan Transp Auth
Transit Fac Svc Ser C-E I J N
& Part of Ser A B F G H ... **BBB**
New York City .... **BBB+**
New York St Hsg Fin Agy
Multifam Ins Mtg Ser 85 A .. **AA-**
New York St Job Dev Auth..... **A-**
New York St Med Care Fac Fin
Agy (Mental Hlth Svc Fac Imp)
Spl Oblig Rfd Ser 87....... **AAA**
New York St Med
Care Fac Fin Agy
Hosp Insd Mtg (Presbyterian
Hosp Main Campus &
Cmnty Hosp) Rfdg Ser ..... **AA**
Insd Hosp Mtg Rev (Doctors
Hospital) Ser 85 A .... **A-**
Insd Hosp Mtg Rev
(Long Beach Memorial
Hosp) Ser 84 D........... **AAA**
Insd Hosp Mtg Rev (St.
Francis Hosp) Ser 84 C ..... **A-**
Insd Hosp Mtg Rev (St. John's
Riverside Hosp) Ser84 B .... **A-**
Insd Hosp Mtg Rev (St.
Joseph's Hosp) Ser 84 A .... **A**
Secd Hosp Ser 87
A 89 91 A94 A .... **BBB**
New York St Thruway
Auth Gtd Rev .... **A-**
New York City Mun Asst
Corp 2nd Resol Ser 45
57 59-62 64-68 .... **AA-**
New York City Mun Wtr
Fin Auth Wtr & Swr .... **A-**
New York St Hsg Fin
Agy FHA Ins Multi
Fam Hsg Ser 95 B......... **AAA**
New York St Med Care Fac Fin
Agy (Mental Hlth Svcs) .... **BBB+**
New York St Pwr
Auth Gen Purp.............. **AA-**
Port Auth of New York & New
Jersey Cons Nts & Bnds.... **AA-**
Syracuse Sr Citizens Hsg
Corp (East Hill Vill Apts)
Sect 8 Asst Ser 79............ **A**

NORTH CAROLINA .... **AAA**

North Carolina Hsg Fin Agy Sin
Fam Mtg Purch Ser 76 A B . **AA+**
North Carolina Mun Pwr Agy #1
(Catawba Elec) Ser 78 79 81 A
85 A B 81-86 88 89 90 92 93 . **A-**
North Carolina Hsg Fin Agy
FHA Ins Multifam Rev Bnds
Ser 84 A G F 85 C D 86 E **AA**
Sin Fam Ser 85 B
86 C 87 D 88 E F ...... **A+/NR**

NORTH DAKOTA .... **NR**

Mercer Cnty (Basin Elec Pwr Coop-Antelope Vy Stn) Poll Ctl .... **A**
North Dakota Hsg Fin Agy Sin Fam Mtg Ser 83 B-C 84 A 85 A 86 A 87 A-C 88 A 89 A B 90 A-C 91 A 92 A B 93 A 94 A-C .... **A+**
North Dakota Mun Bnd Bank Ser 79 A Due 93-2000 .... **A**

OHIO .... **AA**

Cleveland .... **A**
Columbus .... **AAA**
Cincinnati .... **AA+**
Montgomery-Knolls Hsg Dev Corp (Knolls II) FHA Ins Mtg Ser 85 .... **A**
Ohio Bldg Auth
(St Correctional Fac) Rfd Ser 85 A .... **NR**
(St Correctional Fac) Rfd Ser 86 A .... **NR**
Ohio Cert of Part Rfd Dtd 9-15-83 .... **NR**
Ohio Hsg Fin Agy
(Beehive & Doan Classroom Apts) FHA Ins Mtg Ser 85 A . **A+**
(Detroit Terr) GNMA Collat Mtg Ser 85 .... **AA-**
(Northridge Apts) FHA Ins Multifam Mtg Ser 85 .... **A+**
(Oakleaf-Toledo Apts) GNMA Collat Ser 85 .... **AA-**
(West Pk II) FHA Ins Multifam Mtg Ser 84 E .... **A+**
FHA Title 1 Ins Home Imp Ser 84 .... **A**
Sin Fam Mtg Ser 83 B .... **A**
Sin Fam Mtg Ser 84 A .... **A**
Ohio Hwy Oblig .... **AAA**
Ohio Pub Fac Com
Hgr Ed Fac .... **A+**
Mental Hlth Fac .... **A+**
Pks & Recre Fac .... **A+**
Ohio Bldg Auth (Local Jail Grant) Ser 86A 87A 89A 94A .... **NR**

OKLAHOMA .... **AA**

Oklahoma Cap Imp Auth (State Office Bldg) .... **A**

OREGON .... **AA-**

Oregon Hsg & Comnty Svcs Dept
Hsg Fin Rev Bnds (Asst or Ins Multi-Unit Prog) Ser 81 A B 91 A-C 93 A .... **A+**
Sin Fam Mtg Prog Ser 77 A 78 A B 80 A B 82 A 83 A 85B C .... **A+**
Oregon
Vet Welfare Var Rate Dem Ser 73 E **A-1**
Vet Welfare Var Rate Dem Ser 73 F .... **A-1+**
Vet Welfare Var Rate Dem Ser 73 G **A-1**
Vet Welfare Var Rate Dem Ser 73 H **A-1**

PENNSYLVANIA .... **NR**

Pennsylvania Gen St Auth Rfd Ser 16-21 23 25-29 .... **AAA**
Pennsylvania Hgr Ed Fac Auth (Temple Univ) FHA Ins Rfd Ser A .... **NR**
Pennsylvania Hsg Fin Agy
FHA Ins Multifam Hsg Ser 85 A B .... **AAA**
FHA Ins Multifam Ser 82 B Taxable 90 T-2 92A .... **AAA**
Moderate Rehab Iss 84 A 85 B .... **AA**
Resid Dev Bnds Iss D ...... **NR**
Resid Dev Iss & Taxable Ser 90T-1 Taxable Ser 91 T-3 91A N P .... **NR**
Resid Dev Iss A .... **NR**
Resid Dev Iss B .... **NR**
Resid Dev Iss C .... **NR**
Resid Dev Iss G .... **NR**
Pennsylvania Hwy & Br Auth . **AA-**
Philadelphia .... **BBB-**
Philadelphia Sch Dist .... **A**
Philadelphia Arpt .... **A-**
Philadelphia Pkg Auth .... **BBB-**
Philadelphia Gas Wks Ser 3-5 7 11 13 14 15 ..... **BBB**

PUERTO RICO .... **A**

Puerto Rico Elec Pwr Auth
Elec .... **A**
Pwr .... **A-**
Puerto Rico Govt Dev Bank Var Rate Dem Cons Ser 85 A ... **NR**
Puerto Rico Hsg Fin Corp Coll Mtg Oblig Ser 86 A .... **AAA**
Puerto Rico Hwy Auth Hwy Ser A B D-G N O Q Due 92-2010 R-V W X .... **A**
Puerto Rico Indl Dev Com Ser 64 67 78 91 ...... **BBB+**
Puerto Rico Mun Fin Agy Ser 74 A 88 A .... **A-**
Puerto Rico Pub Bldgs Auth .... **A**
Puerto Rico Tel Auth Ser A-M .. **A+**
Univ of Puerto Rico (Univ Sys) . **A**

RHODE ISLAND .... **NR**

Rhode Island Hsg & Mtg Fin Corp
Multifam Hsg Ins Mtg Bnd Prog Ser 76 A .... **AAA**
Rev Bnd Prog Ser 84 A .... **A+**
Mtg Fin Rev Bnds .... **A+/NR**
Multifam .... **A+**

SOUTH CAROLINA .... **AA+**

South Carolina Pub Svc Auth Elec Expansion Ser 73-88 A .... **AA-**
South Carolina St Hsg Fin & Dev Auth
Homeownership Mtg Rev Bnds Ser 82A 83AB 84A 85AB 87A 88 A-C2 90A-C 91A .... **AA**
Multifam Rental Hsg Rev Bnds Ser 84 A .. **AAA/A-1+**
Sin Fam Mtg Rev Bnds Ser 79 A B .... **AA**

SOUTH DAKOTA .... **NR**

South Dakota Bldg Auth Lse Rfd Ser 87 A .... **NR**
South Dakota Hsg Dev Auth
Multifam Hsg Ser 77 A 78 A 79 A 80 A 82 A 92 A-C .... **A+**
Home Ownership Mtg .... **AA+**

TENNESSEE .... **AA+**

Nashville & Davidson Cnty Metro Govt
Elec Sys Rec Ser 86 A 92 A B .... **AA**
Wtr & Swr Rfdg Ser 85 A 86 93 .... **A**
Wtr & Swr Rfdg Ser 85 A 86 93 .... **AA**
Tennessee Local Dev Auth Ser 85 86 91 A Rfdg 93 A .. **AA-**
Tennessee St Sch Bnd Auth . **AA**
Tennessee Hsg Dev Agy Homeownership Prog Iss ... **AA**

TEXAS .... **NR**

Austin
Comb Util Sr Lien .... **A**
Comb Util Subord Lien .... **A-**
Comb Util Subord Lien ...... **AA**
Dallas Cnty .... **AAA**
Dallas-Fort Worth Regl Arpt Spl Fac Fuel Sys Ser 71 ...... **A-**
Dallas .... **AAA**
Wtrwks & Swr .... **AA**
Dallas-Fort Worth Regl Arpt .... **A**
Fort Worth .... **AA**
Harris Cnty .... **AA**
Houston .... **AA-**
Wtr & Swr Sys Prior Lien Exchange .... **A**
Lower Colorado River Auth Prior Lien Rfdg Ser 87 91 ... **AA-**
San Antonio .... **AA**
(San Antonio Wtr Brd) Prior Lien Ser 80-84 86 86 A 87 89 90 A 91 .... **A+**
Arpt Ser 80 83 92 .... **A**
Prior Lien Swr Sys Ser 80 82 84 86 87 .... **A+**
Elec & Gas .... **AA**
Tarrant Cnty .... **AA+**
Texas Dept of Hsg & Comnty Affairs Sin Fam Mtg Ser 83 A 84 A B 85 A-C 86 A B 87 B 91 A Jr Lien 94 A B .... **A+**
Texas
Vets Hsg Asst .... **AA**
Vets Land .... **AA**
Hgr Ed Coordinating Brd Coll .... **AA**
Texas Wtr Dev Brd (Texas) .. **AA**

UTAH .... **AAA**

Utah Hsg Fin Agy
FHA Ins Sect 8 Asst Multifam Hsg Bnds Ser 79 A .... **AA**
Multifam Mtg Rev Bnds FNMA Mtg Bckd Rfd Secs Prog Ser 85 B ...... **AAA**
Multifam Mtg Rev Bnds FNMA Mtg Bckd Secs Prog Ser 85 A .... **AAA**
Sin Fam Mtg Bnds Ser 83 A .... **AA**
Sin Fam Mtg Bnds Ser 84 A .... **AA**
Sin Fam Mtg Purch Bnds Ser 77 A 78 A 86 A 86 B 87 A 89 D .... **AA**
Sin Fam Mtg Sr 87 Iss E .... **AA/NR**
Sin Fam Resid Mtg Bnds Ser 83 A .... **AA**

VERMONT .... **AA-**

Vermont Hsg Fin Agy
Multifam Mtg Ser 77 A B 78 A 79 A 86 A 88 A .... **AA-**
Multifam Hsg Prog Sect 8 ..... **A+**
Sin Fam Ins Mtg Ser 1976 A 1977 A .... **AA-**
Vermont Mun Bnd Bank Ser 89-1 92-1 92-2 93-1 94-1 72 Resol .... **A-**

VIRGINIA .... **NR**

Virginia Hsg Dev Auth
Bldg .... **AA+**
Collat Mtg Ser 87 A .... **AAA**

Virginia (Continued)
Multifam Mtg
Purch Ser 73 A .... **AA**
Multifam Mtg Ser 77
A B 78 A B 85 A .... **AA+**
Virginia Pub Schs Auth (87
Resol) Ser 63 87 88 88 B
89 A B 90 A B 91 A-C 92
A B 93A Rfdg B 93 C .... **AA**
Virginia Resources Auth
(Upper Occoquan Swg
Auth) Swr Sys Ser 85 .... **AA**
Wtr & Swr Ser 85 A B .... **AA**
Wtr & Swr Sys Pooled
Ln Prog Fix Rate Ser
86 A Due 2016 .... **AA**
Wtr & Swr Sys Pooled
Ln Prog Fix Rate Ser
86 A Due 2017 .... **AA**
Virginia Hsg Dev
Auth Multifam .... **AA+**

WASHINGTON .... **AA**

Seattle .... **AA+**
Washington Pub Pwr Supp Sys
(Nuclear Proj #1) .... **AA**
(Nuclear Proj #2) .... **AA**
(Nuclear Proj #3) .... **AA**
(Packwood Lake Hydroelec) .. **A**
Washington St Capitol Fac
Rev 69 Ch 273 Ex Sess 69 ... **A**
Washington St Hsg Fin Com
Multifam Mtg Rev Bnds
FHA Ins Ser 85 A .... **A+**
Multifam Mtg Rev Bnds
FNMA Mtg Bckd Secs
Prog Ser 85 E .... **AAA**
Multifam Rev Bnds FNMA Mtg
Bckd Prog Rfd Ser 84 A ... **NR**
Washington Pub Pwr Supp
Sys (Nuclear Proj #4 #5) .... **D**

WEST VIRGINIA .... **A+**

West Virginia Wtr Dev Auth
Ser 85 A 86 A 88 A 89 A B
90 A 91 A 93 A-II 93 B-Ii ... **BBB+**
West Virginia Hsg Dev Fd
Mtg Purch Prog Bnds .... **AAA**

WISCONSIN .... **AA**

Milwaukee Cnty .... **AA-**
Milwaukee Metro Swr Dist .... **AA**
Milwaukee .... **AA+**
Wisconsin Hlth Fac Auth
(Middleton Vill Assn)
FHA Ins Mtg Ser 86 .... **AAA**
Wisconsin Hsg & Econ Dev Auth
FHA Ins Homeownership
Ser 85 I Ii .... **AA-/NR**
Homeownership Rev
Bnds Ser 86 A .... **A+/NR**
Homeownership Rev
Bnds Ser 86 B .... **A+**
Hsg Rehab Ln Rev Bnds Ser
79 A 81 A 83 A 84 A 85 A .. **NR**
Vets Hsg Rev Bnds
Ser 74 A 75 A .... **NR**
Wisconsin St Agy Bldg Corp ... **A+**
Wisconsin St Coll
Bldg Corp Lse Rent .... **A+**
Wisconsin Hsg & Econ Dev Auth
Homeownership Rev Bnds
Taxable Ser 1995 E .... **AA**
Homewnership Mtg In Rev .. **AA**
Hsg Rev .... **A**
Wisconsin Univ Bldg Corp
(Wisconsin) Lse Rent Oblig ... **A+**

WYOMING .... **NR**

Convertible Bonds

EXPLANATION OF COLUMN HEADINGS AND FOOTNOTES

EXCHANGE: Unlisted except where symbols are used:
●—New York Stock Exchange ◆—American Stock Exchange.

ISSUE TITLE: Name of Bond at time of offering; otherwise issue footnoted with name change of obligor. Minor changes with old title indicated in brackets, i.e. Midlantic (Banks) Corp.
§ Int. and/or prin. in default.

S&P DEBT RATING: See pages xxi & xxii for definitions.

BOND FORM: Letters are used to indicate form of bond: BE—Book-Entry; C—Coupon only; CR—Coupon or Registered, interchangeable; R—Registered only.

CONVERSION EXPIRES: Denotes the year in which the conversion privilege expires. When privilege will expire within the next 12 months, the month, day and year are given.

DIVIDEND INCOME PER BOND: If $1,000 Bond were converted, the annual amount of dividends expected to be paid by the company on the stock based on most recent indication of annual rate of payment.

STOCK VALUE OF BOND: Price at which the bond must sell to equal the price of the stock, i.e., number of shares received on conversion times price of the stock.

CONVERSION PARITY: Price at which stock must sell to equal bond price, i.e., price of bond dividend by number of shares received on conversion.

P/E RATIO: (Price-Earnings Ratio) Ratio is derived by dividing current stock price by estimated new year earnings or last 12 months if no estimate is available.

EARNINGS, in general, are per share as reported by company. **FOR YEARS INDICATED:** Fiscal years ending prior to March 31 are shown under preceding year. Foreign issues traded ADR are dollars per share, converted at prevailing exchange rate. Specific footnotes used:

△ – Excl extra-ord income	† – Partial Year	P – Preliminary
▲ – Incl extra-ord income	‡ – New Year Earns	p – Pro forma
□ – Excl extra-ord charges	d – Deficit	R – Fully diluted
■ – Incl extra-ord charges	E – S&P Estimate	n/r – Not reported
⋆ – Excl tax credits	j – Currency of origin	
± – Combined various classes	n/a – Not available	

LAST 12 Mos. indicates earnings through period indicated by superior number preceding figure: ^{1} for Jan., ^{2} for Feb., etc. Figure without superior number indicates fiscal year end.

Exchange ↓ Issue, Rate, Interest Dates and Maturity	S&P Debt Rating	Bond Form	Outstdg. Mil-$	Conv. Ex-pires	Shares per $1,000 Bond	Price per Share	Div. Income per Bond	1995 Price Range High	1995 Price Range Low	Curr Bid Sale(s) Ask(A)	Curr. Yield	Yield to Mat	Stock Value of Bond	Conv Parity	Stock Data Month End	Stock Data P/E Ratio	EPS Yr. End	EPS 1994	EPS 1995	EPS Last 12 Mos
• [1]ADT[2]Operations[3](Zero) [4] 2010	BB+	R	[5]776	2010	[6]28.23	....	....	47¼	39	47	....	5.27	42⅜	16¾	•15	18	Dc	0.76	....	[9]0.83
◆Advanced Medical[7]Inc[8] 7¼s Jj15 2002	CCC–	R	16.2	2002	55.13	18.14	....	71¼	53	65	....	Flat	16⅝	11⅞	◆3	6	Dc	0.34	....	[9]0.46
• Advest Group 9s Ms15 2008	NR	R	21.0	2008	73.69	13.57	....	104	87	s100½	8.96	8.93	62¾	13¾	•8½	11	Sp	0.34	0.73	0.73
◆Aeroflex Inc 7½s QJun15 2004	NR	R	10.0	2004	177.78	5.625	....	106	89	98½	7.61	7.74	75⅝	5⅝	•4¼	7	Je	0.57	0.57	[9]0.56
AES Corp[9] 6½s Ms15 2002	B+	R	50.0	2002	38.146	26.215	....	106⅝	91¼	106⅝	6.10	5.23	91⅛	28	23⅞	17	Dc	Δ1.30	....	[9]1.39
Ag Services of America[7] 7s Mn31 2003	NR	R	13.8	2003	108.10	9.25	....	110	97	109	6.42	5.51	102¾	10⅛	9½	12	Fb	0.66	....	[11]0.78
• AGCO Corp[7] 6½s Jd 2008	BB–	R	66.8	2008	78.95	12.67	3.16	358½	290	402¾	1.61	....	402¾	51⅛	•51	7	Dc	6.13	....	[9]6.77
Agnico-Eagle Mines[10](Sr)[11] . 5¾s $Jj27 2004	B+	R	[5]127	2004	55.762	....	5.58	88¼	66½	82¾	6.95	8.77	69¾	14⅞	•12½	..	Dc	0.38	....	[9]j0.52
Air & Water Tech[12] 8s Mn15 2015	B–	R	115	2015	[13]33.333	30.00	....	84⅛	53¼	84⅛	9.51	9.85	20½	25¼	◆6⅛	d	Oc	□d9.23	Pd0.35	d0.35
◆Air Express Int'l[14] 6s Jj15 2003	BB–	R	74.8	2003	29.36	34.0625	5.87	121¾	96	s108	5.56	4.65	67⅝	36⅞	23	15	Dc	1.28	E1.50	[9]1.47
[15]Air Wis Services 7¾s Jd15 2010	NR	R	33.0	2010	[16]3.86	259.08	....	91⅜	61½	91⅜	8.48	8.82	69	236¾	•178½	6	Dc	□0.76	E27.00	[9]25.40
• Airborne Freight[17] 6¾s fA15 2001	BBB–	R	115	2001	28.169	35.50	8.45	103	91¼	s100½	6.72	6.64	75	35¾	•26⅝	26	Dc	1.81	E1.00	[9]1.05
• Alaska Air Gr(Sr) 6½s Jd15 2005	B–	R	115	2005	46.512	21.50	....	109⅝	91⅛	101½	6.40	6.29	75⅝	21⅞	•16¼	16	Dc	1.68	E1.00	[9]0.95
Alaska Air Gr 7¾s Jd15 2010	B–	R	14.4	2010	35.40	28.25	....	94⅞	83¾	89⅝	8.65	9.05	57⅝	25⅜	•16¼	16	Dc	1.68	E1.00	[9]0.95
• Alaska Air Gr[7] 6⅞s Jd15 2014	B–	R	54.0	2014	29.76	33.60	....	88¼	74	s81	8.49	9.00	48⅜	27¼	•16¼	16	Dc	1.68	E1.00	[9]0.95
• Albany Int'l[18] 5¼s Ms15 2002	BB–	R	[5]150	2002	38.083	....	15.23	103½	84	s89	5.90	7.50	69⅛	23⅜	•18⅛	13	Dc	±0.80	....	[9]1.31
◆Alexander Haagen Prop('A') 7½s jJ15 2001	NR	R	75.0	2001	55.56	18.00	80.01	91	80¾	84¼	8.90	11.72	68⅛	15¼	◆12¼	d	Dc	0.14	....	[9]d0.12
All Amer Communications[19] ... 6½s aO 2003	NR	R	60.0	2003	86.957	11.50	....	121¾	67	96	6.77	7.18	83¾	11⅛	9⅝	8	Dc	±0.07	....	[9]1.11
• Allegheny Ludlum 5⅞s Ms15 2002	CALL	BE	90.0	1-2-96	49.38	20.25	25.68	114	100½	103¾	5.66	Call	91⅜	21⅛	•18½	11	Dc	0.26	E1.65	[9]1.61
• Allwaste Inc[7] 7¼s Jd 2014	B+	R	30.0	2014	83.75	11.94	....	91½	82	s84½	8.58	8.99	39⅞	10⅛	•4¾	d	Au	0.36	d0.03	d0.03
• ALZA Corp[20](Zero)[21] 2014	BBB–	R	[5]825	2014	12.987	....	....	40¾	35	41	....	4.87	31⅞	31⅝	•24½	28	Dc	0.71	E0.87	[9]0.83
Amer Travellers 6½s aO 2005	BB–	R	104	2005	43.96	22.75	....	138½	100	123¾	5.25	3.59	123¾	28¼	28⅛	14	Dc	1.71	....	[9]1.98
• AMR Corp 6⅛s [22]QNov 2024	BB–	R	1000	2004	12.658	79.00	....	108½	82½	102¾	5.96	5.92	94	81¼	•74¼	10	Dc	2.26	E7.00	[9]4.31
• AMSCO Int'l[7] 6½s aO15 2002	BB+	R	100	2002	33.22	30.10	....	96½	76½	95¾	6.79	7.30	49½	28⅞	•14⅞	14	Dc	□d1.64	E1.00	[9]0.76
• Anacomp,[23]Inc[24] 13⅞s §Jj15 2002	D	R	[5]23.2	2002	57.14	17.50	....	102	6	s9¾	....	Flat	⅞	1¾	•⅛	d	Sp	Δ0.10	....	[6]d3.17
• Analog Devices[7] 3½s jD 2000	BBB	R	230	2000	Conv 60 days fr 12-18-95[25]			104½	100	104½	3.35	2.52	....	....	•35⅜	23	Oc	0.97	P1.50	1.50
Andersen Group 10½s aO15 2002	NR	R	8.04	2002	61.84	16.17	....	87¼	74⅞	83½	12.57	14.37	26⅜	13⅝	4¼	d	Fb	□d0.49	....	[8]d1.28
[27]Apollo Computer 7¼s Fa 2011	AA	R	105	2011	Conv into $729.17			99	90	99	7.32	7.36	....	....	....	..		....	....	....
Argosy Gaming[19] 12s Jd 2001	B–	R	100	2001	56.50	17.70	....	108½	89¼	90¾	13.22	14.52	43⅛	16⅛	7⅝	16	Dc	0.40	....	[9]0.47
• Arvin Indus 7½s QSep30 2014	BB+	R	90.3	2014	35.08	28.51	26.66	102	94	99¼	7.56	7.57	58	28⅜	•16½	23	Dc	d0.73	E0.70	[9]d1.51
• Ashland[7]Inc[28] 6¾s jJ 2014	BBB–	R	124	2014	19.48	51.34	21.43	101	89¾	s99½	6.78	6.80	68½	51⅛	•35⅛	..	Sp	2.94	0.08	0.08
AST Research[29](Zero)[30] [31] 2013	B–	R	[5]315	2013	12.993	....	....	33¼	28	33	....	6.27	11⅛	25½	8½	d	Je	1.64	d3.07	[9]d4.21
◆Atari Corp[32] 5¼s Apr29 2002	NR	R	43.5	2002	61.31	16.31	....	58	44¼	s47	11.17	20.59	8½	7¾	◆1⅜	d	Dc	0.16	....	[9]d0.04

Uniform Footnote Explanations—See Page 260. Other: [1] Gtd by & data of ADT Ltd. [2] (HRO)To 7-6-02,Chge of Ctr at $383.09&accr OID. [3] (HRO)On 7-2-02 at $599.46. [4] Due 7-6-10. [5] Incl disc. [6] Conv into ADT Ltd com. [7] (HRO)On Chge of Ctrl at 100. [8] Int of 7-15-94 pd 8-17-94. [9] (HRO)For a Redemp Event at 100. [10] Co must offer repurch on Chge of Ctrl. [11] Int of 3.5% pd Jan & Jul 27,bal pd at maturity. [12] (HRO)To 5-15-00 on Chge of Ctrl at 100. [13] Into Cl A com. [14] (HRO)For a Fundamental Chge at declining prices. [15] Mgr into & data of UAL Corp. [16] Conv into UAL Corp com. [17] (HRO)For a Risk Event at 100. [18] (HRO)On Chge of Ctrl at 87.59 & accr OID. [19] (HRO)On Chge of Ctrl at 101. [20] (HRO)To 7-14-99,Ctrl Chge, at $354.71&accr OID. [21] (HRO)On 7-14-99(04&09)$459.63($595.58&$771.74). [22] Co may extend the int pyt period(max 20 qtrs). [23] Default 7-15-95 int. [24] Plan pre-packaged Chapt 11 reorg. [25] To be conv into 23.88 com. [26] To be conv into 23.88 com. [27] Subsid of Hewlett-Packard. [28] Was Ashland Oil. [29] (HRO)On 12-14-98(03&08)at $459.63($595.58&$771.74). [30] (HRO)To 12-14-98 on Chge of Ctrl at $354.71 & accr OID. [31] Due 12-14-13. [32] Offered outside U.S.

Exchange ↓ Issue, Rate, Interest Dates and Maturity	S&P Debt Rating	Bond Form	Outstdg. Mil-$	Conv. Ex-pires	Shares per $1,000 Bond	Price per Share	Div. Income per Bond	1995 Price Range High	1995 Price Range Low	Curr Bid Sale(s) Ask(A)	Curr. Yield	Yield to Mat	Stock Value of Bond	Conv Parity	Stock Data Month End	Stock Data P/E Ratio	Earnings Per Share Yr. End	1994	1995	Last 12 Mos
Atlantic Amer'n 8s Mn15 1997	NR	R	5.63	1997	91.41	10.94	....	85	85	85	9.41	21.07	21¼	9⅜	2⁵⁄₁₆	12	Dc	△0.49	....	[9]0.19
◆Audiovox Corp[1] 6¼s Ms15 2001	CCC+	R	65.0	2001	[2]56.50	17.70	....	80	62	62¼	10.04	17.60	30¾	11⅛	◆5⅜	d	Nv	□2.88	....	[8]d1.14
◆Aurora Electronics[3] 7¾s Ao15 2001	NR	R	10.2	2001	85.70	11.66	....	78¼	46⅛	63	12.30	19.16	17¾	7⅜	◆2¹⁄₁₆	d	Sp	d0.87	Pd1.79	d1.79
• Automatic Data Proc[4](Zero)[5] .... [6] 2012	AA	R	[7]805	2012	12.922	....	10.34	52¾	41¼	s50	....	4.34	96	38¾	•74¼	26	Je	□2.37	2.77	[9]2.85
Baby Superstore[8] .... 4⅞s aO 2000	B–	R	100	2000	18.56	53.875	....	116⅝	99	116⅝	4.18	1.26	105⅞	62⅞	57	93	Ja	0.44	....	[10]0.61
• Baker Hughes (Sr)[9] (Zero) .... [10] 2008	A–	R	385	2008	18.599	....	8.56	62	54	63	....	3.78	45⅜	33⅞	•24⅜	36	Sp	□0.85	□0.67	0.67
Baker (J.) Inc[11] .... 7s Jd 2002	B+	R	70.0	2002	62.02	16.125	3.72	105	68	68½	10.22	14.75	35¾	11⅛	5¾	d	Ja	1.71	....	[10]d2.35
• Bally[12]Entertainment[13] 6s mS15 1998	NR	R	1.85	1998	34.49	28.99	....	98	82	91⅛	....	Flat	48⅜	26½	•14	25	Dc	□d1.08	E0.55	[9]0.12
• Bally Entertainment .... 8s [14]ms15 2000	NR	R	15.4	2000	72.20	13.85	....	106½	97	s106½	....	Flat	101⅛	14⅞	•14	25	Dc	□d1.08	E0.55	[9]0.12
• Bally[12]Entertainment[15] 10s jD15 2006	B+	R	80.0	2006	30.60	32.68	....	99½	76½	s93½	....	Flat	42⅞	30⅝	•14	25	Dc	□d1.08	E0.55	[9]0.12
• Bank of N.Y. 7½s fA15 2001	A–	R	250	2001	51.15	19.55	73.66	240	145	249⅜	3.01	....	249⅜	48⅞	•48¾	10	Dc	3.92	E4.55	[9]4.48
• BBN Corp[16] .... 6s Ao 2012	NR	R	73.5	2012	33.33	30.00	....	157	72	s137	4.38	3.09	137⅛	41⅛	•41⅛	12	Je	d0.48	3.61	[9]3.23
Bell Sports Corp[17] 4¼s mN15 2000	B	R	75.0	2000	18.50	54.06	....	78¼	63	69⅜	6.13	12.90	14⅞	37½	8	d	Je	1.27	d0.42	[9]d0.82
Ben Franklin Retail Strs[18] .... 7½s Jd 2003	B–	R	25.0	2003	129.03	7.75	....	82⅜	65⅝	65⅝	11.43	15.43	35½	5⅛	2¾	12	Mr	P0.28	....	[9]0.22
Benson Eyecare[19] 8s Mn15 2001	CCC+	R	40.0	2001	110.42	9.056	....	132⅞	100¼	114¾	6.97	4.85	99½	10½	•9	d	Dc	0.41	....	[9]d0.09
Benton Oil & Gas[18] .... 8s Mn 2002	NR	R	6.10	2002	[20]101.157	9.89	....	163⅛	101	151¾	5.27	....	151¾	15⅛	15	53	Dc	0.12	....	[9]0.28
• Bergen Brunswig 6⅞s jJ15 2011	BBB+	R	10.6	2011	Conv into apx $520.83			93	83	92	7.47	7.77	....	....	....	..		....	....	....
• Beverly Enterprises 7⅝s Ms15 2003	B	R	67.9	2003	48.85	20.47	....	98½	91½	s95½	7.98	8.47	52	19⅝	•10⅝	16	Dc	□0.79	E0.64	[9]0.74
• Beverly Enterpr(Zero)[21] .... [22] 2003	NR	R	[7]2.70	2003	13.32	....	....	53½	49⅝	53	....	8.59	14¼	39⅞	•10⅝	16	Dc	□0.79	E0.64	[9]0.74
• Beverly Enterprises .... 5½s QAug 2018	B	R	150	2018	75.00	13.33	....	103½	92½	s94½	5.82	5.95	79¾	12⅝	•10⅝	16	Dc	□0.79	E0.64	[9]0.74
Big B, Inc[8] 6½s Ms15 2003	B	R	40.3	2003	81.96	12.20	16.39	132¼	90½	98½	6.60	6.76	82	12⅛	10	10	Ja	0.97	....	[10]0.93
Bindley Western[8] .... 6½s aO 2002	BB–	R	65.0	2002	50.44	19.825	4.04	108	93½	103	6.31	5.95	85¾	20½	•17	12	Dc	1.34	....	[9]1.41
Boston Chicken[8] .... 4½s Fa 2004	B–	R	130	2004	33.36	27.969	....	126¾	70	119	3.78	1.95	107¼	35¾	32⅛	51	Dc	0.38	E0.63	[9]0.59
Boston Chicken[23](Zero)[24] .... [25] 2015	B–	R	[7]720	2015	8.532	....	....	30⅝	20½	28½	....	6.57	27½	33½	32⅛	51	Dc	0.38	E0.63	[9]0.59
Box Energy[8] .... 8¼s jD 2002	B–	R	55.1	2002	[26]90.909	11.00	....	104½	88½	97	8.51	8.84	78½	10¾	8⅝	45	Dc	±0.44	....	[9]0.19
• Brown & Sharpe Mfg 9¼s jD15 2005	NR	R	15.9	2005	38.10	26.25	....	102	86	97	9.54	9.73	39⅛	25½	•10¼	d	Dc	±d2.37	....	[9]d0.68
• Browning-Ferris Ind 6¼s fA15 2012	A–	R	345	2012	24.39	41.00	16.59	103¼	91	s99¾	6.27	6.27	71¾	41	•29⅜	15	Sp	□1.52	1.93	1.93
Builders Transport 8s fA15 2005	B	R	27.0	2005	40.98	24.40	....	95	82½	89	8.99	9.79	31¼	21¾	7⅝	18	Dc	0.81	....	[9]0.41
Builders Transport .... 6½s Mn 2011	B	R	23.5	2011	26.49	37.75	....	75¾	72	72½	8.97	10.05	20¼	27⅜	7⅝	18	Dc	0.81	....	[9]0.41
• Burnham Pacific Prop 8½s Jj15 2002	BBB–	R	25.7	2002	62.50	16.00	62.50	100	88	96¼	8.83	9.28	60¼	15½	•9⅝	13	Dc	0.84	....	[9]0.73
C-Cube Microsystems[27] .... 5⅞s mN 2005	CCC+	R	75.0	2005	32.57	30.70	....	211¾	100	203⅝	2.89	....	203⅝	62⅝	62½	..	Dc	0.16	E0.63	[9]0.52
California Microwave[8] 5¼s jD15 2003	B	R	57.5	2003	35.16	28.4375	....	139⅞	84	84	6.25	8.01	58½	24	16⅝	d	Je	±1.20	d0.51	[9]d0.52
• Camden Property Trust .... 7.33s Ao 2001	NR	R	47.8	2001	41.67	24.00	76.67	99¼	93	99½	7.37	7.44	99	24	•23¾	26	Dc	p0.82	....	[9]0.90

Uniform Footnote Explanations—See Page 260. Other: [1] Co must offer repurch at 101 on Chge of Ctrl. [2] Conv into Cl'A' com. [3] Was BSN Corp. [4] (HRO)To 5-20-97 on Chge of Ctrl. [5] (HRO)2-20-97(02&07)at$459.63($595.58&$771.74). [6] Due 2-20-12. [7] Incl disc. [8] (HRO)On Chge of Ctrl at 100. [9] (HRO)On 5-5-98(03) at $706.83($840.73). [10] Due 5-5-08. [11] (HRO)For a Redemp at 100. [12] Was Bally Mfg. [13] Int arrears fr 3-15-91 pd 9-28-92. [14] Due 12-15-00. [15] Int arrears fr 12-15-90 pd 9-28-92. [16] Was Bolt Beranek/Newman. [17] (HRO)For a Risk Event at 100. [18] (HRO)For a Fundamental Chge at 100. [19] (HRO)On Chge of Ctrl at 101. [20] Fractional shrs in cash. [21] (HRO)On ea Sep 30 at prices as defined. [22] Due 7-16-03. [23] (HRO)On 6-1-00(05&10)at$308.32($456.39&$675.57). [24] (HRO)To 6-1-00 on Ctrl Chge at $208.29 & accr OID. [25] Due 6-1-15. [26] Into Cl'B' com. [27] (HRO)For a Fundamental Chge at declining prices.

Exchange ↓ Issue, Rate, Interest Dates and Maturity	S&P Debt Rating	Bond Form	Outstdg. Mil-$	Conv. Ex-pires	Shares per $1,000 Bond	Price per Share	Div. Income per Bond	1995 Price Range High	1995 Price Range Low	Curr Bid Sale(s) Ask(A)	Curr. Yield	Yield to Mat	Stock Value of Bond	Conv Parity	Stock Data Month End	Stock Data P/E Ratio	Earnings Per Share Yr. End	1994	1995	Last 12 Mos
• [1]Cameron Iron Works 7s Jd15 2012	BBB+	R	0.72	2012	[2]43.478	23.00	69.56	No Sale		96½	7.25	7.37	....	22¼	•....	..	Dc	....	....	....
• Capstone Capital[3] .... 10½s Ao 2002	NR	R	50.0	2002	62.02	16.125	110.40	114	99	118⅝	8.85	6.79	118⅝	19¼	•19⅛	..	Dc	‡0.80	....	[9]....
CareLine Inc[3] .... 8s Mn 2001	BBB	R	75.0	2001	83.33	12.00	....	111½	78½	111½	7.17	5.48	....	13½	....	65	Dc	0.31	....	[6]0.14
• Carnival[4]Corp[5] .... 4½s jJ 1997	BBB+	R	115	1997	[6]57.56	17.375	20.72	153	121	140⅜	3.21	....	140⅜	24½	•24⅜	15	Nv	±1.35	±P1.59	1.59
• [7]Cenco Inc .... 5s mN 1996	NR	R	2.01	11-1-96	Conv into Debs[8]			95	92	96⅛	5.20	9.91	....	....	•35	21	My	1.29	1.51	[11]1.63
• [7]Cenco Inc .... 4¾s mS 1997	NR	R	6.74	1997	Conv into Debs[9]			94½	87⅝	93	5.11	9.36	....	....	•35	21	My	1.29	1.51	[11]1.63
◆Center Point Properties....... 8.22s Jj15 2004	NR	R	44.0	2004	54.79	18.25	85.47	117	98	126¾	6.49	4.26	126¾	23¼	◆23⅛	33	Dc	0.41	....	[9]0.69
Centocor Inc[10] .... 7¼s Fa 2001	CCC	R	107	2001	36.04	27.75	....	119½	84¼	116¾	6.21	3.62	111⅜	32½	30⅞	d	Dc	d2.55	Ed0.90	[9]d1.49
• [11]Chemical Waste Mgmt(Zero)....... [12] 2010	A	R	[13]575	2010	Conv into Cv Nts[14]			41	38¾	s41	....	6.19	....	....	....	..		....	....	....
Chesapeake Utilities[15] .... 8¼s Ms 2014	NR	R	4.23	2014	58.77	17.01	52.89	99	93	98⅜	8.39	8.42	86	16¾	•14⅝	8	Dc	1.23	....	[9]1.77
◆Chock Full O'Nuts................ 8s mS15 2006	B–	R	43.3	2006	128.04	7.81	....	104	88	s94	8.51	8.88	67¼	7⅜	•5¼	11	Jl	0.73	0.45	[10]0.44
• Chock Full O'Nuts..................... 7s Ao 2012	B–	R	51.7	2012	121.51	8.23	....	97⅛	77¾	s86	8.14	8.61	63⅞	7⅛	•5¼	11	Jl	0.73	0.45	[10]0.44
◆[16]CII Financial[3].................... 7½s mS15 2001	NR	R	56.8	2001	16.921	59.10	....	88	64	s87	8.62	10.59	53¾	51½	•31¾	16	Dc	1.71	....	[9]1.90
Cincinnati Fin'l(Sr)[17] .... 5½s Mn 2002	AA–	R	80.0	2002	21.34	46.86	29.02	142½	109	139¼	3.95	....	139¼	65⅜	65¼	15	Dc	3.72	....	[9]4.11
• CNA Income Shrs....................8.08s Jd 1997	NR	R	28.1	1997	85.25	11.73	85.25	No Sale		99	8.16	8.83	87½	11⅝	•10¼	..	Dc	....	....	....
CNB Bancshares[3].................... 7½s mS 2011	NR	R	10.0	2011	52.91	18.90	42.33	162	140¼	150⅞	4.97	3.31	150⅞	28⅝	28½	14	Dc	1.89	....	[9]2.00
• Coeur d'Alene Mines[18] 6⅜s Jj31 2004	B–	R	100	2004	38.80	25.77	5.82	99	78	s94¾	6.73	7.24	66½	24½	•17⅛	..	Dc	d0.26	....	[9]0.04
• [19]Coleman[20]Worldwide[21](SrSec).... [22] 2013	B	R	[13]500	2013	[23]7.853	....	....	32	26	s30	....	7.04	27⅝	38¼	•35⅛	19	Dc	□1.26	....	[9]1.83
Colonial BancGroup[24]......... 7½s Ms31 2011	NR	R	10.0	2011	35.71	28.00	32.14	117⅞	88	115¼	6.51	5.96	115¼	32⅜	•32¼	9	Dc	±2.85	....	[9]3.48
Columbia Banking System...... 7.85s [25] 2002	NR	R	5.75	2002	90.17	11.09	....	115	95	108¼	7.25	6.28	108¼	12⅛	12	17	Dc	□d0.14	....	[9]0.70
Comarco Inc 9¾s Ao15 2000	NR	R	2.98	2000	86.96	11.50	....	335⅞	92	126⅛	7.73	3.19	126⅛	14⅝	14½	19	Ja	0.68	....	[10]0.74
Comcast[26]Corp([27]Step-up) ... 3⅜s mS9 2005	B+	R	250	2005	[28]40.816	24.50	3.67	105⅝	77⅜	93⅜	3.61	....	72	23	17⅝	d	Dc	□±d0.32	....	[9]d0.26
Comcast Corp[29] 1⅛s Ao15 2007	B+	R	[13]542	2007	[30]19.312	....	1.74	53⅞	38⅝	50	2.25	7.90	34⅛	26	17⅝	d	Dc	□±d0.32	....	[9]d0.26
• [31]Compania Tele de Chile[32] . 4½s Jj15 2003	BBB+	BE	71.9	2003	[33]12.28	81.43	23.58	No Sale		101⅞	4.42	....	101⅞	83	•82⅞	19	Dc	±4.42	....	[3]4.16
Comprehensive Care[34] 7½s Ao15 2010	NR	R	9.54	2010	3.851	259.70	....	52½	33½	51	14.71	16.52	3⅜	132½	•8⅝	d	My	d3.60	d5.11	[8]d4.47
Comptronix Corp[3] .... 6¾s Ms 2002	NR	R	29.2	2002	56.34	17.75	....	67	38	49	13.78	22.37	7¾	8¾	1⅜	d	Dc	d1.38	....	[9]d0.26
• Consorcio G Grupo Dina[35]....... 8s jj15 2004	NR	R	164	2004	[36]56.88	17.58	....	65½	24	s36½	21.92	....	10¾	6½	•1⅞	d	Dc	*d2.33	....	[3]d2.97
• Conner Peripherals................ 6¾s Ms 2001	B	R	230	2001	34.48	29.00	....	101¾	69¼	s99	6.82	6.98	72½	28¾	•21	21	Dc	2.10	E1.00	[9]1.41
• Conner Peripherals................ 6½s Ms 2002	B	R	345	2002	41.667	24.00	....	108	69¾	s101½	6.40	6.20	87⅝	24⅜	•21	21	Dc	2.10	E1.00	[9]1.41
• Consol Natural Gas[37]........... 7¼s jD15 2015	A+	R	246	2015	18.52	54.00	35.93	106¼	96¼	s103⅝	7.00	6.91	84⅛	56	•45⅜	..	Dc	1.97	E0.20	[9]0.08
Contl Homes Hldg[3] .... 6⅞s mN 2002	CCC+	R	75.0	2002	42.105	23.75	8.42	117⅛	99⅛	117⅛	5.87	3.99	103¾	27⅞	•24⅝	10	My	2.11	1.99	[11]2.42
Convex Computer .... 6s Ms 2012	NR	R	53.5	2012	45.98	21.75	....	89	46½	89	6.74	7.16	21⅞	19⅜	•4¾	d	Dc	d2.35	....	[9]d1.26
Cooker[3]Restaurant[38] .... 6¾s QOct 2002	NR	R	19.3	2002	46.38	21.5625	2.32	87	62	87	7.76	9.39	52¼	18⅞	•11¼	20	Dc	Δ0.34	....	[9]0.54

Uniform Footnote Explanations—See Page 260. Other: [1] Asmd by & data of Cooper Indus. [2] Into Cooper Indus $1.60 Cv Pfd. [3] (HRO)On Chge of Ctrl at 100. [4] Was Carnival Cruise Lines. [5] (HRO)For a Repurch Event at 100. [6] Into Cl A com. [7] Subsid & data of Manor Care. [8] Into $709.67 prin amt Manor Care 15.5%'02. [9] Into $503.82 prin amt Manor Care 15.5%'02. [10] (HRO)For a Fundamental Chge at 100. [11] (HRO)On any 6-30 at $306.56 plus accr OID. [12] Due 8-16-10. [13] Incl disc. [14] Cv into 0.1440 of 2% Cv Nts'05,fractions in cash. [15] (HRO)For a Designated Event,as defined. [16] Merged into&data of Sierra Health Services. [17] Co must offer to redeem on sale of certain ops. [18] (HRO)For a Designated Event at 100. [19] Conv into & data of Coleman Co. [20] (HRO)5-27-98(03&08)at $343.61($490.58&$700.42). [21] (HRO)For certain events at $240.67 & accr OID. [22] Due 5-27-13. [23] Conv into Coleman Co com. [24] Into Cl'A'. [25] Due 6-30-02:int pd mthly. [26] (HRO)For a Fundamental Chge at curr red prices. [27] Int at 3.375% thru 9-8-97,5.5% aft. [28] Cv into Cl A Spl Com. [29] (HRO)For a Fundamental Chge at prices as defined. [30] Into Cl A Spl com. [31] At maturity Deb red at 112.660% of par. [32] Now Compania de Tele com Chile. [33] Into ADSs (rep 208.77 Cl A com). [34] Plan exch for cash & com. [35] Co may red in whole,at 100,for tax law chge. [36] Into Grupo Dina Ser L ADSs. [37] (HRO)On 12-15-00 at 100. [38] (HRO)On ea 11-1 at 100,ltd,as defined.

Exchange ↓ Issue, Rate, Interest Dates and Maturity	S&P Debt Rating	Bond Form	Outstdg. Mil-$	Conv. Ex-pires	Shares per $1,000 Bond	Price per Share	Div. Income per Bond	1995 Price Range High	1995 Price Range Low	Curr Bid Sale(s) Ask(A)	Curr. Yield	Yield to Mat	Stock Value of Bond	Conv Parity	Stock Data Month End	Stock Data P/E Ratio	Earnings Per Share Yr. End	1994	1995	Last 12 Mos
• Cooper[1]Cos[2] .... 10⅝s Ms 2005	NR	R	9.40	2005	66.67	15.00	....	90	80	s90	....	Flat	50⅛	13½	•7½	..	Oc	d0.45	P0.01	0.01
• Cooper Indus[3] .... 7.05s QJan 2015	BBB+	R	691	2015	24.23	41.272	31.98	105	93¾	s103	6.84	6.77	89⅛	42⅝	•36¾	15	Dc	d0.64	E2.45	[9]0.81
[4]Costco Wholesale[5] 5¾s Mn15 2002	BBB	R	300	2002	24.24	41.25	....	95⅛	80⅜	95⅛	6.04	6.70	37	39¼	15¼	21	Au	d0.51	0.68	[11]0.71
• Cray Research .... 6⅛s Fa 2011	BB–	R	105	2011	12.82	78.00	....	83¾	65	80½	7.61	8.43	31⅝	62⅞	•24⅝	d	Dc	2.16	....	[9]d7.57
• Cross Timbers Oil[3] .... 5¼s mN 2003	B	R	75.0	2003	43.243	23.125	12.97	95	78½	93½	5.61	6.31	76¼	21⅝	•17⅝	60	Dc	0.19	....	[9]0.29
• CUC Int'l (Zero) .... [6] 1996	NR	R	[7]17.6	6-6-96	151.88	....	....	329½	329½	518⅜	....	....	518⅜	34¼	•34⅛	42	Ja	0.67	....	[10]0.81
DAKA Int'l[8] 7s Ms15 2003	NR	R	20.5	2003	83.33	12.00	....	285½	123	229¼	3.05	....	229¼	27⅝	27½	13	Je	1.55	2.03	[9]1.99
• [9]Data-Design[10]Labs 7s Mn15 2001	NR	R	1.31	2001	500.00	2.00	....	95	88¼	131¼	5.33	1.01	131¼	2⅝	•2⅝	23	Je	d0.55	Δd0.15	[9]0.11
• [9]Data-Design[10]Labs .... 8½s fA 2008	NR	R	1.69	2008	94.12	10.625	....	82	59	75	11.33	12.49	24¾	8	•2⅝	23	Je	d0.55	Δd0.15	[9]0.11
• Data General[11] .... 7¾s Jd 2001	B–	R	125	2001	52.08	19.20	....	100½	81	s99	7.83	7.98	71	19⅛	•13⅝	d	Sp	d2.45	Pd1.23	d1.23
[12]Data Switch .... 8¼s Jd 2002	NR	R	16.0	2002	20.747	48.20	19.92	100¾	71⅛	100	8.25	8.25	67¼	48¼	•32⅜	14	Dc	1.71	E2.18	[9]0.33
• Datapoint Corp[13] .... 8⅞s Jd 2006	NR	R	64.4	2006	55.231	18.11	....	52	17	s42	....	Flat	7	7⅝	•1¼	d	Jl	□d6.69	d2.29	[10]d1.92
DBA Systems .... 8¼s mN 2010	NR	R	1.93	2010	51.28	19.50	....	79	76	78	10.58	11.34	22½	15¼	4⅜	14	Je	0.20	0.34	[9]0.31
• Deere & Co. 5½s Jj15 2001	A–	R	2.00	2001	274.73	3.64	219.78	No Sale		968½	0.57	....	968½	35⅜	•35¼	13	Oc	2.34	P2.71	2.71
Delta Air Lines[14] 3.23s Jd15 2003	B+	R	[7]800	2003	12.68	....	2.54	103⅛	69¼	95¼	3.39	3.97	93⅜	75⅛	•73⅝	11	Je	d10.32	Δ4.07	[9]6.54
• Developers Diversified Rlty ... 7s fA15 1999	BBB–	R	60.0	1999	29.96	33.375	64.71	108	92⅛	98½	7.11	7.48	90	33	•30	20	Dc	□1.35	....	[9]1.45
◆Diagnostic/Retr'l Sys .... 8½s fA 1998	NR	R	17.5	1998	[15]66.67	15.00	....	99	95	98¾	8.61	9.05	52⅛	14⅞	◆7¾	13	Mr	±0.50	....	[9]0.57
DiMon[16]Inc[17] 7¾s mS30 2006	B+	R	56.5	2006	74.40	13.44	40.18	139½	102⅜	131¼	5.90	4.12	131¼	17¾	•17⅝	d	Je	pd0.17	d0.79	[9]d0.59
Discovery Zone[18](Zero)[19] .... [20] 2013	CCC	R	255	2013	13.485	....	....	33⅝	23½	25¾	....	7.77	4¼	19⅛	3⅛	4	Dc	□d0.41	E0.65	[9]d2.31
Dixie Yarns 7s Mn15 2012	B+	R	44.8	2012	31.06	32.20	....	75½	66½	75½	9.27	10.09	12⅛	24⅜	3⅞	d	Dc	±d0.24	....	[9]d0.36
[21]DorchesterMasterLtdPtn[22] ..... 8½s jD 2005	NR	R	27.9	2005	Conv into $652.50			69	65¼	68	....	Flat	....	....	....	..		....	....	....
Drug Emporium[23] .... 7¾s aO 2014	NR	R	50.8	2014	65.146	15.35	....	78½	69½	72½	10.69	11.31	26⅞	11¼	4⅛	16	Fb	d0.41	....	[11]0.25
◆Ducommun Inc 7¾s Ms31 2011	NR	R	28.0	2011	100.20	9.98	....	110	79½	104	7.45	7.31	99	10½	◆9⅞	12	Dc	0.48	....	[9]0.79
[24]Durr-Fillauer[25]Med'l .... 7s Ms 2006	BBB+	R	20.9	2006	29.41	34.00	14.12	101	88	101	6.93	6.86	73¼	34⅜	•24⅞	15	Sp	1.45	P1.61	1.61
Eagle Hardware & Garden[16] 6¼s Ms15 2001	CCC+	R	86.2	2001	55.56	18.00	....	77½	63¾	71½	8.74	14.16	41¾	12⅞	7½	d	Ja	d0.28	....	[10]d0.19
EDO Corp[26] 7s jD15 2011	NR	R	29.3	2011	45.45	22.00	....	71¼	51	70½	9.93	10.95	22¾	15⅝	•5	d	Dc	d4.30	....	[9]d2.40
• [27]Elan Int'l Finance[28](Zero)[29] .... [30] 2012	BB+	R	[7]431	2012	[31]10.886	....	....	54½	39¼	53	....	Flat	53	48¾	•48⅝	20	Mr	1.90	E2.40	[9]2.12
• EMC Corp[3] .... 4¼s Jj 2001	B+	R	200	2001	50.40	19.84	....	143½	93	s99¾	4.26	4.31	77½	19⅞	•15⅜	11	Dc	1.18	E1.40	[9]1.37
• [32]Employee Benefit[16]Plans[33] 6¾s jJ31 2006	B–	R	48.6	2006	4.49	222.78	0.45	99⅝	67	A100	6.75	6.75	....	222¾	•....	33	Dc	2.56	E3.05	[9]2.93
• Empresas ICA Sociedad 5s $Ms15 2004	BB–	BE	435	2004	[34]30.17	33.15	3.02	63½	23½	s53½	9.35	15.05	31	17¾	•10¼	85	Dc	0.12	....	0.12
[35]EnClean Inc[36] .... 7½s fA 2001	A	R	46.0	2001	Conv into $375			98	92	98	7.65	7.95	....	....	....	..		....	....	....
[37]Environmental Systems .... 6¾s Mn 2011	NR	R	21.4	2011	Conv into $693.07			72	69⅜	69⅜	9.73	10.90	....	....	....	..		....	....	....
• Equitable Cos .... 6⅛s [38]Qjan22 2024	NR	R	365	2024	40.40	24.75	8.08	116½	95¼	111	5.52	5.37	97	27½	•24	13	Dc	□1.70	E1.75	[9]1.78

Uniform Footnote Explanations—See Page 260. Other: [1] Was CooperVision Inc. [2] Int incr fr 8.625% on 6-29-89. [3] (HRO)On Chge of Ctrl at 100. [4] (HRO)On Chge of Ctrl at 101. [5] Now Price/Costco Inc. [6] Due 6-6-96. [7] Incl disc. [8] (HRO)For Redemp Event at 100. [9] (HRO)For Certain Mgrs/Acquis,at declin'g prices. [10] Now DDL Electronics. [11] (HRO)For a Fundamental Chge,as defined. [12] Mgr into & data of Genl Signal. [13] Int of 12-1-95 pd 12-28-95. [14] (HRO)On Chge of Ctrl at $718.00 & accr OID. [15] Into Cl B. [16] (HRO)For a Risk Event at 100. [17] Was Dibrell Bros. [18] (HRO)On 10-14-98(03&08)at $494.52($625.35&790.79). [19] (HRO)To 10-14-98 on Chge of Ctrl. [20] Due 10-14-13. [21] Merged into Damson Oil. [22] Int of 12-1-86,pd 12-12-86,12-1-87 pd 12-22-87. [23] (HRO)To 10-1-99 at 100 for a Risk Event. [24] Subsid & data of Bergen Brunswig. [25] (HRO)For a Special Red Event at 100. [26] (HRO)On Chge of Ctrl at curr red prices. [27] Gtd by & data of Elan Corp, plc. [28] (HRO)10-16-97(02&07)at $427.27($567.28&$753.17). [29] (HRO)To 10-16-97 on Chge in Ctrl. [30] Due 10-16-12. [31] Into ADS of Elan Corp,plc. [32] Merged into & data of First Fin'l Mgmt. [33] Purch offer, $1000 to Nov 29. [34] Into ADSs. [35] Asmd by & data of WNX Technologies. [36] (HRO)For a Fundamnental Chge at 100. [37] Acq by Brambles USA. [38] Due 12-15-04.

Exchange ↓ Issue, Rate, Interest Dates and Maturity	S&P Debt Rating	Bond Form	Outstdg. Mil-$	Conv. Ex-pires	Shares per $1,000 Bond	Price per Share	Div. Income per Bond	1995 Price Range High	1995 Price Range Low	Curr Bid Sale(s) Ask(A)	Curr. Yield	Yield to Mat	Stock Value of Bond	Conv Parity	Stock Data Month End	Stock Data P/E Ratio	Earnings Per Share Yr. End	1994	1995	Last 12 Mos
• [1]Equitable Gas 9½s Jj15 2006	A–	R	2.66	2006	[2]90.42	11.06	106.70	No Sale		282⅝	3.36	....	282⅝	31⅜	•31¼	24	Dc	1.76	....	[9]1.27
E'town Corp .... 6¾s Fa 2012	A–	R	12.2	2012	25.00	40.00	51.00	94¼	86⅜	92½	7.30	7.56	75⅜	37	•30⅛	13	Dc	1.95	....	[9]2.22
Evans&Southerl'd Comp .... 6s Ms 2012	NR	R	37.1	2012	23.752	42.10	....	84	71	84	7.14	7.75	52⅞	35⅜	22¼	16	Dc	Δd0.65	....	[9]1.36
Executone Info Systems[3] ... 7½s Ms15 2011	NR	R	11.9	2011	94.12	10.625	....	83	77½	83	9.04	9.65	21⅞	8⅞	2⁵⁄₁₆	d	Dc	0.16	....	[9]d0.78
• Fabri-Centers Amer[4] .... 6¼s Ms 2002	B	R	57.0	2002	41.026	24.375	....	89	74½	84	7.44	9.76	54⅜	20½	•13¼	14	Ja	0.63	....	[10]0.91
Farm Fresh Inc .... 7½s Ms 2010	CCC+	R	15.0	2010	Conv into cash & deb[5]			64⅜	55½	58⅝	12.79	14.43	....	....	....	..		....	....	....
• Federal Nat'l Mtg .... 4⅜s aO 1996	NR	R	0.65	10-1-96	152.82	6.54	415.67	No Sale		1893⅛	0.23	....	1893⅛	124	•123⅞	14	Dc	□7.80	E8.60	[9]8.34
• Federated Dept Strs[6] .... 5s aO 2003	BB–	BE	305	2003	29.254	34.1825	....	103⅞	97½	99½	5.03	5.08	79¾	34⅛	•27¼	36	Ja	1.41	E0.75	[10]d0.13
[7]Federated[8]Group[9] .... 7½s §Ao15 2010	NR	R	20.5	2010	Conv into $267.90			27	26	26¾	....	Flat	....	....	....	..		....	....	....
• Fidelity Natl Finl[10](Zero)[11] .... [12] 2009	B+	BE	[13]236	2009	19.177	....	5.91	45¾	33½	s45¾	....	6.05	35¾	23⅞	•18⅝	93	Dc	Δ0.65	....	[9]0.20
• Fieldcrest Cannon 6s Ms15 2012	B+	R	125	2012	22.60	44.25	....	84⅞	66	s68½	8.76	9.95	37⅜	30⅜	•16½	d	Dc	3.02	Ed0.65	[9]0.88
Fifth Third Bancorp 4¼s Jj15 1998	A+	R	144	1998	15.717	63.625	24.52	120¼	92	115¼	3.69	....	115¼	73⅜	73¼	17	Dc	3.80	E4.30	[9]4.20
◆First Central Fin'l .... 9s fA 2000	NR	R	6.76	2000	133.33	7.50	16.00	No Sale		100	9.00	9.00	88⅜	7⅝	◆6⅝	6	Dc	0.97	....	[9]1.02
• [14]First Financial Mgmt[15](Sr) ... 5s jD15 1999	A	R	447	1999	22.98	43.52	2.76	164	104½	153¾	3.25	....	153¾	67	•66⅞	29	Dc	1.87	E2.25	[9]2.10
• First Republic Bancorp .... 7¼s jD 2002	NR	R	34.5	2002	73.15	13.67	....	108	91	97¼	7.46	7.77	96⅛	13⅜	•13⅛	87	Dc	0.92	....	[9]0.15
First State Bancorp .... 7s mN 2003	NR	R	5.00	2003	76.19	13.125	15.24	122	100	118	5.93	4.27	91½	15½	12	10	Dc	1.18	....	[9]1.17
Fischbach (& Moore)[16] .... 4¾s Ao 1997	NR	R	8.97	1997	Conv into $196.43			97⅞	89⅜	97⅞	4.85	6.53	....	....	....	..		....	....	....
Fischbach[16] .... 8½s aO 2005	NR	R	5.30	2005	Conv into $305.56			102¾	86¾	102⅞	8.27	8.07	....	....	....	..		....	....	....
Fisher Scientific[17]Int'l[6] .... 4¾s Ms 2003	BBB–	BE	[13]125	2003	28.47	35.125	2.28	108½	90	108⅛	4.39	....	95⅛	38	•33⅜	53	Dc	2.18	....	[9]0.62
[18]Flagstar[19]Corp[20] .... 10s mN 2014	NR	R	100	2014	[21]41.67	24.00	....	75⅜	54	54	18.52	19.05	13⅛	13	3⅛	d	Dc	□7.38	....	[9]d0.66
Fort Bend Hldg .... 8s jD 2005	NR	R	11.0	2005	46.296	21.60	12.96	100⅞	100	100⅞	7.93	7.87	83⅜	21⅞	18	9	Mr	1.94	....	[9]1.94
• Fremont[22]Gen'l[23](Zero) .... [24] 2013	BB+	R	[13]325	2013	12.858	....	10.29	49	32	47⅜	....	4.24	47⅜	36⅞	•36¾	10	Dc	3.25	....	[9]3.68
• GenCorp Inc[25] .... 8s fA 2002	BB–	R	115	2002	62.247	16.065	37.35	102¼	92	101½	7.88	7.70	76⅜	16⅜	•12¼	..	Nv	□d0.41	....	[8]Nil
• General Host[25] 8s Fa15 2002	CCC+	R	65.0	2002	106.27	9.41	....	98	75½	s80	10.00	12.80	42⅝	7⅝	•4	30	Ja	0.39	....	[10]0.13
• Gen'l Instrument[26] 5s Jd15 2000	BBB–	BE	500	2000	42.10	23.75	....	169	99⅛	s110	4.55	2.61	98½	26¼	•23⅜	18	Dc	□2.01	....	[9]1.26
• General Signal .... 5¾s Jd 2002	A–	BE	100	2002	25.32	39.50	24.31	109	98⅛	103¾	5.54	5.06	82	41	•32⅜	14	Dc	1.71	E2.18	[9]0.33
• Genesis Health Ventures[6] 6s mN30 2003	B	R	86.3	2003	44.138	22.656	....	141	130	161⅛	3.72	....	161⅛	36⅝	•36½	23	Sp	Δ□1.33	P□1.55	1.55
• GenRad, Inc .... 7¼s Mn 2011	NR	R	50.0	2011	69.57	14.375	....	95	63¾	s92¼	7.86	8.14	67⅞	13⅜	•9¾	18	Dc	0.28	....	[9]0.52
[27]Glycomed Inc[4] .... 7½s Jj 2003	NR	BE	50.0	2003	[28]37.71	26.52	....	82⅛	52	77½	9.68	12.40	....	20⅝	....	..	Je	....	....	....
GranCare Inc[6] 6½s Jj15 2003	B	R	60.0	2003	36.84	27.145	....	95½	82	86¼	7.54	9.19	53½	23½	•14½	16	Dc	1.08	....	[9]0.88
GrandeTel[6]Technologies[29] 8s jJ31 2003	NR	R	22.5	2003	83.333	12.00	....	63	46	46	17.39	23.61	4¼	5⅝	½	d	Ja	d4.38	....	[10]jd3.02
Graphic Indus 7s Mn15 2006	NR	R	20.8	2006	61.54	16.25	4.31	98¾	82	98¾	7.09	7.17	75½	16⅛	12¼	13	Ja	0.80	....	[10]0.93
[30]Great Lakes Fed S&L[31] .... 7¼s Ao 2011	BB+	R	11.7	2011	[32]39.03	25.63	....	193½	103½	193½	3.75	0.73	....	49⅝	....	15	Dc	....	....	[9]1.90

Uniform Footnote Explanations—See Page 260. Other: [1] Now Equitable Resources. [2] Into Equitable Resources. [3] Was Vodavi Technology. [4] (HRO)For a Risk Event at 100. [5] Cv into $416 & $119 16.5% Sub Deb'04. [6] (HRO)On Chge of Ctrl at 100. [7] Acq by Atari Corp. [8] Int of 10-15-89,pd 12-7-89:4-15-90,pd 5-29-90. [9] Default 4-15-91 int. [10] (HRO)To 2-15-99 on Chge of Ctrl at $443.14 & accr OID. [11] (HRO)On 2-15-99('04)at $581.25($762.40). [12] Due 2-15-09. [13] Incl disc. [14] Merged into & data of First Data. [15] (HRO)For a Fundamental Chge at declining prices. [16] Merged into American Int'l Group. [17] Int 4.75% to 3-1-96, 6.5% aft. [18] Was TW Food Svcs. [19] (HRO)On Chge of Ctrl at 101. [20] Subsid & data of Flagstar Cos. [21] Into Flagstar Cos com. [22] (HRO)To 10-12-98 on Chge of Ctrl at $372.42 & accr OID. [23] (HRO)On 10-12-98(03&08)at $476.73($610.26&781.19). [24] Due 10-12-13. [25] (HRO)For a Redemp Event at 100. [26] (HRO)For Repurch Event at 100. [27] Subsid&data of Ligand Pharmaceuticals. [28] Into Ligand Pharm com. [29] Was MTC Electronics. [30] Issued in min denom $100T. [31] Now Great Lakes Bancorp FSB. [32] Into Great Lakes Bancorp FSB com.

Exchange ↓ Issue, Rate, Interest Dates and Maturity	S&P Debt Rating	Bond Form	Outstdg. Mil-$	Conv. Expires	Shares per $1,000 Bond	Price per Share	Div. Income per Bond	1995 Price Range High	1995 Price Range Low	Curr Bid Sale(s) Ask(A)	Curr. Yield	Yield to Mat	Stock Value of Bond	Conv Parity	Stock Data Month End	Stock Data P/E Ratio	Earnings Per Share Yr. End	1994	1995	Last 12 Mos
[1]Greenery Rehab Group...... 6½s Jd15 2011	NR	R	26.6	2011	[2]14.425	69.32	....	81⅛	68¼	72⅝	8.95	10.02	36½	50⅜	•25¼	d	My	pd0.66	p0.79	[11]d0.12
[3]Greenery Rehab[1]Group.......... 8¾s Ao 2015	NR	R	28.2	2015	[2]18.518	54.00	....	90	88	88	9.94	10.18	46⅞	47⅝	•25¼	d	My	pd0.66	p0.79	[11]d0.12
Greenwich Air Services[4] 8s ms15 2000	NR	R	13.3	2000	85.47	11.70	....	202	75	196⅝	4.07	....	196⅝	23⅛	23	19	Sp	0.68	P1.21	1.21
◆Greyhound[5]Lines[6].............. 8½s Ms31 2007	NR	R	9.88	2007	80.81	12.375	....	93	52	92½	9.19	9.60	34⅞	11½	◆4¼	d	Dc	Δd7.58	....	[9]d3.14
• Guilford Mills 6s mS15 2012	BBB–	R	66.2	2012	33.90	29.50	20.34	103½	86	s94½	6.35	6.54	69⅛	28	•20⅜	8	Sp	1.82	P2.41	2.41
Hasbro, Inc[5] 6s mN15 1998	A–	R	150	1998	34.09	29.33	10.91	120¼	104⅛	109⅝	5.47	2.51	105¾	32¼	◆31	17	Dc	□2.01	E1.80	[9]1.65
[7]Hazleton Labs 6½s Mn15 2006	A	R	11.4	2006	[8]79.461	12.58	57.21	297	205⅝	254⅜	2.56	....	254⅜	32⅛	•32	d	Dc	1.32	Ed0.29	[10]d0.46
◆Health-Chem 10⅜s Ao15 1999	NR	R	12.5	1999	50.00	20.00	....	101	91	95	10.92	12.25	7½	19	◆1½	50	Dc	Δ0.18	....	[9]0.03
• HEALTHSOUTH[9]Corp[10] .... 5s Ao 2001	B	R	115	2001	53.15	18.813	....	166	105	154⅞	3.23	....	154⅞	29¼	•29⅛	27	Dc	0.70	E1.07	[9]0.67
Hechinger Co........................... 5½s Ao 2012	B	R	123	2012	[11]35.92	27.84	5.75	66¾	42¾	46½	11.83	13.86	15¾	13	4⅜	d	Ja	±d0.24	....	[10]d0.84
Hector Communications[12]... 8½s Fa15 2002	NR	R	11.0	2002	112.50	8.89	....	105	97	100	8.50	8.50	85⅞	9	7⅝	50	Dc	0.97	....	[9]0.15
• Hercules Inc......................... 6½s Jd30 1999	A–	R	5.57	1999	85.71	11.67	78.85	494	494	483¼	1.35	....	483¼	56½	•56⅜	20	Dc	2.29	E2.80	[9]2.95
• Hercules Inc.......................... 8s fA15 2010	A–	R	66.9	2010	67.11	14.90	61.74	253	253	378⅜	2.11	....	378⅜	56½	•56⅜	20	Dc	2.29	E2.80	[9]2.95
Hexcel Corp[13] .... 7s fA 2011	NR	R	25.6	2011	32.55	30.72	....	84	62	83½	8.38	8.99	36⅝	25¾	•11¼	d	Dc	d4.10	....	[9]d0.30
• HFS Inc[5](Sr)[14] .... 4½s aO 1999	A–	R	150	1999	27.56	36.29	....	197	95½	225⅜	2.00	....	225⅜	81⅞	•81¾	61	Dc	1.06	....	[9]1.34
Hollinger[15]Inc[16](Zero)...................... [17] 2013	BB	CR	[18]485	2013	27.143	....	16.29	30¾	26½	30¾	....	6.75	19¾	11⅜	7¼	..	Dc	1.96	....	[9]j0.11
HomeTown Buffet[19]..................... 7s jD 2002	B–	R	40.0	2002	....	13.65	....	100¼	96¼	100¼	6.98	6.95	....	....	11	22	Dc	0.31	....	[10]0.50
• HoraceMann[5]Educators[20]......... 6½s jD 1999	BBB+	BE	100	1999	28.57	35.00	10.29	103¼	93	101½	6.40	6.06	89⅜	35⅝	•31¼	11	Dc	□2.23	....	[9]2.65
[21]Hospital Corp Amer .... 8½s Ms 2008	NR	R	7.59	2008	Conv into $983			109¾	100⅞	103½	8.21	8.04	....	....	....	..		....	....	....
◆Hudson General 7s jJ15 2011	NR	R	30.0	2011	30.53	32.75	15.27	110	71	s105	6.67	6.48	99¼	34½	◆32½	8	Je	Δ5.86	3.69	[9]3.91
• ICN[5]Pharmaceuticals(New) 8½s mN15 1999	B–	R	115	1999	43.51	22.983	12.03	122	84½	s111	7.66	5.32	83⅞	25⅝	•19¼	d	Dc	■d7.92	....	[9]d7.39
• IMC Global[5]Inc[22]........................ 6¼s jD 2001	BB–	R	115	2001	63.00	31.75	20.16	126	88¾	256¾	2.43	....	256¾	40⅞	•40¾	17	Je	□d0.07	□2.15	[9]2.29
• Inco Ltd (Sr)....................... 7¾s $Ms15 2016	BBB–	R	173	2016	26.14	38.25	10.46	112½	97	s107	7.24	7.09	87	41	•33¼	16	Dc	0.15	E2.05	[9]2.20
• Inco Ltd (Sr)............................ 5¾s $jJ 2004	BBB–	R	173	2004	33.33	30.00	13.33	137	104	133	4.32	1.59	110⅞	40	•33¼	16	Dc	0.15	E2.05	[9]2.20
Ingles[5]Markets[23] 10s aO15 2008	B+	R	37.5	2008	[24]90.09	11.10	59.46	108⅛	101⅛	103¾	9.64	9.48	100¼	11⅝	11⅛	12	Sp	Δ±0.90	±0.93	0.93
Integrated Device Tech[25]......... 5½s Jd 2002	B–	R	175	2002	34.93	28.625	....	131⅛	81½	81½	6.75	9.40	45	23⅜	12⅞	7	Mr	1.04	E1.68	[9]1.34
• Integrated Health Svcs[9]........... 5¾s Jj 2001	B–	R	125	2001	30.675	32.60	0.61	110	106½	A100	5.75	5.75	76¾	32⅝	•25	10	Dc	1.96	E2.48	[9]2.39
• Integrated Health Svcs[9].............. 6s Jj 2003	B	R	115	2003	31.13	32.125	0.62	127	95	95	6.32	6.91	77⅞	30⅝	•25	10	Dc	1.96	E2.48	[9]2.39
Int'l Fast Food 9s jD15 2007	NR	R	2.76	2007	117.65	8.50	....	28	15	15	....	....	6¼	1⅜	½	d	Dc	d2.04	....	[9]d0.89
• Interpool,[26]Inc[27] 5¼s jD15 2018	BB+	R	2.00	2018	42.79	23.37	....	92	71	A95	5.53	5.64	76½	22¼	•17⅞	11	Dc	1.39	....	[9]1.59
• Interstate/Johnson Lane..... 7¾s Ms31 2011	NR	R	21.0	2011	56.34	17.75	6.76	92½	79⅝	s90⅛	8.60	8.95	59⅞	16	•10⅝	11	Sp	Δ1.20	0.94	0.94
• IRT Property........................ 7.30s fA15 2003	BB+	R	86.3	2003	88.89	11.25	80.00	95	88	s95	7.68	8.19	82¼	10¾	•9¼	15	Dc	Δ0.35	....	[9]0.60
Jacobson Stores 6¾s jD15 2011	NR	R	34.5	2011	30.61	32.67	15.31	77⅛	67½	71	9.51	10.54	27⅝	23¼	9	37	Ja	0.71	....	[10]0.24

Uniform Footnote Explanations—See Page 260. Other: [1] Merged into & data of Horizon Healthcare. [2] Into Horizon Healthcare com. [3] (HRO)At 100 to 4-1-95 for Risk Events. [4] (HRO)For a Fundamental Chge at 100. [5] (HRO)On Chge of Ctrl at 100. [6] Int of 9-30-94 pd 1-27-95. [7] Cv into & data of Corning Inc. [8] Into Corning Inc com. [9] (HRO)For a Repurch Event at 100. [10] Was HEALTHSOUTH Rehab. [11] Into Cl'A'. [12] Death red benefit,ltd,as defined. [13] Int of 2-1-94 pd 2-9-95. [14] Was Hospitality Franchise Sys. [15] (HRO)On 11-4-98 at $413.95(10-5-03&08 at $553.67&$744.09). [16] (HRO)To 11-4-98 on Chge of Ctrl at $306.55 & accr int. [17] Due 10-5-13 in U.S.$. [18] Incl disc. [19] (HRO)For a Risk Event at 100. [20] Int 4% thru 11-30-94,6.5% aft. [21] Merged into Columbia Hlthcare. [22] Was IMC Fertilizer Group. [23] Int incr fr 9% on 10-15-90. [24] Into Cl A. [25] (HRO)For Designated Event at declining prices. [26] Co may exch for 5.25% Cm Cv Pfd to 12-15-16. [27] (HRO)On Chge of Ctrl at 101.

Exchange / Issue, Rate, Interest Dates and Maturity	S&P Debt Rating	Bond Form	Outstdg. Mil-$	Conv. Ex-pires	Shares per $1,000 Bond	Price per Share	Div. Income per Bond	1995 Price Range High	1995 Price Range Low	Curr Bid Sale(s) Ask(A)	Curr. Yield	Yield to Mat	Stock Value of Bond	Conv Parity	Stock Data Month End	Stock Data P/E Ratio	Yr. End	EPS 1994	EPS 1995	EPS Last 12 Mos
Kaman Corp 6s Ms15 2012	BBB−	R	33.2	2012	[1]42.81	23.36	18.84	83	72	82	7.32	8.00	47¾	19¼	11⅛	d	Dc	±d0.93	....	[9]d0.88
[2]Kelley Oil & Gas Ptnrs[3] 7⅞s jD15 1999	B−	R	[4]36.2	1999	Conv into com/com & pfd[5]			81¾	44½	49⅞	15.79	....	....	....	1 5/16	d	Dc	pd1.54	....	[9]d1.42
◆[7]Kelley Oil & Gas Ptnrs[3] 8½s Ao 2000	B−	R	26.9	2000	Conv into com/com & pfd[8]			91	35	s56	15.18	....	....	....	1 5/16	d	Dc	pd1.54	....	[9]d1.42
• Kellwood Co 9s aO15 1999	NR	R	1.32	1999	157.89	6.33	94.73	No Sale		321¾	2.80	....	321¾	20½	•20⅜	48	Ap	1.71	0.53	[10]0.42
• Kollmorgen Corp 8¾s Mn 2009	NR	R	38.0	2009	29.11	34.35	2.33	100	85¼	99½	8.79	8.81	32⅛	34¼	•11	26	Dc	0.18	....	[9]0.42
L.A. Gear, Inc.[10] 7¾s mN31 2002	CCC	R	50.0	2002	81.30	12.30	....	63¾	39½	41	18.90	....	13¼	5⅛	•1⅝	d	Nv	d1.29	Ed1.15	[8]d1.73
• Lafarge Corp 7s jJ 2013	BBB+	R	100	2013	45.20	22.125	18.08	109	98½	s102¾	6.81	6.73	84¼	22¾	•18⅝	10	Dc	±1.18	....	[9]1.83
Lam Research[11] 6s Mn 2003	B	R	66.0	2003	40.00	25.00	....	293½	149	183	3.28	....	183	45¾	45¾	12	Je	1.55	3.27	[9]3.73
[12]Landmark Bancshrs 8¾s mN 1998	BB−	R	17.3	1998	[13]40.19	24.88	32.15	106⅛	95⅛	102¼	8.56	7.84	95½	25½	23¾	13	Dc	1.69	....	[9]1.81
Laser Indus Ltd 8s mS15 2006	NR	R	7.22	2006	100.00	10.00	....	126¼	67	108¾	7.36	6.83	108¾	10⅞	◆10⅞	13	Dc	0.67	....	[9]0.83
[14]LDDS[15]Communications[16] 5s fA15 2003	B+	R	196	2003	[17]26.28	38.07	....	105	75½	105	4.76	4.23	92¾	40	35¼	25	Dc	d0.95	E1.38	[9]0.40
Legg Mason Inc 5¼s Mn 2003	BBB−	R	68.0	2003	38.76	25.80	18.60	121⅝	91	114⅞	4.57	2.98	106⅝	29¾	•27½	14	Mr	1.30	....	[9]1.93
• Leucadia Nat'l[18] 5¼s Fa 2003	BBB	R	100	2003	34.78	28.75	4.35	112	91½	s101½	5.17	5.00	87	29¼	•25	18	Dc	1.22	....	[9]1.34
• [19]Liberty Property L.P. 8s jJ 2001	NR	BE	200	2001	[20]50.00	20.00	80.00	108½	94	103¾	7.71	7.16	103¾	20¾	•20¾	25	Dc	p0.80	....	[9]0.81
[21]Liebert Corp 8s mN15 2010	AA	R	47.1	2010	[22]37.08	26.97	72.68	303¾	231⅜	303¼	2.64	....	303¼	81⅞	•81¾	19	Sp	□4.04	□4.16	4.16
Lomas[23]Financial[24](Sr)[25] 9s §aO31 2003	D	R	140	2003	57.14	17.50	....	74	5	8	....	Flat	⅛	1½	•....	d	Je	d9.07	d7.63	d7.63
• Lowe's Cos[26] 3s jJ22 2003	A−	R	[4]287	2003	38.32	....	7.66	140	105	128⅜	2.34	....	128⅜	33⅝	•33½	23	Ja	1.44	E1.45	[10]1.45
• LTC Properties 8½s Jj 2000	NR	R	30.0	2000	66.67	15.00	84.00	101½	99	100½	8.46	8.35	100⅛	15⅛	•15	14	Dc	0.99	....	[9]1.07
• LTC Properties 8½s Jj 2001	NR	R	45.0	2001	64.52	15.50	81.30	100	100	97	8.76	9.26	96⅞	15⅛	•15	14	Dc	0.99	....	[9]1.07
• LTC Properties 9¾s jJ 2004	NR	R	11.1	2004	100.00	10.00	126.00	No Sale		150	6.50	3.04	150	15	•15	14	Dc	0.99	....	[9]1.07
LTX Corp 7¼s Ao15 2011	NR	R	7.31	2011	55.56	18.00	....	80	55	75	9.67	10.58	50¾	13½	9⅛	17	Jl	d1.23	0.37	[10]0.53
◆MacNeal-Schwendler 7⅞s [27]ms15 2004	NR	R	56.6	2004	66.006	15.15	42.24	128	82	s112	7.03	6.07	105⅝	17	◆16	13	Ja	d2.27	....	[10]1.21
Magna Group[28] 7s [29]jd 1999	BB−	R	16.4	1999	57.21	17.48	45.77	151	100⅛	135⅞	5.15	....	135⅞	23⅞	23¾	13	Dc	1.69	....	[9]1.81
• Magna[30]Intl[15] 5s $aO15 2002	A−	R	345	2002	[31]13.382	54.40	14.45	104½	100	100½	4.98	4.91	58	75⅛	•43¼	..	Jl	4.18	5.20	[10]j5.04
• MagneTek, Inc[15] 8s mS15 2001	B	R	75.0	2001	62.50	16.00	....	105⅜	88	s89	8.99	10.61	50⅞	14¼	•8⅛	d	Je	d1.84	□0.29	[9]d0.08
• Malan Realty Investors 9½s jJ15 2004	NR	R	64.0	2004	58.82	17.00	99.99	95	79½	s83	11.45	12.83	72⅞	14⅛	•12⅜	..	Dc	p0.64	....	[9]....
Mark Twain Bancshrs[32] 7s Jd 1999	BB+	R	8.78	1999	62.94	15.889	67.98	248⅝	166⅞	244	2.87	....	244	38⅞	38¾	13	Dc	2.54	....	[9]2.85
Marsh Supermarkets[15] 7s Fa15 2003	B	R	20.0	2003	[33]64.52	15.50	28.39	98½	81¾	97	7.22	7.55	85½	15⅛	13¼	12	Mr	±1.02	....	[10]1.10
• Masco Corp 5¼s Fa15 2012	BBB	R	178	2012	23.65	42.28	17.97	97⅞	77½	s96	5.47	5.63	74¼	40⅝	•31⅜	17	Dc	1.22	E1.75	[9]1.20
• MascoTech, Inc 4½s jD15 2003	BB−	R	345	2003	32.26	31.00	5.16	78¾	67	78	5.77	8.34	35⅛	24¼	•10⅞	d	Dc	Δd4.00	....	[9]d4.35
Mastec Inc[34] 12s mN15 2000	NR	R	17.5	2000	59.56	16.79	....	101¾	95½	101¾	11.79	11.51	79	17⅛	13¼	45	Dc	0.47	....	[9]0.29
Max&Erma's Restaurants[15] 8s QSep 2004	NR	R	10.0	2004	101.42	9.86	....	99	89	90	8.89	9.73	59⅝	8⅞	5⅞	11	Oc	0.47	P0.50	0.50
Maxtor Corp 5¾s Ms 2012	CCC+	R	100	2012	25.00	40.00	....	77¾	50½	77	7.47	8.37	16⅝	30⅞	6⅝	d	Mr	d1.63	Ed1.75	[9]d1.40

Uniform Footnote Explanations—See Page 260. Other: [1] Into Cl A com. [2] (HRO)On Chge in Ctrl at $828.89 plus accr OID. [3] Now Kelly Oil & Gas. [4] Incl disc. [5] Into 68.666 com or 34.31 com & 7.155 $2.625 Pfd. [6] Into 68.666 com or 34.31 com & 7.155 $2.625 Pfd. [7] (HRO)For a Redemp Event at 100. [8] Into 51.864 com or 25.932 com & 5.411 $2.625 Pfd. [9] Into 51.864 com or 25.932 com & 5.411 $2.625 Pfd. [10] (HRO)For A Designated Event at 100. [11] (HRO)For a Fundamental Chge at 100. [12] Merged into & data of Magna Group. [13] Into Magna Group com. [14] Now WorldCom Inc. [15] (HRO)On Chge of Ctrl at 100. [16] Was IDB Communications Gr. [17] Into WorldCom Inc com. [18] (HRO)On Chge of Ctrl at 101. [19] Exch for & data of Liberty Prop Trust. [20] Into Liberty Property Trust com. [21] Subsid & data of Emerson Electric. [22] Into Emerson Electric com. [23] (HRO)For a Redemp Event at 101. [24] Filed Bankruptcy Chapt 11. [25] Default 10-31-95 int. [26] (HRO)On Chge of Ctrl at $880.27 & accr OID. [27] Due 8-18-04. [28] Payable in cash/com when due. [29] Due 8-1-99. [30] Co may red in whole,at 100,for tax law chge. [31] Into Cl A Vtg Shrs. [32] To be exch for com when due. [33] Conv into Cl B com. [34] Was Burnup & Sims.

Exchange ↓ Issue, Rate, Interest Dates and Maturity	S&P Debt Rating	Bond Form	Outstdg. Mil-$	Conv. Ex-pires	Shares per $1,000 Bond	Price per Share	Div. Income per Bond	1995 Price Range High	1995 Price Range Low	Curr Bid Sale(s) Ask(A)	Curr. Yield	Yield to Mat	Stock Value of Bond	Conv Parity	Stock Data Month End	Stock Data P/E Ratio	Earnings Per Share Yr. End	1994	1995	Last 12 Mos
• MAXXIM Medical 6¾s Ms 2003	B–	R	28.8	2003	55.56	18.00	....	106⅛	92	s103	6.55	6.22	93⅛	18⅝	•16¾	62	Oc	Δ1.05	....	[7]0.27
• [1]MBL[2]Int'l[3]Finance(Bermuda) 3s mN31 2002	A+	BE	2000	2002	Conv fr 4-2-96[4]			118⅛	100	109	2.75	1.62	....	....	....	..	Mr	....	....	....
• [5]McCrory[6]Corp[7] 6½s §Fa15 1992	D	R	3.37	2-15-92	Conv into Debs & cash[8]			12½	4	4	....	Flat	....	....	....	..	Ja	....	....	....
[9]McKesson Corp 4½s Ms 2004	A	R	180	2004	[10]38.554	25.9375	24.67	98	88	94⅛	4.78	5.40	70	24½	18⅛	19	Mr	1.16	....	[9]0.94
Medalist Indus 7½s jJ 2001	NR	R	7.76	2001	53.33	18.75	....	89	82½	86	8.72	10.95	32	16¼	6	17	Dc	0.02	....	[9]0.35
[11]Medco Containment Svc[12] 6s mS 2001	AAA	BE	28.7	2001	Cv into Cash & Com[13]			216⅝	143¾	216⅜	2.77	....	....	....	•65⅝	24	Dc	2.38	E2.70	[9]2.61
[14]Medical Care Int'l[15] 7s fA 2015	BBB	R	69.0	2015	[16]14.75	67.82	1.77	100	84	99	7.07	7.09	74⅞	67⅛	•50¾	21	Dc	□2.13	E2.37	[9]2.19
• [17]Mediplex Group 6½s fA 2003	NR	R	22.4	2003	[18]40.128	24.92	....	145	140	98½	6.60	6.75	54¼	24⅝	•13½	11	Dc	1.19	....	[9]1.21
• [19]MEDIQ Inc[15] 7½s jJ15 2003	CCC+	R	34.5	2003	[20]65.359	15.30	....	82	77	s79¾	9.40	11.60	58⅞	12¼	9	17	Sp	0.50	0.53	0.53
◆MEDIQ Inc 7¼s Jd 2006	CCC+	R	51.7	2006	94.79	10.55	....	90	64½	s80	9.06	10.44	40⅞	8½	◆4¼	d	Sp	d0.30	Pd0.20	d0.20
• Meditrust 7s Ms 1998	BBB–	R	40.8	1998	32.65	30.625	88.16	101½	100	113⅞	6.15	0.56	113⅞	35	•34⅞	13	Dc	2.28	E2.55	[9]2.49
• Meditrust 7½s Ms 2001	BBB–	R	87.9	2001	27.64	36.18	74.63	105	93	100¼	7.48	7.44	96½	36⅜	•34⅞	13	Dc	2.28	E2.55	[9]2.49
• Meditrust 9s Jj 2002	BBB–	R	18.2	2002	37.04	27.00	100.01	125½	105½	129¼	6.96	3.55	129¼	35	•34⅞	13	Dc	2.28	E2.55	[9]2.49
• Medusa Corp[15] 6s mN15 2003	B+	R	57.5	2003	30.19	33.125	15.10	102	91	98½	6.09	6.24	80⅛	32¾	•26½	11	Dc	1.81	....	[9]2.31
• Mellon Bank([21]Sub Cap Nts) 7¼s mS 1999	BBB+	R	4.50	1999	29.70	33.67	65.34	160	110	159¾	4.54	....	159¾	53⅞	•53¾	11	Dc	2.42	E4.50	[9]3.39
Michaels[22]Stores[15] 4¾s Jj15 2003	B+	BE	97.0	2003	26.32	38.00	....	109⅛	75⅝	79½	5.97	....	36¼	30¼	13¾	..	Ja	1.77	....	[10]0.02
Micropolis Corp 6s Ms15 2012	CCC	R	75.0	2012	20.62	48.50	....	64½	48	48	12.50	14.33	7¾	23⅜	3¾	d	Dc	d2.03	Ed4.00	[9]d3.50
Microsemi Corp[23] 5⅞s §Ms 2012	NR	R	33.3	2012	73.80	13.55	....	108⅞	59½	93⅝	....	Flat	63¾	12¾	8⅝	11	Sp	d0.28	P0.74	0.74
◆Mid-Atlantic Realty Trust 7⅝s mS15 2003	NR	R	60.0	2003	95.24	10.50	87.62	86½	80	s86	8.87	10.30	82¼	9⅛	◆8⅝	15	Dc	0.46	....	[9]0.57
Midlantic(Banks)Corp 8¼s jJ 2010	BBB–	R	73.0	2010	20.83	48.00	26.66	137¾	93	136¾	6.03	4.72	136¾	65¾	65⅝	15	Dc	□5.18	E4.35	[9]4.62
Mobile Telecommun Tech[15] 6¾s Mn15 2002	NR	R	2.79	2002	100.00	10.00	....	363¾	190	213¾	3.16	....	213¾	21⅜	21⅜	d	Dc	d0.76	Ed0.78	[9]d0.80
◆Moog,Inc 9⅞s Jj15 2006	NR	R	22.1	2006	[24]43.71	22.88	....	106	99⅜	s105	9.40	9.10	75½	24⅛	◆17¼	17	Sp	Δ±0.22	P±1.00	1.00
• [25]Moran Energy[26] 8¾s Jj15 2008	NR	R	23.7	2008	[27]57.01	17.54	....	83	64	83	....	Flat	12⅞	14⅝	•2¼	32	Dc	0.02	....	[9]0.07
• Morgan(J.P.)Co.(Sr) 4¾s mN 1998	AA+	R	2.00	1998	50.00	20.00	162.00	No Sale		401¼	1.18	....	401¼	80¼	•80¼	12	Dc	6.02	E6.35	[9]5.59
• Morgan Stanley Group(Zero) [28] 2001	A+	BE	[29]25.0	1998	[30]13.118	....	14.95	83½	83½	81	....	3.54	72½	61¾	•55¼	20	Dc	0.21	E2.70	[9]0.28
• Motorola, Inc[31](Zero) [32] 2009	AA–	R	[29]130	2009	18.268	....	7.31	145	98	109	....	....	104¼	59¾	•57	18	Dc	2.65	E3.14	[9]3.08
• Motorola,Inc[33](Zero)[34] [35] 2013	AA–	R	[29]480	2013	11.178	....	4.47	95½	67¾	s76½	....	1.52	63¾	68½	•57	18	Dc	2.65	E3.14	[9]3.08
• National Education 6½s Mn15 2011	B–	R	57.5	2011	40.00	25.00	....	73	50⅛	69½	9.35	10.55	33	17⅜	•8¼	d	Dc	d2.16	....	[9]d2.74
• Nat'l Health Investors 10s [36]jj 2006	NR	R	110	2006	50.00	20.00	140.00	128⅜	128⅜	165⅝	6.04	2.88	165⅝	33⅛	•33⅛	12	Dc	2.35	....	[9]2.63
◆Nat'l Healthcare L.P.[37] 6s [38]Qmar31 2000	NR	BE	30.0	2000	65.762	15.206	136.79	256	204	256½	2.34	....	256½	39⅛	◆39	15	Dc	2.02	....	[9]2.48
• Nationwide Health Prop(Sr) 6¼s Jj 1999	BBB	BE	65.0	1998	22.31	44.825	64.70	102	91½	s101	6.19	5.88	93¾	45⅜	•42	16	Dc	2.47	....	[9]2.62
Network Equip Tech[39] 7¼s Mn15 2014	NR	R	33.6	2014	31.75	31.50	....	133⅜	87⅞	103⅞	6.98	6.87	87	32¾	•27⅜	14	Mr	1.44	....	[9]1.87
• [40]News[41]America[42]Hldgs(Zero) [43] 2002	BBB–	R	[29]60.0	2002	[44]30.084	....	2.41	No Sale		A70	....	5.78	64⅜	23⅜	•21⅜	15	Je	Δ1.76	Δ1.36	[9]1.37

Uniform Footnote Explanations—See Page 260. Other: [1] Conv into & data of Mitsubishi Bank Ltd. [2] (HRO)For Fundamental Chge at 100. [3] Co may red in whole,at 100,for tax law chge. [4] Into 45.45 ADS of Mitsubishi Bank Ltd. [5] Subsid of Rapid-American. [6] Default 2-15-92 P&I. [7] Prop exch:$200&$800 10.25% Sub Deb in reorg. [8] Into $643 10% Deb'06 & $46.43 cash. [9] Exch for & data of Armor All Products. [10] Into Armor All Products com(or cash equiv). [11] (HRO)For a Designated Event at 100. [12] Cv into & data of Merck & Co. [13] Into $532.79 & 24.877 com of Merck & Co. [14] Merged into & data of Columbia/HCA Hlthcare. [15] (HRO)On Chge of Ctrl at 100. [16] Into Columbia/HCA Healthcare com. [17] Merged into & data of Sun Hlthcre Grp. [18] Into Sun Hlthcre Grp com. [19] Exch for & data of NutraMax Products. [20] Into NutraMax Products com. [21] To be exch for Cap Sec when due. [22] Int at 4.75% to 1-15-96,6.75% aft. [23] Default 3-1-93 int. [24] Into Cl A. [25] Now Kaneb Services. [26] Int arrears paid 3-31-89. [27] Into Kaneb Services com. [28] Due 12-31-01. [29] Incl disc. [30] Into SmithKline Beecham ADRs. [31] (HRO)On 9-7-99('04)at $553.68($744.10). [32] Due 9-7-09. [33] (HRO)To 9-27-98 on Chge of Ctrl at $639.23 & accr OID. [34] (HRO)On 9-27-98(03&08)at$714.90($799.52&$894.16). [35] Due 9-27-13. [36] Due 10-17-06. [37] (HRO)On Chge of Ctrl at 125. [38] Due 7-1-00. [39] (HRO)To 5-15-99 for Fundamental Chge as defined. [40] Gtd by & conv into News Corp Ltd. [41] (HRO)On 3-31-97 at $683.74. [42] (HRO)To 3-31-97,on Chge in Ctrl. [43] Due 3-31-02. [44] Into News Corp Ltd ADSs.

Exchange ↓ Issue, Rate, Interest Dates and Maturity	S&P Debt Rating	Bond Form	Outstdg. Mil-$	Conv. Ex-pires	Shares per $1,000 Bond	Price per Share	Div. Income per Bond	1995 Price Range High	1995 Price Range Low	Curr Bid Sale(s) Ask(A)	Curr. Yield	Yield to Mat	Stock Value of Bond	Conv Parity	Stock Data Month End	Stock Data P/E Ratio	EPS Yr. End	EPS 1994	EPS 1995	EPS Last 12 Mos
Noble Affilates[1] .... 4¼s mN 2003	BBB−	R	230	2003	27.29	36.65	4.37	99¾	82	99¾	4.26	4.29	81⅝	36⅝	•29⅞	d	Dc	0.06	Ed0.01	[9]d0.11
Northwest Natural Gas (Sr).... 7¼s Ms 2012	A−	R	12.9	2012	33.50	29.85	60.30	114¾	93¾	110⅝	6.55	6.20	110⅝	33⅛	33	14	Dc	2.44	....	[9]2.35
• Norwest Corp[2] .... 6¾s jJ 2003	A+	R	0.20	2003	200.00	5.00	192.00	No Sale		660	1.02	....	660	33	•33	11	Dc	2.45	E2.80	[9]2.67
• NovaCare, Inc[1] 5½s Jj15 2000	B	R	175	2000	37.52	26.65	....	89	75¾	s81⅝	6.74	11.28	19¼	21⅞	•5⅛	5	Je	0.90	0.95	[9]0.90
O'Brien Enviro[3]Energy[4] ..... 7¾s §Ms15 2002	NR	R	11.4	2002	[5]210.53	4.75	....	109	29½	109	....	Flat	....	5¼	....	..	Je	d0.98	....	d0.98
O'Brien[4]Enviro[3]Energy[1] ...... 11s §Ms15 2010	NR	R	11.5	2010	[5]180.18	5.55	....	113	29½	113	....	Flat	....	6⅜	....	..	Je	d0.98	....	d0.98
O'Brien[4]Enviro[3]Energy[1] ...... 11s §Ms15 2011	NR	R	26.3	2011	[6]183.15	5.46	....	113	29½	113	....	Flat	....	6¼	....	..	Je	d0.98	....	d0.98
• Office Depot[7](Zero)[8] .... [9] 2007	BB−	BE	[10]316	2007	29.263	....	....	91	69	65	....	3.64	57½	22¼	•19⅝	23	Dc	0.69	....	[9]0.84
• Office[11]Depot[12](Zero) .... [13] 2008	BB−	BE	[10]345	2008	21.234	....	....	71	52	58	....	4.29	41¾	27⅜	•19⅝	23	Dc	0.69	....	[9]0.84
OHM Corp[14] .... 8s aO 2006	B+	R	57.5	2006	41.67	24.00	....	95¼	78	86½	9.25	10.08	30¾	20⅞	•7⅜	d	Dc	d0.49	....	[9]d0.61
Old Nat'l Bancorp(Ind).......... 8s mS15 2012	BBB+	R	38.0	2012	42.517	23.524	39.12	152⅝	143½	147¾	5.41	4.04	147¾	34⅞	34¾	15	Dc	2.08	....	[9]2.20
• Old Republic Int'l 5¾s fA15 2002	A+	R	110	2002	39.024	25.625	20.29	137	95¼	138⅝	4.15	....	138⅝	35⅝	•35½	11	Dc	2.55	....	[9]3.16
• Olsten Corp[15] 4⅞s Mn15 2003	BBB	R	125	2003	28.74	34.80	9.20	120½	100	s115	4.24	2.62	113⅝	40⅛	•39½	19	Dc	±1.67	E2.07	[9]1.99
• Omnicare Inc[1] .... 5¾s aO 2003	B+	R	80.5	2003	69.26	14.438	6.93	314	160	s314	1.83	....	310	45⅜	•44¾	53	Dc	0.60	....	[9]0.84
[16]On-Line Software Intl 6¼s Ms15 2002	NR	R	14.3	2002	Conv into $855.67			95	85½	85⅝	7.30	9.35	....	....	....	..		....	....	....
Orbital Sciences[1] .... 6¾s Ms 2003	B−	R	55.0	2003	69.565	14.375	....	153⅛	99	99	6.82	6.93	88¾	14¼	12¾	..	Dc	0.28	....	[9]0.02
• Oryx Energy Co[17] 7½s Mn15 2014	B+	R	200	2014	25.56	39.125	....	91	69	88½	8.47	8.77	34¼	34⅝	•13⅜	8	Dc	□d0.68	E1.51	[9]1.58
• Outboard Marine[1] .... 7s jJ 2002	B+	R	65.0	2002	44.94	22.25	17.98	110	99	103¾	6.75	6.29	91⅝	23⅛	•20⅜	8	Sp	2.42	2.56	2.56
◆Pacific Gulf Prop 8⅜s Fa15 2001	B	R	56.6	2001	53.70	18.62	85.92	96	87	s93	9.01	10.15	87⅜	17⅜	◆16¼	..	Dc	□‡0.63	....	[9]....
Pacific Physician Svcs 5½s jD15 2003	B−	R	69.0	2003	34.48	29.00	....	96	72½	96	5.73	6.14	62⅛	27⅞	18	26	Jl	0.54	□0.63	[10]0.67
• Pacific Scientific 7¾s Jd15 2003	NR	R	17.3	2003	52.64	19.00	6.32	142	101	131⅝	5.89	2.99	131⅝	25⅛	•25	24	Dc	0.85	....	[9]1.01
Paco Pharm'l Svs .... 6½s Ms 2007	NR	R	4.27	2007	Conv into $505.69			82⅞	70¼	82⅞	7.84	8.95	....	....	....	..		....	....	....
• Patten Corp 8¼s Mn15 2012	CCC	R	34.7	2012	115.571	8.653	....	93½	74½	s90½	9.12	9.40	55	7⅞	•4¾	14	Mr	0.30	....	[9]0.32
• [18]Pennzoil Co[19](Sr) 6½s Jj15 2003	BBB	R	403	2003	11.887	84.125	23.77	127	111	124	5.24	2.73	62⅜	104⅜	•52⅜	18	Dc	2.60	E2.87	[9]3.03
• [20]Pennzoil Co(Sr) .... 4¾s aO 2003	BBB	CR	500	2003	[21]8.502	117.625	17.00	101¾	85½	s101¼	4.69	4.56	44⅝	119⅛	•52⅜	18	Dc	2.60	E2.87	[9]3.03
• Pep Boys-Man,Mo,Jack[1] .... 4s mS 1999	BBB−	R	86.3	1999	24.39	41.00	4.63	102	92	96¼	4.16	5.13	62½	39½	•25⅝	18	Ja	□1.32	E1.40	[10]1.33
• Pfizer Inc 4s Fa15 1997	AAA	R	0.70	1997	168.407	5.938	175.14	No Sale		1061	0.38	....	1061	63⅛	•63	25	Dc	2.09	E2.50	[9]2.39
• Pier 1 Imports[22] .... 6⅞s Ao 2002	B	R	70.0	2002	83.33	12.00	13.33	111½	90	s108	6.37	5.35	94⅞	13	•11⅜	20	Fb	0.60	....	[11]0.57
• Pioneer Financial Svcs[23] 8s jJ15 2000	NR	R	3.10	2000	85.11	11.75	15.32	154	93½	157½	5.08	....	157½	18⅝	•18½	7	Dc	2.36	....	[9]2.46
• [24]Pittston Co .... 4s jJ 1997	BB+	R	14.6	1997	Conv into $157.80			95⅛	89⅛	95⅛	4.20	7.48	....	....	....	..		....	....	....
• Pogo Producing[15] 5½s Ms15 2004	B	R	75.0	2004	45.069	22.188	5.41	118	91¼	127⅜	4.32	1.89	127⅜	28⅜	•28¼	80	Dc	□0.82	E0.35	[9]0.34
• Pogo Producing 8s jD31 2005	B	R	43.5	2005	25.32	39.50	3.04	103½	96	s102½	7.80	7.64	71⅝	40½	•28¼	80	Dc	□0.82	E0.35	[9]0.34
• Potomac Elec Pwr (Sr) .... 5s mS 2002	A−	R	115	2002	29.50	....	48.97	94	79½	93	5.38	6.30	77½	31⅝	•26¼	37	Dc	1.79	E0.70	[9]0.69

Uniform Footnote Explanations—See Page 260. Other: [1] (HRO)On Chge of Ctrl at 100. [2] Was Northwest Bancorp. [3] Was O'Brien Energy Sys. [4] Filed bankruptcy Chapt 11:Default 3-15-94 int. [5] Into Cl 'A' com. [6] Into Cl'A' com. [7] (HRO)On 12-11-97(02) at $610.27($781.19). [8] (HRO)To 12-11-97,Chge in Ctrl,$476.74&accr OID. [9] Due 12-11-07. [10] Incl disc. [11] (HRO)To 11-1-00 on Chge of Ctrl at $552.07 & accr OID. [12] (HRO)On 11-1-00 at $728.41. [13] Due 11-1-08. [14] Was Environmental Treat/Tech. [15] (HRO)For a Repurch Event at 100. [16] Acq by Computer Assoc Int'l. [17] (HRO)For a Risk Event at 100. [18] Exch for & data of Chevron Corp. [19] (HRO)For certain events at 100. [20] Cv into & data of Chevron Corp. [21] Into Chevron Corp com. [22] (HRO)For a Redemp Event at 100. [23] (HRO)For a Fundamental Chge at 100. [24] Now Pittston Svcs Gr.

Exchange ↓ Issue, Rate, Interest Dates and Maturity	S&P Debt Rating	Bond Form	Outstdg. Mil-$	Conv. Ex-pires	Shares per $1,000 Bond	Price per Share	Div. Income per Bond	1995 Price Range High	1995 Price Range Low	Curr Bid Sale(s) Ask(A)	Curr. Yield	Yield to Mat	Stock Value of Bond	Conv Parity	Stock Data Month End	Stock Data P/E Ratio	Earnings Per Share Yr. End	1994	1995	Last 12 Mos
• Potomac Elec Pwr (Sr)[1] 7s Jj15 2018	A−	R	68.8	2018	37.04	27.00	61.49	102½	83	s102½	6.83	6.78	97¼	27¾	•26¼	37	Dc	1.79	E0.70	[9]0.69
◆Presidio[2]Oil[3] .... 9s §Ms15 2015	D	R	50.0	2015	[4]106.61	9.38	....	40	16½	18½	....	Flat	¼	1¾	◆1/32	d	Dc	d0.91	....	[9]d1.11
[5]Preston Corp .... 7s Mn 2011	NR	R	27.8	2011	Conv into apx $158.65			82	72	76	9.21	10.11	....	....	....	..		....	....	....
[2]Price Co[6] .... 6¾s Ms 2001	BBB	R	288	2001	44.37	22.54	....	102¾	89	101¼	6.67	6.46	67¾	22⅞	15¼	21	Au	d0.51	0.68	[11]0.71
[6]Price Co 5½s Fa31 2012	BBB	R	179	2012	42.07	23.77	....	98¼	74½	94¾	5.80	6.01	64¼	22⅝	15¼	21	Au	d0.51	0.68	[11]0.71
• Prime Hospitality[7] 7s Ao15 2002	B−	R	75.0	2002	83.33	12.00	....	111	100	s102½	6.83	6.51	83⅜	12⅜	•10	20	Dc	Δ0.57	E0.50	[9]0.59
Primedex Health Systems...... 10s Qjul 2003	NR	R	22.5	2003	125.00	8.00	....	50	1	4	....	Flat	2½	⅜	3/16	d	Oc	Pd0.52	....	[4]d0.51
◆Professional Bancorp([8]Reset) 8½s Ms 2004	NR	R	5.00	2004	71.42	14.00	....	114	88	105⅜	8.07	....	89⅜	14⅞	◆12½	8	Dc	0.82	....	[9]1.45
Proffitt's Inc .... 4¾s mN 2003	B	R	86.3	2003	23.42	42.70	....	96	73	85	5.59	7.29	61½	36⅜	26¼	15	Ja	1.46	....	[10]1.73
Property Cap Tr.................. 9¾s Mn15 2008	NR	R	2.55	2008	52.63	19.00	25.26	92	80	90	10.83	11.26	45½	17⅛	◆8⅝	8	Jl	0.45	Δ0.58	[10]0.98
Property Cap Tr......................10s jD15 2009	NR	R	30.8	2009	46.08	21.70	22.12	98	79⅜	96⅞	10.32	10.43	39¾	21⅛	◆8⅝	8	Jl	0.45	Δ0.58	[10]0.98
• Quanex Corp[9] 6.88s Jd31 2007	BB−	R	86.3	2007	31.75	31.50	19.05	100	92	s96½	7.13	7.34	61⅝	30½	•19⅜	8	Oc	0.96	□P2.20	2.20
Quantum Corp .... 6⅜s Ao 2002	B+	R	212	2002	55.10	18.15	....	157⅛	93¼	103½	6.16	5.70	88⅞	18⅞	16⅛	9	Mr	1.72	E1.70	[9]0.10
Quantum Hlth Resources[7] ...... 4¾s aO 2000	B+	R	86.3	2000	32.99	30.31	....	109½	71	71	6.69	13.14	32⅜	21⅝	9¾	61	Dc	1.37	E0.16	[9]0.43
Quixote Corp 8s Ao15 2011	NR	R	20.0	2011	52.63	19.00	12.63	94	85	85	9.41	9.92	40⅞	16¼	7¾	d	Je	1.44	0.73	[9]d0.84
Raymond Corp[2] 6½s jD15 2003	B	R	57.5	2003	56.47	17.71	....	138	108	128½	5.06	2.53	128½	22⅞	22¾	12	Dc	1.47	....	[9]1.88
[10]Re Capital Corp(Sr)[11] .... 5½s fA 2000	NR	R	69.0	2000	Conv into $1076.33			108⅜	93⅜	107⅝	5.11	3.68	....	....	....	..	Dc	....	....	....
[12]Recognition Equip............ 7¼s Ao15 2011	B−	R	51.7	2011	59.70	16.75	....	94⅞	71¾	85¾	8.45	8.98	....	14⅜	•....	24	Oc	d1.70	E0.50	[7]0.11
Regal[2]Communications[13] .... 10s §Jd15 2008	NR	R	35.0	2008	132.28	7.56	....	10	4	7	....	Flat	....	⅝	....	..	Sp	....	....	[6]....
• Regency Health Services..... 6½s jJ15 2003	NR	R	50.0	2003	80.81	12.375	....	129	98¼	s99	6.57	6.67	81⅞	12⅜	•10⅛	12	Dc	□0.01	....	[9]0.79
Richardson Electr 7¼s jD15 2006	NR	R	70.8	2006	47.30	21.14	7.57	85¾	74	85	8.53	9.48	50⅞	18	10¾	28	My	d1.75	Δ0.21	[11]0.38
• Rite Aid[14](Zero)[15]............................ [16] 2006	BBB+	R	[17]400	2006	15.933	....	10.83	54	45	54⅝	....	5.80	54⅝	34⅜	•34¼	17	Fb	1.67	E1.95	[11]1.85
• Riverwood Int'l[18] 6¾s mS15 2003	NR	R	125	2003	Conv fr 9-15-96[19]			148	102	107	6.31	5.62	....	....	•19⅛	38	Dc	□0.16	....	[9]0.50
• RLI Corp(Sr).......................... 6s jJ15 2003	BBB−	R	40.0	2003	38.46	26.00	20.00	104	84¾	105	5.71	5.19	96¼	27⅜	•25	33	Dc	d0.67	....	[9]0.74
• Roadmaster Indus[10]............... 8s fA15 2003	B−	R	51.7	2003	250.00	4.00	....	106½	77½	s84	9.52	11.17	59⅜	3⅜	•2⅜	d	Dc	0.16	....	[9]d0.19
◆Rogers Commun'n([20]Dfrd)(Sr)[21] . 5¾s $mN26 2005	BB−	R	225	2005	[22]34.368	....	....	No Sale		52⅞	10.87	15.05	52½	15½	15¼	d	Dc	±d1.16	....	[9]jd1.81
◆Rogers[23]Commun'n[24](Zero)(Sr)[25].. [26] 2013	BB−	R	[17]280	2013	[22]20.675	....	....	35	31	34¾	....	Flat	31⅝	16⅞	15¼	d	Dc	±d1.16	....	[9]jd1.81
• Rohr, Inc[27]........................... 7¾s Mn15 2004	B	R	58.0	2004	96.62	10.35	....	130½	130½	139	5.58	2.55	139	14½	•14⅜	23	Jl	0.38	□0.68	[10]0.61
• Rohr(Indus) Inc......................... 7s aO 2012	B	R	115	2012	23.26	43.00	....	86	67½	85	8.24	8.72	33½	36⅝	•14⅜	23	Jl	0.38	□0.68	[10]0.61
• Royce Value Trust[28]............ 5¾s Jd31 2004	NR	R	40.0	2004	[29]75.19	13.30	2.26	102⅛	93¼	s101½	5.67	5.53	89⅜	13½	•11⅞	..	Dc	....	....	....
RPM, Inc[30](Zero)[31] .... [32] 2012	BBB−	R	[17]400	2012	24.416	....	11.72	43	37⅝	42⅝	....	5.16	40⅜	17½	16½	19	My	0.74	0.86	[8]0.87
◆Saba Petroleum[33] 9s jD15 2005	NR	R	11.0	2005	114.29	8.75	....	101	97	99½	9.05	9.08	87¼	8¾	◆7⅝	63	Dc	0.13	....	[9]0.12
◆Sage Energy[34] 8½s aO15 2005	NR	R	19.8	2005	Conv into $260			86	78¼	s85¾	9.91	10.90	....	....	....	..		....	....	....

Uniform Footnote Explanations—See Page 260. Other: [1] (HRO)At 100,ltd as defined. [2] (HRO)On Chge of Ctrl at 100. [3] Default 9-15-95 int. [4] Into Cl A com. [5] Merged into Yellow Corp. [6] Now Price/Costco Inc. [7] (HRO)For a Risk Event at 100. [8] Int to 3-1-98,adj aft. [9] (HRO)On Chge of Ctrl at curr redemp price. [10] (HRO)For a Repurch Event at 100. [11] Acq by Zurich Reinsurance Ctr. [12] Now Recognition Int'l. [13] Filed bankruptcy Chapt 11:default 6-15-94 int. [14] (HRO)On 7-24-96('01)at $514.86($717.54). [15] To 7-24-96 for Chge in Ctrl at$369.43 &accr OID. [16] Due 7-24-06. [17] Incl disc. [18] Co must offer repurch at 100 on Chge of Ctrl. [19] Into 57.01 com,earliest:9-15-96,Ctrl Chge,com tender. [20] Int of 2% pd in cash, bal deferred. [21] To 11-26-98 Co may offer repurch on Chge of Ctrl. [22] Conv into Cl'B' com. [23] (HRO)6-21-98(5-20-03&08)$445.28($581.33&$762.51). [24] To 5-20-98 Co may offer $337.85&accr OID on Ctrl Chge. [25] May repurch in whole at $337.85&accr OID for tax chge. [26] Due 5-20-13, in U.S.$. [27] Co must offer repurch at 101 on Chge of Ctrl. [28] Terms may be reset for low mkt price to 5-31-99. [29] Not red during last 7 trad'g days in ea Dec. [30] (HRO)9-30-97(02&07)at $459.63($595.58&$771.74). [31] (HRO)To 9-30-97,Chge in Ctrl,$354.7 &accr OID. [32] Due 9-30-12. [33] (HRO)On Chge of Ctrl at 102. [34] Subsid of Sage Acquis.

Exchange ↓ Issue, Rate, Interest Dates and Maturity	S&P Debt Rating	Bond Form	Outstdg. Mil-$	Conv. Ex-pires	Shares per $1,000 Bond	Price per Share	Div. Income per Bond	1995 Price Range High	1995 Price Range Low	Curr Bid Sale(s) Ask(A)	Curr. Yield	Yield to Mat	Stock Value of Bond	Conv Parity	Stock Data Month End	Stock Data P/E Ratio	EPS Yr. End	EPS 1994	EPS 1995	EPS Last 12 Mos
Sanifill, Inc[1] .... 7½s Jd 2006	BB−	R	58.0	2006	34.70	28.82	....	118½	95½	117½	6.38	5.29	115⅞	33⅞	•33⅜	23	Dc	1.12	E1.40	[9]1.35
Savoy Pictures Entertainment.... 7s jJ 2003	B	R	105	2003	53.76	18.60	....	80	68	80	8.75	10.98	34	15	6¼	d	Dc	d2.58	....	[9]d2.63
[2]Scan-Tron Corp.......... 6¾s Jd 2011	NR	R	10.6	2011	[3]39.73	25.17	40.52	97¾	90¼	95¾	7.05	7.21	83	24⅛	•20⅞	13	Dc	1.68	E1.60	[9]1.59
Scandinavian Broadcstg[4]Sys[5]. 7¼s fA 2005	NR	BE	135	2005	34.88	28.67	....	112	100	102¼	7.09	6.92	76⅜	29⅜	21⅞	d	Dc	d0.22	....	[9]d3.12
Schuler Homes[6].......... 6½s Jj15 2003	B	R	50.0	2003	45.81	21.83	....	86½	73¾	80¾	8.05	10.42	35⅞	17¾	7¾	9	Dc	1.47	....	[9]0.81
• Seagate Technology.......... 6¾s Mn 2012	BB+	R	267	2012	23.53	42.50	....	128½	82½	s113	5.97	5.53	111⅞	48⅛	•47½	10	Je	3.08	3.52	[9]4.66
• [7]Seagram & Sons[8](Zero).......... [9] 2006	A−	R	[10]70.7	2006	[11]18.44	....	11.06	68½	50¼	63¾	....	4.47	63⅝	34⅝	•34½	54	Ja	□2.18	E0.63	[10]0.95
Security First[4].......... 6¼s QMay 2008	NR	R	8.50	2008	85.58	11.68	34.23	134⅞	104⅞	122	5.12	3.98	122	14⅜	14¼	9	Mr	P1.61	....	[9]1.55
• Seitel Inc[12].......... 9s Ms31 2002	NR	R	3.50	2002	107.758	9.28	....	No Sale		381¼	2.36	....	381¼	35½	•35⅜	27	Dc	□1.23	....	[9]1.29
• SFP Pipeline Hldgs([13]V/R)... 11.16s QAug15 2010	NR	R	[10]219	2010	Exchangeable[14]			124	118	A119	....	Flat	....	....	•36⅝	11	Dc	3.93	....	[9]3.19
Sholodge, Inc[4].......... 7½s Mn 2004	B+	R	54.0	2004	42.90	23.31	....	104¾	79⅝	81⅝	9.19	10.91	40⅞	19⅛	9½	4	Dc	□0.93	....	[9]2.08
• Shoney's, Inc(Zero).......... [15] 2004	NR	R	[10]201	2004	29.349	....	....	45½	36½	38	....	12.03	30⅛	13	•10¼	15	Oc	□Δ1.52	E0.66	[8]1.06
Sierra Tahoe Bancorp.......... 8½s Fa 2004	NR	R	10.0	2004	100.00	10.00	24.00	120	90	113¾	7.47	6.30	106¼	11⅜	10⅝	11	Dc	1.12	....	[9]0.97
• Sizeler Property Inv.......... 8s jJ15 2003	NR	R	65.0	2003	76.92	13.00	86.15	90½	85	86¼	9.28	10.70	68⅜	11¼	•8⅞	25	Dc	Δ0.58	....	[9]0.35
• Snyder Oil Corp[4].......... 7s Mn15 2001	B+	R	83.7	2001	43.18	23.1575	11.23	95	86¼	s92¾	7.55	8.71	51⅞	21½	•12	d	Dc	0.07	....	[9]d0.68
• Solectron Corp[16](Zero)[17].......... [18] 2012	B+	R	[10]35.0	2012	20.792	....	....	75⅝	55	91¾	....	0.53	91¾	44¼	•44⅛	22	Au	1.32	1.82	[11]1.93
Sports & Recreation[4].......... 4¼s mN 2000	B−	R	74.7	2000	39.21	25.50	....	107	67	69	6.16	13.10	28	17⅝	•7⅛	11	Ja	□0.84	....	[10]0.65
[19]SRI Corp.......... 8¾s Jj 2008	BBB−	R	7.83	2008	[20]70.572	14.17	79.04	270⅞	176⅞	250⅝	3.49	....	250⅝	35⅝	35½	10	Dc	2.76	....	[9]3.56
• Standard Commercial[21]...... 7¼s Ms31 2007	B	R	69.0	2007	31.44	31.81	....	80½	67	s71	10.21	12.01	31⅛	22⅝	•9⅞	d	Mr	d3.52	....	[9]d4.05
Starbucks Corp[4].......... 4¼s mN 2002	B−	R	150	2002	Conv 60 days fr 10-24-95			111½	98⅝	106¼	4.00	3.22	....	....	21	57	Sp	0.17	P0.37	0.37
Starbucks Corp[4].......... 4½s fA 2003	B−	R	80.5	2003	66.67	30.00	....	156¾	90¾	140⅛	3.21	....	140⅛	21⅛	21	57	Sp	0.17	P0.37	0.37
State St Boston.......... 7¾s Mn 2008	A+	R	3.92	2008	173.92	5.75	125.22	804½	497⅞	782¾	0.99	....	782¾	45⅛	•45	15	Dc	2.70	E2.95	[9]2.92
Statesman Group[4].......... 6¼s Mn 2003	NR	R	23.2	2003	Conv into $1000.78[22]			101¼	100	100⅛	6.24	6.23	....	....	....	..	Dc	....	....	....
• Sterling Banc([23]F/R 4th)[24].......... [25]jj 1998	NR	R	14.8	1998	80.00	12.50	22.40	102⅝	96	102⅝	....	Flat	100	12⅞	•12½	15	Dc	0.63	....	[9]0.81
• Sterling Banc([26]F/R 'V').......... jJ 2001	NR	R	7.05	2001	114.29	8.75	32.00	115	97⅞	142⅞	....	....	142⅞	12⅝	•12½	15	Dc	0.63	....	[9]0.81
• Sterling Software[4].......... 5¾s Fa 2003	CALL	R	115	2-5-96	35.27	28.35	....	210	125	220	2.61	Call	220	62½	•62⅜	..	Sp	2.54	0.39	0.39
• Stone Container[4].......... 6¾s Fa15 2007	B	R	115	2007	29.464	33.94	17.68	99	75	s89½	7.54	8.21	42⅜	30½	•14⅜	3	Dc	□d1.60	E4.50	[9]4.08
• Storage Technology[27].......... 8s Mn31 2015	B	R	146	2015	28.369	35.25	....	106	83¼	s97½	8.21	8.26	67¾	34⅜	•23⅞	23	Dc	0.66	E1.00	[9]0.25
[28]Summit Health Ltd[4].......... 7½s Ao 2003	B−	R	37.4	2003	69.444	14.40	....	177⅛	120⅞	158⅞	4.72	....	158⅞	23	22⅞	19	Je	1.20	1.10	[9]1.20
• Sun Co.......... 6¾s Jd15 2012	BBB	R	10.0	2012	24.50	40.81	24.50	100	94	99	6.82	6.85	67⅛	40½	•27⅜	11	Dc	□0.91	E2.41	[9]1.77
• [29]Sunshine[30]Mining.......... 9s jJ15 2008	NR	R	1.52	2008	571.428	1.75	....	No Sale		A100	....	Flat	71½	1⅞	•1¼	d	Dc	d0.08	....	[9]d0.13
• Swift Energy[31].......... 6½s Jd31 2003	NR	R	28.8	2003	81.48	12.27	....	107	88	107	6.07	5.35	97⅞	13¼	•12	33	Dc	□0.56	....	[9]0.36
SysteMed,[32]Inc[33].......... 10s mS15 2002	NR	R	6.32	2002	170.36	5.87	....	136⅜	100	100	10.00	9.99	78⅞	5⅞	4⅝	23	Dc	0.14	....	[9]0.20

Uniform Footnote Explanations—See Page 260. Other: [1] (HRO)To 6-1-01 a Risk Event at 100. [2] Now Scantron Corp sub&data of Harland(John H.). [3] Into Harland (John H.)com. [4] (HRO)On Chge of Ctrl at 100. [5] Co may red in whole,at 100,for tax law chge. [6] (HRO)For a Risk Event at 100. [7] Sub & data of Seagram Co Ltd(guarantor). [8] (HRO)On ea Sep 15. [9] Due 3-5-06. [10] Incl disc. [11] Into Seagram Co Ltd. [12] (HRO)For Designated Event at 100. [13] Int(min 8%)subj to adj,as defined. [14] Into 37.2093 com of Santa Fe Pac PL,restricted. [15] Due 4-11-04. [16] (HRO)To 5-5-97,Chge in Ctrl $252.57 & accr OID. [17] (HRO)On 5-5-97(02&07)at$356.28($502.57&$708.92). [18] Due 5-5-12. [19] Now Selective Insurance Group. [20] Into Selective Insurance Group com. [21] (HRO)For a Special Redemp Event at 100. [22] Excl $131.25 for pending litigation settlement. [23] Int based on prime rate,as defined. [24] Trading 'no int accrual'. [25] Due 11-1-98. [26] Int adj daily. [27] (HRO)For a Redemp Event at declining prices. [28] Exch for & data of Summit Care. [29] Int reset fr 8.875% eff 7-15-91. [30] Now Sunshine Mining & Refin'g. [31] (HRO)On Chge of Ctrl at 100(ltd as defined). [32] Was Newport Pharm Int'l. [33] (HRO)For redemp events,as defined.

Exchange ↓ Issue, Rate, Interest Dates and Maturity	S&P Debt Rating	Bond Form	Outstdg. Mil-$	Conv. Ex-pires	Shares per $1,000 Bond	Price per Share	Div. Income per Bond	1995 Price Range High	1995 Price Range Low	Curr Bid Sale(s) Ask(A)	Curr. Yield	Yield to Mat	Stock Value of Bond	Conv Parity	Stock Data Month End	Stock Data P/E Ratio	Earnings Per Share Yr. End	1994	1995	Last 12 Mos
Systems & Computer Tech[1]... 6¼s mS 2003	B−	R	31.3	2003	66.67	15.00	....	197⅝	116	132⅝	4.71	1.70	132⅝	20	19⅞	90	Sp	0.86	0.22	0.22
◆Teck Corp[2] 3¾s jJ15 2006	BBB−	R	[3]170	2006	[4]46.551	....	9.31	No Sale		124	3.02	1.31	124	26¾	26⅝	27	Dc	±0.77	....	[9]j0.97
Telxon Corp .... 7½s Jd 2012	NR	R	24.7	2012	37.38	26.75	0.37	104	75	102	7.35	7.29	84⅝	27⅜	22⅝	32	Mr	0.57	....	[9]0.70
• Texfi Indus .... 11¼s aO 1997	NR	R	3.54	1997	149.48	6.69	....	90	87	90⅛	12.48	18.02	41⅛	6⅛	•2¾	d	Oc	d1.03	Pd1.96	d1.96
◆[5]Time Warner(Zero)[6](Sr)[7] .... [8] 2012	BBB−	BE	[3]1651	2012	[9]7.301	....	2.34	35	30	34	....	Flat	22¾	46⅝	◆31	17	Dc	□2.01	E1.80	[9]1.65
• Time Warner(Zero)[10](Sr)[11] .... [12] 2013	BBB−	BE	[3]2415	2013	7.759	....	2.79	42	35¼	s41	....	5.17	29½	52⅞	•37⅞	d	Dc	d0.27	Ed0.55	[9]d0.44
• Time Warner .... 8¾s [13]Qjan 2015	BB+	R	1225	2015	20.95	47.73	7.54	105	93¾	s103⅝	8.44	8.37	79⅜	49½	•37⅞	d	Dc	d0.27	Ed0.55	[9]d0.44
• Titan Wheel Int'l[1] .... 4¾s jD 2000	BB−	R	90.0	2000	80.00	12.50	4.80	164	100	130	3.65	....	130	16¼	•16¼	8	Dc	1.14	....	[9]1.84
• [14]Toll Corp[1] 4¾s Jj15 2004	BB−	R	57.5	2004	[15]45.98	21.75	....	104½	67	113	4.20	2.92	105⅞	24⅝	•23	15	Oc	1.08	P1.47	1.47
TPI[1]Enterprises[16] 8¼s jJ15 2002	B−	R	51.6	2002	153.85	6.50	....	102	76	93	8.87	9.72	48⅛	6⅛	3⅛	d	Dc	d0.18	....	[10]d0.34
◆Trans-Lux .... 9s jD 2005	NR	R	4.44	2005	78.74	12.70	11.02	106	100	s105½	8.53	8.18	63	13½	◆8	9	Dc	±1.04	....	[9]0.82
TransAmerican Waste Indus.. 10s jJ29 2003	NR	R	[3]5.80	2003	[17]181.82	5.50	....	71	21	68	14.71	17.86	27⅜	3¾	1½	d	Au	d0.75	d0.34	[11]d0.22
Trenwick Group (Sr)[18] 6s jD15 1999	BBB	R	104	1999	20.62	48.50	23.09	118⅝	98	117½	5.11	1.44	116	57	56¼	13	Dc	3.04	....	[9]4.26
Tridex Corp 12.90s jD15 1999	NR	R	3.29	1999	235.00	4.25	....	240⅞	135⅛	164½	7.84	....	164½	7	7	10	Mr	0.69	....	[9]0.66
• TriMas Corp[1] .... 5s fA 2003	BB−	BE	115	2003	44.20	22.625	8.84	114	98	s98	5.10	5.32	82⅞	22¼	•18¾	12	Dc	1.35	....	[9]1.49
Turner[19]Broadcast'g[20]Sys(Zero).... [21] 2007	BB−	R	[3]582	2007	12.783	....	0.89	45⅝	39⅜	45⅝	....	7.18	33¼	35¾	◆26	65	Dc	±□0.16	E0.40	[9]0.38
• UAL Corp .... 6⅜s QFeb 2025	B+	R	582	2025	Conv into cash & com[22]			101	101	A110	5.80	5.67	....	....	•178½	6	Dc	□0.76	E27.00	[9]25.40
• UNC Inc 7½s Ms31 2006	B	R	69.0	2006	64.94	15.40	....	93	74½	s89	8.43	9.17	39	13¾	•6	d	Dc	d3.89	....	[9]d0.80
Unifi, Inc[1] 6s Ms15 2002	BBB	R	230	2002	33.71	29.67	17.53	104	96¼	100¼	5.99	5.95	75⅛	29¾	•22¼	15	Je	1.08	1.67	[9]1.45
Union Bankshares .... 8.30s Ao 2003	NR	R	6.90	2003	78.68	12.71	....	98	91	98	8.47	8.67	92½	12½	11¾	10	Dc	0.87	....	[9]1.14
• Union Pacific(Sr) .... 4¾s Ao 1999	A−	R	2.02	1999	140.00	7.14	240.80	900	680	924	0.51	....	924	66	•66	21	Dc	2.66	E3.05	[9]4.42
• Unisys Corp[1] .... 8¼s fA 2000	B	R	345	2000	97.68	10.2375	....	118½	80	s89	9.27	11.39	53¾	9⅛	•5½	d	Dc	□d0.07	Ed0.45	[9]d0.69
[23]United Gaming, Inc[24] 7½s Ms15 2003	NR	R	85.0	2003	100.00	10.00	....	80	49	49	15.31	21.20	30⅝	5	3	d	Je	d1.28	d0.95	[9]d1.06
◆U.S. Cellular[25](Zero)[26] .... [27] 2015	BBB−	R	[3]650	2015	9.475	....	....	37½	30⅝	s35	....	5.47	32	37	◆33¾	34	Dc	0.21	....	[9]0.97
U.S.[1]Filter[28] 5s aO15 2000	B+	BE	60.0	2000	48.78	20.50	....	131¾	93	130	3.85	....	130	26¾	•26⅝	39	Mr	0.51	....	[9]0.68
U.S. Home[1] .... 4⅞s mN 2005	B	BE	80.0	2005	28.17	35.50	....	95¾	61⅝	95¾	5.09	5.44	82⅛	34	•29⅛	9	Dc	2.89	E3.07	[9]3.06
• U S[29]WEST[30]Inc[31](Zero)........ [32] 2011	A	R	[3]1569	2011	6.14	....	13.14	34¾	30⅝	s34¾	....	6.94	21⅞	56⅝	•35⅝	15	Dc	p2.53	E2.35	[6]2.52
• URS Corp[33] 6½s Fa15 2012	NR	R	2.15	2012	4.85	206.30	....	70	60	69	9.42	10.53	3½	142⅜	•7	10	Oc	0.60	P0.67	0.67
USF&G Corp[34](Zero)[35] .... [36] 2009	BB+	R	[3]245	2009	29.499	....	5.90	59¾	46⅜	57⅛	....	4.29	49⅞	19⅜	•16⅞	12	Dc	2.14	E1.35	[9]1.79
• USX Corp[37] .... 5¾s jJ 2001	BB−	R	214	2001	Into common[38]			94½	80	s94	6.12	7.08	31⅛	59	•19½	16	Dc	1.10	E1.21	[9]1.09
• USX Corp 7s Jd15 2017	BB−	R	238	2017	Into common[39]			97	81	s95¼	7.35	7.45	51¼	36⅜	•19½	16	Dc	1.10	E1.21	[9]1.09
• USX Corp (Zero)[40] .... [41] 2005	BB+	R	[3]920	2005	Into common[42]			47½	43¾	s46¼	....	8.19	16⅛	56⅜	•19½	16	Dc	1.10	E1.21	[9]1.09
• UtiliCorp United[43] .... 6⅝s [44]mn 2011	BBB−	R	12.2	2011	42.23	23.68	72.64	118½	110	124⅛	5.34	4.45	124⅛	29½	•29⅜	15	Dc	2.08	....	[9]1.96

Uniform Footnote Explanations—See Page 260. Other: [1] (HRO)On Chge of Ctrl at 100. [2] (HRO)To 7-15-99,Ctrl Chge,at $809.41&accr dfd int. [3] Incl disc. [4] Into Cl 'B' Sub Vtg Shrs. [5] (HRO)12-17-97(02&07)at$397.21($540.41&$735.12). [6] (HRO)To12-17-97onChge inCtrl $292.04&accr OID. [7] Exch for & data of Hasbro Inc. [8] Due 12-17-12. [9] Into com of Hasbro Inc. [10] (HRO)6-22-98(03&08)at $476.74($610.27&$781.20). [11] (HRO)To 6-22-98,Chge in Ctrl at $372.43&accr OID. [12] Due 6-22-13. [13] Due 1-10-15. [14] Conv into & data of Toll Bros Inc(guarantor). [15] Into Toll Bros Inc com. [16] Gtd by TPI Restaurants. [17] Automatic conv if com price 165% of conv. [18] (HRO)For a Repurch Event at 100. [19] (HRO)On 2-13-97 at $490.58. [20] (HRO)To2-13-97,Chge in Ctrl at$343.61& accrOID. [21] Due 2-13-07. [22] Cv into $541.90 cash & 3.192 com. [23] (HRO)On Chge of Ctrl at 101. [24] Now Alliance Gaming. [25] (HRO)To 6-15-00 on Ctrl Chge at $306.46 & accr OID. [26] (HRO)On 6-15-00 at $411.99. [27] Due 6-15-15. [28] Issued in min denom $100T. [29] (HRO)To 6-25-96 on Chge in Ctrl. [30] (HRO)On 6-25-01('06)at $490.58($700.42). [31] (HRO)On 6-25-96 at $343.61. [32] Due 6-25-11. [33] Was Thortec Int'l. [34] (HRO)To 3-3-99 onChge of Ctrl at $512.98&accr OID. [35] (HRO)On 3-3-99('04)at $640.82($800.51). [36] Due 3-3-99. [37] Was U.S.Steel. [38] Into 15.94 USX-Marathon & 3.19 USX-Steel com. [39] Into 26.23 USX-Marathon & 5.25 USX-Steel com. [40] (HRO)On 8-9-95 at $466.93(8-9-00,$679.64). [41] Due 8-9-05. [42] Into 8.207 USX-Marathon & 1.64 USX-Steel com. [43] (HRO)Ea May 1, limited,as defined. [44] Due 7-1-11.

Convertible Bonds

Exchange ↓ Issue, Rate, Interest Dates and Maturity	S&P Debt Rating	Bond Form	Outstdg. Mil-$	Conv. Ex-pires	Shares per $1,000 Bond	Price per Share	Div. Income per Bond	1995 Price Range High	1995 Price Range Low	Curr Bid Sale(s) Ask(A)	Curr. Yield	Yield to Mat	Stock Value of Bond	Conv Parity	Stock Data Month End	Stock Data P/E Ratio	Earnings Per Share Yr. End	1994	1995	Last 12 Mos
[1]UTL Corp 6½s jJ 2011	NR	R	28.0	2011	Conv into $158.33			85⅜	73⅜	85⅜	7.61	8.18	....	....	....	..		....	....	....
• [2]Valhi[3]Inc(Zero)[4](Sr Sec) [5] 2007	B	R	[6]379	2007	[7]14.43	....	9.81	37¾	31½	37	....	8.60	35¼	25¾	•24⅜	20	Oc	1.98	P□1.17	1.17
Varlen Corp[8] 6½s Jd 2003	B+	R	69.0	2003	40.24	24.85	16.10	115	94½	100	6.50	6.50	86⅝	24⅞	21½	6	Ja	2.68	....	[10]3.49
VLSI Technology[9] 8¼s aO 2005	B	R	173	2005	18.25	54.80	....	104¼	91¾	91¾	8.99	9.57	33⅛	50⅜	18⅛	17	Dc	±0.85	E1.01	[9]0.92
• Waban Inc[8] 6½s jJ 2002	BB–	R	109	2002	40.40	24.75	....	100½	88	s97½	6.67	6.98	75¼	24¼	•18⅝	8	Ja	1.95	E2.20	[10]2.06
Wainoco Oil 7¾s Jd 2014	CCC+	R	46.0	2014	114.29	8.75	....	87	72	74½	10.40	11.01	37¼	6⅝	•3¼	d	Dc	d0.46	....	[9]d1.12
• [10]Waste Mgmt[11](Zero) [12] 2001	A+	R	[6]27.7	2001	34.88	....	20.93	105	91	103⅞	....	....	103⅞	29⅞	•29¾	18	Dc	1.62	E1.60	[9]1.56
• [10]Waste[11]Mgmt(Zero) [13] 2012	A+	R	[6]1279	2012	Conv into Cv Notes[14]			38	35⅜	38	....	6.03	....	....	....	..		....	....	....
• Waterhouse Investor Svc[8] 6s jD15 2003	B+	R	50.0	2003	42.74	23.40	8.55	114	68½	s107½	5.58	4.85	105⅞	25¼	•24¾	13	Au	1.37	1.68	[11]1.90
• Wendy's Int'l[15] 7s Ao 2006	BBB	R	100	2006	81.30	12.30	19.51	182	124	172⅞	4.05	....	172⅞	21⅜	•21¼	19	Dc	0.93	E1.12	[9]1.08
◆West'n Invt R.E. Tr[16](Sr) 8s [17]Qjan 2008	BBB	R	65.7	2008	44.98	22.23	50.38	100	90	98	8.16	8.26	48⅜	21⅞	◆10¾	18	Dc	0.92	....	[9]0.59
Weston(Roy F.),Inc 7s Ao15 2002	NR	R	25.8	2002	[18]47.33	21.13	....	90	77⅛	88⅝	7.90	9.43	24⅜	18¾	5⅛	30	Dc	±d0.12	....	[9]0.17
Westwood One 6¾s aO15 2011	NR	R	15.4	2011	40.68	24.583	....	92	66½	85	7.94	8.49	57½	21	14⅛	64	Dc	□d0.09	....	[9]0.22
• Whirlpool Corp[19](Zero)[20] [21] 2011	A	R	[6]675	2011	7.237	....	9.84	43	36¼	40	....	6.05	38⅝	55⅜	•53¼	17	Dc	2.10	E3.00	[9]1.35
[22]Winners Corp 8¼s Jd 2003	NR	R	15.6	2003	56.34	17.75	....	98⅝	83½	97	8.51	8.81	53⅝	17¼	•9½	9	Dc	0.90	....	[9]1.00
• WMS Industries 5¾s [23]jd 2002	B	R	57.5	2002	34.48	29.00	....	97¾	83	s87½	6.57	8.15	56½	25½	•16⅜	19	Je	1.19	0.80	[9]0.85
• WMX Technologies[24] 2s Jj24 2005	A	R	[6]550	2005	26.078	38.35	15.65	87	80½	s86	2.33	3.84	77⅝	33	•29¾	18	Dc	1.62	E1.60	[9]1.56
• WorldCorp Inc[8] 7s Mn15 2004	CCC–	R	65.0	2004	90.42	11.06	....	121	89¼	s101	6.93	6.84	90½	11¼	•10	4	Dc	0.54	....	[9]2.32
[25]WorldWay Corp[26] 6¼s Ao15 2011	BBB–	R	50.0	2011	Cv into $231.55			77½	66¾	72	8.68	9.82	....	....	....	..		....	....	....
• Zenith Electronics 6¼s Ao 2011	CCC	R	115	2011	32.00	31.25	....	74	62	s71	8.80	9.99	22	22¼	•6⅞	d	Dc	d0.34	Ed1.65	[9]d1.53

Uniform Footnote Explanations-See Page 260. Other: [1] Acquired by Boeing Co. [2] Exch for & data of Dresser Indus com. [3] (HRO)On 10-20-97(02)at $404.84($636.27). [4] (HRO)On Chge in Ctrl at $257.59 & accr OID. [5] Due 10-20-07. [6] Incl disc. [7] Into Dresser Indus com. [8] (HRO)On Chge of Ctrl at 100. [9] (HRO)For Designated Events at 101. [10] Now WMX Technologies. [11] (HRO)On ea Jun 30,as defined. [12] Due 1-21-01. [13] Due 4-13-12. [14] Cv into 0.2123 of 2% Cv Nts'05,fractions in cash. [15] (HRO)For a Redemp Event at 100. [16] (HRO)On any Jun 30 at 100. [17] Due 6-30-08. [18] Into Cl A com. [19] (HRO)On5-14-96(01&06)at$356.27($502.56&$708.91). [20] (HRO)To 5-14-96 on Chge in Ctrl. [21] Due 5-14-11. [22] Now Volunteer Capital. [23] Due 11-30-02. [24] (HRO)On 3-15-98('00)at $789.95($843.03). [25] Was Carolina Freight. [26] Mgr into & data of Arkansas Best.